P9-DNQ-047

Presented to

___Natalea Olson___

On

___27 February 2019___

From

___Grace Free Church___

Welcome!

Welcome to a very special book—the Bible! Maybe you have read storybook Bibles before, but this might be your first "real" Bible. The Bible is made up of 66 books from Genesis to Revelation. All together these books are known as God's Word. Each book is broken into numbered chapters (just like many other books), and each chapter is made up of numbered verses.

Bible verses are located by book, chapter, and verse. They are written out like this: Genesis 27:2. That means you can find this verse in the book of Genesis, chapter 27, verse 2. Now try it on your own by searching for John 3:16. There is a table of contents in the front of your Bible, just a few pages after this page, to help you. (Hint: John is in the New Testament.)

We are excited for you to explore this Bible and discover just how much God loves you!

Discoverer's Bible (NIV, NIrV, KJV)
Illustrations and artwork Copyright © 2011 by Zondervan

NIrV

Holy Bible

NEW INTERNATIONAL READER'S VERSION

NIrV

Holy Bible

ZONDERVAN®

NIrV Large Print Holy Bible
Copyright © 2000, 2008, 2014 by Zondervan

The Holy Bible, *New International Reader's Version®*
Copyright © 1995, 1996, 1998, 2014 by Biblica, Inc.®
All rights reserved

Published by Zondervan
3900 *Sparks Drive SE*
Grand Rapids, Michigan 49546, U.S.A.

www.zondervan.com

Library of Congress Catalog Card Number 2014939189

The "NIrV" and "New International Reader's Version" are trademarks registered in the United States Patent and Trademark Office by Biblica, Inc.® Use of either trademark requires the permission of Biblica, Inc.®

The NIrV text may be quoted in any form (written, visual, electronic or audio), up to and inclusive of five hundred (500) verses without express written permission of the publisher, providing the verses quoted do not amount to a complete book of the Bible nor do the verses quoted account for 25 percent or more of the total text of the work in which they are quoted.

Notice of copyright must appear on the title or copyright page of the work as follows:

> Scriptures taken from The Holy Bible, *New International Reader's Version®, NIrV®.* Copyright © 1995, 1996, 1998, 2014 by Biblica, Inc.® Used by permission. All rights reserved worldwide.

When quotations from the NIrV text are used in non-saleable media, such as church bulletins, orders of service, posters, transparencies or similar media, a complete copyright notice is not required, but the initials (NIrV) must appear at the end of each quotation.

Any commentary or other biblical reference work produced for commercial sale that uses the New International Reader's Version must obtain written permission for use of the NIrV text.

Permission requests for commercial use within the U.S. and Canada that exceed the above guidelines must be directed to, and approved in writing by, Zondervan, 3900 Sparks Dr SE, Grand Rapids, MI 49546.

Permission requests for commercial use within the U.K., EEC, and EFTA countries that exceed the above guidelines must be directed to, and approved in writing by, Hodder & Stoughton Ltd., a member of the Hodder Headline Plc. Group, 338 Euston Road, London NW1 3BH, England.

Permission requests for non-commercial use that exceed the above guidelines must be directed to, and approved in writing by, Biblica, Inc.®, 1820 Jet Stream Drive, Colorado Springs, CO 80921. www.Biblica.com

Any Internet addresses (websites, blogs, etc.) and telephone numbers in this Bible are offered as a resource. They are not intended in any way to be or imply an endorsement by Zondervan, nor does Zondervan vouch for the content of these sites and numbers for the life of this Bible.

All rights reserved.

Printed in China

18 19 20 21 22 23 24 25 26 /DSC/ 20 19 18 17 16 15 14 13 12 11 10 9 8

You will be pleased to know that a portion of the purchase price of your new NIrV Bible has been provided to Biblica, Inc.® to help spread the gospel of Jesus Christ around the world!

Table of Contents

The Old Testament

The New Testament

Books of the Bible in Alphabetical Order

The books of the New Testament are indicated by *italics*.

Getting to Know Jesus

Question:

How can I get to know Jesus?

Answer:

You can get to know Jesus in the same way you would get to know a new friend: by spending time with him, by learning more about him, by finding out what he did and what he is like. God's Word, the Bible, has wonderful stories for you to read about Jesus' life and everything he did. By talking to Jesus in prayer and reading the Bible, you will get to know your new friend. God already knows you and loves you, and he wants you to know him too.

Question:

Who is Jesus?

Answer:

Jesus is God's Son. Jesus was born about 2,000 years ago, and he lived in a part of the world called Palestine. When he was about thirty years old, he began to preach and to heal. Three or four years later he was nailed to a cross to die. When the people who loved him went to his grave three days later, Jesus' body wasn't there. He had come back to life, just as he said he would.

Question:

Why did Jesus have to die?

Answer:

Because sin came into the world when Adam and Eve disobeyed God, God asked Jesus to come to make things right again. It was all part of God's great plan to make right what had become so wrong because of sin. We all deserve to be punished, but God loves us so much he sent Jesus to take our punishment. Because of Jesus, we can know for sure that God welcomes us into his loving arms — right now and when we die and go to be with him in heaven.

Question:

Where is Jesus now?

Answer:

Jesus is in heaven with his Father. But he has not left us alone here on earth. He sent the Holy Spirit to live with us — to make us strong when we feel like giving up, to help us to care about other people when we sometimes don't feel like it, and to tell us that Jesus will always love us.

Question:

Does Jesus love me?

Answer:

Jesus loves you more than you can imagine.

He loves you when you cry and when you laugh. He loves you when you argue with your brother or when you've had a bad day. He loves you so much that he died for you — but he isn't still dead. He is alive, and he is loving and watching over you every day.

Question:

Will Jesus ever stop loving me?

Answer:

No! No matter what you do, Jesus will always love you. There will be times when you wonder if Jesus is real. There will be times when you wonder if he loves you. There will be times when you do things that you shouldn't do — when you act mean to your sister or lie to your father. But when you pray and tell Jesus that you have times when you doubt; when you pray and tell Jesus that you know you've done wrong and you want to do better — you can be sure that he will never let you down. He will love you your whole life long, and you will live with him forever.

Question:

How do I know I'm a Christian?

Answer:

There are many signs.

When you love Jesus with all the love you can give, when you know deep down that Jesus loves you, when you believe Jesus died to forgive your sins, when you want to live for Jesus — those are good signs that help you know you are a Christian. Sure, you're going to fail sometimes, but God's love for you is so great that it covers those times when you fail. He sees deep into your heart. He knows your desire to live for him, and he loves you.

A Word About The New International Reader's Version

Have You Ever Heard of the New International Version?

We call it the NIV. Many people read the NIV. In fact, more people read the NIV than any other English Bible. They like it because it's easy to read and understand.

And now we are happy to give you another Bible that's easy to read and understand. It's the New International Reader's Version. We call it the NIrV.

Who Will Enjoy Reading the New International Reader's Version?

People who are just starting to read will understand and enjoy the NIrV. Children will be able to read it and understand it. So will older people who are learning how to read. People who are reading the Bible for the first time will be able to enjoy reading the NIrV. So will people who have a hard time understanding what they read. And so will people who use English as their second language. We hope this Bible will be just right for you.

How Is the NIrV Different From the NIV?

The NIrV is based on the NIV. The NIV Committee on Bible Translation (CBT) didn't produce the NIrV. But a few of us who worked on the NIrV are members of CBT. We worked hard to make the NIrV possible. We used the words of the NIV when we could. When the words of the NIV were too long, we used shorter words. We tried to use words that are easy to understand. We also made the sentences of the NIV much shorter.

Why did we do all these things? Because we wanted to make the NIrV very easy to read and understand.

What Other Helps Does the NIrV Have?

We decided to give you a lot of other help too. For example, sometimes a verse is quoted from another place in the Bible. When it is, we tell you the Bible book, chapter and verse it comes from. We put that information right after the verse that quotes from another place.

We separated each chapter into shorter sections. We gave a title to almost every chapter. Sometimes we even gave a title to a section. We did these things to help you understand what the chapter or section is all about.

Another example of a helpful change has to do with the word "Selah" in the Psalms. What this Hebrew word means is still not clear. So, for now, this word is not helpful for readers. The NIV has moved the word to the bottom of the page. We have followed the NIV and removed this Hebrew word from the NIrV. Perhaps one day we will learn what this word means. But until then, the Psalms are easier to read and understand without it.

Sometimes the writers of the Bible used more than one name for the same person or place. For example, in the New Testament the Sea of Galilee is also called the Sea of Gennesaret. Sometimes it is also called the Sea of Tiberias. But in the NIrV we decided to call it the Sea of Galilee everywhere it appears. We called it that because that is its most familiar name.

We also wanted to help you learn the names of people and places in the Bible. So sometimes we provided names even in verses where those names don't actually appear. For example, sometimes the Bible says "the River" where it means "the Euphrates River." In those places, we used the full name "the Euphrates River." Sometimes the word "Pharaoh" in the Bible means "Pharaoh Hophra." In those places, we used his full name "Pharaoh Hophra." We did all these things in order to make the NIrV as clear as possible.

Does the NIrV Say What the First Writers of the Bible Said?

We wanted the NIrV to say just what the first writers of the Bible said. So we kept checking the Greek New Testament as we did our work. That's because the New Testament's first writers used Greek. We also kept checking the Hebrew Old Testament as we did our work. That's because the Old Testament's first writers used Hebrew.

We used the best copies of the Greek New Testament. We also used the best copies of the Hebrew Old Testament. Older English Bibles couldn't use those copies because they had not yet been found. The oldest copies are best because they are closer in time to the ones the first Bible writers wrote. That's why we kept checking the older copies instead of the newer ones.

Some newer copies of the Greek New Testament added several verses that the older ones don't have. Sometimes it's several verses in a row. This occurs at Mark 16:9 – 20 and John 7:53 — 8:11. We have included these verses in the NIrV. Sometimes the newer copies added only a single verse. An example is Mark 9:44. That verse is not in the oldest Greek New Testaments. So we put the verse number 43/44 right before Mark 9:43. You can look on the list below for Mark 9:44 and locate the verse that was added.

Verses That Were Not Found in Oldest Greek New Testaments

Matthew 17:21	But that kind does not go out except by prayer and fasting.
Matthew 18:11	The Son of Man came to save what was lost.
Matthew 23:14	How terrible for you, teachers of the law and Pharisees! You pretenders! You take over the houses of widows. You say long prayers to show off. So God will punish you much more.
Mark 7:16	Everyone who has ears to hear should listen.
Mark 9:44	In hell, / "'the worms don't die, / and the fire doesn't go out.'
Mark 9:46	In hell, / "'the worms don't die, / and the fire doesn't go out.'
Mark 11:26	But if you do not forgive, your Father who is in heaven will not forgive your sins either.
Mark 15:28	Scripture came true. It says, "And he was counted among those who disobey the law."
Luke 17:36	Two men will be in the field. One will be taken and the other left.
Luke 23:17	It was Pilate's duty to let one prisoner go free for them at the Feast.
John 5:4	From time to time an angel of the Lord would come down. The angel would stir up the waters. The first disabled person to go into the pool after it was stirred would be healed.
Acts 8:37	Philip said, "If you believe with all your heart, you can." The official answered, "I believe that Jesus Christ is the Son of God."
Acts 15:34	But Silas decided to remain there.
Acts 24:7	But Lysias, the commander, came. By using a lot of force, he took Paul from our hands.
Acts 28:29	After he said that, the Jews left. They were arguing strongly among themselves.
Romans 16:24	May the grace of our Lord Jesus Christ be with all of you. Amen.

What Is Our Prayer for You?

The Lord has blessed the New International Version in a wonderful way. He has used it to help millions of Bible readers. Many people have put their faith in Jesus after reading it. Many others have become stronger believers because they have read it.

We hope and pray that the New International Reader's Version will help you in the same way. If that happens, we will give God all the glory.

A Word About This Edition

This edition of the New International Reader's Version has been revised to include the changes of the New International Version. Over the years, many helpful changes have been made to the New International Version. Those changes were made because our understanding of the original writings is better. Those changes also include changes that have taken place in the English language. We wanted the New International Reader's Version to include those helpful changes as well. We wanted the New International Reader's Version to be as clear and correct as possible.

We want to thank the people who helped us prepare this new edition. They are Jeannine Brown from Bethel Seminary St. Paul, Yvonne Van Ee from Calvin College, Michael Williams from Calvin Theological Seminary, and Ron Youngblood from Bethel Seminary San Diego. We also want to thank the people at Biblica who encouraged and supported this work.

The
Old Testament

Genesis

Introduction:

Genesis is the first book of the Bible. The word Genesis means "beginnings." This book tells how the world began. Moses wrote the book of Genesis. He wrote about Adam and Eve's sin. He wrote about God's love. This book tells of God's special people. Some of these people are Noah, Abraham, Isaac, Jacob, and Joseph.

The first five books of the Bible are called the books of the law. These books were God's instructions to the people of Israel. Genesis is one of these books because it tells how Israel became God's people.

Outline of contents:

The Beginning

1 In the beginning, God created the heavens and the earth. ² The earth didn't have any shape. And it was empty. There was darkness over the surface of the waves. At that time, the Spirit of God was hovering over the waters.

³ God said, "Let there be light." And there was light. ⁴ God saw that the light was good. He separated the light from the darkness. ⁵ God called the light "day." He called the darkness "night." There was evening, and there was morning. It was day one.

⁶ God said, "Let there be a huge space between the waters. Let it separate water from water." ⁷ And that's exactly what happened. God made the huge space between the waters. He separated the water under the space from the water above it. ⁸ God called the huge space "sky." There was evening, and there was morning. It was day two.

⁹ God said, "Let the water under the sky be gathered into one place. Let dry ground appear." And that's exactly what happened. ¹⁰ God called the dry ground "land." He called all the water that was gathered together "seas." And God saw that it was good.

¹¹ Then God said, "Let the

land produce plants. Let them produce their own seeds. And let there be trees on the land that grow fruit with seeds in it. Let each kind of plant or tree have its own kind of seeds." And that's exactly what happened. ¹²So the land produced plants. Each kind of plant had its own kind of seeds. And the land produced trees that grew fruit with seeds in it. Each kind of tree had its own kind of seeds. God saw that it was good. ¹³There was evening, and there was morning. It was day three.

¹⁴God said, "Let there be lights in the huge space of the sky. Let them separate the day from the night. Let the lights set the times for the holy celebrations and the days and the years. ¹⁵Let them be lights in the huge space of the sky to give light on the earth." And that's exactly what happened. ¹⁶God made two great lights. He made the larger light to rule over the day and the smaller light to rule over the night. He also made the stars. ¹⁷God put the lights in the huge space of the sky to give light on the earth. ¹⁸He put them there to rule over the day and the night. He put them there to separate light from darkness. God saw that it was good. ¹⁹There was evening, and there was morning. It was day four.

²⁰God said, "Let the seas be filled with living things. Let birds fly above the earth across the huge space of the sky." ²¹So God created the great sea creatures. He created every kind of living thing that fills the seas and moves about in them. He created every kind of bird that flies. And God saw that it was good. ²²God blessed them. He said, "Have little ones so that there will be many of you. Fill the water in the seas. Let there be more and more birds on the earth." ²³There was evening, and there was morning. It was day five.

²⁴God said, "Let the land produce every kind of living creature. Let there be livestock, and creatures that move along the ground, and wild animals." And that's exactly what happened. ²⁵God made every kind of wild animal. He made every kind of livestock. He made every kind of creature that moves along the ground. And God saw that it was good.

²⁶Then God said, "Let us make human beings so that they are like us. Let them rule over the fish in the seas and the birds in the sky. Let them rule over the livestock and all the wild animals. And let them rule over all the creatures that move along the ground."

²⁷So God created human
    beings in his own
    likeness.
  He created them to be like
    himself.
  He created them as male
    and female.

²⁸God blessed them. He said to them, "Have children so that there will be many of you.

Fill the earth and bring it under your control. Rule over the fish in the seas and the birds in the sky. Rule over every living creature that moves along the ground."

29 Then God said, "I am giving you every plant on the face of the whole earth that produces its own seeds. I am giving you every tree that has fruit with seeds in it. All of them will be given to you for food. 30 I am giving every green plant as food for all the land animals and for all the birds in the sky. I am also giving the plants to all the creatures that move along the ground. I am giving them to every living thing that breathes." And that's exactly what happened.

31 God saw everything he had made. And it was very good. There was evening, and there was morning. It was day six.

2 So the heavens and the earth and everything in them were completed.

2 By the seventh day God had finished the work he had been doing. So on that day he rested from all his work. 3 God blessed the seventh day and made it holy. He blessed it because on that day he rested from all the work he had done.

Adam and Eve

4 Here is the story of the heavens and the earth when they were created. The LORD God made the earth and the heavens.

5 At that time, bushes had not yet appeared on the earth. Plants had not started to grow. The LORD God had not sent rain on the earth. And there was no one to farm the land. 6 But streams came from the earth. They watered the entire surface of the ground. 7 Then the LORD God formed a man. He made him out of the dust of the ground. God breathed the breath of life into him. And the man became a living person.

8 The LORD God had planted a garden in the east in Eden. He put in the garden the man he had formed. 9 The LORD God made every kind of tree grow out of the ground. The trees were pleasing to look at. Their fruit was good to eat. There were two trees in the middle of the garden. One of them had fruit that let people live forever. The other had fruit that let people tell the difference between good and evil.

10 A river watered the garden. It flowed out of Eden. From there the river separated into four other rivers. 11 The name of the first river is the Pishon. It winds through the whole land of Havilah. Gold is found there. 12 The gold of that land is good. Onyx and sweet-smelling resin are also found there. 13 The name of the second river is the Gihon. It winds through the whole land of Cush. 14 The name of the third river is the Tigris. It runs along the east side of Ashur. And the fourth river is called the Euphrates.

15 The LORD God put the man in the Garden of Eden. He put him there to farm its land and

take care of it. [16] The LORD God gave the man a command. He said, "You may eat fruit from any tree in the garden. [17] But you must not eat the fruit from the tree of the knowledge of good and evil. If you do, you will certainly die."

[18] The LORD God said, "It is not good for the man to be alone. I will make a helper who is just right for him."

[19] The LORD God had formed all the wild animals and all the birds in the sky. He had made all of them out of the ground. He brought them to the man to see what names he would give them. And the name the man gave each living creature became its name. [20] So the man gave names to all the livestock, all the birds in the sky, and all the wild animals.

But Adam didn't find a helper that was just right for him. [21] So the LORD God caused him to fall into a deep sleep. While the man was sleeping, the LORD God took out one of the man's ribs. Then the LORD God closed the opening in the man's side. [22] Then the LORD God made a woman. He made her from the rib he had taken out of the man. And the LORD God brought her to the man.

[23] The man said,

"Her bones have come from
    my bones.
Her body has come from
    my body.
She will be named 'woman,'
    because she was taken out
    of a man."

[24] That's why a man leaves his father and mother and is joined to his wife. The two of them become one.

[25] Adam and his wife were both naked. They didn't feel any shame.

Adam and Eve Fall Into Sin

3 The serpent was more clever than any of the wild animals the LORD God had made. The serpent said to the woman, "Did God really say, 'You must not eat fruit from any tree in the garden'?"

[2] The woman said to the serpent, "We may eat fruit from the trees in the garden. [3] But God did say, 'You must not eat the fruit from the tree in the middle of the garden. Do not even touch it. If you do, you will die.'"

[4] "You will certainly not die," the serpent said to the woman. [5] "God knows that when you eat fruit from that tree, you will know things you have never known before. Like God, you will be able to tell the difference between good and evil."

[6] The woman saw that the tree's fruit was good to eat and pleasing to look at. She also saw that it would make a person wise. So she took some of the fruit and ate it. She also gave some to her husband, who was with her. And he ate it. [7] Then both of them knew things they had never known before. They realized they were naked. So they sewed together fig leaves and made clothes for themselves.

[8] Then the man and his wife heard the LORD God walking in the garden. It was during the coolest time of the day. They hid from the LORD God among the trees of the garden. [9] But the LORD God called out to the man. "Where are you?" he asked.

[10] "I heard you in the garden," the man answered. "I was afraid, because I was naked. So I hid."

[11] The LORD God said, "Who told you that you were naked? Have you eaten fruit from the tree I commanded you not to eat from?"

[12] The man said, "It's the fault of the woman you put here with me. She gave me some fruit from the tree. And I ate it."

[13] Then the LORD God said to the woman, "What have you done?"

The woman said, "The serpent tricked me. That's why I ate the fruit."

[14] So the LORD God spoke to the serpent. He said, "Because you have done this,

"You are set apart from all
　　livestock
　and all wild animals.
I am putting a curse on
　　you.
You will crawl on your belly.
　You will eat dust
　all the days of your life.
[15] I will make you and the
　　woman hate each other.
　Your children and
　　her children will be
　　enemies.
Her son will crush your head.
　And you will bite his heel."

[16] The LORD God said to the woman,

"I will increase your pain
　when you give birth.
You will be in great pain
　when you have children.
You will long for your
　husband.
And he will rule over you."

[17] The LORD God said to Adam, "You listened to your wife's suggestion. You ate fruit from the tree I warned you about. I said, 'You must not eat its fruit.'

"So I am putting a curse on
　the ground because of
　what you did.
All the days of your life you
　will have to work hard.
It will be painful for you
　to get food from the
　ground. [18] You will eat
　plants from the field,
even though the ground
　produces thorns and
　prickly weeds.
[19] You will have to work hard
　and sweat a lot
　to produce the food you
　eat.
You were made out of the
　ground.
　You will return to it when
　you die.
You are dust,
　and you will return to
　dust."

[20] Adam named his wife Eve. She would become the mother of every living person.

[21] The LORD God made clothes out of animal skins for Adam and his wife to wear. [22] The

LORD God said, "Just like one of us, the man can now tell the difference between good and evil. He must not be allowed to reach out and pick fruit from the tree of life and eat it. If he does, he will live forever." ²³ So the LORD God drove the man out of the Garden of Eden. He sent the man to farm the ground he had been made from. ²⁴ The LORD God drove him out and then placed angels on the east side of the garden. He also placed there a flaming sword that flashed back and forth. The angels and the sword guarded the way to the tree of life.

Cain and Abel

4 Adam loved his wife Eve and slept with her. She became pregnant and gave birth to Cain. She said, "With the LORD's help I have had a baby boy." ² Later she gave birth to his brother Abel.

Abel took care of sheep. Cain farmed the land. ³ After some time, Cain gathered some things he had grown. He brought them as an offering to the LORD. ⁴ And Abel also brought an offering. He brought the fattest parts of some animals from his flock. They were the first animals born to their mothers. The LORD was pleased with Abel and his offering. ⁵ But he wasn't pleased with Cain and his offering. So Cain became very angry, and his face was sad.

⁶ Then the LORD said to Cain, "Why are you angry? Why are you looking so sad? ⁷ Do what is right and then you will be accepted. If you don't do what is right, sin is waiting at your door to grab you. It desires to control you. But you must rule over it."

⁸ Cain said to his brother Abel, "Let's go out to the field." So they went out. There Cain attacked his brother Abel and killed him.

⁹ Then the LORD said to Cain, "Where is your brother Abel?"

"I don't know," Cain replied. "Am I supposed to take care of my brother?"

¹⁰ The LORD said, "What have you done? Listen! Your brother's blood is crying out to me from the ground. ¹¹ So I am putting a curse on you. I am driving you away from this ground. It has opened its mouth to receive your brother's blood from your hand. ¹² When you farm the land, it will not produce its crops for you anymore. You will be a restless person who wanders around on the earth."

¹³ Cain said to the LORD, "You are punishing me more than I can take. ¹⁴ Today you are driving me away from the land. I will be hidden from you. I'll be a restless person who wanders around on the earth. Anyone who finds me will kill me."

¹⁵ But the LORD said to him, "No. Anyone who kills you will be paid back seven times." The LORD put a mark on Cain. Then anyone who found him wouldn't kill him. ¹⁶ So Cain went away from the LORD. He lived in the land of Nod. It was east of Eden.

¹⁷ Cain loved his wife and slept with her. She became pregnant

and gave birth to Enoch. At that time Cain was building a city. He named it after his son Enoch. [18] Enoch had a son named Irad. Irad was the father of Mehujael. Mehujael was the father of Methushael. And Methushael was the father of Lamech.

[19] Lamech married two women. One was named Adah, and the other was named Zillah. [20] Adah gave birth to Jabal. He was the father of people who live in tents and raise livestock. [21] His brother's name was Jubal. He was the father of everyone who plays stringed instruments and wind instruments. [22] Zillah also had a son. His name was Tubal-Cain. He made all kinds of tools out of bronze and iron. Tubal-Cain's sister was Naamah.

[23] Lamech said to his wives,

"Adah and Zillah, listen
    to me!
  You wives of Lamech, hear
    my words!
I have killed a man because
    he wounded me.
  I have killed a young man
    because he hurt me.
[24] Anyone who would have
    killed Cain would have
    been paid back seven
    times.
  But anyone who hurts
    me will be paid back 77
    times."

[25] Adam slept with his wife again. She gave birth to a son and named him Seth. She said, "God has given me another child. He will take the place of Abel, because Cain killed him." [26] Seth also had a son and named him Enosh.

Then people began to call on the name of the LORD.

The Family Line of Adam

5 Here is the written story of Adam's family line.

When God created human beings, he made them to be like him. [2] He created them as male and female, and he blessed them. He called them "human beings" when they were created.

[3] When Adam was 130 years old, he had a son who was like him. He named him Seth. [4] Adam lived 800 years after Seth was born. He also had other sons and daughters. [5] Adam lived a total of 930 years. And then he died.

[6] Seth lived 105 years. Then he became the father of Enosh. [7] Seth lived 807 years after Enosh was born. He also had other sons and daughters. [8] Seth lived a total of 912 years. And then he died.

[9] Enosh lived 90 years. Then he became the father of Kenan. [10] Enosh lived 815 years after Kenan was born. He also had other sons and daughters. [11] Enosh lived a total of 905 years. And then he died.

[12] Kenan lived 70 years. Then he became the father of Mahalalel. [13] Kenan lived 840 years after Mahalalel

was born. He also had other sons and daughters. ¹⁴Kenan lived a total of 910 years. And then he died.

¹⁵Mahalalel lived 65 years. Then he became the father of Jared. ¹⁶Mahalalel lived 830 years after Jared was born. He also had other sons and daughters. ¹⁷Mahalalel lived a total of 895 years. And then he died.

¹⁸Jared lived 162 years. Then he became the father of Enoch. ¹⁹Jared lived 800 years after Enoch was born. He also had other sons and daughters. ²⁰Jared lived a total of 962 years. And then he died.

²¹Enoch lived 65 years. Then he became the father of Methuselah. ²²Enoch walked faithfully with God 300 years after Methuselah was born. He also had other sons and daughters. ²³Enoch lived a total of 365 years. ²⁴Enoch walked faithfully with God. And then he couldn't be found, because God took him from this life.

²⁵Methuselah lived 187 years. Then he became the father of Lamech. ²⁶Methuselah lived 782 years after Lamech was born. He also had other sons and daughters. ²⁷Methuselah lived a total of 969 years. And then he died.

²⁸Lamech lived 182 years. Then he had a son ²⁹and named him Noah. Lamech said, "He will comfort us when we are working. He'll comfort us when our hands work so hard they hurt. We have to work hard because the LORD put a curse on the ground." ³⁰Lamech lived 595 years after Noah was born. He also had other sons and daughters. ³¹Lamech lived a total of 777 years. And then he died.

³²After Noah was 500 years old, he became the father of Shem, Ham and Japheth.

The Sins of Everyone on Earth

6 There began to be many human beings on the earth. And daughters were born to them. ²The sons of God saw that the daughters of human beings were beautiful. So they married any of them they chose. ³Then the LORD said, "My Spirit will not struggle with human beings forever. They will have only 120 years to live."

⁴The Nephilim were on the earth in those days. That was when the sons of God went to the daughters of human beings. Children were born to them. The Nephilim were famous heroes who lived long ago. Nephilim were also on the earth later on.

⁵The LORD saw how bad the sins of everyone on earth had become. They only thought

about evil things. ⁶ The LORD was very sad that he had made human beings on the earth. His heart was filled with pain. ⁷ So the LORD said, "I created human beings, but I will wipe them out. I will also destroy the animals, the birds in the sky, and the creatures that move along the ground. I am very sad that I have made human beings." ⁸ But the LORD was very pleased with Noah.

Noah and the Flood

⁹ Here is the story of Noah's family line.

Noah was a godly man. He was without blame among the people of his time. He walked faithfully with God. ¹⁰ Noah had three sons. Their names were Shem, Ham and Japheth.

¹¹ The earth was very sinful in God's eyes. It was full of people who did mean and harmful things. ¹² God saw how sinful the earth had become. All its people were living very sinful lives. ¹³ So God said to Noah, "I am going to put an end to everyone. They have filled the earth with their harmful acts. I am certainly going to destroy them and the earth. ¹⁴ So make yourself an ark out of cypress wood. Make rooms in it. Cover it with tar inside and out. ¹⁵ Here is how I want you to build it. The ark has to be 450 feet long. It has to be 75 feet wide and 45 feet high. ¹⁶ Make a roof for it. Leave below the roof an opening all the way around that is a foot and a half high. Put a door in one side of the ark. Make lower, middle and upper decks. ¹⁷ I am going to bring a flood on the earth. It will destroy all life under the sky. It will destroy every living creature that breathes. Everything on earth will die. ¹⁸ But I will make my covenant with you. You will go into the ark. Your sons and your wife and your sons' wives will enter it with you. ¹⁹ Bring a male and a female of every living thing into the ark. They will be kept alive with you. ²⁰ Two of every kind of bird will come to you. Two of every kind of animal will also come to you. And so will two of every kind of creature that moves along the ground. All of them will be kept alive with you. ²¹ Take every kind of food that you will need. Store it away as food for you and them."

²² Noah did everything just as God commanded him.

7 Then the LORD said to Noah, "Go into the ark with your whole family. I know that you are a godly man among the people of today. ² Take seven pairs of every kind of 'clean' animal with you. Take a male and a female of each kind. Take one pair of every kind of animal that is not 'clean.' Take a male and a female of each kind. ³ Also take seven pairs of every kind of bird. Take a male and a female of each kind. Then every kind will be kept alive. They can spread out again over the whole earth. ⁴ Seven days from now I will send rain on the earth. It will rain for 40 days and 40 nights.

I will destroy from the face of the earth every living creature I have made."

⁵ Noah did everything the LORD commanded him to do.

⁶ Noah was 600 years old when the flood came on the earth. ⁷ He and his sons entered the ark. His wife and his sons' wives went with them. They entered the ark to escape the waters of the flood. ⁸ Male and female pairs of "clean" animals and pairs of animals that were not "clean" came to Noah. So did male and female pairs of birds and of all the creatures that move along the ground. ⁹ All of them came to Noah and entered the ark. Everything happened just as God had commanded Noah. ¹⁰ After seven days the flood came on the earth.

¹¹ Noah was 600 years old. It was the 17th day of the second month of the year. On that day all of the springs at the bottom of the oceans burst open. God opened the windows of the sky. ¹² Rain fell on the earth for 40 days and 40 nights.

¹³ On that same day Noah entered the ark together with his sons Shem, Ham and Japheth. Noah's wife and the wives of his three sons also entered it. ¹⁴ They had every kind of wild animal with them. They had every kind of livestock, creature that moves along the ground, and bird that flies. ¹⁵ Pairs of all living creatures that breathe came to Noah and entered the ark. ¹⁶ The animals going in were male and female of every living thing. Ev-

erything happened just as God had commanded Noah. Then the LORD shut him in.

¹⁷ For 40 days the flood kept coming on the earth. As the waters rose higher, they lifted the ark high above the earth. ¹⁸ The waters rose higher and higher on the earth. And the ark floated on the water. ¹⁹ The waters rose on the earth until all the high mountains under the entire sky were covered. ²⁰ The waters continued to rise until they covered the mountains by more than 20 feet. ²¹ Every living thing that moved on land died. The birds, the livestock and the wild animals died. All of the creatures that fill the earth also died. And so did every human being. ²² Every breathing thing on dry land died. ²³ Every living thing on earth was wiped out. People and animals were destroyed. The creatures that move along the ground and the birds in the sky were wiped out. Everything on earth was destroyed. Only Noah and those with him in the ark were left.

²⁴ The waters flooded the earth for 150 days.

8 But God showed concern for Noah. He also showed concern for all the wild animals and livestock that were with Noah in the ark. So God sent a wind to sweep over the earth. And the waters began to go down. ² The springs at the bottom of the oceans had been closed. The windows of the sky had also been closed. And the rain had stopped falling from the sky. ³ The water on the earth continued to go down. At the end of the 150 days the water had gone down. ⁴On the 17th day of the seventh month, the ark came to rest on the mountains of Ararat. ⁵The waters continued to go down until the tenth month. On the first day of that month, the tops of the mountains could be seen.

⁶After 40 days Noah opened a window he had made in the ark. ⁷He sent out a raven. It kept flying back and forth until the water on the earth had dried up. ⁸Then Noah sent out a dove. He wanted to see if the water on the surface of the ground had gone down. ⁹But the dove couldn't find any place to rest. Water still covered the whole surface of the earth. So the dove returned to Noah in the ark. Noah reached out his hand and took the dove in. He brought it back to himself in the ark. ¹⁰He waited seven more days. Then he sent out the dove again from the ark. ¹¹In the evening the dove returned to him. There in its beak was a freshly picked olive leaf! So Noah knew that the water on the earth had gone down. ¹²He waited seven more days. Then he sent out the dove again. But this time it didn't return to him.

¹³It was the first day of the first month of Noah's 601st year. The water on the earth had dried up. Then Noah removed the covering from the ark. He saw that the surface of the ground was dry. ¹⁴By the 27th day of the second month the earth was completely dry.

¹⁵Then God said to Noah, ¹⁶"Come out of the ark. Bring your wife and your sons and their wives with you. ¹⁷Bring out every kind of living thing that is with you. Bring the birds, the animals, and all the creatures that move along the ground. Then they can multiply on the earth. They can have little ones and the number of them can increase."

¹⁸So Noah came out of the ark. His sons and his wife and his sons' wives were with him. ¹⁹All the animals came out of the ark. The creatures that move along the ground also came out. So did all the birds. Everything that moves on land came out of the ark, one kind after another.

²⁰Then Noah built an altar to honor the LORD. He took some of the "clean" animals and birds. He sacrificed them on the altar as burnt offerings. ²¹The smell of the offerings pleased the LORD. He said to himself, "I will never put a curse on the ground again because of human beings. I will not do it even though their hearts are always directed toward evil. Their thoughts are evil from the time they are young. I will never destroy all living things again, as I have just done.

²²"As long as the earth lasts,
   there will always be a time
      to plant
   and a time to gather the
      crops.
As long as the earth lasts,
   there will always be cold
      and heat.

There will always be summer
and winter,
day and night."

God Makes a Covenant With Noah

9 Then God blessed Noah and his sons. He said to them, "Have children so that there are many of you. Fill the earth. ²All the land animals will be afraid of you. All the birds in the sky will be afraid of you. Every creature that moves along the ground will be afraid of you. So will every fish in the seas. Every living thing is put under your control. ³Everything that lives and moves about will be food for you. I have already given you the green plants for food. Now I am giving you everything.

⁴"But you must not eat meat that still has blood in it. ⁵I will certainly hold someone accountable if you are murdered. I will even hold animals accountable if they kill you. I will also hold anyone accountable who murders another person.

⁶"Anyone who murders a
human being
will be killed by a human
being.
That is because I have made
human beings
so that they are like me.

⁷"Have children so that there will be many of you. Multiply and become many on the earth."

⁸Then God spoke to Noah and to his sons who were with him. He said, ⁹"I am now making my covenant with you and with all your children who will be born after you. ¹⁰I am making it also with every living creature that was with you in the ark. I am making my covenant with the birds, the livestock and all the wild animals. I am making it with all the creatures that came out of the ark with you. In fact, I am making it with every living thing on earth. ¹¹Here is my covenant I am making with you. The waters of a flood will never again destroy all life. A flood will never again destroy the earth."

¹²God continued, "My covenant is between me and you and every living creature with you. It is a covenant for all time to come. Here is the sign of the covenant I am making. ¹³I have put my rainbow in the clouds. It will be the sign of the covenant between me and the earth. ¹⁴Sometimes when I bring clouds over the earth, a rainbow will appear in them. ¹⁵Then I will remember my covenant between me and you and every kind of living creature. The waters will never again become a flood to destroy all life. ¹⁶When the rainbow appears in the clouds, I will see it. I will remember that my covenant will last forever. It is a covenant between me and every kind of living creature on earth."

¹⁷So God said to Noah, "The rainbow is the sign of my covenant. I have made my covenant between me and all life on earth."

The Sons of Noah

18 The sons of Noah who came out of the ark were Shem, Ham and Japheth. Ham was the father of Canaan. 19 The people who were scattered over the earth came from Noah's three sons.

20 Noah was a man who farmed the land. He decided to plant a field that produced grapes for making wine. 21 When he drank some of the wine, it made him drunk. Then he lay down inside his tent without any clothes on. 22 Ham saw his father naked. Then Ham, the father of Canaan, went outside and told his two brothers. 23 But Shem and Japheth picked up a piece of clothing and laid it across their shoulders. Then they walked backward into the tent. They covered their father's body. They turned their faces away because they didn't want to see their father naked.

24 Then Noah woke up from his sleep that was caused by the wine. He found out what his youngest son had done to him. 25 He said,

"May a curse be put on
    Canaan!
He will be the lowest of
    slaves to his brothers."

26 Noah also said,

"May the LORD, the God of
    Shem, be praised.
May Canaan be the slave of
    Shem.
27 May God add land to
    Japheth's territory.
May Japheth live in the
    tents of Shem.

And may Canaan be the
    slave of Japheth."

28 After the flood Noah lived 350 years. 29 Noah lived a total of 950 years. And then he died.

A List of Nations

10 Here is the story of Shem, Ham and Japheth. They were Noah's sons. After the flood, they also had sons.

The Sons of Japheth

2 The sons of Japheth were
    Gomer, Magog, Madai,
    Javan, Tubal, Meshek
    and Tiras.
3 The sons of Gomer were
    Ashkenaz, Riphath and
    Togarmah.
4 The sons of Javan were
    Elishah, Tarshish, the
    Kittites and the Roda-
    nites.
5 From these people came
    the families who lived near
    the Mediterranean Sea.
    Each tribe and nation then
    spread out into its own ter-
    ritory and had its own lan-
    guage.

The Sons of Ham

6 The sons of Ham were
    Cush, Egypt, Put and Ca-
    naan.
7 The sons of Cush were
    Seba, Havilah, Sabtah,
    Raamah and Sabteka.
    The sons of Raamah were
    Sheba and Dedan.
8 Cush was the father of
    Nimrod. Nimrod became
    a mighty hero on the earth.
9 He was a mighty hunter in

the LORD's eyes. That's why people sometimes compare others with Nimrod. They say, "They are like Nimrod, who was a mighty hunter in the LORD's eyes." [10] The first capital cities of Nimrod's kingdom were Babylon, Uruk, Akkad and Kalneh. These cities were in the land of Babylon. [11] From that land he went to Assyria. There he built Nineveh, Rehoboth Ir and Calah. [12] He also built Resen, which is between Nineveh and Calah. Nineveh is the most famous city.

[13] Egypt was the father of the Ludites, Anamites, Lehabites, Naphtuhites, [14] Pathrusites, Kasluhites and Caphtorites. The Philistines came from the Kasluhites.

[15] Canaan was the father of Sidon.

Sidon was his oldest son. Canaan was also the father of the Hittites, [16] Jebusites, Amorites and Girgashites. [17] And he was the father of the Hivites, Arkites, Sinites, [18] Arvadites, Zemarites and Hamathites.

Later the Canaanite tribes scattered. [19] The borders of Canaan reached from Sidon toward Gerar all the way to Gaza. Then they continued toward Sodom, Gomorrah, Admah and Zeboyim all the way to Lasha.

[20] These are the sons of Ham. They are listed by their tribes and languages in their territories and nations.

The Sons of Shem

[21] Sons were also born to Shem, Japheth's younger brother. All the sons of Eber belonged to Shem's family line.

[22] The sons of Shem were Elam, Ashur, Arphaxad, Lud and Aram.

[23] The sons of Aram were Uz, Hul, Gether and Meshek.

[24] Arphaxad was the father of Shelah.

Shelah was the father of Eber.

[25] Eber had two sons.

One was named Peleg. That's because the earth was divided up in his time. His brother was named Joktan.

[26] Joktan was the father of Almodad, Sheleph, Hazarmaveth, Jerah, [27] Hadoram, Uzal, Diklah, [28] Obal, Abimael, Sheba, [29] Ophir, Havilah and Jobab. They were all sons of Joktan.

[30] The area where they lived stretched from Mesha toward Sephar. It was in the eastern hill country.

[31] These are the sons of Shem. They are listed by their tribes and languages in their territories and nations.

32 These are the tribes of Noah's sons. They are listed by their family lines within their nations. From them the nations spread out over the earth after the flood.

The Tower of Babel

11 The whole world had only one language, and everyone spoke it. 2 They moved to the east and found a broad valley in Babylon. There they made their home.

3 They said to one another, "Come on! Let's make bricks and bake them well." They used bricks instead of stones. They used tar to hold the bricks together. 4 Then they said, "Come on! Let's build a city for ourselves. Let's build a tower that reaches to the sky. We'll make a name for ourselves. Then we won't be scattered over the whole earth."

5 But the LORD came down to see the city and the tower the people were building. 6 He said, "All these people are united and speak the same language. That is why they can do all this. Now they will be able to do anything they plan. 7 Come on! Let us go down and mix up their language. Then they will not be able to understand one another."

8 So the LORD scattered them from there over the whole earth. And they stopped building the city. 9 There the LORD mixed up the language of the whole world. That's why the city was called Babel. From there the LORD scattered them over the whole earth.

The Family Line of Shem

10 Here is the story of Shem's family line.

It was two years after the flood. When Shem was 100 years old, he became the father of Arphaxad. 11 After Arphaxad was born, Shem lived 500 years and had other sons and daughters.

12 When Arphaxad had lived 35 years, he became the father of Shelah. 13 After Shelah was born, Arphaxad lived 403 years and had other sons and daughters.

14 When Shelah had lived 30 years, he became the father of Eber. 15 After Eber was born, Shelah lived 403 years and had other sons and daughters.

16 When Eber had lived 34 years, he became the father of Peleg. 17 After Peleg was born, Eber lived 430 years and had other sons and daughters.

18 When Peleg had lived 30 years, he became the father of Reu. 19 After Reu was born, Peleg lived 209 years and had other sons and daughters.

20 When Reu had lived 32 years, he became the father of Serug. 21 After Serug was born, Reu lived 207 years and had other sons and daughters.

22 When Serug had lived 30 years, he became the father of Nahor. 23 After

Nahor was born, Serug lived 200 years and had other sons and daughters.

24 When Nahor had lived 29 years, he became the father of Terah. 25 After Terah was born, Nahor lived 119 years and had other sons and daughters.

26 After Terah was 70 years old, he became the father of Abram, Nahor and Haran.

The Family Line of Abram

27 Here is the story of Terah's family line.

Terah became the father of Abram, Nahor and Haran. And Haran became the father of Lot. 28 Haran died in the city of Ur in Babylonia, the land where he was born. Haran died while his father Terah was still alive. 29 Abram and Nahor both got married. The name of Abram's wife was Sarai. The name of Nahor's wife was Milkah, the daughter of Haran. Haran was the father of Milkah and Iscah. 30 But Sarai wasn't able to have children.

31 Terah left Ur in Babylon. He took with him his son Abram and his grandson Lot, the son of Haran. Terah also took his daughter-in-law Sarai, the wife of his son Abram. All of them left together to go to Canaan. But when they came to Harran, they made their home there.

32 Terah lived for 205 years. And then he died in Harran.

God Chooses Abram

12 The LORD had said to Abram, "Go from your country, your people and your father's family. Go to the land I will show you.

2 "I will make you into a great
  nation.
  And I will bless you.
I will make your name great.
  You will be a blessing to
  others.
3 I will bless those who bless
  you.
  I will put a curse on anyone
  who puts a curse on you.
All nations on earth
  will be blessed because of
  you."

4 So Abram went, just as the LORD had told him. Lot went with him. Abram was 75 years old when he left Harran. 5 He took his wife Sarai and his nephew Lot. They took all the people and possessions they had acquired in Harran. They started out for the land of Canaan. And they arrived there.

6 Abram traveled through the land. He went as far as the large tree of Moreh at Shechem. At that time the Canaanites were living in the land. 7 The LORD appeared to Abram at Shechem. He said, "I will give this land to your family who comes after you." So Abram built an altar there to honor the LORD, who had appeared to him.

8 From there, Abram went on toward the hills east of Bethel. He set up his tent there. Bethel was to the west, and Ai was to

the east. Abram built an altar there and called on the name of the LORD.

⁹ Then Abram left and continued south toward the Negev Desert.

Abram Goes to Egypt

¹⁰ At that time there was not enough food in the land. So Abram went down to Egypt to live there for a while. ¹¹ As he was about to enter Egypt, he spoke to his wife Sarai. He said, "I know what a beautiful woman you are. ¹² The people of Egypt will see you and say, 'This is his wife.' Then they will kill me. But they will let you live. ¹³ Tell them you are my sister. Then I'll be treated well and my life will be spared because of you."

¹⁴ Abram arrived in Egypt. The Egyptians saw that Sarai was a very beautiful woman. ¹⁵ When Pharaoh's officials saw her, they told Pharaoh how beautiful she was. So she was taken into his palace. ¹⁶ Pharaoh treated Abram well because of her. So Abram gained more sheep and cattle and male and female donkeys. He also gained more male and female servants and some camels.

¹⁷ But the LORD sent terrible sicknesses on Pharaoh and everyone in his palace. The LORD did it because of Abram's wife Sarai. ¹⁸ So Pharaoh sent for Abram. "What have you done to me?" he said. "Why didn't you tell me she was your wife? ¹⁹ Why did you say she was your sister? That's why I took her to be my wife. Now then, here's your wife. Take her and go!" ²⁰ Then Pharaoh gave orders to his men about Abram. They sent him on his way. So he left with his wife and everything he had.

Abram and Lot Separate

13 Abram went up from Egypt to the Negev Desert. He took his wife and everything he had. Lot went with him. ² Abram had become very rich. He had a lot of livestock and silver and gold.

³ Abram left the Negev Desert. He went from place to place until he came to Bethel. Then he came to the place between Bethel and Ai where his tent had been earlier. ⁴ There he called on the name of the LORD at the altar he had built.

⁵ Lot was moving around with Abram. Lot also had flocks and herds and tents. ⁶ But the land didn't have enough food for both Abram and Lot. They had large herds and many servants, so they weren't able to stay together. ⁷ The people who took care of Abram's herds and those who took care of Lot's herds began to argue. The Canaanites and Perizzites were also living in the land at that time.

⁸ So Abram said to Lot, "Let's not argue with each other. The people taking care of your herds and those taking care of mine shouldn't argue with one another either. After all, we're part of the same family. ⁹ Isn't the whole land in front of you? Let's separate. If you go to the left, I'll

go to the right. If you go to the right, I'll go to the left."

¹⁰Lot looked around. He saw that the whole Jordan River valley toward the town of Zoar had plenty of water. It was like the garden of the LORD, like the land of Egypt. This was before the LORD destroyed Sodom and Gomorrah. ¹¹So Lot chose the whole Jordan River valley for himself. Then he started out toward the east. The two men separated. ¹²Abram lived in the land of Canaan. Lot lived among the cities of the Jordan River valley. He set up his tents near Sodom. ¹³The people of Sodom were evil. They were sinning greatly against the LORD.

¹⁴The LORD spoke to Abram after Lot had left him. He said, "Look around from where you are. Look north and south, east and west. ¹⁵I will give you all the land you see. I will give it forever to you and your family who comes after you. ¹⁶I will make them like the dust of the earth. Can dust be counted? If it can, then your family can be counted. ¹⁷Go! Walk through the land. See how long and wide it is. I am giving it to you."

¹⁸So Abram went to live near the large trees of Mamre at Hebron. There he pitched his tents and built an altar to honor the LORD.

Abram Saves Lot

14 Amraphel was the king of Babylon. Arioch was the king of Ellasar. Kedorlaomer was the king of Elam. And Tidal was the king of Goyim. ²They went to war against five other kings. They were Bera king of Sodom, Birsha king of Gomorrah, Shinab king of Admah, Shemeber king of Zeboyim, and the king of Bela. Bela was also called Zoar. ³These five kings all gathered their armies together in the Valley of Siddim. It was also called the valley of the Dead Sea. ⁴For 12 years Kedorlaomer had ruled over them. But in the 13th year they opposed him.

⁵So in the 14th year, Kedorlaomer and the kings who helped him went to war. They won the battle against the Rephaites in Ashteroth Karnaim. They also won the battle against the Zuzites in Ham and the Emites in Shaveh Kiriathaim. ⁶They did the same thing to the Horites in the hill country of Seir. They marched all the way to El Paran near the desert. ⁷Then they turned back and went to En Mishpat. En Mishpat was also called Kadesh. They took over the whole territory of the Amalekites. They also won the battle against the Amorites who were living in Hazezon Tamar.

⁸Then the kings of Sodom, Gomorrah, Admah, Zeboyim and Bela marched out. Bela was also called Zoar. They lined up their armies for battle in the Valley of Siddim. ⁹They got ready to fight against Kedorlaomer king of Elam, Tidal king of Goyim, Amraphel king of Babylonia, and Arioch king of Ellasar. There were four kings against five. ¹⁰The Valley of

Siddim was full of tar pits. The kings of Sodom and Gomorrah ran away from the battle. Some of their men fell into the pits, but the rest escaped to the hills. ¹¹The four kings took all the things that belonged to Sodom and Gomorrah. They also took all their food and then left. ¹²They carried away Abram's nephew Lot and the things he owned. Lot was living in Sodom at that time.

¹³A man escaped and came to report everything to Abram. Abram was a Hebrew. He was living near the large trees of Mamre the Amorite. Mamre was a brother of Eshkol and Aner. All of them helped Abram. ¹⁴Abram heard that Lot had been captured. So he called out his 318 trained men. All of them were sons of his servants. Abram and his men chased their enemies as far as Dan. ¹⁵During the night Abram separated his men into groups. They attacked their enemies and drove them away. They chased them north of Damascus as far as Hobah. ¹⁶Abram took back everything the kings had taken. He brought back his nephew Lot and the things Lot owned. He also brought back the women and the other people.

¹⁷After Abram won the battle over Kedorlaomer and the kings who helped him, he returned home. The king of Sodom came out to meet him in the Valley of Shaveh. It was also called the King's Valley.

¹⁸Melchizedek was the king of Jerusalem. He brought out bread and wine. He was the priest of the Most High God. ¹⁹He gave a blessing to Abram. He said,

"May the Most High God
    bless Abram.
  May the Creator of heaven
    and earth bless him.
²⁰Give praise to the Most High
    God.
  He gave your enemies into
    your hand."

Then Abram gave Melchizedek a tenth of everything.

²¹The king of Sodom said to Abram, "Give me the people. Keep everything else for yourself."

²²But Abram said to the king of Sodom, "I have raised my hand to make a promise to the LORD. He is the Most High God. He is the Creator of heaven and earth. ²³I've said I will not accept anything that belongs to you. I will not take even a thread or the strap of a sandal. You will never be able to say, 'I made Abram rich.' ²⁴I'll accept only what my men have eaten and what belongs to Aner, Eshkol and Mamre. These three men went with me. Let them have their share."

God Makes a Covenant With Abram

15 Some time later, Abram had a vision. The LORD said to him,

"Abram, do not be afraid.
  I am like a shield to you.
  I am your very great
    reward."

²But Abram said, "LORD and King, what can you give me? I still don't have any children. My servant Eliezer comes from Damascus. When I die, he will get everything I own." ³Abram continued, "You haven't given me any children. So this servant of mine will get everything I own."

⁴Then a message from the LORD came to Abram. The LORD said, "When you die, what you have will not go to this man. You will have a son of your own. He will get everything you have." ⁵The LORD took Abram outside and said, "Look up at the sky. Count the stars, if you can." Then he said to him, "That's how many children will be born into your family."

⁶Abram believed the LORD. The LORD was pleased with Abram because he believed. So Abram's faith made him right with the LORD.

⁷He also said to Abram, "I am the LORD. I brought you out of Ur in the land of Babylon. I will give you this land to have as your very own."

⁸But Abram said, "LORD and King, how can I know I will have this land as my own?"

⁹So the LORD said to him, "Bring me a young cow, a goat and a ram. Each must be three years old. Bring a dove and a young pigeon along with them."

¹⁰Abram brought all of them to the LORD. Abram cut them in two and placed the halves opposite each other. But he didn't cut the birds in half. ¹¹Then large birds came down to eat the dead bodies of the animals and birds. But Abram chased the large birds away.

¹²As the sun was going down, Abram fell into a deep sleep. A thick and scary darkness covered him. ¹³Then the LORD said to him, "You can be sure of what I am about to tell you. For 400 years, your family who comes after you will be strangers in another country. They will become slaves there and will be treated badly. ¹⁴But I will punish the nation that makes them slaves. After that, they will leave with many possessions. ¹⁵But you will die in peace. You will join the members of your family who have already died. And you will be buried when you are very old. ¹⁶Your children's grandchildren will come back here. That's because the sin of the Amorites has not yet reached the point where I must punish them."

¹⁷The sun set and it became dark. Then a burning torch and a pot filled with smoking coals appeared. They passed between the pieces of the animals that had been cut in two. ¹⁸On that day the LORD made a covenant with Abram. He said, "I am giving this land to your family who comes after you. It reaches from the River of Egypt to the great Euphrates River. ¹⁹It includes the land of the Kenites, Kenizzites, Kadmonites, ²⁰Hittites, Perizzites and Rephaites. ²¹The Amorites, Canaanites, Girgashites and Jebusites also live there."

Hagar and Ishmael

16 Abram's wife Sarai had never had any children by him. But she had a female slave from Egypt named Hagar. ² So she said to Abram, "The LORD has kept me from having children. Go and sleep with my slave. Maybe I can have a family through her."

Abram agreed to what Sarai had said. ³ His wife Sarai gave him her slave Hagar to be his wife. That was after he had been living in Canaan for ten years. ⁴ Then he slept with Hagar, and she became pregnant.

When Hagar knew she was pregnant, she began to look down on the woman who owned her. ⁵ Then Sarai said to Abram, "It's your fault that I'm suffering like this. I put my slave in your arms. Now that she knows she's pregnant, she looks down on me. May the LORD judge between you and me. May he decide which of us is right."

⁶ "Your slave belongs to you," Abram said. "Do with her what you think is best." Then Sarai treated Hagar badly. So Hagar ran away from her.

⁷ The angel of the LORD found Hagar near a spring of water in the desert. The spring was beside the road to Shur. ⁸ The angel said, "Hagar, you are Sarai's slave. Where have you come from? Where are you going?"

"I'm running away from my owner Sarai," she answered.

⁹ Then the angel of the LORD told her, "Go back to the woman who owns you. Obey her." ¹⁰ The angel continued, "I will give you and your family many children. There will be more of them than anyone can count."

¹¹ The angel of the LORD also said to her,

"You are now pregnant
   and will have a son.
You will name him Ishmael,
   because the LORD has
      heard about your
      suffering.
¹² He will be like a wild donkey.
   He will use his power
      against everyone,
   and everyone will be
      against him.
   He will not get along with
      any of his family."

¹³ She gave a name to the LORD who spoke to her. She called him "You are the God who sees me." That's because she said, "I have now seen the One who sees me." ¹⁴ That's why the well was named Beer Lahai Roi. It's still there, between Kadesh and Bered.

¹⁵ So Hagar had a son by Abram and Abram gave him the name Ishmael. ¹⁶ Abram was 86 years old when Hagar had Ishmael by him.

The Covenant of Circumcision

17 When Abram was 99 years old, the LORD appeared to him. He said, "I am the Mighty God. Walk faithfully with me. Live in a way that pleases me. ² I will now act on my covenant between me and you. I will greatly increase the number of your children after you."

³ Abram fell with his face to the ground. God said to him, ⁴ "This is my covenant with you. You will be the father of many nations. ⁵ You will not be called Abram anymore. Your name will be Abraham, because I have made you a father of many nations. ⁶ I will greatly increase the number of your children after you. Nations and kings will come from you. ⁷ I will make my covenant with you last forever. It will be between me and you and your family after you for all time to come. I will be your God. And I will be the God of all your family after you. ⁸ You are now living in Canaan as an outsider. But I will give you the whole land of Canaan. You will own it forever and so will all your family after you. And I will be their God."

⁹ Then God said to Abraham, "You must keep my covenant. You and your family after you must keep it for all time to come. ¹⁰ Here is my covenant that you and your family after you must keep. You and every male among you must be circumcised. ¹¹ That will be the sign of the covenant between me and you. ¹² It must be done for all time to come. Every male among you who is eight days old must be circumcised. That includes those who are born into your own family or outside it. It also includes those bought with money from a stranger. ¹³ So any male born into your family or bought with your money must be circumcised. My covenant will last forever. Your body will have the mark of my covenant on it. ¹⁴ Any male who has not been circumcised will be separated from his people. He has broken my covenant."

¹⁵ God also said to Abraham, "Do not continue to call your wife by the name Sarai. Her name will be Sarah. ¹⁶ I will give her my blessing. You can be sure that I will give you a son by her. I will bless her so that she will be the mother of nations. Kings of nations will come from her."

¹⁷ Abraham fell with his face to the ground. He laughed and said to himself, "Can a 100-year-old man have a son? Can Sarah have a child at the age of 90?" ¹⁸ Abraham said to God, "I really wish Ishmael could receive your blessing!"

¹⁹ Then God said, "Yes, I will bless Ishmael. But your wife Sarah will have a son by you. And you will name him Isaac. I will establish my covenant with him. That covenant will last forever. It will be for Isaac and his family after him. ²⁰ I have heard what you said about Ishmael. I will surely bless him. I will make his family very large. He will be the father of 12 rulers. And I will make him into a great nation. ²¹ But I will establish my covenant with Isaac. By this time next year, Sarah will have a son by you." ²² When God had finished speaking with Abraham, God left him.

²³ On that same day Abraham circumcised his son Ishmael. He also circumcised every male who was born into his family or

bought with his money. He did exactly as God had told him. [24] Abraham was 99 years old when he was circumcised. [25] His son Ishmael was 13. [26] Abraham and his son Ishmael were both circumcised on that same day. [27] And every male in Abraham's household was circumcised along with him. That included those born into his family or bought from a stranger.

Three Men Visit Abraham

18 The LORD appeared to Abraham near the large trees of Mamre. Abraham was sitting at the entrance to his tent. It was the hottest time of the day. [2] Abraham looked up and saw three men standing nearby. So he quickly left the entrance to his tent to greet them. He bowed low to the ground.

[3] He said, "My lord, if you are pleased with me, don't pass me by. [4] Let me get you some water. Then all of you can wash your feet and rest under this tree. [5] Let me get you something to eat to give you strength. Then you can go on your way. I want to do this for you now that you have come to me."

"All right," they answered. "Do as you say."

[6] So Abraham hurried into the tent to Sarah. "Quick!" he said. "Get about 36 pounds of the finest flour. Prepare it and bake some bread."

[7] Then he ran over to the herd. He picked out a choice, tender calf. He gave it to a servant, who hurried to prepare it.

[8] Then he brought some butter and milk and the calf that had been prepared. He served them to the three men. While they ate, he stood near them under a tree.

[9] "Where is your wife Sarah?" they asked him.

"Over there in the tent," he said.

[10] Then one of them said, "I will surely return to you about this time next year. Your wife Sarah will have a son."

Sarah was listening at the entrance to the tent, which was behind him. [11] Abraham and Sarah were already very old. Sarah was too old to have a baby. [12] So she laughed to herself. She thought, "I'm worn out, and my husband is old. Can I really know the joy of having a baby?"

[13] Then the LORD said to Abraham, "Why did Sarah laugh? Why did she say, 'Will I really have a baby, now that I am old?' [14] Is anything too hard for me? I will return to you at the appointed time next year. Sarah will have a son."

[15] Sarah was afraid. So she lied and said, "I didn't laugh."

But the LORD said, "Yes, you laughed."

Abraham Pleads for Sodom

[16] The men got up to leave. They looked down toward Sodom. Abraham walked along with them to see them on their way. [17] Then the LORD said, "Should I hide from Abraham what I am about to do? [18] He will certainly become a great and

powerful nation. All nations on earth will be blessed because of him. [19] I have chosen him. He must direct his children to live in the way that pleases me. And he must direct the members of his family after him to do the same. So he must guide all of them in doing what is right and fair. Then I, the LORD, will do for Abraham what I have promised him."

[20] The LORD also said, "The cries against Sodom and Gomorrah are very great. Their sin is so bad [21] that I will go down and see for myself. I want to see if what they have done is as bad as the cries that have reached me. If it is not, then I will know."

[22] The men turned away and went toward Sodom. But Abraham remained standing in front of the LORD. [23] Then Abraham came up to him. He said, "Will you sweep away godly people along with those who are evil? [24] What if there are 50 godly people in the city? Will you really sweep it away? Won't you spare the place because of the 50 godly people in it? [25] You would never kill godly people along with those who are evil, would you? Would you treat them all alike? You would never do anything like that! Won't the Judge of the whole earth do what is right?"

[26] The LORD said, "If I find 50 godly people in the city of Sodom, I will spare it. I will spare the whole place because of them."

[27] Then Abraham spoke up again. He said, "I have been very bold to speak to the Lord. After all, I'm only dust and ashes. [28] What if the number of godly people is five fewer than 50? Will you destroy the whole city because there are five fewer people?"

"If I find 45 there," he said, "I will not destroy it."

[29] Once again Abraham spoke to him. He asked, "What if only 40 are found there?"

He said, "If there are 40, I will not do it."

[30] Then Abraham said, "Lord, please don't be angry with me. Let me speak. What if only 30 can be found there?"

He answered, "If I find 30, I will not do it."

[31] Abraham said, "I have been very bold to speak to the Lord. What if only 20 can be found there?"

He said, "If I find 20, I will not destroy it."

[32] Then he said, "Lord, please don't be angry with me. Let me speak just one more time. What if only ten can be found there?"

He answered, "If I find ten, I will not destroy it."

[33] When the LORD had finished speaking with Abraham, he left. And Abraham returned home.

The LORD Destroys Sodom and Gomorrah

19 The two angels arrived at Sodom in the evening. Lot was sitting near the gate of the city. When Lot saw the angels, he got up to greet them. He bowed down with his face to the ground. ²"My lords," he said, "please come to my house. You can wash your feet and spend the night there. Then you can go on your way early in the morning."

"No," they answered. "We'll spend the night in the town square."

³But Lot wouldn't give up. So they went with him and entered his house. He prepared a meal for them. He baked bread without using yeast. And they ate. ⁴Before Lot and his guests had gone to bed, all the men came from every part of the city of Sodom. Young and old men alike surrounded the house. ⁵They called out to Lot. They said, "Where are the men who came to you tonight? Bring them out to us. We want to have sex with them."

⁶Lot went outside to meet them. He shut the door behind him. ⁷He said, "No, my friends. Don't do such an evil thing. ⁸Look, I have two daughters that no man has ever slept with. I'll bring them out to you now. Then do to them what you want to. But don't do anything to these men. I've brought them inside so they can be safe."

⁹"Get out of our way!" the men of Sodom replied to Lot. "You came here as an outsider. Now you want to act like a judge! We'll treat you worse than them." They kept trying to force Lot to open the door. Then they moved forward to break it down.

¹⁰But the the angels inside reached out and pulled Lot back into the house and shut the door. ¹¹Then they made the men who were at the door of the house blind. They blinded both young and old men so that they couldn't find the door.

¹²The two angels said to Lot, "Do you have any other family members here? Do you have sons-in-law, sons, daughters or any other relatives in the city? Get them out of here! ¹³We are going to destroy this place. Many have cried out to the LORD against the people of this city. So he has sent us to destroy it."

¹⁴Then Lot went out and spoke to his sons-in-law. They had promised to marry his daughters. He said, "Hurry up! Get out of this place! The LORD is about to destroy the city!" But his sons-in-law thought he was joking.

¹⁵The sun was coming up. So the angels tried to get Lot to leave. They said, "Hurry up! Take your wife and your two daughters who are here. Get out! If you don't, you will be swept away when the city is destroyed."

¹⁶Lot didn't move right away. So the men grabbed him by the hand. They also took hold of the hands of his wife and two daughters. They led all of them safely out of the city. The LORD had mercy on them. ¹⁷As soon as the angels had brought them out, one of them spoke. He said, "Run for your lives! Don't look back! Don't stop anywhere in

the valley! Run to the mountains! If you don't, you will be swept away!"

¹⁸ But Lot said to them, "No, my lords! Please! ¹⁹ You have done me a big favor. You have been very kind to me by sparing my life. But I can't run to the mountains. I won't be able to escape this horrible thing that's going to happen. And then I'll die. ²⁰ Look, here's a town near enough to run to. It's small. Let me run to it. It's very small, isn't it? Then my life will be spared."

²¹ The Lord said to Lot, "All right. I will also give you what you are asking for. I will not destroy the town you are talking about. ²² But run there quickly. I can't do anything until you reach it." The town was named Zoar. Zoar means Small.

²³ By the time Lot reached Zoar, the sun had risen over the land. ²⁴ Then the Lord sent down burning sulfur. It came down like rain on Sodom and Gomorrah. It came from the Lord. It came out of the sky. ²⁵ The Lord destroyed these cities and the whole valley. All the people who were living in the cities were wiped out. So were the plants in the land. ²⁶ But Lot's wife looked back. When she did, she became a pillar made out of salt.

²⁷ Early the next morning Abraham got up. He returned to the place where he had stood in front of the Lord. ²⁸ He looked down toward Sodom and Gomorrah and the whole valley. He saw thick smoke rising from the land. It looked like smoke from a furnace.

²⁹ So when God destroyed the cities of the valley, he showed concern for Abraham. He brought Lot out safely when he destroyed the cities where Lot had lived.

Lot and His Daughters

³⁰ Lot and his two daughters left Zoar. They went to live in the mountains because Lot was afraid to stay in Zoar. So he and his daughters lived in a cave. ³¹ One day the older daughter spoke to the younger one. She said, "Our father is old. People all over the earth have men to marry and have children with. We do not. ³² So let's get our father to drink wine. Then we can sleep with him. We can use our father to continue our family line."

³³ That night they got their father to drink wine. Then the older daughter went in and slept with him. He wasn't aware when she lay down or when she got up.

³⁴ The next day the older daughter spoke to the younger one again. She said, "Last night I slept with my father. Let's get him to drink wine again tonight. Then you go in and sleep with him. We can use our father to continue our family line." ³⁵ So they got their father to drink wine that night also. Then the younger daughter slept with him. Again he wasn't aware when she lay down or when she got up.

³⁶ So both of Lot's daughters

became pregnant by their father. ³⁷ The older daughter had a son. She named him Moab. He's the father of the Moabites of today. ³⁸ The younger daughter also had a son. She named him Ben-Ammi. He's the father of the Ammonites of today.

Abraham and Abimelek

20 Abraham moved south into the Negev Desert. He lived between Kadesh and Shur. For a while he stayed in Gerar. ² There Abraham said about his wife Sarah, "She's my sister." Then Abimelek, the king of Gerar, sent for Sarah and took her.

³ So God appeared to Abimelek in a dream one night. He said to him, "You are as good as dead because of the woman you have taken. She is already married."

⁴ But Abimelek hadn't gone near her. So he said, "Lord, will you destroy a nation that hasn't done anything wrong? ⁵ Didn't Abraham say to me, 'She's my sister'? And didn't she also say, 'He's my brother'? I had no idea I was doing anything wrong."

⁶ Then God spoke to him in the dream. He said, "Yes, I know you had no idea you were doing anything wrong. So I have kept you from sinning against me. That is why I did not let you touch her. ⁷ Now return the man's wife to him. He is a prophet. So he will pray for you, and you will live. But what if you do not return her? Then you can be sure that you and all your people will die."

⁸ Early the next morning Abimelek sent for all his officials. When he told them everything that had happened, they were really afraid. ⁹ Then Abimelek called Abraham in. Abimelek said, "What have you done to us? Have I done something wrong to you? Why have you brought so much guilt on me and my kingdom? You have done things to me that should never be done." ¹⁰ Abimelek also asked Abraham, "Why did you do this?"

¹¹ Abraham replied, "I thought, 'There is no respect for God in this place. They will kill me because of my wife.' ¹² Besides, she really is my sister. She's the daughter of my father, but not the daughter of my mother. And she became my wife. ¹³ God had me wander away from my father's house. So I said to her, 'Here is how you can show your love to me. Everywhere we go, say about me, "He's my brother." ' "

¹⁴ Then Abimelek gave Abraham sheep and cattle and male and female slaves. He also returned his wife Sarah to him. ¹⁵ Abimelek said, "Here is my land. Live anywhere you want to."

¹⁶ He said to Sarah, "I'm giving your brother 25 pounds of silver. This will show everyone with you that I am sorry for what I did to you. You haven't done anything wrong."

¹⁷ Then Abraham prayed to God, and God healed Abimelek. He also healed his wife and his female slaves so they could have

children again. ¹⁸ The LORD had kept all the women in Abimelek's house from having children. He had done it because of Abraham's wife Sarah.

Isaac Is Born

21 The LORD was gracious to Sarah, just as he had said he would be. The LORD did for Sarah what he had promised to do. ² Sarah became pregnant. She had a son by Abraham when he was old. The child was born at the exact time God had promised. ³ Abraham gave the name Isaac to the son Sarah had by him. ⁴ When his son Isaac was eight days old, Abraham circumcised him. He did it exactly as God had commanded him. ⁵ Abraham was 100 years old when his son Isaac was born to him.

⁶ Sarah said, "God has given laughter to me. Everyone who hears about this will laugh with me." ⁷ She also said, "Who would have said to Abraham that Sarah would breast-feed children? But I've had a son by him when he is old."

Abraham Sends Hagar and Ishmael Away

⁸ Isaac grew. The time came for his mother to stop breast-feeding him. On that day Abraham prepared a big celebration. ⁹ But Sarah saw Ishmael making fun of Isaac. Ishmael was the son Hagar had by Abraham. Hagar was Sarah's Egyptian slave. ¹⁰ Sarah said to Abraham, "Get rid of that slave woman! Get rid of her son! That woman's son will never have a share of the family's property. All of it belongs to my son Isaac."

¹¹ What Sarah said upset Abraham very much. After all, Ishmael was his son. ¹² But God said to Abraham, "Do not be so upset about the boy and your slave Hagar. Listen to what Sarah tells you, because your family line will continue through Isaac. ¹³ I will also make the son of your slave into a nation. I will do it because he is your child."

¹⁴ Early the next morning Abraham got some food and a bottle of water. The bottle was made out of animal skin. He gave the food and water to Hagar, placing them on her shoulders. Then he sent her away with the boy. She went on her way and wandered in the Desert of Beersheba.

¹⁵ When the water in the bottle was gone, she put the boy under a bush. ¹⁶ Then she sat down about as far away as a person can shoot an arrow. She thought, "I can't stand to watch the boy die." As she sat there, she began to sob.

¹⁷ God heard the boy crying. Then the angel of God called out to Hagar from heaven. He said to her, "What is the matter, Hagar? Do not be afraid. God has heard the boy crying as he lies there. ¹⁸ Lift up the boy and take him by the hand. I will make him into a great nation."

¹⁹ Then God opened Hagar's eyes, and she saw a well of water. So she went and filled the

bottle with water and gave the boy a drink. ²⁰God was with the boy as he grew up. He lived in the desert and learned to shoot a bow and arrow. ²¹While he was living in the Desert of Paran, his mother got a wife for him from Egypt.

The Agreement at Beersheba

²²At that time Abimelek and his army commander, Phicol, spoke to Abraham. They said to Abraham, "God is with you in everything you do. ²³Now make a promise to me here while God is watching. Give me your word that you will treat me fairly. Promise that you will treat my children and their children the same way. I've been kind to you. Now you be kind to me and the country where you are living as an outsider."

²⁴Abraham said, "I give you my word that I'll do it."

²⁵Then Abraham complained to Abimelek that his servants had taken over a well of water. ²⁶But Abimelek said, "I don't know who has done this. You didn't tell me. And today is the first time I heard about it."

²⁷So Abraham gave Abimelek sheep and cattle. The two men came to an agreement. ²⁸Then Abraham picked out seven female lambs from his flock. ²⁹Abimelek asked Abraham, "What's the meaning of these seven female lambs? Why have you picked them out and set them apart?"

³⁰Abraham replied, "Accept the seven lambs from me. They will be a witness that I dug this well."

³¹So that place was named Beersheba. That's because there the two men came to an agreement.

³²After the agreement had been made at Beersheba, Abimelek went back to the land of the Philistines. His army commander, Phicol, went with him. ³³Abraham planted a tamarisk tree in Beersheba. There he called on the name of the LORD, the God who lives forever. ³⁴Abraham stayed in the land of the Philistines for a long time.

God Tests Abraham

22 Some time later God tested Abraham. He said to him, "Abraham!"

"Here I am," Abraham replied.

²Then God said, "Take your son, your only son. He is the one you love. Take Isaac. Go to the place called Moriah. Give your son to me there as a burnt offering. Sacrifice him on the mountain I will show you."

³Early the next morning Abraham got up and loaded his donkey. He took two of his servants and his son Isaac with him. He cut enough wood for the burnt offering. Then he started out for the place God had shown him. ⁴On the third day Abraham saw the place a long way off. ⁵He said to his servants, "Stay here with the donkey. I and the boy will go over there and worship. Then we'll come back to you."

⁶Abraham had his son Isaac carry the wood for the burnt offering. He himself carried the fire and the knife. And the two of them walked on together. ⁷Then Isaac said to his father Abraham, "Father?"

"Yes, my son?" Abraham replied.

"The fire and wood are here," Isaac said. "But where is the lamb for the burnt offering?"

⁸Abraham answered, "God himself will provide the lamb for the burnt offering, my son." And the two of them walked on together.

⁹They reached the place God had shown Abraham. There Abraham built an altar. He arranged the wood on it. He tied up his son Isaac. Abraham placed him on the altar, on top of the wood. ¹⁰Then he reached out his hand. He picked up the knife to kill his son. ¹¹But the angel of the LORD called out to him from heaven. He said, "Abraham! Abraham!"

"Here I am," Abraham replied.

¹²"Do not lay a hand on the boy," he said. "Do not harm him. Now I know that you would do anything for God. You have not held back from me your son, your only son."

¹³Abraham looked around. There in a bush he saw a ram caught by its horns. He went over and took the ram. He sacrificed it as a burnt offering instead of his son. ¹⁴So Abraham named that place The LORD Will Provide. To this day people say, "It will be provided on the mountain of the LORD."

¹⁵The angel of the LORD called out to Abraham from heaven a second time. ¹⁶He said, "I am giving you my word that I will bless you. I will bless you because of what you have done," announces the LORD. "You have not held back your son, your only son. ¹⁷So I will certainly bless you. I will make the children born into your family as many as the stars in the sky. I will make them as many as the grains of sand on the seashore. They will take over the cities of their enemies. ¹⁸All nations on earth will be blessed because of your children. All these things will happen because you have obeyed me."

¹⁹Then Abraham returned to his servants. They started out together for Beersheba. And Abraham stayed in Beersheba.

Nahor's Sons

²⁰Some time later Abraham was told, "Milkah has become a mother. She has had sons by your brother Nahor.

²¹Uz was born first. Then came his brother Buz. Kemuel was born next. He became the father of Aram.

²²Milkah's other sons are Kesed, Hazo, Pildash, Jidlaph and Bethuel."

²³Bethuel became the father of Rebekah.

Milkah had the eight sons by Abraham's brother Nahor.

²⁴Nahor had a concubine named Reumah. She also had sons.

They were Tebah, Gaham, Tahash and Maakah.

Sarah Dies

23 Sarah lived to be 127 years old. ²She died at Kiriath Arba. Kiriath Arba is also called Hebron. It's in the land of Canaan. Sarah's death made Abraham very sad. He went to the place where her body was lying. There he wept over her.

³Then Abraham got up from beside his wife's body. He said to the Hittites, ⁴"I'm an outsider. I'm a stranger among you. Sell me some property where I can bury those in my family who die. Then I can bury my wife."

⁵The Hittites replied to Abraham, ⁶"Sir, listen to us. You are a mighty prince among us. Bury your wife in the best place we have to bury our dead. None of us will refuse to sell you a place to bury her."

⁷Then Abraham bowed down in front of the Hittites, the people of the land. ⁸He said to them, "If you are willing to let me bury my wife, then listen to me. Speak to Zohar's son Ephron for me. ⁹Ask him to sell me the cave of Machpelah. It belongs to him and is at the end of his field. Ask him to sell it to me for the full price. I want it as a place to bury my dead wife among you."

¹⁰Ephron the Hittite was sitting there among his people. He replied to Abraham. All of the Hittites who had come to the gate of his city heard him. ¹¹"No, sir," Ephron said. "Listen to me. I will give you the field. I'll also give you the cave that's in the field. I will give it to you in front of my people. Bury your wife."

¹²Again Abraham bowed down in front of the people of the land. ¹³He spoke to Ephron so they could hear him. He said, "Please listen to me. I'll pay the price of the field. Accept it from me. Then I can bury my wife there."

¹⁴Ephron answered Abraham, ¹⁵"Sir, listen to me. The land is worth ten pounds of silver. But what's that between the two of us? Bury your wife."

¹⁶Abraham agreed to Ephron's offer. He weighed out for Ephron the price he had named. The Hittites there had heard the amount. The price was ten pounds of silver. Abraham measured it by the weights that were used by merchants.

¹⁷So Ephron sold his field to Abraham. The field was in Machpelah near Mamre. Abraham bought the field and the cave that was in it. He also bought all the trees that were inside the borders of the field. Everything was sold ¹⁸to Abraham as his property. He bought it in front of all the Hittites who had come to the gate of the city. ¹⁹Then Abraham buried his wife Sarah. He buried her in the cave in the field of Machpelah near Mamre in the land of Canaan. Mamre is at Hebron. ²⁰So

the field and the cave that was in it were sold to Abraham by the Hittites. The property became a place to bury those who died in his family.

Abraham's Servant Finds a Wife for Isaac

24 By that time Abraham was very old. The Lord had blessed Abraham in every way. ²The best servant in his house was in charge of everything Abraham had. Abraham said to him, "Put your hand under my thigh. ³The Lord is the God of heaven and the God of earth. I want you to make a promise to me in his name. I'm living among the people of Canaan. But I want you to promise me that you won't get a wife for my son from their daughters. ⁴Instead, promise me that you will go to my country and to my own relatives. Get a wife for my son Isaac from there."

⁵The servant asked Abraham, "What if the woman doesn't want to come back with me to this land? Then should I take your son back to the country you came from?"

⁶"Make sure you don't take my son back there," Abraham said. ⁷"The Lord, the God of heaven, took me away from my father's family. He brought me out of my own land. He made me a promise. He said, 'I will give this land to your family after you.' The Lord will send his angel ahead of you. So you will be able to get a wife for my son from there. ⁸The woman may not want to come back with you. If she doesn't, you will be free from your promise. But don't take my son back there." ⁹So the servant put his hand under Abraham's thigh. He promised to do what his master wanted.

¹⁰The servant chose ten of his master's camels and left. He loaded the camels with all kinds of good things from his master. He started out for Aram Naharaim and made his way to the town of Nahor. ¹¹He stopped near the well outside the town. There he made the camels get down on their knees. It was almost evening, the time when women go out to get water.

¹²Then he prayed, "Lord, you are the God of my master Abraham. Make me successful today. Be kind to my master Abraham. ¹³I'm standing beside this spring. The daughters of the people who live in the town are coming out here to get water. ¹⁴I will speak to a young woman. I'll say to her, 'Please lower your jar so I can have a drink.' Suppose she says, 'Have a drink of water, and I'll get some for your camels too.' Then let her be the one you have chosen for your servant Isaac. That's how I'll know you have been kind to my master."

¹⁵Before he had finished praying, Rebekah came out. She was carrying a jar on her shoulder. She was the daughter of Milkah's son Bethuel. Milkah was the wife of Abraham's brother Nahor. ¹⁶The young woman was very beautiful. No man had ever

slept with her. She went down to the spring. She filled her jar and came up again.

17 The servant hurried to meet her. He said, "Please give me a little water from your jar."

18 "Have a drink, sir," she said. She quickly lowered the jar to her hands and gave him a drink.

19 After she had given him a drink, she said, "I'll get water for your camels too. I'll keep doing it until they have had enough to drink." 20 So she quickly emptied her jar into the stone tub. Then she ran back to the well to get more water. She got enough for all his camels. 21 The man didn't say a word. He watched her closely. He wanted to learn whether the Lord had given him success on the journey he had made.

22 The camels finished drinking. Then the man took out a gold nose ring. It weighed about a fifth of an ounce. He also took out two gold bracelets. They weighed about four ounces. 23 Then he asked, "Whose daughter are you? And please tell me something else. Is there room in your father's house for us? Can we spend the night there?"

24 She answered, "I'm the daughter of Bethuel. He's the son Milkah had by Nahor." 25 She continued, "We have plenty of straw and feed for your camels. We also have room for you to spend the night."

26 Then the man bowed down and worshiped the Lord. 27 He said, "I praise the Lord, the God of my master Abraham. The Lord hasn't stopped being kind and faithful to my master. The Lord has led me on this journey. He has brought me to the house of my master's relatives."

28 The young woman ran home. She told her mother's family what had happened. 29 Rebekah had a brother named Laban. He hurried out to the spring to meet the man. 30 Laban had seen the nose ring. He had seen the bracelets on his sister's arms. And he had heard Rebekah tell what the man had said to her. So Laban went out to the man. He found him standing by the camels near the spring. 31 "The Lord has given you his blessing," he said. "So come with me. Why are you standing out here? I've prepared my house for you. I also have a place for the camels."

32 So the man went to the house. The camels were unloaded. Straw and feed were brought for the camels. And water was brought for him and his men to wash their feet. 33 Then food was placed in front of him. But he said, "I won't eat until I've told you what I have to say."

"Then tell us," Laban said.

34 So he said, "I am Abraham's servant. 35 The Lord has blessed my master greatly, and he has become rich. The Lord has given him sheep and cattle, silver and gold. He has also given him male and female servants, camels and donkeys. 36 My master's wife Sarah had a son by him when she was old. He has

given that son everything he owns. ³⁷My master made me promise him. He said, 'I'm living in the land of the people of Canaan. But promise me that you won't get a wife for my son from their daughters. ³⁸Instead, go to my father's family and to my own relatives. Get a wife for my son there.'

³⁹"Then I asked my master, 'What if the woman won't come back with me?'

⁴⁰"He replied, 'I have walked faithfully with the Lord. He will send his angel with you. He will give you success on your journey. So you will be able to get a wife for my son. She will be from my own relatives and from my father's family. ⁴¹When you go to my relatives, suppose they refuse to give her to you. Then you will be free from the promise you made to me.'

⁴²"Today I came to the spring. I said, 'Lord, you are the God of my master Abraham. Please make me successful on this journey I've made. ⁴³I'm standing beside this spring. A young woman will come out to get water. I'll say to her, "Please let me drink a little water from your jar." ⁴⁴Suppose she says, "Have a drink of water, and I'll get some for your camels too." Then let her be the one the Lord has chosen for my master's son.'

⁴⁵"Before I finished praying in my heart, Rebekah came out. She was carrying a jar on her shoulder. She went down to the spring and got water. I said to her, 'Please give me a drink.'

⁴⁶"She quickly lowered her jar from her shoulder. She said, 'Have a drink, and I'll get water for your camels too.' So I drank. She also got water for the camels.

⁴⁷"I asked her, 'Whose daughter are you?'

"She said, 'The daughter of Bethuel. He's the son Milkah had by Nahor.'

"Then I put the ring in her nose. I put the bracelets on her arms. ⁴⁸And I bowed down and worshiped the Lord. I praised the Lord, the God of my master Abraham. He had led me on the right road. He had led me to get for my master's son the granddaughter of my master's brother. ⁴⁹Now will you be kind and faithful to my master? If you will, tell me. And if you won't, tell me. Then I'll know which way to turn."

⁵⁰Laban and Bethuel answered, "The Lord has done all of this. We can't say anything to you one way or the other. ⁵¹Here is Rebekah. Take her and go. Let her become the wife of your master's son, just as the Lord has said."

⁵²Abraham's servant heard what they said. So he bowed down to the Lord with his face to the ground. ⁵³He brought out gold and silver jewelry and articles of clothing. He gave all of them to Rebekah. He also gave expensive gifts to her brother and her mother. ⁵⁴Then Abraham's servant and the men who were with him ate and drank. They spent the night there.

When they got up the next

morning, Abraham's servant said, "Send me back to my master."

⁵⁵ But her brother and her mother replied, "Let the young woman stay with us ten days or so. Then you can go."

⁵⁶ But he said to them, "Don't make me wait. The LORD has given me success on my journey. Send me on my way so I can go to my master."

⁵⁷ Then they said, "Let's get Rebekah and ask her about it." ⁵⁸ So they sent for her and asked, "Will you go with this man?"

"Yes, I'll go," she said.

⁵⁹ So they sent their sister Rebekah on her way with Abraham's servant and his men. They also sent Rebekah's servant with her. ⁶⁰ And they gave Rebekah their blessing. They said to her,

> "Dear sister, may your family
>   grow
>   by thousands and
>   thousands.
> May they take over
>   the cities of their enemies."

⁶¹ Then Rebekah and her female servants got ready. They got on their camels to go back with the man. So Abraham's servant took Rebekah and left.

⁶² By that time Isaac had come from Beer Lahai Roi. He was living in the Negev Desert. ⁶³ One evening he went out to the field. He wanted to spend some time thinking. When he looked up, he saw camels approaching. ⁶⁴ Rebekah also looked up and saw Isaac. She got down from her camel. ⁶⁵ She asked the servant, "Who is that man in the field coming to meet us?"

"He's my master," the servant answered. So she covered her face with her veil.

⁶⁶ Then the servant told Isaac everything he had done. ⁶⁷ Isaac brought Rebekah into the tent that had belonged to his mother Sarah. And he married Rebekah. She became his wife, and he loved her. So Isaac was comforted after his mother died.

Abraham Dies

25 Abraham had married another woman. Her name was Keturah. ² She had Zimran, Jokshan, Medan, Midian, Ishbak and Shuah by Abraham. ³ Jokshan was the father of Sheba and Dedan. The children of Dedan were the Ashurites, the Letushites and the Leummites. ⁴ The sons of Midian were Ephah, Epher, Hanok, Abida and Eldaah. All of them were members of Keturah's family line.

⁵ Abraham left everything he owned to Isaac. ⁶ But while he was still living, he gave gifts to the sons of his concubines. Then he sent them away from his son Isaac. He sent them to the land of the east.

⁷ Abraham lived a total of 175 years. ⁸ He took his last breath and died when he was very old. He had lived a very long time. Then he joined the members of his family who had already died. ⁹ Abraham's sons

Isaac and Ishmael buried him. They put his body in the cave of Machpelah near Mamre. It was in the field of Ephron, the son of Zohar the Hittite. [10] Abraham had bought the field from the Hittites. He was buried there with his wife Sarah. [11] After Abraham died, God blessed his son Isaac. At that time Isaac was living near Beer Lahai Roi.

The Sons of Ishmael

[12] Here is the story of the family line of Abraham's son Ishmael. Hagar gave birth to Ishmael by Abraham. Hagar was Sarah's slave from Egypt.

[13] Here are the names of the sons of Ishmael. They are listed in the order they were born.

Nebaioth was Ishmael's oldest son. Then came Kedar, Adbeel, Mibsam, [14] Mishma, Dumah, Massa, [15] Hadad, Tema, Jetur, Naphish and Kedemah.

[16] All of them were Ishmael's sons. They were rulers of 12 tribes. They all lived in their own settlements and camps.

[17] Ishmael lived a total of 137 years. Then he took his last breath and died. He joined the members of his family who had already died. [18] His children settled in the area between Havilah and Shur. It was near the eastern border of Egypt, as you go toward Ashur. Ishmael's children weren't friendly toward any of the tribes related to them.

Jacob and Esau

[19] Here is the story of the family line of Abraham's son Isaac.

Abraham was the father of Isaac. [20] Isaac was 40 years old when he married Rebekah. She was the daughter of Bethuel, the Aramean from Paddan Aram. She was also the sister of Laban, the Aramean.

[21] Rebekah couldn't have children. So Isaac prayed to the Lord for her. And the Lord answered his prayer. His wife Rebekah became pregnant. [22] The babies struggled with each other inside her. She said, "Why is this happening to me?" So she went to ask the Lord what she should do.

[23] The Lord said to her,

"Two nations are in your
    body.
  Two tribes that are now
    inside you will be
    separated.
One nation will be stronger
    than the other.
  The older son will serve the
    younger one."

[24] The time came for Rebekah to have her babies. There were twin boys in her body. [25] The first one to come out was red. His whole body was covered with hair. So they named him Esau. [26] Then his brother came out. His hand was holding onto Esau's heel. So he was named Jacob. Isaac was 60 years old when Rebekah had them.

²⁷ The boys grew up. Esau became a skillful hunter. He liked the open country. But Jacob was content to stay at home among the tents. ²⁸ Isaac liked the meat of wild animals. So Esau was his favorite son. But Rebekah's favorite was Jacob.

²⁹ One day Jacob was cooking some stew. Esau came in from the open country. He was very hungry. ³⁰ He said to Jacob, "Quick! I'm very hungry! Let me have some of that red stew!" That's why he was also named Edom.

³¹ Jacob replied, "First sell me the rights that belong to you as the oldest son in the family."

³² "Look, I'm dying of hunger," Esau said. "What good are those rights to me?"

³³ But Jacob said, "First promise to sell me your rights." So Esau promised to do it. He sold Jacob all the rights that belonged to him as the oldest son.

³⁴ Then Jacob gave Esau some bread and some lentil stew. Esau ate and drank. Then he got up and left.

So Esau didn't value the rights that belonged to him as the oldest son.

Isaac and Abimelek

26 There was very little food in the land. The same thing had been true earlier, in Abraham's time. Isaac went to Abimelek in Gerar. Abimelek was the king of the Philistines. ² The Lord appeared to Isaac and said, "Do not go down to Egypt. Live in the land where I tell you to live. ³ Stay there for a while. I will be with you and give you my blessing. I will give all these lands to you and your children after you. And I will keep my word that I gave to your father Abraham. ⁴ I will make your children after you as many as the stars in the sky. And I will give them all these lands. All nations on earth will be blessed because of your children. ⁵ I will do all these things because Abraham obeyed me. He did everything I required. He kept my commands, my rules and my instructions." ⁶ So Isaac stayed in Gerar.

⁷ The men of that place asked him about his wife. He said, "She's my sister." He was afraid to say, "She's my wife." He thought, "The men of this place might kill me because of Rebekah. She's a beautiful woman."

⁸ Isaac had been there a long time. One day Abimelek, the king of the Philistines, looked down from a window. He saw Isaac hugging and kissing his wife Rebekah. ⁹ So Abimelek sent for Isaac. He said, "She's really your wife, isn't she? Why did you say she was your sister?"

Isaac answered him, "I thought I might lose my life because of her."

¹⁰ Then Abimelek said, "What have you done to us? What if one of the men slept with your wife? Then you would have made us guilty."

¹¹ So Abimelek gave orders to all the people. He said, "Anyone

who harms this man or his wife will surely be put to death."

¹²Isaac planted crops in that land. That same year he gathered 100 times more than he planted. That was because the LORD blessed him. ¹³Isaac became rich. His wealth continued to grow until he became very rich. ¹⁴He had many flocks and herds and servants. Isaac had so much that the Philistines became jealous of him. ¹⁵So they stopped up all the wells the servants of his father Abraham had dug. They filled them with dirt.

¹⁶Then Abimelek said to Isaac, "Move away from us. You have become too powerful for us."

¹⁷So Isaac moved away from there. He camped in the Valley of Gerar, where he made his home. ¹⁸Isaac opened up the wells again. They had been dug in the time of his father Abraham. The Philistines had stopped them up after Abraham died. Isaac gave the wells the same names his father had given them.

¹⁹Isaac's servants dug wells in the valley. There they discovered fresh water. ²⁰But the people of Gerar who took care of their own herds argued with the people who took care of Isaac's herds. "The water is ours!" the people of Gerar said. So Isaac named the well Esek. That's because they argued with him. ²¹Then Isaac's servants dug another well. They argued about that one too. So he named it Sitnah. ²²Isaac moved on from there and dug another well. But no one argued about that one. So he named it Rehoboth. He said, "Now the LORD has given us room. Now we will be successful in the land."

²³From there Isaac went up to Beersheba. ²⁴That night the LORD appeared to him. He said, "I am the God of your father Abraham. Do not be afraid. I am with you. I will bless you. I will increase the number of your children because of my servant Abraham."

²⁵Isaac built an altar there and worshiped the LORD. There he set up his tent. And there his servants dug a well.

²⁶During that time, Abimelek had come to him from Gerar. His personal adviser, Ahuzzath, had come with him. So had his army commander, Phicol. ²⁷Isaac asked them, "Why have you come to me? You were angry with me and sent me away."

²⁸They answered, "We saw clearly that the LORD was with you. So we said, 'There should be an agreement between us and you.' We want to make a peace treaty with you. ²⁹Give us your word that you won't harm us. We didn't harm you. We always treated you well. We sent you away peacefully. And now the LORD has blessed you."

³⁰Then Isaac had a feast prepared for them. They ate and drank. ³¹Early the next morning the men made a treaty with each other. Then Isaac sent the men of Gerar on their way. And they left peacefully.

³² That day Isaac's servants came to him. They told him about the well they had dug. They said, "We've found water!" ³³ So he named it Shibah. To this day the name of the town has been Beersheba.

Jacob Takes Esau's Blessing

³⁴ When Esau was 40 years old, he got married to Judith. She was the daughter of Beeri the Hittite. Esau also married Basemath. She was the daughter of Elon the Hittite. ³⁵ Isaac and Rebekah became very upset because Esau had married Hittite women.

27 Isaac had become old. His eyes were so weak he couldn't see anymore. One day he called for his older son Esau. He said to him, "My son."

"Here I am," he answered.

² Isaac said, "I'm an old man now. And I don't know when I'll die. ³ Now then, get your weapons. Get your bow and arrows. Go out to the open country. Hunt some wild animals for me. ⁴ Prepare for me the kind of tasty food I like. Bring it to me to eat. Then I'll give you my blessing before I die."

⁵ Rebekah was listening when Isaac spoke to his son Esau. Esau left for the open country. He went to hunt for a wild animal and bring it back. ⁶ Then Rebekah said to her son Jacob, "Look, I heard your father speaking to your brother Esau. ⁷ He said, 'Bring me a wild animal. Prepare some tasty food for me to eat. Then I'll give you my blessing before I die. The LORD will be my witness.' " ⁸ Rebekah continued, "My son, listen carefully. Do what I tell you. ⁹ Go out to the flock. Bring me two of the finest young goats. I will prepare tasty food for your father. I'll make it just the way he likes it. ¹⁰ I want you to take it to your father to eat. Then he'll give you his blessing before he dies."

¹¹ Jacob said to his mother Rebekah, "My brother Esau's body is covered with hair. But my skin is smooth. ¹² What if my father touches me? He would know I was trying to trick him. He would curse me instead of giving me a blessing."

¹³ His mother said to him, "My son, let the curse be on me. Just do what I say. Go and get the goats for me."

¹⁴ So he went and got the goats. He brought them to his mother. And she prepared some tasty food. She made it just the way his father liked it. ¹⁵ The clothes of her older son Esau were in her house. She took Esau's best clothes and put them on her younger son Jacob. ¹⁶ She covered his hands with the skins of the goats. She also covered the smooth part of his neck with them. ¹⁷ Then she handed to her son Jacob the tasty food and the bread she had made.

¹⁸ He went to his father and said, "My father."

"Yes, my son," Isaac answered. "Who is it?"

¹⁹ Jacob said to his father, "I'm your oldest son Esau. I've done as you told me. Please sit up.

Eat some of my wild meat. Then give me your blessing."

²⁰ Isaac asked his son, "How did you find it so quickly, my son?"

"The LORD your God gave me success," he replied.

²¹ Then Isaac said to Jacob, "Come near so I can touch you, my son. I want to know whether you really are my son Esau."

²² Jacob went close to his father. Isaac touched him and said, "The voice is the voice of Jacob. But the hands are the hands of Esau." ²³ Isaac didn't recognize Jacob. Jacob's hands were covered with hair like those of his brother Esau. So Isaac blessed him. ²⁴ "Are you really my son Esau?" he asked.

"I am," Jacob replied.

²⁵ Isaac said, "My son, bring me some of your wild meat to eat. Then I'll give you my blessing."

Jacob brought it to him. So Isaac ate. Jacob also brought some wine. And Isaac drank. ²⁶ Then Jacob's father Isaac said to him, "Come here, my son. Kiss me."

²⁷ So Jacob went to him and kissed him. When Isaac smelled the clothes, he gave Jacob his blessing. He said,

"It really is the smell of my
     son.
     It's like the smell of a field
         that the LORD has blessed.
²⁸ May God give you dew from
     heaven.
     May he give you the
         richness of the earth.
     May he give you plenty of
         grain and fresh wine.

²⁹ May nations serve you.
     May they bow down to you.
     Rule over your brothers.
     May the sons of your
         mother bow down to you.
     May those who curse you be
         cursed.
     And may those who bless
         you be blessed."

³⁰ When Isaac finished blessing him, Jacob left his father. Just then his brother Esau came in from hunting. ³¹ He too prepared some tasty food. He brought it to his father. Then Esau said to him, "My father, please sit up. Eat some of my wild meat. Then give me your blessing."

³² His father Isaac asked him, "Who are you?"

"I'm your son," he answered. "I'm Esau, your oldest son."

³³ Isaac began to shake all over. He said, "Then who hunted a wild animal and brought it to me? I ate it just before you came. I gave him my blessing. And he will certainly be blessed!"

³⁴ Esau heard his father's words. Then he yelled loudly and bitterly. He said to his father, "Bless me! Bless me too, my father!"

³⁵ But Isaac said, "Your brother came and tricked me. He took your blessing."

³⁶ Esau said, "Isn't Jacob just the right name for him? This is the second time he has taken advantage of me. First, he took my rights as the oldest son. And now he's taken my blessing!" Then Esau asked, "Haven't you saved any blessing for me?"

³⁷ Isaac answered Esau, "I've made him ruler over you. I've made all his relatives serve him. And I've provided him with grain and fresh wine. So what can I possibly do for you, my son?"

³⁸ Esau said to his father, "Do you have only one blessing, my father? Bless me too, my father!" Then Esau wept loudly.

³⁹ His father Isaac answered him,

"You will live far away from
 the fruit of the earth.
You will live far away from
 the dew of heaven above.
⁴⁰ You will live by using the
 sword.
And you will serve your
 brother.
But you will grow restless.
 Then you will throw off the
 heavy load
 he has caused you to
 carry."

⁴¹ Esau was angry with Jacob. He was angry because of the blessing his father had given to Jacob. He said to himself, "The days of sorrow over my father's death are near. Then I'll kill my brother Jacob."

⁴² Rebekah was told what her older son Esau had said. So she sent for her younger son Jacob. She said to him, "Your brother Esau is planning to get back at you by killing you. ⁴³ Now then, my son, do what I say. Run away at once to my brother Laban in Harran. ⁴⁴ Stay with him until your brother's anger calms down. ⁴⁵ When he forgets what you did to him, I'll let you know. Then you can come back from there. Why should I lose both of you in one day?"

⁴⁶ Then Rebekah spoke to Isaac. She said, "I'm sick of living because of Esau's Hittite wives. Suppose Jacob also marries a Hittite woman. If he does, my life won't be worth living."

28 So Isaac called for Jacob and blessed him. Then he commanded him, "Don't get married to a Canaanite woman. ² Go at once to Paddan Aram. Go to the house of your mother's father Bethuel. Find a wife for yourself there. Take her from among the daughters of your mother's brother Laban. ³ May the Mighty God bless you. May he give you children. May he make your family larger until you become a community of nations. ⁴ May he give you and your children after you the blessing he gave to Abraham. Then you can take over the land where you now live as an outsider. It's the land God gave to Abraham." ⁵ Isaac sent Jacob on his way. Jacob went to Paddan Aram. He went to Laban, the son of Bethuel the Aramean. Laban was Rebekah's brother. And Rebekah was the mother of Jacob and Esau.

⁶ Esau found out that Isaac had blessed Jacob and had sent him to Paddan Aram. Isaac wanted him to get a wife from there. Esau heard that when Isaac blessed Jacob, he commanded him, "Don't get married to a woman from Canaan." ⁷ Esau

also learned that Jacob had obeyed his father and mother and had gone to Paddan Aram. [8] Then Esau realized how much his father Isaac disliked Canaanite women. [9] So he went to Ishmael and married Mahalath. She was the sister of Nebaioth and the daughter of Abraham's son Ishmael. Esau added her to the wives he already had.

Jacob Has a Dream at Bethel

[10] Jacob left Beersheba and started out for Harran. [11] He reached a certain place and stopped for the night. The sun had already set. He took one of the stones there and placed it under his head. Then he lay down to sleep. [12] In a dream he saw a stairway standing on the earth. Its top reached to heaven. The angels of God were going up and coming down on it. [13] The LORD stood beside the stairway. He said, "I am the LORD. I am the God of your grandfather Abraham and the God of Isaac. I will give you and your children after you the land you are lying on. [14] They will be like the dust of the earth that can't be counted. They will spread out to the west and to the east. They will spread out to the north and to the south. All nations on earth will be blessed because of you and your children after you. [15] I am with you. I will watch over you everywhere you go. And I will bring you back to this land. I will not leave you until I have done what I have promised you."

[16] Jacob woke up from his sleep. Then he thought, "The LORD is surely in this place. And I didn't even know it." [17] Jacob was afraid. He said, "How holy this place is! This must be the house of God. This is the gate of heaven."

[18] Early the next morning Jacob took the stone he had placed under his head. He set it up as a sacred stone. And he poured olive oil on top of it. [19] He named that place Bethel. But the city used to be called Luz.

[20] Then Jacob made a promise. He said, "May God be with me. May he watch over me on this journey I'm taking. May he give me food to eat and clothes to wear. [21] May he do as he has promised so that I can return safely to my father's home. Then you, LORD, will be my God. [22] This stone I've set up as a sacred stone will be God's house. And I'll give you a tenth of everything you give me."

Jacob Arrives in Paddan Aram

29 Then Jacob continued on his journey. He came to the land where the eastern tribes lived. [2] There he saw a well in the open country. Three flocks of sheep were lying near it. The flocks were given water from the well. The stone over the opening of the well was large. [3] All the flocks would gather there. The shepherds would roll the stone away from the well's opening. They would give water to the sheep. Then they would put the stone back in its place over the opening of the well.

⁴Jacob asked the shepherds, "My friends, where are you from?"

"We're from Harran," they replied.

⁵He said to them, "Do you know Nahor's grandson Laban?"

"Yes, we know him," they answered.

⁶Then Jacob asked them, "How is he?"

"He's fine," they said. "Here comes his daughter Rachel with the sheep."

⁷"Look," he said, "the sun is still high in the sky. It's not time for the flocks to be brought together. Give water to the sheep and take them back to the grasslands."

⁸"We can't," they replied. "We have to wait until all the flocks are brought together. The stone has to be rolled away from the opening of the well. Then we'll give water to the sheep."

⁹He was still talking with them when Rachel came with her father's sheep. It was her job to take care of the flock. ¹⁰Rachel was the daughter of Laban, Jacob's uncle. When Jacob saw Rachel with Laban's sheep, he went over to the well. He rolled the stone away from the opening. He gave water to his uncle's sheep. ¹¹Jacob kissed Rachel. Then he began to cry because he was so happy. ¹²He had told Rachel he was a relative of her father. He had also said he was Rebekah's son. Rachel ran and told her father what Jacob had said.

¹³As soon as Laban heard the news about his sister's son Jacob, he hurried to meet him. Laban hugged Jacob and kissed him. Then Laban brought him to his home. There Jacob told him everything. ¹⁴Then Laban said to him, "You are my own flesh and blood."

Jacob Marries Leah and Rachel

Jacob stayed with Laban for a whole month. ¹⁵Then Laban said to him, "You are one of my relatives. But is that any reason for you to work for me for nothing? Tell me what your pay should be."

¹⁶Laban had two daughters. The name of the older one was Leah. And the name of the younger one was Rachel. ¹⁷Leah was plain, but Rachel was beautiful. She had a nice figure. ¹⁸Jacob was in love with Rachel. He said to Laban, "I'll work for you for seven years so I can marry your younger daughter Rachel."

¹⁹Laban said, "It's better for me to give her to you than to some other man. Stay here with me." ²⁰So Jacob worked for seven years so he could marry Rachel. But they seemed like only a few days to him because he loved her so much.

²¹Then Jacob said to Laban, "Give me my wife. I've completed my time. I want to sleep with her."

²²So Laban brought all the people of the place together and had a feast prepared. ²³But when evening came, he gave his daughter Leah to Jacob. And

Jacob slept with her. ²⁴ Laban gave his female servant Zilpah to his daughter as her servant.

²⁵ When Jacob woke up the next morning, there was Leah next to him! So he said to Laban, "What have you done to me? I worked for you so I could marry Rachel, didn't I? Why did you trick me?"

²⁶ Laban replied, "It isn't our practice here to give the younger daughter to be married before the older one. ²⁷ Complete this daughter's wedding week. Then we'll give you the younger one also. But you will have to work for another seven years."

²⁸ So Jacob completed the week with Leah. Then Laban gave him his daughter Rachel to be his wife. ²⁹ Laban gave his female servant Bilhah to his daughter Rachel as her servant. ³⁰ Jacob slept with Rachel also. He loved Rachel more than he loved Leah. And he worked for Laban for another seven years.

Jacob Becomes the Father of Many Children

³¹ The LORD saw that Jacob didn't love Leah as much as he loved Rachel. So he let Leah have children. But Rachel wasn't able to have children. ³² Leah became pregnant. She had a son. She named him Reuben. She said, "The LORD has seen me suffer. Surely my husband will love me now."

³³ She became pregnant again. She had a son. Then she said, "The LORD heard that Jacob doesn't love me very much.

That's why the LORD gave me this one too." So she named him Simeon.

³⁴ She became pregnant again. She had a son. Then she said, "Now at last my husband will value me. I have had three sons by him." So the boy was named Levi.

³⁵ She became pregnant again. She had a son. Then she said, "This time I'll praise the LORD." So she named him Judah. Then she stopped having children.

30 Rachel saw that she wasn't having any children by Jacob. So she became jealous of her sister. She said to Jacob, "Give me children, or I'll die!"

² Jacob became angry with her. He said, "Do you think I'm God? He's the one who has kept you from having children."

³ Then she said, "Here's my servant Bilhah. Sleep with her so that she can have children for me. Then I too can have a family through her."

⁴ So Rachel gave Jacob her servant Bilhah as a wife. Jacob slept with her. ⁵ And Bilhah became pregnant. She had a son by him. ⁶ Then Rachel said, "God has stood up for my rights. He has listened to my prayer and given me a son." So she named him Dan.

⁷ Rachel's servant Bilhah became pregnant again. She had a second son by Jacob. ⁸ Then Rachel said, "I've had a great struggle with my sister. Now I've won." So she named him Naphtali.

⁹Leah saw that she had stopped having children. So she gave her servant Zilpah to Jacob as a wife. ¹⁰Leah's servant Zilpah had a son by Jacob. ¹¹Then Leah said, "What good fortune!" So she named him Gad.

¹²Leah's servant Zilpah had a second son by Jacob. ¹³Then Leah said, "I'm so happy! The women will call me happy." So she named him Asher.

¹⁴While the wheat harvest was being gathered, Reuben went out into the fields. He found some mandrake plants. He brought them to his mother Leah. Rachel said to Leah, "Please give me some of your son's mandrakes."

¹⁵But Leah said to her, "Isn't it enough that you took my husband away? Are you going to take my son's mandrakes too?"

Rachel said, "All right. Jacob can sleep with you tonight if you give me your son's mandrakes."

¹⁶Jacob came in from the fields that evening. Leah went out to meet him. "You have to sleep with me tonight," she said. "I've traded my son's mandrakes for that time with you." So he slept with her that night.

¹⁷God listened to Leah. She became pregnant and had a fifth son by Jacob. ¹⁸Then Leah said, "God has rewarded me because I gave my female servant to my husband." So she named the boy Issachar.

¹⁹Leah became pregnant again. She had a sixth son by Jacob. ²⁰Then Leah said, "God has given me a priceless gift. This time my husband will treat me with honor. I've had six sons by him." So she named the boy Zebulun.

²¹Some time later she had a daughter. She named her Dinah.

²²Then God listened to Rachel. He showed concern for her. He made it possible for her to have children. ²³She became pregnant and had a son. Then she said, "God has taken away my shame." ²⁴She said, "May the LORD give me another son." So she named him Joseph.

Jacob Becomes the Owner of Large Flocks

²⁵After Rachel had Joseph, Jacob spoke to Laban. He said, "Send me on my way. I want to go back to my own home and country. ²⁶Give me my wives and children. I worked for you to get them. So I'll be on my way. You know how much work I've done for you."

²⁷But Laban said to him, "If you are pleased with me, stay here. I've discovered that the LORD has blessed me because of you." ²⁸He continued, "Name your pay. I'll give it to you."

²⁹Jacob said to him, "You know how hard I've worked for you. You know that your livestock has done better under my care. ³⁰You had only a little before I came. But that little has become a lot. The LORD has blessed you everywhere I've been. But when can I do something for my own family?"

³¹"What should I give you?" Laban asked.

"Don't give me anything," Jacob replied. "Just do one thing for me. Then I'll go on taking care of your flocks and watching over them. ³² Let me go through all your flocks today. Let me remove every speckled or spotted sheep. Let me remove every dark-colored lamb. Let me remove every speckled or spotted goat. They will be my pay. ³³ My honesty will be a witness about me in days to come. It will be a witness every time you check on what you have paid me. Suppose I have a goat that doesn't have speckles or spots. Or suppose I have a lamb that isn't dark colored. Then it will be considered stolen."

³⁴ "I agree," said Laban. "Let's do what you have said." ³⁵ That same day Laban removed all the male goats that had stripes or spots. He removed all the female goats that had speckles or spots. They were the ones that had white on them. He also removed all the dark-colored lambs. He had his sons take care of them. ³⁶ Then he put a journey of three days between himself and Jacob. But Jacob continued to take care of the rest of Laban's flocks.

³⁷ Jacob took freshly cut branches from poplar, almond and plane trees. He made white stripes on the branches by peeling off their bark. ³⁸ Then he placed the peeled branches in all the stone tubs where the animals drank water. He placed them there so they would be right in front of the flocks when they came to drink. The flocks were ready to mate when they came to drink. ³⁹ So they mated in front of the branches. And the flocks gave birth to striped, speckled or spotted little ones. ⁴⁰ Jacob put the little ones of the flock to one side by themselves. But he made the older ones face the striped and dark-colored animals that belonged to Laban. In that way, he made separate flocks for himself. He didn't put them with Laban's animals. ⁴¹ Every time the stronger females were ready to mate, Jacob would place the branches in the stone tubs. He would place them in front of the animals so they would mate near the branches. ⁴² But if the animals were weak, he wouldn't place the branches there. So the weak animals went to Laban. And the strong ones went to Jacob. ⁴³ That's how Jacob became very rich. He became the owner of large flocks. He also had many male and female servants. And he had many camels and donkeys.

Jacob Runs Away From Laban

31 Jacob heard what Laban's sons were saying. "Jacob has taken everything our father owned," they said. "He has gained all this wealth from what belonged to our father." ² Jacob noticed that Laban's feelings toward him had changed.

³ Then the Lord spoke to Jacob. He said, "Go back to your father's land and to your relatives. I will be with you."

[4] So Jacob sent word to Rachel and Leah. He told them to come out to the fields where his flocks were. [5] He said to them, "I see that your father's feelings toward me have changed. But the God of my father has been with me. [6] You know that I've worked for your father with all my strength. [7] But your father has cheated me. He has changed my pay ten times. In spite of everything that's happened, God hasn't let him harm me. [8] Sometimes Laban would say, 'The speckled ones will be your pay.' Then all the flocks had little ones with speckles. At other times he would say, 'The striped ones will be your pay.' Then all the flocks had little ones with stripes. [9] So God has taken away your father's livestock and given them to me.

[10] "Once during the mating season I had a dream. In my dream I looked and saw male goats mating with the flock. The goats had stripes, speckles or spots. [11] The angel of God said to me in the dream, 'Jacob.' I answered, 'Here I am.' [12] He said, 'Look around you. See the male goats mating with the flock. All of them have stripes, speckles or spots. That's because I have seen everything that Laban has been doing to you. [13] I am the God of Bethel. That is where you poured olive oil on a sacred stone. There you made a promise to me. Now leave this land. Go back to your own land.'"

[14] Rachel and Leah replied, "Do we still have any share of our father's property? [15] Doesn't our father think of us as outsiders? First he sold us. Now he has used up what he was paid for us. [16] All the wealth God took away from our father really belongs to us and our children. So do what God has told you to do."

[17] Then Jacob put his children and wives on camels. [18] He drove all his livestock ahead of him. He also took with him everything he had acquired in Paddan Aram. He left to go to his father Isaac in the land of Canaan.

[19] Laban had gone to clip the wool from his sheep. While he was gone, Rachel stole the statues of the family gods that belonged to her father. [20] And that's not all. Jacob tricked Laban, the Aramean. He didn't tell him he was running away. [21] So Jacob ran off with everything he had. He crossed the Euphrates River. And he headed for the hill country of Gilead.

Laban Chases Jacob

[22] On the third day Laban was told that Jacob had run away. [23] He took his relatives with him and went after Jacob. Seven days later he caught up with him in the hill country of Gilead. [24] Then God came to Laban, the Aramean, in a dream at night. He said to him, "Be careful. Do not say anything to Jacob, whether it is good or bad."

[25] Jacob had set up his tent in the hill country of Gilead. That's where Laban caught up with him. Laban and his relatives

camped there too. ²⁶Laban said to Jacob, "What have you done? You have tricked me. You have taken my daughters away like prisoners of war. ²⁷Why did you run away in secret and trick me? Why didn't you tell me? Then I could have sent you away happily. We could have sung to the music of tambourines and harps. ²⁸You didn't even let me kiss my grandchildren and my daughters goodbye. You have done a foolish thing. ²⁹I have the power to harm you. But last night the God of your father spoke to me. He said, 'Be careful. Do not say anything to Jacob, whether it is good or bad.' ³⁰Now you have run away. You longed to go back to your father's home. But why did you have to steal the statues of my gods?"

³¹Jacob answered Laban, "I was afraid. I thought you would take your daughters away from me by force. ³²But if you find anyone who has the statues of your gods, that person will not remain alive. While our relatives are watching, look for yourself. See if there's anything of yours here with me. If you find anything belonging to you, take it." But Jacob didn't know that Rachel had stolen the statues.

³³So Laban went into Jacob's tent and Leah's tent. He went into the tent of their two female servants. But he didn't find anything. After he came out of Leah's tent, he entered Rachel's tent. ³⁴Rachel was the one who had taken the statues of Laban's family gods. She had put them inside her camel's saddle. She was sitting on them. Laban searched the whole tent. But he didn't find anything.

³⁵Rachel said to her father, "I'm sorry, sir. I can't get up for you right now. But don't be angry with me. I'm having my monthly period." So he searched everywhere but couldn't find the statues of his gods.

³⁶Jacob was very angry with Laban. "What is my crime?" he asked. "What have I done to you that you hunt me down like this? ³⁷You have searched through all my things. What have you found that belongs to your family? Put it here in front of your relatives and mine. Let them decide between the two of us.

³⁸"I've been with you for 20 years now. The little ones of your sheep and goats were not dead when they were born. I haven't eaten rams from your flocks. ³⁹I didn't bring you animals torn apart by wild beasts. I made up for the loss myself. Also, you made me pay for anything stolen by day or night. ⁴⁰And what was my life like? The heat burned me in the daytime. And it was so cold at night that I froze. I couldn't sleep. ⁴¹That's what it was like for the 20 years I was living with you. I worked for 14 years to marry your two daughters. I worked for six years to get my share of your flocks. You changed my pay ten times. ⁴²But the God of my father was with me. He is the God of Abra-

ham and the God Isaac worshiped. If he hadn't been with me, you would surely have sent me away without anything to show for all my work. But God has seen my hard times. He has seen all the work my hands have done. So last night he warned you."

⁴³ Laban answered Jacob, "The women are my daughters. The children are my children. The flocks are my flocks. Everything you see is mine. But what can I do today about these daughters of mine? What can I do about the children they've had? ⁴⁴ Come now. Let's make a formal agreement, you and I. Let it be a witness between us."

⁴⁵ So Jacob set up a stone as a way to remember. ⁴⁶ He said to his relatives, "Get some stones." So they took stones and put them in a pile. And they ate there by it. ⁴⁷ Laban named the pile of stones Jegar Sahadutha. Jacob named it Galeed.

⁴⁸ Laban said, "This pile of stones is a witness between you and me today." That's why it was named Galeed. ⁴⁹ It was also called Mizpah. That's because Laban said, "May the Lord keep watch between you and me when we are away from each other. ⁵⁰ Don't treat my daughters badly. Don't get married to any women besides my daughters. There isn't anyone here to see what we're doing. But remember that God is a witness between you and me."

⁵¹ Laban also said to Jacob, "Here is this pile of stones. And here is this stone I've set up. I've set them up between you and me. ⁵² This pile is a witness. And this stone is a witness. They are witnesses that I won't go past this pile to harm you. And they are witnesses that you won't go past this pile and this stone to harm me. ⁵³ The God of Abraham and Nahor is also the God of their father. May their God decide which of us is right."

So Jacob made a promise using the name of the God his father Isaac worshiped. ⁵⁴ He offered a sacrifice there in the hill country. And he invited his relatives to a meal. After they had eaten, they spent the night there.

⁵⁵ Early the next morning Laban kissed his grandchildren and his daughters. He gave them his blessing. Then he left and returned home.

Jacob Gets Ready to Meet Esau

32 Jacob also went on his way. The angels of God met him. ² Jacob saw them. He said, "This is the army of God!" So he named that place Mahanaim.

³ Jacob sent messengers ahead of him to his brother Esau. Esau lived in the land of Seir. It was also called the country of Edom. ⁴ Jacob told the messengers what to do. He said, "Here's what you must tell my master Esau. 'Your servant Jacob says, "I've been staying with Laban. I've remained there until now. ⁵ I have cattle and donkeys and sheep and goats. I also have male and

female servants. Now I'm sending this message to you. I hope I can please you."' "

⁶The messengers came back to Jacob. They said, "We went to your brother Esau. He's coming now to meet you. He has 400 men with him."

⁷Jacob was very worried and afraid. So he separated the people with him into two groups. He also separated the flocks and herds and camels. ⁸He thought, "Esau might come and attack one group. If he does, the group that's left can escape."

⁹Then Jacob prayed, "You are the God of my grandfather Abraham. You are the God of my father Isaac. LORD, you are the one who said to me, 'Go back to your country and your relatives. Then I will give you success.' ¹⁰You have been very kind and faithful to me. But I'm not worthy of any of this. When I crossed this Jordan River, all I had was my walking stick. But now I've become two camps. ¹¹Please save me from the hand of my brother Esau. I'm afraid he'll come and attack me and the mothers with their children. ¹²But you have said, 'I will surely give you success. I will make your children as many as the grains of sand on the seashore. People will not be able to count them.'"

¹³Jacob spent the night there. He chose a gift for his brother Esau from what he had with him. ¹⁴He chose 200 female goats and 20 male goats. He chose 200 female sheep and 20 male sheep.

¹⁵He chose 30 female camels with their little ones. He chose 40 cows and ten bulls. And he chose 20 female donkeys and ten male donkeys. ¹⁶He put each herd by itself. Then he put his servants in charge of them. He said to his servants, "Go on ahead of me. Keep some space between the herds."

¹⁷Jacob spoke to his servant who was leading the way. He said, "My brother Esau will meet you. He'll ask, 'Who is your master? Where are you going? And who owns all these animals in front of you?' ¹⁸Then say to Esau, 'They belong to your servant Jacob. They are a gift to you from him. And Jacob is coming behind us.'"

¹⁹He also spoke to the second and third servants. He told them and all the others who followed the herds what to do. He said, "Say the same thing to Esau when you meet him. ²⁰Make sure you say, 'Your servant Jacob is coming behind us.'" Jacob was thinking, "I'll make peace with him with these gifts I'm sending on ahead. When I see him later, maybe he'll welcome me." ²¹So Jacob's gifts went on ahead of him. But he himself spent the night in the camp.

Jacob Wrestles With God

²²That night Jacob got up. He took his two wives, his two female servants and his 11 sons and sent them across the Jabbok River. ²³After they had crossed the stream, he sent over everything he owned. ²⁴So Jacob was

left alone. A man wrestled with him until morning. ²⁵ The man saw that he couldn't win. So he touched the inside of Jacob's hip. As Jacob wrestled with the man, Jacob's hip was twisted. ²⁶ Then the man said, "Let me go. It is morning."

But Jacob replied, "I won't let you go unless you bless me."

²⁷ The man asked him, "What is your name?"

"Jacob," he answered.

²⁸ Then the man said, "Your name will not be Jacob anymore. Instead, it will be Israel. You have wrestled with God and with people. And you have won."

²⁹ Jacob said, "Please tell me your name."

But he replied, "Why do you want to know my name?" Then he blessed Jacob there.

³⁰ So Jacob named the place Peniel. He said, "I saw God face to face. But I'm still alive!"

³¹ The sun rose above Jacob as he passed by Peniel. He was limping because of his hip. ³² That's why the Israelites don't eat the meat attached to the inside of an animal's hip. They don't eat it to this day. It's because the inside of Jacob's hip was touched.

Jacob Meets Esau

33 Jacob looked and saw Esau coming with his 400 men! So Jacob separated the children. He put them with Leah, Rachel and the two female servants. ² He put the servants and their children in front. He put Leah and her children next. And he put Rachel and Joseph last. ³ He himself went on ahead. As he came near his brother, he bowed down to the ground seven times.

⁴ But Esau ran to meet Jacob. He hugged him and threw his arms around his neck. He kissed him, and they cried for joy. ⁵ Then Esau looked around and saw the women and children. "Who are these people with you?" he asked.

Jacob answered, "They are the children God has so kindly given to me."

⁶ Then the female servants and their children came near and bowed down. ⁷ Next, Leah and her children came and bowed down. Last of all came Joseph and Rachel. They bowed down too.

⁸ Esau asked, "Why did you send all those herds I saw?"

"I hoped I could do something to please you," Jacob replied.

⁹ But Esau said, "I already have plenty, my brother. Keep what you have for yourself."

¹⁰ "No, please!" said Jacob. "If I've pleased you, accept this gift from me. Seeing your face is like seeing the face of God. You have welcomed me so kindly. ¹¹ Please accept the present that was brought to you. God has given me so much. I have everything I need." Jacob wouldn't give in. So Esau accepted it.

¹² Then Esau said, "Let's be on our way. I'll go with you."

¹³ But Jacob said to him, "You know that the children are

young. You also know that I have to take care of the cows and female sheep that are feeding their little ones. If the animals are driven hard for just one day, all of them will die. ¹⁴So you go on ahead of me. I'll move along only as fast as the flocks and herds and the children can go. I'll go slowly until I come to you in Seir."

¹⁵Esau said, "Then let me leave some of my men with you."

"Why do that?" Jacob asked. "I just hope I've pleased you."

¹⁶So that day Esau started on his way back to Seir. ¹⁷But Jacob went to Sukkoth. There he built a place for himself. He also made shelters for his livestock. That's why the place is named Sukkoth.

¹⁸After Jacob came from Paddan Aram, he arrived safely at the city of Shechem in Canaan. He camped where he could see the city. ¹⁹For 100 pieces of silver he bought a piece of land. He got it from Hamor's sons. Hamor was the father of Shechem. Jacob set up his tent on that piece of land. ²⁰He also set up an altar there. He named it El Elohe Israel.

Simeon and Levi Kill the Men of Shechem

34 Dinah was the daughter Leah had by Jacob. Dinah went out to visit the women of the land. ²Hamor, the Hivite, was the ruler of that area. When his son Shechem saw Dinah, he took her and raped her. ³Then he longed for Jacob's daughter Dinah. He fell in love with her and spoke tenderly to her. ⁴Shechem said to his father Hamor, "Get me that young woman. I want her to be my wife."

⁵Jacob heard that his daughter Dinah had been raped. His sons were in the fields with his livestock. So he did nothing about it until they came home.

⁶Then Shechem's father Hamor went out to talk with Jacob. ⁷Jacob's sons had come in from the fields. They came as soon as they heard what had happened. They were shocked and very angry. Shechem had done a very terrible thing. He had forced Jacob's daughter to have sex with him. He had done something that should never be done in Israel.

⁸But Hamor said to Jacob and his sons, "My son Shechem wants your daughter. Please give her to him to be his wife. ⁹Let your people and ours get married to each other. Give us your daughters as our wives. You can have our daughters as your wives. ¹⁰You can live among us. Here is the land. Live in it. Trade in it. Buy property in it."

¹¹Then Shechem spoke to Dinah's father and brothers. He said, "I want to please you. I'll give you anything you ask for. ¹²Make the price for the bride as high as you want to. I'll pay you whatever you ask. Just give me the young woman. I want to marry her."

¹³Their sister Dinah had been raped. So Jacob's sons lied to Shechem and his father Ha-

mor. [14] They said to them, "We can't do it. We can't give our sister to a man who isn't circumcised. That would bring shame on us. [15] We'll agree, but only on one condition. You will have to become like us. You will have to circumcise all your males. [16] Then we'll give you our daughters as your wives. And we'll take your daughters as our wives. We'll live among you and become one big family with you. [17] But if you won't agree to be circumcised, then we'll take our sister and go."

[18] Their offer seemed good to Hamor and his son Shechem. [19] The young man was the most honored of all his father's family. He didn't lose any time in doing what Dinah's father and brothers had said, because he was delighted with Jacob's daughter. [20] Hamor and his son Shechem went to the city gate. They spoke to the other men there. [21] "These men are friendly toward us," they said. "Let them live in our land. Let them trade in it. The land has plenty of room for them. We can marry their daughters. And they can marry ours. [22] But they will agree to live with us as one big family only on one condition. All our males must be circumcised, just as they are. [23] Won't their livestock and their property belong to us? Won't all their animals become ours? So let's say yes to them. Then they'll live among us."

[24] All the men who went out through the city gate agreed with Hamor and his son Shechem. So every male in the city was circumcised.

[25] Three days later, all of them were still in pain. Then Simeon and Levi took their swords. They were Jacob's sons and Dinah's brothers. They attacked the city when the people didn't expect it. They killed every male. [26] They also used their swords to kill Hamor and his son Shechem. Then they took Dinah from Shechem's house and left. [27] Jacob's other sons found the dead bodies. They robbed the city where their sister had been raped. [28] They took the flocks and herds and donkeys. They took everything in the city and in the fields. [29] They carried everything away. And they took all the women and children. They took away everything in the houses.

[30] Then Jacob said to Simeon and Levi, "You have brought trouble on me. Now I'm like a very bad smell to the Canaanites and Perizzites who live in this land. There aren't many of us. They may join together against me and attack me. Then I and my family will be destroyed."

[31] But they replied, "Should Shechem have treated our sister like a prostitute?"

Jacob Returns to Bethel

35 Then God said to Jacob, "Go up to Bethel and live there. Build an altar there to honor me. That's where I appeared to you when you were running away from your brother Esau."

²So Jacob spoke to his family and to everyone with him. He said, "Get rid of the statues of false gods you have with you. Make yourselves pure by washing and changing your clothes. ³Come, let's go up to Bethel. There I'll build an altar to honor God. He answered me when I was in trouble. He's been with me everywhere I've gone." ⁴So they gave Jacob all the statues of false gods they had. They also gave him their earrings. Jacob buried those things under the oak tree at Shechem. ⁵Then Jacob and everyone with him started out. The terror of God fell on the towns all around them. So no one chased them.

⁶Jacob and all the people with him came to Luz. Luz is also called Bethel. It's in the land of Canaan. ⁷Jacob built an altar at Luz. He named the place El Bethel. There God made himself known to Jacob when he was running away from his brother.

⁸Rebekah's attendant Deborah died. They buried her body under the oak tree outside Bethel. So it was called Allon Bakuth.

⁹After Jacob returned from Paddan Aram, God appeared to him again. And God blessed him. ¹⁰God said to him, "Your name is Jacob. But you will not be called Jacob anymore. Your name will be Israel." So he named him Israel.

¹¹God said to him, "I am the Mighty God. Have children so that there will be many of you. You will become the father of a nation and a community of nations. Your later family will include kings. ¹²I am giving you the land I gave to Abraham and Isaac. I will also give it to your children after you." ¹³Then God left him at the place where he had talked with him.

¹⁴Jacob set up a sacred stone at the place where God had talked with him. He poured out a drink offering on it. He also poured olive oil on it. ¹⁵Jacob named the place Bethel. That's where God had talked with him.

Rachel and Isaac Die

¹⁶They moved on from Bethel. Ephrath wasn't very far away when Rachel began to have a baby. She was having a very hard time of it. ¹⁷The woman who helped her saw that she was having problems. So she said to Rachel, "Don't be afraid. You have another son." ¹⁸But Rachel was dying. As she took her last breath, she named her son Ben-Oni. But his father named him Benjamin.

¹⁹So Rachel died. She was buried beside the road to Ephrath. Ephrath was also called Bethlehem. ²⁰Jacob set up a stone marker over her tomb. To this day, the stone marks the place where Rachel was buried.

²¹Israel moved on again. He set up his tent beyond Migdal Eder. ²²While Israel was living in that area, Reuben went in and slept with Bilhah. She was the concubine of Reuben's father. And Israel heard about it.

Here are the 12 sons Jacob had.

23 Leah was the mother of Reuben, Jacob's oldest son.

Her other sons were Simeon, Levi, Judah, Issachar and Zebulun.

24 The sons of Rachel were Joseph and Benjamin.

25 The sons of Rachel's female servant Bilhah were Dan and Naphtali.

26 The sons of Leah's female servant Zilpah were Gad and Asher.

These were Jacob's sons. They were born in Paddan Aram.

27 Jacob came home to his father Isaac in Mamre. Mamre is near Kiriath Arba, where Abraham and Isaac had stayed. The place is also called Hebron. 28 Isaac lived 180 years. 29 Then he took his last breath and died. He was very old when he joined the members of his family who had already died. His sons Esau and Jacob buried him.

The Family Line of Esau

36 Here is the story of the family line of Esau. Esau was also called Edom.

2 Esau got his wives from among the women of Canaan. He married Adah, the daughter of Elon the Hittite. He also married Oholibamah, the daughter of Anah and the granddaughter of Zibeon the Hivite. 3 And he married Basemath, the daughter of Ishmael and the sister of Nebaioth.

4 Adah had Eliphaz by Esau. Basemath had Reuel. 5 Oholibamah had Jeush, Jalam and Korah. All of them were Esau's sons. They were born in Canaan.

6 Esau moved to a land far away from his brother Jacob. Esau took with him his wives, his sons and daughters, and all the people who lived with him. He also took his livestock and all his other animals. He took everything he had acquired in Canaan. 7 Jacob and Esau owned so much that they couldn't remain together. There wasn't enough land for both of them. They had too much livestock. 8 So Esau made his home in the hill country of Seir. Esau was also called Edom.

9 Here is the story of the family line of Esau. He's the father of the people of Edom. They live in the hill country of Seir.

10 Here are the names of Esau's sons.

They are Eliphaz, the son of Esau's wife Adah, and Reuel, the son of Esau's wife Basemath.

11 The sons of Eliphaz were Teman, Omar, Zepho, Gatam and Kenaz.

12 Esau's son Eliphaz also had a concubine named Timna. She had Amalek by Eliphaz. They were grandsons of Esau's wife Adah.

13 The sons of Reuel were Nahath, Zerah, Shammah and Mizzah. They

were grandsons of Esau's wife Basemath.

¹⁴ Esau's wife Oholibamah was the daughter of Anah and the granddaughter of Zibeon.

She had Jeush, Jalam and Korah by Esau.

¹⁵ Here are the chiefs among Esau's sons.

Eliphaz was Esau's oldest son. The sons of Eliphaz were

Chiefs Teman, Omar, Zepho, Kenaz, ¹⁶ Korah, Gatam and Amalek. They were the chiefs in Edom who were sons of Eliphaz. They were Adah's grandsons.

¹⁷ The sons of Esau's son Reuel were

Chiefs Nahath, Zerah, Shammah and Mizzah. They were the chiefs in Edom who were sons of Reuel. They were grandsons of Esau's wife Basemath.

¹⁸ The sons of Esau's wife Oholibamah were

Chiefs Jeush, Jalam and Korah. They were the chiefs who were sons of Esau's wife Oholibamah. She was Anah's daughter.

¹⁹ That was the family line of Esau. And these were the chiefs. Esau was also called Edom.

²⁰ Seir, the Horite, had sons living in the same area. They were Lotan, Shobal, Zibeon, Anah, ²¹ Dishon, Ezer and Dishan. These sons of Seir in Edom were Horite chiefs.

²² The sons of Lotan were Hori and Homam. Timna was Lotan's sister.

²³ The sons of Shobal were Alvan, Manahath, Ebal, Shepho and Onam.

²⁴ The sons of Zibeon were Aiah and Anah.

He was the Anah who discovered the hot springs of water in the desert. He found them while he was taking care of the donkeys that belonged to his father Zibeon.

²⁵ The children of Anah were Dishon and Oholibamah. Oholibamah was the daughter of Anah.

²⁶ The sons of Dishon were Hemdan, Eshban, Ithran and Keran.

²⁷ The sons of Ezer were Bilhan, Zaavan and Akan.

²⁸ The sons of Dishan were Uz and Aran.

²⁹ The Horite chiefs were Lotan, Shobal, Zibeon, Anah, ³⁰ Dishon, Ezer and Dishan.

They were the Horite chiefs in the land of Seir. They are listed tribe by tribe.

The Rulers of Edom

³¹ Before Israel had a king, there were kings who ruled in Edom.

³² Bela became the king of Edom. Bela was the son of Beor. Bela's city was called Dinhabah.

33 When Bela died, Jobab became the next king. Jobab was the son of Zerah from Bozrah.

34 When Jobab died, Husham became the next king. Husham was from the land of the Temanites.

35 When Husham died, Hadad became the next king. Hadad was the son of Bedad. Hadad had won the battle over Midian in the country of Moab. Hadad's city was called Avith.

36 When Hadad died, Samlah became the next king. Samlah was from Masrekah.

37 When Samlah died, Shaul became the next king. Shaul was from Rehoboth on the river.

38 When Shaul died, Baal-Hanan became the next king. Baal-Hanan was the son of Akbor.

39 When Baal-Hanan died, Hadad became the next king. Hadad's city was called Pau. His wife's name was Mehetabel. She was Matred's daughter. Matred was the daughter of Me-Zahab.

40 Here are the chiefs in the family line of Esau. They are listed by name as chiefs in charge of their tribes and territories. They are Timna, Alvah, Jetheth, 41 Oholibamah, Elah, Pinon, 42 Kenaz, Teman, Mibzar, 43 Magdiel and Iram.

They were the chiefs of Edom. They ruled over their settlements in the land where they lived.

That's the end of the story of the family line of Esau. He was the father of the people of Edom.

Joseph Has Two Dreams

37 Jacob lived in the land of Canaan. It's the land where his father had stayed.

2 Here is the story of the family line of Jacob.

Joseph was a young man. He was 17 years old. He was taking care of the flocks with some of his brothers. They were the sons of Bilhah and the sons of Zilpah, the wives of his father Jacob. Joseph brought their father a bad report about his brothers.

3 Israel loved Joseph more than any of his other sons. That's because Joseph had been born to him when he was old. Israel made him a beautiful robe. 4 Joseph's brothers saw that their father loved him more than any of them. So they hated Joseph. They couldn't even speak one kind word to him.

5 Joseph had a dream. When he told it to his brothers, they hated him even more. 6 He said to them, "Listen to the dream I had. 7 We were tying up bundles of grain out in the field. Suddenly my bundle stood up straight. Your bundles gathered around my bundle and bowed down to it."

8 His brothers said to him, "Do

you plan to be king over us? Will you really rule over us?" So they hated him even more because of his dream. They didn't like what he had said.

⁹ Then Joseph had another dream. He told it to his brothers. "Listen," he said. "I had another dream. This time the sun and moon and 11 stars were bowing down to me."

¹⁰ He told his father as well as his brothers. Then his father rebuked him. He said, "What about this dream you had? Will your mother and I and your brothers really do that? Will we really come and bow down to the ground in front of you?" ¹¹ His brothers were jealous of him. But his father kept the dreams in mind.

Joseph Is Sold by His Brothers

¹² Joseph's brothers had gone to take care of their father's flocks near Shechem. ¹³ Israel said to Joseph, "As you know, your brothers are taking care of the flocks near Shechem. Come. I'm going to send you to them."

"All right," Joseph replied.

¹⁴ So Israel said to him, "Go to your brothers. See how they are doing. Also see how the flocks are doing. Then come back and tell me." So he sent him away from the Hebron Valley.

Joseph arrived at Shechem. ¹⁵ A man found him wandering around in the fields. He asked Joseph, "What are you looking for?"

¹⁶ He replied, "I'm looking for my brothers. Can you tell me where they are taking care of their flocks?"

¹⁷ "They've moved on from here," the man answered. "I heard them say, 'Let's go to Dothan.'"

So Joseph went to look for his brothers. He found them near Dothan. ¹⁸ But they saw him a long way off. Before he reached them, they made plans to kill him.

¹⁹ "Here comes that dreamer!" they said to one another. ²⁰ "Come. Let's kill him. Let's throw him into one of these empty wells. Let's say that a wild animal ate him up. Then we'll see whether his dreams will come true."

²¹ Reuben heard them talking. He tried to save Joseph from them. "Let's not take his life," he said. ²² "Don't spill any of his blood. Throw him into this empty well here in the desert. But don't harm him yourselves." Reuben said that to save Joseph from them. He was hoping he could take him back to his father.

²³ When Joseph came to his brothers, he was wearing his beautiful robe. They took it away from him. ²⁴ And they threw him into the well. The well was empty. There wasn't any water in it.

²⁵ Then they sat down to eat their meal. As they did, they saw some Ishmaelite traders coming from Gilead. Their camels were loaded with spices, lotion and myrrh. They were on their way to take them down to Egypt.

26 Judah said to his brothers, "What will we gain if we kill our brother and try to cover up what we've done? 27 Come. Let's sell him to these traders. Let's not harm him ourselves. After all, he's our brother. He's our own flesh and blood." Judah's brothers agreed with him.

28 The traders from Midian came by. Joseph's brothers pulled him up out of the well. They sold him to the Ishmaelite traders for eight ounces of silver. Then the traders took him to Egypt.

29 Later, Reuben came back to the empty well. He saw that Joseph wasn't there. He was so upset that he tore his clothes. 30 He went back to his brothers and said, "The boy isn't there! Now what should I do?"

31 Then they got Joseph's beautiful robe. They killed a goat and dipped the robe in the blood. 32 They took the robe back to their father. They said, "We found this. Take a look at it. See if it's your son's robe."

33 Jacob recognized it. He said, "It's my son's robe! A wild animal has eaten him up. Joseph must have been torn to pieces."

34 Jacob tore his clothes. He put on the rough clothing people wear when they're sad. Then he mourned for his son many days. 35 All Jacob's other sons and daughters came to comfort him. But they weren't able to. He said, "I will continue to mourn until I go down into the grave to be with my son." So Joseph's father mourned for him.

36 But the traders from Midian sold Joseph to Potiphar in Egypt. Potiphar was one of Pharaoh's officials. He was the captain of the palace guard.

Judah and Tamar

38 At that time, Judah left his brothers. He went down to stay with a man named Hirah from the town of Adullam. 2 There Judah met the daughter of a man from Canaan. His name was Shua. Judah married her and slept with her. 3 She became pregnant and had a son. They named him Er. 4 She became pregnant again and had another son. She named him Onan. 5 She had still another son. She named him Shelah. He was born at Kezib.

6 Judah got a wife for his oldest son Er. Her name was Tamar. 7 But Judah's oldest son Er was evil in the LORD's eyes. So the LORD put him to death.

8 Then Judah said to Onan, "Sleep with your brother's wife. After all, you are her brother-in-law. So carry out your duty to her. Provide children for your brother." 9 But Onan knew that the children wouldn't belong to him. So every time he slept with his brother's wife, he spilled his semen on the ground. He did it so he wouldn't provide children for his brother. 10 What he did was evil in the LORD's eyes. So the LORD put him to death also.

11 Then Judah spoke to his daughter-in-law Tamar. He said, "Live as a widow in your father's home. Wait there until my son

Shelah grows up." Judah was thinking, "Shelah might die too, just like his brothers." So Tamar went to live in her father's home.

¹² After a long time Judah's wife died. She was the daughter of Shua. When Judah got over his sadness, he went up to Timnah. His friend Hirah from Adullam went with him. Men were clipping the wool from Judah's sheep at Timnah.

¹³ Tamar was told, "Your father-in-law is on his way to Timnah to clip the wool from his sheep." ¹⁴ So she took off her widow's clothes. She covered her face with a veil so people wouldn't know who she was. Then she sat down at the entrance to Enaim. Enaim is on the road to Timnah. Tamar knew that Shelah had grown up. But she hadn't been given to him as his wife.

¹⁵ Judah saw her. He thought she was a prostitute because she had covered her face with a veil. ¹⁶ He didn't realize that she was his daughter-in-law. He went over to her by the side of the road. He said, "Come. Let me sleep with you."

"What will you give me to sleep with you?" she asked.

¹⁷ "I'll send you a young goat from my flock," he said.

"Will you give me something that belongs to you?" she asked. "I'll keep it until you send the goat."

¹⁸ He said, "What should I give you?"

"Give me your official seal and the string that it hangs from," she answered. "And give me your walking stick." So he gave them to her. Then he slept with her. And she became pregnant by him. ¹⁹ After she left, she took off her veil. She put on her widow's clothes again.

²⁰ Judah sent his friend Hirah with the young goat he had promised. He wanted to get back what he had given to the woman. But his friend Hirah couldn't find her. ²¹ He asked the men who lived at Enaim, "Where's the temple prostitute? She used to sit beside the road here."

"There hasn't been any temple prostitute here," they said.

²² So Hirah went back to Judah. He said, "I couldn't find her. Besides, the men who lived there didn't know anything about her. They said, 'There hasn't been any temple prostitute here.'"

²³ Then Judah said, "Let her keep what she has. I don't want people making fun of us. After all, I did send her this young goat. We can't help it if you couldn't find her."

²⁴ About three months later people brought word to Judah. They said, "Your daughter-in-law Tamar is guilty of being a prostitute. Now she's pregnant."

Judah said, "Bring her out! Have her burned to death!"

²⁵ As Tamar was being brought out, she sent a message to her father-in-law. She said, "I am pregnant by the man who owns these." She continued, "Do you recognize this seal and string

and walking stick? Do you know who they belong to?"

²⁶ Judah recognized them. He said, "She's a better person than I am. I should have given her to my son Shelah, but I didn't." Judah never slept with Tamar again.

²⁷ The time came for Tamar to have her baby. There were twin boys inside her. ²⁸ As the babies were being born, one of them stuck out his hand. So the woman helping Tamar took a bright red thread. The woman tied it on the baby's wrist. She said, "This one came out first." ²⁹ But he pulled his hand back, and his brother came out first instead. She said, "Just look at how you have forced your way out!" So he was called Perez. ³⁰ Then his brother, who had the red thread on his wrist, came out. So he was named Zerah.

Joseph and the Wife of Potiphar

39 Joseph had been taken down to Egypt. An Egyptian named Potiphar had bought him from the Ishmaelite traders who had taken him there. Potiphar was one of Pharaoh's officials. He was the captain of the palace guard.

² The LORD was with Joseph. He gave him great success. Joseph lived in Potiphar's house. ³ Joseph's master saw that the LORD was with him. He saw that the LORD made Joseph successful in everything he did. ⁴ So Potiphar was pleased with Joseph and made him his attendant. He put Joseph in charge of his house. He trusted Joseph to take care of everything he owned. ⁵ From that time on, the LORD blessed Potiphar's family and servants because of Joseph. He blessed everything Potiphar had in his house and field. ⁶ So Joseph took good care of everything Potiphar owned. With Joseph in charge, Potiphar didn't have to worry about anything except the food he ate.

Joseph was strong and handsome. ⁷ After a while, his master's wife noticed Joseph. She said to him, "Come to bed with me!"

⁸ But he refused. "My master has put me in charge," he told her. "Now he doesn't have to worry about anything in the house. He trusts me to take care of everything he owns. ⁹ No one in this house is in a higher position than I am. My master hasn't held anything back from me, except you. You are his wife. So how could I do an evil thing like that? How could I sin against God?" ¹⁰ She spoke to Joseph day after day. But he told her he wouldn't go to bed with her. He didn't even want to be with her.

¹¹ One day Joseph went into the house to take care of his duties. None of the family servants was inside. ¹² Potiphar's wife grabbed him by his coat. "Come to bed with me!" she said. But he left his coat in her hand. And he ran out of the house.

¹³ She saw that he had left his coat in her hand and had run out of the house. ¹⁴ So she called her servants. "Look," she said

to them, "this Hebrew slave has been brought here to make fun of us! He came in here to force me to have sex with him. But I screamed for help. [15] He heard my scream. So he left his coat beside me and ran out of the house."

[16] She kept Joseph's coat with her until Potiphar came home. [17] Then she told him her story. She said, "That Hebrew slave you brought us came to me to rape me. [18] But I screamed for help. So he left his coat beside me and ran out of the house."

[19] Potiphar's wife told him, "That's how your slave treated me." When Joseph's master heard her story, he became very angry. [20] So he put Joseph in prison. It was the place where the king's prisoners were kept.

While Joseph was there in the prison, [21] the LORD was with him. He was kind to him. So the man running the prison was pleased with Joseph. [22] He put Joseph in charge of all the prisoners. He made him responsible for everything done there. [23] The man who ran the prison didn't pay attention to anything in Joseph's care. That's because the LORD was with Joseph. He gave Joseph success in everything he did.

The Wine Taster and the Baker

40 Some time later, the Egyptian king's baker and wine taster did something their master didn't like. [2] So Pharaoh became angry with his two officials, the chief wine taster and the chief baker. [3] He put them in prison in the house of the captain of the palace guard. It was the same prison where Joseph was kept. [4] The captain put Joseph in charge of those men. So Joseph took care of them.

Some time passed while they were in prison. [5] Then each of the two men had a dream. The men were the Egyptian king's baker and wine taster. They were being held in prison. Both of them had dreams the same night. Each of their dreams had its own meaning.

[6] Joseph came to them the next morning. He saw that they were sad. [7] They were Pharaoh's officials, and they were in prison with Joseph in his master's house. So he asked them, "Why do you look so sad today?"

[8] "We both had dreams," they answered. "But no one can tell us what they mean."

Then Joseph said to them, "Only God knows what dreams mean. Tell me your dreams."

[9] So the chief wine taster told Joseph his dream. He said to him, "In my dream I saw a vine in front of me. [10] There were three branches on the vine. As soon as it budded, it flowered. And bunches of ripe grapes grew on it. [11] Pharaoh's cup was in my hand. I took the grapes. I squeezed them into Pharaoh's cup. Then I put the cup in his hand."

[12] "Here's what your dream means," Joseph said to him. "The three branches are three

days. [13] In three days Pharaoh will let you out of prison. He'll give your job back to you. And you will put Pharaoh's cup in his hand. That's what you used to do when you were his wine taster. [14] But when everything is going well with you, remember me. Do me a favor. Speak to Pharaoh about me. Get me out of this prison. [15] I was taken away from the land of the Hebrews by force. Even here I haven't done anything to be put in prison for."

[16] The chief baker saw that Joseph had given a positive meaning to the wine taster's dream. So he said to Joseph, "I had a dream too. There were three baskets of bread on my head. [17] All kinds of baked goods for Pharaoh were in the top basket. But the birds were eating them out of the basket on my head."

[18] "Here's what your dream means," Joseph said. "The three baskets are three days. [19] In three days Pharaoh will cut your head off. Then he will stick a pole through your body and set the pole up. The birds will eat your flesh."

[20] The third day was Pharaoh's birthday. He had a feast prepared for all his officials. He brought the chief wine taster and the chief baker out of prison. He did it in front of his officials. [21] He gave the chief wine taster's job back to him. Once again the wine taster put the cup into Pharaoh's hand. [22] But Pharaoh had a pole stuck through the chief baker's body. Then he had the pole set up. Everything happened just as Joseph had told them when he explained their dreams.

[23] But the chief wine taster didn't remember Joseph. In fact, he forgot all about him.

Pharaoh Has Two Dreams

41 When two full years had passed, Pharaoh had a dream. In his dream, he was standing by the Nile River. [2] Seven cows came up out of the river. They looked healthy and fat. They were eating some of the tall grass growing along the river. [3] After them, seven other cows came up out of the Nile. They looked ugly and skinny. They were standing beside the other cows on the riverbank. [4] The ugly, skinny cows ate up the seven cows that looked healthy and fat. Then Pharaoh woke up.

[5] He fell asleep again and had a second dream. In that dream, seven heads of grain were growing on one stem. They were healthy and good. [6] After them, seven other heads of grain came up. They were thin and dried up by the east wind. [7] The thin heads of grain swallowed up the seven healthy, full heads. Then Pharaoh woke up. It had been a dream.

[8] In the morning he was worried. So he sent for all the magicians and wise men of Egypt. Pharaoh told them his dreams. But no one could tell him what they meant.

[9] Then the chief wine taster spoke up. He said to Pharaoh,

"Now I remember that I've done something wrong. ¹⁰Pharaoh was once angry with his servants. He put me and the chief baker in prison. We were in the house of the captain of the palace guard. ¹¹Each of us had a dream the same night. Each dream had its own meaning. ¹²A young Hebrew servant was there with us. He was a servant of the captain of the guard. We told him our dreams. And he explained them to us. He told each of us the meaning of our dreams. ¹³Things turned out exactly as he said they would. I was given back my job. The other man had a pole stuck through his body."

¹⁴So Pharaoh sent for Joseph. He was quickly brought out of the prison. Joseph shaved and changed his clothes. Then he came to Pharaoh.

¹⁵Pharaoh said to Joseph, "I had a dream. No one can tell me what it means. But I've heard that when you hear a dream you can explain it."

¹⁶"I can't do it," Joseph replied to Pharaoh. "But God will give Pharaoh the answer he wants."

¹⁷Then Pharaoh told Joseph what he had dreamed. He said, "I was standing on the bank of the Nile River. ¹⁸Seven cows came up out of the river. They were fat and looked healthy. They were eating the tall grass growing along the river. ¹⁹After them, seven other cows came up. They were bony and very ugly and thin. I had never seen such ugly cows in the whole land of Egypt. ²⁰The thin, ugly cows ate up the seven fat cows that came up first. ²¹But no one could tell that the thin cows had eaten the fat cows. That's because the thin cows looked just as ugly as they had before. Then I woke up.

²²"In my dream I also saw seven heads of grain. They were full and good. They were all growing on one stem. ²³After them, seven other heads of grain came up. They were weak and thin and dried up by the east wind. ²⁴The thin heads of grain swallowed up the seven good heads. I told my dream to the magicians. But none of them could explain it to me."

²⁵Then Joseph said to Pharaoh, "Both of Pharaoh's dreams have the same meaning. God has shown Pharaoh what he is about to do. ²⁶The seven good cows are seven years. And the seven good heads of grain are seven years. Both dreams mean the same thing. ²⁷The seven thin, ugly cows that came up later are seven years. So are the seven worthless heads of grain dried up by the east wind. They are seven years when there won't be enough food.

²⁸"It's just as I said to Pharaoh. God has shown Pharaoh what he's about to do. ²⁹Seven years with plenty of food are coming to the whole land of Egypt. ³⁰But seven years when there won't be enough food will follow them. Then everyone will forget about all the food Egypt had. Terrible hunger will

destroy the land. [31] There won't be anything left to remind people of the years when there was plenty of food in the land. That's how bad the hunger that follows will be. [32] God gave the dream to Pharaoh in two forms. That's because the matter has been firmly decided by God. And it's because God will do it soon.

[33] "So Pharaoh should look for a wise and understanding man. He should put him in charge of the land of Egypt. [34] Pharaoh should appoint officials to be in charge of the land. They should take a fifth of the harvest in Egypt during the seven years when there's plenty of food. [35] They should collect all the extra food of the good years that are coming. Pharaoh should give them authority to store up the grain. They should keep it in the cities for food. [36] The grain should be stored up for the country to use later. It will be needed during the seven years when there isn't enough food in Egypt. Then the country won't be destroyed just because it doesn't have enough food."

[37] The plan seemed good to Pharaoh and all his officials. [38] So Pharaoh said to them, "The spirit of God is in this man. We can't find anyone else like him, can we?"

[39] Then Pharaoh said to Joseph, "God has made all this known to you. No one is as wise and understanding as you are. [40] You will be in charge of my palace. All my people must obey your orders. I will be greater than you only because I'm the one who sits on the throne."

Joseph Is Put in Charge of Egypt

[41] So Pharaoh said to Joseph, "I'm putting you in charge of the whole land of Egypt." [42] Then Pharaoh took from his finger the ring he used to give his official stamp. He put it on Joseph's finger. He dressed him in robes made out of fine linen. He put a gold chain around Joseph's neck. [43] He also had him ride in a chariot. Joseph was now next in command after Pharaoh. People went in front of Joseph and shouted, "Get down on your knees!" By doing all these things, Pharaoh put Joseph in charge of the whole land of Egypt.

[44] Then Pharaoh said to Joseph, "I am Pharaoh. But unless you give an order, no one will do anything in the whole land of Egypt." [45] Pharaoh gave Joseph the name Zaphenath-Paneah. He gave Joseph a wife. She was Asenath, the daughter of Potiphera. Potiphera was the priest of On. Joseph traveled all over the land of Egypt.

[46] Joseph was 30 years old when he began serving Pharaoh, the king of Egypt. He left Pharaoh's palace and traveled all over Egypt. [47] During the seven years there was plenty of food. The land produced more than the people needed. [48] Joseph collected all the extra food produced in those seven years in Egypt. He stored it in the cities. In each city he stored

up the food grown in the fields around it. ⁴⁹ Joseph stored up huge amounts of grain. There was as much of it as sand by the sea. There was so much grain it couldn't be measured. So Joseph stopped keeping records of it.

⁵⁰ Before the years when there wasn't enough food, two sons were born to Joseph. He had them by Asenath, the daughter of Potiphera. Potiphera was the priest of On. ⁵¹ Joseph named his first son Manasseh. That's because he said, "God has made me forget all my trouble and my father's whole family." ⁵² He named the second son Ephraim. That's because he said, "God has given me children in the land where I've suffered so much."

⁵³ The seven years when there was plenty of food in Egypt came to an end. ⁵⁴ Then the seven years when there wasn't enough food began. It happened just as Joseph had said it would. There wasn't enough food in any of the other lands. But in the whole land of Egypt there was food. ⁵⁵ When all the people of Egypt began to get hungry, they cried out to Pharaoh for food. He told all the Egyptians, "Go to Joseph. Do what he tells you."

⁵⁶ There wasn't enough food anywhere in the country. So Joseph opened the storerooms. He sold grain to the Egyptians because people were very hungry all over Egypt. ⁵⁷ People from all over the world came to Egypt. They came to buy grain from Joseph. That's because people were very hungry everywhere.

Joseph's Brothers Go Down to Egypt

42 Jacob found out that there was grain in Egypt. So he said to his sons, "Why do you just keep looking at one another?" ² He continued, "I've heard there's grain in Egypt. Go down there. Buy some for us. Then we'll live and not die."

³ So ten of Joseph's brothers went down to Egypt to buy grain there. ⁴ But Jacob didn't send Joseph's brother Benjamin with them. He was afraid Benjamin might be harmed. ⁵ Israel's sons were among the people who went to buy grain. There wasn't enough food in the land of Canaan.

⁶ Joseph was the governor of the land. He was the one who sold grain to all its people. When Joseph's brothers arrived, they bowed down to him with their faces to the ground. ⁷ As soon as Joseph saw his brothers, he recognized them. But he pretended to be a stranger. He spoke to them in a mean way. "Where do you come from?" he asked.

"From the land of Canaan," they replied. "We've come to buy food."

⁸ Joseph recognized his brothers, but they didn't recognize him. ⁹ Then Joseph remembered his dreams about them. So he said to them, "You are spies! You have come to see the places where our land isn't guarded very well."

[10] "No, sir," they answered. "We've come to buy food. [11] All of us are the sons of one man. We're honest men. We aren't spies."

[12] "No!" he said to them. "You have come to see the places where our land isn't guarded very well."

[13] But they replied, "We were 12 brothers. All of us were the sons of one man. He lives in the land of Canaan. Our youngest brother is now with our father. And one brother is gone."

[14] Joseph said to them, "I still say you are spies! [15] So I'm going to test you. And here's the test. You can be sure that you won't leave this place unless your youngest brother comes here. You can be just as sure of this as you are sure that Pharaoh lives. I give you my word that you won't leave here unless your brother comes. [16] Send one of you back to get your brother. The rest of you will be kept in prison. I'll test your words. Then we'll find out whether you are telling the truth. You can be sure that Pharaoh lives. And you can be just as sure that if you aren't telling the truth, we'll know that you are spies!" [17] So Joseph kept all of them under guard for three days.

[18] On the third day, Joseph spoke to them again. He said, "Do what I say. Then you will live, because I have respect for God. [19] If you are honest men, let one of your brothers stay here in prison. The rest of you may go and take grain back to your hungry families. [20] But you must bring your youngest brother to me. That will prove that your words are true. Then you won't die." So they did what he said.

[21] They said to one another, "God is surely punishing us because of our brother. We saw how upset he was when he begged us to let him live. But we wouldn't listen. That's why all this trouble has come to us."

[22] Reuben replied, "Didn't I tell you not to sin against the boy? But you wouldn't listen! Now we're being paid back for killing him." [23] They didn't realize that Joseph could understand what they were saying. He was using someone else to explain their words to him in the Egyptian language.

[24] Joseph turned away from his brothers and began to weep. Then he came back and spoke to them again. He had Simeon taken and tied up right there in front of them.

[25] Joseph gave orders to have their bags filled with grain. He had each man's money put back into his sack. He also made sure they were given food for their journey. [26] Then the brothers loaded their grain on their donkeys and left.

[27] When night came, they stopped. One of them opened his sack to get feed for his donkey. He saw his money in the top of his sack. [28] "My money has been given back," he said to his brothers. "Here it is in my sack."

They had a sinking feeling in their hearts. They began to

tremble. They turned to one another and said, "What has God done to us?"

29 They came to their father Jacob in the land of Canaan. They told him everything that had happened to them. They said, 30 "The man who is the governor of the land spoke to us in a mean way. He treated us as if we were spying on the land. 31 But we said to him, 'We're honest men. We aren't spies. 32 We were 12 brothers. All of us were the sons of one father. But now one brother is gone. And our youngest brother is with our father in Canaan.'

33 "Then the man who is the governor of the land spoke to us. He said, 'Here's how I will know whether you are honest men. Leave one of your brothers here with me. Take food for your hungry families and go. 34 But bring your youngest brother to me. Then I'll know that you are honest men and not spies. I'll give your brother back to you. And you will be free to trade in the land.' "

35 They began emptying their sacks. There in each man's sack was his bag of money! When they and their father saw the money bags, they were scared to death. 36 Their father Jacob said to them, "You have taken my children away from me. Joseph is gone. Simeon is gone. Now you want to take Benjamin. Everything is going against me!"

37 Then Reuben spoke to his father. He said, "You can put both of my sons to death if I don't bring Benjamin back to you. Trust me to take care of him. I'll bring him back."

38 But Jacob said, "My son will not go down there with you. His brother is dead. He's the only one left here with me. Suppose he's harmed on the journey you are taking. Then I would die as a sad old man."

Joseph's Brothers Go Down to Egypt Again

43 There still wasn't enough food anywhere in the land. 2 After a while Jacob's family had eaten all the grain the brothers had brought from Egypt. So their father said to them, "Go back. Buy us a little more food."

3 But Judah said to him, "The man gave us a strong warning. He said, 'You won't see my face again unless your brother Benjamin is with you.' 4 So send our brother along with us. Then we'll go down and buy food for you. 5 If you won't send him, we won't go down. The man said to us, 'You won't see my face again unless your brother is with you.' "

6 Israel asked, "Why did you bring this trouble to me? Why did you tell the man you had another brother?"

7 They replied, "The man questioned us closely about ourselves and our family. He asked us, 'Is your father still living? Do you have another brother?' We just answered his questions. How could we possibly know he would say, 'Bring your brother down here'?"

8 Judah spoke to Israel his fa-

ther. "Send the boy along with me," he said. "We'll go right away. Then we and you and our children will live and not die. ⁹I myself promise to keep Benjamin safe. You can blame me if I don't bring him back to you. I'll set him right here in front of you. If I don't, you can put the blame on me for the rest of my life. ¹⁰As it is, we've already waited too long. We could have made the trip to Egypt and back twice by now."

¹¹Then their father Israel spoke to them. He said, "If that's the way it has to be, then do what I tell you. Put some of the best things from our land in your bags. Take them down to the man as a gift. Take some lotion and a little honey. Take some spices and myrrh. Take some pistachio nuts and almonds. ¹²Take twice the amount of money with you. You have to give back the money that was put in your sacks. Maybe it was a mistake. ¹³Also take your brother. Go back to the man at once. ¹⁴May the Mighty God cause him to show you mercy. May the man let your other brother and Benjamin come back with you. And if I lose my sons, I lose them."

¹⁵So the men took the gifts. They took twice the amount of money. They also took Benjamin. They hurried down to Egypt and went to Joseph. ¹⁶When Joseph saw Benjamin with them, he spoke to the manager of his house. "Take these men to my house," he said. "Kill an animal and prepare a meal.

I want them to eat with me at noon."

¹⁷The manager did what Joseph told him to do. He took the men to Joseph's house. ¹⁸They were frightened when they were taken to Joseph's house. They thought, "We were brought here because of the money that was put back in our sacks the first time. He wants to attack us and overpower us. Then he can hold us as slaves and take our donkeys."

¹⁹So they went up to Joseph's manager. They spoke to him at the entrance to the house. ²⁰"Please, sir," they said. "We came down here the first time to buy food. ²¹We opened our sacks at the place where we stopped for the night. Each of us found in our sacks the exact amount of the money we had paid. So we've brought it back with us. ²²We've also brought more money with us to buy food. We don't know who put our money in our sacks."

²³"It's all right," the manager said. "Don't be afraid. Your God, the God of your father, has given you riches in your sacks. I received your money." Then he brought Simeon out to them.

²⁴The manager took the men into Joseph's house. He gave them water to wash their feet. He provided feed for their donkeys. ²⁵The brothers prepared their gifts for Joseph. He was planning to arrive at noon. They had heard that they were going to eat there.

²⁶When Joseph came home,

they gave him the gifts they had brought into the house. They bowed down low in front of him. ²⁷ He asked them how they were. Then he said, "How is your old father you told me about? Is he still living?"

²⁸ They replied, "Your servant our father is still alive and well." And they bowed down to show him honor.

²⁹ Joseph looked around. Then he saw his brother Benjamin, his own mother's son. He asked, "Is this your youngest brother? Is he the one you told me about?" He continued, "May God be gracious to you, my son." ³⁰ It moved him deeply to see his brother. So Joseph hurried out and looked for a place to cry. He went into his own room and cried there.

³¹ Then he washed his face and came out. He calmed down and said, "Serve the food."

³² They served Joseph by himself. They served the brothers by themselves. They also served the Egyptians who ate with Joseph by themselves. Because of their beliefs, Egyptians couldn't eat with Hebrews. ³³ The brothers had been given places in front of Joseph. They had been seated in the order of their ages, from the oldest to the youngest. That made them look at each other in great surprise. ³⁴ While they were eating, some food was brought to them from Joseph's table. Benjamin was given five times as much as anyone else. So all Joseph's brothers ate and drank a lot with him.

A Silver Cup in a Sack

44 Joseph told the manager of his house what to do. "Fill the men's sacks with as much food as they can carry," he said. "Put each man's money in his sack. ² Then put my silver cup in the youngest one's sack. Put it there along with the money he paid for his grain." So the manager did what Joseph told him to do.

³ When morning came, the men were sent on their way with their donkeys. ⁴ They hadn't gone very far from the city when Joseph spoke to his manager. "Go after those men right away," he said. "Catch up with them. Say to them, 'My master was good to you. Why have you paid him back by doing evil? ⁵ Isn't this the cup my master drinks from? Doesn't he also use it to find things out? You have done an evil thing.' "

⁶ When the manager caught up with them, he told them what Joseph had said. ⁷ But they said to him, "Why do you say these things? We would never do anything like that! ⁸ We even brought back to you from Canaan the money we found in our sacks. So why would we steal silver or gold from your master's house? ⁹ If you find out that any of us has the cup, he will die. And the rest of us will become your slaves."

¹⁰ "All right, then," he said. "As you wish. The one found to have the cup will become my slave. But the rest of you will not be blamed."

¹¹ Each of them quickly put his

sack down on the ground and opened it. ¹²Then the manager started to search. He began with the oldest and ended with the youngest. The cup was found in Benjamin's sack. ¹³When that happened, they were so upset they tore their clothes. Then all of them loaded their donkeys and went back to the city.

¹⁴Joseph was still in the house when Judah and his brothers came in. They threw themselves down on the ground in front of him. ¹⁵Joseph said to them, "What have you done? Don't you know that a man like me has ways to find things out?"

¹⁶"What can we say to you?" Judah replied. "What can we say? How can we prove we haven't done anything wrong? God has shown you that we are guilty. We are now your slaves. All of us are, including the one found to have the cup."

¹⁷But Joseph said, "I would never do anything like that! Only the man found to have the cup will become my slave. The rest of you may go back to your father in peace."

¹⁸Then Judah went up to him. He said, "Please, sir. Let me speak a word to you. Don't be angry with me, even though you are equal to Pharaoh himself. ¹⁹You asked us, 'Do you have a father or a brother?' ²⁰We answered, 'We have an old father. A young son was born to him when he was old. His brother is dead. He's the only one of his mother's sons left. And his father loves him.'

²¹"Then you said to us, 'Bring him down to me. I want to see him for myself.' ²²We said to you, 'The boy can't leave his father. If he does, his father will die.' ²³But you told us, 'Your youngest brother must come down here with you. If he doesn't, you won't see my face again.' ²⁴So we went back to my father. We told him what you had said.

²⁵"Then our father said, 'Go back. Buy a little more food.' ²⁶But we said, 'We can't go down. We'll only go if our youngest brother goes there with us. We can't even see the man's face unless our youngest brother goes with us.'

²⁷"Your servant my father said to us, 'You know that my wife had two sons by me. ²⁸One of them went away from me. And I said, "He must have been torn to pieces." I haven't seen him since. ²⁹What if you take this one from me too and he is harmed? Then you would cause me to die as a sad old man. I would go down into the grave full of pain and suffering.'

³⁰"So now, what will happen if the boy isn't with us when I go back to my father? His life depends on the boy's life. ³¹When he sees that the boy isn't with us, he'll die. Because of us, he'll go down into the grave as a sad old man. ³²I promised my father I would keep the boy safe. I said, 'Father, I'll bring him back to you. If I don't, you can put the blame on me for the rest of my life.'

³³"Now then, please let me

stay here. Let me be your slave in place of the boy. Let the boy return with his brothers. ³⁴ How can I go back to my father if the boy isn't with me? No! Don't let me see the pain and suffering that would come to my father."

Joseph Tells His Brothers Who He Is

45 Joseph couldn't control himself anymore in front of all his attendants. He cried out, "Have everyone leave me!" So there wasn't anyone with Joseph when he told his brothers who he was. ² He wept so loudly that the Egyptians heard him. Everyone in Pharaoh's house heard about it.

³ Joseph said to his brothers, "I am Joseph! Is my father still alive?" But his brothers weren't able to answer him. They were too afraid of him.

⁴ Joseph said to his brothers, "Come close to me." So they did. Then he said, "I am your brother Joseph. I'm the one you sold into Egypt. ⁵ But don't be upset. And don't be angry with yourselves because you sold me here. God sent me ahead of you to save many lives. ⁶ For two years now, there hasn't been enough food in the land. And for the next five years, people won't be plowing or gathering crops. ⁷ But God sent me ahead of you to keep some of you alive on earth. He sent me here to save your lives by an act of mighty power.

⁸ "So then, it wasn't you who sent me here. It was God. He made me like a father to Phar-aoh. He made me master of Pharaoh's entire house. God made me ruler of the whole land of Egypt. ⁹ Now hurry back to my father. Say to him, 'Your son Joseph says, "God has made me master of the whole land of Egypt. Come down to me. Don't waste any time. ¹⁰ You will live in the area of Goshen. You, your children and grandchildren, your flocks and herds, and everything you have will be near me. ¹¹ There I will provide everything you need. There are still five years to come when there won't be enough food. If you don't come down here, you and your family and everyone who belongs to you will lose everything."'

¹² "My brothers, I am Joseph. You can see for yourselves that I am the one speaking to you. My brother Benjamin can see it too. ¹³ Tell my father about all the honor given to me in Egypt. Tell him about everything you have seen. And bring my father down here quickly."

¹⁴ Then Joseph threw his arms around his brother Benjamin and wept. Benjamin also hugged him and wept. ¹⁵ Joseph kissed all his brothers and wept over them. After that, his brothers talked with him.

¹⁶ The news reached Pharaoh's palace that Joseph's brothers had come. Pharaoh and all his officials were pleased. ¹⁷ Pharaoh said to Joseph, "Here's what I want you to tell your brothers. Say to them, 'Load your animals. Return to the land of Ca-

naan. [18] Bring your father and your families back to me. I'll give you the best land in Egypt. You can enjoy all the good things in the land.'

[19] "And here's something else I want you to tell them. Say to them, 'Take some carts from Egypt. Your children and your wives can use them. Get your father and come back. [20] Don't worry about the things you have back there. The best of everything in Egypt will belong to you.'"

[21] Then the sons of Israel did so. Joseph gave them carts, as Pharaoh had commanded. He also gave them supplies for their journey. [22] He gave new clothes to each of them. But he gave Benjamin more than seven pounds of silver. He also gave him five sets of clothes. [23] He sent his father ten male donkeys loaded with the best things from Egypt. He also sent ten female donkeys loaded with grain and bread and other supplies for his journey. [24] Then Joseph sent his brothers away. As they were leaving he said to them, "Don't argue on the way!"

[25] So they went up out of Egypt. They came to their father Jacob in the land of Canaan. [26] They told him, "Joseph is still alive! In fact, he is ruler of the whole land of Egypt." Jacob was shocked. He didn't believe them. [27] So they told him everything Joseph had said to them. Jacob saw the carts Joseph had sent to carry him back. That gave new life to their father Jacob. [28] Israel said, "I believe it now! My son Joseph is still alive. I'll go and see him before I die."

Jacob Goes Down to Egypt

46 So Israel started out with everything that belonged to him. When he reached Beersheba, he offered sacrifices to the God of his father Isaac.

[2] God spoke to Israel in a vision at night. "Jacob! Jacob!" he said.

"Here I am," Jacob replied.

[3] "I am God. I am the God of your father," he said. "Do not be afraid to go down to Egypt. There I will make you into a great nation. [4] I will go down to Egypt with you. I will surely bring you back again. And when you die, Joseph will close your eyes with his own hand."

[5] Then Jacob left Beersheba. Israel's sons put their father Jacob and their families in the carts that Pharaoh had sent to carry him. [6] So Jacob and his whole family went to Egypt. They took their livestock with them. And they took everything they had acquired in Canaan. [7] Jacob brought his sons and grandsons with him to Egypt. He also brought his daughters and granddaughters. He brought his whole family with him.

[8] Here are the names of Israel's children and grandchildren who went to Egypt. Jacob and his whole family are included.

Reuben was Jacob's oldest son.

⁹The sons of Reuben were
Hanok, Pallu, Hezron
and Karmi.

¹⁰The sons of Simeon were
Jemuel, Jamin, Ohad, Jakin,
Zohar and Shaul.
Shaul was the son of a
woman from Canaan.

¹¹The sons of Levi were
Gershon, Kohath and
Merari.

¹²The sons of Judah were
Er, Onan, Shelah, Perez
and Zerah.
But Er and Onan had died
in the land of Canaan.
The sons of Perez were
Hezron and Hamul.

¹³The sons of Issachar were
Tola, Puah, Jashub and
Shimron.

¹⁴The sons of Zebulun were
Sered, Elon and Jahleel.

¹⁵These were the sons and
grandsons born to Jacob
and Leah in Paddan Aram.
Leah also had a daughter
by Jacob. Her name was Dinah.
The total number of
people in the family line of
Jacob and Leah was 33.

¹⁶The sons of Gad were
Zephon, Haggi, Shuni,
Ezbon, Eri, Arodi and
Areli.

¹⁷The sons of Asher were
Imnah, Ishvah, Ishvi and
Beriah. Their sister was
Serah.
The sons of Beriah were
Heber and Malkiel.

¹⁸These were the children
and grandchildren born
to Jacob and Zilpah. Laban
had given Zilpah to

his daughter Leah. The total
number of people in the
family line of Jacob and Zilpah
was 16.

¹⁹The sons of Jacob's wife Rachel
were
Joseph and Benjamin.
²⁰In Egypt, Asenath
had Manasseh and
Ephraim by Joseph. Asenath
was the daughter
of Potiphera. Potiphera
was the priest of On.

²¹The sons of Benjamin were
Bela, Beker, Ashbel, Gera,
Naaman, Ehi, Rosh,
Muppim, Huppim and
Ard.

²²These were the sons and
grandsons born to Jacob
and Rachel. The total number
of people in the family
line of Jacob and Rachel
was 14.

²³The son of Dan was
Hushim.

²⁴The sons of Naphtali were
Jahziel, Guni, Jezer and
Shillem.

²⁵These were the sons and
grandsons born to Jacob
and Bilhah. Laban had
given Bilhah to his daughter
Rachel. The total number
of people in the family
line of Jacob and Bilhah
was seven.

²⁶The total number of people
who went to Egypt with Jacob
was 66. That number
includes only his own children
and grandchildren.
It doesn't include his sons'
wives or his grandsons'

wives. 27 The total number of the members of Jacob's family who went to Egypt was 70. That includes the two sons who had been born to Joseph in Egypt.

28 Jacob sent Judah ahead of him to Joseph. He sent him to get directions to Goshen. And so they arrived in the area of Goshen. 29 Then Joseph had his servants get his chariot ready. He went to Goshen to meet his father Israel. As soon as he came to his father, Joseph threw his arms around him. Then Joseph wept for a long time.

30 Israel said to Joseph, "I have seen for myself that you are still alive. Now I'm ready to die."

31 Then Joseph spoke to his brothers and to the rest of his father's family. He said, "I will go up and speak to Pharaoh. I'll say to him, 'My brothers and the rest of my father's family have come to me. They were living in the land of Canaan. 32 The men are shepherds. They take care of livestock. They've brought along their flocks and herds and everything they own.' 33 Pharaoh will send for you. He'll ask, 'What do you do for a living?' 34 You should answer, 'We've taken care of livestock from the time we were boys. We've done just as our fathers did.' It's the practice of the people of Egypt not to mix with shepherds. So Pharaoh will let you settle in the area of Goshen."

47 Joseph went to Pharaoh. He told him, "My father and brothers have come from the land of Canaan. They've brought along their flocks and herds and everything they own. They are now in Goshen." 2 Joseph had chosen five of his brothers to meet with Pharaoh.

3 Pharaoh asked the brothers, "What do you do for a living?"

"We're shepherds," they replied to Pharaoh. "And that's what our fathers were." 4 They also said to him, "We've come to live in Egypt for a while. There isn't enough food anywhere in Canaan. There isn't any grass for our flocks. So please let us live in Goshen."

5 Pharaoh said to Joseph, "Your father and your brothers have come to you. 6 The land of Egypt is open to you. Let your father and brothers live in the best part of the land. Let them live in Goshen. Do any of them have special skills? If they do, put them in charge of my own livestock."

7 Then Joseph brought his father Jacob in to meet Pharaoh. Jacob gave Pharaoh his blessing. 8 Then Pharaoh asked him, "How old are you?"

9 Jacob said to Pharaoh, "The years of my journey through life are 130. My years have been few and hard. They aren't as many as the years of my father and grandfather before me." 10 Jacob gave Pharaoh his blessing. Then he left him.

11 So Joseph helped his father and his brothers make their homes in Egypt. He gave them property in the best part of the land, just as Pharaoh had

directed him to do. That part was known as the territory of Rameses. ¹²Joseph also provided food for his father and brothers. He provided for them and the rest of his father's family. He gave them enough for all their children.

Joseph Saves Many Lives

¹³But there wasn't any food in the whole area. In fact, there wasn't enough food anywhere. The people of Egypt and Canaan lost their strength because there wasn't enough food to go around. ¹⁴Joseph collected all the money in Egypt and Canaan. People paid it to him for the grain they were buying. And Joseph brought it to Pharaoh's palace. ¹⁵When the money of the people of Egypt and Canaan was gone, all the Egyptians came to Joseph. They said, "Give us food. What good would it do you to watch us all die? Our money is all gone."

¹⁶"Then bring your livestock," said Joseph. "You say your money is gone. So I'll trade you food for your livestock." ¹⁷They brought their livestock to Joseph. He traded them food for their animals. They gave him their horses, sheep, goats, cattle and donkeys. He helped the people live through that year by trading them food for all their livestock.

¹⁸When that year was over, they came to him the next year. They said, "We can't hide the truth from you. Our money is gone. Our livestock belongs to you. We don't have anything left to give you except our bodies and our land. ¹⁹What good would it do you to watch us die? Why should our land be destroyed? Trade us food for ourselves and our land. Then we and our land will belong to Pharaoh. Give us some seeds so we can live and not die. We don't want the land to become a desert."

²⁰So Joseph bought all the land in Egypt for Pharaoh. All the people of Egypt sold their fields. They did that because there wasn't enough food anywhere. So the land became Pharaoh's. ²¹Joseph made the people slaves from one end of Egypt to the other. ²²But Joseph didn't buy the land that belonged to the priests. They received a regular share of food from Pharaoh. They had enough food from what Pharaoh gave them. That's why they didn't have to sell their land.

²³Joseph said to the people, "I've bought you and your land today for Pharaoh. So here are some seeds for you to plant in the ground. ²⁴But when the crop comes in, give a fifth of it to Pharaoh. Keep the other four-fifths for yourselves. They will be seeds for the fields. And they will be food for yourselves, your children, and the other people who live with you."

²⁵"You have saved our lives," they said. "If you are pleased with us, we will be Pharaoh's slaves."

²⁶So Joseph made a law about

land in Egypt. It's still the law today. A fifth of the produce belongs to Pharaoh. Only the land belonging to the priests didn't become Pharaoh's.

27 The people of Israel lived in Egypt in the area of Goshen. They received property there. They had children and so became many.

28 Jacob lived 17 years in Egypt. He lived a total of 147 years. 29 The time came near for Israel to die. So he sent for his son Joseph. He said to him, "If you are pleased with me, put your hand under my thigh. Promise me that you will be kind and faithful to me. Don't bury me in Egypt. 30 When I join the members of my family who have already died, carry me out of Egypt. Bury me where they are buried."

"I'll do exactly as you say," Joseph said.

31 "Give me your word that you will do it," Jacob said. So Joseph gave him his word. And Israel worshiped God as he leaned on the top of his walking stick.

Ephraim and Manasseh

48 Some time later Joseph was told, "Your father is sick." So he took his two sons Manasseh and Ephraim along with him. 2 Jacob was told, "Your son Joseph has come to you." So Israel became stronger and sat up in bed.

3 Jacob said to Joseph, "The Mighty God appeared to me at Luz in the land of Canaan. He blessed me there. 4 He said

to me, 'I am going to give you children. I will make your family very large. I will make you a community of nations. And I will give this land to your children after you. It will belong to them forever.'

5 "Now then, two sons were born to you in Egypt. It happened before I came to you here. They will be counted as my own sons. Ephraim and Manasseh will belong to me, in the same way that Reuben and Simeon belong to me. 6 Any children born to you after them will belong to you. Any territory they receive will come from the land that will be given to Ephraim and Manasseh. 7 As I was returning from Paddan, Rachel died. It made me very sad. She died in the land of Canaan while we were still on the way. We weren't very far away from Ephrath. So I buried her body there beside the road to Ephrath." Ephrath was also called Bethlehem.

8 Israel saw Joseph's sons. He asked, "Who are they?"

9 "They are the sons God has given me here," Joseph said to his father.

Then Israel said, "Bring them to me. I want to give them my blessing."

10 Israel's eyes were weak because he was old. He couldn't see very well. So Joseph brought his sons close to him. His father kissed them and hugged them.

11 Israel said to Joseph, "I never thought I'd see your face again. But now God has let me see your children too."

¹²Then Joseph lifted his sons off Israel's knees. Joseph bowed down with his face to the ground. ¹³He placed Ephraim on his right, toward Israel's left hand. He placed Manasseh on his left, toward Israel's right hand. Then he brought them close to Israel. ¹⁴But Israel reached out his right hand and put it on Ephraim's head. He did it even though Ephraim was the younger son. He crossed his arms and put his left hand on Manasseh's head. He did it even though Manasseh was the older son.

¹⁵Then Israel gave Joseph his blessing. He said,

"May God bless these boys.
    He is the God of my
        grandfather Abraham
        and my father Isaac.
    They walked faithfully
        with him.
    He is the God who has been
        my shepherd
    all my life right up to this
        day.
¹⁶He is the Angel who has
        saved me from all harm.
    May he bless these boys.
May they be called by my
        name.
    May they also be called
        by the names of my
        grandfather Abraham
        and my father Isaac.
    And may the number of them
        greatly increase
        on the earth."

¹⁷Joseph saw his father putting his right hand on Ephraim's head. And Joseph didn't like it. So he took hold of his father's hand to move it over to Manasseh's head. ¹⁸Joseph said to him, "No, my father. Here's my older son. Put your right hand on his head."

¹⁹But his father wouldn't do it. He said, "I know, my son. I know. He too will become a nation. He too will become great. But his younger brother will be greater than he is. His children after him will become a group of nations." ²⁰On that day, Jacob gave them his blessing. He said,

"The people of Israel will bless
    others in your name.
They will say, 'May God
    make you like Ephraim
    and Manasseh.' "

So he put Ephraim ahead of Manasseh.

²¹Then Israel said to Joseph, "I'm about to die. But God will be with all of you. He'll take you back to the land of your fathers. ²²But to you, Joseph, I am giving more land than your brothers. I'm giving you the land I took from the Amorites. I took it with my sword and bow."

Jacob Gives Blessings to His Sons

49 Then Jacob sent for his sons. He said, "Gather around me so I can tell you what will happen to you in days to come.

²"Sons of Jacob, come together
    and listen.
    Listen to your father Israel.

³"Reuben, you are my oldest
    son.

You were my first child.
  You were the first sign of
  my strength.
  You were first in honor. You
  were first in power.
⁴But you are as unsteady as
  water. So you won't be
  first anymore.
  You had sex with my
  concubine on my bed.
  You lay on my couch and
  made it 'unclean.'

⁵"Simeon and Levi are
  brothers.
  Their swords have killed a
  lot of people.
⁶I won't share in their plans.
  I won't have anything to do
  with them.
  They became angry and
  killed people.
  They cut the legs of oxen
  just for the fun of it.
⁷May the LORD put a curse on
  them
  because of their terrible
  anger.
  I will scatter them in Jacob's
  land.
  I will spread them around
  in Israel.

⁸"Judah, your brothers will
  praise you.
  Your enemies will be
  brought under your
  control.
  Your father's sons will bow
  down to you.
⁹Judah, you are like a lion's
  cub.
  You return from hunting,
  my son.
  Like a lion, you lie down and
  sleep.

You are like a mother lion.
  Who dares to wake you
  up?
¹⁰The right to rule will not
  leave Judah.
  The ruler's scepter will not
  be taken from between
  his feet.
  It will be his until the king it
  belongs to will come.
  The nations will obey that
  king.
¹¹He will tie his donkey to a
  vine.
  He will tie his colt to the
  very best branch.
  He will wash his clothes in
  wine.
  He will wash his robes in
  the red juice of grapes.
¹²His eyes will be darker than
  wine.
  His teeth will be whiter
  than milk.

¹³"Zebulun will live by the
  seashore.
  He will become a safe
  harbor for ships.
  His border will go out
  toward Sidon.

¹⁴"Issachar is like a wild
  donkey
  lying down among the
  sheep pens.
¹⁵He sees how good his resting
  place is.
  He sees that his land is
  pleasant.
  So he will carry a heavy load
  on his back.
  He will obey when he's
  forced to work.

¹⁶"Dan will do what is fair for
  his people.

He will do it as one of the
   tribes of Israel.
¹⁷ Dan will be a snake by the
   side of the road.
He will be a poisonous
   snake along the path.
It bites the horse's heels
   so that the rider falls off
   backward.

¹⁸ "Lord, I look to you to save
   me.

¹⁹ "Gad will be attacked by a
   group of robbers.
But he will attack them as
   they run away.

²⁰ "Asher's food will be rich and
   sweet.
He will provide food that
   even a king would enjoy.

²¹ "Naphtali is a female deer set
   free
and gives birth to beautiful
   fawns.

²² "Joseph is a vine that grows a
   lot of fruit.
It grows close by a spring.
Its branches climb over a
   wall.
²³ Mean people shot arrows at
   him.
They shot at him because
   they were angry.
²⁴ But his bow remained steady.
His strong arms moved
   freely.
The hand of the Mighty God
   of Jacob was with him.
The Shepherd, the Rock of
   Israel, stood by him.
²⁵ Joseph, your father's God
   helps you.
The Mighty God blesses
   you.

He gives you blessings from
   the sky above.
He gives you blessings
   from the deep springs
   below.
He blesses you with
   children and with a
   mother's milk.
²⁶ Your father's blessings are
   great.
They are greater than the
   blessings from the age-
   old mountains.
They are greater than the
   gifts from the ancient
   hills.
Let all those blessings rest on
   the head of Joseph.
Let them rest on the head
   of the one who is prince
   among his brothers.

²⁷ "Benjamin is a hungry wolf.
In the morning he eats
   what he has killed.
In the evening he shares
   what he has stolen."

²⁸ All these are the 12 tribes of
Israel. That's what their father
said to them when he blessed
them. He gave each one the
blessing that was just right for
him.

Jacob Dies

²⁹ Then Jacob gave directions
to his sons. He said, "I'm about
to join the members of my family who have already died. Bury
me with them in the cave in
the field of Ephron, the Hit-
tite. ³⁰ The cave is in the field of
Machpelah near Mamre in Ca-
naan. Abraham had bought it as
a place where he could bury his

wife's body. He had bought the cave and the field from Ephron, the Hittite. ³¹ The bodies of Abraham and his wife Sarah were buried there. So were the bodies of Isaac and his wife Rebekah. I also buried Leah's body there. ³² Abraham bought the field and the cave from the Hittites."

³³ When Jacob had finished telling his sons what to do, he pulled his feet up into his bed. Then he took his last breath and died. He joined the members of his family who had already died.

50 Joseph threw himself on his father's body. He wept over him and kissed him. ² Then Joseph talked to the doctors who served him. He told them to prepare the body of his father Israel to be buried. So the doctors prepared it. ³ They took 40 days to do it. They needed that much time to prepare a body in the right way. The Egyptians mourned for Jacob 70 days.

⁴ After the days of sadness had passed, Joseph went to Pharaoh's officials. He said to them, "If you are pleased with me, speak to Pharaoh for me. Tell him, ⁵ 'My father made me give my word to him. He said, "I'm about to die. Bury me in the tomb I dug for myself in the land of Canaan." So let me go there and bury my father. Then I'll come back.' "

⁶ Pharaoh said, "Go there and bury your father. Do what he made you promise to do."

⁷ So Joseph went to Canaan to bury his father. All Pharaoh's officials went with him. They were the important people of his court and all the leaders of Egypt. ⁸ Joseph's family also went. His brothers and all the rest of his father's family went. Only their children and their flocks and herds were left in Goshen. ⁹ Chariots and horsemen also went up with him. It was a very large group.

¹⁰ They came to Atad, a place where grain was processed. It was near the Jordan River. There they sobbed loudly and bitterly. Joseph set apart seven days of sadness to honor his father's memory. ¹¹ The Canaanites living in that area saw how sad all of them were. They said, "The Egyptians are having a very special service for the dead." That's why that place near the Jordan River is called Abel of the Egyptians.

¹² So Jacob's sons did exactly as he had commanded them. ¹³ They carried his body to the land of Canaan. They buried it in the cave in the field of Machpelah near Mamre. Abraham had bought the cave as a place where he could bury his wife's body. He had bought the cave and the field from Ephron, the Hittite. ¹⁴ After Joseph buried his father, he went back to Egypt. His brothers and all the others who had gone to help him bury his father went back with him.

Joseph Calms His Brothers' Fears

¹⁵ Now that their father was dead, Joseph's brothers were

worried. They said, "Remember all the bad things we did to Joseph? What if he decides to hold those things against us? What if he pays us back for them?" [16] So they sent a message to Joseph. They said, "Your father gave us directions before he died. [17] He said, 'Here's what you must say to Joseph. Tell him, "I'm asking you to forgive your brothers. Forgive the terrible things they did to you. Forgive them for treating you so badly."' Now then, please forgive our sins. We serve the God of your father." When their message came to Joseph, he wept.

[18] Then his brothers came and threw themselves down in front of him. "We are your slaves," they said.

[19] But Joseph said to them, "Don't be afraid. Do you think I'm God? [20] You planned to harm me. But God planned it for good. He planned to do what is now being done. He wanted to save many lives. [21] So then, don't be afraid. I'll provide for you and your children." He calmed their fears. And he spoke in a kind way to them.

Joseph Dies

[22] Joseph stayed in Egypt, along with all his father's family. He lived 110 years. [23] He lived long enough to see Ephraim's children and grandchildren. When the children of Makir were born, they were placed on Joseph's knees and counted as his own children. Makir was the son of Manasseh.

[24] Joseph said to his brothers, "I'm about to die. But God will surely come to help you. He'll take you up out of this land. He'll bring you to the land he promised to give to Abraham, Isaac and Jacob." [25] Joseph made the Israelites promise him. He said, "God will surely come to help you. Then you must carry my bones up from this place."

[26] So Joseph died at the age of 110. They prepared his body to be buried. Then he was placed in a casket in Egypt.

Exodus

Introduction:

Exodus means "going out." This book tells how God's people, Israel, left Egypt. The story of Israel began in Genesis. In Egypt, God put Moses in charge of his people. Moses was not strong on his own, but God helped him. God sent plagues to Egypt so the king would let God's people go. The last plague made the king let Israel go. Before they left, the people ate the Passover meal, a reminder that God had saved them. Then God led the people through the Red Sea, but they walked on dry ground!

God was with the people on their journey. He led them night and day, and he gave them food to eat. At Mount Sinai, God made a covenant with Israel. This means that Israel was God's special people. God promised to love them and take care of them. He gave them laws so they would know how to live and how to worship him.

Outline of contents:

The Israelites Become Slaves in Egypt

1 Here are the names of Israel's children who went to Egypt with Jacob. Each one went with his family. ² Jacob's sons were

Reuben, Simeon, Levi, Judah,
³ Issachar, Zebulun, Benjamin,
⁴ Dan, Naphtali,
Gad and Asher.

⁵ The total number of Jacob's children and grandchildren was 70. Joseph was already in Egypt.

⁶ Joseph and all his brothers died. So did all their children. ⁷ The people of Israel had many children. The number of them greatly increased. There were so many of them that they filled the land.

⁸ Then a new king came to power in Egypt. Joseph didn't mean anything to him. ⁹ "Look," he said to his people. "The Israelites are far too many for us. ¹⁰ Come. We must deal with them carefully. If we don't, there will be even more of them. Then if war breaks out, they'll join our enemies. They'll fight against us and leave the country."

[11] So the Egyptians put slave drivers over the people of Israel. The slave drivers treated them badly and made them work hard. The Israelites built the cities of Pithom and Rameses so Pharaoh could store things there. [12] But the worse the slave drivers treated the Israelites, the more Israelites there were. So the Egyptians became afraid of them. [13] They made them work hard. They didn't show them any pity. [14] The people suffered because of their hard labor. The slave drivers forced them to work with bricks and mud. And they made them do all kinds of work in the fields. The Egyptians didn't show them any pity at all. They made them work very hard.

[15] There were two Hebrew women named Shiphrah and Puah. They helped other women having babies. The king of Egypt spoke to them. He said, [16] "You are the ones who help the other Hebrew women. Watch them when they get into a sitting position to have their babies. Kill the boys. Let the girls live." [17] But Shiphrah and Puah had respect for God. They didn't do what the king of Egypt had told them to do. They let the boys live. [18] Then the king of Egypt sent for the women. He asked them, "Why have you done this? Why have you let the boys live?"

[19] The women answered Pharaoh, "Hebrew women are not like the women of Egypt. They are strong. They have their babies before we get there."

[20] So God was kind to Shiphrah and Puah. And the number of Israelites became even greater. [21] Shiphrah and Puah had respect for God. So he gave them families of their own.

[22] Then Pharaoh gave an order to all his people. He said, "You must throw every Hebrew baby boy into the Nile River. But let every Hebrew baby girl live."

Moses Is Born

2 A man and a woman from the tribe of Levi got married. [2] She became pregnant and had a son by her husband. She saw that her baby was a fine child. And she hid him for three months. [3] After that, she couldn't hide him any longer. So she got a basket made out of the stems of tall grass. She coated the basket with tar. She placed the child in the basket. Then she put it in the tall grass that grew along the bank of the Nile River. [4] The child's sister wasn't very far away. She wanted to see what would happen to him.

[5] Pharaoh's daughter went down to the Nile River to take a bath. Her attendants were walking along the river bank. She saw the basket in the tall grass. So she sent her female slave to get it. [6] When she opened it, Pharaoh's daughter saw the baby. He was crying. She felt sorry for him. "This is one of the Hebrew babies," she said.

[7] Then his sister spoke to Pharaoh's daughter. She asked, "Do you want me to go and get one of the Hebrew women? She

could breast-feed the baby for you."

8 "Yes. Go," she answered. So the girl went and got the baby's mother. 9 Pharaoh's daughter said to her, "Take this baby and feed him for me. I'll pay you." So the woman took the baby and fed him. 10 When the child grew older, she took him to Pharaoh's daughter. And he became her son. She named him Moses. She said, "I pulled him out of the water."

Moses Escapes to Midian

11 Moses grew up. One day, he went out to where his own people were. He watched them while they were hard at work. He saw an Egyptian hitting a Hebrew man. The man was one of Moses' own people. 12 Moses looked around and didn't see anyone. So he killed the Egyptian. Then he hid his body in the sand. 13 The next day Moses went out again. He saw two Hebrew men fighting. He asked the one who had started the fight a question. He said, "Why are you hitting another Hebrew man?"

14 The man said, "Who made you ruler and judge over us? Are you thinking about killing me as you killed the Egyptian?" Then Moses became afraid. He thought, "People must have heard about what I did."

15 When Pharaoh heard about what had happened, he tried to kill Moses. But Moses escaped from Pharaoh and went to live in Midian. There he sat down by a well. 16 A priest of Midian had

seven daughters. They came to fill the stone tubs with water. They wanted to give water to their father's flock. 17 Some shepherds came along and chased the girls away. But Moses got up and helped them. Then he gave water to their flock.

18 The girls returned to their father Reuel. He asked them, "Why have you returned so early today?"

19 They answered, "An Egyptian saved us from the shepherds. He even got water for us and gave it to the flock."

20 "Where is he?" Reuel asked his daughters. "Why did you leave him? Invite him to have something to eat."

21 Moses agreed to stay with the man. And the man gave his daughter Zipporah to Moses to be his wife. 22 Zipporah had a son by him. Moses named him Gershom. That's because Moses said, "I'm an outsider in a strange land."

23 After a long time, the king of Egypt died. The people of Israel groaned because they were slaves. They also cried out to God. Their cry for help went up to him. 24 God heard their groans. He remembered his covenant with Abraham, Isaac and Jacob. 25 So God looked on the Israelites with concern for them.

Moses and the Burning Bush

3 Moses was taking care of the flock of his father-in-law Jethro. Jethro was the priest of Midian. Moses led the flock

to the western side of the desert. He came to Horeb. It was the mountain of God. ²There the angel of the LORD appeared to him from inside a burning bush. Moses saw that the bush was on fire. But it didn't burn up. ³So Moses thought, "I'll go over and see this strange sight. Why doesn't the bush burn up?"

⁴The LORD saw that Moses had gone over to look. So God spoke to him from inside the bush. He called out, "Moses! Moses!"

"Here I am," Moses said.

⁵"Do not come any closer," God said. "Take off your sandals. The place you are standing on is holy ground." ⁶He continued, "I am the God of your father. I am the God of Abraham. I am the God of Isaac. And I am the God of Jacob." When Moses heard that, he turned his face away. He was afraid to look at God.

⁷The LORD said, "I have seen how my people are suffering in Egypt. I have heard them cry out because of their slave drivers. I am concerned about their suffering. ⁸So I have come down to save them from the Egyptians. I will bring them up out of that land. I will bring them into a good land. It has a lot of room. It is a land that has plenty of milk and honey. The Canaanites, Hittites, Amorites, Perizzites, Hivites and Jebusites live there. ⁹And now Israel's cry for help has reached me. I have seen how badly the Egyptians are treating them. ¹⁰So now, go.

I am sending you to Pharaoh. I want you to bring the Israelites out of Egypt. They are my people."

¹¹But Moses spoke to God. "Who am I that I should go to Pharaoh?" he said. "Who am I that I should bring the Israelites out of Egypt?"

¹²God said, "I will be with you. I will give you a sign. It will prove that I have sent you. When you have brought the people out of Egypt, all of you will worship me on this mountain."

¹³Moses said to God, "Suppose I go to the people of Israel. Suppose I say to them, 'The God of your fathers has sent me to you.' And suppose they ask me, 'What is his name?' Then what should I tell them?"

¹⁴God said to Moses, "I AM WHO I AM. Here is what you must say to the Israelites. Tell them, 'I am has sent me to you.'"

¹⁵God also said to Moses, "Say to the Israelites, 'The LORD is the God of your fathers. He has sent me to you. He is the God of Abraham. He is the God of Isaac. And he is the God of Jacob.' My name will always be The LORD. Call me this name for all time to come.

¹⁶"Go. Gather the elders of Israel together. Say to them, 'The LORD, the God of your fathers, appeared to me. He is the God of Abraham, Isaac and Jacob. God said, "I have watched over you. I have seen what the Egyptians have done to you. ¹⁷I have promised to bring you up out of Egypt where you are suffering.

I will bring you into the land of the Canaanites, Hittites, Amorites, Perizzites, Hivites and Jebusites. It is a land that has plenty of milk and honey." '

18 "The elders of Israel will listen to you. Then you and the elders must go to the king of Egypt. You must say to him, 'The LORD has met with us. He is the God of the Hebrews. Let us take a journey that lasts about three days. We want to go into the desert to offer sacrifices to the LORD our God.' 19 But I know that the king of Egypt will not let you and your people go. Only a mighty hand could make him do that. 20 So I will reach out my hand. I will strike the Egyptians with all the amazing things I will do. After that, their king will let you go.

21 "I will cause the Egyptians to treat you in a kind way. Then when you leave, you will not go with your hands empty. 22 Every woman should ask her neighbor and any woman living in her house for things made out of silver and gold. Ask them for clothes too. Put them on your children. In that way, you will take the wealth of Egypt along with you."

Signs for Moses to Do

4 Moses answered, "What if the elders of Israel won't believe me? What if they won't listen to me? Suppose they say, 'The LORD didn't appear to you.' Then what should I do?"

2 The LORD said to him, "What do you have in your hand?"

"A walking stick," he said.

3 The LORD said, "Throw it on the ground."

So Moses threw it on the ground. It turned into a snake. He ran away from it. 4 Then the LORD said to Moses, "Reach your hand out. Take the snake by the tail." So he reached out and grabbed the snake. It turned back into a walking stick in his hand. 5 The LORD said, "When they see this sign, they will believe that I appeared to you. I am the LORD, the God of their fathers. I am the God of Abraham. I am the God of Isaac. And I am the God of Jacob."

6 Then the LORD said, "Put your hand inside your coat." So Moses put his hand inside his coat. When he took it out, the skin had become as white as snow. His hand was covered with a skin disease.

7 "Now put it back into your coat," the LORD said. So Moses put his hand back into his coat. When he took it out, the skin was healthy again. His hand was like the rest of his skin.

8 Then the LORD said, "Suppose they do not believe you or pay attention to the first sign. Then maybe they will believe the second one. 9 But suppose they do not believe either sign. Suppose they will not listen to you. Then get some water from the Nile River. Pour it on the dry ground. The water you take from the river will turn into blood on the ground."

10 Moses spoke to the LORD. He said, "Lord, I've never been a

good speaker. And I haven't gotten any better since you spoke to me. I don't speak very well at all."

¹¹ The LORD said to him, "Who makes human beings able to talk? Who makes them unable to hear or speak? Who makes them able to see? Who makes them blind? It is I, the LORD. ¹² Now go. I will help you speak. I will teach you what to say."

¹³ But Moses said, "Lord, please send someone else to do it."

¹⁴ Then the LORD became very angry with Moses. He said, "What about your brother, Aaron the Levite? I know he can speak well. He is already on his way to meet you. He will be glad to see you. ¹⁵ Speak to him. Tell him what to say. I will help both of you speak. I will teach you what to do. ¹⁶ He will speak to the people for you. He will be like your mouth. And you will be like God to him. ¹⁷ But take this walking stick in your hand. You will be able to do signs with it."

Moses Returns to Egypt

¹⁸ Then Moses went back to his father-in-law Jethro. He said to him, "Let me return to my own people in Egypt. I want to see if any of them are still alive." Jethro said, "Go. I hope everything goes well with you."

¹⁹ The LORD had said to Moses in Midian, "Go back to Egypt. All those who wanted to kill you are dead." ²⁰ So Moses got his wife and sons. He put them on a donkey. Together they started back to Egypt. And he took the walking stick in his hand. It was the stick God would use in a powerful way.

²¹ The LORD spoke to Moses. He said, "When you return to Egypt, do all the amazing things I have given you the power to do. Do them in the sight of Pharaoh. But I will make him stubborn. He will not let the people go. ²² Then say to Pharaoh, 'The LORD says, "Israel is like an oldest son to me. ²³ I told you, 'Let my son go. Then he will be able to worship me.' But you refused to let him go. So I will kill your oldest son." ' "

²⁴ On the way to Egypt, Moses stopped for the night. There the LORD met him and was about to kill him. ²⁵ But Zipporah got a knife made out of flint. She circumcised her son with it. Then she touched Moses' feet with the skin she had cut off. "Surely, you are a husband who has forced me to spill my son's blood," she said. ²⁶ So the LORD didn't kill Moses. When she said "husband who has forced me to spill my son's blood," she was talking about circumcision.

²⁷ The LORD said to Aaron, "Go into the desert to see Moses." So Aaron greeted Moses at the mountain of God and kissed him. ²⁸ Then Moses told Aaron everything the LORD had sent him to say. Moses also told him about all the signs the LORD had commanded him to do.

²⁹ Moses and Aaron gathered all the elders of Israel together. ³⁰ Aaron told them everything the LORD had said to Moses. He also performed the signs in

the sight of the people. [31] And they believed. They heard that the LORD was concerned about them. He had seen their suffering. So they bowed down and worshiped him.

5 Later on, Moses and Aaron went to Pharaoh. They said, "The LORD is the God of Israel. He says, 'Let my people go. Then they will be able to hold a feast to honor me in the desert.'"

[2] Pharaoh said, "Who is the LORD? Why should I obey him? Why should I let Israel go? I don't even know the LORD. And I won't let Israel go."

[3] Then Moses and Aaron said, "The God of the Hebrews has met with us. Now let us take a journey that lasts about three days. We want to go into the desert to offer sacrifices to the LORD our God. If we don't, he might strike us with plagues. Or he might let us be killed by swords."

[4] But the king of Egypt said, "Moses and Aaron, why are you taking the people away from their work? Get back to work!" [5] Pharaoh continued, "There are large numbers of your people in the land. But you are stopping them from working."

[6] That same day Pharaoh gave orders to the slave drivers and the overseers in charge of the people. [7] He said, "Don't give the people any more straw to make bricks. Let them go and get their own straw. [8] But require them to make the same number of bricks as before. Don't lower the number they have to make. They are lazy. That's why they are crying out, 'Let us go. We want to offer sacrifices to our God.' [9] Make them work harder. Then they will be too busy to pay attention to lies."

[10] The slave drivers and the overseers left. They said to the people, "Pharaoh says, 'I won't give you any more straw. [11] Go and get your own straw anywhere you can find it. But you still have to make the same number of bricks.'" [12] So the people scattered all over Egypt. They went to gather any pieces of straw left in the fields. [13] Pharaoh's slave drivers kept making the people work hard. They said, "Finish the work you are required to do each day. Make the same number of bricks you made when you had straw." [14] The slave drivers whipped the Israelite overseers they had appointed. The slave drivers asked, "Why haven't you made the same number of bricks yesterday or today, just as before?"

[15] Then the Israelite overseers appealed to Pharaoh. They asked, "Why have you treated us like this? [16] You didn't give us any straw. But you told us, 'Make bricks!' We are being whipped. But it's the fault of your own people."

[17] Pharaoh said, "You are lazy! That's why you keep saying, 'Let us go. We want to offer sacrifices to the LORD.' [18] Now get to work. We won't give you any straw. But you still have to make the same number of bricks."

[19] The Israelite overseers realized they were in trouble. They knew it when they were told, "Don't reduce the number of bricks you are required to make each day." [20] When they left Pharaoh, they found Moses and Aaron waiting to meet them. [21] They said to Moses and Aaron, "We want the LORD to look at what you have done! We want him to judge you for it! We are like a very bad smell to Pharaoh and his officials. You have given them an excuse to kill us with their swords."

The LORD Promises to Save the Israelites

[22] Moses returned to talk to the LORD. He said to him, "Why, Lord? Why have you brought trouble on these people? Is this why you sent me? [23] I went to Pharaoh to speak to him in your name. Ever since then, he has brought nothing but trouble on these people. And you haven't saved your people at all."

6 Then the LORD said to Moses, "Now you will see what I will do to Pharaoh. Because of my powerful hand, he will let the people of Israel go. Because of my mighty hand, he will drive them out of his country."

[2] God continued, "I am the LORD. [3] I appeared to Abraham, Isaac and Jacob as the Mighty God. But I did not show them the full meaning of my name, The LORD. [4] I also made my covenant with them. I promised to give them the land of Canaan. That is where they lived as outsiders. [5] Also, I have heard the groans of the Israelites. The Egyptians are keeping them as slaves. But I have remembered my covenant.

[6] "So tell the people of Israel, 'I am the LORD. I will throw off the heavy load the Egyptians have put on your shoulders. I will set you free from being slaves to them. I will reach out my arm and save you with mighty acts when I judge Egypt. [7] I will take you to be my own people. I will be your God. I throw off the load the Egyptians have put on your shoulders. Then you will know that I am the LORD your God. [8] I will bring you to the land I promised to give to Abraham, Isaac and Jacob. I lifted up my hand and promised it to them. The land will belong to you. I am the LORD.'"

[9] Moses reported these things to the Israelites. But they didn't listen to him. That's because they had lost all hope and had to work very hard.

[10] Then the LORD said to Moses, [11] "Go. Tell Pharaoh, the king of Egypt, to let the people of Israel leave his country."

[12] But Moses said to the LORD, "The people won't listen to me. So why would Pharaoh listen to me? After all, I don't speak very well."

The Family Record of Moses and Aaron

[13] The LORD had spoken to Moses and Aaron. He had talked with them about the Israelites and about Pharaoh, the king of

Egypt. He had commanded Moses and Aaron to bring the people of Israel out of Egypt.

[14] Here were the leaders of the family groups of Reuben, Simeon and Levi.

Reuben was the oldest son of Israel. Reuben's sons were Hanok, Pallu, Hezron and Karmi.
These were the family groups of Reuben.

[15] The sons of Simeon were Jemuel, Jamin, Ohad, Jakin, Zohar and Shaul. Shaul was the son of a woman from Canaan.
These were the family groups of Simeon.

[16] Here are the names of the sons of Levi written in their family record. They were Gershon, Kohath and Merari.
Levi lived for 137 years.
[17] The sons of Gershon, by their family groups, were Libni and Shimei.
[18] The sons of Kohath were Amram, Izhar, Hebron and Uzziel.
Kohath lived for 133 years.
[19] The sons of Merari were Mahli and Mushi.
These are the family groups of Levi written in their family record.

[20] Amram married his father's sister Jochebed. Aaron and Moses were members of Amram's family line.
Amram lived for 137 years.
[21] The sons of Izhar were Korah, Nepheg and Zikri.
[22] The sons of Uzziel were Mishael, Elzaphan and Sithri.

[23] Aaron married Elisheba. She was the daughter of Amminadab and the sister of Nahshon. She had Nadab, Abihu, Eleazar and Ithamar by Aaron.

[24] The sons of Korah were Assir, Elkanah and Abiasaph.
These were the family groups of Korah.

[25] Eleazar, the son of Aaron, married one of the daughters of Putiel. She had Phinehas by Eleazar.

These are the leaders of the families of Levi. Their names are written in their family records.

[26] The LORD had spoken to this same Aaron and Moses. He had told them, "Bring the Israelites out of Egypt like an army on the march." [27] They spoke to Pharaoh, the king of Egypt, about bringing the people of Israel out of Egypt. It was this same Moses and Aaron.

Aaron Speaks for Moses

[28] The LORD had spoken to Moses in Egypt. [29] He had told him, "I am the LORD. Tell Pharaoh, the king of Egypt, everything I tell you."

[30] But Moses said to the LORD, "I don't speak very well. So why would Pharaoh listen to me?"

7 Then the LORD said to Moses, "I have made you like God to Pharaoh. And your brother Aaron will be like a prophet to you. [2] You must say everything I command you to say. Then your brother Aaron must tell Pharaoh to let the people of Israel leave his country. [3] But I will make Pharaoh stubborn. I will multiply the signs and amazing things I will do in Egypt. [4] In spite of that, he will not listen to you. So I will use my powerful hand against Egypt. When I judge them with mighty acts, I will bring my people Israel out like an army on the march. [5] Then the Egyptians will know that I am the LORD. I will reach out my powerful hand against them. I will bring the people of Israel out of Egypt."

[6] Moses and Aaron did exactly as the LORD had commanded them. [7] Moses was 80 years old and Aaron was 83 when they spoke to Pharaoh.

Aaron's Walking Stick Becomes a Snake

[8] The LORD spoke to Moses and Aaron. [9] He said, "Pharaoh will say to you, 'Do a miracle.' When he does, speak to Aaron. Tell him, 'Take your walking stick and throw it down in front of Pharaoh.' It will turn into a snake."

[10] So Moses and Aaron went to Pharaoh. They did exactly as the LORD had commanded them. Aaron threw the stick down in front of Pharaoh and his officials. It turned into a snake. [11] Then Pharaoh sent for wise men and people who do evil magic. By doing their magic tricks, the Egyptian magicians did the same things Aaron had done. [12] Each one threw down his walking stick. Each stick turned into a snake. But Aaron's walking stick swallowed theirs up. [13] In spite of that, Pharaoh became stubborn. He wouldn't listen to them, just as the LORD had said.

The Plague of Blood

[14] Then the LORD said to Moses, "Pharaoh is very stubborn. He refuses to let the people go. [15] In the morning Pharaoh will go down to the Nile River. Go and meet him on the bank of the river. Take in your hand the walking stick that turned into a snake. [16] Say to Pharaoh, 'The LORD, the God of the Hebrews, has sent me to you. He says, "Let my people go. Then they will be able to worship me in the desert. But up to now you have not listened."' [17] The LORD says, "Here is how you will know that I am the LORD. I will strike the water of the Nile River with the walking stick that is in my hand. The river will turn into blood. [18] The fish in the river will die. The river will stink. The Egyptians will not be able to drink its water."'"

[19] The LORD said to Moses, "Tell Aaron, 'Get your walking stick. Reach your hand out

over the waters of Egypt. The streams, canals, ponds and all the lakes will turn into blood. There will be blood everywhere in Egypt. It will even be in the wooden buckets and stone jars.'"

20 Moses and Aaron did exactly as the LORD had commanded them. Aaron held out his staff in front of Pharaoh and his officials. He struck the water of the Nile River. And all the water turned into blood. 21 The fish in the Nile died. The river smelled so bad the Egyptians couldn't drink its water. There was blood everywhere in Egypt. 22 But the Egyptian magicians did the same things by doing their magic tricks. So Pharaoh became stubborn. He wouldn't listen to Moses and Aaron, just as the LORD had said. 23 Even that miracle didn't change Pharaoh's mind. In fact, he turned around and went into his palace. 24 All the Egyptians dug holes near the Nile River to get drinking water. They couldn't drink water from the river.

The Plague of Frogs

25 Seven days passed after the LORD struck the Nile River. 8 1 Then the LORD said to Moses, "Go to Pharaoh. Tell him, 'The LORD says, "Let my people go. Then they will be able to worship me. 2 If you refuse to let them go, I will send a plague of frogs on your whole country. 3 The Nile River will be full of frogs. They will come up into your palace. You will have frogs in your bedroom and on your bed. They will be in the homes of your officials and your people. They will be in your ovens and in the bowls for kneading your bread. 4 The frogs will be on you, your people and all your officials."'"

5 Then the LORD spoke to Moses. He said, "Tell Aaron, 'Reach out your hand. Hold your walking stick over the streams, canals and ponds. Make frogs come up on the land of Egypt.'"

6 So Aaron reached out his hand over the waters of Egypt. The frogs came up and covered the land. 7 But the magicians did the same things by doing their magic tricks. They also made frogs come up on the land of Egypt.

8 Pharaoh sent for Moses and Aaron. He said to them, "Pray to the LORD to take the frogs away from me and my people. Then I'll let your people go to offer sacrifices to the LORD."

9 Moses said to Pharaoh, "You can have the honor of setting the time for me to pray. I will pray for you, your officials and your people. I'll pray that the frogs will leave you and your homes. The only frogs left will be the ones in the Nile River."

10 "Tomorrow," Pharaoh said.

Moses replied, "It will happen just as you say. Then you will know that there is no one like the LORD our God. 11 The frogs will leave you and your houses. They will leave your officials and your people. The frogs will remain only in the Nile River."

¹²Moses and Aaron left Pharaoh. Then Moses cried out to the Lord about the frogs he had brought on Pharaoh. ¹³And the Lord did what Moses asked. The frogs died in the houses, courtyards and fields. ¹⁴The Egyptians piled them up. The land smelled very bad because of them. ¹⁵But when Pharaoh saw that the frogs were dead, he became stubborn. He wouldn't listen to Moses and Aaron, just as the Lord had said.

The Plague of Gnats

¹⁶Then the Lord spoke to Moses. He said, "Tell Aaron, 'Reach out your walking stick. Strike the dust on the ground with it.' Then all over the land of Egypt the dust will turn into gnats." ¹⁷So they did it. Aaron reached out the stick that was in his hand. He struck the dust on the ground with it. The dust all over the land of Egypt turned into gnats. They landed on people and animals alike. ¹⁸The magicians tried to produce gnats by doing their magic tricks. But they couldn't.

The gnats stayed on people and animals everywhere. ¹⁹So the magicians said to Pharaoh, "God's powerful finger has done this." But Pharaoh remained stubborn. He wouldn't listen, just as the Lord had said.

The Plague of Flies

²⁰Then the Lord spoke to Moses. He said, "Get up early in the morning. Talk to Pharaoh as he goes down to the Nile River. Say to him, 'The Lord says, "Let my people go. Then they will be able to worship me. ²¹If you do not let my people go, I will send large numbers of flies. I will send them on you and your officials. I will send them on your people and into your homes. The houses of the Egyptians will be full of flies. Even the ground will be covered with them.

²²" ' "But on that day I will treat the area of Goshen differently from yours. That is where my people live. There will not be large numbers of flies in Goshen. Then you will know that I, the Lord, am in this land. ²³I will treat my people differently from yours. This sign will take place tomorrow." ' "

²⁴So the Lord did it. Huge numbers of flies poured into Pharaoh's palace. They came into the homes of his officials. All over Egypt the flies destroyed the land.

²⁵Then Pharaoh sent for Moses and Aaron. He said to them, "Go. Offer sacrifices to your God here in the land."

²⁶But Moses said, "That wouldn't be right. The sacrifices we offer to the Lord our God wouldn't be accepted by the Egyptians because of their beliefs. For that reason, they would throw stones at us and try to kill us. ²⁷We have to take a journey that lasts about three days. We want to go into the desert to offer sacrifices to the Lord our God, just as he commands us."

²⁸Pharaoh said, "I will let you and your people go to offer sac-

rifices. You can offer them to the LORD your God in the desert. But you must not go very far. Now pray for me."

29 Moses replied, "As soon as I leave you, I will pray to the LORD. Tomorrow the flies will leave you. They will also leave your officials and your people. Just be sure you don't try to trick us again. Let the people go to offer sacrifices to the LORD."

30 Then Moses left Pharaoh and prayed to the LORD. 31 And the LORD did what Moses asked. The flies left Pharaoh, his officials and his people. Not one fly remained. 32 But Pharaoh became stubborn this time also. He wouldn't let the people go.

The Plague on Livestock

9 Then the LORD spoke to Moses. He said, "Go to Pharaoh. Tell him, 'The LORD, the God of the Hebrews, says, "Let my people go. Then they will be able to worship me. 2 Do not refuse to let them go. Do not keep holding them back. 3 If you refuse, my powerful hand will bring a terrible plague on you. I will strike your livestock in the fields. I will strike your horses, donkeys, camels, cattle, sheep and goats. 4 But I will treat Israel's livestock differently from yours. No animal that belongs to the people of Israel will die."'"

5 The LORD set a time for the plague. He said, "Tomorrow I will send it on the land." 6 So the next day the LORD sent it. All the livestock of the Egyptians died. But not one animal that belonged to the Israelites died. 7 Pharaoh searched and found out what had happened. He discovered that not even one animal that belonged to the Israelites had died. But he was still very stubborn. He wouldn't let the people go.

The Plague of Boils

8 Then the LORD spoke to Moses and Aaron. He said, "Take handfuls of ashes from a furnace. Have Moses toss them into the air in front of Pharaoh. 9 The ashes will turn into fine dust over the whole land of Egypt. Then painful boils will break out on people and animals all over the land. Their bodies will be covered with them."

10 So Moses and Aaron took ashes from a furnace and stood in front of Pharaoh. Moses tossed them into the air. Then boils broke out on people and animals alike. 11 The bodies of all the Egyptians were covered with boils. The magicians couldn't stand in front of Moses because of the boils that were all over them. 12 But the LORD made Pharaoh stubborn. Pharaoh wouldn't listen to Moses and Aaron, just as the LORD had said to Moses.

The Plague of Hail

13 Then the LORD spoke to Moses. He said, "Get up early in the morning. Go to Pharaoh and say to him, 'The LORD, the God of the Hebrews, says, "Let my people go. Then they will be able to worship me. 14 If you do not let them

go, I will send the full force of my plagues against you this time. They will strike your officials and your people. Then you will know that there is no one like me in the whole earth. ¹⁵ By now I could have reached out my hand. I could have struck you and your people with a plague that would have wiped you off the earth. ¹⁶ But I had a special reason for making you king. I decided to show you my power. I wanted my name to become known everywhere on earth. ¹⁷ But you are still against my people. You will not let them go. ¹⁸ So at this time tomorrow I will send the worst hailstorm ever to fall on Egypt in its entire history. ¹⁹ Give an order now to bring your livestock inside to a safe place. Bring in everything that is outside. The hail will fall on all the people and animals that are left outside. They will die." '"

²⁰ The officials of Pharaoh who had respect for what the LORD had said obeyed him. They hurried to bring their slaves and their livestock inside. ²¹ But others didn't pay attention to what the LORD had said. They left their slaves and livestock outside.

²² Then the LORD spoke to Moses. He said, "Reach out your hand toward the sky. Then hail will fall all over Egypt. It will beat down on people and animals alike. It will strike everything growing in the fields of Egypt." ²³ Moses reached out his walking stick toward the sky. Then the LORD sent thun-der and hail. Lightning flashed down to the ground. The LORD rained hail on the land of Egypt. ²⁴ Hail fell and lightning flashed back and forth. It was the worst storm in Egypt's entire history. ²⁵ Hail struck everything in the fields all over Egypt. It fell on people and animals alike. It beat down everything growing in the fields. It tore all the leaves off the trees. ²⁶ The only place it didn't hail was in the area of Go-shen. That's where the people of Israel were.

²⁷ Then Pharaoh sent for Moses and Aaron. "This time I've sinned," he said to them. "The LORD has done what is right. I and my people have done what is wrong. ²⁸ Pray to the LORD, because we've had enough thunder and hail. I'll let you and your people go. You don't have to stay here any longer."

²⁹ Moses replied, "When I've left the city, I'll lift up my hands and pray to the LORD. The thunder will stop. There won't be any more hail. Then you will know that the earth belongs to the LORD. ³⁰ But I know that you and your officials still don't have any respect for the LORD God."

³¹ The barley was ripe. The flax was in bloom. So they were both destroyed. ³² But the wheat and spelt weren't destroyed. That's because they ripen later.

³³ Then Moses left Pharaoh and went out of the city. Moses lifted up his hands and prayed to the LORD. The thunder and hail stopped. The rain didn't pour down on the land any lon-

ger. ³⁴ Pharaoh saw that the rain, hail and thunder had stopped. So he sinned again. He and his officials became stubborn. ³⁵ So Pharaoh was stubborn. He wouldn't let the people of Israel go, just as the LORD had said through Moses.

The Plague of Locusts

10 Then the LORD said to Moses, "Go to Pharaoh. I have made him stubborn. I have also made his officials stubborn so I can perform my signs among them. ² Then you will be able to tell your children and grandchildren how hard I was on the Egyptians. You can tell them I performed my signs among the people of Egypt. And all of you will know that I am the LORD."

³ So Moses and Aaron went to Pharaoh. They said to him, "The LORD, the God of the Hebrews, says, 'How long will you refuse to obey me? Let my people go. Then they will be able to worship me. ⁴ If you refuse to let them go, I will bring locusts into your country tomorrow. ⁵ They will cover the ground so that it can't be seen. They will eat what little you have left after the hail. That includes every tree growing in your fields. ⁶ They will fill your houses. They will be in the homes of all your officials and your people. Your parents and your people before them have never seen anything like it as long as they have lived here.'" Then Moses turned around and left Pharaoh.

⁷ Pharaoh's officials said to him, "How long will this man be a trap for us? Let the people go. Then they'll be able to worship the LORD their God. After everything that's happened, don't you realize that Egypt is destroyed?"

⁸ Moses and Aaron were brought back to Pharaoh. "Go. Worship the LORD your God," he said. "But tell me who will be going."

⁹ Moses answered, "We'll go with our young people and old people. We'll go with our sons and daughters. We'll take our flocks and herds. We are supposed to hold a feast to honor the LORD."

¹⁰ Pharaoh said, "Suppose I ever let you go, along with your women and children. Then the LORD really will be with all of you! Clearly you are planning to do something bad. ¹¹ No! I'll only allow the men to go and worship the LORD. After all, that's what you have been asking for." Then Pharaoh drove Moses and Aaron out of his sight.

¹² The LORD said to Moses, "Reach out your hand over Egypt so that locusts cover the land. They will eat up everything growing in the fields. They will eat up everything left by the hail."

¹³ So Moses reached out his walking stick over Egypt. Then the LORD made an east wind blow across the land. It blew all that day and all that night. By morning the wind had brought the locusts. ¹⁴ Large numbers of them came down in every part

of Egypt. There had never been a plague of locusts like it before. And there will never be one like it again. ¹⁵ The locusts covered the ground until it was black. They ate up everything left after the hail. They ate up everything growing in the fields. They ate up the fruit on the trees. There was nothing green left on any tree or plant in the whole land of Egypt.

¹⁶ Pharaoh quickly sent for Moses and Aaron. He said, "I have sinned against the LORD your God. I've also sinned against you. ¹⁷ Now forgive my sin one more time. Pray to the LORD your God to take this deadly plague away from me."

¹⁸ After Moses left Pharaoh, he prayed to the LORD. ¹⁹ The LORD changed the wind to a very strong west wind. It picked up the locusts. It blew them into the Red Sea. Not even one locust was left anywhere in Egypt. ²⁰ But the LORD made Pharaoh stubborn. So Pharaoh wouldn't let the people of Israel go.

The Plague of Darkness

²¹ The LORD spoke to Moses. He said, "Reach out your hand toward the sky so that darkness spreads over Egypt. It will be so dark that people can feel it." ²² So Moses reached out his hand toward the sky. Then complete darkness covered Egypt for three days. ²³ No one could see anyone else or go anywhere for three days. But all the people of Israel had light where they lived.

²⁴ Then Pharaoh sent for Moses. He said to him, "Go. Worship the LORD. Even your women and children can go with you. Just leave your flocks and herds behind."

²⁵ But Moses said, "You must allow us to take our animals. We need to offer them as sacrifices and burnt offerings to the LORD our God. ²⁶ Our livestock must also go with us. We have to use some of them to worship the LORD our God. We can't leave even one animal behind. Until we get there, we won't know what we are supposed to use to worship the LORD."

²⁷ But the LORD made Pharaoh stubborn. So he wouldn't let the people go. ²⁸ Pharaoh said to Moses, "Get out of my sight! Make sure you don't come to see me again! If you do, you will die."

²⁹ "I'll do just as you say," Moses replied. "I will never come to see you again."

The LORD Announces the Tenth Plague

11 The LORD had spoken to Moses. He had said, "I will bring one more plague on Pharaoh and on Egypt. After that, he will let you and your people go. When he does, he will drive every one of you away. ² Tell the men and women alike to ask their neighbors for things made out of silver and gold." ³ The LORD caused the Egyptians to treat the Israelites in a kind way. Pharaoh's officials and the people had great respect for Moses.

⁴Moses told Pharaoh, "The LORD says, 'About midnight I will go through every part of Egypt. ⁵Every oldest son in Egypt will die. The oldest son of Pharaoh, who sits on the throne, will die. The oldest son of every female slave, who works at her hand mill, will die. All the male animals born first to their mothers among the cattle will also die. ⁶There will be loud crying all over Egypt. It will be worse than it's ever been before. And nothing like it will ever be heard again. ⁷But among the Israelites not even one dog will bark at any person or animal.' Then you will know that the LORD treats Egypt differently from us. ⁸All your officials will come and bow down to me. They will say, 'Go, you and all the people who follow you!' After that, I will leave." Moses was very angry when he left Pharaoh.

⁹The LORD had spoken to Moses. He had said, "Pharaoh will refuse to listen to you. So I will multiply the amazing things I will do in Egypt." ¹⁰Moses and Aaron performed all these amazing things in the sight of Pharaoh. But the LORD made Pharaoh stubborn. He wouldn't let the people of Israel go out of his country.

The First Passover Sacrifice

12 The LORD spoke to Moses and Aaron in Egypt. ²He said, "From now on, this month will be your first month. Each of your years will begin with it. ³Speak to the whole community of Israel. Tell them that on the tenth day of this month each man must get a lamb from his flock. A lamb should be chosen for each family and home. ⁴Suppose there are not enough people in your family to eat a whole lamb. Then you must share some of it with your nearest neighbor. You must add up the total number of people there are. You must decide how much lamb is needed for each person. ⁵The animals you choose must be males that are a year old. They must not have any flaws. You may choose either sheep or goats. ⁶Take care of them until the 14th day of the month. Then the whole community of Israel must kill them when the sun goes down. ⁷Take some of the blood. Put it on the sides and tops of the doorframes of the houses where you eat the lambs. ⁸That same night eat the meat cooked over a fire. Also eat bitter plants. And eat bread made without yeast. ⁹Do not eat the meat when it is raw. Don't boil it in water. Instead, cook it over a fire. Cook the head, legs and inside parts. ¹⁰Do not leave any of it until morning. If some is left over until morning, burn it up. ¹¹Eat the meat while your coat is tucked into your belt. Put your sandals on your feet. Take your walking stick in your hand. Eat the food quickly. It is the LORD's Passover.

¹²"That same night I will pass through Egypt. I will strike down all those born first among the people and animals. And I

will judge all the gods of Egypt. I am the LORD. ¹³ The blood on your houses will be a sign for you. When I see the blood, I will pass over you. No deadly plague will touch you when I strike Egypt.

¹⁴ "Always remember this day. You and your children after you must celebrate this day as a feast to honor the LORD. You must do this for all time to come. It is a law that will last forever. ¹⁵ For seven days eat bread made without yeast. On the first day remove the yeast from your homes. For the next seven days, anyone who eats anything with yeast in it must be separated from Israel. ¹⁶ On the first and seventh days, come together for a sacred assembly. Do not work at all on these days. The only thing you are allowed to do is prepare food for everyone to eat.

¹⁷ "Celebrate the Feast of Unleavened Bread. I brought you out of Egypt on this very day like an army on the march. It is a law that will last for all time to come. ¹⁸ In the first month eat bread made without yeast. Eat it from the evening of the 14th day until the evening of the 21st day. ¹⁹ For seven days do not let any yeast be found in your homes. Anyone who eats anything with yeast in it must be separated from the community of Israel. That applies to outsiders and Israelites alike. ²⁰ Do not eat anything made with yeast. No matter where you live, eat bread made without yeast."

²¹ Then Moses sent for all the elders of Israel. He said to them, "Go at once. Choose the animals for your families. Each family must kill a Passover lamb. ²² Get a branch of a hyssop plant. Dip it into the blood in the bowl. Put some of the blood on the top and on both sides of the doorframe. None of you can go out of the door of your house until morning. ²³ The LORD will go through the land to strike down the Egyptians. He'll see the blood on the top and sides of the doorframe. He will pass over that house. He won't let the destroying angel enter your homes to strike you down.

²⁴ "Obey all these directions. It's a law for you and your children after you for all time to come. ²⁵ The LORD will give you the land, just as he promised. When you enter it, keep this holy day. ²⁶ Your children will ask you, 'What does this holy day mean to you?' ²⁷ Tell them, 'It's the Passover sacrifice to honor the LORD. He passed over the houses of the Israelites in Egypt. He spared our homes when he struck down the Egyptians.'" Then the Israelites bowed down and worshiped. ²⁸ They did just what the LORD commanded Moses and Aaron.

²⁹ At midnight the LORD struck down every oldest son in Egypt. He killed the oldest son of Pharaoh, who sat on the throne. He killed all the oldest sons of prisoners. He also killed all the male animals born first to their mothers among the livestock. ³⁰ Pharaoh and all his of-

ficials got up during the night. So did all the Egyptians. There was loud crying in Egypt because someone had died in every home.

The Exodus

³¹ During the night, Pharaoh sent for Moses and Aaron. He said to them, "Get out of here! You and the Israelites, leave my people! Go. Worship the LORD, just as you have asked. ³² Go. Take your flocks and herds, just as you have said. And also give me your blessing."

³³ The Egyptians begged the people of Israel to hurry up and leave the country. "If you don't," they said, "we'll all die!" ³⁴ So the people took their dough before the yeast was added to it. They carried it on their shoulders in bowls for kneading bread. The bowls were wrapped in clothes. ³⁵ They did just as Moses had directed them. They asked the Egyptians for things made out of silver and gold. They also asked them for clothes. ³⁶ The LORD had caused the Egyptians to treat the Israelites in a kind way. So the Egyptians gave them what they asked for. The Israelites took many expensive things that belonged to the Egyptians.

³⁷ The Israelites traveled from Rameses to Sukkoth. There were about 600,000 men old enough to go into battle. The women and children went with them. ³⁸ So did many other people. The Israelites also took large flocks and herds with them. ³⁹ The Israelites brought dough from Egypt. With it they baked loaves of bread without yeast. The dough didn't have any yeast in it. That's because the people had been driven out of Egypt before they had time to prepare their food.

⁴⁰ The Israelites lived in Egypt for 430 years. ⁴¹ Then all the LORD's people marched out of Egypt like an army. That happened at the end of the 430 years, to the exact day. ⁴² The LORD kept watch that night to bring them out of Egypt. So on that same night every year all the Israelites must keep watch. They must do it to honor the LORD for all time to come.

Rules for the Passover

⁴³ The LORD said to Moses and Aaron, "Here are the rules for the Passover meal.

"No one from another country is allowed to eat it. ⁴⁴ Any slave you have bought is allowed to eat it after you have circumcised him. ⁴⁵ But a hired worker or someone who lives with you for a short time is not allowed to eat it.

⁴⁶ "It must be eaten inside the house. Do not take any of the meat outside. Do not break any of the bones. ⁴⁷ The whole community of Israel must celebrate the Passover.

⁴⁸ "Suppose an outsider living among you wants to celebrate the LORD's Passover. Then all the males in that home must be circumcised. After that, the person can take part, just like an Israelite. Only circumcised males

may eat it. ⁴⁹The same law applies to Israelites and to outsiders living among you."

⁵⁰All the people of Israel did just what the LORD had commanded Moses and Aaron. ⁵¹On that day the LORD brought the Israelites out of Egypt like an army on the march.

Setting Apart the Oldest Sons

13 The LORD said to Moses, ²"Set apart for me the first boy born in every family. The oldest son of every Israelite mother belongs to me. Every male animal born first to its mother also belongs to me."

³Then Moses said to the people, "Remember this day. It's the day you came out of Egypt. That's the land where you were slaves. The LORD used his mighty hand to bring you out of Egypt. Don't eat anything with yeast in it. ⁴You are leaving today. It's the month of Aviv. ⁵The LORD will bring you into the land of the Canaanites, Hittites, Amorites, Hivites and Jebusites. He promised your people of long ago that he would give that land to you. It's a land that has plenty of milk and honey. When you get there, celebrate this holy day in this month. ⁶For seven days eat bread made without yeast. On the seventh day hold a feast to honor the LORD. ⁷Eat bread made without yeast during those seven days. Nothing with yeast in it should be found among you. No yeast should be seen anywhere inside your borders. ⁸On that day talk to your child. Say, 'I'm doing this because of what the LORD did for me when I came out of Egypt.' ⁹When you celebrate this holy day, it will be like a mark on your hand. It will be like a reminder on your forehead. This law of the LORD must be on your lips. The LORD used his mighty hand to bring you out of Egypt. ¹⁰Obey this law at the appointed time year after year.

¹¹"The LORD will bring you into the land of Canaan. He will give it to you, just as he promised he would. He gave his word to you and your people of long ago. ¹²After you arrive in the land, give to the LORD the oldest son of every mother. Every male animal born first to its mother among your livestock belongs to the LORD. ¹³By sacrificing a lamb, buy back every male donkey born first to its mother. But if you don't buy the donkey back, break its neck. Buy back every oldest son.

¹⁴"In days to come, your child will ask you, 'What does this mean?' Say to them, 'The LORD used his mighty hand to bring us out of Egypt. That's the land where we were slaves. ¹⁵Pharaoh was stubborn. He refused to let us go. So the LORD killed every oldest son in Egypt. He also killed all those born first among the people and animals. That's why I sacrifice to the LORD every male animal born first. And that's why I buy back each of my oldest sons for the LORD.' ¹⁶This holy day will be like a mark on your hand. It will be like a sign

on your forehead. It will remind you that the LORD used his mighty hand to bring us out of Egypt."

Israel Goes Through the Red Sea

[17] Pharaoh let the people go. The shortest road from Goshen to Canaan went through the Philistine country. But God didn't lead them that way. God said, "If they have to go into battle, they might change their minds. They might return to Egypt." [18] So God led the people toward the Red Sea by taking them on a road through the desert. The Israelites were ready for battle when they went up out of Egypt.

[19] Moses took the bones of Joseph along with him. Joseph had made the Israelites give their word to do this. He had said, "God will surely come to help you. When he does, you must carry my bones up from this place with you." *(Genesis 50:25)* [20] The people left Sukkoth. They camped at Etham on the edge of the desert. [21] By day the LORD went ahead of them in a pillar of cloud. It guided them on their way. At night he led them with a pillar of fire. It gave them light. So they could travel by day or at night. [22] The pillar of cloud didn't leave its place in front of the people during the day. And the pillar of fire didn't leave its place at night.

14 Then the LORD spoke to Moses. [2] He said, "Tell the people of Israel to turn back. Have them camp near Pi Ha-

hiroth between Migdol and the Red Sea. They must camp by the sea, right across from Baal Zephon. [3] Pharaoh will think, 'The Israelites are wandering around the land. They don't know which way to go. The desert is all around them.' [4] I will make Pharaoh stubborn. He will chase them. But I will gain glory for myself because of what will happen to Pharaoh and his whole army. And the Egyptians will know that I am the LORD." So the Israelites camped by the Red Sea.

[5] The king of Egypt was told that the people had escaped. Then Pharaoh and his officials changed their minds about them. They said, "What have we done? We've let the people of Israel go! We've lost our slaves and all the work they used to do for us!" [6] So he had his chariot made ready. He took his army with him. [7] He took 600 of the best chariots in Egypt. He also took along all the other chariots. Officers were in charge of all of them. [8] The LORD made Pharaoh, the king of Egypt, stubborn. So he chased the Israelites as they were marching out boldly. [9] The Egyptians went after the Israelites. All Pharaoh's horses and chariots and horsemen and troops chased them. They caught up with the Israelites as they camped by the sea. The Israelites were near Pi Hahiroth, across from Baal Zephon.

[10] As Pharaoh approached, the Israelites looked back. There

were the Egyptians marching after them! The Israelites were terrified. They cried out to the LORD. ¹¹They said to Moses, "Why did you bring us to the desert to die? Weren't there any graves in Egypt? What have you done to us by bringing us out of Egypt? ¹²We told you in Egypt, 'Leave us alone. Let us serve the Egyptians.' It would have been better for us to serve the Egyptians than to die here in the desert!"

¹³Moses answered the people. He said, "Don't be afraid. Stand firm. You will see how the LORD will save you today. Do you see those Egyptians? You will never see them again. ¹⁴The LORD will fight for you. Just be still."

¹⁵Then the LORD spoke to Moses. He said, "Why are you crying out to me? Tell the people of Israel to move on. ¹⁶Hold out your walking stick. Reach out your hand over the Red Sea to divide the water. Then the people can go through the sea on dry ground. ¹⁷I will make the Egyptians stubborn. They will go in after the Israelites. I will gain glory for myself because of what will happen to Pharaoh, his army, chariots and horsemen. ¹⁸The Egyptians will know that I am the LORD. I will gain glory because of what will happen to Pharaoh, his chariots and his horsemen."

¹⁹The angel of God had been traveling in front of Israel's army. Now he moved back and went behind them. The pillar of cloud also moved away from in front of them. Now it stood behind them. ²⁰It came between the armies of Egypt and Israel. All through the night the cloud brought darkness to one side and light to the other. Neither army went near the other all night long.

²¹Then Moses reached out his hand over the Red Sea. All that night the LORD pushed the sea back with a strong east wind. He turned the sea into dry land. The waters were divided. ²²The people of Israel went through the sea on dry ground. There was a wall of water on their right side and on their left.

²³The Egyptians chased them. All Pharaoh's horses and chariots and horsemen followed them into the sea. ²⁴Near the end of the night the LORD looked down from the pillar of fire and cloud. He saw the Egyptian army and threw it into a panic. ²⁵He jammed the wheels of their chariots. That made the chariots hard to drive. The Egyptians said, "Let's get away from the Israelites! The LORD is fighting for Israel against Egypt."

²⁶Then the LORD spoke to Moses. He said, "Reach out your hand over the sea. The waters will flow back over the Egyptians and their chariots and horsemen." ²⁷So Moses reached out his hand over the sea. At sunrise the sea went back to its place. The Egyptians tried to run away from the sea. But the LORD swept them into it. ²⁸The water flowed back and covered the chariots and horsemen. It

covered the entire army of Pharaoh that had followed the people of Israel into the sea. Not one of the Egyptians was left. ²⁹ But the Israelites went through the sea on dry ground. There was a wall of water on their right side and on their left. ³⁰ That day the Lord saved Israel from the power of Egypt. The Israelites saw the Egyptians lying dead on the shore. ³¹ The Israelites saw the amazing power the Lord showed against the Egyptians. So the Israelites had great respect for the Lord and put their trust in him. They also put their trust in his servant Moses.

The Song of Moses and Miriam

15 Here is the song that Moses and the people of Israel sang to the Lord. They said,

"I will sing to the Lord.
　　He is greatly honored.
He has thrown Pharaoh's
　　horses and chariot drivers
　　into the Red Sea.
² The Lord gives me strength
　　and protects me.
He has saved me.
He is my God, I will praise
　　him.
He is my father's God, and I
　　will honor him.
³ The Lord goes into battle.
　　The Lord is his name.
⁴ He has thrown Pharaoh's
　　chariots and army
　　into the Red Sea.
Pharaoh's best officers
　　drowned in the sea.
⁵ The deep waters covered them.
　　They sank to the bottom
　　like a stone.

⁶ "Lord, your right hand
　　was majestic and powerful.
Lord, your right hand
　　destroyed your enemies.
⁷ Because of your great
　　majesty,
　　you threw down those who
　　opposed you.
Your burning anger blazed
　　out.
　　It burned them up like
　　straw.
⁸ The powerful blast from your
　　nose
　　piled up the waters.
The rushing waters stood
　　firm like a wall.
The deep waters stood up
　　in the middle of the sea.

⁹ "Your enemies bragged,
　　'We will chase Israel and
　　will catch them.
We'll divide up what we take
　　from them.
　　We'll eat them alive.
We'll pull our swords out.
　　Our powerful hands will
　　destroy them.'
¹⁰ But you blew with your
　　breath.
　　The Red Sea covered your
　　enemies.
They sank like lead
　　in the mighty waters.

¹¹ "Lord, who among the gods
　　is like you?
　　Who is like you?
You are majestic and holy.
Your glory fills me with
　　wonder.
　　You do amazing things.
¹² You reach out your right hand.
　　The earth swallows up
　　your enemies.

13 "Because your love is faithful,
  you will lead the people
    you have set free.
  Because you are so strong,
    you will guide them to the
      holy place where you
        live.
14 The nations will hear about it
    and tremble.
  Pain and suffering
    will take hold of the
      Philistines.
15 The chiefs of Edom will be
    terrified.
  The leaders of Moab will
    tremble with fear.
  The people of Canaan will
    melt away.
16   Fear and terror will fall on
      them.
  Your powerful arm
    will make them as still as a
      stone.
  Then your people will pass
    by, Lord.
  Then the people you
    created will pass by.
17 You will bring them in.
  You will plant them on
    the mountain you gave
      them.
  Lord, you have made that
    place your home.
  Lord, your hands have
    made your holy place
      secure.

18 "The Lord rules
  for ever and ever."

19 Pharaoh's horses, chariots
and horsemen went into the Red
Sea. The Lord brought the waters of the sea back over them.
But the people of Israel walked
through the sea on dry ground.

20 Aaron's sister Miriam was a
prophet. She took a tambourine in her hand. All the women
followed her. They played tambourines and danced. 21 Miriam
sang to them,

  "Sing to the Lord.
    He is greatly honored.
  He has thrown Pharaoh's
    horses and chariot drivers
      into the Red Sea."

The Waters of Marah and Elim

22 Then Moses led Israel away
from the Red Sea. They went
into the Desert of Shur. For three
days they traveled in the desert.
They didn't find any water there.
23 When they came to Marah,
they couldn't drink its water. It
was bitter. That's why the place
is named Marah. 24 The people
told Moses they weren't happy
with him. They said, "What are
we supposed to drink?"

25 Then Moses cried out to the
Lord. The Lord showed him
a stick. Moses threw it into the
water. The water became fit to
drink.

There the Lord gave a ruling
and instruction for the people.
And there he tested them. 26 He
said, "I am the Lord your God.
Listen carefully to me. Do what
is right in my eyes. Pay attention
to my commands. Obey all my
rules. If you do, I will not send
on you any of the sicknesses I
sent on the Egyptians. I am the
Lord who heals you."

27 The people came to Elim.
It had 12 springs and 70 palm
trees. They camped there near
the water.

The LORD Gives Israel Food Every Day

16 The whole community of Israel started out from Elim. They came to the Desert of Sin. It was between Elim and Sinai. They arrived there on the 15th day of the second month after they had come out of Egypt. ² In the desert the whole community told Moses and Aaron they weren't happy with them. ³ The Israelites said to them, "We wish the LORD had put us to death in Egypt. There we sat around pots of meat. We ate all the food we wanted. But you have brought us out into this desert. You must want this entire community to die of hunger."

⁴ Then the LORD spoke to Moses. He said, "I will rain down bread from heaven for you. The people must go out each day. Have them gather enough bread for that day. Here is how I will test them. I will see if they will follow my directions. ⁵ On the sixth day they must prepare what they bring in. On that day they must gather twice as much as on the other days."

⁶ So Moses and Aaron spoke to all the people of Israel. They said, "In the evening you will know that the LORD brought you out of Egypt. ⁷ And in the morning you will see the glory of the LORD. He has heard you say you aren't happy with him. Who are we? Why are you telling us you aren't happy with us?" ⁸ Moses also said, "You will know that the LORD has heard you speak against him. He will give you meat to eat in the evening. He'll give you all the bread you want in the morning. But who are we? You aren't speaking against us. You are speaking against the LORD."

⁹ Then Moses told Aaron, "Talk to the whole community of Israel. Say to them, 'Come to the LORD. He has heard you speak against him.'"

¹⁰ While Aaron was talking to the whole community of Israel, they looked toward the desert. There was the glory of the LORD appearing in the cloud!

¹¹ The LORD said to Moses, ¹² "I have heard the people of Israel talking about how unhappy they are. Tell them, 'When the sun goes down, you will eat meat. In the morning you will be filled with bread. Then you will know that I am the LORD your God.'"

¹³ That evening quail came and covered the camp. In the morning the ground around the camp was covered with dew. ¹⁴ When the dew was gone, thin flakes appeared on the desert floor. They looked like frost on the ground. ¹⁵ The people of Israel saw the flakes. They asked each other, "What's that?" They didn't know what it was.

Moses said to them, "It's the bread the LORD has given you to eat. ¹⁶ Here is what the LORD has commanded. He has said, 'Everyone should gather as much as they need. Take three pounds for each person who lives in your tent.'"

¹⁷ The people of Israel did as

they were told. Some gathered a lot, and some gathered a little. ¹⁸ When they measured it out, the one who gathered a lot didn't have too much. And the one who gathered a little had enough. Everyone gathered only what they needed.

¹⁹ Then Moses said to them, "Don't keep any of it until morning."

²⁰ Some of them didn't pay any attention to Moses. They kept part of it until morning. But it was full of maggots and began to stink. So Moses became angry with them.

²¹ Each morning everyone gathered as much as they needed. But by the hottest time of the day, the thin flakes had melted away. ²² On the sixth day, the people gathered twice as much. It amounted to six pounds for each person. The leaders of the community came and reported that to Moses. ²³ He said to them, "Here is what the LORD commanded. He said, 'Tomorrow will be a day of rest. It will be a holy Sabbath day. It will be set apart for the LORD. So bake what you want to bake. Boil what you want to boil. Save what is left. Keep it until morning.' "

²⁴ So they saved it until morning, just as Moses commanded. It didn't stink or get maggots in it. ²⁵ "Eat it today," Moses said. "Today is a Sabbath day to honor the LORD. You won't find any flakes on the ground today. ²⁶ Gather them for six days. But on the seventh day there won't be any. It's the Sabbath day."

²⁷ In spite of what Moses said, some of the people went out on the seventh day to gather the flakes. But they didn't find any. ²⁸ Then the LORD spoke to Moses. He said, "How long will all of you refuse to obey my commands and my teachings? ²⁹ Keep in mind that I have given you the Sabbath day. That is why on the sixth day I give you bread for two days. Everyone must stay where they are on the seventh day. No one can go out." ³⁰ So the people rested on the seventh day.

³¹ The people of Israel called the bread manna. It was white like coriander seeds. It tasted like wafers made with honey. ³² Moses said, "Here is what the LORD has commanded. He has said, 'Get three pounds of manna. Keep it for all time to come. Then those who live after you will see the bread I gave you to eat in the desert. I gave it to you when I brought you out of Egypt.' "

³³ So Moses said to Aaron, "Get a jar. Put three pounds of manna in it. Then place it in front of the LORD. Keep it there for all time to come."

³⁴ Aaron did exactly as the LORD had commanded Moses. He put the manna with the tablets of the covenant law. He put it there so it would be kept for all time to come. ³⁵ The Israelites ate manna for 40 years. They ate it until they came to a land where people were living. They ate it until they reached the border of Canaan.

³⁶ The jar had three pounds of manna in it.

Water Out of the Rock

17 The whole community of Israel started out from the Desert of Sin. They traveled from place to place, just as the LORD commanded. They camped at Rephidim. But there wasn't any water for the people to drink. ² So they argued with Moses. They said, "Give us water to drink."

Moses replied, "Why are you arguing with me? Why are you testing the LORD?"

³ But the people were thirsty for water there. So they told Moses they weren't happy with him. They said, "Why did you bring us up out of Egypt? Did you want us, our children and our livestock to die of thirst?"

⁴ Then Moses cried out to the LORD. He said, "What am I going to do with these people? They are almost ready to kill me by throwing stones at me."

⁵ The LORD answered Moses. "Go out in front of the people. Take some of the elders of Israel along with you. Take in your hand the walking stick you used when you struck the Nile River. Go. ⁶ I will stand there in front of you by the rock at Mount Horeb. Hit the rock. Then water will come out of it for the people to drink." So Moses hit the rock while the elders of Israel watched. ⁷ Moses called the place Massah and Meribah. That's because the people of Israel argued with him there.

They also tested the LORD. They asked, "Is the LORD among us or not?"

Joshua Wins the Battle Over the Amalekites

⁸ The Amalekites came and attacked the Israelites at Rephidim. ⁹ Moses said to Joshua, "Choose some of our men. Then go out and fight against the Amalekites. Tomorrow I will stand on top of the hill. I'll stand there holding the walking stick God gave me."

¹⁰ So Joshua fought against the Amalekites, just as Moses had ordered. Moses, Aaron and Hur went to the top of the hill. ¹¹ As long as Moses held up his hand, the Israelites were winning. But every time he lowered his hands, the Amalekites began to win. ¹² When Moses' arms got tired, Aaron and Hur got a stone and put it under him. Then he sat on it. Aaron and Hur held up his hands. Aaron was on one side, and Hur was on the other. Moses' hands remained steady until sunset. ¹³ So Joshua destroyed the Amalekite army with swords.

¹⁴ Then the LORD said to Moses, "This is something to be remembered. So write it on a scroll. Make sure Joshua knows you have done it. I will completely erase the memory of the Amalekites from the earth."

¹⁵ Then Moses built an altar. He called it The LORD Is My Banner. ¹⁶ He said, "The Amalekites opposed the authority of the LORD. So the LORD

will fight against the Amalekites for all time to come."

Jethro Visits Moses

18 Moses' father-in-law Jethro was the priest of Midian. He heard about everything God had done for Moses and for his people Israel. Jethro heard how the LORD had brought Israel out of Egypt.

2 Moses had sent his wife Zipporah to his father-in-law. So Jethro welcomed her 3 and her two sons. One son was named Gershom. That's because Moses had said, "I'm an outsider in a strange land." 4 The other was named Eliezer. That's because Moses had said, "My father's God helped me. He saved me from Pharaoh's sword."

5 Moses' father-in-law Jethro came to Moses in the desert. Moses' sons and wife came with Jethro. Moses was camped near the mountain of God. 6 Jethro had sent a message to him. It said, "I, your father-in-law Jethro, am coming to you. I'm bringing your wife and her two sons."

7 So Moses went out to meet his father-in-law. Moses bowed down and kissed him. They greeted each other. Then they went into the tent. 8 Moses told Jethro everything the LORD had done to Pharaoh and the Egyptians. The LORD did all of this because of how much he loved Israel. Moses told Jethro about all their hard times along the way. He told him about how the LORD had saved them.

9 Jethro was delighted to hear about all the good things the LORD had done for Israel. He heard about how God had saved them from the power of the Egyptians. 10 He said, "I praise the LORD. He saved you and your people from the power of the Egyptians and of Pharaoh. 11 Now I know that the LORD is greater than all other gods. See what he did to those who looked down on Israel." 12 Then Moses' father-in-law Jethro brought a burnt offering and other sacrifices to God. Aaron came with all the elders of Israel. They ate a meal with Moses' father-in-law in the sight of God.

13 The next day Moses took his seat to serve the people as their judge. They stood around him from morning until evening. 14 His father-in-law saw everything Moses was doing for the people. So he said, "Aren't you trying to do too much for the people? You are the only judge. And all these people are standing around you from morning until evening."

15 Moses answered, "The people come to me to find out what God wants them to do. 16 Anytime they don't agree with one another, they come to me. I decide between them. I tell them about God's rules and instructions."

17 Moses' father-in-law replied, "What you are doing isn't good. 18 You will just get worn out. And so will these people who come to you. There's too much work for you. You can't possibly handle it by yourself.

¹⁹ Listen to me. I'll give you some advice, and may God be with you. You must speak to God for the people. Take their problems to him. ²⁰ Teach them his rules and instructions. Show them how to live and what to do. ²¹ But choose men of ability from all the people. They must have respect for God. You must be able to trust them. They must not try to get money by cheating others. Appoint them as officials over thousands, hundreds, fifties and tens. ²² Let them serve the people as judges. But have them bring every hard case to you. They can decide the easy ones themselves. That will make your load lighter. They will share it with you. ²³ If this is what God wants and if you do it, then you will be able to carry the load. And all these people will go home satisfied."

²⁴ Moses listened to his father-in-law. He did everything Jethro said. ²⁵ He chose men of ability from the whole community of Israel. He made them leaders of the people. They became officials over thousands, hundreds, fifties and tens. ²⁶ They judged the people at all times. They brought the hard cases to Moses. But they decided the easy ones themselves.

²⁷ Moses sent his father-in-law on his way. So Jethro returned to his own country.

Israel Comes to Mount Sinai

19 Exactly three months after the people of Israel left Egypt, they came to the Desert of Sinai. ² After they started out from Rephidim, they entered the Desert of Sinai. They camped there in the desert in front of the mountain.

³ Then Moses went up to God. The Lord called out to him from the mountain. He said, "Here is what I want you to say to my people, who belong to Jacob's family. Tell the Israelites, ⁴ 'You have seen for yourselves what I did to Egypt. You saw how I carried you on the wings of eagles and brought you to myself. ⁵ Now obey me completely. Keep my covenant. If you do, then out of all the nations you will be my special treasure. The whole earth is mine. ⁶ But you will be a kingdom of priests to serve me. You will be my holy nation.' That is what you must tell the Israelites."

⁷ So Moses went back. He sent for the elders of the people. He explained to them everything the Lord had commanded him to say. ⁸ All the people answered together. They said, "We will do everything the Lord has said." So Moses brought their answer back to the Lord.

⁹ The Lord spoke to Moses. He said, "I am going to come to you in a thick cloud. The people will hear me speaking with you. They will always put their trust in you." Then Moses told the Lord what the people had said.

¹⁰ The Lord said to Moses, "Go to the people. Today and tomorrow set them apart for me. Have them wash their clothes. ¹¹ Have the people ready by the

third day. On that day the LORD will come down on Mount Sinai. Everyone will see it. ¹²Put limits for the people around the mountain. Tell them, 'Be careful that you do not go near the mountain. Do not even touch the foot of it. Whoever touches the mountain must be put to death. ¹³Do not lay a hand on any of them. Kill them with stones or shoot them with arrows. Whether they are people or animals, do not let them live.' They may go near the mountain only when the ram's horn gives out a long blast."

¹⁴Moses went down the mountain to the people. After he set them apart for the LORD, they washed their clothes. ¹⁵Then he spoke to the people. He said, "Get ready for the third day. Don't have sex."

¹⁶On the morning of the third day there was thunder and lightning. A thick cloud covered the mountain. A trumpet gave out a very loud blast. Everyone in the camp trembled with fear. ¹⁷Then Moses led the people out of the camp to meet with God. They stood at the foot of the mountain. ¹⁸Smoke covered Mount Sinai, because the LORD came down on it in fire. The smoke rose up from it like smoke from a furnace. The whole mountain trembled and shook. ¹⁹The sound of the trumpet got louder and louder. Then Moses spoke. And the voice of God answered him.

²⁰The LORD came down to the top of Mount Sinai. He told Moses to come to the top of the mountain. So Moses went up. ²¹The LORD said to him, "Go down and warn the people. They must not force their way through to see the LORD. If they do, many of them will die. ²²The priests approach the LORD when they serve him. But even they must set themselves apart for the LORD. If they do not, his anger will break out against them."

²³Moses said to the LORD, "The people can't come up Mount Sinai. You yourself warned us. You said, 'Put limits around the mountain. Set it apart as holy.'"

²⁴The LORD replied, "Go down. Bring Aaron up with you. But the priests and the people must not force their way through. They must not come up to the LORD. If they do, his anger will break out against them."

²⁵So Moses went down to the people and told them.

God Gives His People the Ten Commandments

20 Here are all the words God spoke. He said,

²"I am the LORD your God. I brought you out of Egypt. That is the land where you were slaves.

³"Do not put any other gods in place of me.

⁴"Do not make for yourself statues of gods that look like anything in the sky. They may not look like anything on the earth or in the waters either. ⁵Do not

bow down to them or worship them. I, the LORD your God, am a jealous God. I cause the sins of the parents to affect their children. I will cause the sins of those who hate me to affect even their grandchildren and great-grandchildren. ⁶But for all time to come I show love to all those who love me and keep my commandments.

⁷"Do not misuse the name of the LORD your God. The LORD will find guilty anyone who misuses his name.

⁸"Remember to keep the Sabbath day holy. ⁹Do all your work in six days. ¹⁰But the seventh day is a sabbath to honor the LORD your God. Do not do any work on that day. The same command applies to your sons and daughters, your male and female servants, and your animals. It also applies to any outsiders who live in your towns. ¹¹In six days the LORD made the heavens, the earth, the sea and everything in them. But he rested on the seventh day. So the LORD blessed the Sabbath day and made it holy.

¹²"Honor your father and mother. Then you will live a long time in the land the LORD your God is giving you.

¹³"Do not murder.

¹⁴"Do not commit adultery.

¹⁵"Do not steal.

¹⁶"Do not be a false witness against your neighbor.

¹⁷"Do not want to have anything your neighbor owns. Do not want to have your neighbor's house, wife, male or female servant, ox or donkey."

¹⁸The people saw the thunder and lightning. They heard the trumpet. They saw the mountain covered with smoke. They trembled with fear and stayed a long way off. ¹⁹They said to Moses, "Speak to us yourself. Then we'll listen. But don't let God speak to us. If he does, we'll die."

²⁰Moses said to the people, "Don't be afraid. God has come to test you. He wants you to have respect for him. That will keep you from sinning."

²¹Moses approached the thick darkness where God was. But the people remained a long way off.

Worship the LORD

²²Then the LORD said to Moses, "Here is what you must tell the people of Israel. Say to them, 'You have seen for yourselves what I said to you from heaven. ²³Do not put any other gods in place of me. Do not make silver or gold statues of them for yourselves.

²⁴"'Make an altar out of dirt for me. Sacrifice your burnt offerings and friendship offerings on it. Sacrifice your sheep, goats and cattle on it. I will come to you and bless you everywhere I cause my name to be honored.

25 If you make an altar out of stones to honor me, do not build it with blocks of stone. You will make it "unclean" if you use a tool on it. 26 Do not walk up steps to my altar. If you do, someone might see your naked body under your robes.'

Other Laws

21 "Here are the laws you must explain to the people of Israel.

Set Your Hebrew Servants Free

2 "Suppose you buy a Hebrew servant. He must serve you for six years. But in the seventh year, you must set him free. He does not have to pay anything. 3 If he does not have a wife when he comes, he must go free alone. But if he has a wife when he comes, she must go with him. 4 Suppose his master gives him a wife. And suppose she has sons or daughters by him. Then only the man will go free. The woman and her children will belong to her master.

5 "But suppose the servant says, 'I love my master and my wife and children. I don't want to go free.' 6 Then his master must take him to the judges. His master must take him to the door or doorpost of his master's house. His master must poke a hole through his servant's earlobe into the door or doorpost. Then he will become his servant for life.

7 "Suppose a man sells his daughter as a servant. Then she can't go free as male servants do. 8 But what if the master who has chosen her does not like her? Then he must let the man buy her back. He has no right to sell her to strangers. He has broken his promise to her. 9 What if he chooses her to marry his son? Then he must grant her the rights of a daughter. 10 What if her master marries another woman? He must still give the first one her food and clothes and sleep with her. 11 If he does not provide her with those three things, she can go free. She does not have to pay anything.

Laws About Harming Others

12 "Anyone who hits and kills someone else must be put to death. 13 Suppose they did not do it on purpose. Suppose I let it happen. Then they can escape to a place I will choose. 14 But suppose they kill someone on purpose. Then take them away from my altar and put them to death.

15 "Anyone who attacks their father or mother must be put to death.

16 "Anyone who kidnaps and sells another person must be put to death. If they still have the person with them when they are caught, they must be put to death.

17 "Anyone who asks for something bad to happen to their father or mother must be put to death.

18 "Suppose two people get into a fight and argue with each other. One hits the other with a stone or his fist. And the per-

Noah's Ark

GENESIS 7:1–24

Creation

GENESIS 1:1–31

son who was hit does not die but has to stay in bed. ¹⁹ And later that person gets up and walks around outside with a walking stick. Then the person who hit the other person will not be held responsible. But that person must pay the one who was hurt for the time spent in bed. The one who hit the other person must be sure that person is completely healed.

²⁰ "Suppose a person beats their male or female slave to death with a club. That person must be punished. ²¹ But they will not be punished if the slave gets up after a day or two. After all, the slave is their property.

²² "Suppose some people are fighting and one of them hits a pregnant woman. And suppose she has her baby early but is not badly hurt. Then the one who hurt her must pay a fine. That person must pay what the woman's husband asks for and the court allows. ²³ But if someone is badly hurt, a life must be taken for a life. ²⁴ An eye must be put out for an eye. A tooth must be knocked out for a tooth. A hand must be cut off for a hand and a foot for a foot. ²⁵ A burn must be given for a burn, a wound for a wound, and a bruise for a bruise.

²⁶ "Suppose an owner hits a male or female slave in the eye and destroys it. Then the owner must let the slave go free to pay for the eye. ²⁷ Suppose an owner knocks out the tooth of a male or female slave. Then he must let the slave go free to pay for the tooth.

²⁸ "Suppose a bull kills a man or woman with its horns. Then you must kill the bull by throwing stones at it. Its meat must not be eaten. But the owner of the bull will not be held accountable. ²⁹ But suppose the bull has had the habit of attacking people. And suppose the owner has been warned but has not kept it fenced in. Then if it kills a man or woman, you must kill it with stones. The owner must also be put to death. ³⁰ But suppose payment is required of him instead. Then the owner can save his life by paying what is required. ³¹ The same law applies if the bull wounds a son or daughter with its horns. ³² Suppose the bull wounds a male or female slave. Then the owner must pay the slave's master about 12 ounces of silver. You must kill the bull with stones.

³³ "Suppose someone uncovers a pit or digs one and does not cover it. And suppose an ox or donkey falls into it. ³⁴ Then the person who opened the pit must pay the animal's owner for the loss. The dead animal will belong to the person who opened the pit.

³⁵ "Suppose someone's bull wounds a neighbor's bull and it dies. Then the owner and the neighbor must sell the live one. And they must share the money and the dead animal equally. ³⁶ But suppose people knew that the bull had the habit of attacking. And suppose the owner did not keep it fenced in. Then the owner must give another

animal to pay for the dead animal. And the dead animal will belong to the owner.

Laws About Keeping Property Safe

22 "Suppose someone steals an ox or a sheep. And suppose that person kills it or sells it. Then the thief must pay back five oxen for the ox. Or the thief must pay back four sheep for the sheep.

2 "Suppose you catch a thief breaking into your house at night. And suppose you hit the thief and the thief dies. Then you are not guilty of murder. 3 But suppose it happens after the sun has come up. Then you are guilty of murder.

"Anyone who steals must pay for whatever they steal. But suppose the thief does not have anything. Then the thief must be sold to pay for what was stolen. 4 What if the stolen ox, donkey or sheep is found alive with the thief? Then the thief must pay back twice as much.

5 "Suppose someone lets their livestock eat grass in someone else's field or vineyard. Then they must pay that person back from the best crops of their own field or vineyard.

6 "Suppose a fire breaks out and spreads into bushes. Suppose it burns cut and stacked grain or grain that is still growing. Or suppose it burns the whole field. Then the one who started the fire must pay for the loss.

7 "Suppose someone gives a neighbor silver or other things to keep safe. And suppose they are stolen from the neighbor's house. The thief, if caught, must pay back twice as much as was stolen. 8 But suppose the thief is not found. Then the neighbor must go to the judges. They will decide whether the neighbor has stolen the other person's property. 9 Suppose you have an ox, donkey, sheep or clothing that does not belong to you. Or you have other property lost by someone else. And suppose someone says, 'That belongs to me.' Then both people must bring their case to the judges. The one the judges decide is guilty must pay back twice as much to the other person.

10 "Suppose someone asks their neighbor to take care of a donkey, ox, sheep or any other animal. And suppose the animal dies or gets hurt. Or suppose it is stolen while no one is looking. 11 Then the problem will be settled by promising the LORD to tell the truth. Suppose the neighbor says, 'I didn't steal your property.' Then the owner must accept what the neighbor says. No payment is required. 12 But suppose the animal really was stolen. Then the neighbor must pay the owner back. 13 Or suppose it was torn to pieces by a wild animal. Then the neighbor must bring in what is left as proof. No payment is required.

14 "Suppose someone borrows an animal from their neighbor. And it gets hurt or dies while the owner is not there. Then the borrower must pay for it. 15 But

suppose the owner is with the animal. Then the borrower will not have to pay. If the borrower hired the animal, the money paid to hire it covers the loss.

Laws About Social Problems

16 "Suppose a man meets a virgin who is not engaged. And he talks her into having sex with him. Then he must pay her father the price for a bride. And he must marry her. 17 But suppose her father absolutely refuses to give her to him. Then he must still pay the price for getting married to a virgin.

18 "Do not let a woman who does evil magic stay alive. Put her to death.

19 "Anyone who has sex with an animal must be put to death.

20 "Anyone who sacrifices to any god other than the LORD must be destroyed.

21 "Do not treat outsiders badly. Do not give them a hard time. Remember, you were outsiders in Egypt.

22 "Do not take advantage of widows. Do not take advantage of children whose fathers have died. 23 If you do, they might cry out to me. I will certainly hear them. 24 And I will get angry. I will kill you with a sword. Your wives will become widows. Your children's fathers will die.

25 "Suppose you lend money to one of my people among you who is in need. Then do not treat it like a business deal. Do not charge any interest at all. 26 Suppose your neighbor owes you money and gives you a coat as a promise to pay it back. Then return it by sunset. 27 That coat is the only thing your neighbor owns to wear or sleep in. When they cry out to me, I will listen, because I am loving and kind.

28 "Do not speak evil things against God. Do not curse the ruler of your people.

29 "Do not keep for yourself your grain offerings or wine offerings.

"You must give me the oldest of your sons. 30 Do the same with your cattle and sheep. Let them stay with their mothers for seven days. But give them to me on the eighth day.

31 "I want you to be my holy people. So do not eat the meat of any animal that has been torn by wild animals. Throw it to the dogs.

Laws About Mercy and Fairness

23 "Do not spread reports that are false. Do not help a guilty person by telling lies in court.

2 "Do not follow the crowd when they do what is wrong. When you are a witness in court, do not turn what is right into what is wrong. Do not go along with the crowd. 3 Do not show favor to a poor person in court.

4 "Suppose you come across your enemy's ox or donkey wandering away. Then be sure to return it. 5 Suppose you see that the donkey of someone who hates you has fallen down under its load. Then do not leave it there. Be sure you help them with it.

⁶ "Be fair to your poor people in their court cases. ⁷ Do not have anything to do with a false charge. Do not put to death people not guilty of doing anything wrong. I will not let guilty people go free.

⁸ "Do not take money from people who want special favors. It makes you blind to the truth. It twists the words of good people.

⁹ "Do not treat outsiders badly. You yourselves know how it feels to be outsiders. Remember, you were outsiders in Egypt.

Sabbath Laws

¹⁰ "For six years plant your fields and gather your crops. ¹¹ But during the seventh year do not plow your land or use it. Then the poor people among you can get food from it. The wild animals can eat what is left over. Do the same thing with your vineyards and your groves of olive trees.

¹² "Do all your work in six days. But do not do any work on the seventh day. Then your oxen and donkeys can rest. The slaves born in your house can be renewed. And so can the outsiders who live among you.

¹³ "Be careful to do everything I have said to you. Do not speak the names of other gods. Do not even let them be heard on your lips.

Laws About Celebrating the Three Main Feasts

¹⁴ "Three times a year you must celebrate a feast in my honor.

¹⁵ "Celebrate the Feast of Unleavened Bread. For seven days, eat bread made without yeast, just as I commanded you. Do it at the appointed time in the month of Aviv. You came out of Egypt in that month.

"You must not come to worship me with your hands empty.

¹⁶ "Celebrate the Feast of Weeks. Bring the first share of your crops from your fields.

"Celebrate the Feast of Booths. Hold it in the fall when you gather in your crops from your fields.

¹⁷ "Three times a year all your men must come to worship me. I am your LORD and King.

¹⁸ "Do not include anything made with yeast when you offer me the blood of a sacrifice.

"Suppose the fat from sacrifices is left over from my feasts. Then do not keep it until morning.

¹⁹ "Bring the best of the first share of your crops to my house. I am the LORD your God.

"Do not cook a young goat in its mother's milk.

God's Angel Will Prepare the Way

²⁰ "I am sending an angel ahead of you. He will guard you along the way. He will bring you to the place I have prepared. ²¹ Pay attention to him. Listen to what he says. Do not refuse to obey him. He will not forgive you if you turn against him. He has my full authority. ²² Listen carefully to what he says. Do everything I say. Then I will be an

enemy to your enemies. I will fight against those who fight against you. ²³ My angel will go ahead of you. He will bring you into the land of the Amorites, Hittites, Perizzites, Canaanites, Hivites and Jebusites. I will wipe them out. ²⁴ Do not do what they do. Do not bow down to their gods or worship them. You must destroy the statues of their gods. You must break their sacred stones to pieces. ²⁵ Worship the Lord your God. Then he will bless your food and water. I, the Lord, will take away any sickness you may have. ²⁶ In your land no woman will give birth to a dead baby. Every woman will be able to have children. I will give you a long life.

²⁷ "I will send my terror ahead of you. I will throw every nation you meet into a panic. I will make all your enemies turn their backs and run away. ²⁸ I will send hornets ahead of you. They will drive the Hivites, Canaanites and Hittites out of your way. ²⁹ But I will not drive them out in just one year. If I did, the land would be deserted. There would be too many wild animals for you. ³⁰ I will drive them out ahead of you little by little. I will do that until there are enough of you to take control of the land.

³¹ "I will make your borders secure from the Red Sea to the Mediterranean Sea. They will go from the desert to the Euphrates River. I will hand over to you the people who live in the land. You will drive them out to

make room for yourselves. ³² Do not make a covenant with them or with their gods. ³³ Do not let them live in your land. If you do, they will cause you to sin against me. If you worship their gods, that will certainly be a trap for you."

The Blood of the Covenant

24 The Lord said to Moses, "You and Aaron, Nadab and Abihu, and 70 of the elders of Israel must come to worship the Lord. Do not come close when you worship. ² Only Moses can come close to me. The others must not come near. And the people may not go up with him."

³ Moses went and told the people all the Lord's words and laws. They answered with one voice. They said, "We will do everything the Lord has told us to do." ⁴ Then Moses wrote down everything the Lord had said.

Moses got up early the next morning. He built an altar at the foot of the mountain. He set up 12 stone pillars. They stood for the 12 tribes of Israel. ⁵ Then he sent young Israelite men to sacrifice burnt offerings. They also sacrificed young bulls as friendship offerings to the Lord. ⁶ Moses put half of the blood in bowls. He splashed the other half against the altar. ⁷ Then he took the Book of the Covenant and read it to the people. They answered, "We will do everything the Lord has told us to do. We will obey him."

⁸ Then Moses took the blood and sprinkled it on the people.

He said, "This is the blood that puts the covenant into effect. The LORD has made this covenant with you in keeping with all these words."

9 Moses and Aaron, Nadab and Abihu, and the 70 elders of Israel went up. 10 They saw the God of Israel. Under his feet was something like a street made out of lapis lazuli. It was as bright blue as the sky itself. 11 But God didn't destroy those Israelite leaders when they saw him. They ate and drank.

12 The LORD said to Moses, "Come up to me on the mountain. Stay here. I will give you the stone tablets. They contain the law and commandments I have written to teach the people."

13 Then Moses and Joshua, his helper, started out. Moses went up on the mountain of God. 14 He said to the elders, "Wait for us here until we come back to you. Aaron and Hur are with you. Anyone who has a problem can go to them."

15 Moses went up on the mountain. Then the cloud covered it. 16 The glory of the LORD settled on Mount Sinai. The cloud covered the mountain for six days. On the seventh day the LORD called out to Moses from inside the cloud. 17 The people of Israel saw the glory of the LORD. It looked like a fire burning on top of the mountain. 18 Moses entered the cloud as he went on up the mountain. He stayed on the mountain for 40 days and 40 nights.

Offerings for the Holy Tent

25 The LORD said to Moses, 2 "Tell the people of Israel to bring me an offering. You must receive the offering for me from everyone whose hearts move them to give.

3 "Here are the offerings you must receive from them.

"gold, silver and bronze 4 blue, purple and bright red yarn and fine linen goat hair 5 ram skins that are dyed red another kind of strong leather acacia wood 6 olive oil for the lights spices for the anointing oil and for the sweet-smelling incense 7 onyx stones and other jewels for the linen apron and chest cloth

8 "Have them make a sacred tent for me. I will live among them. 9 Make the holy tent and everything that belongs to it. Make them exactly like the pattern I will show you.

The Ark of the Covenant Law

10 "Have them make an ark out of acacia wood. It must be a chest three feet nine inches long and two feet three inches wide and high. 11 Cover it inside and outside with pure gold. Put a strip of gold around it. 12 Make four gold rings for it. Join them to its four bottom corners. Put two rings on one side and two rings on the other. 13 Then make poles out of acacia wood. Cover

them with gold. ¹⁴ Put the poles through the rings on the sides of the ark to carry it. ¹⁵ The poles must remain in the rings of the ark. Do not remove them. ¹⁶ I will give you the tablets of the covenant law. When I do, put them into the ark.

¹⁷ "Make its cover out of pure gold. The cover is the place where sin will be paid for. Make it three feet nine inches long and two feet three inches wide. ¹⁸ Make two cherubim out of hammered gold at the ends of the cover. ¹⁹ Put one of the cherubim on each end of it. Make the cherubim part of the cover itself. ²⁰ They must have their wings spread up over the cover. The cherubim must face each other and look toward the cover. ²¹ Place the cover on top of the ark. I will give you the tablets of the covenant law. Put them in the ark. ²² The ark is where the tablets of the covenant law are kept. I will meet with you above the cover between the two cherubim that are over the ark. There I will give you all my commands for the Israelites.

The Table for the Holy Bread

²³ "Make a table out of acacia wood. Make it three feet long, one foot six inches wide and two feet three inches high. ²⁴ Cover it with pure gold. Put a strip of gold around it. ²⁵ Also make a rim around it three inches wide. Put a strip of gold around the rim. ²⁶ Make four gold rings for the table. Join them to the four corners, where the four legs are.

²⁷ The rings must be close to the rim. They must hold the poles that will be used to carry the table. ²⁸ Make the poles out of acacia wood. Cover them with gold. Use them to carry the table. ²⁹ Make its plates and dishes out of pure gold. Also make its pitchers and bowls out of pure gold. Use the pitchers and bowls to pour out drink offerings. ³⁰ Put the holy bread on the table. It must be near my holy throne on the ark of the covenant law at all times.

The Gold Lampstand

³¹ "Make a lampstand out of pure gold. Hammer out its base and stem. Its buds, blossoms and cups must branch out from it. They must be part of the lampstand itself. ³² Six branches must come out from the sides of the lampstand. Make three on one side and three on the other. ³³ On one branch make three cups that are shaped like almond flowers with buds and blossoms. Then put three on the next branch. Do the same with all six branches that come out from the lampstand. ³⁴ On the lampstand there must be four cups that are shaped like almond flowers with buds and blossoms. ³⁵ One bud must be under the first pair of branches that come out from the lampstand. Put a second bud under the second pair. And put a third bud under the third pair. Make a total of six branches. ³⁶ The buds and branches must come out from the lampstand. The whole

lampstand must be one piece hammered out of pure gold.

37 "Then make its seven lamps. Set them up on it so that they light the space in front of it. 38 The trays and wick cutters must be made out of pure gold. 39 Use 75 pounds of pure gold to make the lampstand and everything used with it. 40 Be sure to make everything just like the pattern I showed you on the mountain.

The Holy Tent

26 "Make ten curtains out of finely twisted linen for the holy tent. Make them with blue, purple and bright red yarn. Have a skilled worker sew cherubim into the pattern. 2 Make all the curtains the same size. They must be 42 feet long and six feet wide. 3 Join five of the curtains together. Do the same thing with the other five. 4 Make loops out of blue strips of cloth along the edge of the end curtain in one set. Do the same thing with the end curtain in the other set. 5 Make 50 loops on the end curtain of the one set. Do the same thing on the end curtain of the other set. Put the loops across from each other. 6 Make 50 gold hooks. Use them to join the curtains together so that the holy tent is all one piece.

7 "Make a total of 11 curtains out of goat hair to put over the holy tent. 8 Make all 11 curtains the same size. They must be 45 feet long and six feet wide. 9 Join five of the curtains together into one set. Do the same thing with the other six. Fold the sixth curtain in half at the front of the tent. 10 Make 50 loops along the edge of the end curtain in the one set. Do the same thing with the other set. 11 Then make 50 bronze hooks. Put them in the loops to join the tent together all in one piece. 12 Let the extra half curtain hang down at the rear of the holy tent. 13 The tent curtains will be 18 inches longer on both sides. What is left over will hang over the sides of the holy tent and cover it. 14 Make a covering for the tent. Make it out of ram skins that are dyed red. Put a covering of the other strong leather over that.

15 "Make frames out of acacia wood for the holy tent. 16 Make each frame 15 feet long and two feet three inches wide. 17 Add two small wooden pins to each frame. Make the pins stick out so that they are even with each other. Make all the frames for the holy tent in the same way. 18 Make 20 frames for the south side of the holy tent. 19 And make 40 silver bases to go under them. Make two bases for each frame. Put one under each pin that sticks out. 20 For the north side of the holy tent make 20 frames 21 and 40 silver bases. Put two bases under each frame. 22 Make six frames for the west end of the holy tent. 23 Make two frames for the corners at the far end. 24 At those two corners the frames must be double from top to bottom. They must be fitted into a single ring. Make both of

them the same. [25] There will be eight frames and 16 silver bases. There will be two bases under each frame.

[26] "Also make crossbars out of acacia wood. Make five for the frames on one side of the holy tent. [27] Make five for the frames on the other side. And make five for the frames on the west, at the far end of the holy tent. [28] The center crossbar must reach from end to end at the middle of the frames. [29] Cover the frames with gold. Make gold rings to hold the crossbars. Also cover the crossbars with gold.

[30] "Set up the holy tent in keeping with the plan I showed you on the mountain.

[31] "Make a curtain out of blue, purple and bright red yarn and finely twisted linen. Have a skilled worker sew cherubim into the pattern. [32] Hang the curtain with gold hooks on four posts that are made out of acacia wood. Cover the posts with gold. Stand them on four silver bases. [33] Hang the curtain from the hooks. Place the ark of the covenant law behind the curtain. The curtain will separate the Holy Room from the Most Holy Room. [34] Put the cover on the ark of the covenant law in the Most Holy Room. The cover will be the place where sin is paid for. [35] Place the table outside the curtain on the north side of the holy tent. And put the lampstand across from it on the south side.

[36] "Make a curtain for the entrance to the tent. Make it out of blue, purple and bright red yarn and finely twisted linen. Have a person who sews skillfully make it. [37] Make gold hooks for the curtain. Make five posts out of acacia wood. Cover them with gold. And make five bronze bases for them.

The Altar for Burnt Offerings

27 "Build an altar out of acacia wood. It must be four feet six inches high and seven feet six inches square. [2] Make a horn stick out from each of its upper four corners. The horns and the altar must be all one piece. Cover the altar with bronze. [3] Make everything for the altar out of bronze. Make its pots to remove the ashes. Make its shovels, sprinkling bowls, meat forks, and pans for carrying ashes. [4] Make a bronze grate for the altar. Make a bronze ring for each of the four corners of the grate. [5] Put the grate halfway up the altar on the inside. [6] Make poles out of acacia wood for the altar. Cover them with bronze. [7] Put the poles through the rings. They will be on two sides of the altar for carrying it. [8] Make the altar out of boards. Leave it hollow. It must look just like what I showed you on the mountain.

The Courtyard

[9] "Make a courtyard for the holy tent. The south side must be 150 feet long. It must have curtains that are made out of finely twisted linen. [10] The curtains must be hung on 20 posts

that have 20 bronze bases. The posts must have silver hooks and bands on them. [11] The north side must also be about 150 feet long. It must have curtains with 20 posts that have 20 bronze bases. The posts must have silver hooks and bands on them.

[12] "The west end of the courtyard must be 75 feet wide. It must have curtains with ten posts that have ten bases. [13] The east end of the courtyard, toward the sunrise, must also be 75 feet wide. [14] On one side of the entrance you must put curtains that are 22 feet six inches long. Hang them on three posts. Each post must have a base. [15] On the other side you must also put curtains that are 22 feet six inches long. Hang them on three posts. Each post must have a base.

[16] "For the entrance to the courtyard, provide a curtain 30 feet long. Make it out of blue, purple and bright red yarn and finely twisted linen. Have someone who sews skillfully make it. Hang it on four posts. Each post must have a base. [17] All the posts that are around the courtyard must have silver bands and hooks. They must also have bronze bases. [18] The courtyard must be 150 feet long and 75 feet wide. It must have curtains that are made out of finely twisted linen. They must be seven feet six inches high. The posts must have bronze bases. [19] Make out of bronze all the other things used for any purpose in the holy tent. That includes all the

tent stakes for the tent and the courtyard.

Oil for the Lampstand

[20] "Command the Israelites to bring you clear oil made from pressed olives. Use it to keep the lamps burning and giving light. [21] Aaron and his sons must keep the lamps burning in the tent of meeting. The lamps will be outside the curtain in front of the tablets of the covenant law. The lamps must be kept burning in front of the LORD from evening until morning. This is a law for the Israelites that will last for all time to come.

The Clothes for the Priests

28 "Have your brother Aaron brought to you from among the Israelites. His sons Nadab, Abihu, Eleazar and Ithamar must also be brought. They will serve me as priests. [2] Make sacred clothes for your brother Aaron. When he is wearing them, people will honor him. They will have respect for him. [3] Speak to all the skilled workers. I have given them the skill to do this kind of work. Tell them to make clothes for Aaron. He will wear them when he is set apart to serve me as priest. [4] The workers must make a chest cloth, a linen apron and an outer robe. They must also make an inner robe, a turban and a belt. They must make sacred clothes for your brother Aaron and his sons. Then they will serve me as priests. [5] Have the workers use thin gold wire, and blue, pur-

ple and bright red yarn, and fine linen.

The Linen Apron

6 "Make the linen apron out of thin gold wire, and out of blue, purple and bright red yarn, and out of finely twisted linen. Have a skilled worker make it. 7 It must have two shoulder straps joined to two of its corners. 8 Its skillfully made waistband must be like the apron. The waistband must be part of the apron itself. Make the waistband out of thin gold wire, and out of blue, purple and bright red yarn, and out of finely twisted linen.

9 "Get two onyx stones. Carve the names of the sons of Israel on them. 10 Arrange them in the order of their birth. Carve six names on one stone and six on the other. 11 Carve the names of the sons of Israel on the two stones the way a jewel cutter would carve them. Then put the stones in fancy gold settings. 12 Connect them to the shoulder straps of the linen apron. The stones will stand for the sons of Israel. Aaron must carry the names on his shoulders as a constant reminder while he is serving the LORD. 13 Make fancy gold settings. 14 Make two braided chains out of pure gold. Make them like ropes. Join the chains to the settings.

The Chest Cloth

15 "Make a chest cloth that will be used for making decisions. Have a skilled worker make it. Make it like the linen apron. Use thin gold wire, and blue, purple and bright red yarn, and finely twisted linen. 16 Make it nine inches square. Fold it in half. 17 Put four rows of valuable jewels on it. Put carnelian, chrysolite and beryl in the first row. 18 Put turquoise, lapis lazuli and emerald in the second row. 19 Put jacinth, agate and amethyst in the third row. 20 And put topaz, onyx and jasper in the fourth row. Put them in fancy gold settings. 21 Use a total of 12 stones. Use one for each of the names of the sons of Israel. Each stone must be carved with the name of one of the 12 tribes.

22 "Make braided chains out of pure gold for the chest cloth. Make them like ropes. 23 Make two gold rings for the chest cloth. Connect them to two corners of it. 24 Join the two gold chains to the rings at the corners of the chest cloth. 25 Join the other ends of the chains to the two settings. Join them to the shoulder straps on the front of the linen apron. 26 Make two gold rings. Connect them to the other two corners of the chest cloth. Put them on the inside edge next to the apron. 27 Make two more gold rings. Connect them to the bottom of the shoulder straps on the front of the apron. Put them close to the seam. Put them right above the waistband of the apron. 28 The rings of the chest cloth must be tied to the rings of the apron. Tie them to the waistband with blue cord. Then the chest cloth will

not swing out from the linen apron.

29 "When Aaron enters the Holy Room, he will carry the names of the sons of Israel over his heart. Their names will be on the chest cloth of decision. They will be a continuing reminder while he is serving the LORD. 30 Also put the Urim and Thummim into the chest cloth. Then they will be over Aaron's heart when he comes to serve the LORD. In that way, Aaron will always have what he needs to make decisions for the people of Israel. He will carry the Urim and Thummim over his heart while he is serving the LORD.

More Clothes for the Priests

31 "Make the outer robe of the linen apron completely out of blue cloth. 32 In the center of the robe, make an opening for the head of the priest. Make an edge like a collar around the opening. Then it will not tear. 33 Make pomegranates out of blue, purple and bright red yarn. Sew them around the hem of the robe. Sew gold bells between them. 34 Sew a gold bell between every two pomegranates all around the hem of the robe. 35 Aaron must wear the robe when he serves as priest. The bells will jingle when he enters the Holy Room while he is serving the LORD. And they will jingle when he goes out. Then he will not die.

36 "Make a plate out of pure gold. Carve words on it as if it were an official seal. Carve the words

SET APART FOR THE LORD.

37 Tie the plate to the front of the turban with a blue cord. 38 Aaron must wear this plate on his forehead all the time. He will be held responsible for all the sacred gifts the Israelites set apart. Then the LORD will accept the gifts.

39 "Make the inner robe out of fine linen. And make the turban out of fine linen. The belt must be made by a person who sews skillfully. 40 Make inner robes, belts and caps for Aaron's sons. When they are wearing them, people will honor his sons. They will also have respect for them. 41 Put all these clothes on your brother Aaron and his sons. Then pour olive oil on them and prepare them to serve me. Set them apart to serve me as priests.

42 "Make linen underwear that reaches from the waist to the thigh. 43 Aaron and the priests in his family line must wear it when they enter the tent of meeting. They must also wear it when they approach the altar to serve in the Holy Room. Then they will not be found guilty and die.

"For all time to come, that will be a law for Aaron and the priests in his family line.

Directions for Setting Apart the Priests

29 "Here is what you must do to set apart Aaron and his sons to serve me as priests. Get a young bull and two rams. They must not have any flaws.

2 Get the finest wheat flour. Make round loaves of bread that do not have yeast in them. Make thick loaves of bread that do not have yeast in them. Mix olive oil into the thick loaves of bread. Also make thin loaves of bread that do not have yeast in them. Brush the thin loaves with olive oil. 3 Put everything in a basket. Offer them along with the bull and the two rams. 4 Then bring Aaron and his sons to the entrance to the tent of meeting. Wash them with water. 5 Take the inner robe, the outer robe of the linen apron, the apron itself and the chest cloth. Dress Aaron in them. Take the skillfully made waistband and tie the apron on him with it. 6 Put the turban on his head. Connect the sacred plate to the turban. 7 Take the anointing oil and pour it on his head. 8 Bring his sons and dress them in their inner robes. 9 Put caps on their heads. Tie belts on Aaron and his sons. The work of the priests belongs to them. This is my law that will last for all time to come.

"Then you must prepare Aaron and his sons to serve me.

10 "Bring the bull to the front of the tent of meeting. Have Aaron and his sons place their hands on its head. 11 Kill it in front of the LORD at the entrance to the tent of meeting. 12 Dip your finger into some of the bull's blood. Put it on the horns that stick out from the upper four corners of the altar. Pour the rest of it out at the base of the altar. 13 Then take all the fat on the inside parts.

Take the long part of the liver. Get both kidneys with the fat on them. And burn all of it on the altar. 14 But burn the bull's meat, hide and guts outside the camp. It is a sin offering.

15 "Get one of the rams. Have Aaron and his sons place their hands on its head. 16 Kill it. Take the blood and splash it against the sides of the altar. 17 Cut the ram into pieces. Wash the inside parts and the legs. Put them with the head and the other pieces. 18 Then burn the whole ram on the altar. It is a burnt offering to me. It has a pleasant smell. It is a food offering presented to the LORD.

19 "Get the other ram. Have Aaron and his sons place their hands on its head. 20 Kill it. Put some of its blood on the right earlobes of Aaron and his sons. Put some on the thumbs of their right hands. Also put some on the big toes of their right feet. Then splash the blood against the sides of the altar. 21 Get some of the blood from the altar. Also get some of the anointing oil. Sprinkle both of them on Aaron and his clothes and on his sons and their clothes. Then he and his sons and their clothes will be set apart to serve the LORD.

22 "Here is what you must take from this second ram. Take the fat, the fat tail and the fat around the inside parts. Take the long part of the liver. Also take both kidneys with the fat on them, and the right thigh. It is the ram you must use when you prepare the priests to serve the LORD.

²³ Get one round loaf of bread and one thick loaf of bread with olive oil mixed in. Also get one thin loaf of bread. Take them from the basket of bread made without yeast. It is the one in front of the LORD. ²⁴ Put all these things in the hands of Aaron and his sons. Tell them to lift them up and wave them in front of the LORD as a wave offering. ²⁵ Then take all these things from their hands. Burn them on the altar along with the burnt offering. Its smell pleases the LORD. It is a food offering presented to the LORD. ²⁶ Get the breast of the ram used when you prepare Aaron to serve the LORD. Wave it in front of the LORD as a wave offering. It will be your share of the meat.

²⁷ "Here are the parts of the second ram that belong to Aaron and his sons. You must set apart the breast that was waved and the thigh that was offered. ²⁸ It will be the regular share from the Israelites for Aaron and his sons. The people must give it to the LORD from their friendship offerings.

²⁹ "Aaron's sacred clothes will belong to his sons who will come after him. Then they can wear them when you anoint them and prepare them to serve the LORD. ³⁰ The son who comes after Aaron as priest must wear them seven days. He will come and serve in the Holy Room in the tent of meeting.

³¹ "Get the ram sacrificed when you prepare Aaron and his sons to serve the LORD. Cook the meat in a sacred place. ³² Aaron and his sons must eat the ram's meat. And they must eat the bread in the basket. They must eat all of it at the entrance to the tent of meeting. ³³ These are the offerings to pay for their sins. They must eat them. The offerings must be made when Aaron and his sons are set apart and prepared to serve the LORD. No one else can eat them. They are sacred. ³⁴ When you prepare Aaron and his sons to serve me, you will sacrifice the ram and the bread. If any parts of the ram or bread are left until morning, burn them up. They must not be eaten. They are sacred.

³⁵ "Do everything I have commanded you to do for Aaron and his sons. Take seven days when you prepare them to serve the LORD. ³⁶ Sacrifice a bull each day. It is a sin offering to pay for their sins. Make the altar pure. Pour olive oil on it to set it apart. ³⁷ Take seven days to make the altar pure. Set it apart. Then the altar will be a very holy place. Anything that touches it will be holy.

³⁸ "Every day sacrifice on the altar two lambs that are a year old. ³⁹ Sacrifice one in the morning and the other one when the sun goes down. ⁴⁰ Along with the first lamb, offer three and a half pounds of fine flour. Mix it with a quart of oil made from pressed olives. Along with that, sacrifice a quart of wine as a drink offering. ⁴¹ Sacrifice the other lamb when the sun goes down. Sacrifice it along with the same grain

offering and its drink offering as you do in the morning. It has a pleasant smell. It is a food offering presented to the LORD.

⁴² "For all time to come, this burnt offering must be sacrificed regularly. Sacrifice it at the entrance to the tent of meeting in front of the LORD. There I will meet with you and speak to you. ⁴³ There I will also meet with the people of Israel. My glory will make the place holy.

⁴⁴ "So I will set apart the tent of meeting and the altar. And I will set apart Aaron and his sons to serve me as priests. ⁴⁵ Then I will live among the people of Israel. And I will be their God. ⁴⁶ They will know that I am the LORD their God. They will know that I brought them out of Egypt so I could live among them. I am the LORD their God.

The Altar for Burning Incense

30 "Make an altar for burning incense. Make it out of acacia wood. ² It must be one and a half feet square and three feet high. Make a horn stick out from each of its upper four corners. ³ Cover the top, sides and horns with pure gold. Put a strip of gold around it. ⁴ Make two gold rings for the altar below the strip. Put the rings across from each other. They will hold the poles that are used to carry it. ⁵ Make the poles out of acacia wood. Cover them with gold. ⁶ Put the altar in front of the curtain that hangs in front of the ark. The ark is where the tablets of the covenant law are kept.

The ark will have a cover. It will be the place where sin is paid for. There I will meet with you.

⁷ "Aaron must burn sweet-smelling incense on the altar. He must do it every morning when he takes care of the lamps. ⁸ He must burn incense again when he lights the lamps at sunset. Incense must be burned regularly in front of the LORD. Do it for all time to come. ⁹ Do not burn any other incense on the altar. Do not use the altar for burnt offerings or grain offerings. And do not pour drink offerings on it. ¹⁰ Once a year Aaron must put the blood of a sin offering on the horns of the altar. He must do this to make the altar pure. He must do this on the day Israel's sin is paid for. Do this for all time to come. The altar is a very holy place to me."

Money to Pay for the People's Lives

¹¹ Then the LORD spoke to Moses. He said, ¹² "Make a list of the Israelites and count them. When you do, each one must pay the LORD for his life at the time he is counted. Then a plague will not come on them when you count them. ¹³ Each one counted must pay a fifth of an ounce of silver. It must be weighed out in keeping with the standard weights that are used in the sacred tent. The payment is an offering to the LORD. ¹⁴ Each one counted must be 20 years old or more. He must give an offering to the LORD. ¹⁵ When you make the offering, rich people must not give

more than a fifth of an ounce of silver. And poor people must not give less. The offering you give to the LORD will pay for your lives. ¹⁶ Receive the money from the people of Israel. Use it for any purpose in the tent of meeting. It will remind the people that they are paying me for their lives."

The Large Bowl for Washing

¹⁷ Then the LORD spoke to Moses. He said, ¹⁸ "Make a large bronze bowl for washing. Make a bronze stand to put it on. Place the bowl between the tent of meeting and the altar. Put water in it. ¹⁹ Aaron and his sons must wash their hands and feet with water from it. ²⁰ When they enter the tent of meeting, they must wash with water so that they will not die. They will come to the altar to serve me. They will bring a food offering to the LORD. ²¹ When they do, they must wash their hands and feet so that they will not die. For all time to come, that will be a law for Aaron and the priests in his family line."

Anointing Oil

²² Then the LORD said to Moses, ²³ "Get some fine spices. Get 12 pounds eight ounces of liquid myrrh. Get six pounds four ounces of sweet-smelling cinnamon and the same amount of sweet-smelling calamus. ²⁴ Also get 12 pounds eight ounces of cassia. All the spices must be weighed out in keeping with the standard weights that are used in the sacred tent. And get a gallon of olive oil. ²⁵ Have a person who makes perfume mix everything into a sacred anointing oil. It will smell sweet. ²⁶ Then use it to anoint the tent of meeting and the ark where the tablets of the covenant law are kept. ²⁷ Anoint the table for the holy bread and all its things. Anoint the lampstand and the things that are used with it. Anoint the altar for burning incense. ²⁸ Anoint the altar for burnt offerings and all its tools. And anoint the large bowl together with its stand. ²⁹ You must set them apart so that they will be very holy. Anything that touches them will be holy.

³⁰ "Anoint Aaron and his sons. Set them apart so that they can serve me as priests. ³¹ Say to the people of Israel, 'This will be my sacred anointing oil for all time to come. ³² Do not pour it on anyone else's body. Do not make any other oil in the same way. It is sacred. So you must think of it as sacred. ³³ Suppose a person makes perfume in the same way. And suppose that person puts it on someone who is not a priest. Then that person must be separated from their people.' "

Incense

³⁴ Then the LORD said to Moses, "Get some sweet-smelling spices. Get some gum resin, onycha and galbanum. Also get some pure frankincense. Make sure everything is in equal amounts. ³⁵ Have a person who

makes perfume mix it all up into a sweet-smelling incense. It must have salt in it. It will be pure and sacred. ³⁶ Grind some of it into powder. Place it in front of the ark of the covenant law in the tent of meeting. There I will meet with you. The incense will be very holy to you. ³⁷ Do not make any incense for yourselves in the same way. Think of it as holy to the LORD. ³⁸ Whoever makes incense in the same way to enjoy its sweet smell must be separated from their people."

Bezalel and Oholiab

31 Then the LORD spoke to Moses. ² He said, "I have chosen Bezalel, the son of Uri. Uri is the son of Hur. Bezalel is from the tribe of Judah. ³ I have filled him with the Spirit of God. I have filled Bezalel with wisdom, with understanding, with knowledge and with all kinds of skill. ⁴ He can make beautiful patterns in gold, silver and bronze. ⁵ He can cut and set stones. He can work with wood. In fact, he can work in all kinds of crafts. ⁶ I have also appointed Oholiab, the son of Ahisamak, to help him. Oholiab is from the tribe of Dan. I have given ability to all the skilled workers. They can make everything I have commanded you to make. Here is the complete list.

⁷ "the tent of meeting
the ark where the tablets of
    the covenant law are kept
the cover for the ark
⁸ the table for the holy bread
    and its things

the pure gold lampstand
    and everything used
    with it
the altar for burning in-
    cense
⁹ the altar for burnt offerings
    and all its tools
the large bowl with its stand
¹⁰ the sacred clothes for Aaron
    the priest
the clothes for his sons
    when they serve as
    priests
¹¹ the anointing oil
the sweet-smelling incense
    for the Holy Room

"The skilled workers must make them just as I commanded you."

The Sabbath Day

¹² Then the LORD spoke to Moses. ¹³ He said, "Tell the people of Israel, 'You must always keep my Sabbath days. That will be the sign of the covenant I have made between me and you for all time to come. Then you will know that I am the LORD. I am the one who makes you holy.

¹⁴ "'Keep the Sabbath day. It is holy to you. Those who misuse it must be put to death. Those who do any work on that day must be separated from their people. ¹⁵ Do your work in six days. But the seventh day is a day of sabbath rest. You must rest on it. It is set apart for the LORD. Those who work on the Sabbath day must be put to death. ¹⁶ The Israelites must keep the Sabbath day. They must celebrate it for all time to come. It will be a covenant that lasts forever. ¹⁷ It

will be the sign of the covenant I have made between me and the Israelites forever. The LORD made the heavens and the earth in six days. But on the seventh day he did not work. He rested.' "

18 The LORD finished speaking to Moses on Mount Sinai. Then he gave him the two tablets of the covenant law. They were made out of stone. The words on them were written by the finger of God.

Israel Worships a Golden Calf

32 The people saw that Moses took a long time to come down from the mountain. So they gathered around Aaron. They said to him, "Come. Make us a god that will lead us. This fellow Moses brought us up out of Egypt. But we don't know what has happened to him."

2 Aaron answered them, "Take the gold earrings off your wives, your sons and your daughters. Bring the earrings to me." 3 So all the people took off their earrings. They brought them to Aaron. 4 He took what they gave him and made it into a metal statue of a god. It looked like a calf. Aaron shaped it with a tool. Then the people said, "Israel, here is your god who brought you up out of Egypt."

5 When Aaron saw what they were doing, he built an altar in front of the calf. He said, "Tomorrow will be a feast day to honor the LORD." 6 So the next day the people got up early. They sacrificed burnt offerings and brought friendship offerings. They sat down to eat and drink. Then they got up to dance wildly in front of their god.

7 The LORD spoke to Moses. He said, "Go down. Your people you brought up out of Egypt have become very sinful. 8 They have quickly turned away from what I commanded them. They have made themselves a metal statue of a god in the shape of a calf. They have bowed down and sacrificed to it. And they have said, 'Israel, here is your god who brought you up out of Egypt.'

9 "I have seen these people," the LORD said to Moses. "They are stubborn. 10 Now leave me alone. I will destroy them because of my great anger. Then I will make you into a great nation."

11 But Moses asked the LORD his God to have mercy on the people. "LORD," he said, "why should you destroy your people in anger? You used your great power and mighty hand to bring them out of Egypt. 12 Why should the Egyptians say, 'He brought them out to hurt them. He wanted to kill them in the mountains. He wanted to wipe them off the face of the earth'? Turn away from your great anger. Please take pity on your people. Don't destroy them! 13 Remember your servants Abraham, Isaac and Israel. You made a promise to them in your own name. You said, 'I will make your children after you as many as the stars in the sky. I will give them all this land

I promised them. It will belong to them forever.'" [14] Then the LORD took pity on his people. He didn't destroy them as he had said he would.

[15] Moses turned and went down the mountain. He had the two tablets of the covenant law in his hands. Words were written on both sides of the tablets, front and back. [16] The tablets were the work of God. The words had been written by God. They had been carved on the tablets.

[17] Joshua heard the noise of the people shouting. So he said to Moses, "It sounds like war in the camp."

[18] Moses replied,

"It's not the sound of
       winning.
   It's not the sound of losing.
   It's the sound of singing
       that I hear."

[19] As Moses approached the camp, he saw the calf. He also saw the people dancing. So he was very angry. He threw the tablets out of his hands. They broke into pieces at the foot of the mountain. [20] He took the calf the people had made. He burned it in the fire. Then he ground it into powder. He scattered it on the water. And he made the Israelites drink it.

[21] He said to Aaron, "What did these people do to you? How did they make you lead them into such terrible sin?"

[22] "Please don't be angry," Aaron answered. "You know how these people like to do what is evil. [23] They said to me, 'Make us a god that will lead us. This fellow Moses brought us up out of Egypt. But we don't know what has happened to him.' [24] So I told them, 'Anyone who has any gold jewelry, take it off.' They gave me the gold. I threw it into the fire. And out came this calf!"

[25] Moses saw that the people were running wild. Aaron had let them get out of control. The people had become a joke to their enemies. [26] Moses stood at the entrance to the camp. He said, "Anyone on the LORD's side, come to me." All the Levites joined him.

[27] Then he spoke to them. He said, "The LORD, the God of Israel, says, 'Each man must put on his sword. Then he must go back and forth through the camp from one end to the other. Each man must kill his brother and friend and neighbor.'" [28] The Levites did as Moses commanded. About 3,000 of the people died that day. [29] Then Moses said to the Levites, "You have been set apart for the LORD today. You fought against your own sons and brothers. And he has blessed you this day."

[30] The next day Moses said to the people, "You have committed a terrible sin. But now I will go up to the LORD. Maybe if I pray to him, he will forgive your sin."

[31] So Moses went back to the LORD. He said, "These people have committed a terrible sin. They have made a god out

of gold for themselves. ³²Now please forgive their sin. But if you won't, then erase my name out of the book you have written."

³³The Lord replied to Moses. The Lord said, "I will erase out of my book only the names of those who have sinned against me. ³⁴Now go. Lead the people to the place I spoke about. My angel will go ahead of you. But when the time comes for me to punish, I will punish them for their sin."

³⁵The Lord struck the people with a plague. That's because of what they did with the calf Aaron had made.

33 Then the Lord said to Moses, "Leave this place. You and the people you brought up out of Egypt must leave it. Go up to the land I promised to give to Abraham, Isaac and Jacob. I said to them, 'I will give it to your children after you.' ²I will send an angel ahead of you. I will drive out the Canaanites, Amorites, Hittites, Perizzites, Hivites and Jebusites. ³Go up to the land that has plenty of milk and honey. But I will not go with you. You are stubborn. I might destroy you on the way."

⁴When the people heard these painful words, they began to mourn. No one put on any jewelry. ⁵The Lord had said to Moses, "Tell the Israelites, 'You are stubborn. If I went with you even for a moment, I might destroy you. Now take off your jewelry. Then I will decide what to do with you.'" ⁶So the people took off their jewelry at Mount Horeb.

The Tent of Meeting

⁷Moses used to take a tent and set it up far outside the camp. He called it the "tent of meeting." Anyone who wanted to ask the Lord a question would go to the tent of meeting outside the camp. ⁸When Moses would go out to the tent, everyone would get up and stand at the entrances to their tents. They would watch Moses until he entered the tent. ⁹As Moses would go into the tent, the pillar of cloud would come down. It would stay at the entrance while the Lord spoke with Moses. ¹⁰The people would see the pillar of cloud standing at the entrance to the tent. Then all of them would stand and worship at the entrances to their tents. ¹¹The Lord would speak to Moses face to face like one would speak to a friend. Then Moses would return to the camp. But Joshua, his young helper, didn't leave the tent. Joshua was the son of Nun.

Moses and the Glory of the Lord

¹²Moses said to the Lord, "You have been telling me, 'Lead these people.' But you haven't let me know whom you will send with me. You have said, 'I know your name. I know all about you. And I am pleased with you.' ¹³If you are pleased with me, teach me more about yourself. Then I can know you. And I can continue to please

you. Remember that this nation is your people."

¹⁴The Lord replied, "I will go with you. And I will give you rest."

¹⁵Then Moses said to him, "If you don't go with us, don't send us up from here. ¹⁶How will anyone know that you are pleased with me and your people? You must go with us. How else will we be different from all the other people on the face of the earth?"

¹⁷The Lord said to Moses, "I will do exactly what you have asked. I am pleased with you. And I know your name. I know all about you."

¹⁸Then Moses said, "Now show me your glory."

¹⁹The Lord said, "I will make all my goodness pass in front of you. And I will announce my name, the Lord, in front of you. I will have mercy on whom I have mercy. And I will show love to those I love. ²⁰But you can't see my face," he said. "No one can see me and stay alive."

²¹The Lord continued, "There is a place near me where you can stand on a rock. ²²When my glory passes by, I will put you in an opening in the rock. I will cover you with my hand until I have passed by. ²³Then I will remove my hand. You will see my back. But my face must not be seen."

The New Stone Tablets

34 The Lord said to Moses, "Cut out two stone tablets that are just like the first ones. I will write on them the words that were on the first tablets, which you broke. ²Be ready in the morning. Then come up on Mount Sinai. Meet with me there on top of the mountain. ³No one must come with you. No one must be seen anywhere on the mountain. Not even the flocks and herds must be allowed to eat grass in front of the mountain."

⁴So Moses carved out two stone tablets just like the first ones. Early in the morning he went up Mount Sinai. He carried the two stone tablets in his hands. He did as the Lord had commanded him to do. ⁵Then the Lord came down in the cloud. He stood there with Moses and announced his name, the Lord. ⁶As he passed in front of Moses, he called out. He said, "I am the Lord, the Lord. I am the God who is tender and kind. I am gracious. I am slow to get angry. I am faithful and full of love. ⁷I continue to show my love to thousands of people. I forgive those who do evil. I forgive those who refuse to obey me. And I forgive those who sin. But I do not let guilty people go without punishing them. I cause the sins of the parents to affect their children, grandchildren and great-grandchildren."

⁸Moses bowed down to the ground at once and worshiped. ⁹"Lord," he said, "if you are pleased with me, then go with us. Even though these people are stubborn, forgive the evil things we have done. Forgive

our sin. And accept us as your people."

¹⁰ Then the LORD said, "I am making a covenant with you. I will do wonderful things in front of all your people. I will do amazing things that have never been done before in any nation in the whole world. The people you live among will see the things that I, the LORD, will do for you. And they will see how wonderful those things really are. ¹¹ Obey what I command you today. I will drive out the Amorites, Canaanites, Hittites, Perizzites, Hivites and Jebusites to make room for you. ¹² Be careful. Do not make a peace treaty with those who live in the land where you are going. They will be a trap to you. ¹³ Break down their altars. Smash their sacred stones. Cut down the poles they use to worship the female god named Asherah. ¹⁴ Do not worship any other god. The LORD is a jealous God. In fact, his name is Jealous.

¹⁵ "Be careful not to make a peace treaty with the people living in the land. They commit sin by offering sacrifices to their gods. They will invite you to eat their sacrifices, and you will do it. ¹⁶ You will choose some of their daughters as wives for your sons. And those daughters will commit sin by worshiping their gods. Then they will lead your sons to do the same thing.

¹⁷ "Do not make any statues of gods.

¹⁸ "Celebrate the Feast of Unleavened Bread. For seven days eat bread made without yeast, just as I commanded you. Do it at the appointed time in the month of Aviv. You came out of Egypt in that month.

¹⁹ "Every male animal born first to its mother belongs to me. That includes your livestock. It includes herds and flocks alike. ²⁰ Sacrifice a lamb to buy back every male donkey born first to its mother. But if you do not buy the donkey back, break its neck. Buy back all your oldest sons.

"You must not come to worship me with your hands empty.

²¹ "Do your work in six days. But you must rest on the seventh day. Even when you are plowing your land or gathering your crops, you must rest on the seventh day.

²² "Celebrate the Feast of Weeks. Bring the first share of your wheat crop. Celebrate the Feast of Booths. Hold it in the fall. ²³ Three times a year all your men must come to worship me. I am your LORD and King, the God of Israel. ²⁴ I will drive out nations ahead of you. I will increase your territory. Go up three times a year to worship me. While you are doing that, I will keep others from wanting to take any of your land for themselves. I am the LORD your God.

²⁵ "Do not include anything made with yeast when you offer me the blood of a sacrifice. You must not keep any of the meat from the sacrifice of the Passover Feast until morning.

26 "Bring the best of the first share of your crops to the house of the LORD your God.

"Do not cook a young goat in its mother's milk."

27 Then the LORD said to Moses, "Write down the words I have spoken. I have made a covenant with you and with Israel in keeping with those words." 28 Moses was there with the LORD for 40 days and 40 nights. He didn't eat any food or drink any water. The LORD wrote on the tablets the words of the covenant law. Those words are the Ten Commandments.

The Face of Moses Shines

29 Moses came down from Mount Sinai. He had the two tablets of the covenant law in his hands. His face was shining because he had spoken with the LORD. But he didn't realize it. 30 Aaron and all the people of Israel saw Moses. His face was shining. So they were afraid to come near him. 31 But Moses called out to them. So Aaron and all the leaders of the community came to him. And Moses spoke to them. 32 After that, all the Israelites came near him. And he gave them all the commands the LORD had given him on Mount Sinai.

33 Moses finished speaking to them. Then he covered his face with a veil. 34 But when he would go to speak with the LORD, he would remove the veil. He would keep it off until he came out. Then he would tell the people what the LORD had com-

manded. 35 They would see that his face was shining. So Moses would cover his face with the veil again. He would keep it on until he went in again to speak with the LORD.

Rules for the Sabbath Day

35 Moses gathered the whole community of Israel together. He said to them, "Here are the things the LORD has commanded you to do. 2 You must do your work in six days. But the seventh day will be your holy day. It will be a day of sabbath rest to honor the LORD. You must rest on it. Anyone who does any work on it must be put to death. 3 Do not even light a fire in any of your homes on the Sabbath day."

Supplies for the Holy Tent

4 Moses spoke to the whole community of Israel. He said, "Here is what the LORD has commanded. 5 Take an offering for the LORD from what you have. Those who want to can bring an offering to the LORD. Here is what they can bring.

"gold, silver and bronze
6 blue, purple and bright red yarn and fine linen
goat hair
7 ram skins that are dyed red another kind of strong leather
acacia wood
8 olive oil for the lights
spices for the anointing oil and for the sweet-smelling incense
9 onyx stones and other jewels

for the linen apron and the chest cloth

10 "All the skilled workers among you must come. They must make everything the LORD has commanded 11 for the holy tent and its covering. Here is what they must make.

"hooks, frames, crossbars, posts and bases;
12 the ark of the covenant law, the poles and cover for the ark, and the curtain that hides the ark;
13 the table for the holy bread, the poles and all the things for the table, and the holy bread;
14 the lampstand for light and everything used with it, the lamps, and the olive oil that gives light;
15 the altar for burning incense, the poles for the altar, the anointing oil, the sweet-smelling incense and the curtain for the entrance to the holy tent;
16 the altar for burnt offerings with its bronze grate, its poles and all its tools; the large bronze bowl with its stand;
17 the curtains of the courtyard with their posts and bases, and the curtain for the entrance to the courtyard;
18 the ropes and tent stakes for the holy tent and for the courtyard;
19 and the sacred clothes for Aaron the priest and the clothes for his sons when they serve as priests."

20 Then the whole community of Israel left Moses. 21 Everyone who wanted to give offerings to the LORD brought them to him. The offerings were for the work on the tent of meeting. They were also for the sacred clothes and for any other purpose at the tent. 22 Every man and woman who wanted to give came. They brought gold jewelry of all kinds. They brought pins, earrings, rings and other jewelry. All of them gave their gold as a wave offering to the LORD. 23 People brought what they had. They brought blue, purple or bright red yarn or fine linen. They brought goat hair, ram skins dyed red, or the other kind of strong leather. 24 Some brought silver or bronze as an offering to the LORD. Others brought acacia wood for any part of the work. 25 All the skilled women spun yarn with their hands. They brought blue, purple or bright red yarn or fine linen. 26 All the skilled women who wanted to spin the goat hair did so. 27 The leaders brought onyx stones and other jewels for the linen apron and the chest cloth. 28 They also brought spices and olive oil. They brought them for the light, for the anointing oil, and for the sweet-smelling incense. 29 All the men and women of Israel who wanted to bring offerings to the LORD brought them to him. The offerings

were for all the work the LORD had commanded Moses to tell them to do.

Bezalel and Oholiab

30 Then Moses spoke to the people of Israel. He said, "The LORD has chosen Bezalel, the son of Uri. Uri is the son of Hur. Bezalel is from the tribe of Judah. 31 The LORD has filled him with the Spirit of God. He has filled him with wisdom, with understanding, with knowledge and with all kinds of skill. 32 Bezalel can make beautiful patterns in gold, silver and bronze. 33 He can cut and set stones. He can work with wood. In fact, he can work in all kinds of arts and crafts. 34 And the LORD has given both him and Oholiab the ability to teach others. Oholiab, the son of Ahisamak, is from the tribe of Dan. 35 The LORD has filled Bezalel and Oholiab with skill to do all kinds of work. They can carve things and make patterns. They can sew skillfully with blue, purple and bright red yarn and on fine linen. They use thread to make beautiful cloth. Both of them have the skill to work

36 in all kinds of crafts. 1 Bezalel and Oholiab must do the work just as the LORD has commanded. So must every skilled worker to whom the LORD has given skill and ability. They know how to do all the work for every purpose connected with the sacred tent. And that includes setting it up."

2 Then Moses sent for Bezalel and Oholiab. He sent for every skilled worker to whom the LORD had given ability and who wanted to come and do the work. 3 They received from Moses all the offerings the people of Israel had brought. They had brought the offerings for all the work for every purpose connected with the holy tent. That included setting it up. The people kept bringing the offerings they chose to give. They brought them morning after morning. 4 So all the skilled workers working on the holy tent stopped what they were doing. 5 They said to Moses, "The LORD commanded us to do the work. And the people are bringing more than enough for us to do it."

6 Then Moses gave an order. A message was sent through the whole camp. It said, "No man or woman should make anything else and offer it for the holy tent." And so the people were kept from bringing more offerings. 7 There was already more than enough to do all the work.

The Holy Tent

8 All the skilled workers made the holy tent. They made ten curtains out of finely twisted linen. They made them with blue, purple and bright red yarn. A skilled worker sewed cherubim into the pattern. 9 All the curtains were the same size. They were 42 feet long and six feet wide. 10 The workers joined

five of the curtains together. They did the same thing with the other five. [11] Then they made loops out of blue strips of cloth along the edge of the end curtain in one set. They did the same thing with the end curtain in the other set. [12] They also made 50 loops on the end curtain of the one set. They did the same thing on the end curtain of the other set. They put the loops across from each other. [13] Then they made 50 gold hooks. They used them to join the two sets of curtains together so that the holy tent was all one piece.

[14] The workers made a total of 11 curtains out of goat hair to put over the holy tent. [15] All 11 curtains were the same size. They were 45 feet long and six feet wide. [16] The workers joined five of the curtains together into one set. They did the same thing with the other six. [17] Then they made 50 loops along the edge of the end curtain in the one set. They did the same thing with the other set. [18] They made 50 bronze hooks. They used them to join the tent together all in one piece. [19] They made a covering for the tent. They made it out of ram skins dyed red. Over that, they put a covering of another kind of strong leather.

[20] The workers made frames out of acacia wood for the holy tent. [21] Each frame was about 15 feet long and two feet three inches wide. [22] The workers added two small wooden pins to each frame. The pins stuck out so that they were even with each other. The workers made all the frames of the holy tent in the same way. [23] The workers made 20 frames for the south side of the holy tent. [24] And they made 40 silver bases to go under them. They made two bases for each frame. They put one under each pin that stuck out. [25] For the north side of the holy tent they made 20 frames [26] and 40 silver bases. They put two bases under each frame. [27] The workers made six frames for the west end of the holy tent. [28] They made two frames for the corners of the holy tent at the far end. [29] At those two corners the frames were double from top to bottom. They were fitted into a single ring. The workers made both of them the same. [30] So there were eight frames and 16 silver bases. There were two bases under each frame.

[31] The workers also made crossbars out of acacia wood. They made five for the frames on one side of the holy tent. [32] They made five for the frames on the other side. And they made five for the frames on the west, at the far end of the holy tent. [33] The center crossbar reached from end to end at the middle of the frames. [34] The workers covered the frames with gold. They made gold rings to hold the crossbars. They also covered the crossbars with gold.

[35] They made the curtain out of blue, purple and bright red yarn and finely twisted linen. A skilled worker sewed cherubim into the pattern. [36] The work-

ers made four posts out of acacia wood for the curtain. They covered the posts with gold. They made gold hooks and four silver bases for the posts. [37] For the entrance to the tent the workers made a curtain. They made it out of blue, purple and bright red yarn and finely twisted linen. A person who sewed skillfully made it. [38] The workers made five posts with hooks for the curtains. They covered the tops of the posts and their bands with gold. And they made five bronze bases for them.

The Ark of the Covenant Law

37 Bezalel made the ark of the covenant law out of acacia wood. It was three feet nine inches long and two feet three inches wide and high. [2] He covered it inside and outside with pure gold. He put a strip of gold around it. [3] He made four gold rings for it. He joined them to its four bottom corners. He put two rings on one side and two rings on the other. [4] Then he made poles out of acacia wood. He covered them with gold. [5] He put the poles through the rings on the sides of the ark to carry it.

[6] He made its cover out of pure gold. It was three feet nine inches long and two feet three inches wide. The cover is the place where sin is paid for. [7] Then he made two cherubim out of hammered gold at the ends of the cover. [8] He put one of the cherubim on each end of it. [9] He made them as part of the cover itself. Their wings spread up over the cover. The cherubim faced each other and looked toward the cover.

The Table for the Holy Bread

[10] The workers made the table out of acacia wood. It was three feet long, one foot six inches wide and two feet three inches high. [11] Then they covered it with pure gold. They put a strip of gold around it. [12] They also made a rim around it three inches wide. They put a strip of gold around the rim. [13] They made four gold rings for the table. They joined them to the four corners, where the four legs were. [14] The rings were close to the rim. The rings held the poles used to carry the table. [15] The workers made the poles out of acacia wood. They covered them with gold. [16] They made plates, dishes and bowls out of pure gold for the table. They also made pure gold pitchers to pour out drink offerings.

The Gold Lampstand

[17] The workers made the lampstand out of pure gold. They hammered out its base and stem. Its buds, blossoms and cups branched out from it. [18] Six branches came out from the sides of the lampstand. There were three on one side and three on the other. [19] On one branch there were three cups shaped like almond flowers with buds and blossoms. There were three on the next branch. In fact, there were three

on each of the six branches that came out from the lampstand. [20] On the lampstand there were four cups shaped like almond flowers with buds and blossoms. [21] One bud was under the first pair of branches that came out from the lampstand. A second bud was under the second pair. And a third bud was under the third pair. There was a total of six branches. [22] The buds and branches came out from the lampstand. The whole lampstand was one piece hammered out of pure gold.

[23] The workers made its seven lamps out of pure gold. They also made its trays and wick cutters out of pure gold. [24] They used 75 pounds of pure gold to make the lampstand and everything used with it.

The Altar for Burning Incense

[25] The workers made the altar for burning incense. They made it out of acacia wood. It was about one foot six inches square and three feet high. A horn stuck out from each of its upper four corners. [26] The workers covered the top, sides and horns with pure gold. They put a strip of gold around it. [27] They made two gold rings below the strip. They put the rings on the sides across from each other. The rings held the poles used to carry it. [28] The workers made the poles out of acacia wood. They covered them with gold.

[29] They also made the sacred anointing oil and the pure, sweet-smelling incense. A person who makes perfume made them.

The Altar for Burnt Offerings

38 The workers built the altar for burnt offerings out of acacia wood. It was four feet six inches high and seven feet six inches square. [2] They made a horn stick out from each of its four upper corners. They covered the altar with bronze. [3] They made all its tools out of bronze. They made its pots, shovels, sprinkling bowls, meat forks, and pans for carrying ashes. [4] They made a bronze grate for the altar. They put the grate halfway up the altar on the inside. [5] They made a bronze ring for each of the four corners of the grate. [6] They made poles out of acacia wood. They covered them with bronze. [7] They put the poles through the rings. The poles were on two sides of the altar for carrying it. The workers made the altar out of boards. They left it hollow.

The Large Bowl for Washing

[8] The workers made the large bronze bowl and its bronze stand. They made them out of bronze mirrors. The mirrors belonged to the women who served at the entrance to the tent of meeting.

The Courtyard

[9] Next, the workers made the courtyard. The south side was 150 feet long. It had curtains made out of finely twisted linen. [10] The curtains had 20 posts

and 20 bronze bases. The posts had silver hooks and bands on them. [11] The north side was also 150 feet long. Its curtains had 20 posts and 20 bronze bases. The posts had silver hooks and bands on them.

[12] The west end was 75 feet wide. It had curtains with ten posts and ten bases. The posts had silver hooks and bands on them. [13] The east end, toward the sunrise, was also 75 feet wide. [14] Curtains 22 feet six inches long were on one side of the entrance to the courtyard. They were hung on three posts. Each post had a base. [15] Curtains 22 feet six inches long were also on the other side of the entrance. They were hung on three posts. Each post had a base. [16] All the curtains around the courtyard were made out of finely twisted linen. [17] The bases for the posts were made out of bronze. The hooks and bands on the posts were made out of silver. Their tops were covered with silver. So all the posts of the courtyard had silver bands.

[18] The curtain for the courtyard entrance was made out of blue, purple and bright red yarn and finely twisted linen. A person who sewed skillfully made it. It was 30 feet long. Like the curtains of the courtyard, it was seven feet six inches high. [19] It had four posts and four bronze bases. Their hooks and bands were made out of silver. Their tops were covered with silver. [20] All the tent stakes of the holy tent were made out of bronze. So were all the stakes of the courtyard around it.

The Amounts of the Metals Used

[21] Here are the amounts of the metals used for the holy tent, where the tablets of the covenant law were kept. Moses commanded the Levites to record the amounts. The Levites did the work under the direction of Ithamar. Ithamar was the son of Aaron the priest. [22] Bezalel, the son of Uri, made everything the LORD had commanded Moses. Uri was the son of Hur. Bezalel was from the tribe of Judah. [23] Oholiab, the son of Ahisamak, helped Bezalel. Oholiab was from the tribe of Dan. He could carve things and make patterns. And he could sew skillfully with blue, purple and bright red yarn and on fine linen. [24] The total weight of the gold from the wave offering was more than a ton. It was weighed out in keeping with the standard weights used in the sacred tent. The gold was used for all the work done in connection with the sacred tent.

[25] The silver received from the men in the community who were listed and counted weighed almost four tons. It was weighed out in keeping with the weights used in the sacred tent. [26] It amounted to a fifth of an ounce for each person. It was weighed out in keeping with the weights used in the sacred tent. The silver was received from the men who had been listed and counted. All of them were

20 years old or more. Their total number was 603,550. ²⁷ The four tons of silver were used to make the bases for the holy tent and for the curtain. The 100 bases were made from the four tons. Each base used more than 75 pounds of silver. ²⁸ The workers used 45 pounds to make the hooks for the posts, to cover the tops of the posts, and to make their bands.

²⁹ The bronze from the wave offering weighed two and a half tons. ³⁰ The workers used some of it to make the bases for the entrance to the tent of meeting. They used some for the bronze altar for burnt offerings and its bronze grate and all its tools. ³¹ They used some for the bases for the courtyard around the holy tent. They used some for the bases for the courtyard entrance. And they used the rest to make all the tent stakes for the holy tent and the courtyard around it.

The Clothes for the Priests

39 The workers made clothes from the blue, purple and bright red yarn. The clothes were worn by the priests who served in the holy tent. The workers also made sacred clothes for Aaron. They made them just as the Lord had commanded Moses.

The Linen Apron

² The workers made the linen apron. They made it out of thin gold wire, and of blue, purple and bright red yarn, and of finely twisted linen. ³ They hammered out thin sheets of gold. They cut it into thin wire. Then they sewed it into the blue, purple and bright red yarn and fine linen. Skilled workers made it. ⁴ The workers made shoulder straps for the apron. The straps were joined to two of its corners. ⁵ Its skillfully made waistband was made like the apron. The waistband was part of the apron itself. It was made out of thin gold wire, and out of blue, purple and bright red yarn, and out of finely twisted linen. The workers made it just as the Lord had commanded Moses.

⁶ They put the onyx stones in fancy gold settings. They carved the names of the sons of Israel on the stones. They did it the way a jewel cutter would carve them. ⁷ Then they connected them to the shoulder straps of the linen apron. The stones stood for the sons of Israel and were a constant reminder for them. The workers did those things just as the Lord had commanded Moses.

The Chest Cloth

⁸ Skilled workers made the chest cloth. They made it like the linen apron. They used thin gold wire, and blue, purple and bright red yarn, and finely twisted linen. ⁹ The chest cloth was nine inches square. It was folded in half. ¹⁰ The workers put four rows of valuable jewels on it. Carnelian, chrysolite and beryl were in the first

row. [11] Turquoise, lapis lazuli and emerald were in the second row. [12] Jacinth, agate and amethyst were in the third row. [13] And topaz, onyx and jasper were in the fourth row. The workers put them in fancy gold settings. [14] They used a total of 12 stones. There was one stone for each of the names of the sons of Israel. Each stone was carved with the name of one of the 12 tribes.

[15] The workers made braided chains out of pure gold for the chest cloth. They made them like ropes. [16] They made two fancy gold settings and two gold rings. They connected them to two corners of the chest cloth. [17] They joined the two gold chains to the rings at the corners of the chest cloth. [18] They joined the other ends of the chains to the two settings. They joined them to the shoulder straps on the front of the linen apron. [19] The workers made two gold rings. They connected them to the other two corners of the chest cloth. They put them on the inside edge next to the apron. [20] Then they made two more gold rings. They connected them to the bottom of the shoulder straps on the front of the apron. They put them close to the seam. They put them right above the waistband of the apron. [21] They tied the rings of the chest cloth to the rings of the apron with blue cord. That connected it to the waistband. Then the chest cloth would not swing out from the linen apron. The workers did those things just as the LORD had commanded Moses.

More Clothes for the Priests

[22] The workers made the outer robe of the linen apron completely out of blue cloth. The cloth was made by a skillful person. [23] The workers made an opening in the center of the robe. They made an edge like a collar around the opening. Then it couldn't tear. [24] They made pomegranates out of blue, purple and bright red yarn and finely twisted linen. They sewed them around the hem of the robe. [25] They made bells out of pure gold. They sewed them around the hem between the pomegranates. [26] They sewed a bell between every two pomegranates all around the hem of the robe. Aaron had to wear the robe when he served as priest. That's what the LORD commanded Moses.

[27] The workers made inner robes out of fine linen for Aaron and his sons. The linen cloth was made by a skillful person. [28] The workers also made the turban out of fine linen. And they made the caps and the underwear out of finely twisted linen. [29] The belt was made out of finely twisted linen and blue, purple and bright red yarn. A person who sewed skillfully made it. The workers did those things just as the LORD had commanded Moses.

[30] They made the plate out of pure gold. It was a sacred crown.

On the plate, they carved the words

SET APART FOR THE LORD.

31 Then they tied the plate to the turban with a blue cord. They did those things just as the LORD had commanded Moses.

The Holy Tent Is Completed

32 So all the work on the holy tent, the tent of meeting, was completed. The Israelites did everything just as the LORD had commanded Moses. 33 Then they brought the holy tent to Moses along with everything that belonged to it. Here are the things they brought:

hooks, frames, crossbars, posts and bases;
34 the covering of ram skins dyed red, the covering of another kind of strong leather and the curtain that hides the ark;
35 the ark where the tablets of the covenant law are kept, the poles and the cover for the ark;
36 the table for the holy bread with all its things and the holy bread;
37 the pure gold lampstand with its row of lamps and everything used with it, and the olive oil that gives light;
38 the gold altar for burning incense, the anointing oil, the sweet-smelling incense and the curtain for the entrance to the tent;
39 the bronze altar for burnt offerings with its bronze grate, its poles and all its tools;
the large bowl with its stand;
40 the curtains of the courtyard with their posts and bases, and the curtain for the entrance to the courtyard;
the ropes and tent stakes for the courtyard;
everything that belongs to the holy tent, the tent of meeting;
41 and the sacred clothes for Aaron the priest and the clothes for his sons when they serve as priests.

42 The Israelites had done all the work just as the LORD had commanded Moses. 43 Moses looked over the work carefully. He saw that the workers had done it just as the LORD had commanded. So Moses gave them his blessing.

Moses Sets Up the Holy Tent

40 Then the LORD said to Moses, 2 "Set up the holy tent, the tent of meeting. Set it up on the first day of the first month. 3 Place in it the ark where the tablets of the covenant law are kept. Hide the ark with the curtain. 4 Bring in the table for the holy bread. Arrange the loaves of bread on it. Then bring in the lampstand. Set up its lamps. 5 Place the gold altar for burning incense in front of the ark where the tablets of the covenant law are kept. Put up the curtain at the entrance to the holy tent.
6 "Place the altar for burnt of-

ferings in front of the entrance to the holy tent, the tent of meeting. ⁷ Place the large bowl between the tent of meeting and the altar. Put water in the bowl. ⁸ Set up the courtyard around the holy tent. Put the curtain at the entrance to the courtyard.

⁹ "Get the anointing oil. Anoint the holy tent and everything in it. Set apart the holy tent and everything that belongs to it. Then it will be holy. ¹⁰ Anoint the altar for burnt offerings and all its tools. Set apart the altar. Then it will be a very holy place. ¹¹ Anoint the large bowl and its stand. Set them apart.

¹² "Bring Aaron and his sons to the entrance to the tent of meeting. Wash them with water. ¹³ Dress Aaron in the sacred clothes. Anoint him and set him apart. Then he will be able to serve me as priest. ¹⁴ Bring his sons and dress them in their inner robes. ¹⁵ Anoint them just as you anointed their father. Then they will be able to serve me as priests. They will be anointed to do the work of priests. That work will last for all time to come." ¹⁶ Moses did everything just as the LORD had commanded him.

¹⁷ So the holy tent was set up. It was the first day of the first month in the second year. ¹⁸ Moses set up the holy tent. He put the bases in place. He put the frames in them. He put in the crossbars. He set up the posts. ¹⁹ He spread the holy tent over the frames. Then he put the coverings over the tent. Moses did it as the LORD had commanded him.

²⁰ He got the tablets of the covenant law. He placed them in the ark. He put the poles through its rings. And he put the cover on it. The cover was the place where sin is paid for. ²¹ Moses brought the ark into the holy tent. He hung the curtain to hide the ark where the tablets of the covenant law are kept. Moses did it as the LORD had commanded him.

²² Moses placed the table for the holy bread in the tent of meeting. It was on the north side of the holy tent outside the curtain. ²³ He arranged the loaves of bread on it in the sight of the LORD. Moses did it as the LORD had commanded him.

²⁴ Moses placed the lampstand in the tent of meeting. It stood across from the table on the south side of the holy tent. ²⁵ He set up the lamps in front of the LORD. Moses did it as the LORD had commanded him.

²⁶ Moses placed the gold altar for burning incense in the tent of meeting. He placed it in front of the curtain. ²⁷ He burned sweet-smelling incense on it. Moses did it as the LORD had commanded him.

²⁸ Then Moses put up the curtain at the entrance to the holy tent. ²⁹ He set the altar for burnt offerings near the entrance to the holy tent, the tent of meeting. He sacrificed burnt offerings and grain offerings on it. Moses did it as the LORD had commanded him.

³⁰ Moses placed the large bowl between the tent of meeting and

the altar. He put water in the bowl for washing. ³¹ Moses and Aaron and his sons used it to wash their hands and feet. ³² They washed whenever they entered the tent of meeting or approached the altar. They did it as the LORD had commanded Moses.

³³ Then Moses set up the courtyard around the holy tent and altar. He put up the curtain at the entrance to the courtyard. And so Moses completed the work.

The Glory of the LORD

³⁴ Then the cloud covered the tent of meeting. The glory of the LORD filled the holy tent. ³⁵ Moses couldn't enter the tent of meeting because the cloud had settled on it. The glory of the LORD filled the holy tent.

³⁶ The Israelites continued their travels. Whenever the cloud lifted from above the holy tent, they started out. ³⁷ But if the cloud didn't lift, they did not start out. They stayed until the day it lifted. ³⁸ So the cloud of the LORD was above the holy tent during the day. Fire was in the cloud at night. All the Israelites could see the cloud during all their travels.

Leviticus

Introduction:

Leviticus means "about the Levites." The Levites were God's priests. They led the people in worship. This book told the people how to worship God. It told the priests how to give animals to God, and it told the people how to be clean.

Some rules were just for the Levites, but God's law helped all of Israel to worship him. God wants his people to worship him and to be holy. One key statement in this book is, "Be holy, because I am holy." (11:44, 45)

Outline of contents:

Rules for Burnt Offerings

1 The LORD called out to Moses. He spoke to him from the tent of meeting. He said, ² "Speak to the Israelites. Tell them, 'Suppose anyone among you brings an offering to the LORD. They must bring an animal from their herd or flock.

³ " 'If someone brings a burnt offering from the herd, they must offer a male animal. It must not have any flaws. They must bring it to the entrance to the tent of meeting. Then the LORD will accept it. ⁴ They must place their hand on the head of the burnt offering. Then the LORD will accept it in place of them. It will pay for their sin. ⁵ The young bull must be killed there in the sight of the LORD.

Then the priests in Aaron's family line must bring its blood to the altar. They must splash it against the sides of the altar. The altar stands at the entrance to the tent of meeting. ⁶ The skin must be removed from the animal brought for the burnt offering. Then the animal must be cut into pieces. ⁷ The priests in Aaron's family line must build a fire on the altar. They must place wood on the fire. ⁸ Then they must place the pieces of the animal on the burning wood on the altar. The pieces include the head and the fat. ⁹ The inside parts of the animal must be washed with water. The legs must also be washed. The priest must burn all of it on the altar. It is a burnt offering. It is a food offering. Its smell pleases the LORD.

¹⁰ " 'If someone offers a burnt offering from the flock, it must be a male animal. It can be a sheep or a goat. It must not have any flaws. ¹¹ They must kill it at the north side of the altar in the sight of the LORD. The priests in Aaron's family line must splash its blood against the sides of the altar. ¹² They must cut the animal into pieces. The priest must place the pieces on the burning wood on the altar. The pieces include the head and the fat. ¹³ They must wash the inside parts with water. The legs must also be washed. The priest must bring all the parts to the altar. He must burn them there. It is a burnt offering. It is a food offering. Its smell pleases the LORD.

¹⁴ " 'If someone offers to the LORD a burnt offering of birds, it must be a dove or a young pigeon. ¹⁵ The priest must bring it to the altar. He must twist its head off. Then he must burn the rest of the bird on the altar. Its blood must be emptied out on the side of the altar. ¹⁶ The priest must remove the small bag inside the bird's throat. He must also remove the feathers. Then he must throw them to the east side of the altar. That is where the ashes are. ¹⁷ He must take hold of the wings of the bird and tear it open. But he must not tear it in two. Then the priest will burn it on the wood burning on the altar. It is a burnt offering. It is a food offering. Its smell pleases the LORD.

Rules for Grain Offerings

2 " 'Suppose anyone brings a grain offering to the LORD. Then their offering must be made out of the finest flour. They must pour olive oil on it. They must also put incense on it. ² They must take it to the priests in Aaron's family line. A priest must take a handful of the flour and oil. He must mix them with all the incense. Then he must burn that part on the altar. It will be a reminder that all good things come from the LORD. It is a food offering. Its smell pleases the LORD. ³ The rest of the grain offering belongs to Aaron and to the priests in his family line. It is a very holy part of the food offerings presented to the LORD.

⁴ " 'If you bring a grain offering baked in an oven, make it out of the finest flour. It can be thick loaves of bread made without yeast. Mix them with olive oil. Or it can be thin loaves of bread that are made without yeast. Spread olive oil on them. ⁵ If your grain offering is cooked on a metal plate, make your offering out of the finest flour. Mix it with oil. Make it without yeast. ⁶ Break it into pieces. Pour oil on it. It is a grain offering. ⁷ If your grain offering is cooked in a pan, make your offering out of the finest flour and some olive oil. ⁸ Bring to the LORD your grain offering made out of all these things. Give it to the priest. He must take it to the altar. ⁹ All good things come from the LORD. The priest must take out the part of the grain offer-

ing that reminds you of this. He must burn it on the altar. It is a food offering. Its smell pleases the LORD. ¹⁰The rest of the grain offering belongs to Aaron and the priests in his family line. It is a very holy part of the food offerings presented to the LORD.

¹¹ " 'Every grain offering you bring to the LORD must be made without yeast. You must not add any yeast or honey to a food offering presented to the LORD. ¹² You can bring them to the LORD as an offering of the first share of food you gather or produce. But they must not be offered on the altar as a pleasant smell. ¹³ Put salt on all your grain offerings. Salt stands for the lasting covenant between you and your God. So do not leave it out of your grain offerings. Add salt to all your offerings.

¹⁴ " 'Suppose you bring to the LORD a grain offering of the first share of your food. Then offer crushed heads of your first grain that have been cooked in fire. ¹⁵ Put olive oil and incense on the grain. It is a grain offering. ¹⁶ The priest must burn part of the crushed grain and the oil. It will remind you that all good things come from the LORD. The priest must burn it together with all the incense. It is a food offering presented to the LORD.

Rules for Friendship Offerings

3 " 'Suppose someone brings a friendship offering. If they offer an animal from the herd, it can be either male or female. It must not have any flaws. They

must offer it in the sight of the LORD. ² They must place their hand on the animal's head. It must be killed at the entrance to the tent of meeting. Then the priests in Aaron's family line must splash the blood against the sides of the altar. ³ Part of the friendship offering must be given to the LORD as a food offering. It must include all the fat that is connected to them. ⁴ It must include both kidneys with the fat on them next to the lower back muscles. It must also include the long part of the liver. All of it must be removed together with the kidneys. ⁵ Then the priests in Aaron's family line must burn it on the altar. They must burn it on top of the burnt offering that is lying on the burning wood. It is a food offering. Its smell pleases the LORD.

⁶ " 'Suppose someone brings an animal from the flock as a friendship offering to the LORD. It can be either male or female. It must not have any flaws. ⁷ If they bring a lamb, they must offer it in the sight of the LORD. ⁸ They must place their hand on the lamb's head. It must be killed there in front of the tent of meeting. Then the priests in Aaron's family line must splash its blood against the sides of the altar. ⁹ Part of the offering must be brought as a sacrifice presented to the LORD. It must include the lamb's fat and the entire fat tail cut off close to the backbone. It must include all the fat that is connected to them. ¹⁰ It must include both

kidneys with the fat on them next to the lower back muscles. The offering must also include the long part of the liver. That must be removed together with the kidneys. ¹¹ Then the priest must burn the offering on the altar as food. It is a food offering presented to the LORD.

¹² " 'If someone brings a goat, they must offer it in the sight of the LORD. ¹³ They must place their hand on its head. It must be killed there in front of the tent of meeting. Then the priests in Aaron's family line must splash its blood against the sides of the altar. ¹⁴ Part of the offering must be brought as a food offering presented to the LORD. It must include all the fat that is connected to them. ¹⁵ It must include both kidneys with the fat on them next to the lower back muscles. It must also include the long part of the liver. That must be removed together with the kidneys. ¹⁶ Then the priest must burn the offering on the altar as food. It is a food offering. It has a pleasant smell. All the fat belongs to the LORD.

¹⁷ " 'You must not eat any fat or any blood. That is a law that will last for all time to come. It applies no matter where you live.' "

Rules for Sin Offerings

4 The LORD spoke to Moses. He said, ² "Speak to the Israelites. Tell them, 'Suppose someone sins without meaning to. And that person does something the LORD commands us not to do.

³ " 'Suppose it is the anointed priest who sins. And suppose he brings guilt on the people. Then he must bring a young bull to the LORD. It must not have any flaws. He must bring it as a sin offering for the sin he has committed. ⁴ He must bring the bull to the entrance to the tent of meeting in the sight of the LORD. He must place his hand on its head. He must kill it there in the sight of the LORD. ⁵ Then the anointed priest must take some of the bull's blood. He must carry it into the tent of meeting. ⁶ He must dip his finger into the blood. He must sprinkle some of it seven times in the sight of the LORD. He must do it in front of the curtain of the Most Holy Room. ⁷ Then the priest must put some of the blood on the horns of the altar for burning incense. The horns stick out from the upper four corners of the altar. The incense burned on that altar has a sweet smell. The altar stands in front of the LORD in the tent of meeting. The priest must pour out the rest of the bull's blood at the bottom of the altar for burnt offerings. That altar stands at the entrance to the tent. ⁸ He must remove all the fat from the bull for the sin offering. It includes the fat that is connected to the inside parts. ⁹ It includes both kidneys with the fat on them next to the lower back muscles. It also includes the long part of the liver. He must remove all of it together with the kidneys. ¹⁰ He must remove it in the same way the fat is re-

moved from an ox sacrificed as a friendship offering. Then the priest must burn all of it on the altar for burnt offerings. [11] But the bull's hide must be taken away. So must all its meat. So must its head and legs. And so must its inside parts and guts. [12] In other words, all the rest of the bull must be taken away. The priest must take it outside the camp. He must take it to a "clean" place. He must take it to the place where the ashes are thrown. Then he must burn it there in a wood fire on a pile of ashes.

[13] " 'Or suppose the whole community of Israel sins without meaning to. They do something the Lord commands us not to do. Suppose they realize their guilt. [14] And suppose their sin becomes known. Then they must bring a young bull as a sin offering. They must offer it in front of the tent of meeting. [15] The elders of the community must place their hands on the bull's head in the sight of the Lord. The bull must be killed in the sight of the Lord. [16] Then the anointed priest must take some of the bull's blood into the tent of meeting. [17] He must dip his finger into the blood. He must sprinkle it seven times in the sight of the Lord. He must do it in front of the curtain. [18] He must put some of the blood on the horns that stick out from the upper four corners of the altar. The altar stands in front of the Lord in the tent of meeting. The priest must pour out the rest of the blood at the bottom of the altar for burnt offerings. That altar stands at the entrance to the tent. [19] He must remove all the fat from the bull. He must burn it on the altar. [20] He must do the same thing with that bull as he did with the bull for the sin offering. When he does, he will pay for the sin of the community. And they will be forgiven. [21] Then he must take the bull outside the camp. He must burn it just as he burned the first bull. It is the sin offering for the whole community.

[22] " 'Or suppose a leader sins without meaning to. He disobeys any of the commands of the Lord his God. [23] And suppose he realizes his guilt and his sin becomes known. Then he must bring an offering. It must be a male goat. It must not have any flaws. [24] He must place his hand on the goat's head. He must kill it. He must do it at the place where the animals for burnt offerings are killed in the sight of the Lord. His offering is a sin offering. [25] Then the priest must dip his finger into some of the blood of the sin offering. He must put it on the horns that stick out from the upper four corners of the altar for burnt offerings. He must pour out the rest of the blood at the bottom of the altar. [26] He must burn all the fat on the altar. He must burn it in the same way he burned the fat of the friendship offering. When he does, he will pay for the sin of the leader. And the leader will be forgiven.

²⁷ "'Or suppose someone in the community sins without meaning to. They disobey any of the LORD's commands. ²⁸ And suppose they realize their guilt and their sin becomes known. Then they must bring an offering for the sin they have committed. It must be a female goat. It must not have any flaws. ²⁹ They must place their hand on the head of the animal for the sin offering. It must be killed at the place where the animals for burnt offerings are killed. ³⁰ Then the priest must dip his finger into some of the blood. He must put it on the horns that stick out from the upper four corners of the altar for burnt offerings. He must pour out the rest of the blood at the bottom of the altar. ³¹ They must remove all the fat in the same way the fat is removed from the friendship offering. The priest must burn it on the altar. Its smell pleases the LORD. When the priest burns the offering, he will pay for their sin. And they will be forgiven.

³² "'Suppose someone brings a lamb as their sin offering. Then they must bring a female animal. It must not have any flaws. ³³ They must place their hand on its head. They must kill it as a sin offering. They must do it at the place where the animals for burnt offerings are killed. ³⁴ Then the priest must dip his finger into some of the blood of the sin offering. He must put it on the horns that stick out from the upper four corners of the altar for burnt offerings. He must pour out the rest of the blood at the bottom of the altar. ³⁵ They must remove all the fat in the same way the fat is removed from the lamb for the friendship offering. The priest must burn it on the altar on top of the food offerings presented to the LORD. When he does, he will pay for the sin they have committed. And they will be forgiven.

5 "'Suppose someone has been called as a witness to something they have seen or learned about. Then if they do not tell what they know, they have sinned. And they will be held responsible for it.

² "'Or suppose someone touches something not "clean." It could be the dead bodies of wild animals or of livestock. Or it could be the dead bodies of creatures that move along the ground. Even though those people are not aware that they touched them, they have become "unclean." And they are guilty. ³ Or suppose they touch something "unclean" that comes from a human being. It could be anything that would make them "unclean." Suppose they are not aware that they touched it. When they find out about it, they will be guilty. ⁴ Or suppose someone makes a promise to do something without thinking it through. It does not matter what they promised. It does not matter whether they made the promise without thinking about it carefully. And suppose they are not aware that they did not think

it through. When they find out about it, they will be guilty. [5] When someone is guilty in any of those ways, they must admit they have sinned. [6] They must bring a sin offering to pay for the sin they have committed. They must bring to the LORD a female lamb or goat from the flock. The priest will sacrifice the animal. That will pay for the person's sin.

[7] " 'Suppose they can't afford a lamb. Then they must get two doves or two young pigeons. They must bring them to the LORD to pay for their sin. One of them is for a sin offering. The other is for a burnt offering. [8] They must bring them to the priest. The priest will offer the one for the sin offering first. He must twist its head. But he must not twist it off completely. [9] Then he must splash some of the blood of the sin offering against the side of the altar. He must empty out the rest of the blood at the bottom of the altar. It is a sin offering. [10] Then the priest will offer the other bird as a burnt offering. He must do it in the way the law requires. That will pay for the sin they have committed. And they will be forgiven.

[11] " 'But suppose they can't afford two doves or two young pigeons. Then they must bring three and a half pounds of the finest flour as an offering for their sin. It is a sin offering. They must not put olive oil or incense on it. That is because it is a sin offering. [12] They must bring it to the priest. The priest must take a handful of it. He must burn that part on the altar. It will be a reminder that all good things come from the LORD. The priest must burn it on top of the food offerings presented to the LORD. It is a sin offering. [13] In that way the priest will pay for any of the sins they have committed. And they will be forgiven. The rest of the offering will belong to the priest. It is the same as in the case of the grain offering.' "

Rules for Guilt Offerings

[14] The LORD spoke to Moses. He said, [15] "Suppose someone is unfaithful to me and sins. And they do it without meaning to. Here is how they sin against me or my priests. They refuse to give the priests one of the holy things set apart for them. Then they must bring me a ram from the flock. It must not have any flaws. It must be worth the required amount of silver. The silver must be weighed out in keeping with the standard weights that are used in the sacred tent. The ram is a guilt offering. It will pay for their sin. [16] They must also pay for the holy thing they refused to give. They must add a fifth of its value to it. They must give all of it to the priest. The priest will pay for their sin with the ram. It is a guilt offering. And they will be forgiven.

[17] "Suppose someone sins by doing something I command them not to do. Even though they do not know it, they are

guilty. They will be held responsible for it. ¹⁸ They must bring to the priest a ram from the flock as a guilt offering. It must not have any flaws. And it must be worth the required amount of money. The priest will sacrifice the animal. That will pay for what they have done wrong without meaning to. And they will be forgiven. ¹⁹ It is a guilt offering. They have been guilty of doing wrong against me."

6 The LORD spoke to Moses. He said, ² "Suppose someone sins by not being faithful to me. They do it by tricking their neighbors. They trick them in connection with something their neighbors have placed in their care. They steal from their neighbors. Or they cheat them. ³ Or they find something their neighbors have lost and then tell a lie about it. Or they go to court. They promise to tell the truth. But instead they tell a lie when they are a witness about it. Or they lie when they are witnesses about any other sin like those sins. ⁴ When they sin in any of these ways and realize their guilt, they must return what they stole. They must give back what they took by cheating their neighbors. They must return what their neighbors placed in their care. They must return the lost property they found. ⁵ They must return anything they told a lie about when they were witnesses in court. They must pay back everything in full. They must add a fifth of its value to it. They must give all of it to the owner on the day they bring their guilt offering. ⁶ He must bring their guilt offering to the priest to pay for their sin. It is an offering to me. They must bring a ram from the flock. It must not have any flaws. It must be worth the required amount of money. ⁷ The priest will sacrifice the ram to pay for their sin. He will do it in my sight. And they will be forgiven for any of the things they did that made them guilty."

More Rules for Burnt Offerings

⁸ The LORD spoke to Moses. He said, ⁹ "Give Aaron and the priests in his family line a command. Tell them, 'Here are some more rules for burnt offerings. The burnt offering must remain on the altar through the whole night. The fire on the altar must be kept burning until morning. ¹⁰ The priest must put on his linen clothes. He must put on linen underwear next to his body. He must remove the ashes of the burnt offering that the fire has burned up on the altar. He must place them beside the altar. ¹¹ Then he must take his clothes off and put others on. He must carry the ashes outside the camp to a "clean" place. ¹² The fire on the altar must be kept burning. It must not go out. Every morning the priest must add more wood to the fire. He must place the burnt offering on the fire. He must burn the fat of the friendship offerings on it. ¹³ The fire must be kept burning on the altar all the time. It must not go out.

More Rules for Grain Offerings

14 " 'Here are some more rules for grain offerings. The priests in Aaron's family line must bring the grain offering to the LORD in front of the altar. 15 The priest must take a handful of the finest flour and olive oil. He must add to it all the incense on the grain offering. He must burn that part on the altar. It will remind him that all good things come from the LORD. Its smell pleases the LORD. 16 Aaron and the priests in his family line will eat the rest of it. But they must eat it without yeast in the holy area. They must eat it in the courtyard of the tent of meeting. 17 It must not be baked with yeast added to it. The LORD has given it to the priests as their share of the food offerings presented to him. It is very holy, just like the sin offering and the guilt offering. 18 Any priests in Aaron's family line can eat it. It is their share of the food offerings presented to the LORD. It is their share for all time to come. Anyone who touches these offerings will become holy.' "

19 The LORD spoke to Moses. He said, 20 "On the day each high priest in Aaron's family line is anointed, he must bring an offering to me. He must bring three and a half pounds of the finest flour as a regular grain offering. He must bring half of it in the morning. He must bring the other half in the evening. 21 Mix it with olive oil. Cook it on a metal plate. Break it in pieces. Bring it as a grain offering. Its smell pleases the LORD. 22 The son of Aaron who will become the next high priest after him will prepare the grain offering. It is the share that must be given to the LORD for all time to come. It must be completely burned up. 23 Every grain offering a high priest offers must be completely burned up. It must not be eaten."

More Rules for Sin Offerings

24 The LORD spoke to Moses. He said, 25 "Speak to Aaron and the priests in his family line. Tell them, 'Here are some more rules for sin offerings. You must kill the animal for the sin offering in the sight of the LORD. Kill it in the place where the burnt offering is killed. It is very holy. 26 The priest who offers it will eat it. He must eat it in the holy area. He must eat it in the courtyard of the tent of meeting. 27 Anyone who touches any of its meat will become holy. Suppose some of the blood is spilled on someone's clothes. Then you must wash them in the holy area. 28 Break the clay pot the meat is cooked in. But suppose you cook it in a bronze pot. Then you must scrub the pot and rinse it with water. 29 Any male in a priest's family may eat the meat. It is very holy. 30 But suppose some of the blood of a sin offering is brought into the tent of meeting. And that blood is brought into the Holy Room to pay for sin. Then that sin offering must not be eaten. It must be burned up.

More Rules for Guilt Offerings

7 " 'Here are some more rules for guilt offerings. The guilt offering is very holy. ²You must kill the animal for the guilt offering where you kill the animal for the burnt offering. Splash its blood against the sides of the altar. ³Offer all its fat. It must include the fat tail and the fat that covers the inside parts. ⁴It must include both kidneys with the fat on them next to the lower back muscles. It must also include the long part of the liver. Remove all of it together with the kidneys. ⁵The priest must burn all of it on the altar. It is a food offering presented to the LORD. It is a guilt offering. ⁶Any male in a priest's family can eat it. But he must eat it in the holy area. It is very holy.

⁷" 'The same law applies to the sin offering and the guilt offering. Both of them belong to the priest who offers them to pay for sin. ⁸The priest who offers a burnt offering for anyone can keep its hide for himself. ⁹Every grain offering baked in an oven belongs to the priest who offers it. So does every grain offering cooked in a pan or on a metal plate. ¹⁰Every grain offering belongs equally to all the priests in Aaron's family line. That is true whether it is mixed with olive oil or it is dry.

More Rules for Friendship Offerings

¹¹" 'Here are some more rules for friendship offerings anyone may bring to the LORD.

¹²" 'Suppose they offer a friendship offering to show they are thankful. Then together with the thank offering they must offer thick loaves of bread. They must make them without yeast. They must mix them with olive oil. Or they must offer thin loaves of bread made without yeast. They must spread olive oil on them. Or they must offer thick loaves of bread made out of the finest flour. They must add olive oil to it. They must work the flour and prepare it well. ¹³They must bring another friendship offering along with their thank offering. It should be thick loaves of bread made with yeast. ¹⁴They must bring one of each kind of bread as an offering. One kind is made with yeast. The other is not. Both of them are a gift to the LORD. They belong to the priest who splashes the blood of the friendship offering against the altar. ¹⁵The person must eat the meat from their thank offering on the day they offer it. They must not leave any of it until morning.

¹⁶" 'But suppose they bring a friendship offering to keep a promise they have made. Or suppose they bring an offering they choose to give. Then they must eat the sacrifice on the day they offer it. But if anything is left over, they may eat it the next day. ¹⁷They must burn up any meat from the sacrifice left over until the third day. ¹⁸Suppose they eat any meat from the friendship offering on the third day. Then the LORD will

not accept the offering. He will not accept it as a gift from them. It is not pure. If they eat any of it, they will be held responsible for it.

¹⁹ " 'They must not eat meat that touches anything "unclean." They must burn it up. Anyone "clean" may eat any other meat. ²⁰ But suppose an "unclean" person eats any meat from the friendship offering that belongs to the LORD. Then they will be separated from their people. ²¹ Suppose someone touches something "unclean." It does not matter whether it comes from a human being who is not "clean." It does not matter whether it comes from an "unclean" animal. It does not matter whether it comes from something hated and "unclean." And suppose they eat any of the meat from the friendship offering that belongs to the LORD. Then they will be separated from their people.' "

Israel Must Not Eat Fat or Blood

²² The LORD spoke to Moses. He said, ²³ "Speak to the Israelites. Tell them, 'Do not eat any of the fat of cattle, sheep or goats. ²⁴ Do not eat the fat of any animal found dead. Do not eat the fat of an animal that wild animals have torn apart. But you can use the fat for any other purpose. ²⁵ Suppose an animal has been sacrificed as a food offering to the LORD. No one may eat its fat. If they do, they will be separated from their people. ²⁶ No matter where you live,

do not eat the blood of any bird or animal. ²⁷ Anyone who eats blood must be separated from their people.' "

The Share That Belongs to the Priests

²⁸ The LORD spoke to Moses. He said, ²⁹ "Speak to the Israelites. Tell them, 'Suppose someone brings a friendship offering to the LORD. Then they must bring part of it as their special gift to the LORD. ³⁰ They must bring it with their own hands. It is a food offering presented to the LORD. They must bring the fat together with the breast. They must lift the breast up and wave it in front of the LORD as a wave offering. ³¹ The priest will burn the fat on the altar. But the breast belongs to Aaron and the priests in his family line. ³² Give the right thigh from your friendship offerings to the priest as a gift. ³³ The priest who offers the blood and fat from the friendship offering must be given the right thigh. It is his share. ³⁴ I, the LORD, have taken the breast that is waved and the thigh that is given. I have taken them from the friendship offerings of the Israelites. And I have given them to Aaron the priest and the priests in his family line. The offerings will be their share from the Israelites for all time to come.' "

³⁵ That is the part of the food offerings presented to the LORD. It is given to Aaron and the priests in his family line. It was given to Aaron and his sons on

the day they were set apart to serve the LORD as priests. ³⁶ On the day they were anointed, the LORD commanded the Israelites to give that part to them. For all time to come, it will be the share of Aaron and the priests in his family line.

³⁷ These are the rules for burnt offerings, grain offerings, sin offerings, guilt offerings and friendship offerings. They are also the rules for the offerings that are given when priests are being prepared to serve the LORD. ³⁸ They are the rules the LORD gave Moses on Mount Sinai. He gave them on the day he commanded the Israelites to bring their offerings to the LORD. That took place in the Sinai Desert.

Preparing the Priests to Serve the LORD

8 The LORD spoke to Moses. He said, ² "Bring Aaron and his sons to the entrance to the tent of meeting. Bring their clothes and the anointing oil. Bring the bull for the sin offering. Also bring two rams. And bring the basket with the bread made without yeast. ³ Then gather the whole community at the entrance to the tent of meeting." ⁴ Moses did just as the LORD had commanded him. All the people gathered together at the entrance to the tent of meeting.

⁵ Moses said to the people, "Here is what the LORD has commanded us to do." ⁶ Then Moses brought Aaron and his sons to the people. He washed Aaron and his sons with water. ⁷ He put the inner robe on Aaron. He tied the belt around him. He dressed him in the outer robe. He put the linen apron on him. He took the skillfully made waistband and tied the apron on him with it. He wanted to make sure it was securely tied to him. ⁸ Moses placed the chest cloth on Aaron. He put the Urim and Thummim in the chest cloth. ⁹ Then he placed the turban on Aaron's head. On the front of the turban he put the gold plate. It was a sacred crown. Moses did everything just as the LORD had commanded him.

¹⁰ Then Moses took the anointing oil and poured it on the holy tent. He also poured it on everything in it. That's how he set apart those things for the LORD. ¹¹ He sprinkled some of the oil on the altar seven times. He poured oil on the altar and all its tools. He poured it on the large bowl and its stand. He did it to set them apart. ¹² He poured some of the anointing oil on Aaron's head. He anointed him to set him apart to serve the LORD. ¹³ Then Moses brought Aaron's sons to the people. He put the inner robes on them. He tied belts around them. He put caps on their heads. He did everything just as the LORD had commanded him.

¹⁴ Then he brought the bull for the sin offering. Aaron and his sons placed their hands on its head. ¹⁵ Moses killed the bull. He dipped his finger into some

of the blood. He put it on the horns that stick out from the upper four corners of the altar. He did it to make the altar pure. He poured out the rest of the blood at the bottom of the altar. So he set it apart to make it pure. ¹⁶ Moses also removed all the fat around the inside parts of the bull. He removed the long part of the liver. He took both kidneys and their fat. Then he burned all of it on the altar. ¹⁷ But he burned the rest of the bull outside the camp. He burned up its hide, its meat and its guts. He did it just as the LORD had commanded him.

¹⁸ Then Moses brought the ram for the burnt offering. Aaron and his sons placed their hands on its head. ¹⁹ Moses killed the ram. He splashed the blood against the sides of the altar. ²⁰ He cut the ram into pieces. He burned the head, the other pieces and the fat. ²¹ He washed the inside parts and the legs with water. He burned the whole ram on the altar as a burnt offering. It had a pleasant smell. It was a food offering presented to the LORD. Moses did everything just as the LORD had commanded him.

²² Then he brought the other ram. It was sacrificed to prepare the priests for serving the LORD. Aaron and his sons placed their hands on its head. ²³ Moses killed the ram. He put some of its blood on Aaron's right earlobe. He put some on the thumb of Aaron's right hand. He also put some on the big toe of Aar-

on's right foot. ²⁴ Then Moses brought Aaron's sons to the people. He put some of the blood on their right earlobes. He put some on the thumbs of their right hands. He also put some on the big toes of their right feet. Then he splashed the rest of the blood against the sides of the altar. ²⁵ He removed the fat, the fat tail and all the fat around the inside parts. He removed the long part of the liver. He removed both kidneys and their fat. And he removed the right thigh. ²⁶ Then he took a thick loaf of bread from the basket of bread made without yeast. The basket was in front of the LORD. Moses took a thick loaf of bread made with olive oil. He also took a thin loaf of bread. He put all of it on the fat parts of the ram and on its right thigh. ²⁷ He put everything in the hands of Aaron and his sons. He told them to lift it up and wave it in front of the LORD as a wave offering. ²⁸ Then Moses took it from their hands. He burned it on the altar on top of the burnt offering. It was the offering that was sacrificed to prepare the priests for serving the LORD. It had a pleasant smell. It was a food offering presented to the LORD. ²⁹ Moses also lifted up the ram's breast and waved it in front of the LORD as a wave offering. The breast was Moses' share of the ram that was sacrificed to prepare the priests for serving the LORD. Moses did everything just as the LORD had commanded him.

³⁰ Then Moses took some of

the anointing oil. He also took some of the blood from the altar. He sprinkled some of the oil and blood on Aaron and his clothes. He also sprinkled some on Aaron's sons and their clothes. That's how he set apart Aaron and his clothes. And that's how he set apart Aaron's sons and their clothes.

31 Then Moses spoke to Aaron and his sons. He said, "Cook the meat at the entrance to the tent of meeting. Eat it there along with the bread from the basket of the offerings that are brought to prepare the priests for serving the LORD. Do it just as I was commanded. I was told, 'Aaron and his sons must eat it.' 32 Then burn up the rest of the meat and the bread. 33 Don't leave the entrance to the tent of meeting for seven days. Don't leave until the days that are required to prepare you for serving the LORD have been completed. Stay here for the full seven days. 34 The LORD commanded what has been done here today. It was done to pay for your sin. 35 Stay at the entrance to the tent of meeting for seven days. Stay here day and night. Do what the LORD requires. Then you won't die. That's the command the LORD gave me."

36 So Aaron and his sons did everything just as the LORD had commanded through Moses.

The Priests Offer Sacrifices

9 On the eighth day Moses sent for Aaron, his sons and the elders of Israel. 2 He said to Aaron, "Bring a bull calf for your sin offering. Bring a ram for your burnt offering. They must not have any flaws. Offer them to the LORD. 3 Then speak to the Israelites. Tell them, 'Bring a male goat for a sin offering. Bring a calf and a lamb for a burnt offering. Both of them must be a year old. They must not have any flaws. 4 Bring an ox and a ram for a friendship offering. Sacrifice all of them to the LORD. Also bring a grain offering. Mix it with olive oil. Today the LORD will appear to you.'"

5 The people got the things Moses commanded them to get. They took them to the front of the tent of meeting. The whole community came up close to the tent. They stood there in front of the LORD. 6 Then Moses said, "You have done what the LORD has commanded. So the glory of the LORD will appear to you."

7 Moses said to Aaron, "Come to the altar. Sacrifice your sin offering and your burnt offering. Pay for your sin and the sin of the people. Sacrifice the people's offering. Pay for their sin. Do just as the LORD has commanded."

8 So Aaron came to the altar. He killed the calf as a sin offering for himself. 9 His sons brought its blood to him. He dipped his finger into the blood. He put some on the horns that stick out from the upper four corners of the altar. He poured out the rest of the blood at the bottom of the altar. 10 He burned the fat and the kidneys on the altar. He also

burned the long part of the liver. All these parts were from the sin offering. Aaron did just as the LORD had commanded Moses. ¹¹He burned up the meat and the hide outside the camp.

¹²Then he killed the animal for the burnt offering. His sons handed him its blood. He splashed it against the sides of the altar. ¹³They handed him the burnt offering piece by piece. It included the animal's head. Aaron burned everything on the altar. ¹⁴He washed the inside parts and the legs. He burned them on top of the burnt offering on the altar.

¹⁵Then Aaron brought the people's offering. He took the goat for their sin offering and killed it. He offered it for a sin offering. He did just as he had done with his own sin offering. ¹⁶He brought the animal for the burnt offering. He offered it in the way the law requires. ¹⁷He also brought the grain offering. He took a handful of it and burned it on the altar. It was in addition to that morning's burnt offering.

¹⁸Aaron killed the ox and the ram as the friendship offering for the people. His sons handed him the blood. He splashed it against the sides of the altar. ¹⁹His sons also brought the fat parts of the ox and the ram. They included the fat tail and the layer of fat. They also included the kidneys and the long part of the liver. ²⁰Aaron's sons placed everything on the breasts of the animals. Aaron burned the fat on the altar. ²¹He lifted up the breasts and the right thigh and waved them in front of the LORD as a wave offering. He did it just as Moses had commanded.

²²Then Aaron lifted up his hands toward the people. He gave them a blessing. He had already sacrificed the sin offering, the burnt offering and the friendship offering. So he stepped down from the altar.

²³Moses and Aaron went into the tent of meeting. When they came out, they gave the people a blessing. The glory of the LORD appeared to all the people. ²⁴The LORD sent fire on the altar. The fire burned up the burnt offering along with the fat parts. All the people saw it. Then they shouted for joy. They fell with their faces to the ground.

The LORD Kills Nadab and Abihu

10 Nadab and Abihu were two of Aaron's sons. They got their shallow cups for burning incense. They put fire in them. They added incense to it. They made an offering to the LORD by using fire that wasn't allowed. They did it against his command. ²So the LORD sent fire on them. It burned them up. They died in front of the LORD. ³Then Moses spoke to Aaron. He said, "That's what the LORD was talking about when he said,

" 'Among those who
    approach me
  I will show that I am holy.
 In the sight of all the people
  I will be honored.' "

So Aaron remained silent.

⁴ Moses sent for Mishael and Elzaphan. They were sons of Aaron's uncle Uzziel. Moses said to them, "Come here. Carry the bodies of your cousins outside the camp. Take them away from in front of the Holy Room." ⁵ So they came and carried them outside the camp. It was just as Moses had ordered. The bodies of Nadab and Abihu still had their inner robes on them.

⁶ Moses spoke to Aaron and to Eleazar and Ithamar. They were Aaron's sons. Moses said, "Don't let your hair hang loose. Don't tear your clothes. If you do, you will die. And the LORD will be angry with the whole community. But all the Israelites are allowed to show they are sad. They are your relatives. They may mourn for those the LORD has destroyed with fire. ⁷ Don't leave the entrance to the tent of meeting. If you do, you will die. That's because the LORD's anointing oil has made you holy." So they did what Moses told them to do.

⁸ Then the LORD spoke to Aaron. He said, ⁹ "You and your sons will go into the tent of meeting. When you do, you must not drink any kind of wine. If you do, you will die. This is a law that will last for all time to come. ¹⁰ This is so that you can tell the difference between what is holy and what is not. You must be able to tell the difference between what is 'clean' and what is not. ¹¹ Then you will be able to teach the Israelites all the rules I have given them through Moses."

¹² Moses spoke to Aaron and to Eleazar and Ithamar. They were Aaron's two remaining sons. Moses said, "Take the grain offering left over from the food offerings presented to the LORD. It is very holy. Make bread without yeast from it. Eat it beside the altar. ¹³ Eat it in the holy area. It's your share and your sons' share of the food offerings presented to the LORD. These rules are in keeping with the command the LORD gave me. ¹⁴ But you and your sons and your daughters can eat the breast that was waved. You can also eat the thigh that was offered. Eat them in a 'clean' place. They have been given to you and your children. They are your share of the friendship offerings the Israelites bring. ¹⁵ The thigh that was offered must be brought together with the fat parts of the food offerings. The breast that was waved must be brought in the same way. All of it must be lifted up and waved in front of the LORD as a wave offering. It will be the share for you and your children for all time to come. That's what the LORD has commanded."

¹⁶ Moses asked about the goat that was brought as the sin offering. He found out that it had been burned up. So he became angry with Eleazar and Ithamar. They were Aaron's two remaining sons. Moses asked them, ¹⁷ "Why didn't you eat the sin offering in a place near the Holy Room? The offering

is very holy. It was given to you to take the people's guilt away. It paid for their sin in the sight of the LORD. [18] The blood of the offering wasn't taken into the Holy Room. So you should have eaten the goat in a place near the Holy Room. That's what I commanded."

[19] Aaron replied to Moses, "Today the people sacrificed their sin offering to the LORD. They also sacrificed their burnt offerings to him. But a terrible thing has happened to me. Two of my sons have died. Would the LORD have been pleased if I had eaten the sin offering today?" [20] When Moses heard that, he was satisfied.

"Clean" and "Unclean" Food

11 The LORD spoke to Moses and Aaron. He said to them, [2] "Speak to the Israelites. Tell them, 'Many animals live on land. Here are the only ones you can eat. [3] You can eat any animal that has hooves that are separated completely in two. But it must also chew the cud.

[4] " 'Some animals only chew the cud. Some only have hooves that are separated in two. You must not eat those animals. Camels chew the cud. But their hooves are not separated in two. So they are "unclean" for you. [5] Rock badgers chew the cud. But their hooves are not separated in two. So they are "unclean" for you. [6] Rabbits chew the cud. But their hooves are not separated in two. So they are "unclean" for you. [7] Pigs have hooves that are separated completely in two. But they do not chew the cud. So they are "unclean" for you. [8] You must not eat the meat of those animals. You must not even touch their dead bodies. They are "unclean" for you.

[9] " 'Many creatures live in the water of the oceans and streams. You can eat all those that have fins and scales. [10] Treat as "unclean" all the creatures in the oceans or streams that do not have fins and scales. That includes all those that move together in groups and all those that do not. [11] Treat them as "unclean." Do not eat their meat. Treat their dead bodies as "unclean." [12] Regard as "unclean" everything that lives in the water that does not have fins and scales.

[13] " 'Here are the birds you must treat as "unclean." Do not eat them because they are "unclean." The birds include eagles, vultures and black vultures. [14] They include red kites and all kinds of black kites. [15] They include all kinds of ravens. [16] They include horned owls, screech owls, gulls and all kinds of hawks. [17] They include little owls, cormorants and great owls. [18] They include white owls, desert owls and ospreys. [19] They also include storks, hoopoes, bats and all kinds of herons.

[20] " 'Treat as "unclean" every flying insect that walks on all fours. [21] But you can eat some flying insects that walk on all fours. Their legs have joints so they can hop on the ground. [22] Here

are the insects you can eat. You can eat all kinds of locusts, katydids, crickets and grasshoppers. ²³ Treat as "unclean" every other creature with wings and four legs.

²⁴ " 'You will make yourselves "unclean" if you eat these things. If you touch their dead bodies, you will be "unclean" until evening. ²⁵ If a person picks up one of their dead bodies, that person must wash their clothes. They will be "unclean" until evening.

²⁶ " 'Suppose an animal has hooves that are not separated completely in two. Or suppose an animal does not chew the cud. Then these animals are "unclean" for you. If you touch the dead body of any of them, you will be "unclean." ²⁷ Many animals walk on all fours. But those that walk on their paws are "unclean" for you. Anyone who touches their dead bodies will be "unclean" until evening. ²⁸ If a person picks up their dead bodies, that person must wash their clothes. They will be "unclean" until evening. These animals are "unclean" for you.

²⁹ " 'Many animals move along the ground. Here are the ones that are "unclean" for you. They include weasels, rats and all kinds of large lizards. ³⁰ They also include geckos, monitor lizards, wall lizards, skinks and chameleons. ³¹ These are the animals that move around on the ground that are "unclean" for you. If you touch their dead bodies, you will be "unclean" until evening. ³² Suppose one of them dies and falls on something. Then that thing will be "unclean." It does not matter what it is used for. It does not matter whether it is made out of wood, cloth, hide or rough cloth. Put it in water. It will be "unclean" until evening. After that, it will be "clean." ³³ Suppose one of these animals falls into a clay pot. Then everything in the pot will be "unclean." You must break the pot. ³⁴ Any food that could be eaten but has water on it that came from that pot is "unclean." And any liquid that could be drunk from it is "unclean." ³⁵ Anything that the dead body of one of these animals falls on becomes "unclean." If it is an oven or cooking pot, break it. It is "unclean." And you must consider it "unclean." ³⁶ But a spring or a well for collecting water remains "clean." That is true even if the dead body of one of these animals falls into it. But anyone who touches the dead body is not "clean." ³⁷ If the dead body falls on any seeds that have not been planted yet, the seeds remain "clean." ³⁸ But suppose water has already been put on the seeds. And suppose the dead body falls on them. Then they are "unclean" for you.

³⁹ " 'Suppose an animal you are allowed to eat dies. If anyone touches its dead body, they will be "unclean" until evening. ⁴⁰ If they eat part of the dead body, they must wash their clothes. They will be "unclean" until evening. If they pick up the dead body, they must wash their

clothes. They will be "unclean" until evening.

⁴¹ " 'Treat as "unclean" every creature that moves along the ground. Do not eat it. ⁴² Do not eat any of these creatures. It does not matter whether they move on their bellies. It does not matter whether they walk on all fours or on many feet. It is "unclean." ⁴³ Do not make yourselves "unclean" by eating any of these animals. Do not make yourselves "unclean" because of them. Do not let them make you "unclean." ⁴⁴ I am the LORD your God. Set yourselves apart. Be holy, because I am holy. Do not make yourselves "unclean" by eating any creatures that move around on the ground. ⁴⁵ I am the LORD. I brought you up out of Egypt to be your God. So be holy, because I am holy.

⁴⁶ " 'These are the rules about animals and birds. These are the rules about every living thing that moves around in the water. And these are the rules about every creature that moves along the ground. ⁴⁷ You must be able to tell the difference between what is "clean" and what is not. You must also be able to tell the difference between living creatures that can be eaten and those that can't.' "

Becoming "Clean" After Having a Baby

12 The LORD spoke to Moses. He said, ² "Speak to the Israelites. Tell them, 'Suppose a woman becomes pregnant and has a baby boy. Then she will be "unclean" for seven days. It is the same as when she is "unclean" during her monthly period. ³ On the eighth day the boy must be circumcised. ⁴ After that, the woman must wait for 33 days to be made pure from her bleeding. She must not touch anything sacred until the 33 days are over. During that time she must not go to the sacred tent. ⁵ But suppose she has a baby girl. Then she will be "unclean" for two weeks. It is the same as during her period. After the two weeks, she must wait for 66 days to be made pure from her bleeding.

⁶ " 'After she has waited the required number of days to be made pure, she must bring two offerings. She must take them to the priest at the entrance to the tent of meeting. She must bring a lamb a year old for a burnt offering. She must also bring a young pigeon or a dove for a sin offering. ⁷ The priest must offer them to the LORD. They will pay for her sin. Then she will be "clean" from her bleeding.

" 'These are the rules for a woman who has a baby boy or girl. ⁸ But suppose she can't afford a lamb. Then she must bring two doves or two young pigeons. One is for a burnt offering. The other is for a sin offering. The priest will sacrifice those offerings. That will pay for her sin. And she will be "clean." ' "

Rules About Skin Diseases

13 The LORD spoke to Moses and Aaron. He told them to say to the people, ² "Suppose someone's skin has a swelling or a rash or a shiny spot. And suppose it could become a skin disease. Then they must be brought to the priest Aaron. Or they must be brought to a priest in Aaron's family line. ³ The priest must look carefully at the sore on the person's skin. He must see whether the hair in the sore has turned white. He must also see whether the sore seems to be under the skin. If the sore is white and is under the skin, it is a skin disease. When the priest looks that person over carefully, he must announce that the person is 'unclean.' ⁴ Suppose the shiny spot on the skin is white but does not seem to be under the skin. And suppose the hair in the spot has not turned white. Then the priest must make the person stay away from everyone else for seven days. ⁵ On the seventh day the priest must look carefully at the sore again. Suppose it has not changed and has not spread in the skin. Then the priest must make the person stay away from everyone else for another seven days. ⁶ On the seventh day the priest must look carefully at the sore again. If it has faded and has not spread, he must announce that the person is 'clean.' It is only a rash. That person must wash their clothes. They will be 'clean.' ⁷ But suppose the rash spreads in the skin after they have shown themselves to the priest a second time. Then they must appear in front of the priest again. ⁸ The priest must look carefully at the

sore. If the rash has spread, he must announce that the person is 'unclean.' They have a skin disease.

⁹ "When anyone has a skin disease, they must be brought to the priest. ¹⁰ The priest must look them over carefully. Suppose there is a white swelling in the skin. Suppose it has turned the hair white. And suppose there are open sores in the swelling. ¹¹ Then the person has a skin disease that will never go away. The priest must announce that they are 'unclean.' The priest must not make them stay away from everyone else. They are already 'unclean.'

¹² "Suppose the disease breaks out all over their skin. And suppose it covers them from head to foot, as far as the priest can tell. ¹³ Then the priest must look them over carefully. If the disease has covered their whole body, the priest must announce that they are 'clean.' All their skin has turned white. So they are 'clean.' ¹⁴ But when open sores appear on their skin, they will not be 'clean.' ¹⁵ When the priest sees the open sores, he must announce that they are 'unclean.' The open sores are not 'clean.' They have a skin disease. ¹⁶ But if the open sores change and turn white, they must go to the priest. ¹⁷ The priest must look them over carefully. If the sores have turned white, the priest must announce that the person is 'clean.' Then they will be 'clean.'

¹⁸ "Suppose someone has a

boil on their skin and it heals. ¹⁹ And suppose a white swelling or shiny pink spot appears where the boil was. Then they must show themselves to the priest. ²⁰ The priest must look at the boil carefully. Suppose it seems to be under the skin. And suppose the hair in it has turned white. Then the priest must announce that the person is 'unclean.' A skin disease has broken out where the boil was. ²¹ But suppose that when the priest looks at the boil carefully, there is no white hair in it. The boil is not under the skin. And it has faded. Then the priest must make the person stay away from everyone else for seven days. ²² If the boil is spreading in the skin, the priest must announce that the person is 'unclean.' They have a skin disease. ²³ But suppose the spot has not changed. And suppose it has not spread. Then it is only a scar from the boil. And the priest must announce that the person is 'clean.'

²⁴ "Suppose someone has a burn on their skin. And suppose a white or shiny pink spot shows up in the open sores of the burn. ²⁵ Then the priest must look at the spot carefully. Suppose the hair in it has turned white. And suppose the spot seems to be under the skin. Then the person has a skin disease. It has broken out where they were burned. The priest must announce that the person is 'unclean.' They have a skin disease. ²⁶ But suppose the priest looks at the spot carefully. Suppose there is no white hair in it. Suppose the spot is not under the skin. And suppose it has faded. Then the priest must make the person stay away from everyone else for seven days. ²⁷ On the seventh day the priest must look them over carefully. If the spot is spreading in the skin, the priest must announce that the person is 'unclean.' They have a skin disease. ²⁸ But suppose the spot has not changed. It has not spread in the skin. And it has faded. Then the burn has caused it to swell. The priest must announce that the person is 'clean.' It is only a scar from the burn.

²⁹ "Suppose a man or woman has a sore on their head or chin. ³⁰ Then the priest must look at the sore carefully. Suppose it seems to be under the skin. And suppose the hair in the sore is yellow and thin. Then the priest must announce that the person is 'unclean.' The sore is a skin disease on the head or chin. ³¹ But suppose the priest looks carefully at the sore. It does not seem to be under the skin. And there is no black hair in it. Then the priest must make the person stay away from everyone else for seven days. ³² On the seventh day the priest must look at the sore carefully. Suppose it has not spread in the skin. It does not have any yellow hair in it. And it does not seem to be under the skin. ³³ Then the man or woman must shave their head. But they must not shave the area where

the disease is. And the priest must make them stay away from everyone else for another seven days. [34] On the seventh day the priest must look at the sore carefully. Suppose it has not spread in the skin. And suppose it does not seem to be under the skin. Then the priest must announce that the person is 'clean.' They must wash their clothes. They will be 'clean.' [35] But suppose the sore spreads in the skin after the priest announces that the person is 'clean.' [36] Then the priest must look them over carefully. Suppose the sore has spread. Then the priest does not have to look for yellow hair. The person is 'unclean.' [37] But suppose the sore has stopped and black hair has grown there, as far as the priest can tell. Then the person is healed and is 'clean.' The priest must announce that they are 'clean.'

[38] "Suppose a man or woman has white spots on the skin. [39] Then the priest must look at them carefully. Suppose he sees that the spots are dull white. Then a harmless rash has broken out on the skin. That person is 'clean.'

[40] "Suppose a man loses all the hair on his head. Then he is 'clean.' [41] Suppose he loses only the hair on the front of his head. Then he is 'clean.' [42] But suppose he has a shiny pink sore on his head where his hair was. Then he has a skin disease. It is breaking out on his whole head or on the front of his head. [43] The priest must look him over carefully. Suppose the swollen sore on his head or on the front of it is pink and shiny. And suppose it looks like a skin disease. [44] Then he has a skin disease. He is 'unclean.' The priest must announce that the man is 'unclean.' That's because he has a sore on his head.

[45] "Suppose someone has a skin disease that makes them 'unclean.' Then they must wear torn clothes. They must let their hair hang loose. They must cover the lower part of their face. They must cry out, 'Unclean! Unclean!' [46] As long as they have the disease, they remain 'unclean.' They must live alone. They must live outside the camp.

Rules About Mold

[47] "Suppose some clothes have mold on them. The clothes could be made out of wool or linen. [48] Or there could be cloth woven or knitted out of linen or wool. There could be pieces of leather. Or there could be things that are made out of leather. [49] And suppose the mold on the clothes or on the woven or knitted cloth looks green or red. Or suppose the green or red mold is on the pieces of leather or the leather goods. Then it is mold that spreads. It must be shown to the priest. [50] The priest must look at it carefully. He must keep the thing with the mold on it away from everything else for seven days. [51] On the seventh day he must look at it carefully. Suppose the mold has spread in the clothes or in the woven or

knitted cloth. Or suppose it has spread on the pieces of leather or on the leather goods. Then it is mold that destroys. The thing is 'unclean.' [52] The priest must burn everything with the mold in it. He must burn the clothes or the woven or knitted cloth made out of wool or linen. He must burn the leather goods. The mold destroys. So everything must be burned.

[53] "But suppose the priest looks at the thing carefully. The mold has not spread in the clothes. And it has not spread in the woven or knitted cloth or in the leather goods. [54] Then he will order someone to wash the thing with the mold on it. After that, the priest must keep that thing away from everything else for another seven days. [55] After the thing with the mold on it has been washed, the priest must look at it again carefully. Suppose the way the mold looks has not changed. Then even though the mold has not spread, it is 'unclean.' Burn it. It does not matter which side of the thing the mold is on. [56] But suppose the priest looks at it carefully. And suppose the mold has faded after the thing has been washed. Then the priest must tear out the part with mold on it. He must tear it out of the clothes or leather. He must tear it out of the woven or knitted cloth. [57] But suppose it shows up again in the clothes. Or suppose it shows up again in the woven or knitted cloth or in the leather goods. Then it is spreading. Ev-erything with the mold on it must be burned. [58] The clothes that have been washed and do not have any more mold on them must be washed again. So must the woven or knitted cloth or the leather goods. Then they will be 'clean.' "

[59] These are the rules about what to do with anything with mold on it. They apply to clothes that are made out of wool or linen. They apply to woven and knitted cloth and to leather goods. They give a priest directions about when to announce whether something is "clean" or "unclean."

Making People "Clean" From Skin Diseases

14 The LORD spoke to Moses. He told him to say to the people, [2] "Here are the rules for making anyone 'clean' who has had a skin disease. They apply when the person is brought to the priest. [3] The priest must go outside the camp. He must look the person over carefully. Suppose they have been healed of their skin disease. [4] Then the priest will order someone to bring him two live 'clean' birds. He will also order someone to bring him some cedar wood, bright red yarn and branches of a hyssop plant. All these things will be used to make the person 'clean.' [5] The priest will order someone to kill one of the birds. It must be killed over fresh water in a clay pot. [6] Then the priest must take the live bird. He must dip it into the blood of the bird killed over the fresh water. He must dip it into the blood together with the cedar wood, the bright red yarn and the hyssop plant. [7] The priest will sprinkle the blood on the person who had the skin disease. That will make them 'clean.' The priest must sprinkle them seven times. Then the priest must announce that they are 'clean.' After that, the priest must let the live bird go free in the open fields.

[8] "The person must also wash their clothes to be made 'clean.' They must shave off all their hair. They must take a bath. Then they will be 'clean.' After that, they may come into the camp. But they must stay outside their tent for seven days. [9] On the seventh day they must shave off all their hair. They must shave their head. They must shave off their beard. They must also shave off their eyebrows and the rest of their hair. They must wash their clothes. They must take a bath. Then they will be 'clean.'

[10] "On the eighth day they must bring two male lambs and one female lamb as an offering. The female must be a year old. The lambs must not have any flaws. They must also bring 11 pounds of the finest flour as a grain offering. They must mix it with olive oil. They must also bring 11 ounces of oil. [11] The priest who announces that the person is 'clean' must bring them and their offerings to me. He must do it at the entrance to the tent of meeting.

[12] "Then the priest must take one of the male lambs. He must offer it as a guilt offering. He must offer it along with 11 ounces of oil. He must lift all of it up and wave it in front of me as a wave offering. [13] He must kill the lamb in the holy area where sin offerings and burnt offerings are killed. The guilt offering belongs to the priest, just as the sin offering does. The guilt offering is very holy. [14] The priest must take some of the blood from the guilt offering and put it on the person's right earlobe. He must put some on the thumb of their right hand. He must also put some on the big toe of their right foot. [15] Then the priest must take some of the oil and pour it into his own left hand. [16] He must dip his right forefinger into the oil in his hand. He must use his finger to sprinkle some of the oil in front of me seven times. [17] The priest must put some of the oil in his hand on the same places he put the blood of the guilt offering. He must put some on the person's right earlobe. He must put some on the thumb of their right hand. He must put some on the big toe of their right foot. [18] He must put on their head the rest of the oil in his hand. It will pay for the person's sin in my sight.

[19] "Then the priest must sacrifice the sin offering. It will pay for the person's sin. They will be made 'clean' after being 'unclean.' After that, the priest will kill the burnt offering. [20] He will offer it on the altar. He will offer

it together with the grain offering. It will pay for the person's sin. Then they will be 'clean.'

21 "But suppose they are poor. Suppose they can't afford all these offerings. Then they must bring one male lamb as a guilt offering. It must be lifted up and waved in front of me to pay for their sin. They must also bring three and a half pounds of the finest flour along with the lamb. They must mix the flour with olive oil. It is a grain offering. They must offer it along with 11 ounces of oil. 22 They must also bring two doves or two young pigeons that they can afford. One is for a sin offering. The other is for a burnt offering.

23 "On the eighth day they must bring them to the priest so they can be made 'clean.' They must bring them to the entrance to the tent of meeting. They must do it in my sight. 24 The priest must take the lamb for the guilt offering. He must take it together with the 11 ounces of oil. He must lift all of it up and wave it in front of me as a wave offering. 25 He must kill the lamb for the guilt offering. He must take some of its blood and put it on the person's right earlobe. He must put some on the thumb of their right hand. He must also put some on the big toe of their right foot. 26 The priest must pour some of the oil into his own left hand. 27 He must dip his right forefinger into the oil in his hand. He must use his finger to sprinkle some of it seven times in front of me. 28 Here is what

he must do with some of the oil in his hand. He must put it on the same places where he put the blood of the guilt offering. He must put some on the person's right earlobe. He must put some on the thumb of their right hand. He must also put some on the big toe of their right foot. 29 He must put on their head the rest of the oil in his hand. It will pay for the person's sin in my sight. 30 The priest will sacrifice the doves or the young pigeons that the person can afford. 31 One is for a sin offering. The other is for a burnt offering. The priest must offer them together with the grain offering. In that way he will pay for the person's sin in my sight. He will do it to make them 'clean.' "

32 These are the rules for anyone who has a skin disease. They are for people who can't afford the regular offerings that are required to make them "clean."

Making Things "Clean" From Mold

33 The LORD spoke to Moses and Aaron. He told them to say to the people, 34 "You will enter the land of Canaan. I am giving it to you as your own. When you enter it, suppose I put mold in one of your houses. And suppose the mold spreads. 35 Then the owner of that house must go and speak to the priest. He must say, 'I've seen something that looks like mold in my house.' 36 The priest must order everything to be taken out of the

house. It must be done before he goes in to look carefully at the mold. If it is not done, the priest must announce that everything in the house is 'unclean.' After the house is empty the priest must go in and check it. [37] He must look carefully at the mold on the walls. Suppose it looks as if it has green or red dents in it. And suppose the dents look as if they are behind the surface of the wall. [38] Then the priest must go out the door. He must close the house up for seven days. [39] On the seventh day the priest will return to check the house. Suppose the mold on the walls has spread. [40] Then he must order someone to tear out the stones that have mold on them. He must have them thrown into an 'unclean' place outside the town. [41] He must have all the inside walls of the house scraped. Everything scraped off must be dumped into an 'unclean' place outside the town. [42] Then other stones must be put in the place of the stones that had mold on them. The inside walls of the house must be coated with new clay.

[43] "Suppose the stones have been torn out. The house has been scraped. And the walls have been coated with new clay. But the mold appears again. [44] Then the priest must go and look things over carefully. Suppose the mold has spread in the house. Then it is the kind of mold that destroys things. The house is not 'clean.' [45] It must be torn down. The stones, the wood and all the clay coating must be torn out. All of it must be taken out of the town to an 'unclean' place.

[46] "Suppose someone goes into the house while it is closed up. Then they will be 'unclean' until evening. [47] If they sleep or eat in the house, they must wash their clothes.

[48] "But suppose the priest comes to look things over carefully. And suppose the mold has not spread after the walls had been coated with new clay. Then he will announce that the house is 'clean.' The mold is gone. [49] To make the house pure, the priest must get two birds. He must also get some cedar wood, bright red yarn and branches of a hyssop plant. [50] He must kill one of the birds over fresh water in a clay pot. [51] Then he must take the cedar wood, the hyssop plant, the bright red yarn and the live bird. He must dip all of them into the blood of the dead bird. He must also dip them into the fresh water. He must sprinkle the house seven times. [52] The priest will use the blood and the water to make the house pure. He will use the live bird to make it pure. He will also use the cedar wood, the hyssop plant and the bright red yarn to make it pure. [53] Then he must let the live bird go free in the open fields outside the town. In that way he will make the house pure. It will be 'clean.' "

[54] These are the rules for skin diseases. They apply to sores. [55] They apply to mold in clothes

or in houses. [56] They also apply to swellings, rashes or shiny red spots on the skin. [57] Use these rules to decide whether something is "clean" or not.

These are the rules for skin diseases and for mold.

Rules About Liquid Body Wastes

15 The LORD said to Moses and Aaron, [2] "Speak to the Israelites. Tell them, 'Suppose liquid waste is flowing out of a man's body. That liquid is not "clean." [3] It does not matter whether it continues to flow out of his body or is blocked. It will make him "unclean." Here is how his liquid body waste will make him "unclean."

[4] "'Any bed the man who has the flow of liquid body waste lies on will be "unclean." Anything he sits on will be "unclean." [5] Anyone who touches the man's bed must wash their clothes. They must take a bath. They will be "unclean" until evening. [6] Suppose someone sits on something the man sat on. Then they must wash their clothes. They must take a bath. They will be "unclean" until evening.

[7] "'Suppose someone touches the man who has the flow of liquid body waste. Then they must wash their clothes. They must take a bath. They will be "unclean" until evening.

[8] "'Suppose someone is "clean." And suppose the man who has the flow of liquid waste spits on them. Then they must wash their clothes. They must take a bath. They will be "unclean" until evening.

[9] "'Everything the man sits on when he is riding will be "unclean." [10] Suppose someone touches any of the things that were under him. Then they will be "unclean" until evening. Even if they pick up those things, they must wash their clothes. They must take a bath. They will be "unclean" until evening.

[11] "'Suppose the man who has the liquid flow touches someone. And suppose he does it without rinsing his hands with water. Then the person he touched must wash their clothes. They must take a bath. They will be "unclean" until evening.

[12] "'Suppose the man touches a clay pot. Then that pot must be broken. Any wooden thing he touches must be rinsed with water.

[13] "'Suppose the man has been healed from his liquid flow. Then he must wait seven days. He must wash his clothes. He must take a bath in fresh water. After that, he will be "clean." [14] On the eighth day he must get two doves or two young pigeons. He must come to the LORD at the entrance to the tent of meeting. There he must give the birds to the priest. [15] The priest must sacrifice them. One is for a sin offering. The other is for a burnt offering. In that way the priest will pay for the man's sin in the sight of the LORD. He will do it because the man had a liquid flow.

[16] "'Suppose semen flows

from a man's body. Then he must wash his whole body with water. He will be "unclean" until evening. ¹⁷ Suppose clothes or leather have semen on them. Then they must be washed with water. They will be "unclean" until evening. ¹⁸ Suppose a man sleeps with a woman. And suppose semen flows from his body and touches both of them. Then they must take a bath. They will be "unclean" until evening.

¹⁹ " 'Suppose a woman is having her regular monthly period. Then for seven days she will be "unclean." Anyone who touches her will be "unclean" until evening.

²⁰ " 'Anything she lies on during her period will be "unclean." Anything she sits on will be "unclean." ²¹ Anyone who touches her bed must wash their clothes. They must take a bath. They will be "unclean" until evening. ²² Anyone who touches anything she sits on must wash their clothes. They must take a bath. They will be "unclean" until evening. ²³ It does not matter whether it was her bed or anything she was sitting on. If anyone touches it, they will be "unclean" until evening.

²⁴ " 'Suppose a man sleeps with that woman. And suppose blood from her monthly period touches him. Then he will be "unclean" for seven days. Any bed he lies on will be "unclean."

²⁵ " 'Suppose blood flows from a woman's body for many days. And it happens at a time other than her monthly period. Or

blood keeps flowing after her period is over. Then she will be "unclean" as long as the blood continues to flow. She will be "unclean," just as she is during the days of her period. ²⁶ Any bed she lies on while her blood continues to flow will be "unclean." It is the same as it is when she is having her period. Anything she sits on will be "unclean." ²⁷ If anyone touches those things, they will be "unclean." They must wash their clothes. They must take a bath. They will be "unclean" until evening.

²⁸ " 'Suppose the woman has been healed from her flow of blood. Then she must wait seven days. After that, she will be "clean." ²⁹ On the eighth day she must get two doves or two young pigeons. She must bring them to the priest at the entrance to the tent of meeting. ³⁰ The priest must sacrifice them. One is for a sin offering. The other is for a burnt offering. In that way he will pay for her sin in the sight of the LORD. He will do it because her flow of blood made her "unclean."

³¹ " 'You must keep the Israelites away from things that make them "unclean." Then they will not die for being "unclean." And they will not die for making the place "unclean" where I, the LORD, live. It is in the middle of the camp.' "

³² These are the rules for a man who has liquid waste flowing out of his body. They apply to a man made "unclean" by semen that flows from his body.

33 They apply to a woman having her monthly period. They apply to a man or woman who has a liquid flow. And they apply to a man who sleeps with a woman who is "unclean."

The Day When Sin Is Paid For

16 The LORD spoke to Moses after two of Aaron's sons had died. They were the sons who died when they came near the LORD. 2 The LORD said to Moses, "Speak to your brother Aaron. Tell him not to come into the Most Holy Room just anytime he wants to. Tell him not to come behind the curtain in front of the cover of the ark. The cover is the place where sin is paid for. If he comes behind the curtain, he will die. That is because I appear in the cloud over the cover.

3 "Aaron must not enter the area of the Most Holy Room without bringing a sacrifice. He must bring a young bull for a sin offering. He must also bring a ram for a burnt offering. 4 He must put on the sacred inner robe made out of linen. He must wear linen underwear next to his body. He must tie the linen belt around him. And he must put the linen turban on his head. Those are sacred clothes. So he must take a bath before he puts them on. 5 The community of Israel must give him two male goats and a ram. The goats are for a sin offering. The ram is for a burnt offering.

6 "Aaron must offer the bull for his own sin offering. It will pay for his own sin and the sin of his whole family. 7 Then he must take the two goats and bring them to me at the entrance to the tent of meeting. 8 He must cast lots for the two goats. One lot is for me. The other is for the goat that carries the people's sins away. 9 Aaron must bring the goat chosen for me by lot. He must sacrifice it for a sin offering. 10 But the goat chosen by the other lot must remain alive. First, it must be brought in to me to pay for the people's sins. Then, it must be sent into the desert as a goat that carries the people's sins away.

11 "Aaron must bring the bull for his own sin offering. It will pay for his own sin and the sin of his whole family. He must kill the bull for his own sin offering. 12 He must take a shallow cup full of burning coals from the altar in my sight. He must get two handfuls of incense completely ground up. The incense must smell sweet. He must take the cup and the incense behind the curtain. 13 He must put the incense on the fire in my sight. The smoke from the incense will hide the cover of the ark where the tablets of the covenant law are kept. The cover is the place where sin is paid for. Aaron must burn the incense so that he will not die. 14 He must dip his finger in the bull's blood. He must sprinkle it on the front of the cover of the ark. He must sprinkle some in front of the cover. He must do it seven times. 15 "Then Aaron must kill the

goat for the sin offering for the people. He must take its blood behind the curtain. There he must do the same thing with it as he did with the bull's blood. He must sprinkle it on the cover of the ark. He must also sprinkle some in front of it. 16 That is how he will make the Most Holy Room pure. He must do it because the Israelites are not 'clean.' They have not obeyed me. They have also committed other sins. Aaron must do the same for the tent of meeting because it stands in the middle of the camp. And the camp is 'unclean.' 17 Aaron will go into the Most Holy Room to pay for the people's sin. While Aaron is there, no one may be in the tent of meeting. No one may enter the tent until Aaron comes out. He will not come out until he has paid for his own sin and the sin of his whole family. He will not come out until he has also paid for the sin of the whole community of Israel.

18 "Then he will come out to the altar for burnt offerings. It is in front of the tent where the ark of the LORD is. He will make the altar pure and clean. He will take some of the bull's blood and some of the goat's blood. Then he will put the blood on all the horns that stick out from the upper four corners of the altar. 19 He will sprinkle some of the blood on it with his finger seven times. He will do it to make the altar pure. He will do it to set it apart from the Israelites. They are 'unclean.'

20 "Aaron will finish making the Most Holy Room pure and 'clean.' He will finish making the tent of meeting and the altar pure. Then he will bring out the live goat. 21 He must place both of his hands on its head. While he does that, he must tell me about all the sins the Israelites have committed. He must tell me about all their evil acts and the times they did not obey me. In that way he puts their sins on the goat's head. Then he will send the goat away into the desert. The goat will be led away by a man appointed to do it. 22 The goat will carry all their sins on itself to a place where there are no people. And the man will set the goat free in the desert.

23 "Then Aaron must go into the tent of meeting. He must take off the linen clothes he put on before he entered the Most Holy Room. He must leave them there. 24 He must take a bath in the holy area. And he must put on his regular clothes. Then he will come out and sacrifice the burnt offering for himself. He will also sacrifice the burnt offering for the people. That will pay for his own sin and the people's sin. 25 He will also burn the fat of the sin offering on the altar.

26 "The man who sets free the goat that carries the people's sins away must wash his clothes. He must take a bath. After that, he can come back into the camp. 27 The bull and the goat for the sin offerings must be taken outside the camp. Their blood was brought into

the Most Holy Room. It paid for sin. The hides, meat and guts of the animals must be burned up. 28 The man who burns them must wash his clothes. He must take a bath. After that, he can come back into the camp.

29 "Here is a law for you that will last for all time to come. On the tenth day of the seventh month you must not eat anything. You must not do any work. It does not matter whether you are Israelites or outsiders. 30 On that day your sin will be paid for. You will be made pure and clean. You will be clean from all your sins in my sight. 31 That day is a sabbath for you. You must rest on it. You must not eat anything on that day. This is a law that will last for all time to come. 32 The high priest must pay for sin. He must make everything pure and clean. He has been anointed and prepared to become the next high priest after his father. He must put on the sacred clothes that are made out of linen. 33 He must make the Most Holy Room, the tent of meeting and the altar pure. And he must pay for the sin of the priests and all the members of the community.

34 "Here is a law for you that will last for all time to come. Once a year you must pay for all the sin of the Israelites."

So it was done, just as the LORD commanded Moses.

Do Not Eat Meat With Blood in It

17 The LORD said to Moses, 2 "Speak to Aaron and his sons. Speak to all the Isra-elites. Tell them, 'Here is what the LORD has commanded. He has said, 3 "Suppose someone sacrifices an ox, a lamb or a goat. They sacrifice it in the camp or outside of it. 4 They do it instead of bringing the animal to the entrance to the tent of meeting. They sacrifice it instead of giving it as an offering to me in front of my holy tent. Then they will be thought of as guilty of spilling blood. Because they have done that, they must be separated from their people. 5 The Israelites are now making sacrifices in the open fields. But they must bring their sacrifices to the priest. They must bring them to me at the entrance to the tent of meeting. There they must sacrifice them as friendship offerings. 6 The priest must splash the blood against my altar. It is the altar at the entrance to the tent of meeting. He must burn the fat. Its smell will please me. 7 The Israelites must stop offering any of their sacrifices to statues of gods that look like goats. When they offer sacrifices to those statues, they are not faithful to me. This is a law for them that will last for all time to come."'

8 "Tell them, 'Suppose someone offers a burnt offering or sacrifice. It does not matter whether they are an Israelite or an outsider. 9 And suppose they do not bring it to the entrance to the tent of meeting to sacrifice it to me. Then they must be separated from their people.

10 " 'Suppose someone eats

meat that still has blood in it. It does not matter whether they are an Israelite or an outsider. I will turn against them if they eat it. I will separate them from their people. ¹¹ The life of each creature is in its blood. So I have given you the blood of animals to pay for your sin on the altar. Blood is life. That is why blood pays for your sin. ¹² So I say to the Israelites, "You must not eat meat that still has blood in it. And an outsider who lives among you must not eat it either."

¹³ " 'Suppose any of you hunts any animal or bird that can be eaten. It does not matter whether you are an Israelite or an outsider. You must let the blood flow out of the animal or bird. You must cover the blood with dirt. ¹⁴ That is because every creature's life is its blood. And that is why I have said to the Israelites, "You must not eat any creature's meat that still has blood in it. Every creature's life is its blood. Anyone who eats that kind of meat must be separated from the community of Israel."

¹⁵ " 'Suppose someone eats anything found dead or torn apart by wild animals. It does not matter whether they are an Israelite or an outsider. They must wash their clothes. They must take a bath. They will be "unclean" until evening. After that, they will be "clean." ¹⁶ But suppose they do not wash their clothes. And suppose they do not take a bath. Then they will be held responsible for what they have done.' "

Do Not Commit Sexual Sins

18 The LORD spoke to Moses. He said, ² "Speak to the Israelites. Tell them, 'I am the LORD your God. ³ Do not do what the people of Egypt do. You used to live there. And do not do what the people of Canaan do. I am bringing you into their land. Do not follow their practices. ⁴ Obey my laws. Be careful to follow my rules. I am the LORD your God. ⁵ Keep my rules and laws. The one who obeys them will benefit from living by them. I am the LORD.

⁶ " 'Do not have sex with any of your close relatives. I am the LORD.

⁷ " 'Do not bring shame on your father by having sex with your mother. Do not have sex with her. She is your mother.

⁸ " 'Do not have sex with any other wife of your father. That would bring shame on your father.

⁹ " 'Do not have sex with your sister. It does not matter whether she is your father's daughter or your mother's daughter. It does not matter whether she was born in the same home as you were or somewhere else.

¹⁰ " 'Do not have sex with your son's daughter or your daughter's daughter. That would bring shame on you.

¹¹ " 'Do not have sex with the daughter of your father's wife. She was born to your father. She is your sister.

¹² "'Do not have sex with your father's sister. She is a close relative on your father's side.

¹³ "'Do not have sex with your mother's sister. She is a close relative on your mother's side.

¹⁴ "'Do not bring shame on your father's brother by having sex with his wife. She is your aunt.

¹⁵ "'Do not have sex with your daughter-in-law. She is your son's wife. Do not have sex with her.

¹⁶ "'Do not have sex with your brother's wife. That would bring shame on your brother.

¹⁷ "'Do not have sex with both a woman and her daughter. Do not have sex with either her son's daughter or her daughter's daughter. They are close relatives on her side. Having sex with them is an evil thing.

¹⁸ "'Do not take your wife's sister as another wife and have sex with her. Do not do it while your wife is still living.

¹⁹ "'Do not have sex with a woman during her monthly period. She is "unclean" at that time.

²⁰ "'Do not have sex with your neighbor's wife. That would make you "unclean."

²¹ "'Do not hand over any of your children to be sacrificed to the god Molek. That would be treating my name as if it were not holy. I am the LORD your God.

²² "'Do not have sex with a man as you would have sex with a woman. I hate that.

²³ "'Do not have sex with an animal. Do not make yourself "unclean" by doing that. A woman must not offer herself to an animal to have sex with it. That is a wrong use of sex.

²⁴ "'Do not make yourselves "unclean" in any of these ways. That is how other nations became "unclean." So I am going to drive those nations out of the land to make room for you. ²⁵ Even their land was not "clean." So I punished it because of its sin. The land itself threw out the people who lived there. ²⁶ But you must keep my rules and my laws. You must not do any of the things I hate. It does not matter whether you are Israelites or outsiders. ²⁷ All these things were done by the people who lived in the land before you. That is how the land became "unclean." ²⁸ If you make the land "unclean," it will throw you out. It will get rid of you just as it got rid of the nations there before you.

²⁹ "'Suppose you do any of the things I hate. Then you must be separated from your people. ³⁰ Do exactly what I require. When you arrive in Canaan, do not follow any of the practices of its people. I hate the things they do. Do not make yourselves "unclean" by doing them. I am the LORD your God.'"

Other Laws

19 The LORD spoke to Moses. He said, ² "Speak to the whole community of Israel. Tell them, 'Be holy, because I am holy. I am the LORD your God.

³ " 'All of you must have respect for your mother and father. You must always keep my Sabbath days. I am the LORD your God.

⁴ " 'Do not turn away from me to worship statues of gods. Do not make for yourselves metal statues of gods. I am the LORD your God.

⁵ " 'Suppose you sacrifice a friendship offering to me. Then do it in the right way. And I will accept it from you. ⁶ You must eat it on the same day you sacrifice it or on the next day. Anything left over until the third day must be burned up. ⁷ If you eat any of it on the third day, it is not pure. I will not accept it. ⁸ Whoever eats it will be held responsible. They have misused what is holy to me. They will be separated from their people.

⁹ " 'Suppose you are harvesting your crops. Then do not harvest all the way to the edges of your field. And do not pick up the grain you missed. ¹⁰ Do not go over your vineyard a second time. Do not pick up the grapes that have fallen to the ground. Leave them for poor people and outsiders. I am the LORD your God.

¹¹ " 'Do not steal.

" 'Do not tell lies.

" 'Do not cheat one another.

¹² " 'Do not give your word in my name and then be a false witness. That would be treating the name of your God as if it were not holy. I am the LORD.

¹³ " 'Do not cheat your neighbor. Do not rob him.

" 'Do not hold back the pay of a hired worker until morning.

¹⁴ " 'Do not ask for bad things to happen to deaf people. Do not put anything in front of blind people that will make them trip. Instead, have respect for me. I am the LORD your God.

¹⁵ " 'Do not make something wrong appear to be right. Treat poor people and rich people in the same way. Do not favor one person over another. Instead, judge everyone fairly.

¹⁶ " 'Do not go around spreading lies among your people.

" 'Do not do anything that puts your neighbor's life in danger. I am the LORD.

¹⁷ " 'Do not hate another Israelite in your heart. Correct your neighbor boldly when they do something wrong. Then you will not share their guilt.

¹⁸ " 'Do not try to get even. Do not hold anything against any of your people. Instead, love your neighbor as you love yourself. I am the LORD.

¹⁹ " 'Obey my rules.

" 'Do not let different kinds of animals mate with each other.

" 'Do not mix two kinds of seeds and then plant them in your field.

" 'Do not wear clothes that are made out of two kinds of cloth.

²⁰ " 'Suppose a man sleeps with a female slave. But she and another man have promised to get married to each other. And her freedom has not yet been paid for or given to her. Then she and the man who slept with her must be punished. But they

must not be put to death, because she had not been set free. ²¹The man must bring a ram to the entrance to the tent of meeting. It is for a guilt offering to me. ²²The priest must take the ram for the guilt offering. He must sacrifice it to pay for the man's sin in my sight. Then his sin will be forgiven.

²³ " 'When you enter the land, suppose you plant a fruit tree. Then do not eat its fruit for the first three years. The fruit is "unclean." ²⁴In the fourth year all the fruit will be holy. Offer it as a way of showing praise to me. ²⁵But in the fifth year you can eat the fruit. Then you will gather more and more fruit. I am the LORD your God.

²⁶ " 'Do not eat any meat that still has blood in it.

" 'Do not practice any kind of evil magic.

²⁷ " 'Do not cut the hair on the sides of your head. Do not clip off the edges of your beard.

²⁸ " 'Do not make cuts on your bodies when someone dies. Do not put marks on your skin. I am the LORD.

²⁹ " 'Do not dishonor your daughter's body by making a prostitute out of her. If you do, the Israelites will start going to prostitutes. The land will be filled with evil.

³⁰ " 'You must always keep my Sabbath days. Have respect for my sacred tent. I am the LORD.

³¹ " 'Do not look for advice from people who get messages from those who have died. Do not go to people who talk to the spirits of the dead. If you do, they will make you "unclean." I am the LORD your God.

³² " 'Stand up in order to show your respect for old people. Also have respect for me. I am the LORD your God.

³³ " 'Suppose an outsider lives with you in your land. Then do not treat them badly. ³⁴Treat them as if they were one of your own people. Love them as you love yourself. Remember that all of you were outsiders in Egypt. I am the LORD your God.

³⁵ " 'Be honest when you measure lengths, weights or amounts. ³⁶Use honest scales and honest weights. Use honest dry measures. And use honest liquid measures. I am the LORD your God. I brought you out of Egypt.

³⁷ " 'Obey all my rules and laws. Follow them. I am the LORD.' "

Israel Will Be Punished for Their Sins

20 The LORD spoke to Moses. He said, ² "Say to the Israelites, 'Suppose a person sacrifices one of his children to the god Molek. It does not matter whether that person is an Israelite or an outsider who lives in Israel. He must be put to death. The members of the community must kill him by throwing stones at him. ³I will turn against that man. I will separate him from his people. That's because he has sacrificed his child to Molek. He has made my sacred tent "unclean." He has treated my name as if it were

not holy. ⁴Suppose the members of the community act like they don't know that the man has sacrificed his child to Molek. And suppose they don't put him to death. ⁵Then I will turn against that man and his family. I will separate them from their people. I will also separate all those who follow him by joining themselves to Molek. They are not faithful to me.

⁶ " 'Suppose someone looks for advice from people who get messages from those who have died. Or they go to people who talk to the spirits of the dead. And they do what those people say. Then they have not been faithful to me. So I will turn against them. I will separate them from their people.

⁷ " 'Set yourselves apart for me. Be holy, because I am the LORD your God. ⁸Obey my rules. Follow them. I am the LORD. I make you holy.

⁹ " 'Anyone who asks for bad things to happen to their father or mother must be put to death. They have cursed their father or mother. So anything that happens to them will be their own fault.

¹⁰ " 'Suppose a man commits adultery with his neighbor's wife. Then the man and the woman must be put to death.

¹¹ " 'Suppose a man has sex with his father's wife. Then he has brought shame on his father. The man and the woman must be put to death. Anything that happens to them will be their own fault.

¹² " 'Suppose a man has sex with his daughter-in-law. Then they must be put to death. They have used sex in the wrong way. Anything that happens to them will be their own fault.

¹³ " 'Suppose a man has sex with another man as he would have sex with a woman. I hate what they have done. They must be put to death. Anything that happens to them will be their own fault.

¹⁴ " 'Suppose a man gets married to both a woman and her mother. That is evil. All of them must be burned to death. Then there will not be any evil among you.

¹⁵ " 'Suppose a man has sex with an animal. Then he must be put to death. You must also kill the animal.

¹⁶ " 'Suppose a woman has sex with an animal. Then kill the woman and the animal. They must be put to death. Anything that happens to them will be their own fault.

¹⁷ " 'Suppose a man gets married to his sister and has sex with her. That is a shameful thing to do. It does not matter whether she is the daughter of his father or of his mother. They must be separated from their community in front of everyone. That man has brought shame on his sister. He will be responsible for what he has done.

¹⁸ " 'Suppose a man has sex with a woman during her monthly period. He has uncovered the place where her bleeding was coming from. And she

has let him do it. So both of them must be separated from their people.

19 " 'Do not have sex with the sister of either your mother or your father. That would bring shame on a close relative. Both of you would be held responsible for what you have done.

20 " 'Suppose a man has sex with his aunt. Then he has brought shame on his uncle. Both of them will be held accountable for what they have done. They will die without having any children.

21 " 'Suppose a man gets married to his brother's wife. That is something that should never be done. He has brought shame on his brother. Neither of them will have any children.

22 " 'Obey all my rules and laws. Follow them. Then the land where I am bringing you to live will not throw you out. 23 To make room for you, I am going to drive out the nations that are in the land. You must not follow the practices of those nations. I hated those nations because they did all those things. 24 But I said to you, "You will take over their land as your own. I will give it to you. It will belong to you. It is a land that has plenty of milk and honey." I am the LORD your God. I have set you apart from the other nations.

25 " 'So you must be able to tell the difference between animals that are "clean" and those that are not. You must know which birds are "clean" and which are not. Do not make yourselves "unclean" by eating any "unclean" animal or bird. Do not make yourselves "unclean" by eating anything that moves along the ground. I have set all of them apart as "unclean" for you. 26 You must be holy. You must be set apart to me. I am the LORD. I am holy. I have set you apart from the other nations to be my own people.

27 " 'Suppose a man or woman gets messages from those who have died. Or suppose a man or woman talks to the spirits of the dead. Then you must put that man or woman to death. You must kill them by throwing stones at them. Anything that happens to them will be their own fault.' "

Rules for Priests

21 The LORD said to Moses, "Speak to the priests, the sons of Aaron. Tell them, 'A priest must not make himself "unclean" by going near the dead body of any of his people. 2 But he can go near the body of a close relative. It could be his mother, father, son, daughter or brother. 3 He can also go near a sister who is not married. She would have depended on him because she did not have a husband. The priest can make himself "unclean" by going near her body. 4 But he must not make himself "unclean" by going near the bodies of people only related to him by marriage. Going near them would make him "unclean."

5 " 'Priests must not shave

any part of their heads. They must not shave off the edges of their beards. They must not make cuts on their bodies when someone dies. 6 Priests must be holy. They must be set apart for me. I am their God. They must not treat my name as if it were not holy. They must be holy because they bring food offerings to me. That is my food.

7 " 'They must not get married to women who are "unclean" because they are prostitutes. They must not marry women who are divorced from their husbands. That is because priests are holy. They are set apart for me. I am their God. 8 Consider them as holy, because they offer up food to me. Consider them as holy, because I am holy. I am the LORD. I make you holy.

9 " 'Suppose a priest's daughter makes herself "unclean" by becoming a prostitute. Then she brings shame on her father. She must be burned to death.

10 " 'The high priest is the one among his brothers whose head has been anointed with olive oil. He has been appointed to wear the priest's clothes. When someone dies, the high priest must not let his own hair hang loose. He must not tear his clothes to show how sad he is. 11 He must not enter a place where there is a dead body. He must not make himself "unclean," even if his father or mother dies. 12 He must not leave the sacred tent of the LORD to take part in burying a body. That would bring shame on the tent. The anointing oil has set the high priest apart. I am the LORD.

13 " 'The woman the high priest gets married to must be a virgin. 14 He must not marry a widow or a woman who is divorced. He must not marry a woman who is "unclean" because she is a prostitute. He must only marry a virgin. She must come from his own people. 15 If he doesn't marry a virgin, he makes the children he has by her "unclean." I am the LORD. I make him holy.' "

16 The LORD said to Moses, 17 "Speak to Aaron. Tell him, 'No man in your family line with any flaws may come near to offer food to the LORD. This is true for all time to come. 18 No man who has any flaws can come near. No man who is blind or disabled can come. No man whose body is scarred or twisted can come. 19 No man whose foot or hand is disabled can come. 20 No man whose back is bent can come. No man who is too short can come. No man who has anything wrong with his eyes can come. No man who has boils or running sores can come. No man whose sex glands are crushed can come. 21 No man with any flaws who is in the family line of Aaron the priest may come near me. He can't come to bring the food offerings to the LORD. If he has any flaws, he must not come near to offer food to the LORD. 22 He can eat the holy food. He can also eat my very holy food. 23 But because he has a flaw, he must not go near the curtain or

approach the altar. If he does, he will make my sacred tent "unclean." I am the LORD. I make everything holy.' "

24 So Moses told all these things to Aaron and his sons. He also told them to all the Israelites.

22 The LORD said to Moses, 2 "Here is what I want you to tell Aaron and his sons. Tell them to treat the sacred offerings with respect. They are the offerings the Israelites set apart to honor me. So Aaron and his sons must never treat my name as if it were not holy. I am the LORD.

3 "Say to them, 'Suppose a man in your family line is "unclean." And suppose he comes near the sacred offerings. They are the offerings the Israelites set apart to honor me. That man must not be allowed to serve me as a priest. That applies for all time to come. I am the LORD.

4 " 'Suppose a man in Aaron's family line has a skin disease. Or suppose liquid waste is flowing out of his body. Then he can't eat the sacred offerings until he is made pure and clean. Suppose he touches something made "unclean" by coming near a dead body. Or suppose he touches someone who has semen flowing from his body. Then he will be "unclean." 5 Or suppose he touches any crawling thing that makes him "unclean." Or suppose he touches any person who makes him "unclean." It does not matter what "unclean" thing he touches. It

will make him "unclean." 6 The one who touches anything of that kind will be "unclean" until evening. He must not eat any of the sacred offerings unless he has taken a bath. 7 When the sun goes down, he will be "clean." After that, he can eat the sacred offerings. They are his food. 8 He must not eat anything found dead or torn apart by wild animals. If he does, it will make him "unclean." I am the LORD.

9 " 'The priests must do what I require. But suppose they make fun of what I require. Then they will become guilty and die. I am the LORD. I make them holy.

10 " 'Only a member of a priest's family can eat the sacred offering. The guest of a priest can't eat it. A priest's hired worker can't eat it either. 11 But suppose a priest buys a slave with money. Or suppose slaves are born in his house. Then they can eat the sacred food. 12 Suppose a priest's daughter marries someone who is not a priest. Then she can't eat any of the food brought as a sacred gift. 13 But suppose the priest's daughter becomes a widow or is divorced. She does not have any children. And she returns to live in her father's house, where she lived when she was young. Then she can eat her father's food. But a person who does not belong to a priest's family can't eat any of it.

14 " 'Suppose someone eats a sacred offering by mistake. Then they must pay back the priest for the offering. They

must also add a fifth of its value to it. ¹⁵The priests must not allow the sacred offerings to become "unclean." They are the offerings the Israelites bring to the LORD. ¹⁶The priests must not allow the offerings to become "unclean" by letting the people eat them. If they do, they will bring guilt on the people. They will have to pay for what they have done. I am the LORD. I make them holy.'"

Sacrifices the LORD Does Not Accept

¹⁷The LORD spoke to Moses. He said, ¹⁸"Speak to Aaron and his sons. Speak to all the Israelites. Tell them, 'Suppose any of you brings a gift for a burnt offering to the LORD. It does not matter whether you are an Israelite or an outsider who lives in Israel. It does not matter whether you bring the offering to keep a promise or because you choose to give it. ¹⁹You must bring a male animal without any flaws if you want the LORD to accept it from you. It does not matter whether it is from your cattle, sheep or goats. ²⁰Do not bring an animal that has any flaws. If you do, the LORD will not accept it from you. ²¹Suppose any of you brings an animal for a friendship offering to the LORD. Then it must not have any flaws at all. If it does, the LORD will not accept it. It does not matter whether the animal is from your herd or flock. It does not matter whether you bring it to keep a promise or because you choose to give it. ²²Do not offer a blind animal to the LORD. Do not bring a hurt or wounded animal. And do not offer one that has warts or boils or running sores. Do not place any of them on the altar as a food offering presented to the LORD. ²³But suppose you bring an offering you choose to give. Then you can bring an ox or a sheep whose body is twisted or too small. But the LORD will not accept it if you offer it to keep a promise. ²⁴You must not offer the LORD a male animal whose sex glands have been hurt. The glands also must not be crushed, torn or cut. You must not offer that kind of animal in your own land. ²⁵And you must not accept that kind of animal from someone who comes from another land. You must not offer it as food for your God. He will not accept it from you. Its body is twisted and has flaws.'"

²⁶The LORD spoke to Moses. He said, ²⁷"When a calf, lamb or goat is born, it must remain with its mother for seven days. From the eighth day on, I will accept it as a food offering presented to me. ²⁸Do not kill a cow and its calf on the same day. Do not kill a female sheep and its lamb on the same day.

²⁹"Sacrifice a thank offering to me in the right way. Then I will accept it from you. ³⁰You must eat it that same day. Do not leave any of it until morning. I am the LORD.

³¹"Obey my commands. Follow them. I am the LORD. ³²Do

not treat my name as if it were not holy. The Israelites must recognize me as the holy God. I am the LORD. I made you holy. [33] I brought you out of Egypt to be your God. I am the LORD."

The Appointed Feast Days

23 The LORD said to Moses, [2] "Speak to the Israelites. Tell them, 'Here are my appointed feast days. They are the appointed feast days of the LORD. Tell the people that they must come together for these sacred assemblies.

The Sabbath Day

[3] " 'There are six days when you can work. But the seventh day is a day of sabbath rest. You must rest on it. Come together on that sacred day. You must not do any work on it. No matter where you live, it is a Sabbath day to honor the LORD.

Passover and Unleavened Bread

[4] " 'Here are the LORD's appointed feasts. Tell the people that they must come together for these sacred gatherings at their appointed times. [5] The LORD's Passover begins when the sun goes down on the 14th day of the first month. [6] The LORD's Feast of Unleavened Bread begins on the 15th day of that month. For seven days you must eat bread made without yeast. [7] On the first day you must come together for a special service. Do not do any regular work on that day. [8] On each of the seven days bring a food offering to the LORD. On the seventh day come together for a special service. Do not do any regular work on that day.' "

The First Share of Israel's Crops Belongs to the LORD

[9] The LORD said to Moses, [10] "Speak to the Israelites. Tell them, 'When you enter the land I am going to give you, bring an offering to the LORD. Gather your crops. Bring the first bundle of grain to the priest. [11] He must lift up the grain and wave it in front of the LORD. Then the LORD will accept it from you. The priest must wave it on the day after the Sabbath. [12] On the day he waves the grain for you, you must sacrifice a burnt offering to me. It must be a lamb that does not have any flaws. It must be a year old. [13] You must bring it together with its grain offering. The grain offering must be seven pounds of the finest flour. Mix it with olive oil. It is a food offering presented to the LORD. It has a pleasant smell. You must offer a drink offering along with the burnt offering. It must be a quart of wine. [14] You must not eat any bread until the day you bring your offering to the LORD your God. You must not eat any cooked grain or any of your first grain until that time. This is a law that will last for all time to come. It applies no matter where you live.

The Feast of Weeks

[15] " 'The day you brought the grain for the wave offering was

the day after the Sabbath. Count off seven full weeks from that day. [16] Count off 50 days up to the day after the seventh Sabbath. On that day bring to the LORD an offering of your first grain. [17] Bring two loaves of bread that are made with seven pounds of the finest flour. They must be baked with yeast. Bring them to me as a wave offering from the first share of your crops. That applies no matter where you live. [18] Together with the bread, bring seven male lambs. Each lamb must be a year old. It must not have any flaws. Also bring one young bull and two rams. They will be a burnt offering to the LORD. They will be offered together with their grain offerings and drink offerings. They are food offerings. Their smell pleases the LORD. [19] Then sacrifice one male goat for a sin offering. Also sacrifice two lambs for a friendship offering. Each of the lambs must be a year old. [20] The priest must lift up the two lambs and wave them in front of me as a wave offering. He must offer them together with the bread made out of the first share of your crops. They are a sacred offering to the LORD. They will be given to the priest. [21] On that same day tell the people that they must come together for a special worship service. They must not do any regular work. That is a law that will last for all time to come. It applies no matter where you live.

[22] " 'Suppose you are gathering your crops. Then do not harvest all the way to the edges of your field. And do not pick up the grain you missed. Leave some for the poor people and the outsiders who live among you. I am the LORD your God.' "

The Feast of Trumpets

[23] The LORD said to Moses, [24] "Say to the Israelites, 'On the first day of the seventh month you must have a day of sabbath rest. It must be a special service announced with trumpet blasts. [25] Do not do any regular work on that day. Instead, bring a food offering to the LORD.' "

The Day When Sin Is Paid For

[26] The LORD spoke to Moses. He said, [27] "The tenth day of the seventh month is the day when sin is paid for. Come together for a special service. Do not eat any food. Bring a food offering to the LORD. [28] Do not do any work on that day. It is the day when sin is paid for. On that day your sin will be paid for in my sight. I am the LORD your God. [29] Suppose you do eat food on that day. Then you will be separated from your people. [30] I will destroy anyone among your people who does any work on that day. [31] You must not do any work at all. This is a law that will last for all time to come. It applies no matter where you live. [32] That day is a day of sabbath rest for you. You must rest on it. You must not eat anything on that day. You must follow the rules of the sabbath rest. Follow them from the evening of the ninth day of the

month until the following evening."

The Feast of Booths

³³ The LORD said to Moses, ³⁴ "Say to the Israelites, 'On the 15th day of the seventh month the LORD's Feast of Booths begins. It lasts for seven days. ³⁵ On the first day you must come together for a special service. Do not do any regular work on that day. ³⁶ On each of the seven days bring a food offering to the LORD. On the eighth day come together for a special service. Bring a food offering to the LORD. That special service is the closing service. Do not do any regular work on that day.

³⁷ " 'These are the LORD's appointed feasts. Tell the people that they must come together for these sacred assemblies. During those times, the people must bring food offerings to the LORD. They are burnt offerings and grain offerings. They are sacrifices and drink offerings. Each offering must be brought at its required time. ³⁸ The offerings are in addition to those of the days of sabbath rest. The offerings are also in addition to your gifts and anything you have promised. They are also in addition to all the offerings you choose to give to the LORD.

³⁹ " 'Begin with the 15th day of the seventh month. That is after you have gathered your crops. On that day celebrate the LORD's Feast of Booths for seven days. The first day is a day of rest. The eighth day is also a day of rest.

⁴⁰ On the first day you must get branches from palms, willows and other leafy trees. You must be filled with joy in front of the LORD your God for seven days. ⁴¹ Celebrate the LORD's Feast of Booths for seven days each year. This is a law that will last for all time to come. Celebrate the feast in the seventh month. ⁴² Live in booths for seven days. All the Israelites must live in booths. ⁴³ Then your children after you will know that I made the Israelites live in booths. I made them do it after I brought them out of Egypt. I am the LORD your God.' "

⁴⁴ So Moses announced to the Israelites the appointed feasts of the LORD.

Olive Oil, Bread and Incense

24 The LORD said to Moses, ² "Command the Israelites to bring you clear oil made from pressed olives. Use it to keep the lamps burning and giving light all the time. ³ Aaron must take care of the lamps in front of the LORD from evening until morning all the time. This is a law that will last for all time to come. The lamps are outside the curtain in front of the tablets of the covenant law in the tent of meeting. ⁴ The lamps are on the pure gold lampstand in front of the LORD. They must be taken care of all the time.

⁵ "Get the finest flour and bake 12 loaves of bread. Use seven pounds of flour for each loaf. ⁶ Arrange them in two stacks. Put six loaves in each stack on the table made out of pure gold.

The table stands in front of the LORD. [7] By each stack put some pure incense. It will remind you that all good things come from the LORD. Burn the incense in place of the bread. The incense is a food offering presented to the LORD. [8] The bread must be set out in front of the LORD regularly. Do it every Sabbath day. It will be Israel's duty to provide it for all time to come. [9] The bread belongs to Aaron and his sons. They must eat it in the holy area. It is a very holy part of their regular share of the food offerings presented to the LORD."

A Person Who Speaks Evil Is Put to Death

[10] There was a man who had an Israelite mother. His father was born in Egypt. The man went out among the Israelites. A fight broke out in the camp between him and an Israelite. [11] The son of the Israelite woman spoke evil things against the LORD by using a curse. So the people brought him to Moses. The name of the man's mother was Shelomith. She was the daughter of Dibri. Dibri was from the tribe of Dan. [12] The people kept her son under guard until they could find out what the LORD wanted them to do.

[13] Then the LORD spoke to Moses. He said, [14] "Get the man who spoke evil things against the LORD. Take him outside the camp. All those who heard him say those things must place their hands on his head. Then the whole community must kill him by throwing stones at him. [15] Say to the Israelites, 'Anyone who curses me will be held accountable. [16] Anyone who speaks evil things against my Name must be put to death. The whole community must kill them by throwing stones at them. It does not matter whether they are an outsider or an Israelite. When they speak evil things against my Name, they must be put to death.

[17] " 'Anyone who kills another human being must be put to death. [18] Anyone who kills someone's animal must pay its owner. A life must be taken for a life. [19] Suppose someone hurts their neighbor. Then what they have done must be done to them. [20] A bone must be broken for a bone. An eye must be put out for an eye. A tooth must be knocked out for a tooth. The one who has hurt his neighbor must be hurt in the same way. [21] Whoever kills an animal must pay its owner. But if they kill a human being, they must be put to death. [22] The same law applies whether they are an outsider or an Israelite. I am the LORD your God.' "

[23] Then Moses spoke to the Israelites. They got the man who had spoken evil things against the LORD. They took him outside the camp. There they killed him by throwing stones at him. The Israelites did just as the LORD had commanded Moses.

The Sabbath Year

25 The LORD spoke to Moses at Mount Sinai. He said, [2] "Speak to the Israelites.

Tell them, 'You will enter the land I am going to give you. When you do, you must honor the LORD every seventh year by not farming the land that year. ³ For six years plant your fields. Trim the branches in your vineyards and gather your crops. ⁴ But the seventh year must be a year of sabbath rest for the land. The land must rest during it. It is a sabbath year to honor the LORD. Do not plant your fields. Do not trim the branches in your vineyards. ⁵ Do not gather what grows without being planted. And do not gather the grapes from the vines you have not taken care of. The land must have a year of rest. ⁶ Anything the land produces during the sabbath year will be food for you. It will be for you and your male and female servants. Your hired workers will eat it. So will people who live with you for a while. ⁷ And so will your livestock and the wild animals that are in your land. Anything the land produces can be eaten.

The Year of Jubilee

⁸ " 'Count off seven sabbath years. Count off seven times seven years. The seven sabbath years add up to a total of 49 years. ⁹ The tenth day of the seventh month is the day when sin is paid for. On that day blow the trumpet all through your land. ¹⁰ Set the 50th year apart. Announce freedom all over the land to everyone who lives there. The 50th year will be a Year of Jubilee for you. Each of you must return to your own family property. And each of you must return to your own tribe. ¹¹ The 50th year will be a Year of Jubilee for you. Do not plant anything. Do not gather what grows without being planted. And do not gather the grapes from the vines you have not taken care of. ¹² It is a Year of Jubilee. It will be holy for you. Eat only what the fields produce.

¹³ " 'In the Year of Jubilee all of you must return to your own property.

¹⁴ " 'Suppose you sell land to any of your own people. Or you buy land from them. Then do not take advantage of each other. ¹⁵ The price you pay must be based on the number of years since the last Year of Jubilee. Here is how the price you charge must be decided. It must be based on the number of years left for gathering crops before the next Year of Jubilee. ¹⁶ When there are many years left, you must raise the price. When there are only a few years left, you must lower the price. That is because what is really being sold to you is the number of crops the land will produce. ¹⁷ Do not take advantage of each other. Instead, have respect for your God. I am the LORD your God.

¹⁸ " 'Follow my rules. Be careful to obey my laws. Then you will live safely in the land. ¹⁹ The land will produce its fruit. You will eat as much as you want. And you will live there in safety. ²⁰ Suppose you say, "In the

seventh year we will not plant anything or gather our crops. So what will we eat?" [21] I will send you a great blessing in the sixth year. The land will produce enough for three years. [22] While you plant during the eighth year, you will eat food from the old crop. You will continue to eat food from it until the crops from the ninth year are gathered.

[23] " 'The land must not be sold without a way of getting it back. That is because it belongs to me. You are only outsiders and strangers in my land. [24] You must make sure that you can buy the land back. That applies to all the land that belongs to you.

[25] " 'Suppose one of your own people becomes poor. And suppose they have to sell some of their land. Then their nearest relative must come and buy back what they have sold. [26] But suppose they do not have anyone to buy it back for them. And suppose things go well for them and they earn enough money to buy it back themselves. [27] Then they must decide how much the crops have become worth since the time they sold the land. They must take that amount off the price the land was sold for. They must give the one selling it back to them the money that is left. Then they can go back to their own property. [28] But suppose they have not earned enough money to pay them back. Then the buyer they sold the land to will keep it until the Year of Ju-

bilee. At that time it will be returned to them. Then they can go back to their property.

[29] " 'Suppose someone sells a house in a city that has a wall around it. Then for a full year after they sell it they have the right to buy it back. [30] But suppose they do not buy it back before the full year has passed. Then the house in the walled city will continue to belong to the buyer and the buyer's children. It will not be returned to the seller in the Year of Jubilee. [31] But houses in villages that do not have walls around them must be treated like property outside walled cities. Those houses can be bought back at any time. And they must be returned in the Year of Jubilee.

[32] " 'The Levites always have the right to buy back their houses in the towns that belong to them. [33] So their property among the Israelites can be bought back. That applies to a house sold in any of their towns. Any house that is sold must be returned to its original owner in the Year of Jubilee. That is because the houses of the Levites will always belong to them. [34] But the grasslands around their towns must never be sold. They will belong to them for all time to come.

[35] " 'Suppose any of your own people become poor. And suppose they can't take care of themselves. Then help them just as you would help an outsider or a stranger. In that way, the poor can continue to live among you.

³⁶ Do not charge them interest of any kind. Instead, have respect for God. Then those who have become poor can continue to live among you. ³⁷ If you lend them money, you must not charge them interest. And you must not sell them food for more than it cost you. ³⁸ I am the LORD your God. I brought you out of Egypt. I did it to give you the land of Canaan. I wanted to be your God.

³⁹ " 'Suppose any of your own people become poor. And suppose they sell themselves to you. Then do not make them work as slaves. ⁴⁰ You must treat them like hired workers. Or you must treat them like those living among you for a while. They must work for you until the Year of Jubilee. ⁴¹ Then they and their children must be set free. They will go back to their own tribes. They will go back to the property their people have always owned. ⁴² The Israelites are my servants. I brought them out of Egypt. So they must not be sold as slaves. ⁴³ Show them pity when you rule over them. Have respect for God.

⁴⁴ " 'You must get your male and female slaves from the nations that are around you. You can buy slaves from them. ⁴⁵ You can also buy as slaves some of the people living among you for a while. You can also buy members of their families born among you. They will become your property. ⁴⁶ You can leave them to your children as their share of your property. You can make them slaves for life. But when you rule over your own people, you must be kind to them.

⁴⁷ " 'Suppose an outsider living among you for a while becomes rich. Then suppose any of your own people become poor. Then they sell themselves to the outsider living among you. Or they sell themselves to a member of the outsider's family. ⁴⁸ Then they keep the right to buy themselves back after they have sold themselves. One of their relatives can buy them back. ⁴⁹ An uncle or a cousin can buy them back after they have sold themselves. In fact, any relative in their tribe can do it. Or suppose things go well for them. Then they can buy themselves back. ⁵⁰ They and their buyer must count the number of years from the time of the sale up to the Year of Jubilee. The price for their freedom must be based on the amount paid to a hired man for that number of years. ⁵¹ Suppose there are many years until the Year of Jubilee. Then for their freedom they must pay a larger share of the price paid for them. ⁵² But suppose there are only a few years left until the Year of Jubilee. Then they must count the number of years that are left. The payment for their freedom must be based on that number. ⁵³ They must be treated as workers hired from year to year. You must make sure that those they must work for are kind to them when they rule over them.

54 " 'Suppose they are not bought back in any of those ways. Then they and their children must still be set free in the Year of Jubilee. 55 That's because the Israelites belong to me. They are my servants. I brought them out of Egypt. I am the LORD your God.

Rewards for Obeying the LORD

26 " 'Do not make statues of gods for yourselves. Do not set up a likeness of a god or a sacred stone for yourselves. Do not place a carved stone in your land and bow down in front of it. I am the LORD your God.

2 " 'You must always keep my Sabbath days. Have respect for my sacred tent. I am the LORD.

3 " 'Follow my rules. Be careful to obey my commands. 4 Then I will send you rain at the right time. The ground will produce its crops. The trees will bear their fruit. 5 You will continue to harvest your grain until you gather your grapes. You will continue to gather your grapes until you plant your crops. You will have all you want to eat. And you will live in safety in your land.

6 " 'I will give you peace in the land. You will be able to sleep because no one will make you afraid. I will remove wild animals from the land. There will not be any war in your country. 7 You will hunt down your enemies. You will kill them with your swords. 8 Five of you will chase 100. And 100 of you will chase 10,000. You will kill your enemies with your swords.

9 " 'I will bless you. I will give you many children so that there will be many of you. And I will be faithful to the covenant I made with you. 10 You will still be eating last year's crops when you will have to make room for new crops. 11 I will live among you. I will not turn away from you. 12 I will walk among you. I will be your God. And you will be my people. 13 I am the LORD your God. I brought you out of Egypt. I did not want you to be slaves in Egypt anymore. I threw off your heavy load. I helped you walk with your heads held high.

Punishment for Not Obeying the LORD

14 " 'On the other hand, suppose you do not listen to me. Suppose you do not carry out all my commands. 15 Suppose you say no to my rules and turn away from my laws. And suppose you break my covenant by failing to carry out all my commands. 16 Then here is what I will do to you. All at once I will bring terror on you. I will send sicknesses that will make you weak. I will send fever that will destroy your sight. It will slowly take your strength away. When you plant seeds, it will not do you any good. Instead, your enemies will eat what you have planted. 17 I will turn against you. Then your enemies will win the battle over you. Those who hate you will rule over you. You will run away even when no one is chasing you.

18 " 'After all that, suppose you

still will not listen to me. Then I will punish you for your sins seven times. [19] I will break down your stubborn pride. I will make the sky above you like iron, and it will not rain. I will make the ground under you like bronze, and you will not be able to farm it. [20] You will work with all your strength, but it will not do you any good. That is because your soil will not produce any crops. The trees of your land will not bear any fruit.

[21] " 'Suppose you continue to be my enemy. And suppose you still refuse to listen to me. Then I will multiply your troubles many times because of your sins. [22] I will send wild animals against you. They will kill your children. They will destroy your cattle. There will be so few of you left that your roads will be deserted.

[23] " 'After all those things, suppose you still do not accept my warnings. And suppose you continue to be my enemy. [24] Then I myself will be your enemy. I will make you suffer again and again for your sins. [25] I will send war against you to punish you for breaking my covenant. When you go back into your cities, I will send a plague among you. You will be handed over to your enemies. [26] I will cut off your supply of bread. Ten women will need only one oven to bake your bread. They will weigh out the bread piece by piece. Even when you eat all of it, it will not be enough to satisfy you.

[27] " 'After all that, suppose you still do not listen to me. And suppose you continue to be my enemy. [28] Then I will be angry with you. I will be your enemy. I myself will again punish you for your sins over and over. [29] You will eat the dead bodies of your sons. You will also eat the dead bodies of your daughters. [30] I will destroy the high places where you worship other gods. I will pull down your incense altars. I will pile up your dead bodies on the lifeless statues of your gods. And I will turn away from you. [31] I will completely destroy your cities. I will destroy your places of worship. The pleasant smell of your offerings will not give me any delight. [32] I myself will destroy your land so completely that your enemies who live there will be shocked. [33] I will scatter you among the nations. I will pull out my sword and hunt you down. Your land and your cities will be completely destroyed. [34] Then the deserted land will enjoy its sabbath years. It will rest. It will not be farmed. It will enjoy its sabbaths. But you will become prisoners in the country of your enemies. [35] The land will rest the whole time it is deserted. It was not able to rest during the sabbaths you lived in it.

[36] " 'Some of you will be left in the lands of your enemies. I will fill your hearts with fear. The sound of a leaf blown by the wind will scare you away. You will run as if you were escaping from swords. You will fall down,

even though no one is chasing you. [37] You will trip over one another as if you were running away from the battle. You will run away, even though no one is chasing you. You will not be able to stand and fight against your enemies. [38] While you are still scattered among the nations, you will die. The lands of your enemies will destroy you. [39] You who are left in those lands will become weaker and weaker. You will die because of your sins and the sins of your people who lived before you.

[40] " 'But suppose you admit that both you and your people who lived before you have sinned. You admit the evil and dishonest things you have done against me. And you admit you have become my enemy. [41] What you did made me become your enemy. I let your enemies take you into their land. But suppose you stop being stubborn. You stop being proud. And you pay for your sin. [42] Then I will remember my covenant with Jacob. I will remember my covenant with Isaac. I will remember my covenant with Abraham. I will remember what I said to them about the land. [43] You will leave the land. It will enjoy its sabbaths while it lies deserted because you are not there. You will pay for your sins because you said no to my laws. You turned away from my rules. [44] But even after all that, I will not say no to you or turn away from you. I will not destroy you completely in the land of your enemies. I will not break my covenant with you. I am the LORD your God. [45] Because of you, I will remember the covenant I made with the people of Israel who lived before you. I brought them out of Egypt to be their God. The nations saw me do it. I am the LORD.' "

[46] These are the orders, the laws and the rules of the covenant the LORD made on Mount Sinai. He made it between himself and the Israelites through Moses.

Keep Your Promises to the LORD

27 The LORD said to Moses, [2] "Speak to the Israelites. Tell them, 'Suppose someone makes a special promise to set a person apart to serve the LORD. Here is how much it will cost to set that person free from the promise to serve. [3] The cost for a male between the ages of twenty and sixty is 20 ounces of silver. It must be weighed out in keeping with the standard weights that are used in the sacred tent. [4] The cost for a female of the same age is 12 ounces of silver. [5] The cost for a male between the ages of five and twenty is 8 ounces of silver. The cost for a female of the same age is 4 ounces of silver. [6] The cost for a male between the ages of one month and five years is 2 ounces of silver. The cost for a female of the same age is 1 ounce of silver. [7] The cost for a male who is sixty years old or more is 6 ounces of silver. The cost for a female of the same age is 4 ounces of silver. [8] But suppose the one who makes the special promise is too poor to pay the required amount. Then they must bring to the priest the person who will be set free. The priest will decide the right value for that person. It will be based on how much the one who makes the promise can afford.

⁹ " 'Suppose what they promised is an animal that the Lord will accept as an offering. Then the animal given to the Lord becomes holy. ¹⁰ The one who makes the promise must not trade it. They must not trade a good animal for a bad one. And they must not trade a bad animal for a good one. Suppose they choose one animal instead of another. Then both animals become holy. ¹¹ Suppose the animal they promised is not "clean." Suppose the Lord will not accept it as an offering. Then the animal must be brought to the priest. ¹² He will decide whether it is good or bad. Its value will be what he decides it will be. ¹³ Suppose the owner wants to buy the animal back. Then a fifth must be added to its cost.

¹⁴ " 'Suppose someone sets apart their house as something holy to the Lord. Then the priest will decide whether it is good or bad. Its value will remain what he decides it will be. ¹⁵ Suppose the person sets apart their house. And suppose later they want to buy it back. Then they must add a fifth to its value. The house will belong to them again. ¹⁶ " 'Suppose someone sets apart a piece of their family's

land to the Lord. Then here is how its value must be decided. It must be based on the number of seeds that are required to grow a full crop on it. That value will be 20 ounces of silver for every 300 pounds of barley seeds. ¹⁷ Suppose they set apart their field during the Year of Jubilee. Then the value that has been decided will not be changed. ¹⁸ But suppose they set apart their field after the Year of Jubilee. Then here is how the priest will decide its value. It will be based on the number of years that are left until the next Year of Jubilee. The value decided will be reduced. ¹⁹ Suppose the one who set apart their field wants to buy it back. Then they must add a fifth to its value. The field will belong to them again. ²⁰ But suppose they do not buy back the field. Instead, suppose they sell it to someone else. Then they can never buy it back. ²¹ When the field is set free in the Year of Jubilee, it will become holy. It will be like a field set apart to the Lord. It will become the property of the priests.

²² " 'Suppose someone sets apart to the Lord a field they have bought. And suppose it is not part of their family's land. ²³ Then here is how the priest will decide its value. It will be based on the number of years that are left until the Year of Jubilee. The owner must pay that value on the day it is decided. The money is holy. It is set apart for the Lord. ²⁴ In the Year of Jubilee the field will go back to

the person it was bought from. That person is the one who had owned the land before. ²⁵ Every amount of money must be weighed out in keeping with the standard weights used in the sacred tent.

²⁶ " 'But no one can set apart the first male animal born to its mother. That animal already belongs to the LORD. It does not matter whether it is an ox or a sheep. It belongs to the LORD. ²⁷ Suppose it is an "unclean" animal. Then the owner may buy it back at the value that has been decided. And they must add a fifth to its value. But suppose it is not bought back. Then it must be sold at the value that has been decided.

²⁸ " 'But nothing a person owns and sets apart to the LORD can be sold or bought back. It does not matter whether it is a human being or an animal or a family's land. Everything set apart to the LORD is very holy to him.

²⁹ " 'No one set apart in a special way to be destroyed can be bought back. They must be put to death.

³⁰ " 'A tenth of everything the land produces belongs to the LORD. That includes grain from the soil and fruit from the trees. It is holy. It is set apart for him. ³¹ Suppose someone wants to buy back some of their tenth. Then they must add a fifth of the cost to it. ³² Every tenth part of herds and flocks will be holy. They will be set apart for the LORD. That includes every tenth animal that its shepherd marks with his wooden staff. ³³ No one may pick out the good animals from the bad. They must not choose one animal instead of another. But if anyone does, both animals become holy. They can't be bought back.' "

³⁴ The LORD gave Moses all these commands on Mount Sinai for the Israelites.

Numbers

Introduction:

This book is called Numbers because it counts the people of Israel. Moses wrote the book of Numbers.

The book of Numbers has three parts. The first part tells about the year Israel spent at Mount Sinai. The second part tells about their trip in the desert. The people walked in the desert for forty years, but God took care of them. The third part tells how God's people got ready to go into their new land.

The people did not always listen to God in the desert. God gave them food and water, but they did not obey him. Sometimes God punished his people, but he still loved them and took care of them.

Outline of contents:

The Men of Israel Are Counted

1 The LORD spoke to Moses in the tent of meeting. It happened in the Desert of Sinai. The LORD spoke to him on the first day of the second month. It was the second year after the Israelites came out of Egypt. The LORD said, ² "Count all the men of Israel. Make a list of them by their tribes and families. List every man by name. List them one by one. ³ Count all the men able to serve in the army. They must be 20 years old or more. I want you and Aaron to make a list of them group by group. ⁴ One man from each tribe must help you. Those who help must be the heads of their families.

⁵ Here are the names of the men who must help you.

"From the tribe of Reuben will come Elizur, the son of Shedeur.
⁶ From the tribe of Simeon will come Shelumiel, the son of Zurishaddai.
⁷ From the tribe of Judah will come Nahshon, the son of Amminadab.
⁸ From the tribe of Issachar will come Nethanel, the son of Zuar.
⁹ From the tribe of Zebulun will come Eliab, the son of Helon.
¹⁰ From the tribe of Ephraim will come Elishama, the son of Ammihud.
From the tribe of Manasseh will come Gamaliel, the son of Pedahzur.
Ephraim and Manasseh are Joseph's two sons.

¹¹ From the tribe of Benjamin will come Abidan, the son of Gideoni.

¹² From the tribe of Dan will come Ahiezer, the son of Ammishaddai.

¹³ From the tribe of Asher will come Pagiel, the son of Okran.

¹⁴ From the tribe of Gad will come Eliasaph, the son of Deuel.

¹⁵ From the tribe of Naphtali will come Ahira, the son of Enan."

¹⁶ These were the men appointed from the community. They were the leaders of the tribes of their people. They were the heads of the major families in Israel.

¹⁷ Moses and Aaron went and got the men whose names had been given to them. ¹⁸ Then Moses and Aaron gathered all the men of Israel together. It was the first day of the second month. The people wrote down the tribe and family they belonged to. The men 20 years old or more were listed by name. They were listed one by one. ¹⁹ Everything was done just as the LORD had commanded Moses. So Moses counted them in the Desert of Sinai.

²⁰ Here is the number of men from the tribe of Reuben. He is Israel's oldest son. All the men able to serve in the army were counted. They were 20 years old or more. They were listed by name. They were listed one by one. They were listed according to the records of their tribes and families. ²¹ The number from the tribe of Reuben was 46,500.

²² Here is the number of men from the tribe of Simeon. All the men able to serve in the army were counted. They were 20 years old or more. They were listed by name. They were listed one by one. They were listed according to the records of their tribes and families. ²³ The number from the tribe of Simeon was 59,300.

²⁴ Here is the number of men from the tribe of Gad. All the men able to serve in the army were counted. They were 20 years old or more. They were listed by name. They were listed according to the records of their tribes and families. ²⁵ The number from the tribe of Gad was 45,650.

²⁶ Here is the number of men from the tribe of Judah. All the men able to serve in the army were counted. They were 20 years old or more. They were listed by name. They were listed according to the records of their tribes and families. ²⁷ The number from the tribe of Judah was 74,600.

²⁸ Here is the number of men from the tribe of Issachar.

All the men able to serve in the army were counted. They were 20 years old or more. They were listed by name. They were listed according to the records of their tribes and families. ²⁹ The number from the tribe of Issachar was 54,400.

³⁰ Here is the number of men from the tribe of Zebulun.

All the men able to serve in the army were counted. They were 20 years old or more. They were listed by name. They were listed according to the records of their tribes and families. ³¹ The number from the tribe of Zebulun was 57,400.

³² Here is the number of men from the tribe of Ephraim. He is the son of Joseph.

All the men able to serve in the army were counted. They were 20 years old or more. They were listed by name. They were listed according to the records of their tribes and families. ³³ The number from the tribe of Ephraim was 40,500.

³⁴ Here is the number of men from the tribe of Manasseh. He is the son of Joseph.

All the men able to serve in the army were counted. They were 20 years old or more. They were listed by name. They were listed according to the records of their tribes and families. ³⁵ The number from the tribe of Manasseh was 32,200.

³⁶ Here is the number of men from the tribe of Benjamin.

All the men able to serve in the army were counted. They were 20 years old or more. They were listed by name. They were listed according to the records of their tribes and families. ³⁷ The number from the tribe of Benjamin was 35,400.

³⁸ Here is the number of men from the tribe of Dan.

All the men able to serve in the army were counted. They were 20 years old or more. They were listed by name. They were listed according to the records of their tribes and families. ³⁹ The number from the tribe of Dan was 62,700.

⁴⁰ Here is the number of men from the tribe of Asher.

All the men able to serve in the army were counted. They were 20 years old or more. They were listed by name. They were listed according to their tribes and families. ⁴¹ The number from the tribe of Asher was 41,500.

⁴² Here is the number of men from the tribe of Naphtali.

All the men able to serve in the army were counted. They were 20 years old or more. They were listed by name. They were listed according to the records of their tribes and families. ⁴³ The number from the tribe of Naphtali was 53,400.

⁴⁴ These were the men counted by Moses and Aaron. The 12 leaders of Israel helped them. There was one leader from each tribe. ⁴⁵ The men who were counted were able to serve in Israel's army. All of them were 20 years old or more. They were counted family by family. ⁴⁶ The total number of men was 603,550.

⁴⁷ But the families of the tribe of Levi were not counted along with the others. ⁴⁸ The LORD had spoken to Moses. He had said, ⁴⁹ "You must not count the men from the tribe of Levi. Do not include them when you list the other men of Israel. ⁵⁰ Instead, put the Levites in charge of the holy tent. That is where the tablets of the covenant law are kept. The Levites will be in charge of everything that belongs to the holy tent. They must carry the tent and everything that belongs to it. They must take care of it.

They must set up camp around it. ⁵¹ When the holy tent must be moved, the Levites must take it down. And when the tent must be set up, the Levites must do it. Anyone else who approaches it must be put to death. ⁵² The Israelites must set up their tents by military groups. All of them must be in their own camps under their own flags. ⁵³ But the Levites must set up their tents around the holy tent. That's where the tablets of the covenant law are kept. Then I will not be angry with the community of Israel. The Levites will be responsible for taking care of the tent."

⁵⁴ The Israelites did everything just as the LORD had commanded Moses.

The Tribes Camp Around the Tent of Meeting

2 The LORD spoke to Moses and Aaron. He said, ² "The Israelites must camp around the tent of meeting. But they must not camp too close to it. All of them must camp under their flags and under the banners of their families."

³ The groups of the camp of Judah must be on the east side. They must set up camp toward the sunrise. They must camp under their flag. The leader of the tribe of Judah is Nahshon, the son of Amminadab. ⁴ There are 74,600 men in Nahshon's group.

⁵ The tribe of Issachar will camp next to them. The leader of the tribe of Is-

sachar is Nethanel, the son of Zuar. [6] There are 54,400 men in Nethanel's group. [7] The tribe of Zebulun will be next. The leader of the tribe of Zebulun is Eliab, the son of Helon. [8] There are 57,400 men in Eliab's group.

[9] So a total of 186,400 men will be set apart for the camp of Judah. They will be arranged group by group. They will start out first.

[10] The groups of the camp of Reuben will be on the south side. They will be under their flag. The leader of the tribe of Reuben is Elizur, the son of Shedeur. [11] There are 46,500 men in Elizur's group.

[12] The tribe of Simeon will camp next to them. The leader of the tribe of Simeon is Shelumiel, the son of Zurishaddai. [13] There are 59,300 men in Shelumiel's group.

[14] The tribe of Gad will be next. The leader of the tribe of Gad is Eliasaph, the son of Deuel. [15] There are 45,650 men in Eliasaph's group.

[16] So a total of 151,450 men will be set apart for the camp of Reuben. They will be arranged group by group. They will start out second.

[17] Then the camp of the Levites will start out. The tent of meeting will go with them. They will march in the middle of the other camps. They will start out in the same order as they do when they set up camp. Each one will be in their own place under their flag.

[18] The groups of the camp of Ephraim will be on the west side. They will be under their flag. The leader of the tribe of Ephraim is Elishama, the son of Ammihud. [19] There are 40,500 men in Elishama's group.

[20] The tribe of Manasseh will be next to them. The leader of the tribe of Manasseh is Gamaliel, the son of Pedahzur. [21] There are 32,200 men in Gamaliel's group.

[22] The tribe of Benjamin will be next. The leader of the tribe of Benjamin is Abidan, the son of Gideoni. [23] There are 35,400 men in Abidan's group.

[24] So a total of 108,100 men will be set apart for the camp of Ephraim. They will be arranged group by group. They will start out third.

[25] The groups of the camp of Dan will be on the north side. They will be under their flag. The leader of the tribe of Dan is Ahiezer, the son of Ammishaddai. [26] There are

62,700 men in Ahiezer's group.

27 The tribe of Asher will camp next to them. The leader of the tribe of Asher is Pagiel, the son of Okran. 28 There are 41,500 men in Pagiel's group.

29 The tribe of Naphtali will be next. The leader of the tribe of Naphtali is Ahira, the son of Enan. 30 There are 53,400 men in Ahira's group.

31 So a total of 157,600 men will be set apart for the camp of Dan. They will start out last. They will march under their flags.

32 Those are the men of Israel. They were counted according to their families. The total number of all the men in the camps is 603,550, group by group. 33 But the Levites weren't counted along with the other men of Israel. That's what the LORD had commanded Moses.

34 So the Israelites did everything the LORD had commanded Moses. That's the way they set up camp under their flags. And that's the way they started out. Each of them marched out with their own tribe and family.

The Levites

3 Here is the story of the family line of Aaron and Moses. It belongs to the time when the LORD spoke to Moses at Mount Sinai.

2 Aaron's oldest son was Nadab. Aaron's other sons were Abihu, Eleazar and Ithamar. 3 Those were the names of Aaron's sons. They were the anointed priests. They were given authority to serve the LORD as priests. 4 But Nadab and Abihu made an offering to the LORD by using fire that wasn't allowed. So they died in front of him. That happened in the Desert of Sinai. They didn't have any sons. Only Eleazar and Ithamar served as priests while their father Aaron was living.

5 The LORD spoke to Moses. He said, 6 "Bring the men of the tribe of Levi to Aaron the priest. They will help him. 7 They must work at the tent of meeting for Aaron and for the whole community. They must do what needs to be done at the holy tent. 8 They must take care of everything connected with the tent of meeting. When they do, they are acting for all the Israelites. 9 Give the Levites to Aaron and his sons. They are the men of Israel who must be given completely to him. 10 Appoint Aaron and his sons to serve as priests. Anyone else who approaches the sacred tent must be put to death."

11 The LORD also said to Moses, 12 "I have taken the Levites from among the Israelites. I have taken them in place of the son born first to each woman in Israel. The Levites belong to me. 13 That's because every male born first to a mother is mine. In Egypt I struck down all the males born first. I did it when I set apart for myself every male

born first to a mother in Israel. That is true for men and animals alike. They belong to me. I am the LORD."

¹⁴ The LORD spoke to Moses in the Desert of Sinai. He said, ¹⁵ "Count the Levites by their family groups. Count every male a month old or more." ¹⁶ So Moses counted them. He did just as the word of the LORD had commanded him.

¹⁷ The sons of Levi were
  Gershon, Kohath and Merari.
¹⁸ The major families from Gershon were
  Libni and Shimei.
¹⁹ The major families from Kohath were
  Amram, Izhar, Hebron and Uzziel.
²⁰ The major families from Merari were
  Mahli and Mushi.

These were the major families of the Levites.

²¹ The families of Libni and Shimei belonged to the family of Gershon.
²² All the males a month old or more were counted. There were 7,500 of them.
²³ The families of Gershon had to camp on the west side. They had to camp behind the holy tent.
²⁴ The leader of the families of Gershon was Eliasaph, the son of Lael.
²⁵ Here are the duties of the families of Gershon at the tent of meeting. They were responsible for tak-

ing care of the holy tent and its coverings. They took care of the curtain at the entrance to the tent of meeting. ²⁶ They took care of the curtains of the courtyard. And they took care of the curtain at the entrance to the courtyard. The courtyard was all around the holy tent and altar. The families of Gershon also took care of the ropes. In fact, they had to take care of everything connected with the use of all those things.

²⁷ The families of Amram, Izhar, Hebron and Uzziel belonged to the family of Kohath.
²⁸ All the males a month old or more were counted. There were 8,600 of them. The families of Kohath were responsible for taking care of the sacred tent.
²⁹ They had to camp on the south side of the holy tent.
³⁰ The leader of the families of Kohath was Elizaphan, the son of Uzziel.
³¹ They were responsible for taking care of the ark of the covenant law. They took care of the table for the holy bread. They took care of the lampstand and the two altars. They took care of the things used for serving in the sacred tent. They also took care of the inner curtain.

In fact, they had to take care of everything connected with the use of all those things.

32 The chief leader of the Levites was Eleazar. He was the son of Aaron the priest. Eleazar was appointed over those responsible for taking care of the sacred tent.

33 The families of Mahli and Mushi belonged to the family of Merari.

34 All the males a month old or more were counted. There were 6,200 of them.

35 The leader of the families of Merari was Zuriel, the son of Abihail.

The families of Merari had to camp on the north side of the holy tent.

36 They were responsible for taking care of the frames of the tent. They took care of its crossbars, posts and bases. They took care of all its supplies. In fact, they had to take care of everything connected with the use of all those things. 37 They also took care of the posts of the courtyard around the holy tent. And they took care of the bases, tent stakes and ropes.

38 Moses, Aaron and Aaron's sons had to camp to the east of the holy tent. They had to camp toward the sunrise in front of the tent of meeting.

They were responsible for taking care of the sacred tent. They had to do it for the Israelites.

Anyone else who approached the tent would be put to death.

39 The total number of the Levite males was 22,000. They were counted family by family. Every male a month old or more was counted. Moses and Aaron counted them, just as the LORD had commanded.

40 The LORD said to Moses, "Count all the Israelite males born first in their families. Count all those a month old or more. Make a list of their names. 41 Take the Levites for me in their place. And take the livestock of the Levites in place of all the male animals in Israel born first to their mothers. I am the LORD."

42 So Moses counted all the oldest sons in Israel. He did just as the LORD had commanded him. 43 There were 22,273 of those sons a month old or more. They were listed by name.

44 The LORD also said to Moses, 45 "Take the Levites in place of all the males born first in Israel. Also take the livestock of the Levites in place of the livestock of Israel. The Levites belong to me. I am the LORD. 46 But there are 273 more males born first in Israel than there are male Levites. 47 Collect two ounces of silver for each of them. Weigh it out according to the standard

weights used in the sacred tent. ⁴⁸ Give the silver to Aaron and his sons. It will buy the freedom of the additional sons in Israel."

⁴⁹ So Moses collected the silver from the additional sons in Israel to buy their freedom. The Levites took the place of all the others. ⁵⁰ Moses collected 35 pounds of silver. It was weighed out according to the weights used in the sacred tent. Moses collected it from the oldest sons in Israel. ⁵¹ He gave the silver to Aaron and his sons. He did just as the LORD had commanded him.

The Families of Kohath

4 The LORD said to Moses and Aaron, ² "Count the Levites who belong to the families of Kohath. Make a list of them family by family. ³ Count all the men 30 to 50 years old. Those are the men who must come and serve at the tent of meeting.

⁴ "Here is the work the men of Kohath must do at the tent of meeting. They must take care of the things that are very holy. ⁵ When the camp is ready to move, Aaron and his sons must go into the tent. They must take down the curtain that hides the ark where the tablets of the covenant law are kept. They must cover the ark with the curtain. ⁶ Then they must cover that with strong leather. They must spread a solid blue cloth over the leather. And they must put the poles in place.

⁷ "They must spread a blue cloth over the table for the holy bread. They must put the plates, dishes and bowls on the cloth. They must also put the jars for drink offerings on it. The bread that is always kept there must remain on it. ⁸ They must spread a bright red cloth over everything. Then they must cover that with the strong leather. And they must put the poles of the table in place.

⁹ "They must get a blue cloth. With it they must cover the lampstand that gives light. They must also cover its lamps, trays and wick cutters. And they must cover all its jars. The jars are for the olive oil used in the lampstand. ¹⁰ Then Aaron and his sons must wrap the lampstand and all the things used with it. They must cover it with the strong leather. And they must put it on a frame to carry it.

¹¹ "They must spread a blue cloth over the gold altar for burning incense. They must cover that with the strong leather. And they must put the poles of the altar in place.

¹² "They must get all the things used for serving in the sacred tent. They must wrap them in a blue cloth. They must cover that with the strong leather. Then they must put those things on a frame to carry them.

¹³ "They must remove the ashes from the bronze altar for burnt offerings. They must spread a purple cloth over it. ¹⁴ Then they must place all the tools on it. The tools are used for serving at the altar. They include the pans for carrying

ashes. They also include the meat forks, shovels and sprinkling bowls. Aaron and his sons must cover the altar with the strong leather. And they must put its poles in place.

15 "Aaron and his sons must cover all the holy things that belong to the holy tent. Only then are the men of Kohath to come and carry everything. They must do so only when the camp is ready to move. But they must not touch the holy things. If they do, they will die. The men of Kohath must carry everything in the tent of meeting.

16 "Eleazar the priest will be in charge of the olive oil for the light. He is the son of Aaron. Eleazar will be in charge of the sweet-smelling incense. He will be in charge of the regular grain offering and the anointing oil. He will be in charge of the entire holy tent. He will also be in charge of everything in it. That includes all the things that belong to the tent."

17 The LORD spoke to Moses and Aaron. He said, 18 "Make sure that the Kohath families are not destroyed from among the Levites. 19 I want them to live and not die when they come near the very holy things. So here is what you must do for them. Aaron and his sons must go into the sacred tent and tell each man what to do. They must tell each man what to carry. 20 But the men of Kohath must not go in and look at the holy things. They must not look at them even for a moment. If they do, they will die."

The Families of Gershon

21 The LORD said to Moses, 22 "Count the families of Gershon. Make a list of them family by family. 23 Count all the men 30 to 50 years old. Those are the men who must come and serve at the tent of meeting.

24 "Here is how the families of Gershon must serve. They must carry things. 25 They must carry the curtains of the holy tent of meeting. They must carry its covering and the outside covering of strong leather. They must carry the curtains that cover the entrance to the tent of meeting. 26 They must carry the curtains of the courtyard. The courtyard is all around the holy tent and altar. They must carry the curtain for the entrance. They must carry the ropes. They must also carry all the supplies used for any purpose in the tent. The families of Gershon must do everything that needs to be done with those things. 27 All their work must be done under the direction of Aaron and his sons. That includes carrying and everything else they do. Aaron and his sons must tell them what to carry. And that will be their work. 28 It is what the families of Gershon must do at the tent of meeting. They must work under the direction of Ithamar the priest. He is the son of Aaron.

The Families of Merari

29 "Count the families of Merari. Count them family by family. 30 Count all the men 30 to 50

years old. Those are the men who must come and serve at the tent of meeting. [31] Here is the work they must do at the tent of meeting. They must carry the frames of the holy tent. They must carry its crossbars, posts and bases. [32] They must also carry the posts of the courtyard. The courtyard is all around the holy tent. And they must carry the bases for the posts as well as their tent stakes and ropes. They must also carry all the supplies and everything connected with their use. Tell each man exactly what to carry. [33] That is the work the families of Merari must do at the tent of meeting. They must work under the direction of Ithamar the priest. He is the son of Aaron."

Counting the Families of the Levites

[34] Moses, Aaron and the leaders of the community counted the men of Kohath. They counted them family by family. [35] They counted all the men from 30 to 50 years old. They were the men who came and served at the tent of meeting. [36] There were 2,750 men. They were counted family by family. [37] That was the total of all the men in the families of Kohath who served at the tent of meeting. Moses and Aaron counted them. They did just as the Lord had commanded through Moses.

[38] The men of Gershon were counted family by family. [39] All the men from 30 to 50 years old were counted. They were the men who came and served at the tent of meeting. [40] There were 2,630 men. They were counted family by family. [41] That was the total of the men in the families of Gershon who served at the tent of meeting. Moses and Aaron counted them. They did just as the Lord had commanded.

[42] The men of Merari were counted family by family. [43] All the men from 30 to 50 years old were counted. They were the men who came and served at the tent of meeting. [44] There were 3,200 men. They were counted family by family. [45] That was the total of the men in the families of Merari. Moses and Aaron counted them. They did just as the Lord had commanded through Moses.

[46] So Moses and Aaron counted all the Levites. The leaders of Israel helped them. They counted the Levites family by family. [47] All the men from 30 to 50 years old were counted. They were the men who came and served at the

tent of meeting. They were also supposed to carry it. [48] The total number of men was 8,580. [49] Everything was done as the LORD had commanded through Moses. Each man was given his work. And each one was told what to carry.

So they were counted, just as the LORD had commanded Moses.

Making the Camp Pure

5 The LORD spoke to Moses. He said, [2] "Tell the Israelites that certain people must be sent away from the camp. Command them to send away anyone who has a skin disease. They must send away all those who have liquid waste coming from their bodies. And they must send away those who are 'unclean' because they have touched a dead body. [3] That applies to men and women alike. Send them out of the camp. They must not make their camp 'unclean.' That is where I live among them."
[4] So the Israelites did what the LORD commanded. They sent out of the camp those who were "unclean." They did just as the LORD had directed Moses.

Sins Against Others Must Be Paid For

[5] The LORD said to Moses, [6] "Speak to the Israelites. Say to them, 'Suppose a man or woman does something wrong to someone else. Then that person is not being faithful to the LORD. People like that are guilty.

[7] They must admit they have committed a sin. They must pay in full for what they did wrong. And they must add a fifth of the value to it. Then they must give all of it to the person they have sinned against. [8] But suppose that person has died. And suppose that person does not have a close relative who can be paid for the sin that was committed. Then what is paid belongs to the LORD. It must be given to the priest. A ram must be given along with it. The ram must be sacrificed to the LORD to pay for the sin. [9] All the sacred gifts the Israelites bring to a priest will belong to him. [10] Sacred gifts belong to their owners. But what they give to the priest will belong to the priest.'"

The Test for an Unfaithful Wife

[11] Then the LORD spoke to Moses again. He said, [12] "Speak to the Israelites. Say to them, 'Suppose a man's wife goes astray. And suppose she is not faithful to her husband. [13] Suppose another man has sex with her. And suppose this is hidden from her husband. No one knows she is not "clean." So there is no witness against her. And she has not been caught in the act. [14] Suppose her husband becomes jealous. He does not trust his wife, and she is really "unclean." Or suppose he does not trust her even though she is "clean." [15] Then he must take his wife to the priest. He must also bring an offering. It must be eight cups of barley flour. The

offering is for his wife. He must not pour olive oil on it. And he must not put incense on it. It is a grain offering for being jealous. It calls attention to the wrong thing a person has done.

16 " 'The priest must have her stand in front of the LORD. 17 He must pour some holy water into a clay jar. He must get some dust from the floor of the holy tent. And he must put it into the water. 18 The priest must have the woman stand in front of the LORD. Then he must untie her hair. He must place in her hands the offering that calls attention to the wrong thing a person has done. It is the grain offering for being jealous. The priest must keep the bitter water with him. It is the water that brings a curse. 19 Then the priest must have the woman give her word. He must say to her, "Suppose no other man has had sex with you. And suppose you haven't gone astray. You have kept yourself pure while you are married to your husband. Then may the bitter water that brings a curse not harm you. 20 But suppose you have gone astray while you are married to your husband. You have made yourself 'unclean.' You have had sex with a man who isn't your husband."

21 At that point the priest must put the woman under the curse that will come if she breaks her word. He must say, "May the LORD cause you to become a curse among your people. You will become a curse when the LORD makes your body unable to have children. 22 May this water that brings a curse enter your body. May it make your body unable to have children."

" 'Then the woman must say, "Amen. Let it happen."

23 " 'The priest must write the curses on a scroll. He must wash them off in the bitter water. 24 It is the water he will make the woman drink. It is bitter water that brings a curse. It will enter her body. And it will cause her to suffer bitterly. 25 The priest must take from her hands the grain offering for being jealous. He must lift it up and wave it in front of the LORD. He must bring it to the altar. 26 Then the priest must take a handful of the grain offering. It is the offering that calls attention to the wrong thing a person has done. The priest must burn it on the altar. After that, he must have the woman drink the water. 27 Suppose she has made herself "unclean." She has not been faithful to her husband. And she has drunk the water that brings a curse. Then it will go into her body. It will cause her to suffer bitterly. It will make her body unable to have children. She will become a curse. 28 Suppose the woman has not made herself "unclean." But suppose she is "clean." Then she will be free of guilt. And she will be able to have children.

29 " 'This is the law about being jealous. It applies to a woman who has gone astray. She has made herself "unclean" while she is married to her husband.

³⁰ And it applies to a man who becomes jealous. He has doubts about his wife. The priest must have her stand in front of the LORD. He must apply the entire law to her. ³¹ The husband will not be guilty of doing anything wrong. But the woman will be punished for her sin.' "

Becoming a Nazirite

6 The LORD said to Moses, ² "Say to the Israelites, 'Suppose a man or woman wants to make a special promise. They want to set themselves apart to the LORD for a certain period of time. They want to be Nazirites. ³ Then they must not drink any kind of wine. They must not drink vinegar made out of wine of any kind. They must not drink grape juice. They must not eat grapes or raisins. ⁴ As long as they are Nazirites, they must not eat anything grapevines produce. They must not even eat the seeds or skins of grapes.

⁵ " 'They must not use razors on their heads. They must not cut their hair during the whole time they have set themselves apart to the LORD. They must be holy until that time is over. They must let the hair on their heads grow long.

⁶ " 'And they must not go near a dead body during that whole time. ⁷ But what if their father or mother dies? Or what if their brother or sister dies? Then they must not make themselves "unclean" because of them. The hair on their heads shows they are set apart for God. ⁸ Dur-ing the whole time they are set apart they are holy to the LORD.

⁹ " 'Suppose someone dies suddenly in front of them. That makes the hair they have set apart to the LORD "unclean." So they must shave their heads on the day they will be made "clean." That is the seventh day. ¹⁰ Then on the eighth day they must bring two doves. Or they can bring two young pigeons. They must bring them to the priest. He will be at the entrance to the tent of meeting. ¹¹ The priest must offer one of the birds as a sin offering. And he must offer the other as a burnt offering. The sacrifices will pay for the sin of the Nazirite man or woman. They sinned by being near a dead body. That same day they must make their heads holy again. ¹² They must set themselves apart to the LORD again. They must do it for the same period of time they had agreed to at first. And they must bring a male lamb a year old as a guilt offering. The days before that do not count. That is because they became "unclean" during the time they were set apart.

¹³ " 'The time when the Nazirites are set apart will come to an end. Here is the law that applies to them at that time. They must be brought to the entrance to the tent of meeting. ¹⁴ There they must present their offerings to the LORD. They must bring a male lamb a year old. It must not have any flaws. It is for a burnt offering. Then they must bring a female lamb a year old.

It must not have any flaws. It is for a sin offering. And they must bring a ram that does not have any flaws. It is for a friendship offering. [15] They must sacrifice the offerings together with their grain offerings and drink offerings. And they must also bring a basket of bread made with the finest flour. The bread must be made without yeast. The offering must include thick loaves with olive oil mixed in. And it must also include thin loaves brushed with olive oil.

[16] " 'The priest must bring all these things to the LORD. He must sacrifice the sin offering and the burnt offering. [17] He must bring the basket of bread made without yeast. And he must sacrifice the ram. It will be a friendship offering to the LORD. The priest must bring it together with its grain offering and drink offering.

[18] " 'Then the Nazirites must shave off the hair that shows they have set themselves apart to the LORD. They must do it at the entrance to the tent of meeting. And they must put the hair in the fire that burns the sacrifice of the friendship offering.

[19] " 'After the Nazirites have shaved off their hair, the priest must take a boiled shoulder of the ram. He must remove one thick loaf and one thin loaf from the basket. They must be made without yeast. And he must place the shoulder and the bread in the hands of the Nazirites. [20] Then he must lift up the shoulder and bread and wave them in front of the LORD. They are a wave offering. They are holy and belong to the priest. Other parts of the ram belong to the priest as well. They are the breast that was waved and the thigh that was offered. After the offering is waved, the Nazirites may drink wine.

[21] " 'This is the law of the Nazirites. They promise to sacrifice offerings to the LORD. They do it when they set themselves apart. And they should bring anything else they can afford. They must fulfill the promises they have made. They must do so according to the law of the Nazirites.' "

How the Priests Bless the People

[22] The LORD spoke to Moses. He said, [23] "Tell Aaron and his sons, 'Here is how I want you to bless the Israelites. Say to them,

[24] " ' "May the LORD bless you
  and take good care of you.
[25] May the LORD smile on you
  and be gracious to you.
[26] May the LORD look on you
    with favor
  and give you peace." '

[27] "In that way they will put the blessing of my name on the Israelites. And I will bless them."

Israel's Leaders Bring Offerings for the Holy Tent

7 Moses finished setting up the holy tent. Then he anointed it with olive oil. He set it apart to the LORD. He did the same thing with everything that belonged to it. He also anointed the altar. And he set apart to

the LORD the altar and all its tools. ²Then the leaders of Israel brought their offerings. The leaders were the heads of the families. They were the leaders of the tribes. They were in charge of the men who had been counted. ³They brought gifts to the LORD. They brought six covered carts and 12 oxen. Each leader gave an ox. And every two leaders gave a cart. They put their gifts in front of the holy tent.

⁴The LORD said to Moses, ⁵"Accept the gifts from the leaders. I want their gifts to be used in the work at the tent of meeting. Give them to the Levites. They need them to do their work."

⁶So Moses gave the carts and the oxen to the Levites. ⁷He gave two carts and four oxen to the men from the family of Gershon. They needed them to do their work. ⁸He gave four carts and eight oxen to the men from the family of Merari. They needed them to do their work. All these men were under the direction of Ithamar the priest. He was the son of Aaron. ⁹But Moses didn't give any carts or oxen to the men from the family of Kohath. They had to carry the holy things on their shoulders. They were responsible for the holy things.

¹⁰When the altar was anointed, the leaders brought their offerings. They placed them in front of the altar. They brought their offerings in order to set apart the altar. ¹¹The LORD had spoken to Moses. He had said, "Each day one leader must bring his offering. He must bring it in order to set apart the altar."

¹²On the first day Nahshon, the son of Amminadab, brought his offering. Nahshon was from the tribe of Judah.

¹³He brought:

one silver plate and one silver sprinkling bowl. The plate weighed three pounds four ounces. The sprinkling bowl weighed one pound 12 ounces. Both were weighed according to the standard weights used in the sacred tent. Each plate and bowl was filled with the finest flour mixed with olive oil. It was a grain offering.

¹⁴He brought one gold dish that weighed four ounces. It was filled with incense.

¹⁵Nahshon brought one young bull, one ram, and one male lamb a year old. They would be sacrificed as a burnt offering.

¹⁶He brought one male goat to be sacrificed as a sin offering.

¹⁷He brought two oxen, five rams and five male goats. He also brought five male lambs a year old. All of them would be sacrificed as a friendship offering.

That was everything that Nahshon, the son of Amminadab, brought as his offering.

18 On the second day Nethanel, the son of Zuar, brought his offering. Nethanel was the leader of the tribe of Issachar.

19 He brought:

one silver plate and one silver sprinkling bowl. The plate weighed three pounds four ounces. The sprinkling bowl weighed one pound 12 ounces. Both were weighed according to the standard weights used in the sacred tent. Each plate and bowl was filled with the finest flour mixed with olive oil. It was a grain offering.

20 He brought one gold dish that weighed four ounces. It was filled with incense.

21 Nethanel brought one young bull, one ram, and one male lamb a year old. They would be sacrificed as a burnt offering.

22 He brought one male goat to be sacrificed as a sin offering.

23 He brought two oxen, five rams and five male goats. He also brought five male lambs a year old. All of them would be sacrificed as a friendship offering.

That was everything that Nethanel, the son of Zuar, brought as his offering.

24 On the third day Eliab, the son of Helon, brought his offering. Eliab was the leader of the people of Zebulun.

25 He brought:

one silver plate and one silver sprinkling bowl. The plate weighed three pounds four ounces. The sprinkling bowl weighed one pound 12 ounces. Both were weighed according to the standard weights used in the sacred tent. Each plate and bowl was filled with the finest flour mixed with olive oil. It was a grain offering.

26 He brought one gold dish that weighed four ounces. It was filled with incense.

27 Eliab brought one young bull, one ram, and one male lamb a year old. They would be sacrificed as a burnt offering.

28 He brought one male goat to be sacrificed as a sin offering.

29 He brought two oxen, five rams and five male goats. He also brought five male lambs a year old. All of them would be sacrificed as a friendship offering.

That was everything that Eliab, the son of Helon, brought as his offering.

30 On the fourth day Elizur, the son of Shedeur, brought his offering. Elizur was the leader of the people of Reuben.

31 He brought:

one silver plate and one silver sprinkling bowl. The plate weighed three pounds four ounces. The sprinkling bowl weighed one pound 12 ounces. Both were weighed according to the standard weights used in the sacred tent. Each plate and bowl was filled with the finest flour mixed with olive oil. It was a grain offering.

32 He brought one gold dish that weighed four ounces. It was filled with incense.

33 Elizur brought one young bull, one ram, and one male lamb a year old. They would be sacrificed as a burnt offering.

34 He brought one male goat to be sacrificed as a sin offering.

35 He brought two oxen, five rams and five male goats. He also brought five male lambs a year old. All of them would be sacrificed as a friendship offering. That was everything that Elizur, the son of Shedeur, brought as his offering.

36 On the fifth day Shelumiel, the son of Zurishaddai, brought his offering. Shelumiel was the leader of the people of Simeon.

37 He brought:
one silver plate and one silver sprinkling bowl. The plate weighed three pounds four ounces. The sprinkling bowl weighed one pound 12 ounces. Both were weighed according to the standard weights used in the sacred tent. Each plate and bowl was filled with the finest flour mixed with olive oil. It was a grain offering.

38 He brought one gold dish that weighed four ounces. It was filled with incense.

39 Shelumiel brought one young bull, one ram, and one male lamb a year old. They would be sacrificed as a burnt offering.

40 He brought one male goat to be sacrificed as a sin offering.

41 He brought two oxen, five rams and five male goats. He also brought five male lambs a year old. All of them would be sacrificed as a friendship offering. That was everything that Shelumiel, the son of Zurishaddai, brought as his offering.

42 On the sixth day Eliasaph, the son of Deuel, brought his offering. Eliasaph was the leader of the people of Gad.

43 He brought:
one silver plate and one silver sprinkling bowl. The plate weighed three pounds four ounces. The sprinkling bowl weighed one pound 12 ounces. Both were weighed according to the standard weights used in the sacred tent. Each plate and

bowl was filled with the finest flour mixed with olive oil. It was a grain offering.

⁴⁴He brought one gold dish that weighed four ounces. It was filled with incense.

⁴⁵Eliasaph brought one young bull, one ram, and one male lamb a year old. They would be sacrificed as a burnt offering.

⁴⁶He brought one male goat to be sacrificed as a sin offering.

⁴⁷He brought two oxen, five rams and five male goats. He also brought five male lambs a year old. All of them would be sacrificed as a friendship offering.

That was everything that Eliasaph, the son of Deuel, brought as his offering.

⁴⁸On the seventh day Elishama, the son of Ammihud, brought his offering. Elishama was the leader of the people of Ephraim.

⁴⁹He brought:

one silver plate and one silver sprinkling bowl. The plate weighed three pounds four ounces. The sprinkling bowl weighed one pound 12 ounces. Both were weighed according to the standard weights used in the sacred tent. Each plate and bowl was filled with the finest flour mixed with olive oil. It was a grain offering.

⁵⁰He brought one gold dish that weighed four ounces. It was filled with incense.

⁵¹Elishama brought one young bull, one ram, and one male lamb a year old. They would be sacrificed as a burnt offering.

⁵²He brought one male goat to be sacrificed as a sin offering.

⁵³He brought two oxen, five rams and five male goats. He also brought five male lambs a year old. All of them would be sacrificed as a friendship offering.

That was everything that Elishama, the son of Ammihud, brought as his offering.

⁵⁴On the eighth day Gamaliel, the son of Pedahzur, brought his offering. Gamaliel was the leader of the people of Manasseh.

⁵⁵He brought:

one silver plate and one silver sprinkling bowl. The plate weighed three pounds four ounces. The sprinkling bowl weighed one pound 12 ounces. Both were weighed according to the standard weights used in the sacred tent. Each plate and bowl was filled with the finest flour mixed with olive oil. It was a grain offering.

⁵⁶He also brought one gold dish that weighed four ounces. It was filled with incense.

⁵⁷Gamaliel brought one young bull, one ram, and one male lamb a year old. They would be sacrificed as a burnt offering. ⁵⁸He brought one male goat to be sacrificed as a sin offering. ⁵⁹He brought two oxen, five rams and five male goats. He also brought five male lambs a year old. All of them would be sacrificed as a friendship offering.

That was everything that Gamaliel, the son of Pedahzur, brought as his offering.

⁶⁰On the ninth day Abidan, the son of Gideoni, brought his offering. Abidan was the leader of the people of Benjamin. ⁶¹He brought:

one silver plate and one silver sprinkling bowl. The plate weighed three pounds four ounces. The sprinkling bowl weighed one pound 12 ounces. Both were weighed according to the standard weights used in the sacred tent. Each plate and bowl was filled with the finest flour mixed with olive oil. It was a grain offering. ⁶²He brought one gold dish that weighed four ounces. It was filled with incense. ⁶³Abidan brought one young bull, one ram, and one male lamb a year old. They would be sacrificed as a burnt offering. ⁶⁴He brought one male goat to be sacrificed as a sin offering. ⁶⁵He brought two oxen, five rams and five male goats. He also brought five male lambs a year old. All of them would be sacrificed as a friendship offering.

That was everything that Abidan, the son of Gideoni, brought as his offering.

⁶⁶On the tenth day Ahiezer, the son of Ammishaddai, brought his offering. Ahiezer was the leader of the people of Dan. ⁶⁷He brought:

one silver plate and one silver sprinkling bowl. The plate weighed three pounds four ounces. The sprinkling bowl weighed one pound 12 ounces. Both were weighed according to the standard weights used in the sacred tent. Each plate and bowl was filled with the finest flour mixed with olive oil. It was a grain offering. ⁶⁸He brought one gold dish that weighed four ounces. It was filled with incense. ⁶⁹Ahiezer brought one young bull, one ram, and one male lamb a year old. They would be sacrificed as a burnt offering. ⁷⁰He brought one male goat to be sacrificed as a sin offering. ⁷¹He brought two oxen, five rams and five male goats. He also brought five male lambs a year old. All of them would be sacrificed as a friendship offering.

That was everything that Ahiezer, the son of Ammishaddai, brought as his offering.

72 On the eleventh day Pagiel, the son of Okran, brought his offering. Pagiel was the leader of the people of Asher.

73 He brought:

one silver plate and one silver sprinkling bowl. The plate weighed three pounds four ounces. The sprinkling bowl weighed one pound 12 ounces. Both were weighed according to the standard weights used in the sacred tent. Each plate and bowl was filled with the finest flour mixed with olive oil. It was a grain offering.

74 He brought one gold dish that weighed four ounces. It was filled with incense.

75 Pagiel brought one young bull, one ram, and one male lamb a year old. They would be sacrificed as a burnt offering.

76 He brought one male goat to be sacrificed as a sin offering.

77 He brought two oxen, five rams and five male goats. He also brought five male lambs a year old. All of them would be sacrificed as a friendship offering.

That was everything that Pagiel, the son of Okran, brought as his offering.

78 On the twelfth day Ahira, the son of Enan, brought his offering. Ahira was the leader of the people of Naphtali.

79 He brought:

one silver plate and one silver sprinkling bowl. The plate weighed three pounds four ounces. The sprinkling bowl weighed one pound 12 ounces. Both were weighed according to the standard weights used in the sacred tent. Each plate and bowl was filled with the finest flour mixed with olive oil. It was a grain offering.

80 He brought one gold dish that weighed four ounces. It was filled with incense.

81 Ahira brought one young bull, one ram, and one male lamb a year old. They would be sacrificed as a burnt offering.

82 He brought one male goat to be sacrificed as a sin offering.

83 He brought two oxen, five rams and five male goats. He also brought five male lambs a year old. All of them would be sacrificed as a friendship offering.

That was everything that Ahira, the son of Enan, brought as his offering.

84 Those were the offerings the Israelite leaders brought. They gave them to set the altar apart when it was anointed with olive oil.

They gave 12 silver plates, 12 silver sprinkling bowls and 12 gold dishes. 85 Each plate weighed three pounds four ounces. Each sprinkling bowl weighed one pound 12 ounces. The total weight of the silver dishes was 60 pounds. Everything was weighed according to the standard weights used in the sacred tent. 86 Each of the 12 gold dishes weighed four ounces. They were filled with incense. They were weighed according to the weights used in the sacred tent. The total weight of the gold dishes was three pounds.

87 The leaders brought 12 young bulls, 12 rams and 12 male lambs a year old. That was the total number of animals they gave for the burnt offering. They gave them together with the grain offering. They brought 12 male goats for the sin offering.

88 The leaders brought 24 oxen, 60 rams, 60 male goats and 60 male lambs a year old. That was the total number of animals sacrificed as the friendship offering.

Those were the offerings they brought to set apart the altar. The leaders brought them after the altar was anointed with oil.

89 Moses entered the tent of meeting. He wanted to speak with the Lord. There Moses heard the Lord talking to him. The Lord's voice was speaking to him from between the two cherubim. The cherubim were over the place where sin is paid for. It was the cover on the ark where the tablets of the covenant law were kept. In this way the Lord spoke to Moses.

Aaron Sets Up the Lamps

8 The Lord said to Moses, 2 "Say to Aaron, 'Set up the seven lamps. They will light up the area in front of the lampstand.'"

3 So Aaron did it. He set up the lamps so that they faced forward on the lampstand. He did just as the Lord had commanded Moses. 4 The lampstand was made out of hammered gold. From its base to its blooms it was made out of hammered gold. The lampstand was made exactly like the pattern the Lord had shown Moses.

Moses Sets Apart the Levites

5 The Lord spoke to Moses. He said, 6 "Take the Levites from among all the Israelites. Make them 'clean' in the usual way. 7 Here is how to make them pure. Sprinkle the special water on them. Then have them shave their whole bodies. Also have

them wash their clothes. That is how they will make themselves pure. ⁸Have them get a young bull along with its grain offering. The offering must be made out of the finest flour mixed with olive oil. Then you must get a second young bull. You must sacrifice it as a sin offering. ⁹Bring the Levites to the front of the tent of meeting. Gather the whole community of Israel together. ¹⁰You must bring the Levites to me. The Israelites must place their hands on them. ¹¹Aaron must bring the Levites to me. They are a wave offering from the Israelites. That is how they will be set apart to do my work.

¹²"Then I want the Levites to place their hands on the heads of the bulls. They must sacrifice one bull as a sin offering to me. And they must sacrifice the other as a burnt offering. The blood of the bulls will pay for the sin of the Levites. ¹³Have the Levites stand in front of Aaron and his sons. Then give them as a wave offering to me. ¹⁴That is how I want you to set apart the Levites from the other Israelites. The Levites will belong to me.

¹⁵"Make the Levites pure. Give them to me as a wave offering. Then they must come to do their work at the tent of meeting. ¹⁶They are the Israelites who will be given to me completely. I have taken them to be my own. I have taken them in place of every son born first in his family in Israel. ¹⁷Every male born first in Israel belongs to me. That is true whether it is a human or an animal. In Egypt I struck down all the males born first to their mothers. Then I set apart for myself all the males born first in Israel. ¹⁸And I have taken the Levites in place of all the sons born first in Israel. ¹⁹I have given the Levites as gifts to Aaron and his sons. I have taken them from among all the Israelites. I have appointed them to do the work at the tent of meeting. They will do it in place of the Israelites. That is how they will keep the Israelites from being guilty when they go near the sacred tent. Then no plague will strike the Israelites when they go near the tent."

²⁰So Moses and Aaron and all the Israelites did with the Levites just as the LORD had commanded Moses. ²¹The Levites made themselves pure. They washed their clothes. Then Aaron gave them to the LORD as a wave offering. That's how he paid for their sin to make them pure. ²²After that, the Levites came to do their work at the tent of meeting. They worked under the direction of Aaron and his sons. And so Moses and Aaron and the whole community of Israel did with the Levites just as the LORD had commanded Moses.

²³The LORD said to Moses, ²⁴"Here is what the Levites must do. Men 25 years old or more must come and take part in the work at the tent of meeting. ²⁵But when they reach the age of 50, they must not work any longer.

They must stop doing their regular work. ²⁶ They can help their brothers with their duties at the tent of meeting. But they themselves should not do the work. That is how you must direct the Levites to do their work."

Israel Celebrates the Passover Feast

9 The LORD spoke to Moses in the Desert of Sinai. It was the first month of the second year after the people came out of Egypt. He said, ² "Tell the Israelites to celebrate the Passover Feast. Have them do it at the appointed time. ³ Celebrate it when the sun goes down on the 14th day of this month. Obey all its rules and laws."

⁴ So Moses told the Israelites to celebrate the Passover Feast. ⁵ They did it in the Desert of Sinai. They celebrated it when the sun went down on the 14th day of the first month. The Israelites did everything just as the LORD had commanded Moses.

⁶ But some of them couldn't celebrate the Passover Feast on that day. That's because they weren't "clean." They had gone near a dead body. So they came to Moses and Aaron that same day. ⁷ They said to Moses, "We went near a dead body. So we aren't 'clean.' But why should we be kept from bringing the LORD's offering at the appointed time? Why shouldn't we bring it along with the other Israelites?"

⁸ Moses answered them, "Wait until I find out what the LORD wants you to do."

⁹ Then the LORD spoke to Moses. He said, ¹⁰ "Tell the Israelites, 'Suppose any of you or your children are "unclean" because they have gone near a dead body. Or suppose they are away on a journey. They must still celebrate the LORD's Passover. ¹¹ They must celebrate it on the 14th day of the second month. They must do so when the sun goes down. They must eat the lamb together with bread made without yeast. They must eat it with bitter plants. ¹² They must not leave any of it until morning. They must not break any of its bones. When they celebrate the Passover Feast, they must follow all the rules. ¹³ But suppose someone is "clean" and not on a journey. And they fail to celebrate the Passover Feast. Then they must be separated from the community of Israel. They did not bring the LORD's offering at the appointed time. They will be punished for their sin.

¹⁴ "'What if there is an outsider living among you? And what if they want to celebrate the LORD's Passover? Then they must obey its rules and laws. You must have the same laws for outsiders as you do for the Israelites.'"

The Cloud Covers the Holy Tent

¹⁵ The holy tent was set up. It was the tent where the tablets of the covenant law were kept. On the day it was set up, the cloud covered it. From evening until morning the cloud above the tent looked like fire. ¹⁶ That's

what continued to happen. The cloud covered the tent. At night the cloud looked like fire. ¹⁷ When the cloud lifted from its place above the tent, the Israelites started out. Where the cloud settled, the Israelites camped. ¹⁸ When the LORD gave the command, the Israelites started out. And when he gave the command, they camped. As long as the cloud stayed above the holy tent, they remained in camp. ¹⁹ Sometimes the cloud remained above the tent for a long time. Then the Israelites obeyed the LORD's order. They didn't start out. ²⁰ Sometimes the cloud was above the tent for only a few days. When the LORD would give the command, they would camp. And when he would give the command, they would start out. ²¹ Sometimes the cloud stayed only from evening until morning. When it lifted in the morning, they started out. It didn't matter whether it was day or night. When the cloud lifted, the people started out. ²² It didn't matter whether the cloud stayed above the holy tent for two days or a month or a year. The Israelites would remain in camp. They wouldn't start out. But when the cloud lifted, they would start out. ²³ When the LORD gave the command, they camped. And when he gave the command, they started out. They obeyed the LORD's order. They obeyed him, just as he had commanded them through Moses.

The Silver Trumpets

10 The LORD said to Moses, ² "Make two trumpets out of hammered silver. Blow them when you want the community to gather together. And blow them when you want the camps to start out. ³ When both trumpets are blown, the whole community must gather in front of you. They must come to the entrance to the tent of meeting. ⁴ Suppose only one trumpet is blown. Then the leaders must gather in front of you. They are the heads of the tribes of Israel. ⁵ When a trumpet blast is blown, the tribes camped on the east side must start out. ⁶ When the second blast is blown, the camps on the south side must start out. The blast will tell them when to start. ⁷ Blow the trumpets to gather the people together. But do not use the same kind of blast.

⁸ "The sons of Aaron, the priests, must blow the trumpets. That is a law for you and your children after you for all time to come. ⁹ Suppose you go into battle in your own land. And suppose it is against an enemy who is treating you badly. Then blow a blast on the trumpets. If you do, I will remember you. I will save you from your enemies. I am the LORD your God. ¹⁰ You must also blow the trumpets when you are happy. Blow them at your appointed feasts. Blow them at your New Moon feasts. Blow them when you sacrifice your burnt offerings. Blow them when you sacrifice

your friendship offerings. They will remind me of you. I am the LORD your God."

The Israelites Leave the Sinai Desert

[11] It was the 20th day of the second month of the second year. On that day the cloud began to move. It went up from above the holy tent where the tablets of the covenant law were kept. [12] Then the Israelites started out from the Desert of Sinai. They traveled from place to place. They kept going until the cloud came to rest in the Desert of Paran. [13] The first time they started out, the LORD commanded Moses to tell them to do it. And they did it.

[14] The groups of the camp of Judah went first. They marched out under their flag. Nahshon was their commander. He was the son of Amminadab. [15] Nethanel was over the group of the tribe of Issachar. Nethanel was the son of Zuar. [16] Eliab was over the group of the tribe of Zebulun. Eliab was the son of Helon. [17] The holy tent was taken down. The men of Gershon and Merari started out. They carried the tent.

[18] The groups of the camp of Reuben went next. They marched out under their flag. Elizur was their commander. He was the son of Shedeur. [19] Shelumiel was over the group of the tribe of Simeon. Shelumiel was the son of Zurishaddai. [20] Eliasaph was over the group of the tribe of Gad. Eliasaph was the son of Deuel. [21] The men of Kohath started out. They carried the holy things. The holy tent had to be set up before they arrived.

[22] The groups of the camp of Ephraim went next. They marched out under their flag. Elishama was their commander. He was the son of Ammihud. [23] Gamaliel was over the group of the tribe of Manasseh. Gamaliel was the son of Pedahzur. [24] Abidan was over the group of the tribe of Benjamin. Abidan was the son of Gideoni.

[25] Finally, the groups of the camp of Dan started out. They marched out under their flag. They followed behind all the other groups and guarded them. Ahiezer was their commander. He was the son of Ammishaddai. [26] Pagiel was over the group of the tribe of Asher. Pagiel was the son of Okran. [27] Ahira was over the group of the tribe of Naphtali. Ahira was the son of Enan. [28] As the groups of Israel started out, that was the order they marched in.

[29] Moses spoke to Hobab, the son of Reuel. Reuel was Moses' father-in-law. Reuel was from Midian. Moses said to Hobab, "We're starting out for the place the LORD promised to us. He said to us, 'I will give it to you.' So come with us. We'll treat you well. The LORD has promised to give good things to Israel."

[30] Hobab answered, "No. I can't go. I'm going back to my own land. I'm returning to my own people."

[31] But Moses said, "Please don't leave us. You know where we should camp in the desert. You can be our guide. [32] So come with us. The LORD will give us good things. We'll share them with you."

[33] So they started out from the mountain of the LORD. They traveled for three days. The ark of the covenant of the LORD went in front of them during those three days. It went ahead of them to find a place for them to rest. [34] They started out from the camp by day. And the cloud of the LORD was above them.

[35] When the ark started out, Moses said,

"LORD, rise up!
　Let your enemies be
　　scattered.
　Let them run away from
　　you."

[36] When the ark stopped, Moses said,

"LORD, return.
　Return to the many
　　thousands of people in
　　Israel."

The LORD Sends Fire Among the People

11 The people weren't happy about the hard times they were having. The LORD heard what they were saying. It made him very angry. Then the LORD sent fire on them. It blazed out among the people. It burned up some of the outer edges of the camp. [2] The people cried out to Moses. Then he prayed to the LORD. And the fire died down.

[3] So that place was named Taberah. That's because fire from the LORD had blazed out among them there.

The LORD Sends Quail for the People to Eat

[4] Some people with them began to wish for other food. Again the Israelites began to cry out. They said, "We wish we had meat to eat. [5] We remember the fish we ate in Egypt. It didn't cost us anything. We also remember the cucumbers, melons, leeks, onions and garlic. [6] But now we've lost all interest in eating. We never see anything but this manna!"

[7] The manna was like coriander seeds. It looked like sap from a tree. [8] The people went around gathering it. Then they ground it up in a small mill they held in their hands. Or they crushed it in a stone bowl. They cooked it in a pot. Or they made loaves out of it. It tasted like something made with olive oil. [9] When the dew came down on the camp at night, the manna also came down.

[10] Moses heard people from every family crying at the entrances to their tents. The LORD became very angry. So Moses became upset. [11] He asked the LORD, "Why have you brought this trouble on me? Why aren't you pleased with me? Why have you loaded me down with the troubles of all these people? [12] Am I like a mother to them? Are they my children? Why do you tell me to carry them in my

arms? Do I have to carry them the way a nurse carries a baby? Do I have to carry them to the land you promised? You promised the land to their people of long ago. ¹³ Where can I get meat for all these people? They keep crying out to me. They say, 'Give us meat to eat!' ¹⁴ I can't carry all these people by myself. The load is too heavy for me. ¹⁵ Is this how you are going to treat me? If you are pleased with me, just put me to death right now. Don't let me live if I have to see myself destroyed anyway."

¹⁶ The LORD said to Moses, "Bring me 70 of Israel's elders. Bring men that you know are leaders and officials among the people. Have them come to the tent of meeting. I want them to stand there with you. ¹⁷ I will come down and speak with you there. I will take some of the power of the Spirit that is on you. And I will put it on them. They will share the responsibility of these people with you. Then you will not have to carry it alone.

¹⁸ "Tell the people, 'Set yourselves apart for tomorrow. At that time you will eat meat. The LORD heard you when you cried out. You said, "We wish we had meat to eat. We were better off in Egypt. Now the LORD will give you meat. And you will eat it. ¹⁹ You will not eat it for just one or two days. You will not eat it for just five, ten or 20 days. ²⁰ Instead, you will eat it for a whole month. You will eat it until it comes out of your noses. You will eat it until you hate it. The

LORD is among you. But you have turned your back on him. You have cried out while he was listening. You have said, "Why did we ever leave Egypt?" ' "

²¹ But Moses said to the LORD, "Here I am among 600,000 men on the march. And you say, 'I will give them meat to eat for a whole month'! ²² Would they have enough if flocks and herds were killed for them? Would they have enough even if all the fish in the ocean were caught for them?"

²³ The LORD answered Moses, "Am I not strong enough? Now you will see whether what I say will come true for you."

²⁴ So Moses went out. He told the people what the LORD had said. He gathered 70 of their elders together. He had them stand around the tent of meeting. ²⁵ Then the LORD came down in the cloud. He spoke with Moses. He took some of the power of the Spirit that was on Moses. And he put it on the 70 elders. When the Spirit came on them, they prophesied. But they didn't do it again.

²⁶ Two men had remained in the camp. Their names were Eldad and Medad. They were listed among the elders. But they didn't go out to the tent of meeting. In spite of that, the Spirit came on them too. So they prophesied in the camp. ²⁷ A young man ran up to Moses. He said, "Eldad and Medad are prophesying in the camp."

²⁸ Joshua spoke up. He was the son of Nun. Joshua had been Moses' helper from the time he

was young. He said, "Moses! Please stop them!"

²⁹ But Moses replied, "Are you jealous for me? I wish that all the LORD's people were prophets. And I wish that the LORD would put his Spirit on them." ³⁰ Then Moses and the elders of Israel returned to the camp.

³¹ The LORD sent out a wind. It drove quail in from the Red Sea. It scattered them all around the camp. They were about three feet above the ground. They could be seen in every direction as far as a person could walk in a day. ³² The people went out all day and gathered quail. They gathered them all night and all the next day. No one gathered less than 60 bushels. Then they spread the quail out all around the camp. ³³ But while the meat was still in their mouths, the LORD acted. Before the people could swallow it, he became very angry with them. He struck them with a terrible plague. ³⁴ So the place was named Kibroth Hattaavah. That's where the bodies of the people who had wished for other food were buried.

³⁵ From Kibroth Hattaavah the people traveled to Hazeroth. And they stayed there.

Miriam and Aaron Speak Against Moses

12 Miriam and Aaron began to say bad things about Moses. That's because Moses had married a woman from Cush. ² "Has the LORD spoken only through Moses?" they asked. "Hasn't he also spoken through us?" The LORD heard what they said.

³ Moses was a very humble man. In fact, he was more humble than anyone else on the face of the earth.

⁴ The LORD spoke to Moses, Aaron and Miriam. He said, "All three of you, come out to the tent of meeting." So they did. ⁵ Then the LORD came down in a pillar of cloud. He stood at the entrance to the tent. And he told Aaron and Miriam to come to him. The two of them stepped forward. ⁶ Then the LORD said, "Listen to my words.

"Suppose there is a prophet
    among you.
I, the LORD, make myself
    known to them in visions.
I speak to them in dreams.
⁷ But this is not true of my
    servant Moses.
He is faithful in everything
    he does in my house.
⁸ With Moses I speak face to face.
I speak with him clearly. I
    do not speak in riddles.
I let him see something of
    what I look like.
So why were you not afraid
    to speak against my
        servant Moses?"

⁹ The LORD was very angry with them. And he left them.

¹⁰ When the cloud went up from above the tent, there stood Miriam. She had a disease that made her skin as white as snow. Aaron turned toward her. He saw that she had a skin disease. ¹¹ So he said to Moses, "We have committed a very foolish sin.

Please don't hold it against us. [12] Don't let Miriam be like a baby that was born dead. Don't let her look like a dead baby whose body is half eaten away."

[13] So Moses cried out to the LORD. He said, "Please, God, heal her!"

[14] The LORD answered Moses. He said, "Suppose her father had spit in her face. Then she would have been put to shame for seven days. So keep her outside the camp for seven days. After that, you can bring her back." [15] So Miriam was kept outside the camp for seven days. The people didn't move on until she was brought back.

[16] After that, the people left Hazeroth. They camped in the Desert of Paran.

Twelve Men Check Out the Land of Canaan

13 The LORD said to Moses, [2] "Send some men to check out the land of Canaan. I am giving it to the Israelites. Send one leader from each of Israel's tribes."

[3] So Moses sent them out from the Desert of Paran. He sent them as the LORD had commanded. All of them were leaders of the Israelites.

[4] Here are their names.

There was Shammua from the tribe of Reuben. Shammua was the son of Zakkur.
[5] There was Shaphat from the tribe of Simeon. Shaphat was the son of Hori.

[6] There was Caleb from the tribe of Judah. Caleb was the son of Jephunneh.
[7] There was Igal from the tribe of Issachar. Igal was the son of Joseph.
[8] There was Hoshea from the tribe of Ephraim. Hoshea was the son of Nun.
[9] There was Palti from the tribe of Benjamin. Palti was the son of Raphu.
[10] There was Gaddiel from the tribe of Zebulun. Gaddiel was the son of Sodi.
[11] There was Gaddi from the tribe of Manasseh. Gaddi was the son of Susi. Manasseh was a tribe of Joseph.
[12] There was Ammiel from the tribe of Dan. Ammiel was the son of Gemalli.
[13] There was Sethur from the tribe of Asher. Sethur was the son of Michael.
[14] There was Nahbi from the tribe of Naphtali. Nahbi was the son of Vophsi.
[15] There was Geuel from the tribe of Gad. Geuel was the son of Maki.

[16] Those are the men Moses sent to check out the land. He gave the name Joshua to Hoshea, the son of Nun.

[17] Moses sent the 12 men to check out Canaan. He said, "Go up through the Negev Desert. Go on into the central hill country. [18] See what the land is like. See whether the people who live there are strong or weak. See whether they are few or many.

¹⁹ What kind of land do they live in? Is it good or bad? What kind of towns do they live in? Do the towns have high walls around them or not? ²⁰ How is the soil? Is it rich land or poor land? Are there trees in it or not? Do your best to bring back some of the fruit of the land." It was the season for the first ripe grapes.

²¹ So the men went up and checked out the land. They went from the Desert of Zin as far as Rehob. It was in the direction of Lebo Hamath. ²² They went up through the Negev Desert and came to Hebron. That's where Ahiman, Sheshai and Talmai lived. They belonged to the family line of Anak. Hebron had been built seven years before Zoan. Zoan was a city in Egypt. ²³ The men came to the Valley of Eshkol. There they cut off a branch that had a single bunch of grapes on it. Two of them carried it on a pole between them. They carried some pomegranates and figs along with it. ²⁴ That place was called the Valley of Eshkol. That's because the men of Israel cut off a bunch of grapes there. ²⁵ At the end of 40 days, the men returned from checking out the land.

The Men Report on What They Found

²⁶ The men came back to Moses, Aaron and the whole community of Israel. The people were at Kadesh in the Desert of Paran. There the men reported to Moses and Aaron and all the people. They showed them the fruit of the land. ²⁷ They gave Moses their report. They said, "We went into the land you sent us to. It really does have plenty of milk and honey! Here's some fruit from the land. ²⁸ But the people who live there are powerful. Their cities have high walls around them and are very large. We even saw members of the family line of Anak there. ²⁹ The Amalekites live in the Negev Desert. The Hittites, Jebusites and Amorites live in the central hill country. The Canaanites live near the Mediterranean Sea. They also live along the Jordan River."

³⁰ Then Caleb interrupted the men speaking to Moses. He said, "We should go up and take the land. We can certainly do it."

³¹ But the men who had gone up with him spoke. They said, "We can't attack those people. They are stronger than we are." ³² The men spread a bad report about the land among the Israelites. They said, "The land we checked out destroys those who live in it. All the people we saw there are very big and tall. ³³ We saw the Nephilim there. We seemed like grasshoppers in our own eyes. And that's also how we seemed to them." The family line of Anak came from the Nephilim.

The People Refuse to Obey the LORD

14 That night all the members of the community raised their voices. They wept out loud. ² The Israelites spoke against Moses and Aaron. The whole community said to them, "We wish we had died in Egypt or even in this desert. ³Why is the LORD bringing us to this land? We're going to be killed by swords. Our enemies will capture our wives and children. Wouldn't it be better for us to go back to Egypt?" ⁴They said to one another, "We should choose another leader. We should go back to Egypt."

⁵Then Moses and Aaron fell with their faces to the ground. They did it in front of the whole community of Israel gathered there. ⁶Joshua, the son of Nun, tore his clothes. So did Caleb, the son of Jephunneh. Joshua and Caleb were two of the men who had checked out the land. ⁷They spoke to the whole community of Israel. They said, "We passed through the land and checked it out. It's very good. ⁸If the LORD is pleased with us, he'll lead us into that land. It's a land that has plenty of milk and honey. He'll give it to us. ⁹But don't refuse to obey him. And don't be afraid of the people of the land. We will swallow them up. The LORD is with us. So nothing can save them. Don't be afraid of them."

¹⁰But all the people talked about killing Joshua and Caleb by throwing stones at them. Then the glory of the LORD appeared at the tent of meeting. All the Israelites saw it. ¹¹The LORD said to Moses, "How long will these people not respect me? How long will they refuse to believe in me? They refuse even though I have done many signs among them. ¹²So I will strike them down with a plague. I will destroy them. But I will make you into a greater and stronger nation than they are."

¹³Moses said to the LORD, "Then the Egyptians will hear about it. You used your power to bring these people up from among them. ¹⁴And the Egyptians will tell the people who live in Canaan about it. LORD, they have already heard a lot about you. They've heard that you are with these people. They've heard that you have been seen face to face. They've been told that your cloud stays over them. They've heard that you go in front of them in a pillar of cloud by day. They've been told that you go in front of them in a pillar of fire at night. ¹⁵Suppose you put all these people to death and leave none alive. Then the nations who have heard these things about you will talk. They'll say, ¹⁶'The LORD promised to give these people the land of Canaan. But he wasn't able to bring them into it. So he killed them in the desert.'

¹⁷"Now, Lord, show your strength. You have said, ¹⁸'I am the LORD. I am slow to get angry. I am full of love. I forgive those who sin. I forgive those who refuse to obey. But I do not let guilty people go without punishing them. I cause the sin of the parents to affect their children, grandchildren and

great-grandchildren.' ¹⁹ LORD, your love is great. So forgive the sin of these people. Forgive them just as you have done from the time they left Egypt until now."

²⁰ The LORD replied, "I have forgiven them, just as you asked. ²¹ You can be sure that I live. You can be just as sure that my glory fills the whole earth. ²² And here is what you can be just as sure of. Not one of these people will see the land I promised to give them. They have seen my glory. They have seen the signs I did in Egypt. And they have seen what I did in the desert. But they did not obey me. And they have tested me ten times. ²³ So not even one of them will ever see the land I promised to give to their people of long ago. The person who has not respected me will never see it. ²⁴ But my servant Caleb has a different spirit. He follows me with his whole heart. So I will bring him into the land he went to. And his children after him will receive land there. ²⁵ The Amalekites and the Canaanites are living in the valleys. So turn back tomorrow. Start out toward the desert. Go along the way that leads to the Red Sea."

²⁶ The LORD said to Moses and Aaron, ²⁷ "How long will this evil community speak against me? I have heard these Israelites talk about how unhappy they are. ²⁸ So tell them, 'Here is what I am announcing. I am the LORD. You can be sure that I live. And here is what you can be just as sure of. I will do to you the very thing that I heard you say. ²⁹ You will die in this desert. Every one of you 20 years old or more will die. Every one of you who was counted in the list of the people will die. Every one of you who has spoken out against me will be wiped out. ³⁰ I lifted up my hand and promised to make this land your home. But now not all of you will enter the land. Caleb, the son of Jephunneh, will enter it. So will Joshua, the son of Nun. They are the only ones who will enter the land. ³¹ You have said that your enemies would capture your children. But I will bring your children in to enjoy the land you have turned your backs on. ³² As for you, you will die in the desert. ³³ Your children will be shepherds here for 40 years. They will suffer because you were not faithful. They will suffer until the last of your bodies lies here in the desert. ³⁴ For 40 years you will suffer for your sins. That is one year for each of the 40 days you checked out the land. You will know what it is like to have me against you.' ³⁵ I, the LORD, have spoken. I will surely do these things to this entire evil community of Israel. They have joined together against me. They will meet their end in this desert. They will die here."

³⁶ So the LORD struck down the men Moses had sent to check out the land. They had returned and had spread a bad report about the land. And that had made the whole

community speak out against Moses. ³⁷Those men were to blame for spreading the bad report. So the LORD struck them down. They died of a plague. ³⁸Only two of the men who went to check out the land remained alive. One of them was Joshua, the son of Nun. The other was Caleb, the son of Jephunneh.

³⁹Moses reported to all the Israelites what the LORD had said. And they became very sad. ⁴⁰Early the next morning they set out for the highest point in the hill country. "We have sinned," they said. "Now we are ready to go up to the land the LORD promised to give us."

⁴¹But Moses said, "Why aren't you obeying the LORD's command? You won't succeed. ⁴²So don't go up. The LORD isn't with you. Your enemies will win the battle over you. ⁴³The Amalekites and the Canaanites will meet you on the field of battle. You have turned away from the LORD. So he won't be with you. And you will be killed by swords."

⁴⁴But they wouldn't listen. They still went up toward the highest point in the hill country. They went up even though Moses didn't move from the camp. They went even though the ark of the LORD's covenant didn't move from the camp. ⁴⁵Then the Amalekites and the Canaanites who lived in that hill country came down. They attacked the Israelites. They won the battle over them. They chased the Israelites all the way to Hormah.

Other Offerings

15 Here is what the LORD said to Moses. ²"Say to the Israelites, 'You are going to enter the land I am giving you as a home. ³When you do, you will present food offerings to the LORD. The animals must come from your herd or flock. The smell of the offerings will please the LORD. They can be either burnt offerings or sacrifices. They can be either for special promises or for feast offerings. Or they can be for offerings you choose to give. ⁴With each of the offerings, the person who brings it must present to the LORD a grain offering. It must be eight cups of the finest flour. It must be mixed with a quart of olive oil. ⁵Also prepare a quart of wine as a drink offering. You must present it with each lamb that you bring for the burnt offering or the sacrifice.

⁶"'Prepare a grain offering to present along with a ram. The grain offering must be 16 cups of the finest flour. It must be mixed with two and a half pints of olive oil. ⁷You must bring two and a half pints of wine as a drink offering. Offer everything as a smell that pleases the LORD.

⁸"'Suppose you prepare a young bull as a burnt offering or sacrifice. You prepare it to keep a special promise to the LORD. Or you prepare it to present as a friendship offering. ⁹Then bring a grain offering with the bull. The grain offering must be 24 cups of the finest flour. It must be mixed with two quarts of ol-

ive oil. ¹⁰Also bring two quarts of wine as a drink offering. It will be a food offering. Its smell will please the LORD. ¹¹Each bull or ram must be prepared in the same way. Each lamb or young goat must also be prepared in that way. ¹²Do it for each animal. Do it for as many animals as you prepare.

¹³ "'Everyone in Israel must do those things in that way. He must do them when he presents a food offering. The smell of offerings like that pleases the LORD. ¹⁴Everyone must always do what the law requires. It does not matter whether they are an outsider or anyone else living among you. They must do exactly as you do when they present a food offering. The smell of offerings like that pleases the LORD. ¹⁵The community must have the same rules for you and for any outsider living among you. This law will last for all time to come. In the sight of the LORD, the law applies both to you and any outsider. ¹⁶The same laws and rules will apply to you and to any outsider living among you.'"

¹⁷The LORD said to Moses, ¹⁸"Speak to the Israelites. Say to them, 'You are going to enter the land I am taking you to. ¹⁹You will eat its food. When you do, present part of it as an offering to the LORD. ²⁰Present a loaf made from the first flour you grind. Present it as an offering from the threshing floor. ²¹You must present the offering to the LORD. You must present it from the first grain you grind. You must do it for all time to come.

Offerings for Sins That Aren't Committed on Purpose

²² "'Suppose you as a community fail to keep any of the commands the LORD gave Moses. And suppose you do it without meaning to. ²³That applies to any of the commands the LORD told Moses to give you. And they are in effect from the day the LORD gave them and for all time to come. ²⁴Suppose the community sins without meaning to. And suppose they do not know they have sinned. Then the whole community must offer a young bull. They must sacrifice it for a burnt offering. Its smell will please the LORD. Along with it, they must offer its required grain offering and drink offering. They must also sacrifice a male goat for a sin offering. ²⁵With it the priest will pay for the sin of the whole community of Israel. Then they will be forgiven. They did not mean to commit that sin. And they have presented to the LORD a food offering for the wrong thing they did. They have brought a sin offering with it. ²⁶The LORD will forgive the whole community of Israel and the outsiders living among them. All the people had a part in the sin, even though they did not mean to do it.

²⁷ "'But suppose just one person sins without meaning to. Then that person must bring a female goat for a sin offering. It must be a year old. ²⁸With it

the priest will pay for the person's sin in front of the LORD. The priest will do it for the one who did wrong by sinning without meaning to. When the sin is paid for, that person will be forgiven. ²⁹ The same law applies to everyone who sins without meaning to. It does not matter whether they are an Israelite or an outsider.

³⁰ " 'But suppose someone sins on purpose. It does not matter whether they are an Israelite or an outsider. They speak evil things against the LORD. They must be separated from the community of Israel. ³¹ They have not respected what the LORD has said. They have broken the LORD's commands. They must certainly be separated from the community. They are still guilty.' "

A Man Works on the Sabbath Day

³² The Israelites were in the desert. One Sabbath day, people saw a man gathering wood. ³³ They brought him to Moses and Aaron and the whole community. ³⁴ They kept him under guard. It wasn't clear what should be done to him. ³⁵ Then the LORD said to Moses, "The man must die. The whole community must kill him by throwing stones at him. They must do it outside the camp." ³⁶ So the people took the man outside the camp. There they killed him by throwing stones at him. They did just as the LORD had commanded Moses.

Tassels on Clothes

³⁷ The LORD said to Moses, ³⁸ "Say to the Israelites, 'You must make tassels on the corners of your clothes. A blue cord must be on each tassel. You must do it for all time to come. ³⁹ You will have the tassels to look at. They will remind you to obey all the LORD's commands. Then you will be faithful to him. You will not chase after what your own hearts and eyes wish for. ⁴⁰ You will remember to obey all my commands. And you will be set apart for your God. ⁴¹ I am the LORD your God. I brought you out of Egypt to be your God. I am the LORD your God.' "

Korah, Dathan and Abiram

16 Korah was the son of Izhar, the son of Kohath. Kohath was the son of Levi. Korah and certain men from the tribe of Reuben turned against Moses. The men from Reuben were Dathan, Abiram and On. Dathan and Abiram were the sons of Eliab. On was the son of Peleth. ² All those men rose up against Moses. And 250 men of Israel joined them. All of them were known as leaders in the community. They had been appointed as members of the ruling body. ³ They came as a group to oppose Moses and Aaron. They said to Moses and Aaron, "You have gone too far! The whole community is holy. Every one in it is holy. And the LORD is with them. So why do you put yourselves above the LORD's people?"

⁴When Moses heard what they said, he fell with his face to the ground. ⁵Then he spoke to Korah and all his followers. He said, "In the morning the LORD will show who belongs to him. He will show who is holy. He'll bring that person near him. He'll bring the man he chooses near him. ⁶Korah, here's what you and all your followers must do. Get some shallow cups for burning incense. ⁷Tomorrow put burning coals and incense in them. Offer it to the LORD. The man the LORD chooses will be the one who is holy. You Levites have gone too far!"

⁸Moses also said to Korah, "Listen, you Levites! ⁹The God of Israel has separated you from the rest of the community of Israel. He has brought you near him to work at the LORD's holy tent. He has given you to the people so that you can serve them. Isn't all that enough for you? ¹⁰He has already brought you and all the other Levites near him. But now you want to be priests too. ¹¹You and all your followers have joined together against the LORD. Why are you telling Aaron you aren't happy with him?"

¹²Then Moses sent for Dathan and Abiram, the sons of Eliab. But they said, "We won't come! ¹³You have brought us up out of a land that has plenty of milk and honey. You have brought us here to kill us in this desert. Isn't that enough? Now do you also want to act as if you were ruling over us? ¹⁴Besides, you haven't brought us into a land that has plenty of milk and honey. You haven't given us fields and vineyards of our own. Do you want to treat these men like slaves? No! We won't come!"

¹⁵Then Moses became very angry. He said to the LORD, "Don't accept their offering. I haven't taken even a donkey from them. In fact, I haven't done anything wrong to any of them."

¹⁶Moses said to Korah, "You and all your followers must stand in front of the LORD tomorrow. You must appear there along with Aaron. ¹⁷Each man must get his shallow cup. He must put incense in it. There will be a total of 250 incense cups. Each man must bring his cup to the LORD. You and Aaron must also bring your cups." ¹⁸So each of them got his cup. He put burning coals and incense in it. All the men came with Moses and Aaron. They stood at the entrance to the tent of meeting. ¹⁹Korah gathered all his followers together at the entrance to the tent. They opposed Moses and Aaron. Then the glory of the LORD appeared to the whole community. ²⁰The LORD said to Moses and Aaron, ²¹"Separate yourselves from these people. Then I can put an end to all of them at once."

²²But Moses and Aaron fell with their faces to the ground. They cried out, "God, you are the God who gives life and breath to all living things. Will you be angry with the whole community when only one man sins?"

²³ Then the LORD spoke to Moses. He said, ²⁴ "Tell the community, 'Move away from the tents of Korah, Dathan and Abiram.'"

²⁵ Moses got up. He went to Dathan and Abiram. The elders of Israel followed him. ²⁶ Moses warned the community. He said, "Move away from the tents of these evil men! Don't touch anything that belongs to them. If you do, the LORD will sweep you away because of all their sins." ²⁷ So they moved away from the tents of Korah, Dathan and Abiram. Dathan and Abiram had already come out. They were standing at the entrances to their tents. Their wives, children and little ones were standing there with them.

²⁸ Then Moses said, "What is about to happen wasn't my idea. The LORD has sent me to do everything I'm doing. Here is how you will know I'm telling you the truth. ²⁹ These men won't die a natural death. Something will happen to them that doesn't usually happen to people. If what I'm telling you doesn't happen, then you will know that the LORD hasn't sent me. ³⁰ But the LORD will make something totally new happen. The ground will open its mouth and swallow them up. It will swallow up everything that belongs to them. They will be buried alive. When that happens, you will know that these men have disrespected the LORD."

³¹ As soon as Moses finished saying all these words, what he had said came true. The ground under them broke open. ³² It opened its mouth. It swallowed up those men. In fact, it swallowed up everyone who lived in their houses. It swallowed all Korah's men. And it swallowed up everything they owned. ³³ They went down into the grave alive. Everything they owned went down with them. The ground closed over them and they died. And so they disappeared from the community. ³⁴ All the Israelites around them heard their cries. They ran away from them. They shouted, "The ground is going to swallow us up too!"

³⁵ Then the LORD sent down fire. It burned up the 250 men offering the incense.

³⁶ The LORD said to Moses, ³⁷ "Speak to Eleazar the priest. He is the son of Aaron. Remind him that the shallow cups are holy. He must take them out of the ashes. He must scatter the burning coals away from there. ³⁸ The men who sinned used those cups. And it cost them their lives. Hammer the cups into bronze sheets that will cover the altar. The cups were offered to the LORD. They have become holy. Let them serve as a warning to the Israelites."

³⁹ So the priest Eleazar collected the bronze incense cups. They had been brought by the men who had been burned to death. He had them hammered out to cover the altar. ⁴⁰ He did just as the LORD had directed Moses to tell him to do. The covering would be a reminder to

the Israelites. It would remind them that no one except a son of Aaron should come and burn incense to the LORD. If people other than priests did that, they would become like Korah and his followers.

⁴¹ The next day the whole community of Israel told Moses and Aaron they weren't happy with them. "You have killed the LORD's people," they said.

⁴² The community gathered together to oppose Moses and Aaron. The people walked toward the tent of meeting. Suddenly the cloud covered it. The glory of the LORD appeared. ⁴³ Then Moses and Aaron went to the front of the tent of meeting. ⁴⁴ The LORD said to Moses, ⁴⁵ "Get away from these people. Then I can put an end to all of them at once." And Moses and Aaron fell with their faces to the ground.

⁴⁶ Moses said to Aaron, "Take your incense cup. Put incense in it. And put burning coals from the altar in it. Then hurry to the people and pay for their sin. The LORD has begun to show his anger. The plague has started." ⁴⁷ So Aaron did as Moses said. He ran in among the people. The plague had already started among them. But Aaron offered the incense and paid for their sin. ⁴⁸ He stood between those alive and those dead. And the plague stopped. ⁴⁹ But 14,700 people died from the plague. That doesn't include those who had died because of what Korah did. ⁵⁰ Then Aaron returned to Moses at the entrance to the tent of meeting. The plague had stopped.

Aaron's Walking Stick Produces Buds

17 The LORD said to Moses, ² "Speak to the Israelites. Get 12 walking sticks from them. Get one from the leader of each of Israel's tribes. Write the name of each man on his walking stick. ³ Write Aaron's name on Levi's walking stick. There must be one stick for the head of each of Israel's tribes. ⁴ Put the walking sticks in the tent of meeting. Place them in front of the ark where the tablets of the covenant law are kept. That is where I meet with you. ⁵ The walking stick that belongs to the man I choose will begin to grow new shoots. The Israelites are never happy with what you do. I will put an end to what they are saying."

⁶ So Moses spoke to the Israelites. Their leaders gave him 12 walking sticks. They gave one for the leader of each of Israel's tribes. Aaron's walking stick was among them. ⁷ Moses put the sticks in front of the LORD in the tent where the tablets of the covenant law were kept.

⁸ The next day Moses entered the tent. He looked at Aaron's walking stick. It stood for the tribe of Levi. Moses saw that it had begun to grow new shoots. It had also produced buds and flowers and almonds. ⁹ Then Moses brought out all the walking sticks from in front of the

Lord. He brought them to all the Israelites. They looked at them. And each man took his own walking stick.

¹⁰ The Lord said to Moses, "Put Aaron's walking stick back in front of the ark where the tablets of the covenant law are kept. The stick will be kept there as a warning to those who refuse to obey. They are never happy with what I do. Aaron's walking stick will put an end to what they are saying. Then they will not die." ¹¹ Moses did just as the Lord commanded him.

¹² The Israelites said to Moses, "We'll die! We are lost! All of us are lost! ¹³ Anyone who even comes near the Lord's holy tent will die. Are all of us going to die?"

Duties of Priests and Levites

18 The Lord spoke to Aaron. He said, "You, your sons and your family are in charge of the sacred tent. You will be responsible for sins connected with the tent. And you and your sons alone will be responsible for sins connected with the office of priest. ² Bring the Levites from your tribe to join you. They will help you when you and your sons serve at the tent of meeting. That is where the tablets of the covenant law are kept. ³ The Levites will work for you. They must do everything that needs to be done at the tent. But they must not go near anything that belongs to the sacred tent. And they must not go near the altar. If they do, they and you will die.

⁴ They will help you take care of the tent of meeting. They will join you in all the work at the tent. No one else can come near you there.

⁵ "You will be responsible for taking care of the sacred tent and the altar. Then I will not be angry with the Israelites again. ⁶ I myself have chosen the Levites. I have chosen them from among the Israelites. They are a gift to you. I have set them apart to do the work at the tent of meeting. ⁷ But only you and your sons can serve as priests. Only you and your sons can work with everything at the altar and behind the curtain. I am letting you serve as priests. It is a gift from me. Anyone else who comes near the sacred tent must be put to death."

Offerings for Priests and Levites

⁸ Then the Lord spoke to Aaron. He said, "I have put you in charge of the offerings brought to me. The Israelites will give me holy offerings. I will give all their offerings to you and your sons. They are the part that belongs to you. They are your share for all time to come. ⁹ You will have a part of the very holy offerings. It is the part not burned in the fire. That part belongs to you and your sons. You will have a part of all the gifts the people bring me as very holy offerings. It does not matter whether they are grain offerings or sin offerings or guilt offerings. ¹⁰ Eat your part as something that is very holy.

Every male will eat it. You must consider it holy.

11 "Part of the gifts the Israelites bring as wave offerings will be set aside. That part will also belong to you. I will give it to you and your sons and daughters. It is your share for all time to come. Everyone in your home who is 'clean' can eat it.

12 "I will give you all the finest olive oil and grain the people give me. And I will give you all the finest fresh wine they give me. They give all those things as the first share of their harvest. 13 All the first shares of the harvest they bring me will belong to you. Everyone in your home who is 'clean' can eat it.

14 "Everything in Israel that is set apart to me belongs to you. 15 Offer to me every male born first to its mother. It belongs to you. That includes humans and animals alike. But you must buy back every oldest son. Suppose certain animals are 'unclean.' Then you must buy back every male born first to its mother. 16 When they are a month old, you must buy them back. You must pay the price to buy them back. The price is set at two ounces of silver. It must be weighed out according to the standard weights used in the sacred tent.

17 "But you must not buy back any male calf, sheep or goat born first. They are holy. Splash their blood against the altar. And burn their fat as a food offering. Its smell pleases me. 18 The meat will belong to you.

It is just like the breast and the right thigh of the wave offering. Those parts belong to you. 19 Part of the holy offerings the Israelites bring to me will be set aside. No matter what it is, I will give it to you and your sons and daughters. It is your share for all time to come. It is a covenant of salt from me. The salt means that the covenant will last for all time to come for you and your children."

20 The LORD spoke to Aaron. He said, "You will not receive any part of the land I am giving to Israel. You will not have any share among them. I am your share. I am what you will receive among the Israelites.

21 "The Israelites will give me a tenth of everything they produce. And I will give it to the Levites. They serve at the tent of meeting. I will give them the tenth for the work they do there. 22 From now on the Israelites must not go near the tent of meeting. If they do, they will be punished for their sin. They will die. 23 The Levites will do the work at the tent of meeting. They will be responsible for any sins connected with the tent. This is a law that will last for all time to come. The Levites will not receive any share among the Israelites. 24 Instead, I will give the Levites the tenth as their share. It is the tenth that the Israelites bring me as an offering. That is why I said the Levites would not have any share of land among the Israelites."

25 The LORD said to Moses,

26 "Speak to the Levites. Say to them, 'You will receive the tenth from the Israelites. I will give it to you as your share. When I do, you must give a tenth of that tenth as an offering to the LORD. 27 Your offering will be considered as if you gave grain from a threshing floor. It will be considered as juice from a winepress. 28 In that way, you also will bring an offering to the LORD. You will bring it from the tenth you receive from the Israelites. You must give the LORD's part to the priest Aaron. You must bring it from the tenth you receive. 29 You must bring to the LORD a part of everything given to you. It must be the best and holiest part.'

30 "Say to the Levites, 'You must bring the best part. Then it will be considered as if you gave grain from a threshing floor. It will be considered as juice from a winepress. 31 You and your families can eat the rest of it anywhere. It is your pay for your work at the tent of meeting. 32 Bring the best part of what you receive. Then you will not be guilty of holding anything back. You will not make the holy offerings of the Israelites "unclean." You will not die.' "

The Special Water That Makes People "Clean"

19 The LORD spoke to Moses and Aaron. He said, 2 "Here is what the law I have commanded requires. Tell the Israelites to bring you a young red cow. It must not have any flaws at all. It must never have pulled a load. 3 Give it to Eleazar the priest. It must be taken outside the camp and killed in front of him. 4 Then Eleazar the priest must put some of its blood on his finger. He must sprinkle the blood toward the front of the tent of meeting. He must do it seven times. 5 While he watches, the young cow must be burned. Its hide, meat, blood and guts must be burned. 6 The priest must get some cedar wood, branches of a hyssop plant, and bright red wool. He must throw them on the young cow as it burns. 7 After that, the priest must wash his clothes. He must also take a bath. Then he can come into the camp. But he will be 'unclean' until evening. 8 The man who burns the young cow must wash his clothes. He must also take a bath. He too will be 'unclean' until evening. 9 "A man who is 'clean' will gather up the ashes of the young cow. He must put them in a place that is 'clean.' The place must be outside the camp. The ashes must be kept by the community of Israel. They will be added to the special water. The water will be used to make people pure from their sin. 10 The man who gathers up the ashes of the young cow must wash his clothes. He too will be 'unclean' until evening. This law is for the Israelites. It is also for the outsiders living among them. The law will last for all time to come. 11 "Anyone who touches a dead person's body will be 'un-

Joseph and His Beautiful Robe
GENESIS 37:1–4

Baby Moses in a Basket
EXODUS 2:1–10

clean' for seven days. ¹²They must make themselves pure and 'clean' with the special water. They must do it on the third day. They must also do it on the seventh day. Then they will be 'clean.' But suppose they do not make themselves pure and 'clean' on the third and seventh days. Then they will not be 'clean.' ¹³Anyone who touches a dead person's body and does not make themselves pure and 'clean' makes my holy tent 'unclean.' They must be separated from Israel. The special water has not been sprinkled on them. So they are 'unclean.' And they remain 'unclean.'

¹⁴"Here is the law that applies when a person dies in a tent. Anyone who enters the tent will be 'unclean' for seven days. Anyone in the tent will also be 'unclean' for seven days. ¹⁵And anything in it that is open and has no lid will be 'unclean.'

¹⁶"Suppose someone is out in the country. And suppose they touch someone who has been killed by a sword. Or they touch someone who has died a natural death. Or they touch a human bone or a grave. Then anyone who touches any of those things will be 'unclean' for seven days.

¹⁷"Here is what I want you to do for someone who is 'unclean.' Put some ashes from the burned young cow into a jar. Pour fresh water on the ashes. ¹⁸Then a man who is 'clean' must dip branches of a hyssop plant in the water. He must sprinkle the tent with it. Everything that belongs to the tent must be sprinkled with it. The people in the tent must also be sprinkled. Anyone who has touched a human bone or a grave must be sprinkled. So must anyone who has touched someone who has been killed. And so must anyone who has touched someone who has died a natural death. ¹⁹The man who is 'clean' must sprinkle those who are 'unclean.' That must be done on the third and seventh days. On the seventh day those who are 'unclean' must be made pure and 'clean.' Those being made 'clean' must wash their clothes. They must take a bath. Then that evening they will be 'clean.' ²⁰But what if those who are 'unclean' do not make themselves pure and 'clean?' Then they must be separated from the community. They have made my holy tent 'unclean.' The special water has not been sprinkled on them. They are 'unclean.' ²¹This law will apply to all those people for all time to come.

"The man who sprinkles the special water must also wash his clothes. Anyone who touches the water will be 'unclean' until evening. ²²Anything that an 'unclean' person touches becomes 'unclean.' And anyone who touches it becomes 'unclean' until evening."

The Lord Gives Israel Water Out of the Rock

20 In the first month the whole community of Israel arrived at the Desert of Zin.

They stayed at Kadesh. Miriam died and was buried there.

2 The people didn't have any water. So they gathered together to oppose Moses and Aaron. 3 They argued with Moses. They said, "We wish we had died when our people fell dead in front of the LORD. 4 Why did you bring the LORD's people into this desert? We and our livestock will die here. 5 Why did you bring us up out of Egypt? Why did you bring us to this terrible place? It doesn't have any grain or figs. It doesn't have any grapes or pomegranates. There isn't even any water for us to drink!"

6 Moses and Aaron left the people. They went to the entrance to the tent of meeting. There they fell with their faces to the ground. Then the glory of the LORD appeared to them. 7 The LORD said to Moses, 8 "Get your walking stick. You and your brother Aaron gather the people together. Then speak to that rock while everyone is watching. It will pour out its water. You will bring water out of the rock for the community. Then they and their livestock can drink it."

9 So Moses took the walking stick from the tent. He did just as the LORD had commanded him. 10 He and Aaron gathered the people together in front of the rock. Moses said to them, "Listen, you who refuse to obey! Do we have to bring water out of this rock for you?" 11 Then Moses raised his arm. He hit the rock twice with his walking stick. Water poured out. And the people and their livestock drank it.

12 But the LORD spoke to Moses and Aaron. He said, "You did not trust in me enough to honor me. You did not honor me as the holy God in front of the Israelites. So you will not bring this community into the land I am giving them."

13 Those were the waters of Meribah. That's where the Israelites argued with the LORD. And that's where he was proven to be holy among them.

Edom Doesn't Let Israel Pass Through Its Territory

14 Moses sent messengers from Kadesh to the king of Edom. The messengers said,

"The nation of Israel is your brother. They say, 'You know about all the hard times we've had. 15 Long ago our people went down into Egypt. We lived there for many years. The Egyptians treated us and our people badly. 16 But we cried out to the LORD. He heard our cry. He sent an angel and brought us out of Egypt.

" 'Now here we are at the town of Kadesh. It's on the edge of your territory. 17 Please let us pass through your country. We won't go through any field or vineyard. We won't drink water from any well. We'll travel along the King's Highway. We won't turn to the right or the left. We'll just go straight through your territory.' "

18 But the people of Edom answered,

"We won't let you pass through here. If you try to, we'll march out against you. We'll attack you with our swords."

19 The Israelites replied,

"We'll go along the main road. We and our livestock won't drink any of your water. If we do, we'll pay for it. We only want to walk through your country. That's all we ask."

20 Again the people of Edom answered,

"We won't let you pass through here."

Then the people of Edom marched out against them. They came with a large and powerful army. 21 Edom refused to let Israel go through their territory. So Israel turned away from them.

Aaron Dies

22 The whole community of Israel started out from Kadesh. They arrived at Mount Hor. 23 It was near the border of Edom. There the LORD spoke to Moses and Aaron. He said, 24 "Aaron will join the members of his family who have already died. He will not enter the land I am giving to the Israelites. Both of you refused to obey my command. You did it at the waters of Meribah. 25 So get Aaron and his son Eleazar. Take them up Mount Hor. 26 Take Aaron's official robes off of him. Put them on his son Eleazar. Aaron will die on Mount Hor. He will join the members of his family who have already died."

27 Moses did just as the LORD had commanded. The three men went up Mount Hor while the whole community was watching. 28 Moses took Aaron's official robes off of him. He put them on Aaron's son Eleazar. And Aaron died there on top of the mountain. Then Moses and Eleazar came down from the mountain. 29 The whole community found out that Aaron had died. So all the Israelites mourned for him for 30 days.

Israel Destroys Arad

21 The Canaanite king of the city of Arad lived in the Negev Desert. He heard that Israel was coming along the road to Atharim. So he attacked the Israelites. He captured some of them. 2 Then Israel made a promise to the LORD. They said, "Hand these people over to us. If you do, we will set their cities apart to you in a special way to be destroyed." 3 The LORD gave Israel what they asked for. He handed the Canaanites over to them. Israel completely destroyed them and their towns. So that place was named Hormah.

Moses Makes a Bronze Snake

4 The Israelites traveled from Mount Hor along the way to

the Red Sea. They wanted to go around Edom. But they grew tired on the way. [5] So they spoke against God and against Moses. They said, "Why have you brought us up out of Egypt? Do you want us to die here in the desert? We don't have any bread! We don't have any water! And we hate this awful food!"

[6] Then the LORD sent poisonous snakes among the Israelites. The snakes bit them. Many of the people died. [7] The others came to Moses. They said, "We sinned when we spoke against the LORD and against you. Pray that the LORD will take the snakes away from us." So Moses prayed for the people.

[8] The LORD said to Moses, "Make a snake. Put it up on a pole. Then anyone who is bitten can look at it and remain alive." [9] So Moses made a bronze snake. He put it up on a pole. Then anyone who was bitten by a snake and looked at the bronze snake remained alive.

The People Continue On to Moab

[10] The Israelites moved on. They camped at Oboth. [11] Then they started out from Oboth. They camped in Iye Abarim. It's in the desert on the eastern border of Moab. [12] From there they moved on. They camped in the Zered Valley. [13] They started out from there and camped by the Arnon River. It's in the desert that spreads out into the territory of the Amorites. The Arnon is the border of Moab. It's between Moab and the Amorites.

[14] Here is what the Book of the Wars of the LORD says about it.

"Sing about Zahab in Suphah
    and the valleys.
  Sing about the Arnon [15] and
    the slopes of the valleys.
They lead to the settlement
    called Ar.
  They lie along the border of
    Moab."

[16] From there the Israelites continued on to Beer. That was the well where the LORD spoke to Moses. He said, "Gather the people together. I will give them water to drink."

[17] Then Israel sang a song. They said,

"Spring up, you well!
    Sing about it.
[18] Sing about the well the
    princes dug.
  Sing about the well the
    nobles of the people dug.
  All their rulers were
    holding their scepters
    and walking sticks."

Then the Israelites went from the desert to Mattanah. [19] They went from Mattanah to Nahaliel. They went from Nahaliel to Bamoth. [20] And they went from Bamoth to a valley in Moab. It's the valley where the highest slopes of Pisgah look out over a dry and empty land.

Israel Wins the Battle Over Sihon and Og

[21] The Israelites sent messengers to speak to Sihon. He was the king of the Amorites. The messengers said to him,

²² "Let us pass through your country. We won't go off the road into any field or vineyard. We won't drink water from any well. We'll travel along the King's Highway. We'll just go straight through your territory."

²³ But Sihon wouldn't let Israel pass through his territory. He gathered his whole army together. Then he marched out into the desert against Israel. When he reached Jahaz, he fought against Israel. ²⁴ But Israel put him to death with their swords. They took over his land. They took everything from the Arnon River to the Jabbok River. But they didn't take over any of the land of the Ammonites. That's because the Ammonites had built strong forts along their border. ²⁵ The Israelites captured all the cities of the Amorites. Then they settled down in them. They captured the city of Heshbon. They also captured all the settlements around it. ²⁶ Sihon, the king of the Amorites, ruled in Heshbon. He had fought against an earlier king of Moab. Sihon had taken from him all his land all the way to the Arnon River.

²⁷ That's why the poets say,

"Come to Heshbon. Let it be built again.
    Let Sihon's city be made as good as new.

²⁸ "Fire went out from Heshbon.
    A blaze went out from the city of Sihon.

It burned up Ar in Moab.
    It burned up the citizens who lived on Arnon's hills.

²⁹ Moab, how terrible it is for you!
    People of Chemosh, you are destroyed!

Chemosh has deserted his sons and daughters.
    His sons have run away from the battle.

His daughters have become prisoners.
    He has handed all of them over to Sihon,
    the king of the Amorites.

³⁰ "But we have taken them over.
    Heshbon's rule has been destroyed all the way to Dibon.

We have destroyed them as far as Nophah.
    Nophah goes all the way to Medeba."

³¹ So Israel settled in the land of the Amorites.

³² Moses sent spies to the city of Jazer. The Israelites captured the settlements around it. They drove out the Amorites who were there. ³³ Then they turned and went up along the road toward Bashan. Og was the king of Bashan. He and his whole army marched out. They went to fight against Israel at Edrei.

³⁴ The LORD said to Moses, "Do not be afraid of Og. I have handed him over to you. I have given you his whole army. I have also given you his land. Do to him what you did to Sihon, the

king of the Amorites. He ruled in Heshbon."

35 So the Israelites struck down Og and his sons. And they wiped out his whole army. They didn't leave anyone alive. They took over his land for themselves.

Balak Sends For Balaam

22 Then the Israelites traveled to the plains of Moab. They camped along the Jordan River across from Jericho.

2 Balak saw everything that Israel had done to the Amorites. Balak was the son of Zippor. 3 The Moabites were terrified because there were so many Israelites. In fact, the Moabites were filled with panic because of the Israelites.

4 The Moabites spoke to the elders of Midian. They said, "This huge mob is going to destroy everything around us. They'll lick it up as an ox licks up all the grass in the fields."

Balak, the son of Zippor, was the king of Moab at that time. 5 He sent messengers to get Balaam. Balaam was the son of Beor. Balaam was at the city of Pethor near the Euphrates River. Pethor was in the land where Balaam had been born. Balak told the messengers to say to Balaam,

"A nation has come out of Egypt. They are covering the face of the land. They've set up camp next to me. 6 So come and put a curse on these people. They are too powerful for me. Maybe I'll be able to win the battle over them. Maybe I'll be able to drive them out of the land. I know that whoever you bless is blessed. And I know that whoever you cursed is cursed."

7 The elders of Moab and Midian left. They took with them the money they knew Balaam would ask for. They wanted him to use evil magic to figure things out for them. They came to where Balaam was. And they told him what Balak had said.

8 "Spend the night here," Balaam said to them. "I'll report back to you with the answer the Lord gives me." So the Moabite officials stayed with him.

9 God came to Balaam. He asked, "Who are these men with you?"

10 Balaam said to God, "Balak king of Moab, the son of Zippor, sent me a message. 11 He said, 'A nation has come out of Egypt. They are covering the whole surface of the land. So come and put a curse on them for me. Maybe I'll be able to fight them. Maybe I'll be able to drive them away.'"

12 But God said to Balaam, "Do not go with them. You must not put a curse on those people. I have blessed them."

13 The next morning Balaam got up. He said to Balak's officials, "Go back to your own country. The Lord won't let me go with you."

14 So the Moabite officials returned to Balak. They said, "Balaam wouldn't come with us."

[15] Then Balak sent other officials. They were more important than the first ones. And there were more of them. [16] They came to Balaam. They said,

"Balak, the son of Zippor, says, 'Don't let anything keep you from coming to me. [17] I'll make you very rich. I'll do anything you say. So come and put a curse on those people for me.'"

[18] But Balaam gave them his answer. He said, "Balak could give me all the silver and gold in his palace. Even then, I still couldn't do anything at all that goes beyond what the LORD my God commands. [19] Now spend the night here so that I can find out what else the LORD will tell me."

[20] That night God came to Balaam. He said, "These men have come to get you. So go with them. But do only what I tell you to do."

Balaam's Donkey

[21] Balaam got up in the morning. He put a saddle on his donkey. Then he went with the Moabite officials. [22] But God was very angry when Balaam went. So the angel of the LORD stood in the road to oppose him. Balaam was riding on his donkey. His two servants were with him. [23] The donkey saw the angel of the LORD standing in the road. The angel was holding a sword. He was ready for battle. So the donkey left the road and went into a field. Balaam hit the donkey. He wanted to get it back on the road.

[24] Then the angel of the LORD stood in a narrow path. The path went through the vineyards. There were walls on both sides. [25] The donkey saw the angel of the LORD. So it moved close to the wall. It crushed Balaam's foot against the wall. So he hit the donkey again.

[26] Then the angel of the LORD moved on ahead. He stood in a narrow place. There was no room to turn, either right or left. [27] The donkey saw the angel of the LORD. So it lay down under Balaam. That made him angry. He hit the donkey with his walking stick. [28] Then the LORD opened the donkey's mouth. It said to Balaam, "What have I done to you? Why did you hit me these three times?"

[29] Balaam answered the donkey. He said, "You have made me look foolish! I wish I had a sword in my hand. If I did, I'd kill you right now."

[30] The donkey said to Balaam, "I'm your own donkey. I'm the one you have always ridden. Haven't you been riding me to this very day? Have I ever made you look foolish before?"

"No," he said.

[31] Then the LORD opened Balaam's eyes. He saw the angel of the LORD standing in the road. He saw that the angel was holding a sword. The angel was ready for battle. So Balaam bowed down. He fell with his face to the ground.

³² The angel of the LORD spoke to him. He asked him, "Why have you hit your donkey three times? I have come here to oppose you. What you are doing is foolish. ³³ The donkey saw me. It turned away from me three times. Suppose it had not turned away. Then I would certainly have killed you by now. But I would have spared the donkey."

³⁴ Balaam said to the angel of the LORD, "I have sinned. I didn't realize you were standing in the road to oppose me. Tell me whether you are pleased with me. If you aren't, I'll go back."

³⁵ The angel of the LORD said to Balaam, "Go with the men. But say only what I tell you to say." So Balaam went with Balak's officials.

³⁶ Balak heard that Balaam was coming. So he went out to meet him. They met at a Moabite town near the Arnon River. The town was on the border of Balak's territory. ³⁷ Balak said to Balaam, "Didn't I send messengers to you? I wanted you to come quickly. So why didn't you come? I can make you very rich."

³⁸ "Well, I've come to you now," Balaam replied. "But I can't say whatever I please. I can only speak the words God puts in my mouth."

³⁹ Then Balaam went with Balak to Kiriath Huzoth. ⁴⁰ Balak sacrificed cattle and sheep. He gave some to Balaam. He also gave some to the officials with him. ⁴¹ The next morning Balak took Balaam up to Bamoth Baal. From there he could see the outer edges of the Israelite camp.

Balaam's First Message From God

23 Balaam said to Balak, "Build me seven altars here. Prepare seven bulls and seven rams for me to sacrifice." ² Balak did just as Balaam said. The two of them offered a bull and a ram on each altar.

³ Then Balaam said to Balak, "Stay here beside your offering. I'll go and try to find out what the LORD wants me to do. Maybe he'll come and meet with me. Then I'll tell you what he says to me." So Balaam went off to a bare hilltop.

⁴ God met with him there. Balaam said, "I've prepared seven altars. On each altar I've offered a bull and a ram."

⁵ The LORD put a message in Balaam's mouth. The LORD said, "Go back to Balak. Give him my message."

⁶ So Balaam went back to him. He found Balak standing beside his offering. All the Moabite officials were with him. ⁷ Then Balaam spoke the message he had received from God. He said,

"Balak brought me from the
     land of Aram.
The king of Moab sent for
     me from the mountains
     in the east.
'Come,' he said. 'Put a curse
     on Jacob's people for me.
Come. Speak against
     Israel.'

⁸But how can I put a curse on
    people God hasn't cursed?
How can I speak against
    people the LORD hasn't
    spoken against?
⁹I see them from the rocky
    peaks.
    I view them from the hills.
I see a group of people who
    live by themselves.
    They don't consider
    themselves to be one of
    the nations.
¹⁰Jacob's people are like the
    dust of the earth.
    Can dust be counted?
Who can count even a
    fourth of the Israelites?
Let me die as godly people die.
    Let my death be like
    theirs!"

¹¹Balak said to Balaam, "What
have you done to me? I brought
you here to put a curse on my
enemies! But all you have done
is give them a blessing!"

¹²He answered, "I have to
speak only the words the LORD
puts in my mouth."

Balaam's Second Message From God

¹³Then Balak said to Balaam,
"Come with me to another
place. You can see the Israelites
from there. You won't see all of
them. You will only see the outer
edges of their camp. From there,
put a curse on them for me." ¹⁴So
Balak took Balaam to the field of
Zophim. It was on the highest
slopes of Pisgah. There Balak
built seven altars. He offered a
bull and a ram on each altar.

¹⁵Balaam said to Balak, "Stay
here beside your offering. I'll
meet with the LORD over there."

¹⁶The LORD met with Balaam.
He put a message in Balaam's
mouth. The LORD said, "Go back
to Balak. Give him my message."

¹⁷So Balaam went to Balak. He
found him standing beside his
offering. The Moabite officials
were with him. Balak asked him,
"What did the LORD say?"

¹⁸Then Balaam spoke the
message he had received from
God. He said,

"Balak, rise up and listen.
    Son of Zippor, hear me.
¹⁹God isn't a mere human. He
    can't lie.
    He isn't a human being. He
    doesn't change his mind.
He speaks, and then he acts.
    He makes a promise, and
    then he keeps it.
²⁰He has commanded me to
    bless Israel.
    He has given them his
    blessing. And I can't
    change it.

²¹"I don't see any trouble
    coming on the people of
    Jacob.
    I don't see any suffering in
    Israel.
The LORD their God is with
    them.
    The shout of the King is
    among them.
²²God brought them out of
    Egypt.
    They are as strong as a
    wild ox.
²³There isn't any magic that
    can hurt the people of
    Jacob.

No one can use magic
    words to harm Israel.
Here is what will be said
    about the people of Jacob.
Here is what will be said
    about Israel.
People will say, 'See what
    God has done!'
24 The Israelites are going to
    wake up like a female
    lion.
They are going to get up
    like a male lion.
They are like a lion that won't
    rest
    until it eats what it has
    caught.
They are like a lion that won't
    rest
    until it drinks the blood of
    what it has killed."

25 Then Balak said to Balaam,
"Don't put a curse on them at
all! And don't give them a blessing at all!"

26 Balaam answered, "Didn't I
tell you that I must do only what
the LORD says?"

Balaam's Third Message From God

27 Then Balak said to Balaam,
"Come. Let me take you to another place. Perhaps God will be
pleased to let you put a curse on
the Israelites for me from there."
28 Balak took Balaam to the top
of Mount Peor. It looks out over
a dry and empty land.
29 Balaam said, "Build me
seven altars here. Prepare seven
bulls and seven rams for me to
sacrifice." 30 Balak did just as
Balaam said. He offered a bull
and a ram on each altar.

24 Balaam saw that the
LORD was pleased to
give his blessing to Israel. So he
didn't try to use evil magic as
he had done at other times. Instead, he turned and looked toward the desert. 2 He looked out
and saw Israel. They had set up
their camps tribe by tribe. The
Spirit of God came on him. 3 Balaam spoke the message he had
received from God. He said,

"Here is the message God
    gave Balaam, the son of
    Beor.
It's the message God gave
    to the one who sees
    clearly.
4 It's the message God gave to
    the one who hears the
    words of God.
He sees a vision from the
    Mighty One.
He falls down flat with his
    face toward the
    ground.
His eyes have been opened
    by the LORD.

5 "People of Jacob, your tents
    are very beautiful.
Israel, the places where you
    live are very beautiful.

6 "They spread out like
    valleys.
They are like gardens
    beside a river.
They are like aloes the LORD
    has planted.
They are like cedar trees
    beside a stream.
7 Their water buckets will run
    over.
Their seeds will have
    plenty of water.

"Their king will be greater
    than King Agag.
    Their kingdom will be
    honored.

8 "God brought them out of
    Egypt.
    They are as strong as a
    wild ox.
    They destroy nations at war
    with them.
    They break their bones in
    pieces.
    They wound them with
    their arrows.
9 Like a male lion they lie
    down and sleep.
    They are like a female
    lion.
    Who dares to wake
    them up?

"May those who bless you be
    blessed!
    May those who curse you
    be cursed!"

10 Then Balak became very
angry with Balaam. He slapped
his hands together. He said to
Balaam, "I sent for you to put a
curse on my enemies. But you
have given them a blessing three
times. 11 Get out of here right
away! Go home! I said I'd make
you very rich. But the LORD has
kept you from getting rich."

12 Balaam answered Balak,
"Here is what I told the messengers you sent me. 13 I said, 'Balak could give me all the silver
and gold in his palace. Even if
I wanted to, I still couldn't do
anything at all that goes beyond
what the LORD commands. I
must say only what the LORD
tells me to say.' 14 Now I'm going

back to my people. But come.
Let me warn you about what
these people will do to your
people in days to come."

Balaam's Fourth Message From God

15 Then Balaam spoke the
message he had received from
God. He said,

"Here is the message God
    gave Balaam, the son of
    Beor.
    It's the message God gave
    to the one who sees
    clearly.
16 It's the message God gave to
    the one who hears the
    words of God.
    The Most High God has
    given him knowledge.
    He sees a vision from the
    Mighty One.
    He falls down flat with his
    face toward the ground.
    His eyes have been opened
    by the LORD.

17 "I see him, but I don't see him
    now.
    I view him, but he isn't
    near.
    A star will come from among
    the people of Jacob.
    A king will rise up out of
    Israel.
    He'll crush the foreheads of
    the people of Moab.
    He'll crush the heads of all
    the people of Sheth.
18 He'll win the battle over
    Edom.
    He'll win the battle over
    his enemy Seir.
    But Israel will grow strong.

¹⁹A ruler will come from
    among the people of
    Jacob.
    He'll destroy those from
    the city who are still
    alive."

Balaam's Fifth Message From God

²⁰Then Balaam saw the Amalekites. He spoke the message he had received from God. He said,

"Amalek was the first nation
    to attack Israel.
    But their end will be total
    destruction."

Balaam's Sixth Message From God

²¹Then Balaam saw the Kenites. He spoke the message he had received from God. He said,

"The place where you live is
    safe.
    Your nest is on a high cliff.
²²But you Kenites will be
    destroyed.
    Ashur will take you as
    prisoners."

Balaam's Seventh Message From God

²³Then Balaam spoke the message he had received from God. He said,

"Who can live when God
    does this?
²⁴   Ships will come from the
    shores of Cyprus.
    They will bring Ashur and
    Eber under their control.
    But they themselves will
    also be destroyed."

²⁵Then Balaam got up and returned home. And Balak went on his way.

Moab Leads Israel Astray

25 Israel was staying in Shittim. The men of Israel began to commit sexual sins with the women of Moab. ²The women invited the men to feasts and sacrifices to honor their gods. The people ate the sacrifices and bowed down in front of the statues of those gods. ³So Israel joined in worshiping the god named Baal that was worshiped at Peor. The LORD became very angry with Israel.

⁴The LORD said to Moses, "Take all the leaders of these people. Kill them. Put their dead bodies out in the open. I want to see you do it in the middle of the day. Then I will not be angry with Israel."

⁵So Moses spoke to Israel's judges. He said, "Some of your people have joined in worshiping the god named Baal that is worshiped at Peor. Each of you must kill the people in your tribe who have done that."

⁶Then an Israelite man brought into the camp a Midianite woman. He did it right in front of the eyes of Moses and the whole community of Israel. They were weeping at the entrance to the tent of meeting. ⁷Phinehas was a priest. He was the son of Eleazar, the son of Aaron. When Phinehas saw what had happened, he left the people. He took a spear in his

hand. [8] He followed the man into the tent. Phinehas stuck the spear through the man and into the woman's stomach. Then the LORD stopped the plague against the Israelites. [9] But the plague had already killed 24,000 of them.

[10] The LORD said to Moses, [11] "Phinehas is a priest. He is the son of Eleazar, the son of Aaron. Phinehas has turned my anger away from the Israelites. I am committed to making sure I am honored among them. And he is as committed as I am. So even though I was angry with them, I did not put an end to them. [12] So tell Phinehas I am making my covenant with him. It is my promise to give him peace. [13] He and his sons after him will have a covenant to be priests forever. That is because he was committed to making sure that I, his God, was honored. In that way he paid for the sin of the Israelites."

[14] The name of the Israelite man who was killed was Zimri. He was the son of Salu. Zimri was killed along with the Midianite woman. Salu was a family leader in the tribe of Simeon. [15] The name of the Midianite woman who was killed was Kozbi. She was the daughter of Zur. He was the chief of a Midianite family.

[16] The LORD spoke to Moses. He said, [17] "Treat the Midianites just as you would treat enemies. Kill them. [18] After all, they treated you like enemies. They tricked you into worshiping the god named Baal that is worshiped at Peor. They also tricked you because of what Kozbi did. She was the woman killed when the plague came that was connected with Peor. Kozbi was the daughter of a Midianite leader."

The Men of Israel Are Counted a Second Time

26 After the plague, the LORD spoke to Moses and Eleazar the priest. Eleazar was the son of Aaron. The LORD said, [2] "Count all the men of Israel. Make a list of them by their families. Count all the men who are able to serve in Israel's army. They must be 20 years old or more." [3] At that time the Israelites were on the plains of Moab. They were by the Jordan River across from Jericho. Moses and Eleazar the priest spoke with them. They said, [4] "Count all the men 20 years old or more. Do it just as the LORD commanded Moses."

Here are the men of Israel who came out of Egypt.

[5] Reuben was Israel's oldest son. Here are the names of his sons.
The Hanokite family came from Hanok.
The Palluite family came from Pallu.
[6] The Hezronite family came from Hezron.
The Karmite family came from Karmi.
[7] These were the families of Reuben. The number of men was 43,730.

⁸Eliab was the son of Pallu. ⁹Eliab's sons were Nemuel, Dathan and Abiram. Dathan and Abiram were the same community officials who refused to obey Moses and Aaron. They were among the followers of Korah who refused to obey the Lᴏʀᴅ. ¹⁰The ground opened its mouth. It swallowed them up along with Korah. The followers of Korah died when fire burned up 250 men. Their deaths were a warning to the rest of Israel. ¹¹But the family line of Korah didn't die out completely.

¹²Here are the names of Simeon's sons. They are listed by their families.
The Nemuelite family came from Nemuel.
The Jaminite family came from Jamin.
The Jakinite family came from Jakin.
¹³The Zerahite family came from Zerah.
The Shaulite family came from Shaul.
¹⁴These were the families of Simeon. The number of the men counted was 22,200.

¹⁵Here are the names of Gad's sons. They are listed by their families.
The Zephonite family came from Zephon.
The Haggite family came from Haggi.
The Shunite family came from Shuni.
¹⁶The Oznite family came from Ozni.
The Erite family came from Eri.
¹⁷The Arodite family came from Arodi.
The Arelite family came from Areli.
¹⁸These were the families of Gad. The number of the men counted was 40,500.

¹⁹Er and Onan were sons of Judah. But they died in Canaan.
²⁰Here are the names of Judah's sons. They are listed by their families.
The Shelanite family came from Shelah.
The Perezite family came from Perez.
The Zerahite family came from Zerah.
²¹Here are the names of the sons of Perez.
The Hezronite family came from Hezron.
The Hamulite family came from Hamul.
²²These were the families of Judah. The number of the men counted was 76,500.

²³Here are the names of Issachar's sons. They are listed by their families.
The Tolaite family came from Tola.
The Puite family came from Puah.
²⁴The Jashubite family came from Jashub.
The Shimronite family came from Shimron.
²⁵These were the families

of Issachar. The number of the men counted was 64,300.

26 Here are the names of Zebulun's sons. They are listed by their families.

The Seredite family came from Sered.

The Elonite family came from Elon.

The Jahleelite family came from Jahleel.

27 These were the families of Zebulun. The number of the men counted was 60,500.

28 Here are the names of Joseph's sons. They are listed by their families. The families came from Manasseh and Ephraim, the sons of Joseph.

29 Here are the names of Manasseh's sons.

The Makirite family came from Makir. Makir was the father of Gilead.

The Gileadite family came from Gilead.

30 Here are the names of Gilead's sons.

The Iezerite family came from Iezer.

The Helekite family came from Helek.

31 The Asrielite family came from Asriel.

The Shechemite family came from Shechem.

32 The Shemidaite family came from Shemida.

The Hepherite family came from Hepher.

33 Zelophehad was the son of Hepher. Zelophehad didn't have any sons. All he had was daughters. Their names were Mahlah, Noah, Hoglah, Milkah and Tirzah.

34 These were the families of Manasseh. The number of the men counted was 52,700.

35 Here are the names of Ephraim's sons. They are listed by their families.

The Shuthelahite family came from Shuthelah.

The Bekerite family came from Beker.

The Tahanite family came from Tahan.

36 The sons of Shuthelah were the Eranite family. They came from Eran.

37 These were the families of Ephraim. The number of the men counted was 32,500.

These were the sons of Joseph. They are listed by their families.

38 Here are the names of Benjamin's sons. They are listed by their families.

The Belaite family came from Bela.

The Ashbelite family came from Ashbel.

The Ahiramite family came from Ahiram.

39 The Shuphamite family came from Shupham.

The Huphamite family came from Hupham.

40 Bela's sons came from Ard and Naaman.

The Ardite family came from Ard.

The Naamite family came from Naaman.

41 These were the families of Benjamin. The number of the men counted was 45,600.

42 Here is the name of Dan's son. He is listed by his family.

The Shuhamite family came from Shuham.

This was the family of Dan. 43 All the men in Dan's family were Shuhamites. The number of the men counted was 64,400.

44 Here are the names of Asher's sons. They are listed by their families.

The Imnite family came from Imnah.

The Ishvite family came from Ishvi.

The Beriite family came from Beriah.

45 Here are the names of the families that came from Beriah's sons.

The Heberite family came from Heber.

The Malkielite family came from Malkiel.

46 Asher also had a daughter named Serah.

47 These were the families of Asher. The number of the men counted was 53,400.

48 Here are the names of Naphtali's sons. They are listed by their families.

The Jahzeelite family came from Jahzeel.

The Gunite family came from Guni.

49 The Jezerite family came from Jezer.

The Shillemite family came from Shillem.

50 These were the families of Naphtali. The number of the men counted was 45,400.

51 The total number of the men of Israel was 601,730.

52 The LORD said to Moses, 53 "I will give the land to them. The amount of land each family receives will be based on the number of its men. 54 Give a larger share to a larger family. Give a smaller share to a smaller family. Each family will receive its share based on the number of men listed in it.

55 "Be sure that you cast lots when you give out the land. What each family receives will be based on the number of men listed in its tribe. 56 Cast lots when you give out each share. Cast lots for the larger and smaller families alike."

57 Here are the names of the Levites. They are listed by their families.

The Gershonite family came from Gershon.

The Kohathite family came from Kohath.

The Merarite family came from Merari.

58 Here are the names of the other Levite families. They are
the Libnite family,
the Hebronite family,
the Mahlite family,

the Mushite family,
the Korahite family.
Amram came from the Kohathite family. [59] The name of Amram's wife was Jochebed. She was from the family line of Levi. She was born to the Levites in Egypt. Aaron, Moses and their sister Miriam were born in the family line of Amram and Jochebed. [60] Aaron was the father of Nadab and Abihu. He was also the father of Eleazar and Ithamar. [61] But Nadab and Abihu made an offering to the LORD by using fire that wasn't allowed. So they died.

[62] The number of male Levites a month old or more was 23,000. They weren't listed along with the other men of Israel. That's because they didn't receive a share among them.

[63] These are the men counted by Moses and Eleazar the priest. At that time the Israelites were on the plains of Moab. They were by the Jordan River across from Jericho. [64] The men of Israel had been counted before in the Sinai Desert by Moses and Aaron the priest. But not one of them was among the men counted this time. [65] The LORD had told the Israelites at Kadesh Barnea that they would certainly die in the desert. Not one of them was left alive except Caleb and Joshua. Caleb was the son of Jephunneh, and Joshua was the son of Nun.

Zelophehad's Daughters

27 The daughters of Zelophehad belonged to the family groups of Manasseh. Zelophehad was the son of Hepher. Hepher was the son of Gilead. Gilead was the son of Makir. Makir was the son of Manasseh. And Manasseh was the son of Joseph. The names of Zelophehad's daughters were Mahlah, Noah, Hoglah, Milkah and Tirzah. They approached [2] the entrance to the tent of meeting. There they stood in front of Moses and Eleazar the priest. The leaders and the whole community were there too. Zelophehad's daughters said, [3] "Our father died in the Sinai Desert. But he wasn't one of the men who followed Korah. He wasn't one of those who joined together against the LORD. Our father died because of his own sin. He didn't leave any sons. [4] Why should our father's name disappear from his family just because he didn't have a son? Give us property among our father's relatives."

[5] So Moses brought their case to the LORD. [6] The LORD said to him, [7] "What Zelophehad's daughters are saying is right. You must certainly give them property. Give them a share among their father's relatives. Give their father's property to them.

[8] "Say to the Israelites, 'Suppose a man dies who doesn't

have a son. Then give his property to his daughter. ⁹Suppose the man doesn't have a daughter. Then give his property to his brothers. ¹⁰Suppose the man doesn't have any brothers. Then give his property to his father's brothers. ¹¹Suppose his father doesn't have any brothers. Then give his property to the nearest male relative in his family group. It will belong to him. That is what the law will require of the Israelites. It is just as the LORD commanded me.' "

Joshua Becomes Israel's New Leader

¹²Then the LORD said to Moses, "Go up this mountain in the Abarim Range. See the land I have given the Israelites. ¹³After you have seen it, you too will join the members of your family who have already died. You will die, just as your brother Aaron did. ¹⁴The community refused to obey me at the waters of Meribah Kadesh in the Desert of Zin. At that time, you and Aaron did not obey my command. You did not honor me in front of them as the holy God."

¹⁵Moses spoke to the LORD. He said, ¹⁶"LORD, you are the God who gives life and breath to all living things. Please put someone in charge of this community. ¹⁷Have that person lead them and take care of them. Then your people won't be like sheep without a shepherd."

¹⁸So the LORD said to Moses, "Joshua, the son of Nun, has the ability to be a wise leader. Get him and place your hand on him. ¹⁹Have him stand in front of Eleazar the priest and the whole community. Put him in charge while everyone is watching. ²⁰Give him some of your authority. Then the whole community of Israel will obey him. ²¹Joshua will stand in front of Eleazar the priest. Eleazar will help him make decisions. Eleazar will get help from me by using the Urim. Joshua and the whole community of Israel must not make any move at all unless I command them to."

²²Moses did just as the LORD commanded him. He got Joshua and had him stand in front of Eleazar the priest and the whole community. ²³Then Moses placed his hands on Joshua. And he put him in charge of the people. He did just as the LORD had directed through Moses.

Offerings That Israel Must Bring Each Day

28 The LORD said to Moses, ²"Here is a command I want you to give the Israelites. Tell them, 'Make sure to present to me my food offerings. Do it at the appointed time. Their smell will please me.' ³Tell them, 'Here is the food offering you must present to the LORD. Present to him two lambs a year old. They must not have any flaws. Present them as a regular burnt offering each day. ⁴Offer one lamb in the morning. Offer the other when the sun goes down. ⁵Present a grain offering along with them. It must have eight cups

of the finest flour. Mix it with a quart of oil made from pressed olives. [6] It is the regular burnt offering. The LORD established it at Mount Sinai. It has a pleasant smell. It is a food offering presented to the LORD. [7] Along with that, offer a quart of wine as a drink offering. It must be given along with each lamb. Pour out the drink offering to the LORD at the sacred tent. [8] Offer the second lamb when the sun goes down. Sacrifice it along with the same kind of grain offering and drink offering that you present in the morning. It is a food offering. Its smell pleases the LORD.

Offerings That Israel Must Bring on the Sabbath Day

[9] "'On the Sabbath day, make an offering of two lambs. They must be a year old. They must not have any flaws. Sacrifice them along with their drink offering. Sacrifice them along with a grain offering of 16 cups of the finest flour. Mix it with olive oil. [10] It is the burnt offering for every Sabbath day. It is in addition to the regular burnt offering and its drink offering.

Offerings That Israel Must Bring Every Month

[11] "'On the first day of every month, bring to the LORD a burnt offering. Bring two young bulls and one ram. Also bring seven male lambs a year old. They must not have any flaws. [12] Present a grain offering along with each bull. It must have 24 cups of the finest flour. Mix it with olive oil. Present a grain offering along with the ram. It must have 16 cups of the finest flour. Mix it with oil. [13] Present a grain offering along with each lamb. It must have eight cups of the finest flour. Mix it with oil. It is for a burnt offering. It has a pleasant smell. It is a food offering presented to the LORD. [14] Present a drink offering along with each bull. It must have two quarts of wine. Offer two and a half pints along with the ram. And offer one quart along with each lamb. It is the burnt offering for each month. It must be made on the day of each New Moon feast during the year. [15] One male goat must be sacrificed to the LORD as a sin offering. It is in addition to the regular burnt offering and its drink offering.

The Passover Feast

[16] "'The LORD's Passover Feast must be held on the 14th day of the first month. [17] On the 15th day of the month there must be a feast. For seven days eat bread made without yeast. [18] On the first day come together for a special service. Do not do any regular work. [19] Present to the LORD a food offering. Present a burnt offering of two young bulls and one ram. Also present seven male lambs a year old. They must not have any flaws. [20] Present a grain offering along with each bull. The offering must have 24 cups of the finest flour. Mix it with olive oil. Offer 16 cups along with the ram. [21] Offer eight cups along with each of the seven lambs.

²²Include a male goat as a sin offering. It will pay for your sin. ²³Offer everything in addition to the regular morning burnt offering. ²⁴Present the food offering every day for seven days. The smell of the offering will please the LORD. You must present the offering in addition to the regular burnt offering and its drink offering. ²⁵On the seventh day come together for a special service. Do not do any regular work.

The Feast of Weeks

²⁶" 'On the day you gather the first share of your crops, present to the LORD an offering of your first grain. Do it during the Feast of Weeks. Come together for a special service. Do not do any regular work. ²⁷Sacrifice a burnt offering of two young bulls and one ram. Also sacrifice seven male lambs a year old. The smell of the offering will please the LORD. ²⁸Present a grain offering along with each bull. It must have 24 cups of the finest flour. Mix it with olive oil. Offer 16 cups along with the ram. ²⁹Offer eight cups along with each of the seven lambs. ³⁰Include a male goat to pay for your sin. ³¹Present everything along with the drink offerings. Do it in addition to the regular burnt offering and its grain offering. Be sure the animals do not have any flaws.

The Feast of Trumpets

29 " 'On the first day of the seventh month, come together for a special service. Do not do any regular work. Blow the trumpets on that day. ²Sacrifice a burnt offering. Its smell will please the LORD. Sacrifice one young bull and one ram. Also sacrifice seven male lambs a year old. They must not have any flaws. ³Present a grain offering along with the bull. It must have 24 cups of the finest flour. Mix it with olive oil. Offer 16 cups along with the ram. ⁴Offer eight cups along with each of the seven lambs. ⁵Include a male goat as a sin offering. It will pay for your sin. ⁶Each month and each day you must sacrifice burnt offerings. Sacrifice them along with their grain offerings and drink offerings as they are required. The offerings for the Feast of Trumpets are in addition to the monthly and daily burnt offerings. They are food offerings presented to the LORD. They have a pleasant smell.

The Day When Sin Is Paid For

⁷" 'On the tenth day of the seventh month, come together for a special service. You must not eat anything on that day. You must not do any work on it. ⁸Sacrifice a burnt offering. Its smell will please the LORD. Sacrifice one young bull and one ram. Also sacrifice seven male lambs a year old. They must not have any flaws. ⁹Present a grain offering along with the bull. The offering must have 24 cups of the finest flour. Mix it with olive oil. Offer 16 cups along with the ram. ¹⁰Offer eight cups along with each of the seven lambs. ¹¹Include a male goat as a sin offering. It is in

addition to the offering that pays for sin. It is in addition to the regular burnt offering along with its grain offering. It is also in addition to their drink offerings.

The Feast of Booths

12 " 'On the 15th day of the seventh month, come together for a special service. Do not do any regular work. Celebrate the Feast of Booths for seven days to honor the LORD. 13 Present a food offering. Its smell will please the LORD. Sacrifice a burnt offering of 13 young bulls and two rams. Also sacrifice 14 male lambs a year old. They must not have any flaws. 14 Present a grain offering along with each of the 13 bulls. It must have 24 cups of the finest flour. Mix it with olive oil. Offer 16 cups along with each of the two rams. 15 Offer eight cups along with each of the 14 lambs. 16 Include a male goat as a sin offering. It is in addition to the regular burnt offering. It is also in addition to its grain offering and drink offering.

17 " 'On the second day sacrifice 12 young bulls and two rams. Also sacrifice 14 male lambs a year old. They must not have any flaws. 18 Present their grain offerings and drink offerings. Present them along with the bulls, rams and lambs. Present them according to the required number. 19 Include a male goat as a sin offering. It is in addition to the regular burnt offering along with its grain offering. It is also in addition to their drink offerings.

20 " 'On the third day sacrifice 11 bulls and two rams. Also sacrifice 14 male lambs a year old. They must not have any flaws. 21 Present their grain offerings and drink offerings. Present them along with the bulls, rams and lambs. Present them according to the required number. 22 Include a male goat as a sin offering. It is in addition to the regular burnt offering. It is also in addition to its grain offering and drink offering.

23 " 'On the fourth day sacrifice ten bulls and two rams. Also sacrifice 14 male lambs a year old. They must not have any flaws. 24 Present their grain offerings and drink offerings. Present them along with the bulls, rams and lambs. Present them according to the required number. 25 Include a male goat as a sin offering. It is in addition to the regular burnt offering. It is also in addition to its grain offering and drink offering.

26 " 'On the fifth day sacrifice nine bulls and two rams. Also sacrifice 14 male lambs a year old. They must not have any flaws. 27 Present their grain offerings and drink offerings. Present them along with the bulls, rams and lambs. Present them according to the required number. 28 Include a male goat as a sin offering. It is in addition to the regular burnt offering. It is also in addition to its grain offering and drink offering.

29 " 'On the sixth day sacrifice eight bulls and two rams. Also sacrifice 14 male lambs a year

old. They must not have any flaws. [30] Present their grain offerings and drink offerings. Present them along with the bulls, rams and lambs. Present them according to the required number. [31] Include a male goat as a sin offering. It is in addition to the regular burnt offering. It is also in addition to its grain offering and drink offering.

[32] " 'On the seventh day sacrifice seven bulls and two rams. Also sacrifice 14 male lambs a year old. They must not have any flaws. [33] Present their grain offerings and drink offerings. Present them along with the bulls, rams and lambs. Present them according to the required number. [34] Include a male goat as a sin offering. It is in addition to the regular burnt offering. It is also in addition to its grain offering and drink offering.

[35] " 'On the eighth day come together for a closing sacred service. Do not do any regular work. [36] Present a food offering. Its smell will please the LORD. Sacrifice a burnt offering of one bull and one ram. Also sacrifice seven male lambs a year old. They must not have any flaws. [37] Present their grain offerings and drink offerings. Present them along with the bull, the ram and the lambs. Present them according to the required number. [38] Include a male goat as a sin offering. It is in addition to the regular burnt offering. It is also in addition to its grain offering and drink offering.

[39] " 'Here are the offerings you must present to the LORD at your appointed feasts. They are burnt offerings, grain offerings, drink offerings and friendship offerings. They are in addition to the offerings you bring to keep a special promise you make to the LORD. They are also in addition to the offerings you choose to give.' "

[40] Moses told the Israelites everything the LORD had commanded him.

Special Promises

30 Moses spoke to the heads of the tribes of Israel. He said, "Here is what the LORD commands. [2] Suppose a man makes a special promise to the LORD. Or suppose he gives his word to do something. Then he must keep his promise. He must do everything he said he would do.

[3] "Suppose a young woman is still living in her father's house. She makes a special promise to the LORD. Or she gives her word to do something. [4] Suppose her father hears about her promise. And he doesn't say anything to her about it. Then she must keep her promise. She must do what she agreed to do. [5] But suppose her father doesn't allow her to keep her promises when he hears about them. Then she doesn't have to do what she promised or agreed to do. The LORD will set her free. He'll do it because her father hasn't allowed her to keep her promises.

[6] "Suppose she gets married after she makes a special prom-

ise. Or she gets married after agreeing to do something without thinking it through. ⁷ Suppose her husband hears about what she did. And he doesn't say anything to her about it. Then she must keep her promise. She must do what she agreed to do. ⁸ But suppose her husband doesn't allow her to keep her promises when he hears about them. Then she doesn't have to do what she promised. She doesn't have to do what she agreed to do without thinking it through. The LORD will set her free.

⁹ "Suppose a widow makes a special promise. Or suppose she gives her word to do something. Then she must keep her promise. She must do what she agreed to do. The same rules apply to a woman who has been divorced.

¹⁰ "Suppose a woman living with her husband makes a special promise. Or she gives her word to do something. ¹¹ Suppose her husband hears about what she did. He doesn't say anything to her about it. And he doesn't try to stop her from keeping her promises. Then she must keep all of them. She must do what she agreed to do. ¹² But suppose her husband doesn't allow her to keep her promises when he hears about them. Then she doesn't have to do what she promised. She doesn't have to do what she agreed to do. Her husband has kept her from doing what she said she would do. The LORD will set her free. ¹³ Her husband can let her keep any special promise she makes. Or he can refuse to let her keep it. Suppose she gives her word not to eat anything. Then her husband can let her keep her promise. Or he can refuse to let her keep it. ¹⁴ But suppose day after day her husband doesn't say anything to her about what she did. Then he lets her keep all her promises. He lets her do everything she agreed to do. That's because he didn't say anything to her when he heard about what she had done. ¹⁵ But suppose some time after he hears about her promises he doesn't let her keep them. Then she will be guilty. But he will bear the consequences for her guilt."

¹⁶ These are the rules the LORD gave Moses about a man and his wife. And these are the rules the LORD gave about a father and his young daughter still living at home.

The LORD Punishes the Midianites

31 The LORD spoke to Moses. He said, ² "Pay the Midianites back for what they did to the Israelites. After that, you will join the members of your family who have already died."

³ So Moses said to the people, "Prepare some of your men for battle. They must go to war against Midian. They will carry out the LORD's plan to punish Midian. ⁴ Send 1,000 men from each of the tribes of Israel into battle." ⁵ So Moses prepared

12,000 men for battle. There were 1,000 from each tribe. They came from the families of Israel. [6] Moses sent them into battle. He sent 1,000 from each tribe. Phinehas the priest went along with them. Phinehas was the son of Eleazar. Phinehas took some things from the sacred tent with him. He also took the trumpets. The trumpet blasts would tell the people what to do and when to do it.

[7] They fought against Midian, just as the LORD had commanded Moses. They killed every man. [8] Evi, Rekem, Zur, Hur and Reba were among the men they killed. Those men were the five kings of Midian. The Israelites also killed Balaam with their swords. Balaam was the son of Beor. [9] The Israelites captured the Midianite women and children. They took for themselves all the herds, flocks and goods. [10] They burned down all the towns where the Midianites lived. They also burned all their camps. [11] They carried off everything they had taken. That included the people and the animals. [12] They brought back to Israel's camp the prisoners and everything else they had taken. They took them to Moses and to Eleazar the priest. They brought them to the whole community. Israel was camped on the plains of Moab. They were by the Jordan River across from Jericho.

[13] Moses and Eleazar the priest went to meet them outside the camp. So did all the leaders of the community. [14] Moses was angry with the officers of the army who had returned from the battle. Some of them were the commanders of thousands of men. Others were the commanders of hundreds.

[15] "Have you let all the women remain alive?" Moses asked them. [16] "The women followed Balaam's advice. They caused the Israelites to be unfaithful to the LORD. The people worshiped the god named Baal that was worshiped at Peor. So a plague struck them. [17] Kill all the boys. And kill every woman who has slept with a man. [18] But save for yourselves every woman who has never slept with a man.

[19] "Anyone who has killed a person must stay outside the camp for seven days. And anyone who has touched a person who was killed must do the same thing. On the third and seventh days you must make yourselves pure. You must also make your prisoners pure. [20] Make all your clothes pure and 'clean.' Everything made out of leather, goat hair or wood must be made pure and 'clean.'"

[21] Then Eleazar the priest spoke to the soldiers who had gone into battle. He said, "Here is what the law the LORD gave Moses requires. [22] All your gold, silver, bronze, iron, tin and lead [23] must be put through fire. So must everything else that doesn't burn up. Then those things will be 'clean.' But they must also be made pure with the special water. In fact, everything that won't burn up

must be put through that water. ²⁴ On the seventh day wash your clothes. And you will be 'clean.' Then you can come into the camp."

The People Divide Up What They Had Taken

²⁵ The LORD spoke to Moses. He said, ²⁶ "Here is what you and Eleazar the priest and the family leaders of the community must do. You must count all the people and animals you captured. ²⁷ Divide up some of what you took with the soldiers who fought in the battle. Divide up the rest with the others in the community. ²⁸ Set apart a gift for me. Take something from the soldiers who fought in the battle. Set apart one out of every 500 people, cattle, donkeys or sheep. ²⁹ Take my gift from the soldiers' half. Give it to Eleazar the priest. It is my share. ³⁰ Also take something from the half that belongs to the Israelites. Choose one out of every 50 people, cattle, donkeys, sheep or other animals. Give them to the Levites. They are responsible for taking care of my holy tent." ³¹ So Moses and Eleazar the priest did just as the LORD had commanded Moses.

³² What the soldiers took included 675,000 sheep. ³³ There were also 72,000 cattle ³⁴ and 61,000 donkeys. ³⁵ And there were 32,000 women who had never slept with a man.

³⁶ Here is the half that belonged to those who had fought in the battle.

There were 337,500 sheep. ³⁷ From among them, the LORD's gift was 675. ³⁸ There were 36,000 cattle. From among them, the LORD's gift was 72. ³⁹ There were 30,500 donkeys. From among them, the LORD's gift was 61. ⁴⁰ There were 16,000 women. From among them, the LORD's gift was 32.

⁴¹ Moses gave the gift to Eleazar the priest. It was the LORD's share. Moses did just as the LORD had commanded him.

⁴² The other half belonged to the Israelites. Moses set it apart from what belonged to the fighting men. ⁴³ The community's half was 337,500 sheep, ⁴⁴ 36,000 cattle, ⁴⁵ 30,500 donkeys ⁴⁶ and 16,000 women. ⁴⁷ Moses chose one out of every 50 people and animals. He gave them to the Levites. They were accountable for taking care of the LORD's holy tent. Moses did just as the LORD had commanded him.

⁴⁸ Then the army officers went to Moses. Some of them were the commanders of thousands of men. Others were the commanders of hundreds. ⁴⁹ All of them said to Moses, "We have counted the soldiers under our command. Not a single one is missing. ⁵⁰ So we've brought an offering to the LORD. We've brought the gold each of us took in the battle. That includes armbands, bracelets, rings, earrings and necklaces. We've brought them in front of the LORD to pay for our sin."

⁵¹Moses and Eleazar the priest accepted the beautiful gold things from the army officers. ⁵²The gold received from the commanders of thousands and commanders of hundreds weighed 420 pounds. Moses and Eleazar offered all of it as a gift to the LORD. ⁵³Each soldier had taken things from the battle for himself. ⁵⁴Moses and Eleazar the priest accepted the gold from all the commanders. They brought it into the tent of meeting. It reminded the LORD of the Israelites.

The Tribes on the East Side of the Jordan River

32 The tribes of Reuben and Gad had very large herds and flocks. They looked at the lands of Jazer and Gilead. They saw that those lands were just right for livestock. ²So they came to Moses and Eleazar the priest. They also came to the leaders of the community. They said, ³"We have seen the cities of Ataroth, Dibon, Jazer, Nimrah and Heshbon. We've seen Elealeh, Sebam, Nebo and Beon. ⁴All of them are in the land the LORD has brought under Israel's control. This land is just right for livestock. And we have livestock. ⁵We hope you are pleased with us," they continued. "If you are, please give us this land. Then it will belong to us. But don't make us go across the Jordan River."

⁶Moses spoke to the people of Gad and Reuben. He said, "Should the rest of us go to war while you stay here? ⁷The LORD has given the land of Canaan to the Israelites. So why would you want to keep them from going over into it? ⁸That's what your fathers did. I sent them from Kadesh Barnea to check out the land. ⁹They went up to the Valley of Eshkol and looked at the land. Then they talked the Israelites out of entering the land the LORD had given them. ¹⁰The LORD's anger was stirred up that day. So he made a promise. He said, ¹¹'Not one of those who were 20 years old or more when they came up out of Egypt will see the land. They have not followed me with their whole heart. I promised to give the land to Abraham, Isaac and Jacob. ¹²But not one of the people who came up out of Egypt will see the land except Caleb and Joshua. Caleb is the son of Jephunneh, the Kenizzite. And Joshua is the son of Nun. They will see the land. They followed the LORD with their whole heart.' ¹³The LORD became very angry with Israel. He made them wander around in the desert for 40 years. They wandered until all the people who had done evil in his sight had died.

¹⁴"Now here you are, you bunch of sinners! You have taken the place of your fathers. And you are making the LORD even angrier with Israel. ¹⁵What if you turn away from following him? Then he'll leave all these people in the desert again. And it will be your fault when they are destroyed."

¹⁶Then they came up to Mo-

ses. They said, "We would like to build pens here for our livestock. We would also like to build cities for our women and children. ¹⁷ But we will prepare ourselves for battle. We're even ready to go ahead of the Israelites. We'll march out with them until we've brought them to their place. While we're gone, our women and children will live in cities that have high walls around them. That will keep them safe from the people living in this land. ¹⁸ We won't return to our homes until each of the Israelites has received their share of the land. ¹⁹ We won't receive any share with them on the west side of the Jordan River. We've already received our share here on the east side."

²⁰ Then Moses said to them, "Do what you have promised to do. Get ready to fight for the LORD. ²¹ Prepare yourselves and go across the Jordan River. Fight for the LORD until he has driven out his enemies in front of him. ²² When the land is under the LORD's control, you can come back here. Your duty to the LORD and Israel will be over. Then the LORD will give you this land as your own.

²³ "But what if you fail to do your duty? Then you will be sinning against the LORD. And you may be sure that your sin will be discovered. It will be brought out into the open. ²⁴ So build up cities for your women and children. Make sheep pens for your flocks. But do what you have promised to do."

²⁵ The people of Gad and Reuben spoke to Moses. They said, "We will do just as you command. ²⁶ Our children and wives will remain here in the cities of Gilead. So will our flocks and herds. ²⁷ But we will prepare ourselves for battle. We'll go across the Jordan River and fight for the LORD. We will do just as you have said."

²⁸ Then Moses gave orders about them to Eleazar the priest. He gave the same orders to Joshua, the son of Nun. He also spoke to the family leaders of the Israelite tribes. ²⁹ He said, "The men of Gad and Reuben must get ready for battle. They must go across the Jordan River with you. They must help you fight for the LORD. They must stay with you until the land has been brought under your control. If they do, you must give them the land of Gilead as their own. ³⁰ But what if they don't get ready for battle? What if they don't go across the Jordan with you? Then they must accept a share with you in Canaan."

³¹ The people of Gad and Reuben gave their answer. They said, "We will do what the LORD has said. ³² We'll get ready for battle. We'll go across the Jordan into Canaan. We'll fight for the LORD there. But the property we receive will be on this side of the Jordan River."

³³ Then Moses gave their land to them. He gave it to the tribes of Gad and Reuben and half of the tribe of Manasseh. Manasseh was Joseph's son. One part

of that land had belonged to the kingdom of Sihon. He was the king of the Amorites. The other part had belonged to the kingdom of Og. He was the king of Bashan. Moses gave that whole land to those two and a half tribes. It included its cities and the territory around them.

34 The people of Gad built up the cities of Dibon, Ataroth and Aroer. 35 They built up Atroth Shophan, Jazer, Jogbehah, 36 Beth Nimrah and Beth Haran. They built a high wall around each of those cities. They also built sheep pens for their flocks. 37 The people of Reuben built up Heshbon, Elealeh and Kiriathaim. 38 They also built up Nebo, Baal Meon and Sibmah. They gave new names to the cities they had built up.

39 The people of Makir, the son of Manasseh, went to the land of Gilead. They captured it. They drove out the Amorites living there. 40 So Moses gave Gilead to the people of Makir, the son of Manasseh. And they settled there. 41 Jair was from the family line of Manasseh. Jair captured Gilead's settlements. He called them Havvoth Jair. 42 Nobah captured Kenath and the settlements around it. He named it after himself.

The Places Where Israel Camped During Their Journey

33 Here are the places where the Israelites camped during their journey. When they came out of Egypt, they marched in groups like an army. Moses and Aaron led them. 2 The LORD commanded Moses to record their journey. Here are the places where they camped.

3 The Israelites started out from Rameses on the 15th day of the first month. It was the day after the Passover Feast. They marched out boldly in plain sight of all the Egyptians. 4 The Egyptians were burying all their oldest sons. The LORD had struck them down. He had done it when he punished their gods.

5 The Israelites left Rameses and camped at Sukkoth.

6 They left Sukkoth and camped at Etham. Etham was on the edge of the desert.

7 They left Etham and turned back to Pi Hahiroth. It was east of Baal Zephon. They camped near Migdol.

8 They left Pi Hahiroth. Then they passed through the Red Sea into the desert. They traveled for three days in the Desert of Etham. Then they camped at Marah.

9 They left Marah and went to Elim. Twelve springs and 70 palm trees were there. So they camped at Elim.

10 They left Elim and camped by the Red Sea.

11 They left the Red Sea and camped in the Desert of Sin.

¹²They left the Desert of Sin and camped at Dophkah.

¹³They left Dophkah and camped at Alush.

¹⁴They left Alush and camped at Rephidim. But there was no water there for the people to drink.

¹⁵They left Rephidim and camped in the Desert of Sinai.

¹⁶They left the Desert of Sinai and camped at Kibroth Hattaavah.

¹⁷They left Kibroth Hattaavah and camped at Hazeroth.

¹⁸They left Hazeroth and camped at Rithmah.

¹⁹They left Rithmah and camped at Rimmon Perez.

²⁰They left Rimmon Perez and camped at Libnah.

²¹They left Libnah and camped at Rissah.

²²They left Rissah and camped at Kehelathah.

²³They left Kehelathah and camped at Mount Shepher.

²⁴They left Mount Shepher and camped at Haradah.

²⁵They left Haradah and camped at Makheloth.

²⁶They left Makheloth and camped at Tahath.

²⁷They left Tahath and camped at Terah.

²⁸They left Terah and camped at Mithkah.

²⁹They left Mithkah and camped at Hashmonah.

³⁰They left Hashmonah and camped at Moseroth.

³¹They left Moseroth and camped at Bene Jaakan.

³²They left Bene Jaakan and camped at Hor Haggidgad.

³³They left Hor Haggidgad and camped at Jotbathah.

³⁴They left Jotbathah and camped at Abronah.

³⁵They left Abronah and camped at Ezion Geber.

³⁶They left Ezion Geber and camped at Kadesh. Kadesh was in the Desert of Zin.

³⁷They left Kadesh and camped at Mount Hor. It was on the border of Edom.

³⁸Aaron the priest went up Mount Hor when the LORD commanded him to. That's where he died. It happened on the first day of the fifth month. It was the 40th year after the Israelites came out of Egypt. ³⁹Aaron was 123 years old when he died on Mount Hor.

⁴⁰The Canaanite king of Arad lived in the Negev Desert in Canaan. He heard that the Israelites were coming.

⁴¹They left Mount Hor and camped at Zalmonah.

⁴²They left Zalmonah and camped at Punon.

⁴³They left Punon and camped at Oboth.

⁴⁴They left Oboth and camped at Iye Abarim. It was on the border of Moab.

⁴⁵They left Iye Abarim and camped at Dibon Gad.

⁴⁶ They left Dibon Gad and camped at Almon Diblathaim.

⁴⁷ They left Almon Diblathaim and camped in the mountains of Abarim near Nebo.

⁴⁸ They left the mountains of Abarim and camped on the plains of Moab. That area was by the Jordan River across from Jericho. ⁴⁹ They camped there along the Jordan River from Beth Jeshimoth to Abel Shittim.

⁵⁰ On the plains of Moab the LORD spoke to Moses. He spoke to him by the Jordan River across from Jericho. The LORD said, ⁵¹ "Speak to the Israelites. Tell them, 'Go across the Jordan River into Canaan. ⁵² Drive out all those living in the land. The statues of their gods are made out of stone and metal. Destroy all those statues. And destroy all the high places where they are worshiped. ⁵³ Take the land as your own. Make your homes in it. I have given it to you. ⁵⁴ Cast lots when you divide up the land. Do it based on the number of people in each tribe and family. Give a larger share to a larger group. And give a smaller group a smaller share. The share they receive by casting lots will belong to them. Give out the shares based on the number of people in Israel's tribes.

⁵⁵ " 'But suppose you do not drive out the people living in the land. Then those you allow to remain there will become like needles in your eyes. They will become like thorns in your sides. They will give you trouble in the land where you will live. ⁵⁶ Then I will do to you what I plan to do to them.' "

Israel Arrives at the Borders of Canaan

34 The LORD said to Moses, ² "Give the Israelites a command. Tell them, 'You are going to enter Canaan. The land will be given to you as your own. Here are the borders it must have.

³ " 'Your southern border will include part of the Desert of Zin. It will be along the border of Edom. Your southern border will start in the east from the southern end of the Dead Sea. ⁴ It will cross south of Scorpion Pass. It will continue on to Zin. From there it will go south of Kadesh Barnea. Then it will go to Hazar Addar and over to Azmon. ⁵ There it will turn and join the Wadi of Egypt. It will come to an end at the Mediterranean Sea.

⁶ " 'Your western border will be the coast of the Mediterranean Sea. That will be your border on the west.

⁷ " 'For your northern border, run a line from the Mediterranean Sea to Mount Hor. ⁸ Continue it from Mount Hor to Lebo Hamath. Then the bor-

der will go to Zedad. ⁹ It will continue to Ziphron. It will come to an end at Hazar Enan. That will be your border on the north.

¹⁰ " 'For your eastern border, run a line from Hazar Enan to Shepham. ¹¹ The border will go down from Shepham to Riblah. Riblah is on the east side of Ain. From there the border will continue along the slopes east of the Sea of Galilee. ¹² Then the border will go down along the Jordan River. It will come to an end at the Dead Sea.

" 'That will be your land. And those will be its borders on every side.' "

¹³ Moses gave the Israelites a command. He said, "Cast lots when you divide up the land. Each tribe will have its own share. The LORD has ordered it to be given to the nine and a half tribes. ¹⁴ The families of the tribes of Reuben and Gad have already received their shares. The families of half of the tribe of Manasseh have also received their share. ¹⁵ Those two and a half tribes have received their shares east of the Jordan River. It flows near Jericho. Their land is toward the sunrise."

¹⁶ The LORD spoke to Moses. He said, ¹⁷ "Here are the names of the men who will give out the shares of the land to your people. They are Eleazar the priest and Joshua, the son of Nun. ¹⁸ Also appoint one leader from each of the nine and a half tribes. They will help you give out the land.

¹⁹ Here are their names.

"Caleb, the son of Jephunneh, is from the tribe of Judah.
²⁰ Shemuel, the son of Ammihud, is from the tribe of Simeon.
²¹ Elidad, the son of Kislon, is from the tribe of Benjamin.
²² Bukki, the son of Jogli, is the leader from the tribe of Dan.
²³ Hanniel, the son of Ephod, is the leader from the tribe of Manasseh. Manasseh was the son of Joseph.
²⁴ Kemuel, the son of Shiphtan, is the leader from the tribe of Ephraim. Ephraim was the son of Joseph.
²⁵ Elizaphan, the son of Parnak, is the leader from the tribe of Zebulun.
²⁶ Paltiel, the son of Azzan, is the leader from the tribe of Issachar.
²⁷ Ahihud, the son of Shelomi, is the leader from the tribe of Asher.
²⁸ Pedahel, the son of Ammihud, is the leader from the tribe of Naphtali."

²⁹ These are the men the LORD commanded to give out the shares of the land. They were commanded to give them to Israel in the land of Canaan.

The Levites Receive Their Towns

35 On the plains of Moab, the LORD spoke to Moses. It was by the Jordan River across from Jericho. The LORD said, ² "Command the Israelites to give the Levites towns to live in. The towns must come from the shares of land the people will have as their own. Also give the Levites the grasslands around the towns. ³ Then the Levites will have towns to live in. They will also have grasslands for their cattle and all their other livestock.

⁴ "The grasslands around each town you give them will go out to 1,500 feet from the town wall. ⁵ Outside each town, the east side will measure 3,000 feet. So will the south side, the west side and the north side. The town must be in the center. And the Levites will own the grasslands around each town.

Cities to Run to for Safety

⁶ "Six of the towns you give the Levites will be cities to go to for safety. A person who has killed someone can run to one of them. Also give the Levites 42 other towns. ⁷ You must give the Levites a total of 48 towns. Also give them the grasslands around those towns. ⁸ The towns you give the Levites must come from the land the Israelites have as their own. So the number you give from each tribe will depend on the size of that tribe's share. Take many towns from a tribe that has many towns. But take only a few towns from a tribe that has only a few."

⁹ Then the LORD said to Moses, ¹⁰ "Speak to the Israelites. Tell them, 'You will soon go across the Jordan River. You will enter Canaan. ¹¹ When you do, choose the cities to go to for safety. People who have killed someone by accident can run to one of those cities. ¹² They will be places of safety for them. People will be safe there from those who want to kill them. Then anyone charged with murder will not die before their case has been brought to the community court. ¹³ Six towns will be the cities you can go to for safety. ¹⁴ Three will be east of the Jordan River. The other three will be in Canaan. ¹⁵ Those six towns will be places where the Israelites can go for safety. Outsiders living in Israel can also go to them for safety. So anyone who has killed another person by accident can run there.

¹⁶ " 'Suppose a person uses an iron object to hit and kill someone. Then that person is a murderer and must be put to death. ¹⁷ Or suppose a person is holding a stone that could kill. And they use it to hit and kill someone. Then that person is a murderer and must be put to death. ¹⁸ Or suppose a person is holding a wooden object that could kill. And they use it to hit and kill someone. Then that person is a murderer and must be put to death. ¹⁹ The dead person's nearest male relative must kill the murderer. When he

meets up with him, he must kill the murderer. ²⁰What if a person makes evil plans against someone else? And what if that person pushes them so that they die? Or what if that person throws something at them so that they die? ²¹Or what if that person hits another person with a fist so that the other dies? Then the person who does any of those things must be put to death. That person is a murderer. The dead person's nearest male relative must kill the murderer. When he meets up with him, he must kill the murderer. ²²"'But what if a person suddenly pushes someone else without being angry? Or what if that person throws something at someone else without meaning to? ²³Or what if that person does not see the other person and drops a stone on them that kills them? He was not the dead person's enemy. He did not mean to harm them. ²⁴Then the court must decide between the person who did the act and the nearest male relative of the one who was killed. Here are the rules the court must follow. ²⁵The court must provide a safe place for the person accused of murder. It must keep the one accused of murder safe from those who want to kill them. The court must send the accused person back to the city they ran to for safety. The accused person must stay there until the high priest dies. That priest has been anointed with holy oil. ²⁶"'But suppose the accused person goes outside that city. ²⁷And suppose the dead person's nearest male relative finds them outside the city. Then the relative can kill the accused person. The relative will not be guilty of murder. ²⁸The accused person must stay in that city until the high priest dies. Only then may they return home.

²⁹"'This is what the law requires of you for all time to come. It will apply to you no matter where you live.

³⁰"'Suppose a person kills someone. Then that person must be put to death as a murderer. But do it only when there are witnesses who can tell what happened. Do not put anyone to death if only one witness tells what happened.

³¹"'Do not accept payment for a murderer's life. A murderer deserves to die. They must certainly be put to death.

³²"'Do not accept payment for anyone who has run to a city for safety. Do not let them buy their freedom to return home. They must not go back and live on their own land before the high priest dies.

³³"'Do not pollute the land where you are. Murder pollutes the land. Only one thing can pay to remove the pollution in the land where murder has been committed. The blood of the one who spilled another's blood must be spilled. ³⁴So do not make the land where you live "unclean," because I live there too. I, the LORD, live among the Israelites.'"

*The Property Zelophehad's
Daughters Will Receive*

36 The heads of the families of Gilead came to Moses. Gilead was the son of Makir. The family heads were from the tribe of Manasseh. So they were in the family line of Joseph. They spoke to Moses in front of the leaders of the families of Israel. ² They said, "The LORD commanded you to give shares of the land to the Israelites. He told you to cast lots when you do it. At that time the LORD ordered you to give our brother Zelophehad's share to his daughters. ³ Suppose they marry men from other tribes in Israel. Then their share will be taken away from our family's land. It will be added to the land of the tribe they marry into. So a part of the share given to us will be taken away. ⁴ The Year of Jubilee for the Israelites will come. Then their share will be added to the land of the tribe they marry into. Their land will be taken away from the share given to our tribe."

⁵ Then the LORD gave a command to Moses. He told Moses to give an order to the Israelites. Moses said, "What the tribe in the family line of Joseph is saying is right. ⁶ Here is what the LORD commands for Zelophehad's daughters. They can marry anyone they want to. But they have to marry someone in their own family's tribe. ⁷ Property in Israel must not pass from one tribe to another. Everyone in Israel must keep their family's share of their tribe's land. ⁸ Suppose a daughter in any tribe of Israel receives land from her parents. Then she must marry someone in her father's family and tribe. In that way, every family's share will remain in its family line in Israel. ⁹ Property can't pass from one tribe to another. Each tribe of Israel must keep the land it receives."

¹⁰ So Zelophehad's daughters did just as the LORD commanded Moses. ¹¹ The names of the daughters were Mahlah, Tirzah, Hoglah, Milkah and Noah. All of them married their cousins on their father's side. ¹² They married men in the family line of Manasseh, the son of Joseph. So the land they received remained in their father's family and tribe.

¹³ These are the commands and rules the LORD gave through Moses. He gave them to the Israelites on the plains of Moab. They were by the Jordan River across from Jericho.

Deuteronomy

Introduction:

Deuteronomy is the last book of the law. In this book, Moses gave two speeches. The people were going into a new land. Moses knew he was about to die. He had to remind the children of God to do what God said.

In the first speech, Moses reminded the people how good God had been to them. In the second speech, Moses told the people to obey God's law. He wanted the people to love God with all their heart. God was going to give his people a home, but they needed to follow him.

Near the end of the book, Joshua is picked to take Moses' place. Moses dies before the people go to the new land.

Outline of contents:

The LORD Commands Israel to Leave Mount Horeb

1 These are the words Moses spoke to all the Israelites. At that time, they were in the desert east of the Jordan River. It's in the Arabah Valley across from Suph. The people were between Paran and Tophel, Laban, Hazeroth and Dizahab. ² It takes 11 days to go from Mount Horeb to Kadesh Barnea if you travel on the Mount Seir road.

³ It was the 40th year since the Israelites had left Egypt. On the first day of the 11th month, Moses spoke to them. He told them everything the LORD had commanded him to tell them. ⁴ They had already won the battle over Sihon. Sihon was the king of the Amorites. He had ruled in Heshbon. Israel had also won the battle over Og at Edrei. Og was the king of Bashan. He had ruled in Ashtaroth.

⁵ The people were east of the Jordan River in the territory of Moab. There Moses began to explain the law. Here is what he said.

⁶ The LORD our God spoke to us at Mount Horeb. He said, "You have stayed long enough at this mountain. ⁷ Take your tents down. Go into the hill country of the Amorites. Go to all the people who are their neighbors. Go

to the people who live in the Arabah Valley. Travel to the mountains and the western hills. Go to the people in the Negev Desert and along the coast. Travel to the land of Canaan and to Lebanon. Go as far as the great Euphrates River. ⁸I have given you all this land. Go in and take it as your own. The LORD promised he would give the land to your fathers. He promised it to Abraham, Isaac and Jacob. He also said he would give it to their children after them."

*Some Officials Are Chosen
to Help Moses*

⁹At that time I spoke to you. I said, "You are too heavy a load for me to carry alone. ¹⁰The LORD your God has caused there to be many of you. Today you are as many as the stars in the sky. ¹¹The LORD is the God of your people. May he cause there to be a thousand times more of you. May he bless you, just as he promised he would. ¹²But I can't handle your problems and troubles all by myself. I can't settle your arguments. ¹³So choose some wise men from each of your tribes. They must understand how to give good advice. The people must have respect for them. I will appoint those men to have authority over you."

¹⁴You answered me, "Your suggestion is good."

¹⁵So I chose the leading men of your tribes who were wise and respected. I appointed them to have authority over you. I made them command-ers of thousands, hundreds, fifties and tens. I appointed them to be officials over the tribes. ¹⁶Here is what I commanded your judges at that time. I said, "Listen to your people's cases when they argue with one another. Judge them fairly. It doesn't matter whether the case is between two Israelites or between an Israelite and an outsider living among you. ¹⁷When you judge them, treat everyone the same. Listen to those who are important and those who are not. Don't be afraid of anyone. God is the highest judge. Bring me any case that is too hard for you. I'll listen to it." ¹⁸At that time I told you everything you should do.

*Twelve Men Check Out the
Land of Canaan*

¹⁹The LORD our God commanded us to start out from Mount Horeb. So we did. We went toward the hill country of the Amorites. We traveled all through the huge and terrible desert you saw. Finally, we reached Kadesh Barnea. ²⁰Then I said to you, "You have reached the hill country of the Amorites. The LORD our God is giving it to us. ²¹The LORD your God has given you the land. Go up and take it. Do what the LORD says. He's the God of your people. Don't be afraid. Don't lose hope."

²²Then all of you came to me. You said, "Let's send some men ahead of us. They can check out the land for us and bring back a report. They can suggest to us

which way to go. They can tell us about the towns we'll come to."

²³ That seemed like a good idea to me. So I chose 12 of you. I picked one man from each tribe. ²⁴ They left and went up into the hill country. There they came to the Valley of Eshkol. They checked it out. ²⁵ They got some of the fruit of that land. Then they brought it down to us and gave us their report. They said, "The Lord our God is giving us a good land."

Israel Refuses to Obey the Lord

²⁶ But you wouldn't go up. You refused to obey the command of the Lord your God. ²⁷ You spoke against him in your tents. You said, "The Lord hates us. That's why he brought us out of Egypt to hand us over to the Amorites. He wanted to destroy us. ²⁸ Where can we go? The men who checked out the land have made us afraid. They say, 'The people are stronger and taller than we are. The cities are large. They have walls that reach up to the sky. We even saw the Anakites there.'"

²⁹ Then I said to you, "Don't be terrified. Don't be afraid of them. ³⁰ The Lord your God will go ahead of you. He will fight for you. With your own eyes you saw how he fought for you in Egypt. ³¹ You also saw how the Lord your God brought you through the desert. He carried you everywhere you went, just as a father carries his son. And now you have arrived here."

³² In spite of that, you didn't trust in the Lord your God. ³³ He went ahead of you on your journey. He was in the fire at night and in the cloud during the day. He found places for you to camp. He showed you the way you should go.

³⁴ The Lord heard what you said. So he became angry. He made a promise. He said, ³⁵ "I promised to give this good land to your people of long ago. But no one alive today will see it. ³⁶ Only Caleb will see the land. He is the son of Jephunneh. I will give him and his children after him the land he walked on. He followed me with his whole heart."

³⁷ Because of you, the Lord became angry with me also. He said, "You will not enter the land either. ³⁸ But Joshua, the son of Nun, is your helper. Joshua will enter the land. Help him to be brave. Give him hope. He will lead Israel to take the land as their own. ³⁹ You said your little ones would be taken prisoner. But they will enter the land. They do not yet know right from wrong. But I will give them the land. They will take it as their own. ⁴⁰ As for you, turn around. Start out toward the desert. Go along the road that leads to the Red Sea."

⁴¹ Then you replied, "We have sinned against the Lord. We will go up and fight. We'll do just as the Lord our God has commanded us." So all of you got your swords and put them on. You thought it would be easy to go up into the hill country.

⁴²But the LORD spoke to me. He said, "Tell them, 'Do not go up and fight. I will not be with you. Your enemies will win the battle over you.'"

⁴³So I told you what the LORD said. But you wouldn't listen. You refused to obey his command. You were so filled with pride that you marched up into the hill country. ⁴⁴The Amorites who lived in those hills came out and attacked you. Like large numbers of bees they chased you. They beat you down from Seir all the way to Hormah. ⁴⁵You came back and wept in front of the LORD. But he didn't pay any attention to your weeping. He wouldn't listen to you. ⁴⁶So you stayed in Kadesh for many years. You spent a long time in that area.

Israel Wanders in the Desert

2 We turned back and started out toward the desert. We went along the road that leads to the Red Sea. That's how the LORD had directed me. For a long time we made our way around the hill country of Seir. ²Then the LORD spoke to me. He said, ³"You have made your way around this hill country long enough. So now turn north. ⁴Here are the orders I want you to give the people. Tell them, 'You are about to pass through the territory of your relatives. They are from the family line of Esau. They live in Seir. They will be afraid of you. But be very careful. ⁵Do not make them angry. If you do, they will go to war against you. I will not give you any of their land. You will not have even enough to put your foot on. I have given Esau's people the hill country of Seir as their own. ⁶Pay them with silver for the food you eat and the water you drink.'"

⁷The LORD your God has blessed you in everything your hands have done. He watched over you when you traveled through that huge desert. For these 40 years the LORD your God has been with you. So you have had everything you need.

⁸We went on past our relatives. They are from the family line of Esau. They live in Seir. We turned away from the Arabah Valley road. It comes up from Elath and Ezion Geber. We traveled along the desert road of Moab.

⁹Then the LORD said to me, "Do not attack the Moabites. Do not even make them angry. If you do, they will go to war against you. I will not give you any part of their land. I have given Moab to the people in the family line of Lot. I have given it to them as their own."

¹⁰The Emites used to live there. They were strong people. There were large numbers of them. They were as tall as the Anakites. ¹¹Like the Anakites, they too were thought of as Rephaites. But the Moabites called them Emites. ¹²The Horites used to live in Seir. But the people of Esau drove them out. They destroyed the Horites to make room for themselves.

Then they settled in their territory. They did just as Israel has done in the land the LORD gave them as their own.

13 The LORD said, "Now get up. Go across the Zered Valley." So we went across it.

14 Between the time we left Kadesh Barnea and the time we went across the Zered Valley, 38 years had passed. By then, all the fighting men who had been in our camp from the beginning had died. The LORD had warned them that it would happen. 15 He used his power against them until he had gotten rid of all of them. Not one was left in the camp.

16 Finally, the last of the fighting men among the people died. 17 Then the LORD said to me, 18 "Today you must pass near the border of Moab. Moab is also called Ar. 19 When you come to the Ammonites, do not attack them. Do not make them angry. If you do, they will go to war against you. I will not give you any of their land as your own. I have given it to the people in the family line of Lot. I have given it to them as their own."

20 That land was also thought of as a land of the Rephaites. They used to live there. But the Ammonites called them Zamzummites. 21 The Rephaites were strong people. There were large numbers of them. They were as tall as the Anakites. The LORD destroyed the Rephaites to make room for the Ammonites. So the Ammonites drove them out. Then they settled in the territory of the Rephaites. 22 The LORD had done the same thing for the people of Esau. They lived in Seir. The LORD destroyed the Horites to make room for Esau's people. They drove the Horites out. So the people of Esau have lived in Seir in the territory of the Horites to this very day. 23 The Avvites lived in villages as far away as Gaza. But people came from Crete and destroyed the Avvites. Then the people of Crete made their home in the territory of the Avvites.

Israel Wins the Battle Over Sihon

24 The LORD said, "Start out and go across the valley of the Arnon River. I have handed Sihon over to you. He is the Amorite king of Heshbon. I have also given you his country. Begin to take it as your own. Go to war against him. 25 This very day I will bring fear and terror on all the nations because of you. They will hear about you. They will tremble with fear. Pain and suffering will grip them because of you."

26 I sent messengers from the Desert of Kedemoth. I told them to go to Sihon, the king of Heshbon. They offered him peace. They said, 27 "Let us pass through your country. We'll stay on the main road. We won't turn off it to one side or the other. 28 We'll pay you the right amount of silver for food to eat and water to drink. Just let us walk through your country. 29 The

people of Esau, who live in Seir, allowed us to do that. The people of Moab, who live in Ar, also allowed us to do it. So let us walk through until we go across the Jordan River. Then we'll be able to go into the land the LORD our God is giving us." ³⁰ But Sihon, the king of Heshbon, refused to let us walk through. The LORD your God had made him stubborn in his heart and spirit. The LORD wanted to hand him over to you. And that's exactly what he has done.

³¹ The LORD said to me, "I have begun to hand Sihon and his country over to you. So begin the battle to take his land as your own."

³² Sihon and his whole army came out to fight against us at Jahaz. ³³ But the LORD our God handed him over to us. We struck him down together with his sons and his whole army. ³⁴ At that time we took all his towns. We completely destroyed them. We killed all the men, women and children. We didn't leave any of them alive. ³⁵ But we took for ourselves the livestock and everything else from the towns we had captured. ³⁶ Not a single town was too strong for us. That includes all the towns from Aroer on the rim of the Arnon River valley all the way to Gilead. It also includes the town in the valley. The LORD our God gave us all of them. ³⁷ And you obeyed the LORD's command. You didn't go near any part of the land of the Ammonites. That includes the land along the Jabbok River. It also includes the land around the towns in the hills.

Israel Wins the Battle Over Og

3 Next, we turned and went up along the road toward Bashan. Og marched out with his whole army. They fought against us at Edrei. Og was the king of Bashan. ² The LORD said to me, "Do not be afraid of Og. I have handed him over to you. I have also handed over his whole army and his land. Do to him what you did to Sihon. Sihon was the Amorite king who ruled in Heshbon."

³ So the LORD our God also handed Og, the king of Bashan, and his whole army over to us. We struck them down. We didn't leave any of them alive. ⁴ At that time we took all his cities. There were 60 of them. We took the whole area of Argob. That was Og's kingdom in Bashan. ⁵ All those cities had high walls around them. The city gates were made secure with heavy metal bars. There were also large numbers of villages that didn't have walls. ⁶ We completely destroyed them. We did to them just as we had done to Sihon, the king of Heshbon. We destroyed all their cities. We destroyed the men, women and children. ⁷ But we kept for ourselves the livestock and everything else we took from their cities.

⁸ So at that time we took the territory east of the Jordan River. We captured it from those

two Amorite kings. The territory goes all the way from the Arnon River valley to Mount Hermon. [9] Hermon is called Sirion by the people of Sidon. The Amorites call it Senir. [10] We captured all the towns on the high plains. We took the whole land of Gilead. And we captured the whole land of Bashan as far away as Salekah and Edrei. Those were towns that belonged to Og's kingdom in Bashan. [11] Og, the king of Bashan, was the only Rephaite left. His bed was decorated with iron. It was more than 13 feet long and six feet wide. It is still in the Ammonite city of Rabbah.

Moses Divides Up the Land

[12] I divided up the land we took over at that time. I gave the tribes of Reuben and Gad the territory north of Aroer by the Arnon River valley. It includes half of the hill country of Gilead together with its towns. [13] I gave the rest of Gilead to half of the tribe of Manasseh. I also gave them the whole land of Bashan, the kingdom of Og. The whole area of Argob in Bashan used to be known as a land of the Rephaites. [14] Jair took the whole area of Argob. He was from the family line of Manasseh. Argob goes all the way to the border of the people of Geshur and Maakah. It was named after Jair. So Bashan is called Havvoth Jair to this very day. [15] I gave Gilead to Makir. [16] But I gave to the tribes of Reuben and Gad the territory that reaches from Gilead down to the Arnon River valley. It goes all the way to the Jabbok River. The Jabbok is the northern border of Ammon. The middle of the Arnon River valley is its southern border. [17] The western border of Reuben and Gad is the Jordan River in the Arabah Valley. It reaches from the Sea of Galilee to the Dead Sea. It runs below the slopes of Pisgah.

[18] Here is the command I gave at that time to the tribes of Reuben and Gad and half of the tribe of Manasseh. I said, "The LORD your God has given you this land as your very own. But all your strong men must be prepared for battle. They must cross over ahead of the rest of the Israelites. [19] But your wives and children can stay in the towns I've given you. You can keep your livestock there too. I know you have a lot of livestock. [20] The LORD has given you peace and rest. Then let your families and livestock stay in those towns until the LORD gives peace and rest to the other tribes. And let your families stay until the other tribes have taken over the land the LORD your God is giving them. That land is across the Jordan River. After that, each of you may go back to the land I've given you as your very own."

The LORD Will Not Allow Moses to Cross the Jordan River

[21] At that time I gave Joshua a command. I said, "Your own eyes have seen everything the LORD your God has done to

Sihon and Og. He will do the same thing to all the kingdoms in the land where you are going. ²² Don't be afraid of them. The LORD your God himself will fight for you."

²³ At that time I made my appeal to the LORD. I said, ²⁴ "LORD and King, you have begun to show me how great you are. You have shown me how strong your hand is. You do great works and mighty acts. There isn't any god in heaven or on earth who can do what you do. ²⁵ Let me go across the Jordan River. Let me see the good land beyond it. I want to see that fine hill country and Lebanon."

²⁶ But the LORD was angry with me because of what you did. He wouldn't listen to me. "That is enough!" the LORD said. "Do not speak to me anymore about this matter. ²⁷ Go up to the highest slopes of Pisgah. Look west and north and south and east. Look at the land with your own eyes. But you are not going to go across this Jordan River. ²⁸ So appoint Joshua as the new leader. Help him to be brave. Give him hope and strength. He will take these people across the Jordan. You will see the land. But he will lead them into it to take it as their own." ²⁹ So we stayed in the valley near Beth Peor.

Obey the LORD

4 Now, Israel, listen to the rules and laws I'm going to teach you. Obey them and you will live. You will go in and take over the land. The LORD was the God of your people of long ago. He's giving you the land. ² Don't add to what I'm commanding you. Don't subtract from it either. Instead, obey the commands of the LORD your God that I'm giving you.

³ Your own eyes saw what the LORD your God did at Baal Peor. He destroyed every one of your people who worshiped the Baal that was worshiped at Peor. ⁴ But all of you who remained true to the LORD your God are still alive today.

⁵ I have taught you rules and laws, just as the LORD my God commanded me. Obey them in the land you are entering to take as your very own. ⁶ Be careful to keep them. That will show the nations how wise and understanding you are. They will hear about all these rules. They'll say, "That great nation certainly has wise and understanding people." ⁷ The LORD our God is near us every time we pray to him. What other nation is great enough to have its gods that close to them? ⁸ I'm giving you the laws of the LORD today. What other nation is great enough to have rules and laws as fair as these?

⁹ Don't be careless. Instead, be very careful. Don't forget the things your eyes have seen. As long as you live, don't let them slip from your mind. Teach them to your children and their children after them. ¹⁰ Remember the day you stood at Mount Horeb. The LORD your God was

there. He said to me, "Bring the people to me to hear my words. I want them to learn to have respect for me as long as they live in the land. I want them to teach my words to their children." [11] You came near and stood at the foot of the mountain. It blazed with fire that reached as high as the very heavens. There were black clouds and deep darkness. [12] Then the LORD spoke to you out of the fire. You heard the sound of his words. But you didn't see any shape or form. You only heard a voice. [13] He announced his covenant to you. That covenant is the Ten Commandments. He commanded you to obey them. Then he wrote them down on two stone tablets. [14] At that time the LORD directed me to teach you his rules and laws. You must obey them in the land you are crossing the Jordan River to take as your own.

Don't Make or Worship Statues of Gods

[15] The LORD spoke to you at Mount Horeb out of the fire. But you didn't see any shape or form that day. So be very careful. [16] Make sure you don't commit a horrible sin. Don't make for yourselves a statue of a god. Don't make a god that looks like a man or woman or anything else. [17] Don't make one that looks like any animal on earth or any bird that flies in the sky. [18] Don't make a statue that looks like any creature that moves along the ground or any fish that swims in the water. [19] When you look up at the heavens, you will see the sun and moon. And you will see huge numbers of stars. Don't let anyone tempt you to bow down to the sun, moon or stars. Don't worship things the LORD your God has provided for all the nations on earth. [20] Egypt was like a furnace that melts iron down and makes it pure. But the LORD took you and brought you out of Egypt. He wanted you to be his very own people. And that's exactly what you are.

[21] The LORD was angry with me because of what you did. He promised that he would never let me go across the Jordan River. He promised that I would never enter that good land. It's the land the LORD your God is giving you as your own. [22] I'll die here in this land. I won't go across the Jordan. But you are about to cross over it. You will take that good land as your own. [23] Be careful. Don't forget the covenant the LORD your God made with you. Don't make for yourselves a statue of any god at all. He has told you not to. So don't do it. [24] The LORD your God is like a fire that burns everything up. He wants you to worship only him.

[25] So don't make a statue of a god. Don't commit that horrible sin. Don't do it even after you have had children and grandchildren. Don't do it even after you have lived in the land a long time. If you do, that will be an evil thing in the sight of the LORD your God. You will make him

angry. [26] Today I'm calling out to the heavens and the earth to be witnesses against you. Suppose you do these things. Then you will quickly die in the land you are going across the Jordan River to take over. You won't live there very long. You will certainly be destroyed. [27] The LORD will drive you out of your land. He will scatter you among the nations. Only a few of you will remain alive there. [28] There you will worship gods that men have made out of wood and stone. Those gods can't see, hear, eat or smell. [29] Perhaps while you are there, you will seek the LORD your God. You will find him if you seek him with all your heart and with all your soul. [30] All the things I've told you about might happen to you. And you will be in trouble. But later you will return to the LORD your God. You will obey him. [31] The LORD your God is tender and loving. He won't leave you or destroy you. He won't forget the covenant he made with your people of long ago. He gave his word when he made it.

The LORD Is God

[32] Ask now about the days of long ago. Find out what happened long before your time. Ask about what has happened since the time God created human beings on the earth. Ask from one end of the world to the other. Has anything as great as this ever happened? Has anything like it ever been heard of? [33] You heard the voice of God speaking out of fire. And you lived! Has that happened to any other people? [34] Has any god ever tried to take one nation out of another to be his own? Has any god done it by testing his people? Has any god done it with signs and amazing deeds or with war? Has any god reached out his mighty hand and powerful arm? Or has any god shown his people his great and wonderful acts? The LORD your God did all those things for you in Egypt. With your very own eyes you saw him do them.

[35] The LORD showed you those things so that you might know he is God. There is no other God except him. [36] From heaven he made you hear his voice. He wanted to teach you. On earth he showed you his great fire. You heard his words coming out of the fire. [37] He loved your people of long ago. He chose their children after them. So he brought you out of Egypt. He used his great strength to do it. [38] He drove out nations to make room for you. They were greater and stronger than you are. He will bring you into their land. He wants to give it to you as your very own. The whole land is as good as yours right now.

[39] The LORD is God in heaven above and on the earth below. Today you must agree with that and take it to heart. There is no other God. [40] I'm giving you his rules and commands today. Obey them. Then things will go well with you and your children after you. You will live a long time in the land. The LORD your

God is giving you the land for all time to come.

Cities to Run to for Safety

⁴¹ Then Moses set apart three cities east of the Jordan River. ⁴² Suppose someone killed a person they didn't hate and without meaning to do it. That person could run to one of those cities and stay alive. ⁴³ Here are the names of the cities. Bezer was for the people of Reuben. It was in the high plains in the desert. Ramoth was for the people of Gad. It was in Gilead. Golan was for the people of Manasseh. It was in Bashan.

Moses Gives the Law to Israel

⁴⁴ Here is the law Moses gave the Israelites. ⁴⁵ Here are its terms, rules and laws. Moses gave them to the people when they came out of Egypt. ⁴⁶ They were now east of the Jordan River in the valley near Beth Peor. They were in the land of Sihon, the king of the Amorites. He ruled in Heshbon. But Moses and the Israelites won the battle over him after we came out of Egypt. ⁴⁷ They captured his land and made it their own. They also took the land of Og, the king of Bashan. Sihon and Og were the two Amorite kings east of the Jordan River. ⁴⁸ Their land reached from Aroer on the rim of the Arnon River valley to Mount Hermon. ⁴⁹ It included the whole Arabah Valley east of the Jordan. It included land all the way to the Dead Sea below the slopes of Pisgah.

The Ten Commandments

5 Moses sent for all the Israelites. Here is what he said to them.

Israel, listen to me. Here are the rules and laws I'm announcing to you today. Learn them well. Be sure to obey them. ² The LORD our God made a covenant with us at Mount Horeb. ³ He didn't make it only with our people of long ago. He also made it with us. In fact, he made it with all of us who are alive here today. ⁴ The LORD spoke to you face to face. His voice came out of the fire on the mountain. ⁵ At that time I stood between the LORD and you. I announced to you the LORD's message. I did it because you were afraid of the fire. You didn't go up the mountain. The LORD said,

⁶ "I am the LORD your God. I brought you out of Egypt. That is the land where you were slaves.

⁷ "Do not put any other gods in place of me.

⁸ "Do not make statues of gods that look like anything in the sky or on the earth or in the waters. ⁹ Do not bow down to them or worship them. I am the LORD your God. I want you to worship only me. I cause the sins of the parents to affect their children. I will cause the sins of those who hate me to affect even their grandchildren and great-grandchildren.

¹⁰ But for all time to come I show love to all those who love me and keep my commandments.

¹¹ "Do not misuse the name of the LORD your God. The LORD will find guilty anyone who misuses his name.

¹² "Keep the Sabbath day holy. Do this just as the LORD your God has commanded you. ¹³ Do all your work in six days. ¹⁴ But the seventh day is a sabbath to honor the LORD your God. Do not do any work on that day. The same command applies to your sons and daughters, your male and female servants, your oxen, your donkeys and your other animals. It also applies to any outsiders who live in your towns. I want your male and female servants to rest, just as you do. ¹⁵ Remember that you were slaves in Egypt. The LORD your God reached out his mighty hand and powerful arm and brought you out of there. So the LORD your God has commanded you to keep the Sabbath day holy.

¹⁶ "Honor your father and mother, just as the LORD your God has commanded you. Then you will live a long time in the land he is giving you. And things will go well with you there.

¹⁷ "Do not murder.

¹⁸ "Do not commit adultery.

¹⁹ "Do not steal.

²⁰ "Do not be a false witness against your neighbor.

²¹ "Do not want to have your neighbor's wife. Do not desire anything your neighbor owns. Do not desire to have your neighbor's house or land, male or female servant, ox or donkey."

²² These are the commandments the LORD announced in a loud voice to your whole community. He gave them to you there on the mountain. He spoke out of the fire, cloud and deep darkness. He didn't add anything else. Then he wrote the commandments on two stone tablets. And he gave them to me.

²³ The mountain was blazing with fire. You heard the voice coming out of the darkness. So your elders and all the leaders of your tribes came to me. ²⁴ You said, "The LORD our God has shown us his glory and majesty. We have heard his voice coming out of the fire. Today we have seen that a person can still stay alive even if God speaks with them. ²⁵ But why should we die? This great fire will burn us up. We'll die if we hear the voice of the LORD our God again. ²⁶ We have heard the voice of the living God. We've heard him speaking out of the fire. Has any other human being ever heard him speak like that and stayed alive? ²⁷ Go near and listen to everything the LORD our God says. Then tell us

what he tells you. We will listen and obey."

28 The LORD heard you when you spoke to me. He said to me, "I have heard what these people said to you. Everything they said was good. 29 But I wish they would always have respect for me in their hearts. I wish they would always obey all my commands. Then things would go well with them and their children forever.

30 "Go and tell them to return to their tents. 31 But you stay here with me. Then I will give you all my commands, rules and laws. You must teach the people to obey them in the land I am giving them as their very own."

32 So be careful to do what the LORD your God has commanded you. Don't turn away from his commands to the right or the left. 33 Live exactly as the LORD your God has commanded you to live. Then you will enjoy life in the land you will soon own. Things will go well with you there. You will live there for a long time.

Love the LORD Your God

6 The LORD your God has directed me to teach you his commands, rules and laws. Obey them in the land you will take over when you go across the Jordan River. 2 Then you, your children and their children after them will honor the LORD your God as long as you live. Obey all his rules and commands I'm giving you. If you do, you will enjoy long life. 3 Israel, listen to me. Make sure you obey me. Then things will go well with you. The number of your people will increase greatly in a land that has plenty of milk and honey. That's what the LORD, the God of your parents, promised you.

4 Israel, listen to me. The LORD is our God. The LORD is the one and only God. 5 Love the LORD your God with all your heart and with all your soul. Love him with all your strength. 6 The commandments I give you today must be in your hearts. 7 Make sure your children learn them. Talk about them when you are at home. Talk about them when you walk along the road. Speak about them when you go to bed. And speak about them when you get up. 8 Write them down and tie them on your hands as a reminder. Also tie them on your foreheads. 9 Write them on the doorframes of your houses. Also write them on your gates.

10 The LORD your God will bring you into the land of Canaan. He gave his word. He promised he would give the land to your fathers, to Abraham, Isaac and Jacob. The land has large, wealthy cities you didn't build. 11 It has houses filled with all kinds of good things you didn't provide. The land has wells you didn't dig. And it has vineyards and groves of olive trees you didn't plant. You will have plenty to eat. 12 But be careful that you don't forget the LORD. Remem-

ber that he brought you out of Egypt. That's the land where you were slaves.

¹³ Worship the LORD your God. He is the only one you should serve. When you make promises, do so in his name. ¹⁴ Don't serve the gods of the nations around you. ¹⁵ The LORD your God is among you. He wants you to worship only him. If you worship other gods, God will be very angry with you. And he will destroy you from the face of the land. ¹⁶ Don't test the LORD your God as you did at Massah. ¹⁷ Be sure to obey the LORD's commands. Obey the terms and rules he has given you. ¹⁸ Do what is right and good in the LORD's eyes. Then things will go well with you. You will go in and take over the land. It's the good land the LORD promised to your people of long ago. ¹⁹ You will drive out all your enemies to make room for you. That's what the LORD said would happen.

²⁰ Later on, your child might ask you, "What is the meaning of the terms, rules and laws the LORD our God has commanded you to obey?" ²¹ If they do ask you, tell them, "We were Pharaoh's slaves in Egypt. But the LORD used his mighty hand to bring us out of Egypt. ²² With our own eyes we saw the LORD send amazing signs. They were great and terrible. He sent them on Egypt and Pharaoh and everyone in his house. ²³ But the LORD brought us out of Egypt. He planned to bring us into the land of Canaan and give it to us.

It's the land he promised to our people of long ago. ²⁴ The LORD our God commanded us to obey all his rules. He commanded us to honor him. If we do, we will always succeed and be kept alive. That's what is happening today. ²⁵ We must make sure we obey the whole law in the sight of the LORD our God. That's what he has commanded us to do. If we obey his law, we'll be doing what he requires of us."

The LORD Will Drive Out Many Nations

7 The LORD your God will bring you into the land. You are going to enter it and take it as your own. He'll drive out many nations to make room for you. He'll drive out the Hittites, Girgashites, Amorites, Canaanites, Perizzites, Hivites and Jebusites. Those seven nations are larger and stronger than you are. ² The LORD your God will hand them over to you. You will win the battle over them. You must completely destroy them. Don't make a peace treaty with them. Don't show them any mercy. ³ Don't marry any of their people. Don't give your daughters to their sons. And don't take their daughters for your sons. ⁴ If you do, those people will turn your children away from serving the LORD. Then your children will serve other gods. The LORD will be very angry with you. He will quickly destroy you. ⁵ So here is what you must do to those people. Break down their altars. Smash their sacred stones.

Cut down the poles they use to worship the female god named Asherah. Burn the statues of their gods in the fire. ⁶You are a holy nation. The LORD your God has set you apart for himself. He has chosen you to be his special treasure. He chose you out of all the nations on the face of the earth to be his people.

⁷The LORD chose you because he loved you very much. He didn't choose you because you had more people than other nations. In fact, you had the smallest number of all. ⁸The LORD chose you because he loved you. He wanted to keep the promise he had made to your people of long ago. That's why he used his mighty hand to bring you out of Egypt. He bought you back from the land where you were slaves. He set you free from the power of Pharaoh, the king of Egypt. ⁹So I want you to realize that the LORD your God is God. He is the faithful God. He keeps his covenant for all time to come. He keeps it with those who love him and obey his commandments. He shows them his love. ¹⁰But he will pay back those who hate him. He'll destroy them. He'll quickly pay back those who hate him. ¹¹So be careful to obey the commands, rules and laws I'm giving you today.

¹²Pay attention to the laws of the LORD your God. Be careful to obey them. Then he will keep his covenant of love with you. That's what he promised to your people of long ago. ¹³The LORD will love you and bless you. He'll cause there to be many of you. He'll give you many children. He'll bless the crops of your land. He'll give you plenty of grain, olive oil and fresh wine. He'll bless your herds with many calves. He'll give your flocks many lambs. He'll do all these things for you in the land of Canaan. It's the land he promised your people of long ago that he would give you. ¹⁴He will bless you more than any other nation. All your men and women will have children. All your livestock will have little ones. ¹⁵The LORD will keep you from getting sick. He won't send on you any of the horrible sicknesses you saw all around you in Egypt. But he'll send them on everyone who hates you. ¹⁶You must destroy all the nations the LORD your God hands over to you. Don't feel sorry for them. Don't serve their gods. If you do, they will be a trap for you.

¹⁷You might say to yourselves, "These nations are stronger than we are. How can we drive them out?" ¹⁸But don't be afraid of them. Be sure to remember what the LORD your God did to Pharaoh and all the Egyptians. ¹⁹With your own eyes you saw what the LORD did to them. You saw the signs and amazing things he did. He reached out his mighty hand and powerful arm. The LORD your God used all those things to bring you out. You are now afraid of the nations that are in the land the LORD promised you. But the LORD your God will do to them

the same things he did to Egypt. ²⁰The LORD your God will also send hornets among those nations. Some of the people left alive will hide from you. But even they will die. ²¹So don't be terrified by them. The LORD your God is with you. He is a great and wonderful God. ²²The LORD your God will drive out those nations to make room for you. But he will do it little by little. You won't be allowed to get rid of them all at once. If you did, wild animals would multiply all around you. ²³But the LORD your God will hand those nations over to you. He will throw them into a panic until they are destroyed. ²⁴He will hand their kings over to you. You will wipe out their names from the earth. No one will be able to stand up against you. You will destroy them. ²⁵Burn the statues of their gods in the fire. Don't wish for the silver and gold on those statues. Don't take it for yourselves. If you do, it will be a trap for you. The LORD your God hates it. ²⁶Don't bring anything he hates into your house. If you do, you will be completely destroyed along with it. So hate it with all your heart. It is set apart to be destroyed.

Remember What the LORD Has Done

8 Make sure you obey every command I'm giving you today. Then you will live, and there will be many of you. You will enter the land and take it as your own. It's the land the LORD promised to your people of long ago. ²Remember how the LORD your God led you all the way. He guided you in the desert for these 40 years. He wanted to take your pride away. He wanted to test you to know what was in your hearts. He wanted to see whether you would obey his commands. ³He took your pride away. He let you go hungry. Then he gave you manna to eat. You and your parents had never even known anything about manna before. He tested you to teach you that man doesn't live only on bread. He also lives on every word that comes from the mouth of the LORD. ⁴Your clothes didn't wear out during these 40 years. Your feet didn't swell. ⁵Here is what I want you to know in your hearts. The LORD your God guides you, just as parents guide their children.

⁶Obey the commands of the LORD your God. Live as he wants you to live. Have respect for him. ⁷The LORD your God is bringing you into a good land. It has brooks, streams and deep springs of water. Those springs flow in its valleys and hills. ⁸It has wheat, barley, vines, fig trees, pomegranates, olive oil and honey. ⁹There is plenty of food in that land. You will have everything you need. Its rocks have iron in them. And you can dig copper out of its hills. ¹⁰When you have eaten and are satisfied, praise the LORD your God. Praise him for the good land he has given you. ¹¹Make sure you don't forget

the Lord your God. Don't fail to obey his commands, laws and rules. I'm giving them to you today. [12] But suppose you don't obey his commands. And suppose you have plenty to eat. You build fine houses and live in them. [13] The number of your herds and flocks increases. You also get more and more silver and gold. And everything you have multiplies. [14] Then your hearts will become proud. And you will forget the Lord your God. The Lord brought you out of Egypt. That's the land where you were slaves. [15] He led you through that huge and terrible desert. It was a dry land. It didn't have any water. It had poisonous snakes and scorpions. The Lord gave you water out of solid rock. [16] He gave you manna to eat in the desert. Your people had never even known anything about manna before. The Lord took your pride away. He tested you. He did it so that things would go well with you in the end. [17] You might say to yourself, "My power and my strong hands have made me rich." [18] But remember the Lord your God. He gives you the ability to produce wealth. That shows he stands by the terms of the covenant he made with you. He promised it to your people of long ago. And he's still faithful to his covenant today.

[19] Don't forget the Lord your God. Don't serve other gods. Don't worship them and bow down to them. I am a witness against you today that if you do, you will certainly be destroyed. [20] You will be destroyed just like the nations the Lord your God is destroying to make room for you. That's what will happen if you don't obey him.

Why the Lord Gave Canaan to Israel

9 Israel, listen to me. You are now about to go across the Jordan River. You will take over the land of the nations that live there. Those nations are greater and stronger than you are. Their large cities have walls that reach up to the sky. [2] The people who live there are Anakites. They are strong and tall. You know all about them. You have heard people say, "Who can stand up against the Anakites?" [3] But today you can be sure the Lord your God will go over there ahead of you. He is like a fire that will burn them up. He'll destroy them. He'll bring them under your control. You will drive them out. You will put an end to them quickly, just as the Lord has promised you.

[4] The Lord your God will drive them out to make room for you. When he does, don't say to yourself, "The Lord has done it because I am godly. That's why he brought me here to take over this land." That isn't true. The Lord is going to drive out those nations to make room for you because they are very evil. [5] You are not going in to take over their land because you have done what is right or honest. It's because those nations

are so evil. That's why the LORD your God will drive them out to make room for you. He will do what he said he would do. He made a promise to your fathers, to Abraham, Isaac and Jacob. ⁶ The LORD your God is giving you this good land to take as your own. But you must understand that it isn't because you are a godly nation. In fact, you are stubborn.

Israel Worshiped the Golden Calf

⁷ Here is something you must remember. Never forget it. You made the LORD your God angry in the desert. You refused to obey him from the day you left Egypt until you arrived here. ⁸ At Mount Horeb you made the LORD angry enough to destroy you. ⁹ I went up the mountain. I went there to receive the tablets of the covenant law. They were made out of stone. It was the covenant the LORD had made with you. I stayed on the mountain for 40 days and 40 nights. I didn't eat any food or drink any water. ¹⁰ The LORD gave me two stone tablets. The words on them were written by the finger of God. All the commandments the LORD gave you were written on the tablets. He announced them to you out of the fire on the mountain. He wrote them on the day you gathered together there.

¹¹ The 40 days and 40 nights came to an end. Then the LORD gave me the two stone tablets. They were the tablets of the cov-

enant law. ¹² The LORD told me, "Go down from here right away. The people you brought out of Egypt have become very sinful. They have quickly turned away from what I commanded them. They have made a statue of a god for themselves."

¹³ The LORD also said to me, "I have seen these people. They are so stubborn! ¹⁴ Do not try to stop me. I am going to destroy them. I will wipe them out from the earth. Then I will make you into a great nation. Your people will be stronger than they were. There will be more of you than there were of them."

¹⁵ So I turned and went down the mountain. It was blazing with fire. I was carrying the two tablets of the covenant law. ¹⁶ When I looked, I saw that you had sinned against the LORD your God. You had made for yourselves a metal statue of a god. It looked like a calf. You had quickly turned away from the path the LORD had commanded you to follow. ¹⁷ So I threw the two tablets out of my hands. You watched them break into pieces.

¹⁸ Then once again I fell down flat in front of the LORD with my face toward the ground. I lay there for 40 days and 40 nights. I didn't eat any food or drink any water. You had committed a terrible sin. You had done an evil thing in the LORD's sight. You had made him angry. ¹⁹ I was afraid of the LORD's great anger. He was so angry with you he wanted to destroy you. But the LORD listened to me again.

20 And he was so angry with Aaron he wanted to destroy him too. But at that time I prayed for Aaron. 21 I also got that sinful calf you had made. I burned it in the fire. I crushed it and ground it into fine powder. Then I threw the powder into a stream that was flowing down the mountain.

22 You also made the LORD angry at Taberah, Massah and Kibroth Hattaavah.

23 The LORD sent you out from Kadesh Barnea. He said, "Go up and take over the land I have given you." But you refused to do what the LORD your God had commanded you to do. You didn't trust him or obey him. 24 You have been refusing to obey the LORD as long as I've known you.

25 I lay down in front of the LORD with my face toward the ground for 40 days and 40 nights. I did it because the LORD had said he would destroy you. 26 I prayed to him. "LORD and King," I said, "don't destroy your people. They belong to you. You set them free by your great power. You used your mighty hand to bring them out of Egypt. 27 Remember your servants Abraham, Isaac and Jacob. Forgive the Israelites for being so stubborn. Don't judge them for the evil and sinful things they've done. 28 If you do, the Egyptians will say, 'The LORD wasn't able to take them into the land he had promised to give them. He hated them. So he brought them out of Egypt to put them to death in the desert.' 29 But they are your people. They belong to you. You used your great power to bring them out of Egypt. You reached out your mighty arm and saved them."

The New Stone Tablets

10 At that time the LORD spoke to me. He said, "Carve out two stone tablets, just like the first ones. Then come up to me on the mountain. Also make a wooden ark. 2 I will write on the tablets the words that were on the first tablets, which you broke. Then you must put the tablets in the ark."

3 So I made the ark out of acacia wood. I carved out two stone tablets that were just like the first ones. I went up the mountain. I carried the two tablets in my hands. 4 The LORD wrote on the tablets what he had written before. It was the Ten Commandments. He had announced them to you out of the fire on the mountain. It was on the day you had gathered together there. So the LORD gave the tablets to me. 5 Then I came back down the mountain. I put the tablets in the ark I had made, just as the LORD had commanded me. And that's where they are now.

6 Remember how the Israelites traveled from the wells of Bene Jaakan to Moserah. That's where Aaron died. And his body was buried there. His son Eleazar became the next priest after him. 7 From Moserah the people traveled to Gudgodah. Then they went on to Jotbathah. That

land has streams of water. ⁸At that time the LORD set the tribe of Levi apart. He appointed them to carry the ark of the covenant of the LORD. He wanted them to serve him. He told them to bless the people in his name. And they still do it today. ⁹That's why the Levites don't have any part of the land the LORD gave the other tribes in Israel. They don't have any share among them. The LORD himself is their share. That's what the LORD your God told them.

¹⁰I had stayed on the mountain for 40 days and 40 nights, just as I did the first time. The LORD listened to me that time also. He didn't want to destroy you. ¹¹"Go," the LORD said to me. "Lead the people on their way. Then they can enter the land and take it over. I have given my word. I promised I would give the land to their fathers, to Abraham, Isaac and Jacob."

Honor the LORD

¹²And now, Israel, what is the LORD your God asking you to do? Honor him. Live exactly as he wants you to live. Love him. Serve him with all your heart and with all your soul. ¹³Obey the LORD's commands and rules. I'm giving them to you today for your own good.

¹⁴The heavens belong to the LORD your God. Even the highest heavens belong to him. He owns the earth and everything in it. ¹⁵But the LORD loved your people of long ago very much. You are their children. And he chose you above all the other nations. His love and his promise remain with you to this very day. ¹⁶So don't be stubborn anymore. Obey the LORD. ¹⁷The LORD your God is the greatest God of all. He is the greatest LORD of all. He is the great God. He is mighty and wonderful. He treats everyone the same. He doesn't accept any money from those who want special favors. ¹⁸He stands up for widows and for children whose fathers have died. He loves outsiders living among you. He gives them food and clothes. ¹⁹So you also must love outsiders. Remember that you yourselves were outsiders in Egypt. ²⁰Honor the LORD your God. Serve him. Remain true to him. When you make promises, do so in his name. ²¹He is the one you should praise. He's your God. With your own eyes you saw the great and amazing things he did for you. ²²Long ago, your people went down into Egypt. The total number of them was 70. And now the LORD your God has made you as many as the stars in the sky.

Love and Obey the LORD

11 Love the LORD your God. Do what he requires. Always obey his rules, laws and commands. ²Remember today that your children weren't the ones the LORD your God guided and corrected. They didn't see his majesty. They weren't in Egypt when he reached out his mighty hand and powerful arm. ³They didn't see the signs and the other things he did in Egypt. They didn't see what he did to Pharaoh, the king of Egypt, and to his whole country. 4 They weren't there when the LORD destroyed the army of Egypt and its horses and chariots. He swept the waters of the Red Sea over the Egyptians while they were chasing you. He wiped them out forever. 5 Your children didn't see what he did for you in the desert before you arrived here. 6 They didn't see what he did to Dathan and Abiram, the sons of Eliab. Eliab was from the tribe of Reuben. The earth opened its mouth right in the middle of the Israelite camp. It swallowed up Dathan and Abiram. It swallowed them up together with their families, tents and every living thing that belonged to them. 7 But with your own eyes you saw all the great things the LORD has done.

8 So obey all the commands I'm giving you today. Then you will be strong enough to go in and take over the land. You will go across the Jordan River and take the land as your own. 9 You will live there for a long time. It's the land the LORD promised to give to Abraham, Isaac and Jacob and their children after them. He gave his word when he made that promise. The land has plenty of milk and honey. 10 You will enter it and take it over. It isn't like the land of Egypt. That's where you came from. You planted your seeds there. You had to water them, just as you have to water a vegetable garden. 11 But you will soon go across the Jordan River. The land you are going to take over has mountains and valleys in it. It drinks rain from heaven. 12 It's a land the LORD your God takes care of. His eyes always look on it with favor. He watches over it from the beginning of the year to its end.

13 So be faithful. Obey the commands the LORD your God is giving you today. Love him. Serve him with all your heart and with all your soul. 14 Then the LORD will send rain on your land at the right time. He'll send rain in the fall and in the spring. You will be able to gather your grain. You will also be able to make olive oil and fresh wine. 15 He'll provide grass in the fields for your cattle. You will have plenty to eat.

16 But be careful. Don't let anyone tempt you to do something wrong. Don't turn away and worship other gods. Don't bow down to them. 17 If you do, the LORD will be very angry with you. He'll close up the sky. It won't rain. The ground won't produce its crops. Soon you will die. You won't live to enjoy the good land the LORD is giving you. 18 So keep my words in your hearts and minds. Write them down and tie them on your hands as a reminder. Also tie them on your foreheads. 19 Teach them to your children. Talk about them when you are at home. Talk about them when you walk along the road. Speak about them when you go to bed.

And speak about them when you get up. ²⁰ Write them on the doorframes of your houses. Also write them on your gates. ²¹ Then you and your children will live for a long time in the land. The LORD promised to give the land to Abraham, Isaac and Jacob. Your family line will continue as long as the heavens remain above the earth.

²² So be careful. Obey all the commands I'm giving you to follow. Love the LORD your God. Live exactly as he wants you to live. Remain true to him. ²³ Then the LORD will drive out all the nations to make room for you. They are larger and stronger than you are. But you will take their land. ²⁴ Every place you walk on will belong to you. Your territory will go all the way from the desert to Lebanon. It will go from the Euphrates River to the Mediterranean Sea. ²⁵ No one will be able to stand up against you. The LORD your God will throw the whole land into a panic because of you. He'll do it everywhere you go, just as he promised you.

²⁶ Listen to me. I'm setting a blessing and a curse in front of you today. ²⁷ I'm giving you the commands of the LORD your God today. You will be blessed if you obey them. ²⁸ But you will be cursed if you don't obey them. So don't turn away from the path I'm now commanding you to take. Don't turn away by worshiping other gods you didn't know before. ²⁹ The LORD your God will bring you into the land to take it over. When he does, you must announce the blessings from Mount Gerizim. You must announce the curses from Mount Ebal. ³⁰ As you know, those mountains are across the Jordan River. They are on the west side of the Jordan toward the setting sun. They are near the large trees of Moreh. The mountains are in the territory of the Canaanites, who live in the Arabah Valley near Gilgal. ³¹ You are about to go across the Jordan River. You will enter the land and take it over. The LORD your God is giving it to you. You will take it over and live there. ³² When you do, make sure you obey all the rules and laws I'm giving you today.

Worship Only Where the LORD Wants You To

12 Here are the rules and laws you must obey. Be careful to obey them in the land the LORD has given you to take as your own. He's the God of your people who lived long ago. Obey these rules and laws as long as you live in the land. ² You will soon drive the nations out of it. Completely destroy all the places where they worship their gods. Destroy them on the high mountains, on the hills and under every green tree. ³ Break down their altars. Smash their sacred stones. Burn up the poles they use to worship the female god named Asherah. Cut down the statues of their gods. Wipe out the names of their gods from those places.

⁴You must not worship the LORD your God the way those nations worship their gods. ⁵Instead, go to the special place he will choose from among all your tribes. He will put his Name there. That's where you must go. ⁶Take your burnt offerings and sacrifices to that place. Bring your special gifts and a tenth of everything you produce. Take with you what you have promised to give. Bring any other offerings you choose to give. And bring the male animals among your livestock that were born first to their mothers. ⁷You and your families will eat at the place the LORD your God will choose. He will be with you there. You will find joy in everything you have done. That's because he has blessed you.

⁸You must not do as we're doing here today. All of us are doing only what we think is right. ⁹That's because you haven't yet reached the place the LORD is giving you. Your God will give you peace and rest there. ¹⁰But first you will go across the Jordan River. You will settle in the land he's giving you. It will belong to you as your share. He will give you peace and rest from all your enemies around you. You will live in safety. ¹¹The LORD your God will choose a special place. He will put his Name there. That's where you must bring everything I command you to bring. That includes your burnt offerings and sacrifices. It includes your special gifts and a tenth of everything

you produce. It also includes all the things of value that you promised to give to the LORD. ¹²Be filled with joy there in the sight of the LORD your God. Your children should also be joyful. So should your male and female servants. And so should the Levites from your towns. The Levites won't receive any part of the land as their share. ¹³Be careful not to sacrifice your burnt offerings anywhere you want to. ¹⁴Offer them only at the place the LORD will choose in one of your tribes. There you must obey everything I command you.

¹⁵But you can kill your animals in any of your towns. You can eat as much of the meat as you want to. You can eat it as if it were antelope or deer meat. That is part of the blessing the LORD your God is giving you. Those who are "clean" and those who are not can eat it. ¹⁶But you must not eat meat that still has blood in it. Pour the blood out on the ground like water. ¹⁷Here are the things you must not eat in your own towns. You must not eat the tenth part of your grain, olive oil and fresh wine. It belongs to the LORD. You must not eat the male animals among your livestock that were born first to their mothers. Don't eat anything you have promised to give. Don't eat any offerings you have chosen to give. And you must not eat any of your special gifts. ¹⁸Instead, you must eat all those things in the sight of the LORD your God. Do it at

the place he will choose. You, your children, your male and female servants and the Levites from your towns can eat them. Be filled with joy in the sight of the LORD your God. Be joyful in everything you do. ¹⁹ Don't forget to take care of the Levites as long as you live in your land.

²⁰ The LORD your God will increase your territory, just as he has promised you. When he does, you might get hungry for meat. You might say, "I'd really like some meat." Then you can eat as much of it as you want to. ²¹ The LORD your God will choose a special place. He will put his Name there. But suppose that place is too far away from you. Then you can kill animals from the herds and flocks the LORD has given you. Do it just as I have commanded you. In your own towns you can eat as much of the meat as you want to. ²² Eat it as you would eat antelope or deer meat. Those who are "clean" and those who are not can eat it. ²³ But be sure you don't eat meat that still has blood in it. The blood is the animal's life. So you must not eat the life along with the meat. ²⁴ You must not eat the blood. Pour it out on the ground like water. ²⁵ Don't eat it. Then things will go well with you and your children after you. You will be doing what is right in the eyes of the LORD.

²⁶ But go to the place the LORD will choose. Take with you the things you have set apart for him. Bring what you have promised to give him. ²⁷ Sacrifice your burnt offerings on the altar of the LORD your God. Offer the meat and the blood there. The blood of your sacrifices must be poured out beside his altar. But you can eat the meat. ²⁸ Make sure you obey all the rules I'm giving you. Then things will always go well with you and your children after you. That's because you will be doing what is good and right in the eyes of the LORD your God.

²⁹ You are about to attack the land and take it over as your own. When you do, the LORD your God will destroy the nations who live there. He will do it to make room for you. You will drive them out. You will settle in their land. ³⁰ They will be destroyed to make room for you. But when they are destroyed, be careful. Don't be trapped. Don't ask questions about their gods. Don't say, "How do these nations serve their gods? We'll do it in the same way." ³¹ You must not worship the LORD your God the way they worship their gods. When they worship, they do all kinds of evil things the LORD hates. They even burn up their children in the fire as sacrifices to their gods.

³² Be sure you do everything I am commanding you to do. Do not add anything to my commands. And do not take anything away from them.

Do Not Worship Other Gods

13 Suppose a prophet appears among you. Or someone comes who uses dreams to tell what's going to happen. He tells you that a sign or something amazing is going to take place. ²The sign or amazing thing he has spoken about might really take place. And then the prophet might say, "Let's serve other gods. Let's worship them." But you haven't known anything about those gods before. ³So you must not listen to what that prophet or dreamer has said. The Lord your God is testing you. He wants to know whether you love him with all your heart and with all your soul. ⁴You must worship him. You must honor him. Keep his commands. Obey him. Serve him. Remain true to him. ⁵That prophet or dreamer must be put to death. He told you not to obey the Lord your God. The Lord brought you out of Egypt. He set you free from the land where you were slaves. He commanded you to live the way he wants you to. But that prophet or dreamer has tried to get you to be unfaithful to the Lord. Get rid of that evil person.

⁶Suppose your very own brother or sister secretly tempts you to do something wrong. Or your child or the wife you love tempts you. Or your closest friend does it. Suppose one of them says, "Let's go and worship other gods." But you and your people of long ago hadn't known anything about those gods before. ⁷They are the gods of the nations around you. Those nations might be near or far away. In fact, they might reach from one end of the land to the other. ⁸Don't give in to those who are tempting you. Don't listen to them. Don't feel sorry for them. Don't spare them or save them. ⁹You must certainly put them to death. You must be the first to throw stones at them. Then all the people must do the same thing. ¹⁰Put them to death by throwing stones at them. They tried to turn you away from the Lord your God. He brought you out of Egypt. That's the land where you were slaves. ¹¹After you kill those who tempted you, all the Israelites will hear about it. And they will be too scared to do an evil thing like that again.

¹²The Lord your God is giving you towns to live in. But suppose you hear something bad about one of those towns. ¹³You hear that people who cause trouble have appeared among you. They've tried to get the people of their town to do something wrong. They've said, "Let's go and worship other gods." But you haven't known anything about those gods before. ¹⁴So you must ask people some questions. You must check out the matter carefully. If it's true, an evil thing has really happened among you. It's something the Lord hates. ¹⁵Then you must certainly kill with your swords everyone who lives in that town. You must destroy it completely. You must wipe out its people and livestock. ¹⁶You must gather all the goods of that town into the middle of the main street. You must burn the town completely.

You must burn up everything in it. It's a whole burnt offering to the LORD your God. The town must remain a pile of stones forever. It must never be built again. ¹⁷ Don't keep anything that should be destroyed. Then the LORD will turn away from his great anger. He will show you mercy. He'll have deep concern for you. He'll cause there to be many of you. That's what he promised your people of long ago. He gave his word when he made the promise. ¹⁸ The LORD your God will do those things if you obey him. I'm giving you his commands today. And you must obey all of them. You must do what is right in his eyes.

"Clean" and "Unclean" Food

14 You are the children of the LORD your God. Don't cut yourselves to honor the dead. Don't shave the front of your heads to honor the dead. ² You are a holy nation. The LORD your God has set you apart for himself. He has chosen you to be his special treasure. He chose you out of all the nations on the face of the earth.

³ Don't eat anything the LORD hates. ⁴ Here are the only animals you can eat. You can eat oxen, sheep, goats, ⁵ deer, gazelles, roe deer, wild goats, ibexes, antelope and mountain sheep. ⁶ You can eat any animal that has a divided hoof. But it must also chew the cud. ⁷ Some animals only chew the cud. Others only have a divided hoof. The camel, rabbit and rock badger chew the cud, but they don't have a divided hoof. So you can't eat them. They are not "clean" for you. ⁸ Pigs aren't "clean" for you either. They have a divided hoof, but they don't chew the cud. So don't eat their meat. And don't touch their dead bodies.

⁹ Many creatures live in water. You can eat all the ones that have fins and scales. ¹⁰ But don't eat anything that doesn't have fins and scales. It isn't "clean" for you.

¹¹ You can eat any "clean" bird. ¹² But there are many birds you can't eat. They include eagles, vultures, and black vultures. ¹³ They include red kites, black kites and all kinds of falcons. ¹⁴ They include all kinds of ravens. ¹⁵ They include horned owls, screech owls, gulls and all kinds of hawks. ¹⁶ They include little owls, great owls, white owls ¹⁷ and desert owls. They include ospreys and cormorants. ¹⁸ They include storks and all kinds of herons. They also include hoopoes and bats.

¹⁹ All flying insects are "unclean" for you. So don't eat them. ²⁰ But you can eat any creature that has wings and is "clean."

²¹ If you find something that's already dead, don't eat it. You can give it to an outsider living in any of your towns. They may eat it. Or you can sell it to someone from another country. But you are a holy nation. The LORD your God has set you apart for himself.

Don't cook a young goat in its mother's milk.

Give a Tenth of What You Produce

²² Be sure to set apart a tenth of everything your fields produce each year. ²³ Here are the things you should eat in the sight of the LORD your God. You should eat a tenth part of your grain, olive oil and fresh wine. You should also eat the male animals among your livestock that were born first to their mothers. Eat all these things at the special place the LORD your God will choose. He will put his Name there. You will learn to honor him always. ²⁴ But suppose the place the LORD will choose for his Name is too far away from you. And suppose your God has blessed you. And your tenth part is too heavy for you to carry. ²⁵ Then sell it for silver. Take the silver with you. Go to the place the LORD your God will choose. ²⁶ Use the silver to buy anything you like. It can be cattle or sheep. It can be any kind of wine. In fact, it can be anything else you wish. Then you and your family can eat there in the sight of the LORD your God. You can be filled with joy. ²⁷ Don't forget to take care of the Levites who will live in your towns. They won't receive any part of the land as their share.

²⁸ At the end of every three years, bring a tenth of everything you produce that year. Store it in your towns. ²⁹ Then the Levites can come and eat. That's because they won't receive any part of the land as their share. The outsiders and widows who live in your towns can come. So can the children whose fathers have died. Everyone can have plenty to eat. Then the LORD your God will bless you in everything you do.

The Year for Forgiving People What They Owe

15 At the end of every seven years you must forgive people what they owe you. ² Have you made a loan to one of your own people? Then forgive what is owed to you. You can't require that person to pay you back. The LORD's time to forgive what is owed has been announced. ³ You can require someone from another nation to pay you back. But you must forgive what any of your own people owes you. ⁴ There shouldn't be any poor people among you. The LORD will greatly bless you in the land he is giving you. You will take it over as your own. ⁵ The LORD your God will bless you if you obey him completely. Be careful to follow all the commands I'm giving you today. ⁶ The LORD your God will bless you, just as he has promised. You will lend money to many nations. But you won't have to borrow from any of them. You will rule over many nations. But none of them will rule over you.

⁷ Suppose someone is poor among you. And suppose they live in one of the towns in the land the LORD your God is giving you. Then don't be mean to them. They are poor. So don't hold back money from them.

⁸ Instead, open your hands and lend them what they need. Do it freely. ⁹ Be careful not to have an evil thought in your mind. Don't say to yourself, "The seventh year will soon be here. It's the year for forgiving people what they owe." If you think like that, you might treat the needy people among you badly. You might not give them anything. Then they might make their appeal to the LORD against you. And he will find you guilty of sin. ¹⁰ So give freely to needy people. Let your heart be tender toward them. Then the LORD your God will bless you in all your work. He will bless you in everything you do. ¹¹ There will always be poor people in the land. So I'm commanding you to give freely to those who are poor and needy in your land. Open your hands to them.

Set Your Hebrew Servants Free

¹² Suppose any Hebrew men or women sell themselves to you. If they do, they will serve you for six years. Then in the seventh year you must let them go free. ¹³ But when you set them free, don't send them away without anything to show for all their work. ¹⁴ Freely give them some animals from your flock. Also give them some of your grain and wine. The LORD your God has blessed you richly. Give to them as he has given to you. ¹⁵ Remember that you were slaves in Egypt. The LORD your God set you free. That's why I'm giving you this command today.

¹⁶ But suppose your servant says to you, "I don't want to leave you." He loves you and your family. And you are taking good care of him. ¹⁷ Then take him to the door of your house. Poke a hole through his earlobe into the doorpost. And he will become your servant for life. Do the same with your female servant.

¹⁸ Don't think you are being cheated when you set your servants free. After all, they have served you for six years. The service of each of them has been worth twice as much as the service of a hired worker. And the LORD your God will bless you in everything you do.

Male Animals Born First to Their Mothers

¹⁹ Set apart every male animal among your livestock that was born first to its mother. Set it apart to the LORD your God. Don't put a firstborn cow to work. Don't clip the wool from a firstborn sheep. ²⁰ Each year you and your family must eat them. Do it in front of the LORD your God at the place he will choose. ²¹ Suppose an animal has something wrong with it. It might not be able to see or walk. Or it might have a bad flaw. Then you must not sacrifice it to the LORD your God. ²² You must eat it in your own towns. Those who are "clean" and those who are "unclean" can eat it. Eat it as if it were antelope or deer meat. ²³ But you must not eat meat that still has blood in it. Pour the

blood out on the ground like water.

The Passover Feast

16 Celebrate the Passover Feast of the LORD your God in the month of Aviv. In that month he brought you out of Egypt at night. [2] Sacrifice an animal from your flock or herd. It is the Passover sacrifice to honor the LORD your God. Sacrifice it at the special place the LORD will choose. He will put his Name there. [3] Don't eat the animal along with bread made with yeast. Instead, for seven days eat bread made without yeast. It's the bread that reminds you of how much you suffered. Remember that you left Egypt in a hurry. Remember it all the days of your life. Don't forget the day you left Egypt. [4] Don't keep any yeast anywhere in your land for seven days. You will sacrifice the Passover animal on the evening of the first day. Do not let any of its meat be left over until the next morning.

[5] You must not sacrifice the Passover animal in just any town the LORD your God is giving you. [6] Sacrifice it only in the special place he will choose for his Name. Sacrifice it there in the evening when the sun goes down. Do it on the same day every year. Be sure it's the day you left Egypt. [7] Cook the animal and eat it. Do it at the place the LORD your God will choose. Then in the morning return to your tents. [8] For six days eat bread made without yeast. On the seventh day come together for a service to honor the LORD your God. Don't do any work on that day.

The Feast of Weeks

[9] Count off seven weeks from the time you begin to cut your grain in the field. [10] Then celebrate the Feast of Weeks to honor the LORD your God. Give to the LORD anything you choose to give as an offering. Give, just as the LORD has given to you. [11] Be filled with joy in the sight of the LORD your God. Be joyful at the special place he will choose for his Name. You, your children, and your male and female servants should be joyful. So should the Levites living in your towns. So should the outsiders and widows living among you. And so should the children whose fathers have died. [12] Remember that you were slaves in Egypt. Be careful to obey the rules I'm giving you.

The Feast of Booths

[13] Gather the grain from your threshing floors. Take the fresh wine from your winepresses. Then celebrate the Feast of Booths for seven days. [14] Be filled with joy at your feast. You, your children, and your male and female servants should be joyful. So should the Levites, the outsiders, and the widows living in your towns. And so should the children whose fathers have died. [15] For seven days celebrate the feast to honor the LORD your God. Do it at the place he will

choose. The LORD will bless you when you gather all your crops. He'll bless you in everything you do. And you will be full of joy. [16] All your men must appear in front of the LORD your God at the holy tent. They must go to the place he will choose. They must do it three times a year. They must go there to celebrate the Feast of Unleavened Bread, the Feast of Weeks and the Feast of Booths. None of your men should appear in front of the LORD without bringing something with him. [17] Each of you must bring a gift. Give to the LORD your God, just as he has given to you.

Appoint Judges and Officials

[18] Appoint judges and officials for each of your tribes. Do it in every town the LORD your God is giving you. They must judge the people fairly. [19] Do what is right. Treat everyone the same. Don't take money from people who want special favors. It makes those who are wise close their eyes to the truth. It twists the words of those who have done nothing wrong. [20] Do only what is right. Then you will live. You will take over the land the LORD your God is giving you.

Don't Worship Other Gods

[21] Don't set up a wooden pole used to worship the female god named Asherah. Don't set it up beside the altar you build to worship the LORD your God. [22] Don't set up a sacred stone to honor another god. The LORD your God hates Asherah poles and sacred stones.

17 Suppose an ox or sheep has anything at all wrong with it. Then don't sacrifice it to the LORD your God. He hates it.

[2] Someone living among you might do what is evil in the sight of the LORD your God. It might happen in one of the towns the LORD is giving you. That person is breaking the LORD's covenant. [3] The person might have worshiped or bowed down to other gods. That person might have bowed down to the sun or moon or stars in the sky. I have commanded you not to do these things. [4] When you hear that people have done something like that, check the matter out carefully. If it's true, an evil thing has been done in Israel. The LORD hates that. [5] So take the person who has done that evil thing to your city gate. Put that person to death by throwing stones at them. [6] Two or three witnesses are required to put someone to death. No one can be put to death because of what only one witness says. Two or three witnesses are required. [7] The witnesses must throw the first stones. Then the rest of the people must also throw stones. Get rid of that evil person.

Law Courts

[8] People will bring their cases to your courts. But some cases will be too hard for you to judge. They might be about murders, attacks or other crimes. Then take those hard cases to the

place the LORD your God will choose. ⁹Go to a priest, who is a Levite. And go to the judge who is in office at that time. Ask them for their decision. They will give it to you. ¹⁰They'll hand down their decisions at the place the LORD will choose. You must do what they decide. Be careful to do everything they tell you to do. ¹¹Act according to whatever they teach you. Accept the decisions they give you. Don't turn away from what they tell you. Don't turn to the right or the left. ¹²Someone might show that they don't respect the judge. Or they will show that they don't respect the priest. The priest will serve the LORD your God at the place God will choose. If anyone doesn't show respect for these people, that person must be put to death. Remove that evil person from Israel. ¹³All the Israelites will hear about it. And they will be afraid to disrespect a judge or priest again.

Appoint the King the LORD Chooses

¹⁴You will enter the land the LORD your God is giving you. You will take it as your own. You will make your homes in it. When you do, you will say, "Let's appoint a king over us, just like all the nations around us." ¹⁵When that happens, make sure you appoint over yourselves a king the LORD your God chooses. He must be from among your own people. Don't appoint over yourselves someone from another country. Don't

choose anyone who isn't from one of the tribes of Israel. ¹⁶The king must not get large numbers of horses for himself. He must not make the people return to Egypt to get more horses. The LORD has told you, "You must not go back there again." ¹⁷The king must not have many wives. If he does, they will lead him astray. He must not store up large amounts of silver and gold.

¹⁸When he sits on the throne of his kingdom, he must make for himself a copy of the law. He must write on a scroll the law that I am teaching you. He must copy it from the scroll of a priest, who is a Levite. ¹⁹The king must keep the scroll close to him at all times. He must read it all the days of his life. Then he can learn to have respect for the LORD his God. He can carefully obey all the words of this law and these rules. ²⁰He won't think of himself as being better than his people are. He won't turn away from the law. He won't turn to the right or the left. Then he and his sons after him will rule over his kingdom in Israel for a long time.

Offerings for Priests and Levites

18 The priests, who are Levites, won't receive any part of the land of Israel. That also applies to the whole tribe of Levi. They will eat the food offerings presented to the LORD. That will be their share. ²They won't have any part of the land the LORD gave the other tribes in Israel. The LORD himself is their share, just as he promised them.

³ Anyone who sacrifices a bull or a sheep owes a share of it to the priests. Their share is the shoulder, the inside parts and the meat from the head. ⁴ You must give the priests the first share of the harvest of your grain, olive oil and fresh wine. You must also give them the first wool you clip from your sheep. ⁵ The LORD your God has chosen the Levites and their sons after them to serve him in his name always. He hasn't chosen priests from any of your other tribes.

⁶ Sometimes a Levite will move from the town in Israel where he's living. And he will come to the place the LORD will choose. He'll do it because he really wants to. ⁷ Then he can serve in the name of the LORD his God. He'll be like all the other Levites who serve the LORD there. ⁸ He must have an equal share of the good things they have. That applies even if he has already received money by selling things his family owned.

Practices the LORD Hates

⁹ You will enter the land the LORD your God is giving you. When you do, don't copy the practices of the nations there. The LORD hates those practices. ¹⁰ Here are things you must not do. Don't sacrifice your children in the fire to other gods. Don't practice any kind of evil magic at all. Don't use magic to try to explain the meaning of warn-ings in the sky or of any other signs. Don't take part in worshiping evil powers. ¹¹ Don't put a spell on anyone. Don't get messages from those who have died. Don't talk to the spirits of the dead. Don't get advice from the dead. ¹² The LORD your God hates it when anyone does these things. The nations in the land he's giving you do these things he hates. So he will drive out those nations to make room for you. ¹³ You must be without blame in the sight of the LORD your God.

The Prophet of the LORD

¹⁴ You will take over the nations that are in the land the LORD is giving you. They listen to those who practice all kinds of evil magic. But you belong to the LORD your God. He says you must not do these things. ¹⁵ The LORD your God will raise up for you a prophet like me. He will be one of your own people. You must listen to him. ¹⁶ At Mount Horeb you asked the LORD your God for a prophet. You asked him on the day you gathered together. You said, "We don't want to hear the voice of the LORD our God. We don't want to see this great fire anymore. If we do, we'll die."

¹⁷ The LORD said to me, "What they are saying is good. ¹⁸ I will raise up for them a prophet like you. He will be one of their own people. I will put my words in his mouth. He will tell them everything I command him to say. ¹⁹ The prophet will speak in my

name. But someone might not listen to what I say through the prophet. I will hold that person responsible for not listening. [20] But suppose a prophet dares to speak in my name something I have not commanded. Or he speaks in the name of other gods. Then that prophet must be put to death."

[21] You will say to yourselves, "How can we know when a message hasn't been spoken by the Lord?" [22] Sometimes a prophet will announce something in the name of the Lord. And it won't take place or come true. Then that's a message the Lord hasn't told him to speak. That prophet has dared to speak on his own authority. So don't be afraid of what he says.

Cities to Run to for Safety

19 The Lord your God will destroy the nations whose land he is giving you. You will drive them out. And you will make your homes in their towns and their houses. [2] When you do, set apart for yourselves three cities in the land. It's the land the Lord your God is giving you to take as your own. [3] Figure out the distances and then separate the land into three parts. Then anyone who kills another person can run to one of these cities for safety. They are in the land the Lord your God is giving you as your own.

[4] Here is the rule about a person who kills someone. That person can run to one of those cities for safety. The rule applies to anyone who kills a neighbor they didn't hate and didn't mean to kill. [5] For example, suppose a man goes into a forest with his neighbor to cut wood. When he swings his ax to chop down a tree, the head of the ax flies off. And it hits his neighbor and kills him. Then that man can run to one of those cities and save his life. [6] If he doesn't go to one of those cities, the dead man's nearest male relative might become very angry. He might chase the man. If the city is too far away, he might catch him and kill him. But the man running to the city isn't worthy of death, because he didn't hate his neighbor. [7] That's why I command you to set apart for yourselves three cities.

[8] The Lord your God will increase the size of your territory. He promised your people of long ago that he would do it. He will give you the whole land he promised them. [9] But he'll do it only if you are careful to obey all the laws I'm commanding you today. I command you to love the Lord your God. You must always live as he wants you to live. Suppose you are careful to obey, and the Lord your God gives you more land. Then you must set apart three more cities. [10] Do it to protect those not guilty of murder. Then you won't spill their blood in your land. It's the land the Lord your God is giving you as your own.

[11] But suppose a man hates his neighbor. So he hides and waits for him. Then he attacks

him and kills him. And he runs to one of those cities for safety. ¹²If he does, the elders of his own town must send for him. He must be brought back from the city. He must be handed over to the dead man's nearest male relative. Then the relative will kill him. ¹³Don't feel sorry for him. He has killed someone who hadn't done anything wrong. Crimes like that must be punished in Israel. Then things will go well with you.

¹⁴Don't move your neighbor's boundary stone. It was set up by people who lived there before you. It marks the border of a field in the land you will receive as your own. The LORD your God is giving you that land. You will take it over.

Witnesses

¹⁵Suppose someone is charged with committing a crime of any kind. Then one witness won't be enough to prove that person is guilty. Every matter must be proved by the words of two or three witnesses.

¹⁶Suppose a witness who tells lies goes to court and brings charges against someone. The witness says someone committed a crime. ¹⁷Then the two people in the case must stand in front of the LORD. They must stand in front of the priests and the judges who are in office at that time. ¹⁸The judges must check out the matter carefully. And suppose the witness is proved to be lying. Then he has said something false in court

against another Israelite. ¹⁹So do to the lying witness what he tried to do to the other person. Get rid of that evil witness. ²⁰The rest of the people will hear about it. And they will be afraid. They won't allow such an evil thing to be done among them again. ²¹Don't feel sorry for that evil person. A life must be taken for a life. An eye must be put out for an eye. A tooth must be knocked out for a tooth. A hand must be cut off for a hand and a foot for a foot.

Going to War

20 When you go to war against your enemies, you might see that they have horses and chariots. They might even have an army stronger than yours. But don't be afraid of them. The LORD your God will be with you. After all, he brought you up out of Egypt. ²Just before you go into battle, the priest will come forward. He'll speak to the army. ³He'll say, "Men of Israel, listen to me. Today you are going into battle against your enemies. Don't be scared. Don't be afraid. Don't panic or be terrified by them. ⁴The LORD your God is going with you. He'll fight for you. He'll help you win the battle over your enemies."

⁵The officers will speak to the army. They will say, "Has anyone built a new house and not started to live in it? Let him go home. If he doesn't, he might die in battle. Then someone else will live in his house. ⁶Has

anyone planted a vineyard and not started to enjoy it? Let him go home. If he doesn't, he might die in battle. Then someone else will enjoy his vineyard. ⁷ Has anyone promised to be married to a woman but hasn't done it yet? Let him go home. If he doesn't, he might die in battle. Then someone else will marry her." ⁸ The officers will continue, "Is anyone afraid or scared? Let him go home. Then the other soldiers won't lose hope too." ⁹ The officers will finish speaking to the army. When they do, they'll appoint commanders over it.

¹⁰ Suppose you march up to attack a city. Before you attack it, offer to make peace with its people. ¹¹ Suppose they accept your offer and open their gates. Then force all the people in the city to be your slaves. They will have to work for you. ¹² But suppose they refuse your offer of peace and prepare for battle. Then surround that city. Get ready to attack it. ¹³ The Lord your God will hand it over to you. When he does, kill all the men with your swords. ¹⁴ But you can take the women and children for yourselves. You can also take the livestock and everything else in the city. What you have captured from your enemies you can use for yourselves. The Lord your God has given it to you. ¹⁵ That's how you must treat all the cities far away from you. Those cities don't belong to the nations that are nearby.

¹⁶ But what about the cities the Lord your God is giving you as your own? Kill everything that breathes in those cities. ¹⁷ Completely destroy them. Wipe out the Hittites, Amorites, Canaanites, Perizzites, Hivites and Jebusites. That's what the Lord your God commanded you to do. ¹⁸ If you don't destroy them, they'll teach you to do all the things the Lord hates. He hates the way they worship their gods. If you do those things, you will sin against the Lord your God.

¹⁹ Suppose you surround a city and get ready to attack it. And suppose you fight against it for a long time in order to capture it. Then don't chop down its trees and destroy them. You can eat their fruit. So don't cut them down. Are the trees people? So why should you attack them? ²⁰ But you can cut down trees that you know aren't fruit trees. You can build war machines out of their wood. You can use them until you capture the city you are fighting against.

What to Do When You Don't Know Who Killed Someone

21 Suppose you find someone who has been killed. The body is lying in a field in the land the Lord your God is giving you as your own. But no one knows who the killer was. ² Then your elders and judges will go out to the field. They will measure the distance from the body to the nearby towns. ³ The elders from the town that is nearest to the body will get a young cow. It must never have been used for work. It must never have pulled a load. [4] The elders must lead it down into a valley. The valley must not have been farmed. There must be a stream flowing through it. There in the valley the elders must break the cow's neck. [5] The priests, who are sons of Levi, will step forward. The LORD your God has chosen them to serve him. He wants them to bless the people in his name. He wants them to decide all cases that have to do with people arguing and attacking others. [6] Then all the elders from the town that is nearest to the body will wash their hands. They will wash them over the young cow whose neck they broke in the valley. [7] They'll say to the LORD, "We didn't kill that person. We didn't see it happen. [8] Accept this payment for the sin of your people Israel. LORD, you have set your people free. Don't hold them guilty for spilling the blood of someone who hasn't done anything wrong." That will pay for the death of that person. [9] So you will get rid of the guilt of killing someone who didn't do anything wrong. That's because you have done what is right in the LORD's eyes.

Marrying a Woman Who Is Your Prisoner

[10] Suppose you go to war against your enemies. And the LORD your God hands them over to you and you take them as prisoners. [11] Then you notice a beautiful woman among them. If you like her, you may marry her. [12] Bring her home. Have her shave her head and cut her nails. [13] Have her throw away the clothes she was wearing when she was captured. Let her live in your house and mourn the loss of her parents for a full month. Then you can go to her and be her husband. And she will be your wife. [14] But suppose you aren't pleased with her. Then let her go where she wants to. You must not sell her. You must not treat her as a slave. You have already brought shame on her.

The Rights of the Oldest Son

[15] Suppose a man has two wives. He loves one but not the other. And both of them have sons by him. But the oldest son is the son of the wife the man doesn't love. [16] Someday he'll leave his property to his sons. When he does, he must not give the rights of the oldest son to the son of the wife he loves. He must give those rights to his oldest son. He must do it even though his oldest son is the son of the wife he doesn't love. [17] He must recognize the full rights of the oldest son. He must do it, even though that son is the son of the wife he doesn't love. He must give that son a double share of everything he has. That son is the first sign of his father's strength. So the rights of the oldest son belong to him.

A Stubborn Son

[18] Suppose someone has a very stubborn son. He doesn't

obey his father and mother. And he won't listen to them when they try to correct him. ¹⁹ Then his parents will take hold of him and bring him to the elders at the gate of his town. ²⁰ They will say to the elders, "This son of ours is very stubborn. He won't obey us. He eats too much. He's always getting drunk." ²¹ Then all the people in his town will put him to death by throwing stones at him. Get rid of that evil person. All the Israelites will hear about it. And they will be afraid to disobey their parents.

Several Other Laws

²² Suppose someone is put to death for a crime worthy of death. And a pole is stuck through their body and set up where people can see it. ²³ Then you must not leave the body on the pole all night. Make sure you bury it that same day. Everyone who is hung on a pole is under God's curse. You must not make the land "unclean." The LORD your God is giving it to you as your own.

22 Suppose you see your neighbor's ox or sheep wandering away. Then don't act as if you didn't see it. Instead, make sure you take it back to its owner. ² Its owner might not live near you. Or you might not know who owns it. So take the animal home with you. Keep it until the owner comes looking for it. Then give it back to them. ³ Do the same thing if you find their donkey, coat or anything they have lost. Don't act as if you didn't see it.

⁴ Suppose you see your neighbor's donkey or ox that has fallen down on the road. Then don't act as if you didn't see it. Help the owner get it up on its feet again.

⁵ A woman must not wear men's clothes. And a man must not wear women's clothes. The LORD your God hates it when anyone does this.

⁶ Suppose you happen to find a bird's nest beside the road. It might be in a tree or on the ground. And suppose the mother bird is sitting on her little birds or on the eggs. Then don't take the mother along with the little ones. ⁷ You can take the little ones. But make sure you let the mother go. Then things will go well with you. You will live for a long time.

⁸ If you build a new house, put a low wall around the edge of your roof. Then you won't be responsible if someone falls off your roof and dies.

⁹ Don't plant two kinds of seeds in your vineyard. If you do, the crops you grow there will be impure. Your grapes will also be impure.

¹⁰ Don't let an ox and a donkey pull the same plow together.

¹¹ Don't wear clothes made out of wool and linen woven together.

¹² Make tassels on the four corners of the coat you wear.

Breaking Marriage Laws

¹³ Suppose a man marries a woman and sleeps with her. But then he doesn't like her. ¹⁴ So he tells lies about her and says she's

a bad woman. He says, "I married this woman. But when I slept with her, I discovered she wasn't a virgin." ¹⁵ Then the young woman's parents must bring proof that she was a virgin. They must give the proof to the elders at the gate of the town. ¹⁶ Her father will speak to the elders. He'll say, "I gave my daughter to this man to be his wife. But he doesn't like her. ¹⁷ So now he has told lies about her. He has said, 'I discovered that your daughter wasn't a virgin.' But here's the proof that my daughter was a virgin." Then her parents will show the elders of the town the cloth that has her blood on it. ¹⁸ The elders will punish the man. ¹⁹ They'll make him weigh out two and a half pounds of silver. They'll give it to the young woman's father. That's because the man has said an Israelite virgin is a bad woman. She will continue to be his wife. He must not divorce her as long as he lives.

²⁰ But suppose the charge is true. And there isn't any proof that the young woman was a virgin. ²¹ Then she must be brought to the door of her father's house. There the people of her town will put her to death by throwing stones at her. She has done a very terrible thing in Israel. She has slept with a man before she was married. Get rid of that evil person.

²² Suppose a man is seen sleeping with another man's wife. Then the man and the woman must both die. Get rid of those evil people.

²³ Suppose a man happens to see a virgin in a town. And she has promised to marry another man. But the man who happens to see her sleeps with her. ²⁴ Then you must take both of them to the gate of that town. You must put them to death by throwing stones at them. You must kill the young woman because she was in a town and didn't scream for help. And you must kill the man because he slept with another man's wife. Get rid of those evil people.

²⁵ But suppose a man happens to see a young woman out in the country. And she has promised to marry another man. But the man who happens to see her rapes her. Then only the man who has done that will die. ²⁶ Don't do anything to the woman. She hasn't committed a sin worthy of death. That case is like the case of someone who attacks and murders a neighbor. ²⁷ The man found the young woman out in the country. And she screamed for help. But there wasn't anyone around who could save her.

²⁸ Suppose a man happens to see a virgin who hasn't promised to marry another man. And the man who happens to see her rapes her. But someone discovers them. ²⁹ Then the man must weigh out 20 ounces of silver. He must give it to her father. The man must marry the young woman, because he raped her. And he can never divorce her as long as he lives.

³⁰ A man must not marry his stepmother. He must not bring

shame on his father by sleeping with her.

Who Can Join in Worship With the LORD's People?

23 No man whose sex organs have been crushed or cut can join in worship with the LORD's people.

2 No one born to an unmarried woman can join in worship with the LORD's people. That also applies to the person's children for all time to come.

3 The people of Ammon and Moab can't join in worship with the LORD's people. That also applies to their children after them for all time to come. 4 The Ammonites and Moabites didn't come to meet you with food and water on your way out of Egypt. They even hired Balaam from Pethor in Aram Naharaim to put a curse on you. Balaam was the son of Beor. 5 The LORD your God wouldn't listen to Balaam. Instead, he turned the curse into a blessing for you. He did it because he loves you. 6 So don't make a peace treaty with the Ammonites and Moabites as long as you live.

7 Don't hate the people of Edom. They are your relatives. Don't hate the people of Egypt. After all, you lived as outsiders in their country. 8 The great-grandchildren of the Edomites and Egyptians can join in worship with the LORD's people.

Keep the Camp of the Soldiers Pure and "Clean"

9 There will be times when you are at war with your ene-mies. And your soldiers will be in camp. Then keep away from anything that isn't pure and "clean." 10 Suppose semen flows from the body of one of your soldiers during the night. Then that will make him "unclean." He must go outside the camp and stay there. 11 But as evening approaches, he must wash himself. When the sun goes down, he can return to the camp.

12 Choose a place outside the camp where you can go to the toilet. 13 Keep a shovel among your tools. When you go to the toilet, dig a hole. Then cover up your waste. 14 The LORD your God walks around in your camp. He's there to keep you safe. He's also there to hand your enemies over to you. So your camp must be holy. Then he won't see anything among you that is shameful. He won't turn away from you.

Several Other Laws

15 If a slave comes to you for safety, don't hand them over to their master. 16 Let them live among you anywhere they want to. Let them live in any town they choose. Don't treat them badly.

17 A man or woman in Israel must not become a temple prostitute. 18 The LORD your God hates the money that men and women get for being prostitutes. So don't take that money into the house of the LORD to pay what you promised to give.

19 Don't charge your own people any interest. Don't charge

them when they borrow money, food or anything else. ²⁰ You can charge interest to people from another country. But don't charge your own people. Then the LORD your God will bless you in everything you do. He will bless you in the land you are entering to take as your own.

²¹ Don't put off giving to the LORD your God everything you promise him. He will certainly require it from you. And you will be guilty of committing a sin. ²² But if you don't make a promise, you won't be guilty. ²³ Make sure you do what you promised to do. With your own mouth you made the promise to the LORD your God. No one forced you to do it.

²⁴ When you enter your neighbor's vineyard, you can eat all the grapes you want. But don't put any of them in your basket. ²⁵ When you enter your neighbor's field, you can pick heads of grain. But don't cut down their standing grain.

24 Suppose a man marries a woman. But later he decides he doesn't like her. He finds something shameful about her. So he gives her a letter of divorce and sends her away from his house. ² Then after she leaves his house she becomes another man's wife. ³ But her second husband doesn't like her either. So he gives her a letter of divorce and sends her away from his house. Or perhaps he dies. ⁴ Then her first husband isn't allowed to marry her again. The LORD would hate

that. When her first husband divorced her, she became "unclean." Don't bring sin on the land the LORD your God is giving you as your own.

⁵ Suppose a man has just married his wife. Then don't send him into battle. Don't give him any other duty either. He's free to stay home for one year. He needs time to make his new wife happy.

⁶ Someone might borrow money from you and give you two millstones to keep until you are paid back. Don't keep them. Don't even keep the upper one. That person needs both millstones to make a living.

⁷ Suppose someone is caught kidnapping another Israelite. And they sell or treat that person as a slave. Then the kidnapper must die. Get rid of that evil person.

⁸ What about skin diseases? Be very careful to do exactly what the priests, who are Levites, tell you to do. You must be careful to obey the commands I've given them. ⁹ Remember what the LORD your God did to Miriam on your way out of Egypt.

¹⁰ Suppose your neighbor borrows something from you. And he offers you something to keep until you get paid back. Then don't go into their house to get it. ¹¹ Stay outside. Let the neighbor bring it out to you. ¹² The neighbor might be poor. You might be given their coat to keep until you get paid back. Don't go to sleep while you still have it.

¹³ Return it before the sun goes down. They need it to sleep in and will thank you for returning it. The LORD your God will see it and know that you have done the right thing.

¹⁴ Don't take advantage of any hired worker who is poor and needy. That applies to your own people. It also applies to outsiders living in one of your towns. ¹⁵ Give them their pay every day. They are poor and are counting on it. If you don't pay them, they might cry out to the LORD against you. Then you will be guilty of committing a sin.

¹⁶ Parents must not be put to death because of what their children do. And children must not be put to death because of what their parents do. People must die because of their own sins.

¹⁷ Do what is right and fair for outsiders and for children whose fathers have died. Suppose a widow borrows something from you. And she offers to give you her coat until she pays you back. Don't take it. ¹⁸ Remember that you were slaves in Egypt. Remember that the LORD your God set you free from there. That's why I'm commanding you to do those things.

¹⁹ When you are gathering crops in your field, you might leave some grain behind by mistake. Don't go back to get it. Leave it behind for outsiders and widows. Leave it for children whose fathers have died. Then the LORD your God will bless you in everything you do.

²⁰ When you knock olives off your trees, don't go back over the branches a second time. Leave what remains for outsiders and widows. Leave it for children whose fathers have died. ²¹ When you pick grapes in your vineyard, don't go back over the vines a second time. Leave what remains for outsiders and widows. Leave it for children whose fathers have died. ²² Remember that you were slaves in Egypt. That's why I'm commanding you to do these things.

25 Suppose two people don't agree about something. Then they must take their case to court. The judges will decide the case. They will let the one who isn't guilty go free. And they will punish the one who is guilty. ² The guilty one might have done something that's worthy of a beating. Then the judge will make them lie down and be beaten with a whip right there in court. The number of strokes should fit the crime. ³ But the judge must not give the guilty person more than 40 strokes. If more than that are used, you will have disrespected your Israelite neighbor.

⁴ Don't stop an ox from eating while you use it to separate grain from straw.

⁵ Suppose two brothers are living near each other. And one of them dies without having a son. Then his widow must not marry anyone outside the family. Her husband's brother should marry her. That's what a brother-in-law is supposed to

do. ⁶ Her first baby boy will be named after her first husband. Then the dead man's name will continue in Israel.

⁷ But suppose the man doesn't want to marry his brother's wife. Then she will go to the elders at the gate of the town. She will say, "My husband's brother refuses to keep his brother's name alive in Israel. He won't do for me what a brother-in-law is supposed to do." ⁸ Then the elders in his town will send for him. They will talk to him. But he still might say, "I don't want to marry her." ⁹ Then his brother's widow will go up to him in front of the elders. She'll pull one of his sandals off his foot. She'll spit in his face. And she'll say, "That's what we do to a man who won't build up his brother's family line." ¹⁰ That man's family line will be known in Israel as The Family of the Man Whose Sandal Was Pulled Off.

¹¹ Suppose two men are fighting. And the wife of one of them comes to save her husband from his attacker. So she reaches out and grabs hold of his attacker's private parts. ¹² Then you must cut off her hand. Don't feel sorry for her.

¹³ Don't have two different scales. Don't have scales that cause things to seem heavier or lighter than they really are. ¹⁴ And don't have two different sets of measures. Don't have measures that cause things to seem larger or smaller than they really are. ¹⁵ You must use weights and measures that are honest and exact. Then you will live a long time in the land the LORD your God is giving you. ¹⁶ He hates anyone who cheats.

¹⁷ Remember what the Amalekites did to you on your way out of Egypt. ¹⁸ You were tired and worn out. They met up with you on your journey. They attacked everyone who was lagging behind. They didn't have any respect for God. ¹⁹ The LORD your God will give you peace and rest from all the enemies around you. He'll do this in the land he's giving you to take over as your very own. No one on earth will mention the Amalekites ever again because you will destroy them. Do not forget!

Give the LORD His Share

26 You will enter the land the LORD your God is giving you as your own. You will take it over. You will make your homes in the land. ² When you do, get some of the first share of everything your soil produces. Put it in a basket. It's from the land the LORD your God is giving you. Take your gifts and go to the special place he will choose. He will put his Name there. ³ Speak to the priest in office at that time. Tell him, "I announce today to the LORD your God that I have come to this land. It's the land he promised to give us. He promised it to our people of long ago." ⁴ The priest will receive the basket from you. He'll set it down in front of the altar of the LORD your God. ⁵ Then you will speak while the LORD is listening. You will say,

"My father Jacob was a wanderer from the land of Aram. He went down into Egypt with a few people. He lived there and became the father of a great nation. It had huge numbers of people. ⁶ But the people of Egypt treated us badly. They made us suffer. They made us work very hard. ⁷ Then we cried out to the LORD. He is the God of our people who lived long ago. He heard our voice. He saw how much we were suffering. The Egyptians were treating us badly. They were making us work very hard. ⁸ So the LORD used his mighty hand and powerful arm to bring us out of Egypt. He did great and terrifying things. He did signs and amazing things. ⁹ He brought us to this place. He gave us this land. It's a land that has plenty of milk and honey. ¹⁰ Now, LORD, I'm bringing you the first share of crops from the soil. After all, you have given them to me." Place the basket in front of the LORD your God. Bow down to him. ¹¹ Then you and the Levites and the outsiders among you will be full of joy. You will enjoy all the good things the LORD your God has given to you and your family.

¹² You will set apart a tenth of everything you produce in the third year. That's the year for giving the tenth to people who have greater needs. You will give it to the Levites, outsiders and widows. You will also give it to children whose fathers have died. Then all of them will have plenty to eat in your towns.

¹³ Speak to the LORD your God. Say to him, "I have taken your sacred share from my house. I have given it to the Levites, outsiders and widows. I have also given it to children whose fathers have died. I've done everything you commanded me to do. I haven't stopped obeying your commands. I haven't forgotten any of them. ¹⁴ I haven't eaten any part of your sacred share while I mourned over someone who had died. I haven't taken any of it from my house while I was 'unclean.' And I haven't offered any of it to the dead. LORD my God, I've obeyed you. I've done everything you commanded me to do. ¹⁵ Look down from the holy place where you live in heaven. Bless your people Israel. Bless the land you have given us. It's the land you promised to give to our people of long ago. It's a land that has plenty of milk and honey."

Obey the LORD's Commands

¹⁶ This day the LORD your God commands you to obey all these rules and laws. Be careful to obey them with all your heart and with all your soul. ¹⁷ Today you have announced that the LORD is your God. You have said you would live exactly as he wants you to live. You have agreed to keep his rules, commands and laws. And you have said you would listen to him. ¹⁸ Today the LORD has announced that you are his people. He has said that you are his special treasure. He promised

that you would be. He has told you to keep all his commands. ¹⁹ He has announced that he will make you famous. He'll give you more praise and honor than all the other nations he has made. And he has said that you will be a holy nation. The LORD your God has set you apart for himself. That's exactly what he promised to do.

The Altar on Mount Ebal

27 Moses and the elders of Israel gave commands to the people. They said, "Obey all the commands we're giving you today. ² You will go across the Jordan River. You will enter the land the LORD your God is giving you. When you do, set up some large stones. Put a coat of plaster on them. ³ Write all the words of this law on them. Do it when you have crossed over into the land the LORD your God is giving you. It's a land that has plenty of milk and honey. The LORD is the God of your people of long ago. He promised you that you would enter the land. ⁴ After you have gone across the Jordan, set up those stones on Mount Ebal. Put a coat of plaster on them. We're commanding you today to do that. ⁵ Build an altar there to honor the LORD your God. Make it out of stones. Don't use any iron tool on them. ⁶ Use stones you find in the fields to build his altar. Then offer burnt offerings on it to the LORD your God. ⁷ Sacrifice friendship offerings there. Eat them and be filled with joy in the sight of the LORD your God. ⁸ You must write all the words of this law on the stones you have set up. Write the words very clearly."

Curses for Not Obeying the LORD

⁹ Then Moses and the priests, who are Levites, spoke to all the Israelites. They said, "Israel, be quiet! Listen! You have now become the people of the LORD your God. ¹⁰ Obey him. Obey his commands and rules that we're giving you today."

¹¹ Here are the commands Moses gave the people that same day.

¹² You will go across the Jordan River. When you do, six tribes will stand on Mount Gerizim to bless the people. Those tribes are Simeon, Levi, Judah, Issachar, Joseph and Benjamin. ¹³ The other six tribes will stand on Mount Ebal to announce some curses. Those tribes are Reuben, Gad, Asher, Zebulun, Dan and Naphtali.

¹⁴ The Levites will speak to all the Israelites in a loud voice. The Levites will say,

¹⁵ "May anyone who makes a statue of a god and sets it up in secret be under the LORD's curse. That statue is made by a skilled worker. And the LORD hates it."

Then all the people will say, "Amen!"

¹⁶ "May anyone who brings shame on their father or mother be under the LORD's curse."

Then all the people will say, "Amen!"

¹⁷ "May anyone who moves their neighbor's boundary stone be under the LORD's curse."

Then all the people will say, "Amen!"

¹⁸ "May anyone who leads blind people down the wrong road be under the LORD's curse."

Then all the people will say, "Amen!"

¹⁹ "May anyone who treats unfairly outsiders, widows, and children whose fathers have died be under the LORD's curse."

Then all the people will say, "Amen!"

²⁰ "May anyone who sleeps with his stepmother be under the LORD's curse. That man brings shame on his father by doing that."

Then all the people will say, "Amen!"

²¹ "May anyone who has sex with animals be under the LORD's curse."

Then all the people will say, "Amen!"

²² "May anyone who sleeps with his sister be under the LORD's curse. It doesn't matter whether she is his full sister or his half sister."

Then all the people will say, "Amen!"

²³ "May anyone who sleeps with his mother-in-law be under the LORD's curse."

Then all the people will say, "Amen!"

²⁴ "May anyone who kills their neighbor secretly be under the LORD's curse."

Then all the people will say, "Amen!"

²⁵ "May anyone who accepts money to kill someone who isn't guilty of doing anything wrong be under the LORD's curse."

Then all the people will say, "Amen!"

²⁶ "May anyone who doesn't honor the words of this law by obeying them be under the LORD's curse."

Then all the people will say, "Amen!"

Blessings for Obeying the LORD

28 Make sure you obey the LORD your God completely. Be careful to obey all his commands. I'm giving them to you today. If you do these things, the LORD will honor you more than all the other nations on earth. ² If you obey the LORD your God, here are the blessings that will come to you and remain with you.

³ You will be blessed in the cities. You will be blessed out in the country.

⁴ Your children will be blessed. Your crops will be blessed. The young animals among your livestock will be blessed. That includes your calves and lambs.

⁵ Your baskets and bread pans will be blessed.

⁶ You will be blessed no matter where you go.

⁷ Enemies will rise up against you. But the LORD will help you

win the battle over them. They will come at you from one direction. But they'll run away from you in every direction.

8 The Lord your God will bless your barns with plenty of grain and other food. He will bless everything you do. He'll bless you in the land he's giving you.

9 The Lord your God will make you his holy people. He will set you apart for himself. He promised to do this. He promised to do it if you would keep his commands and live exactly as he wants you to live. 10 All the nations on earth will see that you belong to the Lord. And they will be afraid of you. 11 The Lord will give you more than you need. You will have many children. Your livestock will have many little ones. Your crops will do very well. All of that will happen in the land he promised to give you. He promised this to your people of long ago.

12 The Lord will open up the heavens. That's where he stores his riches. He will send rain on your land at just the right time. He'll bless everything you do. You will lend money to many nations. But you won't have to borrow from any of them. 13 The Lord your God will make you leaders, not followers. Pay attention to his commands that I'm giving you today. Be careful to obey them. Then you will always be on top. You will never be on the bottom. 14 Don't turn away from any of the commands

I'm giving you today. Don't turn to the right or the left. Don't follow other gods. Don't worship them.

Curses for Not Obeying the Lord

15 But suppose you don't obey the Lord your God. And you aren't careful to obey all his commands and rules I'm giving you today. Then he will send curses on you. They'll catch up with you. Here are those curses.

16 You will be cursed in the cities. You will be cursed out in the country.

17 Your baskets and bread pans will be cursed.

18 Your children will be cursed. Your crops will be cursed. Your calves and lambs will be cursed.

19 You will be cursed no matter where you go.

20 The Lord will send curses on you. You won't know what's going on. In everything you do, he will be angry with you. You will be destroyed suddenly and completely. This will happen because you did an evil thing when you deserted the Lord. 21 He will send all kinds of sicknesses on you. He'll send them until he has destroyed you. He'll remove you from the land you are entering to take as your own. 22 The Lord will make you sick and very weak. He will strike you with fever and swelling. He'll send burning heat. There won't be any rain. The hot winds will completely dry up your crops. All those things will

happen until you die. ²³ The sky above you will be like bronze. The ground beneath you will be like iron. ²⁴ The LORD will turn the rain of your country into dust and powder. It will come down from the skies until you are destroyed.

²⁵ The LORD will help your enemies win the battle over you. You will come at them from one direction. But you will run away from them in every direction. All the kingdoms on earth will be completely shocked when they see you. ²⁶ Birds and wild animals will eat up your dead bodies. There won't be anyone left to scare them away. ²⁷ The LORD will send boils on you, just like the ones he sent on the Egyptians. You will have growths in your bodies and boils on your skin. You will itch all over. No one will be able to heal you. ²⁸ The LORD will make you lose your mind. He will make you blind. You won't know what's going on. ²⁹ Even at noon you will have to feel your way around like a blind person in the dark. You won't have success in anything you do. Day after day you will be robbed and treated badly. No one will be able to save you.

³⁰ You and a woman will promise to marry each other. But another man will take her and rape her. You will build a house. But you won't live in it. You will plant a vineyard. But you won't eat a single grape from it. ³¹ Your ox will be killed right in front of your eyes. But you won't eat any of it. Your donkey will be taken away from you by force. And you will never get it back. Your sheep will be given to your enemies. No one will be able to save them. ³² Your children will be given to another nation. Day after day you will watch for them to come back. But you will only wear out your eyes. You won't be able to help your children. ³³ A nation you don't know anything about will eat what you work to produce on your land. You will only be treated badly as long as you live. ³⁴ The things you see will make you lose your mind. ³⁵ The LORD will send painful boils on your knees and legs. No one will be able to heal them. They will cover you from head to toe.

³⁶ The LORD will drive you out of the land. And he will drive out the king you place over yourselves. All of you will go to another nation. You and your people of long ago didn't know anything about them. There you will worship other gods. They will be made out of wood and stone. ³⁷ You will look very bad to all the nations where the LORD sends you. They will be completely shocked when they see you. They will mock you and make fun of you.

³⁸ You will plant many seeds in your field. But you will gather very little food. Locusts will eat it up. ³⁹ You will plant vineyards and take care of them. But you won't drink the wine. You won't gather the grapes. Worms will eat them up. ⁴⁰ You will have

olive trees through your whole country. But you won't use the oil. The olives will drop off the trees. ⁴¹ You will have children. But you won't be able to keep them. They'll be taken away as prisoners. ⁴² Large numbers of locusts will eat up the leaves on all your trees. They will also eat up the crops on your land.

⁴³ Outsiders who live among you will become your leaders. They will rise higher and higher. But you will sink lower and lower. ⁴⁴ They will lend money to you. But you won't be able to lend money to them. They will be the leaders. But you will be the followers.

⁴⁵ The Lord your God will send all these curses on you. They will follow you everywhere. They'll catch up with you. You will be under the Lord's curse until you are destroyed. That's because you didn't obey him. You didn't keep the commands and rules he gave you. ⁴⁶ These curses will remain as signs and awful judgments against you and your children after you forever. ⁴⁷ You didn't serve the Lord your God with joy and gladness when times were good. ⁴⁸ So he will send enemies against you. You will have to serve them. You will be hungry and thirsty. You will be naked and poor. The Lord will put the iron chains of slavery around your necks until he has destroyed you.

⁴⁹ The Lord will bring a nation against you from far away. It will come from the ends of the earth. It will dive down on you like an eagle. You won't understand that nation's language. ⁵⁰ Its people will look mean. They won't have any respect for old people. They won't show any kindness to young people. ⁵¹ They will eat up the young animals among your livestock. They'll eat up the crops on your land. They'll destroy you. They won't leave you any grain, olive oil or fresh wine. They won't leave you any calves or lambs. They'll destroy you. ⁵² They'll surround all the cities throughout your whole land. They'll attack those cities until the high, strong walls you trust in fall down. That's what will happen to the cities in the land the Lord your God is giving you.

⁵³ Your enemies will surround you and attack you. They will make you suffer greatly. So you will eat your own children. You will eat the dead bodies of the sons and daughters the Lord your God has given you. ⁵⁴ There may be a gentle and caring man among you. But he will treat his own brother badly. He'll be just as mean to the wife he loves and to any of his children who are still alive. ⁵⁵ He won't give to a single one of them any part of the dead bodies of his children that he's eating. It will be all he has left to eat. That's how much your enemies will make you suffer when they surround all your cities and attack them. ⁵⁶ There may be a gentle and caring woman among you. She wouldn't even touch

the ground with her feet without first putting her sandals on. But she will not share anything with the husband she loves. She won't share with her own children either. ⁵⁷ She will eat what comes out of her body after she has a baby. Then she'll even eat her baby. She won't share it with anyone in her family. In her great hunger she'll plan to eat it in secret. There won't be anything else for her to eat because the city she lives in will be surrounded. That's an example of how much your enemies will make you suffer when they are attacking your cities.

⁵⁸ Be careful to follow all the words of this law. They are written in this scroll. Have respect for the glorious and wonderful name of the Lord your God. If you don't, ⁵⁹ he will send terrible plagues on you and your children after you. He'll send horrible and lasting troubles. He'll make you very sick for a long time. ⁶⁰ He'll bring on you all the sicknesses you were afraid of getting when you were in Egypt. You won't be able to get rid of them. ⁶¹ The Lord will also bring on you all other kinds of sickness and trouble. I haven't even written those down in this Book of the Law. You will be destroyed. ⁶² At one time you were as many as the stars in the sky. But there will only be a few of you left. That's because you didn't obey the Lord your God. ⁶³ It pleased the Lord to give you success and to cause there to be many of you. But it will please

him just as much to wipe you out and destroy you. You will be removed from the land you are entering to take as your own.

⁶⁴ Then the Lord will scatter you among all the nations. He'll spread you around from one end of the earth to the other. There you will worship statues of gods made out of wood and stone. You and your people of long ago hadn't known anything about those gods. ⁶⁵ Among those nations you won't find any peace. There won't be any place where you can make your home and rest your feet. The Lord will give you minds filled with worry. He'll give you eyes worn out from looking for help. You won't have any hope in your hearts. ⁶⁶ Your lives will always be in danger. You will be filled with fear night and day. You will never be sure you are safe. ⁶⁷ In the morning you will say, "We wish it were evening!" In the evening you will say, "We wish it were morning!" Your hearts will be filled with fear. The things you see will terrify you. ⁶⁸ The Lord will send you back to Egypt in ships. He'll send you on a journey I said you should never have to make again. You will offer to sell yourselves to your enemies as slaves in Egypt. But no one will buy you.

Obey the Terms of the Covenant

29 Here are the terms of the covenant the Lord commanded Moses to make with the Israelites in Moab. The terms were added to the covenant he had made with them at Mount Horeb.

2 Moses sent for all the Israelites. Here is what he said to them.

With your own eyes you have seen everything the LORD did in Egypt to Pharaoh. You have seen what he did to all Pharaoh's officials and to his whole land. 3 With your own eyes you saw how the LORD really made them suffer. You saw the signs and amazing things he did. 4 But to this day the LORD hasn't given you a mind that understands. He hasn't given you eyes that see. He hasn't given you ears that hear. 5 Yet the LORD says, "I led you through the desert for 40 years. During that time your clothes didn't wear out. The sandals on your feet didn't wear out either. 6 You didn't eat any bread. You didn't drink any kind of wine. I did all these things because I wanted you to know that I am the LORD your God."

7 When you got here, Sihon and Og came out to fight against us. Sihon was the king of Heshbon. And Og was the king of Bashan. But we won the battle over them. 8 We took their land. We gave it to the tribes of Reuben and Gad and half of the tribe of Manasseh as their share.

9 Be careful to obey the terms of this covenant. Then you will have success in everything you do. 10 Today all of you are standing here in the sight of the LORD your God. Your leaders and chief men are here. Your elders and officials are here. So are all the other men of Israel. 11 Your children and wives are here with you too. So are the outsiders living in your camps. They chop your wood and carry your water. 12 All of you are standing here in order to enter into a covenant with the LORD your God. He is making the covenant with you today. He's giving you his word. 13 Today he wants to show you that you are his people and that he is your God. That's what he promised to Abraham, Isaac and Jacob. 14 I'm making this covenant and the promise that goes along with it. I'm making this covenant with you. 15 You are standing here with us today in front of the LORD our God. And I'm also making this covenant with those who aren't here today.

16 You yourselves know how we lived in Egypt. You also know how we passed through other countries on the way here. 17 You saw the statues of their gods made out of wood, stone, silver and gold. The LORD hates those statues. 18 Make sure there isn't a man or woman among your families or tribes who turns away from the LORD our God. No one must worship the gods of those nations. Make sure that kind of worship doesn't spread like bitter poison through your whole community.

19 Some people who worship those gods will hear the promise that seals the covenant I'm making. They think they can escape trouble by what they're saying. They say, "We'll be safe,

even though we're stubborn and go our own way." But they will bring trouble on the whole land. 20 The LORD will never be willing to forgive those people. His great anger will blaze out against them. All the curses I've written down in this book will fall on them. And the LORD will erase any mention of them from the earth. 21 He will find those people in all the tribes of Israel and give them nothing but trouble. That will agree with all the curses of the covenant. They are written down in this Book of the Law.

22 Even your children's children will see the troubles that have fallen on the land. They'll see the sicknesses the LORD has brought on it. People who come from countries far away will also see those things. 23 The whole land will be burned up. Nothing but salt and sulfur will be left. Nothing will be planted there. Nothing will grow there. In fact, nothing will even start to grow there. The land will be like Sodom, Gomorrah, Admah and Zeboyim after they were destroyed. The LORD wiped out those cities because he was very angry. 24 All the nations will ask, "Why has the LORD done this to the land? What could have made him so very angry?"

25 And they will hear the answer, "It's because the people living there have broken the covenant of the LORD. He's the God of their people of long ago. He made that covenant with them when he brought them out of Egypt. 26 They went off and worshiped other gods. They bowed down to them. They hadn't known anything about those gods before. The LORD hadn't given those gods to them. 27 So the LORD became very angry with this land. He brought on it all the curses written down in this book. 28 The LORD's anger blazed out against his people. So he pulled them up out of their land. He threw them into another land. And that's where they are now."

29 The LORD our God keeps certain things hidden. But he makes other things known to us and to our children forever. He does it so we can obey all the words of this law.

The LORD Will Bless His People

30 I have told you about all these blessings and curses. The LORD your God will bring them on you. Then you will think carefully about the blessings and curses. You will think about them everywhere the LORD your God scatters you among the nations. 2 You and your children will return to the LORD your God. You will obey him with all your heart and with all your soul. That will be according to everything I'm commanding you today. 3 When all that happens, the LORD your God will bless you with great success again. He will be very kind to you. He'll bring you back from all the nations where he scattered you. 4 Suppose you have been forced to go away to the farthest land on earth. The LORD your God will bring you back even from there. ⁵He will bring you to the land that belonged to your people of long ago. You will take it over. He'll make you better off than your people were. He'll cause there to be more of you than there were of them. ⁶The LORD your God will keep you from being stubborn. He'll do the same thing for your children and their children. Then you will love him with all your heart and with all your soul. And you will live. ⁷The LORD your God will put all these curses on your enemies. They hated you and hunted you down. ⁸You will obey the LORD again. You will obey all his commands that I'm giving you today. ⁹Then the LORD your God will give you great success in everything you do. You will have many children. Your livestock will have many little ones. Your crops will do very well. The LORD will take delight in you again. He'll give you success. That's what he did for your people of long ago. ¹⁰But you must obey the LORD your God. You must keep his commands and rules. They are written in this Book of the Law. You must turn to the LORD your God with all your heart and with all your soul.

Choose Life, Not Death

¹¹What I'm commanding you today is not too hard for you. It isn't beyond your reach. ¹²It isn't up in heaven. So you don't have to ask, "Who will go up into heaven to get it? Who will announce it to us so we can obey it?" ¹³And it isn't beyond the ocean. So you don't have to ask, "Who will go across the ocean to get it? Who will announce it to us so we can obey it?" ¹⁴No, the message isn't far away at all. In fact, it's really near you. It's in your mouth and in your heart so that you can obey it.

¹⁵Today I'm giving you a choice. You can have life and success. Or you can have death and harm. ¹⁶I'm commanding you today to love the LORD your God. I'm commanding you to live exactly as he wants you to live. You must obey his commands, rules and laws. Then you will live. There will be many of you. The LORD your God will bless you in the land you are entering to take as your own.

¹⁷Don't let your hearts turn away from the LORD. Instead, obey him. Don't let yourselves be drawn away to other gods. And don't bow down to them and worship them. ¹⁸If you do, I announce to you this day that you will certainly be destroyed. You are about to go across the Jordan River and take over the land. But you won't live there very long.

¹⁹I'm calling for the heavens and the earth to be witnesses against you this very day. I'm offering you the choice of life or death. You can choose either blessings or curses. But I want you to choose life. Then you and

your children will live. ²⁰ And you will love the LORD your God. You will obey him. You will remain true to him. The LORD is your very life. He will give you many years in the land. He promised to give that land to your fathers, to Abraham, Isaac and Jacob.

Joshua Becomes the New Leader

31 Here are the words Moses spoke to all the Israelites. ² He said, "I am now 120 years old. I'm not able to lead you anymore. The LORD has said to me, 'You will not go across the Jordan River.' ³ The LORD your God himself will go across ahead of you. He'll destroy the nations there in order to make room for you. You will take over their land. Joshua will also go across ahead of you, just as the LORD said he would. ⁴ The LORD will do to those nations what he did to Sihon and Og. He destroyed those Amorite kings along with their land. ⁵ The LORD will hand those nations over to you. Then you must do to them everything I've commanded you to do. ⁶ Be strong and brave. Don't be afraid of them. Don't be terrified because of them. The LORD your God will go with you. He will never leave you. He'll never desert you."

⁷ Then Moses sent for Joshua. Moses spoke to him in front of all the Israelites. He said, "Be strong and brave. You must go with these people. They are going into the land the LORD promised to give to their people of long ago. You must divide it up among them. They will each receive their share. ⁸ The LORD himself will go ahead of you. He will be with you. He will never leave you. He'll never desert you. So don't be afraid. Don't lose hope."

The Law Must Be Read to the People

⁹ Moses wrote down this law. He gave it to the priests, who are sons of Levi. They carried the ark of the covenant of the LORD. He also gave the law to all the elders of Israel. ¹⁰ Then Moses commanded them, "You must read this law at the end of every seven years. Do it in the year when you forgive people what they owe. Read it during the Feast of Booths. ¹¹ That's when all the Israelites come to appear in front of the LORD your God at the holy tent. It will be at the place he will choose. You must read this law to them. ¹² Gather the people together. Gather the men, women and children. Also bring together the outsiders living in your towns. Then they can listen and learn to have respect for the LORD your God. And they'll be careful to obey all the words of this law. ¹³ Their children must hear it read too. They don't know this law yet. They too must learn to have respect for the LORD your God. They must honor him as long as you live in the land. You are about to go across the Jordan River and take that land as your very own."

The Israelites Will Refuse to Obey the LORD

¹⁴ The LORD said to Moses, "The day when you will die is near. Have Joshua go to the tent of meeting. Join him there. That is where I will appoint him as the new leader." So Joshua and Moses went to the tent of meeting.

¹⁵ Then the LORD appeared at the tent in a pillar of cloud. It stood over the entrance to the tent. ¹⁶ The LORD spoke to Moses. He said, "You are going to join the members of your family who have already died. The Israelites will not be faithful to me. They will soon join themselves to the false gods that are worshiped in the land they are entering. The people will desert me. They will break the covenant I made with them. ¹⁷ In that day I will become angry with them. I will desert them. I will turn my face away from them. And they will be destroyed. Many horrible troubles and hard times will come on them. On that day they will say, 'Trouble has come on us. Our God isn't with us!' ¹⁸ I will certainly turn away from them on that day. I will do it because they did a very evil thing when they turned to other gods.

¹⁹ "I want you to write down a song and teach it to the Israelites. Have them sing it. It will be my witness against them. ²⁰ I will bring them into a land that has plenty of milk and honey. I promised the land to their people of long ago. In that land they will eat until they have had enough. They will get fat. When they do, they will turn to other gods and worship them. They will turn their backs on me. They will break my covenant. ²¹ Many horrible troubles and hard times will come on them. Then the song I am giving you will be a witness against them. That is because the song will not be forgotten by their children and their children's children. I know what they are likely to do. I know it even before I bring them into the land I promised them." ²² So that day Moses wrote the song down. And Moses taught it to the Israelites.

²³ The LORD gave a command to Joshua, the son of Nun. He said, "Be strong and brave. You will bring the Israelites into the land I promised them. I myself will be with you."

²⁴ Moses finished writing the words of this law in a book. He wrote them down from beginning to end. ²⁵ Then he gave a command to the Levites who carried the ark of the covenant of the LORD. Moses said, ²⁶ "Take this Book of the Law. Place it beside the ark of the covenant of the LORD your God. It will remain there as a witness against you. ²⁷ I know how you refuse to obey the LORD. I know how stubborn you are. You have refused to obey him while I've been living among you. So you will certainly refuse to obey him after I'm dead! ²⁸ Gather together all the elders of your tribes and all your officials. Bring them to me.

Then I can speak these words to them. I can call for the heavens and the earth to be witnesses against them. ²⁹ I know that after I'm dead you will certainly become very sinful. You will turn away from the path I've commanded you to take. In days to come, trouble will fall on you. That's because you will do what is evil in the sight of the LORD. You will make him very angry because of the statues of gods your hands have made."

The Song of Moses

³⁰ Moses spoke the words of this song from beginning to end. The whole community of Israel heard them. Here is what he said.

32 Heavens, listen to me.
　　Then I will speak.
　　Earth, hear the words of
　　　my mouth.
² Let my teaching fall like rain.
　　Let my words come down
　　　like dew.
　　Let them be like raindrops on
　　　new grass.
　　Let them be like rain on
　　　tender plants.

³ I will make known the name
　　of the LORD.
　　Praise God! How great
　　　he is!
⁴ He is the Rock. His works are
　　perfect.
　　All his ways are right.
　　He is faithful. He doesn't do
　　　anything wrong.
　　He is honest and fair.

⁵ Israel, you have sinned
　　against him very much.

It's too bad for you that
　　you aren't his children
　　anymore.
　　You have become a twisted
　　　and evil nation.
⁶ Is that how you thank the
　　LORD?
　　You aren't wise. You are
　　　foolish.
　　Remember, he's your Father.
　　　He's your Creator.
　　He made you. He formed
　　　you.

⁷ Remember the days of long
　　ago.
　　Think about what the
　　　LORD did through those
　　　many years.
　　Ask your father. He will tell
　　　you.
　　Ask your elders. They'll
　　　explain it to you.
⁸ The Most High God gave the
　　nations their lands.
　　He divided up the human
　　　race.
　　He set up borders for the
　　　nations.
　　He did it based on the
　　　number of the angels in
　　　his heavenly court.
⁹ The LORD's people are his
　　share.
　　Jacob is the nation he has
　　　received.

¹⁰ The LORD found Israel in a
　　desert.
　　He found them in an
　　　empty and windy land.
　　He took care of them and
　　　kept them safe.
　　He guarded them as he
　　　would guard his own
　　　eyes.

¹¹ He was like an eagle that stirs
   up its nest.
   It hovers over its little ones.
It spreads out its wings to
   catch them.
   It carries them up in the air
   on its feathers.
¹² The LORD was the only one
   who led Israel.
   No other god was with them.

¹³ The LORD made them ride on
   the highest places in the
   land.
   He fed them what grew in
   the fields.
He gave them the sweetest
   honey.
   He fed them olive oil from
   a rocky hillside.
¹⁴ He gave them butter and
   milk from the herds and
   flocks.
   He fed them the fattest
   lambs and goats.
He gave them the best of
   Bashan's rams.
   He fed them the finest
   wheat.
   They drank the bubbling
   red juice of grapes.

¹⁵ When Israel grew fat, they
   became stubborn.
   When they were filled with
   food, they became fat
   and heavy.
They left the God who made
   them.
   They turned away from the
   Rock who saved them.
¹⁶ They made him jealous by
   serving false gods.
   They made him angry by
   worshiping statues of
   gods.

He hated those gods.
¹⁷ The people sacrificed to
   those false gods, not to
   God.
   They hadn't known
   anything about those
   false gods.
Those gods were new to
   them.
   Their people of long ago
   didn't worship them.
¹⁸ But then they deserted the
   Rock. He was their
   Father.
   They forgot the God who
   created them.

¹⁹ When the LORD saw this, he
   turned away from
   them.
   His sons and daughters
   made him angry.
²⁰ "I will turn my face away
   from them," he said.
   "I will see what will
   happen to them in the
   end.
They are sinful people.
   They are unfaithful
   children.
²¹ They made me jealous by
   serving what is not even
   a god.
   They made me angry by
   worshiping worthless
   statues of gods.
I will use people who are not
   a nation to make them
   jealous.
   A nation that has no
   understanding will
   make them angry.
²² My anger will start a fire.
   It will burn all the way
   down to the kingdom of
   the dead.

It will eat up the earth and its
    crops.
It will set the base of the
    mountains on fire.

23 "I will pile troubles on my
    people.
I will shoot all my arrows
    at them.
24 I will send them hunger. It
    will make them weak.
I will send terrible
    sickness. I will send
    deadly plagues.
I will send wild animals that
    will tear them apart.
Snakes that glide through
    the dust will bite them.
25 In the streets their children
    will be killed by
    swords.
Their homes will be filled
    with terror.
The young men and women
    will die.
The babies and old people
    will die.
26 I said I would scatter them.
I said I would erase their
    name from human
    memory.
27 But I was afraid their
    enemies would make
    fun of that.
I was afraid their attackers
    would not understand.
I was sure they would say,
    'We're the ones who've
    beaten them!
The Lord isn't the one who
    did it.' "
28 Israel is a nation that doesn't
    have any sense.
They can't understand
    anything.

29 I wish they were wise. Then
    they would understand
    what's coming.
They'd realize what would
    happen to them in the
    end.
30 How could one person chase
    a thousand?
How could two make ten
    thousand run away?
It couldn't happen unless
    their Rock had deserted
    them.
It couldn't take place
    unless the Lord had
    given them up.
31 Their rock is not like our
    Rock.
Even our enemies know
    that.
32 Their vine comes from the
    vines of Sodom.
It comes from the
    vineyards of Gomorrah.
Their grapes are filled with
    poison.
Their bunches of grapes
    taste bitter.
33 Their wine is like the poison
    of snakes.
It's like the deadly poison
    of cobras.

34 The Lord says, "I have kept
    all those terrible things
    stored away.
I have kept them sealed up
    in my strongbox.
35 I punish people. I will pay
    them back.
The time will come when
    their feet will slip.
Their day of trouble is
    near.
Very soon they will be
    destroyed."

³⁶The Lord will come to the
   aid of his people.
   He'll show tender love to
      those who serve him.
He will know when their
   strength is gone.
He'll see that no one at all
   is left.
³⁷He'll say, "Where are their
   gods now?
Where is the rock they
   went to for safety?
³⁸Where are the gods who ate
   the fat of their sacrifices?
Where are the gods who
   drank the wine of their
   drink offerings?
Let those gods rise up to help
   you!
Let them keep you safe!

³⁹"Look! I am the One!
   There is no other God
      except me.
I put some people to death. I
   bring others to life.
I have wounded, and I will
   heal.
No one can save you from
   my power.
⁴⁰I raise my hand to heaven.
   Here is the promise I
   make.
You can be sure that I live
   forever.
⁴¹And you can be just as sure
   that I will sharpen my
   flashing sword.
My hand will hold it when I
   judge.
I will get even with my
   enemies.
I will pay back those who
   hate me.
⁴²I will make my arrows drip
   with blood.

My sword will destroy
   people.
It will kill some. It will even
   kill prisoners.
It will cut off the heads of
   enemy leaders."

⁴³You nations, be full of joy.
   Be joyful together with
   God's people.
The Lord will get even
   with his enemies.
He will pay them back for
   killing those who serve
   him.
He will wipe away the sin
   of his land and people.

⁴⁴Moses spoke all the words
of this song to the people.
Joshua, the son of Nun, was
with him. ⁴⁵Moses finished
speaking all these words to all
the Israelites. ⁴⁶Then he said to
them, "Think carefully about
all the words I have announced
to you today. I want you to command your children to be careful to obey all the words of this
law. ⁴⁷They aren't just useless
words for you. They are your
very life. If you obey them, you
will live in the land for a long
time. It's the land you are going
across the Jordan River to take
as your own."

Moses Will Die on Mount Nebo
⁴⁸On that same day the Lord
said to Moses, ⁴⁹"Go up into
the Abarim mountains. Go
to Mount Nebo in Moab. It is
across from Jericho. From there
look out over Canaan. It is the
land I am giving the Israelites
to take as their own. ⁵⁰You will

die there on the mountain you have climbed. You will join the members of your family who have already died. In the same way, your brother Aaron died on Mount Hor. He joined the members of his family who had already died. ⁵¹ You and Aaron disobeyed me in front of the Israelites. It happened at the waters of Meribah Kadesh in the Desert of Zin. You did not honor me among the Israelites as the holy God. ⁵² So you will see the land, but only from far away. You will not enter the land I am giving to the Israelites."

Moses Blesses the Tribes

33 Here is the blessing that Moses, the man of God, gave to the Israelites before he died. ² He said,

> "The LORD came from Mount
>   Sinai.
> Like the rising sun, he
>   shone on his people from
>   Mount Seir.
> He shone on them from
>   Mount Paran.
> He came with large numbers
>   of angels.
> He came from his
>   mountain slopes in the
>   south.
> ³ LORD, I'm sure you love your
>   people.
> All the holy ones are in
>   your hands.
> At your feet all of them bow
>   down.
> And you teach them.
> ⁴ They learn the law Moses
>   gave us.

> It belongs to the
>   community of the
>   people of Jacob.
> ⁵ The LORD was king over
>   Israel
> when the leaders of the
>   people came together.
> The tribes of Israel were
>   also there."

⁶ Here's what Moses said about Reuben.

> "Let Reuben live. Don't let
>   him die.
>   And do not let his people
>   be few."

⁷ Here's what Moses said about Judah.

> "LORD, listen to Judah cry
>   out.
>   Bring him to his people.
> By his own power he stands
>   up for himself.
>   LORD, help him fight
>   against his enemies!"

⁸ Here's what Moses said about Levi.

> "Your Thummim and Urim
>   belong to your faithful
>   servant.
> You tested him at
>   Massah.
> You argued with him at the
>   waters of Meribah.
> ⁹ Levi didn't show special favor
>   to anyone.
> He did not spare his father
>   and mother.
> He didn't excuse his
>   relatives or his children.
> But he watched over your
>   word.
> He guarded your covenant.

10 He teaches your rules to the
    people of Jacob.
    He teaches your law to
        Israel.
    He offers incense to you.
    He sacrifices whole burnt
        offerings on your altar.
11 LORD, bless all his skills.
    Be pleased with everything
        he does.
    Destroy those who rise up
        against him.
    Strike down his enemies
        until they can't get up."

12 Here's what Moses said
about Benjamin.

    "Let the one the LORD loves
        rest safely in him.
    The LORD guards him all
        day long.
    The one the LORD loves
        rests in his arms."

13 Here's what Moses said
about Joseph.

    "May the LORD bless Joseph's
        land.
    May he bless it with
        dew from the highest
        heavens.
    May he bless it with water
        from the deepest oceans.
14 May he bless it with the
        best crops the sun can
        produce.
    May he bless it with the
        finest crops the moon
        can give.
15 May he bless it with the best
        products of the age-old
        mountains.
    May he bless it with the
        many crops of the
        ancient hills.

16 May he bless it with the best
        gifts that fill the earth.
    May he bless it with the
        favor of the God who
        spoke out of the burning
        bush.
    Let all these blessings rest on
        the head of Joseph.
    Let them rest on the head
        of the one who is prince
        among his brothers.
17 His glory is like the glory of
        a bull born first to its
        mother.
    His horns are like the
        horns of a wild ox.
    He will use them to destroy
        the nations.
    He'll wipe out the nations
        that are very far away.
    The ten thousands of men in
        Ephraim's army are like
        the bull and the ox.
    So are the thousands in the
        army of Manasseh."

18 Here's what Moses said
about Zebulun and Issachar.

    "Zebulun, be filled with joy
        when you go out.
    Issachar, be joyful in your
        tents.
19 You will call for other people
        to go to the mountain.
    There you will offer the
        sacrifices of those who
        do what is right.
    You will enjoy the many good
        things your ships bring
        you.
    You will enjoy treasures
        that are hidden in the
        sand."

20 Here's what Moses said
about Gad.

"May the God who gives Gad
　　more land be praised!
Gad lives there like a lion
　　that tears off arms and
　　heads.
21 He chose the best land for his
　　livestock.
The leader's share was kept
　　for him.
The leaders of the people
　　came together.
Then Gad carried out the
　　LORD's holy plan.
He carried out the LORD's
　　decisions for Israel."

22 Here's what Moses said
about Dan.

"Dan is like a lion's cub
　　that charges out of the land
　　of Bashan."

23 Here's what Moses said
about Naphtali.

"The LORD greatly favors
　　Naphtali.
The LORD fills him with his
　　blessing.
Naphtali's land will reach
　　south to the Sea of
　　Galilee."

24 Here's what Moses said
about Asher.

"Asher is the most blessed of
　　sons.
Let his brothers be kind to
　　him.
Let Asher wash his feet
　　with olive oil.
25 The bars of his gates will be
　　made out of iron and
　　bronze.
His strength will last as
　　long as he lives.

26 "There is no one like the God
　　of Israel.
He rides across the
　　heavens to help you.
He rides on the clouds in
　　his glory.
27 God lives forever! You can
　　run to him for safety.
His powerful arms are
　　always there to carry
　　you.
He will drive out your
　　enemies to make room
　　for you.
He'll say to you, 'Destroy
　　them!'
28 So Israel will live in safety.
Jacob will live secure
in a land that has grain and
　　fresh wine.
There the heavens drop
　　their dew.
29 Israel, how blessed you are!
Who is like you?
The LORD has saved you.
He keeps you safe. He helps
　　you.
He's like a glorious sword
　　to you.
Your enemies will bow down
　　to you in fear.
You will walk on the
　　highest places of their
　　lands."

Moses Dies

34 Moses climbed Mount
Nebo. He went up from
the plains of Moab to the highest slopes of Pisgah. It's across
from Jericho. At Pisgah the
LORD showed him the whole
land from Gilead all the way
to Dan. 2 Moses saw the whole
land of Naphtali. He saw the

territory of Ephraim and Manasseh. The LORD showed him the whole land of Judah all the way to the Mediterranean Sea. ³ Moses saw the Negev Desert. He saw the whole area from the Valley of Jericho all the way to Zoar. Jericho was also known as The City of Palm Trees. ⁴ Then the LORD spoke to Moses. He said, "This is the land I promised to Abraham, Isaac and Jacob. I told them, 'I will give this land to your children and their children.' Moses, I have let you see it with your own eyes. But you will not go across the Jordan River to enter it."

⁵ Moses, the servant of the LORD, died there in Moab. It happened just as the LORD had said. ⁶ The LORD buried the body of Moses in Moab. His grave is in the valley across from Beth Peor. But to this day no one knows where his grave is. ⁷ Moses was 120 years old when he died. But his eyesight was still good. He was still very strong. ⁸ The Israelites mourned over Moses on the plains of Moab for 30 days. They did it until their time for weeping and crying was over.

⁹ Joshua, the son of Nun, was filled with wisdom. That's because Moses had placed his hands on him. So the Israelites listened to Joshua. They did what the LORD had commanded Moses.

¹⁰ Since then, Israel has never had a prophet like Moses. The LORD knew him face to face. ¹¹ Moses did many signs and amazing things. The LORD had sent him to do them in Egypt. Moses did them against Pharaoh, against all his officials and against his whole land. ¹² No one has ever had the mighty power Moses had. No one has ever done the wonderful acts he did in the sight of all the Israelites.

Joshua

Introduction:

Joshua was the man who took Moses' place. This book tells his story as he leads God's people into a new land, called Canaan. God told Joshua to be strong and brave. He promised to be with Joshua and to take care of him.

With God's help, the people took over the new land. God led them across the river and into the land. He broke down the walls of strong cities. God kept his promise; he gave the people of Israel a home of their own.

After the people took over the land, Joshua told them to obey God. He wanted the people to remember that God took care of them. He told the people to serve God always.

Outline of contents:

Joshua Becomes Israel's Leader

1 Moses, the servant of the LORD, died. After that, the LORD spoke to Joshua, the son of Nun. Joshua was Moses' helper. The LORD said to Joshua, 2 "My servant Moses is dead. Now then, I want you and all these people to get ready to go across the Jordan River. I want all of you to go into the land I am about to give to the Israelites. 3 I will give all of you every place you walk on, just as I promised Moses. 4 Your territory will reach from the Negev Desert all the way to Lebanon. The great Euphrates River will be to the east. The Mediterranean Sea will be to the west. Your territory will include all the Hittite country. 5 Joshua, no one will be able to oppose you as long as you live. I will be with you, just as I was with Moses. I will never leave you. I will never desert you. 6 Be strong and brave. You will lead these people. They will take the land as their very own. It is the land I promised to give their people of long ago.

7 "Be strong and very brave. Make sure you obey the whole law my servant Moses gave you. Do not turn away from it to the right or the left. Then you will have success everywhere you go. 8 Never stop reading this Book of the Law. Day and night you must think about what it says. Make sure you do everything written in it. Then things will go well with you. And you will have great success. 9 Here

is what I am commanding you to do. Be strong and brave. Do not be afraid. Do not lose hope. I am the LORD your God. I will be with you everywhere you go."

¹⁰ So Joshua gave orders to the officers of the people. He said, ¹¹ "Go through the camp. Tell the people, 'Get your supplies ready. Three days from now you will go across the Jordan River right here. You will go in and take over the land. The LORD your God is giving it to you as your very own.'"

¹² Joshua also spoke to the tribes of Reuben and Gad and half of the tribe of Manasseh. He said to them, ¹³ "Remember what Moses, the servant of the LORD, commanded you. He said, 'The LORD your God is giving you this land. It's a place where you can make your homes and live in peace and rest.' ¹⁴ Your wives, children and livestock can stay here east of the Jordan River. Moses gave you this land. But all your fighting men must get ready for battle. They must go across ahead of the other tribes. You must help them ¹⁵ until the LORD gives them rest. In the same way, he has already given you rest. You must help them until they also have taken over their land. It's the land the LORD your God is giving them. After that, you can come back here. Then you can live in your own land. It's the land that Moses, the servant of the LORD, gave you east of the Jordan River. It's toward the sunrise."

¹⁶ Then the tribes of Reuben and Gad and half of the tribe of Manasseh answered Joshua. They said, "We'll do what you have commanded us to do. We'll go where you send us. ¹⁷ We obeyed Moses completely. And we'll obey you just as completely. But may the LORD your God be with you, just as he was with Moses. ¹⁸ Suppose people question your authority. And suppose they refuse to obey anything you command them to do. Then they will be put to death. Just be strong and brave!"

Rahab Helps the Spies

2 Joshua, the son of Nun, sent two spies from Shittim. He sent them in secret. He said to them, "Go and look over the land. Most of all, check out Jericho." So they went to Jericho. They stayed at the house of a prostitute. Her name was Rahab.

² The king of Jericho was told, "Look! Some of the Israelites have come here tonight. They've come to check out the land." ³ So the king sent a message to Rahab. It said, "Bring out the men who came into your house. They've come to check out the whole land."

⁴ But the woman had hidden the two men. She said, "It's true that the men came here. But I didn't know where they had come from. ⁵ They left at sunset, when it was time to close the city gate. I don't know which way they went. Go after them quickly. You might catch up with them." ⁶ But in fact she

had taken them up on the roof. There she had hidden them under some flax she had piled up. ⁷The king's men left to hunt down the spies. They took the road that leads to where the Jordan River can be crossed. As soon as they had gone out of the city, the gate was shut.

⁸Rahab went up on the roof before the spies settled down for the night. ⁹She said to them, "I know that the LORD has given you this land. We are very much afraid of you. Everyone who lives in this country is weak with fear because of you. ¹⁰We've heard how the LORD dried up the Red Sea for you when you came out of Egypt. We've heard what you did to Sihon and Og, the two Amorite kings. They ruled east of the Jordan River. You completely destroyed them. ¹¹When we heard about it, we were terrified. Because of you, we aren't brave anymore. The LORD your God is the God who rules in heaven above and on the earth below.

¹²"Now then, please give me your word. Promise me in the name of the LORD that you will be kind to my family. I've been kind to you. Promise me ¹³that you will spare the lives of my father and mother. Spare my brothers and sisters. Also spare everyone in their families. Promise that you won't put any of us to death."

¹⁴So the men made a promise to her. "If you save our lives, we'll save yours," they said. "Just don't tell anyone what we're do-ing. Then we'll be kind and faithful to you when the LORD gives us the land."

¹⁵The house Rahab lived in was part of the city wall. So she let the spies down by a rope through the window. ¹⁶She said to them, "Go up into the hills. The men chasing you won't be able to find you. Hide yourselves there for three days until they return. Then you can go on your way."

¹⁷The spies had said to her, "You made us give our word. But we won't keep our promise ¹⁸unless you do what we say. When we enter the land, you must tie this bright red rope in the window. Tie it in the window you let us down through. Bring your father and mother into your house. Also bring in your brothers and everyone else in your family. ¹⁹None of you must go out into the street. If you do, anything that happens to you will be your own fault. We won't be responsible. But if anyone hurts someone who is inside the house with you, it will be our fault. We will be responsible. ²⁰Don't tell anyone what we're doing. If you do, we won't have to keep the promise you asked us to make."

²¹"I agree," Rahab replied. "I'll do as you say."

So she sent them away, and they left. Then she tied the bright red rope in the window.

²²When the spies left, they went up into the hills. They stayed there for three days. By that time the men chasing them

had searched all along the road. They couldn't find them. So they returned. ²³ Then the two spies started back. They went down out of the hills. They went across the Jordan River. They came to Joshua, the son of Nun. They told him everything that had happened to them. ²⁴ They said, "We're sure the LORD has given the whole land over to us. All the people there are weak with fear because of us."

Israel Goes Across the Jordan River

3 Early one morning Joshua and all the Israelites started out from Shittim. They went down to the Jordan River. They camped there before they went across it. ² After three days the officers went all through the camp. ³ They gave orders to the people. They said, "Watch for the ark of the covenant of the LORD your God. The priests, who are Levites, will be carrying it. When you see it, you must move out from where you are and follow it. ⁴ Then you will know which way to go. You have never gone this way before. But don't go near the ark. Stay about 1,000 yards away from it."

⁵ Joshua said to the people, "Set yourselves apart to the LORD. Tomorrow he'll do amazing things among you."

⁶ Joshua said to the priests, "Go and get the ark of the covenant. Walk on ahead of the people." So they went and got it. Then they walked on ahead of them.

⁷ The LORD said to Joshua, "Today I will begin to honor you in the eyes of all the Israelites. Then they will know that I am with you, just as I was with Moses. ⁸ Speak to the priests who carry the ark of the covenant. Tell them, 'When you reach the edge of the Jordan River, go into the water and stand there.'"

⁹ Joshua said to the Israelites, "Come here. Listen to what the LORD your God is saying. ¹⁰ You will soon know that the living God is among you. He will certainly drive out the people now living in the land. He'll do it to make room for you. He'll drive out the Canaanites, Hittites, Hivites, Perizzites, Girgashites, Amorites and Jebusites. ¹¹ The ark will go into the Jordan River ahead of you. It's the ark of the covenant of the Lord of the whole earth. ¹² Choose 12 men from the tribes of Israel. Choose one from each tribe. ¹³ The priests will carry the ark of the LORD. He's the Lord of the whole earth. As soon as the priests step into the Jordan, it will stop flowing. The water that's coming down the river will pile up in one place. That's how you will know that the living God is among you."

¹⁴ So the people took their tents down. They prepared to go across the Jordan River. The priests carrying the ark of the covenant went ahead of them. ¹⁵ The water of the Jordan was going over its banks. It always does that at the time the crops are being gathered. The

priests came to the river. Their feet touched the water's edge. ¹⁶ Right away the water coming down the river stopped flowing. It piled up far away at a town called Adam near Zarethan. The water flowing down to the Dead Sea was completely cut off. So the people went across the Jordan River opposite Jericho. ¹⁷ The priests carried the ark of the covenant of the LORD. They stopped in the middle of the river and stood on dry ground. They stayed there until the whole nation of Israel had gone across on dry ground.

4 After the whole nation had gone across the Jordan River, the LORD spoke to Joshua. He said, ² "Choose 12 men from among the people. Choose one from each tribe. ³ Tell them to get 12 stones from the middle of the river. They must pick them up from right where the priests stood. They must carry the stones over with all of you. And they must put them down at the place where you will stay tonight."

⁴ So Joshua called together the 12 men he had appointed from among the Israelites. There was one man from each tribe. ⁵ He said to them, "Go back to the middle of the Jordan River. Go to where the ark of the LORD your God is. Each one of you must pick up a stone. You must carry it on your shoulder. There will be as many stones as there are tribes in Israel. ⁶ The stones will serve as a reminder to you. In days to come, your children

will ask you, 'What do these stones mean?' ⁷ Tell them that the LORD cut off the flow of water in the Jordan River. Tell them its water stopped flowing when the ark of the covenant of the LORD went across. The stones will always remind the Israelites of what happened there."

⁸ So the Israelites did as Joshua commanded them. They took 12 stones from the middle of the Jordan River. There was one stone for each of the tribes of Israel. It was just as the LORD had told Joshua. The people carried the stones with them to their camp. There they put them down. ⁹ Joshua also piled up 12 stones in the middle of the river. He piled them up right where the priests who carried the ark of the covenant had stood. And they are still there to this very day.

¹⁰ The priests who carried the ark remained standing in the middle of the Jordan River. They stayed there until the people had done everything the LORD had commanded Joshua. It was just as Moses had directed Joshua. All the people went across quickly. ¹¹ As soon as they did, the ark of the LORD and the priests also went across to the other side. The people were watching them. ¹² Among the people who went across the river were men from the tribes of Reuben and Gad and half of the tribe of Manasseh. The men were ready for battle. They went across ahead of the rest of the Israelites. It was just as Moses had

directed them. [13] There were about 40,000 of them. All of them were ready for battle. They went across in front of the ark of the LORD. They marched to the plains around Jericho. They were prepared to go to war.

[14] That day the LORD honored Joshua in the eyes of all the Israelites. They had respect for Joshua as long as he lived. They respected him just as much as they had respected Moses.

[15] Then the LORD spoke to Joshua. He said, [16] "Command the priests to come up out of the Jordan River. They are carrying the ark where the tablets of the covenant law are kept."

[17] So Joshua gave a command to the priests. He said, "Come up out of the Jordan River."

[18] Then the priests came up out of the river. They were carrying the ark of the covenant of the LORD. As soon as they stepped out on dry ground, the water of the Jordan began to flow again. It went over its banks, just as it had done before.

[19] On the tenth day of the first month the people went up out of the Jordan River. They camped at Gilgal on the eastern border of Jericho. [20] Joshua set up the 12 stones at Gilgal. They were the ones the people had taken out of the Jordan. [21] Then he spoke to the Israelites. He said, "In days to come, your children after you will ask their parents, 'What do these stones mean?' [22] Their parents must tell them, 'Israel went across the Jordan River on dry ground.' [23] The LORD your God dried up the Jordan for you until you had gone across it. He did to the Jordan River the same thing he had done to the Red Sea. He dried up the Red Sea ahead of us until we had gone across it. [24] He did it so that all the nations on earth would know that he is powerful. He did it so that you would always have respect for the LORD your God."

5 All the Amorite and Canaanite kings heard how the LORD had dried up the Jordan River. They heard how he had dried it up for the Israelites until they had gone across it. The Amorite kings lived west of the Jordan. The kings of Canaan lived along the Mediterranean Sea. When all those kings heard what the LORD had done, they were terrified. They weren't brave enough to face the Israelites anymore.

Circumcision and Passover at Gilgal

[2] At that time the LORD said to Joshua, "Make knives out of flint. Use them to circumcise the men of Israel." [3] So Joshua made knives out of flint. Then he used them to circumcise the men of Israel at Gibeath Haaraloth.

[4] Here is why Joshua circumcised them. All the men who came out of Egypt had died. They died while they were wandering through the Sinai Desert. They were the men old enough to serve in the army. [5] All the men who came out had been circumcised. But all the men

born in the desert during the journey from Egypt hadn't been circumcised. ⁶The Israelites had moved around in the desert for 40 years. By the end of that time all the men old enough to serve in the army when they left Egypt had died. That's because they hadn't obeyed the LORD. He had made a promise to them. He had told them they wouldn't see the land. It's the land he had promised to their people to give us. It's a land that has plenty of milk and honey. ⁷Because they hadn't obeyed him, he raised up their sons to take their place. They were the ones Joshua circumcised. They hadn't been circumcised yet. That's because no one had circumcised them during the journey. ⁸So Joshua circumcised all those men. The whole nation remained in the camp until the men were healed.

⁹Then the LORD spoke to Joshua. He said, "Today I have taken away from you the shame of being slaves in Egypt." That's why the place where the men were circumcised has been called Gilgal to this very day.

¹⁰The Israelites celebrated the Passover Feast. They observed it on the evening of the 14th day of the month. They did it while they were camped at Gilgal on the plains around Jericho. ¹¹The day after the Passover, they ate some of the food grown in the land. On that same day they ate grain that had been cooked. They also ate bread made without yeast. ¹²The manna stopped coming down the day after they ate the food grown in the land. The Israelites didn't have manna anymore. Instead, that year they ate food grown in Canaan.

Israel Captures Jericho

¹³When Joshua was near Jericho, he looked up and saw a man standing in front of him. The man was holding a sword. He was ready for battle. Joshua went up to him. He asked, "Are you on our side? Or are you on the side of our enemies?"

¹⁴"I am not on either side," he replied. "I have come as the commander of the LORD's army." Then Joshua fell with his face to the ground. He asked the man, "What message does my Lord have for me?"

¹⁵The commander of the LORD's army replied, "Take off your sandals. The place you are standing on is holy ground." So Joshua took them off.

6 The gates of Jericho were shut tight and guarded closely because of the Israelites. No one went out. No one came in.

²Then the LORD said to Joshua, "I have handed Jericho over to you. I have also handed over to you its king and its fighting men. ³March around the city once with all your fighting men. In fact, do it for six days. ⁴Have seven priests get trumpets made out of rams' horns. They must carry them in front of the ark. On the seventh day, march around the city seven times. Tell the priests to blow the trumpets

as you march. ⁵You will hear them blow a long blast on the trumpets. When you do, tell the whole army to give a loud shout. The wall of the city will fall down. Then the whole army will march up to the city. Everyone will go straight in."

⁶So Joshua, the son of Nun, called for the priests. He said to them, "Go and get the ark of the covenant of the LORD. I want seven of you to carry trumpets in front of it." ⁷He gave an order to the army. He said, "Move out! March around the city. Some of the fighting men must march in front of the ark of the LORD."

⁸When Joshua had spoken to the men, the seven priests went forward. They were carrying the seven trumpets as they marched in front of the ark of the LORD. They were blowing the trumpets. The ark of the LORD's covenant was carried behind the priests. ⁹Some of the fighting men marched ahead of the priests who were blowing the trumpets. The others followed behind the ark and guarded all the priests. That whole time the priests were blowing the trumpets. ¹⁰But Joshua had given an order to the army. He had said, "Don't give a war cry. Don't raise your voices. Don't say a word until the day I tell you to shout. Then shout!" ¹¹So he had the ark of the LORD carried around the city once. Then the army returned to camp. They spent the night there.

¹²Joshua got up early the next morning. The priests went and got the ark of the LORD. ¹³The seven priests carrying the seven trumpets started out. They marched in front of the ark of the LORD. They blew the trumpets. Some of the fighting men marched ahead of them. The others followed behind the ark and guarded all of them. The priests kept blowing the trumpets. ¹⁴On the second day they marched around the city once. Then the army returned to camp. They did all those things for six days.

¹⁵On the seventh day, they got up at sunrise. They marched around the city, just as they had done before. But on that day they went around it seven times. ¹⁶On the seventh time around, the priests blew a long blast on the trumpets. Then Joshua gave a command to the army. He said, "Shout! The LORD has given you the city! ¹⁷The city and everything in it must be set apart to the LORD to be destroyed. But the prostitute Rahab and all those with her in her house must be spared. That's because she hid the spies we sent. ¹⁸But keep away from the things that have been set apart to the LORD. If you take any of them, you will be destroyed. And you will bring trouble on the camp of Israel. You will cause it to be destroyed. ¹⁹All the silver and gold is holy. It is set apart to the LORD. So are all the things made out of bronze and iron. All those things must be added to the treasures kept in the LORD's house."

20 The priests blew the trumpets. As soon as the army heard the sound, they gave a loud shout. Then the wall fell down. Everyone charged straight in. So they took the city. 21 They set it apart to the LORD to be destroyed. They destroyed every living thing in it with their swords. They killed men and women. They wiped out young people and old people. They destroyed cattle, sheep and donkeys.

22 Then Joshua spoke to the two men who had gone in to check out the land. He said, "Go into the prostitute's house. Bring her out. Also bring out everyone with her. That's what you promised her you would do." 23 So the young men who had checked out the land went into Rahab's house. They brought her out along with her parents and brothers and sisters. They brought out everyone else there with her. They put them in a place outside the camp of Israel. 24 Then they burned the whole city and everything in it. But they added the silver and gold to the treasures kept in the LORD's house. They also put there the things made out of bronze and iron. 25 But Joshua spared the prostitute Rahab. He spared her family. He also spared everyone else in the house with her. He did it because she hid the spies he had sent to Jericho. Rahab lives among the Israelites to this day.

26 At that time Joshua made a promise and called down a curse. He said, "May the person who tries to rebuild this city of Jericho be under the LORD's curse.

"If that person lays its
 foundations,
 it will cost the life of his
 oldest son.
If he sets up its gates,
 it will cost the life of his
 youngest son."

27 So the LORD was with Joshua. And Joshua became famous everywhere in the land.

Achan Sins Against the LORD

7 But the Israelites weren't faithful to the LORD. They didn't destroy what had been set apart to him. So they did not do what they had been told to do. Achan had taken some of those things. So the LORD became very angry with Israel. Achan was the son of Karmi. Karmi was the son of Zimri. And Zimri was the son of Zerah. Achan and all his relatives were from the tribe of Judah.

2 Joshua sent men from Jericho to Ai. Ai is near Beth Aven east of Bethel. Joshua told the men, "Go up and check out the area around Ai." So the men went up and checked it out. 3 Then they returned to Joshua. They said, "The whole army doesn't have to go up and attack Ai. Send only two or three thousand men. They can take the city. Don't make the whole army go up there. Only a few people live in Ai." 4 So only about 3,000 troops went up. But

the men of Ai drove them away. [5] They chased the Israelites from the city gate all the way to Sheb- arim. They killed about 36 of them on the way down. So the Israelites were terrified.

[6] Joshua and the elders of Is- rael became sad. Joshua tore his clothes. He fell in front of the ark of the LORD with his face to the ground. He remained there un- til evening. The elders did the same thing. They also sprinkled dust on their heads. [7] Joshua said, "LORD and King, why did you ever bring these people across the Jordan River? Did you want to hand us over to the Amorites? Did you want them to destroy us? I wish we had been content to stay on the other side of the Jordan! [8] Lord, our ene- mies have driven us away. What can I say? [9] The Canaanites will hear about it. So will everyone else in the country. They will surround us. They'll erase any mention of our name from the face of the earth. Then what will you do when people don't honor your great name anymore?"

[10] The LORD said to Joshua, "Get up! What are you doing down there on your face? [11] Is- rael has sinned. I made a cov- enant with them. I commanded them to keep it. But they have broken it. They have taken some of the things that had been set apart to me in a special way to be destroyed. They have stolen. They have lied. They have taken the things they stole and have put them with their own things. [12] That is why the Israelites can't

stand up against their enemies. They turn their backs and run. That's because I have decided to let them be destroyed. You must destroy the things you took that had been set apart to me. If you do not, I will not be with you anymore.

[13] "Go and set the people apart. Tell them, 'Make your- selves pure. Get ready for to- morrow. Here is what the LORD, the God of Israel, wants you to do. He says, "People of Israel, you have kept some of the things that had been set apart to me to be destroyed. You can't stand up against your enemies until you get rid of those things."

[14] "'In the morning, come for- ward tribe by tribe. The tribe the LORD chooses will come for- ward group by group. The group the LORD chooses will come forward family by family. And the men in the family the LORD chooses will come forward one by one. [15] Whoever is caught with the things that had been set apart to the LORD will be de- stroyed by fire. Everything that belongs to that person will also be destroyed. He has broken the LORD's covenant. He has done a very terrible thing in Israel!'"

[16] Early the next morning Joshua had Israel come forward by tribes. The tribe of Judah was chosen. [17] The groups of Judah came forward. The group of Ze- rah was chosen. Joshua had the group of Zerah come forward by families. The family of Zimri was chosen. [18] He had their men come forward one by one.

Achan was chosen. Achan was the son of Karmi. Karmi was the son of Zimri. And Zimri was the son of Zerah. Zerah was from the tribe of Judah.

¹⁹ Joshua said to Achan, "My son, the Lord is the God of Israel. So give him glory and honor him by telling the truth! Tell me what you have done. Don't hide it from me."

²⁰ Achan replied, "It's true! I've sinned against the Lord, the God of Israel. Here is what I've done. ²¹ I saw a beautiful robe from Babylonia among the things we had taken. I saw five pounds of silver. And I saw a gold bar that weighed 20 ounces. I wanted them, so I took them. I hid them in the ground inside my tent. The silver is on the bottom."

²² So Joshua sent some messengers. They ran to Achan's tent. And there was everything, hidden in his tent! The silver was on the bottom. ²³ They brought the things out of the tent. They took them to Joshua and all the Israelites. And they spread them out in the sight of the Lord.

²⁴ Then Joshua and all the people grabbed Achan, the son of Zerah. They took the silver, the robe and the gold bar. They took Achan's sons and daughters. They took his cattle, donkeys and sheep. They also took his tent and everything he had. They carried all of it out to the Valley of Achor. ²⁵ Joshua said to Achan, "Why have you brought this trouble on us? The Lord will bring trouble on you today."

Then all the people killed Achan by throwing stones at him. They also killed the rest of his family with stones. They burned all of them up. ²⁶ They placed a large pile of rocks on top of Achan's body. The place has been called the Valley of Achor ever since. That pile is still there to this day. After the people killed Achan, the Lord was no longer angry with them.

Israel Destroys Ai

8 Then the Lord said to Joshua, "Do not be afraid. Do not lose hope. Go up and attack Ai. Take the whole army with you. I have handed the king of Ai over to you. I have given you his people, his city and his land. ² Remember what you did to Jericho and its king. You will do the same thing to Ai and its king. But this time you can keep for yourselves the livestock and everything else you take from them. Have some of your fighting men hide behind the city and take them by surprise."

³ So Joshua and the whole army moved out to attack Ai. He chose 30,000 of his best fighting men. He sent them out at night. ⁴ He gave them orders. He said, "Listen carefully to what I'm saying. You must hide behind the city. Don't go very far away from it. All of you must be ready to attack it. ⁵ I and all those with me will march up to the city. The men of Ai will come out to fight against us, just as they did before. Then we'll run away from them. ⁶ They'll chase us

until we've drawn them away from the city. They'll say, 'They are running away from us, just as they did before.' When we run away from them, ⁷come out of your hiding place. Capture the city. The LORD your God will hand it over to you. ⁸When you have taken it, set it on fire. Do what the LORD has commanded. Make sure you obey my orders."

⁹Then Joshua sent them away. They went to the place where they had planned to hide. They hid in a place west of Ai. It was between Bethel and Ai. But Joshua spent that night with his troops.

¹⁰Early the next morning Joshua brought together his army. He and the leaders of Israel marched in front of them to Ai. ¹¹The whole army that was with him marched up to the city. They stopped in front of it. They set up camp north of Ai. There was a valley between them and the city. ¹²Joshua had chosen about 5,000 soldiers. He had ordered them to hide in a place west of Ai. It was between Bethel and Ai. ¹³The men took up their battle positions. All the men in the camp north of the city took up their positions. So did those who were supposed to hide west of the city. That night Joshua went into the valley.

¹⁴The king of Ai saw what the troops with Joshua were doing. So the king and all his men hurried out of the city early in the morning. They marched out to meet Israel in battle. They went to a place that looked out over the Arabah Valley. The king didn't know that some of Israel's fighting men were hiding behind the city. ¹⁵Joshua and all his men let the men of Ai drive them back. The Israelites ran away toward the desert. ¹⁶All the men of Ai were called out to chase them. They chased Joshua. So they were drawn away from the city. ¹⁷Not even one man remained in Ai or Bethel. All of them went out to chase Israel. When they did, they left the city wide open.

¹⁸Then the LORD said to Joshua, "Hold out toward Ai the javelin that is in your hand. I will give the city to you." So Joshua held out toward the city the javelin in his hand. ¹⁹As soon as he did, the men hiding behind the city got up quickly. They came out of their hiding places and rushed forward. They entered the city and captured it. They quickly set it on fire.

²⁰The men of Ai looked back. They saw smoke rising up from the city into the sky. But they couldn't escape in any direction. The Israelites had been running away toward the desert. But now they turned around to face those chasing them. ²¹Joshua and all his men saw that the men who had been hiding behind the city had captured it. They also saw that smoke was going up from it. So they turned around and attacked the men of Ai. ²²The men who had set Ai on fire came out of the city. They also fought against the men of

Ai. So the men of Ai were caught in the middle. The army of Israel was on both sides of them. Israel struck them down. They didn't let anyone remain alive or get away. ²³ But they captured the king of Ai alive. They brought him to Joshua.

²⁴ Israel finished killing all the men of Ai. They destroyed them in the fields and in the desert where they had chased them. They struck down every one of them with their swords. Then all the Israelites returned to Ai. And they killed those who were left in it. ²⁵ The total number of men and women they killed that day was 12,000. The Israelites put to death all the people of Ai. ²⁶ Joshua continued to hold out his javelin toward Ai. He didn't lower his hand until he and his men had totally destroyed everyone who lived there. ²⁷ But this time Israel kept for themselves the livestock and everything else they had taken from the city. The LORD had directed Joshua to let them do it.

²⁸ So Joshua burned down Ai. He tore it down so it could never be built again. It has been deserted to this very day. ²⁹ Joshua killed the king of Ai. He stuck a pole through the body. Then he set it up where people could see it. He left it there until evening. At sunset, Joshua ordered his men to remove the body from the pole. He told them to throw the body down at the entrance of the city gate. They put a large pile of rocks over the body. That pile is still there to this day.

Joshua Reads the Book of the Law to the People

³⁰ Joshua built an altar to honor the LORD, the God of Israel. He built it on Mount Ebal. ³¹ Moses, the servant of the LORD, had commanded the Israelites to do that. Joshua built the altar according to what is written in the Book of the Law of Moses. Joshua built the altar out of stones that iron tools had never touched. Then the people offered on the altar burnt offerings to the LORD. They also sacrificed friendship offerings on it. ³² Joshua copied the law of Moses on stones. He did it while all the Israelites were watching. ³³ They were standing on both sides of the ark of the covenant of the LORD. All the Israelites, including outsiders and citizens, were there. Israel's elders, officials and judges were also there. All of them faced the priests, who were Levites. They were carrying the ark. Half of the people stood in front of Mount Gerizim. The other half stood in front of Mount Ebal. Moses, the servant of the LORD, had earlier told them to do it. Moses told them to do it when he had given directions to bless the Israelites.

³⁴ Then Joshua read all the words of the law out loud. He read the blessings and the curses. He read them just as they are written in the Book of the Law. ³⁵ Joshua read every word Moses had commanded. He read them to the whole community of Israel. That included the women and children. It also

included the outsiders living among them.

The People of Gibeon Trick Israel

9 All the kings who ruled west of the Jordan River heard about the battles Israel had won. That included the kings who ruled in the central hill country and the western hills. It also included those who ruled along the entire coast of the Mediterranean Sea all the way to Lebanon. They were the kings of the Hittites, Amorites, Canaanites, Perizzites, Hivites and Jebusites. ²They brought their armies together to fight against Joshua and Israel.

³The people of Gibeon heard about what Joshua had done to Jericho and Ai. ⁴So they decided to trick the Israelites. They packed supplies as if they were going on a long trip. They loaded their donkeys with old sacks and old wineskins. The wineskins were cracked but had been mended. ⁵They put worn-out sandals on their feet. The sandals had been patched. They also wore old clothes. All the bread they took along was dry and moldy. ⁶They went to Joshua in the camp at Gilgal. They spoke to him and the Israelites. They said, "We've come from a country that's far away. Make a peace treaty with us."

⁷The Israelites said to the Hivites, "But suppose you live close to us. If you do, we can't make a peace treaty with you."

⁸"We'll serve you," they said to Joshua.

But Joshua asked, "Who are you? Where do you come from?"

⁹They answered, "We've come from a country that's very far away. We've come because the LORD your God is famous. We've heard reports about him. We've heard about everything he did in Egypt. ¹⁰We've heard about everything he did to Sihon and Og. They were the two kings of the Amorites. They ruled east of the Jordan River. Sihon was the king of Heshbon. Og was the king of Bashan. He ruled in Ashtaroth. ¹¹Our elders and all the people living in our country spoke to us. They said, 'Take supplies for your trip. Go and meet the Israelites. Say to them, "We'll serve you. Make a peace treaty with us."' ¹²Look at our bread. It was warm when we packed it. We packed it at home the day we left to come and see you. But look at how dry and moldy it is now. ¹³When we filled these wineskins, they were new. But look at how cracked they are now. And our clothes and sandals are worn out because we've traveled so far."

¹⁴The Israelites looked over the supplies those people had brought. But they didn't ask the LORD what they should do. ¹⁵Joshua made a peace treaty with the people who had come. He agreed to let them live. The leaders of the community gave their word that they agreed with the treaty.

¹⁶So the Israelites made a peace treaty with the people of Gibeon. But three days later they

heard that the people of Gibeon lived close to them. [17] So the Israelites started out to go to the cities of those people. On the third day they came to Gibeon, Kephirah, Beeroth and Kiriath Jearim. [18] But they didn't attack those cities. That's because the leaders of the community had given their word and made a peace treaty with them. They had given their word in the name of the LORD, the God of Israel.

The whole community told the leaders they weren't happy with them. [19] But all the leaders answered, "We've made a peace treaty with them. We've given our word in the name of the LORD, the God of Israel. So we can't touch them now. [20] But here is what we'll do to them. We'll let them live. Then the LORD won't be angry with us because we didn't keep our promise." [21] They continued, "Let them live. But make them cut wood and carry water to serve the whole community." So the leaders kept their promise to them.

[22] Joshua sent for the people of Gibeon. He said to them, "Why did you trick us? You said, 'We live far away from you.' But in fact you live close to us. [23] So now you are under a curse. You will always serve us. You will always cut wood and carry water for the house of my God."

[24] They answered Joshua, "We were clearly told what the LORD your God had commanded his servant Moses to do. He commanded him to give you the whole land. He also ordered him to wipe out all its people to make room for you. So we were afraid you would kill us. That's why we tricked you. [25] We are now under your control. Do to us what you think is good and right."

[26] So Joshua saved the people of Gibeon. He didn't let the Israelites kill them. [27] That day he made them cut wood and carry water. They had to serve the community of Israel. They also had to do work connected with the altar of the LORD. The altar would be at the place the LORD would choose. And they still serve the Israelites to this day.

The Sun Stands Still

10 Adoni-Zedek was the king of Jerusalem. He heard that Joshua had captured Ai. He found out that the city had been set apart to the LORD in a special way to be destroyed. He heard that Joshua had done to Ai and its king the same thing he had done to Jericho and its king. Adoni-Zedek heard that the people of Gibeon had made a peace treaty with Israel. He also found out that they were living among the Israelites. [2] The things he heard alarmed him and his people very much. That's because Gibeon was an important city. It was like one of the royal cities. It was larger than Ai. All its men were good soldiers. [3] So Adoni-Zedek, the king of Jerusalem, made an appeal to Hoham, the king of Hebron. He appealed to Piram, the king of Jarmuth. He appealed to Japhia, the king of

Lachish. He also made an appeal to Debir, the king of Eglon. 4 "Come up and help me attack Gibeon," he said. "Its people have made peace with Joshua and the Israelites."

5 Then the kings of Jerusalem, Hebron, Jarmuth, Lachish and Eglon gathered their armies together. Those five Amorite kings moved all their troops into position to fight against Gibeon. Then they attacked it.

6 Joshua was in the camp at Gilgal. The people of Gibeon sent a message to him there. They said, "Don't desert us. We serve you. Come up to us quickly! Save us! Help us! All the Amorite kings from the central hill country have gathered their armies together to fight against us."

7 So Joshua marched up from Gilgal with his whole army. The army included all his best fighting men. 8 The LORD said to Joshua, "Do not be afraid of them. I have handed them over to you. Not one of them will be able to fight against you and win."

9 Joshua marched all night from Gilgal. He took the Amorite armies by surprise. 10 The LORD threw them into a panic as Israel marched toward them. Then Joshua and the Israelites won a complete victory over them at Gibeon. The Israelites chased them along the road that goes up to Beth Horon. They struck them down all the way to Azekah and Makkedah. 11 The Amorites tried to escape as Israel marched toward them. They ran down the road from Beth Horon to Azekah. Then the LORD threw large hailstones down on them. The hailstones killed more of them than the swords of the Israelites did.

12 So the LORD gave the Amorites over to Israel. On that day Joshua spoke to the LORD while the Israelites were listening. He said,

"Sun, stand still over Gibeon.
And you, moon, stand
    still over the Valley of
    Aijalon."
13 So the sun stood still.
The moon stopped.
They didn't move again
    until the nation won the
    battle over its enemies.

You can read about it in the Book of Jashar.

The sun stopped in the middle of the sky. It didn't go down for about a full day. 14 There has never been a day like it before or since. It was a day when the LORD listened to a mere human being. Surely the LORD was fighting for Israel!

15 Joshua and his whole army returned to the camp at Gilgal.

Joshua Kills the Five Amorite Kings

16 The five Amorite kings had run away. They had hidden in the cave at Makkedah. 17 Joshua was told that the five kings had been found. He was also told that they were hiding in the cave at Makkedah. 18 He said, "Roll some large rocks up to the opening of the cave. Put some

men there to guard it. ¹⁹ But keep on going! Chase your enemies! Attack them from behind. Don't let them get back to their cities. The LORD your God has handed them over to you."

²⁰ So Joshua and the men of Israel had complete victory over them. They killed almost every one of them. But a few escaped. They went back to their cities that had high walls around them. ²¹ Then Israel's whole army returned safely to Joshua. He was in the camp at Makkedah. No one in the land dared to say anything against the Israelites.

²² Joshua said, "Open up the cave. Bring those five kings out to me." ²³ So Joshua's men brought the kings out of the cave. They were the kings of Jerusalem, Hebron, Jarmuth, Lachish and Eglon. ²⁴ The men brought them to Joshua. Then he sent for all the men of Israel. He spoke to the army commanders who had come with him. He said, "Come here. Put your feet on the necks of these kings." So they came forward and placed their feet on the necks of the kings.

²⁵ Joshua said to them, "Don't be afraid. Don't lose hope. Be strong and brave. This is what the LORD will do to all the enemies you are going to fight." ²⁶ Joshua put the five kings to death. He stuck a pole through each of their bodies. Then he set the poles up where people could see the bodies. He left them there until evening.

²⁷ At sunset Joshua ordered his men to take down the bodies. So they took them down from the poles and threw them into the cave where the kings had been hiding. They placed large rocks at the opening of the cave. And the rocks are still there to this day.

The Campaign Against the Cities in the South

²⁸ That day Joshua captured Makkedah. He cut down its people and their king. He totally destroyed everyone in it. He didn't leave anyone alive. He did to the king of Makkedah the same thing he had done to the king of Jericho.

²⁹ Joshua moved on from Makkedah to Libnah. Israel's whole army went with him. They attacked Libnah. ³⁰ The LORD also handed that city and its king over to Israel. Joshua destroyed the city. He and his men killed everyone in it with their swords. He didn't leave anyone alive there. He did to its king the same thing he had done to the king of Jericho.

³¹ Joshua moved on from Libnah to Lachish. Israel's whole army went with him. The men took up their battle positions. Then Joshua attacked Lachish. ³² The LORD handed it over to Israel. Joshua captured the city on the second day of the battle. He destroyed the city. He and his men killed everyone in it with their swords. He had done the same thing to Libnah. ³³ While all that was happening, Horam had come up to help Lachish. He was the king of Gezer. But Joshua

won the battle over him and his army. No one was left alive.

³⁴ Joshua moved on from Lachish to Eglon. Israel's whole army went with him. They took up their battle positions. Then they attacked Eglon. ³⁵ They captured it that same day. They totally destroyed everyone in it with their swords. They had done the same thing to Lachish.

³⁶ Joshua went up from Eglon to Hebron. Israel's whole army went with him. Then they attacked Hebron. ³⁷ They captured the city. They destroyed it and its villages. They killed all its people and their king with their swords. They didn't leave anyone alive. They totally destroyed the city and everyone in it. They had done the same thing at Eglon.

³⁸ Joshua turned back and attacked Debir. Israel's whole army went with him. ³⁹ They captured the city, its king and its villages. They totally destroyed everyone in Debir with their swords. They didn't leave anyone alive. They did to Debir and its king the same thing they had done to Libnah and its king. They had also done the same thing to Hebron.

⁴⁰ So Joshua brought the whole area under his control. That included the central hill country and the Negev Desert. It included the western hills and the mountain slopes. It also included all the kings in that whole area. Joshua didn't leave anyone alive. He totally destroyed everyone who breathed. He did just as the LORD, the God of Israel, had commanded. ⁴¹ Joshua brought everyone from Kadesh Barnea to Gaza under his control. He did the same thing to everyone from the whole area of Goshen to Gibeon. ⁴² He won the battle over all those kings and their lands. He did it in one campaign. That's because the LORD, the God of Israel, fought for Israel.

⁴³ Then Joshua returned to the camp at Gilgal. Israel's whole army went with him.

The Campaign Against the Cities in the North

11 Jabin was the king of Hazor. He heard about the battles Israel had won. So he sent a message to Jobab. Jobab was the king of Madon. Jabin sent the same message to the kings of Shimron and Akshaph. ² He also sent it to many other kings. Some ruled in the mountains in the north. Some ruled in the Arabah Valley south of Kinnereth. Others ruled in the western hills. Still others ruled in Naphoth Dor in the west. ³ Jabin sent the same message to the people of east Canaan and west Canaan. He sent it to the Amorites, Hittites, Perizzites and Jebusites. They lived in the central hill country. He also sent it to the Hivites who lived below Mount Hermon in the area of Mizpah. ⁴ Those kings marched out with all their troops. They had a large number of horses and chariots. It was a huge army. The fighting men were as

many as the grains of sand on the seashore. ⁵All those kings gathered their armies together to fight against Israel. They set up camp together at the Waters of Merom.

⁶The LORD said to Joshua, "Do not be afraid of them. By this time tomorrow I will hand all of them over to Israel. All of them will be killed. You must cut the legs of their horses. You must burn their chariots."

⁷So Joshua and his whole army attacked them suddenly. They fought against them at the Waters of Merom. ⁸The LORD handed them over to Israel. The Israelites won the battle over them. They hunted them down all the way to Greater Sidon. They chased them to Misrephoth Maim. They chased them to the Valley of Mizpah in the east. Not one of them was left alive. ⁹Joshua did to them what the LORD had ordered him to do. He cut the legs of their horses. He burned up their chariots.

¹⁰At that time Joshua turned back. He captured Hazor. He killed its king with his sword. Hazor was the most important city in all those kingdoms. ¹¹The army of Israel killed everyone in Hazor with their swords. Its people had been set apart to the LORD to be destroyed. Israel's army didn't spare anyone who breathed. Then Joshua burned down the city.

¹²Joshua captured all those royal cities and their kings. He and his men killed everyone in those cities with their swords. He totally destroyed them. He did just as Moses, the servant of the LORD, had commanded. ¹³Many cities were built on top of earlier cities that had been destroyed. Israel didn't burn any of those except Hazor. Joshua burned it down. ¹⁴The army of Israel kept for themselves the livestock and everything else they took from those cities. But they killed all the people with their swords. They completely destroyed them. They didn't spare anyone who breathed. ¹⁵The LORD had commanded his servant Moses to do all these things. Moses had passed that command on to Joshua. And Joshua carried it out. He did everything the LORD had commanded Moses.

¹⁶So Joshua captured the whole land. He took over the central hill country and the whole Negev Desert. He took over the whole area of Goshen. He took over the western hills. He took over the Arabah Valley. He took over the mountains of Israel and the hills around them. ¹⁷He took over the area that begins at Mount Halak, which rises toward Seir. The area ends at Baal Gad in the Valley of Lebanon below Mount Hermon. Joshua captured the kings who ruled over that whole land. He put them to death. ¹⁸He fought battles against all those kings for a long time. ¹⁹Only the Hivites who lived in Gibeon made a peace treaty with the Israelites. No other city made a treaty with them. So Israel captured all those cities in battle.

20 The LORD himself made their people stubborn. He made them go to war against Israel so he could totally destroy them. He wanted to wipe them out. He didn't show them any mercy. The LORD had commanded Moses to destroy the Canaanites. 21 At that time Joshua went and destroyed the Anakites. They lived all through the hill country of Judah and Israel. They lived in Hebron, Debir and Anab. Joshua totally destroyed the Anakites and their towns. 22 There weren't any Anakites left alive in Israel's territory. But a few were left alive in Gaza, Gath and Ashdod. 23 So Joshua captured the whole land, just as the LORD had directed Moses. Joshua gave the land to Israel as their very own. He divided it up and gave each tribe its share. Then the land had peace and rest.

Israel Wins the Battle Over the Kings in the Land

12 The Israelites took over the territory east of the Jordan River. The land they captured reached from the Arnon River valley to Mount Hermon. It included the whole east side of the Arabah Valley. Israel won the battle over the kings of that whole territory. Here are the lands Israel captured from the kings they won the battle over.

2 They took over the land of Sihon. He was the king of the Amorites.

He ruled in Heshbon. The land he ruled over begins at Aroer. Aroer is on the rim of the Arnon River valley. Sihon ruled from the middle of the valley to the Jabbok River. The Jabbok is the border of Ammon. Sihon's territory included half of Gilead. 3 He also ruled over the east side of the Arabah Valley. That land begins at the Sea of Galilee. It goes to the Dead Sea and over to Beth Jeshimoth. Then it goes south, below the slopes of Pisgah.

4 Israel also took over the territory of Og. He was the king of Bashan.

He was one of the last of the Rephaites. He ruled in Ashtaroth and Edrei. 5 He ruled over Mount Hermon, Salekah and the whole land of Bashan. Og's kingdom reached all the way to the border of Geshur and Maakah. He ruled over half of Gilead. His land reached the border of Sihon, the king of Heshbon.

6 Moses was the servant of the LORD. Moses and the Israelites won the battle over those two kings. He gave their land to the tribes of Reuben and Gad and half of the tribe of Manasseh. He gave it to them as their share.

7 Joshua and the Israelites won the battle over the kings who

ruled west of the Jordan River. The lands of those kings reached from Baal Gad in the Valley of Lebanon to Mount Halak, which rises toward Seir. Joshua gave their lands to the tribes of Israel as their very own. He divided them up and gave each tribe its share. [8] Those lands included the central hill country, the western hills and the Arabah Valley. They also included the mountain slopes, the Desert of Judah and the Negev Desert. Those lands belonged to the Hittites, Amorites, Canaanites, Perizzites, Hivites and Jebusites.

Here are the kings Israel won the battle over.

[9] the king of Jericho   one
the king of Ai, which is near
     Bethel   one
[10] the king of Jerusalem   one
the king of Hebron   one
[11] the king of Jarmuth   one
the king of Lachish   one
[12] the king of Eglon   one
the king of Gezer   one
[13] the king of Debir   one
the king of Geder   one
[14] the king of Hormah   one
the king of Arad   one
[15] the king of Libnah   one
the king of Adullam   one
[16] the king of Makkedah   one
the king of Bethel   one
[17] the king of Tappuah   one
the king of Hepher   one
[18] the king of Aphek   one
the king of Lasharon   one
[19] the king of Madon   one
the king of Hazor   one
[20] the king of Shimron
     Meron   one
the king of Akshaph   one
[21] the king of Taanach   one
the king of Megiddo   one
[22] the king of Kedesh   one
the king of Jokneam in
     Carmel   one
[23] the king of Dor in
     Naphoth Dor   one
the king of Goyim in
     Gilgal   one
[24] the king of Tirzah   one

The total number of kings was 31.

The Land That Remained to Be Taken Over

13 Joshua was now very old. The LORD said to him, "You are very old. And there are still very large areas of land that have not yet been taken over.

[2] "Here is the land that remains to be taken over.

It includes all the areas of Philistia and Geshur. [3] Those areas begin at the Shihor River in the eastern part of Egypt. They go to the territory of Ekron in the north. All that land is considered Canaanite even though it is controlled by five Philistine rulers. They rule over Gaza, Ashdod, Ashkelon, Gath and Ekron. The Avvites [4] live south of them.

The rest of the land of Canaan that remains to be taken over reaches from Arah all the way to Aphek. Arah belongs to the people of Sidon. The land that remains to be taken reaches the border of Amorite territory. ⁵It includes the area of Byblos.

It also includes all of Lebanon to the east. It reaches from Baal Gad below Mount Hermon all the way to Lebo Hamath.

⁶ "I myself will drive out all the people who live in the mountain areas. Those areas reach from Lebanon to Misrephoth Maim. They include the area where all the people of Sidon live. I myself will drive out those people to make room for the Israelites. Make sure you set that land apart for Israel. Give it to them as their share, just as I have directed you. ⁷Divide it up among the nine tribes and half of the tribe of Manasseh. Give each tribe its share."

Land for the Tribes East of the Jordan River

⁸The other half of Manasseh's tribe had already received the share of land Moses had given them. Their share was east of the Jordan River. The tribes of Reuben and Gad had already received their share too. Moses, the servant of the LORD, had given it to them.

⁹That land starts at Aroer on the rim of the Arnon River valley. It includes the town in the middle of the valley. It includes the high plains of Medeba all the way to Dibon.

¹⁰It also includes all the towns of Sihon, the king of the Amorites. He had ruled in Heshbon. That area reaches to the border of Ammon.

¹¹It also includes Gilead. It includes the territory of Geshur and Maakah. It includes Mount Hermon and the whole land of Bashan all the way to Salekah. ¹²So it includes the entire kingdom of Og in Bashan. Og had ruled in Ashtaroth and Edrei. He was the last of the Rephaites.

Moses had won the battle over Sihon and Og. He had taken over their land. ¹³But the Israelites didn't drive out the people of Geshur and Maakah. So they continue to live among the Israelites to this day.

¹⁴Moses hadn't given any share of the land to the tribe of Levi. That's because the food offerings are their share. Those offerings are presented to the LORD, the God of Israel. Moses gave the Levites what he had promised them.

¹⁵Here is what Moses had given to the tribe of Reuben, according to its family groups. ¹⁶Their territory starts at Aroer on the rim of the Arnon River valley. It includes the town in the middle of the valley. It

includes all of the high plains near Medeba. [17] It includes Heshbon and all its towns on those plains. Those towns include Dibon, Bamoth Baal, Beth Baal Meon, [18] Jahaz, Kedemoth and Mephaath. [19] They include Kiriathaim, Sibmah and Zereth Shahar on the hill in the valley. [20] They also include Beth Peor, Beth Jeshimoth and the slopes of Pisgah. [21] All those towns are on the high plains. The territory includes the whole kingdom of Sihon, the king of the Amorites. He had ruled in Heshbon.

Moses had won the battle over him and over the chiefs of Midian. Those chiefs were Evi, Rekem, Zur, Hur and Reba. They were princes who helped Sihon fight against Israel. They lived in that country. [22] The Israelites killed many of them in battle. They also killed Balaam with their swords. He was the son of Beor. Balaam had used evil magic to find out what was going to happen.

[23] The border of the tribe of Reuben was the bank of the Jordan River. All those towns and their villages were given to the tribe of Reuben as their very own. Each family group received its share.

[24] Here is what Moses had given to the tribe of Gad, according to its family groups. [25] Their territory includes Jazer and all the towns of Gilead. It includes half of the country of Ammon all the way to Aroer, which was near Rabbah. [26] Their territory reaches from Heshbon to Ramath Mizpah and Betonim. It reaches from Mahanaim to the territory of Debir. [27] In the valley their land includes Beth Haram, Beth Nimrah, Sukkoth and Zaphon. It also includes the rest of the kingdom of Sihon. He was the king of Heshbon. His kingdom included the east side of the Jordan River. It reached up to the south end of the Sea of Galilee.

[28] All those towns and their villages were given to the tribe of Gad as their very own. Each family group received its share.

[29] Here is what Moses had given to half of the tribe of Manasseh, according to its family groups. It's what Moses had given to half of Manasseh's family line.

[30] Their territory starts at Mahanaim. It includes the whole land of Bashan. That was the entire kingdom of Og, the king of Bashan. Manasseh's territory includes all the 60

towns of Jair in Bashan. ³¹ It includes half of the land of Gilead. It also includes Ashtaroth and Edrei. They were the royal cities of Og in Bashan.

That land was given to half of the family line of Makir. He was the son of Manasseh. Each family group received its share.

³² Those were the shares of land Moses had given the eastern tribes when he was in the plains of Moab. The plains are across the Jordan River east of Jericho. ³³ But Moses hadn't given any share to the tribe of Levi. The Lord, the God of Israel, is their share. Moses gave the Levites what he had promised them.

Land for the Tribes West of the Jordan River

14 The rest of the tribes of Israel received their shares of land in Canaan. Eleazar the priest and Joshua, the son of Nun, decided what each of the tribes should receive. The leaders of the tribes helped them make these decisions. ² The shares of nine tribes and half of the tribe of Manasseh were decided by casting lots. That's what the Lord had commanded through Moses. ³ Moses had given two tribes and the other half of the tribe of Manasseh their shares east of the Jordan River. But Moses had not given the Levites a share among the other tribes.

⁴ Manasseh and Ephraim were the sons of Joseph. They had become two tribes. The Levites didn't receive any share of the land. They only received towns to live in and grasslands for their flocks and herds. ⁵ So the Israelites divided up the land, just as the Lord had commanded Moses.

Joshua Gives Hebron to Caleb

⁶ The people of Judah approached Joshua at Gilgal. Caleb, the son of Jephunneh the Kenizzite, spoke to Joshua. He said, "You know what the Lord said to Moses, the man of God. He spoke to him at Kadesh Barnea about you and me. ⁷ Moses, the servant of the Lord, sent me from Kadesh Barnea to check out the land. I was 40 years old at that time. I brought back an honest report to him. I told him exactly what I had seen. ⁸ Several other men of Israel went up with me. What they reported terrified the people. But I followed the Lord my God with my whole heart. ⁹ So on that day Moses made a promise to me. He said, 'The land you have walked on will be your share. It will be the share of your children forever. That's because you have followed the Lord my God with your whole heart.' *(Deuteronomy 1:36)*

¹⁰ "The Lord has done just as he promised. He made the promise while Israel was wandering around in the desert. That was 45 years ago. He has kept me alive all this time. So here I am today, 85 years old!

¹¹ I'm still as strong today as I was the day Moses sent me out. I'm just as able to go out to battle now as I was then. ¹² So give me this hill country. The LORD promised it to me that day. At that time you yourself heard that the Anakites were living there. You also heard that their cities were large and had high walls around them. But I'll drive them out, just as the LORD said I would. He will help me do it."

¹³ Then Joshua blessed Caleb, the son of Jephunneh. He gave him Hebron as his share. ¹⁴ So ever since that time Hebron has belonged to Caleb, the son of Jephunneh the Kenizzite. That's because he followed the LORD, the God of Israel, with his whole heart. ¹⁵ Hebron used to be called Kiriath Arba. It was named after Arba. He was the greatest man among the Anakites.

So the land had peace and rest.

Land Is Given to Judah

15 Land was given to the tribe of Judah, according to its family groups. It reached down to the territory of Edom. It went as far south as the Desert of Zin.

² Judah's border on the south started from the bay at the south end of the Dead Sea. ³ It went across to the south of Scorpion Pass. It continued on to Zin. It went over to the south of Kadesh Barnea. Then it ran past Hezron up to

Addar. It curved around to Karka. ⁴ It then went along to Azmon. There it joined the Wadi of Egypt and ended at the Mediterranean Sea. That was the southern border of Judah.

⁵ The border on the east was the Dead Sea. It went north all the way to where the Jordan River enters the sea.

The border on the north started at the bay of the Dead Sea. That's where the Jordan River enters the sea. ⁶ From there it went up to Beth Hoglah. It continued north of Beth Arabah to the Stone of Bohan, the son of Reuben. ⁷ Then it went from the Valley of Achor up to Debir. It turned north to Gilgal. Gilgal faces the Pass of Adummim south of the valley. The border continued along to the springs of En Shemesh. It came to an end at En Rogel. ⁸ Then it ran up the Valley of Ben Hinnom. It went along the south slope of Jerusalem. From there it climbed to the top of the hill west of the Hinnom Valley. The hill is also at the north end of the Valley of Rephaim. ⁹ From the top of the hill the border headed toward the springs of Nephtoah. It went to the towns near Mount Ephron. It went down toward Kiriath Jearim. ¹⁰Then it curved west from Kiriath Jearim to Mount Seir. It ran along the north slope of Mount Kesalon. It continued down to Beth Shemesh and crossed over to Timnah. ¹¹It went to the north slope of Ekron. Then it turned toward Shikkeron. It passed along to Mount Baalah and reached Jabneel. The border came to an end at the Mediterranean Sea. ¹²The border on the west was the coastline of the Mediterranean Sea.

Those were the borders of the family groups of the tribe of Judah.

¹³Joshua gave a part of Judah's share of land to Caleb, the son of Jephunneh. That was according to the LORD's command to Joshua. The share Caleb received was the city of Hebron. It was also called Kiriath Arba. Anak came from the family line of Arba. ¹⁴Caleb drove three Anakites out of Hebron. Their names were Sheshai, Ahiman and Talmai. They were from the family line of Anak. ¹⁵From Hebron, Caleb marched out against the people living in Debir. It used to be called Kiriath Sepher. ¹⁶Caleb said, "I will give my daughter Aksah to be married. She'll be the wife of the man who attacks and captures Kiriath Sepher." ¹⁷Othniel captured it. So Caleb gave his daughter Aksah to him to be his wife. Othniel was the son of Kenaz. He was Caleb's brother.

¹⁸One day Aksah came to Othniel. She begged him to ask her father for a field. When she got off her donkey, Caleb spoke to her. He asked, "What can I do for you?"

¹⁹She replied, "Do me a special favor. You have given me some land in the Negev Desert. Give me springs of water also." So Caleb gave her the upper and lower springs.

²⁰Here is the share of land given to the tribe of Judah, according to its family groups.

²¹The towns farthest south that were given to Judah were in the Negev Desert. They were near the border of Edom. Here is a list of those towns.
Kabzeel, Eder, Jagur, ²²Kinah, Dimonah, Adadah, ²³Kedesh, Hazor, Ithnan, ²⁴Ziph, Telem, Bealoth, ²⁵Hazor Hadattah, Hazor, ²⁶Amam, Shema, Moladah, ²⁷Hazar Gaddah, Heshmon, Beth Pelet, ²⁸Hazar Shual, Beersheba, Biziothiah, ²⁹Baalah, Iyim, Ezem, ³⁰Eltolad, Kesil, Hormah, ³¹Ziklag, Madmannah, Sansannah, ³²Lebaoth, Shilhim, Ain and Rimmon. The total number of towns was 29. Some of them had villages near them.

³³Towns were also given to Judah in the western hills. Here is a list of those towns.

Eshtaol, Zorah, Ashnah, ³⁴Zanoah, En Gannim, Tappuah, Enam, ³⁵Jarmuth, Adullam, Sokoh, Azekah, ³⁶Shaaraim, Adithaim and Gederah. Gederah is also called Gederothaim. The total number of towns was 14. Some of them had villages near them.

³⁷Here's another list of towns given to Judah in the western hills. Zenan, Hadashah, Migdal Gad, ³⁸Dilean, Mizpah, Joktheel, ³⁹Lachish, Bozkath, Eglon, ⁴⁰Kabbon, Lahmas, Kitlish, ⁴¹Gederoth, Beth Dagon, Naamah and Makkedah. The total number of towns was 16. Some of them had villages near them.

⁴²Here's another list of towns given to Judah in the western hills. Libnah, Ether, Ashan, ⁴³Iphtah, Ashnah, Nezib, ⁴⁴Keilah, Akzib and Mareshah. The total number of towns was nine. Some of them had villages near them.

⁴⁵Judah was also given Ekron and the settlements and villages around it. ⁴⁶West of Ekron, Judah was given all the settlements and villages near Ashdod. ⁴⁷Judah was given Ashdod and the settlements and villages around it. And Judah was given Gaza and its settlements and villages. Judah's territory went all the way to the Wadi of Egypt and the coast of the Mediterranean Sea.

⁴⁸Towns were also given to Judah in the central hill country. Here is a list of those towns.

Shamir, Jattir, Sokoh, ⁴⁹Dannah, Debir, ⁵⁰Anab, Eshtemoh, Anim, ⁵¹Goshen, Holon and Giloh. The total number of towns was 11. Some of them had villages near them.

⁵²Here's another list of towns given to Judah in the central hill country. Arab, Dumah, Eshan, ⁵³Janim, Beth Tappuah, Aphekah, ⁵⁴Humtah, Hebron and Zior. The total number of towns was nine. Some of them had villages near them.

⁵⁵Here's another list of towns given to Judah in the central hill country. Maon, Carmel, Ziph, Juttah, ⁵⁶Jezreel, Jokdeam, Zanoah, ⁵⁷Kain, Gibeah and Timnah. The total number of towns was ten. Some of them had villages near them.

⁵⁸Here's another list of towns given to Judah in the central hill country. Halhul, Beth Zur, Gedor,

⁵⁹ Maarath, Beth Anoth and Eltekon. The total number of towns was six. Some of them had villages near them.

⁶⁰ Here's another list of towns given to Judah in the central hill country. Kiriath Jearim and Rabbah. The total number of towns was two. They had villages near them.

⁶¹ Towns were also given to Judah in the desert. Here is a list of those towns.

Beth Arabah, Middin, Sekakah, ⁶² Nibshan, the City of Salt and En Gedi. The total number of towns was six. Some of them had villages near them.

⁶³ Judah couldn't drive out the Jebusites who were living in Jerusalem. So they live there with the people of Judah to this day.

Land Is Given to Ephraim and Manasseh

16 The land given to the two tribes in the family line of Joseph began at the Jordan River. Their border started east of the springs of Jericho. It went up from there through the desert into the hill country of Bethel. ² Bethel is also called Luz. From Bethel the border crossed over to Ataroth. That's where the Arkites live. ³ Then it went west down to the territory of the Japhletites. It went all the way to the area of Lower Beth Horon. It went on to Gezer. The border came to an end at the Mediterranean Sea.

⁴ The tribes of Manasseh and Ephraim were from the family line of Joseph. So they received that land as their share.

⁵ Here is the territory given to the tribe of Ephraim, according to its family groups.

The border of their share of land started at Ataroth Addar in the east. It went to Upper Beth Horon. ⁶ It continued toward the Mediterranean Sea. From Mikmethath on the north, it curved toward the east. It went to Taanath Shiloh. It passed by Taanath Shiloh to Janoah on the east. ⁷ Then it went down from Janoah to Ataroth and Naarah. It touched Jericho and came to an end at the Jordan River. ⁸ From Tappuah the border went west to the Kanah Valley. It came to an end at the Mediterranean Sea. That was the land given to the tribe of Ephraim. Each family group received its share.

⁹ The tribe of Ephraim was also given other towns and villages that were set apart for them. Those towns and villages were in the share of land given to the tribe of Manasseh.

¹⁰ The people of Ephraim didn't drive out the Canaanites living in Gezer. The Canaanites live among the people of Ephraim to this day. But they are forced to work hard for the people of Ephraim.

17 Land was given to the tribe of Manasseh. It was given to Makir. Manasseh was Joseph's oldest son. Makir was Manasseh's oldest son. The people of Gilead came from the family line of Makir. The people of Gilead had received the lands of Gilead and Bashan. That's because the people of Makir were great soldiers. ² So land was given to the rest of the people of Manasseh. It was given to the family groups of Abiezer, Helek, Asriel, Shechem, Hepher and Shemida. They were the other men in the family line of Manasseh, the son of Joseph. Those were their names by their family groups.

³ Makir was the son of Manasseh. Gilead was the son of Makir. Hepher was the son of Gilead. And Zelophehad was the son of Hepher. Zelophehad didn't have any sons. He only had daughters. Their names were Mahlah, Noah, Hoglah, Milkah and Tirzah. ⁴ The daughters of Zelophehad went to Eleazar the priest and to Joshua, the son of Nun. They also went to the other leaders. They said, "The LORD commanded Moses to give us our share of land among our male relatives." So Joshua gave them land along with their male relatives. That was according to what the LORD had commanded. ⁵ Manasseh's share was made up of ten pieces of land. That land was in addition to Gilead and Bashan east of the Jordan River. ⁶ So the five granddaughters of Hepher in the family line of Manasseh received land, just as the other five sons of Manasseh did. The land of Gilead belonged to the rest of the family line of Manasseh.

⁷ The territory of Manasseh reached from Asher to Mikmethath. Mikmethath was east of Shechem. The border ran south from Mikmethath. The people living at En Tappuah were inside the border. ⁸ Manasseh had the land around Tappuah. But the town of Tappuah itself was on the border of Manasseh's land. It belonged to the people of Ephraim. ⁹ The border continued south to the Kanah Valley. Some of the towns that belonged to Ephraim were located among the towns of Manasseh. But the border of Manasseh was the north side of the valley. The border came to an end at the Mediterranean Sea. ¹⁰ The land on the south belonged to Ephraim. The land on the north belonged to Manasseh. The territory of Manas-

seh reached the Mediterranean Sea. The tribe of Asher was the border on the north. The tribe of Issachar was the border on the east.

11 Inside the land given to Issachar and Asher, the towns of Beth Shan and Ibleam belonged to Manasseh. The towns of Dor, Endor, Taanach and Megiddo and their people also belonged to Manasseh. Manasseh was given all those towns and the settlements around them. The third town in the list was also called Naphoth Dor.

12 But the people of Manasseh weren't able to take over those towns. That's because the Canaanites had made up their minds to live in that area. 13 The Israelites grew stronger. Then they forced the Canaanites to work hard for them. But they didn't drive them out completely.

14 The people in the family line of Joseph spoke to Joshua. They said, "Why have you given us only one share of the land to have as our own? There are large numbers of us. The LORD has blessed us greatly."

15 "That's true," Joshua said. "There are large numbers of you. And the hill country of Ephraim is too small for you. So go up into the forest. Clear out some land for yourselves in the territory of the Perizzites and Rephaites."

16 The people in Joseph's family line replied, "The hill country isn't big enough for us. And all the Canaanites who live in the plains use chariots that have iron parts. They include the people of Beth Shan and its settlements. They also include the people who live in the Valley of Jezreel."

17 Joshua spoke again to the people in Joseph's family line. He said to the people of Ephraim and Manasseh, "There are large numbers of you. And you are very powerful. You will have more than one piece of land. 18 You will also have the central hill country. It's covered with trees. Cut them down and clear the land. That whole land from one end to the other will belong to you. The Canaanites use chariots that have iron parts. And those people are strong. But you can drive them out."

The Rest of the Land Is Divided Up

18 The whole community of Israel gathered together at Shiloh. They set up the tent of meeting there. The country was brought under their control. 2 But there were still seven tribes in Israel who had not yet received their shares of land.

3 So Joshua spoke to the Israelites. He said, "The LORD, the God of your people, has given you this land. How long will you wait before you begin to take it over? 4 Appoint three men from

each tribe. I'll send them to map out the land. Then they'll write a report about its features. The report will point out the share of land each tribe will receive. Then the men will return to me. ⁵You must divide the land up into seven shares. Judah must remain in its territory in the south. The people in Joseph's family line must remain in their territory in the north. ⁶Write reports about the features of those seven shares of land. Bring them here to me. Then I'll cast lots for you in the sight of the LORD our God. ⁷But the Levites don't get any share of your land. That's because their share is to serve the LORD as priests. The tribes of Gad and Reuben and half of the tribe of Manasseh have already received their shares. They are on the east side of the Jordan River. Moses, the servant of the LORD, gave their shares to them."

⁸The men started out on their way to map out the land. Joshua directed them, "Go and map out the land. Write a report about its features. Then return to me. I'll cast lots for you here at Shiloh in the sight of the LORD." ⁹So the men left and went through the land. They wrote a report about its features on a scroll. It showed how they divided up the land into seven shares. It listed the towns in each share. The men returned to Joshua in the camp at Shiloh.

¹⁰Then Joshua cast lots for them in Shiloh in the sight of the LORD. There he gave out a share of land to each of the remaining tribes in Israel.

Land Is Given to Benjamin

¹¹The first lot drawn out was for the tribe of Benjamin, according to its family groups. The territory they were given was located between the tribes of the people of Judah and the people of Joseph. Here are the borders of Benjamin's territory. ¹²On the north side their border started at the Jordan River. It went past the north slope of Jericho. Then it headed west into the central hill country. It came to an end at the Desert of Beth Aven. ¹³From there the border crossed to the south slope of Bethel. Then it went down to Ataroth Addar on the hill south of Lower Beth Horon. ¹⁴From the hill that faces Beth Horon on the south the border turned south. Then the border went along the west side of the hill. It came to an end at Kiriath Jearim. That town belongs to the people of Judah. That was the border on the west. ¹⁵The border on the south side started at the west edge of Kiriath Jearim. It came to an end at the springs of Nephtoah. ¹⁶It went down to the foot of the hill that faces the Valley of Ben Hinnom. The hill is north

of the Valley of Rephaim. The border continued down the Hinnom Valley. It went along the south slope of Jerusalem, where the people of Jebus live. It continued on to En Rogel. ¹⁷ Then it curved north. It went to En Shemesh. It continued on to Geliloth. Geliloth faces the Pass of Adummim. The border ran down to the Stone of Bohan, the son of Reuben. ¹⁸ It continued to the north slope of Beth Arabah. It went on down into the Arabah Valley. ¹⁹ From there it went to the north slope of Beth Hoglah. It came to an end at the north bay of the Dead Sea. That's where the Jordan River flows into the Dead Sea. That was the border on the south.

²⁰ The Jordan River formed the border on the east side.

Those were the borders that marked out on all sides the land the family groups of Benjamin received as their share.

²¹ Here is a list of towns given to the tribe of Benjamin, according to its family groups.

Jericho, Beth Hoglah, Emek Keziz, ²² Beth Arabah, Zemaraim, Bethel, ²³ Avvim, Parah, Ophrah, ²⁴ Kephar Ammoni, Ophni and Geba. The total number of towns and their villages was 12.

²⁵ Here is another list of towns given to Benjamin.

Gibeon, Ramah, Beeroth, ²⁶ Mizpah, Kephirah, Mozah, ²⁷ Rekem, Irpeel, Taralah, ²⁸ Zelah, Haeleph, Jerusalem, Gibeah and Kiriath. The total number of towns and their villages was 14.

That was the share of land the family groups of Benjamin received.

Land Is Given to Simeon

19 The second lot drawn out was for the tribe of Simeon, according to its family groups. The share of land they were given was in the territory of Judah. ² Here is what Simeon's share included.

Beersheba, Moladah, ³ Hazar Shual, Balah, Ezem, ⁴ Eltolad, Bethul, Hormah, ⁵ Ziklag, Beth Markaboth, Hazar Susah, ⁶ Beth Lebaoth and Sharuhen. The total number of towns was 13. Some of them had villages near them.

⁷ Here's another list of towns given to Simeon.

Ain, Rimmon, Ether and Ashan. The total number of towns was four. Some of them had villages near them. ⁸ The towns and all the villages around them reached all the way to Ramah in the Negev Desert.

Ten Commandments
for Kids

1   You may not love anyone or anything more than you love God.

2   You may not worship or put more importance on any person or thing other than God. You must worship only the Lord, not a friend, not a movie star or sports hero, not a car or skateboard.

3   You may not swear. Use God's holy name in a loving way, never to express anger or frustration.

4   One day of your week should be set aside for resting and worshiping God.

5   Respect your parents. Love them, and the Lord will reward you in your life.

6   You may not hate other people; don't think of hurting someone else in any way.

7   Keep your thoughts and actions pure. Husbands and wives should share their special love only with each other.

8   Do not take anything that does not belong to you.

9   You may not tell lies, especially when that lie will hurt someone else.

10   Do not be jealous of what others have. You may not be jealous of your friend's new toy or clothes or the big house your neighbor lives in. Be satisfied with what you have.

BASED ON EXODUS 20:1–17 AND DEUTERONOMY 5:7–21

Moses Receives the Ten Commandments

EXODUS 24:12–18

That was the share of land the tribe of Simeon received, according to its family groups.

9 Simeon's share of land was taken from Judah's share. That's because Judah had more land than they needed. So the people of Simeon received their share of land inside the territory of Judah.

Land Is Given to Zebulun

10 The third lot drawn out was for the tribe of Zebulun, according to its family groups. Here are the borders of Zebulun's territory. The border of their share of land went as far as Sarid. 11 It ran west to Maralah and touched Dabbesheth. It reached to the valley near Jokneam. 12 It turned east from Sarid toward the sunrise. It went to the territory of Kisloth Tabor. It went on to Daberath and up to Japhia. 13 Then it continued east to Gath Hepher and Eth Kazin. It came to an end at Rimmon and turned toward Neah. 14 There the border went around on the north to Hannathon. It came to an end at the Valley of Iphtah El. 15 Zebulun's territory included Kattath, Nahalal, Shimron, Idalah and Bethlehem. The total number of towns was 12.

Some of them had villages near them. 16 Those towns and their villages were Zebulun's share, according to its family groups.

Land Is Given to Issachar

17 The fourth lot drawn out was for the tribe of Issachar, according to its family groups. 18 Here is what Issachar's share included. Jezreel, Kesulloth, Shunem, 19 Hapharaim, Shion, Anaharath, 20 Rabbith, Kishion, Ebez, 21 Remeth, En Gannim, En Haddah and Beth Pazzez. 22 The border touched Tabor, Shahazumah and Beth Shemesh. It came to an end at the Jordan River. The total number of towns was 16. Some of them had villages near them. 23 Those towns and their villages were the share the tribe of Issachar received, according to its family groups.

Land Is Given to Asher

24 The fifth lot drawn out was for the tribe of Asher, according to its family groups. 25 Here is what Asher's share included. Helkath, Hali, Beten, Akshaph, 26 Allammelek, Amad and Mishal. On the west the border touched Carmel and Shihor Libnath. 27 Then it turned east toward Beth Dagon.

It touched Zebulun and the Valley of Iphtah El. It went north to Beth Emek and Neiel. It went past Kabul on the left. 28 It went to Abdon, Rehob, Hammon and Kanah. It reached all the way to Greater Sidon. 29 The border then turned back toward Ramah. It went to Tyre, a city that had high walls around it. It turned toward Hosah. It came to an end at the Mediterranean Sea in the area of Akzib, 30 Ummah, Aphek and Rehob.

The total number of towns was 22. Some of them had villages near them. 31 Those towns and their villages were the share the tribe of Asher received, according to its family groups.

Land Is Given to Naphtali

32 The sixth lot drawn out was for Naphtali, according to its family groups. 33 Their border started at Heleph and the large tree in Zaanannim. It went past Adami Nekeb and Jabneel. It went to Lakkum and came to an end at the Jordan River. 34 The border ran west through Aznoth Tabor. It came to an end at Hukkok. It touched Zebulun on the south. It touched Asher on the west. It touched the Jordan on the east. 35 The towns that had high walls around them were Ziddim, Zer, Hammath, Rakkath, Kinnereth, 36 Adamah, Ramah, Hazor, 37 Kedesh, Edrei, En Hazor, 38 Iron, Migdal El, Horem, Beth Anath and Beth Shemesh. The total number of towns was 19. Some of them had villages near them.

39 Those towns and their villages were the share the tribe of Naphtali received, according to its family groups.

Land Is Given to Dan

40 The seventh lot drawn out was for the tribe of Dan, according to its family groups. 41 Here is what Dan's share of land included.

Zorah, Eshtaol, Ir Shemesh, 42 Shaalabbin, Aijalon, Ithlah, 43 Elon, Timnah, Ekron, 44 Eltekeh, Gibbethon, Baalath, 45 Jehud, Bene Berak, Gath Rimmon, 46 Me Jarkon and Rakkon. Dan's share included the area that faces Joppa.

47 The people of Dan lost their territory. So they went up and attacked Leshem. They captured it. They killed its people with their swords. Then they moved into Leshem and made their homes there. They named it Dan. That's because they traced their family line back to him.

48 All those towns and their villages were the share the

tribe of Dan received, according to its family groups.

Land Is Given to Joshua

⁴⁹ The Israelites finished dividing up the shares of land the tribes received. Then they gave a share to Joshua, the son of Nun. ⁵⁰ They did what the Lord had commanded them to do. They gave Joshua the town he asked for. It was Timnath Serah in the hill country of Ephraim. He built up the town and made his home there.

⁵¹ All those territories were given out by casting lots at Shiloh. The lots were drawn out by Eleazar the priest and by Joshua, the son of Nun. The leaders of the tribes of Israel helped them. The lots were drawn out in front of the Lord at the entrance to the tent of meeting. So the work of dividing up the land was finished.

Cities to Run to for Safety

20 Then the Lord spoke to Joshua. He said, ² "Tell the Israelites to choose the cities to go to for safety, just as I directed you through Moses. ³ Anyone who kills a person by accident can run there for safety. So can anyone who kills a person without meaning to. The one charged with murder will be kept safe from the nearest male relative of the person killed. ⁴ Suppose those who are charged with murder run for safety to one of these cities. Then they must stand in the entrance of the city gate. They must state their case in front of the elders of that city. The elders must let them come into their city. The elders must provide a place for them to live in their city. ⁵ Suppose the nearest male relative of the person killed chases the one charged with murder. Then the elders must not hand them over to that relative. That's because that person didn't mean to kill their neighbor. They didn't make evil plans to do it. ⁶ They must stay in that city until their case has been brought to the community court. They must stay there until the high priest serving at that time dies. Then they can go back to their own home. They can return to the town they ran away from."

⁷ So the Israelites set apart Kedesh in Galilee. It's in the hill country of Naphtali. They set apart Shechem. It's in the hill country of Ephraim. They set apart Kiriath Arba. It's in the hill country of Judah. Kiriath Arba is also called Hebron. ⁸ On the east side of the Jordan River near Jericho they chose Bezer. It's in the desert on the high plains. It's in the territory of the tribe of Reuben. They chose Ramoth in Gilead. It's in the territory of the tribe of Gad. They chose Golan in the land of Bashan. It's in the territory of the tribe of Manasseh. ⁹ Suppose you kill someone by accident. Or another Israelite does it. Or an outsider who lives

among you does it. Then any of you can run for safety to one of these cities that have been chosen. There you won't be killed by the nearest male relative of the person killed by accident. First your case must be brought to the community court.

Towns Are Given to the Levites

21 The leaders of the Levite family groups approached Eleazar the priest and Joshua, the son of Nun. They also approached the leaders of the family groups of Israel's other tribes. ²They went to all of them at Shiloh in Canaan. They said to them, "Give us towns to live in. Also give us grasslands for our livestock. That's what the LORD commanded through Moses."

³So the Israelites gave the Levites towns and grasslands out of their own shares of land. They did what the LORD had commanded. Here are the towns the Levites were given.

⁴The first lot drawn out was for the people of Kohath, according to their family groups. Some of the Levites came from the family line of Aaron the priest. They were given 13 towns from the tribes of Judah, Simeon and Benjamin.

⁵The rest of Kohath's family groups were given ten towns. Those towns were from the family groups of the tribes of Ephraim and Dan and half of the tribe of Manasseh.

⁶The family groups of Gershon were given 13 towns. Those towns were from the family groups of the tribes of Issachar, Asher and Naphtali and half of the tribe of Manasseh. That part of Manasseh was in the land of Bashan.

⁷The family groups of Merari received 12 towns from the tribes of Reuben, Gad and Zebulun. Each family group received its share.

⁸So the Israelites gave those towns and their grasslands to the Levites. They did what the LORD had commanded through Moses.

⁹Some towns were given from the territories of the tribes of Judah and Simeon. ¹⁰The Israelites gave them to the members of the family line of Aaron. The towns were given to the family groups of Kohath. They were Levites. The first lot drawn out was for them. Here are the towns the family groups of Kohath were given.

¹¹The Israelites gave them Kiriath Arba and the grasslands around it. Kiriath Arba is also called Hebron. It's in the hill country of Judah. Anak came from the family line of Arba. ¹²But Israel

had already given away the fields and villages around the city. They had given them to Caleb as his share. Caleb was the son of Jephunneh. ¹³So they gave Hebron to the members of the family line of Aaron the priest. Hebron was a city where anyone charged with murder could go for safety. They also gave them Libnah, ¹⁴Jattir, Eshtemoa, ¹⁵Holon, Debir, ¹⁶Ain, Juttah and Beth Shemesh. They gave those towns and their grasslands to the family groups of Kohath. The total number of towns from the tribes of Judah and Simeon came to nine.

¹⁷The Israelites gave some towns from the tribe of Benjamin to the family groups of Kohath.

The towns were Gibeon, Geba, ¹⁸Anathoth and Almon. The total number of these towns and their grasslands came to four.

¹⁹So the total number of towns and their grasslands given to the priests in Aaron's family line came to 13.

²⁰There were other family groups of Kohath among the Levites. They were given towns from the tribe of Ephraim. Here are the towns those other family groups of Kohath were given.

²¹In the hill country of Ephraim they were given Shechem. It was a city where anyone charged with murder could go for safety. They were also given Gezer, ²²Kibzaim and Beth Horon. The total number of these towns and their grasslands came to four.

²³From the tribe of Dan they received

Eltekeh, Gibbethon, ²⁴Aijalon and Gath Rimmon. The total number of these towns and their grasslands came to four.

²⁵From half of the tribe of Manasseh they received Taanach and Gath Rimmon. The total number of these towns and their grasslands came to two.

²⁶So all these ten towns and their grasslands were given to the other family groups of Kohath.

²⁷Here are the towns given to the family groups of Gershon among the Levites.

From half of the tribe of Manasseh they received Golan in the land of Bashan. Golan was a city where anyone charged with murder could go for safety. They also received Be Eshterah. The total number of these towns and their grasslands came to two.

²⁸From the tribe of Issachar they received

Kishion, Daberath, ²⁹Jarmuth and En Gannim. The total number of these towns and their grass-lands came to four.

30 From the tribe of Asher they received

Mishal, Abdon, 31 Helkath and Rehob. The total number of these towns and their grasslands came to four.

32 From the tribe of Naphtali they received

Kedesh in Galilee. Kedesh was a city where anyone charged with murder could go for safety. They also received Hammoth Dor and Kartan. The total number of these towns and their grasslands came to three.

33 So the total number of towns and their grasslands given to the family groups of Gershon came to 13.

34 The rest of the Levites were from the family groups of Merari. Here are the towns they were given.

From the tribe of Zebulun they received

Jokneam, Kartah, 35 Dimnah and Nahalal. The total number of these towns and their grasslands came to four.

36 From the tribe of Reuben they received

Bezer, Jahaz, 37 Kedemoth and Mephaath. The total number of these towns and their grasslands came to four.

38 From the tribe of Gad they received

Ramoth in Gilead. Ramoth was a city where anyone charged with murder could go for safety. They also received Mahanaim, 39 Heshbon and Jazer. The total number of these towns and their grasslands came to four.

40 So the total number of towns given to the family groups of Merari came to 12. That concludes the list of towns the rest of the Levites received.

41 The total number of Levite towns and their grasslands in the territory given to Israel came to 48. 42 Each of those towns had grasslands around it. That was true of all of them.

43 So the LORD gave Israel all the land he had promised to give to Abraham, Isaac and Jacob. And Israel took it over. Then they made their homes there. 44 The LORD gave them peace and rest on every side. He had promised their people of long ago that he would do that. Not one of Israel's enemies was able to fight against them and win. The LORD handed all their enemies over to them. 45 The LORD kept all the good promises he had made to the Israelites. Every one of them came true.

The Eastern Tribes Return Home

22 Joshua sent for the tribes of Reuben and Gad and half of the tribe of Manasseh. 2 He said to them, "You have

done everything that Moses, the servant of the LORD, commanded. You have also obeyed everything I commanded. ³For a long time now you haven't deserted the other Israelites. Instead, you have done what the LORD your God sent you to do. You have obeyed him right up to this day. ⁴Now the LORD your God has given the other tribes peace and rest. That's what he promised to do. So return to your homes. They are in the land that Moses, the servant of the LORD, gave you. It's on the east side of the Jordan River. ⁵Be very careful to obey the law that Moses, the servant of the LORD, gave you. He commanded you to love the LORD your God. He told you to live exactly as the LORD wants you to. He told you to obey the LORD's commands. He told you to remain faithful to the LORD. And he told you to serve the LORD with all your heart and with all your soul."

⁶Joshua gave the eastern tribes his blessing. Then he sent them home. So they went. ⁷Moses had given land in Bashan to half of the tribe of Manasseh. Joshua had given land to the other half of the tribe. He had given it to them along with the other tribes on the west side of the Jordan River. When Joshua sent them home, he blessed them. ⁸He said, "Return to your homes. Take your great wealth with you. Return with your large herds of livestock. Take your silver, gold, bronze and iron with you. Return with all the extra clothes you acquired. Divide up the things you have taken from your enemies. Share them with your people."

⁹So the tribes of Reuben and Gad and half of the tribe of Manasseh went home. They left the other Israelites at Shiloh in Canaan. They returned to Gilead. That was their own land. They had acquired it according to the LORD's command through Moses.

¹⁰The tribes of Reuben and Gad and half of the tribe of Manasseh came to Geliloth. It was near the Jordan River in the land of Canaan. They built a large altar there by the Jordan. ¹¹The rest of the Israelites heard that the eastern tribes had built the altar. They heard that it had been built on the border of Canaan at Geliloth. It was near the Jordan River on the west side. ¹²So the whole community of Israel gathered together at Shiloh. They decided to go to war against the eastern tribes.

¹³The Israelites sent Phinehas the priest to the land of Gilead. Phinehas was the son of Eleazar. They sent him to the tribes of Reuben and Gad and half of the tribe of Manasseh. ¹⁴They sent ten of their leaders with him. There was one from each of the tribes of Israel. Each man was the leader of a family group among the larger family groups of Israel.

¹⁵Those leaders went to the tribes of Reuben and Gad and half of the tribe of Manasseh. Those tribes were in the land

of Gilead. The leaders said to them, [16] "We're speaking for the LORD's whole community. How could you disobey the God of Israel like this? How could you turn away from the LORD? How could you disobey him by building an altar for yourselves? [17] Don't you remember how we sinned at Peor? The LORD struck us with a plague because of what we did. Up to this day we're still suffering because of that sin. [18] Are you turning away from the LORD now?

"Suppose you disobey the LORD today. If you do, he'll be angry with the whole community of Israel tomorrow. [19] If your own land is 'unclean,' come over to the LORD's land. It's where his holy tent stands. Share our land with us. But don't disobey the LORD. Don't turn against us by building an altar for yourselves. Don't build any altar other than the altar of the LORD our God. [20] Remember what happened to Achan, the son of Zerah. Achan wasn't faithful to the LORD. He took the things that had been set apart to the LORD in a special way to be destroyed. Didn't the whole community of Israel experience the LORD's anger? Achan wasn't the only one who died because of his sin."

[21] Then the tribes of Reuben and Gad and half of the tribe of Manasseh replied. They answered the leaders of the family groups of Israel. [22] They said, "The Mighty One, God, the LORD! The Mighty One, God, the LORD! He knows! And we want Israel to know! Have we opposed the LORD? Have we refused to obey him? If we have, don't spare us today. [23] Have we built our own altar so we can turn away from the LORD? Have we built it to offer burnt offerings and grain offerings on it? Have we built it to sacrifice friendship offerings on it? If we have, may the LORD himself hold us accountable.

[24] "No! We built it because we were afraid. Someday your children might speak to our children. We were afraid they might say, 'What do you have to do with the LORD? What do you have to do with the God of Israel? [25] The LORD has made the Jordan River a border between us and you. You people of Reuben! You people of Gad! You don't have anything to do with the LORD.' If your children say that, they might cause our children to stop worshiping the LORD.

[26] "That's why we said to ourselves, 'Let's get ready and build an altar. But let's not build it to offer burnt offerings or sacrifices on it.' [27] So just the opposite is true. The altar will be a witness between us and you. It will be a witness between our children and yours after us. It will also be a witness that we will worship the LORD at his sacred tent. We'll worship him there with our burnt offerings, sacrifices and friendship offerings. Then in days to come your children won't be able to say to ours, 'You don't have anything to do with the LORD.'

[28] "So we said to ourselves,

'Suppose they say that to us sometime. Or suppose they say it to our children after us. Then we'll answer, "Look at this altar. It's exactly like the LORD's altar. Our people built it. They didn't build it to offer burnt offerings and sacrifices on it. Instead, they built it to be a witness between us and you." '

29 "We would never refuse to obey the LORD. We would never turn away from him now. We wouldn't build an altar to offer burnt offerings, grain offerings and sacrifices on it. We wouldn't use any altar other than the altar of the LORD our God. That altar stands in front of his holy tent."

30 Phinehas the priest heard what the tribes of Reuben, Gad and Manasseh had to say. The leaders of the family groups of the community of Israel heard it too. All of them were pleased with what they heard. 31 Phinehas the priest spoke to the tribes of Reuben, Gad and Manasseh. Phinehas was the son of Eleazar. He said, "Today we know that the LORD is with us. That's because you have been faithful to him in this matter. Now you have saved the Israelites from the LORD's anger against them."

32 Then Phinehas the priest, the son of Eleazar, returned to Canaan. So did the leaders. All of them went back from their meeting with the tribes of Reuben and Gad in Gilead. They brought a report back to the Israelites. 33 The people were glad to hear the report. They praised God. They didn't talk anymore about going to war against the eastern tribes. And they didn't talk anymore about destroying the country where the tribes of Reuben and Gad lived.

34 The tribes of Reuben and Gad gave the altar a name. They called it A Witness Between Us that the LORD is God.

Joshua Says Goodbye to the Leaders

23 A long time had passed. The LORD had given Israel peace and rest from all their enemies around them. By that time Joshua was very old. 2 So he sent for all the elders, leaders, judges and officials of Israel. He said to them, "I'm very old. 3 You yourselves have seen everything the LORD your God has done. You have seen what he's done to all these nations because of you. The LORD your God fought for you. 4 Remember how I've given you all the land of the nations that remain here. I've given each of your tribes a share of it. It's the land of the nations I conquered. It's between the Jordan River and the Mediterranean Sea in the west. 5 The LORD your God himself will drive those nations out of your way. He will push them out to make room for you. You will take over their land, just as the LORD your God promised you.

6 "Be very strong. Be careful to obey everything written in the Book of the Law of Moses. Don't turn away from it to the right or the left. 7 Don't have anything to do with the nations that remain

among you. Don't use the names of their gods for any reason at all. Don't give your word and make promises in their names. You must not serve them. You must not bow down to them. ⁸ You must remain true to the LORD your God, just as you have done until now.

⁹ "The LORD has driven out great and powerful nations to make room for you. To this day no one has been able to fight against you and win. ¹⁰ One of you can chase a thousand away. That's because the LORD your God fights for you, just as he promised he would. ¹¹ So be very careful to love the LORD your God.

¹² "But suppose you turn away from him. You mix with the people who are left alive in the nations that remain among you. Later, you and they get married to each other. And you do other kinds of things with them. ¹³ Then you can be sure of what the LORD your God will do. He won't drive out those nations to make room for you anymore. Instead, they will become traps and snares for you. They will be like whips on your backs. They will be like thorns in your eyes. All that will continue until you are destroyed. It will continue until you are removed from this good land. It's the land the LORD your God has given you.

¹⁴ "Now I'm about to die, just as everyone else on earth does. The LORD your God has kept all the good promises he gave you. Every one of them has come

true. Not one has failed to come true. And you know that with all your heart and soul. ¹⁵ Every good thing has come to pass that the LORD your God has promised you. So you know that he can also bring against you all the evil things he has warned you about. He'll do it until he has destroyed you. He'll do it until he has removed you from this good land. It's the land he has given you. ¹⁶ Suppose you break the covenant the LORD your God made with you. He commanded you to obey it. But suppose you go and serve other gods. And you bow down to them. Then the LORD will be very angry with you. You will quickly be destroyed. You will be removed from the good land he has given you."

The Covenant Is Renewed at Shechem

24 Joshua gathered all Israel's tribes together at Shechem. He sent for the elders, leaders, judges and officials of Israel. They came and stood there in the sight of God.

² Joshua spoke to all the people. He said, "The LORD is the God of Israel. He says, 'Long ago your people lived east of the Euphrates River. They worshiped other gods there. Your people included Terah. He was the father of Abraham and Nahor. ³ I took your father Abraham from the land east of the Euphrates. I led him all through Canaan. I gave him many children and grandchildren. I gave him Isaac.

4 To Isaac I gave Jacob and Esau. I gave the hill country of Seir to Esau. But Jacob and his family went down to Egypt.

5 "'Then I sent Moses and Aaron. I made the people of Egypt suffer because of the plagues I sent on them. But I brought you out of Egypt. 6 When I brought your people out, they came to the Red Sea. The people of Egypt chased them with chariots and with men on horses. They chased them all the way to the sea. 7 But your people cried out to me for help. So I put darkness between you and the people of Egypt. I swept them into the sea. It completely covered them. Your own eyes saw what I did to them. After that, you lived in the desert for a long time.

8 "'I brought you to the land of the Amorites. They lived east of the Jordan River. They fought against you. But I handed them over to you. I destroyed them to make room for you. Then you took over their land. 9 Balak, the son of Zippor, prepared to fight against Israel. Balak was the king of Moab. He sent for Balaam, the son of Beor. Balak wanted Balaam to put a curse on you. 10 But I would not listen to Balaam's curses. So he blessed you again and again. And I saved you from his power.

11 "'Then you went across the Jordan River. You came to Jericho. Its people fought against you. So did the Amorites, Perizzites, Canaanites, Hittites, Girgashites, Hivites and Jebusites. But I handed them over to you. 12 I sent hornets ahead of you. They drove your enemies out to make room for you. That included the two Amorite kings. You did not do that with your own swords and bows. 13 So I gave you a land you had never farmed. I gave you cities you had not built. You are now living in them. And you are eating the fruit of vineyards and olive trees you did not plant.'

14 "So have respect for the LORD. Serve him. Be completely faithful to him. Throw away the gods your people worshiped east of the Euphrates River and in Egypt. Serve the LORD. 15 But suppose you don't want to serve him. Then choose for yourselves right now whom you will serve. You can choose the gods your people served east of the Euphrates River. Or you can serve the gods of the Amorites. After all, you are living in their land. But as for me and my family, we will serve the LORD."

16 Then the people answered Joshua, "We would never desert the LORD! We would never serve other gods! 17 The LORD our God himself brought us and our parents up out of Egypt. He brought us out of that land where we were slaves. With our own eyes, we saw those great signs he did. He kept us safe on our entire journey. He kept us safe as we traveled through all the nations. 18 He drove them out to make room for us. That included the Amorites. They also lived in the land. We too will serve the

LORD. That's because he is our God."

¹⁹ Joshua said to the people, "You aren't able to serve the LORD. He is a holy God. He is a jealous God. He won't forgive you when you disobey him. He won't forgive you when you sin against him. ²⁰ Suppose you desert the LORD. Suppose you serve the gods that people in other lands serve. If you do, he will turn against you. He will bring trouble on you. He will destroy you, even though he has been good to you."

²¹ But the people said to Joshua, "No! We will serve the LORD."

²² Then Joshua said, "You are witnesses against yourselves. You have said that you have chosen to serve the LORD."

"Yes. We are witnesses," they replied.

²³ "Now then," said Joshua, "throw away the statues of the gods that are among you. People from other lands serve those gods. Give yourselves completely to the LORD. He is the God of Israel."

²⁴ Then the people said to Joshua, "We will serve the LORD our God. We will obey him."

²⁵ On that day Joshua made a covenant for the people. There at Shechem he reminded them of its rules and laws. ²⁶ He recorded these things in the Book of the Law of God. Then he got a large stone. He set it up in Shechem under the oak tree. It was near the place that had been set apart for the LORD.

²⁷ "Look!" he said to all the people. "This stone will be a witness against us. It has heard all the words the LORD has spoken to us. Suppose you aren't faithful to your God. Then the stone will be a witness against you."

²⁸ Joshua sent the people away. He sent all of them to their own shares of land.

Joshua Is Buried in the Promised Land

²⁹ Then Joshua, the servant of the LORD, died. He was the son of Nun. He was 110 years old when he died. ³⁰ His people buried him at Timnath Serah on his own property. It's north of Mount Gaash in the hill country of Ephraim.

³¹ Israel served the LORD as long as Joshua lived. They also served him as long as the elders lived. Those were the elders who lived longer than Joshua did. They had seen for themselves everything the LORD had done for Israel.

³² The Israelites had brought Joseph's bones up from Egypt. They buried his bones at Shechem in the piece of land Jacob had bought. He had bought it from the sons of Hamor. He had paid 100 pieces of silver for it. Hamor was the father of Shechem. That piece of land became the share that belonged to Joseph's children after him.

³³ Aaron's son Eleazar died. He was buried at Gibeah in the hill country of Ephraim. Gibeah had been given to Eleazar's son Phinehas.

Judges

Introduction:

This book tells the story of Israel after Joshua died. The heroes of this book are called judges. God gave the people judges to help them when things were bad. When the people loved God, things were good. When the people forgot God, things were bad. The stories in this book all follow the same pattern:

1. The people of Israel loved God and lived in peace.
2. The people of Israel forgot God and worshiped false gods.
3. God punished the people. He sent another nation to fight and rule over them.
4. The people of Israel turned to God and asked him to forgive them.
5. God forgave the people and sent a judge to help them.

Twelve judges are mentioned in this book. Deborah, Gideon and Samson are the best-known judges.

Outline of contents:

The Israelites Fight Against the Remaining Canaanites

1 Joshua died. After that, the Israelites spoke to the LORD. They asked him, "Who of us will go up first and fight against the Canaanites?"

2 The LORD answered, "The tribe of Judah will go up. I have handed the land over to them."

3 Then the men of Judah spoke to their fellow Israelites, the men of Simeon. They said, "Come up with us. Come into the territory Joshua gave us. Help us fight against the Canaanites. Then we'll go with you into your territory." So the men of Simeon went with them.

4 When the men of Judah attacked, the LORD helped them. He handed the Canaanites and Perizzites over to them. They struck down 10,000 men at Bezek. 5 The men of Judah found Adoni-Bezek there. They fought against him. They struck down the Canaanites and Perizzites. 6 But Adoni-Bezek ran away. The men of Judah chased him and caught him. Then they cut off his thumbs and big toes.

7 Adoni-Bezek said, "I cut off the thumbs and big toes of 70 kings. I made them pick up scraps under my table. Now God has paid me back for what I did to them." The men of Judah brought Adoni-Bezek to Jerusalem. That's where he died.

⁸The men of Judah attacked Jerusalem and captured it. They set the city on fire. They killed its people with their swords.

⁹After that, the men of Judah went down to fight against some Canaanites. Those Canaanites were living in the central hill country. They also fought against those living in the Negev Desert and the western hills. ¹⁰Then the men of Judah marched out against the Canaanites living in Hebron. Hebron used to be called Kiriath Arba. The men of Judah won the battle over Sheshai, Ahiman and Talmai. ¹¹From Hebron they marched out against the people living in Debir. It used to be called Kiriath Sepher.

¹²Caleb said, "I will give my daughter Aksah to be married. I'll give her to the man who attacks and captures Kiriath Sepher." ¹³Othniel captured it. So Caleb gave his daughter Aksah to him to be his wife. Othniel was the son of Kenaz. He was Caleb's younger brother.

¹⁴One day Aksah came to Othniel. She begged him to ask her father for a field. When she got off her donkey, Caleb asked her, "What can I do for you?"

¹⁵She replied, "Do me a special favor. You have given me some land in the Negev Desert. Give me springs of water also." So Caleb gave her the upper and lower springs.

¹⁶Moses' father-in-law was a Kenite. His family went up from Jericho. Jericho was also known as the City of Palm Trees. His family went up with the people of Judah to the Desert of Judah. They went there to live among its people. Those people were living in the Negev Desert near Arad.

¹⁷The men of Judah marched out with their fellow Israelites, the men of Simeon. They attacked the people of Canaan living in Zephath. They set the city apart to the LORD in a special way to be destroyed. That's why the city was called Hormah. ¹⁸The men of Judah captured Gaza, Ashkelon and Ekron. They also captured the territory around each of those cities.

¹⁹The LORD was with the men of Judah. They took over the central hill country. But they weren't able to drive the people out of the plains. That's because those people used chariots that had some iron parts. ²⁰Moses had promised to give Hebron to Caleb. So Hebron was given to Caleb. He drove the three sons of Anak out of it. ²¹But the people of Benjamin did not drive out the Jebusites living in Jerusalem. So to this day they live there with the people of Benjamin.

²²The tribes of Joseph attacked Bethel. The LORD was with them. ²³They sent men to Bethel to check it out. It used to be called Luz. ²⁴Those who were sent saw a man coming out of the city. They said to him, "Show us how to get into the city. If you do, we'll see that you are treated well." ²⁵So he showed them how to get in. The men of

Joseph killed the people in the city with their swords. But they spared the man from Bethel. They also spared his whole family. [26] Then he went to the land of the Hittites. He built a city there. He called it Luz. That's still its name to this day.

[27] But the tribe of Manasseh didn't drive out the people of Beth Shan. They didn't drive out the people of Taanach, Dor, Ibleam and Megiddo. And they didn't drive out the people of the settlements that are around those cities either. That's because the Canaanites had made up their minds to continue living in that land. [28] Later, Israel became stronger. Then they forced the Canaanites to work hard for them. But Israel never drove them out completely. [29] The tribe of Ephraim didn't drive out the Canaanites living in Gezer. So the Canaanites continued to live there among them. [30] The tribe of Zebulun didn't drive out the Canaanites living in Kitron and Nahalol. So these Canaanites lived among them. But the people of Zebulun forced the Canaanites to work hard for them. [31] The tribe of Asher didn't drive out the people living in Akko and Sidon. They didn't drive out the people of Ahlab, Akzib, Helbah, Aphek and Rehob. [32] So the people of Asher lived among the Canaanites who were in the land. [33] The tribe of Naphtali didn't drive out the people living in Beth Shemesh and Beth Anath. So the people of Naphtali lived among the Canaanites

who were in the land. The people of Beth Shemesh and Beth Anath were forced to work hard for them. [34] The Amorites made the people of Dan stay in the central hill country. They didn't let them come down into the plain. [35] The Amorites made up their minds to stay in Mount Heres. They also stayed in Aijalon and Shaalbim. But the power of the tribes of Joseph grew. Then the Amorites were forced to work hard for them. [36] The border of the Amorites started at Scorpion Pass. It went to Sela and even past it.

The Angel of the LORD Warns Israel at Bokim

2 The angel of the LORD went up from Gilgal to Bokim. There he said to the Israelites, "I brought you up out of Egypt. I led you into this land. It is the land I promised to give to Abraham, Isaac and Jacob. At that time I said, 'I will never break the covenant I made with you. [2] So you must not make a covenant with the people of this land. Instead, you must tear down their altars.' But you have disobeyed me. Why did you do it? [3] I have said something else. I said, 'I will not drive out those people to make room for you. They and their gods will become traps for you.'"

[4] The angel of the LORD spoke these things to all the Israelites. Then the people wept out loud. [5] So that place was called Bokim. The people offered sacrifices there to the LORD.

The People Disobey the Lord and Lose Their Battles

⁶ Joshua sent the Israelites away. Then they went to take over the land. All of them went to their own shares of land. ⁷ The people served the Lord as long as Joshua lived. They also served him as long as the elders lived. Those were the elders who lived longer than Joshua did. They had seen all the great things the Lord had done for Israel.

⁸ Joshua, the servant of the Lord, died. He was the son of Nun. He was 110 years old when he died. ⁹ His people buried him on his own property at Timnath Heres. It's north of Mount Gaash in the hill country of Ephraim.

¹⁰ All the people of Joshua's time joined the members of their families who had already died. Then those who were born after them grew up. They didn't know the Lord and what he had done for Israel. ¹¹ The Israelites did what was evil in the sight of the Lord. They served gods that were named Baal. ¹² They deserted the Lord, the God of their people. He had brought them out of Egypt. But now the Israelites served other gods and worshiped them. They served the gods of the nations that were around them. They made the Lord angry ¹³ because they deserted him. They served Baal. They also served female gods that were named Ashtoreth. ¹⁴ The Lord became angry with the Israelites. So he handed them over to robbers.

The robbers stole everything from them. The Lord handed the Israelites over to their enemies all around them. Israel wasn't able to fight against them anymore and win. ¹⁵ When the Israelites went out to fight, the Lord's power was against them. He let their enemies win the battle over them. The Lord had warned them that it would happen. And now they were suffering terribly.

¹⁶ Then the Lord gave them leaders. The leaders saved them from the power of those robbers. ¹⁷ But the people wouldn't listen to their leaders. They weren't faithful to the Lord. They served other gods and worshiped them. They didn't obey the Lord's commands as their people before them had done. They quickly turned away from the path their people had taken. ¹⁸ When the Lord gave them a leader, he was with that leader. The Lord saved the people from the power of their enemies. He did it as long as the leader lived. The Lord felt very sorry for the people. They groaned because of what their enemies did to them. Their enemies treated them badly. ¹⁹ But when the leader died, the people returned to their evil ways. The things they did were even more sinful than the things their people before them had done. They served other gods and worshiped them. They refused to give up their evil practices. They wouldn't change their stubborn ways.

²⁰ So the Lord became very angry with the Israelites. He said, "This nation has broken my covenant. I made it with their people of long ago. But this nation has not listened to me. ²¹ Joshua left some nations in the land when he died. I will no longer drive out those nations to make room for Israel. ²² I will use those nations to test Israel. I will see whether Israel will live the way I, the Lord, want them to. I will see whether they will be like their people of long ago. I will see whether they will follow my path." ²³ The Lord had let those nations remain in the land. He didn't drive them out right away. He didn't hand them over to Joshua.

3 The Lord left some nations in the land. He left them to test the Israelites who hadn't lived through any of the wars in Canaan. ² He wanted to teach the men in Israel who had never been in battle before. He wanted them to learn how to fight. ³ So he left the five rulers of the Philistines. He left the people of Canaan and the people of Sidon. He left the Hivites living in the Lebanon mountains. They lived in the area between Mount Baal Hermon and Lebo Hamath. ⁴ The Lord left those nations where they were to test the Israelites. He wanted to see whether they would obey his commands. He had given those commands through Moses to their people of long ago.

⁵ So the Israelites lived among the Canaanites, Hittites, Amorites, Perizzites, Hivites and Jebusites. ⁶ They married the daughters of those people. They gave their own daughters to the sons of those people. And they served the gods of those people.

Othniel

⁷ The Israelites did what was evil in the sight of the Lord. They forgot the Lord their God. They served gods that were named Baal. They also served female gods that were named Asherah. ⁸ So the Lord was very angry with Israel. He handed them over to the power of Cushan-Rishathaim, the king of Aram Naharaim. For eight years Israel was under his rule. ⁹ They cried out to the Lord. Then he provided someone to save them. The man's name was Othniel, the son of Kenaz. He was Caleb's younger brother. ¹⁰ The Spirit of the Lord came on Othniel. So he became Israel's leader. He went to war. The Lord handed over to him Cushan-Rishathaim, the king of Aram. Othniel won the battle over him. ¹¹ So the land was at peace for 40 years. Then Othniel, the son of Kenaz, died.

Ehud

¹² Again the Israelites did what was evil in the sight of the Lord. So the Lord gave Eglon power over Israel. Eglon was the king of Moab. ¹³ He got the Ammonites and Amalekites to join him. All of them came and attacked Israel. They captured Jericho. Jericho was also known as The City

of Palm Trees. ¹⁴For 18 years the Israelites were under the rule of Eglon, the king of Moab.

¹⁵Again the Israelites cried out to the LORD. Then he provided someone to save them. The man's name was Ehud, the son of Gera. Ehud was left-handed. He was from the tribe of Benjamin. The Israelites sent Ehud to Eglon, the king of Moab. They sent him to give the king what he required them to bring him. ¹⁶Ehud had made a sword that had two edges. It was about a foot and a half long. He tied it to his right leg under his clothes. ¹⁷Eglon, the king of Moab, was a very fat man. Ehud gave him the gift he had brought. ¹⁸After that, Ehud sent away those who had carried it. ¹⁹When he came to the place where some statues of gods stood near Gilgal, Ehud went back to Eglon. He said, "Your Majesty, I have a secret message for you."

The king said to his attendants, "Leave us!" And all his attendants left him.

²⁰Then Ehud approached him. King Eglon was sitting alone in the upstairs room of his palace. Ehud said, "I have a message from God for you." So the king got up from his seat. ²¹Then Ehud reached out his left hand. He pulled out the sword tied to his right leg. He stuck it into the king's stomach. ²²Even the handle sank in after the blade. Eglon sagged and fell to the floor. Ehud didn't pull out the sword. And the fat closed over it. ²³Ehud went out to the porch. He shut the doors of the upstairs room behind him. Then he locked them.

²⁴After he had gone, the servants came. They found the doors of the upstairs room locked. They said, "Eglon must be going to the toilet in the inside room of the palace." ²⁵They waited for a long time. They waited so long they became worried. But the king still didn't open the doors of the room. So they took a key and unlocked them. There they saw their king. He had fallen to the floor and was dead.

²⁶While Eglon's servants had been waiting, Ehud had gotten away. He passed by the statues of gods and escaped to Seirah. ²⁷There in the hill country of Ephraim he blew a trumpet. Then he led the Israelites down from the hills.

²⁸"Follow me," Ehud ordered. "The LORD has handed your enemy Moab over to you." So they followed him down. They took over the only places where people could go across the Jordan River to get to Moab. They didn't let anyone go across. ²⁹At that time they struck down about 10,000 men of Moab. All those men were strong and powerful. But not even one escaped. ³⁰That day Moab was brought under the rule of Israel. So the land was at peace for 80 years.

Shamgar

³¹After Ehud, Shamgar became the next leader. He was the son of Anath. Shamgar struck

down 600 Philistines with a large, pointed stick used to drive oxen. He too saved Israel.

Deborah

4 After Ehud died, the Israelites once again did what was evil in the sight of the LORD. ² So the LORD handed them over to the power of Jabin. He was a king in Canaan. He ruled in Hazor. The commander of his army was Sisera. He lived in Harosheth Haggoyim. ³ Jabin used 900 chariots that had some iron parts. He treated the Israelites very badly for 20 years. So they cried out to the LORD for help.

⁴ Deborah was a prophet. She was the wife of Lappidoth. She was leading Israel at that time. ⁵ Under the Palm Tree of Deborah she served the people as their judge. That place was between Ramah and Bethel in the hill country of Ephraim. The Israelites went up to her there. They came to have her decide cases for them. She settled matters between them. ⁶ Deborah sent for Barak. He was the son of Abinoam. Barak was from Kedesh in the land of Naphtali. Deborah said to Barak, "The LORD, the God of Israel, is giving you a command. He says, 'Go! Take 10,000 men from the tribes of Naphtali and Zebulun with you. Then lead them up to Mount Tabor. ⁷ I will lead Sisera into a trap. He is the commander of Jabin's army. I will bring him, his chariots and his troops to the Kishon River. There I will hand him over to you.'"

⁸ Barak said to her, "If you go with me, I'll go. But if you don't go with me, I won't go."

⁹ "All right," Deborah said. "I'll go with you. But because of the way you are doing this, you won't receive any honor. Instead, the LORD will hand Sisera over to a woman." So Deborah went to Kedesh with Barak. ¹⁰ There he sent for men from Zebulun and Naphtali. And 10,000 men followed him into battle. Deborah also went with him.

¹¹ Heber, the Kenite, had left the other Kenites. They came from the family line of Hobab. He was the brother-in-law of Moses. Heber set up his tent by the large tree in Zaanannim near Kedesh.

¹² Sisera was told that Barak, the son of Abinoam, had gone up to Mount Tabor. ¹³ So Sisera gathered together his 900 chariots that had some iron parts. He also gathered together all his men. He brought them from Harosheth Haggoyim to the Kishon River.

¹⁴ Then Deborah said to Barak, "Go! Today the LORD will hand Sisera over to you. Hasn't the LORD gone ahead of you?" So Barak went down Mount Tabor. His 10,000 men followed him. ¹⁵ As Barak's men marched out, the LORD drove Sisera away from the field of battle. The LORD scattered all of Sisera's chariots. Barak's men struck down Sisera's army with their swords. Sisera got down from his chariot. He ran away on foot.

16 Barak chased Sisera's chariots and army. Barak chased them all the way to Harosheth Haggoyim. All of Sisera's troops were killed by swords. Not even one was left. 17 But Sisera ran away on foot. He ran to the tent of Jael. She was the wife of Heber, the Kenite. Sisera ran there because there was a treaty between Heber's family and Jabin, the king of Hazor.

18 Jael went out to meet Sisera. "Come in, sir," she said. "Come right in. Don't be afraid." So he entered her tent. Then she covered him with a blanket.

19 "I'm thirsty," he said. "Please give me some water." So Jael opened a bottle of milk. The bottle was made out of animal skin. She gave him a drink of milk. Then she covered him up again.

20 "Stand in the doorway of the tent," he told her. "Someone might come by and ask you, 'Is anyone in there?' If that happens, say 'No.'"

21 But Heber's wife Jael picked up a tent stake and a hammer. She went quietly over to Sisera. He was lying there, fast asleep. He was very tired. She drove the stake through his head right into the ground. So he died.

22 Just then Barak came by because he was chasing Sisera. Jael went out to meet him. "Come right in," she said. "I'll show you the man you are looking for." So he went in with her. Sisera was lying there with the stake through his head. He was dead.

23 On that day God brought Jabin under Israel's control. He was a king in Canaan. 24 Israel's power grew stronger and stronger against King Jabin. The Israelites became so strong that they destroyed him.

The Song of Deborah

5 On that day Deborah and Barak sang a song. Barak was the son of Abinoam. Here is what Deborah and Barak sang.

2 "The princes in Israel lead
    the way.
The people follow them just
    because they want to.
When this happens, praise
    the LORD!

3 "Kings, hear this! Rulers,
    listen!
I will sing to the LORD.
I will praise the LORD in
    song. He is the God of
    Israel.

4 "LORD, you went out from Seir.
    You marched out from the
    land of Edom.
The earth shook. The
    heavens poured.
The clouds poured down
    their water.
5 The mountains shook
    because of the LORD. He
    was at Mount Sinai.
They shook because of the
    LORD. He is the God of
    Israel.

6 "The main roads were
    deserted. So travelers
    used the winding paths.
That happened in the days
    of Shamgar, the son of
    Anath.

It happened in the days of
Jael.

⁷ Those who lived in the
villages of Israel would
not fight.
They held back until I,
Deborah, came.
I came as a mother in
Israel.

⁸   War came to the city gates.
Then God chose new
leaders.
But no shields or spears were
seen anywhere.
There weren't any among
40,000 men in Israel.

⁹ My heart is with the princes
in Israel.
It's with the people who
follow them just because
they want to.
Praise the LORD!

¹⁰ "Some of you ride on white
donkeys.
Some of you sit on your
saddle blankets.
Some of you walk along the
road.
Think about ¹¹ the voices
of the singers at the
watering places.
They sing about the
victories of the LORD.
They sing about the
victories of his people
who live in Israel's
villages.

"The people of the LORD
went down to the city
gates.

¹² 'Wake up, Deborah! Wake
up!' they said.
'Wake up! Wake up! Begin
to sing!

Barak, get up!
Son of Abinoam, capture
your prisoners!'

¹³ "The nobles who were left
came down.
The people of the LORD
came down to me against
the powerful enemy.

¹⁴ Some came from the part of
Ephraim where some
Amalekites lived.
Some from Benjamin were
with the people who
followed Ephraim.
Captains came down from
Makir.
Those who rule like
commanders came
down from Zebulun.

¹⁵ The princes of Issachar were
with Deborah.
The men of Issachar were
with Barak.
They went into the valley
under his command.
In the territories of Reuben,
men looked deeply into
their hearts.

¹⁶ Why did they stay among the
sheep pens?
Why did they stay to hear
shepherds whistling for
the flocks?
In the territories of Reuben,
men looked deeply into
their hearts.

¹⁷ Gilead stayed east of the
Jordan River.
Why did Dan stay near the
ships?
The men of Asher remained
on the coast of the
Mediterranean Sea.
They stayed in their safe
harbors.

¹⁸ The people of Zebulun put
     their very lives in danger.
So did Naphtali on the
     hillside fields.

¹⁹ "Kings came and fought.
The kings of Canaan fought
     at Taanach by the streams
     of Megiddo.
But they didn't carry away
     any silver.
They didn't take anything
     at all.

²⁰ From the heavens the stars
     fought.
From the sky they fought
     against Sisera.

²¹ The Kishon River swept them
     away.
The Kishon is a very old
     river.
My spirit, march on! Be
     strong!

²² The hooves of the horses
     pounded like thunder.
The powerful horses of our
     enemies galloped away.

²³ 'Let Meroz be cursed,' said
     the angel of the LORD.
'Let bitter curses fall on its
     people.
They did not come to help the
     LORD.
They did not come to
     help him against our
     powerful enemies.'

²⁴ "May Jael be the most blessed
     woman of all.
May the wife of Heber, the
     Kenite, be blessed.
May she be the most
     blessed woman of all
     those who live in tents.

²⁵ Sisera asked for water. She
     gave him milk.

In a bowl fit for nobles she
     brought him buttermilk.

²⁶ Her hand reached out for a
     tent stake.
Her right hand reached for
     a hammer.
She hit Sisera. She crushed
     his head.
She drove the stake right
     through his head.

²⁷ He sank down. He fell at her
     feet.
He was lying there.
At her feet he sank down. He
     fell.
He fell where he sank down.
     That's where he died.

²⁸ "Sisera's mother looked out
     through the window.
From behind the wooden
     screen she cried out.
'Why is his chariot taking
     so long to get here?' she
     said.
'Why can't I hear the noise
     of his chariots yet?'

²⁹ Her wisest ladies answer her.
And here's what she keeps
     saying to herself.

³⁰ She says, 'They must be
     finding riches to bring
     back.
They must be dividing
     them up.
Each man is getting a woman
     or two.
They are giving colorful
     clothes to Sisera.
The clothes are very
     beautiful.
He will bring some for me to
     wear.
The men must be finding
     many things to bring
     home.'

³¹ "LORD, may all your enemies
be destroyed.
But may all who love you
be like the morning sun.
May they be like the sun
when it shines the
brightest."

So the land was at peace for 40 years.

Gideon

6 The Israelites did what was evil in the sight of the LORD. So for seven years he handed them over to the people of Midian. ²The Midianites treated the Israelites very badly. That's why they made hiding places for themselves. They hid in holes in the mountains. They also hid in caves and in other safe places. ³Each year the people planted their crops. When they did, the Midianites came into the country and attacked it. So did the Amalekites and other tribes from the east. ⁴They camped on the land. They destroyed the crops all the way to Gaza. They didn't spare any living thing for Israel. They didn't spare sheep or cattle or donkeys. ⁵The Midianites came up with their livestock and tents. They came like huge numbers of locusts. It was impossible to count the men and their camels. They came into the land to destroy it. ⁶The Midianites made the Israelites very poor. So they cried out to the LORD for help.

⁷They cried out to the LORD because of what the Midianites had done. ⁸So he sent a prophet to Israel. The prophet said, "The LORD is the God of Israel. He says, 'I brought you up out of Egypt. That is the land where you were slaves. ⁹I saved you from the power of the Egyptians. I saved you from all those who were treating you badly. I drove out the Canaanites to make room for you. I gave you their land. ¹⁰I said to you, "I am the LORD your God. You are now living in the land of the Amorites. Do not worship their gods." But you have not listened to me.' "

¹¹The angel of the LORD came. He sat down under an oak tree in Ophrah. The tree belonged to Joash. He was from the family line of Abiezer. Gideon was threshing wheat in a winepress at Ophrah. He was the son of Joash. Gideon was threshing in a winepress to hide the wheat from the Midianites. ¹²The angel of the LORD appeared to Gideon. He said, "Mighty warrior, the LORD is with you."

¹³ "Pardon me, sir," Gideon replied, "you say the LORD is with us. Then why has all this happened to us? Where are all the wonderful things he has done? Our people of long ago told us about them. They said, 'Didn't the LORD bring us up out of Egypt?' But now the LORD has deserted us. He has handed us over to Midian."

¹⁴The LORD turned to Gideon. He said to him, "You are strong. Go and save Israel from the power of Midian. I am sending you."

¹⁵ "Pardon me, sir," Gideon replied, "but how can I possibly

save Israel? My family group is the weakest in the tribe of Manasseh. And I'm the least important member of my family."

¹⁶ The LORD answered, "I will be with you. So you will strike down the Midianites. You will leave no one alive."

¹⁷ Gideon replied, "If you are pleased with me, give me a special sign. Then I'll know that it's really you talking to me. ¹⁸ Please don't go away until I come back. I'll bring my offering and set it down in front of you."

The LORD said, "I will wait until you return."

¹⁹ Gideon went inside and prepared a young goat. From 36 pounds of flour he made bread without using yeast. He put the meat in a basket. In a pot he put soup made from the meat. Then he brought all of it and offered it to the LORD under the oak tree.

²⁰ The angel of God said to Gideon, "Take the meat and the bread. Place them on this rock. Then pour out the soup." So Gideon did it. ²¹ The angel of the LORD had a walking stick in his hand. With the tip of the stick he touched the meat and the bread. Fire blazed out of the rock. It burned up the meat and the bread. Then the angel of the LORD disappeared. ²² Gideon realized it was the angel of the LORD. He cried out, "Oh no, my LORD and King, I have seen the angel of the LORD face to face!"

²³ But the LORD said to him, "May peace be with you! Do not be afraid. You are not going to die."

²⁴ So Gideon built an altar there to honor the LORD. He called it The LORD Is Peace. It still stands in Ophrah to this day. Ophrah is in the territory that belongs to the family line of Abiezer.

²⁵ That same night the LORD spoke to Gideon. He said, "Get the second bull from your father's herd. Get the one that is seven years old. Tear down the altar your father built to honor the god named Baal. Cut down the pole beside it. The pole is used to worship the female god named Asherah. ²⁶ Then build the right kind of altar. Build it to honor the LORD your God. Build it on top of this hill. Then use the wood from the Asherah pole you cut down. Sacrifice the second bull as a burnt offering."

²⁷ So Gideon went and got ten of his servants. He did just as the LORD had told him. But he was afraid of his family. He was also afraid of the people in the town. So he did everything at night instead of during the day.

²⁸ In the morning the people in the town got up. They saw that Baal's altar had been torn down. The Asherah pole beside it had been cut down. And the second bull had been sacrificed on the new altar that had been built.

²⁹ They asked each other, "Who did this?"

They looked into the matter carefully. Someone told them, "Gideon, the son of Joash, did it."

³⁰ The people in the town spoke to Joash. They ordered

him, "Bring your son out here. He must die. He has torn down Baal's altar. He has cut down the Asherah pole beside it."

[31] But Joash replied to the angry crowd around him. He asked, "Are you going to stand up for Baal? Are you trying to save him? Those who stand up for him will be put to death by morning! Is Baal really a god? If he is, he can stand up for himself when someone tears down his altar." [32] That's why they gave Gideon the name Jerub-Baal on that day. Gideon had torn down Baal's altar. So they said, "Let Baal take his stand against him."

[33] All the Midianites and Amalekites gathered their armies together. Other tribes from the east joined them. All of them went across the Jordan River. They camped in the Valley of Jezreel. [34] Then the Spirit of the LORD came on Gideon. So Gideon blew a trumpet to send for the men of Abiezer. He told them to follow him. [35] He sent messengers all through Manasseh's territory. He called for the men of Manasseh to fight. He also sent messengers to the men of Asher, Zebulun and Naphtali. So all those men went up to join the others.

[36] Gideon said to God, "You promised you would use me to save Israel. [37] Please do something for me. I'll put a piece of wool on the threshing floor. Suppose dew is only on the wool tomorrow morning. And suppose the ground all around it is dry. Then I will know that you will use me to save Israel. I'll know that your promise will come true." [38] And that's what happened. Gideon got up early the next day. He squeezed the dew out of the wool. The water filled a bowl.

[39] Then Gideon said to God, "Don't be angry with me. Let me ask you for just one more thing. Let me use the wool for one more test. But this time make the wool dry. And let the ground be covered with dew." [40] So that night God did it. Only the wool was dry. The ground all around it was covered with dew.

Gideon Wins the Battle Over the Midianites

7 Early in the morning Jerub-Baal and all his men camped at the spring of Harod. Jerub-Baal was another name for Gideon. The camp of Midian was north of Gideon's camp. It was in the valley near the hill of Moreh. [2] The LORD said to Gideon, "I want to hand Midian over to you. But you have too many men for me to do that. Then Israel might brag, 'My own strength has saved me.' [3] So here is what I want you to announce to the army. Tell them, 'Those who tremble with fear can turn back. They can leave Mount Gilead.'" So 22,000 men left. But 10,000 remained.

[4] The LORD said to Gideon, "There are still too many men. So take them down to the water. There I will reduce the number of them for you. If I say, 'This

one will go with you,' he will go. But if I say, 'That one will not go with you,' he will not go."

⁵ So Gideon took the men down to the water. There the LORD said to him, "Some men will drink the way dogs do. They will lap up the water with their tongues. Separate them from those who get down on their knees to drink." ⁶ Three hundred men brought up the water to their mouths with their hands. And they lapped it up the way dogs do. All the rest got down on their knees to drink.

⁷ The LORD spoke to Gideon. He said, "With the help of the 300 men who lapped up the water I will save you. I will hand the Midianites over to you. Let all the other men go home." ⁸ So Gideon sent those Israelites home. But he kept the 300 men. They took over the supplies and trumpets the others had left.

The Midianites had set up their camp in the valley below where Gideon was. ⁹ During that night the LORD said to Gideon, "Get up. Go down against the camp. I am going to hand it over to you. ¹⁰ But what if you are afraid to attack? Then go down to the camp with your servant Purah. ¹¹ Listen to what they are saying. After that, you will not be afraid to attack the camp." So Gideon and his servant Purah went down to the edge of the camp. ¹² The Midianites had set up their camp in the valley. So had the Amalekites and all the other tribes from the east. There were so many of them that they looked like huge numbers of locusts. Like the grains of sand on the seashore, their camels couldn't be counted.

¹³ Gideon arrived just as a man was telling a friend about his dream. "I had a dream," he was saying. "A round loaf of barley bread came rolling into the camp of Midian. It hit a tent with great force. The tent turned over and fell down flat."

¹⁴ His friend replied, "That can only be the sword of Gideon, the son of Joash. Gideon is from Israel. God has handed the Midianites over to him. He has given him the whole camp."

¹⁵ Gideon heard the man explain what the dream meant. Then Gideon bowed down and worshiped. He returned to the camp of Israel. He called out, "Get up! The LORD has handed the Midianites over to you." ¹⁶ Gideon separated the 300 men into three fighting groups. He put a trumpet and an empty jar into the hands of each man. And he put a torch inside each jar.

¹⁷ "Watch me," he told them. "Do what I do. I'll go to the edge of the enemy camp. Then do exactly as I do. ¹⁸ I and everyone with me will blow our trumpets. Then blow your trumpets from your positions all around the camp. And shout the battle cry, 'For the LORD and for Gideon!' "

¹⁹ Gideon and the 100 men with him reached the edge of the enemy camp. It was about ten o'clock at night. It was just after the guard had been changed.

Gideon and his men blew their trumpets. They broke the jars that were in their hands. ²⁰ The three fighting groups blew their trumpets. They smashed their jars. They held their torches in their left hands. They held in their right hands the trumpets they were going to blow. Then they shouted the battle cry, "A sword for the LORD and for Gideon!" ²¹ Each man stayed in his position around the camp. But all the Midianites ran away in fear. They were crying out as they ran.

²² When the 300 trumpets were blown, the LORD caused all the men in the enemy camp to start fighting one another. They attacked one another with their swords. The army ran away to Beth Shittah toward Zererah. They ran all the way to the border of Abel Meholah near Tabbath. ²³ Israelites from the tribes of Naphtali, Asher and all of Manasseh were called out. They chased the Midianites. ²⁴ Gideon sent messengers through the entire hill country of Ephraim. They said, "Come on down against the Midianites. Take control of the waters of the Jordan River before they get there. Do it all the way to Beth Barah."

So all the men of Ephraim were called out. They took control of the waters of the Jordan all the way to Beth Barah. ²⁵ They also captured Oreb and Zeeb. Those men were two of the Midianite leaders. The men of Ephraim killed Oreb at the rock of Oreb. They killed Zeeb at the winepress of Zeeb. They chased the Midianites. And they brought the heads of Oreb and Zeeb to Gideon. He was by the Jordan River.

Zebah and Zalmunna

8 The men of Ephraim asked Gideon, "Why have you treated us like this? Why didn't you ask us to help you when you went out to fight against Midian?" In anger they challenged Gideon.

² But he answered them, "What I've done isn't anything compared to what you have done. Ephraim's grapes have been gathered. Isn't what is left over better than all the grapes that have been gathered from Abiezer's vines? ³ God handed Oreb and Zeeb over to you. They were Midianite leaders. So what was I able to do compared to what you did?" After Gideon had said that, they didn't feel angry with him anymore.

⁴ Gideon and his 300 men were very tired. But they kept on chasing their enemies. They came to the Jordan River and went across it. ⁵ Gideon said to the men of Sukkoth, "Give my troops some bread. They are worn out. And I'm still chasing Zebah and Zalmunna. They are the kings of Midian."

⁶ But the officials of Sukkoth objected. They said, "Have you already killed Zebah and Zalmunna? Have you cut their hands off and brought them back to prove it? If you haven't,

why should we give bread to your troops?"

⁷ Gideon replied, "The LORD will hand Zebah and Zalmunna over to me. When he does, I'll tear your skin with thorns from desert bushes."

⁸ From there Gideon went up to Peniel. He asked its men for the same thing. But they answered as the men of Sukkoth had. ⁹ So he said to the men of Peniel, "I'll be back after I've won the battle. Then I'll tear down this tower."

¹⁰ Zebah and Zalmunna were in Karkor. They had an army of about 15,000 men. That's all that were left of the armies of the tribes from the east. About 120,000 men who carried swords had died in battle. ¹¹ Gideon went up the trail the people of the desert had made. It ran east of Nobah and Jogbehah. He attacked the army by surprise. ¹² Zebah and Zalmunna ran away. They were the two kings of Midian. Gideon chased them and captured them. He destroyed their whole army.

¹³ Then Gideon, the son of Joash, returned from the battle. He came back through the Pass of Heres. ¹⁴ He caught a young man from Sukkoth. He asked him about the elders of the town. The young man wrote down for him the names of Sukkoth's 77 officials. ¹⁵ Then Gideon came and said to the men of Sukkoth, "Here are Zebah and Zalmunna. You made fun of me because of them. You said, 'Have you already killed Zebah and Zalmunna? Have you cut their hands off and brought them back to prove it? If you haven't, why should we give bread to your tired men?'"

¹⁶ Gideon went and got the elders of the town. Then he taught the men of Sukkoth a lesson. He tore their skin with thorns from desert bushes. ¹⁷ He also pulled down the tower at Peniel. He killed the men in the town.

¹⁸ Then he spoke to Zebah and Zalmunna. He asked, "What were the men like that you killed at Tabor?"

"Men like you," they answered. "Each one walked as if he were a prince."

¹⁹ Gideon replied, "Those were my brothers. They were the sons of my own mother. You can be sure that the LORD lives. And you can be just as sure that if you had spared their lives, I wouldn't kill you." ²⁰ Then Gideon turned to his oldest son Jether. He said, "Kill them!" But Jether didn't pull out his sword. He was only a boy. So he was afraid.

²¹ Zebah and Zalmunna said, "Come on. Do it yourself. 'The older the man, the stronger he is.'" So Gideon stepped forward and killed them. Then he took the gold chains off the necks of their camels.

Gideon's Linen Apron

²² The Israelites said to Gideon, "Rule over us. We want you, your son and your grandson to be our rulers. You have saved us from the power of Midian."

²³ But Gideon told them, "I will not rule over you. My son won't rule over you either. The LORD will rule over you." ²⁴ He continued, "I do ask one thing. I want each of you to give me an earring. I'm talking about the earrings you took from your enemies." It was the practice of the people in the family line of Ishmael to wear gold earrings.

²⁵ The Israelites said, "We'll be glad to give them to you." So they spread out a piece of clothing. Each of them threw a ring on it from what he had taken. ²⁶ The weight of the gold rings Gideon asked for was 43 pounds. That didn't include the moon-shaped necklaces the kings of Midian had worn. It didn't include their other necklaces or their purple clothes. And it didn't include the gold chains that had been on the necks of their camels. ²⁷ Gideon made an object out of all the gold. It looked like the linen apron the high priest of Israel wore. Gideon placed it in Ophrah. That was his hometown. All the Israelites worshiped it there. They weren't faithful to the LORD. So the gold object became a trap to Gideon and his family.

Gideon Dies

²⁸ Israel brought Midian under their control. Midian wasn't able to attack Israel anymore. So the land was at peace for 40 years. The peace lasted as long as Gideon was living.

²⁹ Jerub-Baal, the son of Joash, went back home to live. Jerub-Baal was another name for Gideon. ³⁰ He had 70 sons of his own. That's because he had many wives. ³¹ And he had a concubine who lived in Shechem. She also had a son by him. Gideon named that son Abimelek. ³² Gideon, the son of Joash, died when he was very old. He was buried in the tomb of his father Joash in Ophrah. Ophrah was in the territory that belonged to the family line of Abiezer.

³³ As soon as Gideon had died, the Israelites began serving and worshiping gods that were named Baal. Israel wasn't faithful to the LORD. They worshiped Baal-Berith as their god. ³⁴ They forgot what the LORD their God had done for them. He had saved them from the power of their enemies all around them. ³⁵ Jerub-Baal had done many good things for the Israelites. But they weren't faithful to his family. Jerub-Baal was another name for Gideon.

Abimelek

9 Abimelek was the son of Jerub-Baal. He went to his mother's brothers in Shechem. He spoke to them and to all the members of his mother's family group. He said, ² "Speak to all the citizens of Shechem. Tell them, 'You can have all 70 of Jerub-Baal's sons rule over you. Or you can have just one man rule over you. Which would you rather have?' Remember, I'm your own flesh and blood."

³ The brothers told all of that to the citizens of Shechem. Then

the people decided to follow Abimelek. They said, "He's related to us." [4] They gave him 28 ounces of silver. They had taken it from the temple of the god named Baal-Berith. Abimelek used it to hire some men. They were wild and weren't good for anything. They became his followers. [5] Abimelek went to his father's home in Ophrah. There on a big rock he murdered his 70 brothers. All of them were the sons of Jerub-Baal. But Jotham escaped by hiding. He was Jerub-Baal's youngest son. [6] All the citizens of Shechem and Beth Millo came together. They gathered at the stone pillar that was beside the large tree in Shechem. They wanted to crown Abimelek as their king.

[7] Jotham was told about it. So he climbed up on top of Mount Gerizim. He shouted down to them, "Citizens of Shechem! Listen to me! Then God will listen to you. [8] One day the trees went out to anoint a king for themselves. They said to an olive tree, 'Be our king.'

[9] "But the olive tree answered, 'Should I give up my olive oil? It's used to honor gods and people alike. Should I give that up just to rule over the trees?'

[10] "Next, the trees said to a fig tree, 'Come and be our king.'

[11] "But the fig tree replied, 'Should I give up my fruit? It's so good and sweet. Should I give that up just to rule over the trees?'

[12] "Then the trees said to a vine, 'Come and be our king.'

[13] "But the vine answered, 'Should I give up my wine? It cheers up gods and people alike. Should I give that up just to rule over the trees?'

[14] "Finally, all the trees spoke to a bush that had thorns. They said, 'Come and be our king.'

[15] "The bush asked the trees, 'Do you really want to anoint me as king over you? If you do, come and rest in my shade. But if you don't, I will destroy you! Fire will come out of me and burn up the cedar trees of Lebanon!'

[16] "Did you act in an honest way when you made Abimelek your king? Did you really do the right thing? Have you been fair to Jerub-Baal and his family? Have you given him the honor he's worthy of? [17] Remember that my father fought for you. He put his life in danger for you. He saved you from the power of Midian. [18] But today you have turned against my father's family. You have murdered his 70 sons on a big rock. Abimelek is only the son of my father's female slave. But you have made him king over the citizens of Shechem. You have done that because he's related to you. [19] Have you citizens of Shechem and Beth Millo acted in an honest way toward Jerub-Baal? Have you done the right thing to his family today? If you have, may you be happy with Abimelek! And may he be happy with you! [20] But if you haven't, let fire come out from Abimelek and burn you up! And let fire come

out from you and burn Abimelek up!"

²¹ Then Jotham ran away. He escaped to a town named Beer. He lived there because he was afraid of his brother Abimelek.

²² Abimelek ruled over Israel for three years. ²³ Then God stirred up trouble between Abimelek and the citizens of Shechem. So they turned against Abimelek. They decided not to follow him anymore. ²⁴ God made that happen because of what Abimelek had done to Jerub-Baal's 70 sons. He had spilled their blood. God wanted to punish their brother Abimelek for doing that. He also wanted to punish the citizens of Shechem. They had helped Abimelek murder his brothers. ²⁵ The citizens of Shechem didn't want Abimelek to be their ruler anymore. So they hid some men on top of the hills. They wanted them to attack and rob everyone who passed by. Abimelek was told about it.

²⁶ Gaal and his relatives moved into Shechem. Gaal was the son of Ebed. The citizens of Shechem put their trust in Gaal. ²⁷ The people of Shechem went out into the fields. They gathered the grapes. They pressed the juice out of them by stomping on them. Then they held a feast in the temple of their god. While they were eating and drinking, they cursed Abimelek. ²⁸ Then Gaal, the son of Ebed, said, "Who is Abimelek? And who is Shechem? Why should we citizens of Shechem be under Abimelek's rule? Isn't he Jerub-Baal's son? Isn't Zebul his helper? It would be better to serve the family of Hamor. He was the father of Shechem. So why should we serve Abimelek? ²⁹ I wish these people were under my command. Then I would get rid of Abimelek. I would say to him, 'Call out your whole army!'"

³⁰ Zebul was the governor of Shechem. He heard about what Gaal, the son of Ebed, had said. So he was very angry. ³¹ Zebul secretly sent messengers to Abimelek. They said, "Gaal, the son of Ebed, has come to Shechem. His relatives have come with him. They are stirring up the city against you. ³² So come with your men during the night. Hide in the fields and wait. ³³ In the morning at sunrise, attack the city. Gaal and his men will come out against you. Then take that opportunity to attack them."

³⁴ So Abimelek and all his troops started out at night. They went into their hiding places near Shechem. Abimelek had separated them into four fighting groups. ³⁵ Gaal, the son of Ebed, had already gone out. He was standing at the entrance of the city gate. He had arrived there just as Abimelek and his troops came out of their hiding places.

³⁶ Gaal saw them. He said to Zebul, "Look! People are coming down from the tops of the mountains!"

Zebul replied, "You are wrong. Those aren't people. They are just the shadows of the mountains."

³⁷ But Gaal spoke up again. He said, "Look! People are coming down from the central hill. Another group is coming from the direction of the fortune tellers' tree."

³⁸ Then Zebul said to Gaal, "Where is your big talk now? You said, 'Who is Abimelek? Why should we be under his rule?' Aren't these the people you made fun of? Go out and fight against them!"

³⁹ So Gaal led the citizens out of Shechem. They fought against Abimelek. ⁴⁰ He chased Gaal from the field of battle. Abimelek chased them all the way to the entrance of the city gate. Many men were killed as they ran away. ⁴¹ Abimelek stayed in Arumah. And Zebul drove Gaal and his relatives out of Shechem.

⁴² The next day the people of Shechem went out to work in the fields. Abimelek was told about it. ⁴³ So he gathered his men together. He separated them into three fighting groups. Then he hid them in the fields and told them to wait. When he saw the people coming out of the city, he got up to attack them. ⁴⁴ Abimelek and the men with him ran forward. They placed themselves at the entrance of the city gate. Then the other two groups attacked the people in the fields. There they struck them down. ⁴⁵ Abimelek kept up his attack against the city all day long. He didn't stop until he had captured it. Then he killed its people. He destroyed the city. He scattered salt on it to make sure that nothing would be able to grow there.

⁴⁶ The citizens in the tower of Shechem heard about what was happening. So they went to the safest place in the temple of the god named El-Berith. ⁴⁷ Abimelek heard that they had gathered together there. ⁴⁸ He and all his men went up Mount Zalmon. He got an ax and cut off some branches. He carried them on his shoulders. He ordered the men with him to do the same thing. "Quick!" he said. "Do what you have seen me do!" ⁴⁹ So all the men cut branches and followed Abimelek. They piled them against the place where the people had gone for safety. Then they set the place on fire with the people still inside. There were about 1,000 men and women in the tower of Shechem. All of them died.

⁵⁰ Next, Abimelek went to Thebez. He surrounded it. Then he attacked it and captured it. ⁵¹ But inside the city there was a strong tower. All the people in the city had run to it for safety. All the men and women had gone into it. They had locked themselves in. They had climbed up on the roof of the tower. ⁵² Abimelek went to the tower and attacked it. He approached the entrance to the tower to set it on fire. ⁵³ But a woman dropped a large millstone on him. It broke his head open.

⁵⁴ He quickly called out to

the man carrying his armor. He said, "Pull out your sword and kill me. Then people can't say, 'A woman killed him.' " So his servant stuck his sword through him. And Abimelek died. ⁵⁵ When the Israelites saw he was dead, they went home.

⁵⁶ That's how God punished Abimelek for the evil thing he had done to his father. He had murdered his 70 brothers. ⁵⁷ God also made the people of Shechem pay for all the evil things they had done. The curse of Jotham came down on them. He was the son of Jerub-Baal.

Tola

10 Tola rose up to save Israel. That happened after the time of Abimelek. Tola was from the tribe of Issachar. He was the son of Puah, who was the son of Dodo. Tola lived in Shamir. It's in the hill country of Ephraim. ² Tola led Israel for 23 years. After he died, he was buried in Shamir.

Jair

³ Jair became the leader after Tola. Jair was from the land of Gilead. He led Israel for 22 years. ⁴ He had 30 sons. They rode on 30 donkeys. His sons controlled 30 towns in Gilead. Those towns are called Havvoth Jair to this day. ⁵ After Jair died, he was buried in Kamon.

Jephthah

⁶ Once again the Israelites did what was evil in the sight of the LORD. They served gods that were named Baal. They served female gods that were named Ashtoreth. They worshiped the gods of Aram and Sidon. They served the gods of Moab and Ammon. They also worshiped the gods of the Philistines. The Israelites deserted the LORD. They didn't serve him anymore. ⁷ So the LORD became very angry with them. He handed them over to the Philistines and the Ammonites. ⁸ That year they broke Israel's power completely. They treated the Israelites badly for 18 years. The people who did this lived east of the Jordan River. They lived in Gilead. That was the land of the Amorites. ⁹ The Ammonites also went across the Jordan. They crossed over to fight against the tribes of Judah, Benjamin and Ephraim. Israel was suffering terribly. ¹⁰ Then the Israelites cried out to the LORD. They said, "We have sinned against you. We have deserted our God. We have served gods that are named Baal."

¹¹ The LORD replied, "The Egyptians and Amorites treated you badly. So did the Ammonites and Philistines. ¹² And so did the Amalekites and the people of Sidon and Maon. Each time you cried out to me for help. And I saved you from their power. ¹³ But you have deserted me. You have served other gods. So I will not save you anymore. ¹⁴ Go and cry out to the gods you have chosen. Let them save you when you get into trouble!"

¹⁵ But the Israelites replied to the LORD, "We have sinned.

Do to us what you think is best. But please save us now." ¹⁶ Then they got rid of the false gods that were among them. They served the LORD. And he couldn't stand to see Israel suffer anymore.

¹⁷ The Ammonites were called together to fight. They camped in the land of Gilead. Then the Israelites gathered together. They camped at the city of Mizpah. ¹⁸ The leaders of Gilead spoke to one another. They said, "Who will lead the attack against the Ammonites? That person will be the ruler of all the people who live in Gilead."

11 Jephthah was a mighty warrior. He was from the land of Gilead. His father's name was Gilead. Jephthah's mother was a prostitute. ² Gilead's wife also had sons by him. When they had grown up, they drove Jephthah away. "You aren't going to get any share of our family's property," they said. "You are the son of another woman." ³ So Jephthah ran away from his brothers. He made his home in the land of Tob. A group of men who weren't good for anything gathered around him there. And they followed him.

⁴ Some time later, the Ammonites were fighting against Israel. ⁵ So the elders of Gilead went to get Jephthah from the land of Tob. ⁶ "Come with us," they said. "Be our commander. Then we can fight against the Ammonites."

⁷ Jephthah said to them, "Didn't you hate me? Didn't you drive me away from my father's house? Why are you coming to me only when you are in trouble?"

⁸ The elders of Gilead replied to him. "You are right," they said. "That's why we're turning to you now. Come with us and fight against the Ammonites. Then you will rule over all of us who live in Gilead."

⁹ Jephthah said, "Suppose you take me back to fight against the Ammonites. And suppose the LORD gives me victory over them. Then will I really be your leader?"

¹⁰ The elders of Gilead replied, "The LORD is our witness. We'll certainly do as you say." ¹¹ So Jephthah went with the elders of Gilead. And the people made him their leader and commander. He went to Mizpah. There he repeated to the LORD everything he had said.

¹² Then Jephthah sent messengers to the king of Ammon. They asked, "What do you have against me? Why have you attacked my country?"

¹³ The king of Ammon answered Jephthah's messengers. He said, "Israel came up out of Egypt. At that time they took my land away. They took all the land between the Arnon River and the Jabbok River. It reached all the way to the Jordan River. Now give it back. Then there will be peace."

¹⁴ Jephthah sent messengers back to the king of Ammon. ¹⁵ They said,

"Here is what Jephthah says to you. Israel didn't

take the land of Moab. They didn't take the land of Ammon. ¹⁶ When Israel came up out of Egypt, they went through the desert to the Red Sea. From there they went on to Kadesh. ¹⁷ Then Israel sent messengers to the king of Edom. They said, 'Please let us go through your country.' But the king of Edom wouldn't listen to them. They sent the same message to the king of Moab. But he refused too. So Israel stayed at Kadesh.

¹⁸ "Next, they traveled through the desert. They traveled along the borders of the lands of Edom and Moab. They passed along the east side of the country of Moab. They camped on the other side of the Arnon River. They didn't enter the territory of Moab. The Arnon River was Moab's border.

¹⁹ "Then Israel sent messengers to Sihon. He was the king of the Amorites. He ruled in Heshbon. They said to him, 'Let us pass through your country to our own land.' ²⁰ But Sihon didn't trust Israel to pass through his territory. Instead, he gathered all his troops together. They camped at Jahaz. And they fought against Israel.

²¹ "Then the LORD, the God of Israel, handed Sihon and his whole army over to Israel. Israel won the battle over them. Amorites were living in the country at that time. And Israel took over all their land. ²² Israel captured all the land between the Arnon River and the Jabbok River. It reached from the desert all the way to the Jordan River.

²³ "The LORD, the God of Israel, has driven the Amorites out to make room for his people. So what right do you have to take it over? ²⁴ You will take what your god Chemosh gives you, won't you? In the same way, we will take over what the LORD our God has given us. ²⁵ Are you any better than Balak, the son of Zippor? Balak was the king of Moab. Did he ever argue with Israel? Did he ever fight against them? ²⁶ For 300 years Israel has been living in Heshbon and Aroer. They have been living in the settlements around those cities. They have also been living in all the towns along the Arnon River. Why didn't you take those places back during that time? ²⁷ I haven't done anything wrong to you. But you are doing something wrong to me. You have gone to war against me. The LORD is the Judge. So let him decide our case today. Let him settle matters between the Israelites and the Ammonites."

²⁸ But the king of Ammon didn't pay any attention to the message Jephthah sent him.

²⁹Then the Spirit of the LORD came on Jephthah. He went across the territories of Gilead and Manasseh. He passed through Mizpah in the land of Gilead. From there he attacked the people of Ammon. ³⁰Jephthah made a promise to the LORD. Jephthah said, "Hand the Ammonites over to me. ³¹If you do, here's what I'll do when I come back from winning the battle. Anything that comes out the door of my house to meet me will belong to the LORD. I will sacrifice it as a burnt offering."

³²Then Jephthah went over to fight against the Ammonites. The LORD handed them over to him. ³³Jephthah destroyed 20 towns between Aroer and the area of Minnith. He destroyed them all the way to Abel Keramim. So Israel brought Ammon under their control.

³⁴Jephthah returned to his home in Mizpah. And guess who came out to meet him. It was his daughter! She was dancing to the beat of tambourines. She was his only child. He didn't have any other sons or daughters. ³⁵When Jephthah saw her, he was so upset that he tore his clothes. He cried out, "Oh no, my daughter! You have filled me with trouble and sorrow. I've made a promise to the LORD. And I can't break it."

³⁶"My father," she replied, "you have given your word to the LORD. So do to me just what you promised to do. The Ammonites were your enemies. And the LORD has paid them back for what they did to you. ³⁷But please do one thing for me," she continued. "Give me two months to wander around in the hills. Let me weep there with my friends. I want to do that because I'll never get married."

³⁸"You may go," he said. He let her go for two months. She and her friends went into the hills. They were filled with sadness because she would never get married. ³⁹After the two months were over, she returned to her father. He did to her just what he had promised to do. And she was a virgin.

So that became a practice in Israel. ⁴⁰Each year the young women of Israel go away for four days. They do it in honor of the daughter of Jephthah. He was from the land of Gilead.

Jephthah Wins the Battle Over Ephraim

12 The troops of Ephraim were called out. The troops went across the Jordan River to Zaphon. When they arrived, they said to Jephthah, "You went to fight against the Ammonites. Why didn't you ask us to go with you? We're going to burn down your house over your head."

²Jephthah answered, "I and my people were taking part in a great struggle. We were at war with the Ammonites. I asked you for help. But you didn't come to save me from their power. ³I saw that you wouldn't help. So I put my own life in danger. I

went across the Jordan to fight against the Ammonites. The LORD helped me win the battle over them. So why have you come up today to fight against me?"

⁴Then Jephthah called the men of Gilead together. They fought against Ephraim. The men of Gilead struck them down. The people of Ephraim had said, "You people of Gilead are nothing but deserters from Ephraim and Manasseh." ⁵The men of Gilead captured the places where people go across the Jordan River to get to Ephraim. Some men of Ephraim weren't killed in the battle. When they arrived at the river, they would say, "Let us go across." Then the men of Gilead would ask each one, "Are you from Ephraim?" Suppose he replied, "No." ⁶Then they would say, "All right. Say 'Shibboleth.'" If he said "Sibboleth," the way he said the word would give him away. He couldn't say it correctly. So they would grab him. Then they would kill him at one of the places where people go across the Jordan. At that time, 42,000 men of Ephraim were killed.

⁷Jephthah led Israel for six years. Then he died. He was buried in a town in Gilead. Jephthah was from the land of Gilead.

Ibzan, Elon and Abdon

⁸After Jephthah, Ibzan from Bethlehem led Israel. ⁹He had 30 sons and 30 daughters. He gave his daughters to be married to men who were outside his family group. He brought in 30 young women to be married to his sons. Those women also came from outside his family group. Ibzan led Israel for seven years. ¹⁰Then he died. He was buried in Bethlehem.

¹¹After Ibzan, Elon led Israel. He was from the tribe of Zebulun. Elon led Israel for ten years. ¹²Then he died. He was buried in Aijalon. It was in the land of Zebulun.

¹³After Elon, Abdon led Israel. Abdon was the son of Hillel. Abdon was from Pirathon. ¹⁴He had 40 sons and 30 grandsons. They rode on 70 donkeys. Abdon led Israel for eight years. ¹⁵Then he died. He was buried at Pirathon in Ephraim. Pirathon was in the hill country of the Amalekites. Abdon was the son of Hillel.

Samson Is Born

13 Once again the Israelites did what was evil in the sight of the LORD. So the LORD handed them over to the Philistines for 40 years.

²A certain man from Zorah was named Manoah. He was from the tribe of Dan. Manoah had a wife who wasn't able to have children. ³The angel of the LORD appeared to Manoah's wife. He said, "You are not able to have children. But you are going to become pregnant. You will have a baby boy. ⁴Make sure you do not drink any kind of wine. Also make sure you

do not eat anything that is 'unclean.' ⁵ You will become pregnant. You will have a son. The hair on his head must never be cut. That is because the boy will be a Nazirite. He will be set apart to God from the day he is born. He will take the lead in saving Israel from the power of the Philistines."

⁶ Then the woman went to her husband. She told him, "A man of God came to me. He looked like an angel of God. His appearance was so amazing that it filled me with great wonder. I didn't ask him where he came from. And he didn't tell me his name. ⁷ But he said to me, 'You will become pregnant. You will have a son. So do not drink any kind of wine. Do not eat anything that is "unclean." That is because the boy will be a Nazirite. He will belong to God in a special way from the day he is born until the day he dies.' "

⁸ Then Manoah prayed to the LORD. He said, "Pardon your servant, Lord. I beg you to let the man of God you sent to us come again. He told us we would have a son. We want the man of God to teach us how to bring up the boy."

⁹ God heard Manoah. And the angel of God came again to the woman. He came while she was out in the field. But her husband Manoah wasn't with her. ¹⁰ The woman hurried to her husband. She told him, "He's here! The man who appeared to me the other day is here!"

¹¹ Manoah got up and followed his wife. When he came to the man, he spoke to him. He said, "Are you the man who talked to my wife?"

"I am," he replied.

¹² So Manoah asked him, "What will happen when your words come true? What rules should we follow for the boy's life and work?"

¹³ The angel of the LORD answered him. He said, "Your wife must do everything I have told her to do. ¹⁴ She must not eat anything that comes from grapevines. She must not drink any kind of wine. She must not eat anything that is 'unclean.' She must do everything I have commanded her to do."

¹⁵ Manoah said to the angel of the LORD, "We would like you to stay and eat. We want to prepare a young goat for you."

¹⁶ The angel of the LORD replied, "Even if I stay, I will not eat any of your food. But if you still want to prepare a burnt offering, you must offer it to the LORD." Manoah didn't realize it was the angel of the LORD.

¹⁷ Then Manoah asked the angel of the LORD a question. "What is your name?" he said. "We want to honor you when your word comes true."

¹⁸ The angel replied, "Why are you asking me what my name is? You would not be able to understand it." ¹⁹ Manoah got a young goat. He brought it along with the grain offering. He sacrificed it on a rock to the LORD. Then the LORD did an amazing thing. It happened while Ma-

noah and his wife were watching. ²⁰A flame blazed up from the altar toward heaven. The angel of the LORD rose up in the flame. When Manoah and his wife saw it, they fell with their faces to the ground. ²¹The angel of the LORD didn't show himself again to Manoah and his wife. Then Manoah realized it was the angel of the LORD.

²² "We're going to die!" he said to his wife. "We've seen God!"

²³ But his wife answered, "The LORD doesn't want to kill us. If he did, he wouldn't have accepted a burnt offering and a grain offering from us. He wouldn't have shown us all these things. He wouldn't have told us we're going to have a son."

²⁴ Later, the woman had a baby boy. She named him Samson. As he grew up, the LORD blessed him. ²⁵The Spirit of the LORD began to work in his life. It happened while he was in Mahaneh Dan. That place is between Zorah and Eshtaol.

Samson Marries a Philistine Woman

14 Samson went down to Timnah. There he saw a young Philistine woman. ²When he returned, he spoke to his father and mother. He said, "I've seen a Philistine woman in Timnah. Get her for me. I want her to be my wife."

³ His father and mother replied, "Can't we find a wife for you among your relatives? Isn't there one among any of our people? Do you have to go to the Phi-listines to get a wife? They aren't God's people. They haven't even been circumcised."

But Samson said to his father, "Get her for me. She's the right one for me." ⁴ Samson's parents didn't know that the LORD wanted things to happen this way. He was working out his plans against the Philistines. That's because the Philistines were ruling over Israel at that time.

⁵ Samson went down to Timnah. His father and mother went with him. They approached the vineyards of Timnah. Suddenly a young lion came roaring toward Samson. ⁶ Then the Spirit of the LORD came powerfully on Samson. So he tore the lion apart with his bare hands. He did it as easily as he might have torn a young goat apart. But he didn't tell his father or mother what he had done. ⁷ Then he went down and talked with the woman. He liked her.

⁸ Some time later, he was going back to marry her. But he turned off the road to look at the lion's dead body. He saw large numbers of bees and some honey in it. ⁹ He dug out the honey with his hands. He ate it as he walked along. Then he joined his parents again. He gave them some honey. They ate it too. But he didn't tell them he had taken it from the lion's dead body.

¹⁰ Samson's father went down to see the woman. Samson had a feast prepared there. He was following the practice of young

men when they married their wives. ¹¹ When the people saw Samson, they gave him 30 men to be his companions.

¹² "Let me tell you a riddle," Samson said to the companions. "The feast will last for seven days. Give me the answer to the riddle before the feast ends. If you do, I'll give you 30 linen shirts. I'll also give you 30 sets of clothes. ¹³ But suppose you can't give me the answer. Then you must give me 30 linen shirts. You must also give me 30 sets of clothes."

"Tell us your riddle," they said. "Let's hear it."

¹⁴ Samson replied,

"Out of the eater came
    something to eat.
Out of the strong came
    something sweet."

For three days they couldn't give him the answer.

¹⁵ On the fourth day they spoke to Samson's wife. "Get your husband to explain the riddle for us," they said. "If you don't, we'll burn you to death. We'll burn up everyone in your family. Did you invite us here to steal our property?"

¹⁶ Then Samson's wife threw herself on him. She sobbed, "You hate me! You don't really love me. You have given my people a riddle. But you haven't told me the answer."

"I haven't even explained it to my father or mother," he replied. "So why should I explain it to you?" ¹⁷ She cried during the whole seven days the feast was going on. So on the seventh day he finally told her the answer to the riddle. That's because she kept on asking him to tell her. Then she explained the riddle to her people.

¹⁸ Before sunset on the seventh day of the feast the men of the town spoke to Samson. They said,

"What is sweeter than honey?
    What is stronger than a
        lion?"

Samson said to them,

"You have plowed with my
    young cow.
If you hadn't, you wouldn't
    have known the answer
    to my riddle."

¹⁹ Then the Spirit of the LORD came powerfully on Samson. He went down to Ashkelon. He struck down 30 of their men. He took everything they had with them. And he gave their clothes to those who had explained the riddle. Samson was very angry as he returned to his father's home. ²⁰ Samson's wife was given to someone else. She was given to a companion of Samson. The companion had helped him at the feast.

Samson Gets Even With the Philistines

15 Later on, Samson went to visit his wife. He took a young goat with him. He went at the time the wheat was being gathered. He said, "I'm going to my wife's room." But her father wouldn't let him go in.

² Her father said, "I was sure you hated her. So I gave her to your companion. Isn't her younger sister more beautiful? Take her instead."

³ Samson said to them, "This time I have a right to get even with the Philistines. I'm going to hurt them badly." ⁴ So he went out and caught 300 foxes. He tied them in pairs by their tails. Then he tied a torch to each pair of tails. ⁵ He lit the torches. He let the foxes loose in the fields of grain that belonged to the Philistines. He burned up the grain that had been cut and stacked. He burned up the grain that was still growing. He also burned up the vineyards and olive trees.

⁶ The Philistines asked, "Who did this?" They were told, "Samson did. He's the son-in-law of the man from Timnah. Samson did it because his wife was given to his companion."

So the Philistines went up and burned the woman and her father to death. ⁷ Samson said to the Philistines, "Is that how you act? Then I promise I won't stop until I pay you back." ⁸ He struck them down with heavy blows. He killed many of them. Then he went down and stayed in a cave. It was in the rock of Etam.

⁹ The Philistines went up and camped in Judah. They spread out near Lehi. ¹⁰ The people of Judah asked, "Why have you come to fight against us?"

"We've come to take Samson as our prisoner," they answered. "We want to do to him what he did to us."

¹¹ Then 3,000 men from Judah went to get Samson. They went down to the cave in the rock of Etam. They said to Samson, "Don't you realize the Philistines are ruling over us? What have you done to us?"

Samson answered, "I only did to them what they did to me."

¹² The men of Judah said to him, "We've come to tie you up. We're going to hand you over to the Philistines."

Samson said, "Promise me you won't kill me yourselves."

¹³ "We agree," they answered. "We'll only tie you up and hand you over to them. We won't kill you." So they tied him up with two new ropes. They led him up from the rock. ¹⁴ Samson approached Lehi. The Philistines came toward him shouting. Then the Spirit of the LORD came powerfully on Samson. The ropes on his arms became like burned thread. They dropped off his hands. ¹⁵ He found a fresh jawbone of a donkey. He grabbed it and struck down 1,000 men.

¹⁶ Then Samson said,

"By using a donkey's jawbone
    I've made them look like
        donkeys.
By using a donkey's jawbone
    I've struck down 1,000
        men."

¹⁷ Samson finished speaking. Then he threw the jawbone away. That's why the place was called Ramath Lehi.

¹⁸ Samson was very thirsty. So he cried out to the LORD. He

said, "You have helped me win this great battle. Do I have to die of thirst now? Must I fall into the power of people who haven't even been circumcised? They aren't your people." [19] Then God opened up the hollow place in Lehi. Water came out of it. When Samson drank the water, his strength returned. He felt as good as new. So the spring was called En Hakkore. It's still there in Lehi.

[20] Samson led Israel for 20 years. In those days the Philistines were in the land.

Samson and Delilah

16 One day Samson went to Gaza. There he saw a prostitute. He went in to spend the night with her. [2] The people of Gaza were told, "Samson is here!" So they surrounded the place. They hid and waited for him at the city gate all night long. They didn't make any move against him during the night. They said, "Let's wait until the sun comes up. Then we'll kill him."

[3] But Samson stayed there only until the middle of the night. Then he got up. He took hold of the doors of the city gate. He also took hold of the two doorposts. He tore them loose, together with their metal bar. He picked them up and put them on his shoulders. Then he carried them to the top of the hill that faces Hebron.

[4] Some time later, Samson fell in love again. The woman lived in the Valley of Sorek. Her name was Delilah. [5] The rulers of the Philistines went to her. They said, "See if you can get him to tell you the secret of why he's so strong. Find out how we can overpower him. Then we can tie him up. We can bring him under our control. Each of us will give you 28 pounds of silver."

[6] So Delilah said to Samson, "Tell me the secret of why you are so strong. Tell me how you can be tied up and controlled."

[7] Samson answered her, "Let someone tie me up with seven new bowstrings. They must be strings that aren't completely dry. Then I'll become as weak as any other man."

[8] So the Philistine rulers brought seven new bowstrings to her. They weren't completely dry. Delilah tied Samson up with them. [9] Men were hiding in the room. She called out to him, "Samson! The Philistines are attacking you!" But he snapped the bowstrings easily. They were like pieces of string that had come too close to a flame. So the secret of why he was so strong wasn't discovered.

[10] Delilah spoke to Samson again. "You have made me look foolish," she said. "You told me a lie. Come on. Tell me how you can be tied up."

[11] Samson said, "Let someone tie me tightly with new ropes. They must be ropes that have never been used. Then I'll become as weak as any other man."

[12] So Delilah got some new ropes. She tied him up with

them. Men were hiding in the room. She called out to him, "Samson! The Philistines are attacking you!" But he snapped the ropes off his arms. They fell off just as if they were threads.

¹³ Delilah spoke to Samson again. "All this time you have been making me look foolish," she said. "You have been telling me lies. This time really tell me how you can be tied up."

He replied, "Weave the seven braids of my hair into the cloth on a loom. Then tighten the cloth with a pin. If you do, I'll become as weak as any other man." So while Samson was sleeping, Delilah took hold of the seven braids of his hair. She wove them into the cloth on a loom. ¹⁴ Then she tightened the cloth with a pin.

Again she called out to him, "Samson! The Philistines are attacking you!" He woke up from his sleep. He pulled up the pin and the loom, together with the cloth.

¹⁵ Then she said to him, "How can you say, 'I love you'? You won't even share your secret with me. This is the third time you have made me look foolish. And you still haven't told me the secret of why you are so strong." ¹⁶ She continued to pester him day after day. She nagged him until he was sick and tired of it.

¹⁷ So he told her everything. He said, "My hair has never been cut. That's because I've been a Nazirite since the day I was born. A Nazirite is set apart to God. If you shave my head,

I won't be strong anymore. I'll become as weak as any other man."

¹⁸ Delilah realized he had told her everything. So she sent a message to the Philistine rulers. She said, "Come back one more time. He has told me everything." So the rulers returned. They brought the silver with them. ¹⁹ Delilah got Samson to go to sleep on her lap. Then she called for someone to shave off the seven braids of his hair. That's how she began to bring Samson under her control. And he wasn't strong anymore.

²⁰ She called out, "Samson! The Philistines are attacking you!"

He woke up from his sleep. He thought, "I'll go out just as I did before. I'll shake myself free." But he didn't know that the Lord had left him.

²¹ Then the Philistines grabbed him. They poked his eyes out. They took him down to Gaza. They put bronze chains around him. Then they made him grind grain in the prison. ²² His head had been shaved. But the hair on it began to grow again.

Samson Dies

²³ The rulers of the Philistines gathered together. They were going to offer a great sacrifice to their god Dagon. They were going to celebrate. They said, "Our god has handed our enemy Samson over to us."

²⁴ When the people saw Samson, they praised their god. They said,

"Our god has handed our
enemy over to us.
Our enemy has destroyed
our land.
He has killed large
numbers of our people."

25 After they had drunk a lot of wine, they shouted, "Bring Samson out. Let him put on a show for us." So they called Samson out of the prison. He put on a show for them.

They had him stand near the temple pillars. 26 Then he spoke to the servant who was holding his hand. He said, "Put me where I can feel the pillars. I'm talking about the ones that hold up the temple. I want to lean against them." 27 The temple was crowded with men and women. All the Philistine rulers were there. About 3,000 men and women were on the roof. They were watching Samson put on a show. 28 Then he prayed to the LORD. Samson said, "LORD and King, show me that you still have concern for me. Please, God, make me strong just one more time. Let me pay the Philistines back for what they did to my two eyes. Let me do it with only one blow." 29 Then Samson reached toward the two pillars that were in the middle of the temple. They were the ones that held up the temple. He put his right hand on one of them. He put his left hand on the other. He leaned hard against them. 30 Samson said, "Let me die together with the Philistines!" Then he pushed with all his might. The temple came down on the rulers. It fell on all the people in it. So Samson killed many more Philistines when he died than he did while he lived.

31 Then his brothers went down to get him. So did his father's whole family. All of them brought Samson back home. They buried him in the tomb of his father Manoah. It's between Zorah and Eshtaol. Samson had led Israel for 20 years.

Micah's False Gods

17 A man named Micah lived in the hill country of Ephraim. 2 He said to his mother, "Someone took 28 pounds of silver from you. I heard you curse the one who took it. I have the silver with me. I'm the one who took it."

Then his mother said, "My son, may the LORD bless you!"

3 He gave the 28 pounds of silver back to his mother. She said to him, "I'm making a promise to set apart my silver to the LORD. My son, I want you to use it to cover a statue of a god made out of wood or stone. That's why I'll give the silver back to you."

4 Micah gave the silver back to his mother. Then she gave five pounds of it to a skilled worker who made things out of silver. He used the silver for the statue. The statue was put in Micah's house.

5 That same Micah had a small temple. He made a sacred linen apron and some statues of his family gods. He appointed one of his sons to serve as his priest. 6 In those days Israel didn't have

a king. The people did anything they thought was right.

⁷A young Levite had been living in land that belonged to the tribe of Judah. He was from Bethlehem in Judah. ⁸He left that town to look for some other place to stay. On his way he came to Micah's house. It was in the hill country of Ephraim.

⁹Micah asked him, "Where are you from?"

"I'm a Levite," he said. "I'm from Bethlehem in Judah. I'm looking for a place to stay."

¹⁰Then Micah said to him, "Live with me. Be my father and priest. I'll give you four ounces of silver a year. I'll also give you clothes and food." ¹¹So the Levite agreed to live with him. The young man became just like one of Micah's sons to him. ¹²Then Micah appointed the Levite to serve as his priest. He lived in Micah's house. ¹³Micah said, "Now I know that the LORD will be good to me. This Levite has become my priest."

The People of Dan Make Their Homes in Laish

18 In those days Israel didn't have a king. And in those days the tribe of Dan was looking for a place where they could make their homes. They hadn't been able to take over their own share of land among the tribes of Israel. ²So the people of Dan sent out five of their leading men from Zorah and Eshtaol. They told the men to look over the land and check it out. Those men did it for all the people of Dan. Those people told the men, "Go. Check out the land."

So they entered the hill country of Ephraim. They went to the house of Micah. That's where they spent the night. ³When they came near Micah's house, they recognized a voice. It was the voice of the young Levite. So they turned off the road and stopped there. They asked him, "Who brought you here? What are you doing in this place? Why are you here?"

⁴The Levite told them what Micah had done for him. He said, "He has hired me. I'm his priest."

⁵Then they said to him, "Please ask God for advice. Try to find out whether we'll have success on our journey."

⁶The priest answered them, "Go in peace. The LORD is pleased with your journey."

⁷So the five men left. They came to Laish. There they saw that the people felt secure. They were living in safety. Like the people in Sidon, they were at peace. Their land had everything they needed. Things were going very well for them. They lived a long way from the people of Sidon. And they didn't think they would ever need help from anyone else.

⁸The men returned to Zorah and Eshtaol. Their people asked them, "What did you find out?"

⁹They answered, "Come on! Let's attack them! We've seen the land, and it is very good. Aren't you going to do

something? Don't wait any longer. Go there and take it over. ¹⁰ When you get there, you will find people who aren't expecting anything bad to happen to them. Their land has plenty of room. God has handed it over to you. It's a land that has everything you will ever need."

¹¹ So 600 men from the tribe of Dan started out from Zorah and Eshtaol. They were prepared for battle. ¹² On their way they set up camp. Their camp was near Kiriath Jearim in Judah. That's why the place is called Mahaneh Dan to this day. It's west of Kiriath Jearim. ¹³ From there they went to the hill country of Ephraim. They came to Micah's house.

¹⁴ Then the five men who had looked over the land of Laish spoke to the other members of their tribe. They said, "Don't you know that one of these houses has a sacred linen apron in it? Some statues of family gods are there. That house also has another statue of a god covered with silver. Now you know what to do." ¹⁵ So they turned off the road and stopped there. They went to the house of the young Levite. He was at Micah's place. They greeted the young man. ¹⁶ The 600 men from Dan stood at the entrance of the gate. They were prepared for battle. ¹⁷ The five men who had looked over the land went inside. They took the statue covered with silver. They also took the family gods and the linen apron. During that time, the priest stood at the entrance of the gate. The 600 men stood there with him. They were prepared for battle.

¹⁸ When the five men went into Micah's house and took all those things, the priest spoke to them. He asked, "What are you doing?"

¹⁹ They answered him, "Be quiet! Don't say a word. Come with us. Be our father and priest. You can serve a whole tribe and family group in Israel as our priest. Isn't that better than serving just one man's family?" ²⁰ The priest was very pleased. He took the linen apron and the family gods. He also took the statue of the god that was covered with silver. Then the priest left with the people. ²¹ They put their little children and their livestock in front of them. They also put everything else they owned in front of them. And they turned and went on their way.

²² The men who lived near Micah were called together. Then they left and caught up with the people of Dan. That's because Dan's people hadn't gone very far from Micah's house. ²³ Those who lived near Micah shouted at them. The people of Dan turned around and asked Micah, "What's the matter with you? Why did you call out your men to fight against us?"

²⁴ He replied, "You took away the gods I made. And you took away my priest. What do I have left? So how can you ask, 'What's the matter with you?'"

²⁵ The people of Dan answered, "Don't argue with us.

Some of the men may get angry and attack you. Then you and your family will lose your lives." ²⁶ So the people of Dan went on their way. Micah saw that they were too strong for him. So he turned around and went back home.

²⁷ The people of Dan took what Micah had made. They also took his priest. They continued on their way to Laish. They went there to fight against a people who were at peace and secure. The people of Dan struck them down with their swords. They burned down their city. ²⁸ No one could save those people and their city. They lived a long way from Sidon. And they didn't think they would ever need help from anyone else. Their city was located in a valley near Beth Rehob.

The people of Dan rebuilt the city. Then they made their homes there. ²⁹ They named it Dan. That's because they traced their family line back to Dan. He was a son of Israel. The city used to be called Laish. ³⁰ There the people of Dan set up for themselves the statue of the god that was covered with silver. Jonathan and his sons were priests for the tribe of Dan. Jonathan was the son of Gershom, the son of Moses. Jonathan and his sons were priests until the time when the land was captured. ³¹ The people of Dan continued to use the statue Micah had made. They used it during the whole time the house of God was in Shiloh.

A Levite and His Concubine

19 In those days Israel didn't have a king.

There was a Levite who lived deep in the hill country of Ephraim. He got a concubine from Bethlehem in Judah. ² But she wasn't faithful to him. She left him. She went back to her parents' home in Bethlehem in Judah. She stayed there for four months. ³ Then her husband went to see her. He tried to talk her into coming back with him. He had his servant and two donkeys with him. She took her husband into her parents' home. When her father saw him, he gladly welcomed him. ⁴ His father-in-law, the woman's father, begged him to stay. So the Levite remained with him for three days. He ate, drank and slept there.

⁵ On the fourth day they got up early. The Levite prepared to leave. But the woman's father said to his son-in-law, "Have something to eat. It will give you strength. Then you can go on your way." ⁶ So the two of them sat down. They ate and drank together. After that, the woman's father said, "Please stay tonight. Enjoy yourself." ⁷ The man got up to go. But his father-in-law talked him into staying. So he stayed there that night. ⁸ On the morning of the fifth day, the Levite got up to go. But the woman's father said, "Have something to eat. It will give you strength. Wait until this afternoon!" So the two of them ate together.

⁹ Then the man got up to leave. His concubine and his servant got up when he did. But his father-in-law, the woman's father, spoke to him again. "Look," he said. "It's almost evening. The day is nearly over. So spend another night here. Please stay. Enjoy yourself. Early tomorrow morning you can get up and go back home." ¹⁰ But the man didn't want to stay another night. So he left. He went toward Jebus. Jebus is also called Jerusalem. The Levite had his two donkeys and his concubine with him. The donkeys had saddles on them.

¹¹ By the time the travelers came near Jebus, the day was almost over. So the servant said to his master, "Come. Let's stop at this Jebusite city. Let's spend the night here."

¹² His master replied, "No. We won't go into any city where strangers live. The people there aren't Israelites. We'll continue on to Gibeah." ¹³ He added, "Come. Let's try to reach Gibeah or Ramah. We can spend the night in one of those places." ¹⁴ So they continued on. As they came near Gibeah in Benjamin, the sun went down. ¹⁵ They stopped there to spend the night. They went to the city's main street and sat down. But no one took them home for the night.

¹⁶ That evening an old man came into the city. He had been working in the fields. He was from the hill country of Ephraim. But he was living in Gibeah. The people who lived there were from the tribe of Benjamin. ¹⁷ The old man saw the traveler in the main street. He asked, "Where are you going? Where did you come from?"

¹⁸ The Levite answered, "We've come from Bethlehem in Judah. We're on our way to Ephraim. I live deep in the hill country there. I've been to Bethlehem. Now I'm going to the house of the LORD. But no one has taken me home for the night. ¹⁹ We have straw and feed for our donkeys. We have food and wine for ourselves. We have enough for me, the woman and the young man with us. We don't need anything."

²⁰ "You are welcome at my house," the old man said. "I'd be happy to supply anything you might need. But don't spend the night in the street." ²¹ So the old man took him into his house and fed his donkeys. After the travelers had washed their feet, they had something to eat and drink.

²² They were inside enjoying themselves. But some of the evil men who lived in the city surrounded the house. They pounded on the door. They shouted to the old man who owned the house. They said, "Bring out the man who came to your house. We want to have sex with him."

²³ The owner of the house went outside. He said to them, "No, my friends. Don't do such an evil thing. This man is my guest. So don't do this terrible thing. ²⁴ Look, here is my virgin daughter. And here's the Levite's concubine. I'll bring them out to

you now. You can have them. Do to them what you want to. But don't do such a terrible thing to this man."

25 The men wouldn't listen to him. So the Levite sent his concubine out to them. They forced her to have sex with them. They raped her all night long. As the night was ending, they let her go. 26 At sunrise she went back to the house where her master was staying. She fell down at the door. She stayed there until daylight.

27 Later that morning her master got up. He opened the door of the house. He stepped out to continue on his way. But his concubine was lying there. She had fallen at the doorway of the house. Her hands were reaching out toward the door. 28 He said to her, "Get up. Let's go." But there wasn't any answer. Then he put her dead body on his donkey. And he started out for home.

29 When he reached home, he got a knife. He cut up his concubine. He cut her into 12 pieces. He sent them into all the territories of Israel. 30 Everyone who saw it spoke to one another. They said, "Nothing like this has ever been seen or done before. Nothing like this has happened since the day the Israelites came up out of Egypt. Just imagine! We must do something! So let's hear your ideas!"

The Israelites Punish the Tribe of Benjamin

20 Then all the Israelites came out. They came from the whole land between Dan and Beersheba. They also came from the land of Gilead. All of them gathered together in front of the Lord at Mizpah. 2 The leaders of all the tribes of Israel came. They took their places among the people of God gathered together. There were 400,000 men carrying swords. 3 The tribe of Benjamin heard that the Israelites had gone up to Mizpah. The Israelites said, "Tell us how this awful thing happened."

4 So the Levite spoke. He was the husband of the woman who had been murdered. He said, "I and my concubine went to Gibeah in Benjamin. We spent the night there. 5 During the night the men of Gibeah came after me. They surrounded the house. They were planning to kill me. They raped my concubine, and she died. 6 I took my concubine and cut her into pieces. I sent one piece to each part of Israel's territory. I did it because the men of Gibeah had done a very terrible thing in Israel. 7 All you men of Israel, speak up now. Tell me what you have decided to do."

8 All the men got up together. They said, "None of us will go home. Not one of us will return to his house. 9 Here is what we'll do to Gibeah. We'll cast lots to tell us how to attack the city. 10 We'll take ten men out of every 100 from all the tribes of Israel. We'll take 100 from every 1,000. We'll take 1,000 from every 10,000. The men we take will get supplies for the army. Then

the army will go to Gibeah in Benjamin. They'll give Gibeah exactly what they should get because of the terrible thing they did in Israel." ¹¹ So all the men of Israel came together to fight against the city.

¹² The tribes of Israel sent people to carry a message through the whole tribe of Benjamin. They said, "What about this awful crime that was committed among you? ¹³ Hand over to us those evil men of Gibeah. We'll put them to death. In that way we'll get rid of those evil people."

But the people of Benjamin wouldn't listen to the other Israelites. ¹⁴ They came together at Gibeah from their towns. They came to fight against the other Israelites. ¹⁵ Right away the people of Benjamin gathered together 26,000 men from their towns. They were carrying swords. These men were added to the 700 capable young men from Gibeah. ¹⁶ Among all these men there were 700 who were left-handed. Each of them could sling a stone at a hair and not miss.

¹⁷ Israel gathered 400,000 men together. They were carrying swords. All of them were trained for battle. That number didn't include the tribe of Benjamin.

¹⁸ The Israelites went up to Bethel. There they asked God, "Who should go up first and fight against the people of Benjamin?"

The LORD answered, "The tribe of Judah will go first."

¹⁹ The next morning the Israelites got up. They set up camp near Gibeah. ²⁰ The Israelites went out to fight against the men of Benjamin. They took up their battle positions against them at Gibeah. ²¹ The men of Benjamin came out of Gibeah. They killed 22,000 Israelites on the field of battle that day. ²² But the Israelites cheered one another on. They again took up their positions in the places where they had been the first day. ²³ The Israelites went and wept in front of the LORD until evening. They asked the LORD, "Should we go up again to fight against the men of Benjamin? They are our fellow Israelites."

The LORD answered, "Go up and fight against them."

²⁴ The Israelites came near the men of Benjamin on the second day. ²⁵ The men of Benjamin came out from Gibeah to oppose them. That time they killed 18,000 more Israelites. All the men who died had been carrying swords.

²⁶ Then all the Israelites, the whole army, went up to Bethel. They sat there and wept in front of the LORD. They didn't eat anything that day until evening. Then they brought burnt offerings and friendship offerings to the LORD. ²⁷ Again the Israelites spoke to the LORD. In those days the ark of the covenant of God was there. ²⁸ Phinehas was serving as priest at the ark. He was the son of Eleazar. Eleazar was the son of Aaron. The Israelites asked, "Should we go up again

to fight against the men of Benjamin? They are our fellow Israelites."

The LORD answered, "Go. Tomorrow I will hand them over to you."

²⁹ Then Israel hid some men and had them wait all around Gibeah. ³⁰ They went up to fight against the men of Benjamin on the third day. They took up their positions against Gibeah, just as they had done before. ³¹ The men of Benjamin came out to fight against them. They were drawn away from the city. They began to wound and kill the Israelites just as they had done before. About 30 men fell in battle. They fell in the open fields and on the roads. One of the roads led to Bethel. The other led to Gibeah. ³² The men of Benjamin said, "We're winning the battle over them, just as we did before." But the men of Israel said, "Let's pull back. Let's draw them away from the city to the roads."

³³ All the men of Israel moved away from their places. They took up new battle positions at Baal Tamar. The men who had been hiding charged out. They came from west of Gibeah. ³⁴ Then 10,000 of Israel's capable young men attacked Gibeah. The men of Benjamin didn't realize they were about to be destroyed. The fighting was very heavy. ³⁵ The LORD helped Israel win the battle over Benjamin. On that day the Israelites struck down 25,100 men of Benjamin. All the men who died had been carrying swords. ³⁶ Then the men of Benjamin saw that they had lost the battle.

The men of Israel had moved away from their positions in front of Benjamin. They had depended on the men they had hidden near Gibeah. ³⁷ Suddenly those men who had been hiding rushed into Gibeah. They spread out. Then they killed everyone in the city with their swords. ³⁸ The Israelites had made a plan with those who had been hiding. They had told them to send up a large cloud of smoke from the city. ³⁹ Then the Israelites would turn around and attack.

The men of Benjamin had begun to wound and kill the men of Israel. They had struck down about 30 of them. They had said, "We're winning the battle over them, just as we did the first time." ⁴⁰ But a large cloud of smoke began to go up from the city. The men of Benjamin turned around. They saw the the whole city going up in smoke. ⁴¹ Then the Israelites turned around and attacked them. The men of Benjamin were terrified. They realized they were going to be destroyed. ⁴² So they ran away from the men of Israel. They ran toward the desert. But they couldn't escape the battle. Other Israelites came out of the towns. There they struck down the men of Benjamin. ⁴³ Here's how it happened. The Israelites had surrounded them. They had chased them and easily caught up with them east of Gibeah. ⁴⁴ So 18,000 men of Benjamin fell in battle. All of them were brave fighters. ⁴⁵ Some men of Benjamin turned back. They ran toward the desert to the rock of Rimmon. As they did, the Israelites struck down 5,000 of them along the roads. They kept chasing the men of Benjamin all the way to Gidom. Along the way they struck down 2,000 more.

⁴⁶ On that day 25,000 men of Benjamin fell in battle. They had been carrying swords. All of them were brave fighters. ⁴⁷ But 600 of them turned back. They ran into the desert to the rock of Rimmon. They stayed there for four months. ⁴⁸ The men of Israel went back to Benjamin. In all the towns they killed the people with their swords. They even killed the animals. So they killed everything they found. They set on fire all the towns they came to.

Wives for the Men of Benjamin

21 The men of Israel had made a promise at Mizpah. They had said, "Not one of us will give his daughter to be married to a man from Benjamin."

² The people went to Bethel. They sat there until evening in front of God. They wept loudly and bitterly. ³ "Lord, you are the God of Israel," they cried. "Why has this happened to Israel? Why is one tribe missing from Israel today?"

⁴ Early the next day the people built an altar. They brought burnt offerings and friendship offerings.

⁵ Then the Israelites asked, "Has anyone failed to come here in front of the Lord? Is anyone missing from all the tribes of Israel?" The people had made a promise. They had said that anyone who failed to come to Mizpah in front of the Lord must be put to death.

⁶ The Israelites were very sad because of what had happened to the tribe of Benjamin. After all, they were their fellow Israelites. "Today one tribe has been cut off from Israel," they said. ⁷ "How can we provide wives for the men who are left? We've made a promise in front of the Lord. We've promised not to give any of our daughters to be married to them." ⁸ Then they asked, "Has any tribe of Israel failed to come here to Mizpah in front of the Lord?" They discovered that no one from Jabesh Gilead had come. No one from there had gathered together with the others in the camp. ⁹ They counted the people. They found that none of the people of Jabesh Gilead had come to Mizpah.

¹⁰ So the community sent 12,000 fighting men to Jabesh Gilead. They directed them to take their swords and kill those living there. That included the women and children. ¹¹ "Here is what you must do," they said. "Kill every male. Also kill every woman who is not a virgin." ¹² They found 400 young women in Jabesh Gilead who had never slept with a man. So they took them to the camp at Shiloh in Canaan.

¹³ Then the whole community sent an offer of peace to the men of Benjamin. The men were at the rock of Rimmon. ¹⁴ So the men of Benjamin returned at that time. They were given the women of Jabesh Gilead who had been spared. But there weren't enough women for all of them.

¹⁵ The people were very sad because of what had happened to the tribe of Benjamin. The Lord had left a gap in the tribes of Israel. They weren't complete without Benjamin. ¹⁶ The elders of the community spoke up. They said, "All the women of Benjamin have been wiped out. So how will we find wives for the men who are left? ¹⁷ The men of Benjamin who are still alive need to have children," they said. "If they don't, a tribe of Israel will be wiped out. ¹⁸ But we can't give them our daughters to be their wives. We Israelites have made a promise. We've said, 'May anyone who gives a wife to a man from Benjamin be under the Lord's curse.' ¹⁹ Look, a feast is celebrated every year in Shiloh to honor the Lord. Shiloh is north of Bethel. It's east of the road that goes from Bethel to Shechem. It's south of Lebonah."

²⁰ So they told the men of Benjamin what to do. They said, "Go. Hide in the vineyards ²¹ and watch. The young women of Shiloh will come out. They'll join in the dancing. When they do, run out of the vineyards. Each of you grab a young woman from Shiloh to be your wife. Then return to the land of Benjamin. ²² Their fathers or brothers might not be happy with what we're doing. If they aren't, we'll say to them, 'Do us a favor. Help the men of Benjamin. We didn't get wives for them during the battle. You aren't guilty of doing anything wrong. After all, you didn't give your daughters to them. Your daughters were stolen from you.'"

²³ So that's what the men of Benjamin did. While the young women were dancing, each man caught one. He carried her away to be his wife. Then the men returned to their own share of land. They built the towns again. They made their homes in them.

²⁴ At that time the Israelites also left. They went home to their tribes and family groups. Each one went to his own share of land.

²⁵ In those days Israel didn't have a king. The people did anything they thought was right.

Ruth

Introduction:

This book is named after a woman called Ruth. She was King David's great-grandmother. Ruth's mother-in-law was Naomi. Naomi was from Israel, and Ruth was from Moab.

There wasn't enough food in the land of Israel. Naomi and her family moved to the country of Moab to find food. Naomi's husband died there. Ruth married one of Naomi's sons. Then he died too. Naomi decided to go home, and Ruth went with her.

Back in Israel, Ruth looked for food. God took care of Naomi and Ruth and gave them food. He also gave Ruth a new husband. The book of Ruth teaches us about love. Ruth loved Naomi and stayed with her. God loved Ruth and Naomi and took care of them.

Outline of contents:

Naomi Loses Her Husband and Sons

1 There was a time when Israel didn't have kings to rule over them. But they had leaders to help them. This is a story about some things that happened during that time. There wasn't enough food in the land of Judah. So a man went to live for a while in the country of Moab. He was from Bethlehem in Judah. His wife and two sons went with him. ² The man's name was Elimelek. His wife's name was Naomi. The names of his two sons were Mahlon and Kilion. They were from the tribe of Ephraim. Their home had been in Bethlehem in Judah. They went to Moab and lived there.

³ Naomi's husband Elimelek died. So she was left with her two sons. ⁴ They married women from Moab. One was named Orpah. The other was named Ruth. Naomi's family lived in Moab for about ten years. ⁵ Then Mahlon and Kilion also died. So Naomi was left without her two sons and her husband.

Naomi and Ruth Return to Bethlehem

⁶ While Naomi was in Moab, she heard that the LORD had helped his people. He had begun to provide food for them again. So Naomi and her two daughters-in-law prepared to go from Moab back to her home. ⁷ She left the place where she had been living. Her daughters-in-law went with her. They started out on the road that would take them back to the land of Judah.

[8] Naomi said to her two daughters-in-law, "Both of you go back. Each of you go to your own mother's home. You were kind to your husbands, who have died. You have also been kind to me. So may the LORD be just as kind to you. [9] May the LORD help each of you find rest in the home of another husband."

Then she kissed them goodbye. They broke down and wept loudly. [10] They said to her, "We'll go back to your people with you."

[11] But Naomi said, "Go home, my daughters. Why would you want to come with me? Am I going to have any more sons who could become your husbands? [12] Go home, my daughters. I'm too old to have another husband. Suppose I thought there was still some hope for me. Suppose I married a man tonight. And later I had sons by him. [13] Would you wait until they grew up? Would you stay single until you could marry them? No, my daughters. My life is more bitter than yours. The LORD's power has turned against me!"

[14] When they heard that, they broke down and wept again. Then Orpah kissed her mother-in-law goodbye. But Ruth held on to her.

[15] "Look," said Naomi. "Your sister-in-law is going back to her people and her gods. Go back with her."

[16] But Ruth replied, "Don't try to make me leave you and go back. Where you go I'll go. Where you stay I'll stay. Your people will be my people. Your God will be my God. [17] Where you die I'll die. And there my body will be buried. I won't let even death separate you from me. If I do, may the LORD punish me greatly." [18] Naomi realized that Ruth had made up her mind to go with her. So she stopped trying to make her go back.

[19] The two women continued on their way. At last they arrived in Bethlehem. The whole town was stirred up because of them. The women in the town asked, "Can this possibly be Naomi?"

[20] "Don't call me Naomi," she told them. "Call me Mara. The Mighty One has made my life very bitter. [21] I was full when I went away. But the LORD has brought me back empty. So why are you calling me Naomi? The LORD has made me suffer. The Mighty One has brought trouble on me."

[22] So Naomi returned from Moab. Ruth, her daughter-in-law from Moab, came with her. They arrived in Bethlehem just when people were beginning to harvest the barley.

Ruth Meets Boaz in the Grain Field

2 Naomi had a relative on her husband's side of the family. The relative's name was Boaz. He was a very important man from the family of Elimelek.

[2] Ruth, who was from Moab, spoke to Naomi. Ruth said, "Let me go out to the fields. I'll pick up the grain that has been left. I'll do it behind anyone who is pleased with me."

Naomi said to her, "My daughter, go ahead." ³ So Ruth went out to a field and began to pick up grain. She worked behind those cutting and gathering the grain. As it turned out, she was working in a field that belonged to Boaz. He was from the family of Elimelek.

⁴ Just then Boaz arrived from Bethlehem. He greeted those cutting and gathering the grain. He said, "May the LORD be with you!"

"And may the LORD bless you!" they replied.

⁵ Boaz spoke to the man in charge of his workers. He asked, "Who does that young woman belong to?"

⁶ The man replied, "She's from Moab. She came back from there with Naomi. ⁷ The young woman said, 'Please let me walk behind the workers. Let me pick up the grain that is left.' She came into the field. She has kept on working here from morning until now. She took only one short rest in the shade."

⁸ So Boaz said to Ruth, "Dear woman, listen to me. Don't pick up grain in any other field. Don't go anywhere else. Stay here with the women who work for me. ⁹ Keep your eye on the field where the men are cutting grain. Walk behind the women who are gathering it. Pick up the grain that is left. I've told the men not to bother you. When you are thirsty, go and get a drink. Take water from the jars the men have filled."

¹⁰ When Ruth heard that, she bowed down with her face to the ground. She asked him, "Why are you being so kind to me? In fact, why are you even noticing me? I'm from another country."

¹¹ Boaz replied, "I've been told all about you. I've heard about everything you have done for your mother-in-law since your husband died. I know that you left your father and mother. I know that you left your country. You came to live with people you didn't know before. ¹² May the LORD reward you for what you have done. May the LORD, the God of Israel, bless you richly. You have come to him to find safety under his care."

¹³ "Sir, I hope you will continue to be kind to me," Ruth said. "You have made me feel safe. You have spoken kindly to me. And I'm not even as important as one of your servants!"

¹⁴ When it was time to eat, Boaz spoke to Ruth again. "Come over here," he said. "Have some bread. Dip it in the wine vinegar."

She sat down with the workers. Then Boaz offered her some grain that had been cooked. She ate all she wanted. She even had some left over. ¹⁵ Ruth got up to pick up more grain. Then Boaz gave orders to his men. He said, "Let her take some stalks from what the women have tied up. Don't tell her she can't. ¹⁶ Even pull out some stalks for her. Leave them for her to pick up. Don't tell her she shouldn't do it."

¹⁷ So Ruth picked up grain in the field until evening. Then

she separated the barley from the straw. The barley weighed 30 pounds. [18] She carried it back to town. Her mother-in-law saw how much she had gathered. Ruth also brought out the food left over from the lunch Boaz had given her. She gave it to Naomi.

[19] Her mother-in-law asked her, "Where did you pick up grain today? Where did you work? May the man who noticed you be blessed!"

Then Ruth told her about the man whose field she had worked in. "The name of the man I worked with today is Boaz," she said.

[20] "May the LORD bless him!" Naomi said to her daughter-in-law. "The LORD is still being kind to those who are living and those who are dead." She continued, "That man is a close relative of ours. He's one of our family protectors."

[21] Then Ruth, who was from Moab, said, "He told me more. He even said, 'Stay with my workers until they have finished bringing in all my grain.'"

[22] Naomi replied to her daughter-in-law Ruth. She said, "That will be good for you, my daughter. Go with the women who work for him. You might be harmed if you go to someone else's field."

[23] So Ruth stayed close to the women who worked for Boaz as she picked up grain. She worked until the time when all the barley and wheat had been harvested. And she lived with her mother-in-law.

Ruth and Boaz at the Threshing Floor

3 One day Ruth's mother-in-law Naomi spoke to her. She said, "My daughter, I must find a home for you. It should be a place where you will be provided for. [2] You have been working with the women who work for Boaz. He's a relative of ours. Tonight he'll be separating the straw from his barley on the threshing floor. [3] So wash yourself. Put on some perfume. And put on your best clothes. Then go down to the threshing floor. But don't let Boaz know you are there. Wait until he has finished eating and drinking. [4] Notice where he lies down. Then go over and uncover his feet. Lie down there. He'll tell you what to do."

[5] "I'll do everything you say," Ruth answered. [6] So she went down to the threshing floor. She did everything her mother-in-law had told her to do.

[7] When Boaz had finished eating and drinking, he was in a good mood. He went over to lie down at the far end of the grain pile. Then Ruth approached quietly. She uncovered his feet and lay down there. [8] In the middle of the night, something surprised Boaz and woke him up. He turned and found a woman lying there at his feet!

[9] "Who are you?" he asked.

"I'm Ruth," she said. "You are my family protector. So take good care of me by making me your wife."

[10] "Dear woman, may the

LORD bless you," he replied. "You are showing even more kindness now than you did earlier. You didn't run after the younger men, whether they were rich or poor. [11] Dear woman, don't be afraid. I'll do for you everything you ask. All the people of my town know that you are an excellent woman. [12] It's true that I'm a relative of yours. But there's a family protector who is more closely related to you than I am. [13] So stay here for the night. In the morning if he wants to help you, good. Let him help you. But if he doesn't want to, then I'll do it. You can be sure that the LORD lives. And you can be just as sure that I'll help you. Lie down here until morning."

[14] So she stayed at his feet until morning. But she got up before anyone could be recognized. Boaz thought, "No one must know that a woman came to the threshing floor."

[15] He said to Ruth, "Bring me the coat you have around you. Hold it out." So she did. He poured more than fifty pounds of barley into it and helped her pick it up. Then he went back to town.

[16] Ruth came to her mother-in-law. Naomi asked, "How did it go, my daughter?"

Then Ruth told her everything Boaz had done for her. [17] She said, "He gave me all this barley. He said, 'Don't go back to your mother-in-law with your hands empty.'"

[18] Naomi said, "My daughter, sit down until you find out what happens. The man won't rest until he settles the whole matter today."

Boaz Marries Ruth

4 Boaz went up to the town gate and sat down there. Right then, the family protector he had talked about came by. Then Boaz said, "Come over here, my friend. Sit down." So the man went over and sat down.

[2] Boaz brought ten of the elders of the town together. He said, "Sit down here." So they did. [3] Then he spoke to the family protector. He said, "Naomi has come back from Moab. She's selling the piece of land that belonged to our relative Elimelek. [4] I thought I should bring the matter to your attention. I suggest that you buy the land. Buy it while those sitting here and the elders of my people are looking on as witnesses. If you are willing to buy it back, do it. But if you aren't, tell me. Then I'll know. No one has the right to buy it back except you. And I'm next in line."

"I'll buy it," he said.

[5] Then Boaz said, "When you buy the property from Naomi, you must also marry Ruth. She is from Moab and is the dead man's widow. So you must marry her. That's because his property must continue to belong to his family."

[6] When the family protector heard that, he said, "Then I can't buy the land. If I did, I might put my own property in danger. So you buy it. I can't do it."

[7] In earlier times in Israel,

there was a certain practice. It was used when family land was bought back and changed owners. The practice made the sale final. One person would take his sandal off and give it to the other. That was how people in Israel showed that a business matter had been settled.

⁸ So the family protector said to Boaz, "Buy it yourself." And he took his sandal off.

⁹ Then Boaz said to the elders and all the people, "Today you are witnesses. You have seen that I have bought land from Naomi. I have bought all the property that had belonged to Elimelek, Kilion and Mahlon. ¹⁰ I've also taken Ruth, who is from Moab, to become my wife. She is Mahlon's widow. I've decided to marry her so the dead man's name will stay with his property. Now his name won't disappear from his family line or from his hometown. Today you are witnesses!"

¹¹ Then the elders and all the people at the gate said, "We are witnesses. The woman is coming into your home. May the LORD make her like Rachel and Leah. Together they built up the family of Israel. May you be an important person in Ephrathah. May you be famous in Bethlehem. ¹² The LORD will give you children through this young woman. May your family be like the family of Perez. He was the son Tamar had by Judah."

Naomi Gains a Son

¹³ So Boaz married Ruth. Then he slept with her. The LORD blessed her so that she became pregnant. And she had a son. ¹⁴ The women said to Naomi, "We praise the LORD. Today he has provided a family protector for you. May this child become famous all over Israel! ¹⁵ He will make your life new again. He'll take care of you when you are old. He's the son of your very own daughter-in-law. She loves you. She is better to you than seven sons."

¹⁶ Then Naomi took the child in her arms and took care of him. ¹⁷ The women living there said, "Naomi has a son!" They named him Obed. He was the father of Jesse. Jesse was the father of David.

¹⁸ Here is the family line of Perez.

Perez was the father of Hezron.
¹⁹ Hezron was the father of Ram.
Ram was the father of Amminadab.
²⁰ Amminadab was the father of Nahshon.
Nahshon was the father of Salmon.
²¹ Salmon was the father of Boaz.
Boaz was the father of Obed.
²² Obed was the father of Jesse.
And Jesse was the father of David.

1 Samuel

Introduction:

The book of 1 Samuel tells us about Samuel, Saul and David. Samuel was a man who grew up in God's house and spoke for God. He led Israel for many years.

The people of Israel wanted a king. Samuel, led by God, chose Saul to lead the people. Saul did not obey God, so God rejected him as king. Then God chose David to take Saul's place. David loved God and wanted the things God wanted.

Saul did not want David to be king, so he tried to kill David. But David trusted God to take care of him and protect him.

Outline of contents:

Samuel Is Born

1 A certain man from Ramathaim in the hill country of Ephraim was named Elkanah. He was the son of Jeroham. Jeroham was the son of Elihu. Elihu was the son of Tohu. Tohu was the son of Zuph. Elkanah belonged to the family line of Zuph. Elkanah lived in the territory of Ephraim. ²Elkanah had two wives. One was named Hannah. The other was named Peninnah. Peninnah had children, but Hannah didn't.

³Year after year Elkanah went up from his town to Shiloh. He went there to worship and sacrifice to the Lord who rules over all. Hophni and Phinehas served as priests of the Lord at Shiloh. They were the two sons of Eli. ⁴Every year at Shiloh, the day would come for Elkanah to offer a sacrifice. On that day, he would give a share of the meat to his wife Peninnah. He would also give a share to each of her sons and daughters. ⁵But he would give two shares of meat to Hannah. That's because he loved her. He also gave her two shares because the Lord had kept her from having children. ⁶Peninnah teased Hannah to make her angry. She did it because the Lord had kept Hannah from having children. ⁷Peninnah teased Hannah year after year. Every time Hannah would go up to the house of the Lord, Elkanah's other wife would tease her. She would keep doing it until Hannah cried and wouldn't eat. ⁸Her husband Elkanah would say to her, "Han-

nah, why are you crying? Why don't you eat? Why are you so unhappy? Don't I mean more to you than ten sons?"

⁹ One time when they had finished eating and drinking in Shiloh, Hannah stood up. Eli the priest was sitting on his chair by the doorpost of the LORD's house. ¹⁰ Hannah was very sad. She wept and wept. She prayed to the LORD. ¹¹ She made a promise to him. She said, "LORD, you rule over all. Please see how I'm suffering! Show concern for me! Don't forget about me! Please give me a son! If you do, I'll give him back to the LORD. Then he will serve the LORD all the days of his life. He'll never use a razor on his head. He'll never cut his hair."

¹² As Hannah kept on praying to the LORD, Eli watched her lips. ¹³ She was praying in her heart. Her lips were moving. But she wasn't making a sound. Eli thought Hannah was drunk. ¹⁴ He said to her, "How long are you going to stay drunk? Stop drinking your wine."

¹⁵ "That's not true, sir," Hannah replied. "I'm a woman who is deeply troubled. I haven't been drinking wine or beer. I was telling the LORD all my troubles. ¹⁶ Don't think of me as an evil woman. I've been praying here because I'm very sad. My pain is so great."

¹⁷ Eli answered, "Go in peace. May the God of Israel give you what you have asked him for."

¹⁸ She said, "May you be pleased with me." Then she left and had something to eat. Her face wasn't sad anymore.

¹⁹ Early the next morning Elkanah and his family got up. They worshiped the LORD. Then they went back to their home in Ramah. Elkanah slept with his wife Hannah. And the LORD blessed her. ²⁰ So after some time, Hannah became pregnant. She had a baby boy. She said, "I asked the LORD for him." So she named him Samuel.

Hannah Gives Samuel to the LORD

²¹ Elkanah went up to Shiloh to offer the yearly sacrifice to the LORD. He also went there to keep a promise he had made. His whole family went with him. ²² But Hannah didn't go. She said to her husband, "When the boy doesn't need me to breast-feed him anymore, I'll take him to the LORD's house. I'll give him to the LORD there. He'll stay there for the rest of his life."

²³ Her husband Elkanah told her, "Do what you think is best. Stay here at home until Samuel doesn't need you to breast-feed him anymore. May the LORD make his promise to you come true." So Hannah stayed home. She breast-fed her son until he didn't need her milk anymore.

²⁴ When the boy didn't need her to breast-feed him anymore, she took him with her to Shiloh. She took him there even though he was still very young. She brought him to the LORD's house. She brought along a bull

that was three years old. She brought 36 pounds of flour. She also brought a bottle of wine. The bottle was made out of animal skin. ²⁵ After the bull was sacrificed, Elkanah and Hannah brought the boy to Eli. ²⁶ Hannah said to Eli, "Pardon me, sir. I'm the woman who stood here beside you praying to the LORD. And that's just as sure as you are alive. ²⁷ I prayed for this child. The LORD has given me what I asked him for. ²⁸ So now I'm giving him to the LORD. As long as he lives he'll be given to the LORD." And there Eli worshiped the LORD.

Hannah's Prayer

2 Then Hannah prayed. She said,

"The LORD has filled my
      heart with joy.
He has made me strong.
I can laugh at my enemies.
I'm so glad he saved me.

² "There isn't anyone holy like
      the LORD.
There isn't anyone except
      him.
There isn't any Rock like
      our God.

³ "Don't keep talking so
      proudly.
Don't let your mouth say
      such proud things.
The LORD is a God who
      knows everything.
He judges everything
      people do.

⁴ "The bows of great heroes are
      broken.

But those who trip and fall
      are made strong.
⁵ Those who used to be full
      have to work for food.
But those who used to be
      hungry aren't hungry
      anymore.
The woman who couldn't
      have children has seven
      of them now.
But the woman who has
      had many children is sad
      now because hers have
      died.

⁶ "The LORD causes people to
      die. He also gives people
      life.
He brings people down to
      the grave. He also brings
      people up from death.
⁷ The LORD makes people
      poor. He also makes
      people rich.
He brings people down. He
      also lifts people up.
⁸ He raises poor people up
      from the trash pile.
He lifts needy people out of
      the ashes.
He lets them sit with
      princes.
He gives them places of
      honor.

"The foundations of the earth
      belong to the LORD.
On them he has set the
      world.
⁹ He guards the paths of his
      faithful servants.
But evil people will lie
      silent in their dark
      graves.

"People don't win just
      because they are strong.

¹⁰ Those who oppose the
  LORD will be totally
  destroyed.
The Most High God will
  thunder from heaven.
The LORD will judge the
  earth from one end to
  the other.

"He will give power to his
  king.
He will give honor to his
  anointed one."

¹¹ Then Elkanah went home
to Ramah. But the boy Samuel
served the LORD under the direction of Eli the priest.

Eli's Evil Sons

¹² Eli's sons were good for
nothing. They didn't honor the
LORD. ¹³ When any of the people came to offer a sacrifice,
here is what the priests would
do. While the meat was being
boiled, the servant of the priest
would come with a large fork
in his hand. ¹⁴ He would stick
the fork into the pan or pot or
small or large kettle. Then the
priest would take for himself
everything the fork brought up.
That's how Eli's sons treated all
the Israelites who came to Shiloh. ¹⁵ Even before the fat was
burned, the priest's servant
would come over. He would
speak to the person who was offering the sacrifice. He would
say, "Give the priest some meat
to cook. He won't accept boiled
meat from you. He'll only accept
raw meat."

¹⁶ Sometimes the person
would say to him, "Let the fat
be burned first. Then take what
you want." But the servant
would answer, "No. Hand it over
right now. If you don't, I'll take it
away from you by force."

¹⁷ That sin of Eli's sons was
very great in the LORD's sight.
That's because they were not
treating his offering with respect.

¹⁸ But the boy Samuel served
the LORD. He wore a sacred
linen apron. ¹⁹ Each year his
mother made him a little robe.
She took it to him when she went
up to Shiloh with her husband.
She did it when her husband
went to offer the yearly sacrifice.
²⁰ Eli would bless Elkanah and
his wife. He would say, "May the
LORD give you children by this
woman. May they take the place
of the boy she prayed for and
gave to the LORD." Then they
would go home. ²¹ The LORD was
gracious to Hannah. Over a period of years she had three more
sons and two daughters. During
that whole time the boy Samuel
grew up serving the LORD.

²² Eli was very old. He kept
hearing about everything his
sons were doing to all the Israelites. He also heard how his sons
were sleeping with the women
who served at the entrance to
the tent of meeting. ²³ So Eli said
to his sons, "Why are you doing
these things? All the people are
telling me about the evil things
you are doing. ²⁴ No, my sons.
The report I hear isn't good. And
it's spreading among the LORD's
people. ²⁵ If a person sins against
someone else, God can help

that sinner. But if anyone sins against the LORD, who can help them?" In spite of what their father Eli said, his sons didn't pay any attention to his warning. That's because the LORD had already decided to put them to death.

26 The boy Samuel continued to grow stronger. He also became more and more pleasing to the LORD and to people.

Prophecy Against Eli's Family

27 A man of God came to Eli. He told him, "The LORD says, 'I made myself clearly known to your relatives who lived long ago. I did it when they were in Egypt under Pharaoh's rule. 28 At that time, I chose Aaron from your family line to be my priest. I chose him out of all the tribes of Israel. I told him to go up to my altar. I told him to burn incense. I chose him to wear a linen apron when he served me. I also gave his family all the food offerings presented by the Israelites. 29 Why don't you treat my sacrifices and offerings with respect? I require them to be brought to the house where I live. Why do you honor your sons more than me? Why do you fatten yourselves on the best parts of every offering that is made by my people Israel?'

30 "The LORD is the God of Israel. He announced, 'I promised that members of your family line would serve me as priests forever.' But now the LORD announces, 'I will not let that happen! I will honor those who honor me. But I will turn away from those who look down on me. 31 The time is coming when I will cut your life short. I will also cut short the lives of those in your family line of priests. No one in your family line will grow old. 32 You will see nothing but trouble in the house where I live. Good things will still happen to Israel. But no one in your family line will ever grow old. 33 I will prevent the members of your family from serving me at my altar. I will destroy the eyesight of all of you I allow to live. I will also cause you to lose your strength. And everyone in your family line will die while they are still young.

34 " 'Something is going to happen to your two sons, Hophni and Phinehas. When it does, it will show you that what I am saying is true. They will both die on the same day. 35 I will raise up for myself a faithful priest. He will do what my heart and mind want him to do. I will make his family line of priests very secure. They will always serve as priests to my anointed king. 36 Everyone left in your family line will come and bow down to him. They will beg him for a piece of silver and a loaf of bread. They will say, "Please give me a place to serve among the priests. Then I can have food to eat." ' "

The LORD Calls Out to Samuel

3 The boy Samuel served the LORD under the direction of Eli. In those days the LORD

didn't give many messages to his people. He didn't give them many visions.

² One night Eli was lying down in his usual place. His eyes were becoming so weak he couldn't see very well. ³ Samuel was lying down in the LORD's house. That's where the ark of God was kept. The lamp of God was still burning. ⁴ The LORD called out to Samuel.

Samuel answered, "Here I am." ⁵ He ran over to Eli and said, "Here I am. You called out to me."

But Eli said, "I didn't call you. Go back and lie down." So he went and lay down.

⁶ Again the LORD called out, "Samuel!" Samuel got up and went to Eli. He said, "Here I am. You called out to me."

"My son," Eli said, "I didn't call you. Go back and lie down."

⁷ Samuel didn't know the LORD yet. That's because the LORD still hadn't given him a message.

⁸ The LORD called out for the third time. He said, "Samuel!" Samuel got up and went to Eli. He said, "Here I am. You called out to me."

Then Eli realized that the LORD was calling the boy. ⁹ So Eli told Samuel, "Go and lie down. If someone calls out to you again, say, 'Speak, LORD. I'm listening.'" So Samuel went and lay down in his place.

¹⁰ The LORD came and stood there. He called out, just as he had done the other times. He said, "Samuel! Samuel!"

Then Samuel replied, "Speak. I'm listening."

¹¹ The LORD said to Samuel, "Pay attention! I am about to do something terrible in Israel. It will make the ears of everyone who hears about it tingle. ¹² At that time I will do everything to Eli and his family that I said I would. I will finish what I have started. ¹³ I told Eli I would punish his family forever. He knew his sons were sinning. He knew they were saying bad things about me. In spite of that, he did not stop them. ¹⁴ So I made a promise to the family of Eli. I said, 'The sins of Eli's family will never be paid for by bringing sacrifices or offerings.'"

¹⁵ Samuel lay down until morning. Then he opened the doors of the LORD's house. He was afraid to tell Eli about the vision he had received. ¹⁶ But Eli called out to him. He said, "Samuel, my son."

Samuel answered, "Here I am."

¹⁷ "What did the LORD say to you?" Eli asked. "Don't hide from me anything he told you. If you do, may God punish you greatly." ¹⁸ So Samuel told him everything. He didn't hide anything from him. Then Eli said, "He is the LORD. Let him do what he thinks is best."

¹⁹ As Samuel grew up, the LORD was with him. He made everything Samuel said come true. ²⁰ So all the Israelites recognized that Samuel really was a prophet of the LORD. Everyone from Dan all the way to

Beersheba knew it. ²¹ The LORD continued to appear at Shiloh. There he made himself known to Samuel through the messages he gave him.

4 And Samuel gave those messages to all the Israelites.

The Philistines Capture the Ark

The Israelites went out to fight against the Philistines. The Israelites camped at Ebenezer. The Philistines camped at Aphek. ² The Philistines brought their forces together to fight against Israel. As the fighting spread, the Israelites lost the battle to the Philistines. The Philistines killed about 4,000 of them on the field of battle. ³ The rest of the Israelite soldiers returned to camp. Then the elders asked them, "Why did the LORD let the Philistines win the battle over us today? Let's bring the ark of the LORD's covenant from Shiloh. Let's take it with us. Then the LORD will save us from the power of our enemies."

⁴ So the people sent men to Shiloh. They brought back the ark of the LORD's covenant law. He sits there on his throne between the cherubim. The LORD is the one who rules over all. Eli's two sons, Hophni and Phinehas, were with the ark of God's covenant law. The ark was in Shiloh.

⁵ The ark of the LORD's covenant law was brought into the camp. Then all the Israelites shouted so loudly that the ground shook. ⁶ The Philistines heard the noise. They asked, "What's all that shouting about in the Hebrew camp?"

Then the Philistines found out that the ark of the LORD had come into the camp. ⁷ So they were afraid. "A god has come into their camp," they said. "Oh no! Nothing like this has ever happened before. ⁸ How terrible it will be for us! Who will save us from the power of these mighty gods? They struck down the people of Egypt in the desert. They sent all kinds of plagues on them. ⁹ Philistines, be strong! Fight like men! If you don't, you will come under the control of the Hebrews. You will become their slaves, just as they have been your slaves. Fight like men!"

¹⁰ So the Philistines fought. The Israelites lost the battle, and every man ran back to his tent. A large number of them were killed. Israel lost 30,000 soldiers who were on foot. ¹¹ The ark of God was captured. And Eli's two sons Hophni and Phinehas died.

Eli Dies

¹² That same day a man from the tribe of Benjamin ran from the front lines of the battle. He went to Shiloh. His clothes were torn. He had dust on his head. ¹³ When he arrived, there was Eli sitting on his chair. He was by the side of the road. He was watching because his heart was really concerned about the ark of God. The man entered the town and told everyone what had happened. Then the whole town cried out.

¹⁴Eli heard the people crying out. He asked, "What's the meaning of all this noise?"

The man hurried over to Eli. ¹⁵Eli was 98 years old. His eyes were so bad he couldn't see. ¹⁶The man told Eli, "I've just come from the front lines of the battle. I just ran away from there today."

Eli asked, "What happened, son?"

¹⁷The man who brought the news replied, "Israel ran away from the Philistines. Large numbers of men in the army were wounded or killed. Your two sons Hophni and Phinehas are also dead. And the ark of God has been captured."

¹⁸When the man spoke about the ark of God, Eli fell backward off his chair. He had been sitting by the side of the gate. When he fell, he broke his neck and died. He was old and fat. He had led Israel for 40 years.

¹⁹The wife of Phinehas was pregnant. She was Eli's daughter-in-law. It was near the time for her baby to be born. She heard the news that the ark of God had been captured. She heard that her father-in-law and her husband were dead. So she went into labor and had her baby. Her pain was more than she could bear. ²⁰As she was dying, the women helping her spoke up. They said, "Don't be afraid. You have had a son." But she didn't reply. She didn't pay any attention.

²¹She named the boy Ichabod. She said, "The God of glory has left Israel." She said it because the ark of God had been captured. She also said it because her father-in-law and her husband had died. ²²She said, "The God of glory has left Israel." She said it because the ark of God had been captured.

The Ark in Ashdod and Ekron

5 The Philistines had captured the ark of God. They took it from Ebenezer to Ashdod. ²They carried the ark into the temple of their god Dagon. They set it down beside the statue of Dagon. ³The people of Ashdod got up early the next day. They saw the statue of Dagon. There it was, lying on the ground! It had fallen on its face in front of the ark of the LORD. So they picked up the statue of Dagon. They put it back in its place. ⁴But the following morning when they got up, they saw the statue of Dagon. There it was, lying on the ground again! It had fallen on its face in front of the ark of the LORD. Its head and hands had been broken off. Only the body of the statue was left. Its head and hands were lying in the doorway of the temple. ⁵That's why to this day no one steps on the bottom part of the doorway of Dagon's temple at Ashdod. Not even the priests of Dagon step there.

⁶The LORD's power was against the people of Ashdod and the settlements near it. He destroyed them. He made them suffer with growths in their bodies. ⁷The people of Ashdod

saw what was happening. They said, "The ark of the god of Israel must not stay here with us. His power is against us and against our god Dagon." [8] So they called together all the rulers of the Philistines. They asked them, "What should we do with the ark of the god of Israel?"

The rulers answered, "Have the ark moved to Gath." So they moved it.

[9] But after the people of Ashdod had moved the ark, the LORD's power was against Gath. That threw its people into a great panic. The LORD made them break out with growths in their bodies. It happened to young people and old people alike. [10] So the ark of God was sent to Ekron.

As the ark was entering Ekron, the people of the city cried out. They shouted, "They've brought the ark of the god of Israel to us. They want to kill us and our people." [11] So they called together all the rulers of the Philistines. They said, "Send the ark of the god of Israel away. Let it go back to its own place. If you don't, it will kill us and our people." The death of so many people had filled the city with panic. God's power was against the city. [12] Those who didn't die suffered with growths in their bodies. The people of Ekron cried out to heaven for help.

The Philistines Return the Ark to Israel

6 The ark of the LORD had been in Philistine territory for seven months. [2] The Philistines called for the priests and for those who practice evil magic. They wanted their advice. They said to them, "What should we do with the ark of the LORD? Tell us how we should send it back to its place."

[3] They answered, "If you return the ark of the god of Israel, don't send it back to him without a gift. Be sure you send a guilt offering to their god along with it. Then you will be healed. You will find out why his power has continued to be against you."

[4] The Philistines asked, "What guilt offering should we send to him?"

Their advisers replied, "There are five Philistine rulers. So send five gold rats. Also send five gold models of the growths in your bodies. Do it because the same plague has struck you and your rulers alike. [5] Make models of the rats and the growths that are destroying the country. Give honor to Israel's god. Then perhaps his power will no longer be against you, your gods and your land. [6] Why are you stubborn, as Pharaoh and the people of Egypt were? Israel's god was very hard on them. Only then did they send the Israelites out. Only then did they let them go on their way.

[7] "Now then, get a new cart ready. Get two cows that have just had calves. Be sure the cows have never pulled a cart before. Tie the cart to them. But take their calves away and put them in a pen. [8] Then put the ark of the LORD on the cart. Put the gold

models in a chest beside the ark. Send them back to the LORD as a guilt offering. Send the cart on its way. ⁹ But keep an eye on the cart. See if it goes up toward Beth Shemesh to its own territory. If it does, then it's the LORD who has brought this horrible trouble on us. But if it doesn't, then we'll know it wasn't his hand that struck us. We'll know it happened to us by chance."

¹⁰ So that's what they did. They took the two cows and tied the cart to them. They put the calves in a pen. ¹¹ They placed the ark of the LORD on the cart. They put the chest there along with it. The chest held the gold models of the rats and of the growths. ¹² Then the cows went straight up toward Beth Shemesh. They stayed on the road. They were mooing all the way. They didn't turn to the right or the left. The Philistine rulers followed them all the way to the border of Beth Shemesh.

¹³ The people of Beth Shemesh were working in the valley. They were gathering their wheat crop. They looked up and saw the ark. When they saw it, they were filled with joy. ¹⁴ The cart came to the field of Joshua of Beth Shemesh. It stopped there beside a large rock. The people chopped up the wood the cart was made out of. They sacrificed the cows as a burnt offering to the LORD. ¹⁵ Some Levites had taken the ark of the LORD off the cart. They had also taken off the chest that held the gold models. They placed them on the large rock.

On that day the people of Beth Shemesh offered burnt offerings to the LORD. They also made sacrifices to him. ¹⁶ The five Philistine rulers saw everything that happened. On that same day they returned to Ekron.

¹⁷ The Philistines sent gold models of growths as a guilt offering to the LORD. There was one each for Ashdod, Gaza, Ashkelon, Gath and Ekron. ¹⁸ They also sent five gold models of rats. There was one for each of the Philistine towns that belonged to the five rulers. Each of those towns had high walls around it. The towns also had country villages around them. The Levites set the ark of the LORD on the large rock. To this day the rock is a witness to what happened there. It's in the field of Joshua of Beth Shemesh.

¹⁹ But some of the people of Beth Shemesh looked into the ark of the LORD. So he struck them down. He put 70 of them to death. The rest of the people were filled with sorrow. That's because the LORD had killed so many of them. ²⁰ The people of Beth Shemesh said, "The LORD is a holy God. Who can stand in front of him? Where can the ark go up to from here?"

²¹ Then messengers were sent to the people of Kiriath Jearim. The messengers said, "The Philistines have returned the ark of the LORD. Come down and take it up to your town." **7** ¹ So the men of Kiriath Jearim came and got the ark of the LORD. They brought it up to Abinadab's

house on the hill. They set his son Eleazar apart to guard the ark. ²The ark remained at Kiriath Jearim for a long time. It was there for a full 20 years.

Samuel Brings the Philistines Under Israel's Control

Then all the Israelites turned back to the LORD. ³So Samuel spoke to all the Israelites. He said, "Do you really want to return to the LORD with all your hearts? If you do, get rid of your false gods. Get rid of your statues of female gods that are named Ashtoreth. Commit yourselves to the LORD. Serve him only. Then he will save you from the power of the Philistines." ⁴So the Israelites put away their statues of gods that were named Baal. They put away their statues of female gods that were named Ashtoreth. They served the LORD only.

⁵Then Samuel said, "Gather all the Israelites together at Mizpah. I will pray to the LORD for you." ⁶When the people had come together at Mizpah, they went to the well and got water. They poured it out in front of the LORD. On that day they didn't eat any food. They admitted they had sinned. They said, "We've sinned against the LORD." Samuel was serving as the leader of Israel at Mizpah.

⁷The Philistines heard that Israel had gathered together at Mizpah. So the Philistine rulers came up to attack them. When the Israelites heard about it, they were afraid. ⁸They said to Samuel, "Don't stop crying out to the LORD our God to help us. Keep praying that he'll save us from the power of the Philistines." ⁹Then Samuel got a very young lamb. He sacrificed it as a whole burnt offering to the LORD. He cried out to the LORD to help Israel. And the LORD answered his prayer.

¹⁰The Philistines came near to attack Israel. At that time Samuel was sacrificing the burnt offering. But that day the LORD thundered loudly against the Philistines. He threw them into such a panic that the Israelites were able to chase them away. ¹¹The men of Israel rushed out of Mizpah. They chased the Philistines all the way to a point below Beth Kar. They killed them all along the way.

¹²Then Samuel got a big stone. He set it up between Mizpah and Shen. He named it Ebenezer. He said, "The LORD has helped us every step of the way." ¹³So the Philistines were brought under Israel's control. The Philistines didn't attack their territory again. The LORD used his power against the Philistines as long as Samuel lived. ¹⁴The Philistines had captured many towns between Ekron and Gath. But they had to give all of them back. Israel took back the territories near those towns from the control of the Philistines. During that time Israel and the Amorites were friendly toward each other.

¹⁵Samuel continued to lead Israel all the days of his life.

16 From year to year he traveled from Bethel to Gilgal to Mizpah. He served Israel as judge in all those places. 17 But he always went back to Ramah. That's where his home was. He served Israel as judge there too. And he built an altar there to honor the LORD.

Israel Asks for a King

8 When Samuel became old, he appointed his sons as Israel's leaders. 2 The name of his oldest son was Joel. The name of his second son was Abijah. They served as judges at Beersheba. 3 But his sons didn't live as he did. They were only interested in making money. They accepted money from people who wanted special favors. They made things that were wrong appear to be right.

4 So all the elders of Israel gathered together. They came to Samuel at Ramah. 5 They said to him, "You are old. Your sons don't live as you do. So appoint a king to lead us. We want a king just like the kings all the other nations have."

6 Samuel wasn't pleased when they said, "Give us a king to lead us." So he prayed to the LORD. 7 The LORD told him, "Listen to everything the people are saying to you. You are not the one they have turned their backs on. I am the one they do not want as their king. 8 They are doing just as they have always done. They have deserted me and served other gods. They have done that from the time I brought them up out of Egypt until this day. Now they are deserting you too. 9 Let them have what they want. But give them a strong warning. Let them know what the king who rules over them will expect to be done for him."

10 Samuel told the people who were asking him for a king everything the LORD had said. 11 Samuel told them, "Here's what the king who rules over you will expect to be done for him. He will take your sons. He'll make them serve with his chariots and horses. They will run in front of his chariots. 12 He'll choose some of your sons to be commanders of thousands of men. Some will be commanders of fifties. Others will have to plow his fields and gather his crops. Still others will have to make weapons of war and parts for his chariots. 13 He'll also take your daughters. Some will have to make perfume. Others will be forced to cook and bake. 14 He will take away your best fields and vineyards and olive groves. He'll give them to his attendants. 15 He will take a tenth of your grain and a tenth of your grapes. He'll give it to his officials and attendants. 16 He will also take your male and female servants. He'll take your best cattle and donkeys. He'll use all of them any way he wants to. 17 He will take a tenth of your sheep and goats. You yourselves will become his slaves. 18 When that time comes, you will cry out for help because of the king

you have chosen. But the LORD won't answer you at that time."

¹⁹ In spite of what Samuel said, the people refused to listen to him. "No!" they said. "We want a king to rule over us. ²⁰ Then we'll be like all the other nations. We'll have a king to lead us. He'll go out at the head of our armies and fight our battles."

²¹ Samuel heard everything the people said. He told the LORD about it. ²² The LORD answered, "Listen to them. Give them a king."

Then Samuel said to the Israelites, "Each of you go back to your own town."

Samuel Anoints Saul to Be Israel's King

9 There was a man named Kish from the tribe of Benjamin. Kish was a very important person. He was the son of Abiel, the son of Zeror. Zeror was the son of Bekorath, the son of Aphiah from the tribe of Benjamin. ² Kish had a son named Saul. Saul was a handsome young man. He was more handsome than anyone in Israel. And he was a head taller than anyone else.

³ The donkeys that belonged to Saul's father Kish were lost. So Kish spoke to his son Saul. He said, "Go and look for the donkeys. Take one of the servants with you." ⁴ Saul and his servant went through the hill country of Ephraim. They also went through the area around Shalisha. But they didn't find the donkeys. So they went on

into the area of Shaalim. But the donkeys weren't there either. Then Saul went through the territory of Benjamin. But they still didn't find the donkeys.

⁵ When Saul and the servant with him reached the area of Zuph, Saul spoke to the servant. He said, "Come on. Let's go back. If we don't, my father will stop thinking about the donkeys. Instead, he'll start worrying about us."

⁶ But the servant replied, "There's a man of God here in Ramah. People have a lot of respect for him. Everything he says comes true. So let's go and see him now. Perhaps he'll tell us which way to go."

⁷ Saul said to his servant, "If we go to see the man, what can we give him? There isn't any food in our sacks. We don't have a gift for the man of God. So what can we give him?"

⁸ The servant answered Saul again. "Look," he said. "I've got a tenth of an ounce of silver. I'll give it to the man of God. Then maybe he'll tell us which way to go." ⁹ In Israel, prophets used to be called seers. So if someone wanted to ask God for advice, they would say, "Come on. Let's go to the seer."

¹⁰ Saul said to his servant, "That's a good idea. Come on. Let's go and ask the seer." So they started out for the town where the man of God lived.

¹¹ They were going up the hill toward the town. Along the way they met some young women who were coming out to get wa-

ter from the well. Saul and his servant asked them, "Is the seer here?"

¹² "Yes, he is," they answered. "In fact, he's just up ahead of you. So hurry along. He has just come to our town today. The people are going to offer a sacrifice at the high place where they worship. ¹³ As soon as you enter the town, you will find him. He'll be there until he goes up to the high place to eat. The people won't start eating until he gets there. He must bless the sacrifice first. After that, those who are invited will eat. So go on up. You should find him there just about now."

¹⁴ They went up to the town. As they were entering it, they saw Samuel. He was coming toward them. He was on his way up to the high place.

¹⁵ The LORD had spoken to Samuel the day before Saul came. He had said, ¹⁶ "About this time tomorrow I will send you a man. He is from the land of Benjamin. Anoint him to be the king of my people Israel. He will save them from the power of the Philistines. I have seen how much my people are suffering. Their cry for help has reached me."

¹⁷ When Samuel saw a man coming toward him, the LORD spoke to Samuel again. He said, "He is the man I told you about. His name is Saul. He will govern my people."

¹⁸ Saul approached Samuel at the gate of the town. He asked Samuel, "Can you please show me the seer's house?"

¹⁹ "I'm the seer," Samuel replied. "Go on up to the high place ahead of me. I want you and your servant to eat with me today. Tomorrow morning I'll tell you what's on your mind. Then I'll send you on your way. ²⁰ Don't worry about the donkeys you lost three days ago. They've already been found. But who do all the Israelites want? You and your father's whole family!"

²¹ Saul answered, "But I'm from the tribe of Benjamin. It's the smallest tribe in Israel. And my family group is the least important in the whole tribe of Benjamin. So why are you saying that to me?"

²² Then Samuel brought Saul and his servant into the room where they would be eating. He seated them at the head table. About 30 people had been invited. ²³ Samuel said to the cook, "Bring the piece of meat I gave you. It's the one I told you to put to one side."

²⁴ So the cook went and got a choice piece of thigh. He set it in front of Saul. Samuel said, "Here is what has been kept for you. Eat it. It was put to one side for you for this special occasion. We've saved it for you ever since I invited the guests." And Saul ate with Samuel that day.

²⁵ They came down from the high place to the town. After that, Samuel talked with Saul on the roof of Samuel's house. ²⁶ The next day they got up at about the time the sun was rising. Samuel called out to Saul on the roof. He said, "Get ready.

Then I'll send you on your way." So Saul got ready. And he and Samuel went outside together. [27] As they were on their way down to the edge of town, Samuel spoke to Saul. He said, "Tell the servant to go ahead of us." So the servant went on ahead. Then Samuel continued, "Stay here for a while. I'll give you a message from God."

10 Then Samuel took a bottle of olive oil. He poured it on Saul's head and kissed him. He said, "The LORD has anointed you to be the king of his people. [2] When you leave me today, you will meet two men. They will be near Rachel's tomb at Zelzah on the border of Benjamin. They'll say to you, 'The donkeys you have been looking for have been found. Now your father has stopped thinking about them. Instead, he's worried about you. He's asking, "What can I do to find my son?"'

[3] "You will go on from Zelzah until you come to the large tree at Tabor. Three men will meet you there. They'll be on their way up to Bethel to worship God. One of them will be carrying three young goats. Another will be carrying three loaves of bread. A third will be carrying a bottle of wine. It will be a bottle made out of animal skin. [4] The men will greet you. They'll offer you two loaves of bread. You will accept the loaves from them.

[5] "After that, you will go to Gibeah of God. Some Philistine soldiers are stationed there. As you approach the town, you will meet a group of prophets. They'll be coming down from the high place where they worship. People will be playing lyres, tambourines, flutes and harps at the head of the group. The prophets will be prophesying. [6] The Spirit of the LORD will come powerfully on you. Then you will prophesy along with them. You will become a different person. [7] All these things will happen. Then do what you want to do. God is with you.

[8] "Go down ahead of me to Gilgal. You can be sure that I'll come down to you there. I'll come and sacrifice burnt offerings and friendship offerings. But you must wait there for seven days until I come to you. Then I'll tell you what to do."

Saul Becomes King of Israel

[9] As Saul turned to leave Samuel, God changed Saul's heart. All these things happened that day. [10] When Saul and his servant arrived at Gibeah, a group of prophets met Saul. Then the Spirit of God came powerfully on him. He prophesied along with them. [11] Those who had known Saul before saw him prophesying with the prophets. They asked one another, "What has happened to the son of Kish? Is Saul also one of the prophets?"

[12] A man who lived in Gibeah answered, "Yes, he is. In fact, he's their leader." That's why people say, "Is Saul also one of the prophets?" [13] After Saul

stopped prophesying, he went to the high place to worship.

14 Later, Saul's uncle spoke to him and his servant. He asked, "Where have you been?"

"Looking for the donkeys," Saul said. "But we couldn't find them. So we went to Samuel."

15 Saul's uncle said, "Tell me what Samuel said to you."

16 Saul replied, "He told us the donkeys had been found." But Saul didn't tell his uncle that Samuel had said he would become king.

17 Samuel sent a message to the Israelites. He told them to meet with the Lord at Mizpah. 18 He said to them, "The Lord is the God of Israel. He says, 'Israel, I brought you up out of Egypt. I saved you from their power. I also saved you from the power of all the kingdoms that had treated you badly.' 19 But now you have turned your backs on your God. He saves you out of all your trouble and suffering. In spite of that, you have said, 'We refuse to listen. Place a king over us.' So now gather together to meet with the Lord. Do it tribe by tribe and family group by family group."

20 Then Samuel had each tribe of Israel come forward. The tribe of Benjamin was chosen by casting lots. 21 Next he had the tribe of Benjamin come forward, family group by family group. Matri's group was chosen. Finally Saul, the son of Kish, was chosen. But when people looked for him, they realized he wasn't there. 22 They needed more help

from the Lord. So they asked him, "Has the man come here yet?"

The Lord said, "Yes. He has hidden himself among the supplies."

23 So they ran over there and brought him out. When he stood up, the people saw that he was a head taller than any of them. 24 Samuel spoke to all the people. He said, "Look at the man the Lord has chosen! There isn't anyone like him among all the people."

Then the people shouted, "May the king live a long time!"

25 Samuel explained to the people the rights and duties of the king who ruled over them. He wrote them down in a book. He placed it in front of the Lord in the holy tent. Then he sent the people away. He sent each of them to their own homes.

26 Saul also went to his home in Gibeah. Some brave men whose hearts God had touched went with Saul. 27 But some people who wanted to stir up trouble said, "How can this fellow save us?" They looked down on him. They didn't bring him any gifts. But Saul kept quiet about it.

Saul Rescues the City of Jabesh Gilead

11 Nahash was the king of Ammon. He and his army went up to Jabesh Gilead. They surrounded it and got ready to attack it. All the men of Jabesh spoke to Nahash. They said, "Make a peace treaty with us.

Then we'll be under your control."

² Nahash, the king of Ammon, replied, "I will make a peace treaty with you. But I'll do it only on one condition. You must let me put out the right eye of every one of you. I want to bring shame on the whole nation of Israel."

³ The elders of Jabesh said to him, "Give us seven days to report back to you. We'll send messengers all through Israel. If no one comes to save us, we'll hand ourselves over to you."

⁴ The messengers came to Gibeah of Saul. They reported to the people the terms Nahash had required. Then all the people wept out loud. ⁵ Just then Saul was coming in from the fields. He was walking behind his oxen. He asked, "What's wrong with everyone? Why are they weeping?" He was told what the men of Jabesh had said.

⁶ When Saul heard their words, the Spirit of God came powerfully on him. He became very angry. ⁷ He got a pair of oxen and cut them into pieces. He sent the pieces by messengers all through Israel. They announced, "You must follow Saul and Samuel. If you don't, this is what will happen to your oxen." The terror of the LORD fell on the people. So all of them came together with one purpose in mind. ⁸ Saul brought his army together at Bezek. There were 300,000 men from Israel and 30,000 from Judah.

⁹ The messengers who had come were told, "Go back and report to the men of Jabesh Gilead. Tell them, 'By the hottest time of the day tomorrow, you will be rescued.'" The messengers went and reported it to the men of Jabesh. It made those men very happy. ¹⁰ They said to the people of Ammon, "Tomorrow we'll hand ourselves over to you. Then you can do to us whatever you like."

¹¹ The next day Saul separated his men into three groups. While it was still dark, they broke into the camp of the Ammonite army. They kept killing the men of Ammon until the hottest time of the day. Those who got away were scattered. There weren't two of them left together anywhere.

The People Agree to Have Saul as King

¹² The people said to Samuel, "Who asked, 'Is Saul going to rule over us?' Turn these men over to us. We'll put them to death."

¹³ But Saul said, "No one will be put to death today! After all, this is the day the LORD has rescued Israel."

¹⁴ Then Samuel said to the people, "Come on. Let's go to Gilgal. There we'll agree again to have Saul as our king." ¹⁵ So all the people went to Gilgal. There, with the LORD as witness, they made Saul their king. There they sacrificed friendship offerings to the LORD. And there Saul and all the Israelites celebrated with great joy.

Samuel's Final Speech to Israel

12 Samuel spoke to all the Israelites. He said, "I've done everything you asked me to do. I've placed a king over you. [2] Now you have a king as your leader. But I'm old. My hair is gray. My sons are here with you. I've been your leader from the time I was young until this day. [3] Here I stand. Bring charges against me if you can. The LORD is a witness. And so is his anointed king. Whose ox have I taken? Whose donkey have I taken? Have I cheated anyone? Have I treated anyone badly? Have I accepted money from anyone who wanted special favors? If I've done any of these things, I'll make it right."

[4] "You haven't cheated us," they replied. "You haven't treated us badly. You haven't taken anything from anyone."

[5] Samuel said to them, "The LORD is a witness against you this day. And so is his anointed king. They are witnesses that I haven't taken anything from any of you."

"The LORD is a witness," they said.

[6] Then Samuel said to the people, "The LORD appointed Moses and Aaron. He brought out of Egypt your people who lived long ago. [7] Now then, stand here. I'm going to remind you of all the good things the LORD has done for you and your people. He is a witness.

[8] "After Jacob's family entered Egypt, they cried out to the LORD for help. The LORD sent Moses and Aaron. They brought your people out of Egypt. They had them make their homes in this land.

[9] "But the people forgot the LORD their God. So he put them under the control of Sisera. Sisera was the commander of the army of Hazor. The LORD also put the Israelites under the control of the Philistines and the king of Moab. All those nations fought against Israel. [10] So the people cried out to the LORD. They said, 'We have sinned. We've deserted the LORD. We've served gods that are named Baal. We've served female gods that are named Ashtoreth. But save us now from the power of our enemies. Then we will serve you.' [11] The LORD sent Gideon, Barak, Jephthah and me. He saved you from the power of your enemies who were all around you. So you lived in safety.

[12] "But then you saw that Nahash, the king of Ammon, was about to attack you. So you said to me, 'No! We want a king to rule over us.' You said it even though the LORD your God was your king. [13] Now here is the king you have chosen. He's the one you asked for. The LORD has placed a king over you. [14] But you must have respect for the LORD. You must serve him and obey him. You must not say no to his commands. Both you and the king who rules over you must obey the LORD your God. If you do, that's good. [15] But you must not disobey him. You must not

say no to his commands. If you do, his power will be against you. That's what happened to your people who lived before you.

¹⁶ "So stand still. Watch the great thing the LORD is about to do right here in front of you! ¹⁷ It's time to gather in the wheat, isn't it? I'll call out to the LORD to send thunder and rain. Then you will realize what an evil thing you did in the sight of the LORD. You shouldn't have asked for a king."

¹⁸ Samuel called out to the LORD. That same day the LORD sent thunder and rain. So all the people had great respect for the LORD and for Samuel.

¹⁹ They said to Samuel, "Pray to the LORD your God for us. Pray that we won't die because we asked for a king. That was an evil thing to do. We added it to all our other sins."

²⁰ "Don't be afraid," Samuel replied. "It's true that you have done all these evil things. But don't turn away from the LORD. Serve him with all your heart. ²¹ Don't turn away and worship statues of gods. They are useless. They can't do you any good. They can't save you either. They are completely useless. ²² But the LORD will be true to his great name. He won't turn his back on his people. That's because he was pleased to make you his own people. ²³ I would never sin against the LORD by failing to pray for you. I'll teach you to live in a way that is good and right. ²⁴ But be sure

to have respect for the LORD. Serve him faithfully. Do it with all your heart. Think about the great things he has done for you. ²⁵ But don't be stubborn. Don't continue to do what is evil. If you do, both you and your king will be destroyed."

Samuel Judges Saul's Sin

13 Saul was 30 years old when he became king. He ruled over Israel for 42 years.

² Saul chose 3,000 of Israel's men. Two thousand of them were with him at Mikmash and in the hill country of Bethel. One thousand were with Jonathan at Gibeah in the land of Benjamin. Saul sent the rest back to their homes.

³ Some Philistine soldiers were stationed at Geba. Jonathan attacked them. The other Philistines heard about it. Saul announced, "Let the Hebrew people hear about what has happened!" He had trumpets blown all through the land. ⁴ So all the Israelites heard the news. They were told, "Saul has attacked the Philistine army camp at Geba. Now the Philistines can't stand the Israelites." The Israelites were called out to join Saul at Gilgal.

⁵ The Philistines gathered together to fight against Israel. They had 3,000 chariots and 6,000 chariot drivers. Their soldiers were as many as the grains of sand on the seashore. They went up and camped at Mikmash. It was east of Beth Aven. ⁶ The Israelites saw that

their army was in deep trouble. So they hid in caves. They hid among bushes and rocks. They also hid in pits and empty wells. 7 Some of them even went across the Jordan River. They went to the lands of Gad and Gilead.

Saul remained at Gilgal. All the troops with him were shaking with fear. 8 He waited seven days, just as Samuel had told him to. But Samuel didn't come to Gilgal. And Saul's men began to scatter. 9 So he said, "Bring me the burnt offering and the friendship offerings." Then he offered up the burnt offering. 10 Just as Saul finished offering the sacrifice, Samuel arrived. Saul went out to greet him.

11 "What have you done?" asked Samuel.

Saul replied, "I saw that the men were scattering. I saw that the Philistines were gathering together at Mikmash. You didn't come when you said you would. 12 So I thought, 'Now the Philistines will come down to attack me at Gilgal. And I haven't asked the LORD for his blessing.' So I felt I had to sacrifice the burnt offering."

13 "You have done a foolish thing," Samuel said. "You haven't obeyed the command the LORD your God gave you. If you had, he would have made your kingdom secure over Israel for all time to come. 14 But now your kingdom won't last. The LORD has already looked for a man who is dear to his heart. He has appointed him king of his people. That's because you haven't obeyed the LORD's command."

15 Then Samuel left Gilgal and went up to Gibeah in the land of Benjamin. Saul counted the men who were with him. The total number was about 600.

Israel Doesn't Have Weapons

16 Saul and his son Jonathan were staying in Gibeah in the land of Benjamin. The men who remained in the army were there with them. At the same time, the Philistines camped at Mikmash. 17 Three groups of soldiers went out from the Philistine camp to attack Israel. One group turned and went toward Ophrah in the area of Shual. 18 Another went toward Beth Horon. The third went toward the border that looked out over the Valley of Zeboim. That valley faces the desert.

19 There weren't any blacksmiths in the whole land of Israel. That's because the Philistines had said, "The Hebrews might hire them to make swords or spears!" 20 So all the Israelites had to go down to the Philistines. They had to go to them to get their plows, hoes, axes and sickles sharpened. 21 It cost a fourth of an ounce of silver to sharpen a plow or a hoe. It cost an eighth of an ounce to sharpen a pitchfork or an axe. That's also what it cost to put new tips on the large sticks used to drive oxen.

22 So the Israelite soldiers went out to battle without swords or

spears in their hands. That was true for all of Saul's and Jonathan's soldiers. Only Saul and his son Jonathan had those weapons.

Jonathan Attacks the Philistines

²³ A group of Philistine soldiers had gone out to the pass at Mikmash. ¹ One day Jonathan, the son of Saul, spoke to the young man carrying his armor. "Come on," he said. "Let's go over to the Philistine army camp on the other side of the pass." But he didn't tell his father about it.

² Saul was staying just outside Gibeah. He was under a pomegranate tree in Migron. He had about 600 men with him. ³ Ahijah was one of them. He was wearing a sacred linen apron. He was a son of Ichabod's brother Ahitub. Ahitub was the son of Eli's son Phinehas. Eli had been the LORD's priest in Shiloh. No one was aware that Jonathan had left.

⁴ Jonathan planned to go across the pass to reach the Philistine camp. But there was a cliff on each side of the pass. One cliff was called Bozez. The other was called Seneh. ⁵ One cliff stood on the north side of the pass toward Mikmash. The other stood on the south side toward Geba.

⁶ Jonathan spoke to the young man carrying his armor. He said, "Come on. Let's go over to the camp of those fellows who aren't circumcised. Perhaps the LORD will help us. If he does, it won't matter how many or how few of us there are. That won't keep the LORD from saving us."

⁷ "Go ahead," the young man said. "Do everything you have in mind. I'm with you all the way."

⁸ Jonathan said, "Come on, then. We'll go across the pass toward the Philistines and let them see us. ⁹ Suppose they say to us, 'Wait there until we come to you.' Then we'll stay where we are. We won't go up to them. ¹⁰ But suppose they say, 'Come up to us.' Then we'll climb up. That will show us that the LORD has handed them over to us."

¹¹ So Jonathan and the young man let the soldiers in the Philistine camp see them. "Look!" said the Philistines. "Some of the Hebrews are crawling out of the holes they were hiding in." ¹² The men in the Philistine camp shouted to Jonathan and the young man carrying his armor. They said, "Come on up here. We'll teach you a thing or two."

So Jonathan said to the young man, "Climb up after me. The LORD has handed them over to Israel."

¹³ Using his hands and feet, Jonathan climbed up. The young man was right behind him. Jonathan struck down the Philistines. The young man followed him and killed those who were still alive. ¹⁴ In that first attack, Jonathan and the young man killed about 20 men. They did it in an area of about half an acre.

Israel Chases the Philistines Away

15 Then panic struck the whole Philistine army. It struck those who were in the camp and those in the field. It struck those who were at the edge of the camp. It also struck those who were in the groups that had been sent out to attack Israel. The ground shook. It was a panic that God had sent.

16 Saul's lookouts at Gibeah in the land of Benjamin saw what was happening. They saw the Philistine army melting away in all directions. 17 Then Saul spoke to the men with him. He said, "Bring the troops together. See who has left our camp." When they did, they discovered that Jonathan and the young man carrying his armor weren't there.

18 Saul said to Ahijah the priest, "Bring the ark of God." At that time it was with the Israelites. 19 While Saul was talking to the priest, the noise in the Philistine camp got louder and louder. So Saul said to the priest, "Stop what you are doing."

20 Then Saul and all his men gathered together. They went to the battle. They saw that the Philistines were in total disorder. They were striking one another with their swords. 21 At an earlier time some of the Hebrews had been on the side of the Philistines. They had gone up with them to their camp. But now they changed sides. They joined the Israelites who were with Saul and Jonathan. 22 Some of the Israelites had hidden in the hill country of Ephraim. They heard that the Philistines were running away. They quickly joined the battle and chased after them. 23 So on that day the LORD saved Israel. And the fighting continued on past Beth Aven.

Jonathan Eats Honey

24 The Israelites became very hungry that day. That's because Saul had forced the army to make a promise. He had said, "None of you must eat any food before evening comes. You must not eat until I've paid my enemies back for what they did. If you do, may you be under a curse!" So none of the troops ate any food at all.

25 The whole army entered the woods. There was honey on the ground. 26 When they went into the woods, they saw the honey dripping out of a honeycomb. No one put any of the honey in his mouth. They were afraid of the curse that would come if they broke their promise. 27 But Jonathan hadn't heard that his father had forced the army to make a promise. Jonathan had a long stick in his hand. He reached out and dipped the end of it into the honeycomb. He put some honey in his mouth. It gave him new life. 28 Then one of the soldiers told him, "Your father forced the army to make a promise that everyone must obey. He said, 'None of you must eat any food today. If you do, may you be under a curse!'

That's why the men are weak and ready to faint."

²⁹ Jonathan said, "My father has made trouble for the country. See how I gained new life after I tasted a little of this honey. ³⁰ Our soldiers took food from their enemies today. Suppose they had eaten some of it. How much better off they would have been! Even more Philistines would have been killed."

³¹ That day the Israelites struck down the Philistines. They killed them from Mikmash to Aijalon. By that time they were tired and worn out. ³² They grabbed what they had taken from their enemies. They killed some of the sheep, cattle and calves right there on the ground. They ate the meat while the blood was still in it. ³³ Then someone said to Saul, "Look! The men are sinning against the LORD. They're eating meat that still has blood in it."

Saul said to them, "You have broken your promise. Roll a large stone over here at once." ³⁴ He continued, "Go out among the men. Tell them, 'Each of you bring me your cattle and sheep. Kill them here and eat them. Don't sin against the LORD by eating meat that still has blood in it.'"

So that night everyone brought the ox he had taken and killed it there. ³⁵ Then Saul built an altar to honor the LORD. It was the first time he had done that.

³⁶ Saul said, "Let's go down and chase after the Philistines tonight. Let's not leave even one of them alive. Let's take everything they have before morning."

"Do what you think is best," they replied.

But the priest said, "Let's ask God for advice first."

³⁷ So Saul asked God, "Should I go down and chase after the Philistines? Will you hand them over to Israel?" But God didn't answer him that day.

³⁸ Saul said to the leaders of the army, "Come here. Let's find out what sin has been committed today. ³⁹ The LORD is the one who rescues Israel. You can be sure that the LORD lives. And you can be just as sure that the sinner must die. He must die even if he's my son Jonathan." But no one said anything.

⁴⁰ Then Saul said to all the Israelites, "You stand over there. I and my son Jonathan will stand over here."

"Do what you think is best," they replied.

⁴¹ Then Saul prayed to the LORD, the God of Israel. He said, "Why haven't you answered your servant today? If I or my son Jonathan is to blame, answer with Urim. But if the Israelites are to blame, answer with Thummim." Jonathan and Saul were chosen by casting lots. The other men were cleared of blame. ⁴² Saul said, "Cast the lot to find out whether I or my son Jonathan is to blame." And Jonathan was chosen.

⁴³ Then Saul said to Jonathan, "Tell me what you have done."

So Jonathan told him, "I used

the end of my stick to get a little honey and taste it. And now do I have to die?"

⁴⁴ Saul said, "Jonathan, I must certainly put you to death. If I don't, may God punish me greatly."

⁴⁵ But the men said to Saul, "Should Jonathan be put to death? Never! He has saved Israel in a wonderful way. He did it today with God's help. You can be sure that the LORD lives. And you can be just as sure that not even one hair on Jonathan's head will fall to the ground." So the men rescued Jonathan. He wasn't put to death.

⁴⁶ Then Saul stopped chasing the Philistines. They went back to their own land.

⁴⁷ After Saul became the king of Israel, he fought against Israel's enemies who were all around them. He went to war against Moab, Ammon and Edom. He fought against the kings of Zobah and the Philistines. No matter where he went, he punished his enemies. ⁴⁸ He fought bravely. He won the battle over the Amalekites. He saved Israel from the power of those who had carried off what belonged to Israel.

Saul's Family

⁴⁹ Saul's sons were Jonathan, Ishvi and Malki-Shua. Saul's older daughter was named Merab. His younger daughter was named Michal. ⁵⁰ Saul's wife was named Ahinoam. She was the daughter of Ahimaaz. The commander of Saul's army was named Abner. He was the son of Ner. Ner was Saul's uncle. ⁵¹ Saul's father Kish and Abner's father Ner were sons of Abiel.

⁵² As long as Saul was king, he had to fight hard against the Philistines. So every time Saul saw a strong or brave man, he took him into his army.

The LORD Is Sad That He Made Saul King

15 Samuel said to Saul, "The LORD sent me to anoint you as king over his people Israel. So listen now to a message from him. ² The LORD who rules over all says, 'I will punish the Amalekites because of what they did to Israel. As the Israelites came up from Egypt, the Amalekites attacked them. ³ Now go. Attack the Amalekites. Completely destroy all that belongs to them. Do not spare the Amalekites. Put the men and women to death. Put the children and babies to death. Also kill the cattle, sheep, camels and donkeys.'"

⁴ So Saul brought his men together at Telaim. The total number was 200,000 soldiers on foot from Israel and 10,000 from Judah. ⁵ Saul went to the city of Amalek. Then Saul had some of his men hide and wait in the valley. ⁶ Then Saul said to the Kenites, "You were kind to all the Israelites when they came up out of Egypt. Get away from the Amalekites. Then I won't have to destroy you along with them." So the Kenites moved away from the Amalekites.

7 Saul attacked the Amalekites. He struck them down all the way from Havilah to Shur. Shur was near the eastern border of Egypt. 8 Saul captured Agag, the king of the Amalekites. But he and his men totally destroyed with their swords all Agag's people. 9 So Saul and the army spared Agag. They spared the best of the sheep and cattle. They spared the fat calves and lambs. They spared everything that was valuable. They weren't willing to completely destroy any of those things. But they totally destroyed everything that was worthless and weak.

10 Then the LORD gave Samuel a message. He said, 11 "I am very sad I have made Saul king. He has turned away from me. He has not done what I directed him to do." When Samuel heard that, he was angry. He cried out to the LORD during that whole night.

12 Early the next morning Samuel got up. He went to see Saul. But Samuel was told, "Saul went to Carmel. There he set up a monument in his own honor. Now he has gone on down to Gilgal."

13 When Samuel got there, Saul said, "May the LORD bless you. I've done what he directed me to do."

14 But Samuel said, "Then why do I hear the baaing of sheep? Why do I hear the mooing of cattle?"

15 Saul answered, "The soldiers brought them from the Amalekites. They spared the best of the sheep and cattle. They did it to sacrifice them to the LORD your God. But we totally destroyed everything else."

16 "That's enough!" Samuel said to Saul. "Let me tell you what the LORD said to me last night."

"Tell me," Saul replied.

17 Samuel said, "There was a time when you didn't think you were important. But you became the leader of the tribes of Israel. The LORD anointed you to be king over Israel. 18 He sent you to do something for him. He said, 'Go and completely destroy the Amalekites. Go and destroy those evil people. Fight against them until you have wiped them out.' 19 Why didn't you obey the LORD? Why did you keep for yourselves what you had taken from your enemies? Why did you do what is evil in the sight of the LORD?"

20 "But I did obey the LORD," Saul said. "I went to do what he sent me to do. I completely destroyed the Amalekites. I brought back Agag, their king. 21 The soldiers took sheep and cattle from what had been taken from our enemies. They took the best of what had been set apart to God. They wanted to sacrifice them to the LORD your God at Gilgal."

22 But Samuel replied,

"What pleases the LORD more?
  Burnt offerings and
    sacrifices, or obeying the
    LORD?
It is better to obey than to
  offer a sacrifice.

It is better to do what he
   says than to offer the fat
   of rams.
23 Refusing to obey the LORD
   is as sinful as using evil
   magic.
Being proud is as evil as
   worshiping statues of
   gods.
You have refused to do what
   the LORD told you to do.
So he has refused to have
   you as king."

24 Then Saul said to Samuel, "I have sinned. I've broken the LORD's command. I haven't done what you directed me to do. I was afraid of the men. So I did what they said I should do. 25 Now I beg you, forgive my sin. Come back into town with me so I can worship the LORD."

26 But Samuel said to him, "I won't go back with you. You have refused to do what the LORD told you to do. So he has refused to have you as king over Israel!"

27 Samuel turned to leave. But Saul grabbed the hem of his robe, and it tore. 28 Samuel said to Saul, "The LORD has torn the kingdom of Israel away from you today. He has given it to one of your neighbors. He has given it to someone better than you. 29 The God who is the Glory of Israel does not lie. He doesn't change his mind. That's because he isn't a mere human being. If he were, he might change his mind."

30 Saul replied, "I have sinned. But please honor me in front of the elders of my people and in front of Israel. Come back with me so I can worship the LORD your God." 31 So Samuel went back with Saul. And Saul worshiped the LORD.

32 Then Samuel said, "Bring me Agag, the king of the Amalekites."

Agag was in chains when he came to Samuel. Agag thought, "The time for me to be put to death must have passed by now." 33 But Samuel said,

"Your sword has killed
   the children of other
   women.
   So the child of your mother
     will be killed."

Samuel put Agag to death at Gilgal in front of the LORD.

34 Then Samuel left to go to Ramah. But Saul went up to his home in Gibeah of Saul. 35 Until the day Samuel died, he didn't go to see Saul again. Samuel was filled with sorrow because of Saul. And the LORD was very sad he had made Saul king over Israel.

Samuel Anoints David to Be Israel's King

16 The LORD said to Samuel, "How long will you be filled with sorrow because of Saul? I have refused to have him as king over Israel. Fill your animal horn with olive oil and go on your way. I am sending you to Jesse in Bethlehem. I have chosen one of his sons to be king."

2 But Samuel said, "How can I go? Suppose Saul hears about it. Then he'll kill me."

The LORD said, "Take a young cow with you. Tell the elders of Bethlehem, 'I've come to offer a sacrifice to the LORD.' ³Invite Jesse to the sacrifice. Then I will show you what to do. You must anoint for me the one I point out to you."

⁴Samuel did what the LORD said. He arrived at Bethlehem. The elders of the town met him. They were trembling with fear. They asked, "Have you come in peace?"

⁵Samuel replied, "Yes, I've come in peace. I've come to offer a sacrifice to the LORD. Set yourselves apart to him and come to the sacrifice with me." Then he set Jesse and his sons apart to the LORD. He invited them to the sacrifice.

⁶When they arrived, Samuel saw Eliab. He thought, "This has to be the one the LORD wants me to anoint for him."

⁷But the LORD said to Samuel, "Do not consider how handsome or tall he is. I have not chosen him. The LORD does not look at the things people look at. People look at the outside of a person. But the LORD looks at what is in the heart."

⁸Then Jesse called for Abinadab. He had him walk in front of Samuel. But Samuel said, "The LORD hasn't chosen him either." ⁹Then Jesse had Shammah walk by. But Samuel said, "The LORD hasn't chosen him either." ¹⁰Jesse had seven of his sons walk in front of Samuel. But Samuel said to him, "The LORD hasn't chosen any of them." ¹¹So he asked Jesse, "Are these the only sons you have?"

"No," Jesse answered. "My youngest son is taking care of the sheep."

Samuel said, "Send for him. We won't sit down to eat until he arrives."

¹²So Jesse sent for his son and had him brought in. He looked very healthy. He had a fine appearance and handsome features.

Then the LORD said, "Get up and anoint him. This is the one."

¹³So Samuel got the animal horn that was filled with olive oil. He anointed David in front of his brothers. From that day on, the Spirit of the LORD came powerfully on David. Samuel went back to Ramah.

David Serves Saul

¹⁴The Spirit of the LORD had left Saul. And an evil spirit sent by the LORD terrified him.

¹⁵Saul's attendants said to him, "An evil spirit sent by God is terrifying you. ¹⁶Give us an order to look for someone who can play the harp. He will play it when the evil spirit sent by God comes on you. Then you will feel better."

¹⁷So Saul said to his attendants, "Find someone who plays the harp well. Bring him to me."

¹⁸One of the servants said, "I've seen someone who knows how to play the harp. He is a son of Jesse from Bethlehem. He's a brave man. He would make a good soldier. He's a good speaker. He's very handsome. And the LORD is with him."

¹⁹ Then Saul sent messengers to Jesse. He said, "Send me your son David, the one who takes care of your sheep." ²⁰ So Jesse got some bread and a bottle of wine. The bottle was made out of animal skin. He also got a young goat. He loaded everything on the back of a donkey. He sent all of it to Saul with his son David.

²¹ David went to Saul and began to serve him. Saul liked him very much. David became one of the men who carried Saul's armor. ²² Saul sent a message to Jesse. Saul said, "Let David stay here. I want him to serve me. I'm pleased with him."

²³ When the evil spirit sent by God would come on Saul, David would get his harp and play it. That would help Saul. He would feel better, and the evil spirit would leave him.

David and Goliath

17 The Philistines gathered their army together for war. They came to Sokoh in Judah. They set up camp at Ephes Dammim. It was between Sokoh and Azekah. ² Saul and the army of Israel gathered together. They camped in the Valley of Elah. They lined up their men to fight against the Philistines. ³ The Philistine army was camped on one hill. Israel's army was on another. The valley was between them.

⁴ A mighty hero named Goliath came out of the Philistine camp. He was from Gath. He was more than nine feet tall.

⁵ He had a bronze helmet on his head. He wore bronze armor that weighed 125 pounds. ⁶ On his legs he wore bronze guards. He carried a bronze javelin on his back. ⁷ His spear was as big as a weaver's rod. Its iron point weighed 15 pounds. The man who carried his shield walked along in front of him.

⁸ Goliath stood there and shouted to the soldiers of Israel. He said, "Why do you come out and line up for battle? I'm a Philistine. You are servants of Saul. Choose one of your men. Have him come down and face me. ⁹ If he's able to fight and kill me, we'll become your slaves. But if I win and kill him, you will become our slaves and serve us." ¹⁰ Goliath continued, "This day I dare the soldiers of Israel to send a man down to fight against me." ¹¹ Saul and the whole army of Israel heard what the Philistine said. They were terrified.

¹² David was the son of Jesse, who belonged to the tribe of Ephraim. Jesse was from Bethlehem in Judah. He had eight sons. When Saul was king, Jesse was already very old. ¹³ Jesse's three oldest sons had followed Saul into battle. The oldest son was Eliab. The second was Abinadab. The third was Shammah. ¹⁴ David was the youngest. The three oldest sons followed Saul. ¹⁵ But David went back and forth from Saul's camp to Bethlehem. He went to Bethlehem to take care of his father's sheep.

¹⁶ Every morning and evening

Goliath came forward and stood there. He did it for 40 days.

¹⁷ Jesse said to his son David, "Get at least half a bushel of grain that has been cooked. Also get ten loaves of bread. Take all of it to your brothers. Hurry to their camp. ¹⁸ Take along these ten chunks of cheese to the commander of their military group. Find out how your brothers are doing. Bring me back some word about them. ¹⁹ They are with Saul and all the men of Israel. They are in the Valley of Elah. They are fighting against the Philistines."

²⁰ Early in the morning David left his father's flock in the care of a shepherd. David loaded up the food and started out, just as Jesse had directed. David reached the camp as the army was going out to its battle positions. The soldiers were shouting the war cry. ²¹ The Israelites and the Philistines were lining up their armies for battle. The armies were facing each other. ²² David left what he had brought with the man who took care of the supplies. He ran to the battle lines and asked his brothers how they were. ²³ As David was talking with them, Goliath stepped forward from his line. Goliath was a mighty Philistine hero from Gath. He again dared someone to fight him, and David heard it. ²⁴ Whenever Israel's army saw Goliath, all of them ran away from him. That's because they were so afraid.

²⁵ The Israelites had been saying, "Just look at how this man keeps daring Israel to fight him! The king will make the man who kills Goliath very wealthy. The king will also give his own daughter to be that man's wife. The king won't require anyone in the man's family to pay any taxes in Israel."

²⁶ David spoke to the men standing near him. He asked them, "What will be done for the man who kills this Philistine? Goliath is bringing shame on Israel. What will be done for the one who removes it? This Philistine isn't even circumcised. He dares the armies of the living God to fight him. Who does he think he is?"

²⁷ The men told David what Israel's soldiers had been saying. The men told him what would be done for the man who killed Goliath.

²⁸ David's oldest brother Eliab heard him speaking with the men. So Eliab became very angry with him. Eliab asked David, "Why have you come down here? Who is taking care of those few sheep in the desert for you? I know how proud you are. I know how evil your heart is. The only reason you came down here was to watch the battle."

²⁹ "What have I done now?" said David. "Can't I even speak?" ³⁰ Then he turned away to speak to some other men. He asked them the same question he had asked before. And they gave him the same answer. ³¹ Someone heard what David said and reported it to Saul. So Saul sent for David.

32 David said to Saul, "Don't let anyone lose hope because of that Philistine. I'll go out and fight him."

33 Saul replied, "You aren't able to go out there and fight that Philistine. You are too young. He's been a warrior ever since he was a boy."

34 But David said to Saul, "I've been taking care of my father's sheep. Sometimes a lion or a bear would come and carry off a sheep from the flock. 35 Then I would go after it and hit it. I would save the sheep it was carrying in its mouth. If it turned around to attack me, I would grab its hair. I would strike it down and kill it. 36 In fact, I've killed both a lion and a bear. I'll do the same thing to this Philistine. He isn't even circumcised. He has dared the armies of the living God to fight him. 37 The LORD saved me from the paw of the lion. He saved me from the paw of the bear. And he'll save me from the powerful hand of this Philistine too."

Saul said to David, "Go. And may the LORD be with you."

38 Then Saul dressed David in his own military clothes. He put a coat of armor on him. He put a bronze helmet on his head. 39 David put on Saul's sword over his clothes. He walked around for a while in all that armor because he wasn't used to it.

"I can't go out there in all this armor," he said to Saul. "I'm not used to it." So he took it off. 40 Then David picked up his wooden staff. He went down to a stream and chose five smooth stones. He put them in the pocket of his shepherd's bag. Then he took his sling in his hand and approached Goliath.

41 At that same time, the Philistine kept coming closer to David. The man carrying Goliath's shield walked along in front of him. 42 Goliath looked David over. He saw how young he was. He also saw how healthy and handsome he was. And he hated him. 43 He said to David, "Why are you coming at me with sticks? Do you think I'm only a dog?" The Philistine cursed David in the name of his gods. 44 "Come over here," he said. "I'll feed your body to the birds and wild animals!"

45 David said to Goliath, "You are coming to fight against me with a sword, a spear and a javelin. But I'm coming against you in the name of the LORD who rules over all. He is the God of the armies of Israel. He's the one you have dared to fight against. 46 This day the LORD will give me the victory over you. I'll strike you down. I'll cut your head off. This day I'll feed the bodies of the Philistine army to the birds and wild animals. Then the whole world will know there is a God in Israel. 47 The LORD doesn't rescue people by using a sword or a spear. And everyone here will know it. The battle belongs to the LORD. He will hand all of you over to us."

48 As the Philistine moved closer to attack him, David ran quickly to the battle line to meet

him. ⁴⁹He reached into his bag. He took out a stone. He put it in his sling. He slung it at Goliath. The stone hit him on the forehead and sank into it. He fell to the ground on his face.

⁵⁰So David won the fight against Goliath with a sling and a stone. He struck down the Philistine and killed him. He did it without even using a sword.

⁵¹David ran and stood over him. He picked up Goliath's sword and cut off his head with it.

The Philistines saw that their hero was dead. So they turned around and ran away. ⁵²Then the men of Israel and Judah shouted and rushed forward. They chased the Philistines to the entrance of Gath. They chased them to the gates of Ekron. Bodies of dead Philistines were scattered all along the road to Gath and Ekron. That's the road that leads to Shaaraim. ⁵³Israel's army returned from chasing the Philistines. They had taken everything from the Philistine camp.

⁵⁴David picked up Goliath's head. He brought it to Jerusalem. He put Goliath's weapons in his own tent.

⁵⁵Saul had been watching David as he went out to meet the Philistine. He spoke to Abner, the commander of the army. Saul said to him, "Abner, whose son is that young man?"

Abner replied, "Your Majesty, I don't know. And that's just as sure as you are alive."

⁵⁶The king said, "Find out whose son that young man is."

⁵⁷After David killed Goliath, he returned to the camp. Then Abner brought him to Saul. David was still carrying Goliath's head.

⁵⁸"Young man, whose son are you?" Saul asked him.

David said, "I'm the son of Jesse from Bethlehem."

Saul's Growing Fear of David

18 David finished talking with Saul. After that, Jonathan and David became close friends. Jonathan loved David just as he loved himself. ²From that time on, Saul kept David with him. He didn't let him return home to his family. ³Jonathan made a covenant with David because he loved him just as he loved himself. ⁴Jonathan took off the robe he was wearing and gave it to David. He also gave him his military clothes. He even gave him his sword, his bow and his belt.

⁵David did everything Saul sent him to do. He did it so well that Saul gave him a high rank in the army. That pleased Saul's whole army, including his officers.

⁶After David had killed Goliath, the men of Israel returned home. The women came out of all the towns of Israel to meet King Saul. They danced and sang joyful songs. They played harps and tambourines. ⁷As they danced, they sang,

"Saul has killed thousands of men.
David has killed tens of thousands."

⁸That song made Saul very angry. It really upset him. He said to himself, "They are saying David has killed tens of thousands of men. But they are saying I've killed only thousands. The only thing left for him to get is the kingdom itself." ⁹From that time on, Saul watched David closely.

¹⁰The next day an evil spirit sent by God came powerfully on Saul. Saul began to prophesy in his house. At that same time David began to play the harp, just as he usually did. Saul was holding a spear. ¹¹He threw it at David. As he did, he said to himself, "I'll pin David to the wall." But David got away from him twice.

¹²The LORD had left Saul and was with David. So Saul was afraid of David. ¹³He sent David away. He put him in command of 1,000 men. David led the troops in battle. ¹⁴In everything he did, he was very successful. That's because the LORD was with him. ¹⁵When Saul saw how successful David was, he became afraid of him. ¹⁶But all the troops of Israel and Judah loved David. That's because he led them in battle.

¹⁷Saul said to David, "Here is my older daughter Merab. I'll give her to you to be your wife. Just serve me bravely and fight the LORD's battles." Saul said to himself, "I won't have to lift my hand to strike him down. The Philistines will do that!"

¹⁸But David said to Saul, "Who am I? Is anyone in my whole family that important in Israel? Am I worthy to become the king's son-in-law?" ¹⁹The time came for Saul to give his daughter Merab to David. Instead, Saul gave her to Adriel from Meholah to be his wife.

²⁰Saul's daughter Michal was in love with David. When they told Saul about it, he was pleased. ²¹"I'll give her to David to be his wife," Saul said to himself. "Then maybe she'll trap him. And maybe the Philistines will strike him down." So Saul said to David, "Now you have a second chance to become my son-in-law."

²²Then Saul gave an order to his attendants. He said, "Speak to David in private. Tell him, 'The king likes you. All his attendants love you. So become his son-in-law.'"

²³Saul's attendants spoke those very words to David. But David said, "Do you think it's a small thing to become the king's son-in-law? I'm only a poor man. I'm not very well known."

²⁴Saul's attendants told him what David had said. ²⁵Saul said, "Tell David, 'Here's the price the king wants for the bride. He wants you to kill 100 Philistines. Then bring back the skins you cut off when you circumcise them. That's how Saul will get even with his enemies.'" Saul hoped that the Philistines would strike David down.

²⁶Saul's attendants also told David those things. Then David was pleased to become the king's son-in-law. So before the

wedding day, ²⁷David and his men went out and killed 200 Philistines. They circumcised the Philistines. Then David brought back all the skins. They counted out the full number and gave them to the king. By doing that, David could become the king's son-in-law. So Saul gave David his daughter Michal to be his wife.

²⁸Saul realized that the LORD was with David. He also realized that his daughter Michal loved David. ²⁹So Saul became even more afraid of him. As long as Saul lived, he remained David's enemy.

³⁰The Philistine commanders kept on going out to battle. Every time they did, David had more success against them than the rest of Saul's officers. So his name became well known.

Saul Tries to Kill David

19 Saul told his son Jonathan and all the attendants to kill David. But Jonathan liked David very much. ²So Jonathan warned him, "My father Saul is looking for a chance to kill you. Be very careful tomorrow morning. Find a place to hide and stay there. ³My father and I will come and stand in the field where you are hiding. I'll speak to him about you. Then I'll tell you what I find out."

⁴Jonathan told his father Saul some good things about David. He said to him, "Please don't do anything to harm David. He hasn't done anything to harm you. And what he's done has helped you a lot. ⁵He put his own life in danger when he killed Goliath. The LORD used him to win a great battle for the whole nation of Israel. When you saw it, you were glad. So why would you do anything to harm a man like David? He isn't guilty of doing anything to harm you. Why would you want to kill him without any reason?"

⁶Saul paid attention to Jonathan. Saul made a promise. He said, "You can be sure that the LORD lives. And you can be just as sure that David will not be put to death."

⁷So Jonathan sent for David and told him everything he and Saul had said. Then he brought David to Saul. David served Saul as he had done before.

⁸Once more war broke out. So David went out and fought against the Philistines. He struck them down with so much force that they ran away from him.

⁹But an evil spirit sent by the LORD came on Saul. It happened as he was sitting in his house and holding his spear. While David was playing the harp, ¹⁰Saul tried to pin him to the wall with his spear. But David got away from him just as Saul drove the spear into the wall. That night David escaped.

¹¹Saul sent some men to watch David's house. He told them to kill David the next morning. But David's wife Michal warned him. She said, "You must run for your life tonight. If you don't, tomorrow you will be killed." ¹²So Michal helped David es-

cape through a window. He ran and got away. ¹³Then Michal got a statue of a god. She laid it on David's bed. She covered it with clothes. And she put some goat hair at the place where David's head would have been.

¹⁴Saul sent the men to capture David. But Michal told them, "He's sick."

¹⁵Then Saul sent the men back to see David. He told them, "Bring him up here to me in his bed. Then I'll kill him." ¹⁶But when the men entered, the only thing they found in the bed was the statue. Some goat hair was at the place where David's head would have been.

¹⁷Saul said to Michal, "Why did you trick me like this? Why did you help my enemy escape?"

Michal told him, "He said to me, 'Help me get away. If you don't, I'll kill you.'"

¹⁸After David had run away and escaped, he went to Samuel at Ramah. He told him everything Saul had done to him. Then David and Samuel went to Naioth and stayed there. ¹⁹Saul was told, "David is in Naioth at Ramah." ²⁰So Saul sent some men to capture him. When they got there, they saw a group of prophets who were prophesying. Samuel was standing there as their leader. Then the Spirit of God came on Saul's men. So they also began to prophesy. ²¹Saul was told about it. So he sent some more men. They began to prophesy too. Saul sent some men a third time. And they also began to prophesy.

²²Finally, Saul decided to go to Ramah himself. He went to the large well at Seku. He asked some people, "Where are Samuel and David?"

"Over in Naioth at Ramah," they said.

²³So Saul went to Naioth at Ramah. But the Spirit of God even came on him. He walked along and prophesied until he came to Naioth. ²⁴There he took off his clothes. Then he also prophesied in front of Samuel. He lay there without his clothes on all that day and night. That's why people say, "Is Saul also one of the prophets?"

David and Jonathan

20 David was in Naioth at Ramah. He ran away from there to where Jonathan was. He asked him, "What have I done? What crime have I committed? I haven't done anything to harm your father. So why is he trying to kill me?"

²"That will never happen!" Jonathan replied. "You aren't going to die! My father doesn't do anything at all without letting me know. So why would he hide this from me? He isn't going to kill you!"

³But David strongly disagreed. He said, "Your father knows very well that you are pleased with me. He has said to himself, 'I don't want Jonathan to know I'm planning to kill David. If he finds out, he'll be very sad.' But I'm very close to being killed. And that's just as sure as the LORD and you are alive."

⁴Jonathan said to David, "I'll do anything you want me to do for you."

⁵So David said, "Tomorrow is the time for the New Moon feast. I'm supposed to eat with the king. But let me go and hide in the field. I'll stay there until the evening of the day after tomorrow. ⁶Your father might miss me. If he does, then tell him, 'David begged me to let him hurry home to Bethlehem. A yearly sacrifice is being offered there for his whole family group.' ⁷Your father might say, 'That's all right.' If he does, it will mean I'm safe. But he might become very angry. If he does, you can be sure he's made up his mind to harm me. ⁸Please be kind to me. You have made a covenant with me in front of the LORD. If I'm guilty, kill me yourself! Don't hand me over to your father!"

⁹"I would never do that!" Jonathan said. "Suppose I had even the smallest clue that my father had made up his mind to harm you. Then I would tell you."

¹⁰David asked, "Who will tell me if your father answers you in a mean way?"

¹¹"Come on," Jonathan said. "Let's go out to the field." So they went there together.

¹²Then Jonathan spoke to David. He said, "I promise you that I'll find out what my father is planning to do. I'll find out by this time the day after tomorrow. The LORD, the God of Israel, is my witness. Suppose my father has kind feelings toward you. Then I'll send you a message and let you know. ¹³But suppose he wants to harm you. And I don't let you know about it. Suppose I don't help you get away in peace. Then may the LORD punish me greatly. May he be with you, just as he has been with my father. ¹⁴But always be kind to me, just as the LORD is. Be kind to me as long as I live. Then I won't be killed. ¹⁵And never stop being kind to my family. Don't stop even when the LORD has cut off every one of your enemies from the face of the earth."

¹⁶So Jonathan made a covenant of friendship with David and his family. He said, "May the LORD hold David's enemies responsible for what they've done." ¹⁷Jonathan had David promise his friendship again because he loved him. In fact, Jonathan loved David just as he loved himself.

¹⁸Then Jonathan said to David, "Tomorrow is the time for the New Moon feast. You will be missed, because your seat at the table will be empty. ¹⁹Go to the place where you hid when all this trouble began. Go there the day after tomorrow, when evening is approaching. There's a stone out there called Ezel. ²⁰Wait by it. I'll shoot three arrows to one side of the stone. I'll pretend I'm practicing my shooting. ²¹Then I'll send a boy out there. I'll tell him, 'Go and find the arrows.' Suppose I say to him, 'The arrows are on this side of you. Bring them here.'

Then come. That will mean you are safe. You won't be in any danger. And that's just as sure as the LORD is alive. ²²But suppose I tell the boy, 'The arrows are far beyond you.' Then go. That will mean the LORD is sending you away. ²³And remember what we talked about. Remember that the LORD is a witness between you and me forever."

²⁴So David hid in the field. When the time for the New Moon feast came, the king sat down to eat. ²⁵He sat in his usual place by the wall. Jonathan sat across from him. Abner sat next to Saul. But David's place was empty. ²⁶Saul didn't say anything that day. He said to himself, "Something must have happened to David to make him 'unclean.' That must be why he isn't here." ²⁷But the next day, David's place was empty again. It was the second day of the month. Finally, Saul spoke to his son Jonathan. He said, "Why hasn't the son of Jesse come to the meal? He hasn't been here yesterday or today."

²⁸Jonathan replied, "David begged me to let him go to Bethlehem. ²⁹He said, 'Let me go. Our family is offering a sacrifice in the town. My brother has ordered me to be there. Are you pleased with me? If you are, let me go and see my brothers.' That's why he hasn't come to eat at your table."

³⁰Saul became very angry with Jonathan. He said to him, "You are an evil son. You have refused to obey me. I know that you are on the side of Jesse's son. You should be ashamed of that. And your mother should be ashamed of having a son like you. ³¹You will never be king as long as Jesse's son lives on this earth. And you will never have a kingdom either. So send someone to bring the son of Jesse to me. He must die!"

³²"Why do you want to put him to death?" Jonathan asked his father. "What has he done?" ³³But Saul threw his spear at Jonathan to kill him. Then Jonathan knew that his father wanted to kill David.

³⁴So Jonathan got up from the table. He was very angry. On that second day of the feast, he refused to eat. He was very sad that his father was treating David so badly.

³⁵The next morning Jonathan went out to the field to meet David. He took a young boy with him. ³⁶He said to the boy, "Run and find the arrows I shoot." As the boy ran, Jonathan shot an arrow far beyond him. ³⁷The boy came to the place where Jonathan's arrow had fallen. Then Jonathan shouted to him, "The arrow went far beyond you, didn't it?" ³⁸He continued, "Hurry up! Run fast! Don't stop!" The boy picked up the arrow and returned to his master. ³⁹The boy didn't know what was going on. Only Jonathan and David knew. ⁴⁰Jonathan gave his weapons to the boy. He told him, "Go back to town. Take the weapons with you." ⁴¹After the boy had gone,

David got up from the south side of the stone. He bowed down in front of Jonathan with his face to the ground. He did it three times. Then they kissed each other and cried. But David cried more than Jonathan did.

⁴² Jonathan said to David, "Go in peace. In the name of the LORD we've promised to be friends. We have said, 'The LORD is a witness between you and me. He's a witness between your children and my children forever.'" Then David left, and Jonathan went back to the town.

David at Nob

21 David went to Ahimelek the priest at Nob. Ahimelek trembled with fear when he met him. He asked David, "Why are you alone? Why isn't anyone with you?"

² David answered Ahimelek the priest, "The king gave me a special job to do. He said to me, 'I don't want anyone to know what I'm sending you to do. So don't say anything about it.' I've told my men to meet me at a certain place. ³ Do you have anything for us to eat? Give me five loaves of bread, or anything else you can find."

⁴ But the priest answered David, "I don't have any bread that isn't holy. I only have some holy bread here. But it's for men who haven't slept with women recently."

⁵ David replied, "Well, we haven't slept with women recently. That's the way it is every time I lead my men out to bat-

tle. We keep ourselves holy even when we do jobs that aren't holy. And that's even more true today." ⁶ So the priest gave him the holy bread. It was the only bread he had. It had been removed from the table that was in front of the LORD. On the same day, hot bread had been put in its place.

⁷ One of Saul's servants was there that day. He had been made to stay at the holy tent for a while. He was Doeg from Edom. Doeg was Saul's chief shepherd.

⁸ David asked Ahimelek, "Don't you have a spear or sword here? I haven't brought my sword or any other weapon. That's because the job the king gave me to do had to be done right away."

⁹ The priest replied, "The sword of Goliath, the Philistine, is here. You killed him in the Valley of Elah. His sword is wrapped in a cloth. It's behind the sacred linen apron. If you want it, take it. It's the only sword here."

David said, "There isn't any sword like it. Give it to me."

David at Gath

¹⁰ That day David ran away from Saul. He went to Achish, the king of Gath. ¹¹ But the servants of Achish spoke to him. They said, "Isn't this David, the king of the land? Isn't he the one the Israelites sing about when they dance? They sing,

"'Saul has killed thousands
    of men.
David has killed tens of
    thousands.'"

[12] David paid close attention to what the servants were saying. He became very much afraid of what Achish, the king of Gath, might do. [13] So he pretended to be out of his mind when he was with them. As long as he was in Gath, he acted like a crazy person. He made marks on the doors of the city gate. He let spit run down his beard.

[14] Achish said to his servants, "Just look at the man! He's out of his mind! Why are you bringing him to me? [15] Don't I have enough crazy people around me already? So why do you have to bring this fellow here? Just look at how he's carrying on in front of me! Why do you have to bring this man into my house?"

David at Adullam and Mizpah

22 David left Gath and escaped to the cave of Adullam. His brothers and the other members of his family heard about it. So they went down to join him there. [2] Everyone who was in trouble or owed money or was unhappy gathered around him. He became their commander. About 400 men were with him.

[3] From there David went to Mizpah in Moab. He spoke to the king of Moab. He said, "Please let my father and mother come and stay with you. Let them stay until I learn what God will do for me." [4] So David left his parents with the king of Moab. They stayed with him as long as David was in his usual place of safety.

[5] But the prophet Gad spoke to David. He said, "Don't stay in your usual place of safety. Go into the land of Judah." So David left and went to the forest of Hereth.

Saul Kills the Priests at Nob

[6] Saul heard that the place where David and his men were hiding had been discovered. Saul was sitting under a tamarisk tree on the hill at Gibeah. He was holding his spear. All his officials were standing at his side. [7] Saul said to them, "Men of Benjamin, listen to me! Do you think Jesse's son will give all of you fields and vineyards? Do you think he'll make some of you commanders of thousands of men? Do you think he'll make the rest of you commanders of hundreds? [8] Is that why all of you have joined together against me? No one tells me when my son makes a covenant with Jesse's son. None of you is concerned about me. No one tells me that my son has stirred up Jesse's son to hide and wait to attack me. But that's exactly what's happening now."

[9] Doeg was standing with Saul's officials. He was from Edom. He said, "I saw Jesse's son David come to Ahimelek at Nob. Ahimelek is the son of Ahitub. [10] Ahimelek asked the LORD a question for David. He also gave him food and the sword of Goliath, the Philistine."

[11] Then the king sent for the priest Ahimelek, the son of Ahitub. The king also sent for all the

men in his family. They were the priests at Nob. All of them came to the king. ¹²Saul said, "Son of Ahitub, listen to me."

"Yes, master," he answered.

¹³Saul said to him, "Why have you and Jesse's son joined together against me? Why did you give him bread and a sword? Why did you ask God a question for him? Now he has turned against me. He is hiding and waiting to attack me right now."

¹⁴Ahimelek answered the king, "David is faithful to you. In fact, he's more faithful to you than anyone else who serves you. He's your own son-in-law. He's the captain of your own personal guards. He's highly respected by everyone in your palace. ¹⁵Was that day the first time I asked God a question for him? Of course not! Please don't bring charges against me. Please don't bring charges against anyone in my family. I don't know anything at all about this whole matter."

¹⁶But the king said, "Ahimelek, you will certainly be put to death. You and your whole family will be put to death."

¹⁷Then the king gave an order to the guards at his side. He said, "Go and kill the priests of the LORD. They are on David's side too. They knew he was running away from me. And they didn't even tell me."

But the king's officials wouldn't raise a hand to strike down the priests of the LORD.

¹⁸Then the king ordered Doeg, "You go and strike down the priests." So Doeg, the Edomite, went and struck them down. That day he killed 85 priests who wore linen aprons. ¹⁹He also killed the people of Nob with his sword. Nob was a town where priests lived. Doeg killed its men and women. He killed its children and babies. He also destroyed its cattle, donkeys and sheep.

²⁰But Abiathar, a son of Ahimelek, escaped. Ahimelek was the son of Ahitub. Abiathar ran away and joined David. ²¹He told David that Saul had killed the priests of the LORD. ²²Then David said to Abiathar, "One day I was at Nob. I saw Doeg, the Edomite, there. I knew he would be sure to tell Saul. Your whole family has been killed. And I'm responsible for it. ²³So stay with me. Don't be afraid. The man who wants to kill you wants to kill me too. You will be safe with me."

David Saves the People of Keilah

23 David was told, "The Philistines are fighting against the town of Keilah. They are stealing grain from the threshing floors." ²So he asked the LORD for advice. He said, "Should I go and attack those Philistines?"

The LORD answered him, "Go and attack them. Save Keilah."

³But David's men said to him, "We're afraid here in Judah. Suppose we go to Keilah and fight against the Philistine army. Then we'll be even more afraid."

⁴Once again David asked the LORD what he should do. The LORD answered him, "Go down

to Keilah. I am going to hand the Philistines over to you." [5] So David and his men went to Keilah. They fought against the Philistines and carried off their livestock. David wounded and killed large numbers of Philistines. And he saved the people of Keilah. [6] Abiathar, the son of Ahimelek, had brought down the sacred linen apron with him from Nob. He did it when he ran away to David at Keilah.

Saul Chases David

[7] Saul was told that David had gone to Keilah. He said, "God has handed him over to me. David has trapped himself by entering a town that has gates with metal bars." [8] So Saul brought together all his soldiers to go to battle. He ordered them to go down to Keilah. He told them to surround David and his men. He told them to get ready to attack them.

[9] David learned that Saul was planning to attack him. So he said to Abiathar the priest, "Bring the linen apron." [10] Then David said, "LORD, you are the God of Israel. I know for sure that Saul plans to come to Keilah. He plans to destroy the town because of me. [11] Will the citizens of Keilah hand me over to him? Will Saul come down here, as I've heard he would? LORD, you are the God of Israel. Please answer me."

The LORD said, "He will come down."

[12] Again David asked, "Will the citizens of Keilah hand me and my men over to Saul?"

And the LORD said, "They will." [13] So David and his men left Keilah. The total number of them was about 600. They kept moving from place to place. Saul was told that David had escaped from Keilah. So he didn't go there.

[14] Sometimes David stayed in places of safety in the desert. At other times he stayed in the hills of the Desert of Ziph. Day after day Saul looked for him. But God didn't hand David over to him.

[15] David was at Horesh in the Desert of Ziph. There he learned that Saul had come out to kill him. [16] Saul's son Jonathan went to David at Horesh. He told David that God would make him strong. [17] "Don't be afraid," he said. "My father Saul won't harm you. You will be king over Israel. And I will be next in command. Even my father Saul knows this." [18] The two of them made a covenant of friendship in front of the LORD. Then Jonathan went home. But David remained at Horesh.

[19] The people of Ziph went up to Saul at Gibeah. They said, "David is hiding among us. He's hiding in places of safety at Horesh. Horesh is south of Jeshimon on the hill of Hakilah. [20] Your Majesty, come down when it pleases you to come. It will be our duty to hand David over to you."

[21] Saul replied, "May the LORD bless you because you were concerned about me. [22] Make sure you are right. Go and check

things out again. Find out where David usually goes. Find out who has seen him there. People tell me he's very tricky. ²³ Find out about all the hiding places he uses. Come back to me with all the facts. I'll go with you. Suppose he's in the area. Then I'll track him down among all the family groups of Judah."

²⁴ So they started out. They went to Ziph ahead of Saul. David and his men were in the Desert of Maon. Maon is south of Jeshimon in the Arabah Valley. ²⁵ Saul and his men started out to look for David. David was told about it. So he went down to a rock in the Desert of Maon to hide. Saul heard he was there. So he went into the Desert of Maon to chase David.

²⁶ Saul was going along one side of the mountain. David and his men were on the other side. They were hurrying to get away from Saul. Saul and his army were closing in on David and his men. They were about to capture them. ²⁷ Just then a messenger came to Saul. He said, "Come quickly! The Philistines are attacking the land." ²⁸ So Saul stopped chasing David. He went to fight against the Philistines. That's why they call that place Sela Hammahlekoth. ²⁹ David left that place. He went and lived in places of safety near En Gedi.

David Doesn't Kill Saul When He Has the Chance

24 Saul returned from chasing the Philistines. Then he was told, "David is in the Desert of En Gedi." ² So Saul took 3,000 of the best soldiers from the whole nation of Israel. He started out to look for David and his men. He planned to look near the Rocky Cliffs of the Wild Goats.

³ He came to some sheep pens along the way. A cave was there. Saul went in to go to the toilet. David and his men were far back in the cave. ⁴ David's men said, "This is the day the LORD told you about. He said to you, 'I will hand your enemy over to you. Then you can deal with him as you want to.'" So David came up close to Saul without being seen. He cut off a corner of Saul's robe.

⁵ Later, David felt sorry that he had cut off a corner of Saul's robe. ⁶ He said to his men, "May the LORD keep me from doing a thing like that again to my master. He is the LORD's anointed king. So I promise that I will never lay my hand on him. The LORD has anointed him." ⁷ David said that to correct his men. He wanted them to know that they should never suggest harming the king. He didn't allow them to attack Saul. So Saul left the cave and went on his way.

⁸ Then David went out of the cave. He called out to Saul, "King Saul! My master!" When Saul looked behind him, David bowed down. He lay down flat with his face toward the ground. ⁹ He said to Saul, "Why do you listen when men say, 'David is trying to harm you'? ¹⁰ This day you have seen with your own

eyes how the Lord handed you over to me in the cave. Some of my men begged me to kill you. But I didn't. I said, 'I will never lay my hand on my master. He is the Lord's anointed king.' ¹¹Look, my father! Look at this piece of your robe in my hand! I cut off the corner of your robe. But I didn't kill you. See, there is nothing in my hand that shows I am guilty of doing anything wrong. I haven't turned against you. I haven't done anything to harm you. But you are hunting me down. You want to kill me. ¹²May the Lord judge between you and me. And may the Lord pay you back because of the wrong things you have done to me. But I won't do anything to hurt you. ¹³People say, 'Evil acts come from those who do evil.' So I won't do anything to hurt you.

¹⁴"King Saul, who are you trying to catch? Who do you think you are chasing? I'm nothing but a dead dog or a flea! ¹⁵May the Lord be our judge. May he decide between us. May he consider my case and stand up for me. May he show that I'm not guilty of doing anything wrong. May he save me from you."

¹⁶When David finished speaking, Saul asked him a question. He said, "My son David, is that your voice?" And Saul wept out loud. ¹⁷"You are a better person than I am," he said. "You have treated me well. But I've treated you badly. ¹⁸You have just now told me about the good things you did to me. The Lord handed me over to you. But you didn't kill me. ¹⁹Suppose a man finds his enemy. He doesn't let him get away without harming him. May the Lord reward you with many good things. May he do it because of the way you treated me today. ²⁰I know for sure that you will be king. I know that the kingdom of Israel will be made secure under your control. ²¹Now make a promise in the name of the Lord. Promise me that you won't kill the children of my family. Also promise me that you won't wipe out my name from my family line."

²²So David made that promise to Saul. Then Saul returned home. But David and his men went up to his usual place of safety.

David, Nabal and Abigail

25 When Samuel died, the whole nation of Israel gathered together. They were filled with sorrow because he was dead. They buried him at his home in Ramah. Then David went down into the Desert of Paran.

²A certain man in Maon was very wealthy. He owned property there at Carmel. He had 1,000 goats and 3,000 sheep. He was clipping the wool off the sheep in Carmel. ³His name was Nabal. His wife's name was Abigail. She was a wise and beautiful woman. But her husband was rude and mean in the way he treated others. He was from the family of Caleb.

⁴David was staying in the

Desert of Paran. While he was there, he heard that Nabal was clipping the wool off his sheep. ⁵ So he sent for ten young men. He said to them, "Go up to Nabal at Carmel. Greet him for me. ⁶ Say to him, 'May you live a long time! May everything go well with you and your family! And may things go well with everything that belongs to you!

⁷ " 'I hear that you are clipping the wool off your sheep. When your shepherds were with us, we treated them well. The whole time they were at Carmel nothing that belonged to them was stolen. ⁸ Ask your own servants. They'll tell you. We've come to you now at a happy time of the year. Please be kind to my men. Please give me and my men anything you can find for us.' "

⁹ When David's men arrived, they gave Nabal the message from David. Then they waited.

¹⁰ Nabal answered David's servants, "Who is this David? Who is this son of Jesse? Many servants are running away from their masters these days. ¹¹ Why should I give away my bread and water? Why should I give away the meat I've prepared for those who clip the wool off my sheep? Why should I give food to men who come from who knows where?"

¹² So David's men turned around and went back. When they arrived, they reported to David every word Nabal had spoken. ¹³ David said to his men, "Each of you put on your swords!" So they did. David put his sword on too. About 400 men went up with David. Two hundred men stayed behind with the supplies.

¹⁴ One of the servants warned Abigail, Nabal's wife. He said, "David sent some messengers from the desert to give his greetings to our master. But Nabal shouted at them and was rude to them. ¹⁵ David's men had been very good to us. They treated us well. The whole time we were near them out in the fields, nothing was stolen. ¹⁶ We were taking care of our sheep near them. During that time, they were like a wall around us night and day. They kept us safe. ¹⁷ Now think it over. See what you can do. Horrible trouble will soon come to our master and his whole family. He's such an evil man that no one can even talk to him."

¹⁸ Abigail didn't waste any time. She got 200 loaves of bread and two bottles of wine. The bottles were made out of animal skins. She got five sheep that were ready to be cooked. She got a bushel of grain that had been cooked. She got 100 raisin cakes. And she got 200 cakes of pressed figs. She loaded all of it on the backs of donkeys. ¹⁹ Then she told her servants, "Go on ahead. I'll follow you." But she didn't tell her husband Nabal about it.

²⁰ Abigail rode her donkey into a mountain valley. There she saw David and his men. They were coming down toward her. ²¹ David had just said,

"Everything we've done hasn't been worth a thing! I watched over that fellow's property in the desert. I made sure none of it was stolen. But he has paid me back evil for good. [22] I won't leave even one of his men alive until morning. If I do, may God punish me greatly!"

[23] When Abigail saw David, she quickly got off her donkey. She bowed down in front of David with her face toward the ground. [24] She fell at his feet. She said, "Pardon your servant, sir. Please let me speak to you. Listen to what I'm saying. Let me take the blame myself. [25] Please don't pay any attention to that evil man Nabal. His name means Foolish Person. And that's exactly what he is. He's always doing foolish things. I'm sorry I didn't get a chance to see the men you sent. [26] Sir, the LORD has kept you from killing Nabal and his men. He has kept you from using your own hands to get even. So may what's about to happen to Nabal happen to all your enemies. May it happen to everyone who wants to harm you. And may it happen just as surely as the LORD your God and you are alive. [27] I've brought a gift for you. Give it to the men who follow you.

[28] "Please forgive me if I shouldn't have done that. The LORD your God will certainly give you and your family line a kingdom that will last. That's because you fight the LORD's battles. You won't do anything wrong as long as you live.

[29] Someone may chase you and try to kill you. But the LORD your God will keep your life safe like a treasure hidden in a bag. And he'll destroy your enemies. Their lives will be thrown away, just as a stone is thrown from a sling. [30] The LORD will do for you every good thing he promised to do. He'll appoint you ruler over Israel. [31] When that happens, you won't have this heavy load on your mind. You won't have to worry about how you killed people without any reason. You won't have to worry about how you got even. The LORD your God will give you success. When that happens, please remember me."

[32] David said to Abigail, "Give praise to the LORD. He is the God of Israel. He has sent you today to find me. [33] May the LORD bless you for what you have done. You have shown a lot of good sense. You have kept me from killing Nabal and his men this day. You have kept me from using my own hands to get even. [34] It's a good thing you came quickly to meet me. If you hadn't come, not one of Nabal's men would have been left alive by sunrise. And that's just as sure as the LORD, the God of Israel, is alive. He has kept me from harming you."

[35] Then David accepted from her what she had brought him. He said, "Go home in peace. I've heard your words. I'll do what you have asked."

[36] Abigail went back to Nabal. He was having a dinner party

in the house. It was the kind of dinner a king would have. He had been drinking too much wine. He was very drunk. So she didn't tell him anything at all until sunrise. ³⁷ The next morning Nabal wasn't drunk anymore. Then his wife told him everything. When she did, his heart grew weak. He became like a stone. ³⁸ About ten days later, the LORD struck Nabal down. And he died.

³⁹ David heard that Nabal was dead. So he said, "Give praise to the LORD. Nabal was rude to me. But the LORD stood up for me. He has kept me from doing something wrong. He has paid Nabal back for the wrong things he did."

Then David sent a message to Abigail. He asked her to become his wife. ⁴⁰ His servants went to Carmel. They said to Abigail, "David has sent us to you. He wants you to come back with us and become his wife."

⁴¹ Abigail bowed down with her face toward the ground. She said, "I am your servant. I'm ready to serve him. I'm ready to wash the feet of his servants." ⁴² Abigail quickly got on a donkey and went with David's messengers. Her five female servants went with her. She became David's wife. ⁴³ David had also married Ahinoam from Jezreel. Both of them became his wives. ⁴⁴ But Saul had given his daughter Michal, David's first wife, to Paltiel. Paltiel was from Gallim. He was the son of Laish.

Once Again David Doesn't Kill Saul When He Has the Chance

26 Some people from Ziph went to Saul at Gibeah. They said, "David is hiding on the hill of Hakilah. It faces Jeshimon."

² So Saul went down to the Desert of Ziph. He took 3,000 of the best soldiers in Israel with him. They went to the desert to look for David. ³ Saul set up his camp beside the road. It was on the hill of Hakilah facing Jeshimon. But David stayed in the desert. He saw that Saul had followed him there. ⁴ So he sent out scouts. From them he learned that Saul had arrived.

⁵ Then David started out. He went to the place where Saul had camped. He saw where Saul and Abner were lying down. Saul was lying inside the camp. The army was camped all around him. Abner was commander of the army. He was the son of Ner. ⁶ Then David spoke to Ahimelek, the Hittite. He also spoke to Joab's brother Abishai, the son of Zeruiah. He asked them, "Who will go down with me into the camp to Saul?"

"I'll go with you," said Abishai. ⁷ So that night David and Abishai went into the camp. They found Saul lying asleep inside the camp. His spear was stuck in the ground near his head. Abner and the soldiers were lying asleep around him.

⁸ Abishai said to David, "Today God has handed your enemy over to you. So let me pin him to the ground. I can do it

with one jab of the spear. I won't even have to strike him twice."

9 But David said to Abishai, "Don't destroy him! No one can do any harm to the LORD's anointed king and not be guilty. 10 You can be sure that the LORD lives," he said. "And you can be just as sure that the LORD himself will strike Saul down. Perhaps he'll die a natural death. Or perhaps he'll go into battle and be killed. 11 May the LORD keep me from doing anything to harm his anointed king. Now get the spear and water jug that are near his head. Then let's leave."

12 So David took the spear and water jug that were near Saul's head. Then he and Abishai left. No one saw them. No one knew about what they had done. In fact, no one even woke up. Everyone was sleeping. That's because the LORD had put them into a deep sleep.

13 David went across to the other side of the valley. He stood on top of a hill far away from Saul's camp. There was a wide space between them. 14 He called out to the army and to Abner, the son of Ner. He said, "Abner! Aren't you going to answer me?"

Abner replied, "Who is calling out to the king?"

15 David said, "You are a great soldier, aren't you? There isn't anyone else like you in Israel. So why didn't you guard the king? He's your master, isn't he? Someone came into the camp to destroy him. 16 You didn't guard him. And that isn't good. You can be sure that the LORD lives. And you can be just as sure that you and your men must die. That's because you didn't guard your master. He's the LORD's anointed king. Look around you. Where are the king's spear and water jug that were near his head?"

17 Saul recognized David's voice. He said, "My son David, is that your voice?"

David replied, "Yes it is, King Saul, my master." 18 He continued, "Why are you chasing me? What evil thing have I done? What am I guilty of? 19 King Saul, please listen to what I'm saying. Was it the LORD who made you angry with me? If it was, may he accept my offering. Was it people who made you angry at me? If it was, may the LORD see them cursed. They have driven me today from my share of the LORD's land. By doing that, they might as well have said, 'Go and serve other gods.' 20 Don't spill my blood on the ground far away from where the LORD lives. King Saul, you have come out to look for nothing but a flea. It's as if you were hunting a partridge in the mountains."

21 Then Saul said, "I have sinned. My son David, come back. Today you thought my life was very special. So I won't try to harm you again. I've really acted like a foolish person. I've made a huge mistake."

22 "Here's your spear," David answered. "Send one of your young men over to get

it. 23 The LORD rewards everyone for doing what is right and being faithful. He handed you over to me today. But I wouldn't harm you. You are the LORD's anointed king. 24 Today I thought your life had great value. In the same way, may the LORD think of my life as having great value. May he save me from all trouble."

25 Then Saul said to David, "May the LORD bless you, David my son. You will do great things. You will also have great success."

So David went on his way. And Saul returned home.

David Among the Philistines

27 David thought, "Some day Saul will destroy me. So the best thing I can do is escape. I'll go to the land of the Philistines. Then Saul will stop looking for me everywhere in Israel. His hand won't be able to reach me."

2 So David and his 600 men left Israel. They went to Achish, the king of Gath. He was the son of Maok. 3 David and his men made their homes in Gath near Achish. Each of David's men had his family with him. David had his two wives with him. They were Ahinoam from Jezreel and Abigail from Carmel. Abigail was Nabal's widow. 4 Saul was told that David had run away to Gath. So he didn't look for David anymore.

5 David said to Achish, "If you are pleased with me, give me a place in one of your country towns. I can live there. I don't really need to live near you in the royal city."

6 So on that day Achish gave David the town of Ziklag. It has belonged to the kings of Judah ever since that time. 7 David lived in Philistine territory for a year and four months.

8 Sometimes David and his men would go up and attack the Geshurites. At other times they would attack the Girzites or the Amalekites. All those people had lived in the land that reached all the way to Shur and Egypt. They had been there for a long time. 9 When David would attack an area, he wouldn't leave a man or woman alive. But he would take their sheep, cattle, donkeys, camels and clothes. Then he would return to Achish.

10 Achish would ask, "Who did you attack today?" David would answer, "The people who live in the Negev Desert of Judah." Or he would answer, "The people in the Negev Desert of Jerahmeel." Or he would answer, "The people in the Negev Desert of the Kenites." 11 David wouldn't leave a man or woman alive to be brought back to Gath. He thought, "They might tell on us. They might tell Achish who we really attacked." That's what David did as long as he lived in Philistine territory. 12 Achish trusted David. He thought, "David's own people, the Israelites, can't stand him anymore. So he'll be my servant for life."

28

While David was living in Ziklag, the Philistines gathered their army together. They planned to fight against Israel. Achish said to David, "Here is what you must understand. You and your men must march out with me and my army."

² David said, "I understand. You will see for yourself what I can do."

Achish replied, "All right. I'll make you my own personal guard for life."

Saul and the Woman at Endor

³ Samuel had died. The whole nation of Israel was filled with sorrow because he was dead. They had buried him in his own town of Ramah. Saul had thrown out of the land people who get messages from those who have died. He had also thrown out people who talk to the spirits of the dead. ⁴ The Philistines gathered together and set up camp at Shunem. At the same time, Saul gathered together all the Israelites. They set up camp at Gilboa. ⁵ When Saul saw the Philistine army, he was afraid. Terror filled his heart. ⁶ He asked the LORD for advice. But the LORD didn't answer him through dreams or prophets. He didn't answer him when Saul had the priest cast lots by using the Urim. ⁷ Saul spoke to his attendants. He said, "Find me a woman who gets messages from those who have died. Then I can go and ask her some questions."

"There's a woman like that in Endor," they said.

⁸ Saul put on different clothes so people wouldn't know who he was. At night he and two of his men went to see the woman. "I want you to talk to a spirit for me," he said. "Bring up the spirit of the dead person I choose."

⁹ But the woman said to him, "By now you must know what Saul has done. He has removed everyone who gets messages from those who have died. He has also removed everyone who talks to the spirits of the dead. He has thrown all of them out of the land. Why are you trying to trap me? Why do you want to have me put to death?"

¹⁰ Saul made a promise in the name of the LORD. He said to the woman, "You can be sure that the LORD lives. And you can be just as sure that you won't be punished for helping me."

¹¹ Then the woman asked, "Whose spirit should I bring up for you?"

"Bring Samuel up," he said.

¹² When the woman saw Samuel, she let out a loud scream. She said to Saul, "Why have you tricked me? You are King Saul!"

¹³ He said to her, "Don't be afraid. Tell me what you see."

The woman said, "I see a ghostly figure. He's coming up out of the earth."

¹⁴ "What does he look like?" Saul asked.

"An old man wearing a robe is coming up," she said.

Then Saul knew it was Samuel. He bowed down. He lay

down flat with his face toward the ground.

¹⁵ Samuel said to Saul, "Why have you troubled me by bringing me up from the dead?"

"I'm having big problems," Saul said. "The Philistines are fighting against me. God has left me. He doesn't answer me anymore. He doesn't speak to me through prophets or dreams. So I've called on you to tell me what to do."

¹⁶ Samuel said, "The LORD has left you. He has become your enemy. So why are you asking me what you should do? ¹⁷ The LORD has spoken through me and has done what he said he would do. The LORD has torn the kingdom out of your hands. He has given it to one of your neighbors. He has given it to David. ¹⁸ You didn't obey the LORD. You didn't show his great anger against the Amalekites by destroying them. So he's punishing you today. ¹⁹ He will hand both Israel and you over to the Philistines. Tomorrow you and your sons will be down here with me. The LORD will also hand Israel's army over to the Philistines."

²⁰ Immediately Saul fell flat on the ground. What Samuel had said filled Saul with fear. His strength was gone. He hadn't eaten anything all that day and all that night.

²¹ The woman went over to Saul because she saw that he was very upset. She said, "Look, I've obeyed you. I put my own life in danger by doing what you told me to do. ²² So please lis-ten to me. Let me give you some food. Eat it. Then you will have the strength to go on your way."

²³ But he refused. He said, "I don't want anything to eat."

Then his men joined the woman in begging him to eat. Finally, he paid attention to them. He got up from the ground and sat on a couch.

²⁴ The woman had a fat calf at her house. She killed it at once. She got some flour. She mixed it and baked some bread that didn't have any yeast in it. ²⁵ Then she set the food in front of Saul and his men. They ate it. That same night they got up and left.

Achish Sends David Back to Ziklag

29 The Philistines gathered their whole army together at Aphek. Israel's army camped by the spring of water at Jezreel. ² The Philistine rulers marched out in groups of hundreds and thousands. David and his men were marching with Achish behind the others. ³ The commanders of the Philistines asked, "Why are these Hebrews here?"

Achish replied, "That's David, isn't it? Wasn't he an officer of Saul, the king of Israel? He has already been with me for more than a year. I haven't found any fault in him. That's been true from the day he left Saul until now."

⁴ But the Philistine commanders were angry with Achish. They said, "Send Da-

vid back. Let him return to the town you gave him. He must not go with us into battle. If he does, he'll turn against us during the fighting. In fact, he might even cut off the heads of our own men. What better way could he choose to win back his master's favor? ⁵ Isn't David the one the Israelites sang about when they danced? They sang,

> " 'Saul has killed thousands of men.
> David has killed tens of thousands.' "

⁶ So Achish called David over to him. He said, "You have been faithful to me. And that's just as sure as the LORD is alive. I would be pleased to have you serve with me in the army. I haven't found any fault in you. That's been true from the day you came to me until today. But the Philistine rulers aren't pleased to have you come along. ⁷ So now go back home in peace. Don't do anything that wouldn't please the Philistine rulers."

⁸ "But what have I done?" asked David. "What have you found against me from the day I came to you until now? Why can't I go and fight against your enemies? After all, you are my king and master."

⁹ Achish answered, "You have been as pleasing to me as an angel of God. But the Philistine commanders have said, 'We don't want David to go up with us into battle.' ¹⁰ So get up early in the morning. Take with you the men who used to serve Saul.

Leave as soon as the sun begins to come up."

¹¹ So David and his men got up early in the morning. They went back to the land of the Philistines. And the Philistines went up to Jezreel.

David Destroys the Amalekites

30 On the third day David and his men arrived in Ziklag. The Amalekites had attacked the people of the Negev Desert. They had also attacked Ziklag and burned it. ² They had captured the women and everyone else in Ziklag. They had taken as prisoners young people and old people alike. But they didn't kill any of them. Instead, they carried them off as they went on their way.

³ David and his men reached Ziklag. They saw that it had been destroyed by fire. They found out that their wives and sons and daughters had been captured. ⁴ So David and his men began to weep out loud. They wept until they couldn't weep anymore. ⁵ David's two wives had been captured. Their names were Ahinoam from Jezreel and Abigail from Carmel. Abigail was Nabal's widow. ⁶ David was greatly troubled. His men were even talking about killing him by throwing stones at him. All of them were very bitter because their sons and daughters had been taken away. But David was made strong by the LORD his God.

⁷ Then David spoke to Abiathar the priest, the son of Ahimelek.

He said, "Bring me the linen apron." Abiathar brought it to him. ⁸ David asked the Lord for advice. He said, "Should I chase after the men who attacked Ziklag? If I do, will I catch up with them?"

"Chase after them," the Lord answered. "You will certainly catch up with them. You will succeed in saving those who were captured."

⁹ David and his 600 men came to the Besor Valley. Some of them stayed behind there. ¹⁰ That's because 200 of them were too tired to go across the valley. But David and the other 400 continued the chase.

¹¹ David's men found an Egyptian in a field. They brought him to David. They gave him water to drink and food to eat. ¹² They gave him part of a cake of pressed figs. They also gave him two raisin cakes. After he ate them, he felt as good as new. That's because he hadn't eaten any food for three days and three nights. He hadn't drunk any water during that time either.

¹³ David asked him, "Who do you belong to? Where do you come from?"

The man said, "I'm from Egypt. I'm the slave of an Amalekite. My master deserted me when I became ill three days ago. ¹⁴ We attacked the people in the Negev Desert of the Kerethites. We attacked the territory that belongs to Judah. We attacked the people in the Negev Desert of Caleb. And we burned Ziklag."

¹⁵ David asked him, "Can you lead me down to the men who attacked Ziklag?"

He answered, "Make a promise to me in the name of God. Promise that you won't kill me. Promise that you won't hand me over to my master. Then I'll take you down to them."

¹⁶ He led David down to where the men were. They were scattered all over the countryside. They were eating and drinking and dancing wildly. That's because they had taken a large amount of goods from those they had attacked. They had taken it from the land of the Philistines and from the people of Judah. ¹⁷ David fought against them from sunset until the evening of the next day. None of them escaped except 400 young men. They rode off on camels and got away. ¹⁸ David got everything back that the Amalekites had taken. That included his two wives. ¹⁹ Nothing was missing. Not one young person or old person or boy or girl was missing. None of the goods or anything else the Amalekites had taken was missing. David brought everything back. ²⁰ He brought back all the flocks and herds. His men drove them on ahead of the other livestock. They said, "Here's what David has captured."

²¹ Then David came to the 200 men who had been too tired to follow him. They had been left behind in the Besor Valley. They came out to welcome David and the men with him. As David and

his men approached, he asked them how they were. ²²But some of the men who had gone out with David were evil. They wanted to stir up trouble. They said, "The 200 men didn't go out into battle with us. So we won't share with them the goods we brought back. But each man can take his wife and children and go home."

²³David replied, "No, my friends. You must not hold back their share of what the LORD has given us. He has kept us safe. He has handed over to us the men who attacked us. ²⁴So no one will pay any attention to what you are saying. Each man who stayed with the supplies will receive the same share as each man who went down to the battle. Everyone's share will be the same." ²⁵David made that a law and a rule for Israel. It has been followed from that day until now.

²⁶David reached Ziklag. He sent some of the goods to the elders of Judah. They were his friends. He said, "Here's a gift for you. It's part of the things we took from the LORD's enemies."

²⁷David sent some goods to the elders in Bethel, Ramoth Negev and Jattir. ²⁸He sent some to the elders in Aroer, Siphmoth, Eshtemoa ²⁹and Rakal. He sent some to the elders in the towns of the Jerahmeelites and Kenites. ³⁰He sent some to the elders in Hormah, Bor Ashan, Athak ³¹and Hebron. He also sent some to the elders in all the other places where he and his men had wandered around.

Saul Takes His Own Life

31 The Philistines fought against the Israelites. The Israelites ran away from them. But many Israelites were killed on Mount Gilboa. ²The Philistines kept chasing Saul and his sons. They killed his sons Jonathan, Abinadab and Malki-Shua. ³The fighting was heavy around Saul. Men who were armed with bows and arrows caught up with him. They shot their arrows at him and wounded him badly.

⁴Saul spoke to the man carrying his armor. He said, "Pull out your sword. Stick it through me. If you don't, these fellows who aren't circumcised will come. They'll stick their swords through me and hurt me badly."

But the man was terrified. He wouldn't do it. So Saul took his own sword and fell on it. ⁵The man saw that Saul was dead. So he fell on his own sword and died with him. ⁶Saul and his three sons died together that same day. The man who carried his armor also died with them that day. So did all of Saul's men.

⁷The Israelites who lived along the valley saw that their army had run away. So did those who lived across the Jordan River. They saw that Saul and his sons were dead. So they left their towns and ran away. Then the Philistines came and made their homes in them.

⁸The day after the Philistines had won the battle, they came to take what they wanted from the dead bodies. They found Saul and his three sons dead on

Mount Gilboa. [9] So they cut off Saul's head. They took his armor from his body. Then they sent messengers through the whole land of the Philistines. They announced the news in the temple where they had set up statues of their gods. They also announced it among their people. [10] They put Saul's armor in the temple where they had set up statues of female gods that were named Ashtoreth. They hung his body up on the wall of Beth Shan.

[11] The people of Jabesh Gilead heard about what the Philistines had done to Saul. [12] So all their brave men marched through the night to Beth Shan. They took down the bodies of Saul and his sons from the wall of Beth Shan. They brought them to Jabesh. There they burned them. [13] Then they got the bones of Saul and his sons and buried them under a tamarisk tree at Jabesh. They didn't eat anything for seven days.

2 Samuel

Introduction:

The book of 2 Samuel tells the story of King David. After Saul died, David became king. First, David was king of Judah. Then he became the king of all Israel.

Outline of contents:

David Hears That Saul Has Died

1 After Saul died, David returned to Ziklag. He had won the battle over the Amalekites. He stayed in Ziklag for two days. ²On the third day a man arrived from Saul's camp. His clothes were torn. He had dust on his head. When he came to David, he fell to the ground to show him respect.

³"Where have you come from?" David asked him.

He answered, "I've escaped from Israel's camp."

⁴"What happened?" David asked. "Tell me."

He said, "Israel's men ran away from the battle. Many of them were killed. Saul and his son Jonathan are dead."

⁵David spoke to the young man who brought him the report. He asked him, "How do you know that Saul and his son Jonathan are dead?"

⁶"I just happened to be there on Mount Gilboa," the young man said. "Saul was there too. He was leaning on his spear. The enemy chariots and char-iot drivers had almost caught up with him. ⁷Then he turned around and saw me. He called out to me. I said, 'What do you want me to do?'

⁸"He asked me, 'Who are you?'

"'An Amalekite,' I answered.

⁹"Then he said to me, 'Stand here by me and kill me! I'm close to death, but I'm still alive.'

¹⁰"So I stood beside him and killed him. I did it because I knew that after he had lost the battle he would be killed anyway. So I took the crown that was on his head. I also took his armband. I've brought them here to you. You are my master."

¹¹Then David tore his clothes. And all his men tore their clothes. ¹²All of them were filled with sadness. They mourned over the whole nation of Israel. They didn't eat anything until evening. That's because Saul and Jonathan and the LORD's army had been killed by swords.

¹³David spoke to the young man who had brought him the report. He asked, "Where are you from?"

"I'm the son of an outsider, an Amalekite," he answered.

¹⁴ David asked him, "Why weren't you afraid to lift your hand to kill the Lord's anointed king?"

¹⁵ Then David called for one of his men. He said, "Go! Strike him down!" So he struck the man down, and the man died. ¹⁶ That's because David had said to him, "Anything that happens to you will be your own fault. What your own mouth has spoken is a witness against you. You said, 'I killed the Lord's anointed king.' "

David's Song of Sadness About Saul and Jonathan

¹⁷ David sang a song of sadness about Saul and his son Jonathan. ¹⁸ He ordered that it be taught to the people of Judah. It is a song that is played on a stringed instrument. It is written down in the Book of Jashar. David sang,

¹⁹ "Israel, a gazelle lies dead on your hills.
  Your mighty men have fallen.

²⁰ "Don't announce it in Gath.
  Don't tell it in the streets of Ashkelon.
  If you do, the daughters of the Philistines will be glad.
  The daughters of men who haven't been circumcised will be joyful.

²¹ "Mountains of Gilboa,
  may no dew or rain fall on you.

May no showers fall on your hillside fields.
  The shield of the mighty king wasn't respected there.
  The shield of Saul lies there. It isn't rubbed with oil anymore.

²² The bow of Jonathan didn't turn back.
  The sword of Saul didn't return without being satisfied.
  They spilled the blood of their enemies.
  They killed mighty men.

²³ "When they lived, Saul and Jonathan were loved and respected.
  When they died, they were not parted.
  They were faster than eagles.
  They were stronger than lions.

²⁴ "Daughters of Israel, mourn over Saul.
  He dressed you in the finest clothes.
  He decorated your clothes with ornaments of gold.

²⁵ "Your mighty men have fallen in battle.
  Jonathan lies dead on your hills.

²⁶ My brother Jonathan, I'm filled with sadness because of you.
  You were very special to me.
  Your love for me was wonderful.
  It was more wonderful than the love of women.

27 "Israel's mighty men have fallen.

Their weapons of war are broken."

David Is Anointed to Be King Over Judah

2 After Saul and Jonathan died, David asked the LORD for advice. "Should I go up to one of the towns of Judah?" he asked.

The LORD said, "Go up."

David asked, "Where should I go?"

"To Hebron," the LORD answered.

2 So David went up there with his two wives. Their names were Ahinoam from Jezreel and Abigail from Carmel. Abigail was Nabal's widow. 3 David also took his men and their families with him. They made their homes in Hebron and its towns. 4 Then the men of Judah came to Hebron. There they anointed David to be king over the people of Judah.

David was told that the men from Jabesh Gilead had buried Saul's body. 5 So he sent messengers to them to speak for him. The messengers said, "You were kind to bury the body of your master Saul. May the LORD bless you for that. 6 And may he now be kind and faithful to you. David will treat you well for being kind to Saul's body. 7 Now then, be strong and brave. Your master Saul is dead. And the people of Judah have anointed David to be king over them."

The Armies of David and Saul Fight Each Other

8 Abner, the son of Ner, was commander of Saul's army. Abner had brought Saul's son Ish-Bosheth to Mahanaim. 9 There Abner made Ish-Bosheth king over Gilead, Ashuri and Jezreel. He also made him king over Ephraim, Benjamin and other areas of Israel.

10 Ish-Bosheth was 40 years old when he became king over Israel. He ruled for two years. But the people of Judah remained faithful to David. 11 David was king in Hebron over the people of Judah for seven and a half years.

12 Abner, the son of Ner, left Mahanaim and went to Gibeon. The men of Ish-Bosheth, the son of Saul, went with him. 13 Joab, the son of Zeruiah, and David's men also went out. All of them met at the pool in Gibeon. One group sat down on one side of the pool. The other group sat on the other side.

14 Then Abner said to Joab, "Let's have some of the young men get up and fight. Let's tell them to fight hand to hand in front of us."

"All right. Let them do it," Joab said.

15 So the young men stood up and were counted off. There were 12 on the side of Benjamin and Saul's son Ish-Bosheth. And there were 12 on David's side. 16 Each man grabbed one of his enemies by the head. Each one stuck his dagger into the other man's side. And all of them fell down together and died. So that

place in Gibeon was named Helkath Hazzurim.

17 The fighting that day was very heavy. Abner and the Israelites lost the battle to David's men.

18 The three sons of Zeruiah were there. Their names were Joab, Abishai and Asahel. Asahel was as quick on his feet as a wild antelope. 19 He chased Abner. He didn't turn to the right or the left as he chased him. 20 Abner looked behind him. He asked, "Asahel, is that you?"

"It is," he answered.

21 Then Abner said to him, "Turn to the right or the left. Fight one of the young men. Take his weapons away from him." But Asahel wouldn't stop chasing him.

22 Again Abner warned Asahel, "Stop chasing me! If you don't, I'll strike you down. Then how could I look your brother Joab in the face?"

23 But Asahel refused to give up the chase. So Abner drove the dull end of his spear into Asahel's stomach. The spear came out through his back. He fell and died right there on the spot. Every man stopped when he came to the place where Asahel had fallen and died.

24 But Joab and Abishai chased Abner. As the sun was going down, they came to the hill of Ammah. It was near Giah on the way to the dry and empty land close to Gibeon. 25 The men of Benjamin gathered in a group around Abner. They took their stand on top of a hill.

26 Abner called out to Joab, "Do you want our swords to keep on killing us off? Don't you know that all this fighting will end in bitter feelings? How long will it be before you order your men to stop chasing their fellow Israelites?"

27 Joab answered, "It's a good thing you spoke up. If you hadn't, the men would have kept on chasing them until morning. And that's just as sure as God is alive."

28 So Joab blew a trumpet. All the troops stopped. They didn't chase Israel anymore. They didn't fight anymore either.

29 All that night Abner and his men marched through the Arabah Valley. They went across the Jordan River. All morning long they kept on going. Finally, they came to Mahanaim.

30 Then Joab stopped chasing Abner. He gathered together the whole army. Besides Asahel, only 19 of David's men were missing. 31 But David's men had killed 360 men from Benjamin who were with Abner. 32 They got Asahel's body and buried it in his father's tomb at Bethlehem. Then Joab and his men marched all night. They arrived at Hebron at sunrise.

3 The war between Saul's royal house and David's royal house lasted a long time. David grew stronger and stronger. But the royal house of Saul grew weaker and weaker.

2 Sons were born to David in Hebron.

His first son was Amnon. Amnon's mother was Ahinoam from Jezreel.

³His second son was Kileab. Kileab's mother was Abigail. She was Nabal's widow from Carmel.

The third son was Absalom. His mother was Maakah. She was the daughter of Talmai, the king of Geshur.

⁴The fourth son was Adonijah. His mother was Haggith.

The fifth son was Shephatiah. His mother was Abital.

⁵The sixth son was Ithream. His mother was David's wife Eglah.

Those sons were born to David in Hebron.

Abner Goes Over to David's Side

⁶The fighting continued between David's royal house and Saul's royal house. Abner gained more and more power in the royal house of Saul. ⁷While Saul was still alive, he had a concubine named Rizpah. She was the daughter of Aiah. Ish-Bosheth said to Abner, "Why did you sleep with my father's concubine?"

⁸Abner was very angry because of what Ish-Bosheth said. So Abner answered, "Do you think I'm only a dog's head? Am I on Judah's side? To this day I've been faithful to the royal house of your father Saul. I've been faithful to his family and friends. I haven't handed you over to David. But now you claim that I've sinned with this woman! ⁹I will do for David

what the LORD promised him. If I don't, may God punish me greatly. ¹⁰I'll take the kingdom away from Saul's royal house. I'll set up the throne of David's kingdom over Israel and Judah. He will rule from Dan all the way to Beersheba." ¹¹Ish-Bosheth didn't dare to say another word to Abner. He was much too afraid of him.

¹²Then Abner sent messengers to David to speak for him. They said, "Who will rule over this land? Make a covenant with me. Then I'll help you bring all the Israelites over to your side."

¹³"Good," said David. "I will make a covenant with you. But there's one thing I want you to do. Bring Saul's daughter Michal to me. Don't come to see me unless she's with you." ¹⁴Then David sent messengers to Saul's son Ish-Bosheth. He ordered them to say, "Give me my wife Michal. She was promised to me. I paid for her the price that was demanded. I paid for her with the skins of 100 circumcised Philistines."

¹⁵So Ish-Bosheth gave the order. He sent men who took Michal away from her husband Paltiel. Paltiel was the son of Laish. ¹⁶But her husband followed her to Bahurim. He was crying all the way. Then Abner said to him, "Go back home!" So he did.

¹⁷Abner talked with the elders of Israel. He said, "For some time you have wanted to make David your king. ¹⁸Now do it! The LORD made a promise to David. He said, 'I will rescue my

people Israel from the power of the Philistines. I will also rescue them from all their enemies. I will rescue them through my servant David.' "

¹⁹ Abner also spoke to the people of Benjamin in person. Then he went to Hebron to tell David everything. He told him what Israel and all the people of Benjamin wanted to do. ²⁰ Abner had 20 men with him. They came to David at Hebron. So David prepared a feast for Abner and his men. ²¹ Then Abner said to David, "Let me go right now. I'll gather together all the Israelites for you. After all, you are now my king and master. The people can make a covenant with you. Then you can rule over everyone you want to." So David sent Abner away. And he went in peace.

Joab Murders Abner

²² Just then David's men and Joab came back from attacking their enemies. They brought with them the large amount of goods they had taken. But Abner wasn't with David in Hebron anymore. That's because David had sent him away, and he had gone in peace. ²³ Joab and all the soldiers with him arrived. Then he was told that Abner, the son of Ner, had come to see the king. He was told that the king had sent Abner away. He was also told that Abner had gone in peace.

²⁴ So Joab went to the king. He said, "What have you done? Abner came to you. Why did you let him get away? Now he's gone! ²⁵ You know what Abner, the son of Ner, is like. He came to trick you. He wanted to watch your every move. He came to find out everything you are doing."

²⁶ Then Joab left David. He sent messengers to get Abner. They brought Abner back from the well of Sirah. But David didn't know about it. ²⁷ When Abner returned to Hebron, Joab took him to one side. He brought him into an inside room. Joab acted as if he wanted to speak to him in private. But he really wanted to get even with him. That's because Abner had spilled the blood of Joab's brother Asahel. So Joab stabbed Abner in the stomach, and he died.

²⁸ Later on, David heard about it. He said, "I and the people of my kingdom aren't guilty of spilling the blood of Abner, the son of Ner. We are free of blame forever in the sight of the LORD. ²⁹ May Joab and his whole family line be held accountable for spilling Abner's blood! May Joab's family never be without someone who has an open sore or skin disease. May his family never be without someone who has to use a crutch to walk. May his family never be without someone who gets killed by a sword. And may his family never be without someone who doesn't have enough to eat."

³⁰ Joab and his brother Abishai murdered Abner. They did it because he had killed their brother Asahel in the battle at Gibeon.

³¹David spoke to Joab and all the people with him. He said, "Tear your clothes. Put on the rough clothing people wear when they're sad. Mourn when you walk in front of Abner's body." King David himself walked behind it. ³²Abner's body was buried in Hebron. The king wept out loud at Abner's tomb. So did the rest of the people.

³³King David sang a song of sadness over Abner. He said,

"Should Abner have died as
    sinful people do?
³⁴   His hands were not tied.
    His feet were not chained.
He died as if he had been
    killed by evil people."

All the people mourned over Abner again.

³⁵Then all of them came and begged David to eat something. They wanted him to eat while it was still day. But David made a promise. He said, "I won't taste bread or anything else before the sun goes down. If I do, may God punish me greatly!"

³⁶All the people heard his promise and were pleased. In fact, everything the king did pleased them. ³⁷So on that day all the people there and all the Israelites understood. They knew that the king didn't have anything to do with the murder of Abner, the son of Ner.

³⁸The king spoke to his men. He said, "Don't you realize that a great commander has died in Israel today? ³⁹I'm the anointed king. But today I'm weak. These sons of Zeruiah are too powerful for me. May the LORD pay back the one who killed Abner! May he pay him back for the evil thing he has done!"

Ish-Bosheth Is Murdered

4 Ish-Bosheth, the son of Saul, heard that Abner had died in Hebron. Then he wasn't so brave anymore. And all the Israelites became alarmed. ²Two men in Ish-Bosheth's army led small fighting groups that attacked their enemies. The names of the men were Baanah and Rekab. They were sons of Rimmon from the town of Beeroth. Rimmon was from the tribe of Benjamin. Beeroth is considered to be part of Benjamin. ³That's because the people who used to live in Beeroth had run away to Gittaim. They have lived there as outsiders to this day.

⁴Jonathan, the son of Saul, had a son named Mephibosheth. Both of Mephibosheth's feet were hurt. He was five years old when the news that Saul and Jonathan had died came from Jezreel. His nurse picked him up and ran. But as she hurried to get away, he fell down. That's how his feet were hurt.

⁵Rekab and Baanah started out for the house of Ish-Bosheth. They were the sons of Rimmon from Beeroth. They arrived there during the hottest time of the day. Ish-Bosheth was taking his early afternoon nap. ⁶Rekab and his brother Baanah went into the inside part of the house. They acted as if they

were going to get some wheat. Instead, they stabbed Ish-Bosheth in the stomach. Then they slipped away.

7 They had gone into the house while Ish-Bosheth was lying on his bed in his bedroom. They stabbed him and killed him. Then they cut off his head and took it with them. They traveled all night through the Arabah Valley. 8 They brought the head of Ish-Bosheth to King David at Hebron. They said to him, "Here's the head of Ish-Bosheth, the son of Saul. Saul was your enemy. He often tried to kill you. Today the LORD has paid back Saul and his family. He has let you get even with them. You are our king and master."

9 David gave an answer to Rekab and his brother Baanah. They were the sons of Rimmon from Beeroth. David said, "The LORD has saved me from every trouble. 10 Someone once told me, 'Saul is dead.' He thought he was bringing me good news. But I grabbed him. I had him put to death in Ziklag. That's the reward I gave him for his news! And that's just as sure as the LORD is alive. 11 Now you evil men have killed a man in his own house. He hadn't done anything wrong. You killed him while he was lying on his own bed. You spilled his blood. So shouldn't I spill your blood? Shouldn't I wipe you off the face of the earth?"

12 Then David gave an order to his men. They killed Rekab and Baanah. They cut off their hands and feet. They hung their bodies by the pool in Hebron. But they buried the head of Ish-Bosheth in Abner's tomb at Hebron.

David Becomes King Over Israel

5 All the tribes of Israel came to see David at Hebron. They said, "We are your own flesh and blood. 2 In the past, Saul was our king. But you led Israel on their military campaigns. And the LORD said to you, 'You will be the shepherd over my people Israel. You will become their ruler.'"

3 All the elders of Israel came to see King David at Hebron. There the king made a covenant with them in front of the LORD. They anointed David as king over Israel.

4 David was 30 years old when he became king. He ruled for 40 years. 5 In Hebron he ruled over Judah for seven and a half years. In Jerusalem he ruled over all of Israel and Judah for 33 years.

David Captures Jerusalem

6 The king and his men marched to Jerusalem. They went to attack the Jebusites who lived there. The Jebusites said to David, "You won't get in here. Even people who can't see or walk can keep you from coming in." The Jebusites thought, "David can't get in here." 7 But David captured the fort of Zion. It became known as the City of David.

8 On that day David had said, "Someone might win the bat-

tle over the Jebusites. But they will have to crawl through the water tunnel to get into the city. That's the only way they can reach those enemies of mine that you say can't see or walk." That's why people say, "Those who 'can't see or walk' won't enter David's palace."

⁹ David moved into the fort. He called it the City of David. He built up the area around the fort. He filled in the low places. He started at the bottom and worked his way up. ¹⁰ David became more and more powerful. That's because the LORD God who rules over all was with him.

¹¹ Hiram was king of Tyre. He sent messengers to David. He sent cedar logs along with them. He also sent skilled workers. They worked with wood and stone. They built a palace for David. ¹² Then David knew that the LORD had made his position as king secure. He knew that he had made him king over the whole nation of Israel. He knew that the LORD had greatly honored his kingdom. The LORD had done it because the Israelites were his people.

¹³ After David left Hebron, he got more concubines and wives in Jerusalem. More sons and daughters were born to him there. ¹⁴ Here is a list of the children who were born to him in Jerusalem. Their names were Shammua, Shobab, Nathan, Solomon, ¹⁵ Ibhar, Elishua, Nepheg, Japhia, ¹⁶ Elishama, Eliada and Eliphelet.

David Wins the Battle Over the Philistines

¹⁷ The Philistines heard that David had been anointed king over Israel. So their whole army went to look for him. But David heard about it. He went down to his usual place of safety. ¹⁸ The Philistines had come and spread out in the Valley of Rephaim. ¹⁹ So David asked the LORD for advice. He said, "Should I go and attack the Philistines? Will you hand them over to me?"

The LORD answered him, "Go. I will surely hand over the Philistines to you."

²⁰ So David went to Baal Perazim. There he won the battle over the Philistines. He said, "The LORD has broken through against my enemies when I've attacked them. He has broken through just as water breaks through a dam." That's why the place was called Baal Perazim. ²¹ The Philistines left the statues of their gods there. So David and his men carried off the statues.

²² Once more the Philistines came up. They spread out in the Valley of Rephaim. ²³ So David asked the LORD for advice. The LORD answered, "Do not go straight up. Instead, circle around behind them. Attack them in front of the poplar trees. ²⁴ Listen for the sound of marching in the tops of the trees. Then move quickly. The sound will mean that I have gone out in front of you. I will strike down the Philistine army." ²⁵ So David did just as the LORD had commanded him. He struck down

the Philistines. He struck them down from Gibeon all the way to Gezer.

David Brings the Ark to Jerusalem

6 Again David brought together the best soldiers in Israel. The total number was 30,000. ² He and all his men went to Baalah in Judah. They wanted to bring the ark of God up to Jerusalem from there. The ark is named after the LORD. He is the LORD who rules over all. He sits on his throne between the cherubim that are on the ark. ³ The ark of God was placed on a new cart. Then it was brought from Abinadab's house, which was on a hill. Uzzah and Ahio were guiding the cart. They were the sons of Abinadab. ⁴ The ark of God was on the cart. Ahio was walking in front of it. ⁵ David was celebrating with all his might in front of the LORD. So was the whole community of Israel. All of them were playing castanets, harps, lyres, tambourines, rattles and cymbals.

⁶ They came to the threshing floor of Nakon. The oxen nearly fell there. So Uzzah reached out and took hold of the ark of God. ⁷ Then the LORD was very angry with Uzzah. That's because what Uzzah did showed that he didn't have any respect for the LORD. So God struck him down. He died there beside the ark of God.

⁸ David was angry because the LORD's great anger had broken out against Uzzah. That's why the place is still called Perez Uzzah to this day.

⁹ David was afraid of the LORD that day. He asked, "How can the ark of the LORD ever be brought to me?" ¹⁰ He didn't want to take the ark of the LORD to be with him in the City of David. Instead, he took it to the house of Obed-Edom. Obed-Edom was from Gath. ¹¹ The ark of the LORD remained in Obed-Edom's house for three months. And the LORD blessed him and his whole family.

¹² King David was told, "The LORD has blessed the family of Obed-Edom. He has also blessed everything that belongs to him. That's because the ark of God is in Obed-Edom's house." So David went down there to bring up the ark. With great joy he brought it up from the house of Obed-Edom. He took it to the City of David. ¹³ Those carrying the ark of the LORD took six steps forward. Then David sacrificed a bull and a fat calf. ¹⁴ David was wearing a sacred linen apron. He danced in front of the LORD with all his might. ¹⁵ He did it while he was bringing up the ark of the LORD. The whole community of Israel helped him bring it up. They shouted. They blew trumpets.

¹⁶ The ark of the LORD was brought into the City of David. Saul's daughter Michal was watching from a window. She saw King David leaping and dancing in front of the LORD. That made her hate him in her heart.

[17] The ark of the Lord was brought into Jerusalem. It was put in its place in the tent David had set up for it. David sacrificed burnt offerings and friendship offerings to the Lord. [18] After he finished sacrificing those offerings, he blessed the people in the name of the Lord who rules over all. [19] He gave to each Israelite man and woman a loaf of bread. He also gave each one a date cake and a raisin cake. Then all the people went home.

[20] David returned home to bless his family. Saul's daughter Michal came out to meet him. She said, "You are the king of Israel. You have really brought honor to yourself today, haven't you? You have gone around half-naked right in front of the female slaves of your officials. You acted like a fool!"

[21] David said to Michal, "I did it to honor the Lord. He chose me instead of your father or anyone else in Saul's family. The Lord appointed me ruler over his people Israel. I will celebrate to honor the Lord. [22] And that's not all. I will bring even less honor to myself. I will bring even more shame on myself. But those female slaves you spoke about will honor me."

[23] Saul's daughter Michal didn't have any children as long as she lived.

God's Promise to David

7 The king moved into his palace. The Lord had given him peace and rest from all his enemies around him. [2] Then the king spoke to Nathan the prophet. He said, "Here I am, living in a house that has beautiful cedar walls. But the ark of God remains in a tent."

[3] Nathan replied to the king, "Go ahead and do what you want to. The Lord is with you."

[4] But that night the word of the Lord came to Nathan. The Lord said,

[5] "Go and speak to my servant David. Tell him, 'The Lord says, "Are you the one to build me a house to live in? [6] I brought the Israelites up out of Egypt. But I have not lived in a house from then until now. I have been moving from place to place. I have been living in a tent. [7] I have moved from place to place with all the Israelites. I commanded their rulers to be shepherds over them. I never asked any of those rulers, 'Why haven't you built me a house that has beautiful cedar walls?' " '

[8] "So tell my servant David, 'The Lord who rules over all says, "I took you away from the grasslands. That's where you were taking care of your father's sheep and goats. I made you ruler over my people Israel. [9] I have been with you everywhere you have gone. I have destroyed all your enemies. Now I will make you famous. Your name will be just as respected as the names of the most

important people on earth. [10] I will provide a place where my people Israel can live. I will plant them in the land. Then they will have a home of their own. They will not be bothered anymore. Evil people will no longer crush them, as they did at first. [11] That is what your enemies have done ever since I appointed leaders over my people Israel. But I will give you peace and rest from all of them.

" ' "I tell you that I, the LORD, will set up a royal house for you. [12] Some day your life will come to an end. You will join the members of your family who have already died. Then I will make one of your own sons the next king after you. And I will make his kingdom secure. [13] He is the one who will build a house where I will put my Name. I will set up the throne of his kingdom. It will last forever. [14] I will be his father. And he will be my son. When he does what is wrong, I will use other men to beat him with rods and whips. [15] I took my love away from Saul. I removed him from being king. You were there when I did it. But I will never take my love away from your son. [16] Your royal house and your kingdom will last forever in my sight. Your throne will last forever." ' "

[17] Nathan reported to David all the words that the LORD had spoken to him.

David's Prayer to the LORD

[18] Then King David went into the holy tent. He sat down in front of the LORD. He said,

"LORD and King, who am I? My family isn't important. So why have you brought me this far? [19] I would have thought that you had already done more than enough for me. But now, LORD and King, you have also said what will happen to my royal house in days to come. And, my LORD and King, this promise is for a mere human being!

[20] "What more can I say to you? LORD and King, you know all about me. [21] You have done a wonderful thing. You have made it known to me. You have done it because that's what you said you would do. It's exactly what you wanted to do for me.

[22] "LORD and King, how great you are! There isn't anyone like you. There isn't any God but you. We have heard about it with our own ears. [23] Who is like your people Israel? God, we are the one nation on earth you have saved. You have set us free for yourself. Your name has become famous. You have done great and wonderful things. You have

driven out nations and their gods to make room for your people. You saved us when you set us free from Egypt. [24] You made Israel your very own people forever. LORD, you have become our God.

[25] "And now, LORD God, keep forever the promise you have made to me and my royal house. Do exactly as you promised. [26] Then your name will be honored forever. People will say, 'The LORD rules over all. He is God over Israel.' My royal house will be made secure in your sight.

[27] "LORD who rules over all, you are the God of Israel. Here's what you have shown me. You told me, 'I will build you a royal house.' So I can boldly pray this prayer to you. [28] LORD and King, you are God! Your covenant can be trusted. You have promised many good things to me. [29] Now please bless my royal house. Then it will continue forever in your sight. LORD and King, you have spoken. Because you have given my royal house your blessing, it will be blessed forever."

David Wins Many Battles

8 While David was king of Israel, he won many battles over the Philistines. He brought them under his control. He took Metheg Ammah away from them.

[2] David also won the bat-tle over the people of Moab. He made them lie down on the ground. Then he measured them off with a piece of rope. He put two-thirds of them to death. He let the other third remain alive. So the Moabites were brought under David's rule. They gave him the gifts he required them to bring him.

[3] David fought against Hadad-ezer, the son of Rehob. Hadade-zer was king of Zobah. He had gone to repair his monument at the Euphrates River. [4] David captured 1,000 of Hadadezer's chariots, 7,000 chariot riders and 20,000 soldiers on foot. He cut the legs of all but 100 of the chariot horses.

[5] The Arameans of Damascus came to help Hadadezer, the king of Zobah. But David struck down 22,000 of them. [6] He stationed some soldiers in the Aramean kingdom of Damascus. The people of Aram were brought under his rule. They gave him the gifts he required them to bring him. The LORD helped David win his battles everywhere he went.

[7] David took the gold shields that belonged to the officers of Hadadezer. He brought the shields to Jerusalem. [8] He took a huge amount of bronze from Te-bah and Berothai. Those towns belonged to Hadadezer.

[9] Tou was king of Hamath. He heard that David had won the battle over the entire army of Hadadezer. [10] So Tou sent his son Joram to King David. Joram greeted David. He praised

David because he had won the battle over Hadadezer. Hadadezer had been at war with Tou. So Joram brought with him gifts made out of silver, of gold and of bronze.

¹¹ King David set those gifts apart for the LORD. He had done the same thing with the silver and gold he had taken from the other nations. Those were nations he had brought under his control. ¹² Those nations were Edom, Moab, Ammon, Philistia and Amalek. He also set apart for the LORD what he had taken from Hadadezer, the son of Rehob. Hadadezer was king of Zobah.

¹³ David returned after he had struck down 18,000 men of Edom in the Valley of Salt. He became famous for doing it.

¹⁴ He stationed some soldiers all through Edom. The whole nation of Edom was brought under David's rule. The LORD helped him win his battles everywhere he went.

David's Officials

¹⁵ David ruled over the whole nation of Israel. He did what was fair and right for all his people. ¹⁶ Joab, the son of Zeruiah, was commander over the army. Jehoshaphat, the son of Ahilud, kept the records. ¹⁷ Zadok, the son of Ahitub, was a priest. Ahimelek, the son of Abiathar, was also a priest. Seraiah was the secretary. ¹⁸ Benaiah, the son of Jehoiada, was commander over the Kerethites and Pelethites. And David's sons were priests.

David and Mephibosheth

9 David asked, "Is anyone left from the royal house of Saul? If there is, I want to be kind to him because of Jonathan."

² Ziba was a servant in Saul's family. David sent for him to come and see him. The king said to him, "Are you Ziba?"

"I'm ready to serve you," he replied.

³ The king asked, "Isn't there anyone still alive from the royal house of Saul? God has been very kind to me. I would like to be kind to that person in the same way."

Ziba answered the king, "A son of Jonathan is still living. Both of his feet were hurt so that he can't walk."

⁴ "Where is he?" the king asked.

Ziba answered, "He's in the town of Lo Debar. He's staying at the house of Makir, the son of Ammiel."

⁵ So King David had Mephibosheth brought from Makir's house in Lo Debar.

⁶ Mephibosheth came to David. He was the son of Jonathan, the son of Saul. Mephibosheth bowed down to David to show him respect.

David said, "Mephibosheth!"

"I'm ready to serve you," he replied.

⁷ "Don't be afraid," David told him. "You can be sure that I will be kind to you because of your father Jonathan. I'll give back to you all the land that belonged to your grandfather Saul. And I'll always provide what you need."

⁸Mephibosheth bowed down to David. He said, "Who am I? Why should you pay attention to me? I'm nothing but a dead dog."

⁹Then the king sent for Saul's servant Ziba. He said to him, "I'm giving your master's grandson everything that belonged to Saul and his family. ¹⁰You and your sons and your servants must farm the land for him. You must bring in the crops. Then he'll be taken care of. I'll always provide what he needs." Ziba had 15 sons and 20 servants.

¹¹Then Ziba said to the king, "I'll do anything you command me to do. You are my king and master." So David provided what Mephibosheth needed. He treated him like one of the king's sons.

¹²Mephibosheth had a young son named Mika. All the members of Ziba's family became servants of Mephibosheth. ¹³Mephibosheth lived in Jerusalem. The king always provided what he needed. Both of his feet were hurt so that he could not walk.

David Wins the Victory Over the Ammonites

10 The king of Ammon died. His son Hanun became the next king after him. ²David thought, "I'm going to be kind to Hanun. His father Nahash was kind to me." So David sent messengers to Hanun. He wanted them to tell Hanun how sad he was that Hanun's father had died.

David's messengers went to the land of Ammon. ³The Ammonite commanders spoke to their master Hanun. They said, "David has sent messengers to tell you he is sad. They say he wants to honor your father. But the real reason they've come is to look the city over. They want to destroy it." ⁴So Hanun grabbed David's messengers. He shaved off half of each man's beard. He cut their clothes off just below the waist and left them half naked. Then he sent them away.

⁵David was told about it. So he sent messengers to his men because they were filled with shame. King David said to them, "Stay at Jericho until your beards grow out again. Then come back here."

⁶The Ammonites realized that what they had done had made David very angry with them. So they hired 20,000 Aramean soldiers who were on foot. The soldiers came from Beth Rehob and Zobah. The Ammonites also hired the king of Maakah and 1,000 men. And they hired 12,000 men from Tob. ⁷David heard about it. So he sent Joab out with the entire army of Israel's fighting men. ⁸The Ammonites marched out. They took up their battle positions at the entrance of their city gate. The Arameans of Zobah and Rehob gathered their troops together in the open country. So did the men of Tob and Maakah.

⁹Joab saw that there were lines

of soldiers in front of him and behind him. So he chose some of the best troops in Israel. He sent them to march out against the Arameans. [10] He put the rest of the men under the command of his brother Abishai. Joab sent them to march out against the Ammonites. [11] He said, "Suppose the Arameans are too strong for me. Then you must come and help me. But suppose the Ammonites are too strong for you. Then I'll come and help you. [12] Be strong. Let's be brave as we fight for our people and the cities of our God. The LORD will do what he thinks is best."

[13] Then Joab and the troops with him marched out to attack the Arameans. They ran away from him. [14] The Ammonites realized that the Arameans were running away. So they ran away from Abishai. They went inside the city. After Joab had fought against the Ammonites, he went back to Jerusalem.

[15] The Arameans saw that they had been driven away by Israel. So they brought their troops together. [16] Hadadezer had some Arameans brought from east of the Euphrates River. They went to Helam under the command of Shobak. He was the commander of Hadadezer's army.

[17] David was told about it. So he gathered the whole army of Israel together. They went across the Jordan River to Helam. The Arameans lined up their soldiers to go to war against David. They began to fight against him. [18] But then they ran away from Israel. David killed 700 of their chariot riders. He killed 40,000 of their soldiers who were on foot. He also struck down Shobak, the commander of their army. Shobak died there. [19] All the kings who were under the rule of Hadadezer saw that Israel had won the battle over them. So they made a peace treaty with the Israelites. They were brought under Israel's rule.

After that, the Arameans were afraid to help the Ammonites anymore.

David and Bathsheba

11 It was spring. It was the time when kings go off to war. So David sent Joab out with the king's special troops and the whole army of Israel. They destroyed the Ammonites. They marched to the city of Rabbah. They surrounded it and got ready to attack it. But David remained in Jerusalem.

[2] One evening David got up from his bed. He walked around on the roof of his palace. From the roof he saw a woman taking a bath. She was very beautiful. [3] David sent a messenger to find out who she was. The messenger returned and said, "She is Bathsheba. She's the daughter of Eliam. She's the wife of Uriah. He's a Hittite." [4] Then David sent messengers to get her. She came to him. And he slept with her. Then she went back home. All of that took place after she had already made herself "clean" from her monthly period. [5] Later, Bathsheba found out she was

Balaam's Talking Donkey

NUMBERS 22:21–41

The Walls of Jericho Fall Down
JOSHUA 6:1–21

pregnant. She sent a message to David. She said, "I'm pregnant."

⁶ So David sent a message to Joab. David said, "Send me Uriah, the Hittite." Joab sent him to David. ⁷ Uriah came to David. David asked him how Joab and the soldiers were doing. He also asked him how the war was going. ⁸ David said to Uriah, "Go home and enjoy some time with your wife." So Uriah left the palace. Then the king sent him a gift. ⁹ But Uriah didn't go home. Instead, he slept at the entrance to the palace. He stayed there with all his master's servants.

¹⁰ David was told, "Uriah didn't go home." So he sent for Uriah. David said to him, "You have been away for a long time. Why didn't you go home?"

¹¹ Uriah said to David, "The ark and the army of Israel and Judah are out there in tents. My commander Joab and your special troops are camped in the open country. How could I go to my house to eat and drink? How could I go there and sleep with my wife? I could never do a thing like that. And that's just as sure as you are alive!"

¹² Then David said to him, "Stay here one more day. Tomorrow I'll send you back to the battle." So Uriah remained in Jerusalem that day and the next. ¹³ David invited Uriah to eat and drink with him. David got him drunk. But Uriah still didn't go home. In the evening he went out and slept on his mat. He stayed there among his master's servants.

¹⁴ The next morning David wrote a letter to Joab. He sent it along with Uriah. ¹⁵ In it he wrote, "Put Uriah out in front. That's where the fighting is the heaviest. Then pull your men back from him. When you do, the Ammonites will strike him down and kill him."

¹⁶ So Joab attacked the city. He put Uriah at a place where he knew the strongest enemy fighters were. ¹⁷ The troops came out of the city. They fought against Joab. Some of the men in David's army were killed. Uriah, the Hittite, also died.

¹⁸ Joab sent David a full report of the battle. ¹⁹ He told the messenger, "Tell the king everything that happened in the battle. When you are finished, ²⁰ his anger might explode. He might ask you, 'Why did you go so close to the city to fight against it? Didn't you know that the enemy soldiers would shoot arrows down from the wall? ²¹ Don't you remember how Abimelek, the son of Jerub-Besheth, was killed? A woman dropped a large millstone on him from the wall. That's how he died in Thebez. So why did you go so close to the wall?' If the king asks you that, tell him, 'And your servant Uriah, the Hittite, is also dead.'"

²² The messenger started out for Jerusalem. When he arrived there, he told David everything Joab had sent him to say. ²³ The messenger said to David, "The men in the city were more powerful than we were. They came out to fight against us in the

open. But we drove them back to the entrance of the city gate. ²⁴Then those who were armed with bows shot arrows at us from the wall. Some of your special troops were killed. Your servant Uriah, the Hittite, is also dead."

²⁵David told the messenger, "Tell Joab, 'Don't get upset over what happened. Swords kill one person as well as another. So keep on attacking the city. Destroy it.' Tell that to Joab. It will cheer him up."

²⁶Uriah's wife heard that her husband was dead. She mourned over him. ²⁷When her time of sadness was over, David had her brought to his house. She became his wife. And she had a son by him. But the LORD wasn't pleased with what David had done.

Nathan Tells David He Has Sinned

12 The LORD sent the prophet Nathan to David. When Nathan came to him, he said, "Two men lived in the same town. One was rich. The other was poor. ²The rich man had a very large number of sheep and cattle. ³But all the poor man had was one little female lamb. He had bought it. He raised it. It grew up with him and his children. It shared his food. It drank from his cup. It even slept in his arms. It was just like a daughter to him.

⁴"One day a traveler came to the rich man. The rich man wanted to prepare a meal for him. But he didn't want to kill one of his own sheep or cattle. Instead, he took the little female lamb that belonged to the poor man. Then the rich man cooked it for the traveler who had come to him."

⁵David was very angry with the rich man. He said to Nathan, "The man who did this must die! And that's just as sure as the LORD is alive. ⁶The man must pay back four times as much as that lamb was worth. How could he do such a thing? And he wasn't even sorry he had done it."

⁷Then Nathan said to David, "You are the man! The LORD, the God of Israel, says, 'I anointed you king over Israel. I saved you from Saul. ⁸I gave you everything that belonged to your master Saul. I even put his wives into your arms. I made you king over all the people of Israel and Judah. And if all of that had not been enough for you, I would have given you even more. ⁹Why did you turn your back on what I told you to do? You did what is evil in my sight. You made sure that Uriah, the Hittite, would be killed in battle. You took his wife to be your own. You let the men of Ammon kill him with their swords. ¹⁰So time after time members of your own royal house will be killed with swords. That's because you turned your back on me. You took the wife of Uriah, the Hittite, to be your own.'

¹¹"The LORD also says, 'I am going to bring trouble on you. It

will come from your own family. I will take your wives away. Your own eyes will see it. I will give your wives to a man who is close to you. He will sleep with them in the middle of the day. [12] You committed your sins in secret. But I will make sure that the man commits his sin in the middle of the day. Everyone in Israel will see it.' "

[13] Then David said to Nathan, "I have sinned against the LORD."

Nathan replied, "The LORD has taken away your sin. You aren't going to die. [14] But you have dared to show great disrespect for the LORD. So the son who has been born to you will die."

[15] Nathan went home. Then the LORD made David's child very sick. That was the child David had by Uriah's wife. [16] David begged God to heal the child. David didn't eat anything. He spent his nights lying on the ground. He put on the rough clothes people wear when they're sad. [17] His most trusted servants stood beside him. They wanted him to get up from the ground. But he refused to do it. And he wouldn't eat any food with them.

[18] On the seventh day the child died. David's attendants were afraid to tell him the child was dead. They thought, "While the child was still alive, we spoke to David. But he wouldn't listen to us. So how can we now tell him the child is dead? He might do something terrible to himself."

[19] David saw that his attendants were whispering to one another. Then he realized the child was dead. "Has the child died?" he asked.

"Yes," they replied. "He's dead."

[20] Then David got up from the ground. After he washed himself, he put on lotions. He changed his clothes. He went into the house of the LORD and worshiped him. Then he went to his own house. He asked for some food. They served it to him. And he ate it.

[21] His attendants asked him, "Why are you acting like this? While the child was still alive, you wouldn't eat anything. You cried a lot. But now that the child is dead, you get up and eat!"

[22] He answered, "While the child was still alive, I didn't eat anything. And I cried a lot. I thought, 'Who knows? The LORD might have mercy on me. He might let the child live.' [23] But now he's dead. So why should I continue to go without food? Can I bring him back to life again? Someday I'll go to him. But he won't return to me."

[24] Then David comforted his wife Bathsheba. He went to her and slept with her. Some time later she had a son. He was given the name Solomon. The LORD loved him. [25] So the LORD sent a message through Nathan the prophet. The LORD said, "Name the boy Jedidiah."

[26] During that time, Joab fought against Rabbah. It was

the royal city of the Ammonites. It had high walls around it. Joab was about to capture it. ²⁷ He sent messengers to David. He told them to say, "I have fought against Rabbah. I've taken control of its water supply. ²⁸ So bring the rest of the troops together. Surround the city and get ready to attack it. Then capture it. If you don't, I'll capture it myself. Then it will be named after me."

²⁹ So David brought together the whole army and went to Rabbah. He attacked it and captured it. ³⁰ David took the gold crown off the head of the king of Ammon. Then the crown was placed on David's head. The crown weighed 75 pounds. It had jewels in it. David took a huge amount of goods from the city. ³¹ He brought out the people who were there. He made them work with saws and iron picks and axes. He forced them to make bricks. David did that to all the towns in Ammon. Then he and his entire army returned to Jerusalem.

Amnon and Tamar

13 Some time later, David's son Amnon fell in love with Tamar. She was the beautiful sister of Absalom. He was another one of David's sons.

² Amnon wanted his sister Tamar so much that it made him sick. She was a virgin, and it seemed impossible for him to do what he wanted with her.

³ Amnon had an adviser named Jonadab. He was the son of David's brother Shimeah. Jonadab was a very clever man. ⁴ He asked Amnon, "You are the king's son, aren't you? So why do you look so worn out every morning? Won't you tell me?"

Amnon answered, "I'm in love with Tamar. She's the sister of my brother Absalom."

⁵ "Go to bed," Jonadab said. "Pretend to be sick. Your father will come to see you. When he does, tell him, 'I would like my sister Tamar to come and give me something to eat. Let her prepare the food right here in front of me where I can watch her. Then she can feed it to me.'"

⁶ So Amnon went to bed. He pretended to be sick. The king came to see him. Amnon said to him, "I would like my sister Tamar to come here. I want to watch her make some special bread. Then she can feed it to me."

⁷ David sent a message to Tamar at the palace. He said, "Go to your brother Amnon's house. Prepare some food for him." ⁸ So Tamar went to the house of her brother Amnon. He was lying in bed. She got some dough and mixed it. She shaped the bread right there in front of him. And she baked it. ⁹ Then she took the bread out of the pan and served it to him. But he refused to eat it.

"Send everyone out of here," Amnon said. So everyone left him. ¹⁰ Then he said to Tamar, "Bring the food here into my bedroom. Please feed it to me." So Tamar picked up the bread she had prepared. She brought it to her brother Amnon in his bedroom. [11] She took it to him so he could eat it. But he grabbed her. He said, "My sister, come to bed with me."

[12] "No, my brother!" she said to him. "Don't force me! An evil thing like that should never be done in Israel! Don't do it! [13] What about me? How could I ever get rid of my shame? And what about you? You would be as foolish as any evil person in Israel. Please speak to the king. He won't keep me from marrying you." [14] But Amnon refused to listen to her. He was stronger than she was. So he raped her.

[15] Then Amnon hated Tamar very much. In fact, he hated her more than he had loved her before. He said to her, "Get up! Get out!"

[16] "No!" she said to him. "Don't send me away. That would be worse than what you have already done to me."

But he refused to listen to her. [17] He sent for his personal servant. He said, "Get this woman out of my sight. Lock the door behind her." [18] So his servant threw her out. Then he locked the door behind her. Tamar was wearing a beautiful robe. It was the kind of robe the virgin daughters of the king wore. [19] She put ashes on her head. She tore the beautiful robe she was wearing. She put her hands on her head and went away. She was weeping out loud as she went.

[20] When her brother Absalom saw her, he spoke to her. He said, "Has Amnon, that brother of yours, forced you to go to bed with him? My sister, don't let it upset you. Don't let it bother you. He's your brother." After that, Tamar lived in her brother Absalom's house. She was very lonely.

[21] King David heard about everything that had happened. So he became very angry. [22] And Absalom never said a word of any kind to Amnon. He hated Amnon because he had brought shame on his sister Tamar.

Absalom Kills Amnon

[23] Two years later, Absalom invited all the king's sons to come to Baal Hazor. It was near the border of Ephraim. The workers who clipped the wool off Absalom's sheep were there. [24] Absalom went to the king. He said, "I've had my workers come to clip the wool. Will you and your attendants please join me?"

[25] "No, my son," the king replied. "All of us shouldn't go. It would be too much trouble for you." Although Absalom begged him, the king still refused to go. But he gave Absalom his blessing.

[26] Then Absalom said, "If you won't come, please let my brother Amnon come with us."

The king asked him, "Why should he go with you?" [27] But Absalom begged him. So the king sent Amnon with him. He also sent the rest of his sons.

[28] Absalom ordered his men, "Listen! When Amnon has had too much wine to drink, I'll say

to you, 'Strike Amnon down.' When I do, kill him. Don't be afraid. I've given you an order, haven't I? Be strong and brave." ²⁹ So Absalom's men killed Amnon, just as Absalom had ordered. Then all the king's sons got on their mules and rode away.

³⁰ While they were on their way, a report came to David. It said, "Absalom has struck down all your sons. Not one of them is left alive." ³¹ The king stood up and tore his clothes. Then he lay down on the ground. All his attendants stood near him. They had also torn their clothes.

³² Jonadab, the son of David's brother Shimeah, spoke up. He said, "You shouldn't think that all the princes have been killed. The only one who is dead is Amnon. Absalom had planned to kill him ever since the day Amnon raped his sister Tamar. ³³ You are my king and master. You shouldn't be concerned about this report. It's not true that all your sons are dead. The only one who is dead is Amnon."

³⁴ While all of that was taking place, Absalom ran away.

The man on guard duty at Jerusalem looked up. He saw many people coming on the road west of him. They were coming down the side of the hill. He went and spoke to the king. He said, "I see men coming down the road from Horonaim. They are coming down the side of the hill."

³⁵ Jonadab said to the king, "See, your sons are coming. It has happened just as I said it would."

³⁶ As he finished speaking, the king's sons came in. They were weeping out loud. The king and all his attendants were also weeping very bitterly.

³⁷ When Absalom ran away, he went to Talmai, the son of Ammihud. Talmai was king of Geshur. King David mourned many days for his son Amnon.

³⁸ So Absalom ran away and went to Geshur. He stayed there for three years. ³⁹ After some time the king got over his sorrow because of Amnon's death. Then King David longed to go to Absalom.

Absalom Returns to Jerusalem

14 Joab, the son of Zeruiah, knew that the king longed to see Absalom. ² So Joab sent someone to Tekoa to have a wise woman brought back from there. Joab said to her, "Pretend you are filled with sadness. Put on the rough clothing people wear when they're sad. Don't use any makeup. Act like a woman who has spent many days mourning for someone who has died. ³ Then go to the king. Give him the message I'm about to give you." And Joab told her what to say.

⁴ The woman from Tekoa went to the king. She bowed down with her face toward the ground. She did it to show him respect. She said, "Your Majesty, please help me!"

⁵ The king asked her, "What's bothering you?"

She said, "I'm a widow. My husband is dead. ⁶I had two sons. They got into a fight with each other in a field. No one was there to separate them. One of my sons struck down the other one and killed him. ⁷Now my whole family group has risen up against me. They say, 'Hand over the one who struck down his brother. Then we can put him to death for killing his brother. That will also get rid of the one who will receive the family property.' They want to kill the only living son I have left, just as someone would put out a burning coal. That would leave my husband without any son on the face of the earth to carry on the family name."

⁸The king said to the woman, "Go home. I'll give an order to make sure you are taken care of."

⁹But the woman from Tekoa said to him, "You are my king and master. Please pardon me and my family. You and your royal family won't be guilty of doing anything wrong."

¹⁰The king replied, "If people give you any trouble, bring them to me. They won't bother you again."

¹¹She said, "Please pray to the LORD your God. Pray that he will keep our nearest male relative from killing my other son. Then my son won't be destroyed."

"You can be sure that the LORD lives," the king said. "And you can be just as sure that not one hair of your son's head will fall to the ground."

¹²Then the woman said, "King David, please let me say something else to you."

"Go ahead," he replied.

¹³The woman said, "You are the king. So why have you done something that brings so much harm on God's people? When you do that, you hand down a sentence against yourself. You won't let the son you drove away come back. ¹⁴All of us must die. We are like water spilled on the ground. It can't be put back into the jar. But that is not what God desires. Instead, he finds a way to bring back anyone who was driven away from him.

¹⁵"King David, I've come here to say this to you now. I've done it because people have made me afraid. I thought, 'I'll go and speak to the king. Perhaps he'll do what I'm asking. ¹⁶A man is trying to separate me and my son from the property God gave us. Perhaps the king will agree to save me from that man.'

¹⁷"So now I'm saying, 'May what you have told me prevent that man from doing what he wants. You are like an angel of God. You know what is good and what is evil. May the LORD your God be with you.'"

¹⁸Then the king said to the woman, "I'm going to ask you a question. I want you to tell me the truth."

"Please ask me anything you want to," the woman said.

¹⁹The king asked, "Joab told you to say all of this, didn't he?"

The woman answered, "What you have told me is exactly right.

And that's just as sure as you are alive. It's true that Joab directed me to do this. He told me everything he wanted me to say. 20 He did it to change the way things now are. You are as wise as an angel of God. You know everything that happens in the land."

21 Later the king said to Joab, "All right. I'll do what you want. Go. Bring back the young man Absalom."

22 Joab bowed down with his face toward the ground. He did it to honor the king. And he asked God to bless the king. He said, "You are my king and master. Today I know that you are pleased with me. You have given me what I asked for."

23 Then Joab went to Geshur. He brought Absalom back to Jerusalem. 24 But the king said, "He must go to his own house. I don't want him to come and see me." So Absalom went to his own house. He didn't go to see the king.

25 In the whole land of Israel there wasn't any man as handsome as Absalom was. That's why everyone praised him. From the top of his head to the bottom of his feet he didn't have any flaws. 26 He used to cut his hair once a year when it became too heavy for him. Then he would weigh it. It weighed five pounds in keeping with the standard weights used in the palace.

27 Three sons and a daughter were born to Absalom. His daughter's name was Tamar. She became a beautiful woman.

28 Absalom lived in Jerusalem for two years without going to see the king. 29 Then Absalom sent for Joab. He wanted to send Joab to the king. But Joab refused to come to Absalom. So Absalom sent for him a second time. But Joab still refused to come. 30 Then Absalom said to his servants, "Joab's field is next to mine. He has barley growing there. Go and set it on fire." So Absalom's servants set the field on fire.

31 Joab finally went to Absalom's house. He said to Absalom, "Why did your servants set my field on fire?"

32 Absalom said to Joab, "I sent a message to you. I said, 'Come here. I want to send you to the king. I want you to ask him for me, "Why did you bring me back from Geshur? I would be better off if I were still there!" ' Now then, I want to go and see the king. If I'm guilty of doing anything wrong, let him put me to death."

33 So Joab went to the king and told him that. Then the king sent for Absalom. He came in and bowed down to the king with his face toward the ground. And the king kissed Absalom.

Absalom Makes Secret Plans Against David

15 Some time later, Absalom got a chariot and horses for himself. He also got 50 men to run in front of him. 2 He would get up early. He would stand by the side of the road that led to the city gate. Sometimes a person would come with a case for the king to decide. Then Absalom would call out to him, "What town are you from?" He would answer, "I'm from one of the tribes of Israel." [3] Absalom would say, "Look, your claims are based on the law. So you have every right to make them. But the king doesn't have anyone here who can listen to your case." [4] Absalom would continue, "I wish I were appointed judge in the land! Then anyone who has a case or a claim could come to me. I would make sure they are treated fairly."

[5] Sometimes people would approach Absalom and bow down to him. Then he would reach out his hand. He would take hold of them and kiss them. [6] Absalom did that to all the Israelites who came to the king with their cases or claims. That's why the hearts of the people were turned toward him.

[7] After Absalom had lived in Jerusalem for four years, he went and spoke to the king. He said, "Let me go to Hebron. I want to keep a promise I made to the LORD. [8] When I was living at Geshur in Aram, I made a promise. I said, 'If the LORD takes me back to Jerusalem, I'll go to Hebron and worship him there.'"

[9] The king said to him, "Go in peace." So he went to Hebron.

[10] Then Absalom sent messengers secretly to all the tribes of Israel. They said, "Listen for the sound of trumpets. As soon as you hear them, say, 'Absalom has become king in Hebron.'"

[11] Absalom had taken 200 men from Jerusalem with him to Hebron. He had invited them to be his guests. They went without having any idea what was going to happen. [12] While Absalom was offering sacrifices, he sent for Ahithophel. Ahithophel was David's adviser. He came to Absalom from Giloh, his hometown. The number of people who followed Absalom kept growing. So he became more and more able to carry out his plans against David.

David Runs Away From Absalom

[13] A messenger came and spoke to David. He told him, "The hearts of the Israelites are turned toward Absalom."

[14] Then David spoke to all his officials who were with him in Jerusalem. He said, "Come on! We have to leave right away! If we don't, none of us will escape from Absalom. He'll move quickly to catch up with us. He'll destroy us. His men will kill everyone in the city with their swords."

[15] The king's officials answered him, "You are our king and master. We're ready to do anything you want."

[16] The king started out. Everyone in his whole family went with him. But he left ten concubines behind to take care of the palace. [17] So the king and all those with him left. They stopped at the edge of the city. [18] All of David's officials

marched past him. All the Kerethites and Pelethites marched along with them. And all of the 600 men who had come with him from Gath marched in front of him.

¹⁹ The king spoke to Ittai. He was from Gath. The king said to him, "Why do you want to come along with us? Go back. Stay with King Absalom. You are an outsider. You left your own country. ²⁰ You came to join me only a short time ago. So why should I make you wander around with us now? I don't even know where I'm going. So go on back. Take your people with you. And may the LORD be kind and faithful to you."

²¹ But Ittai replied to the king, "You are my king and master. I want to be where you are. It doesn't matter whether I live or die. And that's just as sure as the LORD and you are alive."

²² David said to Ittai, "Go ahead then. Keep marching with my men." So Ittai, the Gittite, kept marching. All his men and their families marched with him.

²³ All the people in the countryside wept out loud as David and all his followers passed by. The king went across the Kidron Valley. He and all the people with him moved on toward the desert.

²⁴ Zadok also went with them. Some of the Levites went with him. They were carrying the ark of the covenant of God. They set down the ark. Abiathar offered sacrifices until all the people had left the city.

²⁵ Then the king said to Zadok, "Take the ark of God back into the city. If the LORD is pleased with me, he'll bring me back. He'll let me see the ark again. He'll also let me see Jerusalem again. That's the place where he lives. ²⁶ But suppose he says, 'I am not pleased with you.' Then I accept that. Let him do to me what he thinks is best."

²⁷ The king said again to Zadok the priest, "Do you understand? Go back to the city with my blessing. Take your son Ahimaaz with you. Also take Abiathar and his son Jonathan with you. ²⁸ I'll wait at the place in the desert where we can go across the Jordan River. I'll wait there until you send word to let me know what's happening." ²⁹ So Zadok and Abiathar took the ark of God back to Jerusalem. They stayed there.

³⁰ But David went on up the Mount of Olives. He was weeping as he went. His head was covered, and he was barefoot. All the people with him covered their heads too. And they were weeping as they went up. ³¹ David had been told, "Ahithophel, along with Absalom, is one of the people making secret plans against you." So David prayed, "LORD, make Ahithophel's advice look foolish."

³² David arrived at the top of the Mount of Olives. That's where people used to worship God. Hushai, the Arkite, was there to meet him. His robe was torn. There was dust on his head. ³³ David said to him,

"If you go with me, you will be too much trouble for me. ³⁴ So return to the city. Say to Absalom, 'Your Majesty, I'll be your servant. In the past, I was your father's servant. But now I'll be your servant.' If you do that, you can help me by making sure Ahithophel's advice fails. ³⁵ Zadok and Abiathar, the priests, will be there with you. Tell them everything you hear in the king's palace. ³⁶ They have their sons Ahimaaz and Jonathan there with them. Send them to tell me everything you hear."

³⁷ So David's trusted friend Hushai went to Jerusalem. He arrived just as Absalom was entering the city.

David and Ziba

16 David went just beyond the top of the Mount of Olives. Ziba was waiting there to meet him. He was Mephibosheth's manager. He had several donkeys with saddles on them. They were carrying 200 loaves of bread and 100 raisin cakes. They were also carrying 100 fig cakes and a bottle of wine. The bottle was made out of animal skin.

² The king asked Ziba, "Why have you brought all these things?"

Ziba answered, "The donkeys are for the king's family to ride on. The bread and fruit are for the people to eat. The wine will make those who get tired in the desert feel like new again."

³ Then the king asked, "Where is your master's grandson Mephibosheth?"

Ziba said to him, "He's staying in Jerusalem. He thinks, 'Today the Israelites will cause me to rule once again over my grandfather Saul's kingdom.'"

⁴ Then the king said to Ziba, "Everything that belonged to Mephibosheth belongs to you now."

"You are my king and master," Ziba said. "I make myself humble in front of you. I bow down to you. May you be pleased with me."

Shimei Curses David

⁵ King David approached Bahurim. As he did, a man came out toward him. The man was from the same family group that Saul was from. His name was Shimei. He was the son of Gera. As he came out of the town, he cursed David. ⁶ He threw stones at David and all his officials. He did it even though all the troops and the special guard were there. They were to the right and left of David. ⁷ As Shimei cursed, he said, "Get out! Get out, you murderer! You are a worthless and evil man! ⁸ You spilled the blood of a lot of people in Saul's family. You took over his kingdom. Now the LORD is paying you back. He has handed the kingdom over to your son Absalom. You have been destroyed because you are a murderer!"

⁹ Then Abishai, the son of Zeruiah, spoke to the king. He said, "King David, why should we let this dead dog curse you? Let me go over there. I'll cut off his head."

¹⁰ But the king said, "You and Joab are sons of Zeruiah. What does this have to do with you? Maybe the Lord said to him, 'Curse David.' If he did, who can ask him, 'Why are you doing this?'"

¹¹ Then David spoke to Abishai and all his officials. He said, "My very own son Absalom is trying to kill me. How much more should this man from Benjamin want to kill me! Leave him alone. Let him curse. The Lord has told him to do it. ¹² Maybe the Lord will see how much I'm suffering. Maybe he'll bring back to me his covenant blessing instead of his curse I'm hearing today."

¹³ So David and his men kept going along the road. At the same time, Shimei was going along the hillside across from him. He was cursing David as he went. He was throwing stones at David. He was showering him with dirt. ¹⁴ The king and all the people with him came to the place they had planned to go to. They were very tired. So David rested there.

Ahithophel and Hushai Give Advice to Absalom

¹⁵ During that time, Absalom and all the men of Israel came to Jerusalem. Ahithophel was with him. ¹⁶ Then Hushai, the Arkite, went to Absalom. He said to him, "May the king live a long time! May the king live a long time!" Hushai was David's trusted friend.

¹⁷ Absalom said to Hushai, "So this is the way you show love to your friend? If he's your friend, why didn't you go with him?"

¹⁸ Hushai said to Absalom, "Why should I? You are the one the Lord has chosen. These people and all the men of Israel have also chosen you. I want to be on your side. I want to stay with you. ¹⁹ After all, who else should I serve? Shouldn't I serve the king's son? I will serve you, just as I served your father."

²⁰ Absalom said to Ahithophel, "Give us your advice. What should we do?"

²¹ Ahithophel answered, "Your father left some concubines behind to take care of the palace. Go and sleep with them. Then all the Israelites will hear about it. They will hear that you have made your father hate you. Everyone with you will be encouraged to give you more support." ²² So they set up a tent for Absalom on the roof of the palace. He went in and slept with his father's concubines. Everyone in Israel saw it.

²³ In those days the advice Ahithophel gave was as good as advice from someone who asks God for guidance. That's what David and Absalom thought about all of Ahithophel's advice.

17 One day Ahithophel said to Absalom, "Here's what I suggest. Choose 12,000 men. Start out tonight and go after David. ² Attack him while he's tired and weak. Fill him with terror. Then all the people with him will run away. Don't strike down anyone except the king.

3 Bring all the other people back. After the man you want to kill is dead, everyone else will return to you. And none of the people will be harmed." 4 Ahithophel's plan seemed good to Absalom. It also seemed good to all the elders of Israel.

5 But Absalom said, "Send for Hushai, the Arkite. Then we can find out what he suggests as well." 6 Hushai came to him. Absalom said, "Ahithophel has given us his advice. Should we do what he says? If we shouldn't, tell us what you would do."

7 Hushai replied to Absalom, "The advice Ahithophel has given you isn't good this time. 8 You know your father and his men. They are fighters. They are as strong as a wild bear whose cubs have been stolen from her. Besides, your father really knows how to fight. He won't spend the night with his troops. 9 In fact, he's probably hiding in a cave or some other place right now. Suppose he attacks your troops first. When people hear about it, they'll say, 'Many of the troops who followed Absalom have been killed.' 10 Then the hearts of your soldiers will melt away in fear. Even those as brave as a lion will be terrified. That's because everyone in Israel knows that your father is a fighter. They know that those with him are brave.

11 "So here's what I suggest. Bring together all the men of Israel from the town of Dan all the way to Beersheba. They are as many as the grains of sand on the seashore. You yourself should lead them into battle. 12 Then we'll attack David no matter where we find him. As dew completely covers the ground, we'll completely overpower his entire army. We won't leave him or any of his men alive. 13 He might try to get away by going into a city. If he does, all of us will bring ropes to that city. We'll drag the whole city down into the valley. Not even a pebble of that city will be left."

14 Absalom and all the men of Israel agreed. They said, "The advice of Hushai, the Arkite, is better than the advice of Ahithophel." The Lord had decided that Ahithophel's good advice would fail. The Lord wanted to bring horrible trouble on Absalom.

15 Hushai spoke to Zadok and Abiathar, the priests. He said, "Ahithophel has given advice to Absalom and the elders of Israel. He suggested that they should do one thing. But I suggested something else. 16 Send a message right away. Tell David, 'Don't spend the night in the desert at a place where people cross the Jordan River. Make sure you go on across. If you don't, you and all the people with you will be swallowed up.'"

17 Jonathan and Ahimaaz were staying at En Rogel just outside Jerusalem. They knew they would be in danger if anyone saw them entering the city. A female servant was supposed to go and tell them what had happened. Then they were

supposed to go and tell King David. [18] But a young man saw Jonathan and Ahimaaz and told Absalom about it. So the two men left right away. They went to the house of a man in Bahurim. He had a well in his courtyard. They climbed down into it. [19] The man's wife got a covering and spread it out over the opening of the well. Then she scattered grain on the covering. So no one knew that the men were hiding in the well.

[20] Absalom's men came to the house. They asked the woman, "Where are Ahimaaz and Jonathan?"

She answered, "They went across the brook." When the men looked around, they didn't find anyone. So they returned to Jerusalem.

[21] After they had gone, Jonathan and Ahimaaz climbed out of the well. They went to tell King David what they had found out. They said to him, "Go across the river right away. Ahithophel has told Absalom how to come after you and strike you down."

[22] So David and all the people with him started out. They went across the Jordan River. By sunrise, everyone had crossed over.

[23] Ahithophel saw that his advice wasn't being followed. So he put a saddle on his donkey. He started out for his house in his hometown. When he arrived, he made everything ready for his death. He made out his will. Then he killed himself. And so he died and was buried in his father's tomb.

Absalom Dies

[24] David went to Mahanaim. Absalom went across the Jordan River with all the men of Israel. [25] Absalom had made Amasa commander of the army in place of Joab. Amasa was the son of Jether. Jether belonged to the family line of Ishmael. He had married Abigail. She was the daughter of Nahash and the sister of Zeruiah. Zeruiah was the mother of Joab. [26] Absalom and the Israelites camped in the land of Gilead.

[27] David came to Mahanaim. Shobi, the son of Nahash, met him there. Shobi was from Rabbah in the land of Ammon. Makir, the son of Ammiel from Lo Debar, met him there too. So did Barzillai from Rogelim in the land of Gilead. [28] They brought beds, bowls and clay pots. They brought wheat, barley, flour, and grain that had been cooked. They brought beans and lentils. [29] They brought honey, butter, sheep, and cheese that was made from cows' milk. They brought all that food for David and his people to eat. They said, "These people have become tired. They've become hungry and thirsty in the desert."

18 David brought together the men with him. He appointed commanders of thousands over some of them. He appointed commanders of hundreds over the others. [2] Then David sent out his troops in military groups. One group was under the command of Joab. Another was under Joab's brother Abishai, the son of Zeruiah. The last was under Ittai, the Gittite. The king told the troops, "You can be sure that I myself will march out with you."

³ But the men said, "You must not march out. If we are forced to run away, our enemies won't care about us. Even if half of us die, they won't care. But you are worth 10,000 of us. So it would be better for you to stay here in the city. Then you can send us help if we need it."

⁴ The king said, "I'll do what you think is best."

So the king stood beside the city gate. His whole army marched out in groups of hundreds and groups of thousands. ⁵ The king gave an order to Joab, Abishai and Ittai. He commanded them, "Be gentle with the young man Absalom. Do it for me." All the troops heard the king give the commanders that order about Absalom.

⁶ David's army marched out of the city to fight against Israel. The battle took place in the forest of Ephraim. ⁷ There David's men won the battle over Israel's army. A huge number of men were wounded or killed that day. The total number was 20,000. ⁸ The fighting spread out over the whole countryside. But more men were killed in the forest that day than out in the open.

⁹ Absalom happened to come across some of David's men. He was riding his mule. The mule went under the thick branches of a large oak tree. Absalom's hair got caught in the tree. He was left hanging in the air. The mule he was riding kept on going.

¹⁰ One of David's men saw what had happened. He told Joab, "I just saw Absalom hanging in an oak tree."

¹¹ Joab said to the man, "What! You saw him? Why didn't you strike him down right there? Then I would have had to give you four ounces of silver and a soldier's belt."

¹² But the man replied, "I wouldn't do anything to hurt the king's son. I wouldn't do it even for 25 pounds of silver. We heard the king's command to you and Abishai and Ittai. He said, 'Be careful not to hurt the young man Absalom. Do it for me.' ¹³ Suppose I had put my life in danger by killing him. The king would have found out about it. Nothing is hidden from him. And you wouldn't have stood up for me."

¹⁴ Joab said, "I'm not going to waste any more time on you." So he got three javelins. Then he went over and plunged them into Absalom's heart. He did it while Absalom was still hanging there alive in the oak tree. ¹⁵ Ten of the men carrying Joab's armor surrounded Absalom. They struck him and killed him.

¹⁶ Then Joab blew his trumpet. He ordered his troops to stop chasing Israel's army. ¹⁷ Joab's men threw Absalom into a big pit in the forest. They covered him with a large pile of rocks.

While all of that was going on, all the Israelites ran back to their homes.

¹⁸ Earlier in his life Absalom had set up a pillar in the King's Valley. He had put it up as a monument to himself. He thought, "I don't have a son to carry on the memory of my name." So he named the pillar after himself. It is still called Absalom's Monument to this day.

David Mourns Over Absalom

¹⁹ Ahimaaz, the son of Zadok, said to Joab, "Let me run and take the news to the king. Let me tell him that the LORD has shown that David is in the right. The LORD has done this by saving David from his enemies."

²⁰ "I don't want you to take the news to the king today," Joab told him. "You can do it some other time. But you must not do it today, because the king's son is dead."

²¹ Then Joab said to a man from Cush, "Go. Tell the king what you have seen." The man bowed down in front of Joab. Then he ran off.

²² Ahimaaz, the son of Zadok, spoke again to Joab. He said, "I don't care what happens to me. Please let me run behind the man from Cush."

But Joab replied, "My son, why do you want to go? You don't have any news that will bring you a reward."

²³ He said, "I don't care what happens. I want to run."

So Joab said, "Run!" Then Ahimaaz ran across the plain of the Jordan River. As he ran, he passed the man from Cush.

²⁴ David was sitting in the area between the inner and outer gates of the city. The man on guard duty went up to the roof over the entrance of the gate by the wall. As he looked out, he saw someone running alone. ²⁵ The guard called out to the king and reported it.

The king said, "If the runner is alone, he must be bringing good news." The runner came closer and closer.

²⁶ Then the man on guard duty saw another runner. He called out to the man guarding the gate. He said, "Look! There's another man running alone!"

The king said, "He must be bringing good news too."

²⁷ The man on guard duty said, "I can see that the first one runs like Ahimaaz, the son of Zadok."

"He's a good man," the king said. "He's bringing good news."

²⁸ Then Ahimaaz called out to the king, "Everything's all right!" He bowed down in front of the king with his face toward the ground. He said, "You are my king and master. Give praise to the LORD your God! He has handed over to you those who lifted their hands to kill you."

²⁹ The king asked, "Is the young man Absalom safe?"

Ahimaaz answered, "I saw total disorder. I saw it just as Joab was about to send the king's servant and me to you. But I don't know what it was all about."

³⁰ The king said, "Stand over

there and wait." So he stepped over to one side and stood there.

31 Then the man from Cush arrived. He said, "You are my king and master. I'm bringing you some good news. The LORD has shown that you are in the right. He has done this by rescuing you today from all those trying to kill you."

32 The king asked the man from Cush, "Is the young man Absalom safe?"

The man replied, "King David, may your enemies be like that young man. May all those who rise up to harm you be like him."

33 The king was very upset. He went up to the room over the entrance of the gate and wept. As he went, he said, "My son Absalom! My son, my son Absalom! I wish I had died instead of you. Absalom! My son, my son!"

19

Someone told Joab, "The king is weeping and mourning for Absalom. He's filled with sadness because his son has died." 2 The army had won a great battle that day. But their joy turned into sadness. That's because someone had told the troops, "The king is filled with sorrow because his son is dead." 3 The men came quietly into the city that day. They were like fighting men who are ashamed because they've run away from a battle. 4 The king covered his face. He cried loudly, "My son Absalom! Absalom, my son, my son!"

5 Then Joab went into the king's house. He said to him,

"Today you have made all your men feel ashamed. They have just saved your life. They have saved the lives of your sons and daughters. And they have saved the lives of your wives and concubines. 6 You love those who hate you. You hate those who love you. The commanders and their troops don't mean anything to you. You made that very clear today. I can see that you would be pleased if Absalom were alive today and all of us were dead. 7 Now go out there and cheer up your men. If you don't, you won't have any of them left with you by sunset. That will be worse for you than all the troubles you have ever had in your whole life. That's what I promise you in the LORD's name."

8 So the king got up and took his seat in the entrance of the city gate. His men were told, "The king is sitting in the entrance of the gate." Then all of them came and stood in front of him.

While all of that was going on, the Israelites had run back to their homes.

David Returns to Jerusalem

9 People from all the tribes of Israel began to argue among themselves. They were saying, "The king saved us from the power of our enemies. He saved us from the power of the Philistines. But now he has left the country to escape from Absalom. 10 We anointed Absalom to rule over us. But he has died in

battle. So why aren't any of you talking about bringing the king back?"

¹¹ King David sent a message to Zadok and Abiathar, the priests. David said, "Speak to the elders of Judah. Tell them I said, 'News has reached me where I'm staying. People all over Israel are talking about bringing me back to my palace. Why should you be the last to do something about it? ¹² You are my relatives. You are my own flesh and blood. So why should you be the last to bring me back?' ¹³ Say to Amasa, 'Aren't you my own flesh and blood? You will be the commander of my army for life in place of Joab. If that isn't true, may God punish me greatly.' "

¹⁴ So the hearts of all the men of Judah were turned toward David. All of them had the same purpose in mind. They sent a message to the king. They said, "We want you to come back. We want all your men to come back too." ¹⁵ Then the king returned. He went as far as the Jordan River.

The men of Judah had come to Gilgal to welcome the king back. They had come to bring him across the Jordan. ¹⁶ Shimei, the son of Gera, was among them. Shimei was from Bahurim in the territory of Benjamin. He hurried down to welcome King David back. ¹⁷ There were 1,000 people from Benjamin with him. Ziba, the manager of Saul's house, was with him too. And so were Ziba's 15 sons and 20 servants. All of them rushed down to the Jordan River. That's where the king was. ¹⁸ They went across at the place where people usually cross it. Then they brought the king's family back over with them. They were ready to do anything he wanted them to do.

Shimei, the son of Gera, had also gone across the Jordan. When he did, he fell down flat with his face toward the ground in front of the king. ¹⁹ He said to him, "You are my king and master. Please don't hold me guilty. Please forgive me for the wrong things I did on the day you left Jerusalem. Please forget all about them. ²⁰ I know I've sinned. But today I've come down here to welcome you. I'm the first member of Joseph's whole family to do it."

²¹ Then Abishai, the son of Zeruiah, said, "Shouldn't Shimei be put to death for what he did? He cursed you. And you are the LORD's anointed king."

²² But David replied, "You and Joab are sons of Zeruiah. What does this have to do with you? What right do you have to interfere? Should anyone be put to death in Israel today? Don't I know that today I am king over Israel again?" ²³ So the king made a promise to Shimei. He said to him, "You aren't going to be put to death."

²⁴ Mephibosheth was Saul's grandson. He had also gone down to welcome the king back. He had not taken care of his feet. He hadn't trimmed his mus-

tache or washed his clothes. He hadn't done any of those things from the day the king left Jerusalem until the day he returned safely. 25 He came from Jerusalem to welcome the king. The king asked him, "Mephibosheth, why didn't you go with me?"

26 He said, "You are my king and master. I'm not able to walk. So I thought, 'I'll have a saddle put on my donkey. I'll ride on it. Then I can go with the king.' But my servant Ziba turned against me. 27 He has told you lies about me. King David, you are like an angel of God. So do what you wish. 28 You should have put all the members of my grandfather's family to death, including me. Instead, you always provided what I needed. So what right do I have to make any more appeals to you?"

29 The king said to him, "You don't have to say anything else. I order you and Ziba to divide up Saul's land between you."

30 Mephibosheth said to the king, "I'm happy that you have returned home safely. So just let Ziba have everything."

31 Barzillai had also come down to go across the Jordan River with the king. He wanted to send the king on his way from there. Barzillai was from Rogelim in the land of Gilead. 32 He was very old. He was 80 years old. He had given the king everything he needed while the king was staying in Mahanaim. That's because Barzillai was very wealthy. 33 The king said to Barzillai, "Come across the river with me. Stay with me in Jerusalem. I'll take good care of you."

34 But Barzillai said to the king, "I won't live for many more years. So why should I go up to Jerusalem with you? 35 I'm already 80 years old. I can hardly tell the difference between what is enjoyable and what isn't. I can hardly taste what I eat and drink. I can't even hear the voices of male and female singers anymore. So why should I add my problems to yours? 36 I'll go across the Jordan River with you for a little way. Why should you reward me by taking care of me? 37 Let me go back home. Then I can die in my own town. I can be buried there in the tomb of my father and mother. But let Kimham take my place. Let him go across the river with you. Do for him whatever you wish."

38 The king said, "Kimham will go across with me. I'll do for him whatever you wish. And I'll do for you anything you wish."

39 So all the people went across the Jordan River. Then the king crossed over. The king kissed Barzillai and said goodbye to him. And Barzillai went back home.

40 After the king had gone across the river, he went to Gilgal. Kimham had gone across with him. All the troops of Judah and half of the troops of Israel had taken the king across.

41 Soon all the men of Israel were coming to the king. They were saying to him, "Why did the men of Judah take you away

from us? They are our relatives. What right did they have to bring you and your family across the Jordan River? What right did they have to bring all your men over with you?"

⁴²All the men of Judah answered the men of Israel. They said, "We did that because the king is our close relative. So why should you be angry about what happened? Have we eaten any of the king's food? Have we taken anything for ourselves?"

⁴³Then the men of Israel answered the men of Judah. They said, "We have ten of the 12 tribes in the kingdom. So we have a stronger claim on David than you have. Why then are you acting as if you hate us? Weren't we the first ones to talk about bringing back our king?"

But the men of Judah argued their side even more forcefully than the men of Israel.

Sheba Urges Israel Not to Follow David

20 An evil man who always stirred up trouble happened to be in Gilgal. His name was Sheba, the son of Bikri. Sheba was from the tribe of Benjamin. He blew his trumpet. Then he shouted,

"We don't have any share in
    David's kingdom!
Jesse's son is not our king!
Men of Israel, every one of
    you go back home!"

²So all the men of Israel deserted David. They followed Sheba, the son of Bikri. But the men of Judah stayed with their king. They remained with him from the Jordan River all the way to Jerusalem.

³David returned to his palace in Jerusalem. He had left ten concubines there to take care of the palace. He put them in a house and kept them under guard. He gave them what they needed. But he didn't sleep with them. They were kept under guard until the day they died. They lived as if they were widows.

⁴The king said to Amasa, "Send for the men of Judah. Tell them to come to me within three days. And be here yourself." ⁵So Amasa went to get the men of Judah. But he took longer than the time the king had set for him.

⁶David said to Abishai, "Sheba, the son of Bikri, will do more harm to us than Absalom ever did. Take my men and go after him. If you don't, he'll find cities that have high walls around them. He'll go into one of them and escape from us." ⁷So Joab's men marched out with the Kerethites and Pelethites. They went out with all the mighty soldiers. All of them were under Abishai's command. They marched out from Jerusalem and went after Sheba, the son of Bikri.

⁸They arrived at the great rock in Gibeon. Amasa went there to welcome them. Joab was wearing his military clothes. Over them at his waist he had strapped on a belt that held a

dagger. As he stepped forward, he secretly took the dagger out.

⁹Joab said to Amasa, "How are you, my friend?" Then Joab reached out his right hand. He took hold of Amasa's beard to kiss him. ¹⁰Amasa didn't notice the dagger in Joab's left hand. Joab stuck it into his stomach. His insides spilled out on the ground. Joab didn't have to stab him again. Amasa was already dead. Then Joab and his brother Abishai went after Sheba, the son of Bikri.

¹¹One of Joab's men stood beside Amasa's body. He said to the other men, "Are you pleased with Joab? Are you on David's side? Then follow Joab!" ¹²Amasa's body lay covered with his blood in the middle of the road. The man saw that all the troops stopped there. He realized that everyone was stopping to look at Amasa's body. So he dragged it from the road into a field. Then he threw some clothes on top of it. ¹³After that happened, everyone continued on with Joab. They went after Sheba, the son of Bikri.

¹⁴Sheba passed through all the territory of the tribes of Israel. He arrived at the city of Abel Beth Maakah. He had gone through the entire area of the Bikrites. They had gathered together and followed him. ¹⁵Joab and all his troops came to Abel Beth Maakah. They surrounded it because Sheba was there. They built a ramp up to the city. It stood against the outer wall. They pounded the wall with huge logs to bring it down. ¹⁶While that was going on, a wise woman called out from the city. She shouted, "Listen! Listen! Tell Joab to come here. I want to speak to him." ¹⁷So Joab went toward her. She asked, "Are you Joab?"

"I am," he answered.

She said, "Listen to what I have to say."

"I'm listening," he said.

¹⁸She continued, "Long ago people used to say, 'Get your answer at Abel.' And that would settle the matter. ¹⁹We are the most peaceful and faithful people in Israel. You are trying to destroy a city that is like a mother in Israel. Why do you want to swallow up what belongs to the Lord?"

²⁰"I would never do anything like that!" Joab said. "I would never swallow up or destroy what belongs to the Lord! ²¹That isn't what I have in mind at all. There's a man named Sheba, the son of Bikri, in your city. He's from the hill country of Ephraim. He's trying to kill King David. Hand that man over to me. Then I'll pull my men back from your city."

The woman said to Joab, "We'll throw his head down to you from the wall."

²²Then the woman gave her wise advice to all the people in the city. They cut off the head of Sheba, the son of Bikri. They threw it down to Joab. So he blew his trumpet. Then his men pulled back from the city. Each of them returned to his home.

And Joab went back to the king in Jerusalem.

David's Officials

23 Joab was commander over Israel's entire army.

Benaiah, the son of Jehoiada, was commander over the Kerethites and Pelethites.
24 Adoniram was in charge of those who were forced to work hard.

Jehoshaphat, the son of Ahilud, kept the records.
25 Sheva was the secretary.

Zadok and Abiathar were priests.
26 Ira, the Jairite, was David's priest.

David Makes Things Right for the People of Gibeon

21 For three years in a row there wasn't enough food in the land. That was while David was king. So David asked the LORD why he wasn't blessing his people. The LORD said, "It is because Saul and his family committed murder. He put the people of Gibeon to death."

2 The people of Gibeon weren't a part of Israel. Instead, they were some of the Amorites who were still left alive. The Israelites had promised to spare them. But Saul had tried to put an end to them. That's because he wanted to make Israel and Judah strong. So now King David sent for the people of Gibeon and spoke to them. 3 He asked them, "What would you like me to do for you? How can I make up for the wrong things that were done to you? I want you to be able to pray that the LORD will once again bless his land."

4 The people of Gibeon answered him. They said, "No amount of silver or gold can make up for what Saul and his family did to us. And we can't put anyone in Israel to death."

"What do you want me to do for you?" David asked.

5 They answered the king, "Saul nearly destroyed us. He made plans to wipe us out. We don't have anywhere to live in Israel. 6 So let seven of the males in his family line be given to us. We'll kill them. We'll put their dead bodies out in the open in the sight of the LORD. We'll do it at Gibeah of Saul. Saul was the LORD's chosen king."

So King David said, "I'll give seven males to you."

7 The king spared Mephibosheth. He was the son of Jonathan and the grandson of Saul. David had made a promise in front of the LORD. He had promised to be kind to Jonathan and the family line of his father Saul. 8 But the king chose Armoni and another Mephibosheth. They were the two sons of Aiah's daughter Rizpah. Saul was their father. The king also chose the five sons of Saul's daughter Merab. Adriel, the son of Barzillai, was their father. Adriel was from Meholah. 9 King David handed them over to the people of Gibeon. They killed them. They put their dead bodies out in the open on a hill in the sight

of the LORD. All seven of them died together. They were put to death during the first days of the harvest. It happened just when people were beginning to harvest the barley.

10 Aiah's daughter Rizpah took some rough cloth people wear when they're sad. She spread it out for herself on a rock. She stayed there from the beginning of the harvest until it rained. The rain poured down from the sky on the dead bodies of the seven males. She didn't let the birds touch them by day. She didn't let the wild animals touch them at night. 11 Someone told David what Rizpah had done. She was Aiah's daughter and Saul's concubine. 12 David went and got the bones of Saul and his son Jonathan. He got them from the citizens of Jabesh Gilead. They had stolen their bodies from the main street in Beth Shan. That's where the Philistines had hung their bodies up on the city wall. They had done it after they struck Saul down on Mount Gilboa. 13 David brought the bones of Saul and his son Jonathan from Jabesh Gilead. The bones of the seven males who had been killed and put out in the open were also gathered up.

14 The bones of Saul and his son Jonathan were buried in the tomb of Saul's father Kish. The tomb was at Zela in the territory of Benjamin. Everything the king commanded was done. After that, God answered prayer and blessed the land.

Wars Against the Philistines

15 Once again there was a battle between the Philistines and Israel. David went down with his men to fight against the Philistines. He became very tired. 16 Ishbi-Benob belonged to the family line of Rapha. The tip of his bronze spear weighed seven and a half pounds. He was also armed with a new sword. He said he would kill David. 17 But Abishai, the son of Zeruiah, came to save David. He struck down the Philistine and killed him. Then David's men made a promise. They said to David, "We never want you to go out with us to battle again. You are the lamp of Israel's kingdom. We want that lamp to keep on burning brightly."

18 There was another battle against the Philistines. It took place at Gob. At that time Sibbekai killed Saph. Sibbekai was a Hushathite. Saph was from the family line of Rapha.

19 In another battle against the Philistines at Gob, Elhanan killed Goliath's brother. Elhanan was the son of Jair from Bethlehem. Goliath was from the city of Gath. His spear was as big as a weaver's rod.

20 There was still another battle. It took place at Gath. A huge man lived there. He had six fingers on each hand and six toes on each foot. So the total number of his toes and fingers was 24. He was also from the family of Rapha. 21 He made fun of Israel. So Jonathan killed him. Jonathan was the son of David's brother Shimeah.

²² Those four Philistine men lived in Gath. They were from the family line of Rapha. David and his men killed them.

David's Song of Praise

22 David sang the words of this song to the LORD. He sang them when the LORD saved him from the power of all his enemies and of Saul. ² He said,

"The LORD is my rock and my
    fort. He is the God who
    saves me.
³ My God is my rock. I go to
    him for safety.
He is like a shield to me.
    He's the power that
    saves me.
He's my place of safety. I go
    to him for help. He's my
    Savior.
He saves me from those
    who want to hurt me.
⁴ I called out to the LORD. He is
    worthy of praise.
He saved me from my
    enemies.
⁵ "The waves of death were all
    around me.
A destroying flood swept
    over me.
⁶ The ropes of the grave were
    tight around me.
Death set its trap in front
    of me.
⁷ When I was in trouble I
    called out to the LORD.
I called out to my God.
From his temple he heard my
    voice.
My cry for help reached his
    ears.

⁸ "The earth trembled and
    shook.
The pillars of the heavens
    rocked back and forth.
They trembled because the
    LORD was angry.
⁹ Smoke came out of his
    nose.
Flames of fire came out of
    his mouth.
Burning coals blazed out
    of it.
¹⁰ He opened the heavens and
    came down.
Dark clouds were under his
    feet.
¹¹ He got on the cherubim and
    flew.
The wings of the wind
    lifted him up.
¹² He covered himself with
    darkness.
The dark rain clouds of
    the sky were like a tent
    around him.
¹³ From the brightness all
    around him
flashes of lightning blazed
    out.
¹⁴ The LORD thundered from
    heaven.
The voice of the Most High
    God was heard.
¹⁵ He shot his arrows and
    scattered the enemy.
He sent flashes of lightning
    and chased them away.
¹⁶ The bottom of the sea could
    be seen.
The foundations of the
    earth were uncovered.
It happened when the LORD's
    anger blazed out.
It came like a blast of
    breath from his nose.

17 "He reached down from
heaven. He took hold
of me.
He lifted me out of deep
waters.
18 He saved me from my
powerful enemies.
He set me free from those
who were too strong
for me.
19 They stood up to me when I
was in trouble.
But the LORD helped me.
20 He brought me out into a
wide and safe place.
He saved me because he
was pleased with me.

21 "The LORD has been good to
me because I do what is
right.
He has rewarded me
because I lead a pure life.
22 I have lived the way the LORD
wanted me to.
I'm not guilty of turning
away from my God.
23 I keep all his laws in mind.
I haven't turned away from
his commands.
24 He knows that I am without
blame.
He knows I've kept myself
from sinning.
25 The LORD has rewarded me
for doing what is right.
He has rewarded me
because I haven't done
anything wrong.

26 "LORD, to those who are
faithful you show that
you are faithful.
To those who are without
blame you show that you
are without blame.

27 To those who are pure you
show that you are pure.
But to those whose paths
are crooked you show
that you are clever.
28 You save those who aren't
proud.
But you watch the proud to
bring them down.
29 LORD, you are my lamp.
You bring light into my
darkness.
30 With your help I can attack a
troop of soldiers.
With the help of my God I
can climb over a wall.

31 "God's way is perfect.
The LORD's word doesn't
have any flaws.
He protects like a shield
all who go to him for
safety.
32 Who is God except the
LORD?
Who is the Rock except
our God?
33 God gives me strength for the
battle.
He keeps my way secure.
34 He makes my feet like the
feet of a deer.
He causes me to stand on
the highest places.
35 He trains my hands to fight
every battle.
My arms can bend a bow of
bronze.
36 LORD, you shield me with
your saving help.
Your help has made me
great.
37 You give me a wide path to
walk in
so that I don't twist my
ankles.

38 "I chased my enemies and
    crushed them.
  I didn't turn back until
    they were destroyed.
39 I crushed them completely so
    that they couldn't get up.
  They fell under my feet.
40 LORD, you gave me strength
    to fight the battle.
  You caused my enemies to
    be humble in front of me.
41 You made them turn their
    backs and run away.
  So I destroyed my enemies.
42 They cried out for help. But
    there was no one to save
    them.
  They called out to the
    LORD. But he didn't
    answer them.
43 I beat them as fine as the dust
    of the earth.
  I pounded them and
    walked on them like
    mud in the streets.

44 "You saved me when people
    attacked me.
  You have kept me as the
    ruler over nations.
  People I didn't know serve
    me now.
45   People from other lands
    bow down to me in fear.
  As soon as they hear about
    me, they obey me.
46 All of them give up hope.
  They come trembling out
    of their hiding places.

47 "The LORD lives! Give praise
    to my Rock!
  Give honor to my God, the
    Rock! He is my Savior!
48 He is the God who pays back
    my enemies.

He brings the nations
    under my control.
49   He sets me free from my
    enemies.
  You have honored me more
    than them.
  You have saved me from
    a man who wanted to
    hurt me.
50 LORD, I will praise you
    among the nations.
  I will sing your praise.
51 He gives his king great
    victories.
  He shows his faithful love
    to his anointed king.
  He shows it to David and
    his family forever."

David's Last Words

23 Here are David's last
    words. He said,

"I am David, the son of Jesse.
  God has given me a
    message.
  The Most High God has
    greatly honored me.
The God of Jacob anointed
    me as king.
  I am the hero of Israel's
    songs.

2 "The Spirit of the LORD spoke
    through me.
  I spoke his word with my
    tongue.
3 The God of Israel spoke.
  The Rock of Israel said to
    me,
  'A king must rule over people
    in a way that is right.
  He must have respect for
    God when he rules.
4 Then he will be like the light
    of morning at sunrise

when there aren't any
   clouds.
He will be like the bright sun
   after rain
   that makes grass grow on
     the earth.'

5 "Suppose my royal family
   was not right with God.
Then he would not have
   made a covenant with
   me that will last forever.
Every part of it was well
   prepared and made
   secure.
Then God would not have
   saved me completely
   or given me everything I
   longed for.
6 But evil people are like
   thorns that are thrown
   away.
You can't pick them up
   with your hands.
7 Even if you touch them,
   you must use an iron tool
   or a spear.
Thorns are burned up right
   where they are."

David's Mighty Warriors

8 Here are the names of David's mighty warriors.

Josheb-Basshebeth was chief of the three mighty warriors. He was a Tahkemonite. He used his spear against 800 men. He killed all of them at one time.

9 Next to him was Eleazar. He was one of the three mighty warriors. He was the son of Dodai, the Ahohite. Eleazar was with David at Pas Dammim. That's where Israel's army made fun of the Philistines who were gathered there for battle. Then the Israelites pulled back. 10 But Eleazar stayed right where he was. He struck down the Philistines until his hand grew tired. But he still held on to his sword. The Lord helped him win a great battle that day. The troops returned to Eleazar. They came back to him only to take what they wanted from the dead bodies.

11 Next to him was Shammah, the son of Agee. Shammah was a Hararite. The Philistines gathered together at a place where there was a field full of lentils. Israel's troops ran away from the Philistines. 12 But Shammah took his stand in the middle of the field. He didn't let the Philistines capture it. He struck them down. The Lord helped him win a great battle.

13 David was at the cave of Adullam. During harvest time, three of the 30 chief warriors came down to him there. A group of Philistines was camped in the Valley of Rephaim. 14 At that time David was in his usual place of safety. Some Philistine troops were stationed at Bethlehem. 15 David longed for a drink of water. He said, "I wish someone would get me water from the well near the gate of Bethlehem." 16 So the three mighty warriors fought their way past the Philistine guards. They got some water from the well near the gate of Bethlehem. They took the water back to David. But David refused to drink it. Instead, he poured it out as a drink offering to the Lord. 17 "Lord, I

would never drink that water!" David said. "It stands for the blood of these men. They put their lives in danger by going to Bethlehem to get it." So David wouldn't drink it.

Those were some of the brave things the three mighty warriors did.

18 Abishai was chief over the three mighty warriors. He was the brother of Joab, the son of Zeruiah. He used his spear against 300 men. He killed all of them. So he became as famous as the three mighty warriors were. 19 In fact, he was even more honored than the three mighty warriors. He became their commander. But he wasn't included among them.

20 Benaiah was a great hero from Kabzeel. He was the son of Jehoiada. Benaiah did many brave things. He struck down two of Moab's best warriors. He also went down into a pit on a snowy day. He killed a lion there. 21 And he struck down a huge Egyptian. The Egyptian was holding a spear. Benaiah went out to fight against him with a club. He grabbed the spear out of the Egyptian's hand. Then he killed him with it. 22 Those were some of the brave things Benaiah, the son of Jehoiada, did. He too was as famous as the three mighty warriors were. 23 He was honored more than any of the thirty chief warriors. But he wasn't included among the three mighty warriors. David put him in charge of his own personal guards.

24 Here is a list of David's men who were among the thirty chief warriors.

Asahel, the brother of Joab
Elhanan, the son of Dodo, from Bethlehem
25 Shammah, the Harodite
Elika, the Harodite
26 Helez, the Paltite
Ira, the son of Ikkesh, from Tekoa
27 Abiezer from Anathoth
Sibbekai, the Hushathite
28 Zalmon, the Ahohite
Maharai from Netophah
29 Heled, the son of Baanah, from Netophah
Ithai, the son of Ribai, from Gibeah in Benjamin
30 Benaiah from Pirathon
Hiddai from the valleys of Gaash
31 Abi-Albon, the Arbathite
Azmaveth, the Barhumite
32 Eliahba, the Shaalbonite
the sons of Jashen
Jonathan, 33 the son of Shammah, the Hararite
Ahiam, the son of Sharar, the Hararite
34 Eliphelet, the son of Ahasbai, the Maakathite
Eliam, the son of Ahithophel, from Giloh
35 Hezro from Carmel
Paarai, the Arbite
36 Igal, the son of Nathan, from Zobah
the son of Hagri
37 Zelek from Ammon
Naharai from Beeroth, who carried the armor of Joab, the son of Zeruiah
38 Ira, the Ithrite
Gareb, the Ithrite

[39] and Uriah, the Hittite

The total number of men was 37.

David Counts His Fighting Men

24 The LORD was very angry with Israel. He stirred up David against them. He said, "Go! Count the men of Israel and Judah."

[2] So the king spoke to Joab and the army commanders with him. He said, "Go all through the territories of the tribes of Israel. Go from the town of Dan all the way to Beersheba. Count the fighting men. Then I'll know how many there are."

[3] Joab replied to the king. He said, "King David, you are my master. May the LORD your God multiply the troops 100 times. And may you live to see it. But why would you want me to count the fighting men?"

[4] The king's word had more authority than the word of Joab and the army commanders. That was true in spite of what Joab had said. So they left the king and went out to count the fighting men of Israel.

[5] They went across the Jordan River. They camped south of the town in the middle of the Arnon River valley near Aroer. Then they went through Gad and continued on to Jazer. [6] They went to Gilead and the area of Tahtim Hodshi. They continued to Dan Jaan and on around toward Sidon. [7] Then they went toward the fort of Tyre. They went to all the towns of the Hivites and Canaanites. Finally, they went on to Beersheba. It was in the Negev Desert of Judah.

[8] They finished going through the entire land. Then they came back to Jerusalem. They had been gone for nine months and 20 days.

[9] Joab reported to the king how many fighting men he had counted. In Israel there were 800,000 men who were able to handle a sword. In Judah there were 500,000.

[10] David felt sorry that he had counted the fighting men. So he said to the LORD, "I committed a great sin when I counted Judah and Israel's men. LORD, I beg you to take away my guilt. I've done a very foolish thing."

[11] Before David got up the next morning, a message from the LORD came to Gad the prophet. He was David's seer. The message said, [12] "Go and tell David, 'The LORD says, "I could punish you in three different ways. Choose one of them for me to use against you."'"

[13] So Gad went to David. He said to him, "Take your choice. Do you want three years when there won't be enough food in your land? Or do you want three months when you will run away from your enemies while they chase you? Or do you want three days when there will be a plague in your land? Think it over. Then take your pick. Tell me how to answer the one who sent me."

[14] David said to Gad, "I'm suffering terribly. Let us fall into the hands of the LORD. His mercy is

great. But don't let me fall into human hands."

[15] So the LORD sent a plague on Israel. It lasted from that morning until he decided to end it. From Dan all the way to Beersheba 70,000 people died. [16] The angel reached his hand out to destroy Jerusalem. But the LORD stopped sending the plague. So he spoke to the angel who was making the people suffer. He said, "That is enough! Do not kill any more people." The angel of the LORD was at Araunah's threshing floor. Araunah was from the city of Jebus.

[17] David saw the angel who was striking down the people. David said to the LORD, "I'm the one who has sinned. I'm the one who has done what is wrong. I'm like a shepherd for these people. These people are like sheep. What have they done? Let your judgment be on me and my family."

David Builds an Altar

[18] On that day Gad went to David. Gad said to him, "Go up to the threshing floor of Araunah, the Jebusite. Build an altar there to honor the LORD." [19] So David went up and did it. He did what the LORD had commanded through Gad. [20] Araunah looked and saw the king and his officials coming toward him. So he went out to welcome them. He bowed down to the king with his face toward the ground.

[21] Araunah said, "King David, you are my master. Why have you come to see me?"

"To buy your threshing floor," David answered. "I want to build an altar there to honor the LORD. When I do, the plague on the people will be stopped."

[22] Araunah said to David, "Take anything you wish. Offer it up. Here are oxen for the burnt offering. Here are threshing sleds. And here are wooden collars from the necks of the oxen. Use all the wood to burn the offering. [23] Your Majesty, I'll give all of it to you." Araunah continued, "And may the LORD your God accept you."

[24] But the king replied to Araunah, "No. I want to pay you for it. I won't sacrifice to the LORD my God burnt offerings that haven't cost me anything."

So David bought the threshing floor and the oxen. He paid 20 ounces of silver for them. [25] David built an altar there to honor the LORD. He sacrificed burnt offerings and friendship offerings. Then the LORD answered David's prayer and blessed the land. The plague on Israel was stopped.

1 Kings

Introduction:

The book of 1 Kings starts with King Solomon, David's son. Solomon was known for being very wise. While king, he built a house for God and a palace for himself.

Rehoboam was the next king. Israel split into two nations while he was king. The northern nation was called Israel. The southern nation was called Judah. First Kings tells about both nations' kings. Some of these kings were good, and some were bad. The good kings obeyed God, but the bad ones worshiped false gods. So God sent prophets to tell the kings to obey God. Prophets were people who spoke for God.

When the people and their king obeyed God, there was peace. When they did not obey God, there was war.

Outline of contents:

Adonijah Makes Himself King

1 King David was now very old. He couldn't keep warm even when blankets were spread over him. ² So his attendants spoke to him. They said, "You are our king and master. Please let us try to find a young virgin to serve you. She can take care of you. She can lie down beside you to keep you warm."

³ So David's attendants looked all over Israel for a beautiful young woman. They found Abishag. She was from the town of Shunem. They brought her to the king. ⁴ The woman was very beautiful. She took care of the king and served him. But the king didn't have sex with her.

⁵ Adonijah was the son of David and his wife Haggith. He came forward and announced, "I'm going to be the next king." So he got chariots and horses ready. He also got 50 men to run in front of him. ⁶ His father had never tried to stop him from doing what he wanted to. His father had never asked him, "Why are you acting the way you do?" Adonijah was also very handsome. Now that Absalom was dead, Adonijah was David's oldest son.

⁷ Adonijah talked things over with Joab, the son of Zeruiah. He also talked with Abiathar the priest. They agreed to help him. ⁸ But Zadok the priest and

Benaiah, the son of Jehoiada, didn't join Adonijah. Nathan the prophet didn't join him. Shimei and Rei didn't join him. And neither did David's special guard.

⁹Adonijah sacrificed sheep, cattle and fat calves. He sacrificed them at the Stone of Zoheleth near En Rogel. He invited all his brothers, the king's sons, and all the royal officials of Judah. ¹⁰But he didn't invite Benaiah or Nathan the prophet. He didn't invite the special guard or his brother Solomon either.

¹¹Nathan asked Solomon's mother Bathsheba, "Haven't you heard? Adonijah, the son of Haggith, has made himself king. And King David doesn't know anything about it. ¹²So let me tell you what to do to save your life. It will also save the life of your son Solomon. ¹³Go in and see King David. Say to him, 'You are my king and master. You promised me, "You can be sure that your son Solomon will be king after me. He will sit on my throne." If that's really true, why has Adonijah become king?' ¹⁴While you are still talking to the king, I'll come in and support what you have said."

¹⁵So Bathsheba went to see the old king in his room. Abishag, the Shunammite, was taking care of him there. ¹⁶Bathsheba bowed low in front of the king.

"What do you want?" the king asked.

¹⁷She said to him, "My master, you made a promise in the name of the LORD your God. You promised me, 'Your son Solomon will be king after me. He will sit on my throne.' ¹⁸But now Adonijah has made himself king. And you don't even know about it. ¹⁹He has sacrificed large numbers of cattle, fat calves and sheep. He has invited all the king's sons. He has also invited Abiathar the priest and Joab, the commander of the army. But he hasn't invited your son Solomon. ²⁰You are my king and master. All the Israelites are watching to see what you will do. They want to find out from you who will sit on the throne after you. ²¹If you don't do something, I and my son Solomon will be treated like people who have committed crimes. That will happen as soon as you join the members of your family who have already died."

²²While she was still speaking with the king, Nathan the prophet arrived. ²³The king was told, "Nathan the prophet is here." So Nathan went to the king. He bowed down with his face toward the ground.

²⁴Nathan said, "You are my king and master. Have you announced that Adonijah will be king after you? Have you said he will sit on your throne? ²⁵Today he has gone down outside the city. He has sacrificed large numbers of cattle, fat calves and sheep. He has invited all the king's sons. He has also invited the commanders of the army and Abiathar the priest. Even now they are eating and

drinking with him. They are saying, 'May King Adonijah live a long time!' ²⁶ But he didn't invite me. He didn't invite Zadok the priest or Benaiah, the son of Jehoiada. He didn't invite your son Solomon either. ²⁷ King David, have you allowed all of that to happen? Did you do it without letting us know about it? Why didn't you tell us who is going to sit on your throne after you?"

David Makes Solomon King

²⁸ King David said, "Tell Bathsheba to come in." So she came and stood in front of the king. ²⁹ Then the king made a promise. He said, "The LORD has saved me from all my troubles. You can be sure that he lives. ³⁰ And you can be just as sure I will do what I promised. This is the day I will do what I promised in the name of the LORD. He is the God of Israel. I promised you that your son Solomon would be king after me. He will sit on my throne in my place."

³¹ Then Bathsheba bowed down in front of the king. Her face was toward the ground. She said, "King David, you are my master. May you live forever!"

³² King David said, "Tell Zadok the priest and Nathan the prophet to come in. Also tell Benaiah, the son of Jehoiada, to come." So they came to the king. ³³ He said to them, "Take my officials with you. Have my son Solomon get on my own mule. Take him down to the Gihon spring. ³⁴ Have Zadok the priest and Nathan the prophet anoint him as king over Israel there. Blow a trumpet. Shout, 'May King Solomon live a long time!' ³⁵ Then come back up to the city with him. Have him sit on my throne. He will rule in my place. I've appointed him ruler over Israel and Judah."

³⁶ Benaiah, the son of Jehoiada, answered the king. "Amen!" he said. "May the LORD your God make it come true. ³⁷ You are my king and master. The LORD has been with you. May he also be with Solomon. King David, may the LORD make Solomon's kingdom even greater than yours!"

³⁸ So Zadok the priest and Nathan the prophet left the palace. Benaiah, the son of Jehoiada, went with them. So did the Kerethites and Pelethites. They had Solomon get on King David's mule. And they brought him down to the Gihon spring. ³⁹ Zadok the priest had taken an animal horn from the sacred tent. The horn was filled with olive oil. He anointed Solomon with the oil. A trumpet was blown. All the people shouted, "May King Solomon live a long time!" ⁴⁰ Then they went up toward the city. Solomon was leading the way. The people were playing flutes. They were filled with great joy. The ground shook because of all the noise.

⁴¹ Adonijah and all his guests heard it. They were just finishing their meal. Joab heard the sound of the trumpet. So he

asked, "What does all this noise in the city mean?"

⁴²While Joab was still speaking, Jonathan arrived. Jonathan was the son of Abiathar the priest. Adonijah said, "Come in. I have respect for you. You must be bringing good news."

⁴³"No! I'm not!" Jonathan answered. "Our master King David has made Solomon king. ⁴⁴David sent Zadok the priest and Nathan the prophet along with Solomon. He also sent Benaiah, the son of Jehoiada, with him. He sent the Kerethites and Pelethites with him too. They put him on the king's mule. ⁴⁵They took him down to the Gihon spring. There Zadok the priest and Nathan the prophet anointed him as king. Now they've gone back up to the city. They were cheering all the way. The city is filled with the sound of it. That's the noise you hear. ⁴⁶And that's not all. Solomon has taken his seat on the royal throne. ⁴⁷The royal officials came to give their blessing to our master King David. They said, 'May your God make Solomon's name more famous than yours! May he make Solomon's kingdom greater than yours!' While King David was sitting on his bed, he bowed in worship. ⁴⁸He said, 'I praise the LORD. He is the God of Israel. He has let me live to see my son sitting on my throne today as the next king.'"

⁴⁹When all Adonijah's guests heard that, they were terrified. So they got up and scattered.

⁵⁰Adonijah was afraid of what Solomon might do to him. So he went and grabbed the horns of the altar for burnt offerings. Those horns stuck out from its upper corners. ⁵¹Then Solomon was told, "King Solomon, Adonijah is afraid of you. He's holding onto the horns of the altar. He says, 'I want King Solomon to make a promise today. I want him to promise that he won't kill me with his sword.'"

⁵²Solomon replied, "Let him show that he's a man people can respect. Then not even one hair on his head will fall to the ground. But if I find out he's done something evil, he will die." ⁵³King Solomon got some men to bring Adonijah down from the altar. He came and bowed down to King Solomon. Solomon said, "Go on home."

David Gives Orders to Solomon

2 The time came near for David to die. So he gave orders to his son Solomon.

²He said, "I'm about to die, just as everyone else on earth does. So be strong. Show how brave you are. ³Do everything the LORD your God requires. Live the way he wants you to. Obey his orders and commands. Keep his laws and rules. Do everything written in the Law of Moses. Then you will have success in everything you do. You will succeed everywhere you go. ⁴The LORD will keep the promise he made to me. He said, 'Your sons must be careful about how they live. They must be faithful

to me with all their heart and soul. Then you will always have a son from your family line to sit on the throne of Israel.'

⁵ "You yourself know what Joab, the son of Zeruiah, did to me. You know that he killed Abner, the son of Ner, and Amasa, the son of Jether. They were the two commanders of Israel's armies. He killed them in a time of peace. It wasn't a time of war. Joab spilled the blood of Abner and Amasa. With that blood he stained the belt around his waist. He also stained the sandals on his feet. ⁶ You are wise. So I leave him in your hands. Just don't let him live to become an old man. Don't let him die peacefully.

⁷ "But be kind to the sons of Barzillai from Gilead. Provide what they need. They were faithful to me when I had to run away from your brother Absalom.

⁸ "Don't forget that Shimei, the son of Gera, is still around. He's from Bahurim in the territory of Benjamin. Shimei cursed me bitterly. He did it on the day I went to Mahanaim. Later, he came down to welcome me at the Jordan River. At that time I made a promise in the name of the LORD. I promised Shimei, 'I won't put you to death with my sword.' ⁹ But now I want you to think of him as guilty. You are wise. You will know what to do to him. Don't let him live to become an old man. Put him to death."

¹⁰ David joined the members of his family who had already died. He was buried in the City of David. ¹¹ He had ruled over Israel for 40 years. He ruled for seven years in Hebron. Then he ruled for 33 years in Jerusalem. ¹² So Solomon sat on the throne of his father David. His position as king was made secure.

Solomon's Kingdom Is Made Secure

¹³ Adonijah was the son of David's wife Haggith. He went to Bathsheba. She was Solomon's mother. She asked Adonijah, "Have you come in peace?"

He answered, "Yes. I've come in peace." ¹⁴ He continued, "I want to ask you something."

"Go ahead," she replied.

¹⁵ He said, "As you know, the kingdom belonged to me. The whole nation of Israel thought of me as their king. But now things have changed. The kingdom belongs to my brother. The LORD has given it to him. ¹⁶ But I have a favor to ask of you. Don't say no to me."

"Go ahead," she said.

¹⁷ So he continued, "Please ask King Solomon for a favor. He won't say no to you. Ask him to give me Abishag from Shunem to be my wife."

¹⁸ "All right," Bathsheba replied. "I'll speak to the king for you."

¹⁹ So Bathsheba went to King Solomon. She went to him to speak for Adonijah. The king stood up to greet her. He bowed down to her. Then he sat down on his throne. He had a throne

brought for his mother. She sat down at his right side.

²⁰ "I have one small favor to ask of you," she said. "Don't say no to me."

The king replied, "Mother, go ahead and ask. I won't say no to you."

²¹ She said, "Let your brother Adonijah marry Abishag, the Shunammite."

²² King Solomon answered his mother, "Why are you asking me to give Abishag, the Shunammite, to Adonijah? You might as well ask me to give him the whole kingdom! After all, he's my older brother. And he doesn't want the kingdom only for himself. He also wants it for Abiathar the priest and for Joab, the son of Zeruiah."

²³ Then King Solomon made a promise in the name of the Lord. He said, "Adonijah will pay with his life because of what he has asked for. If he doesn't, may God punish me greatly. ²⁴ The Lord has made my position as king secure. I'm sitting on the throne of my father David. The Lord has built a royal house for me, just as he promised. You can be sure that the Lord lives. And you can be just as sure that Adonijah will be put to death today." ²⁵ So King Solomon gave the order to Benaiah, the son of Jehoiada. Benaiah struck down Adonijah, and he died.

²⁶ The king spoke to Abiathar the priest. He said, "Go back to your fields in Anathoth. You should really be put to death. But I won't have it done now. That's because you carried the ark of the Lord and King. You did it for my father David. You shared all of his hard times."

²⁷ So Solomon wouldn't let Abiathar serve as a priest of the Lord anymore. That's how the message the Lord had spoken at Shiloh came true. He had spoken it about the family of Eli.

²⁸ News of what Solomon had done reached Joab. Joab had never made evil plans along with Absalom. But he had joined Adonijah. So he ran to the tent of the Lord. He grabbed the horns that stuck out from the upper corners of the altar for burnt offerings. ²⁹ King Solomon was told that Joab had run to the tent. He was also told that Joab was by the altar. Then Solomon gave the order to Benaiah, the son of Jehoiada. He told him, "Go! Strike him down!"

³⁰ So Benaiah entered the tent of the Lord. He said to Joab, "The king says, 'Come on out!'"

But Joab answered, "No. I'd rather die here."

Benaiah told the king what Joab had said to him.

³¹ Then the king commanded Benaiah, "Do what he says. Strike him down and bury him. Then I and my family line won't be held accountable for the blood Joab spilled. He killed people who weren't guilty of doing anything wrong. ³² The Lord will pay him back for the blood he spilled. Joab attacked two men. He killed them with

his sword. And my father David didn't even know anything about it. Joab killed Abner, the son of Ner. Abner was the commander of Israel's army. Joab also killed Amasa, the son of Jether. Amasa was the commander of Judah's army. Abner and Amasa were better men than Joab is. They were more honest than he is. ³³May Joab and his children after him be held forever accountable for spilling the blood of Abner and Amasa. But may David and his children after him enjoy the LORD's peace and rest forever. May the LORD also give his peace to David's royal house and kingdom forever."

³⁴So Benaiah, the son of Jehoiada, went up to the LORD's tent. There he struck down Joab. And he killed him. Joab was buried at his home out in the country. ³⁵The king put Benaiah in charge of the army. Benaiah took Joab's place. The king also put Zadok the priest in Abiathar's place.

³⁶Then the king sent for Shimei. He said to him, "Build yourself a house in Jerusalem. Live there. Don't go anywhere else. ³⁷You must not leave the city and go across the Kidron Valley. If you do, you can be sure you will die. And it will be your own fault."

³⁸Shimei replied to the king, "You are my king and master. What you say is good. I'll do it." Shimei stayed in Jerusalem for a long time.

³⁹Three years after Solomon had talked with Shimei, two of Shimei's slaves ran off. They went to Achish, the king of Gath. He was the son of Maakah. Shimei was told, "Your slaves are in Gath." ⁴⁰When Shimei heard that, he put a saddle on his donkey. Then he went to Achish at Gath to look for his slaves. Shimei found them and brought them back from Gath.

⁴¹Solomon was told that Shimei had left Jerusalem. He was told he had gone to Gath and had returned. ⁴²So the king sent for Shimei. He said to him, "Didn't I force you to make a promise in the name of the LORD? Didn't I warn you? I said, 'You must not leave the city and go somewhere else. If you do, you can be sure you will die.' At that time you said to me, 'What you say is good. I'll obey your command.' ⁴³So why didn't you keep your promise to the LORD? Why didn't you obey the command I gave you?"

⁴⁴The king continued, "You know all the wrong things you did to my father David. In your heart you know them. Now the LORD will pay you back for what you did. ⁴⁵But I will be blessed. The LORD will make David's kingdom secure forever."

⁴⁶Then the king gave the order to Benaiah, the son of Jehoiada. Benaiah left the palace and struck down Shimei. And he died.

So the kingdom was now made secure in Solomon's hands.

Solomon Asks God for Wisdom

3 Solomon and Pharaoh, the king of Egypt, agreed to help each other. So Solomon married Pharaoh's daughter. He brought her to the City of David. She stayed there until he finished building his palace, the LORD's temple, and the wall around Jerusalem. ² But the people continued to offer sacrifices at the high places where they worshiped. That's because a temple hadn't been built yet where the LORD would put his Name. ³ Solomon showed his love for the LORD. He did it by obeying the laws his father David had taught him. But Solomon offered sacrifices at the high places. He also burned incense there.

⁴ King Solomon went to the city of Gibeon to offer sacrifices. That's where the most important high place was. There he offered 1,000 burnt offerings on the altar. ⁵ The LORD appeared to Solomon at Gibeon. He spoke to him in a dream during the night. God said, "Ask for anything you want me to give you."

⁶ Solomon answered, "You have been very kind to my father David, your servant. That's because he was faithful to you. He did what was right. His heart was honest. And you have continued to be very kind to him. You have given him a son to sit on his throne this day.

⁷ "LORD my God, you have now made me king. You have put me in the place of my father David. But I'm only a little child. I don't know how to carry out my duties. ⁸ I'm here among the people you have chosen. They are a great nation. They are more than anyone can count. ⁹ So give me a heart that understands. Then I can rule over your people. I can tell the difference between what is right and what is wrong. Who can possibly rule over this great nation of yours?"

¹⁰ The Lord was pleased that Solomon had asked for that. ¹¹ So God said to him, "You have not asked to live for a long time. You have not asked to be wealthy. You have not even asked to have your enemies killed. Instead, you have asked for wisdom. You want to do what is right and fair when you judge people. Because that is what you have asked for, ¹² I will give it to you. I will give you a wise and understanding heart. So here is what will be true of you. There has never been anyone like you. And there never will be. ¹³ And that is not all. I will give you what you have not asked for. I will give you wealth and honor. As long as you live, no other king will be as great as you are. ¹⁴ Live the way I want you to. Obey my laws and commands, just as your father David did. Then I will let you live for a long time." ¹⁵ Solomon woke up. He realized he had been dreaming.

He returned to Jerusalem. He stood in front of the ark of the Lord's covenant. He sacrificed burnt offerings and friendship offerings. Then he gave a feast for all his officials.

A Wise Ruling

[16] Two prostitutes came to the king. They stood in front of him. [17] One of them said, "Pardon me, my master, this woman and I live in the same house. I had a baby while she was there with me. [18] Three days after my child was born, this woman also had a baby. We were alone. There wasn't anyone in the house but the two of us.

[19] "During the night this woman's baby died. It happened because she was lying on top of him. [20] So she got up in the middle of the night. She took my son from my side while I was asleep. She put him by her breast. Then she put her dead son by my breast. [21] The next morning, I got up to nurse my son. But he was dead! I looked at him closely in the morning light. And I saw that it wasn't my baby."

[22] The other woman said, "No! The living baby is my son. The dead one belongs to you."

But the first woman said, "No! The dead baby is yours. The living one belongs to me." So they argued in front of the king.

[23] The king said, "One of you says, 'My son is alive. Your son is dead.' The other one says, 'No! Your son is dead. Mine is alive.'"

[24] He continued, "Bring me a sword." So a sword was brought to him. [25] Then he gave an order. He said, "Cut the living child in two. Give half to one woman and half to the other."

[26] The woman whose son was alive was filled with deep love for her son. She said to the king, "My master, please give her the living baby! Don't kill him!"

But the other woman said, "Neither one of us will have him. Cut him in two!"

[27] Then the king made his decision. He said, "Give the living baby to the first woman. Don't kill him. She's his mother."

[28] All the Israelites heard about the decision the king had given. That gave them great respect for him. They saw that God had given him wisdom. They knew that Solomon would do what was right and fair when he judged people.

Solomon's Officials and Governors

4 So King Solomon ruled over the whole nation of Israel.

[2] Here are the names of his chief officials.

Azariah was the priest. He was the son of Zadok.

[3] Elihoreph and Ahijah were secretaries. They were the sons of Shisha.

Jehoshaphat kept the records. He was the son of Ahilud.

[4] Benaiah was the commander in chief. He was the son of Jehoiada.

Zadok and Abiathar were priests.

[5] Azariah was in charge of the local governors. He was the son of Nathan.

Zabud was a priest. He was also the king's adviser. He was the son of Nathan.

⁶Ahishar was in charge of the palace.

Adoniram was in charge of those who were forced to work for the king. He was the son of Abda.

⁷Solomon had 12 local governors over the whole land of Israel. They provided supplies for the king and the royal family. Each governor had to provide supplies for one month out of each year.

⁸Here are their names and areas.

Ben-Hur's area was the hill country of Ephraim.

⁹Ben-Deker's area was Makaz, Shaalbim, Beth Shemesh and Elon Bethhanan.

¹⁰Ben-Hesed's area was Arubboth. Sokoh and the whole land of Hepher were included in his area.

¹¹Ben-Abinadab's area was Naphoth Dor. He married Solomon's daughter Taphath.

¹²Baana's area was Taanach, Megiddo and the whole territory of Beth Shan. Beth Shan was next to Zarethan below Jezreel. Baana's area reached from Beth Shan all the way to Abel Meholah. It also went across to Jokmeam. Baana was the son of Ahilud.

¹³Ben-Geber's area was Ramoth Gilead. The settlements of Jair, the son of Manasseh, were included in his area in Gilead. The area of Argob in Bashan was also included. That area had 60 large cities that had high walls around them. The city gates were made secure with heavy bronze bars.

¹⁴Ahinadab's area was Mahanaim. He was the son of Iddo.

¹⁵Ahimaaz's area was Naphtali. He had married Basemath. She was Solomon's daughter.

¹⁶Baana's area was Asher and Aloth. He was the son of Hushai.

¹⁷Jehoshaphat's area was Issachar. He was the son of Paruah.

¹⁸Shimei's area was Benjamin. He was the son of Ela.

¹⁹Geber's area was Gilead. He was the only governor over the area. He was the son of Uri. Gilead had been the country of Sihon and Og. Sihon had been king of the Amorites. Og had been king of Bashan.

Solomon's Daily Supplies

²⁰There were many people in Judah and Israel. In fact, they were as many as the grains of sand on the seashore. They ate, drank and were happy. ²¹Solomon ruled over all the kingdoms from the Euphrates River to the land of the Philistines. He ruled

as far as the border of Egypt. All those countries brought the gifts he required them to bring him. And Solomon ruled over those countries for his whole life.

22 Here are the supplies Solomon required every day.

    five and a half tons of the finest flour
    11 tons of meal
23 ten oxen that had been fed by hand
    20 oxen that had been fed on grasslands
    100 sheep and goats
    deer, antelopes and roebucks
    the finest birds

24 Solomon ruled over all the kingdoms that were west of the Euphrates River. He ruled from Tiphsah all the way to Gaza. And he had peace and rest on every side. 25 While Solomon was king, Judah and Israel lived in safety. They were secure from Dan all the way to Beersheba. Everyone had their own vine and their own fig tree. 26 Solomon had 4,000 spaces where he kept his chariot horses. He had a total of 12,000 horses. 27 The local governors provided supplies for King Solomon. They provided them for all who ate at the king's table. Each governor provided supplies for one month every year. The governors made sure the king had everything he needed. 28 They also brought barley and straw for the chariot horses and the other horses. Each of the governors brought the amounts required of them. They brought them to the proper places.

God Makes Solomon Very Wise

29 God made Solomon very wise. His understanding couldn't even be measured. It was like the sand on the seashore. People can't measure that either. 30 Solomon's wisdom was greater than the wisdom of all the people of the east. It was greater than all the wisdom of Egypt. 31 Solomon was wiser than anyone else. He was wiser than Ethan, the Ezrahite. He was wiser than Heman, Kalkol and Darda. They were the sons of Mahol. Solomon became famous in all the nations around him. 32 He spoke 3,000 proverbs. He wrote 1,005 songs. 33 He spoke about plants. He knew everything about them, from the cedar trees in Lebanon to the hyssop plants that grow out of walls. He spoke about animals and birds. He also spoke about reptiles and fish. 34 The kings of all the world's nations heard about how wise Solomon was. So they sent their people to listen to him.

Solomon Prepares to Build the Temple

5 Hiram was the king of Tyre. He heard that Solomon had been anointed as king. He heard that Solomon had become the next king after his father David. Hiram had always been David's friend. So Hiram sent his messengers to Solomon. 2 Then

Solomon sent a message back to Hiram. Solomon said,

³ "As you know, my father David had to fight many battles. His enemies attacked him from every side. So he couldn't build a temple where the LORD his God would put his Name. That wouldn't be possible until the LORD had put his enemies under his control. ⁴ But now the LORD my God has given me peace and rest on every side. We don't have any enemies. And we don't have any other major problems either. ⁵ So I'm planning to build a temple. I want to build it for the Name of the LORD my God. That's what he told my father David he wanted me to do. He said, 'I will put your son on the throne in your place. He will build a temple. I will put my Name there.'

⁶ "So give your men orders to cut down cedar trees in Lebanon for me. My men will work with yours. I'll pay you for your men's work. I'll pay any amount you decide on. As you know, we don't have anyone as skilled in cutting down trees as the men of Sidon are."

⁷ When Hiram heard Solomon's message, he was very pleased. He said, "May the LORD be praised today. He has given David a wise son to rule over that great nation."

⁸ So Hiram sent a message to Solomon. Hiram said,

"I have received the message you sent me. I'll do everything you want me to. I'll provide the cedar and juniper logs. ⁹ My men will bring them from Lebanon down to the Mediterranean Sea. I'll make them into rafts. I'll float them to the place you want me to. When the rafts arrive, I'll separate the logs from each other. Then you can take them away. And here's what I want in return. Provide food for all the people in my palace."

¹⁰ So Hiram supplied Solomon with all the cedar and juniper logs he wanted. ¹¹ Solomon gave Hiram 3,600 tons of wheat as food for the people in his palace. He also gave him 120,000 gallons of oil made from pressed olives. He did that for Hiram year after year. ¹² The LORD made Solomon wise, just as he had promised him. There was peace between Hiram and Solomon. The two of them made a peace treaty.

¹³ King Solomon forced men from all over Israel to work hard for him. There were 30,000 of them. ¹⁴ He sent them off to Lebanon in groups of 10,000 each month. They spent one month in Lebanon. Then they spent two months at home. Adoniram was in charge of the people who were forced to work. ¹⁵ Solomon had 70,000 people who

carried things. He had 80,000 who cut stones in the hills. [16] He had 3,300 men in charge of the project. They also directed the workers. [17] The people did what the king commanded. They removed large blocks of the best quality stone from a rock pit. They used them to provide a foundation for the temple. [18] The skilled workers of Solomon and Hiram cut and prepared the logs and stones. They would later be used in building the temple. Workers from Byblos also helped.

Solomon Builds the Temple

6 Solomon began to build the temple of the LORD. It was 480 years after the Israelites came out of Egypt. It was in the fourth year of Solomon's rule over Israel. He started in the second month. That was the month of Ziv.

[2] The temple King Solomon built for the LORD was 90 feet long. It was 30 feet wide. And it was 45 feet high. [3] The temple had a porch in front of the main hall. The porch was as wide as the temple itself. It was 30 feet wide. It came out 15 feet from the front of the temple. [4] Solomon made narrow windows high up in the temple walls. [5] He built side rooms around the temple. They were built against the walls of the main hall and the Most Holy Room. [6] On the first floor the side rooms were seven and a half feet wide. On the second floor they were nine feet wide. And on the third floor they were ten and a half feet wide. Solomon made the walls of the temple thinner as they went up floor by floor. The result was ledges along the walls. So the floor beams of the side rooms rested on the ledges. The beams didn't go into the temple walls.

[7] All the stones used for building the temple were shaped where they were cut. So hammers, chisels and other iron tools couldn't be heard where the temple was being built.

[8] The entrance to the first floor was on the south side of the temple. A stairway led up to the second floor. From there it went on up to the third floor. [9] So Solomon built the temple and finished it. He made its roof out of beams and cedar boards. [10] He built side rooms all along the temple. Each room was seven and a half feet high. They were joined to the temple by cedar beams.

[11] A message came to Solomon from the LORD. The LORD said, [12] "You are now building this temple. Follow my orders. Keep my rules. Obey all my commands. Then I will make the promise I gave your father David come true. I will do it through you. [13] I will live among my people Israel. I will not desert them."

[14] So Solomon built the temple and finished it. [15] He put cedar boards on its inside walls. He covered them from floor to ceiling. He covered the temple floor with juniper boards. [16] He

put up a wall 30 feet from the back of the temple. He made it with cedar boards from floor to ceiling. That formed a room inside the temple. It was the Most Holy Room. ¹⁷ The main hall in front of the room was 60 feet long. ¹⁸ The inside of the temple was covered with cedar wood. Gourds and open flowers were carved on the wood. Everything was cedar. There wasn't any stone showing anywhere.

¹⁹ Solomon prepared the Most Holy Room inside the temple. That's where the ark of the covenant of the LORD would be placed. ²⁰ The Most Holy Room was 30 feet long. It was 30 feet wide. And it was 30 feet high. Solomon covered the inside of it with pure gold. He prepared the cedar altar for burning incense. He covered it with gold. ²¹ Solomon covered the inside of the main hall with pure gold. He placed gold chains across the front of the Most Holy Room. That room was covered with gold. ²² So Solomon covered the inside of the whole temple with gold. He also covered the altar for burning incense with gold. It was right in front of the Most Holy Room.

²³ For the Most Holy Room Solomon made a pair of cherubim. He made them out of olive wood. Each cherub was 15 feet high. ²⁴ One wing of the first cherub was seven and a half feet long. The other wing was also seven and a half feet long. So the wings measured 15 feet from tip to tip. ²⁵ The second cherub's wings also measured 15 feet from tip to tip. The two cherubim had the same size and shape. ²⁶ Each cherub was 15 feet high. ²⁷ Solomon placed the cherubim inside the Most Holy Room in the temple. Their wings were spread out. The wing tip of one cherub touched one wall. The wing tip of the other touched the other wall. The tips of their wings touched each other in the middle of the room. ²⁸ Solomon covered the cherubim with gold.

²⁹ On the walls all around the temple he carved cherubim, palm trees and open flowers. He carved them on the walls of the Most Holy Room and the main hall. ³⁰ He also covered the floors of those two rooms with gold.

³¹ For the entrance to the Most Holy Room he made two doors out of olive wood. Each door was one-fifth of the width of the Most Holy Room. ³² On the two olive wood doors he carved cherubim, palm trees and open flowers. He covered the cherubim and palm trees with hammered gold. ³³ In the same way he made olive wood doorposts for the entrance to the main hall. Each doorpost was one-fourth of the width of the hall. ³⁴ He also made two doors out of juniper wood. Each door had two parts. They turned in bases shaped like cups. ³⁵ He carved cherubim, palm trees and open flowers on the doors. He covered the doors with gold. He hammered the gold evenly over the carvings.

36 He used blocks of stone to build a wall around the inside courtyard. The first three layers of the wall were made out of stone. The top layer was made out of beautiful cedar wood.

37 The foundation of the LORD's temple was laid in Solomon's fourth year. It was in the month of Ziv. 38 The temple was finished in his 11th year. It was in the month of Bul. That was the eighth month. Everything was finished just as the plans required. Solomon had spent seven years building the temple.

Solomon Builds His Palace

7 But it took Solomon 13 years to finish constructing his palace and the other buildings related to it. 2 He built the Palace of the Forest of Lebanon. It was 150 feet long. It was 75 feet wide. And it was 45 feet high. It had four rows of cedar columns. They held up beautiful cedar beams. 3 Above the beams was a roof made out of cedar boards. It rested on the columns. There were three rows of beams with 15 in each row. The total number of beams was 45. 4 The windows of the palace were placed high up in the walls. They were in groups of three. And they faced each other. 5 All the doorways had frames shaped like rectangles. They were in front. They were in groups of three. And they faced each other.

6 Solomon made a covered area. It was 75 feet long. And it was 45 feet wide. Its roof was held up by columns. In front of it was a porch. In front of that were pillars and a roof that went out beyond them.

7 Solomon built the throne hall. It was called the Hall of Justice. That's where he would serve as judge. He covered the hall with cedar boards from floor to ceiling. 8 The palace where he would live was set farther back. Its plan was something like the plan for the hall. Solomon had married Pharaoh's daughter. He made a palace for her. It was like the hall.

9 All those buildings were made out of blocks of good quality stone. They were cut to the right size. They were made smooth on their back and front sides. Those stones were used for the outside of each building and for the large courtyard. They were also used from the foundations up to the roofs. 10 Large blocks of good quality stone were used for the foundations. Some were 15 feet long. Others were 12 feet long. 11 The walls above them were made out of good quality stones. The stones were cut to the right size. On top of them was a layer of cedar beams. 12 The large courtyard had a wall around it. The first three layers of the wall were made out of blocks of stone. The top layer was made out of beautiful cedar wood. The same thing was done with the inside courtyard of the LORD's temple and its porch.

More Facts About the Temple

13 King Solomon sent messengers to Tyre. He wanted them to

bring Huram back with them. [14] Huram's mother was a widow. She was from the tribe of Naphtali. Huram's father was from Tyre. He was skilled in working with bronze. Huram also had great skill, knowledge and understanding in working with bronze. He came to King Solomon and did all the work he was asked to do.

[15] Huram made two bronze pillars. Each of them was 27 feet high. And each was 18 feet around. [16] Each pillar had a decorated top made out of bronze. Each top was seven and a half feet high. [17] Chains that were linked together hung down from the tops of the pillars. There were seven chains for each top. [18] Huram made two rows of pomegranates. They circled the chains. The pomegranates decorated the tops of the pillars. Huram did the same thing for each pillar. [19] The tops on the pillars of the porch were shaped like lilies. The lilies were 6 feet high. [20] On the tops of both pillars were 200 pomegranates. They were in rows all around the tops. They were above the part that was shaped like a bowl. And they were next to the chains. [21] Huram set the pillars up at the temple porch. The pillar on the south he named Jakin. The one on the north he named Boaz. [22] The tops of the pillars were shaped like lilies. So the work on the pillars was finished.

[23] Huram made a huge metal bowl for washing. Its shape was round. It measured 15 feet from rim to rim. It was seven and a half feet high. And it was 45 feet around. [24] Below the rim there was a circle of gourds around the bowl. In every 18 inches around the bowl there were ten gourds. The gourds were arranged in two rows. They were made as part of the bowl itself.

[25] The huge bowl stood on 12 bulls. Three of them faced north. Three faced west. Three faced south. And three faced east. The bowl rested on top of the bulls. Their rear ends were toward the center. [26] The bowl was three inches thick. Its rim was like the rim of a cup. The rim was shaped like the bloom of a lily. The bowl held 12,000 gallons of water.

[27] Huram also made ten stands out of bronze. They could be moved around. Each stand was six feet long. It was six feet wide. And it was four and a half feet high. [28] Here is how the stands were made. They had sides that were joined to posts. [29] On the sides between the posts were lions, bulls and cherubim. They were also on all of the posts. Above and below the lions and bulls were wreaths made out of hammered metal. [30] Each stand had four bronze wheels with bronze axles. Each stand had a bowl that rested on four supports. The stand had wreaths on each side. [31] There was a round opening on the inside of each stand. The opening had a frame 18 inches deep. The sides were 27 inches high from the top of the opening to the bottom of

the base. There was carving around the opening. The sides of the stands were square, not round. ³²The four wheels were under the sides. The axles of the wheels were connected to the stand. Each wheel was 27 inches across. ³³The wheels were made like chariot wheels. All the axles, rims, spokes and hubs were made out of metal.

³⁴Each stand had four handles on it. There was one on each corner. They came out from the stand. ³⁵At the top of the stand there was a round band. It was nine inches deep. The sides and supports were connected to the top of the stand. ³⁶Huram carved cherubim, lions and palm trees on the sides of the stands. He also carved them on the surfaces of the supports. His carving covered every open space. He had also carved wreaths all around. ³⁷That's how he made the ten stands. All of them were made in the same molds. And they had the same size and shape.

³⁸Then Huram made ten bronze bowls. Each one held 240 gallons. The bowls measured six feet across. There was one bowl for each of the ten stands. ³⁹He placed five of the stands on the south side of the temple. He placed the other five on the north side. He put the huge bowl on the south side. It was at the southeast corner of the temple. ⁴⁰He also made the pots, shovels and sprinkling bowls.

So Huram finished all the work he had started for King Solomon. Here's what he made for the LORD's temple.

⁴¹He made the two pillars.
He made the two tops for the pillars. The tops were shaped like bowls.
He made the two sets of chains that were linked together. They decorated the two bowl-shaped tops of the pillars.
⁴²He made the 400 pomegranates for the two sets of chains. There were two rows of pomegranates for each chain. They decorated the bowl-shaped tops of the pillars.
⁴³He made the ten stands with their ten bowls.
⁴⁴He made the huge bowl. He made the 12 bulls that were under it.
⁴⁵He made the pots, shovels and sprinkling bowls.

Huram made all those objects for King Solomon for the LORD's temple. He made them out of bronze. Then he shined them up. ⁴⁶The king had made them in clay molds. It was done on the plain of the Jordan River between Sukkoth and Zarethan. ⁴⁷Solomon didn't weigh any of those things. There were too many of them to weigh. No one even tried to weigh the bronze they were made out of.

⁴⁸Solomon also made everything in the LORD's temple.

He made the golden altar.
He made the golden table for the holy bread.
⁴⁹He made the pure gold

lampstands. There were five on the right and five on the left. They were in front of the Most Holy Room.

He made the gold flowers. He made the gold lamps and tongs. ⁵⁰He made the bowls, wick cutters, sprinkling bowls, dishes, and shallow cups for burning incense. All of them were made out of pure gold.

He made the gold bases for the doors of the inside room. That's the Most Holy Room. He also made gold bases for the doors of the main hall of the temple.

⁵¹King Solomon finished all the work for the LORD's temple. Then he brought in the things his father David had set apart for the LORD. They included the silver and gold and all the other things for the LORD's temple. Solomon placed them with the other treasures that were there.

The Ark Is Brought to the Temple

8 Then King Solomon sent for the elders of Israel. He told them to come to him in Jerusalem. They included all the leaders of the tribes. They also included the chiefs of the families of Israel. Solomon wanted them to bring up the ark of the LORD's covenant from Zion. Zion was the City of David. ²All the Israelites came together to where King Solomon was. It was at the time of the Feast of Booths. The feast was held in the month of Ethanim. That's the seventh month.

³All the elders of Israel arrived. Then the priests picked up the ark and carried it. ⁴They brought up the ark of the LORD. They also brought up the tent of meeting and all the sacred things in the tent. The priests and Levites carried everything up. ⁵The entire community of Israel had gathered around King Solomon. All of them were in front of the ark. They sacrificed huge numbers of sheep and cattle. There were so many animals that they couldn't be recorded. In fact, they couldn't even be counted.

⁶The priests brought the ark of the LORD's covenant law to its place in the Most Holy Room of the temple. They put it under the wings of the cherubim. ⁷Their wings were spread out over the place where the ark was. They covered the ark. They also covered the poles used to carry it. ⁸The poles were very long. Their ends could be seen from the Holy Room in front of the Most Holy Room. But they couldn't be seen from outside the Holy Room. They are still there to this day. ⁹There wasn't anything in the ark except the two stone tablets. Moses had placed them in it at Mount Horeb. That's where the LORD had made a covenant with the Israelites. He made it after they came out of Egypt.

¹⁰The priests left the Holy Room. Then the cloud filled the

temple of the LORD. [11] The priests couldn't do their work because of it. That's because the glory of the LORD filled his temple.

[12] Then Solomon said, "LORD, you have said you would live in a dark cloud. [13] As you can see, I've built a beautiful temple for you. You can live in it forever."

[14] The whole community of Israel was standing there. The king turned around and gave them his blessing. [15] Then he said,

"I praise the LORD. He is the God of Israel. With his own mouth he made a promise to my father David. With his own powerful hand he made it come true. He said, [16] 'I brought my people Israel out of Egypt. Ever since, I haven't chosen a city in any tribe of Israel where a temple could be built for my Name. But I have chosen David to rule over my people Israel.'

[17] "With all his heart my father David wanted to build a temple. He wanted to do it so the LORD could put his Name there. The LORD is the God of Israel. [18] But the LORD spoke to my father David. He said, 'With all your heart you wanted to build a temple for my Name. It is good that you wanted to do that. [19] But you will not build the temple. Instead, your son will build the temple for my Name. He is your own flesh and blood.'

[20] "The LORD has kept the promise he made. I've become the next king after my father David. Now I'm sitting on the throne of Israel. That's exactly what the LORD promised would happen. I've built the temple where the LORD will put his Name. He is the God of Israel. [21] I've provided a place for the ark there. The tablets of the LORD's covenant law are inside it. He made that covenant with our people of long ago. He made it when he brought them out of Egypt."

Solomon Prays to Set the Temple Apart to the LORD

[22] Then Solomon stood in front of the LORD's altar. He stood in front of the whole community of Israel. He spread out his hands toward heaven. [23] He said,

"LORD, you are the God of Israel. There is no God like you in heaven above or on earth below. You keep the covenant you made with us. You show us your love. You do that when we follow you with all our hearts. [24] You have kept your promise to my father David. He was your servant. With your mouth you made a promise. With your powerful hand you have made it come true. And today we can see it.

[25] "LORD, you are the God of Israel. Keep the promises

you made to my father David. Do it for him. He was your servant. Here is what you said to him. 'A son from your family line will sit before me on the throne of Israel. This will always be true if your children after you are careful in everything they do. They must live in my sight faithfully the way you have lived.' [26] God of Israel, let your promise to my father David come true.

[27] "But will you really live on earth? After all, the heavens can't hold you. In fact, even the highest heavens can't hold you. So this temple I've built certainly can't hold you! [28] But please pay attention to my prayer. Lord my God, be ready to help me as I make my appeal to you. Listen to my cry for help. Hear the prayer I'm praying to you today. [29] Let your eyes look toward this temple night and day. You said, 'I will put my Name there.' So please listen to the prayer I'm praying toward this place. [30] Hear me when I ask you to help us. Listen to your people Israel when they pray toward this place. Listen to us from heaven. It's the place where you live. When you hear us, forgive us.

[31] "Suppose someone does something wrong to their neighbor. And the person who has done something wrong is required to give their word. They must tell the truth about what they have done. They must come and do it in front of your altar in this temple. [32] When they do, listen to them from heaven. Take action. Judge between the person and their neighbor. Punish the guilty one. Do to that person what they have done to their neighbor. Deal with the one who isn't guilty in a way that shows they are free from blame. That will prove they aren't guilty.

[33] "Suppose your people Israel have lost the battle against their enemies. And suppose they've sinned against you. But they turn back to you and praise your name. They pray to you in this temple. And they ask you to help them. [34] Then listen to them from heaven. Forgive the sin of your people Israel. Bring them back to the land you gave to their people who lived long ago.

[35] "Suppose your people have sinned against you. And because of that, the sky is closed up and there isn't any rain. But your people pray toward this place. They praise you by admitting they've sinned. And they turn away from their sin because you have made them suffer. [36] Then listen to them from heaven. Forgive the sin of your people

Israel. Teach them the right way to live. Send rain on the land you gave them as their share.

37 "Suppose there isn't enough food in the land. And a plague strikes the land. The hot winds completely dry up our crops. Or locusts or grasshoppers come and eat them up. Or an enemy surrounds one of our cities and gets ready to attack it. Or trouble or sickness comes. 38 But suppose one of your people prays to you. They ask you to help them. They are aware of how much their own heart is suffering. And they spread out their hands toward this temple to pray. 39 Then listen to them from heaven. It's the place where you live. Forgive them. Take action. Deal with everyone in keeping with everything they do. You know their hearts. In fact, you are the only one who knows every human heart. 40 Your people will have respect for you. They will respect you as long as they are in the land you gave our people long ago.

41 "Suppose there are outsiders who don't belong to your people Israel. And they have come from a land far away. They've come because they've heard about your name. 42 When they get here, they will find out even more about your great name. They'll hear about how you reached out your mighty hand and powerful arm. So they'll come and pray toward this temple. 43 Then listen to them from heaven. It's the place where you live. Do what those outsiders ask you to do. Then all the nations on earth will know you. They will have respect for you. They'll respect you just as your own people Israel do. They'll know that your Name is in this house I've built.

44 "Suppose your people go to war against their enemies. It doesn't matter where you send them. And suppose they pray to you toward the city you have chosen. They pray toward the temple I've built for your Name. 45 Then listen to them from heaven. Listen to their prayer for your help. Stand up for them.

46 "Suppose your people sin against you. After all, there isn't anyone who doesn't sin. And suppose you get angry with them. You hand them over to their enemies. They take them as prisoners to their own lands. It doesn't matter whether those lands are near or far away. 47 But suppose your people change their ways in the land where they are held as prisoners. They turn away from their sins. They beg you to help them in the land of

those who won the battle over them. They say, 'We have sinned. We've done what is wrong. We've done what is evil.' ⁴⁸ And they turn back to you with all their heart and soul. Suppose it happens in the land of their enemies who took them away as prisoners. There they pray to you toward the land you gave their people long ago. They pray toward the city you have chosen. And they pray toward the temple I've built for your Name. ⁴⁹ Then listen to them from heaven. It's the place where you live. Listen to their prayer. Listen to them when they ask you to help them. Stand up for them. ⁵⁰ Your people have sinned against you. Please forgive them. Forgive them for all the wrong things they've done against you. And make those who won the battle over them show mercy to them. ⁵¹ After all, they are your people. They belong to you. You brought them out of Egypt. You brought them out of that furnace that melts iron down and makes it pure.

⁵² "Let your eyes be open to me when I ask you to help us. Let them be open to your people Israel when they ask you to help them. Pay attention to them every time they cry out to you. ⁵³ After all, you chose them out of all the nations in the world. You made them your very own people. You did it just as you had announced through your servant Moses. That's when you brought out of Egypt our people of long ago. You are our Lord and King."

⁵⁴ Solomon finished praying. He finished asking the Lord to help his people. Then he got up from in front of the Lord's altar. He had been down on his knees with his hands spread out toward heaven. ⁵⁵ He stood in front of the whole community of Israel. He blessed them with a loud voice. He said,

⁵⁶ "I praise the Lord. He has given peace and rest to his people Israel. That's exactly what he promised to do. He gave his people good promises through his servant Moses. Every single word of those promises has come true. ⁵⁷ May the Lord our God be with us, just as he was with our people who lived long ago. May he never leave us. May he never desert us. ⁵⁸ May he turn our hearts to him. Then we will live the way he wants us to. We'll obey the commands, rules and directions he gave our people of long ago. ⁵⁹ I've prayed these words to the Lord our God. May he keep them close to him day and night. May he stand up for me. May he also stand up for his people Israel. May he

give us what we need every day. [60] Then all the nations on earth will know that the LORD is God. They'll know that there isn't any other god. [61] And may you commit your lives completely to the LORD our God. May you live by his rules. May you obey his commands. May you always do as you are doing now."

The Temple Is Set Apart to the LORD

[62] Then the king and the whole community of Israel offered sacrifices to the LORD. [63] Solomon sacrificed friendship offerings to the LORD. He sacrificed 22,000 oxen. He also sacrificed 120,000 sheep and goats. So the king and the whole community set the temple of the LORD apart to him.

[64] On that same day the king set the middle area of the courtyard apart to the LORD. It was in front of the LORD's temple. There Solomon sacrificed burnt offerings and grain offerings. He also sacrificed the fat of the friendship offerings there. He did it there because the bronze altar that stood in front of the LORD was too small. It wasn't big enough to hold all the burnt offerings, the grain offerings and the fat of the friendship offerings.

[65] At that time Solomon celebrated the Feast of Booths. The whole community of Israel was with him. It was a huge crowd. People came from as far away as Lebo Hamath and the Wadi of Egypt. For seven days they celebrated in front of the LORD our God. The feast continued for seven more days. That made a total of 14 days. [66] On the following day Solomon sent the people away. They asked the LORD to bless the king. Then they went home. The people were glad. Their hearts were full of joy. That's because the LORD had done so many good things for his servant David and his people Israel.

The LORD Appears to Solomon

9 Solomon finished building the LORD's temple and the royal palace. He had accomplished everything he had planned to do. [2] The LORD appeared to him a second time. He had already appeared to him at Gibeon. [3] The LORD said to him,

"I have heard you pray to me. I have heard you ask me to help you. You have built this temple. I have set it apart for myself. My Name will be there forever. My eyes and my heart will always be there.

[4] "But you must walk faithfully with me, just as your father David did. Your heart must be honest. It must be without blame. Do everything I command you to do. Obey my rules and laws. [5] Then I will set up your royal throne over Israel forever. I promised your father David I would do that. I said to him, 'You

will always have a son from your family line on the throne of Israel.'

6 "But suppose all of you turn away from me. Or your children turn away from me. You refuse to obey the commands and rules I have given you. And you go off to serve other gods and worship them. 7 Then I will remove Israel from the land. It is the land I gave them. I will turn my back on this temple. I will do it even though I have set it apart for my Name to be there. Then Israel will be hated by all the nations. They will laugh and joke about Israel. 8 This temple will become a pile of stones. All those who pass by it will be shocked. They will make fun of it. And they will say, 'Why has the LORD done a thing like this to this land and temple?' 9 People will answer, 'Because they have deserted the LORD their God. He brought out of Egypt their people of long ago. But they have been holding on to other gods. They've been worshiping them. They've been serving them. That's why the LORD has brought all this horrible trouble on them.' "

Other Things Solomon Did

10 Solomon built the LORD's temple and the royal palace. It took him 20 years to construct those two buildings. 11 King Solomon gave 20 towns in Galilee to Hiram, the king of Tyre. That's because Hiram had provided him with all the cedar and juniper logs he wanted. He had also provided Solomon with all the gold he wanted. 12 Hiram went from Tyre to see the towns Solomon had given him. But he wasn't pleased with them. 13 "My friend," he asked, "what have you given me? What kind of towns are these?" So he called them the Land of Kabul. And that's what they are still called to this day. 14 Hiram had sent four and a half tons of gold to Solomon.

15 King Solomon forced people to work hard for him. Here is a record of what they did. They built the LORD's temple and Solomon's palace. They filled in the low places. They rebuilt the wall of Jerusalem. They built up Hazor, Megiddo and Gezer. 16 Pharaoh, the king of Egypt, had attacked Gezer and captured it. He had set it on fire. He had killed the Canaanites who lived there. Then he had given Gezer as a wedding gift to his daughter. She was Solomon's wife. 17 Solomon rebuilt Gezer. He built up Lower Beth Horon 18 and Baalath. He built up Tadmor in the desert. All those towns were in his land. 19 He built up all the cities where he could store things. He also built up the towns for his chariots and horses. He built anything he wanted to build in Jerusalem, Lebanon and all the territory he ruled over.

²⁰ There were still many people left in the land who weren't Israelites. They included Amorites, Hittites, Perizzites, Hivites and Jebusites. ²¹ They were children of the people who had lived in the land before the Israelites came. Those people had been set apart to the Lord in a special way to be destroyed. But the Israelites hadn't been able to kill all of them. Solomon forced them to work very hard as his slaves. And they still work for Israel as slaves to this day. ²² But Solomon didn't force any of the Israelites to work as his slaves. Instead, some were his fighting men. Others were his government officials, his officers and his captains. Others were commanders of his chariots and chariot drivers. ²³ Still others were the chief officials in charge of Solomon's projects. There were 550 officials in charge of those who did the work.

²⁴ Pharaoh's daughter moved from the City of David up to the palace Solomon had built for her. After that, he filled in the low places near the palace.

²⁵ Three times a year Solomon sacrificed burnt offerings and friendship offerings. He sacrificed them on the altar he had built to honor the Lord. Along with the offerings, he burned incense to the Lord. So he carried out his duties for the temple.

²⁶ King Solomon also built ships at Ezion Geber. It's near Elath in Edom. It's on the shore of the Red Sea. ²⁷ Hiram sent his men to serve on the ships together with Solomon's men. Hiram's sailors knew the sea. ²⁸ All of them sailed to Ophir. They brought back 16 tons of gold. They gave it to King Solomon.

The Queen of Sheba Visits Solomon

10 The queen of Sheba heard about how famous Solomon was. She also heard about how he served and worshiped the Lord. So she came to test Solomon with hard questions. ² She arrived in Jerusalem with a very large group of attendants. Her camels were carrying spices, huge amounts of gold, and valuable jewels. She came to Solomon and asked him about everything she wanted to know. ³ Solomon answered all her questions. There wasn't anything too hard for the king to explain to her. ⁴ So the queen of Sheba saw how very wise Solomon was. She saw the palace he had built. ⁵ She saw the food on his table. She saw his officials sitting there. She saw the robes of the servants who waited on everyone. She saw his wine tasters. And she saw the burnt offerings Solomon sacrificed at the Lord's temple. She could hardly believe everything she had seen.

⁶ She said to the king, "Back in my own country I heard a report about you. I heard about how much you had accomplished. I also heard about how wise you are. Everything I heard is true. ⁷ But I didn't believe those

things. So I came to see for myself. And now I believe it! You are twice as wise and wealthy as people say you are. The report I heard doesn't even begin to tell the whole story about you. ⁸ How happy your people must be! How happy your officials must be! They always get to serve you and hear the wise things you say. ⁹ May the LORD your God be praised. He takes great delight in you. He placed you on the throne of Israel. The LORD will love Israel for all time to come. That's why he has made you king. He knows that you will do what is fair and right."

¹⁰ She gave the king four and a half tons of gold. She also gave him huge amounts of spices and valuable jewels. No one would ever bring to King Solomon as many spices as the queen of Sheba gave him.

¹¹ Hiram's ships brought gold from Ophir. From there they also brought huge amounts of almugwood and valuable jewels. ¹² The king used the almugwood to make supports for the LORD's temple and the royal palace. He also used it to make harps and lyres for those who played the music. That much almugwood has never been brought into Judah or seen there since that day.

¹³ King Solomon gave the queen of Sheba everything she wanted and asked for. That was in addition to what he had given her out of his royal riches. Then she left. She returned to her own country with her attendants.

Solomon's Greatness

¹⁴ Each year Solomon received 25 tons of gold. ¹⁵ That didn't include the money brought in by business and trade. It also didn't include the money from all the kings of Arabia and the governors of the territories.

¹⁶ King Solomon made 200 large shields out of hammered gold. Each one weighed 15 pounds. ¹⁷ He also made 300 small shields out of hammered gold. Each one weighed seven and a half pounds. The king put all the shields in the Palace of the Forest of Lebanon.

¹⁸ Then he made a large throne. It was covered with ivory. And that was covered with fine gold. ¹⁹ The throne had six steps. Its back had a rounded top. The throne had armrests on both sides of the seat. A statue of a lion stood on each side of the throne. ²⁰ Twelve lions stood on the six steps. There was one at each end of each step. Nothing like that throne had ever been made for any other kingdom. ²¹ All of King Solomon's cups were made out of gold. All the things used in the Palace of the Forest of Lebanon were made out of pure gold. Nothing was made out of silver. When Solomon was king, silver wasn't considered to be worth very much. ²² He had many ships that carried goods to be traded. His ships went to sea along with Hiram's ships. Once every three years the ships returned. They brought gold, silver, ivory, apes and peacocks.

²³ King Solomon was richer than all the other kings on earth. He was also wiser than they were. ²⁴ People from the whole world wanted to meet Solomon in person. They wanted to see for themselves how wise God had made him. ²⁵ Year after year, everyone who came to him brought a gift. They brought gifts made out of silver and gold. They brought robes, weapons and spices. They also brought horses and mules.

²⁶ Solomon had 1,400 chariots and 12,000 horses. He kept some of his horses and chariots in the chariot cities. He kept the others with him in Jerusalem. ²⁷ The king made silver as common in Jerusalem as stones. He made cedar wood as common there as sycamore-fig trees in the western hills. ²⁸ Solomon got horses from Egypt and from Kue. The royal traders bought them from Kue at the current price. ²⁹ They weighed out 15 pounds of silver for a chariot from Egypt. And they weighed out almost four pounds of silver for a horse. They also sold horses and chariots to all the kings of the Hittites and the kings of the Arameans.

Solomon's Wives

11 King Solomon loved many women besides Pharaoh's daughter. They were from other lands. They were Moabites, Ammonites, Edomites, Sidonians and Hittites. ² The LORD had warned Israel about women from other nations. He had said, "You must not marry them. If you do, you can be sure they will turn your hearts toward their gods." But Solomon continued to love them anyway. He wouldn't give them up. ³ He had 700 wives who came from royal families. And he had 300 concubines. His wives led him astray. ⁴ As Solomon grew older, his wives turned his heart toward other gods. He didn't follow the LORD his God with all his heart. So he wasn't like his father David. ⁵ Solomon worshiped Ashtoreth. Ashtoreth was the female god of the Sidonians. He also worshiped Molek. Molek was the god of the Ammonites. The LORD hated that god. ⁶ Solomon did what was evil in the sight of the LORD. He didn't completely obey the LORD. He didn't do what his father David had done.

⁷ There is a hill east of Jerusalem. Solomon built a high place for worshiping Chemosh there. He built a high place for worshiping Molek there too. Chemosh was the god of Moab. Molek was the god of Ammon. The LORD hated both of those gods. ⁸ Solomon also built high places so that all his wives from other nations could worship their gods. Those women burned incense and offered sacrifices to their gods.

⁹ The LORD became angry with Solomon. That's because his heart had turned away from the LORD, the God of Israel. He had appeared to Solomon twice. ¹⁰ He had commanded Solomon not to worship other

gods. But Solomon didn't obey the LORD. ¹¹So the LORD said to Solomon, "You have chosen not to keep my covenant. You have decided not to obey my rules. I commanded you to do what I told you. But you did not do it. So you can be absolutely sure I will tear the kingdom away from you. I will give it to one of your officials. ¹²But I will not do that while you are still living. Because of your father David I will wait. I will tear the kingdom out of your son's hand. ¹³But I will not tear the whole kingdom away from him. I will give him one of the tribes because of my servant David. I will also do it because of Jerusalem. That is the city I have chosen."

Solomon's Enemies

¹⁴Then the LORD brought an enemy against Solomon. The enemy's name was Hadad. He was from Edom. In fact, he belonged to the royal family of Edom. ¹⁵David had fought against Edom. Joab had been the commander of the army. He had gone up to bury the dead bodies of the Israelites who had been killed in battle. At that time he had struck down all the men in Edom. ¹⁶In fact, Joab and all the men of Israel stayed there for six months. During that time they destroyed all the men in Edom. ¹⁷But when Hadad was only a boy, he ran away to Egypt. Some officials from Edom went with him. They had served Hadad's father. ¹⁸They started out from Midian and went to Paran.

They took some people from Paran with them. Then they went to Egypt. They went to Pharaoh, the king of Egypt. He gave Hadad a house and some land. He also supplied him with food.

¹⁹Pharaoh was very pleased with Hadad. Pharaoh's wife was Queen Tahpenes. He gave Hadad her sister to be his wife. ²⁰The sister of Tahpenes had a son by Hadad. The baby was named Genubath. Tahpenes brought him up in the royal palace. Genubath lived there with Pharaoh's own children.

²¹Hadad heard that David had joined the members of his family who had already died. He also heard that Joab, the commander of the army, was dead. Hadad heard those things while he was in Egypt. He said to Pharaoh, "Let me go. I want to return to my own country."

²²"Why do you want to go back to your own country?" Pharaoh asked. "Don't you have everything you need right here?"

"Yes," Hadad replied. "But I want you to let me go anyway!"

²³God brought another enemy against Solomon. The enemy's name was Rezon. He was the son of Eliada. Rezon had run away from his master Hadadezer, the king of Zobah. ²⁴David had destroyed Zobah's army. Then Rezon gathered together some men to follow him. He became their leader. They went to Damascus where they made their homes. They also took control of Damascus. ²⁵Rezon was Israel's enemy as long as Solo-

mon was living. Rezon added to the trouble Hadad had caused. So Rezon ruled in Aram. He was Israel's enemy.

Jeroboam Refuses to Follow Solomon

²⁶ Jeroboam refused to follow King Solomon. He was one of Solomon's officials. He was from Zeredah in the territory of Ephraim. His father was Nebat. His mother was a widow named Zeruah.

²⁷ Here is the story of how Jeroboam refused to follow the king. Solomon had filled in the low places near the palace. He had also repaired the wall of the city of his father David. ²⁸ Jeroboam was a very important young man. Solomon saw how well he did his work. So he put him in charge of all the workers in northern Israel.

²⁹ About that time Jeroboam was going out of Jerusalem. Ahijah the prophet met him on the road. Ahijah was from Shiloh. He was wearing a new coat. The two of them were all alone out in the country. ³⁰ Ahijah grabbed the new coat he had on. He tore it up into 12 pieces. ³¹ Then he said to Jeroboam, "Take ten pieces for yourself. The LORD is the God of Israel. He says, 'I am going to tear the kingdom out of Solomon's hand. I will give you ten of its tribes. ³² Solomon will have one of its tribes. I will let him keep it because of my servant David and because of Jerusalem. I have chosen that city out of all the cities in the tribes of Israel. ³³ I will do these things because the tribes have deserted me. They have worshiped Ashtoreth, the female god of the people of Sidon. They have worshiped Chemosh, the god of the people of Moab. And they have worshiped Molek, the god of the people of Ammon. They have not lived the way I wanted them to. They have not done what is right in my eyes. They have not obeyed my rules and laws as Solomon's father David did.

³⁴ "'But I will not take the whole kingdom out of Solomon's hand. I have made him ruler all the days of his life. I have done it because of my servant David. I chose him, and he obeyed my commands and rules. ³⁵ I will take the kingdom out of his son's hands. And I will give you ten of the tribes. ³⁶ I will give one of the tribes to David's son. Then my servant David will always have a son on his throne in Jerusalem. The lamp of David's kingdom will always burn brightly in my sight. Jerusalem is the city I chose for my Name. ³⁷ But I will make you king over Israel. You will rule over everything your heart desires. So you will be the king of Israel. ³⁸ Do everything I command you to do. Live the way I want you to. Do what is right in my eyes. Obey my rules and commands. That is what my servant David did. If you do those things, I will be with you. I will build you a kingdom. It will last as long as the one I built for David. I will give Israel to you. ³⁹ I will punish

David's family because of what Solomon has done. But I will not punish them forever.' "

⁴⁰ Solomon tried to kill Jeroboam. But Jeroboam ran away to Egypt. He went to Shishak, the king of Egypt. He stayed there until Solomon died.

Solomon Dies

⁴¹ The other events of Solomon's rule are written down. Everything he did and the wisdom he showed are written down. They are written in the official records of Solomon. ⁴² Solomon ruled in Jerusalem over the whole nation of Israel for 40 years. ⁴³ Then he joined the members of his family who had already died. He was buried in the city of his father David. Solomon's son Rehoboam became the next king after him.

Israel Refuses to Follow Rehoboam

12 Rehoboam went to the city of Shechem. All the Israelites had gone there to make him king. ² Jeroboam heard about it. He was the son of Nebat. Jeroboam was still in Egypt at that time. He had gone there for safety. He wanted to get away from King Solomon. But now he returned from Egypt. ³ So the people sent for Jeroboam. He and the whole community of Israel went to Rehoboam. They said to him, ⁴ "Your father put a heavy load on our shoulders. But now make our hard work easier. Make the heavy load on us lighter. Then we'll serve you."

⁵ Rehoboam answered, "Go away for three days. Then come back to me." So the people went away.

⁶ King Rehoboam asked the elders for advice. They had served his father Solomon while he was still living. Rehoboam asked them, "What advice can you give me? How should I answer these people?"

⁷ They replied, "Serve them today. Give them what they are asking for. Then they'll always serve you."

⁸ But Rehoboam didn't accept the advice the elders gave him. Instead, he asked for advice from the young men. They had grown up with him and were now serving him. ⁹ He asked them, "What's your advice? How should I answer these people? They say to me, 'Make the load your father put on our shoulders lighter.' "

¹⁰ The young men who had grown up with him gave their answer. They replied, "These people have said to you, 'Your father put a heavy load on our shoulders. Make it lighter.' Now tell them, 'My little finger is stronger than my father's legs. ¹¹ My father put a heavy load on your shoulders. But I'll make it even heavier. My father beat you with whips. But I'll beat you with bigger whips.' "

¹² Three days later Jeroboam and all the people returned to Rehoboam. That's because the king had said, "Come back to me in three days." ¹³ The king answered the people in a mean

way. He didn't accept the advice the elders had given him. ¹⁴ Instead, he followed the advice of the young men. He said, "My father put a heavy load on your shoulders. But I'll make it even heavier. My father beat you with whips. But I'll beat you with bigger whips." ¹⁵ So the king didn't listen to the people. That's because the LORD had planned it that way. What he had said through Ahijah came true. Ahijah had spoken the LORD's message to Jeroboam, the son of Nebat. Ahijah was from Shiloh.

¹⁶ All the Israelites saw that the king refused to listen to them. So they answered the king. They said,

"We don't have any share in
     David's royal family.
  We don't have any share in
     Jesse's son.
People of Israel, let's go back
     to our homes.
  David's royal family,
     take care of your own
     kingdom!"

So the Israelites went home. ¹⁷ But Rehoboam still ruled over the Israelites living in the towns of Judah.

¹⁸ Adoniram was in charge of those who were forced to work hard for King Rehoboam. The king sent him out among all the Israelites. But they killed Adoniram by throwing stones at him. King Rehoboam was able to get away in his chariot. He escaped to Jerusalem. ¹⁹ Israel has refused to follow the royal family of David to this day.

²⁰ All the Israelites heard that Jeroboam had returned. They sent for him. They wanted him to meet with the whole community. Then they made him king over the entire nation of Israel. Only the tribe of Judah remained true to David's royal family.

²¹ Rehoboam arrived in Jerusalem. He brought together 180,000 capable young men from Judah and the tribe of Benjamin. He had decided to go to war against Israel. Solomon's son Rehoboam wanted his fighting men to get the kingdom of Israel back for him.

²² But a message from God came to Shemaiah. He was a man of God. God said to him, ²³ "Speak to Solomon's son Rehoboam, the king of Judah. Speak to all Judah and the tribe of Benjamin. Also speak to the rest of the people. Tell all of them, ²⁴ 'The LORD says, "Do not go up to fight against the Israelites. They are your relatives. I want every one of you to go back home. Things have happened exactly the way I planned them." ' " So the fighting men obeyed the LORD's message. They went home again, just as he had ordered.

Golden Calves at Bethel and Dan

²⁵ Jeroboam built up the walls of Shechem. It was in the hill country of Ephraim. Jeroboam made Shechem his home. From there he went out and built up Peniel.

²⁶ Jeroboam thought, "My kingdom still isn't secure. It could very easily go back to the royal family of David. ²⁷ Suppose the Israelites go up to Jerusalem to offer sacrifices at the LORD's temple. If they do, they will again decide to follow Rehoboam as their master. Then they'll kill me. They'll return to King Rehoboam. He is king of Judah."

²⁸ So King Jeroboam asked for advice. Then he made two golden statues that looked like calves. He said to the people, "It's too hard for you to go up to Jerusalem. Israel, here are your gods who brought you up out of Egypt." ²⁹ He set up one statue in Bethel. He set up the other one in Dan. ³⁰ What Jeroboam did was sinful. And it caused Israel to sin. The people came to worship the statue at Bethel. They went all the way to Dan to worship the statue that was there.

³¹ Jeroboam built temples for worshiping gods on high places. He appointed all kinds of people as priests. They didn't even have to be Levites. ³² He established a feast. It was on the 15th day of the eighth month. He wanted to make it like the Feast of Booths that was held in Judah. Jeroboam built an altar at Bethel. He offered sacrifices on it. He sacrificed to the calves he had made. He also put priests in Bethel. He did it at the high places he had made. ³³ He offered sacrifices on the altar he had built at Bethel. It was on the 15th day of the eighth month. That's the month he had chosen for it. So he established the feast for the Israelites. And he went up to the altar to sacrifice offerings.

A Man of God From Judah

13 A man of God went from Judah to Bethel. He had received a message from the LORD. He arrived in Bethel just as Jeroboam was standing by the altar to offer a sacrifice. ² The man cried out. He shouted a message from the LORD against the altar. He said, "Altar! Altar! The LORD says, 'A son named Josiah will be born into the royal family of David. Altar, listen to me! Josiah will sacrifice the priests of the high places on you. They will be the children of the priests who are offering sacrifices here. So human bones will be burned on you.'" ³ That same day the man of God spoke about a miraculous sign. He said, "Here is the sign the LORD has announced. This altar will be broken to pieces. The ashes on it will be spilled out."

⁴ The man of God announced that message against the altar at Bethel. When King Jeroboam heard it, he reached out his hand from the altar. He said, "Grab him!" But as he reached out his hand toward the man, it dried up. He couldn't even pull it back. ⁵ Also, the altar broke into pieces. Its ashes spilled out. That happened in keeping with the miraculous sign the man of God had announced. He had received a message from the LORD.

[6] King Jeroboam spoke to the man of God. He said, "Pray to the LORD your God for me. Pray that my hand will be as good as new again." So the man of God prayed to the LORD for the king. And the king's hand became as good as new. It was just as healthy as it had been before.

[7] The king said to the man of God, "Come home with me for a meal. I'll give you a gift."

[8] But the man of God replied to the king. He said, "What if you were to give me half of what you own? Even then I wouldn't go with you. I wouldn't eat bread or drink water here. [9] The LORD gave me a command. He said, 'Do not eat bread or drink water there. Do not return the same way you came.'" [10] So he took another road. He didn't go back on the same road he had taken when he came to Bethel.

[11] An old prophet was living in Bethel. His sons came and spoke to him. They told him everything the man of God had done there that day. They also told their father what the man had said to the king. [12] Their father asked them, "Which way did he go?" His sons showed him the road the man of God from Judah had taken. [13] So he said to his sons, "Put a saddle on the donkey for me." When they had done it, he got on the donkey. [14] He traveled on the same road the man of God had taken. He found the man sitting under an oak tree. He asked him, "Are you the man of God who came from Judah?"

"I am," he replied.

[15] So the prophet said to him, "Come home with me. I'll give you something to eat."

[16] The man of God said, "I can't go back to Bethel with you. I can't eat bread or drink water with you there. [17] I've received a message from the LORD. He told me, 'Do not eat bread or drink water there. Do not return the same way you came.'"

[18] The old prophet answered, "I'm also a prophet, just like you. An angel gave me a message from the LORD. The message said, 'Bring the man of God back with you to your house. Then he can eat bread and drink water with you.'" But the old prophet was telling him a lie. [19] The man of God returned with him. He ate and drank in his house.

[20] They were sitting at the table. The LORD gave a message to the old prophet who had brought the man of God back. [21] He cried out to the man who had come from Judah. He told him, "The LORD says, 'You have not done what I told you to do. You have not obeyed the command I gave you. I am the LORD your God. [22] You came back here and ate bread and drank water. You did it in the place where I told you not to. So your body will not be buried in your family tomb.'"

[23] The man of God finished eating and drinking. Then the old prophet who had brought him back put a saddle on the man's donkey for him. [24] And the man went on his way. A lion

attacked him on the road and killed him. His body was left lying on the road. The donkey and the lion were standing beside it. ²⁵ Some people passed by. They saw the body lying on the road. They saw the lion standing beside the body. Then they went and reported it in the city where the old prophet lived.

²⁶ The prophet who had brought the man back from his journey heard about what had happened. He said, "It's the man of God. He didn't do what the Lord told him to do. So the Lord has given him over to the lion. The lion has attacked him and killed him. Everything has happened just as the Lord's message had warned him it would."

²⁷ The old prophet said to his sons, "Put a saddle on the donkey for me." So they did. ²⁸ Then he went out. He found the body of the man of God lying on the road. The donkey and the lion were standing beside it. The lion hadn't eaten the body. It hadn't attacked the donkey either. ²⁹ So the prophet picked up the man's body. He put it on the donkey. He brought it back to his own city. He wanted to mourn for him and bury him. ³⁰ Then he placed the body in his own tomb. People mourned for him. They said, "Oh, no, my friend! My dear friend!"

³¹ After the old prophet had buried the the man of God, he spoke to his sons. He said, "When I die, bury me in the grave where the man of God is buried. Put my bones next to his bones. ³² I want you to do that because he announced a message from the Lord. He spoke against the altar in Bethel. He also spoke against all the temples that are on the high places. They are in the towns of Samaria. What the man of God said will certainly come true."

³³ Even after all of that happened, Jeroboam still didn't change his evil ways. Once more he appointed priests for the high places. He made priests out of all kinds of people. In fact, he let anyone become a priest who wanted to. He set them apart to serve at the high places. ³⁴ All of that was the great sin the royal family of Jeroboam committed. It led to their fall from power. Because of it, they were destroyed from the face of the earth.

Ahijah's Prophecy Against Jeroboam

14 At that time Abijah became sick. He was the son of Jeroboam. ² Jeroboam said to his wife, "Go. Put on some different clothes. Then no one will recognize you as my wife. Go to Shiloh. That's where Ahijah the prophet is. He told me I would be king over the Israelites. ³ Take ten loaves of bread with you. Take some cakes and a jar of honey. Go to him. He'll tell you what will happen to our son." ⁴ So Jeroboam's wife did what he said. She went to Ahijah's house in Shiloh.

Ahijah couldn't see. He was

blind because he was so old.
⁵ But the LORD had told Ahijah,
"Jeroboam's wife is coming. Her
son is sick. She'll ask you about
him. Give her the answer I give
you. When she arrives, she'll
pretend to be someone else."

⁶ Ahijah heard the sound of
her footsteps at the door. He
said, "Come in. I know that you
are Jeroboam's wife. Why are
you pretending to be someone
else? I have some bad news for
you. ⁷ Go. Tell Jeroboam that
the LORD has a message for
him. The LORD is the God of Israel. He says, 'I chose you from
among the people. I appointed
you king over my people Israel. ⁸ I tore the kingdom away
from the royal house of David.
I gave it to you. But you have
not been like my servant David.
He obeyed my commands. He
followed me with all his heart.
He did only what was right in
my eyes. ⁹ You have done more
evil things than all those who
lived before you. You have
made other gods for yourself.
You have made statues of gods
out of metal. You have made
me very angry. You have turned
your back on me.

¹⁰ " 'Because of that, I am going to bring horrible trouble on
your royal house. I will cut off
from you every male in Israel.
It does not matter whether they
are slaves or free. I will burn up
your royal house, just as someone burns up trash. I will burn
it until it is all gone. ¹¹ Some of
the people who belong to you
will die in the city. Dogs will

eat them up. Others will die in
the country. The birds will eat
them. The LORD has spoken!'

¹² "Now go back home. When
you enter your city, your son
will die. ¹³ All the Israelites will
mourn for him. Then he will be
buried. He is the only one who
belongs to Jeroboam who will
be buried. That is because he is
the only one in Jeroboam's royal
house in whom I have found
anything good. I am the LORD,
the God of Israel.

¹⁴ "I will choose for myself a
king over Israel. He will destroy
the family of Jeroboam. This
day your son will die. Even now
this is beginning to happen. ¹⁵ I,
the LORD, will strike down Israel. Israel will be like tall grass
swaying in the water. I will pull
Israel up from this good land by
the roots. I gave it to their people who lived long ago. I will
scatter Israel to the east side of
the Euphrates River. That is because they made the LORD very
angry. They made poles used to
worship the female god named
Asherah. ¹⁶ I will give Israel up
because of the sins Jeroboam
has committed. He has also
caused Israel to commit those
same sins."

¹⁷ Then Jeroboam's wife got
up and left. She went to the
city of Tirzah. As soon as she
stepped through the doorway
of the house, her son died. ¹⁸ He
was buried and all the Israelites
mourned for him. That's what
the LORD had said would happen. He had said it through his
servant, Ahijah the prophet.

[19] The other events of Jeroboam's rule are written down. His wars and how he ruled are written down. They are written in the official records of the kings of Israel. [20] Jeroboam ruled for 22 years. Then he joined the members of his family who had already died. Jeroboam's son Nadab became the next king after him.

Rehoboam King of Judah

[21] Rehoboam was king in Judah. He was the son of Solomon. Rehoboam was 41 years old when he became king. He ruled for 17 years in Jerusalem. It was the city the LORD had chosen out of all the cities in the tribes of Israel. He wanted to put his Name there. Rehoboam's mother was Naamah from Ammon.

[22] The people of Judah did what was evil in the sight of the LORD. The sins they had committed made the LORD angry. The LORD was angry because they refused to worship only him. They did more to make him angry than their people who lived before them had done. [23] Judah also set up for themselves high places for worship. They set up sacred stones. They set up poles used to worship the female god named Asherah. They did it on every high hill and under every green tree. [24] There were even male prostitutes at the temples in the land. The people took part in all the practices of other nations. The LORD hated those practices.

He had driven those nations out to make room for the Israelites.

[25] Shishak attacked Jerusalem. It was in the fifth year that Rehoboam was king. Shishak was king of Egypt. [26] He carried away the treasures of the LORD's temple. He also carried away the treasures of the royal palace. He took everything. That included all the gold shields Solomon had made. [27] So King Rehoboam made bronze shields to take their place. He gave them to the commanders of the guards on duty at the entrance to the royal palace. [28] Every time the king went to the LORD's temple, the guards carried the shields. Later, they took them back to the room where they were kept.

[29] The other events of Rehoboam's rule are written down. Everything he did is written in the official records of the kings of Judah. [30] Rehoboam and Jeroboam were always at war with each other. [31] Rehoboam joined the members of his family who had already died. He was buried in his family tomb in the City of David. His mother was Naamah from Ammon. Rehoboam's son Abijah became the next king after him.

Abijah King of Judah

15 Abijah became king of Judah. It was in the 18th year of Jeroboam's rule over Israel. Jeroboam was the son of Nebat. [2] Abijah ruled in Jerusalem for three years. His mother's name was Maakah. She was Abishalom's daughter.

³Abijah committed all the sins his father had committed before him. Abijah didn't obey the LORD his God with all his heart. He didn't do what King David had done. ⁴But the LORD still kept the lamp of Abijah's kingdom burning brightly in Jerusalem. He did it by giving him a son to be the next king after him. He also did it by making Jerusalem strong. The LORD did those things because of David. ⁵David had done what was right in the sight of the LORD. He had kept all the LORD's commands. He had obeyed them all the days of his life. But he hadn't obeyed the LORD in the case of Uriah, the Hittite.

⁶There was war between Abijah and Jeroboam all through Abijah's life. ⁷The other events of Abijah's rule are written down. Everything he did is written down. All these things are written in the official records of the kings of Judah. There was war between Abijah and Jeroboam. ⁸Abijah joined the members of his family who had already died. He was buried in the City of David. Abijah's son Asa became the next king after him.

Asa King of Judah

⁹Asa became king of Judah. It was in the 20th year that Jeroboam was king of Israel. ¹⁰Asa ruled in Jerusalem for 41 years. His grandmother's name was Maakah. She was Abishalom's daughter.
¹¹Asa did what was right in the sight of the LORD. That's what King David had done. ¹²Asa threw out of the land the male prostitutes who were at the temples. He got rid of all the statues of gods made by his people of long ago. ¹³He even removed his grandmother Maakah from her position as queen mother. That's because she had made a pole used to worship the female god named Asherah. The LORD hated it. So Asa cut it down. He burned it in the Kidron Valley. ¹⁴Asa didn't remove the high places from Israel. But he committed his whole life completely to the LORD. ¹⁵He and his father had set apart silver, gold and other things to the LORD. Asa brought them into the LORD's temple.

¹⁶There was war between Asa and Baasha, the king of Israel. It lasted the whole time they were kings. ¹⁷Baasha was king of Israel. He marched out against Judah. Baasha built up the walls of Ramah. He did it to keep people from leaving or entering the territory of Asa, the king of Judah.

¹⁸Asa took all the silver and gold left among the treasures of the LORD's temple and his own palace. He put his officials in charge of it. He sent the officials to Ben-Hadad. Ben-Hadad was king of Aram. He was ruling in Damascus. He was the son of Tabrimmon and the grandson of Hezion. ¹⁹"Let's make a peace treaty between us," Asa said. "My father and your father had made a peace treaty between them. Now I'm sending you a

gift of silver and gold. So break your treaty with Baasha, the king of Israel. Then he'll go back home."

20 Ben-Hadad agreed with King Asa. He sent his army commanders against the towns of Israel. He captured Ijon, Dan, Abel Beth Maakah and the whole area of Kinnereth in addition to Naphtali. 21 Baasha heard about it. So he stopped building up Ramah. He went back home to Tirzah. 22 Then King Asa gave an order to all the men of Judah. Everyone was required to help. They carried away from Ramah the stones and wood Baasha had been using there. King Asa used them to build up Geba in the territory of Benjamin. He also used them to build up Mizpah.

23 All the other events of Asa's rule are written down, including the cities he built. Everything he did is written in the official records of the kings of Judah. But when Asa became old, his feet began to give him trouble. 24 He joined the members of his family who had already died. He was buried in his family tomb. It was in the city of King David. Asa's son Jehoshaphat became the next king after him.

Nadab King of Israel

25 Nadab became king of Israel. It was in the second year that Asa was king of Judah. Nadab ruled over Israel for two years. He was the son of Jeroboam. 26 Nadab did what was evil in the sight of the LORD. He lived the way his father had lived. He committed the same sin his father Jeroboam had caused Israel to commit.

27 Baasha was from the tribe of Issachar. He was the son of Ahijah. Baasha made plans against Nadab and struck him down at Gibbethon. It was a Philistine town. Baasha struck him down while Nadab and all the men of Israel were getting ready to attack Gibbethon. 28 He killed Nadab in the third year that Asa was king of Judah. Baasha became the next king after Nadab.

29 As soon as Baasha became king, he killed Jeroboam's whole family. He didn't leave any of them alive. He destroyed every one of them. He did what the LORD had said would happen. The LORD had spoken that message through his servant Ahijah from Shiloh. 30 The LORD judged Jeroboam's family because of the sins Jeroboam had committed. He had also caused Israel to commit those same sins. He had made the LORD very angry. The LORD is the God of Israel.

31 The other events of Nadab's rule are written down. Everything he did is written in the official records of the kings of Israel. 32 There was war between Asa and Baasha, the king of Israel. It lasted the whole time they were kings.

Baasha King of Israel

33 Baasha became king of Israel in Tirzah. It was in the third year that Asa was king of Judah. Baasha ruled for 24 years. He

was the son of Ahijah. ³⁴ Baasha did what was evil in the sight of the LORD. He lived the way Jeroboam had lived. He committed the same sin Jeroboam had caused Israel to commit.

16 The LORD's message about Baasha came to Jehu, the son of Hanani. Here is what the LORD said about Baasha. ² "I lifted you up from the dust. I appointed you king over my people Israel. But you lived the way Jeroboam had lived. You also caused my people Israel to sin. And their sins made me very angry. ³ So I am about to destroy you, Baasha, and your royal house. I will make your house like the royal house of Jeroboam, the son of Nebat. ⁴ Some of the people who belong to you will die in the city. Dogs will eat them up. Others will die in the country. The birds will eat them."

⁵ The other events of Baasha's rule are written down. What he did and what he accomplished are written in the official records of the kings of Israel. ⁶ Baasha joined the members of his family who had already died. He was buried in Tirzah. Baasha's son Elah became the next king after him.

⁷ The LORD's message came through the prophet Jehu, the son of Hanani. It was against Baasha and his royal house. Baasha had done all kinds of evil things in the sight of the LORD. Baasha had also destroyed the royal house of Jeroboam. What Baasha did had made the LORD very angry. So Baasha had become as sinful as the royal house of Jeroboam had been.

Elah King of Israel

⁸ Elah became king of Israel. It was in the 26th year that Asa was king of Judah. Elah ruled in Tirzah for two years. He was the son of Baasha.

⁹ Zimri was one of Elah's officials. He commanded half of Elah's chariot drivers. He made plans against Elah. Elah was in Tirzah at the time. He was getting drunk in the home of Arza. Arza was in charge of the palace at Tirzah. ¹⁰ Zimri came in. He struck Elah down and killed him. It was in the 27th year of Asa, the king of Judah. Zimri became the next king after Elah.

¹¹ As soon as Zimri was seated on the throne as king, he killed off Baasha's whole family. He didn't even spare one male. It didn't matter whether it was a relative or a friend. ¹² So Zimri destroyed the whole family of Baasha. That's what the LORD had said would happen. He had spoken against Baasha through Jehu the prophet. ¹³ Baasha and his son Elah had committed all kinds of sin. They had also caused Israel to commit the same sins. So Israel made the LORD very angry. They did it by worshiping worthless statues of gods. The LORD is the God of Israel.

¹⁴ The other events of Elah's rule are written down. Everything he did is written in the

official records of the kings of Israel.

Zimri King of Israel

15 Zimri ruled in Tirzah for seven days. It was in the 27th year that Asa was king of Judah. The army of Israel had set up camp near Gibbethon. It was a Philistine town. 16 The Israelites in the camp heard that Zimri had made plans against King Elah. They also heard that Zimri had murdered him. So they announced that Omri was king over Israel. He was the commander of the army. They made him king that day in the camp. 17 Then Omri and all his men pulled back from Gibbethon. They marched to Tirzah and surrounded it. They attacked it and captured it. 18 Zimri saw that they had taken over the city. So he went into the safest place in the royal palace. He set the palace on fire all around him. He died there 19 because of the sins he had committed. He had done what was evil in the sight of the LORD. He had lived the way Jeroboam had lived. He had committed the same sin Jeroboam had caused Israel to commit. 20 The other events of Zimri's rule are written down. The way he turned against King Elah and killed him is written down. All these things are written in the official records of the kings of Israel.

Omri King of Israel

21 The Israelites divided up into two groups. Half of them wanted Tibni to be king. He was the son of Ginath. The other half wanted Omri. 22 But Omri's followers were stronger than those of Tibni, the son of Ginath. So Tibni died. And Omri began to rule.

23 Omri became king of Israel. It was in the 31st year that Asa was king of Judah. Omri ruled for 12 years. He ruled in Tirzah for six of those years. 24 He bought the hill of Samaria from Shemer. He weighed out 150 pounds of silver for it. Then he built a city on the hill. He called it Samaria. He named it after Shemer. Shemer had owned the hill before him.

25 But Omri did what was evil in the sight of the LORD. He sinned more than all the kings who had ruled before him. 26 He lived the way Jeroboam, the son of Nebat, had lived. He committed the same sin Jeroboam had caused Israel to commit. Israel made the LORD very angry. They did it by worshiping worthless statues of gods. The LORD is the God of Israel.

27 The other events of Omri's rule are written down. Everything he did and the things he accomplished are written in the official records of the kings of Israel. 28 Omri joined the members of his family who had already died. He was buried in Samaria. Omri's son Ahab became the next king after him.

Ahab King of Israel

29 Ahab became king of Israel. It was in the 38th year that Asa

was king of Judah. Ahab ruled over Israel in Samaria for 22 years. He was the son of Omri. ³⁰ Ahab, the son of Omri, did what was evil in the sight of the LORD. He did more evil things than any of the kings who had ruled before him. ³¹ He thought it was only a small thing to commit the sins Jeroboam, the son of Nebat, had committed. Ahab also married Jezebel. She was Ethbaal's daughter. Ethbaal was king of the people of Sidon. Ahab began to serve the god named Baal and worship him. ³² He set up an altar to honor Baal. He set it up in the temple of Baal that he built in Samaria. ³³ Ahab also made a pole used to worship the female god named Asherah. He made the LORD very angry. Ahab did more to make him angry than all the kings of Israel had done before him. The LORD is the God of Israel.

³⁴ In Ahab's time, Hiel from Bethel rebuilt Jericho. When he laid its foundations, it cost him the life of his oldest son Abiram. When he set up its gates, it cost him the life of his youngest son Segub. That's what the LORD had said would happen. He had spoken it through Joshua, the son of Nun.

Elijah Announces No Dew or Rain

17 Elijah was from Tishbe in the land of Gilead. He said to Ahab, "I serve the LORD. He is the God of Israel. You can be sure that he lives. And you can be just as sure that there won't

be any dew or rain on the whole land. There won't be any during the next few years. It won't come until I say so."

Elijah Is Fed by Ravens

² Then a message came to Elijah from the LORD. He said, ³ "Leave this place. Go east and hide in the Kerith Valley. It is east of the Jordan River. ⁴ You will drink water from the brook. I have directed some ravens to supply you with food there."

⁵ So Elijah did what the LORD had told him to do. He went to the Kerith Valley. It was east of the Jordan River. He stayed there. ⁶ The ravens brought him bread and meat in the morning. They also brought him bread and meat in the evening. He drank water from the brook.

Elijah and the Widow at Zarephath

⁷ Some time later the brook dried up. It hadn't rained in the land for quite a while. ⁸ A message came to Elijah from the LORD. He said, ⁹ "Go right away to Zarephath in the region of Sidon. Stay there. I have directed a widow there to supply you with food." ¹⁰ So Elijah went to Zarephath. He came to the town gate. A widow was there gathering sticks. He called out to her. He asked, "Would you bring me a little water in a jar? I need a drink." ¹¹ She went to get the water. Then he called out to her, "Please bring me a piece of bread too."

¹² "I don't have any bread," she

replied. "And that's just as sure as the LORD your God is alive. All I have is a small amount of flour in a jar and a little olive oil in a jug. I'm gathering a few sticks to take home. I'll make one last meal for myself and my son. We'll eat it. After that, we'll die."

¹³ Elijah said to her, "Don't be afraid. Go home. Do what you have said. But first make a small loaf of bread for me. Make it out of what you have. Bring it to me. Then make some for yourself and your son. ¹⁴ The LORD is the God of Israel. He says, 'The jar of flour will not be used up. The jug will always have oil in it. You will have flour and oil until the day the LORD sends rain on the land.'"

¹⁵ She went away and did what Elijah had told her to do. So Elijah had food every day. There was also food for the woman and her family. ¹⁶ The jar of flour wasn't used up. The jug always had oil in it. That's what the LORD had said would happen. He had spoken that message through Elijah.

¹⁷ Some time later the son of the woman who owned the house became sick. He got worse and worse. Finally he stopped breathing. ¹⁸ The woman said to Elijah, "You are a man of God. What do you have against me? Did you come to bring my sin out into the open? Did you come to kill my son?"

¹⁹ "Give me your son," Elijah replied. He took him from her arms. He carried him to the up-stairs room where he was staying. He put him down on his bed. ²⁰ Then Elijah cried out to the LORD. He said, "LORD my God, I'm staying with this widow. Have you brought pain and sorrow even to her? Have you caused her son to die?" ²¹ Then he lay down on the boy three times. He cried out to the LORD. He said, "LORD my God, give this boy's life back to him!"

²² The LORD answered Elijah's prayer. He gave the boy's life back to him. So the boy lived. ²³ Elijah picked up the boy. He carried him down from the up-stairs room into the house. He gave him to his mother. He said, "Look! Your son is alive!"

²⁴ Then the woman said to Elijah, "Now I know that you are a man of God. I know that the message you have brought from the LORD is true."

Elijah and Obadiah

18 It was now three years since it had rained. A message came to Elijah from the LORD. He said, "Go. Speak to Ahab. Then I will send rain on the land." ² So Elijah went to speak to Ahab.

There wasn't enough food in Samaria. The people there were very hungry. ³ Ahab had sent for Obadiah. He was in charge of Ahab's palace. Obadiah had great respect for the LORD. ⁴ Ahab's wife Jezebel had been killing off the LORD's proph-ets. So Obadiah had hidden 100 prophets in two caves. He had put 50 in each cave. He had supplied them with food and water. [5] Ahab had said to Obadiah, "Go through the land. Go to all the valleys and springs of water. Maybe we can find some grass there. It will keep the horses and mules alive. Then we won't have to kill any of our animals." [6] So they decided where each of them would look. Ahab went in one direction. Obadiah went in another.

[7] As Obadiah was walking along, Elijah met him. Obadiah recognized him. He bowed down to the ground. He said, "My master Elijah! Is it really you?"

[8] "Yes," he replied. "Go and tell your master Ahab, 'Elijah is here.'"

[9] "What have I done wrong?" asked Obadiah. "Why are you handing me over to Ahab to be put to death? [10] My master has sent people to look for you everywhere. There isn't a nation or kingdom where he hasn't sent someone to look for you. Suppose a nation or kingdom would claim you weren't there. Then Ahab would make them give their word that they couldn't find you. And that's just as sure as the LORD your God is alive. [11] But now you are telling me to go to my master. You want me to say, 'Elijah is here.' [12] But the Spirit of the LORD might carry you away when I leave you. Then I won't know where you are. If I go and tell Ahab and he doesn't find you, he'll kill me. But I've worshiped the LORD ever since I was young. [13] My master, haven't you heard what I did? Jezebel was killing the LORD's prophets. But I hid 100 of them in two caves. I put 50 in each cave. I supplied them with food and water. [14] And now you are telling me to go to my master Ahab. You want me to say to him, 'Elijah is here.' Ahab will kill me!"

[15] Elijah said, "I serve the LORD who rules over all. You can be sure that he lives. And you can be just as sure that I will speak to Ahab today."

Elijah on Mount Carmel

[16] Obadiah went back to Ahab. He told Ahab that Elijah wanted to see him. So Ahab went to where Elijah was. [17] When he saw Elijah, he said to him, "Is that you? You are always stirring up trouble in Israel."

[18] "I haven't made trouble for Israel," Elijah replied. "But you and your father's family have. You have turned away from the LORD's commands. You have followed gods that are named Baal. [19] Now send for people from all over Israel. Tell them to meet me on Mount Carmel. And bring the 450 prophets of the god named Baal. Also bring the 400 prophets of the female god named Asherah. All of them eat at Jezebel's table."

[20] So Ahab sent that message all through Israel. He gathered the prophets together on Mount Carmel. [21] Elijah went there and stood in front of the people. He said, "How long will it take you to make up your minds? If the

LORD is the one and only God, worship him. But if Baal is the one and only God, worship him."

The people didn't say anything.

²² Then Elijah said to them, "I'm the only one of the LORD's prophets left. But Baal has 450 prophets. ²³ Get two bulls for us. Let Baal's prophets choose one for themselves. Let them cut it into pieces. Then let them put it on the wood. But don't let them set fire to it. I'll prepare the other bull. I'll put it on the wood. But I won't set fire to it. ²⁴ Then you pray to your god. And I'll pray to the LORD. The god who answers by sending fire down is the one and only God."

Then all the people said, "What you are saying is good."

²⁵ Elijah said to the prophets of Baal, "Choose one of the bulls. There are many of you. So prepare your bull first. Pray to your god. But don't light the fire." ²⁶ So they prepared the bull they had been given.

They prayed to Baal from morning until noon. "Baal! Answer us!" they shouted. But there wasn't any reply. No one answered. Then they danced around the altar they had made.

²⁷ At noon Elijah began to tease them. "Shout louder!" he said. "I'm sure Baal is a god! Perhaps he has too much to think about. Or maybe he has gone to the toilet. Or perhaps he's away on a trip. Maybe he's sleeping. You might have to wake him up." ²⁸ So they shouted louder.

They cut themselves with swords and spears until their blood flowed. That's what they usually did when things really looked hopeless. ²⁹ It was now past noon. The prophets of Baal continued to prophesy with all their might. They did it until the time came to offer the evening sacrifice. But there wasn't any reply. No one answered. No one paid any attention.

³⁰ Then Elijah said to all the people, "Come here to me." So they went to him. He rebuilt the altar of the LORD. It had been torn down. ³¹ Elijah got 12 stones. There was one for each tribe in the family line of Jacob. The LORD's message had come to Jacob. It had said, "Your name will be Israel." ³² Elijah used the stones to build an altar to honor the LORD. He dug a ditch around it. The ditch was large enough to hold 24 pounds of seeds. ³³ He arranged the wood for the fire. He cut the bull into pieces. He placed the pieces on the wood. Then he said to some of the people, "Fill four large jars with water. Pour it on the offering and the wood." So they did.

³⁴ "Do it again," he said. So they did it again.

"Do it a third time," he ordered. And they did it the third time. ³⁵ The water ran down around the altar. It even filled the ditch.

³⁶ When it was time to offer the evening sacrifice, the prophet Elijah stepped forward. He prayed, "LORD, you are the God of Abraham, Isaac and Israel.

Today let everyone know that you are God in Israel. Let them know I'm your servant. Let them know I've done all these things because you commanded me to. ³⁷Answer me. LORD, answer me. Then these people will know that you are the one and only God. They'll know that you are turning their hearts back to you again."

³⁸The fire of the LORD came down. It burned up the sacrifice. It burned up the wood and the stones and the soil. It even dried up the water in the ditch.

³⁹All the people saw it. Then they fell down flat with their faces toward the ground. They cried out, "The LORD is the one and only God! The LORD is the one and only God!"

⁴⁰Then Elijah commanded them, "Grab the prophets of Baal. Don't let a single one of them get away!" So they grabbed them. Elijah had them brought down to the Kishon Valley. There he had them put to death.

⁴¹Elijah said to Ahab, "Go. Eat and drink. I can hear the sound of a heavy rain." ⁴²So Ahab went off to eat and drink. But Elijah climbed to the top of Mount Carmel. He bent down toward the ground. Then he put his face between his knees.

⁴³"Go and look toward the sea," he told his servant. So he went up and looked.

"I don't see anything there," he said.

Seven times Elijah said, "Go back."

⁴⁴The seventh time the servant said, "I see a cloud. It's as small as a man's hand. It's coming up over the sea."

Elijah said, "Go to Ahab. Tell him, 'Tie your chariot to your horse. Go down to Jezreel before the rain stops you.'"

⁴⁵Black clouds filled the sky. The wind came up, and a heavy rain began to fall. Ahab rode off to Jezreel. ⁴⁶The power of the LORD came on Elijah. He tucked his coat into his belt. And he ran ahead of Ahab all the way to Jezreel.

Elijah Runs Away to Mount Horeb

19 Ahab told Jezebel everything Elijah had done. He told her how Elijah had killed all the prophets of Baal with his sword. ²So Jezebel sent a message to Elijah. She said, "You can be sure that I will kill you, just as I killed the other prophets. I'll do it by this time tomorrow. If I don't, may the gods punish me greatly."

³Elijah was afraid. So he ran for his life. He came to Beersheba in Judah. He left his servant there. ⁴Then he traveled for one day into the desert. He came to a small bush. He sat down under it. He prayed that he would die. "LORD, I've had enough," he said. "Take my life. I'm no better than my people of long ago." ⁵Then he lay down under the bush. And he fell asleep.

Suddenly an angel touched him. The angel said, "Get up and eat." ⁶Elijah looked around. Near his head he saw some bread. It had been baked over hot coals. A jar of water was also there. So Elijah ate and drank. Then he lay down again.

[7] The angel of the LORD came to him a second time. He touched him and said, "Get up and eat. Your journey will be long and hard." [8] So he got up. He ate and drank. The food gave him new strength. He traveled for 40 days and 40 nights. He kept going until he arrived at Horeb. It was the mountain of God. [9] There he went into a cave and spent the night.

The LORD Appears to Elijah

A message came to Elijah from the LORD. He said, "Elijah, what are you doing here?"

[10] He replied, "LORD God who rules over all, I've been very committed to you. The Israelites have turned their backs on your covenant. They have torn down your altars. They've put your prophets to death with their swords. I'm the only one left. And they are trying to kill me."

[11] The LORD said, "Go out. Stand on the mountain in front of me. I am going to pass by."

As the LORD approached, a very powerful wind tore the mountains apart. It broke up the rocks. But the LORD wasn't in the wind. After the wind there was an earthquake. But the LORD wasn't in the earthquake. [12] After the earthquake a fire came. But the LORD wasn't in the fire. And after the fire there was only a gentle whisper. [13] When Elijah heard it, he pulled his coat over his face. He went out and stood at the entrance to the cave.

Then a voice said to him, "Elijah, what are you doing here?"

[14] He replied, "LORD God who rules over all, I've been very committed to you. The Israelites have turned their backs on your covenant. They have torn down your altars. They've put your prophets to death with their swords. I'm the only one left. And they are trying to kill me."

[15] The LORD said to him, "Go back the way you came. Go to the Desert of Damascus. When you get there, anoint Hazael as king over Aram. [16] Also anoint Jehu as king over Israel. He is the son of Nimshi. And anoint Elisha from Abel Meholah as the next prophet after you. He is the son of Shaphat. [17] Jehu will put to death anyone who escapes Hazael's sword. And Elisha will put to death anyone who escapes Jehu's sword. [18] But I will keep 7,000 people in Israel for myself. They have not bowed down to Baal. And they have not kissed him."

The LORD Chooses Elisha

[19] Elijah left Mount Horeb. He saw Elisha, the son of Shaphat. Elisha was plowing in a field. He was driving the last of 12 pairs of oxen. Elijah went up to him. He threw his coat around him. [20] Then Elisha left his oxen. He ran after Elijah. "Let me kiss my father and mother goodbye," he said. "Then I'll come with you."

"Go back," Elijah replied. "What have I done to you?"

[21] So Elisha left him and went

back. He got his two oxen and killed them. He burned the plow to cook the meat. He gave it to the people, and they ate it. Then he started to follow Elijah. He became Elijah's servant.

Ben-Hadad Attacks Samaria

20 Ben-Hadad brought his whole army together. He was king of Aram. He went up to Samaria. He took 32 kings and their horses and chariots with him. All of them surrounded Samaria and attacked it. ²Ben-Hadad sent messengers into the city. They spoke to Ahab, the king of Israel. They told him, "Ben-Hadad says, ³'Your silver and gold belong to me. The best of your wives and children also belong to me.'"

⁴The king of Israel replied, "What you say is true. You are my king and master. I belong to you. And everything I have belongs to you."

⁵The messengers came again. They told Ahab, "Ben-Hadad says, 'I commanded you to give me your silver and gold. I also commanded you to give me your wives and children. ⁶But now I'm going to send my officials to you. They will come about this time tomorrow. They'll search your palace. They'll search the houses of your officials. They'll take everything you value. And they'll carry it all away.'"

⁷The king of Israel sent for all the elders of the land. He said to them, "This man is really looking for trouble! He sent for my wives and children. He sent for my silver and gold. And I agreed to give them to him."

⁸All the elders and people answered, "Don't listen to him. Don't agree to give him what he wants."

⁹So Ahab replied to Ben-Hadad's messengers. He said, "Tell my king and master, 'I will do everything you commanded me to do the first time. But this time, I can't do what you want me to do.'" They took Ahab's answer back to Ben-Hadad.

¹⁰Then Ben-Hadad sent another message to Ahab. Ben-Hadad said, "There won't be enough dust left in Samaria to give each of my followers even a handful. If there is, may the gods punish me greatly."

¹¹The king of Israel replied. He said, "Tell him, 'Someone who puts his armor on shouldn't brag like someone who takes it off.'"

¹²Ben-Hadad and the kings were in their tents drinking. That's when he heard the message. He ordered his men, "Get ready to attack." So they prepared to attack the city.

Ahab Wins the Battle Over Ben-Hadad

¹³During that time a prophet came to Ahab, the king of Israel. He announced, "The Lord says, 'Do you see this huge army? I will hand it over to you today. Then you will know that I am the Lord.'"

¹⁴"But who will do it?" Ahab asked.

The prophet answered, "The

LORD says, 'The junior officers who are under the area commanders will do it.' "

"And who will start the battle?" Ahab asked.

The prophet answered, "You will."

15 So Ahab sent for the junior officers who were under the area commanders. The total number of officers was 232. Ahab gathered together the rest of the Israelites. The total number of them was 7,000. 16 They started out at noon. At that time Ben-Hadad and the 32 kings helping him were in their tents. They were getting drunk. 17 The junior officers who were under Ahab's area commanders marched out first.

Ben-Hadad had sent out scouts. They came back and reported, "Men are marching against us from Samaria."

18 Ben-Hadad said, "They might be coming to make peace. If they are, take them alive. Or they might be coming to make war. If they are, take them alive."

19 The junior officers marched out of the city. The army was right behind them. 20 Each man struck down the one fighting against him. When that happened, the army of Aram ran away. The Israelites chased them. But Ben-Hadad, the king of Aram, escaped on a horse. Some of his horsemen escaped with him. 21 The king of Israel attacked them. He overpowered the horses and chariots. Large numbers of the men of Aram were wounded or killed.

22 After that, the prophet came to the king of Israel again. The prophet said, "Make your position stronger. Do what needs to be done. Next spring the king of Aram will attack you again."

23 During that time, the officials of the king of Aram gave him advice. They said, "The gods of Israel are gods of the hills. That's why they were too strong for us. But suppose we fight them on the plains. Then we'll certainly be stronger than they are. 24 Here's what you should do. Don't let any of the kings continue as military leaders. Have other officers take their places. 25 You must also put another army together. It should be just like the one you lost. It should have the same number of horses and chariots. Then we'll be able to fight against Israel on the plains. And we'll certainly be stronger than they are." Ben-Hadad agreed with their advice. He did what they suggested.

26 The next spring Ben-Hadad brought together the men of Aram. They went up to the city of Aphek to fight against Israel. 27 The Israelites were also brought together. They were given supplies. They marched out to fight against their enemies. Israel's army camped across from Aram's army. The Israelites looked like two small flocks of goats that had become separated from the others. But the men of Aram covered the countryside.

28 The man of God came up to

the king of Israel again. He told him, "The LORD says, 'The men of Aram think the LORD is a god of the hills. They do not think he is a god of the valleys. So I, the LORD, will hand their huge army over to you. Then you will know that I am the LORD.' "

²⁹ For seven days the two armies camped across from each other. On the seventh day the battle began. The Israelites wounded or killed 100,000 Aramean soldiers who were on foot. That happened in a single day. ³⁰ The rest of the men of Aram escaped to the city of Aphek. Its wall fell down on 27,000 of them. Ben-Hadad ran to the city. He hid in a secret room.

³¹ His officials said to him, "Look, we've heard that the kings of Israel often show mercy. So let's go to the king of Israel. Let's wear the rough clothing people wear when they're sad. Let's tie ropes around our heads. Perhaps Ahab will spare your life."

³² So they wore rough clothing. They tied ropes around their heads. Then they went to the king of Israel. They told him, "Your servant Ben-Hadad says, 'Please let me live.' "

The king answered, "Is he still alive? He used to be my friend."

³³ The men thought that was good news. So they quickly used the word Ahab had used. "Yes! Your friend Ben-Hadad!" they said.

"Go and get him," the king said. Ben-Hadad came out of the secret room. Then Ahab had him get into his chariot.

³⁴ "I'll return the cities my father took from your father," Ben-Hadad offered. "You can set up your own market areas in Damascus. That's what my father did in Samaria."

Ahab said, "If we sign a peace treaty, I'll set you free." So Ben-Hadad made a treaty with him. Then Ahab let him go.

A Prophet Accuses Ahab

³⁵ There was a group of people called the group of the prophets. A message from the LORD came to one of their members. He said to his companion, "Strike me down with your weapon." But he wouldn't do it.

³⁶ The prophet said, "You haven't obeyed the LORD. So as soon as you leave me, a lion will kill you." The companion went away. And a lion found him and killed him.

³⁷ The prophet found another man. He said, "Please strike me down." So the man struck him down and wounded him. ³⁸ Then the prophet went and stood by the road. He waited for the king to come by. He pulled his headband down over his eyes so no one would recognize him. ³⁹ The king passed by. Then the prophet called out to him. He said, "I went into the middle of the battle. Someone came to me with a prisoner. He said, 'Guard this man. Don't let him get away. If he does, you will pay for his life with yours. Or you can pay 75 pounds of silver.' ⁴⁰ While I was busy here and there, the man disappeared."

The king of Israel spoke to him. He told him, "What you've just said is what will happen to you."

⁴¹ Then the prophet quickly removed the headband from his eyes. The king of Israel recognized him as one of the prophets. ⁴² He told the king, "The LORD says, 'You have set a man free. But I had said he should be set apart to the LORD in a special way to be destroyed. So you must pay for his life with yours. You must pay for his people's lives with the lives of your people.' " ⁴³ The king of Israel was angry. He was in a bad mood. He went back to his palace in Samaria.

Naboth's Vineyard

21 Some time later King Ahab wanted a certain vineyard. It belonged to Naboth from Jezreel. The vineyard was in Jezreel. It was close to the palace of Ahab, the king of Samaria. ² Ahab said to Naboth, "Let me have your vineyard. It's close to my palace. I want to use it for a vegetable garden. I'll trade you a better vineyard for it. Or, if you prefer, I'll pay you what it's worth."

³ But Naboth replied, "May the LORD keep me from giving you the land my family handed down to me."

⁴ So Ahab went home. He was angry. He was in a bad mood because of what Naboth from Jezreel had said. He had told Ahab, "I won't give you the land my family handed down to me."

So Ahab lay on his bed. He was in a very bad mood. He wouldn't even eat anything.

⁵ His wife Jezebel came in. She asked him, "Why are you in such a bad mood? Why won't you eat anything?"

⁶ He answered her, "Because I spoke to Naboth from Jezreel. I said, 'Sell me your vineyard. Or, if you prefer, I'll give you another vineyard in its place.' But he said, 'I won't sell you my vineyard.' "

⁷ His wife Jezebel said, "Is this how the king of Israel acts? Get up! Eat something! Cheer up. I'll get you the vineyard of Naboth from Jezreel."

⁸ So she wrote some letters in Ahab's name. She stamped them with his royal seal. Then she sent them to the elders and nobles who lived in the city where Naboth lived. ⁹ In those letters she wrote,

"Announce a day when people are supposed to go without eating. Have Naboth sit in an important place among the people. ¹⁰ But put two worthless and evil men in seats across from him. Have them bring charges that he has cursed God and the king. Then take him out of the city. Kill him by throwing stones at him."

¹¹ So the elders and nobles who lived in that city did what Jezebel wanted. They did everything she directed in the letters she had written to them.

¹²They announced a day of fasting. They had Naboth sit in an important place among the people. ¹³Then two worthless and evil men came and sat across from him. They brought charges against Naboth in front of the people. The two men said, "Naboth has cursed God and the king." So they took him outside the city. They killed him by throwing stones at him. ¹⁴Then they sent a message to Jezebel. They said, "Naboth is dead. We killed him by throwing stones at him."

¹⁵Jezebel heard that Naboth had been killed. As soon as she heard it, she said to Ahab, "Get up. Take over the vineyard of Naboth from Jezreel. It's the one he wouldn't sell to you. He isn't alive anymore. He's dead." ¹⁶Ahab heard that Naboth was dead. So Ahab got up and went down to take over Naboth's vineyard.

¹⁷Then a message from the Lord came to Elijah, who was from Tishbe. The Lord said, ¹⁸"Go down to see Ahab, the king of Israel. He rules in Samaria. You will find him in Naboth's vineyard. Ahab has gone there to take it over. ¹⁹Tell him, 'The Lord says, "Haven't you murdered a man? Haven't you taken over his property?"' Then tell Ahab, 'The Lord says, "Dogs licked up Naboth's blood. In that same place dogs will lick up your blood. Yes, I said your blood!"'"

²⁰Ahab said to Elijah, "My enemy! You have found me!"

"I have found you," he answered. "That's because you gave yourself over to do evil things. You did what was evil in the sight of the Lord. ²¹So the Lord says, 'I am going to bring horrible trouble on you. I will destroy your children after you. I will destroy every male in Israel who is related to you. It does not matter whether they are slaves or free. ²²I will make your royal house like the house of Jeroboam, the son of Nebat. I will make it like the house of Baasha, the son of Ahijah. You have made me very angry. You have caused Israel to sin.'

²³"The Lord also says, 'Dogs will eat up Jezebel near the wall of Jezreel.'

²⁴"Some of the people who belong to Ahab will die in the city. Dogs will eat them up. Others will die in the country. The birds will eat them."

²⁵There was never anyone like Ahab. He gave himself over to do what was evil in the sight of the Lord. His wife Jezebel talked him into it. ²⁶He acted in the most evil way. He worshiped statues of gods. He was like the Amorites. The Lord drove them out to make room for Israel.

²⁷When Ahab heard what Elijah had said, he tore his clothes. He put on the rough clothing people wear when they're sad. He went without eating. He even slept in his clothes. He went around looking sad.

²⁸Then a message from the Lord came to Elijah, who was from Tishbe. The Lord said,

²⁹ "Have you seen how Ahab has made himself humble in my sight? Because he has done that, I will not bring trouble on him while he lives. But I will bring it on his royal house when his son is king."

Micaiah Prophesies Against Ahab

22 For three years there wasn't any war between Aram and Israel. ²In the third year Jehoshaphat went down to see Ahab, the king of Israel. Jehoshaphat was king of Judah. ³The king of Israel had spoken to his officials. He had said, "Don't you know that Ramoth Gilead belongs to us? And we aren't even doing anything to take it back from the king of Aram."

⁴So Ahab asked Jehoshaphat, "Will you go with me to fight against Ramoth Gilead?"

Jehoshaphat replied to the king of Israel, "Yes. I'll go with you. My men will go with you. My horses will also go with you." ⁵Jehoshaphat continued, "First ask the LORD for advice."

⁶So the king of Israel brought about 400 prophets together. He asked them, "Should I go to war against Ramoth Gilead? Or should I stay here?"

"Go," they answered. "The Lord will hand it over to you."

⁷But Jehoshaphat asked, "Is there no longer a prophet of the LORD here? If there is, ask him what we should do."

⁸The king of Israel answered Jehoshaphat. He said, "There is still one other man we can go to. We can ask the LORD for advice through him. But I hate him. He never prophesies anything good about me. He only prophesies bad things. His name is Micaiah. He's the son of Imlah."

"You shouldn't say bad things about him," Jehoshaphat replied.

⁹So the king of Israel called for one of his officials. He told him, "Bring Micaiah, the son of Imlah, right away."

¹⁰The king of Israel and Jehoshaphat, the king of Judah, were wearing their royal robes. They were sitting on their thrones at the threshing floor. It was near the entrance of the gate of Samaria. All the prophets were prophesying in front of them. ¹¹Zedekiah was the son of Kenaanah. Zedekiah had made horns out of iron. They looked like animal horns. He announced, "The LORD says, 'With these horns you will drive back the men of Aram until they are destroyed.'"

¹²All the other prophets were prophesying the same thing. "Attack Ramoth Gilead," they said. "Win the battle over it. The LORD will hand it over to you."

¹³A messenger went to get Micaiah. He said to him, "Look. The other prophets agree. All of them are saying the king will have success. So agree with them. Say the same thing they do."

¹⁴But Micaiah said, "You can be sure that the LORD lives. And here is something you can be

just as sure of. I can only tell the king what the Lord tells me to say."

¹⁵ When Micaiah arrived, the king spoke to him. He asked, "Should we go to war against Ramoth Gilead, or not?"

"Attack," he answered. "You will win. The Lord will hand Ramoth Gilead over to you."

¹⁶ The king said to him, "I've made you promise to tell the truth many times before. So don't tell me anything but the truth in the name of the Lord."

¹⁷ Then Micaiah answered, "I saw all the Israelites scattered on the hills. They were like sheep that didn't have a shepherd. The Lord said, 'These people do not have a master. Let each of them go home in peace.'"

¹⁸ The king of Israel spoke to Jehoshaphat. He said, "Didn't I tell you he never prophesies anything good about me? He only prophesies bad things."

¹⁹ Micaiah continued, "Listen to the Lord's message. I saw the Lord sitting on his throne. All the angels of heaven were standing around him. Some were standing at his right side. The others were standing at his left side. ²⁰ The Lord said, 'Who will get Ahab to attack Ramoth Gilead? I want him to die there.'

"One angel suggested one thing. Another suggested something else. ²¹ Finally, a spirit came forward and stood in front of the Lord. The spirit said, 'I'll get Ahab to do it.'

²² "'How?' the Lord asked.

"The spirit said, 'I'll go out and put lies in the mouths of all his prophets.'

"'You will have success in getting Ahab to attack Ramoth Gilead,' said the Lord. 'Go and do it.'

²³ "So the Lord has put lies in the mouths of all your prophets. He has said that great harm will come to you."

²⁴ Then Zedekiah, the son of Kenaanah, went up and slapped Micaiah in the face. Zedekiah asked Micaiah, "Do you think the spirit sent by the Lord left me? Do you think that spirit went to speak to you?"

²⁵ Micaiah replied, "You will find out on the day you go to hide in an inside room to save your life."

²⁶ Then the king of Israel gave an order. He said, "Take Micaiah away. Send him back to Amon. Amon is the ruler of the city of Samaria. And send him back to Joash. Joash is a member of the royal court. ²⁷ Tell him, 'The king says, "Put this fellow in prison. Don't give him anything but bread and water until I return safely."'"

²⁸ Micaiah announced, "Do you really think you will return safely? If you do, the Lord hasn't spoken through me." He continued, "All of you people, remember what I've said!"

Ahab Is Killed at Ramoth Gilead

²⁹ So the king of Israel went up to Ramoth Gilead. Jehoshaphat, the king of Judah, went there too. ³⁰ The king of Israel spoke

to Jehoshaphat. He said, "I'll go into battle wearing different clothes. Then people won't recognize me. But you wear your royal robes." So the king of Israel put on different clothes. Then he went into battle.

³¹ The king of Aram had given an order to his 32 chariot commanders. He had said, "Fight only against the king of Israel. Don't fight against anyone else." ³² The chariot commanders saw Jehoshaphat. They thought, "That has to be the king of Israel." So they turned to attack him. But Jehoshaphat cried out. ³³ Then the commanders saw he wasn't the king of Israel after all. So they stopped chasing him.

³⁴ But someone shot an arrow without taking aim. The arrow hit the king of Israel between the parts of his armor. The king told his chariot driver, "Turn the chariot around. Get me out of this battle. I've been wounded." ³⁵ All day long the battle continued. The king kept himself standing up by leaning against the inside of his chariot. He kept his face toward the men of Aram. The blood from his wound ran down onto the floor of the chariot. That evening he died. ³⁶ As the sun was setting, a cry spread through the army. "Every man must go to his own town!" they said. "Every man must go to his own land!"

³⁷ So the king died. He was brought to Samaria. They buried him there. ³⁸ They washed the chariot at a pool in Samaria. It was where the prostitutes took baths. The dogs licked up Ahab's blood. It happened exactly as the LORD had said it would.

³⁹ The other events of Ahab's rule are written down. Everything he did is written down. That includes the palace he built and decorated with ivory. It also includes the cities he built up and put high walls around. All these things are written in the official records of the kings of Israel. ⁴⁰ Ahab joined the members of his family who had already died. Ahab's son Ahaziah became the next king after him.

Jehoshaphat King of Judah

⁴¹ Jehoshaphat began to rule over Judah. It was in the fourth year that Ahab was king of Israel. Jehoshaphat was the son of Asa. ⁴² Jehoshaphat was 35 years old when he became king. He ruled in Jerusalem for 25 years. His mother's name was Azubah. She was the daughter of Shilhi. ⁴³ Jehoshaphat followed all the ways of his father Asa. He didn't wander away from them. He did what was right in the sight of the LORD. But the high places weren't removed. The people continued to offer sacrifices and burn incense at them. ⁴⁴ Jehoshaphat was also at peace with the king of Israel.

⁴⁵ The other events of Jehoshaphat's rule are written down. The brave things he did in battle and everything else he accomplished are written down. All these things are written in the official records of the kings of Judah. ⁴⁶ Jehoshaphat got rid of

the rest of the male prostitutes who were at the temples. They had remained in the land even after the rule of his father Asa. [47] At that time Edom didn't have a king. An area governor was in charge.

[48] Jehoshaphat built many ships that he used to carry goods to be traded. The ships were supposed to go to Ophir for gold. But they never had a chance to sail. They were wrecked at Ezion Geber. [49] At that time Ahaziah, the son of Ahab, spoke to Jehoshaphat. He said, "Let my men sail with yours." But Jehoshaphat refused.

[50] Jehoshaphat joined the members of his family who had already died. He was buried in the family tomb in the city of King David. Jehoshaphat's son Jehoram became the next king after him.

Ahaziah King of Israel

[51] Ahaziah became king of Israel in Samaria. It was in the 17th year that Jehoshaphat was king of Judah. Ahaziah ruled over Israel for two years. He was the son of Ahab. [52] Ahaziah did what was evil in the sight of the LORD. He lived the way his father and mother had lived. He lived the way Jeroboam, the son of Nebat, had lived. Jeroboam had caused Israel to sin. [53] Ahaziah served and worshiped the god named Baal. He made the LORD, the God of Israel, very angry. That's exactly what Ahaziah's father had done.

2 Kings

Introduction:

The book of 2 Kings tells the rest of the stories of the kings of Israel and Judah. Most of the kings in this book are bad kings. They did not do what God wanted. They did not follow his laws, and they worshiped false gods.

God sent prophets to tell the kings to obey God, but the kings did not listen. God told the kings they would be punished if they did not turn away from their sin. Finally, God let kings from other countries take the people captive. The book of 2 Kings tells about the end of both Israel and Judah.

Outline of contents:

The LORD Judges Ahaziah

1 After King Ahab died, Moab refused to remain under Israel's control. ² Ahaziah had fallen through the window of his upstairs room in Samaria. He had hurt himself. So he sent messengers to ask the god named Baal-Zebub for advice. Baal-Zebub was the god of the city of Ekron. Ahaziah said to the messengers, "Go and ask Baal-Zebub whether I will get well again."

³ But the angel of the LORD spoke to Elijah, who was from Tishbe. The angel said, "Go up to see the messengers of Ahaziah, the king of Samaria. Tell them, 'You are on your way to ask Baal-Zebub for advice. He is the god of Ekron. Are you going there to pray to that god? Do you think there is no God in Israel?' ⁴ The LORD says to Ahaziah, 'You will never leave the bed you are lying on. You can be sure that you will die!'" So Elijah went to see the messengers.

⁵ They returned to the king. He asked them, "Why have you come back?"

⁶ "A man met us on our way there," they replied. "He said to us, 'Go back to the king who sent you. Tell him, "The LORD says, 'You are sending messengers to ask Baal-Zebub for advice. He is the god of Ekron. Are you going there to pray to that god? Do you think there is no God in Israel? You will never leave the bed you are lying on. You can be sure that you will die!'"'"

⁷The king asked the messengers, "What kind of man came to see you? Who told you these things?"

⁸They replied, "He was wearing clothes made out of hair. He had a leather belt around his waist."

The king said, "That was Elijah from Tishbe."

⁹Then Ahaziah sent a captain to Elijah. The captain had his group of 50 fighting men with him. Elijah was sitting on top of a hill. The captain went up to him. He said to Elijah, "Man of God, the king says, 'Come down!'"

¹⁰Elijah answered the captain, "If I'm really a man of God, may fire come down from heaven! May it burn up you and your 50 men!" Then fire came down from heaven. It burned up the captain and his men.

¹¹After that happened, the king sent another captain to Elijah. The captain had his 50 men with him. He said to Elijah, "Man of God, the king says, 'Come down at once!'"

¹²Elijah replied, "If I'm really a man of God, may fire come down from heaven! May it burn up you and your 50 men!" Then the fire of God came down from heaven. It burned up the captain and his 50 men.

¹³So the king sent a third captain with his 50 men. The captain went up to Elijah. He fell on his knees in front of him. "Man of God," he begged, "please have respect for my life! Please have respect for the lives of these 50 men! ¹⁴Fire has come down from heaven. It has burned up the first two captains and all their men. But please have respect for my life!"

¹⁵The angel of the LORD said to Elijah, "Go down along with him. Don't be afraid of him." So Elijah got up and went down to the king with the captain.

¹⁶Elijah told the king, "The LORD says, 'You have sent messengers to ask Baal-Zebub for advice. He is the god of Ekron. Did you go there to pray to that god for advice? Do you think there is no God in Israel? You will never leave the bed you are lying on. You can be sure that you will die!'" ¹⁷So King Ahaziah died. It happened just as the LORD had said it would. He had spoken that message through Elijah.

Ahaziah didn't have any sons. So Joram, his younger brother, became the next king after him. It was the second year of Jehoram, the king of Judah. Jehoram was the son of Jehoshaphat. ¹⁸All the other events of Ahaziah's rule are written down. Everything he did is written in the official records of the kings of Israel.

Elijah Is Taken Up to Heaven

2 Elijah and Elisha were on their way from Gilgal. The LORD was going to use a strong wind to take Elijah up to heaven. ²Elijah said to Elisha, "Stay here. The LORD has sent me to Bethel."

But Elisha said, "I won't leave

you. And that's just as sure as the LORD and you are alive." So they went down to Bethel.

³There was a group of prophets at Bethel. They came out to where Elisha was. They asked him, "Do you know what the LORD is going to do? He's going to take your master away from you today."

"Yes, I know," Elisha replied. "So be quiet."

⁴Then Elijah said to him, "Stay here, Elisha. The LORD has sent me to Jericho."

Elisha replied, "I won't leave you. And that's just as sure as the LORD and you are alive." So they went to Jericho.

⁵There was a group of prophets at Jericho. They went up to where Elisha was. They asked him, "Do you know what the LORD is going to do? He's going to take your master away from you today."

"Yes, I know," Elisha replied. "So be quiet."

⁶Then Elijah said to him, "Stay here. The LORD has sent me to the Jordan River."

Elisha replied, "I won't leave you. And that's just as sure as the LORD and you are alive." So the two of them walked on.

⁷Fifty men from the group of prophets followed them. The men stopped and stood not far away from them. They faced the place where Elijah and Elisha had stopped at the Jordan River. ⁸Elijah rolled up his coat. Then he struck the water with it. The water parted to the right and to the left. The two of them

went across the river on dry ground.

⁹After they had gone across, Elijah said to Elisha, "Tell me. What can I do for you before I'm taken away from you?"

"Please give me a double share of your spirit," Elisha replied.

¹⁰"You have asked me for something that's very hard to do," Elijah said. "But suppose you see me when I'm taken away from you. Then you will receive what you have asked for. If you don't see me, you won't receive it."

¹¹They kept walking along and talking together. Suddenly there appeared a chariot and horses made of fire. The chariot and horses came between the two men. Then Elijah went up to heaven in a strong wind. ¹²Elisha saw it and cried out to Elijah, "My father! You are like a father to me! You, Elijah, are the true chariots and horsemen of Israel!" Elisha didn't see Elijah anymore. Then Elisha took hold of his own garment and tore it in two.

¹³He picked up the coat that had fallen from Elijah. He went back and stood on the bank of the Jordan River. ¹⁴Then he struck the water with Elijah's coat. "Where is the power of the LORD?" he asked. "Where is the power of the God of Elijah?" When Elisha struck the water, it parted to the right and to the left. He went across the river.

¹⁵The group of prophets from Jericho were watching.

They said, "The spirit of Elijah has been given to Elisha." They went over to Elisha. They bowed down to him with their faces toward the ground. ¹⁶ "Look," they said. "We have 50 capable men. Let them go and look for your master. Perhaps the Spirit of the LORD has lifted him up. Maybe he has put him down on a mountain or in a valley."

"No," Elisha replied. "Don't send them."

¹⁷ But they kept asking until he felt he couldn't say no. So he said, "Send them." And they sent 50 men. They looked for Elijah for three days. But they didn't find him. ¹⁸ So they returned to Elisha. He was staying in Jericho. Elisha said to them, "Didn't I tell you not to go?"

Elisha Makes Jericho's Water Pure

¹⁹ The people of Jericho said to Elisha, "Look. This town has a good location. You can see that for yourself. But the spring of water here is bad. So the land doesn't produce anything."

²⁰ "Bring me a new bowl," Elisha said. "Put some salt in it." So they brought it to him.

²¹ Then he went out to the spring. He threw the salt into it. He told the people, "The LORD says, 'I have made this water pure. It will never cause death again. It will never keep the land from producing crops again.'" ²² The water has stayed pure to this day. That's what Elisha had said would happen.

Some Boys Make Fun of Elisha

²³ Elisha left Jericho and went up to Bethel. He was walking along the road. Some boys came out of the town. They made fun of him. "Get out of here, baldy!" they said. "Get out of here! You don't even have any hair on your head!" ²⁴ He turned around and looked at them. And he asked for bad things to happen to them. He did it in the name of the LORD. Then two bears came out of the woods. They attacked 42 of the boys. ²⁵ Elisha went on to Mount Carmel. From there he returned to Samaria.

Moab's King Refuses to Obey Israel's King

3 Joram became king of Israel in Samaria. It was in the 18th year that Jehoshaphat was king of Judah. Joram ruled for 12 years. He was the son of Ahab. ² Joram did what was evil in the sight of the LORD. But he wasn't as bad as his father and mother had been. Joram's father had made a sacred stone used to worship the god named Baal. Joram got rid of it. ³ But he kept on committing the sins of Jeroboam, the son of Nebat. Jeroboam had also caused Israel to commit those same sins. Joram didn't turn away from them.

⁴ Mesha raised sheep. He was king of Moab. He had to pay the king of Israel 100,000 lambs a year. He also had to pay him with the wool of 100,000 rams a year. ⁵ After Ahab died, Moab's king refused to obey the next

king of Israel. ⁶ So at that time King Joram started out from Samaria. He gathered together all of Israel's troops. ⁷ He also sent a message to Jehoshaphat, the king of Judah. Joram said, "The king of Moab is refusing to obey me. Will you go with me to fight against Moab?"

"Yes. I'll go with you," Jehoshaphat replied. "My men will go with you. My horses will also go with you."

⁸ "What road should we take to attack Moab?" Joram asked.

"The one that goes through the Desert of Edom," Jehoshaphat answered.

⁹ So the king of Israel marched out. The king of Judah and the king of Edom went with him. Their armies marched around the southern end of the Dead Sea. After seven days they ran out of water. There wasn't any water for the men or their animals.

¹⁰ "What should we do now?" exclaimed the king of Israel. "The LORD has called us three kings together. Did he do it only to hand us over to Moab?"

¹¹ But Jehoshaphat asked, "Isn't there a prophet of the LORD here? Can't we ask the LORD for advice through him?"

An officer of the king of Israel answered, "Elisha is here. He's the son of Shaphat. Elisha used to serve Elijah."

¹² Jehoshaphat said, "The LORD speaks through him." So the king of Israel went down to see Elisha. Jehoshaphat and the king of Edom also went there.

¹³ Elisha said to the king of Israel, "Why do you want to come to me? Go to your father's prophets. Go to your mother's prophets."

"No," the king of Israel answered. "The LORD called us three kings together. He did it to hand us over to Moab."

¹⁴ Elisha said, "I serve the LORD who rules over all. You can be sure that he lives. And you can be just as sure that I have respect for Jehoshaphat, the king of Judah. If I didn't, I wouldn't pay any attention to you. ¹⁵ But now bring me someone who plays the harp."

While that person was playing the harp, the LORD's power came on Elisha. ¹⁶ Elisha announced, "The LORD says, 'I will fill this valley with pools of water.' ¹⁷ This will happen because the LORD says, 'You will not see wind or rain. But this valley will be filled with water. Then you, your cattle and your other animals will have water to drink.' ¹⁸ This is an easy thing for the LORD to do. He will also hand Moab over to you. ¹⁹ You will destroy every city that has high walls around it. You will destroy every major town. You will cut down every good tree. You will stop up all the springs of water. And you will cover every good field with stones."

²⁰ The next day, the time came to offer the morning sacrifice. And then it happened! Water was flowing from the direction of Edom! In fact, the land was filled with water!

²¹ Now all the people of Moab had heard that the kings had come to fight against them. So the king of Moab sent for all Moab's fighting men. It didn't matter whether they were young or old. He sent for everyone who could carry a weapon. All of them were stationed at the border. ²² They got up early in the morning. The sun was already shining on the water. Across the way, the water looked red to the men of Moab. It looked like blood. ²³ "That's blood!" they said. "Those kings must have fought and killed each other. Let's go, Moab! Let's take everything that has any value."

²⁴ So the men of Moab went to the camp of Israel. Just as they arrived there, the men of Israel got ready to fight. They fought against the men of Moab until those men ran away. The men of Israel marched into the land and attacked it. They killed the people of Moab. ²⁵ They destroyed the towns. Each man threw a large stone on every good field. They did that until the fields were covered. They stopped up all the springs of water. And they cut down every good tree. The only town left with any stones in place was Kir Hareseth. But some of the Israelites armed with slings surrounded it. Then they attacked it.

²⁶ The king of Moab saw that the battle had gone against him. So he took with him 700 men who had swords. They tried to break through the battle lines to the king of Edom. But they couldn't do it. ²⁷ Then the king of Moab took his oldest son. He was the son who would become the next king of Moab. But the king offered his son as a sacrifice on the city wall. That shocked and terrified the men of Israel. So they pulled back and returned to their own land.

Elisha Provides Olive Oil for a Widow

4 The wife of a man from the group of the prophets cried out to Elisha. She said, "My husband is dead. You know how much respect he had for the LORD. But he owed money to someone. And now that person is coming to take my two boys away. They will become his slaves."

² Elisha replied to her, "How can I help you? Tell me. What do you have in your house?"

"I don't have anything there at all," she said. "All I have is a small jar of olive oil."

³ Elisha said, "Go around to all your neighbors. Ask them for empty jars. Get as many as you can. ⁴ Then go inside your house. Shut the door behind you and your sons. Pour oil into all the jars. As each jar is filled, put it over to one side."

⁵ The woman left him. Then she shut the door behind her and her sons. They brought the jars to her. And she kept pouring. ⁶ When all the jars were full, she spoke to one of her sons. She said, "Bring me another jar."

But he replied, "There aren't any more left." Then the oil stopped flowing.

[7] She went and told the man of God about it. He said, "Go and sell the oil. Pay what you owe. You and your sons can live on what is left."

The Son of a Woman From Shunem Is Brought Back to Life

[8] One day Elisha went to the town of Shunem. A rich woman lived there. She begged him to stay and have a meal. So every time he came by, he stopped there to eat. [9] The woman said to her husband, "That man often comes by here. I know that he is a holy man of God. [10] Let's make a small room for him on the roof. We'll put a bed and a table in it. We'll also put a chair and a lamp in it. Then he can stay there when he comes to visit us."

[11] One day Elisha came. He went up to his room and lay down there. [12] He said to his servant Gehazi, "Go and get the woman from Shunem." So he did. She stood in front of Elisha. [13] He said to Gehazi, "Tell her, 'You have gone to a lot of trouble for us. Now what can we do for you? Can we speak to the king for you? Or can we speak to the commander of the army for you?'"

She replied, "I live among my own people. I have everything I need here."

[14] After she left, Elisha asked Gehazi, "What can we do for her?"

Gehazi said, "She doesn't have a son. And her husband is old."

[15] Then Elisha said, "Bring her here again." So he did. She stood in the doorway. [16] "You will hold a son in your arms," Elisha said. "It will be about this time next year."

"No, my master!" she objected. "You are a man of God. So please don't lie to me!"

[17] But the woman became pregnant. She had a baby boy. It happened the next year about that same time. That's exactly what Elisha had told her would happen.

[18] The child grew. One day he went out to get his father. His father was with the people who were gathering the crops. [19] The boy said to his father, "My head hurts! It really hurts!"

His father told a servant, "Carry him to his mother." [20] The servant lifted up the boy. He carried him to his mother. The boy sat on her lap until noon. Then he died. [21] She went up to the room on the roof. There she laid him on the bed of the man of God. Then she shut the door and went out.

[22] She sent for her husband. She said, "Please send me one of the servants and a donkey. Then I can go quickly to the man of God and return."

[23] "Why do you want to go to him today?" he asked. "It isn't the time for the New Moon feast. It isn't the Sabbath day."

"Don't let that bother you," she said.

24 She put a saddle on her donkey. She said to her servant, "Let's go. Don't slow down for me unless I tell you to." 25 So she started out. She came to Mount Carmel. That's where the man of God was.

When she was still a long way off, he saw her coming. He said to his servant Gehazi, "Look! There's the woman from Shunem! 26 Run out there to meet her. Ask her, 'Are you all right? Is your husband all right? Is your child all right?' "

"Everything is all right," she said.

27 She came to the man of God at the mountain. Then she took hold of his feet. Gehazi came over to push her away. But the man of God said, "Leave her alone! She is suffering terribly. But the LORD hasn't told me the reason for it. He has hidden it from me."

28 "My master, did I ask you for a son?" she said. "Didn't I tell you, 'Don't make me hope for something that won't happen'?"

29 Elisha said to Gehazi, "Tuck your coat into your belt. Take my walking stick and run to Shunem. Don't say hello to anyone you see. If anyone says hello to you, don't answer. Lay my walking stick on the boy's face."

30 But the child's mother said, "I won't leave you. And that's just as sure as the LORD and you are alive." So Elisha got up and followed her.

31 Gehazi went on ahead. He laid Elisha's walking stick on the boy's face. But there wasn't any sound. The boy didn't move at all. So Gehazi went back to Elisha. He told him, "The boy hasn't awakened."

32 Elisha arrived at the house. The boy was dead. He was lying on Elisha's bed. 33 Elisha went into the room. He shut the door. He was alone with the boy. He prayed to the LORD. 34 Then Elisha got on the bed. He lay down on the boy. His mouth touched the boy's mouth. His eyes touched the boy's eyes. And his hands touched the boy's hands. As Elisha lay on the boy, the boy's body grew warm. 35 Elisha turned away. He walked back and forth in the room. Then he got on the bed again. He lay down on the boy once more. The boy sneezed seven times. After that, he opened his eyes.

36 Elisha sent for Gehazi. He said to him, "Go and get the woman from Shunem." So he did. When she came, Elisha said, "Take your son." 37 She came in and fell at Elisha's feet. She bowed down with her face toward the ground. Then she took her son and went out.

Deadly Food in a Pot

38 Elisha returned to Gilgal. There wasn't enough food to eat in that area. The group of the prophets was meeting with Elisha. So he said to his servant, "Put the large pot over the fire. Cook some stew for these prophets."

39 One of them went out into

the fields to gather herbs. He found a wild vine and picked some of its gourds. He picked as many as he could fit in his coat. Then he cut them up and put them into the pot of stew. But no one knew what they were. 40 The stew was poured out for the men. They began to eat it. But then they cried out, "Man of God, the food in that pot will kill us!" They couldn't eat it.

41 Elisha said, "Get some flour." He put it in the pot. He said, "Serve it to the men to eat." Then there wasn't anything in the pot that could harm them.

Elisha Feeds 100 People

42 A man came from Baal Shalishah. He brought the man of God 20 loaves of barley bread. They had been baked from the first grain that had ripened. The man also brought some heads of new grain. "Give this food to the people to eat," Elisha said.

43 "How can I put this in front of 100 men?" his servant asked.

But Elisha answered, "Give it to the people to eat. Do it because the Lord says, 'They will eat and have some left over.'" 44 Then the servant put the food in front of them. They ate it and had some left over. It happened just as the Lord had said it would.

Naaman Is Healed of a Skin Disease

5 Naaman was army commander of the king of Aram. He was very important to his master and was highly respected. That's because the Lord had helped him win the battle over Aram's enemies. He was a brave soldier. But he had a skin disease.

2 Groups of soldiers from Aram had marched out. They had captured a young girl from Israel. She became a servant of Naaman's wife. 3 The young girl spoke to the woman she was serving. She said, "I wish my master would go and see the prophet who is in Samaria. He would heal my master of his skin disease."

4 Naaman went to see his own master. He told him what the girl from Israel had said. 5 "I think you should go," the king of Aram replied. "I'll give you a letter to take to the king of Israel." So Naaman left. He took 750 pounds of silver with him. He also took 150 pounds of gold. And he took ten sets of clothes. 6 He carried the letter to the king of Israel. It said, "I'm sending my servant Naaman to you with this letter. I want you to heal him of his skin disease."

7 The king of Israel read the letter. As soon as he did, he tore his royal robes. He said, "Am I God? Can I kill people and bring them back to life? Why does this fellow send someone to me to be healed of his skin disease? He must be trying to pick a fight with me!"

8 Elisha, the man of God, heard that the king of Israel had torn his robes. So he sent the king a message. Elisha said, "Why have you torn your

robes? Tell the man to come to me. Then he will know there is a prophet in Israel." ⁹So Naaman went to see Elisha. He took his horses and chariots with him. He stopped at the door of Elisha's house. ¹⁰Elisha sent a messenger out to him. The messenger said, "Go! Wash yourself in the Jordan River seven times. Then your skin will be healed. You will be pure and 'clean' again."

¹¹But Naaman went away angry. He said, "I was sure Elisha would come out to me. I thought he would stand there and pray to the Lord his God. I thought he would wave his hand over my skin. Then I would be healed. ¹²And what about the Abana and Pharpar rivers of Damascus? Aren't they better than all the rivers of Israel? Couldn't I wash in the rivers of Damascus and be made pure and 'clean'?" So he turned and went away. He was very angry.

¹³Naaman's servants went over to him. They said, "You are like a father to us. What if Elisha the prophet had told you to do some great thing? Wouldn't you have done it? But he only said, 'Wash yourself. Then you will be pure and "clean."'" You should be even more willing to do that!" ¹⁴So Naaman went down to the Jordan River. He dipped himself in it seven times. He did exactly what the man of God had told him to do. Then his skin was made pure again. It became "clean" like the skin of a young boy.

¹⁵Naaman and all his attendants went back to the man of God. Naaman stood in front of Elisha. Naaman said, "Now I know that there is no God anywhere in the whole world except in Israel. So please accept a gift from me."

¹⁶The prophet answered, "I serve the Lord. You can be sure that he lives. And you can be just as sure that I won't accept a gift from you." Even though Naaman begged him to take it, Elisha wouldn't.

¹⁷"I can see that you won't accept a gift from me," said Naaman. "But please let me have some soil from your land. Give me as much as a pair of mules can carry. Here's why I want it. I won't ever bring burnt offerings and sacrifices to any other god again. I'll bring them only to the Lord. I'll worship him on his own soil. ¹⁸But there is one thing I hope the Lord will forgive me for. From time to time my master will enter the temple to bow down to his god Rimmon. When he does, he'll lean on my arm. Then I'll have to bow down there also. I hope the Lord will forgive me for that."

¹⁹"Go in peace," Elisha said.

Naaman started out on his way. ²⁰Gehazi was the servant of Elisha, the man of God. Gehazi said to himself, "My master was too easy on Naaman from Aram. He should have accepted the gift Naaman brought. I'm going to run after him. I'm going to get something from him. And that's just as sure as the LORD is alive."

²¹ Gehazi hurried after Naaman. Naaman saw him running toward him. So he got down from the chariot to greet him. "Is everything all right?" he asked.

²² "Everything is all right," Gehazi answered. "My master sent me to say, 'Two young men from the group of the prophets have just come to me. They've come from the hill country of Ephraim. Please give them 75 pounds of silver and two sets of clothes.'"

²³ "I wish you would take twice as much silver," said Naaman. He begged Gehazi to accept it. Then Naaman tied up 150 pounds of silver in two bags. He also gave Gehazi two sets of clothes. He gave all of it to two of his own servants. They carried it ahead of Gehazi. ²⁴ Gehazi came to the hill where Elisha lived. Then the servants handed the things over to Gehazi. He put them away in Elisha's house. He sent the men away, and they left. ²⁵ Then he went back inside the house. He stood in front of his master Elisha.

"Gehazi, where have you been?" Elisha asked.

"I didn't go anywhere," Gehazi answered.

²⁶ But Elisha said to him, "Didn't my spirit go with you? I know that the man got down from his chariot to greet you. Is this the time for you to accept money or clothes? Is it the time to take olive groves, vineyards, flocks or herds? Is it the time to accept male and female slaves? ²⁷ You and your children after you will have Naaman's skin disease forever." Then Gehazi left Elisha. And he had Naaman's skin disease. His skin had become as white as snow.

An Ax Blade Floats

6 The group of the prophets said to Elisha, "Look. The place where we meet with you is too small for us. ² We would like to go to the Jordan River. Each of us can get some wood there. We want to build a place there for us to meet."

Elisha said, "Go."

³ Then one of them said, "Won't you please come with us?"

"I will," Elisha replied. ⁴ And he went with them.

They went to the Jordan River. There they began to cut down trees. ⁵ One of them was cutting down a tree. The iron blade of his ax fell into the water. "Oh no, master!" he cried out. "This ax was borrowed!"

⁶ The man of God asked, "Where did the blade fall?" He showed Elisha the place. Then Elisha cut a stick and threw it there. That made the iron blade float. ⁷ "Take it out of the water," he said. So the man reached out and took it.

Elisha Makes the Soldiers of Aram Blind

⁸ The king of Aram was at war with Israel. He talked things over with his officers. Then he

said, "I'm going to set up my camp in a certain place."

⁹ Elisha, the man of God, sent a message to the king of Israel. Elisha said, "Try to stay away from that place. Aram's army is going to be down there." ¹⁰ The king of Israel checked on the place the man of God had told him about. Time after time Elisha warned the king. So the king was on guard in those places.

¹¹ All of that made the king of Aram very angry. He sent for his officers. He said to them, "Tell me! Which of us is on the side of the king of Israel?"

¹² "You are my king and master," said one of his officers. "None of us is on Israel's side. But Elisha is a prophet in Israel. He tells the king of Israel even the words you speak in your own bedroom."

¹³ "Go and find out where he is," the king ordered. "Then I can send my men and capture him." The report came back. The officers said, "He's in Dothan." ¹⁴ Then the king sent horses and chariots and a strong army there. They went at night and surrounded the city.

¹⁵ The servant of the man of God got up the next morning. He went out early. He saw that an army with horses and chariots had surrounded the city. "Oh no, my master!" the servant said. "What can we do?"

¹⁶ "Don't be afraid," the prophet answered. "Those who are with us are more than those who are with them."

¹⁷ Elisha prayed, "Lord, open my servant's eyes so that he can see." Then the Lord opened his eyes. Elisha's servant looked up and saw the hills. He saw that Elisha was surrounded by horses and chariots made of fire.

¹⁸ Aram's army came down toward Elisha. Then he prayed to the Lord, "Make these soldiers blind." So the Lord made them blind, just as Elisha had prayed.

¹⁹ Elisha told them, "This isn't the right road. This isn't the right city. Follow me. I'll lead you to the man you are looking for." He led them to Samaria.

²⁰ They entered the city. Then Elisha said, "Lord, open the eyes of these men. Help them see again." Then the Lord opened their eyes. They looked around. And there they were, inside Samaria!

²¹ The king of Israel saw them. So he asked Elisha, "Should I kill them? I need your advice. You are like a father to me. Should I kill them?"

²² "Don't kill them," he answered. "Would you kill people you have captured with your own sword or bow? Put some food and water in front of them. Then they can eat and drink. They can go back to their master." ²³ So the king of Israel prepared a great feast for them. After they had finished eating and drinking, he sent them away. They returned to their master. So the groups of fighting men from Aram stopped attacking Israel's territory.

Aram's Army Attacks Samaria and People Go Hungry

²⁴ Some time later, Ben-Hadad gathered his entire army together. Ben-Hadad was the king of Aram. His army marched up and surrounded Samaria. Then they attacked it. ²⁵ There wasn't enough food anywhere in the city. It was surrounded for so long that people had to weigh out two pounds of silver for a donkey's head. They had to weigh out two ounces of silver for half a pint of seed pods.

²⁶ One day the king of Israel was walking on top of the city wall. A woman cried out to him, "You are my king and master. Please help me!"

²⁷ The king replied, "If the LORD doesn't help you, where can I get help for you? From the threshing floor? From the winepress?" ²⁸ He continued, "What's wrong?"

She answered, "A woman said to me, 'Give up your son. Then we can eat him today. Tomorrow we'll eat my son.' ²⁹ So we cooked my son. Then we ate him. The next day I said to her, 'Give up your son. Then we can eat him.' But she had hidden him."

³⁰ When the king heard the woman's words, he tore his royal robes. As he walked along the wall, the people looked up at him. They saw that under his robes he was wearing the rough clothing people wear when they're sad. ³¹ He said, "I'll cut the head of Shaphat's son Elisha off his shoulders today. If I don't, may God punish me greatly!"

³² Elisha was sitting in his house. The elders were sitting there with him. The king went to see Elisha. He sent a messenger on ahead of him. Before the messenger arrived, Elisha spoke to the elders. He said, "That murderer is sending someone here to cut off my head. Can't you see that? When the messenger comes, close the door. Hold it shut against him. Can't you hear his master's footsteps right behind him?"

³³ Elisha was still talking to the elders when the messenger came down to him.

The king also arrived. He said, "The LORD has sent this horrible trouble on us. Why should I wait any longer for him to help us?"

7 Elisha replied, "Listen to a message from the LORD. He says, 'About this time tomorrow, flour won't cost very much. Even 12 pounds of the finest flour will cost less than half of an ounce of silver. You will also be able to buy 20 pounds of barley for the same price. That's all you will have to pay for those things at the gate of Samaria.'"

² The king was leaning on an officer's arm. The officer spoke to the man of God. The officer said, "Suppose the LORD opens the sky and pours down food on us. Even if he does, could what you are saying really happen?"

"You will see it with your own eyes," answered Elisha. "But you won't eat any of it!"

The Attack on Samaria Ends

³ There were four men who had a skin disease. They were at the entrance of the gate of Samaria. They said to one another, "Why should we stay here until we die? ⁴ Suppose we say, 'We'll go into the city.' There isn't any food there, and we'll die. But if we stay here, we'll die anyway. So let's go over to Aram's army camp. Let's give ourselves up. If they spare us, we'll live. If they kill us, we'll die."

⁵ At sunset they got up and went to Aram's army camp. They arrived at the edge of it. But no one was there. ⁶ The Lord had caused the soldiers of Aram to hear a noise. It sounded like chariots and horses and a huge army. So the soldiers said to one another, "Listen! The king of Israel has hired the Hittite and Egyptian kings. He has paid them to attack us!" ⁷ So the soldiers of Aram had run away at sunset. They had left their tents and horses and donkeys behind. They had left the camp just as it was. And they had run for their lives.

⁸ The men who had a skin disease arrived at the edge of the camp. They entered one of the tents. They ate and drank. Then they took silver, gold and clothes. They went off and hid them. They returned and entered another tent. They took some things from it and hid them also.

⁹ But then they said to one another, "What we're doing isn't right. This is a day of good news. And we're keeping it to ourselves. If we wait until sunrise, we'll be punished. Let's go at once. Let's report this to the royal palace."

¹⁰ So they went. They called out to the people who were guarding the city gates. They told them, "We went into Aram's army camp. No one was there. We didn't hear anyone. The horses and donkeys were still tied up. The tents were left just as they were." ¹¹ The people who guarded the gates shouted the news. It was reported inside the palace.

¹² The king of Israel got up in the night. He spoke to his officers. He said, "I'll tell you what the men of Aram have done to us. They know we are very hungry. So they have left the camp to hide in the countryside. They are thinking, 'We are sure they'll come out. Then we'll take them alive. And we'll get into the city.'"

¹³ One of the king's officers said, "A few horses are still left in the city. Have some men get five of them. Those men won't be any worse off than all the other Israelites who are left here. In fact, all of us will soon be dead anyway. So let's send the men to find out what happened."

¹⁴ The men chose two chariots and their horses. The king sent them out to look for Aram's army. He commanded the drivers, "Go and find out what has happened." ¹⁵ They followed the trail of Aram's soldiers all the way to the Jordan River. They

found clothes and supplies all along the road. The soldiers had thrown them down when they ran away. So the men who were sent out returned. They reported to the king what they had seen. [16] Then the people went out of the city. They took everything of value from Aram's army camp. So 12 pounds of the finest flour sold for less than half of an ounce of silver. And 20 pounds of barley sold for the same price. That's exactly what the LORD had said would happen.

[17] The king had put an officer in charge of the city gate. He was the officer on whose arm the king leaned. On their way out of the city, the people knocked the officer down. In the entrance of the gate he was crushed as they walked on top of him. And so he died. That's exactly what the man of God had said would happen. He had said it when the king came down to his house. [18] What Elisha, the man of God, had told the king came true. Elisha had said, "About this time tomorrow, flour won't cost very much. Even 12 pounds of the finest flour will cost less than half of an ounce of silver. You will also be able to buy 20 pounds of barley for the same price. That's all you will have to pay for those things at the gate of Samaria."

[19] The officer had spoken to the man of God. The officer had said, "Suppose the LORD opens the sky and pours down food on us. Even if he does, could what you are saying really happen?" The man of God had replied, "You will see it with your own eyes. But you won't eat any of it!" [20] And that's exactly what happened to the officer. On their way out of the city, the people knocked him down. In the entrance of the gate he was crushed as they walked on top of him. And so he died.

The Woman From Shunem Gets Her Land Back

8 Elisha had brought a woman's son back to life. He had said to her, "Go away with your family. Stay for a while anywhere you can. The LORD has decided that there won't be enough food in the land. That will be true for seven years." [2] The woman did just as the man of God told her to. She and her family went away. They stayed in the land of the Philistines for seven years.

[3] The seven years passed. Then she came back from the land of the Philistines. She went to the king of Israel. She wanted to ask him to get her house and land back. [4] The king was talking to Gehazi. Gehazi was the servant of the man of God. The king had said, "Tell me about all the great things Elisha has done." [5] Gehazi was telling the king how Elisha had brought a dead boy back to life. Just then the woman came to ask the king to get her house and land back. She was the woman whose son Elisha had brought back to life.

Gehazi said, "King Joram, this is the woman I've been telling you about. And this is her son. He's the one Elisha brought back to life." ⁶The king asked the woman about her house and land. And she told him.

Then he appointed an official to look into her case. The king told him, "Give her back everything that belonged to her. That includes all the money that was earned from her land. It was earned from the day she left the country until now."

Hazael Murders Ben-Hadad

⁷Elisha went to Damascus. Ben-Hadad was sick. He was king of Aram. The king was told, "The man of God has come all the way up here." ⁸Then the king said to Hazael, "Take a gift with you. Go and see the man of God. Ask him for the LORD's advice. Ask him whether I will get well again."

⁹Hazael went to see Elisha. Hazael took 40 camels with him as a gift. The camels were loaded with all the finest goods of Damascus. Hazael went into Elisha's house and stood in front of him. Hazael said, "Ben-Hadad has sent me. He is the king of Aram. He asks, 'Will I get well again?'"

¹⁰Elisha answered, "Go and tell him, 'Yes. You will get well again.' But the LORD has shown me that he will in fact die." ¹¹Elisha stared at him without looking away. He did it until Hazael felt uncomfortable. Then the man of God began to weep.

¹²"Why are you weeping?" asked Hazael.

"Because I know how much harm you will do to the people of Israel," Elisha answered. "You will set fire to their cities that have high walls around them. You will kill their young men with your swords. You will smash their little children on the ground. You will rip open their pregnant women."

¹³Hazael said, "How could I possibly do a thing like that? I'm nothing but a dog. I don't have that kind of power."

"You will become king of Aram," Elisha answered. "That's what the LORD has shown me."

¹⁴Then Hazael left Elisha and returned to his master. Ben-Hadad asked, "What did Elisha say to you?" Hazael replied, "He told me you would get well again." ¹⁵But the next day Hazael got a thick cloth. He soaked it in water. He spread it over the king's face. He held it there until the king died. Then Hazael became the next king after him.

Jehoram King of Judah

¹⁶Jehoram began to rule as king over Judah. It was in the fifth year that Joram was king of Israel. Joram was the son of Ahab. Jehoram was the son of Jehoshaphat. ¹⁷Jehoram was 32 years old when he became king. He ruled in Jerusalem for eight years. ¹⁸He followed the ways of the kings of Israel, just as the royal family of Ahab had done. In fact, he married a daughter of Ahab. Jehoram did what was evil in the sight of the LORD. ¹⁹But the LORD didn't want to

destroy Judah. That's because the LORD had made a covenant with his servant David. The LORD had promised to keep the lamp of David's kingdom burning brightly. The LORD had promised that for him and his children after him forever.

²⁰ When Jehoram was king over Judah, Edom refused to remain under Judah's control. Edom set up their own king. ²¹ So Jehoram went to Zair. He took all his chariots with him. The men of Edom surrounded him and his chariot commanders. He got up at night and fought his way out. But his army ran back home. ²² To this day Edom has refused to remain under Judah's control. When Jehoram was Judah's king, Libnah also refused to remain under the control of Judah.

²³ The other events of Jehoram's rule are written down. Everything he did is written in the official records of the kings of Judah. ²⁴ Jehoram joined the members of his family who had already died. He was buried in the family tomb in the City of David. Jehoram's son Ahaziah became the next king after him.

Ahaziah King of Judah

²⁵ Ahaziah began to rule as king over Judah. It was in the 12th year that Joram was king of Israel. Joram was the son of Ahab. Ahaziah was the son of Jehoram. ²⁶ Ahaziah was 22 years old when he became king. He ruled in Jerusalem for one year. His mother's name was Atha-liah. She was a granddaughter of Omri. Omri had been the king of Israel. ²⁷ Ahaziah followed the ways of the royal family of Ahab. Ahaziah did what was evil in the sight of the LORD, just as the family of Ahab had done. That's because he had married into Ahab's family.

²⁸ Ahaziah joined forces with Joram. They went to war against Hazael at Ramoth Gilead. Joram was the son of Ahab. Hazael was king of Aram. The soldiers of Aram wounded King Joram. ²⁹ So he returned to Jezreel to give his wounds time to heal. The soldiers of Aram had wounded him at Ramoth in his battle against Hazael, the king of Aram.

Ahaziah, the son of Jehoram, went down to Jezreel. He went there to see Joram. That's because Joram had been wounded. Ahaziah was king of Judah. Joram was the son of Ahab.

Jehu Is Anointed as King of Israel

9 Elisha the prophet sent for a man from the group of the prophets. Elisha said to him, "Tuck your coat into your belt. Take this bottle of olive oil with you. Go to Ramoth Gilead. ² When you get there, look for Jehu. He's the son of Jehoshaphat, the son of Nimshi. Go to Jehu. Get him away from his companions. Take him into an inside room. ³ Then get the bottle. Pour the oil on his head. Announce to him, 'The LORD says, "I anoint you as king over Israel." ' After that, open the door and run away. Do it quickly!"

⁴So the young prophet went to Ramoth Gilead. ⁵When he arrived, he found the army officers sitting together. "Commander, I have a message for you," he said.

"For which one of us?" asked Jehu.

"For you, commander," he replied.

⁶Jehu got up and went into the house. Then the prophet poured the oil on Jehu's head. He announced, "The LORD is the God of Israel. He says, 'I am anointing you as king over the LORD's people Israel. ⁷You must destroy the royal house of your master Ahab. I will pay them back for spilling the blood of my servants the prophets. I will also pay them back for the blood of all the LORD's servants that Jezebel spilled. ⁸The whole house of Ahab will die out. I will destroy every male in Israel who is related to Ahab. It does not matter whether they are slaves or free. ⁹I will make Ahab's royal house like the house of Jeroboam, the son of Nebat. I will make it like the house of Baasha, the son of Ahijah. ¹⁰Dogs will eat up Jezebel on a piece of land at Jezreel. No one will bury her.' " Then the prophet opened the door and ran away.

¹¹Jehu went out to where the other officers were. One of them asked him, "Is everything all right? Why did that crazy man come to you?"

"You know the man. You know the kinds of things he says," Jehu replied.

¹²"That's not true!" they said. "Tell us."

Jehu said, "Here is what he told me. He announced, 'The LORD says, "I am anointing you as king over Israel." ' "

¹³The officers quickly grabbed their coats. They spread them out under Jehu on the bare steps of the house. Then they blew a trumpet. They shouted, "Jehu is king!"

Jehu Kills Joram and Ahaziah

¹⁴Jehu was the son of Jehoshaphat, the son of Nimshi. Jehu made plans against Joram. During that time Joram and Israel's whole army had been guarding Ramoth Gilead. They had been guarding it against Hazael, the king of Aram. ¹⁵But King Joram had returned to Jezreel. He had gone there to give his wounds time to heal. The soldiers of Aram had wounded him in his battle against Hazael, the king of Aram. Jehu said to his men, "Do you want to make me king? If you do, don't let anyone sneak out of the city. Don't let them go and tell the news in Jezreel." ¹⁶Then Jehu got into his chariot. He rode off to Jezreel. Joram was resting there. And Ahaziah, the king of Judah, had gone down to see him.

¹⁷A lookout was standing on the roof of the tower in Jezreel. He saw Jehu's troops approaching. So he called out, "I see some troops coming."

"Get a horseman," Joram

ordered. "Send him to ride out to them. Have him ask, 'Are you coming in peace?'"

[18] The horseman rode out to where Jehu was. He said, "The king asks, 'Are you coming in peace?'"

"What do you know about peace?" Jehu answered. "Get in line behind me."

The lookout reported, "The messenger has reached them. But he isn't coming back."

[19] So the king sent out a second horseman. When he came to them, he said, "The king asks, 'Are you coming in peace?'"

Jehu replied, "What do you know about peace? Get in line behind me."

[20] The lookout reported, "The second messenger has reached them. But he isn't coming back either. The one driving the chariot drives like Jehu, the son of Nimshi. He's driving like a crazy person."

[21] "Get my chariot ready," King Joram ordered. When it was ready, he rode out. Ahaziah, the king of Judah, rode out with him. Each of them was in his own chariot. They both went to meet Jehu. They met him at the piece of land that had belonged to Naboth from Jezreel. [22] When Joram saw Jehu he asked, "Have you come here in peace, Jehu?"

"Your mother Jezebel worships statues of gods," Jehu replied. "She also worships evil powers. The evil things she does have spread everywhere. As long as all of that goes on, how can there be peace?"

[23] Joram turned around and tried to get away. He called out, "It's treason, Ahaziah!"

[24] Then Jehu shot an arrow at Joram. It hit him between the shoulders. It went through his heart. He sank down slowly in his chariot. [25] Jehu spoke to Bidkar, his chariot officer. Jehu said, "Pick Joram up. Throw him on the field that belonged to Naboth from Jezreel. Remember how you and I were riding together in chariots behind Joram's father Ahab? It was when the LORD spoke this prophecy against him. The LORD announced, [26] 'Yesterday I saw the blood of Naboth and the blood of his sons. You can be sure that I will make you pay for it on this piece of land.' So pick Joram up. Throw him on that piece of land. That's what the LORD said would happen."

[27] Ahaziah, the king of Judah, saw what had happened. So he tried to get away. He went up the road toward Beth Haggan. Jehu chased him. He shouted, "Kill him too!" Jehu's men wounded Ahaziah in his chariot. It happened on the way up to Gur near Ibleam. But Ahaziah escaped to Megiddo. And that's where he died. [28] Ahaziah's servants took him to Jerusalem in his chariot. They buried him in his family tomb in the City of David. [29] Ahaziah had become king of Judah. It was in the 11th year of Joram, the son of Ahab.

Jehu Kills Jezebel

[30] Jehu went to Jezreel. Jezebel heard about it. So she put

makeup on her eyes and fixed her hair. Then she looked out of a window. ³¹ Jehu entered the gate below. Jezebel said to him, "You are just like Zimri. You murdered your master. Have you come here in peace?"

³² Jehu looked up at the window. "Who is on my side?" he called out. "Who?" Two or three officials looked down at him. ³³ "Throw her down!" Jehu said. So they threw her down. Some of her blood splashed on the wall. Some of it splashed on Jehu's chariot horses as they ran over her.

³⁴ Jehu went inside. He ate and drank. "The LORD put a curse on that woman," he said. "Take proper care of her body. Bury her. After all, she was a king's daughter." ³⁵ So they went out to bury her. But all they found was her head, feet and hands. ³⁶ They went back and reported it to Jehu. He told them, "That's what the LORD said would happen. He announced it through his servant Elijah, who was from Tishbe. He said, 'On a piece of land at Jezreel, dogs will eat up Jezebel's body. ³⁷ Her body will end up as garbage on that piece of land. So no one will be able to say, "Here's where Jezebel is buried."'"

Jehu Wipes Out Ahab's Royal House

10 Ahab's royal family in the city of Samaria had a total of 70 sons. Jehu wrote some letters to the officials of the city. He also sent them to the elders there. And he sent them to the people who took care of Ahab's children. Jehu said, ² "Your master's sons are with you. You also have chariots and horses and weapons. And you are living in a city that has high walls around it. As soon as you read this letter, here's what I want you to do. ³ Choose the best and most respected son of your master. Place him on his father Joram's throne. Then fight for your master's royal house."

⁴ The leaders of Samaria were terrified. They said, "King Joram and King Ahaziah couldn't stand up against Jehu. So how can we?"

⁵ The city governor and the person in charge of the palace sent a message to Jehu. The message was also from the elders and the people who took care of Ahab's children. In the message, they said, "We will serve you. We'll do anything you say. We won't appoint anyone to be king. Do what you think is best."

⁶ Then Jehu wrote them a second letter. He said, "You say you are on my side. You say you will obey me. If you really mean it, bring me the heads of your master's sons. Meet me in Jezreel by this time tomorrow."

There were 70 royal princes. They were with the most important men of the city. Those men were in charge of raising them. ⁷ When Jehu's letter arrived, the men went and got the princes. They killed all 70 of them. They put their heads in baskets. Then they sent them to Jehu in Jezreel.

8 When the messenger arrived, he spoke to Jehu. He told him, "The heads of the princes have been brought here."

Then Jehu ordered his men, "Put them in two piles. Stack them up at the entrance of the city gate until morning."

9 The next morning Jehu went out. He stood in front of all the people. He said, "You aren't guilty of doing anything wrong. I'm the one who made plans against my master Joram. I killed him. But who killed all these? 10 I want you to know that the LORD has spoken against Ahab's royal house. Not a word of what he has said will fail. The LORD has done exactly what he announced through his servant Elijah." 11 So Jehu killed everyone from Ahab's family who was in Jezreel. He also killed all Ahab's chief men. And he killed Ahab's close friends and his priests. He didn't leave anyone alive in Ahab's family.

12 Then Jehu started out for Samaria. At Beth Eked of the Shepherds, 13 he saw some people. They were relatives of Ahaziah, the king of Judah. Jehu asked them, "Who are you?"

They said, "We are Ahaziah's relatives. We've come down to visit the families of the king and of his mother."

14 "Take them alive!" Jehu ordered. So his men took them alive. Then they killed them by the well of Beth Eked. They killed a total of 42 of them. Jehu didn't leave anyone alive.

15 Jehu left there. On the way he met Jehonadab. He was the son of Rekab. Jehonadab was on his way to see Jehu. Jehu greeted him. He asked, "Are you my friend? You know I'm your friend."

"I am," Jehonadab answered.

"If that's true," said Jehu, "hold out your hand." So he did. Then Jehu helped him up into the chariot. 16 Jehu said, "Come along with me. See how committed I am to serve the LORD." Jehu had Jehonadab ride along in his chariot.

17 Jehu came to Samaria. He killed everyone there who was left from Ahab's family. And so he completely destroyed Ahab's royal house. That's what the LORD had said would happen. He had spoken that message to Elijah.

Jehu Kills the People Who Serve Baal

18 Then Jehu brought together all the people. He said to them, "Ahab served the god named Baal a little. I will serve him a lot. 19 Send for all of Baal's prophets. Also send for all his priests and the others who serve him. Make sure that not a single one is missing. I'm going to hold a great sacrifice to honor Baal. Anyone who doesn't come will be killed." But Jehu was lying to them. He was planning to destroy everyone who served Baal.

20 Jehu said, "Call everyone together to honor Baal." So they did. 21 Then he sent a message all through Israel. All those who served Baal came. Not a sin-

gle one of them stayed away. They crowded into Baal's temple. It was full from one end to the other. ²² Jehu spoke to the one who took care of the sacred robes. He told him, "Bring robes for everyone who serves Baal." So he brought the robes out for them.

²³ Then Jehu went into Baal's temple. Jehonadab, the son of Rekab, went with him. Jehu said to those who served Baal, "Look around. Make sure that no one who serves the LORD is here with you. Make sure only those who serve Baal are here." ²⁴ So they went in to offer sacrifices and burnt offerings. Jehu had stationed 80 men outside. He warned them, "I'm placing some men in your hands. Don't let a single one of them escape. If you do, you will pay for his life with yours."

²⁵ Jehu finished sacrificing the burnt offering. As soon as he did, he gave an order to the guards and officers. He commanded them, "Go inside and kill everyone. Don't let a single one of them escape." So they cut them down with their swords. The guards and officers threw the bodies outside. Then they entered the most sacred area inside Baal's temple. ²⁶ They brought the sacred stone of Baal outside. They burned it up. ²⁷ So they destroyed Baal's sacred stone. They also tore down Baal's temple. People have used it as a public toilet to this day.

²⁸ So Jehu destroyed the worship of the god named Baal in Israel. ²⁹ But he didn't turn away from the sins of Jeroboam, the son of Nebat. Jeroboam had caused Israel to commit those same sins. Jehu worshiped the golden calves at Bethel and Dan.

³⁰ The LORD said to Jehu, "You have done well. You have accomplished what is right in my eyes. You have done to Ahab's royal house everything I wanted you to do. So your sons after you will sit on the throne of Israel. They will rule until the time of your children's grandchildren." ³¹ But Jehu wasn't careful to obey the law of the LORD. He didn't obey the God of Israel with all his heart. He didn't turn away from the sins of Jeroboam. Jeroboam had caused Israel to commit those same sins.

³² In those days the LORD began to make the kingdom of Israel smaller. Hazael gained control over many parts of Israel. He gained control over all their territory ³³ east of the Jordan River. It included the whole land of Gilead from Aroer by the Arnon River valley all the way to Bashan. That was the territory of Gad, Reuben and Manasseh.

³⁴ The other events of Jehu's rule are written down. Everything he did and accomplished is written in the official records of the kings of Israel.

³⁵ Jehu joined the members of his family who had already died. He was buried in Samaria. His son Jehoahaz became the next king after him. ³⁶ Jehu had

ruled over Israel in Samaria for 28 years.

Athaliah and Joash

11 Athaliah was Ahaziah's mother. She saw that her son was dead. So she began to destroy the whole royal house of Judah. ²But Jehosheba went and got Joash, the son of Ahaziah. Jehosheba was the daughter of King Jehoram and the sister of Ahaziah. She stole Joash away from among the royal princes. All of them were about to be murdered. She put Joash and his nurse in a bedroom. That's how she hid him from Athaliah. And that's why Athaliah didn't kill him. ³The child remained hidden with his nurse at the LORD's temple for six years. Athaliah ruled over the land during that time.

⁴In the seventh year Jehoiada the priest sent for the commanders of military groups of 100 men. They were the commanders over the Carites and the guards. Jehoiada had them brought to him at the temple of the LORD. He made a covenant with them. At the temple he made them promise to be faithful. Then he showed them the king's son. ⁵He gave them a command. He said, "Here's what you must do. There are five groups of you. Some of you are in the three groups that are going on duty on the Sabbath day. A third of you must guard the royal palace. ⁶A third of you must guard the Sur Gate. And a third of you must guard the gate that is behind the guard. All of you must take turns guarding the temple. ⁷The rest of you are in the other two groups. Normally you are not on duty on the Sabbath day. But you also must guard the temple for the king. ⁸Station yourselves around the king. Each of you must have his weapon in his hand. Anyone else who approaches your groups must be put to death. Stay close to the king no matter where he goes."

⁹The commanders of the military groups did just as Jehoiada the priest ordered. Each commander got his men and came to Jehoiada. Some of the men were going on duty on the Sabbath day. Others were going off duty. ¹⁰Then Jehoiada gave weapons to the commanders. He gave them spears and shields. The weapons had belonged to King David. They had been in the LORD's temple. ¹¹The guards stationed themselves around the new king. Each of them had his weapon in his hand. They were near the altar and the temple. They stood from the south side of the temple to its north side.

¹²Jehoiada brought out Ahaziah's son. He put the crown on him. He gave him a copy of the covenant. And he announced that Joash was king. Jehoiada and his sons anointed him. The people clapped their hands. Then they shouted, "May the king live a long time!"

¹³Athaliah heard the noise the guards and the people were

making. So she went to the people at the Lord's temple. [14] She looked, and there was the king! He was standing next to the pillar. That was the usual practice. The officers and trumpet players were standing beside the king. All the people of the land were filled with joy. They were blowing trumpets. Then Athaliah tore her royal robes. She called out, "Treason! It's treason!"

[15] Jehoiada the priest gave an order to the commanders of the military groups of 100 men. The commanders were in charge of the troops. He said to them, "Bring her away from the temple between the line of guards. Use your swords to kill anyone who follows her." The priest had said, "She must not be put to death at the Lord's temple." [16] So they grabbed her as she reached the place where the horses enter the palace grounds. There she was put to death.

[17] Then Jehoiada made a covenant between the Lord and the king and people. He had the king and people promise that they would be the Lord's people. Jehoiada also made a covenant between the king and the people. [18] All the people of the land went to Baal's temple. They tore it down. They smashed to pieces the altars and the statues of gods. They killed Mattan in front of the altars. He was the priest of Baal.

Then Jehoiada the priest stationed guards at the temple of the Lord. [19] Jehoiada took with him the commanders of groups of 100 men. They were the commanders over the Carites and the guards. He also took with him all the people of the land. All of them brought the new king down from the Lord's temple. They went into the palace. They entered it by going through the gate of the guards. Then the king sat down on the royal throne. [20] All the people of the land were filled with joy. And the city was calm. That's because Athaliah had been killed with a sword at the palace.

[21] Joash was seven years old when he became king.

Joash Repairs the Temple

12 Joash became king of Judah. It was in the seventh year of Jehu's rule. Joash ruled in Jerusalem for 40 years. His mother's name was Zibiah. She was from Beersheba. [2] Joash did what was right in the eyes of the Lord. Joash lived that way as long as Jehoiada the priest was teaching him. [3] But the high places weren't removed. The people continued to offer sacrifices and burn incense there.

[4] Joash spoke to the priests. He said, "Collect all the money the people bring as sacred offerings to the Lord's temple. That includes the money collected when the men who are able to serve in the army are counted. It includes the money received from people who make a special promise to the Lord. It also includes the money people bring

to the temple just because they want to. [5] Let each priest receive the money from one of the people in charge of the temple's treasures. Then use all of that money to repair the temple where it needs it."

[6] It was now the 23rd year of the rule of King Joash. And the priests still hadn't repaired the temple. [7] So the king sent for Jehoiada the priest and the other priests. He asked them, "Why aren't you repairing the temple where it needs it? Don't take any more money from the people in charge of the treasures. Instead, hand it over so the temple can be repaired." [8] The priests agreed that they wouldn't collect any more money from the people. They also agreed that they wouldn't repair the temple themselves.

[9] Jehoiada the priest got a chest. He drilled a hole in its lid. He placed the chest beside the altar for burnt offerings. The chest was on the right side as people enter the LORD's temple. Some priests guarded the entrance. They put into the chest all the money the people brought to the temple. [10] From time to time there was a large amount of money in the chest. When that happened, the royal secretary and the high priest came. They counted the money the people had brought to the temple. Then they put it into bags. [11] After they added it all up, they used it to repair the temple. They gave it to the men who had been put in charge of the work.

Those men used it to pay the workers. They paid the builders and those who worked with wood. [12] They paid those who cut stones and those who laid them. They bought lumber and blocks of stone. So they used the money to repair the LORD's temple. They also paid all the other costs to make the temple like new again.

[13] The money the people brought to the LORD's temple wasn't used to make silver bowls. It wasn't used for wick cutters, sprinkling bowls or trumpets. And it wasn't used for any other things made out of gold or silver. [14] Instead, it was paid to the workers. They used it to repair the temple. [15] The royal secretary and the high priest didn't require a report from those who were in charge of the work. That's because they were completely honest. They always paid the workers. [16] Money was received from people who brought guilt offerings and sin offerings. But it wasn't taken to the LORD's temple. It belonged to the priests.

[17] About that time Hazael, the king of Aram, went up and attacked Gath. Then he captured it. After that, he turned back to attack Jerusalem. [18] But Joash, the king of Judah, didn't want to go to war. So he took all the sacred objects. They had been set apart to the LORD by the kings who had ruled over Judah before him. Those kings were Jehoshaphat, Jehoram and Ahaziah. Joash took the gifts he

himself had set apart. He took all the gold that was among the temple treasures. He also took all the gold from the royal palace. He sent all those things to Hazael, the king of Aram. Then Hazael pulled his army back from Jerusalem.

¹⁹ The other events of the rule of Joash are written down. Everything he did is written in the official records of the kings of Judah. ²⁰ The officials of Joash made evil plans against him. They killed him at Beth Millo. It happened on the road that goes down to Silla. ²¹ The officials who murdered him were Jozabad and Jehozabad. Jozabad was the son of Shimeath. Jehozabad was the son of Shomer. After Joash died, he was buried in the family tomb in the City of David. Joash's son Amaziah became the next king after him.

Jehoahaz King of Israel

13 Jehoahaz became king of Israel in Samaria. It was in the 23rd year of the rule of Joash, the king of Judah. Jehoahaz ruled for 17 years. Joash was the son of Ahaziah. Jehoahaz was the son of Jehu. ² Jehoahaz did what was evil in the eyes of the LORD. He committed the sins Jeroboam, the son of Nebat, had committed. Jeroboam had caused Israel to commit those same sins. Jehoahaz didn't turn away from them. ³ So the LORD was very angry with Israel. For a long time he kept them under the power of Hazael, the king of Aram. The LORD also kept them under the power of his son Ben-Hadad.

⁴ Then Jehoahaz asked the LORD for help. The LORD listened to him. The LORD saw how badly the king of Aram was treating Israel. ⁵ The LORD provided someone to save Israel. And they escaped from the power of Aram. So the Israelites lived in their own homes, just as they had before. ⁶ But the people didn't turn away from the sins of the royal house of Jeroboam. He had caused Israel to commit those same sins. The people continued to commit them. And the pole used to worship the female god named Asherah remained standing in Samaria.

⁷ The army of Jehoahaz had almost nothing left. All it had was 50 horsemen, 10 chariots and 10,000 soldiers on foot. The king of Aram had destroyed the rest of them. He had made them like dust at threshing time.

⁸ The other events of the rule of Jehoahaz are written down. Everything he did and accomplished is written in the official records of the kings of Israel. ⁹ Jehoahaz joined the members of his family who had already died. He was buried in Samaria. Jehoahaz's son Jehoash became the next king after him.

Jehoash King of Israel

¹⁰ Jehoash became king of Israel in Samaria. It was in the 37th year that Joash was king

of Judah. Jehoash ruled for 16 years. He was the son of Jehoahaz. [11] Jehoash did what was evil in the eyes of the LORD. Jehoash didn't turn away from any of the sins of Jeroboam, the son of Nebat. Jeroboam had caused Israel to commit those same sins. And Jehoash continued to commit them.

[12] The other events of the rule of Jehoash are written down. That includes his war against Amaziah, the king of Judah. Everything he did and accomplished is written in the official records of the kings of Israel. [13] Jehoash joined the members of his family who had already died. He was buried in the royal tombs in Samaria. Jeroboam became the next king on Israel's throne after him.

[14] Elisha had been suffering from a sickness. Later he would die from it. Jehoash, the king of Israel, went down to see him. Jehoash wept over him. "My father!" he cried. "You are like a father to me! You, Elisha, are the true chariots and horsemen of Israel!"

[15] Elisha said to Jehoash, "Get a bow and some arrows." So he did. [16] "Hold the bow in your hands," Elisha said to the king of Israel. So Jehoash took hold of the bow. Then Elisha put his hands on the king's hands.

[17] "Open the east window," Elisha said. So he did. "Shoot!" Elisha said. So he shot. "That's the LORD's arrow!" Elisha announced. "It means you will win the battle over Aram! You will

completely destroy the men of Aram at Aphek."

[18] Elisha continued, "Get some arrows." So the king did. Elisha told him, "Strike the ground." Jehoash struck it three times. Then he stopped. [19] The man of God was angry with him. He said, "You should have struck the ground five or six times. Then you would have won the war over Aram. You would have completely destroyed them. But now you will win only three battles over them."

[20] Elisha died and was buried.

Some robbers from Moab used to enter the country of Israel every spring. [21] One day some Israelites were burying a man. Suddenly they saw a group of robbers. So they threw the man's body into Elisha's tomb. The body touched Elisha's bones. When it did, the man came back to life again. He stood up on his feet.

[22] Hazael, the king of Aram, treated Israel badly. He did it the whole time Jehoahaz was king. [23] But the LORD helped Israel. He was tender and kind to them. He showed concern for them. He did all these things because of the covenant he had made with Abraham, Isaac and Jacob. To this day he hasn't been willing to destroy Israel. And he hasn't driven them out of his land.

[24] Hazael, the king of Aram, died. His son Ben-Hadad became the next king after him. [25] Then Jehoash won back some towns from Ben-Hadad, the son of Hazael. Ben-Hadad had cap-

tured them in battle from Jehoahaz, the father of Jehoash. Jehoash won three battles over Ben-Hadad. So Jehoash won back the Israelite towns.

Amaziah King of Judah

14 Amaziah began to rule as king over Judah. It was in the second year that Jehoash was king of Israel. He was the son of Jehoahaz. Amaziah was the son of Joash. ² Amaziah was 25 years old when he became king. He ruled in Jerusalem for 29 years. His mother's name was Jehoaddan. She was from Jerusalem. ³ Amaziah did what was right in the eyes of the LORD. But he didn't do what King David had done. He always followed the example of his father Joash. ⁴ But the high places weren't removed. The people continued to offer sacrifices and burn incense there.

⁵ The kingdom was firmly under his control. So he put to death the officials who had murdered his father, the king. ⁶ But he didn't put their children to death. He obeyed what is written in the Book of the Law of Moses. There the LORD commanded, "Parents must not be put to death because of what their children do. And children must not be put to death because of what their parents do. People must die because of their own sins." *(Deuteronomy 24:16)*

⁷ Amaziah won the battle over 10,000 men of Edom. It happened in the Valley of Salt. During the battle he captured the town of Sela. He called it Joktheel. That's the name it still has to this day.

⁸ After the battle, Amaziah sent messengers to Jehoash, the king of Israel. Jehoash was the son of Jehoahaz, the son of Jehu. Amaziah said, "Come on. Let us face each other in battle."

⁹ But Jehoash, the king of Israel, answered Amaziah, the king of Judah. Jehoash said, "A thorn bush in Lebanon sent a message to a cedar tree there. The thorn bush said, 'Give your daughter to be married to my son.' Then a wild animal in Lebanon came along. It crushed the thorn bush by walking on it. ¹⁰ It's true that you have won the battle over Edom. So you are proud. Enjoy your success while you can. But stay home and enjoy it! Why ask for trouble? Why bring yourself crashing down? Why bring Judah down with you?"

¹¹ But Amaziah wouldn't listen. So Jehoash, the king of Israel, attacked. He and Amaziah, the king of Judah, faced each other in battle. The battle took place at Beth Shemesh in Judah. ¹² Israel drove Judah away. Every man ran home. ¹³ Jehoash king of Israel captured Amaziah king of Judah at Beth Shemesh. Amaziah was the son of Joash. Joash was the son of Ahaziah. Jehoash went to Jerusalem. He broke down part of its wall. It's the part that went from the Ephraim Gate to the Corner Gate. That part of the wall was 600 feet long. ¹⁴ Jehoash took all

the gold, silver and objects that were in the LORD's temple. He also took all those same kinds of things that were among the treasures of the royal palace. And he took prisoners. Then he returned to Samaria.

15 The other events of the rule of Jehoash are written down. That includes his war against Amaziah, the king of Judah. Everything he did and accomplished is written in the official records of the kings of Israel. 16 Jehoash joined the members of his family who had already died. He was buried in Samaria in the royal tombs of Israel. Jehoash's son Jeroboam became the next king after him.

17 Amaziah king of Judah lived for 15 years after Jehoash king of Israel died. Amaziah was the son of Joash. Jehoash was the son of Jehoahaz. 18 The other events of Amaziah's rule are written down. They are written in the official records of the kings of Judah.

19 Some people made evil plans against Amaziah in Jerusalem. So he ran away to Lachish. But they sent men to Lachish after him. There they killed him. 20 His body was brought back on a horse. Then he was buried in the family tomb in Jerusalem, the City of David.

21 All the people of Judah made Uzziah king. He was 16 years old. They made him king in place of his father Amaziah. 22 Uzziah rebuilt Elath. He brought it under Judah's control

again. He did it after Amaziah joined the members of his family who had already died.

Jeroboam II King of Israel

23 Jeroboam became king of Israel in Samaria. It was in the 15th year that Amaziah was king of Judah. Jeroboam ruled for 41 years. Amaziah was the son of Joash. Jeroboam was the son of Jehoash. 24 Jeroboam did what was evil in the eyes of the LORD. He didn't turn away from any of the sins the earlier Jeroboam, the son of Nebat, had committed. That Jeroboam had caused Israel to commit those same sins. 25 Jeroboam, the son of Jehoash, made the borders of Israel the same as they were before. They reached from Lebo Hamath all the way to the Dead Sea. That's what the LORD, the God of Israel, had said would happen. He had spoken that message through his servant Jonah. Jonah the prophet was the son of Amittai. Jonah was from the town of Gath Hepher.

26 The LORD had seen how much everyone in Israel was suffering. It didn't matter whether they were slaves or free. They didn't have anyone to help them. 27 The LORD hadn't said he would wipe out Israel's name from the earth. So he saved them by the power of Jeroboam, the son of Jehoash.

28 The other events of the rule of Jeroboam are written down. What he and his army accomplished is written down. That includes how he brought Da-

mascus and Hamath back under Israel's control. Damascus and Hamath had belonged to the territory of Judah. Everything he did is written in the official records of the kings of Israel. [29] Jeroboam joined the members of his family who had already died. He was buried in the royal tombs of Israel. Jeroboam's son Zechariah became the next king after him.

Uzziah King of Judah

15 Uzziah began to rule as king over Judah. It was in the 27th year that Jeroboam was king of Israel. Uzziah was the son of Amaziah. [2] Uzziah was 16 years old when he became king. He ruled in Jerusalem for 52 years. His mother's name was Jekoliah. She was from Jerusalem. [3] Uzziah did what was right in the eyes of the LORD, just as his father Amaziah had done. [4] But the high places weren't removed. The people continued to offer sacrifices and burn incense there.

[5] The LORD caused King Uzziah to suffer from a skin disease until the day he died. He lived in a separate house. His son Jotham was in charge of the palace. Jotham ruled over the people of the land.

[6] The other events of the rule of Uzziah are written down. Everything he did is written in the official records of the kings of Judah. [7] Uzziah joined the members of his family who had already died. He was buried near them in the City of David. Uz-

ziah's son Jotham became the next king after him.

Zechariah King of Israel

[8] Zechariah became king of Israel in Samaria. It was in the 38th year that Uzziah was king of Judah. Zechariah ruled for six months. He was the son of Jeroboam, the son of Jehoash. [9] Zechariah did what was evil in the eyes of the LORD. He did what the kings of Israel before him had done. He didn't turn away from the sins Jeroboam, the son of Nebat, had committed. Jeroboam had caused Israel to commit those same sins.

[10] Shallum made evil plans against Zechariah. He attacked Zechariah in front of the people and killed him. Then he became the next king after him. Shallum was the son of Jabesh. [11] The other events of the rule of Zechariah are written down. They are written in the official records of the kings of Israel. [12] What happened to Zechariah is what the LORD said would happen. He had spoken that message to Jehu. The LORD had said, "Your sons after you will sit on the throne of Israel. They will rule until the time of your children's grandchildren." *(2 Kings 10:30)*

Shallum King of Israel

[13] Shallum became king of Israel. It was in the 39th year that Uzziah was king of Judah. Shallum ruled in Samaria for one month. He was the son of Jabesh. [14] Menahem went from Tirzah up to Samaria. There he

attacked Shallum, the son of Jabesh. Menahem killed him and became the next king after him. Menahem was the son of Gadi.

¹⁵ The other events of Shallum's rule are written down. The evil things he planned are written down. All these things are written in the official records of the kings of Israel.

¹⁶ At that time Menahem started out from Tirzah and attacked Tiphsah. He attacked everyone in the city and the area around it. That's because they refused to open their gates for him. He destroyed Tiphsah. He ripped open all their pregnant women.

Menahem King of Israel

¹⁷ Menahem became king of Israel. It was in the 39th year that Uzziah was king of Judah. Menahem ruled in Samaria for ten years. He was the son of Gadi. ¹⁸ Menahem did what was evil in the eyes of the LORD. During his entire rule he didn't turn away from the sins Jeroboam, the son of Nebat, had committed. Jeroboam had caused Israel to commit those same sins.

¹⁹ Then Tiglath-Pileser marched into the land of Israel. He was king of Assyria. Menahem gave him 38 tons of silver to get his help. He wanted to make his control over the kingdom stronger. ²⁰ Menahem forced Israel to give him that money. Every wealthy person had to give him 20 ounces of silver. All of it went to the king of Assyria. So he pulled his troops back. He didn't stay in the land anymore.

²¹ The other events of the rule of Menahem are written down. Everything he did is written in the official records of the kings of Israel. ²² Menahem joined the members of his family who had already died. Menahem's son Pekahiah became the next king after him.

Pekahiah King of Israel

²³ Pekahiah became king of Israel in Samaria. It was in the 50th year that Uzziah was king of Judah. Pekahiah ruled for two years. He was the son of Menahem. ²⁴ Pekahiah did what was evil in the eyes of the LORD. He didn't turn away from the sins Jeroboam, the son of Nebat, had committed. Jeroboam had caused Israel to commit those same sins. ²⁵ One of Pekahiah's chief officers was Pekah. He was the son of Remaliah. Pekah made evil plans against Pekahiah. He took 50 men from Gilead with him and killed Pekahiah. Pekah also killed Argob and Arieh. He killed all of them in the safest place in the royal palace at Samaria. So Pekah killed Pekahiah. He became the next king after him.

²⁶ The other events of the rule of Pekahiah are written down. Everything he did is written in the official records of the kings of Israel.

Pekah King of Israel

²⁷ Pekah became king of Israel in Samaria. It was in the

52nd year that Uzziah was king of Judah. Pekah ruled for 20 years. He was the son of Remaliah. [28] Pekah did what was evil in the eyes of the Lord. He didn't turn away from the sins Jeroboam, the son of Nebat, had committed. Jeroboam had caused Israel to commit those same sins.

[29] During the rule of Pekah, the king of Israel, Tiglath-Pileser marched into the land again. He was king of Assyria. He captured the towns of Ijon, Abel Beth Maakah, Janoah, Kedesh and Hazor. He also captured the lands of Gilead and Galilee. That included the whole territory of Naphtali. He took the people away from their own land. He sent them off to Assyria. [30] Then Hoshea made evil plans against Pekah, the son of Remaliah. Hoshea was the son of Elah. Hoshea attacked Pekah and killed him. Then Hoshea became the next king after him. It was in the 20th year of the rule of Jotham, the son of Uzziah.

[31] The other events of the rule of Pekah are written down. Everything he did is written in the official records of the kings of Israel.

Jotham King of Judah

[32] Jotham began to rule as king over Judah. It was in the second year that Pekah was king of Israel. He was the son of Remaliah. Jotham was the son of Uzziah. [33] Jotham was 25 years old when he became king. He ruled in Jerusalem for 16 years. His mother's name was Jerusha. She was the daughter of Zadok. [34] Jotham did what was right in the eyes of the Lord, just as his father Uzziah had done. [35] But the high places weren't removed. The people continued to offer sacrifices and burn incense there. Jotham rebuilt the Upper Gate of the Lord's temple.

[36] The other events of the rule of Jotham are written down. Everything he did is written in the official records of the kings of Judah. [37] In those days the Lord began to send Rezin and Pekah against Judah. Rezin was king of Aram. Pekah was the son of Remaliah. [38] Jotham joined the members of his family who had already died. He was buried in the family tomb in the city of King David. Jotham's son Ahaz became the next king after him.

Ahaz King of Judah

16 Ahaz began to rule as king over Judah. It was in the 17th year of the rule of Pekah, the son of Remaliah. Ahaz was the son of Jotham. [2] Ahaz was 20 years old when he became king. He ruled in Jerusalem for 16 years. Ahaz didn't do what was right in the eyes of the Lord his God. He didn't do what King David had done. [3] He followed the ways of the kings of Israel. He even sacrificed his son in the fire to another god. He followed the practices of the nations. The Lord hated those practices. He had driven out those nations to make room for the Israelites. ⁴Ahaz offered sacrifices and burned incense at the high places. He also did it on the tops of hills and under every green tree.

⁵Rezin and Pekah marched up to Jerusalem and surrounded it. Rezin was king of Aram. Pekah, the son of Remaliah, was king of Israel. They attacked Ahaz. But they couldn't overpower him. ⁶At that time Rezin, the king of Aram, won back Elath for Aram. He drove out the people of Judah. Then the people of Edom moved into Elath. And they still live there to this day.

⁷Ahaz sent messengers to Tiglath-Pileser. He was king of Assyria. The message of Ahaz said, "I am your servant. You are my master. Come up and save me from the power of the kings of Aram and Israel. They are attacking me." ⁸Ahaz took the silver and gold that were in the LORD's temple. He also took the silver and gold that were among the treasures in the royal palace. He sent all of it as a gift to the king of Assyria. ⁹So the king of Assyria did what Ahaz asked him to do. He attacked the city of Damascus and captured it. He sent its people away to Kir. And he put Rezin to death.

¹⁰Then King Ahaz went to Damascus. He went there to see Tiglath-Pileser, the king of Assyria. Ahaz saw an altar in Damascus. He sent a drawing of it to Uriah the priest. Ahaz also sent him plans for building it.

¹¹So Uriah the priest built an altar. He followed all the plans King Ahaz had sent from Damascus. He finished it before Ahaz returned. ¹²The king came back from Damascus. When he saw the altar, he approached it. Then he offered sacrifices on it. ¹³He offered up his burnt offering and grain offering. He poured out his drink offering. And he splashed the blood from his friendship offerings against the altar. ¹⁴The bronze altar for burnt offerings stood in front of the LORD. It was between the new altar and the LORD's temple. Ahaz took the bronze altar away from the front of the temple. He put it on the north side of the new altar.

¹⁵Then King Ahaz gave orders to Uriah the priest. He said, "Offer sacrifices on the large new altar. Offer the morning burnt offering and the evening grain offering. Offer my burnt offering and my grain offering. Offer the burnt offering of all the people of the land. Offer their grain offering and their drink offering. Splash against this altar the blood from all the burnt offerings and sacrifices. But I will use the bronze altar to look for advice and direction." ¹⁶Uriah the priest did just as King Ahaz had ordered.

¹⁷Ahaz cut off the sides of the bronze stands. He removed the bowls from the stands. He removed the huge bowl from the bronze bulls it stood on. He placed the bowl on a stone base. ¹⁸He took away the covered area

that had been used on the Sabbath day. It had been built at the LORD's temple. He removed the royal entrance that was outside the temple. Ahaz did all these things to honor the king of Assyria.

¹⁹ The other events of the rule of Ahaz are written down. Everything he did is written in the official records of the kings of Judah. ²⁰ Ahaz joined the members of his family who had already died. He was buried in the family tomb in the City of David. Ahaz's son Hezekiah became the next king after him.

Hoshea the Last King of Israel

17 Hoshea became king of Israel in Samaria. It was in the 12th year that Ahaz was king of Judah. Hoshea ruled for nine years. He was the son of Elah. ² Hoshea did what was evil in the eyes of the LORD. But he wasn't as evil as the kings of Israel who ruled before him.

³ Shalmaneser came up to attack Hoshea. Shalmaneser was king of Assyria. He had been Hoshea's master. He had forced Hoshea to bring him gifts. ⁴ But the king of Assyria found out that Hoshea had turned against him. Hoshea had sent messengers to So, the king of Egypt. Hoshea didn't send gifts to the king of Assyria anymore. He had been sending them every year. So Shalmaneser grabbed him and put him in prison. ⁵ The king of Assyria marched into the whole land of Israel. He marched to Samaria and surrounded it for three years. From time to time he attacked it. ⁶ Finally, the king of Assyria captured Samaria. It was in the ninth year of Hoshea. The king of Assyria took the Israelites away from their own land. He sent them off to Assyria. He made some of them live in Halah. He made others live in Gozan on the Habor River. And he made others live in the towns of the Medes.

Israel Is Forced to Leave the Land Because of Sin

⁷ All of this took place because the Israelites had sinned against the LORD their God. He had brought them up out of Egypt. He had brought them out from under the power of Pharaoh, the king of Egypt. But they worshiped other gods. ⁸ The LORD had driven out other nations to make room for Israel. But they followed the evil practices of those nations. They also followed the practices that the kings of Israel had started. ⁹ The Israelites did things in secret against the LORD their God. What they did wasn't right. They built high places for worship in all their towns. They built them at lookout towers. They also built them at cities that had high walls around them. ¹⁰ They set up sacred stones. And they set up poles used to worship the female god named Asherah. They did that on every high hill and under every green tree. ¹¹ The LORD had driven out nations to make room for

Israel. But the Israelites burned incense at every high place, just as those nations had done. The Israelites did evil things that made the LORD very angry. ¹²They worshiped statues of gods. They did it even though the LORD had said, "Do not do that." ¹³The LORD warned Israel and Judah through all his prophets and seers. He said, "Turn from your evil ways. Keep my commands and rules. Obey every part of my Law. I commanded your people who lived long ago to obey it. And I gave it to you through my servants the prophets."

¹⁴But the people wouldn't listen. They were as stubborn as their people of long ago had been. Those people didn't trust in the LORD their God. ¹⁵They refused to obey his rules. They broke the covenant he had made with them. They didn't pay any attention to the rules he had warned them to keep. They worshiped worthless statues of gods. Then they themselves became worthless. They followed the example of the nations around them. They did it even though the LORD had ordered them not to. He had said, "Do not do as they do."

¹⁶They turned away from all the commands of the LORD their God. They made two statues of gods for themselves. The statues were shaped like calves. They made a pole used to worship the female god named Asherah. They bowed down to all the stars. And they worshiped the god named Baal. ¹⁷They sacrificed their sons and daughters in the fire. They practiced all kinds of evil magic. They gave up following God's rules. They did only what was evil in the eyes of the LORD. All these things made him very angry.

¹⁸So the LORD was very angry with Israel. He removed them from his land. Only the tribe of Judah was left. ¹⁹And even Judah didn't obey the commands of the LORD their God. They followed the practices Israel had started. ²⁰So the LORD turned his back on all the people of Israel. He made them suffer. He handed them over to people who stole everything they had. And finally he threw them out of his land.

²¹The LORD took control of Israel away from the royal house of David. The Israelites made Jeroboam, the son of Nebat, their king. Jeroboam tried to get Israel to stop following the LORD. He caused them to commit a terrible sin. ²²The Israelites were stubborn. They continued to commit all the sins Jeroboam had committed. They didn't turn away from them. ²³So the LORD removed them from his land. That's what he had warned them he would do. He had given that warning through all his servants the prophets. So the people of Israel were taken away from their country. They were forced to go to Assyria. And that's where they still are.

Assyria Makes Other People Live in Samaria

24 The king of Assyria brought people from Babylon, Kuthah, Avva, Hamath and Sepharvaim. He made all of them live in the towns of Samaria. They took the place of the people of Israel. They lived in all the towns of Samaria. 25 When they first lived there, they didn't worship the LORD. So he sent lions among them. And the lions killed some of the people. 26 A report was given to the king of Assyria. He was told, "You forced people to leave their own homes and live in the towns of Samaria. But they don't know what the god of that country requires. So he has sent lions among them. And the lions are killing the people off. That's because the people don't know what that god requires."

27 Then the king of Assyria gave an order. He said, "Get one of the priests you captured from Samaria. Send him back to live there. Have him teach the people what the god of that land requires." 28 So a priest went back to live in Bethel. He was one of the priests who had been forced to leave Samaria. He taught the people of Bethel how to worship the LORD.

29 In spite of that, the people from each nation made statues of their own gods. They made them in all the towns where they had been forced to live. They set up those statues in small temples. The people of Samaria had built the temples at the high places. 30 The people from Babylon made statues of the god named Sukkoth Benoth. Those from Kuthah made statues of the god named Nergal. Those from Hamath made statues of the god named Ashima. 31 The Avvites made statues of the gods named Nibhaz and Tartak. The Sepharvites sacrificed their children in the fire to the gods named Adrammelek and Anammelek. They were the gods of Sepharvaim. 32 So the people of Samaria worshiped the LORD. But they also appointed all kinds of their own people to be their priests. The priests served in the small temples at the high places. 33 The people worshiped the LORD. But they also served their own gods. They followed the evil practices of the nations they had been taken from.

34 The people of Samaria are still stubborn. They continue in their old practices to this day. And now they don't even worship the LORD. They don't follow his directions and rules. They don't obey his laws and commands. The LORD had given all these laws to the family of Jacob. He gave the name Israel to Jacob. 35 The LORD made a covenant with the Israelites. At that time he commanded them, "Do not worship any other gods. Do not bow down to them. Do not serve them or sacrifice to them. 36 The LORD is the one you must worship. The LORD brought you up out of Egypt by his great power. He saved you by reaching out his mighty arm. You

must bow down only to him. You must offer sacrifices only to him. [37]You must always be careful to follow his directions and rules. You must obey the laws and commands he wrote for you. Do not worship other gods. [38]Do not forget the covenant I made with you. And remember, you must not worship other gods. [39]Instead, worship the LORD your God. He will save you from the powerful hand of all your enemies."

[40]But the people wouldn't listen. Instead, they were stubborn. They continued in their old practices. [41]They worshiped the LORD. But at the same time, they served the statues of their gods. And to this day their children and grandchildren continue to do what their people before them did.

Hezekiah King of Judah

18 Hezekiah began to rule as king over Judah. It was in the third year that Hoshea was king of Israel. He was the son of Elah. Hezekiah was the son of Ahaz. [2]Hezekiah was 25 years old when he became king. He ruled in Jerusalem for 29 years. His mother's name was Abijah. She was the daughter of Zechariah. [3]Hezekiah did what was right in the eyes of the LORD, just as King David had done. [4]Hezekiah removed the high places. He smashed the sacred stones. He cut down the poles used to worship the female god named Asherah. He broke into pieces the bronze snake Moses had made. Up to that time the Israelites had been burning incense to it. They called it Nehushtan.

[5]Hezekiah trusted in the LORD, the God of Israel. There was no one like Hezekiah among all the kings of Judah. There was no king like him either before him or after him. [6]Hezekiah remained faithful to the LORD. He didn't stop serving him. He obeyed the commands the LORD had given Moses. [7]The LORD was with Hezekiah. Because of that, Hezekiah was successful in everything he did. He refused to remain under the control of the king of Assyria. He didn't serve him. [8]He won the war against the Philistines. He won battles at their lookout towers. He won battles at their cities that had high walls around them. He won battles against the Philistines all the way to Gaza and its territory.

[9]Shalmaneser marched to Samaria and surrounded it. It was in the fourth year of King Hezekiah. That was the seventh year of Hoshea, the king of Israel. Hoshea was the son of Elah. Shalmaneser was king of Assyria. [10]At the end of three years the army of Assyria captured Samaria. That happened in the sixth year of Hezekiah's rule. It was the ninth year of the rule of Hoshea, the king of Israel. [11]The king of Assyria took the people of Israel away from their own land. He sent them off to Assyria. He made some of them live in Ha-

lah. He made others live in Gozan on the Habor River. And he made others live in the towns of the Medes. ¹²These things happened because the Israelites hadn't obeyed the LORD their God. They had broken the covenant he had made with them. They had refused to do everything Moses, the servant of the LORD, had commanded. They hadn't paid any attention to those commands. They hadn't obeyed them.

¹³Sennacherib attacked and captured all the cities of Judah that had high walls around them. It was in the 14th year of the rule of Hezekiah. Sennacherib was king of Assyria. ¹⁴Hezekiah, the king of Judah, sent a message to the king of Assyria at Lachish. Hezekiah said, "I have done what is wrong. Pull your troops back from me. Then I'll pay you anything you ask me to." The king of Assyria forced Hezekiah, the king of Judah, to give him 11 tons of silver. Hezekiah also had to give him one ton of gold. ¹⁵So Hezekiah gave him all the silver in the LORD's temple. He also gave him all the silver among the treasures in the royal palace.

¹⁶Hezekiah, the king of Judah, had covered the doors and doorposts of the LORD's temple with gold. But now he had to strip it off. He had to give it to the king of Assyria.

Sennacherib Warns Jerusalem

¹⁷The king of Assyria sent his highest commander from Lachish to King Hezekiah at Jerusalem. He also sent his chief officer and his field commander along with a large army. All of them came up to Jerusalem. They stopped at the channel that brings water from the Upper Pool. The channel was on the road to the Washerman's Field. ¹⁸The Assyrians called for King Hezekiah. Eliakim, Shebna and Joah went out to them. Eliakim, the son of Hilkiah, was in charge of the palace. Shebna was the secretary. Joah, the son of Asaph, kept the records.

¹⁹The field commander said to them, "Give Hezekiah this message. Tell him,

" 'Sennacherib is the great king of Assyria. He says, "Why are you putting your faith in what your king says? ²⁰You say you have a military plan. You say you have a strong army. But your words don't mean anything. Who are you depending on? Why don't you want to stay under my control? ²¹Look, I know you are depending on Egypt. Why are you doing that? Egypt is nothing but a broken papyrus stem. Try leaning on it. It will only cut your hand. Pharaoh, the king of Egypt, is just like that to everyone who depends on him. ²²But suppose you say to me, 'We are depending on the LORD our God.' Didn't Hezekiah remove your god's high places and altars? Didn't

Hezekiah say to the people of Judah and Jerusalem, 'You must worship at the altar in Jerusalem'?

23 " ' "Go ahead and make a deal with my master, the king of Assyria. I'll give you 2,000 horses. But only if you can put riders on them! 24 You are depending on Egypt for chariots and horsemen. You can't drive away even the least important officer among my master's officials. 25 Besides, do you think I've come without receiving a message from the LORD? Have I come to attack and destroy this place without a message from him? The LORD himself told me to march out against your country. He told me to destroy it." ' "

26 Then Shebna, Joah and Eliakim, the son of Hilkiah, spoke to the field commander. They said, "Please speak to us in the Aramaic language. We understand it. Don't speak to us in Hebrew. If you do, the people sitting on the city wall will be able to understand you."

27 But the commander replied, "My master sent me to say these things. Are these words only for your master and you to hear? Aren't they also for the people sitting on the wall? They are going to suffer just like you. They'll have to eat their own waste. They'll have to drink their own urine."

28 Then the commander stood up and spoke in the Hebrew language. He called out, "Pay attention to what the great king of Assyria is telling you. 29 He says, 'Don't let Hezekiah trick you. He can't save you from my power. 30 Don't let Hezekiah talk you into trusting in the LORD. Don't believe him when he says, "You can be sure that the LORD will save us. This city will not be handed over to the king of Assyria." '

31 "Don't listen to Hezekiah. The king of Assyria says, 'Make a peace treaty with me. Come over to my side. Then each one of you will eat fruit from your own vine and fig tree. Each one of you will drink water from your own well. 32 You will do that until I come back. Then I'll take you to a land just like yours. It's a land that has a lot of grain and fresh wine. It has plenty of bread and vineyards. It has olive trees and honey. So choose life! Don't choose death!'

"Don't pay any attention to Hezekiah. He's telling you a lie when he says, 'The LORD will save us.' 33 Has the god of any nation ever saved his land from the power of the king of Assyria? 34 Where are the gods of Hamath and Arpad? Where are the gods of Sepharvaim, Hena and Ivvah? Have they saved Samaria from my power? 35 Which one of all the gods of those countries has been able to save his land from me? So how can the LORD save Jerusalem from my power?"

36 But the people remained silent. They didn't say anything.

That's because King Hezekiah had commanded, "Don't answer him."

[37] Then Eliakim, the son of Hilkiah, went to Hezekiah. Eliakim was in charge of the palace. Shebna the secretary went with him. So did Joah, the son of Asaph. Joah kept the records. All of them went to Hezekiah with their clothes torn. They told him what the field commander had said.

Isaiah Prophesies That Jerusalem Will Be Saved

19 When King Hezekiah heard what the field commander had said, he tore his clothes. He put on the rough clothing people wear when they're sad. Then he went into the LORD's temple. [2] Hezekiah sent Eliakim, who was in charge of the palace, to Isaiah the prophet. Isaiah was the son of Amoz. Hezekiah also sent to Isaiah the leading priests and Shebna the secretary. All of them were wearing the same rough clothing. [3] They told Isaiah, "Hezekiah says, 'Today we're in great trouble. The LORD is warning us. He's bringing shame on us. Sometimes babies come to the moment when they should be born. But their mothers aren't strong enough to allow them to be born. Today we are like those mothers. We aren't strong enough to save ourselves. [4] Perhaps the LORD your God will hear everything the field commander has said. His master, the king of Assyria, has sent him to make fun of the living God. Maybe the LORD your God will punish him for what he has heard him say. So pray for the remaining people who are still alive here.'"

[5] King Hezekiah's officials came to Isaiah. [6] Then Isaiah said to them, "Tell your master, 'The LORD says, "Do not be afraid of what you have heard. The officers of the king of Assyria have spoken evil things against me. [7] Listen! I will send him news from his own country. It will make him want to return home. There I will have him killed by a sword."'"

[8] The field commander heard that the king of Assyria had left Lachish. So the commander pulled his troops back from Jerusalem. He went to join the king. He found out that the king was fighting against Libnah.

[9] During that time Sennacherib received a report. He was told that Tirhakah was marching out to fight against him. Tirhakah was the king of Cush. Sennacherib sent messengers again to Hezekiah with a letter. Sennacherib said, [10] "Tell Hezekiah, the king of Judah, 'Don't let the god you depend on trick you. He says, "Jerusalem will not be handed over to the king of Assyria." But don't believe him. [11] I'm sure you have heard about what the kings of Assyria have done to all the other countries. They have destroyed them completely. So do you think you will be saved? [12] The kings who ruled before me destroyed

many nations. Did the gods of those nations save them? Did the gods of Gozan, Harran or Rezeph save them? What about the gods of the people of Eden who were in Tel Assar? ¹³Where is the king of Hamath? Where is the king of Arpad? Where are the kings of Lair, Sepharvaim, Hena and Ivvah?'"

Hezekiah's Prayer

¹⁴When Hezekiah received the letter from the messengers, he read it. Then he went up to the Lord's temple. There he spread the letter out in front of the Lord. ¹⁵Hezekiah prayed to the Lord. He said, "Lord, you are the God of Israel. You sit on your throne between the cherubim. You alone are God over all the kingdoms on earth. You have made heaven and earth. ¹⁶Listen, Lord. Hear us. Open your eyes, Lord. Look at the trouble we're in. Listen to what Sennacherib is saying. You are the living God. And he dares to make fun of you!

¹⁷"Lord, it's true that the kings of Assyria have completely destroyed many nations and their lands. ¹⁸They have thrown the statues of the gods of those nations into the fire. And they have destroyed them. That's because they weren't really gods at all. They were nothing but statues made out of wood and stone. They were made by human hands. ¹⁹Lord our God, save us from the power of Sennacherib. Then all the kingdoms of the earth will know that you alone are the Lord. You alone are God."

Isaiah Prophesies That Sennacherib Will Fall From Power

²⁰Isaiah sent a message to Hezekiah. Isaiah was the son of Amoz. Isaiah said, "The Lord is the God of Israel. The Lord says, 'I have heard your prayer about Sennacherib, the king of Assyria.' ²¹Here is the message the Lord has spoken against him. The Lord says,

" 'You will not win the battle
over Zion.
Its people hate you and
make fun of you.
The people of Jerusalem lift
up their heads proudly
as you run away.
²²Who have you laughed at?
Who have you spoken evil
things against?
Who have you raised your
voice against?
Who have you looked at so
proudly?
You have done it against
me.
I am the Holy One of Israel!
²³Through your messengers
you have dared to make
fun of the Lord.
And you have said,
"I have many chariots.
With them I have gone to the
tops of the mountains.
I've climbed the highest
mountains in Lebanon.
I've cut down its tallest cedar
trees.
I've cut down the best of its
juniper trees.

I've reached its farthest
     parts.
     I've reached its finest
         forests.
24 I've dug wells in strange
     lands.
     I've drunk the water from
         them.
     I've walked through all of
         Egypt's streams.
     I've dried up every one of
         them."

25 " 'But I, the LORD, say,
     "Haven't you heard what
         I have done?
     Long ago I arranged for
         you to do all of that.
     In days of old I planned it.
     Now I have made it
         happen.
     You have turned cities with
         high walls
     into piles of stone.
26 Their people do not have any
     power left.
     They are troubled and put
         to shame.
They are like plants in the
     field.
     They are like new green
         plants.
They are like grass that grows
     on a roof.
     It dries up before it is
         completely grown.
27 " ' "But I know where you are.
     I know when you come and
         go.
     I know how very angry you
         are with me.
28 You roar against me and
     brag.
     And I have heard your
         bragging.

So I will put my hook in your
     nose.
     I will put my bit in your
         mouth.
And I will make you go
     home
     by the same way you
         came." ' "

29 The LORD said, "Hezekiah,
here is a miraculous sign for
you.

     "This year you will eat what
         grows by itself.
     In the second year you will
         eat what grows from
         that.
But in the third year you will
     plant your crops and
         gather them in.
     You will plant your
         grapevines and eat their
         fruit.
30 Those who remain from the
     kingdom of Judah will be
         like plants.
     Once more they will put
         down roots and produce
         fruit.
31 Out of Jerusalem will come
     those who remain.
     Out of Mount Zion will
         come those who
         survive.

     "The LORD's great love will
         make sure that happens.
     He rules over all.

32 "Here is a message from me
about the king of Assyria. The
LORD says,

     " 'The king of Assyria will not
         enter this city.
     He will not even shoot an
         arrow at it.

He will not come near it with
a shield.
He will not build a ramp
in order to climb over its
walls.
³³ By the same way he came he
will go home.
He will not enter this city,'
announces the Lord.
³⁴ " 'I will guard this city and
save it.
I will do it for myself. And I
will do it for my servant
David.' "

³⁵ That night the angel of the Lord went into the camp of the Assyrians. He put to death 185,000 people there. The people of Jerusalem got up the next morning and looked out at the camp. There were all the dead bodies! ³⁶ So Sennacherib, the king of Assyria, took the army tents down. Then he left. He returned to Nineveh and stayed there. ³⁷ One day Sennacherib was worshiping in the temple of his god Nisrok. His sons Adrammelek and Sharezer killed him with their swords. Then they escaped to the land of Ararat. Esarhaddon became the next king after his father Sennacherib.

Hezekiah Becomes Sick

20 In those days Hezekiah became very sick. He was about to die. Isaiah the prophet, the son of Amoz, went to him. Isaiah told Hezekiah, "The Lord says, 'Put everything in order. Make out your will. You are going to die soon. You will not get well again.' "

² Hezekiah turned his face toward the wall. He prayed to the Lord. He said, ³ "Lord, please remember how faithful I've been to you. I've lived the way you wanted me to. I've served you with all my heart. I've done what is good in your sight." And Hezekiah wept bitterly.

⁴ Isaiah was leaving the middle courtyard. Before he had left it, a message came to him from the Lord. He said, ⁵ "Go back and speak to Hezekiah. He is the ruler of my people. Tell him, 'The Lord, the God of King David, says, "I have heard your prayer. I have seen your tears. And I will heal you. On the third day from now you will go up to my temple. ⁶ I will add 15 years to your life. And I will save you and this city from the power of the king of Assyria. I will guard this city. I will do it for myself. And I will do it for my servant David." ' "

⁷ Then Isaiah said, "Press some figs together. Spread them on a piece of cloth." So that's what they did. Then they applied it to Hezekiah's boil. And he got well again.

⁸ Hezekiah had said to Isaiah, "You say the Lord will heal me. You say that I'll go up to his temple on the third day from now. What will the sign be to prove he'll really do that?"

⁹ Isaiah answered, "The Lord will do what he has promised. Here is his sign to you. Do you want the shadow the sun makes to go forward ten steps? Or do you want it to go back ten steps?"

Famous People of the Bible

Abraham	Genesis 12:1—25:10
Adam and Eve	Genesis 2:21—3:19
David	1 Samuel 16–17; 2 Samuel 1–6; 11–12
Deborah	Judges 4–5
Esau	Genesis 25:29–34; 27; Malachi 1:2–3
Esther	Esther 3–8
Gideon	Judges 6–7
Hannah	1 Samuel 1:1—2:21
Isaac	Genesis 24–27
Jacob	Genesis 27–33
Job	Job 1:1—2:13; 42:7–17
John	John 19:26–27; Acts 4:1–31
John the Baptist	Matthew 3; 14:1–12
Joseph	Genesis 37; 39–50
Joshua	Numbers 13:1—14:38; Joshua 1–6
Lazarus	John 11:1–44
Mary the mother of Jesus	Luke 1:26—2:52
Mary and Martha	Luke 10:38–42; John 11:1–5, 19–33
Mary Magdalene	John 20:1–18
Matthew	Mark 2:13–14
Miriam	Exodus 2:1–10; Numbers 12:1–15
Moses	Exodus 2–4; 14–15
Naomi	Ruth 1–4
Noah	Genesis 6:9—9:17
Paul (Saul)	Acts 9:1–19; 21–28
Peter	Matthew 14:22–33; Acts 3:1–10
Philip	Acts 8:4–7, 26–40
Ruth	Ruth 1–4
Samson	Judges 13–16
Samuel	1 Samuel 1–3; 8; 16
Sarah	Genesis 11:29—23:20
Solomon	1 Kings 2:1—3:28; 4:20–34; 10
Timothy	Acts 16:1; 17:14–15; 1 Timothy 1:1–2

David and Goliath
1 SAMUEL 17

¹⁰ "It's easy for the shadow to go forward ten steps," said Hezekiah. "So have it go back ten steps."

¹¹ Then Isaiah the prophet called out to the LORD. And the LORD made the shadow go back ten steps. It went back the ten steps it had gone down on the stairway Ahaz had made.

Messengers Come From Babylon to Hezekiah

¹² At that time Marduk-Baladan, the king of Babylon, sent Hezekiah letters and a gift. He had heard that Hezekiah had been sick. Marduk-Baladan was the son of Baladan. ¹³ Hezekiah received the messengers. He showed them everything in his storerooms. He showed them the silver and gold. He showed them the spices and the fine olive oil. He showed them where he kept his weapons. And he showed them all his treasures. In fact, he showed them everything in his palace and in his whole kingdom.

¹⁴ Then Isaiah the prophet went to King Hezekiah. He asked him, "What did those men say? Where did they come from?"

"They came from a land far away," Hezekiah said. "They came from Babylon."

¹⁵ The prophet asked, "What did they see in your palace?"

"They saw everything in my palace," Hezekiah said. "I showed them all my treasures."

¹⁶ Then Isaiah said to Hezekiah, "Listen to the LORD's message. He says, ¹⁷ 'You can be sure the time will come when everything in your palace will be carried off to Babylon. Everything the kings before you have stored up until this day will be taken away. There will not be anything left,' says the LORD. ¹⁸ 'Some of the members of your family line will be taken away. They will be your own flesh and blood. They will include the children who will be born into your family line in years to come. And they will serve the king of Babylon in his palace.' "

¹⁹ "The message the LORD has spoken through you is good," Hezekiah replied. He thought, "There will be peace and safety while I'm still living."

²⁰ The other events of the rule of Hezekiah are written down. That includes how he made the pool and the tunnel. He used them to bring water into Jerusalem. Everything he accomplished is written in the official records of the kings of Judah. ²¹ Hezekiah joined the members of his family who had already died. Hezekiah's son Manasseh became the next king after him.

Manasseh King of Judah

21 Manasseh was 12 years old when he became king. He ruled in Jerusalem for 55 years. His mother's name was Hephzibah. ² Manasseh did what was evil in the eyes of the LORD. He followed the practices of the nations. The LORD hated those practices. He had driven those nations out to make room

for the Israelites. ³Manasseh rebuilt the high places. His father Hezekiah had destroyed them. Manasseh also set up altars to the god named Baal. He made a pole used to worship the female god named Asherah. Ahab, the king of Israel, had done those same things. Manasseh even bowed down to all the stars. And he worshiped them. ⁴He built altars in the LORD's temple. The LORD had said about his temple, "I will put my Name there in Jerusalem." ⁵In the two courtyards of the LORD's temple Manasseh built altars to honor all the stars. ⁶He sacrificed his own son in the fire to another god. He practiced all kinds of evil magic. He got messages from those who had died. He talked to the spirits of the dead. He did many things that were evil in the eyes of the LORD. Manasseh made the LORD very angry.

⁷Manasseh had carved a pole used to worship the female god named Asherah. He put it in the temple. The LORD had spoken to David and his son Solomon about the temple. He had said, "My Name will be in this temple and in Jerusalem forever. Out of all the cities in the tribes of Israel I have chosen Jerusalem. ⁸I gave this land to your people who lived long ago. I will not make the Israelites wander away from it again. But they must be careful to do everything I commanded them. They must obey the whole Law that my servant Moses gave

them." ⁹But the people didn't pay any attention. Manasseh led them astray. They did more evil things than the nations the LORD had destroyed. He had destroyed them to make room for the Israelites.

¹⁰The LORD spoke through his servants the prophets. He said, ¹¹"Manasseh, the king of Judah, has committed terrible sins. I hate them. Manasseh has done more evil things than the Amorites who were in the land before him. And he has led Judah to commit sin by worshiping his statues of gods. ¹²I am the LORD, the God of Israel. I tell you, 'I am going to bring trouble on Jerusalem and Judah. It will be so horrible that the ears of everyone who hears about it will tingle. ¹³I will measure out punishment against Jerusalem, just as I did against Samaria. I used a plumb line against the royal family of Ahab. I used it to prove that they did not measure up to my standards. I will use the same plumb line against Jerusalem. I will wipe out Jerusalem, just as someone wipes a dish. I will wipe it and turn it upside down. ¹⁴I will desert those who remain among my people. I will hand them over to their enemies. All their enemies will rob them. ¹⁵That's because my people have done what is evil in my sight. They have made me very angry. They have done that from the day their own people came out of Egypt until this day.' "

¹⁶Manasseh also spilled the

blood of many people who weren't guilty of doing anything wrong. He spilled so much blood that he filled Jerusalem with it from one end of the city to the other. And he caused Judah to commit sin. So they also did what was evil in the eyes of the LORD. ¹⁷ The other events of the rule of Manasseh are written down. That includes the sin he committed. Everything he did is written in the official records of the kings of Judah. ¹⁸ Manasseh joined the members of his family who had already died. He was buried in his palace garden. It was called the garden of Uzza. Manasseh's son Amon became the next king after him.

Amon King of Judah

¹⁹ Amon was 22 years old when he became king. He ruled in Jerusalem for two years. His mother's name was Meshullemeth. She was the daughter of Haruz. She was from Jotbah. ²⁰ Amon did what was evil in the eyes of the LORD, just as his father Manasseh had done. ²¹ He lived the way his father had lived. He worshiped the statues of the gods his father had worshiped. He bowed down to them. ²² He deserted the LORD, the God of his people. He didn't obey the LORD.

²³ Amon's officials made plans against him. They murdered the king in his palace. ²⁴ Then the people of the land killed all those officials who had made plans against King Amon. Then

the people of the land made his son Josiah king in his place. ²⁵ The other events of the rule of Amon are written down. Everything he did is written in the official records of the kings of Judah. ²⁶ Amon was buried in his grave in the garden of Uzza. Amon's son Josiah became the next king after him.

Hilkiah Finds the Book of the Law

22 Josiah was eight years old when he became king. He ruled in Jerusalem for 31 years. His mother's name was Jedidah. She was the daughter of Adaiah. She was from Bozkath. ² Josiah did what was right in the eyes of the LORD. He lived the way King David had lived. He didn't turn away from it to the right or the left.

³ King Josiah sent his secretary Shaphan to the LORD's temple. It was in the 18th year of Josiah's rule. Shaphan was the son of Azaliah. Azaliah was the son of Meshullam. Josiah said, ⁴ "Go up to Hilkiah the high priest. Have him add up the money that has been brought into the LORD's temple. The men who guard the doors have collected it from the people. ⁵ Have them put all the money in the care of certain men. These men have been put in charge of the work on the LORD's temple. Have them pay the workers who repair it. ⁶ Have them pay the builders and those who work with wood. Have them pay those who lay the stones. Also have

them buy lumber and blocks of stone to repair the temple. [7] But they don't have to report how they use the money that is given to them. That's because they are completely honest."

[8] Hilkiah the high priest spoke to Shaphan the secretary. Hilkiah said, "I've found the Book of the Law in the LORD's temple." Hilkiah gave it to Shaphan, who read it. [9] Then Shaphan went to King Josiah. Shaphan told him, "Your officials have paid out the money that was in the LORD's temple. They've put it in the care of the workers and directors there." [10] Shaphan continued, "Hilkiah the priest has given me a book." Shaphan read some of it to the king.

[11] The king heard the words of the Book of the Law. When he did, he tore his royal robes. [12] He gave orders to Hilkiah the priest, Ahikam, Akbor, Shaphan the secretary and Asaiah. Ahikam was the son of Shaphan. Akbor was the son of Micaiah. And Asaiah was the king's attendant. Josiah commanded them, [13] "Go. Ask the LORD for advice. Ask him about what is written in this book that has been found. Do it for me. Also do it for the people and the whole nation of Judah. The LORD is very angry with us. That's because our people who have lived before us didn't obey the words of this book. They didn't do everything written there about us."

[14] Hilkiah the priest went to speak to Huldah the prophet. So did Ahikam, Akbor, Shaphan and Asaiah. Huldah was the wife of Shallum. Shallum was the son of Tikvah. Tikvah was the son of Harhas. Shallum took care of the sacred robes. Huldah lived in the New Quarter of Jerusalem.

[15] Huldah said to them, "The LORD is the God of Israel. He says, 'Here is what you must tell the man who sent you to me. [16] Tell him, "The LORD says, 'I am going to bring horrible trouble on this place and its people. Everything written in the book the king of Judah has read will take place. [17] That's because the people have deserted me. They have burned incense to other gods. They have made me very angry because of the statues of gods their hands have made. So my anger will burn like a fire against this place. And the fire of my anger will not be put out.'"' [18] The king of Judah sent you to ask the LORD for advice. Tell him, 'The LORD is the God of Israel. He has a message for you about the things you heard. He says, [19] "Your heart was tender. You made yourself humble in the eyes of the LORD. You heard what I spoke against this place and its people. I said they would be under a curse. I told them they would be destroyed. You tore your royal robes and wept in front of me. And I have heard you," announces the LORD. [20] "You will join the members of your family who have already died. You will be buried in peace. Your eyes will not see all

the trouble I am going to bring on this place."' "

Huldah's answer was taken back to the king.

Josiah Promises Again to Obey the Covenant

23 Then the king called together all the elders of Judah and Jerusalem. ² He went up to the LORD's temple. The people of Judah and Jerusalem went with him. So did the priests and prophets. All of them went, from the least important of them to the most important. The king had all the words of the Book of the Covenant read to them. The book had been found in the LORD's temple. ³ The king stood next to his pillar. He agreed to the terms of the covenant in front of the LORD. The king promised to serve the LORD and obey his commands, directions and rules. He promised to obey them with all his heart and with all his soul. So he agreed to the terms of the covenant written down in that book. Then all the people committed themselves to the covenant as well.

⁴ Certain things in the LORD's temple had been made to honor other gods. They were the god named Baal, the female god named Asherah and all the stars in the sky. The king ordered Hilkiah the high priest to remove those things. The king ordered the priests who were next in rank and the men who guarded the doors to help Hilkiah. Josiah took those things that had been in the LORD's temple and burned them outside Jerusalem. He burned them in the fields in the Kidron Valley. And he took the ashes to Bethel. ⁵ Josiah got rid of the priests who served other gods. The kings of Judah had appointed those priests to burn incense. They burned the incense on the high places of the towns of Judah. And they burned it on the high places around Jerusalem. They burned incense to honor Baal and the sun and moon. They burned it to honor all the stars. ⁶ Josiah removed the Asherah pole from the LORD's temple. It had been used to worship the female god named Asherah. He took it to the Kidron Valley outside Jerusalem. There he burned it. He ground it into powder. And he scattered it over the graves of the ordinary people. ⁷ He also tore down the rooms where the male temple prostitutes stayed. Those rooms were in the LORD's temple. Women had made cloth for Asherah in them.

⁸ Josiah brought all the priests from the towns of Judah and destroyed the high places. He destroyed them from Geba all the way to Beersheba. The priests had burned incense on them. Josiah broke down the gate at the entrance of the Gate of Joshua. It was on the left side of Jerusalem's city gate. Joshua was the city governor. ⁹ The priests of the high places didn't serve at the LORD's altar in Jerusalem. In spite of that, they ate with the other priests. All of them ate bread made without yeast.

[10] Josiah destroyed the high place at Topheth in the Valley of Ben Hinnom. He didn't want anyone to use the high place to sacrifice his son or daughter in the fire to the god named Molek. [11] Josiah removed the statues of horses from the entrance to the Lord's temple. The kings of Judah had set them apart to honor the sun. The statues were in the courtyard. They were near the room of an official named Nathan-Melek. Josiah burned the chariots that had been set apart to honor the sun.

[12] He pulled down the altars the kings of Judah had set up. They had put them on the palace roof near the upstairs room of Ahaz. Josiah also pulled down the altars Manasseh had built. They were in the two courtyards of the Lord's temple. Josiah removed the altars from there. He smashed them to pieces. Then he threw the broken pieces into the Kidron Valley. [13] The king also destroyed the high places that were east of Jerusalem. They were at the southern end of the Mount of Olives. They were the ones Solomon, the king of Israel, had built. He had built a high place for worshiping Ashtoreth. She was the evil female god of the people of Sidon. Solomon had also built one for worshiping Chemosh. He was the evil god of Moab. And Solomon had built one for worshiping Molek. He was the god of the people of Ammon. The Lord hated that god. [14] Josiah smashed the sacred stones.

He cut down the poles used to worship the female god named Asherah. Then he covered all those places with human bones.

[15] There was an altar at Bethel. It was at the high place made by Jeroboam, the son of Nebat. Jeroboam had caused Israel to commit sin. Even that altar and high place were destroyed by Josiah. He burned the high place. He ground it into powder. He also burned the Asherah pole. [16] Then Josiah looked around. He saw the tombs on the side of the hill. He had the bones removed from them. And he burned them on the altar to make it "unclean." That's what the Lord had said would happen. He had spoken that message through a man of God. The man had announced those things long before they took place.

[17] The king asked, "What's that stone on the grave over there?"

The people of the city said, "It marks the tomb where the man of God is buried. He came from Judah. He spoke against the altar at Bethel. He announced the very things you have done to it."

[18] "Leave it alone," Josiah said. "Don't let anyone touch his bones." So they spared his bones. They also spared the bones of the prophet who had come from the northern kingdom of Israel.

[19] Josiah did in the rest of the northern kingdom the same things he had done at Bethel. He removed all the small tem-

ples at the high places. He made them "unclean." The kings of Israel had built them in the towns of the northern kingdom. The people in those towns had made the Lord very angry. ²⁰ Josiah killed all the priests of those high places on the altars. He burned human bones on the altars. Then he went back to Jerusalem.

²¹ The king gave an order to all the people. He said, "Celebrate the Passover Feast to honor the Lord your God. Do what is written in this Book of the Covenant." ²² A Passover Feast like that one had not been held for a long time. There hadn't been any like it in the days of the judges who led Israel. And there hadn't been any like it during the whole time the kings of Israel and Judah were ruling. ²³ King Josiah celebrated the Passover Feast in Jerusalem to honor the Lord. It was in the 18th year of his rule.

²⁴ And that's not all. Josiah got rid of those who got messages from people who had died. He got rid of those who talked to the spirits of people who had died. He got rid of the statues of family gods and the statues of other gods. He got rid of everything else the Lord hates that was in Judah and Jerusalem. He did it to carry out what the law required. That law was written in the book that Hilkiah the priest had found in the Lord's temple. ²⁵ There was no king like Josiah either before him or after him. None of them turned to the

Lord as he did. He obeyed the Lord with all his heart and all his soul. He obeyed him with all his strength. He did everything the Law of Moses required.

²⁶ In spite of that, the Lord didn't turn away from his great anger against Judah. That's because of everything Manasseh had done to make him very angry. ²⁷ So the Lord said, "I will remove Judah from my land. I will do to them what I did to Israel. I will turn my back on Jerusalem. It is the city I chose. I will also turn my back on this temple. I spoke about it. I said, 'I will put my Name there.'" *(1 Kings 8:29)*

²⁸ The other events of the rule of Josiah are written down. Everything he did is written in the official records of the kings of Judah.

²⁹ Pharaoh Necho was king of Egypt. He marched up to the Euphrates River. He went there to help the king of Assyria. It happened while Josiah was king. Josiah marched out to meet Necho in battle. When Necho saw him at Megiddo, he killed him. ³⁰ Josiah's servants brought his body in a chariot from Megiddo to Jerusalem. They buried him in his own tomb. Then the people of the land went and got Jehoahaz. They anointed him as king in place of his father Josiah.

Jehoahaz King of Judah

³¹ Jehoahaz was 23 years old when he became king. He ruled in Jerusalem for three months. His mother's name was Hamutal. She was the daughter of

Jeremiah. She was from Libnah. ³²Jehoahaz did what was evil in the eyes of the LORD. He did just as the kings who had ruled before him had done. ³³Pharaoh Necho put him in chains at Riblah in the land of Hamath. That kept him from ruling in Jerusalem. Necho made the people of Judah pay him a tax of almost four tons of silver and 75 pounds of gold. ³⁴Pharaoh Necho made Eliakim king in place of his father Josiah. Necho changed Eliakim's name to Jehoiakim. But he took Jehoahaz with him to Egypt. And that's where Jehoahaz died. ³⁵Jehoiakim paid Pharaoh Necho the silver and gold he required. To get the money, Jehoiakim taxed the land. He forced the people to give him the silver and gold. He made each one pay him what he required.

Jehoiakim King of Judah

³⁶Jehoiakim was 25 years old when he became king. He ruled in Jerusalem for 11 years. His mother's name was Zebidah. She was the daughter of Pedaiah. She was from Rumah. ³⁷Jehoiakim did what was evil in the eyes of the LORD. He did just as the kings who had ruled before him had done.

24 During Jehoiakim's rule, Nebuchadnezzar marched into the land and attacked it. He was king of Babylon. He became Jehoiakim's master for three years. But then Jehoiakim decided he didn't want to remain under Nebuchadnezzar's control. ²The LORD sent robbers against Jehoiakim from Babylon, Aram, Moab and Ammon. He sent them to destroy Judah. That's what the LORD had said would happen. He had spoken that message through his servants the prophets. ³These things happened to Judah in keeping with what the LORD had commanded. He brought enemies against his people in order to remove them from his land. He removed them because of all the sins Manasseh had committed. ⁴Manasseh had spilled the blood of many people who weren't guilty of doing anything wrong. In fact, he spilled so much of their blood that he filled Jerusalem with it. So the LORD refused to forgive him.

⁵The other events of the rule of Jehoiakim are written down. Everything he did is written in the official records of the kings of Judah. ⁶Jehoiakim joined the members of his family who had already died. Jehoiakim's son Jehoiachin became the next king after him.

⁷The king of Egypt didn't march out from his own country again. That's because the king of Babylon had taken so much of his territory. It reached from the Wadi of Egypt all the way to the Euphrates River.

Jehoiachin King of Judah

⁸Jehoiachin was 18 years old when he became king. He ruled in Jerusalem for three months. His mother's name was Ne-

hushta. She was the daughter of Elnathan. She was from Jerusalem. ⁹Jehoiachin did what was evil in the eyes of the LORD. He did just as his father Jehoiakim had done.

¹⁰At that time the officers of Nebuchadnezzar, the king of Babylon, marched to Jerusalem. They surrounded it and got ready to attack it. ¹¹Nebuchadnezzar himself came up to the city. He arrived while his officers were attacking it. ¹²Jehoiachin, the king of Judah, handed himself over to Nebuchadnezzar. Jehoiachin's mother did the same thing. And so did all his attendants, nobles and officials.

The king of Babylon took Jehoiachin away as his prisoner. It was in the eighth year of Nebuchadnezzar's rule. ¹³Nebuchadnezzar removed the treasures from the LORD's temple. He also removed the treasures from the royal palace. He cut up the gold objects that Solomon, the king of Israel, had made for the temple. That's what the LORD had announced would happen. ¹⁴Nebuchadnezzar took all the people of Jerusalem to the land of Babylon as prisoners. That included all the officers and fighting men. It also included all the skilled workers. The total number of prisoners was 10,000. Only the poorest people were left in the land.

¹⁵Nebuchadnezzar took Jehoiachin to Babylon as his prisoner. He also took the king's mother from Jerusalem to Babylon. And he took Jehoiachin's wives, his officials and the most important people of the land. ¹⁶The king also forced the whole army of 7,000 soldiers to go away to the land of Babylon. Those men were strong and able to go to war. And the king forced 1,000 skilled workers to go to Babylon. ¹⁷Nebuchadnezzar made Jehoiachin's uncle Mattaniah king in his place. And Nebuchadnezzar changed Mattaniah's name to Zedekiah.

Zedekiah King of Judah

¹⁸Zedekiah was 21 years old when he became king. He ruled in Jerusalem for 11 years. His mother's name was Hamutal. She was the daughter of Jeremiah. She was from Libnah. ¹⁹Zedekiah did what was evil in the eyes of the LORD. He did just as Jehoiakim had done. ²⁰The enemies of Jerusalem and Judah attacked them because the LORD was angry. In the end the LORD threw them out of his land.

The Fall of Jerusalem

Zedekiah also refused to remain under the control of Nebuchadnezzar.

25 Nebuchadnezzar was king of Babylon. He marched out against Jerusalem. His whole army went with him. It was in the ninth year of the rule of Zedekiah. It was on the tenth day of the tenth month. Nebuchadnezzar set up camp outside the city. He brought in war machines all around it. ²It was surrounded until the 11th year of King Zedekiah's rule.

³ By the ninth day of the fourth month, there wasn't any food left in the city. So the people didn't have anything to eat. ⁴ Then the Babylonians broke through the city wall. Judah's whole army ran away at night. They went out through the gate between the two walls near the king's garden. They escaped even though the Babylonians surrounded the city. Judah's army ran toward the Arabah Valley. ⁵ But the Babylonian army chased King Zedekiah. They caught up with him in the plains near Jericho. All his soldiers were separated from him. They had scattered in every direction. ⁶ The king was captured.

He was taken to the king of Babylon at Riblah. That's where Nebuchadnezzar decided how he would be punished. ⁷ Nebuchadnezzar's men killed the sons of Zedekiah. They forced him to watch it with his own eyes. Then they poked out his eyes. They put him in bronze chains. And they took him to Babylon.

⁸ Nebuzaradan was an official of the king of Babylon. In fact, he was commander of the royal guard. He came to Jerusalem. It was in the 19th year that Nebuchadnezzar was king of Babylon. It was on the seventh day of the fifth month. ⁹ Nebuzaradan set the LORD's temple on fire. He also set fire to the royal palace and all the houses in Jerusalem.

He burned down every important building. ¹⁰ The whole Babylonian army broke down the walls around Jerusalem. That's what the commander told them to do. ¹¹ Some people still remained in the city. But Nebuzaradan the commander took them away as prisoners. He also took the rest of the people of the land. That included those who had joined the king of Babylon. ¹² But the commander left behind some of the poorest people of the land. He told them to work in the vineyards and fields.

¹³ The Babylonian army destroyed the LORD's temple. They broke the bronze pillars into pieces. They broke up the bronze stands that could be moved around. And they broke up the huge bronze bowl. Then they carried the bronze away to Babylon. ¹⁴ They also took away the pots, shovels, wick cutters and dishes. They took away all the bronze objects used for any purpose in the temple. ¹⁵ The commander of the royal guard took away the shallow cups for burning incense. He took away the sprinkling bowls. So he took away everything made out of pure gold or silver.

¹⁶ The bronze was more than anyone could weigh. It included the bronze from the two pillars, the huge bowl and the stands. Solomon had made all those things for the LORD's temple. ¹⁷ Each pillar was 27 feet high. The bronze top of one pillar was four and a half feet high. It was decorated with a set of bronze

chains and pomegranates all around it. The other pillar was just like it. It also had a set of chains.

¹⁸ The commander of the guard took some prisoners. They included Seraiah the chief priest and Zephaniah the priest who was next in rank. They also included the three men who guarded the temple doors. ¹⁹ Some people were still left in the city. The commander took as a prisoner the officer who was in charge of the fighting men. He took the five men who gave advice to the king. He also took the secretary. He was the chief officer in charge of getting the people of the land to serve in the army. And he took 60 of those people serving in the army who were still in the city. ²⁰ Nebuzaradan the commander took all of them away. He brought them to the king of Babylon at Riblah. ²¹ There the king had them put to death. Riblah was in the land of Hamath.

So the people of Judah were taken as prisoners. They were taken far away from their own land.

²² Nebuchadnezzar, the king of Babylon, had left some people behind in Judah. He appointed Gedaliah to govern them. Gedaliah was the son of Ahikam. Ahikam was the son of Shaphan. ²³ All of Judah's army officers and their men heard about what had happened. They heard that the king had appointed Gedaliah as governor. So they came to Gedaliah at Mizpah. Ishmael,

the son of Nethaniah, came. So did Johanan, the son of Kareah. Seraiah, the son of Tanhumeth, also came. And so did Jaazaniah, the son of the Maakathite. All their men came too. Seraiah was from Netophah. ²⁴ Gedaliah promised to help them and their men. He spoke in a kind way to them. He said, "Don't be afraid of the Babylonian officials. Make your homes in the land of Judah. Serve the king of Babylon. Then things will go well with you."

²⁵ But in the seventh month Ishmael, the son of Nethaniah, came with ten men. He killed Gedaliah. He also killed the people of Judah and the Babylonians who were with Gedaliah at Mizpah. Nethaniah was the son of Elishama. Ishmael was a member of the royal family. ²⁶ After he had killed Gedaliah, all the people ran away to Egypt. Everyone from the least important of them to the most important ran away. The army officers went with them. All of them went to Egypt because they were afraid of the Babylonians.

Jehoiachin Is Set Free

²⁷ Awel-Marduk set Jehoiachin, the king of Judah, free from prison. It was in the 37th year after Jehoiachin had been taken away to Babylon. It was also the year Awel-Marduk became king of Babylon. It was on the 27th day of the 12th month. ²⁸ Awel-Marduk spoke kindly to Jehoiachin. He gave him a place

of honor. Other kings were with Jehoiachin in Babylon. But his place was more important than theirs. ^{29} So Jehoiachin put his prison clothes away. For the rest of Jehoiachin's life the king provided what he needed. ^{30} The king did that for Jehoiachin day by day as long as he lived.

1 Chronicles

Introduction:

The book of 1 Chronicles tells about King David. It starts with lists of many different families within God's special people, including David's family. Then it tells about David's life.

First and 2 Chronicles used to be one book. It was written after kings from other countries took Judah and Israel captive. After this, some of the people were allowed to go home. This book reminded them that they were still God's people.

Outline of contents:

A List of Names From Adam to Abraham

A List of Names From Adam to the Sons of Noah

1 Adam, Seth, Enosh, ² Kenan, Mahalalel, Jared, ³ Enoch, Methuselah, Lamech, Noah.

⁴ The sons of Noah were Shem, Ham and Japheth.

The Sons of Japheth

⁵ The sons of Japheth were Gomer, Magog, Madai, Javan, Tubal, Meshek and Tiras.
⁶ The sons of Gomer were Ashkenaz, Riphath and Togarmah.
⁷ The sons of Javan were Elishah, Tarshish, the Kittites and the Rodanites.

The Sons of Ham

⁸ The sons of Ham were Cush, Egypt, Put and Canaan.

⁹ The sons of Cush were Seba, Havilah, Sabta, Raamah and Sabteka.
The sons of Raamah were Sheba and Dedan.
¹⁰ Cush was the father of Nimrod. Nimrod became a mighty hero on the earth.
¹¹ Egypt was the father of the Ludites, Anamites, Lehabites and Naphtuhites. ¹² He was also the father of the Pathrusites, Kasluhites and Caphtorites. The Philistines came from the family line of the Kasluhites.
¹³ Canaan was the father of Sidon. Sidon was his oldest son.
Canaan was also the father of the Hittites, ¹⁴ Jebusites, Amorites and Girgashites. ¹⁵ And he was the father of the Hivites, Arkites, Sinites,

¹⁶ Arvadites, Zemarites and Hamathites.

The Sons of Shem

¹⁷ The sons of Shem were
Elam, Ashur, Arphaxad, Lud and Aram.
The sons of Aram were
Uz, Hul, Gether and Meshek.
¹⁸ Arphaxad was the father of Shelah.
Shelah was the father of Eber.
¹⁹ Eber was the father of two sons.
One was named Peleg. That's because the earth was divided up in his time. His brother was named Joktan.
²⁰ Joktan was the father of Almodad, Sheleph, Hazarmaveth and Jerah.
²¹ He was also the father of Hadoram, Uzal, Diklah, ²² Obal, Abimael, Sheba, ²³ Ophir, Havilah and Jobab. All of them were sons of Joktan.

²⁴ Shem, Arphaxad, Shelah,
²⁵ Eber, Peleg, Reu,
²⁶ Serug, Nahor, Terah,
²⁷ Abram. Abram was also called Abraham.

The Family of Abraham

²⁸ The sons of Abraham were Isaac and Ishmael.

The Family Line of Hagar

²⁹ Here are the members of the family line of Hagar.
Nebaioth was Ishmael's oldest son. Then came Kedar, Adbeel, Mibsam, ³⁰ Mishma, Dumah, Massa, Hadad, Tema, ³¹ Jetur, Naphish and Kedemah.
All of them were Ishmael's sons.

The Family Line of Keturah

³² Here are the sons born to Abraham's concubine Keturah.
They were Zimran, Jokshan, Medan, Midian, Ishbak and Shuah.
The sons of Jokshan were Sheba and Dedan.
³³ The sons of Midian were Ephah, Epher, Hanok, Abida and Eldaah.
All of them were from the family line of Keturah.

The Family Line of Sarah

³⁴ Abraham was the father of Isaac.
The sons of Isaac were Esau and Israel.

The Sons of Esau

³⁵ The sons of Esau were Eliphaz, Reuel, Jeush, Jalam and Korah.
³⁶ The sons of Eliphaz were Teman, Omar, Zepho, Gatam and Kenaz.
Timna had Amalek by Eliphaz.
³⁷ The sons of Reuel were Nahath, Zerah, Shammah and Mizzah.

The People of Seir in Edom

³⁸ The sons of Seir were Lotan, Shobal, Zibeon,

Anah, Dishon, Ezer and Dishan.

³⁹ The sons of Lotan were Hori and Homam. Timna was Lotan's sister.

⁴⁰ The sons of Shobal were Alvan, Manahath, Ebal, Shepho and Onam.

The sons of Zibeon were Aiah and Anah.

⁴¹ The son of Anah was Dishon.

The sons of Dishon were Hemdan, Eshban, Ithran and Keran.

⁴² The sons of Ezer were Bilhan, Zaavan and Akan.

The sons of Dishan were Uz and Aran.

The Rulers of Edom

⁴³ Before Israel had a king, there were kings who ruled in Edom.

Bela was the son of Beor. Bela's city was called Dinhabah.

⁴⁴ When Bela died, Jobab became the next king. Jobab was the son of Zerah from Bozrah.

⁴⁵ When Jobab died, Husham became the next king. Husham was from the land of the people of Teman.

⁴⁶ When Husham died, Hadad became the next king. Hadad was the son of Bedad. Hadad had won the battle over Midian in the country of Moab. Hadad's city was called Avith.

⁴⁷ When Hadad died, Samlah became the next king. Samlah was from Masrekah.

⁴⁸ When Samlah died, Shaul became the next king. Shaul was from the town of Rehoboth. It was by a river.

⁴⁹ When Shaul died, Baal-Hanan became the next king. Baal-Hanan was the son of Akbor.

⁵⁰ When Baal-Hanan died, Hadad became the next king. Hadad's city was called Pau. His wife's name was Mehetabel. She was the daughter of Matred. Matred was the daughter of Me-Zahab.

⁵¹ Hadad also died.

The chiefs of Edom were Timna, Alvah, Jetheth, ⁵² Oholibamah, Elah, Pinon, ⁵³ Kenaz, Teman, Mibzar, ⁵⁴ Magdiel and Iram.

They were the chiefs of Edom.

The Sons of Israel

2 Here are the names of the sons of Israel. Reuben, Simeon, Levi, Judah, Issachar, Zebulun, ² Dan, Joseph, Benjamin, Naphtali, Gad, Asher.

The Family of Judah

The Family Line From Judah's Sons to Hezron's Sons

³ The sons of Judah were Er, Onan and Shelah. A woman from Canaan had these three sons by

him. She was the daughter of Shua.

Er was Judah's oldest son. He was evil in the LORD's sight. So the LORD put him to death.

⁴Tamar was Judah's daughter-in-law. She had Perez and Zerah by him. The total number of Judah's sons was five.

⁵The sons of Perez were Hezron and Hamul.

⁶The sons of Zerah were Zimri, Ethan, Heman, Kalkol and Darda. The total number of Zerah's sons was five.

⁷The son of Karmi was Achar. He brought trouble on Israel. Some things that had been set apart to the LORD in a special way to be destroyed. He took some of those things. When he did that, he disobeyed the LORD's command.

⁸The son of Ethan was Azariah.

⁹Hezron was the father of Jerahmeel, Ram and Caleb.

The Family Line of Ram

¹⁰Ram was the father of Amminadab.

Amminadab was the father of Nahshon. Nahshon was the leader of the people of Judah.

¹¹Nahshon was the father of Salmon.

Salmon was the father of Boaz.

¹²Boaz was the father of Obed.

And Obed was the father of Jesse.

¹³Jesse's first son was Eliab. His second son was Abinadab.

The third was Shimea.

¹⁴The fourth was Nethanel.

The fifth was Raddai.

¹⁵The sixth was Ozem.

And the seventh was David.

¹⁶Their sisters were Zeruiah and Abigail.

Zeruiah's three sons were Abishai, Joab and Asahel.

¹⁷Abigail was the mother of Amasa. Amasa's father was Jether. Jether belonged to the family line of Ishmael.

The Family Line of Caleb

¹⁸Caleb was the son of Hezron. Caleb's wife Azubah had children by him. Jerioth also had children by him. Azubah's sons were Jesher, Shobab and Ardon.

¹⁹When Azubah died, Caleb married Ephrath. She had Hur by him.

²⁰Hur was the father of Uri. And Uri was the father of Bezalel.

²¹When he was 60 years old, Hezron married the daughter of Makir. Makir was the father of Gilead. Hezron slept with his

wife, and she had Segub by him.

²² Segub was the father of Jair. Jair controlled 23 towns in Gilead.

²³ But Geshur and Aram captured Havvoth Jair. They also captured Kenath and the settlements around it. The total number of towns captured was 60.

Hezron, Segub and Jair belonged to the family line of Makir. Makir was the father of Gilead.

²⁴ Hezron died in Caleb Ephrathah. Abijah was Hezron's wife. She had Ashhur by him. Ashhur was born after Hezron died. Ashhur was the father of Tekoa.

The Family Line of Jerahmeel

²⁵ Here are the sons of Jerahmeel. He was the oldest son of Hezron.

Ram was Jerahmeel's oldest son. Then came Bunah, Oren, Ozem and Ahijah. ²⁶ Jerahmeel had another wife. Her name was Atarah. She was the mother of Onam.

²⁷ Here are the sons of Ram. He was the oldest son of Jerahmeel. The sons of Ram were Maaz, Jamin and Eker.

²⁸ The sons of Onam were Shammai and Jada.

The sons of Shammai were Nadab and Abishur. ²⁹ Abishur's wife was named Abihail. She had Ahban and Molid by him.

³⁰ The sons of Nadab were Seled and Appaim. Seled died without having any children.

³¹ The son of Appaim was Ishi. Ishi was the father of Sheshan. Sheshan was the father of Ahlai.

³² The sons of Jada were Jether and Jonathan. Jada was Shammai's brother. Jether died without having any children.

³³ The sons of Jonathan were Peleth and Zaza.

They belonged to the family line of Jerahmeel.

³⁴ Sheshan didn't have any sons. All he had was daughters.

He had a servant from Egypt named Jarha. ³⁵ Sheshan gave his daughter to be married to his servant Jarha. She had Attai by Jarha.

³⁶ Attai was the father of Nathan.

Nathan was the father of Zabad.

³⁷ Zabad was the father of Ephlal.

Ephlal was the father of Obed.

³⁸ Obed was the father of Jehu. Jehu was the father of Azariah.

³⁹ Azariah was the father of Helez.

Helez was the father of Eleasah.

⁴⁰ Eleasah was the father of Sismai.

Sismai was the father of Shallum.

⁴¹ Shallum was the father of Jekamiah.

And Jekamiah was the father of Elishama.

The Family Groups of Caleb

⁴² Caleb was the brother of Jerahmeel.

Caleb's oldest son was Mesha. Mesha was the father of Ziph.

Caleb had another son named Mareshah. Mareshah was the father of Hebron.

⁴³ The sons of Hebron were Korah, Tappuah, Rekem and Shema.

⁴⁴ Shema was the father of Raham.

Raham was the father of Jorkeam.

Rekem was the father of Shammai.

⁴⁵ The son of Shammai was Maon.

Maon was the father of Beth Zur.

⁴⁶ Caleb had a concubine named Ephah.

She was the mother of Haran, Moza and Gazez. Haran was the father of Gazez.

⁴⁷ The sons of Jahdai were Regem, Jotham, Geshan, Pelet, Ephah and Shaaph.

⁴⁸ Caleb had a concubine named Maakah.

She was the mother of Sheber and Tirhanah.

⁴⁹ She was also the mother of Shaaph and Sheva. Shaaph was the father of Madmannah. Sheva was the father of Makbenah and Gibea.

Caleb's daughter was Aksah.

⁵⁰ All of them belonged to the family line of Caleb.

Hur was the oldest son of Ephrathah.

Hur was the brother of Shobal. Shobal was the father of Kiriath Jearim.

⁵¹ Hur was the father of Salma. Salma was the father of Bethlehem. Hur was also the father of Hareph. Hareph was the father of Beth Gader.

⁵² Here is the family line of Shobal, the father of Kiriath Jearim. It included Haroeh and half of the people of Manahath. ⁵³ It also included the family groups of Kiriath Jearim. They were the Ithrites, Puthites, Shumathites and Mishraites. The people of Zorah and Eshtaol belonged to these family groups.

⁵⁴ Here is the family line of Salma. It included Bethlehem, the people of Netophah, Atroth Beth Joab, half of the people of Manahath, and the Zorites. ⁵⁵ It also included the family groups of secretaries who lived at Jabez. They were the Tirathites, Shimeathites and Sucathites. They

were the Kenites who belonged to the family line of Hammath. Hammath was the father of the family line of Rekab.

The Sons of David

3 Here are the sons of David who were born to him in Hebron.

His first son was Amnon. Amnon's mother was Ahinoam from Jezreel. The second son was Daniel. His mother was Abigail from Carmel. ²The third son was Absalom. His mother was Maakah. She was the daughter of Talmai, the king of Geshur. The fourth son was Adonijah. His mother was Haggith. ³The fifth son was Shephatiah. His mother was Abital. The sixth son was Ithream. David's wife Eglah had Ithream by him.

⁴These six sons were born to David in Hebron. He ruled there for seven and a half years.

After that, he ruled in Jerusalem for 33 years. ⁵Children were born to him there. They included Shammua, Shobab, Nathan and Solomon. The mother of these four sons was Bathsheba. She was the daughter of Ammiel.

⁶David's children also included Ibhar, Elishua, Eliphelet, ⁷Nogah, Nepheg, Japhia, ⁸Elishama, Eliada and Eliphelet. There were nine of them.

⁹David was the father of all these sons. His concubines also had sons by him. David's sons had a sister named Tamar.

The Kings of Judah

¹⁰Solomon's son was Rehoboam. Abijah was the son of Rehoboam. Asa was the son of Abijah. Jehoshaphat was the son of Asa. ¹¹Jehoram was the son of Jehoshaphat. Ahaziah was the son of Jehoram. Joash was the son of Ahaziah. ¹²Amaziah was the son of Joash. Azariah was the son of Amaziah. Jotham was the son of Azariah. ¹³Ahaz was the son of Jotham. Hezekiah was the son of Ahaz. Manasseh was the son of Hezekiah. ¹⁴Amon was the son of Manasseh. Josiah was the son of Amon. ¹⁵Josiah's first son was Johanan. Jehoiakim was his second son.

Zedekiah was the third son.

Shallum was the fourth son.
¹⁶The next king after Jehoiakim was his son Jehoiachin.

After that, Josiah's son Zedekiah became king.

The Royal Family Line After Jehoiachin

¹⁷Here are the members of the family line of Jehoiachin. He was taken as a prisoner to Babylon.

His sons were Shealtiel, ¹⁸Malkiram, Pedaiah, Shenazzar, Jekamiah, Hoshama and Nedabiah.
¹⁹The sons of Pedaiah were Zerubbabel and Shimei.

The sons of Zerubbabel were Meshullam and Hananiah. Shelomith was their sister. ²⁰There were also five other sons. They were Hashubah, Ohel, Berekiah, Hasadiah and Jushab-Hesed.
²¹The family line of Hananiah included Pelatiah and Jeshaiah. It also included the sons of Rephaiah, Arnan, Obadiah and Shekaniah.
²²The family line of Shekaniah included Shemaiah and his sons. They were Hattush, Igal, Bariah, Neariah and Shaphat. The total number of men was six.
²³The sons of Neariah were Elioenai, Hizkiah and Azrikam. The total number of sons was three.
²⁴The sons of Elioenai were Hodaviah, Eliashib, Pelaiah, Akkub, Johanan, Delaiah and Anani. The total number of sons was seven.

Other Family Groups of Judah

4 The family line of Judah included

Perez, Hezron, Karmi, Hur and Shobal.
²Reaiah was the son of Shobal and the father of Jahath. Jahath was the father of Ahumai and Lahad. These were the family groups of the people of Zorah.
³The sons of Etam were Jezreel, Ishma and Idbash. Their sister was named Hazzelelponi.
⁴Penuel was the father of Gedor. Ezer was the father of Hushah.

These people belonged to the family line of Hur. He was the oldest son of Ephrathah and the father of Bethlehem.

⁵Ashhur was the father of Tekoa. Ashhur had two wives. Their names were Helah and Naarah.
⁶Naarah had Ahuzzam, Hepher, Temeni and Haahashtari by Ashhur. They belonged to the family line of Naarah.
⁷The sons of Helah were Zereth, Zohar, Ethnan ⁸and Koz. Koz was the father of Anub and Haz-

zobebah. He was also the father of the family groups of Aharhel. Aharhel was the son of Harum.

⁹ Jabez was more respected than his brothers. His mother had named him Jabez. She had said, "I was in a lot of pain when he was born." ¹⁰ Jabez cried out to the God of Israel. He said, "I wish you would bless me. I wish you would give me more territory. Let your power protect me. Keep me from harm. Then I won't have any pain." God gave him what he asked for.

¹¹ Kelub was the brother of Shuhah and the father of Mehir. Mehir was the father of Eshton. ¹² Eshton was the father of Beth Rapha, Paseah and Tehinnah. Tehinnah was the father of Ir Nahash. These were the men of Rekah.

¹³ The sons of Kenaz were Othniel and Seraiah.

The sons of Othniel were Hathath and Meonothai. ¹⁴ Meonothai was the father of Ophrah.

Seraiah was the father of Joab. Joab was the father of Ge Harashim.

Ge Harashim was called by that name because all its people were skilled workers.

¹⁵ The sons of Caleb were Iru, Elah and Naam. Caleb was the son of Jephunneh.

The son of Elah was Kenaz.

¹⁶ The sons of Jehallelel were Ziph, Ziphah, Tiria and Asarel.

¹⁷ The sons of Ezrah were Jether, Mered, Epher and Jalon.

One of Mered's wives had Miriam, Shammai and Ishbah by him. Ishbah was the father of Eshtemoa. ¹⁸ These were the children of Pharaoh's daughter Bithiah. Mered had married her.

His wife from the tribe of Judah had Jered, Heber and Jekuthiel by him. Jered was the father of Gedor. Heber was the father of Soko. Jekuthiel was the father of Zanoah.

¹⁹ Hodiah's wife was the sister of Naham. Her sons were the father of Keilah the Garmite and Eshtemoa the Maakathite.

²⁰ The sons of Shimon were Amnon, Rinnah, Ben-Hanan and Tilon.

The family line of Ishi included Zoheth and Ben-Zoheth.

²¹ Shelah was the son of Judah. The sons of Shelah were Er and Laadah. Er was the father of Lekah. Laadah was the father of Mareshah. He was also the father of the family groups of the linen workers who lived in Beth Ashbea. ²² Other sons of Shelah were Jokim, Joash, Saraph and the men

of Kozeba. Moab and Jashubi Lehem were ruled by sons of Shelah. The records of all these matters are very old.

²³ Some of Shelah's sons were potters who lived in Netaim and Gederah. They stayed there and worked for the king.

The Family Line of Simeon

²⁴ The family line of Simeon included
Nemuel, Jamin, Jarib, Zerah and Shaul. ²⁵ Shallum was Shaul's son. Mibsam was Shallum's son. Mishma was Mibsam's son.

²⁶ The family line of Mishma included Hammuel. Hammuel was Mishma's son. Zakkur was Hammuel's son. Shimei was Zakkur's son.

²⁷ Shimei had 16 sons and six daughters. But his brothers didn't have many children. So their whole family group didn't have as many people as Judah had. ²⁸ Shimei's family group lived in Beersheba, Moladah, Hazar Shual, ²⁹ Bilhah, Ezem, Tolad, ³⁰ Bethuel, Hormah, Ziklag, ³¹ Beth Markaboth, Hazar Susim, Beth Biri and Shaaraim. These were their towns until David became king. ³² Five of the villages around these towns were Etam, Ain, Rimmon, Token and Ashan. ³³ The territory of all the villages around these towns reached all the way to Baalath. These were their settlements.

The tribe of Simeon kept its own family history.

³⁴ Simeon's family line included Meshobab, Jamlech and Joshah. Joshah was the son of Amaziah. ³⁵ Simeon's family line also included Joel and Jehu. Jehu was the son of Joshibiah. Joshibiah was the son of Seraiah. Seraiah was the son of Asiel. ³⁶ And the family line included Elioenai, Jaakobah, Jeshohaiah, Asaiah, Adiel, Jesimiel, Benaiah ³⁷ and Ziza. Ziza was the son of Shiphi. Shiphi was the son of Allon. Allon was the son of Jedaiah. Jedaiah was the son of Shimri. And Shimri was the son of Shemaiah.

³⁸ The men whose names are listed above were leaders of their family groups.

Their families greatly increased their numbers. ³⁹ They spread out all the way to the edge of Gedor east of the valley. They looked for grasslands for their flocks. ⁴⁰ They found grasslands that were rich and good. The land had plenty of room. It was peaceful and quiet. Some of the people of Ham had lived there before.

⁴¹ The men whose names are listed lived at the time when Hezekiah was king of Judah. They came and attacked the Hamites in their homes. They also attacked the Meunites

who were there. And they completely destroyed them. What happened to them is clear even to this day. The men of Simeon made their homes where the Meunites had lived. That's because in that place there were enough grasslands for their flocks. ⁴²Five hundred of these men came into the hill country of Seir and attacked it. They were led by Pelatiah, Neariah, Rephaiah and Uzziel. These four men were the sons of Ishi. ⁴³They killed the rest of the Amalekites who had escaped. And they still live there to this day.

The Family Line of Reuben

5 Reuben was the oldest son of Israel.

But he slept with his father's concubine. By doing that, he made his father's bed "unclean." That's why his rights as the oldest son were given to the sons of Joseph, the son of Israel. So Reuben isn't listed in the family history as the one who had the rights of the oldest son. ²Judah also did not have the rights of the oldest son. Judah didn't have them even though he was the leader among his brothers. And a ruler came from his family line. But the rights of the oldest son belonged to Joseph.

³Reuben was the oldest son of Israel. Reuben's sons were

Hanok, Pallu, Hezron and Karmi.

⁴The family line of Joel includes

his son Shemaiah. Gog was the son of Shemaiah. Shimei was the son of Gog. ⁵Micah was the son of Shimei.

Reaiah was the son of Micah. Baal was the son of Reaiah.

⁶And Beerah was the son of Baal. Beerah was a leader of the people of Reuben. Tiglath-Pileser took Beerah as a prisoner to another country. Tiglath-Pileser was the king of Assyria.

⁷Here are the relatives of the family groups of Reuben. They are listed in their family history.

They include Chief Jeiel, Zechariah ⁸and Bela. Bela was the son of Azaz. Azaz was the son of Shema. Shema was the son of Joel.

All of them made their homes in the area from Aroer to Nebo and Baal Meon. ⁹To the east they made their homes in the land up to the edge of the desert. That desert reaches all the way to the Euphrates River. They made their homes there because their livestock had increased in Gilead.

¹⁰While Saul was king, the people of Reuben went to war against the Hagrites. They won the battle over them. Then they lived in the houses of the Hagrites. The people of Reuben lived in the entire area east of Gilead.

The Family Line of Gad

¹¹ The people of Gad lived next to the people of Reuben in Bashan. They spread out all the way to Salekah.

¹² Joel was their chief. Shapham was next. Then came Janai and Shaphat in Bashan.

¹³ Here are their relatives family by family. They included Michael, Meshullam, Sheba, Jorai, Jakan, Zia and Eber. The total number of them was seven.

¹⁴ These were the sons of Abihail. Abihail was the son of Huri. Huri was the son of Jaroah. Jaroah was the son of Gilead. Gilead was the son of Michael. Michael was the son of Jeshishai. Jeshishai was the son of Jahdo. And Jahdo was the son of Buz.

¹⁵ Ahi was the leader of some of the families of Gad. Ahi was the son of Abdiel. Abdiel was the son of Guni.

¹⁶ The people of Gad lived in the land of Gilead. They lived in the villages of Bashan. They also lived on all the grasslands of Sharon as far as they reached.

¹⁷ All these names were written down in the family history. They were written during the time when Jotham was king of Judah and Jeroboam was king of Israel.

¹⁸ The tribes of Reuben, Gad and half the tribe of Manasseh had 44,760 men able to serve in the army. Each one was able to handle a shield and sword. Each was also able to use a bow. Each was trained for battle. ¹⁹ They went to war against the Hagrites, Jetur, Naphish and Nodab. ²⁰ God helped his people fight against the Hagrites and all who were helping them. He handed over all those enemies to his people. That's because they cried out to him during the battle. He answered their prayers, because they trusted in him. ²¹ They captured the livestock of the Hagrites. They captured 50,000 camels, 250,000 sheep and 2,000 donkeys. They also took 100,000 people as prisoners. ²² Many others were killed, because God won the battle over them. His people lived in the land until they themselves were taken as prisoners to other countries.

The Family Line of Half of the Tribe of Manasseh

²³ The people in half of the tribe of Manasseh became a very large group. They made their homes in the land from Bashan to Baal Hermon. Baal Hermon is also called Senir. Another name for it is Mount Hermon.

²⁴ Here are the leaders of their families. They included Epher, Ishi, Eliel, Azriel, Jeremiah, Hodaviah and Jahdiel. They were brave fighting men. They were also famous and were leaders of their families. ²⁵ But they weren't faithful to

the God of their people. They joined themselves to the gods of the nations of the land and worshiped them. God had destroyed those nations to make room for his people. ²⁶So the God of Israel stirred up the spirit of Pul. He was king of Assyria. He was also called Tiglath-Pileser. He took the tribes of Reuben and Gad and half of the tribe of Manasseh to other countries as his prisoners. He took them to Halah, Habor, Hara and the river of Gozan. And that's where they still are to this day.

The Family Line of Levi

6 The sons of Levi were Gershon, Kohath and Merari.
²The sons of Kohath were Amram, Izhar, Hebron and Uzziel.
³Aaron, Moses and Miriam were born into the family line of Amram.
The sons of Aaron were Nadab, Abihu, Eleazar and Ithamar.

⁴Eleazar was the father of Phinehas.
Phinehas was the father of Abishua.
⁵Abishua was the father of Bukki.
Bukki was the father of Uzzi.
⁶Uzzi was the father of Zerahiah.
Zerahiah was the father of Meraioth.
⁷Meraioth was the father of Amariah.

Amariah was the father of Ahitub.
⁸Ahitub was the father of Zadok.
Zadok was the father of Ahimaaz.
⁹Ahimaaz was the father of Azariah.
Azariah was the father of Johanan.
¹⁰Johanan was the father of Azariah. Azariah served as priest in the temple Solomon built in Jerusalem.
¹¹Azariah was the father of Amariah.
Amariah was the father of Ahitub.
¹²Ahitub was the father of Zadok.
Zadok was the father of Shallum.
¹³Shallum was the father of Hilkiah.
Hilkiah was the father of Azariah.
¹⁴Azariah was the father of Seraiah.
And Seraiah was the father of Jozadak.
¹⁵Jozadak was taken away from his own land. The LORD took the people of Judah and Jerusalem to the land of Babylon. He used Nebuchadnezzar to take them there as prisoners.

¹⁶The sons of Levi were Gershon, Kohath and Merari.
¹⁷The names of the sons of Gershon were Libni and Shimei.
¹⁸The sons of Kohath were

Amram, Izhar, Hebron and Uzziel.

¹⁹ The sons of Merari were Mahli and Mushi.

Here are the members of the family groups of the Levites. They are listed under the names of their fathers.

²⁰ Gershon was the father of Libni.
Jahath was Libni's son.
Zimmah was Jahath's son.

²¹ Joah was Zimmah's son.
Iddo was Joah's son.
Zerah was Iddo's son.
And Jeatherai was Zerah's son.

²² The family line of Kohath included his son Amminadab.
Korah was Amminadab's son.
Assir was Korah's son.

²³ Elkanah was Assir's son.
Ebiasaph was Elkanah's son.
Assir was Ebiasaph's son.

²⁴ Tahath was Assir's son.
Uriel was Tahath's son.
Uzziah was Uriel's son.
And Shaul was Uzziah's son.

²⁵ The family line of Elkanah included his son Amasai.
Amasai was the father of Ahimoth.

²⁶ Elkanah was Ahimoth's son.
Zophai was Elkanah's son.
Nahath was Zophai's son.

²⁷ Eliab was Nahath's son.
Jeroham was Eliab's son.

Elkanah was Jeroham's son.
And Samuel was Elkanah's son.

²⁸ The sons of Samuel were his first son Joel
and his second son Abijah.

²⁹ The family line of Merari included his son Mahli.
Libni was Mahli's son.
Shimei was Libni's son.
Uzzah was Shimei's son.

³⁰ Shimea was Uzzah's son.
Haggiah was Shimea's son.
And Asaiah was Haggiah's son.

The Levites Who Were in Charge of the Music

³¹ Here are the Levites David put in charge of the music in the house of the LORD. He did it after the ark was placed there. ³² The men used their music to serve in front of the holy tent, the tent of meeting. They served there until Solomon built the temple of the LORD in Jerusalem. They did their work according to the rules they had been given.

³³ Here are the men who served. The list also includes their sons.

The family line of Kohath included
Heman. He led the music.
He was the son of Joel.
Joel was the son of Samuel.

³⁴ Samuel was the son of Elkanah.

Elkanah was the son of Jeroham.

Jeroham was the son of Eliel.

Eliel was the son of Toah. [35] Toah was the son of Zuph.

Zuph was the son of Elkanah.

Elkanah was the son of Mahath.

Mahath was the son of Amasai. [36] Amasai was the son of Elkanah.

Elkanah was the son of Joel.

Joel was the son of Azariah.

Azariah was the son of Zephaniah. [37] Zephaniah was the son of Tahath.

Tahath was the son of Assir.

Assir was the son of Ebiasaph.

Ebiasaph was the son of Korah. [38] Korah was the son of Izhar.

Izhar was the son of Kohath.

Kohath was the son of Levi.

And Levi was the son of Israel. [39] Heman had a relative named Asaph. Asaph served as Heman's helper at his right side.

Asaph was the son of Berekiah.

Berekiah was the son of Shimea.

[40] Shimea was the son of Michael.

Michael was the son of Baaseiah.

Baaseiah was the son of Malkijah. [41] Malkijah was the son of Ethni.

Ethni was the son of Zerah.

Zerah was the son of Adaiah. [42] Adaiah was the son of Ethan.

Ethan was the son of Zimmah.

Zimmah was the son of Shimei. [43] Shimei was the son of Jahath.

Jahath was the son of Gershon.

And Gershon was the son of Levi.

[44] Here are the Levites in the family line of Merari who served as Heman's helpers at his left side. They were relatives of the Kohathites.

Ethan was the son of Kishi.

Kishi was the son of Abdi.

Abdi was the son of Malluk. [45] Malluk was the son of Hashabiah.

Hashabiah was the son of Amaziah.

Amaziah was the son of Hilkiah. [46] Hilkiah was the son of Amzi.

Amzi was the son of Bani.

Bani was the son of Shemer.

⁴⁷Shemer was the son of Mahli.

Mahli was the son of Mushi.

Mushi was the son of Merari.

And Merari was the son of Levi.

⁴⁸The rest of the Levites were appointed to do all the other work at the holy tent. It was the house of God. ⁴⁹Aaron and his sons after him brought the offerings. They sacrificed them on the altar of burnt offering. They also burned incense on the altar of incense. That was part of what they did in the Most Holy Room. That's how they paid for the sin of Israel. They did everything just as Moses, the servant of God, had commanded.

⁵⁰Here are the members of the family line of Aaron.

Eleazar was Aaron's son.

Phinehas was Eleazar's son.

Abishua was Phinehas's son.

⁵¹Bukki was Abishua's son.

Uzzi was Bukki's son.

Zerahiah was Uzzi's son.

⁵²Meraioth was Zerahiah's son.

Amariah was Meraioth's son.

Ahitub was Amariah's son.

⁵³Zadok was Ahitub's son.

And Ahimaaz was Zadok's son.

⁵⁴Here were the places where they made their homes.

These places were given to them as their territory. Some were given to the children of Aaron who were from the family group of Kohath. They were given out by casting lots. The first lot was for Kohath. ⁵⁵In Judah the Kohathites were given Hebron. They also received the grasslands around Hebron. ⁵⁶But the fields and villages around the city were given to Caleb, the son of Jephunneh. ⁵⁷So the people in the family line of Aaron received Hebron. It was a city where people could go for safety. Aaron's family line received Libnah, Jattir, Eshtemoa, ⁵⁸Hilen and Debir. ⁵⁹They also received Ashan, Juttah and Beth Shemesh. They were given all these towns together with their grasslands. ⁶⁰From the tribe of Benjamin they received Gibeon, Geba, Alemeth and Anathoth. They received these towns together with their grasslands.

All these towns were handed out to the family groups of Kohath. The total number of towns was 13.

⁶¹The rest of the members of the family line of Kohath were given ten towns. The towns were from the family groups of half of the tribe of Manasseh.

⁶²The members of the family line of Gershon were given 13 towns. They received them family group by family group. Most of the towns were from the tribes of Issachar, Asher and Naphtali. The rest were from the other half of the tribe of Manasseh. It's in Bashan.

⁶³The members of the family line of Merari were given 12 towns. They received them family group by family group. The towns were from the tribes of Reuben, Gad and Zebulun.

⁶⁴So the Israelites gave the Levites all these towns and their grasslands.

⁶⁵They gave other towns to them from the tribes of Judah, Simeon and Benjamin.

⁶⁶Some of the family groups of Kohath were given towns from the tribe of Ephraim as their territory.

⁶⁷In the hill country of Ephraim they received Shechem. Shechem was a city where people could go for safety. The Kohathites also received Gezer, ⁶⁸Jokmeam, Beth Horon, ⁶⁹Aijalon and Gath Rimmon. They were given all these towns together with their grasslands.

⁷⁰From half of the tribe of Manasseh the people of Israel gave the towns of Aner and Bileam. They gave them to the rest of the family groups of Kohath. They gave them together with their grasslands.

⁷¹Here is what the members of the family line of Gershon were given.

From half of the tribe of Manasseh they received Golan in Bashan and also Ashtaroth. They received them together with their grasslands.

⁷²From the tribe of Issachar they received Kedesh, Daberath, ⁷³Ramoth and Anem. They received them together with their grasslands.

⁷⁴From the tribe of Asher they received Mashal, Abdon, ⁷⁵Hukok and Rehob. They received them together with their grasslands.

⁷⁶From the tribe of Naphtali they received Kedesh in Galilee. They also received Hammon and Kiriathaim. They were given all these towns together with their grasslands.

⁷⁷The members of the family line of Merari make up the rest of the Levites. Here is what they were given.

From the tribe of Zebulun they received Jokneam, Kartah, Rimmono and Tabor. They received them together with their grasslands.

78 The tribe of Reuben was across the Jordan River east of Jericho. From that tribe the Merarites received Bezer in the desert, Jahzah, 79 Kedemoth and Mephaath. They received them together with their grasslands.

80 From the tribe of Gad they received Ramoth in Gilead. They also received Mahanaim, 81 Heshbon and Jazer. They received all these towns together with their grasslands.

The Family Line of Issachar

7 The sons of Issachar were Tola, Puah, Jashub and Shimron. The total number of sons was four.

2 The sons of Tola were Uzzi, Rephaiah, Jeriel, Jahmai, Ibsam and Samuel. They were the leaders of their families. The total number of fighting men who were listed in the history of the family line of Tola was 22,600. That was when David was king.

3 The son of Uzzi was Izrahiah.

The sons of Izrahiah were Michael, Obadiah, Joel and Ishiah. All five of them were chiefs. 4 According to their family history, 36,000 of their men were ready for bat-

tle. That's because they had many wives and children.

5 The total number of fighting men who belonged to all the family groups of Issachar was 87,000. The men were listed in their family history.

The Family Line of Benjamin

6 The three sons of Benjamin were
Bela, Beker and Jediael.

7 The sons of Bela were
Ezbon, Uzzi, Uzziel, Jerimoth and Iri. They were the leaders of their families. The total number of sons was five. Their family history listed 22,034 fighting men.

8 The sons of Beker were
Zemirah, Joash, Eliezer, Elioenai, Omri, Jeremoth, Abijah, Anathoth and Alemeth. All of them were the sons of Beker. 9 Their family history listed the leaders of their families. It also listed 20,200 fighting men.

10 The son of Jediael was
Bilhan.

The sons of Bilhan were
Jeush, Benjamin, Ehud, Kenaanah, Zethan, Tarshish and Ahishahar. 11 All these sons of Jediael were the leaders of their families. There were 17,200 fighting men who were ready to go to war.

12 The Shuppites and Huppites belonged to the family

line of Ir. The Hushites belonged to the family line of Aher.

The Family Line of Naphtali

[13] The sons of Naphtali were Jahziel, Guni, Jezer and Shillem. They belonged to the family line of Bilhah.

The Family Line of Manasseh

[14] Here is the family line of Manasseh.

He had a concubine who was from the land of Aram. She had Asriel and Makir by him. Makir was the father of Gilead. [15] Makir married a woman from among the Huppites and Shuppites. He had a sister named Maakah.

Another member of Manasseh's family line was Zelophehad. All he had was daughters. [16] Makir's wife Maakah had a son by him. She named the boy Peresh. He had a brother named Sheresh. The sons of Sheresh were Ulam and Rakem. [17] The son of Ulam was Bedan.

These were the members of the family line of Makir, the son of Manasseh. Gilead was the son of Makir. [18] Gilead's sister was Hammoleketh. She was the mother of Ishhod, Abiezer and Mahlah. [19] The sons of Shemida were Ahian, Shechem, Likhi and Aniam.

The Family Line of Ephraim

[20] Here are the members of the family line of Ephraim.

Shuthelah was Ephraim's son.

Bered was Shuthelah's son.

Tahath was Bered's son.

Eleadah was Tahath's son.

Tahath was Eleadah's son. [21] Zabad was Tahath's son.

And Shuthelah was Zabad's son.

Men from Gath killed Ezer and Elead when they went down to steal their livestock. [22] Their father Ephraim mourned for them for many days. His relatives came to comfort him. [23] Then he slept with his wife. She became pregnant and had a baby boy. Ephraim named him Beriah. That's because something bad had happened in his family. [24] His daughter was Sheerah. She built Lower and Upper Beth Horon. She also built Uzzen Sheerah. [25] Rephah was Beriah's son.

Resheph was Rephah's son.

Telah was Resheph's son.

Tahan was Telah's son. [26] Ladan was Tahan's son.

Ammihud was Ladan's son.

Elishama was Ammihud's son. [27] Nun was Elishama's son. And Joshua was the son of Nun.

[28] The lands and settlements of the members of Ephraim's line included Bethel and the villages around it. Naaran was on the east. Gezer and its villages were on the west. The lands and settlements included Shechem. They also included the villages around Shechem all the way to Ayyah and its villages. [29] Along the borders of Manasseh were Beth Shan, Taanach, Megiddo and Dor, together with their villages. The members of the family line of Joseph lived in these towns. Joseph was the son of Israel.

The Family Line of Asher

[30] The sons of Asher were Imnah, Ishvah, Ishvi and Beriah. They had a sister named Serah.

[31] The sons of Beriah were Heber and Malkiel. Malkiel was the father of Birzaith.

[32] Heber was the father of Japhlet, Shomer, Hotham and their sister Shua.

[33] The sons of Japhlet were Pasak, Bimhal and Ashvath. They were Japhlet's sons.

[34] The sons of Shomer were Ahi, Rohgah, Hubbah and Aram.

[35] The sons of Shomer's brother Helem were Zophah, Imna, Shelesh and Amal.

[36] The sons of Zophah were Suah, Harnepher, Shual, Beri, Imrah, [37] Bezer, Hod, Shamma, Shilshah, Ithran and Beera.

[38] The sons of Jether were Jephunneh, Pispah and Ara.

[39] The sons of Ulla were Arah, Hanniel and Rizia.

[40] All of them were members of the family line of Asher. They were the leaders of their families. They were fine men. They were brave fighting men. They were outstanding leaders. The total number of men who were ready for battle was 26,000. They were listed in their family history.

The Family History of Saul

8 Benjamin was the father of Bela. Bela was his first son. Ashbel was his second son. Aharah was the third. [2] Nohah was the fourth. And Rapha was the fifth.

[3] The sons of Bela were Addar, Gera, Abihud, [4] Abishua, Naaman, Ahoah, [5] Gera, Shephuphan and Huram.

[6] Here are the members of the family line of Ehud. They were the leaders of the families who were living in Geba. Later,

they were taken away from their own land. They were forced to go to Manahath. ⁷The sons of Ehud were Naaman, Ahijah and Gera. Gera took them away from their land. He was the father of Uzza and Ahihud.

⁸Sons were born to Shaharaim in Moab. That happened after he had divorced his wives Hushim and Baara. ⁹His wife Hodesh had sons by him. Their names were Jobab, Zibia, Mesha, Malkam, ¹⁰Jeuz, Sakia and Mirmah. His sons were the leaders of their families. ¹¹His wife Hushim had Abitub and Elpaal by him.

¹²The sons of Elpaal were Eber, Misham and Shemed. Shemed built Ono and Lod and the villages around it. ¹³Beriah and Shema were also sons of Elpaal. They were the leaders of the families who were living in Aijalon. Beriah and Shema drove out the people who were living in Gath.

¹⁴Ahio, Shashak, Jeremoth, ¹⁵Zebadiah, Arad, Eder, ¹⁶Michael, Ishpah and Joha were the sons of Beriah.

¹⁷Zebadiah, Meshullam, Hizki, Heber, ¹⁸Ishmerai, Izliah and Jobab were other sons of Elpaal.

¹⁹Jakim, Zikri, Zabdi, ²⁰Elienai, Zillethai, Eliel, ²¹Adaiah, Beraiah and Shimrath were the sons of Shimei.

²²Ishpan, Eber, Eliel, ²³Abdon, Zikri, Hanan, ²⁴Hananiah, Elam, Anthothijah, ²⁵Iphdeiah and Penuel were the sons of Shashak.

²⁶Shamsherai, Shehariah, Athaliah, ²⁷Jaareshiah, Elijah and Zikri were the sons of Jeroham.

²⁸All these men were the leaders of their families. They were listed as chiefs in their family history. They lived in Jerusalem.

²⁹Jeiel lived in the city of Gibeon. He was the father of Gibeon.

Jeiel had a wife named Maakah. ³⁰His oldest son was Abdon. His other sons were Zur, Kish, Baal, Ner, Nadab, ³¹Gedor, Ahio, Zeker ³²and Mikloth. Mikloth was the father of Shimeah. Mikloth and Shimeah also lived in Jerusalem. They lived near their relatives.

³³Ner was the father of Kish. Kish was the father of Saul. Saul was the father of Jonathan, Malki-Shua, Abinadab and Esh-Baal.

³⁴The son of Jonathan was Merib-Baal. Merib-Baal was the father of Micah.

³⁵The sons of Micah were Pithon, Melek, Tarea and Ahaz. ³⁶Ahaz was the

father of Jehoaddah. Jehoaddah was the father of Alemeth, Azmaveth and Zimri. Zimri was the father of Moza. [37] Moza was the father of Binea. Raphah was Binea's son. Eleasah was Raphah's son. And Azel was Eleasah's son.

[38] Azel had six sons. Their names were

Azrikam, Bokeru, Ishmael, Sheariah, Obadiah and Hanan. All of them were the sons of Azel.

[39] Here are the sons of Azel's brother Eshek.

Ulam was his first son. Jeush was the second. Eliphelet was the third. [40] The sons of Ulam were brave fighting men. They could use a bow. They had many sons and grandsons. The total number of sons and grandsons was 150.

All these men belonged to the family line of Benjamin.

9 The whole community of Israel was listed in their family histories. They were written down in the records of the kings of Israel and Judah. The people of Judah were taken away from their own land. They were taken as prisoners to Babylon. That's because they weren't faithful to the LORD.

The People Who Lived in Jerusalem

[2] The first people who came back from Babylon were some Israelites, priests, Levites and temple servants. They made their homes again in their own towns on their own property.

[3] Some of them lived in Jerusalem. They included people from Judah, Benjamin, Ephraim and Manasseh.

[4] They included Uthai. He was the son of Ammihud. Ammihud was the son of Omri. Omri was the son of Imri. Imri was the son of Bani. Bani belonged to the family line of Perez. Perez was the son of Judah.

[5] The family line of Shelah included

his oldest son Asaiah. It also included the sons of Asaiah.

[6] The family line of Zerah included

Jeuel.

The total number of the people of Judah was 690.

[7] The family line of Benjamin included

Sallu. He was the son of Meshullam. Meshullam was the son of Hodaviah. Hodaviah was the son of Hassenuah.

[8] Ibneiah was the son of Jeroham.

Elah was the son of Uzzi. Uzzi was the son of Mikri.

Meshullam was the son of Shephatiah. Shephatiah was the son of Reuel. Reuel was the son of Ibnijah.

⁹The total number of the people of Benjamin was 956. They were listed in their family history. All these men were the leaders of their families.

¹⁰The family line of the priests included
Jedaiah, Jehoiarib and Jakin.
¹¹It also included Azariah. He was the son of Hilkiah. Hilkiah was the son of Meshullam. Meshullam was the son of Zadok. Zadok was the son of Meraioth. Meraioth was the son of Ahitub. Azariah was the official who was in charge of the house of God.
¹²Adaiah was the son of Jeroham. Jeroham was the son of Pashhur. Pashhur was the son of Malkijah.
Maasai was the son of Adiel. Adiel was the son of Jahzerah. Jahzerah was the son of Meshullam. Meshullam was the son of Meshillemith. Meshillemith was the son of Immer.
¹³The total number of priests was 1,760. They were the leaders of their families. They were able men. It was their duty to serve in the house of God.
¹⁴The family line of the Levites included
Shemaiah. He was the son of Hasshub. Hasshub was the son of Azrikam.

Azrikam was the son of Hashabiah. Shemaiah belonged to the family line of Merari.
¹⁵The family line of the Levites also included Bakbakkar, Heresh, Galal and Mattaniah. Mattaniah was the son of Mika. Mika was the son of Zikri. Zikri was the son of Asaph.
¹⁶Obadiah was the son of Shemaiah. Shemaiah was the son of Galal. Galal was the son of Jeduthun.
Berekiah was the son of Asa. Asa was the son of Elkanah. He lived in the villages of the people of Netophah.

¹⁷The men who guarded the gates were
Shallum, Akkub, Talmon, Ahiman and other Levites. Shallum was their chief. ¹⁸He was stationed at the King's Gate on the east side. That duty has continued to this day. These guards belonged to the camp of the Levites.
¹⁹Shallum was the son of Kore. Kore was the son of Ebiasaph. Ebiasaph was the son of Korah. Shallum and the other Levites in his family belonged to the family line of Korah. They had the duty of guarding the entrances to the tent. From long ago, their people

had the duty of guarding the entrance to the house of the LORD.

²⁰ Long ago Phinehas, the son of Eleazar, was in charge of those who guarded the gate. And the LORD was with him.

²¹ Zechariah guarded the entrance to the tent of meeting. He was the son of Meshelemiah.

²² The total number of the men who were chosen to guard the entrances was 212. They were listed in their family history in their villages.

David and Samuel the prophet had appointed them to their positions. They appointed them because they trusted them. ²³ These Levites and their children after them were in charge of guarding the gates of the house of the LORD. The house of the LORD was also called the tent of meeting. ²⁴ The men who guarded the gates were on the four sides of the tent. They were on the east, west, north and south sides. ²⁵ From time to time, their relatives in their villages had to come to help them. They had to share their duties for a week at a time. ²⁶ But the four main men who guarded the gates were Levites. They were trusted with the duty of taking care of the storerooms and the other rooms in the house of God. ²⁷ They spent the night in their positions around the house of God. That's because they had to guard it. They were in charge of the key that opened it each morning.

²⁸ Some Levites were in charge of the objects that were used when they served at the temple. They counted the objects when they were brought in. They also counted them when they were taken out. ²⁹ Other Levites were appointed to take care of all the other things that belonged to the temple. They also took care of the special flour, wine, olive oil, incense and spices. ³⁰ Some of the priests took care of mixing the spices. ³¹ There was a Levite named Mattithiah. He was the oldest son of Shallum. Shallum belonged to the family line of Korah. Mattithiah was trusted with the duty of baking the offering bread. ³² The bread was placed on the table every Sabbath day. Some Levites in the family line of Kohath were in charge of preparing the bread.

³³ Those who led the music lived in rooms in the temple. They were the leaders of their Levite families. Their only duty was to lead the music. They had to do that work day and night.

³⁴ All of them were the leaders of their Levite families. They were listed as chiefs in their family history. They lived in Jerusalem.

The Family History of Saul

³⁵ Jeiel lived in the city of Gibeon. He was the father of Gibeon.

Jeiel had a wife named Maakah. ³⁶ His oldest son was Abdon. His other sons were Zur, Kish, Baal, Ner, Nadab, 37 Gedor, Ahio, Zechariah and Mikloth. 38 Mikloth was the father of Shimeam. Mikloth and Shimeam lived near their relatives in Jerusalem. 39 Ner was the father of Kish. Kish was the father of Saul. Saul was the father of Jonathan, Malki-Shua, Abinadab and Esh-Baal. 40 The son of Jonathan was Merib-Baal. Merib-Baal was the father of Micah. 41 The sons of Micah were Pithon, Melek, Tahrea and Ahaz. 42 Ahaz was the father of Jadah. Jadah was the father of Alemeth, Azmaveth and Zimri. Zimri was the father of Moza. 43 Moza was the father of Binea. Rephaiah was Binea's son. Eleasah was Rephaiah's son. And Azel was Eleasah's son. 44 Azel had six sons. Their names were Azrikam, Bokeru, Ishmael, Sheariah, Obadiah and Hanan. They were the sons of Azel.

Saul Takes His Own Life

10 The Philistines fought against Israel. The men of Israel ran away from them. But many Israelites were killed on Mount Gilboa. 2 The Philistines kept chasing Saul and his sons. They killed his sons Jonathan, Abinadab and Malki-Shua.

3 The fighting was heavy around Saul. Men armed with bows and arrows caught up with him. They shot their arrows at him and wounded him badly.

4 Saul spoke to the man who was carrying his armor. He said, "Pull out your sword and stick it through me. If you don't, these men who aren't circumcised will come and hurt me badly."

But the man was terrified. He wouldn't do it. So Saul took his own sword and fell on it. 5 The man saw that Saul was dead. So he fell on his own sword and died. 6 Saul and his three sons died. All of them died together.

7 All the Israelites who lived in the valley saw that their army had run away. They saw that Saul and his sons were dead. So the Israelites left their towns and ran away. Then the Philistines came and lived in them.

8 The day after the Philistines had won the battle, they came to take what they wanted from the dead bodies. They found Saul and his sons dead on Mount Gilboa. 9 So they took what they wanted from Saul's body. They cut off his head and took his armor. Then they sent messengers through the whole land of the Philistines. They announced the news to the statues of their gods. They also announced it among their people. 10 They put Saul's armor in the temple of their gods. They hung up his head in the temple of their god Dagon.

11 The people of Jabesh Gilead heard what the Philistines had

done to Saul. ¹²So all the brave men of Jabesh Gilead went and got the bodies of Saul and his sons. They brought them to Jabesh. Then they buried the bones of Saul and his sons under the great tree that was there. They didn't eat anything for seven days.

¹³Saul died because he wasn't faithful to the LORD. He didn't obey the word of the LORD. He even asked for advice from a person who gets messages from people who have died. ¹⁴He didn't ask the LORD for advice. So the LORD put him to death. He turned the kingdom over to David. David was the son of Jesse.

David Becomes King Over Israel

11 The whole community of Israel came together to see David at Hebron. They said, "We are your own flesh and blood. ²In the past, Saul was our king. But you led the men of Israel in battle. The LORD your God said to you, 'You will be the shepherd over my people Israel. You will become their ruler.' "

³All the elders of Israel came to see King David at Hebron. There he made a covenant with them in front of the LORD. They anointed David as king over Israel. It happened just as the LORD had promised through Samuel.

David Captures Jerusalem

⁴David and all the men of Israel marched to Jerusalem. Jerusalem was also called Jebus. The Jebusites who lived there ⁵said to David, "You won't get in here." But David captured the fort of Zion. It became known as the City of David.

⁶David had said, "Anyone who leads the attack against the Jebusites will become the commander of Israel's army." Joab went up first. So he became the commander of the army. He was the son of Zeruiah.

⁷David moved into the fort. So it was called the City of David. ⁸He built up the city around the fort. He filled in the low places. He built a wall around it. During that time, Joab built up the rest of the city. ⁹David became more and more powerful. That's because the LORD who rules over all was with him.

David's Mighty Warriors

¹⁰The chiefs of David's mighty warriors and the whole community of Israel helped David greatly. They helped him become king over the entire land. That's exactly what the LORD had promised him. ¹¹Here is a list of David's mighty warriors.

Jashobeam was chief of the officers. He was a Hakmonite. He used his spear against 300 men. He killed all of them at one time.

¹²Next to him was Eleazar. He was one of the three mighty warriors. He was the son of Dodai, the Ahohite. ¹³Jashobeam was with David at Pas Dammim. The Philistines had gathered there for battle. Israel's troops ran away from the Phi-

listines. At the place where that happened, there was a field full of barley. ¹⁴ The three mighty warriors took their stand in the middle of the field. They didn't let the Philistines capture it. They struck them down. The LORD helped them win a great battle.

¹⁵ David was near the rock at the cave of Adullam. Three of the 30 chiefs came down to him there. A group of Philistines was camped in the Valley of Rephaim. ¹⁶ At that time David was in his usual place of safety. Some Philistine troops were stationed at Bethlehem. ¹⁷ David really wanted some water. He said, "I wish someone would get me a drink of water from the well near the gate of Bethlehem!" ¹⁸ So the three mighty warriors fought their way past the Philistine guards. They got some water from the well near the gate of Bethlehem. They took the water back to David. But David refused to drink it. Instead, he poured it out as a drink offering to the LORD. ¹⁹ "I would never drink that water!" David said. "It would be like drinking the blood of these men. They put their lives in danger by going to Bethlehem." The men had put their lives in danger by bringing the water back. So David wouldn't drink it.

Those were some of the brave things the three mighty warriors did.

²⁰ Abishai was chief over the three mighty warriors. He was the brother of Joab. Abishai used his spear against 300 men. He killed all of them. So he became as famous as the three mighty warriors. ²¹ He was honored twice as much as the three mighty warriors. He became their commander. But he wasn't included among them.

²² Benaiah was a great hero from Kabzeel. He was the son of Jehoiada. Benaiah did many brave things. He struck down two of Moab's best fighting men. He also went down into a pit on a snowy day. He killed a lion there. ²³ And Benaiah struck down an Egyptian who was seven and a half feet tall. The Egyptian was holding a spear as big as a weaver's rod. Benaiah went out to fight against him with a club. He grabbed the spear out of the Egyptian's hand. Then he killed him with it. ²⁴ Those were some of the brave things Benaiah, the son of Jehoiada, did. He too was as famous as the three mighty warriors. ²⁵ He was honored more than any of the 30 chiefs. But he wasn't included among the three mighty warriors. And David put him in charge of his own personal guards.

²⁶ Here is a list of David's mighty warriors.

Asahel, the brother of Joab
Elhanan, the son of Dodo, from Bethlehem
²⁷ Shammoth, the Harorite
Helez, the Pelonite
²⁸ Ira, the son of Ikkesh, from Tekoa
Abiezer from Anathoth
²⁹ Sibbekai, the Hushathite

Ilai, the Ahohite
30 Maharai from Netophah
Heled, the son of Baanah,
from Netophah
31 Ithai, the son of Ribai, from
Gibeah in Benjamin
Benaiah from Pirathon
32 Hurai from the valleys of
Gaash
Abiel, the Arbathite
33 Azmaveth, the Baharumite
Eliahba, the Shaalbonite
34 the sons of Hashem, the Gi-
zonite
Jonathan, the son of Sha-
gee, the Hararite
35 Ahiam, the son of Sakar,
the Hararite
Eliphal, the son of Ur
36 Hepher, the Mekerathite
Ahijah, the Pelonite
37 Hezro from Carmel
Naarai, the son of Ezbai
38 Joel, the brother of Nathan
Mibhar, the son of Hagri
39 Zelek from Ammon
Naharai, from Beeroth,
who carried the armor of
Joab, the son of Zeruiah
40 Ira, the Ithrite
Gareb, the Ithrite
41 Uriah, the Hittite
Zabad, the son of Ahlai
42 Adina, the son of Shiza, the
Reubenite, who was chief
of the Reubenites and the
30 men with him
43 Hanan, the son of Maakah
Joshaphat, the Mithnite
44 Uzzia, the Ashterathite
Shama and Jeiel, the sons of
Hotham from Aroer
45 Jediael, the son of Shimri
his brother Joha, the Tizite
46 Eliel, the Mahavite

Jeribai and Joshaviah, the
sons of Elnaam
Ithmah from Moab
47 Eliel
Obed
Jaasiel, the Mezobaite

Fighting Men Join David

12 Some fighting men
came to David at Ziklag.
They were among those who
helped him in battle. David
had been forced to hide from
Saul, the son of Kish. 2 The
men were armed with bows.
They were able to shoot arrows or throw stones from a
sling with either hand. They
were relatives of Saul from
the tribe of Benjamin. Here
is a list of them.

3 Their chief Ahiezer and Jo-
ash, the sons of Shemaah
the Gibeathite
Jeziel and Pelet, the sons of
Azmaveth
Berakah
Jehu from Anathoth
4 Ishmaiah, the Gibeonite,
who was a mighty war-
rior among the 30 chiefs
and a leader of the 30
chiefs
Jeremiah
Jahaziel
Johanan
Jozabad from Gederah
5 Eluzai
Jerimoth
Bealiah
Shemariah
Shephatiah, the Haruphite
6 the Korahites Elkanah, Ish-
iah, Azarel, Joezer and
Jashobeam

⁷Joelah and Zebadiah, the sons of Jeroham from Gedor

⁸Some men of Gad went over to David's side at his usual place of safety in the desert. They were brave fighting men. They were ready for battle. They were able to use shields and spears. Their faces were like the faces of lions. They could run as fast as antelopes in the mountains.

⁹Ezer was their chief.
  Obadiah was next in command. Eliab was third.
¹⁰Mishmannah was fourth. Jeremiah was fifth.
¹¹Attai was sixth. Eliel was seventh.
¹²Johanan was eighth. Elzabad was ninth.
¹³Jeremiah was tenth. And Makbannai was eleventh.

¹⁴All these men of Gad were army commanders. The least important of them was equal to 100 men. The most important was equal to 1,000. ¹⁵They went across the Jordan River when it was flowing over its banks. That happened in the first month of spring. They chased away everyone who lived in the valleys. They chased them away from the east and west sides of the river.

¹⁶Some men from the territories of Benjamin and Judah also came to David at his usual place of safety. ¹⁷David went out to meet them. He said to them, "Have you come to me in peace? Have you come to help me? If you have, I'm ready for you to join me. But suppose you have come to hand me over to my enemies when I haven't even harmed anyone. Then may the God of our people see it and judge you."

¹⁸The Spirit of God came on Amasai. He was leader of the 30 chiefs. He said,

"David, we belong to you!
  Son of Jesse, we're on your
    side!
May you have great success.
  May those who help you
    also have success.
  Your God will help you."

So David welcomed them. He made them leaders in his army.

¹⁹Some people from the tribe of Manasseh went over to David's side. They did this when he marched out with the Philistines to fight against Saul. But David and his men didn't help the Philistines. That's because after all the Philistine rulers had discussed the matter, they sent him away. They said, "Suppose he deserts to his master Saul. Then our heads will be cut off!" ²⁰So David went to Ziklag. Here are the men of Manasseh who went over to his side. They were Adnah, Jozabad, Jediael, Michael, Jozabad, Elihu and Zillethai. They were leaders of groups of 1,000 men in Manasseh. ²¹They helped David fight against enemy armies. All the men of Manasseh were brave fighting men. They were commanders in David's army. ²²Day after day men came to

help David. Soon he had a large army. It was like the army of God.

Other Fighting Men Join David at Hebron

23 Large numbers of men came to David at Hebron. They were prepared for battle. They came to hand Saul's kingdom over to him, just as the LORD had said. Here are the numbers of the men who came.

24 The men from Judah carried shields and spears. They were prepared for battle. The total number of them was 6,800.

25 The fighting men from Simeon were ready for battle. The total number of them was 7,100.

26 The total number of men from Levi was 4,600. 27 They included Jehoiada. He was the leader of the family of Aaron. He came with 3,700 men. 28 The men from Levi also included Zadok. He was a brave young fighter. He came with 22 officers from his family.

29 The men from Benjamin were from Saul's tribe. Most of them had remained faithful to Saul's family until that time. The total number of them was 3,000.

30 The men from Ephraim were brave fighting men. They were famous in their own family groups. The total number of them was 20,800.

31 The men from half of the tribe of Manasseh had been chosen by name to come and make David king. The total number of them was 18,000.

32 The men from Issachar understood what was going on at that time. They knew what Israel should do. The total number of their chiefs was 200. They came with all their relatives who were under their command.

33 The men from Zebulun knew how to fight well. That's because they had done it many times before. They were prepared for battle. They had every kind of weapon. They came to help David with their whole heart. The total number of them was 50,000.

34 The total number of officers from Naphtali was 1,000. They came with 37,000 men who carried shields and spears.

35 The men from Dan were ready for battle. The total number of them was 28,600.

36 The men from Asher knew how to fight well. That's because they had done it many times before. They were prepared for battle. The total number of them was 40,000.

37 The men from the tribes of

Reuben, Gad and half the tribe of Manasseh were armed with every kind of weapon. The men came from the east side of the Jordan River. The total number of them was 120,000.

38 All these fighting men offered to serve in the army.

Before they came to Hebron, they had agreed completely to make David king over all the Israelites. All the rest of the people also agreed to make David king. 39 The men spent three days there with David. They ate and drank what their families had given them. 40 Their neighbors also brought food. They brought it on donkeys, camels, mules and oxen. They came from as far away as the territories of Issachar, Zebulun and Naphtali. There was plenty of flour, fig cakes, raisin cakes, wine, olive oil, cattle and sheep. The Israelites brought all these things because they were so happy.

David Brings Back the Ark

13 David talked with each of his officers. He wanted to get their advice. Some of them were commanders of thousands of men. Others were commanders of hundreds. 2 David spoke to the whole community of Israel. He said, "Let's send word to the rest of our people no matter how far away they live. They live in all the territories of Israel. Let's also send word to the priests and Levites who are with them in their towns and on their grasslands. Let's invite everyone to come and join us. Let's do it if it seems good to you and if that's what the LORD our God wants. 3 Let's bring the ark of our God back here to us. We didn't use it to ask God for advice during the whole time Saul was king." 4 So that's what the whole community agreed to do. It seemed right to them.

5 David gathered together all the Israelites. They came from the area between the Shihor River in Egypt and Lebo Hamath. They came to bring the ark of God from Kiriath Jearim to Jerusalem. 6 David went to Baalah of Judah. The whole community of Israel went with him. Baalah is also called Kiriath Jearim. All the people went there to get the ark of God the LORD. He sits on his throne between the cherubim. The ark is named after the LORD.

7 The ark of God was placed on a new cart. Then it was moved from Abinadab's house. Uzzah and Ahio were guiding it. 8 David was celebrating with all his might in front of God. So was the whole community of Israel. All of them were singing songs. They were also playing harps, lyres, tambourines, cymbals and trumpets.

9 They came to the threshing floor of Kidon. The oxen nearly fell there. So Uzzah reached out his hand to hold the ark steady. 10 Then the LORD became very angry with Uzzah. The LORD struck him down because he

had put his hand on the ark. So Uzzah died there in front of God.

¹¹ David was angry because the LORD's great anger had broken out against Uzzah. That's why the place is still called Perez Uzzah to this day.

¹² David was afraid of God that day. David asked, "How can I ever bring the ark of God back here to me?" ¹³ So he didn't take the ark to be with him in the City of David. Instead, he took it to the house of Obed-Edom. Obed-Edom was from Gath. ¹⁴ The ark of God remained with the family of Obed-Edom. It stayed in his house for three months. And the LORD blessed his family. He also blessed everything that belonged to him.

David's Palace and Family

14 Hiram was king of Tyre. He sent messengers to David. He sent cedar logs along with them. He also sent skilled workers to build a palace for David. They worked with stone and wood. ² David knew that the LORD had made his position as king secure. He knew that the LORD had made him king over the whole nation of Israel. He knew that the LORD had greatly honored his kingdom. The LORD had done it because the Israelites were his people.

³ In Jerusalem David married more women. He also became the father of more sons and daughters. ⁴ Here is a list of the children born to him in Jerusalem. Their names were Shammua, Shobab, Nathan, Solomon, ⁵ Ibhar, Elishua, Elpelet, ⁶ Nogah, Nepheg, Japhia, ⁷ Elishama, Beeliada and Eliphelet.

David Wins the Battle Over the Philistines

⁸ The Philistines heard that David had been anointed king over the entire nation of Israel. So the whole Philistine army went to look for him. But David heard about it. He went out to where they were. ⁹ The Philistines had come and attacked the people in the Valley of Rephaim. ¹⁰ So David asked God for advice. David asked, "Should I go and attack the Philistines? Will you hand them over to me?"

The LORD answered him, "Go. I will hand them over to you."

¹¹ So David and his men went up to Baal Perazim. There David won the battle over the Philistines. He said, "God has broken through against my enemies, just as water breaks through a dam." That's why the place was called Baal Perazim. ¹² The Philistines had left statues of their gods there. So David gave orders to burn them up.

¹³ Once more the Philistines attacked the people in the valley. ¹⁴ So David asked God for advice again. God answered him, "Do not go straight after them. Instead, circle around them. Attack them in front of the poplar trees. ¹⁵ Listen for the sound of marching in the tops of the trees. Then move out to fight. The sound will mean that I have gone out in front of you.

I will strike down the Philistine army." ¹⁶ So David did just as God had commanded him. He and his men struck down the Philistine army. They struck them down from Gibeon all the way to Gezer.

¹⁷ So David became famous in every land. The LORD made all the nations afraid of him.

David Brings the Ark to Jerusalem

15 David constructed buildings for himself in the City of David. Then he prepared a place for the ark of God. He set up a tent for it. ² He said, "Only Levites can carry the ark of God. That's because the LORD chose them to carry his ark. He chose them to serve him forever in front of the place where his throne is."

³ David gathered the whole community of Israel together in Jerusalem. He wanted to carry up the ark of the LORD to the place he had prepared for it.

⁴ He called together the members of the family line of Aaron. He also called the Levites together. Here are the men who came from the families of the Levites.

⁵ From the families of Kohath
came the leader Uriel and 120 relatives.
⁶ From the families of Merari
came the leader Asaiah and 220 relatives.
⁷ From the families of Gershon

came the leader Joel and 130 relatives.
⁸ From the families of Elizaphan
came the leader Shemaiah and 200 relatives.
⁹ From the families of Hebron
came the leader Eliel and 80 relatives.
¹⁰ From the families of Uzziel
came the leader Amminadab and 112 relatives.

¹¹ David sent for Zadok and Abiathar, the priests. He also sent for Uriel, Asaiah, Joel, Shemaiah, Eliel and Amminadab. They were Levites. ¹² He said to them, "You are the leaders of the families of Levi. You and the other Levites must set yourselves apart to serve the LORD and his people. You must carry up the ark of the LORD. He is the God of Israel. Put the ark in the place I've prepared for it. ¹³ Remember when the anger of the LORD our God broke out against us? That's because it wasn't you Levites who tried to carry up the ark the first time. We didn't ask the LORD how to do it in the way the law requires." ¹⁴ So the priests and Levites set themselves apart. Then they carried up the ark of the LORD. He is the God of Israel. ¹⁵ This time the Levites used the poles to carry on their shoulders the ark of God. That's what Moses had commanded in keeping with the word of the LORD.

¹⁶ David told the Levite leaders to appoint other Levites as musicians. He wanted them to

make a joyful sound with lyres, harps and cymbals. [17] So the Levites appointed Heman, the son of Joel. From his relatives they chose Asaph, the son of Berekiah. Other relatives were from the family of Merari. From them they chose Ethan, the son of Kushaiah. [18] Along with them they chose their relatives who were next in rank. Their names were Zechariah, Jaaziel, Shemiramoth, Jehiel, Unni, Eliab, Benaiah, Maaseiah, Mattithiah, Eliphelehu, Mikneiah, Obed-Edom and Jeiel. They guarded the gates. [19] Heman, Asaph and Ethan played the bronze cymbals. [20] Zechariah, Jaaziel, Shemiramoth, Jehiel, Unni, Eliab, Maaseiah and Benaiah played the lyres according to alamoth. [21] Mattithiah, Eliphelehu, Mikneiah, Obed-Edom, Jeiel and Azaziah played the harps according to sheminith. [22] Kenaniah was the leader of the Levites. He was in charge of the singing because he was good at it.

[23] Berekiah and Elkanah guarded the ark. [24] Some of the priests blew trumpets in front of the ark of God. Their names were Shebaniah, Joshaphat, Nethanel, Amasai, Zechariah, Benaiah and Eliezer. Obed-Edom and Jehiah also helped guard the ark.

[25] David and the elders of Israel went to carry up the ark of the covenant of the LORD. So did the commanders of military groups of 1,000 men. With great joy they carried up the ark from the house of Obed-Edom. [26] God had helped the Levites who were carrying the ark of the covenant of the LORD. So seven bulls and seven rams were sacrificed. [27] David was wearing a robe made out of fine linen. So were all the Levites who were carrying the ark. And so were the musicians and the choir director Kenaniah. David was also wearing a sacred linen apron. [28] So the whole community of Israel brought up the ark of the covenant of the LORD. They shouted. They blew rams' horns and trumpets. They played cymbals, lyres and harps.

[29] The ark of the covenant of the LORD was brought into the City of David. Saul's daughter Michal was watching from a window. She saw King David dancing and celebrating. That made her hate him in her heart.

Serving God in Front of the Ark

16 The ark of God was carried into Jerusalem. It was put in the tent David had set up for it. The priests brought burnt offerings and friendship offerings to God. [2] After David finished sacrificing those offerings, he blessed the people in the name of the LORD. [3] He gave to each Israelite man and woman a loaf of bread. He also gave each one a date cake and a raisin cake.

[4] He appointed some of the Levites to serve in front of the ark of the LORD. David wanted

them to give honor, thanks and praise to the LORD. He is the God of Israel. ⁵Asaph was the leader of those Levites. Zechariah was next in rank. Then came Jaaziel, Shemiramoth, Jehiel, Mattithiah, Eliab, Benaiah, Obed-Edom and Jeiel. They played the lyres and harps. Asaph played the cymbals. ⁶Benaiah and Jahaziel, the priests, blew the trumpets. They blew them at regular times in front of the ark of the covenant of God.

⁷That day was the first time David appointed Asaph and his helpers. He appointed them to give praise to the LORD with these words.

⁸Give praise to the LORD.
     Make his name known.
     Tell the nations what he
          has done.
⁹Sing to him. Sing praise to
          him.
     Tell about all the
          wonderful things he has
          done.
¹⁰Honor him, because his
          name is holy.
     Let the hearts of those who
          trust in the LORD be
          glad.
¹¹Look to the LORD and to his
          strength.
     Always look to him.
¹²Remember the wonderful
          things he has done.
     Remember his miracles
          and how he judged our
          enemies.
¹³Remember, you his servants,
          the children of Israel.

Remember, you people of
     Jacob. Remember, you
     who are chosen by God.

¹⁴He is the LORD our God.
     He judges the whole
          earth.
¹⁵He will keep his covenant
          forever.
     He will keep his promise
          for all time to come.
¹⁶He will keep the covenant he
          made with Abraham.
     He will keep the promise
          he made to Isaac.
¹⁷He made it stand as a law for
          Jacob.
     He made it stand as a
          covenant for Israel. It
          will last forever.
¹⁸He said, "I will give you the
          land of Canaan.
     It will belong to you."

¹⁹At first there weren't very
          many of God's people.
     There were only a few. And
          they were strangers in
          the land.
²⁰They wandered from nation
          to nation.
     They wandered from one
          kingdom to another.
²¹But God didn't allow anyone
          to treat them badly.
     To keep them safe, he gave
          a command to kings.
²²He said to them, "Do not
          touch my anointed ones.
     Do not harm my prophets."

²³All you people of the earth,
          sing to the LORD.
     Day after day tell about
          how he saves us.
²⁴Tell the nations about his
          glory.

Tell all people about the
wonderful things he has
done.
25 The Lord is great. He is
really worthy of praise.
People should have respect
for him as the greatest
God of all.
26 All the gods of the nations are
like their statues.
They can't do anything.
But the Lord made the
heavens.
27 Glory and majesty are all
around him.
Strength and joy are in the
place where he lives.
28 Praise the Lord, all you
nations.
Praise the Lord for his
glory and strength.
29   Praise the Lord for the
glory that belongs to
him.
Bring an offering and come
to him.
Worship the Lord because
of his beauty and
holiness.
30 All you people of the earth,
tremble when you are
with him.
The world is firmly set in
place. It can't be moved.
31 Let the heavens be filled with
joy. Let the earth be
glad.
Let them say among the
nations, "The Lord
rules!"
32 Let the ocean and everything
in it roar.
Let the fields and
everything in them be
glad.

33 Let the trees in the forest sing
with joy.
They will sing before the
Lord.
He will judge the people of
the world.
34 Give thanks to the Lord,
because he is good.
His faithful love continues
forever.
35 Cry out, "Save us, God our
Savior.
Save us. Bring us back from
among the nations.
Then we will give thanks to
you, because your name
is holy.
We will celebrate by
praising you."
36 Give praise to the Lord, the
God of Israel,
for ever and ever.

Then all the people said,
"Amen!" They also said, "Praise
the Lord."

37 David left Asaph and his
helpers to serve in front of the
ark of the covenant of the Lord.
They served there at regular
times. They did it as they were
required to do each day. 38 David also left Obed-Edom and
his 68 helpers to serve with
them. Obed-Edom and Hosah
guarded the gates. Obed-Edom
was the son of Jeduthun.
39 David left Zadok the priest
and some other priests in front
of the holy tent of the Lord. It
was at the high place in Gibeon.
40 David left them there to sacrifice burnt offerings to the Lord
on the altar every morning and
evening. They did it accord-

ing to everything written in the Law of the LORD. That's the Law he had given to Israel. ⁴¹ Heman and Jeduthun were with the priests. So were the rest of those who had been chosen by name and appointed to serve. They had been chosen to give thanks to the LORD, "because his faithful love continues forever." ⁴² It was the duty of Heman and Jeduthun to blow the trumpets. They also had the duty of playing the cymbals and other instruments for the sacred songs. The sons of Jeduthun were stationed at one of the gates.

⁴³ All the people left. Everyone went home. And David returned home to bless his family.

God Makes a Promise to David

17 David moved into his palace. Then he spoke to Nathan the prophet. He said, "Here I am, living in a house that has beautiful cedar walls. But the ark of the covenant of the LORD is under a tent."

² Nathan replied to David, "Do what you want to. God is with you."

³ But that night a message came to Nathan from God. He said,

⁴ "Go and speak to my servant David. Tell him, 'The LORD says, "You are not the one who will build me a house to live in. ⁵ I have not lived in a house from the day I brought Israel up out of Egypt until now. I have moved my tent from one place to another.

I have moved my home from one place to another. ⁶ I have moved from place to place with all the Israelites. I commanded their leaders to be shepherds over my people. I never asked any of those leaders, 'Why haven't you built me a house that has beautiful cedar walls?' " '

⁷ "So tell my servant David, 'The LORD who rules over all says, "I took you away from the grasslands. That is where you were taking care of your father's sheep and goats. I appointed you ruler over my people Israel. ⁸ I have been with you everywhere you have gone. I destroyed all your enemies when you were attacking them. Now I will make you famous. Your name will be just as respected as the names of the most important people on earth. ⁹ I will provide a place where my people Israel can live. I will plant them in the land. Then they will have a home of their own. They will not be bothered anymore. Sinful people will no longer crush them, as they did at first. ¹⁰ That is what your enemies have done ever since I appointed leaders over my people Israel. But I will bring all your enemies under your control.

" ' "I tell you that I, the LORD, will build a royal

house for your family. [11] Some day your life will come to an end. You will join the members of your family who have already died. Then I will give you one of your own sons to become the next king after you. I will make his kingdom secure. [12] He is the one who will build me a house. I will set up his throne. It will last forever. [13] I will be his father. And he will be my son. I took my love away from the man who ruled before you. But I will never take my love away from your son. [14] I will place him over my house and my kingdom forever. His throne will last forever." ' "

[15] Nathan reported to David all the words that the LORD had spoken to him.

David's Prayer

[16] Then King David went into the holy tent. He sat down in front of the LORD. He said,

"LORD God, who am I? My family isn't important. So why have you brought me this far? [17] I would have thought that you had already done more than enough for me. But now, my God, you have spoken about my royal house. You have said what will happen to it in days to come. LORD God, you have treated me as if I were the most honored man of all.

[18] "What more can I say to you for honoring me? You know all about me. [19] LORD, you have done a wonderful thing. You have given me many great promises. All of them are for my good. They are exactly what you wanted to give me.

[20] "LORD, there isn't anyone like you. There isn't any God but you. We have heard about it with our own ears. [21] Who is like your people Israel? God, we are the one nation on earth you have saved. You have set us free for yourself. Your name has become famous. You have done great and wonderful things. You have driven out nations to make room for your people. You saved us when you set us free from Egypt. [22] You made Israel your very own people forever. LORD, you have become our God.

[23] "And now, LORD, let the promise you have made to me and my royal house stand forever. Do exactly as you promised. [24] When your promise comes true, your name will be honored forever. People will say, 'The LORD rules over all. He is the God over Israel. He is Israel's God!' My royal house will be made secure in your sight.

[25] "My God, you have shown me that you will build me a royal house. So I can pray to you boldly. [26] You, LORD, are God! You

have promised many good things to me. ²⁷You have been pleased to bless my royal house. Now it will continue forever in your sight. LORD, you have blessed it. And it will be blessed forever."

David Wins Many Battles

18 While David was king of Israel, he won many battles over the Philistines. He brought them under his control. He took Gath away from the Philistines. He also captured the villages around Gath.

²David also won the battle over the people of Moab. They were brought under his rule. They gave him the gifts he required them to bring him.

³David fought against Hadadezer in the area of Hamath. Hadadezer was king of Zobah. He had gone to set up his monument at the Euphrates River. ⁴David captured 1,000 of Hadadezer's chariots, 7,000 chariot riders and 20,000 soldiers on foot. He cut the legs of all but 100 of the chariot horses.

⁵The Arameans of Damascus came to help Hadadezer, the king of Zobah. But David struck down 22,000 of them. ⁶David stationed some soldiers in the Aramean kingdom of Damascus. The people of Aram were brought under his rule. They gave him the gifts he required them to bring him. The LORD helped David win his battles wherever he went.

⁷David took the gold shields carried by the officers of Hadadezer. He brought the shields to Jerusalem. ⁸He took a huge amount of bronze from Tebah and Kun. Those towns belonged to Hadadezer. Later, Solomon used the bronze to make the huge bronze bowl for washing. He also used it to make the pillars and many other bronze objects for the temple.

⁹Tou was king of Hamath. He heard that David had won the battle over the entire army of Hadadezer, the king of Zobah. ¹⁰So Tou sent his son Hadoram to King David. Hadoram greeted David. He praised him because David had won the battle over Hadadezer. Hadadezer had been at war with Tou. So Hadoram brought David all kinds of things made out of gold, of silver and of bronze.

¹¹King David set those things apart for the LORD. He had done the same thing with the silver and gold he had taken from other nations. The nations were Edom, Moab, Ammon, Philistia and Amalek.

¹²Abishai struck down 18,000 men of Edom in the Valley of Salt. Abishai was the son of Zeruiah. ¹³Abishai stationed some soldiers in Edom. The whole nation of Edom was brought under his rule. The LORD helped David win his battles wherever he went.

David's Officials

¹⁴David ruled over the whole nation of Israel. He did what was fair and right for all his people.

15 Joab, the son of Zeruiah, was commander over the army.

Jehoshaphat, the son of Ahilud, kept the records. 16 Zadok, the son of Ahitub, was a priest. Ahimelek, the son of Abiathar, was also a priest.

Shavsha was the secretary. 17 Benaiah, the son of Jehoiada, was commander over the Kerethites and Pelethites.

And King David's sons were the chief officials who served at his side.

David Wins the Battle Over the Ammonites

19 Nahash was king of Ammon. After he died, his son became the next king after him. 2 David thought, "I'm going to be kind to Hanun. His father Nahash was kind to me." So David sent messengers to Hanun. He wanted them to tell Hanun how sad he was that Hanun's father had died. David's messengers went to the land of Ammon. They told Hanun how sad David was.

3 The Ammonite commanders spoke to Hanun. They said, "David has sent messengers to tell you he is sad. They say he wants to honor your father. But the real reason they've come is to look the land over. They want to destroy it." 4 So Hanun grabbed David's messengers. He shaved them. He cut off their clothes just below the waist and left them half naked. Then he sent them away.

5 Someone came and told David what had happened to his men. So David sent messengers to them because they were filled with shame. King David said to them, "Stay at Jericho until your beards grow out again. Then come back here."

6 The Ammonites realized that what they had done had made David very angry with them. So Hanun and the Ammonites got 38 tons of silver. They used it to hire chariots and chariot riders from Aram Naharaim, Aram Maakah and Zobah. 7 They hired 32,000 chariots and riders. They also hired the king of Maakah and his troops. All of them came out and camped near Medeba. At the same time the Ammonites brought their troops together from their towns. Then they marched out to fight.

8 David heard about it. So he sent Joab out with the entire army of Israel's fighting men. 9 The Ammonites marched out. They took up their battle positions at the entrance to their city. The kings who came to help them gathered their troops together in the open country. 10 Joab saw that there were lines of soldiers in front of him and behind him. So he chose some of the best troops in Israel. He sent them to march out against the Arameans. 11 He put the rest of the men under the command of his brother Abishai. They were sent to march out against the Ammonites. 12 Joab said, "Suppose the

Arameans are too strong for me. Then you must come and help me. But suppose the Ammonites are too strong for you. Then I'll come and help you. ¹³ Be strong. Let's be brave as we fight for our people and the cities of our God. The LORD will do what he thinks is best."

¹⁴ Then Joab and the troops with him marched out to attack the Arameans. They ran away from him. ¹⁵ The Ammonites realized that the Arameans were running away. So they also ran away from Joab's brother Abishai. They went inside the city. Then Joab went back to Jerusalem.

¹⁶ The Arameans saw that they had been driven away by Israel. So they sent messengers to get some Arameans from east of the Euphrates River. The Arameans were under the command of Shophak. He was the commander of Hadadezer's army.

¹⁷ David was told about it. So he gathered together the whole army of Israel. They went across the Jordan River. David marched out against the Arameans. He lined up his soldiers opposite them. He lined them up to meet the Arameans in battle. The Arameans began to fight against him. ¹⁸ But then they ran away from Israel. David killed 7,000 of their chariot riders. He killed 40,000 of their soldiers who were on foot. He also killed Shophak, the commander of their army.

¹⁹ The people who were under the rule of Hadadezer saw that Israel had won the battle over them. So they made a peace treaty with David. They were brought under his rule.

After that, the Arameans wouldn't help the Ammonites anymore.

Joab Captures the City of Rabbah

20 In the spring, Joab led Israel's army out. It was the time when kings march out to war. Joab destroyed the land of Ammon. He went to the city of Rabbah. He surrounded it and got ready to attack it. But David remained in Jerusalem. Later, Joab attacked Rabbah and completely destroyed it. ² David took the gold crown off the head of the king of Ammon. The crown weighed 75 pounds. It had jewels in it. It was placed on David's head. He took a huge amount of goods from the city. ³ He brought out the people who were there. He made them work with saws and iron picks and axes. David did that to all the towns in Ammon. Then he and his entire army returned to Jerusalem.

Israel Goes to War Against the Philistines

⁴ War broke out at Gezer against the Philistines. At that time Sibbekai killed Sippai. So the Philistines were brought under Israel's control. Sibbekai was a Hushathite. Sippai was from the family line of Rapha.

⁵ In another battle against the Philistines, Elhanan killed

Lahmi. Elhanan was the son of Jair. Lahmi was the brother of Goliath. Goliath was from the city of Gath. Lahmi's spear was as big as a weaver's rod.

⁶ There was still another battle. It took place at Gath. A huge man lived there. He had six fingers on each hand and six toes on each foot. So the total number of his toes and fingers was 24. He was also from the family line of Rapha. ⁷ He made fun of Israel. So Jonathan killed him. Jonathan was the son of David's brother Shimea.

⁸ Those Philistine men lived in Gath. They were from the family line of Rapha. David and his men killed them.

David Counts His Fighting Men

21 Satan rose up against Israel. He stirred up David to count the men of Israel. ² So David said to Joab and the commanders of the troops, "Go! Count the men of Israel from Beersheba all the way to Dan. Report back to me. Then I'll know how many there are."

³ Joab replied, "May the LORD multiply his troops 100 times. King David, you are my master. Aren't all the men under your control? Why would you want me to count them? Do you want to make Israel guilty?"

⁴ In spite of what Joab said, the king's order had more authority than Joab's reply did. So Joab left and went all through Israel. Then he came back to Jerusalem. ⁵ Joab reported to David how many fighting men he had counted. In the whole land of Israel there were 1,100,000 men who could use their swords well. That included 470,000 men in Judah.

⁶ But Joab didn't include the tribes of Levi and Benjamin in the total number. The king's command was sickening to Joab. ⁷ It was also evil in the sight of God. So he punished Israel.

⁸ Then David said to God, "I committed a great sin when I counted Israel's men. I beg you to take away my guilt. I've done a very foolish thing."

⁹ The LORD spoke to Gad, David's prophet. The LORD said, ¹⁰ "Go and tell David, 'The LORD says, "I could punish you in three different ways. Choose one of them for me to punish you with." '"

¹¹ So Gad went to David. Gad said to him, "The LORD says, 'Take your choice. ¹² You can have three years when there will not be enough food in the land. You can have three months when your enemies will sweep you away. They will catch up with you. They will destroy you with their swords. Or you can have three days when the sword of the LORD will punish you. That means there would be three days of plague in the land. My angel would strike down people in every part of Israel.' So take your pick. Tell me how to answer the one who sent me."

¹³ David said to Gad, "I'm suffering terribly. Let me fall into the hands of the LORD. His

mercy is very great. But don't let me fall into human hands."

¹⁴ So the LORD sent a plague on Israel. And 70,000 Israelites died. ¹⁵ God sent an angel to destroy Jerusalem. But as the angel was doing it, the LORD saw it. The LORD decided to end the plague he had sent. So he spoke to the angel who was destroying the people. He said, "That is enough! Do not kill any more people!" The angel of the LORD was standing at Araunah's threshing floor. Araunah was from the city of Jebus.

¹⁶ David looked up. He saw the angel of the LORD standing between heaven and earth. The angel was holding out a sword over Jerusalem. David and the elders fell with their faces to the ground. They were wearing the rough clothing people wear when they're sad.

¹⁷ David said to God, "I ordered the fighting men to be counted. I'm the one who has sinned. I am the shepherd of these people. I'm the one who has done what is wrong. These people are like sheep. What have they done? LORD my God, punish me and my family. But don't let this plague continue to strike your people."

David Builds an Altar

¹⁸ Then the angel of the LORD ordered Gad to tell David to go up to the threshing floor of Araunah, the Jebusite. He wanted David to build an altar there to honor the LORD. ¹⁹ So David went up and did it. He obeyed the message that Gad had spoken in the LORD's name. ²⁰ Araunah was threshing wheat. He turned and saw the angel. Araunah's four children were with him. They hid themselves. ²¹ David approached the threshing floor. Araunah looked up and saw him. So Araunah left the threshing floor. He bowed down to David with his face toward the ground.

²² David said to him, "Let me have the property your threshing floor is on. I want to build an altar there to honor the LORD. When I do, the plague on the people will be stopped. Sell the threshing floor to me for the full price."

²³ Araunah said to David, "Take it! King David, you are my master. Do what you please. I'll even provide the oxen for the burnt offerings. Use boards from the threshing sleds for the wood. Use the wheat for the grain offering. I'll give it all to you."

²⁴ But King David replied to Araunah, "No! I want to pay the full price. I won't take what belongs to you and give it to the LORD. I won't sacrifice a burnt offering that hasn't cost me anything."

²⁵ So David paid Araunah 15 pounds of gold for the property. ²⁶ David built an altar there to honor the LORD. He sacrificed burnt offerings and friendship offerings. He called out to the LORD. The LORD answered him by sending fire from heaven on the altar for burnt offerings.

27 Then the LORD spoke to the angel. And the angel put his sword away. 28 When the angel did that, David was still at the threshing floor of Araunah, the Jebusite. David saw that the LORD had answered him. So he offered sacrifices there. 29 At that time, the LORD's holy tent was at the high place in Gibeon. The altar for burnt offerings was there too. Moses had made the holy tent in the desert. 30 David couldn't go to the tent to pray to God. That's because he was afraid of the sword of the angel of the LORD.

22 David announced, "The house of the LORD God will be built here. Israel's altar for burnt offerings will also be here."

David Makes Plans for Building the Temple

2 David gave orders to bring together the outsiders who were living in Israel. He appointed some of them to cut stones. He wanted them to prepare blocks of stone for building the house of God. 3 David provided a large amount of iron to make nails. They were for the doors of the gateways and for the fittings. He provided more bronze than anyone could weigh. 4 He also provided more cedar logs than anyone could count. The people of Sidon and Tyre brought large numbers of logs to David.

5 David said, "My son Solomon is young. He's never done anything like this before. The house that will be built for the LORD should be very grand and wonderful. All the nations should consider it to be famous and beautiful. I'll get things ready for it." So David got many things ready before he died.

6 Then he sent for his son Solomon. He told him to build a house for the LORD, the God of Israel. 7 David said to Solomon, "My son, with all my heart I wanted to build a house for the LORD my God. That's where his Name will be. 8 But a message from the LORD came to me. It said, 'You have spilled the blood of many people. You have fought many wars. You are not the one who will build a house for my Name. That is because I have seen you spill the blood of many people on the earth. 9 But you are going to have a son. He will be a man of peace. And I will give him peace and rest from all his enemies on every side. His name will be Solomon. I will give Israel peace and quiet while he is king. 10 He will build a house for my Name. He will be my son. And I will be his father. I will make his kingdom secure over Israel. It will last forever.'

11 "My son, may the LORD be with you. May you have success. May you build the house of the LORD your God, just as he said you would. 12 May the LORD give you good sense. May he give you understanding when he makes you king over Israel. Then you will keep the law of the LORD your God. 13 Be careful to obey

the rules and laws the LORD gave Moses for Israel. Then you will have success. Be strong and brave. Don't be afraid. Don't lose hope.

14 "I've tried very hard to provide for the LORD's temple. I've provided 3,750 tons of gold and 37,500 tons of silver. I've provided more bronze and iron than anyone can weigh. I've also given plenty of wood and stone. You can add to it. 15 You have a lot of workers. You have people who can cut stones and people who can lay the stones. You have people who can work with wood. You also have people who are skilled in every other kind of work. 16 Some of them can work with gold and silver. Others can work with bronze and iron. There are more workers than anyone can count. So begin the work. May the LORD be with you."

17 Then David ordered all Israel's leaders to help his son Solomon. 18 He said to them, "The LORD your God is with you. He's given you peace and rest on every side. He's handed over to me the people who are living in the land. The land has been brought under the control of the LORD and his people. 19 So be committed to the LORD your God with all your heart and soul. Start building the temple of the LORD God. Then bring the ark of the covenant of the LORD into it. Also bring in the sacred objects that belong to God. The temple will be built for the Name of the LORD."

The Family Line of Levi

23 David had become very old. So he made his son Solomon king over Israel.

2 He gathered together all the leaders of Israel. He also gathered the priests and the Levites together. 3 The Levites who were 30 years old or more were counted. The total number of men was 38,000. 4 David said, "From them, 24,000 will be in charge of the work of the LORD's temple. And 6,000 will be officials and judges. 5 Another 4,000 will guard the gates. And 4,000 will praise the LORD with the instruments of music I've provided for that purpose."

6 David separated the Levites into groups. He did it according to the sons of Levi. The sons were Gershon, Kohath and Merari.

The Family of Gershon

7 Ladan and Shimei belonged to the family of Gershon.

8 The sons of Ladan were Jehiel, Zetham and Joel. Jehiel was the oldest son. The total number of sons was three.

9 The sons of Shimei were Shelomoth, Haziel and Haran. The total number of sons was three. They were the leaders of the families of Ladan.

10 The sons of Shimei were Jahath, Ziza, Jeush and Beriah. The total number of the sons of Shimei was four.

¹¹ Jahath was the first son. Ziza was the second son. But Jeush and Beriah didn't have many sons. So they were counted as one family. They had only one task.

The Family of Kohath

¹² The sons of Kohath were Amram, Izhar, Hebron and Uzziel. The total number of sons was four. ¹³ The sons of Amram were Aaron and Moses.

Aaron and his family line were set apart forever as the LORD's priests. They had the duty of setting the most holy things apart to the LORD. They offered sacrifices to the LORD. They served him. They gave blessings in his name forever. ¹⁴ The sons of Moses, the man of God, were counted as part of the tribe of Levi. ¹⁵ The sons of Moses were Gershom and Eliezer. ¹⁶ Shubael was the oldest son in the family line of Gershom. ¹⁷ Rehabiah was the oldest son in the family line of Eliezer.

Eliezer didn't have any other sons. But Rehabiah had a great many sons. ¹⁸ Shelomith was the oldest son of Izhar. ¹⁹ Jeriah was the first son of Hebron.

Amariah was his second son. Jahaziel was the third. Jekameam was the fourth. ²⁰ Micah was the first son of Uzziel.

Ishiah was his second son.

The Family of Merari

²¹ The sons of Merari were Mahli and Mushi.

The sons of Mahli were Eleazar and Kish. ²² Eleazar died without having any sons. All he had was daughters. They married their cousins. The cousins were the sons of Kish. ²³ The sons of Mushi were Mahli, Eder and Jerimoth. The total number of sons was three.

²⁴ Those were the family lines of Levi. They were recorded under the names of the family leaders. Each worker who was 20 years old or more was counted. They served in the LORD's temple. ²⁵ David had said, "The LORD is the God of Israel. He has given peace and rest to his people. He has come to Jerusalem to live there forever. ²⁶ So the Levites don't need to carry the holy tent anymore. They don't need to carry any of its objects anymore. Those were the things that were used to serve there." ²⁷ The Levites who were 20 years old or more were counted. That was in keeping with David's final directions.

28 The Levites had the duty of helping the members of Aaron's family line. They helped them serve in the LORD's temple. They were in charge of the courtyards and the side rooms. They made all the sacred things pure and "clean." They also had other duties at the house of God. 29 They were in charge of setting the holy bread out on the table. They prepared the special flour for the grain offerings. They made the thin loaves without using any yeast. They did the baking and the mixing. They measured the amount and size of everything. 30 They stood every morning to thank and praise the LORD. They did the same thing every evening. 31 They also did it every time burnt offerings were brought to the LORD. Those offerings were brought every Sabbath day. They were also brought at every New Moon feast and during the appointed yearly feasts. The Levites served in front of the LORD at regular times. The proper number of Levites was always used when they served. They served in the way the law required. 32 So the Levites carried out their duties for the tent of meeting and for the Holy Room. They worked under their relatives who were in the family line of Aaron. They helped them serve at the LORD's temple.

The Groups of Priests

24 The priests in the family line of Aaron were separated into groups. The groups were separated according to the sons of Aaron.

The sons of Aaron were Nadab, Abihu, Eleazar and Ithamar. 2 But Nadab and Abihu died before their father did. They didn't have any sons. So Eleazar and Ithamar served as the priests. 3 With the help of Zadok and Ahimelek, David separated the priests into groups. Each group served in its appointed order and time. Zadok belonged to the family line of Eleazar. Ahimelek belonged to the family line of Ithamar. 4 More leaders were found among Eleazar's family line than among Ithamar's. So the priests were separated into their groups based on that fact. There were 16 family leaders from Eleazar's line. There were eight family leaders from Ithamar's line. 5 The priests were separated into their groups by casting lots. That was the fair way to do it. The priests were officials of the temple and officials of God. They came from the family lines of Eleazar and Ithamar.

6 Shemaiah was a Levite. He was the son of Nethanel. Shemaiah was the writer who recorded the names of the priests. He wrote them down in front of the king and the officials. The officials included Zadok the priest and Ahimelek. Ahimelek was the son of Abiathar. The officials also included the leaders of the families of the priests and the Levites. One family was chosen by lot from Eleazar's group.

Then one was chosen from Ithamar's group.

⁷The 1st lot chosen was for Jehoiarib.
The 2nd was for Jedaiah.
⁸The 3rd was for Harim.
The 4th was for Seorim.
⁹The 5th was for Malkijah.
The 6th was for Mijamin.
¹⁰The 7th was for Hakkoz.
The 8th was for Abijah.
¹¹The 9th was for Jeshua.
The 10th was for Shekaniah.
¹²The 11th was for Eliashib.
The 12th was for Jakim.
¹³The 13th was for Huppah.
The 14th was for Jeshebeab.
¹⁴The 15th was for Bilgah.
The 16th was for Immer.
¹⁵The 17th was for Hezir.
The 18th was for Happizzez.
¹⁶The 19th was for Pethahiah.
The 20th was for Jehezkel.
¹⁷The 21st was for Jakin.
The 22nd was for Gamul.
¹⁸The 23rd was for Delaiah.
The 24th was for Maaziah.

¹⁹That was their appointed order for serving when they entered the LORD's temple. That order was based on the rules Aaron had given them long ago. Everything was done exactly as the LORD had commanded Aaron. The LORD is the God of Israel.

The Rest of the Levites

²⁰Here are the other members of the family line of Levi.

From the sons of Amram came Shubael.
From the sons of Shubael came Jehdeiah.
²¹From the sons of Rehabiah came Ishiah. Ishiah was the oldest.
²²From the people of Izhar came Shelomoth.
From the sons of Shelomoth came Jahath.
²³Jeriah was the first son of Hebron. Amariah was his second son. Jahaziel was the third. Jekameam was the fourth.
²⁴The son of Uzziel was Micah.
From the sons of Micah came Shamir.
²⁵The brother of Micah was Ishiah.
From the sons of Ishiah came Zechariah.
²⁶The sons of Merari were Mahli and Mushi.
The son of Jaaziah was Beno.
²⁷The sons of Merari from Jaaziah were Beno, Shoham, Zakkur and Ibri.
²⁸From Mahli came Eleazar. Eleazar didn't have any sons.
²⁹From Kish came Jerahmeel. Jerahmeel was the son of Kish.
³⁰The sons of Mushi were Mahli, Eder and Jerimoth.

Those were the Levites, family by family.

³¹They cast lots just as their relatives had done. Their rela-

tives were in the family line of Aaron. They cast lots in front of King David, Zadok and Ahimelek. They did it in front of the family leaders of the priests. They also did it in front of the family leaders of the Levites. The families of the oldest brother were treated in the same way as the families of the youngest.

The Musicians

25 David and the commanders of the army set apart some of the sons of Asaph, Heman and Jeduthun. They set them apart to serve the LORD by prophesying while harps, lyres and cymbals were being played. Here is the list of the men who served in that way.

2 From the sons of Asaph came
Zakkur, Joseph, Nethaniah and Asarelah. The sons of Asaph were under the direction of Asaph. He prophesied under the king's direction.

3 From the sons of Jeduthun came
Gedaliah, Zeri, Jeshaiah, Shimei, Hashabiah and Mattithiah. The total number was six. They were under the direction of their father Jeduthun. He prophesied while playing the harp. He used it to thank and praise the LORD.

4 From the sons of Heman came
Bukkiah, Mattaniah, Uz-ziel, Shubael, Jerimoth, Hananiah, Hanani, Eliathah, Giddalti, Romamti-Ezer, Joshbekashah, Mallothi, Hothir and Mahazioth. 5 All of them were sons of the king's prophet Heman. They were given to Heman to bring him honor. That's what God had promised. God gave him 14 sons and three daughters.

6 All of them were under the direction of their father. They played music for the LORD's temple. They served at the house of God by playing cymbals, lyres and harps. Asaph, Jeduthun and Heman were under the king's direction.
7 All of them were trained and skilled in playing music for the LORD. Their total number was 288. That included their relatives. 8 Young and old alike cast lots for their duties. That was true for students as well as teachers.

9 The 1st lot chosen was for Asaph. It was for Joseph and his sons and relatives. The total number was 12.
The 2nd lot was for Gedaliah and his relatives and sons. The total number was 12.
10 The 3rd was for Zakkur and his sons and relatives. The total number was 12.
11 The 4th was for Izri and his sons and relatives. The total number was 12.

¹²The 5th was for Nethaniah and his sons and relatives. The total number was 12. ¹³The 6th was for Bukkiah and his sons and relatives. The total number was 12. ¹⁴The 7th was for Jesarelah and his sons and relatives. The total number was 12. ¹⁵The 8th was for Jeshaiah and his sons and relatives. The total number was 12. ¹⁶The 9th was for Mattaniah and his sons and relatives. The total number was 12. ¹⁷The 10th was for Shimei and his sons and relatives. The total number was 12. ¹⁸The 11th was for Azarel and his sons and relatives. The total number was 12. ¹⁹The 12th was for Hashabiah and his sons and relatives. The total number was 12. ²⁰The 13th was for Shubael and his sons and relatives. The total number was 12. ²¹The 14th was for Mattithiah and his sons and relatives. The total number was 12. ²²The 15th was for Jerimoth and his sons and relatives. The total number was 12. ²³The 16th was for Hananiah and his sons and rela-

tives. The total number was 12. ²⁴The 17th was for Joshbekashah and his sons and relatives. The total number was 12. ²⁵The 18th was for Hanani and his sons and relatives. The total number was 12. ²⁶The 19th was for Mallothi and his sons and relatives. The total number was 12. ²⁷The 20th was for Eliathah and his sons and relatives. The total number was 12. ²⁸The 21st was for Hothir and his sons and relatives. The total number was 12. ²⁹The 22nd was for Giddalti and his sons and relatives. The total number was 12. ³⁰The 23rd was for Mahazioth and his sons and relatives. The total number was 12. ³¹The 24th was for Romamti-Ezer and his sons and relatives. The total number was 12.

The Men Who Guarded the Gates

26 Here are the groups of men who guarded the gates.

From the family of Korah came Meshelemiah, the son of Kore. Kore was one of the sons of Asaph. ²Meshelemiah had sons.

Zechariah was his first son.
Jediael was his second son.
Zebadiah was the third.
Jathniel was the fourth.
³ Elam was the fifth.
Jehohanan was the sixth.
And Eliehoenai was the seventh.
⁴ Obed-Edom also had sons.
Shemaiah was his first son.
Jehozabad was his second son.
Joah was the third.
Sakar was the fourth.
Nethanel was the fifth.
⁵ Ammiel was the sixth.
Issachar was the seventh.
And Peullethai was the eighth.
God had blessed Obed-Edom.
⁶ Obed-Edom's son Shemaiah also had sons. They were leaders in their family. That's because they were men of great ability. ⁷ The sons of Shemaiah were
Othni, Rephael, Obed and Elzabad.
Elzabad's relatives Elihu and Semakiah were also capable men.
⁸ All of them belonged to the family line of Obed-Edom. They and their sons and relatives were capable men. They were strong enough to do their work. The total number of men in the family line of Obed-Edom was 62.

⁹ Meshelemiah's sons and relatives were capable men. Their total number was 18.

¹⁰ Hosah belonged to the family line of Merari. Hosah's first son was
Shimri. But Shimri wasn't the oldest son. His father had made him the first.
¹¹ Hilkiah was Hosah's second son.
Tabaliah was the third.
Zechariah was the fourth.
The total number of Hosah's sons and relatives was 13.

¹² Those groups of men guarded the gates. They worked under their leaders. They served at the LORD's temple, just as their relatives had served. ¹³ Lots were cast for each gate, family by family. Young and old alike were chosen.
¹⁴ The lot chosen for the East Gate was for Shelemiah.
Then lots were cast for his son Zechariah, who gave wise advice. The lot chosen for the North Gate was for Zechariah.
¹⁵ The lot chosen for the South Gate was for Obed-Edom. The lot chosen for the storeroom was for his sons.
¹⁶ Lots were chosen for the West Gate and the Shalleketh Gate on the upper road. Those lots were chosen for Shuppim and Hosah.

One guard stood next to another.

¹⁷There were six Levites a day on the east.

There were four a day on the north.

There were four a day on the south.

And there were two at a time at the storeroom.

¹⁸Two Levite guards were at the courtyard to the west. And four were at the road.

¹⁹Those were the groups of the men who guarded the gates. They belonged to the family lines of Korah and Merari.

Other Officials

²⁰Men were in charge of the treasures in the house of God. They were the Levite relatives of the men who guarded the gates. These men were also in charge of other treasures that had been set apart for God. ²¹Ladan was from the family line of Gershon. Some leaders of families belonged to Ladan's family line. One of them was Jehieli. ²²The sons of Jehieli were Zetham and his brother Joel. They were in charge of the treasures in the LORD's temple.

²³Here are the officials who were from the family lines of Amram, Izhar, Hebron and Uzziel.

²⁴Shubael was from the family line of Moses' son Gershom. Shubael was the official in charge of the treasures. ²⁵His relatives through Eliezer included his son Rehabiah. Jeshaiah was Rehabiah's son. Joram was Jeshaiah's son. Zikri was Joram's son. And Shelomith was Zikri's son. ²⁶Shelomith and his relatives were in charge of all the treasures that had been set apart for God. King David had set those treasures apart. Some family leaders had also set them apart. They were the commanders of thousands of men and commanders of hundreds. The treasures had also been set apart by other army commanders. ²⁷Some of the goods that had been taken in battle were set apart to repair the LORD's temple. ²⁸Samuel the prophet had set apart some things for God. Saul, the son of Kish, had set apart other things. So had Abner, the son of Ner. And so had Joab, the son of Zeruiah. All these things and everything else that had been set apart were taken care of by Shelomith and his relatives.

²⁹From the family line of Izhar came Kenaniah and his sons. They were given duties that were away from the temple. They were offi-

cials and judges over Israel.

30 From the family line of Hebron came Hashabiah and his relatives. They were capable men. The total number was 1,700. It was their duty to serve the king in Israel west of the Jordan River. It was also their duty to do all the LORD's work there. 31 Jeriah was the chief of the family line of Hebron. That's based on their family history.

In the 40th year of David's rule, a search was made in the records. That's how capable men were found in the family line of Hebron at Jazer in Gilead. 32 Jeriah had 2,700 relatives. They were capable men and family leaders. King David had put them in charge of the tribes of Reuben and Gad and half of the tribe of Manasseh. They were in charge of matters having to do with God and the king.

The Groups of Fighting Men in the Army

27 Here is the list of the Israelites who served in the king's army. They included leaders of families. They included commanders of thousands of men and commanders of hundreds. They also included other officers. All of them served the king in everything concerning the army's fighting groups. These groups were on duty month by month all through the year. The total number of men in each group was 24,000.

2 Jashobeam was in charge of the first fighting group for the first month. He was the son of Zabdiel. The total number of men in Jashobeam's group was 24,000. 3 He belonged to the family line of Perez. He was chief of all the army officers for the first month.

4 Dodai was in charge of the second fighting group for the second month. He belonged to the family line of Ahoah. Mikloth was the leader of Dodai's group. The total number of men in Dodai's group was 24,000.

5 The third army commander for the third month was Benaiah the priest, the son of Jehoiada. Benaiah was the chief. The total number of men in Benaiah's fighting group was 24,000.

6 That same Benaiah was a mighty warrior among the 30 chiefs. In fact, he was leader over the 30 chiefs. His son Ammizabad was in charge of Benaiah's group.

7 The fourth commander for the fourth month was

Joab's brother Asahel. Asahel's son Zebadiah was the next commander after him. The total number of men in Asahel's fighting group was 24,000.

⁸ The fifth commander for the fifth month was Shamhuth. He was an Izrahite. The total number of men in Shamhuth's fighting group was 24,000.

⁹ The sixth commander for the sixth month was Ira. He was the son of Ikkesh from Tekoa. The total number of men in Ira's fighting group was 24,000.

¹⁰ The seventh commander for the seventh month was Helez. He was a Pelonite from Ephraim. The total number of men in Helez's fighting group was 24,000.

¹¹ The eighth commander for the eighth month was Sibbekai. He was a Hushathite from Zerah. The total number of men in Sibbekai's fighting group was 24,000.

¹² The ninth commander for the ninth month was Abiezer. He was from Anathoth in Benjamin. The total number of men in Abiezer's fighting group was 24,000.

¹³ The tenth commander for the tenth month was Maharai. He was a Netoph-athite from Zerah. The total number of men in Maharai's fighting group was 24,000.

¹⁴ The 11th commander for the 11th month was Benaiah. He was from Pirathon in Ephraim. The total number of men in Benaiah's fighting group was 24,000.

¹⁵ The 12th commander for the 12th month was Heldai. He was a Netophathite from the family line of Othniel. The total number of men in Heldai's fighting group was 24,000.

The Leaders of the Tribes

¹⁶ Here are the leaders of the tribes of Israel.

Over the tribe of Reuben was Eliezer, the son of Zikri.
Over Simeon was Shephatiah, the son of Maakah.
¹⁷ Over Levi was Hashabiah, the son of Kemuel.
Over Aaron was Zadok.
¹⁸ Over Judah was Elihu. He was David's brother.
Over Issachar was Omri, the son of Michael.
¹⁹ Over Zebulun was Ishmaiah, the son of Obadiah.
Over Naphtali was Jerimoth, the son of Azriel.
²⁰ Over Ephraim was Hoshea, the son of Azaziah.
Over half of the tribe of Manasseh was Joel, the son of Pedaiah.
²¹ Over the half of the tribe of

Manasseh in Gilead was Iddo, the son of Zechariah.

Over Benjamin was Jaasiel, the son of Abner. 22 Over Dan was Azarel, the son of Jeroham.

These were the leaders of the tribes of Israel.

23 David didn't count the men who were 20 years old or less. That's because the LORD had promised to make the people of Israel as many as the stars in the sky. 24 Joab, the son of Zeruiah, began to count the men. But he didn't finish. The LORD was angry with Israel because David had begun to count the men. So the number wasn't written down in the official records of King David.

Other Officials of the King

25 Azmaveth was in charge of the royal storerooms. He was the son of Adiel.

Jonathan was in charge of the storerooms in the fields, towns, villages and lookout towers. He was the son of Uzziah. 26 Ezri was in charge of the workers who farmed the land. He was the son of Kelub. 27 Shimei was in charge of the vineyards. He was from Ramah.

Zabdi was in charge of the grapes from the vineyards. He was also in charge of storing the wine. He was a Shiphmite.

28 Baal-Hanan was in charge of the olive trees and sycamore-fig trees in the western hills. He was from Geder.

Joash was in charge of storing the olive oil. 29 Shitrai was in charge of the herds that ate grass in Sharon. He was from Sharon.

Shaphat was in charge of the herds in the valleys. He was the son of Adlai. 30 Obil was in charge of the camels. He was from the family line of Ishmael.

Jehdeiah was in charge of the donkeys. He was from Meronoth. 31 Jaziz was in charge of the flocks. He was a Hagrite.

All these men were the officials in charge of King David's property.

32 Jonathan was David's uncle. He gave good advice. He was a man of understanding. He was also a secretary.

Jehiel took care of the king's sons. He was the son of Hakmoni. 33 Ahithophel was the king's adviser.

Hushai was the king's trusted friend. He was an Arkite. 34 Jehoiada and Abiathar became the next advisers after Ahithophel. Jehoiada was the son of Benaiah.

Joab was the commander of the royal army.

David's Plans for the Temple

28

David asked all the officials of Israel to come together at Jerusalem. He sent for the officers who were over the tribes. He sent for the commanders of the military groups who served the king. He sent for the commanders of thousands of men and commanders of hundreds. He sent for the officials who were in charge of all the royal property and livestock. They belonged to the king and his sons. He sent for the palace officials and the warriors. He also sent for all the brave fighting men.

² King David stood up. He said, "All of you Israelites, listen to me. With all my heart I wanted to build a house for the LORD. I wanted it to be a place of peace and rest for the ark of the covenant of the LORD. The ark is the stool for our God's feet. I made plans to build the LORD's house. ³ But God said to me, 'You are not the one who will build a house for my Name. That is because you are a fighting man. You have spilled people's blood.'

⁴ "But the LORD chose me. He is the God of Israel. He chose me from my whole family to be king over Israel forever. He chose Judah to lead the tribes. From the tribe of Judah he chose my family. From my father's sons he chose me. He was pleased to make me king over the whole nation of Israel. ⁵ The LORD has given me many sons. From all of them he has chosen my son Solomon. He wants Solomon to sit on the throne of the LORD's kingdom. He wants him to rule over Israel. ⁶ The LORD said to me, 'Your son Solomon is the one who will build my house and my courtyards. I have chosen him to be my son. And I will be his father. ⁷ I will make his kingdom secure. It will last forever. That will happen if he continues to obey my commands and laws. He must continue to obey them, just as he is doing now.'

⁸ "So I'm giving you a command in the sight of all the people of Israel. The LORD's community is watching. And our God is listening. I command you to be careful to follow all the commands of the LORD your God. Then you will own this good land. You will pass it on to your children after you as their share forever.

⁹ "My son Solomon, always remember the God of your father. Serve him with all your heart. Do it with a mind that wants to obey him. The LORD looks deep down inside every heart. He understands every desire and every thought. If you look to him, you will find him. But if you desert him, he will turn his back on you forever. ¹⁰ Think about it. The LORD has chosen you to build a house as a holy place where he can live. So be strong. Get to work."

¹¹ Then David gave his son Solomon the plans for the porch of the temple. He gave him the plans for its buildings and its storerooms. He gave him the

plans for its upper parts and its inside rooms. He gave him the plans for the place where sin is paid for and forgiven. ¹²He gave him the plans for everything the Spirit of the LORD had put in his mind. There were plans for the courtyards of the LORD's temple. There were plans for all the rooms around it. There were plans for the places where the treasure of God's temple would be kept. There were plans for the places where the things set apart for God would be kept. ¹³David told Solomon how to separate the priests and Levites into groups. He gave him directions for all the work they should do when they served in the LORD's temple. David also showed Solomon how all the objects should be used at the temple. ¹⁴Different things were used for different purposes. David told Solomon how much gold should be used for each gold object. He also told him how much silver should be used for each silver object. ¹⁵He told him how much gold should be used to make each gold lampstand and its lamps. He told him how much silver should be used to make each silver lampstand and its lamps. The amount depended on how each lampstand would be used. ¹⁶David told Solomon how much gold should be used to make each table for holy bread. He told him how much silver should be used to make the silver tables. ¹⁷He told him how much pure gold should be used to make the forks, sprinkling bowls and pitchers. He told him how much gold should be used to make each gold dish. He told him how much silver should be used to make each silver dish. ¹⁸And David told Solomon how much pure gold should be used to make the altar for burning incense. He also gave Solomon the plan for the chariot of the gold cherubim. The cherubim spread their wings over the ark of the covenant of the LORD.

¹⁹David said, "I have written everything down. I wrote it all down as the LORD guided me. He helped me understand every part of the plan."

²⁰David also said to his son Solomon, "Be strong and brave. Get to work. Don't be afraid. Don't lose hope. The LORD God is my God. He is with you. He won't fail you. He won't desert you until all the work for serving in the LORD's temple is finished. ²¹The groups of the priests and Levites are ready to do all the work on God's temple. Every person who is willing and skilled can help you do all the work. The officials and all the people will obey every command you give them."

Gifts Are Brought for Building the Temple

29 Then King David spoke to the whole community. He said, "God has chosen my son Solomon. But Solomon is young. He's never done anything like this before. The task is huge. This grand and wonderful temple won't be built for human beings. It will be built for the LORD God. ² With all my riches I've done everything I could for the temple of my God. I've provided gold for the gold work and silver for the silver work. I've provided bronze for the bronze work and iron for the iron work. I've given wood for the things that will be made out of wood. I've given onyx and turquoise for the settings. I've given stones of different colors and all kinds of fine stone and marble. I've provided everything in huge amounts. ³ With all my heart I want the temple of my God to be built. So I'm giving my personal treasures of gold and silver for it. I'm adding them to everything else I've provided for the holy temple. ⁴ I'm giving 110 tons of gold and 260 tons of pure silver. Cover the walls of the buildings with it. ⁵ Use it for the gold work and the silver work. Use it for everything the skilled workers will do. How many of you are willing to set yourselves apart to the LORD today?"

⁶ Many people were willing to give. They included the leaders of families and the officers of the tribes of Israel. They included the commanders of thousands of men and commanders of hundreds. They also included the officials who were in charge of the king's work. ⁷ All of them gave to the work on God's temple. They gave more than 190 tons of gold and 380 tons of silver. They also gave 675 tons of bronze and 3,800 tons of iron. ⁸ Anyone who had valuable jewels added them to the treasure for the LORD's temple. Jehiel was in charge of the temple treasure. He was from the family line of Gershon. ⁹ The people were happy when they saw what their leaders had been willing to give. The leaders had given freely. With their whole heart they had given everything to the LORD. King David was filled with joy.

David's Prayer

¹⁰ David praised the LORD in front of the whole community. He said,

"LORD, we give you praise.
  You are the God of our
    father Israel.
  We give you praise for ever
    and ever.
¹¹ LORD, you are great and
    powerful.
  Glory, majesty and beauty
    belong to you.
  Everything in heaven and
    on earth belongs to you.
  LORD, the kingdom belongs
    to you.
  You are honored as the one
    who rules over all.
¹² Wealth and honor come from
    you.
  You are the ruler of all
    things.
  In your hands are strength
    and power.
  You can give honor and
    strength to everyone.
¹³ Our God, we give you thanks.
  We praise your glorious
    name.

14 "But who am I? And who are my people? Without your help we wouldn't be able to give this much. Everything comes from you. We've given back to you only what comes from you. 15 We are outsiders and strangers in your sight. So were all of our people who lived long ago. Our days on this earth are like a shadow. We don't have any hope. 16 LORD our God, we've given more than enough. We've provided it to build you a temple where you will put your holy Name. But all of it comes from you. All of it belongs to you. 17 My God, I know that you tested our hearts. And you are pleased when we are honest. I've given all these things just because I wanted to. When I did it, I was completely honest with you. Your people here have also been willing to give to you. And I've been happy to see this. 18 LORD, you are the God of our fathers Abraham, Isaac and Israel. Keep these desires and thoughts in the hearts of your people forever. Keep their hearts faithful to you. 19 Help my son Solomon serve you with all his heart. Then he will keep your commands and rules. He will do what you require. He'll do everything to build the grand and wonderful temple I've provided for."

20 Then David said to the whole community, "Praise the LORD your God." So all of them praised the LORD. He's the God of their people who lived long ago. The whole commu-nity bowed low. They fell down flat with their faces toward the ground. They did it in front of the LORD and the king.

Solomon Becomes the Next King

21 The next day they offered sacrifices to the LORD. They brought burnt offerings to him. They sacrificed 1,000 bulls, 1,000 rams and 1,000 male lambs. They also brought the required drink offerings. And they offered many other sacri-fices for the whole community of Israel. 22 They ate and drank with great joy that day. They did it in front of the LORD. Then they announced a second time that Solomon was king. He was the son of David. They anointed Solomon in front of the LORD. They anointed him to be ruler. They also anointed Zadok to be priest.

23 So Solomon sat on the throne of the LORD. He ruled as king in place of his father Da-vid. Things went well with him. All the people of Israel obeyed him. 24 All the officers and war-riors promised to be completely faithful to King Solomon. So did all of King David's sons.

25 The LORD greatly honored Solomon in the sight of all the people. He gave him royal maj-esty. Solomon was given more glory than any king over Israel ever had before.

David Dies

26 David was king over the whole nation of Israel. He was the son of Jesse. 27 He ruled over

Israel for 40 years. He ruled for seven years in Hebron and for 33 years in Jerusalem. [28] He died when he was very old. He had enjoyed a long life. He had enjoyed wealth and honor. David's son Solomon became the next king after him.

[29] The events of King David's rule from beginning to end are written down. They are written in the records of Samuel, Nathan and Gad, the prophets. [30] The records tell all about David's rule and power. They tell about what happened concerning him and Israel and the kingdoms of all the other lands.

2 Chronicles

Introduction:

The book of 2 Chronicles tells about David's sons. This book was written to help the people of Israel. It reminded them about their past. God always loved them. God still loved them.

God made a promise to David's sons. If they did what God said, they would have peace. If they did not do what God said, they would have war. This book tells about the good and bad kings. But it tells more about the good kings than the bad ones.

The people and their kings did not stay faithful to God. So God let a king named Nebuchadnezzar take the people captive. But God still loved his people. At the end of the book, God let his people go home.

Outline of contents:

Solomon Asks God for Wisdom

1 Solomon was the son of David. Solomon made his position secure over his kingdom. The LORD his God was with him. He made Solomon very great.

² Solomon spoke to the whole community of Israel. He spoke to the commanders of thousands of men and commanders of hundreds. He spoke to the judges and all the leaders in Israel. He spoke to the leaders of Israel's families. ³ Solomon and the whole community went to the high place at Gibeon. That's because God's tent of meeting was there. The LORD's servant Moses had made the tent in the desert. ⁴ David had carried up the ark of God from Kiriath Jearim. He had brought it to the place he had prepared for it. He had set up a tent for it in Jerusalem. ⁵ But the bronze altar that Bezalel had made was in Gibeon. Bezalel was the son of Uri. Uri was the son of Hur. The altar was in front of the LORD's holy tent. So Solomon and the whole community asked the LORD for advice in Gibeon. ⁶ Solomon went up to the bronze altar in front of the LORD at the tent of meeting. Solomon sacrificed 1,000 burnt offerings on the altar.

⁷ That night God appeared to Solomon. He said to him, "Ask for anything you want me to give you."

⁸ Solomon answered God, "You were very kind to my father David. Now you have made me king in his place. ⁹ LORD God, let

the promise you gave to my father David come true. You have made me king. My people are as many as the dust of the earth. They can't be counted. ¹⁰ Give me wisdom and knowledge. Then I'll be able to lead these people. Without your help, who would be able to rule this great nation of yours?"

¹¹ God said to Solomon, "I am glad that those are the things you really want. You have not asked for wealth, possessions or honor. You have not even asked to have your enemies killed. You have not asked to live for a long time. Instead, you have asked for wisdom and knowledge. You want to be able to rule my people wisely. I have made you king over them. ¹² So wisdom and knowledge will be given to you. I will also give you wealth, possessions and honor. You will have more than any king before you ever had. And no king after you will have as much."

¹³ Then Solomon left the high place at Gibeon. He went from the tent of meeting there to Jerusalem. And he ruled over Israel.

¹⁴ Solomon had 1,400 chariots and 12,000 horses. He kept some of them in the chariot cities. He kept others with him in Jerusalem. ¹⁵ The king made silver and gold as common in Jerusalem as stones. He made cedar wood as common there as sycamore-fig trees in the western hills. ¹⁶ Solomon got horses from Egypt and Kue. The king's buyers purchased them from Kue at the current price. ¹⁷ They could get a chariot from Egypt for 15 pounds of silver. They could get a horse for less than four pounds of silver. They sold horses and chariots to all the Hittite and Aramean kings.

Solomon Prepares to Build the Temple

2 Solomon gave orders to build a temple. That's where the LORD would put his Name. Solomon also gave orders to build a royal palace for himself. ² He chose 70,000 men to carry things. He chose 80,000 to cut stones in the hills. He put 3,600 men in charge of them.

³ Solomon sent a message to Hiram. Hiram was king of Tyre. Solomon said,

"Send me cedar logs, just as you did for my father David. You sent him cedar to build a palace to live in. ⁴ Now I'm about to build a temple. The Name of the LORD my God will be there. I'll set the temple apart for him. Sweet-smelling incense will be burned in front of him there. The holy bread will be set out at regular times. Burnt offerings will be sacrificed there every morning and evening. They will be sacrificed every Sabbath day. They will be sacrificed at every New Moon feast. And they will be sacrificed at every yearly appointed feast of the LORD our God. That's a law for Israel that will last for all time to come.

5 "The temple I'm going to build will be beautiful. That's because our God is greater than all other gods. 6 So who is able to build a temple for him? After all, the heavens can't hold him. In fact, not even the highest heavens can hold him. So who am I to build a temple for him? It will only be a place to burn sacrifices in front of him.

7 "Send me a man skilled at working with gold, silver, bronze and iron. He must also be able to work with purple, blue and bright red yarn. He must be skilled in the art of carving. Send him to work in Judah and Jerusalem with my skilled workers. My father David provided them to help me.

8 "Also send me cedar, juniper and algum logs from Lebanon. I know that your servants are skilled in cutting wood there. My servants will work with yours. 9 They'll provide me with plenty of lumber. That's because the temple I'm building must be large and beautiful. 10 I'll pay your servants. They will cut the wood. I'll pay them 3,600 tons of wheat that has been ground up. I'll pay them 3,000 tons of barley. I'll also pay them 120,000 gallons of wine and 120,000 gallons of olive oil."

11 King Hiram of Tyre replied to Solomon. He wrote a letter to him. In it Hiram said,

"The LORD loves his people. That's why he has made you their king."

12 Hiram continued,

"I praise the LORD. He is the God of Israel. He made heaven and earth. He has given King David a wise son. You have good sense. You understand what is right. You will build a temple for the LORD. You will also build a palace for yourself.

13 "I'm sending Huram-Abi to you. He is very skillful. 14 His mother was from Dan. His father was from Tyre. He is trained to work with gold, silver, bronze and iron. He knows how to work with stone and wood. He can also work with purple, blue and bright red yarn and fine linen. He's skilled in all kinds of carving. He can follow any pattern you give him. He'll work with your skilled workers. He'll also work with those of your father David. David was my master.

15 "Now please send us what you promised. Send us the wheat, barley, olive oil and wine. 16 And we'll cut all the logs from Lebanon that you need. We'll make rafts out of them. We'll float them by sea down to Joppa. Then you can take them up to Jerusalem."

¹⁷ Solomon counted all the outsiders who were living in Israel. He did it after his father David had counted them. There were 153,600 of them. ¹⁸ He chose 70,000 to carry things. He chose 80,000 to cut stones in the hills. He put 3,600 men in charge of the people to keep them working.

Solomon Builds the Temple

3 Then Solomon began to build the temple of the LORD. He built it on Mount Moriah in Jerusalem. That's where the LORD had appeared to Solomon's father David. The LORD had appeared at the threshing floor of Araunah. Araunah was from Jebus. David had provided the threshing floor. ² Solomon began building the temple on the second day of the second month. It was in the fourth year of his rule.

³ Solomon laid the foundation for God's temple. It was 90 feet long and 30 feet wide. Solomon's men followed the standard measure used at that time. ⁴ The porch in front of the temple was 30 feet across and 30 feet high.

Solomon covered the inside of the temple with pure gold. ⁵ He covered the inside of the main hall with juniper boards. Then he covered the boards with fine gold. He decorated the hall with palm tree patterns and chain patterns. ⁶ He decorated the temple with valuable jewels. The gold he used came from Parvaim. ⁷ He covered the ceiling beams, doorframes, walls and doors of the temple with gold. He carved cherubim on the walls.

⁸ He built the Most Holy Room. It was as long as the temple was wide. It was 30 feet long and 30 feet wide. He covered the inside of the Most Holy Room with 23 tons of fine gold. ⁹ He also covered the upper parts with gold. The gold on the nails weighed 20 ounces.

¹⁰ For the Most Holy Room, Solomon made a pair of carved cherubim. He covered them with gold. ¹¹ The total length of the cherubim's wings from tip to tip was 30 feet. One wing of the first cherub was seven and a half feet long. Its tip touched the temple wall. The other wing was also seven and a half feet long. Its tip touched the wing tip of the other cherub. ¹² In the same way one wing of the second cherub was seven and a half feet long. Its tip touched the other temple wall. The other wing was also seven and a half feet long. Its tip touched the wing tip of the first cherub. ¹³ So the total length of the wings of the two cherubim was 30 feet from tip to tip. The cherubim stood facing the main hall.

¹⁴ Solomon made the curtain out of blue, purple and bright red yarn and fine linen. A skilled worker sewed cherubim into its pattern.

¹⁵ For the front of the temple, Solomon made two pillars. Each pillar was 26 feet tall. Each had a decorated top seven and a half feet high. ¹⁶ Solomon made

chains that were linked together. He put them on top of the pillars. He also made 100 pomegranates. He fastened them to the chains. ¹⁷ Solomon set the pillars up in front of the temple. One was on the south. The other was on the north. He named the one on the south Jakin. The one on the north he named Boaz.

More Facts About the Temple

4 Solomon made a bronze altar 30 feet long, 30 feet wide and 15 feet high. ² He made a huge metal bowl for washing. Its shape was round. It measured 15 feet from rim to rim. It was seven and a half feet high. And it was 45 feet around. ³ Below the rim there was a circle of bull figures around the bowl. In every 18 inches around the bowl there were ten bulls. The bulls were arranged in two rows. They were made as part of the bowl itself.

⁴ The bowl stood on 12 bulls. Three of them faced north. Three faced west. Three faced south. And three faced east. The bowl rested on top of them. Their rear ends were toward the center. ⁵ The bowl was three inches thick. Its rim was like the rim of a cup. The rim was shaped like the bloom of a lily. The bowl held 18,000 gallons of water.

⁶ Solomon made ten smaller bowls for washing. He placed five of them on the south side of the huge bowl. He placed the other five on the north side. The things used for the burnt offerings were rinsed in the smaller bowls. But the priests used the huge bowl for washing.

⁷ Solomon made ten gold lampstands. He followed the pattern the Lord had given him. He placed the lampstands in the temple. He put five of them on the south side. He put the other five on the north side.

⁸ He made ten tables. He placed them in the temple. He put five of them on the south side. He put the other five on the north side. He also made 100 gold sprinkling bowls.

⁹ He made the courtyard of the priests. He also made the large courtyard. He made doors for it. He covered the doors with bronze. ¹⁰ He placed the huge bowl on the south side of the courtyard. He put it at the southeast corner.

¹¹ And Huram also made the pots, shovels and sprinkling bowls.

So Huram finished the work he had started for King Solomon. Here's what he made for God's temple.

¹² He made the two pillars.
He made the two tops for the pillars. The tops were shaped like bowls.
He made the two sets of chains that were linked together. They decorated the two bowl-shaped tops of the pillars.
¹³ He made the 400 pomegranates for the two sets of chains. There were two rows of pomegranates for each chain. They

decorated the bowl-shaped tops of the pillars.
¹⁴He made the stands and their bowls.
¹⁵He made the huge bowl. He made the 12 bulls that were under it.
¹⁶He made the pots, shovels and meat forks. He also made all the things used with them.

Huram-Abi made all these objects for King Solomon for the LORD's temple. He made them out of bronze. Then he shined them up. ¹⁷The king had them made in clay molds. It was done on the plains of the Jordan River between Sukkoth and Zarethan. ¹⁸Solomon made huge numbers of these things. There were too many of them to weigh. In fact, it was impossible to add up the weight of all the bronze.

¹⁹Solomon also made all the objects that were in God's temple.

He made the golden altar.
He made the tables for the holy bread.
²⁰He made the pure gold lampstands and their lamps. The lamps burned in front of the Most Holy Room, just as the law required.
²¹He made the gold flowers. He made the gold lamps and tongs. They were made out of solid gold.
²²He made the wick cutters, sprinkling bowls, dishes, and shallow cups for burning incense. All of them were made out of pure gold. He made the gold doors of the temple. They were the inner doors to the Most Holy Room and the doors of the main hall.

5 Solomon finished all the work for the LORD's temple. Then he brought in the things his father David had set apart for the LORD. They included the silver and gold and all the objects for God's temple. Solomon placed them there with the other treasures.

The Ark Is Brought to the Temple

²Then Solomon sent for the elders of Israel. He told them to come to Jerusalem. They included all the leaders of the tribes. They also included the chiefs of the families of Israel. Solomon wanted them to bring up the ark of the LORD's covenant from Zion. Zion was the City of David. ³All the Israelites came together to where the king was. It was at the time of the Feast of Booths. The feast was held in the seventh month.

⁴All the elders of Israel arrived. Then the Levites picked up the ark and carried it. ⁵They brought up the ark. They also brought up the tent of meeting and all the sacred things in the tent. The priests, who were Levites, carried up everything. ⁶The entire community of Israel had gathered around King Solomon. All of them were in front of the ark. They sacrificed huge numbers of sheep and cattle.

There were so many animals that they couldn't be recorded. In fact, they couldn't even be counted.

7 The priests brought the ark of the LORD's covenant to its place in the Most Holy Room of the temple. They put it under the wings of the cherubim. 8 The cherubim's wings were spread out over the place where the ark was. They covered the ark. They also covered the poles used to carry it. 9 The poles reached out from the ark. They were so long that their ends could be seen from in front of the Most Holy Room. But they couldn't be seen from outside the Holy Room. They are still there to this day. 10 There wasn't anything in the ark except the two tablets. Moses had placed them in it at Mount Horeb. That's where the LORD had made a covenant with the Israelites. He made it after they came out of Egypt.

11 The priests left the Holy Room. All the priests who were there had set themselves apart to the LORD. It didn't matter what group they were in. 12 All the Levites who played music stood near the east side of the altar. They included Asaph, Heman, Jeduthun and their sons and relatives. They were dressed in fine linen. They were playing cymbals, harps and lyres. They were joined by 120 priests who were blowing trumpets. 13 The trumpet players and other musicians played their instruments together. They praised the LORD and gave

thanks to him. The singers sang to the music of the trumpets, cymbals and other instruments. They sang in praise to the LORD,

"The LORD is good.
His faithful love continues forever."

Then a cloud filled the temple of the LORD. 14 The priests couldn't do their work. That's because the cloud of the LORD's glory filled God's temple.

6 Then Solomon said, "LORD, you have said you would live in a dark cloud. 2 I've built a beautiful temple for you. You can live in it forever."

3 The whole community of Israel was standing there. The king turned around and gave them his blessing. 4 Then he said,

"I praise the LORD. He is the God of Israel. With his mouth he made a promise to my father David. With his powerful hands he made it come true. He said, 5 'I brought my people out of Egypt. Since then, a temple for my Name has not been built. I have not chosen a city in any tribe of Israel for that purpose. And I have not chosen anyone to be ruler over my people Israel. 6 But now I have chosen Jerusalem. I will put my Name there. And I have chosen David to rule over my people Israel.'

7 "With all his heart my father David wanted to build a temple. He wanted

to do it so the Name of the LORD could be there. The LORD is the God of Israel. ⁸But the LORD spoke to my father David. He said, 'With all your heart you wanted to build a temple for my Name. It is good that you wanted to do that. ⁹But you will not build the temple. Instead, your son will build the temple for my Name. He is your own flesh and blood.'

¹⁰ "The LORD has kept the promise he made. I've become the next king after my father David. Now I'm sitting on the throne of Israel. That's exactly what the LORD promised would happen. I've built the temple for the Name of the LORD. He is the God of Israel. ¹¹I've placed the ark there. The tablets of the LORD's covenant are inside it. He made that covenant with the people of Israel."

Solomon Prays to Set the Temple Apart to the LORD

¹²Then Solomon stood in front of the LORD's altar. He stood in front of the whole community of Israel. He spread out his hands to pray. ¹³He had made a bronze stage. It was seven and a half feet long and seven and a half feet wide. It was four and a half feet high. He had placed it in the center of the outer courtyard. He stood on the stage. Then he got down on his knees in front of the whole community of Israel.

He spread out his hands toward heaven. ¹⁴He said,

"LORD, you are the God of Israel. There is no God like you in heaven or on earth. You keep the covenant you made with us. You show us your love. You do that when we follow you with all our hearts. ¹⁵You have kept your promise to my father David. He was your servant. With your mouth you made a promise. With your powerful hand you have made it come true. And today we can see it.

¹⁶ "LORD, you are the God of Israel. Keep the promises you made to my father David. Do it for him. He was your servant. You said to him, 'You will always have a son from your family line to sit on Israel's throne. He will sit in front of the Most Holy Room, where my own throne is. That will be true only if your children after you are careful in everything they do. They must live the way my law tells them to. That is the way you have lived.' ¹⁷LORD, you are the God of Israel. So let your promise to your servant David come true.

¹⁸ "But will God really live on earth with human beings? After all, the heavens can't hold you. In fact, even the highest heavens can't hold you. So this temple I've built certainly can't hold you! ¹⁹But please pay atten-

tion to my prayer. LORD my God, be ready to help me as I make my appeal to you. Listen to my cry for help. Hear the prayer I'm praying to you. [20] Let your eyes look toward this temple day and night. You said you would put your Name here. Listen to the prayer I'm praying toward this place. [21] Hear me when I ask you to help us. Listen to your people Israel when they pray toward this place. Listen to us from heaven. It's the place where you live. When you hear us, forgive us.

[22] "Suppose someone does something wrong to their neighbor. And the person who has done something wrong is required to give their word. They must tell the truth about what they have done. They must come and do it in front of your altar in this temple. [23] When they do, listen to them from heaven. Take action. Judge between the person and their neighbor. Pay back the guilty one. Do to them what they have done to their neighbor. Deal with the one who isn't guilty in a way that shows they are free from blame. That will prove they aren't guilty.

[24] "Suppose your people Israel have lost the battle against their enemies. And suppose they've sinned against you. But they turn back to you and praise your name. They pray to you in this temple. And they ask you to help them. [25] Then listen to them from heaven. Forgive the sin of your people Israel. Bring them back to the land you gave to them and their people who lived long ago.

[26] "Suppose your people have sinned against you. And because of that, the sky is closed up and there isn't any rain. But your people pray toward this place. They praise you by admitting they've sinned. And they turn away from their sin because you have made them suffer. [27] Then listen to them from heaven. Forgive the sin of your people Israel. Teach them the right way to live. Send rain on the land you gave them as their share.

[28] "Suppose there isn't enough food in the land. And a plague strikes the land. The hot winds completely dry up our crops. Or locusts or grasshoppers come and eat them up. Or enemies surround one of our cities and get ready to attack it. Or trouble or sickness comes. [29] But suppose one of your people prays to you. They ask you to help them. They are aware of how much they are suffering. And they spread out their hands toward this temple to pray. [30] Then

listen to them from heaven. It's the place where you live. Forgive them. Deal with everyone in keeping with everything they do. You know their hearts. In fact, you are the only one who knows every human heart. ³¹ Your people will have respect for you. They will live the way you want them to. They'll live that way as long as they are in the land you gave our people long ago.

³² "Suppose an outsider who doesn't belong to your people Israel has come from a land far away. They have come because they've heard about your great name. They have heard that you reached out your mighty hand and powerful arm. So they come and pray toward this temple. ³³ Then listen to them from heaven. It's the place where you live. Do what that outsider asks you to do. Then all the nations on earth will know you. They will have respect for you. They'll respect you just as your own people Israel do. They'll know that your Name is in this house I've built.

³⁴ "Suppose your people go to war against their enemies. It doesn't matter where you send them. And suppose they pray to you toward this city you have chosen. They pray toward the temple I've built for your Name. ³⁵ Then listen to them from heaven. Listen to their prayer. Listen to them when they ask you to help them. Stand up for them.

³⁶ "Suppose they sin against you. After all, there isn't anyone who doesn't sin. And suppose you get angry with them. You hand them over to their enemies. They take them as prisoners to another land. It doesn't matter whether that land is near or far away. ³⁷ But suppose your people change their ways in the land where they are held as prisoners. They turn away from their sins. They beg you to help them in the land where they are prisoners. They say, 'We have sinned. We've done what is wrong. We've done what is evil.' ³⁸ And they turn back to you with all their heart and soul. Suppose it happens in the land where they were taken as prisoners. There they pray toward the land you gave their people long ago. They pray toward the city you have chosen. And they pray toward the temple I've built for your Name. ³⁹ Then listen to them from heaven. It's the place where you live. Listen to their prayer. Listen to them when they ask you to help them. Stand up for them. Your people have sinned against you. Please forgive them.

⁴⁰ "My God, let your eyes

see us. Let your ears pay attention to the prayers offered in this place.

⁴¹ "LORD God, rise up and come
to your resting place.
Come in together with the
ark.
It's the sign of your power.
LORD God, may your priests
put on salvation as if it
were their clothes.
May your faithful people
be glad because you are
so good.
⁴² LORD God, don't turn your
back on your anointed
king.
Remember the great love
you promised to your
servant David."

*The Temple Is Set Apart
to the LORD*

7 Solomon finished praying. Then fire came down from heaven. It burned up the burnt offering and the sacrifices. The glory of the LORD filled the temple. ² The priests couldn't enter the temple of the LORD because his glory filled it. ³ All the Israelites saw the fire coming down. They saw the glory of the LORD above the temple. So they got down on their knees in the courtyard with their faces toward the ground. They worshiped the LORD. They gave thanks to him and said,

"The LORD is good.
His faithful love continues
forever."

⁴ Then the king and all the people offered sacrifices to the

LORD. ⁵ King Solomon sacrificed 22,000 oxen and 120,000 sheep and goats. So the king and all the people set the temple of God apart. ⁶ The priests and Levites took their positions. The Levites played the LORD's musical instruments. King David had made them for praising the LORD. They were used when he gave thanks to the LORD. He said, "His faithful love continues forever." Across from where the Levites were, the priests blew their trumpets. All the people of Israel were standing.

⁷ Solomon set the middle area of the courtyard apart to the LORD. It was in front of the LORD's temple. There Solomon sacrificed burnt offerings. He also sacrificed the fat of the friendship offerings there. He did it there because the bronze altar he had made couldn't hold it all. It couldn't hold the burnt offerings, the grain offerings and the fat parts.

⁸ At that time Solomon celebrated the Feast of Booths for seven days. The whole community of Israel was with him. It was a huge crowd. People came from as far away as Lebo Hamath and the Wadi of Egypt. ⁹ On the eighth day they held a special service. For seven days they had celebrated by setting the altar apart to honor God. The feast continued for seven more days. ¹⁰ Then Solomon sent the people home. It was the 23rd day of the seventh month. The people were glad. Their hearts were full of joy. That's because

the LORD had done good things for David and Solomon and his people Israel.

The LORD Appears to Solomon

[11] Solomon finished the LORD's temple and the royal palace. He had done everything he had planned to do in the LORD's temple and his own palace. [12] The LORD appeared to him at night. The LORD said,

"I have heard your prayer. I have chosen this place for myself. It is a temple where sacrifices will be offered. [13] "Suppose I close up the sky and there isn't any rain. Suppose I command locusts to eat up the crops. And I send a plague among my people. [14] But they make themselves humble in my sight. They pray and look to me. And they turn from their evil ways. Then I will listen to them from heaven. I will forgive their sin. And I will heal their land. After all, they are my people. [15] Now my eyes will see them. My ears will pay attention to the prayers they offer in this place. [16] I have chosen this temple. I have set it apart for myself. My Name will be there forever. My eyes and my heart will always be there.

[17] "But you must walk faithfully with me, just as your father David did. Do everything I command you to do. Obey my rules and laws. [18] Then I will set up

your royal throne. I made a covenant with your father David to do that. I said to him, 'You will always have a son from your family line to rule over Israel.'

[19] "But suppose all of you turn away from me. You refuse to obey the rules and commands I have given you. And you go off to serve other gods and worship them. [20] Then I will remove Israel from my land. It is the land I gave them. I will turn my back on this temple. I will do it even though I have set it apart for my Name to be there. I will make all the nations hate it. They will laugh and joke about it. [21] This temple will become a pile of stones. All those who pass by it will be shocked. They will say, 'Why has the LORD done a thing like this to this land and temple?' [22] People will answer, 'Because they have deserted the LORD. He is the God of their people who lived long ago. He brought them out of Egypt. But they have been holding on to other gods. They've been worshiping them. They've been serving them. That's why the LORD has brought all this horrible trouble on them.'"

Other Things Solomon Did

8 Solomon built the LORD's temple and his own palace. It took him 20 years to build them.

After that, ² Solomon rebuilt the villages Hiram had given him. Solomon had Israelites make their homes in them. ³ Then Solomon went to Hamath Zobah. He captured it. ⁴ He also built up Tadmor in the desert. He built up all the cities in Hamath where he could store things. ⁵ He rebuilt Upper Beth Horon and Lower Beth Horon. He put up high walls around them. He made their city gates secure with heavy metal bars. ⁶ He rebuilt Baalath and all the cities where he could store things. He also rebuilt all the cities for his chariots and horses. Solomon built anything he wanted in Jerusalem, Lebanon and all the territory he ruled.

⁷ There were still many people left in the land who weren't Israelites. They included Hittites, Amorites, Perizzites, Hivites and Jebusites. ⁸ They were children of the people who had lived in the land before the Israelites came. The people of Israel hadn't destroyed them. Solomon forced them to work very hard as his slaves. And they still work for Israel to this day. ⁹ But Solomon didn't force the Israelites to work as his slaves. Instead, some were his fighting men. Others were commanders of his captains, chariots and chariot drivers. ¹⁰ Still others were King Solomon's chief officials. There were 250 officials in charge of the other men.

¹¹ Solomon brought Pharaoh's daughter up from the City of David to the palace he had built for her. Solomon said, "My wife must not live in the palace of David, who was the king of Israel. It's one of the places the ark of the LORD has entered. That makes it holy."

¹² Solomon had built the LORD's altar. It stood in front of the temple porch. On that altar Solomon sacrificed burnt offerings to the LORD. ¹³ Each day he sacrificed what the Law of Moses required. He sacrificed the required offerings every Sabbath day. He also sacrificed them at each New Moon feast and during the three yearly feasts. Those three were the Feast of Unleavened Bread, the Feast of Weeks and the Feast of Booths. ¹⁴ Solomon followed the orders his father David had given him. He appointed the groups of priests for their duties. He appointed the Levites to lead the people in praising the LORD. They also helped the priests do their required tasks each day. Solomon appointed the groups of men who guarded all the gates. That's what David, the man of God, had ordered. ¹⁵ The king's commands were followed completely. They applied to the priests and Levites. They also applied to the temple treasure.

¹⁶ All of Solomon's work was carried out. It started the day the foundation of the LORD's temple was laid. It ended when the LORD's temple was finished.

¹⁷ Solomon went to Ezion Geber and Elath on the coast of Edom. ¹⁸ Hiram sent him ships that his own officers

commanded. They were sailors who knew the sea. Together with Solomon's men they sailed to Ophir. They brought back 17 tons of gold. They gave it to King Solomon.

The Queen of Sheba Visits Solomon

9 The queen of Sheba heard about how famous Solomon was. So she came to Jerusalem to test him with hard questions. She arrived with a very large group of attendants. Her camels were carrying spices, huge amounts of gold, and valuable jewels. She came to Solomon and asked him about everything she wanted to know. ² He answered all her questions. There wasn't anything too hard for him to explain to her. ³ So the queen of Sheba saw how wise Solomon was. She saw the palace he had built. ⁴ She saw the food on his table. She saw his officials sitting there. She saw the robes of the servants who waited on everyone. She saw the robes the wine tasters were wearing. And she saw the burnt offerings Solomon sacrificed at the Lord's temple. She could hardly believe everything she had seen.

⁵ She said to the king, "Back in my own country I heard a report about you. I heard about how much you had accomplished. I also heard about how wise you are. Everything I heard is true. ⁶ But I didn't believe what people were saying. So I came to see for myself. And now I believe it!

You are twice as wise as people say you are. The report I heard doesn't even begin to tell the whole story about you. ⁷ How happy your people must be! How happy your officials must be! They always get to serve you and hear the wise things you say. ⁸ May the Lord your God be praised. He takes great delight in you. He placed you on his throne as king. He put you there to rule for him. Your God loves Israel very much. He longs to take good care of them forever. That's why he has made you king over them. He knows that you will do what is fair and right."

⁹ She gave the king four and a half tons of gold. She also gave him huge amounts of spices and valuable jewels. There had never been as many spices as the queen of Sheba gave to King Solomon.

¹⁰ The servants of Hiram and the servants of Solomon brought gold from Ophir. They also brought algumwood and valuable jewels. ¹¹ The king used the algumwood to make steps for the Lord's temple and the royal palace. He also used it to make harps and lyres for those who played the music. No one had ever seen anything like those instruments in Judah before.

¹² King Solomon gave the queen of Sheba everything she wanted and asked for. In fact, he gave her more than she had brought to him. Then she left. She returned to her own country with her attendants.

Solomon's Greatness

¹³ Each year Solomon received 25 tons of gold. ¹⁴ That didn't include the money brought in by business and trade. All the kings of Arabia also brought gold and silver to Solomon. So did the governors of the territories.

¹⁵ King Solomon made 200 large shields out of hammered gold. Each one weighed 15 pounds. ¹⁶ He also made 300 small shields out of hammered gold. Each one weighed almost eight pounds. The king put all the shields in the Palace of the Forest of Lebanon.

¹⁷ Then he made a large throne. It was covered with ivory. And that was covered with pure gold. ¹⁸ The throne had six steps. A gold stool for the king's feet was connected to it. The throne had armrests on both sides of the seat. A statue of a lion stood on each side of the throne. ¹⁹ Twelve lions stood on the six steps. There was one at each end of each step. Nothing like that throne had ever been made for any other kingdom. ²⁰ All of King Solomon's cups were made out of gold. All the things used in the Palace of the Forest of Lebanon were made out of pure gold. Nothing was made out of silver. When Solomon was king, silver wasn't considered to be worth very much. ²¹ He had many ships that carried goods to be traded. The crews of those ships were made up of Hiram's servants. Once every three years the ships returned. They brought gold, silver, ivory, apes and peacocks.

²² King Solomon was richer than all the other kings on earth. He was also wiser than they were. ²³ All these kings wanted to meet Solomon in person. They wanted to see for themselves how wise God had made him. ²⁴ Year after year, everyone who came to him brought a gift. They brought gifts made out of silver and gold. They brought robes, weapons and spices. They also brought horses and mules.

²⁵ Solomon had 4,000 spaces where he kept his horses and chariots. He had 12,000 horses. He kept some of his horses and chariots in the chariot cities. He kept the others with him in Jerusalem. ²⁶ Solomon ruled over all the kings from the Euphrates River to the land of the Philistines. He ruled all the way to the border of Egypt. ²⁷ The king made silver as common in Jerusalem as stones. He made cedar wood as common there as sycamore-fig trees in the western hills. ²⁸ Solomon got horses from Egypt. He also got them from many other countries.

Solomon Dies

²⁹ The other events of Solomon's rule from beginning to end are written down. They are written in the records of Nathan the prophet. They are written in the prophecy of Ahijah. He was from Shiloh. They are also written in the records of the visions of Iddo the prophet about

Jeroboam. Jeroboam was the son of Nebat. ³⁰ Solomon ruled in Jerusalem over the whole nation of Israel for 40 years. ³¹ Then he joined the members of his family who had already died. He was buried in the city of his father David. Solomon's son Rehoboam became the next king after him

Israel Refuses to Follow Rehoboam

10 Rehoboam went to the city of Shechem. All the Israelites had gone there to make him king. ² Jeroboam heard about it. He was the son of Nebat. Jeroboam was in Egypt at that time. He had gone there for safety. He wanted to get away from King Solomon. But now he returned from Egypt. ³ So the people sent for Jeroboam. He and all the people went to Rehoboam. They said to him, ⁴ "Your father put a heavy load on our shoulders. But now make our hard work easier. Make the heavy load on us lighter. Then we'll serve you."

⁵ Rehoboam answered, "Come back to me in three days." So the people went away.

⁶ Then King Rehoboam asked the elders for advice. They had served his father Solomon while he was still living. Rehoboam asked them, "What advice can you give me? How should I answer these people?"

⁷ They replied, "Be kind to them. Please them. Give them what they are asking for. Then they'll always serve you."

⁸ But Rehoboam didn't accept the advice the elders gave him. He asked for advice from the young men who had grown up with him and were now serving him. ⁹ He asked them, "What's your advice? How should I answer these people? They said to me, 'Make the load your father put on our shoulders lighter.'"

¹⁰ The young men who had grown up with him gave their answer. They replied, "The people have said to you, 'Your father put a heavy load on our shoulders. Make it lighter.' Now tell them, 'My little finger is stronger than my father's legs. ¹¹ My father put a heavy load on your shoulders. But I'll make it even heavier. My father beat you with whips. But I'll beat you with bigger whips.'"

¹² Three days later Jeroboam and all the people returned to Rehoboam. That's because the king had said, "Come back to me in three days." ¹³ The king answered them in a mean way. He didn't accept the advice of the elders. ¹⁴ Instead, he followed the advice of the young men. He said, "My father put a heavy load on your shoulders. But I'll make it even heavier. My father beat you with whips. But I'll beat you with bigger whips." ¹⁵ So the king didn't listen to the people. That's because God had planned it that way. What the LORD had said through Ahijah came true. Ahijah had spoken the LORD's message to Jeroboam, the son of Nebat. Ahijah was from Shiloh.

[16] All the Israelites saw that the king refused to listen to them. So they answered the king. They said,

"We don't have any share in
    David's royal family.
We don't have any share in
    Jesse's son.
People of Israel, let's go back
    to our homes.
David's royal family,
    take care of your own
    kingdom!"

So all the Israelites went home. [17] But Rehoboam still ruled over the Israelites who were living in the towns of Judah.

[18] Adoniram was in charge of those who were forced to work hard for King Rehoboam. The king sent him out among the Israelites. But they killed Adoniram by throwing stones at him. Rehoboam was able to get away in his chariot. He escaped to Jerusalem. [19] Israel has refused to follow the royal family of David to this day.

11 Rehoboam arrived in Jerusalem. He brought together 180,000 capable young men from the tribes of Judah and Benjamin. He had decided to go to war against Israel. He wanted his fighting men to get the kingdom of Israel back for him.

[2] But a message came to Shemaiah from the LORD. Shemaiah was a man of God. The LORD said to him, [3] "Speak to Solomon's son Rehoboam, the king of Judah. Speak to all the people of Israel in Judah and Benjamin. Tell them, [4] 'The LORD says, "Do not go up to fight against your relatives. I want every one of you to go back home. Things have happened exactly the way I planned them."' " So the young men obeyed the LORD's message. They turned back. They didn't march out against Jeroboam.

Rehoboam Builds Up Judah's Towns

[5] Rehoboam lived in Jerusalem. He made Judah more secure by building up its towns. [6] He built up Bethlehem, Etam, Tekoa, [7] Beth Zur, Soko and Adullam. [8] He also built up Gath, Mareshah, Ziph, [9] Adoraim, Lachish, Azekah, [10] Zorah, Aijalon and Hebron. All of them were cities in Judah and Benjamin that had high walls around them. [11] Rehoboam made those cities even more secure. He put commanders in them. He gave the cities plenty of food, olive oil and wine. [12] He put shields and spears in all those cities. He made them very strong. So he ruled over Judah and Benjamin.

[13] The priests and Levites were on Rehoboam's side. They came from their territories all over Israel. [14] The Levites even left their grasslands and other property behind. They came to Judah and Jerusalem. That's because Jeroboam and his sons had refused to accept them as priests of the LORD. [15] Jeroboam had appointed his own priests to serve at the high places. He had made statues of gods that looked like

goats and calves. His priests served those gods. [16] Some people from every tribe in Israel followed the Levites to Jerusalem. With all their hearts they wanted to worship the LORD. He is the God of Israel. They came to Jerusalem to offer sacrifices to him. He was the God of their people of long ago. [17] All those who came to Jerusalem made the kingdom of Judah strong. They helped Solomon's son Rehoboam for three years. During that time they lived the way David and Solomon had lived.

Rehoboam's Family

[18] Rehoboam married Mahalath. She was the daughter of David's son Jerimoth. Her mother was Abihail. Abihail was the daughter of Jesse's son Eliab. [19] Mahalath had sons by Rehoboam. Their names were Jeush, Shemariah and Zaham. [20] Then Rehoboam married Maakah. She was the daughter of Absalom. She had sons by Rehoboam. Their names were Abijah, Attai, Ziza and Shelomith. [21] Rehoboam loved Absalom's daughter Maakah. In fact, he loved her more than any of his other wives and concubines. He had a total of 18 wives and 60 concubines. And he had a total of 28 sons and 60 daughters.

[22] Rehoboam appointed Maakah's son Abijah to be the chief prince among his brothers. He did it because he wanted to make him king. [23] Rehoboam acted wisely. He scattered some of his sons through all the territories of Judah and Benjamin. He put them in all the cities that had high walls around them. He gave them plenty of food and everything else they needed. He also gave them many wives.

Shishak Attacks Jerusalem

12 Rehoboam had made his position as king secure. He had become very strong. Then he turned away from the law of the LORD. So did all the people of Judah. [2] They hadn't been faithful to the LORD. So Shishak attacked Jerusalem. It was in the fifth year that Rehoboam was king. Shishak was king of Egypt. [3] He came with 1,200 chariots and 60,000 horsemen. Troops of Libyans, Sukkites and Cushites came with him from Egypt. There were so many of them they couldn't be counted. [4] Shishak captured the cities of Judah that had high walls around them. He came all the way to Jerusalem.

[5] Then Shemaiah the prophet came to Rehoboam and the leaders of Judah. They had gathered together in Jerusalem. They were afraid of Shishak. Shemaiah said to them, "The LORD says, 'You have left me. So now I am leaving you to Shishak.'"

[6] The king and the leaders of Israel made themselves humble in the LORD's sight. They said, "The LORD does what is right and fair."

[7] The LORD saw they had made themselves humble. So he gave a message to Shema-

iah. The LORD said, "They have made themselves humble in my sight. So I will not destroy them. Instead, I will soon save them. Even though I am very angry with Jerusalem, I will not use Shishak to destroy them. ⁸But the people of Jerusalem will be brought under his control. Then they will learn the difference between serving me and serving the kings of other lands."

⁹Shishak, the king of Egypt, attacked Jerusalem. He carried away the treasures of the LORD's temple. He also carried the treasures of the royal palace away. He took everything. That included the gold shields Solomon had made. ¹⁰So King Rehoboam made bronze shields to take their place. He gave them to the commanders of the guards who were on duty at the entrance to the royal palace. ¹¹Every time the king went to the LORD's temple, the guards went with him. They carried the shields. Later, they took them back to the room where they were kept.

¹²Rehoboam had made himself humble in the LORD's sight. So the LORD turned his anger away from him. Rehoboam wasn't totally destroyed. In fact, some good things happened in Judah.

¹³King Rehoboam had made his position secure in Jerusalem. He continued as king. He was 41 years old when he became king. He ruled for 17 years in Jerusalem. It was the city the LORD had chosen out of all the cities in the tribes of Is-rael. He wanted to put his Name there. The name of Rehoboam's mother was Naamah from Ammon. ¹⁴Rehoboam did what was evil. That's because he hadn't worshiped the LORD with all his heart.

¹⁵The events of Rehoboam's rule from beginning to end are written down. They are written in the records of Shemaiah and Iddo, the prophets. The records deal with family histories. Rehoboam and Jeroboam were always at war with each other. ¹⁶Rehoboam joined the members of his family who had already died. He was buried in the City of David. Rehoboam's son Abijah became the next king after him.

Abijah King of Judah

13 Abijah became king of Judah. It was in the 18th year of Jeroboam's rule over Is-rael. ²Abijah ruled in Jerusalem for three years. His mother's name was Maakah. She was a daughter of Uriel. Uriel was from Gibeah.

There was war between Abi-jah and Jeroboam. ³Abijah went into battle with an army of 400,000 capable fighting men. Jeroboam lined up his soldiers against them. He had 800,000 able troops.

⁴Abijah stood on Mount Zem-araim. It's in the hill country of Ephraim. Abijah said, "Jero-boam and all you Israelites, lis-ten to me! ⁵The LORD is the God of Israel. Don't you know that he has placed David and his

sons after him on Israel's throne forever? The LORD made a covenant of salt with David. The salt means the covenant will last for all time to come. ⁶ Jeroboam, the son of Nebat, was an official of David's son Solomon. But he refused to obey his master. ⁷ Some worthless and evil men gathered around him. They opposed Solomon's son Rehoboam. At that time Rehoboam was young. He couldn't make up his mind. He wasn't strong enough to stand up against those men.

⁸ "Now you plan to stand up against the kingdom of the LORD. His kingdom is in the hands of men in David's family line. It's true that you have a huge army. You have the statues of the golden calves that Jeroboam made to be your gods. ⁹ But you drove out the priests of the LORD, the sons of Aaron. You also drove out the Levites. You appointed your own priests. That's what the people of other nations do. Anyone can come and set himself apart. All he has to do is sacrifice a young bull and seven rams. Then he becomes a priest of gods that aren't really gods at all!

¹⁰ "But the LORD is our God. We haven't deserted him. The priests who serve the LORD belong to the family line of Aaron. The Levites help them. ¹¹ Every morning and evening the priests bring burnt offerings and sweet-smelling incense to the LORD. They set out the holy bread on the table. That table is 'clean.' They light the lamps on the gold lampstand every evening. We always do what the LORD our God requires in his law. But you have deserted him. ¹² God is with us. He's our leader. His priests will blow their trumpets. They will sound the battle cry against you. People of Israel, don't fight against the LORD. He's the God of your people who lived long ago. You can't possibly succeed."

¹³ Jeroboam had sent some troops behind Judah's battle lines. He told them to hide and wait there. He and his men stayed in front of Judah's lines. ¹⁴ Judah turned and saw that they were being attacked from the front and from the back. Then they cried out to the LORD. The priests blew their trumpets. ¹⁵ The men of Judah shouted the battle cry. When they did, God drove Jeroboam and all the Israelites away from Abijah and Judah. ¹⁶ The Israelites ran away from them. God handed Israel over to Judah. ¹⁷ Abijah and his troops wounded and killed large numbers of them. In fact, 500,000 of Israel's capable men lay dead or wounded. ¹⁸ So at that time the Israelites were brought under Judah's control. The people of Judah won the battle over them. That's because they trusted in the LORD, the God of their people.

¹⁹ Abijah chased Jeroboam. He captured from him the towns of Bethel, Jeshanah and Ephron. He also captured the villages around them. ²⁰ Jeroboam didn't get his power back

during the time of Abijah. In fact, the Lord struck Jeroboam down, and he died.

²¹ But Abijah grew stronger. He married 14 wives. He had 22 sons and 16 daughters.

²² The other events of Abijah's rule are written down. The things he did and said are written in the notes of Iddo the prophet.

14 Abijah joined the members of his family who had already died. He was buried in the City of David. Abijah's son Asa became the next king after him. While Asa was king, the country had peace and rest for ten years.

Asa Becomes King of Judah

² Asa did what was good and right in the eyes of the Lord his God. ³ Asa removed the altars where false gods were worshiped. He took away the high places. He smashed the sacred stones. He cut down the poles used to worship the female god named Asherah. ⁴ He commanded Judah to worship the Lord, the God of their people. He commanded them to obey the Lord's laws and commands. ⁵ Asa removed the high places and incense altars from every town in Judah. The kingdom had peace and rest under his rule. ⁶ He built up the cities of Judah that had high walls around them. The land was at peace. No one was at war with Asa during those years. That's because the Lord gave him peace and rest.

⁷ "Let's build up our towns," Asa said to the people of Judah. "Let's put walls around them. Let's provide them with towers. Let's make them secure with gates that have heavy metal bars. The land still belongs to us. That's because we've trusted in the Lord our God. We trusted in him, and he has given us peace and rest on every side." So they built. And things went well for them.

⁸ Asa had an army of 300,000 men from Judah. They carried spears and large shields. There were 280,000 men from Benjamin. They were armed with bows and small shields. All these men were brave soldiers.

⁹ Zerah marched out against them. He was from Cush. He had a huge army of thousands. He also had 300 chariots. They came all the way to Mareshah. ¹⁰ Asa went out to meet Zerah in battle. They took up their positions in the Valley of Zephathah. It's near Mareshah.

¹¹ Then Asa called out to the Lord his God. He said, "Lord, there isn't anyone like you. You help the weak against the strong. Lord our God, help us. We trust in you. In your name we have come out to fight against this huge army. Lord, you are our God. Don't let mere human beings win the battle over you."

¹² The Lord struck down the men of Cush for Asa and Judah. The Cushites ran away. ¹³ Asa and his army chased them all the way to Gerar. A large number of Cushites fell down wounded or dead. So they couldn't fight

back. The LORD and his army crushed them. The men of Judah carried off a large amount of goods. ¹⁴ They destroyed all the villages around Gerar. The LORD had made the people in those villages afraid of him. The men of Judah took everything from all the villages. ¹⁵ They also attacked the camps of those who took care of the herds. They carried off large numbers of sheep, goats and camels. Then they returned to Jerusalem.

Asa Makes Judah a Better Nation

15 The Spirit of God came on Azariah. He was the son of Oded. ² Azariah went out to meet Asa. He said to him, "Asa and all you people of Judah and Benjamin, listen to me. The LORD is with you when you are with him. If you really look for him, you will find him. But if you desert him, he will desert you. ³ For a long time Israel didn't worship the true God. They didn't have a priest who taught them. So they didn't know God's law. ⁴ But when they were in trouble, they turned to the LORD, the God of Israel. When they did, they found him. ⁵ In those days it wasn't safe to travel around. The people who lived in all the areas of the land were having a lot of trouble. ⁶ One nation was crushing another. One city was crushing another. That's because God was causing them to suffer terribly. ⁷ But be strong. Don't give up. God will reward you for your work."

⁸ Asa heard that prophecy. He paid attention to the words of Azariah the prophet, the son of Oded. So Asa became bolder than ever. He removed the statues of gods from the whole land of Judah and Benjamin. He also removed them from the towns he had captured in the hills of Ephraim. He did it because the LORD hated those gods. Asa repaired the altar of the LORD. It was in front of the porch of the LORD's temple.

⁹ Then Asa gathered together all the people of Judah and Benjamin. He also gathered together the people from Ephraim, Manasseh and Simeon who were living among them. Large numbers of people had come over to him from Israel. They came because they saw that the LORD his God was with him.

¹⁰ They gathered in Jerusalem. It was the third month of the 15th year of Asa's rule. ¹¹ At that time they sacrificed to the LORD 700 oxen and 7,000 sheep and goats. The animals were among the things they had taken after the battle. ¹² They made a covenant to obey the LORD, the God of their people. They would obey him with all their heart and soul. ¹³ All those who wouldn't obey the LORD, the God of Israel, would be killed. It wouldn't matter how important they were. It wouldn't matter whether they were men or women. ¹⁴ They made a promise to the LORD. They praised him out loud. They shouted. They

blew trumpets and horns. ¹⁵All the people of Judah were happy about the promise they had made. They turned to God with all their heart. When they did, they found him. So the LORD gave them peace and rest on every side.

¹⁶King Asa also removed his grandmother Maakah from her position as queen mother. That's because she had made a pole used to worship the female god named Asherah. The LORD hated it. So Asa cut it down. He broke it up. He burned it in the Kidron Valley. ¹⁷Asa didn't remove the high places from Israel. But he committed his whole life completely to the LORD. ¹⁸He and his father had set apart silver, gold and other things to the LORD. Asa brought them into God's temple.

¹⁹There weren't any more wars until the 35th year of Asa's rule.

Asa's Last Years

16 Baasha was king of Israel. He marched out against Judah. It was in the 36th year of Asa's rule over Judah. Baasha built up the walls of Ramah. He did it to keep people from leaving or entering the territory of Asa, the king of Judah.

²Asa took the silver and gold from among the treasures of the LORD's temple and his own palace. He sent it to Ben-Hadad. Ben-Hadad was king of Aram. He was ruling in Damascus. ³"Let's make a peace treaty between us," Asa said. "My fa-

ther and your father had made a peace treaty between them. Now I'm sending you silver and gold. So break your treaty with Baasha, the king of Israel. Then he'll go back home."

⁴Ben-Hadad agreed with King Asa. He sent his army commanders against the towns of Israel. His army captured Ijon, Dan, Abel Maim and all the cities in Naphtali where Baasha stored things. ⁵Baasha heard about it. So he stopped building up Ramah and left that place. ⁶Then King Asa brought all the men of Judah to Ramah. They carried away the stones and wood Baasha had been using. Asa used them to build up Geba and Mizpah.

⁷At that time Hanani the prophet came to Asa, the king of Judah. He said to him, "You trusted the king of Aram. You didn't trust in the LORD your God. So the army of the king of Aram has escaped from you. ⁸The people of Cush and Libya had a strong army. They had large numbers of chariots and horsemen. But you trusted in the LORD. So he handed them over to you. ⁹The LORD looks out over the whole earth. He gives strength to those who commit their lives completely to him. You have done a foolish thing. From now on you will be at war."

¹⁰Asa was angry with the prophet because of what he had said. In fact, he was so angry he put him in prison. At the same time, Asa treated some of his own people very badly.

¹¹ The events of Asa's rule from beginning to end are written down. They are written in the records of the kings of Judah and Israel. ¹² In the 39th year of Asa's rule his feet began to hurt. The pain was terrible. But even though he was suffering, he didn't look to the LORD for help. All he did was go to the doctors. ¹³ In the 41st year of Asa's rule he joined the members of his family who had already died. ¹⁴ He was buried in a tomb. He had cut it out for himself in the City of David. His body was laid on a wooden frame. It was covered with spices and different mixes of perfume. A huge fire was made to honor him.

Jehoshaphat King of Judah

17 Jehoshaphat was the son of Asa. Jehoshaphat became the next king after him. He made his kingdom strong in case Israel would attack him. ² He placed troops in all the cities of Judah that had high walls around them. He stationed some soldiers in Judah. He also put some in the towns of Ephraim that his father Asa had captured. ³ The LORD was with Jehoshaphat. That's because he lived the way King David had lived. He didn't ask for advice from the gods that were named Baal. ⁴ Instead, Jehoshaphat obeyed the God of his father. He obeyed the LORD's commands instead of the practices of Israel. ⁵ The LORD made the kingdom secure under Jehoshaphat's control. All the people of Judah brought gifts to Jehoshaphat. So he had great wealth and honor. ⁶ His heart was committed to living the way the LORD wanted him to. He removed the high places from Judah. He also removed the poles used to worship the female god named Asherah.

⁷ In the third year of his rule, he sent his officials to teach in the towns of Judah. The officials were Ben-Hail, Obadiah, Zechariah, Nethanel and Micaiah. ⁸ Some Levites were with them. Their names were Shemaiah, Nethaniah, Zebadiah, Asahel, Shemiramoth, Jehonathan, Adonijah, Tobijah and Tob-Adonijah. Elishama and Jehoram, the priests, were also with them. ⁹ They taught people all through Judah. They took the Book of the Law of the LORD with them. They went around to all the towns of Judah. And they taught the people.

¹⁰ All the kingdoms of the lands around Judah became afraid of the LORD. So they didn't go to war against Jehoshaphat. ¹¹ Some Philistines brought to Jehoshaphat the gifts and silver he required of them. The Arabs brought him their flocks. They brought him 7,700 rams and 7,700 goats.

¹² Jehoshaphat became more and more powerful. He built forts in Judah. He also built cities in Judah where he could store things. ¹³ He had large supplies in the towns of Judah. In Jerusalem he kept men who knew how to fight well. ¹⁴ Here is a list of them, family by family.

From Judah there were commanders of groups of 1,000.

One of them was Adnah. He commanded 300,000 fighting men. ¹⁵ Another was Jehohanan. He commanded 280,000. ¹⁶ Another was Amasiah, the son of Zikri. Amasiah commanded 200,000. He had offered to serve the LORD.

¹⁷ From Benjamin there were also commanders.

One of them was Eliada. He was a brave soldier. He commanded 200,000 men. They were armed with bows and shields. ¹⁸ Another was Jehozabad. He commanded 180,000 men. They were prepared for battle.

¹⁹ These were the men who served the king. He stationed some other men in the cities all through Judah. The cities had high walls around them.

Micaiah Prophesies Against Ahab

18 Jehoshaphat had great wealth and honor. He joined forces with Ahab by marrying Ahab's daughter. ² Some years later he went down to see Ahab in Samaria. Ahab killed a lot of sheep and cattle for Jehoshaphat and the people with him. Ahab tried to get Jehoshaphat to attack Ramoth Gilead. ³ Ahab was the king of Israel. He spoke to Jehoshaphat, the king of Judah. He asked, "Will you go with me to fight against Ramoth Gilead?"

Jehoshaphat replied, "Yes. I'll go with you. My men will also go with your men. We'll join you in the war." ⁴ He continued, "First ask the LORD for advice."

⁵ So the king of Israel brought 400 prophets together. He asked them, "Should we go to war against Ramoth Gilead, or not?"

"Go," they answered. "God will hand it over to you."

⁶ But Jehoshaphat asked, "Is there no longer a prophet of the LORD here? If there is, ask him what we should do."

⁷ The king of Israel answered Jehoshaphat. He said, "There is still one prophet we can go to. We can ask the LORD for advice through him. But I hate him. He never prophesies anything good about me. He only prophesies bad things. His name is Micaiah. He's the son of Imlah."

"You shouldn't say bad things about him," Jehoshaphat replied.

⁸ So the king of Israel called for one of his officials. He told him, "Bring Micaiah, the son of Imlah, right away."

⁹ The king of Israel and Jehoshaphat, the king of Judah, were wearing their royal robes. They were sitting on their thrones at the threshing floor. It was near the entrance of the gate of Samaria. All the prophets were prophesying in front of them. ¹⁰ Zedekiah was the son of Kenaanah. Zedekiah had made horns out of iron. They looked like animal horns. He announced, "The

LORD says, 'With these horns you will drive back the men of Aram until they are destroyed.' "

[11] All the other prophets were prophesying the same thing. "Attack Ramoth Gilead," they said. "Win the battle over it. The LORD will hand it over to you."

[12] A messenger went to get Micaiah. He said to him, "Look. The other prophets agree. All of them are saying the king will have success. So agree with them. Say the same thing they do."

[13] But Micaiah said, "You can be sure that the LORD lives. And you can be just as sure that I can only tell the king what my God says."

[14] When Micaiah arrived, the king spoke to him. He asked, "Should we go to war against Ramoth Gilead, or not?"

"Attack," he answered. "You will win. The people of Ramoth Gilead will be handed over to you."

[15] The king said to him, "I've made you promise to tell the truth many times before. So don't tell me anything but the truth in the name of the LORD."

[16] Then Micaiah answered, "I saw all the Israelites scattered on the hills. They were like sheep that didn't have a shepherd. The LORD said, 'These people do not have a master. Let each of them go home in peace.' "

[17] The king of Israel spoke to Jehoshaphat. He said, "Didn't I tell you he never prophesies anything good about me? He only prophesies bad things."

[18] Micaiah continued, "Listen to the LORD's message. I saw the LORD sitting on his throne. Some of the angels of heaven were standing at his right side. The others were standing at his left side. [19] The LORD said, 'Who will get Ahab, the king of Israel, to attack Ramoth Gilead? I want him to die there.'

"One angel suggested one thing. Another suggested something else. [20] Finally, a spirit came forward and stood in front of the LORD. The spirit said, 'I'll get Ahab to do it.'

" 'How?' the LORD asked.

[21] "The spirit said, 'I'll go and put lies in the mouths of all his prophets.'

" 'You will have success in getting Ahab to attack Ramoth Gilead,' said the LORD. 'Go and do it.'

[22] "So the LORD has put lies in the mouths of your prophets. He has said that great harm will come to you."

[23] Then Zedekiah, the son of Kenaanah, went up and slapped Micaiah in the face. Zedekiah asked Micaiah, "Do you think the spirit sent by the LORD left me? Do you think that spirit went to speak to you?"

[24] Micaiah replied, "You will find out on the day you go to hide in an inside room to save your life."

[25] Then the king of Israel gave an order. He said, "Take Micaiah away. Send him back to Amon. Amon is the ruler of the city of Samaria. And send Micaiah back to Joash. Joash is a member

of the royal court. ²⁶ Tell them, 'The king says, "Put this fellow in prison. Don't give him anything but bread and water until I return safely." ' ".

²⁷ Micaiah announced, "Do you really think you will return safely? If you do, the LORD hasn't spoken through me." He continued, "All you people, remember what I've said!"

Ahab Is Killed at Ramoth Gilead

²⁸ So the king of Israel went up to Ramoth Gilead. Jehoshaphat, the king of Judah, went there too. ²⁹ The king of Israel spoke to Jehoshaphat. He said, "I'll go into battle wearing different clothes. Then people won't recognize me. But you wear your royal robes." So the king of Israel put on different clothes. Then he went into battle.

³⁰ The king of Aram had given an order to his chariot commanders. He had said, "Fight only against the king of Israel. Don't fight against anyone else."

³¹ The chariot commanders saw Jehoshaphat. They thought, "That's the king of Israel." So they turned to attack him. But Jehoshaphat cried out. And the LORD helped him. God drew the commanders away from him.

³² They saw he wasn't the king of Israel after all. So they stopped chasing him.

³³ But someone shot an arrow without taking aim. The arrow hit the king of Israel between the parts of his armor. The king told the chariot driver, "Turn the chariot around. Get me out of this battle. I've been wounded."

³⁴ All day long the battle continued. The king of Israel kept himself standing up by leaning against the inside of his chariot. He kept his face toward the men of Aram until evening. At sunset he died.

19 Jehoshaphat, the king of Judah, returned safely to his palace in Jerusalem. ² Jehu the prophet went out to meet him. He was the son of Hanani. Jehu said to the king, "You shouldn't help evil people. You shouldn't love those who hate the LORD. The LORD is angry with you. ³ But there's some good in you. You have removed all the poles in the land used to worship the female god named Asherah. And you have worshiped God with all your heart."

Jehoshaphat Appoints Judges

⁴ Jehoshaphat lived in Jerusalem. He went out again among the people. He went from Beersheba to the hill country of Ephraim. He turned the people back to the LORD, the God of Israel. ⁵ Jehoshaphat appointed judges in the land. He put them in all the cities of Judah that had high walls around them. ⁶ He told the judges, "Think carefully about what you do. After all, you aren't judging for human beings. You are judging for the LORD. He's with you every time you make a decision. ⁷ Have respect for the LORD. Judge carefully. He is always right. He treats everyone the same. Our God doesn't want his judges to

take money from people who want special favors."

⁸ In Jerusalem, Jehoshaphat chose some Levites and priests. He also chose some leaders of Israelite families. He appointed all of them to apply the law of the LORD fairly. He wanted them to decide cases. He wanted them to settle matters between people. All those judges lived in Jerusalem. ⁹ Here are the orders Jehoshaphat gave them. He said, "Have respect for the LORD. Serve him faithfully. Do it with all your heart. ¹⁰ Cases will come to you from your people who live in the other cities. The cases might be about murder or other matters dealt with by the law, commands, directions and rules. Warn the people not to sin against the LORD. If you don't warn them, he will be angry with you and your people. Do what I say. Then you won't sin.

¹¹ "Amariah the chief priest will be over you in any matter that concerns the LORD. Zebadiah is the leader of the tribe of Judah. He is the son of Ishmael. Zebadiah will be over you in any matter that concerns the king. The Levites will serve as your officials. Be brave. And may the LORD be with those of you who do well."

Jehoshaphat Wins the Battle Over Moab and Ammon

20 After that, the Moabites, Ammonites and some Meunites went to war against Jehoshaphat.

² Some people came and told him, "A huge army is coming from Edom to fight against you. They have come across the Dead Sea. They are already in Hazezon Tamar." Hazezon Tamar is also called En Gedi. ³ Jehoshaphat was alarmed. So he decided to ask the LORD for advice. He told all the people of Judah to go without eating. ⁴ The people came together to ask the LORD for help. In fact, they came from every town in Judah to pray to him.

⁵ Then Jehoshaphat stood up among the people of Judah and Jerusalem. He was in front of the new courtyard at the LORD's temple. ⁶ He said,

"LORD, you are the God of our people who lived long ago. You are the God who is in heaven. You rule over all the kingdoms of the nations. You are strong and powerful. No one can fight against you and win. ⁷ Our God, you drove out the people who lived in this land. You drove them out to make room for your people Israel. You gave this land forever to those who belong to the family line of your friend Abraham. ⁸ They have lived in this land. They've built a temple here for your Name. They have said, ⁹ 'Suppose trouble comes on us. It doesn't matter whether it's a punishing sword, or plague or hunger. We'll serve you. We'll stand in front of this temple where your Name is. We'll cry out to you when we're in trouble. Then you will hear us. You will save us.'

10 "But here are men from Ammon, Moab and Mount Seir. You wouldn't allow Israel to march in and attack their territory when the Israelites came from Egypt. So Israel turned away from them. They didn't destroy them. 11 See how they are paying us back. They are coming to drive us out. They want to take over the land you gave us as our share. 12 Our God, won't you please judge them? We don't have the power to face this huge army that's attacking us. We don't know what to do. But we're looking to you to help us."

13 All the men of Judah stood there in front of the LORD. Their wives, children and little ones were with them.

14 Then the Spirit of the LORD came on Jahaziel. He was standing among the people of Israel. He was the son of Zechariah. Zechariah was the son of Benaiah. Benaiah was the son of Jeiel. Jeiel was the son of Mattaniah. Jahaziel was a Levite. He was from the family line of Asaph.

15 Jahaziel said, "King Jehoshaphat, listen! All you who live in Judah and Jerusalem, listen! The LORD says to you, 'Do not be afraid. Do not lose hope because of this huge army. The battle is not yours. It is God's. 16 Tomorrow march down against them. They will be climbing up by the Pass of Ziz. You will find them at the end of the valley in the Desert of Jeruel. 17 You will not have to fight this battle. Take your positions. Stand firm. You will see how the LORD will save you. Judah and Jerusalem, do not be afraid. Do not lose hope. Go out and face them tomorrow. The LORD will be with you.'"

18 Jehoshaphat bowed down with his face toward the ground. All the people of Judah and Jerusalem also bowed down. They worshiped the LORD. 19 Then some Levites from the families of Kohath and Korah stood up. They praised the LORD, the God of Israel. They praised him with very loud voices.

20 Early in the morning all the people left for the Desert of Tekoa. As they started out, Jehoshaphat stood up. He said, "Judah, listen to me! People of Jerusalem, listen to me! Have faith in the LORD your God. He'll take good care of you. Have faith in his prophets. Then you will have success." 21 Jehoshaphat asked the people for advice. Then he appointed men to sing to the LORD. He wanted them to praise the LORD because of his glory and holiness. They marched out in front of the army. They said,

"Give thanks to the LORD.
    His faithful love continues
    forever."

22 They began to sing and praise him. Then the LORD hid some men and told them to wait. He wanted them to attack the people of Ammon, Moab

and Mount Seir. They had gone into Judah and attacked it. But they lost the battle. ²³ The Ammonites and Moabites rose up against the men from Mount Seir. They destroyed them. They put an end to them. When they finished killing the men from Seir, they destroyed one another.

²⁴ The men of Judah came to the place that looks out over the desert. They turned to look down at the huge army. But all they saw was dead bodies lying there on the ground. No one had escaped. ²⁵ So Jehoshaphat and his men went down there to carry off anything of value. Among the dead bodies they found a large amount of supplies, clothes and other things of value. There was more than they could take away. There was so much it took three days to collect all of it. ²⁶ On the fourth day they gathered together in the Valley of Berakah. There they praised the LORD. That's why it's called the Valley of Berakah to this day.

²⁷ Then all the men of Judah and Jerusalem returned to Jerusalem. They were filled with joy. Jehoshaphat led them. The LORD had made them happy because all their enemies were dead. ²⁸ They entered Jerusalem and went to the LORD's temple. They were playing harps, lyres and trumpets.

²⁹ All the surrounding kingdoms began to have respect for God. They had heard how the LORD had fought against Israel's enemies. ³⁰ The kingdom of Jehoshaphat was at peace. His God had given him peace and rest on every side.

Jehoshaphat's Rule Comes to an End

³¹ So Jehoshaphat ruled over Judah. He was 35 years old when he became Judah's king. He ruled in Jerusalem for 25 years. His mother's name was Azubah. She was the daughter of Shilhi. ³² Jehoshaphat followed the ways of his father Asa. He didn't wander away from them. He did what was right in the eyes of the LORD. ³³ But the high places weren't removed. The people still hadn't worshiped the God of Israel with all their hearts.

³⁴ The other events of Jehoshaphat's rule from beginning to end are written down. They are written in the official records of Jehu, the son of Hanani. They are written in the records of the kings of Israel.

³⁵ Jehoshaphat king of Judah and Ahaziah king of Israel agreed to be friends. Ahaziah did what was evil. ³⁶ Jehoshaphat agreed with him to build a lot of ships. They were built at Ezion Geber. They carried goods that were traded for other goods. ³⁷ Eliezer was the son of Dodavahu from Mareshah. Eliezer prophesied against Jehoshaphat. He said, "You have joined forces with Ahaziah. So the LORD will destroy what you have made." The ships were wrecked. They were never able to sail or trade goods.

21

Jehoshaphat joined the members of his family who had already died. He was buried in the family tomb in the City of David. Jehoshaphat's son Jehoram became the next king after him. ² Jehoram's brothers, the sons of Jehoshaphat, were Azariah, Jehiel, Zechariah, Azariahu, Michael and Shephatiah. All of them were sons of Jehoshaphat, the king of Israel. ³ Their father had given them many gifts. He had given them silver, gold and other things of value. He had also given them cities in Judah that had high walls around them. But he had made Jehoram king. That's because Jehoram was his oldest son.

Jehoram King of Judah

⁴ Jehoram made his position secure over his father's kingdom. Then he killed all his brothers with his sword. He also killed some of the officials of Israel. ⁵ Jehoram was 32 years old when he became king. He ruled in Jerusalem for eight years. ⁶ He followed the ways of the kings of Israel, just as the royal family of Ahab had done. In fact, he married a daughter of Ahab. Jehoram did what was evil in the eyes of the LORD. ⁷ But the LORD didn't want to destroy the royal family of David. That's because the LORD had made a covenant with him. The LORD had promised to keep the lamp of David's kingdom burning brightly. The LORD had promised that for David and his children after him forever.

⁸ When Jehoram was king over Judah, Edom refused to remain under Judah's control. They set up their own king. ⁹ So Jehoram went to Edom. He took his officers and all his chariots with him. The men of Edom surrounded him and his chariot commanders. But he got up at night and fought his way out. ¹⁰ To this day Edom has refused to remain under Judah's control.

At that same time, Libnah also refused to remain under the control of Judah. That's because Jehoram had deserted the LORD, the God of his people. ¹¹ Jehoram had also built high places on the hills of Judah. He had caused the people of Jerusalem to worship other gods. They weren't faithful to the LORD. Jehoram had led Judah down the wrong path.

¹² Jehoram received a letter from Elijah the prophet. In it, Elijah said,

"The LORD is the God of your father David. The LORD says, 'You have not followed the ways of your own father Jehoshaphat or of Asa, the king of Judah. ¹³ Instead, you have followed the ways of the kings of Israel. You have led Judah and the people of Jerusalem to worship other gods, just as the royal family of Ahab did. Also, you have murdered your own brothers. They were members of your own family. They were better men than you are. ¹⁴ So now the LORD is about to strike down your people with a heavy blow. He will strike down your sons, your wives and everything that belongs to you. ¹⁵ And you yourself will be very sick for a long time. The sickness will finally cause your insides to come out.' "

¹⁶ The LORD stirred up the anger of the Philistines against Jehoram. He also stirred up the anger of the Arabs. They lived near the people of Cush. ¹⁷ The Philistines and Arabs attacked Judah. They went in and carried off all the goods they found in the king's palace. They also took his sons and wives. The only son he had left was Ahaziah. He was the youngest son.

¹⁸ After all of that, the LORD made Jehoram very sick. He couldn't be healed. ¹⁹ After he had been sick for two years, the sickness caused his insides to come out. He died in great pain. His people didn't make a funeral fire to honor him. They had made funeral fires to honor the kings who ruled before him.

²⁰ Jehoram was 32 years old when he became king. He ruled in Jerusalem for eight years. No one was sorry when he passed away. He was buried in the City of David. But he wasn't placed in the tombs of the kings.

Ahaziah King of Judah

22 The people of Jerusalem made Ahaziah king in place of Jehoram. Ahaziah was Jehoram's youngest son. Robbers had come with the Arabs into Jehoram's camp. The robbers had killed all his older sons. So Ahaziah, the king of Judah, began to rule. He was the son of Jehoram.

² Ahaziah was 22 years old when he became king. He ruled in Jerusalem for one year. His mother's name was Athaliah. She was a granddaughter of Omri.

³ Ahaziah also followed the ways of the royal family of Ahab. That's because Ahaziah's mother gave him bad advice. She told him to do what was wrong. ⁴ So he did what was evil in the eyes of the LORD. He did what the family of Ahab had done. After Ahaziah's father died, the members of Ahab's family became his advisers. That's what destroyed him. ⁵ He also followed their advice when he joined forces with Joram, the king of Israel. They went to war against Hazael at Ramoth Gilead. Joram was the son of Ahab. Hazael was king of Aram. The soldiers of Aram wounded Joram. ⁶ So he returned to Jezreel to give his wounds time to heal. His enemies had wounded him at Ramoth in his battle against Hazael, the king of Aram.

Ahaziah, the son of Jehoram, went down to Jezreel. He went there to see Joram. That's because Joram had been wounded. Ahaziah was king of Judah. Joram was the son of Ahab.

⁷ Through Ahaziah's visit to Joram, God caused Ahaziah to fall from power. When Ahaziah arrived, he rode out with Joram to meet Jehu, the son of Nim-

shi. The LORD had anointed Jehu to destroy the royal family of Ahab. ⁸ So Jehu punished Ahab's family, just as the LORD had told him to. While he was doing it, he found the officials of Judah and the sons of Ahaziah's relatives. They had been serving Ahaziah. So Jehu killed them. ⁹ Then he went to look for Ahaziah. Jehu's men captured him while he was hiding in Samaria. Ahaziah was brought to Jehu and put to death. People buried him, because they said, "He was a grandson of Jehoshaphat, who followed the LORD with all his heart." So no one in the royal family of Ahaziah was powerful enough to keep the kingdom.

Athaliah and Joash

¹⁰ Athaliah was Ahaziah's mother. She saw that her son was dead. So she began to wipe out the whole royal family of Judah. ¹¹ But Jehosheba went and got Joash, the son of Ahaziah. Jehosheba was the daughter of King Jehoram. She stole Joash away from among the royal princes. All of them were about to be murdered. She put Joash and his nurse in a bedroom. Jehosheba, the daughter of King Jehoram, was the wife of Jehoiada the priest. She was also Ahaziah's sister. So Jehosheba hid the child from Athaliah. That's why Athaliah couldn't kill him. ¹² The child remained hidden with the priest and his wife at God's temple for six years. Athaliah ruled over the land during that time.

23 When Joash was seven years old, Jehoiada showed how strong he was. He made a covenant with the commanders of groups of 100 men. The commanders were Azariah son of Jeroham, Ishmael son of Jehohanan, Azariah son of Obed, Maaseiah son of Adaiah, and Elishaphat son of Zikri. ² They went all through Judah. They gathered together the Levites and the leaders of Israelite families from all the towns. They came to Jerusalem. ³ The whole community made a covenant with the new king at God's temple.

Jehoiada said to them, "Ahaziah's son will rule over Judah. That's what the LORD promised concerning the family line of David. ⁴ Here's what I want you to do. A third of you priests and Levites who are going on duty on the Sabbath day must guard the doors. ⁵ A third of you must guard the royal palace. And a third of you must guard the Foundation Gate. All the other men must guard the courtyards of the LORD's temple. ⁶ Don't let anyone enter the temple except the priests and Levites who are on duty. They can enter because they are set apart to the LORD. But all the other men must obey the LORD's command not to enter. ⁷ The Levites must station themselves around the new king. Each man must have his weapon in his hand. Anyone else who enters the temple must be put to death. Stay close to the king no matter where he goes."

⁸ The Levites did just as Jehoiada the priest ordered. So did all the men of Judah. Each commander got his men. Some of the men were going on duty on the Sabbath day. Others were going off duty. Jehoiada didn't let any of the groups go. ⁹ Then he gave weapons to the commanders of the groups. He gave them spears, large shields and small shields. The weapons had belonged to King David. They had been in God's temple. ¹⁰ Jehoiada stationed all the men around the new king. Each man had his weapon in his hand. They were standing near the altar and the temple. They stood from the south side of the temple to its north side.

¹¹ Jehoiada and his sons brought Ahaziah's son out. They put the crown on him. They gave him a copy of the covenant. And they announced that he was king. They anointed him. Then they shouted, "May the king live a long time!"

¹² Athaliah heard the noise of the people running and cheering the new king. So she went to them at the LORD's temple. ¹³ She looked, and there was the king! He was standing next to his pillar at the entrance. The officers and trumpet players were standing beside the king. All the people of the land were filled with joy. They were blowing trumpets. Musicians with their musical instruments were leading the songs of praise. Then Athaliah tore her royal robes. She shouted, "Treason! It's treason!"

¹⁴ Jehoiada the priest sent out the commanders of the groups of 100 men. They were in charge of the troops. He said to them, "Bring her away from the temple between the line of guards. Use your swords to kill anyone who follows her." The priest had said, "Don't put her to death at the LORD's temple." ¹⁵ So they grabbed her as she reached the entrance of the Horse Gate on the palace grounds. There they put her to death.

¹⁶ Then Jehoiada made a covenant. He promised that he, the people and the king would be the LORD's people. ¹⁷ All the people went to Baal's temple. They tore it down. They smashed the altars and the statues of gods. They killed Mattan in front of the altars. He was the priest of Baal.

¹⁸ Then Jehoiada put the priests, who were Levites, in charge of the LORD's temple. David had given them their duties in the temple. He had appointed them to sacrifice burnt offerings to the LORD. He wanted them to do it in keeping with what was written in the Law of Moses. David wanted them to sing and be full of joy. ¹⁹ Jehoiada stationed guards at the gates of the LORD's temple. No one who was "unclean" in any way could enter.

²⁰ Jehoiada took with him the commanders of hundreds, the nobles, the rulers of the people, and all the people of the land. He brought the new king down from the LORD's temple. They went into the palace through the

Upper Gate. Then they seated the king on the royal throne. ²¹ All the people of the land were filled with joy. And the city was calm. That's because Athaliah had been killed by a sword.

Joash Repairs the Temple

24 Joash was seven years old when he became king. He ruled in Jerusalem for 40 years. His mother's name was Zibiah. She was from Beersheba. ² Joash did what was right in the eyes of the LORD. Joash lived that way as long as Jehoiada the priest was alive. ³ Jehoiada chose two wives for Joash. They had sons and daughters by Joash.

⁴ Some time later Joash decided to make the LORD's temple look like new again. ⁵ He called together the priests and Levites. He said to them, "Go to the towns of Judah. Collect the money that the nation of Israel owes every year. Use it to repair the temple of your God. Do it now." But the Levites didn't do it right away.

⁶ So the king sent for Jehoiada the chief priest. He said to him, "Why haven't you required the Levites to bring in the tax from Judah and Jerusalem? It was set up by the LORD's servant Moses and the whole community of Israel. It was used for the tent where the tablets of the covenant law were kept."

⁷ The children of that evil woman Athaliah had broken into God's temple. They had used even its sacred objects for the gods that were named Baal.

⁸ King Joash commanded that a wooden chest be made. It was placed outside near the gate of the LORD's temple. ⁹ Then a message went out in Judah and Jerusalem. It said that the people should bring the tax to the LORD. God's servant Moses had required Israel to pay that tax when they were in the desert. ¹⁰ All the officials and people gladly brought their money. They dropped it into the chest until it was full. ¹¹ The chest was brought in by the Levites to the king's officials. Every time the officials saw there was a large amount of money in the chest, it was emptied out. The royal secretary and the officer of the chief priest came and emptied it. Then they carried it back to its place. They did it regularly. They collected a great amount of money. ¹² The king and Jehoiada gave it to the people who were doing the work on the LORD's temple. They hired people who could lay the stones and people who could work with wood. They also hired people who could work with iron and bronze. They hired all of them to repair the temple.

¹³ The men in charge of the work did their best. The repairs went very well under them. They rebuilt God's temple. They did it in keeping with its original plans. They made the temple even stronger. ¹⁴ So they finished the work. Then they brought the rest of the money to the king and Jehoiada. It was used to pay for the objects that were made for

the LORD's temple. The objects were used for serving at the temple. They were also used for the burnt offerings. The objects included dishes and other things made out of gold and silver. As long as Jehoiada lived, burnt offerings were sacrificed continually at the LORD's temple. ¹⁵ Jehoiada had become very old. He died at the age of 130. ¹⁶ He was buried with the kings in the City of David. That's because he had done so many good things in Israel for God and his temple.

The Evil Things Joash Did

¹⁷ After Jehoiada died, the officials of Judah came to King Joash. They bowed down to him. He listened to them. ¹⁸ They turned their backs on the temple of the LORD, the God of their people. They worshiped poles made to honor the female god named Asherah. They also worshiped statues of other gods. Because Judah and Jerusalem were guilty of sin, God became angry with them. ¹⁹ The LORD sent prophets to the people to bring them back to him. The prophets told the people what they were doing wrong. But the people wouldn't listen. ²⁰ Then the Spirit of God came on Zechariah the priest. He was the son of Jehoiada. Zechariah stood in front of the people. He told them, "God says, 'Why do you refuse to obey my commands? You will not have success. You have deserted me. So I have deserted you.'"

²¹ But the people made evil plans against Zechariah. The king ordered them to kill Zechariah by throwing stones at him. They did it in the courtyard of the LORD's temple. ²² King Joash didn't remember how kind Zechariah's father Jehoiada had been to him. So he killed Jehoiada's son. As Zechariah was dying he said, "May the LORD see this. May he hold you responsible."

²³ In the spring, the army of Aram marched into Judah and Jerusalem against Joash. They killed all the leaders of the people. They took a large amount of goods from Judah. They sent it to their king in Damascus. ²⁴ The army of Aram had come with only a few men. But the LORD allowed them to win the battle over a much larger army. Judah had deserted the LORD, the God of their people. That's why the LORD punished Joash. ²⁵ The army of Aram pulled back. They left Joash badly wounded. His officials planned to do evil things to him. That's because he murdered the son of Jehoiada the priest. They killed Joash in his bed. So he died. He was buried in the City of David. But he wasn't placed in the tombs of the kings.

²⁶ Those who made the plans against Joash were Zabad and Jehozabad. Zabad was the son of Shimeath. She was from Ammon. Jehozabad was the son of Shimrith. She was from Moab. ²⁷ The story of the sons of Joash is written in the notes on the

records of the kings. The many prophecies about him are written there too. So is the record of how he made God's temple look like new again. Joash's son Amaziah became the next king after him.

Amaziah King of Judah

25 Amaziah was 25 years old when he became king. He ruled in Jerusalem for 29 years. His mother's name was Jehoaddan. She was from Jerusalem. ² Amaziah did what was right in the eyes of the LORD. But he didn't do it with all his heart. ³ The kingdom was firmly under his control. So he put to death the officials who had murdered his father, the king. ⁴ But he didn't put their children to death. He obeyed what is written in the Law, the Book of Moses. There the LORD commanded, "Parents must not be put to death because of what their children do. And children must not be put to death because of what their parents do. People must die because of their own sins." *(Deuteronomy 24:16)*

⁵ Amaziah called the people of Judah together. He arranged them by families under commanders of thousands and commanders of hundreds. He did it for all the people of Judah and Benjamin. Then he brought together the men who were 20 years old or more. He found out there were 300,000 men who were able to serve in the army. They could handle spears and shields. ⁶ He also hired 100,000 fighting men from Israel. He had to pay them almost four tons of silver.

⁷ But a man of God came to him. He said, "Your Majesty, these troops from Israel must not march out with you. The LORD is not with Israel. He isn't with any of the people of Ephraim. ⁸ Go and fight bravely in battle if you want to. But God will destroy you right in front of your enemies. God has the power to help you or destroy you."

⁹ Amaziah asked the man of God, "But what about all that silver I paid for these Israelite troops?"

The man of God replied, "The LORD can give you much more than that."

¹⁰ So Amaziah let the troops go who had come to him from Ephraim. He sent them home. They were very angry with Judah. They were still very angry when they went home.

¹¹ Then Amaziah showed how strong he was. He led his army to the Valley of Salt. There he killed 10,000 men of Seir. ¹² The army of Judah also captured 10,000 men alive. The army of Judah took them to the top of a cliff. Then they threw them down. All of them were smashed to pieces.

¹³ The troops Amaziah had sent back attacked some towns that belonged to Judah. Amaziah hadn't allowed the troops to take part in the war. They attacked towns from Samaria to Beth Horon. They killed 3,000

people. They carried off huge amounts of goods. ¹⁴ Amaziah returned from killing the men of Edom. He brought back the statues of the gods of Seir. He set them up as his own gods. He bowed down to them. He burned sacrifices to them. ¹⁵ The LORD was very angry with Amaziah. He sent a prophet to him. The prophet said, "Why do you ask the gods of those people for advice? They couldn't even save their own people from your power!" ¹⁶ While the prophet was still speaking, the king spoke to him. He said, "Did I ask you for advice? Stop! If you don't, you will be struck down."

So the prophet stopped. But then he said, "I know that God has decided to destroy you. That's because you have worshiped other gods. You haven't listened to my advice."

¹⁷ Amaziah, the king of Judah, spoke to his advisers. Then he sent a message to Jehoash, the king of Israel. Jehoash was the son of Jehoahaz. Jehoahaz was the son of Jehu. Amaziah dared Jehoash, "Come on! Let us face each other in battle!"

¹⁸ But Jehoash, the king of Israel, answered Amaziah, the king of Judah. Jehoash said, "A thorn bush in Lebanon sent a message to a cedar tree there. The thorn bush said, 'Give your daughter to be married to my son.' Then a wild animal in Lebanon came along. It crushed the thorn bush by walking on it. ¹⁹ You brag that you have won the battle over Edom. You are very proud. But stay home! Why ask for trouble? Why bring yourself crashing down? Why bring Judah down with you?"

²⁰ But Amaziah wouldn't listen. That's because God had planned to hand Judah over to Jehoash. After all, they had asked the gods of Edom for advice. ²¹ So Jehoash, the king of Israel, attacked. He and Amaziah, the king of Judah, faced each other in battle. The battle took place at Beth Shemesh in Judah. ²² Israel drove Judah away. Every man ran home. ²³ Jehoash king of Israel captured Amaziah king of Judah at Beth Shemesh. Amaziah was the son of Joash. Joash was the son of Ahaziah. Jehoash brought Amaziah to Jerusalem. Jehoash broke down part of its wall. It's the part that went from the Ephraim Gate to the Corner Gate. That part of the wall was 600 feet long. ²⁴ Jehoash took all the gold and silver. He took all the objects he found in God's temple. Obed-Edom had been in charge of them. Jehoash also took the palace treasures and the prisoners. Then he returned to Samaria.

²⁵ Amaziah king of Judah lived for 15 years after Jehoash king of Israel died. Amaziah was the son of Joash. Jehoash was the son of Jehoahaz. ²⁶ The other events of Amaziah's rule from beginning to end are written down. They are written in the records of the kings of Judah and Israel. ²⁷ Amaziah turned away from obeying the LORD. From

that time on, some people made evil plans against him in Jerusalem. So he ran away to Lachish. But they sent men after him to Lachish. There they killed him. 28 His body was brought back on a horse to Jerusalem, the City of Judah. There he was buried in the family tomb.

Uzziah King of Judah

26 All the people of Judah made Uzziah king. He was 16 years old. They made him king in place of his father Amaziah. 2 Uzziah rebuilt Elath. He brought it under Judah's control again. He did it after Amaziah joined the members of his family who had already died.

3 Uzziah was 16 years old when he became king. He ruled in Jerusalem for 52 years. His mother's name was Jekoliah. She was from Jerusalem. 4 Uzziah did what was right in the eyes of the LORD, just as his father Amaziah had done. 5 He tried to obey God during the days of Zechariah. Zechariah taught him to have respect for God. As long as Uzziah obeyed the LORD, God gave him success.

6 Uzziah went to war against the Philistines. He broke down the walls of Gath, Jabneh and Ashdod. Then he rebuilt some towns that were near Ashdod. He also rebuilt some other towns where Philistines lived. 7 God helped him fight against the Philistines. He also helped him fight against the Meunites and against the Arabs who lived in Gur Baal. 8 The Ammonites brought to Uzziah the gifts he required of them. He became famous all the way to the border of Egypt. That's because he had become very powerful.

9 Uzziah built towers in Jerusalem. They were at the Corner Gate, the Valley Gate and the angle of the wall. He made the towers very strong. 10 He also built towers in the desert. He dug many wells, because he had a lot of livestock. The livestock were in the western hills and on the plains. Uzziah had people working in his fields and vineyards in the hills and in the rich lands. That's because he loved the soil.

11 Uzziah's army was well trained. It was ready to march out by military groups according to their numbers. Jeiel and Maaseiah brought them together. Jeiel was the secretary. Maaseiah was the officer. They were under the direction of Hananiah. He was one of the royal officials. 12 The total number of family leaders who were over the fighting men was 2,600. 13 An army of 307,500 men was under their command. The men were trained for war. They were a powerful force. They helped the king against his enemies. 14 Uzziah provided the entire army with shields, spears, helmets, coats of armor, bows, and stones for their slings. 15 In Jerusalem he invented machines to be used on the towers and on the corners of city walls. These machines were used by men who shot arrows from the walls.

The machines were also used by men to throw large stones from the walls. Uzziah became famous everywhere. God greatly helped him until he became powerful.

16 But after Uzziah became powerful, his pride brought him down. He wasn't faithful to the LORD his God. He entered the LORD's temple to burn incense on the altar for burning incense. 17 Azariah the priest followed him in. So did 80 other brave priests of the LORD. 18 They stood up to Uzziah. They said, "Uzziah, it isn't right for you to burn incense to the LORD. Only the priests are supposed to do that. They are members of the family line of Aaron. They have been set apart to burn incense. So get out of here. Leave the temple. You haven't been faithful. The LORD God won't honor you."

19 Uzziah was holding a shallow cup. He was ready to burn incense in it. He became angry. He shouted at the priests in the LORD's temple. He did it near the altar for burning incense. While he was shouting, a skin disease suddenly broke out on his forehead. 20 Azariah the chief priest and all the other priests looked at him. They saw that Uzziah had a skin disease on his forehead. So they hurried him out of the temple. Actually, he himself really wanted to leave. He knew that the LORD was making him suffer.

21 King Uzziah had the skin disease until the day he died. He lived in a separate house because he had the disease. And he wasn't allowed to enter the LORD's temple. Uzziah's son Jotham was in charge of the palace. Jotham ruled over the people of the land.

22 The other events of Uzziah's rule from beginning to end were written down by Isaiah the prophet. Isaiah was the son of Amoz. 23 Uzziah joined the members of his family who had already died. He was buried near them in a royal burial ground. People said, "He had a skin disease." Uzziah's son Jotham became the next king after him.

Jotham King of Judah

27 Jotham was 25 years old when he became king. He ruled in Jerusalem for 16 years. His mother's name was Jerusha. She was the daughter of Zadok. 2 Jotham did what was right in the eyes of the LORD, just as his father Uzziah had done. But Jotham didn't enter the LORD's temple as Uzziah had done. The people, however, continued to do very sinful things. 3 Jotham rebuilt the Upper Gate of the LORD's temple. He did a lot of work on the wall at the hill of Ophel. 4 He built towns in the hill country of Judah. He also built forts and towers in areas that had a lot of trees in them.

5 Jotham went to war against the king of Ammon. He won the battle over the Ammonites. That year they paid Jotham almost four tons of silver. They paid him 1,800 tons of wheat and

1,500 tons of barley. They also brought him the same amount in the second and third years. ⁶ Jotham became powerful. That's because he had worshiped the LORD his God with all his heart.

⁷ The other events of Jotham's rule are written down. That includes all his wars and the other things he did. All these things are written in the records of the kings of Israel and Judah. ⁸ Jotham was 25 years old when he became king. He ruled in Jerusalem for 16 years. ⁹ Jotham joined the members of his family who had already died. He was buried in the City of David. Jotham's son Ahaz became the next king after him.

Ahaz King of Judah

28 Ahaz was 20 years old when he became king. He ruled in Jerusalem for 16 years. He didn't do what was right in the eyes of the LORD. He didn't do what King David had done. ² He followed the ways of the kings of Israel. He also made statues of gods that were named Baal. ³ He burned sacrifices in the Valley of Ben Hinnom. He sacrificed his children in the fire to other gods. He followed the practices of the nations. The LORD hates these practices. The LORD had driven out those nations to make room for the people of Israel. ⁴ Ahaz offered sacrifices and burned incense at the high places. He also did it on the tops of hills and under every green tree.

⁵ So the LORD his God handed him over to the king of Aram. The men of Aram won the battle over him. They took many of his people as prisoners. They brought them to Damascus.

God also handed Ahaz over to Pekah. Pekah was king of Israel. His army wounded or killed many of the troops of Ahaz. ⁶ In one day Pekah, the son of Remaliah, killed 120,000 soldiers in Judah. That's because Judah had deserted the LORD, the God of their people. ⁷ Zikri was a fighting man from Ephraim. He killed Maaseiah, Azrikam and Elkanah. Maaseiah was the king's son. Azrikam was the officer who was in charge of the palace. And Elkanah was next in command after the king. ⁸ The men of Israel captured 200,000 wives, sons and daughters from their relatives in Judah. They also took a large amount of goods. They carried all of it back to Samaria.

⁹ But a prophet of the LORD was there. His name was Oded. When the army returned to Samaria, he went out to meet them. He said to them, "The LORD is the God of your people. He was very angry with Judah. So he handed them over to you. But you have killed them. Your anger reached all the way to heaven. ¹⁰ Now you are planning to make the men and women of Judah and Jerusalem your slaves. But aren't you also guilty of sins against the LORD your God? ¹¹ Listen to me! You have taken your relatives from

Judah as prisoners. The LORD is very angry with you. So send your relatives back."

¹²Then some of the leaders in Ephraim stood up to those who were returning from the war. The leaders were Azariah, Berekiah, Jehizkiah and Amasa. Azariah was the son of Jehohanan. Berekiah was the son of Meshillemoth. Jehizkiah was the son of Shallum. And Amasa was the son of Hadlai. ¹³"Don't bring those prisoners here," they said. "If you do, we'll be guilty in the sight of the LORD. Do you really want to add to our sin and guilt? We're already very guilty. The LORD is very angry with Israel."

¹⁴So the soldiers gave up the prisoners and the goods they had taken. They did it in front of the officials and the whole community. ¹⁵Azariah, Berekiah, Jehizkiah and Amasa received the prisoners. From the goods that had been taken, they gave clothes to everyone who was naked. They gave them clothes, sandals, food, drink and healing lotion. They put all the weak people on donkeys. They took them back to their relatives at Jericho. Then they returned to Samaria. Jericho was also known as the City of Palm Trees.

¹⁶At that time King Ahaz sent men to the king of Assyria to get help. ¹⁷The men of Edom had come and attacked Judah again. They had carried away prisoners. ¹⁸At the same time the Philistines had attacked towns in the western hills and in the Negev Desert of Judah. They had captured Beth Shemesh, Aijalon and Gederoth. They had also captured Soko, Timnah and Gimzo and the villages around them. They had settled down in all of them. ¹⁹The LORD had made Judah less powerful because of Ahaz, their king. Ahaz had stirred up the people of Judah to do evil things. He hadn't been faithful to the LORD at all. ²⁰Tiglath-Pileser came to Ahaz. But he gave Ahaz trouble instead of help. Tiglath-Pileser was king of Assyria. ²¹Ahaz took some things from the LORD's temple. He also took some from the royal palace and from the officials. He gave all of them to the king of Assyria. But that didn't help Ahaz.

²²When King Ahaz was in trouble, he became even more unfaithful to the LORD. ²³Ahaz offered sacrifices to the gods of Damascus. They had won the battle over him. Ahaz thought, "The gods of the kings of Aram have helped them. So I'll sacrifice to those gods. Then they'll help me." But those gods only caused his ruin. In fact, those gods caused the ruin of the whole nation of Israel.

²⁴Ahaz gathered together everything that belonged to God's temple. He cut all of it in pieces. Ahaz shut the doors of the LORD's temple. He set up altars at every street corner in Jerusalem. ²⁵In every town in Judah he built high places. Sacrifices were burned there to other gods. That made the LORD, the God of his people, very angry.

²⁶ The other events of the rule of Ahaz and all his evil practices from beginning to end are written down. They are written in the records of the kings of Judah and Israel. ²⁷ Ahaz joined the members of his family who had already died. He was buried in the city of Jerusalem. But he wasn't placed in the tombs of the kings of Israel. Ahaz's son Hezekiah became the next king after him.

Hezekiah Purifies the Temple

29 Hezekiah was 25 years old when he became king. He ruled in Jerusalem for 29 years. His mother's name was Abijah. She was the daughter of Zechariah. ² Hezekiah did what was right in the eyes of the LORD, just as King David had done.

³ In the first month of Hezekiah's first year as king, he opened the doors of the LORD's temple. He repaired them. ⁴ He brought the priests and Levites in. He gathered them together in the open area on the east side of the temple. ⁵ He said, "Levites, listen to me! Set yourselves apart to the LORD. Set apart the temple of the LORD. He's the God of your people who lived long ago. Remove anything 'unclean' from the temple. ⁶ Our people weren't faithful. They did what was evil in the eyes of the LORD our God. They deserted him. They turned their faces away from the place where he lives. They turned their backs on him. ⁷ They also shut the doors of the temple porch. They put the lamps out. They didn't burn incense at the temple. They didn't sacrifice burnt offerings there to the God of Israel. ⁸ So the LORD has become angry with Judah and Jerusalem. He has made them look so bad that everyone is shocked when they see them. They laugh at them. You can see it with your own eyes. ⁹ That's why our fathers have been killed by swords. That's why our sons and daughters and wives have become prisoners. ¹⁰ So I'm planning to make a covenant with the LORD, the God of Israel. Then he'll stop being angry with us. ¹¹ My sons, don't fail to obey the LORD. He has chosen you to stand in front of him and work for him. He wants you to serve him and burn incense to him."

¹² Here are the Levites who went to work.

Mahath and Joel were from the family line of Kohath. Mahath was the son of Amasai. Joel was the son of Azariah.

Kish and Azariah were from the family line of Merari. Kish was the son of Abdi. Azariah was the son of Jehallelel.

Joah and Eden were from the family line of Gershon. Joah was the son of Zimmah. Eden was the son of Joah.

¹³ Shimri and Jeiel were from

the family line of Eliza-
phan.
Zechariah and Mattaniah
were from
the family line of Asaph.
¹⁴ Jehiel and Shimei were
from
the family line of Heman.
Shemaiah and Uzziel were
from
the family line of Jedu-
thun.

¹⁵ All these Levites gathered the other Levites together. They set themselves apart to the Lord. Then they went in to purify the Lord's temple. That's what the king had ordered them to do. They did what the Lord told them to. ¹⁶ The priests went into the Lord's temple to make it pure. They brought out to the temple courtyard everything that was "unclean." They had found "unclean" things in the Lord's temple. The Levites took them and carried them out to the Kidron Valley. ¹⁷ On the first day of the first month they began to set everything in the temple apart to the Lord. By the eighth day of the month they reached the Lord's porch. For eight more days they set the Lord's temple itself apart to him. They finished on the 16th day of the first month.

¹⁸ Then they went to King Hezekiah. They reported, "We've purified the whole temple of the Lord. That includes the altar for burnt offerings and all its tools. It also includes the table for the holy bread and all its objects. ¹⁹ We've prepared all the things King Ahaz had removed. We've set them apart to the Lord. Ahaz had removed them while he was king. He wasn't faithful to the Lord. Those things are now in front of the Lord's altar."

²⁰ Early the next morning King Hezekiah gathered together the city officials. They all went up to the Lord's temple. ²¹ They brought seven bulls, seven rams, seven male lambs and seven male goats with them. They sacrificed the animals as a sin offering for the kingdom, for the temple and for Judah. The king commanded the priests to offer them on the Lord's altar. The priests were from the family line of Aaron. ²² They killed the bulls. Then they splashed the blood against the altar. Next they killed the rams and splashed the blood against the altar. Then they killed the lambs and splashed the blood against the altar. ²³ The goats for the sin offering were brought to the king and the whole community. They placed their hands on them. ²⁴ Then the priests killed the goats. They put the blood on the altar as a sin offering. It paid for the sin of the whole nation of Israel. The king had ordered the burnt offering and the sin offering for the whole nation.

²⁵ Hezekiah stationed the Levites in the Lord's temple. They had cymbals, harps and lyres. They did everything in the way King David, his prophet Gad, and Nathan the prophet had required. The Lord had given commands about all these

things through his prophets.
²⁶ So the Levites stood ready
with David's musical instruments. And the priests had their
trumpets ready.

²⁷ Hezekiah gave the order to
sacrifice the burnt offering on
the altar. The offering began.
Singing to the Lord also began.
The singing was accompanied
by the trumpets and by the instruments of David. He had
been king of Israel. ²⁸ The whole
community bowed down. They
worshiped the Lord. At the
same time the musicians played
their musical instruments. The
priests blew their trumpets. All
of that continued until the burnt
offering had been sacrificed.

²⁹ So the offerings were finished. King Hezekiah got down
on his knees. He worshiped the
Lord. So did everyone who was
with him. ³⁰ The king and his
officials ordered the Levites to
praise the Lord. They used the
words of David and Asaph the
prophet. They sang praises with
joy. They bowed down and worshiped the Lord.

³¹ Then Hezekiah said, "You
have set yourselves apart to
the Lord. Come and bring sacrifices and thank offerings to
his temple." So the whole community brought sacrifices and
thank offerings. Everyone who
wanted to brought burnt offerings.

³² The whole community
brought 70 bulls, 100 rams and
200 male lambs. They brought
all of them as burnt offerings to
the Lord. ³³ The total number of
animals set apart as sacrifices
to the Lord was 600 bulls and
3,000 sheep and goats. ³⁴ But
there weren't enough priests
to skin all the burnt offerings.
So their relatives, the Levites,
helped them. They worked until the task was finished. By that
time other priests had been set
apart to the Lord. The Levites
had been more careful than
the priests when they set themselves apart. ³⁵ There were large
numbers of burnt offerings,
along with the drink offerings
and the fat from the friendship
offerings. They were offered
along with the burnt offerings.

So the service of the Lord's
temple was started up again.
³⁶ Hezekiah and all the people were filled with joy. That's
because everything had been
done so quickly. God had provided for his people in a wonderful way.

*Hezekiah Celebrates the
Passover Feast*

30 Hezekiah sent a message
to all the people of Israel
and Judah. He also wrote letters to the tribes of Ephraim and
Manasseh. He invited everyone
to come to the Lord's temple in
Jerusalem. He wanted them to
celebrate the Passover Feast to
honor the Lord. He is the God
of Israel. ² The king, his officials
and the whole community in
Jerusalem decided to celebrate
the Passover Feast in the second month. ³ They hadn't been
able to celebrate it at the regular time. That's because there

weren't enough priests who had set themselves apart to the LORD. Also, the people hadn't gathered together in Jerusalem. ⁴ The plan seemed good to the king and the whole community. ⁵ They decided to send a message all through Israel. It was sent out from Beersheba all the way to Dan. The message invited the people to come to Jerusalem. It invited them to celebrate the Passover Feast to honor the LORD, the God of Israel. The Passover Feast hadn't been celebrated by large numbers of people for a long time. It hadn't been done in keeping with what was written in the law.

⁶ Messengers went all through Israel and Judah. They carried letters from the king and his officials. The king had ordered them to do that. The letters said,

"People of Israel, return to the LORD. He is the God of Abraham, Isaac and Israel. Return to him. Then he will return to you who are left in the land. You have escaped from the power of the kings of Assyria. ⁷ Don't be like your parents and the rest of your people. They weren't faithful to the LORD, the God of their people. That's why he punished them. He made them look so bad that everyone was shocked when they saw them. You can see it for yourselves. ⁸ Don't be stubborn. Don't be as your people were. Obey the LORD. Come to his temple. He has set it apart to himself forever. Serve the LORD your God. Then he'll stop being angry with you. ⁹ Suppose you return to the LORD. Then those who captured your relatives and children will be kind to them. In fact, your relatives and children will come back to this land. The LORD your God is kind and tender. He won't turn away from you if you return to him."

¹⁰ The messengers went from town to town in Ephraim and Manasseh. They went all the way to Zebulun. But people laughed and made fun of them. ¹¹ In spite of that, some people from Asher, Manasseh and Zebulun made themselves humble. They went to Jerusalem. ¹² God helped the people of Judah. He helped them agree with one another. So they did what the king and his officials had ordered. They did what the LORD told them to do.

¹³ A very large crowd of people gathered together in Jerusalem. They went there to celebrate the Feast of Unleavened Bread. It took place in the second month. ¹⁴ They removed the altars in Jerusalem. They cleared away the altars for burning incense. They threw all the altars into the Kidron Valley.

¹⁵ They killed the Passover lamb on the 14th day of the second month. The priests and Levites were ashamed of how they had lived. They set themselves

apart to the LORD. They brought burnt offerings to his temple. [16] Then they did their regular tasks just as the Law of Moses, the man of God, required. The Levites gave the blood of the animals to the priests. The priests splashed it against the altar. [17] Many people in the crowd hadn't set themselves apart to the LORD. They weren't "clean." They couldn't set apart their lambs to him. So the Levites had to kill the Passover lambs for all of them. [18] Many people came from Ephraim, Manasseh, Issachar and Zebulun. Most of them hadn't made themselves pure and "clean." But they still ate the Passover meal. That was against what was written in the law. But Hezekiah prayed for them. He said, "The LORD is good. May he forgive everyone [19] who wants to worship God with all their heart. God is the LORD, the God of their people. May God forgive them even if they aren't 'clean' in keeping with the rules of the temple." [20] The LORD answered Hezekiah's prayer. He healed the people.

[21] The people of Israel who were in Jerusalem celebrated the Feast of Unleavened Bread. They celebrated for seven days with great joy. The Levites and priests praised the LORD every day. They praised the LORD with loud musical instruments. The instruments had been set apart to the LORD.

[22] Hezekiah spoke words that gave hope to all the Levites. They understood how to serve the LORD well. For the seven days of the feast they ate the share given to them. They also sacrificed friendship offerings. They praised the LORD, the God of their people.

[23] Then the whole community agreed to celebrate the feast for seven more days. So for another seven days they celebrated with joy. [24] Hezekiah, the king of Judah, provided 1,000 bulls and 7,000 sheep and goats for the community. The officials provided 1,000 bulls and 10,000 sheep and goats for them. A large number of priests set themselves apart to the LORD. [25] The entire community of Judah was filled with joy. So were the priests and Levites. And so were all the people who had gathered together from Israel. That included the outsiders who had come from Israel. It also included those who lived in Judah. [26] There was great joy in Jerusalem. There hadn't been anything like it in Israel since the days of Solomon, the son of David. Solomon had been king of Israel. [27] The priests and Levites gave their blessing to the people. God heard them. Their prayer reached all the way to heaven. It's the holy place where God lives.

31 The Passover Feast came to an end. The people of Israel who were in Jerusalem went out to the towns of Judah. They smashed the sacred stones. They cut down the poles used to worship the female god named Asherah. They destroyed the high places and the altars. They did those things all through Judah and Benjamin. They also did them in Ephraim and Manasseh. They destroyed all the objects used to worship other gods. Then the Israelites returned to their own towns and property.

The People Bring Gifts to the LORD

2 Hezekiah put the priests and Levites in groups based on their duties. The priests sacrificed burnt offerings and friendship offerings. The Levites served the LORD by giving thanks and singing praises at the gates of his house. 3 The king gave some of his own possessions to the temple. He gave them for the morning and evening burnt offerings. He gave them for the burnt offerings for every Sabbath day. He gave them for the burnt offerings for every New Moon feast. And he gave them for the burnt offerings for every yearly appointed feast. He did it in keeping with what is written in the Law of the LORD. 4 Hezekiah gave an order to the people who were living in Jerusalem. He commanded them to give to the priests and Levites the share they owed them. Then the priests and Levites could give their full attention to the Law of the LORD. 5 The order went out. Right away the people of Israel began to give freely. They gave the first share of the harvest of their grain, fresh wine, olive oil and honey. They also gave the first share of everything else their fields produced. They brought a large amount. It was a tenth of everything. 6 Here is what the people of Israel and Judah who lived in the towns of Judah brought. They brought a tenth of their herds and flocks. They also brought a tenth of the holy things they had set apart to the LORD their God. They put them in piles. 7 They began doing it in the third month. They finished in the seventh month. 8 Hezekiah and his officials came and saw the piles. When they did, they praised the LORD. And they blessed his people Israel.

9 Hezekiah asked the priests and Levites about the piles. 10 Azariah the chief priest answered him. He said, "The people have been bringing their gifts to the LORD's temple. Ever since they began to bring them, we've had enough to eat. We have even had plenty to spare. That's because the LORD has blessed his people. So we have a large amount left over." Azariah was from the family line of Zadok.

11 Hezekiah gave orders to prepare storerooms in the LORD's temple. And it was done. 12 The people were faithful. They brought in their offerings and a tenth of everything they produced. They also brought the gifts they had set apart to the LORD. Konaniah the Levite was in charge of everything they brought. His brother Shimei was next in command

after him. [13] Konaniah and his brother Shimei had helpers who worked with them. Their names were Jehiel, Azaziah, Nahath, Asahel, Jerimoth, Jozabad, Eliel, Ismakiah, Mahath and Benaiah. King Hezekiah and Azariah had appointed them. Azariah was the official in charge of God's temple.

[14] Kore the Levite guarded the East Gate. He was in charge of the offerings people chose to give to God. He handed out the offerings made to the LORD. He also handed out the gifts that had been set apart to the LORD. Kore was the son of Imnah. [15] Eden, Miniamin, Jeshua, Shemaiah, Amariah and Shekaniah helped Kore. They were faithful in helping him in the towns of the priests. They handed out gifts to their brother priests, group by group. They gave the gifts to old men and young men alike.

[16] In addition to that, they handed out gifts to the males who were three years old or more. The names of those males were listed in their family history. All of them would enter the LORD's temple. They would carry out their duties each day. Each group did all the different things it was supposed to do. [17] Kore and his Levite companions also handed out gifts to the priests. The priests were listed by their families in their family history. Those Levites also handed out gifts to the Levites who were 20 years old or more. Each group did all the different things it was supposed to do. [18] Those groups included all the little ones, the wives, and the sons and daughters of the whole community. All of them were listed in their family history. They were faithful in setting themselves apart to serve the LORD.

[19] Some of the priests lived in other towns or on farms around their towns. They were from the family line of Aaron. Men were chosen by name to hand out shares to those priests. They gave a share to every male among them. They also gave a share to everyone whose name was written down in the family history of the Levites.

[20] That's what Hezekiah did all through Judah. He did what was good and right. He was faithful to the LORD his God. [21] He tried to obey his God. He worked for him with all his heart. That's the way he worked in everything he did to serve God's temple. He obeyed the law. He followed the LORD's commands. So he had success.

Sennacherib Warns Jerusalem

32 Hezekiah had been completely faithful to the LORD. However, Sennacherib king of Assyria came and marched into Judah. Sennacherib surrounded the cities that had high walls around them. He got ready to attack them. He thought he could win the battle over them. He thought he could take them for himself. [2] Hezekiah saw that Sennacherib had come to Jerusalem to fight against it. ³ So he asked his officials and military leaders for advice. He asked them about blocking off the water from the springs outside the city. They gave him the advice he asked for. ⁴ They gathered together a large group of people. They blocked all the springs. They also blocked the stream that flowed through the land. "Why should the kings of Assyria come and find plenty of water?" they asked. ⁵ Then Hezekiah worked hard repairing all the broken parts of the wall. He built towers on it. He built another wall outside that one. He built up the areas that had been filled in around the City of David. He also made large numbers of weapons and shields.

⁶ He appointed military officers over the people. He gathered the officers together in front of him in the open area at the city gate. He gave them words of hope. He said, ⁷ "Be strong. Be brave. Don't be afraid. Don't lose hope. The king of Assyria has a huge army with him. But there's a greater power with us than there is with him. ⁸ The only thing he has is human strength. But the LORD our God is with us. He will help us. He'll fight our battles." The people had great faith in what Hezekiah, the king of Judah, said.

⁹ Later Sennacherib, the king of Assyria, and all his forces surrounded Lachish. They prepared to attack it. At that time, Sennacherib sent his officers to Jerusalem. They went there with a message for Hezekiah, the king of Judah. The message was also for all the people of Judah who were there. The message said,

¹⁰ "Sennacherib, the king of Assyria, says, 'Why are you putting your faith in what your king says? Why do you remain in Jerusalem when you are surrounded? ¹¹ Hezekiah says, "The LORD our God will save us from the power of the king of Assyria." But he isn't telling you the truth. If you listen to him, you will die of hunger and thirst. ¹² Didn't Hezekiah himself remove your god's high places and altars? Didn't Hezekiah say to the people of Judah and Jerusalem, "You must worship at one altar. You must burn sacrifices on it"?

¹³ " 'Don't you know what I and the kings who ruled before me have done? Don't you know what we've done to all the peoples of the other lands? Were the gods of those nations ever able to save their lands from my power? ¹⁴ The kings who ruled before me destroyed many nations. Which one of the gods of those nations has been able to save his people from me? So how can your god save you from my power? ¹⁵ Don't let Hezekiah trick you. He's telling you lies. Don't believe him. No god of any nation

or kingdom has been able to save his people from my power. No god has been able to save his people from the power of the kings who ruled before me. So your god won't save you from my power either!' "

16 Sennacherib's officers spoke even more things against the LORD God and his servant Hezekiah. 17 The king also wrote letters against the LORD. His letters made fun of the God of Israel. They said, "The peoples of other lands have their gods. But those gods didn't save their people from my power. So the god of Hezekiah won't save his people from my power either." 18 Then the officers called out in the Hebrew language to the people of Jerusalem who were on the wall. They were trying to scare them and make them afraid. That's because they wanted to capture the city. 19 They were comparing the God of Jerusalem to the gods of the other nations of the world. But those gods were only statues. They had been made by human hands.

20 King Hezekiah cried out in prayer to God in heaven. He prayed about the problem Jerusalem was facing. So did Isaiah the prophet. He was the son of Amoz. 21 The LORD sent an angel. The angel wiped out all the enemy's fighting men, commanders and officers. He put an end to them right there in the camp of the Assyrian king. So Sennacherib went back to his own land in shame. He went

into the temple of his god. There some of his own sons, the people closest to him, killed him with their swords.

22 So the LORD saved Hezekiah and the people of Jerusalem. He saved them from the power of Sennacherib, the king of Assyria. He also saved them from all their other enemies. He took care of them on every side. 23 Many people brought offerings to Jerusalem for the LORD. They brought expensive gifts for Hezekiah, the king of Judah. From then on, all the nations thought well of him.

Hezekiah's Pride, Success and Death

24 In those days Hezekiah became sick. He knew he was about to die. So he prayed to the LORD. And the LORD answered him. He gave him a miraculous sign. 25 But Hezekiah's heart was proud. He didn't give thanks for the many kind things the LORD had done for him. So the LORD became angry with him. He also became angry with Judah and Jerusalem. 26 Then Hezekiah had a change of heart. He was sorry he had been proud. The people of Jerusalem were also sorry they had sinned. So the LORD wasn't angry with them as long as Hezekiah was king.

27 Hezekiah was very rich. He received great honor. He made storerooms for his silver and gold. He also made them for his jewels, spices, shields and all kinds of expensive things. 28 He

made buildings to store the harvest of grain, fresh wine and olive oil. He made barns for all kinds of cattle. He made sheep pens for his flocks. ²⁹ He built villages. He gained large numbers of flocks and herds. God had made him very rich.

³⁰ Hezekiah blocked up the upper opening of the Gihon spring. He directed the water to flow down to the west side of the City of David. He had success in everything he did. ³¹ The rulers of Babylon sent messengers to him. They asked him about the miraculous sign that had taken place in the land. Then God left Hezekiah to test him. God wanted to know everything in Hezekiah's heart.

³² Hezekiah did many things that showed he was faithful to the LORD. Those things and the other events of his rule are written down. They are written in the record of the vision of the prophet Isaiah, the son of Amoz. That record is part of the records of the kings of Judah and Israel. ³³ Hezekiah joined the members of his family who had already died. He was buried on the hill where the tombs of David's family are. The whole nation of Judah honored him when he died. So did the people of Jerusalem. Hezekiah's son Manasseh became the next king after him.

Manasseh King of Judah

33 Manasseh was 12 years old when he became king. He ruled in Jerusalem for 55 years. ² Manasseh did what was evil in the eyes of the LORD. He followed the practices of the nations. The LORD hated those practices. The LORD had driven out those nations to make room for the Israelites. ³ Manasseh rebuilt the high places. His father Hezekiah had destroyed them. Manasseh also set up altars to the gods that were named Baal. He made poles used to worship the female god named Asherah. He even bowed down to all the stars and worshiped them. ⁴ He built altars in the LORD's temple. The LORD had said about his temple, "My Name will remain in Jerusalem forever." ⁵ In the two courtyards of the LORD's temple Manasseh built altars to honor all the stars in the sky. ⁶ He sacrificed his children in the fire to other gods. He did it in the Valley of Ben Hinnom. He practiced all kinds of evil magic. He took part in worshiping evil powers. He got messages from people who had died. He talked to the spirits of people who have died. He did many things that were evil in the eyes of the LORD. Manasseh made the LORD very angry.

⁷ Manasseh had carved a statue of a god. He put it in God's temple. God had spoken to David and his son Solomon about the temple. He had said, "My Name will be in this temple and in Jerusalem forever. Out of all the cities in the tribes of Israel I have chosen Jerusalem. ⁸ I gave this land to your people who lived long ago. I will not make

the Israelites leave it again. But they must be careful to do everything I commanded them. They must follow all the laws, directions, and rules I gave them through Moses." ⁹ But Manasseh led Judah and the people of Jerusalem astray. They did more evil things than the nations the Lord had destroyed to make room for the Israelites.

¹⁰ The Lord spoke to Manasseh and his people. But they didn't pay any attention to him. ¹¹ So the Lord brought the army commanders of the king of Assyria against them. They took Manasseh as a prisoner. They put a hook in his nose. They put him in bronze chains. And they took him to Babylon. ¹² When Manasseh was in trouble, he asked the Lord his God to help him. He made himself very humble in the sight of the God of his people. ¹³ Manasseh prayed to him. When he did, the Lord felt sorry for him. He answered his prayer. The Lord brought Manasseh back to Jerusalem and his kingdom. Then Manasseh knew that the Lord is God.

¹⁴ After that, Manasseh rebuilt the outer wall of the City of David. It was west of the Gihon spring in the valley. It reached all the way to the entrance of the Fish Gate. It went around the entire hill of Ophel. Manasseh also made the wall much higher. He stationed military commanders in all the cities in Judah that had high walls around them.

¹⁵ Manasseh got rid of the false gods. He removed the statue of one of those gods from the Lord's temple. He also removed all the altars he had built on the temple hill and in Jerusalem. He threw them out of the city. ¹⁶ Then he made the Lord's altar look like new again. He sacrificed friendship offerings and thank offerings on it. He told the people of Judah to serve the Lord, the God of Israel. ¹⁷ The people continued to offer sacrifices at the high places. But they offered them only to the Lord their God.

¹⁸ The other events of Manasseh's rule are written down in the official records of the kings of Judah. These records include his prayer to his God. They also include the words the prophets spoke to him in the name of the Lord, the God of Israel. ¹⁹ Everything about Manasseh is written in the records of the prophets. That includes his prayer and the fact that God felt sorry for him. It includes everything he did before he made himself humble in the Lord's sight. It includes all his sins and the fact that he wasn't faithful to the Lord. It includes the locations where he built high places. It includes the places where he set up poles used to worship the female god named Asherah. And it includes the places where he set up statues of other gods. ²⁰ Manasseh joined the members of his family who had already died. He was buried in his palace. Manasseh's son Amon became the next king after him.

Amon King of Judah

²¹ Amon was 22 years old when he became king. He ruled in Jerusalem for two years. ²² Amon did what was evil in the eyes of the LORD, just as his father Manasseh had done. Amon worshiped and offered sacrifices to all the statues of gods that Manasseh had made. ²³ He didn't make himself humble in the LORD's sight as his father Manasseh had done. So Amon became even more guilty.

²⁴ Amon's officials made plans against him. They murdered him in his palace. ²⁵ Then the people of the land killed all those who had made plans against King Amon. They made his son Josiah king in his place.

Josiah Makes Judah a Better Nation

34 Josiah was eight years old when he became king. He ruled in Jerusalem for 31 years. ² He did what was right in the eyes of the LORD. He lived the way King David had lived. He didn't turn away from it to the right or the left.

³ While he was still young, he began to worship the God of King David. It was the eighth year of Josiah's rule. In his 12th year Josiah began to get rid of the high places in Judah and Jerusalem. He removed the poles used to worship the female god named Asherah. He also removed the statues of other false gods. ⁴ He ordered the altars of the gods that were named Baal to be torn down. Josiah cut to pieces the altars above them that were used for burning incense. He smashed the Asherah poles. He also smashed the statues of other false gods. Josiah broke all of them to pieces. He scattered the pieces over the graves of those who had offered sacrifices to those gods. ⁵ He burned the bones of the priests on their altars. That's the way he made Judah and Jerusalem pure and "clean." ⁶ Josiah went to the towns of Manasseh, Ephraim and Simeon. He went all the way to Naphtali. He also went to the destroyed places around all those towns. ⁷ Everywhere Josiah went he tore down the altars and the Asherah poles. He crushed the statues of gods to powder. He cut to pieces all the altars for burning incense. He destroyed all those things everywhere in Israel. Then he went back to Jerusalem.

⁸ In the 18th year of Josiah's rule, he decided to make the land and temple pure and "clean." So he sent Shaphan, Maaseiah and Joah to repair the temple of the LORD his God. Shaphan was the son of Azaliah. Maaseiah was ruler of the city. And Joah, the son of Joahaz, kept the records.

⁹ These men went to Hilkiah the high priest. They gave him the money that had been brought into God's temple. The Levites who guarded the gates had collected it. They had received some of the money from the people of Manasseh and Ephraim. They had also re-

ceived some from the other people who remained in Israel. The rest of the money came from other people. It came from all the people of Judah and Benjamin and the people living in Jerusalem. ¹⁰ Men were appointed to direct the work on the LORD's temple. All the money collected was given to them. These men paid the workers who repaired the temple. They made it look like new again. ¹¹ They also gave money to the builders and those who worked with wood. The workers used it to buy lumber and blocks of stone. The lumber was used for the supports and beams for the buildings. The kings of Judah had let the buildings fall down.

¹² The workers were faithful in doing the work. Jahath and Obadiah directed them. They were Levites from the family line of Merari. Zechariah and Meshullam also directed them. They were from the family line of Kohath. The Levites were skilled in playing musical instruments. ¹³ They were in charge of the laborers. They directed all the workers from job to job. Some of the Levites were secretaries and writers. Other Levites guarded the gates.

Hilkiah Finds the Book of the Law

¹⁴ The money that had been taken into the LORD's temple was being brought out. At that time Hilkiah the priest found the Book of the Law of the LORD. It had been given through Mo-

ses. ¹⁵ Hilkiah spoke to Shaphan the secretary. Hilkiah said, "I've found the Book of the Law in the LORD's temple." Hilkiah gave the book to Shaphan.

¹⁶ Then Shaphan took the book to King Josiah. He told him, "Your officials are doing everything they've been asked to do. ¹⁷ They have paid out the money that was in the LORD's temple. They've put it in the care of the directors and workers." ¹⁸ Shaphan continued, "Hilkiah the priest has given me a book." Shaphan read some of it to the king.

¹⁹ The king heard the words of the Law. When he did, he tore his royal robes. ²⁰ He gave orders to Hilkiah, Ahikam, Abdon, Shaphan the secretary and Asaiah. Ahikam was the son of Shaphan. Abdon was the son of Micah. And Asaiah was the king's attendant. Josiah commanded them, ²¹ "Go. Ask the LORD for advice. Ask him about what is written in this book that has been found. Do it for me. Also do it for the people who remain in Israel and Judah. The LORD has been very angry with us. That's because our people before us didn't obey what the LORD had said. They didn't do everything written in this book."

²² Hilkiah and the people the king had sent with him went to speak to Huldah the prophet. She was the wife of Shallum. Shallum was the son of Tokhath. Tokhath was the son of Hasrah. Shallum took care of the sacred

robes. Huldah lived in the New Quarter of Jerusalem.

23 Huldah said to them, "The LORD is the God of Israel. He says, 'Here is what you should tell the man who sent you to me. 24 "The LORD says, 'I am going to bring horrible trouble on this place and its people. There are curses written down in the book that has been read to the king of Judah. All those curses will take place. 25 That's because the people have deserted me. They have burned incense to other gods. They have made me very angry because of everything their hands have made. So my anger will burn like a fire against this place. And the fire of my anger will not be put out.' " ' 26 The king of Judah sent you to ask for advice. Tell him, 'The LORD is the God of Israel. He has a message for you about the things you heard. 27 The LORD says, "Your heart was tender. You made yourself humble in my sight. You heard what I spoke against this place and its people. So you made yourself humble. You tore your royal robes and wept. And I have heard you," announces the LORD. 28 You will join the members of your family who have already died. You will be buried in peace. You will not see all the trouble I am going to bring. I am going to bring trouble on this place and the people who live here.' "

Huldah's answer was taken back to the king.

29 Then the king called together all the elders of Judah and Jerusalem. 30 He went up to the LORD's temple. The people of Judah and Jerusalem went with him. So did the priests and Levites. All of them went, from the least important of them to the most important. The king had all the words of the Book of the Covenant read to them. The book had been found in the LORD's temple. 31 The king stood next to his pillar. He agreed to the terms of the covenant in front of the LORD. The king promised to serve the LORD and obey his commands, directions and rules. He promised to obey them with all his heart and with all his soul. So the king promised to obey the terms of the covenant that were written in that book.

32 Then he had everyone in Jerusalem and in Benjamin commit themselves to the covenant. The people of Jerusalem did it in keeping with the covenant of the God of Israel.

33 Josiah removed all the statues of false gods from the whole territory that belonged to the Israelites. The LORD hated those statues. Josiah had everyone in Israel serve the LORD their God. As long as he lived, they didn't fail to follow the LORD, the God of their people.

Josiah Celebrates the Passover Feast

35 Josiah celebrated the Passover Feast in Jerusalem to honor the LORD. The Passover lamb was killed on the 14th day of the first month.

Elijah Is Taken Up to Heaven
2 KINGS 2:1–14

Daniel in the Lions' Den

DANIEL 6

[2] Josiah appointed the priests to their duties. He cheered them up as they served the LORD at his temple. [3] The Levites taught all the people of Israel. The Levites had been set apart to the LORD. Josiah said to them, "Put the sacred ark of the covenant in the temple Solomon built. He was the son of David and king of Israel. The ark must not be carried around on your shoulders. Serve the LORD your God. Serve his people Israel. [4] Prepare yourselves by families in your groups. Do it based on the directions written by David, the king of Israel, and by his son Solomon.

[5] "Stand at the temple. Stand there with a group of Levites for each group of families among your people. [6] Kill the Passover lambs. Set yourselves apart to the LORD. Prepare the lambs for your people. Do what the LORD commanded through Moses."

[7] Josiah provided animals for the Passover offerings. He gave them for all the people who were there. He gave a total of 30,000 lambs and goats and 3,000 oxen. He gave all of them from his own possessions.

[8] His officials also gave freely. They gave to the people and the priests and Levites. Hilkiah, Zechariah and Jehiel were in charge of God's temple. They gave the priests 2,600 Passover lambs and 300 oxen. [9] Konaniah and his brothers Shemaiah and Nethanel also gave offerings. So did Hashabiah, Jeiel and Jozabad. All of them were the leaders of the Levites. They gave 5,000 Passover lambs and 500 oxen for the Levites.

[10] The Passover service was arranged. The priests stood in their places. The Levites were in their groups. That's what the king had ordered. [11] The Passover lambs were killed. The priests splashed against the altar the blood handed to them. The Levites skinned the animals. [12] They set the burnt offerings to one side. These offerings were for the smaller family groups to offer to the LORD. That's what was written in the Book of Moses. The Levites did the same thing with the oxen. [13] They cooked the Passover animals over the fire, just as the law required. They boiled the holy offerings in pots, large kettles and pans. They served the offerings quickly to all the people. [14] After that, they got things ready for themselves and the priests. That's because the priests, who were from the family line of Aaron, were busy until dark. They were sacrificing the burnt offerings and the fat parts. The Levites got things ready for themselves and for the priests, who belonged to Aaron's family line.

[15] Those who played music were from the family line of Asaph. They were in the places that had been set up by David, Asaph, Heman and Jeduthun. Jeduthun had been the king's prophet. The guards at each gate didn't have to leave their places. That's because their brother Levites got things ready for them.

¹⁶So at that time the entire service to honor the Lord was carried out. The Passover Feast was celebrated. The burnt offerings were sacrificed on the Lord's altar. That's what King Josiah had ordered. ¹⁷The Israelites who were there celebrated the Passover Feast at that time. They observed the Feast of Unleavened Bread for seven days. ¹⁸The Passover Feast hadn't been observed like that in Israel since the days of Samuel the prophet. None of the kings of Israel had ever celebrated a Passover Feast like Josiah's. He celebrated it with the priests and Levites. All the people of Judah and Israel were there along with the people of Jerusalem. He celebrated it with them too. ¹⁹That Passover Feast was celebrated in the 18th year of Josiah's rule.

Josiah Dies

²⁰Josiah had put the temple in order. After all of that, Necho went up to fight at Carchemish. He was king of Egypt. Carchemish was on the Euphrates River. Josiah marched out to meet Necho in battle. ²¹But Necho sent messengers to him. They said, "Josiah king of Judah, there isn't any trouble between you and me. I'm not attacking you at this time. I'm at war with another country. God told me to hurry. He's with me. So stop opposing him. If you don't, he'll destroy you."

²²But Josiah wouldn't turn away from Necho. Josiah wore different clothes so people wouldn't recognize him. He wanted to go to war against Necho. He wouldn't listen to what God had commanded Necho to say. Instead, Josiah went out to fight him on the plains of Megiddo.

²³Men who had bows shot arrows at King Josiah. After he was hit, he told his officers, "Take me away. I'm badly wounded." ²⁴So they took him out of his chariot. They put him in his other chariot. They brought him to Jerusalem. There he died. He was buried in the tombs of his family. All the people of Judah and Jerusalem mourned for him.

²⁵Jeremiah wrote songs of sadness about Josiah. To this day all the male and female singers remember Josiah by singing those songs. That became a practice in Israel. The songs are written down in the Book of the Songs of Sadness.

²⁶Josiah did many things that showed he was faithful to the Lord. Those things and the other events of Josiah's rule were in keeping with what is written in the Law of the Lord. ²⁷All the events from beginning to end are written down. They are written in the records of the kings of Israel and Judah. **36** ¹The people of the land went and got Jehoahaz. He was the son of Josiah. The people made Jehoahaz king in Jerusalem in place of his father.

Jehoahaz King of Judah

²Jehoahaz was 23 years old when he became king. He ruled

in Jerusalem for three months. ³ The king of Egypt removed him from his throne in Jerusalem. The king of Egypt made the people of Judah pay him a huge tax. The tax was almost four tons of silver and 75 pounds of gold. ⁴ Necho, the king of Egypt, made Eliakim king over Judah and Jerusalem. Eliakim was a brother of Jehoahaz. Necho changed Eliakim's name to Jehoiakim. But Necho took Eliakim's brother Jehoahaz with him to Egypt.

Jehoiakim King of Judah

⁵ Jehoiakim was 25 years old when he became king. He ruled in Jerusalem for 11 years. He did what was evil in the eyes of the LORD his God. ⁶ Nebuchadnezzar attacked him. Nebuchadnezzar was king of Babylon. He put Jehoiakim in bronze chains. And he took him to Babylon. ⁷ Nebuchadnezzar also took to Babylon objects from the LORD's temple. He put them in his own temple there.

⁸ The other events of Jehoiakim's rule are written in the records of the kings of Israel and Judah. He did things the LORD hated. Those things and everything that happened to him are also written in those records. Jehoiakim's son Jehoiachin became the next king after him.

Jehoiachin King of Judah

⁹ Jehoiachin was 18 years old when he became king. He ruled in Jerusalem for three months and ten days. He did what was evil in the eyes of the LORD. ¹⁰ In the spring, King Nebuchadnezzar sent for him. He brought him to Babylon. He also brought things of value from the LORD's temple. He made Zedekiah king over Judah and Jerusalem. Zedekiah was Jehoiachin's uncle.

Zedekiah King of Judah

¹¹ Zedekiah was 21 years old when he became king. He ruled in Jerusalem for 11 years. ¹² He did what was evil in the eyes of the LORD his God. He didn't pay any attention to the message the LORD spoke through Jeremiah the prophet. ¹³ Zedekiah also refused to remain under the control of King Nebuchadnezzar. The king had forced Zedekiah to make a promise in God's name. But Zedekiah's heart became very stubborn. He wouldn't turn to the LORD, the God of Israel. ¹⁴ And that's not all. The people and all the leaders of the priests became more and more unfaithful. They followed all the practices of the nations. The LORD hated those practices. The people and leaders made the LORD's temple "unclean." The LORD had set the temple in Jerusalem apart in a special way for himself.

The Fall of Jerusalem

¹⁵ The LORD, the God of Israel, sent word to his people through his messengers. He sent it to them again and again. He took pity on his people. He also took pity on the temple where he lived. ¹⁶ But God's people made

fun of his messengers. They hated his words. They laughed at his prophets. Finally the LORD's great anger was stirred up against his people. Nothing could save them. [17] The LORD brought the king of the Babylonians against them. The Babylonian army killed their young people with their swords at the temple. They didn't spare young men or young women. They didn't spare the old people or weak people either. God handed all of them over to Nebuchadnezzar. [18] Nebuchadnezzar carried off to Babylon all the objects from God's temple. Some of those things were large. Others were small. He carried off the treasures of the temple. He also carried off the treasures that belonged to the king and his officials. [19] The Babylonians set God's temple on fire. They broke down the wall of Jerusalem. They burned all the palaces. They destroyed everything of value there.

[20] Nebuchadnezzar took the rest of the people to Babylon as prisoners. They had escaped from being killed by swords. They served him and those who ruled after him. That lasted until the kingdom of Persia came to power. [21] The land of Israel enjoyed its sabbath years. It rested. That deserted land wasn't farmed for a full 70 years. What the LORD had spoken through Jeremiah came true.

[22] It was the first year of the rule of Cyrus. He was king of Persia. The LORD inspired him to send a message all through his kingdom. It happened so that what the LORD had spoken through Jeremiah would come true. The message was written down. It said,

[23] "Cyrus, the king of Persia, says,

" 'The LORD is the God of heaven. He has given me all the kingdoms on earth. He has appointed me to build a temple for him at Jerusalem in Judah. Any of his people among you may go up to Jerusalem. And may the LORD their God be with them.' "

Ezra

Introduction:

Ezra was a priest and a teacher of God's law.

The book of Ezra tells about the Israelites who went back to their land. King Nebuchadnezzar had attacked them and taken them to Babylonia. Later, King Cyrus said they were free to go back home. The people went home and rebuilt the city of Jerusalem. They rebuilt the temple too.

Then Ezra came and told them to obey God. Ezra was a good and wise leader. He helped the people turn away from their sin and love God.

Outline of contents:

Cyrus Helps the Jews to Return to Jerusalem

1 It was the first year of the rule of Cyrus. He was king of Persia. The LORD inspired him to send a message all through his kingdom. It happened so that what the LORD had spoken through Jeremiah would come true. The message was written down. It said,

2 "Cyrus, the king of Persia, says,

" 'The LORD is the God of heaven. He has given me all the kingdoms on earth. He has appointed me to build a temple for him at Jerusalem in Judah. 3 Any of his people among you may go up to Jerusalem and build the LORD's temple. He is the God of Israel. He is the God who is in Jerusalem. And may their God be with them. 4 The people still left alive in every place must bring gifts to the people going. They must provide silver and gold to the people going up to Jerusalem. The people must bring goods and livestock. They should also bring any offerings they choose to. All those gifts will be for God's temple in Jerusalem.' "

5 Then everyone God had inspired prepared to go. They wanted to go up to Jerusalem and build the LORD's temple there. They included the family leaders of Judah and Benjamin. They also included the priests and Levites. 6 All their neighbors helped them. They gave them silver and gold objects.

They gave them goods and livestock. And they gave them gifts of great value. All those things were added to the other offerings the people chose to give.

⁷King Cyrus also brought out the objects that belonged to the LORD's temple. Nebuchadnezzar had carried them off from Jerusalem. He had put them in the temple of his own god. ⁸Cyrus, the king of Persia, told Mithredath to bring them out. Mithredath was in charge of the temple treasures. He counted those objects. Then he gave them to Sheshbazzar, the prince of Judah.

⁹Here is a list of the objects.

There were 30 gold dishes.
There were 1,000 silver dishes.
There were 29 silver pans.
¹⁰There were 30 gold bowls.
There were 410 matching silver bowls.
There were 1,000 other objects.
¹¹The total number of gold and silver objects was 5,400.

Sheshbazzar brought all of these back with him to Jerusalem. So Sheshbazzar and the Jews who had been forced to leave Judah came up from Babylon to Jerusalem.

The List of the Jews Who Returned to Judah

2 Nebuchadnezzar had taken many Jews away from the land of Judah. He had forced them to go to Babylon as prisoners. Now they returned to Jerusalem and Judah. All of them went back to their own towns. Nebuchadnezzar was king of Babylon. ²The leaders of the Jews included Zerubbabel, Joshua, Nehemiah, Seraiah and Reelaiah. They also included Mordecai, Bilshan, Mispar, Bigvai, Rehum and Baanah.

Here is a list of the men of Israel who returned home.
³There were 2,172 from the family line of Parosh.
⁴There were 372 from Shephatiah.
⁵There were 775 from Arah.
⁶There were 2,812 from Pahath-Moab through the family line of Jeshua and Joab.
⁷There were 1,254 from Elam.
⁸There were 945 from Zattu.
⁹There were 760 from Zakkai.
¹⁰There were 642 from Bani.
¹¹There were 623 from Bebai.
¹²There were 1,222 from Azgad.
¹³There were 666 from Adonikam.
¹⁴There were 2,056 from Bigvai.
¹⁵There were 454 from Adin.
¹⁶There were 98 from Ater through the family line of Hezekiah.
¹⁷There were 323 from Bezai.
¹⁸There were 112 from Jorah.
¹⁹There were 223 from Hashum.

²⁰There were 95 from Gibbar.
²¹There were 123 from the men of Bethlehem.
²²There were 56 from Netophah.
²³There were 128 from Anathoth.
²⁴There were 42 from Azmaveth.
²⁵There were 743 from Kiriath Jearim, Kephirah and Beeroth.
²⁶There were 621 from Ramah and Geba.
²⁷There were 122 from Mikmash.
²⁸There were 223 from Bethel and Ai.
²⁹There were 52 from Nebo.
³⁰There were 156 from Magbish.
³¹There were 1,254 from the other Elam.
³²There were 320 from Harim.
³³There were 725 from Lod, Hadid and Ono.
³⁴There were 345 from Jericho.
³⁵There were 3,630 from Senaah.

³⁶Here is a list of the priests.
There were 973 from the family line of Jedaiah through the line of Jeshua.
³⁷There were 1,052 from Immer.
³⁸There were 1,247 from Pashhur.
³⁹There were 1,017 from Harim.

⁴⁰Here is a list of the Levites.
There were 74 from the family lines of Jeshua and Kadmiel. Kadmiel was from the line of Hodaviah.

⁴¹Here is a list of the musicians.
There were 128 from the family line of Asaph.

⁴²Here is a list of the men who guarded the gates.
There were 139 from the family lines of Shallum, Ater, Talmon, Akkub, Hatita and Shobai.

⁴³Here is a list of the members of the family lines of the temple servants.
Ziha, Hasupha, Tabbaoth,
⁴⁴Keros, Siaha, Padon,
⁴⁵Lebanah, Hagabah, Akkub,
⁴⁶Hagab, Shalmai, Hanan,
⁴⁷Giddel, Gahar, Reaiah,
⁴⁸Rezin, Nekoda, Gazzam,
⁴⁹Uzza, Paseah, Besai,
⁵⁰Asnah, Meunim, Nephusim,
⁵¹Bakbuk, Hakupha, Harhur,
⁵²Bazluth, Mehida, Harsha,
⁵³Barkos, Sisera, Temah,
⁵⁴Neziah, Hatipha

⁵⁵Here is a list of the members of the family lines of the servants of Solomon.
Sotai, Hassophereth, Peruda,
⁵⁶Jaala, Darkon, Giddel,
⁵⁷Shephatiah, Hattil, Pokereth-Hazzebaim, Ami
⁵⁸The total number of the members of the family lines of the temple servants and the servants of Solomon was 392.

⁵⁹ Many people came up to Judah from the towns of Tel Melah, Tel Harsha, Kerub, Addon and Immer. But they weren't able to prove that their families belonged to the people of Israel.

⁶⁰ There were 652 of them from the family lines of Delaiah, Tobiah and Nekoda.

⁶¹ Here is a list of the members of the family lines of the priests.

They were Hobaiah, Hakkoz and Barzillai. Barzillai had married a daughter of Barzillai from Gilead. So he was also called Barzillai.

⁶² The priests looked for their family records. But they couldn't find them. So they weren't able to serve as priests. They were "unclean." ⁶³ The governor gave them an order. He told them not to eat any of the most sacred food. They had to wait until there was a priest who could use the Urim and Thummim. The priest would use them to find out what the LORD wanted the people to do.

⁶⁴ The total number of the entire group that returned was 42,360. ⁶⁵ That didn't include their 7,337 male and female slaves. There were also 200 male and female singers. ⁶⁶ And there were 736 horses, 245 mules, ⁶⁷ 435 camels and 6,720 donkeys.

⁶⁸ All the people arrived at the place in Jerusalem where the LORD's temple would be rebuilt. Then some of the leaders of the families brought offerings they chose to give. They would be used for rebuilding the house of God. It would stand in the same place it had been before. ⁶⁹ The people gave money for the work. It was based on how much they had. They gave 1,100 pounds of gold. They also gave three tons of silver. And they gave 100 sets of clothes for the priests. All of that was added to the temple treasure.

⁷⁰ The priests and Levites made their homes in their own towns. So did the musicians, the men who guarded the gates, and the temple servants. The rest of the Israelites also made their homes in their own towns.

The People Rebuild the Altar

3 The Israelites had made their homes in their towns. In the seventh month all of them gathered together in Jerusalem. ² Then Joshua began to build the altar for burnt offerings to honor the God of Israel. Joshua was the son of Jozadak. The other priests helped Joshua. So did Zerubbabel and his men. They built the altar according to what is written in the Law of Moses. Moses was a man of God. Zerubbabel was the son of Shealtiel. ³ The people who built the altar were afraid of the nations around them. But they built it anyway. They set it up where it had stood before. They sacrificed burnt

offerings on it to the LORD. They offered the morning and evening sacrifices on it. ⁴ Then they celebrated the Feast of Booths. They did it according to what is written in the Law. They sacrificed the number of burnt offerings required for each day. ⁵ After they celebrated the Feast of Booths, they sacrificed the regular burnt offerings. They offered the New Moon sacrifices. They also offered the sacrifices for all the appointed sacred feasts of the LORD. And they sacrificed the offerings the people chose to give him. ⁶ On the first day of the seventh month they began to offer burnt offerings to the LORD. They did it even though the foundation of the LORD's temple hadn't been laid yet.

The People Begin to Rebuild the Temple

⁷ The people gave money to those who worked with stone and those who worked with wood. They gave food and drink and olive oil to the people of Sidon and Tyre. Then those people brought cedar logs down from Lebanon to the Mediterranean Sea. They floated them down to Joppa. Cyrus, the king of Persia, authorized them to do it.

⁸ It was the second month of the second year after they had arrived at the house of God in Jerusalem. Zerubbabel, the son of Shealtiel, began the work. Joshua, the son of Jozadak, helped him. So did everyone else. That included the priests and Levites. It also included the rest of those who had returned to Jerusalem. They had been prisoners in the land of Babylon. Levites who were 20 years old or more were appointed to be in charge of building the LORD's house. ⁹ Those who joined together to direct the work included Joshua and his sons and brothers. They also included Kadmiel and his sons. And they included the sons of Henadad and their sons and brothers. All those men were Levites. Kadmiel and his sons were members of the family line of Hodaviah.

¹⁰ The builders laid the foundation of the LORD's temple. Then the priests came. They were wearing their special clothes. They brought their trumpets with them. The Levites who belonged to the family line of Asaph also came. They brought their cymbals with them. The priests and Levites took their places to praise the LORD. They did everything just as King David had required them to. ¹¹ They sang to the LORD. They praised him. They gave thanks to him. They said,

"The LORD is good.
    His faithful love to Israel
    continues forever."

All the people gave a loud shout. They praised the LORD. They were glad because the foundation of the LORD's temple had been laid. ¹² But many of the older priests and Levites and family leaders wept out loud.

They had seen the first temple. So when they saw the foundation of the second temple being laid, they wept. Others shouted with joy. ¹³ No one could tell the difference between the shouts of joy and the sounds of weeping. That's because the people made so much noise. The sound was heard far away.

Enemies Oppose the Rebuilding of the Temple

4 The people who had returned from Babylon were building a temple to honor the LORD. He is the God of Israel. The enemies of Judah and Benjamin heard about it. ² Then those enemies came to Zerubbabel. The family leaders of Israel were with him. The enemies said, "We want to help you build. We're just like you. We worship your God. We offer sacrifices to him. We've been doing that ever since the time of Esarhaddon. He was king of Assyria. He brought our people here."

³ Zerubbabel and Joshua answered them. So did the rest of the family leaders of Israel. They said, "You can't help us build a temple to honor our God. You aren't part of us. We'll build it ourselves. We'll do it to honor the LORD, the God of Israel. Cyrus, the king of Persia, commanded us to build it."

⁴ Then the nations around Judah tried to make its people lose hope. They wanted to make them afraid to go on building. ⁵ So those nations paid some of the Jewish officials to work against the people of Judah. They wanted their plans to fail. They did it during the whole time Cyrus was king of Persia. They kept doing it until Darius became king.

Later Enemies Also Oppose the Jews

⁶ The enemies of the Jews brought charges against the people of Judah and Jerusalem. It happened when Xerxes began to rule over Persia.

⁷ Then Artaxerxes became king of Persia. During his rule, Bishlam, Mithredath, Tabeel and their friends wrote a letter to Artaxerxes. It was written in the Aramaic language. And it used the Aramaic alphabet.

⁸ Rehum and Shimshai also wrote a letter to King Artaxerxes. Rehum was the commanding officer. Shimshai was the secretary. Their letter was against the people of Jerusalem. It said,

⁹ We, Rehum and Shimshai, are writing this letter. Rehum is the commanding officer. Shimshai is the secretary. Our friends join us in writing. They include the judges, officials and managers in charge of the people from Persia, Uruk and Babylon. They are also over the Elamites from Susa. ¹⁰ And they are over those who were forced to leave their countries. The great King Ashurbanipal, who is worthy of honor, forced them to leave. He moved

them to the city of Samaria. He also moved them to other places west of the Euphrates River.

[11] Here is a copy of the letter sent to Artaxerxes.

We are sending this letter to you, King Artaxerxes.

It is from your servants who live west of the Euphrates River.

[12] We want you to know about the people who left you and have come up to us. They have gone to Jerusalem and are rebuilding that evil city. It has caused trouble for a long time. Those people are making its walls like new again. They are repairing the foundations. [13] Here is something else we want you to know. Suppose this city is rebuilt. And suppose its walls are made like new again. Then no more taxes, gifts or fees will be collected. And sooner or later there will be less money for you. [14] We owe a lot to you. We don't want to see dishonor brought on you. So we're sending this letter to tell you what is going on. [15] Then you can have a search made in the official records. Have someone check the records of the kings who ruled before you. If you do, you will find out that Jerusalem is an evil city. It causes trouble for kings and countries.

For a long time the city has refused to let anyone rule over it. That's why it was destroyed. [16] We want you to know that this city shouldn't be rebuilt. Its walls shouldn't be made like new again. If that happens, you won't have anything left west of the Euphrates River.

[17] The king replied,

I am writing this letter to Rehum, the commanding officer. I am also writing it to Shimshai the secretary. And I am writing it to your friends living in Samaria and in other places west of the Euphrates River.

I give you my greetings.

[18] The letter you sent us has been read to me. It has been explained to me in my language. [19] I gave an order. I had a search made. Here is what we found out. Jerusalem has a long history of turning against the kings of the countries that have ruled over it. It has refused to remain under their control. It is always stirring up trouble. [20] Jerusalem has had powerful kings. Some of them ruled over everything west of the Euphrates. Taxes, gifts and fees were paid to them. [21] So give an order to those men. Make them stop their work. Then the city won't be rebuilt until I give the order.

²² Pay careful attention to this matter. Why should we let this danger grow? That would not be in our best interests.

²³ The copy of the letter of King Artaxerxes was read to Rehum and Shimshai the secretary. It was also read to their friends. Right away they went to the Jews in Jerusalem. They forced them to stop their work.

²⁴ And so the work on the house of God in Jerusalem came to a stop. No more work was done on it until the second year that Darius was king of Persia.

Tattenai's Letter to King Darius

5 Haggai and Zechariah, the prophets, prophesied to the Jews in Judah and Jerusalem. They spoke to them in the name of the God of Israel. God had spoken to those prophets. Zechariah belonged to the family line of Iddo. ² Zerubbabel, the son of Shealtiel, began to work. So did Joshua, the son of Jozadak. They began to rebuild the house of God in Jerusalem. The prophets of God were right there with them. They were helping them.

³ At that time Tattenai was governor of the land west of the Euphrates River. He and Shethar-Bozenai and their friends went to the Jews. They asked them, "Who authorized you to rebuild this temple? Who told you that you could finish it?" ⁴ They also asked, "What are the names of the people who are putting up this building?" ⁵ But the God of the Jews was watching over their elders. So they didn't have to stop their work. First a report would have to be sent to Darius. Then they would have to receive his answer in writing.

⁶ Here is a copy of the letter sent to King Darius. It was from Tattenai, the governor of the land west of the Euphrates. Shethar-Bozenai joined him in writing it. So did their friends. They were officials of that land. ⁷ The report they sent to the king said,

We are sending this letter to you, King Darius.

We give you our most friendly greetings.

⁸ We want you to know that we went to the land of Judah. We went to the temple of the great God. The people are building it with large stones. They are putting wooden beams in the walls. The people are working hard. The work is moving ahead very quickly under the direction of the people.

⁹ We asked the elders some questions. We said to them, "Who authorized you to rebuild this temple? Who told you that you could finish it?" ¹⁰ We also asked them what their names were. We wanted to write down the names of their leaders for your information.

[11] Here is the answer they gave us. They said,

"We serve the God of heaven and earth. We are rebuilding the temple that was built many years ago. The great King Solomon built it and finished it. [12] But our people made the God of heaven angry. So he handed them over to Nebuchadnezzar from Chaldea. He was king of Babylon. He destroyed this temple. He forced the Jews to leave their own country. He took them away to Babylon. [13] "But King Cyrus gave an order to rebuild this house of God. He gave it in the first year he was king of Babylon. [14] He even removed some gold and silver objects from the temple of Babylon. Nebuchadnezzar had brought them there from the house of God in Jerusalem. He had taken them to the temple in Babylon. Then King Cyrus brought the objects out. He gave them to a man named Sheshbazzar. Cyrus had appointed him as governor. [15] Cyrus told him, 'Take these objects with you. Go and put them in the temple in Jerusalem. Rebuild the house of God in the same place where it stood before.'

[16] "So Sheshbazzar made the trip to Jerusalem. He laid the foundations of the house of God there. From that day until now the people have been working on it. But they haven't finished it yet."

[17] If it pleases you, King Darius, let a search be made in the royal records. Search the official records of the kings of Babylon. Find out whether King Cyrus really did give an order to rebuild this house of God in Jerusalem. Then tell us what you decide to do.

King Darius's Reply to Tattenai

6 King Darius gave an order. He had a search made in the official records stored among the treasures at Babylon. [2] A book was found in a safe storeroom at Ecbatana in the land of Media. Here is what was written on it.

This is my official reply to your letter.

[3] In the first year that Cyrus was king, he gave an order. It concerned God's temple in Jerusalem. King Cyrus said,

Rebuild the temple. Then the Jews can offer sacrifices there. Lay its foundations. The temple must be 90 feet high and 90 feet wide. [4] Its walls must have three layers of large stones. They must also have a layer of beautiful wood. Use money from the royal treasures to pay for everything. [5] The gold and silver objects from the house of God must be returned. Nebuchadnezzar had taken them from the first temple in Jerusalem. And he had brought them to Babylon. Now they must be returned to their places in the temple at Jerusalem. They must be put in the house of God there.

⁶Tattenai, you are governor of the land west of the Euphrates River. I want you to stay away from the temple in Jerusalem. I also want you, Shethar-Bozenai, and you other officials of that area to stay away from it. ⁷Don't try to stop the work on the temple of God. Let the governor of the Jews and their elders rebuild the house of their God. Let them build it in the same place where it stood before.

⁸Here is what I want you to do for the elders of the Jews. Here is how you must help them to build the house of their God.

Pay all their expenses from the royal treasures. Use the money you collect from the people who live west of the Euphrates. Don't let the work on the temple stop. ⁹Don't fail to give the priests in Jerusalem what they ask for each day. Give them what they need. Give them young bulls, rams and male lambs. The priests can use them to sacrifice burnt offerings to the God of heaven. Also give them wheat, salt, wine and olive oil. ¹⁰Give them those things so they can offer sacrifices that please the God of heaven. And I want them to pray that things will go well for me and my sons.

¹¹Don't change this order. If anyone tries to change it, they must be put to death. A pole must be pulled from their house. The pole must be stuck through their body. Because that person tried to change my royal order, their house must be broken to pieces. ¹²God has chosen to put his Name in the temple at Jerusalem. May he wipe out any king or nation that lifts a hand to change this order. May he also wipe out anyone who tries to destroy the temple in Jerusalem.

That's what I have ordered. I am King Darius. Make sure you carry out my order.

The Temple Is Completed and Set Apart to God

¹³The governor Tattenai and Shethar-Bozenai carried out King Darius's order. And so did their friends. ¹⁴The elders of the Jews continued to build the temple. They enjoyed great success because of the preaching of Haggai and Zechariah, the prophets. Zechariah belonged to the family line of Iddo. The people finished building the temple. That's what the God of Israel had commanded them to do. Cyrus and Darius had

given orders allowing them to do it. Later, Artaxerxes supplied many things that were needed in the temple. Those three men were kings of Persia. ¹⁵ So the temple was completed on the third day of the month of Adar. It was in the sixth year that Darius was king.

¹⁶ When the house of God was set apart, the people of Israel celebrated with joy. The priests and Levites joined them. So did the rest of those who had returned from the land of Babylon. ¹⁷ When the house of God was set apart to him, the people sacrificed 100 bulls. They also sacrificed 200 rams and 400 male lambs. As a sin offering for the whole nation of Israel, the people sacrificed 12 male goats. One goat was sacrificed for each tribe in Israel. ¹⁸ The priests were appointed to their groups. And the Levites were appointed to their groups. All of them served God at Jerusalem. They served him in keeping with what is written in the Book of Moses.

The People Celebrate the Passover Feast

¹⁹ The people who had returned from the land of Babylon celebrated the Passover Feast. It was on the 14th day of the first month. ²⁰ The priests and Levites had made themselves pure and "clean." The Levites killed Passover lambs for the people who had returned from Babylon. They also did it for themselves and their relatives, the priests. ²¹ So the Israelites who had returned ate the Passover lamb. They ate it together with all those who had separated themselves from the practices of their Gentile neighbors. Those practices were "unclean." The people worshiped the LORD. He is the God of Israel. ²² For seven days they celebrated the Feast of Unleavened Bread with joy. That's because the LORD had filled them with joy. They were glad because he had changed the mind of the king of Persia. So the king had helped them with the work on the house of the God of Israel.

Ezra Comes to Jerusalem

7 After all these things had happened, Ezra came up to Jerusalem from Babylon. It was during the rule of Artaxerxes. He was king of Persia. Ezra was the son of Seraiah. Seraiah was the son of Azariah. Azariah was the son of Hilkiah. ² Hilkiah was the son of Shallum. Shallum was the son of Zadok. Zadok was the son of Ahitub. ³ Ahitub was the son of Amariah. Amariah was the son of Azariah. Azariah was the son of Meraioth. ⁴ Meraioth was the son of Zerahiah. Zerahiah was the son of Uzzi. Uzzi was the son of Bukki. ⁵ Bukki was the son of Abishua. Abishua was the son of Phinehas. Phinehas was the son of Eleazar. And Eleazar was the son of Aaron the chief priest. ⁶ So Ezra came up from Babylon. He was a teacher who knew the Law of Moses very well. The LORD, the God of

Israel, had given Israel that law. The king had given Ezra everything he asked for. That's because the LORD his God helped him. ⁷ Some of the Israelites came up to Jerusalem too. They included priests, Levites and musicians. They also included the temple servants and those who guarded the temple gates. It was in the seventh year that Artaxerxes was king.

⁸ Ezra arrived in Jerusalem in the fifth month of the seventh year of the king's rule. ⁹ Ezra had begun his journey from Babylon on the first day of the first month. He arrived in Jerusalem on the first day of the fifth month. That's because God was gracious to him and helped him. ¹⁰ Ezra had committed himself to study and obey the Law of the LORD. He also wanted to teach the LORD's rules and laws in Israel.

King Artaxerxes's Letter to Ezra

¹¹ Ezra was a priest and teacher of the Law. He was an educated man. He knew the LORD's commands and rules for Israel very well. Here is a copy of a letter King Artaxerxes had given to Ezra. It said,

¹² I, Artaxerxes, am writing this letter. I am the greatest king of all.

I have given it to Ezra the priest. He is the teacher of the Law of the God of heaven.

I give you my greetings.

¹³ Ezra, I am giving an order about the Israelites in my kingdom. Any of them who want to go to Jerusalem with you may go. The order also allows priests and Levites to go with you. ¹⁴ I and my seven advisers are sending you to see how things are going in Judah and Jerusalem. Find out whether the people there are obeying the Law of your God. You have a copy of that law with you. ¹⁵ I and my advisers have freely given some silver and gold to the God of Israel. He is the God who lives in Jerusalem. Take that silver and gold with you. ¹⁶ Also take any other silver and gold you can get from the land of Babylon. And take the offerings the people and priests choose to give for the temple of their God in Jerusalem. ¹⁷ Make sure you use the money to buy bulls, rams and male lambs. Also buy their grain offerings and drink offerings. Then sacrifice them on the altar of the temple of your God in Jerusalem.

¹⁸ You and the other Jews can do what you think is best with the rest of the silver and gold. Do what your God wants you to do. ¹⁹ Give to the God of Jerusalem all the things you are responsible for. Use them for worshiping your God in his temple. ²⁰ You might need to supply some other things

for the temple of your God. If you do, take them from among the royal treasures.

21 I, King Artaxerxes, also give this order. It applies to all those who are in charge of the treasures west of the Euphrates River. Make sure you provide anything Ezra the priest might ask you to give. He is the teacher of the Law of the God of heaven. 22 Give Ezra up to three and three-fourths tons of silver. Give him up to 18 tons of wheat. Give him up to 600 gallons of wine and up to 600 gallons of olive oil. And give him as much salt as he needs. 23 Work hard for the temple of the God of heaven. Do everything he has required. I don't want him to be angry with my kingdom and the kingdom of my sons. 24 Here is something else I want you to know. You have no authority to collect taxes, gifts or fees from these people. You may not collect them from the priests, Levites or musicians. You may not collect them from those who guard the temple gates. You may not collect them from the temple servants. And you may not collect them from other workers at the house of God in Jerusalem.

25 Ezra, appoint judges and other court officials. When you do it, use the wisdom your God gives you. Those you appoint should do what is right and fair when they judge people. They should do it for everyone who lives west of the Euphrates River. They should do it for everyone who knows the laws of your God. And I want you to teach the people who don't know those laws. 26 Anyone who doesn't obey the law of your God must be punished. The same thing applies to anyone who doesn't obey my law. The people must be punished in keeping with the laws they have broken. Some of them must be put to death. Others must be forced to leave the places where they live. Others must have their property taken away from them. Still others must be put in prison.

27 So here is what I, Ezra, say to you people of Israel. "Give praise to the Lord. He is the God of our people who lived long ago. He has put it in the king's heart to bring honor to the Lord's temple in Jerusalem. The king has honored the Lord in his letter. 28 The Lord has been kind to me. He has caused the king and his advisers to be kind to me. In fact, all the king's powerful officials have been kind to me. The strong hand of the Lord my God helped me. That gave me new strength. So I gathered together leaders from Israel to go up to Jerusalem with me."

*The Family Leaders Who
Returned to Jerusalem With Ezra*

8 Many family leaders came up to Jerusalem with me from Babylon. So did others who were listed with them. It was during the time when Artaxerxes was king. Here is a list of those who came.

2 Gershom came from the family line of Phinehas.
Daniel came from the family line of Ithamar.
Hattush came from the family line of David. 3 Hattush also belonged to the family of Shekaniah.
Zechariah came from the family line of Parosh. The total number of men who were listed with him was 150.
4 Eliehoenai came from the family line of Pahath-Moab. Eliehoenai was the son of Zerahiah. The total number of men with him was 200.
5 Shekaniah came from the family line of Zattu. Shekaniah was the son of Jahaziel. The total number of men with him was 300.
6 Ebed came from the family line of Adin. Ebed was the son of Jonathan. The total number of men with him was 50.
7 Jeshaiah came from the family line of Elam. Jeshaiah was the son of Athaliah. The total number of men with him was 70.

8 Zebadiah came from the family line of Shephatiah. Zebadiah was the son of Michael. The total number of men with him was 80.
9 Obadiah came from the family line of Joab. Obadiah was the son of Jehiel. The total number of men with him was 218.
10 Shelomith came from the family line of Bani. Shelomith was the son of Josiphiah. The total number of men with him was 160.
11 Zechariah came from the family line of Bebai. Zechariah was the son of Bebai. The total number of men with him was 28.
12 Johanan came from the family line of Azgad. Johanan was the son of Hakkatan. The total number of men with him was 110.
13 Eliphelet, Jeuel and Shemaiah came from the family line of Adonikam. Some members of their family had gone up to Jerusalem before them. The total number of men with them was 60.
14 Uthai and Zakkur came from the family line of Bigvai. The total number of men with them was 70.

*Ezra Leads Many Jews Back
to Jerusalem*

15 I gathered the people together at the canal that flows toward Ahava. We camped

there for three days. I looked for Levites among the people and priests. But I didn't find any. [16] So I sent for Eliezer, Ariel, Shemaiah, Elnathan and Jarib. I also sent for Elnathan, Nathan, Zechariah and Meshullam. All of them were leaders. And I sent for Joiarib and Elnathan. They were very well educated. [17] I ordered all those men to go to Iddo. He was the leader in Kasiphia. He and his Levite relatives were temple servants there. I told my men what to say to them. I wanted Iddo and his Levite relatives to bring some attendants to us for the house of our God. [18] God was gracious to us and helped us. So they brought us Sherebiah, a very capable man. He came from the family line of Mahli. Mahli was the son of Levi. Levi was a son of Israel. They also brought us Sherebiah's sons and brothers. The total number of men was 18. [19] And they brought Hashabiah and his brothers and nephews. They brought them together with Jeshaiah. He came from the family line of Merari. The total number of men was 20. [20] They also brought 220 of the temple servants. That was a special group David and his officials had established. They were supposed to help the Levites. All of them were listed by name.

[21] By the canal that flows toward Ahava, I announced a fast. I told the people not to eat any food. In that way, we made ourselves humble in God's sight. We prayed that he would give us and our children a safe journey. We asked him to keep safe everything we owned. [22] I was ashamed to ask King Artaxerxes for soldiers and horsemen. They could have kept us safe from enemies on the road. But we had told the king that our God would keep us safe. We had said, "Our God is gracious and helps everyone who looks to him. But he becomes very angry with anyone who deserts him." [23] So we didn't eat anything. We prayed to our God about all these matters. And he answered our prayers.

[24] Then I set apart 12 of the leading priests. They were Sherebiah, Hashabiah and ten of their relatives. [25] I weighed out to them the offering of silver and gold and other things. They had been given for the house of our God. The king, his advisers and officials, and all the Israelites who were there had given them. [26] I weighed out 24 tons of silver and gave it to those men. I weighed out almost four tons of silver things. I weighed out almost four tons of gold. [27] I weighed out 20 gold bowls. They weighed 19 pounds. I also weighed out two fine objects. The bronze they were made out of was highly polished. They were as priceless as gold.

[28] I said to those men, "You are set apart to the LORD. So are these things. The silver and gold were offered to the LORD by those who chose to give them. He is the God of your people. [29] Guard all these things

carefully until you weigh them out. Weigh them in the special rooms of the LORD's temple in Jerusalem. Do this in front of the leading priests and the Levites. Make sure the family leaders of Israel are watching."

30 Then the priests and Levites received the silver and gold and sacred objects. All of them had been weighed out. They were going to be taken to the house of our God in Jerusalem.

31 On the 12th day of the first month we started out. We left the canal that flows toward Ahava. And we headed for Jerusalem. Our God helped us. He kept us safe from enemies and robbers along the way. 32 So we arrived in Jerusalem. There we rested for three days.

33 On the fourth day we weighed out the silver and gold. We also weighed out the sacred objects. We weighed everything in the house of our God. We handed all of it over to Meremoth the priest. He was the son of Uriah. Eleazar, Jozabad and Noadiah were with him. Eleazar was the son of Phinehas. Jozabad was the son of Jeshua. Noadiah was the son of Binnui. Jozabad and Noadiah were Levites. 34 Everything was listed by number and weight. And the total weight was recorded at that time.

35 Then the people sacrificed burnt offerings to the God of Israel. They had returned from Babylon. They offered 12 bulls for the whole nation of Israel. They offered 96 rams and 77 male lambs. All of that was a burnt offering to the LORD. They sacrificed 12 male goats as a sin offering. 36 They also handed over the king's orders. They gave them to the royal officials and governors who ruled over the land west of the Euphrates River. Then those men helped the people. They also did many things for the house of God.

Ezra Prays for the People

9 After all these things had been done, the leaders came to me. They said, "The people of Israel have committed sins. Even the priests and Levites have sinned. They haven't kept themselves separate from the nations around them. The LORD hates the practices of those nations. He hates what the Canaanites, Hittites, Perizzites and Jebusites do. He also hates what the Ammonites, Moabites, Egyptians and Amorites do. 2 The men of Israel have married the daughters of some of those people. They've also taken some of those women for their sons to marry. So they've mixed our holy nation with the nations around us. We leaders and officials have also married women who don't worship the LORD. By doing this, we have led the way in breaking our covenant with the LORD."

3 When I heard that, I tore my inner robe and my coat. I pulled hair from my head and beard. I was so shocked I sat down. 4 Then everyone who trembled with fear at God's words gath-

ered around me. That's because the people who had returned from Babylon had not been faithful. So I was very upset. I just sat there until the time of the evening sacrifice.

⁵ Then I got up. I had been very sad for quite a while. My inner robe and my coat were torn. I fell down on my knees. I spread my hands out to the LORD my God. ⁶ I prayed,

"I'm filled with shame and dishonor, my God. I can hardly look to you and pray. That's because our sins are piled up above our heads. Our guilt reaches all the way to the heavens. ⁷ We are filled with it. It has been like that ever since the days of our people who lived long ago. Kings of other countries have killed many of us and our kings and priests with their swords. They've forced others to leave their own land. They've taken them away as prisoners. They've robbed others. They've made still others feel ashamed and dishonored. All these things have happened to us because we've committed so many sins. And that's how things still are to this day.

⁸ "But you are the LORD our God. Now you have shown us your kindness for a short time. That's because you have allowed a few of us to remain here. Your temple has given us new hope. So you have made things eas-ier for us. You have given us a little rest from our slavery. ⁹ We are still slaves. But you are our God. You haven't turned away from us. You haven't left us in our slavery. You have been kind to us. The kings of Persia have seen it. You have given us new life to repair your temple and rebuild it. You have given us a place of safety in Judah and Jerusalem.

¹⁰ "You are our God. What can we say after the way you have blessed us? We have turned away from your commands. ¹¹ You gave us your commands through your servants the prophets. You said, 'You are entering the land to take it as your own. The sinful practices of its people have made the land impure. They have filled it with their "unclean" acts from one end to the other. The LORD hates all their practices. ¹² So don't let your daughters marry their sons. And don't let their daughters marry your sons. Don't make a peace treaty with them at any time. Then you will be strong. You will eat the good things the land produces. And you will leave all of it to your children as their share. They and their children after them will enjoy it forever.'

¹³ "Our evil acts and our terrible sins have brought about the things that have

happened to us. You are our God. Because we sinned so much, you should have punished us even more than you have. But you have left many of your people alive. ¹⁴ Suppose we don't obey your commands again. And suppose we continue to marry people who commit sins that you hate. If we do, you will be so angry with us that you will destroy us. You won't leave us even a few people. You won't leave anyone alive. ¹⁵ LORD, you are the God of Israel. You are holy. You always do what is right. Today you have left many of your people alive. Here we are with all our guilt. You see the guilt of our sin. Because we have sinned, not one of us can stand in front of you."

The People Admit They Have Sinned

10 Ezra was praying and admitting to God that his people had sinned. He was weeping and throwing himself down in front of the house of God. Then a large crowd of Israelites gathered around him. Men, women and children were there. They too wept bitterly. ² Shekaniah spoke to Ezra. Shekaniah was the son of Jehiel. He belonged to the family line of Elam. Shekaniah said, "We haven't been faithful to our God. We've married women from the nations around us. In spite of that, there is still hope for Israel. ³ So let's make a covenant in front of our God. Let's promise to send away all these women and their children. That's what you have advised us to do. Those who respect our God's commands have given us the same advice. We want to do what the Law says. ⁴ Get up, Ezra. This matter is in your hands. Do what you need to. We will be behind you all the way. Be brave and do it."

⁵ So Ezra got up. He made the leading priests and Levites and all the Israelites make a promise. He made them promise they would do what Shekaniah had suggested. And they made that promise. ⁶ Then Ezra left the house of God. He went to Jehohanan's room. Jehohanan was the son of Eliashib. While Ezra was there, he didn't eat any food. He didn't drink any water. That's because he was filled with sadness. He mourned because the people weren't faithful to the LORD's commands. Those people were the ones who had returned from the land of Babylon.

⁷ Then an announcement was sent all through Judah and Jerusalem. All the people who had returned were told to gather together in Jerusalem. ⁸ They were supposed to come there before three days had passed. If they didn't, they would lose all their property. They would also be removed from the community of those who had returned. That's what the officials and elders had decided.

⁹Before the three days were over, all the men of Judah and Benjamin had gathered together in Jerusalem. It was the 20th day of the ninth month. They were sitting in the open area in front of the house of God. They were very upset by what they knew would happen. And they were upset because it was raining. ¹⁰Then Ezra the priest stood up. He said, "You haven't been faithful to the LORD. You have married women from other lands. So you have added to Israel's guilt. ¹¹Now honor the LORD, the God of your people. Then do what he wants you to do. Separate yourselves from the nations around you. Send away your wives from other lands."

¹²The whole community answered with a loud voice. They said, "You are right! We must do as you say. ¹³But there are a lot of people here. And it's the rainy season. So we can't stand outside. Besides, this matter can't be taken care of in just a day or two. That's because we have sinned terribly by what we've done. ¹⁴Our officials can act for the whole community. Have everyone in our towns who has married a woman from another land come at a certain time. Tell them to come together with the elders and judges of each town. Then our God will no longer be angry with us concerning this whole matter." ¹⁵Only a few men opposed that. They included Jonathan and Jahzeiah. Meshullam and Shabbethai the Levite joined them. Jonathan was the son of Asahel. Jahzeiah was the son of Tikvah.

¹⁶So those who had returned did what had been suggested. Ezra the priest chose some family leaders. There was one from each family group. All of them were chosen by name. They sat down to check out each case. They started on the first day of the tenth month. ¹⁷By the first day of the first month they were finished. They had handled all the cases of the men who had married women from other lands.

A List of Those Who Had Married Women From Other Lands

¹⁸Among the family lines of the priests, here are the men who had married women from other lands.
Maaseiah, Eliezer, Jarib and Gedaliah
came from the family line of Joshua and his brothers. Joshua was the son of Jozadak. ¹⁹All of them made a firm promise to send their wives away. Each of these men brought a ram from his flock as a guilt offering.
²⁰Hanani and Zebadiah
came from the family line of Immer.
²¹Maaseiah and Elijah
came from the family line of Harim. So did Shemaiah, Jehiel and Uzziah.
²²Elioenai, Maaseiah and Ishmael

came from the family line of Pashhur. So did Nethanel, Jozabad and Elasah.

²³ Among the Levites, here are the men who had married women from other lands. There were Jozabad, Shimei and Kelaiah. There were also Pethahiah, Judah and Eliezer. Kelaiah's other name was Kelita.
²⁴ Eliashib came from the musicians.

Shallum, Telem and Uri came from the men who guarded the temple gates.

²⁵ Among the other Israelites, here are the men who had married women from other lands.

Ramiah, Izziah, Malkijah and Mijamin
came from the family line of Parosh. So did Eleazar, Malkijah and Benaiah.
²⁶ Mattaniah, Zechariah and Jehiel
came from the family line of Elam. So did Abdi, Jeremoth and Elijah.
²⁷ Elioenai, Eliashib and Mattaniah
came from the family line of Zattu. So did Jeremoth, Zabad and Aziza.
²⁸ Jehohanan, Hananiah, Zabbai and Athlai
came from the family line of Bebai.
²⁹ Meshullam, Malluk and Adaiah
came from the family

line of Bani. So did Jashub, Sheal and Jeremoth.
³⁰ Adna, Kelal, Benaiah and Maaseiah
came from the family line of Pahath-Moab. So did Mattaniah, Bezalel, Binnui and Manasseh.
³¹ Eliezer, Ishijah, Malkijah, Shemaiah and Shimeon
came from the family line of Harim. ³² So did Benjamin, Malluk and Shemariah.
³³ Mattenai, Mattattah, Zabad and Eliphelet
came from the family line of Hashum. So did Jeremai, Manasseh and Shimei.
³⁴ Maadai, Amram and Uel
came from the family line of Bani. ³⁵ So did Benaiah, Bedeiah, Keluhi, ³⁶ Vaniah, Meremoth, Eliashib, ³⁷ Mattaniah, Mattenai and Jaasu.
³⁸ Shimei
came from the family line of Binnui. ³⁹ So did Shelemiah, Nathan, Adaiah, ⁴⁰ Maknadebai, Shashai, Sharai, ⁴¹ Azarel, Shelemiah, Shemariah, ⁴² Shallum, Amariah and Joseph.
⁴³ Jeiel, Mattithiah, Zabad and Zebina
came from the family line of Nebo. So did Jaddai, Joel and Benaiah.

⁴⁴ All these men had married women from other lands. Some of them had even had children by those wives.

Nehemiah

Introduction:

This book tells about the Israelites who went home to Jerusalem. They rebuilt the city walls. Nehemiah worked for the king of Persia, but he wanted to help the people. He gave up his job and went home. Nehemiah helped the people in Jerusalem rebuild the city walls. He also helped the people turn back to God.

Outline of contents:

Nehemiah Prays to the LORD

1 These are the words of Nehemiah. He was the son of Hakaliah.

I was in the fort of Susa. I was there in the 20th year that Artaxerxes was king. It was in the month of Kislev. ² At that time Hanani came from Judah with some other men. He was one of my brothers. I asked him and the other men about the Jews who were left alive in Judah. They had returned from Babylon. I also asked him about Jerusalem.

³ He and the men with him said to me, "Some of the people who returned are still alive. They are back in the land of Judah. But they are having a hard time. They are ashamed. The wall of Jerusalem is broken down. Its gates have been burned with fire."

⁴ When I heard about these things, I sat down and wept. For several days I was very sad. I didn't eat any food. And I prayed to the God of heaven. ⁵ I said,

"LORD, you are the God of heaven. You are a great and wonderful God. You keep the covenant you made with those who love you and obey your commandments. You show them your love. ⁶ Please pay careful attention to my prayer. See how your people are suffering. Please listen to me. I'm praying to you day and night. I'm praying for the people of Israel. We Israelites have committed sins against you. All of us admit it. I and my family have also sinned against you. ⁷ We've done some very evil things. We haven't obeyed the commands, rules and laws you gave your servant Moses.

⁸ "Remember what you told him. You said, 'If you people are not faithful, I

will scatter you among the nations. ⁹But if you return to me, I will bring you back. If you obey my commands, I will gather you together again. I will bring you back from the farthest places on earth. I will bring you to the special place where I have chosen to put my Name.'

¹⁰ "LORD, they are your people. They serve you. You used your great strength and mighty hand to set them free from Egypt. ¹¹Lord, please pay careful attention to my prayer. Listen to the prayers of all of us. We take delight in bringing honor to your name. Give me success today when I bring my request to King Artaxerxes."

I was the king's wine taster.

Artaxerxes Sends Nehemiah to Jerusalem

2 Wine was brought in for King Artaxerxes. It was the month of Nisan in the 20th year of his rule. I got the wine and gave it to him. I hadn't been sad in front of him before. But now I was. ²So the king asked me, "Why are you looking so sad? You aren't sick. You must be feeling very sad."

I was really afraid. ³But I said to the king, "May you live forever! Why shouldn't I look sad? The city where my people of long ago are buried has been destroyed. And fire has burned up its gates."

⁴The king said to me, "What do you want?"

I prayed to the God of heaven. ⁵Then I answered the king, "Are you pleased with me, King Artaxerxes? If it pleases you, send me to Judah. Let me go to the city of Jerusalem. That's where my people are buried. I want to rebuild it."

⁶The queen was sitting beside the king. He turned and asked me, "How long will your journey take? When will you get back?" It pleased the king to send me. So I chose a certain time.

⁷I also said to him, "If it pleases you, may I take some letters with me? I want to give them to the governors of the land west of the Euphrates River. Then they'll help me travel safely through their territory until I arrive in Judah. ⁸May I also have a letter to Asaph? He takes care of the royal park. I want him to give me some logs so I can make beams out of them. I want to use them for the gates of the fort that is by the temple. Some of the logs will also be used in the city wall. And I'll need some for the house I'm going to live in." God was kind to me and helped me. So the king gave me what I asked for. ⁹Then I went to the governors of the land west of the Euphrates River. I gave them the king's letters. He had also sent army officers and horsemen along with me.

¹⁰Sanballat and Tobiah heard about what was happening. Sanballat was a Horonite. Tobiah was an official from Am-

mon. They were very upset that someone had come to help the Israelites.

Nehemiah Checks Out the Walls of Jerusalem

[11] I went to Jerusalem and stayed there for three days. [12] Then at night I took a few other people with me to check out the walls. I hadn't told anyone what my God wanted me to do for Jerusalem. There weren't any donkeys with me except the one I was riding on.

[13] That night I went out through the Valley Gate. I went toward the Jackal Well and the Dung Gate. I checked out the walls of Jerusalem. They had been broken down. I also checked the city gates. Fire had burned them up. [14] I moved on toward the Fountain Gate and the King's Pool. But there wasn't enough room for my donkey to get through. [15] It was still night. I went up the Kidron Valley. I kept checking the wall. Finally, I turned back. I went back in through the Valley Gate. [16] The officials didn't know where I had gone or what I had done. That's because I hadn't said anything to anyone yet. I hadn't told the priests or nobles or officials. And I hadn't spoken to any other Jews who would be rebuilding the wall.

[17] I said to them, "You can see the trouble we're in. Jerusalem has been destroyed. Fire has burned up its gates. Come on. Let's rebuild the wall of Jerusalem. Then people won't be ashamed anymore." [18] I also told them how my gracious God was helping me. And I told them what the king had said to me.

They replied, "Let's start rebuilding." So they began that good work.

[19] But Sanballat, the Horonite, heard about it. So did Tobiah, the official from Ammon. Geshem, the Arab, heard about it too. All of them laughed at us. They made fun of us. "What do you think you are doing?" they asked. "Are you turning against the king?"

[20] I answered, "The God of heaven will give us success. We serve him. So we'll start rebuilding the walls. But you don't have any share in Jerusalem. You don't have any claim to it. You don't have any right to worship here."

A List of the People Who Repaired the Wall

3 Eliashib the high priest and the other priests went to work. They rebuilt the Sheep Gate. They set it apart to God. They put its doors in place. They continued to rebuild the wall up to the Tower of the Hundred. They set the tower apart to God. Then they continued to rebuild the wall all the way to the Tower of Hananel. [2] Some men from Jericho rebuilt the next part of the wall. And Zakkur rebuilt the next part. He was the son of Imri.

[3] The sons of Hassenaah rebuilt the Fish Gate. They laid its beams. They put in place its

doors with their metal bolts and bars. [4] Meremoth repaired the next part of the wall. He was the son of Uriah. Uriah was the son of Hakkoz. Next to Meremoth, Meshullam made some repairs. He was the son of Berekiah. Berekiah was the son of Meshezabel. Next to Meshullam, Zadok also made some repairs. He was the son of Baana. [5] Some men from Tekoa repaired the next part of the wall. But their nobles refused to do any work at all. They didn't pay any attention to the people who were in charge of the work.

[6] Joiada and Meshullam repaired the Jeshanah Gate. Joiada was the son of Paseah. Meshullam was the son of Besodeiah. Joiada and Meshullam laid the beams of the gate. They put in place its doors with their metal bolts and bars. [7] Next to them, some from Gibeon and Mizpah made repairs. They included Melatiah from Gibeon and Jadon from Meronoth. Those places were under the authority of the governor of the land west of the Euphrates River. [8] Uzziel repaired the next part of the wall. He made his living by working with gold. He was the son of Harhaiah. Hananiah made repairs on the next part. He made his living by making perfume. So the wall of Jerusalem was made like new again all the way to the Broad Wall. [9] Rephaiah repaired the next part. He was the son of Hur. Rephaiah ruled over half of the territory where Jerusalem was located. [10] Jedaiah repaired the part of the wall that was across from his house. He was the son of Harumaph. Hattush made repairs next to Jedaiah. Hattush was the son of Hashabneiah. [11] Malkijah and Hasshub repaired another part of the wall. They also repaired the Tower of the Ovens. Malkijah was the son of Harim. Hasshub was the son of Pahath-Moab. [12] Shallum repaired the next part. His daughters helped him. He was the son of Hallohesh. Shallum ruled over the other half of the territory where Jerusalem was located.

[13] Hanun repaired the Valley Gate. Some people who lived in Zanoah helped him. They rebuilt it. They put in place its doors with their metal bolts and bars. They also repaired 1,500 feet of the wall. They repaired it all the way to the Dung Gate.

[14] Malkijah repaired the Dung Gate. He was the son of Rekab. Malkijah ruled over the territory where Beth Hakkerem was located. He rebuilt the gate. He put in place its doors with their metal bolts and bars.

[15] Shallun repaired the Fountain Gate. He was the son of Kol-Hozeh. Shallun ruled over the territory where Mizpah was located. He rebuilt the gate. He put a roof over it. And he put in place the doors of the gate with their metal bolts and bars. He also repaired the wall by the Pool of Siloam. It was near the King's Garden. Shallun repaired

the wall as far as the steps that go down from the City of David. [16] Next to Shallun, Nehemiah made some repairs. He was the son of Azbuk. Nehemiah ruled over half of the territory where Beth Zur was located. He repaired the wall up to the part that was across from the tombs of David. He repaired it all the way to the man-made pool and the House of the Heroes.

[17] Next to Nehemiah, some Levites made repairs. They worked under the direction of Rehum. He was the son of Bani. Next to Rehum, Hashabiah made repairs for his territory. He ruled over half of the territory where Keilah was located. [18] Next to him, other Levites made some repairs. They worked under the direction of Binnui. He was the son of Henadad. Binnui ruled over the other half of the territory where Keilah was located. [19] Next to Binnui, Ezer repaired another part of the wall. He was the son of Jeshua. Ezer ruled over Mizpah. He repaired the part across from the place that went up to the storeroom where the weapons were kept. He repaired the wall up to the angle of the wall. [20] Next to Ezer, Baruch worked hard to repair another part of the wall. He was the son of Zabbai. He repaired the part from the angle of the wall to the entrance to Eliashib's house. Eliashib was the high priest. [21] Next to Baruch, Meremoth repaired another part. He was the son of Uriah. Uriah was the son of Hakkoz. Meremoth

repaired the part from the entrance to Eliashib's house to the end of the house.

[22] Next to Meremoth, some priests from the surrounding area made repairs. [23] Next to them, Benjamin and Hasshub repaired the part of the wall that was in front of their house. Next to them, Azariah repaired the part that was beside his house. He was the son of Maaseiah. Maaseiah was the son of Ananiah. [24] Next to Azariah, Binnui made repairs on another part. Binnui was the son of Henadad. Binnui repaired the wall from Azariah's house to the angle and the corner. [25] Palal worked across from the angle. He was the son of Uzai. Palal also worked across from the tower that was part of the upper palace. It was near the courtyard of the guard. Next to him, Pedaiah made some repairs. He was the son of Parosh. [26] The temple servants who lived on the hill of Ophel helped Pedaiah. They repaired the wall up to the part that was across from the Water Gate. It was toward the east and the palace tower. [27] Next to the temple servants, the men from Tekoa repaired another part. They made repairs from the large palace tower to the wall of Ophel.

[28] The priests made repairs above the Horse Gate. Each priest repaired the part of the wall that was in front of his own house. [29] Next to them, Zadok made repairs across from his house. He was the son of

Immer. Next to Zadok, Shemaiah made some repairs. He was the son of Shekaniah. Shemaiah guarded the East Gate. [30] Next to him, Hananiah and Hanun repaired another part of the wall. Hananiah was the son of Shelemiah. Hanun was the sixth son of Zalaph. Next to Hananiah and Hanun, Meshullam made some repairs. He was the son of Berekiah. Meshullam repaired the part that was across from where he lived. [31] Next to him, Malkijah made some repairs. He made his living by working with gold. He repaired the wall up to the house of the temple servants and the traders. It was across from the Inspection Gate. He also repaired the wall as far as the room above the corner. [32] The traders and those who made their living by working with gold made some repairs. They repaired the wall from the room above the corner to the Sheep Gate.

Nehemiah's Enemies Oppose the Rebuilding

4 Sanballat heard that we were rebuilding the wall. So he became very angry and upset. He made fun of the Jews. [2] He spoke to his friends and the army of Samaria. He said, "What are those Jews trying to do? Can they make their city wall like new again? Will they offer sacrifices? Can they finish everything in a single day? The stones from their city wall and buildings are piled up like trash. And everything has been badly burned. Can they use those stones to rebuild everything again?"

[3] Tobiah from Ammon was at Sanballat's side. He said, "What are they building? They're putting up a stone wall. But suppose a fox climbs on top of it. Even that will break it down!"

[4] I prayed to God. I said, "Our God, please listen to our prayer. Some people hate us. They're saying bad things about us. So let others say bad things about them. Let them be carried off like stolen goods. Let them be taken to another country as prisoners. [5] Don't hide your eyes from their guilt. Don't forgive their sins. They have said bad things about the builders."

[6] So we rebuilt the wall. We repaired it until all of it was half as high as we wanted it to be. The people worked with all their heart.

[7] But Sanballat and Tobiah heard that Jerusalem's walls continued to be repaired. The Arabs, the Ammonites and the people of Ashdod heard about it too. They heard that the gaps in the wall were being filled in. So they were very angry. [8] All of them made evil plans to come and fight against Jerusalem. They wanted to stir up trouble against it. [9] But we prayed to our God. We put guards on duty day and night to watch out for danger. [10] During that time, the people in Judah spoke up. They said, "The workers are getting

weaker and weaker all the time. Broken stones are piled up everywhere. They are in our way. So we can't rebuild the wall."

[11] And our enemies said, "We will be right there among them. We'll kill them. We'll put an end to their work. We'll do it before they even know it or see us."

[12] Then the Jews who lived near our enemies came to us. They told us ten times, "No matter where you are, they'll attack us."

[13] So I stationed some people behind the lowest parts of the wall. That's where our enemies could easily attack us. I stationed the people family by family. They had their swords, spears and bows with them. [14] I looked things over. Then I stood up and spoke to the nobles, the officials and the rest of the people. I said, "Don't be afraid of your enemies. Remember the Lord. He is great and powerful. So fight for your families. Fight for your sons and daughters. Fight for your wives and homes."

[15] Our enemies heard that we knew what they were trying to do. They heard that God had blocked their evil plans. So all of us returned to the wall. Each of us did our own work.

[16] From that day on, half of my men did the work. The other half were given spears, shields, bows and armor. The officers stationed themselves behind all the people of Judah. [17] The people continued to build the wall. The people who carried supplies did their work with one hand. They held a weapon in the other hand. [18] Each of the builders wore his sword at his side as he worked. But the man who blew the trumpet stayed with me.

[19] Then I spoke to the nobles, the officials and the rest of the people. I said, "This is a big job. It covers a lot of territory. We're separated too far from one another along the wall. [20] When you hear the sound of the trumpet, join us at that location. Our God will fight for us!"

[21] So we continued the work. Half of the men held spears. We worked from the first light of sunrise until the stars came out at night. [22] At that time I also spoke to the people. I told them, "Have every man and his helper stay inside Jerusalem at night. Then they can guard us at night. And they can work during the day." [23] My relatives and I didn't take off our clothes. My men and the guards didn't take theirs off either. Each man kept his weapon with him, even when he went to get water.

Nehemiah Helps Some Poor People

5 Some men and their wives cried out against their Jewish brothers and sisters. [2] Some of them were saying, "There are now many of us. We have many sons and daughters. We have to get some grain so we can eat and stay alive."

[3] Others were saying, "We're being forced to sell our fields,

vineyards and homes. We have to do it to buy grain. There isn't enough food for everyone."

⁴Still others were saying, "We've had to borrow money. We needed it to pay the king's tax on our fields and vineyards. ⁵We belong to the same family lines as the rest of our people. Our children are as good as theirs. But we've had to sell them off as slaves. Some of our daughters have already been made slaves. But we can't do anything about it. That's because our fields and vineyards now belong to others."

⁶I heard them when they cried out. And I was very angry when I heard what they were saying. ⁷I thought it over for a while. Then I accused the nobles and officials of breaking the law. I told them, "You are charging your own people interest!" So I called together a large group of people to handle the matter. ⁸I said, "Our Jewish brothers and sisters were sold to other nations. We've done everything we could to buy them back and bring them home. But look at what you are doing! You are actually selling your own people! Now we'll have to buy them back too!" The people kept quiet. They couldn't think of anything to say.

⁹So I continued, "What you are doing isn't right. Shouldn't you show respect for our God? Shouldn't you live in a way that will keep our enemies from saying bad things about us? ¹⁰I'm lending the people money and grain. So are my relatives and my men. But we must stop charging interest! ¹¹Give the people's fields back to them. Give them back their vineyards, olive groves and houses. Do it right away. Give everything back to them. Also give them back the one percent on the money, grain, fresh wine and olive oil you have charged them."

¹²"We'll give it back," they said. "And we won't require anything more from them. We'll do exactly as you say."

Then I sent for the priests. I made the nobles and officials promise to do what they had said. ¹³I also shook out my pockets and emptied them. I said, "Someone might decide not to keep this promise they have made. If that happens, may God shake them out of their house! May he empty them of everything they own!"

The whole community said, "Amen." They praised the LORD. And the leaders did what they had promised to do.

¹⁴And that's not all. I was appointed as governor of Judah in the 20th year that Artaxerxes was king of Persia. I remained in that position until his 32nd year. During those 12 years, I and my relatives didn't eat the food that was provided for my table. ¹⁵But there had been governors before me. They had put a heavy load on the people. They had taken a pound of silver from each of them. They had also taken food and wine from them. Their officials had acted like high and

mighty rulers over them. But because of my great respect for God, I didn't act like that. [16] Instead, I spent all my time working on this wall. All my men were gathered there to work on it too. We didn't receive any land for ourselves.

[17] Many people ate at my table. They included 150 Jews and officials. They also included leaders who came to us from the nations that were around us. [18] Each day one ox, six of the best sheep and some birds were prepared for me. Every ten days plenty of wine of all kinds was brought in as well. In spite of all that, I never asked for the food that was provided for my table. That's because the people were already paying too many taxes.

[19] You are my God. Please remember me and help me. Keep in mind everything I've done for these people.

Nehemiah's Enemies Continue to Oppose the Rebuilding

6 Sanballat, Tobiah and Geshem, the Arab, heard about what I had done. So did the rest of our enemies. All of them heard I had rebuilt the wall. In fact, they heard there weren't any gaps left in it. But up to that time I hadn't put up the gates at the main entrances to the city. [2] Sanballat and Geshem sent me a message. They said, "Come. Let's talk with one another. Let's meet in one of the villages on the plain of Ono."

But they were planning to harm me. [3] So I sent messengers to them with my answer. I replied, "I'm working on a huge project. So I can't get away. Why should the work stop while I leave it? Why should I go down and talk with you?" [4] They sent me the same message four times. And I gave them the same answer each time.

[5] Sanballat sent his helper to me a fifth time. He brought the same message. He was carrying a letter that wasn't sealed. [6] It said,

"A report is going around among the nations. Geshem says it's true. We hear that you and the other Jews are planning to turn against the Persian rulers. And that's why you are building the wall. It's also reported that you are about to become their king. [7] People say that you have even appointed prophets to make an announcement about you. In Jerusalem they are going to say, 'Judah has a king!' That report will get back to the king of Persia. So come. Let's meet together."

[8] I sent a reply to Sanballat. I said, "What you are saying isn't really happening. You are just making it up."

[9] All of them were trying to frighten us. They thought, "Their hands will get too weak to do the work. So it won't be completed."

But I prayed to God. I said, "Make my hands stronger."

[10] One day I went to Shemaiah's house. He was the son of Delaiah. Delaiah was the son of Mehetabel. Shemaiah had shut himself up in his home. He said, "Let's go to God's house. Let's meet inside the temple and close the doors. Some men are coming at night to kill you."

[11] But I said, "Should a man like me run away? Should someone like me go into the temple just to save his life? No! I won't go!" [12] I realized that God hadn't sent Shemaiah. Tobiah and Sanballat had hired him. That's why he had prophesied lies about me. [13] They had hired him to scare me. They wanted me to commit a sin by doing what he said. That would give me a bad name in the community. People would find fault with me and my work.

[14] You are my God. Remember what Tobiah and Sanballat have done. Also remember the prophet Noadiah. She and the rest of the prophets have been trying to scare me. [15] So the city wall was completed on the 25th day of the month of Elul. It was finished in 52 days.

Nehemiah's Enemies Oppose the Completed Wall

[16] All our enemies heard about it. All the nations around us became afraid. They weren't sure of themselves anymore. They realized that our God had helped us finish the work. [17] In those days the nobles of Judah sent many letters to Tobiah. And replies from Tobiah came back to them. [18] Many people in Judah had promised that they would be faithful to him. That's because he was Shekaniah's son-in-law. Shekaniah was the son of Arah. Tobiah's son Jehohanan had married Meshullam's daughter. Meshullam was the son of Berekiah. [19] Tobiah's friends kept reporting to me the good things he did. They also kept telling him what I said. And Tobiah himself sent letters to scare me.

7 The wall had been rebuilt. I had put up the gates at the main entrances to the city. The people who guarded the gates were appointed to their positions. So were the musicians and the Levites. [2] I put my brother Hanani in charge of Jerusalem. Hananiah helped him. Hananiah was commander of the fort that was by the temple. Hanani was an honest man. He had more respect for God than most people do. [3] I said to Hanani and Hananiah, "Don't open the gates of Jerusalem until the hottest time of the day. Tell the men who guard the gates to shut them before they go off duty. Make sure they lock them up tight. Also appoint as guards some people who live in Jerusalem. Station some of them at their appointed places. Station others near their own homes."

A List of People Who Returned to Judah

[4] Jerusalem was large. It had a lot of room. But only a few people lived there. The houses hadn't

been rebuilt yet. ⁵So my God gave me the idea and encouraged me to gather the people together. He also encouraged me to gather the nobles and officials together with them. He wanted me to list them by families. I found the family history of those who had been the first to return. Here is what I found written in it.

⁶Nebuchadnezzar had taken many Jews away from the land of Judah. He had forced them to go to Babylon as prisoners.

Now they returned to Jerusalem and Judah. All of them went back to their own towns. Nebuchadnezzar was king of Babylon. ⁷The leaders of the Jews included Zerubbabel, Joshua, Nehemiah, Azariah, Raamiah and Nahamani. They also included Mordecai, Bilshan, Mispereth, Bigvai, Nehum and Baanah.

Here is a list of the men of Israel who returned home. ⁸There were 2,172 from the family line of Parosh. ⁹There were 372 from Shephatiah. ¹⁰There were 652 from Arah. ¹¹There were 2,818 from Pahath-Moab through the family line of Jeshua and Joab. ¹²There were 1,254 from Elam. ¹³There were 845 from Zattu. ¹⁴There were 760 from Zakkai.

¹⁵There were 648 from Binnui. ¹⁶There were 628 from Bebai. ¹⁷There were 2,322 from Azgad. ¹⁸There were 667 from Adonikam. ¹⁹There were 2,067 from Bigvai. ²⁰There were 655 from Adin. ²¹There were 98 from Ater through the family line of Hezekiah. ²²There were 328 from Hashum. ²³There were 324 from Bezai. ²⁴There were 112 from Hariph. ²⁵There were 95 from Gibeon. ²⁶There were 188 from the men of Bethlehem and Netophah. ²⁷There were 128 from Anathoth. ²⁸There were 42 from Beth Azmaveth. ²⁹There were 743 from Kiriath Jearim, Kephirah and Beeroth. ³⁰There were 621 from Ramah and Geba. ³¹There were 122 from Mikmash. ³²There were 123 from Bethel and Ai. ³³There were 52 from the other Nebo. ³⁴There were 1,254 from the other Elam. ³⁵There were 320 from Harim. ³⁶There were 345 from Jericho. ³⁷There were 721 from Lod, Hadid and Ono.

³⁸There were 3,930 from Senaah.

³⁹Here is a list of the priests.
There were 973 from the family line of Jedaiah through the line of Jeshua.
⁴⁰There were 1,052 from Immer.
⁴¹There were 1,247 from Pashhur.
⁴²There were 1,017 from Harim.

⁴³The Levites belonged to the family line of Jeshua through Kadmiel through the line of Hodaviah. The total number of men was 74.
⁴⁴The musicians belonged to the family line of Asaph. The total number of men was 148.
⁴⁵The men who guarded the temple gates belonged to the family lines of Shallum, Ater, Talmon, Akkub, Hatita and Shobai. The total number of men was 138.

⁴⁶Here is a list of the members of the family lines of the temple servants.
Ziha, Hasupha, Tabbaoth,
⁴⁷Keros, Sia, Padon,
⁴⁸Lebana, Hagaba, Shalmai,
⁴⁹Hanan, Giddel, Gahar,
⁵⁰Reaiah, Rezin, Nekoda,
⁵¹Gazzam, Uzza, Paseah,
⁵²Besai, Meunim, Nephusim,
⁵³Bakbuk, Hakupha, Harhur,
⁵⁴Bazluth, Mehida, Harsha,
⁵⁵Barkos, Sisera, Temah,
⁵⁶Neziah, Hatipha

⁵⁷Here is a list of the members of the family lines of the servants of Solomon.
Sotai, Sophereth, Perida,
⁵⁸Jaala, Darkon, Giddel,
⁵⁹Shephatiah, Hattil, Pokereth-Hazzebaim, Amon
⁶⁰The total number of the members of the family lines of the temple servants and the servants of Solomon was 392.

⁶¹Many people came up to Judah from the towns of Tel Melah, Tel Harsha, Kerub, Addon and Immer. But they weren't able to prove that their families belonged to the people of Israel.
⁶²There were 642 of them from the family lines of Delaiah, Tobiah and Nekoda.

⁶³Here is a list of the members of the family lines of the priests.
They were
Hobaiah, Hakkoz and Barzillai. Barzillai had married a daughter of Barzillai from Gilead. So he was also called Barzillai.
⁶⁴The priests looked for their family records. But they couldn't find them. So they weren't able to serve as priests. They weren't "clean." ⁶⁵The governor gave them an order. He told them not to eat any of the most sacred food. They had to wait until there was a priest who could use the

Urim and Thummim. The priest would use them to get decisions from the LORD.

⁶⁶ The total number of the entire group that returned was 42,360. ⁶⁷ That didn't include their 7,337 male and female slaves. There were also 245 male and female singers. ⁶⁸ And there were 736 horses, 245 mules, ⁶⁹ 435 camels and 6,720 donkeys.

⁷⁰ Some of the family leaders helped pay for the work. The governor gave 19 pounds of gold to be added to the temple treasure. He also gave 50 bowls and 530 sets of clothes for the priests. ⁷¹ Some of the family leaders gave 375 pounds of gold for the work. They also gave one and a third tons of silver. All of that was added to the temple treasure. ⁷² The rest of the people gave a total of 375 pounds of gold and one and a fourth tons of silver. They also gave 67 sets of clothes for the priests.

⁷³ The priests and Levites made their homes in their own towns. So did the musicians, the temple servants and the men who guarded the gates. The rest of the Israelites also made their homes in their own towns.

Ezra Reads the Law to the People

The Israelites had made their homes in their towns. In the

8 seventh month, ¹ all of them gathered together. They went to the open area in front of the Water Gate. They told Ezra to bring out the Book of the Law of Moses. The LORD had given Israel that Law so they would obey him. Ezra was the teacher of the Law.

² Ezra the priest brought the Law out to the whole community. It was the first day of the seventh month. The group was made up of men, women, and children old enough to understand what Ezra was going to read. ³ He read the Law to them from sunrise until noon. He did it as he faced the open area in front of the Water Gate. He read it to the men, the women, and the children old enough to understand. And all the people paid careful attention as Ezra was reading the Book of the Law.

⁴ Ezra, the teacher of the Law, stood on a high wooden stage. It had been built for the occasion. Mattithiah, Shema and Anaiah stood at his right side. So did Uriah, Hilkiah and Maaseiah. Pedaiah, Mishael and Malkijah stood at his left side. So did Hashum, Hashbaddanah, Zechariah and Meshullam.

⁵ Ezra opened the book. All the people could see him. That's because he was standing above them. As he opened the book, the people stood up. ⁶ Ezra praised the LORD. He is the great God. All the people lifted up their hands and said, "Amen! Amen!" Then they bowed down. They turned their faces toward the ground and worshiped the LORD.

7 The Levites taught the Law to the people. They remained standing while the Levites taught them. The Levites who were there included Jeshua, Bani, Sherebiah, Jamin, Akkub, Shabbethai and Hodiah. They also included Maaseiah, Kelita, Azariah, Jozabad, Hanan and Pelaiah. 8 All these Levites read to the people parts of the Book of the Law of God. They made it clear to them. They told them what it meant. So the people understood what was being read.

9 Nehemiah was the governor. Ezra was a priest and the teacher of the Law. They spoke up. So did the Levites who were teaching the people. All these men said to the people, "This day is set apart to honor the LORD your God. So don't weep. Don't be sad." All the people had been weeping as they listened to the words of the Law.

10 Nehemiah said, "Go and enjoy some good food and sweet drinks. Send some of it to people who don't have any. This day is holy to our Lord. So don't be sad. The joy of the LORD makes you strong."

11 The Levites calmed all the people down. They said, "Be quiet. This is a holy day. So don't be sad."

12 Then all the people went away to eat and drink. They shared their food with others. They celebrated with great joy. Now they understood the words they had heard. That's because everything had been explained to them.

13 All the family leaders gathered around Ezra, the teacher. So did the priests and Levites. All of them paid attention to the words of the Law. It was the second day of the month. 14 The LORD had given the Law through Moses. He wanted the Israelites to obey it. It is written there that they were supposed to live in booths during the Feast of Booths. That feast was celebrated in the seventh month. 15 They were also supposed to spread the message all through their towns and in Jerusalem. They were supposed to announce, "Go out into the central hill country. Bring back some branches from olive and wild olive trees. Also bring some from myrtle, palm and shade trees. Use the branches to make booths."

16 So the people went out and brought back some branches. They built themselves booths on their own roofs. They made them in their courtyards. They put them up in the courtyards of the house of God. They built them in the open area in front of the Water Gate. And they built them in the open area in front of the Gate of Ephraim. 17 All the people who had returned from the land of Babylon made booths. They lived in them during the Feast of Booths. They hadn't celebrated the feast with so much joy for a long time. In fact, they had never celebrated it like that from the days of Joshua, the son of Nun, until that day. So their joy was very great.

[18] Day after day, Ezra read parts of the Book of the Law of God to them. He read it out loud from the first day to the last. They celebrated the Feast of Booths for seven days. On the eighth day they gathered together. They followed the required rules for celebrating the feast.

The Israelites Admit They Have Sinned

9 It was the 24th day of the seventh month. The Israelites gathered together again. They didn't eat any food. They wore the rough clothing people wear when they're sad. They put dust on their heads. [2] The Israelites separated themselves from everyone else. They stood and admitted they had sinned. They also admitted that their people before them had sinned. [3] They stood where they were. They listened while the Levites read parts of the Book of the Law of the LORD their God. They listened for a fourth of the day. They spent another fourth of the day admitting their sins. They also worshiped the LORD their God. [4] Some people were standing on the stairs of the Levites. They included Jeshua, Bani, Kadmiel, Shebaniah, Bunni, Sherebiah, Bani and Kenani. With loud voices they called out to the LORD their God. [5] Then some Levites spoke up. They included Jeshua, Kadmiel, Bani, Hashabneiah, Sherebiah, Hodiah, Shebaniah and Pethahiah. They said to the people, "Stand up. Praise the LORD your God. He lives for ever and ever!"

So the people said, "LORD, may your glorious name be praised. May it be lifted high above every other name that is blessed and praised. [6] You are the one and only LORD. You made the heavens. You made even the highest heavens. You created all the stars in the sky. You created the earth and everything on it. And you made the oceans and everything in them. You give life to everything. Every living being in heaven worships you.

[7] "You are the LORD God. You chose Abram. You brought him out of Ur in the land of Babylon. You named him Abraham. [8] You knew that his heart was faithful to you. And you made a covenant with him. You promised to give to his children after him a land of their own. It was the land of the Canaanites, Hittites and Amorites. The Perizzites, Jebusites and Girgashites also lived there. You have kept your promise. That's because you always do what is right and fair.

[9] "You saw how our people of long ago suffered in Egypt. You heard them cry out to you at the Red Sea. [10] You sent signs and wonders against Pharaoh. You sent plagues on all his

officials. In fact, you sent them on all the people of Egypt. You knew how they treated our people. They looked down on them. But you made a name for yourself. That name remains to this very day. ¹¹ You parted the waters of the Red Sea for the Israelites. They passed through it on dry ground. But you threw into the sea those who chased them. They sank down like a stone into the mighty waters. ¹² By day you led the Israelites with a pillar of cloud. At night you led them with a pillar of fire. It gave them light to show them the way you wanted them to go.

¹³ "You came down on Mount Sinai. From heaven you spoke to our people. You gave them rules and laws. Those laws are right and fair. You gave them orders and commands that are good. ¹⁴ You taught them about your holy Sabbath day. You gave them commands, orders and laws. You did it through your servant Moses. ¹⁵ When the people were hungry, you gave them bread from heaven. When they were thirsty, you brought them water out of a rock. You told them to go into the land of Canaan. You told them to take it as their own. It was the land you had promised to give them.

¹⁶ "But our people before us became proud and stubborn. They didn't obey your commands. ¹⁷ They refused to listen to you. They forgot the miracles you had done among them. So they became stubborn. When they refused to obey you, they appointed a leader for themselves. They wanted to go back to being slaves in Egypt. But you are a God who forgives. You are gracious. You are tender and kind. You are slow to get angry. You are full of love. So you didn't desert them. ¹⁸ They made for themselves a metal statue of a god that looked like a calf. They said to one another, 'Here is your god. He brought you up out of Egypt.' And they did evil things that dishonored you. But you still didn't desert them.

¹⁹ "Because you loved them so much, you didn't leave them in the desert. During the day the pillar of cloud didn't stop guiding them on their path. At night the pillar of fire didn't stop shining on the way you wanted them to go. ²⁰ You gave them your good Spirit to teach them. You didn't hold back your manna from their mouths. And you gave them water when they were thirsty. ²¹ For 40 years you took good care of them in the desert. They had everything they needed. Their

clothes didn't wear out. And their feet didn't swell up.

²² "You gave them kingdoms and nations. You even gave them lands far away. They took over the country of Sihon. He was the king of Heshbon. They also took over the country of Og. He was the king of Bashan. ²³ You gave them as many children as there are stars in the sky. You told their parents to enter the land. You told them to take it over. And you brought their children into it. ²⁴ Their children went into the land. They took it as their own. You brought the Canaanites under Israel's control. The Canaanites lived in the land. But you handed them over to Israel. You also handed over their kings and the other nations in the land to Israel. You allowed Israel to deal with them just as they wanted to. ²⁵ Your people captured cities that had high walls around them. They also took over the rich land in Canaan. They took houses filled with all kinds of good things. They took over wells that had already been dug. They took many vineyards, olive groves and fruit trees. They ate until they were very full and satisfied. They were filled with joy because you were so good to them.

²⁶ "But they didn't obey you. Instead, they turned against you. They turned their backs on your law. They killed your prophets. The prophets had warned them to return to you. But they did very evil things that dishonored you. ²⁷ So you handed them over to their enemies, who treated them badly. Then they cried out to you. From heaven you heard them. You loved them very much. So you sent leaders to help them. The leaders saved them from the power of their enemies.

²⁸ "Then the people were enjoying peace and rest again. That's when they did what you did not want them to do. Then you handed them over to their enemies. So their enemies ruled over them. When they cried out to you again, you heard them from heaven. You loved them very much. So you saved them time after time.

²⁹ "You warned them so that they would obey your law again. But they became proud. They didn't obey your commands. They sinned against your rules. You said, 'Anyone who obeys my rules will live by them.' But the people didn't care about that. They turned their backs on you. They became very stubborn. They refused to listen to you. ³⁰ For many

years you put up with them. By your Spirit you warned them through your prophets. In spite of that, they didn't pay any attention. So you handed them over to the nations that were around them. ³¹ But you loved them very much. So you didn't put an end to them. You didn't desert them. That's because you are a gracious God. You are tender and kind.

³² "Our God, you are the great God. You are mighty and wonderful. You keep the covenant you made with us. You show us your love. So don't let all our suffering seem like a small thing to you. We've suffered greatly. So have our kings and leaders. So have our priests and prophets. Our people who lived long ago also suffered. And all your people are suffering right now. In fact, we've been suffering from the time of the kings of Assyria until today. ³³ In spite of everything that has happened to us, you have been fair. You have been faithful in what you have done. But we did what was evil. ³⁴ Our kings and leaders didn't follow your law. Our priests and our people before us didn't follow it either. They didn't pay any attention to your commands or rules that you warned them to keep. ³⁵ They didn't serve you.

They didn't turn from their evil ways. They didn't obey you even when they had a kingdom. You were very good to them. And they enjoyed it. You gave them a rich land. It had plenty of room in it. But they still didn't serve you.

³⁶ "Now look at us. We are slaves today. We're slaves in the land you gave our people of long ago. You gave it to them so they could eat its fruit and the other good things it produces. ³⁷ But we have sinned against you. So its great harvest goes to the kings of Persia. You have placed them over us. They rule over our bodies and cattle just as they please. And we are suffering terribly.

The People Agree to Obey God's Law

³⁸ "So we are making a firm agreement. We're writing it down. Our leaders are putting their official marks on it. And so are our Levites and priests."

10 Here are the names of those who put their official marks on the agreement.

Nehemiah, the son of Hakaliah
He was the governor.

Zedekiah, ² Seraiah, Azariah, Jeremiah,

³ Pashhur, Amariah, Malkijah,

⁴ Hattush, Shebaniah, Malluk,

⁵Harim, Meremoth, Obadiah,
⁶Daniel, Ginnethon, Baruch,
⁷Meshullam, Abijah, Mijamin,
⁸Maaziah, Bilgai, Shemaiah
They were the priests.
⁹Here are the names of the Levites.

Jeshua, the son of Azaniah,
Binnui, one of the sons of Henadad,
Kadmiel
¹⁰Here are the names of those who helped them.

Shebaniah, Hodiah, Kelita, Pelaiah, Hanan,
¹¹Mika, Rehob, Hashabiah,
¹²Zakkur, Sherebiah, Shebaniah,
¹³Hodiah, Bani, Beninu
¹⁴Here are the names of the leaders of the people.

Parosh, Pahath-Moab, Elam, Zattu, Bani,
¹⁵Bunni, Azgad, Bebai,
¹⁶Adonijah, Bigvai, Adin,
¹⁷Ater, Hezekiah, Azzur,
¹⁸Hodiah, Hashum, Bezai,
¹⁹Hariph, Anathoth, Nebai,
²⁰Magpiash, Meshullam, Hezir,
²¹Meshezabel, Zadok, Jaddua,
²²Pelatiah, Hanan, Anaiah,
²³Hoshea, Hananiah, Hasshub,
²⁴Hallohesh, Pilha, Shobek,
²⁵Rehum, Hashabnah, Maaseiah,
²⁶Ahiah, Hanan, Anan,
²⁷Malluk, Harim, Baanah

²⁸The rest of the people gathered together. They included the priests, the Levites and the men who guarded the gates. They included the musicians and temple servants. They also included all the people who separated themselves from the surrounding nations to obey the Law of God. All these men brought their wives with them. And they brought all their sons and daughters who were old enough to understand what was being agreed to. ²⁹All the men joined the nobles of their people. They made a firm agreement. They made a promise and said they would be cursed if they didn't keep it. They promised to follow the Law of God. It had been given through Moses, the servant of God. They promised to obey carefully all the commands, rules and laws of the LORD our Lord.

³⁰Here is what the priests, Levites and people said. "We promise not to let our daughters marry men from the nations around us. And we promise not to let their daughters marry our sons.

³¹"The people around us will bring goods and grain to sell on the Sabbath day. But we won't buy anything from them on the Sabbath day. In fact, we won't buy anything from them on any holy day. Every seventh year we won't farm the

land. And we'll forgive people what they owe us.

32 "We will be accountable for carrying out the commands for serving in the house of our God. Each of us will give an eighth of an ounce of silver every year. 33 It will pay for the holy bread that is placed on the table in the temple. It will pay for the regular grain offerings and burnt offerings. It will pay for the offerings on the Sabbath days. It will pay for the offerings at the New Moon feasts and at the appointed feasts. It will pay for the holy offerings. It will be used for sin offerings to pay for the sins of Israel. It will also pay for everything else that needs to be done at the house of our God.

34 "We are the priests, Levites and people. Each of our families should bring a gift of wood to the house of our God. We have cast lots to decide when they will do that. They will bring it at certain appointed times every year. The wood will be burned on the altar of the LORD our God. That's what the Law requires.

35 "We will also be accountable for bringing the first share of our crops each year. And we'll bring the first share of every fruit tree. We'll bring them to the LORD's house.

36 "Each of us will bring our oldest son to the priests who serve there. We'll also bring the male animals that were born first to their mothers among our cattle, herds and flocks. We'll bring them to the house of our God. That's what the Law requires.

37 "We will also bring the first part of the meal we grind. We'll bring the first of our grain offerings. We'll bring the first share of fruit from all our trees. And we'll bring the first share of our olive oil and fresh wine. We'll give all those things to the priests. They'll put them in the storerooms of the house of our God. And we'll give a tenth of our crops to the Levites. They collect the tenth shares. They do it in all the towns where we work. 38 A priest from Aaron's family line must go with the Levites when they receive the tenth shares. And the Levites must bring a tenth of those shares up to the house of our God. They must put it in the rooms where the treasures are stored. 39 The people of Israel, including the Levites, must bring their gifts. They must bring grain, olive oil and fresh wine. They must put them in the storerooms where the objects for the temple are kept. That's also where the objects are kept for the priests serving at the tem-

ple, the musicians and the men who guard the gates.

"We won't forget to take care of the house of our God."

People Are Chosen to Live in Jerusalem

11 The leaders of the people made their homes in Jerusalem. The rest of the people cast lots. They did it to choose one person out of every ten of them. That person was chosen to live in the holy city of Jerusalem. The other nine had to stay in their own towns. ² The people thanked everyone who agreed to live in Jerusalem.

³ Here are the leaders from different parts of the country who made their homes in Jerusalem.

Some Israelites, priests and Levites lived in the towns of Judah. So did some temple servants and some members of the family lines of Solomon's servants. All of them lived on their own property in the towns of Judah. ⁴ At the same time, other people from the tribes of Judah and Benjamin lived in Jerusalem.

Here are the leaders from the family line of Judah. There was Athaiah. He was the son of Uzziah. Uzziah was the son of Zechariah. Zechariah was the son of Amariah. Amariah was the son of Shephatiah. Shephatiah was the son of Mahalalel. Mahalalel belonged to the family line of Perez.

⁵ There was also Maaseiah. He was the son of Baruch. Baruch was the son of Kol-Hozeh. Kol-Hozeh was the son of Hazaiah. Hazaiah was the son of Adaiah. Adaiah was the son of Joiarib. Joiarib was the son of Zechariah. Zechariah belonged to the family line of Shelah.

⁶ Many important men who belonged to the family line of Perez lived in Jerusalem. The total number of them was 468.

⁷ Here are the leaders from the family line of Benjamin.

There was Sallu. He was the son of Meshullam. Meshullam was the son of Joed. Joed was the son of Pedaiah. Pedaiah was the son of Kolaiah. Kolaiah was the son of Maaseiah. Maaseiah was the son of Ithiel. Ithiel was the son of Jeshaiah. ⁸ There were also Gabbai and Sallai. They were Sallu's followers. The total number of men was 928.

⁹ Joel was their chief officer. He was the son of Zikri. A man named Judah was in charge of the New Quarter of Jerusalem. He was the son of Hassenuah.

¹⁰Here are the leaders from among the priests.

There were Jedaiah, Jakin and the son of Joiarib. ¹¹There was also Seraiah. He was the son of Hilkiah. Hilkiah was the son of Meshullam. Meshullam was the son of Zadok. Zadok was the son of Meraioth. Meraioth was the son of Ahitub. Ahitub was the official in charge of God's house. ¹²There were also people who helped them. They carried out the work for the temple. The total number of men was 822.

There was also Adaiah. He was the son of Jeroham. Jeroham was the son of Pelaliah. Pelaliah was the son of Amzi. Amzi was the son of Zechariah. Zechariah was the son of Pashhur. Pashhur was the son of Malkijah. ¹³There were also people who helped Adaiah. They were family leaders. The total number of men was 242.

There was also Amashsai. He was the son of Azarel. Azarel was the son of Ahzai. Ahzai was the son of Meshillemoth. Meshillemoth was the son of Immer. ¹⁴There were also people who helped Amashsai. They were important men. The total number of them was 128.

Their chief officer was Zabdiel. He was the son of Haggedolim.

¹⁵Here are the leaders from among the Levites.

There was Shemaiah. He was the son of Hasshub. Hasshub was the son of Azrikam. Azrikam was the son of Hashabiah. Hashabiah was the son of Bunni.

¹⁶There were also Shabbethai and Jozabad. They were two of the leaders of the Levites. They were in charge of the work that was done outside God's house.

¹⁷There was also Mattaniah. He led in prayer and in giving thanks. He was the son of Mika. Mika was the son of Zabdi. Zabdi was the son of Asaph.

There was also Bakbukiah. He was second among those who helped Mattaniah.

And there was Abda. He was the son of Shammua. Shammua was the son of Galal. Galal was the son of Jeduthun.

¹⁸The total number of Levites in the holy city was 284.

¹⁹Here are the leaders from among the men who guarded the gates.

There were Akkub, Talmon and those who helped them. They stood guard at the gates. The total number of men was 172.

20 The rest of the Israelites were in all the towns of Judah. The priests and Levites were with them. All of them lived on their own family property.

21 The temple servants lived on the hill of Ophel. Ziha and Gishpa were in charge of them.

22 Uzzi was the chief officer of the Levites in Jerusalem. He was the son of Bani. Bani was the son of Hashabiah. Hashabiah was the son of Mattaniah. Mattaniah was the son of Mika. Uzzi was one of the members of Asaph's family line. They were musicians in charge of the worship services at the house of God. 23 The musicians received their orders from the Persian king. He told them what they should do every day.

24 Pethahiah worked for the king in all matters that were connected with the people. He was the son of Meshezabel. Meshezabel belonged to the family line of Zerah. Zerah was the son of Judah.

25 Many of the people of Judah lived in villages that had fields around them. Some of them lived in Kiriath Arba and the settlements that were around it. Others lived in Dibon and its settlements. Others lived in Jekabzeel and its villages. 26 Others lived in Jeshua, Moladah and Beth Pelet. 27 Others lived in Hazar Shual and in Beersheba and its settlements. 28 Others lived in Ziklag and in Mekonah and its settlements. 29 Others lived in En Rimmon and Zorah. Others lived in Jarmuth, 30 Zanoah and Adullam and their villages. Others lived in Lachish and its fields. Still others lived in Azekah and its settlements. So the people of Judah were living all the way from Beersheba to the Valley of Hinnom.

31 Some of the members of the family line of Benjamin who were from Geba lived in Mikmash. Others lived in Aija and in Bethel and its settlements. 32 Others lived in Anathoth, Nob and Ananiah. 33 Others lived in Hazor, Ramah and Gittaim. 34 Others lived in Hadid, Zeboim and Neballat. 35 Others lived in Lod and Ono. Still others lived in Ge Harashim.

36 Some of the groups of the Levites from Judah made their homes in the territory of Benjamin.

The Priests and Levites Who Returned to Judah

12 Some priests and Levites returned to Judah with Zerubbabel and Joshua. Zerubbabel was the son of Shealtiel. Here are the names of those priests and Levites.

Seraiah, Jeremiah, Ezra, 2 Amariah, Malluk, Hattush, 3 Shekaniah, Rehum, Meremoth, 4 Iddo, Ginnethon, Abijah, 5 Mijamin, Moadiah, Bilgah, 6 Shemaiah, Joiarib, Jedaiah, 7 Sallu, Amok, Hilkiah, Jedaiah

All of them were the leaders of the priests and those who

helped them. They lived in the days of Joshua.

⁸ The Levites were Jeshua, Binnui, Kadmiel, Sherebiah and Judah. There were also Mattaniah and those who helped him. They were in charge of the songs for giving thanks. ⁹ Bakbukiah and Unni helped them. They stood and sang across from them during the services.

¹⁰ Joshua was the father of Joiakim.

Joiakim was the father of Eliashib.

Eliashib was the father of Joiada.

¹¹ Joiada was the father of Jonathan.

And Jonathan was the father of Jaddua.

¹² Here are the names of the family leaders of the priests. They were the leaders in the days of Joiakim.

Meraiah was from Seraiah's family.

Hananiah was from Jeremiah's family.

¹³ Meshullam was from Ezra's family.

Jehohanan was from Amariah's family.

¹⁴ Jonathan was from Malluk's family.

Joseph was from Shekaniah's family.

¹⁵ Adna was from Harim's family.

Helkai was from Meremoth's family.

¹⁶ Zechariah was from Iddo's family.

Meshullam was from Ginnethon's family.

¹⁷ Zikri was from Abijah's family.

Piltai was from Miniamin's and Moadiah's family.

¹⁸ Shammua was from Bilgah's family.

Jehonathan was from Shemaiah's family.

¹⁹ Mattenai was from Joiarib's family.

Uzzi was from Jedaiah's family.

²⁰ Kallai was from Sallu's family.

Eber was from Amok's family.

²¹ Hashabiah was from Hilkiah's family.

And Nethanel was from Jedaiah's family.

²² The names of the family leaders of the Levites in the days of Eliashib, Joiada, Johanan and Jaddua were written down. So were the names of the family leaders of the priests. That happened while Darius ruled over Persia. ²³ The names of the leaders in Levi's family line up to the time of Johanan were written down. They were written in the official records. Johanan was the son of Eliashib. ²⁴ The leaders of the Levites were Hashabiah, Sherebiah and Jeshua. Jeshua was the son of Kadmiel. Those who helped them stood across from them to sing praises and give thanks. One group would sing back to the other. That's what David, the man of God, had ordered.

²⁵ Mattaniah, Bakbukiah,

Obadiah, Meshullam, Talmon and Akkub stood at the gates of the temple. They guarded the storerooms at the gates. 26 They served in the days of Joiakim. He was the son of Joshua. Joshua was the son of Jozadak. They also served in the days of Nehemiah and Ezra. Nehemiah was the governor. Ezra was a priest and the teacher of the Law.

The Wall of Jerusalem Is Set Apart to God

27 The wall of Jerusalem was set apart to God. For that occasion, the Levites were gathered together from where they lived. They were brought to Jerusalem to celebrate that happy occasion. They celebrated the fact that the wall was being set apart to God. They did it by singing and giving their thanks to him. They celebrated by playing music on cymbals, harps and lyres. 28 The musicians were also brought together. Some of them came in from the area around Jerusalem. Others came from the villages where the people of Netophah lived. 29 Others came from Beth Gilgal. Still others came from the area of Geba and Azmaveth. The musicians had built villages for themselves around Jerusalem. 30 The priests and Levites made themselves pure. Then they made the people, the gates and the wall pure and "clean."

31 I, Nehemiah, had the leaders of Judah go up on top of the wall. I also appointed two large choirs to sing and give thanks. I told one of them to walk south on top of the wall. That was toward the Dung Gate. 32 Hoshaiah and half of the leaders of Judah followed them. 33 Azariah, Ezra, Meshullam, 34 Judah, Benjamin, Shemaiah and Jeremiah also followed them. 35 Some priests who had trumpets followed them. So did Zechariah. He was the son of Jonathan. Jonathan was the son of Shemaiah. Shemaiah was the son of Mattaniah. Mattaniah was the son of Micaiah. Micaiah was the son of Zakkur. Zakkur was the son of Asaph. 36 Those who helped Zechariah also marched along. They were Shemaiah, Azarel, Milalai, Gilalai, Maai, Nethanel, Judah and Hanani. They brought musical instruments with them. That's what David, the man of God, had ordered. Ezra led the group that was marching south. He was the teacher of the Law. 37 At the Fountain Gate they continued straight up the steps of the City of David. The steps went up to the wall. Then the group passed above the place where David's palace had been. They continued on to the Water Gate on the east.

38 The second choir went north. I followed them on top of the wall. Half of the people went with me. They went past the Tower of the Ovens. They went to the Broad Wall. 39 They marched over the Gate of Ephraim. They went over the Jeshanah Gate and the Fish Gate. They went past the Tower

of Hananel and the Tower of the Hundred. They continued on to the Sheep Gate. At the Gate of the Guard they stopped.

⁴⁰ Then the two choirs that sang and gave thanks took their places in God's house. So did I. So did half of the officials. ⁴¹ And so did the priests. They were Eliakim, Maaseiah, Miniamin, Micaiah, Elioenai, Zechariah and Hananiah. They had their trumpets with them. ⁴² Maaseiah, Shemaiah, Eleazar, Uzzi, Jehohanan, Malkijah, Elam and Ezer were also there. The choirs sang under the direction of Jezrahiah. ⁴³ On that day large numbers of sacrifices were offered. The people were glad because God had given them great joy. The women and children were also very happy. The joyful sound in Jerusalem could be heard far away.

Nehemiah Makes Some Final Changes

⁴⁴ At that time some men were put in charge of the storerooms. That's where all the gifts the people brought were placed. Those gifts included the first shares of their crops. They also included a tenth of everything the Law required. Crops were harvested from the fields around the towns. The people had to bring the shares of those crops that were required by the Law. They gave them to the priests and Levites. That's because the people of Judah were pleased with the priests and Levites who were serving God.

⁴⁵ The priests and Levites did everything their God wanted them to do. They made things pure and "clean." The musicians and the men who guarded the temple gates also served God. Everything was done just as David and his son Solomon had commanded. ⁴⁶ A long time ago there had been directors for the musicians. There had also been directors for the songs for giving thanks and praise to God. It was in the time of David and Asaph. ⁴⁷ So now in the days of Zerubbabel and Nehemiah, all the people of Israel brought their gifts. They gave the musicians and the men who guarded the gates what they were supposed to give them every day. They also set apart the shares for the other Levites. And the Levites set apart the shares for the priests in the family line of Aaron.

13 At that time the Book of Moses was read out loud. All the people heard it. It was written there that no Ammonite or Moabite could ever become a member of God's community. ² That's because they hadn't given the people of Israel food and water. Instead, they had hired Balaam to put a curse on them. But our God turned the curse into a blessing. ³ When that law was read, the people of Judah obeyed it. They sent out of Israel everyone who was from another nation.

⁴ Eliashib the priest had been put in charge of the storerooms in the house of our God. He had

worked closely with Tobiah. ⁵ He had also provided a large room for Tobiah. It had been used to store the grain offerings. The incense and the objects for the temple had been put there. And a tenth of the grain, olive oil and fresh wine had been kept there. That's what the Law required for the Levites. That's also what it required for the musicians and the men who guarded the temple gates. The gifts for the priests had been kept there too.

⁶ But I wasn't in Jerusalem while all of that was going on. I had returned to the Persian King Artaxerxes, the king of Babylon. I went to him in the 32nd year of his rule. Some time later I asked him to let me return to Jerusalem. ⁷ When I got back, I learned about the evil thing Eliashib had done. He had provided a room for Tobiah. It was in the courtyards of God's house. ⁸ So I was very unhappy. I threw all of Tobiah's things out of the room. ⁹ I gave orders to make the rooms pure and "clean" again. Then I put the supplies from God's house back into them. That included the grain offerings and the incense.

¹⁰ I also learned that the shares the Levites were supposed to receive hadn't been given to them. So all the Levites and musicians had to leave their regular temple duties. They had to go back and farm their own fields. ¹¹ I gave a warning to the officials. I asked them, "Why aren't you taking care of God's house?" Then I brought the Levites and musicians together. I stationed them in their proper places. I put them back to work.

¹² All the people of Judah brought a tenth of the grain, olive oil and fresh wine. They took it to the storerooms. ¹³ I put some men in charge of the storerooms. They were Shelemiah, Zadok and Pedaiah. Shelemiah was a priest. Zadok was a teacher of the law. And Pedaiah was a Levite. I made Hanan their assistant. He was the son of Zakkur. Zakkur was the son of Mattaniah. I knew that these men could be trusted. They were put in charge of handing out the supplies to the other Levites.

¹⁴ You are my God. Remember me because of what I've done. I've worked faithfully for your temple and its services. So please don't forget the good things I've done.

¹⁵ In those days I saw some people of Judah stomping on grapes in winepresses. They were doing it on the Sabbath day. Other people were bringing in grain. They were loading it on donkeys. Still other people were loading up wine, grapes, figs and other kinds of things. They were bringing all of it into Jerusalem on the Sabbath day. So I warned them not to sell food on that day. ¹⁶ People from Tyre who lived in Jerusalem were bringing in fish. In fact, they were bringing in all kinds of goods. They were selling them in Jerusalem on the

Sabbath day. The people of Judah were buying them. [17] I gave a warning to the nobles of Judah. I said, "Why are you doing such an evil thing? You are misusing the Sabbath day! [18] Your people of long ago did the very same things. That's why our God has brought all this trouble on us. That's why he's making this city suffer so much. Now you are making him even angrier against Israel. You are misusing the Sabbath day."

[19] Evening shadows fell on the gates of Jerusalem before the Sabbath day started. So I ordered the gates to be shut. They had to remain closed until the Sabbath day was over. I stationed some of my own men at the gates. I told them not to let anything be brought in on the Sabbath day. [20] Once or twice some traders and sellers spent the night outside Jerusalem. They were hoping to sell all kinds of goods. [21] But I gave them a warning. I said, "Why are you spending the night by the wall? If you do this again, I'll arrest you." So from that time on they didn't come on the Sabbath day anymore. [22] I commanded the Levites to make themselves pure. Then I told them to go and guard the gates. I wanted the Sabbath day to be kept holy.

You are my God. Remember me because of the good things I've done. Be kind to me according to your great love.

[23] In those days I also saw that some men of Judah had married women from Ashdod. Others had married women from Ammon or Moab. [24] Half of their children spoke the language of Ashdod. Or they spoke the language of one of the other nations. They didn't even know how to speak the language of Judah. [25] So I gave them a warning. I cursed them. I beat up some of them. I pulled their hair out. I had them make a promise in God's name. I said, "You must promise not to give your daughters to be married to their sons. You must promise not to let their daughters marry your sons. And you must not marry their daughters either. [26] That's how Solomon, the king of Israel, sinned. He married women from other nations. There wasn't a king like him anywhere. His God loved him. In fact, God made him king over the whole nation of Israel. But even he was led into sin by women from other lands. [27] Now I hear that you too are doing all of the same terrible and evil things. You aren't being faithful to our God. You are marrying women from other lands."

[28] One of the sons of Joiada was the son-in-law of Sanballat the Horonite. Joiada, the son of Eliashib, was the high priest. I drove Joiada's son away from me.

[29] You are my God. Remember what those priests have done. They have brought shame to their own work. They have also brought shame to the covenant

that God made with the priests and Levites long ago.

³⁰ So I made the priests and Levites pure. I made them pure from every practice that had come from other countries and had made them impure. I gave them their duties. Each one had his own job to do. ³¹ I also made plans for gifts of wood to be brought at certain appointed times. And I made plans for the first share of the crops to be brought.

You are my God. Please remember me with kindness.

Esther

Introduction:

This book is named for a girl called Esther. Esther was a Jew. She lived in a country called Persia. She was very beautiful. The king made Esther his queen.

Esther's parents died. So she was raised by her cousin Mordecai. Haman, a friend of the king, hated Mordecai. He wanted to kill Mordecai's people, the Jews. Esther was very brave, so she went to the king for help. She saved her people from being killed.

God's name is not used in this book. But God is at work. God took care of Esther. He took care of the Jews too. God always cares for his people.

Outline of contents:

Esther is made queen (1:1—2:23)
Haman tries to kill the Jews (3:1—5:14)
The Jews win (6:1—10:3)

Vashti Is Removed From Her Position as Queen

1 King Xerxes ruled over the 127 territories in his kingdom. They reached from India all the way to Cush. Here is what happened during the time Xerxes ruled over the whole Persian kingdom. ²He was ruling from his royal throne in the fort of Susa. ³In the third year of his rule King Xerxes gave a feast. It was for all his nobles and officials. The military leaders of Persia and Media were there. So were the princes and the nobles of the territories he ruled over.

⁴Every day for 180 days he showed his guests the great wealth of his kingdom. He also showed them how glorious his kingdom was. ⁵When those days were over, the king gave another feast. It lasted for seven days. It was held in the garden of the king's courtyard. It was for all the people who lived in the fort of Susa. Everyone from the least important person to the most important was invited. ⁶The garden was decorated with white and blue linen banners. They hung from ropes that were made out of white linen and purple cloth. The ropes were connected to silver rings on marble pillars. There were gold and silver couches in the garden. They were placed on a floor that was made out of small stones. The floor had purple crystal, marble, mother-of-pearl and other stones of great value. ⁷Royal wine was served in gold cups. Each cup was different from all the others. There was plenty of wine. The king always provided as much as his guests

wanted. [8] He commanded that they should be allowed to drink as much or as little as they wished. He directed all his servants to give his guests what they asked for.

[9] Queen Vashti also gave a feast. Only women were invited. It was held in the royal palace of King Xerxes.

[10] On the seventh day Xerxes was in a good mood because he had drunk a lot of wine. So he gave a command to the seven officials who served him. They were Mehuman, Biztha, Harbona, Bigtha, Abagtha, Zethar and Karkas. [11] King Xerxes told them to bring Queen Vashti to him. He wanted her to come wearing her royal crown. He wanted to show off her beauty to the people and nobles. She was lovely to look at. [12] The attendants told Queen Vashti what the king had ordered her to do. But she refused to come. So the king became very angry.

[13] It was the king's practice to ask for advice about matters of law and fairness. So he spoke with the wise men who understood what was going on at that time. [14] They were the men closest to the king. Their names were Karshena, Shethar, Admatha, Tarshish, Meres, Marsena and Memukan. They were the seven nobles of Persia and Media. They were the king's special advisers and the most important men in the kingdom. [15] "You know the law," the king said. "What should I do to Queen Vashti? She hasn't obeyed my command. The officials told her what I ordered her to do, didn't they?"

[16] Then Memukan gave a reply to the king and the nobles. He said, "Queen Vashti has done what is wrong. But she didn't do it only against you, King Xerxes. She did it also against all the nobles. And she did it against the people in all the territories you rule over. [17] All the women will hear about what the queen has done. Then they won't respect their husbands. They'll say, 'King Xerxes commanded Queen Vashti to be brought to him. But she wouldn't come.' [18] Here is what will start today. The leading women in Persia and Media who have heard about the queen's actions will act in the same way. They'll disobey all your nobles, just as she disobeyed you. They won't have any respect for their husbands. They won't honor them.

[19] "So if it pleases you, send out a royal order. Let it be written down in the laws of Persia and Media. Those laws can never be changed. Let the royal order say that Vashti can never see you again. Also let her position as queen be given to someone who is better than she is. [20] And let your order be announced all through your entire kingdom. Then all women will have respect for their husbands, from the least important to the most important."

[21] The king and his nobles were pleased with that advice. So he did what Memukan had

suggested. ²² The king sent messages out to every territory in the kingdom. He sent them to each territory in its own writing. He sent them to every nation in its own language. The messages announced that every man should rule over his own family, using his own language.

Esther Becomes Queen of Persia

2 Later, the great anger of King Xerxes calmed down. Then he remembered Vashti and what she had done. He also remembered the royal order he had sent out concerning her. ² At that time the king's personal attendants made a suggestion. They said, "King Xerxes, let a search be made for some beautiful young virgins for you. ³ Appoint some officials in every territory in your kingdom. Have them bring all these beautiful young women into the fort of Susa. Put them in the special place where the virgins stay. Then put Hegai in charge of them. He's the official who serves you. He's in charge of the women. Let beauty care be given to the new group of women. ⁴ Then let the young woman who pleases you the most become queen in Vashti's place." The king liked that advice. So he followed it.

⁵ There was a Jew living in the fort of Susa. He was from the tribe of Benjamin. His name was Mordecai. He was the son of Jair. Jair was the son of Shimei. Shimei was the son of Kish. ⁶ Nebuchadnezzar had forced Mordecai to leave Jerusalem. He was among the prisoners who were carried off along with Jehoiachin. Jehoiachin had been king of Judah. Nebuchadnezzar was king of Babylon. ⁷ Mordecai had a cousin named Hadassah. He had raised her because she didn't have a father or mother. Hadassah was also called Esther. She had a lovely figure and was very beautiful. Mordecai had adopted her as his own daughter. He had done it when her father and mother died.

⁸ After the king's order and law were announced, many young women were brought to the fort of Susa. Hegai was put in charge of them. Esther was also taken to the king's palace. She was put under the control of Hegai. He was in charge of the place where the virgins stayed. ⁹ Esther pleased him. He showed her how happy he was with her. Right away he provided her with her beauty care and special food. He appointed seven female attendants to help her. They were chosen from the king's palace. He moved her and her attendants into the best part of the place where the virgins stayed.

¹⁰ Esther hadn't told anyone who her people were. She hadn't talked about her family. That's because Mordecai had told her not to. ¹¹ Mordecai tried to find out how Esther was getting along. He wanted to know what was happening to her. So he walked back and forth near the courtyard by the place where

the virgins stayed. He did it every day.

[12] Each young woman had to complete 12 months of beauty care. They used oil of myrrh for six months. And they used perfume and makeup for the other six months. A virgin's turn to go in to King Xerxes could come only after a full 12 months had passed. [13] And here is how she would go to the king. She would be given anything she wanted from the place where the virgins stayed. She could take it with her to the king's palace. [14] In the evening she would go there. In the morning she would leave. Then she would go to the special place where the king's concubines stayed. She would be put under the control of Shaashgaz. He was the king's official who was in charge of the concubines. She would never return to the king unless he was pleased with her. He had to send for her by name before she could go to him again.

[15] Mordecai had adopted Esther. She had been the daughter of his uncle Abihail. Her turn came to go in to the king. She only asked for what Hegai suggested. He was the king's official who was in charge of the place where the virgins stayed. Everyone who saw Esther was pleased with her. [16] She was taken to King Xerxes in the royal house. It was now the tenth month. That was the month of Tebeth. It was the seventh year of the rule of Xerxes.

[17] The king liked Esther more than he liked any of the other women. She pleased him more than any of the other virgins. So he put a royal crown on her head. He made her queen in Vashti's place. [18] Then the king gave a feast to honor Esther. All his nobles and officials were invited. He announced a holiday all through the territories he ruled over. He freely gave many gifts in keeping with his royal wealth.

Mordecai Uncovers a Plan to Kill the King

[19] The virgins were gathered together a second time. At that time Mordecai was sitting at the palace gate. [20] Esther had kept her family history a secret. She hadn't told anyone who her people were. Mordecai had told her not to. She continued to follow his directions. That's what she had always done when he was bringing her up.

[21] Bigthana and Teresh were two of the king's officers. They guarded the door of the royal palace. They became angry with King Xerxes. So they decided to kill him. They made their evil plans while Mordecai was sitting at the palace gate. [22] So Mordecai found out about it and told Queen Esther. Then she reported it to the king. She told him that Mordecai had uncovered the plans against him. [23] Some people checked Esther's report. And they found out it was true. So the two officials were put to death. Then poles were stuck through them. They

were set up where people could see them. All of that was written in the official records. It was written down while the king was watching.

Haman Plans to Destroy the Jews

3 After those events, King Xerxes honored Haman. Haman was the son of Hammedatha. He was from the family line of Agag. The king gave Haman a higher position than he had before. He gave him a seat of honor. It was higher than the positions any of the other nobles had. ² All the royal officials at the palace gate got down on their knees. They gave honor to Haman. That's because the king had commanded them to do it. But Mordecai refused to get down on his knees. He wouldn't give Haman any honor at all.

³ The royal officials at the palace gate asked Mordecai a question. They said, "Why don't you obey the king's command?" ⁴ Day after day they spoke to him. But he still refused to obey. So they told Haman about it. They wanted to see whether he would let Mordecai get away with what he was doing. Mordecai had told them he was a Jew.

⁵ Haman noticed that Mordecai wouldn't get down on his knees. He wouldn't give Haman any honor. So Haman was very angry. ⁶ But he had found out who Mordecai's people were. So he didn't want to kill only Mordecai. He also looked for a way to destroy all Mordecai's peo-

ple. They were Jews. He wanted to kill all of them everywhere in the kingdom of Xerxes.

⁷ The lot was cast in front of Haman. The lot was called Pur. It was cast in the first month of the 12th year that Xerxes was king. That month was called Nisan. The lot was cast to choose a day and a month. The month chosen was the 12th month. That month was called Adar.

⁸ Then Haman said to King Xerxes, "Certain people are scattered among the nations. They live in all the territories in your kingdom. They keep themselves separate from everyone else. Their practices are different from the practices of all other people. They don't obey your laws. It really isn't good for you to put up with them. ⁹ If it pleases you, give the order to destroy them. I'll even add 375 tons of silver to the king's officials for the royal treasures."

¹⁰ So the king took his ring off his finger. The ring had his royal seal on it. He gave the ring to Haman. Haman was the son of Hammedatha, the Agagite. Haman was the enemy of the Jews. ¹¹ "Keep the money," the king said to Haman. "Do what you want to with those people."

¹² The king sent for the royal secretaries. It was the 13th day of the first month. The secretaries wrote down all Haman's orders. They wrote them down in the writing of each territory in the kingdom. They also wrote them in the language of each nation. The orders were sent

to the royal officials and to the governors of the territories. And the orders were also sent to the nobles of the nations. The orders were written in the name of King Xerxes himself. And they were stamped with his own official mark. ¹³ They were carried by messengers. They were sent to all the king's territories. The orders commanded people to destroy, kill and wipe out all the Jews. That included young people and old people alike. It included women and children. All the Jews were supposed to be killed on a single day. That day was the 13th day of the 12th month. It was the month of Adar. The orders also commanded people to take everything that belonged to the Jews. ¹⁴ A copy of the order had to be sent out as law. It had to be sent to every territory in the kingdom. It had to be announced to the people of every nation. Then they would be ready for that day. ¹⁵ The king commanded the messengers to go out. So they did. The order was sent out from the fort of Susa. Then the king and Haman sat down to drink wine. But the people in the city were bewildered.

Mordecai Talks Esther Into Helping the Jews

4 Mordecai found out about everything that had been done. So he tore his clothes. He put on the rough clothing people wear when they're sad. He sat down in ashes. Then he went out into the city. He wept out loud. He cried bitter tears. ² But he only went as far as the palace gate. That's because no one dressed in that rough clothing was allowed to go through it. ³ All the Jews were very sad. They didn't eat anything. They wept and cried. Many of them put on the rough clothing people wear when they're sad. They were lying down in ashes. They did all these things in every territory where the king's order and law had been sent.

⁴ Esther's male and female attendants came to her. They told her about Mordecai. So she became very troubled. She wanted him to take off his rough clothing. So she sent him other clothes to wear. But he wouldn't accept them. ⁵ Then Esther sent for Hathak. He was one of the king's officials. He had been appointed to take care of her. She ordered him to find out what was troubling Mordecai. She wanted to know why he was so upset.

⁶ So Hathak went out to see Mordecai. He was in the open area in front of the palace gate. ⁷ Mordecai told him everything that had happened to him. He told him about the exact amount of money Haman had promised to add to the royal treasures. He said Haman wanted it to be used to pay some men to destroy the Jews. ⁸ Mordecai also gave Hathak a copy of the order. It commanded people to wipe out the Jews. The order had been sent from Susa. Mordecai told Hathak to show the order to Esther.

He wanted Hathak to explain it to her. Mordecai told him to tell her to go and beg the king for mercy. Mordecai wanted her to make an appeal to the king for her people.

9 Hathak went back and reported to Esther what Mordecai had said. 10 Then Esther directed him to give an answer to Mordecai. She told him to say, 11 "There is a certain law that everyone knows about. All the king's officials know about it. The people in the royal territories know about it. It applies to any man or woman who approaches the king in the inner courtyard without being sent for. It says they must be put to death. But there is a way out. Suppose the king reaches out his gold scepter toward them. Then their lives will be spared. But 30 days have gone by since the king sent for me."

12 Esther's words were reported to Mordecai. 13 Then he sent back an answer. He said, "You live in the king's palace. But don't think that just because you are there you will be the only Jew who will escape. 14 What if you don't say anything at this time? Then help for the Jews will come from another place. But you and your family will die. Who knows? It's possible that you became queen for a time just like this."

15 Then Esther sent a reply to Mordecai. She said, 16 "Go. Gather together all the Jews who are in Susa. And fast for my benefit. Don't eat or drink anything for three days. Don't do it night or day. I and my attendants will fast just as you do. Then I'll go to the king. I'll do it even though it's against the law. And if I have to die, I'll die."

17 So Mordecai went away. He carried out all Esther's directions.

Esther Asks the King for a Favor

5 On the third day Esther put on her royal robes. She stood in the inner courtyard of the palace. It was in front of the king's hall. The king was sitting on his royal throne in the hall. He was facing the entrance. 2 He saw Queen Esther standing in the courtyard. He was pleased with her. So he reached out toward her the gold scepter that was in his hand. Then Esther approached him. She touched the tip of the scepter.

3 The king asked, "What is it, Queen Esther? What do you want? I'll give it to you. I'll even give you up to half of my kingdom."

4 Esther replied, "King Xerxes, if it pleases you, come to a feast today. I've prepared it for you. Please have Haman come with you."

5 "Bring Haman at once," the king said to his servants. "Then we'll do what Esther asks."

So the king and Haman went to the feast Esther had prepared. 6 As they were drinking wine, the king asked Esther the same question again. He said, "What do you want? I'll give it to you. What do you want me to do for you? I'll even give you up to half of my kingdom."

7 Esther replied, "Here is what I want. Here is my appeal to you. 8 I hope you will be pleased to give me what I want. And I hope you will be pleased to listen to my appeal. If you are, I'd like you and Haman to come tomorrow to the feast I'll prepare for you. Then I'll answer your question."

Haman Is Very Angry With Mordecai

9 That day Haman was happy. So he left the palace in a good mood. But then he saw Mordecai at the palace gate. He noticed that Mordecai didn't stand up when he walked by. In fact, Mordecai didn't have any respect for him at all. So he was very angry with him. 10 But Haman was able to control himself. He went on home.

Haman called together his friends and his wife Zeresh. 11 He bragged to them about how rich he was. He talked about how many sons he had. He spoke about all the ways the king had honored him. He bragged about how the king had given him a high position. It was higher than the position of any of the other nobles and officials. 12 "And that's not all," Haman added. "I'm the only person Queen Esther invited to come with the king to the feast she gave. Now she has invited me along with the king tomorrow. 13 But even all of that doesn't satisfy me. I won't be satisfied as long as I see that Jew Mordecai sitting at the palace gate."

14 Haman's wife Zeresh and all his friends said to him, "Get a pole. In the morning, ask the king to have Mordecai put to death. Have the pole stuck through his body. Set it up at a place where it will be 75 feet above the ground. Everyone will be able to see it there. Then go to the feast with the king. Have a good time." Haman was delighted with that suggestion. So he got the pole ready.

The King Honors Mordecai

6 That night the king couldn't sleep. So he ordered the official records of his rule to be brought in. He ordered someone to read them to him. 2 What Mordecai had done was written there. He had uncovered the plans of Bigthana and Teresh. They were two of the king's officers who guarded the door of the royal palace. They had decided to kill King Xerxes.

3 "What great honor has Mordecai received for doing that?" the king asked.

"Nothing has been done for him," his attendants answered.

4 The king asked, "Who is in the courtyard?" Haman had just entered the outer courtyard of the palace. He had come to speak to the king about putting Mordecai to death. He wanted to talk about putting Mordecai's body on the pole he had prepared for him.

5 The king's attendants said to

him, "Haman is standing in the courtyard."

"Bring him in," the king ordered.

⁶ Haman entered. Then the king asked him, "What should be done for the man I want to honor?"

Haman said to himself, "Is there anyone the king would rather honor than me?" ⁷ So he answered the king. He said, "Here is what you should do for the man you want to honor. ⁸ Have your servants get a royal robe you have worn. Have them bring a horse you have ridden on. Have a royal mark placed on its head. ⁹ Then give the robe and horse to one of your most noble princes. Let the robe be put on the man you want to honor. Let him be led on the horse through the city streets. Let people announce in front of him, 'This is what is done for the man the king wants to honor!' "

¹⁰ "Go right away," the king commanded Haman. "Get the robe. Bring the horse. Do exactly what you have suggested. Do it for Mordecai the Jew. He's sitting out there at the palace gate. Make sure you do everything you have suggested."

¹¹ So Haman got the robe and the horse. He put the robe on Mordecai. And he led him on horseback through the city streets. He walked along in front of him and announced, "This is what is done for the man the king wants to honor!"

¹² After that, Mordecai returned to the palace gate. But Haman rushed home. He covered his head because he was very sad. ¹³ He told his wife Zeresh everything that had happened to him. He also told all his friends.

His advisers and his wife Zeresh spoke to him. They said, "Your fall from power started with Mordecai. He's a Jew. So now you can't stand up against him. You are going to be destroyed!" ¹⁴ They were still talking with him when the king's officials arrived. They hurried Haman away to the feast Esther had prepared.

Haman Is Put to Death

7 So the king and Haman went to Queen Esther's feast. ² They were drinking wine on the second day. The king again asked, "What do you want, Queen Esther? I'll give it to you. What do you want me to do for you? I'll even give you up to half of my kingdom."

³ Then Queen Esther answered, "Your Majesty, I hope you will be pleased to let me live. That's what I want. Please spare my people. That's my appeal to you. ⁴ My people and I have been sold to be destroyed. We've been sold to be killed and wiped out. Suppose we had only been sold as male and female slaves. Then I wouldn't have said anything. That kind of suffering wouldn't be a good enough reason to bother you."

⁵ King Xerxes asked Queen Esther, "Who is the man who

has dared to do such a thing? And where is he?"

⁶ Esther said, "The man hates us! He's our enemy! He's this evil Haman!"

Then Haman was terrified in front of the king and queen. ⁷ The king got up. He was very angry. He left his wine and went out into the palace garden. But Haman realized that the king had already decided what he was going to do to him. So he stayed behind to beg Queen Esther for his life.

⁸ The king returned from the palace garden to the dinner hall. Just then he saw Haman falling on the couch where Esther was lying.

The king shouted, "Will he even treat the queen like this? Will he harm her while she's right here with me in the palace?"

As soon as the king finished speaking, his men covered Haman's face. ⁹ Then Harbona said, "There's a pole standing near Haman's house. He has prepared it for Mordecai. Mordecai is the one who spoke up to help you. Haman had planned to have him put to death. He was going to have the pole stuck through his body. Then he was going to set it up at a place where it would be 75 feet above the ground." Harbona was one of the officials who attended the king.

The king said to his men, "Put Haman to death! Stick the pole through his body! Set it up where everyone can see it!" ¹⁰ So they did. And they used the pole Haman had prepared for Mordecai. Then the king's anger calmed down.

The King Allows the Jews to Fight for Their Lives

8 That same day King Xerxes gave Queen Esther everything Haman had owned. Haman had been the enemy of the Jews. Esther had told the king that Mordecai was her cousin. So Mordecai came to see the king. ² The king took his ring off. It had his royal mark on it. He had taken it back from Haman. Now he gave it to Mordecai. And Esther put Mordecai in charge of everything Haman had owned.

³ Esther made another appeal to the king. She fell at his feet and wept. She begged him to put an end to the evil plan of Haman, the Agagite. He had decided to kill the Jews. ⁴ The king reached out his gold scepter toward Esther. She got up and stood in front of him.

⁵ She said, "King Xerxes, I hope you will think what I'm asking is the right thing to do. I hope you are pleased with me. If you are, and if it pleases you, let an order be written. Let it take the place of the messages Haman wrote. Haman was the son of Hammedatha, the Agagite. He planned to kill the Jews. He wrote orders to destroy us in all your territories. ⁶ I couldn't stand by and see the horrible trouble that would fall on my people! I couldn't stand to see my family destroyed!"

7 King Xerxes gave a reply to Queen Esther and Mordecai the Jew. He said, "Haman attacked the Jews. So I've given Esther everything he owned. My men have stuck a pole through his dead body. And they've set it up where everyone can see it. 8 Now write another order in my name. Do it for the benefit of the Jews. Do what seems best to you. Stamp the order with my royal mark. Nothing that is written in my name and stamped with my mark can ever be changed."

9 Right away the king sent for the royal secretaries. It was the 23rd day of the third month. That was the month of Sivan. They wrote down all Mordecai's orders to the Jews. They also wrote them to the royal officials, the governors and the nobles of the 127 territories in his kingdom. The territories reached from India all the way to Cush. The orders were written down in the writing of each territory. They were written in the language of each nation. They were also written to the Jews in their own writing and language. 10 Mordecai wrote the orders in the name of King Xerxes. He stamped them with the king's royal mark. He sent them by messengers on horseback. They rode fast horses that were raised just for the king.

11 The Jews in every city could now gather together and fight for their lives. The king's order gave them that right. But suppose soldiers from any nation or territory attacked them, their women or children. Then the Jews could destroy, kill and wipe out those soldiers. They could also take the goods that belonged to their enemies. 12 A day was appointed for the Jews to do that in all the king's territories. It was the 13th day of the 12th month. That was the month of Adar. 13 A copy of the order was sent out as law in every territory. It was announced to the people of every nation. So the Jews would be ready on that day. They could pay back their enemies.

14 The messengers rode on the royal horses. They raced along. That's what the king commanded them to do. The order was also sent out in the fort of Susa.

The Jews Win the Battle Over Their Enemies

15 Mordecai left the king and went on his way. Mordecai was wearing royal clothes when he went. They were blue and white. He was also wearing a large gold crown. And he was wearing a purple coat. It was made out of fine linen. The city of Susa celebrated with great joy. 16 The Jews were filled with joy and happiness. They were very glad because now they were being honored. 17 They celebrated and enjoyed good food. They were glad and full of joy. That was true everywhere the king's order came. It was true in every territory and every city. Many people from other nations announced that they had become

Jews. That's because they were so afraid of the Jews.

9 The king's order had to be carried out on the 13th day of the 12th month. That was the month of Adar. On that day the enemies of the Jews had hoped to win the battle over them. But now everything had changed. The Jews had gained the advantage over those who hated them. ² The Jews gathered together in their cities. They gathered in all the territories King Xerxes ruled over. They came together to attack those who were trying to destroy them. No one could stand up against them. The people from all the other nations were afraid of them. ³ All the nobles in the territories helped the Jews. So did the royal officials, the governors and the king's officers. That's because they were so afraid of Mordecai. ⁴ He was well known in the palace. His fame spread all through the territories. So he became more and more important.

⁵ The Jews struck down with swords all their enemies. They killed them and destroyed them. They did what they pleased to those who hated them. ⁶ The Jews killed 500 men. They destroyed them in the fort of Susa. ⁷ They also killed Parshandatha, Dalphon, Aspatha, ⁸ Poratha, Adalia, Aridatha, ⁹ Parmashta, Arisai, Aridai and Vaizatha. ¹⁰ They were the ten sons of Haman. He was the son of Hammedatha. Haman had been the enemy of the Jews. They didn't take anything that belonged to their enemies.

¹¹ A report was brought to the king that same day. He was told how many men had been killed in the fort of Susa. ¹² He said to Queen Esther, "The Jews have killed 500 men. They destroyed them in the fort of Susa. They also killed the ten sons of Haman there. What have they done in the rest of my territories? Now what do you want? I'll give it to you. What do you want me to do for you? I'll do that too."

¹³ "If it pleases you," Esther answered, "let the Jews in Susa carry out today's order tomorrow also. Stick poles through the dead bodies of Haman's ten sons. Set them up where everyone can see them."

¹⁴ So the king commanded that it be done. An order was sent out in Susa. And the king's men did to the bodies of Haman's sons everything they were told to do. ¹⁵ The Jews in Susa came together on the 14th day of the month of Adar. They put 300 men to death in Susa. But they didn't take anything that belonged to those men.

¹⁶ During that time, the rest of the Jews also gathered together. They lived in the king's territories. They came together to fight for their lives. They didn't want their enemies to bother them anymore. They wanted to get some peace and rest. So they killed 75,000 of their enemies. But they didn't take anything that belonged to them. ¹⁷ It happened on the 13th of Adar. On the 14th day they rested. They made it a day to celebrate

with great joy. And they enjoyed good food.

¹⁸ But the Jews in Susa had gathered together on the 13th and 14th. Then on the 15th they rested. They made it a day to celebrate with great joy. And they enjoyed good food.

¹⁹ That's why Jews who live out in the villages celebrate on the 14th of Adar. They celebrate that day with great joy. And they enjoy good food. They also give presents to each other on that day.

Purim Is Celebrated

²⁰ Mordecai wrote down these events. He sent letters to all the Jews all through the territories of King Xerxes. It didn't matter whether the Jews lived nearby or far away. ²¹ Mordecai told them to celebrate the 14th and 15th days of the month of Adar. He wanted them to do it every year. ²² Mordecai told the Jews to celebrate the time when they got rest from their enemies. That was the month when their sadness was turned into joy. It was when their weeping turned into a day for celebrating. He wrote the letters to celebrate those days as times of joy. He wanted the people to enjoy good food. He told them to give presents of food to one another. He also wanted them to give gifts to people who were poor.

²³ So the Jews agreed to continue the celebrating they had started. They kept doing what Mordecai had written to them. ²⁴ Haman was the son of Ham-medatha, the Agagite. He had been the enemy of all the Jews. He had planned to destroy them. He had cast the lot to destroy them completely. The lot was called Pur. ²⁵ But the king had found out about Haman's evil plan. So the king had sent out written orders. He had ordered that Haman's evil plan against the Jews should happen to him instead. The king also commanded that poles be stuck through the dead bodies of Haman and his sons. Then they should be set up where everyone could see them. ²⁶ The days the Jews were celebrating were called Purim. Purim comes from the word Pur. Pur means Lot. Now the Jews celebrate these two days every year. They do it because of everything that was written in Mordecai's letter. They also do it because of what they had seen and what had happened to them. ²⁷ So they established it as a regular practice. They decided they would always observe these two days of the year. They would celebrate in the required way. And they would celebrate at the appointed time. They and their children after them would always observe these days. And so would all who join them. ²⁸ The days should be remembered and celebrated. They should be remembered by every family for all time to come. They should be celebrated in every territory and in every city. The Jews should never stop celebrating the days of Purim. Their children after

them should always remember these days.

²⁹ So Queen Esther, the daughter of Abihail, wrote a second letter. She wrote it together with Mordecai the Jew. They wanted to give their full authority to this second letter about Purim. ³⁰ Mordecai sent letters to all the Jews in the 127 territories of the kingdom of Xerxes. The letters had messages of kindness and hope in them. ³¹ The letters established the days of Purim at their appointed times. They spoke about what Mordecai the Jew and Queen Esther had ordered the people to do. Everything should be done in keeping with the directions the Jews had set up for themselves and their children after them. The directions applied to their times of fasting and sadness. ³² Esther's order established the rules about Purim. It was written down in the records.

The Greatness of Mordecai

10 King Xerxes required people all through his kingdom to bring gifts. King Xerxes required gifts from its farthest shores. ² All the king's powerful and mighty acts are written down. That includes the whole story of how important Mordecai was. The king had given him a position of great honor. All these things are written in the official records of the kings of Media and Persia. ³ The position of Mordecai the Jew was second only to the position of King Xerxes. Mordecai was the most important Jew. All the other Jews had the highest respect for him. That's because he worked for the good of his people. And he spoke up for the benefit of all the Jews.

Job

Introduction:

There are five books of poems and wisdom in the Bible. Job is the first of these books. Job was a rich man. He loved God very much. But some bad things happened to him. Had Job done something wrong?

Job had three friends. They said Job had done something bad and made God angry. They said that was why bad things happened to him. But Job did not agree. He said he still loved God very much.

The book of Job tells us that sometimes God lets bad things happen to his people. But he still loves us and takes care of us. In the end, God takes care of all things.

Outline of contents:

The Story Begins

1 There was a man who lived in the land of Uz. His name was Job. He was honest. He did what was right. He had respect for God and avoided evil. ² Job had seven sons and three daughters. ³ He owned 7,000 sheep and 3,000 camels. He owned 500 pairs of oxen and 500 donkeys. He also had a large number of servants. He was the most important man among all the people in the east.

⁴ His sons used to give feasts in their homes on their birthdays. They would invite their three sisters to eat and drink with them. ⁵ The time for enjoying good food would end. Then Job would make plans for his children to be made pure and "clean." He would sacrifice a burnt offering for each of them. He would do it early in the morning. He would think, "Perhaps my children have sinned. Maybe they have spoken evil things against God in their hearts." That's what Job always did for his children when he felt they had sinned.

⁶ One day angels came to the LORD. Satan also came with them. ⁷ The LORD said to Satan, "Where have you come from?"

Satan answered, "From traveling all around the earth. I've

been going from one end of it to the other."

⁸ Then the LORD said to Satan, "Have you thought about my servant Job? There isn't anyone on earth like him. He is honest. He does what is right. He has respect for God and avoids evil."

⁹ "You always give Job everything he needs," Satan replied. "That's why he has respect for you. ¹⁰ Haven't you guarded him and his family? Haven't you taken care of everything he has? You have blessed everything he does. His flocks and herds are spread all through the land. ¹¹ But now reach out your hand and strike down everything he has. Then I'm sure he will speak evil things against you. In fact, he'll do it right in front of you."

¹² The LORD said to Satan, "All right. I am handing everything he has over to you. But do not touch the man himself."

Then Satan left the LORD and went on his way.

¹³ One day Job's sons and daughters were at their oldest brother's house. They were enjoying good food and drinking wine. ¹⁴ During that time a messenger came to Job. He said, "The oxen were plowing. The donkeys were eating grass near them. ¹⁵ Then the Sabeans attacked us and carried off the animals. They killed some of the servants with their swords. I'm the only one who has escaped to tell you!"

¹⁶ While he was still speaking, a second messenger came. He said, "God sent lightning from the sky. It struck the sheep and killed them. It burned up some of the servants. I'm the only one who has escaped to tell you!"

¹⁷ While he was still speaking, a third messenger came. He said, "The Chaldeans separated themselves into three groups. They attacked your camels and carried them off. They killed the rest of the servants with their swords. I'm the only one who has escaped to tell you!"

¹⁸ While he was still speaking, a fourth messenger came. He said, "Your sons and daughters were at their oldest brother's house. They were enjoying good food and drinking wine. ¹⁹ Suddenly a strong wind blew in from the desert. It struck the four corners of the house. The house fell down on your children. Now all of them are dead. I'm the only one who has escaped to tell you!"

²⁰ After Job heard all these reports, he got up and tore his robe. He shaved his head. Then he fell to the ground and worshiped the LORD. ²¹ He said,

"I was born naked.
    And I'll leave here naked.
The LORD has given, and the
    LORD has taken away.
May the name of the LORD
    be praised."

²² In spite of everything, Job didn't sin by blaming God for doing anything wrong.

2 On another day angels came to the LORD. Satan also came to him along with them. ² The LORD said to Satan, "Where have you come from?"

Satan answered, "From traveling all around the earth. I've been going from one end of it to the other."

3 Then the LORD said to Satan, "Have you thought about my servant Job? There isn't anyone on earth like him. He is honest. He does what is right. He has respect for God and avoids evil. You tried to turn me against him. You wanted me to destroy him without any reason. But he still continues to be faithful."

4 Satan replied, "A man will give everything he has to save himself. So Job is willing to give up the lives of his family to save his own life. 5 But now reach out your hand and strike his flesh and bones. Then I'm sure he will speak evil things against you. In fact, he'll do it right in front of you."

6 The LORD said to Satan, "All right. I am handing him over to you. But you must spare his life."

7 Then Satan left the LORD and went on his way. He sent painful sores on Job. They covered him from the bottom of his feet to the top of his head. 8 He got part of a broken pot. He used it to scrape his skin. He did it while he was sitting in ashes.

9 His wife said to him, "Are you still continuing to be faithful to the LORD? Speak evil things against him and die!"

10 Job replied, "You are talking like a foolish woman. We accept good things from God. So we should also accept trouble when he sends it."

In spite of everything, Job didn't say anything that was sinful.

11 Job had three friends named Eliphaz the Temanite, Bildad the Shuhite, and Zophar the Naamathite. They heard about all the troubles that had come to Job. So they started out from their homes. They had agreed to meet together. They wanted to go and show their concern for Job. They wanted to comfort him. 12 When they got closer to where he lived, they could see him. But they could hardly recognize him. They began to weep out loud. They tore their robes and sprinkled dust on their heads. 13 Then they sat down on the ground with him for seven days and seven nights. No one said a word to him. That's because they saw how much he was suffering.

Job Wishes He Had Never Been Born

3 After a while, Job opened his mouth to speak. He cursed the day he had been born. 2 He said,

3 "May the day I was born be
   wiped out.
   May the night be wiped
      away when people said,
      'A boy is born!'
4 May that day turn into
      darkness.
   May God in heaven not
      care about it.
   May no light shine on it.
5 May gloom and total
      darkness take it back.
   May a cloud settle over it.
   May blackness cover it up.

⁶May deep darkness take over
the night I was born.
May it not be included
among the days of the
year.
May it never appear in any
of the months.
⁷May no children ever have
been born on that night.
May no shout of joy be
heard in it.
⁸May people say evil things
about that day.
May people ready to
wake the sea monster
Leviathan say evil things
about that day.
⁹May its morning stars
become dark.
May it lose all hope of ever
seeing daylight.
May it not see the first light
of the morning sun.
¹⁰It didn't keep my mother
from letting me be born.
It didn't keep my eyes from
seeing trouble.
¹¹"Why didn't I die when I was
born?
Why didn't I die as I came
out of my mother's body?
¹²Why was I placed on her
knees?
Why did her breasts give
me milk?
¹³If all of that hadn't happened,
I would be lying down in
peace.
I'd be asleep and at rest in
the grave.
¹⁴I'd be with the earth's kings
and rulers.
They had built for
themselves places that
are now destroyed.

¹⁵I'd be with princes who used
to have gold.
They had filled their
houses with silver.
¹⁶Why wasn't I buried like
a baby who was born
dead?
Why wasn't I buried like a
child who never saw the
light of day?
¹⁷In the grave, sinful people
don't cause trouble
anymore.
And there tired people find
rest.
¹⁸Prisoners also enjoy peace
there.
They don't hear a slave
driver shouting at them
anymore.
¹⁹The least important and most
important people are
there.
And there the slaves are set
free from their owners.
²⁰"Why should those who
suffer ever be born?
Why should life be given to
those whose spirits are
bitter?
²¹Why is life given to those
who long for death that
doesn't come?
Why is it given to those
who would rather search
for death
than for hidden treasure?
²²Why is life given to those who
are actually happy and
glad
when they reach the grave?
²³Why is life given to a man
like me?
God hasn't told me what
will happen to me.

He has surrounded me
　　with nothing but trouble.
24 Sighs have become my food
　　every day.
　　Groans pour out of me like
　　water.
25 What I was afraid of has
　　come on me.
　　What I worried about has
　　happened to me.
26 I don't have any peace and
　　quiet.
　　I can't find any rest. All I
　　have is trouble."

The First Speech of Eliphaz

4 Then Eliphaz the Temanite
replied,

2 "Job, suppose someone tries
　　to talk to you.
　　Will that make you uneasy?
　　I can't keep from speaking
　　up.
3 Look, you taught many people.
　　You made weak hands
　　strong.
4 Your words helped those who
　　had fallen down.
　　You made shaky knees
　　strong.
5 Now trouble comes to you.
　　And you are unhappy
　　about it.
　　It strikes you down. And
　　you are afraid.
6 Shouldn't you worship God
　　and trust in him?
　　Shouldn't your honest life
　　give you hope?

7 "Here's something to think
　　about.
　　Have people who aren't
　　guilty ever been wiped
　　out?

Have honest people
　　ever been completely
　　destroyed?
8 Here's what I've observed.
　　People gather a crop from
　　what they plant.
　　If they plant evil and
　　trouble, that's what they
　　will harvest.
9 The breath of God destroys
　　them.
　　The blast of his anger
　　wipes them out.
10 Powerful lions might roar
　　and growl.
　　But their teeth are broken.
11 Lions die because they don't
　　have any food.
　　Then their cubs are
　　scattered.

12 "A message came to me in
　　secret.
　　It was as quiet as a whisper.
13 I had a scary dream one
　　night.
　　I was sound asleep.
14 Fear and trembling seized
　　me.
　　That made every bone in
　　my body shake.
15 A spirit glided past my face.
　　The hair on my body stood
　　on end.
16 Then the spirit stopped.
　　But I couldn't tell what it
　　was.
　　Something stood there in
　　front of me.
　　I heard a soft voice.
17 It said, 'Can a human being
　　be more right than
　　God?
　　Can even a strong man be
　　more pure than the God
　　who made him?

18 God doesn't trust those who
serve him.
He even brings charges
against his angels.
19 So he'll certainly find fault
with human beings.
After all, they are made out
of dust.
They can be crushed more
easily than a moth.
20 Between sunrise and sunset
they are broken to
pieces.
Nobody even notices. They
disappear forever.
21 Like a tent that falls down,
they get weak.
They die because they
didn't follow God's
wisdom.' "

5 Eliphaz continued,

"Call out if you want to, Job.
But who will answer you?
Which one of the holy
angels will you turn to?
2 Anger kills foolish people.
Jealousy destroys those
who are childish.
3 I saw that foolish people were
having success.
But suddenly harm came
to their their homes.
4 Their children aren't safe
at all.
They lose their case in
court.
No one speaks up for them.
5 Hungry people eat up the
crops of the foolish.
They even take the food
that grows among
thorns.
Thirsty people long for the
wealth of the foolish.

6 Hard times don't just grow
out of the soil.
Trouble doesn't jump out
of the ground.
7 People are born to have
trouble.
And that's just as sure as
sparks fly up.
8 "If I were you, I'd make my
appeal to God.
I'd bring my case to be
judged by him.
9 He does wonderful things
that can't be
understood.
He does miracles that can't
even be counted.
10 He sends rain on the earth.
He sends water on the
countryside.
11 He lifts up people who are
lowly in spirit.
He lifts up those who are
sad.
He keeps them safe.
12 He stops the evil plans of
those who are clever.
The work of their hands
doesn't succeed.
13 Some people think they are
so wise.
But God catches them in
their own tricks.
He sweeps away the evil
plans of sinful people.
14 Darkness covers them in the
daytime.
At noon they feel their
way around as if it were
night.
15 God saves needy people from
the cutting words of
their enemies.
He saves them from their
power.

16 So poor people have hope.
And God shuts the mouths
of those who don't treat
others fairly.

17 "Blessed is the person God
corrects.
So don't hate the Mighty
One's training.
18 He wounds. But he also
bandages up those he
wounds.
He harms. But his hands
also heal those he
harms.
19 From six troubles he will save
you.
Even if you are in trouble
seven times, no harm
will come to you.
20 When there isn't enough
food, God will keep you
from dying.
When you go into battle, he
won't let a sword strike
you down.
21 He will keep you safe from
words that can hurt you.
You won't need to be
afraid
when everything is being
destroyed.
22 You will laugh when things
are being destroyed.
You will enjoy life even
when there isn't enough
food.
You won't be afraid of wild
animals.
23 You will make a covenant
with the stones in the
fields.
They won't keep your crops
from growing.
Even wild animals will be
at peace with you.

24 You will know that the tent
you live in is secure.
You will check out your
property.
You will see that nothing is
missing.
25 You can be sure you will have
a lot of children.
They will be as many as
the blades of grass on the
earth.
26 You will go down to the grave
while you are still very
strong.
You will be like a crop that
is gathered at the right
time.

27 "We have carefully studied
all these things.
And they are true.
So pay attention to them.
Apply them to yourself."

Job's Reply

6 Job replied,

2 "I wish my great pain could
be weighed!
I wish all my suffering
could be weighed on
scales!
3 I'm sure it would weigh more
than the grains of sand
on the seashore.
No wonder I've been so
quick to speak!
4 The Mighty One has shot me
with his arrows.
I have to drink their
poison.
God's terrors are aimed at
me.
5 Does a wild donkey cry out
when it has enough
grass?

Does an ox call out when it
has plenty of food?
⁶ Is food that doesn't have any
taste eaten without salt?
Is there any flavor in the
sap of a mallow plant?
⁷ I refuse to touch that kind of
food.
It makes me sick.

⁸ "I wish I could have what I'm
asking for!
I wish God would give me
what I'm hoping for!
⁹ I wish he would crush me!
I wish he would just cut off
my life!
¹⁰ Then I'd still have one thing
to comfort me.
It would be that I haven't
said no to the Holy One's
commands.
That would give me joy
in spite of my pain that
never ends.

¹¹ "I'm so weak that I no longer
have any hope.
Things have gotten so bad
that I can't wait for help
anymore.
¹² Am I as strong as stone?
Is my body made out of
bronze?
¹³ I don't have the power to help
myself.
All hope of success has
been taken away from
me.

¹⁴ "A person shouldn't stop
being kind to a friend.
Anyone who does that
stops showing respect
for the Mighty One.
¹⁵ But my friends have stopped
being kind to me.

They are like streams that
only flow for part of the
year.
They are like rivers that
flow over their banks
¹⁶ when the ice begins to
break up.
The streams rise when the
snow starts to melt.
¹⁷ But they stop flowing when
the dry season comes.
They disappear from their
stream beds when the
weather warms up.
¹⁸ Groups of traders turn away
from their usual paths.
They go off into the dry
and empty land.
And they die there.
¹⁹ Traders from Tema look for
water.
Traveling merchants
from Sheba also hope
to find it.
²⁰ They become troubled
because they had
expected to find some.
But when they arrive at the
stream beds,
they don't find any water
at all.
²¹ And now, my friends, you
haven't helped me either.
You see the horrible
condition I'm in.
And that makes you
afraid.
²² I've never said, 'Give me
something to help me.
Use your wealth to set me
free.
²³ Save me from the power of
my enemy.
Rescue me from the power
of mean people.'

24 "Teach me. Then I'll be quiet.
Show me what I've done
wrong.
25 Honest words are so painful!
But your reasoning doesn't
prove anything.
26 Are you trying to correct
what I'm saying?
Are you treating my
hopeless words like
nothing but wind?
27 You would even cast lots for
those whose fathers have
died.
You would even trade away
your closest friend.

28 "But now please look at me.
Would I tell you a lie right
here in front of you?
29 Stop what you are saying.
Don't be so unfair.
Think it over again.
You are trying to take my
honesty away from me.
30 Has my mouth spoken
anything that is evil?
Do my lips say things that
are hateful?"

7 Job continued,

"Don't all human beings have
to work hard on this earth?
Aren't their days like the
days of hired workers?
2 I've been like a slave
who longs for the evening
shadows to come.
I've been like a hired worker
who is waiting to be paid.
3 I've been given several
months that were useless
to me.
My nights have been filled
with suffering.

4 When I lie down I think,
'How long will it be before I
can get up?'
The night drags on.
I toss and turn until
sunrise.
5 My body is covered with
worms and sores.
My skin is broken. It has
boils all over it.

6 "My days pass by faster than
a weaver can work.
They come to an end. I
don't have any hope.
7 God, remember that my life
is only a breath.
I'll never be happy again.
8 The eyes that see me now
won't see me anymore.
You will look for me. But I'll
be gone.
9 When a cloud disappears, it's
gone forever.
And anyone who goes
down to the grave never
returns.
10 He never comes home
again.
Even his own family
doesn't remember him.

11 "So I won't keep quiet.
When I'm suffering greatly,
I'll speak out.
When my spirit is bitter, I'll
tell you how unhappy I
am.
12 Am I the ocean? Am I the sea
monster?
If I'm not, why do you
guard me so closely?
13 Sometimes I think my bed
will comfort me.
I think my couch will keep
me from being unhappy.

¹⁴ But even then you send me
   dreams that frighten
   me.
   You send me visions that
   terrify me.
¹⁵ So I would rather choke to
   death.
   That would be better than
   living in this body of
   mine.
¹⁶ I hate my life. I don't want to
   live forever.
   Leave me alone. My days
   don't mean anything
   to me.

¹⁷ "What are human beings that
   you think so much of
   them?
   What are they that you pay
   so much attention to
   them?
¹⁸ You check up on them every
   morning.
   You test them every
   moment.
¹⁹ Won't you ever look away
   from me?
   Won't you leave me alone
   even for one second?
²⁰ If I've really sinned, tell me
   what I've done to you.
   You see everything we do.
   Why do you shoot your
   arrows at me?
   Have I become a problem
   to you?
²¹ Why don't you forgive the
   wrong things I've
   done?
   Why don't you forgive me
   for my sins?
   I'll soon lie down in the dust
   of my grave.
   You will search for me. But
   I'll be gone."

The First Speech of Bildad

8 Then Bildad the Shuhite replied,

² "Job, how long will you talk
   like that?
   Your words don't have any
   meaning.
³ Does God ever treat people
   unfairly?
   Does the Mighty One make
   what is wrong
   appear to be right?
⁴ Your children sinned against
   him.
   So he punished them for
   their sin.
⁵ But seek God with all your
   heart.
   Make your appeal to the
   Mighty One.
⁶ Be pure and honest.
   And he will rise up and
   help you now.
   He'll give you everything
   you had before.
⁷ In the past, things went well
   with you.
   But in days to come, things
   will get even better.

⁸ "Find out what our parents
   taught.
   Discover what those
   who lived before them
   learned.
⁹ After all, we were born only
   yesterday.
   So we don't know
   anything.
   Our days on this earth
   are like a shadow that
   disappears.
¹⁰ Won't your people of long
   ago teach you and tell
   you?

Won't the things they said
help you understand?
¹¹ Can grass grow tall where
there isn't any swamp?
Can plants grow well
where there isn't any
water?
¹² While they are still growing
and haven't been cut,
they dry up faster than
grass does.
¹³ The same thing happens to
everyone who forgets
God.
The hope of ungodly
people dies out.
¹⁴ What they trust in is very
weak.
What they depend on is
like a spider's web.
¹⁵ They lean on it, but it falls
apart.
They hold on to it, but it
gives way.
¹⁶ They are like a plant in the
sunshine
that receives plenty of
water.
It spreads its new growth
all over the garden.
¹⁷ It wraps its roots around a
pile of rocks.
It tries to find places to
grow among the stones.
¹⁸ But when the plant is pulled
up from its spot,
that place says, 'I never saw
you.'
¹⁹ The life of that plant is sure to
dry up.
But from the same soil
other plants will grow.
²⁰ "I'm sure God doesn't turn
his back on anyone who
is honest.

And he doesn't help those
who do what is evil.
²¹ He will fill your mouth with
laughter.
Shouts of joy will come
from your lips.
²² Your enemies will put on
shame as if it were
clothes.
The tents of sinful people
will be gone."

Job's Reply

9 Job replied,

² "I'm sure that what you have
said is true.
But how can human beings
prove to God they are
not guilty?
³ They might wish to argue
with him.
But they couldn't answer
him
even once in a thousand
times.
⁴ His wisdom is deep. His
power is great.
No one opposes him and
comes away unharmed.
⁵ He moves mountains, and
they don't even know it.
When he is angry, he turns
them upside down.
⁶ He shakes the earth loose
from its place.
He makes its pillars tremble.
⁷ When he tells the sun not to
shine, it doesn't.
He turns off the light of the
stars.
⁸ He's the only one who can
spread out the heavens.
He alone can walk on the
waves of the ocean.

⁹ He made the Big Dipper and
  Orion.
 He created the Pleiades
  and the southern stars.
¹⁰ He does wonderful things
  that can't be understood.
 He does miracles that can't
  even be counted.
¹¹ When he passes by me, I can't
  see him.
 When he goes past me, I
  can't recognize him.
¹² If he takes something, who
  can stop him?
 Who would dare to ask
  him, 'What are you
  doing?'
¹³ God doesn't hold back his
  anger.
 Even the helpers of the sea
  monster Rahab
 bowed in fear at his feet.

¹⁴ "So how can I disagree with
  God?
 How can I possibly argue
  with him?
¹⁵ Even if I hadn't done
  anything wrong,
 I couldn't answer him.
 I could only beg my Judge
  to have mercy on me.
¹⁶ Suppose I called out to him
  and he answered.
 I don't believe he'd listen
  to me.
¹⁷ He would send a storm to
  crush me.
 He'd increase my wounds
  without any reason.
¹⁸ He wouldn't let me catch my
  breath.
 He'd make my life very
  bitter.
¹⁹ If it's a matter of strength, he
  is mighty!

 And if it's a matter of being
  fair,
 who would dare to bring
  charges against him?
²⁰ Even if I hadn't sinned, what
  I said would prove me
  guilty.
 Even if I were honest, my
  words would show that
  I'm wrong.

²¹ "Even though I'm honest,
  I'm not concerned about
  myself.
 I hate my own life.
²² It all amounts to the same
  thing. That's why I say,
 'God destroys honest
  people and sinful people
  alike.'
²³ Suppose a plague brings
  sudden death.
 Then he laughs when those
  who haven't sinned lose
  hope.
²⁴ Suppose a nation falls into
  the power of sinful
  people.
 Then God makes its judges
  blind to the truth.
 If he isn't the one doing it,
  who is?

²⁵ "God, my days race by like a
  runner.
 They fly away without
  seeing any joy.
²⁶ They speed along like
  papyrus boats.
 They are like eagles
  swooping down on their
  food.
²⁷ Suppose I say, 'I'll forget
  about all my problems.
 I'll change my frown into a
  smile.'

²⁸ Then I'd still be afraid I'd go
on suffering.
That's because I know you
would say
I had done something
wrong.
²⁹ In fact, you have already said
I'm guilty.
So why should I struggle
without any reason?
³⁰ Suppose I clean myself with
soap.
Suppose I wash my hands
with cleanser.
³¹ Even then you would throw
me into a muddy pit.
And even my clothes
would hate me.
³² "God isn't a mere human
being like me. I can't
answer him.
We can't take each other to
court.
³³ I wish someone would settle
matters between us.
I wish someone would
bring us together.
³⁴ I wish someone would keep
God from punishing me.
Then his terror wouldn't
frighten me anymore.
³⁵ I would speak up without
being afraid of him.
But as things stand now, I
can't do that.

10 "I'm sick of living.
So I'll talk openly about
my problems.
I'll speak out because my
spirit is bitter.
² I say to God, 'Don't find me
guilty.
Instead, tell me what charges
you are bringing against me.

³ Does it make you happy
when you crush me?
Does it please you to turn
your back on what you
have made?
While you do those things,
you smile on the plans of
sinful people!
⁴ You don't have human eyes.
You don't see as people see.
⁵ Your days aren't like the days
of a mere human being.
Your years aren't even like
the years of a strong man.
⁶ So you search for my mistakes.
You look for my sin.
⁷ You already know I'm not
guilty.
No one can save me from
your power.
⁸ " 'Your hands shaped me and
made me.
So are you going to destroy
me now?
⁹ Remember, you molded me
like clay.
So are you going to turn me
back into dust?
¹⁰ Didn't you pour me out like
milk?
Didn't you form me like
cheese?
¹¹ Didn't you put skin and flesh
on me?
Didn't you sew me together
with bones and muscles?
¹² You gave me life. You were
kind to me.
You took good care of me.
You watched over me.
¹³ " 'But here's what you hid in
your heart.
Here's what you had on
your mind.

¹⁴ If I sinned, you would be
　　watching me.
　　You wouldn't let me go
　　without punishing me.
¹⁵ If I were guilty, how terrible
　　that would be for me!
　　Even if I haven't sinned,
　　I can't be proud of what I've
　　done.
　　That's because I'm so full of
　　shame.
　　I'm drowning in my
　　suffering.
¹⁶ If I become proud, you hunt
　　me down like a lion.
　　You show your mighty
　　power against me.
¹⁷ You bring new witnesses
　　against me.
　　You become more and
　　more angry with me.
　　You use your power against
　　me again and again.
¹⁸ " 'Why did you bring me out
　　of my mother's body?
　　I wish I had died before
　　anyone saw me.
¹⁹ I wish I'd never been born!
　　I wish I'd been carried
　　straight from my
　　mother's body to the
　　grave!
²⁰ Aren't my few days almost
　　over?
　　Leave me so I can have a
　　moment of joy.
²¹ Turn away before I go to the
　　place I can't return from.
　　It's the land of gloom and
　　total darkness.
²² It's the land of darkest night
　　and total darkness and
　　disorder.
　　There even the light is like
　　darkness.' "

The First Speech of Zophar

11 Then Zophar the Naama-
　　thite replied,

² "Don't all your words require
　　an answer?
　　I'm sure that what you are
　　saying can't be right.
³ Your useless talk won't keep
　　us quiet.
　　Someone has to correct
　　you when you make fun
　　of truth.
⁴ You say to God, 'My beliefs
　　are perfect.
　　I'm pure in your sight.'
⁵ I wish God would speak.
　　I wish he'd answer you.
⁶ I wish he'd show you the
　　secrets of wisdom.
　　After all, true wisdom has
　　two sides.
　　Here's what I want you to know.
　　God has forgotten some of
　　your sins.

⁷ "Do you know how deep the
　　mysteries of God are?
　　Can you discover the limits
　　of the Mighty One's
　　knowledge?
⁸ They are higher than the
　　heavens above.
　　What can you do?
　　They are deeper than the
　　deepest parts of the
　　earth below.
　　What can you know?
⁹ They are longer than the earth.
　　They are wider than the
　　ocean.

¹⁰ "Suppose God comes along
　　and puts you in prison.
　　Suppose he takes you to
　　court.
　　Then who can oppose him?

¹¹ He certainly knows when
people tell lies.
When he sees evil, he pays
careful attention to it.
¹² A wild donkey's colt can't be
born a human being.
And it's just as impossible
that a person without
sense can become wise.

¹³ "So commit yourself to God
completely.
Reach out your hands to
him for help.
¹⁴ Get rid of all the sin you
have.
Don't let anything that is
evil stay in your tent.
¹⁵ Then, free of those things,
you can face others.
You can stand firm without
being afraid.
¹⁶ You can be sure you will
forget your troubles.
They will be like water that
has flowed on by.
¹⁷ Life will be brighter than the
sun at noon.
And darkness will become
like morning.
¹⁸ You will be secure, because
there is hope.
You will look around you
and find a safe place to
rest.
¹⁹ You will lie down, and no one
will make you afraid.
Many people will want you
to help them.
²⁰ But sinful people won't find
what they are looking
for.
They won't be able to
escape.
All they can hope for is to
die."

Job's Reply

12 Job replied,

² "You people think you are the
only ones who matter!
You are sure that wisdom
will die with you!
³ But I have a brain, just like you.
I'm as clever as you are.
In fact, everyone knows as
much as you do.

⁴ "My friends laugh at me all
the time,
even though I called out to
God and he answered.
My friends laugh at me,
even though I'm honest
and right.
⁵ People who have an easy life
look down on those who
have problems.
They think trouble comes
only to those whose feet
are slipping.
⁶ Why doesn't anyone bother
the tents of robbers?
Why do those who make
God angry remain
secure?
They are in God's hands!

⁷ "But ask the animals what
God does.
They will teach you.
Or ask the birds in the sky.
They will tell you.
⁸ Or speak to the earth. It will
teach you.
Or let the fish in the ocean
educate you.
⁹ Are there any of these
creatures that don't
know
what the powerful hand of
the LORD has done?

¹⁰He holds the life of every
creature in his hand.
He controls the breath of
every human being.
¹¹Our tongues tell us what tastes
good and what doesn't.
And our ears tell us what's
true and what isn't.
¹²Old people are wise.
Those who live a long time
have understanding.
¹³"Wisdom and power belong
to God.
Advice and understanding
also belong to him.
¹⁴What he tears down can't be
rebuilt.
The people he puts in
prison can't be set free.
¹⁵If he holds back the water,
everything dries up.
If he lets the water loose, it
floods the land.
¹⁶Strength and understanding
belong to him.
Those who tell lies and
those who believe them
also belong to him.
¹⁷He removes the wisdom of
rulers and leads them
away.
He makes judges look
foolish.
¹⁸He sets people free from the
chains that kings put on
them.
Then he dresses the kings
in the clothes of slaves.
¹⁹He removes the authority of
priests and leads them
away.
He removes from their
positions
officials who have been in
control for a long time.

²⁰He shuts the mouths of
trusted advisers.
He takes away the
understanding of
elders.
²¹He looks down on proud
leaders.
He takes away the strength
of those who are
mighty.
²²He tells people the secrets of
darkness.
He brings total darkness
out into the light.
²³He makes nations great, and
then he destroys them.
He makes nations grow,
and then he scatters
them.
²⁴He takes away the
understanding of the
leaders of the earth.
He makes them wander in
a desert where no one
lives.
²⁵Without any light, they
feel their way along in
darkness.
God makes them unsteady
like those who get
drunk.

13

"My eyes have seen
everything God has
done.
My ears have heard it and
understood it.
²What you know, I also know.
I'm as clever as you are.
³In fact, I long to speak to the
Mighty One.
I want to argue my case
with God.
⁴But you spread lies about me
and take away my good
name.

If you are trying to heal me,
    you aren't very good
    doctors!
⁵ I wish you would keep your
    mouths shut!
  Then people would think
    you were wise.
⁶ Listen to my case.
  Listen as I make my appeal.
⁷ Will you say evil things in
    order to help God?
  Will you tell lies for him?
⁸ Do you want to be on God's
    side?
  Will you argue his case for
    him?
⁹ Would it turn out well if
    he looked you over
    carefully?
  Could you fool him as
    you might fool human
    beings?
¹⁰ He would certainly hold you
    responsible
  if you took his side in
    secret.
¹¹ Wouldn't his glory terrify you?
  Wouldn't the fear of him
    fall on you?
¹² Your sayings are as useless as
    ashes.
  The answers you give are
    as weak as clay.

¹³ "So be quiet and let me
    speak.
  Then I won't care what
    happens to me.
¹⁴ Why do I put myself in
    danger?
  Why do I take my life in my
    hands?
¹⁵ Even if God kills me, I'll still
    put my hope in him.
  I'll argue my case in front
    of him.

¹⁶ No matter how things turn
    out,
  I'm sure I'll still be saved.
  After all, no ungodly person
    would dare to come into
    his court.
¹⁷ Listen carefully to what I'm
    saying.
  Pay close attention to my
    words.
¹⁸ I've prepared my case.
  And I know I'll be proved
    right.
¹⁹ Can others bring charges
    against me?
  If they can, I'll keep quiet
    and die.

²⁰ "God, I won't hide from
    you.
  Here are the only two
    things I want.
²¹ Stop treating me this way.
  And stop making me so
    afraid.
²² Then send for me, and I'll
    answer.
  Or let me speak, and you
    reply.
²³ How many things have I
    done wrong?
  How many sins have I
    committed?
  Show me my crime. Show
    me my sin.
²⁴ Why do you turn your face
    away from me?
  Why do you think of me as
    your enemy?
²⁵ I'm already like a leaf that is
    blown by the wind.
  Are you going to terrify me
    even more?
  I'm already like dry straw.
  Are you going to keep on
    chasing me?

26 You write down bitter things
against me.
You make me suffer for the
sins
I committed when I was
young.
27 You put my feet in chains.
You watch every step I
take.
You do it by putting marks
on the bottom of my
feet.

28 "People waste away like
something that is rotten.
They are like clothes that
are eaten by moths.

14 ¹Human beings have only
a few days to live.
Their lives are full of
trouble.
2 They grow like flowers, and
then they dry up.
They are like shadows that
quickly disappear.

3 "God, do you even notice
them?
Will you let them appear in
your court?
4 Who can bring what is pure
from something that
isn't pure?
No one!
5 You decide how long anyone
will live.
You have established the
number of his months.
You have set a limit to the
number of his days.
6 So look away from him.
Leave him alone.
Let him put in his time like
a hired worker.

7 "At least there is hope for a
tree.

If it's cut down, it will begin
to grow again.
New branches will appear
on it.
8 Its roots may grow old in the
ground.
Its stump may die in the
soil.
9 But when it smells water, it
will begin to grow.
It will send out new growth
like a plant.
10 No man is like that. When
he dies, he is buried in a
grave.
He takes his last breath.
Then he is gone.
11 Water dries up from lakes.
Riverbeds become empty
and dry.
12 In the same way, people lie
down and never get up.
People won't wake or rise
from their sleep
until the heavens are
gone.

13 "I wish you would hide me in
a grave!
I wish you would cover
me up until your anger
passes by!
I wish you would set the time
for me to spend in the
grave
and then bring me back up!
14 If someone dies, will they live
again?
All the days of my hard
work
I will wait for the time when
you give me new life.
15 You will call out to me, and I
will answer you.
You will long for the person
your hands have made.

16 Then you will count every
step I take.
But you won't keep track of
my sin.
17 The wrong things I've done
will be sealed up in a
bag.
You will wipe out my sins
by forgiving them.
18 "A mountain wears away and
crumbles.
A rock is moved from its
place.
19 Water wears away stones.
Storms wash away soil.
In the same way, you
destroy a person's hope.
20 You overpower them
completely, and then
they're gone.
You change the way they
look and send them to
their graves.
21 If their children are honored,
they don't even know it.
If their children are
dishonored, they don't
even see it.
22 All they feel is the pain of
their own bodies.
They are full of sadness
only for themselves."

The Second Speech of Eliphaz

15 Then Eliphaz the Temanite replied,

2 "Job, would a wise person
answer with a lot of
meaningless talk?
Would they fill their
stomach with the hot
east wind?
3 Would they argue with
useless words?
Would they give worthless
speeches?
4 But you even cause others to
lose their respect for God.
You make it hard for them
to be faithful to him.
5 Your sin makes you say evil
things.
You talk like people who
twist the truth.
6 Your own mouth judges you,
not mine.
Your own lips witness
against you.

7 "Are you the first man who
was ever born?
Were you created before
the hills?
8 Do you listen in when God
speaks with his angels?
Do you think you are the
only wise person?
9 What do you know that we
don't know?
What understanding do you
have that we don't have?
10 People who are old and gray
are on our side.
And they are even older
than your parents!
11 Aren't God's words of comfort
enough for you?
He speaks them to you
gently.
12 Why have you let your wild
ideas carry you away?
Why do your eyes flash
with anger?
13 Why do you get so angry with
God?
Why do words like those
pour out of your mouth?
14 "Can human beings really be
pure?

Can those who are born
really be right with
God?
15 God doesn't trust his holy
angels.
Even the heavens aren't
pure in his sight.
16 So he'll certainly find fault
with human beings.
After all, they are evil and
sinful.
They drink up evil as if it
were water.

17 "Listen to me. I'll explain
things to you.
Let me tell you what I've
seen.
18 I'll tell you what those who
are wise have said.
They don't hide anything
they've received
from their people of long
ago.
19 The land was given only to
those people.
Their wisdom didn't come
from outsiders.
And here's what those who
are wise have said.
20 Sinful people always suffer
pain.
Mean people suffer all
their lives.
21 Terrifying sounds fill their
ears.
When everything seems to
be going well,
robbers attack them.
22 They lose all hope of
escaping the darkness of
death.
They will certainly be
killed by swords.
23 Like vultures, they look
around for food.

They know that the day
they will die is near.
24 Suffering and pain terrify
them.
Their troubles overpower
them,
like a king ready to attack
his enemies.
25 They shake their fists at
God.
They brag about
themselves and oppose
the Mighty One.
26 They boldly charge against
him
with their thick, strong
shields.

27 "Their faces are very fat.
Their stomachs hang
out.
28 They'll live in towns that
have been destroyed.
They'll live in houses
where no one else lives.
The houses will crumble to
pieces.
29 They won't be rich anymore.
Their wealth won't last.
Their property will no
longer spread out over
the land.
30 They won't escape the
darkness of death.
A flame will dry up
everything they have.
The breath of God will
blow them away.
31 Don't let them fool
themselves
by trusting in what is
worthless.
They won't get anything
out of it.
32 Even before they die, they
will dry up.

No matter what they do, it
won't succeed.
³³ They'll be like vines
that are stripped of their
unripe grapes.
They'll be like olive trees
that drop their flowers.
³⁴ People who are ungodly
won't have any children.
Fire will burn up the tents
of people who accept
money
from those who want
special favors.
³⁵ Instead of having children,
ungodly people create
suffering.
All they produce is evil.
They are full of lies."

Job's Reply

16
Job replied,

² "I've heard many of these
things before.
All of you are terrible at
comforting me!
³ Your speeches go on forever.
Won't they ever end?
What's wrong with you?
Why do you keep on
arguing?
⁴ If you and I changed places,
I could say the same things
you are saying.
I could make fine speeches
against you.
I could shake my head at you.
⁵ But what I might say would
give you hope.
My words of comfort would
help you.

⁶ "If I speak, it doesn't help me.
And if I keep quiet, my
pain doesn't go away.

⁷ God has worn me out
completely.
He has destroyed my whole
family.
⁸ People can see the condition
he has put me in.
My thin body stands as a
witness against me.
⁹ God is angry with me.
He attacks me and tears
me up.
He grinds his teeth at me.
He stares at me as if he
were my enemy.
¹⁰ People make fun of me.
They slap my face and
laugh at me.
All of them join together
against me.
¹¹ God has turned me over to
sinful people.
He has handed me over to
them.
¹² Everything was going well
with me.
But he broke me into
pieces like a clay pot.
He grabbed me by the neck
and crushed me.
He has taken aim at me.
¹³ He shoots his arrows at me
from all sides.
Without pity, he stabs me in
the kidneys.
He spills my insides on the
ground.
¹⁴ He smashes through me as if
I were a wall.
He rushes at me like a
fighting man.

¹⁵ "I've sewed rough clothing
over my skin.
All I can do is sit here in the
dust.
¹⁶ My face is red from crying.

I have dark circles under
my eyes.
17 But I haven't harmed anyone.
My prayers to God are
pure.

18 "Earth, please don't cover up
my blood!
May God always hear my
cry for help!
19 Even now my witness is in
heaven.
The one who speaks up for
me is there.
20 My go-between is my friend
as I pour out my tears to
God.
21 He makes his appeal to God
to help me
as a person pleads for a
friend.
22 "Only a few years will pass by.
Then I'll take the path of
no return.

17 1 My strength is almost
gone.
I won't live much longer.
A grave is waiting for me.
2 People who make fun of me
are all around me.
I'm forced to watch as they
attack me with their
words.

3 "God, please pay the price to
have me set free.
Who else would put up
money for me?
4 You have closed the minds of
those who are trying to
comfort me.
They don't understand that
I haven't done anything
wrong.
So don't let them win the
argument.

5 Suppose someone tells lies
about their friends to get
a reward.
Then their own children
will suffer for it.

6 "God has made an example
of me.
People spit in my face.
7 My eyes have grown weak
because I'm so sad.
My body is so thin it hardly
casts a shadow.
8 People who claim to be
honest
are shocked when they
see me.
Those who think they haven't
sinned
are stirred up against me.
They think I'm ungodly.
9 But godly people will keep
doing what is right.
Those who have clean
hands will grow
stronger.

10 "Come on, all of you! Try
again!
I can't find a wise person
among you.
11 My life is almost over. My
plans are destroyed.
Yet the desires of my heart
12 turn night into day.
Even though it's dark,
'Light is nearby.'
13 Suppose the only home I can
hope for is a grave.
And suppose I make my
bed in the darkness of
death.
14 Suppose I say to the grave,
'You are like a father to me.'
And suppose I say to its
worms,

'You are like a mother or
    sister to me.'
¹⁵ Then what hope do I have?
    Who can give me any hope?
¹⁶ Will hope go down to the
    gates of death with me?
    Will we go down together
    into the dust of the
    grave?"

The Second Speech of Bildad

18 Then Bildad the Shuhite
    replied,

² "Job, when will you stop
    these speeches of yours?
    Be reasonable! Then we
    can talk.
³ Why do you look at us as if we
    were cattle?
    Why do you think of us as
    being stupid?
⁴ Your anger is tearing you to
    pieces.
    Does the earth have to be
    deserted just to prove
    you are right?
    Must all the rocks be
    moved from their
    places?

⁵ "The lamps of sinful people
    are blown out.
    Their flames will never
    burn again.
⁶ The lights in their tents
    become dark.
    The lamps beside those
    who are evil go out.
⁷ They walk more slowly than
    they used to.
    Their own evil plans make
    them fall.
⁸ Their feet take them into a
    net.
    They wander right into it.

⁹ A trap grabs hold of their
    heels.
    It refuses to let them go.
¹⁰ A trap lies in their path.
    A rope to catch them
    is hidden on the
    ground.
¹¹ Terrors alarm them on every
    side.
    They follow them every
    step of the way.
¹² Trouble would like to eat
    them up.
    Danger waits for them
    when they fall.
¹³ It eats away parts of their
    skin.
    Death itself feeds on their
    arms and legs.
¹⁴ They are torn away from the
    safety of their tents.
    They are marched off to
    the one who rules over
    death.
¹⁵ Fire races through their
    tents.
    Burning sulfur is scattered
    over their homes.
¹⁶ Their roots dry up under
    them.
    Their branches dry up
    above them.
¹⁷ No one on earth remembers
    them.
    Their names are forgotten
    in the land.
¹⁸ They are driven from
    light into the place of
    darkness.
    They are thrown out of the
    world.
¹⁹ Their family dies out among
    their people.
    No one is left where they
    used to live.

²⁰What has happened to them
  shocks the people in the
  west.
    It terrifies the people in the
    east.
²¹Now you know what the
  homes of sinners are
  like.
    Those who don't know God
    live in places like that."

Job's Reply

19 Job replied,

²"How long will you people
  make me suffer?
    How long will you crush
    me with your words?
³You have already accused me
  many times.
    You have attacked me
    without feeling any
    shame.
⁴Suppose it's true that I've
  gone down the wrong
  path.
    Then it's my concern, not
    yours.
⁵Suppose you want to place
  yourselves above me.
    Suppose you want to use
    my shame to prove I'm
    wrong.
⁶Then I want you to know that
  God hasn't treated me
  right.
    In fact, he has captured me
    in his net.
⁷"I cry out, 'Someone harmed
  me!'
    But I don't get any reply.
    I call out for help.
    But I'm not treated fairly.
⁸God has blocked my way, and
  I can't get through.

He has made my paths so
  dark I can't see where
  I'm going.
⁹He has taken my wealth away
  from me.
    He has stripped me of my
    honor.
¹⁰He tears me down on every
  side until I'm gone.
    He pulls up the roots of my
    hope as if I were a tree.
¹¹His anger burns against me.
    He thinks I'm one of his
    enemies.
¹²His troops march toward me
  in force.
    They come at me from
    every direction.
    They camp around my tent.

¹³"God has caused my family
  to desert me.
    The people I used to know
    are now strangers to me.
¹⁴My relatives have gone away.
    My closest friends have
    forgotten me.
¹⁵My guests and my female
  servants think of me as a
  stranger.
    They look at me as if I were
    an outsider.
¹⁶I send for my servant, but he
  doesn't answer.
    He doesn't come, even
    though I beg him to.
¹⁷My wife can't stand the way
  my breath smells.
    My own family won't have
    anything to do with me.
¹⁸Even little children mock me.
    When I appear, they make
    fun of me.
¹⁹All my close friends hate me.
    Those I love have turned
    against me.

20 I'm nothing but skin and
      bones.
    I've barely escaped death.

21 "Have pity on me, my friends!
      Please have pity!
    God has struck me down
      with his powerful hand.
22 Why do you chase after me as
      he does?
    Aren't you satisfied with
      what you have done to
      me already?

23 "I wish my words were
      written down!
    I wish they were written in
      a book!
24 I wish they were cut into lead
      with an iron tool!
    I wish they were carved in
      rock forever!
25 I know that my redeemer
      lives.
    In the end he will stand on
      the earth.
26 Though my skin will be
      destroyed,
    in my body I'll see God.
27 I myself will see him with my
      own eyes.
    I'll see him, and he won't
      be a stranger to me.
    How my heart longs for
      that day!

28 "You might say, 'Let's keep
      bothering Job.
    After all, he's the cause of
      all his suffering.'
29 But you should be afraid
      when God comes to
      judge you.
    He'll be angry. He'll punish
      you with his sword.
    Then you will know that he
      is the Judge."

The Second Speech of Zophar

20 Then Zophar the Naama-
      thite replied,

2 "My troubled thoughts force
      me to answer you.
    That's because I'm very
      upset.
3 What you have just said
      dishonors me.
    So I really have to reply to
      you.

4 "I'm sure you must know how
      things have always been.
    They've been that way
      ever since human beings
      were placed on this earth.
5 Those who are evil are happy
      for only a short time.
    The joy of ungodly people
      lasts only for a moment.
6 Their pride might reach all the
      way up to the heavens.
    Their heads might touch
      the clouds.
7 But they will disappear
      forever,
    like the waste from their
      own bodies.
    Anyone who has seen them
      will say,
    'Where did they go?'
8 Like a dream they will fly
      away.
    They will never be seen
      again.
    They will be driven away
      like visions in the night.
9 The eyes that saw them won't
      see them anymore.
    Even their own families
      won't remember them.
10 Their children must pay back
      what they took from
      poor people.

Their own hands must give back the wealth they stole.
11 They might feel young and very strong.
But they will soon lie down in the dust of their graves.

12 "Anything that is evil tastes sweet to them.
They keep it under their tongues for a while.
13 They can't stand to let it go.
So they hold it in their mouths.
14 But their food will turn sour in their stomachs.
It will become like the poison of a serpent inside them.
15 They will spit out the rich food they swallowed.
God will make their stomachs throw it up.
16 They will suck the poison of a serpent.
The fangs of an adder will kill them.
17 They won't enjoy streams that flow with honey.
They won't enjoy rivers that flow with cream.
18 What they worked for they must give back
before they can eat it.
They won't enjoy what they have earned.
19 They've crushed poor people and left them with nothing.
They've taken over houses they didn't even build.
20 "No matter how much they have,

they always long for more.
But their treasure can't save them.
21 There isn't anything left for them to eat up.
Their success won't last.
22 While they are enjoying the good life,
trouble will catch up with them.
Terrible suffering will come on them.
23 When they've filled their stomachs,
God will pour out his great anger on them.
He'll strike them down with blow after blow.
24 They might run away from iron weapons.
But arrows that have bronze tips will wound them.
25 They will pull the arrows out of their backs.
They will remove the shining tips from their livers.
They will be filled with terror.
26 Total darkness hides and waits for their treasures.
God will send a fire that will destroy them.
It will burn up everything that's left in their tents.
27 Heaven will show their guilt to everyone.
The earth will be a witness against them.
28 A flood will carry their houses away.
Rushing water will wash them away
on the day when God judges.

²⁹Now you know what God will
do to sinful people.
Now you know what he has
planned for them."

Job's Reply

21 Job replied,

²"Listen carefully to what I'm
saying.
Let that be the comfort you
people give me.
³Put up with me while I
speak.
After I've spoken, you can
make fun of me!

⁴"I'm not arguing with mere
human beings.
So why shouldn't I be
angry and uneasy?
⁵Look at me and be shocked.
Put your hand over your
mouth and stop
talking!
⁶When I think about these
things, I'm terrified.
My whole body trembles.
⁷Why do sinful people keep on
living?
The older they grow, the
richer they get.
⁸They see their children grow
up around them.
They watch their family
grow larger.
⁹Their homes are safe.
They don't have to be
afraid.
God isn't punishing
them.
¹⁰Every time their bulls mate,
their cows become
pregnant.
And the calves don't die
before they are born.

¹¹Sinful people send their
children out like a flock
of lambs.
Their little ones dance
around.
¹²They sing to the music
of tambourines and
lyres.
They have a good time
while flutes are being
played.
¹³Those who are evil spend
their years living well.
They go down to their
graves in peace.
¹⁴But they say to God, 'Leave us
alone!
We don't want to know how
you want us to live.
¹⁵Who is the Mighty One? Why
should we serve him?
What would we get if we
prayed to him?'
¹⁶But they aren't in control of
their own success.
So I don't pay any attention
to their plans.

¹⁷"How often are their lamps
blown out?
How often does trouble
come on them?
How often does God
punish them when he's
angry?
¹⁸How often are they like straw
blowing in the wind?
How often are they like
tumbleweeds swept
away by a storm?
¹⁹People say, 'God stores up
the punishment of
evil people for their
children.'
But let God punish the evil
people themselves.

Then they'll learn a lesson
　from it.
20 Let their own eyes see how
　they are destroyed.
Let them drink the wine of
　the Mighty One's anger.
21 What do they care about
　the families they leave
　behind?
What do they care about
　them
when their lives come to
　an end?

22 "Can anyone teach God
　anything?
After all, he judges even
　the angels in heaven.
23 Some people die while they
　are still very strong.
They are completely
　secure. They have an
　easy life.
24 They are well fed.
Their bodies are healthy.
25 Others die while their spirits
　are bitter.
They've never enjoyed
　anything good.
26 Side by side they lie in the
　dust of death.
The worms in their graves
　cover all of them.

27 "I know exactly what you
　people are thinking.
I know you are planning to
　do bad things to me.
28 You are saying to yourselves,
　'Where is the great man's
　house now?
Where are the tents where
　his evil family lived?'
29 Haven't you ever asked
　questions of those who
　travel?

Haven't you paid any
　attention to their stories?
30 They'll tell you that sinful
　people
are spared from the day of
　trouble.
They'll say that those
　people
are saved from the day
when God will judge.
31 Who speaks against them for
　the way they act?
Who pays them back for
　what they've done?
32 Their bodies will be carried
　to their graves.
Guards will watch over
　their tombs.
33 The soil in the valley will be
　pleasant
to those who have died.
Many people will walk along
　behind their bodies.
Many others will walk in
　front of them.

34 "So how can you comfort me
　with your speeches?
They don't make any sense
　at all.
Your answers are nothing
　but lies!"

The Third Speech of Eliphaz

22 Then Eliphaz the Teman-
　ite replied,

2 "Can any person be of benefit
　to God?
Can even a wise person be
　of any help to him?
3 Job, what pleasure would it
　give the Mighty One if
　you were right?
What would he get if you
　were completely honest?

4 "You say you have respect for
   him.
      Is that why he corrects you?
      Is that why he brings
      charges against you?
5 Haven't you done many evil
   things?
      Don't you sin again and
      again?
6 You took clothes away from
   your relatives
      just because they owed you
      some money.
      You left them naked for no
      reason at all.
7 You didn't give any water to
   people who were tired.
      You held food back from
      those who were hungry.
8 You did it even though you
   were honored and
   powerful.
      You owned land and lived
      on it.
9 But you sent widows away
   without anything.
      You mistreated children
      whose fathers had died.
10 That's why traps have been
   set all around you.
      That's why sudden danger
      terrifies you.
11 That's why it's so dark you
   can't even see.
      That's why a flood covers
      you up.

12 "Isn't God in the highest
   parts of heaven?
      See how high the highest
      stars are!
13 But you still say, 'What does
   God know?
      Can he see through the
      darkest clouds to judge
      us?

14 He goes around in the
   highest heavens.
      Thick clouds keep him
      from seeing us.'
15 Will you stay on the old
   path
      that sinful people have
      walked on?
16 They were carried off even
   before they died.
      Their foundations were
      washed away by a flood.
17 They said to God, 'Leave us
   alone!
      What can you do to us, you
      Mighty One?'
18 But he was the one who filled
   their houses with good
   things.
      So I don't pay any attention
      to the plans of evil people.

19 Those who do what is right
   are joyful
      when they see sinners
      destroyed.
      Those who haven't done
      anything wrong make
      fun of them.
20 They say, 'Our enemies are
   completely destroyed.
      Fire has burned up their
      wealth.'

21 "Job, obey God and be at
   peace with him.
      Then he will help you
      succeed.
22 Do what he teaches you
   to do.
      Keep his words in your
      heart.
23 If you return to the Mighty
   One,
      you will have what you had
      before.

But first you must remove everything that is evil far from your tent.
²⁴ You must throw your gold nuggets away.
You must toss your gold from Ophir into a valley.
²⁵ Then the Mighty One himself will be your gold.
He'll be like the finest silver to you.
²⁶ You will find delight in the Mighty One.
You will honor God and trust in him.
²⁷ You will pray to him, and he will hear you.
You will keep the promises you made to him.
²⁸ What you decide to do will be done.
Light will shine on the path you take.
²⁹ When people are brought low you will say, 'Lift them up!'
Then God will help them.
³⁰ He'll even save those who are guilty.
He'll save them because your hands are clean."

Job's Reply

23

Job replied,

² "Even today my problems are more than I can handle.
In spite of my groans, God's hand is heavy on me.
³ I wish I knew where I could find him!
I wish I could go to the place where he lives!

⁴ I would state my case to him.
I'd give him all my arguments.
⁵ I'd find out what his answers would be.
I'd think about what he would say to me.
⁶ Would he strongly oppose me?
No. He wouldn't bring charges against me.
⁷ There honest people can prove to him they're not guilty.
There my Judge would tell me once and for all that I'm not guilty.

⁸ "But if I go to the east, God isn't there.
If I go to the west, I don't find him.
⁹ When he's working in the north, I don't see him there.
When he turns to the south, I don't see him there either.
¹⁰ But he knows every step I take.
When he has tested me, I'll come out as pure as gold.
¹¹ My feet have closely followed his steps.
I've stayed on his path without turning away.
¹² I haven't disobeyed his commands.
I've treasured his words more than my daily bread.

¹³ "But he's the only God. Who can oppose him?
He does anything he wants to do.

14 He carries out his plans
against me.
And he still has many other
plans just like them.
15 That's why I'm so terrified.
When I think about all of
this, I'm afraid of him.
16 God has made my heart
weak.
The Mighty One has filled
me with terror.
17 But even the darkness of
death won't make me
silent.
When the darkness of the
grave covers my face, I
won't be quiet.

24 "Why doesn't the Mighty
One set a time for
judging sinful people?
Why do those who know
him have to keep waiting
for that day?
2 People move their neighbor's
boundary stones.
They steal their neighbor's
flocks.
3 They take away the donkeys
that belong to children
whose fathers have died.
They take a widow's ox
until she has paid what
she owes.
4 They push those who are
needy out of their way.
They force all the poor
people in the land to go
into hiding.
5 The poor are like wild
donkeys in the desert.
They have to go around
looking for food.
The dry and empty land
provides the only food
for their children.

6 The poor go to the fields and
get a little grain.
They gather up what is
left in the vineyards of
sinners.
7 The poor don't have any
clothes. So they spend
the night naked.
They don't have anything
to cover themselves in
the cold.
8 They are soaked by
mountain rains.
They hug the rocks
because they don't have
anything to keep them
warm.
9 Children whose fathers have
died
are torn away from their
mothers.
A poor person's baby is
taken away to pay back
what is owed.
10 The poor don't have any
clothes. They go around
naked.
They carry bundles of
grain, but they still go
hungry.
11 They work very hard as they
crush olives.
They stomp on grapes in
winepresses,
but they are still thirsty.
12 The groans of those who are
dying are heard from the
city.
Those who are wounded
cry out for help.
But God doesn't charge
anyone with doing what
is wrong.

13 "Some people hate it when
daylight comes.

In the daytime they never
walk outside.
[14] When daylight is gone,
murderers get up.
They kill poor people and
those who are in need.
In the night they sneak
around like robbers.
[15] Those who commit adultery
wait until the sun goes
down.
They think, 'No one will
see us.'
They keep their faces
hidden.
[16] In the dark, thieves break
into houses.
But by day they shut
themselves in.
They don't want anything
to do with the light.
[17] Midnight is like morning to
them.
The terrors of darkness are
their friends.

[18] "But sinners are like bubbles
on the surface of water.
Their share of the land is
under God's curse.
So no one goes to their
vineyards.
[19] Melted snow disappears
when the air is hot and
dry.
And sinners disappear
when they go down into
their graves.
[20] Even their mothers forget
them.
The worms in their graves
eat them up.
No one remembers sinful
people anymore.
They are cut down like
trees.

[21] They mistreat women who
aren't able to have
children.
They aren't kind to
widows.
[22] But God is powerful.
He even drags away people
who are strong.
When he rises up against
them,
they can never be sure they
are safe.
[23] God might let them rest and
feel secure.
But his eyes see how they
live.
[24] For a little while they are
honored.
Then they are gone.
They are brought low.
And they die like everyone
else.
They are cut off like heads
of grain.

[25] "Who can prove that what
I'm saying is wrong?
Who can prove that my
words aren't true?"

The Third Speech of Bildad

25 Then Bildad the Shuhite
replied,

[2] "God is King. He should be
feared.
He establishes peace in the
highest parts of heaven.
[3] Can anyone count his
troops?
Is there anyone his light
doesn't shine on?
[4] How can human beings be
right with God?
How can mere people
really be pure?

5 Even the moon isn't bright
  and the stars aren't pure in
  God's eyes.
6 So how about human beings?
  They are like maggots.
  How about mere people?
  They are like worms."

Job's Reply

26 Job replied,

2 "Bildad, you haven't helped
  people who aren't
  strong!
  You haven't saved people
  who are weak!
3 You haven't offered advice to
  those who aren't wise!
  In fact, you haven't
  understood anything at
  all!
4 Who helped you say these
  things?
  Whose spirit was speaking
  through you?

5 "The spirits of the dead are
  suffering greatly.
  So are those that are under
  the waters.
  And so are all those that
  live in them.
6 The place of the dead is
  naked in the sight of
  God.
  The grave lies open in front
  of him.
7 He spreads out the northern
  skies over empty space.
  He hangs the earth over
  nothing.
8 He wraps up water in his
  clouds.
  They are heavy, but they
  don't burst.

9 He covers the face of the full
  moon.
  He spreads his clouds
  over it.
10 He marks out the place where
  the sky meets the sea.
  He marks out the
  boundary between light
  and darkness.
11 The pillars of the heavens
  shake.
  They are terrified when his
  anger blazes out.
12 With his power he stirred up
  the oceans.
  In his wisdom he cut the
  sea monster Rahab to
  pieces.
13 His breath made the skies
  bright and clear.
  His hand wounded the
  serpent that glides
  through the sea.
14 Those are only on the edges
  of what he does.
  They are only the soft
  whispers that we hear
  from him.
  So who can understand
  how very powerful
  he is?"

Job's Final Reply to His Friends

27 Job continued to speak.
He said,

2 "God hasn't treated me
  fairly.
  The Mighty One has made
  my life bitter.
  You can be sure that God
  lives.
  And here's something else
  you can be sure of.
3 As long as I have life
  and God gives me breath,

⁴my mouth won't say evil
things.
My lips won't tell lies.
⁵I'll never admit you people
are right.
Until I die, I'll say I'm
telling the truth.
⁶I'll continue to say I'm right.
I'll never let go of that.
I won't blame myself as
long as I live.

⁷"May my enemies suffer like
sinful people!
May my attackers be
punished like those who
aren't fair!
⁸What hope do ungodly
people have when their
lives are cut short?
What hope do they have
when God takes away
their lives?
⁹God won't listen to their cry
when trouble comes on
them.
¹⁰They won't take delight in the
Mighty One.
They'll never call out to
God.

¹¹"I'll teach all of you about
God's power.
I won't hide the things the
Mighty One does.
¹²You have seen those things
yourselves.
So why do you continue
your useless talk?

¹³"Here's what God does to
sinful people.
Here's what those who are
mean receive from the
Mighty One.
¹⁴All their children will be
killed by swords.

They'll never have enough
to eat.
¹⁵A plague will kill those who
are left alive.
The widows of sinful
men
won't even weep over their
own children.
¹⁶Sinners might store up silver
like dust
and clothes like piles of
clay.
¹⁷But people who do what is
right will wear those
clothes.
People who haven't done
anything wrong
will divide up that silver.
¹⁸The house an evil person
builds is like a moth's
cocoon.
It's like a hut that's made
by someone on guard
duty.
¹⁹Sinful people lie down
wealthy, but their wealth
is taken away.
When they open their eyes,
everything is gone.
²⁰Terrors sweep over them like
a flood.
A storm takes them away
during the night.
²¹The east wind carries them
off, and they are gone.
It sweeps them out of their
houses.
²²It blows against them without
mercy.
They try to escape from its
power.
²³It claps its hands and makes
fun of them.
It hisses them out of their
houses."

The Place Where Wisdom Is Found Is Explained

28 There are mines where silver is found.
There are places where gold is purified.
[2] Iron is taken out of the earth.
Copper is melted down from ore.
[3] Human beings light up the darkness.
They search for ore in the deepest pits.
They look for it in the blackest darkness.
[4] Far from where people live they cut a tunnel.
They do it in places where other people don't go.
Far away from people they swing back and forth on ropes.
[5] Food grows on the surface of the earth.
But far below, the earth is changed as if by fire.
[6] Lapis lazuli is taken from the rocky earth.
Its dust contains nuggets of gold.
[7] No bird knows that hidden path.
No falcon's eye has seen it.
[8] Proud animals don't walk on it.
Lions don't prowl there.
[9] Human hands attack the hardest rock.
Their strong hands uncover the base of the mountains.
[10] They tunnel through the rock.
Their eyes see all its treasures.
[11] They search the places where the rivers begin.
They bring hidden things out into the light.
[12] But where can wisdom be found?
Where does understanding live?
[13] No human being understands how much it's worth.
It can't be found anywhere in the world.
[14] The ocean says, "It's not in me."
The sea says, "It's not here either."
[15] It can't be bought with the finest gold.
Its price can't be weighed out in silver.
[16] It can't be bought with gold from Ophir.
It can't be bought with priceless onyx or lapis lazuli.
[17] Gold or crystal can't compare with it.
It can't be bought with jewels made of gold.
[18] Don't bother to talk about coral and jasper.
Wisdom is worth far more than rubies.
[19] A topaz from Cush can't compare with it.
It can't be bought with the purest gold.
[20] So where does wisdom come from?
Where does understanding live?
[21] It's hidden from the eyes of every living thing.

Even the birds in the sky
    can't find it.
²² Death and the Grave say,
    "Only reports about it have
    reached our ears."
²³ But God understands the way
    to it.
    He is the only one who
    knows where it lives.
²⁴ He sees from one end of the
    earth to the other.
    He views everything in the
    world.
²⁵ He made the mighty wind.
    He measured out the
    waters.
²⁶ He gave orders for the rain to
    fall.
    He made paths for the
    thunderstorms.
²⁷ Then he looked at wisdom
    and set its price.
    He established it and
    tested it.
²⁸ He said to human beings,
    "Have respect for the Lord.
    That will prove you are
    wise.
    Avoid evil. That will show
    you have understanding."

Job's Final Speech

29 Job continued to speak.
    He said,

² "How I long for the times
    when things were
    better!
    That's when God watched
    over me.
³ The light of his lamp shone
    on me.
    I walked through darkness
    by his light.
⁴ Those were the best days of
    my life.

That's when God's
    friendship blessed my
    house.
⁵ The Mighty One was still
    with me.
    My children were all
    around me.
⁶ The path in front of me was
    like sweet cream.
    It was as if the rock poured
    out olive oil for me.

⁷ "In those days I went to the
    city gate.
    I took my seat as a member
    of the council.
⁸ Young people who saw me
    stepped to one side.
    Old people stood up as I
    approached.
⁹ The leaders stopped
    speaking.
    They covered their mouths
    with their hands.
¹⁰ The voices of the nobles
    became quiet.
    Their tongues stuck to the
    roofs of their mouths.
¹¹ Everyone who heard me said
    good things about me.
    Those who saw me
    honored me.
¹² That's because I saved poor
    people who cried out for
    help.
    I saved helpless children
    whose fathers had
    died.
¹³ Those who were dying gave
    me their blessing.
    I made the hearts of
    widows sing.
¹⁴ I put on a godly life as if it
    were my clothes.
    Fairness was my robe and
    my turban.

15 I was like eyes for those who
were blind.
I was like feet for those who
couldn't walk.
16 I was like a father to needy
people.
I stood up for strangers in
court.
17 Sinners are like animals that
have powerful teeth.
But I took from their
mouths the people they
had caught.

18 "I thought, 'I'll die in my own
house.
The days of my life will be
as many as the grains of
sand.
19 My roots will reach down to
the water.
The dew will lie all night
on my branches.
20 I will remain healthy and
strong.
My bow will stay as good as
new in my hand.'

21 "People wanted to hear what
I had to say.
They waited silently for the
advice I gave them.
22 After I had spoken, they
didn't speak anymore.
My words fell gently on
their ears.
23 They waited for me just as
they would wait for rain
showers.
They drank my words just
as they would drink the
spring rain.
24 When I smiled at them, they
could hardly believe it.
The light of my face lifted
their spirits.

25 I chose the way they should
go. I sat as their chief.
I lived as a king lives
among his troops.
I was like someone who
comforts those who are
sad.

30 "But now those who are
younger than I am make
fun of me.
I wouldn't even put their
parents with my sheep
dogs!
2 Their strong hands couldn't
give me any help.
That's because their
strength was gone.
3 They were weak because they
were needy and
hungry.
They wandered through
dry and empty deserts at
night.
4 Among the bushes they
gathered salty plants.
They ate the roots of desert
bushes.
5 They were driven away from
human society.
They were shouted at as if
they were robbers.
6 They were forced to live in
dry stream beds.
They had to stay among
rocks
and in holes in the
ground.
7 Like donkeys they cried out
among the bushes.
There they crowded
together and hid.
8 They were so foolish that no
one respected them.
They were driven out of the
land.

⁹ "Now their children laugh
at me.
They make fun of me with
their songs.
¹⁰ They hate me. They stay away
from me.
They even dare to spit in
my face.
¹¹ God has made my body
weak.
It's like a tent that has
fallen down.
So those children do what
they want to in front of
me.
¹² Many people attack me on
my right side.
They lay traps for my feet.
They come at me from
every direction.
¹³ They tear up the road I walk
on.
They succeed in destroying
me.
They say, 'No one can help
him.'
¹⁴ They attack me like troops
smashing through a
wall.
Among the destroyed
buildings they come
rolling in.
¹⁵ Terrors sweep over me.
My honor is driven away as
if by the wind.
My safety vanishes like a
cloud.
¹⁶ "Now my life is slipping away.
Days of suffering grab hold
of me.
¹⁷ At night my bones hurt.
My aches and pains never
stop.
¹⁸ God's great power becomes
like clothes to me.

He chokes me like the neck
of my shirt.
¹⁹ He throws me down into the
mud.
I'm nothing but dust and
ashes.
²⁰ "God, I cry out to you. But
you don't answer me.
I stand up. But all you do is
look at me.
²¹ You do mean things to me.
You attack me with your
mighty power.
²² You pick me up and blow me
away with the wind.
You toss me around in the
storm.
²³ I know that you will bring me
down to death.
That's what you have
appointed for everyone.
²⁴ "No one would crush
people
when they cry out for help
in their trouble.
²⁵ Haven't I wept for those who
are in trouble?
Haven't I felt sorry for poor
people?
²⁶ I hoped good things would
happen, but something
evil came.
I looked for light, but all I
saw was darkness.
²⁷ My insides are always
churning.
Nothing but days of
suffering are ahead
of me.
²⁸ My skin has become dark,
but the sun didn't do it.
I stand up in the
community and cry out
for help.

²⁹I've become a brother to wild
dogs.
Owls are my companions.
³⁰My skin grows black and peels.
My body burns with fever.
³¹My lyre is tuned to sadness.
My flute makes a sound
like weeping.

31

"I made an agreement
with my eyes.
I promised not to look at
a young woman with
impure thoughts.
²What do we receive from God
above?
What do we get from the
Mighty One in heaven?
³Sinful people are destroyed.
Trouble comes to those
who do what is wrong.
⁴Doesn't God see how I live?
Doesn't he count every
step I take?

⁵"I haven't told any lies.
My feet haven't hurried to
cheat others.
⁶So let God weigh me in
honest scales.
Then he'll know I haven't
done anything wrong.
⁷Suppose my steps have
turned away from the
right path.
Suppose my heart has
wanted what my eyes
have seen.
Or suppose my hands have
become 'unclean.'
⁸Then may others eat what
I've planted.
May my crops be pulled up
by the roots.

⁹"Suppose my heart has been
tempted by a woman.

Or suppose I've prowled
around my neighbor's
home.
¹⁰Then may my wife grind
another man's grain.
May other men sleep with
her.
¹¹Wanting another woman
would have been an evil
thing.
It would have been a sin
that should be judged.
¹²It's like a fire that burns
down to the grave.
It would have caused my
crops to be pulled up by
the roots.

¹³"Suppose I haven't treated
any of my male and
female servants fairly
when they've brought
charges against me.
¹⁴Then what will I do when
God opposes me?
What answer will I give
him
when he asks me to explain
myself?
¹⁵Didn't he who made me
make my servants also?
Didn't the same God form
us inside our mothers?

¹⁶"I haven't said no to what
poor people have
wanted.
I haven't let widows lose
their hope.
¹⁷I haven't kept my bread to
myself.
I've shared it with children
whose fathers had died.
¹⁸From the time I was young,
I've helped those
widows.

I've raised those children
  as a father would.
¹⁹ Suppose I've seen people
    dying
  because they didn't have
    enough clothes.
  I've seen needy people
    who didn't have enough to
    keep warm.
²⁰ And they didn't give me their
    blessing
  when I warmed them with
    wool from my sheep.
²¹ Suppose I've raised my
    hand
  against children whose
    fathers have died.
  And I did it because I knew
    I had power in the
    courts.
²² Then let my arm fall from my
    shoulder.
  Let it be broken off at the
    joint.
²³ I was afraid God would
    destroy me.
  His glory terrifies me.
  So I'd never do things like
    that.
²⁴ "Suppose I've put my trust in
    gold.
  I've said to pure gold, 'You
    make me feel secure.'
²⁵ And I'm happy because I'm
    so wealthy.
  I'm glad because my hands
    have earned so much.
²⁶ Suppose I've worshiped the
    sun in all its glory.
  I've bowed down to the
    moon in all its beauty.
²⁷ My heart has been secretly
    tempted.
  My hand has thrown kisses
    to the sun and moon.

²⁸ Then these things would
    have been sins that
    should be judged.
  And I wouldn't have
    been faithful to God in
    heaven.
²⁹ "I wasn't happy when hard
    times came to my
    enemies.
  I didn't enjoy seeing the
    trouble they had.
³⁰ I didn't allow my mouth to
    sin
  by asking for bad things to
    happen to them.
³¹ The workers in my house
    always said,
  'Job always gives plenty of
    food to everyone.'
³² No stranger ever had to
    spend the night in the
    street.
  My door was always open
    to travelers.
³³ I didn't hide my sin as other
    people do.
  I didn't hide my guilt in my
    heart.
³⁴ I was never afraid of the
    crowd.
  I never worried that my
    relatives might hate me.
  I didn't have to keep quiet
    or stay inside.
³⁵ "I wish someone would listen
    to me!
  I'm signing my name to
    everything I've said.
  I hope the Mighty One will
    give me his answer.
  I hope the one who brings
    charges against me will
    write them down.

36 I'll wear them on my
     shoulder.
   I'll put them on my head
     like a crown.
37 I'll give that person a report
     of every step I take.
   I'll present it to him like I
     would to a ruler.

38 "Suppose my land cries out
     against me.
   And all its soil is wet with
     tears.
39 Suppose I've used up its
     crops without paying for
     them.
   Or I've broken the spirit of
     its renters.
40 Then let thorns grow instead
     of wheat.
   Let stinkweed come up
     instead of barley."

   The words of Job end here.

The Speech of Elihu

32 So the three men stopped
answering Job, because
he thought he was right. 2 But
Elihu the Buzite was very angry
with Job. That's because Job said
he himself was right instead of
God. Elihu was the son of Barakel. He was from the family of
Ram. 3 Elihu was also very angry
with Job's three friends. They
hadn't found any way to prove
that Job was wrong. But they
still said he was guilty. 4 Elihu
had waited before he spoke to
Job. That's because the others
were older than he was. 5 But he
saw that the three men didn't
have anything more to say. So
he was very angry.

6 Elihu the Buzite, the son of
Barakel, said,

   "I'm young, and you are old.
     So I was afraid to tell you
       what I know.
7 I thought, 'Those who are
     older should speak first.
   Those who have lived for
     many years
     should teach people how to
       be wise.'
8 But the spirit in people gives
     them understanding.
   The breath of the Mighty
     One gives them wisdom.
9 Older people aren't the only
     ones who are wise.
   They aren't the only ones
     who understand what is
       right.

10 "So I'm saying you should
     listen to me.
   I'll tell you what I know.
11 I waited while you men
     spoke.
   I listened to your
     reasoning.
   While you were searching for
     words,
12   I paid careful attention to
       you.
   But not one of you has proved
     that Job is wrong.
   None of you has answered
     his arguments.
13 Don't claim, 'We have
     enough wisdom to
     answer Job.'
   Let God, not a mere man,
     prove that he's wrong.
14 Job hasn't directed his words
     against me.
   I won't answer him with
     your arguments.

15 "Job, these men are afraid.
　They don't have anything
　　else to say.
　They've run out of words.
16 Do I have to keep on waiting,
　now that they are
　　silent?
　They are just standing
　　there with nothing to
　　say.
17 I too have something to say.
　I too will tell what I know.
18 I'm full of words.
　My spirit inside me forces
　　me to speak.
19 Inside I'm like wine that is
　bottled up.
　I'm like new wineskins
　　ready to burst.
20 I must speak so I can feel
　better.
　I must open my mouth and
　　reply.
21 I'll treat everyone the same.
　I won't praise anyone
　　without meaning it.
22 If I weren't honest when I
　praised people,
　my Maker would soon take
　　me from this life.

33 "Job, listen now to my
　　words.
　Pay attention to everything
　　I say.
2 I'm about to open my mouth.
　My words are on the tip of
　　my tongue.
3 What I say comes from an
　honest heart.
　My lips speak only what I
　　know is true.
4 The Spirit of God has made
　me.
　The breath of the Mighty
　　One gives me life.

5 So answer me if you can.
　Stand up and argue your
　　case in front of me.
6 To God I'm just the same as
　you.
　I too am a piece of clay.
7 You don't have to be afraid
　of me.
　My hand won't be too
　　heavy on you.

8 "But I heard what you said.
　And here are the exact
　　words I heard.
9 You said, 'I'm pure. I have
　done no wrong.
　I'm clean. I'm free from sin.
10 But God has found fault with
　me.
　He thinks I'm his enemy.
11 He puts my feet in chains.
　He watches every step I
　　take.'

12 "But I'm telling you that you
　aren't right when you
　　talk like that.
　After all, God is greater
　　than any human being.
13 Why do you claim that God
　never answers anybody's
　　questions?
14 He speaks in one way and
　then another.
　But we do not even realize it.
15 He might speak in a dream or
　in a vision at night.
　That's when people are
　　sound asleep in their
　　beds.
16 He might speak in their ears.
　His warnings might terrify
　　them.
17 He warns them in order to
　turn them away from
　　sinning.

He wants to keep them
from being proud.
¹⁸ He wants to stop them from
going down into the
grave.
He doesn't want them to be
killed by swords.
¹⁹ Someone might be punished
by suffering in bed.
The pain in their bones
might never go away.
²⁰ They might feel so bad they
can't eat anything.
They might even hate the
finest food.
²¹ Their body might waste away
to nothing.
Their bones might have
been hidden.
But now they stick out.
²² They might approach the
very edge of the grave.
The messengers of death
might come for them.
²³ But suppose there is an angel
who will speak up for him.
The angel is very special.
He's one out of a
thousand.
He will tell that person
how to do what is right.
²⁴ That angel will be gracious to
them. He'll say to God,
'Spare them from going
down into the grave.
I know a way that can set
them free.'
²⁵ Then their body is made like
new again.
They become as strong and
healthy as when they
were young.
²⁶ Then that person can pray to
God and be blessed by
him.

They will see God's face
and shout for joy.
God will make them well
and happy again.
²⁷ Then that person will come
to others and say,
'I sinned. I made what is
wrong appear to be right.
But I wasn't punished as I
should have been.
²⁸ God has set me free. He has
kept me from going
down into the darkness
of the grave.
So I'll live to enjoy the light
of life.'

²⁹ "God does all these things to
people.
In fact, he does them again
and again.
³⁰ He wants to stop people from
going down into the
darkness of the grave.
Then the light of life will
shine on them.

³¹ "Pay attention, Job! Listen to
me!
Be quiet so I can speak.
³² If you have anything to say,
answer me.
Speak up. I want to help
you be cleared of all
charges.
³³ But if you don't have
anything to say, listen to
me.
Be quiet so I can teach you
how to be wise."

34

Elihu continued,
² "Hear what I'm saying, you
wise men.
Listen to me, you who have
learned so much.

³ Our tongues tell us what
    tastes good and what
    doesn't.
And our ears tell us what's
    true and what isn't.
⁴ So let's choose for ourselves
    what is right.
Let's learn together what is
    good.

⁵ "Job says, 'I'm not guilty of
    doing anything wrong.
But God doesn't treat me
    fairly.
⁶ Even though I'm right,
    he thinks I'm a liar.
Even though I'm not guilty,
    his arrows give me wounds
    that can't be healed.'
⁷ Is there anyone like Job?
    He accuses God as easily
    as he drinks water.
⁸ He's a companion of those
    who do evil.
He spends his time with
    sinful people.
⁹ He asks, 'What good is it
    to try to please God?'

¹⁰ "So listen to me, you
    men who have
    understanding.
God would never do what
    is evil.
The Mighty One would
    never do what is
    wrong.
¹¹ He pays back everyone for
    what they've done.
He gives them exactly what
    they should get.
¹² It isn't possible for God to do
    wrong.
The Mighty One would
    never treat people
    unfairly.

¹³ Who appointed him to rule
    over the earth?
Who put him in charge of
    the whole world?
¹⁴ If he really wanted to,
    he could hold back his
    spirit and breath.
¹⁵ Then everyone would die
    together.
They would return to the
    dust.

¹⁶ "Job, if you have
    understanding, listen
    to me.
Pay attention to what I'm
    saying.
¹⁷ Can someone who hates to
    be fair govern?
Will you bring charges
    against the holy and
    mighty God?
¹⁸ He says to kings, 'You are
    worthless.'
He says to nobles, 'You are
    evil.'
¹⁹ He doesn't favor princes.
    He treats rich people and
    poor people the same.
His hands created all of
    them.
²⁰ They die suddenly in the
    middle of the night.
God strikes them down,
    and they pass away.
Even people who are
    mighty are removed, but
    not by human hands.

²¹ "His eyes see how people live.
    He watches every step they
    take.
²² There is no deep shadow or
    total darkness
where those who do what
    is evil can hide.

23 God doesn't need to bring
    charges against anyone.
    He knows they are guilty.
    So he doesn't need to have
    them appear in his court
    to be judged.
24 He destroys the mighty
    without asking them
    questions in court.
    Then he sets others up in
    their places.
25 He knows what they do.
    So he crushes them during
    the night.
26 He punishes them for the
    sins they commit.
    He does it where everyone
    can see them.
27 That's because they turned
    away from following
    him.
    They didn't have respect
    for anything he does.
28 They caused poor people to
    cry out to him.
    He heard the cries of those
    who were in need.
29 But if he remains silent, who
    can judge him?
    If he turns his face away,
    who can see him?
    He rules over individual
    people and nations
    alike.
30   He keeps those who are
    ungodly from ruling.
    He keeps them from laying
    traps for others.

31 "Someone might say to God,
    'I'm guilty of sinning,
    but I won't do it anymore.
32 Show me my sins that I'm not
    aware of.
    If I've done what is wrong,
    I won't do it again.'

33 But you refuse to turn away
    from your sins.
    So God won't treat you
    the way you want to be
    treated.
    You must decide, Job. I can't
    do it for you.
    So tell me what you
    know.

34 "You men who have
    understanding have
    spoken.
    You wise men who hear me
    have said to me,
35 'Job doesn't know what he's
    talking about.
    The things he has said
    don't make any sense.'
36 I wish Job would be given the
    hardest test possible!
    He answered like someone
    who is evil.
37 To his sin he adds even more
    sin.
    He claps his hands and
    makes fun of us.
    He multiplies his words
    against God."

35 Elihu continued,

2 "Job, do you think it's fair for
    you to say,
    'I am the one who is right,
    not God'?
3 You ask him, 'What good is it
    for me not to sin?
    What do I get by not
    sinning?'

4 "I'd like to reply to you
    and to your friends who
    are with you.
5 Look up at the heavens.
    Observe the clouds that are
    high above you.

6 If you sin, what does that
mean to God?
If you sin many times, what
does that do to him?
7 If you do what is right, how
does that help him?
What does he get from
you?
8 The evil things you do only
hurt people like yourself.
The right things you do
only help other human
beings.

9 "People cry out when they
are treated badly.
They beg to be set free
from the power of those
who are over them.
10 But no one says, 'Where is the
God who made me?
He gives us songs even
during the night.
11 He teaches us more than
he teaches the wild
animals.
He makes us wiser than
the birds in the sky.'
12 He doesn't answer sinful
people when they cry out
to him.
That's because they are so
proud.
13 In fact, God doesn't listen to
their empty cries.
The Mighty One doesn't
pay any attention to
them.
14 So he certainly won't listen to
you.
When you say you don't see
him, he won't hear you.
He won't listen when you
state your case to him.
He won't pay attention
even if you wait for him.

15 When you say his anger never
punishes sin, he won't
hear you.
He won't listen when you
say he doesn't pay any
attention to evil.
16 So you say things that don't
mean anything.
You use a lot of words,
but you don't know what
you are talking about."

36

Elihu continued,
2 "Put up with me a little
longer.
I'll show you I can speak up
for God even more.
3 I get my knowledge from far
away.
I'll announce that the God
who made me is fair.
4 You can be sure that my
words are true.
One who has perfect
knowledge is talking
to you.

5 "God is mighty, but he
doesn't hate people.
He's mighty, and he knows
exactly what he's going
to do.
6 He doesn't keep alive those
who are evil.
Instead, he gives suffering
people their rights.
7 He watches over those who
do what is right.
He puts them on thrones as
if they were kings.
He honors them forever.
8 But some people are held by
chains.
Their pain ties them up
like ropes.

⁹God tells them what they've
done.
He tells them they've
become proud and
sinned against him.
¹⁰He makes them listen when
he corrects them.
He commands them to
turn away
from the evil things they've
done.
¹¹If they obey him and serve
him,
they'll enjoy a long and
happy life.
Things will go well with
them.
¹²But if they don't listen to him,
they'll be killed by swords.
They'll die because they
didn't want to know
anything about him.

¹³"Those whose hearts are
ungodly are always
angry.
Even when God puts them
in chains,
they don't cry out for help.
¹⁴They die while they are still
young.
They die among the
male prostitutes at the
temples.
¹⁵But God saves suffering
people while they suffer.
He speaks to them while
they are hurting.

¹⁶"Job, he wants to take you out
of the jaws of trouble.
He wants to bring you to a
wide and safe place.
He'd like to seat you at a
table that is loaded with
the best food.

¹⁷But now you are loaded down
with the punishment
sinners will receive.
You have been judged
fairly.
¹⁸Be careful that no one tempts
you with riches.
Don't take money from
people who want special
favors,
no matter how much it is.
¹⁹Can your wealth keep you
out of trouble?
Can all your mighty efforts
keep you going?
²⁰Don't wish for the night to
come
so you can drag people
away from their homes.
²¹Be careful not to do what is
evil.
You seem to like evil better
than suffering!

²²"God is honored because he
is so powerful.
There is no teacher equal
to him.
²³Who has told him what he
can do?
Who has said to him,
'You have done what is
wrong'?
²⁴Remember to thank him for
what he's done.
People have praised him
with their songs.
²⁵Every human being has seen
his work.
People can see it from far
away.
²⁶How great God is! We'll never
completely understand
him.
We'll never find out how
long he has lived.

27 "He makes mist rise from the
water.
Then it falls as rain into the
streams.
28 The clouds pour down their
moisture.
Rain showers fall on
people everywhere.
29 Who can understand how
God spreads out the
clouds?
Who can explain how he
thunders from his home
in heaven?
30 See how he scatters his
lightning around him!
He lights up the deepest
parts of the ocean.
31 The rain he sends makes
things grow for the
nations.
He provides them with
plenty of food.
32 He holds lightning bolts in
his hands.
He commands them to
strike their marks.
33 His thunder announces that
a storm is coming.
Even the cattle let us know
it's approaching.

37 "When I hear the
thunder, my heart
pounds.
It beats faster inside me.
2 Listen! Listen to the roar of
his voice!
Listen to the thunder that
comes from him!
3 He sends his lightning across
the sky.
It reaches from one end of
the earth to the other.
4 Next comes the sound of his
roaring thunder.

He thunders with his
majestic voice.
When his voice fills the air,
he doesn't hold anything
back.
5 God's voice thunders in
wonderful ways.
We'll never understand the
great things he does.
6 He says to the snow, 'Fall on
the earth.'
He tells the rain, 'Pour down
your mighty waters.'
7 He stops everyone from
working.
He wants them to see his
work.
8 The animals go inside.
They remain in their
dens.
9 The storm comes out of
its storeroom in the
heavens.
The cold comes from the
driving winds.
10 The breath of God produces
ice.
The shallow water freezes
over.
11 He loads the clouds with
moisture.
He scatters his lightning
through them.
12 He directs the clouds to
circle
above the surface of the
whole earth.
They do everything he
commands them to do.
13 He tells the clouds to punish
people.
Or he brings them to water
his earth and show his
love.
14 "Job, listen to me.

Stop and think about the
wonderful things God
does.
¹⁵ Do you know how he controls
the clouds?
Do you understand how
he makes his lightning
flash?
¹⁶ Do you know how the clouds
stay up in the sky?
Do you understand the
wonders of the God who
has perfect knowledge?
¹⁷ Even your clothes are too hot
for you
when the land lies quiet
under the south wind.
¹⁸ Can you help God spread out
the skies?
They are as hard as a mirror
that's made out of bronze.

¹⁹ "Job, tell us what we should
say to God.
We can't prepare our case
because our minds are
dark.
²⁰ Should he be told that I want
to speak?
Would anyone ask to be
destroyed by him?
²¹ No one can look at the sun.
It's too bright after the
wind has swept the skies
clean.
²² Out of the north, God comes
in his shining glory.
He comes in all his
wonderful majesty.
²³ We can't reach up to the
Mighty One.
He is lifted high because of
his power.
Everything he does is fair
and right.
So he doesn't crush people.

²⁴ That's why they have respect
for him.
He cares about all those
who are wise."

The LORD Speaks

38 The LORD spoke to Job
out of a storm. He said,

² "Who do you think you are to
disagree with my plans?
You do not know what you
are talking about.
³ Get ready to stand up for
yourself.
I will ask you some
questions.
Then I want you to answer
me.

⁴ "Where were you when I laid
the earth's foundation?
Tell me, if you know.
⁵ Who measured it? I am sure
you know!
Who stretched a measuring
line across it?
⁶ What was it built on?
Who laid its most
important stone?
⁷ When it happened, the
morning stars sang
together.
All the angels shouted with
joy.

⁸ "Who created the ocean?
Who caused it to be
born?
⁹ I put clouds over it as if they
were its clothes.
I wrapped it in thick
darkness.
¹⁰ I set limits for it.
I put its doors and metal
bars in place.
¹¹ I said, 'You can come this far.

But you can't come any
farther.
Here is where your proud
waves have to stop.'

12 "Job, have you ever
commanded the
morning to come?
Have you ever shown the
sun where to rise?
13 The daylight takes the earth
by its edges
as if it were a blanket.
Then it shakes sinful
people out of it.
14 The earth takes shape like
clay stamped with an
official's mark.
Its features stand out
like the different parts of
your clothes.
15 Sinners would rather have
darkness than light.
When the light comes,
their power is broken.

16 "Have you traveled to the
springs at the bottom of
the ocean?
Have you walked in its
deepest parts?
17 Have the gates of death been
shown to you?
Have you seen the gates of
the deepest darkness?
18 Do you understand how big
the earth is?
Tell me, if you know all
these things.

19 "Where does light come from?
And where does darkness
live?
20 Can you take them to their
places?
Do you know the paths to
their houses?

21 I am sure you know! After all,
you were already born!
You have lived so many
years!

22 "Have you entered the places
where the snow is kept?
Have you seen the
storerooms for the hail?
23 I store up snow and hail for
times of trouble.
I keep them for days of war
and battle.
24 Where does lightning come
from?
Where do the east winds
live that blow across the
earth?
25 Who tells the rain where it
should fall?
Who makes paths for the
thunderstorms?
26 They bring water to places
where no one lives.
They water deserts that do
not have anyone in them.
27 They satisfy the needs of dry
and empty lands.
They make grass start
growing there.
28 Does the rain have a father?
Who is the father of the
drops of dew?
29 Does the ice have a mother?
Who is the mother of
the frost from the
heavens?
30 The waters become as hard
as stone.
The surface of the ocean
freezes over.

31 "Can you tie up the cords of
the Pleiades?
Can you untie the belt that
Orion wears?

³² Can you bring out all the
　　stars in their seasons?
　Can you lead out the Big
　　Dipper and the Little
　　Dipper?
³³ Do you know the laws that
　　govern the heavens?
　Can you rule over the earth
　　the way I do?
³⁴ "Can you give orders to the
　　clouds?
　Can you make them pour
　　rain down on you?
³⁵ Do you send the lightning
　　bolts on their way?
　Do they report to you,
　　'Here we are'?
³⁶ Who gives the ibis wisdom?
　Who gives the rooster
　　understanding?
³⁷ Who is wise enough to count
　　the clouds?
　Who can tip over the water
　　jars of the heavens?
³⁸ I tip them over when the
　　ground becomes
　　hard.
　I do it when the dirt sticks
　　together.
³⁹ "Do you hunt for food for
　　mother lions?
　Do you satisfy the hunger
　　of their cubs?
⁴⁰ Some of them lie low in their
　　dens.
　Others lie waiting in the
　　bushes.
⁴¹ Who provides food for
　　ravens
　when their babies cry out
　　to me?
　They wander around
　　because they do not have
　　anything to eat.

39 "Job, do you know when
mountain goats have
their babies?
　Do you watch when female
　　deer give birth?
² Do you count the months
　　until the animals have
　　their babies?
　Do you know the time
　　when they give birth?
³ They bend their back legs
　　and have their babies.
　Then their labor pains
　　stop.
⁴ Their little ones grow strong
　　and healthy in the wild.
　They leave and do not
　　come home again.

⁵ "Who let the wild donkeys go
　　free?
　Who untied their ropes?
⁶ I gave them the dry and
　　empty land as their
　　home.
　I gave them salt flats to
　　live in.
⁷ They laugh at all the noise in
　　town.
　They do not hear the
　　shouts of the donkey
　　drivers.
⁸ They wander over the hills to
　　look for grass.
　They search for anything
　　green to eat.

⁹ "Job, will wild oxen agree to
　　serve you?
　Will they stay by your feed
　　box at night?
¹⁰ Can you keep them in
　　straight rows with
　　harnesses?
　Will they plow the valleys
　　behind you?

¹¹ Will you depend on them for
their great strength?
Will you let them do your
heavy work?
¹² Can you trust them to haul in
your grain?
Will they bring it to your
threshing floor?

¹³ "The wings of ostriches flap
with joy.
But they can't compare
with the wings and
feathers of storks.
¹⁴ Ostriches lay their eggs on
the ground.
They let them get warm in
the sand.
¹⁵ They do not know that
something might step on
them.
A wild animal might walk
all over them.
¹⁶ Ostriches are mean to their
little ones.
They treat them as if they
did not belong to them.
They do not care that their
work was useless.
¹⁷ I did not provide ostriches
with wisdom.
I did not give them good
sense.
¹⁸ But when they spread their
feathers to run,
they laugh at a horse and
its rider.

¹⁹ "Job, do you give horses their
strength?
Do you put flowing manes
on their necks?
²⁰ Do you make them jump like
locusts?
They terrify others with
their proud snorting.

²¹ They paw the ground
wildly.
They are filled with joy.
They charge at their
enemies.
²² They laugh at fear. They are
not afraid of anything.
They do not run away from
swords.
²³ Many arrows rattle at their
sides.
Flashing spears and
javelins are also there.
²⁴ They are so excited that they
race over the ground.
They can't stand still when
trumpets are blown.
²⁵ When they hear the trumpets
they snort, 'Aha!'
They catch the smells of
battle far away.
They hear the shouts of
commanders and the
battle cries.

²⁶ "Job, are you wise enough to
teach hawks where to
fly?
They spread their wings
and fly toward the
south.
²⁷ Do you command eagles to
fly so high?
They build their nests as
high as they can.
²⁸ They live on cliffs and stay
there at night.
High up on the rocks they
think they are safe.
²⁹ From there they look for their
food.
They can see it from far away.
³⁰ Their little ones like to eat
blood.
Eagles gather where they
see dead bodies."

40

The LORD continued,

2 "I am the Mighty One.
  Will the man who argues
    with me correct me?
  Let him who brings
    charges against me
    answer me!"

3 Job replied to the LORD,

4 "I'm not worthy. How can I
    reply to you?
  I'm putting my hand over
    my mouth. I'll stop
    talking.
5 I spoke once. But I really
    don't have any answer.
  I spoke twice. But I won't
    say anything else."

6 Then the LORD spoke to Job
out of the storm. He said,

7 "Get ready to stand up for
    yourself.
  I will ask you some more
    questions.
  Then I want you to answer
    me.

8 "Would you dare to claim
    that I am not being fair?
  Would you judge me in
    order to make yourself
    seem right?
9 Is your arm as powerful as
    mine is?
  Can your voice thunder as
    mine does?
10 Then put on glory and beauty
    as if they were your
    clothes.
  Also put on honor and
    majesty.
11 Let loose your great anger.
  Look at those who are proud
    and bring them low.

12 Look at proud people and
    make them humble.
  Crush evil people right
    where they are.
13 Bury their bodies together in
    the dust.
  Cover their faces in the
    grave.
14 Then I myself will admit to
    you
  that your own right hand
    can save you.

15 "Look at Behemoth. It is a
    huge animal.
  I made both of you.
  It eats grass like an ox.
16 Look at the strength it has in
    its hips!
  What power it has in the
    muscles of its stomach!
17 Its tail sways back and forth
    like a cedar tree.
  The tendons of its thighs
    are close together.
18 Its bones are like tubes made
    out of bronze.
  Its legs are like rods made
    out of iron.
19 It ranks first among my
    works.
  I made it. I can approach it
    with my sword.
20 The hills produce food
    for it.
  All the other wild animals
    play near it.
21 It lies under lotus plants.
  It hides in tall grass in the
    swamps.
22 The lotus plants hide it in
    their shade.
  Poplar trees near streams
    surround it.
23 It is not afraid when the river
    roars.

It is secure even when the Jordan River rushes against its mouth.
²⁴ Can anyone capture it by its eyes?
Can anyone trap it and poke a hole through its nose?

41 "Job, can you pull Leviathan out of the sea with a fishhook?
Can you tie down its tongue with a rope?
² Can you put a rope through its nose?
Can you stick a hook through its jaw?
³ Will it keep begging you for mercy?
Will it speak gently to you?
⁴ Will it make an agreement with you?
Can you make it your slave for life?
⁵ Can you make a pet out of it like a bird?
Can you put it on a leash for the young women in your house?
⁶ Will traders offer you something for it?
Will they divide it up among the merchants?
⁷ Can you fill its body with harpoons?
Can you throw fishing spears into its head?
⁸ If you touch it, it will fight you.
Then you will remember never to touch it again!
⁹ No one can possibly control Leviathan.
Just looking at it will terrify you.

¹⁰ No one dares to wake it up.
So who can possibly stand up to me?
¹¹ Who has a claim against me that I must pay?
Everything on earth belongs to me.

¹² "Now I will speak about the Leviathan's legs.
I will talk about its strength and its graceful body.
¹³ Who can strip off its outer coat?
Who would try to pierce its double coat of armor?
¹⁴ Who dares to open its jaws?
Its mouth is filled with terrifying teeth.
¹⁵ Its back has rows of shields that are close together.
¹⁶ Each one is so close to the next one
that not even air can pass between them.
¹⁷ They are joined tightly to one another.
They stick together and can't be forced apart.
¹⁸ Leviathan's snorting throws out flashes of light.
Its eyes shine like the first light of day.
¹⁹ Flames spray out of its mouth.
Sparks of fire shoot out.
²⁰ Smoke pours out of its nose.
It is like smoke from a boiling pot over burning grass.
²¹ Its breath sets coals on fire.
Flames fly out of its mouth.
²² Its neck is very strong.
People run to get out of its way.

²³ Its rolls of fat are close
together.
They are firm and can't be
moved.
²⁴ Its chest is as hard as rock.
It is as hard as a lower
millstone.
²⁵ When Leviathan rises up,
even mighty people are
terrified.
They run away when it
moves around wildly.
²⁶ A sword that strikes it has no
effect.
Neither does a spear or
dart or javelin.
²⁷ It treats iron as if it were straw.
It crushes bronze as if it
were rotten wood.
²⁸ Arrows do not make it run
away.
Stones that are thrown
from slings are like straw
hitting it.
²⁹ A club seems like a piece of
straw to it.
It laughs when it hears a
javelin rattling.
³⁰ Its undersides are like broken
pieces of pottery.
It leaves a trail in the mud
like a threshing sled.
³¹ It makes the ocean churn like
a boiling pot.
It stirs up the sea like
perfume someone is
making.
³² It leaves a shiny trail behind
it.
You would think the ocean
had white hair.
³³ Nothing on earth is equal to
Leviathan.
That creature is not afraid
of anything.

³⁴ It looks down on proud
people.
It rules over all those who
are proud.' "

Job's Reply

42 Job replied to the LORD,

² "I know that you can do
anything.
No one can keep you from
doing what you plan to do.
³ You asked me, 'Who do you
think you are to disagree
with my plans?
You do not know what you
are talking about.'
I spoke about things I didn't
completely understand.
I talked about things that
were too wonderful for
me to know.

⁴ "You said, 'Listen now, and I
will speak.
I will ask you some
questions.
Then I want you to answer
me.'
⁵ My ears had heard about you.
But now my own eyes have
seen you.
⁶ So I hate myself.
I'm really sorry for what I
said about you.
That's why I'm sitting in
dust and ashes."

The Story Ends

⁷ After the LORD finished
speaking to Job, he spoke to Eliphaz the Temanite. He said, "I
am angry with you and your two
friends. You have not said what
is true about me, as my servant
Job has. ⁸ So now get seven bulls

and seven rams. Go to my servant Job. Then sacrifice a burnt offering for yourselves. My servant Job will pray for you. And I will accept his prayer. I will not punish you for saying the foolish things you said. You have not said what is true about me, as my servant Job has." ⁹ So Eliphaz the Temanite, Bildad the Shuhite, and Zophar the Naamathite did what the LORD told them to do. And the LORD accepted Job's prayer.

¹⁰ After Job had prayed for his friends, the LORD made him successful again. He gave him twice as much as he had before. ¹¹ All his brothers and sisters and everyone who had known him before came to see him. They ate with him in his house. They showed their concern for him. They comforted him because of all the troubles the LORD had brought on him. Each one gave him a piece of silver and a gold ring.

¹² The LORD blessed the last part of Job's life even more than the first part. He gave Job 14,000 sheep and 6,000 camels. He gave him 1,000 pairs of oxen and 1,000 donkeys. ¹³ Job also had seven sons and three daughters. ¹⁴ He named the first daughter Jemimah. He named the second Keziah. And he named the third Keren-Happuch. ¹⁵ Job's daughters were more beautiful than any other women in the whole land. Their father gave them a share of property along with their brothers.

¹⁶ After all of that happened, Job lived for 140 years. He saw his children, his grandchildren and his great-grandchildren. ¹⁷ And so Job died. He had lived for a very long time.

Psalms

Introduction:

Psalms is a book of poems. Some of the poems were songs, and some were prayers. Some praised God, and some thanked him. Some of the psalms asked God for forgiveness, and some asked God for help. David wrote many of the psalms.

The book of Psalms says that God is the great King. The poems say that he made all things. They say people can trust God. The poems say we should be thankful to God. The poems tell us God loves us.

Outline of contents:

BOOK I

Psalms 1–41

Psalm 1

¹ Blessed is the person who
    obeys the law of the
    LORD.
  They don't follow the
    advice of evil people.
  They don't make a habit of
    doing what sinners do.
  They don't join those who
    make fun of the LORD
    and his law.
² Instead, the law of the LORD
    gives them joy.
  They think about his law
    day and night.
³ That kind of person is like a
    tree that is planted near
    a stream of water.
  It always bears its fruit at
    the right time.

  Its leaves don't dry up.
  Everything godly people
    do turns out well.
⁴ Sinful people are not like that
    at all.
  They are like straw
    that the wind blows away.
⁵ When the LORD judges them,
    their life will come to an
    end.
  Sinners won't have any
    place among those who
    are godly.

⁶ The LORD watches over the
    lives of godly people.
  But the lives of sinful people
    will lead to their death.

Psalm 2

¹ Why do the nations plan evil
    together?
  Why do they make useless
    plans?

² The kings of the earth rise up
    against the LORD.
The rulers of the earth
    join together against his
    anointed king.
³ "Let us break free from their
    chains," they say.
"Let us throw off their
    ropes."

⁴ The God who sits on his
    throne in heaven laughs.
The Lord makes fun of
    those rulers and their
    plans.
⁵ When he is angry, he warns
    them.
When his anger blazes out,
    he terrifies them.
⁶ He says to them,
    "I have placed my king on
    my holy mountain of
    Zion."

⁷ I will announce what the
LORD has promised.

He said to me, "You are my
    son.
Today I have become your
    father.
⁸ Ask me, and I will give the
    nations to you.
All nations on earth will
    belong to you.
⁹ You will break them with an
    iron scepter.
You will smash them to
    pieces like clay pots."

¹⁰ Kings, be wise!
Rulers of the earth, be
    warned!
¹¹ Serve the LORD and have
    respect for him.
Celebrate his rule with
    trembling.

¹² Obey the son completely, or
    he will be angry.
Your way of life will lead to
    your death.
His anger can blaze out at
    any moment.
Blessed are all those who
    go to him for safety.

Psalm 3

*A psalm of David when he ran
away from his son Absalom.*

¹ LORD, I have so many
    enemies!
So many people are rising
    up against me!
² Many are saying about me,
    "God will not save him."

³ LORD, you are like a shield
    that keeps me safe.
You bring me honor.
    You help me win the
    battle.
⁴ I call out to the LORD.
    He answers me from his
    holy mountain.

⁵ I lie down and sleep.
    I wake up again, because
    the LORD takes care of
    me.
⁶ I won't be afraid even though
    tens of thousands
    attack me on every side.

⁷ LORD, rise up!
    My God, save me!
Strike all my enemies in the
    face.
Break the teeth of sinful
    people.

⁸ LORD, you are the one who
    saves.
May your blessing be on
    your people.

Psalm 4

For the director of music.
A psalm of David to be played
on stringed instruments.

¹ My faithful God,
  answer me when I call out
  to you.
Give me rest from my trouble.
Have mercy on me. Hear
  my prayer.

² How long will you people
  turn my glory into
  shame?
How long will you love
  what will certainly fail
  you?
How long will you pray to
  statues of gods?

³ Remember that the LORD
  has set apart his faithful
  servant for himself.
The LORD hears me when I
  call out to him.

⁴ Tremble and do not sin.
When you are in bed,
look deep down inside
  yourself and be silent.

⁵ Offer to the LORD the
  sacrifices that godly
  people offer.
Trust in him.

⁶ LORD, many are asking,
  "Who will make us
  successful?"
LORD, may you do good
  things for us.

⁷ Fill my heart with joy
  when the people have lots
  of grain and fresh wine.

⁸ In peace I will lie down and
  sleep.
LORD, you alone keep me
  safe.

Psalm 5

For the director of music. A psalm
of David to be played on flutes.

¹ LORD, listen to my words.
Pay attention when I
  mourn.

² My King and my God,
  hear me when I cry for help.
I pray to you.

³ LORD, in the morning you
  hear my voice.
In the morning I pray to
  you.
I wait for you in hope.

⁴ For you, God, aren't happy
  with anything that is
  evil.
Those who do what is
  wrong can't live where
  you are.

⁵ Those who are proud can't
  stand in front of you.
You hate everyone who
  does what is evil.

⁶ You destroy those who tell
  lies.
LORD, you hate murderers
  and those who cheat
  others.

⁷ Because of your great love
  I can come into your
  house.
With deep respect I bow
  down
toward your holy temple.

⁸ LORD, I have many enemies.
Lead me in your right path.
Make your way smooth
  and straight for me.

⁹ Not a word from their mouths
  can be trusted.
Their hearts are filled with
  a desire to hurt others.

Their throats are like open
graves.
With their tongues they tell
lies.
¹⁰ God, show that they are
guilty.
Let their evil plans bring
them down.
Send them away because of
their many sins.
They have refused to obey
you.
¹¹ But let all those who go to you
for safety be glad.
Let them always sing for
joy.
Spread your cover over them
and keep them safe.
Then those who love you
will be glad because of
you.
¹² Surely, LORD, you bless those
who do what is right.
Like a shield, your loving
care keeps them safe.

Psalm 6

*For the director of music. According
to sheminith. A psalm of David to be
played on stringed instruments.*

¹ LORD, don't correct me when
you are angry.
Don't punish me when you
are very angry.
² LORD, have mercy on me. I'm
so weak.
LORD, heal me. My body is
full of pain.
³ My soul is very troubled.
LORD, how long will it be
until you save me?
⁴ LORD, turn to me and help me.
Save me. Your love never
fails.

⁵ Dead people can't call out
your name.
How can they praise you
when they are in the
grave?
⁶ My groaning has worn me
out.
All night long my tears
flood my bed.
My bed is wet because of
my crying.
⁷ I'm so sad I can't see very
well.
My eyesight gets worse
because of all my
enemies.
⁸ Get away from me, all you
who do evil.
The LORD has heard my
weeping.
⁹ The LORD has heard my cry
for his mercy.
The LORD accepts my
prayer.
¹⁰ All my enemies will be
covered with shame and
trouble.
They will turn back in
shame. It will happen
suddenly.

Psalm 7

*A shiggaion of David. He sang
it to the LORD about Cush, who was
from the tribe of Benjamin.*

¹ LORD my God, I go to you for
safety.
Help me. Save me from all
those who are chasing
me.
² If you don't, they will tear
me apart as if they were
lions.

They will rip me to pieces
   so that no one can save
   me.

³ Lord my God, suppose I
   have done something
   wrong.
   Suppose I am guilty.
⁴ Or I have done evil to my
   friend.
   Or I have robbed my
   enemy without any
   reason.
⁵ Then let my enemy chase me
   and catch me.
   Let him stomp me into the
   ground.
   Let him bury me in the
   dust.

⁶ Lord, rise up in your anger.
   Rise up against the great
   anger of my enemies.
   My God, wake up.
   Command that the right
   thing be done.
⁷ Let all the people of the earth
   gather around you.
   Rule over them from your
   throne in heaven.
⁸   Lord, judge all people.
  Lord, show that I have done
   what is right.
   Most High God, remember
   that I am honest.
⁹ God, you always do what is
   right.
   You look deep down inside
   the hearts and minds of
   people.
  Bring to an end the terrible
   things sinful people do.
   Make godly people safe.

¹⁰ The Most High God is like
   a shield that keeps me
   safe.

He saves those whose
   hearts are honest.
¹¹ God judges fairly.
   He shows his anger every
   day.
¹² If evil people don't change
   their ways,
   God will sharpen his sword.
   He will get his bow ready to
   use.
¹³ He has prepared his deadly
   weapons.
   He has made his flaming
   arrows ready.

¹⁴ Whoever is full of evil
   plans trouble and ends up
   telling lies.
¹⁵ Whoever digs a hole and
   shovels it out
   falls into the pit they have
   made.
¹⁶ The trouble they cause
   comes back on them.
   The terrible things they do
   will happen to them.

¹⁷ I will give thanks to the Lord
   because he does what is
   right.
   I will sing the praises of the
   name of the Lord Most
   High.

Psalm 8

*For the director of music. According
to* gittith. *A psalm of David.*

¹ Lord, our Lord,
   how majestic is your name
   in the whole earth!

You have set your glory
   in the heavens.
² You have made sure that
   children
   and infants praise you.

Jonah and the Big Fish
JONAH 1:1–17

Reading the Bible

People read the Bible in different ways. Some people like to read it like any other book, from the beginning to the end. Other people like to read one book at a time, like the Gospel of Mark. Still others choose to read about a special theme in the Bible, like Jesus' life. Here's an example you might want to try:

The Life and Teachings of Jesus

❏ Luke 1: Preparing for Jesus' arrival

❏ Luke 2: The story of Jesus' birth

❏ Mark 1: The beginning of Jesus' ministry

❏ Mark 9: A day in the life of Jesus

❏ Matthew 5: The Sermon on the Mount

❏ Matthew 6: The Sermon on the Mount (continued)

❏ Luke 15: Parables of Jesus

❏ John 3: A conversation with Jesus

❏ John 14: Jesus' final instructions

❏ John 17: Jesus' prayer for his disciples

❏ Matthew 26: Jesus' betrayal and arrest

❏ Matthew 27: Jesus dies on a cross

❏ John 20: Jesus' resurrection

❏ Luke 24: Jesus appears after his resurrection

Their praise is a wall
that stops the talk of your
enemies.
³I think about the heavens.
I think about what your
fingers have created.
I think about the moon and
stars
that you have set in place.
⁴What are human beings that
you think about them?
What is a son of man that
you take care of him?
⁵You have made them a little
lower than the angels.
You placed on them a
crown of glory and
honor.
⁶You made human beings rule
over everything your
hands created.
You put everything under
their control.
⁷They rule over all flocks and
herds
and over the wild animals.
⁸They rule over the birds in
the sky
and over the fish in the
ocean.
They rule over everything
that swims in the
oceans.
⁹LORD, our Lord,
how majestic is your name
in the whole earth!

Psalm 9

For the director of music.
A psalm of David to the tune
of "The Death of the Son."

¹LORD, I will give thanks to
you with all my heart.
I will tell about all the
wonderful things you
have done.
²I will be glad and full of joy
because of you.
Most High God, I will sing
the praises of your name.
³My enemies turn back.
They fall down and die
right in front of you.
⁴You have proved that I
haven't done anything
wrong.
You have sat on your
throne and judged
fairly.
⁵You have punished the
nations. You have
destroyed evil people.
You have erased their
names from your book
for ever and ever.
⁶My enemies have been
destroyed forever.
You have leveled their
cities to the ground.
Even the memory of them
is gone.
⁷The LORD rules forever.
He has set up his throne so
that he can judge people.
⁸He rules the world in keeping
with what is right.
He judges all its people
fairly.
⁹The LORD is a place of safety
for those who have been
treated badly.
He keeps them safe in
times of trouble.
¹⁰LORD, those who know you
will trust in you.
You have never deserted
those who look to you.

11 Sing the praises of the LORD.
 He rules from his throne
 in Zion.
 Tell among the nations
 what he has done.
12 The God who pays back
 murderers remembers.
 He doesn't forget the cries
 of those who are hurting.

13 LORD, see how badly my
 enemies treat me!
 Help me! Don't let me go
 down to the gates of
 death!
14 Then I can give praise to you
 at the gates of the city of
 Zion.
 There I will be full of joy
 because you have saved
 me.
15 The nations have fallen into
 the pit they have dug.
 Their feet are caught in the
 net they have hidden.
16 The LORD is known to be fair
 by the things he does.
 Evil people are trapped by
 what they have done.
17 Sinful people go down to the
 place of the dead.
 So do all the nations that
 forget God.
18 But God will never forget
 needy people.
 The hope of those who are
 hurting will never die.

19 LORD, rise up. Don't let
 people win the battle.
 Let the nations come to
 you and be judged.
20 LORD, strike them with
 terror.
 Let the nations know they are
 only human beings.

Psalm 10

1 LORD, why are you so far
 away?
 Why do you hide yourself
 in times of trouble?

2 An evil person is proud and
 hunts down those who
 are weak.
 He catches weak people by
 making clever plans.
3 He brags about what his
 heart desires.
 He speaks well of those
 who always want
 more.
 He attacks the LORD with
 his words.
4 Because he is proud, that evil
 person doesn't turn to
 the LORD.
 There is no room for God
 in any of his thoughts.
5 Everything always goes well
 for him.
 So he is proud.
 He doesn't want to have
 anything to do with
 God's laws.
 He makes fun of all his
 enemies.
6 He says to himself, "I will
 always be secure."
 He promises himself,
 "No one will ever harm
 me."
7 His mouth is full of lies and
 warnings.
 With his tongue he speaks
 evil and makes trouble.

8 Sinful people hide and wait
 near the villages.
 From their hiding places
 they murder people who
 aren't guilty.

They watch in secret for those they want to attack.
⁹They hide and wait like a lion in the bushes.
From their hiding places they wait to catch those who are helpless.
They catch them and drag them off in their nets.
¹⁰Those they have attacked are beaten up. They fall to the ground.
They fall because their attackers are too strong for them.
¹¹Sinful people say to themselves, "God will never notice.
He covers his face. He never sees us."

¹²Lord, rise up! God, show your power!
Don't forget those who are helpless.
¹³Why do sinful people attack you with their words?
Why do they say to themselves,
"He won't hold us accountable"?
¹⁴God, you see the problems of people in trouble.
You take note of their pain. You do something about it.
So those who are attacked place themselves in your care.
You help children whose fathers have died.
¹⁵Take away the power of sinful people.
Hold them accountable for the evil things they do.

Uncover all the evil they have done.
¹⁶The Lord is King for ever and ever.
The nations will disappear from his land.
¹⁷Lord, you hear the desires of those who are hurting.
You cheer them up and give them hope.
You listen to their cries.
¹⁸You stand up for those whose fathers have died
and for those who have been treated badly.
You do it so that mere human beings made of dust
may not terrify others anymore.

Psalm 11

For the director of music.
A psalm of David.

¹I run to the Lord for safety.
So how can you say to me,
"Fly away like a bird to your mountain.
²Look! Evil people are bending their bows.
They are placing their arrows against the strings.
They are planning to shoot from the shadows
at those who have honest hearts.
³When law and order are being destroyed,
what can godly people do?"

⁴The Lord is in his holy temple.
The Lord is on his throne in heaven.

He watches everyone on
   earth.
His eyes study them.
5 The LORD watches over those
   who do what is right.
But he really hates sinful
   people and those who
   love to hurt others.
6 He will pour out flaming
   coals and burning
   sulfur
on those who do what is
   wrong.
A hot and dry wind will
   destroy them.

7 The LORD always does what
   is right.
So he loves it when people
   do what is fair.
Those who are honest will
   enjoy his blessing.

Psalm 12

*For the director of music. According
to* sheminith. *A psalm of David.*

1 Help, LORD! No one does
   what is right anymore.
Those who are faithful
   have disappeared from
   the human race.
2 Everyone tells lies to their
   neighbors.
With their lips they praise
   others, but they don't
   really mean it.

3 May the LORD close all lips
   that don't mean what
   they say.
May he stop every tongue
   that brags.
4 They say, "What we speak
   with our tongues will
   win the battle.

What we say with our lips
   will keep us safe. No one
   will have victory over
   us."

5 The LORD says, "The poor are
   being robbed.
Those who are in need
   groan.
So I will stand up to help
   them.
I will keep them safe from
   those who tell lies about
   them."
6 The words of the LORD are
   perfect.
They are like silver made
   pure in a clay furnace.
They are like gold made
   pure seven times over.

7 LORD, you will keep needy
   people safe.
You will always keep
   sinners from hurting us.
8 Proud and sinful people walk
   around openly
when the evil they do is
   praised by the human
   race.

Psalm 13

*For the director of music.
A psalm of David.*

1 LORD, how long must I wait?
   Will you forget me
   forever?
How long will you turn
   your face away from me?
2 How long must I struggle
   with my thoughts?
How long must my heart be
   sad day after day?
How long will my enemies
   keep winning the battle
   over me?

3 LORD my God, look at me and
answer me.
Give me new life, or I will
die.
4 Then my enemies will say,
"We have beaten him."
They will be filled with joy
when I die.

5 But I trust in your faithful
love.
My heart is filled with joy
because you will save
me.
6 I will sing praise to the
LORD.
He has been so good to me.

Psalm 14

For the director of music.
A psalm of David.

1 Foolish people say in their
hearts,
"There is no God."
They do all kinds of horrible
and evil things.
No one does anything
good.

2 The LORD looks down from
heaven
on all people.
He wants to see if there are
any who understand.
He wants to see if there are
any who trust in God.
3 All of them have turned
away.
They have all become evil.
No one does anything good,
no one at all.

4 Do all these people who do
evil know nothing?
They eat up my people as if
they were eating bread.

They never call out to the
LORD.
5 But just look at them! They
are filled with terror
because God is among
those who do right.
6 You who do evil keep poor
people from succeeding.
But the LORD is their place
of safety.

7 How I pray that the God who
saves Israel will come
out of Zion!
Then the LORD will bless
his people with great
success again.
So let the people of Jacob
be filled with joy! Let
Israel be glad!

Psalm 15

A psalm of David.

1 LORD, who can live in your
sacred tent?
Who can stay on your holy
mountain?

2 Anyone who lives without
blame
and does what is right.
They speak the truth from
their heart.
3   They don't tell lies about
other people.
They don't do wrong to their
neighbors.
They don't say anything
bad about them.
4 They hate evil people.
But they honor those who
have respect for the
LORD.
They keep their promises
even when it hurts.

They do not change their
  mind.
5 They lend their money to
    poor people without
    charging interest.
  They don't accept money
    to harm those who aren't
    guilty.

Anyone who lives like that
  will always be secure.

Psalm 16

A miktam of David.

1 My God, keep me safe.
  I go to you for safety.

2 I say to the LORD, "You are
    my Lord.
  Without you, I don't have
    anything that is good."
3 I say about God's people who
    live in our land, "They
    are the noble ones.
  I take great delight in
    them."
4 Those who run after other
    gods
  will suffer more and
    more.
  I will not pour out offerings of
    blood to those gods.
  My lips will not speak their
    names.

5 LORD, you alone are
    everything I need.
  You make my life secure.
6 I am very pleased with what
    you have given me.
  I am very happy with what
    I've received from you.
7 I will praise the LORD. He
    gives me good advice.
  Even at night my heart
    teaches me.

8 I keep my eyes always on the
    LORD.
  He is at my right hand.
  So I will always be secure.

9 So my heart is glad. Joy is on
    my tongue.
  My body also will be
    secure.
10 You will not leave me in the
    place of the dead.
  You will not let your
    faithful one rot away.
11 You always show me the path
    of life.
  You will fill me with joy
    when I am with you.
  You will make me happy
    forever at your right
    hand.

Psalm 17

A prayer of David.

1 LORD, hear me, because I ask
    for what is right.
  Listen to my cry for help.
  Hear my prayer.
    It doesn't come from lips
    that tell lies.
2 When you hand down your
    sentence, may it be in
    my favor.
  May your eyes see what is
    right.

3 Look deep down into my
    heart.
  Study me carefully at night
    and test me.
  You won't find anything
    wrong.
  I have planned nothing evil.
  My mouth has not said
    sinful things.

4 Though evil people tried to
pay me to do wrong,
I have not done what they
wanted.
Instead I have done what you
commanded.
5 My steps have stayed on your
paths.
My feet have not slipped.

6 My God, I call out to you
because you will answer
me.
Listen to me. Hear my
prayer.
7 Show me the wonders of your
great love.
By using your great power,
you save those who go to
you for safety from their
enemies.
8 Take good care of me, just as
you would take care of
your own eyes.
Hide me in the shadow of
your wings.
9 Save me from the sinful
people who want to
destroy me.
Save me from my deadly
enemies who are all
around me.

10 They make their hearts hard
and stubborn.
Their mouths speak with
pride.
11 They have tracked me down.
They are all around me.
Their eyes watch for a
chance to throw me to
the ground.
12 They are like a hungry lion,
waiting to attack.
They are like a powerful
lion, hiding in the bushes.

13 LORD, rise up. Oppose them
and bring them down.
With your sword, save me
from those evil people.
14 LORD, by your power save me
from people like that.
They belong to this world.
They get their reward in
this life.

May what you have stored up
for evil people fill their
bellies.
May their children's
stomachs be filled with
it.
And may there even be
leftovers for their little
ones.
15 You will show that I am
right; I will enjoy your
blessing.
When I wake up, I will be
satisfied because I will
see you.

Psalm 18

*For the director of music. A psalm
of David, the servant of the LORD.
He sang the words of this song to
the LORD. He sang them when the
LORD saved him. He saved him
from the power of all his enemies
and of Saul. David said,*

1 I love you, LORD.
You give me strength.

2 The LORD is my rock and my
place of safety. He is the
God who saves me.
My God is my rock. I go to
him for safety.
He is like a shield to me.
He's the power that saves
me. He's my place of
safety.

³I called out to the LORD. He is
worthy of praise.
He saved me from my
enemies.

⁴The ropes of death were
almost wrapped around
me.
A destroying flood swept
over me.

⁵The ropes of the grave were
tight around me.
Death set its trap in front of
me.

⁶When I was in trouble, I
called out to the LORD.
I cried to my God for help.
From his temple he heard my
voice.
My cry for help reached his
ears.

⁷The earth trembled and
shook.
The base of the mountains
rocked back and forth.
It trembled because the
LORD was angry.

⁸Smoke came out of his nose.
Flames of fire came out of
his mouth.
Burning coals blazed out of
it.

⁹He opened the heavens and
came down.
Dark clouds were under his
feet.

¹⁰He stood on the cherubim
and flew.
The wings of the wind
lifted him up.

¹¹He covered himself with
darkness.
The dark rain clouds of
the sky were like a tent
around him.

¹²Clouds came out of the
brightness that was all
around him.
They came with hailstones
and flashes of lightning.

¹³The LORD thundered from
heaven.
The voice of the Most High
God was heard.

¹⁴He shot his arrows and
scattered our enemies.
He sent great flashes of
lightning and chased the
enemies away.

¹⁵The bottom of the sea could
be seen.
The foundations of the
earth were uncovered.
LORD, it happened when your
anger blazed out.
It came like a blast of
breath from your nose.

¹⁶He reached down from
heaven. He took hold
of me.
He lifted me out of deep
waters.

¹⁷He saved me from my
powerful enemies.
He set me free from those
who were too strong for
me.

¹⁸They opposed me when I was
in trouble.
But the LORD helped me.

¹⁹He brought me out into a
wide and safe place.
He saved me because he
was pleased with me.

²⁰The LORD has been good to
me because I do what is
right.
He has rewarded me
because I lead a pure life.

²¹ I have lived the way the LORD
 wanted me to.
 I am not guilty of turning
 away from my God.
²² I keep all his laws in mind.
 I haven't turned away from
 his commands.
²³ He knows that I am without
 blame.
 He knows I've kept myself
 from sinning.
²⁴ The LORD has rewarded me
 for doing what is right.
 He has rewarded me
 because I haven't done
 anything wrong.
²⁵ LORD, to those who are
 faithful you show that
 you are faithful.
 To those who are without
 blame you show that you
 are without blame.
²⁶ To those who are pure you
 show that you are
 pure.
 But to those whose paths
 are crooked you show
 that you are clever.
²⁷ You save those who aren't
 proud.
 But you bring down those
 whose eyes are proud.
²⁸ LORD, you keep the lamp
 of my life burning
 brightly.
 You are my God. You bring
 light into my darkness.
²⁹ With your help I can attack a
 troop of soldiers.
 With the help of my God I
 can climb over a wall.
³⁰ God's way is perfect.
 The LORD's word doesn't
 have any flaws.

He is like a shield
 to all who go to him for
 safety.
³¹ Who is God except the LORD?
 Who is the Rock except our
 God?
³² God gives me strength for the
 battle.
 He keeps my way secure.
³³ He makes my feet like the
 feet of a deer.
 He causes me to stand on
 the highest places.
³⁴ He trains my hands to fight
 every battle.
 My arms can bend a bow of
 bronze.
³⁵ LORD, you are like a shield
 that keeps me safe.
 Your strong right hand
 keeps me going.
 Your help has made me
 great.
³⁶ You give me a wide path to
 walk on
 so that I don't twist my
 ankles.
³⁷ I chased my enemies and
 caught them.
 I didn't turn back until
 they were destroyed.
³⁸ I crushed them so that they
 couldn't get up.
 They fell under my feet.
³⁹ LORD, you gave me strength
 to fight the battle.
 You made my enemies
 humble in front of me.
⁴⁰ You made them turn their
 backs and run away.
 So I destroyed my
 enemies.
⁴¹ They cried out for help. But
 there was no one to save
 them.

They called out to the
LORD. But he didn't
answer them.
⁴² I beat them as fine as dust
blown by the wind.
I stomped on them like
mud in the streets.
⁴³ You saved me when my own
people attacked me.
You made me the ruler
over nations.
People I didn't know serve
me now.
⁴⁴ People from other lands bow
down to me in fear.
As soon as they hear me,
they obey me.
⁴⁵ All of them give up hope.
They come trembling
out of their hiding
places.
⁴⁶ The LORD lives! Give praise to
my Rock!
Give honor to God my
Savior!
⁴⁷ He is the God who pays back
my enemies.
He brings the nations
under my control.
⁴⁸ He saves me from my
enemies.
You have honored me more
than them.
You have saved me from a
man who wanted to hurt
me.
⁴⁹ LORD, I will praise you
among the nations.
I will sing the praises of
your name.
⁵⁰ The LORD helps his king win
great battles.
He shows his faithful love
to his anointed king.

He shows it to David and to
his family forever.

Psalm 19

For the director of music.
A psalm of David.

¹ The heavens tell about the
glory of God.
The skies show that his
hands created them.
² Day after day they speak
about it.
Night after night they
make it known.
³ But they don't speak or use
words.
No sound is heard from
them.
⁴ Yet their voice goes out into
the whole earth.
Their words go out from
one end of the world to
the other.

God has set up a tent in the
heavens for the sun.
⁵   The sun is like a groom
leaving the room of his
wedding night.
The sun is like a great
runner who takes delight
in running a race.
⁶ It rises at one end of the
heavens.
Then it moves across to the
other end.
Everything enjoys its
warmth.

⁷ The law of the LORD is
perfect.
It gives us new strength.
The laws of the LORD can be
trusted.
They make childish people
wise.

8 The rules of the LORD are
  right.
    They give joy to our hearts.
  The commands of the LORD
    shine brightly.
    They give light to our
      minds.
9 The law that brings respect
    for the LORD is pure.
    It lasts forever.
  The commands the LORD
    gives are true.
    All of them are completely
      right.
10 They are more priceless than
    gold.
    They have greater value
      than huge amounts of
      pure gold.
    They are sweeter than honey
      that is taken from the
      honeycomb.
11 Your servant is warned by
    them.
    When people obey
      them, they are greatly
      rewarded.
12 But who can know their own
    mistakes?
    Forgive my hidden faults.
13 Also keep me from the sins I
    want to commit.
    May they not be my
      master.
    Then I will be without blame.
    I will not be guilty of any
      great sin against your
      law.
14 LORD, may these words of my
    mouth please you.
    And may these thoughts of
      my heart please you also.
    You are my Rock and my
      Redeemer.

Psalm 20

For the director of music.
A psalm of David.

1 May the LORD answer you
    when you are in trouble.
  May the God of Jacob keep
    you safe.
2 May he send you help from
    the sacred tent.
  May he give you aid from
    Zion.
3 May he remember all your
    sacrifices.
  May he accept your burnt
    offerings.
4 May he give you what your
    heart wishes for.
  May he make all your plans
    succeed.
5 May we shout for joy over
    your victory.
  May we lift up our flags in
    the name of our God.
  May the LORD give you
    everything you ask for.

6 Now I know that the LORD
    gives victory to his
    anointed king.
  He answers him from his
    sacred home in heaven.
  The power of God's right
    hand gives victory to the
    king.
7 Some trust in chariots. Some
    trust in horses.
  But we trust in the LORD
    our God.
8 They are brought to their
    knees and fall down.
  But we get up and stand
    firm.
9 LORD, give victory to the king!
  Answer us when we call
    out to you!

Psalm 21

For the director of music.
A psalm of David.

[1] LORD, the king is filled with
joy because you are
strong.
How great is his joy
because you help him
win his battles!
[2] You have given him what his
heart wished for.
You haven't kept back from
him what his lips asked
for.
[3] You came to greet him with
rich blessings.
You placed a crown of pure
gold on his head.
[4] He asked you for life, and you
gave it to him.
You promised him days
that would never end.
[5] His glory is great because
you helped him win his
battles.
You have honored him
with glory and majesty.
[6] You have given him blessings
that will never end.
You have made him glad
and joyful because you
are with him.
[7] The king trusts in the LORD.
The faithful love of the
Most High God
will keep the king secure.

[8] You, the king, will capture all
your enemies.
Your right hand will take
hold of them.
[9] When you appear for battle,
you will burn them up like
they were in a flaming
furnace.

The LORD will swallow them
up in his great anger.
His fire will burn them up.
[10] You will wipe their children
from the face of the
earth.
You will remove them from
the human race.
[11] Your enemies make evil
plans against you.
They think up evil things
to do. But they can't
succeed.
[12] You will make them turn
their backs and run
away
when you aim your arrows
at them.

[13] LORD, may you be honored
because you are strong.
We will sing and praise
your might.

Psalm 22

For the director of music.
A psalm of David to the tune
of "The Doe of the Morning."

[1] My God, my God, why have
you deserted me?
Why do you seem so far
away when I need you to
save me?
Why do you seem so far
away that you can't hear
my groans?
[2] My God, I cry out in the
daytime. But you don't
answer.
I cry out at night. But you
don't let me sleep.

[3] But you rule from your
throne as the Holy One.
You are the God Israel
praises.

⁴Our people of long ago put
　　their trust in you.
　They trusted in you, and
　　you saved them.
⁵They cried out to you and
　　were saved.
　They trusted in you, and
　　you didn't let them
　　down.

⁶Everyone treats me like a
　　worm and not a man.
　They hate me and look
　　down on me.
⁷All those who see me laugh
　　at me.
　They shout at me and
　　make fun of me.
　They shake their heads
　　at me.
⁸They say, "He trusts in the
　　Lord.
　Let the Lord help him.
　If the Lord is pleased with
　　him,
　　let him save him."

⁹But you brought me out of my
　　mother's body.
　You made me trust in you
　　even when I was at my
　　mother's breast.
¹⁰From the time I was born,
　　you took good care
　　of me.
　Ever since I came out of my
　　mother's body, you have
　　been my God.
¹¹Don't be far away from me.
　Trouble is near,
　and there is no one to
　　help me.
¹²Many enemies are all around
　　me.
　They are like strong bulls
　　from the land of Bashan.

¹³They are like roaring lions
　　that tear to pieces what
　　they kill.
　They open their mouths
　　wide to attack me.
¹⁴My strength is like water
　　that is poured out on the
　　ground.
　I feel as if my bones aren't
　　connected.
　My heart has turned to wax.
　It has melted away inside
　　me.
¹⁵My mouth is dried up like a
　　piece of broken pottery.
　My tongue sticks to the
　　roof of my mouth.
　You bring me down to the
　　edge of the grave.
¹⁶A group of sinful people has
　　closed in on me.
　They are all around me like
　　a pack of dogs.
　They have pierced my
　　hands and my feet.
¹⁷Everyone can see all my
　　bones right through my
　　skin.
　People stare at me. They
　　laugh when I suffer.
¹⁸They divide up my clothes
　　among them.
　They cast lots for what I am
　　wearing.

¹⁹Lord, don't be so far away
　　from me.
　You give me strength. Come
　　quickly to help me.
²⁰Save me from being killed by
　　the sword.
　Save the only life I have.
　Save me from the power
　　of those dogs.
²¹Save me from the mouths of
　　those lions.

Save me from the horns of
those wild oxen.

22 I will announce your name to
my people.
I will praise you among
those who are gathered
to worship you.
23 You who have respect for the
LORD, praise him!
All you people of Jacob,
honor him!
All you people of Israel,
worship him!
24 He has not forgotten the one
who is hurting.
He has not turned away
from his suffering.
He has not turned his face
away from him.
He has listened to his cry
for help.

25 Because of what you have
done,
I will praise you in the
whole community of
those who worship you.
In front of those who respect
you,
I will keep my promises.
26 Those who are poor will eat
and be satisfied.
Those who seek the LORD
will praise him.
May their hearts be filled
with new hope!
27 People from one end of the
earth to the other
will remember and turn to
the LORD.
The people of all the nations
will bow down in front of
him.
28 The LORD is King.
He rules over the nations.

29 All rich people of the earth
will feast and worship
God.
All who go down to the
grave will kneel in front
of him.
Those who cannot keep
themselves alive will
kneel.
30 Those who are not yet born
will serve him.
Those who are born later
will be told about the
Lord.
31 And they will tell people who
have not yet been born,
"The Lord has done what is
right!"

Psalm 23

A psalm of David.

1 The LORD is my shepherd.
He gives me everything I
need.
2　He lets me lie down in
fields of green grass.
He leads me beside quiet
waters.
3　He gives me new strength.
He guides me in the right
paths
for the honor of his name.
4 Even though I walk
through the darkest
valley,
I will not be afraid.
You are with me.
Your shepherd's rod and staff
comfort me.

5 You prepare a feast for me
right in front of my
enemies.
You pour oil on my head.
My cup runs over.

⁶I am sure that your goodness
and love will follow me
all the days of my life.
And I will live in the house of
the Lord
forever.

Psalm 24

A psalm of David.

¹The earth belongs to the
Lord. And so does
everything in it.
The world belongs to him.
And so do all those who
live in it.
²He set it firmly on the oceans.
He made it secure on the
waters.

³Who can go up to the temple
on the mountain of the
Lord?
Who can stand in his holy
place?
⁴Anyone who has clean hands
and a pure heart.
Anyone who does not trust
in the statue of a god.
Anyone who doesn't
use the name of that
god when he makes a
promise.
⁵People like that will receive
the Lord's blessing.
When God their Savior
hands down his
sentence, it will be in
their favor.
⁶The people who look to God
are like that.
God of Jacob, they look to
you.

⁷Open wide, you gates.
Open up, you ancient
doors.

Then the King of glory will
come in.
⁸Who is the King of glory?
The Lord, who is strong
and mighty.
The Lord, who is mighty
in battle.
⁹Open wide, you gates.
Open wide, you ancient
doors.
Then the King of glory will
come in.
¹⁰Who is he, this King of glory?
The Lord who rules over
all.
He is the King of glory.

Psalm 25

A psalm of David.

¹In you, Lord my God, I put
my trust.
² I trust in you.
Don't let me be put to shame.
Don't let my enemies win
the battle over me.
³Those who put their hope in
you
will never be put to shame.
But those who lie to other
people for no reason
will be put to shame.

⁴Lord, show me your ways.
Teach me how to follow
you.
⁵Guide me in your truth.
Teach me.
You are God my Savior.
I put my hope in you all
day long.
⁶Lord, remember your great
mercy and love.
You have shown them to
your people for a long
time.

⁷Don't remember the sins I
committed when I was
young.
Don't remember how often
I refused to obey you.
Remember me because you
love me.
LORD, you are good.
⁸The LORD is honest and
good.
He teaches sinners to walk
in his ways.
⁹He shows those who aren't
proud how to do what is
right.
He teaches them his ways.
¹⁰All the LORD's ways are
loving and faithful
toward those who obey
what his covenant
commands.
¹¹LORD, be true to your name.
Forgive my sin, even
though it is great.
¹²Who are the people who have
respect for the LORD?
God will teach them
the ways they should
choose.
¹³Things will always go well for
them.
Their children will be
given the land.
¹⁴The LORD shares his plans
with those who have
respect for him.
He makes his covenant
known to them.
¹⁵My eyes always look to the
LORD.
He alone can set my feet
free from the trap.
¹⁶Turn to me and help me.
I am lonely and hurting.

¹⁷Take away the troubles of my
heart.
Set me free from my great
pain.
¹⁸Look at how I'm hurting! See
how much I suffer!
Take away all my sins.
¹⁹Look at how many enemies I
have!
See how terrible their
hatred is for me!
²⁰Guard my life. Save me.
Don't let me be put to
shame.
I go to you for safety.
²¹May my honest and good life
keep me safe.
LORD, I have put my hope
in you.
²²God, set Israel free
from all their troubles!

Psalm 26

A psalm of David.

¹LORD, when you hand down
your sentence, let it be in
my favor.
I have lived without blame.
I have trusted in the LORD.
I have never doubted him.
²LORD, test me. Try me out.
Look deep down into my
heart and mind.
³I have always remembered
your love that never fails.
I have always depended
on the fact that you are
faithful.
⁴I don't spend time with
people who tell lies.
I don't keep company with
pretenders.
⁵I hate to be with a group of
sinful people.

I refuse to spend time with
  those who are evil.
⁶ I wash my hands to show that
    I'm not guilty.
  Lord, I come near your
    altar.
⁷ I shout my praise to you.
  I tell about all the
    wonderful things you
    have done.
⁸ Lord, I love the house where
    you live.
  I love the place where your
    glory is.

⁹ Don't destroy me together
    with sinners.
  Don't take away my life
    along with murderers.
¹⁰ Their hands are always
    planning to do evil.
  Their right hands are
    full of money that has
    bought their help.
¹¹ But I live without blame.
  Save me from harm and
    treat me with kindness.

¹² My feet stand on level
    ground.
  In the whole community I
    will praise the Lord.

Psalm 27

A psalm of David.

¹ The Lord is my light, and he
    saves me.
  Why should I fear anyone?
  The Lord is my place of
    safety.
  Why should I be afraid?
² My enemies are evil.
  They will trip and fall
when they attack me
  and try to swallow
    me up.

³ Even if an army attacks me,
  my heart will not be afraid.
Even if war breaks out
    against me,
  I will still trust in God.

⁴ I'm asking the Lord for only
    one thing.
  Here is what I want.
  I want to live in the house of
    the Lord
  all the days of my life.
  I want to look at the beauty of
    the Lord.
  I want to worship him in
    his temple.
⁵ When I'm in trouble,
  he will keep me safe in his
    house.
He will hide me in the safety
    of his holy tent.
He will put me on a rock
    that is very high.
⁶ Then I will win the battle
  over my enemies who are
    all around me.
At his holy tent I will offer my
    sacrifice with shouts of
    joy.
  I will sing and make music
    to the Lord.

⁷ Lord, hear my voice when I
    call out to you.
  Treat me with kindness
    and answer me.
⁸ My heart says, "Seek him!"
  Lord, I will seek you.
⁹ Don't turn your face away
    from me.
  Don't turn me away
    because you are angry.
  You have helped me.
God my Savior, don't say no
    to me.
  Don't desert me.

¹⁰ My father and mother may
  desert me,
  but the LORD will accept me.
¹¹ LORD, teach me your ways.
  Lead me along a straight
  path.
  There are many people
  who treat me badly.
¹² My enemies want to harm
  me. So don't turn me
  over to them.
  Witnesses who tell lies are
  rising up against me.
  They say all sorts of evil
  things about me.

¹³ Here is something I am still
  sure of.
  I will see the LORD's
  goodness
  while I'm still alive.
¹⁴ Wait for the LORD.
  Be strong and don't lose
  hope.
  Wait for the LORD.

Psalm 28

A psalm of David.

¹ LORD, my Rock, I call out to
  you.
  Pay attention to me.
  If you remain silent, I will die.
  I will be like those who go
  down into the grave.
² Hear my cry for your favor
  when I call out to you for
  help.
  Hear me when I lift up my
  hands in prayer
  toward your Most Holy
  Room.

³ Don't drag me away with
  sinners.
  Don't drag me away with
  those who do evil.

They speak in a friendly way
  to their neighbors.
  But their hearts are full of
  hate.
⁴ Pay them back for their evil
  actions.
  Pay them back for what
  their hands have done.
  Give them exactly what
  they should get.
⁵ They don't care about the
  LORD's mighty acts.
  They don't care about what
  his hands have done.
  So he will tear them down.
  He will never build them
  up again.

⁶ Give praise to the LORD.
  He has heard my cry for his
  favor.
⁷ The LORD gives me strength.
  He is like a shield that
  keeps me safe.
  My heart trusts in him, and
  he helps me.
  My heart jumps for joy.
  With my song I praise
  him.

⁸ The LORD gives strength to
  his people.
  He guards and saves his
  anointed king.
⁹ Save your people. Bless those
  who belong to you.
  Be their shepherd. Take
  care of them forever.

Psalm 29

A psalm of David.

¹ Praise the LORD, you angels
  in heaven.
  Praise the LORD for his
  glory and strength.

²Praise the LORD for the glory
that belongs to him.
Worship the LORD because
of his beauty and
holiness.
³The voice of the LORD is
heard over the waters.
The God of glory thunders.
The LORD thunders over
the mighty waters.
⁴The voice of the LORD is
powerful.
The voice of the LORD is
majestic.
⁵The voice of the LORD breaks
the cedar trees.
The LORD breaks the
cedars of Lebanon into
pieces.
⁶He makes the mountains of
Lebanon leap like a calf.
He makes Mount Hermon
jump like a young wild
ox.
⁷The voice of the LORD
strikes
with flashes of lightning.
⁸The voice of the LORD shakes
the desert.
The LORD shakes the
Desert of Kadesh.
⁹The voice of the LORD twists
the oak trees.
It strips the forests bare.
And in his temple everyone
cries out, "Glory!"
¹⁰The LORD on his throne rules
over the flood.
The LORD rules from his
throne as King forever.
¹¹The LORD gives strength to
his people.
The LORD blesses his
people with peace.

Psalm 30

*A psalm of David. A song for setting
apart the completed temple to God.*

¹LORD, I will give you honor.
You brought me out of deep
trouble.
You didn't give my enemies
the joy of seeing me die.
²LORD my God, I called out to
you for help.
And you healed me.
³LORD, you brought me up
from the place of the
dead.
You kept me from going
down into the pit.

⁴Sing the praises of the LORD,
you who are faithful to
him.
Praise him, because his
name is holy.
⁵His anger lasts for only a
moment.
But his favor lasts for a
person's whole life.
Weeping can stay for the
night.
But joy comes in the
morning.

⁶When I felt safe, I said,
"I will always be secure."
⁷LORD, when you gave me
your help,
you made Mount Zion
stand firm.
But when you took away your
help,
I was terrified.

⁸LORD, I called out to you.
I cried to you for mercy.
⁹I said, "What good will come
if I become silent in
death?

What good will come if I go
    down into the grave?
Can the dust of my dead body
    praise you?
Can it tell how faithful you
    are?
¹⁰ Lord, hear me. Have mercy
    on me.
    Lord, help me."
¹¹ You turned my loud crying
    into dancing.
    You removed my clothes of
    sadness and dressed me
    with joy.
¹² So my heart will sing your
    praises. I can't keep
    silent.
    Lord, my God, I will praise
    you forever.

Psalm 31

For the director of music.
A psalm of David.

¹ Lord, I have come to you for
    safety.
    Don't let me ever be put to
    shame.
    Save me, because you do
    what is right.
² Pay attention to me.
    Come quickly to help me.
    Be the rock I go to for safety.
    Be the strong fort that
    saves me.
³ You are my rock and my fort.
    Lead me and guide me for
    the honor of your name.
⁴ Keep me free from the trap
    that is set for me.
    You are my place of safety.
⁵ Into your hands I commit my
    very life.
    Lord, set me free. You are
    my faithful God.

⁶ I hate those who worship
    worthless statues of
    gods.
    But I trust in the Lord.
⁷ I will be glad and full of joy
    because you love me.
    You saw that I was hurting.
    You took note of my great
    pain.
⁸ You have not handed me over
    to the enemy.
    You have put me in a wide
    and safe place.

⁹ Lord, have mercy on me. I'm
    in deep trouble.
    I'm so sad I can hardly see.
    My whole body grows weak
    with sadness.
¹⁰ Pain has taken over my life.
    My years are spent in
    groaning.
    I have no strength because
    I'm hurting so much.
    My body is getting weaker
    and weaker.
¹¹ My neighbors make fun of
    me
    because I have so many
    enemies.
    My closest friends are afraid
    of me.
    People who see me on
    the street run away
    from me.
¹² No one remembers me. I
    might as well be dead.
    I have become like broken
    pottery.
¹³ I hear many people
    whispering,
    "There is terror all around
    him!"
    Many have joined together
    against me.
    They plan to kill me.

14 But I trust in you, Lord.
   I say, "You are my God."
15 My whole life is in your
   hands.
     Save me from the hands of
     my enemies.
     Save me from those who
     are chasing me.
16 May you look on me with
   favor.
     Save me because your love
     is faithful.
17 Lord, I have cried out to
   you.
     Don't let me be put to
     shame.
   But let sinners be put to
   shame.
     Let them lie silent in the
     place of the dead.
18 Their lips tell lies. Let them
   be silenced.
     They speak with pride
     against those who do
     right.
     They make fun of them.

19 You have stored up so many
   good things.
     You have stored them
     up for those who have
     respect for you.
   You give those things while
   everyone watches.
     You give them to people
     who run to you for
     safety.
20 They are safe because you
   are with them.
     You hide them from
     the evil plans of their
     enemies.
   In your house you keep them
   safe
     from those who bring
     charges against them.

21 Give praise to the Lord.
     He showed me his
     wonderful love
     when my enemies attacked
     the city I was in.
22 I was afraid and said,
     "I've been cut off from you!"
   But you heard my cry for your
   favor.
     You heard me when I
     called out to you for help.

23 Love the Lord, all you who
   are faithful to him!
     The Lord keeps safe those
     who are faithful to him.
     But he completely pays
     back those who are
     proud.
24 Be strong, all you who put
   your hope in the Lord.
     Never give up.

Psalm 32

A maskil *of David.*

1 Blessed is the person whose
   lawless acts are forgiven.
     Their sins have been taken
     away.
2 Blessed is the person whose
   sin the Lord never
   counts against them.
     That person doesn't want
     to cheat anyone.

3 When I kept silent about my
   sin,
     my body became weak
     because I groaned all day
     long.
4 Day and night
     you punished me.
   I became weaker and weaker
   as I do in the heat of
   summer.

⁵ Then I admitted my sin to
you.
I didn't cover up the wrong
I had done.
I said, "I will admit my
lawless acts to the
LORD."
And you forgave the guilt
of my sin.

⁶ Let everyone who is faithful
pray to you
while they can still look to
you.
When troubles come like a
flood,
they certainly won't reach
those who are faithful.
⁷ You are my hiding place.
You will keep me safe from
trouble.
You will surround me with
songs sung by those who
praise you
because you save your
people.
⁸ I will guide you and teach
you the way you should
go.
I will give you good advice
and watch over you with
love.
⁹ Don't be like a horse or a
mule.
They can't understand
anything.
They have to be controlled by
bits and bridles.
If they aren't, they won't
come to you.
¹⁰ Sinful people have all kinds
of trouble.
But the LORD's faithful love
is all around those who
trust in him.

¹¹ Be glad because of what the
LORD has done for you.
Be joyful, you who do what
is right!
Sing, all you whose hearts
are honest!

Psalm 33

¹ You who are godly, sing with
joy to the LORD.
It is right for honest people
to praise him.
² With the harp, praise the
LORD.
With the lyre that has ten
strings, make music to
him.
³ Sing a new song to him.
Play with skill, and shout
with joy.
⁴ What the LORD says is right
and true.
He is faithful in everything
he does.
⁵ The LORD loves what is right
and fair.
The earth is full of his
faithful love.
⁶ The heavens were made when
the LORD commanded it
to happen.
All the stars were created
by the breath of his
mouth.
⁷ He gathers together the
waters of the sea.
He puts the oceans in their
places.
⁸ Let the whole earth have
respect for the LORD.
Let all the people in the
world honor him.
⁹ He spoke, and the world
came into being.

He commanded, and it
　　stood firm.
¹⁰ The Lord blocks the sinful
　　plans of the nations.
　　He keeps them from doing
　　what they want to do.
¹¹ But the plans of the Lord
　　stand firm forever.
　　What he wants to do will
　　last for all time.

¹² Blessed is the nation whose
　　God is the Lord.
　　Blessed are the people he
　　chose to be his own.
¹³ From heaven the Lord looks
　　down
　　and sees everyone.
¹⁴ From his throne he watches
　　all those who live on the
　　earth.
¹⁵ He creates the hearts of all
　　people.
　　He is aware of everything
　　they do.
¹⁶ A king isn't saved just
　　because his army is
　　big.
　　A soldier doesn't escape
　　just because he is very
　　strong.
¹⁷ People can't trust a horse to
　　save them either.
　　Though it is very strong, it
　　can't save them.
¹⁸ But the Lord looks with favor
　　on those who respect
　　him.
　　He watches over those who
　　put their hope in his
　　faithful love.
¹⁹ He watches over them to save
　　them from death.
　　He wants to keep them
　　alive when there is no
　　food in the land.

²⁰ We wait in hope for the
　　Lord.
　　He helps us. He is like a
　　shield that keeps us safe.
²¹ Our hearts are full of joy
　　because of him.
　　We trust in him, because
　　he is holy.
²² Lord, may your faithful love
　　be with us.
　　We put our hope in you.

Psalm 34

*A psalm of David when he was
with Abimelek and pretended to be
out of his mind. Abimelek drove
him away, and David left.*

¹ I will thank the Lord at all
　　times.
　　My lips will always praise
　　him.
² I will find my glory in
　　knowing the Lord.
　　Let those who are hurting
　　hear me and be joyful.
³ Join me in giving glory to the
　　Lord.
　　Let us honor him together.

⁴ I looked to the Lord, and he
　　answered me.
　　He saved me from
　　everything I was
　　afraid of.
⁵ Those who look to him have
　　joyful faces.
　　They are never covered
　　with shame.
⁶ This poor man called out,
　　and the Lord heard
　　him.
　　He saved him out of all his
　　troubles.
⁷ The angel of the Lord stands
　　guard

around those who have
respect for him.
And he saves them.

8 Taste and see that the LORD
is good.
Blessed is the person who
goes to him for safety.
9 You holy people of God, have
respect for the LORD.
Those who respect him
have everything they
need.
10 The lions may grow weak and
hungry.
But those who look to the
LORD have every good
thing they need.

11 My children, come. Listen to
me.
I will teach you to have
respect for the LORD.
12 Do you love life
and want to see many good
days?
13 Then keep your tongues from
speaking evil.
Keep your lips from telling
lies.
14 Turn away from evil, and do
good.
Look for peace, and go
after it.

15 The LORD looks with favor on
those who are godly.
His ears are open to their
cry.
16 But the LORD doesn't look
with favor on those who
do evil.
He removes all memory of
them from the earth.

17 Godly people cry out, and the
LORD hears them.

He saves them from all
their troubles.
18 The LORD is close to those
whose hearts have been
broken.
He saves those whose spirits
have been crushed.
19 The person who does what
is right may have many
troubles.
But the LORD saves him
from all of them.
20 The LORD watches over all
his bones.
Not one of them will be
broken.

21 Sinners will be killed by their
own evil.
The enemies of godly
people will be judged.
22 The LORD will save those
who serve him.
No one who goes to him
for safety will be found
guilty.

Psalm 35

A psalm of David.

1 LORD, stand up against those
who stand up against
me.
Fight against those who
fight against me.
2 Pick up your shield and your
armor.
Rise up and help me.
3 Get your spear and javelin
ready to fight
against those who are
chasing me.
Say to me, "I will save you."
4 Let those who are trying to
kill me

be brought down in
dishonor.
Let those who plan to
destroy me
be turned back in terror.
⁵Let them be like straw
blowing in the wind,
while the angel of the Lord
drives them away.
⁶Let their path be dark and
slippery,
while the angel of the Lord
chases them.
⁷They set a trap for me
without any reason.
Without any reason they
dug a pit to catch me.
⁸So let them be destroyed
without warning.
Let the trap they set for me
catch them.
Let them fall into the pit
and be destroyed.
⁹Then I will be full of joy
because of what the
Lord has done.
I will be glad because he
has saved me.
¹⁰My whole being will cry
out,
"Who is like you, Lord?
You save poor people from
those who are too strong
for them.
You save poor and needy
people from those who
rob them."
¹¹Mean people come forward
to speak against me.
They ask me things I
don't know anything
about.
¹²They pay me back with evil,
even though I was good
to them.

They leave me like
someone who has lost a
family member.
¹³But when they were sick, I
put on the clothing of
sadness.
I made myself humble by
going without food.
My prayers for them weren't
always answered.
¹⁴ So I went around crying
as if I were mourning over
my friend or relative.
I bowed my head in sadness
as if I were weeping over
my mother.
¹⁵But when I tripped and fell,
they were all very happy.
Attackers gathered against
me when I didn't even
know it.
They kept on telling lies
about me.
¹⁶Like ungodly people, they
were mean and made
fun of me.
They ground their teeth at
me in hate.
¹⁷Lord, how much longer will
you just look on?
Save me from their deadly
attacks.
Save the only life I have.
Save me from these lions.
¹⁸I will give you thanks in the
whole community.
Among all your people I
will praise you.
¹⁹Don't let those who are my
enemies without any
reason
laugh at me and make fun
of me.
Don't let those who hate me
without any reason

wink at me with an evil
purpose.
20 They don't speak words of
peace.
They make up false charges
against those who live
quietly in the land.
21 They make fun of me.
They say, "With our own
eyes we have seen what
you did."
22 LORD, you have seen this.
Don't be silent.
Lord, don't be far away
from me.
23 Wake up! Rise up to help me!
My God and Lord, stand up
for me.
24 LORD my God, when you
hand down your
sentence, let it be in my
favor.
You always do what is right.
Don't let my enemies have
the joy of seeing me fall.
25 Don't let them think,
"That's exactly what we
wanted!"
Don't let them say, "We
have swallowed him up."
26 Let all those who laugh at me
because I'm in trouble
be ashamed and
bewildered.
Let all who think they are
better than I am
put on shame and
dishonor as if they were
clothes.
27 Let those who are happy
when my name is
cleared
shout with joy and
gladness.

Let them always say, "May
the LORD be honored.
He is pleased when
everything goes well
with the one who serves
him."
28 You always do what is right.
My tongue will speak
about it
and praise you all day
long.

Psalm 36

*For the director of music. A psalm
of David, the servant of the LORD.*

1 I have a message from God in
my heart.
It is about the evil ways of
anyone who sins.
They don't have any
respect for God.
2 They praise themselves so
much
that they can't see their sin
or hate it.
3 Their mouths speak words
that are evil and false.
They do not act wisely or
do what is good.
4 Even as they lie in bed they
make evil plans.
They commit themselves
to a sinful way of life.
They never say no to what
is wrong.
5 LORD, your love is as high as
the heavens.
Your faithful love reaches
up to the skies.
6 Your holiness is as great as
the height of the highest
mountains.
You are as honest as the
oceans are deep.

Lord, you keep people and
   animals safe.
7 How priceless your faithful
   love is!
   People find safety in the
     shadow of your wings.
8 They eat well because there
    is more than enough in
    your house.
   You let them drink from
    your river that flows with
    good things.
9 You have the fountain of life.
   We are filled with light
    because you give us
    light.

10 Keep on loving those who
    know you.
   Keep on doing right to
    those whose hearts are
    honest.
11 Don't let the feet of those who
    are proud step on me.
   Don't let the hands of those
    who are evil drive me
    away.
12 See how those who do evil
    have fallen!
   They are thrown down and
    can't get up.

Psalm 37

A psalm of David.

1 Don't be upset because of
    sinful people.
   Don't be jealous of those
    who do wrong.
2 Like grass, they will soon dry
    up.
   Like green plants, they will
    soon die.

3 Trust in the Lord and do
   good.

Then you will live in the
   land and enjoy its food.
4 Find your delight in the
   Lord.
   Then he will give you
    everything your heart
    really wants.

5 Commit your life to the
   Lord.
   Here is what he will do if
    you trust in him.
6 He will make the reward for
    your godly life shine like
    the dawn.
   He will make the proof of
    your honest life shine
    like the sun at noon.

7 Be still and wait patiently for
    the Lord to act.
   Don't be upset when other
    people succeed.
   Don't be upset when they
    carry out their evil
    plans.

8 Turn away from anger and
    don't give in to wrath.
   Don't be upset, because
    that only leads to evil.
9 Sinful people will be
    destroyed.
   But those who put their
    hope in the Lord will
    receive the land.

10 In a little while, there won't
    be any more sinners.
   Even if you look for them,
    you won't be able to find
    them.
11 But those who are free of
    pride will be given the
    land.
   They will enjoy peace and
    success.

¹²Sinful people make plans to
    harm those who do what
    is right.
  They grind their teeth at
    them.
¹³But the Lord laughs at those
    who do evil.
  He knows the day is
    coming when he will
    judge them.
¹⁴Sinners pull out their
    swords.
  They bend their bows.
  They want to kill poor and
    needy people.
  They plan to murder those
    who lead honest lives.
¹⁵But they will be killed by
    their own swords.
  Their own bows will be
    broken.

¹⁶Those who do what is right
    may have very little.
  But it's better than the
    wealth of many
    sinners.
¹⁷The power of those who are
    evil will be broken.
  But the Lord takes good
    care of those who do
    what is right.

¹⁸Those who are without
    blame spend their days
    in the Lord's care.
  What he has given them
    will last forever.
¹⁹When trouble comes to them,
    they will have what they
    need.
  When there is little food in
    the land, they will still
    have plenty.
²⁰But sinful people will die.

The Lord's enemies may
    be like flowers in the
    field.
  But they will be swallowed
    up.
  They will disappear like
    smoke.

²¹Sinful people borrow and
    don't pay back.
  But those who are godly
    give freely to others.
²²The Lord will give the land
    to those he blesses.
  But he will destroy those
    he curses.

²³The Lord makes secure the
    footsteps
  of the person who delights in
    him,
²⁴Even if that person trips, he
    won't fall.
  The Lord's hand takes
    good care of him.

²⁵I once was young, and now
    I'm old.
  But I've never seen godly
    people deserted.
  I've never seen their
    children begging for
    bread.
²⁶The godly are always giving
    and lending freely.
  Their children will be a
    blessing.

²⁷Turn away from evil and do
    good.
  Then you will live in the
    land forever.
²⁸The Lord loves those who
    are honest.
  He will not desert those
    who are faithful to
    him.

Those who do wrong will be completely destroyed. The children of sinners will die.
²⁹ Those who do what is right will be given the land. They will live in it forever.

³⁰ The mouths of those who do what is right speak words of wisdom. They say what is honest.
³¹ God's law is in their hearts. Their feet do not slip.

³² Those who are evil hide and wait for godly people. They want to kill them.
³³ But the LORD will not leave the godly in their power. He will not let them be found guilty when they are brought into court.

³⁴ Put your hope in the LORD. Live as he wants you to. He will honor you by giving you the land. When sinners are destroyed, you will see it.

³⁵ I saw a mean and sinful person. He was doing well, like a green tree in its own land.
³⁶ But he soon passed away and was gone. Even though I looked for him, I couldn't find him.

³⁷ Consider honest people who are without blame. People who seek peace will have a tomorrow.
³⁸ But all sinners will be destroyed.

Those who are evil won't have a tomorrow.
³⁹ The LORD saves those who do what is right. He is their place of safety when trouble comes.
⁴⁰ The LORD helps them and saves them. He saves them from sinful people because they go to him for safety.

Psalm 38

A psalm of David. A prayer.

¹ LORD, don't correct me when you are angry. Don't punish me when you are burning with anger.
² You have wounded me with your arrows. You have struck me with your hand.
³ Because of your anger, my whole body is sick. Because of my sin, I'm not healthy.
⁴ My guilt has become too much for me. It is a load too heavy to carry.

⁵ My wounds are ugly. They stink. I've been foolish. I have sinned.
⁶ I am bent over. I've been brought very low. All day long I go around weeping.
⁷ My back is filled with burning pain. My whole body is sick.

⁸I am weak and feel as if I've
been broken in pieces.
I groan because of the
great pain in my heart.
⁹Lord, everything I really
want is clearly known to
you.
You always hear me when I
sigh.
¹⁰My heart pounds, and my
strength is gone.
My eyes can hardly see.
¹¹My friends and companions
avoid me because of my
wounds.
My neighbors stay far away
from me.
¹²Those who are trying to kill
me set their traps.
Those who want to harm
me talk about destroying
me.
All day long they make
their plans and tell their
lies.
¹³Like a deaf person, I can't
hear.
Like someone who can't
speak, I can't say a word.
¹⁴I'm like someone who doesn't
hear.
I'm like someone whose
mouth can't make any
reply.
¹⁵Lord, I wait for you to help me.
Lord my God, I know you
will answer.
¹⁶I said, "Don't let my enemies
have the joy of seeing me
fall.
Don't let them brag when
my feet slip."
¹⁷I am about to fall.
My pain never leaves me.

¹⁸I admit that I have done
wrong.
I am troubled by my sin.
¹⁹Though I have done nothing
to cause it, many people
have become my
enemies.
They hate me without any
reason.
²⁰They pay me back with evil,
even though I was good
to them.
They bring charges against
me, though I try only to
do what is good.
²¹Lord, don't desert me.
My God, don't be far away
from me.
²²Lord my Savior,
come quickly to help me.

Psalm 39

*For the director of music. For
Jeduthun. A psalm of David.*

¹I said, "I will be careful about
how I live.
I will not sin by what I say.
I will keep my mouth closed
when I am near sinful
people."
²So I was completely silent.
I didn't even say anything
good.
But the pain inside me
grew worse.
³My heart was deeply
troubled.
As I thought about what
was happening to me,
I became even more
troubled.
Then I spoke out.
⁴I said, "Lord, show me when
my life will end.

Show me how many days I
    have left.
Tell me how short my life
    will be.
⁵ You have given me only a few
    days to live.
My whole life doesn't seem
    like anything to you.
No one lasts any longer
    than a breath.
This is true even for those
    who feel secure.
⁶ People are only shadows as
    they go here and there.
They rush around, but it
    doesn't mean anything.
They pile up wealth, but
    they don't know who will
    finally get it.

⁷ "Lord, what can I look
    forward to now?
You are the only hope I
    have.
⁸ Save me from all the wrong
    things I've done.
Don't let foolish people
    make fun of me.
⁹ I keep silent. I don't open my
    mouth.
You are the one who
    has caused all this to
    happen.
¹⁰ Please stop beating me.
I'm about to die from the
    blows of your hand.
¹¹ You correct and punish
    people for their sin.
Then, just as a moth eats
    cloth, you destroy their
    wealth.
No one lasts any longer
    than a breath.
¹² "LORD, hear my prayer.
Listen to my cry for help.

Pay attention to my
    weeping.
I'm like an outsider in your
    home.
I'm just a stranger, like
    all my family who lived
    before me.
¹³ Leave me alone.
Let me enjoy life again
    before I die."

Psalm 40

For the director of music.
A psalm of David.

¹ I was patient while I waited
    for the LORD.
He turned to me and heard
    my cry for help.
² I was sliding down into the
    pit of death, and he
    pulled me out.
He brought me up out of
    the mud and dirt.
He set my feet on a rock.
He gave me a firm place to
    stand on.
³ He gave me a new song to
    sing.
It is a hymn of praise to our
    God.
Many people will see and
    have respect for the
    LORD.
They will put their trust in
    him.

⁴ Blessed is the person
    who trusts in the LORD.
They don't trust in proud
    people.
Those proud people
    worship statues of gods.
⁵ LORD my God,
no one can compare with
    you.

You have done many
  wonderful things.
You have planned to do
  these things for us.
There are too many of them
  for me to talk about.

6 You didn't want sacrifices
  and offerings.
You didn't require burnt
  offerings and sin
  offerings.
You opened my ears so
  that I could hear you and
  obey you.
7 Then I said, "Here I am.
It is written about me in
  the book.
8 My God, I have come to do
  what you want.
Your law is in my heart."

9 I have told the whole
  community of those who
  worship you.
I have told them what you
  have done to save me.
LORD, you know
  that I haven't kept quiet.
10 I haven't kept to myself that
  what you did for me was
  right.
I have spoken about how
  faithful you were when
  you saved me.
I haven't hidden your love
  and your faithfulness
  from the whole community.

11 LORD, don't hold back your
  mercy from me.
May your love and
  faithfulness always keep
  me safe.
12 There are more troubles all
  around me than I can
  count.

My sins have caught up
  with me, and I can't see
  any longer.
My sins are more than the
  hairs of my head.
I have lost all hope.

13 LORD, please save me.
  LORD, come quickly to help
    me.
14 Let all those who are trying
    to kill me be put to
    shame.
Let them lose their way.
Let all those who want to
    destroy me
  be turned back in shame.
15 Some people make fun
    of me.
Let them be shocked when
    their plans fail.
16 But let all those who seek
    you
  be joyful and glad because
    of what you have done.
Let those who count on you
    to save them always say,
  "The LORD is great!"

17 But I am poor and needy.
May the Lord be concerned
    about me.
You are the God who helps
    me and saves me.
You are my God, so don't
    wait any longer.

Psalm 41

For the director of music.
A psalm of David.

1 Blessed are those who care
    about weak people.
When they are in trouble,
    the LORD saves them.
2 The LORD guards them and
    keeps them alive.

They are counted among those who are blessed in the land.
The LORD won't hand them over to the wishes of their enemies.
³ The LORD will take care of them when they are lying sick in bed.
He will make them well again.
⁴ I said, "LORD, have mercy on me.
Heal me, because I have sinned against you."
⁵ My enemies are saying bad things about me.
They say, "When will he die and his name be forgotten?"
⁶ When one of them comes to see me,
he says things that aren't true.
At the same time, he thinks up lies to tell against me.
Then he goes out and spreads those lies around.
⁷ All my enemies whisper to each other about me.
They want something terrible to happen to me.
⁸ They say, "He is sick and will die very soon.
He will never get up from his bed again."
⁹ Even my close friend, someone I trusted, has failed me.
I even shared my bread with him.
¹⁰ But LORD, may you have mercy on me.

Make me well, so I can pay them back.
¹¹ Then I will know that you are pleased with me,
because my enemies haven't won the battle over me.
¹² You will take good care of me because I've been honest.
You will let me be with you forever.

¹³ Give praise to the LORD, the God of Israel,
for ever and ever.
Amen and Amen.

BOOK II

Psalms 42–72

Psalm 42

For the director of music. A maskil *of the Sons of Korah.*

¹ A deer longs for streams of water.
God, I long for you in the same way.
² I am thirsty for God. I am thirsty for the living God.
When can I go and meet with him?
³ My tears have been my food day and night.
All day long people say to me, "Where is your God?"
⁴ When I remember what has happened,
I tell God all my troubles.
I remember how I used to walk to the house of God.
The Mighty One guarded my steps.

We shouted with joy and
  praised God
as we went along with the
  joyful crowd.

5 My spirit, why are you so sad?
  Why are you so upset deep
    down inside me?
Put your hope in God.
  Once again I will have
    reason to praise him.
  He is my Savior and my God.

6 My spirit is very sad deep
    down inside me.
  So I will remember you
    here where the Jordan
    River begins.
  I will remember you here on
    the Hermon mountains
    and on Mount Mizar.
7 You have sent wave upon
    wave of trouble over me.
  It roars down on me like a
    waterfall.
  All your waves and breakers
    have rolled over me.

8 During the day the LORD
    sends his love to me.
  During the night I sing
    about him.
  I say a prayer to the God
    who gives me life.

9 I say to God my Rock,
  "Why have you forgotten
    me?
  Why must I go around in
    sorrow?
  Why am I treated so badly
    by my enemies?"
10 My body suffers deadly pain
    as my enemies make fun of
    me.
  All day long they say to me,
  "Where is your God?"

11 My spirit, why are you so sad?
  Why are you so upset deep
    down inside me?
Put your hope in God.
  Once again I will have
    reason to praise him.
  He is my Savior and my God.

Psalm 43

1 My God, when you hand
    down your decision, let it
    be in my favor.
  Stand up for me against an
    unfaithful nation.
  Save me from those lying
    and sinful people.
2 You are God, my place of
    safety.
  Why have you turned your
    back on me?
  Why must I go around in
    sorrow?
  Why am I beaten down by
    my enemies?
3 Send me your light and your
    faithful care.
  Let them lead me.
  Let them bring me back to
    your holy mountain,
  to the place where you live.
4 Then I will go to the altar of
    God.
  I will go to God. He is my
    joy and my delight.
  God, you are my God.
  I will praise you by playing
    the lyre.

5 My spirit, why are you so sad?
  Why are you so upset deep
    down inside me?
Put your hope in God.
  Once again I will have
    reason to praise him.
  He is my Savior and my God.

Psalm 44

*For the director of music. A maskil
of the Sons of Korah.*

¹ God, we have heard what you
did.
Those who came before us
have told us
what you did in their days,
in days long ago.
² By your power you drove out
the nations.
You gave our people homes
in the land.
You crushed the people who
were there.
And you made our people
do well.
³ They didn't win the land with
their swords.
They didn't gain success by
their own power.
Your powerful right hand
and your mighty arm
gave them victory.
You gave them success
because you loved them.

⁴ You are my King and my
God.
You give victories to the
people of Jacob.
⁵ With your help we push back
our enemies.
By your power we walk all
over them.
⁶ I put no trust in my bow.
My sword doesn't bring me
victory.
⁷ But you give us victory over
our enemies.
You put them to shame.
⁸ All day long we talk about
how great God is.
We will praise your name
forever.

⁹ But now you have turned
your back on us and
made us humble.
You don't march out with
our armies anymore.
¹⁰ You made us turn and run
from our enemies.
They have taken what
belongs to us.
¹¹ You handed us over to be
eaten up like sheep.
You have scattered us
among the nations.
¹² You sold your people for very
little.
You didn't gain anything
when you sold them.
¹³ You have made us something
that our neighbors
laugh at.
Those who live around
us make fun of us and
tease us.
¹⁴ The nations make jokes
about us.
They shake their heads at
us.
¹⁵ All day long I have to live
with my shame.
My face is covered
with it.
¹⁶ That's because they laugh at
me and attack me with
their words.
They want to get even
with me.
¹⁷ All of this happened to us,
even though we had not
forgotten you.
We had not broken the
covenant you made
with us.
¹⁸ Our hearts had not turned
away from you.

Our feet had not wandered
from your path.
¹⁹ But you crushed us and left
us to the wild dogs.
You covered us over with
deep darkness.
²⁰ We didn't forget our God.
We didn't spread out our
hands in prayer to a false
god.
²¹ If we had, God would have
discovered it.
He knows the secrets of
our hearts.
²² But because of you, we face
death all day long.
We are considered as
sheep to be killed.
²³ Lord, wake up! Why are you
sleeping?
Get up! Don't say no to us
forever.
²⁴ Why do you turn your face
away from us?
Why do you forget our pain
and troubles?
²⁵ We are brought down to the
dust.
Our bodies lie flat on the
ground.
²⁶ Rise up and help us.
Save us because of your
faithful love.

Psalm 45

For the director of music. A maskil
*of the Sons of Korah. A wedding
song to the tune of "Lilies."*

¹ My heart is full of beautiful
words
as I say my poem for the
king.
My tongue is like the pen of
a skillful writer.

² You are the most excellent of
men.
Your lips have been given
the ability to speak
gracious words.
God has blessed you
forever.
³ Mighty one, put your sword
at your side.
Put on glory and majesty as
if they were your
clothes.
⁴ In your majesty ride out with
power
to fight for what is true,
humble and fair.
Let your right hand do
wonderful things.
⁵ Shoot your sharp arrows
into the hearts of your
enemies.
Let the nations come under
your control.
⁶ Your throne is the very
throne of God.
Your kingdom will last for
ever and ever.
You will rule by treating
everyone fairly.
⁷ You love what is right and
hate what is evil.
So your God has placed
you above your
companions.
He has filled you with joy
by pouring the sacred oil
on your head.
⁸ Myrrh and aloes and cassia
make all your robes
smell good.
In palaces decorated with
ivory
the music played on
stringed instruments
makes you glad.

⁹Daughters of kings are
        among the women you
        honor.
    At your right hand is the
        royal bride dressed in
        gold from Ophir.
¹⁰Royal bride, listen and pay
        careful attention.
    Forget about your people
        and the home you came
        from.
¹¹Let the king be charmed by
        your beauty.
    Honor him. He is now your
        master.
¹²The people of Tyre will come
        with gifts.
    Wealthy people will try to
        gain your favor.
¹³In her room, the princess
        looks glorious.
    Her gown has gold threads
        running through it.
¹⁴Dressed in beautiful clothes,
        she is led to the king.
    Her virgin companions
        follow her.
    They have been brought to
        be with her.
¹⁵They are led in with joy and
        gladness.
    They enter the palace of
        the king.
¹⁶Your sons will rule just
        as your father and
        grandfather did.
    You will make them
        princes through the
        whole land.
¹⁷I will make sure that people
        will always remember
        you.
    The nations will praise you
        for ever and ever.

Psalm 46

For the director of music.
A song of the Sons of Korah.
According to alamoth.

¹God is our place of safety. He
        gives us strength.
    He is always there to help
        us in times of trouble.
²The earth may fall apart.
    The mountains may fall into
        the middle of the sea.
    But we will not be afraid.
³The waters of the sea may
        roar and foam.
    The mountains may shake
        when the waters rise.
    But we will not be afraid.

⁴God's blessings are like a
        river. They fill the city of
        God with joy.
    That city is the holy place
        where the Most High
        God lives.
⁵Because God is there, the city
        will not fall.
    God will help it at the
        beginning of the day.
⁶Nations are in disorder.
    Kingdoms fall.
    God speaks, and the
        people of the earth melt
        in fear.

⁷The LORD who rules over all
        is with us.
    The God of Jacob is like a
        fort to us.

⁸Come and see what the LORD
        has done.
    See the places he has
        destroyed on the earth.
⁹He makes wars stop from one
        end of the earth to the
        other.

He breaks every bow. He
snaps every spear.
He burns every shield with
fire.
¹⁰ He says, "Be still, and know
that I am God.
I will be honored among
the nations.
I will be honored in the
earth."
¹¹ The LORD who rules over all
is with us.
The God of Jacob is like a
fort to us.

Psalm 47

*For the director of music. A psalm
of the Sons of Korah.*

¹ Clap your hands, all you
nations.
Shout to God with cries of
joy.
² Do this because the LORD
Most High is wonderful.
He is the great King over
the whole earth.
³ He brought nations under
our control.
He made them fall under
us.
⁴ He chose our land for us.
The people of Jacob are
proud of their land,
and God loves them.

⁵ God went up to his throne
while his people were
shouting with joy.
The LORD went up while
trumpets were playing.
⁶ Sing praises to God. Sing
praises.
Sing praises to our King.
Sing praises.

⁷ God is the King of the whole
earth.
Sing a psalm of praise to
him.
⁸ God rules over the nations.
He is seated on his holy
throne.
⁹ The nobles of the nations
come together.
They are now part of the
people of the God of
Abraham.
The kings of the earth belong
to God.
He is greatly honored.

Psalm 48

A song. A psalm of the Sons of Korah.

¹ The LORD is great. He is
really worthy of praise.
Praise him in the city
of our God, his holy
mountain.
² Mount Zion is high and
beautiful.
It brings joy to everyone on
earth.
Mount Zion is like the
highest parts of Mount
Zaphon.
It is the city of the Great
King.
³ God is there to keep it safe.
He has shown himself to
be like a fort to the city.

⁴ Many kings joined forces.
They entered Israel
together.
⁵ But when they saw Mount
Zion, they were
amazed.
They ran away in terror.
⁶ Trembling took hold of
them.

They felt pain like a
 woman giving birth.
⁷ LORD, you destroyed them
 like ships of Tarshish
 that were torn apart by an
 east wind.

⁸ What we heard we have also
 seen.
 We have seen it
in the city of the LORD who
 rules over all.
 We have seen it in the city
 of our God.
 We have heard and seen
 that God makes it secure
 forever.

⁹ God, inside your temple
 we think about your
 faithful love.
¹⁰ God, your fame reaches from
 one end of the earth to
 the other.
 So people praise you from
 one end of the earth to
 the other.
 You use your power to do
 what is right.
¹¹ Mount Zion is filled with joy.
 The villages of Judah are
 glad.
 That's because you judge
 fairly.
¹² Walk all around Zion.
 Count its towers.
¹³ Think carefully about its
 outer walls.
 Just look at how safe it is!
 Then you can tell its people
 that God keeps them
 safe.
¹⁴ This God is our God for ever
 and ever.
 He will be our guide to the
 very end.

Psalm 49

*For the director of music. A psalm
 of the Sons of Korah.*

¹ Hear this, all you nations.
 Listen, all you who live in
 this world.
² Listen, people, whether
 you are ordinary or
 important.
 Listen, people, whether
 you are rich or poor.
³ My mouth will speak wise
 words.
 What I think about in
 my heart will give you
 understanding.
⁴ I will pay attention to a
 proverb.
 I will explain my riddle as I
 play the harp.

⁵ Why should I be afraid when
 trouble comes?
 Why should I fear when
 sinners are all around
 me?
 They are the kind of
 people who want to take
 advantage of me.
⁶ They trust in their wealth.
 They brag about how rich
 they are.
⁷ No one can pay for the life of
 anyone else.
 No one can give God what
 that would cost.
⁸ The price for a life is very high.
 No payment is ever
 enough.
⁹ No one can pay enough to
 live forever
 and not rot in the grave.
¹⁰ Everyone can see that even
 wise people die.

People who are foolish and
who have no sense also
pass away.
All of them leave their
wealth to others.
[11] Their tombs will remain their
houses forever.
Their graves will be their
homes for all time to
come.
Naming lands after
themselves won't help
either.

[12] Even though people may be
very rich, they don't live
on and on.
They are like the animals.
They die.
[13] That's what happens to
those who trust in
themselves.
It also happens to their
followers, who agree
with what they say.
[14] They are like sheep and will
end up in the grave.
Death will be their
shepherd.
But when honest people
come to power, a new
day will dawn.
The bodies of sinners will
waste away in the
grave.
They will end up far away
from their princely
houses.
[15] But God will save me from
the place of the dead.
He will certainly take me
to himself.

[16] Don't get too upset when
other people become
rich.

Don't be troubled when
they become more and
more wealthy.
[17] They won't take anything
with them when they
die.
Their riches won't go down
to the grave with them.
[18] While they lived, they
believed they were
blessed.
People praised them when
things were going well
for them.
[19] But they will die, like their
people of long ago.
They will never again see
the light of life.

[20] People who have riches but
don't understand
are like the animals.
They die.

Psalm 50

A psalm of Asaph.

[1] The Mighty One, God, the
Lord, speaks.
He calls out to the earth
from the sunrise in the east
to the sunset in the west.
[2] From Zion, perfect and
beautiful,
God's glory shines out.
[3] Our God comes, and he won't
be silent.
A burning fire goes ahead
of him.
A terrible storm is all
around him.
[4] He calls out to heaven and
earth to be his witnesses.
Then he judges his people.
[5] He says, "Gather this holy
people around me.

They made a covenant
with me by offering a
sacrifice."
⁶ The heavens announce that
what God decides is
right.
That's because he is a God
of justice.
⁷ God says, "Listen, my people,
and I will speak.
I will be a witness against
you, Israel.
I am God, your God.
⁸ I don't bring charges against
you because of your
sacrifices.
I don't bring charges
because of the burnt
offerings you always
bring me.
⁹ I don't need a bull from your
barn.
I don't need goats from
your pens.
¹⁰ Every animal in the forest
already belongs to me.
And so do the cattle on a
thousand hills.
¹¹ I own every bird in the
mountains.
The insects in the fields
belong to me.
¹² If I were hungry, I wouldn't
tell you.
The world belongs to me.
And so does everything
in it.
¹³ Do I eat the meat of bulls?
Do I drink the blood of
goats?
¹⁴ Bring me thank offerings,
because I am your God.
Carry out the promises you
made to me, because I
am the Most High God.

¹⁵ Call out to me when trouble
comes.
I will save you. And you
will honor me."

¹⁶ But here is what God says to
a sinful person.
"What right do you have to
speak the words of my
laws?
How dare you speak the
words of my covenant!
¹⁷ You hate my teaching.
You turn your back on
what I say.
¹⁸ When you see a thief, you
join him.
You make friends with
those who commit
adultery.
¹⁹ You use your mouth to speak
evil.
You use your tongue to
spread lies.
²⁰ You are a witness against
your brother.
You always tell lies about
your own mother's son.
²¹ When you did these things, I
kept silent.
So you thought I was just
like you.
But now I'm going to bring
you to court.
I will bring charges against
you.

²² "You who forget God, think
about this.
If you don't, I will tear you
to pieces.
No one will be able to save
you.
²³ People who sacrifice thank
offerings to me honor
me.

To those who are without
　　blame I will show my
　　power to save."

Psalm 51

*For the director of music. A psalm
of David when the prophet Nathan
came to him. Nathan came to him
after David had committed adultery
with Bathsheba.*

¹ God, have mercy on me
　　according to your faithful
　　love.
Because your love is so
　　tender and kind,
　　wipe out my lawless acts.
² Wash away all the evil things
　　I've done.
　　Make me pure from my
　　sin.

³ I know the lawless acts I've
　　committed.
　　I can't forget my sin.
⁴ You are the one I've really
　　sinned against.
　　I've done what is evil in
　　your sight.
So you are right when you
　　sentence me.
　　You are fair when you
　　judge me.
⁵ I know I've been a sinner ever
　　since I was born.
　　I've been a sinner ever
　　since my mother became
　　pregnant with me.
⁶ I know that you wanted
　　faithfulness even when
　　I was in my mother's
　　body.
　　You taught me wisdom in
　　that secret place.

⁷ Sprinkle me with hyssop,
　　then I will be clean.
Wash me, then I will be
　　whiter than snow.
⁸ Let me hear you say, "Your
　　sins are forgiven."
　　That will bring me joy and
　　gladness.
Let the body you have
　　broken be glad.
⁹ Take away all my sins.
　　Wipe away all the evil
　　things I've done.

¹⁰ God, create a pure heart in
　　me.
　　Give me a new spirit that is
　　faithful to you.
¹¹ Don't send me away from
　　you.
　　Don't take your Holy Spirit
　　away from me.
¹² Give me back the joy that
　　comes from being saved
　　by you.
　　Give me a spirit that obeys
　　you so that I will keep
　　going.

¹³ Then I will teach your ways
　　to those who commit
　　lawless acts.
　　And sinners will turn back
　　to you.
¹⁴ You are the God who saves
　　me.
　　I have committed murder.
　　God, take away my guilt.
Then my tongue will sing
　　about how right you are
　　no matter what you do.
¹⁵ Lord, open my lips so that I
　　can speak.
　　Then my mouth will praise
　　you.
¹⁶ You don't take delight in
　　sacrifice.
　　If you did, I would bring it.

You don't take pleasure in
    burnt offerings.
¹⁷The greatest sacrifice you
    want is a broken spirit.
God, you will gladly accept
    a heart
    that is broken because of
    sadness over sin.
¹⁸May you be pleased to give
    Zion success.
    May it please you to
    build up the walls of
    Jerusalem.
¹⁹Then you will delight in the
    sacrifices of those who
    do what is right.
    Whole burnt offerings will
    bring delight to you.
    And bulls will be offered
    on your altar.

Psalm 52

*For the director of music. A maskil
of David when Doeg, who was from
Edom, had gone to Saul. Doeg had
told Saul, "David has gone to the
house of Ahimelek."*

¹You think you are such a big,
    strong man!
    Why do you brag about the
    evil things you've done?
    You are a dishonor to God
    all the time.
²You plan ways to destroy
    others.
    Your tongue is like a blade
    that has a sharp edge.
    You are always telling lies.
³You love evil instead of good.
    You would rather lie than
    tell the truth.
⁴   You love to harm others
    with your words, you
    liar!

⁵So God will destroy you
    forever.
    He will grab you and pluck
    you from your tent.
    He will remove you from
    this life.
⁶Those who do what is right
    will see it and learn a
    lesson from it.
    They will laugh at you and
    say,
⁷"Just look at this fellow!
    He didn't depend on God
    for his safety.
    He put his trust in all his
    wealth.
    He grew strong by
    destroying others!"

⁸But I am like a healthy olive
    tree.
    My roots are deep in the
    house of God.
    I trust in your faithful love
    for ever and ever.
⁹I will praise you forever for
    what you have done.
    I will praise you when
    I'm with your faithful
    people.
    I will put my hope in you
    because you are good.

Psalm 53

*For the director of music. According
to mahalath. A maskil of David.*

¹Foolish people say in their
    hearts,
"There is no God."
    They do all kinds of horrible
    and evil things.
    No one does anything
    good.

²God looks down from heaven
    on all people.

He wants to see if there are
   any who understand.
He wants to see if there are
   any who trust in God.
³ All of them have turned
   away.
   They have all become evil.
No one does anything good,
   no one at all.

⁴ Don't these people who do
   evil know anything?
They eat up my people as if
   they were eating bread.
They never call out to God
   for help.
⁵ Just look at them! They are
   filled with terror
even when there is nothing
   to be afraid of!
People of Israel, God
   scattered the bones of
   those who attacked you.
You put them to shame,
   because God hated
   them.

⁶ How I pray that the God who
   saves Israel will come
   out of Zion!
God will bless his people
   with great success again.
Then let the people of
   Jacob be filled with joy!
Let Israel be glad!

Psalm 54

*For the director of music. To be
played on stringed instruments. A
maskil of David when the men from
Ziph had gone to Saul. They had
said, "Isn't David hiding among us?"*

¹ God, save me by your power.
   Set me free by your might.
² God, hear my prayer.
   Listen to what I'm saying.

³ Enemies who are proud are
   attacking me.
Mean people are trying to
   kill me.
They don't care about God.

⁴ But I know that God helps me.
The Lord is the one who
   keeps me going.

⁵ My enemies tell lies about me.
Do to them the evil things
   they planned against me.
God, be faithful and
   destroy them.

⁶ I will sacrifice an offering to
   you
   just because I choose to.
LORD, I will praise your name
   because it is good.
⁷ You have saved me from all
   my troubles.
With my own eyes I have
   seen you win the battle
   over my enemies.

Psalm 55

*For the director of music.
A maskil of David to be played
on stringed instruments.*

¹ God, listen to my prayer.
   Pay attention to my cry for
   help.
²   Hear me and answer me.
My thoughts upset me. I'm
   very troubled.
³   I'm troubled by what my
      enemies say about me.
I'm upset because they say
   they will harm me.
They cause me all kinds of
   suffering.
When they are angry, they
   attack me with their
   words.

⁴I feel great pain deep down
  inside me.
The terrors of death have
  fallen on me.
⁵Fear and trembling have
  taken hold of me.
Panic has overpowered
  me.
⁶I said, "I wish I had wings like
  a dove!
Then I would fly away and
  be at rest.
⁷I would escape to a place far
  away.
I would stay out in the
  desert.
⁸I would hurry to my place of
  safety.
It would be far away from
  the winds and storms
  I'm facing."

⁹Lord, confuse the sinners
  and keep them from
  understanding one
  another.
I see people destroying
  things and fighting in
  the city.
¹⁰Day and night they prowl
  around on top of its
  walls.
The city is full of crime and
  trouble.
¹¹Forces that destroy are at
  work inside it.
Its streets are full of people
  who cheat others and
  take advantage of them.
¹²If an enemy were making fun
  of me,
I could stand it.
If he were getting ready to
  oppose me,
I could hide.

¹³But it's you, someone like
  myself.
It's my companion, my
  close friend.
¹⁴We used to enjoy good
  friendship at the house
  of God.
We used to walk together
  among those who came
  to worship.

¹⁵Let death take my enemies by
  surprise.
Let them be buried alive,
  because their hearts and
  homes are full of evil.

¹⁶But I call out to God.
And the LORD saves me.
¹⁷Evening, morning and noon
  I groan and cry out.
And he hears my voice.
¹⁸Even though many enemies
  are fighting against me,
he brings me safely back
  from the battle.
¹⁹God has been on his throne
  since ancient times and
  does not change.
He will hear my enemies
  and make them humble.
That's because they have
  no respect for God.

²⁰My companion attacks his
  friends.
He breaks his promise.
²¹His talk is as smooth as
  butter.
But he has war in his heart.
His words flow like olive oil.
But they are like swords
  ready for battle.

²²Turn your worries over to the
  LORD.
He will keep you going.

He will never let godly
    people be shaken.
²³ God, you will bring sinners
    down to the grave.
Murderers and liars
    won't live out even half of
    their lives.

But I trust in you.

Psalm 56

For the director of music. A miktam
*of David after the Philistines had
captured him in Gath. To the tune of
"A Dove on Distant Oak Trees."*

¹ Help me, God. Men are
    chasing me.
All day long they keep
    attacking me.
² My enemies chase me all day
    long.
Many proud people are
    attacking me.
³ When I'm afraid,
    I put my trust in you.
⁴ I trust in God. I praise his
    word.
I trust in God. I am not
    afraid.
What can mere people do
    to me?
⁵ All day long they twist my
    words.
They are always making
    plans to destroy me.
⁶ They get together and
    hide.
They watch my steps.
They hope to kill me.
⁷ Because they are so evil,
    make sure you don't let
    them escape.
God, bring down the
    nations in your anger.

⁸ Make a record of my sadness.
List my tears in your book.
Aren't you making a record
    of them?
⁹ My enemies will turn back
    when I call out to you for
    help.
Then I will know that God
    is on my side.
¹⁰ I trust in God. I praise his
    word.
I trust in the LORD. I praise
    his word.
¹¹ I trust in God. I am not
    afraid.
What can mere people do
    to me?
¹² God, I have made promises
    to you.
I will bring my thank
    offerings to you.
¹³ You have saved me from the
    darkness of death.
You have kept me from
    tripping and falling.
Now I can live with you
    in the light of life.

Psalm 57

For the director of music. A miktam
*of David when he had run away
from Saul into the cave. To the
tune of "Do Not Destroy."*

¹ Have mercy on me, God.
    Have mercy on me.
I go to you for safety.
I will find safety in the
    shadow of your wings.
There I will stay until the
    danger is gone.
² I cry out to God Most High.
I cry out to God, and he
    shows that I am right.

³ He answers from heaven and
saves me.
He puts to shame those
who chase me.
He shows his love and that
he is faithful.

⁴ Men who are like lions are all
around me.
I am forced to lie down
among people who are
like hungry animals.
Their teeth are like spears
and arrows.
Their tongues are like
sharp swords.

⁵ God, may you be honored
above the heavens.
Let your glory be over the
whole earth.

⁶ My enemies spread a net to
catch me by the feet.
I felt helpless.
They dug a pit in my path.
But they fell into it
themselves.

⁷ God, my heart feels secure.
My heart feels secure.
I will sing and make music
to you.

⁸ My spirit, wake up!
Harp and lyre, wake up!
I want to sing and make
music before the sun
rises.

⁹ Lord, I will praise you among
the nations.
I will sing about you
among the people of the
earth.

¹⁰ Great is your love. It reaches
to the heavens.
Your truth reaches to the
skies.

¹¹ God, may you be honored
above the heavens.
Let your glory be over the
whole earth.

Psalm 58

For the director of music.
A miktam of David to the tune
of "Do Not Destroy."

¹ Are you rulers really fair
when you speak?
Do you judge people
honestly?

² No, in your hearts you plan to
be unfair.
With your hands you do
terrible things on the
earth.

³ Even from birth those who
are evil go down the
wrong path.
From the day they are born
they go the wrong way
and spread lies.

⁴ Their words are like the
poison of a snake.
They are like the poison of
a cobra that has covered
up its ears.

⁵ It won't listen to a snake
charmer's tune,
even if the charmer plays
very well.

⁶ God, break the teeth in the
mouths of those
sinners!
LORD, tear out the sharp
teeth of those lions!

⁷ Let those people disappear
like water that flows
away.
When they draw their
bows, let their arrows
fall short of the target.

8 Let them be like a slug that
    melts away as it moves
    along.
 Let them be like a baby
    that is born dead and
    never sees the sun.

9 Evil people will be swept
    away before burning
    thorns can heat a pot.
 And it doesn't matter if the
    thorns are green or dry.

10 Godly people will be glad
    when those who have
    hurt them are paid back.
 They will dip their feet in
    the blood of those who
    do evil.

11 Then people will say,
    "The godly will get their
    reward.
 There really is a God who
    judges the earth."

Psalm 59

*For the director of music. A miktam
of David when Saul had sent men
to watch David's house. Saul sent
the men to kill David. To the tune
of "Do Not Destroy."*

1 God, save me from my
    enemies.
 Keep me safe from people
    who are attacking me.

2 Save me from those who do
    evil.
 Save me from people who
    want to kill me.

3 See how they hide and wait
    for me!
 LORD, angry people plan to
    harm me,
 even though I haven't
    hurt them in any way or
    sinned against them.

4 I haven't done anything
    wrong to them. But they
    are ready to attack me.
 Rise up and help me! Look
    at what I'm up against!

5 LORD God who rules over all,
    rise up. God of Israel,
    punish all the nations.
 Don't show any mercy to
    those sinful people
 who have turned against
    me.

6 My enemies are like a pack of
    barking dogs
 that come back to the city
    in the evening.
 They prowl around the
    city.

7 Listen to what pours out of
    their mouths.
 The words from their lips
    are like swords.
 They think, "Who can hear
    us?"

8 But you laugh at them,
    LORD.
 You make fun of all those
    nations.

9 You give me strength. I look
    to you.
 God, you are like a fort to
    me. 10 You are my God,
    and I can depend on you.

 God will march out in front
    of me.
 He will let me look down
    on those who tell lies
    about me.

11 Lord, you are like a shield
    that keeps us safe.
 Don't kill my enemies all at
    once.
 If you do, my people will
    forget about it.

Use your power to pull my
　　enemies up by the roots
　　like weeds.
　　Destroy them.
[12] They have sinned with their
　　mouths.
　　Their lips have spoken evil
　　words.
　　They have cursed me and
　　lied.
　　Let them be caught in their
　　pride.
[13] Burn them up in your anger.
　　Burn them up until there
　　isn't anything left of
　　them.
　　Then everyone from one end
　　of the earth to the other
　　will know
　　that God rules over the
　　people of Jacob.
[14] My enemies are like a pack of
　　barking dogs
　　that come back into the
　　city in the evening.
　　They prowl around the
　　city.
[15] They wander around looking
　　for food.
　　They groan if they don't
　　find something that will
　　satisfy them.
[16] But I will sing about your
　　strength.
　　In the morning I will sing
　　about your love.
　　You are like a fort to me.
　　You keep me safe in times
　　of trouble.
[17] You give me strength. I sing
　　praise to you.
　　God, you are like a fort to
　　me. You are my God, and
　　I can depend on you.

Psalm 60

*For the director of music. For
teaching. A miktam of David
when he fought against Aram
Naharaim and Aram Zobah. That
was when Joab returned and struck
down 12,000 people from Edom
in the Valley of Salt. To the tune
of "The Lily of the Covenant."*

[1] God, you have turned away
　　from us. You have
　　attacked us.
　　You have been angry. Now
　　turn back to us!
[2] You have shaken the land
　　and torn it open.
　　Fix its cracks, because it is
　　falling apart.
[3] You have shown your people
　　hard times.
　　You have made us drink
　　the wine of your anger.
　　Now we can't even walk
　　straight.
[4] But you lead into battle those
　　who have respect for you.
　　You give them a flag
　　to wave against the
　　enemy's weapons.
[5] Save us and help us by your
　　power.
　　Do this so that those you
　　love may be saved.
[6] God has spoken from his
　　temple.
　　He has said, "I will win the
　　battle.
　　Then I will divide up the land
　　around Shechem.
　　I will divide up the Valley
　　of Sukkoth.
[7] Gilead belongs to me.
　　So does the land of
　　Manasseh.

Ephraim is the strongest
tribe.
It is like a helmet for my
head.
Judah is the royal tribe.
It is like a ruler's scepter.
⁸ Moab serves me like one who
washes my feet.
I toss my sandal on Edom
to show that I own it.
I shout to Philistia that I
have won the battle."

⁹ Who will bring me to the
city that has high walls
around it?
Who will lead me to the
land of Edom?
¹⁰ God, isn't it you, even though
you have now turned
away from us?
Isn't it you, even though
you don't lead our
armies into battle
anymore?
¹¹ Help us against our
enemies.
The help people give
doesn't amount to
anything.
¹² With your help we will win
the battle.
You will walk all over our
enemies.

Psalm 61

For the director of music.
A psalm of David to be played
on stringed instruments.

¹ God, hear my cry for help.
Listen to my prayer.

² From a place far away I call
out to you.
I call out as my heart gets
weaker.

Lead me to the safety of a
rock that is high above
me.
³ You have always kept me safe
from my enemies.
You are like a strong tower
to me.

⁴ I long to live in your holy tent
forever.
There I find safety in the
shadow of your wings.
⁵ God, you have heard my
promises.
You have given me what
belongs to those who
worship you.

⁶ Add many days to the king's
life.
Let him live on and on for
many years.
⁷ May he always enjoy your
blessing as he rules.
Let your love and truth
keep him safe.

⁸ Then I will always sing praise
to you.
I will keep my promises
day after day.

Psalm 62

For the director of music.
For Jeduthun. A psalm of David.

¹ It is surely true that I find my
rest in God.
He is the God who saves
me.
² It is surely true that he is my
rock. He is the God who
saves me.
He is like a fort to me. I will
always be secure.

³ How long will you enemies
attack me?

Will all of you throw me
  down?
I'm like a leaning wall.
I'm like a fence about to
  fall.
⁴Surely my enemies only want
  to pull me down
  from my place of honor.
They take delight in telling
  lies.
They bless me with what they
  say.
But in their hearts they ask
  for bad things to happen
  to me.

⁵Yes, I must find my rest in
  God.
He is the God who gives
  me hope.
⁶It is surely true that he is my
  rock and the God who
  saves me.
He is like a fort to me, so I
  will always be secure.
⁷I depend on God to save me
  and to honor me.
He is my mighty rock and
  my place of safety.
⁸Trust in him at all times, you
  people.
Tell him all your troubles.
God is our place of
  safety.

⁹Surely ordinary people are
  only a breath.
Important people are not
  what they seem to be.
If they were weighed on a
  scale, they wouldn't
  amount to anything.
Together they are only a
  breath.
¹⁰Don't trust in money you
  have taken from others.

Don't put false hope in
  things you have stolen.
Even if your riches grow,
  don't put your trust in
  them.

¹¹God, I have heard you say
  two things.
One is that power belongs
  to you, God.
¹²   The other is that your love,
  Lord, never ends.
You will reward everyone
  in keeping with what they
  have done.

Psalm 63

*A psalm of David when he was
in the Desert of Judah.*

¹God, you are my God.
I seek you with all my
  heart.
With all my strength I thirst
  for you
  in this dry desert
  where there isn't any
  water.

²I have seen you in the sacred
  tent.
There I have seen your
  power and your glory.
³Your love is better than life.
So I will bring glory to you
  with my lips.
⁴I will praise you as long as I
  live.
I will call on your name
  when I lift up my hands
  in prayer.
⁵I will be as satisfied as if I
  had eaten the best food
  there is.
I will sing praise to you
  with my mouth.

⁶As I lie on my bed I
remember you.
I think of you all night
long.
⁷Because you have helped
me,
I sing in the shadow of your
wings.
⁸I hold on to you tightly.
Your powerful right hand
takes good care of me.

⁹Those who want to kill me
will be destroyed.
They will go down into the
grave.
¹⁰They will be killed by
swords.
They will become food for
wild dogs.

¹¹But the king will be filled
with joy because of what
God has done.
All those who make
promises in God's name
will be able to brag.
But the mouths of liars will
be shut.

Psalm 64

*For the director of music.
A psalm of David.*

¹God, hear me as I tell you my
problem.
Don't let my enemies kill
me.
²Hide me from evil people
who talk about how to
harm me.
Hide me from those people
who are planning to do
evil.

³They make their tongues like
sharp swords.

They aim their mean
words like deadly
arrows.
⁴They shoot from their hiding
places at people who
aren't guilty.
They shoot quickly and
aren't afraid of being
caught.

⁵They help one another make
evil plans.
They talk about hiding
their traps.
They say, "Who can see
what we are doing?"
⁶They make plans to do what
is evil.
They say, "We have
thought up a perfect
plan!"
The hearts and minds of
people are so clever!

⁷But God will shoot my
enemies with his
arrows.
He will suddenly strike
them down.
⁸He will turn their own words
against them.
He will destroy them.
All those who see them will
shake their heads
and look down on them.

⁹All people will respect
God.
They will tell about his
works.
They will think about what
he has done.
¹⁰Godly people will be full of
joy because of what the
LORD has done.
They will go to him for
safety.

All those whose hearts are
honest will be proud of
what he has done.

Psalm 65

*For the director of music. A psalm
of David. A song.*

¹ Our God, we look forward to
praising you in Zion.
We will keep our promises
to you.
² All people will come to you,
because you hear and
answer prayer.
³ When our sins became too
much for us,
you forgave our lawless
acts.
⁴ Blessed are those you
choose
and bring near to worship
you.
You bring us into the
courtyards of your holy
temple.
There in your house we are
filled with all kinds of
good things.
⁵ God our Savior, you answer
us with right and
wonderful deeds.
People all over the world
and beyond the farthest
oceans
put their hope in you.
⁶ You formed the mountains
by your power.
You showed how strong
you are.
⁷ You calmed the oceans and
their roaring waves.
You calmed the angry
words and actions of the
nations.

⁸ Everyone on earth is amazed
at the wonderful things
you have done.
What you do makes people
from one end of the
earth to the other sing
for joy.
⁹ You take care of the land and
water it.
You make it able to grow
many crops.
You fill your streams with
water.
You do that to provide the
people with grain.
That's what you have
decided to do for the
land.
¹⁰ You water its rows.
You smooth out its bumps.
You soften it with showers.
And you bless its crops.
¹¹ You bring the year to a close
with huge crops.
You provide more than
enough food.
¹² The grass grows thick even in
the desert.
The hills are dressed with
gladness.
¹³ The meadows are covered
with flocks and herds.
The valleys are dressed
with grain.
They sing and shout for joy.

Psalm 66

*For the director of music.
A song. A psalm.*

¹ Shout to God for joy,
everyone on earth!
² Sing about the glory of his
name!
Give him glorious praise!

³ Say to God, "What wonderful
things you do!
Your power is so great
that your enemies bow
down to you in fear.
⁴ Everyone on earth bows
down to you.
They sing praise to you.
They sing the praises of
your name."

⁵ Come and see what God has
done.
See what wonderful things
he has done for people!
⁶ He turned the Red Sea into
dry land.
The people of Israel passed
through the waters on
foot.
Come, let us be full of joy
because of what he did.
⁷ He rules by his power
forever.
His eyes watch the nations.
Let no one who refuses to
obey him rise up against
him.

⁸ Praise our God, all you
nations.
Let the sound of the praise
you give him be heard.
⁹ He has kept us alive.
He has kept our feet from
slipping.
¹⁰ God, you have tested us.
You put us through fire to
make us like silver.
¹¹ You put us in prison.
You placed heavy loads on
our backs.
¹² You let our enemies ride their
chariots over our heads.
We went through fire and
water.

But you brought us to a place
where we have everything
we need.

¹³ I will come to your temple
with burnt offerings.
I will keep my promises to
you.
¹⁴ I made them with my lips.
My mouth spoke them
when I was in trouble.
¹⁵ I will sacrifice fat animals to
you as burnt offerings.
I will offer rams, bulls and
goats to you.

¹⁶ Come and hear, all you who
have respect for God.
Let me tell you what he has
done for me.
¹⁷ I cried out to him with my
mouth.
I praised him with my
tongue.
¹⁸ If I had enjoyed having sin in
my heart,
the Lord would not have
listened.
¹⁹ But God has surely listened.
He has heard my prayer.
²⁰ Give praise to God.
He has accepted my
prayer.
He has not held back his
love from me.

Psalm 67

*For the director of music.
A psalm. A song to be played
on stringed instruments.*

¹ God, have mercy on us and
bless us.
May you be pleased with
us.
² Then your ways will be
known on earth.

All nations will see that you
  have the power to save.
3 God, may the nations praise
  you.
    May all the people on earth
    praise you.
4 May the nations be glad and
  sing for joy.
    You rule the people of the
    earth fairly.
    You guide the nations of
    the earth.
5 God, may the nations praise
  you.
    May all the people on earth
    praise you.
6 The land produces its crops.
    God, our God, blesses us.
7 May God continue to bless us.
    Then people from one end
    of the earth to the other
    will have respect for him.

Psalm 68

*For the director of music. A psalm
    of David. A song.*

1 May God rise up and scatter
  his enemies.
    May they turn and run
    away from him.
2   May you, God, blow them
    away like smoke.
  As fire melts wax,
    so may God destroy sinful
    people.
3 But may those who do what is
  right be glad
    and filled with joy when
    they are with him.
    May they be happy and
    joyful.
4 Sing to God, sing praise to his
  name.

Lift up a song to the God
  who rides on the clouds.
    Be glad when you are with
    him.
    His name is the LORD.
5 God is in his holy temple.
    He is a father to children
    whose fathers have died.
    He takes care of women
    whose husbands have
    died.
6 God gives lonely people a
  family.
    He sets prisoners free, and
    they go out singing.
  But those who refuse to obey
  him
    live in a land that is baked
    by the sun.

7 God, you led your people out.
    You marched through the
    desert.
8 The ground shook
    when you, the God of Sinai,
    appeared.
  The heavens poured down
  rain
    when you, the God of
    Israel, appeared.
9 God, you gave us plenty of
  rain.
    You renewed your worn-
    out land.
10 God, your people made their
  homes in it.
    From all your riches, you
    provided for those who
    were poor.

11 The Lord gives the message.
    The women who make it
    known are a huge
    group.
12 They said, "Kings and armies
    are running away.

The women at home are
dividing up
the things the army took
from their enemies.
[13] Even while the soldiers sleep
near the sheep pens,
God wins the battle for
them.
He gives the enemy's silver
and gold
to Israel, his dove."
[14] The Mighty One has
scattered the kings
around the land.
It was like snow falling on
Mount Zalmon.

[15] Mount Bashan is a majestic
mountain.
Mount Bashan is a very
rocky mountain.
[16] Why are you jealous of
Mount Zion, you rocky
mountain?
That's where God chooses
to rule.
That's where the LORD
himself will live
forever.
[17] God has come with tens
of thousands of his
chariots.
He has come with
thousands and
thousands of them.
The Lord has come from
Mount Sinai.
He has entered his holy
place.
[18] When he went up to his place
on high,
he took many prisoners.
He received gifts from
people,
even from those who
refused to obey him.

The LORD God went up to
live on Mount Zion.
[19] Give praise to the Lord. Give
praise to God our Savior.
He carries our heavy loads
day after day.
[20] Our God is a God who saves.
He is the King and the
LORD. He saves us from
death.
[21] God will certainly smash the
heads of his enemies.
He will break the hairy
heads of those who keep
on sinning.
[22] The Lord says, "I will bring
your enemies from
Bashan.
I will bring them up from
the bottom of the sea.
[23] Then your feet can wade in
their blood.
The tongues of your dogs
can lick up all the blood
they want."
[24] God, those who worship you
come marching into
view.
My God and King, those
who follow you have
entered the sacred tent.
[25] The singers are walking in
front.
Next come the musicians.
Young women playing
tambourines are with
them.
[26] The leaders sing, "Praise God
among all those who
worship him.
Praise the LORD in the
community of Israel."
[27] The little tribe of Benjamin
leads the worshipers.

Next comes the great
crowd of Judah's princes.
Then come the princes of
Zebulun and the princes
of Naphtali.
28 God, show us your power.
Show us your strength.
God, do as you have done
before.
29 Do it from your temple at
Jerusalem,
where kings will bring you
gifts.
30 Give a strong warning to
Egypt, that beast among
the tall grass.
It is like a herd of bulls
among the calves.
May that beast bow down
before you with gifts of
silver.
Scatter the nations who
like to make war.
31 Messengers will come from
Egypt.
The people of Cush will
be quick to bring gifts to
you.
32 Sing to God, you kingdoms of
the earth.
Sing praise to the Lord.
33 He rides across the highest
places in heaven.
He rides across the ancient
skies above.
He thunders with his
mighty voice.
34 Tell how powerful God is.
He rules as king over
Israel.
The skies show how
powerful he is.
35 How wonderful is God in his
holy place!

The God of Israel gives
power and strength to
his people.

Give praise to God!

Psalm 69

*For the director of music. A psalm of
David to the tune of "Lilies."*

1 God, save me.
My troubles are like a
flood.
I'm up to my neck in them.
2 I'm sinking in deep mud.
I have no firm place to
stand.
I am out in deep water.
The waves roll over me.
3 I'm worn out from calling for
help.
My throat is very dry.
My eyes grow tired
looking for my God.
4 Those who hate me without
any reason
are more than the hairs on
my head.
Many people who don't have
any reason to be my
enemies
are trying to destroy me.
They force me to give back
what I didn't steal.

5 God, you know how foolish
I've been.
My guilt is not hidden from
you.

6 Lord, you are the LORD who
rules over all.
May those who put their
hope in you not be
dishonored because of
me.
You are the God of Israel.

May those who worship
you not be put to shame
because of me.
⁷ Because of you, people laugh
at me.
My face is covered with
shame.
⁸ I'm an outsider to my own
family.
I'm a stranger to my own
mother's children.
⁹ My great love for your house
destroys me.
Those who make fun of
you make fun of me also.
¹⁰ When I weep and go without
eating,
they laugh at me.
¹¹ When I put on rough clothing
to show how sad I am,
people make jokes about
me.
¹² Those who gather in public
places make fun of me.
Those who get drunk make
up songs about me.

¹³ But LORD, I pray to you.
May this be the time you
help me.
God, answer me because you
love me so much.
Save me, as you always do.
¹⁴ Save me from the trouble I'm
in.
It's like slippery mud, so
don't let me sink in it.
Save me from those who hate
me.
Save me from the deep
water I'm in.
¹⁵ Don't let the floods cover me.
Don't let the deep water
swallow me up.
Don't let the grave close its
mouth over me.

¹⁶ LORD, answer me because
your love is so good.
Turn to me because you
are so kind.
¹⁷ Don't turn your face away
from me.
Answer me quickly. I'm in
trouble.
¹⁸ Come near and save me.
Set me free from my
enemies.

¹⁹ You know how they make fun
of me.
They dishonor me and put
me to shame.
You know all about my
enemies.
²⁰ They have broken my heart
by saying evil things
about me.
It has left me helpless.
I looked for pity, but I didn't
find any.
I looked for someone to
comfort me, but I didn't
find anyone.
²¹ They put bitter spices in my
food.
They gave me vinegar
when I was thirsty.

²² Let their feast be a trap and a
snare.
Let my enemies get what's
coming to them.
²³ Let their eyes grow weak so
they can't see.
Let their backs be bent
forever.
²⁴ Pour out your anger on
them.
Let them feel what it is like.
²⁵ May their homes be deserted.
May no one live in their
tents.

26 They attack those you have
wounded.
They talk about the pain of
those you have hurt.
27 Charge them with one crime
after another.
Don't save them.
28 May their names be erased
from the book of life.
Don't include them in the
list of those who do
right.
29 I'm in pain. I'm in deep
trouble.
God, save me and keep me
safe.
30 I will praise God's name by
singing to him.
I will bring him glory by
giving him thanks.
31 That will please the LORD
more than offering him
an ox.
It will please him more
than offering him a
bull with its horns and
hooves.
32 Poor people will see it and be
glad.
The hearts of those who
worship God will be
strengthened.
33 The LORD hears those who
are in need.
He doesn't forget his
people in prison.
34 Let heaven and earth praise
him.
Let the oceans and
everything that moves in
them praise him.
35 God will save Zion.
He will build the cities of
Judah again.

Then people will live in them
and own the land.
36 The children of those who
serve God will receive it.
Those who love him will
live there.

Psalm 70

For the director of music.
A prayer of David.

1 God, hurry and save me.
LORD, come quickly and
help me.
2 Let those who are trying to
kill me be put to shame.
Let them not be honored.
Let all those who want to
destroy me
be turned back in shame.
3 Some people make fun of me.
Let them be turned back
when their plans fail.
4 But let all those who seek you
be joyful and glad because
of what you have done.
Let those who want you to
save them always say,
"The LORD is great!"

5 But I am poor and needy.
God, come quickly to me.
You are the God who helps
me and saves me.
LORD, please don't wait any
longer.

Psalm 71

1 LORD, I have gone to you for
safety.
Let me never be put to
shame.
2 You do what is right, so save
me and help me.
Pay attention to me and
save me.

³ Be my rock of safety
that I can always go to.
Give the command to save
me.
You are my rock and my
fort.
⁴ My God, save me from the
power of sinners.
Save me from the hands
of those who are mean
and evil.
⁵ You are the King and the
LORD. You have always
been my hope.
I have trusted in you ever
since I was young.
⁶ From the time I was born I
have depended on you.
You brought me out of my
mother's body.
I will praise you forever.
⁷ To many people I am an
example of how much
you care.
You are my strong place of
safety.
⁸ My mouth is filled with
praise for you.
All day long I will talk
about your glory.
⁹ Don't push me away when
I'm old.
Don't desert me when my
strength is gone.
¹⁰ My enemies speak against
me.
Those who want to kill me
get together and make
evil plans.
¹¹ They say, "God has deserted
him.
Go after him and grab
him.
No one will save him."

¹² God, don't be far away from
me.
My God, come quickly and
help me.
¹³ May those who bring charges
against me die in shame.
May those who want to
harm me
be covered with shame
and dishonor.
¹⁴ But I will always have hope.
I will praise you more and
more.
¹⁵ I will tell other people about
all the good things you
have done.
All day long I will talk
about how you have
saved your people.
But there's no way I could
say how many times
you've done this.
¹⁶ LORD and King, I will come
and announce your
mighty acts.
I will announce all the
good things that you
alone do.
¹⁷ God, ever since I was young
you have taught me.
To this very day I tell about
your wonderful acts.
¹⁸ God, don't leave me
even when I'm old and
have gray hair.
Let me live to tell my children
about your power.
Let me tell all of them
about your mighty acts.
¹⁹ God, your saving acts reach
to the skies.
You have done great
things.
God, who is like you?

20 You have sent many bitter
    troubles my way.
  But you will give me new
    life.
  Even if I'm almost in the
    grave,
    you will bring me back.
21 You will honor me more and
    more.
  You will comfort me once
    again.
22 My God, I will use the harp to
    praise you
  because you are always
    faithful.
  Holy One of Israel,
    I will use the lyre to sing
    praise to you.
23 My lips will shout with joy
    when I sing praise to you.
  You have saved me.
24 All day long my tongue will
    say
    that you have done what is
    right.
  Those who wanted to harm
    me have been put to
    shame.
  They have not been
    honored.

Psalm 72

A psalm of Solomon.

1 God, give the king the ability
    to judge fairly.
  He is your royal son. Help
    him to do what is right.
2 May he rule your people in
    the right way.
  May he be fair to those
    among your people who
    are hurting.
3 May the mountains and the
    hills produce rich crops,

because the people will do
    what is right.
4 May the king stand up for
    those who are hurting.
  May he save the children of
    those who are in need.
  May he crush those who
    treat others badly.

5 May the king rule as long as
    the sun shines
  and the moon gives its
    light.
  May he rule for all time to
    come.
6 May he be like rain falling on
    the fields.
  May he be like showers
    watering the earth.
7 May godly people do well as
    long as he rules.
  May they have more than
    they need as long as the
    moon lasts.

8 May the king rule from sea to
    sea.
  May his kingdom reach
    from the Euphrates River
    to the ends of the earth.
9 May the desert tribes bow
    down to him.
  May his enemies lick the
    dust.
10 May the kings of Tarshish
    and of places far away
  bring him gifts.
  May the kings of Sheba and
    Seba
  give him presents.
11 May all kings bow down to
    him.
  May all nations serve him.

12 The king will save needy
    people who cry out to
    him.

He will save those who are
hurting and have no one
else to help.
13 He will take pity on those
who are weak and in
need.
He will save them from
death.
14 He will save them from
people who treat others
badly.
He will save them from
people who do mean
things to them.
Their lives are very special
to him.

15 May the king live a long
time!
May gold from Sheba be
given to him.
May people always pray for
him.
May they ask the LORD to
bless him all day long.
16 May there be plenty of grain
everywhere in the land.
May it sway in the wind on
the tops of the hills.
May the crops grow well, like
those in Lebanon.
May they grow like the
grass of the field.
17 May the king's name be
remembered forever.
May his fame last as long
as the sun shines.

Then all nations will be
blessed because of him.
They will call him blessed.

18 Give praise to the LORD God,
the God of Israel.
Only he can do wonderful
things.

19 Give praise to his glorious
name forever.
May his glory fill the whole
earth.
Amen and Amen.

20 The prayers of David, the son
of Jesse, end here.

BOOK III

Psalms 73–89

Psalm 73

A psalm of Asaph.

1 God is truly good to Israel.
He is good to those who
have pure hearts.

2 But my feet had almost
slipped.
I had almost tripped and
fallen.
3 I saw that proud and sinful
people were doing well.
And I began to long for
what they had.
4 They don't have any
troubles.
Their bodies are healthy
and strong.
5 They don't have the problems
most people have.
They don't suffer as other
people do.
6 Their pride is like a necklace.
They put on meanness as if
it were their clothes.
7 Many sins come out of their
hard and stubborn
hearts.
There is no limit to the evil
things they can think up.
8 They laugh at others and
speak words of hatred.

They are proud. They warn
　　others about the harm
　　they can do to them.
⁹They brag as if they owned
　　heaven itself.
　　They talk as if they
　　controlled the earth.
¹⁰So people listen to them.
　　They lap up their words
　　like water.
¹¹They say, "How would God
　　know what we're doing?
　　Does the Most High God
　　know anything?"
¹²Here is what sinful people
　　are like.
　　They don't have a care in
　　the world.
　　They keep getting richer
　　and richer.
¹³It seems as if I have kept my
　　heart pure for no reason.
　　It didn't do me any good to
　　wash my hands
　　to show that I wasn't
　　guilty of doing anything
　　wrong.
¹⁴Day after day I've been in
　　pain.
　　God has punished me in a
　　new way every morning.
¹⁵What if I had talked like
　　that?
　　Then I wouldn't have
　　been faithful to God's
　　children.
¹⁶I tried to understand it all.
　　But it was more than I
　　could handle.
¹⁷It troubled me until I entered
　　God's temple.
　　Then I understood what
　　will finally happen to
　　bad people.

¹⁸God, I'm sure you will make
　　them slip and fall.
　　You will throw them down
　　and destroy them.
¹⁹It will happen very suddenly.
　　A terrible death will take
　　them away completely.
²⁰A dream goes away when a
　　person wakes up.
　　Lord, it will be like that
　　when you rise up.
　　It will be as if those people
　　were only a dream.
²¹At one time my heart was sad
　　and my spirit was bitter.
²²I didn't have any sense. I
　　didn't know anything.
　　I acted like a wild animal
　　toward you.
²³But I am always with you.
　　You hold me by my right
　　hand.
²⁴You give me wise advice to
　　guide me.
　　And when I die, you will
　　take me away
　　into the glory of heaven.
²⁵I don't have anyone in heaven
　　but you.
　　I don't want anything on
　　earth besides you.
²⁶My body and my heart may
　　grow weak.
　　God, you give strength to
　　my heart.
　　You are everything I will
　　ever need.
²⁷Those who don't want
　　anything to do with you
　　will die.
　　You destroy all those who
　　aren't faithful to you.
²⁸But I am close to you. And
　　that's good.

Lord and King, I have made
you my place of safety.
I will talk about everything
you have done.

Psalm 74

A maskil of Asaph.

1 God, why have you turned
your back on us for so
long?
Why are you so angry with
us? We are your very
own sheep.
2 Remember the nation that
you chose as your own
so long ago.
Remember that you set us
free from slavery to be
your very own people.
Remember Mount Zion,
where you lived.
3 Walk through this place that
has been torn down
beyond repair.
See how completely your
enemies have destroyed
the temple!

4 In the place where you used
to meet with us,
your enemies have
shouted, "We've won the
battle!"
They have set up their
flags to show they have
beaten us.
5 They acted like people
cutting down a forest
with axes.
6   They smashed all the
beautiful wooden walls
with their axes and
hatchets.
7 They burned your temple to
the ground.

They polluted the place
where your Name is.
8 They had said in their hearts,
"We will crush them
completely!"
They burned every
place where you were
worshiped in the
land.
9 We don't get signs from God
anymore.
There aren't any prophets
left.
None of us knows how long
that will last.

10 God, how long will your
enemies make fun of
you?
Will they attack you with
their words forever?
11 Why don't you help us? Why
do you hold back your
power?
Use your strong power to
destroy your enemies!

12 God, you have been my king
for a long time.
You are the only God who
can save anyone on
earth.
13 You parted the waters of the
Red Sea by your power.
You broke the heads of that
sea monster in Egypt.
14 You crushed the heads of the
sea monster Leviathan.
You fed it to the creatures
of the desert.
15 You opened up streams and
springs.
You dried up rivers that
flow all year long.
16 You rule over the day and the
night.

You created the sun and
the moon.
¹⁷You decided where the
borders of the earth
would be.
You made both summer
and winter.
¹⁸LORD, remember how your
enemies have made fun
of you.
Remember how foolish
people have attacked
you with their words.
¹⁹Don't hand over Israel, your
dove, to those wild
animals.
Don't forget your suffering
people forever.
²⁰Honor the covenant you
made with us.
Horrible things are
happening in every dark
corner of the land.
²¹Don't let your suffering
people be put to shame.
May those who are poor
and needy praise you.
²²God, rise up. Stand up for
your cause.
Remember how foolish
people make fun of you
all day long.
²³Pay close attention to the
shouts of your enemies.
The trouble they cause
never stops.

Psalm 75

*For the director of music. A psalm
of Asaph. A song to the tune of
"Do Not Destroy."*

¹God, we praise you.
We praise you because you
are near to us.

People talk about the
wonderful things you
have done.
²You say, "I choose the
appointed time to judge
people.
And I judge them fairly.
³When the earth and all its
people tremble,
I keep everything from
falling to pieces.
⁴To the proud I say, 'Don't brag
anymore.'
To sinners I say, 'Don't
show off your power.
⁵Don't show it off against
me.
Don't talk back to me.' "

⁶No one from east or west or
north or south
can judge themselves.
⁷God is the one who judges.
He says to one person,
"You are guilty."
To another he says, "You
are not guilty."
⁸In the hand of the LORD is a
cup.
It is full of wine mixed with
spices.
It is the wine of his anger.
He pours it out. All the evil
people on earth
drink it down to the very
last drop.
⁹I will speak about this
forever.
I will sing praise to the God
of Jacob.
¹⁰God says, "I will destroy
the power of all sinful
people.
But I will make godly
people more powerful."

Psalm 76

*For the director of music. A psalm
of Asaph. A song to be played on
stringed instruments.*

¹ In the land of Judah, God is
  well known.
  In Israel, his name is
  great.
² His tent is in Jerusalem.
  The place where he lives is
  on Mount Zion.
³ There he broke the deadly
  arrows of his enemies.
  He broke their shields and
  swords.
  He broke their weapons of
  war.
⁴ God, you shine like a very
  bright light.
  You are more majestic than
  mountains full of wild
  animals.
⁵ Brave soldiers have been
  robbed of everything
  they had.
  Now they lie there,
  sleeping in death.
  Not one of them can even
  lift his hands.
⁶ God of Jacob, at your
  command
  both horse and chariot lie
  still.
⁷ People should have respect
  for you alone.
  Who can stand in front of
  you when you are
  angry?
⁸ From heaven you handed
  down your sentence.
  The land was afraid and
  became quiet.
⁹ God, that happened when
  you rose up to judge.

It happened when you
  came to save all your
  suffering people in the
  land.
¹⁰ Your anger against sinners
  brings you praise.
  Those who live through
  your anger gather to
  worship you.
¹¹ Make promises to the LORD
  your God and keep
  them.
  Let all the neighboring
  nations
  bring gifts to the God who
  should be respected.
¹² He breaks the proud spirit of
  rulers.
  The kings of the earth have
  respect for him.

Psalm 77

*For the director of music.
For Jeduthun. A psalm of Asaph.*

¹ I cried out to God for help.
  I cried out to God to hear
  me.
² When I was in trouble, I
  looked to the Lord for
  help.
  During the night I lifted up
  my hands in prayer.
  But I refused to be
  comforted.

³ God, I remembered you, and
  I groaned.
  I thought about you, and I
  became weak.
⁴ You kept me from going to
  sleep.
  I was so troubled I couldn't
  speak.
⁵ I thought about days
  gone by.

I thought about the years of
   long ago.
⁶ I remembered how I used to
   sing praise to you in the
   night.
I thought about it, and here
   is what I asked myself.
⁷ "Will the Lord turn away
   from us forever?
Won't he ever show us his
   kindness again?
⁸ Has his faithful love
   disappeared forever?
Has his promise failed for
   all time?
⁹ Has God forgotten to help
   us?
Has he held back his tender
   love because he was
   angry?"
¹⁰ Then I thought, "Here is what
   gives me hope.
For many years the Most
   High God showed how
   powerful he is.
¹¹ LORD, I will remember what
   you did.
Yes, I will remember your
   miracles of long ago.
¹² I will spend time thinking
   about everything you
   have done.
I will consider all your
   mighty acts."
¹³ God, everything you do is
   holy.
What god is as great as our
   God?
¹⁴ You are the God who does
   miracles.
You show your power
   among the nations.
¹⁵ With your mighty arm you
   set your people free.

You set the children of
   Jacob and Joseph free.
¹⁶ God, the water of the Red Sea
   saw you.
It saw you and boiled up.
The deepest waters were
   stirred up.
¹⁷ The clouds poured down
   rain.
The skies rumbled with
   thunder.
Lightning flashed back and
   forth like arrows.
¹⁸ Your thunder was heard in
   the windstorm.
Your lightning lit up the
   world.
The earth trembled and
   shook.
¹⁹ Your path led through the
   Red Sea.
You walked through the
   mighty waters.
But your footprints were
   not seen.
²⁰ You led your people like a
   flock.
You led them by the hands
   of Moses and Aaron.

Psalm 78

A maskil of Asaph.

¹ My people, listen to my
   teaching.
Pay attention to what I say.
² I will open my mouth and tell
   a story.
I will speak about things
   that were hidden.
They happened a long time
   ago.
³ We have heard about them
   and we know them.

Our people who lived
    before us have told us
    about them.
⁴We won't hide them from our
    children.
We will tell them to those
    who live after us.
We will tell them what the
    LORD has done that is
    worthy of praise.
We will talk about
    his power and the
    wonderful things he has
    done.
⁵He gave laws to the people of
    Jacob.
He gave Israel their law.
He commanded our people
    who lived before us
    to teach his laws to their
    children.
⁶Then those born later would
    know his laws.
Even their children yet to
    come would know
    them.
And they in turn would tell
    their children.
⁷Then they would put their
    trust in God.
They would not forget what
    he had done.
They would obey his
    commands.
⁸They would not be like their
    people who lived long
    ago.
Those people were
    stubborn. They refused
    to obey God.
They turned away from him.
Their spirits were not
    faithful to him.
⁹The soldiers of Ephraim were
    armed with bows.

But they ran away on the
    day of battle.
¹⁰They didn't keep the
    covenant God had made
    with them.
They refused to live by his
    law.
¹¹They forgot what he had
    done.
They didn't remember the
    wonders he had shown
    them.
¹²He did miracles right in front
    of their people who lived
    long ago.
At that time they were
    living in Egypt, in the
    area of Zoan.
¹³God parted the Red Sea and
    led them through it.
He made the water stand
    up like a wall.
¹⁴He guided them with the
    cloud during the day.
He led them with the light
    of a fire all night long.
¹⁵He broke the rocks open in
    the desert.
He gave them as much
    water as there is in the
    oceans.
¹⁶He brought streams out of a
    rocky cliff.
He made water flow down
    like rivers.

¹⁷But they continued to sin
    against him.
In the desert they refused
    to obey the Most High
    God.
¹⁸They were stubborn and
    tested God.
They ordered him to give
    them the food they
    wanted.

¹⁹ They spoke against God.
They said,
"Can God really put food
on a table in the desert?
²⁰ It is true that he struck the
rock, and streams of
water poured out.
Huge amounts of water
flowed down.
But can he also give us
bread?
Can he supply meat for his
people?"
²¹ When the LORD heard what
they said, he was very
angry.
His anger broke out like
fire against the people of
Jacob.
He became very angry
with Israel.
²² That was because they didn't
believe in God.
They didn't trust in his
power to save them.
²³ But he gave a command to
the skies above.
He opened the doors of the
heavens.
²⁴ He rained down manna for
the people to eat.
He gave them the grain of
heaven.
²⁵ Mere human beings ate the
bread of angels.
He sent them all the food
they could eat.
²⁶ He made the east wind blow
from the heavens.
By his power he caused the
south wind to blow.
²⁷ He rained down meat on
them like dust.
He sent them birds like
sand on the seashore.

²⁸ He made the birds come
down inside their
camp.
The birds fell all around
their tents.
²⁹ People ate until they couldn't
eat any more.
He gave them what they
had wanted.
³⁰ But even before they had
finished eating, God
acted.
He did it while the food
was still in their mouths.
³¹ His anger rose up against
them.
He put to death the
strongest among them.
He struck down Israel's
young men.
³² But even after all that, they
kept on sinning.
Even after the wonderful
things he had done, they
still didn't believe.
³³ So he brought their days
to an end like a puff of
smoke.
He ended their years with
terror.
³⁴ Every time God killed some
of them, the others
would seek him.
They gladly turned back to
him again.
³⁵ They remembered that God
was their Rock.
They remembered that
God Most High had set
them free.
³⁶ But they didn't mean it when
they praised him.
They lied to him when they
spoke.
³⁷ They turned away from him.

They weren't faithful to the
covenant he had made
with them.
38 But he was full of tender
love.
He forgave their sins
and didn't destroy his
people.
Time after time he held back
his anger.
He didn't let all his burning
anger blaze out.
39 He remembered that they
were only human.
He remembered they were
only a breath of air
that drifts by and doesn't
return.
40 How often they refused to
obey him in the desert!
How often they caused him
sorrow in that dry and
empty land!
41 Again and again they tested
God.
They made the Holy One of
Israel sad and angry.
42 They didn't remember his
power.
They forgot the day he set
them free
from those who had
treated them so badly.
43 They forgot how he had
shown them his signs in
Egypt.
They forgot his miracles in
the area of Zoan.
44 He turned the river of Egypt
into blood.
The people of Egypt
couldn't drink water
from their streams.
45 He sent large numbers of flies
that bit them.

He sent frogs that
destroyed their land.
46 He gave their crops to the
grasshoppers.
He gave their food to the
locusts.
47 He destroyed their vines with
hail.
He destroyed their fig trees
with sleet.
48 He killed their cattle with
hail.
Their livestock were struck
by lightning.
49 Because he was so angry
with Egypt, he caused
them to have great
trouble.
In his great anger he
sent destroying angels
against them.
50 God prepared a path for his
anger.
He didn't spare their lives.
He gave them over to the
plague.
51 He killed the oldest son of
each family in Egypt.
He struck down the oldest
son in every house in the
land of Ham.
52 But he brought his people out
like a flock.
He led them like sheep
through the desert.
53 He guided them safely, and
they weren't afraid.
But the Red Sea swallowed
up their enemies.
54 And so he brought his people
to the border of his holy
land.
He led them to the central
hill country he had
taken by his power.

⁵⁵ He drove out the nations
    to make room for his
    people.
He gave to each family a
    piece of land to pass on
    to their children.
He gave the tribes of Israel
    a place to make their
    homes.
⁵⁶ But they tested God.
They refused to obey the
    Most High God.
They didn't keep his laws.
⁵⁷ They were like their people
    who lived long ago.
They turned away from
    him and were not
    faithful.
They were like a bow that
    doesn't shoot straight.
They couldn't be trusted.
⁵⁸ They made God angry by
    going to their high
    places.
They made him jealous by
    worshiping the statues of
    their gods.
⁵⁹ When God saw what the
    people were doing, he
    was very angry.
He turned away from them
    completely.
⁶⁰ He deserted the holy tent at
    Shiloh.
He left the tent he had set
    up among his people.
⁶¹ He allowed the ark to be
    captured.
Into the hands of his
    enemies he sent the ark
    where his glory rested.
⁶² He let his people be killed by
    swords.
He was very angry with
    them.

⁶³ Fire destroyed their young
    men.
Their young women had
    no one to marry.
⁶⁴ Their priests were killed by
    swords.
Their widows weren't able
    to weep.
⁶⁵ Then the Lord woke up as if
    he had been sleeping.
He was like a warrior
    waking up from the deep
    sleep caused by wine.
⁶⁶ He drove back his enemies.
He put them to shame that
    will last forever.
⁶⁷ He turned his back on the
    tents of the people of
    Joseph.
He didn't choose to live in
    the tribe of Ephraim.
⁶⁸ Instead, he chose to live in
    the tribe of Judah.
He chose Mount Zion,
    which he loved.
⁶⁹ There he built his holy place
    as secure as the
    heavens.
He built it to last forever,
    like the earth.
⁷⁰ He chose his servant David.
He took him from the
    sheep pens.
⁷¹ He brought him from tending
    sheep
to be the shepherd of his
    people Jacob.
He made him the shepherd
    of Israel, his special
    people.
⁷² David cared for them with
    a faithful and honest
    heart.
With skilled hands he led
    them.

Psalm 79

A psalm of Asaph.

¹ God, an army from the
nations has attacked
your land.
They have polluted your
holy temple.
They have completely
destroyed Jerusalem.
² They have left the dead
bodies of your people.
They have left them as food
for the birds in the sky.
They have left the bodies of
your faithful people.
They have left them for the
wild animals.
³ They have poured out the
blood of your people like
water.
It is all around Jerusalem.
No one is left to bury the
dead.
⁴ We are something our
neighbors joke about.
The nations around us
laugh at us and make
fun of us.
⁵ LORD, how long will you be
angry with us? Will it be
forever?
How long will your
jealousy burn like fire?
⁶ Bring your great anger
against the nations
that don't pay any attention
to you.
Bring it against the
kingdoms
that don't worship you.
⁷ They have swallowed up the
people of Jacob.
They have destroyed
Israel's homeland.

⁸ Don't hold against us the sins
of our people who lived
before us.
May you be quick to show
us your tender love.
We are in great need.
⁹ God our Savior, help us.
Then glory will come to
you.
Save us and forgive our sins.
Then people will honor
your name.
¹⁰ Why should the nations say,
"Where is their God?"
Show the nations that you
punish those who kill
your people.
We want to see it happen.
¹¹ Listen to the groans of the
prisoners.
Use your strong arm
to save people sentenced to
death.
¹² Lord, our neighbors have
laughed at you.
Pay them back seven times
for what they have
done.
¹³ We are your people, your very
own sheep.
We will praise you forever.
For all time to come
we will keep on praising
you.

Psalm 80

For the director of music.
A psalm of Asaph to the tune
of "The Lilies of the Covenant."

¹ Shepherd of Israel, hear us.
You lead the people of
Joseph like a flock.
You sit on your throne
between the cherubim.

Show your glory
2 to the people of Ephraim,
Benjamin and Manasseh.
Call your strength into action.
Come and save us.

3 God, make us new again.
May you be pleased with
us.
Then we will be saved.

4 LORD God, you rule over all.
How long will you be
angry?
Will you be angry with
your people even when
they pray to you?
5 You have given us tears as
our food.
You have made us drink
tears by the bowlful.
6 You have let our neighbors
mock us.
Our enemies laugh at us.

7 God who rules over all, make
us new again.
May you be pleased with
us.
Then we will be saved.

8 You brought Israel out of
Egypt.
Israel was like a vine.
After you drove the nations
out of Canaan,
you planted the vine in
their land.
9 You prepared the ground
for it.
It took root and spread out
over the whole land.
10 The mountains were covered
with its shade.
The shade of its branches
covered the mighty
cedar trees.

11 Your vine sent its branches
out all the way to the
Mediterranean Sea.
They reached as far as the
Euphrates River.
12 Why have you broken down
the walls around your
vine?
Now all who pass by it can
pick its grapes.
13 Wild pigs from the forest
destroy it.
Insects from the fields feed
on it.
14 God who rules over all,
return to us!
Look down from heaven
and see us!
Watch over your vine.
15 Guard the root you have
planted with your
powerful right hand.
Take care of the branch
you have raised up for
yourself.
16 Your vine has been cut
down and burned in
the fire.
You have been angry with
us, and we are dying.
17 May you honor the people at
your right hand.
May you honor the nation
you have raised up for
yourself.
18 Then we won't turn away
from you.
Give us new life. We will
worship you.

19 LORD God who rules over all,
make us new again.
May you be pleased with
us.
Then we will be saved.

Psalm 81

For the director of music. According to gittith. A psalm of Asaph.

¹ Sing joyfully to God! He gives us strength.
  Give a loud shout to the God of Jacob!
² Let the music begin. Play the tambourines.
  Play sweet music on harps and lyres.

³ Blow the ram's horn on the day of the New Moon feast.
  Blow it again when the moon is full and the Feast of Booths begins.
⁴ This is an order given to Israel.
  It is a law of the God of Jacob.
⁵ He gave it as a covenant law for the people of Joseph.
  It was given when God went out to punish Egypt.
  There I heard a voice I didn't recognize.

⁶ The voice said, "I removed the load from your shoulders.
  I set your hands free from carrying heavy baskets.
⁷ You called out when you were in trouble, and I saved you.
  I answered you out of a thundercloud.
  I tested you at the waters of Meribah.
⁸ "My people, listen and I will warn you.
  Israel, I wish you would listen to me!
⁹ Don't have anything to do with the gods of other nations.
  Don't bow down and worship any god other than me.
¹⁰ I am the LORD your God.
  I brought you up out of Egypt.
  Open your mouth wide, and I will fill it with good things.

¹¹ "But my people wouldn't listen to me.
  Israel wouldn't obey me.
¹² So I let them go their own stubborn way.
  I let them follow their own sinful plans.

¹³ "I wish my people would listen to me!
  I wish Israel would live as I want them to live!
¹⁴ Then I would quickly bring their enemies under control.
  I would use my power against their attackers.
¹⁵ Those who hate me would bow down to me in fear.
  They would be punished forever.
¹⁶ But you would be fed with the finest wheat.
  I would satisfy you with the sweetest honey."

Psalm 82

A psalm of Asaph.

¹ God takes his place at the head of a large gathering of leaders.

He announces his decisions among them.

2 He says, "How long will you stand up for those who aren't fair to others?
How long will you show mercy to sinful people?
3 Stand up for the weak and for children whose fathers have died.
Protect the rights of people who are poor or treated badly.
4 Save those who are weak and needy.
Save them from the power of sinful people.

5 "You leaders don't know anything.
You don't understand anything.
You are in the dark about what is right.
Law and order have been destroyed all over the world.

6 "I said, 'You leaders are like gods.
You are all children of the Most High God.'
7 But you will die, like mere human beings.
You will die like every other leader."

8 God, rise up. Judge the earth.
All the nations belong to you.

Psalm 83

A song. A psalm of Asaph.

1 God, don't remain silent.
Don't refuse to listen.
Do something, God.
2 See how your enemies are growling like dogs.
See how they are rising up against you.
3 They make clever plans against your people.
They make evil plans against those you love.
4 "Come," they say. "Let's destroy that whole nation.
Then the name of Israel won't be remembered anymore."

5 All of them agree on the evil plans they have made.
They join forces against you.
6 Their forces include the people of Edom, Ishmael, Moab and Hagar.
7 They also include the people of Byblos, Ammon, Amalek, Philistia and Tyre.
8 Even Assyria has joined them to give strength to the people of Moab and Ammon.

9 Do to them what you did to the people of Midian.
Do to them what you did to Sisera and Jabin at the Kishon River.
10 Sisera and Jabin died near the town of Endor.
Their bodies were left on the ground like human waste.
11 Do to the nobles of your enemies what you did to Oreb and Zeeb.
Do to all their princes what you did to Zebah and Zalmunna.

¹²They said, "Let's take over the grasslands that belong to God."

¹³My God, make them like straw that the wind blows away.
Make them like tumbleweed.
¹⁴Destroy them as fire burns up a forest.
Destroy them as a flame sets mountains on fire.
¹⁵Chase them with your mighty winds.
Terrify them with your storm.
¹⁶Lord, put them to shame so that they will seek you.

¹⁷May they always be filled with terror and shame.
May they die in dishonor.
¹⁸May you, the Lord, let your enemies know who you are.
You alone are the Most High God over the whole earth.

Psalm 84

For the director of music. According to gittith. *A psalm of the Sons of Korah.*

¹Lord who rules over all, how lovely is the place where you live!
²I can't wait to be in the courtyards of the Lord's temple.
I really want to be there.
My whole being cries out for the living God.

³Lord who rules over all, even the sparrow has found a home near your altar.

My King and my God, the swallow also has a nest there, where she may have her young.
⁴Blessed are those who live in your house.
They are always praising you.
⁵Blessed are those whose strength comes from you.
They have firmly decided to travel to your temple.
⁶As they pass through the dry Valley of Baka, they make it a place where water flows.
The rain in the fall covers it with pools.
⁷Those people get stronger as they go along, until each of them appears in Zion, where God lives.

⁸Lord God who rules over all, hear my prayer.
God of the people of Jacob, listen to me.
⁹God, may you be pleased with your anointed king.
You appointed him to be like a shield that keeps us safe.

¹⁰A single day in your courtyards is better than a thousand anywhere else.
I would rather guard the door of the house of my God than live in the tents of sinful people.
¹¹The Lord God is like the sun that gives us light.

He is like a shield that
keeps us safe.
The LORD blesses us with
favor and honor.
He doesn't hold back
anything good
from those whose lives are
without blame.
12 LORD who rules over all,
blessed is the person who
trusts in you.

Psalm 85

*For the director of music. A psalm
of the Sons of Korah.*

1 LORD, you were good to your
land.
You blessed the people of
Jacob with great success
again.
2 You forgave the evil things
your people did.
You took away all their
sins.
3 You stopped being angry
with them.
You turned your great
anger away from them.

4 God our Savior, make us new
again.
Stop being unhappy with
us.
5 Will you be angry with us
forever?
Will you be angry for all
time to come?
6 Won't you give us new life
again?
Then we'll be joyful
because of what you
have done.
7 LORD, show us your faithful
love.
Save us.

8 I will listen to what God the
LORD says.
He promises peace to his
faithful people.
But they must not turn to
foolish ways.
9 I know he's ready to save
those who have respect
for him.
Then his glory can be seen
in our land.

10 God's truth and faithful love
join together.
His peace and holiness kiss
each other.
11 His truth springs up from the
earth.
His holiness looks down
from heaven.
12 The LORD will certainly give
what is good.
Our land will produce its
crops.
13 God's holiness leads the way
in front of him.
It prepares the way for his
coming.

Psalm 86

A prayer of David.

1 LORD, hear me and answer
me.
I am poor and needy.
2 Keep my life safe, because I
am faithful to you.
Save me, because I trust
in you.
You are my God.
3 Lord, have mercy on me.
I call out to you all day
long.
4 Bring joy to me.
Lord, I put my trust
in you.

⁵Lord, you are forgiving and
good.
You are full of love for all
who call out to you.
⁶LORD, hear my prayer.
Listen to my cry for
mercy.
⁷When I'm in trouble, I will
call out to you.
And you will answer me.
⁸Lord, there's no one like you
among the gods.
No one can do what you
do.
⁹Lord, all the nations you have
made
will come and worship
you.
They will bring glory to
you.
¹⁰You are great. You do
wonderful things.
You alone are God.

¹¹LORD, teach me how you
want me to live.
Do this so that I will
depend on you, my
faithful God.
Give me a heart that doesn't
want anything
more than to worship you.
¹²Lord my God, I will praise
you with all my heart.
I will bring glory to you
forever.
¹³Great is your love for me.
You have kept me from
going down into the
place of the dead.

¹⁴God, proud people are
attacking me.
A gang of mean people is
trying to kill me.
They don't care about you.

¹⁵But Lord, you are a God who
is tender and kind.
You are gracious.
You are slow to get angry.
You are faithful and full
of love.
¹⁶Come to my aid and have
mercy on me.
Show your strength by
helping me.
Save me because I serve
you just as my mother
did.
¹⁷Prove your goodness to me.
Then my enemies will see
it and be put to shame.
LORD, you have helped me
and given me comfort.

Psalm 87

A psalm of the Sons of Korah. A song.

¹The LORD has built his city
on the holy mountain.
²He loves the city of Zion
more than all the other
places
where the people of Jacob
live.
³City of God,
the LORD says glorious
things about you.
⁴He says, "I will include Egypt
and Babylon
in a list of nations who
recognize me as king.
I will also include Philistia
and Tyre, along with
Cush.
I will say about them, 'They
were born in Zion.'"

⁵Certainly it will be said about
Zion,
"This nation and that
nation were born in it.

The Most High God
　　himself will make it
　　secure."
6 Here is what the LORD will
　　write in his list of the
　　nations.
　　"Each of them was born in
　　Zion."
7 As they make music they will
　　sing,
　　"Zion, all our blessings
　　come from you."

Psalm 88

*For the director of music. According
to* mahalath leannoth. *A song.
A psalm of the Sons of Korah.
A maskil of Heman the Ezrahite.*

1 LORD, you are the God who
　　saves me.
　　Day and night I cry out
　　to you.
2 Please hear my prayer.
　　Pay attention to my cry for
　　help.

3 I have so many troubles
　　I'm about to die.
4 People think my life is over.
　　I'm like someone who
　　doesn't have any
　　strength.
5 People treat me as if I were
　　dead.
　　I'm like those who have
　　been killed and are now
　　in the grave.
You don't even remember
　　them anymore.
　　They are cut off from your
　　care.
6 It's as if you have put me deep
　　down in the grave.
　　It's as if you have put me in
　　that deep, dark place.

7 Your great anger lies heavy
　　on me.
　　All the waves of your anger
　　have crashed over me.
8 You have taken my closest
　　friends away from me.
　　You have made me
　　sickening to them.
I feel trapped and can't
　　escape.
9 　I'm crying so much I can't
　　see very well.

LORD, I call out to you every
　　day.
　　I lift up my hands to you in
　　prayer.
10 Do you do wonderful things
　　for those who are dead?
　　Do their spirits rise up and
　　praise you?
11 Do those who are dead speak
　　about your love?
　　Do those who are in the
　　grave tell how faithful
　　you are?
12 Are your wonderful deeds
　　known in that dark
　　place?
　　Are your holy acts known
　　in that land where the
　　dead are forgotten?

13 LORD, I cry out to you for
　　help.
　　In the morning I pray to you.
14 LORD, why do you say no
　　to me?
　　Why do you turn your face
　　away from me?

15 I've been in pain ever since I
　　was young.
　　I've been close to death.
You have made me suffer
　　terrible things.
　　I have lost all hope.

¹⁶ Your great anger has swept
over me.
Your terrors have
destroyed me.
¹⁷ All day long they surround
me like a flood.
They have closed in all
around me.
¹⁸ You have taken my friends
and neighbors away
from me.
Darkness is my closest
friend.

Psalm 89

A maskil of Ethan the Ezrahite.

¹ Lord, I will sing about your
great love forever.
For all time to come, I will
tell how faithful you are.
² I will tell everyone that your
love stands firm forever.
I will tell them that you are
always faithful, even in
heaven itself.

³ You said, "Here is the
covenant I have made
with my chosen one.
Here is the promise I have
made to my servant
David.
⁴ 'I will make your family line
continue forever.
I will make your kingdom
secure for all time to
come.' "

⁵ Lord, the heavens praise
you for your wonderful
deeds.
When your holy angels
gather together,
they praise you for how
faithful you are.

⁶ Who in the skies above can
compare with the Lord?
Who among the angels is
like the Lord?
⁷ God is highly respected
among his holy angels.
He's more wonderful than
all those who are around
him.
⁸ Lord God who rules over all,
who is like you?
Lord, you are mighty.
You are faithful in
everything you do.

⁹ You rule over the stormy
sea.
When its waves rise up, you
calm them down.
¹⁰ You crushed Egypt and killed
her people.
With your powerful arm
you scattered your
enemies.
¹¹ The heavens belong to you.
The earth is yours also.
You made the world and
everything that is in it.
¹² You created everything from
north to south.
Mount Tabor and Mount
Hermon sing to you with
joy.
¹³ Your arm is powerful.
Your hand is strong.
Your right hand is mighty.

¹⁴ Your kingdom is built on
what is right and fair.
Your faithful love leads the
way in front of you.
¹⁵ Blessed are those who have
learned to shout praise
to you.
Lord, they live in the light
of your kindness.

¹⁶ All day long they are full of joy
        because of who you are.
    They celebrate the fact that
        you do what is right.
¹⁷ You bring them glory and
        give them strength.
    You are pleased to honor
        our king.
¹⁸ Our king is like a shield that
        keeps us safe.
    He belongs to the LORD.
    He belongs to the Holy One
        of Israel.

¹⁹ You once spoke to your faithful
        people in a vision.
    You said, "I have given
        strength to a soldier.
    I have raised up a young
        man from among the
        people.
²⁰ I have found my servant
        David.
    I have poured my sacred
        oil on his head.
²¹ My powerful hand will keep
        him going.
    My mighty arm will give
        him strength.
²² No enemy will have the
        victory over him.
    No evil person will treat
        him badly.
²³ I will crush the king's
        enemies.
    I will completely destroy
        them.
²⁴ I will love him and be faithful
        to him.
    Because of me his power
        will increase.
²⁵ I will give him a great
        kingdom.
    It will reach from the
        Mediterranean Sea to
        the Euphrates River.

²⁶ He will call out to me, 'You
        are my Father.
    You are my God. You are
        my Rock and Savior.'
²⁷ I will also make him my
        oldest son.
    Among all the kings of
        the earth, he will be the
        most important one.
²⁸ I will continue to love him
        forever.
    I will never break my
        covenant with him.
²⁹ I will make his family line
        continue forever.
    His kingdom will last as
        long as the heavens.

³⁰ "What if his sons turn away
        from my laws
    and do not follow them?
³¹ What if they disobey my
        orders
    and fail to keep my
        commands?
³² Then I will punish them for
        their sins.
    I will strike them with a
        rod.
    I will whip them for their
        evil acts.
³³ But I will not stop loving
        David.
    I will always be faithful to
        him.
³⁴ I will not break my covenant.
    I will not go back on my
        word.
³⁵ Once and for all, I have made
        a promise.
    It is based on my holiness.
    And I will not lie to David.
³⁶ His family line will continue
        forever.
    His kingdom will last as
        long as the sun.

37 It will last forever like the
moon,
that faithful witness in the
sky."

38 But you have turned your
back on your anointed
king.
You have been very angry
with him.
39 You have broken the
covenant you made with
him.
You have thrown your
servant's crown into the
dirt.
40 You have broken through the
walls around his city.
You have completely
destroyed his secure
places.
41 All those who pass by
have carried off what
belonged to him.
His neighbors make fun of
him.
42 You have made his enemies
strong.
You have made all of them
happy.
43 You have made his sword
useless.
You have not helped him in
battle.
44 You have put an end to his
glory.
You have knocked his
throne to the ground.
45 You have cut short the days of
his life.
You have covered him with
shame.
46 LORD, how long will you
hide yourself? Will it be
forever?

How long will your anger
burn like fire?
47 Remember how short my
life is.
You have created all
people for such a useless
purpose!
48 Who can live and not die?
Who can escape the power
of the grave?
49 Lord, where is the great love
you used to have?
You faithfully promised it
to David.
50 Lord, remember how my
enemies have made fun
of me.
I've had to put up with
mean words from all the
nations.
51 LORD, your enemies have
said mean things.
They have laughed
at everything your
anointed king has done.

52 Give praise to the LORD
forever!
Amen and Amen.

BOOK IV

Psalms 90–106

Psalm 90

A prayer of Moses, the man of God.

1 Lord, from the very
beginning
you have been like a home
to us.
2 Before you created the
whole world and the
mountains were made,
from the beginning to the
end you are God.

3 You turn human beings back
  to dust.
  You say to them, "Return to
  dust."
4 To you a thousand years
  are like a day that has just
  gone by.
  They are like a few hours of
  the night.
5 Yet you sweep people away,
  and they die.
  They are like new grass
  that grows in the
  morning.
6 In the morning it springs up
  new,
  but by evening it's all
  dried up.
7 Your anger destroys us.
  Your burning anger
  terrifies us.
8 You have put our sins right in
  front of you.
  You have placed our secret
  sins where you can see
  them clearly.
9 You have been angry with us
  all of our days.
  We groan as we come to
  the end of our lives.
10 We live to be about 70.
  Or we may live to be 80, if
  we stay healthy.
  But even our best days are
  filled with trouble and
  sorrow.
  The years quickly pass,
  and we are gone.
11 If only we knew the power of
  your anger!
  It's as great as the respect
  we should have for you.
12 Teach us to realize how short
  our lives are.

Then our hearts will
  become wise.
13 LORD, please stop punishing
  us!
  How long will you keep it up?
  Be kind to us.
14 Satisfy us with your faithful
  love every morning.
  Then we can sing for joy
  and be glad all our days.
15 Make us glad for as many
  days as you have made
  us suffer.
  Give us joy for as many
  years as we've had
  trouble.
16 Show us your mighty acts.
  Let our children see your
  glorious power.
17 May the Lord our God always
  be pleased with us.
  Lord, make what we do
  succeed.
  Please make what we do
  succeed.

Psalm 91

1 Whoever rests in the shadow
  of the Most High God
  will be kept safe by the
  Mighty One.
2 I will say about the LORD,
  "He is my place of safety.
  He is like a fort to me.
  He is my God. I trust in
  him."
3 He will certainly save you
  from hidden traps
  and from deadly sickness.
4 He will cover you with his
  wings.
  Under the feathers of his
  wings you will find
  safety.

He is faithful. He will keep
you safe like a shield or a
tower.
⁵You won't have to be afraid
of the terrors that come
during the night.
You won't have to fear the
arrows that come at you
during the day.
⁶You won't have to be afraid of
the sickness that attacks
in the darkness.
You won't have to fear the
plague that destroys at
noon.
⁷A thousand may fall dead at
your side.
Ten thousand may fall near
your right hand.
But no harm will come to
you.
⁸You will see with your own
eyes
how God punishes sinful
people.

⁹Suppose you say, "The LORD
is the one who keeps me
safe."
Suppose you let the Most
High God be like a home
to you.
¹⁰Then no harm will come to
you.
No terrible plague will
come near your tent.
¹¹The LORD will command his
angels
to take good care of you.
¹²They will lift you up in their
hands.
Then you won't trip over a
stone.
¹³You will walk on lions and
cobras.

You will crush mighty lions
and poisonous snakes.
¹⁴The LORD says, "I will save
the one who loves me.
I will keep him safe,
because he trusts in me.
¹⁵He will call out to me, and I
will answer him.
I will be with him in times
of trouble.
I will save him and honor
him.
¹⁶I will give him a long and full
life.
I will save him."

Psalm 92

A psalm. A song for the Sabbath day.

¹LORD, it is good to praise you.
Most High God, it is good
to make music to honor
you.
²It is good to sing every
morning about your love.
It is good to sing every
night about how faithful
you are.
³I sing about it to the music
of the lyre that has ten
strings.
I sing about it to the music
of the harp.

⁴LORD, you make me glad by
your deeds.
I sing for joy about what
you have done.
⁵LORD, how great are the
things you do!
How wise your thoughts
are!
⁶Here is something that
people without sense
don't know.

Here is what foolish people
  don't understand.
⁷ Those who are evil spring up
  like grass.
Those who do wrong
  succeed.
But they will be destroyed
  forever.

⁸ But LORD, you are honored
  forever.
⁹ LORD, your enemies will
  certainly die.
All those who do evil will
  be scattered.
¹⁰ You have made me as strong
  as a wild ox.
You have poured the finest
  olive oil on me.
¹¹ I've seen my evil enemies
  destroyed.
I've heard that they have
  lost the battle.

¹² Those who do what is right will
  grow like a palm tree.
They will grow strong like
  a cedar tree in Lebanon.
¹³ Their roots will be firm in the
  house of the LORD.
They will grow strong
  and healthy in the
  courtyards of our God.
¹⁴ When they get old, they will
  still bear fruit.
Like young trees they will
  stay fresh and strong.
¹⁵ They will say to everyone,
  "The LORD is honest.
He is my Rock, and there is
  no evil in him."

Psalm 93

¹ The LORD rules.
He puts on majesty as if it
  were clothes.

The LORD puts on majesty
  and strength.
Indeed, the world has been
  set in place.
It is firm and secure.
² LORD, you began to rule a
  long time ago.
You have always existed.

³ LORD, the seas have lifted up
  their voice.
They have lifted up their
  pounding waves.
⁴ But LORD, you are more
  powerful than the roar of
  the ocean.
You are stronger than the
  waves of the sea.
LORD, you are powerful in
  heaven.

⁵ Your laws do not change,
  LORD.
Your temple will be holy
  for all time to come.

Psalm 94

¹ The LORD is a God who
  punishes.
Since you are the one who
  punishes, come and
  show your anger.
² Judge of the earth, rise up.
Pay back proud people for
  what they have done.
³ LORD, how long will those
  who are evil be glad?
How long will they be full
  of joy?

⁴ Proud words pour out of their
  mouths.
All those who do evil are
  always bragging.
⁵ LORD, they crush your people.
They treat badly those who
  belong to you.

⁶They kill outsiders. They kill
widows.
They murder children
whose fathers have died.
⁷They say, "The LORD doesn't
see what's happening.
The God of Jacob doesn't
pay any attention to it."

⁸You who aren't wise, pay
attention.
You foolish people, when
will you become wise?
⁹Does he who made the ear
not hear?
Does he who formed the
eye not see?
¹⁰Does he who corrects nations
not punish?
Does he who teaches
human beings not know
anything?
¹¹The LORD knows what people
think.
He knows that their
thoughts don't amount
to anything.

¹²LORD, blessed is the person
you correct.
Blessed is the person you
teach from your law.
¹³You give them rest from
times of trouble,
until a pit is dug to trap
sinners.
¹⁴The LORD won't say no to his
people.
He will never desert those
who belong to him.
¹⁵He will again judge people
in keeping with what is
right.
All those who have honest
hearts will follow the
right way.

¹⁶Who will rise up for me
against sinful people?
Who will stand up for me
against those who do
evil?
¹⁷Suppose the LORD had not
helped me.
Then I would soon have
been lying quietly in the
grave.
¹⁸I said, "My foot is slipping."
But LORD, your faithful love
kept me from falling.
¹⁹I was very worried.
But your comfort brought
me joy.

²⁰Can you have anything to do
with rulers who aren't
fair?
Can those who make laws
that cause suffering be
friends of yours?
²¹Evil people join together
against those who do
what is right.
They sentence to death
those who aren't guilty of
doing anything wrong.
²²But the LORD has become
like a fort to me.
My God is my rock. I go to
him for safety.
²³He will pay them back for
their sins.
He will destroy them for
their evil acts.
The LORD our God will
destroy them.

Psalm 95

¹Come, let us sing for joy to
the LORD.
Let us give a loud shout to
the Rock who saves us.

² Let us come to him and give
　　him thanks.
　Let us praise him with
　　music and song.

³ The LORD is the great God.
　He is the greatest King.
　He rules over all the gods.
⁴ He owns the deepest parts of
　　the earth.
　The mountain peaks
　　belong to him.
⁵ The ocean is his, because he
　　made it.
　He formed the dry land
　　with his hands.

⁶ Come, let us bow down and
　　worship him.
　Let us fall on our knees in
　　front of the LORD our
　　Maker.
⁷ He is our God.
　We are the sheep
　　belonging to his flock.
　We are the people he takes
　　good care of.

　If only you would listen to his
　　voice today.
⁸　He says, "Don't be
　　stubborn as you were at
　　Meribah.
　Don't be stubborn as you
　　were that day at Massah
　　in the desert.
⁹ There your people of long ago
　　really tested me.
　They did it even though
　　they had seen what I had
　　done for them.
¹⁰ For 40 years I was angry with
　　them.
　I said, 'Their hearts are
　　always going astray.
　They do not know how I
　　want them to live.'

¹¹ So when I was angry, I made
　　a promise.
　I said, 'They will never
　　enjoy the rest I planned
　　for them.'"

Psalm 96

¹ Sing a new song to the LORD.
　All you people of the earth,
　　sing to the LORD.
² Sing to the LORD. Praise
　　him.
　Day after day tell about
　　how he saves us.
³ Tell the nations about his
　　glory.
　Tell all people about the
　　wonderful things he has
　　done.

⁴ The LORD is great. He is
　　really worthy of praise.
　People should have respect
　　for him as the greatest
　　God of all.
⁵ All the gods of the nations are
　　like their statues.
　They can't do anything.
　But the LORD made the
　　heavens.
⁶ Glory and majesty are all
　　around him.
　Strength and glory can be
　　seen in his temple.

⁷ Praise the LORD, all you
　　nations.
　Praise the LORD for his
　　glory and strength.
⁸ Praise the LORD for the glory
　　that belongs to him.
　Bring an offering and come
　　into the courtyards of his
　　temple.
⁹ Worship the LORD because of
　　his beauty and holiness.

All you people of the earth,
  tremble when you are
  with him.
¹⁰ Say to the nations, "The LORD
  rules."
The world is firmly set in
  place. It can't be moved.
The LORD will judge the
  people of the world
  fairly.
¹¹ Let the heavens be full of joy.
  Let the earth be glad.
Let the ocean and
  everything in it roar.
¹²   Let the fields and
  everything in them be
  glad.
Let all the trees in the forest
  sing for joy.
¹³   Let all creation be full
  of joy in front of the
  LORD,
  because he is coming to
  judge the earth.
He will faithfully judge the
  people of the world
  in keeping with what is
  right.

Psalm 97

¹ The LORD rules. Let the earth
  be glad.
Let countries that are far
  away be full of joy.
² Clouds and thick darkness
  surround him.
His rule is built on what is
  right and fair.
³ The LORD sends fire ahead of
  him.
It burns up his enemies all
  around him.
⁴ His lightning lights up the
  world.

The earth sees it and
  trembles.
⁵ The mountains melt like wax
  when the LORD is near.
He is the Lord of the whole
  earth.
⁶ The heavens announce that
  what he does is right.
All people everywhere see
  his glory.

⁷ All who worship statues of
  gods or brag about them
  are put to shame.
All you gods, worship the
  LORD!

⁸ Zion hears about it and is
  filled with joy.
LORD, the villages of Judah
  are glad
because of how you
  judge.
⁹ LORD, you are the Most High
  God.
You rule over the whole
  earth.
You are honored much
  more than all gods.

¹⁰ Let those who love the LORD
  hate evil.
He guards the lives of
  those who are faithful
  to him.
He saves them from the
  power of sinful people.
¹¹ Good things come to those
  who do what is right.
Joy comes to those whose
  hearts are honest.
¹² You who are godly, be glad
  because of what the
  LORD has done.
Praise him, because his
  name is holy.

Psalm 98

A psalm.

¹ Sing a new song to the LORD.
He has done wonderful
things.
By the power of his right
hand and his holy arm
he has saved his people.
² The LORD has made known
his power to save.
He has shown the nations
that he does what is
right.
³ He has shown his faithful
love
to the people of Israel.
People from one end of the
earth to the other
have seen that our God has
saved us.
⁴ Shout for joy to the LORD,
everyone on earth.
Burst into joyful songs and
make music.
⁵ Make music to the LORD with
the harp.
Sing and make music with
the harp.
⁶ Blow the trumpets. Give a
blast on the ram's horn.
Shout for joy to the LORD.
He is the King.

⁷ Let the ocean and everything
in it roar.
Let the world and all who
live in it shout.
⁸ Let the rivers clap their
hands.
Let the mountains sing
together with joy.
⁹ Let them sing to the LORD,
because he is coming to
judge the earth.

He will judge the nations of
the world
in keeping with what is
right and fair.

Psalm 99

¹ The LORD rules.
Let the nations tremble.
He sits on his throne between
the cherubim.
Let the earth shake.
² Great is the LORD in Zion.
He is honored over all the
nations.
³ Let them praise his great and
wonderful name.
He is holy.

⁴ The King is mighty and loves
justice.
He has set up the rules for
fairness.
He has done what is right and
fair
for the people of Jacob.
⁵ Honor the LORD our God.
Worship at his feet.
He is holy.

⁶ Moses and Aaron were two of
his priests.
Samuel was one of those
who worshiped him.
They called out to the LORD.
And he answered them.
⁷ He spoke to them from the
pillar of cloud.
They obeyed his laws and
the orders he gave them.

⁸ LORD our God, you answered
them.
You showed Israel that you
are a God who forgives.
But when they did wrong,
you punished them.

9 Honor the LORD our God.
　　Worship at his holy
　　　mountain.
　　The LORD our God is holy.

Psalm 100

A psalm for giving grateful praise.

1 Shout for joy to the LORD,
　　everyone on earth.
2 　Worship the LORD with
　　　gladness.
　　Come to him with songs
　　　of joy.
3 Know that the LORD is God.
　　He made us, and we belong
　　　to him.
　　We are his people.
　　We are the sheep
　　　belonging to his flock.

4 Give thanks as you enter the
　　gates of his temple.
　　Give praise as you enter its
　　　courtyards.
　　Give thanks to him and
　　　praise his name.
5 The LORD is good. His
　　faithful love continues
　　　forever.
　　It will last for all time to
　　　come.

Psalm 101

A psalm of David.

1 I will sing about your love
　　and fairness.
　　LORD, I will sing praise to
　　　you.
2 I will be careful to lead a life
　　that is without blame.
　　When will you come and
　　　help me?

　In my own home I will lead
　　a life

that is without blame.
3 　I won't look at anything
　　that is evil and call it
　　　good.

　I hate the acts of people who
　　aren't faithful to you.
　I won't have anything to do
　　with those things.
4 I will stay away from those
　　whose hearts are twisted.
　　I won't have anything to do
　　with what is evil.

5 I will get rid of anyone
　　who tells lies about their
　　　neighbor in secret.
　I won't put up with anyone
　　whose eyes and heart are
　　　proud.

6 I will look with favor on the
　　faithful people in the
　　　land.
　　They will live with me.
　　Those whose lives are
　　　without blame will serve
　　　me.

7 No one who lies and cheats
　　will live in my house.
　No one who tells lies
　　will serve me.

8 Every morning I will get rid of
　　all the sinful people in the
　　　land.
　I will remove from the city of
　　the LORD
　　everyone who does what is
　　　evil.

Psalm 102

*A prayer of a suffering person who
has become weak. They pour out
their problems to the LORD.*

1 LORD, hear my prayer.
　　Listen to my cry for help.

2 Don't turn your face away
      from me
   when I'm in trouble.
   Pay attention to me.
      When I call out for help,
      answer me quickly.
3 My days are disappearing
      like smoke.
   My body burns like
      glowing coals.
4 My strength has dried up like
      grass.
   I even forget to eat my
      food.
5 I groan out loud because of
      my suffering.
   I'm nothing but skin and
      bones.
6 I'm like a desert owl.
   I'm like an owl among
      destroyed buildings.
7 I can't sleep. I've become
      like a bird alone on a roof.
8 All day long my enemies
      laugh at me.
   Those who make fun of me
      use my name as a curse.
9 I eat ashes as my food.
   My tears fall into what I'm
      drinking.
10 You were very angry with me.
   So you picked me up and
      threw me away.
11 The days of my life are like an
      evening shadow.
   I dry up like grass.

12 But LORD, you are seated on
      your throne forever.
   Your fame will continue for
      all time to come.
13 You will rise up and show
      deep concern for Zion.
   The time has come for you
      to help Zion.

14 The stones of your destroyed
      city are priceless to us.
   Even its dust brings deep
      concern to us.
15 The nations will worship the
      LORD.
   All the kings on earth will
      respect his glorious
      power.
16 The LORD will build Zion
      again.
   He will appear in his glory.
17 He will answer the prayer
      of those who don't have
      anything.
   He won't say no to their cry
      for help.
18 Let this be written down for
      those born after us.
   Then people who are not
      yet born can praise the
      LORD.
19 Here is what should be
      written.
   "The LORD looked down
      from his temple in
      heaven.
   From heaven he viewed
      the earth.
20 He heard the groans of the
      prisoners.
   He set free those who were
      sentenced to death."
21 So people will talk about him
      in Zion.
   They will praise him in
      Jerusalem.
22 Nations and kingdoms
   will gather there to
      worship the LORD.
23 When I was still young, he
      took away my strength.
   He wasn't going to let me
      live much longer.

24 So I said, "My God, don't let
    me die in the middle of
    my life.
  You will live for all time to
    come.
25 In the beginning you made
    the earth secure.
  You placed it on its
    foundations.
  Your hands created the
    heavens.
26 They will pass away. But you
    will remain.
  They will all wear out like a
    piece of clothing.
  You will make them like
    clothes
  that are taken off and
    thrown away.
27 But you remain the same.
  Your years will never end.
28 Our children will live with
    you.
  Their sons and daughters
    will be safe in your
    care."

Psalm 103

A psalm of David.

1 I will praise the LORD.
  Deep down inside me, I
    will praise him.
  I will praise him, because
    his name is holy.
2 I will praise the LORD.
  I won't forget anything he
    does for me.
3 He forgives all my sins.
  He heals all my sicknesses.
4 He saves my life from going
    down into the grave.
  His faithful and tender
    love makes me feel like a
    king.

5 He satisfies me with the good
    things I desire.
  Then I feel young and
    strong again, just like an
    eagle.
6 The LORD does what is right
    and fair
  for all who are treated badly.
7 He told Moses all about his
    plans.
  He let the people of Israel
    see his mighty acts.
8 The LORD is tender and kind.
    He is gracious.
  He is slow to get angry. He
    is full of love.
9 He won't keep bringing
    charges against us.
  He won't stay angry with
    us forever.
10 He doesn't punish us for
    our sins as much as we
    should be punished.
  He doesn't pay us back in
    keeping with the evil
    things we've done.
11 He loves those who have
    respect for him.
  His love is as high as the
    heavens are above the
    earth.
12 He has removed our sins
    from us.
  He has removed them as
    far as the east is from the
    west.
13 A father is tender and kind to
    his children.
  In the same way, the LORD
    is tender and kind
  to those who have respect
    for him.
14 He knows what we are
    made of.

He remembers that we are
dust.
¹⁵ The life of human beings is
like grass.
People grow like the
flowers in the field.
¹⁶ When the wind blows on
them, they are gone.
No one can tell that they
had ever been there.
¹⁷ But the LORD's love
for those who have respect
for him
lasts for ever and ever.
Their children's children will
know
that he always does what is
right.
¹⁸ He always loves those who
keep his covenant.
He always does what is
right for those who
remember to obey his
commands.
¹⁹ The LORD has set up his
throne in heaven.
His kingdom rules over
all.
²⁰ Praise the LORD, you angels
of his.
Praise him, you mighty
ones
who carry out his orders
and obey his word.
²¹ Praise the LORD, all you
angels in heaven.
Praise him, all you who
serve him and do what
he wants.
²² Let everything the LORD has
made praise him
everywhere in his
kingdom.

I will praise the LORD.

Psalm 104

¹ I will praise the LORD.

LORD my God, you are very
great.
You are dressed in glory
and majesty.
² The LORD wraps himself in
light as if it were a
robe.
He spreads out the heavens
like a tent.
³　He builds his palace high
in the heavens.
He makes the clouds serve as
his chariot.
He rides on the wings of
the wind.
⁴ He makes the winds serve as
his messengers.
He makes flashes of
lightning serve him.

⁵ He placed the earth on its
foundations.
It can never be moved.
⁶ You, LORD, covered it with
the oceans like a
blanket.
The waters covered the
mountains.
⁷ But you commanded the
waters, and they ran
away.
At the sound of your
thunder they rushed off.
⁸ They flowed down the
mountains.
They went into the
valleys.
They went to the place you
appointed for them.
⁹ You drew a line they can't
cross.
They will never cover the
earth again.

¹⁰ The LORD makes springs
pour water into the
valleys.
It flows between the
mountains.
¹¹ The springs give water to all
the wild animals.
The wild donkeys satisfy
their thirst.
¹² The birds in the sky build
nests by the waters.
They sing among the
branches.
¹³ The LORD waters the
mountains from his
palace high in the
clouds.
The earth is filled with the
things he has made.
¹⁴ He makes grass grow for the
cattle
and plants for people to
take care of.
That's how they get food
from the earth.
¹⁵ There is wine to make people
glad.
There is olive oil to make
their skin glow.
And there is bread to make
them strong.
¹⁶ The cedar trees of Lebanon
belong to the LORD.
He planted them and gave
them plenty of water.
¹⁷ There the birds make their
nests.
The stork has its home in
the juniper trees.
¹⁸ The high mountains belong
to the wild goats.
The cliffs are a safe place
for the rock badgers.
¹⁹ The LORD made the moon to
mark off the seasons.

The sun knows when to go
down.
²⁰ You, LORD, bring darkness,
and it becomes night.
Then all the animals of the
forest prowl around.
²¹ The lions roar while they
hunt.
All their food comes from
God.
²² The sun rises, and they slip
away.
They return to their dens
and lie down.
²³ Then people get up and go to
work.
They keep working until
evening.
²⁴ LORD, you have made so
many things!
How wise you were when
you made all of them!
The earth is full of your
creatures.
²⁵ Look at the ocean, so big and
wide!
It is filled with more
creatures than people
can count.
It is filled with living
things, from the largest
to the smallest.
²⁶ Ships sail back and forth on
it.
Leviathan, the sea monster
you made, plays in it.
²⁷ All creatures depend on you
to give them their food
when they need it.
²⁸ When you give it to them,
they eat it.
When you open your hand,
they are satisfied with
good things.

²⁹When you turn your face
away from them,
they are terrified.
When you take away their
breath,
they die and turn back into
dust.
³⁰When you send your Spirit,
you create them.
You give new life to the
ground.
³¹May the glory of the LORD
continue forever.
May the LORD be happy
with what he has made.
³²When he looks at the earth, it
trembles.
When he touches the
mountains, they pour
out smoke.
³³I will sing to the LORD all my
life.
I will sing praise to my God
as long as I live.
³⁴May these thoughts of mine
please him.
I find my joy in the LORD.
³⁵But may sinners be gone
from the earth.
May evil people disappear.

I will praise the LORD.
Praise the LORD.

Psalm 105

¹Give praise to the LORD and
announce who he is.
Tell the nations what he
has done.
²Sing to him, sing praise to
him.
Tell about all the
wonderful things he has
done.

³Praise him, because his
name is holy.
Let the hearts of those who
trust in the LORD be
glad.
⁴Seek the LORD and the
strength he gives.
Always seek him.

⁵Remember the wonderful
things he has done.
Remember his miracles
and how he judged our
enemies.
⁶Remember what he has
done, you children of his
servant Abraham.
Remember it, you people
of Jacob, God's chosen
ones.
⁷He is the LORD our God.
He judges the whole earth.

⁸He will keep his covenant
forever.
He will keep his promise
for all time to come.
⁹He will keep the covenant he
made with Abraham.
He will keep the promise
he made to Isaac.
¹⁰He made it stand as a law for
Jacob.
He made it stand as a
covenant for Israel that
will last forever.
¹¹He said, "I will give you the
land of Canaan.
It will belong to you."

¹²At first there weren't very
many of God's people.
There were only a few, and
they were strangers in
the land.
¹³They wandered from nation
to nation.

They wandered from one
    kingdom to another.
¹⁴ But God didn't allow anyone
    to treat them badly.
To keep them safe, he gave
    a command to kings.
¹⁵ He said to them, "Do not
    touch my anointed ones.
Do not harm my prophets."

¹⁶ He made the people in the
    land go hungry.
He destroyed all their food
    supplies.
¹⁷ He sent a man ahead of them
    into Egypt.
That man was Joseph. He
    had been sold as a slave.
¹⁸ The Egyptians put his feet in
    chains.
They put an iron collar
    around his neck.
¹⁹ He was in prison until what
    he said would happen
    came true.
The word of the LORD
    proved that he was right.
²⁰ The king of Egypt sent for
    Joseph and let him out of
    prison.
The ruler of many nations
    set him free.
²¹ He put Joseph in charge of
    his palace.
He made him ruler over
    everything he owned.
²² Joseph was in charge of
    teaching the princes.
He taught the elders how to
    think and live wisely.
²³ Then the rest of Jacob's
    family went to Egypt.
The people of Israel lived
    as outsiders in the land
    of Ham.

²⁴ The LORD gave his people so
    many children
that there were too many of
    them for their enemies.
²⁵ He made the Egyptians hate
    his people.
The Egyptians made evil
    plans against them.
²⁶ The LORD sent his servant
    Moses to the king of
    Egypt.
He sent Aaron, his chosen
    one, along with him.
²⁷ The LORD gave them the
    power to do signs among
    the Egyptians.
They did his wonders in
    the land of Ham.
²⁸ The LORD sent darkness over
    the land.
He did it because the
    Egyptians had refused to
    obey his words.
²⁹ He turned their rivers and
    streams into blood.
He caused the fish in them
    to die.
³⁰ Their land was covered with
    frogs.
Frogs even went into the
    bedrooms of the rulers.
³¹ The LORD spoke, and large
    numbers of flies came.
Gnats filled the whole
    country.
³² He turned their rain into
    hail.
Lightning flashed all
    through their land.
³³ He destroyed their vines and
    fig trees.
He broke down the trees in
    Egypt.
³⁴ He spoke, and the locusts
    came.

There were so many of
them they couldn't be
counted.
35 They ate up every green
thing in the land.
They ate up what the land
produced.
36 Then he killed the oldest son
of every family in Egypt.
He struck down the oldest
of all their sons.

37 He brought the people of
Israel out of Egypt.
The Egyptians loaded
them down with silver
and gold.
From among the tribes of
Israel no one got tired or
fell down.
38 The Egyptians were glad
when the people of Israel
left.
They were terrified
because of Israel.
39 The LORD spread out a cloud
to cover his people.
He gave them a fire to light
up the night.
40 They asked for meat, and he
brought them quail.
He fed them well with
manna, the bread of
heaven.
41 He broke open a rock, and
streams of water poured
out.
They flowed like a river in
the desert.
42 He remembered the holy
promise
he had made to his servant
Abraham.
43 His chosen people shouted
for joy

as he brought them out of
Egypt.
44 He gave them the lands of
other nations.
He let them take over what
others had worked for.
45 He did it so they might obey
his rules
and follow his laws.

Praise the LORD.

Psalm 106

1 Praise the LORD.

Give thanks to the LORD,
because he is good.
His faithful love continues
forever.
2 Who can speak enough about
the mighty acts of the
LORD?
Who can praise him as
much as he should be
praised?
3 Blessed are those who always
do what is fair.
Blessed are those who keep
doing what is right.
4 LORD, remember me when
you bless your people.
Help me when you save
them.
5 Then I will enjoy the good
things you give your
chosen ones.
I will be joyful together
with your people.
I will join them when they
praise you.

6 We have sinned, just as our
people of long ago did.
We too have done what is
evil and wrong.
7 When our people were in
Egypt,

they forgot about the
LORD's miracles.
They didn't remember his
many kind acts.
At the Red Sea they refused
to obey him.
⁸ But he saved them for the
honor of his name.
He did it to make his
mighty power known.
⁹ He ordered the Red Sea to
dry up, and it did.
He led his people through
it as if it were a desert.
¹⁰ He saved them from the
power of their enemies.
He set them free from their
control.
¹¹ The waters covered their
enemies.
Not one of them escaped
alive.
¹² Then his people believed his
promises
and sang praise to him.
¹³ But they soon forgot what he
had done.
They didn't wait for what
he had planned to
happen.
¹⁴ In the desert they longed for
food.
In that dry and empty land
they tested God.
¹⁵ So he gave them what they
asked for.
But he also sent a sickness
that killed many of
them.
¹⁶ In their camp some of them
became jealous of Moses
and Aaron.
Aaron had been set apart
to serve the LORD.

¹⁷ The ground opened up and
swallowed Dathan.
It buried Abiram and his
followers.
¹⁸ Fire blazed among all of
them.
Flames destroyed those
evil people.
¹⁹ At Mount Horeb they made
a metal statue of a bull
calf.
They worshiped that statue
of a god.
²⁰ They traded their glorious
God
for a statue of a bull that
eats grass.
²¹ They forgot the God who
saved them.
They forgot the God who
had done great things in
Egypt.
²² They forgot the miracles he
did in the land of Ham.
They forgot the wonderful
things he did by the Red
Sea.
²³ So he said he would destroy
them.
But Moses, his chosen one,
stood up for them.
He kept God's anger from
destroying them.

²⁴ Later on, they refused to
enter the pleasant land
of Canaan.
They didn't believe God's
promise.
²⁵ In their tents they told the
LORD how unhappy they
were.
They didn't obey him.
²⁶ So he lifted up his hand and
promised

that he would make them
die in the desert.
²⁷ He promised he would
scatter their children's
children among the
nations.
He would make them die
in other lands.
²⁸ They joined in worshiping
the Baal that was
worshiped at Peor.
They ate food that had
been offered to gods that
aren't even alive.
²⁹ Their evil ways made the
LORD angry.
So a plague broke out
among them.
³⁰ But Phinehas stood up and
took action.
Then the plague stopped.
³¹ What Phinehas did made
him right with the
LORD.
It will be remembered for
all time to come.

³² By the waters of Meribah the
LORD's people made him
angry.
Moses got in trouble
because of them.
³³ They refused to obey the
Spirit of God.
So Moses spoke without
thinking.

³⁴ They didn't destroy the
nations in Canaan
as the LORD had
commanded them.
³⁵ Instead, they mixed with
those nations
and adopted their ways.
³⁶ They worshiped statues of
their gods.

That became a trap for
them.
³⁷ They sacrificed their sons
and daughters
as offerings to false gods.
³⁸ They killed those who
weren't guilty of doing
anything wrong.
They killed their own sons
and daughters.
They sacrificed them as
offerings to statues of the
gods of Canaan.
The land became
"unclean" because of
the blood of their
children.
³⁹ The people made themselves
impure by what they had
done.
They weren't faithful to the
LORD.

⁴⁰ So the LORD became angry
with his people.
He turned away from his
own children.
⁴¹ He handed them over to the
nations.
Their enemies ruled over
them.
⁴² Their enemies treated them
badly
and kept them under their
power.
⁴³ Many times the LORD saved
them.
But they refused to obey
him.
So he destroyed them
because of their sins.

⁴⁴ Yet he heard them when they
cried out.
He paid special attention
to their suffering.

⁴⁵Because they were his
    people, he remembered
    his covenant.
  Because of his great love,
    he felt sorry for them.
⁴⁶He made all those who held
    them as prisoners
  have mercy on them.

⁴⁷LORD our God, save us.
  Bring us back from among
    the nations.
  Then we will give thanks to
    you, because your name
    is holy.
  We will celebrate by
    praising you.

⁴⁸Give praise to the LORD, the
    God of Israel,
  for ever and ever.
  Let all the people say,
    "Amen!"

  Praise the LORD.

BOOK V

Psalms 107–150

Psalm 107

¹Give thanks to the LORD,
    because he is good.
  His faithful love continues
    forever.
²Let those who have been
    set free by the LORD tell
    their story.
  He set them free from the
    power of the enemy.
³He brought them back from
    other lands.
  He brought them back
    from east and west, from
    north and south.

⁴Some of them wandered in
    deserts that were dry
    and empty.
  They couldn't find a city
    where they could make
    their homes.
⁵They were hungry and
    thirsty.
  Their lives were slipping
    away.
⁶Then they cried out to the
    LORD because of their
    problems.
  And he saved them from
    their troubles.
⁷He led them straight
    to a city where they could
    make their homes.
⁸Let them give thanks to the
    LORD for his faithful
    love.
  Let them give thanks for
    the wonderful things he
    does for people.
⁹He gives those who are
    thirsty all the water they
    want.
  He gives those who are
    hungry all the good food
    they can eat.

¹⁰Others lived in the deepest
    darkness.
  They suffered as prisoners
    in iron chains.
¹¹That's because they hadn't
    obeyed the commands
    of God.
  They had refused to follow
    the plans of the Most
    High God.
¹²So he made them do work
    that was hard and bitter.
  They tripped and fell, and
    there was no one to help
    them.

¹³ Then they cried out to the
    Lord because of their
    problems.
And he saved them from
    their troubles.
¹⁴ He brought them out of the
    deepest darkness.
He broke their chains off.
¹⁵ Let them give thanks to the
    Lord for his faithful
    love.
Let them give thanks for
    the wonderful things he
    does for people.
¹⁶ He breaks down gates that
    are made of bronze.
He cuts through bars that
    are made of iron.

¹⁷ Others were foolish. They
    suffered because of their
    sins.
They suffered because they
    wouldn't obey the
    Lord.
¹⁸ They refused to eat anything.
They came close to passing
    through the gates of
    death.
¹⁹ Then they cried out to the
    Lord because of their
    problems.
And he saved them from
    their troubles.
²⁰ He gave his command and
    healed them.
He saved them from the
    grave.
²¹ Let them give thanks to the
    Lord for his faithful
    love.
Let them give thanks for
    the wonderful things he
    does for people.
²² Let them sacrifice thank
    offerings.

Let them talk about what
    he has done as they sing
    with joy.

²³ Some people sailed out on
    the ocean in ships.
They traded goods on the
    mighty waters.
²⁴ They saw the works of the
    Lord.
They saw the wonderful
    deeds he did on the
    ocean.
²⁵ He spoke and stirred up a
    storm.
It lifted the waves high.
²⁶ They rose up to the
    heavens. Then they went
    down deep into
    the ocean.
In that kind of danger
    the people's boldness
    melted away.
²⁷ They were unsteady like
    people who have
    become drunk.
They didn't know what to
    do.
²⁸ Then they cried out to the
    Lord because of their
    problems.
And he brought them out
    of their troubles.
²⁹ He made the storm as quiet
    as a whisper.
The waves of the ocean
    calmed down.
³⁰ The people were glad when
    the ocean became
    calm.
Then he guided them to
    the harbor they were
    looking for.
³¹ Let them give thanks to the
    Lord for his faithful
    love.

Let them give thanks for
the wonderful things he
does for people.
³² Let them honor him among
his people who gather
for worship.
Let them praise him in the
meeting of the elders.

³³ He turned rivers into a
desert.
He turned flowing springs
into thirsty ground.
³⁴ He turned land that
produced crops into a
salty land where nothing
could grow.
He did it because the
people who lived there
were evil.
³⁵ He turned the desert into
pools of water.
He turned the dry and
cracked ground into
flowing springs.
³⁶ He brought hungry people
there to live.
They built a city where
they could make their
homes.
³⁷ They planted fields and
vineyards
that produced large crops.
³⁸ He blessed the people, and
they greatly increased
their numbers.
He kept their herds from
getting smaller.

³⁹ Then the number of God's
people got smaller.
They were made humble
by trouble, suffering and
sorrow.
⁴⁰ The God who looks down on
proud nobles

made them wander in a
desert where no one
lives.
⁴¹ But he lifted needy people
out of their suffering.
He made their families
increase like flocks of
sheep.
⁴² Honest people see it and are
filled with joy.
But no one who is evil has
anything to say.
⁴³ Let those who are wise pay
attention to these
things.
Let them think about
the loving deeds of the
LORD.

Psalm 108

A song. A psalm of David.

¹ God, my heart feels secure.
I will sing and make music
to you with all my heart.
² Harp and lyre, wake up!
I want to sing and make
music before the sun
rises.
³ LORD, I will praise you
among the nations.
I will sing about you
among the people of the
earth.
⁴ Great is your love. It is higher
than the heavens.
Your truth reaches to the
skies.
⁵ God, may you be honored
above the heavens.
Let your glory be over the
whole earth.

⁶ Save us. Help us with your
powerful right hand,

so that those you love may
be saved.
7 God has spoken from his
temple.
He has said, "I will win the
battle.
Then I will divide up the land
around Shechem.
I will divide up the Valley
of Sukkoth.
8 Gilead belongs to me, and
so does the land of
Manasseh.
Ephraim is the strongest
tribe. It is like a helmet
for my head.
Judah is the royal tribe. It is
like a ruler's scepter.
9 Moab serves me like one who
washes my feet.
I toss my sandal on Edom
to show that I own it.
I shout to Philistia that I
have won the battle."
10 Who will bring me to the
city that has high walls
around it?
Who will lead me to the
land of Edom?
11 God, isn't it you, even though
you have now turned
away from us?
Isn't it you, even though
you don't lead our
armies into battle
anymore?
12 Help us against our
enemies.
The help people give
doesn't amount to
anything.
13 With your help we will win
the battle.
You will walk all over our
enemies.

Psalm 109

For the director of music.
A psalm of David.

1 God, I praise you.
Don't remain silent.
2 Sinful people who lie and
cheat have spoken
against me.
They have used their
tongues to tell lies about
me.
3 They gather all around me
with their words of
hatred.
They attack me without
any reason.
4 They bring charges against
me,
even though I love them
and pray for them.
5 They pay me back with evil
for the good things I do.
They pay back my love
with hatred.

6 Appoint an evil person to
take my enemies to
court.
Let him stand at their right
hand and bring charges
against them.
7 When they are tried, let them
be found guilty.
May even their prayers
judge them.
8 May their days be few.
Let others take their places
as leaders.
9 May their children's fathers
die.
May their wives become
widows.
10 May their children be driven
from their destroyed
homes.

May they wander around
like beggars.
¹¹ May everything those people
own be taken away to
pay for what they owe.
May strangers rob them
of everything they've
worked for.
¹² May no one be kind to
them
or take pity on the children
they leave behind.
¹³ May their family line come
to an end.
May their names be
forgotten by those who
live after them.
¹⁴ May the LORD remember the
evil things their fathers
have done.
May he never erase the sins
of their mothers.
¹⁵ May the LORD never forget
their sins.
Then he won't let people
remember the names of
my enemies anymore.

¹⁶ They never thought about
doing anything kind.
Instead, they drove those
who were poor and
needy to their deaths.
They did the same thing to
those whose hearts were
broken.
¹⁷ They loved to curse others.
May their curses come
back on them.
They didn't find any pleasure
in giving anyone their
blessing.
May no blessing ever come
to them.
¹⁸ They cursed others as easily
as they put on clothes.

Cursing was as natural to
them as getting a drink
of water
or putting olive oil on their
bodies.
¹⁹ May their curses cover them
like coats.
May their curses be
wrapped around them
like a belt forever.
²⁰ May that be the LORD's way of
paying back
those who bring charges
against me.
May it happen to those who
say
evil things about me.

²¹ But LORD and King,
help me so that you bring
honor to yourself.
Because your love is so
good, save me.
²² I am poor and needy.
My heart is wounded deep
down inside me.
²³ I fade away like an evening
shadow.
I'm like a locust that
someone brushes off.
²⁴ My knees are weak because
I've gone without food.
My body is very thin.
²⁵ Those who bring charges
against me laugh at me.
When they see me, they
shake their heads at me.

²⁶ LORD my God, help me.
Save me because of your
faithful love.
²⁷ LORD, let my enemies know
that you yourself have
saved me.
You have done it with your
own hand.

28 They may curse me.
But may you bless me.
May those who attack me be
put to shame.
But may I be filled with
joy.
29 May those who bring charges
against me be clothed
with dishonor.
May they be wrapped in
shame as if it were a
coat.
30 With my mouth I will
continually praise the
LORD.
I will praise him when all
his people gather for
worship.
31 He stands ready to help those
who need it.
He saves them from
those who are ready to
sentence them to death.

Psalm 110

A psalm of David.

1 The LORD says to my lord,
"Sit at my right hand
until I put your enemies
under your control."
2 The LORD will make your
royal authority spread
out from Zion to other
lands.
He says, "Rule over your
enemies who are all
around you."
3 Your troops will be willing to
fight for you
on the day of battle.
Your young men will be
wrapped in holy
majesty.

They will come to you like
the fresh dew that falls
early in the morning.
4 The LORD has made a
promise.
He will not change his
mind.
He has said, "You are a priest
forever,
just like Melchizedek."
5 The Lord is at your right hand.
He will crush kings on the
day when he is angry.
6 He will judge the nations. He
will pile up dead bodies
on the field of battle.
He will crush the rulers of
the whole earth.
7 He will drink from a brook
along the way and
receive new strength.
And so he will win the
battle.

Psalm 111

1 Praise the LORD.

I will praise the LORD with all
my heart.
I will praise him where
honest people gather for
worship.
2 The LORD has done great
things.
All who take delight in
those things think
deeply about them.
3 What he does shows his glory
and majesty.
He will always do what is
right.
4 The LORD causes his wonders
to be remembered.
He is kind and tender.

5 He provides food for those
who have respect for
him.
He remembers his
covenant forever.
6 He has shown his people
what his power can do.
He has given them the
lands of other nations.
7 He is faithful and right in
everything he does.
All his rules can be
trusted.
8 They will stand firm for ever
and ever.
They were given by the
LORD.
He is faithful and honest.
9 He set his people free.
He made a covenant
with them that will last
forever.
His name is holy and
wonderful.

10 If you really want to become
wise,
you must begin by having
respect for the LORD.
All those who follow
his rules have good
understanding.
People should praise him
forever.

Psalm 112

1 Praise the LORD.

Blessed are those who have
respect for the LORD.
They find great delight
when they obey God's
commands.
2 Their children will be
powerful in the land.

Because they are honest,
their children will be
blessed.
3 Their family will have wealth
and riches.
They will always be
blessed for doing what is
right.
4 Even in the darkness light
shines on honest people.
It shines on those who are
kind and tender and
godly.
5 Good things will come to
those who are willing to
lend freely.
Good things will come
to those who are fair in
everything they do.
6 Those who do what is right
will always be secure.
They will be remembered
forever.
7 They aren't afraid when bad
news comes.
They stand firm because
they trust in the LORD.
8 Their hearts are secure. They
aren't afraid.
In the end they will see
their enemies destroyed.
9 They have spread their gifts
around to poor people.
Their good works continue
forever.
They will be powerful and
honored.

10 Evil people will see it and be
upset.
They will grind their teeth
and become weaker and
weaker.
What evil people long to do
can't succeed.

Psalm 113

¹ Praise the LORD.

Praise him, you who serve
    the LORD.
    Praise the name of the LORD.
² Let us praise the name of the
    LORD,
    both now and forever.
³ From the sunrise in the east
    to the sunset in the west,
    may the name of the LORD
    be praised.

⁴ The LORD is honored over all
    the nations.
    His glory reaches to the
    highest heavens.
⁵ Who is like the LORD our God?
    He sits on his throne in
    heaven.
⁶ He bends down to look
    at the heavens and the
    earth.
⁷ He raises poor people up
    from the trash pile.
    He lifts needy people out of
    the ashes.
⁸ He causes them to sit with
    princes.
    He causes them to sit with
    the princes of his people.
⁹ He gives children to the
    woman who doesn't
    have any children.
    He makes her a happy
    mother in her own home.

Praise the LORD.

Psalm 114

¹ The people of Israel came out
    of Egypt.
    The people of Jacob left a
    land where a different
    language was spoken.

² Then Judah became the holy
    place where God lived.
    Israel became the land he
    ruled over.

³ The Red Sea saw him and
    parted.
    The Jordan River stopped
    flowing.
⁴ The mountains leaped like
    rams.
    The hills skipped like
    lambs.

⁵ Red Sea, why did you part?
    Jordan River, why did you
    stop flowing?
⁶ Why did you mountains leap
    like rams?
    Why did you hills skip like
    lambs?

⁷ Earth, tremble with fear
    when the Lord comes.
    Tremble when the God of
    Jacob is near.
⁸ He turned the rock into a
    pool.
    He turned the hard rock
    into springs of water.

Psalm 115

¹ LORD, may glory be given to
    you, not to us.
    You are loving and
    faithful.

² Why do the nations ask,
    "Where is their God?"
³ Our God is in heaven.
    He does anything he wants
    to do.
⁴ But the statues of their gods
    are made out of silver
    and gold.
    They are made by human
    hands.

⁵They have mouths but can't
speak.
They have eyes but can't
see.
⁶They have ears but can't
hear.
They have noses but can't
smell.
⁷They have hands but can't
feel.
They have feet but can't
walk.
They have throats but can't
say anything.
⁸Those who make statues of
gods will be like them.
So will all those who trust
in them.

⁹All you Israelites, trust in the
LORD.
He helps you like a shield
that keeps you safe.
¹⁰Priests of Aaron, trust in the
LORD.
He helps you like a shield
that keeps you safe.
¹¹You who have respect for the
LORD, trust in him.
He helps you like a shield
that keeps you safe.

¹²The LORD remembers us and
will bless us.
He will bless Israel, his
people.
He will bless the priests of
Aaron.
¹³The LORD will bless those
who have respect for
him.
He will bless important
and unimportant people
alike.
¹⁴May the LORD give you many
children.

May he give them to you
and to your children
after you.
¹⁵May the LORD bless you.
He is the Maker of heaven
and earth.
¹⁶The highest heavens belong
to the LORD.
But he has given the earth
to human beings.
¹⁷Dead people don't praise the
LORD.
Those who lie quietly in
the grave don't praise
him.
¹⁸But we who are alive praise
the LORD,
both now and forever.

Praise the LORD.

Psalm 116

¹I love the LORD, because he
heard my voice.
He heard my cry for his
help.
²Because he paid attention to
me,
I will call out to him as long
as I live.
³The ropes of death were
wrapped around me.
The horrors of the grave
came over me.
I was overcome by sadness
and sorrow.
⁴Then I called out to the
LORD.
I cried out, "LORD, save
me!"

⁵The LORD is holy and kind.
Our God is full of tender
love.

⁶ The Lord takes care of those
who are not aware of
danger.
When I was in great need,
he saved me.
⁷ I said to myself, "Be calm.
The Lord has been good to
me."
⁸ Lord, you have saved me
from death.
You have dried the tears
from my eyes.
You have kept me from
tripping and falling.
⁹ So now I can enjoy life here
with you
while I'm still living.
¹⁰ I trusted in the Lord even
when I said to myself,
"I am in great pain."
¹¹ When I was terrified, I said to
myself,
"No one tells the truth."
¹² The Lord has been so good
to me!
How can I ever pay him
back?
¹³ I will bring an offering of
wine to the Lord
and thank him for saving
me.
I will worship him.
¹⁴ In front of all the Lord's
people,
I will do what I promised
him.
¹⁵ The Lord pays special
attention
when his faithful people
die.
¹⁶ Lord, I serve you.
I serve you just as my
mother did.

You have set me free
from the chains of my
suffering.
¹⁷ Lord, I will sacrifice a thank
offering to you.
I will worship you.
¹⁸ In front of all the Lord's
people,
I will do what I promised
him.
¹⁹ I will keep my promise in the
courtyards of the Lord's
temple.
I will keep my promise in
Jerusalem itself.

Praise the Lord.

Psalm 117

¹ All you nations, praise the
Lord.
All you people on earth,
praise him.
² Great is his love for us.
The Lord is faithful
forever.

Praise the Lord.

Psalm 118

¹ Give thanks to the Lord,
because he is good.
His faithful love continues
forever.

² Let the people of Israel say,
"His faithful love continues
forever."
³ Let the priests of Aaron say,
"His faithful love continues
forever."
⁴ Let those who have respect
for the Lord say,
"His faithful love continues
forever."

5 When I was in great trouble, I
cried out to the LORD.
He answered me and set
me free from my trouble.
6 The LORD is with me. I will
not be afraid.
What can mere human
beings do to me?
7 The LORD is with me. He
helps me.
I win the battle over my
enemies.

8 It is better to go to the LORD
for safety
than to trust in mere
human beings.
9 It is better to go to the LORD
for safety
than to trust in human
leaders.

10 The nations were all around
me.
But by the LORD's power I
destroyed them.
11 They were around me on
every side.
But by the LORD's power I
destroyed them.
12 They attacked me like
swarms of bees.
But they were burned up
as quickly as thorns in a
fire.
By the LORD's power I
destroyed them.
13 I was pushed back and about
to be killed.
But the LORD helped me.
14 The LORD gives me strength
and makes me secure.
He has saved me.
15 Shouts of joy ring out in the
tents of godly people.

They praise him for his
help in battle.
They shout, "The LORD's
powerful right hand has
done mighty things!
16 The LORD's powerful right
hand has won the battle!
The LORD's powerful right
hand has done mighty
things!"

17 I will not die but live.
I will talk about what the
LORD has done.
18 The LORD has really
punished me.
But he didn't let me die.

19 Open for me the gates where
the godly can go in.
I will enter and give thanks
to the LORD.
20 This is the gate of the LORD.
Only those who do what is
right can go through it.
21 LORD, I will give thanks
to you, because you
answered me.
You have saved me.

22 The stone the builders didn't
accept
has become the most
important stone of all.
23 The LORD has done it.
It is wonderful in our eyes.
24 The LORD has done it on this
day.
Let us be joyful today and
be glad.

25 LORD, save us.
LORD, give us success.
26 Blessed is the one who comes
in the name of the LORD.
From the temple of the
LORD we bless you.

²⁷The LORD is God.
He has been good to us.
Take branches in your hands.
Join in the march on the
day of the feast.
March up to the corners of
the altar.
²⁸You are my God, and I will
praise you.
You are my God, and I will
honor you.
²⁹Give thanks to the LORD,
because he is good.
His faithful love continues
forever.

Psalm 119

א Aleph

¹Blessed are those who live
without blame.
They live in keeping with
the law of the LORD.
²Blessed are those who obey
his covenant laws.
They trust in him with all
their hearts.
³They don't do anything
wrong.
They live as he wants them
to live.
⁴You have given me rules
that I must obey
completely.
⁵I hope I will always stand
firm
in following your orders.
⁶Then I won't be put to shame
when I think about all your
commands.
⁷I will praise you with an
honest heart
as I learn about how fair
your decisions are.

⁸I will obey your orders.
Please don't leave me all
alone.

ב Beth

⁹How can a young person
keep their life pure?
By living according to your
word.
¹⁰I trust in you with all my heart.
Don't let me wander away
from your commands.
¹¹I have hidden your word in
my heart
so that I won't sin against
you.
¹²LORD, I give praise to you.
Teach me your orders.
¹³With my lips I talk about
all the decisions you have
made.
¹⁴Following your covenant
laws gives me joy
just as great riches give joy
to others.
¹⁵I spend time thinking about
your rules.
I consider how you want
me to live.
¹⁶I take delight in your orders.
I won't fail to obey your
word.

ג Gimel

¹⁷Be good to me while I am
alive.
Do this so that I may obey
your word.
¹⁸Open my eyes so that I can
see
the wonderful truths in
your law.
¹⁹I'm a stranger on earth.
Don't hide your commands
from me.

²⁰ My heart is filled with
longing
for your laws at all times.
²¹ You correct proud people.
They are under your
curse.
They wander away from
your commands.
²² I obey your covenant laws.
So don't let evil people
laugh at me or hate me.
²³ Even if rulers sit together and
tell lies about me,
I will spend time thinking
about your orders.
²⁴ Your covenant laws are my
delight.
They give me wise advice.

ד Daleth

²⁵ I lie in the dust. I'm about to
die.
Keep me alive as you have
promised.
²⁶ I told you how I've lived,
and you gave me your
answer.
Teach me your orders.
²⁷ Help me understand how
your rules direct me to
live.
Then I may think deeply
about the wonderful
things you have done.
²⁸ My sadness has worn me
out.
Give me strength as you
have promised.
²⁹ Keep me from cheating and
telling lies.
Be kind to me and teach
me your law.
³⁰ I have chosen to be faithful to
you.
I put my trust in your laws.

³¹ LORD, I'm careful to obey
your covenant laws.
Don't let me be put to shame.
³² I am quick to follow your
commands,
because you have added to
my understanding.

ה He

³³ LORD, teach me how your
orders direct me to live.
Then I will live that way to
the very end.
³⁴ Help me understand your law
so that I may follow it.
I will obey it with all my
heart.
³⁵ Teach me to live as you
command,
because that makes me
very happy.
³⁶ Make me want to follow your
covenant laws
instead of wanting to gain
things only for myself.
³⁷ Turn my eyes away from
things that are worthless.
Keep me alive as you have
promised.
³⁸ Keep your promise to me.
Then other people will
have respect for you.
³⁹ Please don't let me be put to
shame.
Your laws are good.
⁴⁰ I really want to follow your
rules.
Keep me alive, because
you do what is right.

ו Waw

⁴¹ LORD, show me your faithful
love.
Save me as you have
promised.

⁴²Then I can answer anyone
who makes fun of me,
because I trust in your
word.
⁴³Help me always to tell the
truth about how faithful
you are.
I have put my hope in your
laws.
⁴⁴I will always obey your law,
for ever and ever.
⁴⁵I will lead a full and happy life,
because I've tried to obey
your rules.
⁴⁶I will talk about your
covenant laws to kings.
I will not be put to shame.
⁴⁷I take delight in obeying your
commands
because I love them.
⁴⁸I reach out for your
commands that I love.
I do this so that I may
think deeply about your
orders.

ז Zayin

⁴⁹Remember what you have
said to me.
You have given me hope.
⁵⁰Even when I suffer, I am
comforted
because you promised to
keep me alive.
⁵¹Proud people make fun of me
without mercy.
But I don't turn away from
your law.
⁵²LORD, I remember the laws
you gave long ago.
I find comfort in them.
⁵³I am very angry
because evil people have
turned away from your
law.

⁵⁴No matter where I live,
I sing about your orders.
⁵⁵LORD, during the night I
remember who you are.
That's why I keep your
law.
⁵⁶I have really done my best
to obey your rules.

ח Heth

⁵⁷LORD, you are everything I
need.
I have promised to obey
your words.
⁵⁸I have looked to you with all
my heart.
Be kind to me as you have
promised.
⁵⁹I have thought about the way
I live.
And I have decided to
follow your covenant
laws.
⁶⁰I won't waste any time.
I will be quick to obey your
commands.
⁶¹Evil people may tie me up
with ropes.
But I won't forget to obey
your law.
⁶²At midnight I get up to give
you thanks
because your decisions are
very fair.
⁶³I'm a friend to everyone who
has respect for you.
I'm a friend to everyone
who follows your rules.
⁶⁴LORD, the earth is filled with
your love.
Teach me your orders.

ט Teth

⁶⁵LORD, be good to me
as you have promised.

⁶⁶ Increase my knowledge and
     give me good sense,
   because I trust your
     commands.
⁶⁷ Before I went through
     suffering, I went down
     the wrong path.
   But now I obey your word.
⁶⁸ You are good, and what you
     do is good.
   Teach me your orders.
⁶⁹ The lies of proud people have
     taken away my good
     name.
   But I follow your rules with
     all my heart.
⁷⁰ Their unfeeling hearts are
     hard and stubborn.
   But I take delight in your
     law.
⁷¹ It was good for me to suffer.
   That's what helped me to
     understand your orders.
⁷² The law you gave is worth
     more to me
   than thousands of pieces of
     silver and gold.

י Yodh

⁷³ You made me and formed
     me with your own
     hands.
   Give me understanding
     so that I can learn your
     commands.
⁷⁴ May those who have respect
     for you be filled with joy
     when they see me.
   I have put my hope in your
     word.
⁷⁵ Lord, I know that your laws
     are right.
   You were faithful to your
     promise when you made
     me suffer.

⁷⁶ May your faithful love
     comfort me
   as you have promised me.
⁷⁷ Show me your tender love so
     that I can live.
   I take delight in your law.
⁷⁸ May proud people be put to
     shame for treating me
     badly for no reason.
   I will think deeply about
     your rules.
⁷⁹ May those who have respect
     for you come to me.
   Then I can teach them
     your covenant laws.
⁸⁰ May I follow your orders with
     all my heart.
   Then I won't be put to
     shame.

כ Kaph

⁸¹ I deeply long for you to save me.
   I have put my hope in your
     word.
⁸² My eyes grow tired looking
     for what you have
     promised.
   I say, "When will you
     comfort me?"
⁸³ I'm as useless as a wineskin
     that smoke has dried up.
   But I don't forget to follow
     your orders.
⁸⁴ How long do I have to wait?
   When will you punish
     those who attack me?
⁸⁵ Proud people do what is
     against your law.
   They dig pits for me to fall
     into.
⁸⁶ All your commands can be
     trusted.
   Help me, because people
     attack me without any
     reason.

[87] They almost wiped me off the
face of the earth.
But I have not turned away
from your rules.
[88] Keep me alive, because of
your faithful love.
Do this so that I may obey
the covenant laws you
have given.

ל Lamedh

[89] LORD, your word lasts
forever.
It stands firm in the
heavens.
[90] You will be faithful for all
time to come.
You made the earth, and it
continues to exist.
[91] Your laws continue to this
very day,
because all things serve
you.
[92] If I had not taken delight in
your law,
I would have died because
of my suffering.
[93] I will never forget your rules.
You have kept me alive,
because I obey them.
[94] Save me, because I belong to
you.
I've tried to obey your
rules.
[95] Sinful people are waiting to
destroy me.
But I will spend time
thinking about your
covenant laws.
[96] I've learned that everything
has its limits.
But your commands
are perfect. They are
always there when I
need them.

מ Mem

[97] LORD, I really love your law!
All day long I spend time
thinking about it.
[98] Your commands make me
wiser than my enemies,
because your commands
are always in my heart.
[99] I know more than all my
teachers do,
because I spend time
thinking about your
covenant laws.
[100] I understand more than the
elders do,
because I obey your rules.
[101] I've kept my feet from every
path that sinners take
so that I might obey your
word.
[102] I haven't turned away from
your laws,
because you yourself have
taught me.
[103] Your words are very sweet to
my taste!
They are sweeter than
honey to me.
[104] I gain understanding from
your rules.
So I hate every path that
sinners take.

נ Nun

[105] Your word is like a lamp that
shows me the way.
It is like a light that guides
me.
[106] I have made a promise
to follow your laws,
because they are right.
[107] I have suffered very much.
LORD, keep me alive as you
have promised.

108 LORD, accept the praise I
freely give you.
Teach me your laws.
109 I keep putting my life in
danger.
But I won't forget to obey
your law.
110 Evil people have set a trap for
me.
But I haven't wandered
away from your rules.
111 Your covenant laws are your
gift to me forever.
They fill my heart with joy.
112 I have decided to obey your
orders
to the very end.

ס Samekh

113 I hate people who can't make
up their minds.
But I love your law.
114 You are my place of safety.
You are like a shield that
keeps me safe.
I have put my hope in your
word.
115 Get away from me, you who
do evil!
Then I can do what my
God commands me to
do.
116 My God, keep me going as
you have promised.
Then I will live.
Don't let me lose all hope.
117 Take good care of me, and I
will be saved.
I will always honor your
orders.
118 You turn your back on all
those who wander away
from your orders.
Their wrong thoughts will
be proved to be wrong.

119 You throw away all the
sinners on earth as if
they were trash.
So I love your covenant laws.
120 My body trembles because I
have respect for you.
I have great respect for
your laws.

ע Ayin

121 I have done what is right and
fair.
So don't leave me to those
who treat me badly.
122 Make sure that everything
goes well with me.
Don't let proud people treat
me badly.
123 My eyes grow tired as I look
to you to save me.
Please save me as you have
promised.
124 Be good to me, because you
love me.
Teach me your orders.
125 I serve you, so help me to
understand what is right.
Then I will understand
your covenant laws.
126 LORD, it's time for you to act.
People are breaking your
law.
127 I love your commands more
than gold.
I love them more than pure
gold.
128 I consider all your rules to be
right.
So I hate every path that
sinners take.

פ Pe

129 Your covenant laws are
wonderful.
So I obey them.

¹³⁰When your words are made
clear, they bring light.
They bring understanding
to childish people.
¹³¹I open my mouth and pant
like a dog,
because I long to know
your commands.
¹³²Turn to me and have mercy
on me.
That's what you've always
done for those who love
you.
¹³³Teach me how to live as you
have promised.
Don't let any sin be my
master.
¹³⁴Set me free from people who
treat me badly.
Then I will obey your
rules.
¹³⁵Have mercy on me.
Teach me your orders.
¹³⁶Streams of tears flow from
my eyes,
because people don't obey
your law.

צ Tsadhe

¹³⁷LORD, you do what is fair.
And your laws are right.
¹³⁸The laws you have made are
fair.
They can be completely
trusted.
¹³⁹My anger is wearing me
out,
because my enemies don't
pay any attention to your
words.
¹⁴⁰Your promises have proved
to be true.
I love them.
¹⁴¹I'm not important. People
look down on me.

But I don't forget to obey
your rules.
¹⁴²You always do what is
right.
And your law is true.
¹⁴³I've had my share of trouble
and suffering.
But your commands give
me delight.
¹⁴⁴Your covenant laws are
always right.
Help me to understand
them. Then I will live.

ק Qoph

¹⁴⁵LORD, I call out to you with
all my heart.
Answer me, and I will obey
your orders.
¹⁴⁶I call out to you.
Save me, and I will keep
your covenant laws.
¹⁴⁷I get up before the sun rises.
I cry out for help.
I've put my hope in your
word.
¹⁴⁸My eyes stay open all night
long.
I spend my time thinking
about your promises.
¹⁴⁹Listen to me, because you
love me.
LORD, keep me alive as you
have promised.
¹⁵⁰Those who think up evil
plans are near.
They have wandered far
away from your law.
¹⁵¹But LORD, you are near.
All your commands are
true.
¹⁵²Long ago I learned from your
covenant laws
that you made them to last
forever.

ר **Resh**

153 Look at how I'm suffering!
   Save me, because I haven't
      forgotten to obey your
      law.
154 Stand up for me and set me
      free.
   Keep me alive as you have
      promised.
155 Those who are evil are far
      from being saved.
   They don't want to obey
      your orders.
156 LORD, you have deep
      concern for me.
   Keep me alive as you have
      promised.
157 Many enemies attack me.
   But I haven't turned away
      from your covenant
      laws.
158 I get very angry when I
      see people who aren't
      faithful to you.
   They don't obey your
      word.
159 See how I love your rules!
   LORD, keep me alive,
      because you love me.
160 All your words are true.
   All your laws are right.
      They last forever.

ש **Sin and Shin**

161 Rulers attack me for no
      reason.
   But I tremble because of
      your word.
162 I'm filled with joy because of
      your promise.
   It's like finding a great
      fortune.
163 I hate lies with a deep hatred.
   But I love your law.

164 Seven times a day I praise
      you
   for your laws, because they
      are right.
165 Those who love your law
      enjoy great peace.
   Nothing can make them
      trip and fall.
166 LORD, I wait for you to save
      me.
   I follow your commands.
167 I obey your covenant laws,
      because I love them
      greatly.
168 I obey your rules and your
      covenant laws,
   because you know all
      about how I live.

ת **Taw**

169 LORD, may you hear my
      cry.
   Give me understanding,
      just as you said you
      would.
170 May you hear my prayer.
   Save me, just as you
      promised.
171 May my lips pour out praise
      to you,
   because you teach me your
      orders.
172 May my tongue sing about
      your word,
   because all your
      commands are right.
173 May your hand be ready to
      help me,
   because I have chosen to
      obey your rules.
174 LORD, I long for you to save
      me.
   Your law gives me delight.
175 Let me live so that I can
      praise you.

May your laws keep me going.
¹⁷⁶ Like a lost sheep, I've gone down the wrong path.
Come and look for me, because I haven't forgotten to obey your commands.

Psalm 120

A song for those who go up to Jerusalem to worship the Lord.

¹ I call out to the Lord when I'm in trouble, and he answers me.
² Lord, save me from people whose lips tell lies.
Save me from people whose tongues don't tell the truth.

³ What will the Lord do to you, you lying tongue?
And what more will he do?
⁴ He will punish you with the sharp arrows of a soldier.
He will punish you with burning coals from a desert bush.

⁵ How terrible it is for me to live in the tents of the people of Meshek!
How terrible to live in the tents of the people of Kedar!
⁶ I have lived too long among those who hate peace.
⁷ I want peace.
But when I speak, they want war.

Psalm 121

A song for those who go up to Jerusalem to worship the Lord.

¹ I look up to the mountains.
Where does my help come from?
² My help comes from the Lord.
He is the Maker of heaven and earth.

³ He won't let your foot slip.
He who watches over you won't get tired.
⁴ In fact, he who watches over Israel
won't get tired or go to sleep.

⁵ The Lord watches over you.
The Lord is like a shade tree at your right hand.
⁶ The sun won't harm you during the day.
The moon won't harm you during the night.

⁷ The Lord will keep you from every kind of harm.
He will watch over your life.
⁸ The Lord will watch over your life no matter where you go,
both now and forever.

Psalm 122

A song for those who go up to Jerusalem to worship the Lord. A psalm of David.

¹ I was very glad when they said to me,
"Let us go up to the house of the Lord."

2 Jerusalem, our feet are
   standing
   inside your gates.
3 Jerusalem is built like a city
   where everything is close
   together.
4 The tribes of the LORD go
   there to praise his name.
   They do it in keeping with
   the law he gave to Israel.
5 The thrones of the family line
   of David are there.
   That's where the people
   are judged.

6 Pray for the peace of
   Jerusalem. Say,
   "May those who love you
   be secure.
7 May there be peace inside
   your walls.
   May your people be kept
   safe."
8 I'm concerned for my family
   and friends.
   So I say to Jerusalem, "May
   you enjoy peace."
9 I'm concerned about the
   house of the LORD our
   God.
   So I pray that things will go
   well with Jerusalem.

Psalm 123

*A song for those who go up to
Jerusalem to worship the LORD.*

1 I look up and pray to you.
   Your throne is in heaven.
2 Slaves depend on their
   masters.
   A female slave depends on
   the woman she works
   for.
In the same way, we depend
   on the LORD our God.

We wait for him to have
   mercy on us.
3 LORD, have mercy on us.
   Have mercy on us,
because people haven't
   stopped making fun of
   us.
4 We have had to put up with
   a lot from those who are
   proud.
   They were always laughing
   at us.

Psalm 124

*A song for those who go up to
Jerusalem to worship the LORD.
A psalm of David.*

1 Here is what Israel should
   say.
   Suppose the LORD had not
   been on our side.
2 Suppose the LORD had not
   been on our side
   when our enemies
   attacked us.
3 Suppose he had not been on
   our side
   when their burning anger
   blazed out against us.
   Then they would have
   swallowed us alive.
4 They would have been like a
   flood that drowned us.
   They would have swept
   over us like a rushing
   river.
5 They would have washed us
   away
   like a swollen stream.

6 Give praise to the LORD.
   He has not let our enemies
   chew us up.
7 We have escaped like a bird
   from a hunter's trap.

The trap has been broken,
and we have escaped.
[8] Our help comes from the
LORD.
He is the Maker of heaven
and earth.

Psalm 125

*A song for those who go up to
Jerusalem to worship the LORD.*

[1] Those who trust in the LORD
are like Mount Zion.
They will always be secure.
They will last forever.
[2] Like the mountains around
Jerusalem,
the LORD is all around his
people
both now and forever.

[3] Evil people will not always
rule
the land the LORD gave to
those who do right.
If they did, those who do
right
might do what is evil.
[4] LORD, do good to those who
are good.
Do good to those whose
hearts are honest.
[5] But the LORD will drive out
those who have taken
crooked paths.
He will drive them out
with those who do evil
things.

May Israel enjoy peace.

Psalm 126

*A song for those who go up to
Jerusalem to worship the LORD.*

[1] Our enemies took us away
from Zion.

But when the LORD
brought us home,
it seemed like a dream
to us.
[2] Our mouths were filled with
laughter.
Our tongues sang with
joy.
Then the people of other
nations said,
"The LORD has done great
things for them."
[3] The LORD has done great
things for us.
And we are filled with joy.

[4] LORD, bless us with great
success again,
as rain makes streams flow
in the Negev Desert.
[5] Those who cry as they plant
their crops
will sing with joy when
they gather them in.
[6] Those who go out weeping
as they carry seeds to
plant
will come back singing with
joy.
They will bring the new
crop back with them.

Psalm 127

*A song for those who go up to
Jerusalem to worship the LORD.
A psalm of Solomon.*

[1] If the LORD doesn't build a
house,
the work of the builders is
useless.
If the LORD doesn't watch
over a city,
it's useless for those on
guard duty to stand
watch over it.

2 It's useless for you to work
    from early morning
until late at night
just to get food to eat.
    God provides for those he
    loves even while they
    sleep.

3 Children are a gift from the
    LORD.
    They are a reward from
    him.
4 Children who are born to
    people when they are
    young
are like arrows in the
    hands of a soldier.
5 Blessed are those
    who have many children.
They won't be put to shame
    when they go up against
    their enemies in court.

Psalm 128

*A song for those who
go up to Jerusalem to
worship the LORD.*

1 Blessed are all those who
    have respect for the
    LORD.
    They live as he wants them
    to live.
2 Your work will give you what
    you need.
    Blessings and good things
    will come to you.
3 As a vine bears a lot of fruit,
    so may your wife have
    many children by you.
May they sit around your
    table
like young olive trees.
4 Only a man who has respect
    for the LORD
will be blessed like that.

5 May the LORD bless you from
    Zion.
May you enjoy the good
    things that come to
    Jerusalem
all the days of your life.
6   May you live to see your
    grandchildren.

May Israel enjoy peace.

Psalm 129

*A song for those who
go up to Jerusalem to
worship the LORD.*

1 Here is what Israel should
    say.
    "My enemies have treated
    me badly ever since I
    was a young nation.
2 My enemies have treated me
    badly ever since I was a
    young nation.
    But they haven't won the
    battle.
3 They have made deep
    wounds in my back.
    It looks like a field a farmer
    has plowed.
4 The LORD does what is
    right.
    Sinners had tied me up
    with ropes. But the LORD
    has set me free."

5 May all those who hate Zion
    be driven back in shame.
6 May they be like grass that
    grows on the roof of a
    house.
    It dries up before it can
    grow.
7 There isn't enough of it to fill
    a person's hand.
    There isn't enough to tie up
    and carry away.

8 May no one who passes by
say to those who hate
Zion,
"May the blessing of the
LORD be on you.
We bless you in the name
of the LORD."

Psalm 130

*A song for those who
go up to Jerusalem to
worship the LORD.*

1 LORD, I cry out to you
because I'm suffering so
deeply.
2 Lord, listen to me.
Pay attention to my cry for
your mercy.
3 LORD, suppose you kept a
close watch on sins.
Lord, who then wouldn't
be found guilty?
4 But you forgive.
So we can serve you with
respect.
5 With all my heart I wait for
the LORD to help me.
I put my hope in his word.
6 I wait for the Lord to help me.
I want his help more than
night watchmen want
the morning to come.
I'll say it again.
I want his help more than
night watchmen want
the morning to come.
7 Israel, put your hope in the
LORD,
because the LORD's love
never fails.
He sets his people
completely free.
8 He himself will set Israel
free from all their sins.

Psalm 131

*A song for those who go up to
Jerusalem to worship the LORD.
A psalm of David.*

1 LORD, my heart isn't proud.
My eyes aren't proud
either.
I don't concern myself with
important matters.
I don't concern myself
with things that are too
wonderful for me.
2 I have made myself calm and
content
like a young child in its
mother's arms.
Deep down inside me, I
am as content as a young
child.

3 Israel, put your hope in the
LORD
both now and forever.

Psalm 132

*A song for those who
go up to Jerusalem to
worship the LORD.*

1 LORD, remember David
and all the times he didn't
do what he wanted.

2 LORD, he made a promise.
Mighty One of Jacob, he
made a promise to you.
3 He said, "I won't enter my
house
or go to bed.
4 I won't let my eyes sleep.
I won't close my eyelids
5 until I find a place for the
LORD.
I want to build a house
for the Mighty One of
Jacob."

⁶ Here are the words we heard
    in Ephrathah.
  We heard them again in the
    fields of Kiriath Jearim.
⁷ "Let us go to the LORD's
    house.
  Let us worship at his feet.
  Let us say,
⁸ 'LORD, rise up and come to
    your resting place.
  Come in together with the
    ark. It's the sign of your
    power.
⁹ May your priests put on
    godliness as if it were
    their clothes.
  May your faithful people
    sing for joy.' "
¹⁰ In honor of your servant
    David,
  don't turn your back on
    your anointed king.
¹¹ The LORD made a promise to
    David.
  It is a firm promise that he
    will never break.
  He said, "After you die,
  I will place one of your own
    sons on your throne.
¹² If your sons keep my
    covenant
  and the laws I teach them,
  then their sons will sit
    on your throne for ever and
    ever."
¹³ The LORD has chosen Zion.
  That's the place where he
    wants to live.
¹⁴ He has said, "This will be my
    resting place for ever and
    ever.
  Here I will sit on my
    throne, because that's
    what I want.

¹⁵ I will greatly bless Zion with
    everything it needs.
  I will give plenty of food to
    the poor people living
    there.
¹⁶ I will put salvation on its
    priests as if it were their
    clothes.
  God's faithful people will
    always sing for joy.
¹⁷ "Here in Jerusalem I will
    raise up a mighty king
    from the family of
    David.
  I will set up the lamp of
    David's kingdom for my
    anointed king.
  Its flame will burn brightly
    forever.
¹⁸ I will put shame on his
    enemies as if it were
    their clothes.
  But he will wear on his
    head a shining crown."

Psalm 133

A song for those who go up to
Jerusalem to worship the LORD.
A psalm of David.

¹ How good and pleasant it is
    when God's people live
    together in peace!
² It's like the special olive oil
    that was poured on Aaron's
    head.
  It ran down on his beard
    and on the collar of his
    robe.
³ It's as if the dew of Mount
    Hermon
  were falling on Mount
    Zion.
  There the LORD gives his
    blessing.

He gives life that never
ends.

Psalm 134

*A song for those who
go up to Jerusalem to
worship the LORD.*

1 All you who serve the LORD,
praise the LORD.
All you who serve at night
in the house of the LORD,
praise him.
2 Lift up your hands in the
temple
and praise the LORD.

3 May the LORD bless you from
Zion.
He is the Maker of heaven
and earth.

Psalm 135

1 Praise the LORD.

Praise the name of the LORD.
You who serve the LORD,
praise him.
2 You who serve in the house of
the LORD, praise him.
You who serve in the
courtyards of the temple
of our God, praise him.

3 Praise the LORD, because he
is good.
Sing praise to his name,
because that is pleasant.
4 The LORD has chosen the
people of Jacob to be his
own.
He has chosen Israel to be
his special treasure.

5 I know that the LORD is great.
I know that our Lord is
greater than all gods.

6 The LORD does anything he
wants to do
in the heavens and on the
earth.
He does it even in the
deepest parts of the
oceans.
7 He makes clouds rise from
one end of the earth to
the other.
He sends lightning with
the rain.
He brings the wind out of
his storerooms.

8 He killed the oldest son of
each family in Egypt.
He struck down the oldest
males that were born to
people and animals.
9 He did miraculous signs in
Egypt.
He did wonders against
Pharaoh and everyone
who served him.
10 He destroyed many
nations.
He killed mighty kings.
11 He killed Sihon, the king of
the Amorites,
and Og, the king of
Bashan.
He killed all the kings of
Canaan.
12 He gave their land as a gift
to his people Israel.

13 LORD, your name continues
forever.
LORD, your fame will last
for all time to come.
14 When the LORD hands down
his sentence, it will be in
his people's favor.
He will show deep concern
for those who serve him.

15 The statues of the nations'
gods are made out of
silver and gold.
They are made by human
hands.
16 They have mouths but can't
speak.
They have eyes but can't
see.
17 They have ears but can't
hear.
They have mouths but
can't breathe.
18 Those who make statues of
gods will be like them.
So will all those who trust
in them.
19 People of Israel, praise the
LORD.
Priests of Aaron, praise the
LORD.
20 Tribe of Levi, praise the
LORD.
You who have respect for
the LORD, praise him.
21 Give praise to the LORD in
Zion.
Give praise to the God who
lives in Jerusalem.

Praise the LORD.

Psalm 136

1 Give thanks to the LORD,
because he is good.
*His faithful love continues
forever.*
2 Give thanks to the greatest
God of all.
*His faithful love continues
forever.*
3 Give thanks to the most
powerful Lord of all.
*His faithful love continues
forever.*

4 Give thanks to the only
one who can do great
miracles.
*His faithful love continues
forever.*
5 By his understanding he
made the heavens.
*His faithful love continues
forever.*
6 He spread out the earth on
the waters.
*His faithful love continues
forever.*
7 He made the great lights in
the sky.
*His faithful love continues
forever.*
8 He made the sun to rule over
the day.
*His faithful love continues
forever.*
9 He made the moon and stars
to rule over the night.
*His faithful love continues
forever.*
10 Give thanks to the God who
killed the oldest son of
each family in Egypt.
*His faithful love continues
forever.*
11 He brought the people of
Israel out of Egypt.
*His faithful love continues
forever.*
12 He did it by reaching out
his mighty hand and
powerful arm.
*His faithful love continues
forever.*
13 Give thanks to the God who
parted the waters of the
Red Sea.
*His faithful love continues
forever.*

¹⁴ He brought Israel through
the middle of it.
*His faithful love continues
forever.*

¹⁵ But he swept Pharaoh and his
army into the Red Sea.
*His faithful love continues
forever.*

¹⁶ Give thanks to the God who
led his people through
the desert.
*His faithful love continues
forever.*

¹⁷ He killed great kings.
*His faithful love continues
forever.*

¹⁸ He struck down mighty
kings.
*His faithful love continues
forever.*

¹⁹ He killed Sihon, the king of
the Amorites.
*His faithful love continues
forever.*

²⁰ He killed Og, the king of
Bashan.
*His faithful love continues
forever.*

²¹ He gave their land as a gift.
*His faithful love continues
forever.*

²² He gave it as a gift to his
servant Israel.
*His faithful love continues
forever.*

²³ Give thanks to the God who
remembered us when
things were going badly.
*His faithful love continues
forever.*

²⁴ He set us free from our
enemies.
*His faithful love continues
forever.*

²⁵ He gives food to every
creature.
*His faithful love continues
forever.*

²⁶ Give thanks to the God of
heaven.
*His faithful love continues
forever.*

Psalm 137

¹ We were sitting by the rivers
of Babylon.
We wept when we
remembered what had
happened to Zion.

² On the nearby poplar trees
we hung up our harps.

³ Those who held us as
prisoners asked us to
sing.
Those who enjoyed
hurting us ordered us to
sing joyful songs.
They said, "Sing one of the
songs of Zion to us!"

⁴ How can we sing the songs of
the LORD
while we are in another
land?

⁵ Jerusalem, if I forget you,
may my right hand never
be able to play the harp
again.

⁶ If I don't remember you,
may my tongue stick to the
roof of my mouth so I
can't sing.
May it happen if I don't
consider Jerusalem
to be my greatest joy.

⁷ LORD, remember what the
people of Edom did
on the day Jerusalem fell.

"Tear it down!" they cried.
"Tear it down to the
ground!"

8 People of Babylon, you
are sentenced to be
destroyed.
Happy is the person who
pays you back
according to what you have
done to us.
9 Happy is the person who
grabs your babies
and smashes them against
the rocks.

Psalm 138

A psalm of David.

1 LORD, I will praise you with
all my heart.
In front of those who think
they are gods
I will sing praise to you.
2 I will bow down facing your
holy temple.
I will praise your name,
because you are always
loving and faithful.
You have honored your holy
word
even more than your own
fame.
3 When I called out to you, you
answered me.
You made me strong and
brave.

4 LORD, may all the kings on
earth praise you
when they hear about what
you have decided.
5 LORD, may they sing about
what you have done,
because your glory is
great.

6 Though the LORD is high
above all, he cares for
the lowly.
Though he is in heaven
above, he sees them on
earth below.
7 Trouble is all around me,
but you keep me alive.
You reach out your hand to
put a stop to the anger of
my enemies.
With your powerful right
hand you save me.
8 LORD, you will show that I
was right to trust you.
LORD, your faithful love
continues forever.
You have done so much for
us, so don't stop now.

Psalm 139

For the director of music.
A psalm of David.

1 LORD, you have seen what is
in my heart.
You know all about me.
2 You know when I sit down
and when I get up.
You know what I'm
thinking even though
you are far away.
3 You know when I go out to
work and when I come
back home.
You know exactly how I
live.
4 LORD, even before I speak a
word,
you know all about it.

5 You are all around me,
behind me and in front
of me.
You hold me safe in your
hand.

The Birth of Jesus
LUKE 2:1–20

Jesus Walks on the Water

MATTHEW 14:22–23

⁶ I'm amazed at how well you
      know me.
   It's more than I can
      understand.

⁷ How can I get away from your
      Spirit?
   Where can I go to escape
      from you?
⁸ If I go up to the heavens, you
      are there.
   If I lie down in the deepest
      parts of the earth, you
      are also there.
⁹ Suppose I were to rise with
      the sun in the east.
   Suppose I travel to the west
      where it sinks into the
      ocean.
¹⁰ Your hand would always be
      there to guide me.
   Your right hand would still
      be holding me close.

¹¹ Suppose I were to say, "I'm
      sure the darkness will
      hide me.
   The light around me will
      become as dark as
      night."
¹² Even that darkness would not
      be dark to you.
   The night would shine like
      the day,
   because darkness is like
      light to you.

¹³ You created the deepest parts
      of my being.
   You put me together inside
      my mother's body.
¹⁴ How you made me is
      amazing and wonderful.
   I praise you for that.
   What you have done is
      wonderful.
   I know that very well.

¹⁵ None of my bones was
      hidden from you
   when you made me inside
      my mother's body.
   That place was as dark as
      the deepest parts of the
      earth.
   When you were putting me
      together there,
¹⁶   your eyes saw my body
      even before it was
      formed.
   You planned how many days
      I would live.
   You wrote down the
      number of them in your
      book
   before I had lived through
      even one of them.

¹⁷ God, your thoughts about me
      are priceless.
   No one can possibly add
      them all up.
¹⁸ If I could count them,
      they would be more than
      the grains of sand.
   If I were to fall asleep
      counting and then wake
      up,
   you would still be there
      with me.

¹⁹ God, I wish you would kill
      the people who are
      evil!
   I wish those murderers
      would get away from me!
²⁰ They are your enemies. They
      misuse your name.
   They misuse it for their
      own evil purposes.
²¹ Lord, I really hate those who
      hate you!
   I really hate those who rise
      up against you!

22 I have nothing but hatred for
them.
I consider them to be my
enemies.

23 God, see what is in my heart.
Know what is there.
Test me.
Know what I'm thinking.
24 See if there's anything in my
life you don't like.
Help me live in the way
that is always right.

Psalm 140

For the director of music.
A psalm of David.

1 LORD, save me from sinful
people.
Keep me safe from those
who want to hurt me.
2 They make evil plans in their
hearts.
They are always starting
fights.
3 Their tongues are as deadly as
the tongue of a serpent.
The words from their lips
are like the poison of a
snake.

4 LORD, keep me safe from the
hands of sinful people.
Protect me from those who
want to hurt me.
They plan ways to trip me
up and make me fall.
5 Proud people have hidden
their traps to catch me.
They have spread out their
nets.
They have set traps for me
along my path.

6 I say to the LORD, "You are
my God."

LORD, hear my cry for
mercy.
7 LORD and King, you save me
because you are strong.
You are like a shield that
keeps me safe in the day
of battle.
8 LORD, don't give sinners what
they want.
Don't let their plans succeed.

9 Those who are all around
me proudly raise their
heads.
May the trouble they
planned for me happen
to them.
10 May burning coals fall on
people like that.
May they be thrown into
the fire.
May they be thrown into
muddy pits and never get
out.
11 Don't let people who lie about
me be secure in the land.
May trouble hunt down
those who want to hurt
me.

12 I know that the LORD makes
sure that poor people
are treated fairly.
He stands up for those who
are in need.
13 I'm sure that those who do
right will praise your
name.
Those who are honest will
live with you.

Psalm 141

A psalm of David.

1 I call out to you, LORD. Come
quickly to help me.

Listen to me when I call out
to you.
[2] May my prayer come to you
like the sweet smell of
incense.
When I lift up my hands in
prayer, may it be like the
evening sacrifice.

[3] LORD, guard my mouth.
Keep watch over the door
of my lips.
[4] Don't let my heart be drawn
to what is evil.
Don't let me join with
people who do evil.
Don't let me eat their fancy
food.

[5] If a godly person hit me,
it would be an act of
kindness.
If they would correct me,
it would be like pouring
olive oil on my head.
I wouldn't say no to it.

I will always pray against the
things that sinful people
do.
[6]　　When their rulers are
thrown down from the
rocky cliffs,
those evil people will
realize that my words
were true.
[7] They will say, "As clumps of
dirt are left from plowing
up the ground,
so our bones will be
scattered near an open
grave."
[8] But LORD and King, I keep
looking to you for help.
I go to you for safety. Don't
let me die.

[9] Keep me from the traps of
those who do evil.
Save me from the traps
they have set for me.
[10] Let evil people fall into their
own nets.
But let me go safely on my
way.

Psalm 142

*A prayer of David when he was
in the cave. A* maskil.

[1] I call out to the LORD.
I pray to him for mercy.
[2] I pour out my problem to
him.
I tell him about my trouble.

[3] When I grow weak,
you are watching over my
life.
In the path where I walk,
people have hidden a trap
to catch me.
[4] Look and see that no one is
on my right side to help
me.
No one is concerned about
me.
I have no place of safety.
No one cares whether I live
or die.

[5] LORD, I cry out to you.
I say, "You are my place of
safety.
You are everything I need
in this life."
[6] Listen to my cry.
I am in great need.
Save me from those who are
chasing me.
They are too strong for me.
[7] My troubles are like a prison.
Set me free so I can praise
your name.

Then those who do what is
　　right will gather around
　　me
because you have been
　　good to me.

Psalm 143

A psalm of David.

1 LORD, hear my prayer.
　　Listen to my cry for
　　mercy.
You are faithful and right.
　　Come and help me.
2 Don't take me to court and
　　judge me,
because in your eyes no
　　living person does what
　　is right.
3 My enemies chase me.
　　They crush me down to the
　　ground.
They make me live in the
　　darkness
like those who died long
　　ago.
4 So I grow weak.
　　Deep down inside me, I'm
　　afraid.
5 I remember what happened
　　long ago.
I spend time thinking
　　about all your acts.
I consider what your hands
　　have done.
6 I spread out my hands to you
　　in prayer.
I'm thirsty for you, just as
　　dry ground is thirsty for
　　rain.
7 LORD, answer me quickly.
　　I'm growing weak.
Don't turn your face away
　　from me,

or I will be like those who
　　go down into the grave.
8 In the morning let me hear
　　about your faithful
　　love,
because I've put my trust
　　in you.
Show me the way I should
　　live,
because I trust you with
　　my life.
9 LORD, save me from my
　　enemies,
because I go to you for
　　safety.
10 Teach me to do what you
　　want,
because you are my God.
May your good Spirit
　　lead me on a level path.

11 LORD, bring yourself honor
　　by keeping me alive.
Because you do what
　　is right, get me out of
　　trouble.
12 Because your love is faithful,
　　put an end to my
　　enemies.
Destroy all of them,
　　because I serve you.

Psalm 144

A psalm of David.

1 Give praise to the LORD, my
　　Rock.
He trains my hands for
　　war.
He trains my fingers for
　　battle.
2 He is my loving God and is
　　like a fort to me.
He is my place of safety
　　and the God who saves
　　me.

He is like a shield that keeps
    me safe.
He brings nations under
    my control.

³ Lord, what are human
    beings that you take care
    of them?
What are mere people that
    you think about them?
⁴ Their lives don't last any
    longer than a breath.
Their days are like a
    shadow that quickly
    disappears.

⁵ Lord, open up your heavens
    and come down.
Touch the mountains,
    and they will pour out
    smoke.
⁶ Send flashes of lightning and
    scatter my enemies.
Shoot your arrows and
    chase them away.
⁷ My enemies are like a mighty
    flood.
Reach down from heaven
    and save me.
Save me from outsiders
    who attack me.
⁸ They tell all kinds of lies with
    their mouths.
Even when they make a
    promise by raising their
    right hands, they don't
    mean it.
⁹ My God, I will sing a new
    song to you.
I will make music to you
    on a lyre that has ten
    strings.
¹⁰ You are the God who helps
    kings win battles.
You save your servant
    David.

From death by the sword
¹¹ save me.
Set me free from outsiders
    who attack me.
They tell all kinds of lies with
    their mouths.
Even when they make a
    promise by raising their
    right hands, they don't
    mean it.

¹² While our sons are young,
    they will be like healthy
    plants.
Our daughters will be like
    pillars
    that have been made to
    decorate a palace.
¹³ Our storerooms will be
    filled
    with every kind of food.
The sheep in our fields will
    increase by thousands.
They will increase by tens
    of thousands.
¹⁴   Our oxen will pull heavy
    loads.
None of our city walls will be
    broken down.
No one will be carried off
    as a prisoner.
No cries of pain will be
    heard in our streets.
¹⁵ Blessed is the nation about
    whom all these things
    are true.
Blessed is the nation whose
    God is the Lord.

Psalm 145

A psalm of praise. A psalm of David.

¹ I will honor you, my God the
    King.
I will praise your name for
    ever and ever.

2 Every day I will praise you.
I will praise your name for
ever and ever.

3 LORD, you are great. You are
really worthy of praise.
No one can completely
understand how great
you are.
4 Parents praise your works to
their children.
They tell about your
mighty acts.
5 They speak about your
glorious majesty.
I will spend time thinking
about your wonderful
deeds.
6 They speak about the
powerful and wonderful
things you do.
I will talk about the great
things you have done.
7 They celebrate your great
goodness.
They sing for joy about
your holy acts.
8 The LORD is gracious, kind
and tender.
He is slow to get angry and
full of love.
9 The LORD is good to all.
He shows deep concern for
everything he has made.
10 LORD, all your works praise
you.
Your faithful people praise
you.
11 They tell about your glorious
kingdom.
They speak about your
power.
12 Then all people will know
about the mighty things
you have done.

They will know about the
glorious majesty of your
kingdom.
13 Your kingdom is a kingdom
that will last forever.
Your rule will continue for
all time to come.

The LORD will keep all his
promises.
He is faithful in everything
he does.
14 The LORD takes good care of
all those who fall.
He lifts up all those who
feel helpless.
15 Every living thing looks to
you for food.
You give it to them exactly
when they need it.
16 You open your hand
and satisfy the needs of
every living creature.

17 The LORD is right in
everything he does.
He is faithful in everything
he does.
18 The LORD is ready to help
all those who call out to
him.
He helps those who really
mean it when they call
out to him.
19 He satisfies the needs of
those who have respect
for him.
He hears their cry and
saves them.
20 The LORD watches over all
those who love him.
But he will destroy all
sinful people.
21 I will praise the LORD with
my mouth.

Let every creature praise
his holy name
for ever and ever.

Psalm 146

[1] Praise the LORD.

I will praise the LORD.
[2]   I will praise the LORD all
my life.
I will sing praise to my God
as long as I live.

[3] Don't put your trust in
human leaders.
Don't trust in people who
can't save you.
[4] When they die, they return to
the ground.
On that day their plans
come to nothing.

[5] Blessed are those who
depend on the God of
Jacob for help.
Blessed are those who put
their hope in the LORD
their God.
[6] He is the Maker of heaven
and earth and the
ocean.
He made everything in
them.
He remains faithful
forever.
[7] He stands up for those who
are treated badly.
He gives food to hungry
people.
The LORD sets prisoners free.
[8]   The LORD gives sight to
those who are blind.
The LORD lifts up those who
feel helpless.
The LORD loves those who
do what is right.

[9] The LORD watches over the
outsiders who live in our
land.
He takes good care of
children whose fathers
have died.
He also takes good care of
widows.
But he causes evil people to
fail
in everything they do.
[10] The LORD rules forever.
The God of Zion will rule
for all time to come.

Praise the LORD.

Psalm 147

[1] Praise the LORD.

How good it is to sing praises
to our God!
How pleasant and right it is
to praise him!

[2] The LORD builds up
Jerusalem.
He gathers the scattered
people of Israel.
[3] He heals those who have
broken hearts.
He takes care of their
wounds.

[4] He decides how many stars
there should be.
He gives each one of them
a name.
[5] Great is our Lord. His power
is mighty.
There is no limit to his
understanding.
[6] The LORD gives strength to
those who aren't proud.
But he throws evil people
down to the ground.

⁷ Sing to the LORD and give
  him grateful praise.
    Make music to our God on
      the harp.
⁸ He covers the sky with
    clouds.
    He supplies the earth with
      rain.
    He makes grass grow on
      the hills.
⁹ He provides food for the
    cattle.
    He provides for the young
      ravens when they cry
      out.

¹⁰ He doesn't take pleasure in
    the strength of horses.
    He doesn't take delight
      in the strong legs of
      warriors.
¹¹ The LORD takes delight in
    those who have respect
    for him.
    They put their hope in his
      faithful love.

¹² Jerusalem, praise the
    LORD.
    Zion, praise your God.
¹³ He makes the metal bars of
    your gates stronger.
    He blesses the people who
      live inside you.
¹⁴ He keeps your borders safe
    and secure.
    He satisfies you with the
      finest wheat.

¹⁵ He sends his command to
    the earth.
    His word arrives there
      quickly.
¹⁶ He spreads the snow like
    wool.
    He scatters the frost like
      ashes.

¹⁷ He throws down his hail like
    pebbles.
    No one can stand his icy
      blast.
¹⁸ He gives his command, and
    the ice melts.
    He stirs up his winds, and
      the waters flow.
¹⁹ He has made his word
    known to the people
    of Jacob.
    He has made his laws and
      rules known to Israel.
²⁰ He hasn't done that for any
    other nation.
    They don't know his laws.

  Praise the LORD.

Psalm 148

¹ Praise the LORD.

  Praise the LORD from the
    heavens.
    Praise him in the heavens
      above.
² Praise him, all his angels.
    Praise him, all his angels
      in heaven.
³ Praise him, sun and moon.
    Praise him, all you shining
      stars.
⁴ Praise him, you highest
    heavens.
    Praise him, you waters
      above the skies.
⁵ Let all of them praise the
    name of the LORD,
    because at his command
      they were created.
⁶ He established them for ever
    and ever.
    He gave them laws they
      will always have to
      obey.

⁷Praise the LORD from the
earth,
you great sea creatures and
all the deepest parts of
the ocean.
⁸Praise him, lightning and
hail, snow and clouds.
Praise him, you stormy
winds that obey him.
⁹Praise him, all you
mountains and hills.
Praise him, all you fruit
trees and cedar trees.
¹⁰Praise him, all you wild
animals and cattle.
Praise him, you small
creatures and flying
birds.
¹¹Praise him, you kings of the
earth and all nations.
Praise him, all you princes
and rulers on earth.
¹²Praise him, young men and
women.
Praise him, old men and
children.

¹³Let them praise the name of
the LORD.
His name alone is
honored.
His glory is higher than
the earth and the
heavens.
¹⁴He has given his people a
strong king.
All his faithful people
praise him for that gift.
All the people of Israel are
close to his heart.

Praise the LORD.

Psalm 149

¹Praise the LORD.

Sing a new song to the LORD.

Sing praise to him in the
assembly of his faithful
people.
²Let Israel be filled with joy
because God is their
Maker.
Let the people of Zion be
glad because he is their
King.
³Let them praise his name
with dancing.
Let them make music to
him with harps and
tambourines.
⁴The LORD takes delight in his
people.
He awards with victory
those who are humble.
⁵Let his faithful people be
filled with joy because
of that honor.
Let them sing for joy even
when they are lying in
bed.

⁶May they praise God with
their mouths.
May they hold in their
hands a sword that has
two edges.
⁷Let them pay the nations
back.
Let them punish the
people of the earth.
⁸Let them put the kings
of those nations in
chains.
Let them put their nobles
in iron chains.
⁹Let them carry out God's
sentence against those
nations.
This will bring glory to all
his faithful people.

Praise the LORD.

Psalm 150

[1] Praise the Lord.

Praise God in his holy
    temple.
Praise him in his mighty
    heavens.
[2] Praise him for his powerful
    acts.
Praise him because he is
    greater than anything
    else.
[3] Praise him by blowing
    trumpets.
Praise him with harps and
    lyres.
[4] Praise him with tambourines
    and dancing.
Praise him with stringed
    instruments and flutes.
[5] Praise him with clashing
    cymbals.
Praise him with clanging
    cymbals.

[6] Let everything that has
    breath praise the Lord.

Praise the Lord.

Proverbs

Introduction:

The book of Proverbs is full of wise sayings. These proverbs tell many truths about life. Solomon wrote some of these wise words. He told people how to live a good life. He wrote, "If you really want to gain knowledge, you must begin by having respect for the LORD." (1:7)

The words of Proverbs help make people wiser. If people do what God says, they will be wise. They cannot be wise and do bad things. They cannot be wise if they do not love God.

Outline of contents:

Purpose

1 These are the proverbs of Solomon. He was the son of David and the king of Israel.

² Proverbs teach you wisdom
and instruct you.
They help you understand
wise sayings.
³ They provide you with
instruction and help you
live wisely.
They lead to what is right
and honest and fair.
⁴ They give understanding to
childish people.
They give knowledge and
good sense to those who
are young.
⁵ Let wise people listen and
add to what they have
learned.
Let those who understand
what is right get
guidance.

⁶ What I'm teaching also helps
you understand proverbs
and stories.
It helps you understand the
sayings and riddles of
those who are wise.

⁷ If you really want to gain
knowledge, you must
begin by having respect
for the LORD.
But foolish people hate
wisdom and instruction.

Think and Live Wisely

A Warning Against Sinful Men

⁸ My son, listen to your father's
advice.
Don't turn away from your
mother's teaching.
⁹ What they teach you will be
like a beautiful crown on
your head.
It will be like a chain to
decorate your neck.

¹⁰ My son, if sinful men tempt
  you,
    don't give in to them.
¹¹ They might say, "Come along
  with us.
    Let's hide and wait to kill
      someone who hasn't
      done anything wrong.
    Let's catch some harmless
      person in our trap.
¹² Let's swallow them alive, as
  the grave does.
    Let's swallow them whole,
      like those who go down
      into the pit.
¹³ We'll get all kinds of valuable
  things.
    We'll fill our houses with
      what we steal.
¹⁴ Cast lots with us for what
  they own.
    We'll share everything we
      take from them."
¹⁵ My son, don't go along with
  them.
    Don't even set your feet on
      their paths.
¹⁶ They are always in a hurry
  to sin.
    They are quick to spill
      someone's blood.
¹⁷ How useless it is to spread
  a net
    where every bird can see it!
¹⁸ Those who hide and wait will
  spill their own blood.
    They will be caught in their
      own trap.
¹⁹ That's what happens to
  everyone
    who goes after money in
      the wrong way.
    That kind of money takes
      away
      the life of those who get it.

Wisdom's Warning

²⁰ Out in the open wisdom calls
  out.
    She raises her voice in a
      public place.
²¹ On top of the city wall she
  cries out.
    Here is what she says near
      the gate of the city.
²² "How long will you childish
  people love your childish
  ways?
    How long will you rude
      people enjoy making fun
      of God and others?
    How long will you foolish
      people hate knowledge?
²³ Pay attention to my
  warning!
    Then I will pour out my
      thoughts to you.
    I will make known to you
      my teachings.
²⁴ But you refuse to listen when
  I call out to you.
    No one pays attention
      when I reach out my
      hand.
²⁵ You turn away from all my
  advice.
    And you do not accept my
      warning.
²⁶ So I will laugh at you when
  you are in danger.
    I will make fun of you
      when hard times come.
²⁷ I will laugh when hard times
  hit you like a storm.
    I will laugh when danger
      comes your way like a
      windstorm.
    I will make fun of you
      when suffering and
      trouble come.

28 "Then you will call to me. But
I won't answer.
You will look for me. But
you won't find me.
29 You hated knowledge.
You didn't choose to have
respect for the LORD.
30 You wouldn't accept my
advice.
You turned your backs on
my warnings.
31 So you will eat the fruit of the
way you have lived.
You will choke on the
fruit of what you have
planned.

32 "The wrong path that
childish people take will
kill them.
Foolish people will be
destroyed by being
satisfied with the way
they live.
33 But those who listen to me
will live in safety.
They will be at ease and
have no fear of being
harmed."

Good Things Come From Wisdom

2 My son, accept my words.
Store up my commands
inside you.
2 Let your ears listen to
wisdom.
Apply your heart to
understanding.
3 Call out for the ability to be
wise.
Cry out for understanding.
4 Look for it as you would look
for silver.
Search for it as you would
search for hidden
treasure.

5 Then you will understand
how to have respect for
the LORD.
You will find out how to
know God.
6 The LORD gives wisdom.
Knowledge and
understanding come
from his mouth.
7 He stores up success for
honest people.
He is like a shield to those
who live without blame.
8 He guards the path of those
who are honest.
He watches over the way of
his faithful ones.

9 You will understand what is
right and honest and fair.
You will understand the
right way to live.
10 Your heart will become wise.
Your mind will delight in
knowledge.
11 Good sense will keep you
safe.
Understanding will guard
you.

12 Wisdom will save you from
the ways of evil men.
It will save you from men
who twist their words.
13 Men like that have left the
straight paths
to walk in dark ways.
14 They take delight in doing
what is wrong.
They take joy in twisting
everything around.
15 Their paths are crooked.
Their ways are not straight.
16 Wisdom will save you from
a woman who commits
adultery.

It will save you from a
sinful woman and her
tempting words.
¹⁷ She has left the man she
married when she was
young.
She has broken the
promise she made in
front of God.
¹⁸ Surely her house leads down
to death.
Her paths lead to the spirits
of the dead.
¹⁹ No one who goes to her
comes back
or reaches the paths of
life.
²⁰ You will walk in the ways of
good people.
You will follow the paths of
those who do right.
²¹ Honest people will live in the
land.
Those who are without
blame will remain in it.
²² But sinners will be cut off
from the land.
Those who aren't faithful
will be torn away from it.

*More Good Things Come
From Wisdom*

3 My son, do not forget my
teaching.
Keep my commands in
your heart.
² They will help you live for
many years.
They will bring you peace
and success.
³ Don't let love and truth ever
leave you.
Tie them around your
neck.

Write them on the tablet of
your heart.
⁴ Then you will find favor and
a good name
in the eyes of God and
people.
⁵ Trust in the LORD with all
your heart.
Do not depend on your
own understanding.
⁶ In all your ways obey him.
Then he will make your
paths smooth and
straight.
⁷ Don't be wise in your own
eyes.
Have respect for the LORD
and avoid evil.
⁸ That will bring health to your
body.
It will make your bones
strong.
⁹ Honor the LORD with your
wealth.
Give him the first share of
all your crops.
¹⁰ Then your storerooms will
be so full they can't hold
everything.
Your huge jars will spill
over with fresh wine.
¹¹ My son, do not hate the
LORD's training.
Do not object when he
corrects you.
¹² The LORD trains those he loves.
He is like a father who
trains the son he is
pleased with.
¹³ Blessed is the one who finds
wisdom.
Blessed is the one who
gains understanding.

¹⁴ Wisdom pays better than
silver does.
She earns more than gold
does.
¹⁵ She is worth more than
rubies.
Nothing you want can
compare with her.
¹⁶ Long life is in her right hand.
In her left hand are riches
and honor.
¹⁷ Her ways are pleasant ways.
All her paths lead to peace.
¹⁸ She is a tree of life to those
who take hold of her.
Those who hold her close
will be blessed.

¹⁹ By wisdom the LORD laid the
earth's foundations.
Through understanding he
set the heavens in place.
²⁰ By his knowledge the seas
were separated,
and the clouds dropped
their dew.
²¹ My son, do not let wisdom
and understanding out
of your sight.
Hold on to good sense and
the understanding of
what is right.
²² They will be life for you.
They will be like a gracious
necklace around your
neck.
²³ Then you will go on your way
in safety.
You will not trip and fall.
²⁴ When you lie down, you
won't be afraid.
When you lie down, you
will sleep soundly.
²⁵ Don't be terrified by sudden
trouble.

Don't be afraid when
sinners are destroyed.
²⁶ The LORD will be at your side.
He will keep your feet from
being caught in a trap.

²⁷ Don't hold back good from
those who are worthy of
it.
Don't hold it back when
you can help.
²⁸ Suppose you already have
something to give.
Don't say to your neighbor,
"Come back tomorrow.
I'll give it to you then."

²⁹ Don't plan to harm your
neighbor.
He lives near you and
trusts you.
³⁰ Don't bring charges against
anyone for no reason.
They have not harmed
you.
³¹ Don't be jealous of a person
who hurts others.
Don't choose any of their
ways.
³² The LORD really hates sinful
people.
But he makes honest
people his closest
friends.

³³ The LORD puts a curse on the
houses of sinners.
But he blesses the homes
of those who do what is
right.
³⁴ He makes fun of proud
people who make fun of
others.
But he gives grace to those
who are humble and
treated badly.

³⁵ Wise people receive honor.
 But foolish people get only
 shame.

Get Wisdom at Any Cost

4 My sons, listen to a father's
 teaching.
 Pay attention and gain
 understanding.
² I give you good advice.
 So don't turn away from
 what I teach you.
³ I, too, was once a young boy
 in my father's house.
 And my mother loved me
 deeply.
⁴ Then my father taught me.
 He said to me, "Take hold
 of my words with all your
 heart.
 Keep my commands, and
 you will live.
⁵ Get wisdom, and get
 understanding.
 Don't forget my words or
 turn away from them.
⁶ Stay close to wisdom, and she
 will keep you safe.
 Love her, and she will
 watch over you.
⁷ To start being wise you must
 first get wisdom.
 No matter what it costs, get
 understanding.
⁸ Value wisdom highly, and
 she will lift you up.
 Hold her close, and she will
 honor you.
⁹ She will set a beautiful crown
 on your head.
 She will give you a glorious
 crown."
¹⁰ My son, listen. Accept what I
 say.

Then you will live for many
 years.
¹¹ I instruct you in the way of
 wisdom.
 I lead you along straight
 paths.
¹² When you walk, nothing will
 slow you down.
 When you run, you won't
 trip and fall.
¹³ Hold on to my teaching and
 don't let it go.
 Guard it well, because it is
 your life.
¹⁴ Don't take the path of evil
 people.
 Don't live the way sinners
 do.
¹⁵ Stay away from their path
 and don't travel on it.
 Turn away from it and go
 on your way.
¹⁶ Sinners can't rest until they
 do what is evil.
 They can't sleep until they
 make someone sin.
¹⁷ They do evil just as easily as
 they eat food.
 They hurt others as easily
 as they drink wine.
¹⁸ The path of those who do
 right is like the sun in
 the morning.
 It shines brighter and
 brighter until the full
 light of day.
¹⁹ But the way of those who
 do what is wrong is like
 deep darkness.
 They don't know what
 makes them trip and fall.
²⁰ My son, pay attention to what
 I say.
 Listen closely to my words.

²¹ Don't let them out of your
sight.
Keep them in your heart.
²² They are life to those who
find them.
They are health to a
person's whole body.
²³ Above everything else, guard
your heart.
Everything you do comes
from it.
²⁴ Don't speak with twisted
words.
Keep evil talk away from
your lips.
²⁵ Let your eyes look straight
ahead.
Keep looking right in front
of you.
²⁶ Think carefully about the
paths that your feet walk
on.
Always choose the right
ways.
²⁷ Don't turn to the right
or left.
Keep your feet from the
path of evil.

A Warning Against Committing Adultery

5 My son, pay attention to my
wisdom.
Listen carefully to my wise
sayings.
² Then you will continue to
have good sense.
Your lips will keep on
speaking words of
knowledge.
³ A woman who commits
adultery has lips that
drip honey.
What she says is smoother
than olive oil.

⁴ But in the end she is like
bitter poison.
She cuts like a sword that
has two edges.
⁵ Her feet go down to death.
Her steps lead straight to
the grave.
⁶ She doesn't give any thought
to her way of life.
Her paths have no
direction, but she
doesn't realize it.

⁷ My sons, listen to me.
Don't turn away from what
I say.
⁸ Stay on a path far away from
that evil woman.
Don't even go near the
door of her house.
⁹ If you do, you will lose your
honor to other people.
You will give your self-
respect to someone who
is mean.
¹⁰ Strangers will use up all your
wealth.
Your hard work will make
someone else rich.
¹¹ At the end of your life you
will groan.
Your skin and your body
will be worn out.
¹² You will say, "How I hated to
take advice!
How my heart refused to
be corrected!
¹³ I would not obey my
teachers.
I wouldn't listen to those
who taught me.
¹⁴ I was soon in deep trouble.
It happened right in front
of the whole assembly of
God's people."

15 Drink water from your own
    well.
  Drink running water from
    your own spring.
16 Should your springs pour out
    into the streets?
  Should your streams of
    water pour out in public
    places?
17 No! Let them belong to you
    alone.
  Never share them with
    strangers.
18 May your fountain be
    blessed.
  May the wife you married
    when you were young
    make you happy.
19 She is like a loving doe, a
    graceful deer.
  May her breasts always
    satisfy you.
  May you always be
    captured by her love.
20 My son, why be captured by
    another man's wife?
  Why hug a woman who has
    gone astray?
21 The LORD watches your
    ways.
  He studies all your paths.
22 Sinners are trapped by their
    own evil acts.
  They are held tight by the
    ropes of their sins.
23 They will die because they
    refused to be corrected.
  Their sins will capture
    them because they were
    very foolish.

Warnings Against Foolish Acts

6 My son, don't promise
    to pay for what your
    neighbor owes.

Don't agree to pay a
    stranger's bill.
2 Don't be trapped by what you
    have said.
  Don't be caught by the
    words of your mouth.
3 Instead, my son, do
    something to free
    yourself.
  Don't fall into your
    neighbor's hands.
  Go until you can't go
    anymore.
  Don't let your neighbor
    rest.
4 Don't let your eyes go to
    sleep.
  Don't let your eyelids close.
5 As a deer frees itself from a
    hunter, free yourself.
  As a bird frees itself from a
    trapper, free yourself.

6 You people who don't want
    to work, think about the
    ant!
  Consider its ways and be
    wise!
7 It has no commander.
  It has no leader or ruler.
8 But it stores up its food in
    summer.
  It gathers its food at
    harvest time.
9 You lazy people, how long
    will you lie there?
  When will you get up from
    your sleep?
10 You might sleep a little or
    take a little nap.
  You might even fold your
    hands and rest.
11 Then you would be poor, as
    if someone had robbed
    you.

You would have little, as
if someone had stolen
from you.
12 An evil troublemaker
goes around saying twisted
things with his mouth.
13   He winks with his eyes.
He makes signals with his
feet.
He motions with his
fingers.
14   His plans are evil, and he
has lies in his heart.
He is always stirring up
fights.
15 Trouble will catch up with
him in an instant.
He will suddenly be
destroyed, and nothing
can save him.

16 There are six things the
LORD hates.
In fact, he hates seven
things.
17 The LORD hates proud
eyes,
a lying tongue,
and hands that kill
those who aren't guilty.
18 He also hates hearts
that make evil plans
and feet that are quick
to do evil.
19 He hates any witness
who pours out lies
and anyone who stirs
up conflict in the com-
munity.

A Warning Against Committing Adultery

20 My son, keep your father's
command.
Don't turn away from your
mother's teaching.

21 Always tie them on your
heart.
Put them around your
neck.
22 When you walk, they will
guide you.
When you sleep, they will
watch over you.
When you wake up, they
will speak to you.
23 Your father's command is
like a lamp.
Your mother's teaching is
like a light.
And whatever instructs and
corrects you
leads to life.
24 It keeps you from your
neighbor's wife.
It keeps you from the
smooth talk of a woman
who commits adultery.
25 Don't hunger in your heart
after her beauty.
Don't let her eyes capture
you.
26 A prostitute can be bought
for only a loaf of bread.
But another man's wife
hunts your very life.
27 You can't shovel fire into your
lap
without burning your
clothes.
28 You can't walk on hot coals
without burning your
feet.
29 It's the same for anyone who
has sex with another
man's wife.
Anyone who touches her
will be punished.

30 People don't hate a thief who
steals
to fill his empty stomach.

³¹ But when he is caught, he
must pay seven times as
much as he stole.
It may even cost him
everything he has.
³² A man who commits adultery
has no sense.
Anyone who does it
destroys himself.
³³ He will be beaten up and
dishonored.
His shame will never be
wiped away.
³⁴ Jealousy stirs up a husband's
anger.
He will show no mercy
when he gets even.
³⁵ He won't accept any
payment.
He won't take any money,
no matter how much he
is offered.

*A Warning Against a Woman
Who Commits Adultery*

7 My son, obey my words.
Store up my commands
inside you.
² Obey my commands and you
will live.
Guard my teachings as you
would guard your own
eyes.
³ Tie them on your fingers.
Write them on the tablet of
your heart.
⁴ Say to wisdom, "You are my
sister."
Say to understanding, "You
are a member of my
family."
⁵ They will keep you from a
woman who commits
adultery.

They will keep you from
the smooth talk of a
sinful wife.
⁶ I stood at the window of my
house.
I looked down through it.
⁷ Among those who were
childish
I saw a young man who
had no sense.
⁸ He went down the street
near that sinful woman's
corner.
He walked toward her
house.
⁹ The sun had gone down, and
the day was fading.
The darkness of night was
falling.
¹⁰ A woman came out to meet
him.
She was dressed like a
prostitute and had a
clever plan.
¹¹ She was wild and pushy.
She never stayed at home.
¹² Sometimes she's in the
streets. Sometimes she's
at other places.
At every corner she waits.
¹³ She took hold of the young
man and kissed him.
With a bold face she spoke
to him. She said,
¹⁴ "Today I offered what I
promised I would.
At home I have meat left
over from my fellowship
offering.
¹⁵ So I came out to meet you.
I looked for you and have
found you!
¹⁶ I have covered my bed

with colored sheets from
    Egypt.
¹⁷ I've perfumed my bed with
    spices.
    I used myrrh, aloes and
        cinnamon.
¹⁸ Come, let's drink our fill of
    love until morning.
    Let's enjoy ourselves by
        sleeping together!
¹⁹ My husband isn't home.
    He's gone on a long
        journey.
²⁰ He took his bag full of money.
    He won't be home for
        several days."
²¹ She led him astray with her
    clever words.
    She charmed him with her
        smooth talk.
²² All at once he followed her.
    He was like an ox going to
        be killed.
    He was like a deer stepping
        into a trap
²³   until an arrow struck its
        liver.
    He was like a bird rushing
        into a trap.
    Little did he know it would
        cost him his life!
²⁴ My sons, listen to me.
    Pay attention to what I say.
²⁵ Don't let your hearts turn to
    her ways.
    Don't step onto her paths.
²⁶ She has brought down a lot of
    men.
    She has killed a huge
        crowd.
²⁷ Her house is a road to the
    grave.
    It leads down to the place
        of the dead.

Wisdom Calls Out

8 Doesn't wisdom call out?
    Doesn't understanding
        raise her voice?
² At the highest point along the
    way,
    she takes her place where
        the paths meet.
³ Beside the gate leading into
    the city,
    she cries out at the
        entrance. She says,
⁴ "People, I call out to you.
    I raise my voice to all
        human beings.
⁵ You who are childish, get
    some good sense.
    You who are foolish, set
        your hearts on getting it.
⁶ Listen! I have things to
    say that you can
        depend on.
    I open my lips to speak
        what is right.
⁷ My mouth speaks what is
    true.
    My lips hate evil.
⁸ All the words of my mouth
    are honest.
    None of them is twisted or
        sinful.
⁹ To those who have
    understanding, all my
        words are right.
    To those who have found
        knowledge, they are
        true.
¹⁰ Choose my teaching instead
    of silver.
    Choose knowledge rather
        than fine gold.
¹¹ Wisdom is worth more than
    rubies.
    Nothing you want can
        compare with her.

12 "I, wisdom, live together with
understanding.
I have knowledge and good
sense.
13 To have respect for the LORD
is to hate evil.
I hate pride and bragging.
I hate evil ways and
twisted words.
14 I have good sense and give
good advice.
I have understanding and
power.
15 By me kings rule.
Leaders make laws that are
fair.
16 By me princes and nobles
govern.
It is by me that anyone
rules on earth.
17 I love those who love me.
Those who look for me find
me.
18 With me are riches and
honor.
With me are lasting wealth
and success.
19 My fruit is better than fine
gold.
My gifts are better than the
finest silver.
20 I walk in ways that are
honest.
I take paths that are
right.
21 I leave riches to those who
love me.
I give them more than they
have room for.
22 "The LORD created me as the
first of his works,
before his acts of long
ago.
23 I was formed a long, long
time ago.

I was formed at the very
beginning, when the
world was created.
24 Before there were any
oceans, I was born.
It was before there were
springs flowing with
water.
25 Before the mountains were
settled in place, I was
born.
Before there were any hills,
I was born.
26 It happened before the LORD
made the world and its
fields.
It was before he made the
dust of the earth.
27 I was there when he set the
heavens in place.
When he marked out the
place where the sky
meets the sea, I was
there.
28 That was when he put the
clouds above.
It was when he fixed the
ocean springs in place.
29 It was when he set limits for
the sea
so that the waters had to
obey his command.
When the LORD marked out
the foundations of the
earth, I was there.
30 I was constantly at his
side.
I was filled with delight day
after day.
I was always happy to be
with him.
31 His whole world filled me
with joy.
I took delight in all human
beings.

32 "My children, listen to me.
    Blessed are those who keep
        my ways.
33 Listen to my teaching and be
        wise.
    Don't turn away from it.
34 Blessed are those who listen
        to me.
    They watch every day at
        my doors.
    They wait beside my
        doorway.
35 Those who find me find life.
    They receive blessing from
        the LORD.
36 But those who don't find me
    harm only themselves.
    Everyone who hates me
        loves death."

Wisdom and Foolishness Call Out

9 Wisdom has built her
    house.
    She has set up its seven
        pillars.
2 She has prepared her meat
        and mixed her wine.
    She has also set her table.
3 She has sent out her servants.
    She calls out from the
        highest point of the
        city.
4 She says, "Let all who are
        childish come to my
        house!"
    She speaks to those who
        have no sense. She says,
5 "Come and eat my food.
    Drink the wine I have
        mixed.
6 Leave your childish ways and
        you will live.
    Walk in the way of
        understanding."

7 When you correct someone
        who makes fun of others,
    you might be laughed at.
    When you warn a sinner,
        you might get hurt.
8 Don't warn those who make
        fun of others, or they will
        hate you.
    Warn those who are wise,
        and they will love you.
9 Teach a wise person, and
        they will become even
        wiser.
    Teach a person who does
        right, and they will learn
        even more.

10 If you want to become wise,
        you must begin by
        respecting the LORD.
    To know the Holy One is to
        gain understanding.
11 Through wisdom, you will
        live a long time.
    Years will be added to your
        life.
12 If you are wise, your wisdom
        will reward you.
    If you make fun of others,
        you alone will suffer.
13 The woman called
        Foolishness is wild.
    She is childish and knows
        nothing.
14 She sits at the door of her
        house.
    She sits at the highest point
        of the city.
15 She calls out to those who
        pass by.
    She calls out to those who
        go straight on their way.
    She says,
16 "Let all who are childish
        come to my house!"

She speaks to those who
have no sense.
[17] She says, "Stolen water is sweet.
Food eaten in secret tastes
good!"
[18] But they don't know that
dead people are there.
They don't know that her
guests are deep in the
place of the dead.

The Proverbs of Solomon

10 These are the proverbs of
Solomon.

A wise son makes his father
glad.
But a foolish son brings
sorrow to his mother.
[2] Riches that are gained by
sinning aren't worth
anything.
But doing what is right
saves you from death.
[3] The LORD gives those who do
right the food they need.
But he lets those who do
wrong go hungry.
[4] Hands that don't want to
work make you poor.
But hands that work hard
bring wealth to you.
[5] A child who gathers crops in
summer is wise.
But a child who sleeps
at harvest time brings
shame.
[6] Blessings are like crowns on
the heads of those who
do right.
But the trouble caused
by what sinners say
destroys them.

[7] The names of those who
do right are used in
blessings.
But the names of those
who do wrong will rot.
[8] A wise heart accepts
commands.
But foolish chattering
destroys you.
[9] Anyone who lives without
blame walks safely.
But anyone who takes a
crooked path will get
caught.
[10] An evil wink gets you into
trouble.
And foolish chattering
destroys you.
[11] The mouths of those who do
right pour out life like a
fountain.
But the mouths of sinners
hide their evil plans.
[12] Hate stirs up fights.
But love erases all sins by
forgiving them.
[13] Wisdom is found on the lips
of those who understand
what is right.
But those who have no
sense are punished.
[14] Wise people store up
knowledge.
But the mouths of foolish
people destroy them.
[15] The wealth of rich people is
like a city that makes
them feel safe.
But having nothing
destroys those who are
poor.

16 People who do what is right
  earn life.
But sinners earn sin and
  death.

17 Anyone who pays attention
  to correction
  shows the path to life.
But anyone who refuses to be
  corrected
  leads others down the
  wrong path.

18 Anyone who hides hatred
  with lying lips
and spreads lies is foolish.

19 Sin is not ended by using
  many words.
But those who are wise
  control their tongues.

20 The tongues of those who do
  right are like fine silver.
But the hearts of those who
  do wrong aren't worth
  very much.

21 The words of those who do
  right benefit many people.
But those who are foolish
  die because they have no
  sense.

22 The blessing of the LORD
  brings wealth.
And it comes without
  painful work.

23 A foolish person finds
  pleasure in evil plans.
But a person who has
  understanding takes
  delight in wisdom.

24 What sinners are afraid of
  will catch up with them.
But those who do right will
  get what they want.

25 When the storm is over,
  sinners are gone.
But those who do right
  stand firm forever.

26 Those who don't want to
  work hurt those who
  send them.
They are like vinegar on
  the teeth or smoke in the
  eyes.

27 Having respect for the LORD
  leads to a longer life.
But the years of evil people
  are cut short.

28 Those who do right can
  expect joy.
But the hopes of sinners
  are bound to fail.

29 The way of the LORD is a safe
  place for those without
  blame.
But that way destroys those
  who do evil.

30 Those who do right will never
  be removed from the
  land.
But those who do wrong
  will not remain in it.

31 The mouths of those who do
  right produce wisdom.
But tongues that speak
  twisted words will be
  made silent.

32 Those who do right know the
  proper thing to say.
But those who do wrong
  speak only twisted
  words.

11 The LORD hates it when
  people use scales to
  cheat others.

But he is delighted when
people use honest
weights.

2 When pride comes, shame
follows.
But wisdom comes to those
who are not proud.

3 Those who do what is right
are guided by their
honest lives.
But those who aren't
faithful are destroyed by
their lies.

4 Wealth isn't worth anything
when God judges you.
But doing what is right
saves you from death.

5 The ways of honest people
are made straight
because they do what is
right.
But those who do what is
wrong are brought down
by their own sins.

6 Godly people are saved by
doing what is right.
But those who aren't
faithful are trapped by
evil longings.

7 Hopes placed in human
beings will die with them.
Everything their power
promised comes to
nothing.

8 Those who do right are saved
from trouble.
But trouble comes on those
who do wrong.

9 With their words ungodly
people destroy their
neighbors.

But those who do what is
right escape because of
their knowledge.

10 When those who do right
succeed, their city is
glad.
When those who do wrong
die, people shout for joy.

11 The blessing of honest people
builds up a city.
But the words of sinners
destroy it.

12 Whoever makes fun of their
neighbor has no sense.
But the one who has
understanding controls
their tongue.

13 Those who talk about others
will tell secrets.
But those who can be
trusted keep the secrets
of others.

14 Without guidance a nation
falls.
But many good advisers
can bring victory to a
nation.

15 Whoever promises to pay for
what someone else owes
will certainly suffer.
But a person who doesn't
agree to pay someone
else's bill is safe.

16 A woman who has a kind
heart gains honor.
But men who are not kind
gain only wealth.

17 Those who are kind benefit
themselves.
But mean people bring
ruin on themselves.

¹⁸ An evil person really earns
    nothing.
But the one who plants
    what is right will
    certainly be rewarded.

¹⁹ Surely right living leads to
    life.
But whoever runs after evil
    finds death.

²⁰ The LORD hates those whose
    hearts are twisted.
But he is pleased with
    those who live without
    blame.

²¹ You can be sure that sinners
    will be punished.
And you can also be sure
    that godly people will go
    free.

²² A beautiful woman who has
    no sense
is like a gold ring in a pig's
    nose.

²³ What godly people long for
    ends only in what is
    good.
But what sinners hope for
    ends only in God's anger.

²⁴ One person gives freely but
    gets even richer.
Another person doesn't
    give what they should
    but gets even poorer.

²⁵ Anyone who gives a lot will
    succeed.
Anyone who renews others
    will be renewed.

²⁶ People ask for bad things
    to happen to those
    who store up grain for
    themselves.

But people ask for God's
    blessing on those who
    are willing to sell.

²⁷ Anyone who looks for what is
    good will be blessed.
But bad things will happen
    to a person who plans to
    do evil.

²⁸ Those who trust in their
    riches will fall.
But those who do right will
    be as healthy as a green
    leaf.

²⁹ Those who bring ruin on
    their families will receive
    nothing but wind.
And foolish people will
    serve wise people.

³⁰ The fruit that godly people
    bear is like a tree of life.
And those who are wise
    save lives.

³¹ Godly people get what they
    should get on earth.
So ungodly people and
    sinners will certainly get
    what they should get!

12 Anyone who loves
    correction loves
    knowledge.
Anyone who hates to be
    corrected is stupid.

² The LORD blesses anyone
    who does good.
But he judges anyone who
    plans to do evil.

³ No one can become strong
    and steady by doing evil.
But if people do what
    is right, they can't be
    removed from the land.

⁴ An excellent woman is her
husband's crown.
But a wife who brings
shame is like sickness in
his bones.

⁵ The plans of godly people are
right.
But the advice of sinners
will lead you the wrong
way.

⁶ The words of those who are
evil hide and wait to spill
people's blood.
But the speech of those
who are honest saves
them from traps like
that.

⁷ Sinners are destroyed and
taken away.
But the houses of godly
people stand firm.

⁸ A person is praised for how
wise they are.
But people hate anyone
who has a twisted mind.

⁹ Being nobody and having a
servant
is better than pretending to
be somebody and having
no food.

¹⁰ Those who do what is right
take good care of their
animals.
But the kindest acts of
those who do wrong are
mean.

¹¹ Those who farm their land
will have plenty of food.
But those who chase
dreams have no sense.

¹² Those who do what is wrong
are safe for just a while.

But those who do what is
right last forever.

¹³ Those who do evil are
trapped by their sinful
talk.
But those who have done
no wrong escape trouble.

¹⁴ Many good things come from
what people say.
And the work of their
hands rewards them.

¹⁵ The way of foolish people
seems right to them.
But those who are wise
listen to advice.

¹⁶ Foolish people are easily
upset.
But wise people pay no
attention to hurtful
words.

¹⁷ An honest witness tells the
truth.
But a dishonest witness
tells lies.

¹⁸ The words of thoughtless
people cut like swords.
But the tongue of wise
people brings healing.

¹⁹ Truthful words last forever.
But lies last for only a
moment.

²⁰ There are lies in the hearts of
those who plan evil.
But there is joy for those
who work to bring peace.

²¹ No harm comes to godly
people.
But sinners have all the
trouble they can handle.

²² The LORD hates those whose
lips tell lies.

But he is pleased with
people who tell the
truth.

23 Wise people keep their
knowledge to
themselves.
But the hearts of foolish
people shout foolish
things.

24 Hands that work hard will
rule.
But people who are lazy
will be forced to work.

25 Worry makes the heart
heavy.
But a kind word cheers it
up.

26 Godly people are careful
about the friends they
choose.
But the way of sinners
leads them down the
wrong path.

27 Lazy people do not even cook
what they catch.
But those who work hard
eat their fill of what is
hunted.

28 There is life in doing what is
right.
Along that path you will
never die.

13 A wise son pays attention
to what his father
teaches him.
But anyone who makes fun
of others doesn't listen to
warnings.

2 The good things people say
benefit them.
But liars love to hurt others.

3 Those who guard what they
say guard their lives.
But those who speak
without thinking will be
destroyed.

4 People who refuse to work
want things and get
nothing.
But the desires of people
who work hard are
completely satisfied.

5 Those who do right hate what
is false.
But those who do wrong
stink and bring shame
on themselves.

6 Doing right guards those
who are honest.
But evil destroys those who
are sinful.

7 Some people pretend to be
rich but have nothing.
Others pretend to be poor
but have great wealth.

8 A person's riches might save
their life.
But a poor person is not
able to do anything
about danger.

9 The lights of godly people
shine brightly.
But the lamps of sinners
are blown out.

10 Where there is arguing, there
is pride.
But those who take advice
are wise.

11 Money gained in the wrong
way disappears.
But money gathered little
by little grows.

¹² Hope that is put off makes
    one sick at heart.
  But a desire that is met is
    like a tree of life.

¹³ Anyone who hates what they
    are taught will pay for it
    later.
  But a person who respects
    a command will be
    rewarded.

¹⁴ The teaching of wise people
    is like a fountain that
    gives life.
  It turns those who listen to
    it away from the jaws of
    death.

¹⁵ Good judgment wins favor.
  But the way of liars leads to
    their ruin.

¹⁶ Wise people act with
    knowledge.
  But foolish people show
    how foolish they are.

¹⁷ An evil messenger gets into
    trouble.
  But a trusted messenger
    brings healing.

¹⁸ Those who turn away from
    their training become
    poor and ashamed.
  But those who accept
    warnings are honored.

¹⁹ A desire that is met is like
    something that tastes
    sweet.
  But foolish people hate to
    turn away from evil.

²⁰ Walk with wise people and
    become wise.
  A companion of foolish
    people suffers harm.

²¹ Hard times chase those who
    are sinful.
  But those who do right
    are rewarded with good
    things.

²² A good person leaves
    what they own to
    their children and
    grandchildren.
  But a sinner's wealth is
    stored up for those who
    do right.

²³ An unplowed field produces
    food for poor people.
  But those who treat them
    badly destroy it all.

²⁴ Those who don't correct their
    children hate them.
  But those who love them
    are careful to correct
    them.

²⁵ Those who do right eat until
    they are full.
  But the stomachs of
    those who do wrong go
    hungry.

14 A wise woman builds her
    house.
  But a foolish woman tears
    hers down with her own
    hands.

² Whoever has respect for the
    Lord lives a good life.
  But those who hate him
    walk down an evil path.

³ The proud words of a foolish
    person sting like a whip.
  But the things wise people
    say keep them safe.

⁴ Where there are no oxen, the
    feed box is empty.

But a strong ox brings in
huge harvests.

5 An honest witness does not lie.
But a dishonest witness
pours out lies.

6 Those who make fun of
others look for wisdom
and don't find it.
But knowledge comes
easily to those who
understand what is right.

7 Stay away from a foolish
person.
You won't find knowledge
in what they say.

8 People are wise and
understanding when
they think about the way
they live.
But people are foolish
when their foolish ways
trick them.

9 Foolish people laugh at
making things right
when they sin.
But honest people try to do
the right thing.

10 Each heart knows its own
sadness.
And no one else can share
its joy.

11 The houses of sinners will be
destroyed.
But the tents of honest
people will stand firm.

12 There is a way that appears to
be right.
But in the end it leads to
death.

13 Even when you laugh, your
heart can be hurting.

And your joy can end in
sadness.

14 Those who aren't faithful will
be paid back
for what they've done.
And good people will receive
rewards
for how they've lived.

15 A childish person believes
anything.
But a wise person thinks
about how they live.

16 A wise person has respect
for the LORD and avoids
evil.
But a foolish person has a
bad temper and yet feels
secure.

17 Anyone who gets angry
quickly does foolish
things.
And a person who is tricky
is hated.

18 Childish people act in
keeping with their
foolish ways.
But knowledge makes wise
people feel like kings.

19 Evil people will bow down in
front of good people.
And those who do wrong
will bow down at the
gates of those who do
right.

20 Poor people are avoided even
by their neighbors.
But rich people have many
friends.

21 It is a sin to hate your neighbor.
But blessed is the person
who is kind to those in
need.

22 Those who plan evil go down
the wrong path.
But those who plan good
find love and truth.

23 All hard work pays off.
But if all you do is talk, you
will be poor.

24 The wealth of wise people is
their crown.
But the foolish ways of
foolish people lead to
what is foolish.

25 An honest witness saves
lives.
But a dishonest witness
tells lies.

26 Anyone who shows respect
for the LORD has a strong
tower.
It will be a safe place for
their children.

27 Respect for the LORD is like a
fountain that gives life.
It turns you away from the
jaws of death.

28 A large population is a king's
glory.
But a prince without
followers is destroyed.

29 Anyone who is patient has
great understanding.
But anyone who gets angry
quickly shows how
foolish they are.

30 A peaceful heart gives life to
the body.
But jealousy rots the
bones.

31 Anyone who crushes poor
people makes fun of
their Maker.

But anyone who is kind
to those in need honors
God.

32 When trouble comes, sinners
are brought down.
But godly people seek
safety in God even as
they die.

33 Wisdom rests in the hearts of
those who understand
what is right.
And even among foolish
people she makes herself
known.

34 Doing what is right lifts
people up.
But sin brings judgment to
any nation.

35 A king is pleased with a wise
servant.
But a servant who is full of
shame stirs up the king's
anger.

15 A gentle answer turns
anger away.
But mean words stir up
anger.

2 The tongues of wise people
use knowledge well.
But the mouths of foolish
people pour out foolish
words.

3 The eyes of the LORD are
everywhere.
They watch those who are
evil and those who are
good.

4 A tongue that calms is like a
tree of life.
But a tongue that tells lies
produces a broken spirit.

5 A foolish person turns their back on their parent's correction.
But anyone who accepts correction shows understanding.

6 The houses of those who do what is right hold great wealth.
But those who do what is wrong earn only ruin.

7 The lips of wise people spread knowledge.
But the hearts of foolish people are not honest.

8 The LORD hates the sacrifice of sinful people.
But the prayers of honest people please him.

9 The LORD hates how sinners live.
But he loves those who run after what is right.

10 Hard training is in store for anyone who leaves the right path.
A person who hates to be corrected will die.

11 Death and the Grave lie open in front of the LORD.
So human hearts certainly lie open to him!

12 People who make fun of others don't like to be corrected.
So they stay away from wise people.

13 A happy heart makes a face look cheerful.
But a sad heart produces a broken spirit.

14 A heart that understands what is right looks for knowledge.
But the mouths of foolish people feed on what is foolish.

15 All the days of those who are crushed are filled with pain and suffering.
But a cheerful heart enjoys a good time that never ends.

16 It is better to have respect for the LORD and have little than to be rich and have trouble.

17 A few vegetables where there is love
are better than the finest meat where there is hatred.

18 A person with a bad temper stirs up conflict.
But a person who is patient calms things down.

19 The way of people who don't want to work is blocked with thorns.
But the path of honest people is a wide road.

20 A wise son makes his father glad.
But a foolish son hates his mother.

21 A person who has no sense enjoys doing foolish things.
But a person who has understanding walks straight ahead.

22 Plans fail without good advice.

But they succeed when
there are many advisers.

23 Joy is found in giving the
right answer.
And how good is a word
spoken at the right time!

24 The path of life leads up for
those who are wise.
It keeps them from going
down to the place of the
dead.

25 The LORD tears down the
proud person's house.
But he keeps the widow's
property safe.

26 The LORD hates the thoughts
of sinful people.
But he considers kind
words to be pure.

27 Those who always want
more bring ruin to their
households.
But a person who refuses to
be paid to lie will live.

28 The hearts of those who do
right think about how
they will answer.
But the mouths of those
who do wrong pour out
evil.

29 The LORD is far away from
those who do wrong.
But he hears the prayers of
those who do right.

30 The cheerful look of a
messenger brings joy to
your heart.
And good news gives
health to your body.

31 Whoever listens to a warning
that gives life

will be at home among
those who are wise.

32 Those who turn away
from correction hate
themselves.
But anyone who accepts
correction gains
understanding.

33 Wisdom teaches you to have
respect for the LORD.
So don't be proud if you
want to be honored.

16 People make plans in
their hearts.
But the LORD puts the
correct answer on their
tongues.

2 Everything a person does
might seem pure to them.
But the LORD knows why
they do what they do.

3 Commit to the LORD
everything you do.
Then he will make your
plans succeed.

4 The LORD works everything
out to the proper end.
Even those who do wrong
were made for a day of
trouble.

5 The LORD hates all those who
have proud hearts.
You can be sure that they
will be punished.

6 Through love and truth sin is
paid for.
People avoid evil when
they have respect for the
LORD.

7 When the way you live
pleases the LORD,

he makes even your
enemies live at peace
with you.

⁸ It is better to have a little and
do right
than to have a lot and be
unfair.

⁹ In their hearts human beings
plan their lives.
But the LORD decides
where their steps will
take them.

¹⁰ A king speaks as if his words
come from God.
And what he says does not
turn right into wrong.

¹¹ Honest scales and balances
belong to the LORD.
He made all the weights in
the bag.

¹² A king hates it when his
people do what is wrong.
A ruler is made secure when
they do what is right.

¹³ Kings are pleased when what
you say is honest.
They value people who
speak what is right.

¹⁴ An angry king can order your
death.
But a wise person will try
to calm him down.

¹⁵ When a king's face is happy,
it means life.
His favor is like rain in the
spring.

¹⁶ It is much better to get
wisdom than gold.
It is much better to choose
understanding than
silver.

¹⁷ The path of honest people
takes them away from
evil.
Those who guard their
ways guard their lives.

¹⁸ If you are proud, you will be
destroyed.
If you are proud, you will
fall.

¹⁹ Suppose you are lowly in
spirit along with those
who are treated badly.
That's better than sharing
stolen goods with those
who are proud.

²⁰ If anyone pays attention to
what they're taught, they
will succeed.
Blessed is the person who
trusts in the LORD.

²¹ Wise hearts are known for
understanding what is
right.
Kind words make people
want to learn more.

²² Understanding is like a
fountain of life to those
who have it.
But foolish people are
punished for the foolish
things they do.

²³ The hearts of wise people
guide their mouths.
Their words make people
want to learn more.

²⁴ Kind words are like honey.
They are sweet to the spirit
and bring healing to the
body.

²⁵ There is a way that appears to
be right.

But in the end it leads to death.

26 The hunger of workers makes them work.
Their hunger drives them on.

27 A worthless person plans to do evil things.
Their words are like a burning fire.

28 A twisted person stirs up conflict.
Anyone who talks about others separates close friends.

29 A person who wants to hurt others tries to get them to sin.
That person leads them down a path that isn't good.

30 Whoever winks with their eye is planning to do wrong.
Whoever closes their lips tightly is up to no good.

31 Gray hair is a glorious crown.
You get it by living the right way.

32 It is better to be patient than to fight.
It is better to control your temper than to take a city.

33 Lots are cast into the lap to make decisions.
But everything they decide comes from the LORD.

17 It is better to eat a dry crust of bread in peace and quiet

than to eat a big dinner in a house full of fighting.

2 A wise servant will rule over a shameful child.
He will be given part of the property as if he were a family member.

3 Fire tests silver, and heat tests gold.
But the LORD tests our hearts.

4 Evil people listen to lies.
Lying people listen to evil.

5 Anyone who laughs at those who are poor makes fun of their Maker.
Anyone who is happy when others suffer will be punished.

6 Grandchildren are like a crown to older people.
And children are proud of their parents.

7 Fancy words don't belong in the mouths of ungodly fools.
And lies certainly don't belong in the mouths of rulers!

8 Those who give money think it will buy them favors.
They think that no matter where they turn, they will succeed.

9 Whoever wants to show love forgives a wrong.
But those who talk about it separate close friends.

10 A person who understands what is right learns more from just a warning

than a foolish person
learns from 100 strokes
with a whip.

¹¹ An evil person tries to keep
others from obeying
God.
The messenger of death
will be sent against
them.

¹² It is better to meet a bear
whose cubs have been
stolen
than to meet a foolish
person who is acting
foolishly.

¹³ Evil will never leave the
house
of anyone who pays back
evil for good.

¹⁴ Starting to argue is like
making a crack in a dam.
So drop the matter before a
fight breaks out.

¹⁵ The LORD hates two things.
He hates it when the guilty
are set free.
He also hates it when those
who aren't guilty are
punished.

¹⁶ Why should a foolish person
try to buy wisdom?
They are not even able to
understand it.

¹⁷ A friend loves at all times.
They are there to help
when trouble comes.

¹⁸ A person who has no sense
agrees to pay what other
people owe.
It isn't wise to promise to
pay other people's bills.

¹⁹ The one who loves to argue
loves to sin.
The one who builds a high
gate is just asking to be
destroyed.

²⁰ If your heart is twisted, you
won't succeed.
If your tongue tells lies, you
will get into trouble.

²¹ It is sad to have a foolish child.
The parents of a godless
fool have no joy.

²² A cheerful heart makes you
healthy.
But a broken spirit dries
you up.

²³ Anyone who does wrong
accepts favors in secret.
Then they turn what is
right into what is wrong.

²⁴ Anyone who understands
what is right keeps
wisdom in view.
But the eyes of a foolish
person look everywhere
else.

²⁵ A foolish child makes his
father sad
and his mother sorry.

²⁶ It isn't good to fine those who
aren't guilty.
So it certainly isn't good
to whip officials just
because they are honest.

²⁷ Anyone who has knowledge
controls their words.
Anyone who has
understanding is not
easily upset.

²⁸ We think even foolish people
are wise if they keep
silent.

We think they understand
what is right if they
control their tongues.

18 A person who isn't
friendly looks out only
for themselves.
They oppose all good sense
by starting fights.

2 Foolish people don't want to
understand.
They take delight in saying
only what they think.

3 People hate it when evil
comes.
And they refuse to honor
those who bring shame.

4 The words of a person's
mouth are like deep
water.
But the fountain of wisdom
is like a flowing stream.

5 It isn't good to favor those
who do wrong.
That would keep justice
from those who aren't
guilty.

6 What foolish people say leads
to arguing.
They are just asking for a
beating.

7 The words of foolish people
drag them down.
They are trapped by what
they say.

8 The words of anyone who
talks about others are
like tasty bites of food.
They go deep down inside
you.

9 Anyone who doesn't want to
work

is like someone who
destroys.

10 The name of the LORD is like
a strong tower.
Godly people run to it and
are safe.

11 The wealth of rich people is
like a city that makes
them feel safe.
They think of it as a city
with walls that can't be
climbed.

12 If a person's heart is proud,
they will be destroyed.
So don't be proud if you
want to be honored.

13 To answer before listening
is foolish and shameful.

14 A cheerful spirit gives
strength even during
sickness.
But you can't keep going if
you have a broken spirit.

15 Those whose hearts
understand what is right
get knowledge.
That's because the ears of
those who are wise listen
for it.

16 A gift opens the door
and helps the giver meet
important people.

17 In court, the first one to
speak seems right.
Then someone else comes
forward and questions
him.

18 Casting lots will put a stop to
arguing.
It will keep the strongest
enemies apart.

¹⁹ A broken friendship is harder
to handle than a city with
high walls around it.
And arguing is like the
locked gates of a mighty
city.

²⁰ Because of what they say
a person can fill their
stomach.
What their words produce
can satisfy them.

²¹ Your tongue has the power of
life and death.
Those who love to talk
will eat the fruit of their
words.

²² The one who finds a wife
finds what is good.
He receives favor from the
LORD.

²³ Poor people beg for mercy.
But rich people answer in a
mean way.

²⁴ A person with unfaithful
friends soon comes to
ruin.
But there is a friend who
sticks closer than a
brother.

19 It is better to be poor and
to live without blame
than to be foolish and to
twist words around.

² Getting excited about
something without
knowledge isn't good.
It's even worse to be in a
hurry and miss the way.

³ A person's own foolish acts
destroy their life.
But their heart is angry
with the LORD.

⁴ Wealth brings many
friends.
But even the closest
friend of a poor person
abandons them.

⁵ A dishonest witness will be
punished.
And whoever pours out lies
will not go free.

⁶ Many try to win the favor of
rulers.
And everyone is the friend
of a person who gives
gifts.

⁷ Poor people are avoided by
their whole family.
Their friends avoid them
even more.
The poor person runs after
his friends to beg for
help.
But they can't be found.

⁸ Anyone who gets wisdom
loves life.
Anyone who values
understanding will soon
succeed.

⁹ A dishonest witness will be
punished.
And those who pour out
lies will die.

¹⁰ It isn't proper for a foolish
person to live in great
comfort.
And it is much worse
when a slave rules over
princes!

¹¹ A person's wisdom makes
them patient.
They will be honored if
they forgive someone
who sins against them.

¹² A king's anger is like a lion's
   roar.
   But his favor is like dew on
   the grass.

¹³ A foolish child is a father's
   ruin.
   A nagging wife is like
   dripping that never
   stops.

¹⁴ You will receive houses
   and wealth from your
   parents.
   But a wise wife is given by
   the LORD.

¹⁵ Anyone who doesn't want to
   work sleeps his life away.
   And a person who refuses
   to work goes hungry.

¹⁶ Those who keep
   commandments keep
   their lives.
   But those who don't care
   how they live will die.

¹⁷ Anyone who is kind to poor
   people lends to the
   LORD.
   God will reward them for
   what they have done.

¹⁸ Train your children, because
   then there is hope.
   Don't do anything to bring
   about their deaths.

¹⁹ A person with a bad temper
   must pay for it.
   If you save them, you will
   have to do it again.

²⁰ Listen to advice and accept
   correction.
   In the end you will be
   counted among those
   who are wise.

²¹ A person may have many
   plans in their heart.
   But the LORD's purpose
   wins out in the end.

²² Everyone longs for love that
   never fails.
   It is better to be poor than
   to be a liar.

²³ Having respect for the LORD
   leads to life.
   Then you will be content
   and free from trouble.

²⁴ A person who doesn't want to
   work leaves his hand in
   the dish.
   He won't even bring it back
   up to his mouth!

²⁵ If you whip a person who
   makes fun of others,
   childish people will learn
   to be wise.
   If you warn those who
   already understand what
   is right,
   they will gain even more
   knowledge.

²⁶ Anyone who robs their father
   and drives out their
   mother
   is a child who brings
   shame and dishonor.

²⁷ My son, if you stop listening
   to what I teach you,
   you will wander away from
   the words of knowledge.

²⁸ A dishonest witness makes
   fun of what is right.
   The mouths of those who
   do wrong gulp down evil.

²⁹ Those who make fun of
   others will be judged.

Foolish people will be
    punished.

20 Wine causes you to make
    fun of others, and beer
    causes you to start fights.
    Anyone who is led astray
    by them is not wise.

² A king's anger brings terror
    like a lion's roar.
    Anyone who makes him
    angry may lose their life.

³ Avoiding a fight brings honor
    to a person.
    But every foolish person is
    quick to argue.

⁴ Anyone who refuses to work
    doesn't plow in the right
    season.
    When they look for a crop
    at harvest time, they
    don't find it.

⁵ The purposes of a person's
    heart are like deep
    water.
    But one who has
    understanding brings
    them out.

⁶ Many claim to have love that
    never fails.
    But who can find a faithful
    person?

⁷ Those who do what is right
    live without blame.
    Blessed are their children
    after them.

⁸ A king sits on his throne to
    judge.
    He gets rid of all evil when
    he sees it.

⁹ No one can say, "I have kept
    my heart pure.

I'm 'clean,' and I haven't
    sinned."

¹⁰ The LORD hates two things.
    He hates weights that
    weigh things heavier or
    lighter than they really
    are.
    He also hates measures
    that measure things
    larger or smaller than
    they really are.

¹¹ Even small children are
    known by their actions.
    So is their conduct really
    pure and right?

¹² The LORD has made two
    things.
    He has made ears that
    hear.
    He has also made eyes that
    see.

¹³ Don't love sleep, or you will
    become poor.
    Stay awake, and you will
    have more food than you
    need.

¹⁴ "It's no good. It's no good!"
    says a buyer.
    Then off they go and brag
    about what they
    bought.

¹⁵ There is gold, and there are
    plenty of rubies.
    But lips that speak
    knowledge are a
    priceless jewel.

¹⁶ Take the coat of one who puts
    up money for what a
    stranger owes.
    Hold it until you get paid
    back if it is done for an
    outsider.

17 Food gained by cheating
     tastes sweet.
   But you will end up with a
     mouth full of gravel.
18 Plans are made by asking for
     guidance.
   So if you go to war, get
     good advice.
19 A person who talks about
     others tells secrets.
   So avoid anyone who talks
     too much.
20 If anyone asks for bad things
     to happen to their father
     or mother,
   that person's lamp will
     be blown out in total
     darkness.
21 Property that you claim too
     soon
   will not be blessed in the
     end.
22 Don't say, "I'll get even with
     you for the wrong you
     did to me!"
   Wait for the LORD, and he
     will make things right
     for you.
23 The LORD hates weights that
     weigh things heavier or
     lighter than they really
     are.
   Scales that are not honest
     don't please him.
24 The LORD directs a person's
     steps.
   So how can anyone
     understand their own
     way?
25 A person is trapped if they
     make a hasty promise to
     God

and only later thinks about
     what they said.
26 A wise king gets rid of evil
     people.
   He runs the threshing
     wheel over them.
27 The spirit of a person is the
     lamp of the LORD.
   It lights up what is deep
     down inside them.
28 Love and truth keep a king
     safe.
   Faithful love makes his
     throne secure.
29 Young men are proud of their
     strength.
   Gray hair brings honor to
     old men.
30 Blows and wounds scrub evil
     away.
   And beatings make you
     pure deep down inside.

21 In the LORD's hand the
     king's heart is like a
     stream of water.
   The LORD directs it toward
     all those who please him.

2 A person might think their
     own ways are right.
   But the LORD knows what
     they are thinking.

3 Do what is right and fair.
   The LORD accepts that
     more than sacrifices.

4 The proud eyes and hearts of
     sinful people are like a
     field not plowed.
   Those things produce
     nothing good.

5 The plans of people who
     work hard succeed.

You can be just as sure
   that those in a hurry will
   become poor.

⁶ A fortune made by people
   who tell lies
   amounts to nothing and
   leads to death.

⁷ The harmful things that evil
   people do will drag them
   away.
   They refuse to do what is
   right.

⁸ The path of those who are
   guilty is crooked.
   But the conduct of those
   who are not guilty is
   honest.

⁹ It is better to live on a corner
   of a roof
   than to share a house with
   a nagging wife.

¹⁰ Sinful people long to do evil.
   They don't show their
   neighbors any mercy.

¹¹ When you punish someone
   who makes fun of others,
   childish people get wise.
   By paying attention to wise
   people, the childish get
   knowledge.

¹² The Blameless One knows
   where sinners live.
   And he destroys them.

¹³ Whoever refuses to listen to
   the cries of poor people
   will also cry out and not be
   answered.

¹⁴ A secret gift calms down
   anger.
   A hidden favor softens
   great anger.

¹⁵ When you do what is fair, you
   make godly people glad.
   But you terrify those who
   do what is evil.

¹⁶ Whoever leaves the path of
   understanding
   ends up with those who are
   dead.

¹⁷ Anyone who loves pleasure
   will become poor.
   Anyone who loves wine
   and olive oil will never
   be rich.

¹⁸ Evil people become the
   payment for setting
   godly people free.
   Those who aren't faithful
   are the payment for
   honest people.

¹⁹ It is better to live in a desert
   than to live with a nagging
   wife who loves to argue.

²⁰ Wise people store up the best
   food and olive oil.
   But foolish people eat up
   everything they have.

²¹ Anyone who wants to be
   godly and loving
   finds life, success and
   honor.

²² A wise person can attack a
   strong city.
   They can pull down the
   place of safety its people
   trust in.

²³ Those who are careful about
   what they say
   keep themselves out of
   trouble.

²⁴ A proud person is called a
   mocker.

He thinks much too highly
of himself.

25 Some people will die while
they are still hungry.
That's because their hands
refuse to work.

26 All day long they hunger for
more.
But godly people give
without holding back.

27 God hates sacrifices that are
brought by evil people.
He hates it even more
when they bring them
for the wrong reason.

28 Witnesses who aren't honest
will die.
But anyone who listens
carefully will be a
successful witness.

29 Sinful people try to look as if
they were bold.
But honest people think
about how they live.

30 No wisdom, wise saying or
plan
can succeed against the
LORD.

31 You can prepare a horse for
the day of battle.
But the power to win
comes from the LORD.

22 You should want a good
name more than you
want great riches.
To be highly respected is
better than having silver
or gold.

2 The LORD made rich people
and poor people.
That's what they have in
common.

3 Wise people see danger and
go to a safe place.
But childish people keep
going and suffer for it.

4 Being humble comes from
having respect for the
LORD.
This will bring you wealth
and honor and life.

5 Thorns and traps lie in the
paths of evil people.
But those who value their
lives stay far away from
them.

6 Start children off on the right
path.
And even when they are
old, they will not turn
away from it.

7 Rich people rule over those
who are poor.
Borrowers are slaves to
lenders.

8 Anyone who plants evil
gathers a harvest of
trouble.
Their power to treat others
badly will be destroyed.

9 Those who give freely will be
blessed.
That's because they share
their food with those
who are poor.

10 If you drive away those who
make fun of others,
fighting also goes away.
Arguing and unkind words
will stop.

11 A person who has a pure and
loving heart and speaks
kindly
will be a friend of the king.

¹² The eyes of the LORD keep
watch over knowledge.
But he does away with
the words of those who
aren't faithful.

¹³ People who don't want to
work say, "There's a lion
outside!"
Or they say, "I'll be
murdered if I go out into
the streets!"

¹⁴ The mouth of a woman who
commits adultery is like
a deep pit.
Any man the LORD is angry
with falls into it.

¹⁵ Children are going to do
foolish things.
But correcting them will
drive that foolishness far
away.

¹⁶ You might treat poor people
badly or give gifts to rich
people.
Trying to get rich in these
ways will instead make
you poor.

30 Sayings of Wise People

Saying 1

¹⁷ Pay attention and listen
to the sayings of wise
people.
Apply your heart to the
sayings I teach.

¹⁸ It is pleasing when you
keep them in your
heart.
Have all of them ready on
your lips.

¹⁹ You are the one I am teaching
today.

That's because I want you
to trust in the LORD.

²⁰ I have written 30 sayings for
you.
They will give you
knowledge and good
advice.

²¹ I am teaching you to be
honest and to speak the
truth.
Then you can give honest
reports to those you
serve.

Saying 2

²² Don't take advantage of poor
people just because they
are poor.
Don't treat badly those
who are in need by
taking them to court.

²³ The LORD will stand up for
them in court.
He will require the lives of
people who have taken
the lives of those in
need.

Saying 3

²⁴ Don't be a friend of a person
who has a bad temper.
Don't go around with a
person who gets angry
easily.

²⁵ You might learn their habits.
And then you will be
trapped by them.

Saying 4

²⁶ Don't agree to pay for what
someone else owes.
And don't agree to pay their
bills for them.

²⁷ If you don't have the money
to pay,

your bed will be taken
  right out from under you!

Saying 5

28 Don't move old boundary
    stones
  set up by your people of
    long ago.

Saying 6

29 Do you see someone who
    does good work?
  That person will serve
    kings.
  That person won't serve
    officials of lower rank.

Saying 7

23 When you sit down to eat
  with a ruler,
  look carefully at what's in
    front of you.
2 Put a knife to your throat
  if you like to eat too much.
3 Don't long for his fancy food.
  It can fool you.

Saying 8

4 Don't wear yourself out to get
    rich.
  Don't trust how wise you
    think you are.
5 When you take even a quick
    look at riches, they are
    gone.
  They grow wings and fly
    away into the sky like an
    eagle.

Saying 9

6 Don't eat the food of anyone
    who doesn't want to
    share it.
  Don't long for his fancy
    food.

7 He is the kind of person
  who is always thinking
    about how much it costs.
  "Eat and drink," he says to
    you.
  But he doesn't mean it.
8 You will throw up what little
    you have eaten.
  You will have wasted your
    words of praise.

Saying 10

9 Don't speak to foolish people.
  They will laugh at your
    wise words.

Saying 11

10 Don't move old boundary
    stones.
  Don't try to take over the
    fields of children whose
    fathers have died.
11 That's because the God who
    guards them is strong.
  He will stand up for them
    in court against you.

Saying 12

12 Apply your heart to what you
    are taught.
  Listen carefully to words of
    knowledge.

Saying 13

13 Don't hold back correction
    from a child.
  If you correct them, they
    won't die.
14 So correct them.
  Then you will save them
    from death.

Saying 14

15 My son, if your heart is wise,
  my heart will be very glad.

¹⁶ Deep down inside, I will be
    happy
    when you say what is right.

Saying 15

¹⁷ Do not long for what sinners
    have.
    But always show great
    respect for the LORD.
¹⁸ There really is hope for you in
    days to come.
    So your hope will not be
    cut off.

Saying 16

¹⁹ My son, listen and be wise.
    Set your heart on the right
    path.
²⁰ Don't join those who drink
    too much wine.
    Don't join those who stuff
    themselves with meat.
²¹ Those who drink or eat too
    much will become poor.
    If they sleep too much,
    they'll have to wear
    rags.

Saying 17

²² Listen to your father, who
    gave you life.
    Don't hate your mother
    when she is old.
²³ Buy the truth and don't sell it.
    Get wisdom, instruction
    and understanding as
    well.
²⁴ The father of a godly child is
    very happy.
    A man who has a wise son
    is glad.
²⁵ May your father and mother
    be glad.
    May the woman who gave
    birth to you be joyful.

Saying 18

²⁶ My son, give me your heart.
    May you be happy living
    the way you see me live.
²⁷ An unfaithful wife is like a
    deep pit.
    A wife who commits
    adultery is like a narrow
    well.
²⁸ She hides and waits like a
    thief.
    She causes many men to
    sin.

Saying 19

²⁹ Who has trouble? Who has
    sorrow?
    Who argues? Who has
    problems?
    Who has wounds for no
    reason? Who has red
    eyes?
³⁰ Those who spend too much
    time with wine.
    Or those who like to taste
    wine mixed with spices.
³¹ Don't look at wine when it is
    red.
    Don't look at it when it
    bubbles in the cup.
    And don't look at it when it
    goes down smoothly.
³² In the end it bites like a
    snake.
    It bites like a poisonous
    serpent.
³³ Your eyes will see strange
    sights.
    Your mind will imagine
    weird things.
³⁴ You will feel like someone
    sleeping on the ocean.
    You will think you are lying
    among the ropes in a
    boat.

35 "They hit me," you will say.
    "But I'm not hurt!
    They beat me. But I don't
        feel it!
    When will I wake up
        so I can find another
        drink?"

Saying 20

24 Do not want what evil
    people have.
    Don't long to be with
        them.
2 In their hearts they plan to
    hurt others.
    With their lips they talk
        about making trouble.

Saying 21

3 By wisdom a house is built.
    Through understanding it
        is made secure.
4 Through knowledge its
    rooms are filled
    with priceless and
        beautiful things.

Saying 22

5 Wise people have success by
    means of great power.
    Those who have
        knowledge gather
        strength.
6 If you go to war, you surely
    need guidance.
    If you want to win, you
        need many good
        advisers.

Saying 23

7 Wisdom is too high for
    foolish people.
    They shouldn't speak
        when people meet at
        the city gate to conduct
        business.

Saying 24

8 Anyone who thinks up sinful
    things to do
    will be known as one who
        plans evil.
9 Foolish plans are sinful.
    People hate those who
        make fun of others.

Saying 25

10 If you grow weak when
    trouble comes,
    your strength is very small!
11 Save those who are being led
    away to death.
    Hold back those who are
        about to be killed.
12 Don't say, "But we didn't
    know anything about
        this."
    Doesn't the God who
        knows what you are
        thinking see it?
    Doesn't the God who guards
        your life know it?
    He will pay back everyone
        for what they have done.

Saying 26

13 Eat honey, my son, because it
    is good.
    Honey from a honeycomb
        has a sweet taste.
14 I want you to know that
    wisdom is like honey for
        you.
    If you find it, there is hope
        for you tomorrow.
    So your hope will not be
        cut off.

Saying 27

15 Don't hide and wait like a
    burglar near a godly
        person's house.
    Don't rob their home.

16 Even if godly people fall
down seven times, they
always get up.
But those who are evil trip
and fall when trouble
comes.

Saying 28

17 Don't be happy when your
enemy falls.
When he trips, don't let
your heart be glad.
18 The LORD will see it, but he
won't be pleased.
He might turn his anger
away from your enemy.

Saying 29

19 Don't be upset because of evil
people.
Don't long for what sinners
have.
20 Tomorrow evil people won't
have any hope.
The lamps of sinners will
be blown out.

Saying 30

21 My son, have respect for the
LORD and the king.
Don't join with officials
who disobey them.
22 The LORD and the king will
suddenly destroy them.
Who knows what trouble
those two can bring?

More Sayings of Wise People

23 Here are more sayings of
wise people.

Taking sides in court is not
good.
24   A curse will fall on those
who say the guilty are
not guilty.

Nations will ask for bad
things to happen to
them.
People will speak against
them.
25 But it will go well with those
who sentence guilty
people.
Rich blessings will come to
them.

26 An honest answer
is like a kiss on the lips.

27 Put your outdoor work in
order.
Get your fields ready.
After that, build your
house.

28 Don't be a witness against
your neighbor for no
reason.
Would you use your lips to
tell lies?
29 Don't say, "I'll do to them
what they have done to
me.
I'll get even with them for
what they did."

30 I went past the field of
someone who didn't
want to work.
I went past the vineyard
of someone who didn't
have any sense.
31 Thorns had grown up
everywhere.
The ground was covered
with weeds.
The stone wall had fallen
down.
32 I applied my heart to what I
observed.
I learned a lesson from
what I saw.

33 You might sleep a little or
　　take a little nap.
　　You might even fold your
　　hands and rest.
34 Then you would be poor, as
　　if someone had robbed
　　you.
　　You would have little, as
　　if someone had stolen
　　from you.

More Proverbs of Solomon

25 These are more proverbs
of Solomon. They were
gathered together by the men of
Hezekiah, the king of Judah.

2 When God hides a matter, he
　　gets glory.
　　When kings figure out a
　　matter, they get glory.

3 The heavens are high and the
　　earth is deep.
　　In the same way, the minds
　　of kings are impossible
　　to figure out.

4 Remove the scum from the
　　silver.
　　Then the master worker
　　can make something out
　　of it.

5 Remove ungodly officials
　　from where the king is.
　　Then the king can make
　　his throne secure
　　because of the godliness
　　around him.

6 Don't brag in front of the
　　king.
　　Don't claim a place among
　　his great men.

7 Let the king say to you,
　　"Come up here."

That's better than for him
　　to shame you in front of
　　his nobles.

What you have seen with
　　your own eyes
8 　don't bring too quickly to
　　court.
What will you do in the end
　　if your neighbor puts you to
　　shame?

9 If you take your neighbor to
　　court,
　　don't tell others any secrets
　　you promised to keep.

10 If you do, someone might
　　hear it and put you to
　　shame.
　　And the charge against you
　　will stand.

11 The right ruling at the right
　　time
　　is like golden apples in
　　silver jewelry.

12 A wise judge's warning to a
　　listening ear
　　is like a gold earring or
　　jewelry made of fine
　　gold.

13 A messenger trusted by the
　　one who sends him
　　is like a drink cooled by
　　snow at harvest time.
　　He renews the spirit of his
　　master.

14 A person who brags about
　　gifts never given
　　is like wind and clouds that
　　don't produce rain.

15 If you are patient, you can
　　win an official over to
　　your side.

And gentle words can
break a bone.

16 If you find honey, eat just
enough.
If you eat too much of it,
you will throw up.
17 Don't go to your neighbor's
home very often.
If they see too much of you,
they will hate you.

18 A person who is a false witness
against a neighbor
is like a club, a sword or a
sharp arrow.

19 Trusting someone who is not
faithful when trouble
comes
is like a broken tooth or a
disabled foot.

20 You may sing songs to a
troubled heart.
But that's like taking a coat
away on a cold day.
It's like pouring vinegar on
a wound.

21 If your enemy is hungry, give
him food to eat.
If he is thirsty, give him
water to drink.
22 By doing these things, you
will pile up burning
coals on his head.
And the LORD will reward
you.

23 Like a north wind that brings
rain you didn't expect
is a crafty tongue that
brings looks of shock.

24 It is better to live on a corner
of a roof
than to share a house with
a nagging wife.

25 Hearing good news from a
land far away
is like drinking cold water
when you are tired.

26 Sometimes godly people give
in to those who are evil.
Then they become like a
muddy spring of water or
a polluted well.

27 It isn't good for you to eat too
much honey.
And you shouldn't try to
search out matters too
deep for you.

28 A person without self-control
is like a city whose walls
are broken through.

26 It isn't proper to honor a
foolish person.
That's like having snow
in summer or rain at
harvest time.

2 A curse given for no reason is
like a wandering bird or
a flying sparrow.
It doesn't go anywhere.

3 A whip is for a horse, and a
harness is for a donkey.
And a beating is for the
backs of foolish people.

4 Don't answer a foolish person
in keeping with their
foolish acts.
If you do, you yourself will
be just like them.

5 Answer a foolish person
in keeping with their
foolish acts.
If you do not, they will
be wise in their own
eyes.

6 Sending a message in the
hand of a foolish person
is like cutting off your feet
or drinking poison.

7 A proverb in the mouth of a
foolish person
is like disabled legs that are
useless.

8 Giving honor to a foolish
person
is like tying a stone in a
slingshot.

9 A proverb in the mouth of a
foolish person
is like a thorn in the hand
of someone who is
drunk.

10 Anyone who hires a foolish
person or someone who
is passing by
is like a person who shoots
arrows at just anybody.

11 Foolish people who do the
same foolish things
again
are like a dog that returns to
where it has thrown up.

12 Do you see a person who is
wise in their own eyes?
There is more hope for a
foolish person than for
them.

13 A person who doesn't want to
work says, "There's a lion
in the road!
There's an angry lion
wandering in the streets!"

14 A person who doesn't want to
work turns over in bed
just like a door that swings
back and forth.

15 A person who doesn't want to
work leaves his hand in
his plate.
He acts as if he is too tired
to bring his hand back
up to his mouth.

16 A person who doesn't want to
work is wiser in his own
eyes
than seven people who
give careful answers.

17 Don't be quick to get mixed
up in someone else's
fight.
That's like grabbing a stray
dog by its ears.

18 Suppose a crazy person
shoots
flaming arrows that can kill.
19 Someone who lies to their
neighbor
and says, "I was only
joking!" is just like that
crazy person.

20 If you don't have wood, your
fire goes out.
If you don't talk about
others, arguing dies
down.

21 Coal glows, and wood
burns.
And a person who argues
stirs up conflict.

22 The words of anyone who
talks about others are
like tasty bites of food.
They go deep down inside
you.

23 Warm words that come from
an evil heart
are like a shiny coating on
a clay pot.

²⁴Enemies use their words as a
mask.
They hide their evil plans
in their hearts.
²⁵Even though what they say
can be charming, don't
believe them.
That's because seven
things God hates fill that
person's heart.
²⁶Their hatred can be hidden
by lies.
But their evil plans will be
shown to everyone.

²⁷Whoever digs a pit will fall
into it.
If someone rolls a big
stone, it will roll back on
them.

²⁸A tongue that tells lies hates
the people it hurts.
And words that seem to
praise you destroy you.

27 Don't brag about
tomorrow.
You don't know what a day
will bring.

²Let another person praise
you, and not your own
mouth.
Let an outsider praise you,
and not your own lips.

³Stones are heavy, and sand
weighs a lot.
But letting a foolish person
make you angry is a
heavier load than both of
them.

⁴Anger is mean, and great
anger overpowers you.
But who can face
jealousy?

⁵Being warned openly is
better
than being loved in
secret.

⁶Wounds from a friend can be
trusted.
But an enemy kisses you
many times.

⁷When you are full, you even
hate honey.
When you are hungry,
even what is bitter tastes
sweet.

⁸Anyone who runs away from
home
is like a bird that flies away
from its nest.

⁹Perfume and incense bring
joy to your heart.
And the sweetness of a
friend comes from their
honest advice.

¹⁰Don't desert your friend or a
friend of your family.
And don't go to your
relative's house when
trouble strikes you.
A neighbor nearby is better
than a relative far away.

¹¹My son, be wise and bring joy
to my heart.
Then I can answer anyone
who makes fun of me.

¹²Wise people see danger and
go to a safe place.
But childish people keep
on going and suffer
for it.

¹³Take the coat of one who puts
up money for what a
stranger owes.

Hold it until you get paid
back if it is done for an
outsider.

[14] Suppose you loudly bless
your neighbor early in
the morning.
Then you might as well be
cursing him.

[15] A nagging wife is like the
dripping
of a leaky roof in a
rainstorm.

[16] Stopping her is like trying to
stop the wind.
It's like trying to grab olive
oil with your hand.

[17] As iron sharpens iron,
so one person sharpens
another.

[18] A person who guards a fig
tree will eat its fruit.
And a person who protects
their master will be
honored.

[19] When you look into water,
you see a likeness of your
face.
When you look into your
heart, you see what you
are really like.

[20] Death and the Grave are
never satisfied.
People's eyes are never
satisfied either.

[21] Fire tests silver, and heat tests
gold.
But people are tested
by the praise they
receive.

[22] Suppose you could grind a
foolish person in a mill.

Suppose you could grind
them as you would grind
grain with a tool.
Even then you could not
remove their foolishness
from them.

[23] Be sure you know how your
flocks are doing.
Pay careful attention to
your herds.

[24] Riches don't last forever.
And a crown is not secure
for all time to come.

[25] The hay is removed, and new
growth appears.
The grass from the hills is
gathered in.

[26] Then your lambs will provide
you with clothes.
And the money from
selling your goats will
buy you a field.

[27] You will have plenty of goats'
milk to feed your
family.
It will also feed your
female servants.

28

Sinners run away even
when no one is chasing
them.
But those who do what is
right are as bold as
lions.

[2] A country has many rulers
when its people don't
obey.
But an understanding
ruler knows how to keep
order.

[3] A ruler who treats poor
people badly
is like a pounding rain that
leaves no crops.

⁴Those who turn away from
instruction praise
sinners.
But those who learn from it
oppose them.

⁵Sinful people don't
understand what is right.
But those who worship
the LORD understand it
completely.

⁶It is better to be poor and live
without blame
than to be rich and follow a
crooked path.

⁷A child who understands
what is right learns from
instruction.
But a child who likes to eat
too much brings shame
on his father.

⁸Someone might get rich by
taking interest or profit
from poor people.
But that person only piles
up wealth for someone
who will be kind to poor
people.

⁹If you don't pay attention to
my instruction,
even your prayers are hated.

¹⁰Those who lead honest people
down an evil path
will fall into their own trap.
But those who are without
blame
will receive good things.

¹¹Rich people may think they
are wise.
But a poor person with
understanding knows
that rich people are
fooling themselves.

¹²When godly people win,
everyone is very happy.
But when sinners take
charge, everyone hides.

¹³Anyone who hides their sins
doesn't succeed.
But anyone who admits
their sins and gives them
up finds mercy.

¹⁴Blessed is the one who
always trembles in front
of God.
But anyone who makes
their heart stubborn will
get into trouble.

¹⁵An evil person who rules over
helpless people
is like a roaring lion or an
angry bear.

¹⁶A ruler who is mean to his
people takes money
from them by force.
But one who hates money
gained in the wrong way
will rule a long time.

¹⁷Anyone troubled by the guilt
of murder
will seek to escape their
guilt by death.
No one should keep them
from it.

¹⁸Anyone who lives without
blame is kept safe.
But anyone whose path is
crooked will fall into the
pit.

¹⁹Those who work their land
will have plenty of food.
But those who chase
dreams will be very poor.

²⁰A faithful person will be
richly blessed.

But anyone who wants to
get rich will be punished.

²¹ Favoring one person over
another is not good.
But a person will do wrong
for a piece of bread.

²² Those who won't share what
they have want to get
rich.
They don't know they are
going to be poor.

²³ It is better to warn a person
than to pretend to praise
them.
In the end that person will
be more pleased with
you.

²⁴ Anyone who steals from their
parents and says, "It's
not wrong,"
is just like someone who
destroys.

²⁵ People who always want
more stir up conflict.
But those who trust in the
LORD will succeed.

²⁶ Those who trust in
themselves are foolish.
But those who live wisely
are kept safe.

²⁷ Those who give to poor
people will have all they
need.
But those who close their
eyes to the poor will
receive many curses.

²⁸ When those who are evil take
charge, other people
hide.
But when those who are
evil die, godly people
grow stronger.

29 Whoever still won't
obey after being warned
many times
will suddenly be destroyed.
Nothing can save them.

² When those who do right
grow stronger, the
people are glad.
But when those who do
wrong become rulers,
the people groan.

³ A man who loves wisdom
makes his father glad.
But a man who spends
time with prostitutes
wastes his father's
wealth.

⁴ By doing what is fair, a king
makes a country secure.
But those who only want
money tear it down.

⁵ Those who only pretend to
praise their neighbors
are spreading a net to catch
them by the feet.

⁶ Sinful people are trapped by
their own sin.
But godly people shout for
joy and are glad.

⁷ Those who do what is right
want to treat poor people
fairly.
But those who do what is
wrong don't care about
the poor.

⁸ Those who make fun of
others stir up a city.
But wise people turn anger
away.

⁹ Suppose a wise person goes
to court with a foolish
person.

Then the foolish person
gets mad and pokes fun,
and there is no peace.

¹⁰ Murderers hate honest
people.
They try to kill those who
do what is right.

¹¹ Foolish people let their anger
run wild.
But wise people keep
themselves under
control.

¹² If rulers listen to lies,
all their officials become
evil.

¹³ The Lord gives sight to the
eyes of poor people and
those who treat others
badly.
That's what they both have
in common.

¹⁴ If a king judges poor people
fairly,
his throne will always be
secure.

¹⁵ If a child is corrected, they
become wise.
But a child who is not
corrected brings shame
to their mother.

¹⁶ When those who do wrong
grow stronger, so does sin.
But those who do right will
see them destroyed.

¹⁷ If you correct your children,
they will give you peace.
They will bring you the
delights you desire.

¹⁸ Where there is no message
from God, people don't
control themselves.

But blessed is the one
who obeys wisdom's
instruction.

¹⁹ Servants can't be corrected
only by words.
Even if they understand,
they won't obey.

²⁰ Have you seen someone
who speaks without
thinking?
There is more hope for
foolish people than for
that person.

²¹ A servant who has been
spoiled from youth
will have no respect for you
later on.

²² An angry person stirs up
fights.
And a person with a bad
temper commits many
sins.

²³ Pride brings a person low.
But those whose spirits are
low will be honored.

²⁴ To help a thief is to become
your own enemy.
When you go to court,
you won't dare to say
anything.

²⁵ If you are afraid of people, it
will trap you.
But if you trust in the Lord,
he will keep you safe.

²⁶ Many people want to meet a
ruler.
But only the Lord sees
that people are treated
fairly.

²⁷ Those who do what is right
hate dishonest people.

Those who do what is wrong hate honest people.

The Sayings of Agur

30 These sayings are the words of Agur, son of Jakeh. These sayings came from God.

This man said to Ithiel:

"I am weary, God.
But I can still have success.
² Surely I am only a dumb animal and not a man.
I don't understand as other men do.
³ I haven't learned wisdom.
And I don't know the things the Holy One knows.
⁴ Who has gone up to heaven and come down?
Whose hands have gathered up the wind?
Who has wrapped up the waters in a coat?
Who has set in place all the boundaries of the earth?
What is his name? What is his son's name?
Surely you know!

⁵ "Every word of God is perfect.
He is like a shield to those who trust in him.
He keeps them safe.
⁶ Don't add to his words.
If you do, he will correct you.
He will prove that you are a liar.

⁷ "Lord, I ask you for two things.
Don't refuse me before I die.
⁸ Keep lies far away from me.
Don't make me either poor or rich,
but give me only the bread I need each day.
⁹ If you don't, I might have too much.
Then I might say I don't know you.
I might say, 'Who is the Lord?'
Or I might become poor and steal.
Then I would bring shame to the name of my God.

¹⁰ "Don't tell lies about a servant when you talk to their master.
If you do, they will curse you, and you will pay for your lies.

¹¹ "Some people curse their fathers.
Others don't bless their mothers.
¹² Some are pure in their own eyes.
But their dirty sins haven't been washed away.
¹³ Some have eyes that are very proud.
They look down on others.
¹⁴ Some people have teeth like swords.
The teeth in their jaws are as sharp as knives.
They are ready to eat up the poor people of the earth.
They are ready to eat up those who are the most needy.

¹⁵ "A leech has two daughters.
They cry out, 'Give! Give!'

"Three things are never
satisfied.
Four things never say,
'Enough!'
¹⁶ The first is the grave.
The second is a woman
who can't have a baby.
The third is land, which
never gets enough wa-
ter.
And the fourth is fire,
which never says,
'Enough!'

¹⁷ "One person makes fun of
their father.
Another doesn't honor
their mother when she is
old.
The ravens of the valley will
peck out their eyes.
Then the vultures will eat
them.

¹⁸ "Three things are too
amazing for me.
There are four things I
don't understand.
¹⁹ The first is the way of
an eagle in the sky.
The second is the way
of a snake on a rock.
The third is the way of
a ship on the ocean.
And the fourth is the
way of a man with a
young woman.

²⁰ "This is the way of a woman
who commits adultery.
She eats and wipes her
mouth.
Then she says, 'I haven't
done anything wrong.'

²¹ "Under three things the
earth shakes.
Under four things it can't
stand up.
²² The first is a servant
who becomes a king.
The second is a foolish
and ungodly person
who gets plenty to eat.
²³ The third is a mean
woman who gets mar-
ried.
And the fourth is a
servant who takes the
place of the woman
she works for.

²⁴ "Four things on earth are
small.
But they are very wise.
²⁵ The first are ants, which
aren't very strong.
But they store up their
food in the summer.
²⁶ The second are hyraxes,
which aren't very power-
ful.
But they make their
home among the rocks.
²⁷ The third are locusts,
which don't have a king.
But they all march for-
ward in ranks.
²⁸ And the fourth are lizards, which your hand
can catch.
But you will find them
in kings' palaces.

²⁹ "Three things walk as if
they were kings.
Four things move as kings
do.
³⁰ The first is a lion, which
is mighty among the
animals. It doesn't

back away from any-
thing.
31 The second is a rooster,
which walks proudly.
The third is a billy goat.
And the fourth is a king,
who is secure against
any who might oppose
him.

32 "Do you do foolish things?
Do you think you are better
than others?
Do you plan evil?
If you do, put your hand
over your mouth and
stop talking!
33 If you churn cream, you will
produce butter.
If you twist a nose, you will
produce blood.
And if you stir up anger,
you will produce a fight."

The Sayings of King Lemuel

31 These are the sayings of
King Lemuel. His mother
taught them to him. These sayings came from God.

2 Listen, my son! Listen, my
very own son!
Listen, you who are the
answer to my prayers!
3 Don't waste your strength on
women.
Don't waste it on those who
destroy kings.

4 Lemuel, it isn't good for kings
to drink wine.
It isn't good for rulers to
long for beer.
5 If they do, they might drink
and forget what has been
commanded.

They might take away the
rights of all those who
are treated badly.
6 Let beer be for those who are
dying.
Let wine be for those who
are sad and troubled.
7 Let them drink and forget
how poor they are.
Let them forget their
suffering.

8 Speak up for those who can't
speak for themselves.
Speak up for the rights of
all those who are poor.
9 Speak up and judge fairly.
Speak up for the rights of
those who are poor and
needy.

The Excellent Woman

10 Who can find an excellent
woman?
She is worth far more than
rubies.
11 Her husband trusts her
completely.
She gives him all the
important things he
needs.
12 She brings him good, not harm,
all the days of her life.
13 She chooses wool and flax.
She loves to work with her
hands.
14 She is like the ships of traders.
She brings her food from
far away.
15 She gets up while it is still
night.
She provides food for her
family.
She also gives some to her
female servants.

16 She considers a field and
   buys it.
   She uses some of the
   money she earns to plant
   a vineyard.
17 She gets ready to work hard.
   Her arms are strong.
18 She sees that her trading
   earns a lot of money.
   Her lamp doesn't go out at
   night.
19 With one hand she holds the
   wool.
   With the other she spins
   the thread.
20 She opens her arms to those
   who are poor.
   She reaches out her hands
   to those who are needy.
21 When it snows, she's not
   afraid for her family.
   All of them are dressed in
   the finest clothes.
22 She makes her own bed
   coverings.
   She is dressed in fine linen
   and purple clothes.
23 Her husband is respected at
   the city gate.
   There he takes his seat
   among the elders of the
   land.

24 She makes linen clothes and
   sells them.
   She supplies belts to the
   traders.
25 She puts on strength and
   honor as if they were her
   clothes.
   She can laugh at the days
   that are coming.
26 She speaks wisely.
   She teaches faithfully.
27 She watches over family
   matters.
   She is busy all the time.
28 Her children stand up and
   call her blessed.
   Her husband also rises up,
   and he praises her.
29 He says, "Many women do
   excellent things.
   But you are better than all
   the others."
30 Charm can fool you. Beauty
   fades.
   But a woman who has
   respect for the LORD
   should be praised.
31 Give her honor for all that her
   hands have done.
   Let everything she has
   done bring praise to her
   at the city gate.

Ecclesiastes

Introduction:
The book of Ecclesiastes tells what makes life good. The person who wrote this book is called the Teacher. The Teacher says the things of this world are no good without God. Money, work, pleasure and wisdom will not make people happy. Without God life is empty.

The Teacher wanted to find the good life. He tried to find it in wisdom and pleasure. He tried to find it in success and money. But he could not find it in any of these things. Instead, the Teacher learned the most important thing in life. "Have respect for God and obey his commandments." (12:13)

Outline of contents:

Everything Is Meaningless

1 These are the words of the Teacher. He was the son of David. He was also the king in Jerusalem.

2 "Meaningless! Everything is
    meaningless!"
says the Teacher.
"Everything is completely
    meaningless!
Nothing has any meaning."

3 What do people get for all
    their work?
Why do they work so hard
    on this earth?
4 People come and people go.
But the earth remains
    forever.
5 The sun rises. Then it sets.
And then it hurries back to
    where it rises.
6 The wind blows to the
    south.
Then it turns to the north.
Around and around it goes.
It always returns to where
    it started.
7 Every stream flows into the
    ocean.
But the ocean never gets
    full.
The streams return
to the place they came
    from.
8 All things are tiresome.
They are more tiresome
    than anyone can say.
But our eyes never see
    enough of anything.

Our ears never hear
   enough.
9 Everything that has ever
   been will come back
   again.
Everything that has ever
   been done will be done
   again.
Nothing is new on earth.
10 There isn't anything about
   which someone can
   say,
"Look! Here's something
   new."
It was already here long ago.
It was here before we
   were.
11 No one remembers the
   people of long ago.
Even those who haven't
   been born yet
won't be remembered
   by those who will be born
   after them.

Wisdom Is Meaningless

12 I, the Teacher, was king over Israel in Jerusalem. 13 I decided to study things carefully. I used my wisdom to check everything out. I looked into everything that is done on earth. What a heavy load God has put on human beings! 14 I've seen what is done on this earth. All of it is meaningless. It's like chasing the wind.

15 People can't straighten
     things that are crooked.
They can't count things
     that don't even exist.

16 I said to myself, "Look, I've now grown wiser than anyone who ruled over Jerusalem in the past. I have a lot of wisdom and knowledge." 17 Then I used my mind to understand what it really means to be wise. And I wanted to know what foolish pleasure is all about. But I found out that it's also like chasing the wind.

18 A lot of human wisdom leads
   to a lot of sorrow.
More knowledge only
   brings more sadness.

Pleasure Is Meaningless

2 I said to myself, "Come on. I'll try out pleasure. I want to find out if it is good." But it also proved to be meaningless. 2 "Laughter doesn't make any sense," I said. "And what can pleasure do for me?" 3 I tried cheering myself up by drinking wine. I even tried living in a foolish way. But wisdom was still guiding my mind. I wanted to see what was good for people to do on earth during their short lives.

4 So I started some large projects. I built houses for myself. I planted vineyards. 5 I made gardens and parks. I planted all kinds of fruit trees in them. 6 I made lakes to water groves of healthy trees. 7 I bought male and female slaves. And I had other slaves who were born in my house. I also owned more herds and flocks than anyone in Jerusalem ever had before. 8 I stored up silver and gold for myself. I gathered up the treasures of kings and their kingdoms. I got some male and female singers. I also got many women

for myself. Women delight the hearts of men. ⁹ I became far more important than anyone in Jerusalem had ever been before. And in spite of everything, I didn't lose my wisdom.

¹⁰ I gave myself everything my
    eyes wanted.
There wasn't any pleasure
    that I refused to give
    myself.
I took delight in everything I
    did.
And that was what I got for
    all my work.
¹¹ But then I looked over
    everything my hands
    had done.
I saw what I had worked so
    hard to get.
And nothing had any
    meaning.
It was like chasing the
    wind.
Nothing was gained on
    this earth.

Wisdom and Foolish Pleasure Are Meaningless

¹² I decided to think about
    wisdom.
I also thought about foolish
    pleasure.
What more can a new king
    do?
Can he do anything more
    than others have already
    done?
¹³ I saw that wisdom is better
    than foolishness,
    just as light is better than
    darkness.
¹⁴ The eyes of a wise person see
    things clearly.

A person who is foolish
    lives in darkness.
But I finally realized that
    death catches up
    with both of them.

¹⁵ Then I said to myself,

"What happens to a foolish
    person will catch up
    with me too.
So what do I gain by being
    wise?"
I said to myself,
"That doesn't have any
    meaning either."
¹⁶ Like a foolish person, a
    wise person won't be
    remembered very long.
The days have already
    come when both of them
    have been forgotten.
Like a person who is foolish,
    a wise person must die
    too!

Work Is Meaningless

¹⁷ So I hated life. That's because the work done on this earth made me sad. None of it has any meaning. It's like chasing the wind. ¹⁸ I hated everything I had worked for on earth. I'll have to leave all of it to someone who lives after me. ¹⁹ And who knows whether that person will be wise or foolish? Either way, they'll take over everything on earth I've worked so hard for. That doesn't have any meaning either. ²⁰ So I began to lose hope because of all my hard work on this earth. ²¹ A person might use wisdom, knowledge and skill to do their work. But then they have to

leave everything they own to someone who hasn't worked for it. That doesn't have any meaning either. In fact, it isn't fair. [22] What do people get for all their hard work on earth? What do they get for all their worries? [23] As long as they live, their work is nothing but pain and sorrow. Even at night their minds can't rest. That doesn't have any meaning either.

[24] A person can't do anything better than eat, drink and be satisfied with their work. I'm finally seeing that those things also come from the hand of God. [25] Without his help, who can eat or find pleasure? [26] God gives wisdom, knowledge and happiness to the person who pleases him. But to a sinner he gives the task of gathering and storing up wealth. Then the sinner must hand it over to the one who pleases God. That doesn't have any meaning either. It's like chasing the wind.

There Is a Time for Everything

3 There is a time for everything.
There's a time for everything that is done on earth.
[2] There is a time to be born.
And there's a time to die.
There is a time to plant.
And there's a time to pull up what is planted.
[3] There is a time to kill.
And there's a time to heal.
There is a time to tear down.
And there's a time to build up.

[4] There is a time to weep.
And there's a time to laugh.
There is a time to be sad.
And there's a time to dance.
[5] There is a time to scatter stones.
And there's a time to gather them.
There is a time to embrace someone.
And there's a time not to embrace.
[6] There is a time to search.
And there's a time to stop searching.
There is a time to keep.
And there's a time to throw away.
[7] There is a time to tear.
And there's a time to mend.
There is a time to be silent.
And there's a time to speak.
[8] There is a time to love.
And there's a time to hate.
There is a time for war.
And there's a time for peace.

[9] What do workers get for their hard work? [10] I've seen the heavy load God has put on human beings. [11] He has made everything beautiful in its time. He has also given people a sense of who he is. But they can't completely understand what God has done from beginning to end. [12] People should be happy and do good while they live. I know there's nothing better for them to do than that. [13] Each of them should eat and drink. People should

be satisfied with all their hard work. That is God's gift to them. ¹⁴ I know that everything God does will last forever. Nothing can be added to it. And nothing can be taken from it. God does that so people will have respect for him.

¹⁵ Everything that now exists
    has already been.
And what is coming has
    existed before.
God will judge those who
    treat others badly.

¹⁶ Here's something else I saw on earth.

Where people should be
    treated right,
    they are treated wrong.
Where people should be
    treated fairly,
    they are treated unfairly.

¹⁷ I said to myself,

"God will judge
    godly and sinful people
    alike.
He has a time for every act.
    He has a time to judge
    everything that is
    done."

¹⁸ I also said to myself, "God tests human beings. He does this so they can see that in certain ways they are like animals. ¹⁹ Surely what happens to animals happens to people too. Death waits for people and animals alike. People die, just as animals do. All of them have the same breath. People don't have any advantage over animals. Nothing has any mean-ing. ²⁰ People and animals go to the same place. All of them come from dust. And all of them return to dust. ²¹ Who can know whether the spirit of a person goes up? Who can tell whether the spirit of an animal goes down into the earth?"

²² So a person should enjoy their work. That's what God made them for. I saw that there's nothing better for them to do than that. After all, who can show them what will happen af-ter they are gone?

Suffering, Hard Work and No Friends

4 I looked and saw how much people were suffering on this earth.

I saw the tears of those who
    are suffering.
    They don't have anyone to
    comfort them.
Power is on the side of those
    who treat them badly.
    Those who are suffering
    don't have anyone to
    comfort them.
² Then I announced that those
    who have already died
are happier than those
    who are still alive.
³ But someone who hasn't
    been born yet
is better off than the dead
    or the living.
That's because that person
    hasn't seen the evil
    things
    that are done on earth.

⁴ I also saw that a person works hard and accomplishes a

lot. But they do it only because they want what another person has. That doesn't have any meaning either. It's like chasing the wind.

5 Foolish people fold their
　　hands and don't work.
　　And that destroys them.
6 One handful with peace and
　　quiet
　is better than two handfuls
　　with hard work.
　Working too hard is like
　　chasing the wind.

7 Again I saw something on earth that didn't mean anything.

8 A man lived all by himself.
　　He didn't have any sons or
　　brothers.
　His hard work never ended.
　　But he wasn't happy with
　　what he had.
　"Who am I working so hard
　　for?" he asked.
　　"Why don't I get the things
　　I enjoy?"
　That doesn't have any
　　meaning either.
　　In fact, it's a very bad
　　deal!

9 Two people are better than
　　one.
　They can help each other
　　in everything they do.
10 Suppose either of them falls
　　down.
　Then the one can help the
　　other one up.
　But suppose a person falls
　　down and doesn't
　　have anyone to help
　　them up.

Then feel sorry for that
　　person!
11 Or suppose two people lie
　　down together.
　Then they'll keep warm.
　But how can one person
　　keep warm alone?
12 One person could be
　　overpowered.
　But two people can stand
　　up for themselves.
　And a rope made out of
　　three cords isn't easily
　　broken.

Getting Ahead Is Meaningless

13 A poor but wise young man is better off than an old but foolish king. That king doesn't pay attention to a warning anymore. 14 The young man might have come from prison to become king. Or he might have been born poor within the kingdom but still became king. 15 I saw that everyone was following the young man who had become the new king. 16 At first, all the people served him when he became king. But those who came later weren't pleased with the way he was ruling. That doesn't have any meaning either. It's like chasing the wind.

Keep Your Promise to God

5 Be careful what you say when you go to God's house. Go there to listen. Don't be like foolish people when you offer your sacrifice. They do what is wrong and don't even know it.

2 Don't be too quick to speak.
　　Don't be in a hurry to say
　　anything to God.

God is in heaven. You are on
   earth.
So use only a few words
   when you speak.
³ Many worries result in
   dreams.
Many words result in
   foolish talk.

⁴ When you make a promise
to God, don't wait too long to
carry it out. He isn't pleased with
foolish people. So do what you
have promised. ⁵ It is not good to
make a promise and not keep it.
It is better to make no promise at
all. ⁶ Don't let your mouth cause
you to sin. Don't say to the temple messenger, "My promise was
a mistake." Why should God be
angry with what you say? Why
should he destroy what you have
done? ⁷ Dreaming too much and
talking too much are meaningless. So have respect for God.

Riches Are Meaningless

⁸ Suppose you see poor people
being mistreated somewhere.
And what is being done to them
isn't right or fair. Don't be surprised by that. One official is
watched by a higher one. Officials who are even higher are
watching both of them. ⁹ All of
them take what the land produces. And the king himself
takes his share from the fields.

¹⁰ Anyone who loves money
   never has enough.
Anyone who loves wealth
   is never satisfied with
   what they get.
That doesn't have any
   meaning either.

¹¹ As more and more goods are
   made,
more and more people use
   them up.
So how can those goods
   benefit their owners?
All they can do is look at
   them with desire.

¹² The sleep of a worker is
   sweet.
It doesn't matter whether
   they eat a little or a lot.
But the wealth of rich
   people
keeps them awake at
   night.

¹³ I've seen something very
evil on earth.

It's when wealth is stored up
   and then brings harm to its
   owners.
¹⁴ It's also when wealth is lost
   because of an unwise
   business deal.
Then there won't be anything
   left
for the owners' children.
¹⁵ Everyone is born naked.
   They come into the world
   with nothing.
And they go out of it with
   nothing.
They don't get anything from
   their work
that they can take with
   them.

¹⁶ Here's something else that
is very evil.

Everyone is born, and
   everyone dies.
And what do they get for
   their work?

Nothing. It's like working for the wind.

¹⁷ All their lives they eat in
darkness.
Their lives are full of
trouble, suffering and
anger.

¹⁸ I have seen what is good. It is good for a person to eat and drink. It's good for them to be satisfied with their hard work on this earth. That's what they should do during the short life God has given them. That's what God made them for. ¹⁹ Sometimes God gives a person wealth and possessions. God makes it possible for that person to enjoy them. God helps them accept the life he has given them. God helps them to be happy in their work. All these things are gifts from God. ²⁰ A person like that doesn't have to think about how their life is going. That's because God fills their heart with joy.

6 I've seen another evil thing on this earth. And it's a heavy load on human beings. ² God gives some people wealth, possessions and honor. They have everything their hearts desire. But God doesn't let them enjoy those things. Instead, strangers enjoy them. This doesn't have any meaning. It's a very evil thing.

³ A man might have a hundred children. He might live a long time. But suppose he can't enjoy his wealth. And suppose he isn't buried in the proper way. Then it doesn't matter how long he lives. I'm telling you

that a baby that is born dead is better off than that man is. ⁴ That kind of birth doesn't have any meaning. The baby dies in darkness and leaves this world. And in darkness it is forgotten. ⁵ It didn't even see the sun. It didn't know anything at all. But it has more rest than that man does. ⁶ And that's true even if he lives for 2,000 years but doesn't get to enjoy his wealth. All people die and go to the grave, don't they?

⁷ People eat up everything
they work to get.
But they are never
satisfied.
⁸ What advantage do wise
people have
over those who are foolish?
What do poor people gain
by knowing how to act
toward others?
⁹ Being satisfied with what you
have
is better than always
wanting more.
That doesn't have any
meaning either.
It's like chasing the wind.

¹⁰ God has already planned
what now exists.
He has already decided
what a human being is.
No one can argue with
someone
who is stronger.
¹¹ The more words people use,
the less meaning there is.
And that doesn't help
anyone.

¹² Who knows what's good for a person? They live for only

a few meaningless days. They
pass through life like a shadow.
Who can tell them what will
happen on earth after they are
gone?

Good Advice About How to Live

7 A good name is better than
fine perfume.
People can learn more
from mourning when
someone dies
than from being happy
when someone is born.
² So it's better to go where
people are mourning
than to go where people
are having a good time.
Everyone will die someday.
Those who are still living
should really think about
that.
³ Not being able to figure
things out is better than
laughter.
That's because sorrow is
good for the heart.
⁴ Those who are wise are
found where there is
sorrow.
But foolish people are
found where there is
pleasure.
⁵ Pay attention to a wise
person's warning.
That's better than listening
to the songs of those who
are foolish.
⁶ A foolish person's laughter
is like the crackling of
thorns burning under a
pot.
That doesn't have any
meaning either.

⁷ When a wise person takes
wealth by force, they
become foolish.
It is sinful to take money
from people who want
special favors.
⁸ The end of a matter is better
than its beginning.
So it's better to be patient
than proud.
⁹ Don't become angry quickly.
Anger lives in the hearts of
foolish people.
¹⁰ Don't say, "Why were things
better in the good old
days?"
It isn't wise to ask that kind
of question.
¹¹ Wisdom is a good thing.
It's like getting a share of
the family wealth.
It benefits those who live
on this earth.
¹² Wisdom provides safety,
just as money provides
safety.
But here's the advantage of
wisdom.
It guards those who
have it.

¹³ Think about what God has
done.
Who can make straight
what he has made
crooked?
¹⁴ When times are good, be
happy.
But when times are bad,
here's something to
think about.
God has made bad times.
He has also made good
times.

So no one can find out
anything
about what's ahead for
them.

¹⁵ In my meaningless life
here's what I've seen.

I've seen godly people dying
even though they are
godly.
And I've seen sinful people
living a long time
even though they are
sinful.
¹⁶ Don't claim to be better than
you are.
And don't claim to be wiser
than you are.
Why destroy yourself?
¹⁷ Don't be too sinful.
And don't be foolish.
Why die before your time
comes?
¹⁸ It's good to hold on to both of
those things.
Don't let go of either one.
Whoever has respect for God
will avoid
going too far in either
direction.

¹⁹ Wisdom makes one wise
person more powerful
than ten rulers in a city.

²⁰ It is true that there isn't
anyone on earth
who does only what is right
and never sins.

²¹ Don't pay attention to
everything people say.
If you do, you might hear
your servant cursing
you.
²² Many times you yourself
have cursed others.

Deep down inside, you
know that's true.

²³ I used wisdom to test all
these things. I said,

"I've made up my mind to be
wise."
But it was more than I
could accomplish.
²⁴ Whatever exists is far away
and very deep.
Who can find it?
²⁵ So I tried to understand
wisdom more
completely.
I wanted to study it and
figure it out.
I tried to find out
everything I could about
it.
I tried to understand why it's
foolish to be evil.
I wanted to see why
choosing foolishness is
so unwise.
²⁶ A woman who hunts a man
down
is more painful than
death.
Her heart is like a trap.
Her hands are like chains.
A man who pleases God will
try to get away from her.
But she will trap a sinner.

²⁷ "Look," says the Teacher.
"Here's what I've discovered.

"I added one thing to another
to find out
everything I could about
wisdom.
²⁸ I searched and searched
but found very little.
I did find one honest man
among a thousand.

But I didn't find one
honest woman among a
thousand.
[29] Here's the only other thing I
found.
God created human beings
as honest.
But they've made many
evil plans."

8

Who is like a wise person?
Who knows how to explain
things?
A person's wisdom makes
their face bright.
It softens the look on their
face.

Obey the King

[2] I'm telling you to obey the king's command. You promised to serve him. You made a promise to God. [3] Don't be in a hurry to quit your job in the palace. Don't stand up for something the king doesn't like. He'll do anything he wants to. [4] The king has the final word. So who can ask him, "What are you doing?"

[5] No one who obeys his
command will be
harmed.
Those who are wise will
know the proper time and
way to approach him.
[6] There's a proper time and
way for people to do
everything.
That's true even though
a person might be
suffering greatly.
[7] No one knows what lies ahead.
So who can tell someone
else what's going to
happen?

[8] No one can stop the wind
from blowing.
And no one has the power
to decide when they will
die.
No one is let out of the army
in times of war.
And evil won't let go of
those who practice it.

[9] I understood all these things. I used my mind to study everything that's done on earth. A man sometimes makes life hard for others. But he ends up hurting himself. [10] I also saw sinful people being buried. They used to come and go from the place of worship. And others praised them in the city where they worshiped. That doesn't have any meaning either. [11] Sometimes the sentence for a crime isn't carried out quickly. So people make plans to commit even more crimes. [12] An evil person may be guilty of a hundred crimes. Yet they may still live a long time. But I know that things will go better with those who have great respect for God. [13] Sinful people don't respect God. So things won't go well with them. Like a shadow, they won't be around very long.

[14] Here's something else on this earth that doesn't have any meaning. Sometimes godly people get what sinful people should receive. And sinful people get what godly people should receive. Here's what I'm telling you. That doesn't have any meaning either. [15] So I advise everyone to enjoy life. A person on this earth can't do anything

better than eat and drink and be glad. Then they will enjoy their work. They'll be happy all the days of the life God has given them on earth.

¹⁶ I used my mind to understand what it really means to be wise. I wanted to observe the hard work people do on earth. They don't close their eyes and go to sleep day or night. ¹⁷ I saw everything God has done. No one can understand what happens on earth. People might try very hard to figure it out. But they still can't discover what it all means. Wise people might claim they know. But they can't really understand it either.

Everyone Dies

9 I thought about all these things. I realized that those who are wise and do what is right are under God's control. What they do is also under his control. But no one knows whether they will be loved or hated. ² Everyone will die someday. Death comes to godly and sinful people alike. It comes to good and bad people alike. It comes to "clean" and "unclean" people alike. Those who offer sacrifices and those who don't offer them also die.

A good person dies,
　　and so does a sinner.
Those who make promises
　　die.
　　So do those who are afraid
　　to make them.

³ Here's what is so bad about everything that happens on this earth. Death catches up with all of us. Also, the hearts of people are full of evil. They live in foolish pleasure. After that, they join those who have already died. ⁴ Anyone who is still living has hope. Even a live dog is better off than a dead lion!

⁵ People who are still alive
　　know they'll die.
But those who have died
　　don't know anything.
They don't receive any more
　　rewards.
And even their name is
　　forgotten.
⁶ Their love, hate and jealousy
　　disappear.
They will never share
　　again
　　in anything that happens
　　on earth.

⁷ Go and enjoy your food. Be joyful as you drink your wine. God has aleady approved what you do. ⁸ Always wear white clothes to show you are happy. Anoint your head with olive oil. ⁹ You love your wife. So enjoy life with her. Do it all the days of this meaningless life God has given you on earth. That's what he made you for. That's what you get for all your hard work on earth. ¹⁰ No matter what you do, work at it with all your might. Remember, you are going to the place of the dead. And there isn't any work or planning or knowledge or wisdom there.

¹¹ Here's something else I've seen on this earth.

Races aren't always won by
　　those who run fast.

Battles aren't always won
by those who are strong.
Wise people don't always
have plenty of food.
Clever people aren't always
wealthy.
Those who have learned
a lot aren't always
successful.
God controls the timing of
every event.
He also controls how
things turn out.

¹² No one knows when trouble
will come to them.

Fish are caught in nets.
Birds are taken in traps.
And people are trapped by
hard times
that come when they don't
expect them.

Being Wise Is Better Than Being Foolish

¹³ Here's something else I
saw on this earth. I saw an example of wisdom that touched
me deeply. ¹⁴ There was once
a small city. Only a few people
lived there. A powerful king attacked it. He brought in war machines all around it. ¹⁵ A certain
man lived in that city. He was
poor but wise. He used his wisdom to save the city. But no one
remembered that poor man.
¹⁶ So I said, "It's better to be wise
than to be powerful." But people look down on the poor man's
wisdom. No one pays any attention to what he says.

¹⁷ People should listen to the
quiet words
of those who are wise.

That's better than paying
attention to the shouts
of a ruler of foolish
people.
¹⁸ Wisdom is better than
weapons of war.
But one sinner destroys a
lot of good.

10 Dead flies give perfume a
bad smell.
And a little foolishness
can make a lot of
wisdom useless.
² The hearts of wise people
lead them on the right
path.
But the hearts of foolish
people take them down
the wrong path.
³ Foolish people don't have any
sense at all.
They show everyone they
are foolish.
They do it even when they
are walking along the
road.
⁴ Suppose a ruler gets very
angry with you.
If he does, don't quit your
job in the palace.
Being calm can overcome
what you have done
against him.

⁵ Here's something evil I've
seen on this earth.
And it's the kind of
mistake that rulers
make.
⁶ Foolish people are given
many important jobs.
Rich people are given
unimportant ones.
⁷ I've seen slaves on
horseback.

I've also seen princes who
were forced to walk as if
they were slaves.

8 Anyone who digs a pit might
fall into it.
Anyone who breaks
through a wall might be
bitten by a snake.
9 Anyone who removes stones
from rock pits might get
hurt.
Anyone who cuts logs
might get wounded.
10 Suppose the blade of an ax is
dull.
And its edge hasn't been
sharpened.
Then more effort is needed to
use it.
But skill will bring
success.
11 Suppose a snake bites before
it is charmed.
Then the snake charmer
receives no payment.
12 Wise people say gracious
things.
But foolish people are
destroyed by what their
own lips speak.
13 At first what they say is
foolish.
In the end their words are
very evil.
14 They talk too much.

No one knows what lies
ahead.
Who can tell someone else
what will happen after
they are gone?

15 The work foolish people do
makes them tired.

They don't even know the
way to town.

16 How terrible it is for a land
whose king used to be a
servant!
How terrible if its princes
get drunk in the
morning!
17 How blessed is the land
whose king was born
into the royal family!
How blessed if its princes
eat and drink at the
proper time!
How blessed if they eat and
drink to become strong
and not to get drunk!
18 When a person won't work,
the roof falls down.
Because of hands that
aren't busy, the house
leaks.
19 People laugh at a dinner
party.
And wine makes life
happy.
People think money can
buy everything.
20 Don't say bad things about
the king.
Don't even think about
those things.
Don't curse rich people.
Don't even curse them in
your bedroom.
A bird might fly away and
carry your words.
It might report what you
said.

Do Many Things to Succeed

11 Sell your grain in the
market overseas.

After a while you might
earn something from it.
2 Try to succeed by doing
many things.
After all, you don't know
what great trouble might
come on the land.

3 Clouds that are full of water
pour rain down on the
earth.
A tree might fall to the south
or the north.
It will stay in the place
where it falls.
4 Anyone who keeps on
watching the wind won't
plant seeds.
Anyone who keeps looking
at the clouds won't
gather crops.
5 You don't know the path the
wind takes.
You don't know how a
baby is made inside its
mother.
So you can't understand how
God works either.
He made everything.
6 In the morning plant your
seeds.
In the evening keep your
hands busy.
You don't know what will
succeed.
It may be one or the
other.
Or both might do equally
well.

Remember Your Creator While You Are Young

7 Light is sweet.
People enjoy being out in
the sun.

8 No matter how many years
anyone might live,
let them enjoy all of
them.
But let them remember the
dark days.
There will be many of
those.
Nothing that's going to
happen will have any
meaning.

9 You young people, be happy
while you are still
young.
Let your heart be joyful
while you are still
strong.
Do what your heart tells you
to do.
Go after what your eyes
look at.
But I want you to know
that God will judge you for
everything you do.
10 So drive worry out of your
heart.
Get rid of all your
troubles.
Being young and strong
doesn't have any
meaning.

12 Remember your Creator.
Remember him while
you are still young.
Think about him before your
times of trouble come.
The years will come when
you will say,
"I don't find any pleasure
in them."
2 That's when the sunlight will
become dark.
The moon and the stars
will also grow dark.

And the clouds will return
after it rains.
3 Remember your Creator
before those who guard
the house tremble with
old age.
That's when strong men
will be bent over.
The women who grind grain
will stop because there
are so few of them left.
Those who look through
the windows won't be
able to see very well.
4 Remember your Creator
before the front doors
are closed.
That's when the sound of
grinding will fade
away.
Old people will rise up when
they hear birds singing.
But they will barely hear
any of their songs.
5 Remember your Creator
before you become
afraid of places that are
too high.
You will also be terrified
because of danger in the
streets.
Remember your Creator
before the almond trees
have buds on them.
That's when grasshoppers
will drag themselves
along.
Old people will lose their
desire.
That's when people will go to
their dark homes in the
grave.
And those who mourn
for the dead will walk
around in the streets.

6 Remember your Creator
before the silver cord is
cut.
Remember him before the
golden bowl is broken.
The wheel will be broken at
the well.
The pitcher will be
smashed at the spring.
7 Remember your Creator
before you return to the
dust you came from.
Remember him before
your spirit goes back to
God who gave it.

8 "Meaningless! Everything is
meaningless!"
says the Teacher.
"Nothing has any
meaning."

Have Respect for God and Obey His Commandments

9 The Teacher was wise. He gave knowledge to people. He tried out many proverbs. He thought about them carefully. Then he wrote them down in order. 10 He did his best to find just the right words. And what he wrote was honest and true.

11 The sayings of those who are wise move people to take action. Their collected sayings are like nails pounded in firm and deep. These sayings are given to us by one shepherd. 12 My son, be careful not to pay attention to anything added to them.

Books will never stop being written. Too much studying makes people tired.

13 Everything has now been heard.

And here's the final thing I
want to say.
Have respect for God
and obey his
commandments.
This is what he expects of
all human beings.

[14]God will judge everything
people do.
That includes everything
they try to hide.
He'll judge everything,
whether it's good or
evil.

Song of Songs

Introduction:

Song of Songs is the last book of poems and wisdom in the Bible. It is a beautiful love poem. In Song of Songs a woman sings her poem of love to a man. The man sings his poem of love back to the woman. Even their friends sing poems.

Song of Songs shows what makes a good marriage. It is a beautiful picture of the love a husband and wife should have.

Outline of contents:

1 This is the greatest song Solomon ever wrote.

A Shulammite woman says to King Solomon,

2 "I long for your lips to kiss me!
    Your love makes me happier than wine does.
3 The lotion you have on pleases me.
    Your name is like perfume that is poured out.
    No wonder the young women love you!
4 Take me away with you. Let us hurry!
    King Solomon, bring me into your palace."

The other women say,

"King Solomon, you fill us with joy. You make us happy.
    We praise your love more than we praise wine."

The woman says to the king,

"It is right for them to love you!

5 "Women of Jerusalem, my skin is dark but lovely.
It is dark like the tents in Kedar.
    It's like the curtains of Solomon's tent.
6 Don't stare at me because I'm dark.
    The sun has made my skin look like this.
My brothers were angry with me.
    They made me take care of the vineyards.
    I haven't even taken care of my own vineyard.

7 "King Solomon, I love you.

So tell me where you take
    care of your flock.
Tell me where you rest your
    sheep at noon.
Why should I have to act like
    a prostitute
near the flocks of your
    friends?"

The other women say,

8 "You are the most beautiful
    woman of all.
Don't you know where to
    find the king?
Follow the tracks the sheep
    make.
Take care of your young
    goats
near the tents of the
    shepherds."

King Solomon says to the
Shulammite woman,

9 "You are my love.
    You are like a mare among
        Pharaoh's chariot horses.
10 Your earrings make your
        cheeks even more
        beautiful.
    Your strings of jewels make
        your neck even more
        lovely.
11 We will make gold earrings
        for you.
    We'll decorate them with
        silver."

The woman says,

12 "The king was at his table.
    My perfume gave off a
        sweet smell.
13 The one who loves me is like
        a small bag of myrrh
    resting between my
        breasts.

14 He is like henna flowers
        from the vineyards of En
        Gedi."

The king says,

15 "You are so beautiful, my
        love!
    So beautiful!
    Your eyes are like doves."

The woman says,

16 "You are so handsome, my
        love!
    So charming!
    The green field is our bed."

The king says,

17 "Cedar trees above us are the
        beams of our house.
    Fir trees overhead are its
        rafters."

2 The woman says,

"I am like a rose on the coast
    of Sharon.
I'm like a lily in the
    valleys."

The king says,

2 "My love, among the young
        women
    you are like a lily among
        thorns."

The woman says,

3 "My love, among the young
        men
    you are like an apple tree
        among the trees of the
        forest.
I'm happy to sit in your
    shade.
    Your fruit tastes so sweet to
        me.
4 Lead me to the dinner hall.

Let your banner of love be
lifted high above me.
⁵Give me some raisins to
make me strong.
Give me some apples to
make me feel like new
again.
Our love has made me
weak.
⁶Your left arm is under my
head.
Your right arm is around
me.
⁷Women of Jerusalem, make
me a promise.
Let the antelopes and the
does serve as witnesses.
Don't stir up love.
Don't wake it up until it's
ready.

⁸"Listen! I hear my love!
Look! Here he comes!
He's leaping across the
mountains.
He's coming over the hills.
⁹The one who loves me is like
an antelope or a young
deer.
Look! There he stands
behind our wall.
He's gazing through the
window.
He's peering through the
screen.
¹⁰He said to me, 'Rise up, my
love.
Come with me, my
beautiful one.
¹¹Look! The winter is past.
The rains are over and
gone.
¹²Flowers are appearing on the
earth.
The season for singing has
come.

The cooing of doves
is heard in our land.
¹³The fig trees are producing
their early fruit.
The flowers on the vines
are giving off their sweet
smell.
Rise up and come, my love.
Come with me, my
beautiful one.' "

The king says,

¹⁴"You are like a dove in an
opening in the rocks.
You are like a dove in
a hiding place on a
mountainside.
Show me your face.
Let me hear your voice.
Your voice is so sweet.
Your face is so lovely.
¹⁵Catch the foxes for us.
Catch the little foxes.
They destroy our
vineyards.
The vineyards are in
bloom."

The woman says,

¹⁶"My love belongs to me, and I
belong to him.
Like an antelope, he eats
among the lilies.
¹⁷Until the day begins
and the shadows fade
away,
turn to me, my love.
Be like an antelope
or like a young deer
on the rocky hills.

3 "All night long on my bed
I searched for the one my
heart loves.
I looked for him but didn't
find him.

2 I will get up and go around in
  the city.
  I'll look through all of its
  streets.
I'll search for the one my
  heart loves.
  So I looked for him but
  didn't find him.
3 Those on guard duty found
  me
  as they were walking
  around in the city.
  'Have you seen the one my
  heart loves?' I asked.
4 As soon as I had passed by
  them
  I found the one my heart
  loves.
I threw my arms around him
  and didn't let him go
until I had brought him to
  my mother's house.
I took him to my mother's
  room.
5 Women of Jerusalem, make
  me a promise.
  Let the antelopes and the
  does serve as witnesses.
Don't stir up love.
  Don't wake it up until it's
  ready.

6 "Who is this man coming up
  from the desert
  like a column of smoke?
He smells like myrrh and
  incense
  made from all the spices of
  the trader.
7 Look! There's Solomon's
  movable throne.
  Sixty soldiers accompany
  it.
  They have been chosen
  from the best warriors in
  Israel.

8 All of them are wearing
  swords.
  They have fought many
  battles.
Each one has his sword at his
  side.
  Each is prepared for the
  terrors of the night.
9 King Solomon made the
  movable throne for
  himself.
  He made it out of wood
  from Lebanon.
10 He formed its posts out of
  silver.
  He made its base out of
  gold.
Its seat was covered with
  purple cloth.
  It was decorated inside
  with love.
Women of Jerusalem,
11 come out.
Look, you women of Zion.
Look at King Solomon
  wearing his crown.
  His mother placed it on
  him.
She did it on his wedding
  day.
  His heart was full of joy."

4 The king says to the Shulammite woman,

"You are so beautiful, my
  love!
  So beautiful!
  Your eyes behind your veil
  are like doves.
Your hair flows like a flock of
  black goats
  coming down from the
  hills of Gilead.
2 Your teeth are as clean as a
  flock of sheep.

Their wool has just been clipped.
They have just come up from being washed.
Each of your teeth has its twin.
Not one of them is alone.
³ Your lips are like a bright red ribbon.
Your mouth is so lovely.
Your cheeks behind your veil
are like the halves of a pomegranate.
⁴ Your neck is strong and beautiful like the tower of David.
That tower is built with rows of stones.
A thousand shields are hanging on it.
All of them belong to mighty soldiers.
⁵ Your breasts are lovely.
They are like two young antelopes
that eat among the lilies.
⁶ I will go to the mountain of myrrh.
I'll go to the hill of incense.
I'll stay there until the day begins
and the shadows fade away.
⁷ Every part of you is so beautiful, my love.
There is no flaw in you.

⁸ "Come with me from Lebanon, my bride.
Come with me from Lebanon.
Come down from the top of Mount Amana.
Come down from the top of Senir.

Come to me from the peak of Mount Hermon.
Leave the dens where the lions live.
Leave the places in the mountains where the leopards stay.
⁹ My bride, you have stolen my heart
with one glance of your eyes.
My sister, you have stolen my heart
with one jewel in your necklace.
¹⁰ My bride, your love is so delightful.
My sister, your love makes me happier than wine does.
Your perfume smells better than any spice.
¹¹ Your lips are as sweet as honey, my bride.
Milk and honey are under your tongue.
Your clothes smell like the cedar trees in Lebanon.
¹² My bride, you are like a garden that is locked up.
My sister, you are like a spring of water that has a fence around it.
You are like a fountain that is sealed up.
¹³ You are like trees whose branches are loaded
with pomegranates, fine fruits, henna and nard,
¹⁴   with nard and saffron,
cane and cinnamon.
You are like every kind of incense tree.
You have myrrh, aloes and all the finest spices.

15 You are like a fountain in a
      garden.
   You are like a well of
      flowing water
      streaming down from
      Lebanon."

The woman says,

16 "Wake up, north wind!
      Come, south wind!
   Blow on my garden.
      Then its sweet smell will
      spread everywhere.
   Let my love come into his
      garden.
      Let him taste its fine
      fruits."

5 The king says,

   "My bride, I have come into
      my garden.
      My sister, I've gathered my
      myrrh and my spice.
   I've eaten my honeycomb
      and my honey.
   I've drunk my wine and my
      milk."

The other women say to the
Shulammite woman and to Solomon,

   "Friends, eat and drink.
      Drink up all the love you
      want."

The woman says,

2 "I slept, but my heart was
      awake.
      Listen! The one who loves
      me is knocking.
   He says, 'My sister, I love you.
      Open up so I can come in.
   You are my dove.
      You are perfect in every
      way.

My head is soaked with dew.
   The night air has made my
      hair wet.'

3 "But I've taken off my robe.
      Must I put it on again?
   I've washed my feet.
      Must I get them dirty
      again?
4 My love put his hand through
      the opening.
   My heart began to pound
      for him.
5 I got up to open the door for
      my love.
   My hands dripped with
      myrrh.
   It flowed from my fingers
      onto the handles of the
      lock.
6 I opened the door for my love.
      But he had left and was
      gone.
   My heart sank because he
      had left.
   I looked for him but didn't
      find him.
   I called out to him, but he
      didn't answer.
7 Those on guard duty found
      me
      as they were walking
      around in the city.
   They beat me. They hurt me.
      Those on guard duty at the
      walls
      took my coat away from
      me.
8 Women of Jerusalem, make
      me a promise.
   If you find the one who
      loves me,
      tell him our love has made
      me weak."

The other women say,

⁹ "You are the most beautiful
   woman of all.
   How is the one you love
   better than others?
   How is he better than anyone
   else?
   Why do you ask us to make
   you this promise?"

The woman says,

¹⁰ "The one who loves me is
   tanned and handsome.
   He's the finest man among
   10,000.
¹¹ His head is like the purest
   gold.
   His hair is wavy and as
   black as a raven.
¹² His eyes are like doves
   by streams of water.
   They look as if they've been
   washed in milk.
   They are set like jewels in
   his head.
¹³ His cheeks are like beds of
   spice
   giving off perfume.
   His lips are like lilies
   dripping with myrrh.
¹⁴ His arms are like rods of
   gold
   set with topaz.
   His body is like polished
   ivory
   decorated with lapis lazuli.
¹⁵ His legs are like pillars of
   marble
   set on bases of pure gold.
   He looks like the finest cedar
   tree
   in the mountains of
   Lebanon.
¹⁶ His mouth is very sweet.
   Everything about him is
   delightful.

That's what the one who
   loves me is like.
   That's what my friend
   is like, women of
   Jerusalem."

6 The other women say,

"You are the most beautiful
   woman of all.
   Where has the one who
   loves you gone?
   Which way did he turn?
   We'll help you look for
   him."

The woman says,

² "My love has gone down to
   his garden.
   He's gone to the beds of
   spices.
   He's eating in the gardens.
   He's gathering lilies.
³ I belong to my love, and he
   belongs to me.
   He's eating among the
   lilies."

The king says,

⁴ "My love, you are as beautiful
   as the city of Tirzah.
   You are as lovely as
   Jerusalem.
   You are as majestic as
   troops carrying their
   banners.
⁵ Turn your eyes away from me.
   They overpower me.
   Your hair flows like a flock of
   black goats
   coming down from the
   hills of Gilead.
⁶ Your teeth are as clean as a
   flock of sheep
   coming up from being
   washed.

Each of your teeth has its
twin.
Not one of them is missing.
⁷ Your cheeks behind your veil
are like the halves of a
pomegranate.
⁸ There might be 60 queens
and 80 concubines.
There might be more
virgins than anyone can
count.
⁹ But you are my perfect dove.
There isn't anyone like you.
You are your mother's
favorite daughter.
The young women see you
and call you blessed.
The queens and
concubines praise you."

The other women say,

¹⁰ "Who is this woman?
She is like the sunrise in all
its glory.
She is as beautiful as the
moon.
She is as bright as the sun.
She is as majestic as the
stars traveling across the
sky."

The king says,

¹¹ "I went down to a grove of nut
trees.
I wanted to look at the new
plants growing in the
valley.
I wanted to find out whether
the vines had budded.
I wanted to see if the
pomegranate trees had
bloomed.
¹² Before I realized it,
I was among the royal
chariots of my people."

The other women say,

¹³ "Come back to us.
Come back, Shulammite
woman.
Come back to us.
Come back. Then we can
look at you."

The king says to the women,

"Why do you want to look at
the Shulammite woman
as you would watch a
dancer at Mahanaim?"

7 The king says to the Shulammite woman,

"You are like a prince's
daughter.
Your feet in sandals are so
beautiful.
Your graceful legs are like
jewels.
The hands of an artist must
have shaped them.
² Your navel is like a round bowl
that always has mixed
wine in it.
Your waist is like a mound of
wheat
surrounded by lilies.
³ Your two breasts are lovely.
They are like two young
antelopes.
⁴ Your neck is smooth and
beautiful like an ivory
tower.
Your eyes are like the pools of
Heshbon
by the gate of Bath Rabbim.
Your nose is like the towering
mountains of Lebanon
that face the city of
Damascus.
⁵ Your head is like a crown on
you.

It is as beautiful as Mount
Carmel.
Your hair is as smooth as
purple silk.
I am captured by your
flowing curls.
⁶ You are so beautiful! You
please me so much!
You are so delightful, my
love!
⁷ You are as graceful as a palm
tree.
Your breasts are as sweet
as the freshest fruit.
⁸ I said, 'I will climb the palm
tree.
I'll take hold of its fruit.'
May your breasts be as sweet
as grapes on the vine.
May your breath smell like
the tastiest apples.
⁹   May your lips be like the
finest wine."

The woman says,

"May my wine go straight to
you, my love.
May it flow gently over our
lips as we sleep.

¹⁰ "I belong to you, my love.
And you long for me.
¹¹ Come, my love. Let's go to the
country.
Let's spend the night in the
villages.
¹² Let's go out to the vineyards
early.
Let's go and see if the vines
have budded.
Let's find out whether their
flowers have opened.
Let's see if the
pomegranate trees are
blooming.

There I will give you my
love.
¹³ The mandrake flowers
give off their strong
smell.
All the best things are
waiting for us,
new and old alike.
I've stored them up for you,
my love.

8 "I wish you were like a
brother to me.
I wish my mother's breasts
had nursed you.
Then if I found you outside,
I could kiss you.
No one would look down
on me.
² I'd bring you to my mother's
house.
She taught me everything I
know.
I'd give you spiced wine to
drink.
It's the juice of my
pomegranates.
³ Your left arm is under my
head.
Your right arm is around
me.
⁴ Women of Jerusalem, make
me a promise.
Don't stir up love.
Don't wake it up until it's
ready."

The other women say,

⁵ "Who is this woman coming
up from the desert?
She's leaning on the one
who loves her."

The woman says to the king,

"Under the apple tree I woke
you up.

That's where your mother
  became pregnant with
  you.
She went into labor, and
  you were born there.
⁶ Hold me close to your heart
  where your royal seal is
  worn.
Keep me as close to
  yourself as the bracelet
  on your arm.
My love for you is so strong it
  won't let you go.
Love is as powerful as death.
Love's jealousy is as strong
  as the grave.
Love is like a blazing fire.
Love burns like a mighty
  flame.
⁷ No amount of water can put it
  out.
Rivers can't sweep it away.
Suppose someone offers
  all their wealth to buy love.
That won't even come close
  to being enough."

The woman's brothers say,

⁸ "We have a little sister.
Her breasts are still small.
What should we do for our
  sister
  when she gets engaged?
⁹ If she were a wall,
  we'd build silver towers on
  her.
If she were a door,

we'd cover her with cedar
  boards."

The woman says to the king,

¹⁰ "I am a wall.
My breasts are like well-
  built towers.
So in your eyes I've become
  like someone who makes
  you happy.
¹¹ Solomon, you had a vineyard
  in Baal Hamon.
You rented your vineyard
  to others.
They had to pay 25 pounds
  of silver for its fruit.
¹² But I can give my own
  vineyard to anyone I
  want to.
So I give my 25 pounds of
  silver to you, Solomon.
Give 5 pounds to those who
  take care of its fruit."

The king says,

¹³ "My love, you live in the
  gardens.
My friends listen for your
  voice.
But let me hear it now."

The woman says,

¹⁴ "Come away with me, my love.
Be like an antelope
or like a young deer
  on mountains that are full
  of spices."

Isaiah

Introduction:

Isaiah wrote this book. He was a prophet in the land of Judah. He told the people what God had said. Isaiah brought sad news. The people of Israel had sinned against God, so God was going to punish them. War was going to come and destroy the cities. The Israelites would have to leave their land. But God still loved his people, so he promised to send a time of peace too. He promised to let his people go home someday. God also promised to send someone to help them. He would send a suffering servant to save people. Isaiah was talking about Jesus.

Outline of contents:

1 Here is the vision about Judah and Jerusalem that Isaiah saw. It came to him when Uzziah, Jotham, Ahaz and Hezekiah were ruling. They were kings of Judah. Isaiah was the son of Amoz.

The Nation Refuses to Obey the LORD

2 Listen to me, you heavens!
  Pay attention to me,
    earth!
  The LORD has said,
  "I raised children. I brought
    them up.
  But they have refused to
    obey me.
3 The ox knows its master.
  The donkey knows where
    its owner feeds it.
  But Israel does not know me.
  My people do not
    understand me."

4 How terrible it will be for this
    sinful nation!
  They are loaded down with
    guilt.
  They are people who do
    nothing but evil.
  They are children who are
    always sinning.
  They have deserted the LORD.
  They have turned against
    the Holy One of Israel.
  They have turned their
    backs on him.

5 Israel, why do you want to be
    beaten all the time?
  Why do you always refuse
    to obey the LORD?

Your head is covered with
wounds.
Your whole heart is weak.
⁶There isn't a healthy spot on
your body.
You are not healthy from
the bottom of your feet to
the top of your head.
You have nothing but
wounds, cuts
and open sores.
They haven't been cleaned
up or bandaged
or treated with olive oil.

⁷Your country has been
deserted.
Your cities have been
burned down.
The food from your fields
is being eaten up by
outsiders.
They are doing it right in
front of you.
Your land has been
completely destroyed.
It looks as if strangers have
taken it over.
⁸The city of Zion is left like a
shed
where someone stands
guard in a vineyard.
It is left like a hut in a
cucumber field.
It's like a city being attacked.
⁹The Lord who rules over all
has let some people live
through that time of
trouble.
If he hadn't, we would have
become like Sodom.
We would have been like
Gomorrah.

¹⁰Rulers of Sodom,
hear the Lord's message.

People of Gomorrah,
listen to the instruction of
our God.
¹¹"Do you think I need any
more of your sacrifices?"
asks the Lord.
"I have more than enough of
your burnt offerings.
I have more than enough
of rams
and the fat of your fattest
animals.
I do not find any pleasure
in the blood of your bulls,
lambs and goats.
¹²Who asked you to bring all
these animals
when you come to worship
me?
Who asked you and your
animals
to walk all over my
courtyards?
¹³Stop bringing offerings that
do not mean anything to
me!
I hate your incense.
I can't stand your worthless
gatherings.
I can't stand the way you
celebrate your New
Moon feasts,
Sabbath days and special
services.
¹⁴Your New Moon feasts and
your other appointed
feasts
I hate with my whole being.
They have become a heavy
load to me.
I am tired of carrying it.
¹⁵You might spread out your
hands toward me when
you pray.
But I do not look at you.

You might even offer many
prayers.
But I am not listening to
them.
Your hands are covered with
the blood of the people
you have murdered.
16 So wash and make
yourselves clean.
Get your evil actions out of
my sight!
Stop doing what is wrong!
17 Learn to do what is right!
Treat people fairly.
Help those who are treated
badly.
Stand up in court for children
whose fathers have
died.
And do the same thing for
widows.
18 "Come. Let us settle this
matter,"
says the Lord.
"Even though your sins are
bright red,
they will be as white as
snow.
Even though they are deep
red,
they will be white like
wool.
19 But you have to be willing to
change and obey me.
If you are, you will eat the
good things that grow on
the land.
20 But if you are not willing to
obey me,
you will be killed by
swords."
The Lord has spoken.
21 See how the faithful city of
Jerusalem

has become like a
prostitute!
Once it was full of people
who treated others
fairly.
Those who did what was
right used to live in it.
But now murderers live
there!
22 Jerusalem, your silver isn't
pure anymore.
Your best wine has been
made weak with water.
23 Your rulers refuse to obey the
Lord.
They join forces with
robbers.
All of them love to accept
money from those who
want special favors.
They are always looking for
gifts from other people.
They don't stand up in court
for children whose
fathers have died.
They don't do it for widows
either.
24 The Lord is the Mighty One
of Israel.
The Lord who rules over
all announces,
"Israel, you have become my
enemies.
I will act against you in my
anger.
I will pay you back for what
you have done.
25 I will turn my power against
you.
I will make you completely
'clean.'
I will remove everything
that is not pure.
26 I will give you leaders like the
ones you had long ago.

I will give you rulers like
  those you had at the
  beginning.
Then you will be called
  the City That Does What Is
  Right.
You will also be called the
  Faithful City."

27 Zion will be saved when
  justice is done.
Those who are sorry for
  their sins will be saved
  when what is right is
  done.
28 But sinners and those who
  refuse to obey the LORD
  will be destroyed.
And those who desert the
  LORD will die.

29 "Israel, you take delight in
  worshiping among the
  sacred oak trees.
You will be full of shame
  for doing that.
You have chosen to worship
  in the sacred gardens.
You will be dishonored for
  doing that.
30 You will be like an oak tree
  whose leaves are
  dying.
You will be like a garden
  that doesn't have any
  water.
31 Your strongest men will
  become like dry pieces
  of wood.
Their worship of other
  gods will be the spark
  that lights the fire.
Everything will be burned
  up.
No one will be there to put
  the fire out."

People From Many Nations Will Worship at Mount Zion

2 Here is a vision that Isaiah,
  the son of Amoz, saw about
Judah and Jerusalem.

2 In the last days

the mountain where the
  LORD's temple is located
  will be famous.
It will be the highest
  mountain of all.
It will be raised above the
  hills.
All the nations will go
  to it.

3 People from many nations
will go there. They will say,

"Come. Let us go up to the
  LORD's mountain.
Let's go to the temple of
  Jacob's God.
He will teach us how we
  should live.
Then we will live the way
  he wants us to."
The law of the LORD will be
  taught at Zion.
His message will go out
  from Jerusalem.
4 He will judge between the
  nations.
He'll settle problems
  among many of them.
They will hammer their
  swords into plows.
They'll hammer their
  spears into pruning
  tools.
Nations will not go to war
  against one another.
They won't even train to
  fight anymore.

5 People of Jacob, come.

Let us live the way the
　　LORD has taught us to.

The Day of the LORD Is Coming

⁶ LORD, you have deserted the
　　people of Jacob.
They are your people.
The land is full of false beliefs
　　from the east.
The people practice
　　evil magic, just as the
　　Philistines do.
They do what ungodly
　　people do.
⁷ Their land is full of silver and
　　gold.
There is no end to their
　　treasures.
Their land is full of horses.
There is no end to their
　　chariots.
⁸ Their land is full of statues of
　　gods.
Their people bow down to
　　what their own hands
　　have made.
They bow down to what
　　their fingers have
　　shaped.
⁹ So people will be brought
　　low.
Everyone will be made
　　humble.
Do not forgive them.

¹⁰ Go and hide in caves in the
　　rocks, you people!
Hide in holes in the
　　ground.
Hide from the terrifying
　　presence of the LORD!
Hide when he comes in
　　glory and majesty!
¹¹ Anyone who brags will be
　　brought low.

Anyone who is proud will
　　be made humble.
The LORD alone will be
　　honored at that time.

¹² The LORD who rules over all
　　has set apart a day when
　　he will judge.
He has set it apart for all
　　those who are proud
　　and think they are
　　important.
He has set it apart for all
　　those who brag about
　　themselves.
All of them will be brought
　　low.
¹³ The LORD has set that day
　　apart for all the cedar
　　trees in Lebanon.
They are very tall.
He has set that day apart
　　for all the oak trees in
　　Bashan.
¹⁴ He has set it apart for all the
　　towering mountains.
He has set it apart for all
　　the high hills.
¹⁵ He has set it apart for every
　　high tower
and every strong wall.
¹⁶ He has set it apart for every
　　trading ship
and every beautiful
　　boat.
¹⁷ Anyone who brags will be
　　brought low.
Anyone who is proud will
　　be made humble.
The LORD alone will be
　　honored at that time.
¹⁸ 　And the statues of gods will
　　totally disappear.
¹⁹ People will run and hide in
　　caves in the rocks.

They will go into holes in
the ground.
They will run away from the
terrifying presence of
the LORD.
They will run when he
comes in glory and
majesty.
When he comes, he will
shake the earth.

²⁰ People had made some
statues of gods out of
silver.
They had made others out
of gold.
Then they worshiped
them.
But when the LORD comes,
they will throw the statues
away to the moles and
bats.

²¹ Those people will run and
hide in caves in the rocks.
They will go into holes in
the cliffs.
They will run away from the
terrifying presence of
the LORD.
They will run when he
comes in glory and
majesty.
When he comes, he will
shake the earth.

²² Stop trusting in mere human
beings, who can't help
you.
They only live for a little
while.
What good are they?

The LORD Will Judge Jerusalem and Judah

3 Here is what
the LORD who rules over all
is about to do.

The LORD will take away from
Jerusalem and Judah
supplies and help alike.
He will take away all the
supplies of food and
water.

² He'll take away heroes and
soldiers.
He'll take away judges and
prophets.
He'll take away fortune
tellers and elders.

³ He'll take away captains of
group of 50 men.
He'll take away
government leaders.
He'll take away advisers,
skilled workers
and those who are clever at
doing evil magic.

⁴ The LORD will make mere
youths their leaders.
Children will rule over
them.

⁵ People will treat one another
badly.
They will fight against one
another.
They will fight against
their neighbors.
Young people will attack old
people.
Ordinary people will
attack those who are
more important.

⁶ A man will grab one of his
brothers
in his father's house. He
will say,
"You have a coat. So you be
our leader.
Take charge of all these
broken-down
buildings!"

[7] But at that time the brother
will cry out,
"I can't help you.
I don't have any food or
clothing in my house.
Don't make me the leader
of these people."

[8] Jerusalem is about to fall.
And so is Judah.
They say and do things
against the LORD.
They dare to disobey him
to his very face.
[9] The look on their faces is a
witness against them.
They show off their sin, just
as the people of Sodom
did.
They don't even try to
hide it.
How terrible it will be for
them!
They have brought trouble
on themselves.

[10] Tell those who do what is
right that things will go
well with them.
They will enjoy the results
of the good things
they've done.
[11] But how terrible it will be for
those who do what is
evil!
Trouble is about to fall on
them.
They will be paid back for
the evil things they've
done.

[12] Those who are young treat
my people badly.
Women rule over them.
My people, your leaders have
taken you down the
wrong path.

They have turned you away
from the right path.

[13] The LORD takes his place in
court.
He stands up to judge the
people.
[14] He judges the elders and
leaders of his people.
He says to them,
"My people are like a
vineyard.
You have destroyed them.
The things you have taken
from poor people are in
your houses.
[15] What do you mean by
crushing my people?
Why are you grinding the
faces of the poor into the
dirt?"
announces the Lord.
He is the LORD who rules
over all.

[16] The LORD continues,
"The women in Zion are
very proud.
They walk along with their
noses in the air.
They tease men with their
eyes.
They sway their hips as they
walk along.
Little chains jingle on their
ankles.
[17] So I will put sores on the
heads of Zion's women.
And I will remove the hair
from their heads."

[18] At that time the Lord will
take away the beautiful things
they wear. He will take away
their decorations, headbands
and moon-shaped necklaces.
[19] He'll take away their earrings,

bracelets and veils. ²⁰ He'll remove their headdresses, anklets and belts. He'll take away their perfume bottles and charms. ²¹ He'll remove the rings they wear on their fingers and in their noses. ²² He'll take away their fine robes and their capes and coats. He'll take away their purses ²³ and mirrors. And he'll take away their linen clothes, turbans and shawls.

²⁴ Instead of smelling sweet,
  the women will smell bad.
Instead of wearing belts,
  they will wear ropes.
Instead of having beautiful
    hair,
  they won't have any hair at
    all.
Instead of wearing fine
    clothes,
  they'll wear rough clothes
    to show how sad they
    are.
Instead of being beautiful,
  on their bodies they'll
    have the marks of their
    owners.
²⁵ Jerusalem, your men will be
    killed by swords.
  Your soldiers will die in
    battle.
²⁶ The city of Zion will be very
    sad.
  Like a widow, she will lose
    everything.
  She will sit on the ground
    and mourn.

4 ¹ At that time seven women will grab hold of one man. They'll say to him, "We will eat our own food. We'll provide our own clothes.

Just let us become your wives. Take away our shame!"

The Branch of the LORD

² At that time Israel's king will be beautiful and glorious. He will be called The Branch of the LORD. The fruit of the land will be the pride and glory of those who are still left alive in Israel. ³ Those who are left in Zion will be called holy. They will be recorded among those who are alive in Jerusalem. ⁴ The Lord will wash away the sin of the women in Zion. He will clean up the blood that was spilled there. He will judge those who spilled that blood. His burning anger will blaze out at them. ⁵ Then the LORD will create over Jerusalem a cloud of smoke by day. He will also create a glow of flaming fire at night. The cloud and fire will appear over all of Mount Zion. They will also appear over the people who gather together there. The LORD's glory will be like a tent over everything. ⁶ It will cover the people and give them shade from the hot sun all day long. It will be a safe place where they can hide from storms and rain.

The Song of the Vineyard

5 I will sing a song for the LORD.
  He is the one I love.
  It's a song about his
    vineyard Israel.
The one I love had a
    vineyard.
  It was on a hillside that had
    rich soil.

² He dug up the soil and
　　removed its stones.
He planted the very best
　　vines in it.
He built a lookout tower
　　there.
He also cut out a winepress
　　for it.
Then he kept looking for a
　　crop of good grapes.
But the vineyard produced
　　only bad fruit.

³ So the LORD said, "People of
　　Jerusalem and Judah,
　　you be the judge between
　　me and my vineyard.
⁴ What more could I have done
　　for my vineyard?
I did everything I could.
I kept looking for a crop of
　　good grapes.
So why did it produce only
　　bad ones?
⁵ Now I will tell you
　　what I am going to do to
　　my vineyard.
I will take away its fence.
　　And the vineyard will be
　　destroyed.
I will break down its wall.
　　And people will walk all
　　over my vineyard.
⁶ I will turn my vineyard
　　into a dry and empty
　　desert.
It will not be pruned or
　　taken care of.
Thorns and bushes will
　　grow there.
I will command the clouds
　　not to rain on it."

⁷ The vineyard of the LORD
　　who rules over all
　　is the nation of Israel.

The people of Judah
　　are the vines he took
　　delight in.
He kept looking for them to
　　do what is fair.
But all he saw was blood
　　being spilled.
He kept looking for them to
　　do what is right.
But all he heard were cries
　　of suffering.

The LORD Judges His Vineyard

⁸ How terrible it will be for
　　you who get too many
　　houses!
How terrible for you who
　　get too many fields!
Finally there won't be any
　　space left in the land.
Then you will live all alone.

⁹ I heard the LORD who rules
over all announce a message.
He said,

"You can be sure that the
　　great houses will
　　become empty.
The fine homes will be left
　　with no one living in
　　them.
¹⁰ A ten-acre vineyard will
　　produce only six gallons
　　of wine.
360 pounds of seeds will
　　produce only 36 pounds
　　of grain."

¹¹ How terrible it will be for
　　those who get up early in
　　the morning
　　to start drinking!
How terrible for those who
　　stay up late at night
　　until they are drunk with
　　wine!

12 They have harps and lyres at
　　their banquets.
　　They have tambourines,
　　　flutes and wine.
　　But they don't have any
　　　concern for the mighty
　　　acts of the LORD.
　　They don't have any
　　　respect for what his
　　　power has done.
13 So my people will be taken
　　away as prisoners.
　　That's because they don't
　　　understand what the
　　　LORD has done.
　　Their nobles will die of
　　　hunger.
　　The rest of the people
　　　won't have any water
　　　to drink.
14 So Death opens its jaws to
　　receive them.
　　Its mouth is open wide to
　　　swallow them up.
　　Their nobles and the rest of
　　　the people will go down
　　　into it.
　　They will go there together
　　　with all those who have
　　　wild parties.
15 So people will be brought
　　low.
　　Everyone will be made
　　　humble.
　　Those who brag will be
　　　brought down.
16 But the LORD who rules over
　　all will be honored
　　because he judges fairly.
　　The holy God will prove that
　　　he is holy
　　by doing what is right.
17 Then sheep will graze as if
　　they were in their own
　　grasslands.

Lambs will eat grass
　　among the destroyed
　　buildings
　　where rich people used to
　　live.

18 How terrible it will be for
　　those who continue to
　　sin
　　and lie about it!
　　How terrible for those who
　　　keep on doing what is
　　　evil
　　as if they were tied to it!
19 How terrible for those who
　　say,
　　"Let God hurry up and do
　　　what he says he will.
　　We want to see it
　　　happen.
　　Let us see the plan of the
　　　Holy One of Israel.
　　We want to know what
　　　it is."

20 How terrible it will be for
　　those who say
　　that what is evil is good!
　　How terrible for those who
　　　say
　　that what is good is evil!
　　How terrible for those who
　　　say
　　that darkness is light
　　and light is darkness!
　　How terrible for those who
　　　say
　　that what is bitter is sweet
　　and what is sweet is
　　　bitter!

21 How terrible it will be for
　　those who think they are
　　wise!
　　How terrible for those who
　　　think they are really
　　　clever!

²² How terrible it will be for
those
who are heroes at drinking
wine!
How terrible for those
who are heroes at mixing
drinks!
²³ How terrible for those
who take money to set
guilty people free!
How terrible for those
who don't treat good
people fairly!
²⁴ Flames of fire burn up
straw.
Dry grass sinks down into
those flames.
Evil people will be like plants
whose roots rot away.
They will be like flowers
that are blown away like
dust.
That's because they have said
no to the law of the LORD
who rules over all.
They have turned against
the message of the Holy
One of Israel.
²⁵ So the LORD is angry with his
people.
He raises his hand against
them and strikes them
down.
The mountains shake.
The bodies of dead people
lie in the streets like
trash.
Even then, the LORD is still
angry.
His hand is still raised
against them.
²⁶ He lifts up a banner to gather
the nations that are far
away.

He whistles for them to
come
from the farthest places on
earth.
Here they come.
They are moving very
quickly.
²⁷ None of them grows tired.
None of them falls down.
None of them sleeps or
even takes a nap.
All of them are ready for
battle.
Every belt is pulled
tight.
Not a single sandal strap is
broken.
²⁸ The enemies' arrows are
sharp.
All their bows are ready.
The hooves of their horses
are as hard as rock.
Their chariot wheels turn
like a twister.
²⁹ The sound of their army is
like the roar of lions.
It's like the roar of young
lions.
They growl as they
capture what they
were chasing.
They carry it off.
No one can take it away
from them.
³⁰ At that time the enemy
army will roar over
Israel.
It will sound like the
roaring of the ocean.
If someone looks at the land
of Israel,
there is only darkness and
trouble.
The clouds will make even
the sun become dark.

The Lord Appoints Isaiah to Speak for Him

6 In the year that King Uzziah died, I saw the Lord. He was seated on his throne. His long robe filled the temple. He was highly honored. ² Above him were seraphs. Each of them had six wings. With two wings they covered their faces. With two wings they covered their feet. And with two wings they were flying. ³ They were calling out to one another. They were saying,

> "Holy, holy, holy is the LORD
>   who rules over all.
> The whole earth is full of
>   his glory."

⁴ The sound of their voices caused the stone doorframe to shake. The temple was filled with smoke.

⁵ "How terrible it is for me!" I cried out. "I'm about to be destroyed! My mouth speaks sinful words. And I live among people who speak sinful words. Now I have seen the King with my own eyes. He is the LORD who rules over all."

⁶ A seraph flew over to me. He was holding a hot coal. He had used tongs to take it from the altar. ⁷ He touched my mouth with the coal. He said, "This has touched your lips. Your guilt has been taken away. Your sin has been paid for."

⁸ Then I heard the voice of the Lord. He said, "Who will I send? Who will go for us?"

I said, "Here I am. Send me!"

⁹ So he said, "Go and speak to these people. Tell them,

> " 'You will hear but never
>   understand.
> You will see but never
>   know what you are
>   seeing.'
¹⁰ Make the hearts of these
>   people stubborn.
> Plug up their ears.
> Close their eyes.
> Otherwise they might see
>   with their eyes.
> They might hear with their
>   ears.
> They might understand
>   with their hearts.
> And they might turn to me
>   and be healed."

¹¹ Then I said, "Lord, how long will it be like that?"

He answered,

> "It will last until the cities of
>   Israel are destroyed.
> It will last until no one is
>   living in them.
> It will last until the houses
>   are deserted.
> The fields will be
>   completely destroyed.
¹² It will last until the LORD has
>   sent everyone far away.
> The land will be totally
>   deserted.
¹³ Suppose only a tenth of the
>   people remain there.
> Even then the land will be
>   completely destroyed
>   again.
> But when oak trees and
>   terebinth trees
>   are cut down, stumps are
>   left.
> And my holy people will be
>   like stumps
>   that begin to grow again."

The Sign of Immanuel

7 Ahaz was king of Judah. Rezin was king of Aram. And Pekah was king of Israel. Rezin and Pekah marched up to fight against Jerusalem. But they couldn't overpower it. Ahaz was the son of Jotham and the grandson of Uzziah. Pekah was the son of Remaliah.

² The royal family of Ahaz was told, "The army of Aram has joined forces with Ephraim's army." So the hearts of Ahaz and his people trembled with fear. They shook just as trees in the forest shake when the wind blows through them.

³ The LORD said to Isaiah, "Go out and see Ahaz. Take your son Shear-Jashub with you. Meet Ahaz at the end of the channel that brings water from the Upper Pool. It is on the road to the Washerman's Field. ⁴ Tell Ahaz, 'Be careful. Stay calm. Do not be afraid. Do not lose hope because of the great anger of Rezin, Aram and the son of Remaliah. After all, they are nothing but two pieces of smoking firewood. ⁵ Aram, Ephraim and Remaliah's son have planned to destroy you. They said, ⁶ "Let's march into Judah and attack it. Let's tear everything down. Then we can share the land among ourselves. And we can make Tabeel's son king over it." ⁷ But I am the LORD and King. I say,

" ' "That will not happen.
It will not take place.
⁸ The capital of Aram is
Damascus.

And the ruler of Damascus
is only Rezin.
Do not worry about the
people of Ephraim.
They will be too crushed
to be considered a
people.
That will happen before 65
years are over.
⁹ The capital of Ephraim is
Samaria.
And the ruler of Samaria is
only Remaliah's son.
If you do not stand firm in
your faith,
you will not stand at all." ' "

¹⁰ The LORD spoke to Ahaz through Isaiah again. He said, ¹¹ "I am the LORD your God. Ask me to give you a sign. It can be anything in the deepest grave or in the highest heaven."

¹² But Ahaz said, "I won't ask. I won't test the LORD."

¹³ Then Isaiah said, "Listen, you members of the royal family of David! Isn't it enough for you to test the patience of human beings? Are you also going to test the patience of my God? ¹⁴ The Lord himself will give you a sign. The virgin is going to have a baby. She will give birth to a son. And he will be called Immanuel. ¹⁵ He will still be very young when he can decide between right and wrong. ¹⁶ Even before then, the lands of the two kings you fear will be ruined. ¹⁷ The LORD will also bring the king of Assyria against you. And he will bring him against your people and the whole royal family. That will be a time of trouble. It will be unlike any since

the people of Ephraim broke away from Judah."

The LORD Uses Assyria to Judge Judah

18 At that time the LORD will whistle for the Egyptians. They will come like flies from the Nile River in Egypt. He will also whistle for the Assyrians. They will come from their country like bees. 19 All of them will come and camp in the deep valleys. They will camp in caves in the rocks. And they'll camp near bushes and water holes. 20 At that time the Lord will use the Assyrians to punish you. Ahaz had hired them earlier from east of the Euphrates River. Now their king will be like a razor in the Lord's hand. He will shave the hair from your head and private parts. He will also shave off your beards. 21 At that time a person may only be able to keep alive one young cow and two goats. 22 But they will give plenty of milk to live on. In fact, everyone left in the land will only have milk curds and honey to eat. 23 The land used to have vineyards with 1,000 vines worth 25 pounds of silver. But soon the whole land will be covered with thorns and bushes. 24 Hunters will go there with bows and arrows. That's because it will be covered with bushes and thorns. 25 All the hills used to be plowed with hoes. But you won't go there anymore. That's because you will be afraid of the thorns and bushes. Cattle will be turned loose on those hills. Sheep will also run there.

Isaiah and His Children Are Signs

8 The LORD said to me, "Get a large sheet of paper. Write 'Maher-Shalal-Hash-Baz' on it with a pen." 2 So I sent for Zechariah and Uriah the priest. Zechariah is the son of Jeberekiah. Zechariah and Uriah were witnesses for me whom I could trust. 3 Then I went and slept with my wife, who was a prophet. She became pregnant and had a baby boy. The LORD said to me, "Name him Maher-Shalal-Hash-Baz. 4 The king of Assyria will carry off the wealth of Damascus. He will also carry away the goods that were taken from Samaria. That will happen before the boy knows how to say 'My father' or 'My mother.' "

5 The LORD continued,

6 "I am like the gently flowing
    stream of Siloam.
But the people of Judah
    have turned their backs
    on me.
They are filled with joy
    because of the fall of
    Rezin
    and the son of Remaliah.
7 So I am about to bring
    against these people
    the king of Assyria and his
    whole army.
The Assyrians will be like the
    mighty Euphrates River
    when it is flooding.
They will run over
    everything in their
    path.

⁸They will sweep on into
Judah like a flood.
They will pass through
Judah and reach all the
way to Jerusalem.
Immanuel, they will attack
your land like an eagle.
Their wings will spread out
and cover it."

⁹Sound the battle cry, you
nations!
But you will be torn
apart.
Listen, all you lands far
away!
Prepare for battle! But you
will be torn apart.
Prepare for battle! But you
will be torn apart.

¹⁰Make your battle plans! But
you won't succeed.
Give your orders! But they
won't be carried out.
That's because God is
with us.

¹¹The LORD speaks to me
while his powerful hand is on
me. He is warning me not to live
the way these people live. He
says,

¹²"People of Judah, do not
agree with those who say
Isaiah is guilty of treason.
Do not fear what they fear.
Do not be afraid.

¹³The LORD rules over all.
So you must think about
him as holy.
You must have respect for
him.
You must fear him.

¹⁴Then the LORD will be a holy
place of safety for you.
But that's not true for many
people in Israel and
Judah.
He will be a stone that
causes them to trip.
He will be a rock that
makes them fall.
And for the people of
Jerusalem
he will be a trap and a
snare.

¹⁵Many of them will trip.
They will fall and be
broken.
They will be trapped and
captured."

¹⁶Tie up and seal this warning
that the LORD said to you
through me.
Preserve among my
followers what he taught
you through me.

¹⁷I will wait for the LORD.
He is turning his face away
from Jacob's people.
I will put my trust in him.

¹⁸Here I am. Here are the children the LORD has given me. We
are signs and reminders to Israel from the LORD who rules
over all. He lives on Mount Zion.

The Darkness Turns to Light

¹⁹There are people who get
messages from those who have
died. But these people only
whisper words that are barely
heard. Suppose someone tells
you to ask for advice from these
people. Shouldn't you ask for
advice from your God instead?
Why should you get advice
from dead people to help those
who are alive? ²⁰Follow what

the LORD taught you and said to you through me. People who don't speak in keeping with these words will have no hope in the morning. ²¹ They will suffer and be hungry. They'll wander through the land. When they are very hungry, they will become angry. They'll look up toward heaven. They'll ask for bad things to happen to their king and their God. ²² Then they will look at the earth. They'll see nothing but suffering and darkness. They'll see terrible sadness. They'll be driven into total darkness.

9 But there won't be any more sadness for those who were suffering. In the past the LORD brought shame on the land of Zebulun. He also brought shame on the land of Naphtali. But in days to come he will honor Galilee, where people from other nations live. He will honor the land along the Mediterranean Sea. And he will honor the territory east of the Jordan River.

² The people who are now
     living in darkness
   will see a great light.
   They are now living in a very
     dark land.
   But a light will shine on
     them.
³ LORD, you will make our
     nation larger.
   You will increase their joy.
   They will show you how glad
     they are.
   They will be as glad as
     people are at harvest
     time.

They will be as glad as
     warriors are
   when they share the things
     they've taken after a
     battle.
⁴ You set Israel free from
     Midian long ago.
   In the same way, you will
     break
the heavy yoke that weighs
     Israel down.
   You will break the wooden
     beams that are on their
     shoulders.
   You will break the rods of
     those who strike them
     down.
⁵ Every fighting man's boot
     that he wore in battle
   will be burned up.
   So will every piece of
     clothing covered with
     blood.
   All of them will be thrown
     into the fire.
⁶ A child will be born to us.
   A son will be given to us.
   He will rule over us.
And he will be called
   Wonderful Adviser and
     Mighty God.
He will also be called Father
   Who Lives Forever
and Prince Who Brings
     Peace.
⁷ There will be no limit to how
     great his authority is.
   The peace he brings will
     never end.
He will rule on David's
     throne
   and over his kingdom.
He will make the
   kingdom strong
     and secure.

His rule will be based on
what is fair and right.
It will last forever.
The LORD's great love
will make sure that
happens.
He rules over all.

The LORD Is Angry With Israel

8 The Lord has sent a message
against Jacob's people.
He will punish Israel.
9 All the people will know
about it.
Ephraim's people and
those who live in
Samaria will know
about it.
Their hearts are very proud.
They say,
10 "The brick buildings have
fallen down.
But we will rebuild them
with blocks of stone.
The fig trees have been
chopped down.
But we'll plant cedar trees
in place of them."
11 In spite of that, the LORD has
made Rezin's enemies
stronger.
He has stirred up Assyria
to fight against Israel.
12 Arameans from the east
have opened their mouths
and swallowed up Israel.
So have Philistines from
the west.

Even then, the LORD is still
angry.
His hand is still raised
against them.
13 But his people have not
returned

to the God who struck
them down.
They haven't turned for help
to the LORD who rules over
all.
14 So he will cut off from Israel
heads and tails alike.
In a single day he will cut
off palm branches and
tall grass alike.
The palm branches are the
people who rule over
others.
The tall grass is the people
who bow down to them.
15 The elders and important
leaders are the heads.
The prophets who teach
lies are the tails.
16 Those who guide the people
of Israel are leading
them down the wrong
path.
So those who follow them
aren't on the right road.
17 The Lord will not be pleased
with the young men.
He won't take pity on
widows and on children
whose fathers have died.
All of them are ungodly and
evil.
They say foolish things
with their mouths.

Even then, the LORD is still
angry.
His hand is still raised
against them.
18 What is evil burns like a fire.
It burns up bushes and
thorns.
It sets the forest on fire.
It sends up a huge column
of smoke.

¹⁹ The LORD rules over all.
When he gets angry, he
will burn up the land.
The people will burn in the
fire.
They will not spare one
another.
²⁰ People will eat up everything
they can find on their
right.
But they'll still be hungry.
They will eat everything they
can find on their left.
But they won't be satisfied.
So they will eat the dead
bodies of their children.
²¹ That's what Manasseh's
people will do to
Ephraim.
And that's what Ephraim's
people will do to
Manasseh.
Together they will turn
against Judah.

Even then, the LORD is still
angry.
His hand is still raised
against them.

10 How terrible it will be for
you
who make laws that aren't
fair!
How terrible for you
who write laws that make
life hard for others!
² You take away the rights of
poor people.
You hold back what is fair
from my people who are
suffering.
You take for yourselves what
belongs to widows.
You rob children whose
fathers have died.

³ What will you do on the day
when the LORD punishes
you?
On that day trouble will
come from far away.
Who will you run to for help?
Who will you trust your
riches with?
⁴ All you can do is bow down
in fear among the
prisoners.
All you can do is fall
among those who have
died in battle.

Even then, the LORD is still
angry.
His hand is still raised
against them.

The LORD Will Judge Assyria

⁵ The LORD says, "How terrible
it will be for the people of
Assyria!
They are the war club that
carries out my anger.
⁶ I will send them against the
ungodly nation of Judah.
I will order them to fight
against my own people.
My people make me angry.
I will order Assyria to take
their goods and carry
them away.
I will order Assyria to walk
on my people
as if they were walking on
mud.
⁷ But that is not what the king
of Assyria plans.
It is not what he has in
mind.
His purpose is to destroy
many nations.
His purpose is to put an
end to them.

8 'Aren't all my commanders
       kings?' he says.
9   'I took over Kalno just as I
       took Carchemish.
   I took over Hamath just as I
       did Arpad.
   I took Samaria just as I did
       Damascus.
10 My powerful hand grabbed
       hold of kingdoms
   whose people worship
       statues of gods.
   They had more gods than
       Jerusalem and Samaria
       did.
11 I took over Samaria and its
       statues of gods.
   In the same way, I will
       take Jerusalem and
       its gods.' "

12 The Lord will finish everything he has planned to do
against Mount Zion and Jerusalem. Then he'll say, "Now I will
punish the king of Assyria. I will
punish him because his heart
and his eyes are so proud. 13 The
king of Assyria says,

" 'By my power
       I have taken over all these
       nations.
   I am very wise.
   I have great
       understanding.
   I have wiped out the borders
       between nations.
   I've taken their treasures.
   Like a great hero I've
       brought their kings
       under my control.
14 I've taken the wealth of the
       nations.
   It was as easy as reaching
       into a bird's nest.

I've gathered the riches of all
       these countries.
   It was as easy as gathering
       eggs
   that have been left in a
       nest.
Not a single baby bird
       flapped its wings.
   Not one of them opened its
       mouth to chirp.' "

15 Does an ax claim to be more
       important
   than the person who
       swings it?
Does a saw brag that it is
       better
   than the one who uses it?
That would be like a stick
       swinging the person who
       picks it up!
It would be like a war club
       waving the one who
       carries it!
16 So the LORD who rules
       over all will send a
       sickness.
   The Lord will send it on the
       king of Assyria's strong
       fighting men.
   It will make them weaker
       and weaker.
The army he was so proud
       of will be completely
       destroyed.
   It will be as if it had been
       burned up in a fire.
17 The LORD is the Light of
       Israel.
   He will become a fire.
   Israel's Holy One will
       become a flame.
In a single day he will burn
       up all Assyria's bushes.
   He will destroy all their
       thorns.

18 He will completely destroy
    the beauty
  of their forests and rich
    farm lands.
  The Assyrian army will be
    like a sick person
  who becomes weaker and
    weaker.
19 It will be like the trees of their
    forests.
  So few of them will be left
    standing
  that even a child could
    count them.

The Israelites Who Are Left Alive

20 In days to come, some people
    will still be left alive in
    Israel.
  They will be from Jacob's
    family line.
  But they won't depend any
    longer on
  the nation that struck them
    down.
  Instead, they will truly
    depend on the LORD.
  He is the Holy One of
    Israel.
21 The people of Jacob who are
    still alive
  will return to the Mighty
    God.
22 Israel, your people might be
    as many as the grains of
    sand by the sea.
  But only a few of them will
    return.
  The LORD has handed down
    a death sentence.
  He will destroy his people.
  What he does is right.
23 The LORD who rules over
    all will carry out his
    sentence.

The Lord will destroy the
    whole land.
24 The LORD rules over all. The
Lord says,

  "My people who live in Zion,
    do not be afraid of the
    Assyrian army.
  They beat you with rods.
  They lift up war clubs
    against you,
  just as the Egyptians did.
25 Very soon I will not be angry
    with you anymore.
  I will turn my anger
    against the Assyrians.
  I will destroy them."

26 The LORD who rules over all
    will beat them with a
    whip.
  He will strike them down
    as he struck down
    Midian at the rock of
    Oreb.
  And he will stretch out his
    walking stick over the
    waters.
  That's what he did in
    Egypt.
27 People of Zion, in days to
    come he will help you.
  He will lift the heavy load
    of the Assyrians from
    your shoulders.
  He will remove their yokes
    from your necks.
  Their yokes will be broken
    because you have become
    so strong.

28 The Assyrian army has
    entered the town of
    Aiath.
  They have passed through
    Migron.

They have stored up
supplies at Mikmash.
²⁹ They have marched through
the pass there. They said,
"Let's camp for the night at
Geba."
The people of Ramah tremble
with fear.
Those who live in Gibeah
of Saul run away.
³⁰ Town of Gallim, cry out!
Laishah, listen!
Poor Anathoth!
³¹ The people of Madmenah are
running away.
Those who live in Gebim
are hiding.
³² Today the Assyrians have
stopped at Nob.
They are shaking their fists
at Mount Zion in the city of
Jerusalem.
³³ The Assyrian soldiers are like
trees in a forest.
The LORD who rules over all
will chop them down.
The Lord will cut off their
branches
with his great power.
He will chop the tall trees
down.
He will cut down even the
highest ones.
³⁴ The Mighty One will chop
down the forest with his
ax.
He will cut down the cedar
trees in Lebanon.

A Branch Will Come From Jesse's Family Line

11 Jesse's family is like a tree
that has been cut down.
A new little tree will grow
from its stump.
From its roots a Branch
will grow and produce
fruit.
² The Spirit of the LORD will
rest on that Branch.
The Spirit will help
him to be wise and
understanding.
The Spirit will help him make
wise plans and carry
them out.
The Spirit will help him
know the LORD and have
respect for him.
³ The Branch will take
delight
in respecting the LORD.

He will not judge things only
by the way they look.
He won't make decisions
based simply on what
people say.
⁴ He will always do what is
right
when he judges those who
are in need.
He'll be completely fair
when he makes decisions
about poor people.
When he commands that
people be punished,
it will happen.
When he orders that evil
people be put to death,
it will take place.
⁵ He will put on godliness as if
it were his belt.
He'll wear faithfulness
around his waist.

⁶ Wolves will live with lambs.
Leopards will lie down
with goats.
Calves and lions will eat
together.

And little children will lead
  them around.
7 Cows will eat with bears.
  Their little ones will lie
   down together.
  And lions will eat straw
   like oxen.
8 A baby will play near a hole
   where cobras live.
  A young child will put its
   hand into a nest
  where poisonous snakes
   live.
9 None of those animals
   will harm or destroy
   anything or anyone
  on my holy mountain of
   Zion.
The oceans are full of water.
  In the same way, the earth
   will be filled
  with the knowledge of the
   LORD.

10 At that time, here is what
the man who is called the Root
of Jesse will do. He will be like
a banner that brings nations together. They will come to him.
And the place where he rules
will be glorious. 11 At that time
the Lord will reach out his hand.
He will gather his people a second time. He will bring back
those who are left alive. He'll
bring them back from Assyria,
Lower Egypt, Upper Egypt and
Cush. He'll bring them from
Elam, Babylon and Hamath. He
will also bring them from the islands of the Mediterranean Sea.

12 He will lift up a banner.
  It will show the nations
   that he is gathering the
   people of Israel.

He'll bring back those who
  had been taken away as
   prisoners.
He'll gather together the
  scattered people of
   Judah.
He'll bring them back from
  all four directions.
13 Ephraim's people won't be
  jealous anymore.
  Judah's attackers will be
   destroyed.
Ephraim won't be jealous of
  Judah.
  And Judah won't attack
   Ephraim.
14 Together they will rush down
  the slopes of Philistia to
   the west.
  They'll take what belongs
   to the people of the
   east.
They'll take over Edom and
  Moab.
  The people of Ammon
   will be under their
   control.
15 The LORD will dry up
  the Red Sea in Egypt.
By his power he'll send a
  burning wind
  to sweep over the
   Euphrates River.
He will break it up into many
  streams.
  Then people will be able
   to go across it wearing
   sandals.
16 There was a road the people
  of Israel used
  when they came up from
   Egypt.
In the same way, there will be
  a wide road coming out
   of Assyria.

It will be used by the LORD's people who are left alive there.

Two Songs of Praise

12 In days to come, the people of Israel will sing,

"LORD, we will praise you.
You were angry with us.
But now your anger has
turned away from us.
And you have brought us
comfort.
² God, you are the one who
saves us.
We will trust in you.
Then we won't be afraid.
LORD, you are the one who
gives us strength.
You are the one who keeps
us safe.
LORD, you have saved us."
³ People of Israel, he will save
you.
That will bring you joy like
water brought up from
wells.

⁴ In days to come, the people of Israel will sing,

"Give praise to the LORD.
Make his name known.
Tell the nations what he
has done.
Announce how honored
he is.
⁵ Sing to the LORD. He has
done glorious things.
Let it be known all over the
world.
⁶ People of Zion, give a loud shout!
Sing for joy!
The Holy One of Israel is
among you.
And he is great."

A Prophecy Against Babylon

13 Here is the prophecy against Babylon that Isaiah, the son of Amoz, saw.

² Lift up a banner on the top of
a bare hill.
Shout to the enemy
soldiers.
Wave for them to enter the
gates
that are used by the nobles
of Babylon.
³ The LORD has commanded
the soldiers he prepared
for battle.
He has sent for them to
carry out his anger
against Babylon.
They will be happy when
he wins the battle for
them.

⁴ Listen! I hear a noise in the
mountains.
It sounds like a huge
crowd.
Listen! I hear a loud noise
among the kingdoms.
It sounds like nations
gathering together.
The LORD who rules over all
is bringing
an army together for war.
⁵ They come from lands far
away.
They come from the
farthest places on
earth.
The LORD and those weapons
of his anger
are coming to destroy
the whole country of
Babylon.

⁶ Cry out! The day of the LORD
is near.

The Mighty One is
coming to destroy the
Babylonians.
⁷Their hands won't be able to
help them.
Everyone's heart will melt
away in fear.
⁸The people will be filled with
terror.
Pain and suffering will
grab hold of them.
They will groan with pain
like a woman having a
baby.
They'll look at one another in
terror.
Their faces will burn with
shame.
⁹The day of the LORD is
coming.
It will be a terrible day.
The LORD's burning anger
will blaze out.
He will make the land dry
and empty.
He'll destroy the sinners
in it.
¹⁰All the stars in the sky
will stop giving their light.
The sun will be darkened as
soon as it rises.
The moon will not shine.
¹¹The LORD will punish the
world because it is so
evil.
He will punish evil people
for their sins.
He'll put an end to the
bragging of those who
are proud.
He'll bring down the pride
of those who don't show
any pity.
¹²He'll make people harder to
find than pure gold.

They will be harder to find
than gold from Ophir.
¹³He will make the heavens
tremble.
He'll shake the earth out of
its place.
The LORD who rules over all
will show how angry he
is.
At that time his burning
anger will blaze out.

¹⁴Outsiders who live in
Babylon will scatter
like antelope that are
chased by a hunter.
They are like sheep that
don't have a shepherd.
All of them will return to
their own people.
They will run back to their
own countries.
¹⁵Those who are captured
will have spears stuck
through them.
Those who are caught will
be killed by swords.
¹⁶Their babies will be smashed
to pieces
right in front of their
eyes.
Their houses will be robbed.
Their wives will be raped.

¹⁷The LORD will stir up the
Medes to attack the
Babylonians.
They aren't interested in
getting silver.
They don't want gold.
¹⁸Instead, they will use their
bows and arrows
to strike down the young
men.
They won't even show any
mercy to babies.

They won't take pity on
  children.
19 The city of Babylon is the
  jewel of kingdoms.
It is the pride and glory of
  the Babylonians.
But God will destroy it
  just as he did Sodom and
  Gomorrah.
20 No one will ever live in
  Babylon again.
No one will live there for
  all time to come.
Those who wander in the
  desert will never set up
  their tents there.
Shepherds will never rest
  their flocks there.
21 But desert creatures will lie
  down there.
Wild dogs will fill its
  houses.
Owls will live there.
Wild goats will jump
  around in it.
22 Hyenas will live in its forts.
Wild dogs will live in its
  beautiful palaces.
The time for Babylon to be
  punished is near.
Its days are numbered.

14 The LORD will show
  tender love toward
  Jacob's people.
Once again he will choose
  Israel.
He'll give them homes in
  their own land.
Outsiders will join them.
They and the people of
  Jacob will become one
  people.
2 Nations will help Israel
  return to their own land.

Israel will possess other
  nations.
They will serve Israel
  as male and female
  servants in the LORD's
  land.
The Israelites will make
  prisoners of those
  who had held them as
  prisoners.
Israel will rule over those
  who had crushed them.

3 The LORD will put an end to
Israel's suffering and trouble.
They will no longer be forced
to do hard labor. At that time,
4 they will make fun of the king
of Babylon. They will say,

"See how the one who
  crushed others has
  fallen!
See how his anger has
  come to an end!
5 The LORD has taken away the
  authority of evil people.
He has broken the power of
  rulers.
6 When they became angry,
  they struck down
  nations.
Their blows never stopped.
In their anger they brought
  nations under their
  control.
They attacked them again
  and again.
7 All the lands now enjoy peace
  and rest.
They break out into
  singing.
8 Even the juniper trees show
  how happy they are.
The cedar trees of Lebanon
  celebrate too.

They say, 'Babylon, you have
fallen.
Now no one comes and
cuts us down.'

⁹ "King of Babylon, many
people in the place of the
dead are really excited.
They're excited about
meeting you when you
go down there.
The spirits of the dead get up
to welcome you.
At one time all of them were
leaders in the world.
They were kings over the
nations.
They get up from their
thrones.
¹⁰ All of them call out to you.
They say,
'You have become weak, just
as we are.
You have become like us.'
¹¹ Your grand show of power
has been brought down
to the grave.
The noise of your harps has
come down here along
with your power.
Maggots are spread out
under you.
Worms cover you.

¹² "King of Babylon, you
thought you were the
bright morning star.
But now you have fallen
from heaven!
You once brought down
nations.
But now you have been
thrown down to the
earth!
¹³ You said in your heart,
'I will go up to the heavens.

I'll raise my throne
above the stars of God.
I'll sit as king on the
mountain where the
gods meet.
I'll set up my throne on the
highest slopes of Mount
Zaphon.
¹⁴ I will rise above the tops of
the clouds.
I'll make myself like the
Most High God.'
¹⁵ But now you have been
brought down to the
place of the dead.
You have been thrown into
the deepest part of the
pit.

¹⁶ "Those who see you stare at
you.
They think about what has
happened to you.
They say to themselves,
'Is this the man who shook
the earth?
Is he the one who made
kingdoms tremble with
fear?
¹⁷ Did he turn the world into a
desert?
Did he destroy its cities?
Did he refuse to let his
prisoners go home?'

¹⁸ "All the kings of the nations
are buried with honor.
Each of them lies in his
own tomb.
¹⁹ But you have been thrown
out of your tomb.
You are like a branch that
is cut off and thrown
away.
You are covered with the
bodies

of those who have been
killed by swords.
You have been tossed into
a stony pit along with
them.
You are like a dead body that
people have walked on.
20 You won't be buried like
other kings.
That's because you have
destroyed your land.
You have killed your
people.

"Let the children of that evil
man be killed.
Let none of them be left
to carry on the family
name.
21 So prepare a place to kill his
children.
Kill them because of the
sins of the rulers
who lived before them.
They must not rise to power.
They must not rule over
the world.
They must not cover the
earth with their cities."

22 "I will rise up against them,"
announces the LORD who
rules over all.
"I will destroy Babylon.
It will not be remembered
anymore.
No one will be left alive
there.
I will destroy its people
and their children after
them,"
announces the LORD.
23 "I will turn it into a place
where nothing but owls
can live.
I will turn it into a swamp.

I will sweep through it like
a broom and destroy
everything,"
announces the LORD who
rules over all.

24 The LORD who rules over
all has made a promise. He has
said,

"You can be sure that what
I have planned will
happen.
What I have decided will
take place.
25 I will crush the Assyrians in
my land.
On my mountains I will
walk all over them.
The yokes they put on my
people will be removed.
The heavy load they put on
their shoulders will be
taken away."

26 That's how the LORD carries
out his plan all over the
world.
That's how he reaches out
his powerful hand to
punish all the nations.
27 The LORD who rules over all
has planned it.
Who can stop him?
He has reached out his
powerful hand.
Who can keep him from
using it?

A Prophecy Against the Philistines

28 This prophecy came to me
from the LORD in the year King
Ahaz died. The LORD said,

29 "The rod of Assyria has struck
all of you Philistines.

But do not be glad that it is broken.
That rod is like a snake that will produce an even more poisonous snake.
It will produce a darting, poisonous serpent.
³⁰ Even the poorest people in Israel will have plenty to eat.
Those who are in need will lie down in safety.
But I will destroy your families.
They will die of hunger.
I will kill any of them who are still left alive.

³¹ "Cities of Philistia, cry out for help! Scream in pain!
All you Philistines, melt away in fear!
An army is coming from the north in a cloud of dust.
No one in its ranks is falling behind.
³² What answer should be given to the messengers from that nation?
Tell them, 'The LORD has made Zion secure.
His suffering people will find safety there.' "

A Prophecy Against Moab

15 Here is a prophecy against Moab that the LORD gave me.

The city of Ar in Moab is destroyed.
It happened in a single night.
Kir in Moab is also destroyed.
It happened in a single night.

² The people of Dibon go up to their temple to worship.
They go to their high places to weep.
The people of Moab cry over the cities of Nebo and Medeba.
All their heads are shaved.
All their beards have been cut off.
³ In the streets they wear the rough clothing people wear when they're sad.
On their roofs and in the market places
all of them are crying.
They fall down flat with their faces toward the ground.
And they weep.
⁴ The people of Heshbon and Elealeh cry out.
Their voices are heard all the way to Jahaz.
So the fighting men of Moab cry out.
Their hearts are weak.

⁵ My heart cries out over Moab.
Some who run away get as far as Zoar.
Others run all the way to Eglath Shelishiyah.
Others go up the hill to Luhith.
They are weeping as they go.
Still others travel the road to Horonaim.
They sing a song of sadness because their town is being destroyed.
⁶ The waters at Nimrim are dried up.
And so is the grass.
The plants have died.
Nothing green is left.

7 The people are trying to
  escape
  through the Valley of the
  Poplar Trees.
They are carrying with them
  the wealth
  they have collected and
  stored up.
8 Their loud cries echo along
  the border of Moab.
They reach as far as
  Eglaim.
Their songs of sadness
  reach all the way to Beer
  Elim.
9 The waters of the city of
  Dimon are full of blood.
But the LORD will bring
  even more trouble on
  Dimon.
He will bring lions against
  those who run away
  from Moab.
They will also attack those
  who remain in the
  land.

16 People of Moab, send
       lambs as a gift
to the ruler of Judah.
Send them from Sela.
Send them across the
  desert.
Send them to Mount Zion
  in the city of Jerusalem.
2 The women of Moab are at
  the places
  where people go across the
  Arnon River.
They are like birds that flap
  their wings
  when they are pushed from
  their nest.
3 The Moabites say to the
  rulers of Judah,

"Make up your mind. Make
  a decision.
Cover us with your shadow.
  Make it like night even at
  noon.
Hide those of us who are
  running away.
Don't turn them over to
  their enemies.
4 Let those who have run away
  from Moab stay with
  you.
Keep them safe from those
  who are trying to destroy
  them."

Those who crush others will
  be destroyed.
The killing will stop.
The attackers will
  disappear from the
  earth.
5 A man from the royal house
  of David will sit on
  Judah's throne.
He will rule with faithful
  love.
When he judges he will do
  what is fair.
He will be quick to do what
  is right.
6 We have heard all about
  Moab's pride.
We have heard how very
  proud they are.
They think they are so
  much better than others.
They brag about themselves.
But all their bragging
  is nothing but empty
  words.
7 So the people of Moab cry
  out.
All of them cry over their
  country.

Sing a song of sadness.
  Weep that you can no
    longer enjoy the raisin
    cakes of Kir Hareseth.
8 The fields of Heshbon
    dry up.
  So do the vines of Sibmah.
  The rulers of the nations
    have walked all over its
    finest vines.
  Those vines once reached as
    far as Jazer.
  They spread out toward the
    desert.
  Their new growth went
    all the way to the
    Dead Sea.
9 Jazer weeps for the vines of
    Sibmah.
  And so do I.
  Heshbon and Elealeh,
  I soak you with my tears!
  There isn't any ripe fruit for
    people to shout about.
  There isn't any harvest to
    make them happy.
10 Joy and gladness are taken
    away from the orchards.
  No one sings or shouts in
    the vineyards.
  No one stomps on grapes at
    the winepresses.
  That's because the LORD
    has put an end to the
    shouting.
11 My heart mourns over Moab
    like a song of sadness
    played on a harp.
  Deep down inside me
    I mourn over Kir
    Hareseth.
12 Moab's people go to their
    high place to pray.
  But all they do is wear
    themselves out.

  Their god Chemosh can't
    help them at all.

13 That's the message the LORD
has already spoken against
Moab. 14 But now he says, "In
exactly three years, people will
look down on Moab's glory. Now
Moab has many people. But by
that time only a few of them will
be left alive. And even they will
be weak."

Prophecies Against Damascus and Israel

17 Here is a prophecy against
Damascus that the LORD
gave me. He said,

  "Damascus will not be a city
    anymore.
  Instead, all its buildings
    will be knocked down.
2 The cities of Aroer will be
    deserted.
  They will be left to the
    flocks that lie down
    there.
  No one will make them
    afraid.
3 Ephraim's people will no
    longer have cities with
    high walls around them.
  Royal power will disappear
    from Damascus.
  Those who are left alive in
    Aram
  will be like the glory of the
    people of Israel,"
    announces the LORD
    who rules over all.

4 "In days to come, the glory
    of Jacob's people will
    fade.
  Their strength will get
    weaker and weaker.

⁵ It will be as when workers cut
and gather grain
in the Valley of Rephaim.
They gather up stalks in their
arms.
Only a few heads of grain
are left.
⁶ In the same way, only a
few people will be left
alive.
It will be as when workers
knock olives off the
trees.
Only two or three olives
are left on the highest
branches.
Four or five at most are
left on the limbs that
produce fruit,"
announces the LORD,
the God of Israel.

⁷ In days to come, people will
look to their Maker for
help.
They will turn their eyes to
the Holy One of Israel.
⁸ They won't trust in the
altars
they made with their own
hands.
They won't pay any attention
to the poles they used
to worship the female god
named Asherah.
And they won't depend on
the incense altars
they made with their own
fingers.

⁹ At that time the strong cities
in Israel will be deserted. They
will be as they were when the
Israelites drove the Canaanites
away. They will be like places
that are taken over by bushes

and weeds. The whole land will
become dry and empty.

¹⁰ Israel, you have forgotten
God, who saves you.
You have not remembered
the Rock, who keeps you
safe.
You might set out the finest
plants.
You might plant vines from
other lands.
¹¹ The plants might start to
grow on the day you set
them out.
The vines might begin to
bud on the morning you
plant them.
But even if they do, there
won't be any harvest.
Instead, there will be
sickness and pain that
won't go away.

¹² How terrible it will be for
the nations that attack
us!
The noise of their armies
is like the sound of the
ocean.
How terrible it will be for
the nations who fight
against us!
They are as loud as huge
waves crashing on the
shore.
¹³ They sound like the roar of
rushing waters.
But when the LORD speaks
out against them, they
run far away.
The wind blows them away
like straw on the hills.
A strong wind drives
them along like
tumbleweeds.

14 In the evening, the nations
terrify us.
But before morning comes,
they are gone.
That's what happens to
those who steal our
goods.
That's what happens to
those who take what
belongs to us.

A Prophecy Against Cush

18 How terrible it will be for
the land
whose armies are like
large numbers of flying
insects!
That land is along the
rivers of Cush.
2 Its people send messengers
on the Nile River.
They travel over the water
in papyrus boats.

Messengers, hurry back
home!
Go back to your people,
who are tall and have
smooth skin.
Everyone is afraid of them.
They are warriors whose
language is different
from ours.
Their land is divided up by
rivers.

3 Pay attention, all you people
of the world!
Listen, all you who live on
earth!
Banners will be lifted up on
the mountains.
And you will see them.
Trumpets will be blown.
And you will hear them.
4 The LORD says to me,

"I will look down from
heaven, where I live.
I will be as quiet as summer
heat in the sunshine.
I will be as quiet as a cloud
of dew in the heat of
harvest."
5 A farmer cuts off new growth
with pruning knives.
He cuts down spreading
branches and takes them
away.
He does it before the grapes
are harvested.
That's when the blooms
are gone and the grapes
are ripe.
In the same way, the LORD
will cut off the nations
that are gathered against
his people.
6 Their dead bodies will be
left for the birds of the
mountains to eat.
They will be left for the
wild animals.
The birds will eat the dead
bodies all summer long.
The wild animals will eat
them all through the
winter.

7 At that time gifts will be
brought to the LORD who rules
over all.

The people who are tall and
have smooth skin will
bring them.
Everyone is afraid of those
people.
They are warriors whose
language is different
from ours.
Their land is divided up by
rivers.

They will bring their gifts to
Mount Zion. That's where the
LORD who rules over all has put
his Name.

A Prophecy Against Egypt

19 Here is a prophecy
against Egypt that the
LORD gave me.

The LORD is coming to
Egypt.
He's riding on a cloud that
moves very fast.
The statues of the gods in
Egypt tremble with fear
because of him.
The hearts of the people
there melt with fear.
²The LORD says, "I will stir up
one Egyptian against
another.
Relatives will fight against
relatives.
Neighbors will fight
against one another.
Cities will fight against
cities.
Kingdoms will fight
against one another.
³The people of Egypt will lose
hope.
I will keep them from
doing what they plan to
do.
They will ask their gods for
advice.
They will turn to the spirits
of dead people for help.
They will go to people who
get messages from those
who have died.
They will ask for advice
from people who talk to
the spirits of the dead.

⁴I will hand the Egyptians over
to a mean and unkind
master.
A powerful king will rule
over them," announces
the LORD.
He is the LORD who rules
over all.

⁵The waters of the Nile River
will dry up.
The bottom of it will be
cracked and dry.
⁶Its canals will stink.
And the streams of Egypt
will get smaller and
smaller
until they dry up.
The tall grass that grows
along the river will dry
up.
⁷   So will the plants along the
banks of the Nile.
Even the planted fields along
the Nile will dry up.
Everything that grows
there will blow away and
disappear.
⁸The fishermen will moan.
All those who drop hooks
into the Nile will weep.
Those who throw their nets
on the water
will become very sad.
⁹Those who make clothes out
of flax will lose hope.
So will those who weave
fine linen.
¹⁰Those who work with cloth
will be unhappy.
And all those who work
for money will be sick at
heart.
¹¹The officials of the city of
Zoan are very foolish.

Pharaoh's wise men give
advice that doesn't make
any sense.
How can they dare to say to
Pharaoh,
"We're among the wise
men"?
How can they say to him,
"We're like the advisers to
the kings of long ago"?
¹²Pharaoh, where are your wise
men now?
Let them tell you
what the LORD who rules
over all
has planned against
Egypt.
¹³The officials of Zoan have
become foolish.
The leaders of Memphis
have been lied to.
The most important leaders
in Egypt
have led its people astray.
¹⁴The LORD has given them
a spirit that makes them
feel dizzy.
They make Egypt unsteady
in everything it does.
Egypt is like a person who
drinks too much.
He throws up and then
walks around in the
mess he's made.
¹⁵No one in Egypt can do
anything to help them.
Its elders and important
leaders can't help them.
Its prophets and priests can't
do anything.
Those who rule over others
can't help.
And those who bow down
to them can't help
either.

¹⁶In days to come, the people of Egypt will become weak. The LORD who rules over all will raise his hand against them. Then they will tremble with fear. ¹⁷The people of Judah will bring terror to the Egyptians. Everyone in Egypt who hears the name of Judah will be terrified. That's because of what the LORD who rules over all is planning to do to them.

¹⁸At that time the people of five cities in Egypt will worship the LORD. He is the LORD who rules over all. They will use the Hebrew language when they worship him. They will promise to be faithful to him. One of those cities will be called the City of the Sun.

¹⁹At that time there will be an altar to the LORD in the middle of Egypt. There will be a monument to him at its border. ²⁰They will remind people that the LORD who rules over all is worshiped in Egypt. The people there will cry out to the LORD. They will cry out because of those who treat them badly. He will send someone to stand up for them and save them. And he will set them free. ²¹So the LORD will make himself known to the people of Egypt. At that time they will recognize that he is the LORD. They will worship him by bringing sacrifices and grain offerings to him. They will make promises to the LORD. And they will keep them. ²²The LORD will strike Egypt with a plague. But then he will heal them. They will turn to the LORD. And he

will answer their prayers and heal them.

²³ At that time there will be a wide road from Egypt to Assyria. The people of Assyria will go to Egypt. And the people of Egypt will go to Assyria. The people of Egypt and Assyria will worship the LORD together. ²⁴ At that time Egypt, Assyria and Israel will be a blessing to the whole earth. ²⁵ The LORD who rules over all will bless those three nations. He will say, "Let the Egyptians be blessed. They are my people. Let the Assyrians be blessed. My hands created them. And let the Israelites be blessed. They are my very own people."

A Prophecy Against Egypt and Cush

20 Sargon, the king of Assyria, sent his highest commander to the city of Ashdod. He attacked it and captured it. ² Three years earlier the LORD had spoken to Isaiah, the son of Amoz. The LORD had said, "Take off the rough clothing you are wearing. And take off your sandals." So Isaiah did. He went around barefoot and naked.

³ After Ashdod was captured, the LORD said, "My servant Isaiah has gone around barefoot and naked for three years. He is a sign and reminder to Egypt and Cush about what will happen to them. ⁴ The king of Assyria will lead prisoners away from Egypt and Cush. Young people and old people alike will be taken away.

Like Isaiah, they will be barefoot and naked. Their backsides will be bare. So the Egyptians will be put to shame. ⁵ People trusted in Cush to help them. They bragged about what Egypt could do for them. But they will lose heart and be put to shame. ⁶ At that time the people who live on the coast of Philistia will speak up. They will say, 'See what has happened to those we depended on! We ran to them for help. We wanted them to save us from the king of Assyria. Now how can we escape?'"

A Prophecy Against Babylon

21 Here is a prophecy against Babylon that the LORD gave me. Babylon is known as the Desert by the Sea.

An attack is coming through
     the desert.
   It is coming from a land of
     terror.
   It's sweeping along like
     a windstorm blowing
     across the Negev Desert.

² I have seen a vision about
     something terrible that
     will happen.
   People are turning against
     Babylon.
   Robbers are taking its
     goods.
   Elamites, attack the city!
     Medes, surround it!
   The LORD will put an
     end to all the suffering
     Babylon has caused.

³ The vision fills my body with
     pain.
   Pains take hold of me.

They are like the pains of a
  woman having a baby.
I am shaken by what I hear.
  I'm terrified by what I see.
⁴ My heart grows weak.
  Fear makes me tremble.
I longed for evening to come.
  But it brought me horror
    instead of rest.

⁵ In my vision the Babylonians
    set the tables.
  They spread out the rugs.
  They eat and drink.
Get up, you officers!
  Rub your shields with oil!

⁶ The Lord said to me,

"Go. Put a guard on duty on
    Jerusalem's walls.
  Have him report what he
    sees.
⁷ Tell him to watch for
    chariots
  that are pulled by teams of
    horses.
Tell him to watch for men
    riding on donkeys or
    camels.
  Make sure he stays awake.
  Make sure he stays wide
    awake."

⁸ "My master!" the guard
shouts back.

"Day after day I stand here on
    the lookout tower.
  Every night I stay here on
    duty.
⁹ Look! Here comes a man in a
    chariot!
  It's being pulled by a team
    of horses.
He's calling out the news,
  'Babylon has fallen! It has
    fallen!

All the statues of its gods
  lie broken in pieces on the
    ground!' "

¹⁰ My people, you have been
    crushed
  like grain on a threshing
    floor.
But now I'm telling you the
    good news I've heard.
It comes from the LORD
  who rules over all.
He is the God of Israel.

A Prophecy Against Edom

¹¹ Here is a prophecy against
Edom that the LORD gave me.

Someone is calling out to me
  from the land of Seir. He
    says,
  "Guard, when will the
    night be over?
  Guard, how soon will it
    end?"
¹² The guard answers,
  "Morning is coming, but
    the night will return.
  If you want to ask again,
  come back and ask."

A Prophecy Against Arabia

¹³ Here is a prophecy against
Arabia that the LORD gave me.

He told me to give orders to
    traders from Dedan.
  They were camping in the
    bushes of Arabia.
¹⁴ I told them to bring water
    for those who are
    thirsty.
I also gave orders to those
  who live in Tema.
  I told them to bring food for
    those who are running
    away.

¹⁵They are running away from
where the fighting is
heaviest.
That's where the swords
are ready to strike.
That's where the bows are
ready to shoot.

¹⁶The Lord spoke to me. He said, "In exactly one year, Kedar's splendor will come to an end. ¹⁷Only a few of Kedar's soldiers who shoot arrows will be left alive." The LORD has spoken. He is the God of Israel.

A Prophecy Against Jerusalem

22 Here is a prophecy against Jerusalem that the LORD gave me. Jerusalem is also known as the Valley of Vision.

People of Jerusalem, what's
the matter with you?
Why have all of you gone
up on the roofs of your
houses?
²Why is your town so full of
noise?
Why is your city so full
of the sound of wild
parties?
Those among you who died
weren't killed by swords.
They didn't die in battle.
³All your leaders have run
away.
They've been captured
without a single arrow
being shot.
All you who were caught
were taken away as
prisoners.
You ran off while your
enemies were still far
away.

⁴So I said, "Leave me alone.
Let me weep bitter tears.
Don't try to comfort me.
My people have been
destroyed."

⁵The LORD who rules over all
sent the noise of battle
against you.
The Lord brought disorder
and terror
to the Valley of Vision.
The walls of the city were
knocked down.
Cries for help were heard
in the mountains.
⁶Soldiers from Elam came
armed with bows and
arrows.
They came with their
chariots and horses.
Soldiers from Kir got their
shields ready.
⁷Your rich valleys filled up
with chariots.
Horsemen took up their
battle positions at your
city gates.
⁸ The Lord made Judah a
place where it wasn't safe
to live anymore.

At that time, you depended
on the weapons in the
Palace of the Forest of
Lebanon.
⁹You saw that the walls of the
City of David
were broken through in
many places.
You stored up water
in the Lower Pool.
¹⁰You picked out the weaker
buildings in Jerusalem.
You tore them down and
used their stones

to strengthen the city walls
against attack.
¹¹ You built a pool between the
two walls.
You used it to save the
water
that was running down
from the Old Pool.
But you didn't look to the
God who made it all
possible.
You didn't pay any
attention to the God
who planned everything
long ago.
¹² The LORD who rules over all
called out to you at that
time.
The Lord told you to weep
and cry.
He told you to tear your
hair out.
And he told you to put
on the rough clothing
people wear when
they're sad.
¹³ Instead, you are enjoying
yourselves at wild
parties!
You are killing cattle and
sheep.
You are eating their meat
and drinking wine.
You are saying, "Let's eat and
drink,
because tomorrow we'll
die."

¹⁴ I heard the LORD who rules
over all speaking. "Your sin can
never be paid for as long as you
live," says the Lord.

¹⁵ The LORD who rules over all
speaks. The Lord says,

"Go and speak to Shebna, the
head servant.
He is in charge of the
palace. Tell him,
¹⁶ 'What are you doing here
outside the city?
Who allowed you to cut out
a tomb for yourself here?
Who said you could carve
out your grave on the
hillside?
Who allowed you to cut out
your resting place in the
rock?
¹⁷ " 'Watch out, you mighty
man!
The LORD is about to grab
you.
He is about to throw you
away.
¹⁸ He will roll you up tightly like
a ball.
He will throw you into a
very large country.
There you will die.
And that's where the
chariots you were so
proud of will be.
Those chariots will then
bring nothing but shame
on your master's family!
¹⁹ The LORD will remove you
from your job.
You will be brought down
from your high position.

²⁰ " 'At that time he will send
for his servant Eliakim. He is
the son of Hilkiah. ²¹ The LORD
will put your robe on Eliakim.
He will tie your belt around
him. He will hand your authority over to him. Eliakim will be
like a father to the people of Jerusalem and Judah. ²² The LORD

will give Eliakim the key of authority in David's royal house. No one can shut what he opens. And no one can open what he shuts. ²³ The LORD will set him firmly in place like a peg driven into a wall. He will hold a position of honor in his family. ²⁴ The good name of his whole family will depend on him. They will be like bowls and jars hanging on a peg.

²⁵ " 'But a new day is coming,' " announces the LORD who rules over all. " 'At that time the peg that was driven into the wall will give way. It will break off and fall down. And the heavy load hanging on it will also fall.' " The LORD has spoken.

A Prophecy Against Tyre

23 Here is a prophecy against Tyre that the LORD gave me.

Men in the ships of Tarshish,
    cry out!
The city of Tyre is
    destroyed.
Its houses and harbor are
    gone.
That's the message you have
    received
from the island of Cyprus.

² People on the island of Tyre,
    be silent.
Traders from the city of
    Sidon, be quiet.
Those who sail on the
    Mediterranean Sea have
    made you rich.
³ Grain from Egypt
    came across the mighty
    waters.

The harvest of the Nile
    River brought wealth
    to Tyre.
It became the market place
    of the nations.

⁴ Sidon, be ashamed. Mighty
    Tyre out in the sea, be
    ashamed.
The sea has spoken. It has
    said,
"It's as if I had never felt labor
    pains or had children.
It's as if I had never brought
    up sons or daughters.
It's as if the city of Tyre had
    never existed."
⁵ The Egyptians will hear
    about what has
    happened to Tyre.
They'll be very sad and
    troubled.

⁶ People of the island of Tyre,
    cry out!
Go across the sea to
    Tarshish.
⁷ Just look at Tyre.
It's no longer the old, old
    city that was known for
    its wild parties.
It no longer sends its people
    out
    to make their homes in
    lands far away.
⁸ Tyre was a city that produced
    kings.
Its traders were princes.
They were honored all over
    the earth.
So who planned to destroy
    such a city?
⁹ The LORD who rules over all
    planned to do it.
He wanted to bring down
    all its pride and glory.

He wanted to shame those
who were honored all
over the earth.

¹⁰ People of Tarshish, farm your
land
as they do along the Nile
River.
That's because you
don't have a harbor
anymore.
¹¹ The LORD has reached his
powerful hand out over
the sea.
He has made its kingdoms
tremble with fear.
He has given a command
concerning Phoenicia.
He has ordered that its
forts be destroyed.
¹² He said, "No more wild
parties for you!
People of Sidon, you are
now destroyed!

"Leave your city. Go across
the sea to Cyprus.
Even there you will not
find any rest."
¹³ Look at the land of the
Babylonians.
No one lives there
anymore.
The Assyrians have turned it
into a place for desert
creatures.
They built their towers in
order to attack it.
They took everything out
of its forts.
They knocked down all its
buildings.
¹⁴ Men in the ships of Tarshish,
cry out!
Mighty Tyre is destroyed!

¹⁵ A time is coming when people will forget about Tyre for
70 years. That's the length of
a king's life. But at the end of
those 70 years, Tyre will be like
the prostitute that people sing
about. They say,

¹⁶ "Forgotten prostitute, pick up
a harp.
Walk through the city.
Play the harp well. Sing many
songs.
Then you will be
remembered."

¹⁷ At the end of the 70 years,
the LORD will punish Tyre. He
will let it return to its way of life
as a prostitute. It will earn its
living with all the kingdoms on
the face of the earth. ¹⁸ But the
money it earns will be set apart
for the LORD. The money won't
be stored up or kept for Tyre. Instead, it will go to those who live
the way the LORD wants them
to. It will pay for plenty of food
and fine clothes for them.

The LORD Will Destroy the Earth

24 The LORD is going to
completely destroy
everything on earth.
He will twist its surface.
He'll scatter those who live
on it.
² Priests and people alike will
suffer.
So will masters and their
servants.
And so will women and
their female servants.
Sellers and buyers alike will
suffer.

The Lord's Prayer

Our Father which art in heaven,
Hallowed be thy name.

Thy kingdom come,
Thy will be done
On earth, as it is in heaven.

Give us this day our daily bread.
And forgive us our debts
As we forgive our debtors.

And lead us not into temptation,
But deliver us from evil.

For thine is the kingdom,
And the power,
And the glory, forever.

Amen.

These words of the Lord's Prayer are found in Matthew 6:9–13 in the King James Version. Different Bible translations use different words, but this is the most commonly memorized version of this prayer.

Love Passage for Kids
Based on 1 Corinthians 13

If I can speak beautifully and sing like an angel but don't love others, I sound like a child banging on a piano or a screeching radio. If I'm very smart—almost a genius—but don't love others, I am nothing.

Love will stand in line and wait its turn.

Love looks for the good in others.

Love doesn't always want what others have, and it doesn't brag about what it does have.

Love is polite, even when the other person is rude.

Love doesn't have to be first.

Love doesn't get angry over small things, and it doesn't remember one reason after another to be hurt.

Love isn't happy when someone else fails but is happy with the truth.

Love will always protect others, especially those who are often picked on or teased.

Love always believes the best about others and is steady and true.

Love never gives up.

The three most important things to have
are faith, hope, and love.
But the greatest of them is love.

So will those who borrow
and those who lend.
And so will those who owe
money and those who
lend it.
³ The earth will be completely
destroyed.
Everything of value will be
taken out of it.
That's what the LORD
has said.

⁴ The earth will dry up
completely.
The world will dry up and
waste away.
The heavens will fade away
along with the earth.
⁵ The earth is polluted by its
people.
They haven't obeyed the
laws of the LORD.
They haven't done what he
told them to do.
They've broken the
covenant that will last
forever.
⁶ So the LORD will send a curse
on the earth.
Its people will pay for what
they've done.
They will be burned up.
Very few of them will be
left.
⁷ The vines and fresh wine will
dry up completely.
Those who used to have a
good time will groan.
⁸ The happy sounds of
tambourines will be
gone.
The noise of those who
enjoy wild parties will
stop.
The joyful music of harps
will become silent.

⁹ People will no longer sing as
they drink wine.
Beer will taste bitter to
those who drink it.
¹⁰ Destroyed cities will lie
empty.
People will lock themselves
inside their houses.
¹¹ In the streets people will cry
out for wine.
All joy will turn into
sadness.
All joyful sounds will be
driven out of the earth.
¹² All the buildings will be
knocked down.
Every city gate will be
smashed to pieces.
¹³ That's how it will be on the
earth.
And that's how it will be
among the nations.
It will be as when workers
knock all but a few olives
off the trees.
It will be like a vine that
has only a few grapes left
after the harvest.
¹⁴ Those who are left alive will
shout for joy.
People from the west will
praise the LORD because
he is the King.
¹⁵ So give glory to him, you who
live in the east.
Honor the name of the
LORD, you who are in the
islands of the sea.
He is the God of Israel.
¹⁶ From one end of the earth
to the other we hear
singing.
People are saying,
"Give glory to the God who
always does what is right."

But I said, "I feel very bad.
  I'm getting weaker and
    weaker.
  How terrible it is for me!
People turn against one
    another.
  They can't be trusted.
  So they turn against one
    another."
17 Listen, you people of the
    earth.
  Terror, a pit and a trap are
    waiting for you.
18 Anyone who runs away from
    the terror
  will fall into the pit.
  Anyone who climbs out of
    the pit
  will be caught in the trap.

The LORD will open the
    windows of the skies.
  He will flood the land.
  The foundations of the
    earth will shake.
19 The earth will be broken up.
  It will split open.
  It will be shaken to pieces.
20 The earth will be unsteady
    like someone who is
    drunk.
  It will sway like a tent in
    the wind.
  Its sin will weigh so heavily
    on it that it will fall.
  It will never get up again.

21 At that time the LORD will
    punish
  the spiritual forces of evil
    in the heavens above.
  He will also punish the
    kings on the earth
    below.
22 They will be brought together
    like prisoners in chains.

They'll be locked up in
    prison.
  After many days the LORD
    will punish them.
23 The LORD who rules over all
    will rule
  on Mount Zion in
    Jerusalem.
  The elders of the city will be
    there.
  They will see his great
    glory.
  His rule will be so glorious
    that the sun and moon
  will be too ashamed to
    shine.

A Song of Praise to the LORD

25 LORD, you are my God.
  I will honor you.
  I will praise your name.
  You have been perfectly
    faithful.
  You have done wonderful
    things.
  You had planned them
    long ago.
2 You have turned cities into
    piles of trash.
  You have pulled down the
    high walls that were
    around them.
  You have destroyed our
    enemies' forts.
  They will never be rebuilt.
3 Powerful nations will honor
    you.
  Even sinful people from
    their cities will have
    respect for you.
4 Poor people have come to
    you for safety.
  You have kept needy
    people safe when they
    were in trouble.

You have been a place to hide
when storms came.
You have been a shade
from the heat of the sun.
Evil people attack us.
They are like a storm
beating against a wall.
5   They are like the heat of
the desert.
You stopped the noisy shouts
of our enemies.
You kept them from
winning the battle over
us and singing about it.
You are like the shadow
of a cloud that cools the
earth.

[6] On Mount Zion the Lord
who rules over all will
prepare
a feast for all the nations.
The best and richest foods
and the finest aged wines
will be served.
[7] On that mountain the Lord
will destroy
the veil of sadness that
covers all the nations.
He will destroy the gloom
that is spread over
everyone.
8   He will swallow up death
forever.
The Lord and King will wipe
away the tears
from everyone's face.
He will remove the shame of
his people
from the whole earth.
    The Lord has spoken.
[9] At that time they will say,

"He is our God.
We trusted in him, and he
saved us.

He is the Lord. We trusted in
him.
Let us be filled with joy
because he saved us."

[10] The Lord's power will keep
Mount Zion safe.
But the people of Moab
will be crushed in their
land.
They will be crushed just
as straw is crushed in
animal waste.
[11] They will try to swim their
way out of it.
They will spread out their
hands in it,
just as swimmers spread
out their hands to swim.
But God will bring down
Moab's pride.
None of their skill will help
them.
[12] He will pull down their high,
strong walls.
He will bring them down
to the ground.
He'll bring them right
down to the dust.

Another Song of Praise

26
At that time a song will
be sung in the land of Judah. It will say,

"We have a strong city.
God's saving power
surrounds it
like walls and towers.
[2] Open its gates
so that those who do what
is right can enter.
They are the people who
remain faithful to God.
[3] Lord, you will give perfect
peace

to those who commit
themselves to be faithful
to you.
That's because they trust
in you.

4 "Trust in the LORD forever.
The LORD himself is the
Rock.
The LORD will keep us safe
forever.
5 He brings down those who
are proud.
He pulls down cities that
have high walls.
They fall down flat on the
ground.
He throws them down to
the dust.
6 The feet of those who were
treated badly stomp on
them.
Those who were poor walk
all over them."

7 The path of godly people is
level.
You are the God who does
what is right.
You make their way smooth.
8 LORD, we are living the way
your laws command us
to live.
We are waiting for you to
act.
We want your honor and
fame to be known.
9 My heart longs for you at
night.
My spirit longs for you in
the morning.
You will come and judge the
earth.
Then the people of the
world will learn to do
what is right.

10 Sometimes grace is shown to
sinful people.
But they still don't learn to
do what is right.
They keep on doing evil even
in a land where others
are honest and fair.
They don't have any
respect for the majesty of
the LORD.
11 LORD, you have raised your
hand high to punish
them.
But they don't even see it.
Let them see how much you
love your people.
Then they will be put to
shame.
Let the fire you are saving
for your enemies burn
them up.

12 LORD, you give us peace.
You are the one who has
done everything we've
accomplished.
13 LORD, you are our God.
Other masters besides you
have ruled over us.
But your name is the only
one we honor.
14 Those other masters are now
dead.
They will never live
again.
Their spirits won't rise
from the dead.
You punished them and
destroyed them.
You wiped out all memory
of them.
15 LORD, you have made our
nation grow.
You have made it larger.
You have gained glory for
yourself.

You have increased the
size of our land.

16 LORD, when your people were
suffering, they came to
you.
When you punished them,
they could barely whisper
a prayer.
17 LORD, you made us like a
woman who is about to
have a baby.
She groans and cries out in
pain.
18 We were pregnant and
groaned with pain.
But nothing was born.
We didn't bring your saving
power to the earth.
And the people of the
world have not come
to life.
19 LORD, your people who have
died will live again.
Their bodies will rise from
the dead.
Let those who lie in the
grave
wake up and shout for joy.
You give life, LORD, like the
dew of the morning.
So the earth will give up its
dead people.
20 My people, go into your
houses.
Shut the doors behind you.
Hide yourselves for a little
while.
Do it until the LORD's anger
is over.
21 He is coming from the place
where he lives.
He will punish the people
of the earth for their
sins.

The blood spilled on the
earth will be brought out
into the open.
The ground will no longer
hide those who have
been killed.

Israel Will Be Saved

27 At that time

the LORD will punish
Leviathan with his
sword.
His great, powerful and
deadly sword will punish
the serpent that glides
through the sea.
He will kill that twisting
sea monster.

2 At that time the LORD will
sing about his fruitful vineyard.
He will say,

3 "I am the LORD. I watch over
my vineyard.
I water it all the time.
I guard it day and night.
I do it so no one can
harm it.
4 I am not angry with my
vineyard.
I wish thorns and bushes
would come up in it.
Then I would march out
against them in battle.
I would set all of them on
fire.
5 So the enemies of my people
should come to me for
safety.
They should make peace
with me.
I will say it again.
They should make peace
with me."

⁶In days to come, Jacob's
     people will put down
     roots like a vine.
  Israel will bud and bloom.
  They will fill the whole
     world with fruit.

⁷The LORD struck down
     those who struck down
     Israel.
  But he hasn't punished
     Israel as much.
  The LORD killed those who
     killed many of his
     people.
  But he hasn't punished his
     people as much.
⁸The LORD will use war to
     punish Israel.
  He will make them leave
     their land.
  With a strong blast of his
     anger he will drive them
     out.
  It will be as if the east wind
     were blowing.
⁹The people of Jacob will have
     to pay for their sin.
  Here is how they will show
     that their sin has been
     removed.
  They will make all the altar
     stones like limestone.
  They will crush them to
     pieces.
  No poles used to worship
     the female god named
     Asherah will be left
     standing.
  No incense altars will be
     left either.
¹⁰Cities that have high walls
     around them will
     become empty.
  They will be settlements
     with no one in them.

  They will be like a desert.
  Calves will eat and lie down
     in them.
  They will strip bare the
     branches of their trees.
¹¹When their twigs are dry,
     they will be broken off.
  Then women will come and
     make fires with them.
  The people of Jacob don't
     understand the LORD.
  So the God who made
     them won't be
     concerned about them.
  Their Creator won't be kind
     to them.

¹²At that time the LORD will
separate Israel from other people. He will gather the Israelites together one by one. He will
gather them from the Euphrates
River to the Wadi of Egypt. ¹³At
that time a loud trumpet will be
blown. Those who were dying in
Assyria will come and worship
the LORD. So will those who
were taken away to Egypt. All of
them will worship the LORD on
his holy mountain in Jerusalem.

The LORD Will Judge the Leaders of Ephraim and Judah

28 How terrible it will be for
     the city of Samaria!
  It sits on a hill like a wreath
     of flowers.
  The leaders of Ephraim are
     drunk.
  They take pride in their
     city.
  It sits above a valley that has
     rich soil.
  How terrible it will be for
     the glorious beauty of
     that fading flower!

²The Lord will bring the
strong and powerful
king of Assyria against
Samaria.
The Lord will throw that
city down to the ground
with great force.
It will be like a hailstorm.
It will be like a wind that
destroys everything.
It will be like a driving rain
and a flooding storm.
³That city is like a wreath.
The leaders of Ephraim are
drunk.
They take pride in their city.
But its enemies will walk
all over it.
⁴It sits on a hill above a rich
valley.
The city is like a wreath of
flowers whose glorious
beauty is fading away.
But it will become like figs
that are ripe before
harvest.
As soon as people see
them,
they pick them and
swallow them.

⁵At that time the LORD who
rules over all
will be like a glorious
crown.
He will be like a beautiful
wreath
for those of his people who
will be left alive.
⁶He will help those
who are fair when they
judge.
He will give strength to
those
who turn back their
enemies at the city gate.

⁷Israel's leaders are drunk
from wine.
They can't walk straight.
They are drunk from beer.
They are unsteady on their
feet.
Priests and prophets drink
beer.
They can't walk straight.
They are mixed up from
drinking too much
wine.
They drink too much beer.
They are unsteady on their
feet.
The prophets see visions but
don't really understand
them.
The priests aren't able to
make good decisions.
⁸They throw up. All the tables
are covered
with the mess they've
made.
There isn't one spot on the
tables
that isn't smelly and dirty.
⁹The LORD's people are
making fun of him. They
say,
"Who does he think he's
trying to teach?
Who does he think he's
explaining his message
to?
Is it to children who do not
need their mother's milk
anymore?
Is it to those who have just
been taken from her
breast?
¹⁰Here is how he teaches.
Do this and do that.
There is a rule for this and a
rule for that.

Learn a little here and
learn a little there."

11 All right then, these people
won't listen to me.
So God will speak to them.
He will speak by using people
who speak unfamiliar
languages.
He will speak by using the
mouths of strangers.
12 He said to his people,
"I am offering you a resting
place.
Let those who are tired rest."
He continued, "I am offering
you a place of peace and
quiet."
But they wouldn't listen.
13 So then, here is what the
LORD's message will
become to them.
Do this and do that.
There is a rule for this and a
rule for that.
Learn a little here and
learn a little there.
So when they try to go
forward,
they'll fall back and be
wounded.
They'll be trapped and
captured.
14 Listen to the LORD's message,
you who make fun of the
truth.
Listen, you who rule
over these people in
Jerusalem.
15 You brag, "We have entered
into a covenant with the
place of the dead.
We have made an
agreement with the
grave.

When a terrible plague
comes to punish us,
it can't touch us.
That's because we depend on
lies to keep us safe.
We hide behind what isn't
true."
16 So the LORD and King
speaks. He says,

"Look! I am laying a stone in
Zion.
It is a stone that has been
tested.
It is the most important stone
for a firm foundation.
The one who depends on
that stone will never be
shaken.
17 I will use a measuring line to
prove that you have not
been fair.
I will use a plumb line to
prove that you have not
done what is right.
Hail will sweep away the lies
you depend on to keep
you safe.
Water will flood your
hiding place.
18 Your covenant with death
will be called off.
The agreement you made
with the place of the
dead will not stand.
When the terrible plague
comes to punish you,
you will be struck down
by it.
19 As often as it comes, it will
carry you away.
Morning after morning,
day and night,
it will come to punish
you."

If you understand this
 message,
  it will bring you absolute
   terror.
20 You will be like someone
  whose bed is too short to
  lie down on.
 You will be like those
  whose blankets are
  too small to wrap
  themselves in.
21 The LORD will rise up to
  judge, just as he did at
  Mount Perazim.
 He will get up to act, just
  as he did in the Valley of
  Gibeon.
 He'll do his work, but it will
  be strange work.
  He'll carry out his task, but
  it will be an unexpected
  one.
22 Now stop making fun of me.
 If you don't, your chains
  will become heavier.
 The LORD who rules over all
  has spoken to me.
 The Lord has told me
  he has ordered that
  the whole land be
  destroyed.
23 Listen and hear my voice.
 Pay attention to what I'm
  saying.
24 When a farmer plows in
  order to plant, does he
  plow without stopping?
 Does he keep on breaking
  up the soil and making
  the field level?
25 When he's made the surface
  even, doesn't he plant
  caraway seeds?
 Doesn't he scatter cumin
  seeds?

Doesn't he plant wheat in its
  proper place?
 Doesn't he plant barley
  where it belongs?
 Doesn't he plant spelt
  along the edge of the
  field?
26 His God directs him.
 He teaches him the right
  way to do his work.

27 Caraway seeds are beaten out
  with a rod.
 They aren't separated out
  under a threshing sled.
 Cumin seeds are beaten out
  with a stick.
 The wheel of a cart isn't
  rolled over them.
28 Grain must be ground up to
  make bread.
 A farmer separates it out.
 But he doesn't go on doing
  it forever.
 He drives the wheels of a
  threshing cart over it.
 But he doesn't use horses
  to grind the grain.
29 All these insights come from
  the LORD who rules over
  all.
 His advice is wonderful.
 His wisdom is glorious.

The LORD Will Judge Jerusalem

29 Jerusalem, how terrible
  it will be for you!
 Ariel, you are the city
  where David made his
  home.
 The years will come
  and go.
 Keep on celebrating your
  regular feasts.
2 The LORD says, "Ariel, I will
  surround you.

Jerusalem, I will get ready
    to attack you.
Your people will mourn.
    They will sing songs of
        sadness.
I will make you like the front
    of an altar
    covered with blood.
³ I will be like an army camped
    against you on all sides.
    I will surround you with
        towers in order to attack
        you.
    I will build my ramps all
        around you and set up
        my ladders.
⁴ You will be brought down to
    the grave.
    You will speak from deep
        down inside the
        ground.
    Your words will be barely
        heard out of the dust.
    Your voice will sound like the
        voice of a ghost
        coming from under the
        ground.
    Your words will sound
        like a whisper out of the
        dust."

⁵ Jerusalem, all your enemies
    will become like fine
    dust.
    Their terrifying armies will
        become like straw
    that the wind blows away.
    All of a sudden, in an instant,
⁶   the LORD who rules over all
        will come.
He will come with thunder,
    earthquakes and a lot of
    noise.
    He'll bring windstorms
        and rainstorms with
        him.

He'll send a blazing
    fire that will burn up
    everything.
⁷ Armies from all the nations
    will fight against Ariel.
    They will attack it and its
        fort.
    They'll surround it
        completely.
But suddenly those armies
    will disappear like a
    dream.
    They will vanish like a
        vision in the night.
⁸ It will be as when a hungry
    person dreams of eating,
    but wakes up still hungry.
It will be as when a thirsty
    person dreams of
    drinking,
    but wakes up weak and
        still thirsty.
In the same way, the armies
    from all the nations
    that fight against Mount
        Zion will disappear.

⁹ People of Jerusalem, be
    shocked and amazed.
    Make yourselves blind so
        you can't see anything.
Get drunk, but not from
    wine.
    Be unsteady on your feet,
        but not because of beer.
¹⁰ The LORD has made you fall
    into a deep sleep.
    He has closed the eyes of
        your prophets.
    He has covered the heads
        of your seers so they
        can't see.

¹¹ For you, this whole vision
is like words that are sealed up
in a scroll. Suppose you give it

to someone who can read. And suppose you say, "Please read this for us." Then they'll answer, "I can't. It's sealed up." ¹² Or suppose you give the scroll to someone who can't read. And suppose you say, "Please read this for us." Then they'll answer, "I don't know how to read."

¹³ The Lord says,

"These people worship me
only with their words.
They honor me by what
they say.
But their hearts are far
away from me.
Their worship doesn't mean
anything to me.
They teach nothing but
human rules that they
have been taught.
¹⁴ So once more I will shock
these people
with many wonderful
acts.
I will destroy the wisdom of
those who think they are
so wise.
I will do away with the
cleverness of those who
think they are so smart."
¹⁵ How terrible it will be for
people who try hard
to hide their plans from the
Lord!
They do their work in
darkness.
They think, "Who sees us?
Who will know?"
¹⁶ They turn everything upside
down.
How silly they are to think
that potters are like the
clay they work with!

Can what is made say to the
one who made it,
"You didn't make me"?
Can the pot say to the potter,
"You don't know
anything"?

¹⁷ In a very short time, Lebanon
will be turned into rich
farm lands.
The rich farm lands will
seem like a forest.
¹⁸ At that time those who can't
hear will hear what is
read from the scroll.
Those who are blind will
come out of gloom and
darkness.
They will be able to see.
¹⁹ Those who aren't proud will
once again find their joy
in the Lord.
And those who are in need
will find their joy in the
Holy One of Israel.
²⁰ Those who don't show any
pity will vanish.
Those who make fun of
others will disappear.
All those who look for ways
to do what is evil will be
cut off.
²¹ Without any proof, they
claim that a person is
guilty.
In court they try to trap
the one who speaks up for
others.
By using dishonest witnesses
they keep people who
aren't guilty
from being treated fairly.

²² Long ago the Lord saved Abraham from trouble. Now he says to Jacob's people,

"You will not be ashamed
anymore.
Your faces will no longer
grow pale with fear.
23 You will see your children
living among you.
I myself will give you those
children.
Then you will honor my
name.
You will recognize how
holy I am.
I am the Holy One of
Jacob.
You will have great respect
for me.
I am the God of Israel.
24 I will give understanding to
you
who find yourselves going
stray.
You who are always speaking
against others
will accept what I teach
you."

The LORD Will Judge His Stubborn People

30 "How terrible it will
be for these stubborn
children of mine!"
announces the LORD.
"How terrible for those who
carry out plans that did
not come from me!
Their agreement with
Egypt did not come from
my Spirit.
So they pile up one sin on
top of another.
2 They go down to Egypt
without asking me for
advice.
They look to Pharaoh to help
them.

They ask Egypt to keep
them safe.
3 But looking to Pharaoh
will only bring them
shame.
Asking Egypt for help will
bring them dishonor.
4 Their officials have gone to
the city of Zoan.
Their messengers have
arrived in Hanes.
5 But the people of Judah will
be put to shame.
That's because they are
trusting in a nation that
is useless to them.
Egypt will not bring them
any help or advantage.
Instead, it will bring them
shame and dishonor."

6 Here is a prophecy the LORD
gave me about the animals in
the Negev Desert.

Judah's messengers carry
their riches on the backs
of donkeys.
They carry their treasures
on the humps of
camels.
They travel through a land
of danger and suffering.
It's a land filled with lions.
Poisonous snakes are also
there.
The messengers travel to a
nation
that can't do them any
good.
7 They travel to Egypt, whose
help is totally useless.
That's why I call it Rahab
the Do-Nothing.

8 The LORD said to me, "Go
now.

Write on a tablet for the
people of Judah
what I am about to say.
Also write it on a scroll.
In days to come
it will be a witness that
lasts forever.
⁹ That's because these people
of Judah refuse to obey
me.
They are children who tell
lies.
They will not listen to what
I want to teach them.
¹⁰ They say to the seers,
'Don't see any more
visions!'
They say to the prophets,
'Don't give us any more
visions of what is right!
Tell us pleasant things.
Prophesy things we want
to hear even if they aren't
true.
¹¹ Get out of our way!
Get off our path!
Keep the Holy One of Israel
away from us!' "

¹² So the Holy One of Israel
speaks. He says,

"You have turned your backs
on what I have said.
You have depended on
telling people lies.
You have crushed others.
¹³ Those sins are like cracks in a
high wall.
They get bigger and bigger.
Suddenly the wall breaks
apart.
Then it quickly falls down.
¹⁴ It breaks into small pieces
like a clay pot.
It breaks up completely.
Not one piece is left big
enough
for taking coals from a
fireplace.
Not one piece is left for
dipping water out of a
well."

¹⁵ The LORD and King is the
Holy One of Israel. He says,

"You will find peace and rest
when you turn away from
your sins and depend on
me.
You will receive the strength
you need
when you stay calm and
trust in me.
But you do not want to do
what I tell you to.
¹⁶ You said, 'No. We'll escape on
horses.'
So you will have to escape!
You said, 'We'll ride off on
fast horses.'
So those who chase you
will use faster horses!
¹⁷ When one of them dares you
to fight,
a thousand of you will run
away.
When five of them dare you,
all of you will run away.
So few of you will be left that
you will be
like a flagpole on top of a
mountain.
You will be like only one
banner on a hill."

¹⁸ But the LORD wants to have
mercy on you.
So he will rise up to give
you his tender love.
The LORD is a God who is
always fair.

Blessed are all those who
wait for him to act!

19 People of Zion, who live
in Jerusalem, you won't weep
anymore. When you cry out to
the LORD for help, he will have
mercy on you. As soon as he
hears you, he'll answer you. 20 He
might treat you like prisoners.
You might eat the bread of trouble. You might drink the water
of suffering. But he will be your
Teacher. He won't hide himself
anymore. You will see him with
your own eyes. 21 You will hear
your Teacher's voice behind you.
You will hear it whether you turn
to the right or the left. It will say,
"Here is the path I want you to
take. So walk on it." 22 Then you
will get rid of the silver statues of
your gods. You won't have anything to do with the gold statues
either. All of them are "unclean."
So you will throw them away
like dirty rags. You will say to
them, "Get away from us!"

23 The LORD will send rain
on the seeds you plant in the
ground. The crops that grow
will be rich and plentiful. At
that time your cattle will eat
grass in rolling meadows. 24 The
oxen and donkeys that work the
soil will eat the finest feed and
crushed grain. The farmers will
use pitchforks and shovels to
separate it from the straw. 25 At
that time the towers of your enemies will fall down. Their soldiers will die. Streams of water
will flow on every high mountain and hill. 26 The moon will
shine like the sun. And the sunlight will be seven times brighter
than usual. It will be like the
light of seven full days. That will
happen when the LORD ban-
dages and heals the wounds
and bruises he has brought on
his people.

27 The LORD will come from far
  away
  in all his power and glory.
He will show his burning
  anger.
  Thick clouds of smoke will
  be all around him.
His mouth will speak angry
  words.
  The words from his tongue
  will be like a destroying
  fire.
28 His breath will be like a
  rushing flood
  that rises up to the neck.
He'll separate out the nations
  he is going to destroy.
He'll place a bit in their
  jaws.
  It will lead them down the
  road to death.
29 You will sing
  as you do on the night you
  celebrate a holy feast.
Your hearts will be filled with
  joy.
  You will be as joyful as
  people playing their
  flutes
as they go up to the mountain
  of the LORD.
  He is the Rock of Israel.
30 The LORD will cause people
  to hear his powerful
  voice.
  He will make them see his
  arm coming down to
  punish them.

It will come down with
burning anger and
destroying fire.
It will come down with
rain, thunderstorms and
hail.
[31] The voice of the LORD will
tear the Assyrians apart.
He will strike them down
with his scepter.
[32] He will strike them
with his club to punish
them.
Each time he does, his people
will celebrate
with the music of harps
and tambourines.
He will use his powerful arm
to strike down the
Assyrians in battle.
[33] In the Valley of Ben Hinnom,
Topheth has been
prepared for a long time.
It has been made ready for
the king of Assyria.
Its fire pit has been made
deep and wide.
It has plenty of wood for
the fire.
The breath of the LORD
will be like a stream of
burning sulfur.
It will set the wood on fire.

The LORD Will Judge Those Who Depend on Egypt

31 How terrible it will be for
those who go down to
Egypt for help!
How terrible for those who
depend on horses!
They trust in how many
chariots they have.
They trust in how strong
their horsemen are.

But they don't look to the
Holy One of Israel.
They don't ask the LORD for
his help.
[2] He too is wise. He can bring
horrible trouble.
He does what he says he'll
do.
He'll rise up against that evil
nation.
He'll fight against those
who help them.
[3] The men of Egypt are only
human beings.
They aren't God.
Their horses are only flesh
and blood.
They aren't spirits.
The LORD will reach out his
powerful hand
to punish everyone.
The Egyptians provide help.
But they will be tripped up.
The people of Judah receive
the help.
But they will fall down.
All of them will be destroyed.

[4] The LORD says to me,

"A powerful lion stands over
its food and growls.
A lot of shepherds can be
brought together to drive
it away.
But the lion is not frightened
by their shouts.
It is not upset by the noise
they make.
In the same way, I will come
down from heaven.
I will fight on Mount Zion
and on its hills.
Nothing will drive me away.
I am the LORD who rules
over all.

⁵Like a bird hovering over
  its nest, I will guard
  Jerusalem.
  I will keep it safe.
  I will 'pass over' it and save it.
  I am the LORD who rules
  over all."

⁶People of Israel, return to the
LORD. He's the God you have so
strongly opposed. ⁷You sinned
when you made your gods out
of silver and gold. The time will
come when all of you will turn
away from them.

⁸The LORD says, "The
  Assyrians will be killed
  by swords.
  But the swords that kill
  them will not be used by
  human beings.
  The Assyrians will run away
  from those swords.
  But their young men will
  be caught
  and forced to work hard.
⁹Their hiding places will be
  destroyed
  when terror strikes them.
  Their commanders will see
  their enemy's battle flags.
  Then they will be filled
  with panic,"
  announces the LORD.
  His fire blazes out from
  Mount Zion.
  His furnace burns in
  Jerusalem.

The King Who Will Do What Is Right

32 A king will come who
  will do what is right.
  His officials will govern
  fairly.

²Each official will be like a
  place to get out of the
  wind.
  He will be like a place to
  hide from storms.
  He'll be like streams of
  water flowing in the
  desert.
  He'll be like the shadow of
  a huge rock in a dry and
  thirsty land.

³Then the eyes of those who
  see won't be closed
  anymore.
  The ears of those who
  hear will listen to the
  truth.
⁴People who are afraid
  will know and
  understand.
  Tongues that stutter will
  speak clearly.
⁵Foolish people won't be
  considered noble
  anymore.
  Those who are worthless
  won't be highly
  respected.
⁶Foolish people say foolish
  things.
  Their minds are set on
  doing evil things.
  They don't do what is right.
  They tell lies about the
  LORD.
  They don't give hungry
  people any food.
  They don't let thirsty
  people have any water.
⁷Those who are worthless use
  sinful methods.
  They make evil plans
  against poor people.
  They destroy them with their
  lies.

They do it even when those
people are right.
8 But those who are noble
make noble plans.
And by doing noble things
they succeed.

The Sinful Women in Jerusalem
9 You women who are so
contented,
pay attention to me.
You who feel so secure,
listen to what I have to
say.
10 You feel secure now.
But in a little over a year
you will tremble with
fear.
The grape harvest will fail.
There won't be any fruit.
11 So tremble, you contented
women.
Tremble with fear, you who
feel so secure.
Take off your fine clothes.
Wrap yourselves in rags.
12 Beat your chests to show how
sad you are.
The pleasant fields have
been destroyed.
The fruitful vines have
dried up.
13 My people's land is
overgrown with thorns
and bushes.
Mourn for all the houses
that were once filled
with joy.
Cry over this city that
used to be full of wild
parties.
14 The royal palace will be left
empty.
The noisy city will be
deserted.

The fort and lookout tower
will become
a dry and empty desert
forever.
Donkeys will enjoy being
there.
Flocks will eat there.
15 That will continue until the
Holy Spirit
is poured out on us from
heaven.
Then the desert will be
turned into rich farm
lands.
The rich farm lands will
seem like a forest.
16 In the desert, the LORD will
make sure people do
what is right.
In the rich farm lands he
will make sure they treat
one another fairly.
17 Doing what is right will bring
peace and rest.
When my people do that,
they will stay calm
and trust in the LORD
forever.
18 They will live in a peaceful
land.
Their homes will be secure.
They will enjoy peace and
quiet.
19 Hail might strip the forests
bare.
Cities might be completely
destroyed.
20 But how blessed you people
will be!
You will plant your seeds
by every stream.
You will let your cattle and
donkeys
wander anywhere they
want to.

*Trouble for Assyria and Help
for God's People*

33

How terrible it will be
for you, you who destroy
others!
Assyria, you haven't been
destroyed yet.
How terrible for you, you who
turn against others!
Others haven't turned
against you yet.
When you stop destroying,
you will be destroyed.
When you stop turning
against others,
others will turn against
you.

2 LORD, have mercy on us.
We long for you to
help us.
Make us strong every
morning.
Save us when we're in
trouble.
3 At the roar of your army, the
nations run away.
When you rise up against
them, they scatter.
4 Nations, what you have
taken in battle is
destroyed.
It's as if young locusts had
eaten it up.
Like large numbers of
locusts,
people rush to get it.

5 The LORD is honored. He
lives in heaven.
He will make sure Zion's
people only do what is
fair and right.
6 He will be the firm
foundation for their
entire lives.

He will give them all the
wisdom, knowledge and
saving power they will
ever need.
Respect for the LORD is the
key to that treasure.

7 Look! Judah's brave men
cry out loud in the
streets.
The messengers who were
sent to bring peace weep
bitter tears.
8 The wide roads are
deserted.
No one travels on them.
Our peace treaty with Assyria
is broken.
Those who witnessed it are
looked down on.
No one is respected.
9 The land dries up and wastes
away.
Lebanon is full of shame
and dries up.
The rich land of Sharon is
like the Arabah Desert.
The trees of Bashan and
Carmel drop their
leaves.

10 "Now I will take action," says
the LORD.
"Now I will be honored.
Now I will be respected.
11 Assyria, your plans and
actions are like straw.
Your anger is a fire that will
destroy you.
12 The nations will be burned to
ashes.
They will be like bushes
that are cut down and
set on fire.

13 "You nations far away, listen
to what I have done!

My people who are near,
    recognize how powerful
    I am!
[14] The sinners in Zion are
    terrified.
    They tremble with fear.
They say, 'Who of us can
    live through the LORD's
    destroying fire?
Who of us can live through
    the fire that burns
    forever?'
[15] People must do what is right.
    They must be honest and
    tell the truth.
    They must not get rich by
    cheating others.
    Their hands must not
    receive money from
    those who want special
    favors.
    They must not let their ears
    listen to plans to commit
    murder.
    They must close their eyes
    to even thinking about
    doing what is evil.
[16] People like that will be kept
    safe.
    It will be as if they
    were living on high
    mountains.
    It will be as if they were
    living in a mountain fort.
    They will have all the food
    they need.
    And they will never run out
    of water."

[17] People of Judah, you will see
    the king in all his glory
    and majesty.
    You will view his kingdom
    spreading far and wide.
[18] You will think about what
    used to terrify you.

You will say to yourself,
    "Where is that chief officer
    of Assyria?
Where is the one who forced
    us to send gifts to his
    king?
Where is the officer in
    charge of the towers
    that were used when we
    were attacked?"
[19] You won't see those proud
    people anymore.
    They spoke a strange
    language.
    None of us could
    understand it.

[20] Just look at Zion! It's the city
    where we celebrate our
    regular feasts.
    Turn your eyes toward
    Jerusalem.
    It will be a peaceful place to
    live in.
    It will be like a tent that
    will never be moved.
    Its stakes will never be
    pulled up.
    None of its ropes will be
    broken.
[21] There the LORD will be our
    Mighty One.
    It will be like a place of
    wide rivers and streams.
    No boat with oars will travel
    on them.
    No mighty ship will sail on
    them.
[22] That's because the LORD is
    our judge.
    The LORD gives us our law.
    The LORD is our king.
    He will save us.
[23] The ropes on your ship hang
    loose.

The mast isn't very secure.
    The sail isn't spread out.
But the LORD will strike
    down the Assyrians.
Then a large amount of
    goods will be taken
    from them and divided
    up.
Even people who are
    disabled will carry off
    some of it.
24 No one living in Zion will
    ever say again, "I'm sick."
And the sins of those
    who live there will be
    forgiven.

The LORD Will Judge the Nations

34 Nations, come near and
    listen to me!
Pay attention to what I'm
    about to say.
Let the earth and everything
    in it listen.
Let the world and
    everything that comes
    out of it pay attention.
2 The LORD is angry with all
    the nations.
His anger is against all
    their armies.
He will totally destroy
    them.
He will have them killed.
3 Those who are killed won't
    be buried.
Their dead bodies will be
    thrown on the ground.
They will stink.
Their blood will cover the
    mountains.
4 All the stars in the sky will
    vanish.
The heavens will be rolled
    up like a scroll.

All the stars in the sky will
    fall like dried-up leaves
    from a vine.
They will drop like
    wrinkled figs from a fig
    tree.

5 The sword of the LORD will
    finish its deadly work in
    the sky.
Then it will come down to
    strike Edom.
He will totally destroy that
    nation.
6 His sword will be red with
    blood.
It will be covered with
    fat.
The blood will flow like the
    blood
    of lambs and goats being
    sacrificed.
The fat will be like the fat
    taken from the kidneys of
    rams.
That's because the LORD will
    offer a sacrifice
    in the city of Bozrah.
He will kill many people in
    the land of Edom.
7 The people and their leaders
    will be killed
    like wild oxen and young
    bulls.
Their land will be wet with
    their blood.
The dust will be covered
    with their fat.

8 That's because the LORD has
    set aside a day to pay
    Edom back.
He has set aside a year to
    pay them back. He will
    pay them back for what
    they did to Zion.

⁹ The streams of Edom will be
   turned into tar.
   Its dust will be turned into
   blazing sulfur.
   Its land will become
   burning tar.
¹⁰ The fire will keep burning
   night and day.
   It can't be put out.
   Its smoke will go up
   forever.
   Edom will lie empty for all
   time to come.
   No one will ever travel
   through it again.
¹¹ The desert owl and screech
   owl will make it their
   home.
   The great owl and the
   raven will build their
   nests there.
   God will use his measuring
   line
   to show how completely
   Edom will be destroyed.
   He will use his plumb line
   to show how empty Edom
   will become.
¹² Edom's nobles won't have
   anything left there
   that can be called a
   kingdom.
   All its princes will
   vanish.
¹³ Thorns will cover its forts.
   Bushes and weeds will
   cover its safest places.
   It will become a home for
   wild dogs.
   It will become a place
   where owls live.
¹⁴ Desert creatures will meet
   with hyenas.
   Wild goats will call out to
   each other.

Night creatures will also lie
   down there.
   They will find places where
   they can rest.
¹⁵ Owls will make their nests
   and lay their eggs there.
   And they will hatch
   them.
   They will take care of their
   little ones
   under the shadow of their
   wings.
   Male and female falcons
   will also gather there.

¹⁶ Look in the book of the
LORD. Here is what you will read
there.

None of those animals will
   be missing.
   Male and female alike will
   be there.
   The LORD himself has
   commanded it.
   And his Spirit will gather
   them together.
¹⁷ The LORD will decide what
   part of the land goes to
   each animal.
   Then he will give each one
   its share.
   It will belong to them forever.
   And they will live there for
   all time to come.

The Joy of the LORD's People

35 The desert and the dry
   ground will be glad.
   The dry places will be full
   of joy.
   Flowers will grow there.
   Like the first crocus in the
   spring,
² the desert will bloom with
   flowers.

It will be very glad and
shout for joy.
The glorious beauty of
Lebanon will be given
to it.
It will be as beautiful as the
rich lands
of Carmel and Sharon.
Everyone will see the glory of
the LORD.
They will see the beauty of
our God.

3 Strengthen the hands of
those who are weak.
Help those whose knees
give way.
4 Say to those whose hearts are
afraid,
"Be strong and do not fear.
Your God will come.
He will pay your enemies
back.
He will come to save you."

5 Then the eyes of those who
are blind will be opened.
The ears of those who can't
hear will be unplugged.
6 Those who can't walk will
leap like a deer.
And those who can't speak
will shout for joy.
Water will pour out in dry
places.
Streams will flow in the
desert.
7 The burning sand will
become a pool of water.
The thirsty ground will
become bubbling
springs.
In the places where wild dogs
once lay down,
tall grass and papyrus will
grow.

8 A wide road will go through
the land.
It will be called the Way of
Holiness.
Only those who lead a holy
life can use it.
"Unclean" and foolish
people can't walk on it.
9 No lions will use it.
No hungry wild animals
will be on it.
None of them will be
there.
Only people who have been
set free will walk on it.
10 Those the LORD has saved
will return to their land.
They will sing as they enter
the city of Zion.
Joy that lasts forever will be
like beautiful crowns on
their heads.
They will be filled with
gladness and joy.
Sorrow and sighing will be
gone.

Sennacherib Warns Jerusalem

36 Sennacherib attacked
and captured all the cit-
ies of Judah that had high walls
around them. It was in the 14th
year of the rule of Hezekiah.
Sennacherib was king of Assyria. 2 He sent his field commander from Lachish to King
Hezekiah at Jerusalem. He sent
him along with a large army.
The commander stopped at the
channel that brings water from
the Upper Pool. It was on the
road to the Washerman's Field.
3 Eliakim, Shebna and Joah
went out to him. Eliakim, the
son of Hilkiah, was in charge of

the palace. Shebna was the secretary. Joah, the son of Asaph, kept the records.

[4] The field commander said to them, "Give Hezekiah this message. Tell him,

" 'Sennacherib is the great king of Assyria. He says, "Why are you putting your faith in what your king says? [5] You say you have a military plan. You say you have a strong army. But your words don't mean anything. Who are you depending on? Why don't you want to stay under my control? [6] Look, I know you are depending on Egypt. Why are you doing that? Egypt is nothing but a broken papyrus stem. Try leaning on it. It will only cut your hand. Pharaoh, the king of Egypt, is just like that to everyone who depends on him. [7] But suppose you say to me, 'We are depending on the Lord our God.' Didn't Hezekiah remove your god's high places and altars? Didn't Hezekiah say to the people of Judah and Jerusalem, 'You must worship at the altar in Jerusalem'?

[8] " ' "Come on. Make a deal with my master, the king of Assyria. I'll give you 2,000 horses. But only if you can put riders on them! [9] You are depending on Egypt for chariots and horsemen. You can't drive away even the least important officer among my master's officials. [10] Besides, do you think I've come without being sent by the Lord? Have I come to attack and destroy this land without receiving a message from him? The Lord himself told me to march out against your country. He told me to destroy it." ' "

[11] Then Eliakim, Shebna and Joah spoke to the field commander. They said, "Please speak to us in the Aramaic language. We understand it. Don't speak to us in Hebrew. If you do, the people on the wall will be able to understand you."

[12] But the commander replied, "My master sent me to say these things. Are these words only for your master and you to hear? Aren't they also for the people sitting on the wall? They are going to suffer just like you. They'll have to eat their own waste. They'll have to drink their own urine."

[13] Then the commander stood up and spoke in the Hebrew language. He called out, "Pay attention to what the great king of Assyria is telling you. [14] He says, 'Don't let Hezekiah trick you. He can't save you! [15] Don't let Hezekiah talk you into trusting in the Lord. Don't believe him when he says, "You can be sure that the Lord will save us. This city will not be handed over to the king of Assyria." '

[16] "Don't listen to Hezekiah. The king of Assyria says, 'Make a peace treaty with me. Come over to my side. Then each one

of you will eat fruit from your own vine and fig tree. Each one of you will drink water from your own well. ¹⁷ You will do that until I come back. Then I'll take you to a land just like yours. It's a land that has a lot of grain and fresh wine. It has plenty of bread and vineyards.

¹⁸ " 'Don't let Hezekiah fool you. He's telling you a lie when he says, "The LORD will save us." Have the gods of any nations ever saved their lands from the power of the king of Assyria? ¹⁹ Where are the gods of Hamath and Arpad? Where are the gods of Sepharvaim? Have they saved Samaria from my power? ²⁰ Which one of all the gods of those countries has been able to save their lands from me? So how can the LORD save Jerusalem from my power?' "

²¹ But the people remained silent. They didn't say anything. That's because King Hezekiah had commanded, "Don't answer him."

²² Then Eliakim, the son of Hilkiah, went to Hezekiah. Eliakim was in charge of the palace. Shebna the secretary went with him. So did Joah, the son of Asaph. Joah kept the records. All of them went to Hezekiah with their clothes torn. They told him what the field commander had said.

Isaiah Prophesies That Jerusalem Will Be Saved

37 When King Hezekiah heard what the field commander had said, he tore his clothes. He put on the rough clothing people wear when they're sad. Then he went into the LORD's temple. ² Hezekiah sent Eliakim, who was in charge of the palace, to Isaiah the prophet, the son of Amoz. He also sent the leading priests and Shebna the secretary to him. All of them were wearing rough clothing. ³ They told Isaiah, "Hezekiah says, 'Today we're in great trouble. The LORD is warning us. He's bringing shame on us. Sometimes babies come to the moment when they should be born. But their mothers aren't strong enough to give birth to them. Today we are like those mothers. We aren't strong enough to save ourselves. ⁴ Perhaps the LORD your God will hear everything the field commander has said. His master, the king of Assyria, has sent him to make fun of the living God. Maybe the LORD your God will punish him for what he has heard him say. So pray for the remaining people who are still alive here.' "

⁵ King Hezekiah's officials came to Isaiah. ⁶ Then he said to them, "Tell your master, 'The LORD says, "Do not be afraid of what you have heard. The officers who are under the king of Assyria have spoken evil things against me. ⁷ Listen! I will send him news from his own country. It will make him want to return home. There I will have him cut down by a sword." ' "

⁸ The field commander heard that the king of Assyria had left

Lachish. So the commander pulled his troops back from Jerusalem. He went to join the king. He found out that the king was fighting against Libnah.

⁹ During that time Sennacherib received a report. He was told that Tirhakah was marching out to fight against him. Tirhakah was the king of Cush. When Sennacherib heard the report, he sent messengers again to Hezekiah with a letter. It said, ¹⁰ "Tell Hezekiah, the king of Judah, 'Don't let the god you depend on trick you. He says, "Jerusalem will not be handed over to the king of Assyria." But don't believe him. ¹¹ I'm sure you have heard about what the kings of Assyria have done to all the other countries. They have destroyed them completely. So do you think you will be saved? ¹² The kings who ruled before me destroyed many nations. Did the gods of those nations save them? Did the gods of Gozan, Harran or Rezeph save them? What about the gods of the people of Eden who were in Tel Assar? ¹³ Where is the king of Hamath? Where is the king of Arpad? Where are the kings of Lair, Sepharvaim, Hena and Ivvah?' "

Hezekiah Prays to the LORD

¹⁴ When Hezekiah received the letter from the messengers, he read it. Then he went up to the LORD's temple. There he spread the letter out in front of the LORD. ¹⁵ Hezekiah prayed to the LORD. He said, ¹⁶ "LORD who rules over all, you are the God of Israel. You sit on your throne between the cherubim. You alone are God over all the kingdoms on earth. You have made heaven and earth. ¹⁷ Listen, LORD. Hear us. Open your eyes, LORD. Look at the trouble we're in. Listen to what Sennacherib is saying. You are the living God. And he dares to make fun of you!

¹⁸ "LORD, it's true that the kings of Assyria have completely destroyed many nations and their lands. ¹⁹ They have thrown the statues of the gods of those nations into the fire. And they have destroyed them. That's because they weren't really gods at all. They were nothing but statues made out of wood and stone. They were made by human hands. ²⁰ LORD our God, save us from the power of Sennacherib. Then all the kingdoms of the earth will know that you are the only God."

Sennacherib Falls From Power

²¹ Isaiah sent a message to Hezekiah. Isaiah said, "The LORD is the God of Israel. He says, 'You have prayed to me about Sennacherib, the king of Assyria. ²² So here is the message the LORD has spoken against him. The LORD is telling him,

" ' "You will not win the battle
　　over Zion.
　Its people hate you and
　　make fun of you.
The people of Jerusalem lift
　　up their heads proudly
　as you run away.

23 Who have you laughed at?
     Who have you spoken evil
       things against?
     Who have you raised your
       voice against?
     Who have you looked at so
       proudly?
     You have done it against
       me.
     I am the Holy One of
       Israel!
24 Through your messengers
     you have laughed at me
     again and again.
   And you have said,
     'I have many chariots.
   With them I have climbed
       to the tops of the
       mountains.
     I've climbed the highest
       mountains in Lebanon.
   I've cut down its tallest cedar
       trees.
     I've cut down the best of its
       juniper trees.
   I've reached its farthest
       mountains.
     I've reached its finest
       forests.
25 I've dug wells in other
       lands.
     I've drunk the water from
       them.
   I've walked through all the
       streams of Egypt.
     I've dried up every one of
       them.'

26 " ' "But I, the LORD, say,
     'Haven't you heard what
       I have done?
     Long ago I arranged for
       you to do this.
   In days of old I planned it.
     Now I have made it
       happen.

You have turned cities with
       high walls
     into piles of stone.
27 Their people do not have any
       power left.
     They are troubled and put
       to shame.
   They are like plants in the
       field.
     They are like new green
       plants.
   They are like grass that grows
       on a roof.
     It dries up before it is
       completely grown.

28 " ' " 'But I know where you
       are.
     I know when you come and
       go.
     I know how very angry you
       are with me.
29 You roar against me and
       brag.
     And I have heard your
       bragging.
   So I will put my hook in your
       nose.
     I will put my bit in your
       mouth.
   And I will make you go home
       by the same way you
       came.' " ' "

30 The LORD said, "Hezekiah,
here is a sign for you.

"This year you will eat what
       grows by itself.
     Next year you will eat what
       grows from that.
   But in the third year you will
       plant your crops and
       gather them in.
   You will plant your
       grapevines and eat their
       fruit.

³¹ The people of the kingdom of
    Judah who are still alive
    will be like plants.
    Once more they will put
    down roots and produce
    fruit.
³² Out of Jerusalem will come
    the people who remain.
    Out of Mount Zion will
    come those who are still
    left alive.
    My great love will make sure
    that happens.
    I rule over all.

³³ "Here is a message from me
about the king of Assyria. I say,

    " 'He will not enter this city.
    He will not even shoot an
    arrow at it.
    He will not come near it with
    a shield.
    He will not build a ramp
    in order to climb over its
    walls.
³⁴ By the way that he came he
    will go home.
    He will not enter this city,'
        announces the Lord.
³⁵ 'I will guard this city and
    save it.
    I will do it for myself.
    And I will do it for my
    servant David.' "

³⁶ Then the angel of the Lord
went into the camp of the Assyrians. He put to death 185,000
soldiers there. The people of Jerusalem got up the next morning. They looked out and saw all
the dead bodies. ³⁷ So Sennacherib, the king of Assyria, took
the army tents down. Then he
left. He returned to Nineveh and
stayed there.

³⁸ One day Sennacherib was
worshiping in the temple of his
god Nisrok. His sons Adrammelek and Sharezer killed him with
their swords. Then they escaped
to the land of Ararat. Esarhaddon became the next king after
his father Sennacherib.

*Hezekiah Becomes Sick and
Is Healed*

38 In those days Hezekiah
became very sick. He
knew he was about to die. Isaiah
went to see him. Isaiah was the
son of Amoz. Isaiah told Hezekiah, "The Lord says, 'Put everything in order. Make out your
will. You are going to die soon.
You will not get well again.' "

² Hezekiah turned his face toward the wall. He prayed to the
Lord. He said, ³ "Lord, please
remember how faithful I've
been to you. I've lived the way
you wanted me to. I've served
you with all my heart. I've done
what is good in your sight." And
Hezekiah wept bitterly.

⁴ A message from the Lord
came to Isaiah. The Lord said,
⁵ "Go and speak to Hezekiah.
Tell him, 'The Lord, the God of
King David, says, "I have heard
your prayer. I have seen your
tears. I will add 15 years to your
life. ⁶ And I will save you and
this city from the power of the
king of Assyria. I will guard this
city.

⁷ " ' "Here is a sign from me.
It will show you that I will heal
you, just as I promised I would.
⁸ The shadow that was made by
the sun has gone down ten steps

on the stairway of Ahaz. I will make it go back up those ten steps.' ' " So the shadow went back up the ten steps it had gone down.

⁹ Here is a song of praise that was written by Hezekiah, the king of Judah. He wrote it after he was sick and had gotten well again.

¹⁰ I said, "I'm enjoying the best
        years of my life.
    Must I now go through the
        gates of death?
    Will the rest of my years be
        taken away from me?"
¹¹ I said, "LORD, I'll never see
        you again
    while I'm still alive.
I'll never see people
        anymore.
    I'll never again be with
        those who live in this
        world.
¹² My body is like a shepherd's
        tent.
    It has been pulled down
        and carried off.
My life is like a piece of cloth
        that I've rolled up.
    You have cut it off from the
        loom.
    In a short period of time
        you have brought my life
        to an end.
¹³ I waited patiently until
        sunrise.
    But like a lion you broke all
        my bones.
    In a short period of time
        you have brought my life
        to an end.
¹⁴ I cried softly like a weak little
        bird.

    I sounded like a dove as I
        mourned.
My eyes grew tired as I
        looked up toward
        heaven.
    Lord, my life is in danger.
        Please come and help
        me!
¹⁵ "But what can I say?
    You have promised to heal
        me.
    And you yourself have
        done it.
Once I was proud and bitter.
    But now I will live the rest
        of my life free of pride.
¹⁶ Lord, people find the will to
        live because you keep
        your promises.
    And my spirit also finds life
        in your promises.
You brought me back to
        health.
    You let me live.
¹⁷ I'm sure it was for my
        benefit
    that I suffered such great
        pain.
You love me. You kept me
        from going down into the
        pit of death.
You have put all my sins
        behind your back.
¹⁸ People in the grave can't
        praise you.
    Dead people can't sing
        praise to you.
Those who go down to the
        grave
    can't hope for you to be
        faithful to them.
¹⁹ It is those who are alive who
        praise you.
    And that's what I'm doing
        today.

Parents tell their children
about how faithful you are.
²⁰"The LORD will save me.
So we will sing and play
music on stringed
instruments.
We will sing all the days of
our lives
in the LORD's temple."

²¹When Hezekiah was sick, Isaiah had said, "Press some figs together. Spread them on a piece of cloth. Apply them to Hezekiah's boil. Then he'll get well again."

²²At that time Hezekiah had asked, "What will the sign be to prove I'll go up to the LORD's temple?" That's when the LORD had made the shadow go back ten steps.

Messengers Come From Babylon to Hezekiah

39 At that time Marduk-Baladan, the king of Babylon, sent Hezekiah letters and a gift. He had heard that Hezekiah had been sick but had gotten well again. Marduk-Baladan was the son of Baladan. ²Hezekiah gladly received the messengers. He showed them what was in his storerooms. He showed them the silver and gold. He took them to where the spices and the fine olive oil were kept. He showed them where he kept all his weapons. And he showed them all his treasures. In fact, he showed them everything that was in his palace and in his whole kingdom.

³Then Isaiah the prophet went to King Hezekiah. Isaiah asked him, "What did those men say? Where did they come from?"

"They came from a land far away," Hezekiah said. "They came to me from Babylon."

⁴Isaiah asked, "What did they see in your palace?"

"They saw everything in my palace," Hezekiah said. "I showed them all my treasures."

⁵Then Isaiah said to Hezekiah, "Listen to the message of the LORD who rules over all. He says, ⁶'You can be sure the time will come when everything in your palace will be carried off to Babylon. Everything the kings before you have stored up until this day will be taken away. There will not be anything left,' says the LORD. ⁷'Some of the members of your family line will be taken away. They will be your own flesh and blood. They will include the children who will be born into your family line. And they will serve the king of Babylon in his palace.'"

⁸"The message the LORD has spoken through you is good," Hezekiah replied. He thought, "There will be peace and safety while I'm still living."

God Comforts His People

40 "Comfort my people," says your God.
"Comfort them.
²Speak tenderly to the people of Jerusalem.
Announce to them
that their hard labor has been completed.

Tell them that their sin has
been paid for.
Tell them the LORD has
punished them enough
for all their sins."

3 A messenger is calling out,
"In the desert prepare
the way for the LORD.
Make a straight road through
it
for our God.
4 Every valley will be filled in.
Every mountain and hill
will be made level.
The rough ground will be
smoothed out.
The rocky places will be
made flat.
5 Then the glory of the LORD
will appear.
And everyone will see it
together.
The LORD has spoken."
6 Another messenger says,
"Cry out."
And I said, "What should I
cry?"

"Cry out, 'All people are like
grass.
They don't stay faithful
to me any longer than
wildflowers last.
7 The grass dries up. The
flowers fall to the ground.
That happens when the
LORD makes his wind
blow on them.
So people are just like
grass.
8 The grass dries up. The
flowers fall to the
ground.
But what our God says will
stand forever.' "

9 Zion, you are bringing good
news to your people.
Go up on a high mountain
and announce it.
Jerusalem, you are bringing
good news to them.
Shout the message loudly.
Shout it out loud. Don't be
afraid.
Say to the towns of Judah,
"Your God is coming!"
10 The LORD and King is coming
with power.
He rules with a powerful
arm.
He has set his people free.
He is bringing them back
as his reward.
He has won the battle over
their enemies.
11 He takes care of his flock like
a shepherd.
He gathers the lambs in his
arms.
He carries them close to his
heart.
He gently leads those that
have little ones.

12 Who has measured the
oceans by using the
palm of his hand?
Who has used the width of
his hand to mark off the
sky?
Who has measured out the
dust of the earth in a
basket?
Who has weighed the
mountains on scales?
Who has weighed the hills
in a balance?
13 Who can ever understand the
Spirit of the LORD?
Who can ever give him
advice?

14 Did the LORD have to ask
anyone to help him
understand?
Did he have to ask
someone to teach him
the right way?
Who taught him what he
knows?
Who showed him how to
understand?
15 The nations are only a drop
in a bucket to him.
He considers them as
nothing but dust on the
scales.
He weighs the islands as if
they were only fine dust.
16 Lebanon doesn't have
enough trees to keep his
altar fires burning.
It doesn't have enough
animals to sacrifice as
burnt offerings to him.
17 To him, all the nations don't
amount to anything.
He considers them to be
worthless.
In fact, they are less than
nothing in his sight.
18 So who will you compare
God with?
Is there any other god like
him?
19 Will you compare him with a
statue of a god?
Anyone who works with
metal can make a statue.
Then another worker covers
it with gold
and makes silver chains for
it.
20 But someone who is too poor
to bring that kind of
offering

will choose some wood
that won't rot.
Then they look for a skilled
worker.
They pay the worker to
make a statue of a god
that won't fall over.
21 Don't you know who made
everything?
Haven't you heard about
him?
Hasn't it been told to you
from the beginning?
Haven't you understood it
ever since the earth was
made?
22 God sits on his throne high
above the earth.
Its people look like
grasshoppers to him.
He spreads out the heavens
like a cover.
He sets it up like a tent to
live in.
23 He takes the power of princes
away from them.
He reduces the rulers of
this world to nothing.
24 They are planted.
They are scattered like
seeds.
They put down roots in the
ground.
But as soon as that happens,
God blows on them and
they dry up.
Then a windstorm
sweeps them away like
straw.
25 "So who will you compare
me with?
Who is equal to me?" says
the Holy One.
26 Look up toward the sky.

Who created everything
you see?
The LORD causes the stars
to come out at night one
by one.
He calls out each one of
them by name.
His power and strength are
great.
So none of the stars is
missing.

27 Family of Jacob, why do you
complain,
"The LORD doesn't notice
our condition"?
People of Israel, why do you
say,
"Our God doesn't pay any
attention to our rightful
claims"?
28 Don't you know who made
everything?
Haven't you heard about
him?
The LORD is the God who
lives forever.
He created everything on
earth.
He won't become worn out or
get tired.
No one will ever know
how great his
understanding is.
29 He gives strength to those
who are tired.
He gives power to those
who are weak.
30 Even young people
become worn out and
get tired.
Even the best of them trip
and fall.
31 But those who trust in the
LORD
will receive new strength.

They will fly as high as
eagles.
They will run and not get
tired.
They will walk and not
grow weak.

The LORD Helps Israel

41 The LORD says, "People
who live on the islands,
come and stand quietly in
front of me.
Let the nations gain new
strength
in order to state their case.
Let them come forward and
speak.
Let us go to court and find
out who is right.

2 "Who has stirred up a king
from the east?
Who has helped him win
his battles?
I hand nations over to him.
I bring kings under his
control.
He turns them into dust with
his sword.
With his bow he turns
them into straw blowing
in the wind.
3 He hunts them down. Then
he moves on unharmed.
He travels so fast that his
feet
don't seem to touch the
ground.
4 Who has made that happen?
Who has carried it out?
Who has created all the
people who have ever
lived?
I, the LORD, have done it.
I was with the first of
them.

And I will be with the last
of them."

5 The people on the islands
have seen that king
coming.
And it has made them
afraid.
People tremble with fear
from one end of the
earth to the other.
They come and gather
together.
6   They help one another.
They say to one another,
"Be strong!"
7 One skilled worker makes a
statue of a god.
Another covers it with
gold.
The first worker says to the
second,
"You have done a good
job."
Another worker smooths
out the metal with a
hammer.
Still another gives the
statue its final shape.
The one who hammers says
to the one who shapes,
"You have done a good
job."
Then they nail the statue
down so it won't fall
over.

8 The LORD says, "People
of Israel, you are my
servants.
Family of Jacob, I have
chosen you.
You are the children of my
friend Abraham.
9 I gathered you from one end
of the earth to the other.

From the farthest places
on earth I brought you
together.
I said, 'You are my servants.'
I have chosen you.
I have not turned my back
on you.
10 So do not be afraid. I am with
you.
Do not be terrified. I am
your God.
I will make you strong and
help you.
I will hold you safe in my
hands.
I always do what is right.

11 "All those who are angry with
you will be put to shame.
And they will be
dishonored.
Those who oppose you will
be destroyed.
And they will vanish.
12 You might search for your
enemies.
But you will not find
them.
Those who go to war against
you
will completely disappear.
13 I am the LORD your God.
I take hold of your right
hand.
I say to you, 'Do not be afraid.
I will help you.'
14 Family of Jacob, you are as
weak as a worm.
But do not be afraid.
People of Israel, there are
only a few of you.
But do not be afraid.
I myself will help you,"
announces the LORD.
He is the one who sets his
people free.

He is the Holy One of
Israel.
15 He says, "I will make you into
a threshing sled.
It will be new and sharp.
It will have many teeth.
You will grind the mountains
down and crush them.
You will turn the hills into
nothing but straw.
16 You will toss them in the air.
A strong wind will catch
them and blow them
away.
You will be glad because I
will make that happen.
You will praise me.
I am the Holy One of Israel.

17 "Those who are poor and
needy search for water.
But there isn't any.
Their tongues are dry
because they are thirsty.
But I will help them. I am the
LORD.
I will not desert them.
I am Israel's God.
18 I will make streams flow on
the bare hilltops.
I will make springs come
up in the valleys.
I will turn the desert into
pools of water.
I will turn the dry and
cracked ground into
flowing springs.
19 I will make trees grow in the
desert.
I will plant cedar and
acacia trees there.
I will plant myrtle and
olive trees there.
I will make juniper trees
grow in the dry and
empty desert.

I will plant fir and cypress
trees there.
20 Then people will see and
know
that my powerful hand has
done it.
They will consider and
understand
that I have created it.
I am the Holy One of
Israel."

21 The LORD says to the nations
and their gods,
"State your case."
Jacob's King says to them,
"Prove your case to me.
22 Tell us, you false gods,
what is going to happen.
Tell us what happened in the
past.
Then we can check it out
and see if it is really true.
Or announce to us the things
that will take place.
23   Tell us what will happen in
the days ahead.
Then we will know that
you are gods.
Do something. It does not
matter whether it is good
or bad.
Then we will be terrified
and filled with fear.
24 But you false gods are less
than nothing.
Your actions are
completely worthless.
I hate it when people
worship you.

25 "I have stirred up a king
who will come from the
north.
He lives in the east.
He will bring honor to me.

He walks all over rulers as if
they were mud.
He steps on them just as a
potter stomps on clay.
²⁶Which one of you false gods
said those things
would happen before they
did?
Who told us about them
so we could know them?
Who told us ahead of time?
Who told us so we could
say,
'You are right'?
None of you false gods told us
about them.
None of you told us ahead
of time.
In fact, no one heard you
say anything at all.
²⁷I was the first to tell Zion.
I said, 'Look! The people
of Israel are coming
back!'
I sent a messenger to
Jerusalem with the good
news.
²⁸I look, but there is no one
among the gods that can
give me advice.
None of them can answer
when I ask them the
simplest question.
²⁹So they are not really gods at
all.
What they do does not
amount to anything.
They are as useless as
wind.

The LORD's Chosen Servant

42 "Here is my servant. I
take good care of him.
I have chosen him. I am
very pleased with him.
I will put my Spirit on him.
He will bring justice to the
nations.
²He will not shout or cry out.
He will not raise his voice
in the streets.
³He will not break a bent
twig.
He will not put out a dimly
burning flame.
He will be faithful and make
everything right.
⁴ He will not grow weak or
lose hope.
He will not give up until he
brings justice to the
earth.
The islands will put their
hope in his teaching."

⁵God created the heavens and
stretches them out.
The LORD spreads out the
earth with everything
that grows on it.
He gives breath to its
people.
He gives life to those who
walk on it.
He says to his servant,
⁶"I, the LORD, have chosen you
to do what is right.
I will take hold of your
hand.
I will keep you safe.
You will put into effect
my covenant with the
people of Israel.
And you will be a light for
the Gentiles.
⁷You will open eyes that can't
see.
You will set prisoners free.
Those who sit in darkness
will come out of their
cells.

8 "I am the LORD. That is my
    name!
  I will not let any other god
      share my glory.
  I will not let statues of gods
      share my praise.
9 What I said would happen
      has taken place.
  Now I announce new
      things to you.
  Before they even begin to
      happen,
    I announce them to you."

A Song of Praise to the LORD

10 Sing a new song to the LORD.
  Sing praise to him from
      one end of the earth to
      the other.
  Sing, you who sail out on the
      ocean.
    Sing, all you creatures in it.
  Sing, you islands.
    Sing, all you who live there.
11 Let the desert and its towns
      raise their voices.
  Let those who live in the
      settlements of Kedar be
      glad.
  Let the people of Sela sing for
      joy.
  Let them shout from the
      tops of the mountains.
12 Let them give glory to the
      LORD.
  Let them praise him in the
      islands.
13 The LORD will march out like
      a mighty warrior.
  He will stir up his anger
      like a soldier getting
      ready to fight.
  He will shout the battle cry.
  And he will win the battle
      over his enemies.

14 The LORD says, "For a long
      time I have kept silent.
  I have been calm and
      quiet.
  But now, like a woman
      having a baby,
    I cry out. I gasp and pant.
15 I will completely destroy the
      mountains and hills.
  I will dry up everything
      that grows there.
  I will turn rivers into dry
      land.
  I will dry up the pools.
16 Israel is blind.
  So I will lead them along
      paths
    they had not known before.
  I will guide them on roads
      they are not familiar
      with.
  I will turn the darkness
      into light as they travel.
  I will make the rough
      places smooth.
  Those are the things I
      will do.
  I will not desert my people.
17 Some people trust in statues
      of gods.
  They say to them, 'You are
      our gods.'
  But they will be dishonored.
  They will be put to shame.

Israel Can't See or Hear

18 "Israel, listen to me! You can
      hear,
    but you do not understand.
  Look to me! You can see,
    but you do not know what
      you are seeing.
19 The people of Israel serve me.
  But who is more blind
      than they are?

Who is more deaf than the
　messengers I send?
Who is more blind than the
　one who has promised to
　be faithful to me?
Who is more blind than the
　servant of the LORD?
20 Israel, you have seen many
　things.
　But you do not pay any
　attention to me.
Your ears are open.
　But you do not listen to
　anything I say."
21 The LORD wanted his people
　to see
how great and glorious his
　law is.
He wanted to show them
　that he always does what
　is right.
22 Enemies have carried off
　everything they own.
　All my people are trapped
　in pits
or hidden away in
　prisons.
They themselves have
　become like stolen
　goods.
No one can save them.
They have been carried off.
And there is no one who
　will say, "Send them
　back."
23 Family of Jacob, who among
　you will listen to what
　I'm saying?
People of Israel, which
　one of you will pay close
　attention in days to
　come?
24 Who allowed you to be
　carried off like stolen
　goods?

Who handed you over to
　robbers?
The LORD did it!
　We have sinned against
　him.
Israel, you wouldn't follow
　his ways.
　You didn't obey his law.
25 So he poured out his great
　anger on you.
He had many of you killed
　in battle.
You were surrounded by
　flames.
But you didn't realize what
　was happening.
Many of you were destroyed.
But you didn't learn
　anything from it.

The LORD Saves Israel

43 Family of Jacob, the
　LORD created you.
　People of Israel, he formed
　you.
He says, "Do not be afraid.
　I will set you free.
I will send for you by name.
　You belong to me.
2 You will pass through deep
　waters.
　But I will be with you.
You will pass through the
　rivers.
　But their waters will not
　sweep over you.
You will walk through fire.
　But you will not be
　burned.
The flames will not harm
　you.
3 I am the LORD your God.
　I am the Holy One of Israel.
　I am the one who saves
　you.

I will give up Egypt to set you
free.
I will give up Cush and
Seba for you.
⁴You are priceless to me.
I love you and honor you.
So I will trade other people
for you.
I will give up other nations
to save your lives.
⁵Do not be afraid. I am with
you.
I will bring your people
back from the east.
I will gather you from the
west.
⁶I will say to the north, 'Let
them go!'
And I will say to the south,
'Do not hold them back.'
Bring my sons from far away.
Bring my daughters from
the farthest places on
earth.
⁷Bring back everyone who
belongs to me.
I created them to bring
glory to me.
I formed them and made
them."

⁸Lead my people into court.
They have eyes but can't
see.
Bring those who have ears
but can't hear.
⁹All the nations are gathering
together.
All of them are coming.
Which one of their gods said
ahead of time
that the people of Israel
would return?
Which of them told us
anything at all about the
past?

Let them bring in their
witnesses to prove they
were right.
Then others will hear
them. And they will say,
"What they said is true."
¹⁰"People of Israel, you are my
witnesses," announces
the LORD.
"I have chosen you to be
my servant.
I wanted you to know me and
believe in me.
I wanted you to
understand that I am the
one and only God.
Before me, there was no other
god at all.
And there will not be any
god after me.
¹¹I am the one and only LORD.
I am the only one who can
save you.
¹²I have made known what
would happen.
I saved you. I have told you
about it.
I did this. It was not some
other god you worship.
You are my witnesses that I
am God," announces the
LORD.
¹³"And that is not all! I have
always been God,
and I always will be.
No one can save people from
my power.
When I do something, who
can undo it?"

*The LORD Is Full of Mercy
but Israel Is Unfaithful*

¹⁴The LORD sets his people free.
He is the Holy One of
Israel. He says,

"People of Israel, I will send
an army to Babylon to
save you.
I will cause all the
Babylonians to run
away.
They will try to escape in
the ships they were so
proud of.
15 I am your LORD and King.
I am your Holy One.
I created you."

16 Long ago the LORD opened
a way for his people to go
through the Red Sea.
He made a path through
the mighty waters.
17 He caused Egypt to send
out its chariots and
horses.
He sent its entire army to
its death.
Its soldiers lay down there.
They never got up again.
They were destroyed.
They were blown out like a
dimly burning flame.
But the LORD says,
18 "Forget the things that
happened in the past.
Do not keep on thinking
about them.
19 I am about to do something
new.
It is beginning to happen
even now.
Don't you see it coming?
I am going to make a way for
you to go through the
desert.
I will make streams of
water in the dry and
empty land.
20 Even wild dogs and owls
honor me.

That is because I provide
water in the desert
for my people to drink.
I cause streams to flow
in the dry and empty
land
for my chosen ones.
21 I do it for the people I made
for myself.
I want them to sing praise
to me.

22 "Family of Jacob, you have
not prayed to me as you
should.
People of Israel, you have
not worn yourselves out
for me.
23 You have not brought
me sheep for burnt
offerings.
You have not honored me
with your sacrifices.
I have not loaded you down
by requiring grain
offerings.
I have not made you tired
by requiring you to burn
incense.
24 But you have not bought any
sweet-smelling cane for
me.
You have not given me the
fattest parts
of your animal sacrifices.
Instead, you have loaded me
down with your sins.
You have made me tired
with the wrong things
you have done.

25 "I am the one who wipes out
your lawless acts.
I do it because of who I am.
I will not remember your
sins anymore.

26 But let us go to court
together.
Remind me of what you
have done.
State your case.
Prove to me that you are
not guilty.
27 Your father Jacob sinned.
The people I sent to teach
you refused to obey me.
28 So I put the high officials of
your temple to shame.
I let Jacob's family be
totally destroyed.
And I let people make fun
of Israel.

The LORD Chooses Israel

44 "Family of Jacob, listen
to me. You are my
servant.
People of Israel, I have
chosen you.
2 I made you. I formed you
when you were born as a
nation.
I will help you.
So listen to what I am
saying.
Family of Jacob, do not
be afraid. You are my
servant.
People of Israel, I have
chosen you.
3 I will pour out water on the
thirsty land.
I will make streams flow
on the dry ground.
I will pour out my Spirit on
your children.
I will pour out my blessing
on their children after
them.
4 They will spring up like grass
in a meadow.

They will grow like poplar
trees near flowing
streams.
5 Some will say, 'We belong to
the LORD.'
Others will call themselves
by Jacob's name.
Still others will write on their
hands,
'We belong to the LORD.'
And they will be called by
the name of Israel.

*Worship the LORD, Not False
Gods*

6 "I am Israel's King. I set them
free.
I am the LORD who rules
over all.
So listen to what I am
saying.
I am the first and the last.
I am the one and only God.
7 Who is like me? Let him
come forward and speak
boldly.
Let him tell me everything
that has happened
since I created my people
long ago.
And let him tell me what has
not happened yet.
Let him announce ahead
of time what is going to
take place.
8 Do not tremble with fear. Do
not be afraid.
Didn't I announce
everything that has
happened?
Didn't I tell you about it
long ago?
You are my witnesses. Is
there any other God
but me?

No! There is no other Rock.
  I do not know even one."

⁹ Those who make statues of
    gods don't amount to
    anything.
  And the statues they
    think so much of are
    worthless.
  Those who would speak up
    for them are blind.
  They don't know anything.
  So they will be put to
    shame.
¹⁰ People make statues of gods.
  But those gods can't do any
    good.
¹¹ People who do that will be
    put to shame.
  Those who make statues
    of gods are mere human
    beings.
  Let all of them come together
    and state their case.
  They will be terrified and
    put to shame.
¹² A blacksmith gets his tool.
  He uses it to shape metal
    over the burning coals.
  He uses his hammers to
    make a statue of a god.
  He forms it with his
    powerful arm.
  He gets hungry and loses his
    strength.
  He doesn't drink any
    water.
  He gets weaker and
    weaker.
¹³ A carpenter measures a piece
    of wood with a line.
  He draws a pattern on it
    with a marker.
  He cuts out a statue with
    sharp tools.

He marks it with
  compasses.
He shapes it into the form
  of a beautiful human
  being.
He does this so he can put
  it in a temple.
¹⁴ He cuts down a cedar tree.
  Or perhaps he takes a
    cypress or an oak tree.
  It might be a tree that grew in
    the forest.
  Or it might be a pine tree
    he planted.
  And the rain made it grow.
¹⁵ A man gets wood from trees
    to burn.
  He uses some of it to warm
    himself.
  He starts a fire and bakes
    bread.
  But he also uses some of it to
    make a god and worship
    it.
  He makes a statue of a god
    and bows down to it.
¹⁶ He burns half of the wood in
    the fire.
  He prepares a meal over it.
  He cooks meat over it.
  He eats until he is full.
  He also warms himself. He
    says,
  "Good! I'm getting warm.
  The fire is nice and hot."
¹⁷ From the rest of the wood he
    makes a statue.
  It becomes his god.
  He bows down and
    worships it.
  He prays to it. He says,
  "Save me! You are my god!"
¹⁸ People like that don't even
    know what they are
    doing.

Their eyes are shut so that
they can't see the truth.
Their minds are closed
so that they can't
understand it.
¹⁹ No one even stops to think
about this.
No one has any sense or
understanding.
If anyone did, they would
say,
"I used half of the wood for
fuel.
I even baked bread over
the fire.
I cooked meat. Then I ate
it.
Should I now make a statue
of a god
out of the wood that's left
over?
Should I bow down to a block
of wood?
The LORD would hate
that."
²⁰ That's as foolish as eating
ashes!
The mind of someone like
that
has led him astray.
He can't save himself.
He can't bring himself to
say,
"This thing I'm holding in my
right hand
isn't really a god at all."

²¹ The LORD says, "Family of
Jacob, remember these
things.
People of Israel, you are my
servant.
I have made you. You are my
servant.
Israel, I will not forget
you.

²² I will sweep your sins away as
if they were a cloud.
I will blow them away as if
they were the morning
mist.
Return to me.
Then I will set you free."

²³ Sing for joy, you heavens!
The LORD does wonderful
things.
Shout out loud, you earth!
Burst into song, you
mountains!
Sing, you forests and all
your trees!
The LORD sets the family of
Jacob free.
He shows his glory in
Israel.

People Will Live in Jerusalem Again

²⁴ The LORD says,
"People of Israel, I set you
free.
I formed you when you
were born as a nation.

"I am the LORD. I am the
Maker of everything.
I alone stretch out the
heavens.
I spread out the earth by
myself.

²⁵ "Some prophets are not really
prophets at all.
I show that their signs are
fake.
I make those who practice
evil magic look foolish.
I destroy the learning of
those who think they are
wise.
Their knowledge does not
make any sense at all.

26 I make the words of my
        servants the prophets
        come true.
    I carry out what my
        messengers say will
        happen.

"I say about Jerusalem,
    'My people will live there
        again.'
I say about the towns of
        Judah,
    'They will be rebuilt.'
I say about their broken-
        down buildings,
    'I will make them like new
        again.'
27 I say to the deep waters,
    'Dry up. Let your streams
        become dry.'
28 I say about Cyrus,
    'He is my shepherd.
    He will accomplish
        everything I want
        him to.
He will say about Jerusalem,
    "Let it be rebuilt."
And he will say about the
        temple,
    "Let its foundations be
        laid."'

45 "Cyrus is my anointed
        king.
    I take hold of his right
        hand.
I give him the power
    to bring nations under his
        control.
I help him strip kings of their
        power
    to go to war against him.
I break city gates open
    so he can go through
        them.
I say to him,

2 'I will march out ahead of
        you.
    I will make the mountains
        level.
I will break down bronze
        gates.
    I will cut through their
        heavy iron bars.
3 I will give you treasures that
        are hidden away.
    I will give you riches that
        are stored up in secret
        places.
Then you will know that I am
        the LORD.
    I am the God of Israel.
    I am sending for you by
        name.
4 Cyrus, I am sending for you
        by name.
    I am doing it for the good of
        the family of Jacob.
    They are my servant.
I am doing it for Israel.
    They are my chosen
        people.
You do not know anything
        about me.
    But I am giving you a title
        of honor.
5 I am the LORD. There is no
        other LORD.
    I am the one and only God.
You do not know anything
        about me.
    But I will make you
        strong.
6 Then people will know there
        is no God but me.
    Everyone from where the
        sun rises in the east
    to where it sets in the west
        will know it.
I am the LORD.
    There is no other LORD.

7 I cause light to shine. I also
    create darkness.
  I bring good times. I also
    create hard times.
  I do all these things. I am
    the LORD.

8 " 'Rain down my godliness,
    you heavens above.
  Let the clouds shower it
    down.
  Let the earth open wide to
    receive it.
  Let freedom spring to life.
  Let godliness grow richly
    along with it.
  I have created all these
    things.
  I am the LORD.' "

9 How terrible it will be for
    anyone who argues with
    their Maker!
  They are like a broken
    piece of pottery lying on
    the ground.
  Does clay say to a potter,
    "What are you making?"
  Does a pot say,
    "The potter doesn't have
    any skill"?

10 How terrible it will be for
    anyone who says to a
    father,
  "Why did you give me life?"
  How terrible for anyone who
    says to a mother,
  "Why have you brought me
    into the world?"

11 The LORD is the Holy One of
    Israel.
  He made them.
  He says to them,
    "Are you asking me about
    what will happen to my
    children?

Are you telling me what I
    should do with what my
    hands have made?

12 I made the earth.
  I created human beings to
    live there.
  My own hands spread out the
    heavens.
  I put all the stars in their
    places.

13 I will stir up Cyrus and help
    him win his battles.
  I will make all his roads
    straight.
  He will rebuild Jerusalem.
  My people have been
    taken away from their
    country.
  But he will set them free.
  I will not pay him to do it.
  He will not receive a
    reward for it,"
  says the LORD who rules
    over all.

14 The LORD says to the people
of Jerusalem,

"You will get everything
    Egypt produces.
  You will receive everything
    the people of Cush
and the tall Sabeans get in
    trade.
  All of it will belong to you.
And all these people will
    walk behind you as
    slaves.
  They will be put in chains
    and come over to you.
  They will bow down to you.
  They will admit,
'God is with you.
  There is no other God.' "

15 You are a God who has been
    hiding yourself.

You are the God of Israel.
  You save us.
¹⁶ All those who make statues
    of gods will be put to
    shame.
  They will be dishonored.
  They will be led away in
    shame together.
¹⁷ But the LORD will save
    Israel.
  He will save them forever.
  They will never be put to
    shame or dishonored.
  That will be true for all
    time to come.

¹⁸ The LORD created the
    heavens.
  He is God.
  He formed the earth and
    made it.
  He set it firmly in place.
  He didn't create it to be
    empty.
  Instead, he formed it for
    people to live on.
  He says, "I am the LORD.
  There is no other LORD.
¹⁹ I have not spoken in secret.
  I have not spoken from a
    dark place.
  I have not said to Jacob's
    people,
  'It is useless to look for me.'
  I am the LORD. I always speak
    the truth.
  I always say what is right.

²⁰ "Come together, you people
    of the nations
  who escaped from
    Babylon.
  Gather together and come
    into court.
  Only people who do not
    know anything

would carry around gods
    that are made out of
    wood.
  They pray to false gods that
    can't save them.
²¹ Tell me what will happen.
  State your case.
  Talk it over together.
  Who spoke long ago about
    what would happen?
  Who said it a long time
    ago?
  I did. I am the LORD.
  I am the one and only God.
  I always do what is right.
  I am the one who saves.
  There is no God but me.

²² "All you who live anywhere
    on earth,
  turn to me and be saved.
  I am God. There is no other
    God.
²³ I have made a promise in my
    own name.
  I have spoken with
    complete honesty.
  I will not take back a single
    word. I said,
  'Everyone will kneel down to
    me.
  Everyone's mouth will
    make promises in my
    name.'
²⁴ They will say, 'The LORD is
    the only one who can
    save us.
  Only he can make us
    strong.' "
  All those who have been
    angry with the LORD will
    come to him.
  And they will be put to
    shame.
²⁵ But the LORD will save all the
    people of Israel.

And so they will boast
about the LORD.

The False Gods of Babylon

46 The gods named Bel and
Nebo are brought down
in shame.
The statues of them are
being carried away on
the backs of animals.
They used to be carried
around by the people
who worshiped them.
But now they've become
a heavy load for tired
animals.
2 The gods named Bel and
Nebo are brought down
in shame together.
They aren't able to save
their own statues.
They themselves are
carried off as prisoners.

3 The LORD says, "Family of
Jacob, listen to me.
Pay attention, you people
of Israel who are left
alive.
I have taken good care of you
since your life began.
I have carried you since
you were born as a
nation.
4 I will continue to carry
you even when you
are old.
I will take good care of you
even when your hair is
gray.
I have made you, and I will
carry you.
I will take care of you, and I
will save you.
I am the LORD.

5 "Who will you compare me
with?
Who is equal to me?
What am I like?
Who can you compare me
with?
6 Some people pour out gold
from their bags.
They weigh out silver on
the scales.
They hire someone who
works with gold to make
it into a god.
They bow down to it and
worship it.
7 They lift it up on their
shoulders and carry it.
They set it up in its place,
and there it stands.
It can't move from that
spot.
Someone might cry out to it.
But it does not answer.
It can't save them from
their troubles.
8 So remember this, you who
refuse to obey me.
Keep it in your minds and
hearts.

9 "Remember what happened
in the past.
Think about what took
place long ago.
I am God. There is no other
God.
I am God. There is no one
like me.
10 Before something even
happens, I announce
how it will end.
In fact, from times long ago
I announced what was
still to come.
I say, 'My plan will succeed.

I will do anything I want
     to do.'
¹¹ I will send for a man from
     the east to carry out my
     plan.
From a land far away, he
     will come like a bird that
     kills its food.
I will bring about what I have
     said.
I will do what I have
     planned.
¹² Listen to me, you stubborn
     people.
Pay attention, you who
     now refuse to do what I
     have said is right.
¹³ The time is almost here for
     me to make everything
     right.
It is not far away.
The time for me to save you
     will not be put off.
I will save the city of Zion.
I will bring honor to
     Israel.

Babylon Will Fall

47 "City of Babylon,
     go down and sit in the
     dust.
Leave your throne and sit
     on the ground.
Queen city of the
     Babylonians,
     your life will not be
     comfortable
and easy anymore.
² Get millstones and grind
     some flour like a female
     slave.
Take off your veil.
Lift up your skirts. Make your
     legs bare.
Wade through the streams.

³ Everyone will see your naked
     body.
Everyone will see your
     shame.
I will pay you back for what
     you did.
I will not spare any of your
     people."

⁴ The one who sets us free is
     the Holy One of Israel.
His name is the Lord Who
     Rules Over All.

⁵ The Lord says, "Queen city
     of the Babylonians,
go into a dark prison. Sit
     there quietly.
You will not be called
     the queen of kingdoms
     anymore.
⁶ I was angry with my people.
I treated them as if they did
     not belong to me.
I handed them over to you.
And you did not show them
     any pity.
You even placed heavy loads
     on their old people.
⁷   You said, 'I am queen
     forever!'
But you did not think about
     what you were doing.
You did not consider how
     things might turn out.

⁸ "So listen, you who love
     pleasure.
You think you are safe and
     secure.
You say to yourself,
     'I am like a god.
No one is greater than I
     am.
I'll never be a widow.
And my children will never
     be taken away from me.'

⁹ But both of these things
    will happen to you in a
    moment.
  They will take place on a
    single day.
  You will lose your children.
  And you will become a
    widow.
  That is what will happen to
    you.
  All your evil magic
    and powerful spells will
    not save you.
¹⁰ You have felt secure in your
    evil ways.
  You have said, 'No one sees
    what I'm doing.'
  Your wisdom and knowledge
    lead you astray.
  You say to yourself,
  'I am like a god. No one is
    greater than I am.'
¹¹ So horrible trouble will come
    on you.
  You will not know how to
    use your evil magic to
    make it go away.
  Great trouble will fall on you.
  No amount of money can
    keep it away.
  Something terrible will
    happen to you all at
    once.
  You will not see it coming
    ahead of time.
¹² "So keep on casting your
    magic spells.
  Keep on practicing your
    evil magic.
  You have been doing those
    things ever since you
    were a child.
  Perhaps they will help you.
  Maybe they will scare your
    enemies away.

¹³ All the advice you have
    received
  has only worn you out!
  Let those who study the
    heavens come forward.
  They claim to know what is
    going to happen
  by watching the stars every
    month.
  So let them save you from the
    trouble
  that is coming on you.
¹⁴ They are just like straw.
  Fire will burn them up.
  They can't even save
    themselves
  from the powerful flames.
  These are not like coals that
    can warm anyone.
  This is not like a fire to
    sit by.
¹⁵ They can't do you any good.
  You have done business
    with them ever since you
    were a child.
  You have always asked
    them for advice.
  All of them are bewildered
    and continue in their
    own ways.
  None of them can save you."

Israel Is Stubborn

48 People of Jacob, listen to
    me.
  You are called by the name
    of Israel.
  You come from the family
    line of Judah.
  You make promises in the
    name of the LORD.
  You pray to Israel's God.
  But you aren't honest.
  You don't mean what you
    say.

2 You call yourselves citizens
   of the holy city of
   Jerusalem.
You say you depend on
   Israel's God.
His name is the LORD
   Who Rules Over All.
He says,
3 "Long ago I told you ahead
   of time what would
   happen.
I announced it and made it
   known.
Then all of a sudden I acted.
And those things took
   place.
4 I knew how stubborn you
   were.
Your neck muscles were as
   unbending as iron.
Your forehead was as hard
   as bronze.
5 So I told you those things
   long ago.
Before they happened I
   announced them to you.
I did it so you would not be
   able to say,
'My statues of gods did
   them.
My wooden and metal
   gods made them
   happen.'
6 You have heard me tell you
   these things.
Think about all of them.
Won't you admit they have
   taken place?

"From now on I will tell you
   about new things that
   will happen.
I have not made them
   known to you before.
7 These things are taking place
   right now.

They did not happen long
   ago.
You have not heard of them
   before today.
So you can't say,
'Oh, yes. I already knew
   about them.'
8 You have not heard or
   understood what I said.
Your ears have been plugged
   up for a long time.
I knew very well that you
   would turn against me.
From the day you were
   born, you have refused
   to obey me.
9 For the honor of my own
   name I wait to show my
   anger.
I hold it back from you so
   people will continue to
   praise me.
I do not want to destroy
   you completely.
10 I have tested you in the
   furnace of suffering.
I have tried to make you
   pure.
But I did not use as much
   heat as it takes to make
   silver pure.
11 I tried to purify you for my
   own honor.
I did it for the honor of my
   name.
How can I let myself be
   dishonored?
I will not give up my glory
   to any other god.

Israel Is Set Free

12 "Family of Jacob, listen to me.
People of Israel, pay
   attention.
I have chosen you.

I am the first and the last.
I am the LORD.
13 With my own hand I laid
the foundations of the
earth.
With my right hand I
spread out the heavens.
When I send for them,
they come and stand ready
to obey me.

14 "People of Israel, come
together and listen to
me.
What other god has said
ahead of time that
certain things would
happen?
I have chosen Cyrus.
He will carry out my plans
against Babylon.
He will use his power
against the Babylonians.
15 I myself have spoken.
I have chosen him to carry
out my purpose.
I will bring him to Babylon.
He will succeed in what I
tell him to do.

16 "Come close and listen to
me.

"From the first time I said
Cyrus was coming,
I did not do it in secret.
When he comes, I will be
there."

The LORD and King has filled
me with his Spirit.
People of Israel, he has sent
me to you.

17 The LORD is the Holy One of
Israel.
He sets his people free. He
says to them,

"I am the LORD your God.
I teach you what is best for
you.
I direct you in the way you
should go.
18 I wish you would pay
attention to my
commands.
If you did, peace would
flow over you like a river.
Godliness would sweep
over you like the waves
of the ocean.
19 Your family would be like the
sand.
Your children after you
would be as many as
the grains of sand by
the sea.
It would be impossible to
count them.
I would always accept the
members of your family
line.
They would never
disappear or be
destroyed."

20 People of Israel, leave
Babylon!
Hurry up and get away
from the Babylonians!
Here is what I want you to
announce.
Make it known with shouts
of joy.
Send the news out from one
end of the earth to the
other.
Say, "The LORD has set free
his servant Jacob."
21 They didn't get thirsty when
he led them through the
deserts.
He made water flow out of
the rock for them.

He broke the rock open,
    and water came out of it.
22 "There is no peace for those
    who are evil," says the
    LORD.

The Servant of the LORD

49 People who live on the
    islands, listen to me.
    Pay attention, you nations
        far away.
    Before I was born the LORD
        chose me to serve him.
    Before I was born the LORD
        spoke my name.
2 He made my words like a
        sharp sword.
    He hid me in the palm of
        his hand.
    He made me into a
        sharpened arrow.
    He took good care of me
        and kept me safe.
3 He said to me, "You are my
        true servant Israel.
    I will show my glory
        through you."
4 But I said, "In spite of my
        hard work,
    I feel as if I haven't
        accomplished
        anything.
    I've used up all my strength.
    It seems as if everything
        I've done is worthless.
    But the LORD will give me
        what I should receive.
    My God will reward me."
5 The LORD formed me in my
        mother's body to be his
        servant.
    He wanted me to bring the
        family of Jacob back to
        him.

He wanted me to gather
    the people of Israel to
    himself.
The LORD will honor me.
My God will give me
    strength.

6 Here is what the LORD says
to me.

    "It is not enough for you as
        my servant
    to bring the tribes of Jacob
        back to their land.
    It is not enough for you to
        bring back
    the people of Israel I have
        kept alive.
    I will also make you a light
        for the Gentiles.
    Then you will make it
        possible for the whole
        world to be saved."

7 The LORD sets his people free.
    He is the Holy One of Israel.
    He speaks to his servant, who
        is looked down on and
        hated by the nations.
    He speaks to the servant of
        rulers. He says to him,
    "Kings will see you and stand
        up to honor you.
    Princes will see you and
        bow down to show you
        their respect.
    I am the LORD. I am faithful.
    I am the Holy One of Israel.
    I have chosen you."

Israel Is Brought Back
to Their Land

8 The LORD says to his servant,

    "When it is time to have
        mercy on you, I will
        answer your prayers.

When it is time to save you,
I will help you.
I will keep you safe.
You will put into effect
my covenant with the
people of Israel.
Then their land will be made
like new again.
Each tribe will be sent back
to its territory that was
left empty.
9 I want you to say to the
prisoners, 'Come out.'
Tell those who are in their
dark cells, 'You are free!'

"On their way home they will
eat beside the roads.
They will find plenty to eat
on every bare hill.
10 They will not get hungry or
thirsty.
The heat from the desert
sun will not beat down
on them.
The God who has tender
love for them will guide
them.
Like a shepherd, he will
lead them beside springs
of water.
11 I will make roads across the
mountains.
I will build wide roads for
my people.
12 They will come from far
away.
Some of them will come
from the north.
Others will come from the
west.
Still others will come from
Aswan in the south."

13 Shout for joy, you heavens!
Be glad, you earth!
Burst into song, you
mountains!
The LORD will comfort his
people.
He will show his tender
love to those who are
suffering.

14 But the city of Zion said, "The
LORD has deserted me.
The Lord has forgotten me."

15 The LORD answers, "Can a
mother forget the baby
who is nursing at her
breast?
Can she stop having tender
love
for the child who was born
to her?
She might forget her child.
But I will not forget you.
16 I have written your name on
the palms of my hands.
Your walls are never out of
my sight.
17 Your people will hurry back.
Those who destroyed you
so completely will leave
you.
18 Look up. Look all around
you.
All your people are getting
together
to come back to you.
You can be sure that I live,"
announces the LORD.
"And you can be just as sure
that your people
will be like decorations you
will wear.
Like a bride, you will wear
them proudly.

19 "Zion, you were destroyed.
Your land was left empty.

It was turned into a dry
and empty desert.
But now you will be too small
to hold all your people.
And those who destroyed
you will be far away.
²⁰ The children born during
your time of sorrow
will speak to you. They will
say,
'This city is too small for us.
Give us more space to live
in.'
²¹ Then you will say to yourself,
'Whose children are these?
I lost my children.
And I couldn't have any
more.
My children were taken far
away from me.
And no one wanted them.
Who brought these
children up?
I was left all alone.
So where have these
children come from?' "

²² The LORD and King continues,

"I will call out to the nations.
I will give a signal to them.
They will bring back your
sons in their arms.
They will carry your
daughters on their hips.
²³ Their kings will become like
fathers to you.
Their queens will be like
mothers who nurse you.
They will bow down to you
with their faces toward
the ground.
They will kiss the dust at
your feet to show you
their respect.

Then you will know that I am
the LORD.
Those who put their
hope in me will not be
ashamed."

²⁴ Can goods that were stolen
by soldiers be taken
away from them?
Can prisoners be set free
from the powerful
Babylonians?

²⁵ "Yes, they can," the LORD
answers.

"Prisoners will be taken away
from soldiers.
Stolen goods will be taken
back from the powerful
Babylonians.
Zion, I will fight against those
who fight against you.
And I will save your
people.
²⁶ I will make those who treat
you badly eat the flesh of
others.
They will drink blood and
get drunk on it as if it
were wine.
Then everyone on earth will
know
that I am the one who
saves you.
I am the LORD. I set you free.
I am the Mighty One of
Jacob."

Israel Sins but the LORD's Servant Obeys

50 The LORD says to the
people in Jerusalem,

"Do you think I divorced
your people who lived
before you?

Is that why I sent them
away?
If it is, show me the letter of
divorce.
I did not sell you into
slavery to pay someone I
owe.
You were sold because you
sinned against me.
Your people were sent
away because of their
lawless acts.
²When I came to save you,
why didn't anyone
welcome me?
When I called out to you,
why didn't anyone
answer me?
Wasn't I powerful enough to
set you free?
Wasn't I strong enough to
save you?
I dry up the sea with a single
command.
I turn rivers into a desert.
Then fish rot because they do
not have any water.
They die because they are
thirsty.
³I make the sky turn dark.
It looks as if it's dressed
in clothing sad people
wear."

⁴The Lord and King has
taught me what to say.
He has taught me how to
help those who are
tired.
He wakes me up every
morning.
He makes me want to listen
like a good student.
⁵The Lord and King has
unplugged my ears.
I've always obeyed him.

I haven't turned away from
him.
⁶I let my enemies beat me on
my bare back.
I let them pull the hair out
of my beard.
I didn't turn my face away
when they made fun of me
and spit on me.
⁷The Lord and King helps me.
He won't let me be
dishonored.
So I've made up my mind to
keep on serving him.
I know he won't let me be
put to shame.
⁸He is near. He will prove I
haven't done anything
wrong.
So who will bring charges
against me?
Let's face each other in
court!
Who can bring charges
against me?
Let him come and face
me!
⁹The Lord and King helps me.
So who will judge me?
My enemies will be like
clothes that moths have
eaten up.
My enemies will disappear.

¹⁰Does anyone among you
have respect for the
Lord?
Does anyone obey the
message of the Lord's
servant?
Let the person who walks in
the dark
trust in the Lord.
Let the one who doesn't have
any light to guide them
depend on their God.

¹¹ But all you sinners who light
    fires
  should go ahead and walk
    in their light.
You who carry flaming
    torches
  should walk in their light.
Here's what I'm going to do to
    you.
  I'll make you lie down in
    great pain.

The LORD's Saving Power
for Zion Lasts Forever

51 The LORD says, "Listen to
    me, you who want to do
    what is right.
  Pay attention, you who
    look to me.
Consider the rock you were
    cut out of.
  Think about the rock pit
    you were dug from.
² Consider Abraham. He is the
    father of your people.
  Think about Sarah. She is
    your mother.
When I chose Abraham,
    he did not have any
    children.
  But I blessed him and gave
    him many of them.
³ You can be sure that I will
    comfort Zion's people.
  I will look with loving
    concern on all their
    destroyed buildings.
I will make their deserts like
    Eden.
  I will make their dry and
    empty land like the
    garden of the LORD.
Joy and gladness will be there.
  People will sing and give
    thanks to me.

⁴ "Listen to me, my people.
  Pay attention, my nation.
My instruction will go out to
    the nations.
  I make everything right.
  That will be a guiding light
    for them.
⁵ The time for me to set you
    free is near.
  I will soon save you.
My powerful arm will
    make everything right
    among the nations.
The islands will put their
    hope in me.
  They will wait for my
    powerful arm to act.
⁶ Look up toward the
    heavens.
  Then look at the earth.
The heavens will vanish like
    smoke.
  The earth will wear out
    like clothes.
Those who live there will
    die like flies.
But I will save you forever.
  My saving power will never
    end.
⁷ "Listen to me, you who know
    what is right.
  Pay attention, you
    who have taken my
    instruction to heart.
Do not be afraid when mere
    human beings make fun
    of you.
  Do not be terrified when
    they laugh at you.
⁸ They will be like clothes that
    moths have eaten up.
  They will be like wool that
    worms have chewed up.
But my saving power will last
    forever.

I will save you for all time
   to come."

9 Wake up, arm of the LORD!
      Wake up!
   Dress yourself with
      strength as if it were your
      clothes!
Wake up, just as you did in
      the past.
   Wake up, as you did long
      ago.
Didn't you cut Rahab to
      pieces?
   Didn't you stab that sea
      monster to death?
10 Didn't you dry up the Red
      Sea?
   Didn't you dry up those
      deep waters?
You made a road on the
      bottom of that sea.
   Then those who were set
      free went across.
11 Those the LORD has saved
      will return to their land.
   They will sing as they enter
      the city of Zion.
   Joy that lasts forever will be
      like beautiful crowns on
      their heads.
They will be filled with
      gladness and joy.
   Sorrow and sighing will be
      gone.
12 The LORD says to his people,
      "I comfort you because of
      who I am.
   Why are you afraid of mere
      human beings?
   They are like grass that
      dries up.
13 How can you forget me? I
      made you.
   I stretch out the heavens.

I lay the foundations of the
      earth.
Why are you terrified every
      day?
   Is it because those who
      are angry with you are
      crushing you?
   Is it because they are
      trying to destroy you?
Their anger can't harm you
      anymore.
14   You prisoners who are so
      afraid will soon be set
      free.
You will not die in your
      prison cells.
   You will not go without
      food.
15 I am the LORD your God.
   I stir up the ocean. I make
      its waves roar.
   My name is the LORD Who
      Rules Over All.
16 I have put my words in your
      mouth.
   I have kept you safe in the
      palm of my hand.
I set the heavens in place.
   I laid the foundations of
      the earth.
   I say to Zion, 'You are my
      people.' "

*The Cup of the LORD's Great
Anger*
17 Wake up, Jerusalem!
      Wake up! Get up!
The LORD has handed you
      the cup of his great
      anger.
   And you have drunk from it.
That cup makes people
      unsteady on their feet.
   And you have drunk from
      it to the very last drop.

¹⁸ Among all the children who
    were born to you
  there was none to guide
    you.
  Among all the children you
    brought up
  there was none to lead you
    by the hand.
¹⁹ Nothing but trouble has
    come to you.
  You have been wiped out
    and destroyed.
  And you have suffered
    hunger and war.
  No one feels sorry for you.
  No one can comfort you.
²⁰ Your children have fainted.
  They lie helpless at every
    street corner.
  They are like antelope that
    have been caught in a
    net.
  They have felt the full force of
    the Lord's great anger.
  Jerusalem, your God had to
    warn them strongly.
²¹ So listen to me, you suffering
    people of Jerusalem.
  You have been made
    drunk, but not by
    drinking wine.
²² Your Lord and King speaks.
  He is your God.
  He stands up for his people.
  He says,
  "I have taken from you
    the cup of my great
    anger.
  It made you unsteady on
    your feet.
  But you will never drink
    from that cup again.
²³ Instead, I will give it to those
    who made you suffer.
  They said to you,

'Fall down flat on the
    ground.
  Then we can walk all over
    you.'
  And that is exactly what you
    did.
  You made your back like a
    street to be walked on."

52 Wake up! Zion, wake up!
  Dress yourself with
  strength as if it were your
  clothes.
  Holy city of Jerusalem,
    put on your clothes of
    glory.
  Those who haven't been
    circumcised will never
    enter you again.
  Neither will those who are
    "unclean."
² Get up, Jerusalem! Shake off
    your dust.
  Take your place on your
    throne.
  Captured people of Zion,
    remove the chains from
    your neck.

³ The Lord says,

"When you were sold as
    slaves, no one paid
    anything for you.
  Now no one will pay any
    money to set you free."

⁴ The Lord and King continues,

"Long ago my people went
    down to Egypt.
  They lived there for a
    while.
  Later, Assyria crushed
    them without any
    reason.

5 "Now look at what has happened to them," announces the LORD.

"Once again my people have
      been taken away.
And no one paid anything
      for them.
Those who rule over them
      brag about it,"
            announces the LORD.
"All day long without
      stopping,
people speak evil things
      against my name.
6 So the day will come when
      my people will really
      know the meaning of my
      name.
They will know what kind
      of God I am.
They will know that I told
      them ahead of time they
      would return to their
      land.
They will know that it
      was I."

7 What a beautiful sight it is
      to see messengers coming
      with good news!
How beautiful to see them
      coming down from the
      mountains
with a message about
      peace!
How wonderful it is when
      they bring the good news
      that we are saved!
How wonderful when they
      say to Zion,
"Your God rules!"
8 Listen! Those on guard duty
      are shouting out the
      message.
With their own eyes

they see the LORD returning
      to Zion.
So they shout for joy.
9 Burst into songs of joy
      together,
you broken-down
      buildings in Jerusalem.
The LORD has comforted his
      people.
He has set Jerusalem free.
10 The LORD will use the power
      of his holy arm to save
      his people.
All the nations will see him
      do it.
Everyone from one end of
      the earth to the other
      will see it.

11 You who carry the objects
      that belong to the
      LORD's temple, leave
      Babylon!
Leave it! Get out of there!
Don't touch anything that
      isn't pure and "clean."
Come out of Babylon and
      be pure.
12 But this time you won't have
      to leave in a hurry.
You won't have to rush
      away.
The LORD will go ahead of
      you and lead you.
The God of Israel will
      follow behind you and
      guard you.

The Suffering and Glory of the LORD's Servant

13 The LORD says, "My servant
      will act wisely and
      accomplish his task.
He will be highly honored.
He will be greatly
      respected.

14 Many people were shocked
   when they saw him.
He was so scarred that he
   no longer looked like a
   person.
His body was so twisted
   that he did not look
   like a human being
   anymore.
15 But many nations will be
   surprised when they see
   what he has done.
Kings will be so amazed
   that they will not be able
   to say anything.
They will understand things
   they were never told.
They will know the
   meaning of things they
   never heard."

53 Who has believed what
   we've been saying?
Who has seen the LORD's
   saving power?
2 His servant grew up like a
   tender young plant.
He grew like a root coming
   up out of dry ground.
He didn't have any beauty
   or majesty that made us
   notice him.
There wasn't anything
   special about the way he
   looked that drew us to
   him.
3 People looked down on him.
   They didn't accept him.
He knew all about pain
   and suffering.
He was like someone people
   turn their faces away
   from.
We looked down on him.
We didn't have any
   respect for him.

4 He suffered the things we
   should have suffered.
He took on himself the
   pain that should have
   been ours.
But we thought God was
   punishing him.
We thought God was
   wounding him and
   making him suffer.
5 But the servant was pierced
   because we had sinned.
He was crushed because
   we had done what was
   evil.
He was punished to make us
   whole again.
His wounds have healed us.
6 All of us are like sheep. We
   have wandered away
   from God.
All of us have turned to our
   own way.
And the LORD has placed on
   his servant
   the sins of all of us.
7 He was treated badly and
   made to suffer.
But he didn't open his
   mouth.
He was led away like a lamb
   to be killed.
Sheep are silent while their
   wool is being cut off.
In the same way, he didn't
   open his mouth.
8 He was arrested and
   sentenced to death.
Then he was taken away.
He was cut off from this
   life.
He was punished for the sins
   of my people.
Who among those who
   were living at that time

tried to stop what was
happening?

9 He was given a grave with
those who were evil.
But his body was buried
in the tomb of a rich
man.
He was killed even though he
hadn't harmed anyone.
And he had never lied to
anyone.

10 The Lord says, "It was my
plan to crush him
and cause him to suffer.
I made his life an offering
to pay for sin.
But he will see all his
children after him.
In fact, he will continue to
live.
My plan will be brought
about through him.
11 After he has suffered, he will
see the light of life.
And he will be satisfied.
My godly servant will make
many people godly
because of what he will
accomplish.
He will be punished for
their sins.
12 So I will give him a place of
honor among those who
are great.
He will be rewarded just
like others who win the
battle.
That's because he was willing
to give his life as a
sacrifice.
He was counted among
those who had
committed crimes.
He took the sins of many
people on himself.

And he gave his life for
those who had done
what is wrong."

Jerusalem Will Be Glorious

54 "Jerusalem, sing!
You are now like a
woman who never had a
child.
Burst into song! Shout for
joy!
You who have never had
labor pains,
you are now all alone.
But you will have more
children than a woman
who still has a husband,"
says the Lord.
2 "Make a large area for your
tent.
Spread out its curtains.
Go ahead and make your
tent wider.
Make its ropes longer.
Drive the stakes down
deeper.
3 You will spread out to the
right and the left.
Your children after you
will drive out the nations
that are now living in
your land.
They will make their
homes in the deserted
cities of those nations.

4 "Do not be afraid. You will
not be put to shame
anymore.
Do not be afraid of being
dishonored.
People will no longer make
fun of you.
You will forget the time when
you suffered as slaves in
Egypt.

You will no longer
    remember the shame
of being a widow in
    Babylon.
5 I made you. I am now your
    husband.
My name is the LORD Who
    Rules Over All.
I am the Holy One of Israel.
I have set you free.
I am the God of the whole
    earth.
6 You were like a wife who was
    deserted.
And her heart was broken.
You were like a wife who
    married young.
And her husband sent her
    away.
But now I am calling you
    to come back," says your
    God.
7 "For a brief moment I left you.
But because I love you so
    much, I will bring you
    back.
8 For a moment I turned my
    face away from you.
I was very angry with you.
But I will show you my loving
    concern.
My faithful love will
    continue forever,"
says the LORD. He is the
    one who set you free.
9 "During Noah's time I made
    a promise.
I said I would never cover
    the earth with water
    again.
In the same way, I have
    promised not to be angry
    with you.
I will never punish you
    again.

10 The mountains might shake.
The hills might be
    removed.
But my faithful love for you
    will never be shaken.
And my covenant that
    promises peace to you
    will never be removed,"
says the LORD. He shows
    you his loving concern.
11 "Suffering city, you have been
    beaten by storms.
You have not been
    comforted.
I will rebuild you with
    turquoise stones.
I will rebuild your
    foundations with lapis
    lazuli.
12 I will line the top of your city
    wall with rubies.
I will make your gates out
    of gleaming jewels.
And I will make all your
    walls out of precious
    stones.
13 I will teach all your children.
And they will enjoy great
    peace.
14 When you do what is right,
    you will be made secure.
Your leaders will not be mean
    to you.
You will not have anything
    to be afraid of.
You will not be terrified
    anymore.
Terror will not come near
    you.
15 People might attack you. But
    I will not be the cause of
    it.
Those who attack you will
    give themselves up to
    you.

16 "I created blacksmiths.
    They fan the coals into
        flames of fire.
    They make weapons that are
        fit for their work.
    I also created those who
        destroy others.
17   But no weapon used
        against you will succeed.
People might bring charges
        against you.
    But you will prove that they
        are wrong.
    Those are the things I do for
        my servants.
    I make everything right for
        them,"
            announces the LORD.

The LORD Invites Thirsty People to Come to Him

55 "Come, all you who are
        thirsty.
    Come and drink the water
        I offer to you.
You who do not have any
        money, come.
    Buy and eat the grain I give
        you.
Come and buy wine and
        milk.
    You will not have to pay
        anything for it.
2 Why spend money on what is
        not food?
    Why work for what does
        not satisfy you?
Listen carefully to me.
    Then you will eat what is
        good.
    You will enjoy the richest
        food there is.
3 Listen and come to me.
    Pay attention to me.
    Then you will live.

I will make a covenant
    with you that will last
        forever.
I will give you my faithful
        love.
    I promised it to David.
4 I made him a witness to the
        nations.
    He became a ruler and
        commander over them.
5 You too will send for nations
        you do not know.
    Even though you do not
        know them,
    they will come running to
        you.
That is what I will do. I am
    the LORD your God.
I am the Holy One of
        Israel.
I have honored you."

6 Turn to the LORD before it's
        too late.
    Call out to him while he's
        still ready to help you.
7 Let those who are evil stop
        doing evil things.
    And let them quit thinking
        evil thoughts.
Let them turn to the LORD.
    The LORD will show them
        his tender love.
Let them turn to our God.
    He is always ready to
        forgive.
8 "My thoughts are not like
        your thoughts.
    And your ways are not like
        my ways,"
            announces the LORD.
9 "The heavens are higher than
        the earth.
    And my ways are higher
        than your ways.

My thoughts are higher
than your thoughts.
[10] The rain and the snow
come down from the
sky.
They do not return to it
without watering the
earth.
They make plants come up
and grow.
The plants produce seeds
for farmers.
They also produce food for
people to eat.
[11] The words I speak are like
that.
They will not return to
me without producing
results.
They will accomplish what I
want them to.
They will do exactly what I
sent them to do.
[12] "My people, you will go out
of Babylon with joy.
You will be led out of it in
peace.
The mountains and hills
will burst into song as
you go.
And all the trees in the
fields
will clap their hands.
[13] Juniper trees will grow
where there used to be
bushes that had thorns
on them.
And myrtle trees will grow
where there used to be
thorns.
That will bring me great
fame.
It will be a lasting reminder
of what I can do.
It will stand forever."

The LORD Will Save Those Who Come to Him

56 The LORD says,

"Do what is fair and right.
I will soon come and save
you.
Soon everyone will know
that what I do is right.
[2] Blessed is the person who
does what I want them to.
They are faithful in
keeping the Sabbath day.
They do not misuse it.
They do not do what is evil
on that day."

[3] Suppose an outsider wants to
follow the LORD.
Then that person shouldn't
say,
"The LORD won't accept me
as one of his people."
And a eunuch shouldn't say,
"I'm like a dry tree
that doesn't bear any fruit."

[4] The LORD says,

"Suppose some eunuchs
keep my Sabbath days.
They choose to do what
pleases me.
And they are faithful in
keeping my covenant.
[5] Then I will set up a
monument in the area of
my temple.
Their names will be
written on it.
That will be better for them
than having sons and
daughters.
The names of the eunuchs
will be remembered
forever.
They will never be forgotten.

6 "Suppose outsiders want to
    follow me
   and serve me.
  They want to love me
    and worship me.
  They keep the Sabbath day
    and do not misuse it.
  And they are faithful in
    keeping my covenant.
7 Then I will bring them to my
    holy mountain of Zion.
  I will give them joy in my
    house.
  They can pray there.
  I will accept their burnt
    offerings and sacrifices
    on my altar.
  My house will be called
    a house where people from
    all nations can pray."
8 The LORD and King will
    gather
   those who were taken away
    from their homes in
    Israel.
  He announces, "I will gather
    them to myself.
  And I will gather others to
    join them."

The LORD Judges Israel's Evil Leaders

9 Come, all you enemy nations!
    Come like wild animals.
  Come and destroy like
    animals in the forest.
10 Israel's prophets are blind.
   They don't know the
    LORD.
  All of them are like
    watchdogs that can't
    even bark.
  They just lie around and
    dream.
  They love to sleep.

11 They are like dogs that love to
    eat.
  They never get enough.
  They are like shepherds
    who don't have any
    understanding.
  All of them do as they
    please.
  They only look for
    what they can get for
    themselves.
12 "Come!" they shout. "Let's get
    some wine!
  Let's drink all the beer we
    can!
  Tomorrow we'll do the same
    thing.
  And that will be even
    better than today."

57 Those who are right with
    God die.
  And no one really cares
    about it.
  People who are faithful to the
    LORD are swept away by
    trouble.
  And no one understands
    why that happens
   to those who do what is
    right.
2 Those who lead honest lives
    will enjoy peace and rest
    when they die.

3 The LORD says, "Come here,
    you children of women
    who practice evil
    magic!
  You are children of
    prostitutes and those
    who commit adultery.
4 Who are you making fun of?
  Who are you laughing at?
  Who are you sticking your
    tongue out at?

You are people who refuse to
　　obey me.
You are just a bunch of
　　liars!
5 You burn with sinful desire
　　among the oak trees.
You worship your gods
　　under every green tree.
You sacrifice your children in
　　the valleys.
You also do it under the
　　cliffs.
6 You have chosen some of the
　　smooth stones in the
　　valleys to be your gods.
You have joined yourselves
　　to them.
You have even poured out
　　drink offerings to them.
You have given grain
　　offerings to them.
So why should I take pity
　　on you?
7 You have made your bed on a
　　very high hill.
You went up there to offer
　　your sacrifices.
8 You have set up statues to
　　remind you of your
　　gods.
You have put them
　　behind your doors and
　　doorposts.
You deserted me. You invited
　　other lovers into your
　　bed.
You climbed into it and
　　welcomed them.
You made a deal with them.
And you looked with desire
　　at their naked bodies.
9 You took olive oil to the god
　　named Molek.
You took a lot of perfume
　　along with you.

You sent your messengers to
　　places far away.
You even sent them down
　　to the place of the dead.
10 You wore yourself out with all
　　your efforts.
But you would not say, 'It's
　　hopeless.'
You received new strength.
So you did not give up.

11 "Who are you so afraid of
　　that you have not been
　　faithful to me?
You have not remembered me.
　　What you do doesn't even
　　bother you.
I have not punished you for a
　　long time.
That is why you are not
　　afraid of me.
12 You have not done what is
　　right or good.
I will let everyone know
　　about it.
And that will not be of any
　　benefit to you.
13 Go ahead and cry out for help
　　to all the statues of your
　　gods.
See if they can save you!
The wind will carry them off.
Just a puff of air will blow
　　them away.
But anyone who comes to me
　　for safety
will receive the land.
They will possess my holy
　　mountain of Zion."

The LORD Comforts People Who Are Sorry for Their Sins

14 A messenger says,

"Build up the road! Build it
　　up! Get it ready!

Remove anything that
     would keep my people
     from coming back."
15 The God who is highly
     honored lives forever.
   His name is holy. He says,
"I live in a high and holy
     place.
   But I also live with anyone
     who turns away from
     their sins.
   I live with anyone who is
     not proud.
   I give new life to them.
   I give it to anyone who
     turns away from their
     sins.
16 I will not find fault with my
     people forever.
   I will not always be angry
     with them.
   If I were, I would cause their
     spirits to grow weak.
   The people I created would
     faint away.
17 I was very angry with them.
   They always longed for
     more and more of
     everything.
   So I punished them for that
     sin.
   I turned my face away
     from them because I was
     angry.
   But they kept on wanting
     their own way.
18 I have seen what they have
     done.
   But I will heal them.
   I will guide them.
   I will give those who
     mourn in Israel the
     comfort they had
     before.
19   Then they will praise me.

I will give perfect peace to
     those who are far away
     and those who are near.
   And I will heal them," says
     the LORD.
20 But those who are evil are
     like the rolling sea.
   It never rests.
   Its waves toss up mud and
     sand.

21 "There is no peace for those
     who are evil," says my
     God.

What True Worship Is All About

58 The LORD told me,

"Shout out loud. Do not hold
     back.
   Raise your voice like a
     trumpet.
   Tell my people that they have
     refused to obey me.
   Tell the family of Jacob
     how much they have
     sinned.
2 Day after day they worship
     me.
   They seem ready and
     willing to know how I
     want them to live.
   They act as if they were a
     nation that does what is
     right.
   They act as if they have not
     turned away from my
     commands.
   They claim to want me to
     give them fair decisions.
   They seem ready and
     willing to come near and
     worship me.
3 'We have gone without food,'
     they say.
   'Why haven't you noticed it?

We have made ourselves
   suffer.
   Why haven't you paid any
      attention to us?'

"On the day when you fast,
      you do as you please.
   You take advantage of all
      your workers.
⁴When you fast, it ends in
      arguing and fighting.
   You hit one another with
      your fists.
   That is an evil thing to do.
The way you are now fasting
      keeps your prayers from
      being heard in heaven.
⁵Do you think that is the way I
      want you to fast?
   Is it only a time for people
      to make themselves
      suffer?
Is it only for people to bow
      their heads like tall grass
      bent by the wind?
   Is it only for people to
      lie down in ashes and
      clothes of mourning?
   Is that what you call a fast?
      Do you think I can accept
      that?
⁶"Here is the way I want you to
      fast.

"Set free those who are held
      by chains without any
      reason.
   Untie the ropes that hold
      people as slaves.
Set free those who are
      crushed.
   Break every evil chain.
⁷Share your food with hungry
      people.
   Provide homeless people
      with a place to stay.

Give naked people clothes to
      wear.
   Provide for the needs of
      your own family.
⁸Then the light of my blessing
      will shine on you like the
      rising sun.
   I will heal you quickly.
I will march out ahead of you.
   And my glory will follow
      behind you and guard
      you.
   That's because I always do
      what is right.
⁹You will call out to me for
      help.
   And I will answer you.
You will cry out.
   And I will say, 'Here I am.'

"Get rid of the chains you use
      to hold others down.
   Stop pointing your finger
      at others as if they had
      done something wrong.
   Stop saying harmful things
      about them.
¹⁰Work hard to feed hungry
      people.
   Satisfy the needs of those
      who are crushed.
Then my blessing will light
      up your darkness.
   And the night of your
      suffering will become
      as bright as the noonday
      sun.
¹¹I will always guide you.
   I will satisfy your needs in
      a land baked by the sun.
I will make you stronger.
You will be like a garden that
      has plenty of water.
You will be like a spring
      whose water never runs
      dry.

¹²Your people will rebuild
the cities that were
destroyed long ago.
And you will build again
on the old foundations.
You will be called One Who
Repairs Broken Walls.
You will be called One
Who Makes City Streets
Like New Again.

¹³ "Do not work on the Sabbath
day.
Do not do just anything you
want to on my holy day.
Make the Sabbath a day you
can enjoy.
Honor the LORD's holy day.
Do not work on it.
Do not do just anything
you want to.
Do not talk about things
that are worthless.
¹⁴Then you will find your joy in
me.
I will give you control over
the most important
places in the land.
And you will enjoy all the
good things
in the land I gave your
father Jacob."
The LORD has spoken.

The LORD Sets His People Free

59 People of Israel, the
LORD's arm is not too
weak to save you.
His ears aren't too deaf to
hear your cry for help.
²But your sins have separated
you from your God.
They have caused him to
turn his face away from
you.
So he won't listen to you.

³Your hands and fingers are
stained with blood.
You are guilty of
committing murder.
Your mouth has told lies.
Your tongue says evil
things.
⁴People aren't fair when they
present cases in court.
They aren't honest when
they state their case.
They depend on weak
arguments. They tell lies.
They plan to make trouble.
Then they carry it out.
⁵The plans they make are like
the eggs of poisonous
snakes.
Anyone who eats those
eggs will die.
When one of them is broken,
a snake comes out.
⁶Those people weave their
evil plans together like a
spider's web.
But the webs they make
can't be used as clothes.
They can't cover
themselves with what
they make.
Their acts are evil.
They do things to harm
others.
⁷They are always in a hurry to
sin.
They run quickly to
murder those who aren't
guilty.
They love to think up evil
plans.
They leave a trail of
harmful actions.
⁸They don't know how to live
at peace with others.
What they do isn't fair.

They lead twisted lives.
No one who lives like that
will enjoy peace and
rest.

9 We aren't being treated
fairly.
We haven't been set free
yet.
The God who always does
what is right
hasn't come to help us.
We look for light, but we see
nothing but darkness.
We look for brightness,
but we walk in deep
shadows.
10 Like blind people we feel our
way along the wall.
We are like those who can't
see.
At noon we trip and fall as if
the sun had already set.
Compared to those who
are healthy, we are like
dead people.
11 All of us growl like hungry
bears.
We sound like doves as we
mourn.
We want the LORD to do what
is fair and save us.
But he doesn't do it.
We long for him to set us free.
But the time for that seems
far away.
12 That's because we've done
so many things he
considers wrong.
Our sins prove that we are
guilty.
The wrong things we've done
are always troubling us.
We admit that we have
sinned.

13 We've refused to obey the
LORD.
We've made evil plans
against him.
We've turned our backs on
our God.
We've stirred up conflict and
refused to follow him.
We've told lies that came
from our own minds.
14 So people stop others from
doing what is fair.
They keep them from
doing what is right.
No one tells the truth in court
anymore.
No one is honest there.
15 In fact, truth can't be found
anywhere.
Those who refuse to do evil
are attacked.

The LORD sees that people
aren't treating others
fairly.
That makes him unhappy.
16 He sees that there is no one
who helps his people.
He is shocked that no one
stands up for them.
So he will use his own
powerful arm to save
them.
He has the strength to do it
because he is holy.
17 He will put the armor of
holiness on his chest.
He'll put the helmet of
salvation on his head.
He'll pay people back for the
wrong things they do.
He'll wrap himself in anger
as if it were a coat.
18 He will pay his enemies
back for what they have
done.

He'll pour his anger out on
them.
He'll punish those who
attack him.
He'll give the people in the
islands what they have
coming to them.
19 People in the west will show
respect for the LORD's
name.
People in the east will
worship him because of
his glory.
The LORD will come like a
rushing river that was
held back.
His breath will drive it along.
20 "I set my people free. I will
come to Mount Zion.
I will come to those in
Jacob's family who turn
away from their sins,"
announces the LORD.

21 "Here is the covenant I will
make with them," says the LORD.
"My Spirit is on you and will not
leave you. I have put my words
in your mouth. They will never
leave your mouth. And they will
never leave the mouths of your
children or their children after
them. That will be true for all
time to come," says the LORD.

Zion Will Be Glorious

60 "People of Jerusalem, get
up.
Shine, because your light
has come.
The glory of the LORD will
shine on you.
2 Darkness covers the earth.
Thick darkness spreads
over the nations.

But I will rise and shine on
you.
My glory will appear over
you.
3 Nations will come to your
light.
Kings will come to the
brightness of your new
day.
4 "Look up. Look all around
you.
All your people are getting
together to come back to
you.
Your sons will come from far
away.
Your daughters will be
carried on the hip like
little children.
5 Then your face will glow with
joy.
Your heart will beat fast
because you are so
happy.
Wealth from across the
ocean will be brought
to you.
The riches of the nations
will come to you.
6 Herds of young camels will
cover your land.
They will come from
Midian and Ephah.
They will also come from
Sheba.
They'll carry gold and
incense.
And people will shout
praises to me.
7 All of Kedar's flocks will be
gathered to you.
The rams of Nebaioth will
serve as your sacrifices.
I will accept them as
offerings on my altar.

That is how I will bring
honor to my glorious
temple.

8 "Whose ships are these that
sail along like clouds?
They fly like doves to their
nests.
9 People from the islands are
coming to me.
The ships of Tarshish are
out in front.
They are bringing your
children back from far
away.
Your children are bringing
their silver and gold with
them.
They are coming to honor
me.
I am the LORD your God.
I am the Holy One of Israel.
I have honored you.

10 "People from other lands
will rebuild your walls.
Their kings will serve
you.
When I was angry with you, I
struck you.
But now I will show you my
tender love.
11 Your gates will always stand
open.
They will never be shut,
day or night.
Then people can bring
you the wealth of the
nations.
Their kings will come
along with them.
12 The nation or kingdom that
will not serve you will be
destroyed.
It will be completely wiped
out.

13 "Lebanon's glorious trees will
be brought to you.
Its junipers, firs and
cypress trees will be
brought.
They will be used to make
my temple beautiful.
And I will bring glory to
the place where my
throne is.
14 The children of those who
crush you will come and
bow down to you.
All those who hate you will
kneel down at your feet.
Jerusalem, they will call you
the City of the LORD.
They will name you Zion,
the City of the Holy One
of Israel.

15 "You have been deserted and
hated.
No one even travels
through you.
But I will make you into
something to be proud of
forever.
You will be a place of joy
for all time to come.
16 You will get everything you
need from kings and
nations.
You will be like children
who are nursing
at their mother's breasts.
Then you will know that I am
the one who saves you.
I am the LORD. I set you
free.
I am the Mighty One of
Jacob.
17 Instead of bronze I will bring
you gold.
In place of iron I will give
you silver.

Instead of wood I will bring
you bronze.
In place of stones I will give
you iron.
I will make peace govern you.
I will make godliness rule
over you.
18 People will no longer harm
one another in your
land.
They will not wipe out or
destroy anything inside
your borders.
You will call your walls
Salvation.
And you will name your
gates Praise.
19 You will not need the light of
the sun by day anymore.
The bright light of the
moon will no longer
have to shine on you.
I will be your light forever.
My glory will shine on you.
I am the LORD your God.
20 Your sun will never set again.
Your moon will never lose
its light.
I will be your light forever.
Your days of sorrow will
come to an end.
21 Then all your people will do
what is right.
The land will belong to
them forever.
They will be like a young tree
I have planted.
My hands have created
them.
They will show how
glorious I am.
22 The smallest family among
you will become a tribe.
The smallest tribe will
become a mighty nation.

I am the LORD.
When it is the right time, I
will act quickly."

The Year When the LORD Sets His People Free

61 The Spirit of the LORD
and King is on me.
The LORD has anointed me
to announce good news to
poor people.
He has sent me to comfort
those whose hearts have
been broken.
He has sent me to announce
freedom
for those who have been
captured.
He wants me to set prisoners
free
from their dark cells.
2 He has sent me to announce
the year
when he will set his people
free.
He wants me to announce
the day
when he will pay his
enemies back.
Our God has sent me to
comfort all those who
are sad.
3 He wants me to help those
in Zion who are filled
with sorrow.
I will put beautiful crowns on
their heads
in place of ashes.
I will anoint them with olive
oil to give them joy
instead of sorrow.
I will give them a spirit of
praise
in place of a spirit of
sadness.

They will be like oak trees
    that are strong and
    straight.
The LORD himself will
    plant them in the land.
That will show how
    glorious he is.
⁴ They will rebuild the places
    that were destroyed long
    ago.
They will repair the
    buildings that have been
    broken down for many
    years.
They will make the destroyed
    cities like new again.
They have been broken
    down for a very long
    time.
⁵ Outsiders will serve you
    by taking care of your
    flocks.
People from other lands
    will work in your fields
    and vineyards.
⁶ You will be called priests of
    the LORD.
You will be named workers
    for our God.
You will enjoy the wealth of
    nations.
You will brag about getting
    their riches.

⁷ Instead of being put to
    shame
you will receive a double
    share of wealth.
Instead of being dishonored
    you will be glad to be in
    your land.
You will receive a double
    share of riches there.
And you'll be filled with joy
    that will last forever.

⁸ The LORD says, "I love
    those who do what
    is right.
I hate it when people steal
    and do other sinful
    things.
So I will be faithful to my
    people.
And I will bless them.
I will make a covenant with
    them
    that will last forever.
⁹ Their children after them
    will be famous among
    the nations.
Their families will be
    praised by people
    everywhere.
All those who see them will
    agree
    that I have blessed them."

¹⁰ The people of Jerusalem will
    say,
    "We take great delight in
    the LORD.
We are joyful because we
    belong to our God.
He has dressed us with
    salvation as if it were our
    clothes.
He has put robes of
    godliness on us.
We are like a groom who
    is dressed up for his
    wedding.
We are like a bride who
    decorates herself with
    her jewels.
¹¹ The soil makes the young
    plant come up.
A garden causes seeds to
    grow.
In the same way, the LORD
    and King will make
    godliness grow.

And all the nations will
praise him."

The LORD Gives Zion a New Name

62 The LORD says, "For the good of Zion I will not keep silent.
For Jerusalem's benefit I
will not remain quiet.
I will not keep silent until
what I will do for them
shines like the sunrise.
I will not remain quiet until
they are saved
and shine like a blazing
torch.
2 Jerusalem, the nations will
see
that I have made
everything right for you.
All their kings will see your
glory.
You will be called by a new
name.
I myself will give it to you.
3 You will be like a glorious
crown in my strong
hand.
You will be like a royal
crown in my powerful
hand.
4 People will not call you
Deserted anymore.
They will no longer name
your land Empty.
Instead, you will be called
One the LORD Delights
In.
Your land will be named
Married One.
That's because the LORD will
take delight in you.
And your land will be
married.

5 As a young man marries a
young woman,
so your Builder will marry
you.
As a groom is happy with his
bride,
so your God will be full of
joy over you."

6 Jerusalem, I have stationed
guards on your walls.
They must never be silent
day or night.
You who call out to the LORD
must not give yourselves
any rest.
7 And don't give him any rest
until he makes Jerusalem
secure.
Don't give him any peace
until people all over the
earth praise that city.

8 The LORD has made a promise.
He has lifted up his right
hand and mighty arm.
He has promised, "I will
never give your grain
to your enemies for food
again.
Outsiders will never again
drink the fresh wine
you have worked so hard for.
9 Instead, those who gather
the grain will eat it
themselves.
And they will praise me.
Those who gather grapes
to make the wine will
enjoy it.
They will drink it in
the courtyards of my
temple."

10 Go out through your gates,
people of Jerusalem! Go
out!

Prepare the way for the rest
of your people to return.
Build up the road! Build it up!
Remove the stones.
Raise a banner over the city
for the nations to see.

11 The LORD has announced a
message
from one end of the earth
to the other.
He has said, "Tell the people
of Zion,
'Look! Your Savior is
coming!
He is bringing his people
back as his reward.
He has won the battle over
their enemies.' "

12 They will be called the Holy
People.
They will be called the
People the LORD Set
Free.
And Jerusalem will be named
the City the LORD Cares
About.
It will be named the City
No Longer Deserted.

God Will Save His People and Punish Their Enemies

63 Who is this man coming
from the city of Bozrah
in Edom?
His clothes are stained
bright red.
Who is he? He is dressed up
in all his glory.
He is marching toward us
with great strength.

The LORD answers, "It is I.
I have won the battle.
I am mighty.
I have saved my people."

2 Why are your clothes red?
They look as if you have
been stomping
on grapes in a winepress.

3 The LORD answers, "I have
been stomping on the
nations
as if they were grapes.
No one was there to help me.
I walked all over the nations
because I was angry.
That is why I stomped on
them.
Their blood splashed all over
my clothes.
So my clothes were stained
bright red.

4 I decided it was time to pay
back Israel's enemies.
The year for me to set my
people free had come.

5 I looked around, but no one
was there to help me.
I was shocked that no one
gave me any help.
So I used my own power to
save my people.
I had the strength to do it
because I was angry.

6 I walked all over the nations
because I was angry with
them.
I made them drink from the
cup of my great anger.
I poured out their blood on
the ground."

Isaiah Praises the LORD and Prays to Him

7 I will talk about the kind
things the LORD has
done.
I'll praise him for
everything he's done
for us.

He has done many good
    things
  for the nation of Israel.
  That's because he loves us
    and is very kind to us.
⁸In the past he said, "They are
    my people.
  They are children who will
    be faithful to me."
  So he saved them.
⁹When they suffered, he
    suffered with them.
  He sent his angel to save
    them.
He set them free because he
    is loving and kind.
  He lifted them up and
    carried them.
  He did it again and again
    in days long ago.
¹⁰But they refused to obey him.
  They made his Holy Spirit
    sad.
So he turned against them
    and became their
    enemy.
  He himself fought against
    them.

¹¹Then his people remembered
    what he did long ago.
  They recalled the days of
    Moses and his people.
They asked, "Where is the
    God who brought
  Israel through the Red Sea?
  Moses led them as the
    shepherd of his flock.
Where is the God who put
    his Holy Spirit among
    them?
¹²He used his glorious and
    powerful arm
  to help Moses.
He parted the waters of the
    sea in front of them.

That mighty act made him
    famous forever.
¹³ He led them through that
    deep sea.
Like a horse in open country,
    they didn't trip and fall.
¹⁴They were like cattle that
    are taken down to the
    plains.
  They were given rest by the
    Spirit of the Lord."
That's how he guided his
    people.
  So he made a glorious
    name for himself.

¹⁵Lord, look down from
    heaven.
  Look down from your holy
    and glorious throne.
Where is your great love for
    us?
  Where is your power?
Why don't you show us
    your tender love and
    concern?
¹⁶You are our Father.
  Abraham might not accept
    us as his children.
  Jacob might not recognize
    us as his family.
But you are our Father,
    Lord.
  Your name is One Who
    Always Sets Us Free.
¹⁷Lord, why do you let us
    wander away from you?
  Why do you let us become
    so stubborn
  that we don't respect you?
Come back and help us.
  We are the tribes that
    belong to you.
¹⁸For a little while your holy
    people possessed the
    land.

But now our enemies have
    torn your temple down.
¹⁹ We are like people you never
    ruled over.
We are like those who don't
    belong to you.

64 I wish you would open
    up your heavens
and come down to us!
I wish the mountains would
    tremble
when you show your
    power!
² Be like a fire that causes
    twigs to burn.
It also makes water boil.
So come down and make
    yourself known to your
    enemies.
Cause the nations to shake
    with fear
when they see your power!
³ Long ago you did some
    wonderful things we
    didn't expect.
You came down, and the
    mountains trembled
when you showed your
    power.
⁴ No one's ears have ever heard
    of a God like you.
No one's eyes have ever
    seen a God who is
    greater than you.
No God but you acts for the
    good
of those who trust in him.
⁵ You come to help those who
    enjoy doing what is right.
You help those who thank
    you for teaching them
    how to live.
But when we continued to
    disobey you,

you became angry with us.
So how can we be saved?
⁶ All of us have become
    like someone who is
    "unclean."
All the good things we do
    are like dirty rags to you.
All of us are like leaves that
    have dried up.
Our sins sweep us away
    like the wind.
⁷ No one prays to you.
No one asks you for help.
You have turned your face
    away from us.
You have let us feel the
    effects of our sins.

⁸ Lord, you are our Father.
    We are the clay. You are the
    potter.
Your hands made all of us.
⁹ Don't be so angry with us,
    Lord.
Don't remember our sins
    anymore.
Please have mercy on us.
    All of us belong to you.
¹⁰ Your sacred cities have
    become a desert.
Even Zion is a desert.
Jerusalem is a dry and
    empty place.
¹¹ Our people of long ago used
    to praise you in our holy
    and glorious temple.
But now it has been burned
    down.
Everything we treasured
    has been destroyed.
¹² Lord, won't you help us even
    after everything that's
    happened?
Will you keep silent and
    punish us more than we
    can stand?

The Lord Judges and Saves

65 The Lord says, "I made myself known to those who were not asking for me.

I was found by those who were not trying to find me.

I spoke to a nation that did not pray to me.

'Here I am,' I said. 'Here I am.'

² All day long I have held out my hands

to welcome a stubborn nation.

They lead sinful lives.

They go where their evil thoughts take them.

³ They are always making me very angry.

They do it right in front of me.

They offer sacrifices in the gardens of other gods.

They burn incense on altars that are made out of bricks.

⁴ They sit among the graves.

They spend their nights talking to the spirits of the dead.

They eat the meat of pigs.

Their cooking pots hold soup that has 'unclean' meat in it.

⁵ They say, 'Keep away! Don't come near us!

We are too sacred for you!'

Those people are like smoke in my nose.

They are like a fire that keeps burning all day.

⁶ "I will judge them. I have even written it down.

I will not keep silent.

Instead, I will pay them back for all their sins.

⁷ I will punish them for their sins.

I will also punish them for the sins of their people before them."

This is what the Lord says.

"They burned sacrifices on the mountains.

They disobeyed me by worshiping other gods on the hills.

So I will make sure they are fully punished

for all the sins they have committed."

⁸ The Lord says,

"Sometimes juice is still left in grapes that have been crushed.

So people say, 'Don't destroy them.

They are still of some benefit.'

That is what I will do for the good of those who serve me.

I will not destroy all my people.

⁹ I will give children to the families of Jacob and Judah.

They will possess my entire land.

My chosen people will be given all of it.

Those who serve me will live there.

¹⁰ Their flocks will eat in the rich grasslands of Sharon.

Their herds will rest in the
　Valley of Achor.
That is what I will do for
　my people who follow
　me.

11 "But some of you have
　deserted me.
You no longer worship on
　my holy mountain of
　Zion.
You spread a table for the god
　called Good Fortune.
You offer bowls of mixed
　wine to the god named
　Fate.
12 So I will make it your fate to
　be killed by swords.
All of you will die in the
　battle.
That's because I called out
　to you, but you did not
　answer me.
I spoke to you, but you did
　not listen.
You did what is evil in my
　sight.
You chose to do what does
　not please me."

13 So the LORD and King says,

"Those who serve me will
　have food to eat.
But you will be hungry.
My servants will have plenty
　to drink.
But you will be thirsty.
Those who serve me will be
　full of joy.
But you will be put to
　shame.
14 My servants will sing
　with joy in their hearts.
But you will cry out
　because of the great pain
　in your hearts.

You will cry because your
　spirits are sad.
15 My chosen ones will use your
　names
　when they curse others.
I am your LORD and King.
　I will put you to death.
But I will give new names
　to those who serve me.
16 They will ask me to bless
　their land.
They will do it in my
　name.
I am the one true God.
They will make promises in
　their land.
They will do it in my
　name.
I am the one true God.
The troubles of the past will
　be forgotten.
They will be hidden from
　my eyes.

*The LORD Will Create New
Heavens and a New Earth*

17 "I will create new heavens
　and a new earth.
The things that have
　happened before will not
　be remembered.
They will not even enter
　your minds.
18 So be glad and full of joy
　forever
　because of what I will
　create.
I will cause others to take
　delight in Jerusalem.
They will be filled with joy
　when they see its people.
19 And I will be full of joy
　because of Jerusalem.
I will take delight in my
　people.

Weeping and crying
will not be heard there
anymore.

20 "Babies in Jerusalem will no longer
live only a few days.
Old people will not fail
to live for a very long time.
Those who live to the age of 100
will be thought of as mere
children when they die.
Those who die before they are 100
will be considered as
having been under God's
curse.
21 My people will build houses
and live in them.
They will plant vineyards
and eat their fruit.
22 They will no longer build houses
only to have others live in
them.
They will no longer plant crops
only to have others eat
them.
My people will live to be as
old as trees.
My chosen ones will enjoy
for a long time
the things they have
worked for.
23 Their work will not be
worthless anymore.
They will not have children
who are sure to face
sudden terror.
Instead, I will bless them.
I will also bless their
children after them.
24 Even before they call out to
me, I will answer them.

While they are still
speaking, I will hear
them.
25 Wolves and lambs will eat
together.
Lions will eat straw like
oxen.
Serpents will not bite
anyone.
They will eat nothing but
dust.
None of those animals will
harm or destroy
anything or anyone on my
holy mountain of Zion,"
says the LORD.

The LORD Judges Some People and Blesses Others

66 The LORD says,

"Heaven is my throne.
The earth is under my
control.
So how could you ever build
a house for me?
Where would my resting
place be?
2 Didn't I make everything by
my power?
That is how all things were
created,"
announces the LORD.

"The people I value are not
proud.
They are sorry for the
wrong things they have
done.
They have great respect for
what I say.
3 But others are not like that.
They sacrifice bulls to me,
but at the same time they
kill people.
They offer lambs to me,

but they also sacrifice dogs
to other gods.
They bring grain offerings to
me,
but they also offer pig's
blood to other gods.
They burn incense to me,
but they also worship
statues of gods.
They have chosen to go their
own way.
They take delight in things
I hate.
⁴ So I have also made a
choice.
I will make them suffer
greatly.
I will bring on them what
they are afraid of.
When I called out to them, no
one answered me.
When I spoke to them, no
one listened.
They did what is evil in my
sight.
They chose to do what
displeases me."

⁵ Listen to the word of the
LORD.
Listen, you who tremble
with fear when he
speaks. He says,
"Some of your own people
hate you.
They turn their backs on
you because you are
faithful to me.
They make fun of you and
say,
'Let the LORD show his glory
by saving you.
Then we can see how
happy you are.'
But they will be put to
shame.

⁶ Hear the loud sounds coming
from the city!
Listen to the noise coming
from the temple!
I am the one causing it.
I am paying back my
enemies for everything
they have done.

⁷ "Zion is like a woman who
has a baby
before she goes into labor.
She has a son
even before her labor pains
begin.
⁸ Who has ever heard of
anything like that?
Who has ever seen such a
thing?
Can a country be born in a
day?
Can a nation be created in
a moment?
But as soon as Zion goes into
labor,
there are many more of her
people.
⁹ Zion, would I bring you to the
moment of birth
and not let it happen?" says
the LORD.
"Would I close up a mother's
body
when it is time for her baby
to be born?" says your
God.
¹⁰ "Be glad along with
Jerusalem, all you who
love her.
Be filled with joy because
of her.
Take great delight in her,
all you who mourn over her.
¹¹ You will nurse at her
comforting breasts.
And you will be satisfied.

You will drink until you are
full.
And you will delight in her
rich and plentiful supply."

12 The LORD continues,

"I will cause peace to flow
over her like a river.
I will make the wealth of
nations sweep over her
like a flooding stream.
You will nurse and be carried
in her arms.
You will play on her lap.
13 As a mother comforts her
child,
I will comfort you.
You will find comfort in
Jerusalem."

14 When you see that happen,
your hearts will be filled
with joy.
Just as grass grows quickly,
you will succeed.
The LORD will show his
power to those who
serve him.
But he will pour out his
anger on his enemies.
15 The LORD will judge them
with fire.
His chariots are coming
like a windstorm.
He will pour out his burning
anger on his enemies.
It will blaze out like flames
of fire.
16 The LORD will judge with fire
and with his sword.
He will judge all people.
He will put many people to
death.

17 "Some people set themselves
apart and make themselves

pure. They do it so they can
go into the gardens to worship
other gods. They follow what the
worship leader tells them to do.
They are among those who eat
the meat of pigs and rats. They
also eat other 'unclean' things.
Those people and the one they
follow will come to a horrible
end," announces the LORD.

18 "They have planned to do
many evil things. And they have
carried out their plans. So I will
come and gather the people of
every nation and language. They
will see my glory when I act.

19 "I will give them a sign. I
will send to the nations some
of those who are left alive. I will
send some of them to the people of Tarshish, Libya and Lydia,
who are famous for using bows.
I will send others to Tubal and
Greece. And I will send still others to islands far away. The people who live there have not heard
about my fame. They have not
seen my glory. But when I act,
those I send will tell the nations
about my glory. 20 And they will
bring back all the people of Israel
from all those nations. They will
bring them to my holy mountain
in Jerusalem. My people will ride
on horses, mules and camels.
They will come in chariots and
wagons," says the LORD. "Those
messengers will bring my people
as an offering to me. They will
bring them to my temple, just as
the Israelites bring their grain offerings in bowls that are 'clean.'
21 And I will choose some of them
to be priests and Levites," says
the LORD.

²² "I will make new heavens and a new earth. And they will last forever," announces the LORD. "In the same way, your name and your children after you will last forever. ²³ Everyone will come and bow down to me. They will do it at every New Moon feast and on every Sabbath day," says the LORD. ²⁴ "When they go out of Jerusalem, they will see the dead bodies of those who refused to obey me. The worms that eat their bodies will not die. The fire that burns them will not be put out. It will make everyone sick just to look at them."

Jeremiah

Introduction:

Jeremiah was a man who spoke for God. He lived in Judah. Jeremiah told the people not to sin. He told them to love God instead. His words made people angry. They wanted to kill Jeremiah. But Jeremiah did not stop speaking God's words to the people.

Jeremiah told the people what God was going to do. He told the people they would have war because they did not stop sinning. He also told the people God would forgive their sin and take care of them after the war.

Outline of contents:

1 These are the words Jeremiah received from the LORD. Jeremiah was the son of Hilkiah. Jeremiah was one of the priests at Anathoth. That's a town in the territory of Benjamin. ²A message from the LORD came to Jeremiah. It came in the 13th year that Josiah was king over Judah. Josiah was the son of Amon. ³After Josiah, his son Jehoiakim was king over Judah. The LORD's message also came to Jeremiah during the whole time Jehoiakim ruled. The LORD continued to speak to Jeremiah while Zedekiah was king over Judah. He did this until the fifth month of the 11th year of Zedekiah's rule. That's when the people of Jerusalem were forced to leave their country. Zedekiah was the son of Josiah. Here is what Jeremiah said.

The LORD Appoints Jeremiah to Speak for Him

⁴A message from the LORD came to me. The LORD said,

⁵"Before I formed you in your
    mother's body I chose
    you.
Before you were born I set
    you apart to serve me.
I appointed you to be a
    prophet to the nations."

⁶"You are my LORD and King," I said. "I don't know how to speak. I'm too young."

⁷ But the LORD said to me, "Do not say, 'I'm too young.' You must go to everyone I send you to. You must say everything I command you to say. ⁸ Do not be afraid of the people I send you to. I am with you. I will save you," announces the LORD.

⁹ Then the LORD reached out his hand. He touched my mouth and spoke to me. He said, "I have put my words in your mouth. ¹⁰ Today I am appointing you to speak to nations and kingdoms. I give you authority to pull them up by the roots and tear them down. I give you authority to destroy them and crush them. I give you authority to build them up and plant them."

¹¹ A message from the LORD came to me. The LORD asked me, "What do you see, Jeremiah?"

"The branch of an almond tree," I replied.

¹² The LORD said to me, "You have seen correctly. I am watching to see that my word comes true."

¹³ Another message from the LORD came to me. The LORD asked me, "What do you see?"

"A pot that has boiling water in it," I answered. "It's leaning toward us from the north."

¹⁴ The LORD said to me, "Something very bad will be poured out on everyone who lives in this land. It will come from the north. ¹⁵ I am about to send for all the armies in the northern kingdoms," announces the LORD.

"Their kings will come to Jerusalem.

They will set up their
thrones at the very gates
of the city.
They will attack all the walls
that surround the city.
They will go to war against
all the towns of Judah.
¹⁶ I will judge my people.
They have done many evil
things.
They have deserted me.
They have burned incense to
other gods.
They have worshiped the
gods
their own hands have made.

¹⁷ "So get ready! Stand up! Tell them everything I command you to. Do not let them terrify you. If you do, I will terrify you in front of them. ¹⁸ Today I have made you like a city that has a high wall around it. I have made you like an iron pillar and a bronze wall. Now you can stand up against the whole land. You can stand against the kings and officials of Judah. You can stand against its priests and its people. ¹⁹ They will fight against you. But they will not win the battle over you. I am with you. I will save you," announces the LORD.

Israel Deserts the LORD

2 A message from the LORD came to me. The LORD said, ² "Go. Announce my message to the people in Jerusalem. I want everyone to hear it. Tell them,

"Here is what the LORD says.

" 'I remember how faithful
you were to me when
you were young.

You loved me as if you were
my bride.
You followed me through the
desert.
Nothing had been planted
there.
³Your people were holy to me.
They were the first share of
my harvest.
All those who destroyed
them were held guilty.
And trouble came to their
enemies,' "
announces the LORD.

⁴People of Jacob, hear the
LORD's message.
Listen, all you tribes of
Israel.

⁵The LORD says,

"What did your people of
long ago find wrong with
me?
Why did they wander so far
away from me?
They worshiped worthless
statues of gods.
Then they themselves
became worthless.
⁶They did not ask, 'Where is
the LORD?
He brought us up out of
Egypt.
He led us through a dry and
empty land.
He guided us through
deserts and deep
valleys.
It was a land of total darkness
where there wasn't any
rain.
No one lived or traveled
there.'
⁷But I brought you into a land
that has rich soil.

I gave you its fruit and its
finest food.
In spite of that, you made my
land impure.
You turned it into
something I hate.
⁸The priests did not ask,
'Where is the LORD?'
Those who taught my law did
not know me.
The leaders refused to
obey me.
The prophets prophesied in
the name of Baal.
They worshiped worthless
statues of gods.

⁹"So I am bringing charges
against you again,"
announces the LORD.
"And I will bring charges
against your children's
children.
¹⁰Go over to the coasts of
Cyprus and look.
Send people to the land of
Kedar and have them
look closely.
See if there has ever been
anything like this.
¹¹Has a nation ever changed its
gods?
Actually, they are not even
gods at all.
But my people have traded
away their glorious
God.
They have traded me for
worthless statues of
gods.
¹²Sky above, be shocked over
this.
Tremble with horror,"
announces the LORD.
¹³"My people have sinned
twice.

They have deserted me,
  even though I am the
  spring of water that gives
  life.
And they have dug their own
  wells.
  But those wells are broken.
  They can't hold any water.
¹⁴ Are you people of Israel
  servants?
  You were not born as
  slaves, were you?
  Then why have you been
  carried off like stolen
  goods?
¹⁵ Lions have roared.
  They have growled at you.
They have destroyed your
  land.
  Your towns are burned and
  deserted.
¹⁶ The men of Memphis and
  Tahpanhes
  have cracked your skulls.
¹⁷ Haven't you brought this on
  yourselves?
  I am the Lord your God,
  but you deserted me.
  You left me even while I
  was leading you.
¹⁸ Why do you go to Egypt
  to drink water from the
  Nile River?
Why do you go to Assyria
  to drink from the
  Euphrates River?
¹⁹ You will be punished
  because you have
  sinned.
  You will be corrected for
  turning away from me.
I am the Lord your God.
  If you desert me, bad
  things will happen to
  you.

If you do not respect me, you
  will suffer bitterly.
I want you to understand
  that,"
    announces the Lord
    who rules over all.
²⁰ "Long ago you broke off the
  yoke I put on you.
  You tore off the ropes I tied
  you up with.
  You said, 'I won't serve you!'
In fact, on every high hill
  you lay down like a
  prostitute.
  You worshiped other gods
  under every green tree.
²¹ You were like a good vine
  when I planted you.
  You were a healthy plant.
Then how did you turn
  against me?
  How did you become a
  bad, wild vine?
²² You might wash yourself with
  soap.
  You might use plenty of
  strong soap.
  But I can still see the stains
  your guilt covers you
  with,"
    announces the Lord
    and King.
²³ "You say, 'I am "clean."
  I haven't followed the gods
  that are named Baal.'
How can you say that?
  Remember how you acted
  in the valley.
Consider what you have
  done.
  You are like a female camel
  running quickly here
  and there.
²⁴ You are like a wild donkey
  that lives in the desert.

She smells the wind when
    she longs for a mate.
Who can hold her back?
The males that run after
    her do not need to wear
    themselves out.
    At mating time they will
    easily find her.
25 Do not run after other gods
    until your sandals are
    worn out and your throat
    is dry.
But you said, 'It's no use!
    I love those gods.
    I must go after them.'

26 "A thief is dishonored when
    he is caught.
    And you people of Israel
    are filled with shame.
Your kings and officials are
    dishonored.
    So are your priests and
    your prophets.
27 You say to a piece of wood,
    'You are my father.'
You say to a stone, 'You are
    my mother.'
You have turned your backs
    to me.
    You refuse to look at me.
But when you are in trouble,
    you say,
    'Come and save us!'
28 Then where are the gods you
    made for yourselves?
Let them come when you
    are in trouble!
Let them save you if they
    can!
Judah, you have as many
    gods
    as you have towns.

29 "Why do you bring charges
    against me?

All of you have refused to
    obey me,"
    announces the LORD.
30 "I punished your people. But
    it did not do them any
    good.
They did not pay attention
    when they were
    corrected.
You have killed your prophets
    by swords.
You have swallowed them
    up like a hungry lion.

31 "You who are now living,
consider my message. I am saying,

    "Have I been like a desert to
    Israel?
    Have I been like a land of
    deep darkness?
Why do my people say, 'We
    are free to wander.
    We won't come to you
    anymore'?
32 Does a young woman forget
    all about her jewelry?
Does a bride forget her
    wedding jewels?
But my people have forgotten
    me
    more days than anyone
    can count.
33 You are very skilled at
    chasing after love!
Even the worst of women
    can learn from how you
    act.
34 The blood of those you have
    killed is on your clothes.
You have destroyed poor
    people who were not
    guilty.
You did not catch them in
    the act of breaking in.

In spite of all this,
35   you say, 'I'm not guilty of
         doing anything wrong.
      The LORD isn't angry with
         me.'
   But I will judge you.
      That's because you say, 'I
         haven't sinned.'
36 Why do you keep on
         changing your ways so
         much?
   Assyria did not help you.
      And Egypt will not help
         you either.
37 So you will also leave Egypt
         with your hands tied
         together above your
         heads.
   I have turned my back on
         those you trust.
      They will not help you.

3   "Suppose a man divorces
         his wife.
   What if she then marries
         another man?
      Should her first husband
         return to her again?
   If he does, won't the land
         become completely
         'unclean'?
   People of Israel, you have
         lived like a prostitute.
      You have loved many other
         gods.
   So do you think you can
         return to me now?"
               announces the LORD.
2 "Look up at the bare hilltops.
      Is there any place where
         you have not worshiped
         other gods?
   You have been unfaithful
         to me like a wife
         committing adultery.

By the side of the road you sat
         waiting for lovers.
   You sat there like someone
         who wanders in the
         desert.
   You have made the land
         impure.
      You are like a sinful
         prostitute.
3 So I have held back the
         showers.
      I have kept the spring rains
         from falling.
   But you still have the bold
         face of a prostitute.
      You refuse to blush with
         shame.
4 You have just now called out
         to me.
      You said,
   'My Father, you have been my
         friend
      ever since I was young.
5 Will you always be angry
         with me?
      Will your anger continue
         forever?'
   This is how you talk.
      But you do all the evil
         things you can."

Israel Is Not Faithful to the LORD

6 During the time Josiah was
king, the LORD spoke to me.
He said, "Have you seen what
the people of Israel have done?
They have not been faithful to
me. They have committed adultery with other gods. They worshiped them on every high hill
and under every green tree.
7 I thought that after they had
done all this, they would return
to me. But they did not. Their
sister nation Judah saw them

doing this. And they were not faithful to me either. [8] I gave Israel their letter of divorce. I sent them away because they were unfaithful to me so many times. But I saw that their sister nation Judah did not have any respect for me. They were not faithful to me either. They also went out and committed adultery with other gods. [9] Israel was not faithful to me, but that did not bother them at all. They made the land 'unclean.' They worshiped gods that were made out of stone and wood. [10] In spite of all this, their sister nation Judah did not come back to me. They were not faithful to me either. They did not return with all their heart. They only pretended to," announces the LORD.

[11] The LORD said to me, "Israel and Judah have not been faithful to me. But Israel was not as bad as Judah was. [12] Go. Announce this message to the people in the north. Tell them,

" 'Israel, you have not been
    faithful,' announces the
    LORD.
  'Return to me. Then I will
    do good things for you
    again.
That's because I am faithful,'
    announces the LORD.
  'I will not be angry with
    you forever.
[13] Admit that you are guilty of
    doing what is wrong.
  You have refused to obey
    me. I am the LORD your
    God.
  You have committed adultery
    with other gods.
  You worshiped them under
    every green tree.
  And you have not obeyed
    me,' "
        announces the LORD.

[14] "You people have not been faithful," announces the LORD. "Return to me. I am your husband. I will choose one of you from each town. I will choose two from each territory. And I will bring you to the city of Zion. [15] Then I will give you shepherds who are dear to my heart. Their knowledge and understanding will help them lead you. [16] In those days there will be many more of you in the land," announces the LORD. "Then people will not talk about the ark of the covenant of the LORD anymore. It will never enter their minds. They will not remember it. The ark will not be missed. And another one will not be made. [17] At that time they will call Jerusalem The Throne of the LORD. All the nations will gather together there. They will go there to honor me. They will no longer do what their stubborn and evil hearts want them to do. [18] In those days the people of Judah will join the people of Israel. Together they will come from a land in the north. They will come to the land I gave to your people of long ago. I wanted them to have it as their very own.

[19] "I myself said,

" 'I would gladly treat you like
    my children.
  I would give you a pleasant
    land.

It is the most beautiful land
    any nation could have.'
I thought you would call me
    'Father.'
I hoped you would always
    obey me.
20 But you people are like
    a woman who is not
    faithful to her husband.
Israel, you have not been
    faithful to me,"
        announces the LORD.
21 A cry is heard on the bare
    hilltops.
The people of Israel are
    weeping and begging for
    help.
That's because their lives are
    so twisted.
They've forgotten the LORD
    their God.
22 "You have not been faithful,"
    says the LORD.
"Return to me. I will heal
    you.
Then you will not turn
    away from me anymore."

"Yes," the people say. "We
    will come to you.
You are the LORD our God.
23 The gods we worship on the
    hills
    and mountains are useless.
You are the LORD our God.
    You are the only one who
    can save us.
24 From our earliest years
    shameful gods have
    harmed us.
They have eaten up
    everything our people of
    long ago worked for.
They have eaten up our
    flocks and herds.

They've destroyed our sons
    and daughters.
25 Let us lie down in our shame.
Let our dishonor cover us.
You are the LORD our God.
    But we have sinned
    against you.
We and our people of long
    ago have sinned.
We haven't obeyed you
    from our earliest years
    until now."

4 "If you, Israel, will return,
    then return to me,"
        announces the LORD.
"Put the statues of your gods
    out of my sight.
I hate them.
Stop going astray.
2 Make all your promises in my
    name.
When you promise say,
    'You can be sure that the
    LORD is alive.'
Be truthful, fair and honest
    when you make these
    promises.
Then the nations will ask for
    blessings from me.
And they will boast about
    me."

3 Here is what the LORD is telling the people of Judah and Jerusalem. He says,

"Your hearts are as hard as a
    field
    that has not been plowed.
So change your ways and
    produce good crops.
Do not plant seeds among
    thorns.
4 People of Judah and you who
    live in Jerusalem, obey
    me.

Do not let your hearts be
stubborn.
If you do, my anger will blaze
out against you.
It will burn like fire
because of the evil
things you have done.
No one will be able to put it
out.

Trouble Will Come From the North

⁵ "Announce my message in
Judah.
Tell it in Jerusalem.
Say, 'Blow trumpets all
through the land!'
Give a loud shout and say,
'Gather together!
Let's run to cities that have
high walls around them!'
⁶ Warn everyone to go to Zion!
Run for safety! Do not wait!
I am bringing trouble from
the north.
Everything will be totally
destroyed."

⁷ Lions have come out of their
dens.
Those who destroy nations
have begun to march
out.
They have left their place
to destroy your land
completely.
Your towns will be broken to
pieces.
No one will live in them.
⁸ So put on the clothes of
sadness.
Mourn and weep over what
has happened.
The LORD hasn't turned
his great anger away from
us.

⁹ "A dark day is coming,"
announces the LORD.
"The king and his officials
will lose hope.
The priests will be shocked.
And the prophets will be
terrified."

¹⁰ Then I said, "You are my
LORD and King. You have completely tricked the people of Judah and Jerusalem! You have
told them, 'You will have peace
and rest.' But swords are pointed
at our throats!"

¹¹ At that time the people of
Judah and Jerusalem will be
warned. They will be told, "A
hot and dry wind is coming,
my people. It is blowing toward
you from the bare hilltops in the
desert. But it does not separate
straw from grain. ¹² It is much
too strong for that. The wind is
coming from me. I am making
my decision against you."

¹³ Look! Our enemies are
approaching like the
clouds.
Their chariots are coming
like a strong wind.
Their horses are faster than
eagles.
How terrible it will be for us!
We'll be destroyed!
¹⁴ People of Jerusalem, wash
your sins from your
hearts and be saved.
How long will you hold on
to your evil thoughts?
¹⁵ A voice is speaking all the
way from the city of Dan.
From the hills of Ephraim
it announces
that trouble is coming.

16 "Tell the nations.
    Make an announcement
        concerning Jerusalem.
    Say, 'An army will attack Judah.
        It is coming from a land far
            away.
    It will shout a war cry
        against the cities of Judah.
17 It will surround them like
        people who guard a field.
    Judah has refused to obey
        me,' "
            announces the LORD.
18 "The army will attack you
        because of your conduct
        and actions.
    This is how you will be
        punished.
    It will be so bitter!
    It will cut deep down into
        your hearts!"

19 I'm suffering! I'm really
        suffering!
    I'm hurting badly.
    My heart is suffering so
        much!
    It's pounding inside me.
    I can't keep silent.
    I've heard the sound of
        trumpets.
    I've heard the battle cry.
20 One trouble follows another.
    The whole land is destroyed.
    In an instant my tents are
        gone.
    My home disappears in a
        moment.
21 How long must I look at our
        enemy's battle flag?
    How long must I hear the
        sound of the trumpets?

22 The LORD says, "My people
        are foolish.
    They do not know me.

They are children who do not
    have any sense.
They have no
    understanding at all.
They are skilled in doing
    what is evil.
They do not know how to
    do what is good."

23 I looked at the earth.
    It didn't have any shape.
    And it was empty.
    I looked at the sky.
    Its light was gone.
24 I looked at the mountains.
    They were shaking.
    All the hills were swaying.
25 I looked. And there weren't
        any people.
    Every bird in the sky had
        flown away.
26 I looked. And the fruitful land
        had become a desert.
    All its towns were
        destroyed.
    The LORD had done all
        this because of his great
        anger.

27 The LORD says,

"The whole land will be
    destroyed.
    But I will not destroy it
        completely.
28 So the earth will be filled
        with sadness.
    The sky above will grow
        dark.
    I have spoken, and I will not
        take pity on them.
    I have made my decision,
        and I will not change my
        mind."

29 People can hear the sound of
        horsemen.

Men armed with bows are
   coming.
The people in every town
   run away.
Some of them go into the
   bushes.
Others climb up among
   the rocks.
All the towns are deserted.
   No one is living in them.

30 What are you doing, you who
   are destroyed?
Why do you dress yourself
   in bright red clothes?
Why do you put on jewels
   of gold?
Why do you put makeup on
   your eyes?
You make yourself
   beautiful for no reason at
   all.
Your lovers hate you.
   They want to kill you.

31 I hear a cry like the cry of a
   woman having a baby.
I hear a groan like
   someone having her first
   child.
It's the cry of the people
   of Zion struggling to
   breathe.
They reach out their hands
   and say,
"Help us! We're fainting!
   Murderers are about to kill
   us!"

No One Is Honest

5 The Lord says, "Go up
   and down the streets of
   Jerusalem.
Look around.
   Think about what you see.
Search through the market.

See if you can find one
   honest person who tries
   to be truthful.
If you can, I will forgive
   this city.
2 They make their promises in
   my name.
They say, 'You can be sure
   that the Lord is alive.'
But their promises can't be
   trusted."

3 Lord, don't your eyes look for
   truth?
You struck down your
   people.
But they didn't feel any
   pain.
You crushed them.
   But they refused to be
   corrected.
They made their faces harder
   than stone.
They refused to turn away
   from their sins.
4 I thought, "The people of
   Jerusalem are foolish.
They don't know how the
   Lord wants them to live.
They don't know what their
   God requires of them.
5 So I will go to the leaders.
   I'll speak to them.
They should know how the
   Lord wants them to live.
They must know what their
   God requires of them."
But all of them had broken off
   the yoke the Lord had
   put on them.
They had torn off the ropes
   he had tied them up
   with.
6 So a lion from the forest will
   attack them.

A wolf from the desert will
   destroy them.
A leopard will hide and wait
   near their towns.
   It will tear to pieces anyone
   who dares to go out.
Again and again they have
   refused to obey the
   LORD.
   They have turned away
   from him many times.

7 The LORD says, "Jerusalem,
   why should I forgive
   you?
   Your people have deserted
   me.
They have made their
   promises in the names of
   gods
   that are not really gods at
   all.
I supplied everything they
   needed.
   But they committed
   adultery.
   Large crowds went to the
   houses of prostitutes.
8 Your people are like stallions
   that have plenty to eat.
   Their sinful desires are out
   of control.
   Each of them goes after
   another man's wife.
9 Shouldn't I punish them for
   this?"
   announces the LORD.
   "Shouldn't I pay back the
   nation
   that does these things?

10 "Armies of Babylon, go
   through their vineyards
   and destroy them.
   But do not destroy them
   completely.

Strip off their branches.
   These people do not belong
   to me.
11 The people of Israel and the
   people of Judah
   have not been faithful to
   me at all,"
      announces the LORD.
12 They have told lies about the
   LORD.
   They said, "He won't do
   anything!
No harm will come to us.
   We will never see war or be
   hungry.
13 The prophets are nothing but
   wind.
   Their message doesn't
   come from the LORD.
   So let what they say will
   happen be done to
   them."

14 The LORD God rules over
all. He says to me,

"The people have spoken
   these words.
So my words will be like
   fire in your mouth.
I will make the people like
   wood.
   And the fire will burn them
   up."

15 "People of Israel, listen to
   me,"
   announces the LORD.
"I am bringing against you
   a nation from far away.
It is an old nation. And it will
   last for a long time.
   Its people speak a language
   you do not know.
   You can't understand what
   they are saying.

¹⁶ The bags they carry their
arrows in are like an
open grave.
All their soldiers are
mighty.
¹⁷ They will eat up your crops
and your food.
They will strike down your
sons and daughters.
They will kill your sheep and
cattle.
They will destroy your
vines and fig trees.
You trust in your cities that
have high walls around
them.
But the people in them will
be killed by swords.

¹⁸ "In spite of that, even in those
days I will not destroy you completely," announces the LORD.
¹⁹ 'Jeremiah,' the people will ask,
'Why has the LORD our God done
all this to us?' Then you will tell
them, 'You have deserted the
LORD. You have served other
gods in your own land. So now
you will serve another nation in
a land that is not your own.'

²⁰ "Here is what I want you to
announce
to the people of Jacob.
Tell it in Judah.
Tell them I say,
²¹ 'Listen to this, you foolish
people,
who do not have any sense.
You have eyes, but you do not
see.
You have ears, but you do
not hear.
²² Shouldn't you have respect
for me?' announces the
LORD.

'Shouldn't you tremble
with fear in front of me?
I made the sand to hold the
ocean back.
It will do that forever.
The ocean can't go past it.
The waves might roll, but
they can't sweep over it.
They might roar, but they
can't go across it.
²³ But you people have
stubborn hearts.
You refuse to obey me.
You have turned away from
me.
You have gone astray.
²⁴ You do not say to yourselves,
"Let us have respect for the
LORD our God.
He sends rain in the fall and
the spring.
He promises us that the
harvest will come
at the same time each
year."
²⁵ But the things you have done
wrong
have robbed you of these
gifts.
Your sins have kept these
good things
far away from you.'

²⁶ "Jeremiah, some of my
people are evil.
They hide and wait just
as people hide to catch
birds.
They set traps for people.
²⁷ A hunter uses tricks to fill his
cage with birds.
And my people have filled
their houses with a lot of
goods.
They have become rich and
powerful.

28 They have grown fat and
    heavy.
  There is no limit to the evil
    things they do.
  In court they do not seek
    justice.
  They don't protect the
    rights of children whose
    fathers have died.
  They do not stand up for
    poor people.
29 Shouldn't I punish them for
    this?"
  announces the LORD.
  "Shouldn't I pay back the
    nation that does these
    things?

30 "Something horrible and
    shocking
  has happened in the land.
31 The prophets prophesy lies.
  The priests rule by their
    own authority.
  And my people love it this
    way.
  But what will you do in the
    end?"

The Babylonians Will Attack Jerusalem

6 The LORD says, "People of
    Benjamin, run for safety!
  Run away from Jerusalem!
  Blow trumpets in the city of
    Tekoa!
  Warn everyone in Beth
    Hakkerem!
  Horrible trouble is coming
    from the north.
  The Babylonians will
    destroy everything with
    awful power.
2 I will destroy the city of Zion,
    even though it is very
    beautiful.

3 Shepherds will come against
    it with their flocks.
  They will set up their tents
    around it.
  All of them will take care of
    their own sheep."

4 The Babylonians say,
  "Prepare for battle
    against Judah!
  Get up! Let's attack them at
    noon!
  But the daylight is fading.
  The shadows of evening
    are getting longer.
5 So get up! Let's attack them at
    night!
  Let's destroy their
    strongest forts!"

6 The LORD who rules over all
speaks to the Babylonians. He
says,

  "Cut down some trees.
  Use the wood to build
    ramps against
    Jerusalem's walls.
  I must punish that city.
  It is filled with people who
    treat others badly.
7 Wells keep giving fresh water.
  And Jerusalem keeps on
    sinning.
  Its people are always fighting
    and causing trouble.
  When I look at them,
  I see nothing but sickness
    and wounds.
8 Jerusalem, listen to my
    warning.
  If you do not, I will turn
    away from you.
  Your land will become a
    desert.
  No one will be able to live
    there."

⁹ The LORD rules over all. He says to me,

> "People gather the few grapes
>   left on a vine.
> So let Israel's enemies
>   gather the few people left
>   alive in the land
> Look carefully at the
>   branches again.
> Do this like someone who
>   gathers the last few
>   grapes."

¹⁰ Who can I speak to? Who can I warn?

> Who will even listen to me?
> Their ears are closed
>   so they can't hear.
> The LORD's message
>   displeases them.
> They don't take any delight
>   in it.

¹¹ But the LORD's anger burns inside me.

> I can no longer hold it in.

The LORD says to me, "Pour
>   out my anger on the
>   children in the street.
> Pour it out on the young
>   men who are gathered
>   together.
> Husband and wife alike will
>   be caught in it.
> So will those who are very
>   old.

¹² I will reach out my hand
>   against those who live in
>   the land,"
>   announces the LORD.

> "Then their houses will be
>   turned over to others.
> So will their fields and
>   their wives.

¹³ Everyone wants to get richer
>   and richer,

> from the least important
>   of them to the most
>   important.
> Prophets and priests alike
>   try to fool everyone they
>   can.

¹⁴ They bandage the wounds of
>   my people
> as if they were not very
>   deep.

> 'Peace, peace,' they say.
> But there isn't any peace.

¹⁵ Are they ashamed of their
>   hateful actions?
> No. They do not feel any
>   shame at all.
> They do not even know
>   how to blush.
> So they will fall like others
>   who have already fallen.
> They will be brought down
>   when I punish them,"
>   says the LORD.

¹⁶ The LORD tells the people of Judah,

> "Stand where the roads cross,
>   and look around.
> Ask where the old paths are.
> Ask for the good path, and
>   walk on it.
> Then your hearts will find
>   rest in me.
> But you said, 'We won't
>   walk on it.'

¹⁷ I appointed prophets to warn
>   you. I said,
> 'Listen to the sound of the
>   trumpets!'
> But you said, 'We won't
>   listen.'

¹⁸ So pay attention, you nations.
> You are witnesses for me.
> Watch what will happen to
>   my people.

¹⁹ Earth, pay attention.
I am going to bring trouble
on them.
I will punish them because
of the evil things they
have done.
They have not listened to my
words.
They have said no to my
law.
²⁰ What do I care about incense
from the land of Sheba?
Why should I bother with
sweet-smelling cane
from a land far away?
I do not accept your burnt
offerings.
Your sacrifices do not
please me."

²¹ So the LORD says,

"I will bring an army against
the people of Judah.
Parents and children alike
will trip and fall.
Neighbors and friends will
die."

²² The LORD says to Jerusalem,

"Look! An army is coming
from the land of the north.
I am stirring up a great
nation.
Its army is coming from
a land that is very far
away.
²³ Its soldiers are armed with
bows and spears.
They are mean. They do
not show any mercy at
all.
They come riding in on their
horses.
They sound like the
roaring ocean.
They are lined up for battle.
They are marching out
to attack you, city of Zion."

²⁴ We have heard reports about
them.
And our hands can't help
us.
We are suffering greatly.
It's like the pain of a
woman having a baby.
²⁵ Don't go out to the fields.
Don't walk on the roads.
Our enemies have swords.
And there is terror on every
side.
²⁶ My people, put on the clothes
of sadness.
Roll among the ashes.
Mourn with bitter weeping
just as you would mourn
for an only son.
The one who is going to
destroy us
will come suddenly.

²⁷ The LORD says to me, "I have
made you like one who
tests metals.
My people are the ore.
I want you to watch them
and test the way they live.
²⁸ All of them are used to
disobeying me.
They go around telling lies
about others.
They are like bronze mixed
with iron.
All of them do very sinful
things.
²⁹ The fire is made very hot
so the lead will burn away.
But it is impossible to make
these people pure.
Those who are evil are not
removed.

³⁰ They are like silver that is
    thrown away.
    That is because I have not
    accepted them."

Worshiping Other Gods Is Worthless

7 A message from the LORD came to Jeremiah. The LORD said, ² "Stand at the gate of my house. Announce my message to the people there. Say,

" 'Listen to the LORD's message, all you people of Judah. You always come through these gates to worship the LORD. ³ The God of Israel is speaking to you. He is the LORD who rules over all. He says, "Change the way you live and act. Then I will let you live in this place. ⁴ Do not trust in lies. Do not say, 'This is the temple of the LORD! This is the temple of the LORD! This is the temple of the LORD!' ⁵ You must really change the way you live and act. Treat one another fairly. ⁶ Do not treat outsiders or widows badly in this place. Do not take advantage of children whose fathers have died. Do not kill those who are not guilty of doing anything wrong. Do not worship other gods. That will only bring harm to you. ⁷ If you obey me, I will let you live in this place. It is the land I gave your people of long ago. It was promised to them for ever and ever. ⁸ But look! You are trusting in worthless lies.

⁹ " ' "You continue to steal and commit murder. You commit adultery. You tell lies in court. You burn incense to Baal. You worship other gods you didn't know before. ¹⁰ Then you come and stand in front of me. You keep coming to this house where I have put my Name. You say, 'We are safe.' You think you are safe when you do so many things I hate. ¹¹ My Name is in this house. But you have made it a den for robbers! I have been watching you!" announces the LORD.

¹² " ' "Go now to the town of Shiloh. Go to the place where I first made a home for my Name. See what I did to it because of the evil things my people Israel were doing. ¹³ I spoke to you again and again," announces the LORD. "I warned you while you were doing all these things. But you did not listen. I called out to you. But you did not answer. ¹⁴ So what I did to Shiloh I will now do to the house where my Name is. It is the temple you trust in. It is the place I gave to you and your people of long ago. ¹⁵ But I will throw you out of my land. That is exactly what I did to the people of Ephraim. And they are your relatives." '

¹⁶ "Jeremiah, do not pray for these people. Do not make any appeal or request for them. Do not beg me. I will not listen to you. ¹⁷ Don't you see what they are doing? They are worshiping other gods in the towns of Judah. They are offering sacrifices to them in the streets of Jerusalem. ¹⁸ The children go out and gather wood. The fathers light the fire. The women mix the dough. They make flat cakes of

bread to offer to the female god called the Queen of Heaven. They pour out drink offerings to other gods. That makes me very angry. ¹⁹ But am I the one they are hurting?" announces the LORD. "Aren't they only harming themselves? They should be ashamed of it."

²⁰ So the LORD and King says, "I will pour out my burning anger on this place. It will strike people and animals alike. It will destroy the trees in the fields and the crops in your land. It will burn, and no one will be able to put it out."

²¹ The LORD who rules over all is the God of Israel. He says, "Go ahead! Add your burnt offerings to your other sacrifices. Eat the meat yourselves! ²² When I brought your people out of Egypt, I spoke to them. But I did not just give them commands about burnt offerings and sacrifices. ²³ I also gave them another command. I said, 'Obey me. Then I will be your God. And you will be my people. Live the way I command you to live. Then things will go well with you.' ²⁴ But they did not listen. They refused to pay any attention to me. Instead, they did what their stubborn and evil hearts wanted them to do. They went backward and not forward. ²⁵ Again and again I sent my servants the prophets to you. They came to you day after day. They prophesied from the time your people left Egypt until now. ²⁶ But your people of long ago did not listen. They refused to pay any attention to me. They were stubborn. They did more evil things than their people who lived before them.

²⁷ "Jeremiah, when you tell them all this, they will not listen to you. When you call out to them, they will not answer. ²⁸ So say to them, 'You are a nation that has not obeyed the LORD your God. You did not pay attention when you were corrected. Truth has died out. You do not tell the truth anymore.' "

²⁹ The LORD says to the people of Jerusalem, "Cut off your hair. Throw it away. Sing a song of sadness on the bare hilltops. I am very angry with you. I have turned my back on you. I have deserted you.

The Valley of Death

³⁰ "The people of Judah have done what is evil in my eyes," announces the LORD. "They have set up statues of their gods. They have worshiped them in the house where my Name is. They have made my house 'unclean.' I hate those statues. ³¹ The people have built the high places of Topheth in the Valley of Ben Hinnom. There they worship other gods. And there they sacrifice their children in the fire. That is something I did not command. It did not even enter my mind. ³² So watch out!" announces the LORD. "The days are coming when people will not call it Topheth anymore. And they will not call it the Valley of Ben Hinnom either. Instead, they will call it the Valley of Death.

They will bury the dead bodies of some people in Topheth. But they will run out of room. ³³ Then they will not be able to bury the bodies of other people there. So the bodies will become food for birds and wild animals. And no one will scare them away. ³⁴ I will put an end to the sounds of joy and gladness. The voices of brides and grooms will not be heard anymore. There will be no sounds of joy in the towns of Judah. And there will be no joy in the streets of Jerusalem. The land will become a desert.

8 "At that time the tombs will be opened," announces the LORD. "The bones of the kings and officials of Judah will be brought out. The bones of the priests and prophets will be removed. So will the bones of the people of Jerusalem. ² They will lie outside under the sun, moon and all the stars. All these people had loved and served these things. They had followed them and worshiped them. They had asked them for advice. So the bones of these people will not be gathered up or buried again. Instead, they will be like human waste lying there on the ground. ³ Everyone left alive in this evil nation will want to die rather than live. That is what they will long for in the lands where I force them to go." The LORD who rules over all announces this.

The LORD Punishes His Sinful People

⁴ "Jeremiah, tell them, 'The LORD says,

" ' "When people fall down, don't they get up again? When someone turns away, don't they come back? ⁵ Then why have the people of Jerusalem turned away from me? Why do they always turn away? They keep on telling lies. They refuse to come back to me. ⁶ I have listened carefully. But they do not say what is right. They refuse to turn away from their sins. None of them says, 'What have I done?' Each of them goes their own way. They are like horses charging into battle. ⁷ Storks know when to fly south. So do doves, swifts and thrushes. But my people do not know what I require them to do. ⁸ " ' "How can you people say, 'We are wise. We have the law of the LORD'? Actually, the teachers of the law have told lies about it. Their pens have not written what is true. ⁹ Those who think they are wise will be put to shame. They will become terrified. They will be trapped.

They have not accepted my
message.
So what kind of wisdom do
they have?
¹⁰ I will give their wives to other
men.
I will give their fields to
new owners.
Everyone wants to get richer
and richer.
Everyone is greedy, from
the least important to
the most important.
Prophets and priests alike
try to fool everyone they
can.
¹¹ They bandage the wounds of
my people
as if they were not very
deep.
'Peace, peace,' they say.
But there isn't any peace.
¹² Are they ashamed of their
hateful actions?
No. They do not feel any
shame at all.
They do not even know
how to blush.
So they will fall like others
who have already fallen.
They will be brought down
when I punish them,"
says the LORD.

¹³ " ' "I will take away their
harvest,"
announces the LORD.
"There will not be any
grapes on the vines.
The trees will not bear any
figs.
The leaves on the trees will
dry up.
What I have given my people
will be taken away from
them." ' "

¹⁴ Why are we sitting here?
Let's gather together!
Let's run to the cities that
have high walls around
them!
Let's die there!
The LORD our God has
sentenced us to death.
He has given us poisoned
water to drink.
That's because we've
sinned against him.
¹⁵ We hoped peace would come.
But nothing good has
happened to us.
We hoped we would finally
be healed.
But there is only terror.
¹⁶ When our enemy's horses
snort,
the noise is heard all the
way from the city of Dan.
When their stallions neigh,
the whole land trembles
with fear.
They have come to destroy
the land and everything
in it.
The city and everyone
who lives there will be
destroyed.

¹⁷ "People of Judah, I will send
poisonous snakes among
you.
No one will be able to
charm them.
And they will bite you,"
announces the LORD.

¹⁸ LORD, my heart is weak
inside me.
You comfort me when I'm
sad.
¹⁹ Listen to the cries of my people
from a land far away.

They cry out, "Isn't the LORD
in Zion?
Isn't its King there anymore?"

The LORD says, "Why have
they made me so angry
by worshiping their
wooden gods?
Why have they made me
angry
with their worthless
statues
of gods from other lands?"

20 The people say, "The harvest
is over.
The summer has ended.
And we still haven't been
saved."

21 My people are crushed, so I
am crushed.
I mourn, and I am filled
with horror.
22 Isn't there any healing lotion
in Gilead?
Isn't there a doctor there?
Then why doesn't someone
heal
the wounds of my people?

9 1 I wish my head were a
spring of water!
I wish my eyes were a
fountain of tears!
I would weep day and night
for my people who have
been killed.
2 I wish I had somewhere to go
in the desert
where a traveler could stay!
Then I could leave my
people.
I could get away from
them.
All of them commit adultery
by worshiping other
gods.

They aren't faithful to the
LORD.

3 "They get ready to use
their tongues like bows,"
announces the LORD.
"Their mouths shoot out lies
like arrows.
They tell lies to gain power
in the land.
They go from one sin to
another.
They do not pay any
attention to me.
4 Be on guard against your
friends.
Do not trust the members
of your own family.
Every one of them cheats.
Every friend tells lies.
5 One friend cheats another.
No one tells the truth.
They have taught their
tongues how to lie.
They wear themselves out
sinning.
6 Jeremiah, you live among
people who tell lies.
When they lie, they refuse to
pay any attention to me,"
announces the LORD.

7 So the LORD who rules over
all says,

"I will put them through the
fire to test them.
What else can I do?
My people are so sinful!
8 Their tongues are like deadly
arrows.
They tell lies.
With their mouths all of them
speak kindly to their
neighbors.
But in their hearts they set
traps for them.

⁹Shouldn't I punish them for
    this?"
announces the Lord.
"Shouldn't I pay back the
    nation
    that does these things?"

¹⁰I will cry and mourn over the
    mountains.
    I will sing a song of
      sadness about the desert
      grasslands.
They are dry and empty.
    No one travels through
      them.
The mooing of cattle isn't
    heard there.
The birds have flown away.
    All the animals are gone.

¹¹The Lord says, "I will knock
    down all of Jerusalem's
    buildings.
I will make it a home for
    wild dogs.
The towns of Judah will be
    completely destroyed.
    No one will be able to live
      in them."

¹²Who is wise enough to understand these things? Who has been taught by the Lord? Who can explain them? Why has the land been destroyed so completely? Why has it become like a desert that no one can go across? ¹³The Lord answered me, "Because my people have turned away from my law. I gave it to them. But they have not kept it. They have not obeyed me. ¹⁴Instead, they have done what their stubborn hearts wanted them to do. They have worshiped the gods that are named Baal. They have done what their people have taught them to do through the years." ¹⁵So now the Lord who rules over all speaks. He is the God of Israel. He says, "I will make these people eat bitter food. I will make them drink poisoned water. ¹⁶I will scatter them among the nations. They and their people before them didn't know about these nations. With swords I will chase these people. I will hunt them down until I have destroyed them."

¹⁷The Lord rules over all. He says,

"Here is something I want
    you to think about.
Send for the women who
    mourn for the dead.
Send for the most skilled
    among them."
¹⁸Let them come quickly
    and weep for us.
Let them cry until tears flow
    from our eyes.
Let them weep until water
    pours out of our eyes.
¹⁹People are heard weeping in
    Zion.
They are saying, "We are
    destroyed!
We are filled with shame!
We must leave our land.
Our houses have been torn
    down."
²⁰You women, hear the Lord's
    message.
Listen to what he's saying.
Teach your daughters how to
    mourn for the dead.
Teach one another a song
    of sadness.

21 Death has climbed in
     through our windows.
   It has entered our forts.
   Death has removed the
     children from the
     streets.
   It has taken the young men
     out of the market.

22 Say, "The LORD announces,

" 'Dead bodies will be like
     human waste
   lying in the open fields.
   They will lie there like grain
     that is cut down at harvest
     time.
   No one will gather them
     up.' "

23 The LORD says,

"Do not let wise people brag
     about how wise they are.
   Do not let strong people
     boast about how strong
     they are.
   Do not let rich people brag
     about how rich they are.
24 But here is what the one
     who brags should boast
     about.
   They should brag that they
     have the understanding
     to know me.
   I want them to know that I
     am the LORD.
   No matter what I do on
     earth, I am always kind,
     fair and right.
   And I take delight in this,"
          announces the LORD.

25 "The days are coming when
I will judge people," announces
the LORD. "I will punish all
those who are circumcised only
in their bodies. 26 That includes

the people of Egypt, Judah,
Edom, Ammon and Moab. It
also includes all those who live
in the desert in places far away.
None of the people in these nations is really circumcised. And
not even the people of Israel are
circumcised in their hearts."

The LORD Is the Only True God

10 People of Israel, listen to
     what the LORD is telling
you. 2 He says,

"Do not follow the practices
     of other nations.
   Do not be terrified by
     warnings in the sky.
   Do not be afraid, even
     though the nations are
     terrified by them.
3 The practices of these
     nations are worthless.
   People cut a tree out of the
     forest.
   A skilled worker shapes the
     wood with a sharp tool.
4 Others decorate it with silver
     and gold.
   They use a hammer to nail
     it to the floor.
   They want to keep it from
     falling down.
5 The statues of their gods can't
     speak.
   They are like scarecrows in
     a field of cucumbers.
   Their statues have to be
     carried around
   because they can't walk.
   So do not be afraid of their
     gods.
   They can't do you any
     harm.
   And they can't do you any
     good either."

⁶Lord, no one is like you.
　You are great.
　You are mighty and
　　powerful.
⁷King of the nations,
　everyone should have
　　respect for you.
　That's what people should
　　give you.
　Among all the wise leaders of
　　the nations
　there is no one like you.
　No one can compare
　　with you in all their
　　kingdoms.
⁸All of them are foolish. They
　　don't have any sense.
　They think they are taught
　　by worthless wooden
　　gods.
⁹Hammered silver is brought
　　from Tarshish.
　Gold is brought from
　　Uphaz.
　People skilled in working
　　with wood and gold
　　make a statue.
　Then they put blue and
　　purple clothes on it.
　The whole thing is made by
　　skilled workers.
¹⁰But you are the only true
　　God.
　You are the only living
　　God.
　You are the King who rules
　　forever.
　When you are angry, the
　　earth trembles with fear.
　The nations can't stand up
　　under your anger.

¹¹The Lord speaks to the
Jews living in Babylon. He says,
"Here is what you must tell the
people of the nations. Tell them,

'Your gods did not make the
heavens and the earth. In fact,
these gods will disappear from
the earth. They will vanish from
under the heavens.'"

¹²But God used his power to
　　make the earth.
　His wisdom set the world
　　in place.
　His understanding spread
　　out the heavens.
¹³When he thunders, the waters
　　in the heavens roar.
　He makes clouds rise from
　　one end of the earth to
　　the other.
　He sends lightning along
　　with the rain.
　He brings the wind out
　　from his storerooms.

¹⁴No one has any sense or
　　knows anything at all.
　Everyone who works with
　　gold is put to shame by
　　his gods.
　The metal gods he has made
　　are fakes.
　They can't even breathe.
¹⁵They are worthless things
　　that people make fun of.
　When the Lord judges
　　them, they will be
　　destroyed.
¹⁶The God of Jacob is not like
　　them.
　He gives his people
　　everything they need.
　He made everything that
　　exists.
　And that includes Israel.
　They are the people who
　　belong to him.
　His name is the Lord Who
　　Rules Over All.

The Land Will Be Destroyed

17 People of Jerusalem,
  your enemies have
  surrounded you.
  They are attacking you.
So gather up what belongs to
  you.
  Then leave the land.
18 The LORD says,
  "I am about to throw out of
  this land
  everyone who lives in it.
I will bring trouble on them.
They will be captured."

19 How terrible it will be for me!
  I've been wounded!
  And my wound can't be
  healed!
In spite of that, I said to
  myself,
  "I'm sick. But I'll have to
  put up with it."
20 Jerusalem is like a tent that
  has been destroyed.
  All its ropes have snapped.
My people have gone away
  from me.
  Now no one is left to set up
  my tent.
I have no one to set up my
  shelter.
21 The leaders of my people are
  like shepherds
  who don't have any sense.
  They don't ask the LORD for
  advice.
That's why they don't
  succeed.
  And that's why their whole
  flock
  is scattered like sheep.
22 Listen! A message is coming!
  I hear the sound of a great
  army

marching down from the
  north!
It will turn Judah's towns into
  a desert.
  They will become a home
  for wild dogs.

Jeremiah Prays to the LORD

23 LORD, I know that a person
  doesn't control their own
  life.
  They don't direct their own
  steps.
24 Correct me, LORD, but please
  be fair.
  Don't correct me when you
  are angry.
  If you do, nothing will be
  left of me.
25 Pour out your great anger on
  the nations.
  They don't pay any
  attention to you.
  They refuse to worship
  you.
They have destroyed the
  people of Jacob.
  They've wiped them out
  completely.
  They've also destroyed the
  land they lived in.

The LORD's People Have Broken His Covenant

11 A message from the LORD came to Jeremiah. The LORD said, 2 "Listen to the terms of the covenant I made with my people of long ago. Tell Judah the terms still apply to them. Tell those who live in Jerusalem that they must obey them too. 3 I am the LORD, the God of Israel. So let the people know what I want them to do. Here is what I

want you to tell them. 'May the person who does not obey the terms of the covenant be under my curse. ⁴I gave those terms to your people of long ago. That was when I brought them out of Egypt. I saved them out of that furnace that melts down iron and makes it pure.' I said, 'Obey me. Do everything I command you to do. Then you will be my people. And I will be your God. ⁵I raised my hand and made a promise to your people of long ago. I promised them I would give them a land that had plenty of milk and honey.' It is the land you own today. I kept my promise."

I replied, "Amen, Lord."

⁶The Lord said to me, "Here is what I want you to announce in the towns of Judah. Say it also in the streets of Jerusalem. Tell the people, 'Listen to the terms of my covenant. Obey them. ⁷Long ago I brought your people up from Egypt. From that time until today, I warned them again and again. I said, "Obey me." ⁸But they did not listen. They did not pay any attention to me. Instead, they did what their stubborn and evil hearts wanted them to do. So I brought down on them all the curses of the covenant. I commanded them to obey it. But they refused.' "

⁹The Lord continued, "The people of Judah have made some evil plans. So have those who live in Jerusalem. ¹⁰All of them have returned to the sins their people of long ago committed.

Those people refused to listen to what I told them. And now the people of Israel and Judah alike have worshiped other gods and served them. They have broken the covenant I made with their people who lived before them. ¹¹So I say, 'I will bring trouble on them. They will not be able to escape it. They will cry out to me. But I will not listen to them. ¹²The people of Jerusalem and of the towns of Judah will cry out. They will cry out to the gods they burn incense to. But those gods will not help them at all when trouble strikes them. ¹³Judah, you have as many gods as you have towns. And in Jerusalem you have set up as many altars as there are streets. You are burning incense to that shameful god named Baal.'

¹⁴"Jeremiah, do not pray for these people. Do not make any appeal or request for them. They will call out to me when they are in trouble. But I will not listen to them.

¹⁵"I love the people of Judah.
  But they are working out
    their evil plans along
    with many others.
  So what are they doing in
    my temple?
  Can meat that is offered
    to me keep me from
    punishing you?
  When you do evil things,
    you get a lot of pleasure
    from them."

¹⁶People of Judah, the Lord
  once called you a
  healthy olive tree.

He thought its fruit was
beautiful.
But now he will come with
the roar of a mighty
storm.
He will set the tree on fire.
And its branches will be
broken.

¹⁷ The LORD who rules over all
planted you. But now he has ordered your enemies to destroy
you. The people of Israel and
Judah have both done what is
evil. They have made the LORD
very angry by burning incense
to Baal.

Jeremiah's Enemies Make Evil Plans Against Him

¹⁸ The LORD told me about
the evil plans of my enemies.
That's how I knew about them.
He showed me what they were
doing. ¹⁹ I had been like a gentle
lamb led off to be killed. I didn't
realize they had made plans
against me. They had said,

"Let's destroy the tree and its
fruit.
Let's take away his life.
Then his name won't be
remembered anymore."
²⁰ But LORD, you rule over all.
You always judge fairly.
You test people's hearts
and minds.
So pay them back for what
they've done.
I've committed my cause
to you.

²¹ The LORD says, "Jeremiah,
here is what I am telling you
about the people of Anathoth.
They say they're going to kill
you. They are saying, 'Don't
prophesy in the LORD's name.
If you do, we will kill you with
our own hands.' " ²² So the LORD
who rules over all says, "I will
punish them. Their young men
will be killed by swords. Their
sons and daughters will die of
hunger. ²³ Only a few people will
be left alive. I will judge the people of Anathoth. I will destroy
them when the time comes to
punish them."

Jeremiah Complains to the LORD

12 LORD, when I bring a
matter to you,
you always do what is
right.
But now I would like to speak
with you
about whether you are
being fair.
Why are sinful people
successful?
Why do those who can't
be trusted have an easy
life?
² You have planted them.
Their roots are deep in the
ground.
They grow and produce
fruit.
They honor you by what they
say.
But their hearts are far
away from you.
³ LORD, you know me and see
me.
You test my thoughts about
you.
Drag those people off like
sheep to be killed!
Set them apart for the day
of their death!

⁴ How long will the land be
thirsty for water?
How long will the grass in
every field be dry?
The people who live in the
land are evil.
So the animals and birds
have died.
And that's not all. The people
are saying,
"The LORD won't see what
happens to us."

The LORD Answers Jeremiah

⁵ The LORD says, "Suppose
you have raced against
people.
And suppose they have
worn you out.
Then how would you be
able to race against
horses?
Suppose you feel safe only in
open country.
Then how would you get
along in the bushes near
the Jordan River?
⁶ Even your relatives have
turned against you.
They are members of your
own family.
They have shouted loudly
at you.
They might say nice things
about you.
But do not trust them.

⁷ "I will turn my back on my
people.
I will desert my land.
I love the people of Judah.
In spite of that, I will
hand them over to their
enemies.
⁸ My land has become to me
like a lion in the forest.

It roars at me.
So I hate it.
⁹ My own land has become
like a spotted hawk.
And other hawks surround
it and attack it.
Come, all you wild animals!
Gather together!
Come together to eat up
my land.
¹⁰ Many shepherds will destroy
my vineyard.
They will walk all over it.
They will turn my pleasant
vineyard
into a dry and empty land.
¹¹ My vineyard will become a
desert.
It will be dry and empty in
my sight.
The whole land will be
completely destroyed.
And no one even cares.
¹² Many will come to destroy it.
They will gather on the
bare hilltops in the
desert.
I will use them as my sword
to destroy my people.
They will kill them from
one end of the land to
the other.
No one will be safe.
¹³ People will plant wheat. But
all they will gather is
thorns.
They will wear themselves
out. But they will not
have anything to show
for it.
I am very angry with them.
So they will be ashamed of
the crop they gather."

¹⁴ Here is what the LORD says.
"All my evil neighbors have

taken over the land I gave my people Israel. So I will pull them up by their roots from the lands they live in. And I will pull up the roots of the people of Judah from among them. ¹⁵ But after I pull up those nations, I will give my tender love to them again. I will bring all of them back to their own lands. I will take all of them back to their own countries. ¹⁶ Suppose those nations learn to follow the practices of my people. And they make their promises in my name. When they promise, they say, 'You can be sure that the Lord is alive.' They do this just as they once taught my people to make promises in Baal's name. Then I will give them a place among my people. ¹⁷ But what if one of those nations does not listen? Then you can be sure of this. I will pull it up by the roots and destroy it," announces the Lord.

A Linen Belt

13 The Lord said to me, "Go and buy a linen belt. Put it around your waist. But do not let it get wet." ² So I bought a belt, just as the Lord had told me to do. And I put it around my waist.

³ Then another message from the Lord came to me. The Lord said, ⁴ "Take off the belt you bought and are wearing around your waist. Go to Perath. Hide the belt there in a crack in the rocks." ⁵ So I went and hid it at Perath. I did just as the Lord had told me to do.

⁶ Many days later the Lord said to me, "Go to Perath. Get the belt I told you to hide there." ⁷ So I went to Perath. I dug up the belt. I took it from the place where I had hidden it. But it had rotted. It was completely useless.

⁸ Then another message from the Lord came to me. The Lord said, ⁹ "In the same way, I will destroy Judah's pride. And I will destroy the great pride of Jerusalem. ¹⁰ These people are evil. They refuse to listen to what I say. They do what their stubborn hearts want them to do. They chase after other gods. They serve them and worship them. So they will be like this belt. They will be completely useless. ¹¹ A belt is tied around a person's waist. In the same way, I tied all the people of Israel to me. I also tied all the people of Judah to me like a belt. I wanted them to be my people. They should have brought me fame and praise and honor. But they have not listened to me," announces the Lord.

Wineskins

¹² "Tell them, 'The Lord is the God of Israel. He says, "Every wineskin should be filled with wine."' Here is what the people might say to you. 'Don't we know that every wineskin should be filled with wine?' ¹³ If they do, here is what you must tell them. 'The Lord says, "I am going to fill with wine everyone who lives in this land. I will make the kings who sit on David's throne drunk. And I will fill with wine

the priests, the prophets and everyone who lives in Jerusalem. ¹⁴ I will smash them against one another. I will punish parents and children alike," announces the LORD. "I will not feel sorry for them. I will not show them any kindness. My tender love for them will not keep me from destroying them." ' "

Judah Will Be Taken Away From Their Land

¹⁵ People of Judah, listen to me.
  Pay attention and don't be
    proud.
  The LORD has spoken.
¹⁶ Give glory to the LORD your
    God.
  Honor him before he sends
    darkness to cover the land.
  Do this before you trip and
    fall
    on the darkened hills.
  You hope that light will
    come.
  But he will turn it into
    thick darkness.
  He will change it to deep
    shadows.
¹⁷ If you don't listen,
  I will weep in secret.
  Because you are so proud,
  I will weep bitterly.
  Tears will flow from my
    eyes.
  The LORD's flock will be
    taken away as prisoners.
¹⁸ Speak to the king and his
    mother. Tell them,
  "Come down from your
    thrones.
  Your glorious crowns
    are about to fall from your
    heads."

¹⁹ The gates of the cities in the
    Negev Desert will be
    shut tight.
  There won't be anyone to
    open them.
  Everyone in Judah will
    be carried away as
    prisoners.
  You will be completely
    taken away.

²⁰ Jerusalem, look up!
  Your enemies are coming
    from the north.
  Where is the flock you were
    supposed to take care of?
  Where are the sheep you
    were so proud of?
²¹ You have worked hard to
    make special friends.
  But the LORD will let them
    rule over you.
  Then what will you say?
  Suffering will take hold of
    you.
  It will be like the pain of a
    woman having a baby.
²² Suppose you ask yourself,
  "Why has this happened to
    me?"
  It's because you have
    committed so many
    sins.
  That's the reason your skirt
    has been torn off.
  That's why your body has
    been treated so badly.
²³ Can people from Ethiopia
    change their skin?
  Can leopards change their
    spots?
  It's the same with you.
  You have always done what
    is evil.
  So how can you do what is
    good?

24 The LORD says, "I will scatter
     you like straw
   that the desert wind blows
     away.
25 This is what will happen to
     you.
   I have appointed it for you,"
     announces the LORD.
"You have forgotten me.
   You have trusted in other
     gods.
26 So I will pull your skirt up
     over your face.
   Then people will see the
     shame of your naked
     body.
27 They will see that you have
     not been faithful to me.
   You have committed
     adultery with other gods.
And you have acted like a
     prostitute
   who does not have any
     shame.
I have seen what you did
   on the hills and in the
     fields.
   And I hate it.
How terrible it will be for you,
     Jerusalem!
   How long will you choose
     to be 'unclean'?"

War and Hunger

14 A message from the LORD
     came to Jeremiah. He told
Jeremiah there wouldn't be any
rain in the land. The LORD said,

2 "Judah is filled with sadness.
   Its cities are wasting away.
The people weep for the land.
   Crying is heard in
     Jerusalem.
3 The nobles send their
     servants to get water.

They go to the wells.
   But they do not find any
     water.
They return with empty jars.
   They are terrified. They do
     not have any hope.
   They cover their heads.
4 The ground is dry and
     cracked.
   There isn't any rain in the
     land.
   The farmers are terrified.
   They cover their heads.
5 Even the female deer in the
     fields
   desert their newborn
     fawns.
   There isn't any grass to eat.
6 Wild donkeys stand on the
     bare hilltops.
   They long for water as wild
     dogs do.
Their eyesight fails
   because they do not have
     any food to eat."

7 LORD, our sins are a witness
     against us.
   But do something for the
     honor of your name.
We have often turned away
     from you.
   We've sinned against you.
8 You are Israel's only hope.
   You save us when we're in
     trouble.
Why are you like a stranger to
     us?
   Why are you like a traveler
     who stays for only one
     night?
9 Why are you like a man taken
     by surprise?
   Why are you like a soldier
     who can't save anyone?
LORD, you are among us.

And we are your people.
Please don't desert us!

¹⁰ The LORD gave Jeremiah a message about these people. The LORD said,

"They really love to wander
away from me.
Their feet go down the
wrong path.
I do not accept these people.
I will remember the evil
things they have done.
I will punish them for their
sins."

¹¹ The LORD continued, "Do not pray that things will go well with them. ¹² Even if they go without food, I will not listen to their cry for help. They might sacrifice burnt offerings and grain offerings. But I will not accept them. Instead, I will destroy them with war, hunger and plague."

¹³ But I said, "LORD and King, the prophets keep telling them something else. They say, 'You won't have to suffer from war or hunger. Instead, the LORD will give you peace and rest in this place.' "

¹⁴ Then the LORD said to me, "The prophets are prophesying lies in my name. I have not sent them or appointed them. I have not even spoken to them. Everything they tell you about their visions or secret knowledge is a lie. They pretend to bring you messages from other gods. They try to get you to believe their own mistaken ideas. ¹⁵ So here is what I am saying about the prophets who are prophesying in my name. I did not send them. But they are saying, 'No war or hunger will come to this land.' Those same prophets will die because of war and hunger. ¹⁶ And the people they are prophesying to will be thrown out into the streets of Jerusalem. They will die because of hunger and war. No one will bury them. No one will bury their wives and children. I will pour out trouble on them. That is exactly what they should get.

¹⁷ "Jeremiah, give them this message. Tell them,

" 'Let tears flow from my
eyes.
Let them pour out night
and day.
Never let them stop.
The people of my own nation
have suffered a terrible
wound.
They have been crushed.
¹⁸ Suppose I go into the
country.
Then I see people who
have been killed by
swords.
Or suppose I go into the city.
Then I see people who
have died of hunger.
Prophet and priest alike have
gone to a land
they hadn't known about
before.' "

¹⁹ LORD, have you completely
turned your back on
Judah?
Do you hate the city of Zion?
Why have you made us
suffer?
We can't be healed.

We hoped peace would
    come.
But nothing good has
    happened to us.
We hoped we would finally
    be healed.
But all we got was terror.
20 LORD, we admit we've done
    evil things.
We also admit that our
    people of long ago were
    guilty.
It's true that we've sinned
    against you.
21 For the honor of your name,
    don't turn your back
    on us.
Don't bring shame on your
    glorious throne in the
    temple.
Remember the covenant you
    made with us.
Please don't break it.
22 Do any of the worthless gods
    of the nations bring rain?
Do the skies send
    down showers all by
    themselves?
No. LORD our God, you send
    the rain.
So we put our hope in you.
You are the one who does
    all these things.

15 Then the LORD said to
me, "Suppose Moses and
Samuel were standing in front of
me. Even then my heart would
not feel sorry for these people.
Send them away from me! Let
them go! ² Suppose these people
ask you, 'Where should we go?'
Then tell them, 'The LORD says,

   " ' "Those I have appointed to
    die will die.

Those I have appointed to be
    killed by swords
    will be killed by swords.
Those I have appointed to die
    of hunger
    will die of hunger.
Those I have appointed to
    be taken away as
    prisoners
    will be taken away." '

³ "I will send four kinds of
destroyers against them," announces the LORD. "Swords will
kill them. Dogs will drag them
away. Birds will eat them up.
And wild animals will destroy
them. ⁴ I will make all the kingdoms on earth hate them. That
will happen because of what
Manasseh did in Jerusalem. He
was king of Judah and the son of
Hezekiah.

⁵ "Jerusalem, who will have
    pity on you?
Who will mourn for you?
Who will stop to ask how
    you are doing?
⁶ You have said no to me,"
    announces the LORD.
"You keep on turning away
    from me.
So I will reach out and
    destroy you.
I am tired of showing you
    pity.
⁷ I will stand at the city gates of
    the land.
I will separate the straw
    from the grain.
I will destroy my people. I
    will bring great sorrow
    on them.
They have not changed
    their ways.

⁸ I will increase the number of
　　their widows.
　　There will be more of them
　　　than the grains of sand
　　　on the seashore.
　At noon I will bring a
　　destroyer
　　against the mothers of the
　　　young men among my
　　　people.
　All at once I will bring down
　　on them
　　great suffering and terror.
⁹ Mothers who have many
　　children will grow
　　weak.
　They will take their last
　　breath.
　The sun will set on them
　　while it is still day.
　They will be dishonored
　　and put to shame.
　All those who are left alive I
　　will kill by swords.
　I will have their enemies
　　do this,"
　　　announces the LORD.

¹⁰ My mother, I wish I had never
　　been born!
　The whole land opposes
　　me.
　They fight against me.
　I haven't made loans to
　　anyone.
　And I haven't borrowed
　　anything.
　But everyone curses me
　　anyway.

¹¹ The LORD said,

"Jeremiah, I will keep you
　　safe for a good purpose.
　I will make your enemies
　　ask you to pray for
　　them.

They will make their appeal
　　to you
　　when they are in great
　　trouble.

¹² "People of Judah, the armies
　　of Babylon
　　will come from the north.
　They are as strong as iron
　　and bronze.
　Can anyone break their
　　power?
¹³ I will give away your wealth
　　and your treasures.
　Your enemies will carry off
　　everything.
　And they will not pay
　　anything for it.
　That will happen because
　　you have sinned so
　　much.
　You have done it
　　throughout your
　　country.
¹⁴ I will make you slaves to your
　　enemies.
　You will serve them in a
　　land
　　you have not known about
　　before.
　My anger will start a fire
　　that will burn you up."

¹⁵ LORD, you understand how
　　much I'm suffering.
　Show concern for me. Take
　　care of me.
　Pay back those who are
　　trying to harm me.
　You are patient. Don't take
　　my life away from me.
　Think about how much
　　shame I suffer because
　　of you.
¹⁶ When I received your words,
　　I ate them.

They filled me with joy.
My heart took delight in
them.
Lord God who rules over all,
I belong to you.
17 I never sat around with those
who go to wild parties.
I never had a good time
with them.
I sat alone because you had
put your powerful hand
on me.
Your anger against sin was
burning inside me.
18 Why does my pain never end?
Why is my wound so deep?
Why can't I ever get well?
To me you are like a stream
that runs dry.
You are like a spring that
doesn't have any water.

19 So the Lord says to Jeremiah,

"If you turn away from your
sins, I will heal you.
And then you will be able
to serve me.
Speak words that are worthy,
not worthless.
Then you will be speaking
for me.
Let these people turn to you.
But you must not turn to
them.
20 I will make you like a wall to
them.
I will make you like a
strong bronze wall.
The people will fight against
you.
But they will not overcome
you.
I am with you.
I will save you,"
announces the Lord.

21 "I will save you from the
hands of evil people.
I will set you free from
those who treat you
badly."

Times of Trouble Are Coming

16 A message from the Lord came to me. He said, 2 "Jeremiah, you must not get married. You must not have any sons or daughters in this land." 3 Here is the Lord's message about the children born in this place. He says about them and their parents, 4 "Some of them will die of deadly sicknesses. No one will mourn for them. Their bodies will not be buried. Instead, they will be like human waste lying there on the ground. Others will die because of war and hunger. Their bodies will not be buried. Instead, they will become food for the birds and the wild animals."

5 The Lord says, "Jeremiah, suppose a meal is being served because someone has died. Do not enter any house where that is happening. Do not go there to mourn or to comfort the family. I will not bless these people anymore. I have taken my love and pity away from them," announces the Lord. 6 "Important and unimportant people alike will die in this land. Their bodies will not be buried. No one will mourn for them. No one will cut themselves or shave their head for the dead. 7 No one will offer food or drink to comfort those who mourn for the dead. No one will do this even if

someone's father or mother has died.

8 "Do not enter a house where a feast is being held. Do not sit down there to eat and drink. 9 I am the LORD who rules over all. I am the God of Israel. I am telling you, 'In your days I will judge your people. You will see it with your own eyes. I will put an end to the sounds of joy and gladness here in Jerusalem. The voices of brides and grooms will not be heard anymore.'

10 "Tell these people all these things. They will ask you, 'Why has the LORD decided to send so much trouble on us? We haven't done anything wrong. We haven't committed any sins against the LORD our God.' 11 When they say this, here is what you should tell them. 'I did it because your people of long ago deserted me,' announces the LORD. 'They followed other gods. They served them and worshiped them. They deserted me. They did not obey my law. 12 But you have done more evil things than they did. All of you are doing what your stubborn and evil hearts want you to do. You are not obeying me. 13 So I will throw you out of this land. I will send you away to another land. Neither you nor your people of long ago have known about it. There you will serve other gods day and night. And I will not give you any help.'

14 "But a new day is coming," announces the LORD. "At that time here is what people will no longer say. 'As sure as he is alive, the LORD brought the Israelites up out of Egypt.' 15 Instead, they will say, 'The LORD brought the Israelites up out of the land of the north. He gathered them out of all the countries where he had forced them to go. And that's just as sure as he is alive.' I will bring them back to the land I gave their people of long ago.

16 "But now I will send for many fishermen," announces the LORD. "They will catch some of these people. After that, I will send for many hunters. They will hunt down the others on every mountain and hill. They will bring them out of the cracks in the rocks. 17 My eyes see everything these people do. What they do is not hidden from me. I always see their sin. 18 I will pay them back double for their sin and the evil things they have done. They have made my land 'unclean.' They have set up lifeless statues of their evil gods. They have filled my land with them. I hate those gods."

19 LORD, you give me strength.
　　You are like a fort to me.
When I'm in trouble,
　　I go to you for safety.
The nations will come to you
　　from one end of the earth
　　　　to the other.
　　They will gather together
　　　　and say,
"Our people of long ago
　　didn't own anything
　　　　except statues of gods.
The statues were worthless.
　　They didn't do them any
　　　　good.

20 Do human beings really
    make their own gods?
    Yes. But they aren't really
    gods at all!"

21 The LORD says, "So I will
    teach them about
    myself.
    This time I will show
    them
    how powerful and mighty I
    am.
    Then they will know
    that I am the LORD.

17 "Judah's sin is carved
    with an iron tool.
    It is written with the flint
    point of the tool.
    It is carved on the tablets of
    their hearts.
    It is written on the horns
    that stick out
    from the corners of their
    altars.
2 Even their children offer
    sacrifices
    to other gods on those
    altars.
    They use the poles that were
    made
    to worship the female god
    named Asherah.
    They worship strange gods
    beside the green trees
    and on the high hills.
3 I will give away my holy
    Mount Zion to the
    Babylonians.
    Your enemies will carry off
    your wealth
    and all your treasures.
    I will give away your high
    places.
    That will happen because
    you have sinned.

You have done it
    throughout your
    country.
4 You will lose the land I gave
    you.
    And it will be your own
    fault.
    I will make you slaves to your
    enemies.
    You will serve them in a
    land you didn't know
    about before.
    You have set my anger on
    fire.
    It will burn forever."

5 The LORD says,

"Those who trust in human
    beings are under my
    curse.
    They depend on human
    strength.
    Their hearts turn away
    from me.
6 They will be like a bush in a
    dry and empty land.
    They will not enjoy success
    when it comes.
    They will live in dry places in
    the desert.
    It is a land of salt where no
    one else lives.

7 "But I will bless anyone who
    trusts in me.
    I will do good things for
    the person who depends
    on me.
8 They will be like a tree
    planted near water.
    It sends out its roots beside
    a stream.
    It is not afraid when heat
    comes.
    Its leaves are always
    green.

It does not worry when there
is no rain.
It always bears fruit."

9 A human heart is more
dishonest than anything
else.
It can't be healed.
Who can understand it?

10 The LORD says, "I look deep
down inside human
hearts.
I see what is in people's
minds.
I reward each person in
keeping with their
conduct.
I bless them based on what
they have done."

11 Some people get rich by
doing sinful things.
They are like a partridge
that hatches eggs it
didn't lay.
When their lives are half
over, their riches will
desert them.
In the end they will prove
how foolish they have
been.

12 Our temple is where the
LORD's glorious throne
is.
From the beginning it has
been high and lifted up.

13 LORD, you are Israel's only
hope.
Everyone who deserts you
will be put to shame.
The names of those who turn
away from you will be
listed among the dead.
LORD, they have deserted
you.

You are the spring of water
that gives life.

14 LORD, heal me. Then I will be
healed.
Save me from my enemies.
Then I will be saved.
You are the one I praise.

15 They keep saying to me,
"What has happened to the
message the LORD gave
you?
Let it come true right now!"

16 I haven't run away from
being the shepherd of
your people.
You know I haven't wanted
the day of Jerusalem's
fall to come.
You are aware of every
word that comes from
my lips.

17 Don't be a terror to me.
When I'm in trouble, I go to
you for safety.

18 Let those who attack me be
put to shame.
But keep me from shame.
Let them be terrified.
But keep me from terror.
Bring the day of trouble on
them.
Destroy them once and for
all.

Keep the Sabbath Day Holy

19 The LORD said to me, "Go.
Stand at the city gate called
the Gate of the People. That is
where the kings of Judah go in
and out. Then stand at all the
other gates of Jerusalem. 20 Say,
'Listen to the LORD's message,
you kings of Judah and all you
people of Judah and Jerusalem.
You always come through these

gates. ²¹ The LORD says, "Make sure you do not carry a load on the Sabbath day. Do not bring it through the gates of Jerusalem. ²² Do not bring a load out of your houses on the Sabbath day. Do not do any work on that day. Instead, keep the Sabbath day holy. Do as I commanded your people of long ago. ²³ But they did not listen. They did not pay any attention to me. They were stubborn. They would not listen or pay attention when I corrected them. ²⁴ Be careful to obey me," announces the LORD. "Do not bring a load through the gates of this city on the Sabbath day. Instead, keep the Sabbath day holy. Do not do any work on it. ²⁵ Then kings who sit on David's throne will come through the gates of this city. They and their officials will come riding in chariots and on horses. The people of Judah and Jerusalem will come along with them. And this city will always have people living in it. ²⁶ Some will come from the towns of Judah. And some will come in from the villages around Jerusalem. Others will come from the territory of Benjamin. And others will come in from the western hills. Still others will come from the central hill country and the Negev Desert. All of them will bring burnt offerings and sacrifices. They will come bringing grain offerings, incense and thank offerings. They will take all these offerings to my house. ²⁷ But what if you do not obey me? Suppose you do not keep the Sabbath day holy. And suppose you carry a load through the gates of Jerusalem on the Sabbath day. Then I will start a fire that can't be put out. It will begin at the gates of Jerusalem. It will destroy its mighty towers." ' "

The LORD Sends Jeremiah to the Potter's House

18 A message from the LORD came to me. He said, ² "Jeremiah, go down to the potter's house. I will give you my message there." ³ So I went down to the potter's house. I saw him working at his wheel. ⁴ His hands were shaping a pot out of clay. But he saw that something was wrong with it. So he formed it into another pot. He shaped it in the way that seemed best to him.

⁵ Then the LORD's message came to me. ⁶ "People of Israel, I can do with you just as this potter does," announces the LORD. "The clay is in the potter's hand. And you are in my hand, people of Israel. ⁷ Suppose I announce that something will happen to a nation or kingdom. Suppose I announce that it will be pulled up by the roots. And I announce that it will be torn down and destroyed. ⁸ But suppose the nation I warned turns away from its sins. Then I will not do what I said I would. I will not bring trouble on it as I had planned. ⁹ But suppose I announce that a nation or kingdom is going to be built up and planted. ¹⁰ And then it does

what is evil in my eyes. It does not obey me. Then I will think again about the good things I had wanted to do for it.

¹¹ "So speak to the people of Judah and Jerusalem. Tell them, 'The LORD says, "Look! I am making plans against you. I am going to bring trouble on you. So each one of you must turn from your evil ways. Change the way you live and act." ' ¹² But they will reply, 'It's no use. We will continue to do what we've already planned. All of us will do what our stubborn and evil hearts want us to do.' "

¹³ So the LORD says,

"Ask the nations a question.
    Say to them,
    'Who has ever heard
        anything like this?
The people of Israel have
        done
    a very horrible thing.
¹⁴ Does the snow ever
        disappear
    from Lebanon's rocky
        slopes?
Do its cool waters ever stop
    flowing from places far
        away?
¹⁵ But my people have forgotten
        me.
    They burn incense to
        worthless gods.
Their gods made them trip
        and fall
    as they walked on the old
        paths.
They made them use side
        roads
    instead of roads that were
        built up.

¹⁶ So their land will become a
        horrible thing.
    People will make fun of it
        again and again.
All those who pass by it will
        be shocked.
    They will shake their
        heads.
¹⁷ I will sweep over my people
    like a wind from the east.
I will use the Babylonians
    to scatter them.
I will show them my back
    and not my face.
I will desert them when
    their day of trouble
        comes.' "

¹⁸ They said, "Come on. Let's make plans against Jeremiah. We'll still have priests to teach us the law. We'll always have wise people to give us advice. We'll have prophets to bring us messages from the LORD. So come on. Let's speak out against Jeremiah. We shouldn't pay any attention to what he says."

¹⁹ LORD, please listen to me!
    Hear what my enemies are
        saying about me!
²⁰ Should the good things I've
        done be paid back with
        evil?
    But my enemies have dug a
        pit for me.
Remember that I stood in
        front of you
    and spoke up for them.
I tried to turn your anger
    away from them.
²¹ So let their children die of
        hunger.
    Let my enemies be killed in
        war.

Let their wives lose their
children and husbands.
Let their men be put to
death.
Let their young men be
killed in battle.
22 Bring their enemies against
them without warning.
Let cries be heard from
their houses.
They have dug a pit to
capture me.
They have hidden traps for
my feet.
23 But LORD, you know
all about their plans to kill
me.
Don't forgive their crimes.
Don't erase their sins from
your sight.
Destroy my enemies.
Punish them when the
time to show your anger
comes.

19 The LORD said to Jeremiah, "Go and buy a clay
jar from a potter. Take along
some of the elders of the people.
Also tell some of the priests to go
with you. 2 Go out to the Valley
of Ben Hinnom. Stand near the
entrance of the gate where broken pieces of pottery are thrown
away. There announce the message I give you. 3 Tell the people,
'Listen to the LORD's message,
you kings of Judah and people of
Jerusalem. The LORD who rules
over all is the God of Israel. He
says, "Listen! I am going to bring
trouble on Jerusalem. It will be so
horrible that it will make the ears
of everyone who hears about it
ring. 4 My people have deserted
me. They have made this city a
place where other gods are worshiped. They have burned incense to them here. They, their
people of long ago and the kings
of Judah had never known these
gods. My people have also filled
this place with the blood of those
who aren't guilty. 5 They have
built the high places where they
worship Baal. There they sacrifice their children in the fire as
offerings to Baal. That is something I did not command or
talk about. It did not even enter
my mind. 6 So watch out!" announces the LORD. "The days
are coming when people will
not call this place Topheth anymore. And they will not call it the
Valley of Ben Hinnom either. Instead, they will call it the Valley
of Death.

7 ' ' "In this place I will make
the plans of Judah and Jerusalem as useless as a broken jar.
I will use their enemies to kill
my people by swords. They will
die at the hands of those who
want to take their lives. I will
give their dead bodies as food
to the birds and the wild animals. 8 I will completely destroy
this city. I will make it a horrible
thing. People will make fun of
it. All those who pass by it will
be shocked. They will laugh at
its people because of all their
wounds. 9 I will make the people of this city eat their sons and
daughters. And they will eat
one another. They will do this
because things will be so bad
during the attack. The enemies
who want to take their lives will
bring all this trouble on them." '

¹⁰ "Jeremiah, break the jar while those who go with you are watching. ¹¹ Tell them, 'Here is what the LORD who rules over all says. "This potter's jar is smashed and can't be repaired. And I will smash this nation and this city. People will bury their dead in Topheth. But they will run out of room. ¹² Here is what I will do to Jerusalem and those who live here," ' announces the LORD. ' "I will make this city like Topheth. ¹³ The houses in Jerusalem will be made 'unclean' like Topheth. So will the houses of the kings of Judah. All these people burned incense on their roofs to all the stars. They poured out drink offerings to other gods." ' "

¹⁴ Then Jeremiah returned from Topheth. That's where the LORD had sent him to prophesy. Jeremiah stood in the courtyard of the LORD's temple. He spoke to all the people. He said, ¹⁵ "The LORD who rules over all is the God of Israel. He says, 'Listen! I am going to punish this city and all the villages around it. I am going to bring against them all the trouble I have announced. That's because my people were stubborn. They would not listen to what I said.' "

Jeremiah and Pashhur

20 Pashhur the priest was the official in charge of the LORD's temple. He was the son of Immer. Pashhur heard Jeremiah prophesying that Jerusalem would be destroyed. ² So he had Jeremiah the prophet beaten. Then Pashhur put him in prison at the Upper Gate of Benjamin at the LORD's temple. ³ The next day Pashhur set him free. Jeremiah said to him, "The LORD's name for you isn't Pashhur. The LORD's name for you is Terror on Every Side. ⁴ The LORD says to you, 'I will make you a terror to yourself. You will also be a terror to all your friends. With your own eyes you will see them die. Their enemies will kill them with swords. I will hand over all the people of Judah to the king of Babylon. He will carry them away to Babylon or kill them with swords. ⁵ I will hand over all the wealth of this city to Judah's enemies. I will give them all its products and everything of value. I will turn over to them all the treasures that belonged to the kings of Judah. They will take these things and carry them off to Babylon. ⁶ Pashhur, you and everyone who lives in your house will also be forced to go there. You have prophesied lies to all your friends. So all of you will die and be buried in Babylon.' "

Jeremiah Complains to the LORD

⁷ You tricked me, LORD, and I
    was tricked.
  You overpowered me and
    won.
  People make fun of me all
    day long.
  Everyone laughs at me.
⁸ Every time I speak, I cry out.
  All you ever tell me to talk
    about
  is fighting and trouble.

Your message has brought
me nothing but
dishonor.
It has made me suffer
shame all day long.
9 Sometimes I think, "I won't
talk about his message
anymore.
I'll never speak in his name
again."
But then your message burns
in my heart.
It's like a fire deep inside
my bones.
I'm tired of holding it in.
In fact, I can't.
10 I hear many people
whispering,
"There is terror on every
side!
Bring charges against
Jeremiah! Let's bring
charges against him!"
All my friends
are waiting for me to slip.
They are saying, "Perhaps he
will be tricked
into making a mistake.
Then we'll win out over him.
We'll get even with him."
11 But you are with me like a
mighty warrior.
So those who are trying to
harm me will trip and
fall.
They won't win out over
me.
They will fail. They'll be
totally put to shame.
Their dishonor will never
be forgotten.
12 LORD, you rule over all.
You test those who do what
is right.

You see what is in people's
hearts and minds.
So pay them back for what
they've done.
I've committed my cause
to you.
13 Sing to the LORD, you people!
Give praise to him!
He saves the lives of people in
need.
He saves them from the
power of sinful people.
14 May the day I was born be
cursed!
May the day I was born
to my mother not be
blessed!
15 May the man who brought
my father the news be
cursed!
He's the one who made my
father very glad.
He said, "You have had a
baby! It's a boy!"
16 May that man be like the
towns
the LORD destroyed
without pity.
May that man hear loud
weeping in the morning.
May he hear a battle cry at
noon.
17 He should have killed me in
my mother's body.
He should have made my
mother my grave.
He should have let her
body stay large forever.
18 Why did I ever come out of
my mother's body?
I've seen nothing but
trouble and sorrow.
My days will end in
shame.

The LORD Refuses Zedekiah's Appeal

21 A message from the LORD came to Jeremiah. It came when King Zedekiah sent Pashhur to Jeremiah. Pashhur was the son of Malkijah. Zedekiah sent Zephaniah the priest along with him. Zephaniah was the son of Maaseiah. They said to Jeremiah, ² "Ask the LORD to help us. Nebuchadnezzar king of Babylon is attacking us. In the past the LORD did wonderful things for us. Maybe he'll do them again. Then Nebuchadnezzar will pull his armies back from us."

³ But Jeremiah answered them, "Tell Zedekiah and his people, ⁴ 'The LORD is the God of Israel. He says, "The king of Babylon and his armies are all around this city. They are getting ready to attack you. You have weapons of war in your hands to fight against them. But I am about to turn your weapons against you. And I will bring your enemies inside this city. ⁵ I myself will fight against you. I will reach out my powerful hand and mighty arm. I will come against you with all my great anger. ⁶ I will strike down those who live in this city. I will kill people and animals alike. They will die of a terrible plague. ⁷ After that, I will hand you over to your enemies. They want to kill you," announces the LORD. "I will hand over Zedekiah, the king of Judah, and his officials. I will also hand over the people in this city who live through the plague, war and hunger. All of them will be handed over to Nebuchadnezzar, the king of Babylon. He will kill them with swords. He will show them no mercy. He will not feel sorry for them. In fact, he will not have any concern for them at all." '

⁸ "Tell the people, 'The LORD says, "I am offering you a choice. You can choose the way that leads to life. Or you can choose the way that leads to death. ⁹ Those who stay in this city will die of war, hunger or plague. But suppose some go out and give themselves up to the Babylonians attacking you. They will live. They will escape with their lives. ¹⁰ I have decided to do this city harm and not good," announces the LORD. "It will be handed over to the king of Babylon. And he will destroy it with fire." '

¹¹ "Also speak to Judah's royal family. Tell them, 'Listen to the LORD's message. ¹² Here is what the LORD says to you who belong to David's royal house.

" ' "Every morning do what is
　　right and fair.
Save those who have been
　　robbed.
Set them free from the
　　people who have treated
　　them badly.
If you do not, my anger will
　　blaze out against you.
It will burn like fire
　　because of the evil
　　things you have done.
No one will be able to put it
　　out.
¹³ Jerusalem, I am against you,"
　　announces the LORD.
"You live above this valley.

You are on a high, rocky
    plain.
And you say, 'Who can come
    against us?
    Who can enter our place of
    safety?'
[14] But I will punish you in
    keeping with what you
    have done,"
        announces the LORD.
"I will start a fire in your
    forests.
    It will burn down
    everything around
    you." ' "

The LORD Judges Evil Kings

22 The LORD said to Jeremiah, "Go down to the palace of the king of Judah. Announce my message there. Tell him, [2] 'King of Judah, listen to the LORD's message. You are sitting on David's throne. You and your officials and your people come through these gates. [3] The LORD says, "Do what is fair and right. Save those who have been robbed. Set them free from the people who have treated them badly. Do not do anything wrong to outsiders or widows in this place. Do not harm children whose fathers have died. Do not kill those who are not guilty of doing anything wrong. [4] Be careful to obey these commands. Then kings who sit on David's throne will come through the gates of this palace. They will come riding in chariots and on horses. Their officials and their people will come along with them. [5] But suppose you do not obey these commands,"

announces the LORD. "Then I promise you that this palace will be destroyed. You can be as sure of this promise as you are sure that I live." ' "

[6] The LORD speaks about the palace of the king of Judah. He says,

"You are like the land of
    Gilead to me.
    You are like the highest
    mountain in Lebanon.
But I will make you like a
    desert.
    You will become like towns
    that no one lives in.
[7] I will send destroyers against
    you.
    All of them will come with
    their weapons.
They will cut up your fine
    cedar beams.
    They will throw them into
    the fire.

[8] "People from many nations will pass by this city. They will ask one another, 'Why has the LORD done such a thing to this great city?' [9] And the answer will be, 'This happened because of what its people have done. They have turned away from the covenant the LORD their God made with them. They have worshiped other gods. And they have served them.' "

[10] Don't weep over dead King
    Josiah.
    Don't be sad because he's
    gone.
Instead, weep bitterly over
    King Jehoahaz.
    He was forced to leave his
    country.

Parable of the Lost Sheep

LUKE 15:1-7

The Parable of the Lost Son
LUKE 15:11–32

He will never return.
He'll never see his own
    land again.

¹¹ Jehoahaz became king of Judah after his father Josiah. But he has gone away from this place. That's because the LORD says about him, "He will never return. ¹² He will die in Egypt. That is where he was taken as a prisoner. He will not see this land again."

¹³ The LORD says, "How terrible
    it will be for King
    Jehoiakim!
He builds his palace
by mistreating his people.
He builds its upstairs rooms
    with money gained by
    sinning.
He makes his own people
    work for nothing.
He does not pay them for
    what they do.
¹⁴ He says, 'I will build myself a
    great palace.
It will have large rooms
    upstairs.'
So he makes big windows in
    it.
He covers its walls with
    cedar boards.
He decorates it with red
    paint.
¹⁵ "Jehoiakim, does having
    more and more cedar
    boards
make you a king?
Your father Josiah had
    enough to eat and drink.
He did what was right and
    fair.
So everything went well
    with him.

¹⁶ He stood up for those who
    were poor or needy.
So everything went well
    with him.
That is what it means to know
    me,"
announces the LORD.
¹⁷ "Jehoiakim, the only thing on
    your mind
is to get rich by cheating
    others.
You would even kill people
    who are not guilty
of doing anything wrong.
You would mistreat them.
    You would take everything
    they own."

¹⁸ So the LORD speaks about King Jehoiakim, the son of Josiah. He says,

"His people will not mourn
    for him.
They will not say,
    'My poor brother! My poor
    sister!'
They will not mourn for
    him.
They will not say,
    'My poor master! How sad
    that his glory is gone!'
¹⁹ In fact, he will be buried like
    a donkey.
His body will be dragged
    away and thrown
outside the gates of
    Jerusalem."

²⁰ The LORD says, "People of
    Jerusalem, go up to
    Lebanon.
Cry out for help.
Let your voice be heard in
    the land of Bashan.
Cry out from the mountains
    of Abarim.

All those who were going
to help you are crushed.
²¹ When you felt secure, I
warned you.
But you said, 'I won't
listen!'
You have acted like that ever
since you were young.
You have not obeyed me.
²² The wind will drive away all
your shepherds.
All those who were going
to help you will be
carried off as prisoners.
Then you will be dishonored
and put to shame.
That will happen because
you have been so sinful.
²³ Some of you live in Jerusalem
in the Palace of the
Forest of Lebanon.
You are comfortable in
your cedar buildings.
But you will groan when pain
comes on you.
It will be like the pain of a
woman having a baby.

²⁴ "King Jehoiachin, you are the son of Jehoiakim," announces the LORD. "Suppose you were a ring on my right hand. And suppose the ring even had my royal mark on it. Then I would still pull you off my finger. And that is just as sure as I am alive. ²⁵ I will hand you over to those who want to kill you. I will hand you over to people you are afraid of. I will give you to Nebuchadnezzar, the king of Babylon. I will hand you over to his armies. ²⁶ I will throw you out into another country. I will throw your mother out. Neither of you was born in that country. But both of you will die there. ²⁷ You will never come back to the land you long to return to."

²⁸ This man Jehoiachin is like a
broken pot.
Everyone hates him. No
one wants him.
Why will he and his children
be thrown out of this
land?
Why will they be sent to a
land
they don't know about?
²⁹ Land, land, land,
listen to the LORD's
message!
³⁰ The LORD says,
"Let the record say that this
man did not have any
children.
Let it report that he did
not have any success
in life.
None of his children will
have success either.
None of them will sit on
David's throne.
None of them will ever rule
over Judah.

The Godly Branch

23 "How terrible it will be for the shepherds who lead my people astray!" announces the LORD. "They are destroying and scattering the sheep that belong to my flock." ² So the LORD, the God of Israel, speaks to the shepherds who take care of my people. He tells them, "You have scattered my sheep. You have driven them away. You have not taken good care of them. So I will punish you for the evil things you have done," announces the LORD. [3] "I myself will gather together those who are left alive in my flock. I will gather them out of all the countries where I have driven them. And I will bring them back to their own land. There my sheep will have many lambs. There will be many more of them. [4] I will place shepherds over them who will take good care of them. My sheep will not be afraid or terrified anymore. And none of them will be missing," announces the LORD.

[5] "A new day is coming,"
    announces the LORD.
  "At that time I will raise up
    for David's royal line
    a godly Branch.
  He will be a King who will
    rule wisely.
  He will do what is fair and
    right in the land.
[6] In his days Judah will be
    saved.
  Israel will live in safety.
  And the Branch will be called
  The LORD Who Makes Us
    Right With Himself.

[7] Other days are also coming," announces the LORD. "At that time people will no longer say, 'The LORD brought the Israelites up out of Egypt. And that's just as sure as he is alive.' [8] Instead, they will say, 'The LORD brought the Israelites up out of the land of the north. He gathered them out of all the countries where he had forced them to go. And that's just as sure as he is alive.' Then they will live in their own land."

Prophets Who Tell Lies

[9] Here is my message about the prophets.

  My heart is broken inside me.
    All my bones tremble with
      fear.
  I am like a man who is
    drunk.
    I am like a strong man who
      has had too much wine.
  That's what the LORD's holy
    words
    have done to me.
[10] The land is full of people
    who aren't faithful to the
      LORD.
  Now the land is under his
    curse.
    And that's why it is thirsty
      for water.
    That's why the desert
      grasslands are dry.
  The prophets are leading
    sinful lives.
    They don't use their power
      in the right way.
[11] "Prophets and priests alike
    are ungodly,"
      announces the LORD.
  "Even in my temple I find
    them sinning.
[12] So their path will become
    slippery.
  They will be thrown out
    into darkness.
  There they will fall.
  I will bring trouble on them
    when the time to punish
      them comes,"
      announces the LORD.

[13] "Among the prophets of
    Samaria
  I saw something I can't
    stand.

They were prophesying in
the name of Baal.
They were leading my
people Israel astray.
[14] I have also seen something
horrible among
Jerusalem's prophets.
They are not faithful to me.
They are not living by the
truth.
They strengthen the hands of
those who do evil.
So not one of them turns
from their sinful ways.
All of them are like the
people of Sodom to me.
They are just like the
people of Gomorrah."

[15] So the LORD who rules over
all speaks about the prophets.
He says,

"I will make them eat bitter
food.
I will make them drink
poisoned water.
The prophets of Jerusalem
have spread
their ungodly ways all
through the land."

[16] The LORD who rules over all
says to the people of Judah,

"Do not listen to what the
prophets are saying to
you.
They fill you with false
hopes.
They talk about visions that
come from their own
minds.
What they say does not
come from my mouth.
[17] They keep speaking to those
who hate me. They say,

'The LORD says you will
have peace.'
They speak to all those who
do
what their stubborn hearts
want them to do.
They tell them, 'No harm
will come to you.'
[18] But which of them has ever
stood in my courts?
Have they been there to
see a vision or hear my
message?
Who has listened and
heard my message
there?
[19] A storm will burst out
because of my great anger.
A windstorm will sweep
down
on the heads of sinful
people.
[20] My anger will not turn back.
I will accomplish
everything
I plan to do.
In days to come
you will understand it
clearly.
[21] I did not send these
prophets.
But they have run to tell
you their message
anyway.
I did not speak to them.
But they have still
prophesied.
[22] Suppose they had stood in
my courts.
Then they would have
announced my message
to my people.
They would have turned my
people from their evil
ways.

They would have turned them away from their sins.

23 "Am I only a God who is nearby?"
announces the Lord.
"Am I not a God who is also far away?
24 Who can hide in secret places
so that I can't see them?"
announces the Lord.
"Don't I fill heaven and earth?"
announces the Lord.

25 "I have heard what the prophets are saying. They prophesy lies in my name. They say, 'I had a dream! The Lord has given me a dream!' 26 How long will that continue in the hearts of these prophets who tell lies? They try to get others to believe their own mistaken ideas. 27 They tell one another their dreams. They think that will make my people forget my name. In the same way, their people of long ago forgot my name when they worshiped Baal. 28 Let the prophet who has a dream describe the dream. But let the one who has my message speak it faithfully. Your prophets have given you straw to eat instead of grain," announces the Lord. 29 "My message is like fire," announces the Lord. "It is like a hammer that breaks a rock in pieces.

30 "So I am against these prophets," announces the Lord. "I am against those who steal messages from one another.

They claim that the messages come from me. 31 Yes," announces the Lord. "I am against the prophets who speak their own words. But they still say, 'Here is what the Lord says.' 32 I am against prophets who talk about dreams that did not come from me," announces the Lord. "They tell foolish lies. Their lies lead my people astray. But I did not send these prophets. I did not appoint them. They do not help my people in the least," announces the Lord.

Prophets Who Give Messages That Are Not From the Lord

33 "Jeremiah, these people might ask you a question. Or a prophet or priest might do this. They might ask, 'What message have you received from the Lord?' Then tell them, 'You ask, "What message?" Here it is. "I will desert you," announces the Lord.' 34 A prophet or priest might make a claim. Or someone else might do this. He might claim, 'This is a message from the Lord.' Then I will punish them and their family. 35 Here is what each of you people keeps on saying to your friends and other Israelites. You ask, 'What is the Lord's answer?' Or you ask, 'What has the Lord spoken?' 36 But you must not talk about 'a message from the Lord' again. That's because each person's own words become their message. And so you twist the Lord's words. He is the living God. He is the Lord who rules over all. And he is our God. 37 Here is what you

keep saying to a prophet. You ask, 'What is the LORD's answer to you?' Or you ask, 'What has the LORD spoken?' ³⁸ You claim, 'This is a message from the LORD.' But here is what the LORD says. 'You used the words, "This is a message from the LORD." But I told you that you must not claim, "This is a message from the LORD." ' ³⁹ So you can be sure I will forget you. I will throw you out of my sight. I will also destroy the city I gave you and your people of long ago. ⁴⁰ I will bring on you shame that will last forever. It will never be forgotten.' "

Judah Is Like Two Baskets of Figs

24 King Jehoiachin was forced to leave Jerusalem. He was the son of Jehoiakim. Jehoiachin was taken to Babylon by Nebuchadnezzar, the king of Babylon. The officials and all the skilled workers were forced to leave with him. After they left, the LORD showed me two baskets of figs. They were in front of his temple. ² One basket had very good figs in it. They were like figs that ripen early. The other basket had very bad figs in it. In fact, they were so bad they couldn't even be eaten.

³ Then the LORD asked me, "What do you see, Jeremiah?"

"Figs," I answered. "The good ones are very good. But the others are so bad they can't be eaten."

⁴ Then a message from the LORD came to me. The LORD said, ⁵ "I am the LORD, the God of Israel. I say, 'I consider the people who were forced to leave Judah to be like these good figs. I sent them away from this place. I forced them to go to Babylon. ⁶ My eyes will watch over them. I will be good to them. And I will bring them back to this land. I will build them up. I will not tear them down. I will plant them. I will not pull them up by the roots. ⁷ I will change their hearts. Then they will know that I am the LORD. They will be my people. And I will be their God. They will return to me with all their heart.

⁸ " 'But there are also bad figs. In fact, they are so bad they can't be eaten,' says the LORD. 'Zedekiah, the king of Judah, is like these bad figs. So are his officials and the people of Jerusalem who are still left alive. I will punish them whether they remain in this land or live in Egypt. ⁹ I will make all the kingdoms on earth displeased with them. In fact, they will hate them a great deal. They will shake their heads at them. They will curse them and make fun of them. All this will happen no matter where I force them to go. ¹⁰ I will send war, hunger and plague against them. They will be destroyed from the land I gave them and their people of long ago.' "

Seventy Years in Babylon

25 A message from the LORD about all the people of Judah came to Jeremiah. It came in the fourth year that Jehoiakim was the king of Judah. It was the first year that Nebuchadnezzar was the king of Babylon. Jehoiakim was the son of Josiah. ² Jeremiah, the LORD's prophet, spoke to all the people of Judah and Jerusalem. He said, ³ "For 23 years the LORD's messages have been coming to me. They began to come in the 13th year that Josiah was king of Judah. He was the son of Amon. The LORD's messages still come to me today. I've spoken to you people again and again. But you haven't listened to me.

⁴ "The LORD has sent all his servants the prophets to you. They've come to you again and again. But you haven't listened. You haven't paid any attention to them. ⁵ They said, 'Each of you must turn from your evil ways and practices. Then you can stay in the land forever. It's the land the LORD gave you and your people of long ago. ⁶ Don't follow other gods. Don't serve them or worship them. Don't make the LORD angry with the gods your own hands have made. Then he won't harm you.'

⁷ " 'But you did not listen to me,' announces the LORD. 'You have made me very angry with the gods your hands have made. And you have brought harm on yourselves.'

⁸ "The LORD who rules over all says, 'You have not listened to my words. ⁹ So I will send for all the nations in the north. And I will send for my servant Nebuchadnezzar, the king of Babylon,' announces the LORD. 'I will bring all of them against this land and against you who live here. They will march out against all the nations that are around this land. I will set apart Judah and the nations around it in a special way to be destroyed. People will be shocked because of them. And they will make fun of them. Those nations will be destroyed forever. ¹⁰ I will put an end to the sounds of joy and gladness. I will put an end to the voices of brides and grooms. The sound of grinding millstones will not be heard anymore. And lamps will not be lit anymore. ¹¹ This whole country will become dry and empty. And these nations will serve the king of Babylon for 70 years.

¹² " 'But I will punish that king and his nation because they are guilty. I will do this when the 70 years are over,' announces the LORD. 'I will make that land a desert forever. ¹³ I have spoken against that land. And I will make all these things happen to it. Everything will happen that is written in this book. And I will make everything Jeremiah prophesied against all the nations come true. ¹⁴ The people of Babylon will become slaves of many other nations and great kings. I will pay them back for what they have done.' "

The Cup of God's Great Anger

¹⁵ The LORD is the God of Israel. He said to me, "Take this cup from my hand. It is filled with the wine of my great anger. Make all the nations to which I

send you drink it. ¹⁶When they drink it, they will not even be able to walk straight. It will drive them out of their minds. I am going to send war against them."

¹⁷So I took the cup from the LORD's hand. I made all the nations to which he sent me drink from it.

¹⁸He sent me to Judah's kings and officials. He told me to go to Jerusalem and the towns of Judah. He wanted me to tell them they would be destroyed. Then people would be shocked because of them. They would make fun of them. They would use their name in a curse. And that's how things still are today.

¹⁹Here is a list of the other kings and nations he sent me to.

Pharaoh, the king of Egypt
his attendants, his officials,
  all his people
²⁰all the people from other
  lands who lived there
all the kings of Uz
the Philistine kings of Ashkelon, Gaza and Ekron
the Philistines still living in
  Ashdod
²¹Edom, Moab, Ammon
²²all the kings of Tyre and Sidon
the kings of the islands and
  other lands along the
  Mediterranean Sea
²³Dedan, Teman, Buz
all the other places far away
  in the east
²⁴all the kings of Arabia

all the other kings of people
  who live in the desert
²⁵all the kings of Zimri, Elam
  and Media
²⁶all the kings in the north,
  near and far

So he sent me to all the kingdoms on the face of the earth, one after the other. They will all drink from the cup of the LORD's anger. After they drink, the king of Babylon will drink from it too.

²⁷The LORD says, "Tell them, 'The LORD who rules over all is the God of Israel. He says, "Drink from this cup. Get drunk and throw up. Fall down and do not get up again. I am going to send war against you."' ²⁸But they might refuse to take the cup from your hand. They might not want to drink from it. Then tell them, 'The LORD who rules over all says, "You must drink from it! ²⁹I am beginning to bring trouble on the city where I have put my Name. You might think you will not be punished. But you will certainly be punished. I am sending war against everyone who lives on earth," announces the LORD who rules over all.'

³⁰"Jeremiah, prophesy against them. Tell them,

" 'The LORD will roar from
    heaven like a lion.
  His voice will sound like
    thunder
  from his holy temple there.
He will roar loudly against
    his land.
  He will shout like those
    who stomp on grapes in
    winepresses.

He will shout against everyone who lives on earth.
31 The noise of battle will be heard
from one end of the earth to the other.
That's because the LORD will bring charges against the nations.
He will judge every human being.
He will kill sinful people with his sword,' "
announces the LORD.

32 The LORD who rules over all says,

"Look! Horrible trouble is spreading
from one nation to another.
A mighty storm is rising.
It is coming from a place that is very far away."

33 At that time those the LORD kills will be lying around everywhere. They will be found from one end of the earth to the other. No one will mourn for them. Their dead bodies will not be gathered up or buried. Instead, they will be like human waste lying there on the ground.

34 Weep and cry, you shepherds.
Roll in the dust, you leaders of the flock.
Your time to be killed has come.
You will fall like the best of the rams.
35 The shepherds won't have any place to run to.
The leaders of the flock won't be able to escape.
36 Listen to the cries of the shepherds.
Hear the weeping of the leaders of the flock.
The LORD is destroying their grasslands.
37 Their peaceful meadows will be completely destroyed because of the LORD's great anger.
38 Like a lion he will leave his den.
The land of those leaders will become a desert.
That's because the sword of the LORD brings great harm.
His anger will burn against them.

Jeremiah's Enemies Try to Have Him Killed

26 A message from the LORD came to Jeremiah. It was shortly after Jehoiakim became king of Judah. He was the son of Josiah. 2 The LORD said to Jeremiah, "Stand in the courtyard of my house. Speak to the people of the towns in Judah. Speak to all those who come to worship in my house. Tell them everything I command you. Do not leave out a single word. 3 Perhaps they will listen. Maybe they will turn from their evil ways. Then I will not do what I said I would. I will not bring trouble on them. I had planned to punish them because of the evil things they had done. 4 Tell them, 'The LORD says, "Listen to me. Obey my law that I gave you. 5 And listen to the words my servants the prophets are speaking. I have sent them

to you again and again. But you have not listened to them. ⁶ So I will make this house like Shiloh. All the nations on earth will use the name of this city in a curse.' "

⁷ Jeremiah spoke these words in the LORD's house. The priests, the prophets and all the people heard him. ⁸ Jeremiah finished telling all the people everything the LORD had commanded him to say. But as soon as he did, the priests, the prophets and all the people grabbed him. They said, "You must die! ⁹ Why do you prophesy these things in the LORD's name? Why do you say that this house will become like Shiloh? Why do you say that this city will be empty and deserted?" And all the people crowded around Jeremiah in the LORD's house.

¹⁰ The officials of Judah heard what had happened. So they went up from the royal palace to the LORD's house. There they took their places at the entrance of the New Gate. ¹¹ Then the priests and prophets spoke to the officials and all the people. They said, "This man should be sentenced to death. He has prophesied against this city. You have heard it with your own ears!"

¹² Then Jeremiah spoke to all the officials and people. He said, "The LORD sent me to prophesy against this house and this city. He told me to say everything you have heard. ¹³ So change the way you live and act. Obey the LORD your God. Then he won't do what

he said he would. He won't bring on you the trouble he said he would bring. ¹⁴ As for me, I'm in your hands. Do to me what you think is good and right. ¹⁵ But you can be sure of one thing. If you put me to death, you will be held responsible for spilling my blood. And I haven't even done anything wrong. You will bring guilt on yourselves and this city and those who live in it. The LORD has sent me to you. He wanted me to say all these things so you could hear them. And that's the truth."

¹⁶ Then the officials and all the people spoke to the priests and prophets. They said, "This man shouldn't be sentenced to death! He has spoken to us in the name of the LORD our God."

¹⁷ Some of the elders of the land stepped forward. They spoke to the whole community gathered there. They said, ¹⁸ "Micah from Moresheth prophesied. It was during the time Hezekiah was king over Judah. Micah spoke to all the people of Judah. He told them, 'The LORD who rules over all says,

" ' "Zion will be plowed up
      like a field.
   Jerusalem will be turned
      into a pile of trash.
   The temple hill will be
      covered with bushes and
      weeds." '   *(Micah 3:12)*

¹⁹ Did King Hezekiah or anyone else in Judah put Micah to death? Hezekiah had respect for the LORD and tried to please him. And the LORD didn't judge

Jerusalem as he said he would. He didn't bring on it the trouble he said he would bring. But we are about to bring horrible trouble on ourselves!"

20 Uriah was another man who prophesied in the name of the LORD. He was from Kiriath Jearim. He was the son of Shemaiah. Uriah prophesied against this city and this land. He said the same things Jeremiah did. 21 King Jehoiakim and all his officers and officials heard Uriah's words. So the king decided to put him to death. But Uriah heard about it. He was afraid. And he ran away to Egypt. 22 So King Jehoiakim sent Elnathan to Egypt. He also sent some other men along with him. Elnathan was the son of Akbor. 23 Those men brought Uriah out of Egypt. They took him to King Jehoiakim. Then the king had Uriah struck down with a sword. He had Uriah's body thrown into one of the graves of the ordinary people.

24 In spite of that, Ahikam stood up for Jeremiah. Ahikam was the son of Shaphan. Because of Ahikam, Jeremiah wasn't handed over to the people to be put to death.

Judah Will Serve Nebuchadnezzar

27 A message from the LORD came to Jeremiah. It was shortly after Zedekiah became king of Judah. He was the son of Josiah. 2 The LORD said, "Make a yoke out of ropes and wooden boards. Put it on your neck.

3 Then write down a message for the kings of Edom, Moab, Ammon, Tyre and Sidon. Give it to their messengers who have come to Jerusalem. They have come to see Zedekiah, the king of Judah. 4 Give them a message for the kings who sent them. It should say, 'The LORD who rules over all is the God of Israel. He says, "Here is what I want you to tell your masters. 5 I reached out my great and powerful arm. I made the earth. I made its people and animals. And I can give the earth to anyone I please. 6 Now I will hand over all your countries to my servant Nebuchadnezzar. He is the king of Babylon. I will put even the wild animals under his control. 7 All the nations will serve him and his son and grandson. After that, I will judge his land. Then many nations and great kings will make him serve them.

8 " ' "But suppose any nation or kingdom will not serve Nebuchadnezzar, the king of Babylon. And suppose it refuses to put its neck under his yoke. Then I will punish that nation with war, hunger and plague," announces the LORD. "I will punish it until his powerful hand destroys it. 9 So do not listen to your prophets. Do not listen to those who claim to have secret knowledge. Do not listen to those who try to explain your dreams. Do not listen to those who get messages from people who have died. Do not listen to those who practice evil magic. All of them will tell you, 'You won't serve the king of

Babylon.' ¹⁰ But they prophesy lies to you. If you listen to them, you will be removed far away from your lands. I will drive you away from them. And you will die. ¹¹ But suppose any nation will put its neck under the yoke of the king of Babylon. And suppose it serves him. Then I will let that nation remain in its own land. I will let its people plow the land and live there,"'" announces the LORD.

¹² I gave the same message to Zedekiah, the king of Judah. I said, "Put your neck under the yoke of the king of Babylon. Obey him. Serve his people. Then you will live. ¹³ Why should you and your people die? Why should you die of war, hunger and plague? That's what the LORD said would happen to any nation that won't serve the king of Babylon. ¹⁴ Don't listen to the words of the prophets who say to you, 'You won't serve the king of Babylon.' They are prophesying lies to you. ¹⁵ 'I have not sent them,' announces the LORD. 'They are prophesying lies in my name. So I will drive you away from your land. And you will die. So will the prophets who prophesy to you.'"

¹⁶ Then I spoke to the priests and all these people. I said, "The LORD says, 'Do not listen to the prophets who speak to you. They say, "Very soon the objects from the LORD's house will be brought back from Babylon." Those prophets are prophesying lies to you. ¹⁷ Do not listen to them. Serve the king of Babylon. Then you will live. Why should this city be destroyed? ¹⁸ If they are prophets and have received a message from me, let them pray to me. I am the LORD who rules over all. Those prophets should pray that what is still in Jerusalem will remain here. They should pray that the objects in my house and the king's palace will not be taken to Babylon. ¹⁹ I am the LORD who rules over all. Do you know what these objects are? They include the two pillars in front of the temple. They include the huge bronze bowl. They include the bronze stands that can be moved around. And they include the other things left in this city. ²⁰ Nebuchadnezzar, the king of Babylon, did not take these things away at first. That was when he took King Jehoiachin from Jerusalem to Babylon. Jehoiachin is the son of Jehoiakim. Nebuchadnezzar also took all the nobles of Judah and Jerusalem along with Jehoiachin. ²¹ I am the LORD who rules over all. I am the God of Israel. Here is what will happen to the things that are left in my house, the king's palace and Jerusalem. ²² They will be taken to Babylon. They will remain there until the day I come for them,' announces the LORD. 'Then I will bring them back. I will return them to this place.'"

The False Prophet Hananiah Opposes Jeremiah

28 The false prophet Hananiah spoke to me, Jeremiah, in the LORD's house.

Hananiah was from Gibeon. He was the son of Azzur. It was shortly after Zedekiah became king of Judah. It was in the fifth month of his fourth year. In front of the priests and all the people Hananiah spoke to me. He said, 2 "The LORD who rules over all is the God of Israel. He says, 'I will break the yoke of the king of Babylon. 3 Nebuchadnezzar, the king of Babylon, removed all the objects that belong to my house. He took them to Babylon. Before two years are over, I will bring them back to this place. 4 I will also bring King Jehoiachin back. He is the son of Jehoiakim. And I will bring back all the others who were taken from Judah to Babylon,' announces the LORD. 'I will break the yoke of the king of Babylon.' "

5 Then Jeremiah the prophet replied to the false prophet Hananiah. Jeremiah spoke to him in front of the priests and all the people. They were standing in the LORD's house. 6 Jeremiah said, "Amen, Hananiah! May the LORD do those things! May he make the words you have prophesied come true. May he bring back from Babylon the objects that belong to the LORD's house. May he bring back to this place all the people who were taken away. 7 But listen to what I have to say. I want you and all the people to hear it. 8 There have been prophets long before you and I were ever born. They have prophesied against many countries and great kingdoms. They have spoken about war,

trouble and plague. 9 But what if a prophet says peace will come? And suppose peace really does come? Only then will he be recognized as a prophet truly sent by the LORD."

10 The false prophet Hananiah took the yoke off the neck of Jeremiah the prophet. Then Hananiah broke the yoke. 11 In front of all the people he said, "The LORD says, 'In the same way, I will break the yoke of Nebuchadnezzar, the king of Babylon. Before two years are over, I will remove it from the necks of all the nations.' " When Jeremiah the prophet heard this, he went on his way.

12 A message from the LORD came to Jeremiah. It was after the false prophet Hananiah had broken the yoke off Jeremiah's neck. The message said, 13 "Go. Tell Hananiah, 'The LORD says, "You have broken a wooden yoke. But in its place you will get an iron yoke." 14 The LORD who rules over all is the God of Israel. He says, "I will put an iron yoke on the necks of all these nations. I will make them serve Nebuchadnezzar, the king of Babylon. So they will serve him. I will even give him control over the wild animals." ' "

15 Then Jeremiah the prophet spoke to the false prophet Hananiah. Jeremiah said, "Listen, Hananiah! The LORD hasn't sent you. But you have tricked these people. Now they trust in lies. 16 So the LORD says, 'I am about to remove you from the face of the earth. Before this

year is over, you will die. You have taught the people to turn against me.'"

¹⁷ In the seventh month of that very year, the false prophet Hananiah died.

Jeremiah's Letter to the Jews in Babylon

29 Jeremiah the prophet sent a letter from Jerusalem to Babylon. It was for the Jewish elders still alive there. It was also for the priests and prophets in Babylon. And it was for all the other people Nebuchadnezzar had taken from Jerusalem to Babylon. ² It was sent to them after King Jehoiachin had been forced to leave Jerusalem. His mother and the court officials were taken with him. The leaders of Judah and Jerusalem had been forced to go to Babylon. All the skilled workers had also been forced to go. ³ Jeremiah gave the letter to Elasah and Gemariah. Elasah was the son of Shaphan. Gemariah was the son of Hilkiah. Zedekiah, the king of Judah, had sent Elasah and Gemariah to King Nebuchadnezzar in Babylon. Here is what the letter said.

⁴ The LORD who rules over all is the God of Israel. He speaks to all those he forced to go from Jerusalem to Babylon. He says, ⁵ "Build houses and make your homes there. Plant gardens and eat what they produce. ⁶ Get married. Have sons and daughters. Find wives for your sons.

Give your daughters to be married. Then they too can have sons and daughters. Let there be many more of you and not fewer. ⁷ Also work for the success of the city I have sent you to. Pray to the LORD for that city. If it succeeds, you too will enjoy success." ⁸ The LORD who rules over all is the God of Israel. He says, "Do not let the prophets trick you. Do not be fooled by those who claim to have secret knowledge. Do not listen to people who try to explain their dreams to you. ⁹ All of them are prophesying lies to you in my name. I have not sent them," announces the LORD.

¹⁰ The LORD says, "You will be forced to live in Babylon for 70 years. After they are over, I will come to you. My good promise to you will come true. I will bring you back home. ¹¹ I know the plans I have for you," announces the LORD. "I want you to enjoy success. I do not plan to harm you. I will give you hope for the years to come. ¹² Then you will call out to me. You will come and pray to me. And I will listen to you. ¹³ When you look for me with all your heart, you will find me. ¹⁴ I will be found by you," announces the LORD. "And I will bring you back from where you were taken as prisoners. I will gather

you from all the nations. I will gather you from the places where I have forced you to go," announces the LORD. "I will bring you back to the place I sent you away from."

¹⁵ You might say, "The LORD has given us prophets in Babylon." ¹⁶ But here is what the LORD says about the king who now sits on David's throne. He also says it about all the people who remain in this city. And he says it about all those who did not go with you to Babylon. ¹⁷ The LORD who rules over all says, "I will send war, hunger and plague against them. I will make them like bad figs. They are so bad they can't be eaten. ¹⁸ I will hunt them down with war, hunger and plague. I will make all the kingdoms on earth displeased with them. They will use their name in a curse. All the nations where I drive them will be shocked at them. They will make fun of them. And they will bring shame on them. ¹⁹ That's because they have not listened to my words," announces the LORD. "I sent messages to them again and again. I sent them through my servants the prophets. And you who were taken to Babylon have not listened either," announces the LORD.

²⁰ So listen to the LORD's message. Listen, all you whom he has sent away from Jerusalem to Babylon. ²¹ The LORD who rules over all is the God of Israel. He speaks about Ahab and Zedekiah. Ahab is the son of Kolaiah. Zedekiah is the son of Maaseiah. They are prophesying lies to you in my name. The LORD says about Ahab and Zedekiah, "I will hand them over to Nebuchadnezzar, the king of Babylon. He will put them to death. You will see it with your own eyes. ²² Because of what happens to them, people will use their names when they curse someone. All those who have been taken from Judah to Babylon will use their names in that way. They will say, 'May the LORD treat you like Zedekiah and Ahab. The king of Babylon burned them in the fire.' ²³ That will happen because they have done awful things in Israel. They have committed adultery with their neighbors' wives. They have spoken lies in my name. I did not give them the authority to speak those things. I know what they have done. And I am a witness to it," announces the LORD.

Shemaiah Opposes Jeremiah

²⁴ Tell Shemaiah, the Nehelamite, ²⁵ "The LORD who rules over all is the God of Israel. He

says, 'You sent letters in your own name to all the people in Jerusalem. You also sent them to Zephaniah the priest. He is the son of Maaseiah. And you sent them to all the other priests. You said to Zephaniah, 26 "The LORD has appointed you priest in place of Jehoiada. He has put you in charge of the LORD's house. You are supposed to arrest any crazy person who claims to be a prophet. You should put him in prison. You should put iron bands around his neck. 27 So why haven't you punished Jeremiah from Anathoth? He claims to be a prophet among you. 28 He has sent a message to us in Babylon. It says, 'You will be there a long time. So build houses and make your homes there. Plant gardens and eat what they produce.' " ' "

29 But Zephaniah the priest read the letter to me. 30 Then a message from the LORD came to me. The LORD said, 31 "Send a message to all the people who were taken away. Tell them, 'The LORD speaks about Shemaiah, the Nehelamite. He says, "Shemaiah has prophesied to you. But I did not send him. He has made you trust in lies. 32 So I say, 'I will certainly punish Shemaiah, the Nehelamite. I will also punish his children after him. He will not have any children left among these people. I will do good things for my people. But he will not see them,' " ' " announces the LORD. " ' " "That's because he has taught people to turn against me.' " ' "

Israel Will Return to the LORD

30 A message from the LORD came to Jeremiah. The LORD said, 2 "I am the LORD. I am the God of Israel. I say, 'Write in a book all the words I have spoken to you. 3 A new day is coming,' " announces the LORD. " 'At that time I will bring my people Israel and Judah back from where they have been taken as prisoners. I will bring them back to this land. I gave it to their people of long ago to have as their own,' " says the LORD.

4 Here are the words the LORD spoke about Israel and Judah. He said, 5 "I am the LORD. I say,

" 'Cries of fear are heard.
    There is terror. There isn't
      any peace.
6 Ask and see.
    Can a man give birth to
      children?
Then why do I see every
      strong man
    with his hands on his
      stomach?
Each of them is acting like a
      woman having a baby.
    Every face is as pale as
      death.
7 How awful that day will be!
    No other day will be
      like it.
It will be a time of trouble for
      the people of Jacob.
    But they will be saved out
      of it.
8 " 'At that time I will break the
      yoke off their necks,'
    announces the LORD who
      rules over all.

'I will tear off the ropes that
hold them.
People from other lands
will not make them
slaves anymore.
⁹ Instead, they will serve me.
And they will serve David
their king.
I will raise him up for them.
I am the LORD their God.

¹⁰ " 'People of Jacob, do not be
afraid.
You are my servant.
Israel, do not be terrified,' "
announces the LORD.
" 'You can be sure that I will
save you.
I will bring you out of a
place far away.
I will bring your children
back
from the land where they
were taken.
Your people will have peace
and security again.
And no one will make
them afraid.
¹¹ I am with you. I will save
you,' "
announces the LORD.
" 'I will completely destroy all
the nations
among which I scatter
you.
But I will not completely
destroy you.
I will correct you. But I will
be fair.
I will not let you go without
any punishment.' "

¹² The LORD says,

"Your wound can't be cured.
Your pain can't be healed.
¹³ No one will stand up for you.

There isn't any medicine
for your sore.
There isn't any healing for
you.
¹⁴ All those who were going to
help you have forgotten
you.
They do not care about you.
I have struck you as if I were
your enemy.
I have punished you as if I
were very mean.
That is because your guilt is
so great.
You have sinned so much.
¹⁵ Why do you cry out about
your wound?
Your pain can't be healed.
Your guilt is very great.
And you have committed
many sins.
That is why I have done all
these things to you.

¹⁶ "But everyone who destroys
you will be destroyed.
All your enemies will be
forced
to leave their countries.
Those who steal from you
will be stolen from.
I will take the belongings
of those who take things
from you.
¹⁷ But I will make you healthy
again.
I will heal your wounds,"
announces the LORD.
"That's because you have
been thrown out.
You are called Zion, the
one no one cares about."

¹⁸ The LORD says,

"I will bless Jacob's people
with great success again.

I will show tender love to
Israel.
Jerusalem will be rebuilt
where it was destroyed.
The palace will stand in its
proper place.
¹⁹ From those places the songs
of people giving thanks
will be heard.
The sound of great joy will
come from there.
I will cause there to be more
of my people.
There will not be fewer of
them.
I will bring them honor.
People will have respect for
them.
²⁰ Things will be as they used to
be for Jacob's people.
I will make their
community firm and
secure.
I will punish everyone who
treats them badly.
²¹ Their leader will be one of
their own people.
Their ruler will rise up
from among them.
I will bring him near.
And he will come close to
me.
He will commit himself to
serve me,"
announces the LORD.
²² "So you will be my people.
And I will be your God."

²³ A storm will burst out
because of the LORD's great
anger.
A strong wind will sweep
down
on the heads of evil people.
²⁴ The LORD's great anger won't
turn back.

He will accomplish
everything
his heart plans to do.
In days to come
you will understand this.

31

"At that time I will be the
God of all the families of
Israel," announces the LORD.
"And they will be my people."
² The LORD says,

"Some of my people will live
through
everything their enemies
do to them.
They will find help in the
desert.
I will come to give peace
and rest to Israel."

³ The LORD appeared to us in
the past. He said,

"I have loved you with a love
that lasts forever.
I have kept on loving you
with a kindness that
never fails.
⁴ I will build you up again.
Nation of Israel, you will be
rebuilt.
Once again you will use
your tambourines to
celebrate.
You will go out and dance
with joy.
⁵ Once again you will plant
vineyards
on the hills of Samaria.
Farmers will plant them.
They will enjoy their fruit.
⁶ There will be a day when
those on guard duty will
cry out.
They will stand on the hills
of Ephraim.
And they will shout,

'Come! Let's go up to Zion.
Let's go up to where the
LORD our God is.' "

⁷ The LORD says,

"Sing for joy because the
people of Jacob are
blessed.
Shout because the LORD
has made them the
greatest nation.
Make your praises heard.
Say, 'LORD, save your
people.
Save the people who are
left alive in Israel.'
⁸ I will bring them from the
land of the north.
I will gather them from one
end of the earth to the
other.
Even those who are blind and
those who can't walk
will be among them.
Pregnant women and women
having their babies
will be among them also.
Many of them will return.
⁹ Their eyes will be filled with
tears as they come.
They will pray as I bring
them back.
I will lead them beside
streams of water.
I will lead them on a level
path
where they will not trip or
fall.
I am Israel's father.
And Ephraim is my oldest
son.
¹⁰ "Listen to my message, you
nations.
Announce it on shores far
away.

Say, 'He who scattered Israel
will gather them.
He will watch over his
flock like a shepherd.'
¹¹ I will set the people of Jacob
free.
I will save them from those
who are stronger than
they are.
¹² They will come and shout for
joy on Mount Zion.
They will be joyful because
of everything I give
them.
I give them grain, olive oil
and fresh wine.
I give them the young
animals in their flocks
and herds.
Israel will be like a garden
that has plenty of
water.
And they will not be sad
anymore.
¹³ Then young women will
dance and be glad.
And so will the men, young
and old alike.
I will turn their mourning
into gladness.
I will comfort them.
And I will give them joy
instead of sorrow.
¹⁴ I will satisfy the priests. I will
give them more than
enough.
And my people will be
filled with the good
things I give them,"
announces the LORD.

¹⁵ The LORD says,

"A voice is heard in Ramah.
It is the sound of weeping
and deep sadness.

Rachel is weeping for her
children.
She refuses to be
comforted,
because they are gone."

¹⁶ The LORD says,
"Do not weep anymore.
Do not let tears fall from
your eyes.
I will reward you for your
work,"
announces the LORD.
"Your children will return
from the land of the
enemy.
¹⁷ So there is hope for your
children,"
announces the LORD.
"Your children will return
to their own land.

¹⁸ "I have heard the groans of
Ephraim's people. They
say,
'You corrected us like a calf
you were training.
And we have been trained.
Bring us back to you, and we
will come back.
You are the LORD our God.
¹⁹ After we wandered away
from you,
we turned away from our
sins.
After we learned our lesson,
we beat our chests in
sorrow.
We were full of shame.
What we did when we were
young brought dishonor
on us.'
²⁰ Aren't the people of Ephraim
my dear children?
Aren't they the children I
take delight in?

I often speak against them.
But I still remember them.
So my heart longs for them.
I love them with a tender
love,"
announces the LORD.
²¹ The LORD says, "Put up road
signs.
Set up stones to show the
way.
Look carefully for the
highway.
Look for the road you will
take.
Return, people of Israel.
Return to your towns.
²² How long will you wander,
my people Israel, who are
not faithful to me?
I will create a new thing on
earth.
The woman will return to
the man.'"

²³ The LORD who rules over all
is the God of Israel. He says, "I
will bring them back from the
place where they were taken.
Here is what the people in Judah and its towns will say once
again. 'May the LORD bless
you, you successful city. Sacred
mountain, may he bless you.'
²⁴ People will live together in Judah and all its towns. Farmers
and shepherds will live there.
²⁵ I will give rest to those who
are tired. I will satisfy those who
are weak."

²⁶ When I heard this, I woke
up and looked around. My sleep
had been pleasant to me.

²⁷ Here is what the LORD announces. "The days are coming
when I will plant the kingdoms

of Israel and Judah again. I will plant them with children and young animals. ²⁸ I watched over Israel and Judah to pull them up by the roots. I tore them down. I crushed them. I destroyed them. I brought horrible trouble on them. But now I will watch over them to build them up and plant them," announces the LORD. ²⁹ "In those days people will no longer say,

" 'The parents have eaten
    sour grapes.
But the children have
    a bitter taste in their
    mouths.'

³⁰ Instead, everyone will die for their own sin. The one who eats sour grapes will taste how bitter they are.

³¹ "The days are coming,"
    announces the LORD.
"I will make a new
    covenant
with the people of Israel.
    I will also make it with the
    people of Judah.
³² It will not be like the
    covenant
I made with their people of
    long ago.
That was when I took them
    by the hand.
I led them out of Egypt.
But they broke my covenant.
    They did it even though I
    was like a husband to
    them,"
    announces the LORD.
³³ "This is the covenant I will
    make with Israel
after that time," announces
    the LORD.

"I will put my law in their
    minds.
I will write it on their
    hearts.
I will be their God.
    And they will be my
    people.
³⁴ They will not need to teach
    their neighbor anymore.
And they will not need
    to teach one another
    anymore.
They will not need to say,
    'Know the LORD.'
That's because everyone will
    know me.
From the least important
    of them to the most
    important,
all of them will know me,"
    announces the LORD.
"I will forgive their evil ways.
I will not remember their
    sins anymore."

³⁵ The LORD speaks.

He makes the sun
    shine by day.
He orders the moon and stars
    to shine at night.
He stirs up the ocean.
    He makes its waves roar.
    His name is the LORD Who
    Rules Over All.
³⁶ "Suppose my orders for
    creation disappear from
    my sight,"
    announces the LORD.
"Only then will the people of
    Israel stop being
a nation in my sight."

³⁷ The LORD says,

"Suppose the sky above
    could be measured.

Suppose the foundations
of the earth below
could be completely
discovered.
Only then would I turn away
the people of Israel.
Even though they have
committed many sins,
I will still accept them,"
announces the LORD.

38 "The days are coming," announces the LORD. "At that time Jerusalem will be rebuilt for me. It will be rebuilt from the Tower of Hananel to the Corner Gate. 39 The measuring line will reach out from there. It will go straight to the hill of Gareb. Then it will turn and reach as far as Goah. 40 There is a valley where dead bodies and ashes are thrown. That whole valley will be holy to me. The side of the Kidron Valley east of the city will be holy to me. It will be holy all the way to the corner of the Horse Gate. The city will never again be pulled up by the roots. It will never be destroyed."

Jeremiah Buys a Field

32 A message from the LORD came to Jeremiah. It came in the 10th year that Zedekiah was king of Judah. It was in the 18th year of the rule of Nebuchadnezzar. 2 The armies of the king of Babylon were getting ready to attack Jerusalem. Jeremiah the prophet was being held as a prisoner. He was kept in the courtyard of the guard. It was part of Judah's royal palace. 3 Zedekiah, the king of Judah, had made Jeremiah a pris-

oner there. Zedekiah had said to him, "Why do you prophesy as you do? You say, 'The LORD says, "I am about to hand over this city to the king of Babylon. He will capture it. 4 Zedekiah, the king of Judah, will not escape from the powerful hands of the armies of Babylon. He will certainly be handed over to the king of Babylon. Zedekiah will speak with him face to face. He will see him with his own eyes. 5 Nebuchadnezzar will take Zedekiah to Babylon. Zedekiah will remain there until I deal with him," announces the LORD. "Suppose you fight against the armies of Babylon. If you do, you will not succeed." ' "

6 Jeremiah said, "A message from the LORD came to me. The LORD said, 7 'Hanamel is going to come to you. He is the son of your uncle Shallum. Hanamel will say, "Buy my field at Anathoth. You are my closest relative. So it's your right and duty to buy it." '

8 "Then my cousin Hanamel came to me. I was in the courtyard of the guard. It happened just as the LORD had said it would. Hanamel said, 'Buy my field at Anathoth. It is in the territory of Benjamin. It is your right to buy it and own it. So buy it for yourself.'

"I knew that this was the LORD's message. 9 So I bought the field at Anathoth from my cousin Hanamel. I weighed out seven ounces of silver for him. 10 I signed and sealed the deed of purchase. I had some people witness everything. And I weighed out the silver on the scales. ¹¹ There were two copies of the deed. One was sealed and the other wasn't. The deed included the terms and conditions of the sale. ¹² I gave Baruch the copies of the deed. My cousin Hanamel saw me do this. The witnesses who had signed the deed were there too. So were all the Jews who were sitting in the courtyard of the guard. Baruch was the son of Neriah. Neriah was the son of Mahseiah.

¹³ "I gave Baruch directions in front of all of them. I said, ¹⁴ 'The LORD who rules over all is the God of Israel. He says, "Take this deed of purchase. Take the sealed and unsealed copies. Put them in a clay jar. Then they will last a long time." ¹⁵ The LORD who rules over all is the God of Israel. He says, "Houses, fields and vineyards will again be bought in this land." '

¹⁶ "I gave the deed of purchase to Baruch, the son of Neriah. Then I prayed to the LORD. I said,

¹⁷ " 'LORD and King, you have reached out your great and powerful arm. You have made the heavens and the earth. Nothing is too hard for you. ¹⁸ You show your love to thousands of people. But you cause the sins of parents to affect even their children. Great and powerful God, your name is the LORD Who Rules Over All. ¹⁹ Your purposes are great. Your acts are mighty. Your eyes see everything people do. You reward each one of them in keeping with their conduct. You do this based on what they have done. ²⁰ You performed signs and wonders in Egypt. And you have continued to do them to this day. You have done them in Israel and among all people. You are still known for doing them. ²¹ You brought your people Israel out of Egypt. You did it with signs and wonders. You reached out your mighty hand and powerful arm. You did great and wonderful things. ²² You gave Israel this land that you promised to their people of long ago. It is a land that has plenty of milk and honey. ²³ Israel came in and took it over. But they did not obey you. They didn't follow your law. They didn't do what you commanded them to do. So you brought all this trouble on them.

²⁴ " 'See how ramps are built up against Jerusalem's walls to attack it. The city will be handed over to the armies of Babylon. They are attacking it. It will fall because of war, hunger and plague. What you said would happen is now happening, as you can see. ²⁵ LORD and King, the city will be handed over to the armies of Babylon. In spite of that, you tell me to buy a field. You say, "Pay for it

with silver. And have the sale witnessed."'"

26 Then a message from the LORD came to Jeremiah. The LORD said, 27 "I am the LORD. I am the God of all people. Is anything too hard for me?" 28 So the LORD says, "I am about to hand this city over to the armies of Babylon. I will give it to Nebuchadnezzar, the king of Babylon. He will capture it. 29 The armies of Babylon are now attacking this city. They will come in and set it on fire. They will burn it down. They will burn down the houses where the people made me very angry. They burned incense on their roofs to the god named Baal. And they poured out drink offerings to other gods.

30 "The people of Israel and Judah have done nothing but evil in my eyes. They have done it since the nation was young. In fact, they have done nothing but make me very angry. They have worshiped statues of gods their own hands have made," announces the LORD. 31 "This city has always stirred up my great anger. It has done it since the day it was built. Now I must remove it from my sight. 32 The people of Israel and Judah have made me very angry. They have done many evil things. They, their kings and officials have sinned. So have their priests and prophets. And the people of Judah and Jerusalem have also sinned. 33 They turned their backs to me. They would not face me. I taught them again and again. But they would not listen or pay attention when they were corrected. 34 They set up the hateful statues of their gods. They did it in the house where I have put my Name. They made my house 'unclean.' 35 The people built high places for Baal in the Valley of Ben Hinnom. That is where they sacrifice their children to Molek in the fire. That is something I did not command. It did not even enter my mind. They did something I hate. They made Judah sin."

36 Here is what you people of Judah are saying about this city. "By war, hunger and plague it will be handed over to the king of Babylon." But here is what the LORD, the God of Israel, says: 37 "You can be sure that I will gather my people again. I will send them away when my burning anger blazes out against them. But I will bring them back to this place. And I will let them live in safety. 38 They will be my people. And I will be their God. 39 I will give them a single purpose in life. Then, they will always have respect for me. Then all will go well for them. And it will also go well for their children after them. 40 I will make a covenant with them that will last forever. I promise that I will never stop doing good to them. I will cause them to respect me. Then they will never turn away from me again. 41 I will take pleasure in doing good things for them. I will certainly plant them in this land. I will do these

things with all my heart and soul."

⁴²The LORD says, "I have brought all this horrible trouble on these people. But now I will give them all the good things I have promised them. ⁴³Once more fields will be bought in this land. It is the land about which you now say, 'It is a dry and empty desert. It doesn't have any people or animals in it. It has been handed over to the armies of Babylon.' ⁴⁴Fields will be bought with silver. Deeds will be signed, sealed and witnessed. That will be done in the territory of Benjamin. It will be done in the villages around Jerusalem and in the towns of Judah. It will also be done in the towns of the central hill country. And it will be done in the towns of the western hills and the Negev Desert. I will bless their people with great success again," announces the LORD.

The LORD Promises to Heal His People

33 Jeremiah was still being held as a prisoner. He was kept in the courtyard of the guard. Then another message from the LORD came to him. The LORD said, ²"I made the earth. I formed it. And I set it in place. The LORD is my name. ³Call out to me. I will answer you. I will tell you great things you do not know. And unless I do, you wouldn't be able to find out about them." ⁴The LORD is the God of Israel. He speaks about the houses in Jerusalem.

He talks about the royal palaces of Judah. The people had torn down many of them. They had used their stones to strengthen the city walls against attack. ⁵That was during their fight with the armies of Babylon. The LORD says, "The houses will be filled with dead bodies. They will be the bodies of the people I will kill. I will kill them when I am very angry with them. I will hide my face from this city. That's because its people have committed so many sins.

⁶"But now I will bring health and healing to Jerusalem. I will heal my people. I will let them enjoy great peace and security. ⁷I will bring Judah and Israel back from the places where they have been taken. I will build up the nation again. It will be just as it was before. ⁸I will wash from its people all the sins they have committed against me. And I will forgive all the sins they committed when they turned away from me. ⁹Then this city will bring me fame, joy, praise and honor. All the nations on earth will hear about the good things I do for this city. They will see the great success and peace I give it. Then they will be filled with wonder. And they will tremble with fear."

¹⁰The LORD says, "You say about this place, 'It's a dry and empty desert. It doesn't have any people or animals in it.' The towns of Judah and the streets of Jerusalem are now deserted. So they do not have any people or animals living in them.

But happy sounds will be heard there once more. ¹¹ They will be the sounds of joy and gladness. The voices of brides and grooms will fill the streets. And the voices of those who bring thank offerings to my house will be heard there. They will say,

" 'Give thanks to the LORD
   who rules over all,
   because he is good.
His faithful love continues
   forever.'

That's because I will bless this land with great success again. It will be as it was before," says the LORD.

¹² The LORD who rules over all says, "This place is a desert. It does not have any people or animals in it. But there will again be grasslands near all its towns. Shepherds will rest their flocks there. ¹³ Flocks will again pass under the hands of shepherds as they count their sheep," says the LORD. "That will be done in the towns of the central hill country. It will be done in the western hills and the Negev Desert. It will be done in the territory of Benjamin. And it will be done in the villages around Jerusalem and in the towns of Judah.

¹⁴ "The days are coming," announces the LORD. "At that time I will fulfill my good promise to my people. I made it to the people of Israel and Judah.

¹⁵ "Here is what I will do in those
   days and at that time.
I will make a godly Branch
   grow from David's royal
   line.

He will do what is fair and
   right in the land.
¹⁶ In those days Judah will be
   saved.
Jerusalem will live in
   safety.
And it will be called
   The LORD Who Makes Us
   Right With Himself."

¹⁷ The LORD says, "David will always have a son to sit on the throne of Israel. ¹⁸ The priests, who are Levites, will always have a man to serve me. He will sacrifice burnt offerings. He will burn grain offerings. And he will offer sacrifices."

¹⁹ A message from the LORD came to Jeremiah. ²⁰ The LORD said, "Could you ever break my covenant with the day? Could you ever break my covenant with the night? Could you ever stop day and night from coming at their appointed times? ²¹ Only then could my covenant with my servant David be broken. Only then could my covenant with the Levites who serve me as priests be broken. Only then would David no longer have someone from his family line to rule on his throne. ²² Here is what I will do for my servant David. And here is what I will do for the Levites who serve me. I will make their children after them as many as the stars in the sky. And I will make them as many as the grains of sand on the seashore. It will be impossible to count them."

²³ A message from the LORD came to Jeremiah. The LORD said, ²⁴ "Haven't you noticed

what these people are saying? They say, 'The LORD once chose the two kingdoms of Israel and Judah. But now he has turned his back on them.' So they hate my people. They do not think of them as a nation anymore. ²⁵ I say, 'What if I had not made my covenant with day and night? What if I had not established the laws of heaven and earth? ²⁶ Only then would I turn my back on the children of Jacob and my servant David. Only then would I not choose one of David's sons to rule over the children of Abraham, Isaac and Jacob. But I will bless my people with great success again. I will love them with tender love.'"

Zedekiah Is Warned

34 Nebuchadnezzar, the king of Babylon, and all his armies were fighting against Jerusalem. They were also fighting against all the towns around it. All the kingdoms and nations Nebuchadnezzar ruled over were helping him. At that time a message from the LORD came to Jeremiah. The LORD said, ² "I am the LORD, the God of Israel. Go to Zedekiah, the king of Judah. Tell him, 'The LORD says, "I am about to hand this city over to the king of Babylon. He will burn it down. ³ You will not escape from his power. You will certainly be captured. You will be handed over to him. You will see the king of Babylon with your own eyes. He will speak with you face to face. And you will go to Babylon.

⁴ " ' "But listen to the LORD's promise to you, Zedekiah king of Judah. I say that you will not be killed by a sword. ⁵ You will die in a peaceful way. People made fires to honor the kings who died before you. In the same way, they will make a fire in your honor. They will mourn for you. They will say, 'My poor master!' I myself make this promise," announces the LORD.' "

⁶ Then Jeremiah the prophet told all this to King Zedekiah in Jerusalem. ⁷ At that time Nebuchadnezzar's armies were fighting against Jerusalem. They were also fighting against Lachish and Azekah. These two cities were still holding out. They were the only cities left in Judah that had high walls around them.

The People Set Their Slaves Free

⁸ A message from the LORD came to Jeremiah. King Zedekiah had made a covenant with all the people in Jerusalem. He had told them to set their Hebrew slaves free. ⁹ All of them had to do this. That applied to male and female slaves alike. No one was allowed to hold another Hebrew as a slave. ¹⁰ So all the officials and people entered into this covenant. They agreed to set their male and female slaves free. They agreed not to hold them as slaves anymore. Instead, they set them free. ¹¹ But later they changed their minds. They took back the people they had set free. They made them slaves again.

¹²Then a message from the LORD came to Jeremiah. ¹³The LORD is the God of Israel. He says, "I made a covenant with your people of long ago. I brought them out of Egypt. That is the land where they were slaves. I said, ¹⁴'Every seventh year you must set your people free. Each of you must set free all the Hebrews who have sold themselves to you. Let them serve you for six years. Then you must let them go free.' *(Deuteronomy 15:12)* But your people of long ago did not listen to me. They did not pay any attention to me. ¹⁵Recently you turned away from your sins. You did what is right in my eyes. Each of you set your Hebrew slaves free. You even made a covenant in front of me. You did it in the house where I have put my Name. ¹⁶But now you have turned around. You have treated my name as if it were not holy. Each of you has taken back your male and female slaves. You had set them free to go where they wished. But now you have forced them to become your slaves again."

¹⁷So the LORD says, "You have not obeyed me. You have not set your Hebrew slaves free. So now I will set you free," announces the LORD. "I will set you free to be destroyed by war, plague and hunger. I will make all the kingdoms on earth displeased with you. ¹⁸Those people who have broken my covenant will be punished. They have not lived up to the terms of the covenant they made in front of me.

When you made that covenant, you cut a calf in two. Then you walked between its pieces. Now I will cut you to pieces. ¹⁹That includes all of you who walked between the pieces of the calf. It includes the leaders of Judah and Jerusalem, the court officials and the priests. It also includes some of the people of the land. ²⁰So I will hand over all those people to their enemies who want to kill them. Their dead bodies will become food for the birds and the wild animals.

²¹"I will hand over King Zedekiah and his officials to their enemies. I will hand them over to those who want to kill them. I will hand them over to the armies of the king of Babylon. They have now pulled back from you. ²²But I am going to give an order," announces the LORD. "I will bring them back to this city. They will fight against it. They will capture it and burn it down. And I will completely destroy the towns of Judah. No one will be able to live there."

The Family Line of Rekab

35 A message from the LORD came to Jeremiah. It came during the time Jehoiakim was king over Judah. Jehoiakim was the son of Josiah. The message said, ²"Go to the members of the family line of Rekab. Invite them to come to one of the side rooms in my house. Then give them wine to drink." ³So I went to get Jaazaniah. He was the son of Jeremiah.

Jeremiah was the son of Habazziniah. I also went to get Jaazaniah's brothers and all his sons. That included all the members of the family line of Rekab. ⁴I brought them into the LORD's house. I took them into the room of the sons of Hanan. He was the son of Igdaliah. He was also a man of God. His room was next to the room of the officials. Their room was above the room of Maaseiah. He was the son of Shallum. He also was one of those who guarded the temple doors. ⁵Then I got bowls full of wine and some cups. I set them down in front of the men from the family line of Rekab. I said to them, "Drink some wine."

⁶But they replied, "We don't drink wine. That's because Jehonadab gave us a command. He was the son of Rekab. He was also one of our own people from long ago. He commanded, 'You and your children after you must never drink wine. ⁷Also you must never build houses. You must never plant crops or vineyards. You must never have any of these things. Instead, you must always live in tents. Then you will live a long time in the land where you are wandering around.' ⁸We have done everything Jehonadab, the son of Rekab, commanded us to do. So we and our wives and our children have never drunk wine. ⁹We have never built houses to live in. We've never had vineyards, fields or crops. ¹⁰We've always lived in tents. We've completely obeyed everything Jehonadab commanded our people of long ago. ¹¹But Nebuchadnezzar, the king of Babylon, marched into this land. Then we said, 'Come. We must go to Jerusalem. There we can escape the armies of Babylon and Aram.' So we have remained in Jerusalem."

¹²Then a message from the LORD came to Jeremiah. It said, ¹³"The LORD who rules over all is the God of Israel. He says, 'Go. Speak to the people of Judah and Jerusalem. Tell them, "Won't you ever learn a lesson? Won't you ever obey my words?" announces the LORD. ¹⁴"Jehonadab, the son of Rekab, ordered his children not to drink wine. And they have kept his command. To this day they do not drink wine. They obey the command Jehonadab gave their people long ago. But I have spoken to you again and again. In spite of that, you have not obeyed me. ¹⁵Again and again I sent all my servants the prophets to you. They said, 'Each of you must turn from your evil ways. You must change the way you act. Do not worship other gods. Do not serve them. Then you will live in the land. I gave it to you and your people of long ago.' But you have not paid any attention. You have not listened to me. ¹⁶The children of Jehonadab, the son of Rekab, have obeyed the command Jehonadab gave them long ago. But the people of Judah have not obeyed me." '"

¹⁷So the LORD God who rules

over all speaks. The God of Israel says, "Listen! I am going to bring horrible trouble on Judah. I will also bring it on everyone who lives in Jerusalem. I will bring on them every trouble I said I would. I spoke to them. But they did not listen. I called out to them. But they did not answer."

18 Then Jeremiah spoke to the members of the family line of Rekab. Jeremiah said, "The LORD who rules over all is the God of Israel. He says, 'You have obeyed the command Jehonadab gave your people of long ago. You have followed all his directions. You have done everything he ordered.' 19 So the LORD who rules over all speaks. The God of Israel says, 'Jehonadab, the son of Rekab, will always have someone from his family line to serve me.'"

Jehoiakim Burns Up Jeremiah's Scroll

36 A message from the LORD came to Jeremiah. It came in the fourth year that Jehoiakim was king of Judah. He was the son of Josiah. The message said, 2 "Get a scroll. Write on it all the words I have spoken to you. Write down what I have said about Israel, Judah and all the other nations. Write what I have said to you from the time of King Josiah until now. 3 The people of Judah will hear about all the trouble I plan to bring on them. Maybe then each of them will turn from their evil ways. If they do, I will forgive their sins

and the evil things they have done."

4 So Jeremiah sent for Baruch, the son of Neriah. Jeremiah told him to write down all the words the LORD had spoken to him. And Baruch wrote them on the scroll. 5 Then Jeremiah said to him, "I'm not allowed to go to the LORD's temple. 6 So you go there. Go on a day when the people are fasting. Read to them from the scroll. Read the words of the LORD you wrote down as I gave them to you. Read them to all the people of Judah who come in from their towns. 7 They will hear what the LORD will do to them when his burning anger blazes out against them. Then perhaps they will pray to him. And maybe each of them will turn from their evil ways."

8 Baruch, the son of Neriah, did everything Jeremiah the prophet told him to do. He went to the LORD's temple. There he read the words of the LORD from the scroll. 9 It was in the fifth year that Jehoiakim, the son of Josiah, was king of Judah. It was the ninth month of that year. A time of fasting at the LORD's temple had been ordered. All the people in Jerusalem were told to take part in it. So were those who had come in from the towns of Judah. 10 Baruch read to all the people who were at the LORD's temple. He read Jeremiah's words from the scroll. He was in the room of Gemariah the secretary. It was located in the upper courtyard at the entrance of the New Gate of the

temple. Gemariah was the son of Shaphan.

¹¹ Micaiah was the son of Gemariah, the son of Shaphan. Micaiah heard Baruch reading all the LORD's words that were written on the scroll. ¹² Then he went down to the secretary's room in the royal palace. All the officials were sitting there. They included the secretary Elishama and Delaiah, the son of Shemaiah. Elnathan, the son of Akbor, was also there. So was Gemariah, the son of Shaphan. Zedekiah, the son of Hananiah, was there too. And so were all the other officials. ¹³ Micaiah told all of them what he had heard. He told them everything Baruch had read to the people from the scroll. ¹⁴ All the officials sent Jehudi to speak to Baruch, the son of Neriah. Jehudi was the son of Nethaniah. Nethaniah was the son of Shelemiah. Shelemiah was the son of Cushi. Jehudi said to Baruch, "Come. Bring the scroll you have read to the people." So Baruch went to them. He carried the scroll with him. ¹⁵ The officials said to him, "Please sit down. Read the scroll to us."

So Baruch read it to them. ¹⁶ They heard all its words. Then they looked at one another in fear. They said to Baruch, "We must report all these words to the king." ¹⁷ They said to Baruch, "Tell us. How did you happen to write all these things? Did Jeremiah tell you to do this?"

¹⁸ "Yes," Baruch replied. "He told me to write down all these words. So I wrote them in ink on the scroll."

¹⁹ Then the officials spoke to Baruch. They said, "You and Jeremiah must go and hide. Don't let anyone know where you are."

²⁰ The officials put the scroll in the room of Elishama the secretary. Then they went to the king in the courtyard. They reported everything to him. ²¹ The king sent Jehudi to get the scroll. Jehudi brought it from the room of Elishama the secretary. Jehudi read it to the king. All the officials were standing beside the king. So they heard it too. ²² It was the ninth month. The king was sitting in his winter apartment. A fire was burning in the fire pot in front of him. ²³ Jehudi read three or four sections from the scroll. Then the king cut them off with a secretary's knife. He threw them into the fire pot. He did that until the entire scroll was burned up in the fire. ²⁴ The king and some of his attendants heard all these words. But they weren't afraid. They didn't tear their clothes. ²⁵ Elnathan, Delaiah and Gemariah begged the king not to burn the scroll. But he wouldn't listen to them. ²⁶ Instead, the king commanded three men to arrest Baruch the secretary and Jeremiah the prophet. But the LORD had hidden them. The three men were Jerahmeel, Seraiah and Shelemiah. Jerahmeel was a member of the royal court. Seraiah was the son of Azriel. And Shelemiah was the son of Abdeel.

²⁷ A message from the LORD came to Jeremiah. It came after the king burned the scroll. On the scroll were the words Baruch had written down. Jeremiah had told him to write them. The message said, ²⁸ "Get another scroll. Write on it all the words that were on the first one. King Jehoiakim burned that one up. ²⁹ Also tell King Jehoiakim, 'The LORD says, "You burned that scroll. You said to Baruch, 'Why did you write that the king of Babylon would certainly come? Why did you write that he would destroy this land? And why did you write that he would remove from it people and animals alike?' " ³⁰ So now the LORD has something to say about Jehoiakim, the king of Judah. He says, "No one from Jehoiakim's family line will sit on David's throne. Jehoiakim's body will be thrown out. It will lie outside in the heat by day and in the frost at night. ³¹ I will punish him and his children and his attendants. I will punish them for their sinful ways. I will bring on them all the trouble I said I would. And I will bring it on the people of Jerusalem and Judah. They have not listened to me." ' "

³² So Jeremiah got another scroll. He gave it to Baruch the secretary. He was the son of Neriah. Jeremiah told Baruch what to write on it. Baruch wrote down all the words that were on the scroll King Jehoiakim had burned up in the fire. And many more words were written on it. They were similar to those that had already been written.

Jeremiah Is Put in Prison

37 Nebuchadnezzar, the king of Babylon, appointed Zedekiah to be king of Judah. He was the son of Josiah. Zedekiah ruled in place of Jehoiachin, the son of Jehoiakim. ² Zedekiah and his attendants didn't pay any attention to what the LORD had said through Jeremiah the prophet. And the people of the land didn't pay any attention either.

³ But King Zedekiah sent Jehukal to Jeremiah the prophet. Zedekiah sent Zephaniah the priest along with him. Jehukal was the son of Shelemiah. Zephaniah was the son of Maaseiah. Jehukal and Zephaniah brought the king's message to Jeremiah. It said, "Please pray to the LORD our God for us."

⁴ At that time Jeremiah was free to come and go among the people. Jeremiah had not yet been put in prison. ⁵ The armies of Babylon were attacking Jerusalem. They received a report that Pharaoh's army had marched out of Egypt to help Zedekiah. So armies of Babylon pulled back from Jerusalem.

⁶ A message from the LORD came to Jeremiah. ⁷ The LORD is the God of Israel. He says, "The king of Judah has sent you to ask me for advice. Tell him, 'Pharaoh's army has marched out to help you. But it will go back to its own land. It will return to Egypt. ⁸ Then the armies of Bab-

ylon will come back here. They will attack this city. They will capture it. Then they will burn it down.'

9 "The LORD says, 'Do not fool yourselves. You think, "The Babylonians will leave us alone." But they will not! 10 Suppose you destroy all the armies of Babylon that are attacking you. Suppose only wounded men are left in their tents. Even then they will come out and burn down this city.'"

11 The armies of Babylon had pulled back from Jerusalem because of Pharaoh's army. 12 So Jeremiah started to leave the city. He was planning to go to the territory of Benjamin. Jeremiah wanted to get his share of the property among the people there. 13 He got as far as the Benjamin Gate. But the captain of the guard arrested him. He said, "You are going over to the side of the Babylonians!" The captain's name was Irijah, the son of Shelemiah. Shelemiah was the son of Hananiah.

14 Jeremiah said to Irijah, "That isn't true! I'm not going to the side of the Babylonians." But Irijah wouldn't listen to him. Instead, he arrested Jeremiah. He brought Jeremiah to the officials. 15 They were angry with him. So they had him beaten. Then they took him to the house of Jonathan the secretary. It had been made into a prison. That's where they put Jeremiah.

16 Jeremiah was put into a prison cell below ground level. He remained there a long time.

17 Then King Zedekiah sent for him. King Zedekiah had Jeremiah brought to the palace. There the king spoke to him in private. The king asked, "Do you have a message from the LORD for me?"

"Yes," Jeremiah replied. "You will be handed over to the king of Babylon."

18 Then Jeremiah continued, "Why have you put me in prison? What crime have I committed against you? What have I done to your attendants or these people? 19 Where are your prophets who prophesied to you? They said, 'The king of Babylon won't attack you. He won't march into this land.' 20 But now please listen, my king and master. Let me make my appeal to you. Please don't send me back to the house of Jonathan the secretary. If you do, I'll die there."

21 Then King Zedekiah gave the order. His men put Jeremiah in the courtyard of the guard. They gave him a loaf of bread from the street of the bakers. They did it every day until all the bread in the city was gone. So Jeremiah remained in the courtyard of the guard.

Jeremiah Is Thrown Into an Empty Well

38 Shephatiah, Gedaliah, Jehukal and Pashhur heard what Jeremiah was telling all the people. Shephatiah was the son of Mattan. Gedaliah was the son of Pashhur. Jehukal was the son of Shelemiah. And Pashhur was the son of

Malkijah. These four men heard Jeremiah say, ² "The LORD says, 'Those who stay in this city will die of war, hunger or plague. But those who go over to the side of the Babylonians will live. They will escape with their lives. They will remain alive.' ³ The LORD also says, 'This city will certainly be handed over to the armies of the king of Babylon. They will capture it.' "

⁴ Then these officials said to the king, "This man should be put to death. What he says is making the soldiers who are left in this city lose hope. It's making all the people lose hope too. He isn't interested in what is best for the people. In fact, he's trying to destroy them."

⁵ "He's in your hands," King Zedekiah answered. "I can't do anything to oppose you."

⁶ So they took Jeremiah and put him into an empty well. It belonged to Malkijah. He was a member of the royal court. His well was in the courtyard of the guard. Zedekiah's men lowered Jeremiah by ropes into the well. It didn't have any water in it. All it had was mud. And Jeremiah sank down into the mud.

⁷ Ebed-Melek was an official in the royal palace. He was from the land of Cush. He heard that Jeremiah had been put into the well. The king was sitting by the Benjamin Gate at that time. ⁸ Ebed-Melek went out of the palace. He said to the king, ⁹ "My king and master, everything these men have done to Jeremiah the prophet is evil. They have thrown him into an empty well. Soon there won't be any more bread in the city. Then he'll starve to death."

¹⁰ So the king gave an order to Ebed-Melek the Cushite. He said, "Take with you 30 men from here. Lift Jeremiah the prophet out of the well before he dies."

¹¹ Then Ebed-Melek took the men with him. He went to a room in the palace. It was under the place where the treasures were stored. He got some old rags and worn-out clothes from there. Then he let them down with ropes to Jeremiah in the well. ¹² Ebed-Melek the Cushite told Jeremiah what to do. Ebed-Melek said, "Put these old rags and worn-out clothes under your arms. They'll pad the ropes." So Jeremiah did. ¹³ Then the men pulled him up with the ropes. They lifted him out of the well. And Jeremiah remained in the courtyard of the guard.

Zedekiah Questions Jeremiah Again

¹⁴ Then King Zedekiah sent for Jeremiah the prophet. The king had him brought to the third entrance to the LORD's temple. "I want to ask you something," the king said to Jeremiah. "Don't hide anything from me."

¹⁵ Jeremiah said to Zedekiah, "Suppose I give you an answer. You will kill me, won't you? Suppose I give you good advice. You won't listen to me, will you?"

¹⁶ But King Zedekiah promised Jeremiah secretly, "I won't

kill you. And I won't hand you over to those who want to kill you. That's just as sure as the LORD is alive. He's the one who has given us breath."

[17] So Jeremiah said to Zedekiah, "The LORD God who rules over all is the God of Israel. He says, 'Give yourself up to the officers of the king of Babylon. Then your life will be spared. And this city will not be burned down. You and your family will remain alive. [18] But what if you do not give yourself up to them? Then this city will be handed over to the Babylonians. They will burn it down. And you yourself will not escape from them.' "

[19] King Zedekiah said to Jeremiah, "I'm afraid of some of the Jews. They are the ones who have gone over to the side of the Babylonians. The Babylonians might hand me over to them. And those Jews will treat me badly."

[20] "They won't hand you over to them," Jeremiah replied. "Obey the LORD. Do what I tell you to do. Then things will go well with you. Your life will be spared. [21] Don't refuse to give yourself up. The LORD has shown me what will happen if you do. [22] All the women who are left in your palace will be brought out. They'll be given to the officials of the king of Babylon. Those women will say to you,

" 'Your trusted friends have
    tricked you.
They have gotten the best
    of you.

Your feet are sunk down in
    the mud.
Your friends have deserted
    you.'

[23] "All your wives and children will be brought out to the Babylonians. You yourself won't escape from them. You will be captured by the king of Babylon. And this city will be burned down."

[24] Then Zedekiah said to Jeremiah, "Don't let anyone know about the talk we've had. If you do, you might die. [25] Suppose the officials find out that I've talked with you. And suppose they come to you and say, 'Tell us what you said to the king. Tell us what the king said to you. Don't hide it from us. If you do, we'll kill you.' [26] Then tell them, 'I was begging the king not to send me back to Jonathan's house. I don't want to die there.' "

[27] All the officials came to Jeremiah. And they questioned him. He told them everything the king had ordered him to say. None of them had heard what he told the king. So they didn't say anything else to him.

[28] Jeremiah remained in the courtyard of the guard. He stayed there until the day Jerusalem was captured.

Jerusalem Is Destroyed

39 Here is how Jerusalem was captured. [1] Nebuchadnezzar, the king of Babylon, marched out against Jerusalem. He came with all his armies and attacked it. It was in the ninth year that Zedekiah was king of Judah. It was in the tenth month. ² The city wall was broken through. It happened on the ninth day of the fourth month. It was in the 11th year of Zedekiah's rule. ³ All the officials of the king of Babylon came. They took seats near the Middle Gate. Nergal-Sharezer from Samgar was there. Nebo-Sarsekim, a chief officer, was also there. So was Nergal-Sharezer, a high official. And all the other officials of the king of Babylon were there too. ⁴ King Zedekiah and all the soldiers saw them. Then they ran away. They left the city at night. They went by way of the king's garden. They went out through the gate between the two walls. And they headed toward the Arabah Valley.

⁵ But the armies of Babylon chased them. They caught up with Zedekiah in the plains near Jericho. They captured him there. And they took him to Nebuchadnezzar, the king of Babylon. He was at Riblah in the land of Hamath. That's where Nebuchadnezzar decided how Zedekiah would be punished. ⁶ The king of Babylon killed the sons of Zedekiah at Riblah. He forced Zedekiah to watch it with his own eyes. He also killed all the nobles of Judah. ⁷ Then he poked out Zedekiah's eyes. He put him in bronze chains. And he took him to Babylon.

⁸ The Babylonians set the royal palace on fire. They also set fire to the houses of the people. And they broke down the walls of Jerusalem. ⁹ Nebuzaradan was commander of the royal guard. Some people still remained in the city. But he took them away to Babylon as prisoners. He also took along those who had gone over to his side. And he took the rest of the people. ¹⁰ Nebuzaradan, the commander of the guard, left some of the poor people of Judah behind. They didn't own anything. So at that time he gave them vineyards and fields.

¹¹ Nebuchadnezzar, the king of Babylon, had given orders about Jeremiah. He had given them to Nebuzaradan, the commander of the royal guard. Nebuchadnezzar had said, ¹² "Take him. Look after him. Don't harm him. Do for him anything he asks." ¹³ So that's what Nebuzaradan, the commander of the guard, did. Nebushazban and Nergal-Sharezer were with him. So were all the other officers of the king of Babylon. Nebushazban was a chief officer. Nergal-Sharezer was a high official. All these men ¹⁴ sent for Jeremiah. They had him taken out of the courtyard of the guard. They turned him over to Gedaliah. Gedaliah was the son of Ahikam, the son of Shaphan. They told Gedaliah to take Jeremiah back to his home. So Jeremiah remained among his own people.

¹⁵ A message from the LORD came to Jeremiah. It came while he was being kept in the courtyard of the guard. The LORD said, ¹⁶ "Go. Speak to

Ebed-Melek the Cushite. Tell him, 'The LORD who rules over all is the God of Israel. He says, "I am about to make the words I spoke against this city come true. I will not give success to it. Instead, I will bring horrible trouble on it. At that time my words will come true. You will see it with your own eyes. ¹⁷ But I will save you on that day," announces the LORD. "You will not be handed over to those you are afraid of. ¹⁸ I will save you. You will not be killed by a sword. Instead, you will escape with your life. That's because you trust in me," announces the LORD.' "

Jeremiah Is Set Free From His Chains

40 A message from the LORD came to Jeremiah. It came after Nebuzaradan, the commander of the royal guard, had set him free at Ramah. Jeremiah was being held by chains when Nebuzaradan found him. Jeremiah was among all the prisoners from Jerusalem and Judah. They were being taken to Babylon. ² But the commander of the guard found Jeremiah. The commander said to him, "The LORD your God ordered that this place be destroyed. ³ And now he has brought it about. He has done exactly what he said he would do. All these things have happened because you people sinned against the LORD. You didn't obey him. ⁴ But today I'm setting you free from the chains on your wrists. Come with me to Babylon if you want to. I'll take good care of you there. But if you don't want to come, then don't. The whole country lies in front of you. Go anywhere you want to." ⁵ But before Jeremiah turned to go, Nebuzaradan continued, "Go back to Gedaliah, the son of Ahikam. The king of Babylon has appointed Gedaliah to be over the towns of Judah. Go and live with him among your people. Or go anywhere else you want to." Ahikam was the son of Shaphan.

The commander gave Jeremiah food and water. He also gave him a gift. Then he let Jeremiah go. ⁶ So Jeremiah went to Mizpah to see Gedaliah, the son of Ahikam. Jeremiah stayed with him. Jeremiah lived among the people who were left behind in the land.

Gedaliah Is Murdered

⁷ Some of Judah's army officers and their men were still in the open country. They heard that the king of Babylon had appointed Gedaliah as governor over Judah. Gedaliah was the son of Ahikam. The king had put Gedaliah in charge of the men, women and children who were still there. They were the poorest people in the land. They hadn't been taken to Babylon. ⁸ When the army officers and their men heard these things, they came to Gedaliah at Mizpah. Ishmael, the son of Nethaniah, came. So did Johanan and Jonathan, the sons of Kareah. Seraiah, the son of Tanhumeth,

also came. The sons of Ephai from Netophah came too. And so did Jaazaniah, the son of the Maakathite. All their men came with them. ⁹ Gedaliah, the son of Ahikam, the son of Shaphan, made a promise. He made the promise to give hope to all these men. He spoke in a kind way to them. He said, "Don't be afraid to serve the Babylonians. Make your homes in the land of Judah. Serve the king of Babylon. Then things will go well with you. ¹⁰ I myself will stay at Mizpah. I'll speak for you to the officials of Babylon who come to us. But you must harvest the wine, summer fruit and olive oil. Put them in your jars. Store them up. And live in the towns you have taken over."

¹¹ All the Jews in Moab, Ammon and Edom heard what had happened. So did the Jews in all the other countries. They heard that the king of Babylon had left some people behind in Judah. They also heard that he had appointed Gedaliah, the son of Ahikam, as governor over them. Ahikam was the son of Shaphan. ¹² When they heard these things, all of them came back to the land of Judah. They went to Gedaliah at Mizpah. They came from all the countries where they had been scattered. And they harvested a large amount of wine and summer fruit.

¹³ Johanan and all the other army officers still in the open country came to Gedaliah at Mizpah. Johanan was the son of Kareah. ¹⁴ The officers spoke to Gedaliah. They said, "Don't you know that Baalis has sent someone to take your life? Baalis is the king of Ammon. He has sent Ishmael, the son of Nethaniah." But Gedaliah, the son of Ahikam, didn't believe them.

¹⁵ Then Johanan, the son of Kareah, spoke in private to Gedaliah in Mizpah. He said, "Let me go and kill Ishmael, the son of Nethaniah. No one will know about it. Why should he take your life? Why should he cause all the Jews gathered around you to be scattered? Why should he cause the people who remain in Judah to die?"

¹⁶ But Gedaliah, the son of Ahikam, spoke to Johanan, the son of Kareah. He said, "Don't do an awful thing like that! What you are saying about Ishmael isn't true."

41 In the seventh month Ishmael came with ten men to Gedaliah, the son of Ahikam, at Mizpah. Ishmael was the son of Nethaniah. Nethaniah was the son of Elishama. Ishmael was a member of the royal family. He had been one of the king's officers. Ishmael and his ten men were eating together at Mizpah. ² They got up and struck down Gedaliah, the son of Ahikam, with their swords. They killed him even though the king of Babylon had appointed him as governor over Judah. Ahikam was the son of Shaphan. ³ Ishmael also killed all the men of Judah who were with Gedaliah at Mizpah. And

he killed the Babylonian soldiers who were there.

⁴ On the next day, people still hadn't found out that Gedaliah had been murdered. ⁵ On that day 80 men came from Shechem, Shiloh and Samaria. They had shaved off their beards. They had torn their clothes. And they had cut themselves. They brought grain offerings and incense with them. They took them to the LORD's house. ⁶ Ishmael, the son of Nethaniah, went out from Mizpah to meet them. He was weeping as he went. When he met them, he said, "Come to Gedaliah, the son of Ahikam." ⁷ They went with him into the city. Then Ishmael, the son of Nethaniah, and the men who were with him killed them. And they threw them into an empty well. ⁸ But ten of the men had spoken to Ishmael. They had said, "Don't kill us! We have some wheat and barley. We also have olive oil and honey. We've hidden all of it in a field." So he didn't kill them along with the others. ⁹ But he had thrown into the empty well all the bodies of the men he had killed. That included Gedaliah's body. The well was the one King Asa had made. He had made it when he strengthened Mizpah against attack by Baasha, the king of Israel. Ishmael, the son of Nethaniah, filled it with the bodies of those he had killed.

¹⁰ Nebuzaradan was the commander of the royal guard. He had appointed Gedaliah son of Ahikam over all the people at Mizpah. But Ishmael made prisoners of the people left at Mizpah. These prisoners included women who were members of the royal court. The prisoners also included everyone else left at Mizpah. Then Ishmael started out to go across the Jordan River to the land of Ammon.

¹¹ Johanan, the son of Kareah, was told what had happened. And so were all the other army officers with him. They heard about all the crimes Ishmael, the son of Nethaniah, had committed. ¹² So they brought all their men together. Then they went to fight against Ishmael, the son of Nethaniah. They caught up with him near the large pool in Gibeon. ¹³ Ishmael had many people with him. They saw Johanan, the son of Kareah. And they saw the other army officers who were with him. So the people who had been forced to go with Ishmael were glad. ¹⁴ Ishmael had taken those people from Mizpah as prisoners. But now they turned and went over to the side of Johanan, the son of Kareah. ¹⁵ But Ishmael, the son of Nethaniah, and eight of his men escaped from Johanan. They ran away to the land of Ammon.

Some Jews Take Jeremiah to Egypt

¹⁶ Then Johanan, the son of Kareah, led away all the people of Mizpah who were still alive. All the other army officers with Johanan helped him do this. He had taken them away from

Ishmael, the son of Nethaniah. That happened after Ishmael had murdered Gedaliah, the son of Ahikam. The people Johanan had taken away included soldiers, women, children and court officials. He had brought them from Gibeon. ¹⁷ They went on their way. They stopped at Geruth Kimham near Bethlehem. They were going to Egypt. ¹⁸ They wanted to get away from the Babylonians. They were afraid of them. That's because Ishmael, the son of Nethaniah, had killed Gedaliah, the son of Ahikam. The king of Babylon had appointed Gedaliah as governor over Judah.

42 Then all the army officers approached Jeremiah. They included Johanan, the son of Kareah, and Jezaniah, the son of Hoshaiah. All the people from the least important of them to the most important also came. ² All of them said to Jeremiah the prophet, "Please listen to our appeal. Pray to the LORD your God. Pray for all of us who are left here. Once there were many of us. But as you can see, only a few of us are left now. ³ So pray to the LORD your God. Pray that he'll tell us where we should go. Pray that he'll tell us what we should do."

⁴ "I've heard you," Jeremiah the prophet replied. "I'll certainly pray to the LORD your God. I'll do what you have asked me to do. In fact, I'll tell you everything the LORD says. I won't keep anything back from you."

⁵ Then they said to Jeremiah, "We'll do everything the LORD your God sends you to tell us to do. If we don't, may he be a true and faithful witness against us. ⁶ It doesn't matter whether what you say is in our favor or not. We're asking you to pray to the LORD our God. And we'll obey him. Things will go well with us. That's because we will obey the LORD our God."

⁷ Ten days later a message came to Jeremiah from the LORD. ⁸ So Jeremiah sent for Johanan, the son of Kareah, and all the other army officers with him. Jeremiah also gathered together all the people from the least important of them to the most important. ⁹ He said to all of them, "The LORD is the God of Israel. You asked me to present your appeal to him. He told me, ¹⁰ 'Stay in this land. Then I will build you up. I will not tear you down. I will plant you. I will not pull you up by the roots. I have decided to stop bringing trouble on you. ¹¹ Do not be afraid of the king of Babylon. You are afraid of him now. Do not be,' announces the LORD. 'I am with you. I will keep you safe. I will save you from his power. ¹² I will show you my loving concern. Then he will have concern for you. And he will let you return to your land.'

¹³ "But suppose you say, 'We won't stay in this land.' If you do, you will be disobeying the LORD your God. ¹⁴ And suppose you say, 'No! We'll go and live in Egypt. There we won't have to face war anymore. We won't

hear the trumpets of war. And we won't get hungry.' ¹⁵ Then listen to what the LORD says to you who are left in Judah. He is the LORD who rules over all. He is the God of Israel. He says, 'Have you already made up your minds to go to Egypt? Are you going to make your homes there? ¹⁶ Then the war you fear will catch up with you there. The hunger you are afraid of will follow you into Egypt. And you will die there. ¹⁷ In fact, that will happen to all those who go and make there homes in Egypt. All of them will die of war, hunger and plague. Not one of them will live. None of them will escape the trouble I will bring on them.' ¹⁸ He is the LORD who rules over all. He is the God of Israel. He says, 'My great anger has been poured out on those who used to live in Jerusalem. In the same way, it will be poured out on you when you go to Egypt. People will use your name in a curse. They will be shocked at you. They will say bad things about you. And they will say you are shameful. You will never see this place again.'

¹⁹ "The LORD has spoken to you who are left in Judah. He has said, 'Do not go to Egypt.' Here is something you can be sure of. I am warning you about it today. ²⁰ You made a big mistake when you asked me to pray to the LORD your God. You said, 'Pray to the LORD our God for us. Tell us everything he says. We'll do it.' ²¹ I have told you today what the LORD your God wants you to do. But you still haven't obeyed him. You haven't done anything he sent me to tell you to do. ²² So here is something else you can be sure of. You will die of war, hunger and plague. You want to go and make your homes in Egypt. But you will die there."

43 Jeremiah finished telling the people everything the LORD their God had said. Jeremiah told them everything the LORD had sent him to tell them. ² After that, Azariah, the son of Hoshaiah, and Johanan, the son of Kareah, spoke to Jeremiah. And all the proud men joined them. They said, "You are lying! The LORD our God hasn't sent you to speak to us. He hasn't told you to say, 'You must not go to Egypt and make your homes there.' ³ But Baruch, the son of Neriah, is turning you against us. He wants us to be handed over to the Babylonians. Then they can kill us. Or they can take us away to Babylon."

⁴ So Johanan, the son of Kareah, disobeyed the LORD's command. So did all the other army officers and all the people. They didn't stay in the land of Judah. ⁵ Instead Johanan, the son of Kareah, and all the other army officers led away all the people who were left in Judah. Those people had returned to Judah from all the nations where they had been scattered. ⁶ Johanan and the other officers also led away many people Nebuzaradan had left at Mizpah. They included men, women and children. They also included

the king's daughters. Nebuzaradan had left them with Gedaliah, the son of Ahikam. They also took Jeremiah the prophet and Baruch son of Neriah along with them. Nebuzaradan was commander of the royal guard. Ahikam was the son of Shaphan. ⁷ So the Jewish leaders disobeyed the LORD. They took everyone to Egypt. They went all the way to Tahpanhes.

⁸ In Tahpanhes a message from the LORD came to Jeremiah. The LORD said, ⁹ "Make sure the Jews are watching you. Then get some large stones. Go to the entrance to Pharaoh's house in Tahpanhes. Bury the stones in the clay under the brick walkway there. ¹⁰ Then tell the Jews, 'The LORD who rules over all is the God of Israel. He says, "I will send for my servant Nebuchadnezzar, the king of Babylon. And I will set his throne over these stones that are buried here. He will set up his royal tent over them. ¹¹ He will come and attack Egypt. He will bring death to those I have appointed to die. He will take away as prisoners those I have appointed to be taken away. And he will kill with swords those I have appointed to be killed. ¹² He will set the temples of the gods of Egypt on fire. He will burn down their temples. He will take away the statues of their gods. Nebuchadnezzar will be like a shepherd who picks his coat clean of lice. Nebuchadnezzar will pick Egypt clean and then depart. ¹³ At Heliopolis in Egypt he will smash the sacred pillars to pieces. And he will burn down the temples of the gods of Egypt." ' "

Worshiping Other Gods Brings Horrible Trouble

44 A message from the LORD came to Jeremiah. It was about all the Jews living in Lower Egypt. They were living in Migdol, Tahpanhes and Memphis. It was also about all the Jews living in Upper Egypt. ² The LORD who rules over all is the God of Israel. He said, "You saw all the trouble I brought on Jerusalem. I also brought it on all the towns in Judah. Today they lie there deserted and destroyed. ³ That's because of the evil things their people did. They made me very angry. They burned incense to other gods. And they worshiped them. They and you and your people of long ago never knew those gods. ⁴ Again and again I sent my servants the prophets. They said, 'Don't worship other gods! The LORD hates it!' ⁵ But the people didn't listen. They didn't pay any attention. They didn't turn from their sinful ways. They didn't stop burning incense to other gods. ⁶ So my burning anger was poured out. It blazed out against the towns of Judah and the streets of Jerusalem. It made them the dry and empty places they are today."

⁷ The LORD God who rules over all is the God of Israel. He says, "Why do you want to bring all this trouble on yourselves?

You are removing from Judah its men and women, its children and babies. Not one of you will be left. [8] Why do you want to make me angry with the gods your hands have made? Why do you burn incense to the gods of Egypt, where you now live? You will destroy yourselves. All the nations on earth will use your name as a curse. They will say you are shameful. [9] Have you forgotten the evil things done by your people of long ago? The kings and queens of Judah did those same things. So did you and your wives. They were done in the land of Judah and the streets of Jerusalem. [10] To this day the people of Judah have not made themselves humble in my sight. They have not shown any respect for me. They have not obeyed my law. They have not followed the rules I gave you and your people of long ago."

[11] The LORD who rules over all is the God of Israel. He says, "I have decided to bring horrible trouble on you. I will destroy the whole land of Judah. [12] I will destroy the people of Judah who are left. They had decided to go to Egypt and make their homes there. But all of them will die in Egypt. They will die of war or hunger. All of them will die, from the least important of them to the most important. They will die of war or hunger. People will use their name as a curse. They will be shocked at them. They will say bad things about them. And they will say they are shameful. [13] I will use war, hunger and plague to punish the Jews who live in Egypt. I punished Jerusalem in the same way. [14] None of the people of Judah who have gone to live in Egypt will escape. Not one of them will live to return to Judah. They long to return and live there. But only a few will escape from Egypt and go back."

[15] All the Jews who were living in Lower and Upper Egypt gathered to give Jeremiah their answer. A large crowd had come together. It included men who knew that their wives were burning incense to other gods. Their wives were there with them. All of them said to Jeremiah, [16] "We won't listen to the message you have spoken to us in the LORD's name! [17] We will certainly do everything we said we would. We'll burn incense to the female god called the Queen of Heaven. We'll pour out drink offerings to her. We'll do just as we and our people of long ago have done. Our kings and our officials also did it. All of us did it in the towns of Judah and the streets of Jerusalem. At that time we had plenty of food. We were well off. We didn't suffer any harm. [18] But then we stopped burning incense to the Queen of Heaven. We stopped pouring out drink offerings to her. And ever since that time we haven't had anything. Instead, we've been dying of war and hunger."

[19] The women added, "We burned incense to the Queen of Heaven. We poured out drink offerings to her. And our

husbands knew we were making cakes that looked like her. They knew we were pouring out drink offerings to her."

²⁰ Then Jeremiah spoke to all the people who were answering him. He spoke to men and women alike. He said, ²¹ "Didn't the Lord know you were burning incense in the towns of Judah? Didn't he care that you were also doing it in the streets of Jerusalem? You and your people of long ago were doing it. Your kings and officials were doing it too. So were the rest of the people in the land. ²² The Lord couldn't put up any longer with the evil things you were doing. He hated the things you did. So your land became a curse. It became a dry and empty desert. No one lived there. And that's the way it still is today. ²³ You have burned incense to other gods. You have sinned against the Lord. You haven't obeyed him or his law. You haven't followed his rules. You haven't lived up to the terms of the covenant he made with you. That's why all this trouble has come on you. You have seen it with your own eyes."

²⁴ Then Jeremiah spoke to all the people. That included the women. He said, "All you people of Judah in Egypt, listen to the Lord's message. ²⁵ The Lord who rules over all is the God of Israel. He says, 'You and your wives have done what you promised you would do. You said, "We will certainly keep the promises we made to the Queen of Heaven. We'll burn incense to her. We'll pour out drink offerings to her." '

"Go ahead then. Do what you said you would! Keep your promises! ²⁶ But listen to the Lord's message. Listen, all you Jews living in Egypt. 'I make a promise by my own great name,' says the Lord. 'Here is what I promise. "No one from Judah who lives anywhere in Egypt will ever again pray in my name. None of them will ever make this promise. They will never say, 'You can be sure that the Lord and King is alive.' " ²⁷ I am watching over them to do them harm and not good. The Jews in Egypt will die of war and hunger until all of them are destroyed. ²⁸ Some will not be killed. They will return to Judah from Egypt. But they will be very few. Then all the people of Judah who came to live in Egypt will know the truth. They will know whether what I say or what they say will come true.

²⁹ " 'I will give you a sign that I will punish you in this place,' announces the Lord. 'Then you can be sure that my warnings of harm against you will come true.' ³⁰ The Lord says, 'I am going to hand over Pharaoh Hophra king of Egypt. I will hand him over to his enemies who want to kill him. In the same way, I handed over King Zedekiah to Nebuchadnezzar, the king of Babylon. He was the enemy who wanted to kill Zedekiah.' "

The LORD Speaks to Baruch

45 Jeremiah talked to Baruch, the son of Neriah. It was in the fourth year that Jehoiakim, the son of Josiah, was king of Judah. It was when Baruch had written down on a scroll the words Jeremiah the prophet told him to write. Jeremiah had said, ² "The LORD is the God of Israel. Baruch, he says to you, ³ 'You have said, "How terrible it is for me! The LORD has added sorrow to my pain. I'm worn out from all my groaning. I can't find any rest." ' ⁴ But here is what the LORD has told me to say to you, Baruch. 'The LORD says, "I will destroy what I have built up. I will pull up by the roots what I have planted. I will do this throughout the earth. ⁵ So should you seek great things for yourself? Do not seek them. I will bring trouble on everyone," announces the LORD. "But no matter where you go, I will let you escape with your life." ' "

A Message About Egypt

46 A message from the LORD came to Jeremiah the prophet. It was about the nations.

² Here is what the LORD says about Egypt.

Here is his message against the army of Pharaoh Necho. He was king of Egypt. Nebuchadnezzar, the king of Babylon, won the battle over Necho's army. That happened at Carchemish on the Euphrates River. It was in the fourth year that Jehoiakim was king of Judah. He was the son of Josiah. The message says,

³ "Egyptians, prepare your
    shields!
Prepare large and small
    shields alike!
March out for battle!
⁴ Get the horses and chariots
    ready to ride!
Take up your battle
    positions!
Put on your helmets!
Shine up your spears!
Put on your armor!
⁵ What do I see?
The Egyptians are
    terrified.
They are pulling back.
Their soldiers are losing.
They run away as fast as they
    can.
They do not look back.
There is terror on every
    side,"
      announces the LORD.
⁶ "Those who run fast can't get
    away.
Those who are strong can't
    escape.
In the north by the Euphrates
    River
    they trip and fall.

⁷ "Who is this that rises like
    the Nile River?
Who rises like rivers of
    rushing waters?
⁸ Egypt rises like the Nile
    River.
It rises like rivers of
    rushing waters.
Egypt says, 'I will rise and
    cover the earth.
I'll destroy cities and their
    people.'

⁹Charge, you horses!
Drive fast, you chariot
drivers!
March on, you soldiers!
March on, you men of
Cush and Put who carry
shields.
March on, you men of
Lydia who shoot
arrows.
¹⁰But that day belongs to me.
I am the LORD who rules
over all.
It is a day for me to pay
back my enemies.
My sword will eat until it is
satisfied.
It will drink until it is
not thirsty for blood
anymore.
I am the Lord. I am the LORD
who rules over all.
I will offer a sacrifice.
I will offer it in the land of the
north
by the Euphrates River.

¹¹ "People of Egypt,
go up to Gilead and get
some healing lotion.
You may try many medicines,
but you will not be
healed.
There isn't any healing for
you.
¹²The nations will hear about
your shame.
Your cries of pain will fill
the earth.
One soldier will trip over
another.
Both of them will fall down
together."

¹³Nebuchadnezzar, the king
of Babylon, was coming to attack Egypt. Here is the message
the LORD spoke to Jeremiah the
prophet about it. He said,

¹⁴ "Egyptians, here is what I
want you to announce in
your land.
Announce it in the city of
Migdol.
Also announce it
in Memphis and
Tahpanhes.
Say, 'Take up your battle
positions! Get ready!
The sword eats up those
around you.'
¹⁵Why are your soldiers lying
on the ground?
They can't stand, because I
bring them down.
¹⁶They will trip again and
again.
They will fall over one
another.
They will say, 'Get up. Let's go
back home.
Let's return to our own
people and our own
lands.
Let's get away from the
swords
that will bring us great
harm.'
¹⁷The Egyptian soldiers will
cry out,
'Pharaoh, our king, is only
a loud noise.
He has missed his chance
to win the battle.'

¹⁸ "I am the King.
My name is the LORD Who
Rules Over All.
Someone will come who is
like Mount Tabor among
the mountains.

He is like Mount Carmel
  by the Mediterranean
  Sea.
And that is just as sure as I
  am alive,"
  announces the King.
19 "So pack your belongings,
  you who live in Egypt.
You will be taken away
  from your land.
Memphis will be completely
  destroyed.
  Its buildings will be broken
  down.
No one will live there.

20 "Egypt is like a beautiful
  young cow.
But Nebuchadnezzar is
  coming against her from
  the north.
He will bite her like a fly.
21 Hired soldiers are in Egypt's
  army.
They are like fat calves.
All of them will turn and run
  away.
They will not hold their
  positions.
The day of trouble is coming
  on them.
The time for them to be
  punished is near.
22 The Egyptians will hiss like a
  snake that is trying to get
  away.
A powerful army will
  advance against them.
Their enemies will come
  against them with axes.
They will be like those who
  cut down trees.
23 Egypt is like a thick forest.
But they will chop it
  down,"
  announces the LORD.

"There are more of their
  enemies than there are
  locusts.
In fact, they can't even be
  counted.
24 The nation of Egypt will be
  put to shame.
It will be handed over
  to the people of the
  north."

25 The LORD who rules over all
is the God of Israel. He says, "I
am about to punish Amon, the
god of Thebes. I will also punish Pharaoh. I will punish Egypt
and its gods and kings. And I
will punish those who depend
on Pharaoh. 26 I will hand them
over to those who want to kill
them. I will give them to Nebuchadnezzar, the king of Babylon, and his officers. But later,
many people will live in Egypt
again as in times past," announces the LORD.

27 "People of Jacob, do not be
  afraid.
You are my servant.
Israel, do not be terrified.
I will bring you safely out of a
  place far away.
I will bring your children
  back
from the land where they
  were taken.
Your people will have peace
  and security again.
And no one will make
  them afraid.
28 People of Jacob, do not be
  afraid.
You are my servant.
I am with you," announces
  the LORD.

"I will completely destroy all
        the nations
    among which I scatter
        you.
    But I will not completely
        destroy you.
    I will correct you. But I will
        be fair.
    I will not let you go without
        any punishment."

A Message About the Philistines

47 A message from the LORD
came to Jeremiah the
prophet. It was about the Philistines before Pharaoh attacked
the city of Gaza.

² The LORD said,

"The armies of Babylon are
        like waters rising in the
        north.
    They will become a great
        flood.
    They will flow over the land
        and everything in it.
    They will flow over the
        towns and those who
        live in them.
    The people will cry out.
    All those who live in the
        land will weep.
³ They will weep when they
        hear galloping horses.
    They will weep at the noise
        of enemy chariots.
    They will weep at the
        rumble of their wheels.
    Parents will not even try to
        help their children.
    Their hands will not be
        able to help them.
⁴ The day has come
    to destroy all the
        Philistines.

The time has come to remove
        all those
    who could help Tyre and
        Sidon.
I am about to destroy the
        Philistines.
    I will not leave anyone
        alive
    who came from the coasts
        of Crete.
⁵ The people of Gaza will be so
        sad
    they will shave their heads.
    And Ashkelon's people will
        be silent.
You who remain on the plain,
    how long will you cut
        yourselves?

⁶ " 'Sword of the LORD!' you cry
        out.
    'How long will it be until
        you rest?
Return to the place you came
        from.
    Stop killing us! Be still!'
⁷ But how can his sword rest
    when the LORD has given it
        a command?
He has ordered it
    to attack Ashkelon and the
        Philistine coast."

A Message About Moab

48 Here is what the LORD
says about Moab.

The LORD who rules over all is
the God of Israel. He says,

"How terrible it will be for the
        city of Nebo!
    It will be destroyed.
Kiriathaim will be captured.
    It will be put to shame.
Its fort will be broken down.
    It will be put to shame.

² Moab will not be praised
anymore.
In Heshbon people will
plan its fall from power.
They will say, 'Come.
Let's put an end to that
nation.'
City of Madmen, you too will
be silent.
My sword will hunt you
down.
³ Cries of sorrow come from
Horonaim.
The town is being
completely destroyed.
⁴ Moab will be broken.
Her little ones will cry out.
⁵ The people go up the hill to
Luhith.
They are weeping bitterly
as they go.
Loud cries are heard on the
road down to Horonaim.
People cry out because the
town is being destroyed.
⁶ People of Moab, run away!
Run for your lives!
Become like a lonely bush
in the desert.
⁷ You trust in the things you
can do.
You trust in your riches.
So you too will be taken
away as prisoners.
Your god named Chemosh
will be carried away.
So will its priests and
officials.
⁸ The one who is going to
destroy you
will come against every
town.
Not even one of them will
escape.
The valley and the high plain

will be destroyed.
The Lord has spoken.
⁹ Sprinkle salt all over Moab.
It will be completely
destroyed.
Its towns will be a dry and
empty desert.
No one will live in them.

¹⁰ "May anyone who is lazy
when they do the Lord's
work
be under my curse!
May anyone who keeps their
sword from killing
be under my curse!

¹¹ "Moab has been at peace
and rest from its earliest
days.
It is like wine that has not
been shaken up.
It has not been poured from
one jar to another.
Moab's people have not
been taken away from
their land.
They are like wine that tastes
as it always did.
Its smell has not changed
at all.
¹² But other days are coming,"
announces the Lord.
"At that time I will send
people who pour wine
from pitchers.
They will pour Moab out
like wine.
They will empty its pitchers.
They will smash its jars.
¹³ Then Moab's people will be
ashamed of their god
named Chemosh.
They will be ashamed just
as the people of Israel
were

when they trusted in their
   false god at Bethel.

¹⁴ "How can you say, 'We are
      soldiers.
   We are men who are brave
      in battle'?
¹⁵ Moab will be destroyed.
   Its enemies will march into
      its towns.
   Its finest young men will die
      in battle,"
   announces the King.
   His name is the LORD Who
      Rules Over All.
¹⁶ "The fall of Moab is near.
   Its time of trouble will
      come quickly.
¹⁷ All you who live around it,
      mourn for its people.
   Be sad, you who know how
      famous Moab is.
   Say, 'Its powerful ruler's
      scepter is broken!
   His glorious scepter is
      smashed.'

¹⁸ "Come down from your
      glorious city, you who
      live in Dibon.
   Come and sit on the thirsty
      ground.
   The one who destroys Moab
      will come up and attack
      you.
   Your enemies will destroy
      your cities
      that have high walls
      around them.
¹⁹ Stand by the road and
      watch,
   you who live in Aroer.
   Ask the men who are
      running away.
   Ask the women who are
      escaping.

Ask them, 'What has
   happened?'
²⁰ Moab has been put to shame.
   It has been destroyed.
   Weep and cry out!
   Tell everyone Moab has been
      destroyed.
   Announce it by the Arnon
      River.
²¹ The high plain has been
      judged.
   So have Holon, Jahzah and
      Mephaath.
²² Dibon, Nebo and Beth
      Diblathaim have been
      judged.
²³   So have Kiriathaim, Beth
      Gamul and Beth Meon.
²⁴ Kerioth and Bozrah have also
      been judged.
   And so have all the towns
      of Moab, far and near
      alike.
²⁵ Moab's power is gone.
   Its strength is broken,"
      announces the LORD.

²⁶ "Moab's people think they
      are better than I am.
   So let their enemies make
      them drunk.
   Let the people get sick and
      throw up.
   Let them roll around in the
      mess they have made.
   Let people laugh at them.
²⁷ Moab, you laughed at Israel,
      didn't you?
   Were Israel's people caught
      among robbers?
   Is that why you shake your
      head at them?
   Is that why you make fun
      of them
      every time you talk about
      them?

28 Leave your towns,
    you who live in Moab.
    Go and live among the
        rocks.
    Be like a dove that makes its
        nest
    at the entrance of a cave.
29 "We have heard all about
        Moab's pride.
    We have heard how very
        proud they are.
    They think they are so much
        better than others.
    Their pride reaches deep
        down inside their hearts.
30 I know how rude they are.
    But it will not get them
        anywhere,"
            announces the LORD.
    "Their bragging does not
        accomplish anything.
31 So I weep over Moab.
    I cry for all Moab's people.
    I groan for the people of Kir
        Hareseth.
32 I weep for you as Jazer weeps,
    you vines of Sibmah.
    Your branches used to spread
        out.
    They went all the way
        down to the Dead Sea.
    They reached as far as the
        sea of Jazer.
    The one who destroys your
        country
    has taken away your
        grapes and ripe fruit.
33 Joy has left your orchards.
    Gladness is gone from your
        fields.
    I have stopped the flow
        of juice from your
        winepresses.
    No one stomps on your
        grapes with shouts of joy.

There are shouts.
    But they are not shouts of
        joy.
34 "The sound of their cry rises
        from Heshbon.
    It rises as far as Elealeh and
        Jahaz.
    It rises from Zoar.
It goes all the way to
        Horonaim and Eglath
        Shelishiyah.
    Even the waters at Nimrim
        are dried up.
35 In Moab people sacrifice
        offerings on the high
        places.
    They burn incense to their
        gods.
    But I will put an end to
        those people,"
            announces the LORD.
36 "Like a flute my heart sings
        a song of sadness for
        Moab.
    It sings like a flute for the
        people of Kir Hareseth.
    The wealth they had
        acquired is gone.
37 Every head is shaved.
    Every beard is cut off.
Every hand is cut.
    And every waist is covered
        with the clothes of
        sadness.
38 Weeping is the only sound in
        Moab.
    It is heard on all its roofs.
    It is heard in the market.
    I have broken Moab
    like a jar that no one
        wants,"
            announces the LORD.
39 "How broken Moab is! How
        the people weep!
    They turn away from others

because they are so
   ashamed.
All those around them laugh
   at them.
They are shocked at them.'"

40 The LORD says,

"Look! Nebuchadnezzar
   is like an eagle diving
   down.
He is spreading his wings
   over Moab.
41 Kerioth will be captured.
   Its forts will be taken.
At that time the hearts of
   Moab's soldiers will
   tremble in fear.
They will be like the heart
   of a woman having a
   baby.
42 Moab will be destroyed as a
   nation.
That is because its people
   thought
they were better than the
   LORD.
43 You people of Moab,"
      announces the LORD,
"terror, a pit and a trap are
   waiting for you.
44 Anyone who runs away from
   the terror
will fall into the pit.
Anyone who climbs out of
   the pit
will be caught in the
   trap.
The time is coming
   when I will punish Moab,"
      announces the LORD.
45 "In the shadow of Heshbon
   those who are trying to
   escape stand helpless.
A fire has blazed out from
   Heshbon.

Flames have come out
   from Sihon's city.
It burns the foreheads of
   Moab's people.
It burns the skulls of those
   who brag loudly.
46 How terrible it will be for you,
   Moab!
Those who worship
   Chemosh are destroyed.
Your sons are being taken to
   another country.
Your daughters are taken
   away as prisoners.

47 "But in days to come
   I will bless Moab with great
   success again,"
      announces the LORD.

This ends the report about
how the LORD would judge
Moab.

A Message About Ammon

49 Here is what the LORD
   says about the people of
Ammon.

He says,

"Doesn't Israel have any
   sons?
Doesn't Israel have anyone
   to take over the family
   property?
Then why has the god named
   Molek taken over Gad?
Why do those who worship
   him live in its towns?
2 But a new day is coming,"
   announces the LORD.
"At that time I will sound the
   battle cry.
I will sound it against
   Rabbah in the land of
   Ammon.

It will become a pile of
broken-down buildings.
The villages around it will
be set on fire.
Then Israel will drive out
those who drove her out,"
says the LORD.
³ "Heshbon, weep for Ai! It is
destroyed!
Cry out, you who live in
Rabbah!
Put on the clothes of sadness
and mourn.
Run here and there inside
the walls.
Your god named Molek will
be carried away.
So will its priests and
officials.
⁴ Why do you brag about your
valleys?
You brag that they produce
so many crops.
Ammon, you are an
unfaithful country.
You trust in your riches.
You say,
'Who will attack me?'
⁵ I will bring terror on you.
It will come from all those
around you,"
announces the Lord. He is the
LORD who rules over all.
"Every one of you will be
driven away.
No one will bring back
those who escape.

⁶ "But after that, I will bless the
people of Ammon
with great success again,"
announces the LORD.

A Message About Edom
⁷ Here is what the LORD says
about Edom.

The LORD who rules over all
says,

"Isn't there wisdom in the
town of Teman anymore?
Can't those who are wise
give advice?
Has their wisdom
disappeared completely?
⁸ Turn around and run away,
you who live in Dedan.
Hide in deep caves.
I will bring trouble on Esau's
family line.
I will do this at the time I
punish them.
⁹ Edom, suppose grape pickers
came to harvest your
vines.
They would still leave a few
grapes.
Suppose robbers came at
night.
They would steal only as
much as they wanted.
¹⁰ But I will strip everything
away from Esau's people.
I will uncover their hiding
places.
They will not be able to
hide anywhere.
Their army is destroyed.
Their friends and
neighbors are destroyed.
So there is no one to say,
¹¹ 'Leave your children whose
fathers have died.
I will keep them alive.
Your widows can also
depend on me.'"

¹² The LORD says, "What if
those who do not have to drink
the cup must drink it anyway? Then shouldn't you be
punished? You will certainly be

punished. You must drink the cup. ¹³ I make a promise in my own name. Bozrah will be destroyed," announces the LORD. "People will be shocked at it. They will say Bozrah is a shameful place. They will use its name as a curse. And all its towns will be destroyed forever."

¹⁴ I've heard a message from the
 LORD.
 A messenger was sent to
  the nations. The LORD
  told him to say,
 "Gather yourselves together
  to attack Edom!
 Prepare for battle!"

¹⁵ The LORD says to Edom, "I
  will make you weak
  among the nations.
 They will hate you.
¹⁶ You live in the safety of the
  rocks.
 You live on top of the hills.
 But the terror you stir up has
  now turned against you.
 Your proud heart has
  tricked you.
 You build your nest as high as
  an eagle does.
 But I will bring you down
  from there,"
    announces the LORD.
¹⁷ "People of Edom,
 all those who pass by you
  will be shocked.
 They will make fun of you
  because of all your
  wounds.
¹⁸ Sodom and Gomorrah were
  destroyed.
 So were the towns that
  were near them,"
    says the LORD.

"You will be just like them.
 No one will live in your
  land.
 No human beings will stay
  there.

¹⁹ "I will be like a lion coming
  up
 from the bushes by the
  Jordan River.
 I will hunt in rich
  grasslands.
 I will chase you from your
  land in an instant.
 What nation will I choose
  to do this?
 Which one will I appoint?
 Is anyone like me?
 Who would dare to argue
  with me?
 What leader can stand
  against me?"
²⁰ So listen to what the LORD
  has planned
 against the people of
  Edom.
 Hear what he has planned
  against those who live in
  Teman.
 Edom's young people will be
  dragged away.
 Their grasslands will be
  shocked at their fate.
²¹ When the earth hears Edom
  fall, it will shake.
 The people's cries will be
  heard all the way to the
  Red Sea.
²² Look! An enemy is coming.
 It's like an eagle diving
  down.
 It will spread its wings over
  Bozrah.
 At that time the hearts of
  Edom's soldiers
 will tremble in fear.

They'll be like the heart of
a woman having a baby.

A Message About Damascus

23 Here is what the LORD says
about Damascus. He says,

"The people of Hamath and
Arpad are terrified.
They have heard bad news.
They have lost all hope.
They are troubled like the
rolling sea.
24 The people of Damascus
have become weak.
They have turned to run
away.
Panic has taken hold of
them.
Suffering and pain have
taken hold of them.
Their pain is like the pain
of a woman having a
baby.
25 Why hasn't the famous city
been deserted?
It is the town I take delight
in.
26 You can be sure its young
men will fall dead in the
streets.
All its soldiers will be put
to death at that time,"
announces the LORD
who rules over all.
27 "I will set the walls of
Damascus on fire.
It will burn down the
strong towers of King
Ben-Hadad."

A Message About Kedar and Hazor

28 Here is what the LORD says
about the people of Kedar and
the kingdoms of Hazor. Nebuchadnezzar, the king of Babylon, was planning to attack
them.

The LORD says to the armies
of Babylon,

"Prepare for battle. Attack
Kedar.
Destroy the people of the
east.
29 Their tents and flocks will be
taken away from them.
Their tents will be carried
off.
All their goods and camels
will be stolen.
People will shout to them,
'There is terror on every
side!'

30 "Run away quickly!
You who live in Hazor, stay
in deep caves,"
announces the LORD.
"Nebuchadnezzar, the king
of Babylon,
has made plans against
you.
He has decided to attack
you.

31 "Armies of Babylon, prepare
for battle.
Attack a nation that feels
secure.
Its people do not have any
worries,"
announces the LORD.
"That nation does not have
gates or bars that lock
them.
Its people live far from
danger.
32 Their camels will be stolen.
Their large herds will be
taken away.

I will scatter to the winds
   those who are in places
   far away.
I will bring trouble on
   them from every side,"
     announces the LORD.
33 "Hazor will become a home
   for wild dogs.
It will be a dry and empty
   desert forever.
No one will live in that land.
   No human beings will stay
   there."

A Message About Elam

34 A message from the LORD
came to Jeremiah the prophet. It
was about Elam. It came shortly
after Zedekiah became king of
Judah.

35 The LORD who rules over all
said,

"Elam's bow is the secret of
   its strength.
But I will break it.
36 I will bring the four winds
   against Elam.
I will bring them from all
   four directions.
I will scatter Elam's people to
   the four winds.
They will be taken away
   to every nation on earth.
37 I will use Elam's enemies to
   smash them.
Those who want to kill
   them will kill them.
I will bring trouble on Elam's
   people.
My anger will be great
   against them,"
     announces the LORD.
"I will chase them with
   swords.

I will hunt them down
   until I have destroyed
   them.
38 I will set up my throne in
   Elam.
I will destroy its king and
   officials,"
     announces the LORD.
39 "But in days to come I will
   bless Elam
with great success again,"
     announces the LORD.

A Message About Babylon

50 Here is the message the
LORD spoke through Jer-
emiah the prophet. It was about
the city of Babylon and the land
of Babylon. He said,

2 "Announce this message
   among the nations.
Lift up a banner.
Let the nations hear the
   message.
Do not keep anything back.
Say, 'Babylon will be
   captured.
The god named Bel will be
   put to shame.
The god named Marduk
   will be filled with terror.
Babylon's gods will be put to
   shame.
The gods its people made
   will be filled with terror.'
3 A nation from the north will
   attack it.
That nation will destroy
   Babylon.
No one will live there.
   People and animals alike
   will run away.
4 "The days are coming,"
     announces the LORD.

"At that time the people of
Israel and Judah will
gather together.
They will come in tears to
me.
I am the LORD their God.
⁵ They will ask how to get to
Zion.
Then they will turn their
faces toward it.
They will come and join
themselves to me.
They will enter into the
covenant I make with
them.
It will last forever.
It will never be forgotten.

⁶ "My people have been like
lost sheep.
Their shepherds have led
them astray.
They have caused them
to wander in the
mountains.
They have wandered over
mountains and hills.
They have forgotten that
I am their true resting
place.
⁷ Everyone who found them
destroyed them.
Their enemies said, 'We
aren't guilty.
They sinned against the
LORD.
He gave them everything
they needed.
He has always been Israel's
hope.'
⁸ "People of Judah, run away
from Babylon.
Leave the land of Babylon.
Be like the goats that lead
the flock.

⁹ I will stir up great nations
that will join forces against
Babylon.
I will bring them from the
land of the north.
They will take up their
battle positions against
Babylon.
They will come from the
north and capture it.
Their arrows will be like
skilled soldiers.
They will not miss their
mark.
¹⁰ So the riches of Babylon will
be taken away.
All those who steal from
it will have more than
enough,"
announces the LORD.

¹¹ "People of Babylon, you have
stolen what belongs to
me.
That has made you glad
and full of joy.
You dance around like
a young cow on a
threshing floor.
You neigh like stallions.
¹² Because of that, you will
bring great shame on
your land.
Your whole nation will be
dishonored.
It will become the least
important of the
nations.
It will become a dry and
empty desert.
¹³ Because I am angry with it,
no one will live there.
It will be completely
deserted.
All those who pass by
Babylon will be shocked.

They will make fun of
it because of all its
wounds.

14 "All you who shoot arrows,
take up your battle
positions around
Babylon.
Shoot at it! Do not spare any
arrows!
Its people have sinned
against me.
15 Shout against them on every
side!
They are giving up.
The towers of the city are
falling.
Its walls are being pulled
down.
The LORD is paying back its
people.
So pay them back
yourselves.
Do to them what they have
done to others.
16 Do not leave anyone in
Babylon to plant the
fields.
Do not leave anyone to
harvest the grain.
Let each of them return to
their own people.
Let them run away to their
own land.
If they don't, their enemy's
sword will bring them
great harm.

17 "Israel is like a scattered
flock
that lions have chased
away.
The first lion that ate them up
was the king of Assyria.
The last one that broke their
bones

was Nebuchadnezzar, the
king of Babylon.''

18 The LORD who rules over all
is the God of Israel. He says,

"I punished the king of
Assyria.
In the same way, I will
punish
the king of Babylon and his
land.
19 But I will bring Israel back to
their own grasslands.
I will feed them on Mount
Carmel and in Bashan.
I will satisfy their hunger
on the hills of Ephraim and
Gilead.
20 The days are coming,"
announces the LORD.
"At that time people will
search for Israel's guilt.
But they will not find any.
They will search for Judah's
sins.
But they will not find any.
That is because I will
forgive the people I have
spared.

21 "Enemies of Babylon,
attack their land of
Merathaim.
Make war against those
who live in Pekod.
Chase them and kill
them. Destroy them
completely,"
announces the LORD.
"Do everything I have
commanded you to do.
22 The noise of battle is heard in
the land.
It is the noise of a great city
being destroyed!
23 It has been broken to pieces.

It was the hammer that
　broke the whole earth.
How empty Babylon is
　among the nations!
24 Babylon, I set a trap for you.
　And you were caught
　　before you knew it.
　You were found and captured.
　That is because you
　　opposed me.
25 I have opened up my
　　storeroom.
　I have brought out the
　　weapons I use when I am
　　angry.
　I am the LORD and King who
　　rules over all.
　I have work to do in the
　　land of the Babylonians.
26 So come against it from far
　　away.
　Open up its storerooms.
　Stack everything up like
　　piles of grain.
　Completely destroy that
　　country.
　Do not leave anyone alive
　　there.
27 Kill all Babylon's strongest
　　warriors.
　Let them die in battle.
　How terrible it will be for
　　them!
　Their time to be judged has
　　come.
　Now they will be punished.
28 Listen to those who have
　　escaped.
　Listen to those who have
　　returned from Babylon.
　They are announcing in Zion
　　how I have paid Babylon
　　back.
　I have paid it back for
　　destroying my temple.

29 "Send for men armed with
　　bows and arrows.
　Send them against
　　Babylon.
　Set up camp all around it.
　　Do not let anyone escape.
　Pay it back for what its people
　　have done.
　Do to them what they have
　　done to others.
　They have dared to disobey
　　me.
　I am the Holy One of Israel.
30 You can be sure its young
　　men will fall dead in the
　　streets.
　All its soldiers will be put
　　to death at that time,"
　　　announces the LORD.
31 "Proud Babylonians, I am
　　against you,"
　　announces the Lord.
　The LORD who rules over all
　　says,
　"Your day to be judged has
　　come.
　It is time for you to be
　　punished.
32 You proud people will trip
　　and fall.
　No one will help you up.
　I will start a fire in your towns.
　It will burn up everyone
　　around you."

33 The LORD who rules over all
says,

"The people of Israel are
　being treated badly.
　So are the people of Judah.
　Those who have captured
　　them are holding them.
　They refuse to let them go.
34 But I am strong and will save
　　them.

My name is the LORD Who
   Rules Over All.
I will stand up for them.
I will bring peace and rest
   to their land.
But I will bring trouble
   to those who live in
   Babylon.
³⁵ "A sword is coming against
   the Babylonians!"
announces the LORD.
"It is coming against those
   who live in Babylon.
It is coming against their
   officials and wise men.
³⁶ A sword is coming against
   their prophets.
But they are not really
   prophets at all!
So they will look foolish.
A sword is coming against
   their soldiers!
They will be filled with
   terror.
³⁷ A sword is coming against
   their horses and chariots!
It is coming against all the
   hired soldiers in their
   armies.
They will become weak.
A sword is coming against
   their treasures!
They will be stolen.
³⁸ There will not be any rain for
   their rivers.
So they will dry up.
Those things will happen
   because their land is full
   of statues of gods.
Those gods will go crazy
   with terror.
³⁹ "Desert creatures and hyenas
   will live in Babylon.
And so will owls.

People will never live there
   again.
It will not be lived in for all
   time to come.
⁴⁰ I destroyed Sodom and
   Gomorrah.
I also destroyed the towns
   that were near them,"
   announces the LORD.
"Babylon will be just like
   them.
No one will live there.
No human beings will stay
   there.
⁴¹ "Look! An army is coming
   from the north.
I am stirring up a great
   nation and many kings.
They are coming from
   a land that is very far
   away.
⁴² Their soldiers are armed with
   bows and spears.
They are mean.
They do not show any
   mercy at all.
They come riding in on their
   horses.
They sound like the
   roaring ocean.
They are lined up for battle.
They are coming to attack
   you, city of Babylon.
⁴³ The king of Babylon has
   heard reports about
   them.
His hands can't help him.
He is in great pain.
It is like the pain of a
   woman having a baby.
⁴⁴ I will be like a lion coming up
   from the bushes by the
   Jordan River.
I will hunt in rich
   grasslands.

I will chase the people of
    Babylon from their land
    in an instant.
    What nation will I choose
      to do this?
    Which one will I appoint?
    Is anyone like me? Who
      would dare to argue
      with me?
    What leader can stand
      against me?"
45 So listen to what the LORD
    has planned against
    Babylon.
    Hear what he has planned
      against the land of the
      Babylonians.
    Their young people will be
      dragged away.
    Their grasslands will be
      shocked at their fate.
46 At the news of Babylon's
    capture,
    the earth will shake.
    The people's cries will be
      heard among the nations.

51

The LORD says,

"I will stir up the spirits of
    destroyers.
    They will march out
      against Babylon and its
      people.
2 I will send other nations
    against it
    to separate the straw from
      the grain.
    I will send them to destroy
      Babylon completely.
    They will oppose it on every
      side.
    At that time it will be
      destroyed.
3 Do not let its soldiers get their
    bows ready to use.

Do not let them put on
    their armor.
Do not spare their young
    men.
    Destroy their armies
      completely.
4 They will fall down dead in
    Babylon.
    They will receive deadly
      wounds in its streets.
5 The land of Israel and Judah
    is full of guilt.
    Its people have sinned
      against me.
But I have not deserted them.
    I am their God.
    I am the LORD who rules
      over all.
    I am the Holy One of Israel.

6 "People of Judah, run away
    from Babylon!
    Run for your lives!
    Do not be destroyed
      because of the sins of its
      people.
It is time for me to pay them
    back.
    I will punish them for what
      they have done.
7 Babylon was like a gold cup
    in my hand.
    That city made the whole
      earth drunk.
The nations drank its wine.
    So now they have gone
      crazy.
8 Babylon will suddenly fall
    and be broken.
    Weep for it!
Get healing lotion for its pain.
    Perhaps it can be healed.

9 "The nations say, 'We would
    have healed Babylon.
    But it can't be healed.

So let's leave it. Let's each go
   to our own land.
   Babylon's sins reach all the
      way to the skies.
   They rise up as high as the
      heavens.'
¹⁰ "The people of Judah say,
   'The LORD has made things
      right for us again.
So come. Let's tell in Zion
   what the LORD our God has
      done.'
¹¹ "I have stirred up you kings
   of the Medes.
   So sharpen your arrows!
Get your shields!
   I plan to destroy Babylon.
I will pay the Babylonians
      back.
   They have destroyed my
      temple.
¹² Lift up a banner! Attack
   Babylon's walls!
   Put more guards on duty!
Station more of them to
      watch over you!
   Hide and wait to attack
      them!
I will do what I have
      planned.
   I will do what I have
      decided to do
   against the people of
      Babylon.
¹³ You who live by the rivers of
   Babylon,
   your end has come.
You who are rich in treasures,
   it is time for you to be
      destroyed.
¹⁴ I am the LORD who rules over
   all.
   I have made a promise in
      my own name.

I have said, 'I will certainly
   fill your land with
      soldiers.
   They will be as many
      as a huge number of
      locusts.
They will win the battle over
      you.
   They will shout for joy.'
¹⁵ "I used my power to make the
   earth.
   I used my wisdom to set
      the world in place.
   I used my understanding
      to spread out the
      heavens.
¹⁶ When I thunder, the waters
   in the heavens roar.
   I make clouds rise from
      one end of the earth to
      the other.
I send lightning with the
   rain.
   I bring out the wind from
      my storerooms.
¹⁷ "No one has any sense.
   No one knows anything.
Everyone who works with
      gold is put to shame
   by his wooden gods.
His metal gods are fakes.
   They can't even breathe.
¹⁸ They are worthless, and
      people make fun of
      them.
   When I judge them, they
      will be destroyed.
¹⁹ But I, the God of Jacob, am
      not like them.
   I give my people
      everything they need.
   I can do this because
      I made everything,
      including Israel.

They are the people who
  belong to me.
  My name is the LORD Who
  Rules Over All.

20 "Babylon, you are my war
  club.
  You are my weapon for
  battle.
  I use you to destroy nations.
  I use you to wipe out
  kingdoms.
21 I use you to destroy horses
  and their riders.
  I use you to destroy
  chariots and their
  drivers.
22 I use you to destroy men and
  women.
  I use you to destroy old
  people and young
  people.
  I use you to destroy
  young men and young
  women.
23 I use you to destroy
  shepherds and their
  flocks.
  I use you to destroy
  farmers and their oxen.
  I use you to destroy
  governors and officials.

24 "Judah, I will pay Babylon
back. You will see it with your
own eyes. I will pay back all
those who live in Babylon. I will
pay them back for all the wrong
things they have done in Zion,"
announces the LORD.

25 "Babylon, I am against you.
  Your kingdom is like a
  destroying mountain.
  You have destroyed the
  whole earth,"
    announces the LORD.

"I will reach out my hand
  against you.
  I will roll you off the cliffs.
  I will make you like a
  mountain that has been
  burned up.
26 No rock will be taken from
  you to be used
  as the most important
  stone for a building.
No stones will be taken from
  you
  to be used for a foundation.
  Your land will be empty
  forever,"
    announces the LORD.

27 "Nations, lift up a banner in
  the land of Babylon!
  Blow a trumpet among
  yourselves!
Prepare yourselves for battle
  against Babylon.
  Send the kingdoms
  of Ararat, Minni and
  Ashkenaz against it.
Appoint a commander
  against it.
  Send many horses against it.
  Let them be as many as a
  huge number of locusts.
28 Prepare yourselves for battle
  against Babylon.
  Prepare the kings of the
  Medes.
Prepare their governors and
  all their officials.
  Prepare all the countries
  they rule over.
29 The Babylonians tremble and
  shake with fear.
  My plans against them
  stand firm.
  I plan to destroy their land
  completely.
  Then no one will live there.

30 Babylon's soldiers have
      stopped fighting.
   They remain in their forts.
   Their strength is all gone.
   They have become weak.
   Their buildings are set on
      fire.
   The metal bars that lock
      their gates are broken.
31 One messenger after another
      comes to the king of
      Babylon.
   All of them announce that
      his entire city is captured.
32 The places where people go
      across the Euphrates
      River have been
      captured.
   The swamps have been set
      on fire.
   And the soldiers are
      terrified."

33 The LORD who rules over all
is the God of Israel. He says,

   "The city of Babylon is like a
      threshing floor
   when cattle are walking
      on it.
   The time to destroy it will
      soon come."

34 The people of Jerusalem say,
   "Nebuchadnezzar, the
      king of Babylon, has
      destroyed us.
   He has thrown us into a
      panic.
   He has emptied us out like
      a jar.
   Like a snake he has
      swallowed us up.
   He has filled his stomach
      with our rich food.
   Then he has spit us out of
      his mouth."

35 The people continue, "May
      the people of Babylon
   pay for the harmful things
      they have done to us.
   May those who live in
      Babylon
   pay for spilling the blood of
      our people."
   That's what the people who
      live in Zion say.

36 So the LORD says,

   "I will stand up for you.
   I will pay the Babylonians
      back for what they did to
      you.
   I will dry up their water
      supply.
   I will make their springs
      run dry.
37 Babylon will have all its
      buildings knocked
      down.
   It will be a home for wild
      dogs.
   No one will live there.
   People will be shocked at it.
   They will make fun of it.
38 All its people roar like young
      lions.
   They growl like lion cubs.
39 They are stirred up.
   So I will set a feast in front
      of them.
   I will make them drunk.
   And they will shout and laugh.
   But then they will lie down
      and die.
   They will never wake up,"
      announces the LORD.
40 "I will lead them down like
      lambs to be put to death.
   They will be like rams and
      goats that have been
      killed.

⁴¹ "Babylon will be captured!
    The whole earth was very
        proud of it.
    But it will be taken over by
        others!
    It will be a deserted place
        among the nations.
⁴² Babylon's enemies will sweep
        over it like an ocean.
    Like roaring waves they
        will cover it.
⁴³ The towns of Babylon will be
        empty.
    It will become a dry and
        desert land.
    No one will live there.
    No one will even travel
        through it.
⁴⁴ I will punish the god named
        Bel in Babylon.
    I will make Bel spit out
        what he has swallowed.
    The nations will not come
        and worship him
        anymore.
    And Babylon's walls will
        fall down.
⁴⁵ "Come out of there, my
        people!
    Run for your lives!
    Run away from my great
        anger.
⁴⁶ You will hear about terrible
        things
        that are happening in
        Babylon.
    But do not lose hope. Do
        not be afraid.
    You will hear one thing this
        year.
    And you will hear
        something else next
        year.
    You will hear about awful
        things in the land.

You will hear about one
        ruler fighting against
        another.
⁴⁷ I will punish the gods of
        Babylon.
    That time will certainly
        come.
    Then the whole land will be
        full of shame.
    Its people will lie down
        and die there.
⁴⁸ So heaven and earth and
        everything in them will
        shout for joy.
    They will be glad because
        of what will happen to
        Babylon.
    Armies will attack it from the
        north.
    And they will destroy it,"
        announces the LORD.

⁴⁹ "Babylon's people have killed
        my people Israel.
    They have also killed
        people all over the
        earth.
    So now Babylon itself must
        fall.
⁵⁰ You who have not been
        killed in the war against
        Babylon,
    leave! Do not wait!
    In a land far away remember
        me.
    And think about
        Jerusalem."

⁵¹ The people of Judah reply,
    "No one honors us
        anymore.
    People make fun of us.
    Our faces are covered with
        shame.
    People from other lands have
        entered

the holy places of the LORD's house."

52 "But the days are coming,"
    announces the LORD.
  "At that time I will punish
    the gods of Babylon.
  And all through its land
    wounded people will
    groan.
53 What if Babylon reached all
    the way to the heavens?
  What if it made its high
    walls even stronger?
  I would still send
    destroyers against it,"
        announces the LORD.

54 "The noise of people
    screaming comes from
    Babylon.
  A terrible sound comes
    from its land.
  It is the sound of a mighty
    city being destroyed.
55 I will destroy Babylon.
  I will put an end to all its
    noise.
  Waves of enemies will sweep
    through it like great
    waters.
  The roar of their voices will
    fill the air.
56 A destroying army will come
    against Babylon.
  The soldiers in the city will
    be captured.
  Their bows will be broken.
  I am the LORD God who pays
    people back.
  I will pay them back in full.
57 I will make Babylon's officials
    and wise men drunk.
  I will do the same thing to
    its governors, officers
    and soldiers.

They will lie down and die.
  They will never wake up,"
    announces the King. His
    name is the LORD Who
    Rules Over All.

58 The LORD who rules over all
says,

  "Babylon's thick walls will
    fall down flat.
  Its high gates will be set on
    fire.
  The nations wear themselves
    out for no reason at all.
  Their hard work will only
    be burned up in the
    flames."

59 Jeremiah the prophet gave a message to the staff officer Seraiah, the son of Neriah. Neriah was the son of Mahseiah. Jeremiah told Seraiah to take the message with him to Babylon. Seraiah went there with Zedekiah, the king of Judah. He left in the fourth year of Zedekiah's rule. 60 Jeremiah had written about all the trouble that would come on Babylon. He had written it down on a scroll. It included everything that had been recorded about Babylon. 61 Jeremiah said to Seraiah, "When you get to Babylon, here's what I want you to do. Make sure that you read all these words out loud. 62 Then say, 'LORD, you have said you will destroy this place. You have said that no people or animals will live here. It will be empty forever.' 63 Finish reading the scroll. Tie a stone to it. Throw it into the Euphrates River. 64 Then say, 'In the same way, Babylon will sink down. It

will never rise again. That is because I will bring such horrible trouble on it. And its people will fall along with it.' "

The words of Jeremiah end here.

Nebuchadnezzar Destroys Jerusalem

52 Zedekiah was 21 years old when he became king. He ruled in Jerusalem for 11 years. His mother's name was Hamutal. She was the daughter of Jeremiah. She was from Libnah. ² Zedekiah did what was evil in the eyes of the LORD. He did just as Jehoiakim had done. ³ The enemies of Jerusalem and Judah attacked them because the LORD was angry. In the end he threw them out of his land.

Zedekiah refused to obey the king of Babylon.

⁴ Nebuchadnezzar was the king of Babylon. He marched out against Jerusalem. All his armies went with him. It was in the ninth year of the rule of Zedekiah. It was on the tenth day of the tenth month. The armies set up camp outside the city. They set up ladders and built ramps and towers all around it. ⁵ It was surrounded until the 11th year of King Zedekiah's rule.

⁶ By the ninth day of the fourth month, there wasn't any food left in the city. So the people didn't have anything to eat. ⁷ Then the Babylonians broke through the city wall. Judah's whole army ran away. They left the city at night. They went out through the gate between the two walls that were near the king's garden. They escaped even though the Babylonians surrounded the city. Judah's army ran toward the Arabah Valley. ⁸ But the armies of Babylon chased King Zedekiah. They caught up with him in the plains near Jericho. All his soldiers were separated from him. They had scattered in every direction. ⁹ The king was captured.

He was taken to the king of Babylon at Riblah. Riblah was in the land of Hamath. That's where Nebuchadnezzar decided how Zedekiah would be punished. ¹⁰ At Riblah the king of Babylon killed the sons of Zedekiah. He forced him to watch it with his own eyes. Nebuchadnezzar also killed all the officials of Judah. ¹¹ Then he poked out Zedekiah's eyes. He put him in bronze chains. And he took him to Babylon. There he put Zedekiah in prison until the day he died.

¹² Nebuzaradan served the king of Babylon. In fact, he was commander of the royal guard. He came to Jerusalem. It was in the 19th year that Nebuchadnezzar was king of Babylon. It was on the tenth day of the fifth month. ¹³ Nebuzaradan set the LORD's temple on fire. He also set fire to the royal palace and all the houses in Jerusalem. He burned down every important building. ¹⁴ The armies of Babylon broke down all the walls around Jerusalem. That's what the commander told them to do. ¹⁵ Some of the poorest people

still remained in the city along with the others. But the commander Nebuzaradan took them away as prisoners. He also took the rest of the skilled workers. That included the people who had joined the king of Babylon. ¹⁶ But Nebuzaradan left the rest of the poorest people of the land behind. He told them to work in the vineyards and fields.

¹⁷ The armies of Babylon destroyed the LORD's temple. They broke the bronze pillars into pieces. They broke up the bronze stands that could be moved around. And they broke up the huge bronze bowl. Then they carried away all the bronze to Babylon. ¹⁸ They also took away the pots, shovels, wick cutters, sprinkling bowls and dishes. They took away all the bronze objects that were used for any purpose in the temple. ¹⁹ The commander of the royal guard took away the bowls and the shallow cups for burning incense. He took away the sprinkling bowls, the pots, the lampstands and the dishes. He took away the bowls used for drink offerings. So he took away everything made out of pure gold or silver.

²⁰ The bronze was more than anyone could weigh. It included the bronze from the two pillars. It included the bronze from the huge bowl and the 12 bronze bulls under it. It also included the stands. King Solomon had made all those things for the LORD's temple. ²¹ Each pillar was 27 feet high and 18 feet around. The pillars were hollow. The metal in each of them was three inches thick. ²² The bronze top of one pillar was seven and a half feet high. It was decorated with a set of bronze chains and pomegranates all around it. The other pillar was just like it. It also had pomegranates. ²³ There were 96 pomegranates on the sides of each of the two tops. The total number of pomegranates above the bronze chains around each top was 100.

²⁴ The commander of the guard took many prisoners. They included Seraiah the chief priest and Zephaniah the priest who reported to him. They also included the three men who guarded the temple doors. ²⁵ Some people were still left in the city. The commander took as a prisoner the officer in charge of the fighting men. He took the seven men who gave advice to the king. He also took the secretary who was the chief officer in charge of getting the people of the land to serve in the army. There were 60 people of the land still in the city. ²⁶ The commander Nebuzaradan took all of them away. He brought them to the king of Babylon at Riblah. ²⁷ There the king had them put to death. Riblah was in the land of Hamath.

So the people of Judah were taken as prisoners. They were taken far away from their own land.

²⁸ Here is the number of the people Nebuchadnezzar took to Babylon as prisoners.

In the seventh year of his rule,
he took 3,023 Jews.
²⁹ In his 18th year,
he took 832 people from Jerusalem.
³⁰ In Nebuchadnezzar's 23rd year,
Nebuzaradan, the commander of the royal guard, took 745 Jews to Babylon.

The total number of people taken to Babylon was 4,600.

Jehoiachin Is Set Free

³¹ Awel-Marduk set Jehoiachin, the king of Judah, free from prison. It was in the 37th year after Jehoiachin had been taken away to Babylon. It was also the year Awel-Marduk became king of Babylon. It was on the 25th day of the 12th month. ³² Awel-Marduk spoke kindly to Jehoiachin. He gave him a place of honor. Other kings were with Jehoiachin in Babylon. But his place was more important than theirs. ³³ So Jehoiachin put away his prison clothes. For the rest of Jehoiachin's life the king of Babylon provided what he needed. ³⁴ The king did that for Jehoiachin day by day as long as he lived. He did it until the day Jehoiachin died.

Lamentations

Introduction:

Lamentations is a book of poems. Its name means "songs for the dead." Jeremiah wrote this book. Some of the poems in Lamentations are very sad.

Lamentations tells about Jerusalem's fall. The walls were knocked down, and the city was destroyed. God was angry because the people had sinned. They had turned away from God. But now Jeremiah asked God to help the people. He wanted the Jews to know that God was good. God is good even when times are bad.

Outline of contents:

1 The city of Jerusalem is so
    empty!
    She used to be full of people.
But now she's like a woman
    whose husband has died.
    She used to be great among
      the nations.
She was like a queen among
    the kingdoms.
    But now she is a slave.

² Jerusalem weeps bitterly at
    night.
    Tears run down her
      cheeks.
    None of her friends
      comforts her.
All those who were going to
    help her
have turned against her.
    They have become her
      enemies.

³ After Judah's people had
    suffered greatly,
they were taken away as
    prisoners.
Now they live among the
    nations.
    They can't find any place to
      rest.
All those who were chasing
    them have caught up
      with them.
    And they can't get away.

⁴ The roads to Zion are
    empty.
    No one travels to her
      appointed feasts.
All the public places near her
    gates are deserted.
    Her priests groan.
Her young women are sad.
    And Zion herself weeps
      bitterly.

⁵ Her enemies have become
    her masters.
    They have an easy life.

The Lord has brought
   suffering to Jerusalem
because her people have
   committed so many
   sins.
Her children have been taken
   away as prisoners.
Her enemies have forced
   her people to leave their
   homes.

6 The city of Zion used to be
   full of glory.
But now her glory has
   faded away.
Her princes are like deer.
   They can't find anything to
   eat.
They are almost too weak to
   get away
from those who hunt them
   down.

7 Jerusalem's people
   are suffering and
   wandering.
They remember all the
   treasures
they used to have.
But they fell into the hands of
   their enemies.
And no one was there to
   help them.
Their enemies looked at
   them.
They laughed because
   Jerusalem had been
   destroyed.

8 Her people have committed
   many sins.
They have become impure.
All those who honored
   Jerusalem now look
   down on her.
They all look at her as if she
   were a naked woman.

The city groans and turns
   away in shame.

9 Her skirts are dirty.
She didn't think about how
   things might turn out.
Her fall from power amazed
   everyone.
And no one was there to
   comfort her.
She said, "Lord, please pay
   attention to how much
   I'm suffering.
My enemies have won the
   battle over me."

10 Jerusalem's enemies took
   away
all her treasures.
Her people saw outsiders
   enter her temple.
The Lord had commanded
   them
not to do that.

11 All Jerusalem's people
   groan
as they search for bread.
They trade their treasures for
   food
just to stay alive.
Jerusalem says, "Lord, look
   at me.
Think about my condition.
Everyone looks down on
   me."

12 Jerusalem also says, "All you
   who are passing by,
don't you care about what
   has happened to me?
Just look at my condition.
Has anyone suffered the way
   I have?
The Lord has brought all
   this on me.
He has made me suffer.

His anger has burned
against me.

13 "He sent down fire from
heaven.
It went deep down into my
bones.
He spread a net to catch me
by the feet.
He stopped me right where
I was.
He made me empty.
I am sick all the time.

14 "My sins have been made
into a heavy yoke.
They were woven together
by his hands.
They have been placed on my
neck.
The Lord has taken away
my strength.
He has handed me over to my
enemies.
I can't win the battle over
them.

15 "The Lord has refused to
accept
any of my soldiers.
He has sent for an army
to crush my young men.
I am like grapes in the Lord's
winepress.
He has stomped on me,
even though I am his very
own.

16 "That's why I am weeping.
Tears are flowing from my
eyes.
No one is near to comfort me.
No one can heal my spirit.
My children don't have
anything.
My enemies are much too
strong for me."

17 Zion reaches out her hands.
But no one is there to
comfort her people.
The Lord has ordered that
the neighbors of Jacob's
people would become
their enemies.
Jerusalem has become
impure among them.

18 Jerusalem says, "The Lord
always does what is
right.
But I refused to obey his
commands.
Listen, all you nations.
Pay attention to how much
I'm suffering.
My young men and women
have been taken away as
prisoners.

19 "I called out to those who
were going to help me.
But they turned against
me.
My priests and elders
died in the city.
They were searching for
food
just to stay alive.

20 "Lord, see how upset I am!
I am suffering deep down
inside.
My heart is troubled.
Again and again I have
refused to obey you.
Outside the city, people are
being killed by swords.
Inside, there is nothing but
death.

21 "People have heard me
groan.
But no one is here to
comfort me.

My enemies have heard
   about all my troubles.
What you have done makes
   them happy.
So please judge them, just as
   you said you would.
Let them become like me.

22 "Please pay attention to all
   their sinful ways.
Punish them as you have
   punished me.
You judged me because I
   had committed so many
   sins.
I groan all the time.
   And my heart is weak."

2 See how the Lord covered
   the city of Zion
with the cloud of his anger!
He threw Israel's glory down
   from heaven to earth.
When he was angry, he
   turned his back
   on his own city.

2 Without pity the Lord
   swallowed up
all the homes of Jacob's
   people.
When he was angry, he tore
   down
   the forts of the people of
   Judah.
He brought down their
   kingdom and princes
   to the ground in dishonor.

3 When he was very angry,
   he took away Israel's
   power.
He pulled back his powerful
   right hand
   as the enemy approached.
His burning anger blazed out
   in Jacob's land.

It burned up everything
   near it.
4 Like an enemy the Lord got
   his bow ready to use.
He had a sword in his right
   hand.
Like an enemy he destroyed
   everything that used to be
   pleasing to him.
His anger blazed out like fire.
It burned up the homes in
   the city of Zion.

5 The Lord was like an enemy.
He swallowed up Israel.
He swallowed up all of its
   palaces.
He destroyed its forts.
He filled the people of Judah
   with sorrow and sadness.

6 The LORD's temple was like a
   garden.
But he completely
   destroyed it.
He destroyed the place
   where he used to meet with
   his people.
He made Zion's people forget
   their appointed feasts and
   Sabbath days.
When he was very angry, he
   turned his back on
   king and priest alike.

7 The Lord deserted his altar.
He left his temple.
He gave the walls of
   Jerusalem's palaces
   into the hands of her
   enemies.
They shouted loudly in the
   house of the LORD.
You would have thought it
   was the day
   of an appointed feast.

⁸The LORD decided to tear
down
the walls around the city of
Zion.
He measured out what he
wanted to destroy.
Then he destroyed
Jerusalem by his power.
He made even her towers
and walls sing songs of
sadness.
All of them fell down.

⁹Her gates sank down into the
ground.
He broke the metal bars
that locked her gates,
and he destroyed them.
Her king and princes were
taken away to other
nations.
There is no law anymore.
Jerusalem's prophets no
longer receive
visions from the LORD.

¹⁰The elders of the city of Zion
sit silently on the ground.
They have sprinkled dust on
their heads.
They've put on the clothes
of sadness.
The young women of
Jerusalem
have bowed their heads
toward the ground.

¹¹I've cried so much I can't see
very well.
I'm suffering deep down
inside.
My heart is broken
because my people are
destroyed.
Children and babies are
fainting
in the streets of the city.

¹²They say to their mothers,
"Where can we find
something to eat and
drink?"
They faint like wounded
soldiers
in the streets of the city.
Their lives are slipping
away
in their mothers' arms.

¹³City of Jerusalem, what can I
say about you?
What can I compare you
to?
People of Zion, what are you
like?
I want to comfort you.
Your wound is as deep as the
ocean.
Who can heal you?

¹⁴The visions of your prophets
were lies.
They weren't worth
anything.
They didn't show you the sins
you had committed.
So that's why you were
captured.
The messages they gave you
were lies.
They led you astray.

¹⁵All those who pass by
clap their hands and make
fun of you.
They laugh at you and shake
their heads
at the city of Jerusalem.
They say, "Could that be the
city
that was called perfect and
beautiful?
Is that the city that brought
joy to everyone on
earth?"

16 All your enemies open their
  mouths
 wide against you.
They laugh at you and grind
  their teeth.
They say, "We have
 swallowed up
 Jerusalem's people.
This is the day we've waited
  for.
And we've lived to see it."

17 The Lord has done what he
  planned to do.
He has made what he said
  come true.
He gave the command long
  ago.
He has destroyed you
  without pity.
He has let your enemies
  laugh at you.
He has made them
  stronger than you are.

18 People in the city of Zion,
  cry out from your heart to
  the Lord.
Let your tears flow like a river
  day and night.
Don't stop at all.
  Don't give your eyes any rest.

19 Get up. Cry out as the night
  begins.
Tell the Lord all your
  troubles.
Lift up your hands to him.
  Pray that the lives of your
  children will be spared.
At every street corner they
  faint
 because they are so hungry.

20 Jerusalem says, "Lord, look
  at me.
Think about my condition.

Have you ever treated
 anyone else like this?
Should women have to eat
  their babies?
Should they eat the
 children they've taken
 care of?
Should priests and prophets
  be killed
 in your own temple?

21 "Young people and old
  people alike
 lie dead in the dust of my
  streets.
My young men and women
  have been killed by
  swords.
You killed them when you
  were angry.
You put them to death
  without pity.

22 "You sent for terrors to come
  against me on every side.
It was as if you were
 inviting people to enjoy a
  feast day.
Because you were angry, no
  one escaped.
No one was left alive.
I took good care of my
 children and brought
  them up.
But my enemies have
 destroyed them."

3 I am a man who has
  suffered greatly.
The Lord has used the
  Babylonians
 to punish my people.
2 He has driven me away. He
  has made me walk
 in darkness instead of
  light.

³ He has turned his powerful
hand against me.
He has done it again and
again, all day long.
⁴ He has worn out my body.
He has broken my bones.
⁵ He has surrounded me and
attacked me.
He has made me suffer
bitterly.
He has made things hard
for me.
⁶ He has made me live in
darkness
like those who are dead
and gone.

⁷ He has built walls around
me, so I can't escape.
He has put heavy chains
on me.
⁸ I call out and cry for help.
But he won't listen to me
when I pray.
⁹ He has put up a stone wall to
block my way.
He has made my paths
crooked.

¹⁰ He has been like a bear
waiting to attack me.
He has been like a lion
hiding in the bushes.
¹¹ He has dragged me off the
path.
He has torn me to pieces.
And he has left me
helpless.
¹² He has gotten his bow ready
to use.
He has shot his arrows at
me.
¹³ The arrows from his bag
have gone through my
heart.

¹⁴ My people laugh at me all the
time.
They sing and make fun of
me all day long.
¹⁵ The LORD has made my life
bitter.
He has made me suffer
bitterly.

¹⁶ He made me chew stones
that broke my teeth.
He has walked all over me
in the dust.
¹⁷ I have lost all hope of ever
having any peace.
I've forgotten what good
times are like.
¹⁸ So I say, "My glory has faded
away.
My hope in the LORD is
gone."

¹⁹ I remember how I suffered
and wandered.
I remember how bitter my
life was.
²⁰ I remember it very well.
My spirit is very sad deep
down inside me.
²¹ But here is something else I
remember.
And it gives me hope.

²² The LORD loves us very
much.
So we haven't been
completely destroyed.
His loving concern never
fails.
²³ His great love is new every
morning.
LORD, how faithful you are!
²⁴ I say to myself, "The LORD
is everything I will ever
need.
So I will put my hope in
him."

25 The LORD is good to those
who put their hope in
him.
He is good to those who
look to him.
26 It is good when people wait
quietly
for the LORD to save them.
27 It is good for a man to carry a
heavy load of suffering
while he is young.

28 Let him sit alone and not say
anything.
The LORD has placed that
load on him.
29 Let him bury his face in the
dust.
There might still be hope
for him.
30 Let him turn his cheek
toward those who would
slap him.
Let him be filled with
shame.

31 The Lord doesn't turn his
back
on people forever.
32 He might bring suffering.
But he will also show
loving concern.
How great his faithful love
is!
33 He doesn't want to bring
pain
or suffering to anyone.

34 Every time people crush
prisoners under their
feet,
the Lord knows all about it.
35 When people refuse to give
someone what they
should,
the Most High God knows
it.

36 When people don't treat
someone fairly,
the Lord knows it.

37 Suppose people order
something to happen.
It won't happen unless the
Lord has planned it.
38 Troubles and good things
alike come to people
because the Most High
God has commanded
them to come.
39 A person who is still alive
shouldn't blame God
when God punishes them
for their sins.

40 Let's take a good look at the
way we're living.
Let's return to the LORD.
41 Let's lift up our hands to God
in heaven.
Let's pray to him with all
our hearts.
42 Let's say, "We have sinned.
We've refused to obey you.
And you haven't forgiven us.

43 "You have covered yourself
with the cloud of your
anger.
You have chased us.
You have killed us without
pity.
44 You have covered yourself
with the cloud of your
anger.
Our prayers can't get
through to you.
45 You have made us become
like trash and garbage
among the nations.

46 "All our enemies have opened
their mouths wide
to swallow us up.

⁴⁷We are terrified and trapped.
  We are broken and
    destroyed."
⁴⁸Streams of tears flow from
    my eyes.
  That's because my people
    are destroyed.
⁴⁹Tears will never stop flowing
    from my eyes.
  My eyes can't get any rest.
⁵⁰I'll weep until the LORD looks
    down from heaven.
  I'll cry until he notices my
    tears.
⁵¹What I see brings pain to my
    spirit.
  All the women of my city
    are mourning.
⁵²Those who were my enemies
    for no reason at all
  hunted me down as if I
    were a bird.
⁵³They tried to end my life
    by throwing me into a deep
      pit.
  They threw stones down at
    me.
⁵⁴The water rose and covered
    my head.
  I thought I was going to
    die.
⁵⁵LORD, I called out to you.
  I called out from the
    bottom of the pit.
⁵⁶I prayed, "Please don't close
    your ears
  to my cry for help."
  And you heard my appeal.
⁵⁷You came near when I called
    out to you.
  You said, "Do not be afraid."
⁵⁸Lord, you stood up for me in
    court.

You saved my life and set
    me free.
⁵⁹LORD, you have seen the
    wrong things
  people have done to me.
  Stand up for me again!
⁶⁰You have seen how my
    enemies
  have tried to get even with
    me.
  You know all about their
    plans against me.
⁶¹LORD, you have heard them
    laugh at me.
  You know all about their
    plans against me.
⁶²You have heard my enemies
    whispering among
      themselves.
  They speak against me all
    day long.
⁶³Just look at them sitting and
    standing there!
  They sing and make fun of
    me.
⁶⁴LORD, pay them back.
  Punish them for what their
    hands have done.
⁶⁵Cover their minds with a veil.
  Put a curse on them!
⁶⁶LORD, get angry with them
    and hunt them down.
  Wipe them off the face of
    the earth.

4 Look at how the gold has
    lost its brightness!
  See how dull the fine gold
    has become!
  The sacred jewels are
    scattered
    at every street corner.

²The priceless children of
    Zion

were worth their weight in
  gold.
But now they are thought of
    as clay pots
  made by the hands of a
    potter.

³ Even wild dogs
  nurse their young pups.
But my people are as mean
  as ostriches in the desert.

⁴ When the babies get thirsty,
    their tongues stick to the
    roofs of their mouths.
When the children beg for
    bread,
  no one gives them any.

⁵ Those who once ate fine food
  are dying in the streets.
Those who wore royal clothes
  are now lying on piles of
    trash.

⁶ My people have been punished
  more than Sodom was.
It was destroyed in a
    moment.
  No one offered it a helping
    hand.

⁷ Jerusalem's princes were
    brighter than snow.
  They were whiter than
    milk.
Their bodies were redder
    than rubies.
  They looked like lapis lazuli.

⁸ But now they are blacker
    than coal.
  No one even recognizes
    them in the streets.
Their skin is wrinkled on
    their bones.
  It has become as dry as a
    stick.

⁹ Those killed by swords are
    better off
  than those who die of
    hunger.
Those who are hungry waste
    away to nothing.
  They don't have any food
    from the fields.

¹⁰ With their own hands, loving
    mothers
  have had to cook even their
    own children.
They ate their children
  when my people were
    destroyed.

¹¹ The LORD has become very
    angry.
  He has poured out his
    burning anger.
He started a fire in Zion.
  It burned its foundations.

¹² The kings of the earth
    couldn't believe what
    was happening.
  Neither could any of the
    peoples of the world.
Enemies actually attacked
    and entered
  the gates of Jerusalem.

¹³ It happened because
    Jerusalem's prophets had
    sinned.
  Her priests had done evil
    things.
All of them spilled the
    blood
  of those who did what was
    right.

¹⁴ Now those prophets and
    priests
  have to feel their way along
    the streets
  as if they were blind.

The blood of those they
    killed has made them
    "unclean."
So no one dares to touch
    their clothes.

¹⁵ "Go away! You are 'unclean'!"
    people cry out to them.
"Go away! Get out of here!
    Don't touch us!"
So they run away and wander
    around.
    Then people among the
        nations say,
    "They can't stay here
        anymore."

¹⁶ The LORD himself has
    scattered them.
He doesn't watch over
    them anymore.
No one shows the priests any
    respect.
No one honors the elders.

¹⁷ And that's not all. Our eyes
    grew tired.
We looked for help that
    never came.
We watched from our
    towers.
    We kept looking for a
        nation that couldn't save
        us.

¹⁸ People hunted us down no
    matter where we went.
We couldn't even walk in
    our streets.
Our end was near, so we only
    had a few days to live.
Our end had come.

¹⁹ Those who were hunting us
    down were faster
    than eagles in the sky.
They chased us over the
    mountains.

They hid and waited for us
    in the desert.

²⁰ Zedekiah, the LORD's
    anointed king, was our
    last hope.
But he was caught in their
    traps.
We thought he would keep us
    safe.
    We expected to continue
        living among the
        nations.

²¹ People of Edom, be joyful.
    You who live in the land of
        Uz, be glad.
But the cup of the LORD's
    anger will also be passed
    to you.
    Then you will become
        drunk.
    Your clothes will be
        stripped off.

²² People of Zion, the time for
    you to be punished
    will come to an end.
The LORD won't keep you
    away from your land any
    longer.
But he will punish your sin,
    people of Edom.
He will show everyone
    the evil things you have
    done.

5 LORD, think about what has
    happened to us.
Look at the shame our
    enemies have brought
    on us.

² The land you gave us has
    been turned over to
    outsiders.
Our homes have been
    given to strangers.

³ Our fathers have been killed.
　 Our mothers don't have
　 　 husbands.
⁴ We have to buy the water we
　 　 drink.
　 We have to pay for the
　 　 wood we use.
⁵ Those who chase us are right
　 　 behind us.
　 We're tired and can't get
　 　 any rest.
⁶ We put ourselves under the
　 　 control of Egypt and
　 　 Assyria
　 just to get enough bread.
⁷ Our people of long ago
　 　 sinned.
　 And they are now dead.
　 We are being punished
　 　 because of their sins.
⁸ Slaves rule over us.
　 No one can set us free
　 　 from their power.
⁹ We put our lives in danger
　 　 just to get some bread to
　 　 eat.
　 Robbers in the desert
　 　 might kill us with their
　 　 swords.
¹⁰ Our skin is as hot as an oven.
　 We are so hungry we're
　 　 burning up with fever.
¹¹ Our women have been
　 　 treated badly in Zion.
　 Our virgins have been
　 　 treated badly in the
　 　 towns of Judah.
¹² Our princes have been hung
　 　 up by their hands.
　 No one shows our elders
　 　 any respect.

¹³ Our young men are forced
　 　 to grind grain at the
　 　 mill.
　 Our boys almost fall down
　 　 as they carry heavy loads
　 　 of wood.
¹⁴ Our elders don't go to the city
　 　 gate anymore.
　 Our young men have
　 　 stopped playing their
　 　 music.
¹⁵ There isn't any joy in our
　 　 hearts.
　 Our dancing has turned
　 　 into mourning.
¹⁶ All of our honor is gone.
　 How terrible it is for us
　 　 because we have sinned!
¹⁷ So our hearts are weak.
　 Our eyes can't see very
　 　 clearly.
¹⁸ Mount Zion has been
　 　 deserted.
　 Wild dogs are prowling all
　 　 around on it.

¹⁹ LORD, you rule forever.
　 Your throne will last for all
　 　 time to come.
²⁰ Why do you always forget us?
　 Why have you deserted us
　 　 for so long?
²¹ LORD, please bring us back to
　 　 you.
　 Then we can return.
　 Make our lives like new
　 　 again.
²² Or have you completely
　 　 turned away from us?
　 Are you really that angry
　 　 with us?

Ezekiel

Introduction:

Ezekiel was a priest and prophet for God. His name means "God is strong." Ezekiel lived when Jerusalem was destroyed. He wrote this book for the Jews who had to move away from their land. He told the people about their sin. But he also told them about God's promise. God still loved his people. He promised to care for them and protect them.

Outline of contents:

The LORD Gives Ezekiel Visions of His Glory

1 I was 30 years old. I was with my people. We had been taken away from our country. We were by the Kebar River in the land of Babylon. On the fifth day of the fourth month, the heavens were opened. I saw visions of God.

² It was the fifth day of the month. Jehoiachin had been king of Judah. It was the fifth year since he had been brought to Babylon as a prisoner. ³ A message from the LORD came to me. I was by the Kebar River in Babylon. The power of the LORD came on me there. I am Ezekiel the priest, the son of Buzi.

⁴ I looked up and saw a windstorm coming from the north. I saw a huge cloud. The fire of lightning was flashing out of it. Bright light surrounded it. The center of the fire looked like glowing metal. ⁵ I saw in the fire something that looked like four living creatures. They appeared to have the shape of a human being. ⁶ But each of them had four faces and four wings. ⁷ Their legs were straight. Their feet looked like the feet of a calf. They were as bright as polished bronze. ⁸ The creatures had human hands under their wings on their four sides. All four of them had faces and wings. ⁹ The wings of one touched the wings of another. Each of the creatures went straight ahead. They didn't change their direction as they moved.

¹⁰ Here's what their faces looked like. Each of the four creatures had the face of a human being. On the right side each had the face of a lion. On the left each had the face of an ox. Each one also had an eagle's face. ¹¹ That's what their faces

looked like. They each had two wings that spread out and lifted up. Each wing touched the wing of another creature on either side. They each had two other wings that covered their bodies. [12] All the creatures went straight ahead. Anywhere their spirits would lead them to go, they would go. They didn't change their direction as they went. [13] The living creatures looked like burning coals of fire or like torches. Fire moved back and forth among the creatures. It was bright. Lightning flashed out of it. [14] The creatures raced back and forth like flashes of lightning.

[15] As I looked at the living creatures, I saw wheels on the ground beside them. Each creature had four faces. [16] Here's how the wheels looked and worked. They gleamed like topaz. All four of them looked alike. Each one seemed to be made like a wheel inside another wheel at right angles. [17] The wheels could go in any one of the four directions the creatures faced. The wheels didn't change their direction as the creatures moved. [18] Their rims were high and terrifying. All four rims were full of eyes all the way around them.

[19] When the living creatures moved, the wheels beside them moved. When the creatures rose from the ground, the wheels also rose. [20] Anywhere their spirits would lead them to go, they would go. And the wheels would rise along with them. That's because the spir-its of the living creatures were in the wheels. [21] When the living creatures moved, the wheels also moved. When the creatures stood still, they also stood still. When the creatures rose from the ground, the wheels rose along with them. That's because the spirits of the living creatures were in the wheels.

[22] Something that looked like a huge space was spread out above the heads of the living creatures. It gleamed like crystal. It was terrifying. [23] The wings of the creatures were spread out under the space. They reached out toward one another. Each creature had two wings covering its body. [24] When the living creatures moved, I heard the sound of their wings. It was like the roar of rushing waters. It sounded like the thundering voice of the Mighty God. It was like the loud noise an army makes. When the creatures stood still, they lowered their wings.

[25] Then a voice came from above the huge space over their heads. They stood with their wings lowered. [26] Above the space over their heads was something that looked like a throne made out of lapis lazuli. On the throne high above was a figure that appeared to be a man. [27] From his waist up he looked like glowing metal that was full of fire. From his waist down he looked like fire. Bright light surrounded him. [28] The glow around him looked like a rainbow in the clouds on a rainy day.

That's what the glory of the LORD looked like. When I saw it, I fell with my face toward the ground. Then I heard the voice of someone speaking.

The LORD Appoints Ezekiel to Speak for Him

2 He said to me, "Son of man, stand up on your feet. I will speak to you." [2] As he spoke, the Spirit of the LORD came into me. He raised me to my feet. I heard him speaking to me.

[3] He said, "Son of man, I am sending you to the people of Israel. That nation has refused to obey me. They have turned against me. They and their people of long ago have been against me to this day. [4] The people I am sending you to are very stubborn. Tell them, 'Here is what the LORD and King says.' [5] They might listen, or they might not. After all, they refuse to obey me. But whether they listen or not, they will know that a prophet was among them. [6] Son of man, do not be afraid of them or of what they say. Do not be afraid, even if thorns and bushes are all around you. Do not be afraid, even if you live among scorpions. Do not be afraid of what they say. Do not be terrified by them. They always refuse to obey me. [7] You must give them my message. They might listen, or they might not. After all, they refuse to obey me. [8] Son of man, listen to what I tell you. Do not be like those who refuse to obey me. Open your mouth. Eat what I give you."

[9] Then I looked up. I saw a hand reach out to me. A scroll was in it. [10] He unrolled it in front of me. Both sides had words written on them. They spoke about sadness, sorrow and trouble.

3 The LORD said to me, "Son of man, eat what is in front of you. Eat this scroll. Then go and speak to the people of Israel." [2] So I opened my mouth. And he gave me the scroll to eat.

[3] Then he said to me, "Son of man, eat this scroll I am giving you. Fill your stomach with it." So I ate it. And it tasted as sweet as honey in my mouth.

[4] Then he said to me, "Son of man, go to the people of Israel. Give them my message. [5] I am not sending you to people who speak another language that is hard to learn. Instead, I am sending you to the people of Israel. [6] You are not being sent to many nations whose people speak other languages that are hard to learn. You would not be able to understand them. Suppose I had sent you to them. Then they certainly would have listened to you. [7] But the people of Israel do not want to listen to you. That is because they do not want to listen to me. All the Israelites are very stubborn. [8] But I will make you just as stubborn as they are. [9] I will make you very brave. So do not be afraid of them. Do not let them terrify you, even though they refuse to obey me."

[10] He continued, "Son of man, listen carefully. Take to heart

everything I tell you. ¹¹ Go now to your own people who were brought here as prisoners. Speak to them. Tell them, 'Here is what the LORD and King says.' Speak to them whether they listen or not."

¹² Then the Spirit of the LORD lifted me up. I heard a loud rumbling sound behind me. The sound was made when the glory of the LORD rose up. It rose up from the place it had been standing. ¹³ The sound was made by the wings of the living creatures. They were brushing against one another. The sound was also made by the wheels beside them. It was a loud rumbling sound. ¹⁴ Then the Spirit lifted me up and took me away. My spirit was bitter. I was very angry. The power of the LORD was on me. ¹⁵ I came to my people who had been brought as prisoners to Tel Aviv. It was near the Kebar River. I went to where they were living. There I sat among them for seven days. I was very sad and scared about everything that had happened.

The LORD Has Appointed Ezekiel to Warn Israel

¹⁶ After seven days, a message from the LORD came to me. ¹⁷ The LORD said, "Son of man, I have appointed you as a prophet to warn the people of Israel. So listen to my message. Give them a warning from me. ¹⁸ Suppose I say to a sinful person, 'You can be sure you will die.' And you do not warn them. You do not try to get them to change their evil ways in order to save their life. Then that sinful person will die because they have sinned. And I will hold you responsible for their death. ¹⁹ But suppose you do warn that sinful person. And they do not turn away from their sin or their evil ways. Then they will die because they have sinned. But you will have saved yourself.

²⁰ "Or suppose a godly person turns away from their godliness and does what is evil. And suppose I put something in their way that will trip them up. Then they will die. Since you did not warn them, they will die for their sin. The godly things that person did will not be remembered. And I will hold you responsible for their death. ²¹ But suppose you do warn a godly person not to sin. And they do not sin. Then you can be sure that they will live because they listened to your warning. And you will have saved yourself."

²² The power of the LORD was on me. He said, "Get up. Go out to the plain. I will speak to you there." ²³ So I got up and went out to the plain. The glory of the LORD was standing there. It was just like the glory I had seen by the Kebar River. So I fell with my face toward the ground.

²⁴ Then the Spirit of the LORD came into me. He raised me to my feet. He said to me, "Go, son of man. Shut yourself inside your house. ²⁵ Some people will tie you up with ropes. So you will not be able to go out among your people. ²⁶ I will make your

tongue stick to the roof of your mouth. Then you will be silent. You will not be able to correct them. That's because they always refuse to obey me. ²⁷But later I will speak to you. I will open your mouth. Then you will tell them, 'Here is what the LORD and King says.' Those who listen will listen. And those who refuse to listen will refuse. They always refuse to obey me.

An Attack on Jerusalem Is Pictured

4 "Son of man, get a block of clay. Put it in front of you. Draw the city of Jerusalem on it. ²Then pretend to surround it and attack it. Make some little models of war machines. Build a ramp up to it. Set camps up around it. Surround it with models of logs to be used for knocking down its gates. ³Then get an iron pan. Put it between you and the city. Pretend it is an iron wall. Turn your face toward the city. It will be under attack when you begin to attack it. That will show the people of Israel what is going to happen to Jerusalem.

⁴"Next, lie down on your left side. Pretend that you are putting Israel's sin on yourself. Keep their sin on you for the number of days you lie on your side. ⁵Let each day you lie there stand for one year of their sin. So you will keep Israel's sin on you for 390 days.

⁶"After you have finished this, lie down again. This time lie on your right side. Pretend that you

are putting Judah's sin on yourself. Lie there for 40 days. That is one day for each year of their sin. ⁷Next, turn your face toward the model of Jerusalem under attack. Uncover your arm as if you were a soldier ready to fight. Prophesy against the city. ⁸I will tie you up with ropes. Then you will not be able to turn from one side to the other. You will stay that way until you have finished attacking Jerusalem.

⁹"Get some wheat and barley. Also get some beans and lentils. And get some millet and spelt. Put everything in a storage jar. Use it to make some bread for yourself. Eat it during the 390 days you are lying down on your side. ¹⁰Weigh out eight ounces of food to eat each day. Eat it at your regular mealtimes. ¹¹Also measure out two-thirds of a quart of water. Drink it at your regular mealtimes. ¹²Eat your food as you would eat a loaf of barley bread. Bake it over human waste in front of the people." ¹³The LORD said, "That is how the people of Israel will eat 'unclean' food. They will eat it in the nations where I will drive them."

¹⁴Then I said, "No, LORD and King! I won't do this! I've never eaten anything 'unclean.' From the time I was young until now, I've never eaten anything that was found dead. And I've never eaten anything torn apart by wild animals. 'unclean' meat has never entered my mouth."

¹⁵"All right," he said. "I will let you bake your bread over waste

from cows. You can use that instead of human waste."

¹⁶ He continued, "Son of man, I am about to cut off the food supply in Jerusalem. The people will be worried as they eat their tiny share of food. They will not have any hope as they drink their tiny share of water. ¹⁷ There will be very little food and water. The people will be shocked as they look at one another. They will become weaker and weaker because of their sin.

God's Judgment Will Be Like a Barber's Razor

5 "Son of man, get a sharp sword. Use it as a barber's razor. Shave your head and beard with it. Then get a set of scales and weigh the hair. Separate it into three piles. ² Burn up a third of the hair inside the city. Do this when you stop attacking the model of Jerusalem. Next, get another third of the hair. Strike it with a sword all around the city. Then scatter the last third to the winds. That is because I will chase the people with a sword that is ready to strike them down. ³ But save a few hairs. Tuck them away in the clothes you are wearing. ⁴ Next, get a few more hairs. Throw them into the fire. Burn them up. The fire will spread to all the people of Israel."

⁵ The LORD and King says, "What you do with the hair stands for what I will do with Jerusalem's people. I have placed that city in the center of the nations. Countries are all around it. ⁶ But its people are sinful. They have refused to obey my laws and rules. They have turned their backs on my laws. They have not followed my rules. These people are worse than the nations and countries around them."

⁷ The LORD and King continues, "You people have been worse than the nations around you. You have not lived by my rules or kept my laws. You have not even lived up to the standards of the nations around you."

⁸ The LORD and King continues, "Jerusalem, I myself am against you. I will punish you in the sight of the nations. ⁹ I will do to you what I have never done before and will never do again. That is because you worship statues of gods. I hate them. ¹⁰ So parents will eat their own children inside the city. And children will eat their parents. I will punish you. And I will scatter to the winds anyone who is left alive. ¹¹ You have made my temple 'unclean.' You have set up statues of all your evil gods. You have done other things I hate. So I will cut you off just like Ezekiel cut off his hair. I will not spare you or feel sorry for you. And that is just as sure as I am alive," announces the LORD and King. ¹² A third of your people will die of the plague inside your walls. Or they will die of hunger there. Another third will be killed by swords outside your walls. And I will scatter the last third of your people to the winds. I will chase

them with a sword that is ready to strike them down.

¹³ "Then I will not be angry anymore. My great anger against them will die down. And I will be satisfied. Then they will know that I have spoken with strong feelings. And my great anger toward them will come to an end. I am the LORD.

¹⁴ "I will destroy you. I will bring shame on you in the sight of the nations around you. All those who pass by will see it. ¹⁵ You will be put to shame. The nations will make fun of you. You will serve as a warning to others. They will be shocked when they see you. So I will punish you because I am very angry with you. You will feel the sting of my warning. I have spoken. I am the LORD. ¹⁶ I will shoot at you with my deadly, destroying arrows of hunger. I will shoot to kill. I will bring more and more hunger on you. I will cut off your food supply. ¹⁷ I will send hunger and wild animals against you. They will destroy all your children. Plague and murder will sweep over you. And I will send swords to kill you. I have spoken. I am the LORD."

Ezekiel Prophesies Against the Mountains of Israel

6 A message from the LORD came to me. The LORD said, ² "Son of man, turn your attention to the mountains of Israel. Prophesy against them. ³ Say, 'Mountains of Israel, listen to the message of the LORD and King. Here is what he says to the mountains and hills. And here is what he says to the canyons and valleys. He tells them, "I will send swords to kill your people. I will destroy the high places where you worship other gods. ⁴ Your altars will be torn down. Your incense altars will be smashed. And I will kill your people in front of the statues of your gods. ⁵ I will put the dead bodies of Israelites in front of those statues. I will scatter your bones around your altars. ⁶ No matter where you live, the towns will be destroyed. The high places will be torn down. So your altars will be completely destroyed. The statues of your gods will be smashed to pieces. Your incense altars will be broken down. And everything you have made will be wiped out. ⁷ Your people will fall down dead among you. Then you will know that I am the LORD.

⁸ " ' "But I will spare some of you. Some will escape from being killed by swords. You will be scattered among other lands and nations. ⁹ You will be taken away to those nations as prisoners. Those of you who escape will remember me. You will recall how much pain your unfaithful hearts gave me. You turned away from me. Your eyes longed to see the statues of your gods. You will hate yourselves because of all the evil things you have done. I hate those things too. ¹⁰ You will know that I am the LORD. I said I would bring trouble on you. And my warning came true." ' "

¹¹ The LORD and King said to me, "Clap your hands. Stamp your feet. Cry out, 'How sad!' Do this because the people of Israel have done so many evil things. I hate those things. Israel will be destroyed by war, hunger and plague. ¹² The one who is far away will die of the plague. The one who is near will be killed by swords. Anyone who is left alive and is spared will die of hunger. And in this way I will pour out my great anger on them. ¹³ Then they will know that I am the LORD. Their people will lie dead among the statues of their gods around their altars. Their bodies will lie on every high hill and every mountaintop. They will lie under every green tree and leafy oak tree. They used to offer sweet-smelling incense to all their gods at those places. ¹⁴ I will reach out my powerful hand against them. The land will become dry and empty. Those people will live from the desert all the way to Diblah. They will know that I am the LORD."

The End Has Come

7 A message from the LORD came to me. The LORD said, ² "Son of man, I am the LORD and King. I say to the land of Israel, 'The end has come! It has come on the four corners of the land. ³ The end has now come for you. I will pour out my anger on you. I will judge you based on how you have lived. I will pay you back for all your evil practices. I hate them.

⁴ " 'I will not feel sorry for you. I will not spare you. You can be sure that I will pay you back for how you have lived. I will judge you for your evil practices. I hate them. You will know that I am the LORD.'

⁵ "I am the LORD and King. I say, 'Horrible trouble is coming! No one has ever heard of anything like it. It is here!

⁶ " 'The end has come! The end has come! It has stirred itself up against you. It is here!
⁷ Death has come on you who live in the land. The time for you to be destroyed has come. The day when it will happen is near. There is no joy on your mountains. There is nothing but panic.

⁸ " 'I am about to pour out all my great anger on you. I will judge you based on how you have lived. I will pay you back for all your evil practices. I hate them.

⁹ " 'I will not feel sorry for you. I will not spare you. I will pay you back for how you have lived. I will judge you for your evil practices. I hate them. You will know that I am the one who strikes you down. I am the LORD.

¹⁰ " 'The day for me to punish you is here! It is here! Death has arrived. The time is ripe for you to be judged. Your pride has grown so much that you will be destroyed. ¹¹ Your mean and harmful acts have become like a rod. I will use it to punish those who do evil. None of them will be left. None of their wealth or anything of value will remain.

¹² " 'The time has come! The

day has arrived! I will soon pour out my great anger on the whole crowd of you. Do not let the buyer be happy. Do not let the seller be sad. ¹³ The seller will not get back the land that was sold. That will be true as long as both the buyer and seller are alive.

" 'Ezekiel, the vision I gave you about that whole crowd will come true. They have committed many sins. So not one of them will be able to save their life. ¹⁴ They have blown trumpets. They have made everything ready. But no one will go into battle. I will soon pour out my great anger on the whole crowd.

¹⁵ " 'There is trouble everywhere. War is outside the city. Plague and hunger are inside it. Those out in the country will die in battle. Those in the city will be destroyed by hunger and plague. ¹⁶ All those who escape and are left alive will run to the mountains. They will sound like doves of the valley when they cry over their sins.

¹⁷ " 'Their hands will be powerless to help them. They will wet themselves. ¹⁸ They will put on the rough clothing people wear when they're sad. They will put on terror as if it were their clothes. Every face will be covered with shame. Every head will be shaved.

¹⁹ " 'They will throw their silver into the streets. They will treat their gold like an "unclean" thing. Their silver and gold won't be able to save them on the day I pour out my an-

ger. It will not be able to satisfy their hunger. Their stomachs can't be filled with it. Their silver and gold have tripped them up. It has made them fall into sin. ²⁰ My people were so proud of their beautiful jewelry. They used it to make statues of their evil gods. I hate those gods. So I will turn their jewelry into an "unclean" thing for them.

²¹ " 'I will hand over their wealth to outsiders. I will turn it over to sinful people in other countries. They will make it "unclean." ²² I will turn my face away from my people. Robbers will make "unclean" the temple I love. They will enter it and make it "unclean."

²³ " 'Ezekiel, get ready to put my people in chains. The land is full of murderers. They are harming one another all over Jerusalem. ²⁴ I will bring the most evil nations against them. They will take over the houses in the city. I will put an end to the pride of those who are mighty. Their holy places will be made "unclean."

²⁵ " 'When terror comes, they will look for peace. But there will not be any. ²⁶ Trouble after trouble will come. One report will follow another. But they will not be true. The people will go searching for a vision from the prophets. But there will not be any. The teaching of the law by the priests will be gone. Advice from the elders will come to an end.

²⁷ " 'The king will be filled with sadness. The princes will

lose all hope. The hands of the people of the land will tremble. I will punish them based on how they have lived. I will judge them by their own standards. Then they will know that I am the LORD.' "

The People Worship Other Gods in the Temple

8 It was the sixth year since King Jehoiachin had been brought to Babylon as a prisoner. On the fifth day of the sixth month, I was sitting in my house. The elders of Judah were sitting there with me. The power of the LORD and King came on me there. [2] I looked up and saw a figure that appeared to be human. From his waist down he looked like fire. From his waist up he looked as bright as glowing metal. [3] He reached out what appeared to be a hand. He took hold of me by the hair of my head. The Spirit of the LORD lifted me up between earth and heaven. In visions God gave me, the Spirit took me to Jerusalem. He brought me to the entrance of the north gate of the inner courtyard. The statue of a god was standing there. It made God very angry. [4] There in front of me was the glory of the God of Israel. It looked just as it did in the vision I had seen on the plain.

[5] Then the LORD said to me, "Son of man, look toward the north." So I did. I saw a statue that made God angry. It was in the entrance of the gate north of the altar.

[6] He said to me, "Son of man, do you see what the Israelites are doing here? They are doing things I hate very much. Those things will cause me to go far away from my temple. But you will see things I hate even more."

[7] Then he brought me to the entrance to the courtyard. I looked up and saw a hole in the wall. [8] He said to me, "Son of man, dig into the wall." So I did. And I saw a door there.

[9] He continued, "Go through it. Look at the evil things they are doing here. I hate those things." [10] So I went in and looked. All over the walls were pictures of all kinds of crawling things and "unclean" animals. The LORD hates it when people worship those things. There were also carvings of the gods of the people of Israel. [11] In front of them stood 70 elders of Israel. Jaazaniah was standing there among them. He is the son of Shaphan. Each elder was holding a shallow cup. A sweet-smelling cloud of incense was rising from the cups.

[12] The LORD spoke to me. He said, "Son of man, do you see what the elders of Israel are doing in the dark? Each of them is in his own room worshiping his own god. They say, 'The LORD doesn't see us. He has deserted the land.' " [13] He continued, "You will see them doing things I hate even more."

[14] Then he brought me to the entrance of the north gate of the LORD's house. I saw women sitting there. They were mourning

for the god named Tammuz. [15] The LORD said to me, "Son of man, do you see what they are doing? You will see things I hate even more."

[16] Then he brought me into the inner courtyard of the LORD's house. About 25 men were there. They were at the entrance to the LORD's temple between the porch and the altar. Their backs were turned toward the temple. Their faces were turned toward the east. And they were bowing down to the sun.

[17] He said to me, "Son of man, have you seen all of this? The people of Judah are doing things here that I hate. This is a very serious matter. They are harming one another all through the land. They continue to make me very angry. Just look at them making fun of me! [18] So I am angry with them. I will punish them. I will not spare them or feel sorry for them. They might even shout in my ears. But I will not listen to them."

The LORD Judges Those Who Worship Other Gods

9 Then I heard the LORD call out in a loud voice. He said, "Bring here those who are appointed to bring my judgment on the city. Make sure each of them has a weapon in his hand." [2] I saw six men coming from the direction of the upper gate. It faces north. Each of them had a deadly weapon in his hand. A man wearing linen clothes came along with them. He was carrying a writing kit at his side.

They came in and stood beside the bronze altar.

[3] The glory of the God of Israel had been above the cherubim. It moved from there to the doorway of the temple. Then the LORD called to the man who was dressed in linen clothes. He had the writing kit. [4] The LORD said to him, "Go all through Jerusalem. Look for those who are sad and sorry about all the things being done there. I hate those things. Put a mark on the foreheads of those people."

[5] I heard him speak to the six men. He said, "Follow him through the city. Do not show any pity or concern. [6] Kill the old men and women, the young men and women, and the children. But do not touch anyone who has the mark. Start at my temple." So they began with the old men who were in front of the temple.

[7] Then he said to the men, "Make the temple 'unclean.' Fill the courtyards with dead bodies. Go!" So they went out and started killing people all through the city. [8] While they were doing it, I was left alone. I fell with my face toward the ground. I cried out, "LORD and King, are you going to destroy all the Israelites who are still left alive? Will you pour out your great anger on all those who remain in Jerusalem?"

[9] He answered me, "The sin of Israel and Judah is very great. The land is full of murderers. Its people are not being fair to one another anywhere in Jerusalem.

They say, 'The Lord has deserted the land. He doesn't see us.' ¹⁰ So I will not spare them or feel sorry for them. Anything that happens to them will be their own fault."

¹¹ Then the man wearing linen clothes returned. He had the writing kit. He reported, "I've done what you commanded."

The Glory of the Lord Moves Out of the Temple

10 I looked up and saw something that appeared to be a throne made out of lapis lazuli. It was above the huge space that was spread out over the heads of the cherubim. ² The Lord spoke to the man who was wearing linen clothes. He said, "Go in among the wheels beneath the cherubim. Fill your hands with burning coals from the fire that is among the cherubim. Scatter the coals over the city." As I watched, he went in.

³ The cherubim were standing on the south side of the temple when the man went in. A cloud filled the inner courtyard. ⁴ Then the glory of the Lord rose from above the cherubim. It moved to the doorway of the temple. The cloud filled the temple. And the courtyard was full of the brightness of the glory of the Lord. ⁵ The sound the wings of the cherubim made could be heard as far away as the outer courtyard. It was like the voice of the Mighty God when he speaks.

⁶ The Lord gave a command to the man who was dressed in linen clothes. He said, "Get some coals of fire from among the wheels. Take them from among the cherubim." So the man went in and stood beside a wheel. ⁷ Then one of the cherubim reached out his hand. He picked up some of the burning coals that were among the wheels. He handed them to the man who was wearing linen clothes. The man took them and left. ⁸ I saw what looked like human hands. They were under the wings of the cherubim.

⁹ I looked up and saw four wheels beside the cherubim. One wheel was beside each of them. The wheels gleamed like topaz. ¹⁰ All four of them looked alike. Each wheel appeared to be inside another wheel at right angles. ¹¹ The wheels could go in any one of the four directions the cherubim faced. The wheels didn't change their direction as the cherubim moved. The cherubim went in the direction their heads faced. They didn't change their direction as they moved. ¹² Their whole bodies were completely covered with eyes. That included their backs, hands and wings. Their four wheels were covered with eyes too. ¹³ I heard someone tell the wheels to start spinning around. ¹⁴ Each of the cherubim had four faces. One face was the face of a cherub. The second was the face of a human being. The third was the face of a lion. And the fourth was an eagle's face.

¹⁵ The cherubim rose from the ground. They were the same

living creatures I had seen by the Kebar River. ¹⁶ When the cherubim moved, the wheels beside them moved. The cherubim spread their wings to rise from the ground. As they did, the wheels didn't leave their side. ¹⁷ When the cherubim stood still, the wheels also stood still. When the cherubim rose, the wheels rose along with them. That's because the spirits of the living creatures were in the wheels.

¹⁸ Then the glory of the LORD moved away from the doorway of the temple. It stopped above the cherubim. ¹⁹ While I watched, they spread their wings. They rose from the ground. As they went, the wheels went along with them. They stopped at the entrance of the east gate of the LORD's house. And the glory of the God of Israel was above them.

²⁰ These were the same living creatures I had seen by the Kebar River. I had seen them beneath the God of Israel. I realized that they were cherubim. ²¹ Each one had four faces and four wings. Under their wings was what looked like human hands. ²² Their faces looked the same as the ones I had seen by the Kebar River. Each of the cherubim went straight ahead.

The LORD's Judgment of Jerusalem Is Certain

11 Then the Spirit of the LORD lifted me up. He brought me to the east gate of the LORD's house. There were 25 men at the entrance of the gate. I saw Jaazaniah and Pelatiah among them. They were leaders of the people. Jaazaniah is the son of Azzur. Pelatiah is the son of Benaiah. ² The LORD said to me, "Son of man, these men are making evil plans. They are giving bad advice to the city. ³ They say, 'Haven't our houses just been built again? The city is like a pot used for cooking. And we are the meat in it.' ⁴ So prophesy against them. Prophesy, son of man."

⁵ Then the Spirit of the LORD came on me. He told me to tell them, "The LORD says, 'You leaders in Israel, that is what you are saying. But I know what you are thinking. ⁶ You have killed many people in this city. In fact, you have filled its streets with dead bodies.'

⁷ "So the LORD and King says, 'The bodies you have thrown there are the meat. And the city is the cooking pot. But I will drive you out of it. ⁸ You are afraid of the swords of war. But I will bring them against you,' announces the LORD and King. ⁹ 'I will drive you out of the city. I will hand you over to outsiders. And I will punish you. ¹⁰ You will be killed by swords. I will judge you at the borders of Israel. Then you will know that I am the LORD. ¹¹ This city will not be a pot for you. And you will not be the meat in it. I will judge you at the borders of Israel. ¹² Then you will know that I am the LORD. You have not obeyed my rules. You have not

kept my laws. Instead, you have lived by the standards of the nations around you.'"

¹³ Pelatiah, the son of Benaiah, died as I was prophesying. Then I fell with my face toward the ground. I cried out in a loud voice. I said, "LORD and King, will you destroy all the Israelites who are still left alive?"

The LORD Will Bring His People Back Home

¹⁴ A message from the LORD came to me. The LORD said, ¹⁵ "Son of man, the people of Jerusalem have spoken about you. They have spoken about the others the Babylonians have taken away. They have also spoken about all the other people of Israel. The people of Jerusalem have said, 'Those people are far away from the LORD. This land was given to us. And it belongs to us.'

¹⁶ "So tell them, 'The LORD and King says, "I sent some of my people far away among the nations. I scattered them among the countries. But for a little while I have been their temple in the countries where they have gone."'

¹⁷ "Tell them, 'The LORD and King says, "I will gather you from the nations. I will bring you back from the countries where you have been scattered. I will give you back the land of Israel."'

¹⁸ "They will return to it. They will remove all its statues of evil gods. I hate those gods. ¹⁹ I will give my people hearts that are completely committed to me. I will give them a new spirit that is faithful to me. I will remove their stubborn hearts from them. And I will give them hearts that obey me. ²⁰ Then they will follow my rules. They will be careful to keep my laws. They will be my people. And I will be their God. ²¹ But some people have hearts that are committed to worshiping the statues of their evil gods. I hate those gods. Anything that happens to those people will be their own fault," announces the LORD and King.

²² Then the cherubim spread their wings. The wheels were beside them. The glory of the God of Israel was above them. ²³ The glory of the LORD went up from the city. It stopped above the Mount of Olives east of the city. ²⁴ The Spirit of God lifted me up. He took me to those who had been brought to Babylon as prisoners. These are the things that happened in the visions the Spirit gave me.

Then the visions I had seen were gone. ²⁵ I told my people everything the LORD had shown me.

Ezekiel Gives a Picture of What Will Happen

12 A message from the LORD came to me. The LORD said, ² "Son of man, you are living among people who refuse to obey me. They have eyes that can see. But they do not really see. They have ears that can hear. But they do not really hear. They refuse to obey me.

³ "Son of man, pack your belongings as if you were going on a long trip. Leave in the daytime. Let the people see you. Start out from where you are. Go to another place. Perhaps they will understand the meaning of what you are doing. But they will still refuse to obey me. ⁴ Bring out your belongings packed for a long trip. Do this during the daytime. Let the people see you. Then in the evening, pretend you are being forced to leave home. Let the people see you. ⁵ While the people are watching, dig through the mud bricks of your house. Then take your belongings out through the hole in the wall. ⁶ Put them on your shoulder. Carry them out at sunset. Let the people see you. Cover your face so you can't see the land. All of that will show the Israelites what is going to happen to them."

⁷ So I did just as he commanded me. During the day I brought out my things as if I were going on a long trip. In the evening I dug through the wall of my house with my hands. At sunset I took my belongings out. I put them on my shoulders. The people watched what I was doing.

⁸ In the morning a message from the LORD came to me. The LORD said, ⁹ "Son of man, didn't the Israelites ask you, 'What are you doing?' They always refuse to obey me.

¹⁰ "Tell them, 'The LORD and King says, "This prophecy is about Zedekiah, the prince in Jerusalem. It is also about all the Israelites who still live there."'

¹¹ Tell them, 'The things I've done are a picture of what's going to happen to you.

"'So what I've done will happen to you. You will be forced to leave home. You will be taken to Babylon as prisoners.'

¹² "The prince among them will put his things on his shoulder and leave. He will do this at sunset. Someone will dig a hole in the city wall for him to go through. He will cover his face so he can't see the land. ¹³ I will spread out my net to catch him. He will be caught in my trap. I will bring him to Babylon. It is the land where the Chaldeans live. But he will not see it. He will die there. ¹⁴ I will scatter to the winds all those around him. I will scatter his officials and all his troops. And I will chase them with a sword that is ready to strike them down.

¹⁵ "They will know that I am the LORD when I scatter them among the nations. I will send them to other countries. ¹⁶ But I will spare a few of them. I will save them from war, hunger and plague. In those countries they will admit they have done all kinds of evil things. I hate those things. They will know that I am the LORD."

¹⁷ A message from the LORD came to me. The LORD said, ¹⁸ "Son of man, tremble with fear as you eat your food. Tremble as you drink your water. ¹⁹ Speak to the people of the land. Say to them, 'Here is what the LORD

and King says. He says this about those who live in Jerusalem and Israel. "They will be worried as they eat their food. They will not have any hope as they drink their water. Their land will be stripped of everything in it because all those who live there are harming one another. ²⁰ The towns where people live will be completely destroyed. The land will become a dry and empty desert. Then you will know that I am the LORD." ' "

The LORD's Judgment Will Come Soon

²¹ A message from the LORD came to me. The LORD said, ²² "Son of man, you have a proverb in the land of Israel. It says, 'The days go by, and not even one vision comes true.' ²³ Tell them, 'The LORD and King says, "I am going to put an end to this proverb. They will not use that saying in Israel anymore." ' Tell them, 'The days are coming soon when every vision will come true. ²⁴ There will be no more false visions. People will no longer use magic to find out whether good things are going to happen in Israel. ²⁵ I am the LORD. So I will say what I want to. And it will come true when I want it to. In your days I will do everything I say I will. But you people always refuse to obey me,' announces the LORD and King."

²⁶ A message from the LORD came to me. The LORD said, ²⁷ "Son of man, the Israelites are saying, 'The vision Ezekiel sees won't come true for many years.

He is prophesying about a time that is a long way off.'

²⁸ "So tell them, 'The LORD and King says, "Everything I say will come true. It will happen when I want it to," announces the LORD and King.' "

The LORD Punishes Those Who Pretend to Be True Prophets

13 A message from the LORD came to me. The LORD said, ² "Son of man, prophesy against those who are now prophesying in Israel. What they prophesy comes out of their own minds. Tell them, 'Listen to the LORD's message! ³ The LORD and King says, "How terrible it will be for you foolish prophets! You say what your own minds tell you to. Your visions do not come from me. ⁴ Israel, your prophets are like wild dogs that live among broken-down buildings. ⁵ You have not repaired the cracks in the city wall for the people of Israel. So it will not stand firm in the battle on the day I judge you. ⁶ The visions of those prophets are false. They use magic to try to find out what is going to happen. But their magic tricks are lies. They say, 'The LORD announces.' But I have not sent them. In spite of that, they expect him to make their words come true. ⁷ You prophets have seen false visions. You have used magic to try to find out what is going to happen. But your magic tricks are lies. So you lied when you said, 'The LORD announces.' I did not even speak to you at all."

⁸ " 'The LORD and King says, "I am against you prophets. Your messages are false. Your visions do not come true," announces the LORD and King. ⁹ Israel, my power will be against the prophets who see false visions. Their magic tricks are lies. They will not be among the leaders of my people. They will not be listed in the records of Israel. In fact, they will not even enter the land. Then you will know that I am the LORD and King.

¹⁰ " ' "They lead my people away from me. They say, 'Peace.' But there isn't any peace. They are like people who build a weak wall. They try to cover up the weakness by painting the wall white. ¹¹ Tell those who do this that their wall is going to fall. Heavy rains will come. I will send hailstones crashing down. Powerful winds will blow. ¹² The wall will fall down. Then people will ask them, 'Now where is the paint you covered it with?' "

¹³ " 'So the LORD and King speaks. He says, "When I am very angry, I will send a powerful wind. Hailstones and heavy rains will come. They will fall with great force. ¹⁴ I will tear down the wall you prophets painted over. I will knock it down. The only thing left will be its foundation. When it falls, you will be destroyed along with it. Then you will know that I am the LORD. ¹⁵ So I will pour out all my great anger on the wall. I will also send it against you prophets who painted it. I will say to you, 'The wall is gone. You who painted it will be gone too. ¹⁶ You prophets of Israel prophesied to Jerusalem. You saw visions of peace for its people. But there wasn't any peace,' announces the LORD and King." '

¹⁷ "Son of man, turn your attention to the daughters of your people. What they prophesy comes out of their own minds. So prophesy against them. ¹⁸ Tell them, 'Here is what the LORD and King says. "How terrible it will be for you women who sew magic charms to put around your wrists! You make veils of different lengths to put on your heads. You do these things to trap people. You trap my people. But you will also be trapped. ¹⁹ You have treated me as if I were not holy. You did it among my very own people. You did it for a few handfuls of barley and scraps of bread. You told lies to my people. They like to listen to lies. You killed those who should have lived. And you spared those who should have died."

²⁰ " 'So the LORD and King says, "I am against your magic charms. You use them to trap people as if they were birds. I will tear them off your arms. I will set free the people you trap like birds. ²¹ I will tear your veils off your heads. I will save my people from your power. They will no longer be under your control. Then you will know that I am the LORD. ²² I had not made godly people sad. But when you told them lies, you made them lose all hope. You

advised sinful people not to turn from their evil ways. You did not want them to save their lives. ²³ So you will never see false visions again. You will not use your magic tricks anymore. I will save my people from your power. Then you will know that I am the LORD." ' "

The LORD Judges Those Who Worship Other Gods

14 Some of the elders of Israel came to see me. They sat down with me. ² Then a message from the LORD came to me. The LORD said, ³ "Son of man, these men have thought about nothing but other gods. They have fallen into the evil trap of worshiping them. Should I let these men ask me for any advice? ⁴ Speak to them. Tell them, 'The LORD and King says, "Suppose any of the Israelites think about other gods. And they fall into the evil trap of worshiping them. Then they go to a prophet to ask for advice. If they do, I myself will tell the prophet to answer them in keeping with their worship of many gods. ⁵ I will win back the hearts of the people of Israel. All of them have deserted me for their other gods." '

⁶ "So speak to the people of Israel. Tell them, 'The LORD and King says, "Turn away from your sins! Also turn away from your gods. Give up all the evil things you have done. I hate them.

⁷ " ' "Suppose any of the Israelites or any outsiders who live in Israel separate themselves from me. And they think about other gods. They fall into the evil trap of worshiping them. Then they go to a prophet to ask me for advice. If they do, I myself will tell the prophet to answer them. ⁸ I will turn against them. I will make an example out of them. People will talk about the bad things that happen to them. I will remove them from you. Then you will know that I am the LORD.

⁹ " ' "Suppose that prophet is stirred up to give a prophecy. Then I am the one who has stirred him up. And I will reach out my powerful hand against him. I will destroy him from among my people Israel. ¹⁰ The prophet will be as much to blame as the one who asks him for advice. Both of them will be guilty. ¹¹ Then the people of Israel will no longer wander away from me. And they will not make themselves 'unclean' anymore with their many sins. They will be my people. And I will be their God," ' announces the LORD and King."

Jerusalem Can't Escape the LORD's Judgment

¹² A message from the LORD came to me. The LORD said, ¹³ "Son of man, suppose the people in a certain country sin against me. And they are not faithful to me. So I reach out my powerful hand against them. I cut off their food supply. I make them very hungry. I kill them and their animals. ¹⁴ And suppose Noah, Daniel and

Job were in that country. Then these three men could save only themselves by doing what is right," announces the LORD and King.

¹⁵ "Or suppose I send wild animals through that country. And they kill all its children. It becomes a dry and empty desert. No one can pass through it because of the animals. ¹⁶ And suppose these three men were in that country. Then they could not save their own sons or daughters. They alone would be saved. But the land would become a dry and empty desert. And that is just as sure as I am alive," announces the LORD and King.

¹⁷ "Or suppose I send swords to kill the people in that country. And I say, 'Let swords sweep all through the land.' And I kill its people and their animals. ¹⁸ And suppose these three men were in that country. Then they could not save their own sons or daughters. They alone would be saved. And that is just as sure as I am alive," announces the LORD and King.

¹⁹ "Or suppose I send a plague into that land. And I pour out my great anger on it by spilling blood. I kill its people and their animals. ²⁰ And suppose Noah, Daniel and Job were in that land. Then they could not save their own sons or daughters. They could save only themselves by doing what is right. And that is just as sure as I am alive," announces the LORD and King.

²¹ The LORD and King says, "It will get much worse. I will punish Jerusalem in four horrible ways. There will be war, hunger, wild animals and plague. They will destroy the people and their animals. ²² But some people will be left alive. Some children will be brought out of the city. They will come to you. You will see how they act and the way they live. And you will be comforted in spite of all the trouble I brought on Jerusalem. ²³ You will be comforted when you see how they act and the way they live. Then you will know that I did not do anything there without a reason," announces the LORD and King.

Jerusalem Is Like a Useless Vine

15 A message from the LORD came to me. Here is what the LORD said. ² "Son of man, how is the wood of a vine different from the wood of any tree in the forest? ³ Can its wood ever be made into anything useful? Can pegs be made from it to hang things on? ⁴ Suppose it is thrown in the fire to be burned. And the fire burns both ends and blackens the middle. Then is the wood useful for anything? ⁵ It was not useful when it was whole. So how can it be made into something useful now? The fire has burned it and blackened it."

⁶ Here is what the LORD and King says. "Instead of the wood of any tree in the forest, I have given the vine to burn in the fire. I will treat the people who live in Jerusalem the same way. ⁷ I will turn against them. They

might have come out of the fire. But the fire will destroy them anyway. I will turn against them. Then you will know that I am the LORD. ⁸ I will make the land a dry and empty desert. My people have not been faithful to me," announces the LORD and King.

Jerusalem Is Like an Unfaithful Wife

16 A message from the LORD came to me. The LORD said, ² "Son of man, tell the people of Jerusalem the evil things they have done. I hate those things. ³ Tell them, 'The LORD and King speaks to Jerusalem. He says, "Your history in the land of Canaan goes back a long way. Your father was an Amorite. Your mother was a Hittite. ⁴ On the day you were born your cord was not cut. You were not washed with water to clean you up. You were not rubbed with salt. And you were not wrapped in large strips of cloth. ⁵ No one took pity on you. No one was concerned enough to do any of these things for you. Instead, you were thrown out into an open field. You were hated on the day you were born.

⁶ " ' "I was passing by. I saw you kicking around in your blood. As you were lying there, I said to you, 'Live!' ⁷ I made you grow like a plant in a field. Soon you had grown up. You became a young adult. Your breasts had formed. Your hair had grown. But you were completely naked.

⁸ " ' "Later, I was passing by again. I looked at you. I saw that you were old enough for love. So I married you and took good care of you. I covered your naked body. I made a firm promise to you. I entered into a covenant with you. And you became mine," announces the LORD and King.

⁹ " ' "I bathed you with water. I washed the blood off you. And I put lotions on you. ¹⁰ I put a beautiful dress on you. I gave you sandals made out of fine leather. I dressed you in fine linen. I covered you with expensive clothes. ¹¹ I decorated you with jewelry. I put bracelets on your arms. I gave you a necklace for your neck. ¹² I put rings on your nose and ears. And I gave you a beautiful crown for your head. ¹³ So you were decorated with gold and silver. Your clothes were made out of fine linen. They were made out of expensive and beautiful cloth. Your food was made out of honey, olive oil and the finest flour. You became very beautiful. You became a queen. ¹⁴ You were so beautiful that your fame spread among the nations. The glory I had given you made your beauty perfect," announces the LORD and King.

¹⁵ " ' "But you trusted in your beauty. You used your fame to become a prostitute. You offered your body freely to anyone who passed by. In fact, you gave yourself to anyone who wanted you. ¹⁶ You used some of your clothes to make high places colorful. That is where people worshiped

other gods. You were a prostitute there. You went to your lover and he took your beauty. ¹⁷ I had given you fine jewelry. It was made out of gold and silver. You used it to make for yourself statues of male gods. You worshiped those gods. You were not faithful to me. ¹⁸ You put your beautiful clothes on them. You offered my oil and incense to them. ¹⁹ You also offered them food. It was made out of olive oil, honey and the finest flour. I had given it to you to eat. You offered it as sweet-smelling incense to them. That is what you did," announces the LORD and King.

²⁰ " ' "Then you took your sons and daughters who belonged to me. And you sacrificed them as food to other gods. Wasn't it enough for you to be a prostitute? ²¹ You killed my children. You sacrificed them to other gods. ²² You did not remember the days when you were young. At that time you were completely naked. You were kicking around in your blood. But now you have done evil things. I hate them. You have worshiped other gods. You have not been faithful to me.

²³ " ' "How terrible it will be for you!" announces the LORD and King. "How terrible for you! You continued to sin against me. ²⁴ Your people built up mounds for themselves in every market. They put little places of worship on them. ²⁵ They set them up at every street corner. Jerusalem, you misused your beauty. You offered your body to anyone who passed by. You did it again and again. ²⁶ You committed shameful acts with the people of Egypt. They were your neighbors who were ready to have sex with you. You offered yourself to them again and again. That made me very angry. ²⁷ So I reached out my powerful hand against you. I made your territory smaller. I handed you over to your Philistine enemies. The people in their towns were shocked by your impure conduct. ²⁸ You also committed shameful acts with the people of Assyria. Nothing ever seemed to satisfy you. You could never get enough. ²⁹ Then you offered yourself to the people of Babylon. But that did not satisfy you either. There are many traders in the land of Babylon.

³⁰ " ' "I am filled with great anger against you," announces the LORD and King. "Just look at all the things you are doing! You are acting like a prostitute who has no shame at all. ³¹ Your people built up mounds at every street corner. You put little places of worship on them in every market. But you did not really act like a prostitute. That's because you refused to let your lovers pay you anything.

³² " ' "You unfaithful wife! You would rather be with strangers than with your own husband! ³³ Every prostitute receives gifts. Instead, you give gifts to all your lovers. You offer them money to come to you from everywhere. You want them to sleep with you. You are not faithful to me.

³⁴ As a prostitute, you are the opposite of others. No one runs after you to sleep with you. You are exactly the opposite. You pay them. They do not pay you.' ' "

³⁵ You prostitute, listen to the LORD's message. ³⁶ The LORD and King says, "You poured out your desire on your lovers. You took off your clothing and slept with them. You did it again and again. You worshiped other gods. I hate them. You even sacrificed your children to them. ³⁷ So I am going to gather together all the lovers you found pleasure with. They include those you loved and those you hated. I will gather them against you from everywhere. I will take your clothes off right in front of them. Then they will see you completely naked. ³⁸ I will hand down my sentence against you. You will be punished like women who commit adultery and sacrifice their children to other gods. I am so angry with you. So I will sentence you to death for everything you have done. ³⁹ Then I will hand you over to your lovers. They will tear down those mounds you built. They will destroy the little places of worship you put on them. They will take your clothes off. They will remove your fine jewelry. And they will leave you completely naked. ⁴⁰ They will bring a crowd against you. The crowd will put you to death by throwing stones at you. And they will chop you to pieces with their swords. ⁴¹ They will burn down your houses and punish you. Many women

will see it. I will not let you be a prostitute anymore. You will no longer pay your lovers. ⁴² Then my great anger against you will die down. My jealous anger will turn away from you. I will be calm. I will not be angry anymore.

⁴³ "You did not remember the days when you were young. The things you did made me very angry. So anything that happens to you will be your own fault," announces the LORD and King. "You added impure conduct to all the other evil things you did. I hate all those things.

⁴⁴ "All those who use proverbs will use this one about you. They will say, 'Like mother, like daughter.' ⁴⁵ You are a true daughter of your mother. She hated her husband and children. And you are a true sister of your sisters. They hated their husbands and children. Your mother was a Hittite. Your father was an Amorite. ⁴⁶ Your older sister was Samaria. She lived north of you with her daughters. Your younger sister was Sodom. She lived south of you with her daughters. ⁴⁷ You lived exactly the way they did. You copied their evil practices. I hate those practices. Everything you did was so sinful that you soon became even worse than they were. ⁴⁸ Your sister Sodom and her daughters never did what you and your daughters have done. And that is just as sure as I am alive," announces the LORD and King. ⁴⁹ "Here is the sin your sister

Sodom committed. She and her daughters were proud. They ate too much. They were not concerned about others. They did not help those who were poor and in need. ⁵⁰ They were very proud. They did many things that were evil in my eyes. I hated those things. So I got rid of Sodom and her daughters, just as you have seen. ⁵¹ Samaria did not commit half the sins you did. You sinned even more than they did. I hate those sins. Compared to what you did, you made your sisters seem godly. ⁵² So you will be dishonored. You have given your sisters an excuse for what they did. Your sins were far worse than theirs. In fact, your sisters appear to be more godly than you. So then, be ashamed. You will be dishonored. You have made them appear to be godly.

⁵³ "I will not only give you back what you had before. I will also do the same thing for Sodom and her daughters. And I will do the same for Samaria and her daughters. ⁵⁴ That will make you feel dishonored. You will be ashamed of everything you have done. You have made them feel better because you sinned more and were punished more than they were. ⁵⁵ Your sisters Sodom and Samaria and their daughters will return to what they were before. And you and your daughters will return to what you were before. ⁵⁶ In the past you would not even mention your sister Sodom. You were proud at that time. ⁵⁷ That was before your sin was un-

covered. Now the daughters of Edom make fun of you. So do all her neighbors and the daughters of the Philistines. Everyone who lives around you hates you. ⁵⁸ You will be punished for your impure conduct. I will also punish you for the other evil things you have done. I hate all those things," announces the LORD.

⁵⁹ The LORD and King says, "I will punish you in keeping with what you have done. I sealed with a promise the covenant I made with you. You hated that promise. And you broke my covenant. ⁶⁰ But I will remember my covenant with you. I made it with you when you were young. Now I will make a new covenant with you. It will last forever. ⁶¹ Then you will remember how you have lived. You will be ashamed when I give you Samaria and Sodom. Samaria is your older sister. Sodom is your younger one. I will give them and their daughters to you as daughters. That can't happen based on my old covenant with you. ⁶² So I will make my new covenant with you. Then you will know that I am the LORD. ⁶³ I will pay for all the sins you have committed. Then you will remember what you have done. You will be ashamed of it. Because of your shame, you will never speak against me again," announces the LORD and King.

Two Eagles and a Vine

17 A message from the LORD came to me. The LORD said, ² "Son of man, tell the people of Israel a story about their kings. Let them know what will happen to them. ³Tell them, 'The LORD and King says, "A great eagle came to the city of 'Lebanon.' It had powerful wings and a lot of long feathers. The feathers were colorful and beautiful. The eagle landed in the top of a cedar tree. ⁴It broke off the highest twig. The eagle carried it away to the land of Babylon. There are many traders in that land. The eagle planted the twig in the city of Babylon.

⁵"'"Then it took from the land a seed that had just sprouted. It put it in rich soil near plenty of water. It planted the seed like a willow tree. ⁶The seed grew into a low, spreading vine. Its branches turned toward the eagle. And its roots remained under the eagle. So the seed became a vine. It produced branches and put out leaves.

⁷"'"But there was another great eagle. It also had powerful wings and a lot of feathers. The vine now sent out its roots toward that eagle. It sent them out from the place where it was planted. And it reached out its branches to the eagle for water. ⁸The seed had been planted in good soil near plenty of water. Then it could produce branches and bear fruit. It could become a beautiful vine."'

⁹"Ezekiel, tell the Israelites, 'The LORD and King asks, "Will the vine grow? Won't it be pulled up by its roots? Won't all its fruit be stripped off? Won't it

dry up? All its new growth will dry up. It will not take a strong arm or many people to pull it up. ¹⁰It has been planted, but will it grow? No. It will dry up completely when the east wind strikes it. It will dry up in the place where it grew."'"

¹¹A message from the LORD came to me. The LORD said, ¹²"These people refuse to obey me. Ask them, 'Don't you know what these things mean?' Tell them, 'Nebuchadnezzar went to Jerusalem. He was the king of Babylon. He carried off King Jehoiachin and the nobles. He brought them back with him to the city of Babylon. ¹³Then Nebuchadnezzar made a peace treaty with Zedekiah. He was a member of Jerusalem's royal family. Nebuchadnezzar made him promise he would keep the treaty. He also took away the leading men of the land as prisoners. ¹⁴He did it to bring down their kingdom. It would not rise again. In fact, it would be able to last only by keeping his treaty. ¹⁵But Zedekiah turned against him. He sent messengers to Egypt. They went there to get horses and a large army. Will he succeed? Will he who does things like that escape? Can he break the peace treaty and still escape?

¹⁶"'Zedekiah will die in Babylon,' announces the LORD and King. 'And that is just as sure as I am alive. He will die in the land of King Nebuchadnezzar, who put him on the throne. Zedekiah didn't keep his promise

to Nebuchadnezzar and broke his treaty. ¹⁷ So Nebuchadnezzar will build ramps against the walls of Jerusalem. He will set up war machines to destroy many lives. Pharaoh will not be able to help Zedekiah during the war. The huge and mighty army of Egypt will not be of any help. ¹⁸ Zedekiah didn't keep his promise to Nebuchadnezzar and broke his treaty. Zedekiah had made a firm promise to keep it. But he broke it anyway. So he will not escape.

¹⁹ " 'The LORD and King says, "Zedekiah didn't keep the promise he made in my name. He broke the treaty. So I will pay him back. And that is just as sure as I am alive. ²⁰ I will spread out my net to catch him. He will be caught in my trap. I will bring him to Babylon. I will judge him there because he was not faithful to me. ²¹ All Zedekiah's best troops will be killed by swords. Those who are left alive will be scattered to the winds. Then you will know that I have spoken. I am the LORD."

²² " 'The LORD and King says, "I myself will get a twig from the very top of a cedar tree and plant it. I will break off the highest twig. I will plant it on a very high mountain. ²³ I will plant it on the high mountains of Israel. It will produce branches and bear fruit. It will become a beautiful cedar tree. All kinds of birds will make their nests in it. They will live in the shade of its branches. ²⁴ All the trees in the forest will know that I bring

down tall trees. I make short trees grow tall. I dry up green trees. And I make dry trees green."

" 'I have spoken. I will do this. I am the LORD.' "

People Will Die Because of Their Own Sins

18 A message from the LORD came to me. The LORD said, ² "You people have a proverb about the land of Israel. What do you mean by it? It says,

" 'The parents eat sour
    grapes.
But the children have
    a bitter taste in their
    mouths.'

³ "You will not use that proverb in Israel anymore," announces the LORD and King. "And that is just as sure as I am alive. ⁴ Everyone belongs to me. Parents and children alike belong to me. A person will die because of their own sins.

⁵ "Suppose there is a godly
    man
who does what is fair and
    right.
⁶ And he does not eat at the
    mountain temples.
He does not worship the
    statues of Israel's gods.
He does not sleep with
    another man's wife.
He does not have sex with
    his own wife
during her monthly period.
⁷ He does not treat anyone
    badly.
Instead, he always returns
    things he takes

to make sure loans are
    paid back.
He does not steal.
Instead, he gives his food
    to hungry people.
He provides clothes for
    those who are naked.
⁸ He does not charge interest
    when he lends money to
    them.
He does not make money
    from them.
He keeps himself from
    doing what is wrong.
He judges cases fairly.
⁹ He obeys my rules.
He is faithful in keeping
    my laws.
He always does what is right.
    You can be sure he will live,"
        announces the LORD
          and King.

¹⁰ "But suppose he has a mean son who harms other people. The son commits murder. Or he does some other things that are wrong. ¹¹ Suppose he does these things even though his father never did.

"Suppose the son eats at the
    mountain temples.
And he sleeps with another
    man's wife.
¹² He treats poor and needy
    people badly.
He steals.
He does not pay back what he
    owes.
He worships statues of gods.
He does other things I hate.
¹³   He charges interest when
    he lends money to poor
    people. He makes money
    from them.

Will a man like that live? He will not! He must be put to death. And what happens to him will be his own fault. He did many things I hate.

¹⁴ "But suppose this son has a son of his own. And the son sees all the sins his father commits. He sees them, but he does not do them.

¹⁵ "Suppose he does not eat at
    the mountain temples.
And he does not worship
    the statues of Israel's
    gods.
He does not sleep with
    another man's wife.
¹⁶ He does not treat anyone
    badly.
He does not make people
    give him something
    to prove they will pay back
    what they owe him.
He does not steal.
Instead, he gives his food
    to hungry people.
He provides clothes for
    those who are naked.
¹⁷ He keeps himself from
    committing sins.
He does not charge interest
    when he lends money to
    poor people.
He does not make money
    from them.
He keeps my laws and
    obeys my rules.

He will not die because of his father's sin. You can be sure he will live. ¹⁸ But his father will die because of his own sin. He got rich by cheating others. He robbed his relatives. He also did what was wrong among his people.

¹⁹ "But you still ask, 'Is the son guilty along with his father?' No! The son did what was fair and right. He was careful to obey all my rules. So you can be sure he will live. ²⁰ A person will die because of their own sins. A child will not be guilty because of what their parent did. And a parent will not be guilty because of what their child did. The right things a godly person does will be added to their account. The wrong things a sinful person does will be charged against them.

²¹ "But suppose a sinful person turns away from all the sins they have committed. And they obey all my rules. They do what is fair and right. Then you can be sure they will live. They will not die. ²² None of the sins they have committed will be held against them. Because of the godly things they have done, they will live. ²³ When sinful people die, it does not give me any joy," announces the LORD and King. "But when they turn away from their sins and live, that makes me very happy.

²⁴ "Suppose a godly person stops doing what is right. And they sin. They do the same evil things a sinful person does. They do things I hate. Then they will not live. I will not remember any of the right things they have done. They have not been faithful to me. They have also committed many other sins. So they are guilty. They will die.

²⁵ "But you say, 'What the Lord does isn't fair.' Listen to me, you Israelites. What I do is always fair. What you do is not. ²⁶ Suppose a godly person stops doing what is right. And they sin. Then they will die because of it. They will die because of the sin they have committed. ²⁷ But suppose a sinful person turns away from the evil things they have done. And they do what is fair and right. Then they will save their life. ²⁸ They think about all the evil things they have done. And they turn away from them. So you can be sure they will live. They will not die. ²⁹ But the Israelites still say, 'What the Lord does isn't fair.' People of Israel, what I do is always fair. What you do is not.

³⁰ "So I will judge you Israelites. I will judge each of you in keeping with what you have done," announces the LORD and King. "Turn away from your sins! Turn away from all the evil things you have done. Then sin will not bring you down. ³¹ Get rid of all the evil things you have done. Let me give you a new heart and a new spirit. Then you will be faithful to me. Why should you die, people of Israel? ³² When anyone dies, it does not give me any joy," announces the LORD and King. "So turn away from your sins. Then you will live!

A Song of Sadness About Israel's Princes

19 "Sing a song of sadness about Israel's princes. ² Say to Israel,

" 'You were like a mother lion
  to your princes.
She lay down among the
  lions.
She brought up her cubs.
³ One of them was Jehoahaz.
He became a strong lion.
He learned to tear apart what
  he caught.
And he became a man-
  eater.
⁴ The nations heard about
  him.
They trapped him in their
  pit.
They put hooks in his face.
And they led him away to
  Egypt.
⁵ " 'The mother lion looked and
  waited.
But all her hope was gone.
So she got another one of her
  cubs.
She made him into a strong
  lion.
⁶ He prowled with the lions.
He became very strong.
He learned to tear apart what
  he caught.
And he became a man-
  eater.
⁷ He broke down their forts.
He completely destroyed
  their towns.
The land and all those who
  were in it
were terrified when he
  roared.
⁸ Then nations came against
  him.
They came from all around
  him.
They spread out their net to
  catch him.
He was trapped in their pit.
⁹ They used hooks to pull him
  into a cage.
They brought him to the
  king of Babylon.
They put him in prison.
So his roar was not heard
  anymore
on the mountains of
  Israel.
¹⁰ " 'Israel, you were like a vine
  in a vineyard.
It was planted near water.
It had a lot of fruit and many
  branches.
There was plenty of water.
¹¹ Its branches were strong.
Each was good enough to
  be made into a ruler's
  scepter.
The vine grew high
above all the leaves.
It stood out because it was so
  tall
and had so many
  branches.
¹² But Nebuchadnezzar became
  angry.
He pulled it up by its
  roots.
He threw it to the ground.
The east wind dried it up.
Its fruit was stripped off.
Its strong branches dried
  up.
And fire destroyed them.
¹³ Now it is planted in the
  Babylonian desert.
It is in a dry and thirsty
  land.
¹⁴ One of its main branches was
  Zedekiah.
Fire spread from it and
  burned up its fruit.
None of its branches is good
  enough

to be made into a ruler's scepter.'

This is a song of sadness. And that is how it should be used.

The LORD Judges Sinful Israel

20 It was the seventh year since King Jehoiachin had been brought to Babylon as a prisoner. On the tenth day of the fifth month, some of the elders of Israel came to ask the LORD for advice. They sat down with me.

² Then a message from the LORD came to me. The LORD said, ³ "Son of man, speak to the elders of Israel. Tell them, 'The LORD and King says, "Have you come to ask me for advice? I will not let you do that," announces the LORD and King. "And that is just as sure as I am alive." '

⁴ "Are you going to judge them, son of man? Will you judge them? Tell them the evil things done by their people of long ago. I hate those things. ⁵ Tell them, 'The LORD and King says, "I chose Israel. On that day I raised my hand and made a promise. I made a promise to the members of Jacob's family line. I made myself known to them in Egypt. I raised my hand and told them, 'I am the LORD your God.' ⁶ On that day I promised I would bring them out of Egypt. I told them I would take them to a land I had found for them. It had plenty of milk and honey. It was the most beautiful land of all. ⁷ I said to them, 'Each of you must get rid of the statues of the evil gods you worship. Do not make yourselves "unclean" by worshiping the gods of Egypt. I am the LORD your God.'

⁸ " ' "But they refused to obey me. They would not listen to me. They did not get rid of the evil gods they worshiped. And they did not turn away from Egypt's gods. So I said I would pour out all my great anger on them in Egypt. ⁹ I wanted my name to be honored. So I brought my people out of Egypt. I did it to keep my name from being treated as if it were not holy. I didn't want this to happen in front of the nations around my people. I had made myself known to Israel in the sight of those nations. ¹⁰ So I led them out of Egypt. I brought them into the Desert of Sinai. ¹¹ I gave them my rules. I made my laws known to them. The person who obeys them will live by them. ¹² I also told them to observe my Sabbath days. That is the sign of the covenant I made with them. I wanted them to know that I made them holy. I am the LORD.

¹³ " ' "But in the desert the people of Israel refused to obey me. They did not follow my rules. They turned their backs on my laws. The person who obeys them will live by them. They totally misused my Sabbath days. So I said I would pour out my great anger on them. I would destroy them in the desert. ¹⁴ But I wanted my name to be honored. I kept it from being treated as if it were not holy. I did not want that to happen in front of the nations. They had seen

me bring Israel out of Egypt. [15] I also raised my hand and made a promise in the desert. I told my people I would not bring them into the land I had given them. It had plenty of milk and honey. It was the most beautiful land of all. [16] But they turned their backs on my laws. They did not obey my rules. They misused my Sabbath days. Their hearts were committed to worshiping the statues of their gods. [17] Then I felt sorry for them. So I did not destroy them. I did not put an end to them in the desert. [18] I spoke to their children there. I said, 'Do not follow the rules your parents gave you. Do not obey their laws. Do not make yourselves "unclean" by worshiping their gods. [19] I am the LORD your God. So follow my rules. Be careful to obey my laws. [20] Keep my Sabbath days holy. That is the sign of the covenant I made with you. You will know that I am the LORD your God.'

[21] " ' "But their children refused to obey me. They did not follow my rules. They were not careful to keep my laws. The person who obeys them will live by them. They misused my Sabbath days. So I said I would pour out all my great anger on them in the desert. [22] But I kept myself from punishing them at that time. I wanted my name to be honored. So I kept it from being treated as if it were not holy. I did not want that to happen in front of the nations. They had seen me bring Israel out of Egypt. [23] I also raised my hand and made a promise in the desert. I told my people I would scatter them among the nations. I would send them to other countries. [24] They had not obeyed my laws. They had turned their backs on my rules. They had misused my Sabbath days. They only wanted to worship the statues of their parents' gods. [25] So I let them follow other rules. Those other rules were not good. I let them have laws they could not live by. [26] I let them become 'unclean' by offering sacrifices to other gods. They even sacrificed the first male child born in each family. I wanted to fill them with horror. Then they would know that I am the LORD." '

[27] "Son of man, speak to the people of Israel. Tell them, 'The LORD and King says, "Your people spoke evil things against me long ago. They were unfaithful to me. [28] But I brought them into the land. I had promised to give the land to them. Then they offered sacrifices that made me very angry. They did it on every high hill and under every green tree. There they brought their sweet-smelling incense. And there they poured out their drink offerings. [29] Then I said to them, 'What is this high place you go to?' " ' " That high place is called Bamah to this day.

The LORD Makes Israel New Again

[30] The LORD said to me, "Speak to the Israelites. Tell them, 'Here is what the LORD and King says.

"Are you going to make yourselves 'unclean' the way your
people of long ago did? Are you
also going to want to worship
the statues of their evil gods?
³¹ You make yourselves 'unclean' by offering sacrifices to
other gods. You even sacrifice
your children in the fire. You
continue to do these things to
this day. People of Israel, should
I let you ask me for advice? I will
not let you do that," announces
the LORD and King. "And that is
just as sure as I am alive.

³² " ' "You say, 'We want to be
like the other nations. We want
to be like all the other people
in the world. They serve gods
made out of wood and stone.'
But what you have in mind will
never happen. ³³ I will rule over
you by reaching out my mighty
hand and powerful arm. I will
pour my great anger out on
you," announces the LORD and
King. "And that is just as sure
as I am alive. ³⁴ I will bring you
back from the nations. I will
gather you together from the
countries where you have been
scattered. I will reach out my
mighty hand and powerful arm.
I will pour my great anger out
on you. ³⁵ I will send you among
the nations. There I will judge
you face to face. It will be as if I
were judging you in the desert
again. ³⁶ Long ago, I judged your
people in the desert of Egypt. In
the same way, I will judge you,"
announces the LORD and King.
³⁷ "I will take note of you as you
pass under my shepherd's stick.
I will separate those who obey

me from those who do not. And
I will give the blessings of the
covenant to those of you who
obey me. ³⁸ I will get rid of those
among you who turn against
me. They refuse to obey me. I
will bring them out of the land
where they are living. But they
will not enter the land of Israel.
Then you will know that I am
the LORD.

³⁹ " ' "People of Israel, the
LORD and King says, 'Go, every
one of you! Serve your gods. But
later you will listen to me. You
will no longer treat my name as
if it were not holy. You will not
offer sacrifices to other gods
anymore. ⁴⁰ People of Israel, you
will all serve me,' announces
the LORD and King. 'You will
serve me on my high and holy
mountain in Jerusalem. There
I will accept you. I will require
your offerings and your finest
gifts. I want you to bring them
along with all your other holy
sacrifices. ⁴¹ I will bring you back
from the nations. I will gather
you together from the countries
where you have been scattered.
Then I will accept you as if you
were sweet-smelling incense. I
will show that I am holy among
you. The nations will see it. ⁴² I
will bring you into the land of
Israel. Then you will know that
I am the LORD. Long ago I raised
my hand and made a promise.
I promised to give that land to
your people of long ago. ⁴³ There
you will remember your conduct. You will think about everything you did that made you
"unclean." And you will hate

yourselves because of all the evil things you have done. ⁴⁴People of Israel, I will deal with you for the honor of my name. I will not deal with you based on your evil conduct and sinful practices. Then you will know that I am the LORD,' announces the LORD and King.' ' "

Ezekiel Prophesies Against the South

⁴⁵A message from the LORD came to me. The LORD said, ⁴⁶"Son of man, turn your attention to Judah in the south. Preach against it. Prophesy against its forests. ⁴⁷Tell them, 'Listen to the LORD's message. The LORD and King says, "I am about to set you on fire. The fire will destroy all your trees. It will burn down green trees and dry trees alike. The blazing flame will not be put out. The faces of everyone from south to north will be burned by it. ⁴⁸Everyone will see that I started the fire. It will not be put out. I am the LORD."'"

⁴⁹Then I said, "LORD and King, people are talking about me. They are saying, 'Isn't he just telling stories?'"

God Uses the Babylonians to Judge Israel

21 A message from the LORD came to me. The LORD said, ²"Son of man, turn your attention to Jerusalem. Preach against the temple. Prophesy against the land of Israel. ³Tell them, 'The LORD says, "I am against you. I will pull out my

sword. I will remove from you godly people and sinful people alike. ⁴Because I am going to remove them, my sword will be ready to use. I will strike down everyone from south to north. ⁵Then all people will know that I have pulled out my sword. I will not put it back. I am the LORD."'

⁶"Groan, son of man! Groan in front of your people. Groan with a broken heart and bitter sorrow. ⁷They will ask you, 'Why are you groaning?' Then you will say, 'Because of the news that is coming. The hearts of all the people will melt away in fear. Their hands will not be able to help them. Their spirits will grow weak. And they will be so afraid they'll wet themselves.' The news is coming! You can be sure those things will happen," announces the LORD and King.

⁸A message from the LORD came to me. The LORD said, ⁹"Son of man, prophesy. Say, 'The Lord says,

" ' "A sword! A sword!
    A sharp and shiny sword is
      coming from Babylon!
¹⁰It is sharpened to kill people.
    It flashes like lightning."'"

The people say, "Should we take delight in the scepter of the LORD's royal son? The sword looks down on every scepter like this." ¹¹The LORD says,

"I have told Nebuchadnezzar
    to shine his sword.
It is in his hand.
It has been sharpened and
    shined.

It is ready for the killer's
hand.
¹²Son of man, cry out and
weep.
The sword is against my
people.
It is against all the princes
of Israel.
It will kill them
along with the rest of my
people.
So beat your chest in
sorrow.

¹³"You can be sure that testing will come. Why does the
sword look down on the scepter? Because even the scepter
will not continue to rule," announces the LORD and King.

¹⁴"Son of man, prophesy.
Clap your hands.
Let the sword strike twice.
Let it strike even three
times.
It is a sword to kill people.
It is a sword to kill many
people.
It is closing in on them
from every side.
¹⁵People's hearts will melt
away in fear.
Many will be wounded or
killed.
I have prepared the sword to
kill people
at all their city gates.
Look! It strikes like lightning.
It is in the killer's hand.
¹⁶Sword, cut to the right.
Then cut to the left.
Strike down people
everywhere your blade is
turned.
¹⁷I too will clap my hands.

I won't be so angry
anymore.
I have spoken. I am the
LORD."

¹⁸A message from the LORD
came to me. The LORD said,
¹⁹"Son of man, mark out on a
map two roads for the sword
to take. The sword belongs to
the king of Babylon. Both roads
start from the same country. Put
up a sign where the road turns
off to the city of Rabbah. ²⁰Mark
out one road for the sword to
take against Rabbah in Ammon. Mark out another against
Judah and the walls of Jerusalem. ²¹The king of Babylon will
stop at the place where the two
roads meet. He will look for a
special sign. He will cast lots by
pulling arrows out of a bag. He
will ask his gods for advice. And
he will look carefully at the liver
of a sheep. ²²His right hand will
pull out the arrow for Jerusalem. There he will get huge logs
ready to knock down its gates.
He will give the command to
kill its people. He will sound the
battle cry. He will build a ramp
up to the city wall. He will bring
in his war machines. ²³The decision to attack Jerusalem will
seem like the wrong advice to
those who made a treaty with
Nebuchadnezzar. But he will remind them that they are guilty.
And he will take them away as
prisoners."

²⁴So the LORD and King says,
"You people have reminded everyone of how guilty you are.
You have done it by refusing to
obey me or any other authority.

Everything you do clearly shows how sinful you are. So you will be taken away as prisoners."

²⁵ King Zedekiah, your day has come. You are an unholy and evil prince in Israel. The day for you to be punished is here. ²⁶ The Lord and King says, "Take off your turban. Remove your crown. Things will not be as they were in the past. Those who are considered not important will be honored. And those who are honored will be considered not important. ²⁷ Jerusalem will fall. I will destroy it. It will not be re-built until the true king comes. After all, the kingdom belongs to him. I will give it to him.

²⁸ "Son of man, prophesy. Say, 'The Lord and King speaks about the Ammonites. He also talks about the way they laugh because of Jerusalem's fall. He says,

" ' "A sword! A sword!
    Nebuchadnezzar's sword is
      ready to kill you.
  It is shined to destroy you.
  It flashes like lightning.
²⁹ The visions of your prophets
    are false.
  They use magic to try to
      find out
    what is going to happen to
      you.
  But their magic tricks are lies.
  The sword will strike
    the necks of you sinful
      people.
  You will be killed.
  The day for you to be
      punished has finally
      come.
  Your time is up.

³⁰ Ammon, return your sword
    to its place.
  In the land where you were
    created, I will judge you.
  That is where you came
    from.
³¹ I will pour out my anger on
    you.
  I will breathe out my
    burning anger against
    you.
  I will hand you over to mean
    people.
  They are skilled at
    destroying others.
³² You will be burned in the fire.
  Your blood will be spilled
    in your land.
  You will not be remembered
    anymore.
  I have spoken. I am the
    Lord." ' "

The Lord Judges Jerusalem for Its Sins

22 A message from the Lord came to me. The Lord said,

² "Son of man, are you going to judge Jerusalem? Will you judge this city that has so many murderers in it? Then tell its people they have done many evil things. I hate those things. ³ Tell them, 'The Lord and King says, "Your city brings death on itself. You spill blood inside its walls. You make yourselves 'unclean' by making statues of gods. ⁴ You are guilty of spilling blood. Your statues have made you 'unclean.' You have brought your days to a close. The end of your years has come. So the nations will make fun of you.

All the countries will laugh at you. ⁵ Those who are near you will tell jokes about you. So will those who are far away. Trouble fills the streets of your sinful city.

⁶ " ' "The princes of Israel are in your city. All of them use their power to spill blood. ⁷ They have made fun of fathers and mothers alike. They have crushed outsiders. They have treated badly the children whose fathers have died. They have done the same thing to widows. ⁸ You have looked down on the holy things that were set apart to me. You have misused my Sabbath days. ⁹ You have spread lies about others so you can spill someone's blood. You eat at the mountain temples. You commit impure acts. ¹⁰ You bring shame on your fathers by having sex with their wives. You have sex with women during their monthly period. That is when they are 'unclean.' ¹¹ One of you has sex with another man's wife. I hate that sin. Another brings shame on his daughter-in-law by having sex with her. Still another has sex with his sister, even though she is his own father's daughter. ¹² You accept money from people who want special favors. You do this to spill someone's blood. You charge interest to poor people when you lend them money. You make money from them. You get rich by cheating your neighbors. And you have forgotten me," announces the LORD and King.

¹³ " ' "I will clap my hands because I am so angry. You got rich by cheating others. You spilled blood inside the walls of your city. ¹⁴ Will you be brave on the day I deal with you? Will you be strong at that time? I have spoken. I will do this. I am the LORD. ¹⁵ I will scatter you among the nations. I will send you to other countries. I will put an end to your 'uncleanness.' ¹⁶ You will be 'unclean' in the sight of the nations. Then you will know that I am the LORD." ' "

¹⁷ A message from the LORD came to me. The LORD said, ¹⁸ "Son of man, the people of Israel have become like scum to me. All of them are like the copper, tin, iron and lead left inside a furnace. They are only the scum that is removed from silver." ¹⁹ So the LORD and King says, "People of Israel, all of you have become like scum. So I will gather you together in Jerusalem. ²⁰ People put silver, copper, iron, lead and tin into a furnace. They melt it with a blazing fire. In the same way, I will gather you. I will pour out my burning anger on you. I will put you inside the city and melt you. ²¹ I will gather you together. My burning anger will blaze out at you. And you will be melted inside Jerusalem. ²² Silver is melted in a furnace. And you will be melted inside the city. Then you will know that I have poured out my burning anger on you. I am the LORD."

²³ Another message from the LORD came to me. The LORD said, ²⁴ "Son of man, speak to

the land. Tell it, 'You have not been washed clean with rain. That's because I am angry with you.' ²⁵ Ezekiel, the princes of the land are like a roaring lion that tears its food apart. They eat people up. They take treasures and other valuable things. They cause many women in the land to become widows. ²⁶ Its priests break my law. They treat things set apart to me as if they were not holy. They treat holy and common things as if they were the same. They teach that there is no difference between things that are 'clean' and things that are not. They refuse to keep my Sabbath days. So they treat me as if I were not holy. ²⁷ The officials in the land are like wolves that tear their food apart. They spill blood and kill people to get rich. ²⁸ The prophets cover up these acts for them. The visions of these prophets are false. They use magic to try to find out what is going to happen. But their magic tricks are lies. They say, 'The LORD and King says.' But I have not spoken to them. ²⁹ The people of the land get rich by cheating others. They steal. They crush those who are poor and in need. They treat outsiders badly. They refuse to be fair to them.

³⁰ "I looked for someone among them who would stand up for Jerusalem. I tried to find someone who would pray to me for the land. Then I would not have to destroy it. But I could not find anyone who would pray for it. ³¹ So I will pour out my anger on its people. I will destroy

them because of my great anger against them. And anything that happens to them will be their own fault," announces the LORD and King.

Samaria and Jerusalem Are Like Two Impure Sisters

23 A message from the LORD came to me. The LORD said, ² "Son of man, once there were two women. They had the same mother. ³ They became prostitutes in Egypt. They have been unfaithful to me since they were young. In that land they allowed their breasts to be touched. They permitted their virgin breasts to be kissed. ⁴ The older sister was named Oholah. The younger one was Oholibah. They belonged to me. Sons and daughters were born to them. Oholah stands for Samaria. And Oholibah stands for Jerusalem.

⁵ "Oholah was unfaithful to me even while she still belonged to me. She longed for her Assyrian lovers. They included soldiers ⁶ who wore blue uniforms. They also included governors and commanders. All of them were young and handsome. They rode horses. ⁷ She gave herself as a prostitute to all Assyria's finest warriors. She made herself impure with the statues of the gods of everyone she longed for. ⁸ She started being a prostitute in Egypt. And she never stopped. When she was young, men had sex with her. They kissed her virgin breasts. They used up all their sinful desires on her.

9 "So I handed her over to her Assyrian lovers. She longed for them. 10 They stripped her naked. They took away her sons and daughters. And they killed her with their swords. Other women laughed when that happened. I was the one who had punished her.

11 "Her sister Oholibah saw it. But her evil desire for sexual sin was worse than her sister's. 12 She too longed for the men of Assyria. They included governors and commanders. They included soldiers who wore fancy uniforms. They also included men who rode horses. All of them were young and handsome. 13 I saw that she too made herself impure. So both sisters did the same evil things.

14 "But Oholibah went even further with her sexual sins. She saw pictures of men drawn on a wall. They were figures of Babylonians drawn in red. 15 They had belts around their waists. They wore flowing turbans on their heads. All of them looked like Babylonian chariot officers. They were from the land of the Chaldeans. 16 As soon as she saw the pictures, she longed for the men. So she sent messengers to them in Babylon. 17 Then the Babylonians came to her. They went to bed with her. They had sex with her. They made her impure when they had sex with her. After they did it, she became sick of them. So she turned away from them. 18 She acted like a prostitute who had no shame at all. She openly showed her na-

ked body. I became sick of what she was doing. So I turned away from her. I had also turned away from her sister. 19 But Oholibah offered her body to her lovers again and again. She remembered the days when she was a young prostitute in Egypt. 20 There she had longed for her lovers. Their private parts seemed as big as those of donkeys. And their flow of semen appeared to be as much as that of horses. 21 So you wanted to return to the days when you were young. You longed for the time when you first became impure in Egypt. That was when you allowed your breasts to be kissed. And you permitted your young breasts to be touched."

22 So the LORD and King says, "Oholibah, I will stir up your lovers against you. You became sick of them. You turned away from them. But I will bring them against you from every side. 23 They include the Babylonians and all the Chaldeans. They include the men from Pekod, Shoa and Koa. They also include all the Assyrians. They are young and handsome. Some of them are governors and commanders. Others are chariot officers. Still others are very high officials. All of them ride horses. 24 So a huge army will come against you with weapons, chariots and wagons. They will take up positions against you on every side. They will carry large and small shields. They will wear helmets. I will turn you over to them to be punished. They will

punish you in their own way. [25] I will pour out my jealous anger on you. And the army's anger will burn against you. They will cut off your noses and ears. Some of you who are left will be killed by swords. They will take away your sons and daughters. Others of you who are left will be burned up. [26] The army will also strip off your clothes. They will take your fine jewelry away from you. [27] You became an impure prostitute in Egypt. But I will put a stop to all of that. You will no longer want to do any of it. You will not remember Egypt anymore."

[28] The Lord and King says, "I am about to hand you over to people you hate. You became sick of them. You turned away from them. [29] They will punish you because they hate you so much. They will take away from you everything you have worked for. They will leave you completely naked. Then everyone will see that you are a prostitute who has no shame at all. You were impure. You offered your body to your lovers again and again. [30] That is why you will be punished. You longed for lovers in other nations. You made yourself impure by worshiping their gods. [31] You did the same things your sister Oholah did. So I will put her cup in your hand. It is filled with the wine of my anger."

[32] The Lord and King says to Oholibah,

"You will drink from your
　　sister's cup.
It is large and deep.
It is filled with the wine of
　　my anger.
So others will laugh at you.
　　They will make fun of you.
[33] You will become drunk and
　　sad.
The cup of my anger will
　　completely destroy you.
It is the same cup your
　　sister Samaria drank
　　from.
[34] You will drink from it until it
　　is empty.
Then you will chew on its
　　pieces.
And you will claw at your
　　breasts.

I have spoken," announces the Lord and King.

[35] So the Lord and King says, "You have forgotten me. You have turned your back on me. You have been impure. You have acted like a prostitute. So I will punish you."

[36] The Lord said to me, "Son of man, are you going to judge Oholah and Oholibah? Then tell them they have done many evil things. I hate those things. [37] They have committed adultery. Their hands are covered with the blood of the people they have murdered. They have worshiped other gods. They have not been faithful to me. They have even sacrificed their children as food to other gods. Those children belonged to me. [38] Here are some other things the sisters have done to me. They have made my temple 'unclean.' They have misused my Sabbath

days. ³⁹ They have sacrificed their children to their gods. On that same day they entered my temple and made it 'unclean.' That is what they have done in my house.

⁴⁰ "They even sent messengers to bring men from far away. When the men arrived, Oholibah took a bath. She put makeup on her eyes. She put her jewelry on. ⁴¹ She sat down on a beautiful couch. A table was in front of it. There she put the incense and olive oil that belonged to me.

⁴² "The noise of a carefree crowd was all around her. Men who drink too much were brought from the desert. Other men were brought along with them. They put bracelets on the wrists of the two sisters. They put beautiful crowns on their heads. ⁴³ Then I spoke about Oholibah. She was worn out by adultery. I said, 'Let them use her as a prostitute. After all, that is what she is.' ⁴⁴ So they slept with her. In fact, they slept with both of these impure women, Oholah and Oholibah. They slept with them just as men sleep with prostitutes. ⁴⁵ But judges who are right with God will sentence the sisters to be punished. They will be punished in the same way as women who commit adultery and murder. After all, they have committed adultery. And their hands are covered with the blood of the people they have murdered."

⁴⁶ The LORD and King says, "Bring an angry crowd against the sisters. Hand them over to those who will terrify them and steal everything they have. ⁴⁷ The crowd will kill them by throwing stones at them. They will use swords to cut them down. They will kill their sons and daughters. And they will burn down their houses.

⁴⁸ "So I will put an end to impurity in the land. Then all its women will be warned. They will not want to be like the sisters. ⁴⁹ Those sisters will be punished because of the impure things they have done. They will be judged because they have worshiped other gods. Then they will know that I am the LORD and King."

Jerusalem Is Like a Cooking Pot

24 It was the ninth year since King Jehoiachin had been brought to Babylon as a prisoner. On the tenth day of the tenth month, a message from the LORD came to me. The LORD said, ² "Son of man, write down today's date. The king of Babylon has surrounded Jerusalem and attacked it today. ³ Your people refuse to obey me. So tell them a story. Say to them, 'The LORD and King told me,

" ' "Put a cooking pot on the
      fire.
   Pour water into it.
⁴ Put pieces of meat in it.
   Use all the best pieces.
   Use the leg and shoulder.
   Fill it with the best bones.
⁵ Pick the finest animal in the
      flock.
   Pile wood under the pot to
      cook the bones.

Bring the water to a boil.
Cook the bones in it." ' "

6 The LORD and King says,

"How terrible it will be for
this city!
It has so many murderers
in it.
How terrible for the pot that
is coated with scum!
The scum on it will not go
away.
Take the meat out of the pot
piece by piece.
Take it out in whatever
order it comes.

7 "The blood Jerusalem's
people spilled is inside
its walls.
They poured it out on a
bare rock.
They did not pour it on the
ground.
If they had, dust would
have covered it up.
8 So I put their blood on the
bare rock.
I did not want it to be
covered up.
I poured out my great anger
on them.
I paid them back."

9 So the LORD and King said to
me,

"How terrible it will be for
this city!
It has so many murderers
in it.
I too will pile the wood high.
10 So pile on the wood.
Light the fire.
Cook the meat well.
Mix in the spices.
Let the bones be blackened.

11 Then set the empty pot on
the coals.
Let it get hot. Let its copper
glow.
Then what is not pure in it
will melt.
Its scum will be burned
away.
12 But it can't be cleaned up.
Its thick scum has not been
removed.
Even fire can't burn it off.

13 "Jerusalem, you are really
impure. I tried to clean you up.
But you would not let me make
you pure. So you will not be
clean again until I am no longer
so angry with you.

14 "I have spoken. The time
has come for me to act. I will not
hold back. I will not feel sorry
for you. I will do what I said I
would do. You will be judged for
your conduct and actions. I am
the LORD," announces the LORD
and King.

Ezekiel's Wife Dies

15 A message from the LORD
came to me. The LORD said,
16 "Son of man, I will take away
from you the wife you delight
in. It will happen very soon. But
do not sing songs of sadness.
Do not let any tears flow from
your eyes. 17 Groan quietly. Do
not mourn for your wife when
she dies. Keep your turban on
your head. Keep your sandals
on your feet. Do not cover your
mustache and beard. Do not eat
the food people eat to comfort
them when someone dies."
18 So I spoke to my people in

the morning. And in the evening my wife died. The next morning I did what I had been commanded to do.

19 Then the people said to me, "Tell us what these things have to do with us. Why are you acting like this?"

20 So I told them. I said, "A message from the LORD came to me. The LORD said, 21 'Speak to the people of Israel. Tell them, "The LORD and King says, 'I am about to make my temple "unclean." I will let the Babylonians burn it down. It is the beautiful building you are so proud of. You take delight in it. You love it. The sons and daughters you left behind will be killed by swords. 22 So do what Ezekiel did. Do not cover your mustache and beard. Do not eat the food people eat to comfort them when someone dies. 23 Keep your turbans on your heads. Keep your sandals on your feet. Do not mourn or weep. You will waste away because you have sinned so much. You will groan among yourselves. 24 What Ezekiel has done will show you what is going to happen to you. You will do just as he has done. Then you will know that I am the LORD and King.' " '

25 "Son of man, I will take away their beautiful temple. It is their joy and glory. They take delight in it. Their hearts long for it. I will also take away their sons and daughters. 26 On the day I destroy everything, a man will escape. He will come and tell you the news. 27 At that time I will open your mouth. Then you will no longer be silent. You will speak with the man. That will show them what will happen to them. And they will know that I am the LORD."

A Prophecy Against Ammon

25 A message from the LORD came to me. The LORD said, 2 "Son of man, turn your attention to the Ammonites. Prophesy against them. 3 Tell them, 'Listen to the message of the LORD and King. He says, "You laughed when my temple was made 'unclean.' You also laughed when the land of Israel was completely destroyed. You mocked the people of Judah when they were taken away as prisoners. 4 So I am going to hand you over to the people of the east. They will set up their tents in your land. They will camp among you. They will eat your fruit. They will drink your milk. 5 I will turn the city of Rabbah into grasslands for camels. Ammon will become a resting place for sheep. Then you will know that I am the LORD." ' " 6 The LORD and King says, "You clapped your hands. You stamped your feet. Deep down inside, you hated the land of Israel. You were glad because of what happened to it. 7 So I will reach out my powerful hand against you. I will give you and everything you have to the nations. I will bring you to an end among the nations. I will destroy you. Then you will know that I am the LORD."

A Prophecy Against Moab

8 The LORD and King says, "Moab and Edom said, 'Look! Judah has become like all the other nations.' 9 So I will let Moab's enemies attack its lower hills. They will begin at the border towns. Those towns include Beth Jeshimoth, Baal Meon and Kiriathaim. They are the glory of that land. 10 I will hand Moab over to the people of the east. I will also give the Ammonites to them. And the Ammonites will no longer be remembered among the nations. 11 I will punish Moab. Then they will know that I am the LORD."

A Prophecy Against Edom

12 The LORD and King says, "Edom got even with Judah. That made Edom very guilty." 13 The LORD continues, "I will reach out my hand against Edom. I will kill its people and their animals. I will completely destroy it. They will be killed by swords from Teman all the way to Dedan. 14 I will use my people Israel to pay Edom back. They will punish Edom because my anger against it is great. They will know how I pay back my enemies," announces the LORD and King.

A Prophecy Against the Philistines

15 The LORD and King says, "Deep down inside them, the Philistines hated Judah. So the Philistines tried to get even with them. They had been Judah's enemies for many years. So they tried to destroy them." 16 The LORD continues, "I am about to reach out my hand against the Philistines. I will wipe out the Kerethites. I will destroy those who remain along the coast. 17 You can be sure that I will pay them back. I will punish them because my anger against them is great. When I pay them back, they will know that I am the LORD."

A Prophecy Against Tyre

26 It was the first day of the 11th month. It was the 12th year since King Jehoiachin had been brought to Babylon as a prisoner. A message from the LORD came to me. The LORD said, 2 "Son of man, Tyre laughed because of what happened to Jerusalem. The people of Tyre said, 'Jerusalem is the gateway to the nations. But the gate is broken. Its doors have swung open to us. Jerusalem has been destroyed. So now we will succeed.'" 3 The LORD and King says, "But I am against you, Tyre. I will bring many nations against you. They will come in like the waves of the sea. 4 They will destroy your walls. They will pull down your towers. I will clear away the stones of your broken-down buildings. I will turn you into nothing but a bare rock. 5 Out in the Mediterranean Sea your island city will become a place to spread fishnets. I have spoken," announces the LORD and King. "The nations will take you and everything you have. 6 Your

settlements on the coast will be destroyed by war. Then you will know that I am the LORD."

⁷ The LORD and King says, "From the north I am going to bring Nebuchadnezzar against Tyre. He is the king of Babylon. He is the greatest king of all. He will come with horses and chariots. Horsemen and a great army will be brought along with him. ⁸ He will go to war against you. He will destroy your settlements on the coast. He will bring in war machines to attack you. A ramp will be built up to your walls. He will raise his shields against you. ⁹ He will use huge logs to knock down your walls. He will destroy your towers with his weapons. ¹⁰ He will have so many horses that they will cover you with dust. Your walls will shake because of the noise of his war horses, wagons and chariots. He will enter your gates, just as men enter a city whose walls have been broken through. ¹¹ The hooves of his horses will pound in your streets. His swords will kill your people. Your strong pillars will fall to the ground. ¹² His men will take away from you your wealth and anything else you have. They will pull down your walls. They will completely destroy your fine houses. They will throw the stones and lumber of your broken-down buildings into the sea. ¹³ I will put an end to your noisy songs. No one will hear the music of your harps anymore. ¹⁴ I will turn you into nothing but a bare rock. You will

become a place to spread fishnets. You will never be rebuilt. I have spoken. I am the LORD," announces the LORD and King.

¹⁵ The LORD and King speaks to Tyre. He says, "The lands along the coast will shake because of the sound of your fall. Wounded people will groan because so many are dying there. ¹⁶ Then all the princes along the coast will step down from their thrones. They will put their robes away. They will take off their beautiful clothes. They will sit on the ground. They will put on terror as if it were their clothes. They will tremble with fear all the time. They will be shocked because of what has happened to you. ¹⁷ Then they will sing a song of sadness about you. They will say to you,

" 'Famous city, you have been
    completely destroyed!
You were filled with sea
    traders.
You and your citizens
    were a mighty power on
    the seas.
You terrified everyone
    who lived in you.
¹⁸ The lands along the coast
    trembled with fear
    when you fell.
The islands in the sea
    were terrified when you
    were destroyed.' "

¹⁹ The LORD and King says to Tyre, "I will turn you into an empty city. You will be like cities where no one lives anymore. I will cause the ocean to sweep over you. Its mighty waters will

cover you. ²⁰ So I will bring you down together with those who go down into the grave. The people there lived long ago. You will have to live in the earth below. It will be like living in buildings that were destroyed many years ago. You will go down into the grave along with others. And you will never come back. You will not take your place in this world again. ²¹ I will bring you to a horrible end. You will be gone forever. People will look for you. But they will never find you," announces the LORD and King.

A Song of Sadness About Tyre

27 A message from the LORD came to me. The LORD said, ² "Son of man, sing a song of sadness about Tyre. ³ It is located at the gateway to the Mediterranean Sea. It does business with nations on many coasts. Say to it, 'The LORD and King says,

" ' "Tyre, you say,
　'I am perfect and
　　beautiful.'
⁴ You were like a ship that
　ruled over the high seas.
Your builders made you
　perfect and beautiful.
⁵ They cut all your lumber
　from juniper trees on
　　Mount Hermon.
They used a cedar tree from
　Lebanon
to make a mast for you.
⁶ They made your oars
　out of oak trees from
　　Bashan.
They made your deck out of
　cypress wood

from the coasts of Cyprus.
They decorated it with
　ivory.
⁷ Your sail was made out of
　beautiful Egyptian linen.
It served as your banner.
Your shades were made out of
　blue and purple cloth.
They were from the coasts
　of Elishah.
⁸ Men from Sidon and Arvad
　manned your oars.
Tyre, your sailors were
　skillful.
⁹ Very skilled workers from
　Byblos were on board.
They kept you waterproof.
All the ships on the sea and
　their sailors
came up beside you.
They brought their goods
　to trade for yours.

¹⁰ " ' "Men from Persia, Lydia
　and Put
served as soldiers in your
　army, city of Tyre.
They hung their shields and
　helmets on your walls.
That brought glory to you.
¹¹ Men from Arvad and Helek
　guarded your walls on
　　every side.
Men from Gammad
　were in your towers.
They hung their shields
　around your walls.
They made you perfect and
　beautiful.

¹² " ' "Tarshish did business with you because you had so much wealth. They traded silver, iron, tin and lead for your goods. ¹³ " ' "Greece, Tubal and Meshek did business with you.

They traded human beings and bronze objects for your products.

14 " ' "Men from Beth Togarmah traded chariot horses, war horses and mules for your goods.

15 " ' "Men from Rhodes did business with you. Many lands along the coast bought goods from you. They paid you with ivory tusks and ebony wood.

16 " ' "Aram did business with you because you had so many products for sale. They traded turquoise, purple cloth and needlework for your goods. They also traded fine linen, coral and rubies for them.

17 " ' "Judah and Israel did business with you. They traded wheat from Minnith, sweets, honey, olive oil and lotion for your products.

18 " ' "Damascus did business with you. That's because you had so many products and so much wealth. They traded to you wine from Helbon and wool from Zahar. 19 They also traded to you casks of wine from Izal. You traded to them wrought iron, cassia and calamus.

20 " ' "Dedan traded saddle blankets to you.

21 " ' "Arabia and all the princes of Kedar bought goods from you. They traded you lambs, rams and goats for them.

22 " ' "Traders from Sheba and Raamah did business with you. They traded the finest spices, jewels and gold for your goods.

23 " ' "Harran, Kanneh and Eden did business with you. So did traders from Sheba, Ashur and Kilmad. 24 In your market they traded beautiful clothes, blue cloth, and needlework to you. They also traded colorful rugs that had twisted cords and tight knots.

25 " ' "The ships of Tarshish
carry your products.
You are like a ship filled with
a heavy load
as you sail the sea.
26 The sailors who man your
oars take you
out to the high seas.
But the east wind will break
you in pieces
far out at sea.
27 You will be wrecked on that
day.
Your wealth, goods and
products
will sink deep into the
sea.
So will your sailors, officers,
carpenters,
traders and all your
soldiers.
Anyone else on board will
sink too.
28 The lands along the coast
will shake
when your sailors cry out.
29 All those who man the oars
will desert their ships.
The sailors and all the
officers
will stand on the shore.
30 They will raise their
voices.
They will cry bitterly over
you.
They will sprinkle dust on
their heads.
They will roll in ashes.

³¹ They will shave their heads
    because of you.
  And they will put on the
    clothes of sadness.
  They will weep over you.
    Their spirits will be greatly
    troubled.
  They will be very sad.
³² As they weep and mourn
    over you,
  they will sing a song of
    sadness about you.
  They will say, 'Who was ever
    like Tyre?
  It was destroyed in the sea.'
³³ Your goods went out on the
    seas.
  You supplied many nations
    with what they needed.
  You had so much wealth and
    so many products.
  You made the kings of the
    earth rich.
³⁴ Now the sea has torn you
    apart.
  You have sunk deep down
    into it.
  Your products and all your
    people
  have gone down with you.
³⁵ All those who live in the
    lands along the coast
  are shocked because of
    what has happened to
    you.
  Their kings tremble with
    fear.
  Their faces are twisted in
    horror.
³⁶ The traders among the
    nations laugh at you.
  You have come to a
    horrible end.
  And you will be gone
    forever.' ' "

A Prophecy Against the King of Tyre

28 A message from the
    LORD came to me. The
LORD said, ² "Son of man, speak
to Ethbaal. He is the ruler of
Tyre. Tell him, 'The LORD and
King says,

  " ' "In your proud heart
    you say, 'I am a god.
  I sit on the throne of a god
    in the Mediterranean Sea.'
  But you are only a human
    being. You are not a
    god.
  In spite of that, you think
    you are as wise as a god.
³ Are you wiser than Daniel?
  Isn't even one secret
    hidden from you?
⁴ You are wise and
    understanding.
  So you have become very
    wealthy.
  You have piled up gold and
    silver
    among your treasures.
⁵ You have used your great
    skill in trading
    to increase your wealth.
  You are very rich.
    So your heart has become
    proud." ' "

⁶ The LORD and King says,

  "You think you are wise.
    In fact, you claim to be as
    wise as a god.
⁷ So I am going to bring
    outsiders against you.
  They will not show you any
    pity at all.
  They will use their swords
    against your beauty and
    wisdom.

They will strike down your
    shining glory.
⁸ They will bring you down to
    the grave.
  You will die a horrible death
    in the middle of the sea.
⁹ Then will you say, 'I am a
    god'?
  Will you say that to those
    who kill you?
  You will be only a human
    being to those who kill
    you.
  You will not be a god to
    them.
¹⁰ You will die just like those
    who have not been
    circumcised.
  Outsiders will kill you.

I have spoken," announces the
LORD and King.

¹¹ A message from the LORD
came to me. The LORD said,
¹² "Son of man, sing a song of
sadness about the king of Tyre.
Tell him, 'The LORD and King
says,

" ' "You were the model of
    perfection.
  You were full of wisdom.
  You were perfect and
    beautiful.
¹³ You were in Eden.
  It was my garden.
  All kinds of jewels decorated
    you.
  Here is a list of them.
    carnelian, chrysolite and
      emerald
    topaz, onyx and jasper
    lapis lazuli, turquoise and
      beryl
  Your settings and mountings
    were made out of gold.

On the day you were
    created,
  they were prepared.
¹⁴ I appointed you to be like a
    guardian angel.
  I anointed you for that
    purpose.
  You were on my holy
    mountain.
  You walked among the
    gleaming jewels.
¹⁵ Your conduct was without
    blame
  from the day you were
    created.
  But soon you began to sin.
¹⁶ You traded with many
    nations.
  You harmed people
    everywhere.
  And you sinned.
So I sent you away from my
    mountain in shame.
  Guardian angel, I drove
    you away
  from among the gleaming
    jewels.
¹⁷ You thought you were so
    handsome
  that it made your heart
    proud.
  You thought you were so
    glorious
  that it spoiled your
    wisdom.
So I threw you down to the
    earth.
  I made an example out of
    you in front of kings.
¹⁸ Your many sins and
    dishonest trade
  made your holy places
    impure.
So I made you go up in
    flames.

Fruit of the Spirit

Galatians 5:22–23 tells us how God wants us to live. These are the things that God wants us to produce so that everyone around us can see the good fruit that he grows in us!

Love Joy

Peace Patience
(Forbearance, Longsuffering)

Kindness

good-ness

FAITHFULNESS

Gentleness

Self-control
(Temperance)

The Little Children and Jesus

MARK 10:13–16

I turned you into nothing
but ashes on the ground.
I let everyone see it.
[19] All the nations that knew you
are shocked because of
what happened to you.
You have come to a horrible
end.
And you will be gone
forever." ' "

A Prophecy Against Sidon

[20] A message from the LORD
came to me. The LORD said,
[21] "Son of man, turn your attention to the city of Sidon. Prophesy against it. [22] Say, 'The LORD
and King says,

" ' "Sidon, I am against your
people.
Among you I will display
my glory.
I will punish your people.
Among you I will prove
that I am holy.
Then you will know that I
am the LORD.
[23] I will send a plague on you.
I will make blood flow in
your streets.
Those who are killed will fall
inside you.
Swords will strike your
people on every side.
Then they will know that I
am the LORD.
[24] " ' "The people of Israel will
no longer have neighbors who
hate them. Those neighbors
will not be like sharp and painful thorns anymore. Then Israel
will know that I am the LORD
and King." ' "

[25] The LORD and King says, "I
will gather the people of Israel
together from the nations where
they have been scattered. That
will prove that I am holy. I will
let the nations see it. Then Israel
will live in their own land. I gave
it to my servant Jacob. [26] My people will live there in safety. They
will build houses. They will
plant vineyards. They will live
in safety. I will punish all their
neighbors who told lies about
them. Then Israel will know
that I am the LORD their God."

A Prophecy Against Egypt

29 It was the tenth year
since King Jehoiachin
had been brought to Babylon
as a prisoner. On the 12th day
of the tenth month, a message
from the LORD came to me.
The LORD said, [2] "Son of man,
turn your attention to Pharaoh
Hophra. He is king of Egypt.
Prophesy against him and the
whole land of Egypt. [3] Tell him,
'The LORD and King says,

" ' "Pharaoh Hophra, I am
against you.
King of Egypt, you are like
a huge monster
lying among your streams.
You say, 'The Nile River
belongs to me.
I made it for myself.'
[4] But I will put hooks in your
jaws.
I will make the fish in your
streams
stick to your scales.
I will pull you out from
among your streams.
All the fish will stick to
your scales.

⁵ I will leave you out in the
  desert.
All the fish in your streams
  will be there with you.
You will fall down in an open
  field.
You will not be picked up.
I will feed you to the wild
  animals
and to the birds in the sky.

⁶ Then everyone who lives in Egypt will know that I am the LORD.

" ' "You have been like a walking stick made out of a papyrus stem. The people of Israel tried to lean on you. ⁷ They took hold of you. But you broke under their weight. You tore open their shoulders. The people of Israel leaned on you. But you snapped in two. And their backs were broken." ' "

⁸ So the LORD and King says, "I will send Nebuchadnezzar's sword against you. He will kill people and animals alike. ⁹ Egypt will become a dry and empty desert. Then your people will know that I am the LORD.

"You said, 'The Nile River belongs to me. I made it for myself.' ¹⁰ So I am against you and your streams. I will destroy the land of Egypt. I will turn it into a dry and empty desert from Migdol all the way to Aswan. I will destroy everything as far as the border of Cush. ¹¹ No people or animals will travel through Egypt. No one will even live there for 40 years. ¹² Egypt will be more empty than any other land. Its destroyed cities will lie empty for 40 years. I will scatter the people of Egypt among the nations. I will send them to other countries."

¹³ But here is what the LORD and King says. "At the end of 40 years I will gather the Egyptians together. I will bring them back from the nations where they were scattered. ¹⁴ I will bring them back from where they were taken as prisoners. I will return them to Upper Egypt. That is where their families came from. There they will be an unimportant kingdom. ¹⁵ Egypt will be the least important kingdom of all. It will never place itself above the other nations again. I will make it very weak. Then it will never again rule over the nations. ¹⁶ The people of Israel will no longer trust in Egypt. Instead, Egypt will remind them of how they sinned when they turned to it for help. Then they will know that I am the LORD and King."

¹⁷ It was the 27th year since King Jehoiachin had been brought to Babylon as a prisoner. On the first day of the first month, a message from the LORD came to me. Here is what the LORD said. ¹⁸ "Son of man, King Nebuchadnezzar drove his army in a hard military campaign. The campaign was against Tyre. Their helmets rubbed their heads bare. The heavy loads they carried made their shoulders raw. But he and his army did not gain anything from the campaign he led against Tyre. ¹⁹ So I am go-

ing to give Egypt to Nebuchadnezzar, the king of Babylon. He will carry off its wealth. He will take away anything else they have. He will give it to his army. ²⁰ I have given Egypt to him as a reward for his efforts. After all, he and his army attacked Egypt because I told them to," announces the LORD and King.

²¹ "When Nebuchadnezzar wins the battle over Egypt, I will make the Israelites strong again. Ezekiel, I will open your mouth. And you will be able to speak to them. Then they will know that I am the LORD."

30 A message from the LORD came to me. The LORD said, ² "Son of man, prophesy. Say, 'The LORD and King says,

" ' "Cry out,
    'A terrible day is coming!'
³ The day is near.
    The day of the LORD is
        coming.
It will be a cloudy day.
    The nations have been
        sentenced to die.
⁴ I will send Nebuchadnezzar's
    sword against Egypt.
Cush will suffer terribly.
    Many will die in Egypt.
Then its wealth will be
    carried away.
Its foundations will be torn
    down.

⁵ The people of Cush, Libya, Lydia, Kub and the whole land of Arabia will be killed by swords. So will the Jews who live in Egypt. They went there from the covenant land of Israel. And the Egyptians will die too." ' "

⁶ The LORD says,

"Those who were going to
    help Egypt will die.
The strength Egypt was so
    proud of will fail.
Its people will be killed by
    swords
    from Migdol all the way to
        Aswan,"
            announces the LORD
                and King.
⁷ "Egypt will be more empty
    than any other land.
Its cities will be completely
    destroyed.
⁸ I will set Egypt on fire.
All those who came to help
    it will be crushed.
Then they will know that I
    am the LORD.

⁹ "At that time I will send messengers out in ships. They will terrify the people of Cush who are so contented. Cush will suffer greatly when Egypt falls. And you can be sure it will fall."

¹⁰ The LORD and King says,

"I will put an end to the huge
    armies of Egypt.
I will use Nebuchadnezzar,
    the king of Babylon, to
        do this.
¹¹ He and his armies will attack
    the land and destroy it.
They will not show its
    people any pity at all.
They will use their swords
    against Egypt.
They will fill the land with
    dead bodies.
¹² I will dry up the waters of the
    Nile River.
I will sell the land to an evil
    nation.

I will use the power of
   outsiders
to destroy the land and
   everything in it.
I have spoken. I am the LORD."

¹³ The LORD and King says,

"I will destroy the statues of
   Egypt's gods.
I will put an end to the gods
   the people in Memphis
   worship.
Egypt will not have princes
   anymore.
I will spread fear all
   through the land.
¹⁴ I will completely destroy
   Upper Egypt.
I will set Zoan on fire.
I will punish Thebes.
¹⁵ I will pour out my burning
   anger on Pelusium.
It is a fort in eastern Egypt.
I will wipe out the huge
   army of Thebes.
¹⁶ I will set Egypt on fire.
Pelusium will groan with
   terrible pain.
Thebes will be ripped apart.
Memphis will suffer
   greatly
because of everything that
   happens.
¹⁷ The young men of Heliopolis
   and Bubastis
will be killed by swords.
Their people will be taken
   away as prisoners.
¹⁸ I will break Egypt's power
   over other lands.
That will be a dark day for
   Tahpanhes.
There the strength Egypt was
   so proud of
will come to an end.

Egypt will be covered with
   clouds.
The people in its villages
   will be taken away as
   prisoners.
¹⁹ So I will punish Egypt.
Then they will know that I
   am the LORD."

²⁰ It was the 11th year since
King Jehoiachin had been
brought to Babylon as a prisoner. On the seventh day of the
first month, a message from the
LORD came to me. The LORD
said, ²¹ "Son of man, I have broken the powerful arm of Pharaoh Hophra, the king of Egypt.
No bandages have been put on
his arm to heal it. It has not been
put in a cast. So his arm will not
be strong enough to use a sword.
²² I am against Pharaoh, the king
of Egypt. I will break both his
arms. I will break his healthy
arm and his broken one. His
sword will fall from his hand.
²³ I will scatter the people of
Egypt among the nations. I will
send them to other countries.
²⁴ I will make the arms of the
king of Babylon stronger. I will
put my sword in his hand. But
I will break the arms of Pharaoh. And he will groan in front
of Nebuchadnezzar. He will cry
out like someone dying from his
wounds. ²⁵ I will make the arms
of the king of Babylon stronger.
But the arms of Pharaoh will not
be able to help Egypt. I will put
my sword in Nebuchadnezzar's
hand. He will get ready to use
it against Egypt. Then they will
know that I am the LORD. ²⁶ I will
scatter the Egyptians among

the nations. I will send them to other countries. Then they will know that I am the LORD."

31 It was the 11th year since King Jehoiachin had been brought to Babylon as a prisoner. On the first day of the third month, a message from the LORD came to me. The LORD said, 2 "Son of man, speak to Pharaoh Hophra, the king of Egypt. Also speak to his huge army. Tell him,

" 'Who can be compared with
    your majesty?
3   Think about what
    happened to Assyria.
  Once it was like a cedar
    tree in Lebanon.
It had beautiful branches
  that provided shade for the
    forest.
It grew very high.
  Its top was above all the
    leaves.
4 The waters fed it.
  Deep springs made it grow
    tall.
Their streams flowed
  all around its base.
They made their way
  to all the trees in the fields.
5 So it grew higher
  than any other tree in the
    fields.
It grew more limbs.
  Its branches grew long.
  They spread because they
    had plenty of water.
6 All the birds in the sky
  made their nests in its
    limbs.
All the wild animals
  had their babies under its
    branches.

All the great nations
  lived in its shade.
7 Its spreading branches
  made it majestic and
    beautiful.
Its roots went down deep
  to where there was plenty
    of water.
8 The cedar trees in my garden
  were no match for it.
The juniper trees
  could not equal its limbs.
The plane trees
  could not compare with its
    branches.
No tree in my garden
  could match its beauty.
9 I gave it many branches.
  They made it beautiful.
All the trees in my Garden of
    Eden
  were jealous of it.' "

10 So the LORD and King says, "The great cedar tree grew very high. Its top was above all the leaves. It was proud of how tall it was. 11 So I handed it over to the Babylonian ruler of the nations. I wanted him to punish it because it was so evil. I decided to get rid of it. 12 The Babylonians cut it down and left it there. They did not show it any pity at all. Some of its branches fell on the mountains. Others fell in all the valleys. The branches lay broken in all the stream beds in the land. All the nations on earth came out from under its shade. And they went on their way. 13 All the birds settled on the fallen tree. All the wild animals lived among its branches. 14 So trees that receive plenty of water must never grow so high

that it makes them proud. Their tops must never be above the rest of the leaves. No other trees that receive a lot of water must ever grow that high. They are appointed to die and go down into the earth below. They will join human beings, who go down to the place of the dead."

15 The Lord and King says, "Assyria was like a cedar tree. But I brought it down to the place of the dead. On that day I dried up the deep springs of water and covered them. I held its streams back. I shut off its rich supply of water. Because of that, Lebanon was dressed in gloom as if it were clothes. All the trees in the fields dried up. 16 I brought the cedar tree down to the place of the dead. It joined the other nations that go down there. I made the nations on earth shake because of the sound of its fall. Then all the trees of Eden were comforted in the earth below. That included the finest and best trees in Lebanon. And it included all the trees that received plenty of water. 17 Others also went down along with the cedar tree into the place of the dead. They included those who had been killed by swords. They also included the armed men among the nations who lived in its shade.

18 "Which one of the trees of Eden can be compared with you? What tree is as glorious and majestic as you are? But you too will be brought down to the earth below. There you will join the trees of Eden. You will lie down

with those who have not been circumcised. You will be among those who were killed by swords.

"That is what will happen to Pharaoh and his huge armies," announces the Lord and King.

32 It was the 12th year since King Jehoiachin had been brought to Babylon as a prisoner. On the first day of the 12th month, a message from the Lord came to me. The Lord said, 2 "Son of man, sing a song of sadness about Pharaoh Hophra, the king of Egypt. Tell him,

" 'You are like a lion among
    the nations.
  You are like a monster in
    the sea.
You move around wildly in
    your rivers.
  You churn the water with
    your feet.
  You make the streams
    muddy.' "

3 The Lord and King says,

"I will use a large crowd of
    people
  to throw my net over you.
  They will pull you up in it.
4 Then I will throw you on the
    land.
  I will toss you into an open
    field.
I will let all the birds in the
    sky settle on you.
  I will let all the wild
    animals eat you up.
5 I will scatter the parts of
    your body all over the
    mountains.
  I will fill the valleys with
    your remains.

⁶ I will soak the land with your
    blood.
        It will flow all the way to
            the mountains.
        The valleys will be filled
            with the parts of your
            body.
⁷ When I wipe you out,
        I will put a cover over the
            heavens.
        I will darken the stars.
    I will cover the sun with a
        cloud.
        The moon will stop
            shining.
⁸ I will darken all the bright
        lights
        in the sky above you.
    I will bring darkness over
        your land,"
                announces the LORD
                    and King.
⁹ "The hearts of many people
        will be troubled.
        That is because I will
            destroy you among the
            nations.
        You had never known
            anything about those
            lands before.
¹⁰ Many nations will be
        shocked
        when they see what has
            happened to you.
    Their kings will tremble with
        fear
        when they find out about it.
    I will get ready to use
        Nebuchadnezzar
        as my sword against them.
    On the day you fall from
        power,
        each of the kings will
            tremble with fear.
        Each will be afraid he is
            the next to die."

¹¹ The LORD and King says,

"I will send against you
        the sword of the king of
            Babylon.
¹² I will destroy your huge army.
        They will be killed by the
            swords
        of Babylon's mighty
            soldiers.
    The soldiers will not show
        them any pity.
    They will bring Egypt
        down in all its pride.
        Its huge armies will be
            thrown down.
¹³ I will destroy all its cattle
        from the places where they
            have plenty of water.
    Human feet will never stir up
        the water again.
        The hooves of cattle will
            not make it muddy
            anymore.
¹⁴ I will let the waters of Egypt
        settle.
        I will make its streams flow
            like olive oil,"
                announces the LORD
                    and King.
¹⁵ "I will turn Egypt into an
        empty land.
        I will strip away everything
            in it.
    I will strike down everyone
        who lives there.
        Then they will know that I
            am the LORD.

¹⁶ "That is the song of sadness
people will sing about Egypt.
Women from other nations
will sing it. They will weep over
Egypt and its huge armies," announces the LORD and King.

¹⁷ A message from the LORD
came to me. King Jehoiachin

had been brought to Babylon as a prisoner. On the 15th day of a month 12 years after that, the message came. The LORD said, [18] "Son of man, weep over the huge army of Egypt. Tell the Egyptians they will go down into the earth below. The women singers from the other mighty nations will go down into the grave along with them and others. [19] Tell them, 'Are you any better than others? Since you are not, go down there. Lie down with those who have not been circumcised.' [20] They will fall dead among those who were killed by swords. Nebuchadnezzar is ready to use his sword against them. Let Egypt be dragged off together with its huge armies. [21] The mighty leaders who are already in the place of the dead will talk about Egypt. They will also speak about the nations that were going to help it. They will say, 'They have come down here. They are lying down with those who had not been circumcised. They are here with those who were killed by swords.'

[22] "Assyria is there with its whole army. Its king is surrounded by the graves of all its people who were killed by swords. [23] Their graves are deep down in the pit. Assyria's army lies around the grave of its king. All those who spread terror while they were alive are now dead. They were killed by swords.

[24] "Elam is also there. Its huge armies lie around the grave of its king. All those who spread terror while they were alive are now dead. They were killed by swords. They had not been circumcised. They went down into the earth below. Their shame is like the shame of others who go down into the grave. [25] A bed is made for Elam's king among the dead. His huge armies lie around his grave. They had not been circumcised. They were killed by swords. They had spread terror while they were alive. So now their shame is like the shame of others who go down into the grave. They lie down among the dead.

[26] "Meshek and Tubal are also there. Their huge armies lie around the graves of their kings. None of them had been circumcised. They had spread their terror while they were alive. So they were killed by swords. [27] But they do not lie down with the other dead soldiers of long ago. Those soldiers and their weapons had gone down into the place of the dead. Their swords had been placed under their heads. Their shields rest on their bones. The soldiers of Meshek and Tubal do not lie down with them. This is true even though they had also spread terror while they were alive.

[28] "Pharaoh Hophra, you too will be broken. You will lie down among those who had not been circumcised. You will be there with those who were killed by swords.

[29] "Edom is also there. So are its kings and all its princes. In

spite of their power, they lie down with those who were killed by swords. They lie down with those who had not been circumcised. They are there with others who went down into the grave.

³⁰ "All the princes of the north are there too. So are all the people of Sidon. They went down into the grave in dishonor. While they were alive, they used their power to spread terror. They had never been circumcised. But now they lie down there with those who were killed by swords. Their shame is like the shame of others who go down into the grave.

³¹ "Pharaoh and his whole army will see all of them. That will comfort him even though his huge armies were killed by swords." This is what the LORD and King announces. ³² "I let Pharaoh spread terror while he was alive. But now he and his huge armies will be buried with those who had not been circumcised. They will lie down there with those who were killed by swords," announces the LORD and King.

The LORD Again Appoints Ezekiel to Warn Israel

33 A message from the LORD came to me. The LORD said, ² "Son of man, speak to your people. Tell them, 'Suppose I send enemies against a land. And its people choose one of their men to stand guard. ³ He sees the enemies coming against the land. He blows a trumpet to warn the people. ⁴ Someone hears the trumpet. But they do not pay any attention to the warning. The enemies come and kill them. Then what happens to them will be their own fault. ⁵ They heard the sound of the trumpet. But they did not pay any attention to the warning. So what happened to them was their own fault. If they had paid attention, they would have saved themselves. ⁶ But suppose the guard sees the enemies coming. And he does not blow the trumpet to warn the people. The enemies come and kill one of them. Then their life has been taken away from them because they sinned. But I will hold the guard responsible for their death.'

⁷ "Son of man, I have appointed you as a prophet to warn the people of Israel. So listen to my message. Give them a warning from me. ⁸ Suppose I say to a sinful person, 'You can be sure that you will die.' And suppose you do not try to get them to change their ways. Then they will die because they have sinned. And I will hold you responsible for their death. ⁹ But suppose you do warn that sinful person. You tell them to change their ways. But they do not change. Then they will die because they have sinned. But you will have saved yourself.

¹⁰ "Son of man, speak to the Israelites. Tell them, 'You are saying, "Our sins and the wrong things we have done weigh us down. We are wasting away

because we have sinned so much. So how can we live?"'
[11] Tell them, 'When sinful people die, it does not give me any joy. But when they turn away from their sins and live, that makes me very happy. And that is just as sure as I am alive,' announces the LORD and King. 'So turn away from your sins! Change your evil ways! Why should you die, people of Israel?'

[12] "Son of man, speak to your people. Tell them, 'Suppose a godly person does not obey the LORD. Then the right things that person has done in the past count for nothing. Suppose a sinful person turns away from doing wrong things. Then the wrong things that person has done in the past won't bring them judgment. A godly person who sins won't be allowed to live. That's true even though they used to do right things.' [13] Suppose I tell a godly person that they will live. And they trust in the fact that they used to do what is right. But now they do what is evil. Then I will not remember any of the right things they have done. They will die because they have done so many evil things. [14] Suppose I say to a sinful person, 'You can be sure you will die.' And then they turn away from their sin. They do what is fair and right. [15] They return things they take to make sure loans are repaid. They give back what they have stolen. They obey my rules that give life. They do not do what is evil. Then you can be sure they will live. They will not die. [16] None of the sins they have committed will be held against them. They have done what is fair and right. So you can be sure they will live.

[17] "In spite of that, your people say, 'What the Lord does isn't fair.' But it is what you do that is not fair. [18] Suppose a godly person stops doing what is right. And they do what is evil. Then they will die because of it. [19] But suppose a sinful person turns away from the evil things they have done. And they do what is fair and right. Then they will live by doing that. [20] In spite of that, you Israelites say, 'What the Lord does isn't fair.' But I will judge each of you based on how you have lived."

The LORD Explains Why Jerusalem Fell

[21] It was the 12th year since we had been brought to Babylon as prisoners. On the fifth day of the tenth month, a man who had escaped from Jerusalem came to bring me a report. He said, "The city has fallen!" [22] The evening before the man arrived, the power of the LORD came on me. He opened my mouth before the man came to me in the morning. So my mouth was opened. I was no longer silent.

[23] Then a message from the LORD came to me. The LORD said, [24] "Son of man, here is what the people living in Israel's broken-down buildings are saying. 'Abraham was only one man. But he owned the land.

We are many people. The land must certainly belong to us.' ²⁵ So tell them, 'The LORD and King says, "You eat meat that still has blood in it. You worship your statues of gods. You commit murder. So should you still possess the land? ²⁶ You depend on your swords. You do things I hate. Each one of you sleeps with your neighbor's wife. So should you still possess the land?" '

²⁷ "Tell them, 'Here is what the LORD and King says. "The people who are left in those broken-down buildings will be killed by swords. Wild animals will eat up those who are out in the country. Those who are in caves and other safe places will die of a plague. And that is just as sure as I am alive. ²⁸ I will turn the land into a dry and empty desert. The strength Jerusalem is so proud of will come to an end. The mountains of Israel will be deserted. No one will travel across them. ²⁹ So I will turn the land into a dry and empty desert. I will punish my people because of all the evil things they have done. I hate those things. Then they will know that I am the LORD." '

³⁰ "Son of man, your people are talking about you. They are getting together by the walls of their houses and at their doors. They are saying to one another, 'Come. Listen to the LORD's message.' ³¹ My people come to you, just as they usually do. They sit in front of you. They hear what you say. But they do not put it into practice.

With their mouths they say they love me. But in their hearts they want what belongs to others. They try to get rich by cheating them. ³² You are nothing more to them than someone who sings love songs. They say you have a beautiful voice. They think you play an instrument well. They hear what you say. But they do not put it into practice.

³³ "Everything I have told you will come true. You can be sure of it. Then the people will know that a prophet has been among them."

The LORD Will Be the Shepherd of His People

34 A message from the LORD came to me. The LORD said, ² "Son of man, prophesy against the shepherds of Israel. Tell them, 'The LORD and King says, "How terrible it will be for you shepherds of Israel! You only take care of yourselves. You should take good care of your flocks. ³ Instead, you eat the butter. You dress yourselves with the wool. You kill the finest animals. But you do not take care of your flocks. ⁴ You have not made the weak ones in the flock stronger. You have not healed the sick. You have not bandaged those who are hurt. You have not brought back those who have wandered away. You have not searched for the lost. When you ruled over them, you were mean to them. You treated them badly. ⁵ So they were scattered because they did not have a shepherd.

They became food for all of the wild animals. ⁶ My sheep wandered all over the mountains and high hills. They were scattered over the whole earth. No one searched for them. No one looked for them."

⁷ " 'Shepherds, listen to the LORD's message. He says, ⁸ "My flock does not have a shepherd. Many of my sheep have been stolen. They have become food for all the wild animals. My shepherds did not care for my sheep. They did not even search for them. Instead, they only took care of themselves. And that is just as sure as I am alive," announces the LORD and King. ⁹ Shepherds, listen to the LORD's message. ¹⁰ The LORD and King says, "I am against the shepherds. I will hold them responsible for my flock. I will stop them from taking care of the flock. Then they will not be able to feed themselves anymore. I will save my flock from their mouths. My sheep will no longer be food for them." ' "

¹¹ The LORD and King says, "I myself will search for my sheep. I will look after them. ¹² A shepherd looks after his scattered flock when he is with them. And I will look after my sheep. I will save them from all the places where they were scattered on a dark and cloudy day. ¹³ I will bring them out from among the nations. I will gather them together from other countries. I will bring them into their own land. There they will eat grass on the mountains and in the valleys. And they will eat in all the fields of Israel. ¹⁴ I will take care of them in the best grasslands. They will eat grass on the highest mountains of Israel. There they will lie down in the finest grasslands. They will eat grass in the best places on Israel's mountains. ¹⁵ I myself will take care of my sheep. I will let them lie down in safety," announces the LORD and King. ¹⁶ "I will search for the lost. I will bring back those who have wandered away. I will bandage the ones who are hurt. I will make the weak ones stronger. But I will destroy those who are fat and strong. I will take good care of my sheep. I will treat them fairly."

¹⁷ The LORD and King says, "You are my flock. I will judge between one sheep and another. I will judge between rams and goats. ¹⁸ You already eat in the best grasslands. Must you also stomp all over the other fields? You already drink clear water. Must you also make the rest of the water muddy with your feet? ¹⁹ Must my flock have to eat the grass you have stomped on? Must they drink the water you have made muddy?"

²⁰ So the LORD and King speaks to them. He says, "I myself will judge between the fat sheep and the skinny sheep. ²¹ You push the other sheep around with your hips and shoulders. You use your horns to butt all the weak sheep. Finally, you drive them away. ²² But I will save my sheep. They

will not be carried off anymore. I will judge between one sheep and another. ²³ I will place one shepherd over them. He will belong to the family line of my servant David. He will take good care of them. He will look after them. He will be their shepherd. ²⁴ I am the Lord. I will be their God. And my servant from David's family line will be the prince among them. I have spoken. I am the Lord.

²⁵ "I will make a covenant with them. It promises to give them peace. I will get rid of the wild animals in the land. Then my sheep can live safely in the desert. They can sleep in the forests. ²⁶ I will make them and the places surrounding my holy mountain of Zion a blessing. I will send down rain at the right time. There will be showers of blessing. ²⁷ The trees will bear their fruit. And the ground will produce its crops. The people will be secure in their land. I will break the chains that hold them. I will save them from the power of those who made them slaves. Then they will know that I am the Lord. ²⁸ The nations will not carry them off anymore. Wild animals will no longer eat them up. They will live in safety. And no one will make them afraid. ²⁹ I will give them a land that is famous for its crops. They will never again be hungry there. The nations will not make fun of them anymore. ³⁰ Then they will know that I am with them. I am the Lord their God. And the Israelites will know that they are my people," announces the Lord and King. ³¹ "You are my sheep. You belong to my flock. And I am your God," announces the Lord and King.

A Prophecy Against Edom

35 A message from the Lord came to me. The Lord said, ² "Son of man, turn your attention to Mount Seir. Prophesy against it. ³ Tell it, 'The Lord and King says, "Mount Seir, I am against you. I will reach out my powerful hand against you. I will turn you into a dry and empty desert. ⁴ I will destroy your towns. Your land will become empty. Then you will know that I am the Lord.

⁵ " ' "People of Edom, you have been Israel's enemies for a long time. You let many Israelites be killed by swords when they were in great trouble. At that time I used Nebuchadnezzar to punish them and destroy them completely. ⁶ Now I will hand you over to murderers. They will hunt you down. You murdered others. So murderers will chase you. And that is just as sure as I am alive," announces the Lord and King. ⁷ "I will turn Mount Seir into a dry and empty desert. No one will be able to go anywhere or do anything there. ⁸ I will fill your mountains with dead bodies. Some of those who are killed by swords will fall down dead on your hills. Others will die in your valleys and in all your canyons. ⁹ I will make your land empty forever. No one will

live in your towns. Then you will know that I am the LORD.

¹⁰ " ' "You said, 'The nations of Israel and Judah will belong to us. We will take them over.' You said that, even though I was there. I am the LORD. ¹¹ You were full of anger, jealousy and hatred toward my people. So I will punish you. When I judge you, they will know that I am the LORD. And that is just as sure as I am alive," announces the LORD and King. ¹² "You will know that I have heard all the terrible things you said. You said them about those who live in the mountains of Israel. You made fun of them. You said, 'They have been destroyed. They've been handed over to us. Let's wipe them out.' ¹³ You bragged that you were better than I am. You spoke against me. You did not hold anything back. But I heard it." ' " ¹⁴ The LORD and King says, "The whole earth will be glad. But I will make your land empty. ¹⁵ You were happy when the land of Israel became empty. So I will treat you in the same way. Mount Seir, you will be empty. So will the whole land of Edom. Then you will know that I am the LORD."

A Prophecy of Hope for the Mountains of Israel

36 "Son of man, prophesy to the mountains of Israel. Tell them, 'Mountains of Israel, listen to the LORD's message. ² The LORD and King says, "Your enemies made fun of you. They bragged, 'The hills you lived in for a long time belong to us now.' " ' ³ Ezekiel, prophesy. Say, 'The LORD and King says, "Your enemies destroyed you. They crushed you from every side. So the rest of the nations took over your land. People talked about you. They told lies about you." ' " ⁴ Mountains of Israel, listen to the message of the LORD and King. He speaks to you mountains, hills, canyons and valleys. He speaks to you destroyed cities and deserted towns. The rest of the nations around you took away from you everything of value. They made fun of you. ⁵ So the LORD and King says, "I am very angry with those nations. I have spoken against them and the whole land of Edom. They were very happy when they took over my land. Deep down inside them, they hated Israel. They wanted to take its grasslands. ⁶ Ezekiel, prophesy about the land of Israel. Speak to the mountains, hills, canyons and valleys. Tell them, 'The LORD and King says, "I have a jealous anger against the nations. They have laughed at you." ⁷ So the LORD and King says, "I raise my hand and make a promise. I promise that the nations around you will also be laughed at.

⁸ " ' "Mountains of Israel, you will produce branches and bear fruit for my people Israel. They will come home soon. ⁹ I am concerned about you. I will do good things for you. Farmers will plow your ground. They will plant seeds in it. ¹⁰ I will

cause many people to live in Israel. The towns will no longer be empty. Their broken-down houses will be rebuilt. [11] I will cause many people and animals to live in you, Israel. They will have many babies. I will cause people to make their homes in your towns, just as I did in the past. I will help you succeed more than ever before. Then you will know that I am the Lord. [12] I will let my people Israel live there again. They will possess you. They will receive you as their own. You will never take their children away from them again." ' "

[13] The Lord and King says, "People say to you mountains, 'You destroy people. You let your nation's children be taken away.' [14] But I will not let you destroy people anymore. I will no longer let your nation's children be taken away," announces the Lord and King. [15] "You will not have to listen to the nations laughing at you anymore. People will no longer make fun of you. You will not let your nation fall," announces the Lord and King.

Israel Will Surely Be Rebuilt

[16] Another message from the Lord came to me. The Lord said, [17] "Son of man, the people of Israel used to live in their own land. But they made it 'unclean' because of how they acted and the way they lived. To me they were 'unclean' like a woman having her monthly period. [18] They spilled people's blood in the land. They made the land 'unclean' by worshiping other gods. So I poured out my great anger on them. [19] I scattered them among the nations. I sent them to other countries. I judged them based on how they acted and on how they lived. [20] They treated my name as if it were not holy. They did it everywhere they went among the nations. People said about them, 'They are the Lord's people. But they were forced to leave his land.' [21] I was concerned about my holy name. The people of Israel treated it as if it were not holy. They did it everywhere they went among the nations.

[22] "So tell the Israelites, 'The Lord and King speaks. He says, "People of Israel, I will not take action for your benefit. Instead, I will act for the honor of my holy name. You have treated it as if it were not holy. You did it everywhere you went among the nations. [23] But I will show everyone how holy my great name is. You have treated it as if it were not holy. So I will use you to prove to the nations how holy I am. Then they will know that I am the Lord," announces the Lord and King.

[24] " ' "I will take you out of the nations. I will gather you together from all the countries. I will bring you back into your own land. [25] I will sprinkle pure water on you. Then you will be 'clean.' I will make you completely pure and 'clean.' I will take all the statues of your gods away from you. [26] I will give you

new hearts. I will give you a new spirit that is faithful to me. I will remove your stubborn hearts from you. I will give you hearts that obey me. ²⁷ I will put my Spirit in you. I will make you want to obey my rules. I want you to be careful to keep my laws. ²⁸ Then you will live in the land I gave your people of long ago. You will be my people. And I will be your God. ²⁹ I will save you from all your 'uncleanness.' I will give you plenty of grain. You will have more than enough. So you will never be hungry again. ³⁰ I will multiply the fruit on your trees. I will increase the crops in your fields. Then the nations will no longer make fun of you because you are hungry. ³¹ You will remember your evil ways and the sinful things you have done. You will hate yourselves because you have sinned so much. I also hate your evil practices. ³² I want you to know that I am not doing those things for your benefit," announces the LORD and King. "People of Israel, you should be ashamed of yourselves! Your conduct has brought dishonor to you."'"

³³ The LORD and King says, "I will make you pure from all your sins. On that day I will give you homes in your towns again. Your broken-down houses will be rebuilt. ³⁴ The dry and empty land will be farmed again. Everyone who passes through it will see that it is no longer empty. ³⁵ They will say, 'This land was completely destroyed. But now it's like the Garden of Eden. The cities were full of broken-down buildings. They were destroyed and empty. But now they have high walls around them. And people live in them.' ³⁶ Then the nations that remain around you will know that I have rebuilt what was once destroyed. I have planted again the fields that were once empty. I have spoken. And I will do this. I am the LORD."

³⁷ The LORD and King says, "Once again I will answer Israel's prayer. Here is what I will do for them. I will multiply them as if they were sheep. ³⁸ Large flocks of animals are sacrificed at Jerusalem during the appointed feasts there. In the same way, the destroyed cities will be filled with flocks of people. Then they will know that I am the LORD."

The Valley of Dry Bones

37 The power of the LORD came on me. His Spirit brought me away from my home. He put me down in the middle of a valley. It was full of bones. ² He led me back and forth among them. I saw a huge number of bones in the valley. The bones were very dry. ³ The LORD asked me, "Son of man, can these bones live?"

I said, "LORD and King, you are the only one who knows."

⁴ Then he said to me, "Prophesy to these bones. Tell them, 'Dry bones, listen to the LORD's message. ⁵ The LORD and King speaks to you. He says, "I will

put breath in you. Then you will come to life again. ⁶I will attach tendons to you. I will put flesh on you. I will cover you with skin. So I will put breath in you. And you will come to life again. Then you will know that I am the LORD." ' "

⁷So I prophesied just as the LORD commanded me to. As I was prophesying, I heard a noise. It was a rattling sound. The bones came together. One bone connected itself to another. ⁸I saw tendons and flesh appear on them. Skin covered them. But there was no breath in them.

⁹Then the LORD said to me, "Prophesy to the breath. Prophesy, son of man. Tell it, 'The LORD and King says, "Breath, come from all four directions. Go into these people who have been killed. Then they can live." ' " ¹⁰So I prophesied just as he commanded me to. And breath entered them. Then they came to life again. They stood up on their feet. They were like a huge army.

¹¹Then the LORD said to me, "Son of man, these bones stand for all the people of Israel. The people say, 'Our bones are dried up. We've lost all hope. We are destroyed.' ¹²So prophesy. Tell them, 'The LORD and King says, "My people, I am going to open up your graves. I am going to bring you out of them. I will take you back to the land of Israel. ¹³So I will open up your graves and bring you out of them. Then you will know that I am the

LORD. You are my people. ¹⁴I will put my Spirit in you. And you will live again. I will settle you in your own land. Then you will know that I have spoken. I have done it," announces the LORD.' "

Israel Will Be One Nation Under One King

¹⁵A message from the LORD came to me. The LORD said, ¹⁶"Son of man, get a stick of wood. Write on it, 'Belonging to the tribe of Judah and the Israelites who are connected with it.' Then get another stick. Write on it, 'Ephraim's stick. Belonging to the tribes of Joseph and all the Israelites connected with them.' ¹⁷Join them together into one stick in your hand.

¹⁸"Your people will ask you, 'What do you mean by this?' ¹⁹Tell them, 'The LORD and King says, "I am going to get the stick of Joseph and the Israelites connected with it. That stick is in Ephraim's hand. I am going to join it to Judah's stick. I will make them a single stick of wood in my hand." ' ²⁰Show them the sticks you wrote on. ²¹Tell them, 'The LORD and King says, "I will take the Israelites out of the nations where they have gone. I will gather them together from all around. I will bring them back to their own land. ²²There I will make them one nation. They will live on the mountains of Israel. All of them will have one king. They will never be two nations again. They will never again be

separated into two kingdoms. ²³ They will no longer make themselves 'unclean' by worshiping any of their evil gods. They will not do wrong things anymore. They always turn away from me. But I will save them from that sin. I will make them pure and 'clean.' They will be my people. And I will be their God.

²⁴ " ' "A man who belongs to the family line of my servant David will be their king. All of them will have one shepherd. They will obey my laws. And they will be careful to keep my rules. ²⁵ They will live in the land I gave to my servant Jacob. That is where your people of long ago lived. They, their children, their children's children, and their children after them will live there forever. And my servant from David's family line will be their prince forever. ²⁶ I will make a covenant with them. It promises to give them peace. The covenant will last forever. I will make them my people. And I will cause there to be many of them. I will put my temple among them forever. ²⁷ I will live with them. I will be their God. And they will be my people. ²⁸ My temple will be among them forever. Then the nations will know that I make Israel holy. I am the LORD." ' "

The LORD Will Have Great Victory Over the Nations

38 A message from the LORD came to me. The LORD said, ² "Son of man, turn your attention to Gog. He is from the land of Magog. He is the chief prince of Meshek and Tubal. Prophesy against him. ³ Tell him, 'The LORD and King says, "Gog, I am against you. You are the chief prince of Meshek and Tubal. ⁴ But I will turn you around. I will put hooks in your jaws. I will bring you out of your land along with your whole army. Your horses will come with you. Your horsemen will be completely armed. Your huge army will carry large and small shields. All of them will be ready to use their swords. ⁵ The men of Persia, Cush and Put will march out with them. All of them will have shields and helmets. ⁶ Gomer and all its troops will be there too. Beth Togarmah from the far north will also come with all its troops. Many nations will help you.

⁷ " ' "Get ready. Be prepared. Take command of the huge armies gathered around you. ⁸ After many years you will be called together to fight. Later, you will march into a land that has not had war for a while. Its people were gathered together from many nations. They came to the mountains of Israel. No one had lived in those mountains for a long time. So the people had been brought back from other nations. Now all the people live in safety. ⁹ You, all your troops and the many nations with you will march up to attack them. All of you will advance like a storm. You will be like a cloud covering their land."

¹⁰ " 'The LORD and King says, "At that time some ideas will come to you. You will make evil plans. ¹¹ You will say, 'I will march out against a land whose villages don't have walls around them. I'll attack those peaceful people. I'll do this when they aren't expecting it. None of their villages has walls or gates with metal bars on them. ¹² I will rob those people. I'll steal everything they have. Then I'll turn my attention to the destroyed houses where people are living again. They have returned there from other nations. Now they are rich. They have plenty of livestock and all kinds of goods. They are living in Israel. It is the center of the earth.' ¹³ The people of Sheba and Dedan will speak to you. So will the traders of Tarshish and all its villages. They will say, 'Have you come to rob us? Have you gathered your huge army together to steal our silver and gold? Are you going to take away from us our livestock and goods? Do you plan to carry off everything we have?' " '

¹⁴ "Son of man, prophesy. Tell Gog, 'The LORD and King says, "A time is coming when my people Israel will be living in safety. You will see that it is a good time to attack them. ¹⁵ So you will come from your place in the far north. Many nations will join you. All their men will be riding on horses. You will have a huge and mighty army. ¹⁶ They will advance against my people Israel. They will be like a cloud covering their land. Gog, in days to come I will bring you against my land. Then the nations will know me. I will use you to prove to them how holy I am."

¹⁷ " 'Here is what the LORD and King says to Gog. "In the past I spoke about you through my servants, the prophets of Israel. At that time they prophesied for years that I would bring you against them. ¹⁸ Here is what will happen in days to come. You will attack the land of Israel. That will stir up my burning anger," announces the LORD and King. ¹⁹ "At that time my burning anger will blaze out at you. There will be a great earthquake in the land of Israel. ²⁰ The fish in the sea, the birds in the sky and the wild animals will tremble with fear. They will tremble with fear because of what I will do. So will every creature that moves along the ground. And so will all the people on earth. The mountains will come crashing down. The cliffs will break into pieces. Every wall will fall to the ground. ²¹ I will punish you on all my mountains," announces the LORD and King. "Your men will use their swords against one another. ²² I will judge you. I will send a plague against you. A lot of blood will be spilled. I will send heavy rain, hailstones and burning sulfur down to the earth. They will fall on you and your troops. They will also come down on the many nations that are helping you. ²³ That will show how great and holy I am. I will make myself known to many nations.

Then they will know that I am the LORD."'

39 "Son of man, prophesy against Gog. Tell him, 'The LORD and King says, "Gog, I am against you. You are the chief prince of Meshek and Tubal. ² But I will turn you around. I will drag you along. I will bring you from the far north. I will send you against the mountains of Israel. ³ Then I will knock your bow out of your left hand. I will make your arrows drop from your right hand. ⁴ You will fall dead on the mountains of Israel. You and all your troops will die there. So will the nations that join you. I will feed you to all kinds of birds that eat dead bodies. So they and the wild animals will eat you up. ⁵ You will fall dead in the open fields. I have spoken," announces the LORD and King. ⁶ "I will send fire on the land of Magog. It will burn up the people who live in safety on the coast. So they will know that I am the LORD.

⁷ " ' "I will make my holy name known among my people Israel. I will no longer let them treat my name as if it were not holy. Then the nations will know that I am the Holy One in Israel. I am the LORD. ⁸ The day I will judge you is coming. You can be sure of it," announces the LORD and King. "It is the day I have spoken about.

⁹ " ' "At that time those who live in the towns of Israel will go out and light a fire. They will use it to burn up the weapons. That includes small and large shields. It also includes bows and arrows, war clubs and spears. It will take seven years to burn all of them up. ¹⁰ People will not gather wood from the fields. They will not cut down the forests. Instead, they will burn the weapons. And they will rob those who robbed them. They will steal from those who stole from them," announces the LORD and King.

¹¹ " ' "Gog, at that time I will bury you in a grave in Israel. It will be in the valley where people travel east of the Dead Sea. It will block the path of travelers. That's because you and your huge armies will be buried there. So it will be called the Valley of Gog's Armies.

¹² " ' "It will take seven months for the Israelites to bury the bodies. They will do this to make the land 'clean' again. ¹³ All the people in the land will bury them. The day that I show how glorious I am will be a time to remember." This is what the LORD and King announces. ¹⁴ "People will keep being hired to make the land 'clean' again. They will go all through it. They and others will bury any bodies lying on the ground.

" ' "After the seven months they will search even more carefully. ¹⁵ As they go through the land here is what they'll do. When anyone sees a bone, they will put a marker beside it. Then those who dig the graves will take the bone to the Valley of Gog's Armies. There they will bury it. ¹⁶ That is how they will

make the land 'clean' again."'."
Also a town called Gog's Armies
is near there.

[17] The Lord and King said to
me, "Son of man, speak to every kind of bird. Call out to all
the wild animals. Tell them,
'Gather together. Come from
everywhere. Gather around
the sacrifice I am preparing for
you. It is the great sacrifice on
the mountains of Israel. There
you will eat human bodies and
drink human blood. [18] You will
eat the bodies of mighty men.
You will drink the blood of the
princes of the earth. You will
eat their bodies and drink their
blood. You will do this as if they
were rams and lambs, goats and
bulls. You will enjoy it as if you
were eating the fattest animals
from Bashan. [19] So I am preparing a sacrifice for you. You will
eat fat until you are completely
full. You will drink blood until
you are drunk. [20] At my table you
will eat horses, riders, mighty
men and soldiers until you are
full,' announces the Lord and
King.

[21] "'I will show all the nations
my glory. They will see how I
punish them when I use my
power against them. [22] From
that time on, the people of Israel
will know that I am the Lord
their God. [23] The nations will
know that the people of Israel
were taken away as prisoners
because they sinned against me.
They were not faithful to me.
So I turned my face away from
them. I handed them over to
their enemies. All of them were
killed by swords. [24] I punished
them because they were "unclean." They did many things
that were wrong. So I turned my
face away from them.'"

[25] The Lord and King says,
"I will now cause the people of
Jacob to recover from my judgment. I will show my tender love
for all the people of Israel. I will
make sure that my name is kept
holy. [26] My people will forget
the shameful things they have
done. They will not remember
all the ways they were unfaithful to me. They used to live in
safety in their land. At that time
no one made them afraid. [27] So
I will bring them back from the
nations. I will gather them from
the countries of their enemies.
And I will use them to prove to
many nations how holy I am.
[28] Then they will know that I am
the Lord their God. I let the nations take my people away as
prisoners. But now I will bring
them back to their own land. I
will not leave anyone behind. [29] I
will no longer turn my face away
from the people of Israel. I will
pour out my Spirit on them," announces the Lord and King.

The New Temple Area

40 It was the 14th year after
Jerusalem had been cap-
tured. We had been brought to
Babylon as prisoners. It was the
tenth day of a month near the
beginning of the 25th year after
that. On that day the power of
the Lord came on me. He took
me back to my land. [2] In visions
God gave me, he brought me

to the land of Israel. He set me on a very high mountain. Some buildings were on the south side of it. They looked like a city. ³ He took me there. I saw a man who appeared to be made out of bronze. He was standing at the gate of the outer courtyard. He was holding a linen measuring tape and a measuring rod. ⁴ The man said to me, "Son of man, look carefully and listen closely. Pay attention to everything I show you. That is why the LORD brought you here. Tell the people of Israel everything you see."

The East Gate to the Outer Courtyard

⁵ I saw a wall that completely surrounded the temple area. The measuring rod in the man's hand was 11 feet long. He measured the wall with it. The wall was as thick and as high as one measuring rod.

⁶ Then the man went to the east gate. He climbed its steps. He measured the gateway. It was one rod wide. ⁷ The rooms where the guards stood were one rod long and one rod wide. The walls between the rooms were almost nine feet thick. The gateway next to the porch was one rod wide. The porch faced the front of the temple.

⁸ Then the man measured the porch of the gateway. ⁹ It was 14 feet wide. Each of its doorposts was three and a half feet thick. The porch of the gateway faced the front of the temple.

¹⁰ Inside the east gate were three rooms on each side. All the rooms were the same size. The walls on each side of the rooms had the same thickness. ¹¹ Then the man measured the entrance of the gateway. It was 18 feet wide and 23 feet long. ¹² In front of each room was a wall. It was 21 inches high. The rooms measured 11 feet on each side. ¹³ Then he measured the gateway from the back wall of one room to the back wall of the room across from it. It was 44 feet from the top of one wall to the top of the other. ¹⁴ He measured along the front of the side walls all around the inside of the gateway. The total was 105 feet. That didn't include the porch that faced the courtyard. ¹⁵ It was 88 feet from the entrance of the gateway to the far end of its porch. ¹⁶ The rooms and their side walls inside the gateway had narrow openings on top of them. So did the porch. All the openings faced the inside. The front of each side wall was decorated with a palm tree.

The Outer Courtyard

¹⁷ Then the man brought me into the outer courtyard. There I saw some rooms and a sidewalk. They had been built all around the courtyard. Along the sidewalk were 30 rooms. ¹⁸ The sidewalk went all the way up to the sides of the gateways. It was as wide as they were long. This was the lower sidewalk. ¹⁹ Then he measured from the inside of the lower gateway to the outside of the inner courtyard. The east

side measured 175 feet. So did the north side.

The North Gate

²⁰ Then the man measured the north gate. He wanted to show me how long and wide it was. The gate led into the outer courtyard. ²¹ It had three rooms on each side. Their side walls and porch measured the same as the ones at the first gateway. They measured 88 feet long and 44 feet wide. ²² Its openings, porch and palm tree decorations measured the same as the ones at the east gate. Seven steps led up to the north gate. Its porch was across from them. ²³ The inner courtyard had a gate. It faced the gate on the north. It was just like the east gate. He measured from one gate to the one across from it. The total was 175 feet.

The South Gate

²⁴ Then the man led me to the south side of the courtyard. There I saw the south gate. He measured its doorposts and porch. They measured the same as the others. ²⁵ The gateway and its porch had narrow openings all around. The openings were the same as the others had. The side walls and porch measured 88 feet long and 44 feet wide. ²⁶ Seven steps led up to it. Its porch was across from them. The front of each side wall was decorated with a palm tree. ²⁷ The inner courtyard also had a gate that faced south. The man measured from this gate to the outer gate on the south side. The total was 175 feet.

The Gates to the Inner Courtyard

²⁸ Then the man brought me into the inner courtyard. We went through the south gate. He measured it. It was the same size as the others. ²⁹ Its rooms, side walls and porch measured the same as the ones at the other gateways. The gateway and its porch had openings all around. The side walls and porch measured 88 feet long and 44 feet wide. ³⁰ The porches of the gateways around the inner courtyard were 44 feet wide and nine feet long. ³¹ Its porch faced the outer courtyard. Palm trees decorated its doorposts. Eight steps led up to it.

³² Then the man brought me to the east side of the inner courtyard. There he measured the gateway. It was the same size as the others. ³³ Its rooms, side walls and porch measured the same as the ones at the other gateways. The gateway and its porch had openings all around. The side walls and porch measured 88 feet long and 44 feet wide. ³⁴ Its porch faced the outer courtyard. Each doorpost was decorated with a palm tree. Eight steps led up to the porch.

³⁵ Then the man brought me to the north gate. He measured it. It was the same size as the others. ³⁶ Its rooms, side walls and porch measured the same as the ones at the other gateways. It had openings all around. The side walls and the

porch measured 88 feet long and 44 feet wide. ³⁷ The porch faced the outer courtyard. Each doorpost was decorated with a palm tree. Eight steps led up to the porch.

The Rooms for Preparing Sacrifices

³⁸ A room with a doorway was by the porch of each inner gateway. The burnt offerings were washed there. ³⁹ On each side of the porch of the gateway were two tables. The burnt offerings were killed on them. So were the sin offerings and guilt offerings. ⁴⁰ Two more tables were by the outer wall of the gateway porch. They were near the steps at the entrance of the north gateway. Two more tables were on the other side of the steps. ⁴¹ So there were four tables on each side of the gateway. The total number of tables was eight. Animals for sacrifice were killed on all of them. ⁴² There were also four other tables for the burnt offerings. They were made out of blocks of stone. Each table was two and a half feet long and two and a half feet wide. And each was almost two feet high. The tools for killing the burnt offerings and other sacrifices were placed on them. ⁴³ Large hooks hung on the walls all around. Each was three inches long. The meat of the offerings was placed on the tables.

The Rooms for the Priests

⁴⁴ Near the inner gates were two rooms. They were in the inner courtyard. One room was next to the north gate. It faced south. The other one was next to the south gate. It faced north. ⁴⁵ The man said to me, "The room that faces south is for the priests who guard the temple. ⁴⁶ The one that faces north is for the priests who guard the altar. All these priests are the sons of Zadok. They are the only Levites who can approach the LORD to serve him."

⁴⁷ Then the man measured the courtyard. It was square. It measured 175 feet long and 175 feet wide. And the altar was in front of the temple.

The New Temple

⁴⁸ The man brought me to the porch of the temple. He measured the doorposts of the porch. Each of them was almost nine feet wide. The entrance was 24 and a half feet wide. Each of the side walls was a little over five feet wide. ⁴⁹ The porch was 35 feet wide. It was 21 feet from front to back. It was reached by some stairs. Pillars were on each side of the doorposts.

41 Then the man brought me to the main hall. There he measured the doorposts. Each of them was 11 feet wide. ² The entrance was 18 feet wide. Each of its side walls was almost nine feet wide. He also measured the main hall. It was 70 feet long and 35 feet wide.

³ Then he went into the Most Holy Room. There he measured the doorposts at the entrance. Each one of them was three and a half feet wide. The entrance

itself was 11 feet wide. Each of its side walls was a little over 12 feet wide. ⁴He also measured the Most Holy Room. It was 35 feet long and 35 feet wide. He said to me, "This is the Most Holy Room." It was beyond the back wall of the main hall.

⁵Then the man measured the wall of the temple. It was 11 feet thick. Each side room around the temple was seven feet wide. ⁶The side rooms were on three floors. There were 30 rooms on each floor. Ledges had been built all around the wall of the temple. So the floor beams of the side rooms rested on the ledges. The beams didn't go into the temple wall. ⁷The side rooms of the temple were wider as we went up floor by floor. A stairway went from the lowest floor all the way up to the top floor. It passed through the middle floor.

⁸I saw that the temple had a raised base all around it. The base formed the foundation of the side rooms. It was as long as one measuring rod. So it was 11 feet long. ⁹The outer wall of each side room was almost nine feet thick. The open area between the side rooms of the temple ¹⁰and the priests' rooms was 35 feet wide. It went all around the temple. ¹¹The side rooms had entrances from the open area. One was on the north side. Another was on the south. The base next to the open area was almost nine feet wide all around.

¹²There was a large building right behind the temple. It was on the west side of the outer courtyard. It was 123 feet wide. Its wall was almost nine feet thick all around. And it was 158 feet long.

¹³Then the man measured the temple. It was 175 feet long. The open area and the large building behind the temple also measured 175 feet. ¹⁴The east side of the inner courtyard was 175 feet wide. That included the front of the temple.

¹⁵Then the man measured the building that was on the west side of the outer courtyard. It was behind the temple. It was 175 feet long. That included the walkways of the building on each side.

The main hall and the Most Holy Room were covered with wood. ¹⁶And the porch that faced the inner courtyard was covered with wood. So were the gateways, narrow openings and walkways around these three places. The gateways and everything beyond them were covered with wood. The floor, the wall up to the openings, and the openings themselves were also covered. ¹⁷The area above the outside of the entrance to the Most Holy Room was decorated. There were also decorations all around the walls of the Most Holy Room. ¹⁸Carved cherubim and palm trees were used in the decorations. Each cherub had a palm tree next to it. And each palm tree had a cherub next to it. Each cherub had two faces. ¹⁹One was the face of a human being. It looked toward the palm tree on one side. The other was the face of a lion. It looked toward the palm tree on the other side. The decorations were carved all around the whole temple. ²⁰ Cherubim and palm trees decorated the wall of the main hall. They were carved from the floor all the way up to the area above the entrance.

²¹ The main hall had a door-frame shaped like a rectangle. So did the Most Holy Room. ²² A wooden altar stood in the main hall. It was a little over five feet high. It was three and a half feet long and three and a half feet wide. Its corners, base and sides were made out of wood. The man said to me, "This is the table that stands in front of the LORD." ²³ The main hall had double doors. So did the Most Holy Room. ²⁴ Each door had two parts that could swing back and forth. ²⁵ Cherubim and palm trees were carved on the doors of the main hall. The decorations were like the ones on the walls. A wooden roof went out beyond the front of the porch. ²⁶ The side walls of the porch had narrow openings on top of them. Palm trees were carved on each side. A wooden roof went out beyond the entrance to each side room of the temple.

The Rooms for the Priests

42 Then the man led me north into the outer courtyard of the temple. He brought me to the rooms that were across from the inner courtyard. They were across from the outer wall of the temple on the north side. ² The rooms were in a building north of the temple. The building had a door that faced north. It was 175 feet long. It was 88 feet wide. ³ One row of rooms was next to the inner courtyard. The other row was across from the sidewalk of the outer courtyard. Each room was 35 feet long. Walkways in front of each row faced each other on all three floors. ⁴ Between the two rows was an inner sidewalk. It was 18 feet wide and 175 feet long. Each of the rooms had a door on the north side. ⁵ The rooms on the top floor were narrower than the others. The walkways took up more space from these rooms. The walkways took up less space from the rooms on the other two floors. ⁶ The courtyards had pillars. But the rooms on the top floor didn't. So their floor space was smaller than the space in the rooms on the other floors. ⁷ The building had an outer wall. It was even with the outer row of rooms and with the outer courtyard. The wall continued east of the outer row for 88 feet. ⁸ So there were two rows of rooms. The row next to the outer courtyard was 88 feet long. The one closest to the temple was 175 feet long. ⁹ The first floor of the building had an entrance on the east side. It led to the outer courtyard.

¹⁰ There were also two rows of rooms in a building next to the

south side of the inner court-yard. The building was across from the south wall of the outer courtyard. [11] Between the two rows was an inner sidewalk. The rooms were like the ones in the north building. They were as long and wide as the rooms on the north. The doorways of the rooms on the south were like the ones on the north. [12] People entered the south rooms through the doorway at the east end of the inner sidewalk. The south wall continued east of the outer row of rooms.

[13] The man said to me, "The north and south rooms face the inner courtyard. They are the priests' rooms. That is where the priests who approach the LORD will eat the very holy offerings. They will also store them there. That includes the grain offer-ings, sin offerings and guilt of-ferings. This place is holy. [14] The priests who enter these holy rooms must leave behind the clothes they served in. Then they can go into the outer court-yard. The clothes they served in are holy. So the priests must put other clothes on. They have to do that before they go near the places where other people go."

[15] The man finished measur-ing what was inside the tem-ple area. Then he led me out through the east gate. He mea-sured all around the area. [16] He measured the east side with his measuring rod. It was 875 feet long. [17] He measured the north side. It was 875 feet long. [18] He measured the south side.

It was 875 feet long. [19] Finally, he turned and measured the west side. It was 875 feet long. [20] So he measured the area on all four sides. It had a wall around it. The wall was 875 feet long and 875 feet wide. It separated what was holy from what was not.

The Glory of God Returns to the Temple

43 Then the man brought me to the east gate. [2] There I saw the glory of the God of Israel. He was coming from the east. His voice was like the roar of rushing waters. His glory made the land shine brightly. [3] The vision I saw was like the one I had when he came to destroy the city. It was also like the visions I had seen by the Kebar River. I fell with my face toward the ground. [4] The glory of the LORD entered the temple through the east gate. [5] Then the Spirit lifted me up. He brought me into the inner courtyard. The glory of the LORD filled the temple.

[6] The man was standing be-side me. I heard someone speaking to me from inside the temple. [7] He said, "Son of man, this is the place where my throne is. The stool for my feet is also here. I will live here among the people of Israel forever. They will never again treat my name as if it were not holy. They and their kings will not serve other gods anymore. The peo-ple will no longer make funeral offerings for their kings. [8] The people of Israel placed their

own doorway next to my holy doorway. They put their doorposts right beside mine. Nothing but a thin wall separated us. They treated my name as if it were not holy. I hated it when they did that. So I became angry with them and destroyed them. ⁹ Now let them stop serving other gods. Let them stop making funeral offerings for their kings. If they obey me, I will live among them forever.

¹⁰ "Son of man, tell the people of Israel about the temple. Then they will be ashamed of their sins. Let them think carefully about how perfect it is. ¹¹ What if they are ashamed of everything they have done? Then show them all the plans of the temple. Explain to them how it is laid out. Tell them about its exits and entrances. Show them exactly what it will look like. Give them all its rules and laws. Write everything down so they can see it. Then they will be faithful to its plan. And they will obey all its rules.

¹² "Here is the law of the temple. The whole area on top of Mount Zion will be very holy. That is the law of the temple."

The Great Altar Is Rebuilt

¹³ The man said, "Here is the size of the altar. The standard measurement I am using is 21 inches. The altar has a drain on the ground. The drain is 21 inches deep and 21 inches wide. It has a rim that is nine inches wide around the edge. Here is how high the altar is. ¹⁴ From the drain to the lower ledge is three and a half feet. The lower ledge goes around the altar and is 21 inches wide. From the lower ledge to the upper ledge is seven feet. The upper ledge also goes around the altar and is 21 inches wide. ¹⁵ The top part of the altar is where the sacrifices are burned. It is seven feet high. A horn sticks out from each of its four corners. ¹⁶ The top part of the altar is square. It is 21 feet long and 21 feet wide. ¹⁷ The upper ledge is also square. It is 25 feet long and 25 feet wide. The drain goes all the way around the altar. The rim of the drain is 11 inches wide. The steps leading up to the top of the altar face east."

¹⁸ Then the man said to me, "Son of man, the LORD and King speaks. He says, 'Here are the rules for the altar when it is built. Follow them when you sacrifice burnt offerings and splash blood against it. ¹⁹ Give a young bull to the priests as a sin offering. They are Levites from the family of Zadok. They approach me to serve me,' announces the LORD and King. ²⁰ 'Get some of the bull's blood. Put it on the four horns of the altar. Also put it on the four corners of the upper ledge of the altar and all around the rim. That will make the altar pure and "clean." ²¹ Use the bull for the sin offering. Burn it in the proper place outside the temple.

²² "'On the second day offer a male goat. It must not have any flaws. It is a sin offering to

make the altar pure and "clean." So do the same thing with the goat that you did with the bull. 23 When you finish making the altar pure, offer a young bull and a ram from the flock. They must not have any flaws. 24 Offer them to me. The priests must sprinkle salt on them. Then they must sacrifice them as a burnt offering to me.

25 " 'Provide a male goat each day for seven days. It is a sin offering. Also provide a young bull and a ram from the flock. They must not have any flaws. 26 For seven days the priests must make the altar pure and "clean." That is how they will set it apart to me. 27 From the eighth day on, the priests must bring your burnt offerings and friendship offerings. They must sacrifice them on the altar. Then I will accept you,' announces the LORD and King."

The Priesthood Will Be Established Again

44 Then the man brought me back to the outer gate of the temple. It was the one that faced east. It was shut. 2 The LORD said to me, "This gate must remain shut. It must not be opened. No one can enter through it. It must remain shut because I have entered through it. I am the God of Israel. 3 The prince is the only one who can sit in the gateway. There he can eat in front of me. He must enter through the porch of the gateway. And he must go out the same way."

4 Then the man brought me through the north gate. He took me to the front of the temple. I looked up and saw the glory of the LORD. It filled his temple. I fell with my face toward the ground.

5 The LORD said to me, "Son of man, pay attention. Look carefully. Listen closely to everything I tell you. I'm telling you about all the rules and instructions concerning my temple. Pay attention to the entrance to the temple and to all its exits. 6 Speak to the people of Israel. They refuse to obey me. Tell them, 'Here is what the LORD and King says. "People of Israel, I have had enough of your evil practices. I hate them. 7 You brought outsiders into my temple. They were not circumcised. Their hearts were stubborn. You made my temple 'unclean.' But you offered me food, fat and blood anyway. When you did all these things, you broke the covenant I made with you. I hated all the evil things you did. 8 You did not do what I told you to. You did not take care of my holy things. Instead, you put other people in charge of my temple." ' " 9 The LORD and King says, "No outsider whose heart is stubborn can enter my temple. They have not been circumcised. Even if they live among the people of Israel they can't enter my temple.

10 "Some Levites wandered far away from me when Israel went astray. They worshiped the statues of their gods. So they will

be punished because they have sinned. [11] They might serve in my temple. They might be in charge of its gates. They might kill the burnt offerings and sacrifices for the people. And they might stand in front of the people and serve them in other ways. [12] But these Levites served the people of Israel. They served while the Israelites were worshiping the statues of their gods. They made the people fall into sin. So I raised my hand and made a promise. I warned them that I would punish them because of their sin," announces the LORD and King. [13] "They must not approach me to serve me as priests. They must not come near any of my holy things. They must stay away from my very holy offerings. They did many things they should have been ashamed of. I hated those things. [14] But I will still appoint them to guard the temple. They will guard it for all the work that has to be done there.

[15] "But the priests must approach me to serve me. They are Levites from Zadok's family line. They guarded my temple when the people of Israel turned away from me. These priests must serve me by offering sacrifices of fat and blood," announces the LORD and King. [16] "They are the only ones who can enter my temple. Only they can come near to serve me as guards.

[17] "They will enter the gates of the inner courtyard. When they do, they must wear linen clothes. They will serve at the gates of the inner courtyard or inside the temple. When they do, they must not wear any clothes made out of wool. [18] They must have linen turbans on their heads. They must wear linen underwear around their waists. They must not wear anything that makes them sweat. [19] They will go into the outer courtyard where the people are. When they do, they must take off the clothes they have been serving in. They must leave them in the sacred rooms. And they must put other clothes on. Then the people will not be made holy if they happen to touch the priests' clothes.

[20] "The priests must not shave their heads. They must not let their hair grow long. They must keep it cut short. [21] No priest may drink wine when he enters the inner courtyard. [22] They must not get married to widows or divorced women. They may only marry Israelite virgins or the widows of priests. [23] The priests must teach my people the difference between what is holy and what is not. They must show them how to tell the difference between what is 'clean' and what is not.

[24] "When people do not agree, the priests must serve as judges between them. They must make their decisions based on my laws. They must obey my laws and rules for all my appointed feasts. And they must keep my Sabbath days holy.

[25] "A priest must not make

himself 'unclean' by going near a dead person. But suppose the dead person was his father or mother. Or suppose it was his son or daughter or brother or unmarried sister. Then the priest may make himself 'unclean.' ²⁶ After he is pure and 'clean' again, he must wait seven days. ²⁷ Then he may go to the inner courtyard to serve in the temple. But when he does, he must sacrifice a sin offering for himself," announces the LORD and King.

²⁸ "The priests will not receive any part of the land of Israel. I myself will be their only share. ²⁹ They will eat the grain offerings, sin offerings and guilt offerings. Everything in Israel that is set apart to me in a special way will belong to them. ³⁰ The best of every first share of the people's crops will belong to the priests. So will all their special gifts. The people must give the priests the first share of their ground meal. Then I will bless my people's families. ³¹ The priests must not eat any bird or animal that is found dead. They must not eat anything that wild animals have torn apart.

The LORD Establishes Israel Again

45 "People of Israel, you will divide up the land you will receive. When you do, give me my share of it. It will be a sacred area. It will be eight miles long and six and a half miles wide. The entire area will be holy. ² The temple area in it will be 875 feet long and 875 feet wide. An 88-foot strip around it will be open land. ³ In the sacred area, measure off a large strip of land. It will be eight miles long and three and a third miles wide. The temple will be in it. It will be the most holy place of all. ⁴ The large strip will be the sacred share of land for the priests. There they will serve in the temple. And they will approach me to serve me there. Their houses will be built on that land. The holy temple will also be located there. ⁵ So the Levites will serve in the temple. They will have an area eight miles long and three and a third miles wide. The towns they live in will be located there.

⁶ "Give the city an area one and two-thirds miles wide and eight miles long. It will be right next to the sacred area. It will belong to all the people of Israel.

⁷ "The prince will have land on both sides of the sacred area and the city. Its border will run east and west along the land of one of the tribes. ⁸ The prince will own this land in Israel. And my princes will not crush my people anymore. Instead, they will allow the people of Israel to receive their own share of land. It will be divided up based on their tribes."

⁹ The LORD and King says, "Princes of Israel, you have gone far enough! Stop hurting others. Do not crush them. Do what is fair and right. Stop taking my people's land away from them," announces the LORD and King. ¹⁰ "Use weights and measures

that are honest and exact. [11] Use the same standard to measure dry and liquid products. Use a 6-bushel measure for dry products. And use a 60-gallon measure for liquids. [12] Every amount of money must be weighed out in keeping with the standard weights.

[13] "You must offer a special gift. It must be six pounds out of every six bushels of grain. [14] Give two and a half quarts out of every 60 gallons of olive oil. [15] Also give one sheep from every flock of 200 sheep. Get them from the grasslands of Israel that receive plenty of water. Use them for grain offerings, burnt offerings and friendship offerings. They will be used to pay for the sin of the people," announces the LORD and King. [16] "All the people in the land will be required to give this special gift. They must give it to the prince in Israel. [17] He must provide the burnt offerings, grain offerings and drink offerings. They will be for the yearly feasts, New Moon feasts and Sabbath days. So they will be for all the appointed feasts of the people of Israel. The prince will provide the sin offerings, grain offerings, burnt offerings and friendship offerings. They will be used to pay for the sin of the Israelites."

[18] The LORD and King says, "Get a young bull. It must not have any flaws. Use it to make the temple pure and 'clean.' Do this on the first day of the first month. [19] The priest must get some of the blood from the sin offering. He must put some on the doorposts of the temple. He must apply some to the four corners of the upper ledge of the altar. He must put the rest on the gateposts of the inner courtyard. [20] Do the same thing on the seventh day of the month. Do this for those who sin without meaning to. And do this for those who sin without realizing what they are doing. So you will make the temple pure and 'clean.'

[21] "Keep the Passover Feast on the 14th day of the first month. It will last for seven days. During that time you must eat bread made without yeast. [22] The prince must provide a bull as a sin offering. It will be for him and all the people of the land. [23] For each of the seven days of the feast he must provide seven bulls and seven rams. They must not have any flaws. They will be a burnt offering to me. The prince must also provide a male goat for a sin offering. [24] He must bring 35 pounds for each bull or ram. He must also provide four quarts of olive oil for each of them.

[25] "The seven days of the feast begin on the 15th day of the seventh month. During those days the prince must provide the same sin offerings, burnt offerings, grain offerings and olive oil."

46 The LORD and King says, "On the six working days of each week you must keep the east gate of the inner courtyard of the temple shut. But open it on Sabbath days and during New

Moon feasts. ² The prince must enter the temple area through the porch of the gateway. He must stand by the gatepost. The priests must sacrifice his burnt offering and friendship offerings. He must bow down in worship at the entrance of the gateway. Then he must leave. But the gate will not be shut until evening. ³ On Sabbath days and during New Moon feasts the people of the land must gather together. They must gather at the entrance of the temple gateway. That is where they must worship me. ⁴ The prince must bring a burnt offering to me on the Sabbath day. It will be six male lambs and a ram. They must not have any flaws. ⁵ He must offer 35 pounds of grain along with the ram. The grain he offers along with the lambs can be as much as he wants to give. He must also offer four quarts of olive oil for every 35 pounds of grain. ⁶ On the day of the New Moon feast the prince must make another offering. He must offer a young bull, six lambs and a ram. They must not have any flaws. ⁷ He must offer 35 pounds of grain along with the bull or ram. The grain he offers along with the lambs can be as much as he wants to give. He must also offer four quarts of olive oil for every 35 pounds of grain. ⁸ Here is how the prince must enter the temple area. He must go in through the porch of the gateway. And he must leave the same way.

⁹ "The people of the land must worship me at the appointed feasts. Those who enter through the north gate must leave through the south gate. Those who enter through the south gate must leave through the north gate. They must not leave through the same gate they entered. Each one must go out the opposite gate. ¹⁰ The prince must be among them. He must go in when they go in. And he must leave when they leave. ¹¹ At the yearly feasts and other appointed feasts there must be grain offerings. The prince must offer 35 pounds of grain along with a bull or ram. The grain he offers along with the lambs can be as much as he wants to give. He must also offer four quarts of olive oil for every 35 pounds of grain.

¹² "He may also bring another offering to me because he chooses to. It might be a burnt offering or friendship offering. When he brings it, the east gate must be opened for him. He will bring his offering just as he does on the Sabbath day. Then he will leave. After he has gone out, the gate must be shut.

¹³ "Every day you must provide a lamb that is a year old. It must not have any flaws. It is a burnt offering to me. You must provide it every morning. ¹⁴ You must also offer grain along with it every morning. Bring six pounds of grain. Also bring one and a half quarts of olive oil to make the flour a little wet. So you will give the grain offering to me. That will be a law that

will last for all time to come.
¹⁵ Provide the lamb, grain offering and oil every morning. They will be used for a regular burnt offering."

¹⁶ The LORD and King says, "Suppose the prince makes a gift from his share of land. And he gives it to one of his sons. Then the property will also belong to his sons after him. It will be handed down to them. ¹⁷ But suppose he makes a gift from his share of land to one of his servants. Then the servant may keep it until the Year of Jubilee. After that, it will be returned to the prince. His property may be handed down only to his sons. It belongs to them. ¹⁸ The prince must not take any share of land that belongs to the people. He must not drive them off their property. He must give his sons their share out of his own property. Then not one of my people will be separated from their property."

¹⁹ The man brought me through the entrance at the side of the north building. That's where the priests' sacred rooms were located. He showed me a place west of the building. ²⁰ He said to me, "This is where the priests must cook the guilt offerings and sin offerings. They must also bake the grain offerings here. Then they will not have to bring the offerings into the outer courtyard. That will keep the people from touching the offerings and becoming holy."

²¹ Then the man brought me to the outer courtyard. He led me around to its four corners. In each corner I saw another smaller courtyard. ²² So in the four corners of the outer courtyard were walled courtyards. Each one was 70 feet long and 53 feet wide. All of them were the same size. ²³ Around the inside of each of the four courtyards was a stone ledge. Places for fire were built all around under each ledge. ²⁴ The man said to me, "These are the kitchens. Those who serve at the temple must cook the people's sacrifices here."

A River Will Flow From the Temple

47 The man brought me back to the entrance to the temple. I saw water flowing east from under a temple gateway. The temple faced east. The water was coming down from under the south side of the temple. It was flowing south of the altar. ² Then he brought me out through the north gate of the outer courtyard. He led me around the outside to the outer gate that faced east. The water was flowing from the south side of the east gate.

³ Then the man went toward the east. He had a measuring line in his hand. He measured off 1,700 feet. He led me through water that was up to my ankles. ⁴ Then he measured off another 1,700 feet. He led me through water that was up to my knees. Then he measured off another 1,700 feet. He led me through water that was up to my waist. ⁵ Then he

measured off another 1,700 feet. But now it was a river that I could not go across. The water had risen so high that it was deep enough to swim in. ⁶He asked me, "Son of man, do you see this?"

Then he led me back to the bank of the river. ⁷When I arrived there, I saw many trees. They were on both sides of the river. ⁸The man said to me, "This water flows toward the eastern territory. It goes down into the Arabah Valley. There it enters the Dead Sea. When it empties into it, the salt water there becomes fresh. ⁹Many creatures will live where the river flows. It will have many schools of fish. This water flows there and makes the salt water fresh. So where the river flows everything will live. ¹⁰People will stand along the shore to fish. From En Gedi all the way to En Eglaim there will be places for spreading fishnets. The Dead Sea will have many kinds of fish. They will be like the fish in the Mediterranean Sea. ¹¹But none of the swamps will have fresh water in them. They will stay salty. ¹²Fruit trees of all kinds will grow on both banks of the river. Their leaves will not dry up. The trees will always have fruit on them. Every month they will bear fruit. The water from the temple will flow to them. Their fruit will be used for food. And their leaves will be used for healing."

The Borders of the Land

¹³Here is what the LORD and King says. "People of Israel, here are the borders of the land that you will divide up. You will divide up the land among the 12 tribes of Israel. Each tribe will receive a share. But the family of Joseph will have two shares. ¹⁴Divide the land into equal parts. Long ago I raised my hand and made a promise. I promised to give the land to your people of long ago. So all of it will belong to you.

¹⁵"Here are the borders of the land.

"On the north side the border will start at the Mediterranean Sea. It will go by the Hethlon road past Lebo Hamath. Then it will continue on to Zedad, ¹⁶Berothah and Sibraim. Sibraim is between Damascus and Hamath. The border will reach all the way to Hazer Hattikon. It is right next to Hauran. ¹⁷The border will go from the sea to Hazar Enan. It will run north of Damascus and south of Hamath. This will be the northern border.

¹⁸"On the east side the border will run between Hauran and Damascus. It will continue along the Jordan River between Gilead and the land of Israel. It will reach to the Dead Sea and all the way to Tamar. This will be the eastern border.

¹⁹"On the south side the border will start at Tamar. It will reach all the way

to the waters of Meribah Kadesh. Then it will run along the Wadi of Egypt. It will end at the Mediterranean Sea. This will be the southern border.

20 "On the west side, the Mediterranean Sea will be the border. It will go to a point across from Lebo Hamath. This will be the western border.

21 "You must divide up this land among yourselves. Do this based on the number of men in your tribes. 22 Each of the tribes must receive a share of the land. You must also give some land to the outsiders who live among you and who have children. Treat them as if they had been born in Israel. Let them have some land among your tribes. 23 Outsiders can live in the land of any tribe. There you must give them their share," announces the LORD and King.

The Land Will Be Divided Up

48 "Here are the tribes. They are listed by their names.

"Dan will receive one share of land. It will be at the northern border of Israel. The border will follow the Hethlon road to Lebo Hamath. Hazar Enan will be part of the border. So will the northern border of Damascus next to Hamath. Dan's northern border will run from east to west.

2 "Asher will receive one share. It will border the territory of Dan from east to west.

3 "Naphtali will receive one share. It will border the territory of Asher from east to west.

4 "Manasseh will receive one share. It will border the territory of Naphtali from east to west.

5 "Ephraim will receive one share. It will border the territory of Manasseh from east to west.

6 "Reuben will receive one share. It will border the territory of Ephraim from east to west.

7 "Judah will receive one share. It will border the territory of Reuben from east to west.

8 "You must give one share as a special gift to me. It will border the territory of Judah from east to west. It will be eight miles wide. It will be as long as the border of each of the territories of the tribes. Its border will run from east to west. The temple will be in the center of that strip of land.

9 "Give that special share of land to me. It will be eight miles long and three and a third miles wide. 10 It will be the sacred share of land for the priests. It will be eight miles long on the north side. It will be three and a third miles wide on the west side. It will be three and a third miles wide on the east side. And it will be eight miles long on the

south side. My temple will be in the center of it. ¹¹ This share of land will be for the priests who are set apart to me. They will come from the family line of Zadok. The members of that family served me faithfully. They did not go astray as the Levites and other Israelites did. ¹² Their share of land will be a special gift to them. It will be part of the sacred share of the land. It will be very holy. Its border will run along the territory of the Levites.

¹³ "The Levites will receive a share. It will be next to the territory of the priests. The Levites' share will be eight miles long and three and a third miles wide. ¹⁴ They must not sell or trade any of it. It is the best part of the land. It must not be handed over to anyone else. It is set apart to me.

¹⁵ "The area that remains is one and two-thirds miles wide. It is eight miles long. It will not be holy. The people in Jerusalem can build houses there. They can use some of it as grasslands. The city will be in the center of it. ¹⁶ Each of the four sides of the city will be one and a half miles long. ¹⁷ Each of the four sides of the city's grasslands will be 440 feet long. ¹⁸ What remains of the area will be three and a third miles long on the east and west sides. Its border will run along the border of the sacred share. Its crops will supply food for the city workers. ¹⁹ They will farm the area. They will come from all the tribes of Israel. ²⁰ The entire area will be a square. Each of its four sides will be eight miles long. Set the sacred share apart as a special gift to me. Do the same thing with the property of the city.

²¹ "The area that remains on both sides will belong to the prince. So his land does not include the sacred share and the property of the city. The eastern part of his land will reach from the sacred share all the way to the eastern border. The western part will reach from the sacred share to the western border. The sacred share itself is eight miles long on its east and west sides. Both of those areas will be right next to the borders of the two tribes on the north and south sides. They will belong to the prince. The sacred share will be in the center of them. It will have the temple in it. ²² The property of the Levites will lie in the center of the prince's share. So will the property of the city. The prince's land will lie between the borders of the tribes of Judah and Benjamin.

²³ "Here is the land for the rest of the tribes.

"Benjamin will receive one share. It will reach from the eastern border to the western border.
²⁴ "Simeon will receive one share. It will border the territory of Benjamin from east to west.
²⁵ "Issachar will receive one share. It will border the territory of Simeon from east to west.

26 "Zebulun will receive one share. It will border the territory of Issachar from east to west.

27 "Gad will receive one share. It will border the territory of Zebulun from east to west.

28 "The southern border of Gad will run south from Tamar to the waters of Meribah Kadesh. It will continue along the Wadi of Egypt. It will end at the Mediterranean Sea.

29 "This is the land you must divide among the tribes of Israel. And these will be the shares they will receive," announces the LORD and King.

The Gates of the New City

30 "Here is a list of the gates of the city.

Start with its north side. It will be a mile and a half long. 31 The city gates will be named after the tribes of Israel. The north side will have three gates. They will be the gates of Reuben, Judah and Levi.

32 "The east side will be a mile and a half long. It will have three gates. They will be the gates of Joseph, Benjamin and Dan.

33 "The south side will be a mile and a half long. It will have three gates. They will be the gates of Simeon, Issachar and Zebulun.

34 "The west side will be a mile and a half long. It will have three gates. They will be the gates of Gad, Asher and Naphtali.

35 "The city will be six miles around.

"From that time on, its name will be 'The LORD Is There.'"

Daniel

Introduction:

This book tells the story of Daniel. When Daniel was young, the king of Babylon attacked Jerusalem. He broke down the city walls and made all the people leave. Daniel had to move away from his home. The Babylonians took him to their king's palace. But Daniel knew God would take care of him.

Daniel and his friends loved God. They would not worship false gods like other people did. God took care of Daniel for all of his long life.

Daniel wrote this book to tell the Jews to trust God. God was greater than the king of Babylon. He is greater than any king!

Outline of contents:

Daniel Is Trained in Babylon

1 It was the third year that Jehoiakim was king of Judah. Nebuchadnezzar, king of Babylon, came to Jerusalem. His armies surrounded the city and attacked it. ²The Lord handed Jehoiakim, the king of Judah, over to him. Nebuchadnezzar also took some of the objects from God's temple. He carried them off to the temple of his god in Babylon. He put them among the treasures of his god.

³The king gave Ashpenaz an order. Ashpenaz was the chief of Nebuchadnezzar's court officials. The king told him to bring him some of the Israelites. The king wanted them to serve him in his court. He wanted nobles and men from the royal family. ⁴He was looking for young men who were healthy and handsome. They had to be able to learn anything. They had to be well educated. They had to have the ability to understand new things quickly and easily. The king wanted men who could serve in his palace. Ashpenaz was supposed to teach them the Babylonian language and writings. ⁵The king had his servants give them food and wine from his own table. They received a certain amount every day. The young men had to be trained for three years. After that, they could begin to serve the king.

⁶Some of the men chosen were from Judah. Their names were Daniel, Hananiah, Mishael and Azariah. ⁷The chief official gave them new names. He gave Daniel the name Belteshazzar.

He gave Hananiah the name Shadrach. He gave Mishael the name Meshach. And he gave Azariah the name Abednego.

8 Daniel decided not to make himself "unclean" by eating the king's food and drinking his wine. So he asked the chief official for a favor. He wanted permission not to make himself "unclean" with the king's food and wine. 9 God had caused the official to be kind and friendly to Daniel. 10 But the official refused to do what Daniel asked for. He said, "I'm afraid of the king. He is my master. He has decided what you and your three friends must eat and drink. Other young men are the same age as you. Why should he see you looking worse than them? When he sees how you look, he might kill me."

11 So Daniel spoke to one of the guards. The chief official had appointed him over Daniel, Hananiah, Mishael and Azariah. 12 Daniel said to him, "Please test us for ten days. Give us nothing but vegetables to eat. And give us only water to drink. 13 Then compare us with the young men who eat the king's food. See how we look. After that, do what you want to." 14 So the guard agreed. He tested them for ten days.

15 After the ten days Daniel and his friends looked healthy and well fed. In fact, they looked better than any of the young men who ate the king's food. 16 So the guard didn't require them to eat the king's special food. He didn't require them to drink the king's wine either. He gave them vegetables instead.

17 God gave knowledge and understanding to these four young men. So they understood all kinds of writings and subjects. And Daniel could understand all kinds of visions and dreams.

18 The three years the king had set for their training ended. So the chief official brought them to Nebuchadnezzar. 19 The king talked with them. He didn't find anyone equal to Daniel, Hananiah, Mishael and Azariah. So they began to serve the king. 20 He asked them for advice in matters that required wisdom and understanding. The king always found their answers to be the best. Other men in his kingdom claimed to get knowledge by using magic. But the answers of Daniel and his friends were ten times better than theirs.

21 Daniel served in Babylon until the first year Cyrus ruled over the land of Babylon. Cyrus was king of Persia.

Nebuchadnezzar Dreams About a Large Statue

2 In the second year of Nebuchadnezzar's rule, he had a dream. His mind was troubled. He couldn't sleep. 2 So the king sent for those who claimed to get knowledge by using magic. He also sent for those who practiced evil magic and those who studied the heavens. He wanted them to tell him what he had dreamed. They came in and stood in front of the king. 3 He

said to them, "I had a dream. It troubles me. So I want to know what it means."

⁴ Then those who studied the heavens answered the king. They spoke in Aramaic. They said, "King Nebuchadnezzar, may you live forever! Tell us what you dreamed. Then we'll explain what it means."

⁵ The king replied to them, "I have made up my mind. You must tell me what I dreamed. And you must tell me what it means. If you don't, I'll have you cut to pieces. And I'll have your houses turned into piles of trash. ⁶ So tell me what I dreamed. Explain it to me. Then I'll give you gifts. I'll reward you. I'll give you great honor. So tell me the dream. And tell me what it means."

⁷ Once more they replied, "King Nebuchadnezzar, tell us what you dreamed. Then we'll tell you what it means."

⁸ The king answered, "I know what you are doing. You are trying to gain more time. You realize that I've made up my mind. ⁹ You must tell me the dream. If you don't, you will pay for it. You have gotten together and made evil plans. You hope things will change. So you are telling me lies. But I want you to tell me what I dreamed. Then I'll know that you can tell me what it means."

¹⁰ They answered the king, "There is no one on earth who can do what you are asking! No king has ever asked for anything like that. Not even a king

as great and mighty as you has asked for it. Those who get knowledge by using magic have never been asked to do what you are asking. And those who study the heavens haven't been asked to do it either. ¹¹ What you are asking is much too hard. No one can tell you what you dreamed except the gods. And they don't live among human beings."

¹² That made the king very angry. He ordered that all the wise men in Babylon be put to death. ¹³ So the order was given to kill them. Men were sent out to look for Daniel and his friends. They were also supposed to be put to death.

¹⁴ Arioch was the commander of the king's guard. He went out to put the wise men of Babylon to death. So Daniel spoke to him wisely and carefully. ¹⁵ He asked the king's officer, "Why did Nebuchadnezzar give a terrible order like that?" Then Arioch explained to Daniel what was going on. ¹⁶ When Daniel heard that, he went to the king. He told him he would explain the dream to him. But he needed more time.

¹⁷ Then Daniel returned to his house. He explained everything to his friends Hananiah, Mishael and Azariah. ¹⁸ He asked them to pray that the God of heaven would give him mercy. He wanted God to help him understand the mystery of the king's dream. Then he and his friends wouldn't be killed along with Babylon's other wise men. ¹⁹ During that night, God gave

Daniel a vision. He showed him what the mystery was all about. Then Daniel praised the God of heaven. 20 He said,

"May God be praised for ever and ever!
He is wise and powerful.
21 He changes times and seasons.
He removes some kings from power.
He causes other kings to rule.
The wisdom of those who are wise comes from him.
He gives knowledge to those who have understanding.
22 He explains deep and hidden things.
He knows what happens in the darkest places.
And where he is, everything is light.
23 God of my people of long ago, I thank and praise you.
You have given me wisdom and power.
You have made known to me what we asked you for.
You have shown us the king's dream."

Daniel Tells the King What His Dream Means

24 Then Daniel went to Arioch. The king had appointed him to put the wise men of Babylon to death. Daniel said to him, "Don't kill the wise men of Babylon. Take me to the king. I'll tell him what his dream means."
25 So Arioch took Daniel to the king at once. Arioch said, "I have found a man among those you brought here from Judah. He can tell you what your dream means."

26 Nebuchadnezzar spoke to Daniel, who was also called Belteshazzar. The king asked him, "Are you able to tell me what I saw in my dream? And can you tell me what it means?"
27 Daniel replied, "You have asked us to explain a mystery to you. But no wise man can do that. And those who try to figure things out by using magic can't do it either. 28 But there is a God in heaven who can explain mysteries. King Nebuchadnezzar, he has shown you what is going to happen. Here is what you dreamed while lying in bed. And here are the visions that passed through your mind.

29 "Your Majesty, while you were still in bed your mind was troubled. You were thinking about things that haven't happened yet. The God who explains mysteries showed these things to you. 30 Now the mystery has been explained to me. But it isn't because I have greater wisdom than anyone else alive. It's because God wants you to know what the mystery means, Your Majesty. He wants you to understand what went through your mind.

31 "King Nebuchadnezzar, you looked up and saw a large statue standing in front of you. It was huge. It shone brightly. And it terrified you. 32 The head of the statue was made out of pure gold. Its chest and arms were made out of silver. Its stom-

ach and thighs were made out of bronze. ³³ Its legs were made out of iron. And its feet were partly iron and partly baked clay. ³⁴ While you were watching, a rock was cut out. But human hands didn't do it. It struck the statue on its feet of iron and clay. It smashed them. ³⁵ Then the iron and clay were broken to pieces. So were the bronze, silver and gold. All of them were broken to pieces. They became like straw on a threshing floor at harvest time. The wind blew them away without leaving a trace. But the rock that struck the statue became a huge mountain. It filled the whole earth.

³⁶ "This was your dream. Now I will tell you what it means. ³⁷ King Nebuchadnezzar, you are the greatest king of all. The God of heaven has given you authority and power. He has given you might and glory. ³⁸ He has put everyone under your control. He has also given you authority over the wild animals and the birds in the sky. It doesn't matter where they live. He has made you ruler over all of them. You are that head of gold.

³⁹ "After you, another kingdom will take over. It won't be as powerful as yours. Next, a third kingdom will rule over the whole earth. The bronze part of the statue stands for that kingdom. ⁴⁰ Finally, there will be a fourth kingdom. It will be as strong as iron. Iron breaks and smashes everything to pieces.

And the fourth kingdom will crush and break all the others. ⁴¹ You saw that the feet and toes were made out of iron and baked clay. And the fourth kingdom will be divided up. But it will still have some of the strength of iron. That's why you saw iron mixed with clay. ⁴² The toes were partly iron and partly clay. And the fourth kingdom will be partly strong and partly weak. ⁴³ You saw the iron mixed with baked clay. And the fourth kingdom will be made up of all kinds of people. They won't hold together any more than iron mixes with clay.

⁴⁴ "In the time of those kings, the God of heaven will set up a kingdom. It will never be destroyed. And no other nation will ever take it over. It will crush all those other kingdoms. It will bring them to an end. But it will last forever. ⁴⁵ That's what the vision of the rock cut out of a mountain means. Human hands didn't cut out the rock. It broke the statue to pieces. It smashed the iron, bronze, clay, silver and gold.

"The great God has shown you what will take place in days to come. The dream is true. And you can trust the meaning of it that I have explained to you."

⁴⁶ Then King Nebuchadnezzar bowed low in front of Daniel. He wanted to honor him. So he ordered that an offering and incense be offered up to him. ⁴⁷ The king said to Daniel, "I'm sure your God is the greatest God of all. He is the Lord of

kings. He explains mysteries. That's why you were able to explain the mystery of my dream."

⁴⁸ Then the king put Daniel in a position of authority. He gave him many gifts. He made him ruler over the city of Babylon and the towns around it. He put him in charge of all its other wise men. ⁴⁹ The king also did what Daniel asked him to. He appointed Shadrach, Meshach and Abednego to help Daniel govern Babylon and the towns around it. Daniel himself remained at the royal court.

A Gold Statue and a Blazing Furnace

3 King Nebuchadnezzar made a gold statue. It was 90 feet tall and 9 feet wide. He set it up on the plain of Dura near the city of Babylon. ² Then the king sent for the royal rulers, high officials and governors. He sent for the advisers, treasurers, judges and court officers. And he sent for all the other officials of Babylon. He asked them to come to a special gathering to honor the statue he had set up. ³ So the royal rulers, high officials and governors came together. So did the advisers, treasurers, judges and court officers. All the other officials joined them. They came to honor the statue that King Nebuchadnezzar had set up. They stood in front of it.

⁴ Then a messenger called out loudly, "Listen, you people who come from every nation! Pay attention, you who speak other languages! Here is what the king commands you to do. ⁵ You will soon hear the sound of horns and flutes. You will hear zithers, lyres, harps and pipes. In fact, you will hear all kinds of music. When you do, you must fall down and worship the gold statue. That is the statue that King Nebuchadnezzar has set up. ⁶ If you don't, you will be thrown into a blazing furnace right away."

⁷ All the people heard the sound of the horns and flutes. They heard the zithers, lyres, harps and other musical instruments. As soon as they did, they fell down and worshiped Nebuchadnezzar's gold statue. They were people from all nations no matter what language they spoke.

⁸ At this time some people who studied the heavens came forward. They spoke against the Jews. ⁹ They said, "King Nebuchadnezzar, may you live forever! ¹⁰ Your Majesty has commanded everyone to fall down and worship the gold statue. You told them to do it when they heard the horns, flutes, zithers, lyres, harps, pipes and other musical instruments. ¹¹ If they didn't, they would be thrown into a blazing furnace. ¹² But you have appointed some Jews to help Daniel govern Babylon and the towns around it. Their names are Shadrach, Meshach and Abednego. They don't pay any attention to you, King Nebuchadnezzar. They don't serve your gods. And they refuse to worship the gold statue you have set up."

¹³Nebuchadnezzar was very angry. He sent for Shadrach, Meshach and Abednego. So they were brought to him. ¹⁴The king said to them, "Shadrach, Meshach and Abednego, is what I heard about you true? Don't you serve my gods? Don't you worship the gold statue I set up? ¹⁵You will hear the horns, flutes, zithers, lyres, harps, pipes and other musical instruments. When you do, fall down and worship the statue I made. If you will, that's very good. But if you won't, you will be thrown at once into a blazing furnace. Then what god will be able to save you from my power?"

¹⁶Shadrach, Meshach and Abednego replied to him. They said, "King Nebuchadnezzar, we don't need to talk about this anymore. ¹⁷We might be thrown into the blazing furnace. But the God we serve is able to bring us out of it alive. He will save us from your power. ¹⁸But we want you to know this, Your Majesty. Even if we knew that our God wouldn't save us, we still wouldn't serve your gods. We wouldn't worship the gold statue you set up."

¹⁹Then Nebuchadnezzar was very angry with Shadrach, Meshach and Abednego. The look on his face changed. And he ordered that the furnace be heated seven times hotter than usual. ²⁰He also gave some of the strongest soldiers in his army a command. He ordered them to tie up Shadrach, Meshach and Abednego. Then he told his men to throw them into the blazing furnace. ²¹So they were tied up. Then they were thrown into the furnace. They were wearing their robes, pants, turbans and other clothes. ²²The king's command was carried out quickly. The furnace was so hot that its flames killed the soldiers who threw Shadrach, Meshach and Abednego into it. ²³So the three men were firmly tied up. And they fell into the blazing furnace.

²⁴Then King Nebuchadnezzar leaped to his feet. He was so amazed he asked his advisers, "Didn't we tie up three men? Didn't we throw three men into the fire?"

They replied, "Yes, we did, Your Majesty."

²⁵The king said, "Look! I see four men walking around in the fire. They aren't tied up. And the fire hasn't even harmed them. The fourth man looks like a son of the gods."

²⁶Then the king approached the opening of the blazing furnace. He shouted, "Shadrach, Meshach and Abednego, come out! You who serve the Most High God, come here!"

So they came out of the fire. ²⁷The royal rulers, high officials, governors and advisers crowded around them. They saw that the fire hadn't harmed their bodies. Not one hair on their heads was burned. Their robes weren't burned either. And they didn't even smell like smoke. ²⁸Then Nebuchadnezzar said, "May the God of Shadrach,

Meshach and Abednego be praised! He has sent his angel and saved his servants. They trusted in him. They refused to obey my command. They were willing to give up their lives. They would rather die than serve or worship any god except their own God. ²⁹ No other god can save people this way. So I'm giving an order about the God of Shadrach, Meshach and Abednego. No one may say anything against him. That's true no matter what language they speak. If they say anything against him, they'll be cut to pieces. And their houses will be turned into piles of trash."

³⁰ Then the king honored Shadrach, Meshach and Abednego. He gave them higher positions in the city of Babylon and the towns around it.

Nebuchadnezzar Dreams About a Tree

4 I, King Nebuchadnezzar, am writing this letter.

I am sending it to people who live all over the world. I'm sending it to people of every nation no matter what language they speak.

May you have great success!

² I am pleased to tell you what has happened. The Most High God has done miraculous signs and wonders for me.

³ His signs are great.
　His wonders are
　　mighty.
His kingdom will last
　forever.
His rule will never end.

⁴ I was at home in my palace. I was content and very successful. ⁵ But I had a dream that made me afraid. I was lying in bed. Then dreams and visions passed through my mind. They terrified me. ⁶ So I commanded that all the wise men in Babylon be brought to me. I wanted them to tell me what my dream meant. ⁷ Those who try to figure things out by using magic came. So did those who study the heavens. I told all of them what I had dreamed. But they couldn't tell me what it meant. ⁸ Finally, Daniel came to me. He is called Belteshazzar, after the name of my god. The spirit of the holy gods is in him. I told him my dream.

⁹ I said, "Belteshazzar, you are chief of the magicians. I know that the spirit of the holy gods is in you. No mystery is too hard for you to figure out. Here is my dream. Tell me what it means. ¹⁰ Here are the visions I saw while I was lying in bed. I looked up and saw a tree standing in the middle of the land. It was very tall. ¹¹ It had grown to be large and strong. Its top touched the sky. It could be seen anywhere on earth. ¹² Its leaves were beautiful.

It had a lot of fruit on it. It provided enough food for people and animals. Under the tree, the wild animals found safety. The birds lived in its branches. Every creature was fed from that tree. ¹³ "While I was still lying in bed, I looked up. In my visions, I saw a holy one. He was a messenger. He was coming down from heaven. ¹⁴ He called out in a loud voice. He said, 'Cut down the tree. Break off its branches. Strip off its leaves. Scatter its fruit. Let the animals under it run away. Let the birds in its branches fly off. ¹⁵ But leave the stump with its roots in the ground. Let it stay in the field. Put a band of iron and bronze around it.

" 'Let King Nebuchadnezzar become wet with the dew of heaven. Let him live with the animals among the plants of the earth. ¹⁶ Let him no longer have the mind of a man. Instead, let him be given the mind of an animal. Let him stay that way until seven periods of time pass by.

¹⁷ " 'The decision is announced by holy messengers. So all who are alive will know that the Most High God is King. He rules over all kingdoms on earth. He gives them to anyone he wants. Sometimes he puts the least important people in charge of them.'

¹⁸ "This is the dream I, King Nebuchadnezzar, had. Now tell me what it means, Belteshazzar. None of the wise men in my kingdom can explain it to me. But you can. After all, the spirit of the holy gods is in you."

Daniel Explains Nebuchadnezzar's Dream

¹⁹ Daniel, who was also called Belteshazzar, was very bewildered for a while. His thoughts terrified him. So the king said, "Belteshazzar, don't let the dream or its meaning make you afraid."

Belteshazzar answered, "My master, I wish the dream were about your enemies! I wish its meaning had to do with them! ²⁰ You saw a tree. It grew to be large and strong. Its top touched the sky. It could be seen from anywhere on earth. ²¹ Its leaves were beautiful. It had a lot of fruit on it. It provided enough food for people and animals. Under the tree, the wild animals found safety. The birds lived in its branches. ²² Your Majesty, you are that tree! You have become great and strong. Your greatness has grown until it reaches the sky. Your rule has spread to all parts of the earth. ²³ "Your Majesty, you saw a holy one. He was a messenger. He came down from heaven. He said, 'Cut down the tree. Destroy it. But leave the stump with its roots in the ground. Let it stay in the field. Put an iron and bronze band around it. Let King Nebuchadnezzar become wet with the dew of heaven. Let him live with the wild animals. Let him stay that way until seven periods of time pass by.'

²⁴ "Your Majesty, here is what your dream means. The Most High God has given an order against you. ²⁵ You will be driven away from people. You will live with the wild animals. You will eat grass just as an ox does. You will become wet with the dew of heaven. Seven periods of time will pass by for you. Then you will recognize that the Most High God rules over all kingdoms on earth. He gives them to anyone he wants. ²⁶ But he gave a command to leave the stump of the tree along with its roots. That means your kingdom will be given back to you. It will happen when you recognize that the God of heaven rules. ²⁷ So, Your Majesty, I hope you will accept my advice. Stop being sinful. Do what is right. Give up your evil practices. Show kindness to those who are being treated badly. Then perhaps things will continue to go well with you."

Nebuchadnezzar's Dream Comes True

²⁸ All this happened to King Nebuchadnezzar. ²⁹ It took place twelve months later. He was walking on the roof of his palace in Babylon. ³⁰ He said, "Isn't this the great Babylon I have built as a place for my royal palace? I used my mighty power to build it. It shows how glorious my majesty is."

³¹ He was still speaking when he heard a voice from heaven. It said, "King Nebuchadnezzar, here is what has been ordered concerning you. Your royal authority has been taken from you. ³² You will be driven away from people. You will live with the wild animals. You will eat grass just as an ox does. Seven periods of time will pass by for you. Then you will recognize that the Most High God rules over all kingdoms on earth. He gives them to anyone he wants."

³³ What had been said about King Nebuchadnezzar came true at once. He was driven away from people. He ate grass just as an ox does. His body became wet with the dew of heaven. He stayed that way until his hair grew like the feathers of an eagle. His nails became like the claws of a bird.

³⁴ At the end of that time I, Nebuchadnezzar, looked

up toward heaven. My mind became clear again. Then I praised the Most High God. I gave honor and glory to the God who lives forever.

His rule will last forever.
His kingdom will never end.
35 He considers all the nations on earth
to be nothing.
He does as he pleases
with the powers of heaven.
He does what he wants
with the nations of the earth.
No one can hold back his hand.
No one can say to him,
"What have you done?"

36 My honor and glory were returned to me when my mind became clear again. The glory of my kingdom was given back to me. My advisers and nobles came to me. And I was put back on my throne. I became even greater than I had been before. 37 Now I, Nebuchadnezzar, give praise and honor and glory to the King of heaven. Everything he does is right. All his ways are fair. He is able to bring down those who live proudly.

A Hand Writes on the Palace Wall

5 King Belshazzar gave a huge banquet. He invited a thousand of his nobles to it. He drank wine with them. 2 While Belshazzar was drinking his wine, he gave orders to his servants. He commanded them to bring in some gold and silver cups. They were the cups his father Nebuchadnezzar had taken from the temple in Jerusalem. Belshazzar had them brought in so everyone could drink from them. That included the king himself, his nobles, his wives and his concubines. 3 So the servants brought in the gold cups. The cups had been taken from God's temple in Jerusalem. The king and his nobles drank from them. So did his wives and concubines. 4 As they drank the wine, they praised their gods. The statues of those gods were made out of gold, silver, bronze, iron, wood or stone.

5 Suddenly the fingers of a human hand appeared. They wrote something on the plaster of the palace wall. It happened near the lampstand. The king watched the hand as it wrote. 6 His face turned pale. He was so afraid that his legs became weak. And his knees were knocking together.

7 The king sent for those who try to figure things out by using magic. He also sent for those who study the heavens. All of them were wise men in Babylon. Then the king spoke to them. He said, "I want one of you to read this writing. I want you to tell me what it means. Whoever does this will be dressed in purple clothes. A gold chain will be put around his neck. And he will

be made the third highest ruler in the kingdom."

⁸ Then all the king's wise men came in. But they couldn't read the writing. They couldn't tell him what it meant. ⁹ So King Belshazzar became even more terrified. His face grew more pale. And his nobles were bewildered.

¹⁰ The queen heard the king and his nobles talking. So she came into the dining hall. "King Belshazzar, may you live forever!" she said. "Don't be afraid! Don't look so pale! ¹¹ I know a man in your kingdom who has the spirit of the holy gods in him. He has understanding and wisdom and good sense just like the gods. He was chief of those who tried to figure things out by using magic. And he was in charge of those who studied the heavens. Your father, King Nebuchadnezzar, appointed him to that position. ¹² King Nebuchadnezzar did this because he saw what the man could do. This man's name is Daniel. Your father called him Belteshazzar. He has a clever mind and knowledge and understanding. He is also able to tell what dreams mean. He can explain riddles and solve hard problems. Send for him. He'll tell you what the writing means."

¹³ So Daniel was brought to the king. The king said to him, "Are you Daniel? Are you one of the prisoners my father the king brought here from Judah? ¹⁴ I have heard that the spirit of the gods is in you. I've also heard that you have understanding and good sense and special wisdom. ¹⁵ The wise men and those who practice magic were brought to me. They were asked to read this writing and tell me what it means. But they couldn't. ¹⁶ I have heard that you are able to explain things and solve hard problems. I hope you can read this writing and tell me what it means. If you can, you will be dressed in purple clothes. A gold chain will be put around your neck. And you will be made the third highest ruler in the kingdom."

¹⁷ Then Daniel answered the king. He said, "You can keep your gifts for yourself. You can give your rewards to someone else. But I will read the writing for you. I'll tell you what it means.

¹⁸ "Your Majesty, the Most High God was good to your father Nebuchadnezzar. He gave him authority and greatness and glory and honor. ¹⁹ God gave him a high position. Then people from every nation became afraid of the king. That was true no matter what language they spoke. The king put to death anyone he wanted to. He spared anyone he wanted to spare. He gave high positions to anyone he wanted to. And he brought down anyone he wanted to bring down. ²⁰ But his heart became very stubborn and proud. So he was removed from his royal throne. His glory was stripped away from him. ²¹ He was driven away from peo-

ple. He was given the mind of an animal. He lived with the wild donkeys. He ate grass just as an ox does. His body became wet with the dew of heaven. He stayed that way until he recognized that the Most High God rules over all kingdoms on earth. He puts anyone he wants to in charge of them.

22 "But you knew all that, Belshazzar. After all, you are Nebuchadnezzar's son. In spite of that, you are still proud. 23 You have taken your stand against the Lord of heaven. You had your servants bring cups from his temple to you. You and your nobles drank wine from them. So did your wives and concubines. You praised your gods. The statues of those gods are made out of silver, gold, bronze, iron, wood or stone. They can't see or hear or understand anything. But you didn't honor God. He holds in his hand your very life and everything you do. 24 So he sent the hand that wrote on the wall.

25 "Here is what was written.

MENE, MENE, TEKEL, PARSIN

26 "And here is what these words mean.

The word Mene means that God has limited the time of your rule. He has brought it to an end.

27 The word Tekel means that you have been weighed on scales. And you haven't measured up to God's standard.

28 The word Peres means that your authority over your kingdom will be taken away from you. It will be given to the Medes and Persians."

29 Then Belshazzar commanded his servants to dress Daniel in purple clothes. So they did. They put a gold chain around his neck. And he was made the third highest ruler in the kingdom.

30 That very night Belshazzar, the king of Babylon, was killed. 31 His kingdom was given to Darius the Mede. Darius was 62 years old.

Daniel Is Thrown Into a Den of Lions

6 It pleased Darius to appoint 120 royal rulers over his entire kingdom. 2 He placed three leaders over them. One of the leaders was Daniel. The royal rulers were made accountable to the three leaders. Then the king wouldn't lose any of his wealth. 3 Daniel did a better job than the other two leaders or any of the royal rulers. He was an unusually good and able man. So the king planned to put him in charge of the whole kingdom. 4 But the other two leaders and the royal rulers heard about it. So they looked for a reason to bring charges against Daniel. They tried to find something wrong with the way he ran the government. But they weren't able to. They couldn't find any fault with his work. He could always be trusted. He never did anything wrong. And he always

did what he was supposed to. [5] Finally these men said, "We want to bring charges against this man Daniel. But it's almost impossible for us to come up with a reason to do it. If we find a reason, it will have to be in connection with the law of his God."

[6] So the two leaders and the royal rulers went as a group to the king. They said, "King Darius, may you live forever! [7] All the royal leaders, high officials, royal rulers, advisers and governors want to make a suggestion. We've agreed that you should give an order. And you should make sure it's obeyed. Your Majesty, here is the command you should make your people obey for the next 30 days. Don't let any of your people pray to any god or human being except to you. If they do, throw them into the lions' den. [8] Now give the order. Write it down in the law of the Medes and Persians. Then it can't be changed." [9] So King Darius put the order in writing.

[10] Daniel found out that the king had signed the order. In spite of that, he did just as he had always done before. He went home to his upstairs room. Its windows opened toward Jerusalem. He went to his room three times a day to pray. He got down on his knees and gave thanks to his God. [11] Some of the other royal officials went to where Daniel was staying. They saw him praying and asking God for help. [12] So they went to the king. They spoke to him about his royal order. They said,

"Your Majesty, didn't you sign an official order? It said that for the next 30 days your people could pray only to you. They could not pray to anyone else, whether god or human being. If they did, they would be thrown into the lions' den."

The king answered, "The order must still be obeyed. It's what the law of the Medes and Persians requires. So it can't be changed."

[13] Then they spoke to the king again. They said, "Daniel is one of the prisoners from Judah. He doesn't pay any attention to you, Your Majesty. He doesn't obey the order you put in writing. He still prays to his God three times a day." [14] When the king heard this, he was very upset. He didn't want Daniel to be harmed in any way. Until sunset, he did everything he could to save him.

[15] Then the men went as a group to King Darius. They said to him, "Your Majesty, remember that no order or command you give can be changed. That's what the law of the Medes and Persians requires."

[16] So the king gave the order. Daniel was brought out and thrown into the lions' den. The king said to him, "You always serve your God faithfully. So may he save you!"

[17] A stone was brought and placed over the opening of the den. The king sealed it with his own special ring. He also sealed it with the rings of his nobles. Then nothing could

be done to help Daniel. ¹⁸The king returned to his palace. He didn't eat anything that night. He didn't ask for anything to be brought to him for his enjoyment. And he couldn't sleep.

¹⁹As soon as the sun began to rise, the king got up. He hurried to the lions' den. ²⁰When he got near it, he called out to Daniel. His voice was filled with great concern. He said, "Daniel! You serve the living God. You always serve him faithfully. So has he been able to save you from the lions?"

²¹Daniel answered, "Your Majesty, may you live forever! ²²My God sent his angel. And his angel shut the mouths of the lions. They haven't hurt me at all. That's because I haven't done anything wrong in God's sight. I've never done anything wrong to you either, Your Majesty."

²³The king was filled with joy. He ordered his servants to lift Daniel out of the den. So they did. They didn't see any wounds on him. That's because he had trusted in his God.

²⁴Then the king gave another order. The men who had said bad things about Daniel were brought in. They were thrown into the lions' den. So were their wives and children. Before they hit the bottom of the den, the lions attacked them. And the lions crushed all their bones.

²⁵Then King Darius wrote to people of all nations, no matter what language they spoke. He said,

"May you have great success!

²⁶"I order people in every part of my kingdom to respect and honor Daniel's God.

"He is the living God.
　　He will live forever.
His kingdom will not be
　　destroyed.
　　His rule will never end.
²⁷He sets people free and
　　saves them.
He does miraculous
　　signs and wonders.
He does them in the
　　heavens and on the
　　earth.
He has saved Daniel
　　from the power of the
　　lions."

²⁸So Daniel had success while Darius was king. Things went well with Daniel during the rule of Cyrus, the Persian.

Daniel Has a Dream About Four Animals

7 It was the first year that Belshazzar was king of Babylon. Daniel had a dream. He was lying in bed. In his dream, visions passed through his mind. He wrote down what he saw.

²Daniel said, "I had a vision at night. I looked up and saw the four winds of heaven. They were stirring up the Mediterranean Sea. ³Four large animals came up out of the sea. Each one was different from the others.

⁴"The first animal was like a lion. It had the wings of an eagle. I watched until its wings

were torn off. Then it was lifted up from the ground. It stood on two feet like a human being. And the mind of a human being was given to it.

5 "I saw a second animal. It looked like a bear. It was raised up on one of its sides. And it had three ribs between its teeth. It was told, 'Get up! Eat meat until you are full!'

6 "After that, I saw another animal. It looked like a leopard. On its back were four wings like the wings of a bird. The animal I saw had four heads. And it was given authority to rule.

7 "After that, in my vision I looked up and saw a fourth animal. It was terrifying and very powerful. It had large iron teeth. It crushed those it attacked and ate them up. It stomped on anything that was left. It was different from the other animals. And it had ten horns.

8 "I thought about the horns. Then I saw another horn. It was a little one. It grew up among the other horns. Three of the first horns were pulled up by their roots to make room for it. The little horn had eyes like the eyes of a human being. Its mouth was always bragging.

9 "As I watched,

"thrones were set in place.
    The Eternal God took his
        seat.
    His clothes were as white as
        snow.
    The hair on his head was
        white like wool.
    His throne was blazing with
        fire.

And flames were all
    around its wheels.
10 A river of fire was flowing.
    It was coming out from in
        front of God.
Thousands and thousands of
    angels served him.
Millions of them stood in
    front of him.
The court was seated.
    And the books were
        opened.

11 "Then I continued to watch because of the way the horn was bragging. I kept looking until the fourth animal was killed. I watched until its body was destroyed. It was thrown into the blazing fire. 12 The authority of the other animals had been stripped away from them. But they were allowed to live for a period of time.

13 "In my vision I saw one who looked like a son of man. He was coming with the clouds of heaven. He approached the Eternal God. He was led right up to him. 14 And he was given authority, glory and a kingdom. People of all nations, no matter what language they spoke, worshiped him. His authority will last forever. It will not pass away. His kingdom will never be destroyed.

An Angel Tells Daniel What His Dream Means

15 "My spirit was troubled. The visions that passed through my mind upset me. 16 I approached an angel who was standing there. I asked him what all these things really meant.

"So he explained to me what everything meant. ¹⁷ He said, 'The four large animals stand for four kings. The kings will appear on the earth. ¹⁸ But the holy people of the Most High God will receive the kingdom. They will possess it forever. It will belong to them for ever and ever.'

¹⁹ "Then I wanted to know what the fourth animal stood for. It was different from the others. It was the most terrifying of all. It had iron teeth and bronze claws. It crushed everyone it attacked and ate them up. It stomped on anything that was left. ²⁰ I also wanted to know about the ten horns on its head. And I wanted to know about the other horn that grew up later. It caused three of the ten horns to fall out. It appeared to be stronger than the others. It had eyes. And its mouth was always bragging. ²¹ I saw that the horn was at war with God's holy people. It was winning the battle over them. ²² But then the Eternal God came. He decided in favor of his holy people. So the time came when the kingdom was given to them.

²³ "Here's how the angel explained it to me. He said, 'The fourth animal stands for a fourth kingdom. It will appear on earth. It will be different from the other kingdoms. It will eat up the whole earth. It will stomp on it and crush it. ²⁴ The ten horns stand for ten kings. They will come from the fourth kingdom. After them another king will appear. He will be different from the earlier ones. He'll bring three kings under his control. ²⁵ He'll speak against the Most High God. He'll treat God's holy people badly. He will try to change the times and laws that were given by God. God's holy people will be placed under his power for three and a half years.

²⁶ " 'But the court will be seated. And the power of that king will be taken away from him. It will be completely destroyed forever. ²⁷ Then the authority, power and greatness of all the kingdoms on earth will be taken from them. And all they had will be given to the holy people of the Most High God. His kingdom will last forever. Every ruler will worship and obey him.'

²⁸ "That's all I saw. My thoughts deeply troubled me. My face turned pale. But I kept those things to myself."

Daniel Has a Vision About a Ram and a Goat

8 It was the third year of King Belshazzar's rule. After the vision that had already appeared to me, I had another one. ² In my vision I saw myself in the city of Susa. It has high walls around it. It is in the land of Elam. In the vision I was beside the Ulai Canal. ³ I looked up and saw a ram that had two horns. It was standing beside the canal. Its horns were long. One of them was longer than the other. But that horn grew up later. ⁴ I watched the ram as it charged toward the west. It also charged toward the north and the south. No animal could stand up against it. Not one of them could save anyone from its power. It did as it pleased. And it became great.

⁵ I was thinking about all of this. Then a goat suddenly came from the west. It had a large horn between its eyes. The goat raced across the whole earth without even touching the ground. ⁶ It came toward the ram that had the two horns. It was the ram I had seen standing beside the canal. The goat was very angry. It charged at the ram. ⁷ I saw it attack the ram with mighty force. It struck the ram and broke the ram's two horns. The ram didn't have the power to stand up against it. The goat knocked the ram to the ground and stomped on it. No one could save the ram from the goat's power. ⁸ The goat became very great. But when its power was at its greatest, the goat's large horn was broken off. In its place four large horns grew up toward the four winds of heaven.

⁹ Out of one of the four horns came another horn. It was small at first but became more and more powerful. It grew to the south and to the east and toward the beautiful land of Israel. ¹⁰ It grew until it reached the stars in the sky. It threw some of them down to the earth. And it stomped on them. ¹¹ It set itself up to be as great as the commander of the LORD's army. It took away the daily sacrifices

from the LORD. And his temple in Jerusalem was thrown down. ¹² Because many of the LORD's people refused to obey him, they were handed over to the horn. The daily sacrifices were also given over to it. The horn was successful no matter what it did. And true worship of God was thrown down to the ground.

¹³ Then I heard a holy angel speaking. Another holy angel spoke to him. He asked, "How long will it take for the vision to come true? When will the daily sacrifices be stopped? When will those who refuse to obey God be destroyed? When will the temple be handed over to an enemy? And when will some of the LORD's people be stomped on?"

¹⁴ One of the holy angels said to me, "It will take 2,300 evenings and mornings. Then the temple will be made holy again."

Gabriel Tells Daniel What His Vision Means

¹⁵ I was having the vision. And I was trying to understand it. Then I saw someone who looked like a man. ¹⁶ I heard a voice from the Ulai Canal. It called out, "Gabriel, tell Daniel what his vision means."

¹⁷ Gabriel came close to where I was standing. I was terrified and fell down flat with my face toward the ground. Here is what he said to me. "Son of man, I want you to understand the vision. It's about the time of the end."

¹⁸ While he was speaking to me, I was sound asleep. I lay with my face on the ground. Then he touched me. He raised me to my feet.

¹⁹ He said, "I am going to tell you what will happen later. It will take place when God is angry. The vision is about the appointed time of the end. ²⁰ You saw a ram that had two horns. It stands for the kings of Media and Persia. ²¹ The goat stands for the king of Greece. The large horn between its eyes is the first king. ²² Four horns took the horn's place when it was broken off. They stand for four kingdoms that will come from his nation. But those kingdoms will not be as powerful as his.

²³ "Toward the end of their rule, those who refuse to obey God will become completely evil. Then another king will appear. He will have a scary-looking face. He will be a master at making clever plans. ²⁴ He will become very strong. But he will not get that way by his own power. People will be amazed at the way he destroys everything. He will be successful no matter what he does. He will destroy mighty people. Those mighty people are God's holy people. ²⁵ He will tell lies in order to succeed. He will think he is more important than anyone else. When people feel safe, he will destroy many of them. He will stand up against the greatest Prince of all. Then he will be destroyed. But he will not be killed by human beings.

²⁶ "The vision of the evenings and mornings that has been given to you is true. But seal up the vision. It is about a time far off."

²⁷ I, Daniel, was worn out. I was too tired to get up for several days. Then I got up and returned to my work for the king. The vision bewildered me. I couldn't understand it.

Daniel Prays to the LORD

9 It was the first year that Darius was king of Babylon. He was from Media and was the son of Xerxes. ² In that year I learned from the Scriptures that Jerusalem would remain destroyed for 70 years. That was what the LORD had told Jeremiah the prophet. ³ So I prayed to the Lord God. I begged him. I made many appeals to him. I didn't eat anything. I put on the rough clothing people wear when they're sad. And I sat down in ashes.

⁴ I prayed to the LORD my God. I admitted that we had sinned. I said,

"Lord, you are a great and wonderful God. You keep the covenant you made with all those who love you and obey your commandments. You show them your love. ⁵ We have sinned and done what is wrong. We have been evil. We have refused to obey you. We have turned away from your commands and laws. ⁶ We haven't listened to your servants the prophets. They spoke in your name to our kings, our princes and our people of long ago. They also brought your message to all our people in the land. ⁷ "Lord, you always do what is right. But we are covered with shame today. We are the people of Judah and Jerusalem. All of us are Israelites, no matter where we live. We are now living in many countries. You scattered us among the nations because we weren't faithful to you. ⁸ LORD, we are covered with shame. So are our kings and princes, and our people of long ago. We have sinned against you. ⁹ You are the Lord our God. You show us your tender love. You forgive us. But we have turned against you. ¹⁰ You are the LORD our God. But we haven't obeyed you. We haven't kept the laws you gave us through your servants the prophets. ¹¹ All the people of Israel have broken your law and turned away from it. They have refused to obey you.

"Curses and warnings are written down in the Law of Moses. He was your servant. Those curses have been poured out on us. That's because we have sinned against you. ¹² The warnings you gave us and our rulers have come true. You have brought great trouble on us. Nothing like what has been done to Jerusalem has ever happened anywhere else on earth. ¹³ The curses that are written in the Law of Moses have fallen on us. We have received nothing but trouble. You are the LORD our God. But we haven't asked for your favor. We haven't turned away from our sins. We've refused to pay attention to the laws you gave us. ¹⁴ LORD, you didn't hold back from bringing this trouble on us. You always do what is right. But we haven't obeyed you.

¹⁵ "Lord our God, you used your mighty hand to bring your people out of Egypt. You made a name for yourself. It is still great to this day. But we have sinned. We've done what is wrong. ¹⁶ Lord, you saved your people before. So turn your great anger away from Jerusalem again. After all, it is your city. It's your holy mountain. You have made those who live around us think little of Jerusalem and your people. That's because we have sinned. Our people before us did evil things too.

¹⁷ "Our God, hear my prayers. Pay attention to the appeals I make to you. Lord, have mercy on your temple that has been destroyed. Do it for your own honor. ¹⁸ Our God, please listen to us. The city that belongs to you has been

destroyed. Open your eyes and see it. We aren't asking you to answer our prayers because we are godly. Instead, we're asking you to do it because you love us so much. [19] Lord, please listen! Lord, please forgive us! Lord, hear our prayers! Take action for your own honor. Our God, please don't wait. Your city and your people belong to you."

Gabriel Tells Daniel About Seventy "Weeks"

[20] I was speaking and praying. I was admitting that I and my people Israel had sinned. I was making my appeal to the Lord my God. My appeal was about his holy mountain of Zion. [21] While I was still praying, Gabriel came to me. I had seen him in my earlier vision. He flew over to me very quickly. It was about the time when the evening sacrifice is offered. [22] He helped me understand. He said, "Daniel, I have come now to help you know and understand these things. [23] You are highly respected. So as soon as you began to pray, the Lord gave you a message. I have come to tell you what it is. Here is how you must understand the vision.

[24] "The Lord has appointed 70 'weeks' for your people and your holy city. During that time, acts against God's law will be stopped. Sin will come to an end. And the evil things people do will be paid for. Then everyone will always do what is right.

Everything that has been made known in visions and prophecies will come true. And the Most Holy Room in the temple will be anointed.

[25] "Here is what I want you to know and understand. There will be seven 'weeks.' Then there will be 62 'weeks.' The seven 'weeks' will begin when an order is given to rebuild Jerusalem and make it like new again. At the end of the 62 'weeks,' the Anointed King will come. Jerusalem will have streets and a water system when it is rebuilt. But that will be done in times of trouble. [26] After the 62 'weeks,' the Anointed King will be put to death. His followers will desert him. And everything he has will be taken away from him. The army of the ruler who will come will destroy the city and the temple. The end will come like a flood. War will continue until the end. The Lord has ordered that many places be destroyed. [27] A covenant will be put into effect with many people for one 'week.' In the middle of the 'week' sacrifices and offerings will come to an end. And at the temple a hated thing that destroys will be set up. It will remain until that ruler who will come is destroyed. Then he will experience what the Lord has ordered."

Daniel Has a Vision About What Will Happen to Israel

10 It was the third year that Cyrus, the king of Persia, ruled over Babylon. At that time

I was living in Babylon. There the people called me Belteshazzar. A message from God came to me. It was true. It was about a great war. I had a vision that showed me what it meant.

2 At that time I was very sad for three weeks. 3 I didn't eat any rich food. No meat or wine touched my lips. I didn't use any lotions at all until the three weeks were over.

4 I was standing on the bank of the great Tigris River. It was the 24th day of the first month. 5 I looked up and saw a man dressed in linen clothes. He had a belt around his waist. It was made out of fine gold from Uphaz. 6 His body gleamed like topaz. His face shone like lightning. His eyes were like flaming torches. His arms and legs were as bright as polished bronze. And his voice was like the sound of a large crowd.

7 I was the only one who saw the vision. The people who were there with me didn't see it. But they were so terrified that they ran and hid. 8 So I was left alone as I was watching this great vision. I felt very weak. My face turned as pale as death. And I was helpless. 9 Then I heard the man speak. As I listened to him, I fell sound asleep. My face was toward the ground.

10 A hand touched me. It pulled me up on my hands and knees. I began to tremble with fear. 11 The man said, "Daniel, you are highly respected. Think carefully about what I am going to say to you. And stand up. God has sent me to you." When he said that, I trembled as I stood up.

12 He continued, "Do not be afraid, Daniel. You decided to get more understanding. You made yourself humble as you worshiped your God. Since the first day you did those things, your words were heard. I have come to give you an answer. 13 But the prince of Persia opposed me for 21 days. Then Michael came to help me. He is one of the leaders of the angels. He helped me win the battle over the king of Persia. 14 Now I have come to explain the vision to you. I will tell you what will happen to your people. The vision shows what will take place in days to come."

15 While he was telling me these things, I bowed with my face toward the ground. I wasn't able to speak. 16 Then someone who looked like a man touched my lips. I opened my mouth. I began to speak to the one who was standing in front of me. I said, "My master, I'm greatly troubled because of the vision I've seen. And I feel very weak. 17 How can I talk with you? My strength is gone. In fact, I can hardly breathe."

18 The one who looked like a man touched me again. He gave me strength. 19 "Do not be afraid," he said. "You are highly respected. May peace be with you! Be strong now. Be strong."

When he spoke to me, I became stronger. I said, "Speak, my master. You have given me strength."

²⁰ So he said, "Do you know why I have come to you? Soon I will return to fight against the prince of Persia. When I go, the prince of Greece will come. ²¹ But first I will tell you what is written in the Book of Truth. No one gives me any help against those princes except Michael. He

11

is your leader. ¹ I stepped forward to help him and keep him safe. It was the first year that Darius, the Mede, was king.

The Kings of Egypt and Syria

² "Now then, what I'm about to tell you is true. Three more kings will come to power in Persia. Then a fourth one will rule. He will be much richer than all the others. He will use his wealth to gain power. And he will stir up everyone against the kingdom of Greece. ³ After him, a mighty king will come to power. He will rule with great power and do as he pleases. ⁴ Not long after his rule ends, his kingdom will be broken up. It will be divided up into four parts. His children will not receive it when he dies. And it will not be as strong as his kingdom. It will be pulled up by the roots. And it will be given to others.

⁵ "The king of Egypt will become strong. But one of his commanders will become even stronger. He will rule over his own kingdom with great power. ⁶ After many years, the two kingdoms will join forces. The daughter of the next king of Egypt will go to the king of Syria.

She will join forces with him. But she will not hold on to her power. And he and his power will not last either. In those days she and her attendants will die. They will die when the people she trusts lie to her. The same thing will happen to her father and the one who helped her.

⁷ "Someone from her family line will take her place. He will attack the army of the next king of Syria. Then he will enter his fort. He will fight against that army and win. ⁸ He will take the metal statues of their gods. He will also take away their priceless objects of silver and gold. He will carry everything off to Egypt. For many years he will leave the king of Syria alone. ⁹ Then the king of Syria will march into territory that was controlled by Egypt. After that, he will return to his own country. ¹⁰ His sons will prepare for war. They will gather a huge army. It will sweep along like a mighty flood. The army will fight its way as far as one of the Egyptian forts.

¹¹ "Another king of Egypt will march out with mighty force. He will be very angry. By then, another person will have become king in Syria. The king of Egypt will come to fight against him. The king of Syria will gather a huge army. But that army will lose the battle. ¹² His soldiers will be carried off. Then the king of Egypt will be filled with pride. He will kill many thousands of soldiers. But his success will not last. ¹³ The king of

Syria will bring another army together. It will be larger than the first one. After several years, he will march out with a huge army. It will have everything it needs for battle.

¹⁴ "In those times many people will rise up against the next king of Egypt. Lawless people in your own nation will refuse to obey him. That is what you saw in your vision. But they will not succeed. ¹⁵ Then the king of Syria will go to a certain city that has high walls around it. He will build ramps against them. And he will capture that city. The forces of Egypt will not have the power to stop him. Even their best troops will not be strong enough to stand up against him. ¹⁶ He will do anything he wants to. No one will be able to stand up against him. He will take over the beautiful land of Israel. And he will have the power to destroy it. ¹⁷ The king of Syria will decide to come with the might of his entire kingdom. He will join forces with the king of Egypt. And the king of Syria will give his daughter to him to become his wife. The king of Syria will do this in order to take control of Egypt. But his plans will not succeed or help him. ¹⁸ Then he will turn his attention to the lands along the Mediterranean coast. He will take over many of them. But a commander will put an end to his proud actions. He will turn his pride back on him. ¹⁹ After this, the king of Syria will return to the forts in his own country. But he will trip and fall. And he will never be seen again.

²⁰ "The next king after him will send someone out to collect taxes. The taxes will help maintain the glory of his kingdom. But in a few years the king will be destroyed. It will not happen because someone becomes angry with him or kills him in battle.

²¹ "After him, another king will take his place. Many people will hate him. He will not be honored as a king should be. He will lead an army into the kingdom when its people feel secure. He will make clever plans to capture it. ²² Then he will sweep away a huge army. The army and a prince of the covenant will be destroyed. ²³ The king of Syria will make an agreement with that prince. But then the king of Syria will not keep his word. He will rise to even greater power with the help of only a few people. ²⁴ When the people in the richest areas feel secure, he will attack them. He will do what the kings before him could not do. And he will reward his followers with the goods and wealth he takes. He will make clever plans to take over the forts. But that will last for only a short time.

²⁵ "He will become stronger and more confident. He will do that by gathering a large army. Then he will go to war against the next king of Egypt. That king will fight against him with a huge and very powerful army. But the king of Egypt will not be able to stand up against him.

So the plans of the king of Syria will succeed. 26 The trusted advisers of the king of Egypt will try to destroy him. His army will be swept away. Many of his soldiers will be wounded or killed. 27 The kings of Syria and Egypt will sit at the same table. But in their hearts they will plan to do what is evil. And they will tell lies to each other. But it will not do them any good. God will put an end to their plans at his appointed time. 28 The king of Syria will return to his own country. He will go back there with great wealth. But he will make evil plans against the holy temple in Jerusalem. He will do a lot of harm to the temple and the people who worship there. Then he will return to his own country.

29 "At God's appointed time, the king of Syria will march south again. But this time things will turn out differently. 30 Roman ships will oppose him. He will lose hope. Then he will turn back. He will take out his anger against the holy temple. And he will do good to the Jews who desert it.

31 "His army will come and make the temple area 'unclean.' They will put a stop to the daily sacrifices. Then they will set up a hated thing that destroys. 32 He will pretend to praise those who have broken the covenant. He will lead them to do what is evil. But the people who know their God will firmly oppose him.

33 "Those who are wise will teach many others. But for a while, some of the wise will be killed by swords. Others will be burned to death. Still others will be made prisoners. Or they will be robbed of everything they have. 34 When that happens, they will receive a little help. Many who are not honest will join them. 35 So some of the wise people will suffer. They will be made pure in the fire. They will be made spotless until the time of the end. It will still come at God's appointed time.

The King Who Honors Himself

36 "A certain king will do as he pleases. He will honor himself. He will put himself above every god. He will say things against the greatest God of all. Those things have never been heard before. He will have success until God is not angry anymore. What God has decided to do must take place. 37 The king will not show any respect for the gods his people have always worshiped. There is a god desired by women. He will not respect that god either. He will not have respect for any god. Instead, he will put himself above all of them. 38 In place of them, he will worship a god of war. He will honor a god his people have not known before. He will give gold and silver to that god. He will bring jewels and expensive gifts to it. 39 He will attack the strongest forts. A new god will help him do it. He will greatly honor those who recognize him as their leader. He will make them rulers over many people.

And he will give them land as a reward.

40 "A king in the south will go to war against him. It will happen at the time of the end. The king who will honor himself will rush out against him. He will come with chariots and horsemen. He will attack with a lot of ships. He will lead his army into many countries. He will sweep through them like a flood. 41 He will also march into the beautiful land of Israel. Many countries will fall. But Edom, Moab and the leaders of Ammon will be saved from his mighty hand. 42 His power will reach out into many countries. Even Egypt will not escape. 43 He will gain control of all Egypt's riches. He will take their gold and silver treasures. The people of Libya and Cush will be under his control. 44 But reports from the east and the north will terrify him. He will march out with great anger to destroy many people and wipe them out. 45 He will set up his royal tents. He will put them between the Mediterranean Sea and the beautiful holy mountain of Zion. But his end will come. And no one will help him.

The Time of the End

12 "At that time Michael will appear. He is the great prince of the angels. He guards your people. There will be a time of terrible suffering. Things will be worse than at any time since nations began. But at that time of suffering your people will be saved. Their names are written in the book of life. 2 Many people who lie dead in their graves will wake up. Some will rise up to life that will never end. Others will rise up to shame that will never end. 3 Those who are wise will shine like the brightness of the sky. Those who lead many others to do what is right will be like the stars for ever and ever. 4 But I want you to roll up this scroll, Daniel. Seal it until the time of the end. Many people will go here and there to increase their knowledge."

5 Then I looked up and saw two other angels. One was on this side of the Tigris River. And one was on the other side. 6 The man who was dressed in linen was above the waters of the river. One of the angels spoke to him. He asked, "How long will it be before these amazing things come true?"

7 The man raised both hands toward heaven. I heard him make a promise in the name of the God who lives forever. He answered me, "Three and a half years. Then the power of the holy people will finally be broken. And all these things will come true."

8 I heard what he said. But I didn't understand it. So I asked, "My master, what will come of all this?"

9 He answered, "Go on your way, Daniel. The scroll is rolled up. It is sealed until the time of the end. 10 Many people will be made pure in the fire. They will be made spotless. But sinful people will continue to be

evil. Not one sinful person will understand. But those who are wise will.

¹¹ "The daily sacrifices will be stopped. And the hated thing that destroys will be set up. After that, there will be 1,290 days. ¹² Blessed are those who wait for the 1,335 days and reach the end of them.

¹³ "Daniel, go on your way until the end. Your body will rest in the grave. Then at the end of the days you will rise from the dead. And you will receive what God has appointed for you."

Hosea

Introduction:

Hosea was a man who spoke for God. He lived in the northern kingdom called Israel. Sometimes he called his country Ephraim. Most of the people in Israel did not obey God.

This book tells about Hosea's family. His wife would not be true to him, and one day she left him. Hosea found his wife and brought her home because he loved her. He loved her even though she had left him.

Hosea said the Israelites were like his wife. They would not be true to God. They had left God's ways so they could worship false gods. But God still loved his people. Even though he punished the people, God promised to bring them back to him.

Outline of contents:

---

1 A message from the LORD came to Hosea, the son of Beeri. The message came while Uzziah, Jotham, Ahaz and Hezekiah were kings of Judah. It also came while Jeroboam was king of Israel. He was the son of Jehoash. Here is what the LORD said to him.

Hosea's Wife and Children

2 The LORD began to speak through Hosea. He said to him, "Go. Marry a woman who has sex with anyone she wants. Have children with her. Do this because the people of the land are like that kind of wife. They have not been faithful to me." 3 So Hosea married Gomer. She was the daughter of Diblaim. Gomer became pregnant and had a son by Hosea.

4 Then the LORD said to Hosea, "Name him Jezreel. That's because I will soon punish Jehu's royal family. He killed many people at the city of Jezreel. So I will put an end to the kingdom of Israel. 5 At that time I will break their military power. It will happen in the Valley of Jezreel."

6 Gomer became pregnant again. She had a daughter. Then the LORD said to Hosea, "Name her Lo-Ruhamah." Lo-Ruhamah means Not Loved. "That's because I will no longer show love to the people of Israel. I will not forgive them anymore. 7 But I will show love to the people

of Judah. And I will save them. I will not use bows or swords or other weapons of war to do it. I will not save them by using horses and horsemen either. Instead, I will use my own power to save them. I am the LORD their God. And I will save them."

8 Later, Gomer stopped nursing Lo-Ruhamah. After that, she had another son. 9 Then the LORD said, "Name him Lo-Ammi." Lo-Ammi means Not My People. "That's because Israel is no longer my people. And I am no longer their God.

10 "But the time will come when the people of Israel will be like the sand on the seashore. It can't be measured or counted. Now it is said about them, 'You are not my people.' But at that time they will be called 'children of the living God.' 11 The people of Judah and Israel will come together again. They will appoint one leader and come up out of the land. And Jezreel's day will be great.

2 "People of Israel, call your brothers 'My people.' And call your sisters 'My loved ones.'

Israel Is Punished and Brought Back to the LORD

2 "Tell your mother she is wrong.
   Tell her she is wrong.
She isn't acting like a wife to
   me anymore.
   She no longer treats me as
   her husband.
Tell her to stop looking and
   acting like a prostitute.
   Tell her not to let her lovers
   lie on her breasts anymore.

3 If she doesn't stop it, I will
   strip her naked.
   I'll make her as bare as she
   was on the day she was
   born.
I'll make her like a desert.
   She will become like dry
   land.
   And I'll let her die of thirst.

4 "I won't show my love to her
   children.
   They are the children of
   other men.
5 Their mother hasn't been
   faithful to me.
   She who became pregnant
   with them
   has brought shame on
   herself.
She said, 'I will chase after
   my lovers.
   They give me my food and
   water.
   They provide me with wool
   and linen.
   They give me olive oil and
   wine.'
6 So I will block her path with
   bushes that have thorns.
   I'll build a wall around
   her.
   Then she can't go to her
   lovers.
7 She will still chase after her
   lovers.
   But she won't catch them.
   She'll look for them.
   But she won't find them.
Then she'll say,
   'I'll go back to my husband.
   That's where I was at first.
   I was better off then than I
   am now.'
8 She wouldn't admit that I was
   the one

who gave her everything
she had.
I provided her with grain,
olive oil and fresh wine.
I gave her plenty of silver and
gold.
But she used it to make
statues of Baal.

9 "So I will take away my grain
when it gets ripe.
I'll take my fresh wine
when it's ready.
I'll take back my wool and my
linen.
I gave them to her to cover
her naked body.
10 So now I'll uncover her body.
All her lovers will see it.
No one can stop me from
punishing her.
11 I will put a stop to the special
times she celebrates.
I'll bring an end to the
feasts she celebrates
each year.
I'll stop her New Moon feasts
and her Sabbath days.
I'll bring all her appointed
feasts to an end.
12 I will destroy her vines and
her fig trees.
She said they were her pay
from her lovers.
I'll make them like clumps of
bushes and weeds.
Wild animals will eat them
up.
13 Israel burned incense to the
gods
that were named Baal.
I will punish her
for all the times she did
that.
She decorated herself with
rings and jewelry.

Then she went after her
lovers.
But she forgot all about
me,"
declares the LORD.

14 "So now I am going to draw
her back to me.
I will lead her into the
desert.
There I will speak tenderly
to her.
15 I will give her back her
vineyards.
I will make the Valley of
Achor a door of hope for
her.
Then she will love me, as
she did when she was
young.
She will love me just as she
did
when she came up out of
Egypt.
16 "A new day is coming,"
announces the LORD.
"Israel will call me 'my
husband.'
She will no longer call me
'my master.'
17 She will no longer speak
about the gods
that are named Baal.
She will not pray to them
for help anymore.
18 At that time I will make a
covenant
for the good of my people.
I will make it with the wild
animals
and the birds in the sky.
It will also be made with the
creatures
that move along the
ground.

I will remove bows and
    swords
    and other weapons of war
    from the land.
    Then my people can lie
    down in safety.
[19] I will make Israel my own.
    She will belong to me
    forever.
    I will do to her what is right
    and fair.
    I will love her tenderly.
[20] I will be faithful to her.
    And she will recognize me
    as the LORD.

[21] "So at that time I will answer
    her,"
    announces the LORD.
    "I will command the skies
    to send rain on the earth.
[22] Then the earth will produce
    grain, olive oil and fresh
    wine.
    And Israel will be called
    Jezreel.
    That's because I will
    answer her prayers.
[23] I will plant her in the land for
    myself.
    I will show my love to the
    one I called Not My
    Loved One.
    I will say, 'You are my people'
    to those who were called
    Not My People.
    And they will say, 'You are
    my God.' "

Hosea Brings His Wife Back to Himself

3 The LORD said to me, "Go.
Show your love to your wife
again. She is loved by another
man. And she has committed
adultery. But I want you to love

her just as I love the people of
Israel. They turn to other gods.
And they love to offer raisin
cakes to Baal and eat them. In
spite of that, I love my people."
[2] So I bought Gomer for six
ounces of silver and 430 pounds
of barley. [3] Then I told her, "You
must wait for me for a long time.
You must not be a prostitute.
You must not have sex with any
man. And I will be faithful to
you too."

[4] So the people of Israel will
live for a long time without a
king or prince. They won't have
sacrifices or sacred stones. They
won't have sacred linen aprons
or statues of family gods. [5] After that, the people of Israel will
return to the LORD their God.
They will look to him and to a
king from the family line of David. In the last days, they will
tremble with fear as they come
to the LORD. And they will receive his full blessing.

The LORD Brings Charges Against Israel

4 People of Israel, listen to the
    LORD's message.
    He is bringing charges
    against you who live in
    Israel.
    He says, "There is no
    faithfulness
    or love in the land.
    No one recognizes me as
    God.
[2] People curse one another.
    They tell lies and commit
    murder.
    They steal and commit
    adultery.

They break all my laws.
They keep spilling the
blood of other people.
³That is why the land is drying
up.
All those who live in it
are getting weaker and
weaker.
The wild animals and the
birds in the sky are dying.
So are the fish in the
ocean.

⁴"But you priests should not
blame the people.
You should not find fault
with one another.
After all, your people
could also bring charges
against you.
⁵You trip and fall day and
night.
And the prophets fall down
along with you.
So I will destroy your nation.
She is the one who gave
birth to you.
⁶My people are destroyed
because they do not know
me.

"You priests have refused to
obey me.
So I will refuse to accept
you as my priests.
You have not paid any
attention to my law.
So I will not let your
children be my priests.
⁷The more priests there were,
the more they sinned
against me.
They have traded their
glorious God for that
shameful god named
Baal.

⁸They live off the sins of my
people.
And they want them to
keep on sinning.
⁹So here is what I will do.
I will punish people and
priests alike.
I will judge them because of
their sinful lives.
I will pay them back
for the evil things they
have done.

¹⁰"My people will eat.
But they will not have
enough.
They will have sex with
prostitutes.
But they will not have any
children.
That's because they have
deserted me.
They have sex ¹¹with
prostitutes.
They drink old wine and
fresh wine.
Their drinking has
destroyed their ability to
understand.
¹²My people ask a wooden
statue of a god for advice.
They get answers from a
stick of wood.
They are as unfaithful as
prostitutes.
They are not faithful to
their God.
¹³They offer sacrifices on the
mountaintops.
They burn offerings on the
hills.
They worship under oak,
poplar and terebinth
trees.
The trees provide plenty of
shade.

So your daughters become
  prostitutes.
And your daughters-in-law
  commit adultery.

14 "I will not punish your
  daughters
  when they become
  prostitutes.
I will not judge your
  daughters-in-law
  when they commit adultery.
After all, the men themselves
  have sex with sinful
  women.
They offer sacrifices where
  temple prostitutes earn
  their living.
People who can't
  understand will be
  destroyed!

15 "Israel, you are not faithful
  to me.
But I do not want Judah to
  become guilty too.

"My people, do not go to
  Gilgal to offer sacrifices.
Do not go up to Bethel to
  worship other gods.
When you make a promise,
  do not say,
'You can be sure that the
  LORD is alive.'
16 The people of Israel are
  stubborn.
They are as stubborn as a
  young cow.
So how can I take care of
  them
  like lambs in a meadow?
17 The people of Ephraim have
  joined themselves to
  other gods.
And nothing can be done
  to help them.

18 They continue to be
  unfaithful to me
  even when their drinks are
  gone.
And their rulers love to do
  shameful things.
19 A windstorm will blow all of
  them away.
And their sacrifices will
  bring shame on them.

The LORD Judges Israel

5 "Listen to me, you priests!
  Pay attention, people of
  Israel!
Listen, you members of the
  royal family!
Here is my decision against
  you.
You have been like a trap at
  Mizpah.
You have been like a net
  spread out on Mount
  Tabor.
2 You refuse to obey me.
You are knee-deep in
  killing.
So I will punish all of
  you.
3 I know all about the people of
  Ephraim.
What Israel is doing is not
  hidden from me.
Now they have joined
  themselves to other
  gods.
They have made
  themselves 'unclean.'

4 "They can't return to me
  because they have done so
  many evil things.
In their hearts they long to
  act like prostitutes.
They do not recognize me
  as the LORD.

⁵ Israel's pride proves that they
　　are guilty.
The people of Ephraim trip
　　and fall because they
　　have sinned.
Judah falls down along
　　with them.
⁶ Israel will come to worship
　　the Lord.
They will bring their
　　animals to offer as
　　sacrifices.
But they will not find him.
He has turned away from
　　them.
⁷ They are not faithful to the
　　Lord.
　　Their children are not his.
When they celebrate their
　　New Moon feasts,
　　he will destroy their fields.

⁸ "My people, blow trumpets
　　in Gibeah!
Blow horns in Ramah!
Shout the battle cry in Bethel!
Say to the people of
　　Benjamin, 'Lead on into
　　battle!'
⁹ The people of Ephraim will
　　be completely destroyed
　　when it is time for me to
　　punish them.
They can be sure it will
　　happen.
　　I am announcing it among
　　their tribes.
¹⁰ Judah's leaders have stolen
　　some land.
They have moved their
　　borders farther north.
So I will pour out my anger
　　on them
　　like a flood of water.
¹¹ Ephraim will soon be
　　crushed.

The Assyrians will stomp
　　all over them.
It will happen because they
　　have made up their
　　minds
　　to chase after other gods.
¹² I will be like a moth to
　　Ephraim.
I will cause Judah to rot
　　away.

¹³ "The people of Ephraim saw
　　how sick they were.
The people of Judah saw
　　that they were wounded.
Then Ephraim turned to
　　Assyria for help.
They sent gifts to the great
　　King Tiglath-Pileser.
But he is not able to make you
　　well.
He can't heal your wounds.
¹⁴ I will be like a lion to
　　Ephraim.
I will attack Judah like a
　　powerful lion.
I will tear them to pieces.
I will drag them off.
Then I will leave them.
　　No one will be able to save
　　them.
¹⁵ I will go back to my lion's den.
I will stay there until they
　　pay the price for their
　　sin.
Then they will turn to me.
They will suffer so much
　　that they will really want
　　me to help them."

Israel Refuses to Turn Away From Their Sins

6 The people say, "Come.
　　Let us return to the Lord.
He has torn us to pieces.
But he will heal us.

He has wounded us.
  But he'll bandage our
  wounds.
² After two days he will give us
  new life.
  On the third day he'll make
  us like new again.
  Then we will enjoy his
  blessing.
³ Let's recognize him as the
  Lord.
  Let's keep trying to know
  him.
You can be sure the sun will
  rise.
  And you can be just as sure
  the Lord will appear.
He will come to renew us like
  the winter rains.
  He will be like the spring
  rains that water the
  earth."

⁴ The Lord says, "Ephraim,
  what can I do with you?
  And what can I do with
  you, Judah?
Your love for me vanishes like
  the morning mist.
  It soon disappears like the
  early dew.
⁵ So I used the words of my
  prophets to cut you in
  pieces.
  I used my words to put you
  to death.
  Then my judgments blazed
  out like the sun.
⁶ I want mercy and not
  sacrifice.
  I want you to recognize me
  as God
  instead of bringing me
  burnt offerings.
⁷ Just as at the city of Adam,
  they disobeyed me,

they have broken the
  covenant I made with
  them.
  They were not faithful to
  me there.
⁸ Ramoth Gilead is a city
  where sinful people live.
  It is stained with footprints
  of blood.
⁹ On the road to Shechem,
  groups of priests act like
  robbers.
  They hide and wait to
  attack people.
They murder them.
  So they carry out their evil
  plans.
¹⁰ I have seen a horrible thing
  in Israel.
  The people of Ephraim are
  unfaithful to their own
  God.
  The people of Israel are
  'unclean.'

¹¹ "People of Judah, I have also
  appointed a time
  for you to be destroyed.

"I would like to bless my
  people
  with great success again.

7 ¹ I would like to heal Israel.
  But when I try to,
  Ephraim's sins
  are brought out into the
  open.
The crimes of Samaria
  are made known to
  everyone.
The people tell lies.
  They break into houses
  and steal.
  They rob others in the
  streets.
² But they do not realize

that I remember all the evil
things they do.
Their sins pile up and cover
them.
I am always aware of their
sins.

3 "Their evil conduct even
makes the king glad.
Their lies make the princes
happy.
4 But all the people are
unfaithful to the king.
Their anger against him
burns
like the coals in an oven.
The baker does not even
need to stir up the fire
until the dough is ready."

5 On special days to honor our
king,
the princes get drunk with
wine.
And the king enjoys the
party.
He joins hands with those
who pretend to be faithful
to him.
6 Their hearts are as hot as an
oven.
They make evil plans to get
rid of him.
Their anger burns like a slow
fire all night.
In the morning it blazes
out like a flaming fire.
7 All of them are as hot as an
oven.
They destroy their rulers.
All their kings fall from
power.
But none of them calls on
the LORD for help.

8 The people of Ephraim mix
with the nations.

They are like a thin loaf of
bread
that is baked on only one
side.
9 People from other lands
make them weaker and
weaker.
But they don't realize it.
Their hair is becoming gray.
But they don't even notice
it.
10 The pride of Israel proves
that they are guilty.
But in spite of everything,
they don't return to the LORD
their God.
They don't go to him for
help.

11 The LORD says,

"The people of Ephraim are
like a dove.
They are easily tricked.
They do not have any sense
at all.
First they call out to Egypt for
help.
Then they turn to Assyria.
12 When they send for help,
I will throw my net over
them.
I will capture them like the
birds in the sky.
When I hear them
gathering like birds,
I will catch them.
13 How terrible it will be for
them!
They have wandered away
from me.
So they will be destroyed.
That's because they have
refused to obey me.
I long to save them.
But they tell lies about me.

¹⁴ They do not cry out to me
   from their hearts.
Instead, they just lie on
   their beds and sob.
They cut themselves when
   they pray to their gods
for grain and fresh wine.
But they turn away from
   me.
¹⁵ I brought them up and made
   them strong.
But they make evil plans
   against me.
¹⁶ I am the Most High God. But
   they do not turn to me.
They are like a bow that
   does not shoot straight.
Their leaders will be killed by
   swords.
They will die because they
   have spoken too proudly.
The people of Egypt
   will make fun of them."

Israel Will Harvest a Windstorm

8 The LORD said to me,

"Put a trumpet to your lips!
   Give a warning to my
   people!
Assyria is like an eagle.
   It is ready to attack my
   land.
My people have broken the
   covenant I made with
   them.
They have refused to obey
   my law.
² Israel shouts to me,
   'We recognize you as our
   God!'
³ But they have turned away
   from what is good.
So an enemy will chase
   them.

⁴ My people appoint kings I do
   not want.
They choose princes
   without my permission.
They use their silver and
   gold
to make statues of gods.
That is how they destroy
   themselves."
⁵ The LORD says, "People of
   Samaria,
throw out your god that
   looks like a calf!
I am very angry with them.
How long will it be until they
   are able
to remain faithful to me?
⁶ Their calf is not God.
A skilled worker from
   Israel made it.
But that calf of Samaria
   will be broken to pieces."

⁷ The LORD says,

"Worshiping other gods is
   like worshiping the
   wind.
It is like planting worthless
   seeds.
Assyria is like a windstorm.
   That is all my people will
   harvest.
There are no heads of grain
   on the stems that will come
   up.
So they will not produce
   any flour.
Even if they did produce
   grain,
   the Assyrians would eat all
   of it up.
⁸ So the people of Israel are
   swallowed up.
Now they are among the
   nations

like something no one
wants.
⁹ They have gone up to Assyria
for help.
They are like a wild donkey
that wanders around by
itself.
Ephraim's people have sold
themselves
to their Assyrian lovers.
¹⁰ They have sold themselves to
the nations
to get their help.
But now I will gather them
together.
They will get weaker and
weaker.
The mighty kings of
Assyria will crush them.

¹¹ "Ephraim built many altars
where they sacrificed
sin offerings to other
gods.
So their altars have become
places where they commit
sin.
¹² In my law I wrote down many
things for their good.
But they considered those
things as something
strange.
¹³ They offer sacrifices as gifts
to me.
They eat the meat of the
animals they bring.
But the Lord is not pleased
with any of this.
He will remember the evil
things they have done.
He will punish them for
their sins.
And they will return to
Egypt.
¹⁴ Israel has forgotten the God
who made them.

They have built palaces for
themselves.
Judah has built forts in
many towns.
But I will send down fire on
their cities.
It will burn up their forts."

Israel Will Be Punished

9 Israel, don't be joyful.
Don't be glad as the other
nations are.
You haven't been faithful to
your God.
You love to get paid for
being a prostitute.
Your pay is the grain at
every threshing floor.
² But soon there won't be any
grain or wine to feed
you.
There won't even be any
fresh wine.
³ You won't remain in the
Lord's land.
Ephraim, you will return to
Egypt.
You will eat "unclean" food
in Assyria.
⁴ You won't pour out wine
offerings to the Lord.
Your sacrifices won't please
him.
They'll be like the bread
people eat when
someone dies.
Everyone who eats those
sacrifices will be
"unclean."
They themselves will have to
eat that kind of food.
They can't bring it into the
Lord's temple.
⁵ What will you do when your
appointed feasts come?

What will you do on the
Lord's special days?
6 Some of you will escape
without being destroyed.
But you will die in Egypt.
Your bodies will be buried
at Memphis.
Weeds will cover your
treasures of silver.
Thorns will grow up in
your tents.
7 The time when God will
punish you is coming.
The day when he will judge
you is near.
I want Israel to know this.
You have committed many
sins.
And you hate me very
much.
That's why you think the
prophet is foolish.
You think the person the
Lord speaks through is
crazy.
8 People of Ephraim, the
prophet, along with my
God,
is warning you of danger.
But you set traps for him
everywhere he goes.
You hate him so much
you even wait for him in
God's house.
9 You have sunk very deep into
sin,
just as your people did at
Gibeah long ago.
God will remember the evil
things they have done.
He will punish them for
their sins.

10 The Lord says,

"When I first found Israel,

it was like finding grapes in
the desert.
When I saw your people of
long ago,
it was like seeing the early
fruit on a fig tree.
But then they went to Baal
Peor.
There they gave
themselves to that
shameful god named
Baal.
They became as evil as the
god they loved.
11 Ephraim's greatness and
glory will be gone.
It will fly away like a bird.
Women will no longer have
children.
They will not be able to get
pregnant.
12 But suppose they do have
children.
Then I will kill every one of
them.
How terrible it will be for
them
when I turn away from
them!
13 Tyre is planted in a pleasant
place.
And so is Ephraim.
But the Assyrians will kill
Ephraim's children."
14 Lord, what should you do to
Ephraim's people?
Give them women whose
babies die before they
are born.
Give them women whose
breasts have no milk.

15 The Lord says,

"My people did many evil
things in Gilgal.

That is why I hated them
there.
They committed many sins.
So I will drive them out of
my land.
I will not love them anymore.
All their leaders refuse to
obey me.
16 Ephraim is like a worthless
plant.
Its roots are dried up.
It does not produce any
fruit.
Suppose Ephraim's people
have children.
Then I will kill the children
they love so much."

17 My God will turn his back on
his people.
They have not obeyed him.
So they will wander among
other nations.

10 ¹ Israel was like a
spreading vine.
They produced fruit for
themselves.
As they grew more fruit,
they built more altars.
As their land became richer,
they made more beautiful
the sacred stones they
worshiped.
² Their hearts are dishonest.
So now they must pay for
their sins.
The LORD will tear down
their altars.
He'll destroy their sacred
stones.
³ Then they'll say, "We don't
have a king.
That's because we didn't
have
any respect for the LORD.

But suppose we did have a
king.
What could he do for us?"
⁴ They make a lot of promises.
They make agreements
among themselves.
They make promises they
don't mean to keep.
So court cases spring up
like poisonous weeds in a
plowed field.
⁵ The people who live in
Samaria are filled with
fear.
They are afraid for their
god that looks like a
calf.
They're afraid it will be
carried off from Beth
Aven, that evil town.
They will mourn over it.
So will the priests who led
them to worship it.
The priests were full of joy
because their statue was so
glorious.
But it will be captured
and taken far away from
them.
⁶ It will be carried off to
Assyria.
The people of Ephraim will
be forced
to give it to the great king.
They will be dishonored.
Israel will be ashamed
of its agreements with
other nations.
⁷ Samaria's king will be
destroyed.
He will be like a twig swept
away by a river.
⁸ The high places where Israel
worshiped other gods
will be destroyed.

That's where they sinned
against the LORD.
Thorns and weeds will grow
up there.
They will cover the altars.
Then the people will say to the
mountains, "Cover us!"
They'll say to the hills,
"Fall on us!"

⁹ The LORD says,

"Israel, you have done evil
things
ever since your people
sinned at Gibeah long
ago.
And you are still doing
what is evil.
War will come again
to those who sinned at
Gibeah.
¹⁰ I will punish them when I
want to.
Nations will gather
together to fight against
them.
They will put them in chains
because they have
committed so many sins.
¹¹ Ephraim was like a well-
trained young cow.
It loved to thresh grain.
So I will put a yoke
on its pretty neck.
I will make Ephraim do hard
work.
Judah also must plow.
So all the people of Jacob
must break up the ground.
¹² Your hearts are as hard as a
field
that has not been plowed.
If you change your ways,
you will produce good
crops.

So plant the seeds of doing
what is right.
Then you will harvest the
fruit of your faithful love.
It is time to seek the LORD.
When you do, he will come
and shower his blessings
on you.
¹³ But you have planted the
seeds of doing what is
wrong.
So you have harvested
the fruit of your evil
conduct.
You have had to eat the
fruit of your lies.
You have trusted in your own
strength.
You have depended on
your many soldiers.
¹⁴ But the roar of battle will
come against you.
All your forts will be
completely destroyed.
It will happen just as
Shalman
destroyed Beth Arbel in a
battle.
Mothers and their children
were smashed on the
ground.
¹⁵ People of Bethel, that will
happen to you.
You have committed far
too many sins.
When the time comes for me
to punish you,
the king of Israel will be
completely destroyed."

God Loves Israel

11 The LORD continues,

"When Israel was a young
nation, I loved them.

I chose to bring my son out
of Egypt.
2 But the more I called out to
Israel,
the more they went away
from me.
They brought sacrifices to the
statues of the gods
that were named Baal.
And they burned incense
to them.
3 I taught Ephraim to walk.
I took them up in my arms.
But they did not realize
I was the one who took
care of them.
4 I led them with kindness and
love.
I was to them like a person
who lifts
a little child to their cheek.
I bent down and fed them.

5 "But they refuse to turn away
from their sins.
So they will return to
Egypt.
And Assyria will rule over
them.
6 A sword will flash in their
cities.
It will destroy the prophets
who teach lies.
It will bring an end to their
plans.
7 My people have made up
their minds
to turn away from me.
Even if they call me the Most
High God,
I will certainly not honor
them."

8 The LORD continues,

"People of Ephraim, how can
I give you up?

Israel, how can I hand you
over to your enemies?
Can I destroy you as I did the
town of Admah?
Can I treat you like
Zeboyim?
My heart is stirred inside me.
It is filled with pity for you.
9 I will not be so angry with
you anymore.
I will not completely
destroy you again.
After all, I am God.
I am not a mere man.
I am the Holy One among
you.
I will not direct my anger
against their cities.
10 I will roar like a lion against
my enemies.
Then the LORD's people
will follow him.
When he roars, his children
will come home
trembling with fear.
They will return from the
west.
11 They will come from Egypt,
trembling like sparrows.
They will return from
Assyria, flying in like
doves.
I will settle you again in your
homes,"
announces the LORD.

Israel Has Sinned

12 The people of Ephraim tell
me nothing but lies.
Israel has not been honest
with me.
And Judah continues to
wander away from God.
They have deserted the
faithful Holy One.

12

¹The people of Ephraim
look to others for help.
It's like chasing the wind.
The wind they keep chasing
is hot and dry.
They tell more and more
lies.
They are always hurting
others.
They make a peace treaty
with Assyria.
They send olive oil to Egypt
to get help.
²The LORD is bringing charges
against Judah.
He will punish Jacob's
people
because of how they act.
He'll pay them back
for the evil things they've
done.
³Even before Jacob was born,
he was holding on to his
brother's heel.
When he became a man,
he struggled with God.
⁴At Peniel he struggled with
the angel and won.
Jacob wept and begged for
his blessing.
God also met with him at
Bethel.
He talked with him there.
⁵He is the LORD God who
rules over all.
His name is the LORD.
⁶People of Jacob, you must
return to your God.
You must hold on to love
and do what is fair.
You must trust in your God
always.
⁷You are like a trader who uses
dishonest scales.
You love to cheat others.

⁸People of Ephraim, you
brag,
"We are very rich.
We've become wealthy.
And no one can prove we
sinned
to gain all this wealth."
⁹The LORD says,
"I have been the LORD your
God
ever since you came out of
Egypt.
But I will make you live in
tents again.
That is what you did when
you celebrated
the Feast of Booths in the
desert.
¹⁰I spoke to the prophets.
They saw many visions.
I gave you warnings
through them."
¹¹The people of Gilead are
evil!
They aren't worth
anything!
Gilgal's people sacrifice bulls
to other gods.
Their altars will become
like piles of stones
on a plowed field.
¹²Jacob ran away to the
country of Aram.
There Israel served Laban
to get a wife.
He took care of sheep to
pay for her.
¹³The prophet Moses brought
Israel up from Egypt.
The LORD used him to take
care of them.
¹⁴But Ephraim's people have
made the LORD very
angry.

Their Lord will hold them
accountable for the
blood they've spilled.
He'll pay them back for the
shameful things they've
done.

The LORD Is Angry With Israel

13 When the tribe of
Ephraim spoke,
the other tribes trembled
with fear.
Ephraim was honored in
Israel.
But its people sinned by
worshiping Baal.
So they were as good as
dead.
² Now they sin more and
more.
They use their silver
to make statues of gods for
themselves.
The statues come from their
own clever ideas.
Skilled workers make all of
them.
The people pray to these
gods.
They offer human
sacrifices to them.
They kiss the gods that
look like calves.
³ So these people will vanish
like the morning mist.
They will soon disappear
like the early dew.
They will be like straw
that the wind blows
around on a threshing
floor.
They will be like smoke
that escapes through a
window.
⁴ The LORD says,

"People of Israel, I have been
the LORD your God
ever since you came out of
Egypt.
You must not worship any
god but me.
You must not have any
savior except me.
⁵ I took care of you in the
desert.
It was a land of burning
heat.
⁶ I fed them until they were
satisfied.
Then they became proud.
They forgot all about me.
⁷ So I will leap on them like a
lion.
I will hide and wait
beside the road like a
leopard.
⁸ I will attack them like a
bear
that is robbed of her cubs.
I will rip them wide open.
Like a lion I will eat them up.
Like a wild animal I will
tear them apart.

⁹ "Israel, you will be destroyed.
I helped you. But you
turned against me.
¹⁰ Where is your king?
Wasn't he supposed to save
you?
Where are the rulers in all
your towns?
You said, 'Give us a king
and princes.'
¹¹ So I became angry and gave
you a king.
Then I took him away from
you.
¹² Ephraim's guilt is piling up.
I am keeping a record of all
their sins.

¹³They will suffer pain like a
woman having a baby.
They are like foolish
children.
It is time for them to be born.
But they don't have the
sense to come out of
their mother's body.
¹⁴ "I will set these people free
from the power of the
grave.
I will save them from
death.
Death, where are your
plagues?
Grave, where is your power
to destroy?

"I will no longer pity
Ephraim.
¹⁵ Even though they are
doing well among the
other tribes,
trouble will come to them.
I will send a hot and dry wind
from the east.
It will blow in from the
desert.
Their springs will not have
any water.
Their wells will dry up.
All their treasures
will be taken out of their
storerooms.
¹⁶The people of Samaria must
pay for their sins.
They have refused to obey
me.
They will be killed by
swords.
Their little children will be
smashed on the ground.
Their pregnant women
will be ripped wide
open."

The LORD Blesses Those Who Turn Away From Sin

14 Israel, return to the LORD
your God.
Your sins have destroyed
you!
² Tell the LORD you are turning
away from your sins.
Return to him.
Say to him,
"Forgive us for all our sins.
Please be kind to us.
Welcome us back to you.
Then our lips will offer you
our praise.
³ Assyria can't save us.
We won't trust in our war
horses.
Our own hands have made
statues of gods.
But we will never call them
our gods again.
We are like children whose
fathers have died.
But you show us your
tender love."

⁴ Then the LORD will answer,

"My people always wander
away from me.
But I will put an end to
that.
My anger has turned away
from them.
Now I will love them freely.
⁵ I will be like the dew to Israel.
They will bloom like a lily.
They will send their roots
down deep
like a cedar tree in
Lebanon.
⁶ They will spread out like new
branches.
They will be as beautiful as
an olive tree.

They will smell as sweet
as the cedar trees in
Lebanon.
[7] Once again my people will
live
in the safety of my shade.
They will grow like grain.
They will bloom like vines.
And Israel will be as
famous
as wine from Lebanon.
[8] Ephraim will have nothing
more to do with other
gods.
I will answer the prayers of
my people.
I will take good care of
them.

I will be like a healthy juniper
tree to them.
All the fruit they bear will
come from me."

[9] If someone is wise, they will
realize
that what I've said is true.
If they have understanding,
they will know what it
means.
The ways of the Lord are
right.
People who are right with
God live the way he
wants them to.
But those who refuse to
obey him trip and fall.

Joel

Introduction:

Joel was a man who spoke for God. He wrote this book to tell the people to turn back to God. Joel told them that bad things would happen if they did not turn away from their sin.

Joel wrote about locusts that came and ate all the plants. He said this should make the people turn away from their sin. He also said God would let worse things happen if the people did not turn back to him.

Outline of contents:

1 A message from the LORD came to Joel, the son of Pethuel. Here is what Joel said.

Locusts Attack the Land

2 Elders, listen to me.
Pay attention, all you who
live in the land.
Has anything like this ever
happened in your whole
life?
Did it ever happen to your
people
who lived long ago?
3 Tell your children about it.
Let them tell their
children.
And let their children tell it
to those who live after them.
4 The giant locusts have eaten
what the common locusts
have left.
The young locusts have eaten
what the giant locusts have
left.

And other locusts have eaten
what the young locusts
have left.
5 Get up and weep, you people
who drink too much!
Cry, all you who drink
wine!
Cry because the fresh wine
has been taken away from
you.
6 The locusts are like a mighty
army
that has marched into our
land.
There are so many of them
they can't even be counted.
Their teeth are as sharp as a
lion's teeth.
They are like the fangs of a
female lion.
7 The locusts have completely
destroyed our vines.
They have wiped out our
fig trees.

They've stripped off the bark
and thrown it away.
They've left the branches
bare.

8 My people, mourn like a
virgin
who is dressed in the
clothes of sadness.
She is sad because she has
lost
the young man she was
going to marry.
9 No one brings grain offerings
and drink offerings
to the LORD's house
anymore.
So the priests who serve the
LORD
are filled with sorrow.
10 Our fields are wiped out.
The ground is dried up.
The grain is destroyed.
The fresh wine is gone.
And there isn't any more
olive oil.
11 Farmers, be sad.
Cry, you who grow vines.
Mourn because the wheat
and barley are gone.
The crops in the fields are
destroyed.
12 The vines and fig trees are
dried up.
The pomegranate, palm
and apple trees
don't have any fruit on
them.
In fact, all the trees in the
fields are dried up.
And my people's joy has
faded away.

A Call to Mourn

13 Priests, put on the clothing of
sadness and mourn.
Cry, you who serve at the
altar.
Come, you who serve my God
in the temple.
Spend the night dressed in
the clothes of sadness.
Weep because no one brings
grain offerings and drink
offerings
to the house of your God
anymore.
14 Announce a holy fast.
Tell the people not to eat
anything.
Gather them together for a
special service.
Send for the elders
and all who live in the
land.
Have them come to the house
of the LORD your God.
And pray to him.

15 The day of the LORD is near.
How sad it will be on that
day!
The Mighty One is coming
to destroy you.

16 Our food has been taken
away
right in front of our eyes.
There isn't any joy or
gladness
in the house of our God.
17 The seeds have dried up in
the ground.
The grain is also gone.
The storerooms have been
destroyed.
The barns are broken
down.
18 Listen to the cattle groan!
The herds wander around.
They don't have any grass to
eat.

The flocks of sheep are
also suffering.

19 LORD, I call out to you.
Fire has burned up the
desert grasslands.
Flames have destroyed all
the trees in the fields.
20 Even the wild animals cry
out to you for help.
The streams of water have
dried up.
Fire has burned up the
desert grasslands.

The LORD Sends an Army of Locusts

2 Priests, blow the trumpets
in Zion.
Give a warning on my holy
mountain.
Let everyone who lives in the
land tremble with fear.
The day of the LORD is
coming.
It is very near.
2 That day will be dark and
sad.
It will be black and
cloudy.
A huge army of locusts is
coming.
They will spread across the
mountains
like the sun when it rises.
There has never been an
army like it.
And there will never be
another
for all time to come.
3 Like fire they eat up
everything in their path.
Behind them it looks as if
flames have burned the
land.

In front of them the land is
like the Garden of Eden.
Behind them it is a dry and
empty desert.
Nothing escapes them.
4 They look like horses.
Like war horses they
charge ahead.
5 They sound like chariots
as they leap over the
mountaintops.
They crackle like fire
burning up dry weeds.
They are like a mighty army
that is ready for battle.

6 When people see them, they
tremble with fear.
All their faces turn pale.
7 The locusts charge ahead like
warriors.
They climb over walls like
soldiers.
All of them march in line.
They don't turn to the right
or the left.
8 They don't bump into one
another.
Each of them marches
straight ahead.
They charge through
everything that tries to
stop them.
But they still stay in line.
9 They attack a city.
They run along its wall.
They climb into houses.
They enter through
windows like robbers.

10 As they march forward, the
earth shakes.
The heavens tremble as
they approach.
The sun and moon grow dark.
And the stars stop shining.

¹¹ The LORD thunders with his
　　mighty voice
　　as he leads his army.
He has so many forces they
　　can't even be counted.
The army that obeys his
　　commands is mighty.
The day of the LORD is great
　　and terrifying.
Who can live through it?

Let Your Hearts Be Broken

¹² The LORD announces to his
people,

"Return to me with all your
　　heart.
　　There is still time.
Do not eat any food.
Weep and mourn."

¹³ Don't just tear your clothes to
　　show how sad you are.
Let your hearts be broken.
Return to the LORD your God.
He is gracious.
He is tender and kind.
He is slow to get angry.
He is full of love.
He won't bring his judgment.
He won't destroy you.
¹⁴ Who knows? He might turn
　　toward you
　　and not bring his
　　judgment.
He might even give you his
　　blessing.
Then you can bring grain
　　offerings and drink
　　offerings
　　to the LORD your God.

¹⁵ Priests, blow the trumpets in
　　Zion.
Announce a holy fast.
Tell the people not to eat
　　anything.

Gather them together for a
　　special service.
¹⁶ Bring them together.
Set all of them apart to me.
Bring together the elders.
Gather the children and
　　the babies
who are still nursing.
Let the groom leave his
　　bedroom.
Let the bride leave their
　　marriage bed.
¹⁷ Let the priests who serve the
　　LORD weep.
Let them cry between the
　　temple porch and the
　　altar.
Let them say, "LORD, spare
　　your people.
Don't let others make fun
　　of them.
Don't let the nations laugh
　　at them.
Don't let them tease your
　　people and say,
'Where is their God?'"

The LORD Answers the Prayer of His People

¹⁸ Then the LORD was
　　concerned for his land.
He took pity on his people.
¹⁹ He replied,

"I am sending you grain,
　　olive oil and fresh wine.
It will be enough to satisfy
　　you completely.
I will never allow other
　　nations
　　to make fun of you again.

²⁰ "I will drive far away from
　　you
　　the army that comes from
　　the north.

I will send some of its forces
    into a dry and empty land.
Its eastern troops will drown
    in the Dead Sea.
    Its western troops
      will drown in the
      Mediterranean Sea.
    Their dead bodies will
      stink."

The LORD has done great
    things.
21   Land of Judah, don't be
    afraid.
Be glad and full of joy.
    The LORD has done great
      things.
22 Wild animals, don't be
    afraid.
    The desert grasslands are
      turning green again.
The trees are bearing their
    fruit.
    The vines and fig trees are
      producing rich crops.
23 People of Zion, be glad.
    Be joyful because of what
      the LORD your God has
      done.
He has given you the right
    amount of rain in the
    fall.
That's because he is faithful.
    He has sent you plenty of
      showers.
He has sent fall and spring
    rains alike,
    just as he did before.
24 Your threshing floors will be
    covered with grain.
    Olive oil and fresh wine
      will spill over
from the places where they
    are stored.

25 The LORD says,

"I sent a great army of locusts
    to attack you.
    They included common
      locusts, giant locusts,
      young locusts and other
      locusts.
I will make up for the years
    they ate your crops.
26 You will have plenty to eat.
    It will satisfy you
      completely.
Then you will praise me.
    I am the LORD your God.
I have done wonderful things
    for you.
    My people will never again
      be put to shame.
27 You will know that I am with
    you in Israel.
    I am the LORD your God.
There is no other God.
    So my people will never
      again be put to shame.

The Day of the LORD Is Coming

28 "After that, I will pour out my
    Spirit on all people.
    Your sons and daughters
      will prophesy.
Your old men will have
    dreams.
    Your young men will have
      visions.
29 In those days I will pour out
    my Spirit
on those who serve me,
    men and women alike.
30 I will show wonders in the
    heavens and on the
    earth.
    There will be blood and
      fire and clouds of smoke.
31 The sun will become dark.
    The moon will turn red
      like blood.

It will happen before the
great and terrible day of
the LORD comes.
32 Everyone who calls out to me
will be saved.
On Mount Zion and in
Jerusalem
some of my people will be
left alive.
I have chosen them.
That is what I have
promised.

The LORD Judges the Nations

3 "At that time I will bless
Judah and Jerusalem
with great success again.
2 I will gather together all the
nations.
I will bring them down
to the Valley of
Jehoshaphat.
There I will put them on trial.
I will judge them for what
they have done
to my people Israel.
They scattered them among
the nations.
They divided up my land
among themselves.
3 They cast lots for my people.
They sold boys into slavery
to get prostitutes.
They sold girls to buy some
wine to drink.

4 "Tyre and Sidon, why are you
doing things like that to me?
And why are you doing them,
all you people in Philistia? Are
you trying to get even with me
for something I have done? If
you are, I will pay you back for it
in a quick and speedy way. 5 You
took my silver and gold. You
carried off my finest treasures
to your temples. 6 You sold the
people of Judah and Jerusalem
to the Greeks. You wanted to
send them far away from their
own country.

7 "But now I will stir them up
into action. I will bring them
back from the places you sold
them to. And I will do to you
what you did to them. 8 I will sell
your sons and daughters to the
people of Judah. And they will
sell them to the Sabeans. The
Sabeans are a nation that is far
away." The LORD has spoken.

9 Announce this among the
nations.
Tell them to prepare for
battle.
Nations, get your soldiers
ready!
Bring all your fighting men
together
and march out to attack.
10 Hammer your plows into
swords.
Hammer your pruning
tools into spears.
Let anyone who is weak say,
"I am strong!"
11 Come quickly, all you
surrounding nations.
Gather together in the
Valley of Jehoshaphat.

LORD, send down your
soldiers from heaven!

12 The LORD says,

"Stir up the nations into
action!
Let them march into the
valley
where I will judge them.
I will take my seat in court.

I will judge all the
surrounding nations.
13 My soldiers, swing your blades.
The nations are ripe for
harvest.
Come and stomp on them as
if they were grapes.
Crush them until the
winepress of my anger is
full.
Do it until the wine spills over
from the places where it is
stored.
The nations have
committed far too many
sins!"

14 Huge numbers of soldiers are
gathered in the valley
where the LORD will hand
down his sentence.
The day of the LORD is near
in that valley.
15 The sun and moon will
become dark.
The stars won't shine
anymore.
16 The LORD will roar like a lion
from Jerusalem.
His voice will sound like
thunder from Zion.
The earth and the heavens
will tremble.
But the LORD will keep the
people of Israel safe.
He will be a place of safety
for them.

The LORD Blesses His People

17 The LORD says,

"You will know that I am the
LORD your God.

I live in Zion.
It is my holy mountain.
Jerusalem will be my holy
city.
People from other lands
will never again attack it.
18 "At that time fresh wine
will drip from the
mountains.
Milk will flow down from
the hills.
Water will run through all
Judah's valleys.
A fountain will flow out of my
temple.
It will water the places
where acacia trees
grow.
19 But Egypt will be deserted.
Edom will become a dry
and empty desert.
They did terrible harm to the
people of Judah.
My people were not guilty
of doing anything
wrong.
But Egypt and Edom
spilled their blood
anyway.
20 My people will live in
Judah and Jerusalem
forever.
The land will be their
home for all time to
come.
21 Egypt and Edom have spilled
my people's blood.
Should I let them escape
my judgment?
No, I will not."

The LORD lives in Zion!

Amos

Introduction:

Amos was a man who took care of sheep, but God made him a prophet. He spoke to people in the northern kingdom of Israel. Israel was very rich at this time, but no one would help the poor. Amos said this was wrong.

The people Amos spoke to wanted more and more money. They were mean and selfish. They worshiped false gods. All these things made God angry. Amos told the people to turn back to God. He wanted them to be kind to each other and to help the poor. He wanted them to tell the truth and do what is right.

Outline of contents:

1 These are the words of Amos. He was a shepherd from the town of Tekoa. Here is the vision he saw concerning Israel. It came to him two years before the earthquake. At that time Uzziah was king of Judah. Jeroboam, the son of Jehoash, was king of Israel. Here are the words of Amos.

² He said,

"The LORD roars like a lion
    from Jerusalem.
  His voice sounds like
      thunder from Zion.
The grasslands of the
    shepherds turn
    brown.
  The top of Mount Carmel
      dries up."

The LORD Judges Israel's Neighbors

³ The LORD says,

"The people of Damascus
    have sinned again and
    again.
  So I will judge them.
They used threshing sleds
    with iron teeth
  to crush Gilead's people.
⁴ So I will send fire to destroy
    the palace of King Hazael.
  It will burn up the forts of
    his son Ben-Hadad.
⁵ I will break down the city
    gate of Damascus.
  I will kill the king
    who lives in the Valley of
    Aven, that evil place.
He holds the ruler's scepter
    in Beth Eden.

The people of Aram will
  be taken away to Kir as
  prisoners,"
            says the Lord.

⁶ The Lord says,

"The people of Gaza have
  sinned again and again.
  So I will judge them.
They captured whole
  communities.
  They sold them to Edom.
⁷ So I will send fire to destroy
  the walls of Gaza.
  It will burn up its forts.
⁸ I will kill the king of Ashdod.
  He holds the ruler's scepter
  in Ashkelon.
I will use my power against
  Ekron.
  Every single Philistine will
  die,"
            says the Lord and King.

⁹ The Lord says,

"The people of Tyre have
  sinned again and again.
  So I will judge them.
They captured whole
  communities.
  They sold them to Edom.
They did not honor the treaty
  of friendship they had made.
¹⁰ So I will send fire to destroy
  the walls of Tyre.
  It will burn up its forts."

¹¹ The Lord says,

"The people of Edom have
  sinned again and again.
  So I will judge them.
They chased Israel with
  swords
  that were ready to strike
  them down.

They killed the women of
  the land.
They were angry all the
  time.
  Their anger was like a fire
  that blazed out.
  It could not be stopped.
¹² So I will send fire to destroy
  the city of Teman.
  It will burn up Bozrah's
  forts."

¹³ The Lord says,

"The people of Ammon have
  sinned again and again.
  So I will judge them.
They ripped open the
  pregnant women in
  Gilead.
  They wanted to add land to
  their territory.
¹⁴ So I will set fire to destroy the
  walls of Rabbah.
  It will burn up its forts.
War cries will be heard on
  that day of battle.
  Strong winds will blow on
  that stormy day.
¹⁵ Ammon's king will be carried
  away.
  So will his officials,"
            says the Lord.

2 The Lord says,

"The people of Moab have
  sinned again and again.
  So I will judge them.
They burned the bones
  of Edom's king to ashes.
² So I will send fire to destroy
  Moab.
  It will burn up Kerioth's
  forts.
Moab will come crashing
  down with a loud noise.

War cries will be heard.
So will the blast of
trumpets.
³ I will kill Moab's ruler.
I will also kill all its
officials,"
says the LORD.

⁴ The LORD says,

"The people of Judah have
sinned again and again.
So I will judge them.
They have refused to obey
my law.
They have not kept my
rules.
Other gods have led them
astray.
Their people of long ago
worshiped those gods.
⁵ So I will send fire to destroy
Judah.
It will burn up Jerusalem's
forts."

The LORD Judges Israel

⁶ The LORD says,

"The people of Israel have
sinned again and again.
So I will judge them.
They sell into slavery those
who have done no
wrong.
They trade needy people
for a mere pair of sandals.
⁷ They grind the heads of the
poor
into the dust of the
ground.
They refuse to be fair to
those who are crushed.
A father and his son have sex
with the same girl.
They treat my name as if it
were not holy.

⁸ They lie down beside every
altar on clothes they
have taken.
They lie on those clothes
until the owner pays back
what is owed.
In the house of their God
they drink wine that was
paid as fines.

⁹ "Yet I destroyed the Amorites
to make room in the land
for my people.
The Amorites were as tall as
cedar trees.
They were as strong as oak
trees.
But I cut off their fruit above
the ground
and their roots below it.

¹⁰ "People of Israel, I brought
you up out of Egypt.
I led you in the desert for
40 years.
I gave you the land of the
Amorites.
¹¹ I raised up prophets from
among your children.
I also set apart for myself
some of your young
people to be Nazirites.
Isn't that true, people of
Israel?"
announces the LORD.
¹² "But you made the Nazirites
drink wine.
You commanded the
prophets not to
prophesy.

¹³ "A cart that is loaded with
grain
crushes anything it runs
over.
In the same way, I will
crush you.

¹⁴ Your fastest runners will not
     escape.
     The strongest people will
       not get away.
     Even soldiers will not be able
       to save their own lives.
¹⁵ Men who are armed with
       bows will lose the battle.
     Soldiers who are quick on
       their feet will not escape.
     Horsemen will not be able
       to save their own lives.
¹⁶ Even your bravest soldiers
       will run away naked on
       that day,"
          announces the LORD.

The LORD Calls for Witnesses Against Israel

3 People of Israel, listen to the LORD's message. He has spoken his message against you. He has spoken it against the whole family he brought up out of Egypt. He says,

² "Out of all the families on
     earth
     I have chosen only you.
     So I will punish you
       because you have
       committed so many
       sins."

³ Do two people walk together
     unless they've agreed to do
     so?
⁴ Does a lion roar in the bushes
     when it doesn't have any
     food?
     Does it growl in its den
       when it hasn't caught
       anything?
⁵ Does a bird fly down to a trap
     on the ground
     when no bait is there?

Does a net spring up from the
     ground
     when it has not caught
     anything?
⁶ When someone blows a
     trumpet in a city,
     don't the people tremble
       with fear?
     When trouble comes to a city,
     hasn't the LORD caused it?

⁷ The LORD and King never
     does anything
     without telling his servants
       the prophets about it.

⁸ A lion has roared.
     Who isn't afraid?
     The LORD and King has
       spoken.
     Who can do anything but
       prophesy?

⁹ Speak to the people in the
     forts of Ashdod and
     Egypt.
     Tell them, "Gather together
       on the mountains of
       Samaria.
     Look at the great trouble in
       that city.
     Its people are committing
       many crimes."

¹⁰ "They do not know how to do
       what is right,"
     announces the LORD.
     "They store up stolen
       goods in their forts."

¹¹ So the LORD and King says,

"Enemies will take over your
     land.
     They will pull down your
       places of safety.
     They will rob your forts."

¹² The LORD says,

"Suppose a shepherd saves
only two leg bones
from a lion's mouth.
Or he might save only a piece
of an ear.
That is how the Israelites
living in Samaria will be
saved.
They will only have a board
from a bed
and a piece of cloth
from a couch."

13 "Listen to me," announces
the Lord. "Be a witness against
the people of Jacob," says the
LORD God who rules over all.

14 "I will punish Israel for their
sins.
When I do, I will destroy
their altars at Bethel.
The horns that stick out from
the upper corners
of their main altar will be
cut off.
They will fall to the
ground.
15 I will tear down their winter
houses.
I will also pull down their
summer houses.
The houses they have
decorated with ivory will
be destroyed.
And their princely houses
will be torn down,"
announces the LORD.

Israel Has Not Returned
to the LORD

4 Listen to the LORD's
message,
you women who live on the
hill of Samaria.
You treat poor people badly.

You crush those who are in
need.
You say to your husbands,
"Bring us some drinks!"
But you are already as fat
as the cows in Bashan.
2 The LORD and King has made
a promise
by his own holy name.
He says, "You can be sure
that the time will come
when your enemies will put
hooks in your faces.
They will lead every
one of you away with
fishhooks.
3 Each of you will go straight
out
through gaps made in the
wall.
You will be thrown out
toward Harmon,"
announces the LORD.
4 "People of Samaria, go to
Bethel and sin!
Go to Gilgal! Sin there even
more!
Bring your sacrifices every
morning.
Every third year, bring a
tenth
of everything you produce.
5 Bake some bread with
yeast.
Burn it as a thank offering.
Brag about the offerings you
freely give.
This is what you Israelites
love to do,"
announces the LORD and King.

6 "I made sure your stomachs
were empty in every city.
You did not have enough
bread in any of your
towns.

In spite of that, you still
have not returned to me,"
announces the LORD.

7 "I also held back rain from
you.
The time to harvest crops
was still three months
away.
I sent rain on one town.
But I held it back from
another.
One field had rain.
But another had no rain
and dried up.
8 People wandered from town
to town to look for water.
But they did not get enough
to drink.
In spite of that, you still
have not returned to
me,"
announces the LORD.

9 "Many times I kept your
gardens and vineyards
from growing.
I sent hot winds to dry
them up completely.
Locusts ate up your fig and
olive trees.
In spite of that, you still
have not returned to
me,"
announces the LORD.

10 "I sent plagues on you,
just as I did on Egypt.
I killed your young men by
swords.
I also let the horses you
had captured be killed.
I filled your noses with the
stink of your camps.
In spite of that, you still
have not returned to me,"
announces the LORD.

11 "I destroyed some of you,
just as I did Sodom and
Gomorrah.
You were like a burning stick
that was pulled out of
the fire.
In spite of that, you still
have not returned to me,"
announces the LORD.

12 "So, people of Israel, I will
judge you.
Because I will do that to
you, Israel,
prepare to meet your God!"

13 The LORD forms the
mountains.
He creates the wind.
He makes his thoughts
known to human beings.
He turns sunrise into
darkness.
He rules over even the
highest places on earth.
His name is the LORD God
Who Rules Over All.

Mourn and Turn Back
to the LORD

5 People of Israel, listen to the
LORD's message. Hear my
song of sadness about you. I say,

2 "The people of Israel have
fallen.
They will never get up again.
They are deserted in their
own land.
No one can lift them up."

3 Here is what the LORD and
King says to Israel.

"A thousand soldiers will
march out from a city.
But only a hundred will
return.

A hundred soldiers will
    march out from a town.
But only ten will come
    back."

⁴The Lord speaks to the people of Israel. He says,

"Look to me and live.
⁵   Do not look to Bethel.
Do not go to Gilgal.
    Do not travel to Beersheba.
The people of Gilgal will be
    taken away as prisoners.
    Nothing will be left of
    Bethel."

⁶Israel, look to the Lord and
    live.
    If you don't, he will sweep
    through
    the tribes of Joseph like a
    fire.
It will burn everything up.
And Bethel won't have
    anyone to put it out.

⁷There are people among
    you who turn what is
    fair into something
    bitter.
    They throw down to the
    ground what is right.
⁸The Lord made the Pleiades
    and Orion.
    He turns midnight into
    sunrise.
    He makes the day fade into
    night.
He sends for the waters in the
    clouds.
    Then he pours them out on
    the surface of the land.
    His name is the Lord.
⁹With a flash of light he
    destroys places of safety.
    He tears down cities

that have high walls
    around them.
¹⁰There are people among
    you who hate anyone
    who stands for justice in
    court.
    They hate those who tell
    the truth.

¹¹You make poor people pay
    tax on their straw.
    You also tax their grain.
So, even though you have
    built stone houses,
    you won't live in them.
You have planted fruitful
    vineyards.
    But you won't drink the
    wine they produce.
¹²I know how many crimes you
    have committed.
    You have sinned far too
    much.

Among you are people who
    crush those who have
    done no wrong.
    They accept money from
    people who want special
    favors.
    They take away the rights
    of poor people in the
    courts.
¹³So those who are wise
    keep quiet in times
    like these.
    That's because the times
    are evil.

¹⁴Look to what is good, not to
    what is evil.
    Then you will live.
And the Lord God who rules
    over all
    will be with you,
    just as you say he is.
¹⁵Hate evil and love good.

Do what is fair in the
 courts.
Perhaps the LORD God who
 rules over all
will have mercy on you.
After all, you are the only
 ones left
in the family line of Joseph.

¹⁶ The LORD God rules over
all. The Lord says,
"People will weep in all the
 streets.
They will be very sad in
 every market place.
Even farmers will be told to
 cry loudly.
People will mourn for the
 dead.
¹⁷ Workers will cry in all the
 vineyards.
That's because I will
 punish you,"
   says the LORD.

The Day of the LORD Is Coming

¹⁸ How terrible it will be for you
 who long for the day of the
 LORD!
Why do you want it to come?
That day will be dark, not
 light.
¹⁹ It will be like a man running
 away from a lion
only to meet a bear.
He enters his house and rests
 his hand on a wall
only to be bitten by a
 snake.
²⁰ The day of the LORD will be
 dark, not light.
It will be very black.
There won't be a ray of
 sunlight anywhere.

²¹ The LORD says,

"I hate your holy feasts.
I can't stand them.
Your gatherings stink.
²² You bring me burnt offerings
 and grain offerings.
But I will not accept them.
You bring your best
 friendship offerings.
But I will not even look at
 them.
²³ Take the noise of your songs
 away!
I will not listen to the
 music of your harps.
²⁴ I want you to treat others
 fairly.
So let fair treatment roll on
 just as a river does!
Always do what is right.
Let right living flow along
 like a stream that never
 runs dry!

²⁵ "People of Israel, did you
 bring me sacrifices and
 offerings
for 40 years in the desert?
²⁶ Yes. But you have honored
 the place
where your king worshiped
 other gods.
You have carried the stands
 the statues of your gods
 were on.
You have lifted up the
 banners
of the stars you worship as
 gods.
You made all those things
 for yourselves.
²⁷ So I will send you away
 as prisoners beyond
 Damascus,"
says the LORD.
 His name is God Who
 Rules Over All.

How Terrible for Those Who Feel Secure When They Shouldn't

6 How terrible it will be for
you men
who are so contented on
Mount Zion!
How terrible for you who feel
secure
on the hill of Samaria!
You are famous men from the
greatest nation.
The people of Israel come
to you
for help and advice.
² Go and look at the city of
Kalneh.
Go from there to the great
city of Hamath.
Then go down to Gath in
Philistia.
Are those places better
off than your two
kingdoms?
Is their land larger than
yours?
³ You are trying to avoid the
time
when trouble will come.
But you are only bringing
closer
the Assyrian rule of
terror.
⁴ You lie down on beds
that are decorated with
ivory.
You rest on your couches.
You eat the best lambs
and the fattest calves.
⁵ You pluck away on your
harps as David did.
You play new songs on
musical instruments.
⁶ You drink wine by the
bowlful.
You use the finest lotions.

But Joseph's people will soon
be destroyed.
And you aren't even sad
about it.
⁷ So you will be among the
first
to be taken away as
prisoners.
You won't be able to enjoy
good food.
You won't lie around on
couches anymore.

The LORD Hates the Pride of Israel

⁸ The LORD and King has made a promise in his own name. He is the LORD God who rules over all. He announces,

"I hate the pride of Jacob's
people.
I can't stand their forts.
I will hand the city of
Samaria
and everything in it over to
their enemies."

⁹ Ten people might be left in one house. If they are, they will die there. ¹⁰ Relatives might come to burn the dead bodies. If they do, they'll have to carry them out of the house first. They might ask someone still hiding there, "Is anyone else here with you?" If the answer is no, the relatives will go on to say, "Be quiet! We must not pray in the LORD's name."

¹¹ That's because the LORD has
already given an order.
He will smash large houses
to pieces.
He will crush small houses
to bits.

¹² Horses don't run on rocky
      ground.
   People don't plow the sea
      with oxen.
   But you have turned fair
      treatment into poison.
   You have turned the
      fruit of right living into
      bitterness.
¹³ You are happy because you
      captured the town of Lo
      Debar.
   You say, "We were strong
      enough to take Karnaim
      too."
¹⁴ But the LORD God rules
      over all. He announces,
   "People of Israel,
   I will stir up a nation
      against you.
   They will crush you from
      Lebo Hamath
   all the way down to the
      Arabah Valley."

Amos Has Visions of Locusts, Fire and a Plumb Line

7 The LORD and King gave
      me a vision. He was bring-
ing large numbers of locusts on
the land. The king's share had
already been harvested. Now
the later crops were coming up.
² The locusts stripped the land
clean. Then I cried out, "LORD
and King, forgive Israel! How
can Jacob's people continue?
They are such a weak nation!"
³ So the LORD had pity on
them.
   "I will let them continue for
now," he said.
   ⁴ The LORD and King gave me a
second vision. He was using fire
to punish his people. It dried up

the deep waters. It burned the
land up. ⁵ Then I cried out, "LORD
and King, please stop! How can
Jacob's people continue? They
are such a weak nation!"
   ⁶ So the LORD had pity on them.
   "I will let them continue for
now," the LORD and King said.
   ⁷ Then the Lord gave me a
third vision. He was standing by a wall. It had been built
very straight, all the way up and
down. He was holding a plumb
line. ⁸ The LORD asked me,
"What do you see, Amos?"
   "A plumb line," I replied.
   Then the Lord said, "Look at
what I am doing. I am hanging
a plumb line next to my people
Israel. It will show how crooked
they are. I will no longer spare
them.

⁹ "The high places where
      Isaac's people worship
      other gods will be
      destroyed.
   The other places of
      worship in Israel will
      also be torn down.
   I will use my sword to attack
      Jeroboam's royal family."

Amaziah Tells Amos to Stop Prophesying

¹⁰ Amaziah was priest of
Bethel. He sent a message to
Jeroboam, the king of Israel. He
said, "Amos is making evil plans
against you right here in Israel.
The people in the land can't
stand to listen to what he's saying. ¹¹ Amos is telling them,

   " 'Jeroboam will be killed by a
      sword.

The people of Israel will
be taken away as
prisoners.
They will be carried off
from their own land.'"

¹² Then Amaziah said to
Amos, "Get out of Israel, you
prophet! Go back to the land of
Judah. Earn your living there.
Do your prophesying there.
¹³ Don't prophesy here at Bethel
anymore. This is where the king
worships. The main temple in
the kingdom is located here."

¹⁴ Amos answered Amaziah,
"I was not a prophet. I wasn't
even the son of a prophet. I was
a shepherd. I also took care of
sycamore-fig trees. ¹⁵ But the
LORD took me away from taking care of the flock. He said to
me, 'Go. Prophesy to my people
Israel.' ¹⁶ Now then, listen to the
LORD's message. You say,

"'Don't prophesy against
Israel.
Stop preaching against the
people of Isaac.'

¹⁷ "But the LORD says,

"'Your wife will become a
prostitute
in the city of Bethel.
Your sons and daughters
will be killed by swords.
Your land will be measured
and divided up.
And you yourself will die in
another country.
The people of Israel will
surely be taken away as
prisoners.
They will be carried off
from their own land.'"

Amos Has a Vision of a Basket of Ripe Fruit

8 The LORD and King gave me
a vision. He showed me a
basket of ripe fruit. ² "What do
you see, Amos?" he asked.

"A basket of ripe fruit," I replied.

Then the LORD said to me,
"The time is ripe for my people Israel. I will no longer spare them.

³ "The time is coming when
the songs in the temple will turn
to weeping,'" announces the
LORD and King. "Many, many
bodies will be thrown everywhere! So be quiet!"

⁴ Listen to me, you who walk
all over needy people.
You crush those who are
poor in the land.

⁵ You say,

"When will the New Moon
feast be over?
Then we can sell our grain.
When will the Sabbath day
come to an end?
Then people can buy our
wheat."
But you measure out less
than the right amount.
You raise your prices.
You cheat others by using
dishonest scales.
⁶ You buy poor people to make
slaves out of them.
You buy those who are in
need for a mere pair of
sandals.
You even sell the worthless
parts of your wheat.

⁷ People of Jacob, you are
proud that the LORD is your

God. But he has made a promise in his own name. He says, "I will never forget anything Israel has done.

8 "The land will tremble
    because of what will
    happen.
  Everyone who lives in it
    will mourn.
  So the whole land will rise
    like the Nile River.
  It will be stirred up.
  Then it will settle back down
    again
    like that river in Egypt."

9 The LORD and King announces,

  "At that time I will make the
    sun go down at noon.
  The earth will become dark
    in the middle of the day.
10 I will turn your holy feasts
    into times for mourning.
  I will turn all your songs
    into weeping.
  You will have to wear the
    clothing of sadness.
  You will shave your heads.
  I will make you mourn as if
    your only son had died.
  The end of that time will be
    like a bitter day."

11 The LORD and King announces,

  "The days are coming
    when I will send hunger
    through the land.
  But people will not be hungry
    for food.
  They will not be thirsty for
    water.
  Instead, they will be hungry
    to hear a message from me.

12 People will wander from
    the Dead Sea to the
    Mediterranean.
  They will travel from north
    to east.
  They will look for a message
    from me.
  But they will not find it.

13 "At that time

  "the lovely young women and
    strong young men
  will faint because they are
    so thirsty.
14 Some people make promises
    in the name of Samaria's
    god.
  That god has led them
    astray.
  Others say, 'People of Dan,
    you can be sure
    that your god is alive.'
  Still others say, 'You can be
    sure
    that Beersheba's god is
    alive.'
  But all these people will fall
    dead.
  They will never get up
    again."

Israel Will Be Destroyed

9 I saw the Lord standing next to the altar in the temple. He said to me,

  "Strike the tops of the temple
    pillars.
  Then the heavy stones at
    the base of the entrance
    will shake.
  Bring everything down on
    the heads of everyone
    there.
  I will kill with my swords
    those who are left alive.

None of the Israelites will
escape.
None will get away.
² They might dig down deep.
But my powerful hand will
take them out of there.
They might climb up to the
heavens.
But I will bring them down
from there.
³ They might hide on top of
Mount Carmel.
But I will hunt them down
and grab them.
They might hide from me at
the bottom of the
ocean.
But even there I will
command the serpent to
bite them.
⁴ Their enemies might take
them away
as prisoners to another
country.
But there I will command
Israel's enemies
to cut them down with
swords.
I will keep my eye on Israel to
harm them.
I will not help them."

⁵ The LORD rules over all.
The Lord touches the
earth, and it melts.
Everyone who lives in it
mourns.
The whole land rises like the
Nile River.
Then it settles back down
again
like that river in Egypt.
⁶ The LORD builds his palace
high in the heavens.
He lays its foundation on
the earth.

He sends for the waters in the
clouds.
Then he pours them out on
the surface of the land.
His name is the LORD.

⁷ "You Israelites are just like
the people of Cush to me,"
announces the LORD.
"I brought Israel up from
Egypt.
I also brought the
Philistines from Crete
and the Arameans from
Kir.
⁸ "I am the LORD and King.
My eyes are watching the
sinful kingdom of Israel.
I will wipe it off the face of
the earth.
But I will not totally
destroy the people of
Jacob,"
announces the LORD.
⁹ "I will give an order.
I will shake the people of
Israel
among all the nations.
They will be like grain that
is shaken through a
screen.
Not a pebble will fall to the
ground.
¹⁰ All the sinners among my
people
will be killed by swords.
They say, 'Nothing bad will
ever happen to us.'

Israel Will Be Made Like New Again

¹¹ "The time will come when I
will set up
David's fallen shelter.
I will repair its broken walls.

I will rebuild what was
destroyed.
I will make it what it used
to be.
¹² Then my people will take
control of those
who are left alive in
Edom.
They will also possess all the
nations
that belong to me,"
  announces the LORD.
He will do all these things.

¹³ "The days are coming," an-
nounces the LORD.

"At that time those who plow
the land
will catch up with those
who harvest the crops.
Those who stomp on grapes
will catch up with those
who plant the vines.

Fresh wine will drip from the
mountains.
It will flow down from all
the hills.
¹⁴ I will bring my people Israel
back home.
I will bless them with great
success again.
They will rebuild the
destroyed cities and live
in them.
They will plant vineyards
and drink the wine they
produce.
They will make gardens
and eat their fruit.
¹⁵ I will plant Israel in their own
land.
They will never again be
removed
from the land I have given
them,"
  says the LORD your God.

Obadiah

Introduction:

Obadiah spoke for God. His name means "servant of the LORD." His book is the shortest book in the Bible. Obadiah wrote about the nation of Edom. Edom was proud and strong. The people of Edom thought no one could hurt them. They laughed when other nations attacked the Israelites.

All this made God very angry. Edom should have helped the Israelites. They both came from the same family. But Edom and Israel did not get along. Edom made Israel's problems worse. God said Edom would be destroyed.

Outline of contents:

Bad things for Edom (1–14)
The day of the Lord (15–21)

Obadiah's Vision

¹This is the vision about Edom that Obadiah had.

Here is what the LORD and King says about Edom.

We've heard a message from the LORD.
A messenger was sent to the nations.
The LORD told him to say,
"Get up! Let us go and make war against Edom."

²The LORD says to Edom,

"I will make you weak among the nations.
They will look down on you.
³You live in the safety of the rocks.
You make your home high up in the mountains.
But your proud heart has tricked you.
So you say to yourself,
'No one can bring me down to the ground.'
⁴You have built your home as high as an eagle does.
You have made your nest among the stars.
But I will bring you down from there,"
announces the LORD.
⁵"Edom, suppose robbers came to you at night.
They would steal only as much as they wanted.
Suppose grape pickers came to harvest your vines.
They would still leave a few grapes.
But you are facing horrible trouble!
⁶People of Esau, everything will be taken away from you.

Your hidden treasures will
be stolen.
7 All those who are helping you
will force you to leave your
country.
Your friends will trick you
and overpower you.
Those who eat bread with
you
will set a trap for you.
But you will not see it."

8 Here is what the LORD
announces. "At that
time
I will destroy the wise men
of Edom.
I will wipe out the men of
understanding
in the mountains of Esau.
9 People of Teman, your
soldiers will be
terrified.
Everyone in Esau's
mountains
will be cut down by
swords.
10 You did harmful things to the
people of Jacob.
They are your relatives.
So you will be covered with
shame.
You will be destroyed
forever.
11 Outsiders entered the gates of
Jerusalem.
They cast lots to see what
each one would get.
Strangers carried off its
wealth.
When that happened, you
just stood there and did
nothing.
You were like one of them.
12 That was a time of trouble for
your relatives.

So you shouldn't have
been happy about what
happened to them.
The people of Judah were
destroyed.
So you should not have
been happy about it.
You should not have laughed
at them so much
when they were in trouble.
13 You should not have
marched
through the gates of my
people's city
when they were in trouble.
You shouldn't have been
happy about what
happened to them.
You should not have stolen
their wealth
when they were in trouble.
14 You waited where the roads
cross.
You wanted to cut down
those who were running
away.
You should not have done
that.
You handed over to their
enemies
those who were still left
alive.
You should not have done
that.
They were in trouble.

15 "The day of the LORD is near
for all the nations.
Others will do to you
what you have done to
them.
You will be paid back
for what you have done.
16 You Edomites made my
holy mountain of Zion
impure

by drinking and
celebrating there.
So all the nations will drink
from the cup of my anger.
And they will keep on
drinking from it.
They will vanish.
It will be as if they had
never existed.
¹⁷ But on Mount Zion some of
my people will be left
alive.
I will save them.
Zion will be my holy
mountain once again.
And the people of Jacob
will again receive the land
as their own.
¹⁸ They will be like a fire.
Joseph's people will be like
a flame.
The nation of Edom will be
like straw.
Jacob's people will set
Edom on fire and burn it
up.
No one will be left alive
among Esau's people."
The LORD has spoken.

¹⁹ Israelites from the Negev
Desert
will take over Esau's
mountains.
Israelites from the western
hills
will possess the land of the
Philistines.
They'll take over the
territories
of Ephraim and Samaria.
Israelites from the tribe of
Benjamin
will possess the land of
Gilead.
²⁰ Some Israelites were forced
to leave their homes.
They'll come back to
Canaan and possess
it all the way to the town of
Zarephath.
Some people from Jerusalem
were taken
to the city of Sepharad.
They'll return and possess
the towns of the Negev
Desert.
²¹ Leaders from Mount Zion
will go
and rule over the
mountains of Esau.
And the kingdom will
belong to the LORD.

Jonah

Introduction:

Jonah was a prophet. God told Jonah to go to Nineveh. Nineveh was an evil city. The enemies of the Jews lived there. But God wanted the people there to follow him.

Jonah did not want to go to Nineveh. He tried to run away from God, but God used a big fish to bring Jonah back. When Jonah went to Nineveh, the people there turned away from their sin. Jonah was very upset. He did not want God to forgive the people there. But God cared about the people of Nineveh. God wants even the worst people to turn to him.

Outline of contents:

Jonah Runs Away From the LORD

1 A message from the LORD came to Jonah, the son of Amittai. The LORD said, ² "Go to the great city of Nineveh. Preach against it. The sins of its people have come to my attention."

³ But Jonah ran away from the LORD. He headed for Tarshish. So he went down to the port of Joppa. There he found a ship that was going to Tarshish. He paid the fare and went on board. Then he sailed for Tarshish. He was running away from the LORD.

⁴ But the LORD sent a strong wind over the Mediterranean Sea. A wild storm came up. It was so wild that the ship was in danger of breaking apart. ⁵ All the sailors were afraid. Each one cried out to his own god for help.

They threw the ship's contents into the sea. They were trying to make the ship lighter.

But Jonah had gone below deck. There he lay down and fell into a deep sleep. ⁶ The captain went down to him and said, "How can you sleep? Get up and call out to your god for help! Maybe he'll pay attention to what's happening to us. Then we won't die."

⁷ Here is what the sailors said to one another. "Someone is to blame for getting us into all this trouble. Come. Let's cast lots to find out who it is." So they did. And Jonah was picked. ⁸ They asked him, "What terrible thing have you done to bring all this trouble on us? Tell us. What do you do for a living? Where do you come from? What is your

country? What people do you belong to?"

⁹He answered, "I'm a Hebrew. I worship the LORD. He is the God of heaven. He made the sea and the dry land."

¹⁰They found out he was running away from the LORD. That's because he had told them. Then they became terrified. So they asked him, "How could you do a thing like that?"

¹¹The sea was getting rougher and rougher. So they asked him, "What should we do to you to make the sea calm down?"

¹²"Pick me up and throw me into the sea," he replied. "Then it will become calm. I know it's my fault that this terrible storm has come on you."

¹³But the men didn't do what he said. Instead, they did their best to row back to land. But they couldn't. The sea got even rougher than before. ¹⁴Then they cried out to the LORD. They prayed, "Please, LORD, don't let us die for taking this man's life. After all, he might not be guilty of doing anything wrong. So don't hold us responsible for killing him. LORD, you always do what you want to." ¹⁵Then they took Jonah and threw him overboard. And the stormy sea became calm. ¹⁶The men saw what had happened. Then they began to have great respect for the LORD. They offered a sacrifice to him. And they made promises to him.

Jonah Prays to the LORD

¹⁷Now the LORD sent a huge fish to swallow Jonah. And Jonah was in the belly of the fish for three days and three nights.

2 ¹From inside the fish Jonah prayed to the LORD his God. ²He said,

"When I was in trouble, I
    called out to the LORD.
And he answered me.
When I was deep in the place
    of the dead,
I called out for help.
And you listened to my
    cry.
³You threw me deep into the
    Mediterranean Sea.
I was deep down in its
    waters.
They were all around me.
All your rolling waves
    were sweeping over me.
⁴I said, 'I have been driven
    away from you.
But I will look again
    toward your holy temple in
    Jerusalem.'
⁵I had almost drowned in the
    waves.
The deep waters were all
    around me.
Seaweed was wrapped
    around my head.
⁶I sank down to the bottom of
    the mountains.
I thought I had died
    and gone down into the
    grave forever.
But you are the LORD my
    God.
You brought my life up
    from the very edge of the
    pit of death.
⁷"When my life was nearly
    over,
I remembered you, LORD.

My prayer rose up to you.
It reached you in your holy
temple in heaven.

8 "Some people worship the
worthless statues of their
gods.
They turn away from God's
love for them.
9 But I will sacrifice a thank
offering to you.
And I will shout with
thankful praise.
I will do what I have
promised.
I will say, 'Lord, you are
the one who saves.'"

10 The Lord gave the fish a command. And it spit Jonah up onto dry land.

Jonah Goes to Nineveh

3 A message from the Lord came to Jonah a second time. The Lord said, 2 "Go to the great city of Nineveh. Announce to its people the message I give you."

3 Jonah obeyed the Lord. He went to Nineveh. It was a very large city. In fact, it took about three days to go through it. 4 Jonah began by going one whole day into the city. As he went, he announced, "In 40 days Nineveh will be destroyed." 5 The people of Nineveh believed God's warning. So they decided not to eat any food for a while. And all of them put on the rough clothing people wear when they're sad. That's what everyone did, from the least important of them to the most important.

6 Jonah's warning reached the king of Nineveh. He got up from his throne. He took off his royal robes. He also dressed himself in the clothing of sadness. And then he sat down in the dust. 7 Here is the message he sent out to the people of Nineveh.

"I and my nobles give this order.

Don't let people or animals taste anything. That includes your herds and flocks. People and animals must not eat or drink anything. 8 Let people and animals alike be covered with the clothing of sadness. All of you must call out to God with all your hearts. Stop doing what is evil. Don't harm others. 9 Who knows? God might take pity on us. He might not be angry with us anymore. Then we won't die."

10 God saw what they did. He saw that they stopped doing what was evil. So he took pity on them. He didn't destroy them as he had said he would.

Jonah Is Angry That the Lord Spares Nineveh

4 But to Jonah this seemed very wrong. He became angry. 2 He prayed to the Lord. Here is what Jonah said to him. "Lord, isn't this exactly what I thought would happen when I was still at home? That is what I tried to prevent by running away to Tarshish. I knew that you are gracious. You are tender

and kind. You are slow to get angry. You are full of love. You are a God who takes pity on people. You don't want to destroy them. ³ LORD, take away my life. I'd rather die than live."

⁴ But the LORD replied, "Is it right for you to be angry?"

⁵ Jonah had left the city. He had sat down at a place east of it. There he put some branches over his head. He sat in their shade. He waited to see what would happen to the city. ⁶ Then the LORD God sent a leafy plant and made it grow up over Jonah. It gave him more shade for his head. It made him more comfortable. Jonah was very happy he had the leafy plant. ⁷ But before sunrise the next day, God sent a worm. It chewed the plant so much that it dried up. ⁸ When the sun rose, God sent a burning east wind. The sun beat down on Jonah's head. It made him very weak. He wanted to die. So he said, "I'd rather die than live."

⁹ But God spoke to Jonah. God said, "Is it right for you to be angry about the plant?"

"It is," Jonah said. "In fact, I'm so angry I wish I were dead."

¹⁰ But the LORD said, "You have been concerned about this plant. But you did not take care of it. You did not make it grow. It grew up in one night and died the next. ¹¹ And shouldn't I show concern for the great city of Nineveh? It has more than 120,000 people. They can't tell right from wrong. Nineveh also has a lot of animals."

Micah

Introduction:

Micah lived in Judah. He was a man who spoke for God. Micah said God was angry with Israel and Judah. Their leaders were evil. They did not help the poor, and they did not live for God.

Micah warned that God would judge Israel and Judah. He also said that God would send good things. God promised to send a ruler. This ruler will set up God's kingdom. Hundreds of years later, Jesus Christ became that ruler!

Outline of contents:

1 A message from the LORD came to Micah. He was from the town of Moresheth. The message came while Jotham, Ahaz and Hezekiah were kings of Judah. This is the vision Micah saw concerning Samaria and Jerusalem. Here is what he said.

² Listen to me, all you nations!
    Earth and everyone who
        lives in it, pay attention!
The LORD and King will be a
    witness against you.
    The Lord will speak from
        his holy temple in
        heaven.

The LORD Will Judge Samaria and Jerusalem

³ The LORD is about to come
    down
    from his home in heaven.
    He rules over even the
        highest places on earth.

⁴ The mountains will melt
    under him
    like wax near a fire.
The valleys will be broken
    apart
    by water rushing down a
        slope.
⁵ All this will happen because
    Jacob's people have done
        what is wrong.
The people of Israel
    have committed many
        sins.
Who is to blame
    for the wrong things Jacob
        has done?
    Samaria!
Who is to blame for the high
    places
    where Judah's people
        worship other gods?
    Jerusalem!

⁶ So the LORD says,

"I will turn Samaria into a
    pile of trash.

It will become a place for
  planting vineyards.
I will dump its stones down
  into the valley.
And I will destroy it
  down to its very
  foundations.
7 All the statues of Samaria's
  gods
  will be broken to pieces.
All the gifts its people gave to
  temple prostitutes
  will be burned with fire.
I will destroy all the statues
  of its gods.
Samaria collected gifts that
  were paid to temple
  prostitutes.
So the Assyrians will use
  the gifts
to pay their own temple
  prostitutes."

Micah Weeps Over His People

8 I will weep and mourn
    because Samaria will be
    destroyed.
  I'll walk around barefoot
    and naked.
  I'll bark like a wild dog.
  I'll hoot like an owl.
9 Samaria's plague can't be
    healed.
  The plague has spread to
    Judah.
  It has spread right up to the
    gate of my people.
  It has spread to Jerusalem
    itself.
10 Don't tell the people of Gath
    about it.
  Don't let them see you
    weep.
  People in Beth Ophrah, roll
    in the dust.

11 You who live in the town of
    Shaphir,
  leave naked and in shame.
  Those who live in Zaanan
    won't come out to help you.
  The people in Beth Ezel will
    mourn.
  They won't be able to help
    keep you safe any longer.
12 Those who live in Maroth
    will groan with pain
  as they wait for help.
  That's because the LORD will
    bring trouble on them.
  It will reach the very gate of
    Jerusalem.
13 You who live in Lachish,
    get your fast horses ready
    to pull their chariots.
  You trust in military power.
  Lachish was where sin
    began
  for the people of Zion.
  The wrong things Israel did
    were also done by you.
14 People of Judah, you might as
    well say goodbye
  to Moresheth near Gath.
  The town of Akzib won't give
    any help
  to the kings of Israel.
15 An enemy will attack
    you who live in Mareshah.
  Israel's nobles will have to
    run away
  and hide in the cave of
    Adullam.
16 The children you enjoy so
    much
  will be taken away as
    prisoners.
  So shave your heads and
    mourn.
  Make them as bare as the
    head of a vulture.

People's Plans and God's Plans

2 How terrible it will be for
    those
    who plan to harm others!
How terrible for those who
    make evil plans
    before they even get out of
    bed!
As soon as daylight comes,
    they carry out their plans.
That's because they have
    the power to do it.
2 If they want fields or
    houses,
    they take them.
They cheat people out of their
    homes.
    They rob them of their
    property.

3 So the LORD says to them,

"I am planning to send
    trouble on you.
    You will not be able to save
    yourselves from it.
You will not live so proudly
    anymore.
    It will be a time of trouble.
4 At that time people will make
    fun of you.
    They will tease you
    by singing a song of
    sadness.
They will pretend to be you
    and say,
'We are totally destroyed.
    Our enemies have divided
    up our land.
The LORD has taken it away
    from us!
    He has given our fields to
    those
    who turned against us.' "

5 So you won't even have
    anyone left
in the LORD's community
    who can divide up the land
    for you.

Some Prophets Aren't Really Prophets at All

6 "Don't prophesy," the
    people's prophets say.
    "Don't prophesy about bad
    things.
Nothing shameful is going
    to happen to us."
7 People of Jacob, should
    anyone say,
"The LORD is patient,
so he wouldn't do things
    like that"?

The LORD replies, "What I
    promise brings good
    things
    to those who lead honest
    lives.
8 But lately my people have
    attacked one another
    as if they were enemies.
You strip off the rich robes
    from those who happen to
    pass by.
They thought they were as
    safe as men
    returning from a battle
    they had won.
9 You drive the women among
    my people
    out of their pleasant
    homes.
You take away my blessing
    from their children
    forever.
10 Get up! Leave this land!
    It is no longer your resting
    place.
You have made it 'unclean.'
    You have completely
    destroyed it.

11 Suppose a prophet goes
      around telling lies.
    And he prophesies that you
      will have
    plenty of wine and beer.
  Then that kind of prophet
      would be
    just right for this nation!

The LORD Promises to Save His People

12 "People of Jacob, I will gather
      all of you.
    I will bring together
      you who are still left alive
      in Israel.
    I will gather you together like
      sheep in a pen.
    You will be like a flock in
      its grasslands.
    Your country will be filled
      with people.
13 I will open the way for you to
      return.
    I will march in front of you.
    You will break through the
      city gates and go free.
    I am your King. I will pass
      through the gates
    in front of you.
    I, the LORD, will lead the
      way."

The LORD Warns Israel's Leaders and Prophets

3 Then I said,

  "Listen, you leaders of Jacob's
      people!
    Pay attention, you rulers of
      Israel!
  You should want to judge
      others fairly.
2   But you hate what is good.
    And you love what is evil.

You are like someone
    who tears the skin off my
      people.
  You pull the meat off their
      bones.
3 You eat my people's bodies.
    You strip off their skin.
    You break their bones in
      pieces.
  You chop them up like meat.
    You put them in a cooking
      pot."

4 The time will come when
      Israel
    will cry out to the LORD.
    But he won't answer them.
  In fact, he'll turn his face
      away from them.
    They have done what is
      evil.

5 The LORD says,

  "The prophets are those
    who lead my people astray.
  If my people feed them,
    the prophets promise them
      peace.
  If my people do not feed
      them,
    the prophets prepare to go
      to war against them.
6 So night will come on the
      prophets.
    But they will not have any
      visions.
  Darkness will cover them.
    But they will not be able
    to figure out what is going
      to happen.
  The sun will set on the
      prophets.
    The day will become dark
      for them.
7 Those who see visions will be
    put to shame.

Those who try to figure out
what is going to happen
will be dishonored.
All of them will cover their
faces.
I will not answer them."

8 The Spirit of the LORD
has filled me with power.
He helps me do what is fair.
He makes me brave.
Now I'm prepared to tell
Jacob's people
what they've done wrong.
I'm ready to tell Israel
they've sinned.
9 Listen to me, you leaders of
Jacob's people!
Pay attention, you rulers of
Israel!
You hate to do what is fair.
You twist everything that is
right.
10 You build up Zion by spilling
the blood of others.
You build Jerusalem by
doing what is evil.
11 Your judges take money from
people
who want special favors.
Your priests teach only if
they get paid for it.
Your prophets won't tell
fortunes
unless they receive
money.
But you still look for the
LORD's help.
You say, "The LORD is with
us.
No trouble will come on
us."
12 So because of what you have
done,
Zion will be plowed up like
a field.

Jerusalem will be turned into
a pile of trash.
The temple hill will be
covered with bushes and
weeds.

*People From Many Nations Will
Worship at the LORD's Mountain*

4 In the last days

the mountain where the
LORD's temple is located
will be famous.
It will be the highest
mountain of all.
It will be lifted up above the
hills.
And nations will go to it.

2 People from many nations
will go there. They will say,

"Come, let us go up to the
LORD's mountain.
Let's go to the temple of
Jacob's God.
He will teach us how we
should live.
Then we will live the way
he wants us to."
The law of the LORD will be
taught at Zion.
His message will go out
from Jerusalem.
3 He will judge between people
from many nations.
He'll settle problems
among strong nations
everywhere.
They will hammer their
swords into plows.
They'll hammer their
spears into pruning
tools.
Nations will not go to war
against one another.

They won't even train to
fight anymore.
⁴ Everyone will have
their own vine and fig tree.
And no one will make them
afraid.
That's what the LORD
who rules over all has
promised.
⁵ Other nations worship and
trust in their gods.
But we will worship and
obey the LORD.
He will be our God for ever
and ever.

The LORD's Plan

⁶ "The time is coming
when I will gather those
who are disabled,"
announces the LORD.
"I will bring together those
who were taken away as
prisoners.
I will gather those I have
allowed to suffer.
⁷ I will make the disabled my
faithful people.
I will make into a strong
nation those driven away
from their homes.
I will rule over them on
Mount Zion.
I will be their King from
that time on and
forever.
⁸ Jerusalem, you used to be
like a guard tower for my
flock.
City of Zion, you used to be
a place of safety for my
people.
The glorious kingdom you
had before
will be given back to you.

Once again a king will rule
over your people."
⁹ Why are you crying out so
loudly now?
Don't you have a king?
Has your ruler died?
Is that why pain comes on
you
like the pain of a woman
having a baby?
¹⁰ People of Zion, groan with
pain.
Cry out like a woman
having a baby.
Soon you must leave your
city.
You must camp in the open
fields.
You will have to go to the
land of Babylon.
But that's where the LORD
will save you.
There he will set you free
from the power of your
enemies.
¹¹ But now many nations
have gathered together to
attack you.
They say, "Let Jerusalem be
made 'unclean.'
We want to laugh when
Zion suffers!"
¹² But those nations don't
know
what the LORD has in
mind.
They don't understand his
plan.
He has planned to gather
them up like bundles of
grain.
He has planned to take
them to his threshing
floor.

13 The LORD says,

"People of Zion, get up
    and crush your enemies.
I will make you like a
    threshing ox.
I will give you iron horns and
    bronze hooves.
So you will crush many
    nations."

They got their money in the
    wrong way.
    But you will set it apart to
    the LORD.
You will give their wealth
    to the Lord of the whole
    earth.

A Promised Ruler Will Come From Bethlehem

5 Jerusalem, you are being
    attacked.
    So bring your troops
    together.
Our enemies have
    surrounded us.
    They want to slap the face
    of Israel's ruler.

2 The LORD says,

"Bethlehem Ephrathah, you
    might not be
an important town in the
    nation of Judah.
But out of you will come for
    me
    a ruler over Israel.
His family line goes back
    to the early years of your
    nation.
It goes all the way back
    to days of long ago."

3 The LORD will hand over
    his people to their
    enemies.

That will last until the
    pregnant woman bears
    her promised son.
Then the rest of his relatives
    in Judah
    will return to their land.

4 That promised son will stand
    firm
    and be a shepherd for his
    flock.
The LORD will give him the
    strength to do it.
The LORD his God will give
    him
    the authority to rule.
His people will live safely.
    His greatness will reach
    from one end of the earth
    to the other.

5 And he will be our peace
    when the Assyrians attack
    our land.
    They will march through
    our forts.
But we will raise up against
    them many shepherds.
    We'll send out against them
    as many commanders as
    we need to.

6 They will use their swords to
    rule over Assyria.
    They'll rule the land of
    Nimrod
    with swords that are ready
    to strike.
The Assyrians will march
    across our borders
    and attack our land.
    But the promised ruler will
    save us from them.

7 Jacob's people who are still
    left alive
    will be scattered among
    many nations.

They will be like dew the
LORD has sent.
Dew doesn't depend on
any human being.
They will be like rain that
falls on the grass.
Rain doesn't wait for
someone to give it
orders.
8 So Jacob's people will be
scattered
among many nations.
They will be like a lion
among the animals in the
forest.
They'll be like a young lion
among flocks of sheep.
Lions attack and tear apart
their prey as they move
along.
No one can keep them
from killing what they
want.
9 LORD, your power will win
the battle
over your enemies.
All of them will be
destroyed.

10 "At that time I will destroy
your war horses,"
announces the LORD.
"I will smash your
chariots.
11 I will destroy the cities in
your land.
I will tear down all your
forts.
12 I will destroy your worship of
evil powers.
You will no longer be able
to put a spell on anyone.
13 I will destroy the statues of
your gods.
I will take your sacred
stones away from you.

You will no longer bow down
to the gods your hands
have made.
14 I will pull down the poles you
used
to worship the female god
named Asherah.
That will happen when I
completely destroy your
cities.
15 I will pay back the nations
that have not obeyed me.
I will direct my anger
against them."

*The LORD Brings Charges
Against Israel*

6 Israel, listen to the LORD's
message. He says to me,

"Stand up in court.
Let the mountains serve as
witnesses.
Let the hills hear what you
have to say."

2 Hear the LORD's case, you
mountains.
Listen, you age-old
foundations of the earth.
The LORD has a case against
his people Israel.
He is bringing charges
against them.

3 The LORD says,

"My people, what have I done
to you?
Have I made things too
hard for you? Answer
me.
4 I brought your people up out
of Egypt.
I set them free from the
land
where they were slaves.

I sent Moses to lead them.
  Aaron and Miriam helped
    him.
⁵ Remember how Balak, the
    king of Moab,
  planned to put a curse on
    your people.
But Balaam, the son of
    Beor,
  gave them a blessing
    instead.
Remember their journey
  from Shittim to Gilgal.
  I want you to know
  that I always do what is
    right."

⁶ The people of Israel say,

"What should we bring with
    us
  when we go to worship the
    LORD?
What should we offer the
    God of heaven
  when we bow down to
    him?
Should we take burnt
    offerings to him?
  Should we sacrifice calves
    that are a year old?
⁷ Will the LORD be pleased
    with thousands of
    rams?
  Will he take delight in
    10,000 rivers of olive
    oil?
Should we offer our oldest
    sons
  for the wrong things we've
    done?
Should we sacrifice our own
    children
  to pay for our sins?"

⁸ The LORD has shown you
    what is good.

He has told you what he
    requires of you.
You must act with justice.
  You must love to show
    mercy.
And you must be humble as
  you live in the sight of
    your God.

The LORD Will Punish His Guilty People

⁹ The LORD is calling out to
    Jerusalem.
  And it would be wise to pay
    attention to him.
He says, "Listen, tribe of
    Judah
  and you people who are
    gathered in the city.
¹⁰ You sinful people, should I
    forget
  that you got your treasures
    by stealing them?
You use dishonest measures
    to cheat others.
  I have placed a curse on
    that practice.
¹¹ Should I forgive anyone who
    uses dishonest scales?
  They use weights that
    weigh things heavier
  or lighter than they really
    are.
¹² The rich people among you
    harm others.
  You are always telling
    lies.
  You try to fool others by
    what you say.
¹³ So I have begun to strike you
    down.
  I have begun to destroy
    you
  because you have sinned
    so much.

¹⁴ You will eat. But you will not
be satisfied.
Your stomachs will still be
empty.
You will try to save what you
can.
But you will not be able to.
If you do save something,
it will be destroyed in
battle.
¹⁵ You will plant seeds.
But you will not harvest
any crops.
You will press olives.
But you will not use the
oil.
You will crush grapes.
But you will not drink the
wine
that is made from them.
¹⁶ You have followed the evil
practices
of King Omri of Israel.
You have done what the
family
of King Ahab did.
You have followed their bad
example.
So I will let you be
destroyed.
Others will make fun of
you.
The nations will laugh at
you."

Israel's Sin Brings Suffering

7 I'm suffering very much!
I'm like someone who
gathers summer fruit in
a vineyard
after the good fruit has
already been picked.
No grapes are left to eat.
None of the early figs I long
for remain.

² Faithful people have
disappeared from the
land.
Those who are honest are
gone.
Everyone hides and waits
to spill the blood of others.
They use nets to try and
trap one another.
³ They are very good at doing
what is evil.
Rulers require gifts.
Judges accept money from
people
who want special favors.
Those who are powerful
always get what they
want.
All of them make evil plans
together.
⁴ The best of these people are
as harmful as thorns.
The most honest of them
are even worse.
God has come to punish
you.
The time your prophets
warned you about has
come.
Panic has taken hold of
you.
⁵ Don't trust your neighbors.
Don't put your faith in your
friends.
Be careful what you say
even to your own wife.
⁶ Sons don't honor their
fathers.
Daughters refuse to obey
their mothers.
Daughters-in-law are against
their mothers-in-law.
A man's enemies are the
members of his own
family.

7 But I will look to the LORD.
   I'll put my trust in God my
     Savior.
   He will hear me.

Jerusalem Will Be Rebuilt

8 The people of Jerusalem say,

"Don't laugh when we suffer,
   you enemies of ours!
We have fallen.
   But we'll get up.
Even though we sit in the dark,
   the LORD will give us light.
9 We've sinned against the
     LORD.
   So he is angry with us.
His anger will continue until
   he takes up our case.
   Then he'll do what is right
     for us.
He'll bring us out into the
   light.
   Then we'll see him save us.
10 Our enemies will see it too.
   And they will be put to
     shame.
After all, they said to us,
   'Where is the LORD your
     God?'
But we will see them
   destroyed.
   Soon they will be stomped
     on
   like mud in the streets."

11 People of Jerusalem, the time
     will come
   when your walls will be
     rebuilt.
   Land will be added to your
     territory.
12 At that time your people will
     come back to you.
   They'll return from Assyria
     and the cities of Egypt.

They'll come from the
   countries
   between Egypt and the
     Euphrates River.
They'll return from the lands
   between the seas.
They'll come back from the
   countries
   between the mountains.
13 But the rest of the earth will
   be deserted.
   The people who live in it
   have done many evil
     things.

Prayer and Praise

14 LORD, be like a shepherd to
     your people.
   Take good care of them.
They are your flock.
   They live by themselves
   in the safety of a forest.
Rich grasslands are all
   around them.
   Let them eat grass in
     Bashan and Gilead
   just as they did long ago.

15 The LORD says to his people,

"I showed you my wonders
   when you came out of
     Egypt long ago.
   In the same way, I will
   show them to you again."

16 When the nations see those
     wonders,
   they will be put to shame.
All their power will be
   taken away from them.
They will be so amazed
   that they won't be able to
     speak or hear.
17 They'll be forced to eat dust
   like a snake.
   They'll be like creatures

that have to crawl on the
ground.
They'll come out of their
dens
trembling with fear.
They'll show respect for the
LORD our God.
They will also have respect
for his people.
¹⁸LORD, who is a God like you?
You forgive sin.
You forgive your people
when they do what is wrong.
You don't stay angry forever.
Instead, you take delight in
showing
your faithful love to them.

¹⁹Once again you will show
loving concern for us.
You will completely wipe
out
the evil things we've
done.
You will throw all our sins
into the bottom of the sea.
²⁰You will be faithful to Jacob's
people.
You will show your love
to Abraham's children.
You will do what you
promised to do for our
people.
You made that promise
long ago.

Nahum

Introduction:

Nahum wrote about Nineveh. It was a big city and the capital of the Assyrian empire. Jonah went there once. He had told the people to turn to God, and they did. But they soon turned back to sin. Nahum told the people of Nineveh that God was going to punish them. God promised to send another country to attack Nineveh. Nahum reminds us that God rules over all the nations.

Outline of contents:

1 Here is a prophecy the LORD gave Nahum, who was from the town of Elkosh. The prophecy came in a vision and is written in a book. The prophecy is about Nineveh.

The LORD Is Angry With Nineveh

2 The LORD is a jealous God
    who punishes people.
He pays them back for the
    evil things they do.
He directs his anger
    against them.
The LORD punishes his
    enemies.
He holds his anger back
    until the right time to
    use it.
3 The LORD is slow to get angry.
    But he is very powerful.
The LORD will not let guilty
    people go
without punishing them.
When he marches out, he stirs
    up winds and storms.
Clouds are the dust kicked
    up by his feet.

4 He controls the seas. He dries
    them up.
He makes all the rivers run
    dry.
Bashan and Mount Carmel
    dry up.
The flowers in Lebanon
    fade.
5 He causes the mountains to
    shake.
The hills melt away.
The earth trembles because
    he is there.
The world and all those who
    live in it also tremble.
6 Who can stand firm when his
    anger burns?
Who can live when he is
    angry?
His anger blazes out like fire.
He smashes the rocks to
    pieces.

7 The LORD is good.
When people are in
    trouble,
they can go to him for
    safety.

He takes good care of those
who trust in him.
[8] But he will destroy Nineveh
with a powerful flood.
He will chase his enemies
into the place of darkness.
[9] The LORD will put an end
to anything they plan
against him.
He won't allow Assyria to win
the battle
over his people a second
time.
[10] His enemies will be tangled
up among thorns.
Their wine will make them
drunk.
They'll be burned up like
dry straw.
[11] Nineveh, a king has marched
out from you.
He makes evil plans
against the LORD.
He thinks about how he
can do what is wrong.
[12] The LORD says,

"His army has many soldiers.
Other nations are helping
them.
But they will be destroyed
and pass away.
Judah, I punished you.
But I will not do it
anymore.
[13] Now I will break Assyria's
yoke off your neck.
I will tear off the ropes that
hold you."

[14] Nineveh, the LORD has given
an order concerning you.
He has said, "You will not
have any children
to carry on your name.

I will destroy the wooden and
metal statues
that are in the temple of
your gods.
I will get your grave ready for
you.
You are worthless."

[15] Look at the mountains of
Judah!
I see a messenger running
to bring good news!
He's telling us that peace
has come!
People of Judah, celebrate
your feasts.
Carry out your promises.
The evil Assyrians won't
attack you again.
They'll be completely
destroyed.

The LORD Will Destroy Nineveh

2 Nineveh, armies are
coming to attack you.
Guard the forts!
Watch the roads!
Get ready!
Gather all your strength!

[2] Assyria once took everything
of value from God's
people.
Its army destroyed all their
vines.
But the LORD will bring
back
the glory of Jacob's people.
He'll make Israel glorious
again.

[3] The shields of the soldiers are
red.
The warriors are dressed
in bright red uniforms.
The metal on their chariots
flashes

when they are prepared for
   war.
   Their spears made out of
      juniper are ready to use.
⁴The chariots race through
   the main streets.
   They rush back and forth
      through them.
   They look like flaming
      torches.
   They dart around like
      lightning.
⁵Nineveh sends for their
   special troops.
   But they trip and fall on their
      way.
   They run toward the city
      wall.
   They keep their shield in
      front of them.
⁶The attackers open the gates
   that hold back
   the waters of the river.
   And the palace falls
      down.
⁷The attackers order that
   Nineveh's people
   be taken away as
      prisoners.
   The female slaves sound like
      doves as they mourn.
   They beat their chests.
⁸Nineveh is like a pool
   whose water is draining
      away.
   "Stop running away!"
      someone cries out.
   But no one turns back.
⁹"Steal the silver!" the
      attackers shout.
   "Grab the gold!"
   The supply is endless.
   There is plenty of wealth
      among all the city's
      treasures.

¹⁰Nineveh is destroyed, robbed
   and stripped!
   Hearts melt away in fear.
   Knees give way.
   Bodies tremble with fear.
   Everyone's face turns pale.

¹¹Assyria is like a lion.
   Where is the lions' den now?
   Where did they feed their
      cubs?
   Where did all the lions go?
   In their den they had
      nothing to fear.
¹²The lion killed enough for his
      cubs to eat.
   He choked what he caught
      for his mate.
   He filled his home with what
      he had killed.
   He brought to his dens
      what he had caught.

¹³"Nineveh, I am against you,"
   announces the Lord who
      rules over all.
   "I will burn up your chariots
      with fire.
   Your young lions will be
      killed by swords.
   I will leave you nothing on
      earth to catch.
   The voices of your
      messengers
   will no longer be heard."

The Lord Will Judge Nineveh

3 How terrible it will be for
      Nineveh!
   It is a city of murderers!
   It is full of liars!
   It is filled with stolen
      goods!
   The killing never stops!
²Whips crack!
   Wheels clack!

Horses charge!
    Chariots rumble!
³ Horsemen attack!
    Swords flash!
    Spears gleam!
Many people die.
    Dead bodies pile up.
They can't even be counted.
    People trip over them.
⁴ All of that was caused by the
        evil desires
    of the prostitute Nineveh.
That woman who practiced
        evil magic
    was very beautiful.
She used her sinful charms
    to make slaves out of the
        nations.
She worshiped evil powers
    in order to trap others.

⁵ "Nineveh, I am against
        you,"
    announces the LORD who
        rules over all.
"I will pull your skirts up over
        your face.
    I will show the nations
        your naked body.
    Kingdoms will make fun of
        your shame.
⁶ I will throw garbage at you.
    I will look down on you.
    I will make an example out
        of you.
⁷ All those who see you will
        run away from you.
    They will say, 'Nineveh is
        destroyed.
    Who will mourn over it?'
Where can I find someone
    to comfort your people?"

⁸ Nineveh, are you better than
        Thebes
    on the Nile River?

There was water all around
        that city.
    The river helped to keep it
        safe.
    The waters were like a wall
        around it.
⁹ Cush and Egypt gave it all the
        strength it needed.
    Put and Libya also helped
        it.
¹⁰ But Thebes was captured
        anyway.
    Its people were taken away
        as prisoners.
Its babies were smashed to
        pieces
    at every street corner.
The Assyrian soldiers cast
        lots
    for all its nobles.
They put them in chains
    and made slaves out of
        them.
¹¹ People of Nineveh, you too
        will get drunk.
    You will try to hide from
        your enemies.
    You will look for a place of
        safety.

¹² All your forts are like fig trees
    that have their first ripe
        fruit on them.
When the trees are shaken,
    the figs fall into the mouths
    of those who eat them.
¹³ Look at your troops.
    All of them are weak.
The gates of your forts
    are wide open to your
        enemies.
    Fire has destroyed the bars
    that lock your gates.

¹⁴ Prepare for the attack by
    storing up water!

Zacchaeus

LUKE 19:1–10

The Triumphal Entry (Palm Sunday)
MATTHEW 21:1–11

Make your walls as strong
as you can!
Make some bricks out of
clay!
Mix the mud to hold them
together!
Use them to repair the
walls!
[15] In spite of all your hard
work,
fire will burn you up inside
your city.
Your enemies will cut you
down with their swords.
They will destroy you
just as a swarm of locusts
eats up crops.
Multiply like grasshoppers!
Increase your numbers like
locusts!
[16] You have more traders
than the number of stars in
the sky.
But like locusts they strip the
land.
Then they fly away.
[17] Your guards are like
grasshoppers.

Your officials are like
swarms of locusts.
They settle in the walls on
a cold day.
But when the sun appears,
they fly away.
And no one knows where
they go.
[18] King of Assyria, your leaders
are asleep.
Your nobles lie down to
rest.
Your people are scattered on
the mountains.
No one is left to gather
them together.
[19] Nothing can heal your
wounds.
You will die of them.
All those who hear the news
about you clap their
hands.
That's because you have
fallen from power.
Is there anyone who has not
suffered
because of how badly you
treated them?

Habakkuk

Introduction:

Habakkuk talked to God. He asked God why bad people had good things. Habakkuk saw many bad things in his country. He saw rich people who were unkind to poor people. He saw bad kings who did not love God.

God told Habakkuk that he was going to punish the people. Babylon would go to war with Judah. But the people of Babylon were evil too. They were worse than the people of Judah. Habakkuk did not understand why God would do this. God told Habakkuk that he would punish the people of Babylon for their sins too. Habakkuk praised God because God always does what is right.

Outline of contents:

1 This is a prophecy that Habakkuk the prophet received from the LORD. Here is what Habakkuk said.

Habakkuk Complains to the LORD

² LORD, how long do I have to
    call out for help?
    Why don't you listen to me?
How long must I keep telling
    you
    that things are terrible?
    Why don't you save us?
³ Why do you make me watch
    while
    people treat others so
        unfairly?
Why do you put up with the
    wrong things
    they are doing?
I have to look at death.
    People are harming others.

They are arguing and
    fighting all the time.
⁴ The law can't do what it's
    supposed to do.
    Fairness never comes out
        on top.
Sinful people surround those
    who do what is right.
    So people are never treated
        fairly.

The LORD Replies to Habakkuk

⁵ The LORD replies,

"Look at the nations. Watch
    them.
    Be totally amazed at what
        you see.
I am going to do something
    in your days
    that you would never
        believe.
You would not believe it

even if someone told you about it.

6 I am going to send the armies of Babylon to attack you.
They are very mean. They move quickly.
They sweep across the whole earth.
They take over homes that do not belong to them.

7 They terrify others.
They do not recognize any laws but their own.
That is how proud they are.

8 Their horses are faster than leopards.
They are meaner than wolves at sunset.
Their horsemen charge straight into battle.
They ride in from far away.
They come down like an eagle diving for its food.

9 All of them are ready and willing to destroy others.
Their huge armies advance like a wind out of the desert.
They gather prisoners like sand.

10 They mock kings and make fun of rulers.
They laugh at all the cities that have high walls around them.
They build dirt ramps against the walls and capture the cities.

11 They sweep past like the wind.
Then they go on their way.
They are guilty.
They worship their own strength."

Habakkuk Complains to the LORD Again

12 LORD, haven't you existed forever?
You are my holy God.
You will never die.
LORD, you have appointed the Babylonians
to punish your people.
My Rock, you have chosen them to judge us.

13 Your eyes are too pure to look at what is evil.
You can't put up with the wrong things people do.
So why do you put up with those who can't be trusted?
The evil Babylonians swallow up
those who are more godly than themselves.
So why are you silent?

14 You have made people to be like the fish in the sea.
They are like the sea creatures that don't have a ruler.

15 The evil Babylonians pull all of them up with hooks.
They catch them in their nets.
They gather them up.
So they celebrate.
They are glad.

16 They offer sacrifices to their nets.
They burn incense to them.
Their nets allow them to live in great comfort.
They enjoy the finest food.

17 Are you going to let them keep on emptying their nets?

Will they go on destroying
    nations
  without showing them any
    mercy?

2 ¹ I will go up to the lookout
    tower.
  I'll station myself on the
    city wall.
  I'll wait to see how the LORD
    will reply to me.
  Then I'll try to figure out
    how his reply answers
    what I've complained
    about.

The LORD Replies to Habakkuk

² The LORD replies,

"Write down the message I
    am giving you.
  Write it clearly on the
    tablets you use.
  Then a messenger can read it
    and run to announce it.
³ The message I give you
    waits for the time I have
    appointed.
  It speaks about what is going
    to happen.
    And all of it will come true.
  It might take a while.
    But wait for it.
  You can be sure it will come.
    It will happen when I want
    it to.

⁴ "The Babylonians are very
    proud.
  What they want is not
    good.

"But the person who is godly
    will live by his faithfulness.

⁵ "Wine makes the
    Babylonians do foolish
    things.

They are proud. They
    never rest.
Like the grave, they are
    always hungry for more.
Like death, they are never
    satisfied.
They gather all the nations to
    themselves.
  They take all those people
    away as prisoners.

⁶ "Won't those people laugh
at the Babylonians? Won't they
make fun of them? They will say
to them,

" 'How terrible it will be for
    you
  who pile up stolen goods!
You get rich by cheating
    others.
  How long will this go on?'
⁷ Those you owe money to will
    suddenly rise up.
They will wake up
  and make you tremble
    with fear.
Then they will take away
    everything you have.
⁸ You have robbed many
    nations.
  So the nations that are left
    will rob you.
You have spilled human
    blood.
  You have destroyed lands
    and cities
  and everyone in them.

⁹ "How terrible it will be for the
    Babylonians!
They build their kingdom
    with money
  that they gained by
    cheating others.
They have tried to make the
    kingdom

as secure as possible.
After all, they did not want
to be destroyed.
10 They have planned to wipe
out many nations.
But they have brought
shame on their own
kingdom.
So they must pay with their
own lives.
11 The stones in the walls of
their homes will cry out.
And the wooden beams
will echo that cry.

12 "How terrible it will be for the
Babylonians!
They build cities by
spilling the blood of
others.
They establish towns by
doing what is wrong.
13 I am the LORD who rules over
all.
Human effort is no better
than wood that feeds a
fire.
So the nations wear
themselves out for
nothing.
14 The oceans are full of water.
In the same way, the earth
will be filled
with the knowledge of my
glory.

15 "How terrible it will be for the
Babylonians!
They give drinks to their
neighbors.
They pour the drinks from
wineskins
until their neighbors are
drunk.
They want to look at their
naked bodies.

16 But the Babylonians will be
filled
with shame instead of
glory.
So now it is their turn to
drink
and be stripped of their
clothes.
The cup of anger in my
powerful right hand
is going to punish them.
They will be covered with
shame instead of glory.
17 The harm they have done to
Lebanon
will bring them down.
Because they have killed so
many animals,
animals will terrify them.
They have spilled human
blood.
They have destroyed lands
and cities
and everyone in them.

18 "If someone carves a statue
of a god, what is it worth?
What value is there in a
god
that teaches lies?
The one who trusts in this
kind of god
worships his own creation.
He makes statues of gods
that can't speak.
19 How terrible it will be for the
Babylonians!
They say to a wooden god,
'Come to life!'
They say to a stone god,
'Wake up!'
Can those gods give
advice?
They are covered with gold
and silver.
They can't even breathe."

²⁰The LORD is in his holy
      temple.
   Let the whole earth be
      silent in front of him.

Habakkuk Prays to the LORD

3 *This is a prayer of Habakkuk the
   prophet. It is on* shigionoth. *Here
   is what he said.*

²LORD, I know how famous
      you are.
   I have great respect for you
      because of your mighty
      acts.
   Do them again for us.
      Make them known in our
      time.
   When you are angry,
      please have mercy on us.

³God came from Teman.
   The Holy One came from
      Mount Paran.
   His glory covered the
      heavens.
      His praise filled the earth.
⁴His glory was like the
      sunrise.
   Rays of light flashed from
      his mighty hand.
   His power was hidden
      there.
⁵He sent plagues ahead of
      him.
   Sickness followed behind
      him.
⁶When he stood up, the earth
      shook.
   When he looked at the
      nations,
   they trembled with fear.
   The age-old mountains
      crumbled.
   The ancient hills fell down.
   But he marches on forever.

⁷I saw the tents of Cushan in
      trouble.
   The people of Midian were
      suffering greatly.

⁸LORD, were you angry with
      the rivers?
   Were you angry with the
      streams?
   Were you angry with the Red
      Sea?
   You rode your horses and
      chariots
   to overcome it.
⁹You got your bow ready to
      use.
   You asked for many
      arrows.
   You broke up the surface
      of the earth with rivers.
¹⁰The mountains saw you and
      shook.
   Floods of water swept by.
   The sea roared.
      It lifted its waves high.
¹¹The sun and moon stood still
      in the sky.
   They stopped because your
      flying arrows flashed by.
   Your gleaming spear shone
      like lightning.
¹²When you were angry, you
      marched across the
      earth.
   Because of your anger you
      destroyed the nations.
¹³You came out to set your
      people free.
   You saved your chosen
      ones.
   You crushed Pharaoh, the
      leader of that evil land of
      Egypt.
   You stripped him from
      head to foot.

14 His soldiers rushed out to
scatter us.
They were laughing at us.
They thought they would
easily destroy us.
They saw us as weak people
who were trying to hide.
So you wounded Pharaoh's
head with his own spear.
15 Your horses charged into the
Red Sea.
They stirred up the great
waters.

16 I listened and my heart
pounded.
My lips trembled at the
sound.
My bones seemed to rot.
And my legs shook.
But I will be patient.
I'll wait for the day of trouble
to come on Babylon.
It's the nation that is
attacking us.

17 The fig trees might not bud.
The vines might not
produce any grapes.
The olive crop might fail.
The fields might not
produce any food.
There might not be any sheep
in the pens.
There might not be any
cattle in the barns.
18 But I will still be glad
because of what the LORD
has done.
God my Savior fills me
with joy.
19 The LORD and King gives me
strength.
He makes my feet like the
feet of a deer.
He helps me walk on the
highest places.

This prayer is for the director of music. It should be sung while being accompanied by stringed instruments.

Zephaniah

Introduction:

Zephaniah spoke for God. He lived in Judah at the same time as King Josiah. Josiah was a good king, but the people had turned away from God. The king wanted the people to obey God. But they did not do what God said for very long. They turned back to sin.

Zephaniah also told the people to turn back to God. He said that if they didn't, God would send a war. The people would lose their homes. But someday God would stop punishing the people. God promised to bring the people home and take care of them.

Outline of contents:

1 A message from the LORD came to Zephaniah, the son of Cushi. Cushi was the son of Gedaliah. Gedaliah was the son of Amariah. Amariah was the son of King Hezekiah. The LORD spoke to Zephaniah during the rule of Josiah. He was king of Judah and the son of Amon.

The LORD Will Judge the Whole World

2 "I will sweep away
everything
from the face of the
earth,"
announces the LORD.
3 "I will destroy people and
animals alike.
I will wipe out the birds in
the sky
and the fish in the waters.
I will destroy the statues
of gods that cause evil
people to sin.

That will happen when
I destroy all human
beings on the face of the
earth,"
announces the LORD.
4 "I will reach out my powerful
hand against Judah.
I will punish all those who
live in Jerusalem.
I will destroy from this place
what is left of Baal
worship.
The priests who serve other
gods
will be removed.
5 I will destroy those who bow
down on their roofs
to worship all the stars.
I will destroy those who
make promises
not only in my name but
also in the name of
Molek.
6 I will destroy those who stop
following the LORD.

They no longer look to him
    or ask him for advice.
[7] Be silent in front of him.
    He is the LORD and King.
    The day of the LORD is
        near.
    The LORD has prepared a
        sacrifice.
    He has set apart for himself
        the people he has invited.
[8] When the LORD's sacrifice is
        ready to be offered,
    I will punish the officials
        and the king's sons.
    I will also judge all those who
        follow
        the practices of other
            nations.
[9] At that time I will punish
    all those who worship
        other gods.
    They fill the temples of their
        gods
        with lies and other
            harmful things.
[10] "At that time people at the
        Fish Gate in Jerusalem
    will cry out," announces
        the LORD.
    "So will those at the New
        Quarter.
    The buildings on the hills
        will come crashing
            down
        with a loud noise.
[11] Cry out, you who live in the
        market places.
    All your merchants will be
        wiped out.
    Those who trade in silver
        will be destroyed.
[12] At that time I will search
        Jerusalem with lamps.
    I will punish those who are
        so contented.

They are like wine that has
    not been shaken up.
They think, 'The LORD won't
    do anything.
He won't do anything good
    or bad.'
[13] Their wealth will be stolen.
    Their houses will be
        destroyed.
    They will build houses.
    But they will not live in
        them.
    They will plant vineyards.
    But they will not drink the
        wine they produce.
[14] The great day of the LORD is
        near.
    In fact, it is coming quickly.
    The cries on that day are
        bitter.
    The Mighty Warrior shouts
        his battle cry.
[15] At that time I will pour out
        my anger.
    There will be great
        suffering and pain.
    It will be a day of horrible
        trouble.
    It will be a time of darkness
        and gloom.
    It will be filled with the
        blackest clouds.
[16] Trumpet blasts and battle
        cries will be heard.
    Soldiers will attack cities
        that have forts and corner
            towers.
[17] I will bring great trouble on
        all people.
    So they will feel their way
        around like blind people.
    They have sinned against
        the LORD.
    Their blood will be poured
        out like dust.

Their bodies will lie rotting
on the ground.
[18] Their silver and gold
won't save them
on the day the LORD pours
out his anger.
The whole earth will be
burned up
when his jealous anger
blazes out.
Everyone who lives on earth
will come to a sudden
end."

The LORD Will Judge Judah and Jerusalem Along With the Nations

God Calls Judah to Turn Away From Their Sins

2 Gather together,
you shameful nation of
Judah!
Gather yourselves together!
[2] Come together before the
LORD's judgment arrives.
The day of the LORD's
judgment will sweep in
like straw blown by the
wind.
Soon the LORD's great anger
will come against you.
The day of his wrath will
come against you.
[3] So look to him, all you people
in the land
who worship him
faithfully.
You always do what he
commands you to do.
Continue to do what is right.
Don't be proud.
Then perhaps the LORD will
keep you safe
on the day he pours out his
anger on the world.

A Message About Philistia

[4] Gaza will be deserted.
Ashkelon will be
destroyed.
Ashdod will be emptied out
at noon.
Ekron will be pulled up by
its roots.
[5] How terrible it will be for you
Kerethites
who live by the
Mediterranean Sea!
Philistia, the LORD has
spoken against you.
What happened to Canaan
will happen to you.

The LORD says, "I will destroy
you.
No one will be left."

[6] The land by the sea will
become grasslands.
It will have wells for
shepherds and pens for
flocks.
[7] That land will belong to those
who are still left alive
among the people of Judah.
They will find grasslands
there.
They will take over
the houses in Ashkelon
and live in them.
The LORD their God will take
care of them.
He will bless them with
great success again.

A Message About Moab and Ammon

[8] The LORD says,

"I have heard Moab make fun
of my people.
The Ammonites also
laughed at them.

They told them that bad
things
would happen to their
land.
9 So Moab will become like
Sodom,"
announces the LORD who
rules over all.
"Ammon will be like
Gomorrah.
Weeds and salt pits will cover
those countries.
They will be dry and empty
deserts forever.
Those who are still left alive
among my people
will take all their valuable
things.
So they will receive those
lands as their own.
And that is just as sure as I
am alive."
The LORD is the God of
Israel.

10 Moab and Ammon will be
judged
because they are so proud.
They made fun of the LORD's
people.
They laughed at them.
11 The LORD who rules over all
will terrify Moab and
Ammon.
He will destroy all the gods
on earth.
Then distant nations will
bow down to him.
All of them will serve him
in their own lands.

A Message About Cush

12 The LORD says, "People of
Cush,
you too will die by my
sword."

A Message About Assyria

13 The LORD will reach out his
powerful hand against
the north.
He will destroy Assyria.
He'll leave Nineveh totally
empty.
It will be as dry as a desert.
14 Flocks and herds will lie
down there.
So will creatures of every
kind.
Desert owls and screech
owls
will rest on its pillars.
The sound of their hooting
will echo through the
windows.
The doorways will be full
of trash.
The cedar beams will be
showing.
15 Nineveh was a carefree city.
It lived in safety.
It said to itself,
"I am the one!
No one is greater than I
am."
But it has been destroyed.
Wild animals make their
home there.
All those who pass by laugh
and shake their fists at it.

A Message About Jerusalem

3 How terrible it will be for
Jerusalem!
Its people crush others.
They refuse to obey the
LORD.
They are "unclean."
2 They don't obey anyone.
They don't accept the
LORD's warnings.
They don't trust in him.

They don't ask their God
  for his help.
3 Jerusalem's officials are like
    roaring lions.
  Their rulers are like
    wolves that hunt in the
    evening.
  They don't leave anything
    to eat in the morning.
4 Their prophets care about
    nothing.
  They can't be trusted.
  Their priests make the
    temple "unclean."
  They break the law they
    teach others to obey.
5 In spite of that, the LORD is
    good to Jerusalem.
  He never does anything
    that is wrong.
  Every morning he does what
    is fair.
  Each new day he does the
    right thing.
  But those who do what is
    wrong
    aren't even ashamed of it.

Jerusalem Remains Unrepentant

6 The LORD says to his people,

"I have destroyed other
    nations.
  I have wiped out their forts.
  I have left their streets
    deserted.
  No one walks along them.
  Their cities are destroyed.
  They are deserted and
    empty.
7 Here is what I thought about
    Jerusalem.
  'Surely you will have respect
    for me.
  Surely you will accept my
    warning.'

Then the city you think
    is safe would not be
    destroyed.
  And I would not have to
    punish you so much.
  But they still wanted to go
    on sinning
    in every way they could.
8 So wait for me to come as
    judge,"
  announces the LORD.
  "Wait for the day I will stand
    up
    to witness against all
    sinners.
  I have decided to gather the
    nations.
  I will bring the kingdoms
    together.
  And I will pour out all my
    burning anger on them.
  The fire of my jealous
    anger
    will burn the whole world
    up.

Israel Will Trust in the LORD

9 "But then I will purify what
    all the nations say.
  And they will use their
    words to worship me.
  They will serve me
    together.
10 My scattered people will
    come to me
    from beyond the rivers of
    Cush.
  They will worship me.
  They will bring me
    offerings.
11 Jerusalem, you have done
    many wrong things to me.
  But at that time you will
    not be put to shame
    anymore.

That's because I will remove
    from this city
    those who think so highly
      of themselves.
You will never be proud again
    on my holy mountain of
    Zion.
¹² But inside your city I will
    leave
    those who are not proud at
      all.
    Those who are still left
      alive will trust in the
      LORD.
¹³ They will not do anything
    wrong.
    They will not tell any lies.
    They will not say anything
      to fool other people.
    They will eat and lie down in
      peace.
    And no one will make
      them afraid."

¹⁴ People of Zion, sing!
    Israel, shout loudly!
People of Jerusalem, be glad!
    Let your hearts be full of
      joy.
¹⁵ The LORD has stopped
    punishing you.
    He has made your enemies
      turn away from you.
The LORD is the King of
    Israel.
    He is with you.
You will never again be afraid
    that others will harm you.
¹⁶ The time is coming when
    people will say to
    Jerusalem,
    "Zion, don't be afraid.
    Don't give up.

¹⁷ The LORD your God is with
    you.
    He is the Mighty Warrior
      who saves.
He will take great delight in
    you.
    In his love he will no longer
      punish you.
    Instead, he will sing for joy
      because of you."

¹⁸ The LORD says to his people,

"You used to celebrate my
    appointed feasts in
    Jerusalem.
You are sad because you
    can't do that anymore.
Other people make fun of
    you because of that.
That sadness was a heavy
    load for you to carry.
But I will remove that load
    from you.
¹⁹ At that time I will punish
    all those who crushed you.
I will save those among you
    who are disabled.
I will gather those who
    have been taken away.
I will give them praise and
    honor
    in every land where they
      have been put to shame.
²⁰ At that time I will gather you
    together.
    And I will bring you home.
I will give you honor and
    praise
    among all the nations on
      earth.
I will bless you with great
    success again,"
           says the LORD.

Haggai

Introduction:

Haggai was a Jew. He lived in Babylon. He had to go there after Jerusalem fell. Many years later, the king said the Jews could go home. The Jews who went home started to repair the destroyed cities. They built their own houses. But they didn't rebuild God's house, the temple. They laid a new foundation, but then stopped working. They said it wasn't time to finish it yet. Haggai told the Jews to put God first and rebuild the temple. The people did what Haggai said.

Some of the people could remember the temple before it was destroyed, which made them very sad. But God promised that his Spirit would be there. God said, "'The new temple will be more beautiful than the first one was.'" (2:9) What would make this temple more special was that Jesus, the Messiah, would go there!

Outline of contents:

Haggai Tells His People to Rebuild the LORD's Temple

1 A message from the LORD came to Haggai the prophet. Haggai gave it to Zerubbabel and Joshua. Zerubbabel was governor of Judah and the son of Shealtiel. Joshua was high priest and the son of Jozadak. The message came on the first day of the sixth month of the second year that Darius was king of Persia. Here is what Haggai said.

² Here is what the LORD who rules over all says. "The people of Judah say, 'It's not yet time to rebuild the LORD's temple.'"

³ So the message from the LORD came to me. The LORD said, ⁴ "My temple is still destroyed. But you are living in your houses that have beautiful wooden walls."

⁵ The LORD who rules over all says, "Think carefully about how you are living. ⁶ You have planted many seeds. But the crops you have gathered are small. So you eat. But you never have enough. You drink. But you are never full. You put on your clothes. But you are not warm. You earn your pay. But it will not buy everything you need."

⁷ He continues, "Think carefully about how you are living. ⁸ Go up into the mountains.

Bring logs down. Use them to rebuild the temple, my house. Then I will enjoy it. And you will honor me," says the LORD. ⁹ You expected a lot. But you can see what a small amount it turned out to be. I blew away what you brought home. I'll tell you why," announces the LORD who rules over all. "Because my temple is still destroyed. In spite of that, each one of you is busy with your own house. ¹⁰ So because of what you have done, the heavens have held back the dew. And the earth has not produced its crops. ¹¹ I ordered the rain not to fall on the fields and mountains. Then the ground did not produce any grain. There were not enough grapes to make fresh wine. The trees did not bear enough olives to make oil. People and cattle suffered. All your hard work failed."

¹² Zerubbabel was the son of Shealtiel. Joshua the high priest was the son of Jozadak. They obeyed the LORD their God. So did all the LORD's people who were still left alive. The LORD had given his message to them through me. He had sent me to speak to them. And the people had respect for him.

¹³ Haggai was the LORD's messenger. So Haggai gave the LORD's message to the people. He told them, "The LORD announces, 'I am with you.'" ¹⁴ So the LORD stirred up the spirits of Zerubbabel, the governor of Judah, and Joshua the high priest. The LORD also stirred up the

rest of the people to help them. Then everyone began to work on the temple of the LORD who rules over all. He is their God. ¹⁵ It was the 24th day of the sixth month.

The New Temple Will Be Beautiful

In the second year of King Darius, ¹ a second message came from the LORD. It came to Haggai the prophet. The message came on the 21st day of the seventh month. The LORD said, ² "Speak to Zerubbabel, the governor of Judah and the son of Shealtiel. Also speak to Joshua the high priest, the son of Jozadak. And speak to all my people who are still left alive. Ask them, ³ 'Did any of you who are here see how beautiful this temple used to be? How does it look to you now? It doesn't look so good, does it? ⁴ But be strong, Zerubbabel,' announces the LORD. 'Be strong, Joshua. Be strong, all of you people in the land,' announces the LORD. 'Start rebuilding. I am with you,' announces the LORD who rules over all. ⁵ 'That is what I promised you when you came out of Egypt. My Spirit continues to be with you. So do not be afraid.'"

⁶ The LORD says, "In a little while I will shake the heavens and the earth once more. I will also shake the ocean and the dry land. ⁷ I will shake all the nations. Then what is desired by all nations will come to my temple. And I will fill the temple

with glory," says the LORD who rules over all. ⁸ "The silver belongs to me. So does the gold," announces the LORD who rules over all. ⁹ "The new temple will be more beautiful than the first one was," says the LORD. "And in this place I will bring peace," announces the LORD who rules over all.

The LORD Will Make His People Pure and "Clean"

¹⁰ A third message from the LORD came to Haggai the prophet. The message came on the 24th day of the ninth month of the second year that Darius was king. ¹¹ The LORD who rules over all speaks. He says, "Ask the priests what the law says. ¹² Suppose someone carries holy meat in the clothes they are wearing. And the clothes touch some bread or stew. Or they touch some wine, olive oil or other food. Then do these things also become holy?"

The priests answered, "No."

¹³ So Haggai said, "Suppose someone is made 'unclean' by touching a dead body. And then they touch one of these things. Does it become 'unclean' too?"

"Yes," the priests replied. "It does."

¹⁴ Then here is what Haggai said. "The LORD announces, 'That is how I look at these people and this nation. Anything they do and anything they sacrifice on the altar is "unclean."

¹⁵ " 'Think carefully about this from now on. Think about how things were before the LORD's temple was built. This was before one stone was laid on top of another. ¹⁶ People went to get 20 measures of grain. But they could find only 10. They went to where the wine was stored to get 50 measures. But only 20 were there. ¹⁷ You worked very hard to produce all those things. But I struck them with rot, mold and hail. And you still did not return to me,' announces the LORD. ¹⁸ It is the 24th day of the ninth month. From this day on, here is what you should think carefully about. Think about the day when the foundation of my temple was laid. ¹⁹ Are any seeds still left in your barns? Until now, your vines and fig trees have not produced any fruit. Your pomegranate and olive trees have not produced any either.

" 'But from this day on I will bless you.' "

The LORD Compares Zerubbabel to His Royal Ring

²⁰ A final message from the LORD came to Haggai. This message also came on the 24th day of the ninth month. The LORD said, ²¹ "Speak to Zerubbabel, the governor of Judah. Tell him I am going to shake the heavens and the earth. ²² I will throw down royal thrones. I will smash the power of other kingdoms. I will destroy chariots and their drivers. Horses and their riders will fall. They will be killed by the swords of their relatives.

23 " 'Zerubbabel, at that time I will pick you,' announces the LORD. 'You are my servant,' announces the LORD. 'You will be like a ring that has my royal mark on it. I have chosen you,' announces the LORD who rules over all."

Zechariah

Introduction:

Zechariah lived at the same time as Haggai. He spoke to the people about rebuilding the temple. Zechariah told them to stay close to God. He told them to obey God by being fair and kind to each other.

Zechariah wanted the people to know that God loved them. He wrote about the king God would send. This king would save his people. Zechariah was talking about Jesus.

Outline of contents:

The LORD Wants His People to Return to Him

1 A message from the LORD came to Zechariah the prophet. Zechariah was the son of Berekiah. Berekiah was the son of Iddo. It was the eighth month of the second year that Darius was king of Persia. Here is what Zechariah said.

2 The LORD who rules over all was very angry with your people of long ago. 3 And now he says to us, "Return to me. Then I will return to you," announces the LORD. 4 "Do not be like your people of long ago. The earlier prophets gave them my message. I said, 'Stop doing what is evil. Turn away from your sinful practices.' But they would not listen to me. They would not pay any attention," announces the LORD. 5 "Where are those people now? And what about my prophets? Do they live forever? 6 I commanded my servants the prophets what to say. I told them what I planned to do. But your people refused to obey me. So I had to punish them.

"Then they had a change of heart. They said, 'The LORD who rules over all has punished us because of how we have lived. He was fair and right to do that. He has done to us just what he decided to do.'"

A Vision of a Horseman Among Some Myrtle Trees

7 A message from the LORD came to Zechariah the prophet. Zechariah was the son of Berekiah. Berekiah was the son of Iddo. The message came during the second year that Darius was king. It was the 24th day of the 11th month. That's the month of Shebat.

⁸I had a vision at night. I saw a man sitting on a red horse. He was standing among the myrtle trees in a valley. Behind him were red, brown and white horses.

⁹An angel was talking with me. I asked him, "Sir, what are these?"

He answered, "I will show you what they are."

¹⁰Then the man standing among the myrtle trees spoke. He said, "They are the messengers the LORD has sent out. He told them to go all through the earth."

¹¹They brought a report to the angel of the LORD. He was standing among the myrtle trees. They said to him, "We have gone all through the earth. We've found the whole world enjoying peace and rest."

¹²Then the angel of the LORD spoke up. He said, "LORD, you rule over all. How long will you keep from showing your tender love to Jerusalem? How long will you keep it from the towns of Judah? You have been angry with them for 70 years." ¹³So the LORD replied with kind and comforting words. He spoke them to the angel who talked with me.

¹⁴Then the angel said, "Announce this message. Say, 'The LORD who rules over all says, "I am very jealous for my people in Jerusalem and Zion. ¹⁵And I am very angry with the nations that feel secure. I was only a little angry with my people. But the nations went too far and tried to wipe them out."

¹⁶"'So the LORD says, "I will return to Jerusalem. I will show its people my tender love. My temple will be rebuilt there. Workers will use a measuring line when they rebuild Jerusalem," announces the LORD.

¹⁷"'He says, "My towns will be filled with good things once more. I will comfort Zion. And I will choose Jerusalem again."'"

A Vision of Four Horns and Four Skilled Workers

¹⁸Then I looked up and saw four animal horns. ¹⁹I spoke to the angel who was talking with me. "What are these horns?" I asked.

He said, "They are the powerful nations that scattered Judah, Israel and Jerusalem."

²⁰Then the LORD showed me four skilled workers. ²¹I asked, "What are they coming to do?"

He answered, "The horns are the powerful nations that scattered the people of Judah. That made Judah helpless. But these four skilled workers have come to terrify the horns. The workers will destroy the power of those nations. Those nations had used their power to scatter Judah's people."

A Vision of a Man Holding a Measuring Line

2 Then I looked up and saw a man. He was holding a measuring line. ²"Where are you going?" I asked.

"To measure Jerusalem," he answered. "I want to find out how wide and how long it is."

³The angel who was talking with me was leaving. At that

time, another angel came over to him. ⁴ He said to him, "Run! Tell that young man Zechariah, 'Jerusalem will be a city that does not have any walls around it. It will have huge numbers of people and animals in it. ⁵ And I myself will be like a wall of fire around it,' announces the LORD. 'I will be the city's glory.'

⁶ "Israel, I have scattered you," announces the LORD. "I have used the power of the four winds of heaven to do it. Come quickly! Run away from the land of the north," announces the LORD.

⁷ "Come, people of Zion! Escape, you who live in Babylon!" ⁸ The LORD rules over all. His angel says to Israel, "The Glorious One has sent me to punish the nations that have robbed you of everything. That's because anyone who hurts you hurts those the LORD loves and guards. ⁹ So I will raise my powerful hand to strike down your enemies. Their own slaves will rob them of everything. Then you will know that the LORD who rules over all has sent me.

¹⁰ " 'People of Zion, shout and be glad! I am coming to live among you,' announces the LORD. ¹¹ 'At that time many nations will join themselves to me. And they will become my people. I will live among you,' says the LORD. Then you will know that the LORD who rules over all has sent me to you. ¹² He will receive Judah as his share in the holy land. And he will choose Jerusalem again. ¹³ All you people of the world, be still because the LORD is coming. He is getting ready to come down from his holy temple in heaven."

A Vision of the High Priest Dressed in Fine Clothes

3 Then the LORD showed me Joshua the high priest. He was standing in front of the angel of the LORD. Satan was standing to the right of Joshua. He was there to bring charges against the high priest. ² The LORD said to Satan, "May the LORD correct you! He has chosen Jerusalem. So may he correct you! Isn't this man Joshua like a burning stick pulled out of the fire?"

³ Joshua stood in front of the angel. He was wearing clothes that were very dirty. ⁴ The angel spoke to those who were standing near him. He said, "Take his dirty clothes off."

He said to Joshua, "I have taken your sin away. I will put fine clothes on you."

⁵ I added, "Put a clean turban on his head." So they did. And they dressed him while the angel of the LORD stood by.

⁶ Then the angel spoke to Joshua. He said, ⁷ "The LORD who rules over all says, 'You must obey me. You must do what I have commanded. Then you will rule in my temple. You will be in charge of my courtyards. And I will give you a place among these who are standing here.

⁸ " 'High Priest Joshua, pay attention! I want you other priests who are sitting with Joshua to listen also. All you men are signs of things to come. I am go-

ing to bring to you my servant the Branch. [9]Look at the stone I have put in front of Joshua! There are seven eyes on that one stone. I will carve a message on it,' says the Lord who rules over all. 'And I will remove the sin of this land in one day.

[10] " 'At that time each of you will invite your neighbors to visit you. They will sit under your vines and fig trees,' announces the Lord."

A Vision of the Gold Lampstand and Two Olive Trees

4 Then the angel who was talking with me returned. He woke me up. It was as if I had been asleep. [2]"What do you see?" he asked me.

"I see a solid gold lampstand," I answered. "It has a bowl on top of it. There are seven lamps on it. Seven tubes lead to the lamps. [3]There are two olive trees by the lampstand. One is on its right side. The other is on its left."

[4]I asked the angel who was talking with me, "Sir, what are these?"

[5]He answered, "Don't you know what they are?"

"No, sir," I replied.

[6]So he said to me, "A message from the Lord came to Zerubbabel. The Lord said, 'Your strength will not get my temple rebuilt. Your power will not do it either. Only the power of my Spirit will do it,' says the Lord who rules over all.

[7]"So nothing can stop Zerubbabel from completing the temple. Even a mountain of problems will be smoothed out by him. When the temple is finished, he will put its most important stone in place. Then the people will shout, 'God bless it! God bless it!' "

[8]Then a message from the Lord came to me. His angel said, [9]"The hands of Zerubbabel have laid the foundation of this temple. His hands will also complete it. Then you will know that the Lord who rules over all has sent me to you.

[10]"Do not look down on the small amount of work done on the temple so far. The seven eyes of the Lord look over the whole earth. They will see Zerubbabel holding the most important stone. They will be filled with joy when they see it."

[11]Then I said to the angel, "I see two olive trees. One is on the right side of the lampstand. The other is on the left. What are these trees?"

[12]I continued, "I also see two olive branches. They are next to the two gold pipes that pour out golden olive oil. What are these branches?"

[13]He answered, "Don't you know what they are?"

"No, sir," I said.

[14]So he told me, "They are Zerubbabel and Joshua. The Lord of the whole earth has anointed them to serve him."

A Vision of a Flying Scroll

5 I looked up again and saw a flying scroll. [2]"What do you see?" the angel asked me.

"A scroll flying in the air," I replied. "It's 30 feet long and 15 feet wide."

³ He said to me, "A curse sent by the LORD is written on it. It is going out over the whole land. Every thief will be driven out of the land. That is what it says on one side of the scroll. Everyone who lies when promising to tell the truth will also be driven out. That is what it says on the other side. ⁴ The LORD who rules over all announces, 'I will send the curse out. It will enter the house of the thief. It will also enter the house of anyone who lies when making a promise in my name. It will remain in that house and destroy it completely. It will pull down its beams and stones.'"

A Vision of a Woman in a Basket

⁵ Then the angel who was talking with me came forward. He said to me, "Look at what is coming."

⁶ "What is it?" I asked.

"A basket," he replied. "The sins of the people all through the land are in it."

⁷ Then the basket's cover was lifted up. It was made out of lead. A woman was sitting in the basket! ⁸ The angel said, "She stands for everything that is evil." Then he pushed her down into the basket. He put the lead cover back over it.

⁹ I looked up and saw two other women. They had wings like the wings of a stork. A wind sent by the LORD carried them along. They lifted the basket up between heaven and earth.

¹⁰ "Where are they taking the basket?" I asked the angel.

¹¹ He replied, "To the country of Babylon. A temple will be built for it. When the temple is ready, the basket will be set there in its place."

A Vision of Four Chariots

6 I looked up again and saw four chariots. They were coming out from between two mountains. The mountains were made out of bronze. ² The first chariot was pulled by red horses. The second one had black horses. ³ The third had white horses. And the fourth had spotted horses. All the horses were powerful. ⁴ I asked the angel who was talking with me, "Sir, what are these?"

⁵ The angel answered, "The four spirits of heaven. They are going out to serve the Lord of the whole world. ⁶ The chariot pulled by the black horses is going toward the north country. The one with the white horses is going toward the west. And the one with the spotted horses is going toward the south."

⁷ The powerful horses went out. They were in a hurry to go all over the earth. The angel said, "Go all through the earth!" So they did.

⁸ Then the LORD called out to me, "Look! The horses going toward the north have given my Spirit rest in the north country."

A Crown Is Given to Joshua

⁹ A message from the LORD came to me. His angel said,

¹⁰ "Get some silver and gold from Heldai, Tobijah and Jedaiah. They have just come back from Babylon. On that same day go to Josiah's house. He is the son of Zephaniah. ¹¹ Use the silver and gold to make a crown. Set it on the head of Joshua the high priest. He is the son of Jozadak. ¹² Give Joshua a message from the LORD who rules over all. He says, 'Here is the man whose name is the Branch. He will branch out and build my temple. ¹³ That is what he will do. He will be dressed in majesty as if it were his royal robe. He will sit as king on his throne. He will also be a priest there. So he will combine the positions of king and priest in himself.' ¹⁴ The crown will be given to Heldai, Tobijah, Jedaiah and Zephaniah's son Hen. The crown will be kept in the LORD's temple. It will remind everyone that the LORD's promises will come true. ¹⁵ Those who are far away will come to Jerusalem. They will help build the LORD's temple. Then his people will know that the LORD who rules over all has sent me to them. It will happen if they are careful to obey the LORD their God."

Have Justice and Mercy

7 During the fourth year that Darius was king, a message from the LORD came to me. It was the fourth day of the ninth month. That's the month of Kislev. ² The people of Bethel wanted to ask the LORD for his blessing. So they sent Share-zer and Regem-Melek and their men. ³ They went to the prophets and priests at the LORD's temple. They asked them, "Should we mourn and go without eating in the fifth month? That's what we've done for many years."

⁴ Then the message came to me from the LORD who rules over all. He said, ⁵ "Ask the priests and all the people in the land a question for me. Say to them, 'You mourned and fasted in the fifth and seventh months. You did it for the past 70 years. But did you really do it for me? ⁶ And when you were eating and drinking, weren't you just enjoying good food for yourselves? ⁷ Didn't I tell you the same thing through the earlier prophets? That was when Jerusalem and the towns around it were at rest and enjoyed success. People lived in the Negev Desert and the western hills at that time.' "

⁸ Another message from the LORD came to me. ⁹ Here is what the LORD who rules over all said to his people. "Treat everyone with justice. Show mercy and tender concern to one another. ¹⁰ Do not take advantage of widows. Do not mistreat children whose fathers have died. Do not be mean to outsiders or poor people. Do not make evil plans against one another."

¹¹ But they refused to pay attention to the LORD. They were stubborn. They turned their backs and covered their ears. ¹² They made their hearts as hard as the hardest stone. They wouldn't listen to the law. They

wouldn't pay attention to the LORD's messages. So the LORD who rules over all was very angry. After all, his Spirit had spoken to his people through the earlier prophets.

¹³ "When I called, they did not listen," says the LORD. "So when they called, I would not listen. ¹⁴ I used a windstorm to scatter them among all the nations. They were strangers there. The land they left behind became dry and empty. No one could even travel through it. This is how they turned the pleasant land into a dry and empty desert."

The LORD Promises to Bless Jerusalem

8 A message came to me from the LORD who rules over all. He said, ² "I am very jealous for my people in Zion. In fact, I am burning with jealousy for them."

³ He continued, "I will return to Zion. I will live among my people in Jerusalem. Then Jerusalem will be called the Faithful City. And my mountain will be called the Holy Mountain."

⁴ He continued, "Once again old men and women will sit in the streets of Jerusalem. All of them will be using canes because they are old. ⁵ The city streets will be filled with boys and girls. They will be playing there."

⁶ He continued, "All of that might seem hard to believe to the people living then. But it will not be too hard for me."

⁷ He continued, "I will save my people. I will gather them from the countries of the east and the west. ⁸ I will bring them back to live in Jerusalem. They will be my people. I will be their faithful God. I will keep my promises to them."

⁹ The LORD who rules over all says to his people, "Now listen to these words, 'Let your hands be strong so that you can rebuild the temple.' This also was said by the prophets Haggai and Zechariah. They spoke to you when the work on my temple began again. ¹⁰ Before the work was started again, there was no pay for the people. And there was no money to rent animals. People could not go about their business safely because of their enemies. I had turned all of them against one another. ¹¹ But now I will not punish you who are living at this time. I will not treat you as I treated your people before you," announces the LORD who rules over all.

¹² "Your seeds will grow well. Your vines will bear fruit. The ground will produce crops for you. And the heavens will drop their dew on your land. I will give all these things to those who are still left alive here. ¹³ Judah and Israel, in the past you have been a curse among the nations. But now I will save you. You will be a blessing to others. Do not be afraid. Let your hands be strong so that you can do my work."

¹⁴ The LORD who rules over all says, "Your people of long ago

made me angry. So I decided to bring trouble on them. I did not show them any pity. ¹⁵ But now I plan to do good things to Jerusalem and Judah again. So do not be afraid. ¹⁶ Here is what you must do. Speak the truth to one another. Make true and wise decisions in your courts. ¹⁷ Do not make evil plans against one another. When you promise to tell the truth, do not lie. Many people love to do that. But I hate all these things," announces the Lord.

¹⁸ Another message came to me from the Lord who rules over all.

He said, ¹⁹ "You have established special times to go without eating. They are your fasts in the fourth, fifth, seventh and tenth months. They will become days of joy. They will be happy times for Judah. It will happen if you take delight in telling the truth and bringing about peace."

²⁰ He continued, "Many nations will still come to you. And those who live in many cities will also come. ²¹ The people who live in one city will go to another city. They will say, 'Let's go right away to ask the Lord for his blessing. Let's look to him as our God. We ourselves are going.' ²² Large numbers of people and nations will come to Jerusalem. They will look to me. They will ask me to bless them."

²³ He continued, "At that time many people of all nations and languages will take hold of one Jew. They will grab hold of the hem of his robe. And they will say, 'We want to go to Jerusalem with you. We've heard that God is with you.'"

The Lord Destroys Israel's Enemies

9 This is a prophecy. It is the Lord's message
against the land of Hadrak.
He will judge Damascus.
That's because all the tribes
of Israel look to him.
So do all other people.
² The Lord will judge Hamath
too.
It's next to Damascus.
He will also punish Tyre and
Sidon
even though they are very
clever.
³ Tyre's people have built a fort
for themselves.
They've piled up silver like
dust.
They have as much gold as
the dirt in the streets.
⁴ But the Lord will take away
everything they have.
He'll destroy their power
on the Mediterranean
Sea.
And Tyre will be
completely burned up.
⁵ Ashkelon will see it and
become afraid.
Gaza will groan with pain.
So will Ekron. Its hope will
vanish.
Gaza will no longer have a
king.
Ashkelon will be deserted.
⁶ A people who come from
several nations will take
over Ashdod.

The LORD says, "I will put an end to the pride of the Philistines.

⁷ They will no longer drink the blood of their animal sacrifices.
I will remove the 'unclean' food from between their teeth.
The Philistines who are left will belong to our God.
They will become a family group in Judah.
And Ekron will be like the Jebusites.
So the Philistines will become part of Israel.
⁸ But I will camp at my temple.
I will guard it against enemy armies.
No one will ever crush my people again.
I will make sure it does not happen.

A King Comes to Zion

⁹ "City of Zion, be full of joy!
People of Jerusalem, shout!
See, your king comes to you.
He always does what is right.
He has won the victory.
He is humble and riding on a donkey.
He is sitting on a donkey's colt.
¹⁰ I will take the chariots away from Ephraim.
I will remove the war horses from Jerusalem.
I will break the bows that are used in battle.
Your king will announce peace to the nations.
He will rule from ocean to ocean.
His kingdom will reach from the Euphrates River to the ends of the earth.
¹¹ I will set your prisoners free from where their enemies are keeping them.
I will do it because of the blood that put into effect my covenant with you.
¹² Return to your place of safety,
you prisoners who still have hope.
Even now I announce that I will give you back much more than you had before.
¹³ I will bend Judah as I bend my bow.
I will make Ephraim's people my arrows.
Zion, I will stir up your sons.
Greece, they will attack your sons.
My people, I will use you as my sword."

The LORD Will Appear

¹⁴ Then the LORD will appear over his people.
His arrows will flash like lightning.
The LORD and King will blow the trumpet of his thunder.
He'll march out like a storm in the south.
¹⁵ The LORD who rules over all will be like a shield to his people.
They will destroy their enemies.

They'll use slings to throw
stones at them.
They'll drink the blood of
their enemies
as if it were wine.
They'll be full like the bowl
that is used
for sprinkling the corners
of the altar.
16 The LORD their God will save
his people on that day.
He will be like a shepherd
who saves his flock.
They will gleam in his land
like jewels in a crown.
17 How very beautiful they will
be!
Grain and fresh wine
will make the young men
and young women
strong.

The LORD Will Take Care of Judah

10 People of Judah, ask the
LORD
to send rain in the spring.
He is the one who sends
the thunderstorms.
He sends down showers of
rain on all people.
He gives everyone the
plants in the fields.
2 Other gods tell lies.
Those who practice magic
see visions that aren't true.
They tell dreams that fool
people.
They give comfort that
doesn't do any good.
So the people wander around
like sheep.
They are crushed because
they don't have a
shepherd.

3 The LORD who rules over all
says,

"I am very angry with the
shepherds.
I will punish the leaders.
The LORD will take care of his
flock.
They are the people of
Judah.
He will make them like a
proud horse in battle.
4 The most important building
stone
will come from the tribe of
Judah.
The tent stake will also
come from it.
And the bow that is used in
battle will come from it.
In fact, every ruler will
come from it.
5 Together they will be like
warriors in battle.
They will stomp their
enemies
into the mud of the streets.
The LORD will be with them.
So they will fight against
the horsemen
and put them to shame.

6 "I will make the family of
Judah strong.
I will save the tribes of
Joseph.
I will bring them back
because I have tender love
for them.
It will be as if
I had not sent them away.
I am the LORD their God.
I will help them.
7 The people of Ephraim will
become like warriors.
Their hearts will be glad

as if they were drinking
   wine.
Their children will see it
   and be filled with joy.
I will make their hearts
   glad.
[8] I will signal for my people to
   come,
   and I will gather them in.
I will set them free.
   There will be as many of
   them as before.
[9] I have scattered them among
   the nations.
   But in lands far away they
   will remember me.
They and their children will
   be kept alive.
   And they will return.
[10] I will bring them back from
   Egypt.
I will gather them from
   Assyria.
I will bring them to Gilead
   and Lebanon.
   There will not be enough
   room for them.
[11] They will pass through a sea
   of trouble.
The stormy sea will calm
   down.
All the deep places in the
   Nile River will dry up.
Assyria's pride will be
   brought down.
Egypt's right to rule will
   disappear.
[12] I will make my people strong.
They will live in safety
   because of me,"
      announces the LORD.

11

Lebanon, open your
   doors!
Then fire can burn up your
   cedar trees.

[2] Juniper trees, cry out!
The cedar trees have fallen
   down.
The majestic trees are
   destroyed.
Cry out, you oak trees of
   Bashan!
The thick forest has been
   cut down.
[3] Listen to the shepherds cry
   out!
Their rich grasslands are
   destroyed.
Listen to the lions roar!
The trees and bushes along
   the Jordan River are
   gone.

The Two Shepherds

[4] The LORD my God says,
"Take care of the sheep that
are set apart to be sacrificed.
[5] Those who buy them kill them.
And they are not punished for
it. Those who sell them say,
'Praise the LORD! We're rich!'
And their own shepherds do
not spare them. [6] I will no longer have pity on the people in
the land," announces the LORD.
"I will hand all of them over to
their neighbors and their king.
They will destroy the land. And
I will not save anyone from
their power."

[7] So I took care of the sheep
set apart to be sacrificed. I took
special care of those that had
been treated badly. Then I got
two shepherd's staffs. I called
one of them Favor. I called the
other one Union. And I took
care of the flock. [8] In one month
I got rid of three worthless shepherds.

The sheep hated me, and I got tired of them. ⁹ So I said, "I won't be your shepherd anymore. Let those of you who are dying die. Let those who are passing away pass away. Let those who are left eat one another up."

¹⁰ Then I got my staff called Favor. I broke it. That meant the covenant the Lord had made with all the nations was broken. ¹¹ It happened that day. The sheep that had been treated badly were watching me. They knew it was the Lord's message. ¹² I told them, "If you think it is best, give me my pay. But if you don't think so, keep it." So they paid me 30 silver coins.

¹³ The Lord said to me, "Throw those coins to the potter." That amount shows how little they valued me! So I threw the 30 silver coins to the potter at the Lord's temple.

¹⁴ Then I broke my second staff called Union. That broke the family connection between Judah and Israel.

¹⁵ The Lord said to me, "Now pretend to be a foolish shepherd. Get the things you need. ¹⁶ I am going to raise up a shepherd over the land. He will not take care of those that are wounded. He will not look for the young ones. He will not heal those that are hurt. He will not feed the healthy ones. Instead, he will eat the best sheep. He will even tear their hooves off.

¹⁷ "How terrible it will be for
that worthless
shepherd!
He deserts the flock.
May a sword strike his arm
and his right eye!
May his powerful arm
become weak!
May his right eye be totally
blinded!"

The Lord Will Destroy Jerusalem's Enemies

12 This is a prophecy. It is the Lord's message about Israel.

The Lord spreads out the heavens. He lays the foundation of the earth. He creates the human spirit within a person. He says, ² "Jerusalem will be like a cup in my hand. It will make all the surrounding nations drunk from the wine of my anger. Judah will be attacked by its enemies. So will Jerusalem. ³ At that time all the nations on earth will gather together against Jerusalem. Then it will become like a rock that can't be moved. All the nations that try to move it will only hurt themselves. ⁴ On that day I will fill every horse with panic. I will make every rider crazy," announces the Lord. "I will watch over the people of Judah. But I will make all the horses of the nations blind. ⁵ Then the family groups of Judah will say in their hearts, 'The people of Jerusalem are strong. That's because the Lord who rules over all is their God.'

⁶ "At that time Judah's family groups will be like a fire pot in a pile of wood. They will be like a burning torch among bundles of grain. They will destroy all the surrounding nations on

every side. But Jerusalem will remain unharmed in its place.

7 "I will save the houses in Judah first. The honor of David's family line is great. So is the honor of those who live in Jerusalem. But their honor will not be greater than the honor of the rest of Judah. 8 At that time I will be like a shield to those who live in Jerusalem. Then even the weakest among them will be great warriors like David. And David's family line will be like the angel of the LORD who leads them. 9 On that day I will begin to destroy all the nations that attack Jerusalem.

Israel's People Will Mourn Over the One They Pierced

10 "I will pour out a spirit of grace and prayer on David's family line. I will also send it on those who live in Jerusalem. They will look to me. I am the one they have pierced. They will mourn over me as someone mourns over an only child who has died. They will be full of sorrow over me. Their sorrow will be just like someone's sorrow over an oldest son. 11 At that time there will be a lot of weeping in Jerusalem. It will be as great as the weeping of the people at Hadad Rimmon. Hadad Rimmon is in the valley of Megiddo. They were weeping over Josiah's death. 12 Everyone in the land will mourn. Each family will mourn by themselves and their wives by themselves. That will include the family lines of David, Nathan, 13 Levi, Shimei and 14 all the others.

The LORD Makes Israel Pure and "Clean"

13 "At that time a fountain will be opened for the benefit of David's family line. It will also bless the others who live in Jerusalem. It will wash away their sins. It will make them pure and 'clean.'

2 "On that day I will remove the names of other gods from the land. They will not even be remembered anymore," announces the LORD who rules over all. "I will drive the evil prophets out of the land. I will get rid of the spirit that put lies in their mouths. 3 Some people might still prophesy. But their own fathers and mothers will speak to them. They will tell them, 'You must die. You have told lies in the LORD's name.' When they prophesy, their own parents will stab them.

4 "At that time every prophet will be ashamed of the vision they see. They will no longer pretend to be a true prophet. They will not put on clothes that are made out of hair in order to trick people. 5 In fact, each one will say, 'I'm not really a prophet. I'm a farmer. I've farmed the land since I was young.' 6 Suppose someone asks, 'What are these wounds on your body?' Then they will answer, 'I was given these wounds at the house of my friends.'

The Good Shepherd Is Killed and the Sheep Are Scattered

7 "My sword, wake up! Attack my shepherd!

Attack the man who is
close to me,"
announces the LORD who
rules over all.
"Strike down the shepherd.
Then the sheep will be
scattered.
And I will turn my hand
against their little ones.
8 Here is what will happen in
the whole land,"
announces the LORD.
"Two-thirds of the people
will be struck down and
die.
But one-third will be left.
9 I will put this third in the fire.
I will make them as pure as
silver.
I will test them like gold.
They will call out to me.
And I will answer them.
I will say, 'They are my
people.'
And they will say, 'The
LORD is our God.'"

The LORD Will Be King Over the Whole Earth

14 The day of the LORD is
coming, Jerusalem. At
that time your enemies will
steal everything your people own. They will divide it up
within your walls. 2 The LORD will gather all
the nations together. They will
fight against Jerusalem. They'll
capture the city. Its houses will
be robbed. Its women will be
raped. Half of the people will
be taken away as prisoners. But
the rest of them won't be taken.
3 Then the LORD will march out
and fight against those nations.

He will fight as on a day of battle. 4 On that day he will stand
on the Mount of Olives. It's east
of Jerusalem. It will be split in
two from east to west. Half of
the mountain will move north.
The other half will move south.
A large valley will be formed.
5 The people will run away
through that mountain valley.
It will reach all the way to Azel.
They'll run away just as they ran
from the earthquake when Uzziah was king of Judah. Then the
LORD my God will come. All the
holy ones will come with him.
6 There won't be any sunlight
on that day. There will be no
cold, frosty darkness either. 7 It
will be a day unlike any other. It
will be a day known only to the
LORD. It won't be separated into
day and night. After that day is
over, there will be light again.
8 At that time water that gives
life will flow out from Jerusalem. Half of it will run east into
the Dead Sea. The other half
will go west to the Mediterranean Sea. The water will flow in
summer and winter.
9 The LORD will be king over
the whole earth. On that day
there will be one LORD. His
name will be the only name.
10 The whole land south of Jerusalem will be changed. From
Geba to Rimmon it will become
like the Arabah Valley. But Jerusalem will be raised up high. It
will be raised from the Benjamin Gate to the First Gate to the
Corner Gate. It will be raised
from the Tower of Hananel to
the royal winepresses. And it

will remain in its place. ¹¹ People will live in it. Jerusalem will never be destroyed again. It will be secure.

¹² The LORD will punish all the nations that fought against Jerusalem. He'll strike them with a plague. It will make their bodies rot while they are still standing on their feet. Their eyes will rot in their heads. Their tongues will rot in their mouths. ¹³ On that day the LORD will fill people with great panic. They will grab one another by the hand. And they'll attack one another. ¹⁴ Judah will also fight at Jerusalem. The wealth of all the surrounding nations will be collected. Huge amounts of gold, silver and clothes will be gathered up. ¹⁵ The same kind of plague will strike the horses, mules, camels and donkeys. In fact, it will strike all the animals in the army camps.

¹⁶ But some people from all the nations that have attacked Jerusalem will still be left alive. All of them will go up there to worship the King. He is the LORD who rules over all. Year after year these people will celebrate the Feast of Booths. ¹⁷ Some nations might not go up to Jerusalem to worship the King. If they don't, they won't have any rain. ¹⁸ The people of Egypt might not go up there to take part. Then they won't have any rain either. That's the plague the LORD will send on the nations that don't go to celebrate the Feast of Booths. ¹⁹ Egypt will be punished. So will all the other nations that don't celebrate the feast.

²⁰ On that day "Holy to the LORD" will be carved on the bells of the horses. The cooking pots in the LORD's temple will be just like the sacred bowls in front of the altar for burnt offerings. ²¹ Every pot in Jerusalem and Judah will be set apart to the LORD. All those who come to offer sacrifices will get some of the pots and cook in them. At that time there won't be any Canaanites in the LORD's temple. He is the LORD who rules over all.

Malachi

Introduction:

Malachi wrote this book after the Jews came home. The people had repaired God's house, the temple. They had repaired their own houses. But things were not good. The people forgot God. They did not give to God what they should have. They married people who worshiped false gods.

Malachi told the Jews to turn back to God. He warned that God would come to judge the people. Those who do not love God will be judged. But God will take care of those who love and honor him.

Outline of contents:

1 This is a prophecy. It is the LORD's message to Israel through Malachi.

Israel Doubts God's Love

2 "Israel, I have loved you," says the LORD.

"But you ask, 'How have you loved us?'

"Wasn't Esau Jacob's brother?" says the LORD. "But I chose Jacob 3 instead of Esau. I have turned Esau's hill country into a dry and empty land. I left that land of Edom to the wild dogs in the desert."

4 Edom might say, "We have been crushed. But we'll rebuild our cities."

The LORD who rules over all says, "They might rebuild their cities. But I will destroy them. They will be called the Evil Land. My anger will always remain on them. 5 You will see it with your own eyes. You will say, 'The LORD is great! He rules even beyond the borders of Israel!'

Give Your Best to the LORD

6 "A son honors his father. A slave honors his master. If I am a father, where is the honor I should have? If I am a master, where is the respect you should give me?" says the LORD who rules over all.

"You priests look down on me.

"But you ask, 'How have we looked down on you?'

7 "You sacrifice 'unclean' food on my altar.

"But you ask, 'How have we made you "unclean"?'

"You do it by looking down on my altar. 8 You sacrifice blind animals to me. Isn't that wrong? You sacrifice disabled or sick animals. Isn't that wrong? Try offering them to your governor! Would he be pleased with you?

Would he accept you?" says the LORD who rules over all.

9 "Now plead with God to be gracious to us! But as long as you give offerings like those, how can he accept you?" says the LORD.

10 "You might as well shut the temple doors! Then you would not light useless fires on my altar. I am not pleased with you," says the LORD. "I will not accept any of the offerings you bring. 11 My name will be great among the nations. They will worship me from where the sun rises in the east to where it sets in the west. In every place, incense and pure offerings will be brought to me. That's because my name will be great among the nations," says the LORD.

12 "But you treat my name as if it were not holy. You say the LORD's altar is 'unclean.' And you look down on its food. 13 You say, 'What a heavy load our work is!' And you turn up your nose. You act as if you hate working for me," says the LORD who rules over all.

"You bring animals that have been hurt. Or you bring disabled or sick animals. Then you dare to offer them to me as sacrifices! Should I accept them from you?" says the LORD. 14 "Suppose you have a male sheep or goat that does not have any flaws. And you promise to offer it to me. But then you sacrifice an animal that has flaws. When you do that, you cheat me. And anyone who cheats me is under my curse. After all, I am

a great king," says the LORD who rules over all. "The other nations have respect for my name. So why don't you respect it?

The LORD Warns the Priests

2 "Now I am giving this warning to you priests. 2 Listen to it. Honor me with all your heart," says the LORD who rules over all. "If you do not, I will send a curse on you. I will turn your blessings into curses. In fact, I have already done that because you have not honored me with all your heart.

3 "Because of what you have done, I will punish your children. I will smear the waste from your sacrifices on your faces. And you will be carried off to the dump along with it. 4 You will know that I have given you this warning. I have warned you so that my covenant with Levi will continue," says the LORD who rules over all. 5 "My covenant promised Levi life and peace. So I gave them to him. I required him to respect me. And he had great respect for my name. 6 True teaching came from his mouth. Nothing but the truth came from his lips. He walked with me in peace. He did what was right. He turned many people away from their sins.

7 "The lips of a priest should guard knowledge. After all, he is the messenger of the LORD who rules over all. And people seek instruction from his mouth. 8 But you have turned away from the right path. Your teaching has caused many people to trip

and fall. You have broken my covenant with Levi," says the LORD who rules over all. ⁹ "So I have caused all the people to hate you. They have lost respect for you. You have not done what I told you to do. Instead, you have favored one person over another in matters of the law."

Breaking the Covenant Through Divorce

¹⁰ People of Judah, all of us have one Father. One God created us. So why do we break the covenant the LORD made with our people of long ago? We do this by being unfaithful to one another.

¹¹ And Judah has been unfaithful. A hateful thing has been done in Israel and Jerusalem. The LORD loves his temple. But Judah has made it impure. Their men have married women who worship other gods. ¹² May the LORD punish the man who marries a woman like this. It doesn't matter who that man is. May the LORD who rules over all remove him from the tents of Jacob's people. May the LORD remove him even if he brings an offering to him.

¹³ Here's something else you do. You flood the LORD's altar with your tears. You weep and cry because your offerings don't please him anymore. He doesn't accept them with pleasure from your hands. ¹⁴ You ask, "Why?" It's because the LORD is holding you responsible. He watches how you treat the wife you married when you were young. You

have been unfaithful to her. You did it even though she's your partner. You promised to stay married to her. And the LORD was a witness to it.

¹⁵ Hasn't the one God made the two of you one also? Both of you belong to him in body and spirit. And why has the one God made you one? Because he wants his children to be like him. So be careful. Don't be unfaithful to the wife you married when you were young.

¹⁶ "Suppose a man hates and divorces his wife," says the LORD God of Israel. "Then he is harming the one he should protect," says the LORD who rules over all.

So be careful. And don't be unfaithful.

Breaking the Covenant by Treating Others Unfairly

¹⁷ You have worn out the LORD by what you keep saying.

"How have we worn him out?" you ask.

You have done it by saying, "All those who do evil things are good in the LORD's sight. And he is pleased with them." Or you ask, "Is God really fair?"

3 The LORD who rules over all says, "I will send my messenger. He will prepare my way for me. Then suddenly the Lord you are looking for will come to his temple. The messenger of the covenant will come. He is the one you long for."

² But who can live through the day when he comes? Who will be left standing when he

appears? He will be like a fire that makes things pure. He will be like soap that makes things clean. ³ He will act like one who makes silver pure. And he will purify the Levites, just as gold and silver are purified with fire. Then these men will bring proper offerings to the Lord. ⁴ And the offerings of Judah and Jerusalem will be acceptable to him. It will be as it was in days and years gone by.

⁵ "So I will come and put you on trial. I will be quick to bring charges against all of you," says the Lord who rules over all. "I will bring charges against you sinful people who do not have any respect for me. That includes those who practice evil magic. It includes those who commit adultery and those who tell lies in court. It includes those who cheat workers out of their pay. It includes those who treat widows badly. It also includes those who mistreat children whose fathers have died. And it includes those who take away the rights of outsiders in the courts.

Breaking the Covenant by Stealing From God

⁶ "I am the Lord. I do not change. That is why I have not destroyed you members of Jacob's family. ⁷ You have turned away from my rules. You have not obeyed them. You have lived that way ever since the days of your people of long ago. Return to me. Then I will return to you," says the Lord who rules over all.

"But you ask, 'How can we return?'

⁸ "Will a mere human being dare to steal from God? But you rob me!

"You ask, 'How are we robbing you?'

"By holding back your offerings. You also steal from me when you do not bring me a tenth of everything you produce. ⁹ So you are under my curse. In fact, your whole nation is under my curse. That is because you are robbing me. ¹⁰ Bring the entire tenth to the storerooms in my temple. Then there will be plenty of food. Test me this way," says the Lord. "Then you will see that I will throw open the windows of heaven. I will pour out so many blessings that you will not have enough room to store them. ¹¹ I will keep bugs from eating up your crops. And your grapes will not drop from the vines before they are ripe," says the Lord. ¹² "Then all the nations will call you blessed. Your land will be delightful," says the Lord who rules over all.

Israel Speaks With Pride Against the Lord

¹³ "You have spoken with pride against me," says the Lord.

"But you ask, 'What have we spoken against you?'

¹⁴ "You have said, 'It is useless to serve God. What do we gain by obeying his laws? And what do we get by pretending to be sad in front of the Lord? ¹⁵ But now we call proud peo-

ple blessed. Things go well with those who do what is evil. And God doesn't even punish those who test him.'"

Those Who Respect the LORD

¹⁶ Those who had respect for the LORD talked with one another. And the LORD heard them. A list of people and what they did was written in a book in front of him. It included the names of those who respected the LORD and honored him.

¹⁷ "The day is coming when I will judge," says the LORD who rules over all. "On that day they will be my special treasure. I will spare them just as a father loves and spares his son who serves him. ¹⁸ Then once again you will see the difference between godly people and sinful people. And you will see the difference between those who serve me and those who do not.

The Day of the LORD Is Coming

4 "You can be sure the day of the LORD is coming. My anger will burn like a furnace. All those who are proud will be like straw. So will all those who do what is evil. The day that is coming will set them on fire," says the LORD who rules over all. "Not even a root or a branch will be left to them. ² But here is what will happen for you who have respect for me. The sun that brings life will rise. Its rays will bring healing to my people. You will go out and leap for joy like calves that have just been fed. ³ Then you will stomp on sinful people. They will be like ashes under your feet. That will happen on the day I judge," says the LORD.

⁴ "Remember the law my servant Moses gave you. Remember the rules and laws I gave him at Mount Horeb. They were for the whole nation of Israel.

⁵ "I will send the prophet Elijah to you. He will come before the day of the LORD arrives. It will be a great and terrifying day. ⁶ Elijah will bring peace between parents and their children. He will also bring peace between children and their parents. If that does not happen, I will come. And I will completely destroy the land."

The
New Testament

Matthew

Introduction:

Matthew is one of the four Gospels. Gospel means "good news." Matthew tells the good news that Jesus Christ has come. Many years earlier, the prophets had said he would come. God had promised to send someone to save people from their sins. The Jews called that person the Messiah. Matthew wrote to the Jews to tell them that Jesus is the Messiah. Matthew quoted many Old Testament verses. He said they came true in Jesus' life.

Jesus is also a great teacher. Matthew wrote down many of the things Jesus said. Jesus told people about his kingdom. He taught people how to live in his kingdom.

Outline of contents:

The Family Line of Jesus the Messiah

1 This is the written story of the family line of Jesus the Messiah. He is the son of David. He is also the son of Abraham.

2 Abraham was the father of Isaac.

Isaac was the father of Jacob.

Jacob was the father of Judah and his brothers.

3 Judah was the father of Perez and Zerah. Tamar was their mother.

Perez was the father of Hezron.

Hezron was the father of Ram.

4 Ram was the father of Amminadab.

Amminadab was the father of Nahshon.

Nahshon was the father of Salmon.

5 Salmon was the father of

Boaz. Rahab was Boaz's mother.

Boaz was the father of Obed. Ruth was Obed's mother.

Obed was the father of Jesse.

6 And Jesse was the father of King David.

David was the father of Solomon. Solomon's mother had been Uriah's wife.

7 Solomon was the father of Rehoboam.

Rehoboam was the father of Abijah.

Abijah was the father of Asa.

8 Asa was the father of Jehoshaphat.

Jehoshaphat was the father of Jehoram.

Jehoram was the father of Uzziah.

9 Uzziah was the father of Jotham.

Jotham was the father of Ahaz.

Ahaz was the father of Hezekiah.

10 Hezekiah was the father of Manasseh.

Manasseh was the father of Amon.

Amon was the father of Josiah.

11 And Josiah was the father of Jeconiah and his brothers. At that time, the Jewish people were forced to go away to Babylon.

12 After this, the family line continued.

Jeconiah was the father of Shealtiel.

Shealtiel was the father of Zerubbabel.

13 Zerubbabel was the father of Abihud.

Abihud was the father of Eliakim.

Eliakim was the father of Azor.

14 Azor was the father of Zadok.

Zadok was the father of Akim.

Akim was the father of Elihud.

15 Elihud was the father of Eleazar.

Eleazar was the father of Matthan.

Matthan was the father of Jacob.

16 Jacob was the father of Joseph. Joseph was the husband of Mary. And Mary was the mother of Jesus, who is called the Messiah.

17 So there were 14 generations from Abraham to David. There were 14 from David until the Jewish people were forced to go away to Babylon. And there were 14 from that time to the Messiah.

Joseph Accepts Jesus as His Son

18 This is how the birth of Jesus the Messiah came about. His mother Mary and Joseph had promised to get married. But before they started to live together, it became clear that she was going to have a baby. She became pregnant by the power of the Holy Spirit. 19 Her

husband Joseph was faithful to the law. But he did not want to put her to shame in public. So he planned to divorce her quietly.

²⁰ But as Joseph was thinking about this, an angel of the Lord appeared to him in a dream. The angel said, "Joseph, son of David, don't be afraid to take Mary home as your wife. The baby inside her is from the Holy Spirit. ²¹ She is going to have a son. You must give him the name Jesus. That's because he will save his people from their sins."

²² All this took place to bring about what the Lord had said would happen. He had said through the prophet, ²³ "The virgin is going to have a baby. She will give birth to a son. And he will be called Immanuel." *(Isaiah 7:14)* The name Immanuel means "God with us."

²⁴ Joseph woke up. He did what the angel of the Lord commanded him to do. He took Mary home as his wife. ²⁵ But he did not sleep with her until she gave birth to a son. And Joseph gave him the name Jesus.

The Wise Men Visit Jesus

2 Jesus was born in Bethlehem in Judea. This happened while Herod was king of Judea. After Jesus' birth, Wise Men from the east came to Jerusalem. ² They asked, "Where is the child who has been born to be king of the Jews? We saw his star when it rose. Now we have come to worship him."

³ When King Herod heard about it, he was very upset. Everyone in Jerusalem was troubled too. ⁴ So Herod called together all the chief priests of the people. He also called the teachers of the law. He asked them where the Messiah was going to be born. ⁵ "In Bethlehem in Judea," they replied. "This is what the prophet has written. He said,

⁶ " 'But you, Bethlehem, in the
     land of Judah,
   are certainly not the least
     important among the
     towns of Judah.
A ruler will come out of you.
  He will rule my people
     Israel like a shepherd.' "
(Micah 5:2)

⁷ Then Herod secretly called for the Wise Men. He found out from them exactly when the star had appeared. ⁸ He sent them to Bethlehem. He said, "Go and search carefully for the child. As soon as you find him, report it to me. Then I can go and worship him too."

⁹ After the Wise Men had listened to the king, they went on their way. The star they had seen when it rose went ahead of them. It finally stopped over the place where the child was. ¹⁰ When they saw the star, they were filled with joy. ¹¹ The Wise Men went to the house. There they saw the child with his mother Mary. They bowed down and worshiped him. Then they opened their treasures. They gave him gold, frankincense and myrrh. ¹² But God

warned them in a dream not to go back to Herod. So they returned to their country on a different road.

Jesus' Family Escapes to Egypt

13 When the Wise Men had left, Joseph had a dream. In the dream an angel of the Lord appeared to Joseph. "Get up!" the angel said. "Take the child and his mother and escape to Egypt. Stay there until I tell you to come back. Herod is going to search for the child. He wants to kill him."

14 So Joseph got up. During the night, he left for Egypt with the child and his mother Mary. 15 They stayed there until King Herod died. So the words the Lord had spoken through the prophet came true. He had said, "I brought my son out of Egypt." *(Hosea 11:1)*

16 Herod realized that the Wise Men had tricked him. So he became very angry. He gave orders about Bethlehem and the area around it. He ordered all the boys two years old and under to be killed. This agreed with the time when the Wise Men had seen the star. 17 In this way, the words Jeremiah the prophet spoke came true. He had said,

18 "A voice is heard in Ramah.
    It's the sound of crying and
        deep sadness.
    Rachel is crying over her
        children.
    She refuses to be
        comforted,
    because they are gone."
                        (Jeremiah 31:15)

Jesus' Family Returns to Nazareth

19 After Herod died, Joseph had a dream while he was still in Egypt. In the dream an angel of the Lord appeared to him. 20 The angel said, "Get up! Take the child and his mother. Go to the land of Israel. The people who were trying to kill the child are dead."

21 So Joseph got up. He took the child and his mother Mary back to the land of Israel. 22 But then he heard that Archelaus was king of Judea. Archelaus was ruling in place of his father Herod. This made Joseph afraid to go there. Joseph had been warned in a dream. So he went back to the land of Galilee instead. 23 There he lived in a town called Nazareth. So what the prophets had said about Jesus came true. They had said that he would be called a Nazarene.

John the Baptist Prepares the Way

3 In those days John the Baptist came and preached in the Desert of Judea. 2 He said, "Turn away from your sins! The kingdom of heaven has come near." 3 John is the one Isaiah the prophet had spoken about. He had said,

    "A messenger is calling out in
        the desert,
    'Prepare the way for the Lord.
        Make straight paths for
            him.'" *(Isaiah 40:3)*

4 John's clothes were made out of camel's hair. He had a leather

belt around his waist. His food was locusts and wild honey. ⁵People went out to him from Jerusalem and all Judea. They also came from the whole area around the Jordan River. ⁶When they confessed their sins, John baptized them in the Jordan.

⁷John saw many Pharisees and Sadducees coming to where he was baptizing. He said to them, "You are like a nest of poisonous snakes! Who warned you to escape the coming of God's anger? ⁸Live in a way that shows you have turned away from your sins. ⁹Don't think you can say to yourselves, 'Abraham is our father.' I tell you, God can raise up children for Abraham even from these stones. ¹⁰The ax is ready to cut the roots of the trees. All the trees that don't produce good fruit will be cut down. They will be thrown into the fire.

¹¹"I baptize you with water, calling you to turn away from your sins. But after me, someone is coming who is more powerful than I am. I'm not worthy to carry his sandals. He will baptize you with the Holy Spirit and fire. ¹²His pitchfork is in his hand to clear the straw from his threshing floor. He will gather his wheat into the storeroom. But he will burn up the husks with fire that can't be put out."

Jesus Is Baptized

¹³Jesus came from Galilee to the Jordan River. He wanted to be baptized by John. ¹⁴But John tried to stop him. So he told Jesus, "I need to be baptized by you. So why do you come to me?"

¹⁵Jesus replied, "Let it be this way for now. It is right for us to do this. It carries out God's holy plan." Then John agreed.

¹⁶As soon as Jesus was baptized, he came up out of the water. At that moment heaven was opened. Jesus saw the Spirit of God coming down on him like a dove. ¹⁷A voice from heaven said, "This is my Son, and I love him. I am very pleased with him."

Jesus Is Tempted in the Desert

4 The Holy Spirit led Jesus into the desert. There the devil tempted him. ²After 40 days and 40 nights of going without eating, Jesus was hungry. ³The tempter came to him. He said, "If you are the Son of God, tell these stones to become bread."

⁴Jesus answered, "It is written, 'Man must not live only on bread. He must also live on every word that comes from the mouth of God.'" *(Deuteronomy 8:3)*

⁵Then the devil took Jesus to the holy city. He had him stand on the highest point of the temple. ⁶"If you are the Son of God," he said, "throw yourself down. It is written,

"'The Lord will command
　　his angels to take good
　　care of you.
They will lift you up in
　　their hands.
Then you won't trip over a
　　stone.'" *(Psalm 91:11,12)*

[7] Jesus answered him, "It is also written, 'Do not test the Lord your God.'" *(Deuteronomy 6:16)*

[8] Finally, the devil took Jesus to a very high mountain. He showed him all the kingdoms of the world and their glory. [9] "If you bow down and worship me," he said, "I will give you all this."

[10] Jesus said to him, "Get away from me, Satan! It is written, 'Worship the Lord your God. He is the only one you should serve.'" *(Deuteronomy 6:13)*

[11] Then the devil left Jesus. Angels came and took care of him.

Jesus Begins to Preach

[12] John had been put in prison. When Jesus heard about this, he returned to Galilee. [13] Jesus left Nazareth and went to live in the city of Capernaum. It was by the lake in the area of Zebulun and Naphtali. [14] In that way, what the prophet Isaiah had said came true. He had said,

[15] "Land of Zebulun! Land of
    Naphtali!
  Galilee, where Gentiles
    live!
  Land along the
    Mediterranean Sea!
  Territory east of the
    Jordan River!
[16] The people who are now
    living in darkness
  have seen a great light.
  They are now living in a very
    dark land.
  But a light has shined on
    them." *(Isaiah 9:1,2)*

[17] From that time on Jesus began to preach. "Turn away from your sins!" he said. "The kingdom of heaven has come near."

Jesus Chooses His First Disciples

[18] One day Jesus was walking beside the Sea of Galilee. There he saw two brothers, Simon Peter and his brother Andrew. They were throwing a net into the lake, because they were fishermen. [19] "Come and follow me," Jesus said. "I will send you out to fish for people." [20] At once they left their nets and followed him.

[21] Going on from there, he saw two other brothers. They were James, son of Zebedee, and his brother John. They were in a boat with their father Zebedee. As they were preparing their nets, Jesus called out to them. [22] Right away they left the boat and their father and followed Jesus.

Jesus Heals Sick People

[23] Jesus went all over Galilee. There he taught in the synagogues. He preached the good news of God's kingdom. He healed every illness and sickness the people had. [24] News about him spread all over Syria. People brought to him all who were ill with different kinds of sicknesses. Some were suffering great pain. Others were controlled by demons. Some were shaking wildly. Others couldn't move at all. And Jesus healed all of them. [25] Large crowds followed him. People came from Galilee, from the area known as the Ten Cities, and from Jeru-

salem and Judea. Others came from the area across the Jordan River.

Jesus Teaches the Disciples and Crowds

5 Jesus saw the crowds. So he went up on a mountainside and sat down. His disciples came to him. ² Then he began to teach them.

Jesus Gives Blessings

He said,

³ "Blessed are those who are spiritually needy.
The kingdom of heaven belongs to them.
⁴ Blessed are those who are sad.
They will be comforted.
⁵ Blessed are those who are humble.
They will be given the earth.
⁶ Blessed are those who are hungry and thirsty for what is right.
They will be filled.
⁷ Blessed are those who show mercy.
They will be shown mercy.
⁸ Blessed are those whose hearts are pure.
They will see God.
⁹ Blessed are those who make peace.
They will be called children of God.
¹⁰ Blessed are those who suffer for doing what is right.
The kingdom of heaven belongs to them.

¹¹ "Blessed are you when people make fun of you and hurt you because of me. You are also blessed when they tell all kinds of evil lies about you because of me. ¹² Be joyful and glad. Your reward in heaven is great. In the same way, people hurt the prophets who lived long ago.

Salt and Light

¹³ "You are the salt of the earth. But suppose the salt loses its saltiness. How can it be made salty again? It is no longer good for anything. It will be thrown out. People will walk all over it.

¹⁴ "You are the light of the world. A town built on a hill can't be hidden. ¹⁵ Also, people do not light a lamp and put it under a bowl. Instead, they put it on its stand. Then it gives light to everyone in the house. ¹⁶ In the same way, let your light shine so others can see it. Then they will see the good things you do. And they will bring glory to your Father who is in heaven.

Jesus Fulfills the Law

¹⁷ "Do not think I have come to get rid of what is written in the Law or in the Prophets. I have not come to do this. Instead, I have come to fulfill what is written. ¹⁸ What I'm about to tell you is true. Heaven and earth will disappear before the smallest letter disappears from the Law. Not even the smallest mark of a pen will disappear from the Law until everything is completed. ¹⁹ Do not ignore even one of the least important commands.

And do not teach others to ignore them. If you do, you will be called the least important person in the kingdom of heaven. Instead, practice and teach these commands. Then you will be called important in the kingdom of heaven. ²⁰ Here is what I tell you. You must be more godly than the Pharisees and the teachers of the law. If you are not, you will certainly not enter the kingdom of heaven.

Murder

²¹ "You have heard what was said to people who lived long ago. They were told, 'Do not commit murder. *(Exodus 20:13)* Anyone who murders will be judged for it.' ²² But here is what I tell you. Do not be angry with a brother or sister. Anyone who is angry with them will be judged. Again, anyone who says to a brother or sister, 'Raca,' must stand trial in court. And anyone who says, 'You fool!' will be in danger of the fire in hell.

²³ "Suppose you are offering your gift at the altar. And you remember that your brother or sister has something against you. ²⁴ Leave your gift in front of the altar. First go and make peace with them. Then come back and offer your gift.

²⁵ "Suppose someone has a claim against you and is taking you to court. Settle the matter quickly. Do this while you are still together on the way. If you don't, you may be handed over to the judge. The judge may hand you over to the officer to be thrown into prison. ²⁶ What I'm about to tell you is true. You will not get out until you have paid the very last penny!

Adultery

²⁷ "You have heard that it was said, 'Do not commit adultery.' *(Exodus 20:14)* ²⁸ But here is what I tell you. Do not even look at a woman in the wrong way. Anyone who does has already committed adultery with her in his heart. ²⁹ If your right eye causes you to sin, poke it out and throw it away. Your eye is only one part of your body. It is better to lose an eye than for your whole body to be thrown into hell. ³⁰ If your right hand causes you to sin, cut it off and throw it away. Your hand is only one part of your body. It is better to lose a hand than for your whole body to go into hell.

Divorce

³¹ "It has been said, 'Suppose a man divorces his wife. If he does, he must give her a letter of divorce.' *(Deuteronomy 24:1)* ³² But here is what I tell you. Anyone who divorces his wife makes her a victim of adultery. And anyone who gets married to the divorced woman commits adultery. A man may divorce his wife only if she has not been faithful to him.

Promises

³³ "Again, you have heard what was said to your people long ago. They were told, 'Do not break the promises you make to

the Lord. Keep your promises to the Lord that you have made.' ³⁴ But here is what I tell you. Do not make any promises like that at all. Do not make them in the name of heaven. That is God's throne. ³⁵ Do not make them in the name of the earth. That is the stool for God's feet. Do not make them in the name of Jerusalem. That is the city of the Great King. ³⁶ And do not make a promise in your own name. You can't make even one hair of your head white or black. ³⁷ All you need to say is simply 'Yes' or 'No.' Anything more than this comes from the evil one.

Be Kind to Others

³⁸ "You have heard that it was said, 'An eye must be put out for an eye. A tooth must be knocked out for a tooth.' *(Exodus 21:24; Leviticus 24:20; Deuteronomy 19:21)* ³⁹ But here is what I tell you. Do not fight against an evil person. Suppose someone slaps you on your right cheek. Turn your other cheek to them also. ⁴⁰ Suppose someone takes you to court to get your shirt. Let them have your coat also. ⁴¹ Suppose someone forces you to go one mile. Go two miles with them. ⁴² Give to the one who asks you for something. Don't turn away from the one who wants to borrow something from you.

Love Your Enemies

⁴³ "You have heard that it was said, 'Love your neighbor. *(Leviticus 19:18)* Hate your enemy.' ⁴⁴ But here is what I tell

you. Love your enemies. Pray for those who hurt you. ⁴⁵ Then you will be children of your Father who is in heaven. He causes his sun to shine on evil people and good people. He sends rain on those who do right and those who don't. ⁴⁶ If you love those who love you, what reward will you get? Even the tax collectors do that. ⁴⁷ If you greet only your own people, what more are you doing than others? Even people who are ungodly do that. ⁴⁸ So be perfect, just as your Father in heaven is perfect.

Giving to Needy People

6 "Be careful not to do good deeds in front of other people. Don't do those deeds to be seen by others. If you do, your Father in heaven will not reward you.

² "When you give to needy people, do not announce it by having trumpets blown. Do not be like those who only pretend to be holy. They announce what they do in the synagogues and on the streets. They want to be honored by other people. What I'm about to tell you is true. They have received their complete reward. ³ When you give to needy people, don't let your left hand know what your right hand is doing. ⁴ Then your giving will be done secretly. Your Father will reward you, because he sees what you do secretly.

Prayer

⁵ "When you pray, do not be like those who only pretend to

be holy. They love to stand and pray in the synagogues and on the street corners. They want to be seen by other people. What I'm about to tell you is true. They have received their complete reward. ⁶ When you pray, go into your room. Close the door and pray to your Father, who can't be seen. Your Father will reward you, because he sees what you do secretly. ⁷ When you pray, do not keep talking on and on. That is what ungodly people do. They think they will be heard because they talk a lot. ⁸ Do not be like them. Your Father knows what you need even before you ask him.

⁹ "This is how you should pray.

" 'Our Father in heaven,
may your name be
honored.
¹⁰ May your kingdom come.
May what you want to
happen be done
on earth as it is done in
heaven.
¹¹ Give us today our daily
bread.
¹² And forgive us our sins,
just as we also have
forgiven those who sin
against us.
¹³ Keep us from sinning when
we are tempted.
Save us from the evil one.'

¹⁴ Forgive other people when they sin against you. If you do, your Father who is in heaven will also forgive you. ¹⁵ But if you do not forgive the sins of other people, your Father will not forgive your sins.

Fasting

¹⁶ "When you go without eating, do not look gloomy like those who only pretend to be holy. They make their faces look very sad. They want to show people they are fasting. What I'm about to tell you is true. They have received their complete reward. ¹⁷ But when you go without eating, put olive oil on your head. Wash your face. ¹⁸ Then others will not know that you are fasting. Only your Father, who can't be seen, will know it. Your Father will reward you, because he sees what you do secretly.

Gather Riches in Heaven

¹⁹ "Do not gather for yourselves riches on earth. Moths and rats can destroy them. Thieves can break in and steal them. ²⁰ Instead, gather for yourselves riches in heaven. There, moths and rats do not destroy them. There, thieves do not break in and steal them. ²¹ Your heart will be where your riches are.

²² "The eye is like a lamp for the body. Suppose your eyes are healthy. Then your whole body will be full of light. ²³ But suppose your eyes can't see well. Then your whole body will be full of darkness. If the light inside you is darkness, then it is very dark!

²⁴ "No one can serve two masters at the same time. You will hate one of them and love the other. Or you will be faithful to one and dislike the other. You

can't serve God and money at the same time.

Do Not Worry

²⁵ "I tell you, do not worry. Don't worry about your life and what you will eat or drink. And don't worry about your body and what you will wear. Isn't there more to life than eating? Aren't there more important things for the body than clothes? ²⁶ Look at the birds of the air. They don't plant or gather crops. They don't put away crops in storerooms. But your Father who is in heaven feeds them. Aren't you worth much more than they are? ²⁷ Can you add even one hour to your life by worrying?

²⁸ "And why do you worry about clothes? See how the wild flowers grow. They don't work or make clothing. ²⁹ But here is what I tell you. Not even Solomon in all his royal robes was dressed like one of these flowers. ³⁰ If that is how God dresses the wild grass, won't he dress you even better? Your faith is so small! After all, the grass is here only today. Tomorrow it is thrown into the fire. ³¹ So don't worry. Don't say, 'What will we eat?' Or, 'What will we drink?' Or, 'What will we wear?' ³² People who are ungodly run after all those things. Your Father who is in heaven knows that you need them. ³³ But put God's kingdom first. Do what he wants you to do. Then all those things will also be given to you. ³⁴ So don't worry about tomorrow. Tomorrow will worry about itself. Each day has enough trouble of its own.

Be Fair When You Judge Other People

7 "Do not judge other people. Then you will not be judged. ² You will be judged in the same way you judge others. You will be measured in the same way you measure others.

³ "You look at the bit of sawdust in your friend's eye. But you pay no attention to the piece of wood in your own eye. ⁴ How can you say to your friend, 'Let me take the bit of sawdust out of your eye'? How can you say this while there is a piece of wood in your own eye? ⁵ You pretender! First take the piece of wood out of your own eye. Then you will be able to see clearly to take the bit of sawdust out of your friend's eye.

⁶ "Do not give holy things to dogs. Do not throw your pearls to pigs. If you do, they might walk all over them. They might turn around and tear you to pieces.

Ask, Search, Knock

⁷ "Ask, and it will be given to you. Search, and you will find. Knock, and the door will be opened to you. ⁸ Everyone who asks will receive. The one who searches will find. The door will be opened to the one who knocks.

⁹ "Suppose your son asks for bread. Which of you will give him a stone? ¹⁰ Or suppose he asks for a fish. Which of you will

give him a snake? [11] Even though you are evil, you know how to give good gifts to your children. How much more will your Father who is in heaven give good gifts to those who ask him! [12] In everything, do to others what you would want them to do to you. This is what is written in the Law and in the Prophets.

The Large and Small Gates

[13] "Enter God's kingdom through the narrow gate. The gate is large and the road is wide that leads to ruin. Many people go that way. [14] But the gate is small and the road is narrow that leads to life. Only a few people find it.

True and False Prophets

[15] "Watch out for false prophets. They come to you pretending to be sheep. But on the inside they are hungry wolves. [16] You can tell each tree by its fruit. Do people pick grapes from bushes? Do they pick figs from thorns? [17] In the same way, every good tree bears good fruit. But a bad tree bears bad fruit. [18] A good tree can't bear bad fruit. And a bad tree can't bear good fruit. [19] Every tree that does not bear good fruit is cut down. It is thrown into the fire. [20] You can tell each tree by its fruit.

True and False Disciples

[21] "Not everyone who says to me, 'Lord, Lord,' will enter the kingdom of heaven. Only those who do what my Father in heaven wants will en-

ter. [22] Many will say to me on that day, 'Lord! Lord! Didn't we prophesy in your name? Didn't we drive out demons in your name? Didn't we do many miracles in your name?' [23] Then I will tell them clearly, 'I never knew you. Get away from me, you who do evil!'

The Wise and Foolish Builders

[24] "So then, everyone who hears my words and puts them into practice is like a wise man. He builds his house on the rock. [25] The rain comes down. The water rises. The winds blow and beat against that house. But it does not fall. It is built on the rock. [26] But everyone who hears my words and does not put them into practice is like a foolish man. He builds his house on sand. [27] The rain comes down. The water rises. The winds blow and beat against that house. And it falls with a loud crash."

[28] Jesus finished saying all these things. The crowds were amazed at his teaching. [29] That's because he taught like one who had authority. He did not speak like their teachers of the law.

Jesus Heals a Man Who Had a Skin Disease

8 Jesus came down from the mountainside. Large crowds followed him. [2] A man who had a skin disease came and got down on his knees in front of Jesus. He said, "Lord, if you are willing to make me 'clean,' you can do it."

[3] Jesus reached out his hand and touched the man. "I am willing to do it," he said. "Be 'clean'!" Right away the man was healed of his skin disease. [4] Then Jesus said to him, "Don't tell anyone. Go and show yourself to the priest, and offer the gift Moses commanded. It will be a witness to everyone."

A Roman Commander Has Faith

[5] When Jesus entered Capernaum, a Roman commander came to him. He asked Jesus for help. [6] "Lord," he said, "my servant lies at home and can't move. He is suffering terribly."

[7] Jesus said, "Shall I come and heal him?"

[8] The commander replied, "Lord, I am not good enough to have you come into my house. But just say the word, and my servant will be healed. [9] I myself am a man under authority. And I have soldiers who obey my orders. I tell this one, 'Go,' and he goes. I tell that one, 'Come,' and he comes. I say to my slave, 'Do this,' and he does it."

[10] When Jesus heard this, he was amazed. He said to those following him, "What I'm about to tell you is true. In Israel I have not found anyone whose faith is so strong. [11] I say to you that many will come from the east and the west. They will take their places at the feast in the kingdom of heaven. They will sit with Abraham, Isaac and Jacob. [12] But those who think they belong in the kingdom will be thrown outside, into the darkness. There they will weep and grind their teeth." [13] Then Jesus said to the Roman commander, "Go! It will be done just as you believed it would." And his servant was healed at that moment.

Jesus Heals Many People

[14] When Jesus came into Peter's house, he saw Peter's mother-in-law. She was lying in bed. She had a fever. [15] Jesus touched her hand, and the fever left her. She got up and began to serve him.

[16] When evening came, many people controlled by demons were brought to Jesus. He drove out the spirits with a word. He healed all who were sick. [17] This happened so that what Isaiah the prophet had said would come true. He had said,

> "He suffered the things
>   we should have
>   suffered.
> He took on himself the
>   sicknesses that should
>   have been ours."

(Isaiah 53:4)

The Cost of Following Jesus

[18] Jesus saw the crowd around him. So he gave his disciples orders to go to the other side of the Sea of Galilee. [19] Then a teacher of the law came to him. He said, "Teacher, I will follow you no matter where you go."

[20] Jesus replied, "Foxes have dens. Birds have nests. But the Son of Man has no place to lay his head."

[21] Another follower said to

him, "Lord, first let me go and bury my father."

²² But Jesus told him, "Follow me. Let the dead bury their own dead."

Jesus Calms the Storm

²³ Jesus got into a boat. His disciples followed him. ²⁴ Suddenly a terrible storm came up on the lake. The waves crashed over the boat. But Jesus was sleeping. ²⁵ The disciples went and woke him up. They said, "Lord! Save us! We're going to drown!"

²⁶ He replied, "Your faith is so small! Why are you so afraid?" Then Jesus got up and ordered the winds and the waves to stop. It became completely calm.

²⁷ The disciples were amazed. They asked, "What kind of man is this? Even the winds and the waves obey him!"

Jesus Heals Two Men Controlled by Demons

²⁸ Jesus arrived at the other side of the lake in the area of the Gadarenes. Two men controlled by demons met him. They came from the tombs. The men were so wild that no one could pass that way. ²⁹ "Son of God, what do you want with us?" they shouted. "Have you come here to punish us before the time for us to be judged?"

³⁰ Not very far away, a large herd of pigs was feeding. ³¹ The demons begged Jesus, "If you drive us out, send us into the herd of pigs."

³² Jesus said to them, "Go!" So the demons came out of the men and went into the pigs. The whole herd rushed down the steep bank. They ran into the lake and drowned in the water. ³³ Those who were tending the pigs ran off. They went into the town and reported all this. They told the people what had happened to the men who had been controlled by demons. ³⁴ Then the whole town went out to meet Jesus. When they saw him, they begged him to leave their area.

Jesus Forgives and Heals a Man Who Could Not Walk

9 Jesus stepped into a boat. He went over to the other side of the lake and came to his own town. ² Some men brought to him a man who could not walk. He was lying on a mat. Jesus saw that they had faith. So he said to the man, "Don't lose hope, son. Your sins are forgiven."

³ Then some teachers of the law said to themselves, "This fellow is saying a very evil thing!"

⁴ Jesus knew what they were thinking. So he said, "Why do you have evil thoughts in your hearts? ⁵ Is it easier to say, 'Your sins are forgiven'? Or to say, 'Get up and walk'? ⁶ But I want you to know that the Son of Man has authority on earth to forgive sins." So he spoke to the man who could not walk. "Get up," he said. "Take your mat and go home." ⁷ The man got up and went home. ⁸ When the crowd saw this, they were filled with wonder. They praised God for

giving that kind of authority to a human being.

Jesus Chooses Matthew and Eats With Sinners

⁹ As Jesus went on from there, he saw a man named Matthew. He was sitting at the tax collector's booth. "Follow me," Jesus told him. Matthew got up and followed him.

¹⁰ Later Jesus was having dinner at Matthew's house. Many tax collectors and sinners came. They ate with Jesus and his disciples. ¹¹ The Pharisees saw this. So they asked the disciples, "Why does your teacher eat with tax collectors and sinners?"

¹² Jesus heard this. So he said, "Those who are healthy don't need a doctor. Sick people do. ¹³ Go and learn what this means, 'I want mercy and not sacrifice.' *(Hosea 6:6)* I have not come to get those who think they are right with God to follow me. I have come to get sinners to follow me."

Jesus Is Asked About Fasting

¹⁴ One day John's disciples came. They said to Jesus, "We and the Pharisees often go without eating. Why don't your disciples go without eating?"

¹⁵ Jesus answered, "How can the guests of the groom be sad while he is with them? The time will come when the groom will be taken away from them. Then they will fast.

¹⁶ "People don't sew a patch of new cloth on old clothes. The new piece will pull away from the old. That will make the tear worse. ¹⁷ People don't pour new wine into old wineskins. If they do, the skins will burst. The wine will run out, and the wineskins will be destroyed. No, people pour new wine into new wineskins. Then both are saved."

Jesus Heals a Dead Girl and a Suffering Woman

¹⁸ While Jesus was saying this, a synagogue leader came. He got down on his knees in front of Jesus. He said, "My daughter has just died. But come and place your hand on her. Then she will live again." ¹⁹ Jesus got up and went with him. So did his disciples.

²⁰ Just then a woman came up behind Jesus. She had a sickness that made her bleed. It had lasted for 12 years. She touched the edge of his clothes. ²¹ She thought, "I only need to touch his clothes. Then I will be healed."

²² Jesus turned and saw her. "Dear woman, don't give up hope," he said. "Your faith has healed you." The woman was healed at that moment.

²³ When Jesus entered the synagogue leader's house, he saw the noisy crowd and people playing flutes. ²⁴ He said, "Go away. The girl is not dead. She is sleeping." But they laughed at him. ²⁵ After the crowd had been sent outside, Jesus went in. He took the girl by the hand, and she got up. ²⁶ News about what Jesus had done spread all over that area.

Jesus Heals Two Blind Men

²⁷ As Jesus went on from there, two blind men followed him. They called out, "Have mercy on us, Son of David!"

²⁸ When Jesus went indoors, the blind men came to him. He asked them, "Do you believe that I can do this?"

"Yes, Lord," they replied.

²⁹ Then he touched their eyes. He said, "It will happen to you just as you believed." ³⁰ They could now see again. Jesus strongly warned them, "Be sure that no one knows about this." ³¹ But they went out and spread the news. They talked about him all over that area.

³² While they were going out, another man was brought to Jesus. A demon controlled him, and he could not speak. ³³ When the demon was driven out, the man spoke. The crowd was amazed. They said, "Nothing like this has ever been seen in Israel."

³⁴ But the Pharisees said, "He drives out demons by the power of the prince of demons."

There Are Only a Few Workers

³⁵ Jesus went through all the towns and villages. He taught in their synagogues. He preached the good news of the kingdom. And he healed every illness and sickness. ³⁶ When he saw the crowds, he felt deep concern for them. They were treated badly and were helpless, like sheep without a shepherd. ³⁷ Then Jesus said to his disciples, "The harvest is huge. But there are only a few workers. ³⁸ So ask the Lord of the harvest to send workers out into his harvest field."

Jesus Sends Out the Twelve Disciples

10 Jesus called for his 12 disciples to come to him. He gave them authority to drive out evil spirits and to heal every illness and sickness.

² Here are the names of the 12 apostles.

First there were Simon Peter and his brother Andrew.

Then came James, son of Zebedee, and his brother John.

³ Next were Philip and Bartholomew,

and also Thomas and Matthew the tax collector.

Two more were James, son of Alphaeus, and Thaddaeus.

⁴ The last were Simon the Zealot and Judas Iscariot. Judas was the one who was later going to hand Jesus over to his enemies.

⁵ Jesus sent these 12 out with the following orders. "Do not go among the Gentiles," he said. "Do not enter any town of the Samaritans. ⁶ Instead, go to the people of Israel. They are like sheep that have become lost. ⁷ As you go, preach this message, 'The kingdom of heaven has come near.' ⁸ Heal those who are sick. Bring those who are dead back to life. Make those who

have skin diseases 'clean' again. Drive out demons. You have received freely, so give freely.

⁹ "Do not get any gold, silver or copper to take with you in your belts. ¹⁰ Do not take a bag for the journey. Do not take extra clothes or sandals or walking sticks. A worker should be given what he needs. ¹¹ When you enter a town or village, look for someone who is willing to welcome you. Stay at their house until you leave. ¹² As you enter the home, greet those who live there. ¹³ If that home welcomes you, give it your blessing of peace. If it does not, don't bless it. ¹⁴ Some people may not welcome you or listen to your words. If they don't, leave that home or town, and shake the dust off your feet. ¹⁵ What I'm about to tell you is true. On judgment day it will be easier for Sodom and Gomorrah than for that town.

¹⁶ "I am sending you out like sheep among wolves. So be as wise as snakes and as harmless as doves. ¹⁷ Watch out! You will be handed over to the local courts. You will be whipped in the synagogues. ¹⁸ You will be brought to governors and kings because of me. You will be witnesses to them and to the Gentiles. ¹⁹ But when they arrest you, don't worry about what you will say or how you will say it. At that time you will be given the right words to say. ²⁰ It will not be you speaking. The Spirit of your Father will be speaking through you.

²¹ "Brothers will hand over brothers to be killed. Fathers will hand over their children. Children will rise up against their parents and have them put to death. ²² You will be hated by everyone because of me. But anyone who remains strong in the faith will be saved. ²³ When people attack you in one place, escape to another. What I'm about to tell you is true. You will not finish going through the towns of Israel before the Son of Man comes.

²⁴ "The student is not better than the teacher. A slave is not better than his master. ²⁵ It is enough for students to be like their teachers. And it is enough for slaves to be like their masters. If the head of the house has been called Beelzebul, what can the others who live there expect?

²⁶ "So don't be afraid of your enemies. Everything that is secret will be brought out into the open. Everything that is hidden will be uncovered. ²⁷ What I tell you in the dark, speak in the daylight. What is whispered in your ear, shout from the rooftops. ²⁸ Do not be afraid of those who kill the body but can't kill the soul. Instead, be afraid of the one who can destroy both soul and body in hell. ²⁹ Aren't two sparrows sold for only a penny? But not one of them falls to the ground outside your Father's care. ³⁰ He even counts every hair on your head! ³¹ So don't be afraid. You are worth more than many sparrows.

³² "What if someone says in front of others that they know me? I will also say in front of my Father who is in heaven that I know them. ³³ But what if someone says in front of others that they don't know me? I will say in front of my Father who is in heaven that I don't know them.

³⁴ "Do not think that I came to bring peace to the earth. I didn't come to bring peace. I came to bring a sword. ³⁵ I have come to turn

"'sons against their fathers.
Daughters will refuse to
obey their mothers.
Daughters-in-law will be
against their mothers-in-
law.
³⁶   A man's enemies will be
the members of his own
family.'   *(Micah 7:6)*

³⁷ "Anyone who loves their father or mother more than me is not worthy of me. Anyone who loves their son or daughter more than me is not worthy of me. ³⁸ Whoever does not pick up their cross and follow me is not worthy of me. ³⁹ Whoever finds their life will lose it. Whoever loses their life because of me will find it.

⁴⁰ "Anyone who welcomes you welcomes me. And anyone who welcomes me welcomes the one who sent me. ⁴¹ Suppose someone welcomes a prophet as a prophet. They will receive a prophet's reward. And suppose someone welcomes a godly person as a godly person. They will receive a godly person's reward.

⁴² Suppose someone gives even a cup of cold water to a little one who follows me. What I'm about to tell you is true. That person will certainly be rewarded."

Jesus and John the Baptist

11 Jesus finished teaching his 12 disciples. Then he went on to teach and preach in the towns of Galilee.

² John the Baptist was in prison. When he heard about the actions of the Messiah, he sent his disciples to him. ³ They asked Jesus, "Are you the one who is supposed to come? Or should we look for someone else?"

⁴ Jesus replied, "Go back to John. Report to him what you hear and see. ⁵ Blind people receive sight. Disabled people walk. Those who have skin diseases are made 'clean.' Deaf people hear. Those who are dead are raised to life. And the good news is preached to those who are poor. ⁶ Blessed is anyone who does not give up their faith because of me."

⁷ As John's disciples were leaving, Jesus began to speak to the crowd about John. He said, "What did you go out into the desert to see? Tall grass waving in the wind? ⁸ If not, what did you go out to see? A man dressed in fine clothes? No. People who wear fine clothes are in kings' palaces. ⁹ Then what did you go out to see? A prophet? Yes, I tell you, and more than a prophet. ¹⁰ He is the one written about in Scripture. It says,

" 'I will send my messenger
   ahead of you.
He will prepare your way
   for you.' *(Malachi 3:1)*

¹¹ What I'm about to tell you is true. No one more important than John the Baptist has ever been born. But the least important person in the kingdom of heaven is more important than he is. ¹² Since the days of John the Baptist, the kingdom of heaven has been under attack. And violent people are taking hold of it. ¹³ All the Prophets and the Law prophesied until John came. ¹⁴ If you are willing to accept it, John is the Elijah who was supposed to come. ¹⁵ Whoever has ears should listen.

¹⁶ "What can I compare today's people to? They are like children sitting in the markets and calling out to others. They say,

¹⁷ " 'We played the flute for you.
   But you didn't dance.
We sang a funeral song.
   But you didn't become sad.'

¹⁸ When John came, he didn't eat or drink as you do. And people say, 'He has a demon.' ¹⁹ But when the Son of Man came, he ate and drank as you do. And people say, 'This fellow is always eating and drinking far too much. He's a friend of tax collectors and "sinners." ' By wise actions wisdom is shown to be right."

Towns That Do Not Turn Away From Sin

²⁰ Jesus began to speak against the towns where he had done most of his miracles. The people there had not turned away from their sins. So he said, ²¹ "How terrible it will be for you, Chorazin! How terrible for you, Bethsaida! Suppose the miracles done in you had been done in Tyre and Sidon. They would have turned away from their sins long ago. They would have put on clothes for mourning. They would have sat down in ashes. ²² But I tell you this. On judgment day it will be easier for Tyre and Sidon than for you. ²³ And what about you, Capernaum? Will you be lifted to the heavens? No! You will go down to the place of the dead. Suppose the miracles done in you had been done in Sodom. It would still be here today. ²⁴ But I tell you this. On judgment day it will be easier for Sodom than for you."

Rest for All Who Are Tired

²⁵ At that time Jesus said, "I praise you, Father. You are Lord of heaven and earth. You have hidden these things from wise and educated people. But you have shown them to little children. ²⁶ Yes, Father. This is what you wanted to do.

²⁷ "My Father has given all things to me. The Father is the only one who knows the Son. And the only ones who know the Father are the Son and those to whom the Son chooses to make him known.

²⁸ "Come to me, all you who are tired and are carrying heavy loads. I will give you

rest. ²⁹ Become my servants and learn from me. I am gentle and free of pride. You will find rest for your souls. ³⁰ Serving me is easy, and my load is light."

Jesus Is Lord of the Sabbath Day

12 One Sabbath day Jesus walked through the grainfields. His disciples were hungry. So they began to break off some heads of grain and eat them. ² The Pharisees saw this. They said to Jesus, "Look! It is against the Law to do this on the Sabbath day. But your disciples are doing it anyway!"

³ Jesus answered, "Haven't you read about what David did? He and his men were hungry. ⁴ So he entered the house of God. He and his men ate the holy bread. Only priests were allowed to eat it. ⁵ Haven't you read the Law? It tells how every Sabbath day the priests in the temple have to do their work on that day. But they are not considered guilty. ⁶ I tell you that something more important than the temple is here. ⁷ Scripture says, 'I want mercy and not sacrifice.' *(Hosea 6:6)* You don't know what those words mean. If you did, you would not bring charges against those who are not guilty. ⁸ The Son of Man is Lord of the Sabbath day."

⁹ Going on from that place, Jesus went into their synagogue. ¹⁰ A man with a weak and twisted hand was there. The Pharisees were trying to accuse Jesus of a crime. So they asked him, "Does the Law allow us to heal on the Sabbath day?"

¹¹ He said to them, "What if one of your sheep falls into a pit on the Sabbath day? Won't you take hold of it and lift it out? ¹² A person is worth more than sheep! So the Law allows us to do good on the Sabbath day."

¹³ Then Jesus said to the man, "Stretch out your hand." So he stretched it out. It had been made as good as new. It was just as good as the other hand. ¹⁴ But the Pharisees went out and planned how to kill Jesus.

God's Chosen Servant

¹⁵ Jesus knew all about the Pharisees' plans. So he left that place. A large crowd followed him, and he healed all who were sick. ¹⁶ But he warned them not to tell other people about him. ¹⁷ This was to make what was spoken through the prophet Isaiah come true. It says,

¹⁸ "Here is my servant. I have
    chosen him.
  He is the one I love. I
    am very pleased with
    him.
  I will put my Spirit on him.
  He will announce to the
    nations that everything
    will be made right.
¹⁹ He will not argue or cry out.
  No one will hear his voice
    in the streets.
²⁰ He will not break a bent
    twig.
  He will not put out a dimly
    burning flame.
  He will make right win over
    wrong.
²¹   The nations will put their
    hope in him." *(Isaiah 42:1–4)*

Jesus and Beelzebul

²² A man controlled by demons was brought to Jesus. The man was blind and could not speak. Jesus healed him. Then the man could speak and see. ²³ All the people were amazed. They said, "Could this be the Son of David?" ²⁴ The Pharisees heard this. So they said, "This fellow drives out demons by the power of Beelzebul, the prince of demons."

²⁵ Jesus knew what they were thinking. So he said to them, "Every kingdom that fights against itself will be destroyed. Every city or family that is divided against itself will not stand. ²⁶ If Satan drives out Satan, he fights against himself. Then how can his kingdom stand? ²⁷ You say I drive out demons by the power of Beelzebul. Then by whose power do your people drive them out? So then, they will be your judges. ²⁸ But suppose I drive out demons by the Spirit of God. Then the kingdom of God has come to you.

²⁹ "Or think about this. How can you enter a strong man's house and just take what the man owns? You must first tie him up. Then you can rob his house.

³⁰ "Anyone who is not with me is against me. Anyone who does not gather sheep with me scatters them. ³¹ So here is what I tell you. Every kind of sin and every evil word spoken against God will be forgiven. But speaking evil things against the Holy Spirit will not be forgiven.

³² Anyone who speaks a word against the Son of Man will be forgiven. But anyone who speaks against the Holy Spirit will not be forgiven. A person like that won't be forgiven either now or in days to come.

³³ "If you make a tree good, its fruit will be good. If you make a tree bad, its fruit will be bad. You can tell a tree by its fruit. ³⁴ You nest of poisonous snakes! How can you who are evil say anything good? Your mouths say everything that is in your hearts. ³⁵ A good man says good things. These come from the good that is stored up inside him. An evil man says evil things. These come from the evil that is stored up inside him. ³⁶ But here is what I tell you. On judgment day, everyone will have to account for every empty word they have spoken. ³⁷ By your words you will be found guilty or not guilty."

The Sign of Jonah

³⁸ Some of the Pharisees and the teachers of the law came to Jesus. They said, "Teacher, we want to see a sign from you."

³⁹ He answered, "Evil and unfaithful people ask for a sign! But none will be given except the sign of the prophet Jonah. ⁴⁰ Jonah was in the belly of a huge fish for three days and three nights. Something like that will happen to the Son of Man. He will spend three days and three nights in the grave. ⁴¹ The men of Nineveh will stand up on judgment day with the people

now living. And the Ninevites will prove that these people are guilty. The men of Nineveh turned away from their sins when Jonah preached to them. And now something more important than Jonah is here. ⁴² The Queen of the South will stand up on judgment day with the people now living. And she will prove that they are guilty. She came from very far away to listen to Solomon's wisdom. And now something more important than Solomon is here.

⁴³ "What happens when an evil spirit comes out of a person? It goes through dry areas looking for a place to rest. But it doesn't find it. ⁴⁴ Then it says, 'I will return to the house I left.' When it arrives there, it finds the house empty. The house has been swept clean and put in order. ⁴⁵ Then the evil spirit goes and takes with it seven other spirits more evil than itself. They go in and live there. That person is worse off than before. That is how it will be with the evil people of today."

Jesus' Mother and Brothers

⁴⁶ While Jesus was still talking to the crowd, his mother and brothers stood outside. They wanted to speak to him. ⁴⁷ Someone told him, "Your mother and brothers are standing outside. They want to speak to you."

⁴⁸ Jesus replied to him, "Who is my mother? And who are my brothers?" ⁴⁹ Jesus pointed to his disciples. He said, "Here is my mother! Here are my brothers!

⁵⁰ Anyone who does what my Father in heaven wants is my brother or sister or mother."

The Story of the Farmer

13 That same day Jesus left the house and sat by the Sea of Galilee. ² Large crowds gathered around him. So he got into a boat and sat down. All the people stood on the shore. ³ Then he told them many things using stories. He said, "A farmer went out to plant his seed. ⁴ He scattered the seed on the ground. Some fell on a path. Birds came and ate it up. ⁵ Some seed fell on rocky places, where there wasn't much soil. The plants came up quickly, because the soil wasn't deep. ⁶ When the sun came up, it burned the plants. They dried up because they had no roots. ⁷ Other seed fell among thorns. The thorns grew up and crowded out the plants. ⁸ Still other seed fell on good soil. It produced a crop 100, 60 or 30 times more than what was planted. ⁹ Whoever has ears should listen."

¹⁰ The disciples came to him. They asked, "Why do you use stories when you speak to the people?"

¹¹ He replied, "Because you have been given the knowledge of the secrets of the kingdom of heaven. It has not been given to outsiders. ¹² Everyone who has this kind of knowledge will be given more knowledge. In fact, they will have very much. If anyone doesn't have this kind of knowledge, even what little they

have will be taken away from them. [13] Here is why I use stories when I speak to the people. I say,

"They look, but they don't really see.
They listen, but they don't really hear or understand.

[14] In them the words of the prophet Isaiah come true. He said,

" 'You will hear but never understand.
You will see but never know what you are seeing.
[15] The hearts of these people have become stubborn.
They can barely hear with their ears.
They have closed their eyes.
Otherwise they might see with their eyes.
They might hear with their ears.
They might understand with their hearts.
They might turn to the Lord, and then he would heal them.'   *(Isaiah 6:9,10)*

[16] But blessed are your eyes because they see. And blessed are your ears because they hear. [17] What I'm about to tell you is true. Many prophets and godly people wanted to see what you see. But they didn't see it. They wanted to hear what you hear. But they didn't hear it.

[18] "Listen! Here is the meaning of the story of the farmer. [19] People hear the message about the kingdom but do not understand it. Then the evil one comes. He steals what was planted in their hearts. Those people are like the seed planted on a path. [20] The seed that fell on rocky places is like other people. They hear the message and at once receive it with joy. [21] But they have no roots. So they last only a short time. They quickly fall away from the faith when trouble or suffering comes because of the message. [22] The seed that fell among the thorns is like others who hear the message. But then the worries of this life and the false promises of wealth crowd it out. They keep the message from producing fruit. [23] But the seed that fell on good soil is like those who hear the message and understand it. They produce a crop 100, 60 or 30 times more than the farmer planted."

The Story of the Weeds

[24] Jesus told the crowd another story. "Here is what the kingdom of heaven is like," he said. "A man planted good seed in his field. [25] But while everyone was sleeping, his enemy came. The enemy planted weeds among the wheat and then went away. [26] The wheat began to grow and form grain. At the same time, weeds appeared.

[27] "The owner's slaves came to him. They said, 'Sir, didn't you plant good seed in your field? Then where did the weeds come from?'

[28] " 'An enemy did this,' he replied.

"The slaves asked him, 'Do you want us to go and pull up the weeds?'

²⁹ " 'No,' the owner answered. 'While you are pulling up the weeds, you might pull up the wheat with them. ³⁰ Let both grow together until the harvest. At that time I will tell the workers what to do. Here is what I will say to them. First collect the weeds. Tie them in bundles to be burned. Then gather the wheat. Bring it into my storeroom.' "

The Stories of the Mustard Seed and the Yeast

³¹ Jesus told the crowd another story. He said, "The kingdom of heaven is like a mustard seed. Someone took the seed and planted it in a field. ³² It is the smallest of all seeds. But when it grows, it is the largest of all garden plants. It becomes a tree. Birds come and rest in its branches."

³³ Jesus told them still another story. "The kingdom of heaven is like yeast," he said. "A woman mixed it into 60 pounds of flour. The yeast worked its way all through the dough."

³⁴ Jesus spoke all these things to the crowd using stories. He did not say anything to them without telling a story. ³⁵ So the words spoken by the prophet came true. He had said,

"I will open my mouth and
    tell stories.
I will speak about things
    that were hidden since
    the world was made."

(Psalm 78:2)

Jesus Explains the Story of the Weeds

³⁶ Then Jesus left the crowd and went into the house. His disciples came to him. They said, "Explain to us the story of the weeds in the field."

³⁷ He answered, "The one who planted the good seed is the Son of Man. ³⁸ The field is the world. The good seed stands for the people who belong to the kingdom. The weeds are the people who belong to the evil one. ³⁹ The enemy who plants them is the devil. The harvest is judgment day. And the workers are angels.

⁴⁰ "The weeds are pulled up and burned in the fire. That is how it will be on judgment day. ⁴¹ The Son of Man will send out his angels. They will weed out of his kingdom everything that causes sin. They will also get rid of all who do evil. ⁴² They will throw them into the blazing furnace. There people will weep and grind their teeth. ⁴³ Then God's people will shine like the sun in their Father's kingdom. Whoever has ears should listen.

The Stories of the Hidden Treasure and the Pearl

⁴⁴ "The kingdom of heaven is like treasure that was hidden in a field. When a man found it, he hid it again. He was very happy. So he went and sold everything he had. And he bought that field.

⁴⁵ "Again, the kingdom of heaven is like a trader who was looking for fine pearls. ⁴⁶ He found one that was very valu-

able. So he went away and sold everything he had. And he bought that pearl.

The Story of the Net

⁴⁷ "Again, the kingdom of heaven is like a net. It was let down into the lake. It caught all kinds of fish. ⁴⁸ When it was full, the fishermen pulled it up on the shore. Then they sat down and gathered the good fish into baskets. But they threw the bad fish away. ⁴⁹ This is how it will be on judgment day. The angels will come. They will separate the people who did what is wrong from those who did what is right. ⁵⁰ They will throw the evil people into the blazing furnace. There the evil ones will weep and grind their teeth.

⁵¹ "Do you understand all these things?" Jesus asked.

"Yes," they replied.

⁵² He said to them, "Every teacher of the law who has become a disciple in the kingdom of heaven is like the owner of a house. He brings new treasures out of his storeroom as well as old ones."

A Prophet Without Honor

⁵³ Jesus finished telling these stories. Then he moved on from there. ⁵⁴ He came to his hometown of Nazareth. There he began teaching the people in their synagogue. They were amazed. "Where did this man get this wisdom? Where did he get this power to do miracles?" they asked. ⁵⁵ "Isn't this the carpenter's son? Isn't his mother's name Mary? Aren't his brothers James, Joseph, Simon and Judas? ⁵⁶ Aren't all his sisters with us? Then where did this man get all these things?" ⁵⁷ They were not pleased with him at all.

But Jesus said to them, "A prophet is honored everywhere except in his own town and in his own home."

⁵⁸ He did only a few miracles in Nazareth because the people there had no faith.

John the Baptist's Head Is Cut Off

14 At that time Herod, the ruler of Galilee and Perea, heard reports about Jesus. ² He said to his attendants, "This is John the Baptist. He has risen from the dead! That is why he has the power to do miracles."

³ Herod had arrested John. He had tied him up and put him in prison because of Herodias. She was the wife of Herod's brother Philip. ⁴ John had been saying to Herod, "It is against the Law for you to have her as your wife." ⁵ Herod wanted to kill John. But he was afraid of the people, because they thought John was a prophet.

⁶ On Herod's birthday the daughter of Herodias danced for Herod and his guests. She pleased Herod very much. ⁷ So he promised to give her anything she asked for. ⁸ Her mother told her what to say. So the girl said to Herod, "Give me the head of John the Baptist on a big plate." ⁹ The king was very upset. But he thought of his

promise and his dinner guests. So he told one of his men to give her what she asked for. ¹⁰ Herod had John's head cut off in the prison. ¹¹ His head was brought in on a big plate and given to the girl. She then carried it to her mother. ¹² John's disciples came and took his body and buried it. Then they went and told Jesus.

Jesus Feeds Five Thousand

¹³ Jesus heard what had happened to John. He wanted to be alone. So he went in a boat to a quiet place. The crowds heard about this. They followed him on foot from the towns. ¹⁴ When Jesus came ashore, he saw a large crowd. He felt deep concern for them. He healed their sick people.

¹⁵ When it was almost evening, the disciples came to him. "There is nothing here," they said. "It's already getting late. Send the crowds away. They can go and buy some food in the villages."

¹⁶ Jesus replied, "They don't need to go away. You give them something to eat."

¹⁷ "We have only five loaves of bread and two fish," they answered.

¹⁸ "Bring them here to me," he said. ¹⁹ Then Jesus directed the people to sit down on the grass. He took the five loaves and the two fish. He looked up to heaven and gave thanks. He broke the loaves into pieces. Then he gave them to the disciples. And the disciples gave them to the people. ²⁰ All of them ate and were satisfied. The disciples picked up 12 baskets of leftover pieces. ²¹ The number of men who ate was about 5,000. Women and children also ate.

Jesus Walks on the Water

²² Right away Jesus made the disciples get into the boat. He had them go on ahead of him to the other side of the Sea of Galilee. Then he sent the crowd away. ²³ After he had sent them away, he went up on a mountainside by himself to pray. Later that night, he was there alone. ²⁴ The boat was already a long way from land. It was being pounded by the waves because the wind was blowing against it. ²⁵ Shortly before dawn, Jesus went out to the disciples. He walked on the lake. ²⁶ They saw him walking on the lake and were terrified. "It's a ghost!" they said. And they cried out in fear.

²⁷ Right away Jesus called out to them, "Be brave! It is I. Don't be afraid."

²⁸ "Lord, is it you?" Peter asked. "If it is, tell me to come to you on the water."

²⁹ "Come," Jesus said.

So Peter got out of the boat. He walked on the water toward Jesus. ³⁰ But when Peter saw the wind, he was afraid. He began to sink. He cried out, "Lord! Save me!"

³¹ Right away Jesus reached out his hand and caught him. "Your faith is so small!" he said. "Why did you doubt me?"

³² When they climbed into

the boat, the wind died down. [33] Then those in the boat worshiped Jesus. They said, "You really are the Son of God!"

[34] They crossed over the lake and landed at Gennesaret. [35] The men who lived there recognized Jesus. So they sent a message all over the nearby countryside. People brought all those who were sick to Jesus. [36] They begged him to let those who were sick just touch the edge of his clothes. And all who touched his clothes were healed.

What Makes People "Unclean"?

15 Some Pharisees and some teachers of the law came from Jerusalem to see Jesus. They asked, [2] "Why don't your disciples obey what the elders teach? Your disciples don't wash their hands before they eat!"

[3] Jesus replied, "And why don't you obey God's command? You would rather follow your own teachings! [4] God said, 'Honor your father and mother.' *(Exodus 20:12; Deuteronomy 5:16)* He also said, 'Anyone who asks for bad things to happen to their father or mother must be put to death.' *(Exodus 21:17; Leviticus 20:9)* [5] But suppose people have something that might be used to help their parents. You allow them to say it is instead 'a gift set apart for God.' [6] So they do not need to honor their father or mother with their gift. You make the word of God useless in order to follow your own teachings. [7] You pretenders! Isaiah was right when he prophesied about you. He said,

[8] "'These people honor me by
        what they say.
    But their hearts are far
        away from me.
[9] Their worship doesn't mean
        anything to me.
    They teach nothing but
        human rules.'" *(Isaiah 29:13)*

[10] Jesus called the crowd to him. He said, "Listen and understand. [11] What goes into someone's mouth does not make them 'unclean.' It's what comes out of their mouth that makes them 'unclean.'"

[12] Then the disciples came to him. They asked, "Do you know that the Pharisees were angry when they heard this?"

[13] Jesus replied, "They are plants that my Father in heaven has not planted. They will be pulled up by the roots. [14] Leave the Pharisees. They are blind guides. If one blind person leads another blind person, both of them will fall into a pit."

[15] Peter said, "Explain this to us."

[16] "Don't you understand yet?" Jesus asked them. [17] "Don't you see? Everything that enters the mouth goes into the stomach. Then it goes out of the body. [18] But the things that come out of a person's mouth come from the heart. Those are the things that make someone 'unclean.' [19] Evil thoughts come out of a person's heart. So do murder, adultery, and other sexual sins. And so do stealing, false witness, and

telling lies about others. ²⁰ Those are the things that make you 'unclean.' But eating without washing your hands does not make you 'unclean.' "

The Faith of a Woman From Canaan

²¹ Jesus left Galilee and went to the area of Tyre and Sidon. ²² A woman from Canaan lived near Tyre and Sidon. She came to him and cried out, "Lord! Son of David! Have mercy on me! A demon controls my daughter. She is suffering terribly."

²³ Jesus did not say a word. So his disciples came to him. They begged him, "Send her away. She keeps crying out after us."

²⁴ Jesus answered, "I was sent only to the people of Israel. They are like lost sheep."

²⁵ Then the woman fell to her knees in front of him. "Lord! Help me!" she said.

²⁶ He replied, "It is not right to take the children's bread and throw it to the dogs."

²⁷ "Yes it is, Lord," she said. "Even the dogs eat the crumbs that fall from their owner's table."

²⁸ Then Jesus said to her, "Woman, you have great faith! You will be given what you are asking for." And her daughter was healed at that moment.

Jesus Feeds Four Thousand

²⁹ Jesus left there. He walked along the Sea of Galilee. Then he went up on a mountainside and sat down. ³⁰ Large crowds came to him. They brought blind peo-ple and those who could not walk. They also brought disabled people, those who could not speak, and many others. They laid them at his feet, and he healed them. ³¹ The people were amazed. Those who could not speak were speaking. The disabled were made well. Those not able to walk were walking. Those who were blind could see. So the people praised the God of Israel.

³² Then Jesus called for his disciples to come to him. He said, "I feel deep concern for these people. They have already been with me three days. They don't have anything to eat. I don't want to send them away hungry. If I do, they will become too weak on their way home."

³³ His disciples answered him. "There is nothing here," they said. "Where could we get enough bread to feed this large crowd?"

³⁴ "How many loaves do you have?" Jesus asked.

"Seven," they replied, "and a few small fish."

³⁵ Jesus told the crowd to sit down on the ground. ³⁶ He took the seven loaves and the fish and gave thanks. Then he broke them and gave them to the disciples. And the disciples passed them out to the people. ³⁷ All of them ate and were satisfied. After that, the disciples picked up seven baskets of leftover pieces. ³⁸ The number of men who ate was 4,000. Women and children also ate. ³⁹ After Jesus had sent the crowd away, he got into the

boat. He went to the area near Magadan.

Jesus Is Asked for a Sign

16 The Pharisees and Sadducees came to test Jesus. They asked him to show them a sign from heaven.

[2] He replied, "In the evening you look at the sky. You say, 'It will be good weather. The sky is red.' [3] And in the morning you say, 'Today it will be stormy. The sky is red and cloudy.' You know the meaning of what you see in the sky. But you can't understand the signs of what is happening right now. [4] An evil and unfaithful people look for a sign. But none will be given to them except the sign of Jonah." Then Jesus left them and went away.

The Yeast of the Pharisees and Sadducees

[5] The disciples crossed over to the other side of the lake. They had forgotten to take bread. [6] "Be careful," Jesus said to them. "Watch out for the yeast of the Pharisees and Sadducees." [7] The disciples talked about this among themselves. They said, "He must be saying this because we didn't bring any bread."

[8] Jesus knew what they were saying. So he said, "Your faith is so small! Why are you talking to each other about having no bread? [9] Don't you understand yet? Don't you remember the five loaves for the 5,000? Don't you remember how many bas-

kets of pieces you gathered? [10] Don't you remember the seven loaves for the 4,000? Don't you remember how many baskets of pieces you gathered? [11] How can you possibly not understand? I wasn't talking to you about bread. But watch out for the yeast of the Pharisees and Sadducees." [12] Then the disciples understood that Jesus was not telling them to watch out for the yeast used in bread. He was warning them against what the Pharisees and Sadducees taught.

Peter Says That Jesus Is the Messiah

[13] Jesus went to the area of Caesarea Philippi. There he asked his disciples, "Who do people say the Son of Man is?"

[14] They replied, "Some say John the Baptist. Others say Elijah. Still others say Jeremiah, or one of the prophets."

[15] "But what about you?" he asked. "Who do you say I am?"

[16] Simon Peter answered, "You are the Messiah. You are the Son of the living God."

[17] Jesus replied, "Blessed are you, Simon, son of Jonah! No mere human showed this to you. My Father in heaven showed it to you. [18] Here is what I tell you. You are Peter. On this rock I will build my church. The gates of hell will not be strong enough to destroy it. [19] I will give you the keys to the kingdom of heaven. What you lock on earth will be locked in heaven. What you unlock on earth will be

unlocked in heaven." ²⁰ Then Jesus ordered his disciples not to tell anyone that he was the Messiah.

Jesus Speaks About His Coming Death

²¹ From that time on Jesus began to explain to his disciples what would happen to him. He told them he must go to Jerusalem. There he must suffer many things from the elders, the chief priests and the teachers of the law. He must be killed and on the third day rise to life again.

²² Peter took Jesus to one side and began to scold him. "Never, Lord!" he said. "This will never happen to you!"

²³ Jesus turned and said to Peter, "Get behind me, Satan! You are standing in my way. You do not have in mind the things God cares about. Instead, you only have in mind the things humans care about."

²⁴ Then Jesus spoke to his disciples. He said, "Whoever wants to be my disciple must say no to themselves. They must pick up their cross and follow me. ²⁵ Whoever wants to save their life will lose it. But whoever loses their life for me will find it. ²⁶ What good is it if someone gains the whole world but loses their soul? Or what can anyone trade for their soul? ²⁷ The Son of Man is going to come in his Father's glory. His angels will come with him. And he will reward everyone in keeping with what they have done.

²⁸ "What I'm about to tell you is true. Some who are standing here will not die before they see the Son of Man coming in his kingdom."

Jesus' Appearance Is Changed

17 After six days Jesus took Peter, James, and John the brother of James with him. He led them up a high mountain. They were all alone. ² There in front of them his appearance was changed. His face shone like the sun. His clothes became as white as the light. ³ Just then Moses and Elijah appeared in front of them. Moses and Elijah were talking with Jesus.

⁴ Peter said to Jesus, "Lord, it is good for us to be here. If you wish, I will put up three shelters. One will be for you, one for Moses, and one for Elijah."

⁵ While Peter was still speaking, a bright cloud covered them. A voice from the cloud said, "This is my Son, and I love him. I am very pleased with him. Listen to him!"

⁶ When the disciples heard this, they were terrified. They fell with their faces to the ground. ⁷ But Jesus came and touched them. "Get up," he said. "Don't be afraid." ⁸ When they looked up, they saw no one except Jesus.

⁹ They came down the mountain. On the way down, Jesus told them what to do. "Don't tell anyone what you have seen," he said. "Wait until the Son of Man has been raised from the dead." ¹⁰ The disciples asked him,

"Why do the teachers of the law say that Elijah has to come first?"

[11] Jesus replied, "That's right. Elijah is supposed to come and make all things new again. [12] But I tell you, Elijah has already come. People didn't recognize him. They have done to him everything they wanted to do. In the same way, they are going to make the Son of Man suffer." [13] Then the disciples understood that Jesus was talking to them about John the Baptist.

Jesus Heals a Boy Who Is Controlled by a Demon

[14] When they came near the crowd, a man approached Jesus. He got on his knees in front of him. [15] "Lord," he said, "have mercy on my son. He shakes wildly and suffers a great deal. He often falls into the fire or into the water. [16] I brought him to your disciples. But they couldn't heal him."

[17] "You unbelieving and evil people!" Jesus replied. "How long do I have to stay with you? How long do I have to put up with you? Bring the boy here to me." [18] Jesus ordered the demon to leave the boy, and it came out of him. He was healed at that moment.

[19] Then the disciples came to Jesus in private. They asked, "Why couldn't we drive out the demon?"

[20-21] He replied, "Because your faith is much too small. What I'm about to tell you is true.

If you have faith as small as a mustard seed, it is enough. You can say to this mountain, 'Move from here to there.' And it will move. Nothing will be impossible for you."

Jesus Speaks a Second Time About His Coming Death

[22] They came together in Galilee. Then Jesus said to them, "The Son of Man is going to be handed over to men. [23] They will kill him. On the third day he will rise from the dead." Then the disciples were filled with deep sadness.

Jesus Pays the Temple Tax

[24] Jesus and his disciples arrived in Capernaum. There the people who collect the temple tax came to Peter. They asked him, "Doesn't your teacher pay the temple tax?"

[25] "Yes, he does," he replied.

When Peter came into the house, Jesus spoke first. "What do you think, Simon?" he asked. "Who do the kings of the earth collect taxes and fees from? Do they collect them from their own children or from others?"

[26] "From others," Peter answered.

"Then the children don't have to pay," Jesus said to him. [27] "But we don't want to make them angry. So go to the lake and throw out your fishing line. Take the first fish you catch. Open its mouth. There you will find the exact coin you need. Take it and give it to them for my tax and yours."

Who Is the Most Important Person in the Kingdom?

18 At that time the disciples came to Jesus. They asked him, "Then who is the most important person in the kingdom of heaven?"

² Jesus called a little child over to him. He had the child stand among them. ³ Jesus said, "What I'm about to tell you is true. You need to change and become like little children. If you don't, you will never enter the kingdom of heaven. ⁴ Anyone who takes the humble position of this child is the most important in the kingdom of heaven. ⁵ Anyone who welcomes a little child like this one in my name welcomes me.

Do Not Cause People to Sin

⁶ "What if someone causes one of these little ones who believe in me to sin? If they do, it would be better for them to have a large millstone hung around their neck and be drowned at the bottom of the sea. ⁷ How terrible it will be for the world because of the things that cause people to sin! Things like that must come. But how terrible for the person who causes them! ⁸ If your hand or foot causes you to sin, cut it off and throw it away. It would be better to enter the kingdom of heaven with only one hand than go into hell with two hands. It would be better to enter the kingdom of heaven with only one foot than go into hell with two feet. In hell the fire burns forever. ⁹ If your eye causes you to sin, poke it out and throw it away. It would be better to enter the kingdom of heaven with one eye than to have two eyes and be thrown into the fire of hell.

The Story of the Wandering Sheep

¹⁰-¹¹ "See that you don't look down on one of these little ones. Here is what I tell you. Their angels in heaven are always with my Father who is in heaven.

¹² "What do you think? Suppose a man owns 100 sheep and one of them wanders away. Won't he leave the 99 sheep on the hills? Won't he go and look for the one that wandered off? ¹³ What I'm about to tell you is true. If he finds that sheep, he is happier about the one than about the 99 that didn't wander off. ¹⁴ It is the same with your Father in heaven. He does not want any of these little ones to die.

When Someone Sins Against You

¹⁵ "If your brother or sister sins against you, go to them. Tell them what they did wrong. Keep it between the two of you. If they listen to you, you have won them back. ¹⁶ But what if they won't listen to you? Then take one or two others with you. Scripture says, 'Every matter must be proved by the words of two or three witnesses.' *(Deuteronomy 19:15)* ¹⁷ But what if they also refuse to listen to the witnesses? Then tell it to the church. And what if they refuse to listen even to the church? Then don't treat

them as a brother or sister. Treat them as you would treat an ungodly person or a tax collector.

18 "What I'm about to tell you is true. What you lock on earth will be locked in heaven. What you unlock on earth will be unlocked in heaven.

19 "Again, here is what I tell you. Suppose two of you on earth agree about anything you ask for. My Father in heaven will do it for you. 20 Where two or three people gather in my name, I am there with them."

The Servant Who Had No Mercy

21 Peter came to Jesus. He asked, "Lord, how many times should I forgive my brother or sister who sins against me? Up to seven times?"

22 Jesus answered, "I tell you, not seven times, but 77 times.

23 "The kingdom of heaven is like a king who wanted to collect all the money his servants owed him. 24 As the king began to do it, a man who owed him 10,000 bags of gold was brought to him. 25 The man was not able to pay. So his master gave an order. The man, his wife, his children, and all he owned had to be sold to pay back what he owed.

26 "Then the servant fell on his knees in front of him. 'Give me time,' he begged. 'I'll pay everything back.' 27 His master felt sorry for him. He forgave him what he owed and let him go.

28 "But then that servant went out and found one of the other servants who owed him 100 silver coins. He grabbed him and began to choke him. 'Pay back what you owe me!' he said.

29 "The other servant fell on his knees. 'Give me time,' he begged him. 'I'll pay it back.'

30 "But the first servant refused. Instead, he went and had the man thrown into prison. The man would be held there until he could pay back what he owed. 31 The other servants saw what had happened and were very angry. They went and told their master everything that had happened.

32 "Then the master called the first servant in. 'You evil servant,' he said. 'I forgave all that you owed me because you begged me to. 33 Shouldn't you have had mercy on the other servant just as I had mercy on you?' 34 In anger his master handed him over to the jailers. He would be punished until he paid back everything he owed.

35 "This is how my Father in heaven will treat each of you unless you forgive your brother or sister from your heart."

Jesus Teaches About Divorce

19 When Jesus finished saying these things, he left Galilee. He went into the area of Judea on the other side of the Jordan River. 2 Large crowds followed him. He healed them there.

3 Some Pharisees came to test Jesus. They asked, "Does the Law allow a man to divorce his wife for any reason at all?"

4 Jesus replied, "Haven't you read that in the beginning the

Creator 'made them male and female'? *(Genesis 1:27)* ⁵ He said, 'That's why a man will leave his father and mother and be joined to his wife. The two will become one.' *(Genesis 2:24)* ⁶ They are no longer two, but one. So no one should separate what God has joined together."

⁷ They asked, "Then why did Moses command that a man can give his wife a letter of divorce and send her away?"

⁸ Jesus replied, "Moses let you divorce your wives because you were stubborn. But it was not this way from the beginning. ⁹ Here is what I tell you. Anyone who divorces his wife and marries another woman commits adultery. A man may divorce his wife only if she has not been faithful to him."

¹⁰ Here is what the disciples said to him. "If that's the way it is between a husband and wife, it is better not to get married."

¹¹ Jesus replied, "Not everyone can accept the idea of staying single. Only those who have been helped to live without getting married can accept it. ¹² Some men are not able to have children because they were born that way. Some have been made that way by other people. Others have chosen to live that way in order to serve the kingdom of heaven. The one who can accept this should accept it."

Little Children Are Brought to Jesus

¹³ Some people brought little children to Jesus. They wanted him to place his hands on the children and pray for them. But the disciples told them not to do it.

¹⁴ Jesus said, "Let the little children come to me. Don't keep them away. The kingdom of heaven belongs to people like them." ¹⁵ Jesus placed his hands on them to bless them. Then he went on from there.

Rich People and the Kingdom of God

¹⁶ Just then, a man came up to Jesus. He asked, "Teacher, what good thing must I do to receive eternal life?"

¹⁷ "Why do you ask me about what is good?" Jesus replied. "There is only one who is good. If you want to enter the kingdom, obey the commandments."

¹⁸ "Which ones?" the man asked.

Jesus said, " 'Do not murder. Do not commit adultery. Do not steal. Do not be a false witness. ¹⁹ Honor your father and mother.' *(Exodus 20:12-16; Deuteronomy 5:16-20)* And 'love your neighbor as you love yourself.' " *(Leviticus 19:18)*

²⁰ "I have obeyed all those commandments," the young man said. "What else do I need to do?"

²¹ Jesus answered, "If you want to be perfect, go and sell everything you have. Give the money to those who are poor. You will have treasure in heaven. Then come and follow me."

²² When the young man heard this, he went away sad. He was very rich.

23 Then Jesus said to his disciples, "What I'm about to tell you is true. It is hard for someone who is rich to enter the kingdom of heaven. 24 Again I tell you, it is hard for a camel to go through the eye of a needle. But it is even harder for someone who is rich to enter the kingdom of God."

25 When the disciples heard this, they were really amazed. They asked, "Then who can be saved?"

26 Jesus looked at them and said, "With people, this is impossible. But with God, all things are possible."

27 Peter answered him, "We have left everything to follow you! What reward will be given to us?"

28 "What I'm about to tell you is true," Jesus said to them. "When all things are made new, the Son of Man will sit on his glorious throne. Then you who have followed me will also sit on 12 thrones. You will judge the 12 tribes of Israel. 29 Suppose anyone has left houses, brothers or sisters, father or mother, husband or wife, children or fields because of me. Anyone who has done that will receive 100 times as much. They will also receive eternal life. 30 But many who are first will be last. And many who are last will be first.

The Story of the Workers
in the Vineyard

20 "The kingdom of heaven is like a man who owned land. He went out early in the morning to hire workers for his vineyard. 2 He agreed to give them the usual pay for a day's work. Then he sent them into his vineyard.

3 "About nine o'clock in the morning he went out again. He saw others standing in the market doing nothing. 4 He told them, 'You also go and work in my vineyard. I'll pay you what is right.' 5 So they went.

"He went out again about noon and at three o'clock and did the same thing. 6 About five o'clock he went out and found still others standing around. He asked them, 'Why have you been standing here all day long doing nothing?'

7 " 'Because no one has hired us,' they answered.

"He said to them, 'You also go and work in my vineyard.'

8 "When evening came, the owner of the vineyard spoke to the person who was in charge of the workers. He said, 'Call the workers and give them their pay. Begin with the last ones I hired. Then go on to the first ones.'

9 "The workers who were hired about five o'clock came. Each received the usual day's pay. 10 So when those who were hired first came, they expected to receive more. But each of them also received the usual day's pay. 11 When they received it, they began to complain about the owner. 12 'These people who were hired last worked only one hour,' they said. 'You have paid them the same as us. We have done most of the work and have been in the hot sun all day.'

13 "The owner answered one of them. 'Friend,' he said, 'I'm being fair to you. Didn't you agree to work for the usual day's pay? 14 Take your money and go. I want to give the one I hired last the same pay I gave you. 15 Don't I have the right to do what I want with my own money? Do you feel cheated because I gave so freely to the others?'

16 "So those who are last will be first. And those who are first will be last."

Jesus Speaks a Third Time About His Coming Death

17 Jesus was going up to Jerusalem. On the way, he took his 12 disciples to one side to talk to them. 18 "We are going up to Jerusalem," he said. "The Son of Man will be handed over to the chief priests and the teachers of the law. They will sentence him to death. 19 Then they will hand him over to the Gentiles. The people will make fun of him and whip him. They will nail him to a cross. On the third day, he will rise from the dead!"

A Mother Asks a Favor of Jesus

20 The mother of Zebedee's sons came to Jesus. Her sons came with her. Getting on her knees, she asked a favor of him.

21 "What do you want?" Jesus asked.

She said, "Promise me that one of my two sons may sit at your right hand in your kingdom. Promise that the other one may sit at your left hand."

22 "You don't know what you're asking for," Jesus said to them. "Can you drink the cup of suffering I am going to drink?"

"We can," they answered.

23 Jesus said to them, "You will certainly drink from my cup. But it is not for me to say who will sit at my right or left hand. These places belong to those my Father has prepared them for."

24 The other ten disciples heard about this. They became angry at the two brothers. 25 Jesus called them together. He said, "You know about the rulers of the Gentiles. They hold power over their people. Their high officials order them around. 26 Don't be like that. Instead, anyone who wants to be important among you must be your servant. 27 And anyone who wants to be first must be your slave. 28 Be like the Son of Man. He did not come to be served. Instead, he came to serve others. He came to give his life as the price for setting many people free."

Two Blind Men Receive Their Sight

29 Jesus and his disciples were leaving Jericho. A large crowd followed him. 30 Two blind men were sitting by the side of the road. They heard that Jesus was going by. So they shouted, "Lord! Son of David! Have mercy on us!"

31 The crowd commanded them to stop. They told them to be quiet. But the two men shouted even louder, "Lord! Son of David! Have mercy on us!"

³² Jesus stopped and called out to them. "What do you want me to do for you?" he asked. ³³ "Lord," they answered, "we want to be able to see." ³⁴ Jesus felt deep concern for them. He touched their eyes. Right away they could see. And they followed him.

Jesus Comes to Jerusalem as King

21 As they all approached Jerusalem, they came to Bethphage. It was on the Mount of Olives. Jesus sent out two disciples. ² He said to them, "Go to the village ahead of you. As soon as you get there, you will find a donkey tied up. Her colt will be with her. Untie them and bring them to me. ³ If anyone says anything to you, say that the Lord needs them. The owner will send them right away."

⁴ This took place so that what was spoken through the prophet would come true. It says,

⁵ "Say to the city of Zion,
  'See, your king comes to
      you.
He is gentle and riding on a
      donkey.
He is riding on a donkey's
      colt.'"   *(Zechariah 9:9)*

⁶ The disciples went and did what Jesus told them to do. ⁷ They brought the donkey and the colt. They placed their coats on them for Jesus to sit on. ⁸ A very large crowd spread their coats on the road. Others cut branches from the trees and spread them on the road. ⁹ Some of the people went ahead of him, and some followed. They all shouted,

"Hosanna to the Son of David!"

"Blessed is the one who
    comes in the name of the
    Lord!"   *(Psalm 118:26)*

"Hosanna in the highest
    heaven!"

¹⁰ When Jesus entered Jerusalem, the whole city was stirred up. The people asked, "Who is this?" ¹¹ The crowds answered, "This is Jesus. He is the prophet from Nazareth in Galilee."

Jesus Clears Out the Temple

¹² Jesus entered the temple courtyard. He began to drive out all those who were buying and selling there. He turned over the tables of the people who were exchanging money. He also turned over the benches of those who were selling doves. ¹³ He said to them, "It is written that the Lord said, 'My house will be called a house where people can pray.' *(Isaiah 56:7)* But you are making it 'a den for robbers.'" *(Jeremiah 7:11)* ¹⁴ Blind people and those who were disabled came to Jesus at the temple. There he healed them. ¹⁵ The chief priests and the teachers of the law saw the wonderful things he did. They also saw the children in the temple courtyard shouting, "Hosanna to the Son of David!" But when they saw all this, they became angry.

¹⁶ "Do you hear what these children are saying?" they asked him.

"Yes," replied Jesus. "Haven't you ever read about it in Scripture? It says,

" 'Lord, you have made sure
that children and infants
praise you.' " *(Psalm 8:2)*

¹⁷ Then Jesus left the people and went out of the city to Bethany. He spent the night there.

Jesus Makes a Fig Tree Dry Up

¹⁸ Early in the morning, Jesus was on his way back to Jerusalem. He was hungry. ¹⁹ He saw a fig tree by the road. He went up to it but found nothing on it except leaves. Then he said to it, "May you never bear fruit again!" Right away the tree dried up.

²⁰ When the disciples saw this, they were amazed. "How did the fig tree dry up so quickly?" they asked.

²¹ Jesus replied, "What I'm about to tell you is true. You must have faith and not doubt. Then you can do what was done to the fig tree. And you can say to this mountain, 'Go and throw yourself into the sea.' It will be done. ²² If you believe, you will receive what you ask for when you pray."

The Authority of Jesus Is Questioned

²³ Jesus entered the temple courtyard. While he was teaching there, the chief priests and the elders of the people came to him. "By what authority are you doing these things?" they asked. "Who gave you this authority?"

²⁴ Jesus replied, "I will also ask you one question. If you answer me, I will tell you by what authority I am doing these things. ²⁵ Where did John's baptism come from? Was it from heaven? Or did it come from human authority?"

They talked to one another about it. They said, "If we say, 'From heaven,' he will ask, 'Then why didn't you believe him?' ²⁶ But what if we say, 'From human authority'? We are afraid of the people. Everyone believes that John was a prophet."

²⁷ So they answered Jesus, "We don't know."

Jesus said, "Then I won't tell you by what authority I am doing these things either.

The Story of the Two Sons

²⁸ "What do you think about this? A man had two sons. He went to the first and said, 'Son, go and work today in the vineyard.'

²⁹ " 'I will not,' the son answered. But later he changed his mind and went.

³⁰ "Then the father went to the other son. He said the same thing. The son answered, 'I will, sir.' But he did not go.

³¹ "Which of the two sons did what his father wanted?"

"The first," they answered.

Jesus said to them, "What I'm about to tell you is true. Tax collectors and prostitutes will enter the kingdom of God ahead of you. [32] John came to show you the right way to live. And you did not believe him. But the tax collectors and the prostitutes did. You saw this. But even then you did not turn away from your sins and believe him.

The Story of the Renters

[33] "Listen to another story. A man who owned some land planted a vineyard. He put a wall around it. He dug a pit for a winepress in it. He also built a lookout tower. He rented the vineyard out to some farmers. Then he moved to another place. [34] When harvest time approached, he sent his slaves to the renters. He told the slaves to collect his share of the fruit.

[35] "But the renters grabbed his slaves. They beat one of them. They killed another. They threw stones at the third to kill him. [36] Then the man sent other slaves to the renters. He sent more than he did the first time. The renters treated them the same way. [37] Last of all, he sent his son to them. 'They will respect my son,' he said.

[38] "But the renters saw the son coming. They said to one another, 'This is the one who will receive all the owner's property someday. Come, let's kill him. Then everything will be ours.' [39] So they took him and threw him out of the vineyard. Then they killed him.

[40] "When the owner of the vineyard comes back, what will he do to those renters?"

[41] "He will destroy those evil people," they replied. "Then he will rent the vineyard out to other renters. They will give him his share of the crop at harvest time."

[42] Jesus said to them, "Haven't you ever read what the Scriptures say,

" 'The stone the builders
      didn't accept
   has become the most
      important stone of all.
The Lord has done it.
   It is wonderful in our eyes'?

(Psalm 118:22,23)

[43] "So here is what I tell you. The kingdom of God will be taken away from you. It will be given to people who will produce its fruit. [44] Anyone who falls on that stone will be broken to pieces. But the stone will crush anyone it falls on."

[45] The chief priests and the Pharisees heard Jesus' stories. They knew he was talking about them. [46] So they looked for a way to arrest him. But they were afraid of the crowd. The people believed that Jesus was a prophet.

The Story of the Wedding Dinner

22 Jesus told them more stories. He said, [2] "Here is what the kingdom of heaven is like. A king prepared a wedding dinner for his son. [3] He sent his slaves to those who had been invited to the dinner. The slaves told them to come. But they refused.

[4] "Then he sent some more slaves. He said, 'Tell those who

were invited that I have prepared my dinner. I have killed my oxen and my fattest cattle. Everything is ready. Come to the wedding dinner.'

⁵ "But the people paid no attention. One went away to his field. Another went away to his business. ⁶ The rest grabbed his slaves. They treated them badly and then killed them. ⁷ The king became very angry. He sent his army to destroy them. They killed those murderers and burned their city.

⁸ "Then the king said to his slaves, 'The wedding dinner is ready. But those I invited were not fit to come. ⁹ So go to the street corners. Invite to the dinner anyone you can find.' ¹⁰ So the slaves went out into the streets. They gathered all the people they could find, the bad as well as the good. Soon the wedding hall was filled with guests.

¹¹ "The king came in to see the guests. He noticed a man there who was not wearing wedding clothes. ¹² 'Friend,' he asked, 'how did you get in here without wedding clothes?' The man couldn't think of anything to say. ¹³ "Then the king told his slaves, 'Tie up his hands and feet. Throw him outside into the darkness. Out there people will weep and grind their teeth.'

¹⁴ "Many are invited, but few are chosen."

Is It Right to Pay the Royal Tax to Caesar?

¹⁵ The Pharisees went out. They made plans to trap Jesus with his own words. ¹⁶ They sent their followers to him. They sent the Herodians with them. "Teacher," they said, "we know that you are a man of honor. You teach the way of God truthfully. You don't let others tell you what to do or say. You don't care how important they are. ¹⁷ Tell us then, what do you think? Is it right to pay the royal tax to Caesar or not?"

¹⁸ But Jesus knew their evil plans. He said, "You pretenders! Why are you trying to trap me? ¹⁹ Show me the coin people use for paying the tax." They brought him a silver coin. ²⁰ He asked them, "Whose picture is this? And whose words?"

²¹ "Caesar's," they replied.

Then he said to them, "So give back to Caesar what belongs to Caesar. And give back to God what belongs to God."

²² When they heard this, they were amazed. So they left him and went away.

Marriage When the Dead Rise

²³ That same day the Sadducees came to Jesus with a question. They do not believe that people rise from the dead. ²⁴ "Teacher," they said, "here is what Moses told us. If a man dies without having children, his brother must get married to the widow. He must provide children to carry on his brother's name. ²⁵ There were seven brothers among us. The first one got married and died. Since he had no children, he left his wife to his brother. ²⁶ The same

thing happened to the second and third brothers. It happened right on down to the seventh brother. ²⁷ Finally, the woman died. ²⁸ Now then, when the dead rise, whose wife will she be? All seven of them were married to her."

²⁹ Jesus replied, "You are mistaken, because you do not know the Scriptures. And you do not know the power of God. ³⁰ When the dead rise, they won't get married. And their parents won't give them to be married. They will be like the angels in heaven. ³¹ What about the dead rising? Haven't you read what God said to you? ³² He said, 'I am the God of Abraham. I am the God of Isaac. And I am the God of Jacob.' *(Exodus 3:6)* He is not the God of the dead. He is the God of the living."

³³ When the crowds heard this, they were amazed by what he taught.

The Most Important Commandment

³⁴ The Pharisees heard that the Sadducees weren't able to answer Jesus. So the Pharisees got together. ³⁵ One of them was an authority on the law. So he tested Jesus with a question. ³⁶ "Teacher," he asked, "which is the most important commandment in the Law?"

³⁷ Jesus replied, " 'Love the Lord your God with all your heart and with all your soul. Love him with all your mind.' *(Deuteronomy 6:5)* ³⁸ This is the first and most important command-

ment. ³⁹ And the second is like it. 'Love your neighbor as you love yourself.' *(Leviticus 19:18)* ⁴⁰ Everything that is written in the Law and the Prophets is based on these two commandments."

Whose Son Is the Messiah?

⁴¹ The Pharisees were gathered together. Jesus asked them, ⁴² "What do you think about the Messiah? Whose son is he?"

"The son of David," they replied.

⁴³ He said to them, "Then why does David call him 'Lord'? The Holy Spirit spoke through David himself. David said,

⁴⁴ " 'The Lord said to my Lord,
     "Sit at my right hand
until I put your enemies
     under your control." '

(Psalm 110:1)

⁴⁵ So if David calls him 'Lord,' how can he be David's son?" ⁴⁶ No one could give any answer to him. From that day on, no one dared to ask him any more questions.

A Warning Against Doing Things for the Wrong Reasons

23 Jesus spoke to the crowds and to his disciples. ² "The teachers of the law and the Pharisees sit in Moses' seat," he said. ³ "So you must be careful to do everything they say. But don't do what they do. They don't practice what they preach. ⁴ They tie up heavy loads that are hard to carry. Then they put them on other people's shoulders. But they themselves aren't willing to lift a finger to move them.

⁵ "Everything they do is done for others to see. On their foreheads and arms they wear little boxes that hold Scripture verses. They make the boxes very wide. And they make the tassels on their coats very long. ⁶ They love to sit down in the place of honor at dinners. They also love to have the most important seats in the synagogues. ⁷ They love to be greeted with respect in the markets. They love it when people call them 'Rabbi.'

⁸ "But you shouldn't be called 'Rabbi.' You have only one Teacher, and you are all brothers. ⁹ Do not call anyone on earth 'father.' You have one Father, and he is in heaven. ¹⁰ You shouldn't be called 'teacher.' You have one Teacher, and he is the Messiah. ¹¹ The most important person among you will be your servant. ¹² People who lift themselves up will be made humble. And people who make themselves humble will be lifted up.

How Terrible for the Teachers of the Law and the Pharisees

¹³⁻¹⁴ "How terrible it will be for you, teachers of the law and Pharisees! You pretenders! You shut the door of the kingdom of heaven in people's faces. You yourselves do not enter. And you will not let those enter who are trying to.

¹⁵ "How terrible for you, teachers of the law and Pharisees! You pretenders! You travel everywhere to win one person to your faith. Then you make them twice as much a child of hell as you are.

¹⁶ "How terrible for you, blind guides! You say, 'If anyone makes a promise in the name of the temple, it means nothing. But anyone who makes a promise in the name of the gold of the temple must keep that promise.' ¹⁷ You are blind and foolish! Which is more important? Is it the gold? Or is it the temple that makes the gold holy? ¹⁸ You also say, 'If anyone makes a promise in the name of the altar, it means nothing. But anyone who makes a promise in the name of the gift on the altar must keep that promise.' ¹⁹ You are blind! Which is more important? Is it the gift? Or is it the altar that makes the gift holy? ²⁰ So anyone making a promise in the name of the altar makes a promise in the name of it and everything on it. ²¹ And anyone making a promise in the name of the temple makes a promise in the name of it and the one who lives in it. ²² And anyone making a promise in the name of heaven makes a promise in the name of God's throne and the one who sits on it.

²³ "How terrible for you, teachers of the law and Pharisees! You pretenders! You give God a tenth of your spices, like mint, dill and cumin. But you have not practiced the more important things of the law, which are fairness, mercy and faithfulness. You should have practiced

the last things without failing to do the first. ²⁴ You blind guides! You remove the smallest insect from your food. But you swallow a whole camel!

²⁵ "How terrible for you, teachers of the law and Pharisees! You pretenders! You clean the outside of a cup and dish. But on the inside you are full of greed. You only want to satisfy yourselves. ²⁶ Blind Pharisee! First clean the inside of the cup and dish. Then the outside will also be clean.

²⁷ "How terrible for you, teachers of the law and Pharisees! You pretenders! You are like tombs that are painted white. They look beautiful on the outside. But on the inside they are full of the bones of the dead. They are also full of other things that are not pure and 'clean.' ²⁸ It is the same with you. On the outside you seem to be doing what is right. But on the inside you are full of what is wrong. You pretend to be what you are not.

²⁹ "How terrible for you, teachers of the law and Pharisees! You pretenders! You build tombs for the prophets. You decorate the graves of the godly. ³⁰ And you say, 'If we had lived in the days of those who lived before us, we wouldn't have done what they did. We wouldn't have helped to kill the prophets.' ³¹ So you are witnesses against yourselves. You admit that you are the children of those who murdered the prophets. ³² So go ahead and finish the sins that those who lived before you started!

³³ "You nest of poisonous snakes! How will you escape from being sentenced to hell? ³⁴ So I am sending you prophets, wise people, and teachers. You will kill some of them. You will nail some to a cross. Others you will whip in your synagogues. You will chase them from town to town. ³⁵ So you will pay for all the godly people's blood spilled on earth. I mean from the blood of godly Abel to the blood of Zechariah, the son of Berekiah. Zechariah was the one you murdered between the temple and the altar. ³⁶ What I'm about to tell you is true. All this will happen to those who are now living.

³⁷ "Jerusalem! Jerusalem! You kill the prophets and throw stones in order to kill those who are sent to you. Many times I have wanted to gather your people together. I have wanted to be like a hen who gathers her chicks under her wings. And you would not let me! ³⁸ Look, your house is left empty. ³⁹ I tell you, you will not see me again until you say, 'Blessed is the one who comes in the name of the Lord.' " *(Psalm 118:26)*

When the Temple Will Be Destroyed and the Signs of the End

24 Jesus left the temple. He was walking away when his disciples came up to him. They wanted to call his attention to the temple buildings. ² "Do you see all these things?" Jesus asked. "What I'm about to tell you is true. Not one stone here will be left on top of another. Every stone will be thrown down."

³ Jesus was sitting on the Mount of Olives. There the disciples came to him in private. "Tell us," they said. "When will this happen? And what will be the sign of your coming? What will be the sign of the end?"

⁴ Jesus answered, "Keep watch! Be careful that no one fools you. ⁵ Many will come in my name. They will claim, 'I am the Messiah!' They will fool many people. ⁶ You will hear about wars. You will also hear people talking about future wars. Don't be alarmed. Those things must happen. But the end still isn't here. ⁷ Nation will fight against nation. Kingdom will fight against kingdom. People will go hungry. There will be earthquakes in many places. ⁸ All these are the beginning of birth pains.

⁹ "Then people will hand you over to be treated badly and killed. All nations will hate you because of me. ¹⁰ At that time, many will turn away from their faith. They will hate each other. They will hand each other over to their enemies. ¹¹ Many false prophets will appear. They will fool many people. ¹² Because evil will grow, most people's love will grow cold. ¹³ But the one who remains strong in the faith will be saved. ¹⁴ This good news of the kingdom will be preached in the whole world. It will be a witness to all nations. Then the end will come.

¹⁵ "The prophet Daniel spoke about 'the hated thing that destroys.' *(Daniel 9:27; 11:31; 12:11)* Someday you will see it standing in the holy place. The reader should understand this. ¹⁶ Then those who are in Judea should escape to the mountains. ¹⁷ No one on the housetop should go down into the house to take anything out. ¹⁸ No one in the field should go back to get their coat. ¹⁹ How awful it will be in those days for pregnant women! How awful for nursing mothers! ²⁰ Pray that you will not have to escape in winter or on the Sabbath day. ²¹ There will be terrible suffering in those days. It will be worse than any other from the beginning of the world until now. And there will never be anything like it again.

²² "If the time had not been cut short, no one would live. But because of God's chosen people, it will be shortened. ²³ At that time someone may say to you, 'Look! Here is the Messiah!' Or, 'There he is!' Do not believe it. ²⁴ False messiahs and false prophets will appear. They will do great signs and miracles. They will try to fool God's chosen people if possible. ²⁵ See, I have told you ahead of time.

²⁶ "So if anyone tells you, 'He is a long way out in the desert,' do not go out there. Or if anyone says, 'He is deep inside the house,' do not believe it. ²⁷ Lightning that comes from the east can be seen in the west. It will be the same when the Son of Man comes. ²⁸ The vultures will gather wherever there is a dead body.

29 "Right after the terrible suffering of those days,

" 'The sun will be darkened.
The moon will not shine.
The stars will fall from the
sky.
The heavenly bodies will
be shaken.' *(Isaiah 13:10; 34:4)*

30 "Then the sign of the Son of Man will appear in heaven. At that time, all the peoples of the earth will mourn. They will mourn when they see the Son of Man coming on the clouds of heaven. He will come with power and great glory. 31 He will send his angels with a loud trumpet call. They will gather his chosen people from all four directions. They will bring them from one end of the heavens to the other.

32 "Learn a lesson from the fig tree. As soon as its twigs get tender and its leaves come out, you know that summer is near. 33 In the same way, when you see all these things happening, you know that the end is near. It is right at the door. 34 What I'm about to tell you is true. The people living now will certainly not pass away until all these things have happened. 35 Heaven and earth will pass away. But my words will never pass away.

The Day and Hour Are Not Known

36 "But no one knows about that day or hour. Not even the angels in heaven know. The Son does not know. Only the Father knows. 37 Remember how it was in the days of Noah. It will be the same when the Son of Man comes. 38 In the days before the flood, people were eating and drinking. They were getting married. They were giving their daughters to be married. They did all those things right up to the day Noah entered the ark. 39 They knew nothing about what would happen until the flood came and took them all away. That is how it will be when the Son of Man comes. 40 Two men will be in the field. One will be taken and the other left. 41 Two women will be grinding with a hand mill. One will be taken and the other left.

42 "So keep watch. You do not know on what day your Lord will come. 43 You must understand something. Suppose the owner of the house knew what time of night the robber was coming. Then he would have kept watch. He would not have let his house be broken into. 44 So you also must be ready. The Son of Man will come at an hour when you don't expect him.

45 "Suppose a master puts one of his slaves in charge of the other slaves in his house. The slave's job is to give them their food at the right time. The master wants a faithful and wise slave for this. 46 It will be good for the slave if the master finds him doing his job when the master returns. 47 What I'm about to tell you is true. The master will put that slave in charge of everything he owns. 48 But suppose that slave is evil. Suppose

he says to himself, 'My master is staying away a long time.' ⁴⁹ Suppose he begins to beat the other slaves. And suppose he eats and drinks with those who drink too much. ⁵⁰ The master of that slave will come back on a day the slave doesn't expect him. He will return at an hour the slave does not know. ⁵¹ Then the master will cut him to pieces. He will send him to the place where pretenders go. There people will weep and grind their teeth.

The Story of Ten Bridesmaids

25 "Here is what the kingdom of heaven will be like at that time. Ten bridesmaids took their lamps and went out to meet the groom. ² Five of them were foolish. Five were wise. ³ The foolish ones took their lamps but didn't take any olive oil with them. ⁴ The wise ones took oil in jars along with their lamps. ⁵ The groom did not come for a long time. So the bridesmaids all grew tired and fell asleep.

⁶ "At midnight someone cried out, 'Here's the groom! Come out to meet him!'

⁷ "Then all the bridesmaids woke up and got their lamps ready. ⁸ The foolish ones said to the wise ones, 'Give us some of your oil. Our lamps are going out.'

⁹ " 'No,' they replied. 'There may not be enough for all of us. Instead, go to those who sell oil. Buy some for yourselves.'

¹⁰ "So they went to buy the oil. But while they were on their way, the groom arrived. The bridesmaids who were ready went in with him to the wedding dinner. Then the door was shut.

¹¹ "Later, the other bridesmaids also came. 'Sir! Sir!' they said. 'Open the door for us!'

¹² "But he replied, 'What I'm about to tell you is true. I don't know you.'

¹³ "So keep watch. You do not know the day or the hour that the groom will come.

The Story of Three Slaves

¹⁴ "Again, here is what the kingdom of heaven will be like. A man was going on a journey. He sent for his slaves and put them in charge of his money. ¹⁵ He gave five bags of gold to one. He gave two bags to another. And he gave one bag to the third. The man gave each slave the amount of money he knew the slave could take care of. Then he went on his journey. ¹⁶ The slave who had received five bags of gold went at once and put his money to work. He earned five bags more. ¹⁷ The one with the two bags of gold earned two more. ¹⁸ But the man who had received one bag went and dug a hole in the ground. He hid his master's money in it.

¹⁹ "After a long time the master of those slaves returned. He wanted to collect all the money they had earned. ²⁰ The man who had received five bags of gold brought the other five. 'Master,' he said, 'you trusted me with five bags of gold. See, I have earned five more.'

²¹ "His master replied, 'You have done well, good and faithful slave! You have been faithful with a few things. I will put you in charge of many things. Come and share your master's happiness!'

²² "The man with two bags of gold also came. 'Master,' he said, 'you trusted me with two bags of gold. See, I have earned two more.'

²³ "His master replied, 'You have done well, good and faithful slave! You have been faithful with a few things. I will put you in charge of many things. Come and share your master's happiness!'

²⁴ "Then the man who had received one bag of gold came. 'Master,' he said, 'I knew that you are a hard man. You harvest where you have not planted. You gather crops where you have not scattered seed. ²⁵ So I was afraid. I went out and hid your gold in the ground. See, here is what belongs to you.'

²⁶ "His master replied, 'You evil, lazy slave! So you knew that I harvest where I have not planted? You knew that I gather crops where I have not scattered seed? ²⁷ Well then, you should have put my money in the bank. When I returned, I would have received it back with interest.'

²⁸ "Then his master commanded the other slaves, 'Take the bag of gold from him. Give it to the one who has ten bags. ²⁹ Everyone who has will be given more. They will have more than enough. And what about anyone who doesn't have? Even what they have will be taken away from them. ³⁰ Throw that worthless slave outside. There in the darkness, people will weep and grind their teeth.'

The Sheep and the Goats

³¹ "The Son of Man will come in all his glory. All the angels will come with him. Then he will sit in glory on his throne. ³² All the nations will be gathered in front of him. He will separate the people into two groups. He will be like a shepherd who separates the sheep from the goats. ³³ He will put the sheep to his right and the goats to his left.

³⁴ "Then the King will speak to those on his right. He will say, 'My Father has blessed you. Come and take what is yours. It is the kingdom prepared for you since the world was created. ³⁵ I was hungry. And you gave me something to eat. I was thirsty. And you gave me something to drink. I was a stranger. And you invited me in. ³⁶ I needed clothes. And you gave them to me. I was sick. And you took care of me. I was in prison. And you came to visit me.'

³⁷ "Then the people who have done what is right will answer him. 'Lord,' they will ask, 'when did we see you hungry and feed you? When did we see you thirsty and give you something to drink? ³⁸ When did we see you as a stranger and invite you in? When did we see you needing clothes and give them to you?

³⁹ When did we see you sick or in prison and go to visit you?'

⁴⁰ "The King will reply, 'What I'm about to tell you is true. Anything you did for one of the least important of these brothers and sisters of mine, you did for me.'

⁴¹ "Then he will say to those on his left, 'You are cursed! Go away from me into the fire that burns forever. It has been prepared for the devil and his angels. ⁴² I was hungry. But you gave me nothing to eat. I was thirsty. But you gave me nothing to drink. ⁴³ I was a stranger. But you did not invite me in. I needed clothes. But you did not give me any. I was sick and in prison. But you did not take care of me.'

⁴⁴ "They also will answer, 'Lord, when did we see you hungry or thirsty and not help you? When did we see you as a stranger or needing clothes or sick or in prison and not help you?'

⁴⁵ "He will reply, 'What I'm about to tell you is true. Anything you didn't do for one of the least important of these, you didn't do for me.'

⁴⁶ "Then they will go away to be punished forever. But those who have done what is right will receive eternal life."

The Plan to Kill Jesus

26 Jesus finished saying all these things. Then he said to his disciples, ² "As you know, the Passover Feast is two days away. The Son of Man will be handed over to be nailed to a cross."

³ Then the chief priests met with the elders of the people. They met in the palace of Caiaphas, the high priest. ⁴ They made plans to arrest Jesus secretly. They wanted to kill him. ⁵ "But not during the feast," they said. "The people may stir up trouble."

A Woman Pours Perfume on Jesus

⁶ Jesus was in Bethany. He was in the home of Simon, who had a skin disease. ⁷ A woman came to Jesus with a special sealed jar of very expensive perfume. She poured the perfume on his head while he was at the table.

⁸ When the disciples saw this, they became angry. "Why this waste?" they asked. ⁹ "The perfume could have been sold at a high price. The money could have been given to poor people."

¹⁰ Jesus was aware of this. So he said to them, "Why are you bothering this woman? She has done a beautiful thing to me. ¹¹ You will always have poor people with you. But you will not always have me. ¹² She poured the perfume on my body to prepare me to be buried. ¹³ What I'm about to tell you is true. What she has done will be told anywhere this good news is preached all over the world. It will be told in memory of her."

Judas Agrees to Hand Jesus Over

¹⁴ One of the 12 disciples went to the chief priests. His name was Judas Iscariot. ¹⁵ He asked, "What will you give me

if I hand Jesus over to you?" So they counted out 30 silver coins for him. ¹⁶ From then on, Judas watched for the right time to hand Jesus over to them.

The Lord's Supper

¹⁷ It was the first day of the Feast of Unleavened Bread. The disciples came to Jesus. They asked, "Where do you want us to prepare for you to eat the Passover meal?"

¹⁸ He replied, "Go into the city to a certain man. Tell him, 'The Teacher says, "My time is near. I am going to celebrate the Passover at your house with my disciples."'" ¹⁹ So the disciples did what Jesus had told them to do. They prepared the Passover meal.

²⁰ When evening came, Jesus was at the table with his 12 disciples. ²¹ While they were eating, he said, "What I'm about to tell you is true. One of you will hand me over to my enemies."

²² The disciples became very sad. One after the other, they began to say to him, "Surely you don't mean me, Lord, do you?"

²³ Jesus replied, "The one who has dipped his hand into the bowl with me will hand me over. ²⁴ The Son of Man will go just as it is written about him. But how terrible it will be for the one who hands over the Son of Man! It would be better for him if he had not been born."

²⁵ Judas was the one who was going to hand him over. He said, "Surely you don't mean me, Teacher, do you?"

Jesus answered, "You have said so."

²⁶ While they were eating, Jesus took bread. He gave thanks and broke it. He handed it to his disciples and said, "Take this and eat it. This is my body."

²⁷ Then he took a cup. He gave thanks and handed it to them. He said, "All of you drink from it. ²⁸ This is my blood of the covenant. It is poured out to forgive the sins of many people. ²⁹ Here is what I tell you. From now on, I won't drink wine with you again until the day I drink it with you in my Father's kingdom."

³⁰ Then they sang a hymn and went out to the Mount of Olives.

Jesus Says That the Disciples Will Turn Away

³¹ Jesus told them, "This very night you will all turn away because of me. It is written that the Lord said,

" 'I will strike the shepherd down.
    Then the sheep of the flock
        will be scattered.'
                    (Zechariah 13:7)

³² But after I rise from the dead, I will go ahead of you into Galilee."

³³ Peter replied, "All the others may turn away because of you. But I never will."

³⁴ "What I'm about to tell you is true," Jesus answered. "It will happen tonight. Before the rooster crows, you will say three times that you don't know me."

³⁵ But Peter said, "I may have to die with you. But I will never

say I don't know you." And all the other disciples said the same thing.

Jesus Prays in Gethsemane

36 Then Jesus went with his disciples to a place called Gethsemane. He said to them, "Sit here while I go over there and pray." 37 He took Peter and the two sons of Zebedee along with him. He began to be sad and troubled. 38 Then he said to them, "My soul is very sad. I feel close to death. Stay here. Keep watch with me."

39 He went a little farther. Then he fell with his face to the ground. He prayed, "My Father, if it is possible, take this cup of suffering away from me. But let what you want be done, not what I want."

40 Then he returned to his disciples and found them sleeping. "Couldn't you men keep watch with me for one hour?" he asked Peter. 41 "Watch and pray. Then you won't fall into sin when you are tempted. The spirit is willing, but the body is weak."

42 Jesus went away a second time. He prayed, "My Father, is it possible for this cup to be taken away? But if I must drink it, may what you want be done."

43 Then he came back. Again he found them sleeping. They couldn't keep their eyes open. 44 So he left them and went away once more. For the third time he prayed the same thing.

45 Then he returned to the disciples. He said to them, "Are you still sleeping and resting? Look! The hour has come. The Son of Man is about to be handed over to sinners. 46 Get up! Let us go! Here comes the one who is handing me over to them!"

Jesus Is Arrested

47 While Jesus was still speaking, Judas arrived. He was one of the 12 disciples. A large crowd was with him. They were carrying swords and clubs. The chief priests and the elders of the people had sent them. 48 Judas, who was going to hand Jesus over, had arranged a signal with them. "The one I kiss is the man," he said. "Arrest him." 49 So Judas went to Jesus at once. He said, "Greetings, Rabbi!" And he kissed him.

50 Jesus replied, "Friend, do what you came to do."

Then the men stepped forward. They grabbed Jesus and arrested him. 51 At that moment, one of Jesus' companions reached for his sword. He pulled it out and struck the slave of the high priest with it. He cut off the slave's ear.

52 "Put your sword back in its place," Jesus said to him. "All who use the sword will die by the sword. 53 Do you think I can't ask my Father for help? He would send an army of more than 70,000 angels right away. 54 But then how would the Scriptures come true? They say it must happen in this way."

55 At that time Jesus spoke to the crowd. "Am I leading a band of armed men against you?" he asked. "Do you have to come

out with swords and clubs to capture me? Every day I sat in the temple courtyard teaching. And you didn't arrest me. [56] But all this has happened so that the words of the prophets would come true." Then all the disciples left him and ran away.

Jesus Is Taken to the Sanhedrin

[57] Those who had arrested Jesus took him to Caiaphas, the high priest. The teachers of the law and the elders had come together there. [58] Not too far away, Peter followed Jesus. He went right up to the courtyard of the high priest. He entered and sat down with the guards to see what would happen.

[59] The chief priests and the whole Sanhedrin were looking for something to use against Jesus. They wanted to put him to death. [60] But they did not find any proof, even though many false witnesses came forward.

Finally, two other witnesses came forward. [61] They said, "This fellow claimed, 'I am able to destroy the temple of God. I can build it again in three days.'"

[62] Then the high priest stood up. He asked Jesus, "Aren't you going to answer? What are these charges that these men are bringing against you?" [63] But Jesus remained silent.

The high priest said to him, "I am commanding you in the name of the living God. May he judge you if you don't tell the truth. Tell us if you are the Messiah, the Son of God."

[64] "You have said so," Jesus replied. "But here is what I say to all of you. From now on, you will see the Son of Man sitting at the right hand of the Mighty One. You will see the Son of Man coming on the clouds of heaven."

[65] Then the high priest tore his clothes. He said, "He has spoken a very evil thing against God! Why do we need any more witnesses? You have heard him say this evil thing. [66] What do you think?"

"He must die!" they answered.

[67] Then they spit in his face. They hit him with their fists. Others slapped him. [68] They said, "Prophesy to us, Messiah! Who hit you?"

Peter Says He Does Not Know Jesus

[69] Peter was sitting out in the courtyard. A female servant came to him. "You also were with Jesus of Galilee," she said.

[70] But in front of all of them, Peter said he was not. "I don't know what you're talking about," he said.

[71] Then he went out to the gate leading into the courtyard. There another servant saw him. She said to the people, "This fellow was with Jesus of Nazareth."

[72] Again he said he was not. With a curse he said, "I don't know the man!"

[73] After a little while, those standing there went up to Peter. "You must be one of them," they said. "The way you talk gives you away."

⁷⁴ Then Peter began to curse and said to them, "I don't know the man!"

Right away a rooster crowed. ⁷⁵ Then Peter remembered what Jesus had said. "The rooster will crow," Jesus had told him. "Before it does, you will say three times that you don't know me." Peter went outside. He broke down and cried.

Judas Hangs Himself

27 It was early in the morning. All the chief priests and the elders of the people planned how to put Jesus to death. ² So they tied him up and led him away. Then they handed him over to Pilate, who was the governor.

³ Judas, who had handed him over, saw that Jesus had been sentenced to die. He felt deep shame and sadness for what he had done. So he returned the 30 silver coins to the chief priests and the elders. ⁴ "I have sinned," he said. "I handed over a man who is not guilty."

"What do we care?" they replied. "That's your problem."

⁵ So Judas threw the money into the temple and left. Then he went away and hanged himself.

⁶ The chief priests picked up the coins. They said, "It's against the law to put this money into the temple fund. It is blood money. It has paid for a man's death." ⁷ So they decided to use the money to buy a potter's field. People from other countries would be buried there. ⁸ That is why it has been called the Field of Blood to this day. ⁹ Then the words spoken by Jeremiah the prophet came true. He had said, "They took the 30 silver coins. That price was set for him by the people of Israel. ¹⁰ They used the coins to buy a potter's field, just as the Lord commanded me." *(Zechariah 11:12,13; Jeremiah 19:1–13; 32:6–9)*

Jesus Is Brought to Pilate

¹¹ Jesus was standing in front of the governor. The governor asked him, "Are you the king of the Jews?"

"Yes. You have said so," Jesus replied.

¹² But when the chief priests and the elders brought charges against him, he did not answer. ¹³ Then Pilate asked him, "Don't you hear the charges they are bringing against you?" ¹⁴ But Jesus made no reply, not even to a single charge. The governor was really amazed.

¹⁵ It was the governor's practice at the Passover Feast to let one prisoner go free. The people could choose the one they wanted. ¹⁶ At that time they had a well-known prisoner named Jesus Barabbas. ¹⁷ So when the crowd gathered, Pilate asked them, "Which one do you want me to set free? Jesus Barabbas? Or Jesus who is called the Messiah?" ¹⁸ Pilate knew that the leaders wanted to get their own way. He knew this was why they had handed Jesus over to him.

¹⁹ While Pilate was sitting on the judge's seat, his wife sent him a message. It said, "Don't

have anything to do with that man. He is not guilty. I have suffered a great deal in a dream today because of him."

20 But the chief priests and the elders talked the crowd into asking for Barabbas and having Jesus put to death.

21 "Which of the two do you want me to set free?" asked the governor.

"Barabbas," they answered.

22 "Then what should I do with Jesus who is called the Messiah?" Pilate asked.

They all answered, "Crucify him!"

23 "Why? What wrong has he done?" asked Pilate.

But they shouted even louder, "Crucify him!"

24 Pilate saw that he wasn't getting anywhere. Instead, the crowd was starting to get angry. So he took water and washed his hands in front of them. "I am not guilty of this man's death," he said. "You are accountable for that!"

25 All the people answered, "Put the blame for his death on us and our children!"

26 Pilate let Barabbas go free. But he had Jesus whipped. Then he handed him over to be nailed to a cross.

The Soldiers Make Fun of Jesus

27 The governor's soldiers took Jesus into the palace, which was called the Praetorium. All the rest of the soldiers gathered around him. 28 They took off his clothes and put a purple robe on him. 29 Then they twisted thorns together to make a crown. They placed it on his head. They put a stick in his right hand. Then they fell on their knees in front of him and made fun of him. "We honor you, king of the Jews!" they said. 30 They spit on him. They hit him on the head with the stick again and again. 31 After they had made fun of him, they took off the robe. They put his own clothes back on him. Then they led him away to nail him to a cross.

Jesus Is Nailed to a Cross

32 On their way out of the city, they met a man from Cyrene. His name was Simon. They forced him to carry the cross. 33 They came to a place called Golgotha. The word Golgotha means the Place of the Skull. 34 There they mixed wine with bitter spices and gave it to Jesus to drink. After tasting it, he refused to drink it. 35 When they had nailed him to the cross, they divided up his clothes by casting lots. 36 They sat down and kept watch over him there. 37 Above his head they placed the written charge against him. It read,

THIS IS JESUS, THE KING OF THE JEWS.

38 Two rebels against Rome were crucified with him. One was on his right and one was on his left. 39 Those who passed by shouted at Jesus and made fun of him. They shook their heads 40 and said, "So you are going to destroy the temple and build it

again in three days? Then save yourself! Come down from the cross, if you are the Son of God!" 41 In the same way the chief priests, the teachers of the law and the elders made fun of him. 42 "He saved others," they said. "But he can't save himself! He's the king of Israel! Let him come down now from the cross! Then we will believe in him. 43 He trusts in God. Let God rescue him now if he wants him. He's the one who said, 'I am the Son of God.'" 44 In the same way the rebels who were being crucified with Jesus also made fun of him.

Jesus Dies

45 From noon until three o'clock, the whole land was covered with darkness. 46 About three o'clock, Jesus cried out in a loud voice. He said, *"Eli, Eli, lema sabachthani?"* This means "My God, my God, why have you deserted me?" *(Psalm 22:1)* 47 Some of those standing there heard Jesus cry out. They said, "He's calling for Elijah." 48 Right away one of them ran and got a sponge. He filled it with wine vinegar and put it on a stick. He offered it to Jesus to drink. 49 The rest said, "Leave him alone. Let's see if Elijah comes to save him."

50 After Jesus cried out again in a loud voice, he died. 51 At that moment the temple curtain was torn in two from top to bottom. The earth shook. The rocks split. 52 Tombs broke open. The bodies of many holy people who had died were raised to life.

53 They came out of the tombs. After Jesus was raised from the dead, they went into the holy city. There they appeared to many people.

54 The Roman commander and those guarding Jesus saw the earthquake and all that had happened. They were terrified. They exclaimed, "He was surely the Son of God!"

55 Not very far away, many women were watching. They had followed Jesus from Galilee to take care of his needs. 56 Mary Magdalene was among them. Mary, the mother of James and Joseph, was also there. So was the mother of Zebedee's sons.

Jesus Is Buried

57 As evening approached, a rich man came from the town of Arimathea. His name was Joseph. He had become a follower of Jesus. 58 He went to Pilate and asked for Jesus' body. Pilate ordered that it be given to him. 59 Joseph took the body and wrapped it in a clean linen cloth. 60 He placed it in his own new tomb that he had cut out of the rock. He rolled a big stone in front of the entrance to the tomb. Then he went away. 61 Mary Magdalene and the other Mary were sitting there across from the tomb.

The Guards at the Tomb

62 The next day was the day after Preparation Day. The chief priests and the Pharisees went to Pilate. 63 "Sir," they said, "we remember something that liar

said while he was still alive. He claimed, 'After three days I will rise again.' ⁶⁴ So give the order to make the tomb secure until the third day. If you don't, his disciples might come and steal the body. Then they will tell the people that Jesus has been raised from the dead. This last lie will be worse than the first."

⁶⁵ "Take some guards with you," Pilate answered. "Go. Make the tomb as secure as you can." ⁶⁶ So they went and made the tomb secure. They put a royal seal on the stone and placed some guards on duty.

Jesus Rises From the Dead

28 The Sabbath day was now over. It was dawn on the first day of the week. Mary Magdalene and the other Mary went to look at the tomb.

² There was a powerful earthquake. An angel of the Lord came down from heaven. The angel went to the tomb. He rolled back the stone and sat on it. ³ His body shone like lightning. His clothes were as white as snow. ⁴ The guards were so afraid of him that they shook and became like dead men.

⁵ The angel said to the women, "Don't be afraid. I know that you are looking for Jesus, who was crucified. ⁶ He is not here! He has risen, just as he said he would! Come and see the place where he was lying. ⁷ Go quickly! Tell his disciples, 'He has risen from the dead. He is going ahead of you into Galilee. There you will see him.' Now I have told you."

⁸ So the women hurried away from the tomb. They were afraid, but they were filled with joy. They ran to tell the disciples. ⁹ Suddenly Jesus met them. "Greetings!" he said. They came to him, took hold of his feet and worshiped him. ¹⁰ Then Jesus said to them, "Don't be afraid. Go and tell my brothers to go to Galilee. There they will see me."

The Guards Report to the Chief Priests

¹¹ While the women were on their way, some of the guards went into the city. They reported to the chief priests all that had happened. ¹² When the chief priests met with the elders, they came up with a plan. They gave the soldiers a large amount of money. ¹³ They told the soldiers, "We want you to say, 'His disciples came during the night. They stole his body while we were sleeping.' ¹⁴ If the governor hears this report, we will pay him off. That will keep you out of trouble." ¹⁵ So the soldiers took the money and did as they were told. This story has spread all around among the Jews to this day.

Jesus' Final Orders to His Disciples

¹⁶ Then the 11 disciples went to Galilee. They went to the mountain where Jesus had told them to go. ¹⁷ When they saw him, they worshiped him. But some still had their doubts. ¹⁸ Then Jesus came to them. He said, "All authority in heaven

and on earth has been given to me. [19] So you must go and make disciples of all nations. Baptize them in the name of the Father and of the Son and of the Holy Spirit. [20] Teach them to obey everything I have commanded you. And you can be sure that I am always with you, to the very end."

Mark

Introduction:

Mark wrote this Gospel. Although he wasn't one of the twelve disciples, he was a follower of Jesus. Mark worked with Paul and Barnabas on their missionary trips. He learned Jesus' stories from Peter. He wrote these stories in this book.

Mark wrote to tell people who Jesus was. Jesus did many things to prove he is the Son of God. He did many miracles to help people. He also died to save people from their sin. Mark told why Jesus had to die. Mark also told that Jesus rose from the dead.

Outline of contents:

John the Baptist Prepares the Way

1 This is the beginning of the good news about Jesus the Messiah, the Son of God. ² Long ago Isaiah the prophet wrote,

"I will send my messenger
ahead of you.
He will prepare your way."
(Malachi 3:1)
³ "A messenger is calling out in the desert,
'Prepare the way for the Lord.
Make straight paths for him.' " *(Isaiah 40:3)*

⁴ And so John the Baptist appeared in the desert. He preached that people should be baptized and turn away from their sins. Then God would forgive them. ⁵ All the people from the countryside of Judea went out to him. All the people from Jerusalem went too. When they admitted they had sinned, John baptized them in the Jordan River. ⁶ John wore clothes made out of camel's hair. He had a leather belt around his waist. And he ate locusts and wild honey. ⁷ Here is what John was preaching. "After me, there is someone coming who is more powerful than I am. I'm not good enough to bend down and untie his sandals. ⁸ I baptize you with water. But he will baptize you with the Holy Spirit."

Jesus Is Baptized and Tempted

⁹ At that time Jesus came from Nazareth in Galilee. John baptized Jesus in the Jordan River. ¹⁰ Jesus was coming up out of the water. Just then he saw heaven

being torn open. Jesus saw the Holy Spirit coming down on him like a dove. [11] A voice spoke to him from heaven. It said, "You are my Son, and I love you. I am very pleased with you."

[12] At once the Holy Spirit sent Jesus out into the desert. [13] He was in the desert 40 days. There Satan tempted him. The wild animals didn't harm Jesus. Angels took care of him.

Jesus Preaches the Good News

[14] After John was put in prison, Jesus went into Galilee. He preached the good news of God. [15] "The time has come," he said. "The kingdom of God has come near. Turn away from your sins and believe the good news!"

Jesus Chooses His First Disciples

[16] One day Jesus was walking beside the Sea of Galilee. There he saw Simon and his brother Andrew. They were throwing a net into the lake. They were fishermen. [17] "Come and follow me," Jesus said. "I will send you out to fish for people." [18] At once they left their nets and followed him.

[19] Then Jesus walked a little farther. As he did, he saw James, the son of Zebedee, and his brother John. They were in a boat preparing their nets. [20] Right away he called out to them. They left their father Zebedee in the boat with the hired men. Then they followed Jesus.

Jesus Drives Out an Evil Spirit

[21] Jesus and those with him went to Capernaum. When the Sabbath day came, he went into the synagogue. There he began to teach. [22] The people were amazed at his teaching. That's because he taught them like one who had authority. He did not talk like the teachers of the law. [23] Just then a man in their synagogue cried out. He was controlled by an evil spirit. He said, [24] "What do you want with us, Jesus of Nazareth? Have you come to destroy us? I know who you are. You are the Holy One of God!"

[25] "Be quiet!" said Jesus firmly. "Come out of him!" [26] The evil spirit shook the man wildly. Then it came out of him with a scream.

[27] All the people were amazed. So they asked each other, "What is this? A new teaching! And with so much authority! He even gives orders to evil spirits, and they obey him." [28] News about Jesus spread quickly all over Galilee.

Jesus Heals Many People

[29] Jesus and those with him left the synagogue. Right away they went with James and John to the home of Simon and Andrew. [30] Simon's mother-in-law was lying in bed with a fever. They told Jesus about her right away. [31] So he went to her. He took her hand and helped her up. The fever left her. Then she began to serve them.

[32] That evening after sunset, the people brought to Jesus all who were sick. They also brought all who were controlled

by demons. ³³ All the people in town gathered at the door. ³⁴ Jesus healed many of them. They had all kinds of sicknesses. He also drove out many demons. But he would not let the demons speak, because they knew who he was.

Jesus Prays in a Quiet Place

³⁵ It was very early in the morning and still dark. Jesus got up and left the house. He went to a place where he could be alone. There he prayed. ³⁶ Simon and his friends went to look for Jesus. ³⁷ When they found him, they called out, "Everyone is looking for you!"

³⁸ Jesus replied, "Let's go somewhere else. I want to go to the nearby towns. I must preach there also. That is why I have come." ³⁹ So he traveled all around Galilee. He preached in their synagogues. He also drove out demons.

Jesus Heals a Man Who Had a Skin Disease

⁴⁰ A man who had a skin disease came to Jesus. On his knees he begged Jesus. He said, "If you are willing to make me 'clean,' you can do it."

⁴¹ Jesus became angry. He reached out his hand and touched the man. "I am willing to do it," Jesus said. "Be 'clean'!"

⁴² Right away the disease left the man, and he was "clean."

⁴³ Jesus sent him away at once. He gave the man a strong warning. ⁴⁴ "Don't tell this to anyone," he said. "Go and show yourself to the priest. Offer the sacrifices that Moses commanded. It will be a witness to the priest and the people that you are 'clean.'" ⁴⁵ But the man went out and started talking right away. He spread the news to everyone. So Jesus could no longer enter a town openly. He stayed outside in lonely places. But people still came to him from everywhere.

Jesus Forgives and Heals a Man Who Could Not Walk

2 A few days later, Jesus entered Capernaum again. The people heard that he had come home. ² So many people gathered that there was no room left. There was not even room outside the door. And Jesus preached the word to them. ³ Four of those who came were carrying a man who could not walk. ⁴ But they could not get him close to Jesus because of the crowd. So they made a hole by digging through the roof above Jesus. Then they lowered the man through it on a mat. ⁵ Jesus saw their faith. So he said to the man, "Son, your sins are forgiven."

⁶ Some teachers of the law were sitting there. They were thinking, ⁷ "Why is this fellow talking like that? He's saying a very evil thing! Only God can forgive sins!"

⁸ Right away Jesus knew what they were thinking. So he said to them, "Why are you thinking these things? ⁹ Is it easier to say to this man, 'Your sins are

forgiven'? Or to say, 'Get up, take your mat and walk'? [10] But I want you to know that the Son of Man has authority on earth to forgive sins." So Jesus spoke to the man who could not walk. [11] "I tell you," he said, "get up. Take your mat and go home." [12] The man got up and took his mat. Then he walked away while everyone watched. All the people were amazed. They praised God and said, "We have never seen anything like this!"

Jesus Chooses Levi and Eats With Sinners

[13] Once again Jesus went out beside the Sea of Galilee. A large crowd came to him. He began to teach them. [14] As he walked along he saw Levi, the son of Alphaeus. Levi was sitting at the tax collector's booth. "Follow me," Jesus told him. Levi got up and followed him.

[15] Later Jesus was having dinner at Levi's house. Many tax collectors and sinners were eating with him and his disciples. They were part of the large crowd following Jesus. [16] Some teachers of the law who were Pharisees were there. They saw Jesus eating with sinners and tax collectors. So they asked his disciples, "Why does he eat with tax collectors and sinners?"

[17] Jesus heard that. So he said to them, "Those who are healthy don't need a doctor. Sick people do. I have not come to get those who think they are right with God to follow me. I have come to get sinners to follow me."

Jesus Is Asked About Fasting

[18] John's disciples and the Pharisees were going without eating. Some people came to Jesus. They said to him, "John's disciples are fasting. The disciples of the Pharisees are also fasting. But your disciples are not. Why aren't they?"

[19] Jesus answered, "How can the guests of the groom go without eating while he is with them? They will not fast as long as he is with them. [20] But the time will come when the groom will be taken away from them. On that day they will go without eating.

[21] "No one sews a patch of new cloth on old clothes. Otherwise, the new piece will pull away from the old. That will make the tear worse. [22] No one pours new wine into old wineskins. Otherwise, the wine will burst the skins. Then the wine and the wineskins will both be destroyed. No, people pour new wine into new wineskins."

Jesus Is Lord of the Sabbath Day

[23] One Sabbath day Jesus was walking with his disciples through the grainfields. The disciples began to break off some heads of grain. [24] The Pharisees said to Jesus, "Look! It is against the Law to do this on the Sabbath day. Why are your disciples doing it?"

[25] He answered, "Haven't you ever read about what David did? He and his men were hungry. They needed food. [26] It was when Abiathar was high priest. David

entered the house of God and ate the holy bread. Only priests were allowed to eat it. David also gave some to his men."

27 Then Jesus said to them, "The Sabbath day was made for man. Man was not made for the Sabbath day. 28 So the Son of Man is Lord even of the Sabbath day."

Jesus Heals on the Sabbath Day

3 Another time Jesus went into the synagogue. A man with a weak and twisted hand was there. 2 Some Pharisees were trying to find fault with Jesus. They watched him closely. They wanted to see if he would heal the man on the Sabbath day. 3 Jesus spoke to the man with the weak and twisted hand. "Stand up in front of everyone," he said.

4 Then Jesus asked them, "What does the Law say we should do on the Sabbath day? Should we do good? Or should we do evil? Should we save life? Or should we kill?" But no one answered.

5 Jesus looked around at them in anger. He was very upset because their hearts were stubborn. Then he said to the man, "Stretch out your hand." He stretched it out, and his hand had become as good as new. 6 Then the Pharisees went out and began to make plans with the Herodians. They wanted to kill Jesus.

Crowds Follow Jesus

7 Jesus went off to the Sea of Galilee with his disciples. A large crowd from Galilee followed. 8 People heard about all that Jesus was doing. And many came to him. They came from Judea, Jerusalem and Idumea. They came from the lands east of the Jordan River. And they came from the area around Tyre and Sidon. 9 Because of the crowd, Jesus told his disciples to get a small boat ready for him. This would keep the people from crowding him. 10 Jesus had healed many people. So those who were sick were pushing forward to touch him. 11 When people controlled by evil spirits saw him, they fell down in front of him. The spirits shouted, "You are the Son of God!" 12 But Jesus ordered them not to tell people about him.

Jesus Appoints the Twelve Disciples

13 Jesus went up on a mountainside. He called for certain people to come to him, and they came. 14 He appointed 12 of them so that they would be with him. He would also send them out to preach. 15 And he gave them authority to drive out demons. 16 So Jesus appointed the 12 disciples. Simon was one of them. Jesus gave him the name Peter. 17 There were James, son of Zebedee, and his brother John. Jesus gave them the name Boanerges. Boanerges means Sons of Thunder. 18 There were also Andrew, Philip, Bartholomew, Matthew, Thomas, and James, son of Alphaeus. And there were Thaddaeus and Simon the

Zealot. ¹⁹ Judas Iscariot was one of them too. He was the one who was later going to hand Jesus over to his enemies.

Jesus Is Accused by Teachers of the Law

²⁰ Jesus entered a house. Again a crowd gathered. It was so large that Jesus and his disciples were not even able to eat. ²¹ His family heard about this. So they went to take charge of him. They said, "He is out of his mind."

²² Some teachers of the law were there. They had come down from Jerusalem. They said, "He is controlled by Beelzebul! He is driving out demons by the power of the prince of demons."

²³ So Jesus called them over to him. He began to speak to them using stories. He said, "How can Satan drive out Satan? ²⁴ If a kingdom fights against itself, it can't stand. ²⁵ If a family is divided, it can't stand. ²⁶ And if Satan fights against himself, and his helpers are divided, he can't stand. That is the end of him. ²⁷ In fact, none of you can enter a strong man's house unless you tie him up first. Then you can steal things from his house. ²⁸ What I'm about to tell you is true. Everyone's sins and evil words against God will be forgiven. ²⁹ But whoever speaks evil things against the Holy Spirit will never be forgiven. Their guilt will last forever."

³⁰ Jesus said this because the teachers of the law were saying, "He has an evil spirit."

Jesus' Mother and Brothers

³¹ Jesus' mother and brothers came and stood outside. They sent someone in to get him. ³² A crowd was sitting around Jesus. They told him, "Your mother and your brothers are outside. They are looking for you."

³³ "Who is my mother? Who are my brothers?" he asked.

³⁴ Then Jesus looked at the people sitting in a circle around him. He said, "Here is my mother! Here are my brothers! ³⁵ Anyone who does what God wants is my brother or sister or mother."

The Story of the Farmer

4 Again Jesus began to teach by the Sea of Galilee. The crowd that gathered around him was very large. So he got into a boat. He sat down in it out on the lake. All the people were along the shore at the water's edge. ² He taught them many things using stories. In his teaching he said, ³ "Listen! A farmer went out to plant his seed. ⁴ He scattered the seed on the ground. Some fell on a path. Birds came and ate it up. ⁵ Some seed fell on rocky places, where there wasn't much soil. The plants came up quickly, because the soil wasn't deep. ⁶ When the sun came up, it burned the plants. They dried up because they had no roots. ⁷ Other seed fell among thorns. The thorns grew up and crowded out the plants. So the plants did not bear grain. ⁸ Still other seed fell on good soil. It grew up and produced a crop

30, 60, or even 100 times more than the farmer planted."

⁹Then Jesus said, "Whoever has ears should listen."

¹⁰Later Jesus was alone. The 12 disciples asked him about the stories. So did the others around him. ¹¹He told them, "The secret of God's kingdom has been given to you. But to outsiders everything is told using stories. ¹²In that way,

" 'They will see but never know what they are seeing.
They will hear but never understand.
Otherwise they might turn and be forgiven!' "

(Isaiah 6:9,10)

¹³Then Jesus said to them, "Don't you understand this story? Then how will you understand any stories of this kind? ¹⁴The seed the farmer plants is God's message. ¹⁵What is seed scattered on a path like? The message is planted. The people hear the message. Then Satan comes. He takes away the message that was planted in them. ¹⁶And what is seed scattered on rocky places like? The people hear the message. At once they receive it with joy. ¹⁷But they have no roots. So they last only a short time. They quickly fall away from the faith when trouble or suffering comes because of the message. ¹⁸And what is seed scattered among thorns like? The people hear the message. ¹⁹But then the worries of this life come to them. Wealth

comes with its false promises. The people also long for other things. All of these are the kinds of things that crowd out the message. They keep it from producing fruit. ²⁰And what is seed scattered on good soil like? The people hear the message. They accept it. They produce a good crop 30, 60, or even 100 times more than the farmer planted."

A Lamp on a Stand

²¹Jesus said to them, "Do you bring in a lamp to put it under a large bowl or a bed? Don't you put it on its stand? ²²What is hidden is meant to be seen. And what is put out of sight is meant to be brought out into the open. ²³Whoever has ears should listen."

²⁴"Think carefully about what you hear," he said. "As you give, so you will receive. In fact, you will receive even more. ²⁵Whoever has something will be given more. Whoever has nothing, even what they have will be taken away from them."

The Story of the Growing Seed

²⁶Jesus also said, "Here is what God's kingdom is like. A farmer scatters seed on the ground. ²⁷Night and day the seed comes up and grows. It happens whether the farmer sleeps or gets up. He doesn't know how it happens. ²⁸All by itself the soil produces grain. First the stalk comes up. Then the head appears. Finally, the full grain appears in the head.

²⁹ Before long the grain ripens. So the farmer cuts it down, because the harvest is ready."

The Story of the Mustard Seed

³⁰ Again Jesus said, "What can we say God's kingdom is like? What story can we use to explain it? ³¹ It is like a mustard seed, which is the smallest of all seeds on earth. ³² But when you plant the seed, it grows. It becomes the largest of all garden plants. Its branches are so big that birds can rest in its shade."

³³ Using many stories like these, Jesus spoke the word to them. He told them as much as they could understand. ³⁴ He did not say anything to them without using a story. But when he was alone with his disciples, he explained everything.

Jesus Calms the Storm

³⁵ When evening came, Jesus said to his disciples, "Let's go over to the other side of the lake." ³⁶ They left the crowd behind. And they took him along in a boat, just as he was. There were also other boats with him. ³⁷ A wild storm came up. Waves crashed over the boat. It was about to sink. ³⁸ Jesus was in the back, sleeping on a cushion. The disciples woke him up. They said, "Teacher! Don't you care if we drown?"

³⁹ He got up and ordered the wind to stop. He said to the waves, "Quiet! Be still!" Then the wind died down. And it was completely calm.

⁴⁰ He said to his disciples, "Why are you so afraid? Don't you have any faith at all yet?"

⁴¹ They were terrified. They asked each other, "Who is this? Even the wind and the waves obey him!"

Jesus Heals a Man Controlled by Demons

5 They went across the Sea of Galilee to the area of the Gerasenes. ² Jesus got out of the boat. A man controlled by an evil spirit came from the tombs to meet him. ³ The man lived in the tombs. No one could keep him tied up anymore. Not even a chain could hold him. ⁴ His hands and feet had often been chained. But he tore the chains apart. And he broke the iron cuffs on his ankles. No one was strong enough to control him. ⁵ Night and day he screamed among the tombs and in the hills. He cut himself with stones.

⁶ When he saw Jesus a long way off, he ran to him. He fell on his knees in front of him. ⁷ He shouted at the top of his voice, "Jesus, Son of the Most High God, what do you want with me? Swear to God that you won't hurt me!" ⁸ This was because Jesus had said to him, "Come out of this man, you evil spirit!"

⁹ Then Jesus asked the demon, "What is your name?"

"My name is Legion," he replied. "There are many of us." ¹⁰ And he begged Jesus again and again not to send them out of the area.

¹¹ A large herd of pigs was feeding on the nearby hillside.

¹²The demons begged Jesus, "Send us among the pigs. Let us go into them." ¹³Jesus allowed it. The evil spirits came out of the man and went into the pigs. There were about 2,000 pigs in the herd. The whole herd rushed down the steep bank. They ran into the lake and drowned.

¹⁴Those who were tending the pigs ran off. They told the people in the town and countryside what had happened. The people went out to see for themselves. ¹⁵Then they came to Jesus. They saw the man who had been controlled by many demons. He was sitting there. He was now dressed and thinking clearly. All this made the people afraid. ¹⁶Those who had seen it told them what had happened to the man. They told about the pigs as well. ¹⁷Then the people began to beg Jesus to leave their area.

¹⁸Jesus was getting into the boat. The man who had been controlled by demons begged to go with him. ¹⁹Jesus did not let him. He said, "Go home to your own people. Tell them how much the Lord has done for you. Tell them how kind he has been to you." ²⁰So the man went away. In the area known as the Ten Cities, he began to tell how much Jesus had done for him. And all the people were amazed.

Jesus Heals a Dead Girl and a Suffering Woman

²¹Jesus went across the Sea of Galilee in a boat. It landed at the other side. There a large crowd gathered around him. ²²Then a man named Jairus came. He was a synagogue leader. When he saw Jesus, he fell at his feet. ²³He begged Jesus, "Please come. My little daughter is dying. Place your hands on her to heal her. Then she will live." ²⁴So Jesus went with him.

A large group of people followed. They crowded around him. ²⁵A woman was there who had a sickness that made her bleed. It had lasted for 12 years. ²⁶She had suffered a great deal, even though she had gone to many doctors. She had spent all the money she had. But she was getting worse, not better. ²⁷Then she heard about Jesus. She came up behind him in the crowd and touched his clothes. ²⁸She thought, "I just need to touch his clothes. Then I will be healed." ²⁹Right away her bleeding stopped. She felt in her body that her suffering was over.

³⁰At once Jesus knew that power had gone out from him. He turned around in the crowd. He asked, "Who touched my clothes?"

³¹"You see the people," his disciples answered. "They are crowding against you. And you still ask, 'Who touched me?' "

³²But Jesus kept looking around. He wanted to see who had touched him. ³³Then the woman came and fell at his feet. She knew what had happened to her. She was shaking with fear. But she told him the whole truth. ³⁴He said to her, "Dear woman, your faith has healed

you. Go in peace. You are free from your suffering."

³⁵While Jesus was still speaking, some people came from the house of Jairus. He was the synagogue leader. "Your daughter is dead," they said. "Why bother the teacher anymore?"

³⁶Jesus heard what they were saying. He told the synagogue leader, "Don't be afraid. Just believe."

³⁷He let only Peter, James, and John, the brother of James, follow him. ³⁸They came to the home of the synagogue leader. There Jesus saw a lot of confusion. People were crying and sobbing loudly. ³⁹He went inside. Then he said to them, "Why all this confusion and sobbing? The child is not dead. She is only sleeping." ⁴⁰But they laughed at him.

He made them all go outside. He took only the child's father and mother and the disciples who were with him. And he went in where the child was. ⁴¹He took her by the hand. Then he said to her, "*Talitha koum!*" This means, "Little girl, I say to you, get up!" ⁴²The girl was 12 years old. Right away she stood up and began to walk around. They were totally amazed at this. ⁴³Jesus gave strict orders not to let anyone know what had happened. And he told them to give her something to eat.

A Prophet Without Honor

6 Jesus left there and went to his hometown of Nazareth. His disciples went with him.

²When the Sabbath day came, he began to teach in the synagogue. Many who heard him were amazed.

"Where did this man get these things?" they asked. "What's this wisdom that has been given to him? What are these remarkable miracles he is doing? ³Isn't this the carpenter? Isn't this Mary's son? Isn't this the brother of James, Joseph, Judas and Simon? Aren't his sisters here with us?" They were not pleased with him at all.

⁴Jesus said to them, "A prophet is honored everywhere except in his own town. He doesn't receive any honor among his relatives or in his own home." ⁵Jesus placed his hands on a few sick people and healed them. But he could not do any other miracles there. ⁶He was amazed because they had no faith.

Jesus Sends Out the Twelve Disciples

Jesus went around teaching from village to village. ⁷He called the 12 disciples to him. Then he began to send them out two by two. He gave them authority to drive out evil spirits.

⁸Here is what he told them to do. "Take only a walking stick for your trip. Do not take bread or a bag. Take no money in your belts. ⁹Wear sandals. But do not take extra clothes. ¹⁰When you are invited into a house, stay there until you leave town. ¹¹Some places may not welcome you or listen to you. If they don't, leave that place and shake the

dust off your feet. That will be a witness against the people living there."

¹²They went out. And they preached that people should turn away from their sins. ¹³They drove out many demons. They poured olive oil on many sick people and healed them.

John the Baptist's Head Is Cut Off

¹⁴King Herod heard about this. Jesus' name had become well known. Some were saying, "John the Baptist has been raised from the dead! That is why he has the power to do miracles."

¹⁵Others said, "He is Elijah." Still others claimed, "He is a prophet. He is like one of the prophets of long ago."

¹⁶But when Herod heard this, he said, "I had John's head cut off. And now he has been raised from the dead!"

¹⁷In fact, it was Herod himself who had given orders to arrest John. He had him tied up and put in prison. He did this because of Herodias. She was the wife of Herod's brother Philip. But now Herod was married to her. ¹⁸John had been saying to Herod, "It is against the Law for you to be married to your brother's wife." ¹⁹Herodias couldn't forgive John for saying that. She wanted to kill him. But she could not, ²⁰because Herod was afraid of John. So he kept John safe. Herod knew John was a holy man who did what was right. When Herod heard him,

he was very puzzled. But he liked to listen to John.

²¹Finally the right time came. Herod gave a banquet on his birthday. He invited his high officials and military leaders. He also invited the most important men in Galilee. ²²Then the daughter of Herodias came in and danced. She pleased Herod and his dinner guests.

The king said to the girl, "Ask me for anything you want. I'll give it to you." ²³And he gave her his promise. He said to her, "Anything you ask for I will give you. I'll give you up to half my kingdom."

²⁴She went out and said to her mother, "What should I ask for?"

"The head of John the Baptist," she answered.

²⁵At once the girl hurried to ask the king. She said, "I want you to give me the head of John the Baptist on a big plate right now."

²⁶The king was very upset. But he thought about his promise and his dinner guests. So he did not want to say no to the girl. ²⁷He sent a man right away to bring John's head. The man went to the prison and cut off John's head. ²⁸He brought it back on a big plate. He gave it to the girl, and she gave it to her mother. ²⁹John's disciples heard about this. So they came and took his body. Then they placed it in a tomb.

Jesus Feeds Five Thousand

³⁰The apostles gathered around Jesus. They told him all

they had done and taught. ³¹ But many people were coming and going. So they did not even have a chance to eat. Then Jesus said to his apostles, "Come with me by yourselves to a quiet place. You need to get some rest."

³² So they went away by themselves in a boat to a quiet place. ³³ But many people who saw them leaving recognized them. They ran from all the towns and got there ahead of them. ³⁴ When Jesus came ashore, he saw a large crowd. He felt deep concern for them. They were like sheep without a shepherd. So he began teaching them many things.

³⁵ By that time it was late in the day. His disciples came to him. "There is nothing here," they said. "It's already very late. ³⁶ Send the people away. Then they can go to the nearby countryside and villages to buy something to eat."

³⁷ But Jesus answered, "You give them something to eat."

They said to him, "That would take more than half a year's pay! Should we go and spend that much on bread? Are we supposed to feed them?"

³⁸ "How many loaves do you have?" Jesus asked. "Go and see."

When they found out, they said, "Five loaves and two fish."

³⁹ Then Jesus directed them to have all the people sit down in groups on the green grass. ⁴⁰ So they sat down in groups of 100s and 50s. ⁴¹ Jesus took the five loaves and the two fish. He looked up to heaven and gave thanks. He broke the loaves into pieces. Then he gave them to his disciples to pass around to the people. He also divided the two fish among them all. ⁴² All of them ate and were satisfied. ⁴³ The disciples picked up 12 baskets of broken pieces of bread and fish. ⁴⁴ The number of men who had eaten was 5,000.

Jesus Walks on the Water

⁴⁵ Right away Jesus made his disciples get into the boat. He had them go on ahead of him to Bethsaida. Then he sent the crowd away. ⁴⁶ After leaving them, he went up on a mountainside to pray.

⁴⁷ Later that night, the boat was in the middle of the Sea of Galilee. Jesus was alone on land. ⁴⁸ He saw the disciples pulling hard on the oars. The wind was blowing against them. Shortly before dawn, he went out to them. He walked on the lake. When he was about to pass by them, ⁴⁹ they saw him walking on the lake. They thought he was a ghost, so they cried out. ⁵⁰ They all saw him and were terrified.

Right away Jesus said to them, "Be brave! It is I. Don't be afraid." ⁵¹ Then he climbed into the boat with them. The wind died down. And they were completely amazed. ⁵² They had not understood about the loaves. They were stubborn.

⁵³ They went across the lake and landed at Gennesaret. There they tied up the boat. ⁵⁴ As

soon as Jesus and his disciples got out, people recognized him. [55] They ran through that whole area to bring to him those who were sick. They carried them on mats to where they heard he was. [56] He went into the villages, the towns and the countryside. Everywhere he went, the people brought the sick to the market areas. Those who were sick begged him to let them touch just the edge of his clothes. And all who touched his clothes were healed.

What Makes People "Unclean"?

7 The Pharisees gathered around Jesus. So did some of the teachers of the law. All of them had come from Jerusalem. [2] They saw some of his disciples eating food with "unclean" hands. That means they were not washed. [3] The Pharisees and all the Jews do not eat unless they wash their hands to make them "clean." That's what the elders teach. [4] When they come from the market, they do not eat unless they wash. And they follow many other teachings. For example, they wash cups, pitchers, and kettles in a special way. [5] So the Pharisees and the teachers of the law questioned Jesus. "Why don't your disciples live by what the elders teach?" they asked. "Why do they eat their food with 'unclean' hands?"

[6] He replied, "Isaiah was right. He prophesied about you people who pretend to be good. He said,

" 'These people honor me by
    what they say.
But their hearts are far
    away from me.
[7] Their worship doesn't mean
    anything to me.
They teach nothing but
    human rules.'   *(Isaiah 29:13)*

[8] You have let go of God's commands. And you are holding on to teachings that people have made up."

[9] Jesus continued speaking, "You have a fine way of setting aside God's commands! You do this so you can follow your own teachings. [10] Moses said, 'Honor your father and mother.' *(Exodus 20:12; Deuteronomy 5:16)* He also said, 'Anyone who asks for bad things to happen to their father or mother must be put to death.' *(Exodus 21:17; Leviticus 20:9)* [11] But you allow people to say that what might have been used to help their parents is Corban. Corban means A Gift Set Apart for God. [12] So you no longer let them do anything for their parents. [13] You make the word of God useless by putting your own teachings in its place. And you do many things like this."

[14] Again Jesus called the crowd to him. He said, "Listen to me, everyone. Understand this. [15-16] Nothing outside of a person can make them 'unclean' by going into them. It is what comes out of them that makes them 'unclean.' "

[17] Then he left the crowd and entered the house. His disciples asked him about this teaching. [18] "Don't you understand?" Jesus

asked. "Don't you see? Nothing that enters a person from the outside can make them 'unclean.' ¹⁹ It doesn't go into their heart. It goes into their stomach. Then it goes out of the body." In saying this, Jesus was calling all foods "clean."

²⁰ He went on to say, "What comes out of a person is what makes them 'unclean.' ²¹ Evil thoughts come from the inside, from a person's heart. So do sexual sins, stealing and murder. ²² Adultery, greed, hate and cheating come from a person's heart too. So do desires that are not pure, and wanting what belongs to others. And so do telling lies about others and being proud and being foolish. ²³ All these evil things come from inside a person and make them 'unclean.'"

Jesus Honors a Greek Woman's Faith

²⁴ Jesus went from there to a place near Tyre. He entered a house. He did not want anyone to know where he was. But he could not keep it a secret. ²⁵ Soon a woman heard about him. An evil spirit controlled her little daughter. The woman came to Jesus and fell at his feet. ²⁶ She was a Greek, born in Syrian Phoenicia. She begged Jesus to drive the demon out of her daughter.

²⁷ "First let the children eat all they want," he told her. "It is not right to take the children's bread and throw it to the dogs."

²⁸ "Lord," she replied, "even the dogs under the table eat the children's crumbs."

²⁹ Then he told her, "That was a good reply. You may go. The demon has left your daughter."

³⁰ So she went home and found her child lying on the bed. And the demon was gone.

Jesus Heals a Man Who Could Not Hear or Speak

³¹ Then Jesus left the area of Tyre and went through Sidon. He went down to the Sea of Galilee and into the area known as the Ten Cities. ³² There some people brought a man to Jesus. The man was deaf and could hardly speak. They begged Jesus to place his hand on the man.

³³ Jesus took the man to one side, away from the crowd. He put his fingers into the man's ears. Then he spit and touched the man's tongue. ³⁴ Jesus looked up to heaven. With a deep sigh, he said to the man, *"Ephphatha!"* That means "Be opened!" ³⁵ The man's ears were opened. His tongue was freed up, and he began to speak clearly.

³⁶ Jesus ordered the people not to tell anyone. But the more he did so, the more they kept talking about it. ³⁷ People were really amazed. "He has done everything well," they said. "He even makes deaf people able to hear. And he makes those who can't speak able to talk."

Jesus Feeds the Four Thousand

8 During those days another large crowd gathered. They had nothing to eat. So

Jesus called for his disciples to come to him. He said, [2] "I feel deep concern for these people. They have already been with me three days. They don't have anything to eat. [3] If I send them away hungry, they will become too weak on their way home. Some of them have come from far away."

[4] His disciples answered him. "There is nothing here," they said. "Where can anyone get enough bread to feed them?"

[5] "How many loaves do you have?" Jesus asked.

"Seven," they replied.

[6] He told the crowd to sit down on the ground. He took the seven loaves and gave thanks to God. Then he broke them and gave them to his disciples. They passed the pieces of bread around to the people. [7] The disciples also had a few small fish. Jesus gave thanks for them too. He told the disciples to pass them around. [8] The people ate and were satisfied. After that, the disciples picked up seven baskets of leftover pieces. [9] About 4,000 people were there. After Jesus sent them away, [10] he got into a boat with his disciples. He went to the area of Dalmanutha.

[11] The Pharisees came and began to ask Jesus questions. They wanted to test him. So they asked him for a sign from heaven. [12] He sighed deeply. He said, "Why do you people ask for a sign? What I'm about to tell you is true. No sign will be given to you." [13] Then he left them.

He got back into the boat and crossed to the other side of the lake.

The Yeast of the Pharisees and Herod

[14] The disciples had forgotten to bring bread. They had only one loaf with them in the boat. [15] "Be careful," Jesus warned them. "Watch out for the yeast of the Pharisees. And watch out for the yeast of Herod."

[16] They talked about this with each other. They said, "He must be saying this because we don't have any bread."

[17] Jesus knew what they were saying. So he asked them, "Why are you talking about having no bread? Why can't you see or understand? Are you stubborn? [18] Do you have eyes and still don't see? Do you have ears and still don't hear? And don't you remember? [19] Earlier I broke five loaves for the 5,000. How many baskets of pieces did you pick up?"

"Twelve," they replied.

[20] "Later I broke seven loaves for the 4,000. How many baskets of pieces did you pick up?"

"Seven," they answered.

[21] He said to them, "Can't you understand yet?"

Jesus Heals a Blind Man at Bethsaida

[22] Jesus and his disciples came to Bethsaida. Some people brought a blind man to him. They begged Jesus to touch him. [23] He took the blind man by the hand. Then he led him outside

the village. He spit on the man's eyes and placed his hands on him. "Do you see anything?" Jesus asked.

24 The man looked up. He said, "I see people. They look like trees walking around."

25 Once more Jesus put his hands on the man's eyes. Then his eyes were opened so that he could see again. He saw everything clearly. 26 Jesus sent him home. He told him, "Don't even go into the village."

Peter Says That Jesus Is the Messiah

27 Jesus and his disciples went on to the villages around Caesarea Philippi. On the way he asked them, "Who do people say I am?"

28 They replied, "Some say John the Baptist. Others say Elijah. Still others say one of the prophets."

29 "But what about you?" he asked. "Who do you say I am?"

Peter answered, "You are the Messiah."

30 Jesus warned them not to tell anyone about him.

Jesus Tells About His Coming Death

31 Jesus then began to teach his disciples. He taught them that the Son of Man must suffer many things. He taught them that the elders would not accept him. The chief priests and the teachers of the law would not accept him either. He must be killed and after three days rise again. 32 He spoke clearly about this. Peter took Jesus to one side and began to scold him.

33 Jesus turned and looked at his disciples. He scolded Peter. "Get behind me, Satan!" he said. "You are not thinking about the things God cares about. Instead, you are thinking only about the things humans care about."

You Must Pick Up Your Cross

34 Jesus called the crowd to him along with his disciples. He said, "Whoever wants to be my disciple must say no to themselves. They must pick up their cross and follow me. 35 Whoever wants to save their life will lose it. But whoever loses their life for me and for the good news will save it. 36 What good is it if someone gains the whole world but loses their soul? 37 Or what can anyone trade for their soul? 38 Suppose anyone is ashamed of me and my words among these adulterous and sinful people. Then the Son of Man will be ashamed of them when he comes in his Father's glory with the holy angels."

9 Jesus said to them, "What I'm about to tell you is true. Some who are standing here will not die before they see that God's kingdom has come with power."

Jesus' Appearance Is Changed

2 After six days Jesus took Peter, James and John with him. He led them up a high mountain. They were all alone. There in front of them his appearance was changed. 3 His clothes be-

came so white they shone. They were whiter than anyone in the world could bleach them. ⁴ Elijah and Moses appeared in front of Jesus and his disciples. The two of them were talking with Jesus.

⁵ Peter said to Jesus, "Rabbi, it is good for us to be here. Let us put up three shelters. One will be for you, one for Moses, and one for Elijah." ⁶ Peter didn't really know what to say, because they were so afraid.

⁷ Then a cloud appeared and covered them. A voice came from the cloud. It said, "This is my Son, and I love him. Listen to him!"

⁸ They looked around. Suddenly they no longer saw anyone with them except Jesus.

⁹ They came down the mountain. On the way down, Jesus ordered them not to tell anyone what they had seen. He told them to wait until the Son of Man had risen from the dead. ¹⁰ So they kept the matter to themselves. But they asked each other what "rising from the dead" meant.

¹¹ Then they asked Jesus, "Why do the teachers of the law say that Elijah has to come first?"

¹² Jesus replied, "That's right. Elijah does come first. He makes all things new again. So why is it written that the Son of Man must suffer much and not be accepted? ¹³ I tell you, Elijah has come. They have done to him everything they wanted to do. They did it just as it is written about him."

Jesus Heals a Boy Who Is Controlled by an Evil Spirit

¹⁴ When Jesus and those who were with him came to the other disciples, they saw a large crowd around them. The teachers of the law were arguing with them. ¹⁵ When all the people saw Jesus, they were filled with wonder. And they ran to greet him.

¹⁶ "What are you arguing with them about?" Jesus asked.

¹⁷ A man in the crowd answered. "Teacher," he said, "I brought you my son. He is controlled by an evil spirit. Because of this, my son can't speak anymore. ¹⁸ When the spirit takes hold of him, it throws him to the ground. He foams at the mouth. He grinds his teeth. And his body becomes stiff. I asked your disciples to drive out the spirit. But they couldn't do it."

¹⁹ "You unbelieving people!" Jesus replied. "How long do I have to stay with you? How long do I have to put up with you? Bring the boy to me."

²⁰ So they brought him. As soon as the spirit saw Jesus, it threw the boy into a fit. He fell to the ground. He rolled around and foamed at the mouth.

²¹ Jesus asked the boy's father, "How long has he been like this?"

"Since he was a child," he answered. ²² "The spirit has often thrown him into fire or water to kill him. But if you can do anything, take pity on us. Please help us."

²³ " 'If you can'?" said Jesus. "Everything is possible for the one who believes."

²⁴Right away the boy's father cried out, "I do believe! Help me overcome my unbelief!"

²⁵Jesus saw that a crowd was running over to see what was happening. Then he ordered the evil spirit to leave the boy. "You spirit that makes him unable to hear and speak!" he said. "I command you, come out of him. Never enter him again."

²⁶The spirit screamed. It shook the boy wildly. Then it came out of him. The boy looked so lifeless that many people said, "He's dead." ²⁷But Jesus took him by the hand. He lifted the boy to his feet, and the boy stood up.

²⁸Jesus went indoors. Then his disciples asked him in private, "Why couldn't we drive out the evil spirit?"

²⁹He replied, "This kind can come out only by prayer."

Jesus Speaks a Second Time About His Coming Death

³⁰They left that place and passed through Galilee. Jesus did not want anyone to know where they were. ³¹That was because he was teaching his disciples. He said to them, "The Son of Man is going to be handed over to men. They will kill him. After three days he will rise from the dead." ³²But they didn't understand what he meant. And they were afraid to ask him about it.

Who Is the Most Important Person?

³³Jesus and his disciples came to a house in Capernaum.
There he asked them, "What were you arguing about on the road?" ³⁴But they kept quiet. On the way, they had argued about which one of them was the most important person.

³⁵Jesus sat down and called for the 12 disciples to come to him. Then he said, "Anyone who wants to be first must be the very last. They must be the servant of everyone."

³⁶Jesus took a little child and had the child stand among them. Then he took the child in his arms. He said to them, ³⁷"Anyone who welcomes one of these little children in my name welcomes me. And anyone who welcomes me also welcomes the one who sent me."

Anyone Who Is Not Against Us Is for Us

³⁸"Teacher," said John, "we saw someone driving out demons in your name. We told him to stop, because he was not one of us."

³⁹"Do not stop him," Jesus said. "For no one who does a miracle in my name can in the next moment say anything bad about me. ⁴⁰Anyone who is not against us is for us. ⁴¹What I'm about to tell you is true. Suppose someone gives you a cup of water in my name because you belong to the Messiah. That person will certainly not go without a reward.

Leading People to Sin

⁴²"What if someone leads one of these little ones who believe

in me to sin? If they do, it would be better if a large millstone were hung around their neck and they were thrown into the sea. ⁴³⁻⁴⁴ If your hand causes you to sin, cut it off. It would be better for you to enter God's kingdom with only one hand than to go into hell with two hands. In hell the fire never goes out. ⁴⁵⁻⁴⁶ If your foot causes you to sin, cut it off. It would be better to enter God's kingdom with only one foot than to have two feet and be thrown into hell. ⁴⁷ If your eye causes you to sin, poke it out. It would be better for you to enter God's kingdom with only one eye than to have two eyes and be thrown into hell. ⁴⁸ In hell,

" 'The worms that eat them
        do not die.
   The fire is not put out.'
                    (Isaiah 66:24)

⁴⁹ Everyone will be salted with fire.
⁵⁰ "Salt is good. But suppose it loses its saltiness. How can you make it salty again? Have salt among yourselves. And be at peace with each other."

Jesus Teaches About Divorce

10 Jesus left that place and went into the area of Judea and across the Jordan River. Again crowds of people came to him. As usual, he taught them.
² Some Pharisees came to test Jesus. They asked, "Does the Law allow a man to divorce his wife?"
³ "What did Moses command you?" he replied.

⁴ They said, "Moses allowed a man to write a letter of divorce and send her away."
⁵ "You were stubborn. That's why Moses wrote you this law," Jesus replied. ⁶ "But at the beginning of creation, God 'made them male and female.' *(Genesis 1:27)* ⁷ 'That's why a man will leave his father and mother and be joined to his wife. ⁸ The two of them will become one.' *(Genesis 2:24)* They are no longer two, but one. ⁹ So no one should separate what God has joined together."
¹⁰ When they were in the house again, the disciples asked Jesus about this. ¹¹ He answered, "What if a man divorces his wife and gets married to another woman? He commits adultery against her. ¹² And what if she divorces her husband and gets married to another man? She commits adultery."

Little Children Are Brought to Jesus

¹³ People were bringing little children to Jesus. They wanted him to place his hands on them to bless them. But the disciples told them to stop. ¹⁴ When Jesus saw this, he was angry. He said to his disciples, "Let the little children come to me. Don't keep them away. God's kingdom belongs to people like them. ¹⁵ What I'm about to tell you is true. Anyone who will not receive God's kingdom like a little child will never enter it." ¹⁶ Then he took the children in his arms. He placed his hands on them to bless them.

Rich People and the Kingdom of God

17 As Jesus started on his way, a man ran up to him. He fell on his knees before Jesus. "Good teacher," he said, "what must I do to receive eternal life?"

18 "Why do you call me good?" Jesus answered. "No one is good except God. 19 You know what the commandments say. 'Do not murder. Do not commit adultery. Do not steal. Do not be a false witness. Do not cheat. Honor your father and mother.' "

(Exodus 20:12–16; Deuteronomy 5:16–20)

20 "Teacher," he said, "I have obeyed all those commandments since I was a boy."

21 Jesus looked at him and loved him. "You are missing one thing," he said. "Go and sell everything you have. Give the money to those who are poor. You will have treasure in heaven. Then come and follow me."

22 The man's face fell. He went away sad, because he was very rich.

23 Jesus looked around. He said to his disciples, "How hard it is for rich people to enter God's kingdom!"

24 The disciples were amazed at his words. But Jesus said again, "Children, how hard it is to enter God's kingdom! 25 Is it hard for a camel to go through the eye of a needle? It is even harder for someone who is rich to enter God's kingdom!"

26 The disciples were even more amazed. They said to each other, "Then who can be saved?"

27 Jesus looked at them and said, "With people, this is impossible. But not with God. All things are possible with God."

28 Then Peter spoke up, "We have left everything to follow you!"

29 "What I'm about to tell you is true," Jesus replied. "Has anyone left home or family or fields for me and the good news? 30 They will receive 100 times as much in this world. They will have homes and families and fields. But they will also be treated badly by others. In the world to come they will live forever. 31 But many who are first will be last. And the last will be first."

Jesus Speaks a Third Time About His Coming Death

32 They were on their way up to Jerusalem. Jesus was leading the way. The disciples were amazed. Those who followed were afraid. Again Jesus took the 12 disciples to one side. He told them what was going to happen to him. 33 "We are going up to Jerusalem," he said. "The Son of Man will be handed over to the chief priests and the teachers of the law. They will sentence him to death. Then they will hand him over to the Gentiles. 34 They will make fun of him and spit on him. They will whip him and kill him. Three days later he will rise from the dead!"

James and John Ask Jesus for a Favor

35 James and John came to Jesus. They were the sons of Zeb-

edee. "Teacher," they said, "we would like to ask you for a favor."

³⁶ "What do you want me to do for you?" he asked.

³⁷ They replied, "Let one of us sit at your right hand in your glorious kingdom. Let the other one sit at your left hand."

³⁸ "You don't know what you're asking for," Jesus said. "Can you drink the cup of suffering I drink? Or can you go through the baptism of suffering I must go through?"

³⁹ "We can," they answered.

Jesus said to them, "You will drink the cup I drink. And you will go through the baptism I go through. ⁴⁰ But it is not for me to say who will sit at my right or left hand. These places belong to those they are prepared for."

⁴¹ The other ten disciples heard about it. They became angry at James and John. ⁴² Jesus called them together. He said, "You know about those who are rulers of the Gentiles. They hold power over their people. Their high officials order them around. ⁴³ Don't be like that. Instead, anyone who wants to be important among you must be your servant. ⁴⁴ And anyone who wants to be first must be the slave of everyone. ⁴⁵ Even the Son of Man did not come to be served. Instead, he came to serve others. He came to give his life as the price for setting many people free."

Blind Bartimaeus Receives His Sight

⁴⁶ Jesus and his disciples came to Jericho. They were leaving the city. A large crowd was with them. A blind man was sitting by the side of the road begging. His name was Bartimaeus. Bartimaeus means Son of Timaeus. ⁴⁷ He heard that Jesus of Nazareth was passing by. So he began to shout, "Jesus! Son of David! Have mercy on me!"

⁴⁸ Many people commanded him to stop. They told him to be quiet. But he shouted even louder, "Son of David! Have mercy on me!"

⁴⁹ Jesus stopped and said, "Call for him."

So they called out to the blind man, "Cheer up! Get up on your feet! Jesus is calling for you." ⁵⁰ He threw his coat to one side. Then he jumped to his feet and came to Jesus.

⁵¹ "What do you want me to do for you?" Jesus asked him.

The blind man said, "Rabbi, I want to be able to see."

⁵² "Go," said Jesus. "Your faith has healed you." Right away he could see. And he followed Jesus along the road.

Jesus Comes to Jerusalem as King

11 As they all approached Jerusalem, they came to Bethphage and Bethany at the Mount of Olives. Jesus sent out two of his disciples. ² He said to them, "Go to the village ahead of you. Just as you enter it, you will find a donkey's colt tied there. No one has ever ridden it. Untie it and bring it here. ³ Someone may ask you, 'Why are you doing this?' If so, say, 'The Lord needs it. But he will send it back here soon.' "

⁴So they left. They found a colt out in the street. It was tied at a doorway. They untied it. ⁵Some people standing there asked, "What are you doing? Why are you untying that colt?" ⁶They answered as Jesus had told them to. So the people let them go. ⁷They brought the colt to Jesus. They threw their coats over it. Then he sat on it. ⁸Many people spread their coats on the road. Others spread branches they had cut in the fields. ⁹Those in front and those in back shouted,

"Hosanna!"

"Blessed is the one who
    comes in the name of the
    Lord!"   *(Psalm 118:25,26)*

¹⁰"Blessed is the coming
    kingdom of our father
    David!"

"Hosanna in the highest
    heaven!"

¹¹Jesus entered Jerusalem and went into the temple courtyard. He looked around at everything. But it was already late. So he went out to Bethany with the 12 disciples.

Jesus Curses a Fig Tree and Clears Out the Temple Courtyard

¹²The next day as Jesus and his disciples were leaving Bethany, they were hungry. ¹³Not too far away, he saw a fig tree. It was covered with leaves. He went to find out if it had any fruit. When he reached it, he found nothing but leaves. It was not the season for figs. ¹⁴Then Jesus said to the tree, "May no one ever eat fruit from you again!" And his disciples heard him say it.

¹⁵When Jesus reached Jerusalem, he entered the temple courtyard. He began to drive out those who were buying and selling there. He turned over the tables of the people who were exchanging money. He also turned over the benches of those who were selling doves. ¹⁶He would not allow anyone to carry items for sale through the temple courtyard. ¹⁷Then he taught them. He told them, "It is written that the Lord said, 'My house will be called a house where people from all nations can pray.' *(Isaiah 56:7)* But you have made it a 'den for robbers.' " *(Jeremiah 7:11)*

¹⁸The chief priests and the teachers of the law heard about this. They began looking for a way to kill Jesus. They were afraid of him, because the whole crowd was amazed at his teaching.

¹⁹When evening came, Jesus and his disciples left the city.

The Dried-Up Fig Tree

²⁰In the morning as Jesus and his disciples walked along, they saw the fig tree. It was dried up all the way down to the roots. ²¹Peter remembered. He said to Jesus, "Rabbi, look! The fig tree you put a curse on has dried up!"

²²"Have faith in God," Jesus said. ²³"What I'm about to tell you is true. Suppose someone

says to this mountain, 'Go and throw yourself into the sea.' They must not doubt in their heart. They must believe that what they say will happen. Then it will be done for them. ²⁴ So I tell you, when you pray for something, believe that you have already received it. Then it will be yours. ²⁵⁻²⁶ And when you stand praying, forgive anyone you have anything against. Then your Father in heaven will forgive your sins."

The Authority of Jesus Is Questioned

²⁷ Jesus and his disciples arrived again in Jerusalem. He was walking in the temple courtyard. Then the chief priests came to him. The teachers of the law and the elders came too. ²⁸ "By what authority are you doing these things?" they asked. "Who gave you authority to do this?"

²⁹ Jesus replied, "I will ask you one question. Answer me, and I will tell you by what authority I am doing these things. ³⁰ Was John's baptism from heaven? Or did it come from human authority? Tell me!"

³¹ They talked to each other about it. They said, "If we say, 'From heaven,' he will ask, 'Then why didn't you believe him?' ³² But what if we say, 'From human authority'?" They were afraid of the people. Everyone believed that John really was a prophet.

³³ So they answered Jesus, "We don't know."

Jesus said, "Then I won't tell you by what authority I am doing these things either."

The Story of the Renters

12 Jesus began to speak to the people using stories. He said, "A man planted a vineyard. He put a wall around it. He dug a pit for a winepress. He also built a lookout tower. He rented the vineyard out to some farmers. Then he went to another place. ² At harvest time he sent a servant to the renters. He told the servant to collect from them some of the fruit of the vineyard. ³ But they grabbed the servant and beat him up. Then they sent him away with nothing. ⁴ So the man sent another servant to the renters. They hit this one on the head and treated him badly. ⁵ The man sent still another servant. The renters killed him. The man sent many others. The renters beat up some of them. They killed the others.

⁶ "The man had one person left to send. It was his son, and he loved him. He sent him last of all. He said, 'They will respect my son.'

⁷ "But the renters said to each other, 'This is the one who will receive all the owner's property someday. Come, let's kill him. Then everything will be ours.' ⁸ So they took him and killed him. They threw him out of the vineyard.

⁹ "What will the owner of the vineyard do then? He will come and kill those renters. He will give the vineyard to others.

10 Haven't you read what this part of Scripture says,

> " 'The stone the builders
>   didn't accept
>   has become the most
>   important stone of all.
> 11 The Lord has done it.
>   It is wonderful in our
>   eyes'?" *(Psalm 118:22,23)*

12 Then the chief priests, the teachers of the law and the elders looked for a way to arrest Jesus. They knew he had told the story against them. But they were afraid of the crowd. So they left him and went away.

Is It Right to Pay the Royal Tax to Caesar?

13 Later the religious leaders sent some of the Pharisees and Herodians to Jesus. They wanted to trap him with his own words. 14 They came to him and said, "Teacher, we know that you are a man of honor. You don't let other people tell you what to do or say. You don't care how important they are. But you teach the way of God truthfully. Is it right to pay the royal tax to Caesar or not? 15 Should we pay or shouldn't we?"

But Jesus knew what they were trying to do. So he asked, "Why are you trying to trap me? Bring me a silver coin. Let me look at it." 16 They brought the coin. He asked them, "Whose picture is this? And whose words?"

"Caesar's," they replied.

17 Then Jesus said to them, "Give back to Caesar what belongs to Caesar. And give back to God what belongs to God."

They were amazed at him.

Marriage When the Dead Rise

18 The Sadducees came to Jesus with a question. They do not believe that people rise from the dead. 19 "Teacher," they said, "Moses wrote for us about a man who died and didn't have any children. But he did leave a wife behind. That man's brother must get married to the widow. He must provide children to carry on his dead brother's name. 20 There were seven brothers. The first one got married. He died without leaving any children. 21 The second one got married to the widow. He also died and left no child. It was the same with the third one. 22 In fact, none of the seven left any children. Last of all, the woman died too. 23 When the dead rise, whose wife will she be? All seven of them were married to her."

24 Jesus replied, "You are mistaken because you do not know the Scriptures. And you do not know the power of God. 25 When the dead rise, they won't get married. And their parents won't give them to be married. They will be like the angels in heaven. 26 What about the dead rising? Haven't you read in the Book of Moses the story of the burning bush? God said to Moses, 'I am the God of Abraham. I am the God of Isaac. And I am the God of Jacob.' *(Exodus 3:6)* 27 He is not the God of the dead. He is

the God of the living. You have made a big mistake!"

The Most Important Commandment

28 One of the teachers of the law came and heard the Sadducees arguing. He noticed that Jesus had given the Sadducees a good answer. So he asked him, "Which is the most important of all the commandments?"

29 Jesus answered, "Here is the most important one. Moses said, 'Israel, listen to me. The Lord is our God. The Lord is one. 30 Love the Lord your God with all your heart and with all your soul. Love him with all your mind and with all your strength.' *(Deuteronomy 6:4,5)* 31 And here is the second one. 'Love your neighbor as you love yourself.' *(Leviticus 19:18)* There is no commandment more important than these."

32 "You have spoken well, teacher," the man replied. "You are right in saying that God is one. There is no other God but him. 33 To love God with all your heart and mind and strength is very important. So is loving your neighbor as you love yourself. These things are more important than all burnt offerings and sacrifices."

34 Jesus saw that the man had answered wisely. He said to him, "You are not far from God's kingdom." From then on, no one dared to ask Jesus any more questions.

Whose Son Is the Messiah?

35 Jesus was teaching in the temple courtyard. He asked, "Why do the teachers of the law say that the Messiah is the son of David? 36 The Holy Spirit spoke through David himself. David said,

> " 'The Lord said to my
>   Lord,
> "Sit at my right hand
> until I put your enemies
>   under your control." '
>
> *(Psalm 110:1)*

37 David himself calls him 'Lord.' So how can he be David's son?"

The large crowd listened to Jesus with delight.

Warning Against the Teachers of the Law

38 As he taught, he said, "Watch out for the teachers of the law. They like to walk around in long robes. They like to be greeted with respect in the market. 39 They love to have the most important seats in the synagogues. They also love to have the places of honor at dinners. 40 They take over the houses of widows. They say long prayers to show off. God will punish these men very much."

The Widow's Offering

41 Jesus sat down across from the place where people put their temple offerings. He watched the crowd putting their money into the offering boxes. Many rich people threw large amounts into them. 42 But a poor widow came and put in two very small copper coins. They were worth only a few pennies.

43 Jesus asked his disciples to

come to him. He said, "What I'm about to tell you is true. That poor widow has put more into the offering box than all the others. ⁴⁴ They all gave a lot because they are rich. But she gave even though she is poor. She put in everything she had. That was all she had to live on.'"

When the Temple Will Be Destroyed and the Signs of the End

13 Jesus was leaving the temple. One of his disciples said to him, "Look, Teacher! What huge stones! What wonderful buildings!"

² "Do you see these huge buildings?" Jesus asked. "Not one stone here will be left on top of another. Every stone will be thrown down."

³ Jesus was sitting on the Mount of Olives, across from the temple. Peter, James, John and Andrew asked him a question in private. ⁴ "Tell us," they said. "When will these things happen? And what will be the sign that they are all about to come true?"

⁵ Jesus said to them, "Keep watch! Be careful that no one fools you. ⁶ Many will come in my name. They will claim, 'I am he.' They will fool many people. ⁷ You will hear about wars. You will also hear people talking about future wars. Don't be alarmed. These things must happen. But the end still isn't here. ⁸ Nation will fight against nation. Kingdom will fight against kingdom. There will be earthquakes in many places. People will go hungry. All these things are the beginning of birth pains.

⁹ "Watch out! You will be handed over to the local courts. You will be whipped in the synagogues. You will stand in front of governors and kings because of me. In that way you will be witnesses to them. ¹⁰ The good news has to be preached to all nations before the end comes. ¹¹ You will be arrested and brought to trial. But don't worry ahead of time about what you will say. Just say what God brings to your mind at the time. It is not you speaking, but the Holy Spirit.

¹² "Brothers will hand over brothers to be killed. Fathers will hand over their children. Children will rise up against their parents and have them put to death. ¹³ Everyone will hate you because of me. But the one who remains strong in the faith will be saved.

¹⁴ "You will see 'the hated thing that destroys.' *(Daniel 9:27; 11:31; 12:11)* It will stand where it does not belong. The reader should understand this. Then those who are in Judea should escape to the mountains. ¹⁵ No one on the roof should go down into the house to take anything out. ¹⁶ No one in the field should go back to get their coat. ¹⁷ How awful it will be in those days for pregnant women! How awful for nursing mothers! ¹⁸ Pray that this will not happen in winter. ¹⁹ Those days will be worse than

any others from the time God created the world until now. And there will never be any like them again.

20 "If the Lord had not cut the time short, no one would live. But because of God's chosen people, he has shortened it. 21 At that time someone may say to you, 'Look! Here is the Messiah!' Or, 'Look! There he is!' Do not believe it. 22 False messiahs and false prophets will appear. They will do signs and miracles. They will try to fool God's chosen people if possible. 23 Keep watch! I have told you everything ahead of time.

24 "So in those days there will be terrible suffering. After that, Scripture says,

" 'The sun will be darkened.
    The moon will not shine.
25 The stars will fall from the
        sky.
    The heavenly bodies will
        be shaken.' *(Isaiah 13:10; 34:4)*

26 "At that time people will see the Son of Man coming in clouds. He will come with great power and glory. 27 He will send his angels. He will gather his chosen people from all four directions. He will bring them from the ends of the earth to the ends of the heavens.

28 "Learn a lesson from the fig tree. As soon as its twigs get tender and its leaves come out, you know that summer is near. 29 In the same way, when you see these things happening, you know that the end is near. It is right at the door. 30 What I'm

about to tell you is true. The people living now will certainly not pass away until all those things have happened. 31 Heaven and earth will pass away. But my words will never pass away.

The Day and Hour Are Not Known

32 "But no one knows about that day or hour. Not even the angels in heaven know. The Son does not know. Only the Father knows. 33 Keep watch! Stay awake! You do not know when that time will come. 34 It's like a man going away. He leaves his house and puts his servants in charge. Each one is given a task to do. He tells the one at the door to keep watch.

35 "So keep watch! You do not know when the owner of the house will come back. It may be in the evening or at midnight. It may be when the rooster crows or at dawn. 36 He may come suddenly. So do not let him find you sleeping. 37 What I say to you, I say to everyone. 'Watch!' "

A Woman Pours Perfume on Jesus at Bethany

14 The Passover and the Feast of Unleavened Bread were only two days away. The chief priests and the teachers of the law were plotting to arrest Jesus secretly. They wanted to kill him. 2 "But not during the feast," they said. "The people may stir up trouble."

3 Jesus was in Bethany. He was at the table in the home of Simon, who had a skin disease. A woman came with a special

sealed jar. It contained very expensive perfume made out of pure nard. She broke the jar open and poured the perfume on Jesus' head.

⁴ Some of the people there became angry. They said to one another, "Why waste this perfume? ⁵ It could have been sold for more than a year's pay. The money could have been given to poor people." So they found fault with the woman.

⁶ "Leave her alone," Jesus said. "Why are you bothering her? She has done a beautiful thing to me. ⁷ You will always have poor people with you. You can help them any time you want to. But you will not always have me. ⁸ She did what she could. She poured perfume on my body to prepare me to be buried. ⁹ What I'm about to tell you is true. What she has done will be told anywhere the good news is preached all over the world. It will be told in memory of her."

¹⁰ Judas Iscariot was one of the 12 disciples. He went to the chief priests to hand Jesus over to them. ¹¹ They were delighted to hear that he would do this. They promised to give Judas money. So he watched for the right time to hand Jesus over to them.

The Last Supper

¹² It was the first day of the Feast of Unleavened Bread. That was the time to sacrifice the Passover lamb. Jesus' disciples asked him, "Where do you want us to go and prepare for you to eat the Passover meal?"

¹³ So he sent out two of his disciples. He told them, "Go into the city. A man carrying a jar of water will meet you. Follow him. ¹⁴ He will enter a house. Say to its owner, 'The Teacher asks, "Where is my guest room? Where can I eat the Passover meal with my disciples?"' ¹⁵ He will show you a large upstairs room. It will have furniture and will be ready. Prepare for us to eat there."

¹⁶ The disciples left and went into the city. They found things just as Jesus had told them. So they prepared the Passover meal.

¹⁷ When evening came, Jesus arrived with the 12 disciples. ¹⁸ While they were at the table eating, Jesus said, "What I'm about to tell you is true. One of you who is eating with me will hand me over to my enemies."

¹⁹ The disciples became sad. One by one they said to him, "Surely you don't mean me?"

²⁰ "It is one of you," Jesus replied. "It is the one who dips bread into the bowl with me. ²¹ The Son of Man will go just as it is written about him. But how terrible it will be for the one who hands over the Son of Man! It would be better for him if he had not been born."

²² While they were eating, Jesus took bread. He gave thanks and broke it. He handed it to his disciples and said, "Take it. This is my body."

²³ Then he took a cup. He gave thanks and handed it to them. All of them drank from it.

24 "This is my blood of the covenant," he said to them. "It is poured out for many. 25 What I'm about to tell you is true. I won't drink wine with you again until the day I drink it in God's kingdom."

26 Then they sang a hymn and went out to the Mount of Olives.

Jesus Says That the Disciples Will Turn Away

27 "You will all turn away," Jesus told the disciples. "It is written,

"'I will strike the shepherd down.
Then the sheep will be scattered.' (Zechariah 13:7)

28 But after I rise from the dead, I will go ahead of you into Galilee."

29 Peter said, "All the others may turn away. But I will not."

30 "What I'm about to tell you is true," Jesus answered. "It will happen today, in fact tonight. Before the rooster crows twice, you yourself will say three times that you don't know me."

31 But Peter would not give in. He said, "I may have to die with you. But I will never say I don't know you." And all the others said the same thing.

Jesus Prays in Gethsemane

32 Jesus and his disciples went to a place called Gethsemane. Jesus said to them, "Sit here while I pray." 33 He took Peter, James and John along with him. He began to be very upset and troubled. 34 "My soul is very sad.

I feel close to death," he said to them. "Stay here. Keep watch."

35 He went a little farther. Then he fell to the ground. He prayed that, if possible, the hour might pass by him. 36 "*Abba*, Father" he said, "everything is possible for you. Take this cup of suffering away from me. But let what you want be done, not what I want."

37 Then he returned to his disciples and found them sleeping. "Simon," he said to Peter, "are you asleep? Couldn't you keep watch for one hour? 38 Watch and pray. Then you won't fall into sin when you are tempted. The spirit is willing, but the body is weak."

39 Once more Jesus went away and prayed the same thing. 40 Then he came back. Again he found them sleeping. They couldn't keep their eyes open. They did not know what to say to him.

41 Jesus returned the third time. He said to them, "Are you still sleeping and resting? Enough! The hour has come. Look! The Son of Man is about to be handed over to sinners. 42 Get up! Let us go! Here comes the one who is handing me over to them!"

Jesus Is Arrested

43 Just as Jesus was speaking, Judas appeared. He was one of the 12 disciples. A crowd was with him. They were carrying swords and clubs. The chief priests, the teachers of the law, and the elders had sent them.

⁴⁴ Judas, who was going to hand Jesus over, had arranged a signal with them. "The one I kiss is the man," he said. "Arrest him and have the guards lead him away." ⁴⁵ So Judas went to Jesus at once. Judas said, "Rabbi!" And he kissed Jesus. ⁴⁶ The men grabbed Jesus and arrested him. ⁴⁷ Then one of those standing nearby pulled his sword out. He struck the servant of the high priest and cut off his ear.

⁴⁸ "Am I leading a band of armed men against you?" asked Jesus. "Do you have to come out with swords and clubs to capture me? ⁴⁹ Every day I was with you. I taught in the temple courtyard, and you didn't arrest me. But the Scriptures must come true." ⁵⁰ Then everyone left him and ran away.

⁵¹ A young man was following Jesus. The man was wearing nothing but a piece of linen cloth. When the crowd grabbed him, ⁵² he ran away naked. He left his clothing behind.

Jesus Is Taken to the Sanhedrin

⁵³ The crowd took Jesus to the high priest. All the chief priests, the elders, and the teachers of the law came together. ⁵⁴ Not too far away, Peter followed Jesus. He went right into the courtyard of the high priest. There he sat with the guards. He warmed himself at the fire.

⁵⁵ The chief priests and the whole Sanhedrin were looking for something to use against Jesus. They wanted to put him to death. But they did not find

any proof. ⁵⁶ Many witnesses lied about him. But their stories did not agree.

⁵⁷ Then some of them stood up. Here is what those false witnesses said about him. ⁵⁸ "We heard him say, 'I will destroy this temple made by human hands. In three days I will build another temple, not made by human hands.'" ⁵⁹ But what they said did not agree.

⁶⁰ Then the high priest stood up in front of them. He asked Jesus, "Aren't you going to answer? What are these charges these men are bringing against you?" ⁶¹ But Jesus remained silent. He gave no answer.

Again the high priest asked him, "Are you the Messiah? Are you the Son of the Blessed One?"

⁶² "I am," said Jesus. "And you will see the Son of Man sitting at the right hand of the Mighty One. You will see the Son of Man coming on the clouds of heaven."

⁶³ The high priest tore his clothes. "Why do we need any more witnesses?" he asked. ⁶⁴ "You have heard him say a very evil thing against God. What do you think?"

They all found him guilty and said he must die. ⁶⁵ Then some began to spit at him. They blindfolded him. They hit him with their fists. They said, "Prophesy!" And the guards took him and beat him.

Peter Says He Does Not Know Jesus

⁶⁶ Peter was below in the courtyard. One of the high

priest's female servants came by. ⁶⁷When she saw Peter warming himself, she looked closely at him.

"You also were with Jesus, that Nazarene," she said. ⁶⁸But Peter said he had not been with him. "I don't know or understand what you're talking about," he said. He went out to the entrance to the courtyard.

⁶⁹The servant saw him there. She said again to those standing around, "This fellow is one of them." ⁷⁰Again he said he was not.

After a little while, those standing nearby said to Peter, "You must be one of them. You are from Galilee."

⁷¹Then Peter began to curse. He said to them, "I don't know this man you're talking about!" ⁷²Right away the rooster crowed the second time. Then Peter remembered what Jesus had spoken to him. "The rooster will crow twice," he had said. "Before it does, you will say three times that you don't know me." Peter broke down and cried.

Jesus Is Brought to Pilate

15 It was very early in the morning. The chief priests, with the elders, the teachers of the law, and the whole Sanhedrin, made their plans. So they tied Jesus up and led him away. Then they handed him over to Pilate. ²"Are you the king of the Jews?" asked Pilate.

"You have said so," Jesus replied.

³The chief priests brought many charges against him. ⁴So Pilate asked him again, "Aren't you going to answer? See how many things they charge you with."

⁵But Jesus still did not reply. Pilate was amazed.

⁶It was the usual practice at the Passover Feast to let one prisoner go free. The people could choose the one they wanted. ⁷A man named Barabbas was in prison. He was there with some other people who had fought against the country's rulers. They had committed murder while they were fighting against the rulers. ⁸The crowd came up and asked Pilate to do for them what he usually did.

⁹"Do you want me to let the king of the Jews go free?" asked Pilate. ¹⁰He knew that the chief priests had handed Jesus over to him because they wanted to get their own way. ¹¹But the chief priests stirred up the crowd. So the crowd asked Pilate to let Barabbas go free instead.

¹²"Then what should I do with the one you call the king of the Jews?" Pilate asked them. ¹³"Crucify him!" the crowd shouted.

¹⁴"Why? What wrong has he done?" asked Pilate.

But they shouted even louder, "Crucify him!"

¹⁵Pilate wanted to satisfy the crowd. So he let Barabbas go free. He ordered that Jesus be whipped. Then he handed him over to be nailed to a cross.

The Soldiers Make Fun of Jesus

[16] The soldiers led Jesus away into the palace. It was called the Praetorium. They called together the whole company of soldiers. [17] The soldiers put a purple robe on Jesus. Then they twisted thorns together to make a crown. They placed it on his head. [18] They began to call out to him, "We honor you, king of the Jews!" [19] Again and again they hit him on the head with a stick. They spit on him. They fell on their knees and pretended to honor him. [20] After they had made fun of him, they took off the purple robe. They put his own clothes back on him. Then they led him out to nail him to a cross.

Jesus Is Nailed to a Cross

[21] A man named Simon was passing by. He was from Cyrene. He was the father of Alexander and Rufus. Simon was on his way in from the country. The soldiers forced him to carry the cross. [22] They brought Jesus to the place called Golgotha. The word Golgotha means the Place of the Skull. [23] Then they gave him wine mixed with spices. But he did not take it. [24] They nailed him to the cross. Then they divided up his clothes. They cast lots to see what each of them would get.

[25] It was nine o'clock in the morning when they crucified him. [26] They wrote out the charge against him. It read,

THE KING OF THE JEWS.

[27-28] They crucified with him two rebels against Rome. One was on his right and one was on his left. [29] Those who passed by shouted at Jesus and made fun of him. They shook their heads and said, "So you are going to destroy the temple and build it again in three days? [30] Then come down from the cross! Save yourself!" [31] In the same way the chief priests and the teachers of the law made fun of him among themselves. "He saved others," they said. "But he can't save himself! [32] Let this Messiah, this king of Israel, come down now from the cross! When we see that, we will believe." Those who were being crucified with Jesus also made fun of him.

Jesus Dies

[33] At noon, darkness covered the whole land. It lasted three hours. [34] At three o'clock in the afternoon Jesus cried out in a loud voice, *"Eloi, Eloi, lema sabachthani?"* This means "My God, my God, why have you deserted me?" *(Psalm 22:1)*

[35] Some of those standing nearby heard Jesus cry out. They said, "Listen! He's calling for Elijah."

[36] Someone ran and filled a sponge with wine vinegar. He put it on a stick. He offered it to Jesus to drink. "Leave him alone," he said. "Let's see if Elijah comes to take him down."

[37] With a loud cry, Jesus took his last breath.

[38] The temple curtain was

What to Read When . . .

THINGS ARE GOING WELL
Luke 12:13–21; 1 Timothy 6:3–19; Hebrews 13:5

YOU ARE ANGRY
Matthew 5:21–22; Matthew 18:21–35; Ephesians 4:25–27; James 1:19–20

YOU ARE JEALOUS
Numbers 12:1–15; 16:1–35; Galatians 5:13–15, 19–21; James 3:13–18

YOU ARE LONELY
1 Kings 19:1–18; Psalm 41; Matthew 26:36–46; 2 Timothy 4:16–18

YOU ARE PROUD
Mark 10:35–45; Romans 12:3; Philippians 2:1–11

YOU ARE SAD
Isaiah 12; Isaiah 40:1–11; Jeremiah 31:10–13; 2 Corinthians 1:3–7; 7:6–13

YOU ARE SELFISH
Luke 12:13–21; 2 Corinthians 9:6–15; 1 John 3:16–18

YOU ARE STRUGGLING TO BE HONEST
Proverbs 12:17; Proverbs 12:22; Ephesians 4:25

YOU ARE STRUGGLING WITH LAZINESS
Proverbs 6:6–11, 10:4–5; Ephesians 5:15–16; 2 Thessalonians 3:6–15

YOU ARE WORRIED
Luke 12:22–34; Philippians 4:4–9; Hebrews 13:5–6

YOU HAVE BEEN FIGHTING WITH SOMEONE
Proverbs 15:18; Matthew 5:5; Colossians 3:15; James 3:17

YOU HAVE BEEN JUDGING OTHERS
Matthew 7:1–5; 1 Corinthians 4:1–5; James 2:1–13; 4:11–12

YOU NEED ASSURANCE OF SALVATION
Psalm 91:14–16; Micah 7:18–20; John 3:1–21; Acts 16:31

YOU NEED HOPE
Psalm 42; 130; Romans 5:1–11; Colossians 1:3–27; 1 Peter 1:3–9

YOU WANT TO LEARN TO PRAY
Matthew 6:5–15; Mark 11:22–25; Luke 18:9–14

What the Bible has to say about . . .

ANGER
Psalm 4:4; Proverbs 16:32; Ephesians 4:25–5:2

CARING/COMPASSION
Psalm 116:5–6; Micah 6:8; 2 Corinthians 1:3–7

CHILDREN
Psalm 78:1–7; Matthew 18:1–9; Mark 10:13–16; Ephesians 6:1–4

DEATH
Psalm 116:15–16; Isaiah 57:1–2; John 12:23–26; Romans 6:1–23

ETERNAL LIFE
Psalm 23; John 3:1–21

FRIENDSHIP
Proverbs 17:17; 26:6; John 14:23–15:17; Colossians 3:12–17

GIVING
Deuteronomy 15:7–11; Malachi 3:10–12; Matthew 6:1–4

HAPPINESS
Psalm 33; Isaiah 12; 52:7–10; Matthew 5:1–12; Philippians 4:4–9

HEAVEN
Matthew 6:19–21; 25:31–44; Revelation 21

HELL
Luke 16:22–24; Matthew 10:27–29; Mark 9:42–49

JOY
Isaiah 12; 52:7–10; Luke 15; James 1:2–18; 1 Peter 4:12–19

LOVE
Deuteronomy 6:1–5; 1 Corinthians 13; 1 John 4:7–21

THE POOR
Deuteronomy 15:1–11; Amos 5:11–15; James 2:1–13

REVENGE
Proverbs 25:21–22; Matthew 5:38–47; Romans 12:17–21

STEWARDSHIP
1 Chronicles 29:1–9; Matthew 25:14–30; Luke 12:35–48

SWEARING/PROFANITY
Exodus 20:7; Ephesians 4:29–32; James 3:1–12

torn in two from top to bottom. ³⁹ A Roman commander was standing there in front of Jesus. He saw how Jesus died. Then he said, "This man was surely the Son of God!"

⁴⁰ Not very far away, some women were watching. Mary Magdalene was among them. Mary, the mother of the younger James and of Joseph, was also there. So was Salome. ⁴¹ In Galilee these women had followed Jesus. They had taken care of his needs. Many other women were also there. They had come up with him to Jerusalem.

Jesus Is Buried

⁴² It was the day before the Sabbath. That day was called Preparation Day. As evening approached, ⁴³ Joseph went boldly to Pilate and asked for Jesus' body. Joseph was from the town of Arimathea. He was a leading member of the Jewish Council. He was waiting for God's kingdom. ⁴⁴ Pilate was surprised to hear that Jesus was already dead. So he called for the Roman commander. He asked him if Jesus had already died. ⁴⁵ The commander said it was true. So Pilate gave the body to Joseph. ⁴⁶ Then Joseph bought some linen cloth. He took down the body and wrapped it in the linen. He put it in a tomb cut out of rock. Then he rolled a stone against the entrance to the tomb. ⁴⁷ Mary Magdalene and Mary the mother of Joseph saw where Jesus' body had been placed.

Jesus Rises From the Dead

16 The Sabbath day ended. Mary Magdalene, Mary the mother of James, and Salome bought spices. They were going to use them for Jesus' body. ² Very early on the first day of the week, they were on their way to the tomb. It was just after sunrise. ³ They asked each other, "Who will roll the stone away from the entrance to the tomb?"

⁴ Then they looked up and saw that the stone had been rolled away. The stone was very large. ⁵ They entered the tomb. As they did, they saw a young man dressed in a white robe. He was sitting on the right side. They were alarmed.

⁶ "Don't be alarmed," he said. "You are looking for Jesus the Nazarene, who was crucified. But he has risen! He is not here! See the place where they had put him. ⁷ Go! Tell his disciples and Peter, 'He is going ahead of you into Galilee. There you will see him. It will be just as he told you.' "

⁸ The women were shaking and confused. They went out and ran away from the tomb. They said nothing to anyone, because they were afraid.

⁹ Jesus rose from the dead early on the first day of the week. He appeared first to Mary Magdalene. He had driven seven demons out of her. ¹⁰ She went and told those who had been with him. She found them crying. They were very sad. ¹¹ They heard that Jesus was alive and

that she had seen him. But they did not believe it.

¹²After that, Jesus appeared in a different form to two of them. This happened while they were walking out in the country. ¹³The two returned and told the others about it. But the others did not believe them either.

¹⁴Later Jesus appeared to the 11 disciples as they were eating. He spoke firmly to them because they had no faith. They would not believe those who had seen him after he rose from the dead.

¹⁵He said to them, "Go into all the world. Preach the good news to everyone. ¹⁶Anyone who believes and is baptized will be saved. But anyone who does not believe will be punished. ¹⁷Here are the miraculous signs that those who believe will do. In my name they will drive out demons. They will speak in languages they had not known before. ¹⁸They will pick up snakes with their hands. And when they drink deadly poison, it will not hurt them at all. They will place their hands on sick people. And the people will get well."

¹⁹When the Lord Jesus finished speaking to them, he was taken up into heaven. He sat down at the right hand of God. ²⁰Then the disciples went out and preached everywhere. The Lord worked with them. And he backed up his word by the signs that went with it.

Luke

Introduction:

Luke wrote the third Gospel. He was a doctor who traveled with Paul. He wrote this book for a man named Theophilus. Luke and Theophilus were not Jews by birth. Luke wanted him to know that the things he had heard about Jesus were true. Luke wanted people to know that the good news was for everyone, not just the Jews.

Jesus loved all kinds of people. Luke's Gospel helps people see this. Jesus loved those who were treated badly. He cared for the poor. He loved people of different races. He welcomed children. And he was kind to women.

Luke tells about the joy Jesus brought to people. Jesus' birth brought great joy to Mary and the shepherds. Jesus brought joy to his followers when he rose from the dead. Jesus brings joy to all who trust in him and follow him.

Outline of contents:

Luke Writes an Orderly Report

1 Many people have attempted to write about the things that have taken place among us. ² Reports of these things were handed down to us. There were people who saw these things for themselves from the beginning. They saw them and then passed the word on. ³ With this in mind, I myself have carefully looked into everything from the beginning. So I also decided to write down an orderly report of exactly what happened. I am doing this for you, most excellent Theophilus. ⁴ I want you to know that the things you have been taught are true.

The Coming Birth of John the Baptist

⁵ Herod was king of Judea. During the time he was ruling, there was a priest named Zechariah. He belonged to a group of priests named after Abijah. His wife Elizabeth also came from the family line of Aaron. ⁶ Both of them did what was right in the sight of God. They obeyed all the Lord's commands and

rules faithfully. [7] But they had no children, because Elizabeth was not able to have any. And they were both very old.

[8] One day Zechariah's group was on duty. He was serving as a priest in God's temple. [9] He happened to be chosen, in the usual way, to go into the temple of the Lord. There he was supposed to burn incense. [10] The time came for this to be done. All who had gathered to worship were praying outside.

[11] Then an angel of the Lord appeared to Zechariah. The angel was standing at the right side of the incense altar. [12] When Zechariah saw him, he was amazed and terrified. [13] But the angel said to him, "Do not be afraid, Zechariah. Your prayer has been heard. Your wife Elizabeth will have a child. It will be a boy, and you must call him John. [14] He will be a joy and delight to you. His birth will make many people very glad. [15] He will be important in the sight of the Lord. He must never drink wine or other such drinks. He will be filled with the Holy Spirit even before he is born. [16] He will bring back many of the people of Israel to the Lord their God. [17] And he will prepare the way for the Lord. He will have the same spirit and power that Elijah had. He will bring peace between parents and their children. He will teach people who don't obey to be wise and do what is right. In this way, he will prepare a people who are ready for the Lord."

[18] Zechariah asked the angel, "How can I be sure of this? I am an old man, and my wife is old too."

[19] The angel said to him, "I am Gabriel. I serve God. I have been sent to speak to you and to tell you this good news. [20] And now you will have to be silent. You will not be able to speak until after John is born. That's because you did not believe my words. They will come true at the time God has chosen."

[21] During that time, the people were waiting for Zechariah to come out of the temple. They wondered why he stayed there so long. [22] When he came out, he could not speak to them. They realized he had seen a vision in the temple. They knew this because he kept gesturing to them. He still could not speak.

[23] When his time of service was over, he returned home. [24] After that, his wife Elizabeth became pregnant. She stayed at home for five months. [25] "The Lord has done this for me," she said. "In these days, he has been kind to me. He has taken away my shame among the people."

The Coming Birth of Jesus

[26] In the sixth month after Elizabeth had become pregnant, God sent the angel Gabriel to Nazareth, a town in Galilee. [27] He was sent to a virgin. The girl was engaged to a man named Joseph. He came from the family line of David. The virgin's name was Mary. [28] The angel greeted her and said, "The

Lord has blessed you in a special way. He is with you."

29 Mary was very upset because of his words. She wondered what kind of greeting this could be. 30 But the angel said to her, "Do not be afraid, Mary. God is very pleased with you. 31 You will become pregnant and give birth to a son. You must call him Jesus. 32 He will be great and will be called the Son of the Most High God. The Lord God will make him a king like his father David of long ago. 33 The Son of the Most High God will rule forever over his people. They are from the family line of Jacob. That kingdom will never end."

34 "How can this happen?" Mary asked the angel. "I am a virgin."

35 The angel answered, "The Holy Spirit will come to you. The power of the Most High God will cover you. So the holy one that is born will be called the Son of God. 36 Your relative Elizabeth will have a child even though she is old. People thought she could not have children. But she has been pregnant for six months now. 37 That's because what God says will always come true."

38 "I serve the Lord," Mary answered. "May it happen to me just as you said it would." Then the angel left her.

Mary Visits Elizabeth

39 At that time Mary got ready and hurried to a town in Judea's hill country. 40 There she entered Zechariah's home and greeted Elizabeth. 41 When Elizabeth heard Mary's greeting, the baby inside her jumped. And Elizabeth was filled with the Holy Spirit. 42 In a loud voice she called out, "God has blessed you more than other women. And blessed is the child you will have! 43 But why is God so kind to me? Why has the mother of my Lord come to me? 44 As soon as I heard the sound of your voice, the baby inside me jumped for joy. 45 You are a woman God has blessed. You have believed that the Lord would keep his promises to you!"

Mary's Song

46 Mary said,

"My soul gives glory to the
        Lord.
47   My spirit delights in God
        my Savior.
48 He has taken note of me
        even though I am not
        considered important.
    From now on all people will
        call me blessed.
49   The Mighty One has done
        great things for me.
    His name is holy.
50 He shows his mercy to those
        who have respect for
        him,
    from parent to child down
        through the years.
51 He has done mighty things
        with his powerful arm.
    He has scattered those
        who are proud in their
        deepest thoughts.
52 He has brought down rulers
        from their thrones.

But he has lifted up people who are not considered important.

⁵³ He has filled with good things those who are hungry.

But he has sent away empty those who are rich.

⁵⁴ He has helped the people of Israel, who serve him.

He has always remembered to be kind

⁵⁵ to Abraham and his children down through the years.

He has done it just as he promised to our people of long ago."

⁵⁶ Mary stayed with Elizabeth about three months. Then she returned home.

John the Baptist Is Born

⁵⁷ The time came for Elizabeth to have her baby. She gave birth to a son. ⁵⁸ Her neighbors and relatives heard that the Lord had been very kind to her. They shared her joy.

⁵⁹ On the eighth day, they came to have the child circumcised. They were going to name him Zechariah, like his father. ⁶⁰ But his mother spoke up. "No!" she said. "He must be called John."

⁶¹ They said to her, "No one among your relatives has that name."

⁶² Then they motioned to his father. They wanted to find out what he would like to name the child. ⁶³ He asked for something to write on. Then he wrote, "His name is John." Everyone was amazed. ⁶⁴ Right away Zechariah could speak again. Right away he praised God. ⁶⁵ All his neighbors were filled with fear and wonder. Throughout Judea's hill country, people were talking about all these things. ⁶⁶ Everyone who heard this wondered about it. And because the Lord was with John, they asked, "What is this child going to be?"

Zechariah's Song

⁶⁷ John's father Zechariah was filled with the Holy Spirit. He prophesied,

⁶⁸ "Give praise to the Lord, the God of Israel!

He has come to his people and purchased their freedom.

⁶⁹ He has acted with great power and has saved us.

He did it for those who are from the family line of his servant David.

⁷⁰ Long ago holy prophets said he would do it.

⁷¹ He has saved us from our enemies.

We are rescued from all who hate us.

⁷² He has been kind to our people of long ago.

He has remembered his holy covenant.

⁷³ He made a promise to our father Abraham.

⁷⁴ He promised to save us from our enemies.

Then we could serve him without fear.

⁷⁵ He wants us to be holy and godly as long as we live.

[76] "And you, my child, will be
called a prophet of the
Most High God.
You will go ahead of the
Lord to prepare the way
for him.
[77] You will tell his people how
they can be saved.
You will tell them that their
sins can be forgiven.
[78] All of that will happen
because our God is
tender and caring.
His kindness will bring
the rising sun to us from
heaven.
[79] It will shine on those living in
darkness
and in the shadow of
death.
It will guide our feet on the
path of peace."

[80] The child grew up, and his spirit became strong. He lived in the desert until he appeared openly to Israel.

Jesus Is Born

2 In those days, Caesar Augustus made a law. It required that a list be made of everyone in the whole Roman world. [2] It was the first time a list was made of the people while Quirinius was governor of Syria. [3] Everyone went to their own town to be listed.

[4] So Joseph went also. He went from the town of Nazareth in Galilee to Judea. That is where Bethlehem, the town of David, was. Joseph went there because he belonged to the family line of David. [5] He went there with Mary to be listed. Mary was engaged to him. She was expecting a baby. [6] While Joseph and Mary were there, the time came for the child to be born. [7] She gave birth to her first baby. It was a boy. She wrapped him in large strips of cloth. Then she placed him in a manger. That's because there was no guest room where they could stay.

[8] There were shepherds living out in the fields nearby. It was night, and they were taking care of their sheep. [9] An angel of the Lord appeared to them. And the glory of the Lord shone around them. They were terrified. [10] But the angel said to them, "Do not be afraid. I bring you good news. It will bring great joy for all the people. [11] Today in the town of David a Savior has been born to you. He is the Messiah, the Lord. [12] Here is how you will know I am telling you the truth. You will find a baby wrapped in strips of cloth and lying in a manger."

[13] Suddenly a large group of angels from heaven also appeared. They were praising God. They said,

[14] "May glory be given to God in
the highest heaven!
And may peace be given to
those he is pleased with
on earth!"

[15] The angels left and went into heaven. Then the shepherds said to one another, "Let's go to Bethlehem. Let's see this thing that has happened, which the Lord has told us about." [16] So they hurried off and

found Mary and Joseph and the baby. The baby was lying in the manger. ¹⁷ After the shepherds had seen him, they told everyone. They reported what the angel had said about this child. ¹⁸ All who heard it were amazed at what the shepherds said to them. ¹⁹ But Mary kept all these things like a secret treasure in her heart. She thought about them over and over. ²⁰ The shepherds returned. They gave glory and praise to God. Everything they had seen and heard was just as they had been told.

²¹ When the child was eight days old, he was circumcised. At the same time he was named Jesus. This was the name the angel had given him before his mother became pregnant.

Joseph and Mary Take Jesus to the Temple

²² The time came for making Mary "clean" as required by the Law of Moses. So Joseph and Mary took Jesus to Jerusalem. There they presented him to the Lord. ²³ In the Law of the Lord it says, "The first boy born in every family must be set apart for the Lord." *(Exodus 13:2,12)* ²⁴ They also offered a sacrifice. They did it in keeping with the Law, which says, "a pair of doves or two young pigeons." *(Leviticus 12:8)*

²⁵ In Jerusalem there was a man named Simeon. He was a good and godly man. He was waiting for God's promise to Israel to come true. The Holy Spirit was with him. ²⁶ The Spirit had told Simeon that he would

not die before he had seen the Lord's Messiah. ²⁷ The Spirit led him into the temple courtyard. Then Jesus' parents brought the child in. They came to do for him what the Law required. ²⁸ Simeon took Jesus in his arms and praised God. He said,

²⁹ "Lord, you are the King over all.
　Now let me, your servant,
　　go in peace.
　That is what you promised.
³⁰ My eyes have seen your
　　salvation.
³¹　You have prepared it in the
　　sight of all nations.
³² It is a light to be given to the
　　Gentiles.
　It will be the glory of your
　　people Israel."

³³ The child's father and mother were amazed at what was said about him. ³⁴ Then Simeon blessed them. He said to Mary, Jesus' mother, "This child is going to cause many people in Israel to fall and to rise. God has sent him. But many will speak against him. ³⁵ The thoughts of many hearts will be known. A sword will wound your own soul too."

³⁶ There was also a prophet named Anna. She was the daughter of Penuel from the tribe of Asher. Anna was very old. After getting married, she lived with her husband seven years. ³⁷ Then she was a widow until she was 84. She never left the temple. She worshiped night and day, praying and going without food. ³⁸ Anna came up

to Jesus' family at that moment. She gave thanks to God. And she spoke about the child to all who were looking forward to the time when Jerusalem would be set free.

³⁹ Joseph and Mary did everything the Law of the Lord required. Then they returned to Galilee. They went to their own town of Nazareth. ⁴⁰ And the child grew and became strong. He was very wise. He was blessed by God's grace.

The Boy Jesus at the Temple

⁴¹ Every year Jesus' parents went to Jerusalem for the Passover Feast. ⁴² When Jesus was 12 years old, they went up to the feast as usual. ⁴³ After the feast was over, his parents left to go back home. The boy Jesus stayed behind in Jerusalem. But they were not aware of it. ⁴⁴ They thought he was somewhere in their group. So they traveled on for a day. Then they began to look for him among their relatives and friends. ⁴⁵ They did not find him. So they went back to Jerusalem to look for him. ⁴⁶ After three days they found him in the temple courtyard. He was sitting with the teachers. He was listening to them and asking them questions. ⁴⁷ Everyone who heard him was amazed at how much he understood. They also were amazed at his answers. ⁴⁸ When his parents saw him, they were amazed. His mother said to him, "Son, why have you treated us like this? Your father and I have been worried about

you. We have been looking for you everywhere."

⁴⁹ "Why were you looking for me?" he asked. "Didn't you know I had to be in my Father's house?" ⁵⁰ But they did not understand what he meant by that.

⁵¹ Then he went back to Nazareth with them, and he obeyed them. But his mother kept all these things like a secret treasure in her heart. ⁵² Jesus became wiser and stronger. He also became more and more pleasing to God and to people.

John the Baptist Prepares the Way

3 Tiberius Caesar had been ruling for 15 years. Pontius Pilate was governor of Judea. Herod was the ruler of Galilee. His brother Philip was the ruler of Iturea and Traconitis. Lysanias was ruler of Abilene. ² Annas and Caiaphas were high priests. At that time God's word came to John, son of Zechariah, in the desert. ³ He went into all the countryside around the Jordan River. There he preached that people should be baptized and turn away from their sins. Then God would forgive them. ⁴ Here is what is written in the book of Isaiah the prophet. It says,

"A messenger is calling out in the desert,
'Prepare the way for the Lord.
Make straight paths for him.
⁵ Every valley will be filled in.
Every mountain and hill will be made level.

The crooked roads will
become straight.
The rough ways will
become smooth.
⁶ And all people will see God's
salvation.' " *(Isaiah 40:3-5)*

⁷ John spoke to the crowds coming to be baptized by him. He said, "You are like a nest of poisonous snakes! Who warned you to escape the coming of God's anger? ⁸ Live in a way that shows you have turned away from your sins. And don't start saying to yourselves, 'Abraham is our father.' I tell you, God can raise up children for Abraham even from these stones. ⁹ The ax is already lying at the roots of the trees. All the trees that don't produce good fruit will be cut down. They will be thrown into the fire."

¹⁰ "Then what should we do?" the crowd asked.

¹¹ John answered, "Anyone who has extra clothes should share with the one who has none. And anyone who has extra food should do the same."

¹² Even tax collectors came to be baptized. "Teacher," they asked, "what should we do?"

¹³ "Don't collect any more than you are required to," John told them.

¹⁴ Then some soldiers asked him, "And what should we do?"

John replied, "Don't force people to give you money. Don't bring false charges against people. Be happy with your pay."

¹⁵ The people were waiting. They were expecting something. They were all wondering in their hearts if John might be the Messiah. ¹⁶ John answered them all, "I baptize you with water. But one who is more powerful than I am will come. I'm not good enough to untie the straps of his sandals. He will baptize you with the Holy Spirit and fire. ¹⁷ His pitchfork is in his hand to toss the straw away from his threshing floor. He will gather the wheat into his barn. But he will burn up the husks with fire that can't be put out." ¹⁸ John said many other things to warn the people. He also announced the good news to them.

¹⁹ But John found fault with Herod, the ruler of Galilee, because of his marriage to Herodias. She was the wife of Herod's brother. John also spoke strongly to Herod about all the other evil things he had done. ²⁰ So Herod locked John up in prison. Herod added this sin to all his others.

The Baptism and Family Line of Jesus

²¹ When all the people were being baptized, Jesus was baptized too. And as he was praying, heaven was opened. ²² The Holy Spirit came to rest on him in the form of a dove. A voice came from heaven. It said, "You are my Son, and I love you. I am very pleased with you."

²³ Jesus was about 30 years old when he began his special work for God and others.

It was thought that he was
the son of Joseph.
Joseph was the son of Heli.

24 Heli was the son of Matthat.
Matthat was the son of Levi.
Levi was the son of Melki.
Melki was the son of Jannai.
Jannai was the son of Joseph.
25 Joseph was the son of Mattathias.
Mattathias was the son of Amos.
Amos was the son of Nahum.
Nahum was the son of Esli.
Esli was the son of Naggai.
26 Naggai was the son of Maath.
Maath was the son of Mattathias.
Mattathias was the son of Semein.
Semein was the son of Josek.
Josek was the son of Joda.
27 Joda was the son of Joanan.
Joanan was the son of Rhesa.
Rhesa was the son of Zerubbabel.
Zerubbabel was the son of Shealtiel.
Shealtiel was the son of Neri.
28 Neri was the son of Melki.
Melki was the son of Addi.
Addi was the son of Cosam.
Cosam was the son of Elmadam.
Elmadam was the son of Er.
29 Er was the son of Joshua.
Joshua was the son of Eliezer.
Eliezer was the son of Jorim.
Jorim was the son of Matthat.
Matthat was the son of Levi.

30 Levi was the son of Simeon.
Simeon was the son of Judah.
Judah was the son of Joseph.
Joseph was the son of Jonam.
Jonam was the son of Eliakim.
31 Eliakim was the son of Melea.
Melea was the son of Menna.
Menna was the son of Mattatha.
Mattatha was the son of Nathan.
Nathan was the son of David.
32 David was the son of Jesse.
Jesse was the son of Obed.
Obed was the son of Boaz.
Boaz was the son of Salmon.
Salmon was the son of Nahshon.
33 Nahshon was the son of Amminadab.
Amminadab was the son of Ram.
Ram was the son of Hezron.
Hezron was the son of Perez.
Perez was the son of Judah.
34 Judah was the son of Jacob.
Jacob was the son of Isaac.
Isaac was the son of Abraham.
Abraham was the son of Terah.
Terah was the son of Nahor.
35 Nahor was the son of Serug.
Serug was the son of Reu.
Reu was the son of Peleg.
Peleg was the son of Eber.

Eber was the son of Shelah.
36 Shelah was the son of Cainan.
Cainan was the son of Arphaxad.
Arphaxad was the son of Shem.
Shem was the son of Noah.
Noah was the son of Lamech.
37 Lamech was the son of Methuselah.
Methuselah was the son of Enoch.
Enoch was the son of Jared.
Jared was the son of Mahalalel.
Mahalalel was the son of Kenan.
38 Kenan was the son of Enosh.
Enosh was the son of Seth.
Seth was the son of Adam.
Adam was the son of God.

Jesus Is Tempted in the Desert

4 Jesus, full of the Holy Spirit, left the Jordan River. The Spirit led him into the desert. ² There the devil tempted him for 40 days. Jesus ate nothing during that time. At the end of the 40 days, he was hungry.

³ The devil said to him, "If you are the Son of God, tell this stone to become bread."

⁴ Jesus answered, "It is written, 'Man must not live only on bread.' " *(Deuteronomy 8:3)*

⁵ Then the devil led Jesus up to a high place. In an instant, he showed Jesus all the kingdoms of the world. ⁶ He said to Jesus, "I will give you all their authority and glory. It has been given to me, and I can give it to anyone I want to. ⁷ If you worship me, it will all be yours."

⁸ Jesus answered, "It is written, 'Worship the Lord your God. He is the only one you should serve.' " *(Deuteronomy 6:13)*

⁹ Then the devil led Jesus to Jerusalem. He had Jesus stand on the highest point of the temple. "If you are the Son of God," he said, "throw yourself down from here. ¹⁰ It is written,

" 'The Lord will command
     his angels to take good
     care of you.
¹¹ They will lift you up in their
     hands.
     Then you won't trip over a
     stone.' "   *(Psalm 91:11,12)*

¹² Jesus answered, "Scripture says, 'Do not test the Lord your God.' " *(Deuteronomy 6:16)*

¹³ When the devil finished all this tempting, he left Jesus until a better time.

Jesus Is Not Accepted in Nazareth

¹⁴ Jesus returned to Galilee in the power of the Holy Spirit. News about him spread through the whole countryside. ¹⁵ He was teaching in their synagogues, and everyone praised him.

¹⁶ Jesus went to Nazareth, where he had been brought up. On the Sabbath day he went into the synagogue as he usually did. He stood up to read. ¹⁷ And the scroll of Isaiah the prophet was handed to him. Jesus unrolled it and found the right place. There it is written,

18 "The Spirit of the Lord is on me.
   He has anointed me
     to announce the good
      news to poor people.
   He has sent me to announce
     freedom for prisoners.
   He has sent me so that the
     blind will see again.
   He wants me to set free those
     who are treated badly.
19   And he has sent me to
     announce the year when
     he will set his people
     free."   *(Isaiah 61:1,2)*

20 Then Jesus rolled up the scroll. He gave it back to the attendant and sat down. The eyes of everyone in the synagogue were staring at him. 21 He began by saying to them, "Today this passage of Scripture is coming true as you listen."

22 Everyone said good things about him. They were amazed at the gracious words they heard from his lips. "Isn't this Joseph's son?" they asked.

23 Jesus said, "Here is a saying you will certainly apply to me. 'Doctor, heal yourself!' And you will tell me this. 'Do the things here in your hometown that we heard you did in Capernaum.' "

24 "What I'm about to tell you is true," he continued. "A prophet is not accepted in his hometown. 25 I tell you for sure that there were many widows in Israel in the days of Elijah. And there had been no rain for three and a half years. There wasn't enough food to eat anywhere in the land. 26 But Elijah was not sent to any of those widows. Instead, he was sent to a widow in Zarephath near Sidon. 27 And there were many in Israel who had skin diseases in the days of Elisha the prophet. But not one of them was healed except Naaman the Syrian."

28 All the people in the synagogue were very angry when they heard that. 29 They got up and ran Jesus out of town. They took him to the edge of the hill on which the town was built. They planned to throw him off the cliff. 30 But Jesus walked right through the crowd and went on his way.

Jesus Drives Out an Evil Spirit

31 Then Jesus went to Capernaum, a town in Galilee. On the Sabbath day he taught the people. 32 They were amazed at his teaching, because his words had authority.

33 In the synagogue there was a man controlled by a demon, an evil spirit. He cried out at the top of his voice. 34 "Go away!" he said. "What do you want with us, Jesus of Nazareth? Have you come to destroy us? I know who you are. You are the Holy One of God!"

35 "Be quiet!" Jesus said firmly. "Come out of him!" Then the demon threw the man down in front of everybody. And it came out without hurting him.

36 All the people were amazed. They said to each other, "What he says is amazing! With authority and power he gives orders to evil spirits. And they come out!" 37 The news about Jesus spread throughout the whole area.

Jesus Heals Many People

[38] Jesus left the synagogue and went to the home of Simon. At that time, Simon's mother-in-law was suffering from a high fever. So they asked Jesus to help her. [39] He bent over her and commanded the fever to leave, and it left her. She got up right away and began to serve them.

[40] At sunset, people brought to Jesus all who were sick. He placed his hands on each one and healed them. [41] Also, demons came out of many people. The demons shouted, "You are the Son of God!" But he commanded them to be quiet. He would not allow them to speak, because they knew he was the Messiah.

[42] At dawn, Jesus went out to a place where he could be by himself. The people went to look for him. When they found him, they tried to keep him from leaving them. [43] But he said, "I must announce the good news of God's kingdom to the other towns also. That is why I was sent." [44] And he kept on preaching in the synagogues of Judea.

Jesus Chooses His First Disciples

5 One day Jesus was standing by the Sea of Galilee. The people crowded around him and listened to the word of God. [2] Jesus saw two boats at the edge of the water. They had been left there by the fishermen, who were washing their nets. [3] He got into the boat that belonged to Simon. Jesus asked him to go out a little way from shore. Then he sat down in the boat and taught the people.

[4] When he finished speaking, he turned to Simon. Jesus said, "Go out into deep water. Let down the nets so you can catch some fish."

[5] Simon answered, "Master, we've worked hard all night and haven't caught anything. But because you say so, I will let down the nets."

[6] When they had done so, they caught a large number of fish. There were so many that their nets began to break. [7] So they motioned to their partners in the other boat to come and help them. They came and filled both boats so full that they began to sink.

[8] When Simon Peter saw this, he fell at Jesus' knees. "Go away from me, Lord!" he said. "I am a sinful man!" [9] He and everyone with him were amazed at the number of fish they had caught. [10] So were James and John, the sons of Zebedee, who worked with Simon.

Then Jesus said to Simon, "Don't be afraid. From now on you will fish for people." [11] So they pulled their boats up on shore. Then they left everything and followed him.

Jesus Heals a Man Who Had a Skin Disease

[12] While Jesus was in one of the towns, a man came along. He had a skin disease all over his body. When he saw Jesus, the man fell with his face to the ground. He begged him, "Lord,

if you are willing to make me 'clean,' you can do it."

¹³ Jesus reached out his hand and touched the man. "I am willing to do it," he said. "Be 'clean'!" Right away the disease left him.

¹⁴ Then Jesus ordered him, "Don't tell anyone. Go and show yourself to the priest. Offer the sacrifices that Moses commanded. It will be a witness to the priest and the people that you are 'clean.' "

¹⁵ But the news about Jesus spread even more. So crowds of people came to hear him. They also came to be healed of their sicknesses. ¹⁶ But Jesus often went away to be by himself and pray.

Jesus Forgives and Heals a Man Who Could Not Walk

¹⁷ One day Jesus was teaching. Pharisees and teachers of the law were sitting there. They had come from every village of Galilee and from Judea and Jerusalem. They heard that the Lord had given Jesus the power to heal the sick. ¹⁸ So some men came carrying a man who could not walk. He was lying on a mat. They tried to take him into the house to place him in front of Jesus. ¹⁹ They could not find a way to do this because of the crowd. So they went up on the roof. Then they lowered the man on his mat through the opening in the roof tiles. They lowered him into the middle of the crowd, right in front of Jesus.

²⁰ When Jesus saw that they had faith, he spoke to the man. He said, "Friend, your sins are forgiven."

²¹ The Pharisees and the teachers of the law began to think, "Who is this fellow who says such an evil thing? Who can forgive sins but God alone?"

²² Jesus knew what they were thinking. So he asked, "Why are you thinking these things in your hearts? ²³ Is it easier to say, 'Your sins are forgiven'? Or to say, 'Get up and walk'? ²⁴ But I want you to know that the Son of Man has authority on earth to forgive sins." So he spoke to the man who could not walk. "I tell you," he said, "get up. Take your mat and go home." ²⁵ Right away, the man stood up in front of them. He took his mat and went home praising God. ²⁶ Everyone was amazed and gave praise to God. They were filled with wonder. They said, "We have seen unusual things today."

Jesus Chooses Levi and Eats With Sinners

²⁷ After this, Jesus left the house. He saw a tax collector sitting at the tax booth. The man's name was Levi. "Follow me," Jesus said to him. ²⁸ Levi got up, left everything and followed him.

²⁹ Then Levi gave a huge banquet for Jesus at his house. A large crowd of tax collectors and others were eating with them. ³⁰ But the Pharisees and their teachers of the law complained to Jesus' disciples. They said,

"Why do you eat and drink with tax collectors and sinners?"

31 Jesus answered them, "Healthy people don't need a doctor. Sick people do. 32 I have not come to get those who think they are right with God to follow me. I have come to get sinners to turn away from their sins."

Jesus Is Asked About Fasting

33 Some of the people who were there said to Jesus, "John's disciples often pray and go without eating. So do the disciples of the Pharisees. But yours go on eating and drinking."

34 Jesus answered, "Can you make the friends of the groom fast while he is with them? 35 But the time will come when the groom will be taken away from them. In those days they will go without eating."

36 Then Jesus gave them an example. He said, "No one tears a piece out of new clothes to patch old clothes. Otherwise, they will tear the new clothes. Also, the patch from the new clothes will not match the old clothes. 37 No one pours new wine into old wineskins. Otherwise, the new wine will burst the skins. The wine will run out, and the wineskins will be destroyed. 38 No, new wine must be poured into new wineskins. 39 After drinking old wine, no one wants the new. They say, 'The old wine is better.'"

Jesus Is Lord of the Sabbath Day

6 One Sabbath day Jesus was walking through the grain-fields. His disciples began to break off some heads of grain. They rubbed them in their hands and ate them. 2 Some of the Pharisees said, "It is against the Law to do this on the Sabbath day. Why are you doing it?"

3 Jesus answered them, "Haven't you ever read about what David did? He and his men were hungry. 4 He entered the house of God and took the holy bread. He ate the bread that only priests were allowed to eat. David also gave some to his men." 5 Then Jesus said to them, "The Son of Man is Lord of the Sabbath day."

6 On another Sabbath day, Jesus went into the synagogue and was teaching. A man whose right hand was weak and twisted was there. 7 The Pharisees and the teachers of the law were trying to find fault with Jesus. So they watched him closely. They wanted to see if he would heal on the Sabbath day. 8 But Jesus knew what they were thinking. He spoke to the man who had the weak and twisted hand. "Get up and stand in front of everyone," he said. So the man got up and stood there.

9 Then Jesus said to them, "What does the Law say we should do on the Sabbath day? Should we do good? Or should we do evil? Should we save life? Or should we destroy it?"

10 He looked around at all of them. Then he said to the man, "Stretch out your hand." He did, and his hand had been made as good as new. 11 But the Pharisees

and the teachers of the law were very angry. They began to talk to one another about what they might do to Jesus.

Jesus Chooses the Twelve Apostles

12 On one of those days, Jesus went out to a mountainside to pray. He spent the night praying to God. 13 When morning came, he called for his disciples to come to him. He chose 12 of them and made them apostles. 14 Simon was one of them. Jesus gave him the name Peter. There were also Simon's brother Andrew, James, John, Philip and Bartholomew. 15 And there were Matthew, Thomas, and James, son of Alphaeus. There were also Simon who was called the Zealot 16 and Judas, son of James. Judas Iscariot was one of them too. He was the one who would later hand Jesus over to his enemies.

Jesus Gives Blessings and Warnings

17 Jesus went down the mountain with them and stood on a level place. A large crowd of his disciples was there. A large number of other people were there too. They came from all over Judea, including Jerusalem. They also came from the coastland around Tyre and Sidon. 18 They had all come to hear Jesus and to be healed of their sicknesses. People who were troubled by evil spirits were made well. 19 Everyone tried to touch Jesus. Power was coming from him and healing them all.

20 Jesus looked at his disciples. He said to them,

"Blessed are you who are
    needy.
  God's kingdom belongs to
    you.
21 Blessed are you who are
    hungry now.
  You will be satisfied.
  Blessed are you who are sad
    now.
  You will laugh.
22 Blessed are you when people
    hate you,
  when they have nothing to
    do with you
  and say bad things about
    you,
  and when they treat your
    name as something evil.
  They do all this because
    you are followers of the
    Son of Man.

23 "The prophets of long ago were treated the same way. When these things happen to you, be glad and jump for joy. You will receive many blessings in heaven.

24 "But how terrible it will be for
    you who are rich!
  You have already had your
    easy life.
25 How terrible for you who are
    well fed now!
  You will go hungry.
  How terrible for you who
    laugh now!
  You will cry and be sad.
26 How terrible for you when
    everyone says good
    things about you!

Their people treated the false prophets the same way long ago.

Love Your Enemies

27 "But here is what I tell you who are listening. Love your enemies. Do good to those who hate you. 28 Bless those who call down curses on you. And pray for those who treat you badly. 29 Suppose someone slaps you on one cheek. Let them slap you on the other cheek as well. Suppose someone takes your coat. Don't stop them from taking your shirt as well. 30 Give to everyone who asks you. And if anyone takes what belongs to you, don't ask to get it back. 31 Do to others as you want them to do to you.

32 "Suppose you love those who love you. Should anyone praise you for that? Even sinners love those who love them. 33 And suppose you do good to those who are good to you. Should anyone praise you for that? Even sinners do that. 34 And suppose you lend money to those who can pay you back. Should anyone praise you for that? Even a sinner lends to sinners, expecting them to pay everything back. 35 But love your enemies. Do good to them. Lend to them without expecting to get anything back. Then you will receive a lot in return. And you will be children of the Most High God. He is kind to people who are evil and are not thankful. 36 So have mercy, just as your Father has mercy.

Be Fair When You Judge Other People

37 "If you do not judge other people, then you will not be judged. If you do not find others guilty, then you will not be found guilty. Forgive, and you will be forgiven. 38 Give, and it will be given to you. A good amount will be poured into your lap. It will be pressed down, shaken together, and running over. The same amount you give will be measured out to you."

39 Jesus also gave them another example. He asked, "Can a blind person lead another blind person? Won't they both fall into a pit? 40 The student is not better than the teacher. But everyone who is completely trained will be like their teacher.

41 "You look at the bit of sawdust in your friend's eye. But you pay no attention to the piece of wood in your own eye. 42 How can you say to your friend, 'Let me take the bit of sawdust out of your eye'? How can you say this while there is a piece of wood in your own eye? You pretender! First take the piece of wood out of your own eye. Then you will be able to see clearly to take the bit of sawdust out of your friend's eye.

A Tree and Its Fruit

43 "A good tree doesn't bear bad fruit. And a bad tree doesn't bear good fruit. 44 You can tell each tree by the kind of fruit it bears. People do not pick figs from thorns. And they don't pick grapes from bushes. 45 A

good man says good things. These come from the good that is stored up in his heart. An evil man says evil things. These come from the evil that is stored up in his heart. A person's mouth says everything that is in their heart.

The Wise and Foolish Builders

⁴⁶ "Why do you call me, 'Lord, Lord,' and still don't do what I say? ⁴⁷ Some people come and listen to me and do what I say. I will show you what they are like. ⁴⁸ They are like a man who builds a house. He digs down deep and sets it on solid rock. When a flood comes, the river rushes against the house. But the water can't shake it. The house is well built. ⁴⁹ But here is what happens when people listen to my words and do not obey them. They are like a man who builds a house on soft ground instead of solid rock. The moment the river rushes against that house, it falls down. It is completely destroyed."

A Roman Commander Has Faith

7 Jesus finished saying all these things to the people who were listening. Then he entered Capernaum. ² There the servant of a Roman commander was sick and about to die. His master thought highly of him. ³ The commander heard about Jesus. So he sent some elders of the Jews to him. He told them to ask Jesus to come and heal his servant. ⁴ They came to Jesus

and begged him, "This man deserves to have you do this. ⁵ He loves our nation and has built our synagogue." ⁶ So Jesus went with them.

When Jesus came near the house, the Roman commander sent friends to him. He told them to say, "Lord, don't trouble yourself. I am not good enough to have you come into my house. ⁷ That is why I did not even think I was fit to come to you. But just say the word, and my servant will be healed. ⁸ I myself am a man who is under authority. And I have soldiers who obey my orders. I tell this one, 'Go,' and he goes. I tell that one, 'Come,' and he comes. I say to my servant, 'Do this,' and he does it."

⁹ When Jesus heard this, he was amazed at the commander. Jesus turned to the crowd that was following him. He said, "I tell you, even in Israel I have not found anyone whose faith is so strong." ¹⁰ Then the men who had been sent to Jesus returned to the house. They found that the servant was healed.

Jesus Raises a Widow's Son From the Dead

¹¹ Some time later, Jesus went to a town called Nain. His disciples and a large crowd went along with him. ¹² He approached the town gate. Just then, a dead person was being carried out. He was the only son of his mother. She was a widow. A large crowd from the town was with her. ¹³ When the Lord

saw her, he felt sorry for her. So he said, "Don't cry."

¹⁴ Then he went up and touched the coffin. Those carrying it stood still. Jesus said, "Young man, I say to you, get up!" ¹⁵ The dead man sat up and began to talk. Then Jesus gave him back to his mother.

¹⁶ The people were all filled with wonder and praised God. "A great prophet has appeared among us," they said. "God has come to help his people." ¹⁷ This news about Jesus spread all through Judea and the whole country.

Jesus and John the Baptist

¹⁸ John's disciples told him about all these things. So he chose two of them. ¹⁹ He sent them to the Lord. John told them to ask him, "Are you the one who is supposed to come? Or should we look for someone else?"

²⁰ The men came to Jesus. They said, "John the Baptist sent us to ask you, 'Are you the one who is supposed to come? Or should we look for someone else?'"

²¹ At that time Jesus healed many people. They had illnesses, sicknesses and evil spirits. He also gave sight to many who were blind. ²² So Jesus replied to the messengers, "Go back to John. Tell him what you have seen and heard. Blind people receive sight. Disabled people walk. Those who have skin diseases are made 'clean.' Deaf people hear. Those who are dead are raised to life. And the good news is announced to those who are poor. ²³ Blessed is anyone who does not give up their faith because of me."

²⁴ So John's messengers left. Then Jesus began to speak to the crowd about John. He said, "What did you go out into the desert to see? Tall grass waving in the wind? ²⁵ If not, what did you go out to see? A man dressed in fine clothes? No. Those who wear fine clothes and have many expensive things are in palaces. ²⁶ Then what did you go out to see? A prophet? Yes, I tell you, and more than a prophet. ²⁷ He is the one written about in Scripture. It says,

> "'I will send my messenger
> ahead of you.
> He will prepare your way
> for you.'   (Malachi 3:1)

²⁸ I tell you, no one more important than John has ever been born. But the least important person in God's kingdom is more important than John is."

²⁹ All the people who heard Jesus' words agreed that God's way was right. Even the tax collectors agreed. These people had all been baptized by John. ³⁰ But the Pharisees and the authorities on the law did not accept for themselves God's purpose. So they had not been baptized by John.

³¹ Jesus went on to say, "What can I compare today's people to? What are they like? ³² They are like children sitting in the market and calling out to each other. They say,

" 'We played the flute for you.
But you didn't dance.
We sang a funeral song.
But you didn't cry.'

33 That is how it has been with John the Baptist. When he came to you, he didn't eat bread or drink wine. And you say, 'He has a demon.' 34 But when the Son of Man came, he ate and drank as you do. And you say, 'This fellow is always eating and drinking far too much. He's a friend of tax collectors and sinners.' 35 All who follow wisdom prove that wisdom is right."

A Sinful Woman Pours Perfume on Jesus

36 One of the Pharisees invited Jesus to have dinner with him. So he went to the Pharisee's house. He took his place at the table. 37 There was a woman in that town who had lived a sinful life. She learned that Jesus was eating at the Pharisee's house. So she came there with a special jar of perfume. 38 She stood behind Jesus and cried at his feet. And she began to wet his feet with her tears. Then she wiped them with her hair. She kissed them and poured perfume on them.

39 The Pharisee who had invited Jesus saw this. He said to himself, "If this man were a prophet, he would know who is touching him. He would know what kind of woman she is. She is a sinner!"

40 Jesus answered him, "Simon, I have something to tell you."

"Tell me, teacher," he said.

41 "Two people owed money to a certain lender. One owed him 500 silver coins. The other owed him 50 silver coins. 42 Neither of them had the money to pay him back. So he let them go without paying. Which of them will love him more?"

43 Simon replied, "I suppose the one who owed the most money."

"You are right," Jesus said.

44 Then he turned toward the woman. He said to Simon, "Do you see this woman? I came into your house. You did not give me any water to wash my feet. But she wet my feet with her tears and wiped them with her hair. 45 You did not give me a kiss. But this woman has not stopped kissing my feet since I came in. 46 You did not put any olive oil on my head. But she has poured this perfume on my feet. 47 So I tell you this. Her many sins have been forgiven. She has shown that she understands this by her great acts of love. But whoever has been forgiven only a little loves only a little."

48 Then Jesus said to her, "Your sins are forgiven."

49 The other guests began to talk about this among themselves. They said, "Who is this who even forgives sins?"

50 Jesus said to the woman, "Your faith has saved you. Go in peace."

The Story of the Farmer

8 After this, Jesus traveled around from one town and village to another. He announced

the good news of God's kingdom. His 12 disciples were with him. ² So were some women who had been healed of evil spirits and sicknesses. One was Mary Magdalene. Seven demons had come out of her. ³ Another was Joanna, the wife of Chuza. He was the manager of Herod's household. Susanna and many others were there also. These women were helping to support Jesus and the 12 disciples with their own money.

⁴ A large crowd gathered together. People came to Jesus from town after town. As they did, he told a story. He said, ⁵ "A farmer went out to plant his seed. He scattered the seed on the ground. Some fell on a path. People walked on it, and the birds ate it up. ⁶ Some seed fell on rocky ground. When it grew, the plants dried up because they had no water. ⁷ Other seed fell among thorns. The thorns grew up with it and crowded out the plants. ⁸ Still other seed fell on good soil. It grew up and produced a crop 100 times more than the farmer planted."

When Jesus said this, he called out, "Whoever has ears should listen."

⁹ His disciples asked him what the story meant. ¹⁰ He said, "You have been given the chance to understand the secrets of God's kingdom. But to outsiders I speak by using stories. In that way,

" 'They see, but they will
    not know what they are
    seeing.

They hear, but they will not
    understand what they
    are hearing.' *(Isaiah 6:9)*

¹¹ "Here is what the story means. The seed is God's message. ¹² The seed on the path stands for God's message in the hearts of those who hear. But then the devil comes. He takes away the message from their hearts. He does it so they won't believe. Then they can't be saved. ¹³ The seed on rocky ground stands for those who hear the message and receive it with joy. But they have no roots. They believe for a while. But when they are tested, they fall away from the faith. ¹⁴ The seed that fell among thorns stands for those who hear the message. But as they go on their way, they are choked by life's worries, riches and pleasures. So they do not reach full growth. ¹⁵ But the seed on good soil stands for those with an honest and good heart. Those people hear the message. They keep it in their hearts. They remain faithful and produce a good crop.

A Lamp on a Stand

¹⁶ "No one lights a lamp and then hides it in a clay jar or puts it under a bed. Instead, they put it on a stand. Then those who come in can see its light. ¹⁷ What is hidden will be seen. And what is out of sight will be brought into the open and made known. ¹⁸ So be careful how you listen. Whoever has something will be given more. Whoever has nothing, even what they think they

have will be taken away from them."

Jesus' Mother and Brothers

¹⁹ Jesus' mother and brothers came to see him. But they could not get near him because of the crowd. ²⁰ Someone told him, "Your mother and brothers are standing outside. They want to see you."

²¹ He replied, "My mother and brothers are those who hear God's word and do what it says."

Jesus Calms the Storm

²² One day Jesus said to his disciples, "Let's go over to the other side of the lake." So they got into a boat and left. ²³ As they sailed, Jesus fell asleep. A storm came down on the lake. It was so bad that the boat was about to sink. They were in great danger.

²⁴ The disciples went and woke Jesus up. They said, "Master! Master! We're going to drown!"

He got up and ordered the wind and the huge waves to stop. The storm quieted down. It was completely calm. ²⁵ "Where is your faith?" he asked his disciples.

They were amazed and full of fear. They asked one another, "Who is this? He commands even the winds and the waves, and they obey him."

Jesus Heals a Man Controlled by Demons

²⁶ Jesus and his disciples sailed to the area of the Gera-senes across the lake from Galilee. ²⁷ When Jesus stepped on shore, he was met by a man from the town. The man was controlled by demons. For a long time he had not worn clothes or lived in a house. He lived in the tombs. ²⁸ When he saw Jesus, he cried out and fell at his feet. He shouted at the top of his voice, "Jesus, Son of the Most High God, what do you want with me? I beg you, don't hurt me!" ²⁹ This was because Jesus had commanded the evil spirit to come out of the man. Many times the spirit had taken hold of him. The man's hands and feet were chained, and he was kept under guard. But he had broken his chains. And then the demon had forced him to go out into lonely places in the countryside.

³⁰ Jesus asked him, "What is your name?"

"Legion," he replied, because many demons had gone into him. ³¹ And they begged Jesus again and again not to order them to go into the Abyss.

³² A large herd of pigs was feeding there on the hillside. The demons begged Jesus to let them go into the pigs. And he allowed it. ³³ When the demons came out of the man, they went into the pigs. Then the herd rushed down the steep bank. They ran into the lake and drowned.

³⁴ Those who were tending the pigs saw what had happened. They ran off and reported it in the town and countryside.

35 The people went out to see what had happened. Then they came to Jesus. They found the man who was now free of the demons. He was sitting at Jesus' feet. He was dressed and thinking clearly. All this made the people afraid. 36 Those who had seen it told the others how the man who had been controlled by demons was now healed. 37 Then all the people who lived in the area of the Gerasenes asked Jesus to leave them. They were filled with fear. So he got into the boat and left.

38 The man who was now free of the demons begged to go with him. But Jesus sent him away. He said to him, 39 "Return home and tell how much God has done for you." So the man went away. He told people all over town how much Jesus had done for him.

Jesus Heals a Dead Girl and a Suffering Woman

40 When Jesus returned, a crowd welcomed him. They were all expecting him. 41 Then a man named Jairus came. He was a synagogue leader. He fell at Jesus' feet and begged Jesus to come to his house. 42 His only daughter was dying. She was about 12 years old. As Jesus was on his way, the crowds almost crushed him.

43 A woman was there who had a sickness that made her bleed. Her sickness had lasted for 12 years. No one could heal her. 44 She came up behind Jesus and touched the edge of his clothes. Right away her bleeding stopped.

45 "Who touched me?" Jesus asked.

Everyone said they didn't do it. Then Peter said, "Master, the people are crowding and pushing against you."

46 But Jesus said, "Someone touched me. I know that power has gone out from me."

47 The woman realized that people would notice her. Shaking with fear, she came and fell at his feet. In front of everyone, she told why she had touched him. She also told how she had been healed in an instant. 48 Then he said to her, "Dear woman, your faith has healed you. Go in peace."

49 While Jesus was still speaking, someone came from the house of Jairus. Jairus was the synagogue leader. "Your daughter is dead," the messenger said. "Don't bother the teacher anymore."

50 Hearing this, Jesus said to Jairus, "Don't be afraid. Just believe. She will be healed."

51 When he arrived at the house of Jairus, he did not let everyone go in with him. He took only Peter, John and James, and the child's father and mother. 52 During this time, all the people were crying and sobbing loudly over the child. "Stop crying!" Jesus said. "She is not dead. She is sleeping."

53 They laughed at him. They knew she was dead. 54 But he took her by the hand and said, "My child, get up!" 55 Her spirit

returned, and right away she stood up. Then Jesus told them to give her something to eat. ⁵⁶ Her parents were amazed. But Jesus ordered them not to tell anyone what had happened.

Jesus Sends Out the Twelve Disciples

9 Jesus called together the 12 disciples. He gave them power and authority to drive out all demons and to heal sicknesses. ² Then he sent them out to announce God's kingdom and to heal those who were sick. ³ He told them, "Don't take anything for the journey. Do not take a walking stick or a bag. Do not take any bread, money or extra clothes. ⁴ When you are invited into a house, stay there until you leave town. ⁵ Some people may not welcome you. If they don't, leave their town and shake the dust off your feet. This will be a witness against the people living there." ⁶ So the 12 disciples left. They went from village to village. They announced the good news and healed people everywhere.

⁷ Now Herod, the ruler of Galilee, heard about everything that was going on. He was bewildered, because some were saying that John the Baptist had been raised from the dead. ⁸ Others were saying that Elijah had appeared. Still others were saying that a prophet of long ago had come back to life. ⁹ But Herod said, "I had John's head cut off. So who is it that I hear such things about?" And he tried to see Jesus.

Jesus Feeds the Five Thousand

¹⁰ The disciples returned. They told Jesus what they had done. Then he took them with him. They went off by themselves to a town called Bethsaida. ¹¹ But the crowds learned about it and followed Jesus. He welcomed them and spoke to them about God's kingdom. He also healed those who needed to be healed.

¹² Late in the afternoon the 12 disciples came to him. They said, "Send the crowd away. They can go to the nearby villages and countryside. There they can find food and a place to stay. There is nothing here."

¹³ Jesus replied, "You give them something to eat."

The disciples answered, "We have only five loaves of bread and two fish. We would have to go and buy food for all this crowd." ¹⁴ About 5,000 men were there.

But Jesus said to his disciples, "Have them sit down in groups of about 50 each." ¹⁵ The disciples did so, and everyone sat down. ¹⁶ Jesus took the five loaves and the two fish. He looked up to heaven and gave thanks. He broke them into pieces. Then he gave them to the disciples to give to the people. ¹⁷ All of them ate and were satisfied. The disciples picked up 12 baskets of leftover pieces.

Peter Says That Jesus Is the Messiah

18 One day Jesus was praying alone. Only his disciples were with him. He asked them, "Who do the crowds say I am?"

19 They replied, "Some say John the Baptist. Others say Elijah. Still others say that one of the prophets of long ago has come back to life."

20 "But what about you?" he asked. "Who do you say I am?"

Peter answered, "God's Messiah."

Jesus Speaks About His Coming Death

21 Jesus strongly warned them not to tell this to anyone. 22 He said, "The Son of Man must suffer many things. The elders will not accept him. The chief priests and the teachers of the law will not accept him either. He must be killed and on the third day rise from the dead."

23 Then he said to all of them, "Whoever wants to follow me must say no to themselves. They must pick up their cross every day and follow me. 24 Whoever wants to save their life will lose it. But whoever loses their life for me will save it. 25 What good is it if someone gains the whole world but loses or gives up their very self? 26 Suppose someone is ashamed of me and my words. The Son of Man will come in his glory and in the glory of the Father and the holy angels. Then he will be ashamed of that person.

27 "What I'm about to tell you is true. Some who are standing here will not die before they see God's kingdom."

Jesus' Appearance Is Changed

28 About eight days after Jesus said this, he went up on a mountain to pray. He took Peter, John and James with him. 29 As he was praying, the appearance of his face changed. His clothes became as bright as a flash of lightning. 30 Two men, Moses and Elijah, appeared in shining glory. Jesus and the two of them talked together. 31 They talked about how he would be leaving them soon. This was going to happen in Jerusalem. 32 Peter and his companions had been very sleepy. But then they became completely awake. They saw Jesus' glory and the two men standing with him. 33 As the men were leaving Jesus, Peter spoke up. "Master," he said to him, "it is good for us to be here. Let us put up three shelters. One will be for you, one for Moses, and one for Elijah." Peter didn't really know what he was saying.

34 While he was speaking, a cloud appeared and covered them. The disciples were afraid as they entered the cloud. 35 A voice came from the cloud. It said, "This is my Son, and I have chosen him. Listen to him." 36 When the voice had spoken, they found that Jesus was alone. The disciples kept quiet about this. They didn't tell anyone at that time what they had seen.

Jesus Heals a Boy Who Is Controlled by an Evil Spirit

37 The next day Jesus and those who were with him came down from the mountain. A large crowd met Jesus. 38 A man in the crowd called out. "Teacher," he said, "I beg you to look at my son. He is my only child. 39 A spirit takes hold of him, and he suddenly screams. It throws him into fits so that he foams at the mouth. It hardly ever leaves him. It is destroying him. 40 I begged your disciples to drive it out. But they couldn't do it."

41 "You unbelieving and evil people!" Jesus replied. "How long do I have to stay with you? How long do I have to put up with you?" Then he said to the man, "Bring your son here."

42 Even while the boy was coming, the demon threw him into a fit. The boy fell to the ground. But Jesus ordered the evil spirit to leave the boy. Then Jesus healed him and gave him back to his father. 43 They were all amazed at God's greatness.

Jesus Speaks a Second Time About His Coming Death

Everyone was wondering about all that Jesus did. Then Jesus said to his disciples, 44 "Listen carefully to what I am about to tell you. The Son of Man is going to be handed over to men." 45 But they didn't understand what this meant. That was because it was hidden from them. And they were afraid to ask Jesus about it.

Who Is the Most Important Person?

46 The disciples began to argue about which one of them would be the most important person. 47 Jesus knew what they were thinking. So he took a little child and had the child stand beside him. 48 Then he spoke to them. "Anyone who welcomes this little child in my name welcomes me," he said. "And anyone who welcomes me welcomes the one who sent me. The one considered least important among all of you is really the most important."

49 "Master," said John, "we saw someone driving out demons in your name. We tried to stop him, because he is not one of us."

50 "Do not stop him," Jesus said. "Anyone who is not against you is for you."

The Samaritans Do Not Welcome Jesus

51 The time grew near for Jesus to be taken up to heaven. So he made up his mind to go to Jerusalem. 52 He sent messengers on ahead. They went into a Samaritan village to get things ready for him. 53 But the people there did not welcome Jesus. That was because he was heading for Jerusalem. 54 The disciples James and John saw this. They asked, "Lord, do you want us to call down fire from heaven to destroy them?" 55 But Jesus turned and commanded them not to do it. 56 Then Jesus and his disciples went on to another village.

The Cost of Following Jesus

⁵⁷ Once Jesus and those who were with him were walking along the road. A man said to Jesus, "I will follow you no matter where you go."

⁵⁸ Jesus replied, "Foxes have dens. Birds have nests. But the Son of Man has no place to lay his head."

⁵⁹ He said to another man, "Follow me."

But the man replied, "Lord, first let me go and bury my father."

⁶⁰ Jesus said to him, "Let dead people bury their own dead. You go and tell others about God's kingdom."

⁶¹ Still another person said, "I will follow you, Lord. But first let me go back and say goodbye to my family."

⁶² Jesus replied, "Suppose someone starts to plow and then looks back. That person is not fit for service in God's kingdom."

Jesus Sends Out the Seventy-Two

10 After this the Lord appointed 72 others. He sent them out two by two ahead of him. They went to every town and place where he was about to go. ² He told them, "The harvest is huge, but the workers are few. So ask the Lord of the harvest to send out workers into his harvest field. ³ Go! I am sending you out like lambs among wolves. ⁴ Do not take a purse or bag or sandals. And don't greet anyone on the road.

⁵ "When you enter a house, first say, 'May this house be blessed with peace.' ⁶ If some-one there works to bring peace, your blessing of peace will rest on them. If not, it will return to you. ⁷ Stay there, and eat and drink anything they give you. Workers are worthy of their pay. Do not move around from house to house.

⁸ "When you enter a town and are welcomed, eat what is given to you. ⁹ Heal the sick people who are there. Tell them, 'God's kingdom has come near to you.' ¹⁰ But what if you enter a town and are not welcomed? Then go into its streets and say, ¹¹ 'We wipe from our feet even the dust of your town. We do it to warn you. But here is what you can be sure of. God's kingdom has come near.' ¹² I tell you this. On judgment day it will be easier for Sodom than for that town.

¹³ "How terrible it will be for you, Chorazin! How terrible for you, Bethsaida! Suppose the miracles done in you had been done in Tyre and Sidon. They would have turned away from their sins long ago. They would have put on the rough clothing people wear when they're sad. They would have sat down in ashes. ¹⁴ On judgment day it will be easier for Tyre and Sidon than for you. ¹⁵ And what about you, Capernaum? Will you be lifted up to the heavens? No! You will go down to the place of the dead.

¹⁶ "Whoever listens to you listens to me. Whoever does not accept you does not accept me. But whoever does not accept me does not accept the one who sent me."

17 The 72 returned with joy. They said, "Lord, even the demons obey us when we speak in your name."

18 Jesus replied, "I saw Satan fall like lightning from heaven. 19 I have given you authority to walk all over snakes and scorpions. You will be able to destroy all the power of the enemy. Nothing will harm you. 20 But do not be glad when the evil spirits obey you. Instead, be glad that your names are written in heaven."

21 At that time Jesus was full of joy through the Holy Spirit. He said, "I praise you, Father. You are Lord of heaven and earth. You have hidden these things from wise and educated people. But you have shown them to little children. Yes, Father. This is what you wanted to do.

22 "My Father has given all things to me. The Father is the only one who knows who the Son is. And the only ones who know the Father are the Son and those to whom the Son chooses to make the Father known."

23 Then Jesus turned to his disciples. He said to them in private, "Blessed are the eyes that see what you see. 24 I tell you, many prophets and kings wanted to see what you see. But they didn't see it. They wanted to hear what you hear. But they didn't hear it."

The Story of the Good Samaritan

25 One day an authority on the law stood up to test Jesus. "Teacher," he asked, "what must I do to receive eternal life?"

26 "What is written in the Law?" Jesus replied. "How do you understand it?"

27 He answered, " 'Love the Lord your God with all your heart and with all your soul. Love him with all your strength and with all your mind.' (Deuteronomy 6:5) And, 'Love your neighbor as you love yourself.' " (Leviticus 19:18)

28 "You have answered correctly," Jesus replied. "Do that, and you will live."

29 But the man wanted to make himself look good. So he asked Jesus, "And who is my neighbor?"

30 Jesus replied, "A man was going down from Jerusalem to Jericho. Robbers attacked him. They stripped off his clothes and beat him. Then they went away, leaving him almost dead. 31 A priest happened to be going down that same road. When he saw the man, he passed by on the other side. 32 A Levite also came by. When he saw the man, he passed by on the other side too. 33 But a Samaritan came to the place where the man was. When he saw the man, he felt sorry for him. 34 He went to him, poured olive oil and wine on his wounds and bandaged them. Then he put the man on his own donkey. He brought him to an inn and took care of him. 35 The next day he took out two silver coins. He gave them to the owner of the inn. 'Take care of him,' he said. 'When I return, I

will pay you back for any extra expense you may have.'

³⁶ "Which of the three do you think was a neighbor to the man who was attacked by robbers?"

³⁷ The authority on the law replied, "The one who felt sorry for him."

Jesus told him, "Go and do as he did."

Jesus at the Home of Martha and Mary

³⁸ Jesus and his disciples went on their way. Jesus came to a village where a woman named Martha lived. She welcomed him into her home. ³⁹ She had a sister named Mary. Mary sat at the Lord's feet listening to what he said. ⁴⁰ But Martha was busy with all the things that had to be done. She came to Jesus and said, "Lord, my sister has left me to do the work by myself. Don't you care? Tell her to help me!"

⁴¹ "Martha, Martha," the Lord answered. "You are worried and upset about many things. ⁴² But few things are needed. Really, only one thing is needed. Mary has chosen what is better. And it will not be taken away from her."

Jesus Teaches About Prayer

11 One day Jesus was praying in a certain place. When he finished, one of his disciples spoke to him. "Lord," he said, "teach us to pray, just as John taught his disciples."

² Jesus said to them, "When you pray, this is what you should say.

"'Father,
may your name be honored.
May your kingdom come.
³ Give us each day our daily
    bread.
⁴ Forgive us our sins,
    as we also forgive everyone
    who sins against us.
Keep us from falling into sin
    when we are tempted.'"

⁵ Then Jesus said to them, "Suppose you have a friend. You go to him at midnight and say, 'Friend, lend me three loaves of bread. ⁶ A friend of mine on a journey has come to stay with me. I have no food to give him.' ⁷ And suppose the one inside answers, 'Don't bother me. The door is already locked. My children and I are in bed. I can't get up and give you anything.' ⁸ I tell you, that person will not get up. And he won't give you bread just because he is your friend. But because you keep bothering him, he will surely get up. He will give you as much as you need.

⁹ "So here is what I say to you. Ask, and it will be given to you. Search, and you will find. Knock, and the door will be opened to you. ¹⁰ Everyone who asks will receive. The one who searches will find. And the door will be opened to the one who knocks.

¹¹ "Fathers, suppose your son asks for a fish. Which of you will give him a snake instead? ¹² Or suppose he asks for an egg. Which of you will give him a scorpion? ¹³ Even though you are evil, you know how to give

good gifts to your children. How much more will your Father who is in heaven give the Holy Spirit to those who ask him!"

Jesus and Beelzebul

¹⁴ Jesus was driving out a demon. The man who had the demon could not speak. When the demon left, the man began to speak. The crowd was amazed. ¹⁵ But some of them said, "Jesus is driving out demons by the power of Beelzebul, the prince of demons." ¹⁶ Others tested Jesus by asking for a sign from heaven.

¹⁷ Jesus knew what they were thinking. So he said to them, "Any kingdom that fights against itself will be destroyed. A family that is divided against itself will fall. ¹⁸ If Satan fights against himself, how can his kingdom stand? I say this because of what you claim. You say I drive out demons by the power of Beelzebul. ¹⁹ Suppose I do drive out demons with Beelzebul's help. With whose help do your followers drive them out? So then, they will be your judges. ²⁰ But suppose I drive out demons with the help of God's powerful finger. Then God's kingdom has come upon you.

²¹ "When a strong man is completely armed and guards his house, what he owns is safe. ²² But when someone stronger attacks, he is overpowered. The attacker takes away the armor the man had trusted in. Then he divides up what he has stolen.

²³ "Whoever is not with me is against me. And whoever does not gather with me scatters.

²⁴ "What happens when an evil spirit comes out of a person? It goes through dry areas looking for a place to rest. But it doesn't find it. Then it says, 'I will return to the house I left.' ²⁵ When it arrives there, it finds the house swept clean and put in order. ²⁶ Then the evil spirit goes and takes seven other spirits more evil than itself. They go in and live there. That person is worse off than before."

²⁷ As Jesus was saying these things, a woman in the crowd called out. She shouted, "Blessed is the mother who gave you birth and nursed you."

²⁸ He replied, "Instead, blessed are those who hear God's word and obey it."

The Sign of Jonah

²⁹ As the crowds grew larger, Jesus spoke to them. "The people of today are evil," he said. "They ask for a sign from God. But none will be given except the sign of Jonah. ³⁰ He was a sign from God to the people of Nineveh. In the same way, the Son of Man will be a sign from God to the people of today. ³¹ The Queen of the South will stand up on judgment day with the people now living. And she will prove that they are guilty. She came from very far away to listen to Solomon's wisdom. And now something more important than Solomon is here. ³² The men of Nineveh will stand up on judgment day with

the people now living. And the Ninevites will prove that those people are guilty. The men of Nineveh turned away from their sins when Jonah preached to them. And now something more important than Jonah is here.

The Eye Is the Lamp of the Body

33 "No one lights a lamp and hides it. No one puts it under a bowl. Instead, they put a lamp on its stand. Then those who come in can see the light. 34 Your eye is like a lamp for your body. Suppose your eyes are healthy. Then your whole body also is full of light. But suppose your eyes can't see well. Then your body also is full of darkness. 35 So make sure that the light inside you is not darkness. 36 Suppose your whole body is full of light. And suppose no part of it is dark. Then your body will be full of light. It will be just as when a lamp shines its light on you."

Six Warnings

37 Jesus finished speaking. Then a Pharisee invited him to eat with him. So Jesus went in and took his place at the table. 38 But the Pharisee was surprised. He noticed that Jesus did not wash before the meal.

39 Then the Lord spoke to him. "You Pharisees clean the outside of the cup and dish," he said. "But inside you are full of greed and evil. 40 You foolish people! Didn't the one who made the outside make the inside also?

41 Give freely to poor people to show what is inside you. Then everything will be clean for you.

42 "How terrible it will be for you Pharisees! You give God a tenth of your garden plants, such as mint and rue. But you have forgotten to be fair and to love God. You should have practiced the last things without failing to do the first.

43 "How terrible for you Pharisees! You love the most important seats in the synagogues. You love having people greet you with respect in the market.

44 "How terrible for you! You are like graves that are not marked. People walk over them without knowing it."

45 An authority on the law spoke to Jesus. He said, "Teacher, when you say things like that, you say bad things about us too."

46 Jesus replied, "How terrible for you authorities on the law! You put such heavy loads on people that they can hardly carry them. But you yourselves will not lift one finger to help them.

47 "How terrible for you! You build tombs for the prophets. It was your people of long ago who killed them. 48 So you show that you agree with what your people did long ago. They killed the prophets, and now you build the prophets' tombs. 49 So God in his wisdom said, 'I will send prophets and apostles to them. They will kill some. And they will try to hurt others.' 50 So the people of today will be punished. They

will pay for all the prophets' blood spilled since the world began. [51] I mean from the blood of Abel to the blood of Zechariah. He was killed between the altar and the temple. Yes, I tell you, the people of today will be punished for all these things.

[52] "How terrible for you authorities on the law! You have taken away the key to the door of knowledge. You yourselves have not entered. And you have stood in the way of those who were entering."

[53] When Jesus went outside, the Pharisees and the teachers of the law strongly opposed him. They threw a lot of questions at him. [54] They set traps for him. They wanted to catch him in something he might say.

Jesus Gives Words of Warning and Hope

12 During that time a crowd of many thousands had gathered. There were so many people that they were stepping on one another. Jesus spoke first to his disciples. "Be on your guard against the yeast of the Pharisees," he said. "They just pretend to be godly. [2] Everything that is secret will be brought out into the open. Everything that is hidden will be uncovered. [3] What you have said in the dark will be heard in the daylight. What you have whispered to someone behind closed doors will be shouted from the rooftops.

[4] "My friends, listen to me. Don't be afraid of those who kill the body but can't do any more than that. [5] I will show you whom you should be afraid of. Be afraid of the one who has the authority to throw you into hell after you have been killed. Yes, I tell you, be afraid of him. [6] Aren't five sparrows sold for two pennies? But God does not forget even one of them. [7] In fact, he even counts every hair on your head! So don't be afraid. You are worth more than many sparrows.

[8] "What about someone who says in front of others that he knows me? I tell you, the Son of Man will say in front of God's angels that he knows that person. [9] But what about someone who says in front of others that he doesn't know me? I, the Son of Man, will say in front of God's angels that I don't know him. [10] Everyone who speaks a word against the Son of Man will be forgiven. But anyone who speaks evil things against the Holy Spirit will not be forgiven.

[11] "You will be brought before synagogues, rulers and authorities. But do not worry about how to stand up for yourselves or what to say. [12] The Holy Spirit will teach you at that time what you should say."

The Story of the Rich Fool

[13] Someone in the crowd spoke to Jesus. "Teacher," he said, "tell my brother to divide the family property with me."

[14] Jesus replied, "Friend, who made me a judge or umpire between you?" [15] Then he said to

them, "Watch out! Be on your guard against wanting to have more and more things. Life is not made up of how much a person has."

16 Then Jesus told them a story. He said, "A certain rich man's land produced a very large crop. 17 He thought to himself, 'What should I do? I don't have any place to store my crops.'

18 "Then he said, 'This is what I'll do. I will tear down my barns and build bigger ones. I will store my extra grain in them. 19 I'll say to myself, "You have plenty of grain stored away for many years. Take life easy. Eat, drink and have a good time."'

20 "But God said to him, 'You foolish man! Tonight I will take your life away from you. Then who will get what you have prepared for yourself?'

21 "That is how it will be for whoever stores things away for themselves but is not rich in the sight of God."

Do Not Worry

22 Then Jesus spoke to his disciples. He said, "I tell you, do not worry. Don't worry about your life and what you will eat. And don't worry about your body and what you will wear. 23 There is more to life than eating. There are more important things for the body than clothes. 24 Think about the ravens. They don't plant or gather crops. They don't have any barns at all. But God feeds them. You are worth much more than birds! 25 Can you add even one hour to your life by worrying? 26 You can't do that very little thing. So why worry about the rest?

27 "Think about how the wild flowers grow. They don't work or make clothing. But here is what I tell you. Not even Solomon in his royal robes was dressed like one of those flowers. 28 If that is how God dresses the wild grass, how much better will he dress you! After all, the grass is here only today. Tomorrow it is thrown into the fire. Your faith is so small! 29 Don't spend time thinking about what you will eat or drink. Don't worry about it. 30 People who are ungodly run after all those things. Your Father knows that you need them. 31 But put God's kingdom first. Then those other things will also be given to you.

32 "Little flock, do not be afraid. Your Father has been pleased to give you the kingdom. 33 Sell what you own. Give to those who are poor. Provide purses for yourselves that will not wear out. Store up riches in heaven that will never be used up. There, no thief can come near it. There, no moth can destroy it. 34 Your heart will be where your riches are.

Be Ready

35 "Be dressed and ready to serve. Keep your lamps burning. 36 Be like servants waiting for their master to return from a wedding dinner. When he comes and knocks, they can open the door for him at once. 37 It will be good for those ser-

vants whose master finds them ready when he comes. What I'm about to tell you is true. The master will then dress himself so he can serve them. He will have them take their places at the table. And he will come and wait on them. ³⁸ It will be good for those servants whose master finds them ready. It will even be good if he comes in the middle of the night or toward morning. ³⁹ But here is what you must understand. Suppose the owner of the house knew at what hour the robber was coming. He would not have let his house be broken into. ⁴⁰ You also must be ready. The Son of Man will come at an hour when you don't expect him."

⁴¹ Peter asked, "Lord, are you telling this story to us, or to everyone?"

⁴² The Lord answered, "Suppose a master puts one of his servants in charge of his other servants. The servant's job is to give them the food they are to receive at the right time. The master wants a faithful and wise manager for this. ⁴³ It will be good for the servant if the master finds him doing his job when the master returns. ⁴⁴ What I'm about to tell you is true. The master will put that servant in charge of everything he owns. ⁴⁵ But suppose the servant says to himself, 'My master is taking a long time to come back.' Suppose that servant begins to beat the other servants, both men and women. Suppose he feeds himself. And suppose he drinks until he gets drunk. ⁴⁶ The master of that servant will come back on a day the servant doesn't expect him. The master will return at an hour the servant doesn't know. Then the master will cut him to pieces. He will send the servant to the place where unbelievers go.

⁴⁷ "Suppose a servant knows the master's wishes. But the servant doesn't get ready and doesn't do what the master wants. Then that servant will receive a heavy beating. ⁴⁸ But suppose the servant does not know his master's wishes. And suppose the servant does things for which he should be punished. He will receive a lighter beating. Much will be required of everyone who has been given much. Even more will be asked of the person who is supposed to take care of much.

Jesus Will Separate People From One Another

⁴⁹ "I have come to bring fire on the earth. How I wish the fire had already started! ⁵⁰ But I have a baptism of suffering to go through. And I must go through it. ⁵¹ Do you think I came to bring peace on earth? No, I tell you. I have come to separate people. ⁵² From now on there will be five members in a family, each one against the other. There will be three against two and two against three. ⁵³ They will be separated. Father will turn against son and son against father. Mother will turn against daughter and daughter against

mother. Mother-in-law will turn against daughter-in-law and daughter-in-law against mother-in-law."

Understanding the Meaning of What Is Happening

54 Jesus spoke to the crowd. He said, "You see a cloud rising in the west. Right away you say, 'It's going to rain.' And it does. 55 The south wind blows. So you say, 'It's going to be hot.' And it is. 56 You pretenders! You know how to understand the appearance of the earth and the sky. Why can't you understand the meaning of what is happening right now?

57 "Why don't you judge for yourselves what is right? 58 Suppose someone has a claim against you, and you are on your way to court. Try hard to settle the matter on the way. If you don't, that person may drag you off to the judge. The judge may turn you over to the officer. And the officer may throw you into prison. 59 I tell you, you will not get out until you have paid the very last penny!"

Turn Away From Sin or Die

13 Some people who were there at that time told Jesus about certain Galileans. Pilate had mixed their blood with their sacrifices. 2 Jesus said, "These people from Galilee suffered greatly. Do you think they were worse sinners than all the other Galileans? 3 I tell you, no! But unless you turn away from your sins, you will all die too.

4 Or what about the 18 people in Siloam? They died when the tower fell on them. Do you think they were more guilty than all the others living in Jerusalem? 5 I tell you, no! But unless you turn away from your sins, you will all die too."

6 Then Jesus told a story. "A man had a fig tree," he said. "It was growing in his vineyard. When he went to look for fruit on it, he didn't find any. 7 So he went to the man who took care of the vineyard. He said, 'For three years now I've been coming to look for fruit on this fig tree. But I haven't found any. Cut it down! Why should it use up the soil?'

8 " 'Sir,' the man replied, 'leave it alone for one more year. I'll dig around it and feed it. 9 If it bears fruit next year, fine! If not, then cut it down.' "

Jesus Heals a Disabled Woman on the Sabbath Day

10 Jesus was teaching in one of the synagogues on a Sabbath day. 11 A woman there had been disabled by an evil spirit for 18 years. She was bent over and could not stand up straight. 12 Jesus saw her. He asked her to come to him. He said to her, "Woman, you will no longer be disabled. I am about to set you free." 13 Then he put his hands on her. Right away she stood up straight and praised God.

14 Jesus had healed the woman on the Sabbath day. This made the synagogue leader angry. He told the people, "There are six

days for work. So come and be healed on those days. But do not come on the Sabbath day."

15 The Lord answered him, "You pretenders! Doesn't each of you go to the barn and untie your ox or donkey on the Sabbath day? Then don't you lead it out to give it water? 16 This woman is a member of Abraham's family line. But Satan has kept her disabled for 18 long years. Shouldn't she be set free on the Sabbath day from what was keeping her disabled?"

17 When Jesus said this, all those who opposed him were put to shame. But the people were delighted. They loved all the wonderful things he was doing.

The Stories of the Mustard Seed and the Yeast

18 Then Jesus asked, "What is God's kingdom like? What can I compare it to? 19 It is like a mustard seed. Someone took the seed and planted it in a garden. It grew and became a tree. The birds sat in its branches."

20 Again he asked, "What can I compare God's kingdom to? 21 It is like yeast that a woman used. She mixed it into 60 pounds of flour. The yeast worked its way all through the dough."

The Narrow Door

22 Then Jesus went through the towns and villages, teaching the people. He was on his way to Jerusalem. 23 Someone asked him, "Lord, are only a few people going to be saved?"

He said to them, 24 "Try very hard to enter through the narrow door. I tell you, many will try to enter and will not be able to. 25 The owner of the house will get up and close the door. Then you will stand outside knocking and begging. You will say, 'Sir, open the door for us.'

"But he will answer, 'I don't know you. And I don't know where you come from.'

26 "Then you will say, 'We ate and drank with you. You taught in our streets.'

27 "But he will reply, 'I don't know you. And I don't know where you come from. Get away from me, all you who do evil!'

28 "You will weep and grind your teeth together when you see those who are in God's kingdom. You will see Abraham, Isaac and Jacob and all the prophets there. But you yourselves will be thrown out. 29 People will come from east and west and north and south. They will take their places at the feast in God's kingdom. 30 Then the last will be first. And the first will be last."

Jesus' Sadness Over Jerusalem

31 At that time some Pharisees came to Jesus. They said to him, "Leave this place. Go somewhere else. Herod wants to kill you."

32 He replied, "Go and tell that fox, 'I will keep on driving out demons. I will keep on healing people today and tomorrow. And on the third day I will reach my goal.' 33 In any case, I must

keep going today and tomorrow and the next day. Certainly no prophet can die outside Jerusalem!

³⁴ "Jerusalem! Jerusalem! You kill the prophets and throw stones in order to kill those who are sent to you. Many times I have wanted to gather your people together. I have wanted to be like a hen who gathers her chicks under her wings. And you would not let me. ³⁵ Look, your house is left empty. I tell you, you will not see me again until you say, 'Blessed is the one who comes in the name of the Lord.' " *(Psalm 118:26)*

Jesus Eats at a Pharisee's House

14 One Sabbath day, Jesus went to eat in the house of a well-known Pharisee. While he was there, he was being carefully watched. ² In front of him was a man whose body was badly swollen. ³ Jesus turned to the Pharisees and the authorities on the law. He asked them, "Is it breaking the Law to heal on the Sabbath day?" ⁴ But they remained silent. So Jesus took hold of the man and healed him. Then he sent him away.

⁵ He asked them another question. He said, "Suppose one of you has a child or an ox that falls into a well on the Sabbath day. Wouldn't you pull it out right away?" ⁶ And they had nothing to say.

⁷ Jesus noticed how the guests picked the places of honor at the table. So he told them a story.

⁸ He said, "Suppose someone invites you to a wedding feast. Do not take the place of honor. A person more important than you may have been invited. ⁹ If so, the host who invited both of you will come to you. He will say, 'Give this person your seat.' Then you will be filled with shame. You will have to take the least important place. ¹⁰ But when you are invited, take the lowest place. Then your host will come over to you. He will say, 'Friend, move up to a better place.' Then you will be honored in front of all the other guests. ¹¹ All those who lift themselves up will be made humble. And those who make themselves humble will be lifted up."

¹² Then Jesus spoke to his host. "Suppose you give a lunch or a dinner," he said. "Do not invite your friends, your brothers or sisters, or your relatives, or your rich neighbors. If you do, they may invite you to eat with them. So you will be paid back. ¹³ But when you give a banquet, invite those who are poor. Also invite those who can't see or walk. ¹⁴ Then you will be blessed. Your guests can't pay you back. But you will be paid back when those who are right with God rise from the dead."

The Story of the Great Banquet

¹⁵ One of the people at the table with Jesus heard him say those things. So he said to Jesus, "Blessed is the one who will eat at the feast in God's kingdom."

¹⁶ Jesus replied, "A certain man was preparing a great ban-

quet. He invited many guests. [17] Then the day of the banquet arrived. He sent his servant to those who had been invited. The servant told them, 'Come. Everything is ready now.'

[18] "But they all had the same idea. They began to make excuses. The first one said, 'I have just bought a field. I have to go and see it. Please excuse me.'

[19] "Another said, 'I have just bought five pairs of oxen. I'm on my way to try them out. Please excuse me.'

[20] "Still another said, 'I just got married, so I can't come.'

[21] "The servant came back and reported this to his master. Then the owner of the house became angry. He ordered his servant, 'Go out quickly into the streets and lanes of the town. Bring in those who are poor. Also bring those who can't see or walk.'

[22] " 'Sir,' the servant said, 'what you ordered has been done. But there is still room.'

[23] "Then the master told his servant, 'Go out to the roads. Go out to the country lanes. Make the people come in. I want my house to be full. [24] I tell you, not one of those people who were invited will get a taste of my banquet.' "

The Cost of Being a Disciple

[25] Large crowds were traveling with Jesus. He turned and spoke to them. He said, [26] "Anyone who comes to me must hate their father and mother. They must hate their wife and children. They must hate their brothers and sisters. And they must hate even their own life. Unless they do this, they can't be my disciple. [27] Whoever doesn't carry their cross and follow me can't be my disciple.

[28] "Suppose one of you wants to build a tower. Won't you sit down first and figure out how much it will cost? Then you will see whether you have enough money to finish it. [29] Suppose you start building and are not able to finish. Then everyone who sees what you have done will laugh at you. [30] They will say, 'This person started to build but wasn't able to finish.'

[31] "Or suppose a king is about to go to war against another king. And suppose he has 10,000 men, while the other has 20,000 coming against him. Won't he first sit down and think about whether he can win? [32] And suppose he decides he can't win. Then he will send some men to ask how peace can be made. He will do this while the other king is still far away. [33] In the same way, you must give up everything you have. Those of you who don't cannot be my disciple.

[34] "Salt is good. But suppose it loses its saltiness. How can it be made salty again? [35] It is not good for the soil. And it is not good for the trash pile. It will be thrown out.

"Whoever has ears should listen."

The Story of the Lost Sheep

15 The tax collectors and sinners were all gathering

around to hear Jesus. ²But the Pharisees and the teachers of the law were whispering among themselves. They said, "This man welcomes sinners and eats with them."

³Then Jesus told them a story. ⁴He said, "Suppose one of you has 100 sheep and loses one of them. Won't he leave the 99 in the open country? Won't he go and look for the one lost sheep until he finds it? ⁵When he finds it, he will joyfully put it on his shoulders ⁶and go home. Then he will call his friends and neighbors together. He will say, 'Be joyful with me. I have found my lost sheep.' ⁷I tell you, it will be the same in heaven. There will be great joy when one sinner turns away from sin. Yes, there will be more joy than for 99 godly people who do not need to turn away from their sins.

The Story of the Lost Coin

⁸"Or suppose a woman has ten silver coins and loses one. Won't she light a lamp and sweep the house? Won't she search carefully until she finds the coin? ⁹And when she finds it, she will call her friends and neighbors together. She will say, 'Be joyful with me. I have found my lost coin.' ¹⁰I tell you, it is the same in heaven. There is joy in heaven over one sinner who turns away from sin."

The Story of the Lost Son

¹¹Jesus continued, "There was a man who had two sons. ¹²The younger son spoke to his father.

He said, 'Father, give me my share of the family property.' So the father divided his property between his two sons.

¹³"Not long after that, the younger son packed up all he had. Then he left for a country far away. There he wasted his money on wild living. ¹⁴He spent everything he had. Then the whole country ran low on food. So the son didn't have what he needed. ¹⁵He went to work for someone who lived in that country. That person sent the son to the fields to feed the pigs. ¹⁶The son wanted to fill his stomach with the food the pigs were eating. But no one gave him anything.

¹⁷"Then he began to think clearly again. He said, 'How many of my father's hired servants have more than enough food! But here I am dying from hunger! ¹⁸I will get up and go back to my father. I will say to him, "Father, I have sinned against heaven. And I have sinned against you. ¹⁹I am no longer fit to be called your son. Make me like one of your hired servants." ' ²⁰So he got up and went to his father.

"While the son was still a long way off, his father saw him. He was filled with tender love for his son. He ran to him. He threw his arms around him and kissed him.

²¹"The son said to him, 'Father, I have sinned against heaven and against you. I am no longer fit to be called your son.'

²²"But the father said to his servants, 'Quick! Bring the best

robe and put it on him. Put a ring on his finger and sandals on his feet. ²³ Bring the fattest calf and kill it. Let's have a feast and celebrate. ²⁴ This son of mine was dead. And now he is alive again. He was lost. And now he is found.' So they began to celebrate.

²⁵ "The older son was in the field. When he came near the house, he heard music and dancing. ²⁶ So he called one of the servants. He asked him what was going on. ²⁷ 'Your brother has come home,' the servant replied. 'Your father has killed the fattest calf. He has done this because your brother is back safe and sound.'

²⁸ "The older brother became angry. He refused to go in. So his father went out and begged him. ²⁹ But he answered his father, 'Look! All these years I've worked like a slave for you. I have always obeyed your orders. You never gave me even a young goat so I could celebrate with my friends. ³⁰ But this son of yours wasted your money with some prostitutes. Now he comes home. And for him you kill the fattest calf!'

³¹ " 'My son,' the father said, 'you are always with me. Everything I have is yours. ³² But we had to celebrate and be glad. This brother of yours was dead. And now he is alive again. He was lost. And now he is found.' "

The Story of the Clever Manager

16 Jesus told his disciples another story. He said,

"There was a rich man who had a manager. Some said that the manager was wasting what the rich man owned. ² So the rich man told him to come in. He asked him, 'What is this I hear about you? Tell me exactly how you have handled what I own. You can't be my manager any longer.'

³ "The manager said to himself, 'What will I do now? My master is taking away my job. I'm not strong enough to dig. And I'm too ashamed to beg. ⁴ I know what I'm going to do. I'll do something so that when I lose my job here, people will welcome me into their houses.'

⁵ "So he called in each person who owed his master something. He asked the first one, 'How much do you owe my master?'

⁶ " 'I owe 900 gallons of olive oil,' he replied.

"The manager told him, 'Take your bill. Sit down quickly and change it to 450 gallons.'

⁷ "Then he asked the second one, 'And how much do you owe?'

" 'I owe 1,000 bushels of wheat,' he replied.

"The manager told him, 'Take your bill and change it to 800 bushels.'

⁸ "The manager had not been honest. But the master praised him for being clever. The people of this world are clever in dealing with those who are like themselves. They are more clever than God's people. ⁹ I tell you, use the riches of this world

to help others. In that way, you will make friends for yourselves. Then when your riches are gone, you will be welcomed into your eternal home in heaven.

¹⁰ "Suppose you can be trusted with something very little. Then you can also be trusted with something very large. But suppose you are not honest with something very little. Then you will also not be honest with something very large. ¹¹ Suppose you have not been worthy of trust in handling worldly wealth. Then who will trust you with true riches? ¹² Suppose you have not been worthy of trust in handling someone else's property. Then who will give you property of your own?

¹³ "No one can serve two masters at the same time. Either you will hate one of them and love the other. Or you will be faithful to one and dislike the other. You can't serve God and money at the same time."

¹⁴ The Pharisees loved money. They heard all that Jesus said and made fun of him. ¹⁵ Jesus said to them, "You try to make yourselves look good in the eyes of other people. But God knows your hearts. What people think is worth a lot is hated by God.

More Teachings

¹⁶ "The teachings of the Law and the Prophets were preached until John the Baptist came. Since then, the good news of God's kingdom is being preached. And everyone is trying very hard to enter it. ¹⁷ It is easier for heaven and earth to disappear than for the smallest part of a letter to drop out of the Law.

¹⁸ "Anyone who divorces his wife and marries another woman commits adultery. Also, the man who marries a divorced woman commits adultery.

The Rich Man and Lazarus

¹⁹ "Once there was a rich man. He was dressed in purple cloth and fine linen. He lived an easy life every day. ²⁰ A man named Lazarus was placed at his gate. Lazarus was a beggar. His body was covered with sores. ²¹ Even dogs came and licked his sores. All he wanted was to eat what fell from the rich man's table.

²² "The time came when the beggar died. The angels carried him to Abraham's side. The rich man also died and was buried. ²³ In the place of the dead, the rich man was suffering terribly. He looked up and saw Abraham far away. Lazarus was by his side. ²⁴ So the rich man called out, 'Father Abraham! Have pity on me! Send Lazarus to dip the tip of his finger in water. Then he can cool my tongue with it. I am in terrible pain in this fire.'

²⁵ "But Abraham replied, 'Son, remember what happened in your lifetime. You received your good things. Lazarus received bad things. Now he is comforted here, and you are in terrible pain. ²⁶ Besides, a wide space has been placed between us and you. So those who want to go from here to you can't go.

And no one can cross over from there to us.'

27 "The rich man answered, 'Then I beg you, father Abraham. Send Lazarus to my family. 28 I have five brothers. Let Lazarus warn them. Then they will not come to this place of terrible suffering.'

29 "Abraham replied, 'They have the teachings of Moses and the Prophets. Let your brothers listen to them.'

30 " 'No, father Abraham,' he said. 'But if someone from the dead goes to them, they will turn away from their sins.'

31 "Abraham said to him, 'They do not listen to Moses and the Prophets. So they will not be convinced even if someone rises from the dead.' "

Sin, Faith and Duty

17 Jesus spoke to his disciples. "Things that make people sin are sure to come," he said. "But how terrible it will be for anyone who causes those things to come! 2 Suppose people lead one of these little ones to sin. It would be better for those people to be thrown into the sea with a millstone tied around their neck. 3 So watch what you do.

"If your brother or sister sins against you, tell them they are wrong. Then if they turn away from their sins, forgive them. 4 Suppose they sin against you seven times in one day. And suppose they come back to you each time and say, 'I'm sorry.' You must forgive them."

5 The apostles said to the Lord, "Give us more faith!"

6 He replied, "Suppose you have faith as small as a mustard seed. Then you can say to this mulberry tree, 'Be pulled up. Be planted in the sea.' And it will obey you.

7 "Suppose one of you has a servant plowing or looking after the sheep. And suppose the servant came in from the field. Will you say to him, 'Come along now and sit down to eat'? 8 No. Instead, you will say, 'Prepare my supper. Get yourself ready. Wait on me while I eat and drink. Then after that you can eat and drink.' 9 Will you thank the servant because he did what he was told to do? 10 It's the same with you. Suppose you have done everything you were told to do. Then you should say, 'We are not worthy to serve you. We have only done our duty.' "

Jesus Heals Ten Men Who Have a Skin Disease

11 Jesus was on his way to Jerusalem. He traveled along the border between Samaria and Galilee. 12 As he was going into a village, ten men met him. They had a skin disease. They were standing close by. 13 And they called out in a loud voice, "Jesus! Master! Have pity on us!"

14 Jesus saw them and said, "Go. Show yourselves to the priests." While they were on the way, they were healed.

15 When one of them saw that he was healed, he came back.

He praised God in a loud voice. ¹⁶ He threw himself at Jesus' feet and thanked him. The man was a Samaritan.

¹⁷ Jesus asked, "Weren't all ten healed? Where are the other nine? ¹⁸ Didn't anyone else return and give praise to God except this outsider?" ¹⁹ Then Jesus said to him, "Get up and go. Your faith has healed you."

The Coming of God's Kingdom

²⁰ Once the Pharisees asked Jesus when God's kingdom would come. He replied, "The coming of God's kingdom is not something you can see. ²¹ People will not say, 'Here it is.' Or, 'There it is.' That's because God's kingdom is among you."

²² Then Jesus spoke to his disciples. "The time is coming," he said, "when you will long to see one of the days of the Son of Man. But you won't see it. ²³ People will tell you, 'There he is!' Or, 'Here he is!' Don't go running off after them. ²⁴ When the Son of Man comes, he will be like the lightning. It flashes and lights up the sky from one end to the other. ²⁵ But first the Son of Man must suffer many things. He will not be accepted by the people of today.

²⁶ "Remember how it was in the days of Noah. It will be the same when the Son of Man comes. ²⁷ People were eating and drinking. They were getting married. They were giving their daughters to be married. They did all those things right up to the day Noah entered the ark. Then the flood came and destroyed them all.

²⁸ "It was the same in the days of Lot. People were eating and drinking. They were buying and selling. They were planting and building. ²⁹ But on the day Lot left Sodom, fire and sulfur rained down from heaven. And all the people were destroyed.

³⁰ "It will be just like that on the day the Son of Man is shown to the world. ³¹ Suppose someone is on the housetop on that day. And suppose what they own is inside the house. They should not go down to get what they own. No one in the field should go back for anything either. ³² Remember Lot's wife! ³³ Whoever tries to keep their life will lose it. Whoever loses their life will keep it. ³⁴ I tell you, on that night two people will be in one bed. One person will be taken and the other left. ³⁵⁻³⁶ Two women will be grinding grain together. One will be taken and the other left."

³⁷ "Where, Lord?" his disciples asked.

He replied, "The vultures will gather where there is a dead body."

The Story of the Widow Who Would Not Give Up

18 Jesus told his disciples a story. He wanted to show them that they should always pray and not give up. ² He said, "In a certain town there was a judge. He didn't have any respect for God or care about what people thought. ³ A widow lived in that town. She came to the judge again and again. She kept begging him, 'Make things right for me. Someone is treating me badly.'

[4] "For some time the judge refused. But finally he said to himself, 'I don't have any respect for God. I don't care about what people think. [5] But this widow keeps bothering me. So I will see that things are made right for her. If I don't, she will someday come and attack me!' "

[6] The Lord said, "Listen to what the unfair judge says. [7] God's chosen people cry out to him day and night. Won't he make things right for them? Will he keep putting them off? [8] I tell you, God will see that things are made right for them. He will make sure it happens quickly. But when the Son of Man comes, will he find people on earth who have faith?"

The Story of the Pharisee and the Tax Collector

[9] Jesus told a story to some people who were sure they were right with God. They looked down on everyone else. [10] He said to them, "Two men went up to the temple to pray. One was a Pharisee. The other was a tax collector. [11] The Pharisee stood by himself and prayed. 'God, I thank you that I am not like other people,' he said. 'I am not like robbers or those who do other evil things. I am not like those who commit adultery. I am not even like this tax collec-tor. [12] I fast twice a week. And I give a tenth of all I get.'

[13] "But the tax collector stood farther away than the Pharisee. He would not even look up to heaven. He brought his hand to his heart and prayed. He said, 'God, have mercy on me. I am a sinner.'

[14] "I tell you, the tax collector went home accepted by God. But not the Pharisee. All those who lift themselves up will be made humble. And those who make themselves humble will be lifted up."

Little Children Are Brought to Jesus

[15] People were also bringing babies to Jesus. They wanted him to place his hands on the babies. When the disciples saw this, they told the people to stop. [16] But Jesus asked the children to come to him. "Let the little children come to me," he said. "Don't keep them away. God's kingdom belongs to people like them. [17] What I'm about to tell you is true. Anyone who will not receive God's kingdom like a little child will never enter it."

Rich People and the Kingdom of God

[18] A certain ruler asked Jesus a question. "Good teacher," he said, "what must I do to receive eternal life?"

[19] "Why do you call me good?" Jesus answered. "No one is good except God. [20] You know what the commandments say. 'Do not commit adultery. Do not

commit murder. Do not steal. Do not be a false witness. Honor your father and mother.' " *(Exodus 20:12–16; Deuteronomy 5:16–20)*

²¹ "I have obeyed all those commandments since I was a boy," the ruler said.

²² When Jesus heard this, he said to him, "You are still missing one thing. Sell everything you have. Give the money to those who are poor. You will have treasure in heaven. Then come and follow me."

²³ When the ruler heard this, he became very sad. He was very rich. ²⁴ Jesus looked at him. Then he said, "How hard it is for rich people to enter God's kingdom! ²⁵ Is it hard for a camel to go through the eye of a needle? It is even harder for someone who is rich to enter God's kingdom!"

²⁶ Those who heard this asked, "Then who can be saved?"

²⁷ Jesus replied, "Things that are impossible with people are possible with God."

²⁸ Peter said to him, "We have left everything we had in order to follow you!"

²⁹ "What I'm about to tell you is true," Jesus said to them. "Has anyone left home or wife or husband or brothers or sisters or parents or children for God's kingdom? ³⁰ They will receive many times as much in this world. In the world to come they will receive eternal life."

Jesus Speaks a Third Time About His Coming Death

³¹ Jesus took the 12 disciples to one side. He told them, "We are going up to Jerusalem. Everything that the prophets wrote about the Son of Man will come true. ³² He will be handed over to the Gentiles. They will make fun of him. They will laugh at him and spit on him. ³³ They will whip him and kill him. On the third day, he will rise from the dead!"

³⁴ The disciples did not understand any of this. Its meaning was hidden from them. So they didn't know what Jesus was talking about.

A Blind Beggar Receives His Sight

³⁵ Jesus was approaching Jericho. A blind man was sitting by the side of the road begging. ³⁶ The blind man heard the crowd going by. He asked what was happening. ³⁷ They told him, "Jesus of Nazareth is passing by."

³⁸ So the blind man called out, "Jesus! Son of David! Have mercy on me!"

³⁹ Those who led the way commanded him to stop. They told him to be quiet. But he shouted even louder, "Son of David! Have mercy on me!"

⁴⁰ Jesus stopped and ordered the man to be brought to him. When the man came near, Jesus spoke to him. ⁴¹ "What do you want me to do for you?" Jesus asked.

"Lord, I want to be able to see," the blind man replied.

⁴² Jesus said to him, "Receive your sight. Your faith has healed you." ⁴³ Right away he could see.

He followed Jesus, praising God. When all the people saw it, they also praised God.

Zacchaeus the Tax Collector

19 Jesus entered Jericho and was passing through. ²A man named Zacchaeus lived there. He was a chief tax collector and was very rich. ³Zacchaeus wanted to see who Jesus was. But he was a short man. He could not see Jesus because of the crowd. ⁴So he ran ahead and climbed a sycamore-fig tree. He wanted to see Jesus, who was coming that way.

⁵Jesus reached the spot where Zacchaeus was. He looked up and said, "Zacchaeus, come down at once. I must stay at your house today." ⁶So Zacchaeus came down at once and welcomed him gladly.

⁷All the people saw this. They began to whisper among themselves. They said, "Jesus has gone to be the guest of a sinner."

⁸But Zacchaeus stood up. He said, "Look, Lord! Here and now I give half of what I own to those who are poor. And if I have cheated anybody out of anything, I will pay it back. I will pay back four times the amount I took."

⁹Jesus said to Zacchaeus, "Today salvation has come to your house. You are a member of Abraham's family line. ¹⁰The Son of Man came to look for the lost and save them."

The Story of Three Slaves

¹¹While the people were listening to these things, Jesus told them a story. He was near Jerusalem. The people thought that God's kingdom was going to appear right away. ¹²Jesus said, "A man from an important family went to a country far away. He went there to be made king and then return home. ¹³So he sent for ten of his slaves. He gave them each about three months' pay. 'Put this money to work until I come back,' he said.

¹⁴"But those he ruled over hated him. They sent some messengers after him. They were sent to say, 'We don't want this man to be our king.'

¹⁵"But he was made king and returned home. Then he sent for the slaves he had given the money to. He wanted to find out what they had earned with it.

¹⁶"The first one came to him. He said, 'Sir, your money has earned ten times as much.'

¹⁷"'You have done well, my good slave!' his master replied. 'You have been faithful in a very small matter. So I will put you in charge of ten towns.'

¹⁸"The second slave came to his master. He said, 'Sir, your money has earned five times as much.'

¹⁹"His master answered, 'I will put you in charge of five towns.'

²⁰"Then another slave came. He said, 'Sir, here is your money. I have kept it hidden in a piece of cloth. ²¹I was afraid of you. You are a hard man. You take out what you did not put in. You harvest what you did not plant.'

²²"His master replied, 'I will

judge you by your own words, you evil slave! So you knew that I am a hard man? You knew that I take out what I did not put in? You knew that I harvest what I did not plant? ²³ Then why didn't you put my money in the bank? When I came back, I could have collected it with interest.'

²⁴ "Then he said to those standing by, 'Take his money away from him. Give it to the one who has ten times as much.'

²⁵ " 'Sir,' they said, 'he already has ten times as much!'

²⁶ "He replied, 'I tell you that everyone who has will be given more. But here is what will happen to anyone who has nothing. Even what they have will be taken away from them. ²⁷ And what about my enemies who did not want me to be king over them? Bring them here! Kill them in front of me!' "

Jesus Comes to Jerusalem as King

²⁸ After Jesus had said this, he went on ahead. He was going up to Jerusalem. ²⁹ He approached Bethphage and Bethany. The hill there was called the Mount of Olives. Jesus sent out two of his disciples. He said to them, ³⁰ "Go to the village ahead of you. As soon as you get there, you will find a donkey's colt tied up. No one has ever ridden it. Untie it and bring it here. ³¹ Someone may ask you, 'Why are you untying it?' If so, say, 'The Lord needs it.' "

³² Those who were sent ahead went and found the young don-key. It was there just as Jesus had told them. ³³ They were untying the colt when its owners came. The owners asked them, "Why are you untying the colt?"

³⁴ They replied, "The Lord needs it."

³⁵ Then the disciples brought the colt to Jesus. They threw their coats on the young donkey and put Jesus on it. ³⁶ As he went along, people spread their coats on the road.

³⁷ Jesus came near the place where the road goes down the Mount of Olives. There the whole crowd of disciples began to praise God with joy. In loud voices they praised him for all the miracles they had seen. They shouted,

³⁸ "Blessed is the king who
    comes in the name of the
    Lord!"   *(Psalm 118:26)*

"May there be peace and
    glory in the highest
    heaven!"

³⁹ Some of the Pharisees in the crowd spoke to Jesus. "Teacher," they said, "tell your disciples to stop!"

⁴⁰ "I tell you," he replied, "if they keep quiet, the stones will cry out."

⁴¹ He approached Jerusalem. When he saw the city, he began to weep. ⁴² He said, "I wish you had known today what would bring you peace! But now it is hidden from your eyes. ⁴³ The days will come when your enemies will arrive. They will build a wall of dirt up against your city. They will surround you

and close you in on every side. ⁴⁴ You didn't recognize the time when God came to you. So your enemies will smash you to the ground. They will destroy you and all the people inside your walls. They will not leave one stone on top of another."

Jesus Clears Out the Temple

⁴⁵ Then Jesus entered the temple courtyard. He began to drive out those who were selling there. ⁴⁶ He told them, "It is written that the Lord said, 'My house will be a house where people can pray.' *(Isaiah 56:7)* But you have made it a 'den for robbers.' " *(Jeremiah 7:11)*

⁴⁷ Every day Jesus was teaching at the temple. But the chief priests and the teachers of the law were trying to kill him. So were the leaders among the people. ⁴⁸ But they couldn't find any way to do it. All the people were paying close attention to his words.

The Authority of Jesus Is Questioned

20 One day Jesus was teaching the people in the temple courtyard. He was announcing the good news to them. The chief priests and the teachers of the law came up to him. The elders came with them. ² "Tell us by what authority you are doing these things," they all said. "Who gave you this authority?"

³ Jesus replied, "I will also ask you a question. Tell me, ⁴ was John's baptism from heaven? Or did it come from people?"

⁵ They talked to one another about it. They said, "If we say, 'From heaven,' he will ask, 'Why didn't you believe him?' ⁶ But if we say, 'From people,' all the people will throw stones at us and kill us. They believe that John was a prophet."

⁷ So they answered Jesus, "We don't know where John's baptism came from."

⁸ Jesus said, "Then I won't tell you by what authority I am doing these things either."

The Story of the Renters

⁹ Jesus went on to tell the people a story. "A man planted a vineyard," he said. "He rented it out to some farmers. Then he went away for a long time. ¹⁰ At harvest time he sent a slave to the renters. They were supposed to give him some of the fruit of the vineyard. But the renters beat the slave. Then they sent him away with nothing. ¹¹ So the man sent another slave. They beat that one and treated him badly. They also sent him away with nothing. ¹² The man sent a third slave. The renters wounded him and threw him out.

¹³ "Then the owner of the vineyard said, 'What should I do? I have a son, and I love him. I will send him. Maybe they will respect him.'

¹⁴ "But when the renters saw the son, they talked the matter over. 'This is the one who will receive all the owner's property someday,' they said. 'Let's kill him. Then everything will be

ours.' ¹⁵ So they threw him out of the vineyard. And they killed him.

"What will the owner of the vineyard do to the renters? ¹⁶ He will come and kill them. He will give the vineyard to others."

When the people heard this, they said, "We hope this never happens!"

¹⁷ Jesus looked right at them and said, "Here is something I want you to explain the meaning of. It is written,

" 'The stone the builders
　　didn't accept
　has become the most
　　important stone of all.'
(Psalm 118:22)

¹⁸ Everyone who falls on that stone will be broken to pieces. But the stone will crush anyone it falls on."

¹⁹ The teachers of the law and the chief priests looked for a way to arrest Jesus at once. They knew he had told that story against them. But they were afraid of the people.

Is It Right to Pay the Royal Tax to Caesar?

²⁰ The religious leaders sent spies to keep a close watch on Jesus. The spies pretended to be sincere. They hoped they could trap Jesus with something he would say. Then they could hand him over to the power and authority of the governor. ²¹ So the spies questioned Jesus. "Teacher," they said, "we know that you speak and teach what is right. We know you don't favor one person over another. You teach the way of God truthfully. ²² Is it right for us to pay taxes to Caesar or not?"

²³ Jesus saw they were trying to trick him. So he said to them, ²⁴ "Show me a silver coin. Whose picture and words are on it?"

"Caesar's," they replied.

²⁵ He said to them, "Then give back to Caesar what belongs to Caesar. And give back to God what belongs to God."

²⁶ They were not able to trap him with what he had said there in front of all the people. Amazed by his answer, they became silent.

Marriage When the Dead Rise

²⁷ The Sadducees do not believe that people rise from the dead. Some of them came to Jesus with a question. ²⁸ "Teacher," they said, "Moses wrote for us about a man's brother who dies. Suppose the brother leaves a wife but has no children. Then the man must marry the widow. He must provide children to carry on his dead brother's name. ²⁹ There were seven brothers. The first one married a woman. He died without leaving any children. ³⁰ The second one married her. ³¹ And then the third one married her. One after another, the seven brothers married her. They all died. None left any children. ³² Finally, the woman died too. ³³ Now then, when the dead rise, whose wife will she be? All seven brothers were married to her."

³⁴ Jesus replied, "People in this world get married. And their

parents give them to be married. [35] But it will not be like that when the dead rise. Those who are considered worthy to take part in the world to come won't get married. And their parents won't give them to be married. [36] They can't die anymore. They are like the angels. They are God's children. They will be given a new form of life when the dead rise. [37] Remember the story of Moses and the burning bush. Even Moses showed that the dead rise. The Lord said to him, 'I am the God of Abraham. I am the God of Isaac. And I am the God of Jacob.' *(Exodus 3:6)* [38] He is not the God of the dead. He is the God of the living. In his eyes, everyone is alive."

[39] Some of the teachers of the law replied, "You have spoken well, teacher!" [40] And no one dared to ask him any more questions.

Whose Son Is the Messiah?

[41] Jesus said to them, "Why do people say that the Messiah is the son of David? [42] David himself says in the Book of Psalms,

" 'The Lord said to my Lord,
  "Sit at my right hand
[43] until I put your enemies
  under your control." '
(Psalm 110:1)

[44] David calls him 'Lord.' So how can he be David's son?"

Warning Against the Teachers of the Law

[45] All the people were listening. Jesus said to his disciples,

[46] "Watch out for the teachers of the law. They like to walk around in long robes. They love to be greeted with respect in the market. They love to have the most important seats in the synagogues. They also love to have the places of honor at banquets. [47] They take over the houses of widows. They say long prayers to show off. God will punish these men very much."

The Widow's Offering

21 As Jesus looked up, he saw rich people putting their gifts into the temple offering boxes. [2] He also saw a poor widow put in two very small copper coins. [3] "What I'm about to tell you is true," Jesus said. "That poor widow has put in more than all the others. [4] All these other people gave a lot because they are rich. But even though she is poor, she put in everything. She had nothing left to live on."

When the Temple Will Be Destroyed and the Signs of the End

[5] Some of Jesus' disciples were talking about the temple. They spoke about how it was decorated with beautiful stones and with gifts that honored God. But Jesus asked, [6] "Do you see all this? The time will come when not one stone will be left on top of another. Every stone will be thrown down."

[7] "Teacher," they asked, "when will these things happen? And what will be the sign that they are about to take place?"

⁸Jesus replied, "Keep watch! Be careful that you are not fooled. Many will come in my name. They will claim, 'I am he!' And they will say, 'The time is near!' Do not follow them. ⁹Do not be afraid when you hear about wars and about fighting against rulers. Those things must happen first. But the end will not come right away."

¹⁰Then Jesus said to them, "Nation will fight against nation. Kingdom will fight against kingdom. ¹¹In many places there will be powerful earthquakes. People will go hungry. There will be terrible sicknesses. Things will happen that will make people afraid. There will be great and miraculous signs from heaven.

¹²"But before all this, people will arrest you and treat you badly. They will hand you over to synagogues and put you in prison. You will be brought to kings and governors. All this will happen to you because of my name. ¹³And so you will be witnesses about me. ¹⁴But make up your mind not to worry ahead of time about how to stand up for yourselves. ¹⁵I will give you words of wisdom. None of your enemies will be able to withstand them or prove them wrong. ¹⁶Even your parents, brothers, sisters, relatives and friends will hand you over to the authorities. The authorities will put some of you to death. ¹⁷Everyone will hate you because of me. ¹⁸But not a hair on your head will be harmed. ¹⁹Remain strong in the faith, and you will receive eternal life.

²⁰"A time is coming when you will see armies surround Jerusalem. Then you will know that it will soon be destroyed. ²¹Those who are in Judea should then escape to the mountains. Those in the city should get out. Those in the country should not enter the city. ²²This is the time when God will punish Jerusalem. Everything will come true, just as it has been written. ²³How awful it will be in those days for pregnant women! How awful for nursing mothers! There will be terrible suffering in the land. There will be great anger against those people. ²⁴Some will be killed by the sword. Others will be taken as prisoners to all the nations. Jerusalem will be taken over by Gentiles until the times of the Gentiles come to an end.

²⁵"There will be signs in the sun, moon and stars. The nations of the earth will be in terrible pain. They will be puzzled by the roaring and tossing of the sea. ²⁶Terror will make people faint. They will be worried about what is happening in the world. The sun, moon and stars will be shaken from their places. ²⁷At that time people will see the Son of Man coming in a cloud. He will come with power and great glory. ²⁸When these things begin to take place, stand up. Hold your head up with joy and hope. The time when you will be set free will be very close."

²⁹Jesus told them a story.

"Look at the fig tree and all the trees," he said. [30] "When you see leaves appear on the branches, you know that summer is near. [31] In the same way, when you see these things happening, you will know that God's kingdom is near.

[32] "What I'm about to tell you is true. The people living now will certainly not pass away until all these things have happened. [33] Heaven and earth will pass away. But my words will never pass away.

[34] "Be careful. If you aren't, your hearts will be loaded down with wasteful living, drunkenness and the worries of life. Then the day the Son of Man returns will close on you like a trap. It will happen suddenly. [35] That day will come on every person who lives on the whole earth. [36] Always keep watching. Pray that you will be able to escape all that is about to happen. Also, pray that you will not be judged guilty when the Son of Man comes."

[37] Each day Jesus taught at the temple. And each evening he went to spend the night on the hill called the Mount of Olives. [38] All the people came to the temple early in the morning. They wanted to hear Jesus speak.

Judas Agrees to Hand Jesus Over

22 The Feast of Unleavened Bread, called the Passover, was near. [2] The chief priests and the teachers of the law were looking for a way to get rid of Jesus. They were afraid of the people. [3] Then Satan entered Judas, who was called Iscariot. Judas was one of the 12 disciples. [4] He went to the chief priests and the officers of the temple guard. He talked with them about how he could hand Jesus over to them. [5] They were delighted and agreed to give him money. [6] Judas accepted their offer. He watched for the right time to hand Jesus over to them. He wanted to do it when no crowd was around.

The Last Supper

[7] Then the day of Unleavened Bread came. That was the time the Passover lamb had to be sacrificed. [8] Jesus sent Peter and John on ahead. "Go," he told them. "Prepare for us to eat the Passover meal."

[9] "Where do you want us to prepare for it?" they asked.

[10] Jesus replied, "When you enter the city, a man carrying a jar of water will meet you. Follow him to the house he enters. [11] Then say to the owner of the house, 'The Teacher asks, "Where is the guest room? Where can I eat the Passover meal with my disciples?" ' [12] He will show you a large upstairs room with furniture already in it. Prepare for us to eat there."

[13] Peter and John left. They found things just as Jesus had told them. So they prepared the Passover meal.

[14] When the hour came, Jesus and his apostles took their places at the table. [15] He said to

them, "I have really looked forward to eating this Passover meal with you. I wanted to do this before I suffer. [16] I tell you, I will not eat the Passover meal again until it is celebrated in God's kingdom."

[17] After Jesus took the cup, he gave thanks. He said, "Take this cup and share it among yourselves. [18] I tell you, I will not drink wine with you again until God's kingdom comes."

[19] Then Jesus took bread. He gave thanks and broke it. He handed it to them and said, "This is my body. It is given for you. Every time you eat it, do this in memory of me."

[20] In the same way, after the supper he took the cup. He said, "This cup is the new covenant in my blood. It is poured out for you. [21] But someone here is going to hand me over to my enemies. His hand is with mine on the table. [22] The Son of Man will go to his death, just as God has already decided. But how terrible it will be for the one who hands him over!" [23] The apostles began to ask one another about this. They wondered which one of them would do it.

[24] They also started to argue. They disagreed about which of them was thought to be the most important person. [25] Jesus said to them, "The kings of the Gentiles hold power over their people. And those who order them around call themselves Protectors. [26] But you must not be like that. Instead, the most important among you should be like the youngest. The one who rules should be like the one who serves. [27] Who is more important? Is it the one at the table, or the one who serves? Isn't it the one who is at the table? But I am among you as one who serves. [28] You have stood by me during my troubles. [29] And I give you a kingdom, just as my Father gave me a kingdom. [30] Then you will eat and drink at my table in my kingdom. And you will sit on thrones, judging the 12 tribes of Israel.

[31] "Simon, Simon! Satan has asked to sift all of you disciples like wheat. [32] But I have prayed for you, Simon. I have prayed that your faith will not fail. When you have turned back, help your brothers to be strong."

[33] But Simon replied, "Lord, I am ready to go with you to prison and to death."

[34] Jesus answered, "I tell you, Peter, you will say three times that you don't know me. And you will do it before the rooster crows today."

[35] Then Jesus asked the disciples, "Did you need anything when I sent you without a purse, bag or sandals?"

"Nothing," they answered.

[36] He said to them, "But now if you have a purse, take it. And also take a bag. If you don't have a sword, sell your coat and buy one. [37] It is written, 'He was counted among those who had committed crimes.' (Isaiah 53:12) I tell you that what is written about me must come true. Yes, it is already coming true."

38 The disciples said, "See, Lord, here are two swords." "Two swords are enough!" he replied.

Jesus Prays on the Mount of Olives

39 Jesus went out as usual to the Mount of Olives. His disciples followed him. 40 When they reached the place, Jesus spoke. "Pray that you won't fall into sin when you are tempted," he said to them. 41 Then he went a short distance away from them. There he got down on his knees and prayed. 42 He said, "Father, if you are willing, take this cup of suffering away from me. But do what you want, not what I want." 43 An angel from heaven appeared to Jesus and gave him strength. 44 Because he was very sad and troubled, he prayed even harder. His sweat was like drops of blood falling to the ground.

45 After that, he got up from prayer and went back to the disciples. He found them sleeping. They were worn out because they were very sad. 46 "Why are you sleeping?" he asked them. "Get up! Pray that you won't fall into sin when you are tempted."

Jesus Is Arrested

47 While Jesus was still speaking, a crowd came up. The man named Judas was leading them. He was one of the 12 disciples. Judas approached Jesus to kiss him. 48 But Jesus asked him, "Judas, are you handing over the Son of Man with a kiss?"

49 Jesus' followers saw what was going to happen. So they said, "Lord, should we use our swords against them?" 50 One of them struck the slave of the high priest and cut off his right ear. 51 But Jesus answered, "Stop this!" And he touched the man's ear and healed him.

52 Then Jesus spoke to the chief priests, the officers of the temple guard, and the elders. They had all come for him. "Am I leading a band of armed men against you?" he asked. "Do you have to come with swords and clubs? 53 Every day I was with you in the temple courtyard. And you didn't lay a hand on me. But this is your hour. This is when darkness rules."

Peter Says He Does Not Know Jesus

54 Then the men arrested Jesus and led him away. They took him into the high priest's house. Peter followed from far away. 55 Some people there started a fire in the middle of the courtyard. Then they sat down together. Peter sat down with them. 56 A female servant saw him sitting there in the firelight. She looked closely at him. Then she said, "This man was with Jesus."

57 But Peter said he had not been with him. "Woman, I don't know him," he said.

58 A little later someone else saw Peter. "You also are one of them," he said.

"No," Peter replied. "I'm not!"

59 About an hour later, another

person spoke up. "This fellow must have been with Jesus," he said. "He is from Galilee."

⁶⁰ Peter replied, "Man, I don't know what you're talking about!" Just as he was speaking, the rooster crowed. ⁶¹ The Lord turned and looked right at Peter. Then Peter remembered what the Lord had spoken to him. "The rooster will crow today," Jesus had said. "Before it does, you will say three times that you don't know me." ⁶² Peter went outside. He broke down and cried.

The Guards Make Fun of Jesus

⁶³ There were men guarding Jesus. They began laughing at him and beating him. ⁶⁴ They blindfolded him. They said, "Prophesy! Who hit you?" ⁶⁵ They also said many other things to make fun of him.

Jesus Is Brought to Pilate and Herod

⁶⁶ At dawn the elders of the people met together. These included the chief priests and the teachers of the law. Jesus was led to them. ⁶⁷ "If you are the Messiah," they said, "tell us."

Jesus answered, "If I tell you, you will not believe me. ⁶⁸ And if I asked you, you would not answer. ⁶⁹ But from now on, the Son of Man will be seated at the right hand of the mighty God."

⁷⁰ They all asked, "Are you the Son of God then?"

He replied, "You say that I am."

⁷¹ Then they said, "Why do we need any more witnesses? We have heard it from his own lips."

23 Then the whole group got up and led Jesus off to Pilate. ² They began to bring charges against Jesus. They said, "We have found this man misleading our people. He is against paying taxes to Caesar. And he claims to be Messiah, a king."

³ So Pilate asked Jesus, "Are you the king of the Jews?"

"You have said so," Jesus replied.

⁴ Then Pilate spoke to the chief priests and the crowd. He announced, "I find no basis for a charge against this man."

⁵ But they kept it up. They said, "His teaching stirs up the people all over Judea. He started in Galilee and has come all the way here."

⁶ When Pilate heard this, he asked if the man was from Galilee. ⁷ He learned that Jesus was from Herod's area of authority. So Pilate sent Jesus to Herod. At that time Herod was also in Jerusalem.

⁸ When Herod saw Jesus, he was very pleased. He had been wanting to see Jesus for a long time. He had heard much about him. He hoped to see Jesus perform a sign of some kind. ⁹ Herod asked him many questions, but Jesus gave him no answer. ¹⁰ The chief priests and the teachers of the law were standing there. With loud shouts they brought charges against him. ¹¹ Herod and his soldiers laughed at him and made fun

of him. They dressed him in a beautiful robe. Then they sent him back to Pilate. ¹²That day Herod and Pilate became friends. Before this time they had been enemies.

¹³Pilate called together the chief priests, the rulers and the people. ¹⁴He said to them, "You brought me this man. You said he was turning the people against the authorities. I have questioned him in front of you. I have found no basis for your charges against him. ¹⁵Herod hasn't either. So he sent Jesus back to us. As you can see, Jesus has done nothing that is worthy of death. ¹⁶⁻¹⁷So I will just have him whipped and let him go."

¹⁸But the whole crowd shouted, "Kill this man! But let Barabbas go!" ¹⁹Barabbas had been thrown into prison. He had taken part in a struggle in the city against the authorities. He had also committed murder.

²⁰Pilate wanted to let Jesus go. So he made an appeal to the crowd again. ²¹But they kept shouting, "Crucify him! Crucify him!"

²²Pilate spoke to them for the third time. "Why?" he asked. "What wrong has this man done? I have found no reason to have him put to death. So I will just have him whipped and let him go."

²³But with loud shouts they kept calling for Jesus to be crucified. The people's shouts won out. ²⁴So Pilate decided to give them what they wanted. ²⁵He set free the man they asked for.

The man had been thrown in prison for murder and for fighting against the authorities. Pilate handed Jesus over to them so they could carry out their plans.

Jesus Is Nailed to a Cross

²⁶As the soldiers led Jesus away, they took hold of Simon. Simon was from Cyrene. He was on his way in from the country. They put a wooden cross on his shoulders. Then they made him carry it behind Jesus. ²⁷A large number of people followed Jesus. Some were women whose hearts were filled with sorrow. They cried loudly because of him. ²⁸Jesus turned and said to them, "Daughters of Jerusalem, do not weep for me. Weep for yourselves and for your children. ²⁹The time will come when you will say, 'Blessed are the women who can't have children! Blessed are those who never gave birth or nursed babies!' ³⁰It is written,

" 'The people will say to the
    mountains, "Fall on us!"
They'll say to the hills,
    "Cover us!" '   *(Hosea 10:8)*

³¹People do these things when trees are green. So what will happen when trees are dry?"

³²Two other men were also led out with Jesus to be killed. Both of them had broken the law. ³³The soldiers brought them to the place called the Skull. There they nailed Jesus to the cross. He hung between the two criminals. One was on his right and

one was on his left. ³⁴ Jesus said, "Father, forgive them. They don't know what they are doing." The soldiers divided up his clothes by casting lots.

³⁵ The people stood there watching. The rulers even made fun of Jesus. They said, "He saved others. Let him save himself if he is God's Messiah, the Chosen One."

³⁶ The soldiers also came up and poked fun at him. They offered him wine vinegar. ³⁷ They said, "If you are the king of the Jews, save yourself."

³⁸ A written sign had been placed above him. It read,

THIS IS THE KING OF THE JEWS.

³⁹ One of the criminals hanging there made fun of Jesus. He said, "Aren't you the Messiah? Save yourself! Save us!"

⁴⁰ But the other criminal scolded him. "Don't you have any respect for God?" he said. "Remember, you are under the same sentence of death. ⁴¹ We are being punished fairly. We are getting just what our actions call for. But this man hasn't done anything wrong."

⁴² Then he said, "Jesus, remember me when you come into your kingdom."

⁴³ Jesus answered him, "What I'm about to tell you is true. Today you will be with me in paradise."

Jesus Dies

⁴⁴ It was now about noon. Then darkness covered the whole land until three o'clock.

⁴⁵ The sun had stopped shining. The temple curtain was torn in two. ⁴⁶ Jesus called out in a loud voice, "Father, into your hands I commit my life." After he said this, he took his last breath.

⁴⁷ The Roman commander saw what had happened. He praised God and said, "Jesus was surely a man who did what was right." ⁴⁸ The people had gathered to watch this sight. When they saw what happened, they felt very sad. Then they went away. ⁴⁹ But all those who knew Jesus stood not very far away, watching these things. They included the women who had followed him from Galilee.

Jesus Is Buried

⁵⁰ A man named Joseph was a member of the Jewish Council. He was a good and honest man. ⁵¹ Joseph had not agreed with what the leaders had decided and done. He was from Arimathea, a town in Judea. He himself was waiting for God's kingdom. ⁵² Joseph went to Pilate and asked for Jesus' body. ⁵³ Joseph took it down and wrapped it in linen cloth. Then he placed it in a tomb cut in the rock. No one had ever been buried there. ⁵⁴ It was Preparation Day. The Sabbath day was about to begin.

⁵⁵ The women who had come with Jesus from Galilee followed Joseph. They saw the tomb and how Jesus' body was placed in it. ⁵⁶ Then they went home. There they prepared spices and perfumes. But they rested on the

Sabbath day in order to obey the Law.

Jesus Rises From the Dead

24 It was very early in the morning on the first day of the week. The women took the spices they had prepared. Then they went to the tomb. ²They found the stone rolled away from it. ³When they entered the tomb, they did not find the body of the Lord Jesus. ⁴They were wondering about this. Suddenly two men in clothes as bright as lightning stood beside them. ⁵The women were terrified. They bowed down with their faces to the ground. Then the men said to them, "Why do you look for the living among the dead? ⁶Jesus is not here! He has risen! Remember how he told you he would rise. It was while he was still with you in Galilee. ⁷He said, 'The Son of Man must be handed over to sinful people. He must be nailed to a cross. On the third day he will rise from the dead.'" ⁸Then the women remembered Jesus' words.

⁹They came back from the tomb. They told all these things to the 11 apostles and to all the others. ¹⁰Mary Magdalene, Joanna, Mary the mother of James, and the others with them were the ones who told the apostles. ¹¹But the apostles did not believe the women. Their words didn't make any sense to them. ¹²But Peter got up and ran to the tomb. He bent over and saw the strips of linen lying by themselves. Then he went away, wondering what had happened.

On the Road to Emmaus

¹³That same day two of Jesus' followers were going to a village called Emmaus. It was about seven miles from Jerusalem. ¹⁴They were talking with each other about everything that had happened. ¹⁵As they talked about those things, Jesus himself came up and walked along with them. ¹⁶But God kept them from recognizing him.

¹⁷Jesus asked them, "What are you talking about as you walk along?"

They stood still, and their faces were sad. ¹⁸One of them was named Cleopas. He said to Jesus, "Are you the only person visiting Jerusalem who doesn't know? Don't you know about the things that have happened there in the last few days?"

¹⁹"What things?" Jesus asked.

"About Jesus of Nazareth," they replied. "He was a prophet. He was powerful in what he said and did in the sight of God and all the people. ²⁰The chief priests and our rulers handed Jesus over to be sentenced to death. They nailed him to a cross. ²¹But we had hoped that he was the one who was going to set Israel free. Also, it is the third day since all this happened. ²²Some of our women amazed us too. Early this morning they went to the tomb. ²³But they didn't find his body. So they came and told us what they had seen. They saw angels, who said Jesus was alive. ²⁴Then some of our friends went to the tomb. They saw it was empty, just as the women had said. They didn't see Jesus' body there."

²⁵ Jesus said to them, "How foolish you are! How long it takes you to believe all that the prophets said! ²⁶ Didn't the Messiah have to suffer these things and then receive his glory?" ²⁷ Jesus explained to them what was said about himself in all the Scriptures. He began with Moses and all the Prophets.

²⁸ They approached the village where they were going. Jesus kept walking as if he were going farther. ²⁹ But they tried hard to keep him from leaving. They said, "Stay with us. It is nearly evening. The day is almost over." So he went in to stay with them.

³⁰ He joined them at the table. Then he took bread and gave thanks. He broke it and began to give it to them. ³¹ Their eyes were opened, and they recognized him. But then he disappeared from their sight. ³² They said to each other, "He explained to us what the Scriptures meant. Weren't we excited as he talked with us on the road?"

³³ They got up and returned at once to Jerusalem. There they found the 11 disciples and those with them. They were all gathered together. ³⁴ They were saying, "It's true! The Lord has risen! He has appeared to Simon!" ³⁵ Then the two of them told what had happened to them on the way. They told how they had recognized Jesus when he broke the bread.

Jesus Appears to the Disciples

³⁶ The disciples were still talking about this when Jesus himself suddenly stood among them. He said, "May you have peace!"

³⁷ They were surprised and terrified. They thought they were seeing a ghost. ³⁸ Jesus said to them, "Why are you troubled? Why do you have doubts in your minds? ³⁹ Look at my hands and my feet. It's really me! Touch me and see. A ghost does not have a body or bones. But you can see that I do."

⁴⁰ After he said that, he showed them his hands and feet. ⁴¹ But they still did not believe it. They were amazed and filled with joy. So Jesus asked them, "Do you have anything here to eat?" ⁴² They gave him a piece of cooked fish. ⁴³ He took it and ate it in front of them.

⁴⁴ Jesus said to them, "This is what I told you while I was still with you. Everything written about me in the Law of Moses, the Prophets and the Psalms must come true."

⁴⁵ Then he opened their minds so they could understand the Scriptures. ⁴⁶ He told them, "This is what is written. The Messiah will suffer. He will rise from the dead on the third day. ⁴⁷ His followers will preach in his name. They will tell others to turn away from their sins and be forgiven. People from every nation will hear it, beginning at Jerusalem. ⁴⁸ You have seen these things with your own eyes. ⁴⁹ I am going to send you

what my Father has promised. But for now, stay in the city. Stay there until you have received power from heaven."

Jesus Is Taken Up Into Heaven

50 Jesus led his disciples out to the area near Bethany. Then he lifted up his hands and blessed them. 51 While he was blessing them, he left them. He was taken up into heaven. 52 Then they worshiped him. With great joy, they returned to Jerusalem. 53 Every day they went to the temple, praising God.

John

Introduction:

John was one of Jesus' twelve disciples. Jesus loved John very much. John wrote this Gospel so people would believe in Jesus.

John tells about miracles Jesus did. John called them signs. These signs give proof that Jesus is God. John also shows that Jesus was human. Jesus could get hungry, tired or even sad.

Outline of contents:

The Word Became a Human Being

1 In the beginning, the Word was already there. The Word was with God, and the Word was God. ² He was with God in the beginning. ³ All things were made through him. Nothing that has been made was made without him. ⁴ Life was in him, and that life was the light for all people. ⁵ The light shines in the darkness. But the darkness has not overcome the light.

⁶ There was a man sent from God. His name was John. ⁷ He came to be a witness about that light. He was a witness so that all people might believe. ⁸ John himself was not the light. He came only as a witness to the light.

⁹ The true light that gives light to everyone was coming into the world. ¹⁰ The Word was in the world. And the world was made through him. But the world did not recognize him. ¹¹ He came to what was his own. But his own people did not accept him. ¹² Some people did accept him and did believe in his name. He gave them the right to become children of God. ¹³ To be a child of God has nothing to do with human parents. Children of God are not born because of human choice or because a husband wants them to be born. They are born because of what God does.

¹⁴ The Word became a human being. He made his home with us. We have seen his glory. It is the glory of the One and Only, who came from the Father. And the Word was full of grace and truth.

¹⁵ John was a witness about the Word. John cried out and

said, "This was the one I was talking about. I said, 'He who comes after me is more important than I am. He is more important because he existed before I was born.'" [16] God is full of grace. From him we have all received grace in place of the grace already given. [17] In the past, God gave us grace through the law of Moses. Now, grace and truth come to us through Jesus Christ. [18] No one has ever seen God. But the One and Only is God and is at the Father's side. The one at the Father's side has shown us what God is like.

John the Baptist Says That He Is Not the Messiah

[19] The Jewish leaders in Jerusalem sent priests and Levites to ask John who he was. John spoke the truth to them. [20] He did not try to hide the truth. He spoke to them openly. He said, "I am not the Messiah."

[21] They asked him, "Then who are you? Are you Elijah?"

He said, "I am not."

"Are you the Prophet we've been expecting?" they asked.

"No," he answered.

[22] They asked one last time, "Who are you? Give us an answer to take back to those who sent us. What do you say about yourself?"

[23] John replied, using the words of Isaiah the prophet. John said, "I'm the messenger who is calling out in the desert, 'Make the way for the Lord straight.'" *(Isaiah 40:3)*

[24] The Pharisees who had been sent [25] asked him, "If you are not the Messiah, why are you baptizing people? Why are you doing that if you aren't Elijah or the Prophet we've been expecting?"

[26] "I baptize people with water," John replied. "But someone is standing among you whom you do not know. [27] He is the one who comes after me. I am not good enough to untie his sandals."

[28] This all happened at Bethany on the other side of the Jordan River. That was where John was baptizing.

What John Says About Jesus

[29] The next day John saw Jesus coming toward him. John said, "Look! The Lamb of God! He takes away the sin of the world! [30] This is the one I was talking about. I said, 'A man who comes after me is more important than I am. That's because he existed before I was born.' [31] I did not know him. But God wants to make it clear to Israel who this person is. That's the reason I came baptizing with water."

[32] Then John told them, "I saw the Holy Spirit come down from heaven like a dove. The Spirit remained on Jesus. [33] I myself did not know him. But the one who sent me to baptize with water told me, 'You will see the Spirit come down and remain on someone. He is the one who will baptize with the Holy Spirit.' [34] I have seen it happen. I am a witness that this is God's Chosen One."

John's Disciples Follow Jesus

35 The next day John was there again with two of his disciples. 36 He saw Jesus walking by. John said, "Look! The Lamb of God!"

37 The two disciples heard him say this. So they followed Jesus. 38 Then Jesus turned around and saw them following. He asked, "What do you want?"

They said, "Rabbi, where are you staying?" Rabbi means Teacher.

39 "Come," he replied. "You will see."

So they went and saw where he was staying. They spent the rest of the day with him. It was about four o'clock in the afternoon.

40 Andrew was Simon Peter's brother. Andrew was one of the two disciples who heard what John had said. He had also followed Jesus. 41 The first thing Andrew did was to find his brother Simon. He told him, "We have found the Messiah." Messiah means Christ. 42 And he brought Simon to Jesus.

Jesus looked at him and said, "You are Simon, son of John. You will be called Cephas." Cephas means Peter, or Rock.

Jesus Chooses Philip and Nathanael

43 The next day Jesus decided to leave for Galilee. He found Philip and said to him, "Follow me."

44 Philip was from the town of Bethsaida. So were Andrew and Peter. 45 Philip found Nathanael and told him, "We have found the one whom Moses wrote about in the Law. The prophets also wrote about him. He is Jesus of Nazareth, the son of Joseph."

46 "Nazareth! Can anything good come from there?" Nathanael asked.

"Come and see," said Philip.

47 Jesus saw Nathanael approaching. Here is what Jesus said about him. "He is a true Israelite. Nothing about him is false."

48 "How do you know me?" Nathanael asked.

Jesus answered, "I saw you while you were still under the fig tree. I saw you there before Philip called you."

49 Nathanael replied, "Rabbi, you are the Son of God. You are the king of Israel."

50 Jesus said, "You believe because I told you I saw you under the fig tree. You will see greater things than that." 51 Then he said to the disciples, "What I'm about to tell you is true. You will see heaven open. You will see the angels of God going up and coming down on the Son of Man."

Jesus Changes Water Into Wine

2 On the third day there was a wedding. It took place at Cana in Galilee. Jesus' mother was there. 2 Jesus and his disciples had also been invited to the wedding. 3 When the wine was gone, Jesus' mother said to him, "They have no more wine."

4 "Dear woman, why are you telling me about this?" Jesus replied. "The time for me to show who I really am isn't here yet."

⁵His mother said to the servants, "Do what he tells you."

⁶Six stone water jars stood nearby. The Jews used water from that kind of jar for special washings. They did that to make themselves pure and "clean." Each jar could hold 20 to 30 gallons.

⁷Jesus said to the servants, "Fill the jars with water." So they filled them to the top.

⁸Then he told them, "Now dip some out. Take it to the person in charge of the dinner."

They did what he said. ⁹The person in charge tasted the water that had been turned into wine. He didn't realize where it had come from. But the servants who had brought the water knew. Then the person in charge called the groom to one side. ¹⁰He said to him, "Everyone brings out the best wine first. They bring out the cheaper wine after the guests have had too much to drink. But you have saved the best until now."

¹¹What Jesus did here in Cana in Galilee was the first of his signs. Jesus showed his glory by doing this sign. And his disciples believed in him.

¹²After this, Jesus went down to Capernaum. His mother and brothers and disciples went with him. They all stayed there for a few days.

Jesus Clears Out the Temple Courtyard

¹³It was almost time for the Jewish Passover Feast. So Jesus went up to Jerusalem. ¹⁴In the temple courtyard he found people selling cattle, sheep and doves. Others were sitting at tables exchanging money. ¹⁵So Jesus made a whip out of ropes. He chased all the sheep and cattle from the temple courtyard. He scattered the coins of the people exchanging money. And he turned over their tables. ¹⁶He told those who were selling doves, "Get these out of here! Stop turning my Father's house into a market!" ¹⁷His disciples remembered what had been written. It says, "My great love for your house will destroy me." *(Psalm 69:9)*

¹⁸Then the Jewish leaders asked him, "What sign can you show us to prove your authority to do this?"

¹⁹Jesus answered them, "When you destroy this temple, I will raise it up again in three days."

²⁰They replied, "It has taken 46 years to build this temple. Are you going to raise it up in three days?" ²¹But the temple Jesus had spoken about was his body. ²²His disciples later remembered what he had said. That was after he had been raised from the dead. Then they believed the Scripture. They also believed the words that Jesus had spoken.

²³Meanwhile, he was in Jerusalem at the Passover Feast. Many people saw the signs he was doing. And they believed in his name. ²⁴But Jesus did not fully trust them. He knew what

people are like. ²⁵ He didn't need anyone to tell him what people are like. He already knew why people do what they do.

Jesus Teaches Nicodemus

3 There was a Pharisee named Nicodemus. He was one of the Jewish rulers. ²He came to Jesus at night and said, "Rabbi, we know that you are a teacher who has come from God. We know that God is with you. If he weren't, you couldn't do the signs you are doing."

³ Jesus replied, "What I'm about to tell you is true. No one can see God's kingdom unless they are born again."

⁴ "How can someone be born when they are old?" Nicodemus asked. "They can't go back inside their mother! They can't be born a second time!"

⁵ Jesus answered, "What I'm about to tell you is true. No one can enter God's kingdom unless they are born with water and the Holy Spirit. ⁶ People give birth to people. But the Spirit gives birth to spirit. ⁷ You should not be surprised when I say, 'You must all be born again.' ⁸ The wind blows where it wants to. You hear the sound it makes. But you can't tell where it comes from or where it is going. It is the same with everyone who is born with the Spirit."

⁹ "How can this be?" Nicodemus asked.

¹⁰ "You are Israel's teacher," said Jesus. "Don't you understand these things? ¹¹ What I'm about to tell you is true. We speak about what we know. We are witnesses about what we have seen. But still you people do not accept what we say. ¹² I have spoken to you about earthly things, and you do not believe. So how will you believe if I speak about heavenly things? ¹³ No one has ever gone into heaven except the one who came from heaven. He is the Son of Man. ¹⁴ Moses lifted up the snake in the desert. In the same way, the Son of Man must also be lifted up. ¹⁵ Then everyone who believes may have eternal life in him."

¹⁶ God so loved the world that he gave his one and only Son. Anyone who believes in him will not die but will have eternal life. ¹⁷ God did not send his Son into the world to judge the world. He sent his Son to save the world through him. ¹⁸ Anyone who believes in him is not judged. But anyone who does not believe is judged already. They have not believed in the name of God's one and only Son. ¹⁹ Here is the judgment. Light has come into the world, but people loved darkness instead of light. They loved darkness because what they did was evil. ²⁰ Everyone who does evil deeds hates the light. They will not come into the light. They are afraid that what they do will be seen. ²¹ But anyone who lives by the truth comes into the light. They live by the truth with God's help. They come into the light so that it will be easy to see their good deeds.

John the Baptist Is a Witness About Jesus

²²After this, Jesus and his disciples went out into the countryside of Judea. There he spent some time with them. And he baptized people there. ²³John was also baptizing. He was at Aenon near Salim, where there was plenty of water. People were coming and being baptized. ²⁴This was before John was put in prison. ²⁵Some of John's disciples and a certain Jew began to argue. They argued about special washings to make people "clean." ²⁶They came to John and here is what they said to him. "Rabbi, that man who was with you on the other side of the Jordan River is baptizing people. He is the one you told us about. Everyone is going to him."

²⁷John replied, "A person can receive only what God gives them from heaven. ²⁸You yourselves are witnesses that I said, 'I am not the Messiah. I was sent ahead of him.' ²⁹The bride belongs to the groom. The friend who helps the groom waits and listens for him. He is full of joy when he hears the groom's voice. That joy is mine, and it is now complete. ³⁰He must become more important. I must become less important.

³¹"The one who comes from above is above everything. The one who is from the earth belongs to the earth and speaks like someone from the earth. The one who comes from heaven is above everything. ³²He is a witness to what he has seen and heard. But no one accepts what he says. ³³Anyone who has accepted it has said, 'Yes. God is truthful.' ³⁴The one whom God has sent speaks God's words. That's because God gives the Holy Spirit without limit. ³⁵The Father loves the Son and has put everything into his hands. ³⁶Anyone who believes in the Son has eternal life. Anyone who does not believe in the Son will not have life. God's anger remains on them."

Jesus Talks With a Woman From Samaria

4 Now Jesus learned that the Pharisees had heard about him. They had heard that he was gaining and baptizing more disciples than John. ²But in fact Jesus was not baptizing. His disciples were. ³So Jesus left Judea and went back again to Galilee.

⁴Jesus had to go through Samaria. ⁵He came to a town in Samaria called Sychar. It was near the piece of land Jacob had given his son Joseph. ⁶Jacob's well was there. Jesus was tired from the journey. So he sat down by the well. It was about noon.

⁷A woman from Samaria came to get some water. Jesus said to her, "Will you give me a drink?" ⁸His disciples had gone into the town to buy food.

⁹The Samaritan woman said to him, "You are a Jew. I am a Samaritan woman. How can you ask me for a drink?" She said

this because Jews don't have anything to do with Samaritans.

¹⁰ Jesus answered her, "You do not know what God's gift is. And you do not know who is asking you for a drink. If you did, you would have asked him. He would have given you living water."

¹¹ "Sir," the woman said, "you don't have anything to get water with. The well is deep. Where can you get this living water? ¹² Our father Jacob gave us the well. He drank from it himself. So did his sons and his livestock. Are you more important than he is?"

¹³ Jesus answered, "Everyone who drinks this water will be thirsty again. ¹⁴ But anyone who drinks the water I give them will never be thirsty. In fact, the water I give them will become a spring of water in them. It will flow up into eternal life."

¹⁵ The woman said to him, "Sir, give me this water. Then I will never be thirsty. And I won't have to keep coming here to get water."

¹⁶ He told her, "Go. Get your husband and come back."

¹⁷ "I have no husband," she replied.

Jesus said to her, "You are right when you say you have no husband. ¹⁸ The fact is, you have had five husbands. And the man you live with now is not your husband. What you have just said is very true."

¹⁹ "Sir," the woman said, "I can see that you are a prophet. ²⁰ Our people have always worshiped on this mountain. But you Jews claim that the place where we must worship is in Jerusalem."

²¹ Jesus said, "Woman, believe me. A time is coming when you will not worship the Father on this mountain or in Jerusalem. ²² You Samaritans worship what you do not know. We worship what we do know. Salvation comes from the Jews. ²³ But a new time is coming. In fact, it is already here. True worshipers will worship the Father in the Spirit and in truth. They are the kind of worshipers the Father is looking for. ²⁴ God is spirit. His worshipers must worship him in the Spirit and in truth."

²⁵ The woman said, "I know that Messiah is coming." Messiah means Christ. "When he comes, he will explain everything to us."

²⁶ Then Jesus said, "The one you're talking about is the one speaking to you. I am he."

The Disciples Join Jesus Again

²⁷ Just then Jesus' disciples returned. They were surprised to find him talking with a woman. But no one asked, "What do you want from her?" No one asked, "Why are you talking with her?"

²⁸ The woman left her water jar and went back to the town. She said to the people, ²⁹ "Come. See a man who told me everything I've ever done. Could this be the Messiah?" ³⁰ The people came out of the town and made their way toward Jesus.

³¹ His disciples were saying to him, "Rabbi, eat something!"

³²But he said to them, "I have food to eat that you know nothing about."

³³Then his disciples asked each other, "Did someone bring him food?"

³⁴Jesus said, "My food is to do what my Father sent me to do. My food is to finish his work. ³⁵Don't you have a saying? You say, 'It's still four months until harvest time.' But I tell you, open your eyes! Look at the fields! They are ripe for harvest right now. ³⁶Even now the one who gathers the crop is getting paid. They are already harvesting the crop for eternal life. So the one who plants and the one who gathers can now be glad together. ³⁷Here is a true saying. 'One plants and another gathers.' ³⁸I sent you to gather what you have not worked for. Others have done the hard work. You have gathered the benefits of their work."

Many Samaritans Believe in Jesus

³⁹Many of the Samaritans from the town of Sychar believed in Jesus. They believed because of what the woman had said about him. She said, "He told me everything I've ever done." ⁴⁰Then the Samaritans came to him and tried to get him to stay with them. So he stayed two days. ⁴¹Because of what he said, many more people became believers.

⁴²They said to the woman, "We no longer believe just because of what you said. We have now heard for ourselves. We know that this man really is the Savior of the world."

Jesus Heals an Official's Son

⁴³After the two days, Jesus left for Galilee. ⁴⁴He himself had pointed out that a prophet is not respected in his own country. ⁴⁵When he arrived in Galilee, the people living there welcomed him. They had seen everything he had done in Jerusalem at the Passover Feast. That was because they had also been there.

⁴⁶Once more, Jesus visited Cana in Galilee. Cana is where he had turned the water into wine. A royal official was there. His son was sick in bed at Capernaum. ⁴⁷The official heard that Jesus had arrived in Galilee from Judea. So he went to Jesus and begged him to come and heal his son. The boy was close to death.

⁴⁸Jesus told him, "You people will never believe unless you see signs and wonders."

⁴⁹The royal official said, "Sir, come down before my child dies."

⁵⁰"Go," Jesus replied. "Your son will live."

The man believed what Jesus said, and so he left. ⁵¹While he was still on his way home, his slaves met him. They gave him the news that his boy was living. ⁵²He asked what time his son got better. They said to him, "Yesterday, at one o'clock in the afternoon, the fever left him."

⁵³Then the father realized

what had happened. That was the exact time Jesus had said to him, "Your son will live." So he and his whole family became believers.

⁵⁴ This was the second sign that Jesus did after coming from Judea to Galilee.

Jesus Heals a Man at the Pool

5 Some time later, Jesus went up to Jerusalem for one of the Jewish feasts. ² In Jerusalem near the Sheep Gate is a pool. In the Aramaic language it is called Bethesda. It is surrounded by five rows of columns with a roof over them. ³⁻⁴ Here a great number of disabled people used to lie down. Among them were those who were blind, those who could not walk, and those who could hardly move. ⁵ One person was there who had not been able to walk for 38 years. ⁶ Jesus saw him lying there. He knew that the man had been in that condition for a long time. So he asked him, "Do you want to get well?"

⁷ "Sir," the disabled man replied, "I have no one to help me into the pool when an angel stirs up the water. I try to get in, but someone else always goes down ahead of me."

⁸ Then Jesus said to him, "Get up! Pick up your mat and walk." ⁹ The man was healed right away. He picked up his mat and walked.

This happened on a Sabbath day. ¹⁰ So the Jewish leaders said to the man who had been healed, "It is the Sabbath day. The law does not allow you to carry your mat."

¹¹ But he replied, "The one who made me well said to me, 'Pick up your mat and walk.'"

¹² They asked him, "Who is this fellow? Who told you to pick it up and walk?"

¹³ The one who was healed had no idea who it was. Jesus had slipped away into the crowd that was there.

¹⁴ Later Jesus found him at the temple. Jesus said to him, "See, you are well again. Stop sinning, or something worse may happen to you." ¹⁵ The man went away. He told the Jewish leaders it was Jesus who had made him well.

The Authority of the Son

¹⁶ Jesus was doing these things on the Sabbath day. So the Jewish leaders began to oppose him. ¹⁷ Jesus defended himself. He said to them, "My Father is always doing his work. He is working right up to this day. I am working too." ¹⁸ For this reason the Jewish leaders tried even harder to kill him. According to them, Jesus was not only breaking the law of the Sabbath day. He was even calling God his own Father. He was making himself equal with God.

¹⁹ Jesus answered, "What I'm about to tell you is true. The Son can do nothing by himself. He can do only what he sees his Father doing. What the Father does, the Son also does. ²⁰ This is because the Father loves the Son. The Father shows him ev-

erything he does. Yes, and the Father will show the Son even greater works than these. And you will be amazed. ²¹ The Father raises the dead and gives them life. In the same way, the Son gives life to anyone he wants to. ²² Also, the Father does not judge anyone. He has given the Son the task of judging. ²³ Then all people will honor the Son just as they honor the Father. Whoever does not honor the Son does not honor the Father, who sent him.

²⁴ "What I'm about to tell you is true. Anyone who hears my word and believes him who sent me has eternal life. They will not be judged. They have crossed over from death to life. ²⁵ What I'm about to tell you is true. A time is coming for me to give life. In fact, it has already begun. The dead will hear the voice of the Son of God. Those who hear it will live. ²⁶ The Father has life in himself. He has allowed the Son also to have life in himself. ²⁷ And the Father has given him the authority to judge. This is because he is the Son of Man.

²⁸ "Do not be amazed at this. A time is coming when all who are in their graves will hear his voice. ²⁹ They will all come out of their graves. People who have done what is good will rise and live again. People who have done what is evil will rise and be found guilty. ³⁰ I can do nothing by myself. I judge only as I hear. And my judging is fair. I do not try to please myself. I try to please the one who sent me.

Being a Witness About Jesus

³¹ "If I am a witness about myself, what I say is not true. ³² There is someone else who is a witness in my favor. And I know that what he says about me is true.

³³ "You have sent people to John the Baptist. He has been a witness to the truth. ³⁴ I do not accept what a person says. I only talk about what John says so that you can be saved. ³⁵ John was like a lamp that burned and gave light. For a while you chose to enjoy his light.

³⁶ "What I say about myself is more important than what John says about me. I am doing the works the Father gave me to finish. These works are a witness that the Father has sent me. ³⁷ The Father who sent me is himself a witness about me. You have never heard his voice. You have never seen what he really looks like. ³⁸ And his word does not live in you. That's because you do not believe the one he sent. ³⁹ You study the Scriptures carefully. You study them because you think they will give you eternal life. The Scriptures you study are a witness about me. ⁴⁰ But you refuse to come to me and receive life.

⁴¹ "I do not accept praise from human beings. ⁴² But I know you. I know that you do not have love for God in your hearts. ⁴³ I have come in my Father's name, and you do not accept me. But if someone else comes in his own name, you will accept him. ⁴⁴ You accept praise from one

another. But you do not seek the praise that comes from the only God. So how can you believe? [45] "Do not think I will bring charges against you in front of the Father. Moses is the one who does that. And he is the one you build your hopes on. [46] Do you believe Moses? Then you should believe me. He wrote about me. [47] But you do not believe what he wrote. So how are you going to believe what I say?"

Jesus Feeds the Five Thousand

6 Some time after this, Jesus crossed over to the other side of the Sea of Galilee. It is also called the Sea of Tiberias. [2] A large crowd of people followed him. They had seen the signs he had done by healing sick people. [3] Then Jesus went up on a mountainside. There he sat down with his disciples. [4] The Jewish Passover Feast was near.

[5] Jesus looked up and saw a large crowd coming toward him. So he said to Philip, "Where can we buy bread for these people to eat?" [6] He asked this only to test Philip. He already knew what he was going to do.

[7] Philip answered him, "Suppose we were able to buy enough bread for each person to have just a bite. That would take more than half a year's pay!"

[8] Another of his disciples spoke up. It was Andrew, Simon Peter's brother. He said, [9] "Here is a boy with five small loaves of barley bread. He also has two small fish. But how far will that go in such a large crowd?"

[10] Jesus said, "Have the people sit down." There was plenty of grass in that place, and they sat down. About 5,000 men were there. [11] Then Jesus took the loaves and gave thanks. He handed out the bread to those who were seated. He gave them as much as they wanted. And he did the same with the fish.

[12] When all of them had enough to eat, Jesus spoke to his disciples. "Gather the leftover pieces," he said. "Don't waste anything." [13] So they gathered what was left over from the five barley loaves. They filled 12 baskets with the pieces left by those who had eaten.

[14] The people saw the sign that Jesus did. Then they began to say, "This must be the Prophet who is supposed to come into the world." [15] But Jesus knew that they planned to come and force him to be their king. So he went away again to a mountain by himself.

Jesus Walks on the Water

[16] When evening came, Jesus' disciples went down to the Sea of Galilee. [17] There they got into a boat and headed across the lake toward Capernaum. By now it was dark. Jesus had not yet joined them. [18] A strong wind was blowing, and the water became rough. [19] They rowed about three or four miles. Then they saw Jesus coming toward the boat. He was walking on the water. They were frightened. [20] But he said to them, "It is I. Don't be afraid." [21] Then they

agreed to take him into the boat. Right away the boat reached the shore where they were heading.

22 The next day the crowd that had stayed on the other side of the lake realized something. They saw that only one boat had been there. They knew that Jesus had not gotten into it with his disciples. And they knew that the disciples had gone away alone. 23 Then some boats arrived from Tiberias. It was near the place where the people had eaten the bread after the Lord gave thanks. 24 The crowd realized that Jesus and his disciples were not there. So they got into boats and went to Capernaum to look for Jesus.

Jesus Is the Bread of Life

25 They found him on the other side of the lake. They asked him, "Rabbi, when did you get here?"

26 Jesus answered, "What I'm about to tell you is true. You are not looking for me because you saw the signs I did. You are looking for me because you ate the loaves until you were full. 27 Do not work for food that spoils. Work for food that lasts forever. That is the food the Son of Man will give you. For God the Father has put his seal of approval on him."

28 Then they asked him, "What does God want from us? What works does he want us to do?"

29 Jesus answered, "God's work is to believe in the one he has sent."

30 So they asked him, "What sign will you give us? What will you do so we can see it and believe you? 31 Long ago our people ate the manna in the desert. It is written in Scripture, 'The Lord gave them bread from heaven to eat.'" *(Exodus 16:4; Nehemiah 9:15; Psalm 78:24,25)*

32 Jesus said to them, "What I'm about to tell you is true. It is not Moses who has given you the bread from heaven. It is my Father who gives you the true bread from heaven. 33 The bread of God is the bread that comes down from heaven. He gives life to the world."

34 "Sir," they said, "always give us this bread."

35 Then Jesus said, "I am the bread of life. Whoever comes to me will never go hungry. And whoever believes in me will never be thirsty. 36 But it is just as I told you. You have seen me, and you still do not believe. 37 Everyone the Father gives me will come to me. I will never send away anyone who comes to me. 38 I have not come down from heaven to do what I want to do. I have come to do what the one who sent me wants me to do. 39 The one who sent me doesn't want me to lose anyone he has given me. He wants me to raise them up on the last day. 40 My Father wants all who look to the Son and believe in him to have eternal life. I will raise them up on the last day."

41 Then the Jews there began to complain about Jesus. That was because he said, "I am the bread that came down from

heaven." ⁴²They said, "Isn't this Jesus, the son of Joseph? Don't we know his father and mother? How can he now say, 'I came down from heaven'?"

⁴³"Stop complaining among yourselves," Jesus answered. ⁴⁴"No one can come to me unless the Father who sent me brings them. Then I will raise them up on the last day. ⁴⁵It is written in the Prophets, 'God will teach all of them.' *(Isaiah 54:13)* Everyone who has heard the Father and learned from him comes to me. ⁴⁶No one has seen the Father except the one who has come from God. Only he has seen the Father. ⁴⁷What I'm about to tell you is true. Everyone who believes has life forever. ⁴⁸I am the bread of life. ⁴⁹Long ago your people ate the manna in the desert, and they still died. ⁵⁰But here is the bread that comes down from heaven. A person can eat it and not die. ⁵¹I am the living bread that came down from heaven. Everyone who eats some of this bread will live forever. This bread is my body. I will give it for the life of the world."

⁵²Then the Jews began to argue sharply among themselves. They said, "How can this man give us his body to eat?"

⁵³Jesus said to them, "What I'm about to tell you is true. You must eat the Son of Man's body and drink his blood. If you don't, you have no life in you. ⁵⁴Anyone who eats my body and drinks my blood has eternal life. I will raise them up on the last day. ⁵⁵My body is real food. My blood is real drink. ⁵⁶Anyone who eats my body and drinks my blood remains in me. And I remain in them. ⁵⁷The living Father sent me, and I live because of him. In the same way, those who feed on me will live because of me. ⁵⁸This is the bread that came down from heaven. Long ago your people ate manna and died. But whoever eats this bread will live forever." ⁵⁹He said this while he was teaching in the synagogue in Capernaum.

Many Disciples Leave Jesus

⁶⁰Jesus' disciples heard this. Many of them said, "This is a hard teaching. Who can accept it?"

⁶¹Jesus was aware that his disciples were complaining about his teaching. So he said to them, "Does this upset you? ⁶²Then what if you see the Son of Man go up to where he was before? ⁶³The Holy Spirit gives life. The body means nothing at all. The words I have spoken to you are full of the Spirit. They give life. ⁶⁴But there are some of you who do not believe." Jesus had known from the beginning which of them did not believe. And he had known who was going to hand him over to his enemies. ⁶⁵So he continued speaking. He said, "This is why I told you that no one can come to me unless the Father helps them."

⁶⁶From this time on, many of his disciples turned back. They no longer followed him.

⁶⁷ "You don't want to leave also, do you?" Jesus asked the 12 disciples.

⁶⁸ Simon Peter answered him, "Lord, who can we go to? You have the words of eternal life. ⁶⁹ We have come to believe and to know that you are the Holy One of God."

⁷⁰ Then Jesus replied, "Didn't I choose you, the 12 disciples? But one of you is a devil!" ⁷¹ He meant Judas, the son of Simon Iscariot. Judas was one of the 12 disciples. But later he was going to hand Jesus over to his enemies.

Jesus Goes to the Feast of Booths

7 After this, Jesus went around in Galilee. He didn't want to travel around in Judea. That was because the Jewish leaders there were looking for a way to kill him. ² The Jewish Feast of Booths was near. ³ Jesus' brothers said to him, "Leave Galilee and go to Judea. Then your disciples there will see the works that you do. ⁴ No one who wants to be well known does things in secret. Since you are doing these things, show yourself to the world." ⁵ Even Jesus' own brothers did not believe in him.

⁶ So Jesus told them, "The time for me to show who I really am is not here yet. For you, any time would be the right time. ⁷ The people of the world can't hate you. But they hate me. This is because I am a witness that their works are evil. ⁸ You go to the feast. I am not going up to this feast. This is because my time

has not yet fully come." ⁹ After he said this, he stayed in Galilee.

¹⁰ But when his brothers had left for the feast, he went also. But he went secretly, not openly. ¹¹ At the feast the Jewish leaders were watching for Jesus. They were asking, "Where is he?"

¹² Many people in the crowd were whispering about him. Some said, "He is a good man."

Others replied, "No. He fools the people." ¹³ But no one would say anything about him openly. They were afraid of the leaders.

Jesus Teaches at the Feast

¹⁴ Jesus did nothing until halfway through the feast. Then he went up to the temple courtyard and began to teach. ¹⁵ The Jews there were amazed. They asked, "How did this man learn so much without being taught?"

¹⁶ Jesus answered, "What I teach is not my own. It comes from the one who sent me. ¹⁷ Here is how someone can find out whether my teaching comes from God or from me. That person must choose to do what God wants them to do. ¹⁸ Whoever speaks on their own does it to get personal honor. But someone who works for the honor of the one who sent him is truthful. Nothing about him is false. ¹⁹ Didn't Moses give you the law? But not one of you obeys the law. Why are you trying to kill me?"

²⁰ "You are controlled by demons," the crowd answered. "Who is trying to kill you?"

²¹ Jesus said to them, "I did one miracle, and you are all amazed.

22 Moses gave you circumcision, and so you circumcise a child on the Sabbath day. But circumcision did not really come from Moses. It came from Abraham. 23 You circumcise a boy on the Sabbath day. You think that if you do, you won't break the law of Moses. Then why are you angry with me? I healed a man's entire body on the Sabbath day! 24 Stop judging only by what you see. Judge in the right way."

People Don't Agree About Who Jesus Is

25 Then some of the people of Jerusalem began asking questions. They said, "Isn't this the man some people are trying to kill? 26 Here he is! He is speaking openly. They aren't saying a word to him. Have the authorities really decided that he is the Messiah? 27 But we know where this man is from. When the Messiah comes, no one will know where he is from."

28 Jesus was still teaching in the temple courtyard. He cried out, "Yes, you know me. And you know where I am from. I am not here on my own authority. The one who sent me is true. You do not know him. 29 But I know him. I am from him, and he sent me."

30 When he said this, they tried to arrest him. But no one laid a hand on him. The time for him to show who he really was had not yet come. 31 Still, many people in the crowd believed in him. They said, "How will it be when the Messiah comes? Will he do more signs than this man?"

32 The Pharisees heard the crowd whispering things like this about him. Then the chief priests and the Pharisees sent temple guards to arrest him.

33 Jesus said, "I am with you for only a short time. Then I will go to the one who sent me. 34 You will look for me, but you won't find me. You can't come where I am going."

35 The Jews said to one another, "Where does this man plan to go? Does he think we can't find him? Will he go where our people live scattered among the Greeks? Will he go there to teach the Greeks? 36 What did he mean when he said, 'You will look for me, but you won't find me'? And what did he mean when he said, 'You can't come where I am going'?"

37 It was the last and most important day of the feast. Jesus stood up and spoke in a loud voice. He said, "Let anyone who is thirsty come to me and drink. 38 Does anyone believe in me? Then, just as Scripture says, rivers of living water will flow from inside them." 39 When he said this, he meant the Holy Spirit. Those who believed in Jesus would receive the Spirit later. Up to that time, the Spirit had not been given. This was because Jesus had not yet received glory.

40 The people heard his words. Some of them said, "This man must be the Prophet we've been expecting."

41 Others said, "He is the Messiah."

Still others asked, "How can

the Messiah come from Galilee? ⁴²Doesn't Scripture say that the Messiah will come from the family line of David? Doesn't it say that he will come from Bethlehem, the town where David lived?" ⁴³So the people did not agree about who Jesus was. ⁴⁴Some wanted to arrest him. But no one laid a hand on him.

The Jewish Leaders Do Not Believe

⁴⁵Finally the temple guards went back to the chief priests and the Pharisees. They asked the guards, "Why didn't you bring him in?"

⁴⁶"No one ever spoke the way this man does," the guards replied.

⁴⁷"You mean he has fooled you also?" the Pharisees asked. ⁴⁸"Have any of the rulers or Pharisees believed in him? ⁴⁹No! But this mob knows nothing about the law. There is a curse on them."

⁵⁰Then Nicodemus, a Pharisee, spoke. He was the one who had gone to Jesus earlier. He asked, ⁵¹"Does our law find a man guilty without hearing him first? Doesn't it want to find out what he is doing?"

⁵²They replied, "Are you from Galilee too? Look into it. You will find that a prophet does not come out of Galilee."

8 ⁵³Then they all went home. ¹But Jesus went to the Mount of Olives.

²At sunrise he arrived again in the temple courtyard. All the people gathered around him there. He sat down to teach them. ³The teachers of the law and the Pharisees brought in a woman. She had been caught committing adultery. They made her stand in front of the group. ⁴They said to Jesus, "Teacher, this woman was caught sleeping with a man who was not her husband. ⁵In the Law, Moses commanded us to kill such women by throwing stones at them. Now what do you say?" ⁶They were trying to trap Jesus with that question. They wanted to have a reason to bring charges against him.

But Jesus bent down and started to write on the ground with his finger. ⁷They kept asking him questions. So he stood up and said to them, "Has any one of you not sinned? Then you be the first to throw a stone at her." ⁸He bent down again and wrote on the ground.

⁹Those who heard what he had said began to go away. They left one at a time, the older ones first. Soon only Jesus was left. The woman was still standing there. ¹⁰Jesus stood up and asked her, "Woman, where are they? Hasn't anyone found you guilty?"

¹¹"No one, sir," she said.

"Then I don't find you guilty either," Jesus said. "Go now and leave your life of sin."

Challenge to What Jesus Says About Himself

¹²Jesus spoke to the people again. He said, "I am the light of the world. Anyone who follows

me will never walk in darkness. They will have that light. They will have life."

¹³ The Pharisees argued with him. "Here you are," they said, "appearing as your own witness. But your witness does not count."

¹⁴ Jesus answered, "Even if I am a witness about myself, what I say does count. I know where I came from. And I know where I am going. But you have no idea where I come from or where I am going. ¹⁵ You judge by human standards. I don't judge anyone. ¹⁶ But if I do judge, what I decide is true. This is because I am not alone. I stand with the Father, who sent me. ¹⁷ Your own Law says that the witness of two people proves the truth about something. ¹⁸ I am a witness about myself. The other witness about me is the Father, who sent me."

¹⁹ Then they asked him, "Where is your father?"

"You do not know me or my Father," Jesus replied. "If you knew me, you would know my Father also." ²⁰ He spoke these words while he was teaching in the temple courtyard. He was near the place where the offerings were put. But no one arrested him. That's because the time for him to die had not yet come.

Challenge to Who Jesus Claims to Be

²¹ Once more Jesus said to them, "I am going away. You will look for me, and you will die in your sin. You can't come where I am going."

²² This made the Jews ask, "Will he kill himself? Is that why he says, 'You can't come where I am going'?"

²³ But Jesus said, "You are from below. I am from heaven. You are from this world. I am not from this world. ²⁴ I told you that you would die in your sins. This will happen if you don't believe that I am he. If you don't believe, you will certainly die in your sins."

²⁵ "Who are you?" they asked.

"Just what I have been telling you from the beginning," Jesus replied. ²⁶ "I have a lot to say that will judge you. But the one who sent me can be trusted. And I tell the world what I have heard from him."

²⁷ They did not understand that Jesus was telling them about his Father. ²⁸ So Jesus said, "You will lift up the Son of Man. Then you will know that I am he. You will also know that I do nothing on my own. I speak just what the Father has taught me. ²⁹ The one who sent me is with me. He has not left me alone, because I always do what pleases him." ³⁰ Even while Jesus was speaking, many people believed in him.

Challenge to the Claim to Be Children of Abraham

³¹ Jesus spoke to the Jews who had believed him. "If you obey my teaching," he said, "you are really my disciples. ³² Then you will know the truth. And the truth will set you free."

³³ They answered him, "We

are Abraham's children. We have never been slaves of anyone. So how can you say that we will be set free?"

³⁴ Jesus replied, "What I'm about to tell you is true. Everyone who sins is a slave of sin. ³⁵ A slave has no lasting place in the family. But a son belongs to the family forever. ³⁶ So if the Son of Man sets you free, you will really be free. ³⁷ I know that you are Abraham's children. But you are looking for a way to kill me. You have no room for my word. ³⁸ I am telling you what I saw when I was with my Father. You are doing what you have heard from your father."

³⁹ "Abraham is our father," they answered.

Jesus said, "Are you really Abraham's children? If you are, you will do what Abraham did. ⁴⁰ But you are looking for a way to kill me. I am a man who has told you the truth I heard from God. Abraham didn't do the things you want to do. ⁴¹ You are doing what your own father does."

"We have the right to claim to be God's children," they objected. "The only Father we have is God himself."

⁴² Jesus said to them, "If God were your Father, you would love me. I have come here from God. I have not come on my own. God sent me. ⁴³ Why aren't my words clear to you? Because you can't really hear what I say. ⁴⁴ You belong to your father, the devil. You want to obey your father's wishes. From the beginning, the devil was a murderer.

He has never obeyed the truth. There is no truth in him. When he lies, he speaks his natural language. He does this because he is a liar. He is the father of lies. ⁴⁵ But because I tell the truth, you don't believe me! ⁴⁶ Can any of you prove I am guilty of sinning? Am I not telling the truth? Then why don't you believe me? ⁴⁷ Whoever belongs to God hears what God says. The reason you don't hear is that you don't belong to God."

Jesus Makes Claims About Himself

⁴⁸ The Jews answered Jesus, "Aren't we right when we say you are a Samaritan? Aren't you controlled by a demon?"

⁴⁹ "I am not controlled by a demon," said Jesus. "I honor my Father. You do not honor me. ⁵⁰ I am not seeking glory for myself. But there is one who brings glory to me. He is the judge. ⁵¹ What I'm about to tell you is true. Whoever obeys my word will never die."

⁵² Then they cried out, "Now we know you are controlled by a demon! Abraham died. So did the prophets. But you say that whoever obeys your word will never die. ⁵³ Are you greater than our father Abraham? He died. So did the prophets. Who do you think you are?"

⁵⁴ Jesus replied, "If I bring glory to myself, my glory means nothing. You claim that my Father is your God. He is the one who brings glory to me. ⁵⁵ You do not know him. But I know him.

If I said I did not, I would be a liar like you. But I do know him. And I obey his word. ⁵⁶Your father Abraham was filled with joy at the thought of seeing my day. He saw it and was glad."

⁵⁷"You are not even 50 years old," they said to Jesus. "And you have seen Abraham?"

⁵⁸"What I'm about to tell you is true," Jesus answered. "Before Abraham was born, I am!" ⁵⁹When he said this, they picked up stones to kill him. But Jesus hid himself. He slipped away from the temple area.

Jesus Makes Claims About Himself

9 As Jesus went along, he saw a man who was blind. He had been blind since he was born. ²Jesus' disciples asked him, "Rabbi, who sinned? Was this man born blind because he sinned? Or did his parents sin?"

³"It isn't because this man sinned," said Jesus. "It isn't because his parents sinned. He was born blind so that God's power could be shown by what's going to happen. ⁴While it is still day, we must do the works of the one who sent me. Night is coming. Then no one can work. ⁵While I am in the world, I am the light of the world."

⁶After he said this, he spit on the ground. He made some mud with the spit. Then he put the mud on the man's eyes. ⁷"Go," he told him. "Wash in the Pool of Siloam." Siloam means Sent. So the man went and washed. And he came home able to see.

⁸His neighbors and people who had seen him earlier begging asked questions. "Isn't this the same man who used to sit and beg?" they asked. ⁹Some claimed that he was.

Others said, "No. He only looks like him."

But the man who had been blind kept saying, "I am the man."

¹⁰"Then how were your eyes opened?" they asked.

¹¹He replied, "The man they call Jesus made some mud and put it on my eyes. He told me to go to Siloam and wash. So I went and washed. Then I could see."

¹²"Where is this man?" they asked him.

"I don't know," he said.

The Pharisees Want to Know How the Blind Man Was Healed

¹³They brought to the Pharisees the man who had been blind. ¹⁴The day Jesus made the mud and opened the man's eyes was a Sabbath day. ¹⁵So the Pharisees also asked him how he was able to see. "He put mud on my eyes," the man replied. "Then I washed. And now I can see."

¹⁶Some of the Pharisees said, "Jesus has not come from God. He does not keep the Sabbath day."

But others asked, "How can a sinner do such signs?" So the Pharisees did not agree with one another.

¹⁷Then they turned again to the blind man. "What do you have to say about him?" they

asked. "It was your eyes he opened."

The man replied, "He is a prophet."

18 They still did not believe that the man had been blind and now could see. So they sent for his parents. 19 "Is this your son?" they asked. "Is this the one you say was born blind? How is it that now he can see?"

20 "We know he is our son," the parents answered. "And we know he was born blind. 21 But we don't know how he can now see. And we don't know who opened his eyes. Ask him. He is an adult. He can speak for himself." 22 His parents said this because they were afraid of the Jewish leaders. The leaders had already made this decision about Jesus. Anyone who said Jesus was the Messiah would be put out of the synagogue. 23 That was why the man's parents said, "He is an adult. Ask him."

24 Again the Pharisees called the man who had been blind to come to them. "Give glory to God by telling the truth!" they said. "We know that the man who healed you is a sinner."

25 He replied, "I don't know if he is a sinner or not. I do know one thing. I was blind, but now I can see!"

26 Then they asked him, "What did he do to you? How did he open your eyes?"

27 He answered, "I have already told you. But you didn't listen. Why do you want to hear it again? Do you want to become his disciples too?"

28 Then they began to attack him with their words. "You are this fellow's disciple!" they said. "We are disciples of Moses! 29 We know that God spoke to Moses. But we don't even know where this fellow comes from."

30 The man answered, "That is really surprising! You don't know where he comes from, and yet he opened my eyes. 31 We know that God does not listen to sinners. He listens to the godly person who does what he wants them to do. 32 Nobody has ever heard of anyone opening the eyes of a person born blind. 33 If this man had not come from God, he could do nothing."

34 Then the Pharisees replied, "When you were born, you were already deep in sin. How dare you talk like that to us!" And they threw him out of the synagogue.

People Who Can't See the Truth

35 Jesus heard that the Pharisees had thrown the man out of the synagogue. When Jesus found him, he said, "Do you believe in the Son of Man?"

36 "Who is he, sir?" the man asked. "Tell me, so I can believe in him."

37 Jesus said, "You have now seen him. In fact, he is the one speaking with you."

38 Then the man said, "Lord, I believe." And he worshiped him.

39 Jesus said, "I have come into this world to judge it. I have come so that people who are blind will see. I have come so

that people who can see will become blind."

⁴⁰ Some Pharisees who were with him heard him say this. They asked, "What? Are we blind too?"

⁴¹ Jesus said, "If you were blind, you would not be guilty of sin. But since you claim you can see, you remain guilty.

The Good Shepherd and His Sheep

10 "What I'm about to tell you Pharisees is true. What if someone does not enter the sheep pen through the gate but climbs in another way? That person is a thief and a robber. ² The one who enters through the gate is the shepherd of the sheep. ³ The gatekeeper opens the gate for him. The sheep listen to his voice. He calls his own sheep by name and leads them out. ⁴ When he has brought out all his own sheep, he goes on ahead of them. His sheep follow him because they know his voice. ⁵ But they will never follow a stranger. In fact, they will run away from him. They don't recognize a stranger's voice." ⁶ Jesus told this story. But the Pharisees didn't understand what he was telling them.

⁷ So Jesus said again, "What I'm about to tell you is true. I am like a gate for the sheep. ⁸ All who have come before me are thieves and robbers. But the sheep have not listened to them. ⁹ I'm like a gate. Anyone who enters through me will be saved. They will come in and go out. And they will find plenty of food. ¹⁰ A thief comes only to steal and kill and destroy. I have come so they may have life. I want them to have it in the fullest possible way.

¹¹ "I am the good shepherd. The good shepherd gives his life for the sheep. ¹² The hired man is not the shepherd and does not own the sheep. So when the hired man sees the wolf coming, he leaves the sheep and runs away. Then the wolf attacks the flock and scatters it. ¹³ The man runs away because he is a hired man. He does not care about the sheep.

¹⁴ "I am the good shepherd. I know my sheep, and my sheep know me. ¹⁵ They know me just as the Father knows me and I know the Father. And I give my life for the sheep. ¹⁶ I have other sheep that do not belong to this sheep pen. I must bring them in too. They also will listen to my voice. Then there will be one flock and one shepherd. ¹⁷ The reason my Father loves me is that I give up my life. But I will take it back again. ¹⁸ No one takes it from me. I give it up myself. I have the authority to give it up. And I have the authority to take it back again. I received this command from my Father."

¹⁹ The Jews who heard these words could not agree with one another. ²⁰ Many of them said, "He is controlled by a demon. He has gone crazy! Why should we listen to him?"

²¹ But others said, "A person controlled by a demon does not

say things like this. Can a demon open the eyes of someone who is blind?"

Another Challenge to Jesus' Claims

22 Then came the Feast of Hanukkah at Jerusalem. It was winter. 23 Jesus was in the temple courtyard walking in Solomon's Porch. 24 The Jews who were gathered there around Jesus spoke to him. They said, "How long will you keep us waiting? If you are the Messiah, tell us plainly."

25 Jesus answered, "I did tell you. But you do not believe. The works that I do in my Father's name are a witness for me. 26 But you do not believe, because you are not my sheep. 27 My sheep listen to my voice. I know them, and they follow me. 28 I give them eternal life, and they will never die. No one will steal them out of my hand. 29 My Father, who has given them to me, is greater than anyone. No one can steal them out of my Father's hand. 30 I and the Father are one."

31 Again the Jews who had challenged him picked up stones to kill him. 32 But Jesus said to them, "I have shown you many good works from the Father. Which good work are you throwing stones at me for?"

33 "We are not throwing stones at you for any good work," they replied. "We are stoning you for saying a very evil thing. You are only a man. But you claim to be God."

34 Jesus answered them, "Didn't God say in your Law, 'I have said you are "gods" '? *(Psalm 82:6)* 35 We know that Scripture is always true. God spoke to some people and called them 'gods.' 36 If that is true, what about the one the Father set apart as his very own? What about this one the Father sent into the world? Why do you charge me with saying a very evil thing? Is it because I said, 'I am God's Son'? 37 Don't believe me unless I do the works of my Father. 38 But what if I do them? Even if you don't believe me, believe these works. Then you will know and understand that the Father is in me and I am in the Father." 39 Again they tried to arrest him. But he escaped from them.

40 Then Jesus went back across the Jordan River. He went to the place where John had been baptizing in the early days. There he stayed. 41 Many people came to him. They said, "John never performed a sign. But everything he said about this man was true." 42 And in that place many believed in Jesus.

Lazarus Dies

11 A man named Lazarus was sick. He was from Bethany, the village where Mary and her sister Martha lived. 2 Mary would later pour perfume on the Lord. She would also wipe Jesus' feet with her hair. It was her brother Lazarus who was sick in bed. 3 So the sisters sent a message to Jesus.

"Lord," they told him, "the one you love is sick."

⁴When Jesus heard this, he said, "This sickness will not end in death. No, it is for God's glory. God's Son will receive glory because of it." ⁵Jesus loved Martha and her sister and Lazarus. ⁶So after he heard Lazarus was sick, he stayed where he was for two more days. ⁷And then he said to his disciples, "Let us go back to Judea."

⁸"But Rabbi," they said, "a short time ago the Jews there tried to kill you with stones. Are you still going back?"

⁹Jesus answered, "Aren't there 12 hours of daylight? Anyone who walks during the day won't trip and fall. They can see because of this world's light. ¹⁰But when they walk at night, they'll trip and fall. They have no light."

¹¹After he said this, Jesus went on speaking to them. "Our friend Lazarus has fallen asleep," he said. "But I am going there to wake him up."

¹²His disciples replied, "Lord, if he's sleeping, he will get better." ¹³Jesus had been speaking about the death of Lazarus. But his disciples thought he meant natural sleep.

¹⁴So then he told them plainly, "Lazarus is dead. ¹⁵For your benefit, I am glad I was not there. Now you will believe. But let us go to him."

¹⁶Then Thomas, who was also called Didymus, spoke to the rest of the disciples. "Let us go also," he said. "Then we can die with Jesus."

Jesus Comforts the Sisters of Lazarus

¹⁷When Jesus arrived, he found out that Lazarus had already been in the tomb for four days. ¹⁸Bethany was less than two miles from Jerusalem. ¹⁹Many Jews had come to Martha and Mary. They had come to comfort them because their brother was dead. ²⁰When Martha heard that Jesus was coming, she went out to meet him. But Mary stayed at home.

²¹"Lord," Martha said to Jesus, "I wish you had been here! Then my brother would not have died. ²²But I know that even now God will give you anything you ask for."

²³Jesus said to her, "Your brother will rise again."

²⁴Martha answered, "I know he will rise again. This will happen when people are raised from the dead on the last day."

²⁵Jesus said to her, "I am the resurrection and the life. Anyone who believes in me will live, even if they die. ²⁶And whoever lives by believing in me will never die. Do you believe this?"

²⁷"Yes, Lord," she replied. "I believe that you are the Messiah, the Son of God. I believe that you are the one who is supposed to come into the world."

²⁸After she said this, she went back home. She called her sister Mary to one side to talk to her. "The Teacher is here," Martha said. "He is asking for you." ²⁹When Mary heard this, she got up quickly and went to him. ³⁰Jesus had not yet entered the

village. He was still at the place where Martha had met him. ³¹ Some Jews had been comforting Mary in the house. They noticed how quickly she got up and went out. So they followed her. They thought she was going to the tomb to mourn there.

³² Mary reached the place where Jesus was. When she saw him, she fell at his feet. She said, "Lord, I wish you had been here! Then my brother would not have died."

³³ Jesus saw her crying. He saw that the Jews who had come along with her were crying also. His spirit became very sad, and he was troubled. ³⁴ "Where have you put him?" he asked.

"Come and see, Lord," they replied.

³⁵ Jesus wept.

³⁶ Then the Jews said, "See how much he loved him!"

³⁷ But some of them said, "He opened the eyes of the blind man. Couldn't he have kept this man from dying?"

Jesus Raises Lazarus From the Dead

³⁸ Once more Jesus felt very sad. He came to the tomb. It was a cave with a stone in front of the entrance. ³⁹ "Take away the stone," he said.

"But, Lord," said Martha, the sister of the dead man, "by this time there is a bad smell. Lazarus has been in the tomb for four days."

⁴⁰ Then Jesus said, "Didn't I tell you that if you believe, you will see God's glory?"

⁴¹ So they took away the stone. Then Jesus looked up. He said, "Father, I thank you for hearing me. ⁴² I know that you always hear me. But I said this for the benefit of the people standing here. I said it so they will believe that you sent me."

⁴³ Then Jesus called in a loud voice. He said, "Lazarus, come out!" ⁴⁴ The dead man came out. His hands and feet were wrapped with strips of linen. A cloth was around his face.

Jesus said to them, "Take off the clothes he was buried in and let him go."

The Plan to Kill Jesus

⁴⁵ Many of the Jews who had come to visit Mary saw what Jesus did. So they believed in him. ⁴⁶ But some of them went to the Pharisees. They told the Pharisees what Jesus had done. ⁴⁷ Then the chief priests and the Pharisees called a meeting of the Sanhedrin.

"What can we do?" they asked. "This man is performing many signs. ⁴⁸ If we let him keep on doing this, everyone will believe in him. Then the Romans will come. They will take away our temple and our nation."

⁴⁹ One of the Jewish leaders spoke up. His name was Caiaphas. He was high priest at that time. He said, "You don't know anything at all! ⁵⁰ You don't realize what is good for you. It is better if one man dies for the people than if the whole nation is destroyed."

⁵¹ He did not say this on his

own because he was high priest at that time. He prophesied that Jesus would die for the Jewish nation. ⁵²He also prophesied that Jesus would die for God's children scattered everywhere. He would die to bring them together and make them one. ⁵³So from that day on, the Jewish rulers planned to kill Jesus.

⁵⁴Jesus no longer moved around openly among the people of Judea. Instead, he went away to an area near the desert. He went to a village called Ephraim. There he stayed with his disciples.

⁵⁵It was almost time for the Jewish Passover Feast. Many people went up from the country to Jerusalem. They went there for the special washing that would make them pure before the Passover Feast. ⁵⁶They kept looking for Jesus as they stood in the temple courtyard. They asked one another, "What do you think? Isn't he coming to the feast at all?" ⁵⁷But the chief priests and the Pharisees had given orders. They had commanded anyone who found out where Jesus was staying to report it. Then they could arrest him.

Mary Pours Perfume on Jesus at Bethany

12 It was six days before the Passover Feast. Jesus came to Bethany, where Lazarus lived. Lazarus was the one Jesus had raised from the dead. ²A dinner was given at Bethany to honor Jesus. Martha served the food. Lazarus was among the people at the table with Jesus. ³Then Mary took about a pint of pure nard. It was an expensive perfume. She poured it on Jesus' feet and wiped them with her hair. The house was filled with the sweet smell of the perfume.

⁴But Judas Iscariot didn't like what Mary did. He was one of Jesus' disciples. Later he was going to hand Jesus over to his enemies. Judas said, ⁵"Why wasn't this perfume sold? Why wasn't the money given to poor people? It was worth a year's pay." ⁶He didn't say this because he cared about the poor. He said it because he was a thief. Judas was in charge of the money bag. He used to help himself to what was in it.

⁷"Leave her alone," Jesus replied. "The perfume was meant for the day I am buried. ⁸You will always have the poor among you. But you won't always have me."

⁹Meanwhile a large crowd of Jews found out that Jesus was there, so they came. But they did not come only because of Jesus. They also came to see Lazarus. After all, Jesus had raised him from the dead. ¹⁰So the chief priests made plans to kill Lazarus too. ¹¹Because of Lazarus, many of the Jews were starting to follow Jesus. They were believing in him.

Jesus Comes to Jerusalem as King

¹²The next day the large crowd that had come for the

feast heard that Jesus was on his way to Jerusalem. ¹³ So they took branches from palm trees and went out to meet him. They shouted,

"Hosanna! "

"Blessed is the one who
　　comes in the name of the
　　Lord!" *(Psalm 118:25,26)*

"Blessed is the king of Israel!"

¹⁴ Jesus found a young donkey and sat on it. This is just as it is written in Scripture. It says,

¹⁵ "City of Zion, do not be afraid.
　　See, your king is coming.
　　He is sitting on a donkey's
　　colt." *(Zechariah 9:9)*

¹⁶ At first, Jesus' disciples did not understand all this. They realized it only after he had received glory. Then they realized that these things had been written about him. They realized that these things had been done to him.

¹⁷ A crowd had been with Jesus when he called Lazarus from the tomb and raised him from the dead. So they continued to tell everyone about what had happened. ¹⁸ Many people went out to meet him. They had heard that he had done this sign. ¹⁹ So the Pharisees said to one another, "This isn't getting us anywhere. Look how the whole world is following him!"

Jesus Tells About His Coming Death

²⁰ There were some Greeks among the people who went up to worship during the feast. ²¹ They came to ask Philip for a favor. Philip was from Bethsaida in Galilee. "Sir," they said, "we would like to see Jesus." ²² Philip went to tell Andrew. Then Andrew and Philip told Jesus.

²³ Jesus replied, "The time has come for the Son of Man to receive glory. ²⁴ What I'm about to tell you is true. Unless a grain of wheat falls to the ground and dies, it remains only one seed. But if it dies, it produces many seeds. ²⁵ Anyone who loves their life will lose it. But anyone who hates their life in this world will keep it and have eternal life. ²⁶ Anyone who serves me must follow me. And where I am, my servant will also be. My Father will honor the one who serves me.

²⁷ "My soul is troubled. What should I say? 'Father, keep me from having to go through with this'? No. This is the very reason I have come to this point in my life. ²⁸ Father, bring glory to your name!"

Then a voice came from heaven. It said, "I have brought glory to my name. I will bring glory to it again." ²⁹ The crowd there heard the voice. Some said it was thunder. Others said an angel had spoken to Jesus.

³⁰ Jesus said, "This voice was for your benefit, not mine. ³¹ Now it is time for the world to be judged. Now the prince of this world will be thrown out. ³² And I am going to be lifted up from the earth. When I am, I will bring all people to myself."

33 He said this to show them how he was going to die.

34 The crowd spoke up. "The Law tells us that the Messiah will remain forever," they said. "So how can you say, 'The Son of Man must be lifted up'? Who is this 'Son of Man'?"

35 Then Jesus told them, "You are going to have the light just a little while longer. Walk while you have the light. Do this before darkness catches up with you. Whoever walks in the dark does not know where they are going. 36 While you have the light, believe in it. Then you can become children of light." When Jesus had finished speaking, he left and hid from them.

Some Jews Believe and Some Don't

37 Jesus had performed so many signs in front of them. But they still would not believe in him. 38 This happened as Isaiah the prophet had said it would. He had said,

> "Lord, who has believed what
>   we've been saying?
> Who has seen the Lord's
>   saving power?" (Isaiah 53:1)

39 For this reason, they could not believe. As Isaiah says in another place,

40 "The Lord has blinded their
    eyes.
He has closed their
    minds.
So they can't see with their
    eyes.
They can't understand
    with their minds.

They can't turn to the Lord.
    If they could, he would
    heal them." (Isaiah 6:10)

41 Isaiah said this because he saw Jesus' glory and spoke about him.

42 At the same time that Jesus did those signs, many of the Jewish leaders believed in him. But because of the Pharisees, they would not openly admit they believed. They were afraid they would be thrown out of the synagogue. 43 They loved praise from people more than praise from God.

44 Then Jesus cried out, "Whoever believes in me does not believe in me only. They also believe in the one who sent me. 45 The one who looks at me sees the one who sent me. 46 I have come into the world to be its light. So no one who believes in me will stay in darkness.

47 "I don't judge a person who hears my words but does not obey them. I didn't come to judge the world. I came to save the world. 48 But there is a judge for anyone who does not accept me and my words. These words I have spoken will judge them on the last day. 49 I did not speak on my own. The Father who sent me commanded me to say all that I have said. 50 I know that his command leads to eternal life. So everything I say is just what the Father has told me to say."

Jesus Washes His Disciples' Feet

13 It was just before the Passover Feast. Jesus knew that the time had come for him

to leave this world. It was time for him to go to the Father. Jesus loved his disciples who were in the world. So he now loved them to the very end.

2 They were having their evening meal. The devil had already tempted Judas, son of Simon Iscariot. He had urged Judas to hand Jesus over to his enemies. 3 Jesus knew that the Father had put everything under his power. He also knew he had come from God and was returning to God. 4 So he got up from the meal and took off his outer clothes. He wrapped a towel around his waist. 5 After that, he poured water into a large bowl. Then he began to wash his disciples' feet. He dried them with the towel that was wrapped around him.

6 He came to Simon Peter. "Lord," Peter said to him, "are you going to wash my feet?"

7 Jesus replied, "You don't realize now what I am doing. But later you will understand."

8 "No," said Peter. "You will never wash my feet."

Jesus answered, "Unless I wash you, you can't share life with me."

9 "Lord," Simon Peter replied, "not just my feet! Wash my hands and my head too!"

10 Jesus answered, "People who have had a bath need to wash only their feet. The rest of their body is clean. And you are clean. But not all of you are." 11 Jesus knew who was going to hand him over to his enemies. That was why he said not every one was clean.

12 When Jesus finished washing their feet, he put on his clothes. Then he returned to his place. "Do you understand what I have done for you?" he asked them. 13 "You call me 'Teacher' and 'Lord.' You are right. That is what I am. 14 I, your Lord and Teacher, have washed your feet. So you also should wash one another's feet. 15 I have given you an example. You should do as I have done for you. 16 What I'm about to tell you is true. A slave is not more important than his master. And a messenger is not more important than the one who sends him. 17 Now you know these things. So you will be blessed if you do them.

Jesus Tells What Judas Will Do

18 "I am not talking about all of you. I know the ones I have chosen. But this will happen so that this passage of Scripture will come true. It says, 'The one who shared my bread has turned against me.' *(Psalm 41:9)*

19 "I am telling you now, before it happens. When it does happen, you will believe that I am who I am. 20 What I'm about to tell you is true. Anyone who accepts someone I send accepts me. And anyone who accepts me accepts the one who sent me."

21 After he had said this, Jesus' spirit was troubled. He said, "What I'm about to tell you is true. One of you is going to hand me over to my enemies."

22 His disciples stared at one another. They had no idea

which one of them he meant. [23] The disciple Jesus loved was next to him at the table. [24] Simon Peter motioned to that disciple. He said, "Ask Jesus which one he means."

[25] The disciple was leaning back against Jesus. He asked him, "Lord, who is it?"

[26] Jesus answered, "It is the one I will give this piece of bread to. I will give it to him after I have dipped it in the dish." He dipped the piece of bread. Then he gave it to Judas, son of Simon Iscariot. [27] As soon as Judas took the bread, Satan entered into him.

So Jesus told him, "Do quickly what you are going to do." [28] But no one at the meal understood why Jesus said this to him. [29] Judas was in charge of the money. So some of the disciples thought Jesus was telling him to buy what was needed for the feast. Others thought Jesus was talking about giving something to poor people. [30] As soon as Judas had taken the bread, he went out. And it was night.

Peter Says He Does Not Know Jesus

[31] After Judas was gone, Jesus spoke. He said, "Now the Son of Man receives glory. And he brings glory to God. [32] If the Son brings glory to God, God himself will bring glory to the Son. God will do it at once.

[33] "My children, I will be with you only a little longer. You will look for me. Just as I told the Jews, so I am telling you now.

You can't come where I am going.

[34] "I give you a new command. Love one another. You must love one another, just as I have loved you. [35] If you love one another, everyone will know you are my disciples."

[36] Simon Peter asked him, "Lord, where are you going?"

Jesus replied, "Where I am going you can't follow now. But you will follow me later."

[37] "Lord," Peter asked, "why can't I follow you now? I will give my life for you."

[38] Then Jesus answered, "Will you really give your life for me? What I'm about to tell you is true. Before the rooster crows, you will say three times that you don't know me!

Jesus Comforts His Disciples

14 "Do not let your hearts be troubled. You believe in God. Believe in me also. [2] There are many rooms in my Father's house. If this were not true, would I have told you that I am going there? Would I have told you that I would prepare a place for you there? [3] If I go and do that, I will come back. And I will take you to be with me. Then you will also be where I am. [4] You know the way to the place where I am going."

Jesus Is the Way to the Father

[5] Thomas said to him, "Lord, we don't know where you are going. So how can we know the way?"

[6] Jesus answered, "I am the

way and the truth and the life. No one comes to the Father except through me. ⁷ If you really know me, you will know my Father also. From now on, you do know him. And you have seen him."

⁸ Philip said, "Lord, show us the Father. That will be enough for us."

⁹ Jesus answered, "Don't you know me, Philip? I have been among you such a long time! Anyone who has seen me has seen the Father. So how can you say, 'Show us the Father'? ¹⁰ Don't you believe that I am in the Father? Don't you believe that the Father is in me? The words I say to you I do not speak on my own authority. The Father lives in me. He is the one who is doing his work. ¹¹ Believe me when I say I am in the Father. Also believe that the Father is in me. Or at least believe what the works I have been doing say about me. ¹² What I'm about to tell you is true. Anyone who believes in me will do the works I have been doing. In fact, they will do even greater things. That's because I am going to the Father. ¹³ And I will do anything you ask in my name. Then the Father will receive glory from the Son. ¹⁴ You may ask me for anything in my name. I will do it.

Jesus Promises That the Holy Spirit Will Come

¹⁵ "If you love me, obey my commands. ¹⁶ I will ask the Father. And he will give you another friend to help you and to be with you forever. ¹⁷ That friend is the Spirit of truth. The world can't accept him. That's because the world does not see him or know him. But you know him. He lives with you, and he will be in you. ¹⁸ I will not leave you like children who don't have parents. I will come to you. ¹⁹ Before long, the world will not see me anymore. But you will see me. Because I live, you will live also. ²⁰ On that day you will realize that I am in my Father. You will know that you are in me, and I am in you. ²¹ Anyone who has my commands and obeys them loves me. My Father will love the one who loves me. I too will love them. And I will show myself to them."

²² Then Judas spoke. "Lord," he said, "why do you plan to show yourself only to us? Why not also to the world?" The Judas who spoke those words was not Judas Iscariot.

²³ Jesus replied, "Anyone who loves me will obey my teaching. My Father will love them. We will come to them and make our home with them. ²⁴ Anyone who does not love me will not obey my teaching. The words you hear me say are not my own. They belong to the Father who sent me.

²⁵ "I have spoken all these things while I am still with you. ²⁶ But the Father will send the Friend in my name to help you. The Friend is the Holy Spirit. He will teach you all things. He will remind you of everything

I have said to you. [27] I leave my peace with you. I give my peace to you. I do not give it to you as the world does. Do not let your hearts be troubled. And do not be afraid.

[28] "You heard me say, 'I am going away. And I am coming back to you.' If you loved me, you would be glad I am going to the Father. The Father is greater than I am. [29] I have told you now before it happens. Then when it does happen, you will believe. [30] I will not say much more to you. The prince of this world is coming. He has no power over me. [31] But he comes so that the world may learn that I love the Father. They must also learn that I do exactly what my Father has commanded me to do.

"Come now. Let us leave.

The Vine and the Branches

15 "I am the true vine. My Father is the gardener. [2] He cuts off every branch joined to me that does not bear fruit. He trims every branch that does bear fruit. Then it will bear even more fruit. [3] You are already clean because of the word I have spoken to you. [4] Remain joined to me, just as I also remain joined to you. No branch can bear fruit by itself. It must remain joined to the vine. In the same way, you can't bear fruit unless you remain joined to me.

[5] "I am the vine. You are the branches. If you remain joined to me, and I to you, you will bear a lot of fruit. You can't do anything without me. [6] If you don't remain joined to me, you are like a branch that is thrown away and dries up. Branches like those are picked up. They are thrown into the fire and burned. [7] If you remain joined to me and my words remain in you, ask for anything you wish. And it will be done for you. [8] When you bear a lot of fruit, it brings glory to my Father. It shows that you are my disciples.

[9] "Just as the Father has loved me, I have loved you. Now remain in my love. [10] If you obey my commands, you will remain in my love. In the same way, I have obeyed my Father's commands and remain in his love. [11] I have told you this so that you will have the same joy that I have. I also want your joy to be complete. [12] Here is my command. Love one another, just as I have loved you. [13] No one has greater love than the one who gives their life for their friends. [14] You are my friends if you do what I command. [15] I do not call you slaves anymore. Slaves do not know their master's business. Instead, I have called you friends. I have told you everything I learned from my Father. [16] You did not choose me. Instead, I chose you. I appointed you so that you might go and bear fruit that will last. I also appointed you so that the Father will give you what you ask for. He will give you whatever you ask for in my name. [17] Here is my command. Love one another.

The World Hates the Disciples

[18] "My disciples, does the world hate you? Remember that it hated me first. [19] If you belonged to the world, it would love you like one of its own. But you do not belong to the world. I have chosen you out of the world. That is why the world hates you. [20] Remember what I told you. I said, 'A slave is not more important than his master.' *(John 13:16)* If people hated me and tried to hurt me, they will do the same to you. If they obeyed my teaching, they will obey yours also. [21] They will treat you like that because of my name. They do not know the one who sent me. [22] If I had not come and spoken to them, they would not be guilty of sin. But now they have no excuse for their sin. [23] Whoever hates me hates my Father also. [24] I did works among them that no one else did. If I hadn't, they would not be guilty of sin. But now they have seen those works. And still they have hated both me and my Father. [25] This has happened so that what is written in their Law would come true. It says, 'They hated me without any reason.' *(Psalms 35:19; 69:4)*

The Work of the Holy Spirit

[26] "I will send the Friend to you from the Father. He is the Spirit of truth, who comes out from the Father. When the Friend comes to help you, he will be a witness about me. [27] You must also be witnesses about me. That's because you have been with me from the beginning.

16 "I have told you all this so that you will not turn away from the truth. [2] You will be thrown out of the synagogue. In fact, the time is coming when someone may kill you. And they will think they are doing God a favor. [3] They will do things like that because they do not know the Father or me. [4] Why have I told you this? So that when their time comes, you will remember that I warned you about them. I didn't tell you this from the beginning because I was with you. [5] But now I am going to the one who sent me. None of you asks me, 'Where are you going?' [6] Instead, you are filled with sadness because I have said these things. [7] But what I'm about to tell you is true. It is for your good that I am going away. Unless I go away, the Friend will not come to help you. But if I go, I will send him to you. [8] When he comes, he will prove that the world's people are guilty. He will prove their guilt concerning sin and godliness and judgment. [9] The world is guilty as far as sin is concerned. That's because people do not believe in me. [10] The world is guilty as far as godliness is concerned. That's because I am going to the Father, where you can't see me anymore. [11] The world is guilty as far as judgment is concerned. That's because the devil, the prince of this world, has already been judged. [12] "I have much more to say to you. It is more than you can handle right now. ¹³ But when the Spirit of truth comes, he will guide you into all the truth. He will not speak on his own. He will speak only what he hears. And he will tell you what is still going to happen. ¹⁴ He will bring me glory. That's because what he receives from me he will show to you. ¹⁵ Everything that belongs to the Father is mine. That is why I said what the Holy Spirit receives from me he will show to you.

The Disciples' Sadness Will Turn Into Joy

¹⁶ Jesus continued, "In a little while, you will no longer see me. Then after a little while, you will see me."

¹⁷ After they heard this, some of his disciples spoke to one another. They said, "What does he mean by saying, 'In a little while, you will no longer see me. Then after a little while, you will see me'? And what does he mean by saying, 'I am going to the Father'?" ¹⁸ They kept asking, "What does he mean by 'a little while'? We don't understand what he is saying."

¹⁹ Jesus saw that they wanted to ask him about these things. So he said to them, "Are you asking one another what I meant? Didn't you understand when I said, 'In a little while, you will no longer see me. Then after a little while, you will see me'? ²⁰ What I'm about to tell you is true. You will weep and mourn while the world is full of joy. You will be sad, but your sadness will turn into joy. ²¹ A woman giving birth to a baby has pain. That's because her time to give birth has come. But when her baby is born, she forgets the pain. She forgets because she is so happy that a baby has been born into the world. ²² That's the way it is with you. Now it's your time to be sad. But I will see you again. Then you will be full of joy. And no one will take away your joy. ²³ When that day comes, you will no longer ask me for anything. What I'm about to tell you is true. My Father will give you anything you ask for in my name. ²⁴ Until now you have not asked for anything in my name. Ask, and you will receive what you ask for. Then your joy will be complete.

²⁵ "I have not been speaking to you plainly. But a time is coming when I will speak clearly. Then I will tell you plainly about my Father. ²⁶ When that day comes, you will ask for things in my name. I am not saying I will ask the Father instead of you asking him. ²⁷ No, the Father himself loves you because you have loved me. He also loves you because you have believed that I came from God. ²⁸ I came from the Father and entered the world. Now I am leaving the world and going back to the Father."

²⁹ Then Jesus' disciples said, "Now you are speaking plainly. You are using examples that are clear. ³⁰ Now we can see that you know everything. You don't

even need anyone to ask you questions. This makes us believe that you came from God."

³¹ "Do you believe now?" Jesus replied. ³² "A time is coming when you will be scattered and go to your own homes. In fact, that time is already here. You will leave me all alone. But I am not really alone. My Father is with me.

³³ "I have told you these things, so that you can have peace because of me. In this world you will have trouble. But be encouraged! I have won the battle over the world."

Jesus Prays for Himself

17 After Jesus said this, he looked toward heaven and prayed. He said,

"Father, the time has come. Bring glory to your Son. Then your Son will bring glory to you. ² You gave him authority over all people. He gives eternal life to all those you have given him. ³ And what is eternal life? It is knowing you, the only true God, and Jesus Christ, whom you have sent. ⁴ I have brought you glory on earth. I have finished the work you gave me to do. ⁵ So now, Father, give glory to me in heaven where your throne is. Give me the glory I had with you before the world began.

Jesus Prays for His Disciples

⁶ "I have shown you to the disciples you gave me out of the world. They were yours. You gave them to me. And they have obeyed your word. ⁷ Now they know that everything you have given me comes from you. ⁸ I gave them the words you gave me. And they accepted them. They knew for certain that I came from you. They believed that you sent me. ⁹ I pray for them. I am not praying for the world. I am praying for those you have given me, because they are yours. ¹⁰ All I have is yours, and all you have is mine. Glory has come to me because of my disciples. ¹¹ I will not remain in the world any longer. But they are still in the world, and I am coming to you. Holy Father, keep them safe by the power of your name. It is the name you gave me. Keep them safe so they can be one, just as you and I are one. ¹² While I was with them, I guarded them. I kept them safe through the name you gave me. None of them has been lost, except the one who was headed for ruin. It happened so that Scripture would come true.

¹³ "I am coming to you now. But I say these things while I am still in the world. I say them so that those you gave me can have the same joy that I have. ¹⁴ I have given them your word. The world has hated them. That's because they are not

part of the world any more than I am. ¹⁵ I do not pray that you will take them out of the world. I pray that you will keep them safe from the evil one. ¹⁶ They do not belong to the world, just as I do not belong to it. ¹⁷ Use the truth to make them holy. Your word is truth. ¹⁸ You sent me into the world. In the same way, I have sent them into the world. ¹⁹ I make myself holy for them so that they too can be made holy by the truth.

Jesus Prays for All Believers

²⁰ "I do not pray only for them. I pray also for everyone who will believe in me because of their message. ²¹ Father, I pray they will be one, just as you are in me and I am in you. I want them also to be in us. Then the world will believe that you have sent me. ²² I have given them the glory you gave me. I did this so they would be one, just as we are one. ²³ I will be in them, just as you are in me. This is so that they may be brought together perfectly as one. Then the world will know that you sent me. It will also show the world that you have loved those you gave me, just as you have loved me.

²⁴ "Father, I want those you have given me to be with me where I am. I want them to see my glory, the glory you have given me. You gave it to me because you loved me before the world was created.

²⁵ "Father, you are holy. The world does not know you, but I know you. Those you have given me know you have sent me. ²⁶ I have shown you to them. And I will continue to show you to them. Then the love you have for me will be in them. I myself will be in them."

Jesus Is Arrested

18 When Jesus had finished praying, he left with his disciples. They crossed the Kidron Valley. On the other side there was a garden. Jesus and his disciples went into it.

² Judas knew the place. He was going to hand Jesus over to his enemies. Jesus had often met in that place with his disciples. ³ So Judas came to the garden. He was guiding a group of soldiers and some officials. The chief priests and the Pharisees had sent them. They were carrying torches, lanterns and weapons.

⁴ Jesus knew everything that was going to happen to him. So he went out and asked them, "Who do you want?"

⁵ "Jesus of Nazareth," they replied.

"I am he," Jesus said. Judas, who was going to hand Jesus over, was standing there with them. ⁶ When Jesus said, "I am he," they moved back. Then they fell to the ground.

[7] He asked them again, "Who do you want?"

"Jesus of Nazareth," they said.

[8] Jesus answered, "I told you I am he. If you are looking for me, then let these men go." [9] This happened so that the words Jesus had spoken would come true. He had said, "I have not lost anyone God has given me." *(John 6:39)*

[10] Simon Peter had a sword and pulled it out. He struck the high priest's slave and cut off his right ear. The slave's name was Malchus.

[11] Jesus commanded Peter, "Put your sword away! Shouldn't I drink the cup of suffering the Father has given me?"

[12] Then the group of soldiers, their commander and the Jewish officials arrested Jesus. They tied him up [13] and brought him first to Annas. He was the father-in-law of Caiaphas, the high priest at that time. [14] Caiaphas had advised the Jewish leaders that it would be good if one man died for the people.

Peter Says He Is Not Jesus' Disciple

[15] Simon Peter and another disciple were following Jesus. The high priest knew the other disciple. So that disciple went with Jesus into the high priest's courtyard. [16] But Peter had to wait outside by the door. The other disciple came back. He was the one the high priest knew. He spoke to the servant woman who was on duty there. Then he brought Peter in.

[17] She asked Peter, "You aren't one of Jesus' disciples too, are you?"

"I am not," he replied.

[18] It was cold. The slaves and officials stood around a fire. They had made it to keep warm. Peter was also standing with them. He was warming himself.

The High Priest Questions Jesus

[19] Meanwhile, the high priest questioned Jesus. He asked him about his disciples and his teaching.

[20] "I have spoken openly to the world," Jesus replied. "I always taught in synagogues or at the temple, where all the Jews come together. I didn't say anything in secret. [21] Why question me? Ask the people who heard me. They certainly know what I said."

[22] When Jesus said that, one of the officials nearby slapped him in the face. "Is this any way to answer the high priest?" he asked.

[23] "Have I said something wrong?" Jesus replied. "If I have, then tell everyone what it was. But if I spoke the truth, why did you hit me?" [24] Annas sent him, tied up, to Caiaphas, the high priest.

Peter Again Says He Is Not Jesus' Disciple

[25] Meanwhile, Simon Peter was still standing there warming himself by the fire. So they asked him, "You aren't one of Jesus' disciples too, are you?"

He said, "I am not."

[26] One of the high priest's slaves was a relative of the man

whose ear Peter had cut off. He said to Peter, "Didn't I see you with Jesus in the garden?" ²⁷ Again Peter said no. At that exact moment a rooster began to crow.

Jesus Is Brought to Pilate

²⁸ Then the Jewish leaders took Jesus from Caiaphas to the palace of the Roman governor. By now it was early morning. The Jewish leaders did not want to be made "unclean." They wanted to be able to eat the Passover meal. So they did not enter the palace. ²⁹ Pilate came out to them. He asked, "What charges are you bringing against this man?"

³⁰ "He has committed crimes," they replied. "If he hadn't, we would not have handed him over to you."

³¹ Pilate said, "Take him yourselves. Judge him by your own law."

"But we don't have the right to put anyone to death," they complained. ³² This happened so that what Jesus said about how he was going to die would come true.

³³ Then Pilate went back inside the palace. He ordered Jesus to be brought to him. Pilate asked him, "Are you the king of the Jews?"

³⁴ "Is that your own idea?" Jesus asked. "Or did others talk to you about me?"

³⁵ "Am I a Jew?" Pilate replied. "Your own people and chief priests handed you over to me. What have you done?"

³⁶ Jesus said, "My kingdom is not from this world. If it were, those who serve me would fight. They would try to keep the Jewish leaders from arresting me. My kingdom is from another place."

³⁷ "So you are a king, then!" said Pilate.

Jesus answered, "You say that I am a king. In fact, that's the reason I was born. I was born and came into the world to be a witness to the truth. Everyone who is on the side of truth listens to me."

³⁸ "What is truth?" Pilate replied. Then Pilate went out again to the Jews gathered there. He said, "I find no basis for any charge against him. ³⁹ But you have a practice at Passover time. At that time, you ask me to set one prisoner free for you. Do you want me to set 'the king of the Jews' free?"

⁴⁰ They shouted back, "No! Not him! Give us Barabbas!" Barabbas had taken part in an armed struggle against the country's rulers.

Jesus Is Sentenced to Be Crucified

19 Then Pilate took Jesus and had him whipped. ² The soldiers twisted thorns together to make a crown. They put it on Jesus' head. Then they put a purple robe on him. ³ They went up to him again and again. They kept saying, "We honor you, king of the Jews!" And they slapped him in the face.

⁴ Once more Pilate came out.

He said to the Jews gathered there, "Look, I am bringing Jesus out to you. I want to let you know that I find no basis for a charge against him." ⁵ Jesus came out wearing the crown of thorns and the purple robe. Then Pilate said to them, "Here is the man!"

⁶ As soon as the chief priests and their officials saw him, they shouted, "Crucify him! Crucify him!"

But Pilate answered, "You take him and crucify him. I myself find no basis for a charge against him."

⁷ The Jewish leaders replied, "We have a law. That law says he must die. He claimed to be the Son of God."

⁸ When Pilate heard that, he was even more afraid. ⁹ He went back inside the palace. "Where do you come from?" he asked Jesus. But Jesus did not answer him. ¹⁰ "Do you refuse to speak to me?" Pilate said. "Don't you understand? I have the power to set you free or to nail you to a cross."

¹¹ Jesus answered, "You were given power from heaven. If you weren't, you would have no power over me. So the one who handed me over to you is guilty of a greater sin."

¹² From then on, Pilate tried to set Jesus free. But the Jewish leaders kept shouting, "If you let this man go, you are not Caesar's friend! Anyone who claims to be a king is against Caesar!"

¹³ When Pilate heard that, he brought Jesus out. Pilate sat down on the judge's seat. It was at a place called the Stone Walkway. In the Aramaic language it was called Gabbatha. ¹⁴ It was about noon on Preparation Day in Passover Week.

"Here is your king," Pilate said to the Jews.

¹⁵ But they shouted, "Take him away! Take him away! Crucify him!"

"Should I crucify your king?" Pilate asked.

"We have no king but Caesar," the chief priests answered.

¹⁶ Finally, Pilate handed Jesus over to them to be nailed to a cross.

Jesus Is Nailed to a Cross

So the soldiers took charge of Jesus. ¹⁷ He had to carry his own cross. He went out to a place called the Skull. In the Aramaic language it was called Golgotha. ¹⁸ There they nailed Jesus to the cross. Two other men were crucified with him. One was on each side of him. Jesus was in the middle.

¹⁹ Pilate had a notice prepared. It was fastened to the cross. It read,

JESUS OF NAZARETH, THE KING
OF THE JEWS.

²⁰ Many of the Jews read the sign. That's because the place where Jesus was crucified was near the city. And the sign was written in the Aramaic, Latin and Greek languages. ²¹ The chief priests of the Jews argued with Pilate. They said, "Do not write 'The King of the Jews.' Write that this

man claimed to be king of the Jews."

²² Pilate answered, "I have written what I have written."

²³ When the soldiers crucified Jesus, they took his clothes. They divided them into four parts. Each soldier got one part. All that was left was Jesus' long, inner robe. It did not have any seams. It was made out of one piece of cloth from top to bottom.

²⁴ "Let's not tear it," they said to one another. "Let's cast lots to see who will get it."

This happened so that Scripture would come true. It says,

"They divided up my clothes
　　among them.
　They cast lots for what I
　　was wearing." *(Psalm 22:18)*

So that is what the soldiers did.

²⁵ Jesus' mother stood near his cross. So did his mother's sister, Mary the wife of Clopas, and Mary Magdalene. ²⁶ Jesus saw his mother there. He also saw the disciple he loved standing nearby. Jesus said to his mother, "Dear woman, here is your son." ²⁷ He said to the disciple, "Here is your mother." From that time on, the disciple took her into his home.

Jesus Dies

²⁸ Later, Jesus knew that everything had now been finished. He also knew that what Scripture said must come true. So he said, "I am thirsty." ²⁹ A jar of wine vinegar was there. So they soaked a sponge in it. They put the sponge on the stem of a hyssop plant. Then they lifted it up to Jesus' lips. ³⁰ After Jesus drank he said, "It is finished." Then he bowed his head and died.

³¹ It was Preparation Day. The next day would be a special Sabbath day. The Jewish leaders did not want the bodies left on the crosses during the Sabbath day. So they asked Pilate to have the legs broken and the bodies taken down. ³² The soldiers came and broke the legs of the first man who had been crucified with Jesus. Then they broke the legs of the other man. ³³ But when they came to Jesus, they saw that he was already dead. So they did not break his legs. ³⁴ Instead, one of the soldiers stuck his spear into Jesus' side. Right away, blood and water flowed out. ³⁵ The man who saw it has been a witness about it. And what he has said is true. He knows that he tells the truth. He is a witness so that you also may believe. ³⁶ These things happened in order that Scripture would come true. It says, "Not one of his bones will be broken." *(Exodus 12:46; Numbers 9:12; Psalm 34:20)* ³⁷ Scripture also says, "They will look to the one they have pierced." *(Zechariah 12:10)*

Jesus Is Buried

³⁸ Later Joseph asked Pilate for Jesus' body. Joseph was from the town of Arimathea. He was a follower of Jesus. But he followed Jesus secretly because he was afraid of the Jewish leaders.

After Pilate gave him permission, Joseph came and took the body away. ³⁹ Nicodemus went with Joseph. He was the man who had earlier visited Jesus at night. Nicodemus brought some mixed spices that weighed about 75 pounds. ⁴⁰ The two men took Jesus' body. They wrapped it in strips of linen cloth, along with the spices. That was the way the Jews buried people. ⁴¹ At the place where Jesus was crucified, there was a garden. A new tomb was there. No one had ever been put in it before. ⁴² That day was the Jewish Preparation Day, and the tomb was nearby. So they placed Jesus there.

The Tomb Is Empty

20 Early on the first day of the week, Mary Magdalene went to the tomb. It was still dark. She saw that the stone had been moved away from the entrance. ² So she ran to Simon Peter and another disciple, the one Jesus loved. She said, "They have taken the Lord out of the tomb! We don't know where they have put him!"

³ So Peter and the other disciple started out for the tomb. ⁴ Both of them were running. The other disciple ran faster than Peter. He reached the tomb first. ⁵ He bent over and looked in at the strips of linen lying there. But he did not go in. ⁶ Then Simon Peter came along behind him. He went straight into the tomb. He saw the strips of linen lying there. ⁷ He also saw the funeral cloth that had been wrapped around Jesus' head. The cloth was still lying in its place. It was separate from the linen. ⁸ The disciple who had reached the tomb first also went inside. He saw and believed. ⁹ They still did not understand from Scripture that Jesus had to rise from the dead. ¹⁰ Then the disciples went back to where they were staying.

Jesus Appears to Mary Magdalene

¹¹ But Mary stood outside the tomb crying. As she cried, she bent over to look into the tomb. ¹² She saw two angels dressed in white. They were seated where Jesus' body had been. One of them was where Jesus' head had been laid. The other sat where his feet had been placed.

¹³ They asked her, "Woman, why are you crying?"

"They have taken my Lord away," she said. "I don't know where they have put him." ¹⁴ Then she turned around and saw Jesus standing there. But she didn't realize that it was Jesus.

¹⁵ He asked her, "Woman, why are you crying? Who are you looking for?"

She thought he was the gardener. So she said, "Sir, did you carry him away? Tell me where you put him. Then I will go and get him."

¹⁶ Jesus said to her, "Mary."

She turned toward him. Then she cried out in the Aramaic language, "Rabboni!" Rabboni means Teacher.

¹⁷ Jesus said, "Do not hold on to me. I have not yet ascended to the Father. Instead, go to those who believe in me. Tell them, 'I am ascending to my Father and your Father, to my God and your God.' "

¹⁸ Mary Magdalene went to the disciples with the news. She said, "I have seen the Lord!" And she told them that he had said these things to her.

Jesus Appears to His Disciples

¹⁹ On the evening of that first day of the week, the disciples were together. They had locked the doors because they were afraid of the Jewish leaders. Jesus came in and stood among them. He said, "May peace be with you!" ²⁰ Then he showed them his hands and his side. The disciples were very happy when they saw the Lord.

²¹ Again Jesus said, "May peace be with you! The Father has sent me. So now I am sending you." ²² He then breathed on them. He said, "Receive the Holy Spirit. ²³ If you forgive anyone's sins, their sins are forgiven. If you do not forgive them, they are not forgiven."

Jesus Appears to Thomas

²⁴ Thomas was one of the 12 disciples. He was also called Didymus. He was not with the other disciples when Jesus came. ²⁵ So they told him, "We have seen the Lord!"

But he said to them, "First I must see the nail marks in his hands. I must put my finger where the nails were. I must put my hand into his side. Only then will I believe."

²⁶ A week later, Jesus' disciples were in the house again. Thomas was with them. Even though the doors were locked, Jesus came in and stood among them. He said, "May peace be with you!" ²⁷ Then he said to Thomas, "Put your finger here. See my hands. Reach out your hand and put it into my side. Stop doubting and believe."

²⁸ Thomas said to him, "My Lord and my God!"

²⁹ Then Jesus told him, "Because you have seen me, you have believed. Blessed are those who have not seen me but still have believed."

The Purpose of John's Gospel

³⁰ Jesus performed many other signs in front of his disciples. They are not written down in this book. ³¹ But these are written so that you may believe that Jesus is the Messiah, the Son of God. If you believe this, you will have life because you belong to him.

Jesus and the Miracle of Many Fish

21 After this, Jesus appeared to his disciples again. It was by the Sea of Galilee. Here is what happened. ² Simon Peter and Thomas, who was also called Didymus, were there together. Nathanael from Cana in Galilee and the sons of Zebedee were with them. So were two other disciples. ³ "I'm going out to fish," Simon Peter told them. They said, "We'll go with you." So they went out and got into the boat. That night they didn't catch anything.

⁴ Early in the morning, Jesus stood on the shore. But the disciples did not realize that it was Jesus.

⁵ He called out to them, "Friends, don't you have any fish?"

"No," they answered.

⁶ He said, "Throw your net on the right side of the boat. There you will find some fish." When they did, they could not pull the net into the boat. There were too many fish in it.

⁷ Then the disciple Jesus loved said to Simon Peter, "It is the Lord!" As soon as Peter heard that, he put his coat on. He had taken it off earlier. Then he jumped into the water. ⁸ The other disciples followed in the boat. They were towing the net full of fish. The shore was only about 100 yards away. ⁹ When they landed, they saw a fire of burning coals. There were fish on it. There was also some bread.

¹⁰ Jesus said to them, "Bring some of the fish you have just caught." ¹¹ So Simon Peter climbed back into the boat. He dragged the net to shore. It was full of large fish. There were 153 of them. But even with that many fish the net was not torn. ¹² Jesus said to them, "Come and have breakfast." None of the disciples dared to ask him, "Who are you?" They knew it was the Lord. ¹³ Jesus came, took the bread and gave it to them. He did the same thing with the fish. ¹⁴ This was the third time Jesus appeared to his disciples after he was raised from the dead.

Jesus Gives Peter His Task

¹⁵ When Jesus and the disciples had finished eating, Jesus spoke to Simon Peter. He asked, "Simon, son of John, do you love me more than these others do?"

"Yes, Lord," he answered. "You know that I love you."

Jesus said, "Feed my lambs."

¹⁶ Again Jesus asked, "Simon, son of John, do you love me?"

He answered, "Yes, Lord. You know that I love you."

Jesus said, "Take care of my sheep."

¹⁷ Jesus spoke to him a third time. He asked, "Simon, son of John, do you love me?"

Peter felt bad because Jesus asked him the third time, "Do you love me?" He answered, "Lord, you know all things. You know that I love you."

Jesus said, "Feed my sheep. ¹⁸ What I'm about to tell you is true. When you were younger, you dressed yourself. You went wherever you wanted to go. But when you are old, you will stretch out your hands. Someone else will dress you. Someone else will lead you where you do not want to go." ¹⁹ Jesus said this to point out how Peter would die. His death would bring glory to God. Then Jesus said to him, "Follow me!"

²⁰ Peter turned around. He

saw that the disciple Jesus loved was following them. He was the one who had leaned back against Jesus at the supper. He had said, "Lord, who is going to hand you over to your enemies?" [21]When Peter saw that disciple, he asked, "Lord, what will happen to him?"

[22]Jesus answered, "Suppose I want him to remain alive until I return. What does that matter to you? You must follow me." [23]Because of what Jesus said, a false report spread among the believers. The story was told that the disciple Jesus loved wouldn't die. But Jesus did not say he would not die. He only said, "Suppose I want him to remain alive until I return. What does that matter to you?"

[24]This is the disciple who is a witness about these things. He also wrote them down. We know that what he says is true.

[25]Jesus also did many other things. What if every one of them were written down? I suppose that even the whole world would not have room for the books that would be written.

Acts

Introduction:

Acts is the second book that Luke wrote. Acts tells about the start of the Christian church. Jesus told his followers to tell others about him. As Jesus' followers did this, the church grew.

Peter and Paul are two important people in Acts. Peter helped start the church in Jerusalem. Paul was one of the first missionaries. He took many trips. Paul told people in many places about Jesus.

Some people hated the church. The leaders of the Jews did not want people to follow Jesus. Paul was one of these leaders until he learned who Jesus was. Before Paul trusted Jesus, he was called Saul. The more people tried to stop the church, the more it grew.

Outline of contents:

Jesus Is Taken Up Into Heaven

1 Theophilus, I wrote about Jesus in my earlier book. I wrote about all he did and taught ² until the day he was taken up to heaven. Before Jesus left, he gave orders to the apostles he had chosen. He did this through the Holy Spirit. ³ After his suffering and death, he appeared to them. In many ways he proved that he was alive. He appeared to them over a period of 40 days. During that time he spoke about God's kingdom. ⁴ One day Jesus was eating with them. He gave them a command. "Do not leave Jerusalem," he said. "Wait for the gift my Father promised. You have heard me talk about it. ⁵ John baptized with water. But in a few days you will be baptized with the Holy Spirit."

⁶ Then the apostles gathered around Jesus and asked him a question. "Lord," they said, "are you going to give the kingdom back to Israel now?"

⁷ He said to them, "You should not be concerned about times or dates. The Father has set them by his own authority. ⁸ But you

will receive power when the Holy Spirit comes on you. Then you will tell people about me in Jerusalem, and in all Judea and Samaria. And you will even tell other people about me from one end of the earth to the other."

⁹ After Jesus said this, he was taken up to heaven. The apostles watched until a cloud hid him from their sight.

¹⁰ While he was going up, they kept on looking at the sky. Suddenly two men dressed in white clothing stood beside them. ¹¹ "Men of Galilee," they said, "why do you stand here looking at the sky? Jesus has been taken away from you into heaven. But he will come back in the same way you saw him go."

Matthias Is Chosen to Take the Place of Judas Iscariot

¹² The apostles returned to Jerusalem from the hill called the Mount of Olives. It is just over half a mile from the city. ¹³ When they arrived, they went upstairs to the room where they were staying.

Peter, John, James and Andrew were there.
Philip, Thomas, Bartholomew and Matthew were there too.
So were James son of Alphaeus, Simon the Zealot, and Judas son of James.

¹⁴ They all came together regularly to pray. The women joined them too. So did Jesus' mother Mary and his brothers.

¹⁵ In those days Peter stood up among the believers. About 120 of them were there. ¹⁶ Peter said, "Brothers and sisters, a long time ago the Holy Spirit spoke through David. He spoke about Judas Iscariot. What the Scripture said would happen had to come true. Judas was the guide for the men who arrested Jesus. ¹⁷ But Judas was one of us. He shared with us in our work for God."

¹⁸ Judas bought a field with the payment he received for the evil thing he had done. He fell down headfirst in the field. His body burst open. All his insides spilled out. ¹⁹ Everyone in Jerusalem heard about this. So they called that field Akeldama. In their language, Akeldama means the Field of Blood.

²⁰ Peter said, "Here is what is written in the Book of Psalms. It says,

" 'May his home be deserted.
    May no one live in it.'
(Psalm 69:25)

The Psalms also say,

" 'Let someone else take his
    place as leader.'
(Psalm 109:8)

²¹ So we need to choose someone to take his place. It will have to be a man who was with us the whole time the Lord Jesus was living among us. ²² That time began when John was baptizing. It ended when Jesus was taken up from us. The one we choose must join us in telling people that Jesus rose from the dead."

²³ So they suggested the names of two men. One was Joseph, who was called Barsabbas. He was also called Justus. The other man was Matthias. ²⁴ Then the believers prayed. They said, "Lord, you know everyone's heart. Show us which of these two you have chosen. ²⁵ Show us who should take the place of Judas as an apostle. He gave up being an apostle to go where he belongs." ²⁶ Then they cast lots. Matthias was chosen. So he was added to the 11 apostles.

The Holy Spirit Comes at Pentecost

2 When the day of Pentecost came, all the believers gathered in one place. ² Suddenly a sound came from heaven. It was like a strong wind blowing. It filled the whole house where they were sitting. ³ They saw something that looked like fire in the shape of tongues. The flames separated and came to rest on each of them. ⁴ All of them were filled with the Holy Spirit. They began to speak in languages they had not known before. The Spirit gave them the ability to do this.

⁵ Godly Jews from every country in the world were staying in Jerusalem. ⁶ A crowd came together when they heard the sound. They were bewildered because each of them heard their own language being spoken. ⁷ The crowd was really amazed. They asked, "Aren't all these people who are speaking Galileans? ⁸ Then why do we each hear them speaking in our own native language? ⁹ We are Parthians, Medes and Elamites. We live in Mesopotamia, Judea and Cappadocia. We are from Pontus, Asia, ¹⁰ Phrygia and Pamphylia. Others of us are from Egypt and the parts of Libya near Cyrene. Still others are visitors from Rome. ¹¹ Some of the visitors are Jews. Others have accepted the Jewish faith. Also, Cretans and Arabs are here. We hear all these people speaking about God's wonders in our own languages!" ¹² They were amazed and bewildered. They asked one another, "What does this mean?"

¹³ But some people in the crowd made fun of the believers. "They've had too much wine!" they said.

Peter Speaks to the Crowd

¹⁴ Then Peter stood up with the 11 apostles. In a loud voice he spoke to the crowd. "My fellow Jews," he said, "let me explain this to you. All of you who live in Jerusalem, listen carefully to what I say. ¹⁵ You think these people are drunk. But they aren't. It's only nine o'clock in the morning! ¹⁶ No, here is what the prophet Joel meant. ¹⁷ He said,

" 'In the last days, God says,
　I will pour out my Holy
　　Spirit on all people.
Your sons and daughters will
　　prophesy.
　Your young men will see
　　visions.

Your old men will have
dreams.
18 In those days, I will pour
out my Spirit on my
servants.
I will pour out my Spirit on
both men and women.
When I do, they will
prophesy.
19 I will show wonders in the
heavens above.
I will show signs on the
earth below.
There will be blood and
fire and clouds of smoke.
20 The sun will become dark.
The moon will turn red
like blood.
This will happen before
the coming of the great
and glorious day of the
Lord.
21 Everyone who calls
on the name of the Lord
will be saved.' *(Joel 2:28–32)*

22 "Fellow Israelites, listen to
this! Jesus of Nazareth was a
man who had God's approval.
God did miracles, wonders
and signs among you through
Jesus. You yourselves know this.
23 Long ago God planned that
Jesus would be handed over to
you. With the help of evil people, you put Jesus to death. You
nailed him to the cross. 24 But
God raised him from the dead.
He set him free from the suffering of death. It wasn't possible for death to keep its hold on
Jesus. 25 David spoke about him.
He said,

" 'I know that the Lord is
always with me.

Because he is at my right
hand,
I will always be secure.
26 So my heart is glad and joy is
on my tongue.
My whole body will be full
of hope.
27 You will not leave me in the
place of the dead.
You will not let your holy
one rot away.
28 You always show me the path
that leads to life.
You will fill me with joy
when I am with you.'

(Psalm 16:8–11)

29 "Fellow Israelites, you can
be sure that King David died.
He was buried. His tomb is still
here today. 30 But David was a
prophet. He knew that God had
made a promise to him. God
had promised that he would
make someone in David's family line king after him. 31 David
saw what was coming. So he
spoke about the Messiah rising from the dead. He said that
the Messiah would not be left in
the place of the dead. His body
wouldn't rot in the ground.
32 God has raised this same Jesus
back to life. We are all witnesses
of this. 33 Jesus has been given a
place of honor at the right hand
of God. He has received the
Holy Spirit from the Father. This
is what God had promised. It is
Jesus who has poured out what
you now see and hear. 34 David
did not go up to heaven. But he
said,

" 'The Lord said to my Lord,
"Sit at my right hand.

35 I will put your enemies
　　under your control." '

(Psalm 110:1)

36 "So be sure of this, all you people of Israel. You nailed Jesus to the cross. But God has made him both Lord and Messiah."

37 When the people heard this, it had a deep effect on them. They said to Peter and the other apostles, "Brothers, what should we do?"

38 Peter replied, "All of you must turn away from your sins and be baptized in the name of Jesus Christ. Then your sins will be forgiven. You will receive the gift of the Holy Spirit. 39 The promise is for you and your children. It is also for all who are far away. It is for all whom the Lord our God will choose."

40 Peter said many other things to warn them. He begged them, "Save yourselves from these evil people." 41 Those who accepted his message were baptized. About 3,000 people joined the believers that day.

The Believers Share Their Lives Together

42 The believers studied what the apostles taught. They shared their lives together. They ate and prayed together. 43 Everyone was amazed at what God was doing. They were amazed when the apostles performed many wonders and signs. 44 All the believers were together. They shared everything they had. 45 They sold property and other things they owned. They gave to any-one who needed something. 46 Every day they met together in the temple courtyard. They ate meals together in their homes. Their hearts were glad and sincere. 47 They praised God. They were respected by all the people. Every day the Lord added to their group those who were being saved.

Peter Heals a Beggar Who Can't Walk

3 One day Peter and John were going up to the temple. It was three o'clock in the afternoon. It was the time for prayer. 2 A man unable to walk was being carried to the temple gate called Beautiful. He had been that way since he was born. Every day someone put him near the gate. There he would beg from people going into the temple courtyards. 3 He saw that Peter and John were about to enter. So he asked them for money. 4 Peter looked straight at him, and so did John. Then Peter said, "Look at us!" 5 So the man watched them closely. He expected to get something from them.

6 Peter said, "I don't have any silver or gold. But I'll give you what I do have. In the name of Jesus Christ of Nazareth, get up and walk." 7 Then Peter took him by the right hand and helped him up. At once the man's feet and ankles became strong. 8 He jumped to his feet and began to walk. He went with Peter and John into the temple courtyards. He walked

and jumped and praised God. [9] All the people saw him walking and praising God. [10] They recognized him as the same man who used to sit and beg at the temple gate called Beautiful. They were filled with wonder. They were amazed at what had happened to him.

Peter Speaks to the People at the Temple

[11] The man was holding on to Peter and John. All the people were amazed. They came running to them at the place called Solomon's Porch. [12] When Peter saw this, he said, "Fellow Israelites, why does this surprise you? Why do you stare at us? It's not as if we've made this man walk by our own power or godliness. [13] The God of our fathers, Abraham, Isaac and Jacob, has done this. God has brought glory to Jesus, who serves him. But you handed Jesus over to be killed. Pilate had decided to let him go. But you spoke against Jesus when he was in Pilate's court. [14] You spoke against the Holy and Blameless One. You asked for a murderer to be set free instead. [15] You killed the one who gives life. But God raised him from the dead. We are witnesses of this. [16] This man whom you see and know was made strong because of faith in Jesus' name. Faith in Jesus has healed him completely. You can see it with your own eyes.

[17] "My fellow Israelites, I know you didn't realize what you were doing. Neither did your leaders. [18] But God had given a promise through all the prophets. And this is how he has made his promise come true. He said that his Messiah would suffer. [19] So turn away from your sins. Turn to God. Then your sins will be wiped away. The time will come when the Lord will make everything new. [20] He will send the Messiah. Jesus has been appointed as the Messiah for you. [21] Heaven must receive him until the time when God makes everything new. He promised this long ago through his holy prophets. [22] Moses said, 'The Lord your God will raise up for you a prophet like me. He will be one of your own people. You must listen to everything he tells you. [23] Anyone who does not listen to him will be completely cut off from their people.' *(Deuteronomy 18:15,18,19)*

[24] "Beginning with Samuel, all the prophets spoke about this. They said these days would come. [25] What the prophets said was meant for you. The covenant God made with your people long ago is yours also. He said to Abraham, 'All nations on earth will be blessed through your children.' *(Genesis 22:18; 26:4)* [26] God raised up Jesus, who serves him. God sent him first to you. He did it to bless you. He wanted to turn each of you from your evil ways."

Peter and John Are Taken to the Sanhedrin

4 Peter and John were speaking to the people. The priests, the captain of the temple guard, and the Sadducees came up to the apostles. ²They were very upset by what the apostles were teaching the people. The apostles were saying that people can be raised from the dead. They said this can happen because Jesus rose from the dead. ³So the temple authorities arrested Peter and John. It was already evening, so they put them in prison until the next day. ⁴But many who heard the message believed. The number of men who believed grew to about 5,000.

⁵The next day the rulers, the elders and the teachers of the law met in Jerusalem. ⁶Annas, the high priest, was there. So were Caiaphas, John, Alexander and other people in the high priest's family. ⁷They had Peter and John brought to them. They wanted to question them. "By what power did you do this?" they asked. "And through whose name?"

⁸Peter was filled with the Holy Spirit. He said to them, "Rulers and elders of the people! ⁹Are you asking us to explain our actions today? Do you want to know why we were kind to a man who couldn't walk? Are you asking how he was healed? ¹⁰Then listen to this, you and all the people of Israel! You nailed Jesus Christ of Nazareth to the cross. But God raised him from the dead. It is through Jesus' name that this man stands healed in front of you. ¹¹Scripture says that Jesus is

" 'the stone you builders did
   not accept.
But it has become the most
   important stone of all.'
(Psalm 118:22)

¹²You can't be saved by believing in anyone else. God has given people no other name under heaven that will save them."

¹³The leaders saw how bold Peter and John were. They also realized that Peter and John were ordinary men with no training. This surprised the leaders. They realized that these men had been with Jesus. ¹⁴The leaders could see the man who had been healed. He was standing there with them. So there was nothing they could say. ¹⁵They ordered Peter and John to leave the Sanhedrin. Then they talked things over. ¹⁶"What can we do with these men?" they asked. "Everyone living in Jerusalem knows they have performed an unusual miracle. We can't say it didn't happen. ¹⁷We have to stop this thing. It must not spread any further among the people. We have to warn these men. They must never speak to anyone in Jesus' name again."

¹⁸Once again the leaders called in Peter and John. They commanded them not to speak or teach at all in Jesus' name. ¹⁹But Peter and John replied, "Which is right from God's point of view? Should we listen to you? Or should we listen to God? You be the judges! ²⁰There's nothing else we can do. We have to speak about the things we've seen and heard."

²¹ The leaders warned them again. Then they let them go. They couldn't decide how to punish Peter and John. They knew that all the people were praising God for what had happened. ²² The man who had been healed by the miracle was over 40 years old.

The Believers Pray

²³ Peter and John were allowed to leave. They went back to their own people. They reported everything the chief priests and the elders had said to them. ²⁴ The believers heard this. Then they raised their voices together in prayer to God. "Lord and King," they said, "you made the heavens, the earth and the sea. You made everything in them. ²⁵ Long ago you spoke by the Holy Spirit. You spoke through the mouth of our father David, who served you. You said,

" 'Why are the nations angry?
    Why do the people make
        useless plans?
²⁶ The kings of the earth rise
        up.
    The rulers of the earth
        gather together
  against the Lord
    and against his anointed
        king.'   *(Psalm 2:1,2)*

²⁷ In fact, Herod and Pontius Pilate met with the Gentiles in this city. They also met with the people of Israel. All of them made plans against your holy servant Jesus. He is the one you anointed. ²⁸ They did what your power and purpose had already decided should happen. ²⁹ Now, Lord, consider the bad things they say they are going to do. Help us to be very bold when we speak your word. ³⁰ Stretch out your hand to heal. Do signs and wonders through the name of your holy servant Jesus."

³¹ After they prayed, the place where they were meeting was shaken. They were all filled with the Holy Spirit. They were bold when they spoke God's word.

The Believers Share What They Own

³² All the believers were agreed in heart and mind. They didn't claim that anything they had was their own. Instead, they shared everything they owned. ³³ With great power the apostles continued their teaching. They were telling people that the Lord Jesus had risen from the dead. And God's grace was working powerfully in all of them. ³⁴ So there were no needy persons among them. From time to time, those who owned land or houses sold them. They brought the money from the sales. ³⁵ They put it down at the apostles' feet. It was then given out to anyone who needed it.

³⁶ Joseph was a Levite from Cyprus. The apostles called him Barnabas. The name Barnabas means Son of Help. ³⁷ Barnabas sold a field he owned. He brought the money from the sale. He put it down at the apostles' feet.

Ananias and Sapphira

5 A man named Ananias and his wife, Sapphira, also sold some land. [2] He kept part of the money for himself. Sapphira knew he had kept it. He brought the rest of it and put it down at the apostles' feet.

[3] Then Peter said, "Ananias, why did you let Satan fill your heart? He made you lie to the Holy Spirit. You have kept some of the money you received for the land. [4] Didn't the land belong to you before it was sold? After it was sold, you could have used the money as you wished. What made you think of doing such a thing? You haven't lied just to people. You've also lied to God."

[5] When Ananias heard this, he fell down and died. All who heard what had happened were filled with fear. [6] Some young men came and wrapped up his body. They carried him out and buried him.

[7] About three hours later, the wife of Ananias came in. She didn't know what had happened. [8] Peter asked her, "Tell me. Is this the price you and Ananias sold the land for?"

"Yes," she said. "That's the price."

[9] Peter asked her, "How could you agree to test the Spirit of the Lord? Listen! You can hear the steps of the men who buried your husband. They are at the door. They will carry you out also."

[10] At that moment she fell down at Peter's feet and died.

Then the young men came in. They saw that Sapphira was dead. So they carried her out and buried her beside her husband. [11] The whole church and all who heard about these things were filled with fear.

The Apostles Heal Many People

[12] The apostles did many signs and wonders among the people. All the believers used to meet together at Solomon's Porch. [13] No outsider dared to join them. But the people thought highly of them. [14] More and more men and women believed in the Lord. They joined the other believers. [15] So people brought those who were sick into the streets. They placed them on beds and mats. They hoped that at least Peter's shadow might fall on some of them as he walked by. [16] Crowds even gathered from the towns around Jerusalem. They brought their sick people. They also brought those who were suffering because of evil spirits. All of them were healed.

The Apostles Are Treated Badly

[17] The high priest and all his companions were Sadducees. They were very jealous of the apostles. [18] So they arrested them and put them in the public jail. [19] But during the night an angel of the Lord came. He opened the doors of the jail and brought the apostles out. [20] "Go! Stand in the temple courtyard," the angel said. "Tell the people all about this new life."

[21] Early the next day they did

as they had been told. They entered the temple courtyard. There they began to teach the people.

The high priest and his companions arrived. They called the Sanhedrin together. The Sanhedrin was a gathering of all the elders of Israel. They sent for the apostles who were in jail. ²² The officers arrived at the jail. But they didn't find the apostles there. So they went back and reported it. ²³ "We found the jail locked up tight," they said. "The guards were standing at the doors. But when we opened the doors, we didn't find anyone inside." ²⁴ When the captain of the temple guard and the chief priests heard this report, they were bewildered. They wondered what would happen next.

²⁵ Then someone came and said, "Look! The men you put in jail are standing in the temple courtyard. They are teaching the people." ²⁶ So the captain went with his officers and brought the apostles back. But they didn't use force. They were afraid the people would kill them by throwing stones at them.

²⁷ They brought the apostles to the Sanhedrin. The high priest questioned them. ²⁸ "We gave you clear orders not to teach in Jesus' name," he said. "But you have filled Jerusalem with your teaching. You want to make us guilty of this man's death."

²⁹ Peter and the other apostles replied, "We must obey God instead of people! ³⁰ You had Jesus killed by nailing him to a cross. But the God of our people raised Jesus from the dead. ³¹ Now Jesus is Prince and Savior. God has proved this by giving Jesus a place of honor with him. He did it to turn Israel away from their sins and forgive them. ³² We are telling people about these things. And so is the Holy Spirit. God has given the Spirit to those who obey him."

³³ When the leaders heard this, they became very angry. They wanted to put the apostles to death. ³⁴ But a Pharisee named Gamaliel stood up in the Sanhedrin. He was a teacher of the law. He was honored by all the people. He ordered the apostles to be taken outside for a little while. ³⁵ Then Gamaliel spoke to the Sanhedrin. "Men of Israel," he said, "think carefully about what you plan to do to these men. ³⁶ Some time ago Theudas appeared. He claimed he was really somebody. About 400 people followed him. But he was killed. All his followers were scattered. So they accomplished nothing. ³⁷ After this, Judas from Galilee came along. This was in the days when the Romans made a list of all the people. Judas led a gang of men against the Romans. He too was killed. All his followers were scattered. ³⁸ So let me give you some advice. Leave these men alone! Let them go! If their plans and actions only come from people, they will fail. ³⁹ But if their plans come from God, you won't be able to stop these men. You will

only find yourselves fighting against God."

⁴⁰ His speech won the leaders over. They called the apostles in and had them whipped. The leaders ordered them not to speak in Jesus' name. Then they let the apostles go.

⁴¹ The apostles were full of joy as they left the Sanhedrin. They considered it an honor to suffer shame for the name of Jesus. ⁴² Every day they taught in the temple courtyards and from house to house. They never stopped telling people the good news that Jesus is the Messiah.

Seven Leaders Are Chosen

6 In those days the number of believers was growing. The Greek Jews complained about the non-Greek Jews. They said that the widows of the Greek Jews were not being taken care of. They weren't getting their fair share of food each day. ² So the 12 apostles gathered all the believers together. They said, "It wouldn't be right for us to give up teaching God's word. And we'd have to stop teaching to wait on tables. ³ Brothers and sisters, choose seven of your men. They must be known as men who are wise and full of the Holy Spirit. We will turn this important work over to them. ⁴ Then we can give our attention to prayer and to teaching God's word."

⁵ This plan pleased the whole group. They chose Stephen. He was full of faith and of the Holy Spirit. Philip, Procorus, Nica-nor, Timon and Parmenas were chosen too. The group also chose Nicolas from Antioch. He had accepted the Jewish faith. ⁶ The group brought them to the apostles. Then the apostles prayed and placed their hands on them.

⁷ So God's word spread. The number of believers in Jerusalem grew quickly. Also, a large number of priests began to obey Jesus' teachings.

Stephen Is Arrested

⁸ Stephen was full of God's grace and power. He did great wonders and signs among the people. ⁹ But members of the group called the Synagogue of the Freedmen began to oppose him. Some of them were Jews from Cyrene and Alexandria. Others were Jews from Cilicia and Asia Minor. They all began to argue with Stephen. ¹⁰ But he was too wise for them. That's because the Holy Spirit gave Stephen wisdom whenever he spoke.

¹¹ Then in secret they talked some men into lying about Stephen. They said, "We heard Stephen speak evil things against Moses and against God."

¹² So the people were stirred up. The elders and the teachers of the law were stirred up too. They arrested Stephen and brought him to the Sanhedrin. ¹³ They found witnesses who were willing to tell lies. These liars said, "This fellow never stops speaking against this holy place. He also speaks against

the law. [14] We have heard him say that this Jesus of Nazareth will destroy this place. He says Jesus will change the practices that Moses handed down to us."

[15] All who were sitting in the Sanhedrin looked right at Stephen. They saw that his face was like the face of an angel.

Stephen Speaks to the Sanhedrin

7 Then the high priest questioned Stephen. "Is what these people are saying true?" he asked.

[2] "Brothers and fathers, listen to me!" Stephen replied. "The God of glory appeared to our father Abraham. At that time Abraham was still in Mesopotamia. He had not yet begun living in Harran. [3] 'Leave your country and your people,' God said. 'Go to the land I will show you.' *(Genesis 12:1)*

[4] "So Abraham left the land of Babylonia. He settled in Harran. After his father died, God sent Abraham to this land where you are now living. [5] God didn't give him any property here. He didn't even give him enough land to set his foot on. But God made a promise to him and to all his family after him. He said they would possess the land. The promise was made even though at that time Abraham had no child. [6] Here is what God said to him. 'For 400 years your family after you will be strangers in a country not their own. They will be slaves and will be treated badly. [7] But I will punish the nation that makes them slaves,' God said. 'After that, they will leave that country and worship me here.' *(Genesis 15:13,14)* [8] Then God made a covenant with Abraham. God told him that circumcision would show who the members of the covenant were. Abraham became Isaac's father. He circumcised Isaac eight days after he was born. Later, Isaac became Jacob's father. Jacob had 12 sons. They became the founders of the 12 tribes of Israel.

[9] "Jacob's sons were jealous of their brother Joseph. So they sold him as a slave. He was taken to Egypt. But God was with him. [10] He saved Joseph from all his troubles. God made Joseph wise. He helped him to become the friend of Pharaoh, the king of Egypt. So Pharaoh made Joseph ruler over Egypt and his whole palace.

[11] "There was not enough food for all Egypt and Canaan. This brought great suffering. Jacob and his sons couldn't find food. [12] But Jacob heard that there was grain in Egypt. So he sent his sons on their first visit. [13] On their second visit, Joseph told his brothers who he was. Pharaoh learned about Joseph's family. [14] After this, Joseph sent for his father Jacob and his whole family. The total number of people was 75. [15] Then Jacob went down to Egypt. There he and his family died. [16] Some of their bodies were brought back to Shechem. They were placed in a tomb Abraham had bought. He

had purchased it from Hamor's sons at Shechem. He had purchased it for a certain amount of money.

17 "In Egypt the number of our people grew and grew. It was nearly time for God to make his promise to Abraham come true. 18 Then 'a new king came to power in Egypt. Joseph didn't mean anything to him.' *(Exodus 1:8)* 19 The king was very evil and dishonest with our people. He treated them badly. He forced them to throw out their newborn babies to die.

20 "At that time Moses was born. He was not an ordinary child. For three months he was taken care of by his family. 21 Then he was placed outside. But Pharaoh's daughter took him home. She brought him up as her own son. 22 Moses was taught all the knowledge of the people of Egypt. He became a powerful speaker and a man of action.

23 "When Moses was 40 years old, he decided to visit the people of Israel. They were his own people. 24 He saw one of them being treated badly by an Egyptian. So he went to help him. He got even by killing the man. 25 Moses thought his own people would realize that God was using him to save them. But they didn't. 26 The next day Moses saw two Israelites fighting. He tried to make peace between them. 'Men, you are both Israelites,' he said. 'Why do you want to hurt each other?'

27 "But the man who was treating the other one badly pushed Moses to one side. He said, 'Who made you ruler and judge over us? 28 Are you thinking of killing me as you killed the Egyptian yesterday?' *(Exodus 2:14)* 29 When Moses heard this, he escaped to Midian. He lived there as an outsider. He became the father of two sons there.

30 "Forty years passed. Then an angel appeared to Moses in the flames of a burning bush. This happened in the desert near Mount Sinai. 31 When Moses saw the bush, he was amazed. He went over for a closer look. There he heard the Lord say, 32 'I am the God of your fathers. I am the God of Abraham, Isaac and Jacob.' *(Exodus 3:6)* Moses shook with fear. He didn't dare to look.

33 "Then the Lord said to him, 'Take off your sandals. You must do this because the place where you are standing is holy ground. 34 I have seen my people beaten down in Egypt. I have heard their groans. I have come down to set them free. Now come. I will send you back to Egypt.' *(Exodus 3:5,7,8,10)*

35 "This is the same Moses the two men of Israel would not accept. They had said, 'Who made you ruler and judge?' But God himself sent Moses to rule the people of Israel and set them free. He spoke to Moses through an angel. The angel had appeared to him in the bush. 36 So Moses led them out of Egypt. He did wonders and signs in Egypt, at the Red Sea, and for 40 years in the desert.

37 "This is the same Moses who spoke to the Israelites. 'God will send you a prophet,' he said. 'He will be like me. He will come from your own people.' *(Deuteronomy 18:15)* 38 Moses was with the Israelites in the desert. He was with the angel who spoke to him on Mount Sinai. Moses was with our people of long ago. He received living words to pass on to us.

39 "But our people refused to obey Moses. They would not accept him. In their hearts, they wished they were back in Egypt. 40 They told Aaron, 'Make us a god who will lead us. This fellow Moses brought us up out of Egypt. But we don't know what has happened to him!' *(Exodus 32:1)* 41 That was the time they made a statue to be their god. It was shaped like a calf. They brought sacrifices to it. They even enjoyed what they had made with their own hands. 42 But God turned away from them. He let them go on worshiping the sun, moon and stars. This agrees with what is written in the book of the prophets. There it says,

" 'People of Israel, did you
    bring me sacrifices and
    offerings
  for 40 years in the desert?
43 You have taken with you the
    shrine of your false god
    Molek.
  You have taken with you
    the star of your false god
    Rephan.
  You made statues of those
    gods to worship.

So I will send you away from
    your country.' *(Amos 5:25-27)*
God sent them to Babylon and even farther.

44 "Long ago our people were in the desert. They had with them the holy tent. The tent was where the tablets of the covenant law were kept. Moses had made the holy tent as God had commanded him. Moses made it like the pattern he had seen. 45 Our people received the tent from God. Then they brought it with them when they took the land of Canaan. God drove out the nations that were in their way. At that time Joshua was Israel's leader. The tent remained in the land until David's time. 46 David was blessed by God. So David asked if he could build a house for the God of Jacob. 47 But it was Solomon who built the temple for God.

48 "But the Most High God does not live in houses made by human hands. As God says through the prophet,

49 " 'Heaven is my throne.
  The earth is under my
    control.
  What kind of house will you
    build for me?
          says the Lord.
  Where will my resting
    place be?
50 Didn't my hand make all
    these things?' *(Isaiah 66:1,2)*

51 "You stubborn people! You won't obey! You won't listen! You are just like your people of long ago! You always oppose the Holy Spirit! 52 Was there ever a

prophet your people didn't try to hurt? They even killed those who told about the coming of the Blameless One. And now you have handed him over to his enemies. You have murdered him. [53] The law you received was given by angels. But you haven't obeyed it."

Stephen Is Killed

[54] When the members of the Sanhedrin heard this, they became very angry. They were so angry they ground their teeth at Stephen. [55] But he was full of the Holy Spirit. He looked up to heaven and saw God's glory. He saw Jesus standing at God's right hand. [56] "Look!" he said. "I see heaven open. The Son of Man is standing at God's right hand."

[57] When the Sanhedrin heard this, they covered their ears. They yelled at the top of their voices. They all rushed at him. [58] They dragged him out of the city. They began to throw stones at him to kill him. The people who had brought false charges against Stephen took off their coats. They placed them at the feet of a young man named Saul.

[59] While the members of the Sanhedrin were throwing stones at Stephen, he prayed. "Lord Jesus, receive my spirit," he said. [60] Then he fell on his knees. He cried out, "Lord! Don't hold this sin against them!" When he had said this, he died.

8 And Saul had agreed with the Sanhedrin that Stephen should die.

The Church Is Treated Badly and Scattered

On that day the church in Jerusalem began to be attacked and treated badly. All except the apostles were scattered throughout Judea and Samaria. [2] Godly Jews buried Stephen. They mourned deeply for him. [3] But Saul began to destroy the church. He went from house to house. He dragged away men and women and put them in prison.

Philip Goes to Samaria

[4] The believers who had been scattered preached the word everywhere they went. [5] Philip went down to a city in Samaria. There he preached about the Messiah. [6] The crowds listened to Philip and saw the signs he did. All of them paid close attention to what he said. [7] Evil spirits screamed and came out of many people. Many people who were disabled or who couldn't walk were healed. [8] So there was great joy in that city.

Simon the Evil Magician

[9] A man named Simon lived in the city. For quite a while he had practiced evil magic there. He amazed all the people of Samaria. He claimed to be someone great. [10] And all the people listened to him, from the least important of them to the most important. They exclaimed, "It is right to call this man the Great Power of God!" [11] He had amazed them for a long time with his evil magic. So they followed him.

¹² But Philip announced the good news of God's kingdom and the name of Jesus Christ. So men and women believed and were baptized. ¹³ Simon himself believed and was baptized. He followed Philip everywhere. He was amazed by the great signs and miracles he saw.

¹⁴ The apostles in Jerusalem heard that people in Samaria had accepted God's word. So they sent Peter and John to Samaria. ¹⁵ When they arrived there, they prayed for the new believers. They prayed that they would receive the Holy Spirit. ¹⁶ The Holy Spirit had not yet come on any of them. They had only been baptized in the name of the Lord Jesus. ¹⁷ Then Peter and John placed their hands on them. And they received the Holy Spirit.

¹⁸ Simon watched as the apostles placed their hands on them. He saw that the Spirit was given to them. So he offered money to Peter and John. ¹⁹ He said, "Give me this power too. Then everyone I place my hands on will receive the Holy Spirit."

²⁰ Peter answered, "May your money be destroyed with you! Do you think you can buy God's gift with money? ²¹ You have no part or share in this holy work. Your heart is not right with God. ²² Turn away from this evil sin of yours. Pray to the Lord. Perhaps he will forgive you for having such a thought in your heart. ²³ I see that you are very bitter. You are a prisoner of sin."

²⁴ Then Simon answered, "Pray to the Lord for me. Pray that nothing you have said will happen to me."

²⁵ Peter and John continued to preach the word of the Lord and tell people about Jesus. Then they returned to Jerusalem. On the way they preached the good news in many villages in Samaria.

Philip and the Man From Ethiopia

²⁶ An angel of the Lord spoke to Philip. "Go south to the desert road," he said. "It's the road that goes down from Jerusalem to Gaza." ²⁷ So Philip started out. On his way he met an Ethiopian official. The man had an important position in charge of all the wealth of the kandake. Kandake means Queen of Ethiopia. This official had gone to Jerusalem to worship. ²⁸ On his way home he was sitting in his chariot. He was reading the Book of Isaiah the prophet. ²⁹ The Holy Spirit told Philip, "Go to that chariot. Stay near it."

³⁰ So Philip ran up to the chariot. He heard the man reading Isaiah the prophet. "Do you understand what you're reading?" Philip asked.

³¹ "How can I?" he said. "I need someone to explain it to me." So he invited Philip to come up and sit with him.

³² Here is the part of Scripture the official was reading. It says,

"He was led like a sheep to be
    killed.
Just as lambs are silent
    while their wool is being
    cut off,
he did not open his mouth.

³³ When he was treated badly,
he was refused a fair
trial.
Who can say anything
about his children?
His life was cut off from the
earth." *(Isaiah 53:7,8)*

³⁴ The official said to Philip,
"Tell me, please. Who is the
prophet talking about? Himself,
or someone else?" ³⁵ Then Philip
began with that same part of
Scripture. He told him the good
news about Jesus.

³⁶⁻³⁷ As they traveled along the
road, they came to some water.
The official said, "Look! Here is
water! What can stop me from
being baptized?" ³⁸ He gave orders to stop the chariot. Then
both Philip and the official went
down into the water. Philip baptized him. ³⁹ When they came
up out of the water, the Spirit of
the Lord suddenly took Philip
away. The official did not see
him again. He went on his way
full of joy. ⁴⁰ Philip was seen next
at Azotus. From there he trav-
eled all around. He preached
the good news in all the towns.
Finally he arrived in Caesarea.

Saul Becomes a Believer

9 Meanwhile, Saul continued to oppose the Lord's
followers. He said they would
be put to death. He went to the
high priest. ² He asked the priest
for letters to the synagogues in
Damascus. He wanted to find
men and women who belonged
to the Way of Jesus. The letters
would allow him to take them as
prisoners to Jerusalem. ³ On his
journey, Saul approached Da-
mascus. Suddenly a light from
heaven flashed around him.
⁴ He fell to the ground. He heard
a voice speak to him, "Saul! Saul!
Why are you opposing me?"
⁵ "Who are you, Lord?" Saul
asked.

"I am Jesus," he replied. "I
am the one you are opposing.
⁶ Now get up and go into the city.
There you will be told what you
must do."

⁷ The men traveling with
Saul stood there. They weren't
able to speak. They had heard
the sound. But they didn't see
anyone. ⁸ Saul got up from the
ground. He opened his eyes, but
he couldn't see. So they led him
by the hand into Damascus.
⁹ For three days he was blind. He
didn't eat or drink anything.

¹⁰ In Damascus there was a
believer named Ananias. The
Lord called out to him in a vision. "Ananias!" he said.

"Yes, Lord," he answered.

¹¹ The Lord told him, "Go to
the house of Judas on Straight
Street. Ask for a man from Tarsus named Saul. He is praying.
¹² In a vision Saul has seen a
man come and place his hands
on him. That man's name is Ananias. In the vision, Ananias
placed his hands on Saul so he
could see again."

¹³ "Lord," Ananias answered,
"I've heard many reports about
this man. They say he has done
great harm to your holy peo-
ple in Jerusalem. ¹⁴ Now he has
come here to arrest all those
who worship you. The chief

priests have given him authority to do this."

15 But the Lord said to Ananias, "Go! I have chosen this man to work for me. He will announce my name to the Gentiles and to their kings. He will also announce my name to the people of Israel. 16 I will show him how much he must suffer for me."

17 Then Ananias went to the house and entered it. He placed his hands on Saul. "Brother Saul," he said, "you saw the Lord Jesus. He appeared to you on the road as you were coming here. He has sent me so that you will be able to see again. You will be filled with the Holy Spirit." 18 Right away something like scales fell from Saul's eyes. And he could see again. He got up and was baptized. 19 After eating some food, he got his strength back.

Saul in Damascus and Jerusalem

Saul spent several days with the believers in Damascus. 20 Right away he began to preach in the synagogues. He taught that Jesus is the Son of God. 21 All who heard him were amazed. They asked, "Isn't he the man who caused great trouble in Jerusalem? Didn't he make trouble for those who worship Jesus? Hasn't he come here to take them as prisoners to the chief priests?" 22 But Saul grew more and more powerful. The Jews living in Damascus couldn't believe what was happening. Saul proved to them that Jesus is the Messiah.

23 After many days, the Jews had a meeting. They planned to kill Saul. 24 But he learned about their plan. Day and night they watched the city gates closely in order to kill him. 25 But his followers helped him escape by night. They lowered him in a basket through an opening in the wall.

26 When Saul came to Jerusalem, he tried to join the believers. But they were all afraid of him. They didn't believe he was really one of Jesus' followers. 27 But Barnabas took him to the apostles. He told them about Saul's journey. He said that Saul had seen the Lord. He told how the Lord had spoken to Saul. Barnabas also said that Saul had preached without fear in Jesus' name in Damascus. 28 So Saul stayed with the believers. He moved about freely in Jerusalem. He spoke boldly in the Lord's name. 29 He talked and argued with the Greek Jews. But they tried to kill him. 30 The other believers heard about this. They took Saul down to Caesarea. From there they sent him off to Tarsus.

31 Then the church throughout Judea, Galilee and Samaria enjoyed a time of peace. The church was strengthened and grew larger. That's because they worshiped the Lord and the Holy Spirit helped them.

Peter Heals Aeneas and Dorcas

32 Peter traveled around the country. He went to visit the

Lord's people who lived in Lydda. ³³ There he found a disabled man named Aeneas. For eight years the man had spent most of his time in bed. ³⁴ "Aeneas," Peter said to him, "Jesus Christ heals you. Get up! Roll up your mat!" So Aeneas got up right away. ³⁵ Everyone who lived in Lydda and Sharon saw him. They turned to the Lord.

³⁶ In Joppa there was a believer named Tabitha. Her name in the Greek language is Dorcas. She was always doing good and helping poor people. ³⁷ About that time she became sick and died. Her body was washed and placed in a room upstairs. ³⁸ Lydda was near Joppa. The believers heard that Peter was in Lydda. So they sent two men to him. They begged him, "Please come at once!"

³⁹ Peter went with them. When he arrived, he was taken upstairs to the room. All the widows stood around him crying. They showed him the robes and other clothes Dorcas had made before she died. ⁴⁰ Peter sent them all out of the room. Then he got down on his knees and prayed. He turned toward the dead woman. He said, "Tabitha, get up." She opened her eyes. When she saw Peter, she sat up. ⁴¹ He took her by the hand and helped her to her feet. Then he called the believers and especially the widows. He brought her to them. They saw that she was alive. ⁴² This became known all over Joppa. Many people believed in the Lord. ⁴³ Peter stayed in Joppa for some time. He stayed with Simon, a man who worked with leather.

Cornelius Calls for Peter

10 A man named Cornelius lived in Caesarea. He was a Roman commander in the Italian Regiment. ² Cornelius and all his family were faithful and worshiped God. He gave freely to people who were in need. He prayed to God regularly. ³ One day about three o'clock in the afternoon he had a vision. He saw clearly an angel of God. The angel came to him and said, "Cornelius!"

⁴ Cornelius was afraid. He stared at the angel. "What is it, Lord?" he asked.

The angel answered, "Your prayers and gifts to poor people are like an offering to God. So he has remembered you. ⁵ Now send men to Joppa. Have them bring back a man named Simon. He is also called Peter. ⁶ He is staying with another Simon, a man who works with leather. His house is by the sea."

⁷ The angel who spoke to him left. Then Cornelius called two of his servants. He also called a godly soldier who was one of his attendants. ⁸ He told them everything that had happened. Then he sent them to Joppa.

Peter Has a Vision

⁹ It was about noon the next day. The men were on their journey and were approaching the city. Peter went up on the

roof to pray. [10] He became hungry. He wanted something to eat. While the meal was being prepared, Peter had a vision. [11] He saw heaven open up. There he saw something that looked like a large sheet. It was being let down to earth by its four corners. [12] It had all kinds of four-footed animals in it. It also had reptiles and birds in it. [13] Then a voice told him, "Get up, Peter. Kill and eat."

[14] "No, Lord! I will not!" Peter replied. "I have never eaten anything that is not pure and 'clean.' "

[15] The voice spoke to him a second time. It said, "Do not say anything is not pure that God has made 'clean.' "

[16] This happened three times. Right away the sheet was taken back up to heaven.

[17] Peter was wondering what the vision meant. At that very moment the men sent by Cornelius found Simon's house. They stopped at the gate [18] and called out. They asked if Simon Peter was staying there.

[19] Peter was still thinking about the vision. The Holy Spirit spoke to him. "Simon," he said, "three men are looking for you. [20] Get up and go downstairs. Don't let anything keep you from going with them. I have sent them."

[21] Peter went down and spoke to the men. "I'm the one you're looking for," he said. "Why have you come?"

[22] The men replied, "We have come from Cornelius, the Ro-man commander. He is a good man who worships God. All the Jewish people respect him. A holy angel told him to invite you to his house. Then Cornelius can hear what you have to say." [23] Then Peter invited the men into the house to be his guests.

Peter Goes to the House of Cornelius

The next day Peter went with the three men. Some of the believers from Joppa went along. [24] The following day he arrived in Caesarea. Cornelius was expecting them. He had called together his relatives and close friends. [25] When Peter entered the house, Cornelius met him. As a sign of respect, he fell at Peter's feet. [26] But Peter made him get up. "Stand up," he said. "I am only a man myself."

[27] As he was talking with Cornelius, Peter went inside. There he found a large group of people. [28] He said to them, "You know that it is against our law for a Jew to enter a Gentile home. A Jew shouldn't have any close contact with a Gentile. But God has shown me that I should not say anyone is not pure and 'clean.' [29] So when you sent for me, I came without asking any questions. May I ask why you sent for me?"

[30] Cornelius answered, "Three days ago at this very hour I was in my house praying. It was three o'clock in the afternoon. Suddenly a man in shining clothes stood in front of me. [31] He said, 'Cornelius,

God has heard your prayer. He has remembered your gifts to poor people. 32 Send someone to Joppa to get Simon Peter. He is a guest in the home of another Simon, who works with leather. He lives by the sea.' 33 So I sent for you right away. It was good of you to come. Now we are all here. And God is here with us. We are ready to listen to everything the Lord has commanded you to tell us."

34 Then Peter began to speak. "I now realize how true it is that God treats everyone the same," he said. 35 "He accepts people from every nation. He accepts anyone who has respect for him and does what is right. 36 You know the message God sent to the people of Israel. It is the good news of peace through Jesus Christ. He is Lord of all. 37 You know what has happened all through the area of Judea. It started in Galilee after John preached about baptism. 38 You know how God anointed Jesus of Nazareth with the Holy Spirit and with power. Jesus went around doing good. He healed all who were under the devil's power. God was with him.

39 "We are witnesses of everything he did in the land of the Jews and in Jerusalem. They killed him by nailing him to a cross. 40 But on the third day God raised him from the dead. God allowed Jesus to be seen. 41 But he wasn't seen by all the people. He was seen only by us. We are witnesses whom God had already chosen. We ate and drank with him after he rose from the dead. 42 He commanded us to preach to the people. He told us to tell people that he is the one appointed by God to judge the living and the dead. 43 All the prophets tell about him. They say that all who believe in him have their sins forgiven through his name."

44 While Peter was still speaking, the Holy Spirit came on all who heard the message. 45 Some Jewish believers had come with Peter. They were amazed because the gift of the Holy Spirit had been poured out even on the Gentiles. 46 They heard them speaking in languages they had not known before. They also heard them praising God.

Then Peter said, 47 "Surely no one can keep these people from being baptized with water. They have received the Holy Spirit just as we have." 48 So he ordered that they be baptized in the name of Jesus Christ. Then they asked Peter to stay with them for a few days.

Peter Explains His Actions

11 The apostles and the believers all through Judea heard that Gentiles had also received God's word. 2 Peter went up to Jerusalem. There the Jewish believers found fault with him. 3 They said, "You went into the house of Gentiles. You ate with them."

4 Starting from the beginning, Peter told them the whole story. 5 "I was in the city of Joppa praying," he said. "There I had

a vision. I saw something that looked like a large sheet. It was being let down from heaven by its four corners. It came down to where I was. ⁶I looked into it and saw four-footed animals of the earth. There were also wild animals, reptiles and birds. ⁷Then I heard a voice speaking to me. 'Get up, Peter,' the voice said. 'Kill and eat.'

⁸"I replied, 'No, Lord! I will not! Nothing that is not pure and "clean" has ever entered my mouth.'

⁹"A second time the voice spoke from heaven. The voice said, 'Do not say anything is not pure that God has made "clean."' ¹⁰This happened three times. Then the sheet was pulled up into heaven.

¹¹"Just then three men stopped at the house where I was staying. They had been sent to me from Caesarea. ¹²The Holy Spirit told me not to let anything keep me from going with them. These six brothers here went with me. We entered the man's house. ¹³He told us how he had seen an angel appear in his house. The angel said, 'Send to Joppa for Simon Peter. ¹⁴He has a message to bring to you. You and your whole family will be saved through it.'

¹⁵"As I began to speak, the Holy Spirit came on them. He came just as he had come on us at the beginning. ¹⁶Then I remembered the Lord's words. 'John baptized with water,' he had said. 'But you will be baptized with the Holy Spirit.' ¹⁷God

gave them the same gift he gave those of us who believed in the Lord Jesus Christ. So who was I to think that I could stand in God's way?"

¹⁸When they heard this, they didn't object anymore. They praised God. They said, "So then, God has allowed even Gentiles to turn away from their sins. He did this so that they could live."

The Believers in Antioch

¹⁹Some believers had been scattered by the suffering that unbelievers had caused them. They were scattered after Stephen was killed. Those believers traveled as far as Phoenicia, Cyprus and Antioch. But they spread the word only among Jews. ²⁰Some believers from Cyprus and Cyrene went to Antioch. There they began to speak to Greeks also. They told them the good news about the Lord Jesus. ²¹The Lord's power was with them. Large numbers of people believed and turned to the Lord.

²²The church in Jerusalem heard about this. So they sent Barnabas to Antioch. ²³When he arrived and saw what the grace of God had done, he was glad. He told them all to remain true to the Lord with all their hearts. ²⁴Barnabas was a good man. He was full of the Holy Spirit and of faith. Large numbers of people came to know the Lord.

²⁵Then Barnabas went to Tarsus to look for Saul. ²⁶He found him there. Then he brought him

to Antioch. For a whole year Barnabas and Saul met with the church. They taught large numbers of people. At Antioch the believers were called Christians for the first time.

²⁷ In those days some prophets came down from Jerusalem to Antioch. ²⁸ One of them was named Agabus. He stood up and spoke through the Spirit. He said there would not be nearly enough food anywhere in the Roman world. This happened while Claudius was the emperor. ²⁹ The believers decided to provide help for the brothers and sisters living in Judea. All of them helped as much as they could. ³⁰ They sent their gift to the elders through Barnabas and Saul.

An Angel Helps Peter Escape From Prison

12 About this time, King Herod arrested some people who belonged to the church. He planned to make them suffer greatly. ² He had James killed with a sword. James was John's brother. ³ Herod saw that the death of James pleased some Jews. So he arrested Peter also. This happened during the Feast of Unleavened Bread. ⁴ After Herod arrested Peter, he put him in prison. Peter was placed under guard. He was watched by four groups of four soldiers each. Herod planned to put Peter on public trial. It would take place after the Passover Feast. ⁵ So Peter was kept in prison.

But the church prayed hard to God for him.

⁶ It was the night before Herod was going to bring him to trial. Peter was sleeping between two soldiers. Two chains held him there. Lookouts stood guard at the entrance. ⁷ Suddenly an angel of the Lord appeared. A light shone in the prison cell. The angel struck Peter on his side. Peter woke up. "Quick!" the angel said. "Get up!" The chains fell off Peter's wrists.

⁸ Then the angel said to him, "Put on your clothes and sandals." Peter did so. "Put on your coat," the angel told him. "Follow me." ⁹ Peter followed him out of the prison. But he had no idea that what the angel was doing was really happening. He thought he was seeing a vision. ¹⁰ They passed the first and second guards. Then they came to the iron gate leading to the city. It opened for them by itself. They went through it. They walked the length of one street. Suddenly the angel left Peter.

¹¹ Then Peter realized what had happened. He said, "Now I know for sure that the Lord has sent his angel. He set me free from Herod's power. He saved me from everything the Jewish people were hoping would happen."

¹² When Peter understood what had happened, he went to Mary's house. Mary was the mother of John Mark. Many people had gathered in her home. They were praying there. ¹³ Peter knocked at the outer entrance.

A servant named Rhoda came to answer the door. ¹⁴ She recognized Peter's voice. She was so excited that she ran back without opening the door. "Peter is at the door!" she exclaimed.

¹⁵ "You're out of your mind," they said to her. But she kept telling them it was true. So they said, "It must be his angel."

¹⁶ Peter kept on knocking. When they opened the door and saw him, they were amazed. ¹⁷ Peter motioned with his hand for them to be quiet. He explained how the Lord had brought him out of prison. "Tell James and the other brothers and sisters about this," he said. Then he went to another place.

¹⁸ In the morning the soldiers were bewildered. They couldn't figure out what had happened to Peter. ¹⁹ So Herod had them look everywhere for Peter. But they didn't find him. Then Herod questioned the guards closely. He ordered that they be put to death.

Herod Dies

Then Herod went from Judea to Caesarea and stayed there. ²⁰ He had been quarreling with the people of Tyre and Sidon. So they got together and asked for a meeting with him. This was because they depended on the king's country to supply them with food. They gained the support of Blastus and then asked for peace. Blastus was a trusted personal servant of the king.

²¹ The appointed day came. Herod was seated on his throne. He was wearing his royal robes. He made a speech to the people. ²² Then they shouted, "This is the voice of a god. It's not the voice of a man." ²³ Right away an angel of the Lord struck Herod down. Herod had not given praise to God. So he was eaten by worms and died.

²⁴ But God's word continued to spread and many people believed the message.

Barnabas and Saul Are Sent Off

²⁵ Barnabas and Saul finished their task. Then they returned from Jerusalem. They took John Mark with them. **13** ¹ In the church at Antioch there were prophets and teachers. Among them were Barnabas, Simeon, and Lucius from Cyrene. Simeon was also called Niger. Another was Manaen. He had been brought up with Herod, the ruler of Galilee. Saul was among them too. ² While they were worshiping the Lord and fasting, the Holy Spirit spoke. "Set apart Barnabas and Saul for me," he said. "I have appointed them to do special work." ³ The prophets and teachers fasted and prayed. They placed their hands on Barnabas and Saul. Then they sent them off.

Events on Cyprus

⁴ Barnabas and Saul were sent on their way by the Holy Spirit. They went down to Seleucia. From there they sailed to Cyprus. ⁵ They arrived at Salamis. There they preached God's word

Jesus Dies on the Cross

MARK 15:21–41

Jesus Returns to Heaven
ACTS 1:1–11

in the Jewish synagogues. John was with them as their helper. ⁶They traveled all across the island until they came to Paphos. There they met a Jew named Bar-Jesus. He was an evil magician and a false prophet. ⁷He was an attendant of Sergius Paulus, the governor. Paulus was a man of understanding. He sent for Barnabas and Saul. He wanted to hear God's word. ⁸But the evil magician named Elymas opposed them. The name Elymas means Magician. He tried to keep the governor from becoming a believer. ⁹Saul was also known as Paul. He was filled with the Holy Spirit. He looked straight at Elymas. He said to him, ¹⁰"You are a child of the devil! You are an enemy of everything that is right! You cheat people. You use all kinds of tricks. Won't you ever stop twisting the right ways of the Lord? ¹¹Now the Lord's hand is against you. You are going to go blind. For a while you won't even be able to see the light of the sun."

Right away mist and darkness came over him. He tried to feel his way around. He wanted to find someone to lead him by the hand. ¹²When the governor saw what had happened, he believed. He was amazed at what Paul was teaching about the Lord.

Paul Preaches in Pisidian Antioch

¹³From Paphos, Paul and his companions sailed to Perga in Pamphylia. There John Mark left them and returned to Jerusalem. ¹⁴From Perga they went on to Pisidian Antioch. On the Sabbath day they entered the synagogue and sat down. ¹⁵The Law and the Prophets were read aloud. Then the leaders of the synagogue sent word to Paul and his companions. They said, "Brothers, do you have any words of instruction for the people? If you do, please speak."

¹⁶Paul stood up and motioned with his hand. Then he said, "Fellow Israelites, and you Gentiles who worship God, listen to me! ¹⁷The God of Israel chose our people who lived long ago. He blessed them greatly while they were in Egypt. With his mighty power he led them out of that country. ¹⁸He put up with their behavior for about 40 years in the desert. ¹⁹And he destroyed seven nations in Canaan. Then he gave the land to his people as their rightful share. ²⁰All this took about 450 years.

"After this, God gave them judges until the time of Samuel the prophet. ²¹Then the people asked for a king. He gave them Saul, son of Kish. Saul was from the tribe of Benjamin. He ruled for 40 years. ²²God removed him and made David their king. Here is God's witness about him. 'David, son of Jesse, is a man dear to my heart,' he said. 'David will do everything I want him to do.'

²³"From this man's family line God has brought to Israel the

Savior Jesus. This is what he had promised. ²⁴ Before Jesus came, John preached that we should turn away from our sins and be baptized. He preached this to all Israel. ²⁵ John was coming to the end of his work. 'Who do you suppose I am?' he said. 'I am not the one you are looking for. But there is someone coming after me. I am not good enough to untie his sandals.'

²⁶ "Listen, fellow children of Abraham! Listen, you Gentiles who worship God! This message of salvation has been sent to us. ²⁷ The people of Jerusalem and their rulers did not recognize Jesus. By finding him guilty, they made the prophets' words come true. These are read every Sabbath day. ²⁸ The people and their rulers had no reason at all for sentencing Jesus to death. But they asked Pilate to have him killed. ²⁹ They did everything that had been written about Jesus. Then they took him down from the cross. They laid him in a tomb. ³⁰ But God raised him from the dead. ³¹ For many days he was seen by those who had traveled with him from Galilee to Jerusalem. Now they are telling our people about Jesus.

³² "We are telling you the good news. What God promised our people long ago ³³ he has done for us, their children. He has raised up Jesus. This is what is written in the second Psalm. It says,

" 'You are my son.
Today I have become your
father.'   *(Psalm 2:7)*

³⁴ God raised Jesus from the dead. He will never rot in the grave. As God has said,

" 'Holy and sure blessings
were promised to David.
I will give them to you.'
    (Isaiah 55:3)

³⁵ In another place it also says,

" 'You will not let your holy
one rot away.'   *(Psalm 16:10)*

³⁶ "David carried out God's purpose while he lived. Then he died. He was buried with his people. His body rotted away. ³⁷ But the one whom God raised from the dead did not rot away.

³⁸ "My friends, here is what I want you to know. I announce to you that your sins can be forgiven because of what Jesus has done. ³⁹ Through him everyone who believes is set free from every sin. Moses' law could not make you right in God's eyes. ⁴⁰ Be careful! Don't let what the prophets spoke about happen to you. They said,

⁴¹ " 'Look, you who make fun of
the truth!
Wonder and die!
I am going to do something
in your days
that you would never
believe.
You wouldn't believe it
even if someone told
you.' "   *(Habakkuk 1:5)*

⁴² Paul and Barnabas started to leave the synagogue. The people invited them to say more about these things on the next Sabbath day. ⁴³ The people were

told they could leave the service. Many Jews followed Paul and Barnabas. Many Gentiles who faithfully worshiped the God of the Jews did the same. Paul and Barnabas talked with them. They tried to get them to keep living in God's grace.

44 On the next Sabbath day, almost the whole city gathered. They gathered to hear the word of the Lord. 45 When the Jews saw the crowds, they became very jealous. They began to disagree with what Paul was saying. They said evil things against him.

46 Then Paul and Barnabas answered them boldly. "We had to speak God's word to you first," they said. "But you don't accept it. You don't think you are good enough for eternal life. So now we are turning to the Gentiles. 47 This is what the Lord has commanded us to do. He said,

" 'I have made you a light for
　　the Gentiles.
　You will bring salvation to
　　the whole earth.' "
　　　　　　　　(Isaiah 49:6)

48 When the Gentiles heard this, they were glad. They honored the word of the Lord. All who were appointed for eternal life believed.

49 The word of the Lord spread through the whole area. 50 But the Jewish leaders stirred up the important women who worshiped God. They also stirred up the men who were leaders in the city. The Jewish leaders tried to get the women and men to attack Paul and Barnabas. They threw Paul and Barnabas out of that area. 51 Paul and Barnabas shook the dust off their feet. This was a warning to the people who had opposed them. Then Paul and Barnabas went on to Iconium. 52 The believers were filled with joy and with the Holy Spirit.

Paul and Barnabas Preach in Iconium

14 At Iconium, Paul and Barnabas went into the Jewish synagogue as usual. They spoke there with great power. Large numbers of Jews and Greeks became believers. 2 But the Jews who refused to believe stirred up some of the Gentiles who were there. They turned them against the two men and the new believers. 3 So Paul and Barnabas spent a lot of time there. They spoke boldly for the Lord. He gave them the ability to do signs and wonders. In this way the Lord showed that they were telling the truth about his grace. 4 The people of the city did not agree with one another. Some were on the side of the Jews. Others were on the side of the apostles. 5 Jews and Gentiles alike planned to treat Paul and Barnabas badly. Their leaders agreed. They planned to kill them by throwing stones at them. 6 But Paul and Barnabas found out about the plan. They escaped to the Lycaonian cities of Lystra and Derbe and to the surrounding area. 7 There they continued to preach the good news.

Paul Preaches in Lystra

⁸ In Lystra there sat a man who couldn't walk. He hadn't been able to use his feet since the day he was born. ⁹ He listened as Paul spoke. Paul looked right at him. He saw that the man had faith to be healed. ¹⁰ So he called out, "Stand up on your feet!" Then the man jumped up and began to walk.

¹¹ The crowd saw what Paul had done. They shouted in the Lycaonian language. "The gods have come down to us in human form!" they exclaimed. ¹² They called Barnabas Zeus. Paul was the main speaker. So they called him Hermes. ¹³ Just outside the city was the temple of the god Zeus. The priest of Zeus brought bulls and wreaths to the city gates. He and the crowd wanted to offer sacrifices to Paul and Barnabas.

¹⁴ But the apostles Barnabas and Paul heard about this. So they tore their clothes. They rushed out into the crowd. They shouted, ¹⁵ "Friends, why are you doing this? We are only human, just like you. We are bringing you good news. Turn away from these worthless things. Turn to the living God. He is the one who made the heavens and the earth and the sea. He made everything in them. ¹⁶ In the past, he let all nations go their own way. ¹⁷ But he has given proof of what he is like. He has shown kindness by giving you rain from heaven. He gives you crops in their seasons. He provides you with plenty of food. He fills your hearts with joy." ¹⁸ Paul and Barnabas told them all these things. But they had trouble keeping the crowd from offering sacrifices to them.

¹⁹ Then some Jews came from Antioch and Iconium. They won the crowd over to their side. They threw stones at Paul. They thought he was dead, so they dragged him out of the city. ²⁰ The believers gathered around Paul. Then he got up and went back into the city. The next day he and Barnabas left for Derbe.

Paul and Barnabas Return to Antioch

²¹ Paul and Barnabas preached the good news in the city of Derbe. They won large numbers of followers. Then they returned to Lystra, Iconium and Antioch. ²² There they helped the believers gain strength. They told them to remain faithful to what they had been taught. "We must go through many hard times to enter God's kingdom," they said. ²³ Paul and Barnabas appointed elders for them in each church. The elders had trusted in the Lord. Paul and Barnabas prayed and fasted. They placed the elders in the Lord's care. ²⁴ After going through Pisidia, Paul and Barnabas came into Pamphylia. ²⁵ They preached the good news in Perga. Then they went down to Attalia.

²⁶ From Attalia they sailed back to Antioch. In Antioch they had been put in God's care to

preach the good news. They had now completed the work God had given them to do. 27 When they arrived at Antioch, they gathered the church together. They reported all that God had done through them. They told how he had opened a way for the Gentiles to believe. 28 And they stayed there a long time with the believers.

Church Leaders Meet in Jerusalem

15 Certain people came down from Judea to Antioch. Here is what they were teaching the believers. "Moses commanded you to be circumcised," they said. "If you aren't, you can't be saved." 2 But Paul and Barnabas didn't agree with this. They argued strongly with them. So Paul and Barnabas were appointed to go up to Jerusalem. Some other believers were chosen to go with them. They were told to ask the apostles and elders about this question. 3 The church sent them on their way. They traveled through Phoenicia and Samaria. There they told how the Gentiles had turned to God. This news made all the believers very glad. 4 When they arrived in Jerusalem, the church welcomed them. The apostles and elders welcomed them too. Then Paul and Barnabas reported everything God had done through them.

5 Some of the believers were Pharisees. They stood up and said, "The Gentiles must be cir-cumcised. They must obey the law of Moses."

6 The apostles and elders met to consider this question. 7 After they had talked it over, Peter got up and spoke to them. "Brothers," he said, "you know that some time ago God chose me. He appointed me to take the good news to the Gentiles. He wanted them to hear the good news and believe. 8 God knows the human heart. By giving the Holy Spirit to the Gentiles, he showed that he accepted them. He did the same for them as he had done for us. 9 God showed that there is no difference between us and them. That's because he made their hearts pure because of their faith. 10 Now then, why are you trying to test God? You test him when you put a heavy load on the shoulders of Gentiles. Our people of long ago couldn't carry that load. We can't either. 11 No! We believe we are saved through the grace of our Lord Jesus. The Gentiles are saved in the same way."

12 Everyone became quiet as they listened to Barnabas and Paul. They were telling about the signs and wonders God had done through them among the Gentiles. 13 When they finished, James spoke up. "Brothers," he said, "listen to me. 14 Simon Peter has explained to us what God has now done. He has chosen some of the Gentiles to be among his very own people. 15 The prophets' words agree with that. They say,

16 " 'After this I will return
and set up again David's
fallen tent.
I will rebuild what was
destroyed.
I will make it what it used
to be.
17 Then everyone else can look
to the Lord.
This includes all the
Gentiles who belong to
me, says the Lord.
The Lord is the one who
does these things.'
(Amos 9:11,12)
18   The Lord does things that
have been known from
long ago.

19 "Now here is my decision. We should not make it hard for the Gentiles who are turning to God. 20 Here is what we should write to them. They must not eat food that has been made impure by being offered to statues of gods. They must not commit sexual sins. They must not eat the meat of animals that have been choked to death. And they must not drink blood. 21 These laws of Moses have been preached in every city from the earliest times. They are read out loud in the synagogues every Sabbath day."

A Letter Is Written to Gentile Believers

22 Then the apostles, the elders and the whole church decided what to do. They would choose some of their own men who were leaders among the believers. They would send them to Antioch with Paul and Barnabas. So they chose Judas Barsabbas and Silas. They were leaders among the believers. 23 Here is the letter they sent with them.

The apostles and elders, your brothers, are writing this letter.

We are sending it to the Gentile believers in Antioch, Syria and Cilicia.

Greetings.

24 We have heard that some of our people came to you and caused trouble. You were upset by what they said. But we had given them no authority to go. 25 So we all agreed to send our dear friends Barnabas and Paul to you. We chose some other men to go with them. 26 Barnabas and Paul have put their lives in danger. They did it for the name of our Lord Jesus Christ. 27 So we are sending Judas and Silas with them. What they say will agree with this letter. 28 Here is what seemed good to the Holy Spirit and to us. We will not give you a load that is too heavy. So here are a few basic rules. 29 Don't eat food that has been offered to statues of gods. Don't drink blood. Don't eat the meat of animals that have been choked to death. And don't commit sexual sins. You will do well to keep away from these things.

Farewell.

30 So the men were sent down to Antioch. There they gathered the church together. They gave the letter to them. 31 The people read it. They were glad for its message of hope. 32 Judas and Silas were prophets. They said many things to give strength and hope to the believers. 33-34 Judas and Silas stayed there for some time. Then the believers sent them away with the blessing of peace. They sent them back to those who had sent them out. 35 Paul and Barnabas remained in Antioch. There they and many others taught and preached the word of the Lord.

Paul and Barnabas Do Not Agree

36 Some time later Paul spoke to Barnabas. "Let's go back to all the towns where we preached the word of the Lord," he said. "Let's visit the believers and see how they are doing." 37 Barnabas wanted to take John Mark with them. 38 But Paul didn't think it was wise to take him. Mark had deserted them in Pamphylia. He hadn't continued with them in their work. 39 Barnabas and Paul strongly disagreed with each other. So they went their separate ways. Barnabas took Mark and sailed for Cyprus. 40 But Paul chose Silas. The believers asked the Lord to give his grace to Paul and Silas as they went. 41 Paul traveled through Syria and Cilicia. He gave strength to the churches there.

Timothy Joins Paul and Silas

16 Paul came to Derbe. Then he went on to Lystra. A believer named Timothy lived there. His mother was Jewish and a believer. His father was a Greek. 2 The believers at Lystra and Iconium said good things about Timothy. 3 Paul wanted to take him along on the journey. So he circumcised Timothy because of the Jews who lived in that area. They all knew that Timothy's father was a Greek. 4 Paul and his companions traveled from town to town. They reported what the apostles and elders in Jerusalem had decided. The people were supposed to obey what was in the report. 5 So the churches were made strong in the faith. The number of believers grew every day.

Paul's Vision of the Man From Macedonia

6 Paul and his companions traveled all through the area of Phrygia and Galatia. The Holy Spirit had kept them from preaching the word in Asia Minor. 7 They came to the border of Mysia. From there they tried to enter Bithynia. But the Spirit of Jesus would not let them. 8 So they passed by Mysia. Then they went down to Troas. 9 During the night Paul had a vision. He saw a man from Macedonia standing and begging him. "Come over to Macedonia!" the man said. "Help us!" 10 After Paul had seen the vision, we got ready at once to leave for Macedonia. We decided that God had

called us to preach the good news there.

Lydia Becomes a Believer in Philippi

[11] At Troas we got into a boat. We sailed straight for Samothrace. The next day we went on to Neapolis. [12] From there we traveled to Philippi, a Roman colony. It is an important city in that part of Macedonia. We stayed there several days.

[13] On the Sabbath day we went outside the city gate. We walked down to the river. There we expected to find a place of prayer. We sat down and began to speak to the women who had gathered together. [14] One of the women listening was from the city of Thyatira. Her name was Lydia, and her business was selling purple cloth. She was a worshiper of God. The Lord opened her heart to accept Paul's message. [15] She and her family were baptized. Then she invited us to her home. "Do you consider me a believer in the Lord?" she asked. "If you do, come and stay at my house." She succeeded in getting us to go home with her.

Paul and Silas Are Thrown Into Prison

[16] One day we were going to the place of prayer. On the way we were met by a female slave. She had a spirit that helped her tell people what was going to happen. She earned a lot of money for her owners by doing this. [17] She followed Paul and the rest of us around. She shouted, "These men serve the Most High God. They are telling you how to be saved." [18] She kept this up for many days. Finally Paul became upset. Turning around, he spoke to the spirit that was in her. "In the name of Jesus Christ," he said, "I command you to come out of her!" At that very moment the spirit left the woman.

[19] Her owners realized that their hope of making money was gone. So they grabbed Paul and Silas. They dragged them into the market place to face the authorities. [20] They brought them to the judges. "These men are Jews," her owners said. "They are making trouble in our city. [21] They are suggesting practices that are against Roman law. These are practices we can't accept or take part in."

[22] The crowd joined the attack against Paul and Silas. The judges ordered that Paul and Silas be stripped and beaten with rods. [23] They were whipped without mercy. Then they were thrown into prison. The jailer was commanded to guard them carefully. [24] When he received these orders, he put Paul and Silas deep inside the prison. He fastened their feet so they couldn't get away.

[25] About midnight Paul and Silas were praying. They were also singing hymns to God. The other prisoners were listening to them. [26] Suddenly there was a powerful earthquake. It shook the prison from top to bottom. All at once the prison doors flew

open. Everyone's chains came loose. 27 The jailer woke up. He saw that the prison doors were open. He pulled out his sword and was going to kill himself. He thought the prisoners had escaped. 28 "Don't harm yourself!" Paul shouted. "We are all here!"

29 The jailer called out for some lights. He rushed in, shaking with fear. He fell down in front of Paul and Silas. 30 Then he brought them out. He asked, "Sirs, what must I do to be saved?"

31 They replied, "Believe in the Lord Jesus. Then you and everyone living in your house will be saved." 32 They spoke the word of the Lord to him. They also spoke to all the others in his house. 33 At that hour of the night, the jailer took Paul and Silas and washed their wounds. Right away he and everyone who lived with him were baptized. 34 The jailer brought them into his house. He set a meal in front of them. He and everyone who lived with him were filled with joy. They had become believers in God.

35 Early in the morning the judges sent their officers to the jailer. They ordered him, "Let those men go." 36 The jailer told Paul, "The judges have ordered me to set you and Silas free. You can leave now. Go in peace."

37 But Paul replied to the officers. "They beat us in public," he said. "We weren't given a trial. And we are Roman citizens! They threw us into prison. And now do they want to get rid of us quietly? No! Let them come themselves and personally lead us out."

38 The officers reported this to the judges. When the judges heard that Paul and Silas were Roman citizens, they became afraid. 39 So they came and said they were sorry. They led them out of the prison. Then they asked them to leave the city. 40 After Paul and Silas came out of the prison, they went to Lydia's house. There they met with the brothers and sisters. They told them to be brave. Then they left.

Paul and Silas Arrive in Thessalonica

17 Paul and those traveling with him passed through Amphipolis and Apollonia. They came to Thessalonica. A Jewish synagogue was there. 2 Paul went into the synagogue as he usually did. For three Sabbath days in a row he talked with the Jews about the Scriptures. 3 He explained and proved that the Messiah had to suffer and rise from the dead. "This Jesus I am telling you about is the Messiah!" he said. 4 His words won over some of the Jews. They joined Paul and Silas. A large number of Greeks who worshiped God joined them too. So did quite a few important women.

5 But other Jews were jealous. So they rounded up some evil people from the market place. Forming a crowd, they

started all kinds of trouble in the city. The Jews rushed to Jason's house. They were looking for Paul and Silas. They wanted to bring them out to the crowd. ⁶ But they couldn't find them. So they dragged Jason and some other believers to the city officials. "These men have caused trouble all over the world," they shouted. "Now they have come here. ⁷ Jason has welcomed them into his house. They are all disobeying Caesar's commands. They say there is another king. He is called Jesus." ⁸ When the crowd and the city officials heard this, they became very upset. ⁹ They made Jason and the others give them money. The officials did this to make sure they would return to the court. Then they let Jason and the others go.

Paul and Silas Are Sent to Berea

¹⁰ As soon as it was night, the believers sent Paul and Silas away to Berea. When they arrived, they went to the Jewish synagogue. ¹¹ The Berean Jews were very glad to receive Paul's message. They studied the Scriptures carefully every day. They wanted to see if what Paul said was true. So they were more noble than the Thessalonian Jews. ¹² Because of this, many of the Berean Jews believed. A number of important Greek women also became believers. And so did many Greek men.

¹³ But the Jews in Thessalonica found out that Paul was preaching God's word in Berea.

So some of them went there too. They stirred up the crowds and got them all worked up. ¹⁴ Right away the believers sent Paul to the coast. But Silas and Timothy stayed in Berea. ¹⁵ The believers who went with Paul took him to Athens. Then they returned with orders that Silas and Timothy were supposed to join him as soon as they could.

Paul Preaches in Athens

¹⁶ Paul was waiting for Silas and Timothy in Athens. He was very upset to see that the city was full of statues of gods. ¹⁷ So he went to the synagogue. There he talked both with Jews and with Greeks who worshiped God. Each day he spoke with anyone who happened to be in the market place. ¹⁸ A group of Epicurean and Stoic thinkers began to argue with him. Some of them asked, "What is this fellow chattering about?" Others said, "He seems to be telling us about gods we've never heard of." They said this because Paul was preaching the good news about Jesus. He was telling them that Jesus had risen from the dead. ¹⁹ They took him to a meeting of the Areopagus. There they said to him, "What is this new teaching you're giving us? ²⁰ You have some strange ideas we've never heard before. We would like to know what they mean." ²¹ All the people of Athens spent their time talking about and listening to the latest ideas. People from other lands who lived there did the same.

²² Then Paul stood up in the meeting of the Areopagus. He said, "People of Athens! I see that you are very religious in every way. ²³ As I walked around, I looked carefully at the things you worship. I even found an altar with

TO AN UNKNOWN GOD

written on it. So you don't know what you are worshiping. Now I am going to tell you about this 'unknown god.'

²⁴ "He is the God who made the world. He also made everything in it. He is the Lord of heaven and earth. He doesn't live in temples built by human hands. ²⁵ He is not served by human hands. He doesn't need anything. Instead, he himself gives life and breath to all people. He also gives them everything else they have. ²⁶ From one man he made all the people of the world. Now they live all over the earth. He decided exactly when they should live. And he decided exactly where they should live. ²⁷ God did this so that people would seek him. And perhaps they would reach out for him and find him. They would find him even though he is not far from any of us. ²⁸ 'In him we live and move and exist.' As some of your own poets have also said, 'We are his children.'

²⁹ "Yes, we are God's children. So we shouldn't think that God is made out of gold or silver or stone. He isn't a statue planned and made by clever people. ³⁰ In the past, God didn't judge people for what they didn't know. But now he commands all people everywhere to turn away from their sins. ³¹ He has set a day when he will judge the world fairly. He has appointed a man to be its judge. God has proved this to everyone by raising that man from the dead."

³² They heard Paul talk about the dead being raised. Some of them made fun of this idea. But others said, "We want to hear you speak about this again." ³³ So Paul left the meeting of the Areopagus. ³⁴ Some of the people became followers of Paul and believed in Jesus. Dionysius was one of them. He was a member of the Areopagus. A woman named Damaris also became a believer. And so did some others.

Paul Goes to Corinth

18 After this, Paul left Athens and went to Corinth. ² There he met a Jew named Aquila, who was a native of Pontus. Aquila had recently come from Italy with his wife Priscilla. The emperor Claudius had ordered all Jews to leave Rome. Paul went to see Aquila and Priscilla. ³ They were tentmakers, just as he was. So he stayed and worked with them. ⁴ Every Sabbath day he went to the synagogue. He was trying to get both Jews and Greeks to believe in the Lord.

⁵ Silas and Timothy came from Macedonia. Then Paul spent all his time preaching. He was a witness to the Jews that Jesus was the Messiah.

⁶But they opposed Paul. They treated him badly. So he shook out his clothes in protest. Then he said to them, "God's judgment against you will be your own fault! Don't blame me for it! From now on I will go to the Gentiles."

⁷Then Paul left the synagogue and went to the house next door. It was the house of Titius Justus, a man who worshiped God. ⁸Crispus was the synagogue leader. He and everyone living in his house came to believe in the Lord. Many others who lived in Corinth heard Paul. They too believed and were baptized.

⁹One night the Lord spoke to Paul in a vision. "Don't be afraid," he said. "Keep on speaking. Don't be silent. ¹⁰I am with you. No one will attack you and harm you. I have many people in this city." ¹¹So Paul stayed in Corinth for a year and a half. He taught them God's word.

¹²At that time Gallio was governor of Achaia. The Jews of Corinth got together and attacked Paul. They brought him into court. ¹³They made a charge against Paul. They said, "This man is talking people into worshiping God in wrong ways. Those ways are against the law."

¹⁴Paul was about to give reasons for his actions. But just then Gallio spoke to them. He said, "You Jews don't claim that Paul has committed a great or small crime. If you did, it would make sense for me to listen to you. ¹⁵But this is about your own law. It is a question of words and names. Settle the matter yourselves. I will not be a judge of such things." ¹⁶So he made them leave. ¹⁷Then the crowd there turned against Sosthenes, the synagogue leader. They beat him up in front of the governor. But Gallio didn't care at all.

Priscilla and Aquila Teach Apollos

¹⁸Paul stayed in Corinth for some time. Then he left the brothers and sisters and sailed for Syria. Priscilla and Aquila went with him. Before he sailed, he had his hair cut off at Cenchreae. He did this because he had made a promise to God. ¹⁹They arrived at Ephesus. There Paul said goodbye to Priscilla and Aquila. He himself went into the synagogue and talked with the Jews. ²⁰The Jews asked him to spend more time with them. But he said no. ²¹As he left, he made them a promise. "If God wants me to," he said, "I will come back." Then he sailed from Ephesus. ²²When he landed at Caesarea, he went up to Jerusalem. There he greeted the church. He then went down to Antioch.

²³Paul spent some time in Antioch. Then he left and traveled all over Galatia and Phrygia. He gave strength to all the believers there.

²⁴At that time a Jew named Apollos came to Ephesus. He was an educated man from Alexandria. He knew the Scriptures very well. ²⁵Apollos had been taught the way of the Lord.

He spoke with great power. He taught the truth about Jesus. But he only knew about John's baptism. ²⁶ He began to speak boldly in the synagogue. Priscilla and Aquila heard him. So they invited him to their home. There they gave him a better understanding of the way of God.

²⁷ Apollos wanted to go to Achaia. The brothers and sisters agreed with him. They wrote to the believers there. They asked them to welcome him. When he arrived, he was a great help to those who had become believers by God's grace. ²⁸ In public meetings, he argued strongly against Jews who disagreed with him. He proved from the Scriptures that Jesus was the Messiah.

Paul Goes to Ephesus

19 While Apollos was at Corinth, Paul took the road to Ephesus. When he arrived, he found some believers there. ² He asked them, "Did you receive the Holy Spirit when you became believers?"

"No," they answered. "We haven't even heard that there is a Holy Spirit."

³ So Paul asked, "Then what baptism did you receive?"

"John's baptism," they replied.

⁴ Paul said, "John baptized people, calling them to turn away from their sins. He told them to believe in the one who was coming after him. Jesus is that one." ⁵ After hearing this, they were baptized in the name of the Lord Jesus. ⁶ Paul placed his hands on them. Then the Holy Spirit came on them. They spoke in languages they had not known before. They also prophesied. ⁷ There were about 12 men in all.

⁸ Paul entered the synagogue. There he spoke boldly for three months. He gave good reasons for believing the truth about God's kingdom. ⁹ But some of them wouldn't listen. They refused to believe. In public they said evil things about the Way of Jesus. So Paul left them. He took the believers with him. Each day he talked with people in the lecture hall of Tyrannus. ¹⁰ This went on for two years. So all the Jews and Greeks who lived in Asia Minor heard the word of the Lord.

¹¹ God did amazing miracles through Paul. ¹² Even handkerchiefs and aprons that had touched him were taken to those who were sick. When this happened, their sicknesses were healed and evil spirits left them.

¹³ Some Jews went around driving out evil spirits. They tried to use the name of the Lord Jesus to set free those who were controlled by demons. They said, "In Jesus' name I command you to come out. He is the Jesus that Paul is preaching about." ¹⁴ Seven sons of Sceva were doing this. Sceva was a Jewish chief priest. ¹⁵ One day the evil spirit answered them, "I know Jesus. And I know about Paul. But who are you?" ¹⁶ Then the man who had the evil spirit

jumped on Sceva's sons. He overpowered them all. He gave them a terrible beating. They ran out of the house naked and bleeding.

[17] The Jews and Greeks living in Ephesus heard about this. They were all overcome with fear. They held the name of the Lord Jesus in high honor. [18] Many who believed now came and openly admitted what they had done. [19] A number of those who had practiced evil magic brought their scrolls together. They set them on fire out in the open. They added up the value of the scrolls. The scrolls were worth more than someone could earn in two lifetimes. [20] The word of the Lord spread everywhere. It became more and more powerful.

[21] After all this had happened, Paul decided to go to Jerusalem. He went through Macedonia and Achaia. "After I have been to Jerusalem," he said, "I must visit Rome also." [22] He sent Timothy and Erastus, two of his helpers, to Macedonia. But he stayed a little longer in Asia Minor.

Trouble in Ephesus

[23] At that time many people became very upset about the Way of Jesus. [24] There was a man named Demetrius who made things out of silver. He made silver models of the temple of the goddess Artemis. He brought in a lot of business for the other skilled workers there. [25] One day he called them together. He also called others who were in the same kind of business. "My friends," he said, "you know that we make good money from our work. [26] You have seen and heard what this fellow Paul is doing. He has talked to large numbers of people here in Ephesus. Almost everywhere in Asia Minor he has led people away from our gods. He says that the gods made by human hands are not gods at all. [27] Our work is in danger of losing its good name. People's faith in the temple of the great goddess Artemis will be weakened. Now she is worshiped all over Asia Minor and the whole world. But soon she will be robbed of her greatness."

[28] When they heard this, they became very angry. They began shouting, "Great is Artemis of the Ephesians!" [29] Soon people were making trouble in the whole city. They all rushed into the theater. They dragged Gaius and Aristarchus along with them. These two men had come with Paul from Macedonia. [30] Paul wanted to appear in front of the crowd. But the believers wouldn't let him. [31] Some of the officials in Asia Minor were friends of Paul. They sent him a message, begging him not to go into the theater.

[32] The crowd didn't know what was going on. Some were shouting one thing and some another. Most of the people didn't even know why they were there. [33] The Jews in the crowd pushed Alexander to the front. They tried to tell him what to say. But he motioned for them to be

quiet. He was about to give the people reasons for his actions. [34] But then they realized that he was a Jew. So they all shouted the same thing for about two hours. "Great is Artemis of the Ephesians!" they yelled.

[35] The city clerk quieted the crowd down. "People of Ephesus!" he said. "The city of Ephesus guards the temple of the great Artemis. The whole world knows this. They know that Ephesus guards her statue, which fell from heaven. [36] These facts can't be questioned. So calm down. Don't do anything foolish. [37] These men haven't robbed any temples. They haven't said evil things against our female god. But you have brought them here anyhow. [38] Demetrius and the other skilled workers may feel they have been wronged by someone. Let them bring charges. The courts are open. We have our governors. [39] Is there anything else you want to bring up? Settle it in a court of law. [40] As it is, we are in danger of being charged with a crime. We could be charged with causing all this trouble today. There is no reason for it. So we wouldn't be able to explain what has happened." [41] After he said this, he sent the people away.

Paul Travels Through Macedonia and Greece

20 All the trouble came to an end. Then Paul sent for the believers. After encouraging them, he said goodbye. He then left for Macedonia.

[2] He traveled through that area, speaking many words of hope to the people. Finally he arrived in Greece. [3] There he stayed for three months. He was just about to sail for Syria. But some Jews were making plans against him. So he decided to go back through Macedonia. [4] Sopater, son of Pyrrhus, from Berea went with him. Aristarchus and Secundus from Thessalonica, Gaius from Derbe, and Timothy went too. Tychicus and Trophimus from Asia Minor also went with him. [5] These men went on ahead. They waited for us at Troas. [6] But we sailed from Philippi after the Feast of Unleavened Bread. Five days later we joined the others at Troas. We stayed there for seven days.

Eutychus Is Raised From the Dead at Troas

[7] On the first day of the week we met to break bread and eat together. Paul spoke to the people. He kept on talking until midnight because he planned to leave the next day. [8] There were many lamps in the room upstairs where we were meeting. [9] A young man named Eutychus was sitting in a window. He sank into a deep sleep as Paul talked on and on. Sound asleep, Eutychus fell from the third floor. When they picked him up from the ground, he was dead. [10] Paul went down and threw himself on the young man. He put his arms around him. "Don't be alarmed," he told them. "He's alive!" [11] Then

Paul went upstairs again. He broke bread and ate with them. He kept on talking until daylight. Then he left. [12] The people took the young man home. They were greatly comforted because he was alive.

Paul Says Goodbye to the Ephesian Elders

[13] We went on ahead to the ship. We sailed for Assos. There we were going to take Paul on board. He had planned it this way because he wanted to go to Assos by land. [14] So he met us there. We took him on board and went on to Mitylene. [15] The next day we sailed from there. We arrived near Chios. The day after that we crossed over to Samos. We arrived at Miletus the next day. [16] Paul had decided to sail past Ephesus. He didn't want to spend time in Asia Minor. He was in a hurry to get to Jerusalem. If he could, he wanted to be there by the day of Pentecost.

[17] From Miletus, Paul sent for the elders of the church at Ephesus. [18] When they arrived, he spoke to them. "You know how I lived the whole time I was with you," he said. "From the first day I came into Asia Minor, [19] I served the Lord with tears and without pride. I served him when I was greatly tested. I was tested by the evil plans of the Jews who disagreed with me. [20] You know that nothing has kept me from preaching whatever would help you. I have taught you in public and from house to house. [21] I have told both Jews and Greeks that they must turn away from their sins to God. They must have faith in our Lord Jesus.

[22] "Now I am going to Jerusalem. The Holy Spirit compels me. I don't know what will happen to me there. [23] I only know that in every city the Spirit warns me. He tells me that I will face prison and suffering. [24] But my life means nothing to me. My only goal is to finish the race. I want to complete the work the Lord Jesus has given me. He wants me to tell others about the good news of God's grace.

[25] "I have spent time with you preaching about the kingdom. I know that none of you will ever see me again. [26] So I tell you today that I am not guilty if any of you don't believe. [27] I haven't let anyone keep me from telling you everything God wants you to do. [28] Keep watch over yourselves. Keep watch over all the believers. The Holy Spirit has made you leaders over them. Be shepherds of God's church. He bought it with his own blood. [29] I know that after I leave, wild wolves will come in among you. They won't spare any of the sheep. [30] Even men from your own people will rise up and twist the truth. They want to get the believers to follow them. [31] So be on your guard! Remember that for three years I never stopped warning you. Night and day I warned each of you with tears.

[32] "Now I trust God to take

care of you. I commit you to the message about his grace. It can build you up. Then you will share in what God plans to give all his people. ³³ I haven't longed for anyone's silver or gold or clothing. ³⁴ You yourselves know that I have used my own hands to meet my needs. I have also met the needs of my companions. ³⁵ In everything I did, I showed you that we must work hard and help the weak. We must remember the words of the Lord Jesus. He said, 'It is more blessed to give than to receive.'"

³⁶ Paul finished speaking. Then he got down on his knees with all of them and prayed. ³⁷ They all wept as they hugged and kissed him. ³⁸ Paul had said that they would never see him again. That's what hurt them the most. Then they went with him to the ship.

Paul Continues His Journey to Jerusalem

21 After we had torn ourselves away from the Ephesian elders, we headed out to sea. We sailed straight to Kos. The next day we went to Rhodes. From there we continued on to Patara. ² We found a ship crossing over to Phoenicia. So we went on board and headed out to sea. ³ We came near Cyprus and passed to the south of it. Then we sailed on to Syria. We landed at Tyre. There our ship was supposed to unload. ⁴ We looked for the believers there and stayed with them for seven days. The believers tried to keep Paul from going on to Jerusalem. They were led by the Holy Spirit to do this. ⁵ When it was time to leave, we continued on our way. All the believers, including their whole families, went with us out of the city. There on the beach we got down on our knees to pray. ⁶ We said goodbye to each other. Then we went on board the ship. And they returned home.

⁷ Continuing on from Tyre, we landed at Ptolemais. There we greeted the brothers and sisters. We stayed with them for a day. ⁸ The next day we left and arrived at Caesarea. We stayed at the house of Philip the evangelist. He was one of the seven deacons. ⁹ He had four unmarried daughters who prophesied.

¹⁰ We stayed there several days. Then a prophet named Agabus came down from Judea. ¹¹ He came over to us. Then he took Paul's belt and tied his own hands and feet with it. He said, "The Holy Spirit says, 'This is how the Jewish leaders in Jerusalem will tie up the owner of this belt. They will hand him over to the Gentiles.'"

¹² When we heard this, we all begged Paul not to go up to Jerusalem. ¹³ He asked, "Why are you crying? Why are you breaking my heart? I'm ready to be put in prison. In fact, I'm ready to die in Jerusalem for the Lord Jesus." ¹⁴ We couldn't change his mind. So we gave up. We said, "May what the Lord wants to happen be done."

¹⁵ After this, we started on our way to Jerusalem. ¹⁶ Some of the believers from Caesarea went with us. They brought us to Mnason's home. We were supposed to stay there. Mnason was from Cyprus. He was one of the first believers.

Paul Arrives in Jerusalem

¹⁷ When we arrived in Jerusalem, the brothers and sisters gave us a warm welcome. ¹⁸ The next day Paul and the rest of us went to see James. All the elders were there. ¹⁹ Paul greeted them. Then he reported everything God had done among the Gentiles through his work.

²⁰ When they heard this, they praised God. Then they spoke to Paul. "Brother," they said, "you see that thousands of Jews have become believers. All of them try very hard to obey the law. ²¹ They have been told that you teach Jews to turn away from the Law of Moses. You teach this to the Jews who live among the Gentiles. They think that you teach those Jews not to circumcise their children. They think that you teach them to give up our Jewish ways. ²² What should we do? They will certainly hear that you have come. ²³ So do what we tell you. There are four men with us who have made a promise to God. ²⁴ Take them with you. Join them in the Jewish practice that makes people pure and 'clean.' Pay their expenses so they can have their heads shaved. Then everyone will know that these reports about you are not true in any way. They will know that you yourself obey the law. ²⁵ We have already given written directions to the believers who are not Jews. They must not eat food that has been offered to statues of gods. They must not drink blood. They must not eat the meat of animals that have been choked to death. And they must not commit sexual sins."

²⁶ The next day Paul took the men with him. They all made themselves pure and "clean" in the usual way. Then Paul went to the temple. There he reported the date when the days of cleansing would end. At that time the proper offering would be made for each of them.

Paul Is Arrested

²⁷ The seven days of cleansing were almost over. Some Jews from Asia Minor saw Paul at the temple. They stirred up the whole crowd and grabbed Paul. ²⁸ "Fellow Israelites, help us!" they shouted. "This is the man who teaches everyone in all places against our people. He speaks against our law and against this holy place. Besides, he has brought Greeks into the temple. He has made this holy place 'unclean.'" ²⁹ They said this because they had seen Trophimus the Ephesian in the city with Paul. They thought Paul had brought him into the temple.

³⁰ The whole city was stirred up. People came running from all directions. They grabbed

Paul and dragged him out of the temple. Right away the temple gates were shut. ³¹ The people were trying to kill Paul. But news reached the commander of the Roman troops. He heard that people were making trouble in the whole city of Jerusalem. ³² Right away he took some officers and soldiers with him. They ran down to the crowd. The people causing the trouble saw the commander and his soldiers. So they stopped beating Paul.

³³ The commander came up and arrested Paul. He ordered him to be held with two chains. Then he asked who Paul was and what he had done. ³⁴ Some in the crowd shouted one thing, some another. But the commander couldn't get the facts because of all the noise. So he ordered that Paul be taken into the fort. ³⁵ Paul reached the steps. But then the mob became so wild that he had to be carried by the soldiers. ³⁶ The crowd that followed kept shouting, "Get rid of him!"

Paul Speaks to the Crowd

³⁷ The soldiers were about to take Paul into the fort. Then he asked the commander, "May I say something to you?"

"Do you speak Greek?" he replied. ³⁸ "Aren't you the Egyptian who turned some of our people against their leaders? Didn't you lead 4,000 terrorists out into the desert some time ago?"

³⁹ Paul answered, "I am a Jew from Tarsus in Cilicia. I am a cit-izen of an important city. Please let me speak to the people."

⁴⁰ The commander told him he could. So Paul stood on the steps and motioned to the crowd. When all of them were quiet, he spoke to them in the Aramaic language.

22

¹ "Brothers and fathers," Paul began, "listen to me now. I want to give you reasons for my actions."

² When they heard that he was speaking to them in Aramaic, they became very quiet.

Then Paul said, ³ "I am a Jew. I was born in Tarsus in Cilicia, but I grew up here in Jerusalem. I studied with Gamaliel. I was well trained by him in the law given to our people long ago. I wanted to serve God as much as any of you do today. ⁴ I hurt the followers of the Way of Jesus. I sent many of them to their death. I arrested men and women. I threw them into prison. ⁵ The high priest and the whole Council can be witnesses of this themselves. I even had some official letters they had written to their friends in Damascus. So I went there to bring these people as prisoners to Jerusalem to be punished.

⁶ "I had almost reached Damascus. About noon a bright light from heaven suddenly flashed around me. ⁷ I fell to the ground and heard a voice speak to me. 'Saul! Saul!' it said. 'Why are you opposing me?'

⁸ " 'Who are you, Lord?' I asked.

" 'I am Jesus of Nazareth,' he

replied. 'I am the one you are opposing.' ⁹The light was seen by my companions. But they didn't understand the voice of the one speaking to me.

¹⁰ "'What should I do, Lord?' I asked.

"'Get up,' the Lord said. 'Go into Damascus. There you will be told everything you have been given to do.' ¹¹The brightness of the light had blinded me. So my companions led me by the hand into Damascus.

¹² "A man named Ananias came to see me. He was a godly Jew who obeyed the law. All the Jews living there respected him very much. ¹³He stood beside me and said, 'Brother Saul, receive your sight!' At that very moment I was able to see him.

¹⁴ "Then he said, 'The God of our people has chosen you. He wanted to tell you his plans for you. You have seen the Blameless One. You have heard words from his mouth. ¹⁵Now you will tell everyone about what you have seen and heard. ¹⁶So what are you waiting for? Get up and call on his name. Be baptized. Have your sins washed away.'

¹⁷ "I returned to Jerusalem and was praying at the temple. Then it seemed to me that I was dreaming. ¹⁸I saw the Lord speaking to me. 'Quick!' he said. 'Leave Jerusalem at once. The people here will not accept what you tell them about me.'

¹⁹ "'Lord,' I replied, 'these people know what I used to do. I went from one synagogue to another and put believers in prison. I also beat them. ²⁰Stephen was a man who told other people about you. I stood there when he was killed. I had agreed that he should die. I even guarded the coats of those who were killing him.'

²¹ "Then the Lord said to me, 'Go. I will send you far away to people who are not Jews.'"

Paul the Roman Citizen

²²The crowd listened to Paul until he said this. Then they shouted, "Kill him! He isn't fit to live!"

²³They shouted and threw off their coats. They threw dust into the air. ²⁴So the commanding officer ordered that Paul be taken into the fort. He gave orders for Paul to be whipped and questioned. He wanted to find out why the people were shouting at him like this. ²⁵A commander was standing there as they stretched Paul out to be whipped. Paul said to him, "Does the law allow you to whip a Roman citizen who hasn't even been found guilty?"

²⁶When the commander heard this, he went to the commanding officer and reported it. "What are you going to do?" the commander asked. "This man is a Roman citizen."

²⁷So the commanding officer went to Paul. "Tell me," he asked. "Are you a Roman citizen?"

"Yes, I am," Paul answered.

²⁸Then the officer said, "I had to pay a lot of money to become a citizen."

"But I was born a citizen," Paul replied.

²⁹ Right away those who were about to question him left. Even the officer was alarmed. He realized that he had put Paul, a Roman citizen, in chains.

Paul Is Taken to the Sanhedrin

³⁰ The commanding officer wanted to find out exactly what the Jews had against Paul. So the next day he let Paul out of prison. He ordered a meeting of the chief priests and all the members of the Sanhedrin. Then he brought Paul and had him stand in front of them.

23 Paul looked straight at the Sanhedrin. "My brothers," he said, "I have always done my duty to God. To this day I feel that I have done nothing wrong." ² Ananias the high priest heard this. So he ordered the men standing near Paul to hit him on the mouth. ³ Then Paul said to him, "You pretender! God will hit you! You sit there and judge me by the law. But you yourself broke the law when you commanded them to hit me!"

⁴ Those who were standing near Paul spoke to him. They said, "How dare you talk like that to God's high priest!"

⁵ Paul replied, "Brothers, I didn't realize he was the high priest. It is written, 'Do not speak evil about the ruler of your people.'" *(Exodus 22:28)*

⁶ Paul knew that some of them were Sadducees and the others were Pharisees. So he called out to the members of the Sanhedrin. "My brothers," he said, "I am a Pharisee. I come from a family of Pharisees. I believe that people will rise from the dead. That's why I am on trial."

⁷ When he said this, the Pharisees and the Sadducees started to argue. They began to take sides. ⁸ The Sadducees say that people will not rise from the dead. They don't believe there are angels or spirits either. But the Pharisees believe all these things.

⁹ People were causing trouble and making a lot of noise. Some of the teachers of the law who were Pharisees stood up. They argued strongly. "We find nothing wrong with this man," they said. "What if a spirit or an angel has spoken to him?" ¹⁰ The people arguing were getting out of control. The commanding officer was afraid that Paul would be torn to pieces by them. So he ordered the soldiers to go down and take him away from them by force. The officer had told them to bring Paul into the fort.

¹¹ The next night the Lord stood near Paul. He said, "Be brave! You have told people about me in Jerusalem. You must do the same in Rome."

The Plan to Kill Paul

¹² The next morning some Jews gathered secretly to make plans against Paul. They made a promise to themselves. They promised that they would not eat or drink anything until they killed him. ¹³ More than 40 men took

part in this plan. [14] They went to the chief priests and the elders. They said, "We have made a special promise to God. We will not eat anything until we have killed Paul. [15] Now then, you and the Sanhedrin must make an appeal to the commanding officer. Ask him to bring Paul to you. Pretend you want more facts about his case. We are ready to kill him before he gets here."

[16] But Paul's nephew heard about this plan. So he went into the fort and told Paul.

[17] Then Paul called one of the commanders. He said to him, "Take this young man to the commanding officer. He has something to tell him." [18] So the commander took Paul's nephew to the officer.

The commander said, "Paul, the prisoner, sent for me. He asked me to bring this young man to you. The young man has something to tell you."

[19] The commanding officer took the young man by the hand. He spoke to him in private. "What do you want to tell me?" the officer asked.

[20] He said, "Some Jews have agreed to ask you to bring Paul to the Sanhedrin tomorrow. They will pretend they want more facts about him. [21] Don't give in to them. More than 40 of them are waiting in hiding to attack him. They have promised that they will not eat or drink anything until they have killed him. They are ready now. All they need is for you to bring Paul to the Sanhedrin."

[22] The commanding officer let the young man go. But he gave him a warning. "Don't tell anyone you have reported this to me," he said.

Paul Is Taken to Caesarea

[23] Then the commanding officer called for two of his commanders. He ordered them, "Gather a company of 200 soldiers, 70 horsemen and 200 men armed with spears. Get them ready to go to Caesarea at nine o'clock tonight. [24] Provide horses for Paul so that he may be taken safely to Governor Felix."

[25] Here is the letter the officer wrote.

[26] I, Claudius Lysias, am writing this letter.

I am sending it to His Excellency, Governor Felix.

Greetings.

[27] The Jews grabbed Paul. They were about to kill him. But I came with my soldiers and saved him. I had learned that he is a Roman citizen. [28] I wanted to know why they were bringing charges against him. So I brought him to their Sanhedrin. [29] I found out that the charge against him was based on questions about their law. But there was no charge against him worthy of death or prison. [30] Then I was told about a plan against the man. So I sent him to you at once. I also ordered those bringing

charges against him to present their case to you.

[31] The soldiers followed their orders. During the night they took Paul with them. They brought him as far as Antipatris. [32] The next day they let the horsemen go on with him. The soldiers returned to the fort. [33] The horsemen arrived in Caesarea. They gave the letter to the governor. Then they handed Paul over to him. [34] The governor read the letter. He asked Paul where he was from. He learned that Paul was from Cilicia. [35] So he said, "I will hear your case when those bringing charges against you get here." Then he ordered that Paul be kept under guard in Herod's palace.

Paul's Trial in Front of Felix

24 Five days later Ananias the high priest went down to Caesarea. Some elders and a lawyer named Tertullus went with him. They brought their charges against Paul to the governor. [2] So Paul was called in. Tertullus began to bring the charges against Paul. He said to Felix, "We have enjoyed a long time of peace while you have been ruling. You are a wise leader. You have made this a better nation. [3] Most excellent Felix, we gladly admit this everywhere and in every way. And we are very thankful. [4] I don't want to bother you. But would you be kind enough to listen to us for a short time?

[5] "We have found that Paul is a troublemaker. This man stirs up trouble among Jews all over the world. He is a leader of those who follow Jesus of Nazareth. [6-7] He even tried to make our temple impure. So we arrested him. [8] Question him yourself. Then you will learn the truth about all these charges we are bringing against him."

[9] The other Jews said the same thing. They agreed that the charges were true.

[10] The governor motioned for Paul to speak. Paul said, "I know that you have been a judge over this nation for quite a few years. So I am glad to explain my actions to you. [11] About 12 days ago I went up to Jerusalem to worship. You can easily check on this. [12] Those bringing charges against me did not find me arguing with anyone at the temple. I wasn't stirring up a crowd in the synagogues or anywhere else in the city. [13] They can't prove to you any of the charges they are making against me. [14] It is true that I worship the God of our people. I am a follower of the Way of Jesus. Those bringing charges against me call it a cult. I believe everything that is in keeping with the Law. I believe everything that is in keeping with what is written in the Prophets. [15] I have the same hope in God that these men themselves have. I believe that both the godly and the ungodly will rise from the dead. [16] So I always try not to do anything wrong in the eyes of God or in the eyes of people.

[17] "I was away for several

years. Then I came to Jerusalem to bring my people gifts for those who were poor. I also came to offer sacrifices. ¹⁸ They found me doing this in the temple courtyard. I had already been made pure and 'clean' in the usual way. There was no crowd with me. I didn't stir up any trouble. ¹⁹ But there are some other Jews who should be here in front of you. They are from Asia Minor. They should bring charges if they have anything against me. ²⁰ Let the Jews who are here tell you what crime I am guilty of. After all, I was put on trial by the Sanhedrin. ²¹ Perhaps they blame me for what I said when I was on trial. I shouted, 'I believe that people will rise from the dead. That is why I am on trial here today.' "

²² Felix knew all about the Way of Jesus. So he put off the trial for the time being. "Lysias the commanding officer will come," he said. "Then I will decide your case." ²³ He ordered the commander to keep Paul under guard. He told him to give Paul some freedom. He also told him to allow Paul's friends to take care of his needs.

²⁴ Several days later Felix came with his wife Drusilla. She was a Jew. Felix sent for Paul and listened to him speak about faith in Christ Jesus. ²⁵ Paul talked about how to live a godly life. He talked about how people should control themselves. He also talked about the time when God will judge everyone. Then Felix became afraid. "That's enough for now!" he said. "You may leave. When I find the time, I will send for you." ²⁶ He was hoping that Paul would offer him some money to let him go. So he often sent for Paul and talked with him.

²⁷ Two years passed. Porcius Festus took the place of Felix. But Felix wanted to do the Jews a favor. So he left Paul in prison.

Paul's Trial in Front of Festus

25 Three days after Festus arrived, he went up from Caesarea to Jerusalem. ² There the chief priests and the Jewish leaders came to Festus. They brought their charges against Paul. ³ They tried very hard to get Festus to have Paul taken to Jerusalem. They asked for this as a favor. They were planning to hide and attack Paul along the way. They wanted to kill him. ⁴ Festus answered, "Paul is being held at Caesarea. Soon I'll be going there myself. ⁵ Let some of your leaders come with me. If the man has done anything wrong, they can bring charges against him there."

⁶ Festus spent eight or ten days in Jerusalem with them. Then he went down to Caesarea. The next day he called the court together. He ordered Paul to be brought to him. ⁷ When Paul arrived, the Jews who had come down from Jerusalem stood around him. They brought many strong charges against him. But they couldn't prove that these charges were true.

[8] Then Paul spoke up for himself. He said, "I've done nothing wrong against the law of the Jews or against the temple. I've done nothing wrong against Caesar."

[9] But Festus wanted to do the Jews a favor. So he said to Paul, "Are you willing to go up to Jerusalem? Are you willing to go on trial there? Are you willing to face these charges in my court?"

[10] Paul answered, "I'm already standing in Caesar's court. This is where I should go on trial. I haven't done anything wrong to the Jews. You yourself know that very well. [11] If I am guilty of anything worthy of death, I'm willing to die. But the charges brought against me by these Jews are not true. No one has the right to hand me over to them. I make my appeal to Caesar!"

[12] Festus talked it over with the members of his court. Then he said, "You have made an appeal to Caesar. To Caesar you will go!"

Festus Talks With King Agrippa

[13] A few days later King Agrippa and Bernice arrived in Caesarea. They came to pay a visit to Festus. [14] They were spending many days there. So Festus talked with the king about Paul's case. He said, "There's a man here that Felix left as a prisoner. [15] When I went to Jerusalem, the Jewish chief priests and the elders brought charges against the man. They wanted him to be found guilty.

[16] "I told them that this is not the way Romans do things. We don't judge people before they have faced those bringing charges against them. They must have a chance to argue against the charges for themselves. [17] When the Jewish leaders came back with me, I didn't waste any time. I called the court together the next day. I ordered the man to be brought in. [18] Those bringing charges against him got up to speak. But they didn't charge him with any of the crimes I had expected. [19] Instead, they argued with him about their own beliefs. They didn't agree about a man named Jesus. They said Jesus was dead, but Paul claimed Jesus was alive. [20] I had no idea how to look into such matters. So I asked Paul if he would be willing to go to Jerusalem. There he could be tried on these charges. [21] But Paul made an appeal to have the Emperor decide his case. So I ordered him to be held until I could send him to Caesar."

[22] Then Agrippa said to Festus, "I would like to hear this man myself."

Festus replied, "Tomorrow you will hear him."

Paul in Front of Agrippa

[23] The next day Agrippa and Bernice arrived. They were treated like very important people. They entered the courtroom. The most important military officers and the leading men of the city came with them. When Festus gave the command, Paul was brought

in. ²⁴ Festus said, "King Agrippa, and everyone else here, take a good look at this man! A large number of Jews have come to me about him. They came to me in Jerusalem and also here in Caesarea. They keep shouting that he shouldn't live any longer. ²⁵ I have found that he hasn't done anything worthy of death. But he made his appeal to the Emperor. So I decided to send him to Rome. ²⁶ I don't have anything certain to write about him to His Majesty. So I have brought him here today. Now all of you will be able to hear him. King Agrippa, it will also be very good for you to hear him. As a result of this hearing, I will have something to write. ²⁷ It doesn't make sense to send a prisoner on to Rome without listing the charges against him."

26 Agrippa said to Paul, "You may now present your case."

So Paul motioned with his hand. Then he began to present his case. ² "King Agrippa," he said, "I am happy to be able to stand here today. I will answer all the charges brought against me by the Jews. ³ I am very pleased that you are familiar with Jewish ways. You know the kinds of things they argue about. So I beg you to be patient as you listen to me.

⁴ "The Jewish people all know how I have lived ever since I was a child. They know all about me from the beginning of my life. They know how I lived in my own country and in Jerusa-

lem. ⁵ They have known me for a long time. So if they wanted to, they could tell you how I have lived. I have lived by the rules of the Pharisees. Those rules are harder to obey than those of any other Jewish group. ⁶ Today I am on trial because of the hope I have. I believe in what God promised our people of long ago. ⁷ It is the promise that our 12 tribes are hoping to see come true. Because of this hope they serve God with faithful and honest hearts day and night. King Agrippa, it is also because of this hope that these Jews are bringing charges against me. ⁸ Why should any of you think it is impossible for God to raise the dead?

⁹ "I believed that I should oppose the name of Jesus of Nazareth. So I did everything I could to oppose his name. ¹⁰ That's just what I was doing in Jerusalem. On the authority of the chief priests, I put many of the Lord's people in prison. I agreed that they should die. ¹¹ I often went from one synagogue to another to have them punished. I tried to force them to speak evil things against Jesus. All I wanted to do was hurt them. I even went looking for them in the cities of other lands.

¹² "On one of these journeys I was on my way to Damascus. I had the authority and commission of the chief priests. ¹³ About noon, King Agrippa, I was on the road. I saw a light coming from heaven. It was brighter than the sun. It was shining around me

and my companions. [14]We all fell to the ground. I heard a voice speak to me in the Aramaic language. 'Saul! Saul!' it said. 'Why are you opposing me? It is hard for you to go against what you know is right.'

[15]"Then I asked, 'Who are you, Lord?'

"'I am Jesus,' the Lord replied. 'I am the one you are opposing. [16]Now get up. Stand on your feet. I have appeared to you to appoint you to serve me. And you must tell other people about me. You must tell others that you have seen me today. You must also tell them that I will show myself to you again. [17]I will save you from your own people and from the Gentiles. I am sending you to them [18]to open their eyes. I want you to turn them from darkness to light. I want you to turn them from Satan's power to God. I want their sins to be forgiven. They will be forgiven when they believe in me. They will have their place among God's people.'

[19]"So then, King Agrippa, I obeyed the vision that appeared from heaven. [20]First I preached to people in Damascus. Then I preached in Jerusalem and in all Judea. And then I preached to the Gentiles. I told them to turn away from their sins to God. The way they live must show that they have turned away from their sins. [21]That's why some Jews grabbed me in the temple courtyard and tried to kill me. [22]But God has helped me to this day. So I stand here

and tell you what is true. I tell it to everyone, both small and great. I have been saying nothing different from what the prophets and Moses said would happen. [23]They said the Messiah would suffer. He would be the first to rise from the dead. He would bring the message of God's light. He would bring it to his own people and to the Gentiles."

[24]While Paul was still presenting his case, Festus interrupted. "You are out of your mind, Paul!" he shouted. "Your great learning is driving you crazy!"

[25]"I am not crazy, most excellent Festus," Paul replied. "What I am saying is true and reasonable. [26]The king is familiar with these things. So I can speak openly to him. I am certain he knows everything that has been going on. After all, it was not done in secret. [27]King Agrippa, do you believe the prophets? I know you do."

[28]Then Agrippa spoke to Paul. "Are you trying to talk me into becoming a Christian?" he said. "Do you think you can do that in such a short time?"

[29]Paul replied, "I don't care if it takes a short time or a long time. I pray to God for you and all who are listening to me today. I pray that you may become like me, except for these chains."

[30]The king stood up. The governor and Bernice and those sitting with them stood up too. [31]They left the room and began

to talk with one another. "Why should this man die or be put in prison?" they said. "He has done nothing worthy of that!"

[32] Agrippa said to Festus, "This man could have been set free. But he has made an appeal to Caesar."

Paul Sails for Rome

27 It was decided that we would sail for Italy. Paul and some other prisoners were handed over to a Roman commander named Julius. He belonged to the Imperial Guard. [2] We boarded a ship from Adramyttium. It was about to sail for ports along the coast of Asia Minor. We headed out to sea. Aristarchus was with us. He was a Macedonian from Thessalonica.

[3] The next day we landed at Sidon. There Julius was kind to Paul. He let Paul visit his friends so they could give him what he needed. [4] From there we headed out to sea again. We passed the calmer side of Cyprus because the winds were against us. [5] We sailed across the open sea off the coast of Cilicia and Pamphylia. Then we landed at Myra in Lycia. [6] There the commander found a ship from Alexandria sailing for Italy. He put us on board. [7] We moved along slowly for many days. We had trouble getting to Cnidus. The wind did not let us stay on course. So we passed the calmer side of Crete, opposite Salmone. [8] It was not easy to sail along the coast. Then we came to a place called Fair Havens. It was near the town of Lasea.

[9] A lot of time had passed. Sailing had already become dangerous. By now it was after the Day of Atonement, a day of fasting. So Paul gave them a warning. [10] "Men," he said, "I can see that our trip is going to be dangerous. The ship and everything in it will be lost. Our own lives will be in danger also." [11] But the commander didn't listen to what Paul said. Instead, he followed the advice of the pilot and the ship's owner. [12] The harbor wasn't a good place for ships to stay during winter. So most of the people decided we should sail on. They hoped we would reach Phoenix. They wanted to spend the winter there. Phoenix was a harbor in Crete. It faced both southwest and northwest.

The Storm

[13] A gentle south wind began to blow. The ship's crew thought they saw their chance to leave safely. So they pulled up the anchor and sailed along the shore of Crete. [14] Before very long, a wind blew down from the island. It had the force of a hurricane. It was called the Northeaster. [15] The ship was caught by the storm. We could not keep it sailing into the wind. So we gave up and were driven along by the wind. [16] We passed the calmer side of a small island called Cauda. We almost lost the lifeboat that was tied to the side of the ship. [17] So the men lifted the lifeboat on board. Then they

tied ropes under the ship itself to hold it together. They were afraid it would get stuck on the sandbars of Syrtis. So they lowered the sea anchor and let the ship be driven along. ¹⁸ We took a very bad beating from the storm. The next day the crew began to throw the ship's contents overboard. ¹⁹ On the third day, they even threw the ship's tools and supplies overboard with their own hands. ²⁰ The sun and stars didn't appear for many days. The storm was terrible. So we gave up all hope of being saved.

²¹ The men had not eaten for a long time. Paul stood up in front of them. "Men," he said, "you should have taken my advice not to sail from Crete. Then you would have avoided this harm and loss. ²² Now I beg you to be brave. Not one of you will die. Only the ship will be destroyed. ²³ I belong to God and serve him. Last night his angel stood beside me. ²⁴ The angel said, 'Do not be afraid, Paul. You must go on trial in front of Caesar. God has shown his grace by sparing the lives of all those sailing with you.' ²⁵ Men, continue to be brave. I have faith in God. It will happen just as he told me. ²⁶ But we must run the ship onto the beach of some island."

The Ship Is Destroyed

²⁷ On the 14th night the wind was still pushing us across the Adriatic Sea. About midnight the sailors had a feeling that they were approaching land.

²⁸ They measured how deep the water was. They found that it was 120 feet deep. A short time later they measured the water again. This time it was 90 feet deep. ²⁹ They were afraid we would crash against the rocks. So they dropped four anchors from the back of the ship. They prayed that daylight would come. ³⁰ The sailors wanted to escape from the ship. So they let the lifeboat down into the sea. They pretended they were going to lower some anchors from the front of the ship. ³¹ But Paul spoke to the commander and the soldiers. "These men must stay with the ship," he said. "If they don't, you can't be saved." ³² So the soldiers cut the ropes that held the lifeboat. They let it drift away.

³³ Just before dawn Paul tried to get them all to eat. "For the last 14 days," he said, "you have wondered what would happen. You have gone without food. You haven't eaten anything. ³⁴ Now I am asking you to eat some food. You need it to live. Not one of you will lose a single hair from your head." ³⁵ After Paul said this, he took some bread and gave thanks to God. He did this where they all could see him. Then he broke it and began to eat. ³⁶ All of them were filled with hope. So they ate some food. ³⁷ There were 276 of us on board. ³⁸ They ate as much as they wanted. They needed to make the ship lighter. So they threw the rest of the grain into the sea.

39 When daylight came, they saw a bay with a sandy beach. They didn't recognize the place. But they decided to run the ship onto the beach if they could. 40 So they cut the anchors loose and left them in the sea. At the same time, they untied the ropes that held the rudders. They lifted the sail at the front of the ship to the wind. Then they headed for the beach. 41 But the ship hit a sandbar. So the front of it got stuck and wouldn't move. The back of the ship was broken to pieces by the pounding of the waves.

42 The soldiers planned to kill the prisoners. They wanted to keep them from swimming away and escaping. 43 But the commander wanted to save Paul's life. So he kept the soldiers from carrying out their plan. He ordered those who could swim to jump overboard first and swim to land. 44 The rest were supposed to get there on boards or other pieces of the ship. That is how everyone reached land safely.

On Shore at Malta

28 When we were safe on shore, we found out that the island was called Malta. 2 The people of the island were unusually kind. It was raining and cold. So they built a fire and welcomed all of us. 3 Paul gathered some sticks and put them on the fire. A poisonous snake was driven out by the heat. It fastened itself on Paul's hand. 4 The people of the island saw the snake hanging from his hand. They said to one another, "This man must be a murderer. He escaped from the sea. But the female god Justice won't let him live." 5 Paul shook the snake off into the fire. He was not harmed. 6 The people expected him to swell up. They thought he would suddenly fall dead. They waited for a long time. But they didn't see anything unusual happen to him. So they changed their minds. They said he was a god.

7 Publius owned property nearby. He was the chief official on the island. He welcomed us to his home. For three days he took care of us. He treated us with kindness. 8 His father was sick in bed. The man suffered from fever and dysentery. So Paul went in to see him. Paul prayed for him. He placed his hands on him and healed him. 9 Then the rest of the sick people on the island came. They too were healed. 10 The people of the island honored us in many ways. When we were ready to sail, they gave us the supplies we needed.

Paul Arrives in Rome

11 After three months we headed out to sea. We sailed in a ship from Alexandria that had stayed at the island during the winter. On the front of the ship the figures of twin gods were carved. Their names were Castor and Pollux. 12 We landed at Syracuse and stayed there for three days. 13 From there we

sailed to Rhegium. The next day the south wind came up. The day after that, we reached Puteoli. [14] There we found some believers. They invited us to spend a week with them. At last we came to Rome. [15] The believers there had heard we were coming. They traveled as far as the Forum of Appius and the Three Taverns to meet us. When Paul saw these people, he thanked God for them and was encouraged by them. [16] When we got to Rome, Paul was allowed to live by himself. But a soldier guarded him.

Paul Preaches in Rome

[17] Three days later Paul called a meeting of the local Jewish leaders. When they came, Paul spoke to them. He said, "My brothers, I have done nothing against our people. I have also done nothing against what our people of long ago practiced. But I was arrested in Jerusalem. I was handed over to the Romans. [18] They questioned me. And they wanted to let me go. They saw I wasn't guilty of any crime worthy of death. [19] But the Jews objected, so I had to make an appeal to Caesar. I certainly did not mean to bring any charge against my own people. [20] I share Israel's hope. That is why I am held with this chain. So I have asked to see you and talk with you."

[21] They replied, "We have not received any letters from Judea about you. None of our people here from Judea has reported or said anything bad about you. [22] But we want to hear what your ideas are. We know that people everywhere are talking against those who believe as you do."

[23] They decided to meet Paul on a certain day. At that time even more people came to the place where he was staying. From morning until evening, he told them about God's kingdom. Using the Law of Moses and the Prophets, he tried to get them to believe in Jesus. [24] Some believed what he said, and others did not. [25] They didn't agree with one another. They began to leave after Paul had made a final statement. He said, "The Holy Spirit was right when he spoke to your people long ago. Through Isaiah the prophet the Spirit said,

[26] " 'Go to your people. Say to them,
"You will hear but never understand.
You will see but never know what you are seeing."
[27] These people's hearts have become stubborn.
They can barely hear with their ears.
They have closed their eyes.
Otherwise they might see with their eyes.
They might hear with their ears.
They might understand with their hearts.
They might turn, and then I would heal them.'

(Isaiah 6:9,10)

28-29 "Here is what I want you to know. God has sent his salvation to the Gentiles. And they will listen!"

30 For two whole years Paul stayed there in a house he rented. He welcomed all who came to see him. 31 He preached boldly about God's kingdom. He taught people about the Lord Jesus Christ. And no one could keep him from teaching and preaching about these things.

Romans

Introduction:

Romans is one of Paul's letters. Paul liked to send letters to churches. Paul wrote letters to teach people. He also wrote letters to cheer them up and give them hope. Sometimes Paul wrote to correct false teaching.

Paul wrote this letter to teach people about being right with God. Paul said that all people are sinners. No one can be right with God by keeping God's law. All of us break God's law, so the law only shows us how sinful we are.

God loves us, so he made a way for us to be right with him. Jesus came and died for our sins. Jesus is the only person who never sinned. He died on the cross to free others from their sin. When we put our faith in Jesus we are made right with God. Jesus takes away our sin and gives us new life. He takes away the power of sin so we can live for him. Paul wanted God's children to live lives that are "pleasing to God."

Outline of contents:

---

1 I, Paul, am writing this letter. I serve Christ Jesus. I have been appointed to be an apostle. God set me apart to tell others his good news. ² He promised the good news long ago. He announced it through his prophets in the Holy Scriptures. ³ The good news is about God's Son. He was born into the family line of King David. ⁴ By the Holy Spirit, he was appointed to be the mighty Son of God. God did this by raising him from the dead. He is Jesus Christ our Lord. ⁵ We received grace because of what Jesus did. He made us apostles to the Gentiles. We must invite all of them to obey God by trusting in Jesus. We do this to bring glory to him. ⁶ You also are among those Gentiles who are appointed to belong to Jesus Christ.

⁷ I am sending this letter to all of you in Rome. You are loved by God and appointed to be his holy people.

May God our Father and the Lord Jesus Christ give you grace and peace.

Paul Longs to Visit Rome

⁸ First, I thank my God through Jesus Christ for all of you. People all over the world are talking about your faith. ⁹ I serve God with my whole heart. I preach the good news about his Son. God knows that I always remember you ¹⁰ in my prayers. I pray that now at last it may be God's plan to open the way for me to visit you.

¹¹ I long to see you. I want to make you strong by giving you a gift from the Holy Spirit. ¹² I want us to encourage one another in the faith we share. ¹³ Brothers and sisters, I want you to know that I planned many times to visit you. But until now I have been kept from coming. My work has produced results among the other Gentiles. In the same way, I want to see results among you.

¹⁴ I have a duty both to Greeks and to non-Greeks. I have a duty both to wise people and to foolish people. ¹⁵ So I really want to preach the good news also to you who live in Rome.

¹⁶ I want to preach it because I'm not ashamed of the good news. It is God's power to save everyone who believes. It is meant first for the Jews. It is meant also for the Gentiles. ¹⁷ The good news shows God's power to make people right with himself. God's power to be made right with him is given to the person who has faith. It happens by faith from beginning to end. It is written, "The one who is right with God will live by faith." *(Habakkuk 2:4)*

God's Anger Against Sinners

¹⁸ God shows his anger from heaven. It is against all the godless and evil things people do. They are so evil that they say no to the truth. ¹⁹ The truth about God is plain to them. God has made it plain. ²⁰ Ever since the world was created it has been possible to see the qualities of God that are not seen. I'm talking about his eternal power and about the fact that he is God. Those things can be seen in what he has made. So people have no excuse for what they do.

²¹ They knew God. But they didn't honor him as God. They didn't thank him. Their thinking became worthless. Their foolish hearts became dark. ²² They claimed to be wise. But they made fools of themselves. ²³ They would rather have statues of gods than the glorious God who lives forever. Their statues of gods are made to look like people, birds, animals and reptiles.

²⁴ So God let them go. He allowed them to do what their sinful hearts wanted to. He let them commit sexual sins. They made one another's bodies impure by what they did. ²⁵ They chose a lie instead of the truth about God. They worshiped and served created things. They didn't worship the Creator. But he is praised forever. Amen.

²⁶ So God let them continue to have their shameful desires. Their women committed sexual acts that were not natural. ²⁷ In the same way, the men turned

away from their natural love for women. They burned with sexual desire for each other. Men did shameful things with other men. They suffered in their bodies for all the wrong things they did.

²⁸ They didn't think it was important to know God. So God let them continue to have evil thoughts. They did things they shouldn't do. ²⁹ They are full of every kind of sin, evil and ungodliness. They want more than they need. They commit murder. They want what belongs to other people. They fight and cheat. They hate others. They say mean things about other people. ³⁰ They tell lies about them. They hate God. They are rude and proud. They brag. They think of new ways to do evil. They don't obey their parents. ³¹ They do not understand. They can't be trusted. They are not loving and kind. ³² They know that God's commands are right. They know that those who do evil things should die. But they continue to do those very things. They also approve of others who do them.

God Judges Fairly

2 If you judge someone else, you have no excuse for it. When you judge another person, you are judging yourself. You do the same things you blame others for doing. ² We know that when God judges those who do evil things, he judges fairly. ³ Though you are only a human being, you judge others. But you yourself do the same things. So how do you think you will escape when God judges you? ⁴ Do you disrespect God's great kindness and favor? Do you disrespect God when he is patient with you? Don't you realize that God's kindness is meant to turn you away from your sins?

⁵ But you are stubborn. In your heart you are not sorry for your sins. You are storing up anger against yourself. The day of God's anger is coming. Then his way of judging fairly will be shown. ⁶ God "will pay back each person in keeping with what they have done." *(Psalm 62:12; Proverbs 24:12)* ⁷ God will give eternal life to those who keep on doing good. They want glory, honor, and life that never ends. ⁸ But there are others who only look out for themselves. They don't accept the truth. They go astray. God will pour out his great anger on them. ⁹ There will be trouble and suffering for everyone who does evil. That is meant first for the Jews. It is also meant for the Gentiles. ¹⁰ But there will be glory, honor and peace for everyone who does good. That is meant first for the Jews. It is also meant for the Gentiles. ¹¹ God treats everyone the same.

¹² Some people do not know God's law when they sin. They will not be judged by the law when they die. Others do know God's law when they sin. They will be judged by the law. ¹³ Hearing the law does not make a person right with God. People are

considered to be right with God only when they obey the law. ¹⁴Gentiles do not have the law. Sometimes they just naturally do what the law requires. They are a law for themselves. This is true even though they don't have the law. ¹⁵They show that what the law requires is written on their hearts. The way their minds judge them proves this fact. Sometimes their thoughts find them guilty. At other times their thoughts find them not guilty. ¹⁶This will happen on the day God appoints Jesus Christ to judge people's secret thoughts. That's part of my good news.

The Jews and the Law

¹⁷Suppose you call yourself a Jew. You trust in the law. You brag that you know God. ¹⁸You know what God wants. You agree with what is best because the law teaches you. ¹⁹You think you know so much more than the people you teach. You think you're helping blind people. You think you are a light for those in the dark. ²⁰You think you can make foolish people wise. You act like you're teaching little children. You think that the law gives you all knowledge and truth. ²¹You claim to teach others, but you don't even teach yourself! You preach against stealing. But you steal! ²²You say that people should not commit adultery. But you commit adultery! You hate statues of gods. But you rob temples! ²³You brag about the law. But when you break it, you rob God of his

honor! ²⁴It is written, "The Gentiles say evil things against God's name because of you." *(Isaiah 52:5; Ezekiel 36:22)*

²⁵Circumcision has value if you obey the law. But if you break the law, it is just as if you hadn't been circumcised. ²⁶And sometimes those who aren't circumcised do what the law requires. Won't God accept them as if they had been circumcised? ²⁷Many are not circumcised physically, but they obey the law. They will prove that you are guilty. You are breaking the law, even though you have the written law and are circumcised.

²⁸A person is not a Jew if they are a Jew only on the outside. And circumcision is more than just something done to the outside of a man's body. ²⁹No, a person is a Jew only if they are a Jew on the inside. And true circumcision means that the heart has been circumcised by the Holy Spirit. The person whose heart has been circumcised does more than obey the written law. The praise that matters for that kind of person does not come from other people. It comes from God.

God Is Faithful

3 Is there any advantage in being a Jew? Is there any value in being circumcised? ²There is great value in every way! First of all, the Jews have been given the very words of God.

³What if some Jews were not faithful? Will the fact that they weren't faithful keep God from

being faithful? ⁴ Not at all! God is true, even if every human being is a liar. It is written,

"You are right when you
    sentence me.
You are fair when you
    judge me."   *(Psalm 51:4)*

⁵ Doesn't the fact that we are wrong prove more clearly that God is right? Then what can we say? Can we say that God is not fair when he brings his anger down on us? As you can tell, I am just using human ways of thinking. ⁶ God is certainly fair! If he weren't, how could he judge the world? ⁷ Someone might argue, "When I lie, it becomes clearer that God is truthful. It makes his glory shine more brightly. Why then does he find me guilty of sin?" ⁸ Why not say, "Let's do evil things so that good things will happen"? Some people actually lie by reporting that this is what we say. They are the ones who will rightly be found guilty.

No One Is Right With God

⁹ What should we say then? Do we Jews have any advantage? Not at all! We have already claimed that Jews and Gentiles are sinners. Everyone is under the power of sin. ¹⁰ It is written,

"No one is right with God, no
    one at all.
¹¹   No one understands.
    No one trusts in God.
¹² All of them have turned
    away.
    They have all become
    worthless.
    No one does anything good,
    no one at all."

*(Psalms 14:1–3; 53:1–3;
Ecclesiastes 7:20)*

¹³ "Their throats are like open
    graves.
    With their tongues they
    tell lies."   *(Psalm 5:9)*
"The words from their lips
    are like the poison of a
    snake."   *(Psalm 140:3)*
¹⁴   "Their mouths are full of
    curses and bitterness."
        (Psalm 10:7)
¹⁵ "They run quickly to commit
    murder.
¹⁶   They leave a trail of
    harmful actions.
¹⁷ They do not know how to live
    in peace."   *(Isaiah 59:7,8)*
¹⁸   "They don't have any
    respect for God."
        (Psalm 36:1)

¹⁹ What the law says, it says to those who are ruled by the law. Its purpose is to shut every mouth and make the whole world accountable to God. ²⁰ So no one will be considered right with God by obeying the law. Instead, the law makes us more aware of our sin.

Becoming Right With God by Faith

²¹ But now God has shown us his saving power without the help of the law. But the Law and the Prophets tell us about this. ²² We are made right with God by putting our faith in Jesus Christ. This happens to all who believe. It is no different for the Jews than for the Gentiles. ²³ Everyone has sinned. No one

measures up to God's glory. [24] The free gift of God's grace makes us right with him. Christ Jesus paid the price to set us free. [25] God gave Christ as a sacrifice to pay for sins through the spilling of his blood. So God forgives the sins of those who have faith. God did all this to prove that he does what is right. He is a God of mercy. So he did not punish for their sins the people who lived before Jesus lived. [26] God did all this to prove in our own time that he does what is right. He also makes right with himself those who believe in Jesus.

[27] So who can brag? No one! Are people saved by the law that requires them to obey? Not at all! They are saved because of the law that requires faith. [28] We firmly believe that a person is made right with God because of their faith. They are not saved by obeying the law. [29] Or is God the God of Jews only? Isn't he also the God of Gentiles? Yes, he is their God too. [30] There is only one God. When those who are circumcised believe in him, he makes them right with himself. Suppose those who are not circumcised believe in him. Then God also will make them right with himself. [31] Does faith make the law useless? Not at all! We agree with the law.

Abraham's Faith Made Him Right With God

4 What should we say about these things? What did Abraham, the father of our people, discover about being right with God? [2] Did he become right with God because of something he did? If so, he could brag about it. But he couldn't brag to God. [3] What do we find in Scripture? It says, "Abraham believed God. God accepted Abraham's faith, and so his faith made him right with God." *(Genesis 15:6)*

[4] When a person works, their pay is not considered a gift. It is owed to them. [5] But things are different with God. He makes ungodly people right with himself. If people trust in him, their faith is accepted even though they do not work. Their faith makes them right with God. [6] King David says the same thing. He tells us how blessed people are when God makes them right with himself. They are blessed because they don't have to do anything in return. David says,

[7] "Blessed are those
    whose lawless acts are
        forgiven.
Blessed are those
    whose sins are taken away.
[8] Blessed is the person
    whose sin the Lord never
        counts against them."

(Psalm 32:1,2)

[9] Is that blessing only for those who are circumcised? Or is it also for those who are not circumcised? We have been saying that God accepted Abraham's faith. So his faith made him right with God. [10] When did it happen? Was it after Abraham was circumcised, or before? It was before he was circumcised,

not after! [11] He was circumcised as a sign of the covenant God had made with him. It showed that his faith had made him right with God before he was circumcised. So Abraham is the father of all believers who have not been circumcised. God accepts their faith. So their faith makes them right with him. [12] And Abraham is also the father of those who are circumcised and believe. So just being circumcised is not enough. Those who are circumcised must also follow the steps of our father Abraham. He had faith before he was circumcised.

[13] Abraham and his family received a promise. God promised that Abraham would receive the world. It would not come to him because he obeyed the law. It would come because of his faith, which made him right with God. [14] Do those who depend on the law receive the promise? If they do, faith would mean nothing. God's promise would be worthless. [15] The law brings God's anger. Where there is no law, the law can't be broken.

[16] The promise is based on God's grace. The promise comes by faith. All of Abraham's children will certainly receive the promise. And it is not only for those who are ruled by the law. Those who have the same faith that Abraham had are also included. He is the father of us all. [17] It is written, "I have made you a father of many nations." *(Genesis 17:5)* God considers Abraham to be our father. The God that Abraham believed in gives life to the dead. Abraham's God also creates things that did not exist before.

[18] When there was no reason for hope, Abraham believed because he had hope. He became the father of many nations, exactly as God had promised. God said, "That is how many children you will have." *(Genesis 15:5)* [19] Abraham did not become weak in his faith. He accepted the fact that he was past the time when he could have children. At that time Abraham was about 100 years old. He also realized that Sarah was too old to have children. [20] But Abraham kept believing in God's promise. He became strong in his faith. He gave glory to God. [21] He was absolutely sure that God had the power to do what he had promised. [22] That's why "God accepted Abraham because he believed. So his faith made him right with God." *(Genesis 15:6)* [23] The words "God accepted Abraham's faith" were written not only for Abraham. [24] They were written also for us. We believe in the God who raised Jesus our Lord from the dead. So God will accept our faith and make us right with himself. [25] Jesus was handed over to die for our sins. He was raised to life in order to make us right with God.

Peace and Hope

5 We have been made right with God because of our faith. Now we have peace with

him because of our Lord Jesus Christ. ²Through faith in Jesus we have received God's grace. In that grace we stand. We are full of joy because we expect to share in God's glory. ³And that's not all. We are full of joy even when we suffer. We know that our suffering gives us the strength to go on. ⁴The strength to go on produces character. Character produces hope. ⁵And hope will never bring us shame. That's because God's love has been poured into our hearts. This happened through the Holy Spirit, who has been given to us.

⁶At just the right time Christ died for ungodly people. He died for us when we had no power of our own. ⁷It is unusual for anyone to die for a godly person. Maybe someone would be willing to die for a good person. ⁸But here is how God has shown his love for us. While we were still sinners, Christ died for us.

⁹The blood of Christ has made us right with God. So we are even more sure that Jesus will save us from God's anger. ¹⁰Once we were God's enemies. But we have been brought back to him because his Son has died for us. Now that God has brought us back, we are even more secure. We know that we will be saved because Christ lives. ¹¹And that is not all. We are full of joy in God because of our Lord Jesus Christ. Because of him, God has brought us back to himself.

Death Through Adam, Life Through Christ

¹²Sin entered the world because one man sinned. And death came because of sin. Everyone sinned, so death came to all people.

¹³Before the law was given, sin was in the world. This is certainly true. But people are not judged for sin when there is no law. ¹⁴Death ruled from the time of Adam to the time of Moses. Death ruled even over those who did not sin as Adam did. He broke God's command. But Adam also became a pattern of the Messiah. The Messiah was the one who was going to come.

¹⁵God's gift can't be compared with Adam's sin. Many people died because of the sin of that one man. But it was even more sure that God's grace would also come through one man. That man is Jesus Christ. God's gift of grace was more than enough for the whole world. ¹⁶The result of God's gift is different from the result of Adam's sin. That one sin brought God's judgment. But after many sins, God's gift made people right with him. ¹⁷One man sinned, and death ruled over all people because of his sin. What will happen is even more sure than this. Those who receive the rich supply of God's grace will rule with Christ. They will rule in his kingdom. They have received God's gift and have been made right with him. This will happen because of what the one man, Jesus Christ, has done.

¹⁸ So one man's sin brought guilt to all people. In the same way, one right act made people right with God. That one right act gave life to all people. ¹⁹ Many people were made sinners because one man did not obey. But one man did obey. That is why many people will be made right with God.

²⁰ The law was given so that sin would increase. But where sin increased, God's grace increased even more. ²¹ Sin ruled and brought death. But grace rules in the lives of those who are right with God. The grace of God brings eternal life. That's because of what Jesus Christ our Lord has done.

Living a New Life in Christ

6 What should we say then? Should we keep on sinning so that God's grace can increase? ² Not at all! As far as sin is concerned, we are dead. So how can we keep on sinning? ³ All of us were baptized into Christ Jesus. Don't you know that we were baptized into his death? ⁴ By being baptized, we were buried with Christ into his death. Christ has been raised from the dead by the Father's glory. And like Christ we also can live a new life.

⁵ By being baptized, we have been joined with him in a death like his. So we will certainly also be joined with him in a resurrection like his. ⁶ We know that what we used to be was nailed to the cross with him. That happened so our bodies that were ruled by sin would lose their power. So we are no longer slaves of sin. ⁷ That's because those who have died have been set free from sin.

⁸ We died with Christ. So we believe that we will also live with him. ⁹ We know that Christ was raised from the dead and will never die again. Death doesn't control him anymore. ¹⁰ When he died, he died once and for all time. He did this to break the power of sin. Now that he lives, he lives in the power of God.

¹¹ In the same way, consider yourselves to be dead as far as sin is concerned. Now you believe in Christ Jesus. So consider yourselves to be alive as far as God is concerned. ¹² So don't let sin rule your body, which is going to die. Don't obey its evil desires. ¹³ Don't give any part of yourself to serve sin. Don't let any part of yourself be used to do evil. Instead, give yourselves to God. You have been brought from death to life. So give every part of yourself to God to do what is right. ¹⁴ Sin will no longer control you like a master. That's because the law does not rule you. God's grace has set you free.

Slaves to Right Living

¹⁵ What should we say then? Should we sin because we are not ruled by the law but by God's grace? Not at all! ¹⁶ Don't you know that when you give yourselves to obey someone you become that person's slave? If

you are slaves of sin, then you will die. But if you are slaves who obey God, then you will live a godly life. [17] You used to be slaves of sin. But thank God that with your whole heart you obeyed the teachings you were given! [18] You have been set free from sin. You have become slaves to right living.

[19] Because you are human, you find this hard to understand. So I am using an everyday example to help you understand. You used to give yourselves to be slaves to unclean living. You were becoming more and more evil. Now give yourselves to be slaves to right living. Then you will become holy. [20] Once you were slaves of sin. At that time right living did not control you. [21] What benefit did you gain from doing the things you are now ashamed of? Those things lead to death! [22] You have been set free from sin. God has made you his slaves. The benefit you gain leads to holy living. And the end result is eternal life. [23] When you sin, the pay you get is death. But God gives you the gift of eternal life. That's because of what Christ Jesus our Lord has done.

An Example From Marriage

7 Brothers and sisters, I am speaking to you who know the law. Don't you know that the law has authority over someone only as long as they live? [2] For example, by law a married woman remains married as long as her husband lives. But suppose her husband dies. Then the law that joins her to him no longer applies. [3] But suppose that married woman sleeps with another man while her husband is still alive. Then she is called a woman who commits adultery. But suppose her husband dies. Then she is free from that law. She is not guilty of adultery if she marries another man.

[4] My brothers and sisters, when Christ died you also died as far as the law is concerned. Then it became possible for you to belong to him. He was raised from the dead. Now our lives can be useful to God. [5] The power of sin used to control us. The law stirred up sinful desires in us. So the things we did resulted in death. [6] But now we have died to what used to control us. We have been set free from the law. Now we serve in the new way of the Holy Spirit. We no longer serve in the old way of the written law.

The Law and Sin

[7] What should we say then? That the law is sinful? Not at all! Yet I wouldn't have known what sin was unless the law had told me. The law says, "Do not want what belongs to other people." *(Exodus 20:17; Deuteronomy 5:21)* If the law hadn't said that, I would not have known what it was like to want what belongs to others. [8] But the commandment gave sin an opportunity. Sin caused me to want all kinds of things that belong to others. A person can't sin by breaking a law if that

law doesn't exist. ⁹Before I knew about the law, I was alive. But then the commandment came. Sin came to life, and I died. ¹⁰I found that the commandment that was supposed to bring life actually brought death. ¹¹When the commandment gave sin the opportunity, sin tricked me. It used the commandment to put me to death. ¹²So the law is holy. The commandment also is holy and right and good.

¹³Did what is good cause me to die? Not at all! Sin had to be recognized for what it really is. So it used what is good to bring about my death. Because of the commandment, sin became totally sinful.

¹⁴We know that the law is holy. But I am not. I have been sold to be a slave of sin. ¹⁵I don't understand what I do. I don't do what I want to do. Instead, I do what I hate to do. ¹⁶I do what I don't want to do. So I agree that the law is good. ¹⁷As it is, I am no longer the one who does these things. It is sin living in me that does them. ¹⁸I know there is nothing good in my desires controlled by sin. I want to do what is good, but I can't. ¹⁹I don't do the good things I want to do. I keep on doing the evil things I don't want to do. ²⁰I do what I don't want to do. But I am not really the one who is doing it. It is sin living in me that does it.

²¹Here is the law I find working in me. When I want to do good, evil is right there with me. ²²Deep inside me I find joy in God's law. ²³But I see another law working in me. It fights against the law of my mind. It makes me a prisoner of the law of sin. That law controls me. ²⁴What a terrible failure I am! Who will save me from this sin that brings death to my body? ²⁵I give thanks to God who saves me. He saves me through Jesus Christ our Lord.

So in my mind I am a slave to God's law. But sin controls my desires. So I am a slave to the law of sin.

The Holy Spirit Gives Life

8 Those who belong to Christ Jesus are no longer under God's judgment. ²Because of what Christ Jesus has done, you are free. You are now controlled by the law of the Holy Spirit who gives you life. The law of the Spirit frees you from the law of sin that brings death. ³The written law was made weak by the power of sin. But God did what the written law could not do. He made his Son to be like those who live under the power of sin. God sent him to be an offering for sin. Jesus suffered God's judgment against our sin. ⁴Jesus does for us everything the holy law requires. The power of sin should no longer control the way we live. The Holy Spirit should control the way we live.

⁵So don't live under the control of sin. If you do, you will think about what sin wants. Live under the control of the Holy Spirit. If you do, you will think about what the Spirit wants. ⁶The thoughts of a person ruled

by sin bring death. But the mind ruled by the Spirit brings life and peace. ⁷ The mind ruled by the power of sin is at war with God. It does not obey God's law. It can't. ⁸ Those who are under the power of sin can't please God.

⁹ But you are not ruled by the power of sin. Instead, the Holy Spirit rules over you. This is true if the Spirit of God lives in you. Anyone who does not have the Spirit of Christ does not belong to Christ. ¹⁰ If Christ lives in you, you will live. Though your body will die because of sin, the Spirit gives you life. The Spirit does this because you have been made right with God. ¹¹ The Spirit of the God who raised Jesus from the dead is living in you. So the God who raised Christ from the dead will also give life to your bodies. He will do this because of his Spirit who lives in you.

¹² Brothers and sisters, we have a duty. Our duty is not to live under the power of sin. ¹³ If you live under the power of sin, you will die. But by the Spirit's power you can put to death the sins you commit. Then you will live.

¹⁴ Those who are led by the Spirit of God are children of God. ¹⁵ The Spirit you received doesn't make you slaves. Otherwise you would live in fear again. Instead, the Holy Spirit you received made you God's adopted child. By the Spirit's power we call God Abba. Abba means Father. ¹⁶ The Spirit him-self joins with our spirits. Together they tell us that we are God's children. ¹⁷ As his children, we will receive all that he has for us. We will share what Christ receives. But we must share in his sufferings if we want to share in his glory.

Suffering Now and Glory in the Future

¹⁸ What we are suffering now is nothing compared with our future glory. ¹⁹ Everything God created looks forward to the future. That will be the time when his children appear in their full and final glory. ²⁰ The created world was held back from fulfilling its purpose. But this was not the result of its own choice. It was planned that way by the one who held it back. God planned ²¹ to set the created world free. He didn't want it to rot away. Instead, God wanted it to have the same freedom and glory that his children have.

²² We know that all that God created has been groaning. It is in pain as if it were giving birth to a child. The created world continues to groan even now. ²³ And that's not all. We have the Holy Spirit as the promise of future blessing. But we also groan inside ourselves. We do this as we look forward to the time when God adopts us as full members of his family. Then he will give us everything he has for us. He will raise our bodies and give glory to them. ²⁴ That's the hope we had when we were saved. But hope that can be seen

is no hope at all. Who hopes for what they already have? ²⁵ We hope for what we don't have yet. So we are patient as we wait for it.

²⁶ In the same way, the Holy Spirit helps us when we are weak. We don't know what we should pray for. But the Spirit himself prays for us. He prays through groans too deep for words. ²⁷ God, who looks into our hearts, knows the mind of the Spirit. And the Spirit prays for God's people just as God wants him to pray.

²⁸ We know that in all things God works for the good of those who love him. He appointed them to be saved in keeping with his purpose. ²⁹ God planned that those he had chosen would become like his Son. In that way, Christ will be the first and most honored among many brothers and sisters. ³⁰ And those God has planned for, he has also appointed to be saved. Those he has appointed, he has made right with himself. To those he has made right with himself, he has given his glory.

We Are More Than Winners

³¹ What should we say then? Since God is on our side, who can be against us? ³² God did not spare his own Son. He gave him up for us all. Then won't he also freely give us everything else? ³³ Who can bring any charge against God's chosen ones? God makes us right with himself. ³⁴ Then who can sentence us to death? No one. Christ Jesus

is at the right hand of God and is also praying for us. He died. More than that, he was raised to life. ³⁵ Who can separate us from Christ's love? Can trouble or hard times or harm or hunger? Can nakedness or danger or war? ³⁶ It is written,

> "Because of you, we face
>   death all day long.
> We are considered as sheep
>   to be killed." *(Psalm 44:22)*

³⁷ No! In all these things we are more than winners! We owe it all to Christ, who has loved us. ³⁸ I am absolutely sure that not even death or life can separate us from God's love. Not even angels or demons, the present or the future, or any powers can separate us. ³⁹ Not even the highest places or the lowest, or anything else in all creation can separate us. Nothing at all can ever separate us from God's love. That's because of what Christ Jesus our Lord has done.

Paul Mourns for Israel

9 I speak the truth in Christ. I am not lying. My mind tells me that what I say is true. It is guided by the Holy Spirit. ² My heart is full of sorrow. My sadness never ends. ³ I am so concerned about my people, who are members of my own race. I am ready to be cursed, if that would help them. I am even willing to be separated from Christ. ⁴ They are the people of Israel. They have been adopted as God's children. God's glory belongs to them. So do the covenants. They received the law. They were taught to worship in the temple. They were given the promises. [5] The founders of our nation belong to them. The Messiah comes from their family line. He is God over all. May he always be praised! Amen.

God's Free Choice

[6] I do not mean that God's word has failed. Not everyone in the family line of Israel really belongs to Israel. [7] Not everyone in Abraham's family line is really his child. Not at all! Scripture says, "Your family line will continue through Isaac." *(Genesis 21:12)* [8] In other words, God's children are not just in the family line of Abraham. Instead, they are the children God promised to him. They are the ones considered to be Abraham's children. [9] God promised, "I will return at the appointed time. Sarah will have a son." *(Genesis 18:10,14)*

[10] And that's not all. Rebekah's children were born at the same time by the same father. He was our father Isaac. [11] Here is what happened. Rebekah's twins had not even been born. They hadn't done anything good or bad yet. So they show that God's purpose is based firmly on his free choice. [12] It was not because of anything they did but because of God's choice. So Rebekah was told, "The older son will serve the younger one." *(Genesis 25:23)* [13] It is written, "I chose Jacob instead of Esau." *(Malachi 1:2,3)*

[14] What should we say then? Is God unfair? Not at all! [15] He said to Moses,

"I will have mercy on whom I
    have mercy.
I will show love to those I
    love." *(Exodus 33:19)*

[16] So it doesn't depend on what people want or what they do. It depends on God's mercy. [17] In Scripture, God says to Pharaoh, "I had a special reason for making you king. I decided to use you to show my power. I wanted my name to become known everywhere on earth." *(Exodus 9:16)* [18] So God does what he wants to do. He shows mercy to one person and makes another stubborn.

[19] One of you will say to me, "Then why does God still blame us? Who can oppose what he wants to do?" [20] But you are a mere human being. So who are you to talk back to God? Scripture says, "Can what is made say to the one who made it, 'Why did you make me like this?'" *(Isaiah 29:16; 45:9)* [21] Isn't the potter free to make different kinds of pots out of the same lump of clay? Some are for special purposes. Others are for ordinary use.

[22] What if God chose to show his great anger? What if he chose to make his power known? But he put up with the people he was angry with. They were made to be destroyed. [23] What if he put up with them to show the riches of his glory to other people? Those other people are the ones he shows his mercy to. He made them to receive his glory.

24 We are those people. He has chosen us. We do not come only from the Jewish race. Many of us are not Jews. 25 God says in Hosea,

"I will call those who are not
my people 'my people.'
I will call the one who is
not my loved one 'my
loved one.'" *(Hosea 2:23)*

26 He also says,

"Once it was said to them,
'You are not my people.'
In that very place they will
be called 'children of the
living God.'" *(Hosea 1:10)*

27 Isaiah cries out concerning Israel. He says,

"The number of people from
Israel may be like the
sand by the sea.
But only a few of them will
be saved.
28 The Lord will carry out his
sentence.
He will be quick to carry it
out on earth, once and
for all." *(Isaiah 10:22,23)*

29 Earlier Isaiah had said,

"The Lord who rules over all
left us children and
grandchildren.
If he hadn't, we would have
become like Sodom.
We would have been like
Gomorrah." *(Isaiah 1:9)*

Israel Does Not Believe

30 What should we say then? Gentiles did not look for a way to be right with God. But they found it by having faith. 31 The people of Israel tried to obey the law to make themselves right with God. But they didn't reach their goal of being right with God. 32 Why not? Because they tried to do it without faith. They tried to be right with God by what they did. They tripped over the stone that causes people to trip and fall. 33 It is written,

"Look! In Zion I am laying a
stone that causes people
to trip.
It is a rock that makes them
fall.
The one who believes in
him will never be put to
shame." *(Isaiah 8:14; 28:16)*

10 Brothers and sisters, with all my heart I long for the people of Israel to be saved. I pray to God for them. 2 I can tell you for certain that they really want to serve God. But how they are trying to do it is not based on knowledge. 3 They didn't know that God's power makes people right with himself. They tried to get right with God in their own way. They didn't do it in God's way. 4 Christ has fulfilled everything the law was meant to do. So now everyone who believes can be right with God.

5 Moses writes about how the law could help a person do what God requires. He writes, "The person who does these things will live by them." *(Leviticus 18:5)* 6 But the way to do what God requires must begin by having faith in him. Scripture says, "Do not say in your heart, 'Who will go up into heaven?'"

(Deuteronomy 30:12) That means to go up into heaven and bring Christ down. ⁷ "And do not say, 'Who will go down into the grave?' " *(Deuteronomy 30:13)* That means to bring Christ up from the dead. ⁸ But what does it say? "The message is near you. It's in your mouth and in your heart." *(Deuteronomy 30:14)* This means the message about faith that we are preaching. ⁹ Say with your mouth, "Jesus is Lord." Believe in your heart that God raised him from the dead. Then you will be saved. ¹⁰ With your heart you believe and are made right with God. With your mouth you say what you believe. And so you are saved. ¹¹ Scripture says, "The one who believes in him will never be put to shame." *(Isaiah 28:16)* ¹² There is no difference between those who are Jews and those who are not. The same Lord is Lord of all. He richly blesses everyone who calls on him. ¹³ Scripture says, "Everyone who calls on the name of the Lord will be saved." *(Joel 2:32)*

¹⁴ How can they call on him unless they believe in him? How can they believe in him unless they hear about him? How can they hear about him unless someone preaches to them? ¹⁵ And how can anyone preach without being sent? It is written, "How beautiful are the feet of those who bring good news!" *(Isaiah 52:7)*

¹⁶ But not all the people of Israel accepted the good news. Isaiah says, "Lord, who has believed our message?" *(Isaiah 53:1)*

¹⁷ So faith comes from hearing the message. And the message that is heard is the message about Christ. ¹⁸ But I ask, "Didn't the people of Israel hear?" Of course they did. It is written,

> "Their voice has gone out
> into the whole earth.
> Their words have gone
> out from one end of
> the world to the other."
> *(Psalm 19:4)*

¹⁹ Again I ask, "Didn't Israel understand?" First, Moses says,

> "I will use people who are
> not a nation to make you
> jealous.
> I will use a nation that
> has no understanding
> to make you angry."
> *(Deuteronomy 32:21)*

²⁰ Then Isaiah boldly speaks about what God says. God said,

> "I was found by those who
> were not trying to find
> me.
> I made myself known to
> those who were not
> asking for me." *(Isaiah 65:1)*

²¹ But Isaiah also speaks about what God says concerning Israel. God said,

> "All day long I have held out
> my hands.
> I have held them out to a
> stubborn people who do
> not obey me." *(Isaiah 65:2)*

The Israelites Who Are Faithful

11 So here is what I ask. Did God turn his back on his people? Not at all! I myself belong to Israel. I am one of Abraham's children. I am from the tribe of Benjamin. ²God didn't turn his back on his people. After all, he chose them. Don't you know what Scripture says about Elijah? He complained to God about Israel. ³He said, "Lord, they have killed your prophets. They have torn down your altars. I'm the only one left. And they are trying to kill me." *(1 Kings 19:10,14)* ⁴How did God answer him? God said, "I have kept 7,000 people for myself. They have not bowed down to Baal." *(1 Kings 19:18)* ⁵Some are also faithful today. They have been chosen by God's grace. ⁶And if they are chosen by grace, then they can't work for it. If that were true, grace wouldn't be grace anymore.

⁷What should we say then? The people of Israel did not receive what they wanted so badly. Those Israelites who were chosen did receive it. But the rest of the people were made stubborn. ⁸It is written,

"God made it hard for them
    to understand.
He gave them eyes that
    could not see.
He gave them ears that
    could not hear.
And they are still like that
    today."
              (Deuteronomy 29:4; Isaiah 29:10)

⁹David says,

"Let their feast be a trap and
    a snare.
Let them trip and fall. Let
    them get what's coming
    to them.

¹⁰Let their eyes grow dark so
    they can't see.
Let their backs be bent
    forever."   *(Psalm 69:22,23)*

Two Kinds of Olive Branches

¹¹Again, here is what I ask. The Israelites didn't trip and fall once and for all time, did they? Not at all! Because Israel sinned, the Gentiles can be saved. That will make Israel jealous of them. ¹²Israel's sin brought riches to the world. Their loss brings riches to the Gentiles. So then what greater riches will come when all Israel turns to God!

¹³I am talking to you who are not Jews. I am the apostle to the Gentiles. So I take pride in the work I do for God and others. ¹⁴I hope somehow to stir up my own people to want what you have. Perhaps I can save some of them. ¹⁵When they were not accepted, it became possible for the whole world to be brought back to God. So what will happen when they are accepted? It will be like life from the dead. ¹⁶The first handful of dough that is offered is holy. This makes all of the dough holy. If the root is holy, so are the branches.

¹⁷Some of the natural branches have been broken off. You are a wild olive branch. But you have been joined to the tree with the other branches. Now you enjoy the life-giving sap of the olive tree root. ¹⁸So don't think you are better than the other branches. Remember, you don't give life to the root. The root gives life to you. ¹⁹You will

say, "Some branches were broken off so that I could be joined to the tree." ²⁰ That's true. But they were broken off because they didn't believe. You stand only because you do believe. So don't be proud, but tremble. ²¹ God didn't spare the natural branches. He won't spare you either.

²² Think about how kind God is! Also think about how firm he is! He was hard on those who stopped following him. But he is kind to you. So you must continue to live in his kindness. If you don't, you also will be cut off. ²³ If the people of Israel do not continue in their unbelief, they will again be joined to the tree. God is able to join them to the tree again. ²⁴ After all, weren't you cut from a wild olive tree? Weren't you joined to an olive tree that was taken care of? And wasn't that the opposite of how things should be done? How much more easily will the natural branches be joined to their own olive tree!

All Israel Will Be Saved

²⁵ Brothers and sisters, here is a mystery I want you to understand. It will keep you from being proud. Part of Israel has refused to obey God. That will continue until the full number of Gentiles has entered God's kingdom. ²⁶ In this way all Israel will be saved. It is written,

"The God who saves will
     come from Mount Zion.
He will remove sin from
     Jacob's family.

²⁷ Here is my covenant with
     them.
   I will take away their sins."

(Isaiah 59:20,21; 27:9;
Jeremiah 31:33,34)

²⁸ As far as the good news is concerned, the people of Israel are enemies. This is for your good. But as far as God's choice is concerned, the people of Israel are loved. This is because of God's promises to the founders of our nation. ²⁹ God does not take back his gifts. He does not change his mind about those he has chosen. ³⁰ At one time you did not obey God. But now you have received mercy because Israel did not obey. ³¹ In the same way, Israel has not been obeying God. But now they receive mercy because of God's mercy to you. ³² God has found everyone guilty of not obeying him. So now he can have mercy on everyone.

Praise to God

³³ How very rich are God's
     wisdom and knowledge!
   How he judges is more
     than we can understand!
   The way he deals with
     people is more than we
     can know!
³⁴ "Who can ever know what
     the Lord is thinking?
   Or who can ever give him
     advice?"   *(Isaiah 40:13)*
³⁵ "Has anyone ever given
     anything to God,
   so that God has to pay
     them back?"   *(Job 41:11)*
³⁶ All things come from him.
   All things are directed by him.

All things are for his praise.
May God be given the glory
forever! Amen.

Living as a Holy Sacrifice to God

12 Brothers and sisters, God has shown you his mercy. So I am asking you to offer up your bodies to him while you are still alive. Your bodies are a holy sacrifice that is pleasing to God. When you offer your bodies to God, you are worshiping him in the right way. [2] Don't live the way this world lives. Let your way of thinking be completely changed. Then you will be able to test what God wants for you. And you will agree that what he wants is right. His plan is good and pleasing and perfect.

Serving One Another in the Body of Christ

[3] God's grace has been given to me. So here is what I say to every one of you. Don't think of yourself more highly than you should. Be reasonable when you think about yourself. Keep in mind the faith God has given to each of you. [4] Each of us has one body with many parts. And the parts do not all have the same purpose. [5] So also we are many persons. But in Christ we are one body. And each part of the body belongs to all the other parts. [6] We all have gifts. They differ according to the grace God has given to each of us. Do you have the gift of prophecy? Then use it according to the faith you have. [7] If your gift is serving,

then serve. If it is teaching, then teach. [8] Is it encouraging others? Then encourage them. Is it giving to others? Then give freely. Is it being a leader? Then work hard at it. Is it showing mercy? Then do it cheerfully.

Love in Action

[9] Love must be honest and true. Hate what is evil. Hold on to what is good. [10] Love one another deeply. Honor others more than yourselves. [11] Stay excited about your faith as you serve the Lord. [12] When you hope, be joyful. When you suffer, be patient. When you pray, be faithful. [13] Share with the Lord's people who are in need. Welcome others into your homes.

[14] Bless those who hurt you. Bless them, and do not curse them. [15] Be joyful with those who are joyful. Be sad with those who are sad. [16] Agree with one another. Don't be proud. Be willing to be a friend of people who aren't considered important. Don't think that you are better than others.

[17] Don't pay back evil with evil. Be careful to do what everyone thinks is right. [18] If possible, live in peace with everyone. Do that as much as you can. [19] My dear friends, don't try to get even. Leave room for God to show his anger. It is written, "I am the God who judges people. I will pay them back," *(Deuteronomy 32:35)* says the Lord. [20] Do just the opposite. Scripture says,

"If your enemies are hungry,
give them food to eat.

If they are thirsty, give
them something to
drink.
By doing those things, you
will pile up burning
coals on their heads."

(Proverbs 25:21,22)

21 Don't let evil overcome you.
Overcome evil by doing good.

Obey Those in Authority

13 All of you must obey
those who rule over you.
There are no authorities except
the ones God has chosen. Those
who now rule have been chosen
by God. ² So whoever opposes
the authorities opposes leaders whom God has appointed.
Those who do that will be
judged. ³ If you do what is right,
you won't need to be afraid of
your rulers. But watch out if
you do what is wrong! You don't
want to be afraid of those in authority, do you? Then do what is
right, and you will be praised.
⁴ The one in authority serves
God for your good. But if you do
wrong, watch out! Rulers don't
carry a sword for no reason at
all. They serve God. And God is
carrying out his anger through
them. The ruler punishes anyone who does wrong. ⁵ You must
obey the authorities. Then you
will not be punished. You must
also obey them because you
know it is right.
⁶ That's also why you pay
taxes. The authorities serve
God. Ruling takes up all their
time. ⁷ Give to everyone what
you owe them. Do you owe
taxes? Then pay them. Do you

owe anything else to the government? Then pay it. Do you
owe respect? Then give it. Do
you owe honor? Then show it.

Love Fulfills the Law

⁸ Pay everything you owe.
But you can never pay back all
the love you owe one another.
Whoever loves other people
has done everything the law
requires. ⁹ Here are some commandments to think about. "Do
not commit adultery." "Do not
commit murder." "Do not steal."
"Do not want what belongs to
others." *(Exodus 20:13-15,17; Deuteronomy 5:17-19,21)* These and all other
commands are included in one
command. Here's what it is.
"Love your neighbor as you love
yourself." *(Leviticus 19:18)* ¹⁰ Love
does not harm its neighbor. So
love does everything the law requires.

The Day Is Near

¹¹ When you do these things,
keep in mind the times we are
living in. The hour has already
come for you to wake up from
your sleep. The full effects of our
salvation are closer now than
when we first believed in Christ.
¹² The dark night of evil is nearly
over. The day of Christ's return
is almost here. So let us get rid of
the works of darkness that harm
us. Let us do the works of light
that protect us. ¹³ Let us act as
we should, like people living in
the daytime. Have nothing to do
with wild parties, and don't get
drunk. Don't take part in sexual
sins or evil conduct. Don't fight

with each other or be jealous of anyone. ¹⁴ Instead, put on the Lord Jesus Christ as if he were your clothing. Don't think about how to satisfy sinful desires.

The Weak and the Strong

14 Accept the person whose faith is weak. Don't argue with them where you have differences of opinion. ² One person's faith allows them to eat anything. But another person eats only vegetables because their faith is weak. ³ The person who eats everything must not look down on the one who does not. And the one who doesn't eat everything must not judge the person who does. That's because God has accepted them. ⁴ Who are you to judge someone else's servant? Whether they are faithful or not is their own master's concern. And they will be faithful, because the Lord has the power to make them faithful.

⁵ One person considers one day to be more holy than another. Another person thinks all days are the same. Each of them should be absolutely sure in their own mind. ⁶ Whoever thinks that one day is special does so to honor the Lord. Whoever eats meat does so to honor the Lord. They give thanks to God. And whoever doesn't eat meat does so to honor the Lord. They also give thanks to God. ⁷ We don't live for ourselves only. And we don't die for ourselves only. ⁸ If we live, we live to honor the Lord. If we die, we die to honor the Lord. So whether we live or die, we belong to the Lord. ⁹ Christ died and came back to life. He did this to become the Lord of both the dead and the living.

¹⁰ Now then, who are you to judge your brother or sister? Why do you act like you're better than they are? We will all stand in God's courtroom to be judged. ¹¹ It is written,

" 'You can be sure that I live,'
        says the Lord.
'And you can be just as sure
        that everyone will kneel
        down down in front of
        me.
    Every tongue will have
        to tell the truth about
        God.' " (Isaiah 45:23)

¹² So we will all have to explain to God the things we have done. ¹³ Let us stop judging one another. Instead, decide not to put anything in the way of a brother or sister. Don't put anything in their way that would make them trip and fall. ¹⁴ I am absolutely sure that nothing is "unclean" in itself. The Lord Jesus has convinced me of this. But someone may consider a thing to be "unclean." If they do, it is "unclean" for them. ¹⁵ Your brother or sister may be upset by what you eat. If they are, you are no longer acting as though you love them. So don't destroy them by what you eat. Remember that Christ died for them. ¹⁶ So suppose you know something is good. Then don't let it be spoken of as if it were evil. ¹⁷ God's kingdom is

not about eating or drinking. It is about doing what is right and having peace and joy. All this comes through the Holy Spirit. ¹⁸ Those who serve Christ in this way are pleasing to God. They are pleasing to people too.

¹⁹ So let us do all we can to live in peace. And let us work hard to build up one another. ²⁰ Don't destroy the work of God because of food. All food is "clean." But it's wrong to eat anything that might cause problems for someone else's faith. ²¹ Don't eat meat if it causes your brother or sister to sin. Don't drink wine or do anything else that will make them sin.

²² Whatever you believe about these things, keep between yourself and God. Blessed is the person who doesn't feel guilty for what they do. ²³ But whoever has doubts about what they eat is guilty if they eat. That's because their eating is not based on faith. Everything that is not based on faith is sin.

15 We who have strong faith should help the weak with their problems. We should not please only ourselves. ² Each of us should please our neighbors. Let us do what is good for them in order to build them up. ³ Even Christ did not please himself. It is written, "The bad things people have said about you have been aimed at me also." *(Psalm 69:9)* ⁴ Everything written in the past was written to teach us. The Scriptures give us strength to go on. They encourage us and give us hope.

⁵ Our God is a God who strengthens and encourages you. May he give you the same attitude toward one another that Christ Jesus had. ⁶ Then you can give glory to God with one mind and voice. He is the God and Father of our Lord Jesus Christ.

⁷ Christ has accepted you. So accept one another in order to bring praise to God. ⁸ I tell you that Christ has become a servant of the Jews. He teaches us that God is true. He shows us that God will keep the promises he made to the founders of our nation. ⁹ Jesus became a servant of the Jews. He did this so that the Gentiles might give glory to God for his mercy. It is written,

"I will praise you among the
    Gentiles.
I will sing the praises of
    your name."
          (2 Samuel 22:50; Psalm 18:49)

¹⁰ Again it says,

"You Gentiles, be full of joy.
Be joyful together
    with God's people."
          (Deuteronomy 32:43)

¹¹ And again it says,

"All you Gentiles, praise the
    Lord.
Let all the nations sing
    praises to him." *(Psalm 117:1)*

¹² And Isaiah says,

"The Root of Jesse will grow
    up quickly.
He will rule over the
    nations.
The Gentiles will put their
    hope in him." *(Isaiah 11:10)*

[13] May the God who gives hope fill you with great joy. May you have perfect peace as you trust in him. May the power of the Holy Spirit fill you with hope.

Paul Serves the Gentiles

[14] My brothers and sisters, I am sure that you are full of goodness. You are filled with knowledge and able to teach one another. [15] But I have written to you very boldly about some things. I wanted to remind you of them again. The grace of God has allowed me [16] to serve Christ Jesus among the Gentiles. I have the duty of a priest to preach God's good news. Then the Gentiles will become an offering that pleases God. The Holy Spirit will make the offering holy.

[17] Because I belong to Christ Jesus, I can take pride in my work for God. [18] I will speak about what Christ has done through me. I won't try to speak about anything else. He has been leading the Gentiles to obey God. He has been doing this by what I have said and done. [19] He has given me power to do signs and wonders. I can do these things by the power of the Spirit of God. From Jerusalem all the way around to Illyricum I have finished preaching. In those places, I preached the good news about Christ. [20] I have always wanted to preach the good news where Christ was not known. I don't want to build on what someone else has started. [21] It is written,

"Those who were not
    told about him will
    understand.
Those who have not heard
    will know what it all
    means." *(Isaiah 52:15)*

[22] That's why I have often been kept from coming to you.

Paul Plans to Visit Rome

[23] Now there is no more place for me to work in those areas. For many years I have wanted to visit you. [24] So I plan to see you when I go to Spain. I hope to visit you while I am passing through. And I hope you will help me on my journey there. But first I want to enjoy being with you for a while. [25] Now I am on my way to Jerusalem to serve the Lord's people there. [26] The believers in Macedonia and Achaia were pleased to take an offering. It was for those who were poor among the Lord's people in Jerusalem. [27] They were happy to do it. And of course they owe it to them. The Gentiles have shared in the Jews' spiritual blessings. So the Gentiles should share their earthly blessings with the Jews. [28] I want to finish my task. I want to make sure that the poor in Jerusalem have received this offering. Then I will go to Spain. On my way I will visit you. [29] I know that when I come to you, I will come with the full blessing of Christ.

[30] Brothers and sisters, I ask you to join me in my struggle. Join me by praying to God for me. I ask this through the authority of our Lord Jesus Christ.

Pray for me with the love the Holy Spirit provides. [31] Pray that I will be kept safe from those in Judea who do not believe. I am taking the offering to Jerusalem. Pray that it will be welcomed by the Lord's people there. [32] Then I will come to you with joy just as God has planned. We will be renewed by being together. [33] May the God who gives peace be with you all. Amen.

Personal Greetings

16 I would like you to welcome our sister Phoebe. She is a deacon of the church in Cenchreae. [2] I ask you to receive her as one who belongs to the Lord. Receive her in the way God's people should. Give her any help she may need from you. She has been a great help to many people, including me.

[3] Greet Priscilla and Aquila. They work together with me in serving Christ Jesus. [4] They have put their lives in danger for me. I am thankful for them. So are all the Gentile churches.

[5] Greet also the church that meets in the house of Priscilla and Aquila.

Greet my dear friend Epenetus. He was the first person in Asia Minor to become a believer in Christ.

[6] Greet Mary. She worked very hard for you.

[7] Greet Andronicus and Junia, my fellow Jews. They have been in prison with me. They are leaders among the apostles. They became believers in Christ before I did.

[8] Greet Ampliatus, my dear friend in the Lord.

[9] Greet Urbanus. He works together with me in serving Christ. And greet my dear friend Stachys.

[10] Greet Apelles. He remained faithful to Christ even when he was tested.

Greet those who live in the house of Aristobulus.

[11] Greet Herodion, my fellow Jew.

Greet the believers who live in the house of Narcissus.

[12] Greet Tryphena and Tryphosa. Those women work hard for the Lord.

Greet my dear friend Persis. She is another woman who has worked very hard for the Lord.

[13] Greet Rufus. He is a chosen believer in the Lord. And greet his mother. She has been like a mother to me too.

[14] Greet Asyncritus, Phlegon and Hermes. Greet Patrobas, Hermas and the other brothers and sisters with them.

[15] Greet Philologus, Julia, Nereus and his sister. Greet Olympas and all of the Lord's people who are with them.

[16] Greet one another with a holy kiss.

All the churches of Christ send their greetings.

[17] I am warning you, brothers and sisters, to watch out for those who try to keep you from staying together. They want to trip you up. They teach you things opposite to what you have learned. Stay away from them. [18] People like that are not

serving Christ our Lord. They are serving only themselves. With smooth talk and with words they don't mean they fool people who don't know any better. [19] Everyone has heard that you obey God. So you have filled me with joy. I want you to be wise about what is good. And I want you to have nothing to do with what is evil.

[20] The God who gives peace will soon crush Satan under your feet.

May the grace of our Lord Jesus be with you.

[21] Timothy works together with me. He sends his greetings to you. So do Lucius, Jason and Sosipater, my fellow Jews.

[22] I, Tertius, wrote down this letter. I greet you as a believer in the Lord.

[23-24] Gaius sends you his greetings. He has welcomed me and the whole church here into his house.

Erastus is the director of public works here in the city. He sends you his greetings. Our brother Quartus also greets you.

[25] May God receive glory. He is able to strengthen your faith. He does this in keeping with the good news and the message I preach. It is the message about Jesus Christ. This message is in keeping with the mystery hidden for a very long time. [26] The mystery has now been made known through the writings of the prophets. The eternal God commanded that it be made known. God wanted all the Gentiles to obey him by trusting in him. [27] May the only wise God receive glory forever through Jesus Christ. Amen.

1 Corinthians

Introduction:

Paul wrote this letter to the church in Corinth. He wrote it while he was staying in Ephesus. Paul had heard sad news about his friends in Corinth.

Corinth was a wicked city. The church there was new, and it was hard for the Christians not to act like their neighbors. The people in the church were fighting with each other. Some were living very bad lives. Paul wrote this letter to scold them and teach them how Christians should act. He wanted the people to know right from wrong and do what was right.

Paul's letter teaches us about love, gifts of the Holy Spirit and the Lord's Supper. It also tells that since Jesus rose from the dead, Christians will also rise from the dead.

Outline of contents:

---

1 I, Paul, am writing this letter. I have been chosen to be an apostle of Christ Jesus just as God planned. Our brother Sosthenes joins me in writing.

² We are sending this letter to you, the members of God's church in Corinth. You have been made holy because you belong to Christ Jesus. God has chosen you to be his holy people. He has done the same for all people everywhere who pray to our Lord Jesus Christ. Jesus is their Lord and ours.

³ May God our Father and the Lord Jesus Christ give you grace and peace.

Paul Gives Thanks

⁴ I always thank my God for you. I thank him because of the grace he has given to you who belong to Christ Jesus. ⁵ You have been blessed in every way because of him. You have been blessed in all your speech and knowledge. ⁶ God has shown that what we have spoken to you about Christ is true. ⁷ There is no gift of the Holy Spirit that you

don't have. You are full of hope as you wait for our Lord Jesus Christ to come again. [8] God will also keep you strong in faith to the very end. Then you will be without blame on the day our Lord Jesus Christ returns. [9] God is faithful. He has chosen you to share life with his Son, Jesus Christ our Lord.

Taking Sides in the Church

[10] Brothers and sisters, I make my appeal to you. I do this in the name of our Lord Jesus Christ. I ask that all of you agree with one another in what you say. I ask that you don't take sides. I ask that you are in complete agreement in all that you think. [11] My brothers and sisters, I have been told you are arguing with one another. Some people from Chloe's house have told me this. [12] Here is what I mean. One of you says, "I follow Paul." Another says, "I follow Apollos." Another says, "I follow Peter." And still another says, "I follow Christ."

[13] Does Christ take sides? Did Paul die on the cross for you? Were you baptized in the name of Paul? [14] I thank God that I didn't baptize any of you except Crispus and Gaius. [15] No one can say that you were baptized in my name. [16] It's true that I also baptized those who live in the house of Stephanas. Besides that, I don't remember if I baptized anyone else. [17] Christ did not send me to baptize. He sent me to preach the good news. He commanded me not to preach with wisdom and fancy words. That would take all the power away from the cross of Christ.

Christ Is God's Power and Wisdom

[18] The message of the cross seems foolish to those who are lost and dying. But it is God's power to us who are being saved. [19] It is written,

"I will destroy the wisdom of
   those who are wise.
I will do away with the
   cleverness of those who
   think they are so smart."
                    (Isaiah 29:14)

[20] Where is the wise person? Where is the teacher of the law? Where are the great thinkers of our time? Hasn't God made the wisdom of the world foolish? [21] God wisely planned that the world would not know him through its own wisdom. It pleased God to use the foolish things we preach to save those who believe. [22] Jews require signs. Greeks look for wisdom. [23] But we preach about Christ and his death on the cross. That is very hard for Jews to accept. And everyone else thinks it's foolish. [24] But there are those God has chosen, both Jews and Greeks. To them Christ is God's power and God's wisdom. [25] The foolish things of God are wiser than human wisdom. The weakness of God is stronger than human strength.

[26] Brothers and sisters, think of what you were when God

chose you. Not many of you were considered wise by human standards. Not many of you were powerful. Not many of you belonged to important families. ²⁷ But God chose the foolish things of the world to shame the wise. God chose the weak things of the world to shame the strong. ²⁸ God chose the things of this world that are common and looked down on. God chose things considered unimportant to do away with things considered important. ²⁹ So no one can boast to God. ³⁰ Because of what God has done, you belong to Christ Jesus. He has become God's wisdom for us. He makes us right with God. He makes us holy and sets us free. ³¹ It is written, "The one who boasts should boast about what the Lord has done." *(Jeremiah 9:24)*

2 And this was the way it was with me, brothers and sisters. When I came to you, I didn't come with fancy words or human wisdom. I preached to you the truth about God's love. ² My goal while I was with you was to talk about only one thing. And that was Jesus Christ and his death on the cross. ³ When I came to you, I was weak and very afraid and trembling all over. ⁴ I didn't preach my message with clever and compelling words. Instead, my preaching showed the Holy Spirit's power. ⁵ This was so that your faith would be based on God's power. Your faith would not be based on human wisdom.

God's Wisdom Through the Holy Spirit

⁶ The words we speak to those who have grown in the faith are wise. Our words are different from the wisdom of this world. Our words are different from those of the rulers of this world. These rulers are becoming less and less powerful. ⁷ No, we announce God's wisdom. His wisdom is a mystery that has been hidden. But before time began, God planned that his wisdom would bring us heavenly glory. ⁸ None of the rulers of this world understood God's wisdom. If they had, they would not have nailed the Lord of glory to the cross. ⁹ It is written that

"no eye has seen,
  no ear has heard,
and no human mind has
    known." *(Isaiah 64:4)*
  God has prepared these
    things for those who love
    him.

¹⁰ God has shown these things to us through his Spirit.

The Spirit understands all things. He understands even the deep things of God. ¹¹ Who can know the thoughts of another person? Only a person's own spirit can know them. In the same way, only the Spirit of God knows God's thoughts. ¹² What we have received is not the spirit of the world. We have received the Spirit who is from God. The Spirit helps us understand what God has freely given us. ¹³ That is what we speak about. We don't use words taught to us by people. We use words taught to us by the Holy Spirit. We use the words taught by the Spirit to explain spiritual truths. [14] The person without the Spirit doesn't accept the things that come from the Spirit of God. These things are foolish to them. They can't understand them. In fact, such things can't be understood without the Spirit's help. [15] The person who has the Spirit can judge all things. But no human being can judge those who have the Spirit. It is written,

[16] "Who can ever know what is
　　in the Lord's mind?
　Can anyone ever teach
　　him?"　　*(Isaiah 40:13)*

But we have the mind of Christ.

The Church and Its Leaders

3 Brothers and sisters, I couldn't speak to you as people who live by the Holy Spirit. I had to speak to you as people who were still following the ways of the world. You aren't growing as Christ wants you to. You are still like babies. [2] The words I spoke to you were like milk, not like solid food. You weren't ready for solid food yet. And you still aren't ready for it. [3] You are still following the ways of the world. Some of you are jealous. Some of you argue. So aren't you following the ways of the world? Aren't you acting like ordinary human beings? [4] One of you says, "I follow Paul." Another says, "I follow Apollos." Aren't you acting like ordinary human beings?

[5] After all, what is Apollos? And what is Paul? We are only people who serve. We helped you to believe. The Lord has given each of us our own work to do. [6] I planted the seed. Apollos watered it. But God has been making it grow. [7] So the one who plants is not important. The one who waters is not important. It is God who makes things grow. He is the important one. [8] The one who plants and the one who waters have the same purpose. The Lord will give each of them a reward for their work. [9] We work together to serve God. You are like God's field. You are like his building.

[10] God has given me the grace to lay a foundation as a wise builder. Now someone else is building on it. But each one should build carefully. [11] No one can lay any other foundation than what has already been laid. That foundation is Jesus Christ. [12] A person may build on it using gold, silver, jewels, wood, hay or straw. [13] But each person's work will be shown for what it is. On judgment day it will be brought to light. It will be put through fire. The fire will test how good each person's work is. [14] If the building doesn't burn up, God will give the builder a reward for the work. [15] If the building burns up, the builder will lose everything. The builder will be saved, but only like one escaping through the flames.

[16] Don't you know that you yourselves are God's temple? Don't you know that God's Spirit

lives among you? ¹⁷ If anyone destroys God's temple, God will destroy that person. God's temple is holy. And you all together are that temple.

¹⁸ Don't fool yourselves. Suppose some of you think you are wise by the standards of the world. Then you should become "fools" so that you can become wise. ¹⁹ The wisdom of this world is foolish in God's eyes. It is written, "God catches wise people in their own evil plans." *(Job 5:13)* ²⁰ It is also written, "The Lord knows that the thoughts of wise people don't amount to anything." *(Psalm 94:11)* ²¹ So no more bragging about human leaders! All things are yours. ²² That means Paul or Apollos or Peter or the world or life or death or the present or the future. All are yours. ²³ You are joined to Christ and belong to him. And Christ is joined to God.

True Apostles of Christ

4 So here is how you should think of us. We serve Christ. We are trusted with the mysteries God has shown us. ² Those who have been given a trust must prove that they are faithful. ³ I care very little if I am judged by you or by any human court. I don't even judge myself. ⁴ I don't feel I have done anything wrong. But that doesn't mean I'm not guilty. The Lord judges me. ⁵ So don't judge anything before the appointed time. Wait until the Lord returns. He will bring to light what is hidden in the dark. He will show the real reasons why people do what they do. At that time each person will receive their praise from God.

⁶ Brothers and sisters, I have used myself and Apollos as examples to help you. You can learn from us the meaning of the saying, "Don't go beyond what is written." Then you won't be proud that you follow one of us instead of the other. ⁷ Who makes you different from anyone else? What do you have that you did not receive? And if you did receive it, why do you brag as though you did not?

⁸ You already have everything you want, don't you? Have you already become rich? Have you already begun to rule? And did you do that without us? I wish that you really had begun to rule. Then we could also rule with you! ⁹ It seems to me that God has put us apostles on display at the end of a parade. We are like people sentenced to die in front of a crowd. We have been made a show for the whole creation to see. Angels and people are staring at us. ¹⁰ We are fools for Christ. But you are so wise in Christ! We are weak. But you are so strong! You are honored. But we are looked down on! ¹¹ Up to this very hour we are hungry and thirsty. We are dressed in rags. We are being treated badly. We have no homes. ¹² We work hard with our own hands. When others curse us, we bless them. When we are attacked, we put up with it. ¹³ When others say bad things about us, we an-

swer with kind words. We have become the world's garbage. We are everybody's trash, right up to this moment.

Paul Warns Against Pride

[14] I am not writing this to shame you. You are my dear children, and I want to warn you. [15] Suppose you had 10,000 believers in Christ watching over you. You still wouldn't have many fathers. I became your father by serving Christ Jesus and telling you the good news. [16] So I'm asking you to follow my example. [17] That's the reason I have sent Timothy to you. He is like a son to me, and I love him. He is faithful in serving the Lord. He will remind you of my way of life in serving Christ Jesus. And that agrees with what I teach everywhere in every church.

[18] Some of you have become proud. You act as if I weren't coming to you. [19] But I will come very soon, if that's what the Lord wants. Then I will find out how those proud people are talking. I will also find out what power they have. [20] The kingdom of God is not a matter of talk. It is a matter of power. [21] Which do you want? Should I come to you to correct and punish you? Or should I come in love and with a gentle spirit?

Throw Out the Evil Person!

5 It is actually reported that there is sexual sin among you. I'm told that a man is sleeping with his father's wife. Even people who don't know God don't let that kind of sin continue. [2] And you are proud! Shouldn't you be very sad instead? Shouldn't you have thrown out of your church the man doing this? [3] Even though I am not right there with you, I am with you in spirit. And because I am with you in spirit, I have already judged the man doing this. I have judged him in the name of our Lord Jesus. [4] So when you come together, I will be with you in spirit. The power of our Lord Jesus will also be with you. [5] When you come together like this, hand this man over to Satan. Then the power of sin in his life will be destroyed. His spirit will be saved on the day the Lord returns.

[6] Your bragging is not good. It is like yeast. Don't you know that just a little yeast makes the whole batch of dough rise? [7] Get rid of the old yeast. Then you can be like a new batch of dough without yeast. That is what you really are. That's because Christ, our Passover Lamb, has been offered up for us. [8] So let us keep the Feast, but not with the old bread made with yeast. The yeast I'm talking about is hatred and evil. Let us keep the Feast with bread made without yeast. Let us keep it with bread that is honesty and truth.

[9] I wrote a letter to you to tell you to stay away from people who commit sexual sins. [10] I didn't mean the people of this world who sin in this way. I didn't mean those who always want more and more. I

didn't mean those who cheat or who worship statues of gods. In that case you would have to leave this world! [11] But here is what I am writing to you now. You must stay away from anyone who claims to be a believer but does evil things. Stay away from anyone who commits sexual sins. Stay away from anyone who always wants more and more things. Stay away from anyone who worships statues of gods. Stay away from anyone who tells lies about others. Stay away from anyone who gets drunk or who cheats. Don't even eat with people like these.

[12] Is it my business to judge those outside the church? Aren't you supposed to judge those inside the church? [13] God will judge those outside. Scripture says, "Get rid of that evil person!" *(Deuteronomy 17:7; 19:19; 21:21; 22:21,24; 24:7)*

Do Not Take Believers to Court

6 Suppose one of you wants to bring a charge against another believer. Should you take it to ungodly people to be judged? Why not take it to the Lord's people? [2] Or don't you know that the Lord's people will judge the world? Since this is true, aren't you able to judge small cases? [3] Don't you know that we will judge angels? Then we should be able to judge the things of this life even more! [4] So suppose you disagree with one another in matters like this. Who do you ask to decide which of you is right? Do you ask people who live in a way the church disapproves of? Of course not! [5] I say this to shame you. Is it possible that no one among you is wise enough to judge matters between believers? [6] Instead, one believer goes to court against another. And this happens in front of unbelievers!

[7] When you take another believer to court, you have lost the battle already. Why not be treated wrongly? Why not be cheated? [8] Instead, you yourselves cheat and do wrong. And you do it to your brothers and sisters. [9] Don't you know that people who do wrong will not receive God's kingdom? Don't be fooled. Those who commit sexual sins will not receive the kingdom. Neither will those who worship statues of gods or commit adultery. Neither will men who sleep with other men. [10] Neither will thieves or those who always want more and more. Neither will those who are often drunk or tell lies or cheat. People who live like that will not receive God's kingdom. [11] Some of you used to do those things. But your sins were washed away. You were made holy. You were made right with God. All of this was done in the name of the Lord Jesus Christ. It was also done by the Spirit of our God.

Sexual Sins

[12] Some of you say, "I have the right to do anything." But not everything is helpful. Again some of you say, "I have the right

to do anything." But I will not be controlled by anything. [13] Some of you say, "Food is for the stomach, and the stomach is for food. And God will destroy both of them." But the body is not meant for sexual sins. The body is meant for the Lord. And the Lord is meant for the body. [14] By his power God raised the Lord from the dead. He will also raise us up. [15] Don't you know that your bodies belong to the body of Christ? Should I take what belongs to Christ and join it to a prostitute? Never! [16] When you join yourself to a prostitute, you become one with her in body. Don't you know this? Scripture says, "The two will become one." *(Genesis 2:24)* [17] But whoever is joined to the Lord becomes one with him in spirit.

[18] Keep far away from sexual sins. All the other sins a person commits are outside the body. But sexual sins are sins against their own body. [19] Don't you know that your bodies are temples of the Holy Spirit? The Spirit is in you, and you have received the Spirit from God. You do not belong to yourselves. [20] Christ has paid the price for you. So use your bodies in a way that honors God.

Advice for Those Who Are Married

7 Now I want to deal with the things you wrote me about. Some of you say, "It is good for a man not to sleep with a woman." [2] But since sexual sin is happening, each man should sleep with his own wife. And each woman should sleep with her own husband. [3] A husband should satisfy his wife's needs. And a wife should satisfy her husband's needs. [4] The wife's body does not belong only to her. It also belongs to her husband. In the same way, the husband's body does not belong only to him. It also belongs to his wife. [5] You shouldn't stop giving yourselves to each other. You might possibly do this when you both agree to it. And you should only agree to it to give yourselves time to pray. Then you should come together again. In that way, Satan will not tempt you when you can't control yourselves. [6] I say those things to you as my advice, not as a command. [7] I wish all of you were single like me. But you each have your own gift from God. One has this gift, and another has that one.

[8] I speak now to those who are not married. I also speak to widows. It is good for you to stay single like me. [9] But if you can't control yourselves, you should get married. It is better to get married than to burn with desire.

[10] I give a command to those who are married. It is a direct command from the Lord, not from me. A wife must not leave her husband. [11] But if she does, she must not get married again. Or she can go back to her husband. And a husband must not divorce his wife.

[12] I also have something to say to everyone else. It is from

me, not a direct command from the Lord. Suppose a brother has a wife who is not a believer. If she is willing to live with him, he must not divorce her. 13 And suppose a woman has a husband who is not a believer. If he is willing to live with her, she must not divorce him. 14 The unbelieving husband has been made holy through his wife. The unbelieving wife has been made holy through her believing husband. If that were not the case, your children would not be pure and "clean." But as it is, they are holy.

15 But if the unbeliever leaves, let that person go. In that case, the believer does not have to stay married to the unbeliever. God wants us to live in peace. 16 Wife, how do you know if you will save your husband? Husband, how do you know if you will save your wife?

Stay as You Were When God Chose You

17 But each believer should live in whatever situation the Lord has given them. Stay as you were when God chose you. That's the rule all the churches must follow. 18 Was a man already circumcised when God chose him? Then he should not become uncircumcised. Was he uncircumcised when God chose him? Then he should not be circumcised. 19 Being circumcised means nothing. Being uncircumcised means nothing. Doing what God commands is what counts. 20 Each

of you should stay as you were when God chose you. 21 Were you a slave when God chose you? Don't let it trouble you. But if you can get your master to set you free, do it. 22 The person who was a slave when the Lord chose them is now the Lord's free person. The one who was free when God chose them is now a slave of Christ. 23 Christ has paid the price for you. Don't become slaves of human beings. 24 Brothers and sisters, each person is accountable to God. So each person should stay as they were when God chose them.

Advice for Those Who Are Not Married

25 Now I want to say something about virgins. I have no direct command from the Lord. But I give my opinion. Because of the Lord's mercy, I give it as one who can be trusted. 26 Times are hard for you right now. So I think it's good for a man to stay as he is. 27 Are you engaged to a woman? Then don't try to get out of it. Are you free from such a promise? Then don't look for a wife. 28 But if you do marry someone, you have not sinned. And if a virgin marries someone, she has not sinned. But those who marry someone will have many troubles in this life. I want to save you from this.

29 Brothers and sisters, what I mean is that the time is short. From now on, those who have a husband or wife should live as if they did not. 30 Those who mourn should live as if they

did not. Those who are happy should live as if they were not. Those who buy something should live as if it were not theirs to keep. [31] Those who use the things of the world should not become all wrapped up in them. The world as it now exists is passing away.

[32] I don't want you to have anything to worry about. A single man is concerned about the Lord's matters. He wants to know how he can please the Lord. [33] But a married man is concerned about the matters of this world. He wants to know how he can please his wife. [34] His concerns pull him in two directions. A single woman or a virgin is concerned about the Lord's matters. She wants to serve the Lord with both body and spirit. But a married woman is concerned about the matters of this world. She wants to know how she can please her husband. [35] I'm saying those things for your own good. I'm not trying to hold you back. I want you to be free to live in a way that is right. I want you to give yourselves completely to the Lord.

[36] Suppose someone is worried that he is not acting with honor toward the virgin he has promised to marry. Suppose his desires are too strong, and he feels that he should marry her. He should do as he wants. He is not sinning. They should get married. [37] But suppose the man has decided not to marry the virgin. And suppose he has no compelling need to get married and can control himself. If he has made up his mind not to get married, he also does the right thing. [38] So then, the man who marries the virgin does the right thing. But the man who doesn't marry her does a better thing.

[39] A woman has to stay married to her husband as long as he lives. If he dies, she is free to marry anyone she wants to. But the one she marries must belong to the Lord. [40] In my opinion, she is happier if she stays single. And I also think that I am led by the Spirit of God in saying this.

Food Sacrificed to Statues of Gods

8 Now I want to deal with food sacrificed to statues of gods. We know that "We all have knowledge." But knowledge makes people proud, while love builds them up. [2] Those who think they know something still don't know as they should. [3] But whoever loves God is known by God.

[4] So then, here is what I say about eating food sacrificed to statues of gods. We know that "a god made by human hands is really nothing at all in the world." We know that "there is only one God." [5] There may be so-called gods either in heaven or on earth. In fact, there are many "gods" and many "lords." [6] But for us there is only one God. He is the Father. All things came from him, and we live for him. And there is only one Lord. He is Jesus Christ. All things came

because of him, and we live because of him.

⁷ But not everyone knows this. Some people still think that statues of gods are real gods. They might eat food sacrificed to statues of gods. When they do, they think of it as food sacrificed to real gods. And because those people have a weak sense of what is right and wrong, they feel guilty. ⁸ But food doesn't bring us close to God. We are no worse if we don't eat. We are no better if we do eat.

⁹ But be careful how you use your rights. Be sure you don't cause someone weaker than you to fall into sin. ¹⁰ Suppose you, with all your knowledge, are eating in a temple of one of those gods. And suppose someone who has a weak sense of what is right and wrong sees you. Won't that person become bold and eat what is sacrificed to statues of gods? ¹¹ If so, then your knowledge destroys that weak brother or sister for whom Christ died. ¹² Suppose you sin against them in this way. Then you harm their weak sense of what is right and wrong. By doing this, you sin against Christ. ¹³ So suppose what I eat causes my brother or sister to fall into sin. Then what should I do? I will never eat meat again. In that way, I will not cause them to fall.

Paul's Rights as an Apostle

9 Am I not free? Am I not an apostle? Haven't I seen Jesus our Lord? Aren't you the result of my work for the Lord? ² Others may not think of me as an apostle. But I am certainly one to you! You are the proof that I am the Lord's apostle.

³ That is what I say to stand up for myself when people judge me. ⁴ Don't we have the right to eat and drink? ⁵ Don't we have the right to take a believing wife with us when we travel? The other apostles do. The Lord's brothers do. Peter does. ⁶ Or are Barnabas and I the only ones who have to do other work for a living? Are we the only ones who can't just do the work of apostles all the time?

⁷ Who serves as a soldier but doesn't get paid? Who plants a vineyard but doesn't eat any of its grapes? Who takes care of a flock but doesn't drink any of the milk? ⁸ Do I say this only on human authority? The Law says the same thing. ⁹ Here is what is written in the Law of Moses. "Do not stop an ox from eating while it helps separate the grain from the straw." *(Deuteronomy 25:4)* Is it oxen that God is concerned about? ¹⁰ Doesn't he say that for us? Yes, it was written for us. Whoever plows and separates the grain hopes to share the harvest. And it is right for them to hope for this. ¹¹ We have planted spiritual seed among you. Is it too much to ask that we receive from you some things we need? ¹² Others have the right to receive help from you. Don't we have even more right to do so?

But we didn't use that right.

No, we have put up with everything. We didn't want to keep the good news of Christ from spreading.

¹³ People who serve in the temple get their food from the temple. Don't you know this? People who serve at the altar eat from what is offered on the altar. Don't you know this? ¹⁴ So those who preach the good news should also receive their living from their work. That is what the Lord has commanded.

¹⁵ But I haven't used any of those rights. And I'm not writing because I hope you will do things like that for me. I would rather die than allow anyone to take away my pride in my work. ¹⁶ But when I preach the good news, I can't brag. I have to preach it. How terrible it will be for me if I do not preach the good news! ¹⁷ If I preach because I want to, I get a reward. If I preach because I have to, I'm only doing my duty. ¹⁸ Then what reward do I get? Here is what it is. I am able to preach the good news free of charge. And I can do this without using all my rights as a person who preaches the good news.

Paul Uses His Freedom to Share the Good News

¹⁹ I am free and don't belong to anyone. But I have made myself a slave to everyone. I do it to win as many as I can to Christ. ²⁰ To the Jews I became like a Jew. That was to win the Jews. To those under the law I became like one who was under the law. I did this even though I myself am not under the law. That was to win those under the law. ²¹ To those who don't have the law I became like one who doesn't have the law. I did this even though I am not free from God's law. I am under Christ's law. Now I can win those who don't have the law. ²² To those who are weak I became weak. That was to win the weak. I have become all things to all people. I have done this so that in all possible ways I might save some. ²³ I do all this because of the good news. And I want to share in its blessings.

Training to Win the Prize

²⁴ In a race all the runners run. But only one gets the prize. You know that, don't you? So run in a way that will get you the prize. ²⁵ All who take part in the games train hard. They do it to get a crown that will not last. But we do it to get a crown that will last forever. ²⁶ So I do not run like someone who doesn't run toward the finish line. I do not fight like a boxer who hits nothing but air. ²⁷ No, I train my body and bring it under control. Then after I have preached to others, I myself will not break the rules. If I did break them, I would fail to win the prize.

Warnings From Israel's History

10 Brothers and sisters, I want you to know something about our people who lived long ago. They were all led by the cloud. They all walked through the Red Sea. ²They were all baptized into Moses in the cloud and in the sea. ³They all ate the same spiritual food. ⁴They all drank the same spiritual water. They drank from the spiritual rock that went with them. That rock was Christ. ⁵But God was not pleased with most of them. Their bodies were scattered in the desert.

⁶Now those things happened as examples for us. They are supposed to keep us from wanting evil things. The people of Israel wanted these evil things. ⁷So don't worship statues of gods, as some of them did. It is written, "The people sat down to eat and drink. Then they got up to dance wildly in front of their god." *(Exodus 32:6)* ⁸We should not commit sexual sins, as some of them did. In one day 23,000 of them died. ⁹We should not test the Messiah, as some of them did. They were killed by snakes. ¹⁰Don't speak against God. That's what some of the people of Israel did. And they were killed by the destroying angel.

¹¹Those things happened to them as examples for us. They were written down to warn us. That's because we are living at the time when God's work is being completed. ¹²So be careful. When you think you are standing firm, you might fall. ¹³You are tempted in the same way all other human beings are. God is faithful. He will not let you be tempted any more than you can take. But when you are tempted, God will give you a way out. Then you will be able to deal with it.

Sharing in the Lord's Supper

¹⁴My dear friends, run away from statues of gods. Don't worship them. ¹⁵I'm talking to people who are reasonable. Judge for yourselves what I say. ¹⁶We give thanks for the cup at the Lord's Supper. When we do, aren't we sharing in the blood of Christ? When we break the bread, aren't we sharing in the body of Christ? ¹⁷Just as there is one loaf, so we who are many are one body. We all share the one loaf.

¹⁸Think about the people of Israel. Don't those who eat the offerings share in the altar? ¹⁹Do I mean that food sacrificed to a statue of a god is anything? Do I mean that a statue of a god is anything? ²⁰No! But what is sacrificed by those who worship statues of gods is really sacrificed to demons. It is not sacrificed to God. I don't want you to be sharing with demons. ²¹You can't drink the cup of the Lord and the cup of demons too. You can't have a part in both the Lord's table and the table of demons. ²²Are we trying to make the Lord jealous? Are we stronger than he is?

The Believer's Freedom

²³You say, "I have the right to do anything." But not everything is helpful. Again you say, "I have the right to do anything." But not everything builds us

up. ²⁴No one should look out for their own interests. Instead, they should look out for the interests of others.

²⁵Eat anything sold in the meat market. Don't ask if it's right or wrong. ²⁶Scripture says, "The earth belongs to the Lord. And so does everything in it." *(Psalm 24:1)*

²⁷Suppose an unbeliever invites you to a meal and you want to go. Then eat anything that is put in front of you. Don't ask if it's right or wrong. ²⁸But suppose someone says to you, "This food has been sacrificed to a statue of a god." Then don't eat it. Keep in mind the good of the person who told you. And don't eat because of a sense of what is right and wrong. ²⁹I'm talking about the other person's sense of what is right and wrong, not yours. Why is my freedom being judged by what someone else thinks? ³⁰Suppose I give thanks when I eat. Then why should I be blamed for eating food I thank God for?

³¹So eat and drink and do everything else for the glory of God. ³²Don't do anything that causes another person to trip and fall. It doesn't matter if that person is a Jew or a Greek or a member of God's church. ³³Follow my example. I try to please everyone in every way. I'm not looking out for what is good for me. I'm looking out for the interests of others. I do it so that they might be saved. ¹Follow my example, just as I follow the example of Christ.

11

Proper Worship

²I praise you for being faithful in remembering me. I also praise you for staying true to the teachings of the past. You have stayed true to them, just as I gave them to you. ³But I want you to know that the head of every man is Christ. The head of the woman is the man. And the head of Christ is God. ⁴Every man who prays or prophesies with his head covered brings shame on his head. ⁵But every woman who prays or prophesies with her head uncovered brings shame on her head. It is the same as having her head shaved. ⁶What if a woman does not cover her head? She might as well have her hair cut off. But it is shameful for her to cut her hair or shave her head. So she should cover her head.

⁷A man should not cover his head. He is the likeness and glory of God. But woman is the glory of man. ⁸Man did not come from woman. Woman came from man. ⁹Also, man was not created for woman. Woman was created for man. ¹⁰That's why a woman should have authority over her own head. She should have this because of the angels. ¹¹But here is how things are for those who belong to the Lord. Woman is not independent of man. And man is not independent of woman. ¹²Woman came from man, and man is born from woman. But everything comes from God. ¹³You be the judge. Is it proper for a woman to pray to God

without covering her head? ¹⁴Suppose a man has long hair. Doesn't the very nature of things teach you that it is shameful? ¹⁵And suppose a woman has long hair. Doesn't the very nature of things teach you that it is her glory? Long hair is given to her as a covering. ¹⁶If anyone wants to argue about this, we don't have any other practice. And God's churches don't either.

Celebrating the Lord's Supper in the Right Way

¹⁷In the following matters, I don't praise you. Your meetings do more harm than good. ¹⁸First, here is what people are telling me. When you come together as a church, you take sides. And in some ways I believe it. ¹⁹Do you really think you need to take sides? You probably think God favors one side over the other! ²⁰So when you come together, it is not the Lord's Supper you eat. ²¹As you eat, some of you go ahead and eat your own private meals. Because of this, one person stays hungry and another gets drunk. ²²Don't you have homes to eat and drink in? You are shaming those in the church who have nothing. Do you think so little of God's church that you do this? What should I say to you? Should I praise you? Certainly not about the Lord's Supper!

²³I passed on to you what I received from the Lord. On the night the Lord Jesus was handed over to his enemies, he took bread. ²⁴When he had given thanks, he broke it. He said, "This is my body. It is given for you. Every time you eat it, do it in memory of me." ²⁵In the same way, after supper he took the cup. He said, "This cup is the new covenant in my blood. Every time you drink it, do it in memory of me." ²⁶You eat the bread and drink the cup. When you do this, you are announcing the Lord's death until he comes again.

²⁷Eat the bread or drink the cup of the Lord in the right way. Don't do it in a way that isn't worthy of him. If you do, you will be guilty. You'll be guilty of sinning against the body and blood of the Lord. ²⁸Everyone should take a careful look at themselves before they eat the bread and drink from the cup. ²⁹Whoever eats and drinks must recognize the body of Christ. If they don't, judgment will come upon them. ³⁰That is why many of you are weak and sick. That is why a number of you have died. ³¹We should think more carefully about what we are doing. Then we would not be found guilty for this. ³²When the Lord judges us in this way, he corrects us. Then in the end we will not be judged along with the rest of the world.

³³My brothers and sisters, when you come together to eat, you should all eat together. ³⁴Anyone who is hungry should eat something at home. Then when you come together, you will not be judged.

When I come, I will give you more directions.

Gifts of the Holy Spirit

12 Brothers and sisters, I want you to know about the gifts of the Holy Spirit. ² You know that at one time you were unbelievers. You were somehow drawn away to worship statues of gods that couldn't even speak. ³ So I want you to know that no one who is speaking with the help of God's Spirit says, "May Jesus be cursed." And without the help of the Holy Spirit no one can say, "Jesus is Lord."

⁴ There are different kinds of gifts. But they are all given to believers by the same Spirit. ⁵ There are different ways to serve. But they all come from the same Lord. ⁶ There are different ways the Spirit works. But the same God is working in all these ways and in all people.

⁷ The Holy Spirit is given to each of us in a special way. That is for the good of all. ⁸ To some people the Spirit gives a message of wisdom. To others the same Spirit gives a message of knowledge. ⁹ To others the same Spirit gives faith. To others that one Spirit gives gifts of healing. ¹⁰ To others he gives the power to do miracles. To others he gives the ability to prophesy. To others he gives the ability to tell the spirits apart. To others he gives the ability to speak in different kinds of languages they had not known before. And to still others he gives the ability to explain what was said in those languages. ¹¹ All the gifts are produced by one and the same Spirit. He gives gifts to each person, just as he decides.

One Body but Many Parts

¹² There is one body, but it has many parts. But all its many parts make up one body. It is the same with Christ. ¹³ We were all baptized by one Holy Spirit. And so we are formed into one body. It didn't matter whether we were Jews or Gentiles, slaves or free people. We were all given the same Spirit to drink. ¹⁴ So the body is not made up of just one part. It has many parts.

¹⁵ Suppose the foot says, "I am not a hand. So I don't belong to the body." By saying this, it cannot stop being part of the body. ¹⁶ And suppose the ear says, "I am not an eye. So I don't belong to the body." By saying this, it cannot stop being part of the body. ¹⁷ If the whole body were an eye, how could it hear? If the whole body were an ear, how could it smell? ¹⁸ God has placed each part in the body just as he wanted it to be. ¹⁹ If all the parts were the same, how could there be a body? ²⁰ As it is, there are many parts. But there is only one body.

²¹ The eye can't say to the hand, "I don't need you!" The head can't say to the feet, "I don't need you!" ²² In fact, it is just the opposite. The parts of the body that seem to be weaker are the ones we can't do without. ²³ The parts that we think are less important we treat with special honor. The private parts aren't shown. But they are treated

with special care. ²⁴ The parts that can be shown don't need special care. But God has put together all the parts of the body. And he has given more honor to the parts that didn't have any. ²⁵ In that way, the parts of the body will not take sides. All of them will take care of one another. ²⁶ If one part suffers, every part suffers with it. If one part is honored, every part shares in its joy.

²⁷ You are the body of Christ. Each one of you is a part of it. ²⁸ First, God has placed apostles in the church. Second, he has placed prophets in the church. Third, he has placed teachers in the church. Then he has given to the church miracles and gifts of healing. He also has given the gift of helping others and the gift of guiding the church. God also has given the gift of speaking in different kinds of languages. ²⁹ Is everyone an apostle? Is everyone a prophet? Is everyone a teacher? Do all work miracles? ³⁰ Do all have gifts of healing? Do all speak in languages they had not known before? Do all explain what is said in those languages? ³¹ But above all, you should want the more important gifts.

Love Is Necessary

But now I will show you the best way of all.

13 Suppose I speak in the languages of human beings or of angels. If I don't have love, I am only a loud gong or a noisy cymbal. ² Suppose I have the gift of prophecy. Suppose I can understand all the secret things of God and know everything about him. And suppose I have enough faith to move mountains. If I don't have love, I am nothing at all. ³ Suppose I give everything I have to poor people. And suppose I give myself over to a difficult life so I can brag. If I don't have love, I get nothing at all.

⁴ Love is patient. Love is kind. It does not want what belongs to others. It does not brag. It is not proud. ⁵ It does not dishonor other people. It does not look out for its own interests. It does not easily become angry. It does not keep track of other people's wrongs. ⁶ Love is not happy with evil. But it is full of joy when the truth is spoken. ⁷ It always protects. It always trusts. It always hopes. It never gives up.

⁸ Love never fails. But prophecy will pass away. Speaking in languages that had not been known before will end. And knowledge will pass away. ⁹ What we know now is not complete. What we prophesy now is not perfect. ¹⁰ But when what is complete comes, the things that are not complete will pass away. ¹¹ When I was a child, I talked like a child. I thought like a child. I had the understanding of a child. When I became a man, I put the ways of childhood behind me. ¹² Now we see only a dim likeness of things. It is as if we were seeing them in a foggy mirror. But someday we will see clearly. We will see face

to face. What I know now is not complete. But someday I will know completely, just as God knows me completely.

[13] The three most important things to have are faith, hope and love. But the greatest of them is love.

Worship in a Way That Helps People Understand

14 Follow the way of love. You should also want the gifts the Holy Spirit gives. Most of all, you should want the gift of prophecy. [2] Anyone who speaks in a language they had not known before doesn't speak to people. They speak only to God. In fact, no one understands them. What they say by the Spirit remains a mystery. [3] But the person who prophesies speaks to people. That person prophesies to make people stronger, to give them hope, and to comfort them. [4] Anyone who speaks in other languages builds up only themselves. But the person who prophesies builds up the church. [5] I would like all of you to speak in other languages. But I would rather have you prophesy. The person who prophesies is more helpful than those who speak in other languages. But that is not the case if someone explains what was said in the other languages. Then the whole church can be built up.

[6] Brothers and sisters, suppose I were to come to you and speak in other languages. What good would I be to you? None! I would need to come with new truth or knowledge. Or I would need to come with a prophecy or a teaching. [7] Here are some examples. Certain objects make sounds. Take a flute or a harp. No one will know what the tune is unless different notes are played. [8] Also, if the trumpet call isn't clear, who will get ready for battle? [9] It's the same with you. You must speak words that people understand. If you don't, no one will know what you are saying. You will just be speaking into the air. [10] It is true that there are all kinds of languages in the world. And they all have meaning. [11] But if I don't understand what someone is saying, I am a stranger to the person speaking. And that person is a stranger to me. [12] It's the same with you. You want the gifts of the Spirit. So try to do your best in using gifts that build up the church.

[13] So here is what the person who speaks in languages they had not known before should do. They should pray that they can explain what they say. [14] If I pray in another language, my spirit prays. But my mind does not pray. [15] So what should I do? I will pray with my spirit. But I will also pray with my understanding. I will sing with my spirit. But I will also sing with my understanding. [16] Suppose you are praising God in the Spirit. And suppose there are visitors among you who want to know what's going on. How can they say "Amen" when you give thanks? They don't know what

you are saying. ¹⁷You are certainly giving thanks. But no one else is being built up.

¹⁸I thank God that I speak in other languages more than all of you do. ¹⁹In the church, I wouldn't want to speak 10,000 words in an unfamiliar language. I'd rather speak five words in a language people could understand. Then I would be teaching others.

²⁰Brothers and sisters, stop thinking like children. Be like babies as far as evil is concerned. But be grown up in your thinking. ²¹In the law it is written,

"With unfamiliar languages
and through the lips of
outsiders
I will speak to these people.
But even then they will
not listen to me."
(Isaiah 28:11,12)

That is what the Lord says.

²²So speaking in other languages is a sign for those who don't believe. It is not a sign for those who do believe. But prophecy is not for those who don't believe. It is for those who believe. ²³Suppose the whole church comes together and everyone speaks in other languages. And suppose visitors or unbelievers come in. Won't they say you are out of your minds? ²⁴But suppose unbelievers or visitors come in while everyone is prophesying. Then they will feel guilty about their sin. They will be judged by all. ²⁵The secrets of their hearts will be brought out into the open. They will fall down and worship God. They will exclaim, "God is really here among you!"

Proper Worship

²⁶Brothers and sisters, what should we say then? When you come together, each of you brings something. You bring a hymn or a teaching or a message from God. You bring a message in another language or explain what was said in that language. Everything must be done to build up the church. ²⁷No more than two or three people should speak in another language. And they should speak one at a time. Then someone must explain what was said. ²⁸If there is no one to explain, the person speaking should keep quiet in the church. They can speak to themselves and to God.

²⁹Only two or three prophets are supposed to speak. Others should decide if what is being said is true. ³⁰What if a message from God comes to someone else who is sitting there? Then the one who is speaking should stop. ³¹Those who prophesy can all take turns. In that way, everyone can be taught and be given hope. ³²Those who prophesy should control their speaking. ³³God is not a God of disorder. He is a God of peace, just as in all the churches of the Lord's people.

³⁴Women should remain silent in church meetings. They are not allowed to speak. They must follow the lead of those

who are in authority, as the law says. ³⁵ If they have a question about something, they should ask their own husbands at home. It is shameful for women to speak in church meetings.

³⁶ Or did the word of God begin with you? Or are you the only people it has reached? ³⁷ Suppose anyone thinks they are a prophet. Or suppose they think they have other gifts given by the Holy Spirit. They should agree that what I am writing to you is the Lord's command. ³⁸ But anyone who does not recognize this will not be recognized.

³⁹ Brothers and sisters, you should want to prophesy. And don't stop people from speaking in languages they had not known before. ⁴⁰ But everything should be done in a proper and orderly way.

Christ Rose From the Dead

15 Brothers and sisters, I want to remind you of the good news I preached to you. You received it and have put your faith in it. ² Because you believed the good news, you are saved. But you must hold firmly to the message I preached to you. If you don't, you have believed it for nothing.

³ What I received I passed on to you. And it is the most important of all. Here is what it is. Christ died for our sins, just as Scripture said he would. ⁴ He was buried. He was raised from the dead on the third day, just as Scripture said he would be.

⁵ He appeared to Peter. Then he appeared to the 12 apostles. ⁶ After that, he appeared to more than 500 brothers and sisters at the same time. Most of them are still living. But some have died. ⁷ He appeared to James. Then he appeared to all the apostles. ⁸ Last of all, he also appeared to me. I was like someone who wasn't born at the right time.

⁹ I am the least important of the apostles. I'm not even fit to be called an apostle. I tried to destroy God's church. ¹⁰ But because of God's grace I am what I am. And his grace was not wasted on me. No, I have worked harder than all the other apostles. But I didn't do the work. God's grace was with me. ¹¹ So this is what we preach, whether I or the other apostles who preached to you. And that is what you believed.

Believers Will Rise From the Dead

¹² We have preached that Christ has been raised from the dead. So how can some of you say that no one rises from the dead? ¹³ If no one rises from the dead, then not even Christ has been raised. ¹⁴ And if Christ has not been raised, what we preach doesn't mean anything. Your faith doesn't mean anything either. ¹⁵ More than that, we would be lying about God. We are witnesses that God raised Christ from the dead. But he did not raise him if the dead are not raised. ¹⁶ If

the dead are not raised, then Christ has not been raised either. ¹⁷ And if Christ has not been raised, your faith doesn't mean anything. Your sins have not been forgiven. ¹⁸ Those who have died believing in Christ are also lost. ¹⁹ Do we have hope in Christ only for this life? Then people should pity us more than anyone else.

²⁰ But Christ really has been raised from the dead. He is the first of all those who will rise from the dead. ²¹ Death came because of what a man did. Rising from the dead also comes because of what a man did. ²² Because of Adam, all people die. So because of Christ, all will be made alive. ²³ But here is the order of events. Christ is the first of those who rise from the dead. When he comes back, those who belong to him will be raised. ²⁴ Then the end will come after Christ destroys all rule, authority and power. Then he will hand over the kingdom to God the Father. ²⁵ Christ must rule until he has put all his enemies under his control. ²⁶ The last enemy that will be destroyed is death. ²⁷ Scripture says that God "has put everything under his control." *(Psalm 8:6)* It says that "everything" has been put under him. But it is clear that this does not include God himself. That's because God put everything under Christ. ²⁸ When he has done that, the Son also will be under God's rule. God put everything under the Son. In that way, God will be all in all.

²⁹ Suppose no one rises from the dead. Then what will people do who are baptized for the dead? Suppose the dead are not raised at all. Then why are people baptized for them? ³⁰ And why would we put ourselves in danger every hour? ³¹ I face death every day. That's the truth. And here is something you can be just as sure of. I take pride in what Christ Jesus our Lord has done for you through my work. ³² Did I fight wild animals in Ephesus with nothing more than human hopes? Then what have I gotten for it? If the dead are not raised,

"Let us eat and drink,
    because tomorrow we will die."   *(Isaiah 22:13)*

³³ Don't let anyone fool you. "Bad companions make a good person bad." ³⁴ You should come back to your senses and stop sinning. Some of you don't know anything about God. I say this to make you ashamed.

The Body That Rises From the Dead

³⁵ But someone will ask, "How are the dead raised? What kind of body will they have?" ³⁶ How foolish! What you plant doesn't come to life unless it dies. ³⁷ When you plant something, it isn't a completely grown plant that you put in the ground. You only plant a seed. Maybe it's wheat or something else. ³⁸ But God gives the seed a body just as he has planned. And to each kind of seed he gives its own

body. ³⁹ Not all earthly creatures are the same. People have one kind of body. Animals have another. Birds have another kind. Fish have still another. ⁴⁰ There are also heavenly bodies as well as earthly bodies. Heavenly bodies have one kind of glory. Earthly bodies have another. ⁴¹ The sun has one kind of glory. The moon has another kind. The stars have still another. And one star's glory is different from that of another star.

⁴² It will be like that with bodies that are raised from the dead. The body that is planted does not last forever. The body that is raised from the dead lasts forever. ⁴³ It is planted without honor. But it is raised in glory. It is planted in weakness. But it is raised in power. ⁴⁴ It is planted as an earthly body. But it is raised as a spiritual body.

Just as there is an earthly body, there is also a spiritual body. ⁴⁵ It is written, "The first man Adam became a living person." (Genesis 2:7) The last Adam became a spirit that gives life. ⁴⁶ What is spiritual did not come first. What is earthly came first. What is spiritual came after that. ⁴⁷ The first man came from the dust of the earth. The second man came from heaven. ⁴⁸ Those who belong to the earth are like the one who came from the earth. And those who are spiritual are like the heavenly man. ⁴⁹ We are like the earthly man. And we will be like the heavenly man.

⁵⁰ Brothers and sisters, here is what I'm telling you. Bodies made of flesh and blood can't share in the kingdom of God. And what dies can't share in what never dies. ⁵¹ Listen! I am telling you a mystery. We will not all die. But we will all be changed. ⁵² That will happen in a flash, as quickly as you can wink an eye. It will happen at the blast of the last trumpet. Then the dead will be raised to live forever. And we will be changed. ⁵³ Our natural bodies don't last forever. They must be dressed with what does last forever. What dies must be dressed with what does not die. ⁵⁴ In fact, that is going to happen. What does not last will be dressed with what lasts forever. What dies will be dressed with what does not die. Then what is written will come true. It says, "Death has been swallowed up. It has lost the battle." (Isaiah 25:8)

⁵⁵ "Death, where is the
　　victory you thought
　　you had?
　Death, where is your
　　sting?" (Hosea 13:14)

⁵⁶ The sting of death is sin. And the power of sin is the law. ⁵⁷ But let us give thanks to God! He gives us the victory because of what our Lord Jesus Christ has done.

⁵⁸ My dear brothers and sisters, remain strong in the faith. Don't let anything move you. Always give yourselves completely to the work of the Lord. Because you belong to the Lord,

you know that your work is not worthless.

The Offering for the Lord's People

16 Now I want to deal with the offering of money for the Lord's people. Do what I told the churches in Galatia to do. ² On the first day of every week, each of you should put some money away. The amount should be in keeping with how much money you make. Save the money so that you won't have to take up an offering when I come. ³ When I arrive, I will send some people with your gift to Jerusalem. They will be people you consider to be good. And I will give them letters that explain who they are. ⁴ If it seems good for me to go also, they will go with me.

What Paul Asks for Himself

⁵ After I go through Macedonia, I will come to you. I will only be passing through Macedonia. ⁶ But I might stay with you for a while. I might even spend the winter. Then you can help me on my journey everywhere I go. ⁷ I don't want to see you now while I am just passing through. Instead, I hope to spend some time with you, if the Lord allows it. ⁸ But I will stay at Ephesus until the day of Pentecost. ⁹ A door has opened wide for me to do some good work here. There are many people who oppose me.

¹⁰ Timothy will visit you. Make sure he has nothing to worry about while he is with you. He is doing the work of the Lord, just as I am. ¹¹ No one should treat him badly. Send him safely on his way so he can return to me. I'm expecting him to come back along with the others.

¹² I want to say something about our brother Apollos. I tried my best to get him to go to you with the others. But he didn't want to go right now. He will go when he can.

¹³ Be on your guard. Remain strong in the faith. Be brave. ¹⁴ Be loving in everything you do.

¹⁵ You know that the first believers in Achaia were from the family of Stephanas. They have spent all their time serving the Lord's people. Brothers and sisters, I am asking you ¹⁶ to follow the lead of people like them. Follow everyone who joins in the task and works hard at it. ¹⁷ I was glad when Stephanas, Fortunatus and Achaicus arrived. They have supplied me with what you couldn't give me. ¹⁸ They renewed my spirit, and yours also. People like them are worthy of honor.

Final Greetings

¹⁹ The churches in Asia Minor send you greetings.

Aquila and Priscilla greet you warmly because of the Lord's love. So does the church that meets in their house.

²⁰ All the brothers and sisters here send you greetings.

Greet one another with a holy kiss.

²¹ I, Paul, am writing this greeting with my own hand.

²² If anyone does not love the Lord, let a curse be on that person! Come, Lord!

²³ May the grace of the Lord Jesus be with you.

²⁴ I give my love to all of you who belong to Christ Jesus. Amen.

2 Corinthians

Introduction:

Paul's first letter to his friends in Corinth taught them what was right and wrong. Some people were angry about that letter. They didn't think Paul had any right to tell them how to act. They would not change the way they lived. Other people felt sorry when they read Paul's letter. They wanted to change the way they lived.

Paul wrote this letter in two parts. He wrote the first part for his friends who changed and lived the way God wanted. He wrote the second part to the angry people in the church. They had said untrue things about Paul and God. Paul wanted them to know the truth.

Outline of contents:

---

1 I, Paul, am writing this letter. I am an apostle of Christ Jesus just as God planned. Timothy our brother joins me in writing.

We are sending this letter to you, the members of God's church in Corinth. It is also for all God's holy people everywhere in Achaia.

² May God our Father and the Lord Jesus Christ give you grace and peace.

Praise to the God Who Gives Comfort

³ Give praise to the God and Father of our Lord Jesus Christ! He is the Father who gives tender love. All comfort comes from him. ⁴ He comforts us in all our troubles. Now we can comfort others when they are in trouble. We ourselves receive comfort from God. ⁵ We share very much in the sufferings of Christ. So we also share very much in his comfort. ⁶ If we are having trouble, it is so that you will be comforted and renewed. If we are comforted, it is so that you will be comforted. Then you will be able to put up with the same suffering we have gone through. ⁷ Our hope for you remains firm. We know that you suffer just as we do. In the same way, God comforts you just as he comforts us.

⁸ Brothers and sisters, we want you to know about the hard times we had in Asia Minor. We were having a lot of trouble.

It was far more than we could stand. We even thought we were going to die. [9] In fact, we felt as if we were under the sentence of death. But that happened so that we would not depend on ourselves but on God. He raises the dead to life. [10] God has saved us from deadly dangers. And he will continue to do it. We have put our hope in him. He will continue to save us. [11] You must help us by praying for us. Then many people will give thanks because of what will happen to us. They will thank God for his kindness to us in answer to the prayers of many.

Paul Changes His Plans

[12] Here is what we take pride in. Our sense of what is right and wrong tells us how we have acted. We have lived with honor and godly honesty. We have depended on God's grace and not on the world's wisdom. We lived that way most of all when we were dealing with you. [13] We are writing only what you can read and understand. And here is what I hope. [14] Up to this point you have understood some of the things we have said. But now here is what I hope for when the Lord Jesus returns. I hope that your pride in us will be the same as our pride in you. When this happens, you will understand us completely.

[15] Because I was sure of this, I wanted to visit you first. Here is how I thought you would be helped twice. [16] I planned to visit you on my way to Macedonia. I would have come back to you from there. Then you would have sent me on my way to Judea. [17] When I planned all this, was I ready to change my mind for no good reason? No. I don't make my plans the way the world makes theirs. In the same breath the world says both, "Yes! Yes!" and "No! No!"

[18] But just as sure as God is faithful, our message to you is not "Yes" and "No." [19] Silas, Timothy and I preached to you about the Son of God, Jesus Christ. Our message did not say "Yes" and "No" at the same time. The message of Christ has always been "Yes." [20] God has made a great many promises. They are all "Yes" because of what Christ has done. So through Christ we say "Amen." We want God to receive glory. [21] He makes both us and you remain strong in the faith because we belong to Christ. He anointed us. [22] He put his Spirit in our hearts and marked us as his own. We can now be sure that he will give us everything he promised us.

[23] I call God to be my witness. May he take my life if I'm lying. I wanted to spare you, so I didn't return to Corinth. [24] Your faith is not under our control. You remain strong in your own faith. But we work together with you for your joy. [1] So I made up my mind that I would not make another painful visit to you. [2] If I make you sad, who is going to make me glad? Only you, the people I made sad. [3] What I wrote to you I wrote for

a special reason. When I came, I didn't want to be troubled by those who should make me glad. I was sure that all of you would share my joy. ⁴I was very troubled when I wrote to you. My heart was sad. My eyes were full of tears. I didn't want to make you sad. I wanted to let you know that I love you very deeply.

Forgive Those Who Make You Sad

⁵Suppose someone has made us sad. In some ways, he hasn't made me sad so much as he has made all of you sad. But I don't want to put this too strongly. ⁶He has been punished because most of you decided he should be. This punishment is enough. ⁷Now you should forgive him and comfort him. Then he won't be sad more than he can stand. ⁸So I'm asking you to tell him again that you still love him. ⁹I wrote to you for another special reason. I wanted to see if you could stand the test. I wanted to see if you could obey everything asked of you. ¹⁰Anyone you forgive I also forgive. Was there anything to forgive? If so, I have forgiven it for your benefit, knowing that Christ is watching. ¹¹We don't want Satan to outsmart us. We know how he does his evil work.

Serving Under the New Covenant

¹²I went to Troas to preach the good news about Christ. There I found that the Lord had opened a door of opportunity for me. ¹³But I still had no peace of mind. I couldn't find my brother Titus there. So I said goodbye to the believers at Troas and went on to Macedonia.

¹⁴Give thanks to God! He always leads us as if we were prisoners in Christ's victory parade. Through us, God spreads the knowledge of Christ everywhere like perfume. ¹⁵God considers us to be the pleasing smell that Christ is spreading. He is spreading it among people who are being saved and people who are dying. ¹⁶To those who are dying, we are the smell of death. To those who are being saved, we are the perfume of life. Who is able to do this work? ¹⁷Unlike many people, we aren't selling God's word to make money. In fact, it is just the opposite. Because of Christ we speak honestly before God. We speak like people God has sent.

3 Are we beginning to praise ourselves again? Some people need letters that speak well of them. Do we need those kinds of letters, either to you or from you? ²You yourselves are our letter. You are written on our hearts. Everyone knows you and reads you. ³You make it clear that you are a letter from Christ. You are the result of our work for God. You are a letter written not with ink but with the Spirit of the living God. You are a letter written not on tablets made out of stone but on human hearts.

⁴Through Christ, we can be sure of this before God. ⁵In our-

selves we are not able to claim anything for ourselves. The power to do what we do comes from God. ⁶He has given us the power to serve under a new covenant. The covenant is not based on the written Law of Moses. It comes from the Holy Spirit. The written Law kills, but the Spirit gives life.

The Greater Glory of the New Covenant

⁷The Law was written in letters on stone. Even though it was a way of serving God, it led to death. But even that way of serving God came with glory. The glory lasted for only a short time. Even so, the people of Israel couldn't look at Moses' face very long. ⁸Since all this is true, won't the work of the Holy Spirit be even more glorious? ⁹The law that condemns people to death had glory. How much more glory does the work of the Spirit have! His work makes people right with God. ¹⁰The glory of the old covenant is nothing compared with the far greater glory of the new. ¹¹The glory of the old lasts for only a short time. How much greater is the glory of the new! It will last forever.

¹²Since we have that kind of hope, we are very bold. ¹³We are not like Moses. He used to cover his face with a veil. That was to keep the people of Israel from seeing the end of what was passing away. ¹⁴But their minds were made stubborn. To this day, the same veil remains when the old covenant is read. The veil has not been removed. Only faith in Christ can take it away. ¹⁵To this day, when the Law of Moses is read, a veil covers the minds of those who hear it. ¹⁶But when anyone turns to the Lord, the veil is taken away. ¹⁷Now the Lord is the Holy Spirit. And where the Spirit of the Lord is, freedom is also there. ¹⁸None of our faces are covered with a veil. All of us can see the Lord's glory and think deeply about it. So we are being changed to become more like him so that we have more and more glory. And this glory comes from the Lord, who is the Holy Spirit.

A Treasure in Clay Jars

4 So because of God's mercy, we have work to do. He has given it to us. And we don't give up. ²Instead, we have given up doing secret and shameful things. We don't twist God's word. In fact, we do just the opposite. We present the truth plainly. In the sight of God, we make our appeal to everyone's sense of what is right and wrong. ³Suppose our good news is covered with a veil. Then it is veiled to those who are dying. ⁴The god of this world has blinded the minds of those who don't believe. They can't see the light of the good news that makes Christ's glory clear. Christ is the likeness of God. ⁵The message we preach is not about ourselves. Our message is about Jesus Christ. We say that he is Lord. And we say that we serve you because of Jesus.

⁶God said, "Let light shine out of darkness." *(Genesis 1:3)* He made his light shine in our hearts. His light gives us the light to know God's glory. His glory is shown in the face of Christ.

⁷Treasure is kept in clay jars. In the same way, we have the treasure of the good news in these earthly bodies of ours. That shows that the mighty power of the good news comes from God. It doesn't come from us. ⁸We are pushed hard from all sides. But we are not beaten down. We are bewildered. But that doesn't make us lose hope. ⁹Others make us suffer. But God does not desert us. We are knocked down. But we are not knocked out. ¹⁰We always carry around the death of Jesus in our bodies. In that way, the life of Jesus can be shown in our bodies. ¹¹We who are alive are always in danger of death because we are serving Jesus. This happens so that his life can also be shown in our earthly bodies. ¹²Death is at work in us. But life is at work in you.

¹³It is written, "I believed, and so I have spoken." *(Psalm 116:10)* We have that same spirit of faith. So we also believe and speak. ¹⁴We know that God raised the Lord Jesus from the dead. And he will also raise us up with Jesus. And he will present both you and us to himself. ¹⁵All this is for your benefit. God's grace is reaching more and more people. So they will become more and more thankful. They will give glory to God.

¹⁶We don't give up. Our bodies are becoming weaker and weaker. But our spirits are being renewed day by day. ¹⁷Our troubles are small. They last only for a short time. But they are earning for us a glory that will last forever. It is greater than all our troubles. ¹⁸So we don't spend all our time looking at what we can see. Instead, we look at what we can't see. That's because what can be seen lasts only a short time. But what can't be seen will last forever.

Waiting for Our New Bodies

5 We know that the earthly tent we live in will be destroyed. But we have a building made by God. It is a house in heaven that lasts forever. Human hands did not build it. ²During our time on earth we groan. We long to put on our house in heaven as if it were clothing. ³Then we will not be naked. ⁴While we live in this tent of ours, we groan under our heavy load. We don't want to be naked. Instead, we want to be fully dressed with our house in heaven. What must die will be swallowed up by life. ⁵God has formed us for that very purpose. He has given us the Holy Spirit as a down payment. The Spirit makes us sure of what is still to come.

⁶So here is what we can always be certain about. As long as we are at home in our bodies, we are away from the Lord. ⁷We live by believing, not by seeing. ⁸We are certain about that.

We would rather be away from our bodies and at home with the Lord. [9] So we try our best to please him. We want to please him whether we are at home in our bodies or away from them. [10] We must all stand in front of Christ to be judged. Each one of us will be judged for what we do while in our bodies. We'll be judged for the good things and the bad things. Then each of us will receive what we are supposed to get.

Christ Brings Us Back to God

[11] We know what it means to have respect for the Lord. So we try to help other people to understand it. What we are is plain to God. I hope it is also plain to your way of thinking. [12] We are not trying to make an appeal to you again. But we are giving you a chance to take pride in us. Some people take pride in their looks rather than what's in their hearts. If you take pride in us, you will be able to answer them. [13] Are we "out of our minds," as some people say? If so, it is because we want to serve God. Does what we say make sense? If so, it is because we want to serve you. [14] Christ's love controls us. We are sure that one person died for everyone. And so everyone died. [15] Christ died for everyone. He died so that those who live should not live for themselves anymore. They should live for Christ. He died for them and was raised again. [16] So from now on we don't look at anyone the way the world

does. At one time we looked at Christ in that way. But we don't anymore. [17] When anyone lives in Christ, the new creation has come. The old is gone! The new is here! [18] All this is from God. He brought us back to himself through Christ's death on the cross. And he has given us the task of bringing others back to him through Christ. [19] God was bringing the world back to himself through Christ. He did not hold people's sins against them. God has trusted us with the message that people may be brought back to him. [20] So we are Christ's official messengers. It is as if God were making his appeal through us. Here is what Christ wants us to beg you to do. Come back to God! [21] Christ didn't have any sin. But God made him become sin for us. So we can be made right with God because of what Christ has done for us.

6 We work together with God. So we are asking you not to receive God's grace and then do nothing with it. [2] He says,

"When I had mercy on you, I heard you.
    On the day I saved you, I helped you."   *(Isaiah 49:8)*

I tell you, now is the time God has mercy. Now is the day he saves.

Paul's Sufferings

[3] We don't put anything in anyone's way. So no one can find fault with our work for God. [4] Instead, we make it clear that we serve God in every way. We serve

him by standing firm in troubles, hard times and suffering. [5] We don't give up when we are beaten or put in prison. When people stir up trouble in the streets, we continue to serve God. We work hard for him. We go without sleep and food. [6] We remain pure. We understand completely what it means to serve God. We are patient and kind. We serve him in the power of the Holy Spirit. We serve him with true love. [7] We speak the truth. We serve in the power of God. We hold the weapons of godliness in the right hand and in the left. [8] We serve God in times of glory and shame. We serve him whether the news about us is bad or good. We are true to our calling. But people treat us as if we were pretenders. [9] We are known, but people treat us as if we were unknown. We are dying, but we continue to live. We are beaten, but we are not killed. [10] We are sad, but we are always full of joy. We are poor, but we make many people rich. We have nothing, but we own everything.

[11] Believers at Corinth, we have spoken freely to you. We have opened our hearts wide to you. [12] We are not holding back our love from you. But you are holding back your love from us. [13] I speak to you as if you were my children. It is only fair that you open your hearts wide to us also.

Paul Warns Against Worshiping False Gods

[14] Do not be joined to unbelievers. What do right and wrong have in common? Can light and darkness be friends? [15] How can Christ and Satan agree? Or what does a believer have in common with an unbeliever? [16] How can the temple of the true God and the statues of other gods agree? We are the temple of the living God. God has said,

"I will live with them.
I will walk among them.
I will be their God.
And they will be my people."

(Leviticus 26:12; Jeremiah 32:38; Ezekiel 37:27)

[17] So,

"Come out from among them
    and be separate,
        says the Lord.
Do not touch anything that is
    not pure and 'clean.'
Then I will receive you."

(Isaiah 52:11; Ezekiel 20:34,41)

[18] And,

"I will be your Father.
You will be my sons and
    daughters,
        says the Lord
    who rules over all."

(2 Samuel 7:14; 7:8)

7 Dear friends, we have these promises from God. So let us make ourselves pure from everything that makes our bodies and spirits impure. Let us be completely holy. We want to honor God.

Paul Has Joy When the Church Turns Away From Sin

[2] Make room for us in your hearts. We haven't done anything wrong to anyone. We

haven't caused anyone to sin. We haven't taken advantage of anyone. ³I don't say this to judge you. I have told you before that you have an important place in our hearts. We would live or die with you. ⁴I have spoken to you very honestly. I am very proud of you. I am very happy. Even with all our troubles, my joy has no limit.

⁵When we came to Macedonia, we weren't able to rest. We were attacked no matter where we went. We had battles on the outside and fears on the inside. ⁶But God comforts those who are sad. He comforted us when Titus came. ⁷We were comforted not only when he came but also by the comfort you had given him. He told us how much you longed for me. He told us about your deep sadness and concern for me. That made my joy greater than ever.

⁸Even if my letter made you sad, I'm not sorry I sent it. At first I was sorry. I see that my letter hurt you, but only for a little while. ⁹Now I am happy. I'm not happy because you were made sad. I'm happy because your sadness led you to turn away from your sins. You became sad just as God wanted you to. So you were not hurt in any way by us. ¹⁰Godly sadness causes us to turn away from our sins and be saved. And we are certainly not sorry about that! But worldly sadness brings death. ¹¹Look at what that godly sadness has produced in you. You are working hard to clear yourselves. You

are angry and alarmed. You are longing to see me. You are concerned. You are ready to make sure that the right thing is done. In every way you have proved that you are not guilty in that matter. ¹²So even though I wrote to you, it wasn't because of the one who did the wrong. It wasn't because of the one who was hurt either. Instead, I wrote you so that in the sight of God you could see for yourselves how faithful you are to us. ¹³All this encourages us.

We were also very glad to see how happy Titus was. You have all renewed his spirit. ¹⁴I had bragged about you to him. And you have not let me down. Everything we said to you was true. In the same way, our bragging about you to Titus has also turned out to be true. ¹⁵His love for you is even greater when he remembers that you all obeyed his teaching. You received him with fear and trembling. ¹⁶I am glad I can have complete faith in you.

Giving Freely to the Lord's People

8 Brothers and sisters, we want you to know about the grace that God has given to the churches in Macedonia. ²They have suffered a great deal. But in their suffering, their joy was more than full. Even though they were very poor, they gave very freely. ³I tell you that they gave as much as they could. In fact, they gave even more than they could. Completely on their own, [4] they begged us for the chance to share in serving the Lord's people in that way. [5] They did more than we expected. First they gave themselves to the Lord. Then they gave themselves to us because that was what God wanted. [6] Titus had already started collecting money from you. So we asked him to help you finish making your kind gift. [7] You do well in everything else. You do well in faith and in speaking. You do well in knowledge and in complete commitment. And you do well in the love we have helped to start in you. So make sure that you also do well in the grace of giving to others.

[8] I am not commanding you to do it. But I want to test you. I want to find out if you really love God. I want to compare your love with that of others. [9] You know the grace shown by our Lord Jesus Christ. Even though he was rich, he became poor to help you. Because he became poor, you can become rich.

[10] Here is my opinion about what is best for you in that matter. Last year you were the first to give. You were also the first to want to give. [11] So finish the work. Then your desire to do it will be matched by your finishing it. Give on the basis of what you have. [12] Do you really want to give? Then the gift is measured by what someone has. It is not measured by what they don't have.

[13] We don't want others to have it easy at your expense. We want things to be equal. [14] Right now you have plenty in order to take care of what they need. Then they will have plenty to take care of what you need. The goal is to even things out. [15] It is written, "The one who gathered a lot didn't have too much. And the one who gathered a little had enough." *(Exodus 16:18)*

Paul Sends Titus to Corinth to Receive the Offering

[16] God put into the heart of Titus the same concern I have for you. Thanks should be given to God for this. [17] Titus welcomed our appeal. He is also excited about coming to you. It was his own idea. [18] Along with Titus, we are sending another brother. All the churches praise him for his service in telling the good news. [19] He was also chosen by the churches to go with us as we bring the offering. We are in charge of it. We want to honor the Lord himself. We want to show how ready we are to help. [20] We want to keep anyone from blaming us for how we take care of that large gift. [21] We are trying hard to do what both the Lord and people think is right.

[22] We are also sending another one of our brothers with them. He has often proved to us in many ways that he is very committed. He is now even more committed because he has great faith in you. [23] Titus is my helper. He and I work together among you. Our brothers are messengers from the churches. They honor Christ. [24] So show them

that you really love them. Show them why we are proud of you. Then the churches can see it.

9 I don't need to write to you about giving to the Lord's people. [2] I know how much you want to help. I have been bragging about it to the people in Macedonia. I have been telling them that since last year you who live in Achaia were ready to give. You are so excited that it has stirred up most of them to take action. [3] But I am sending the brothers. Then our bragging about you in this matter will have a good reason. You will be ready, just as I said you would be. [4] Suppose people from Macedonia come with me and find out that you are not prepared. Then we, as well as you, would be ashamed of being so certain. [5] So I thought I should try to get the brothers to visit you ahead of time. They will finish the plans for the large gift you had promised. Then it will be ready as a gift freely given. It will not be given by force.

Paul's Advice to Give Freely

[6] Here is something to remember. The one who plants only a little will gather only a little. And the one who plants a lot will gather a lot. [7] Each of you should give what you have decided in your heart to give. You shouldn't give if you don't want to. You shouldn't give because you are forced to. God loves a cheerful giver. [8] And God is able to shower all kinds of blessings on you. So in all things and at all times you will have everything you need. You will do more and more good works. [9] It is written,

"They have spread their gifts
    around to poor people.
Their good works continue
    forever."   *(Psalm 112:9)*

[10] God supplies seed for the person who plants. He supplies bread for food. God will also supply and increase the amount of your seed. He will increase the results of your good works. [11] You will be made rich in every way. Then you can always give freely. We will take your many gifts to the people who need them. And they will give thanks to God.

[12] Your gifts meet the needs of the Lord's people. And that's not all. Your gifts also cause many people to thank God. [13] You have shown yourselves to be worthy by what you have given. So other people will praise God because you obey him. That proves that you really believe the good news about Christ. They will also praise God because you share freely with them and with everyone else. [14] Their hearts will be filled with love for you when they pray for you. God has given you grace that is better than anything. [15] Let us give thanks to God for his gift. It is so great that no one can tell how wonderful it really is!

Paul Speaks Up for His Service to the Church

10 Christ is humble and free of pride. Because of this, I make my appeal to you. I, Paul, am the one you call "shy" when I am face to face with you. But when I am away from you, you think I am "bold" toward you. ²I am coming to see you. Please don't make me be as bold as I expect to be toward some people. They think that I live the way the people of this world live. ³I do live in the world. But I don't fight my battles the way the people of the world do. ⁴The weapons I fight with are not the weapons the world uses. In fact, it is just the opposite. My weapons have the power of God to destroy the camps of the enemy. ⁵I destroy every claim and every reason that keeps people from knowing God. I keep every thought under control in order to make it obey Christ. ⁶Until you have obeyed completely, I will be ready to punish you every time you don't obey.

⁷You are judging only by how things look on the surface. Suppose someone is sure they belong to Christ. Then they should consider again that we belong to Christ just as much as they do. ⁸Do I brag too much about the authority the Lord gave me? If I do, it's because I want to build you up, not tear you down. And I'm not ashamed of that kind of bragging. ⁹Don't think that I'm trying to scare you with my letters. ¹⁰Some say, "His letters sound important. They are powerful. But in person he doesn't seem like much. And what he says doesn't amount to anything." ¹¹People like that have a lot to learn. What I say in my letters when I'm away from you, I will do in my actions when I'm with you.

¹²I don't dare to compare myself with those who praise themselves. I'm not that kind of person. They measure themselves by themselves. They compare themselves with themselves. When they do that, they are not wise. ¹³But I won't brag more than I should. God himself has given me an opportunity for serving. I will only brag about what I have done with that opportunity. This opportunity for serving also includes you. ¹⁴I am not going too far in my bragging. I would be going too far if I hadn't come to where you live. But I did get there with the good news about Christ. ¹⁵And I won't brag about work done by others. If I did, I would be bragging more than I should. As your faith continues to grow, I hope that my work among you will greatly increase. ¹⁶Then I will be able to preach the good news in the areas beyond you. I don't want to brag about work already done in someone else's territory. ¹⁷But, "The one who brags should brag about what the Lord has done." *(Jeremiah 9:24)* ¹⁸Those who praise themselves are not accepted. Those the Lord praises are accepted.

Paul and Those Who Pretend to Be Apostles

11 I hope you will put up with me in a little foolish bragging. Yes, please put up with me! ²My jealousy for

you comes from God himself. I promised to give you to only one husband. That husband is Christ. I wanted to be able to give you to him as if you were a pure virgin. ³ But Eve's mind was tricked by the snake's clever lies. And here's what I'm afraid of. Your minds will also somehow be led astray. They will be led away from your true and pure love for Christ. ⁴ Suppose someone comes to you and preaches about a Jesus different from the Jesus we preached about. Or suppose you receive a spirit different from the Spirit you received before. Or suppose you receive a different message of good news. Suppose it was different from the one you accepted earlier. You put up with those kinds of things easily enough.

⁵ I don't think I'm in any way less important than those "super-apostles." ⁶ It's true that I haven't been trained as a speaker. But I do have knowledge. I've made that very clear to you in every way. ⁷ I preached God's good news to you free of charge. When I did that, I was putting myself down in order to lift you up. Was this a sin? ⁸ I received help from other churches so I could serve you. This was almost like robbing them. ⁹ When I was with you and needed something, I didn't cause you any expense. The believers who came from Macedonia gave me what I needed. I haven't caused you any expense at all. And I won't ever do it. ¹⁰ I'm sure that the truth of Christ is in me. And I'm just as sure that nobody in Achaia will keep me from bragging. ¹¹ Why? Because I don't love you? No! God knows I do!

¹² And I will keep on doing what I'm doing. That will stop those who claim they have things to brag about. They think they have a chance to be considered equal with us. ¹³ People like that are false apostles. They are workers who tell lies. They only pretend to be apostles of Christ. ¹⁴ That comes as no surprise. Even Satan himself pretends to be an angel of light. ¹⁵ So it doesn't surprise us that Satan's servants also pretend to be serving God. They will finally get exactly what they deserve.

Paul Brags About His Sufferings

¹⁶ I will say it again. Don't let anyone think I'm a fool. But if you do, put up with me just as you would put up with a fool. Then I can do a little bragging. ¹⁷ When I brag about myself like this, I'm not talking the way the Lord would. I'm talking like a fool. ¹⁸ Many are bragging the way the people of the world do. So I will brag like that too. ¹⁹ You are so wise! You gladly put up with fools! ²⁰ In fact, you even put up with anyone who makes you a slave or uses you. You put up with those who take advantage of you. You put up with those who claim to be better than you. You put up with those who slap you in the face. ²¹ I'm ashamed to have to say that I was too weak for that!

Whatever anyone else dares to brag about, I also dare to brag about. I'm speaking like a fool! [22] Are they Hebrews? So am I. Do they belong to the people of Israel? So do I. Are they Abraham's children? So am I. [23] Are they serving Christ? I am serving him even more. I'm out of my mind to talk like this! I have worked much harder. I have been in prison more often. I have suffered terrible beatings. Again and again I almost died. [24] Five times the Jews gave me 39 strokes with a whip. [25] Three times I was beaten with sticks. Once they tried to kill me by throwing stones at me. Three times I was shipwrecked. I spent a night and a day in the open sea. [26] I have had to keep on the move. I have been in danger from rivers. I have been in danger from robbers. I have been in danger from my fellow Jews and in danger from Gentiles. I have been in danger in the city, in the country, and at sea. I have been in danger from people who pretended they were believers. [27] I have worked very hard. Often I have gone without sleep. I have been hungry and thirsty. Often I have gone without food. I have been cold and naked. [28] Besides everything else, every day I am concerned about all the churches. It is a very heavy load. [29] If anyone is weak, I feel weak. If anyone is led into sin, I burn on the inside.

[30] If I have to brag, I will brag about the things that show how weak I am. [31] I am not lying. The God and Father of the Lord Jesus knows this. May God be praised forever. [32] In Damascus the governor who served under King Aretas had their city guarded. He wanted to arrest me. [33] But I was lowered in a basket from a window in the wall. So I escaped from the governor.

Paul's Vision and His Painful Problem

12 We can't gain anything by bragging. But I have to do it anyway. I am going to tell you what I've seen. I want to talk about what the Lord has shown me. [2] I know a believer in Christ who was taken up to the third heaven 14 years ago. I don't know if his body was taken up or not. Only God knows. [3] I don't know if that man was in his body or out of it. Only God knows. But I do know that [4] he was taken up to paradise. He heard things there that couldn't be put into words. They were things that no one is allowed to talk about. [5] I will brag about a man like that. But I won't brag about myself. I will brag only about how weak I am. [6] Suppose I decide to brag. That would not make me a fool, because I would be telling the truth. But I don't brag, so that no one will think more of me than they should. People should judge me by what I do and say. [7] God has shown me amazing and wonderful things. People should not think more of me because of it. So I wouldn't become proud of myself, I was given a problem. This problem caused pain in my body. It is a messenger from Satan to make me suffer. [8] Three times I begged the Lord to take it away from me. [9] But he said to me, "My grace is all you need. My power is strongest when you are weak." So I am very happy to brag about how weak I am. Then Christ's power can rest on me. [10] Because of how I suffered for Christ, I'm glad that I am weak. I am glad in hard times. I am glad when people say mean things about me. I am glad when things are difficult. And I am glad when people make me suffer. When I am weak, I am strong.

Paul's Concern for the People of Corinth

[11] I have made a fool of myself. But you made me do it. You should have praised me. Even though I am nothing, I am in no way less important than the "super-apostles." [12] While I was with you, I kept on showing you the actions of a true apostle. These actions include signs, wonders and miracles. [13] How were you less important than the other churches? The only difference was that I didn't cause you any expense. Forgive me for that wrong!

[14] Now I am ready to visit you for the third time. I won't cause you any expense. I don't want what you have. What I really want is you. After all, children shouldn't have to save up for their parents. Parents should save up for their children. [15] So I will be very happy to spend everything I have for you. I will even spend myself. If I love you more, will you love me less? [16] In any case, I haven't caused you any expense. But I'm so tricky! I have caught you by tricking you! Or so you think! [17] Did I take advantage of you through any of the men I sent to you? [18] I asked Titus to go to you. And I sent our brother with him. Titus didn't take advantage of you, did he? Didn't we walk in the same footsteps by the same Spirit?

[19] All this time, have you been thinking that I've been speaking up for myself? No, I've been speaking with God as my witness. I've been speaking like a believer in Christ. Dear friends, everything I do is to help you become stronger. [20] I'm afraid that when I come I won't find you as I want you to be. I'm afraid that you won't find me as you want me to be. I'm afraid there will be arguing, jealousy and fits of anger. I'm afraid each of you will focus only on getting ahead. Then you will tell lies about each other. You will talk about each other. I'm afraid you will be proud and cause trouble. [21] I'm afraid that when I come again my God will put me to shame in front of you. Then I will be sad about many who sinned earlier and have not turned away from it. They have not turned away from uncleanness, sexual sins and wild living. They have done all those things.

Final Warnings

13 This will be my third visit to you. Scripture says, "Every matter must be proved by the words of two or three witnesses." *(Deuteronomy 19:15)* [2] I already warned you during my second visit. I now say it again while I'm away. When I return, I won't spare those who sinned earlier. I won't spare any of the others either. [3] You are asking me to prove that Christ is speaking through me. He is not weak in dealing with you. He is powerful among you. [4] It is true that Christ was nailed to the cross because he was weak. But Christ lives by God's power. In the same way, we share his weakness. But by God's power we will live with Christ as we serve you.

[5] Take a good look at yourselves to see if you are really believers. Test yourselves. Don't you realize that Christ Jesus is in you? Unless, of course, you fail the test! [6] I hope you will discover that I haven't failed the test. [7] I pray to God that you won't do anything wrong. I don't pray so that people will see that I have passed the test. Instead, I pray this so that you will do what is right, even if it seems I have failed. [8] I can't do anything to stop the truth. I can only work for the truth. [9] I'm glad when I am weak but you are strong. I pray that there will be no more problems among you. [10] That's why I write these things before I come to you. Then when I do come, I won't have to be hard on you when I use my authority. The Lord gave me the authority to build you up. He didn't give it to me to tear you down.

Final Greetings

[11] Finally, brothers and sisters, be joyful! Work to make things right with one another. Help one another and agree with one another. Live in peace. And the God who gives love and peace will be with you.

[12] Greet one another with a holy kiss.

[13] All God's people here send their greetings.

[14] May the grace shown by the Lord Jesus Christ be with you all. May the love that God has given us be with you. And may the sharing of life brought about by the Holy Spirit be with you all.

Galatians

Introduction:

Galatia was a part of the land we now call Turkey. Paul wrote this letter to the churches there. The churches were being taught by false teachers. These teachers said wrong things about the good news of Jesus Christ. They taught that people were saved by doing what the Jewish law says.

Paul said people are made right with God by believing in Jesus. No one has ever been made right with God by doing what the law says. Paul said that all who depend on the law instead of faith in Jesus are under a curse.

Paul wanted people to have faith in Jesus. This is the only way to be a child of God. Children of God live by the Holy Spirit, not the law. Paul said those led by the Holy Spirit show the fruit of the Spirit. "The fruit the Holy Spirit produces is love, joy and peace. It is being patient, kind and good. It is being faithful and gentle and having control of oneself." (5:22–23)

Outline of contents:

1 I, Paul, am writing this letter. I am an apostle. People have not sent me. No human authority has sent me. I have been sent by Jesus Christ and by God the Father. God raised Jesus from the dead. ²All the brothers and sisters who are with me join me in writing.

We are sending this letter to you, the members of the churches in Galatia.

³May God our Father and the Lord Jesus Christ give you grace and peace. ⁴Jesus gave his life for our sins. He set us free from this evil world. That was what our God and Father wanted. ⁵Give glory to God for ever and ever. Amen.

There Is No Other Good News

⁶I am amazed. You are so quickly deserting the one who chose you. He chose you to live in the grace that Christ has provided. You are turning to a different "good news." ⁷What you are accepting is really not the good news at all. It seems that some people have gotten you all mixed up. They are trying to twist the good news about

Christ. [8] But suppose even we should preach a different "good news." Suppose even an angel from heaven should preach it. Suppose it is different from the good news we gave you. Then let anyone who does that be cursed by God. [9] I have already said it. Now I will say it again. Suppose someone preaches a "good news" that is different from what you accepted. That person should be cursed by God.

[10] Am I now trying to get people to think well of me? Or do I want God to think well of me? Am I trying to please people? If I were, I would not be serving Christ.

Paul Was Appointed by God

[11] Brothers and sisters, here is what I want you to know. The good news I preached does not come from human beings. [12] No one gave it to me. No one taught it to me. Instead, I received it from Jesus Christ. He showed it to me.

[13] You have heard how I lived earlier in my Jewish way of life. With all my strength I attacked the church of God. I tried to destroy it. [14] I was moving ahead in my Jewish way of life. I went beyond many of my people who were my own age. I held firmly to the teachings passed down by my people. [15] But God set me apart from before the time I was born. He showed me his grace by appointing me. He was pleased [16] to show his Son in my life. He wanted me to preach about Jesus among the Gentiles.

When God appointed me, I decided right away not to ask anyone for advice. [17] I didn't go up to Jerusalem to see those who were apostles before I was. Instead, I went into Arabia. Later I returned to Damascus.

[18] Then after three years I went up to Jerusalem. I went there to get to know Peter. I stayed with him for 15 days. [19] I didn't see any of the other apostles. I only saw James, the Lord's brother. [20] Here is what you can be sure of. And God is even a witness to it. What I am writing you is not a lie.

[21] Then I went to Syria and Cilicia. [22] The members of Christ's churches in Judea did not know me in a personal way. [23] They only heard others say, "The man who used to attack us has changed. He is now preaching the faith he once tried to destroy." [24] And they praised God because of me.

Paul Is Accepted by the Apostles

2 Then after fourteen years, I went up again to Jerusalem. This time I went with Barnabas. I took Titus along also. [2] I went because God showed me what he wanted me to do. I spoke in private to those who are respected as leaders. I told them the good news that I preach among the Gentiles. I wanted to be sure I wasn't running my race for no purpose. And I wanted to know that I had not been running my race for no purpose. [3] Titus

was with me. He was a Greek. But even he was not forced to be circumcised. ⁴This matter came up because some people had slipped in among us. They had pretended to be believers. They wanted to find out about the freedom we have because we belong to Christ Jesus. They wanted to make us slaves again. ⁵We didn't give in to them for a moment. We did this so that the truth of the good news would be kept safe for you.

⁶Some people in Jerusalem were thought to be important. But it makes no difference to me what they were. God does not treat people differently. Those people added nothing to my message. ⁷In fact, it was just the opposite. They recognized the task I had been trusted with. It was the task of preaching the good news to the Gentiles. My task was like Peter's task. He had been trusted with the task of preaching to the Jews. ⁸God was working in Peter as an apostle to the Jews. God was also working in me as an apostle to the Gentiles. ⁹James, Peter and John are respected as pillars in the church. They recognized the special grace given to me. So they shook my hand and the hand of Barnabas. They wanted to show they accepted us. They agreed that we should go to the Gentiles. They would go to the Jews. ¹⁰They asked only one thing. They wanted us to continue to remember poor people. That was what I had wanted to do all along.

Paul Opposes Peter

¹¹When Peter came to Antioch, I told him to his face that I was against what he was doing. He was clearly wrong. ¹²He used to eat with the Gentiles. But certain men came from a group sent by James. When they arrived, Peter began to draw back. He separated himself from the Gentiles. That's because he was afraid of the circumcision group sent by James. ¹³Peter's actions were not honest, and other Jews in Antioch joined him. Even Barnabas was led astray.

¹⁴I saw what they were doing. It was not in line with the truth of the good news. So I spoke to Peter in front of them all. "You are a Jew," I said. "But you live like one who is not. So why do you force Gentiles to follow Jewish ways?"

¹⁵We are Jews by birth. We are not sinful Gentiles. ¹⁶Here is what we know. No one is made right with God by obeying the law. It is by believing in Jesus Christ. So we too have put our faith in Christ Jesus. This is so we can be made right with God by believing in Christ. We are not made right by obeying the law. That's because no one can be made right with God by obeying the law.

¹⁷We are seeking to be made right with God through Christ. As we do, what if we find that we who are Jews are also sinners? Does that mean that Christ causes us to sin? Certainly not! ¹⁸Suppose I build again what I had destroyed. Then I would really be breaking the law.

¹⁹ By the law, I died as far as the law is concerned. I died so that I might live for God. ²⁰ I have been crucified with Christ. I don't live any longer, but Christ lives in me. Now I live my life in my body by faith in the Son of God. He loved me and gave himself for me. ²¹ I do not get rid of the grace of God. What if a person could become right with God by obeying the law? Then Christ died for nothing!

Faith or Obeying the Law

3 You foolish people of Galatia! Who has put you under an evil spell? When I preached, I clearly showed you that Jesus Christ had been nailed to the cross. ² I would like to learn just one thing from you. Did you receive the Holy Spirit by obeying the law? Or did you receive the Spirit by believing what you heard? ³ Are you so foolish? You began by the Holy Spirit. Are you now trying to finish God's work in you by your own strength? ⁴ Have you experienced so much for nothing? And was it really for nothing? ⁵ So I ask you again, how does God give you his Spirit? How does he work miracles among you? Is it by doing what the law says? Or is it by believing what you have heard? ⁶ In the same way, Abraham "believed God. God was pleased with Abraham because he believed. So his faith made him right with God." *(Genesis 15:6)*

⁷ So you see, those who have faith are children of Abraham. ⁸ Long ago, Scripture knew that God would make the Gentiles right with himself. He would do this by their faith in him. He announced the good news ahead of time to Abraham. God said, "All nations will be blessed because of you." *(Genesis 12:3; 18:18; 22:18)* ⁹ So those who depend on faith are blessed along with Abraham. He was the man of faith.

¹⁰ All who depend on obeying the law are under a curse. It is written, "May everyone who doesn't continue to do everything written in the Book of the Law be under God's curse." *(Deuteronomy 27:26)* ¹¹ We know that no one who depends on the law is made right with God. This is because "the one who is right with God will live by faith." *(Habakkuk 2:4)* ¹² The law is not based on faith. In fact, it is just the opposite. It teaches that "the person who does these things will live by them." *(Leviticus 18:5)* ¹³ Christ set us free from the curse of the law. He did it by becoming a curse for us. It is written, "Everyone who is hung on a pole is under God's curse." *(Deuteronomy 21:23)* ¹⁴ Christ Jesus set us free so that the blessing given to Abraham would come to the Gentiles through Christ. He did it so that we might receive the promise of the Holy Spirit. The promised Spirit comes by believing in Christ.

The Law and the Promise

¹⁵ Brothers and sisters, let me give you an example from everyday life. No one can get rid of an official agreement between

people. No one can add to it. It can't be changed after it has been made. It is the same with God's covenant agreement. [16] The promises were given to Abraham. They were also given to his seed. Scripture does not say, "and to seeds." That means many people. It says, "and to your seed." *(Genesis 12:7; 13:15; 24:7)* That means one person. And that one person is Christ. [17] Here is what I mean. The law came 430 years after the promise. But the law does not get rid of God's covenant and promise. The covenant had already been made by God. So the law does not do away with the promise. [18] The great gift that God has for us does not depend on the law. If it did, it would no longer depend on the promise. But God gave it to Abraham as a free gift through a promise.

[19] Then why was the law given at all? It was added because of human sin. And it was supposed to control us until the promised Seed had come. The law was given through angels, and a go-between was put in charge of it. [20] A go-between means that there is more than one side to an agreement. But God didn't use a go-between when he made his promise to Abraham.

[21] So is the law opposed to God's promises? Certainly not! What if a law had been given that could give life? Then people could become right with God by obeying the law. [22] But Scripture has locked up everything under the control of sin. It does so in order that what was promised might be given to those who believe. The promise comes through faith in Jesus Christ.

Children of God

[23] Before faith in Christ came, we were guarded by the law. We were locked up until this faith was made known. [24] So the law was put in charge of us until Christ came. He came so that we might be made right with God by believing in Christ. [25] But now faith in Christ has come. So the law is no longer in charge of us.

[26] So in Christ Jesus you are all children of God by believing in Christ. [27] This is because all of you who were baptized into Christ have put on Christ. You have put him on as if he were your clothes. [28] There is no Jew or Gentile. There is no slave or free person. There is no male or female. That's because you are all one in Christ Jesus. [29] You who belong to Christ are Abraham's seed. So you will receive what God has promised.

4 Here is what I have been saying. As long as your own children are young, they are no different from slaves in your house. They are no different, even though they will own all the property. [2] People are in charge of the property. And other people are in charge of the children. The children remain under their care until they become adults. At that time their fathers give them the property. [3] It is the same with us. When we

were children, we were slaves to the basic spiritual powers of the world. ⁴ But then the chosen time came. God sent his Son. A woman gave birth to him. He was born under the authority of the law. ⁵ He came to set free those who were under the authority of the law. He wanted us to be adopted as children with all the rights children have. ⁶ Because you are his children, God sent the Spirit of his Son into our hearts. He is the Holy Spirit. By his power we call God Abba. Abba means Father. ⁷ So you aren't a slave any longer. You are God's child. Because you are his child, God gives you the rights of those who are his children.

Paul's Concern for the Believers in Galatia

⁸ At one time you didn't know God. You were slaves to gods that are really not gods at all. ⁹ But now you know God. Even better, God knows you. So why are you turning back to those weak and worthless powers? Do you want to be slaves to them all over again? ¹⁰ You are observing special days and months and seasons and years! ¹¹ I am afraid for you. I am afraid that somehow I have wasted my efforts on you.

¹² I make my appeal to you, brothers and sisters. I'm asking you to become like me. After all, I became like you. You didn't do anything wrong to me. ¹³ Remember when I first preached the good news to you? Remember I did that because I was sick. ¹⁴ And my sickness was hard on you. But you weren't mean to me. You didn't make fun of me. Instead, you welcomed me as if I were an angel of God. You welcomed me as if I were Christ Jesus himself. ¹⁵ So why aren't you treating me the same way now? Suppose you could have torn out your own eyes and given them to me. Then you would have done it. I am a witness to this. ¹⁶ Have I become your enemy now by telling you the truth?

¹⁷ Those people are trying hard to win you over. But it is not for your good. They want to take you away from us. They want you to commit yourselves to them. ¹⁸ It is fine to be committed to something, if the purpose is good. And you shouldn't be committed only when I am with you. You should always be committed. ¹⁹ My dear children, I am in pain for you like I was when we first met. I have pain like a woman giving birth. And my pain will continue until Christ makes you like himself. ²⁰ I wish I could be with you now. I wish I could change my tone of voice. As it is, I don't understand you.

Hagar and Sarah

²¹ You who want to be under the authority of the law, tell me something. Don't you know what the law says? ²² It is written that Abraham had two sons. The slave woman gave birth to one of them. The free woman gave birth to the other one. ²³ Abraham's son by the slave woman

was born in the usual way. But his son by the free woman was born because of God's promise.

²⁴ These things are examples. The two women stand for two covenants. One covenant comes from Mount Sinai. It gives birth to children who are going to be slaves. It is Hagar. ²⁵ Hagar stands for Mount Sinai in Arabia. She stands for the present city of Jerusalem. That's because she and her children are slaves. ²⁶ But the Jerusalem that is above is free. She is our mother. ²⁷ It is written,

"Be glad, woman,
    you who have never had
      children.
Shout for joy and cry out
    loud,
    you who have never had
      labor pains.
The woman who is all alone
    has more children
    than the woman who has a
      husband."   *(Isaiah 54:1)*

²⁸ Brothers and sisters, you are children because of God's promise just as Isaac was. ²⁹ At that time, the son born in the usual way tried to hurt the other son. The other son was born by the power of the Holy Spirit. It is the same now. ³⁰ But what does Scripture say? "Get rid of the slave woman. Get rid of her son. The slave woman's son will never have a share of the family's property. He'll never share it with the free woman's son." *(Genesis 21:10)* ³¹ Brothers and sisters, we are not the slave woman's children. We are the free woman's children.

Christ Sets Us Free

5 Christ has set us free to enjoy our freedom. So remain strong in the faith. Don't let the chains of slavery hold you again.

² Here is what I, Paul, say to you. Don't let yourselves be circumcised. If you do, Christ won't be of any value to you. ³ I say it again. Every man who lets himself be circumcised must obey the whole law. ⁴ Some of you are trying to be made right with God by obeying the law. You have been separated from Christ. You have fallen away from God's grace. ⁵ But we long to be made completely holy because of our faith in Christ. Through the Holy Spirit we wait for this in hope. ⁶ Circumcision and uncircumcision aren't worth anything to those who believe in Christ Jesus. The only thing that really counts is faith that shows itself through love.

⁷ You were running a good race. Who has kept you from obeying the truth? ⁸ The God who chooses you does not keep you from obeying the truth. ⁹ You should know that "just a little yeast works its way through the whole batch of dough." ¹⁰ The Lord makes me certain that you will see the truth of this. The one who has gotten you all mixed up will have to pay the price. This will happen no matter who has done it. ¹¹ Brothers and sisters, I no longer preach that people must be circumcised. If I did, why am I still being opposed? If I preached that, then the cross wouldn't upset anyone. ¹² So

then, what about troublemakers who try to get others to be circumcised? I wish they would go the whole way! I wish they would cut off everything that marks them as men!

Living by the Holy Spirit's Power

13 My brothers and sisters, you were chosen to be free. But don't use your freedom as an excuse to live under the power of sin. Instead, serve one another in love. 14 The whole law is fulfilled by obeying this one command. "Love your neighbor as you love yourself." *(Leviticus 19:18)* 15 If you say or do things that harm one another, watch out! You could end up destroying one another.

16 So I say, live by the Holy Spirit's power. Then you will not do what your desires controlled by sin want you to do. 17 The desires controlled by sin do not want what the Spirit delights in. And the Spirit does not want what the desires controlled by sin delight in. The two are at war with each other. That's why you are not supposed to do whatever you want. 18 But if you are led by the Spirit, you are not under the authority of the law.

19 The result of sin's control in our lives is clear. It includes sexual sins, impure acts and wild living. 20 It includes worshiping statues of gods and worshiping evil powers. It also includes hatred and fighting, jealousy and fits of anger. Sinful desire is interested only in getting ahead. It stirs up trouble. It separates people into their own little groups. 21 It wants what others have. It gets drunk and takes part in wild parties. It does many things of that kind. I warn you now as I did before. People who live like this will not receive God's kingdom.

22 But the fruit the Holy Spirit produces is love, joy and peace. It is being patient, kind and good. It is being faithful 23 and gentle and having control of oneself. There is no law against things of that kind. 24 Those who belong to Christ Jesus have nailed their sinful desires to his cross. They don't want these things anymore. 25 Since we live by the Spirit, let us keep in step with the Spirit. 26 Let us not become proud. Let us not make each other angry. Let us not want what belongs to others.

Do Good to Everyone

6 Brothers and sisters, what if someone is caught in a sin? Then you who live by the Spirit should correct that person. Do it in a gentle way. But be careful. You could be tempted too. 2 Carry one another's heavy loads. If you do, you will fulfill the law of Christ. 3 If anyone thinks they are somebody when they are nobody, they are fooling themselves. 4 Each person should test their own actions. Then they can take pride in themselves. They won't be comparing themselves to someone else. 5 Each person should carry their own load. 6 But those who are taught the word should

share all good things with their teacher.

7 Don't be fooled. You can't outsmart God. A man gathers a crop from what he plants. 8 Some people plant to please their desires controlled by sin. From these desires they will harvest death. Others plant to please the Holy Spirit. From the Spirit they will harvest eternal life. 9 Let us not become tired of doing good. At the right time we will gather a crop if we don't give up. 10 So when we can do good to everyone, let us do it. Let's try even harder to do good to the family of believers.

Not Circumcision but the New Creation

11 Look at the big letters I'm using as I write to you with my own hand!

12 Some people are worried about how things look on the outside. They are trying to force you to be circumcised. They do it for only one reason. They don't want to suffer by being connected with the cross of Christ. 13 Even those who are circumcised don't obey the law. But they want you to be circumcised. Then they can brag about what has been done to your body. 14 I never want to brag about anything except the cross of our Lord Jesus Christ. Through that cross the ways of the world have been crucified as far as I am concerned. And I have been crucified as far as the ways of the world are concerned. 15 Circumcision and uncircumcision don't mean anything. What really counts is that the new creation has come. 16 May peace and mercy be given to all who follow this rule. May peace and mercy be given to the Israel that belongs to God.

17 From now on, let no one cause trouble for me. My body has marks that show I belong to Jesus.

18 Brothers and sisters, may the grace of our Lord Jesus Christ be with your spirit. Amen.

Ephesians

Introduction:

Paul wrote this letter from Rome. He was in prison. Paul wrote to his friends in Ephesus. Ephesus was a big city. There were many Christians in the church at Ephesus. There were many other churches near the city too. This letter was passed around to all of them.

Paul wrote this letter about the church. He said the church is a family. God gives his children new life through Jesus. All God's children are part of the same family.

Paul said God's children must love each other. He also said we must let God make us strong so we can fight the devil. We are like soldiers, but we do not use guns or swords. We must "put on all of God's armor" (Ephesians 6:11). We must trust God for help.

Outline of contents:

1 I, Paul, am writing this letter. I am an apostle of Christ Jesus just as God planned.

I am sending this letter to you, God's holy people in Ephesus. Because you belong to Christ Jesus, you are faithful.

² May God our Father and the Lord Jesus Christ give you grace and peace.

Praise God for His Spiritual Blessings in Christ

³ Give praise to the God and Father of our Lord Jesus Christ. He has blessed us with every spiritual blessing. Those blessings come from the heavenly world. They belong to us because we belong to Christ. ⁴ God chose us to belong to Christ before the world was created. He chose us to be holy and without blame in his eyes. He loved us. ⁵ So he decided long ago to adopt us. He adopted us as his children with all the rights children have. He did it because of what Jesus Christ has done. It pleased God to do it. ⁶ All those things bring praise to his glorious grace. God freely gave us his grace because of the One he loves. ⁷ We have been set free because of what Christ has done. Because he bled and died our sins have been forgiven. We have been set free because God's grace is so rich. ⁸ He poured his

grace on us. By giving us great wisdom and understanding, [9] he showed us the mystery of his plan. It was in keeping with what he wanted to do. It was what he had planned through Christ. [10] It will all come about when history has been completed. God will then bring together all things in heaven and on earth under Christ.

[11] We were also chosen to belong to him. God decided to choose us long ago in keeping with his plan. He works out everything to fit his plan and purpose. [12] We were the first to put our hope in Christ. We were chosen to bring praise to his glory. [13] You also became believers in Christ. That happened when you heard the message of truth. It was the good news about how you could be saved. When you believed, he stamped you with an official mark. That official mark is the Holy Spirit that he promised. [14] The Spirit marks us as God's own. We can now be sure that someday we will receive all that God has promised. That will happen after God sets all his people completely free. All these things will bring praise to his glory.

Paul Prays and Gives Thanks

[15] I have heard about your faith in the Lord Jesus. I have also heard about your love for all God's people. That is why [16] I have not stopped thanking God for you. I always remember you in my prayers. [17] I pray to the God of our Lord Jesus Christ. God is the glorious Father. I keep asking him to give you the wisdom and understanding that come from the Holy Spirit. I want you to know God better. [18] I pray that you may understand more clearly. Then you will know the hope God has chosen you to receive. You will know that what God will give his holy people is rich and glorious. [19] And you will know God's great power. It can't be compared with anything else. His power works for us who believe. It is the same mighty strength [20] God showed. He showed this when he raised Christ from the dead. God seated him at his right hand in his heavenly kingdom. [21] There Christ sits far above all who rule and have authority. He also sits far above all powers and kings. He is above every name that is appealed to in this world and in the world to come. [22] God placed all things under Christ's rule. He appointed him to be ruler over everything for the church. [23] The church is Christ's body and is filled by Christ. He fills everything in every way.

God Has Given Us New Life Through Christ

2 You were living in your sins and lawless ways. But in fact you were dead. [2] You used to live as sinners when you followed the ways of this world. You served the one who rules over the spiritual forces of evil. He is the spirit who is now at work in those who don't obey God. [3] At one time we all lived

among them. Our desires were controlled by sin. We tried to satisfy what they wanted us to do. We followed our desires and thoughts. God was angry with us like he was with everyone else. That's because of the kind of people we all were. ⁴But God loves us deeply. He is full of mercy. ⁵So he gave us new life because of what Christ has done. He gave us life even when we were dead in sin. God's grace has saved you. ⁶God raised us up with Christ. He has seated us with him in his heavenly kingdom. That's because we belong to Christ Jesus. ⁷He has done it to show the riches of his grace for all time to come. His grace can't be compared with anything else. He has shown it by being kind to us. He was kind to us because of what Christ Jesus has done. ⁸God's grace has saved you because of your faith in Christ. Your salvation doesn't come from anything you do. It is God's gift. ⁹It is not based on anything you have done. No one can brag about earning it. ¹⁰We are God's creation. He created us to belong to Christ Jesus. Now we can do good works. Long ago God prepared these works for us to do.

God's New Family of Jews and Gentiles

¹¹You who are not Jews by birth, here is what I want you to remember. You are called "uncircumcised" by those who call themselves "circumcised." But they have only been circum-cised in their bodies by human hands. ¹²Before you believed in Christ, you were separated from him. You were not considered to be citizens of Israel. You were not included in what the covenants promised. You were without hope and without God in the world. ¹³At one time you were far away from God. But now you belong to Christ Jesus. He spilled his blood for you. This has brought you near to God.

¹⁴Christ himself is our peace. He has made Jews and Gentiles into one group of people. He has destroyed the hatred that was like a wall between us. ¹⁵Through his body on the cross, Christ set aside the law with all its commands and rules. He planned to create one new people out of Jews and Gentiles. He wanted to make peace between them. ¹⁶He planned to bring both Jews and Gentiles back to God as one body. He planned to do this through the cross. On that cross, Christ put to death their hatred toward one another. ¹⁷He came and preached peace to you who were far away. He also preached peace to those who were near. ¹⁸Through Christ we both come to the Father by the power of one Holy Spirit.

¹⁹So you are no longer outsiders and strangers. You are citizens together with God's people. You are also members of God's family. ²⁰You are a building that is built on the apostles and prophets. They are the foundation. Christ Jesus

himself is the most important stone in the building. ²¹ The whole building is held together by him. It rises to become a holy temple because it belongs to the Lord. ²² And because you belong to him, you too are being built together. You are being made into a house where God lives through his Spirit.

God's Wonderful Plan for the Gentiles

3 I, Paul, am a prisoner because of Christ Jesus. I am in prison because of my work among you who are Gentiles.

² I am sure you have heard that God appointed me to share his grace with you. ³ I'm talking about the mystery God showed me. I have already written a little about it. ⁴ By reading about this mystery, you will be able to understand what I know. You will know about the mystery of Christ. ⁵ The mystery was not made known to people of other times. But now the Holy Spirit has made this mystery known to God's holy apostles and prophets. ⁶ Here is the mystery. Because of the good news, God's promises are for Gentiles as well as for Jews. Both groups are parts of one body. They share in the promise. It belongs to them because they belong to Christ Jesus.

⁷ I now serve the good news because God gave me his grace. His power is at work in me. ⁸ I am by far the least important of all the Lord's holy people. But he gave me the grace to preach to the Gentiles about the unlimited riches that Christ gives. ⁹ God told me to make clear to everyone how the mystery came about. In times past it was kept hidden in the mind of God, who created all things. ¹⁰ He wanted the rulers and authorities in the heavenly world to come to know his great wisdom. The church would make it known to them. ¹¹ That was God's plan from the beginning. He has fulfilled his plan through Christ Jesus our Lord. ¹² Through him and through faith in him we can approach God. We can come to him freely. We can come without fear. ¹³ So here is what I'm asking you to do. Don't lose hope because I am suffering for you. It will lead to the time when God will give you his glory.

Paul Prays for the Ephesians

¹⁴ I bow in prayer to the Father because of my work among you. ¹⁵ From the Father every family in heaven and on earth gets its name. ¹⁶ I pray that he will use his glorious riches to make you strong. May his Holy Spirit give you his power deep down inside you. ¹⁷ Then Christ will live in your hearts because you believe in him. And I pray that your love will have deep roots. I pray that it will have a strong foundation. ¹⁸ May you have power together with all the Lord's holy people to understand Christ's love. May you know how wide and long and high and deep it is. ¹⁹ And may you know his love, even though it can't be known completely. Then

you will be filled with everything God has for you.

20 God is able to do far more than we could ever ask for or imagine. He does everything by his power that is working in us. 21 Give him glory in the church and in Christ Jesus. Give him glory through all time and for ever and ever. Amen.

Growing Up Together in the Body of Christ

4 I am a prisoner because of the Lord. So I am asking you to live a life worthy of what God chose you for. 2 Don't be proud at all. Be completely gentle. Be patient. Put up with one another in love. 3 The Holy Spirit makes you one in every way. So try your best to remain as one. Let peace keep you together. 4 There is one body and one Spirit. You were appointed to one hope when you were chosen. 5 There is one Lord, one faith and one baptism. 6 There is one God and Father of all. He is over everything. He is through everything. He is in everything.

7 But each one of us has received a gift of grace. These gifts are given to us by Christ. 8 That is why Scripture says,

"When he went up to his
    place on high,
he took many prisoners.
He gave gifts to his people."
(Psalm 68:18)

9 What does "he went up" mean? It can only mean that he also came down to the lower, earthly places. 10 The one who came down is the same one who went up. He went up higher than all the heavens. He did it in order to fill all creation. 11 So Christ himself gave the gift of the apostles to the church. He gave the prophets and those who preach the good news. And he also gave the pastors and teachers as a gift to the church. 12 He gave all these people so that they might prepare God's people to serve. Then the body of Christ will be built up. 13 That will continue until we all become one in the faith. We will also become one in the knowledge of God's Son. Then we will be grown up in the faith. We will receive everything that Christ has for us.

14 We will no longer be babies in the faith. We won't be like ships tossed around by the waves. We won't be blown here and there by every new teaching. We won't be blown around by cleverness and tricks. Certain people use them to hide their evil plans. 15 Instead, we will speak the truth in love. So we will grow up in every way to become the body of Christ. Christ is the head of the body. 16 He makes the whole body grow and build itself up in love. Under the control of Christ, each part of the body does its work. It supports the other parts. In that way, the body is joined and held together.

Teachings for Living as Christians

17 Here is what I'm telling you. I am speaking for the Lord as I warn you. You must no longer

live as the Gentiles do. Their thoughts don't have any purpose. ¹⁸ They can't understand the truth. They are separated from the life of God. That's because they don't know him. And they don't know him because their hearts are stubborn. ¹⁹ They have lost all feeling for what is right. So they have given themselves over to all kinds of evil pleasures. They take part in every kind of unclean act. And they are full of greed.

²⁰ But that is not the way of life in Christ that you learned about. ²¹ You heard about Christ and were taught about life in him. What you learned was the truth about Jesus. ²² You were taught not to live the way you used to. You must get rid of your old way of life. That's because it has been made impure by the desire for things that lead you astray. ²³ You were taught to be made new in your thinking. ²⁴ You were taught to start living a new life. It is created to be truly good and holy, just as God is.

²⁵ So each of you must get rid of your lying. Speak the truth to your neighbor. We are all parts of one body. ²⁶ Scripture says, "When you are angry, do not sin." *(Psalm 4:4)* Do not let the sun go down while you are still angry. ²⁷ Don't give the devil a chance. ²⁸ Anyone who has been stealing must never steal again. Instead, they must work. They must do something useful with their own hands. Then they will have something to give to people in need.

²⁹ Don't let any evil talk come out of your mouths. Say only what will help to build others up and meet their needs. Then what you say will help those who listen. ³⁰ Do not make God's Holy Spirit mourn. The Holy Spirit is the proof that you belong to God. And the Spirit is the proof that God will set you completely free. ³¹ Get rid of all hard feelings, anger and rage. Stop all fighting and lying. Don't have anything to do with any kind of hatred. ³² Be kind and tender to one another. Forgive one another, just as God forgave you because of what Christ has done.

5 ¹ You are the children that God dearly loves. So follow his example. ² Lead a life of love, just as Christ did. He loved us. He gave himself up for us. He was a sweet-smelling offering and sacrifice to God.

³ There should not be even a hint of sexual sin among you. Don't do anything impure. And do not always want more and more. These are not the things God's holy people should do. ⁴ There must not be any bad language or foolish talk or dirty jokes. They are out of place. Instead, you should give thanks. ⁵ Here is what you can be sure of. Those who give themselves over to sexual sins are lost. So are people whose lives are impure. The same is true of those who always want more and more. People who do these things might as well worship statues of gods. No one who does them will receive a share

in the kingdom of Christ and of God. ⁶ Don't let anyone fool you with worthless words. People who say things like that aren't obeying God. He is angry with them. ⁷ So don't go along with people like that.

⁸ At one time you were in the dark. But now you are in the light because of what the Lord has done. Live like children of the light. ⁹ The light produces what is completely good, right and true. ¹⁰ Find out what pleases the Lord. ¹¹ Have nothing to do with the acts of darkness. They don't produce anything good. Show what they are really like. ¹² It is shameful even to talk about what people who don't obey do in secret. ¹³ But everything the light shines on can be seen. And everything that the light shines on becomes a light. ¹⁴ That is why it is said,

"Wake up, sleeper.
　　Rise from the dead.
　　Then Christ will shine on
　　　　you."

¹⁵ So be very careful how you live. Do not live like people who aren't wise. Live like people who are wise. ¹⁶ Make the most of every opportunity. The days are evil. ¹⁷ So don't be foolish. Instead, understand what the Lord wants. ¹⁸ Don't fill yourself up with wine. Getting drunk will lead to wild living. Instead, be filled with the Holy Spirit. ¹⁹ Speak to one another with psalms, hymns and songs from the Spirit. Sing and make music from your heart to the Lord.

²⁰ Always give thanks to God the Father for everything. Give thanks to him in the name of our Lord Jesus Christ.

Teachings for Christian Families

²¹ Follow the lead of one another because of your respect for Christ.

²² Wives, follow the lead of your own husbands as you follow the Lord. ²³ The husband is the head of the wife, just as Christ is the head of the church. The church is Christ's body. He is its Savior. ²⁴ The church follows the lead of Christ. In the same way, wives should follow the lead of their husbands in everything.

²⁵ Husbands, love your wives. Love them just as Christ loved the church. He gave himself up for her. ²⁶ He did it to make her holy. He made her clean by washing her with water and the word. ²⁷ He did it to bring her to himself as a brightly shining church. He wants a church that has no stain or wrinkle or any other flaw. He wants a church that is holy and without blame. ²⁸ In the same way, husbands should love their wives. They should love them as they love their own bodies. Any man who loves his wife loves himself. ²⁹ After all, no one ever hated their own body. Instead, they feed and care for their body. And this is what Christ does for the church. ³⁰ We are parts of his body. ³¹ Scripture says, "That's why a man will leave his father and mother and be joined to

his wife. The two will become one." *(Genesis 2:24)* ³²That is a deep mystery. But I'm talking about Christ and the church. ³³A husband also must love his wife. He must love her just as he loves himself. And a wife must respect her husband.

6 Children, obey your parents as believers in the Lord. Obey them because it's the right thing to do. ²Scripture says, "Honor your father and mother." That is the first commandment that has a promise. ³"Then things will go well with you. You will live a long time on the earth." *(Deuteronomy 5:16)*

⁴Fathers, don't make your children angry. Instead, instruct them and teach them the ways of the Lord as you raise them.

⁵Slaves, obey your masters here on earth. Respect them and honor them with a heart that is true. Obey them just as you would obey Christ. ⁶Don't obey them only to please them when they are watching. Do it because you are slaves of Christ. Be sure your heart does what God wants. ⁷Serve your masters with all your heart. Work as serving the Lord and not as serving people. ⁸You know that the Lord will give each person a reward. He will give to them in keeping with the good they do. It doesn't matter whether they are a slave or not.

⁹Masters, treat your slaves in the same way. When you warn them, don't be too hard on them. You know that the God who is their Master and yours is in heaven. And he treats everyone the same.

God's Armor for Believers

¹⁰Finally, let the Lord make you strong. Depend on his mighty power. ¹¹Put on all of God's armor. Then you can remain strong against the devil's evil plans. ¹²Our fight is not against human beings. It is against the rulers, the authorities and the powers of this dark world. It is against the spiritual forces of evil in the heavenly world. ¹³So put on all of God's armor. Evil days will come. But you will be able to stand up to anything. And after you have done everything you can, you will still be standing. ¹⁴So remain strong in the faith. Put the belt of truth around your waist. Put the armor of godliness on your chest. ¹⁵Wear on your feet what will prepare you to tell the good news of peace. ¹⁶Also, pick up the shield of faith. With it you can put out all the flaming arrows of the evil one. ¹⁷Put on the helmet of salvation. And take the sword of the Holy Spirit. The sword is God's word.

¹⁸At all times, pray by the power of the Spirit. Pray all kinds of prayers. Be watchful, so that you can pray. Always keep on praying for all the Lord's people. ¹⁹Pray also for me. Pray that whenever I speak, the right words will be given to me. Then I can be bold as I tell the mystery of the good news. ²⁰Because of the good news, I am being held by chains as the Lord's

messenger. So pray that I will be bold as I preach the good news. That's what I should do.

Final Greetings

[21] Tychicus is a dear brother. He is faithful in serving the Lord. He will tell you everything about me. Then you will know how I am and what I am doing. [22] That's why I am sending him to you. I want you to know how we are. And I want him to encourage you.

[23] May God the Father and the Lord Jesus Christ give peace to the brothers and sisters. May they also give the believers love and faith.

[24] May grace be given to everyone who loves our Lord Jesus Christ with a love that will never die.

Philippians

Introduction:

Paul wrote this letter from Rome. He wrote to his friends in Philippi. Paul was in prison at the time. His friends in Philippi sent him a gift. A man from Philippi named Epaphroditus brought it to Paul. Epaphroditus became very sick while visiting Paul. Paul wrote this letter to tell his friends that Epaphroditus was feeling better. Paul also thanked his friends for the gift.

This letter is full of joy. Paul knew his friends at Philippi loved him. They helped him when they could. He was glad that he could work for the Lord. It did not matter that he was in prison. He could still tell people about Jesus.

Paul told his friends in Philippi to love each other. He told them not to be selfish. Paul wanted his friends to be like Jesus.

Outline of contents:

1 We, Paul and Timothy, are writing this letter. We serve Christ Jesus.

We are sending this letter to you, all God's holy people in Philippi. You belong to Christ Jesus. We are also sending this letter to your leaders and deacons.

² May God our Father and the Lord Jesus Christ give you grace and peace.

Paul Prays and Gives Thanks

³ I thank my God every time I remember you. ⁴ In all my prayers for all of you, I always pray with joy. ⁵ I am happy because you have joined me in spreading the good news. You have done so from the first day until now. ⁶ God began a good work in you. And I am sure that he will carry it on until it is completed. That will be on the day Christ Jesus returns.

⁷ It is right for me to feel this way about all of you. I love you with all my heart. I may be held by chains, or I may be standing up for the truth of the good news. Either way, all of you share in God's grace together with me. ⁸ God is my witness that I long for all of you. I love you with the love that Christ Jesus gives.

⁹ I pray that your love will

grow more and more. And let it be based on knowledge and understanding. [10] Then you will be able to know what is best. Then you will be pure and without blame for the day that Christ returns. [11] You will be filled with the fruit of right living produced by Jesus Christ. All these things bring glory and praise to God.

Paul Spreads the Good News While in Prison

[12] Brothers and sisters, here is what I want you to know. What has happened to me has actually helped to spread the good news. [13] One thing has become clear. I am being held by chains because I am a witness for Christ. All the palace guards and everyone else know it. [14] And because I am a prisoner, most of the believers have become bolder in the Lord. They now dare even more to preach the good news without fear.

[15] It's true that some preach about Christ because they are jealous. But others preach about Christ to help me in my work. [16] The last group acts out of love. They know I have been put here to be a witness for the good news. [17] But the others preach about Christ only to get ahead. They preach Christ for the wrong reasons. They think they can stir up trouble for me while I am being held by chains. [18] But what does it matter? Here is the important thing. Whether for right or wrong reasons, Christ is being preached about. That makes me very glad.

And I will continue to be glad. [19] I know that you are praying for me. I also know that God will give me the Spirit of Jesus Christ to help me. So no matter what happens, I'm sure I will still be set free. [20] I completely expect and hope that I won't be ashamed in any way. I'm sure I will be brave enough. Now as always Christ will receive glory because of what happens to me. He will receive glory whether I live or die. [21] For me, life finds all its meaning in Christ. Death also has its benefits. [22] Suppose I go on living in my body. Then I will be able to carry on my work. It will bear a lot of fruit. But what should I choose? I don't know! [23] I can't decide between the two. I long to leave this world and be with Christ. That is better by far. [24] But it is more important for you that I stay alive. [25] I'm sure of this. So I know I will remain with you. And I will continue with all of you to help you grow in your faith. I will also continue to help you be joyful in what you have been taught. [26] I'm sure I will be with you again. Then you will be able to boast in Christ Jesus even more because of me.

Living to Honor the Good News

[27] No matter what happens, live in a way that brings honor to the good news about Christ. Then I will know that you remain strong together in the one Spirit. I will know this if I come and see you or only hear about

you. I will know that you work together as one person. I will know that you work to spread the teachings about the good news. 28 So don't be afraid in any way of those who oppose you. This will show them that they will be destroyed and that you will be saved. That's what God will do. 29 Here is what he has given you to do for Christ. You must not only believe in him. You must also suffer for him. 30 You are going through the same struggle you saw me go through. As you have heard, I am still struggling.

Being Humble Like Christ

2 So does belonging to Christ help you in any way? Does his love comfort you at all? Do you share anything in common because of the Holy Spirit? Has Christ ever been gentle and loving toward you? 2 If any of these things has happened to you, then agree with one another. Have the same love. Be one in spirit and in the way you think and act. By doing this, you will make my joy complete. 3 Don't do anything only to get ahead. Don't do it because you are proud. Instead, be humble. Value others more than yourselves. 4 None of you should look out just for your own good. Each of you should also look out for the good of others.

5 As you deal with one another, you should think and act as Jesus did.

6 In his very nature he was
God.

Jesus was equal with God.
But Jesus didn't take
advantage of that fact.
7 Instead, he made himself
nothing.
He did this by taking on
the nature of a servant.
He was made just like
human beings.
8 He appeared as a man.
He was humble and
obeyed God completely.
He did this even though it
led to his death.
Even worse, he died on a
cross!
9 So God lifted him up to the
highest place.
God gave him the name
that is above every
name.
10 When the name of Jesus is
spoken, everyone will
kneel down to worship
him.
Everyone in heaven and
on earth and under the
earth will kneel down to
worship him.
11 Everyone's mouth will say
that Jesus Christ is Lord.
And God the Father will
receive the glory.

Live Without Complaining

12 My dear friends, you have always obeyed God. You obeyed while I was with you. And you have obeyed even more while I am not with you. So continue to work out your own salvation. Do it with fear and trembling. 13 God is working in you. He wants your plans and your acts to fulfill his good purpose.

¹⁴ Do everything without complaining or arguing. ¹⁵ Then you will be pure and without blame. You will be children of God without fault among sinful and evil people. Then you will shine among them like stars in the sky. ¹⁶ You will shine as you hold on tight to the word of life. Then I will be able to boast about you on the day Christ returns. I can be happy that I didn't run or work for nothing. ¹⁷ But my life might even be poured out like a drink offering on your sacrifices. I'm talking about the way you serve because you believe. Even so, I am glad. I am joyful with all of you. ¹⁸ So you too should be glad and joyful with me.

Timothy and Epaphroditus

¹⁹ I hope to send Timothy to you soon if the Lord Jesus allows it. Then I will be encouraged when I receive news about you. ²⁰ I have no one else like Timothy. He will truly care about how you are doing. ²¹ All the others are looking out for their own interests. They are not looking out for the interests of Jesus Christ. ²² But you know that Timothy has proved himself. He has served with me like a son with his father in spreading the good news. ²³ So I hope to send him as soon as I see how things go with me. ²⁴ And I'm sure I myself will come soon if the Lord allows it.

²⁵ But I think it's necessary to send Epaphroditus back to you. He is my brother in the Lord. He is a worker and a soldier of Christ together with me. He is also your messenger. You sent him to take care of my needs. ²⁶ He longs for all of you. He is troubled because you heard he was sick. ²⁷ He was very sick. In fact, he almost died. But God had mercy on him. He also had mercy on me. God spared me sadness after sadness. ²⁸ So I want even more to send him to you. Then when you see him again, you will be glad. And I won't worry so much. ²⁹ So then, welcome him as a brother in the Lord with great joy. Honor people like him. ³⁰ He almost died for the work of Christ. He put his life in danger to make up for the help you yourselves couldn't give me.

Do Not Trust in Who You Are or What You Can Do

3 Further, my brothers and sisters, be joyful because you belong to the Lord! It is no trouble for me to write about some important matters to you again. If you know about them, you will have a safe path to follow. ² Watch out for those dogs. They are people who do evil things. When they circumcise, it is nothing more than a useless cutting of the body. ³ But we have been truly circumcised. We serve God by the power of his Spirit. We boast about what Christ Jesus has done. We don't put our trust in who we are or what we can do. ⁴ I have many reasons to trust in who I am and what I have done. Someone else may think they have reasons to trust in these things. But I have even more. ⁵ I was circumcised on the

eighth day. I am part of the people of Israel. I am from the tribe of Benjamin. I am a pure Hebrew. As far as the law is concerned, I am a Pharisee. 6 As far as being committed is concerned, I opposed and attacked the church. As far as keeping the law is concerned, I kept it perfectly.

7 I thought things like that were really something great. But now I consider them to be nothing because of Christ. 8 Even more, I consider everything to be nothing compared to knowing Christ Jesus my Lord. To know him is worth much more than anything else. Because of him I have lost everything. But I consider all of it to be garbage so I can know Christ better. 9 I want to be joined to him. Being right with God does not come from my obeying the law. It comes because I believe in Christ. It comes from God because of faith. 10 I want to know Christ better. Yes, I want to know the power that raised him from the dead. I want to join him in his sufferings. I want to become like him by sharing in his death. 11 Then by God's grace I will rise from the dead.

12 I have not yet received all these things. I have not yet reached my goal. Christ Jesus took hold of me so that I could reach that goal. So I keep pushing myself forward to reach it. 13 Brothers and sisters, I don't consider that I have taken hold of it yet. But here is the one thing I do. I forget what is behind me. I push hard toward what is ahead of me. 14 I push myself forward toward the goal to win the prize. God has appointed me to win it. The heavenly prize is Christ Jesus himself.

Following Paul's Example

15 So all of us who are grown up in the faith should see things this way. Maybe you think differently about something. But God will make it clear to you. 16 Only let us live up to what we have already reached.

17 Brothers and sisters, join together in following my example. You have us as a model. So pay close attention to those who live as we do. 18 I have told you these things many times before. Now I tell you again with tears in my eyes. Many people live like enemies of the cross of Christ. 19 The only thing they have coming to them is death. Their stomach is their god. They brag about what they should be ashamed of. They think only about earthly things. 20 But we are citizens of heaven. And we can hardly wait for a Savior from there. He is the Lord Jesus Christ. 21 He has the power to bring everything under his control. By his power he will change our earthly bodies. They will become like his glorious body.

Remain Strong in the Lord

4 My brothers and sisters, in this way remain strong in the Lord. I love you and long for you. Dear friends, you are my joy and my crown.

2 Here is what I'm asking Euodia and Syntyche to do. I'm

asking them to work together in the Lord. That's because they both belong to the Lord. ³ My true companion, here is what I ask you to do. Help these women, because they have served at my side. They have worked with me to spread the good news. So have Clement and the rest of those who have worked together with me. Their names are all written in the book of life.

Final Commands

⁴ Always be joyful because you belong to the Lord. I will say it again. Be joyful! ⁵ Let everyone know how gentle you are. The Lord is coming soon. ⁶ Don't worry about anything. No matter what happens, tell God about everything. Ask and pray, and give thanks to him. ⁷ Then God's peace will watch over your hearts and your minds. He will do this because you belong to Christ Jesus. God's peace can never be completely understood.

⁸ Finally, my brothers and sisters, always think about what is true. Think about what is noble, right and pure. Think about what is lovely and worthy of respect. If anything is excellent or worthy of praise, think about those kinds of things. ⁹ Do what you have learned or received or heard from me. Follow my example. The God who gives peace will be with you.

Paul Gives Thanks for the Philippians' Gifts

¹⁰ At last you are concerned about me again. That makes me very happy. We belong to the Lord. I know that you were concerned. But you had no chance to show it. ¹¹ I'm not saying this because I need anything. I have learned to be content no matter what happens to me. ¹² I know what it's like not to have what I need. I also know what it's like to have more than I need. I have learned the secret of being content no matter what happens. I am content whether I am well fed or hungry. I am content whether I have more than enough or not enough. ¹³ I can do all this by the power of Christ. He gives me strength.

¹⁴ But it was good of you to share in my troubles. ¹⁵ And you believers at Philippi know what happened when I left Macedonia. Not one church helped me in the matter of giving and receiving. You were the only one that did. That was in the early days when you first heard the good news. ¹⁶ Even when I was in Thessalonica, you sent me help when I needed it. And you did it more than once. ¹⁷ It is not that I want your gifts. What I really want is what is best for you. ¹⁸ I have received my full pay and have more than enough. I have everything I need. That's because Epaphroditus brought me the gifts you sent. They are a sweet-smelling offering. They are a gift that God accepts. He is pleased with it. ¹⁹ My God will meet all your needs. He will meet them in keeping with his wonderful riches. These riches come to you because you belong to Christ Jesus.

²⁰ Give glory to our God and Father for ever and ever. Amen.

Final Greetings

²¹ Greet all God's people. They belong to Christ Jesus.

The brothers and sisters who are with me send greetings.

²² All God's people here send you greetings. Most of all, those who live in the palace of Caesar send you greetings.

²³ May the grace of the Lord Jesus Christ be with your spirit. Amen.

Colossians

Introduction:

Paul wrote this letter from a Roman prison. Paul wrote this letter because of false teachers at Colosse. They said Jesus was not really God. The false teachers followed special rules. They worshiped angels too.

Paul wrote the book of Colossians to tell people the truth. Paul taught that Jesus is God. Only Jesus can save us from our sins. We depend on him, not on human rules, to make us right with God.

Outline of contents:

1 I, Paul, am writing this letter. I am an apostle of Christ Jesus just as God planned. Our brother Timothy joins me in writing.

² We are sending this letter to you, our brothers and sisters in Colossae. You belong to Christ. You are holy and faithful.

May God our Father give you grace and peace.

Paul Prays and Gives Thanks

³ We always thank God, the Father of our Lord Jesus Christ, when we pray for you. ⁴ We thank him because we have heard about your faith in Christ Jesus. We have also heard that you love all God's people. ⁵ Your faith and love are based on the hope you have. What you hope for is stored up for you in heaven. You have already heard about it. You were told about it when the true message was given to you. I'm talking about the good news ⁶ that has come to you. In the same way, the good news is bearing fruit. It is bearing fruit and growing all over the world. It has been doing that among you since the day you heard it. That is when you really understood God's grace. ⁷ You learned the good news from Epaphras. He is dear to us. He serves Christ together with us. He faithfully works for Christ and for us among you. ⁸ He also told us about your love that comes from the Holy Spirit.

⁹ That's why we have not stopped praying for you. We have been praying for you since the day we heard about you. We keep asking God to fill you with the knowledge of what he wants. We pray he will give you

the wisdom and understanding that the Spirit gives. [10] Then you will be able to lead a life that is worthy of the Lord. We pray that you will please him in every way. So we want you to bear fruit in every good thing you do. We pray that you will grow to know God better. [11] We want you to be very strong, in keeping with his glorious power. We want you to be patient. We pray that you will never give up. [12] We want you to give thanks with joy to the Father. He has made you fit to have what he will give to all his holy people. You will all receive a share in the kingdom of light. [13] He has saved us from the kingdom of darkness. He has brought us into the kingdom of the Son he loves. [14] Because of what the Son has done, we have been set free. Because of him, all our sins have been forgiven.

The Son of God Is Better Than Everything Else

[15] The Son is the exact likeness of God, who can't be seen. The Son is first, and he is over all creation. [16] All things were created in him. He created everything in heaven and on earth. He created everything that can be seen and everything that can't be seen. He created kings, powers, rulers and authorities. All things have been created by him and for him. [17] Before anything was created, he was already there. He holds everything together. [18] And he is the head of the body, which is the church. He is the beginning. He is the

first to be raised from the dead. That happened so that he would be far above everything. [19] God was pleased to have his whole nature living in Christ. [20] God was pleased to bring all things back to himself. That's because of what Christ has done. These things include everything on earth and in heaven. God made peace through Christ's blood, by his death on the cross.

[21] At one time you were separated from God. You were enemies in your minds because of your evil ways. [22] But because Christ died, God has brought you back to himself. Christ's death has made you holy in God's sight. So now you don't have any flaw. You are free from blame. [23] But you must keep your faith steady and firm. You must not move away from the hope the good news holds out to you. This is the good news that you heard. It has been preached to every creature under heaven. I, Paul, now serve the good news.

Paul's Work for the Church

[24] I am happy because of what I am suffering for you. My suffering joins with and continues the sufferings of Christ. I suffer for his body, which is the church. [25] I serve the church. God appointed me to bring the complete word of God to you. [26] That word contains the mystery that has been hidden for many ages. But now it has been made known to the Lord's people. [27] God has chosen to make known to them the glorious

riches of that mystery. He has made it known among the Gentiles. And here is what it is. Christ is in you. He is your hope of glory.

²⁸ Christ is the one we preach about. With all the wisdom we have, we warn and teach everyone. When we bring them to God, we want them to be like Christ. We want them to be grown up as people who belong to Christ. ²⁹ That's what I'm working for. I work hard with all the strength of Christ. His strength works powerfully in me.

2 I want you to know how hard I am working for you. I'm concerned for those who are in Laodicea. I'm also concerned for everyone who has not met me in person. ² My goal is that their hearts may be encouraged and strengthened. I want them to be joined together in love. Then their understanding will be rich and complete. They will know the mystery of God. That mystery is Christ. ³ All the treasures of wisdom and knowledge are hidden in him. ⁴ But I don't want anyone to fool you with words that only sound good. ⁵ So even though I am away from you in body, I am with you in spirit. And I am glad to see that you are controlling yourselves. I am happy that your faith in Christ is so strong.

Having All Things in Christ

⁶ You received Christ Jesus as Lord. So keep on living your lives in him. ⁷ Have your roots in him. Build yourselves up in him. Grow strong in what you believe, just as you were taught. Be more thankful than ever before.

⁸ Make sure no one controls you. They will try to control you by using false reasoning that has no meaning. Their ideas depend on human teachings. They also depend on the basic spiritual powers of this world. They don't depend on Christ.

⁹ God's whole nature is living in Christ in human form. ¹⁰ Because you belong to Christ, you have been made complete. He is the ruler over every power and authority. ¹¹ When you received Christ, your circumcision was not done by human hands. Instead, your circumcision was done by Christ. He put away the person you used to be. At that time, sin's power ruled over you. ¹² When you were baptized, you were buried together with Christ. And you were raised to life together with him when you were baptized. You were raised to life by believing in God's work. God himself raised Jesus from the dead.

¹³ At one time you were dead in your sins. Your desires controlled by sin were not circumcised. But God gave you new life together with Christ. He forgave us all our sins. ¹⁴ He wiped out what the law said that we owed. The law stood against us. It judged us. But he has taken it away and nailed it to the cross. ¹⁵ He took away the weapons of the powers and authorities. He made a public show of them. He

won the battle over them by dying on the cross.

Freedom From Human Rules

¹⁶ So don't let anyone judge you because of what you eat or drink. Don't let anyone judge you about holy days. I'm talking about special feasts and New Moons and Sabbath days. ¹⁷ They are only a shadow of the things to come. But what is real is found in Christ. ¹⁸ Some people enjoy pretending they aren't proud. They worship angels. But don't let people like that judge you. These people tell you every little thing about what they have seen. They are proud of their useless ideas. That's because their minds are not guided by the Holy Spirit. ¹⁹ They aren't connected anymore to the head, who is Christ. But the whole body grows from the head. The muscles and tendons hold the body together. And God causes it to grow.

²⁰ Some people still follow the basic spiritual powers of the world. But you died with Christ as far as these powers are concerned. So why do you act as if you still belong to the world? Here are the rules you follow. ²¹ "Do not handle! Do not taste! Do not touch!" ²² Rules like these are about things that will pass away soon. They are based on merely human rules and teachings. ²³ It is true that these rules seem wise. Because of them, people give themselves over to their own kind of worship. They pretend they are humble. They treat their bodies very badly. But rules like these don't help. They don't stop people from chasing after sinful pleasures.

Teachings About Holy Living

3 You have been raised up with Christ. So think about things that are in heaven. That is where Christ is. He is sitting at God's right hand. ² Think about things that are in heaven. Don't think about things that are only on earth. ³ You died. Now your life is hidden with Christ in God. ⁴ Christ is your life. When he appears again, you also will appear with him in heaven's glory.

⁵ So put to death anything that comes from sinful desires. Get rid of sexual sins and impure acts. Don't let your feelings get out of control. Remove from your life all evil desires. Stop always wanting more and more. You might as well be worshiping statues of gods. ⁶ God's anger is going to come because of these things. ⁷ That's the way you lived at one time in your life. ⁸ But now here are the kinds of things you must also get rid of. You must get rid of anger, rage, hate and lies. Let no dirty words come out of your mouths. ⁹ Don't lie to one another. You have gotten rid of your old way of life and its habits. ¹⁰ You have started living a new life. Your knowledge of how that life should have the Creator's likeness is being made new. ¹¹ Here there is no Gentile or Jew. There is no difference between those who are circumcised and those who are not. There is no rude outsider, or even a Scythian.

There is no slave or free person. But Christ is everything. And he is in everything.

[12] You are God's chosen people. You are holy and dearly loved. So put on tender mercy and kindness as if they were your clothes. Don't be proud. Be gentle and patient. [13] Put up with one another. Forgive one another if you are holding something against someone. Forgive, just as the Lord forgave you. [14] And over all these good things put on love. Love holds them all together perfectly as if they were one.

[15] Let the peace that Christ gives rule in your hearts. As parts of one body, you were appointed to live in peace. And be thankful. [16] Let the message about Christ live among you like a rich treasure. Teach and correct one another wisely. Teach one another by singing psalms and hymns and songs from the Spirit. Sing to God with thanks in your hearts. [17] Do everything you say or do in the name of the Lord Jesus. Always give thanks to God the Father through Christ.

Teachings About Christian Families

[18] Wives, follow the lead of your husbands. That's what the Lord wants you to do.

[19] Husbands, love your wives. Don't be mean to them.

[20] Children, obey your parents in everything. That pleases the Lord.

[21] Fathers, don't make your children bitter. If you do, they will lose hope.

[22] Slaves, obey your earthly masters in everything. Don't do it just to please them when they are watching you. Obey them with an honest heart. Do it out of respect for the Lord. [23] Work at everything you do with all your heart. Work as if you were working for the Lord, not for human masters. [24] Work because you know that you will finally receive as a reward what the Lord wants you to have. You are slaves of the Lord Christ. [25] Anyone who does wrong will be paid back for what they do. God treats everyone the same.

4 Masters, give your slaves what is right and fair. Do it because you know that you also have a Master in heaven.

More Teachings

[2] Give a lot of time and effort to prayer. Always be watchful and thankful. [3] Pray for us too. Pray that God will give us an opportunity to preach our message. Then we can preach the mystery of Christ. Because I preached it, I am being held by chains. [4] Pray that I will preach it clearly, as I should. [5] Be wise in the way you act toward outsiders. Make the most of every opportunity. [6] Let the words you speak always be full of grace. Learn how to make your words what people want to hear. Then you will know how to answer everyone.

Final Greetings

[7] Tychicus will tell you all the news about me. He is a dear brother. He is a faithful worker.

He serves the Lord together with us. ⁸I am sending him to you for one reason. I want you to know what is happening here. I want him to encourage you and make your hearts strong. ⁹He is coming with Onesimus, our faithful and dear brother. He is one of you. They will tell you everything that is happening here.

¹⁰Aristarchus is in prison with me. He sends you his greetings. So does Mark, the cousin of Barnabas. You have been given directions about him. If he comes to you, welcome him. ¹¹Jesus, who is called Justus, also sends greetings. They are the only Jews who have worked together with me for God's kingdom. They have been a comfort to me. ¹²Epaphras sends greetings. He is one of you. He serves Christ Jesus. He is always praying hard for you. He prays that you will hold on tightly to all that God has in mind for us. He prays that you will keep growing in your knowledge of what God wants. He also prays that you will be completely sure about it. ¹³I am happy to tell you that he is working very hard for you. He is also working hard for everyone in Laodicea and Hierapolis. ¹⁴Our dear friend Luke, the doctor, sends greetings. So does Demas.

¹⁵Give my greetings to the brothers and sisters in Laodicea. Also give my greetings to Nympha and the church that meets in her house.

¹⁶After this letter has been read to you, send it on. Be sure that it is also read to the church in Laodicea. And be sure that you read the letter from Laodicea.

¹⁷Tell Archippus, "Be sure that you complete the work the Lord gave you to do."

¹⁸I, Paul, am writing this greeting with my own hand. Remember that I am being held by chains. May grace be with you.

1 Thessalonians

Introduction:

Paul started a church in Thessalonica on one of his missionary trips. Some Jews became angry at Paul's teaching. He had to leave after only a short time. He wrote this letter to cheer up the friends he left behind. He wanted to teach them more about Jesus.

The Christians in this city were treated badly. Paul said that they must not give up faith in Jesus. Paul also taught them that Jesus would come again sometime. When he comes back, all Christians will go to live with him. We must work hard until then.

Outline of contents:

1 I, Paul, am writing this letter. Silas and Timothy join me in writing.

We are sending this letter to you, the members of the church in Thessalonica. You belong to God the Father and the Lord Jesus Christ.

May grace and peace be given to you.

Paul Gives Thanks for the Thessalonians' Faith

² We always thank God for all of you. We keep on praying for you. ³ We remember you when we pray to our God and Father. Your work is produced by your faith. Your service is the result of your love. Your strength to continue comes from your hope in our Lord Jesus Christ.

⁴ Brothers and sisters, you are loved by God. We know that he has chosen you. ⁵ Our good news didn't come to you only in words. It came with power. It came with the Holy Spirit's help. He gave us complete faith in what we were preaching. You know how we lived among you for your good. ⁶ We and the Lord were your examples. You followed us. You welcomed our message even when you were suffering terribly. You welcomed it with the joy the Holy Spirit gives. ⁷ So you became a model to all the believers in the lands of Macedonia and Achaia. ⁸ The Lord's message rang out from you. That was true not only in Macedonia and Achaia. Your faith in God has also become known everywhere. So we don't have to say anything about it. ⁹ The believers themselves re-

The ABCs of Becoming a Christian

Becoming a Christian (someone who follows Jesus Christ) is simple. Just follow the ABCs! Find the verses listed by using the table of contents in the front of this Bible. You can read the verses and talk to God right now, right where you are. He is always happy to listen.

A – ADMIT

Admit honestly to God that you are a sinner and have not obeyed him.

Romans 3:23 • Romans 6:23 • 1 John 1:9

B – BELIEVE

Believe that Jesus Christ is God's Son and died on the cross and became alive again. He died for your sins so you can be forgiven.

1 Corinthians 15:3–4 • John 3:16 • Acts 4:12 • Romans 5:8

C – CONFESS

Confess your faith in Jesus. Tell someone you know (like a pastor, parent, or other Christian). Then celebrate! If you don't already attend a church, try to find one. It is important to help you grow in your new life in Christ.

Romans 10:9–10 • Romans 10:13

If you followed these ABCs and decided to follow Jesus, we would love to hear from you! Write to:

Zonderkidz Bible Editors
Zondervan
3900 Sparks Drive SE
Grand Rapids, MI 49546

Children from Every Nation
REVELATION 7:9–10

port the kind of welcome you gave us. They tell about how you turned away from statues of gods. And you turned to serve the living and true God. [10] They tell about how you are waiting for his Son to come from heaven. God raised him from the dead. He is Jesus. He saves us from God's anger, and his anger is sure to come.

Paul's Work for God in Thessalonica

2 Brothers and sisters, you know that our visit to you produced results. [2] You know what happened earlier in the city of Philippi. We suffered, and people treated us very badly there. But God gave us the boldness to tell you his good news. We preached to you even when people strongly opposed us. [3] The appeal we make is based on truth. It comes from a pure heart. We are not trying to trick you. [4] In fact, it is just the opposite. God has approved us to preach. He has trusted us with the good news. We aren't trying to please people. We want to please God. He tests our hearts. [5] As you know, we never praised you if we didn't mean it. We didn't put on a mask to cover up any sinful desire. God is our witness that this is true. [6] We were not expecting people to praise us. We were not looking for praise from you or anyone else. Yet as Christ's apostles, we could have used our authority over you. [7] Instead, we were like young children when we were with you.

As a mother feeds and cares for her little children, [8] we cared for you. We loved you so much. So we were happy to share with you God's good news. We were also happy to share our lives with you. [9] Brothers and sisters, I am sure you remember how hard we worked. We labored night and day while we preached to you God's good news. We didn't want to cause you any expense. [10] You are witnesses of how we lived among you believers. God is also a witness that we were holy and godly and without blame. [11] You know that we treated each of you as a father treats his own children. [12] We gave you hope and strength. We comforted you. We really wanted you to live in a way that is worthy of God. He chooses you to enter his glorious kingdom.

[13] We never stop thanking God for the way you received his word. You heard it from us. But you didn't accept it as a human word. You accepted it for what it really is. It is God's word. It is really at work in you who believe. [14] Brothers and sisters, you became like the members of God's churches in Judea. They are believers in Christ Jesus, just as you are. Your own people made you suffer. You went through the same things the church members in Judea suffered from the Jews. [15] The Jews who killed the Lord Jesus and the prophets also forced us to leave. They do not please God. They are enemies of everyone.

16 They try to keep us from speaking to the Gentiles. These Jews don't want the Gentiles to be saved. In this way, these Jews always increase their sins to the limit. God's anger has come on them at last.

Paul Wants to See the Believers in Thessalonica

17 Brothers and sisters, we were separated from you for a short time. Apart from you, we were like children without parents. We were no longer with you in person. But we kept you in our thoughts. We really wanted to see you. So we tried very hard to do so. 18 We wanted to come to you. Again and again I, Paul, wanted to come. But Satan blocked our way. 19 What is our hope? What is our joy? When our Lord Jesus returns, what is the crown we will delight in? Isn't it you? 20 Yes, you are our glory and our joy.

3 We couldn't wait any longer. So we thought it was best to be left by ourselves in Athens. 2 We sent our brother Timothy to give you strength and hope in your faith. He works together with us in God's service to spread the good news about Christ. 3 We sent him so that no one would be upset by times of testing. You know very well that we have to go through times of testing. 4 In fact, when we were with you, here is what we kept telling you. We were telling you that our enemies would make us suffer. As you know very well, it has turned out that way.

5 That's the reason I sent someone to find out about your faith. I couldn't wait any longer. I was afraid that Satan had tempted you in some way. Then our work among you would have been useless.

Timothy Brings a Good Report

6 But Timothy has come to us from you just now. He has brought good news about your faith and love. He has told us that you always have happy memories of us. He has also said that you desire to see us, just as we desire to see you. 7 Brothers and sisters, in all our trouble and suffering your faith encouraged us. 8 Now we really live, because you are standing firm in the Lord. 9 How can we thank God enough for you? We thank God because of all the joy we have in his presence. We have this joy because of you. 10 Night and day we pray very hard that we will see you again. We want to give you what is missing in your faith.

11 Now may a way be opened up for us to come to you. May our God and Father himself and our Lord Jesus do this. 12 May the Lord make your love grow. May it be like a rising flood. May your love for one another increase. May it also increase for everyone else. May it be just like our love for you. 13 May the Lord give you strength in your hearts. Then you will be holy and without blame in the sight of our God and Father. May that be true when our Lord Jesus comes with all his holy ones.

Living in a Way That Pleases God

4 Now I want to talk about some other matters, brothers and sisters. We taught you how to live in a way that pleases God. In fact, that is how you are living. In the name of the Lord Jesus we ask and beg you to do it more and more. ² You know the directions we gave you. They were given by the authority of the Lord Jesus.

³ God wants you to be made holy. He wants you to stay away from sexual sins. ⁴ He wants all of you to learn to control your own bodies. You must live in a way that is holy. You must live with honor. ⁵ Don't desire to commit sexual sins like people who don't know God. ⁶ None of you should sin against your brother or sister by doing that. You should not take advantage of your brother or sister. The Lord will punish everyone who commits these kinds of sins. We have already told you and warned you about this. ⁷ That's because God chose us to live pure lives. He wants us to be holy. ⁸ Suppose someone refuses to accept our teaching. They are not turning their back on us. They are turning their back on God. This same God gives you his Holy Spirit.

⁹ We don't need to write to you about your love for one another. God himself has taught you to love one another. ¹⁰ In fact, you do love all God's family all around Macedonia. Brothers and sisters, we are asking you to love one another more and more. ¹¹ And do everything you can to live a quiet life. You should mind your own business. And work with your hands, just as we told you to. ¹² Then unbelievers will have respect for your everyday life. And you won't have to depend on anyone.

What Happens to Believers Who Have Died

¹³ Brothers and sisters, we want you to know what happens to those who die. We don't want you to mourn, as other people do. They mourn because they don't have any hope. ¹⁴ We believe that Jesus died and rose again. When he returns, many who believe in him will have died already. We believe that God will bring them back with Jesus. ¹⁵ This agrees with what the Lord has said. When the Lord comes, many of us will still be alive. We tell you that we will certainly not go up before those who have died. ¹⁶ The Lord himself will come down from heaven. We will hear a loud command. We will hear the voice of the leader of the angels. We will hear a blast from God's trumpet. Many who believe in Christ will have died already. They will rise first. ¹⁷ After that, we who are still alive and are left will be caught up together with them. We will be taken up in the clouds. We will meet the Lord in the air. And we will be with him forever. ¹⁸ So encourage one another with these words of comfort.

The Day of the Lord Is Coming

5 Brothers and sisters, we don't have to write to you about times and dates. ² You know very well how the day of the Lord will come. It will come like a thief in the night. ³ People will be saying that everything is peaceful and safe. Then suddenly they will be destroyed. It will happen like birth pains coming on a pregnant woman. None of the people will escape.

⁴ Brothers and sisters, you are not in darkness. So that day should not surprise you as a thief would. ⁵ All of you are children of the light. You are children of the day. We don't belong to the night. We don't belong to the darkness. ⁶ So let us not be like the others. They are asleep. Instead, let us be wide awake and in full control of ourselves. ⁷ Those who sleep, sleep at night. Those who get drunk, get drunk at night. ⁸ But we belong to the day. So let us control ourselves. Let us put on our chest the armor of faith and love. Let us put on the hope of salvation like a helmet. ⁹ God didn't choose us to receive his anger. He chose us to receive salvation because of what our Lord Jesus Christ has done. ¹⁰ Jesus died for us. Some will be alive when he comes. Others will be dead. Either way, we will live together with him. ¹¹ So encourage one another with the hope you have. Build each other up. In fact, that's what you are doing.

Final Teachings

¹² Brothers and sisters, we ask you to accept the godly leaders who work hard among you. They care for you in the Lord. They correct you. ¹³ Have a lot of respect for them. Love them because of what they do. Live in peace with one another. ¹⁴ Brothers and sisters, we are asking you to warn certain people. These people don't want to work. Instead, they make trouble. We are also asking you to encourage those who have lost hope. Help those who are weak. Be patient with everyone. ¹⁵ Make sure that no one pays back one wrong act with another. Instead, always try to do what is good for each other and for everyone else.

¹⁶ Always be joyful. ¹⁷ Never stop praying. ¹⁸ Give thanks no matter what happens. God wants you to thank him because you believe in Christ Jesus.

¹⁹ Don't try to stop what the Holy Spirit is doing. ²⁰ Don't treat prophecies as if they weren't important. ²¹ But test all prophecies. Hold on to what is good. ²² Say no to every kind of evil.

²³ God is the God who gives peace. May he make you holy through and through. May your whole spirit, soul and body be kept free from blame. May you be without blame from now until our Lord Jesus Christ comes. ²⁴ The God who has chosen you is faithful. He will do all these things.

²⁵ Brothers and sisters, pray for us.

²⁶Greet all God's people with a holy kiss.

²⁷While the Lord is watching, here is what I command you.

Have this letter read to all the brothers and sisters.

²⁸May the grace of our Lord Jesus Christ be with you.

2 Thessalonians

Introduction:

Paul wrote this letter to the Thessalonians soon after he wrote the first one. They had not done what Paul wanted them to do. They thought Jesus was coming back very soon. They had stopped working and were just waiting for Jesus. Paul wrote to them again. He told them to keep working and not be lazy.

Paul told them about the second coming of Jesus. Paul called it "the day of the Lord." Paul told the people to work hard until Jesus came back.

Outline of contents:

1 I, Paul, am writing this letter. Silas and Timothy join me in writing.

We are sending this letter to you, the members of the church in Thessalonica. You belong to God our Father and the Lord Jesus Christ.

² May God the Father and the Lord Jesus Christ give you grace and peace.

Paul Prays and Gives Thanks

³ Brothers and sisters, we should always thank God for you. That is only right, because your faith is growing more and more. We also thank God that the love you all have for one another is increasing. ⁴ So among God's churches we brag about the fact that you don't give up easily. We brag about your faith in all the suffering and testing you are going through.

⁵ All of this proves that when God judges, he is fair. So you will be considered worthy to enter God's kingdom. You are suffering for his kingdom. ⁶ God is fair. He will pay back trouble to those who give you trouble. ⁷ He will help you who are troubled. And he will also help us. All these things will happen when the Lord Jesus appears from heaven. He will come in blazing fire. He will come with his powerful angels. ⁸ He will punish those who don't know God. He will punish those who don't obey the good news about our Lord Jesus. ⁹ They will be destroyed forever. They will be shut out of heaven. They will never see the glory of the Lord's strength. ¹⁰ All these things will happen when he comes. On that day his glory will be seen in his holy people. Everyone who has believed will be

amazed when they see him. This includes you, because you believed the witness we gave you.

¹¹ Keeping this in mind, we never stop praying for you. Our God has chosen you. We pray that he will make you worthy of his choice. We pray he will make every good thing you want to do come true. We pray that he will do this by his power. We pray that he will make perfect all that you have done by faith. ¹² We pray this so that the name of our Lord Jesus will receive glory through what you have done. We also pray that you will receive glory through what he has done. We pray all these things in keeping with the grace of our God and the Lord Jesus Christ.

The Man of Sin

2 Brothers and sisters, we want to ask you something. It has to do with the coming of our Lord Jesus Christ. It concerns the time when we will go to be with him. ² What if you receive a message that is supposed to have come from us? What if it says that the day of the Lord has already come? If it does, we ask you not to become easily upset or alarmed. Don't be upset whether that message is spoken or written or prophesied. ³ Don't let anyone trick you in any way. That day will not come until people rise up against God. It will not come until the man of sin appears. He is a marked man. He is headed

for ruin. ⁴ He will oppose everything that is called God. He will oppose everything that is worshiped. He will give himself power over everything. He will set himself up in God's temple. He will announce that he himself is God.

⁵ Don't you remember? When I was with you, I used to tell you these things. ⁶ Now you know what is holding back the man of sin. He is held back so that he can make his appearance at the right time. ⁷ The secret power of sin is already at work. But the one who now holds back that power will keep doing it until he is taken out of the way. ⁸ Then the man of sin will appear. The Lord Jesus will overthrow him with the breath of his mouth. The glorious brightness of Jesus' coming will destroy the man of sin. ⁹ The coming of the man of sin will fit how Satan works. The man of sin will show his power through all kinds of signs and wonders. These signs and wonders will lead people astray. ¹⁰ So people who are dying will be fooled by this evil. These people are dying because they refuse to love the truth. The truth would save them. ¹¹ So God will fool them completely. Then they will believe the lie. ¹² Many will not believe the truth. They will take pleasure in evil. They will be judged.

Remain Strong in the Faith

¹³ Brothers and sisters, we should always thank God for you. The Lord loves you. That's

because God chose you as the first to be saved. Salvation comes through the Holy Spirit's work. He makes people holy. It also comes through believing the truth. [14] He chose you to be saved by accepting the good news that we preach. And you will share in the glory of our Lord Jesus Christ.

[15] Brothers and sisters, remain strong in the faith. Hold on to what we taught you. We passed our teachings on to you by what we preached and wrote.

[16] Our Lord Jesus Christ and God our Father loved us. By his grace God gave us comfort that will last forever. The hope he gave us is good. May our Lord Jesus Christ and God our Father [17] comfort your hearts. May they make you strong in every good thing you do and say.

Paul Asks for Prayer

3 Now I want to talk about some other matters. Brothers and sisters, pray for us. Pray that the Lord's message will spread quickly. Pray that others will honor it just as you did. [2] And pray that we will be saved from sinful and evil people. Not everyone is a believer. [3] But the Lord is faithful. He will strengthen you. He will guard you from the evil one. [4] We trust in the Lord. So we are sure that you are doing the things we tell you to do. And we are sure that you will keep on doing them. [5] May the Lord fill your hearts with God's love. May Christ give you the strength to go on.

Paul Warns Those Who Do Not Want to Work

[6] Brothers and sisters, here is a command we give you. We give it in the name of the Lord Jesus Christ. Keep away from every believer who doesn't want to work and makes trouble. Keep away from any believer who doesn't live up to the teaching you received from us. [7] You know how you should follow our example. We worked when we were with you. [8] We didn't eat anyone's food without paying for it. In fact, it was just the opposite. We worked night and day. We worked very hard so that we wouldn't cause any expense to any of you. [9] We worked, even though we have the right to receive help from you. We did it in order to be a model for you to follow. [10] Even when we were with you, we gave you a rule. We said, "Anyone who won't work shouldn't be allowed to eat."

[11] We hear that some people among you don't want to work and are making trouble. They aren't really busy. Instead, they are bothering others. [12] We belong to the Lord Jesus Christ. So we strongly command people like that to settle down. They have to earn the food they eat. [13] Brothers and sisters, don't ever get tired of doing what is good.

[14] Keep an eye on anyone who doesn't obey the teachings in our letter. Don't have anything to do with that person. Then they will feel ashamed. [15] But don't think of them as an en-

emy. Instead, warn them as you would warn another believer.

Final Greetings

16 May the Lord who gives peace give you peace at all times and in every way. May the Lord be with all of you.

17 I, Paul, write this greeting in my own handwriting. That's how I prove that I am the author of all my letters. I always do it that way.

18 May the grace of our Lord Jesus Christ be with you all.

1 Timothy

Introduction:

Timothy was Paul's friend. He went on missionary trips with Paul. Paul gave Timothy the job of leading the church in Ephesus. Paul wrote this letter while Timothy was there.

Timothy was a young man. Being the church leader was an important job. Paul gave Timothy some advice for his work. He told Timothy how people in a church should act. Paul also wrote about the church leaders. He told how they should act too.

Outline of contents:

---

1 I, Paul, am writing this letter. I am an apostle of Christ Jesus, just as God our Savior commanded. Christ Jesus also commanded it. We have put our hope in him.

² Timothy, I am sending you this letter. You are my true son in the faith.

May God the Father and Christ Jesus our Lord give you grace, mercy and peace.

Paul Warns Timothy to Oppose False Teachers

³ Timothy, stay there in Ephesus. That is what I told you to do when I went into Macedonia. I want you to command certain people not to teach things that aren't true. ⁴ And command them not to spend their time on stories that are made up. They must not waste time on family histories that never end. These things only lead to fights about ideas. They don't help God's work move forward. His work is done by faith. ⁵ Love is the purpose of my command. Love comes from a pure heart. It comes from a good sense of what is right and wrong. It comes from faith that is honest and true. ⁶ Some have turned from these teachings. They would rather talk about things that have no meaning. ⁷ They want to be teachers of the law. And they are very sure about that law. But they don't know what they are talking about.

⁸ We know that the law is good if it is used properly. ⁹ We also know that the law isn't made for godly people. It is made for those who break the law. It is for those who refuse to obey. It is for ungodly and sinful people. It is for those who aren't holy and who don't believe. It is for those who kill their fathers or mothers. It is for murderers. ¹⁰ It is for those

who commit sexual sins. It is for those who commit homosexual acts. It is for people who buy and sell slaves. It is for liars. It is for people who tell lies in court. It is for those who are a witness to things that aren't true. And it is for anything else that is the opposite of true teaching. 11 True teaching agrees with the good news about the glory of the blessed God. He trusted me with that good news.

The Lord Pours Out His Grace on Paul

12 I am thankful to Christ Jesus our Lord. He has given me strength. I thank him that he considered me faithful. I thank him for appointing me to serve him. 13 I used to speak evil things against Jesus. I tried to hurt his followers. I really pushed them around. But God showed me mercy anyway. I did those things without knowing any better. I wasn't a believer. 14 Our Lord poured out more and more of his grace on me. Along with it came faith and love from Christ Jesus.

15 Here is a saying that you can trust. It should be accepted completely. Christ Jesus came into the world to save sinners. And I am the worst sinner of all. 16 But for that very reason, God showed me mercy. And I am the worst of sinners. He showed me mercy so that Christ Jesus could show that he is very patient. I was an example for those who would come to believe in him. Then they would receive eternal life. 17 The eternal King will never die. He can't be seen. He is the only God. Give him honor and glory for ever and ever. Amen.

Paul Commands Timothy

18 My son Timothy, I am giving you this command. It is in keeping with the prophecies once made about you. By remembering them, you can fight the battle well. 19 Then you will hold on to faith. You will hold on to a good sense of what is right and wrong. Some have not accepted this knowledge of right and wrong. So they have destroyed their faith. They are like a ship that has sunk. 20 Hymenaeus and Alexander are among them. I have handed them over to Satan. That will teach them not to speak evil things against God.

Teachings About Worship

2 First, I want you to pray for all people. Ask God to help and bless them. Give thanks for them. 2 Pray for kings. Pray for everyone who is in authority. Pray that we can live peaceful and quiet lives. And pray that we will be godly and holy. 3 This is good, and it pleases God our Savior. 4 He wants all people to be saved. He wants them to come to know the truth. 5 There is only one God. And there is only one go-between for God and human beings. He is the man Christ Jesus. 6 He gave himself to pay for the sins of all people. We have been told this message at just the right time.

[7] I was appointed to be a messenger and an apostle to preach the good news. I am telling the truth. I'm not lying. God appointed me to be a true and faithful teacher of the Gentiles.

[8] So I want the men in every place to pray. I want them to lift up holy hands. I don't want them to be angry when they pray. I don't want them to argue. [9] In the same way, I want the women to be careful how they dress. They should wear clothes that are right and proper. They shouldn't wear their hair in very fancy styles. They shouldn't wear gold or pearls. They shouldn't wear clothes that cost a lot of money. [10] Instead, they should put on good works as if good works were their clothes. This is proper for women who claim to worship God.

[11] When a woman is learning, she should be quiet. She should follow her leaders in every way. [12] I do not let women teach or take authority over a man. They must be quiet. [13] That's because Adam was made first. Then Eve was made. [14] Adam was not the one who was tricked. The woman was tricked and became a sinner. [15] Will women be saved by having children? Only if they keep on believing, loving, and leading a holy life in a proper way.

Rules for Choosing Leaders and Deacons

3 Here is a saying you can trust. If anyone wants to be a leader in the church, they want to do a good work for God and people. [2] A leader must be free from blame. He must be faithful to his wife. In anything he does, he must not go too far. He must control himself. He must be worthy of respect. He must welcome people into his home. He must be able to teach. [3] He must not get drunk. He must not push people around. He must be gentle. He must not be a person who likes to argue. He must not love money. [4] He must manage his own family well. He must make sure that his children obey him. And he must do this in a way that gains him respect. [5] Suppose someone doesn't know how to manage his own family. Then how can he take care of God's church? [6] The leader must not be a new believer. If he is, he might become proud. Then he would be judged just like the devil. [7] The leader must also be respected by those who are outside the church. Then he will not be put to shame. He will not fall into the devil's trap.

[8] In the same way, deacons must be worthy of respect. They must be honest and true. They must not drink too much wine. They must not try to get money by cheating people. [9] They must hold on to the deep truths of the faith. Even their own minds tell them to do that. [10] First they must be tested. Then let them serve as deacons if there is nothing against them.

[11] In the same way, the women must be worthy of respect. They must not say things that harm

others. In anything they do, they must not go too far. They must be worthy of trust in everything.

¹² A deacon must be faithful to his wife. He must manage his children and family well. ¹³ Those who have served well earn the full respect of others. They also become more sure of their faith in Christ Jesus.

Paul's Reasons for Giving Instructions to Timothy

¹⁴ I hope I can come to you soon. But now I am writing these instructions to you. ¹⁵ Then if I have to put off my visit, you will know how people should act in God's family. The family of God is the church of the living God. It is the pillar and foundation of the truth. ¹⁶ There is no doubt that true godliness comes from this great mystery.

Jesus came as a human
being.
The Holy Spirit proved that
he was the Son of God.
He was seen by angels.
He was preached among
the nations.
People in the world believed
in him.
He was taken up to heaven
in glory.

4 The Holy Spirit clearly says that in the last days some people will leave the faith. They will follow spirits that will fool them. They will believe things that demons will teach them. ² Teachings like those come from liars who pretend to be what they are not. Their sense of what is right and wrong has been destroyed. It's as though it has been burned with a hot iron. ³ They do not allow people to get married. They order them not to eat certain foods. But God created those foods. So people who believe and know the truth should receive them and give thanks for them. ⁴ Everything God created is good. You shouldn't turn anything down. Instead, you should thank God for it. ⁵ The word of God and prayer make it holy.

⁶ Point out these things to the brothers and sisters. Then you will serve Christ Jesus well. You will show that you've grown in the truths of the faith. You will show that you've been trained by the good teaching you've obeyed. ⁷ Don't have anything to do with godless stories and silly tales. Instead, train yourself to be godly. ⁸ Training the body has some value. But being godly has value in every way. It promises help for the life you are now living and the life to come. ⁹ This is the truth you can trust and accept completely. ¹⁰ This is why we work and try so hard. It's because we have put our hope in the living God. He is the Savior of all people. Most of all, he is the Savior of those who believe.

¹¹ Command and teach these things. ¹² Don't let anyone look down on you because you are young. Set an example for the believers in what you say and in how you live. Also set an example in how you love and in what

you believe. Show the believers how to be pure. ¹³ Until I come, spend your time reading Scripture out loud to one another. Spend your time preaching and teaching. ¹⁴ Don't fail to use the gift the Holy Spirit gave you. He gave it to you through a prophecy from God. It was given when the elders placed their hands on you.

¹⁵ Keep on doing these things. Give them your complete attention. Then everyone will see how you are coming along. ¹⁶ Be careful of how you live and what you believe. Never give up. Then you will save yourself and those who hear you.

Instructions About Widows, Elders and Slaves

5 Correct an older man in a way that shows respect. Make an appeal to him as if he were your father. Treat younger men as if they were your brothers. ² Treat older women as if they were your mothers. Treat younger women as if they were your sisters. Be completely pure in the way you treat them.

³ Take care of the widows who really need help. ⁴ But suppose a widow has children or grandchildren. They should first learn to put their faith into practice. They should care for their own family. In that way they will pay back their parents and grandparents. That pleases God. ⁵ A widow who really needs help and is left all alone puts her hope in God. Night and day she keeps on praying. Night and day she asks God for help. ⁶ But a widow who lives for pleasure is dead even while she is still living. ⁷ Give these instructions to the people. Then no one can be blamed. ⁸ Everyone should provide for their own relatives. Most of all, everyone should take care of their own family. If they don't, they have left the faith. They are worse than someone who doesn't believe.

⁹ No widow should be put on the list of widows unless she is more than 60 years old. She must also have been faithful to her husband. ¹⁰ She must be well known for the good things she does. That includes bringing up children. It includes inviting guests into her home. It includes washing the feet of the Lord's people. It includes helping those who are in trouble. A widow should spend her time doing all kinds of good things.

¹¹ Don't put younger widows on that kind of list. They might want pleasure more than they want Christ. Then they would want to get married again. ¹² If they do that, they will be judged. They have broken their first promise. ¹³ Besides, they get into the habit of having nothing to do. They go around from house to house. They waste their time. They also bother other people and say things that make no sense. They shouldn't say those things. ¹⁴ So here is the advice I give to younger widows. Get married. Have children. Take care of your own homes. Don't give the enemy the chance to

tell lies about you. [15] In fact, some have already turned away to follow Satan.

[16] Suppose a woman is a believer and takes care of widows. She should continue to help them. She shouldn't let the church pay the expenses. Then the church can help the widows who really need it.

[17] The elders who do the church's work well are worth twice as much honor. That is true in a special way of elders who preach and teach. [18] Scripture says, "Do not stop an ox from eating while it helps separate the grain from the straw." *(Deuteronomy 25:4)* Scripture also says, "Workers are worthy of their pay." *(Luke 10:7)* [19] Don't believe a charge against an elder unless two or three witnesses bring it. [20] But those elders who are sinning should be corrected in front of everyone. This will be a warning to the others. [21] I command you to follow these instructions. I command you in the sight of God and Christ Jesus and the chosen angels. Treat everyone the same. Don't favor one person over another.

[22] Don't be too quick to place your hands on others to set them apart to serve God. Don't take part in the sins of others. Keep yourself pure.

[23] Stop drinking only water. If your stomach is upset, drink a little wine. It can also help the other sicknesses you often have.

[24] The sins of some people are easy to see. They are already being judged. Others will be judged later. [25] In the same way, good works are easy to see. But even good works that are hard to see can't stay hidden forever.

6 All who are forced to serve as slaves should consider their masters worthy of full respect. Then people will not speak evil things against God's name and against what we teach. [2] Some slaves have masters who are believers. They shouldn't show their masters disrespect just because they are also believers. Instead, they should serve them even better. That's because their masters are loved by them as believers. These masters are committed to caring for their slaves.

People Who Teach Lies or Love Money

These are the things you are to teach. Try hard to get the believers to do them. [3] Suppose someone teaches something different than I have taught. Suppose that person doesn't agree with the true teaching of our Lord Jesus Christ. Suppose they don't agree with godly teaching. [4] Then that person is proud and doesn't understand anything. They like to argue more than they should. They can't agree about what words mean. All of this results in wanting what others have. It causes fighting, harmful talk, and evil distrust. [5] It stirs up trouble all the time among people whose minds are twisted by sin. The truth they once had has been taken away from them. They think they can get rich by being godly.

6 You gain a lot when you live a godly life. But you must be happy with what you have. 7 We didn't bring anything into the world. We can't take anything out of it. 8 If we have food and clothing, we will be happy with that. 9 People who want to get rich are tempted. They fall into a trap. They are tripped up by wanting many foolish and harmful things. Those who live like that are dragged down by what they do. They are destroyed and die. 10 Love for money causes all kinds of evil. Some people want to get rich. They have wandered away from the faith. They have wounded themselves with many sorrows.

Paul Gives a Final Command to Timothy

11 But you are a man of God. Run away from all these things. Try hard to do what is right and godly. Have faith, love and gentleness. Hold on to what you believe. 12 Fight the good fight along with all other believers. Take hold of eternal life. You were chosen for it when you openly told others what you believe. Many witnesses heard you. 13 God gives life to everything. Christ Jesus told the truth when he was a witness in front of Pontius Pilate. In the sight of God and Christ, I give you a command. 14 Obey it until our Lord Jesus Christ appears. Obey it completely. Then no one can find fault with it or you. 15 God will bring Jesus back at a time that pleases him. God is the blessed and only Ruler. He is the greatest King of all. He is the most powerful Lord of all. 16 God is the only one who can't die. He lives in light that no one can get close to. No one has seen him. No one can see him. Honor and power belong to him forever. Amen.

17 Command people who are rich in this world not to be proud. Tell them not to put their hope in riches. Wealth is so uncertain. Command those who are rich to put their hope in God. He richly provides us with everything to enjoy. 18 Command the rich to do what is good. Tell them to be rich in doing good things. They must give freely. They must be willing to share. 19 In this way, they will store up true riches for themselves. It will provide a firm basis for the next life. Then they will take hold of the life that really is life.

20 Timothy, guard what God has trusted you with. Turn away from godless chatter. Stay away from opposing ideas that are falsely called knowledge. 21 Some people believe them. By doing that they have turned away from the faith.

May God's grace be with you all.

2 Timothy

Introduction:

Paul wrote this second letter to Timothy. Paul was in prison in Rome again. He knew he was going to die soon. He wrote this letter to cheer Timothy up. Paul also wrote to give Timothy advice. Paul gave Timothy commands to help lead the church. He told Timothy to teach the truth. Paul wanted Timothy to be faithful to Jesus.

Outline of contents:

1 I, Paul, am writing this letter. I am an apostle of Christ Jesus just as God planned. He sent me to tell about the promise of life found in Christ Jesus.

² Timothy, I am sending you this letter. You are my dear son.

May God the Father and Christ Jesus our Lord give you grace, mercy and peace.

Paul Gives Thanks

³ I thank God, whom I serve as did our people of long ago. I serve God, knowing that what I have done is right. Night and day I thank God for you. Night and day I always remember you in my prayers. ⁴ I remember your tears. I long to see you so that I can be filled with joy. ⁵ I remember your honest and true faith. It was alive first in your grandmother Lois and in your mother Eunice. And I am certain that it is now alive in you also.

Paul Encourages Timothy to Be Faithful

⁶ This is why I remind you to help God's gift grow, just as a small spark grows into a fire. God put his gift in you when I placed my hands on you. ⁷ God gave us his Spirit. And the Spirit doesn't make us weak and fearful. Instead, the Spirit gives us power and love. He helps us control ourselves. ⁸ So don't be ashamed of the message about our Lord. And don't be ashamed of me, his prisoner. Instead, join with me as I suffer for the good news. God's power will help us do that. ⁹ God has saved us. He has chosen us to live a holy life. It wasn't because of anything we have done. It was because of his own purpose and grace. Through Christ Jesus, God gave us this grace even before time began. ¹⁰ It has now been made known through the coming of

our Savior, Christ Jesus. He has broken the power of death. Because of the good news, he has brought life out into the light. That life never dies. [11] I was appointed to announce the good news. I was appointed to be an apostle and a teacher. [12] That's why I'm suffering the way I am. But this gives me no reason to be ashamed. That's because I know who I have believed in. I am sure he is able to take care of what I have given him. I can trust him with it until the day he returns as judge.

[13] Follow what you heard from me as the pattern of true teaching. Follow it with faith and love because you belong to Christ Jesus. [14] Guard the truth of the good news that you were trusted with. Guard it with the help of the Holy Spirit who lives in us.

Examples of Faithful and Unfaithful People

[15] You know that all the believers in Asia Minor have deserted me. They include Phygelus and Hermogenes.

[16] May the Lord show mercy to all who live in the house of Onesiphorus. He often encouraged me. He was not ashamed that I was being held by chains. [17] In fact, it was just the opposite. When he was in Rome, he looked everywhere for me. At last he found me. [18] May Onesiphorus find mercy from the Lord on the day Jesus returns as judge! You know very well how many ways Onesiphorus helped me in Ephesus.

Paul Again Encourages Timothy to Be Faithful

2 My son, be strong in the grace that is yours in Christ Jesus. [2] You have heard me teach in front of many witnesses. Pass on to people you can trust the things you've heard me say. Then they will be able to teach others also. [3] Like a good soldier of Christ Jesus, join with me in suffering. [4] A soldier does not take part in things that don't have anything to do with the army. Instead, he tries to please his commanding officer. [5] It is the same for anyone who takes part in a sport. They don't receive the winner's crown unless they play by the rules. [6] The farmer who works hard should be the first to receive a share of the crops. [7] Think about what I'm saying. The Lord will help you understand what all of it means.

[8] Remember Jesus Christ. He came from David's family line. He was raised from the dead. That is my good news. [9] I am suffering for it. I have even been put in chains like someone who has committed a crime. But God's word is not held back by chains. [10] So I put up with everything for the good of God's chosen people. Then they also can be saved. Christ Jesus saves them. He gives them glory that will last forever.

[11] Here is a saying you can trust.

If we died with him,
    we will also live with him.
[12] If we don't give up,
    we will also rule with him.

If we say we don't know him, he will also say he doesn't know us. [13] Even if we are not faithful, he remains faithful. He must be true to himself.

What to Do About False Teachers

[14] Keep reminding God's people of these things. While God is watching, warn them not to argue about words. That doesn't have any value. It only destroys those who listen. [15] Do your best to please God. Be a worker who doesn't need to be ashamed. Teach the message of truth correctly. [16] Stay away from godless chatter. Those who take part in it will become more and more ungodly. [17] Their teaching will spread like a deadly sickness. Hymenaeus and Philetus are two of those teachers. [18] They have turned away from the truth. They say that the time when people will rise from the dead has already come. They destroy the faith of some people. [19] But God's solid foundation stands firm. Here is the message written on it. "The Lord knows who his own people are." *(Numbers 16:5)* Also, "All who say they believe in the Lord must turn away from evil."

[20] In a large house there are things made out of gold and silver. But there are also things made out of wood and clay. Some have special purposes. Others have common purposes. [21] Suppose someone stays away from what is common. Then the Master will be able to use them for special purposes. They will be made holy. They will be ready to do any good work.

[22] Run away from the evil things that young people long for. Try hard to do what is right. Have faith, love and peace. Do these things together with those who call on the Lord from a pure heart. [23] Don't have anything to do with arguing. It is dumb and foolish. You know it only leads to fights. [24] Anyone who serves the Lord must not be hard to get along with. Instead, they must be kind to everyone. They must be able to teach. The one who serves must not hold anything against anyone. [25] They must gently teach those who are against them. Maybe God will give a change of heart to those who are against you. That will lead them to know the truth. [26] Maybe they will come to their senses. Maybe they will escape the devil's trap. He has taken them as prisoners to do what he wanted.

3 Here is what I want you to know. There will be terrible times in the last days. [2] People will love themselves. They will love money. They will brag and be proud. They will tear others down. They will not obey their parents. They won't be thankful or holy. [3] They won't love others. They won't forgive others. They will tell lies about people. They will be out of control. They will be wild. They will hate what is good. [4] They will turn against their friends. They will act without thinking. They will think they are better than others. They will love what pleases them instead of loving God. [5] They will act as if they were serving God. But what they do will show that they have turned their backs on God's power. Have nothing to do with these people.

[6] They are the kind who trick their way into the homes of some women. These women are ready to believe anything. And they take control over these women. These women are loaded down with sins. They give in to all kinds of evil desires. [7] They are always learning. But they are never able to come to know the truth. [8] Jannes and Jambres opposed Moses. In the same way, the teachers I'm talking about oppose the truth. Their minds are twisted. As far as the faith is concerned, God doesn't accept them. [9] They won't get very far. Just like Jannes and Jambres, their foolish ways will be clear to everyone.

Paul Gives a Final Command to Timothy

[10] But you know all about my teaching. You know how I live and what I live for. You know about my faith and love. You know how patient I am. You know I haven't given up. [11] You know that I was treated badly. You know that I suffered greatly. You know what kinds of things happened to me in Antioch, Iconium and Lystra. You know how badly I have been treated.

But the Lord saved me from all my troubles. [12] In fact, everyone who wants to live a godly life in Christ Jesus will be treated badly. [13] Evil people and pretenders will go from bad to worse. They will fool others, and others will fool them. [14] But I want you to continue to follow what you have learned and are sure about. You know the people you learned it from. [15] You have known the Holy Scriptures ever since you were a little child. They are able to teach you how to be saved by believing in Christ Jesus. [16] God has breathed life into all Scripture. It is useful for teaching us what is true. It is useful for correcting our mistakes. It is useful for making our lives whole again. It is useful for training us to do what is right. [17] By using Scripture, the servant of God can be completely prepared to do every good thing.

4 I give you a command in the sight of God and Christ Jesus. Christ will judge the living and the dead. Because he and his kingdom are coming, here is the command I give you. [2] Preach the word. Be ready to serve God in good times and bad. Correct people's mistakes. Warn them. Encourage them with words of hope. Be very patient as you do these things. Teach them carefully. [3] The time will come when people won't put up with true teaching. Instead, they will try to satisfy their own desires. They will gather a large number of teach-

ers around them. The teachers will say what the people want to hear. [4] The people will turn their ears away from the truth. They will turn to stories that aren't true. [5] But I want you to keep your head no matter what happens. Don't give up when times are hard. Work to spread the good news. Do everything God has given you to do.

[6] I am already being poured out like a drink offering. The time when I will leave is near. [7] I have fought the good fight. I have finished the race. I have kept the faith. [8] Now there is a crown waiting for me. It is given to those who are right with God. The Lord, who judges fairly, will give it to me on the day he returns. He will not give it only to me. He will also give it to all those who are longing for him to return.

Personal Words

[9] Do your best to come to me quickly. [10] Demas has deserted me. He has gone to Thessalonica. He left me because he loved this world. Crescens has gone to Galatia. Titus has gone to Dalmatia. [11] Only Luke is with me. Get Mark and bring him with you. He helps me in my work for the Lord. [12] I sent Tychicus to Ephesus. [13] When you come, bring my coat. I left it with Carpus at Troas. Also bring my books. Most of all, bring the ones made out of animal skins.

[14] Remember Alexander, the one who works with metal. He did me a great deal of harm. The Lord will pay him back for what he has done. [15] You too should watch out for him. He strongly opposed our message.

[16] The first time I was put on trial, no one came to help me. Everyone deserted me. I hope they will be forgiven for it. [17] The Lord stood at my side. He gave me the strength to preach the whole message. Then all the Gentiles heard it. I was saved from the lion's mouth. [18] The Lord will save me from every evil attack. He will bring me safely to his heavenly kingdom. Give him glory for ever and ever. Amen.

Final Greetings

[19] Greet Priscilla and Aquila. Greet those who live in the house of Onesiphorus.

[20] Erastus stayed in Corinth. I left Trophimus sick in Miletus. [21] Do your best to get here before winter.

Eubulus greets you. So do Pudens, Linus, Claudia and all the brothers and sisters.

[22] May the Lord be with your spirit. May God's grace be with you all.

Titus

Introduction:

Paul wrote this letter to a man named Titus. Titus was Paul's friend and helper. The two of them visited the island of Crete. Paul had Titus stay there to be the leader of the church.

This letter is like the two letters Paul wrote to Timothy. Paul wanted Titus to know how to lead the church. He told Titus how the church should act. Paul also told Titus what a leader should do. He gave Titus some good advice.

Outline of contents:

1 I, Paul, am writing this letter. I serve God, and I am an apostle of Jesus Christ. God sent me to help his chosen people believe in Christ more and more. God sent me to help them understand even more the truth that leads to godly living. ² That belief and understanding lead to the hope of eternal life. Before time began, God promised to give that life. And he does not lie. ³ Now, at just the right time, he has made his promise clear. He did this through the preaching that he trusted me with. God our Savior has commanded all these things.

⁴ Titus, I am sending you this letter. You are my true son in the faith we share.

May God the Father and Christ Jesus our Savior give you grace and peace.

Choosing Elders Who Love What Is Good

⁵ I left you on the island of Crete. I did this because there were some things that hadn't been finished. I wanted you to put them in order. I also wanted you to appoint elders in every town. I told you how to do it. ⁶ An elder must be without blame. He must be faithful to his wife. His children must be believers. They must not give anyone a reason to say that they are wild and don't obey. ⁷ A church leader takes care of God's family. That's why he must be without blame. He must not look after only his own interests. He must not get angry easily. He must not get drunk. He must not push people around. He must not try to get money by cheating people. ⁸ Instead, a church leader must welcome people into his home.

He must love what is good. He must control his mind and feelings. He must do what is right. He must be holy. He must control the desires of his body. ⁹The message as it has been taught can be trusted. He must hold firmly to it. Then he will be able to use true teaching to comfort others and build them up. He will be able to prove that people who oppose it are wrong.

Warning People Who Fail to Do Good

¹⁰Many people refuse to obey God. All they do is talk about things that mean nothing. They try to fool others. No one does these things more than the circumcision group. ¹¹They must be stopped. They are making trouble for entire families. They do this by teaching things they shouldn't. They do these things to cheat people. ¹²One of Crete's own prophets has a saying. He says, "People from Crete are always liars. They are evil beasts. They don't want to work. They live only to eat." ¹³This saying is true. So give a strong warning to people who refuse to obey God. Then they will understand the faith correctly. ¹⁴Then they will pay no attention to Jewish stories that aren't true. They won't listen to the mere human commands of people who turn away from the truth. ¹⁵To people who are pure, all things are pure. But to those who have twisted minds and don't believe, nothing is pure. In fact, their minds and their sense of what is right

and wrong are twisted. ¹⁶They claim to know God. But their actions show they don't know him. They are hated by God. They refuse to obey him. They aren't fit to do anything good.

Doing Good Because of the Good News

2 But what you teach must agree with true teaching. ²Tell the older men that in anything they do, they must not go too far. They must be worthy of respect. They must control themselves. They must have true faith. They must love others. They must not give up.

³In the same way, teach the older women to lead a holy life. They must not tell lies about others. They must not let wine control them. Instead, they must teach what is good. ⁴Then they can advise the younger women to love their husbands and children. ⁵The younger women must control themselves and be pure. They must take good care of their homes. They must be kind. They must follow the lead of their husbands. Then no one will be able to speak evil things against God's word.

⁶In the same way, help the young men to control themselves. ⁷Do what is good. Set an example for them in everything. When you teach, be honest and serious. ⁸No one can question the truth. So teach what is true. Then those who oppose you will be ashamed. That's because they will have nothing bad to say about us.

⁹Teach slaves to obey their masters in everything they do. Tell them to try to please their masters. They must not talk back to them. ¹⁰They must not steal from them. Instead, they must show that they can be trusted completely. Then they will make the teaching about God our Savior appealing in every way.

¹¹God's grace has now appeared. By his grace, God offers to save all people. ¹²His grace teaches us to say no to godless ways and sinful desires. We must control ourselves. We must do what is right. We must lead godly lives in today's world. ¹³That's how we should live as we wait for the blessed hope God has given us. We are waiting for Jesus Christ to appear in his glory. He is our great God and Savior. ¹⁴He gave himself for us. By doing that, he set us free from all evil. He wanted to make us pure. He wanted us to be his very own people. He wanted us to desire to do what is good.

¹⁵These are the things you should teach. Encourage people and give them hope. Correct them with full authority. Don't let anyone look down on you.

Do What Is Good Because You Are Saved

3 Remind God's people to obey rulers and authorities. Remind them to be ready to do what is good. ²Tell them not to speak evil things against anyone. Remind them to live in peace. They must consider the needs of others. They must always be gentle toward everyone.

³At one time we too acted like fools. We didn't obey God. We were tricked. We were controlled by all kinds of desires and pleasures. We were full of evil. We wanted what belongs to others. People hated us, and we hated one another. ⁴But the kindness and love of God our Savior appeared. ⁵He saved us. It wasn't because of the good things we had done. It was because of his mercy. He saved us by washing away our sins. We were born again. The Holy Spirit gave us new life. ⁶God poured out the Spirit on us freely. That's because of what Jesus Christ our Savior has done. ⁷His grace made us right with God. So now we have received the hope of eternal life as God's children. ⁸You can trust this saying. These things are important. Treat them that way. Then those who trust in God will be careful to commit themselves to doing good. These things are excellent. They are for the good of everyone.

⁹But keep away from foolish disagreements. Don't argue about family histories. Don't make trouble. Don't fight about what the law teaches. Don't argue about things like that. It doesn't do any good. It doesn't help anyone. ¹⁰Warn anyone who tries to get believers to separate from one another. Warn that person more than once. After that, have nothing to do with them. ¹¹You can be sure that

people like this are twisted and sinful. Their own actions judge them.

Final Words

[12] I will send Artemas or Tychicus to you. Then do your best to come to me at Nicopolis. I've decided to spend the winter there. [13] Do everything you can to help Zenas the lawyer and Apollos. Send them on their way. See that they have everything they need.

[14] Our people must learn to commit themselves to doing what is good. Then they can provide for people when they are in great need. If they do that, their lives won't turn out to be useless.

[15] Everyone who is with me sends you greetings.

Greet those who love us in the faith.

May God's grace be with you all.

Philemon

Introduction:

Paul wrote this letter to a man named Philemon. Philemon was Paul's friend. He had a slave named Onesimus. Onesimus stole money from Philemon and ran away. Then he met Paul and became a Christian.

Paul told Onesimus to go home. Paul asked Philemon to forgive Onesimus. He asked Philemon to treat Onesimus like a brother and not like a slave. Paul said he would pay back Philemon for what Onesimus had stolen.

Outline of contents:

---

¹ I, Paul, am writing this letter. I am a prisoner because of Christ Jesus. Our brother Timothy joins me in writing.

Philemon, we are sending you this letter. You are our dear friend. You work together with us. ² We are also sending it to our sister Apphia and to Archippus. He is a soldier of Christ together with us. And we are sending it to the church that meets in your home.

³ May God our Father and the Lord Jesus Christ give you grace and peace.

Paul Prays and Gives Thanks

⁴ I always thank my God when I remember you in my prayers. ⁵ That's because I hear about your love for all God's people. I also hear about your faith in the Lord Jesus. ⁶ I pray that what we share by believing will help you understand even more. Then you will completely understand every good thing we share by believing in Christ. ⁷ Your love has given me great joy. It has encouraged me. My brother, you have renewed the hearts of the Lord's people.

Paul Makes an Appeal for Onesimus

⁸ Because of the authority Christ has given me, I could be bold. I could order you to do what you should do anyway. ⁹ But we love each other. And I would rather appeal to you on the basis of that love. I, Paul, am an old man. I am now also a prisoner because of Christ Jesus. ¹⁰ I am an old man, and I'm in prison. This is how I make my appeal to you for my son Onesimus. He became a

son to me while I was being held in chains. [11] Before that, he was useless to you. But now he has become useful to you and to me. [12] I'm sending Onesimus back to you. All my love for him goes with him. [13] I'm being held in chains because of the good news. So I would have liked to keep Onesimus with me. And he could take your place in helping me. [14] But I didn't want to do anything unless you agreed. Any favor you do must be done because you want to do it, not because you have to. [15] Onesimus was separated from you for a little while. Maybe that was so you could have him back forever. [16] You could have him back not as a slave. Instead, he would be better than a slave. He would be a dear brother. He is very dear to me but even more dear to you. He is dear to you not only as another human being. He is also dear to you as a brother in the Lord.

[17] Do you think of me as a believer who works together with you? Then welcome Onesimus as you would welcome me. [18] Has he done anything wrong to you? Does he owe you anything? Then charge it to me. [19] I'll pay it back. I, Paul, am writing this with my own hand. I won't even mention that you owe me your life. [20] My brother, we both belong to the Lord. So I wish I could receive some benefit from you. Renew my heart. We know that Christ is the one who really renews it. [21] I'm sure you will obey. So I'm writing to you. I know you will do even more than I ask.

[22] There is one more thing. Have a guest room ready for me. I hope I can return to all of you in answer to your prayers.

[23] Epaphras sends you greetings. Together with me, he is a prisoner because of Christ Jesus. [24] Mark, Aristarchus, Demas and Luke work together with me. They also send you greetings.

[25] May the grace of the Lord Jesus Christ be with your spirit.

Hebrews

Introduction:

The book of Hebrews was written to cheer up some Jewish Christians. They had been treated badly. Sometimes they were made fun of in front of others. Some even had their property taken away. Many of these Jewish Christians were scared. They thought about giving up their faith in Jesus. It was hard to be a Christian.

This book tells that believing in Jesus is good. Jesus is from God, and he is God. He is better than the angels. Jesus is better than Moses and Joshua. He is better than any priest. Jesus paid for our sin. Jesus is the only sacrifice for sin.

The book of Hebrews tells of many people who had faith in God. They are our examples. We must believe and trust God too. We must have faith even when it is not easy. We must have faith when people treat us badly.

Outline of contents:

God Speaks His Final Word Through His Son

1 In the past, God spoke to our people through the prophets. He spoke at many times. He spoke in different ways. ² But in these last days, he has spoken to us through his Son. He is the one whom God appointed to receive all things. God also made everything through him. ³ The Son is the shining brightness of God's glory. He is the exact likeness of God's being. He uses his powerful word to hold all things together. He provided the way for people to be made pure from sin. Then he sat down at the right hand of the King, the Majesty in heaven. ⁴ So he became higher than the angels. The name he received is more excellent than theirs.

The Son Is Greater Than the Angels

⁵ God never said to any of the angels,

"You are my Son.
    Today I have become your
        Father." *(Psalm 2:7)*

Or,

"I will be his Father.
And he will be my Son."

(2 Samuel 7:14; 1 Chronicles 17:13)

6 God's first and only Son is over all things. When God brings him into the world, he says,

"Let all God's angels worship him." *(Deuteronomy 32:43)*

7 Here is something else God says about the angels.

"God makes his angels to be like spirits.
He makes those who serve him to be like flashes of lightning." *(Psalm 104:4)*

8 But here is what he says about the Son.

"You are God. Your throne will last for ever and ever.
Your kingdom will be ruled by justice.
9 You have loved what is right and hated what is evil.
So your God has placed you above your companions.
He has filled you with joy by pouring the sacred oil on your head." *(Psalm 45:6,7)*

10 He also says,

"Lord, in the beginning you made the earth secure.
You placed it on its foundations.
The heavens are the work of your hands.
11 They will pass away. But you remain.
They will all wear out like a piece of clothing.

12 You will roll them up like a robe.
They will be changed as a person changes clothes.
But you remain the same.
Your years will never end." *(Psalm 102:25–27)*

13 God never said to an angel,

"Sit at my right hand until I put your enemies under your control." *(Psalm 110:1)*

14 All angels are spirits who serve. God sends them to serve those who will receive salvation.

A Warning to Pay Attention

2 So we must pay the most careful attention to what we have heard. Then we will not drift away from it. 2 Even the message God spoke through angels had to be obeyed. Every time people broke the Law, they were punished. Every time they didn't obey, they were punished. 3 Then how will we escape if we don't pay attention to God's great salvation? The Lord first announced this salvation. Those who heard him gave us the message about it. 4 God showed that this message is true by signs and wonders. He showed that it's true by different kinds of miracles. God also showed that this message is true by the gifts of the Holy Spirit. God gave them out as it pleased him.

Jesus Was Made Fully Human

5 God has not put angels in charge of the world that is going

to come. We are talking about that world. ⁶ There is a place where someone has spoken about this. He said,

> "What are human beings that you think about them?
> What is a son of man that you take care of him?
> ⁷ You made them a little lower than the angels.
> You placed on them a crown of glory and honor.
> ⁸   You have put everything under their control."
>
> *(Psalm 8:4–6)*

So God has put everything under his Son. Everything is under his control. We do not now see everything under his control. ⁹ But we do see Jesus already given a crown of glory and honor. He was made lower than the angels for a little while. He suffered death. By the grace of God, he tasted death for everyone. That is why he was given his crown.

¹⁰ God has made everything. He is now bringing his many sons and daughters to share in his glory. It is only right that Jesus is the one to lead them into their salvation. That's because God made him perfect by his sufferings. ¹¹ And Jesus, who makes people holy, and the people he makes holy belong to the same family. So Jesus is not ashamed to call them his brothers and sisters. ¹² He says,

> "I will announce your name to my brothers and sisters.

> I will sing your praises among those who worship you."
>
> *(Psalm 22:22)*

¹³ Again he says,

> "I will put my trust in him."
>
> *(Isaiah 8:17)*

And again he says,

> "Here I am. Here are the children God has given me."
>
> *(Isaiah 8:18)*

¹⁴ Those children have bodies made out of flesh and blood. So Jesus became human like them in order to die for them. By doing this, he could break the power of the devil. The devil is the one who rules over the kingdom of death. ¹⁵ Jesus could set people free who were afraid of death. All their lives they were held as slaves by that fear. ¹⁶ It is certainly Abraham's children that he helps. He doesn't help angels. ¹⁷ So he had to be made like people, fully human in every way. Then he could serve God as a kind and faithful high priest. And then he could pay for the sins of the people by dying for them. ¹⁸ He himself suffered when he was tempted. Now he is able to help others who are being tempted.

Jesus Is Greater Than Moses

3 Holy brothers and sisters, God chose you to be his people. So keep thinking about Jesus. We embrace him as our apostle and our high priest. ² Moses was faithful in everything he did in the house of God. In the same way, Jesus

was faithful to the God who appointed him. [3] The person who builds a house has greater honor than the house itself. In the same way, Jesus has been found worthy of greater honor than Moses. [4] Every house is built by someone. But God is the builder of everything. [5] "Moses was faithful as one who serves in the house of God." (Numbers 12:7) He was a witness to what God would say in days to come. [6] But Christ is faithful as the Son over the house of God. And we are his house if we hold tightly to what we are certain about. We must also hold tightly to the hope we boast in.

A Warning Against Unbelief

[7] The Holy Spirit says,

"Listen to his voice today.
[8]   If you hear it, don't be
      stubborn.
    You were stubborn when you
      opposed me.
    You did that when you
      were tested in the
      desert.
[9] There your people of long ago
      tested me.
    Yet for 40 years they saw
      what I did.
[10] That is why I was angry with
      them.
    I said, 'Their hearts are
      always going astray.
    They have not known my
      ways.'
[11] So when I was angry, I made
      a promise.
    I said, 'They will never
      enjoy the rest I planned
      for them.'" (Psalm 95:7-11)

[12] Brothers and sisters, make sure that none of you has a sinful heart. Do not let an unbelieving heart turn you away from the living God. [13] But build one another up every day. Do it as long as there is still time. Then none of you will become stubborn. You won't be fooled by sin's tricks. [14] We belong to Christ if we hold tightly to the faith we had at first. But we must hold it tightly until the end. [15] It has just been said,

"Listen to his voice today.
    If you hear it, don't be
      stubborn.
    You were stubborn when
      you opposed me."
                          (Psalm 95:7,8)

[16] Who were those who heard and refused to obey? Weren't they all the people Moses led out of Egypt? [17] Who was God angry with for 40 years? Wasn't it with those who sinned? They died in the desert. [18] God promised that those people would never enjoy the rest he planned for them. God gave his word when he made that promise. Didn't he make that promise to those who didn't obey? [19] So we see that they weren't able to enter. That's because they didn't believe.

God's People Enter His Sabbath Rest

4 God's promise of enjoying his rest still stands. So be careful that none of you fails to receive it. [2] The good news was announced to our people of long

ago. It has also been preached to us. The message they heard didn't have any value for them. That's because they didn't share the faith of those who obeyed. ³ Now we who have believed enjoy that rest. God said,

"When I was angry, I made a promise.
I said, 'They will never enjoy the rest I planned for them.'" *(Psalm 95:11)*

Ever since God created the world, his works have been finished. ⁴ Somewhere he spoke about the seventh day. He said, "On the seventh day God rested from all his works." *(Genesis 2:2)* ⁵ In the part of Scripture I talked about earlier God spoke. He said, "They will never enjoy the rest I planned for them." *(Psalm 95:11)* ⁶ It is still true that some people will enjoy this rest. But those who had the good news announced to them earlier didn't go in. That's because they didn't obey. ⁷ So God again chose a certain day. He named it Today. He did this when he spoke through David a long time later. Here is what was written in the Scripture already given.

"Listen to his voice today.
If you hear it, don't be stubborn." *(Psalm 95:7,8)*

⁸ Suppose Joshua had given them rest. If he had, God would not have spoken later about another day. ⁹ So there is still a Sabbath rest for God's people. ¹⁰ God rested from his work. Those who enjoy God's rest also rest from their works. ¹¹ So let us make every effort to enjoy that rest. Then no one will die by disobeying as they did.

¹² The word of God is alive and active. It is sharper than any sword that has two edges. It cuts deep enough to separate soul from spirit. It can separate bones from joints. It judges the thoughts and purposes of the heart. ¹³ Nothing God created is hidden from him. His eyes see everything. He will hold us responsible for everything we do.

Jesus Is the Great High Priest

¹⁴ We have a great high priest. He has gone up into heaven. He is Jesus the Son of God. So let us hold firmly to what we say we believe. ¹⁵ We have a high priest who can feel it when we are weak and hurting. We have a high priest who has been tempted in every way, just as we are. But he did not sin. ¹⁶ So let us boldly approach God's throne of grace. Then we will receive mercy. We will find grace to help us when we need it.

5 Every high priest is chosen from among the people. He is appointed to act for the people. He acts for them in whatever has to do with God. He offers gifts and sacrifices for their sins. ² Some people have gone astray without knowing it. He is able to deal gently with them. He can do that because he himself is weak. ³ That's why he has to offer sacrifices for his own sins. He must also do it for

the sins of the people. ⁴ And no one can take this honor for himself. Instead, he receives it when he is appointed by God. That is just how it was for Aaron.

⁵ It was the same for Christ. He did not take for himself the glory of becoming a high priest. But God said to him,

"You are my Son.
　Today I have become your
　　Father." *(Psalm 2:7)*

⁶ In another place God said,

"You are a priest forever,
　just like Melchizedek."
　　　　(Psalm 110:4)

⁷ Jesus prayed while he lived on earth. He made his appeal with sincere cries and tears. He prayed to the God who could save him from death. God answered Jesus because he truly honored God. ⁸ Jesus was God's Son. But by suffering he learned what it means to obey. ⁹ In this way he was made perfect. Eternal salvation comes from him. He saves all those who obey him. ¹⁰ God appointed him to be the high priest, just like Melchizedek.

A Warning Against Falling Away

¹¹ We have a lot to say about this. But it is hard to make it clear to you. That's because you are no longer trying to understand. ¹² By this time you should be teachers. But in fact, you need someone to teach you all over again. You need even the simple truths of God's word.

You need milk, not solid food. ¹³ Anyone who lives on milk is still a baby. That person does not want to learn about living a godly life. ¹⁴ Solid food is for those who are grown up. They have trained themselves to tell the difference between good and evil. That shows they have grown up.

6 So let us move beyond the simple teachings about Christ. Let us grow up as believers. Let us not start all over again with the basic teachings. They taught us that we need to turn away from doing things that lead to death. They taught us that we must have faith in God. ² These basic teachings taught us about different ways of becoming "clean." They taught us about placing hands of blessing on people. They taught us that people will rise from the dead. They taught us that God will judge everyone. And they taught us that what he decides will last forever. ³ If God permits, we will go beyond those teachings and grow up.

⁴ What if some people fall away from the faith? It won't be possible to bring them back. It is true that they have seen the light. They have tasted the heavenly gift. They have shared in the Holy Spirit. ⁵ They have tasted the good things of God's word. They have tasted the powers of the age to come. ⁶ But they have fallen away from the faith. So it won't be possible to bring them back. They won't be able to turn away from their sins. They

are losing everything. That's because they are nailing the Son of God to the cross all over again. They are bringing shame on him in front of everyone. ⁷ Some land drinks the rain that falls on it. It produces a crop that is useful to those who farm the land. That land receives God's blessing. ⁸ But other land produces only thorns and weeds. That land isn't worth anything. It is in danger of coming under God's curse. In the end, it will be burned.

⁹ Dear friends, we have to say these things. But we are sure of better things in your case. We are talking about the things that have to do with being saved. ¹⁰ God is fair. He will not forget what you have done. He will remember the love you have shown him. You showed it when you helped his people. And you show it when you keep on helping them. ¹¹ We want each of you to be faithful to the very end. If you are, then what you hope for will fully happen. ¹² We don't want you to slow down. Instead, be like those who have faith and are patient. They will receive what God promised.

God Keeps His Promise

¹³ When God made his promise to Abraham, God gave his word. There was no one greater than himself to promise by. So he promised by making an appeal to himself. ¹⁴ He said, "I will certainly bless you. I will give you many children." *(Genesis 22:17)* ¹⁵ Abraham was patient while he waited. Then he received what God promised him.

¹⁶ People promise things by someone greater than themselves. Giving your word makes a promise certain. It puts an end to all arguing. ¹⁷ So God gave his word when he made his promise. He wanted to make it very clear that his purpose does not change. He wanted those who would receive what was promised to know this. ¹⁸ When God made his promise, he gave his word. He did this so we would have good reason not to give up. Instead, we have run to take hold of the hope set before us. This hope is set before us in God's promise. So God made his promise and gave his word. These two things can't change. He couldn't lie about them. ¹⁹ Our hope is certain. It is something for the soul to hold on to. It is strong and secure. It goes all the way into the Most Holy Room behind the curtain. ²⁰ That is where Jesus has gone. He went there to open the way ahead of us. He has become a high priest forever, just like Melchizedek.

Melchizedek the Priest

7 Melchizedek was the king of Salem. He was the priest of God Most High. He met Abraham, who was returning from winning a battle over some kings. Melchizedek blessed him. ² Abraham gave him a tenth of everything. First, the name Melchizedek means "king of what is right." Also, "king of

Salem" means "king of peace." ³Melchizedek has no father or mother. He has no family line. His days have no beginning. His life has no end. He remains a priest forever. In this way, he is like the Son of God.

⁴Think how great Melchizedek was! Even our father Abraham gave him a tenth of what he had captured. ⁵Now the law lays down a rule for the sons of Levi who become priests. They must collect a tenth from the people. They must collect it from the other Israelites. They must do this, even though all of them belong to the family line of Abraham. ⁶Melchizedek did not trace his family line from Levi. But he collected a tenth from Abraham. Melchizedek blessed the one who had received the promises. ⁷Without a doubt, the more important person blesses the less important one. ⁸In the one case, the tenth is collected by people who die. But in the other case, it is collected by the one who is said to be living. ⁹Levi collects the tenth. But we might say that Levi paid the tenth through Abraham. ¹⁰That's because when Melchizedek met Abraham, Levi was still in Abraham's body.

Jesus Is Like Melchizedek

¹¹The law that was given to the people called for the priestly system. That system began with Levi. Suppose the priestly system could have made people perfect. Then why was there still a need for another priest to come? And why did he need to be like Melchizedek? Why wasn't he from Aaron's family line? ¹²A change of the priestly system requires a change of law. ¹³We are talking about a priest who is from a different tribe. No one from that tribe has ever served at the altar. ¹⁴It is clear that our Lord came from the family line of Judah. Moses said nothing about priests who were from the tribe of Judah. ¹⁵But suppose another priest like Melchizedek appears. Then what we have said is even more clear. ¹⁶He has not become a priest because of a rule about his family line. He has become a priest because of his powerful life. His life can never be destroyed. ¹⁷Scripture says,

"You are a priest forever,
    just like Melchizedek."
(Psalm 110:4)

¹⁸The old rule is set aside. It was weak and useless. ¹⁹The law didn't make anything perfect. Now a better hope has been given to us. That hope brings us near to God.

²⁰The change of priestly system was made with a promise. Others became priests without any promise. ²¹But Jesus became a priest with a promise. God said to him,

"The Lord has given his word
    and made a promise.
He will not change his
    mind. He has said,
'You are a priest forever.'"
(Psalm 110:4)

²²Because God gave his word, Jesus makes certain the promise of a better covenant.

²³There were many priests in Levi's family line. Death kept them from continuing in office. ²⁴But Jesus lives forever. So he always holds the office of priest. ²⁵People now come to God through him. And he is able to save them completely and for all time. Jesus lives forever. He prays for them.

²⁶A high priest like that really meets our need. He is holy, pure and without blame. He isn't like other people. He does not sin. He is lifted high above the heavens. ²⁷He isn't like the other high priests. They need to offer sacrifices day after day. First they bring offerings for their own sins. Then they do it for the sins of the people. But Jesus gave one sacrifice for the sins of the people. He gave it once and for all time. He did it by offering himself. ²⁸The law appoints as high priests men who are weak. But God's promise came after the law. By his promise the Son was appointed. The Son has been made perfect forever.

The High Priest of a New Covenant

8 Here is the main point of what we are saying. We have a high priest like that. He sat down at the right hand of the throne of the King, the Majesty in heaven. ²He serves in the sacred tent. The Lord set up the true holy tent. A mere human being did not set it up.

³Every high priest is appointed to offer gifts and sacrifices. So this priest also had to have something to offer. ⁴What if he were on earth? Then he would not be a priest. There are already priests who offer the gifts required by the law. ⁵They serve at a sacred tent. But it is only a copy and shadow of what is in heaven. That's why God warned Moses when he was about to build the holy tent. God said, "Be sure to make everything just like the pattern I showed you on the mountain." *(Exodus 25:40)* ⁶But Jesus has been given a greater work to do for God. He is the go-between for the new covenant. This covenant is better than the old one. The new covenant is based on better promises.

⁷Suppose nothing had been wrong with that first covenant. Then no one would have looked for another covenant. ⁸But God found fault with the people. He said,

"The days are coming,
    announces the Lord.
I will make a new covenant
  with the people of Israel.
I will also make it with the
    people of Judah.
⁹It will not be like the
    covenant
I made with their people of
    long ago.
That was when I took them
    by the hand.
I led them out of Egypt.
My new covenant will be
    different because they
    didn't remain faithful to
    my old covenant.

So I turned away from
them,
announces the Lord.
¹⁰ This is the covenant I will
establish with the people
of Israel
after that time, says the
Lord.
I will put my laws in their
minds.
I will write them on their
hearts.
I will be their God.
And they will be my
people.
¹¹ People will not teach their
neighbor anymore.
They will not say to one
another, 'Know the
Lord.'
That's because everyone will
know me.
From the least important
to the most important,
all of them will know me.
¹² I will forgive their evil ways.
I will not remember
their sins anymore."

(Jeremiah 31:31–34)

¹³ God called this covenant
"new." So he has done away
with the first one. And what is
out of date and has been done
away with will soon disappear.

Worship in the Holy Tent on Earth

9 The first covenant had rules
for worship. It also had a sacred tent on earth. ² A holy tent
was set up. The lampstand was
in the first room. So was the table with its holy bread. That was
called the Holy Room. ³ Behind
the second curtain was a room
called the Most Holy Room. ⁴ It
had the golden altar for incense.
It also had the wooden chest
called the ark of the covenant.
The ark was covered with gold.
It held the gold jar of manna. It
held Aaron's walking stick that
had budded. It also held the
stone tablets. The words of the
covenant were written on them.
⁵ The cherubim were above the
ark. God showed his glory there.
The cherubim spread their
wings over the place where sin
was paid for. But we can't say
everything about these things
now.

⁶ That's how everything was
arranged in the holy tent. The
priests entered it at regular
times. They went into the outer
room to do their work for God
and others. ⁷ But only the high
priest went into the inner room.
He went in only once a year. He
never entered without taking
blood with him. He offered the
blood for himself. He also offered it for the sins the people
had committed because they
didn't know any better. ⁸ Here is
what the Holy Spirit was showing us. He was telling us that
God had not yet clearly shown
the way into the Most Holy
Room. It would not be clearly
shown as long as the first holy
tent was still being used. ⁹ That's
an example for the present
time. It shows us that the gifts
and sacrifices people offered
were not enough. They were
not able to remove the worshiper's feelings of guilt. ¹⁰ They deal
only with food and drink and

different kinds of special washings. They are rules people had to obey only until the new covenant came.

The Blood of Christ

[11] But Christ came to be the high priest of the good things already here now. When he came, he went through the greater and more perfect holy tent. This tent was not made with human hands. In other words, it is not a part of this creation. [12] He did not enter by spilling the blood of goats and calves. He entered the Most Holy Room by spilling his own blood. He did it once and for all time. In this way, he paid the price to set us free from sin forever. [13] The blood of goats and bulls is sprinkled on people. So are the ashes of a young cow. They are sprinkled on people the law called "unclean." The people are sprinkled to make them holy. That makes them "clean" on the outside. [14] But Christ offered himself to God without any flaw. He did this through the power of the eternal Holy Spirit. So how much cleaner will the blood of Christ make us! It washes away our feelings of guilt for committing sin. Sin always leads to death. But now we can serve the living God.

[15] That's why Christ is the go-between of a new covenant. Now those God calls to himself will receive the eternal gift he promised. They will receive it now that Christ has died to save them. He died to set them free from the sins they committed under the first covenant.

[16] What happens when someone leaves a will? It is necessary to prove that the person who made the will has died. [17] A will is in effect only when somebody has died. It never takes effect while the one who made it is still living. [18] That's why even the first covenant was not put into effect without the spilling of blood. [19] Moses first announced every command of the law to all the people. Then he took the blood of calves. He also took water, bright red wool and branches of a hyssop plant. He sprinkled the Book of the Covenant. He also sprinkled all the people. [20] He said, "This is the blood of the covenant God has commanded you to keep." (Exodus 24:8) [21] In the same way, he sprinkled the holy tent with blood. He also sprinkled everything that was used in worship there. [22] In fact, the law requires that nearly everything be made "clean" with blood. Without the spilling of blood, no one can be forgiven.

[23] So the copies of the heavenly things had to be made pure with these sacrifices. But the heavenly things themselves had to be made pure with better sacrifices. [24] Christ did not enter a sacred tent made with human hands. That tent was only a copy of the true one. He entered heaven itself. He did it to stand in front of God for us. He is there right now. [25] The high priest enters the Most

Holy Room every year. He enters with blood that is not his own. But Christ did not enter heaven to offer himself again and again. 26 If he had, he would have had to suffer many times since the world was created. But he has appeared once and for all time. He has come at the time when God's work is being completed. He has come to do away with sin by offering himself. 27 People have to die once. After that, God will judge them. 28 In the same way, Christ was offered up once. He took away the sins of many people. He will also come a second time. At that time he will not suffer for sin. Instead, he will come to bring salvation to those who are waiting for him.

Christ's Sacrifice Is Once and for All Time

10 The law is only a shadow of the good things that are coming. It is not the real things themselves. The same sacrifices have to be offered over and over again. They must be offered year after year. That's why the law can never make perfect those who come near to worship. 2 If the law could, wouldn't the sacrifices have stopped being offered? The worshipers would have been made "clean" once and for all time. They would not have felt guilty for their sins anymore. 3 But those offerings remind people of their sins every year. 4 It isn't possible for the blood of bulls and goats to take away sins.

5 So when Christ came into the world, he said,

"You didn't want sacrifices
   and offerings.
Instead, you prepared a
   body for me.
6 You weren't pleased
   with burnt offerings and
   sin offerings.
7 Then I said, 'Here I am. It is
   written about me in the
   book.
I have come to do what
   you want, my God.' "

(Psalm 40:6–8)

8 First Christ said, "You didn't want sacrifices and offerings. You didn't want burnt offerings and sin offerings. You weren't pleased with them." He said this even though they were offered in keeping with the law. 9 Then he said, "Here I am. I have come to do what you want." He did away with the shadow of the good things that were coming. He did it to put in place the good things themselves. 10 We have been made holy by what God wanted. We have been made holy because Jesus Christ offered his body once and for all time.

11 Day after day every priest stands and does his special duties. He offers the same sacrifices again and again. But they can never take away sins. 12 Jesus our priest offered one sacrifice for sins for all time. Then he sat down at the right hand of God. 13 And since that time, he waits for his enemies to be put under his control. 14 By

that one sacrifice he has made perfect forever those who are being made holy.

¹⁵ The Holy Spirit also speaks to us about this. First he says,

¹⁶ "This is the covenant I will
make with them
after that time, says the
Lord.
I will put my laws in their
hearts.
I will write my laws on
their minds." *(Jeremiah 31:33)*

¹⁷ Then he adds,

"I will not remember their
sins anymore.
I will not remember the
evil things they have
done." *(Jeremiah 31:34)*

¹⁸ Where these sins have been forgiven, an offering for sin is no longer necessary.

An Appeal and Warning to Remain Faithful

¹⁹ Brothers and sisters, we are not afraid to enter the Most Holy Room. We enter boldly because of the blood of Jesus. ²⁰ His way is new because he lives. It has been opened for us through the curtain. I'm talking about his body. ²¹ We also have a great priest over the house of God. ²² So let us come near to God with a sincere heart. Let us come near boldly because of our faith. Our hearts have been sprinkled. Our minds have been cleansed from a sense of guilt. Our bodies have been washed with pure water. ²³ Let us hold firmly to the hope we claim to have. The God who promised is faithful. ²⁴ Let us consider how we can stir up one another to love. Let us help one another to do good works. ²⁵ And let us not give up meeting together. Some are in the habit of doing this. Instead, let us encourage one another with words of hope. Let us do this even more as you see Christ's return approaching.

²⁶ What if we keep sinning on purpose? What if we do it even after we know the truth? Then there is no offering for our sins. ²⁷ All we can do is to wait in fear for God to judge. His blazing fire will burn up his enemies. ²⁸ Suppose someone did not obey the law of Moses. And suppose two or three witnesses made charges against them. That person would die without mercy. ²⁹ People who deserve even more punishment include those who have hated the Son of God. They include people who have said no to him. They include people who have treated as unholy the blood of the covenant that makes them holy. They also include people who have disrespected the Holy Spirit who brings God's grace. Don't you think people like this should be punished more than anyone else? ³⁰ We know the God who said, "I am the God who judges people. I will pay them back." *(Deuteronomy 32:35)* Scripture also says, "The Lord will judge his people." *(Deuteronomy 32:36; Psalm 135:14)* ³¹ It is a terrible thing to fall into the hands of the living God.

³² Remember those earlier

days after you received the light. You remained strong in a great battle that was full of suffering. ³³ Sometimes people spoke badly about you in front of others. Sometimes you were treated badly. At other times you stood side by side with people being treated like this. ³⁴ You suffered along with people in prison. When your property was taken from you, you accepted it with joy. You knew that God had given you better and more lasting things. ³⁵ So don't throw away your bold faith. It will bring you rich rewards.

³⁶ You need to be faithful. Then you will do what God wants. You will receive what he has promised.

³⁷ "In just a little while,
　he who is coming will
　　come.
　He will not wait any
　　longer."

³⁸ And,

"The one who is right with
　God will live by faith.
And I am not pleased with
　the one who pulls back."

(Habakkuk 2:3,4)

³⁹ But we don't belong to the people who pull back and are destroyed. We belong to the people who believe and are saved.

Faith That Produces Action

11 Faith is being sure of what we hope for. It is being sure of what we do not see. ² That is what the people of long ago were praised for.

³ We have faith. So we understand that everything was made when God commanded it. That's why we believe that what we see was not made out of what could be seen.

⁴ Abel had faith. So he brought to God a better offering than Cain did. Because of his faith Abel was praised as a godly man. God said good things about his offerings. Because of his faith Abel still speaks. He speaks even though he is dead.

⁵ Enoch had faith. So he was taken from this life. He didn't die. "He couldn't be found, because God had taken him away." (Genesis 5:24) Before God took him, Enoch was praised as one who pleased God. ⁶ Without faith it is impossible to please God. Those who come to God must believe that he exists. And they must believe that he rewards those who look to him.

⁷ Noah had faith. So he built an ark to save his family. He built it because of his great respect for God. God had warned him about things that could not yet be seen. Because of his faith Noah showed the world that it was guilty. Because of his faith he was considered right with God.

⁸ Abraham had faith. So he obeyed God. God called him to go to a place he would later receive as his own. So he went. He did it even though he didn't know where he was going. ⁹ Because of his faith he made his home in the land God had promised him. Abraham was

like an outsider in a strange country. He lived there in tents. So did Isaac and Jacob. They received the same promise he did. ¹⁰ Abraham was looking forward to the city that has foundations. He was waiting for the city that God planned and built. ¹¹ And Sarah had faith. So God made it possible for her to become a mother. She became a mother even though she was too old to have children. But Sarah believed that the God who made the promise was faithful. ¹² Abraham was past the time when he could have children. But many children came from that one man. They were as many as the stars in the sky. They were as many as the grains of sand on the seashore. No one could count them.

¹³ All these people were still living by faith when they died. They didn't receive the things God had promised. They only saw them and welcomed them from a long way off. They openly said that they were outsiders and strangers on earth. ¹⁴ People who say things like that show that they are looking for a country of their own. ¹⁵ What if they had been thinking of the country they had left? Then they could have returned to it. ¹⁶ Instead, they longed for a better country. They wanted a heavenly one. So God is pleased when they call him their God. In fact, he has prepared a city for them.

¹⁷ Abraham had faith. So when God tested him, Abraham offered Isaac as a sac-

rifice. Abraham had held on tightly to the promises. But he was about to offer his one and only son. ¹⁸ God had said to him, "Your family line will continue through Isaac." *(Genesis 21:12)* Even so, Abraham was going to offer him up. ¹⁹ Abraham did this, because he believed that God could even raise the dead. In a way, he did receive Isaac back from death.

²⁰ Isaac had faith. So he blessed Jacob and Esau. He told them what was ahead for them.

²¹ Jacob had faith. So he blessed each of Joseph's sons. He blessed them when he was dying. Because of his faith he worshiped God. Jacob worshiped as he leaned on the top of his walking stick.

²² Joseph had faith. So he spoke to the people of Israel about how they would leave Egypt someday. When his death was near, he spoke about where to bury his bones.

²³ Moses' parents had faith. So they hid him for three months after he was born. They saw he was a special child. They were not afraid of the king's command.

²⁴ Moses had faith. So he refused to be called the son of Pharaoh's daughter. That happened after he had grown up. ²⁵ He chose to be treated badly together with the people of God. He chose not to enjoy sin's pleasures. They only last for a short time. ²⁶ He suffered shame because of Christ. He thought it had great value. Moses consid-

ered it better than the riches of Egypt. He was looking ahead to his reward. ²⁷ Because of his faith, Moses left Egypt. It wasn't because he was afraid of the king's anger. He didn't let anything stop him. That's because he saw the God who can't be seen. ²⁸ Because of his faith, Moses was the first to keep the Passover Feast. He commanded the people of Israel to sprinkle blood on their doorways. He did it so that the destroying angel would not touch their oldest sons.

²⁹ The people of Israel had faith. So they passed through the Red Sea. They went through it as if it were dry land. The Egyptians tried to do it also. But they drowned.

³⁰ Israel's army had faith. So the walls of Jericho fell down. It happened after they had marched around the city for seven days.

³¹ Rahab, the prostitute, had faith. So she welcomed the spies. That's why she wasn't killed with those who didn't obey God.

³² What more can I say? I don't have time to tell about all the others. I don't have time to talk about Gideon, Barak, Samson and Jephthah. I don't have time to tell about David and Samuel and the prophets. ³³ Because of their faith they took over kingdoms. They ruled fairly. They received the blessings God had promised. They shut the mouths of lions. ³⁴ They put out great fires. They escaped being killed by swords. Their weakness was turned to strength. They became powerful in battle. They beat back armies from other countries. ³⁵ Women received back their dead. The dead were raised to life again. There were others who were made to suffer greatly. But they refused to be set free. They did this so that after death they would be raised to an even better life. ³⁶ Some were made fun of and even whipped. Some were held by chains. Some were put in prison. ³⁷ Some were killed with stones. Some were sawed in two. Some were killed by swords. They went around wearing the skins of sheep and goats. They were poor. They were attacked. They were treated badly. ³⁸ The world was not worthy of them. They wandered in deserts and mountains. They lived in caves. They lived in holes in the ground.

³⁹ All these people were praised because they had faith. But none of them received what God had promised. ⁴⁰ That's because God had planned something better for us. So they would only be made perfect together with us.

12 A huge cloud of witnesses is all around us. So let us throw off everything that stands in our way. Let us throw off any sin that holds on to us so tightly. And let us keep on running the race marked out for us. ² Let us keep looking to Jesus. He is the one who started this journey of faith. And he is the one who completes the journey of faith. He paid no attention to

the shame of the cross. He suffered there because of the joy he was looking forward to. Then he sat down at the right hand of the throne of God. ³He made it through these attacks by sinners. So think about him. Then you won't get tired. You won't lose hope.

God Trains His Children

⁴You struggle against sin. But you have not yet fought to the point of spilling your blood. ⁵Have you completely forgotten this word of hope? It speaks to you as a father to his children. It says,

"My son, think of the Lord's
    training as important.
Do not lose hope when he
    corrects you.
⁶The Lord trains the one he
    loves.
He corrects everyone he
    accepts as his son."
(Proverbs 3:11,12)

⁷Put up with hard times. God uses them to train you. He is treating you as his children. What children are not trained by their parents? ⁸God trains all his children. But what if he doesn't train you? Then you are not really his children. You are not God's true sons and daughters at all. ⁹Besides, we have all had human fathers who trained us. We respected them for it. How much more should we be trained by the Father of spirits and live! ¹⁰Our parents trained us for a little while. They did what they thought was best. But God trains us for our good. He does this so we may share in his holiness. ¹¹No training seems pleasant at the time. In fact, it seems painful. But later on it produces a harvest of godliness and peace. It does this for those who have been trained by it.

¹²So put your hands to work. Strengthen your legs for the journey. ¹³"Make level paths for your feet to walk on." *(Proverbs 4:26)* Then those who have trouble walking won't be disabled. Instead, they will be healed.

A Warning and an Appeal

¹⁴Try your best to live in peace with everyone. Try hard to be holy. Without holiness no one will see the Lord. ¹⁵Be sure that no one misses out on God's grace. See to it that a bitter plant doesn't grow up. If it does, it will cause trouble. And it will make many people impure. ¹⁶See to it that no one commits sexual sins. See to it that no one is godless like Esau. He sold the rights to what he would receive as the oldest son. He sold them for a single meal. ¹⁷As you know, after that he wanted to receive his father's blessing. But he was turned away. With tears he tried to get the blessing. But he couldn't change what he had done.

The Mountain of Fear and the Mountain of Joy

¹⁸You haven't come to a mountain that can be touched. You haven't come to a mountain burning with fire. You haven't come to darkness, gloom and

storm. [19] You haven't come to a blast from God's trumpet. You haven't come to a voice speaking to you. When people heard that voice long ago, they begged it not to say anything more to them. [20] What God commanded was too much for them. He said, "If even an animal touches the mountain, it must be killed with stones." *(Exodus 19:12,13)* [21] The sight was terrifying. Moses said, "I am trembling with fear." *(Deuteronomy 9:19)*

[22] But you have come to Mount Zion. You have come to the city of the living God. This is the heavenly Jerusalem. You have come to a joyful gathering of angels. There are thousands and thousands of them. [23] You have come to the church of God's people. God's first and only Son is over all things. God's people share in what belongs to his Son. Their names are written in heaven. You have come to God, who is the Judge of all people. You have come to the spirits of godly people who have been made perfect. [24] You have come to Jesus. He is the go-between of a new covenant. You have come to the sprinkled blood. It promises better things than the blood of Abel.

[25] Be sure that you don't say no to the one who speaks. People did not escape when they said no to the one who warned them on earth. And what if we turn away from the one who warns us from heaven? How much less will we escape! [26] At that time his voice shook the earth. But now he has promised, "Once more I will shake the earth. I will also shake the heavens." *(Haggai 2:6)* [27] The words "once more" point out that what can be shaken can be taken away. I'm talking about created things. Then what can't be shaken will remain.

[28] We are receiving a kingdom that can't be shaken. So let us be thankful. Then we can worship God in a way that pleases him. Let us worship him with deep respect and wonder. [29] Our "God is like a fire that burns everything up." *(Deuteronomy 4:24)*

Final Appeals

13 Keep on loving one another as brothers and sisters. [2] Don't forget to welcome outsiders. By doing that, some people have welcomed angels without knowing it. [3] Keep on remembering those in prison. Do this as if you were together with them in prison. And remember those who are treated badly as if you yourselves were suffering.

[4] All of you should honor marriage. You should keep the marriage bed pure. God will judge the person who commits adultery. He will judge everyone who commits sexual sins. [5] Don't be controlled by love for money. Be happy with what you have. God has said,

"I will never leave you.
    I will never desert you."
       (Deuteronomy 31:6)

[6] So we can say boldly,

"The Lord helps me. I will not
    be afraid.

What can mere human beings do to me?"

(Psalm 118:6,7)

⁷ Remember your leaders. They spoke God's word to you. Think about the results of their way of life. Copy their faith. ⁸ Jesus Christ is the same yesterday and today and forever.

⁹ Don't let all kinds of strange teachings lead you astray. It is good that God's grace makes our hearts strong. Don't try to grow strong by eating foods that the law requires. They have no value for the people who eat them. ¹⁰ The priests, who are Levites, worship at the holy tent. But we have an altar that they have no right to eat from.

¹¹ The high priest carries the blood of animals into the Most Holy Room. He brings their blood as a sin offering. But the bodies are burned outside the camp. ¹² Jesus also suffered outside the city gate. He suffered to make the people holy by spilling his own blood. ¹³ So let us go to him outside the camp. Let us be willing to suffer the shame he suffered. ¹⁴ Here we do not have a city that lasts. But we are looking for the city that is going to come. ¹⁵ So let us never stop offering to God our praise through Jesus. Let us talk openly about our faith in him. Then our words will be like an offering to God. ¹⁶ Don't forget to do good. Don't forget to share with others. God is pleased with those kinds of offerings.

¹⁷ Trust in your leaders. Put yourselves under their authority. Do this, because they keep watch over you. They know they are accountable to God for everything they do. Do this, so that their work will be a joy. If you make their work a heavy load, it won't do you any good.

¹⁸ Pray for us. We feel sure we have done what is right. We desire to live as we should in every way. ¹⁹ I beg you to pray that I may return to you soon.

Final Blessing and Greetings

²⁰ Our Lord Jesus is the great Shepherd of the sheep. The God who gives peace brought him back from the dead. He did it because of the blood of the eternal covenant. Now may God ²¹ supply you with everything good. Then you can do what he wants. May he do in us what is pleasing to him. We can do it only with the help of Jesus Christ. Give him glory for ever and ever. Amen.

²² Brothers and sisters, I beg you to accept my word. It tells you to be faithful. Accept my word because I have written to you only a short letter.

²³ I want you to know that our brother Timothy has been set free. If he arrives soon, I will come with him to see you.

²⁴ Greet all your leaders. Greet all the Lord's people.

The believers from Italy send you their greetings.

²⁵ May grace be with you all.

James

Introduction:

James wrote this letter. James was Jesus' brother. Jesus' brothers did not believe in him before he died. They became Christians after he rose from the dead. James lived in Jerusalem. He was a church leader there.

James taught people how to live as Christians. He said we show real faith in how we act. If we only talk like Christians our faith is no good. We must live like Christians too. James wanted us to love rich people and poor people the same. He wanted us to watch what we say. James did not want people to be proud. He wanted us to be patient, even in hard times.

Outline of contents:

Facing all kinds of trouble (1:1–18)
True faith in practice (1:19—3:12)
True wisdom in practice (3:13—5:12)
The prayer of faith (5:13–20)

---

1 I, James, am writing this letter. I serve God and the Lord Jesus Christ.

I am sending this letter to you, the 12 tribes scattered among the nations.

Greetings.

Facing All Kinds of Trouble

2 My brothers and sisters, you will face all kinds of trouble. When you do, think of it as pure joy. 3 Your faith will be tested. You know that when this happens it will produce in you the strength to continue. 4 And you must allow this strength to finish its work. Then you will be all you should be. You will have everything you need. 5 If any of you needs wisdom, you should ask God for it. He will give it to you. God gives freely to everyone and doesn't find fault. 6 But when you ask, you must believe. You must not doubt. That's because a person who doubts is like a wave of the sea. The wind blows and tosses them around. 7 They shouldn't expect to receive anything from the Lord. 8 This kind of person can't make up their mind. They can never decide what to do.

9 Here's what believers who are in low positions in life should be proud of. They should be proud that God has given them a high position in the kingdom. 10 But rich people should take pride in their low positions. That's because they will fade away like wild flowers. 11 The sun rises. Its burning heat dries up the plants. Their

blossoms fall. Their beauty is destroyed. In the same way, rich people will fade away. They fade away even as they go about their business.

¹² Blessed is the person who keeps on going when times are hard. After they have come through hard times, this person will receive a crown. The crown is life itself. The Lord has promised it to those who love him.

¹³ When a person is tempted, they shouldn't say, "God is tempting me." God can't be tempted by evil. And he doesn't tempt anyone. ¹⁴ But each person is tempted by their own evil desires. These desires lead them on and drag them away. ¹⁵ When these desires are allowed to remain, they lead to sin. And when sin is allowed to remain and grow, it leads to death.

¹⁶ My dear brothers and sisters, don't let anyone fool you. ¹⁷ Every good and perfect gift is from God. This kind of gift comes down from the Father who created the heavenly lights. These lights create shadows that move. But the Father does not change like these shadows. ¹⁸ God chose to give us new birth through the message of truth. He wanted us to be the first harvest of his new creation.

Listen to the Word and Do What It Says

¹⁹ My dear brothers and sisters, pay attention to what I say. Everyone should be quick to listen. But they should be slow to speak. They should be slow to get angry. ²⁰ Human anger doesn't produce the holy life God wants. ²¹ So get rid of everything that is sinful. Get rid of the evil that is all around us. Don't be too proud to accept the word that is planted in you. It can save you.

²² Don't just listen to the word. You fool yourselves if you do that. You must do what it says. ²³ Suppose someone listens to the word but doesn't do what it says. Then they are like a person who looks at their face in a mirror. ²⁴ After looking at themselves, they leave. And right away they forget what they look like. ²⁵ But suppose someone takes a good look at the perfect law that gives freedom. And they keep looking at it. Suppose they don't forget what they've heard, but they do what the law says. Then this person will be blessed in what they do.

²⁶ Suppose people think their beliefs and how they live are both right. But they don't control what they say. Then they are fooling themselves. Their beliefs and way of life are not worth anything at all. ²⁷ Here are the beliefs and way of life that God our Father accepts as pure and without fault. When widows are in trouble, take care of them. Do the same for children who have no parents. And don't let the world make you impure.

Treat Everyone the Same

2 My brothers and sisters, you are believers in our glorious Lord Jesus Christ. So treat everyone the same. ²Suppose a man comes into your meeting wearing a gold ring and fine clothes. And suppose a poor man in dirty old clothes also comes in. ³Would you show special attention to the man wearing fine clothes? Would you say, "Here's a good seat for you"? Would you say to the poor man, "You stand there"? Or "Sit on the floor by my feet"? ⁴If you would, aren't you treating some people better than others? Aren't you like judges who have evil thoughts?

⁵My dear brothers and sisters, listen to me. Hasn't God chosen those who are poor in the world's eyes to be rich in faith? Hasn't he chosen them to receive the kingdom? Hasn't he promised it to those who love him? ⁶But you have disrespected poor people. Aren't rich people taking advantage of you? Aren't they dragging you into court? ⁷Aren't they speaking evil things against the worthy name of Jesus? Remember, you belong to him.

⁸The royal law is found in Scripture. It says, "Love your neighbor as you love yourself." (*Leviticus 19:18*) If you really keep this law, you are doing what is right. ⁹But you sin if you don't treat everyone the same. The law judges you because you have broken it. ¹⁰Suppose you keep the whole law but trip over just one part of it. Then you are guilty of breaking all of it. ¹¹God said, "Do not commit adultery." (*Exodus 20:14; Deuteronomy 5:18*) He also said, "Do not commit murder." (*Exodus 20:13; Deuteronomy 5:17*) Suppose you don't commit adultery but do commit murder. Then you have broken the law.

¹²Speak and act like people who are going to be judged by the law that gives freedom. ¹³Those who have not shown mercy will not receive mercy when they are judged. To show mercy is better than to judge.

Show Your Faith by What You Do

¹⁴Suppose a person claims to have faith but doesn't act on their faith. My brothers and sisters, can this kind of faith save them? ¹⁵Suppose a brother or a sister has no clothes or food. ¹⁶Suppose one of you says to them, "Go. I hope everything turns out fine for you. Keep warm. Eat well." And suppose you do nothing about what they really need. Then what good have you done? ¹⁷It is the same with faith. If it doesn't cause us to do something, it's dead.

¹⁸But someone will say, "You have faith. I do good deeds."

Show me your faith that doesn't cause you to do good deeds. And I will show you my faith by the goods deeds I do. ¹⁹You believe there is one God. Good! Even the demons believe that. And they tremble!

²⁰You foolish person! Do you want proof that faith without good deeds is useless? ²¹Our father Abraham offered his son Isaac on the altar. Wasn't he considered to be right with God because of what he did? ²²So you see that what he believed

and what he did were working together. What he did made his faith complete. ²³ That is what Scripture means where it says, "Abraham believed God. God accepted Abraham because he believed. So his faith made him right with God." *(Genesis 15:6)* And that's not all. God called Abraham his friend. ²⁴ So you see that a person is considered right with God by what they do. It doesn't happen only because they believe.

²⁵ Didn't God consider even Rahab the prostitute to be right with him? That's because of what she did for the spies. She gave them a place to stay. Then she sent them off in a different direction. ²⁶ A person's body without their spirit is dead. In the same way, faith without good deeds is dead.

Control What You Say

3 My brothers and sisters, most of you shouldn't become teachers. That's because you know that those of us who teach will be held more accountable. ² All of us get tripped up in many ways. Suppose someone is never wrong in what they say. Then they are perfect. They are able to keep their whole body under control.

³ We put a small piece of metal in the mouth of a horse to make it obey us. We can control the whole animal with it. ⁴ And how about ships? They are very big. They are driven along by strong winds. But they are steered by a very small rudder. It makes them go where the captain wants to go. ⁵ In the same way, the tongue is a small part of a person's body. But it talks big. Think about how a small spark can set a big forest on fire. ⁶ The tongue is also a fire. The tongue is the most evil part of the body. It makes the whole body impure. It sets a person's whole way of life on fire. And the tongue itself is set on fire by hell.

⁷ People have tamed all kinds of wild animals, birds, reptiles and sea creatures. And they still tame them. ⁸ But no one can tame the tongue. It is an evil thing that never rests. It is full of deadly poison.

⁹ With our tongues we praise our Lord and Father. With our tongues we curse people. We do it even though people have been created to be like God. ¹⁰ Praise and cursing come out of the same mouth. My brothers and sisters, it shouldn't be this way. ¹¹ Can fresh water and salt water flow out of the same spring? ¹² My brothers and sisters, can a fig tree produce olives? Can a grapevine produce figs? Of course not. And a saltwater spring can't produce fresh water either.

Two Kinds of Wisdom

¹³ Is anyone among you wise and understanding? That person should show it by living a good life. A wise person isn't proud when they do good deeds. ¹⁴ But suppose your hearts are jealous and bitter. Suppose you are concerned only about get-

ting ahead. Then don't brag about it. And don't say no to the truth. [15] Wisdom like this doesn't come down from heaven. It belongs to the earth. It doesn't come from the Holy Spirit. It comes from the devil. [16] Are you jealous? Are you concerned only about getting ahead? Then your life will be a mess. You will be doing all kinds of evil things.

[17] But the wisdom that comes from heaven is pure. That's the most important thing about it. And that's not all. It also loves peace. It thinks about others. It obeys. It is full of mercy and good fruit. It is fair. It doesn't pretend to be what it is not. [18] Those who make peace plant it like a seed. They will harvest a crop of right living.

Obey God

4 Why do you fight and argue among yourselves? Isn't it because of your sinful desires? They fight within you. [2] You want something, but you don't have it. So you kill. You want what others have, but you can't get what you want. So you argue and fight. You don't have what you want, because you don't ask God. [3] When you do ask for something, you don't receive it. That's because you ask for the wrong reason. You want to spend your money on your sinful pleasures.

[4] You are not faithful to God. Don't you know that to be a friend of the world is to hate God? So anyone who chooses to be the world's friend becomes God's enemy. [5] Don't you know what Scripture says? God wants the spirit in us to belong only to him. God caused this spirit to live in us. Don't you think Scripture has a reason for saying this? [6] But God continues to give us more grace. That's why Scripture says,

"God opposes those who are
    proud.
But he gives grace to
    those who are humble."
(Proverbs 3:34)

[7] So obey God. Stand up to the devil. He will run away from you. [8] Come near to God, and he will come near to you. Wash your hands, you sinners. Make your hearts pure, you who can't make up your minds. [9] Be full of sorrow. Cry and weep. Change your laughter to mourning. Change your joy to sadness. [10] Be humble in front of the Lord. And he will lift you up.

[11] My brothers and sisters, don't speak against one another. Anyone who speaks against a brother or sister speaks against the law. And anyone who judges another believer judges the law. When you judge the law, you are not keeping it. Instead, you are acting as if you were its judge. [12] There is only one Lawgiver and Judge. He is the God who is able to save life or destroy it. But who are you to judge your neighbor?

Bragging About Tomorrow

[13] Now listen, you who say, "Today or tomorrow we will go

to this or that city. We will spend a year there. We will buy and sell and make money." ¹⁴ You don't even know what will happen tomorrow. What is your life? It is a mist that appears for a little while. Then it disappears. ¹⁵ Instead, you should say, "If it pleases the Lord, we will live and do this or that." ¹⁶ As it is, you brag. You brag about the evil plans your pride produces. This kind of bragging is evil. ¹⁷ So suppose someone knows the good deeds they should do. But suppose they don't do them. By not doing these good deeds, they sin.

A Warning to Rich People

5 You rich people, listen to me. Cry and weep, because you will soon be suffering. ² Your riches have rotted. Moths have eaten your clothes. ³ Your gold and silver have lost their brightness. Their dullness will be a witness against you. Your wanting more and more will eat your body like fire. You have stored up riches in these last days. ⁴ You have even failed to pay the workers who mowed your fields. Their pay is crying out against you. The cries of those who gathered the harvest have reached the ears of the Lord. He rules over all. ⁵ You have lived an easy life on earth. You have given yourselves everything you wanted. You have made yourselves fat like cattle that will soon be butchered. ⁶ You have judged and murdered people who aren't guilty. And they weren't even opposing you.

Be Patient When You Suffer

⁷ Brothers and sisters, be patient until the Lord comes. See how the farmer waits for the land to produce its rich crop. See how patient the farmer is for the fall and spring rains. ⁸ You too must be patient. You must remain strong. The Lord will soon come back. ⁹ Brothers and sisters, don't find fault with one another. If you do, you will be judged. And the Judge is standing at the door!

¹⁰ Brothers and sisters, think about the prophets who spoke in the name of the Lord. They are an example of how to be patient when you suffer. ¹¹ As you know, we think that people who don't give up are blessed. You have heard that Job was patient. And you have seen what the Lord finally did for him. The Lord is full of tender mercy and loving concern.

¹² My brothers and sisters, here is what is most important. Don't make a promise by giving your word. Don't promise by heaven or earth. And don't promise by anything else to back up what you say. All you need to say is a simple "Yes" or "No." If you do more than this, you will be judged.

The Prayer of Faith

¹³ Is anyone among you in trouble? Then that person should pray. Is anyone among you happy? Then that person should sing songs of praise. ¹⁴ Is anyone among you sick? Then that person should send for

the elders of the church to pray over them. They should ask the elders to anoint them with olive oil in the name of the Lord. [15] The prayer offered by those who have faith will make the sick person well. The Lord will heal them. If they have sinned, they will be forgiven. [16] So confess your sins to one another. Pray for one another so that you might be healed. The prayer of a godly person is powerful. Things happen because of it.

[17] Elijah was a human being, just as we are. He prayed hard that it wouldn't rain. And it didn't rain on the land for three and a half years. [18] Then he prayed again. That time it rained. And the earth produced its crops.

[19] My brothers and sisters, suppose one of you wanders away from the truth. And suppose someone brings that person back. [20] Then here is what I want you to remember. Anyone who keeps a sinner from going astray will save them from death. God will erase many sins by forgiving them.

1 Peter

Introduction:

Peter was one of Jesus' disciples. He wrote this letter. The Christians he wrote were being hurt for believing in Jesus. Paul wrote to cheer them up.

Peter wanted the people to be brave. He reminded them that Jesus had been hurt too. Jesus was brave. He trusted God. We must trust God too. We are special to God. We must live the way God wants us to live.

Outline of contents:

---

1 I, Peter, am writing this letter. I am an apostle of Jesus Christ.

I am sending this letter to you, God's chosen people. You are people who have had to wander in the world. You are scattered all over the areas of Pontus, Galatia, Cappadocia, Asia and Bithynia. ²You have been chosen in keeping with what God the Father had planned. That happened through the Spirit's work to make you pure and holy. God chose you so that you might obey Jesus Christ. God wanted you to be in a covenant relationship with him. He established this relationship by the blood of Christ.

May more and more grace and peace be given to you.

Peter Praises God for a Living Hope

³Give praise to the God and Father of our Lord Jesus Christ. In his great mercy he has given us a new birth and a living hope. This hope is living because Jesus Christ rose from the dead. ⁴He has given us new birth so that we might share in what belongs to him. This is a gift that can never be destroyed. It can never spoil or even fade away. It is kept in heaven for you. ⁵Through faith you are kept safe by God's power. Your salvation is going to be completed. It is ready to be shown to you in the last days. ⁶Because you know all this, you have great joy. You have joy even though you may have had to suffer for a little while. You may have had to suf-

fer sadness in all kinds of trouble. ⁷ Your troubles have come in order to prove that your faith is real. Your faith is worth more than gold. That's because gold can pass away even when fire has made it pure. Your faith is meant to bring praise, honor and glory to God. This will happen when Jesus Christ returns. ⁸ Even though you have not seen him, you love him. Though you do not see him now, you believe in him. You are filled with a glorious joy that can't be put into words. ⁹ You are receiving the salvation of your souls. This salvation is the final result of your faith.

¹⁰ The prophets searched very hard and with great care to find out about this salvation. They spoke about the grace that was going to come to you. ¹¹ They wanted to find out when and how this salvation would come. The Spirit of Christ in them was telling them about the sufferings of the Messiah. These were his sufferings that were going to come. The Spirit of Christ was also telling them about the glory that would follow. ¹² It was made known to the prophets that they were not serving themselves. Instead, they were serving you when they spoke about the things that you have now heard. Those who have preached the good news to you have told you these things. They have done it with the help of the Holy Spirit sent from heaven. Even angels long to look into these things.

Be Holy

¹³ So be watchful, and control yourselves completely. In this way, put your hope in the grace that lies ahead. This grace will be brought to you when Jesus Christ returns. ¹⁴ You should obey your Father. You shouldn't give in to evil desires. They controlled your life when you didn't know any better. ¹⁵ The God who chose you is holy. So you should be holy in all that you do. ¹⁶ It is written, "Be holy, because I am holy." *(Leviticus 11:44,45; 19:2)*

¹⁷ You call on a Father who judges each person's work without favoring one over another. So live as outsiders during your time here. Live with the highest respect for God. ¹⁸ You were set free from an empty way of life. This way of life was handed down to you by your own people of long ago. You know that you were not bought with things that can pass away, like silver or gold. ¹⁹ Instead, you were bought with the priceless blood of Christ. He is a perfect lamb. He doesn't have any flaws at all. ²⁰ He was chosen before God created the world. But he came into the world for your sake in these last days. ²¹ Because of what Christ has done, you believe in God. It was God who raised him from the dead. And it was God who gave him glory. So your faith and hope are in God.

²² You have made yourselves pure by obeying the truth. So you have an honest and true love for each other. So love one another deeply, from your

hearts. [23] You have been born again by means of the living word of God. His word lasts forever. You were not born again from a seed that will die. You were born from a seed that can't die. [24] It is written,

"All people are like grass.
    All their glory is like the
        flowers in the field.
The grass dries up. The
        flowers fall to the
        ground.
[25]   But the word of the Lord
        lasts forever." *(Isaiah 40:6–8)*

And this is the word that was preached to you.

2 So get rid of every kind of evil, and stop telling lies. Don't pretend to be something you are not. Stop wanting what others have, and don't speak against one another. [2] Like newborn babies, you should long for the pure milk of God's word. It will help you grow up as believers. [3] You can do this now that you have tasted how good the Lord is.

The Living Stone and a Chosen People

[4] Christ is the living Stone. People did not accept him, but God chose him. God places the highest value on him. [5] You also are like living stones. As you come to Christ, you are being built into a house for worship. There you will be holy priests. You will offer spiritual sacrifices. God will accept them because of what Jesus Christ has done. [6] In Scripture it says,

"Look! I am placing a stone in
    Zion.
It is a chosen and very
    valuable stone.
It is the most important
    stone in the building.
The one who trusts in him
    will never be put to
    shame." *(Isaiah 28:16)*

[7] This stone is very valuable to you who believe. But to people who do not believe,

"The stone the builders did
    not accept
has become the most
    important stone of all."
                        (Psalm 118:22)

[8] And,

"It is a stone that causes
    people to trip.
It is a rock that makes them
    fall." *(Isaiah 8:14)*

They trip and fall because they do not obey the message. That is also what God planned for them.

[9] But God chose you to be his people. You are royal priests. You are a holy nation. You are God's special treasure. You are all these things so that you can give him praise. God brought you out of darkness into his wonderful light. [10] Once you were not a people. But now you are the people of God. Once you had not received mercy. But now you have received mercy.

Living Godly Lives Among People Who Don't Believe

[11] Dear friends, you are outsiders and those who wander

in this world. So I'm asking you not to give in to your sinful desires. They fight against your soul. ¹² People who don't believe might say you are doing wrong. But lead good lives among them. Then they will see your good deeds. And they will give glory to God on the day he comes to judge.

¹³ Follow the lead of every human authority. Do this for the Lord's sake. Obey the emperor. He is the highest authority. ¹⁴ Obey the governors. The emperor sends them to punish those who do wrong. He also sends them to praise those who do right. ¹⁵ By doing good you will put a stop to the talk of foolish people. They don't know what they are saying. ¹⁶ Live as free people. But don't use your freedom to cover up evil. Live as people who are God's slaves. ¹⁷ Show proper respect to everyone. Love the family of believers. Have respect for God. Honor the emperor.

¹⁸ Slaves, obey your masters out of deep respect for God. Obey not only those who are good and kind. Obey also those who are not kind. ¹⁹ Suppose a person suffers pain unfairly because they want to obey God. This is worthy of praise. ²⁰ But suppose you receive a beating for doing wrong, and you put up with it. Will anyone honor you for this? Of course not. But suppose you suffer for doing good, and you put up with it. God will praise you for this. ²¹ You were chosen to do good even if you suffer. That's because Christ suffered for you. He left you an example that he expects you to follow. ²² Scripture says,

"He didn't commit any sin.
No lies ever came out of his
mouth." *(Isaiah 53:9)*

²³ People shouted at him and made fun of him. But he didn't do the same thing back to them. When he suffered, he didn't say he would make them suffer. Instead, he trusted in the God who judges fairly. ²⁴ "He himself carried our sins" in his body on the cross. *(Isaiah 53:5)* He did it so that we would die as far as sins are concerned. Then we would lead godly lives. "His wounds have healed you." *(Isaiah 53:5)* ²⁵ "You were like sheep wandering away." *(Isaiah 53:6)* But now you have returned to the Shepherd. He is the one who watches over your souls.

3 Wives, follow the lead of your own husbands. Suppose some of them don't believe God's word. Then let them be won to Christ without words by seeing how their wives behave. ² Let them see how pure you are. Let them see that your lives are full of respect for God. ³ Fancy hairstyles don't make you beautiful. Wearing gold jewelry or fine clothes doesn't make you beautiful. ⁴ Instead, your beauty comes from inside you. It is the beauty of a gentle and quiet spirit. Beauty like this doesn't fade away. God places great value on it. ⁵ This is how the holy women of the past used

to make themselves beautiful. They put their hope in God. And they followed the lead of their own husbands. ⁶Sarah was like that. She obeyed Abraham. She called him her master. Do you want to be like her? Then do what is right. And don't give in to fear.

⁷Husbands, consider the needs of your wives. They are weaker than you. So treat them with respect. Honor them as those who will share with you the gracious gift of life. Then nothing will stand in the way of your prayers.

Suffering for Doing Good

⁸Finally, I want all of you to agree with one another. Be understanding. Love one another. Be kind and tender. Be humble. ⁹Don't pay back evil with evil. Don't pay back unkind words with unkind words. Instead, pay back evil with kind words. This is what you have been chosen to do. You will receive a blessing by doing this. ¹⁰Scripture says,

"Suppose someone wants to love life
    and see good days.
Then they must keep their
    tongues from speaking
    evil.
They must keep their lips
    from telling lies.
¹¹They must turn away from
    evil and do good.
They must look for peace
    and go after it.
¹²The Lord's eyes look on godly
    people, and he blesses
    them.

His ears are open to their
    prayers.
But the Lord doesn't bless
    those who do evil."

(Psalm 34:12–16)

¹³Who is going to hurt you if you really want to do good? ¹⁴But suppose you do suffer for doing what is right. Even then you will be blessed. Scripture says, "Don't fear what others say they will do to hurt you. Don't be afraid." *(Isaiah 8:12)* ¹⁵But make sure that in your hearts you honor Christ as Lord. Always be ready to give an answer to anyone who asks you about the hope you have. Be ready to give the reason for it. But do it gently and with respect. ¹⁶Live so that you don't have to feel you've done anything wrong. Some people may say evil things about your good conduct as believers in Christ. If they do, they will be put to shame for speaking like this about you. ¹⁷God may want you to suffer for doing good. That's better than suffering for doing evil. ¹⁸Christ also suffered once for sins. The one who did what is right suffered for those who don't do right. He suffered to bring you to God. His body was put to death. But the Holy Spirit brought him back to life. ¹⁹After that, Christ went and made an announcement to the spirits in prison. ²⁰Long ago these spirits did not obey. That was when God was patient while Noah was building the ark. And only a few people went into the ark. In fact, there were only eight. Those eight people were

saved through water. [21] The water of the flood is a picture. It is a picture of the baptism that now saves you too. This baptism has nothing to do with removing dirt from your body. Instead, it promises God that you will keep a clear sense of right and wrong. This baptism saves you by the same power that raised Jesus Christ from the dead. [22] He has gone into heaven. He is at God's right hand. Angels, authorities and powers are under his control.

Living for God

4 Christ suffered in his body. So prepare yourselves to think in the same way Christ did. Do this because whoever suffers in their body is finished with sin. [2] As a result, they don't live the rest of their earthly life for evil human desires. Instead, they live to do what God wants. [3] You have spent enough time in the past doing what ungodly people choose to do. You lived a wild life. You longed for evil things. You got drunk. You went to wild parties. You worshiped statues of gods, which the Lord hates. [4] Ungodly people are surprised that you no longer join them in what they do. They want you to join them in their wild and wasteful living. So they say bad things about you. [5] But they will have to explain their actions to God. He is ready to judge those who are alive and those who are dead. [6] That's why the good news was preached even to people who are now dead. It was preached to them for two reasons. It was preached so that their bodies might be judged. This judgment is made by human standards. But the good news was also preached so that their spirits might live. This life comes by means of God's power.

[7] The end of all things is near. So be watchful and control yourselves. Then you may pray. [8] Most of all, love one another deeply. Love erases many sins by forgiving them. [9] Welcome others into your homes without complaining. [10] God's gifts of grace come in many forms. Each of you has received a gift in order to serve others. You should use it faithfully. [11] If anyone speaks, they should do it as one speaking God's words. If anyone serves, they should do it with the strength God provides. Then in all things God will be praised through Jesus Christ. Glory and power belong to him for ever and ever. Amen.

Suffering for Being a Christian

[12] Dear friends, don't be surprised by the terrible things happening to you. The trouble you are having has come to test you. So don't feel as if something strange were happening to you. [13] Instead, be joyful that you are taking part in Christ's sufferings. Then you will have even more joy when Christ returns in glory. [14] Suppose people say bad things about you because you believe in Christ. Then you are blessed, because God's Spirit

rests on you. He is the Spirit of glory. [15] If you suffer, it shouldn't be because you are a murderer. It shouldn't be because you are a thief or someone who does evil things. It shouldn't be because you interfere with other people's business. [16] But suppose you suffer for being a Christian. Then don't be ashamed. Instead, praise God because you are known by the name of Christ. [17] It is time for judgment to begin with the household of God. And since it begins with us, what will happen to people who don't obey God's good news? [18] Scripture says,

> "Suppose it is hard for godly
> people to be saved.
> Then what will happen
> to ungodly people and
> sinners?" *(Proverbs 11:31)*

[19] Here is what people who suffer because of God's plan should do. They should commit themselves to their faithful Creator. And they should continue to do good.

To Older and Younger Believers

5 I'm speaking to the elders among you. I was a witness of Christ's sufferings. And I will also share in the glory that is going to come. I'm making my appeal to you as one who is an elder together with you. [2] Be shepherds of God's flock, the believers under your care. Watch over them, though not because you have to. Instead, do it because you want to. That's what God wants you to do. Don't do it because you want to get money in dishonest ways. Do it because you really want to serve. [3] Don't act as if you were a ruler over those under your care. Instead, be examples to the flock. [4] The Chief Shepherd will come again. Then you will receive the crown of glory. It is a crown that will never fade away.

[5] In the same way, I'm speaking to you who are younger. Follow the lead of those who are older. All of you, put on a spirit free of pride toward one another. Put it on as if it were your clothes. Do this because Scripture says,

> "God opposes those who are
> proud.
> But he gives grace to
> those who are humble." *(Proverbs 3:34)*

[6] So make yourselves humble. Put yourselves under God's mighty hand. Then he will honor you at the right time. [7] Turn all your worries over to him. He cares about you.

[8] Be watchful and control yourselves. Your enemy the devil is like a roaring lion. He prowls around looking for someone to swallow up. [9] Stand up to him. Remain strong in what you believe. You know that you are not alone in your suffering. The family of believers throughout the world is going through the same thing.

[10] God always gives you all the grace you need. So you will only have to suffer for a little while. Then God himself will build

you up again. He will make you strong and steady. And he has chosen you to share in his eternal glory because you belong to Christ. [11] Give him the power for ever and ever. Amen.

Final Greetings

[12] I consider Silas to be a faithful brother. With his help I have written you this short letter. I have written it to encourage you. And I have written to speak the truth about the true grace of God. Remain strong in it.

[13] The members of the church in Babylon send you their greetings. They were chosen together with you. Mark, my son in the faith, also sends you his greetings.

[14] Greet each other with a kiss of friendship.

May God give peace to all of you who believe in Christ.

2 Peter

Introduction:

This is Peter's second letter to Christians in the modern country of Turkey. He had told them to be brave when they were being hurt. Now they were in trouble again. False teachers gave them bad advice. Peter wanted the people to know the truth.

Peter wanted the Christians to have faith. He told them much about God. He told them how God wanted them to act. Peter wanted them to live a holy life. Peter said God would get rid of the false teachers. He also said Jesus would come again.

Outline of contents:

---

1 I, Simon Peter, am writing this letter. I serve Jesus Christ. I am his apostle.

I am sending this letter to you. You are those who have received a faith as valuable as ours. You received it because our God and Savior Jesus Christ does what is right.

² May more and more grace and peace be given to you. May they come to you as you learn more about God and about Jesus our Lord.

Showing That God Has Chosen You

³ God's power has given us everything we need to lead a godly life. All of this has come to us because we know the God who chose us. He chose us because of his own glory and goodness. ⁴ He has also given us his very great and valuable promises. He did it so you could share in his nature. You can share in it because you've escaped from the evil in the world. This evil is caused by sinful desires.

⁵ So you should try very hard to add goodness to your faith. To goodness, add knowledge. ⁶ To knowledge, add the ability to control yourselves. To the ability to control yourselves, add the strength to keep going. To the strength to keep going, add godliness. ⁷ To godliness, add kindness for one another. And to kindness for one another, add love. ⁸ All these things should describe you more and more. They will make you useful and fruitful as you know our Lord Jesus Christ better. ⁹ But what if these things don't describe someone at all? Then that person can't see very well. In fact,

they are blind. They have forgotten that their past sins have been washed away.

[10] My brothers and sisters, try very hard to show that God has appointed you to be saved. Try hard to show that he has chosen you. If you do everything I have just said, you will never trip and fall. [11] You will receive a rich welcome into the kingdom that lasts forever. It is the kingdom of our Lord and Savior Jesus Christ.

Prophecy of Scripture Comes From God

[12] So I will always remind you of these things. I'll do it even though you know them. I'll do it even though you now have deep roots in the truth. [13] I think it is right for me to remind you. It is right as long as I live in this tent. I'm talking about my body. [14] I know my tent will soon be removed. Our Lord Jesus Christ has made that clear to me. [15] I hope that you will always be able to remember these things after I'm gone. I will try very hard to see that you do.

[16] We told you about the time our Lord Jesus Christ came with power. But we didn't make up clever stories when we told you about it. With our own eyes we saw him in all his majesty. [17] God the Father gave him honor and glory. The voice of the Majestic Glory came to him. It said, "This is my Son, and I love him. I am very pleased with him." *(Matthew 17:5; Mark 9:7; Luke 9:35)* [18] We ourselves heard this voice that came from heaven. We were with him on the sacred mountain.

[19] We also have the message of the prophets. This message can be trusted completely. You must pay attention to it. The message is like a light shining in a dark place. It will shine until the day Jesus comes. Then the Morning Star will rise in your hearts. [20] Above all, here is what you must understand. No prophecy in Scripture ever came from a prophet's own understanding of things. [21] Prophecy never came simply because a prophet wanted it to. Instead, the Holy Spirit guided the prophets as they spoke. So, although prophets are human, prophecy comes from God.

False Teachers Will Be Destroyed

2 But there were also false prophets among the people. In the same way there will be false teachers among you. In secret they will bring in teachings that will destroy you. They will even turn against the Lord and Master who died to pay for their sins. So they will quickly destroy themselves. [2] Many people will follow their lead. These people will do the same evil things the false teachers do. They will cause people to think badly about the way of truth. [3] These teachers are never satisfied. They want to get something out of you. So they make up stories to take advantage of you. They have been under a sentence of death for a long time. The God who will destroy them has not been sleeping.

⁴ God did not spare angels when they sinned. Instead, he sent them to hell. He chained them up in dark prisons. He will keep them there until he judges them. ⁵ God did not spare the world's ungodly people long ago. He brought the flood on them. But Noah preached about the right way to live. God kept him safe. He also saved seven others. ⁶ God judged the cities of Sodom and Gomorrah. He burned them to ashes. He made them an example of what is going to happen to ungodly people. ⁷ God saved Lot, a man who did what was right. Lot was shocked by the evil conduct of people who didn't obey God's laws. ⁸ That good man lived among them day after day. He saw and heard the evil things they were doing. They were breaking God's laws. And the godly spirit of Lot was deeply troubled. ⁹ Since all this is true, then the Lord knows how to save godly people. He knows how to keep them safe in times of testing. The Lord also knows how to keep ungodly people under guard. He will do so until the day they will be judged and punished. ¹⁰ Most of all, this is true of people who follow desires that come from sin's power. These people hate to be under authority.

They are bold and proud. So they aren't even afraid to speak evil things against heavenly beings. ¹¹ Now angels are stronger and more powerful than these people. But even angels don't speak evil things against heavenly beings. They don't do this when they bring judgment on them from the Lord. ¹² These people speak evil about things they don't understand. They are like wild animals who can't think. Instead, they do what comes naturally to them. They are born only to be caught and destroyed. Just like animals, these people too will die.

¹³ They will be paid back with harm for the harm they have done. Their idea of pleasure is to have wild parties in the middle of the day. They are like dirty spots and stains. They enjoy their sinful pleasures while they eat with you. ¹⁴ They stare at women who are not their wives. They want to sleep with them. They never stop sinning. They trap those who are not firm in their faith. They have mastered the art of getting what they want. God has placed them under his judgment. ¹⁵ They have left God's way. They have wandered off. They follow the way of Balaam, son of Beor. He loved to get paid for doing his evil work. ¹⁶ But a donkey corrected him for the wrong he did. Animals don't speak. But the donkey spoke with a human voice. It tried to stop the prophet from doing a very dumb thing.

¹⁷ These people are like springs without water. They are like mists driven by a storm. The blackest darkness is reserved for them. ¹⁸ They speak empty, bragging words. They make their appeal to the evil desires that come from sin's power. They

tempt new believers who are just escaping from the company of sinful people. [19] They promise to give freedom to these new believers. But they themselves are slaves to sinful living. That's because "people are slaves to anything that controls them." [20] They may have escaped the sin of the world. They may have come to know our Lord and Savior Jesus Christ. But what if they are once again caught up in sin? And what if it has become their master? Then they are worse off at the end than they were at the beginning. [21] Suppose they had not known the way of godliness. This would have been better than to know godliness and then turn away from it. The way of godliness is the sacred command passed on to them. [22] What the proverbs say about them is true. "A dog returns to where it has thrown up." *(Proverbs 26:11)* And, "A pig that is washed goes back to rolling in the mud."

The Day of the Lord

3 Dear friends, this is now my second letter to you. I have written both of them as reminders. I want to encourage you to think in a way that is pure. [2] I want you to remember the words the holy prophets spoke in the past. Remember the command our Lord and Savior gave through your apostles. [3] Most of all, here is what you must understand. In the last days people will make fun of the truth. They will laugh at it. They will follow their own evil

desires. [4] They will say, "Where is this 'return' he promised? Everything goes on in the same way it has since our people of long ago died. In fact, it has continued this way since God first created everything." [5] Long ago, God's word brought the heavens into being. His word separated the earth from the waters. And the waters surrounded it. But these people forget things like that on purpose. [6] The waters also flooded the world of that time. And so they destroyed the world. [7] By God's word the heavens and earth of today are being reserved for fire. They are being kept for the day when God will judge. Then ungodly people will be destroyed.

[8] Dear friends, here is one thing you must not forget. With the Lord a day is like a thousand years. And a thousand years are like a day. [9] The Lord is not slow to keep his promise. He is not slow in the way some people understand it. Instead, he is patient with you. He doesn't want anyone to be destroyed. Instead, he wants all people to turn away from their sins.

[10] But the day of the Lord will come like a thief. The heavens will disappear with a roar. Fire will destroy everything in them. God will judge the earth and everything done in it.

[11] So everything will be destroyed in this way. And what kind of people should you be? You should lead holy and godly lives. [12] Live like this as you look forward to the day of God.

Living like this will make the day come more quickly. On that day fire will destroy the heavens. Its heat will melt everything in them. [13] But we are looking forward to a new heaven and a new earth. Godliness will live there. All this is in keeping with God's promise.

[14] Dear friends, I know you are looking forward to this. So try your best to be found pure and without blame. Be at peace with God. [15] Remember that while our Lord is waiting patiently to return, people are being saved. Our dear brother Paul also wrote to you about this. God made him wise to write as he did. [16] Paul writes the same way in all his letters. He speaks about what I have just told you. His letters include some things that are hard to understand. People who don't know better and aren't firm in the faith twist what he says. They twist the other Scriptures too. So they will be destroyed.

[17] Dear friends, you have already been warned about this. So be on your guard. Then you won't be led astray by people who don't obey the law. Instead, you will remain safe. [18] Grow in the grace and knowledge of our Lord and Savior Jesus Christ.

Glory belongs to him both now and forever. Amen.

1 John

Introduction:

John wrote this letter. He also wrote the next two letters in the Bible. He wrote the Gospel called John too.

This letter warned about false teachers. The false teachers said Jesus was not God. They said that God did not become human. John wanted Christians to know the truth about Jesus. John said we must know that Jesus is God. We must also know that Jesus was a human being.

John said we must do what God says. We must love each other. We must walk in the light too. This means that we live by the truth and do what is good. If we do these things then we know that we are God's children.

Outline of contents:

The Word of Life Became a Human Being

1 Here is what we announce to everyone about the Word of life. The Word was already here from the beginning. We have heard him. We have seen him with our eyes. We have looked at him. Our hands have touched him. ² This life has appeared. We have seen him. We are witnesses about him. And we announce to you this same eternal life. He was already with the Father. He has appeared to us. ³ We announce to you what we have seen and heard. We do it so you can share life together with us. And we share life with the Father and with his Son, Jesus Christ. ⁴ We are writing this to make our joy complete.

Walking in the Light

⁵ Here is the message we have heard from him and announce to you. God is light. There is no darkness in him at all. ⁶ Suppose we say that we share life with God but still walk in the darkness. Then we are lying. We are not living out the truth. ⁷ But suppose we walk in the light, just as he is in the light. Then we share life with one another. And the blood of Jesus, his Son, makes us pure from all sin.

⁸ Suppose we claim we are without sin. Then we are fooling ourselves. The truth is not in us.

⁹ But God is faithful and fair. If we confess our sins, he will forgive our sins. He will forgive every wrong thing we have done. He will make us pure. ¹⁰ If we claim we have not sinned, we are calling God a liar. His word is not in us.

2 My dear children, I'm writing this to you so that you will not sin. But suppose someone does sin. Then we have a friend who speaks to the Father for us. He is Jesus Christ, the Blameless One. ² He gave his life to pay for our sins. But he not only paid for our sins. He also paid for the sins of the whole world.

Instructions About Loving and Hating Other Believers

³ We know that we have come to know God if we obey his commands. ⁴ Suppose someone says, "I know him." But suppose this person does not do what God commands. Then this person is a liar and is not telling the truth. ⁵ But if anyone obeys God's word, then that person truly loves God. Here is how we know we belong to him. ⁶ Those who claim to belong to him must live just as Jesus did.

⁷ Dear friends, I'm not writing you a new command. Instead, I'm writing one you have heard before. You have had it since the beginning. ⁸ But I am writing what amounts to a new command. Its truth was shown in how Jesus lived. It is also shown in how you live. That's because the darkness is passing away. And the true light is already shining.

⁹ Suppose someone claims to be in the light but hates a brother or sister. Then they are still in the darkness. ¹⁰ Anyone who loves their brother and sister lives in the light. There is nothing in them to make them fall into sin. ¹¹ But anyone who hates a brother or sister is in the darkness. They walk around in the darkness. They don't know where they are going. The darkness has made them blind.

Reasons for Writing

¹² Dear children, I'm writing to you
because your sins have been forgiven.
They have been forgiven because of what Jesus has done.
¹³ Fathers, I'm writing to you because you know the one who is from the beginning.
Young men, I'm writing to you because you have won the battle over the evil one.

¹⁴ Dear children, I'm writing to you because you know the Father.
Fathers, I'm writing to you because you know the one who is from the beginning.
Young men, I'm writing to you because you are strong.
God's word lives in you.
You have won the battle over the evil one.

Do Not Love the World

¹⁵ Do not love the world or anything in it. If anyone loves the world, love for the Father is not in them. ¹⁶ Here is what people who belong to this world do. They try to satisfy what their sinful desires want to do. They long for what their sinful eyes look at. They take pride in what they have and what they do. All of this comes from the world. None of it comes from the Father. ¹⁷ The world and its evil desires are passing away. But whoever does what God wants them to do lives forever.

Warnings About Saying No to the Son

¹⁸ Dear children, we are living in the last days. You have heard that the great enemy of Christ is coming. But even now many enemies of Christ have already come. That's how we know that these are the last days. ¹⁹ These enemies left our community of believers. They didn't really belong to us. If they had belonged to us, they would have remained with us. But by leaving they showed that none of them belonged to us. ²⁰ You have received the Spirit from the Holy One. And all of you know the truth. ²¹ I'm not writing to you because you don't know the truth. I'm writing because you do know it. I'm writing to you because no lie comes from the truth. ²² Who is the liar? It is anyone who says that Jesus is not the Christ. The person who says this is the great enemy of Christ. They say no to the Father and the Son. ²³ The person who says no to the Son doesn't belong to the Father. But anyone who says yes to the Son belongs to the Father also.

²⁴ Make sure that you don't forget what you have heard from the beginning. Then you will remain joined to the Son and to the Father. ²⁵ And here is what God has promised us. He has promised us eternal life.

²⁶ I'm writing these things to warn you. I am warning you about people trying to lead you astray. ²⁷ But you have received the Holy Spirit from God. He continues to live in you. So you don't need anyone to teach you. God's Spirit teaches you about everything. What he says is true. He doesn't lie. Remain joined to Christ, just as you have been taught by the Spirit.

God's Children and Sin

²⁸ Dear children, remain joined to Christ. Then when he comes, we can be bold. We will not be ashamed to meet him when he comes. ²⁹ You know that God is right and always does what is right. And you know that everyone who does what is right is God's child.

3 See what amazing love the Father has given us! Because of it, we are called children of God. And that's what we really are! The world doesn't know us because it didn't know him. ² Dear friends, now we are children of God. He still hasn't let us

know what we will be. But we know that when Christ appears, we will be like him. That's because we will see him as he really is. ³ Christ is pure. All who hope to be like him make themselves pure.

⁴ Everyone who sins breaks the law. In fact, breaking the law is sin. ⁵ But you know that Christ came to take our sins away. And there is no sin in him. ⁶ No one who remains joined to him keeps on sinning. No one who keeps on sinning has seen him or known him.

⁷ Dear children, don't let anyone lead you astray. The person who does what is right is holy, just as Christ is holy. ⁸ The person who does what is sinful belongs to the devil. That's because the devil has been sinning from the beginning. But the Son of God came to destroy the devil's work. ⁹ Those who are God's children will not keep on sinning. God's very nature remains in them. They can't go on sinning. That's because they are God's children. ¹⁰ Here is how you can tell the difference between God's children and the devil's children. Anyone who doesn't do what is right isn't God's child. And anyone who doesn't love their brother or sister isn't God's child either.

More Instructions About Loving and Hating One Another

¹¹ From the beginning we have heard that we should love one another. ¹² Don't be like Cain. He belonged to the evil one. He murdered his brother. And why did he murder him? Because the things Cain had done were wrong. But the things his brother had done were right. ¹³ My brothers and sisters, don't be surprised if the world hates you. ¹⁴ We know that we have left our old dead way of life. And we have entered into new life. We know this because we love one another. Anyone who doesn't love still lives in their old condition. ¹⁵ Anyone who hates their brother or sister is a murderer. And you know that no murderer has eternal life.

¹⁶ We know what love is because Jesus Christ gave his life for us. So we should give our lives for our brothers and sisters. ¹⁷ Suppose someone sees a brother or sister in need and is able to help them. And suppose that person doesn't take pity on these needy people. Then how can the love of God be in that person? ¹⁸ Dear children, don't just talk about love. Put your love into action. Then it will truly be love.

¹⁹ Here's how we know that we hold to the truth. And here's how we put our hearts at rest, knowing that God is watching. ²⁰ If our hearts judge us, we know that God is greater than our hearts. And he knows everything. ²¹ Dear friends, if our hearts do not judge us, we can be bold with God. ²² And he will give us anything we ask. That's because we obey his commands. We do what pleases him. ²³ God has commanded us to believe in the name of his Son, Jesus Christ.

He has also commanded us to love one another. ²⁴The one who obeys God's commands remains joined to him. And he remains joined to them. Here is how we know that God lives in us. We know it because of the Holy Spirit he gave us.

Jesus Came as a Human Being

4 Dear friends, do not believe every spirit. Test the spirits to see if they belong to God. Many false prophets have gone out into the world. ²Here is how you can recognize the Spirit of God. Every spirit agreeing that Jesus Christ came in a human body belongs to God. ³But every spirit that doesn't agree with this does not belong to God. You have heard that the spirit of the great enemy of Christ is coming. Even now it is already in the world.

⁴Dear children, you belong to God. You have not accepted the teachings of the false prophets. That's because the one who is in you is powerful. He is more powerful than the one who is in the world. ⁵False prophets belong to the world. So they speak from the world's point of view. And the world listens to them. ⁶We belong to God. And those who know God listen to us. But those who don't belong to God don't listen to us. That's how we can tell the difference between the Spirit of truth and the spirit of lies.

We Love Because God Loved Us

⁷Dear friends, let us love one another, because love comes from God. Everyone who loves has become a child of God and knows God. ⁸Anyone who does not love does not know God, because God is love. ⁹Here is how God showed his love among us. He sent his one and only Son into the world. He sent him so we could receive life through him. ¹⁰Here is what love is. It is not that we loved God. It is that he loved us and sent his Son to give his life to pay for our sins. ¹¹Dear friends, since God loved us this much, we should also love one another. ¹²No one has ever seen God. But if we love one another, God lives in us. His love is made complete in us.

¹³Here's how we know that we are joined to him and he to us. He has given us his Holy Spirit. ¹⁴The Father has sent his Son to be the Savior of the world. We have seen it and are witnesses to it. ¹⁵God lives in anyone who agrees that Jesus is the Son of God. This kind of person remains joined to God. ¹⁶So we know that God loves us. We depend on it.

God is love. Anyone who leads a life of love is joined to God. And God is joined to them. ¹⁷Suppose love is fulfilled among us. Then we can be without fear on the day God judges the world. Love is fulfilled among us when in this world we are like Jesus. ¹⁸There is no fear in love. Instead, perfect love drives away fear. That's because fear has to do with being punished. The one who fears does not have perfect love.

¹⁹We love because he loved us first. ²⁰Suppose someone claims to love God but hates a brother or sister. Then they are a liar. They don't love their brother or sister, whom they have seen. So they can't love God, whom they haven't seen. ²¹Here is the command God has given us. Anyone who loves God must also love their brother and sister.

Faith in God's Son Who Became a Human Being

5 Everyone who believes that Jesus is the Christ is a child of God. And everyone who loves the Father loves his children as well. ²Here is how we know that we love God's children. We know it when we love God and obey his commands. ³In fact, here is what it means to love God. We love him by obeying his commands. And his commands are not hard to obey. ⁴That's because everyone who is a child of God has won the battle over the world. Our faith has won the battle for us. ⁵Who is it that has won the battle over the world? Only the person who believes that Jesus is the Son of God.

⁶Jesus Christ was born as we are, and he died on the cross. He wasn't just born as we are. He also died on the cross. The Holy Spirit is a truthful witness about him. That's because the Spirit is the truth. ⁷There are three that are witnesses about Jesus. ⁸They are the Holy Spirit, the birth of Jesus, and the death of Jesus. And the three of them agree. ⁹We accept what people say when they are witnesses. But it's more important when God is a witness. That's because it is what God says about his Son. ¹⁰Whoever believes in the Son of God accepts what God says about him. Whoever does not believe God is calling him a liar. That's because they have not believed what God said about his Son. ¹¹Here is what God says about the Son. God has given us eternal life. And this life is found in his Son. ¹²Whoever belongs to the Son has life. Whoever doesn't belong to the Son of God doesn't have life.

Final Words

¹³I'm writing these things to you who believe in the name of the Son of God. I'm writing so you will know that you have eternal life. ¹⁴Here is what we can be sure of when we come to God in prayer. If we ask anything in keeping with what he wants, he hears us. ¹⁵If we know that God hears what we ask for, we know that we have it.

¹⁶Suppose you see any brother or sister commit a sin. But this sin is not the kind that leads to death. Then you should pray, and God will give them life. I'm talking about someone whose sin does not lead to death. But there is a sin that does lead to death. I'm not saying you should pray about that sin. ¹⁷Every wrong thing we do is sin. But there are sins that do not lead to death.

¹⁸We know that those who are children of God do not keep on

sinning. The Son of God keeps them safe. The evil one can't harm them. [19] We know that we are children of God. We know that the whole world is under the control of the evil one. [20] We also know that the Son of God has come. He has given us un-derstanding. So we can know the God who is true. And we be-long to the true God by belong-ing to his Son, Jesus Christ. He is the true God and eternal life.

[21] Dear children, keep away from statues of gods.

2 John

Introduction:

John wrote many letters. He said it was for "the chosen lady and her children." This meant either a Christian woman and her family or a church and its members.

John said some important things. He said Christians should love each other. He said we must do what God says. If we love God we will do what he says. John also wrote about false teachers. The false teachers did not believe the truth about Jesus. John told Christians to stay away from the false teachers.

Outline of contents:

---

¹ I, the elder, am writing this letter.

I am sending it to the lady chosen by God and to her children. I love all of you because of the truth. I'm not the only one who loves you. So does everyone who knows the truth. ² I love you because of the truth that is alive in us. This truth will be with us forever.

³ God the Father and Jesus Christ his Son will give you grace, mercy and peace. These blessings will be with us because we love the truth.

⁴ It has given me great joy to find some of your children living by the truth. That's just what the Father commanded us to do. ⁵ Dear lady, I'm not writing you a new command. I'm writing a command we've had from the beginning. I'm asking that we love one another. ⁶ The way we show our love is to obey God's commands. He commands you to lead a life of love. That's what you have heard from the beginning.

⁷ I say this because many people have tried to fool others. These people have gone out into the world. They don't agree that Jesus Christ came in a human body. People like this try to trick others. These people are like the great enemy of Christ. ⁸ Watch out that you don't lose what we have worked for. Make sure that you get your full reward. ⁹ Suppose someone thinks they know more than we do. So they don't follow Christ's teaching. Then that person doesn't belong to God. But whoever follows Christ's teaching belongs to the Father and the Son. ¹⁰ Suppose someone comes to you and doesn't

teach these truths. Then don't take them into your house or welcome them. [11] Anyone who welcomes them shares in their evil work.

[12] I have a lot to write to you. But I don't want to use paper and ink. I hope I can visit you instead. Then I can talk with you face to face. That will make our joy complete.

[13] The children of your sister, who is chosen by God, send their greetings.

3 John

Introduction:

John wrote this letter to Gaius. Gaius was John's friend. He was a leader in the church. Gaius was kind to other Christians. Another leader in the church was not acting like a friend. His name was Diotrephes. Diotrephes said bad things about John. He was not kind to other Christians.

John wrote to thank Gaius. John also wrote to scold Diotrephes. John said he hoped to visit soon.

Outline of contents:

---

[1] I, the elder, am writing this letter.

I am sending it to you, my dear friend Gaius. I love you because of the truth.

[2] Dear friend, I know that your spiritual life is going well. I pray that you also may enjoy good health. And I pray that everything else may go well with you. [3] Some believers came to me and told me that you are faithful to the truth. They told me that you continue to live by it. This news gave me great joy. [4] I have no greater joy than to hear that my children are living by the truth.

[5] Dear friend, you are faithful in what you are doing for the brothers and sisters. You are faithful even though they are strangers to you. [6] They have told the church about your love. Please help them by sending them on their way in a manner that honors God. [7] They started on their journey to serve Jesus Christ. They didn't receive any help from those who aren't believers. [8] So we should welcome people like them. We should work together with them for the truth.

[9] I wrote to the church. But Diotrephes will not welcome us. He loves to be the first in everything. [10] So when I come, I will point out what he is doing. He is saying evil things that aren't true about us. Even this doesn't satisfy him. So he refuses to welcome other believers. He also keeps others from welcoming them. In fact, he throws them out of the church.

[11] Dear friend, don't be like

those who do evil. Be like those who do good. Anyone who does what is good belongs to God. Anyone who does what is evil hasn't really seen or known God. [12] Everyone says good things about Demetrius. He lives in keeping with the truth. We also say good things about him. And you know that what we say is true.

[13] I have a lot to write to you. But I don't want to write with pen and ink. [14] I hope I can see you soon. Then we can talk face to face.

May you have peace.

The friends here send their greetings.

Greet each one of the friends there.

Jude

Introduction:

Jesus had two brothers. One was James, and the other was Jude. Jude wrote this short letter. He wrote to warn Christians about false teachers. These people taught the same kind of false teaching that Peter wrote about in 2 Peter. Jude reminded Christians about the truth of God's salvation. He told them to stand up for the faith.

The false teachers said Jesus was not God. They said people could live sinful lives. Jude said God would punish the false teachers. God would destroy them.

Outline of contents:

---

¹ I, Jude, am writing this letter. I serve Jesus Christ. I am a brother of James.

I am sending this letter to you who have been chosen by God. You are loved by God the Father. You are kept safe for Jesus Christ.

² May more and more mercy, peace and love be given to you.

A Warning Against the Sin of Ungodly People

³ Dear friends, I really wanted to write to you about the salvation we share. But now I feel I should write and ask you to stand up for the faith. God's holy people were trusted with it once and for all time. ⁴ Certain people have secretly slipped in among you. Long ago it was written that they would be judged. They are ungodly people. They misuse the grace of our God as an excuse for sexual sins. They say no to Jesus Christ, our only Lord and King.

⁵ I want to remind you about some things you already know. The Lord saved his people. At one time he brought them out of Egypt. But later he destroyed those who did not believe. ⁶ Some of the angels didn't stay where they belonged. They didn't keep their positions of authority. The Lord has kept those angels in darkness. They are held by chains that last forever. On judgment day, God will judge them. ⁷ The people of Sodom and Gomorrah and the towns around them also did evil things. They freely committed sexual sins. They committed sins of the worst possible kind. There is a fire that never goes out. Those people are an example of those who are punished with it.

⁸ In the very same way, these

ungodly people act on their evil dreams. So they make their own bodies impure. They don't accept authority. And they say evil things against heavenly beings. [9] But even Michael, the leader of the angels, didn't dare to say these things. He didn't even say these things when he argued with the devil about the body of Moses. Michael didn't dare to judge the devil. He didn't say the devil was guilty of saying evil things. Instead, Michael said, "May the Lord judge you!" [10] But these people say evil things against whatever they don't understand. And the very things they do understand will destroy them. That's because they are like wild animals that can't think for themselves. Instead, they do what comes naturally to them.

[11] How terrible it will be for them! They have followed the way of Cain. They have rushed into the same mistake Balaam made. They did it because they loved money. They are like Korah. He turned against his leaders. These people will certainly be destroyed, just as Korah was.

[12] These ungodly people are like stains at the meals you share. They have no shame. They are shepherds who feed only themselves. They are like clouds without rain. They are blown along by the wind. They are like trees in the fall. Since they have no fruit, they are pulled out of the ground. So they die twice. [13] They are like wild waves of the sea. Their shame rises up like foam. They are like falling stars. God has reserved a place of very black darkness for them forever.

[14] Enoch was the seventh man in the family line of Adam. He gave a prophecy about these people. He said, "Look! The Lord is coming with thousands and thousands of his holy ones. [15] He is coming to judge everyone. He is coming to sentence all of them. He will judge them for all the ungodly acts they have done. They have done them in ungodly ways. He will sentence ungodly sinners for all the things they have said to oppose him." [16] These people complain and find fault with others. They follow their own evil desires. They brag about themselves. They praise others to get what they want.

Remain in God's Love

[17] Dear friends, remember what the apostles of our Lord Jesus Christ said would happen. [18] They told you, "In the last days, some people will make fun of the truth. They will follow their own ungodly desires." [19] They are the people who separate you from one another. They do only what comes naturally. They are not led by the Holy Spirit.

[20] But you, dear friends, build yourselves up in your most holy faith. Let the Holy Spirit guide and help you when you pray. [21] And by doing these things, remain in God's love as you wait. You are waiting for the mercy of our Lord Jesus Christ to bring you eternal life.

22 Show mercy to those who doubt. 23 Save others by pulling them out of the fire. To others, show mercy mixed with fear of sin. Hate even the clothes that are stained by the sins of those who wear them.

Praise to God

24 Give praise to the God who is able to keep you from falling into sin. He will bring you into his heavenly glory without any fault. He will bring you there with great joy. 25 Give praise to the only God our Savior. Glory, majesty, power and authority belong to him. Give praise to him through Jesus Christ our Lord. His praise was before all time, continues now, and will last forever. Amen.

Revelation

Introduction:

John wrote the book of Revelation. The Roman rulers did not like John. They made him leave his home. They put him on an island called Patmos. Jesus gave John a vision while he was living on the island. It was about the battle between God and Satan. John wrote about the vision in the book of Revelation.

John knew it was hard to be a Christian. He wanted Christians to trust God. That is why John wrote this book about his vision. Some things in this book are hard to understand. John makes one thing very clear. John said God takes care of everything on earth. Jesus is in control. He will judge and punish evil. God will also make a new home for his children. They will live with him forever.

Outline of contents:

The Revelation Is Given

1 This is the revelation from Jesus Christ. God gave it to him to show those who serve God what will happen soon. God made it known by sending his angel to his servant John. ² John is a witness to everything he saw. What he saw is God's word and what Jesus Christ has said. ³ Blessed is the one who reads out loud the words of this prophecy. Blessed are those who hear it and think everything it says is important. The time when these things will come true is near.

Greetings and Praise to God

⁴ I, John, am writing this letter.

I am sending it to the seven churches in Asia Minor.

May grace and peace come to you from God. He is the one who is, and who was, and who will come. May grace and peace come to you from the seven spirits. These spirits are in front of God's throne. [5] May grace and peace come to you from Jesus Christ. He is the faithful witness, so what he has shown can be trusted. He was the first to rise from the dead. He rules over the kings of the earth.

Glory and power belong to Jesus Christ who loves us! He has set us free from our sins by pouring out his blood for us. [6] He has made us members of his royal family. He has made us priests who serve his God and Father. Glory and power belong to Jesus Christ for ever and ever! Amen.

[7] "Look! He is coming with the clouds!" *(Daniel 7:13)*
"Every eye will see him.
Even those who pierced him
will see him."
All the nations of the earth
"will mourn because of
him." *(Zechariah 12:10)*
This will really happen! Amen.

[8] "I am the Alpha and the Omega, the Beginning and the End," says the Lord God. "I am the God who is, and who was, and who will come. I am the Mighty One."

John's Vision of Christ

[9] I, John, am a believer like you. I am a friend who suffers like you. As members of Jesus' royal family, we can put up with anything that happens to us. I was on the island of Patmos because I taught God's word and what Jesus said. [10] The Holy Spirit gave me a vision on the Lord's Day. I heard a loud voice behind me that sounded like a trumpet. [11] The voice said, "Write on a scroll what you see. Send it to the seven churches in Asia Minor. They are Ephesus, Smyrna, Pergamum, Thyatira, Sardis, Philadelphia and Laodicea."

[12] I turned around to see who was speaking to me. When I turned, I saw seven golden lampstands. [13] In the middle of them was someone who looked "like a son of man." *(Daniel 7:13)* He was dressed in a long robe with a gold strip of cloth around his chest. [14] The hair on his head was white like wool, as white as snow. His eyes were like a blazing fire. [15] His feet were like bronze metal glowing in a furnace. His voice sounded like rushing waters. [16] He held seven stars in his right hand. Coming out of his mouth was a sharp sword with two edges. His face was like the sun shining in all its brightness.

[17] When I saw him, I fell at his feet as if I were dead. Then he put his right hand on me and said, "Do not be afraid. I am the First and the Last. [18] I am the Living One. I was dead. But now look! I am alive for ever and ever! And I hold the keys to Death and Hell.

[19] "So write down what you have seen. Write about what is happening now and what will happen later. [20] Here is the meaning of the mystery of the seven stars you saw in my right

hand. They are the angels of the seven churches. And the seven golden lampstands you saw stand for the seven churches.

The Letter to the Church in Ephesus

2 "Here is what I command you to write to the church in Ephesus.

Here are the words of Jesus, who holds the seven stars in his right hand. He also walks among the seven golden lampstands. He says, [2]'I know what you are doing. You work long and hard. I know you can't put up with evil people. You have tested those who claim to be apostles but are not. You have found out that they are liars. [3] You have been faithful and have put up with a lot of trouble because of me. You have not given up.

[4]'But here is something I hold against you. You have turned away from the love you had at first. [5] Think about how far you have fallen! Turn away from your sins. Do the things you did at first. If you don't, I will come to you and remove your lampstand from its place. [6] But you do have this in your favor. You hate the way the Nicolaitans act. I hate it too.

[7]'Whoever has ears should listen to what the Holy Spirit says to the churches. Here is what I will do for anyone who has vic-tory over sin. I will let that person eat from the tree of life in God's paradise.'

The Letter to the Church in Smyrna

[8] "Here is what I command you to write to the church in Smyrna.

Here are the words of Jesus, who is the First and the Last. He is the one who died and came to life again. He says, [9]'I know that you suffer and are poor. But you are rich! Some people say they are Jews but are not. I know that their words are evil. Their worship comes from Satan. [10] Don't be afraid of what you are going to suffer. I tell you, the devil will put some of you in prison to test you. You will be treated badly for ten days. Be faithful, even if it means you must die. Then I will give you life as your crown of victory.

[11]'Whoever has ears should listen to what the Holy Spirit says to the churches. Here is what I will do for anyone who has victory over sin. I will not let that person be hurt at all by the second death.'

The Letter to the Church in Pergamum

[12] "Here is what I command you to write to the church in Pergamum.

Here are the words of Jesus, who has the sharp

sword with two edges. He says, [13] 'I know that you live where Satan has his throne. But you remain faithful to me. You did not give up your faith in me. You didn't give it up even in the days of Antipas. Antipas, my faithful witness, was put to death in your city, where Satan lives.

[14] 'But I have a few things against you. Some of your people follow the teaching of Balaam. He taught Balak to lead the people of Israel into sin. So they ate food that had been offered to statues of gods. And they committed sexual sins. [15] You also have people who follow the teaching of the Nicolaitans. [16] So turn away from your sins! If you don't, I will come to you soon. I will fight against those people with the sword that comes out of my mouth.

[17] 'Whoever has ears should listen to what the Holy Spirit says to the churches. Here is what I will do for anyone who has victory over sin. I will give that person hidden manna to eat. I will also give each of them a white stone with a new name written on it. Only the one who receives this name will know what it is.'

The Letter to the Church in Thyatira

[18] "Here is what I command you to write to the church in Thyatira.

Here are the words of the Son of God. He is Jesus, whose eyes are like blazing fire. His feet are like polished bronze. He says, [19] 'I know what you are doing. I know your love and your faith. I know how well you have served. I know you don't give up easily. In fact, you are doing more now than you did at first.

[20] 'But here is what I have against you. You put up with that woman Jezebel. She calls herself a prophet. With her teaching, she has led my servants into sexual sin. She has tricked them into eating food offered to statues of gods. [21] I've given her time to turn away from her sinful ways. But she doesn't want to. [22] She lay down to commit her sin so I will make her lie down in suffering. Those who commit adultery with her will suffer greatly too. Their only way out is to turn away from what she taught them to do. [23] I will strike her children dead. Then all the churches will know that I search hearts and minds. I will pay each of you back for what you have done.

[24] 'I won't ask the rest of you in Thyatira to do anything else. You don't follow the teaching of Jezebel. You haven't learned what some people call Satan's deep secrets. [25] Just hold on to what you have until I come.

²⁶'Here is what I will do for anyone who has victory over sin. I will do it for anyone who carries out my plans to the end. I will give that person authority over the nations. ²⁷It is written, "They will rule them with an iron scepter. They will break them to pieces like clay pots." *(Psalm 2:9)* Their authority is like the authority I've received from my Father. ²⁸I will also give the morning star to all who have victory. ²⁹Whoever has ears should listen to what the Holy Spirit says to the churches.'

The Letter to the Church in Sardis

3 "Here is what I command you to write to the church in Sardis.

Here are the words of Jesus, who holds the seven spirits of God. He has the seven stars in his hand. He says, 'I know what you are doing. People think you are alive, but you are dead. ²Wake up! Strengthen what is left, or it will die. You have not done all that my God wants you to do. ³So remember what you have been taught and have heard. Hold firmly to it. Turn away from your sins. If you don't wake up, I will come like a thief. You won't know when I will come to you.

⁴'But you have a few people in Sardis who are pure. They aren't covered with evil like dirty clothes. They will walk with me, dressed in white, because they are worthy. ⁵Here is what I will do for anyone who has victory over sin. I will dress that person in white like those worthy people. I will never erase their names from the book of life. I will speak of them by name to my Father and his angels. ⁶Whoever has ears should listen to what the Holy Spirit says to the churches.'

The Letter to the Church in Philadelphia

⁷"Here is what I command you to write to the church in Philadelphia.

Here are the words of Jesus, who is holy and true. He holds the key of David. No one can shut what he opens. And no one can open what he shuts. He says, ⁸'I know what you are doing. Look! I have put an open door in front of you. No one can shut it. I know that you don't have much strength. But you have obeyed my word. You have not said no to me. ⁹Some people claim they are Jews but are not. They are liars. Their worship comes from Satan. I will make them come and fall down at your feet. I will make them say in public that I have loved you. ¹⁰You have kept my command to remain strong in the faith no matter what happens. So I will keep you from the time of suffering. That time is going to come to the whole world. It will test those who live on the earth.

¹¹ 'I am coming soon. Hold on to what you have. Then no one will take away your crown. ¹² Here is what I will do for anyone who has victory over sin. I will make that person a pillar in the temple of my God. They will never leave it again. I will write the name of my God on them. I will write the name of the city of my God on them. This is the new Jerusalem, which is coming down out of heaven from my God. I will also write my new name on them. ¹³ Whoever has ears should listen to what the Holy Spirit says to the churches.'

The Letter to the Church in Laodicea

¹⁴ "Here is what I command you to write to the church in Laodicea.

Here are the words of Jesus, who is the Amen. What he speaks is faithful and true. He rules over what God has created. He says, ¹⁵ 'I know what you are doing. I know you aren't cold or hot. I wish you were either one or the other! ¹⁶ But you are lukewarm. You aren't hot or cold. So I am going to spit you out of my mouth. ¹⁷ You say, "I am rich. I've become wealthy and don't need anything." But you don't realize how pitiful and miserable you have become. You are poor, blind and naked. ¹⁸ So here's my advice. Buy from me gold made pure by fire. Then you will become rich. Buy from me white clothes to wear. Then you will be able to cover the shame of your naked bodies. And buy from me healing lotion to put on your eyes. Then you will be able to see.

¹⁹ 'I warn and correct those I love. So be sincere, and turn away from your sins. ²⁰ Here I am! I stand at the door and knock. If anyone hears my voice and opens the door, I will come in. I will eat with that person, and they will eat with me.

²¹ 'Here is what I will do for anyone who has victory over sin. I will give that person the right to sit with me on my throne. In the same way, I had victory. Then I sat down with my Father on his throne. ²² Whoever has ears should listen to what the Holy Spirit says to the churches.'"

The Throne in Heaven

4 After this I looked, and there in front of me was a door standing open in heaven. I heard the voice I had heard be-

fore. It sounded like a trumpet. The voice said, "Come up here. I will show you what must happen after this." ²At once the Holy Spirit gave me a vision. There in front of me was a throne in heaven with someone sitting on it. ³The one who sat there shone like jasper and ruby. Around the throne was a rainbow shining like an emerald. ⁴Twenty-four other thrones surrounded that throne. Twenty-four elders were sitting on them. The elders were dressed in white. They had gold crowns on their heads. ⁵From the throne came flashes of lightning, rumblings and thunder. Seven lamps were blazing in front of the throne. These stand for the seven spirits of God. ⁶There was something that looked like a sea of glass in front of the throne. It was as clear as crystal.

In the inner circle, around the throne, were four living creatures. They were covered with eyes, in front and in back. ⁷The first creature looked like a lion. The second looked like an ox. The third had a man's face. The fourth looked like a flying eagle. ⁸Each of the four living creatures had six wings. Each creature was covered all over with eyes. It had eyes even under its wings. Day and night, they never stop saying,

> " 'Holy, holy, holy
> is the Lord God who rules
> over all.' *(Isaiah 6:3)*
> He was, and he is, and
> he will come."

⁹The living creatures give glory, honor and thanks to the one who sits on the throne. He lives for ever and ever. ¹⁰At the same time, the 24 elders fall down and worship the one who sits on the throne. He lives for ever and ever. They lay their crowns in front of the throne. They say,

> ¹¹ "You are worthy, our Lord
>   and God!
> You are worthy to receive
>   glory and honor and
>   power.
> You are worthy because you
>   created all things.
> They were created and
>   they exist.
> This is the way you
>   planned it."

The Scroll and the Lamb

5 Then I saw a scroll in the right hand of the one sitting on the throne. The scroll had writing on both sides. It was sealed with seven seals. ²I saw a mighty angel calling out in a loud voice. He said, "Who is worthy to break the seals and open the scroll?" ³But no one in heaven or on earth or under the earth could open the scroll. No one could even look inside it. ⁴I cried and cried. That's because no one was found who was worthy to open the scroll or look inside. ⁵Then one of the elders said to me, "Do not cry! The Lion of the tribe of Judah has won the battle. He is the Root of David. He is able to break the seven seals and open the scroll." ⁶Then I saw a Lamb that looked as if he had been put to

death. He stood at the center of the area around the throne. The Lamb was surrounded by the four living creatures and the elders. He had seven horns and seven eyes. The eyes stand for the seven spirits of God, which are sent out into all the earth. [7] The Lamb went and took the scroll. He took it from the right hand of the one sitting on the throne. [8] Then the four living creatures and the 24 elders fell down in front of the Lamb. Each one had a harp. They were holding golden bowls full of incense. They stand for the prayers of God's people. [9] Here is the new song they sang.

"You are worthy to take the scroll
and break open its seals.
You are worthy because you were put to death.
With your blood you bought people for God.
They come from every tribe, people and nation, no matter what language they speak.
[10] You have made them members of a royal family.
You have made them priests to serve our God.
They will rule on the earth."

[11] Then I looked and heard the voice of millions and millions of angels. They surrounded the throne. They surrounded the living creatures and the elders. [12] In a loud voice they were saying,

"The Lamb, who was put to death, is worthy!
He is worthy to receive power and wealth and wisdom and strength!
He is worthy to receive honor and glory and praise!"

[13] All creatures in heaven, on earth, under the earth, and on the sea were speaking. The whole creation was speaking. I heard all of them say,

"Praise and honor belong to the one who sits on the throne and to the Lamb!
Glory and power belong to God for ever and ever!"

[14] The four living creatures said, "Amen." And the elders fell down and worshiped.

The Seals of the Scroll Are Broken

6 I watched as the Lamb broke open the first of the seven seals. Then I heard one of the four living creatures say in a voice that sounded like thunder, "Come!" [2] I looked, and there in front of me was a white horse! Its rider held a bow in his hands. He was given a crown. He rode out like a hero on his way to victory.

[3] The Lamb broke open the second seal. Then I heard the second living creature say, "Come!" [4] Another horse came out. It was red like fire. Its rider was given power to take peace from the earth. He was given power to make people kill each other. He was given a large sword.

⁵The Lamb broke open the third seal. Then I heard the third living creature say, "Come!" I looked, and there in front of me was a black horse! Its rider was holding a pair of scales in his hand. ⁶Next, I heard what sounded like a voice coming from among the four living creatures. It said, "Two pounds of wheat for a day's pay. And six pounds of barley for a day's pay. And leave the olive oil and the wine alone!"

⁷The Lamb broke open the fourth seal. Then I heard the voice of the fourth living creature say, "Come!" ⁸I looked, and there in front of me was a pale horse! Its rider's name was Death. Following close behind him was Hell. They were given power over a fourth of the earth. They were given power to kill people by swords. They could also use hunger, sickness and the earth's wild animals to kill.

⁹The Lamb broke open the fifth seal. I saw souls under the altar. They were the souls of people who had been killed. They had been killed because of God's word and their faithful witness. ¹⁰They called out in a loud voice. "How long, Lord and King, holy and true?" they asked. "How long will you wait to judge those who live on the earth? How long will it be until you pay them back for killing us?" ¹¹Then each of them was given a white robe. "Wait a little longer," they were told. "There are still more of your believing brothers and sisters who will be killed. They will be killed just as you were."

¹²I watched as the Lamb broke open the sixth seal. There was a powerful earthquake. The sun turned black like the clothes people wear when they're sad. Those clothes are made out of goat's hair. The whole moon turned as red as blood. ¹³The stars in the sky fell to earth. They dropped like figs from a tree shaken by a strong wind. ¹⁴The sky rolled back like a scroll. Every mountain and island was moved out of its place.

¹⁵Everyone hid in caves and among the rocks of the mountains. This included the kings of the earth, the princes and the generals. It included rich people and powerful people. It also included everyone else, both slaves and people who were free. ¹⁶They called out to the mountains and rocks, "Fall on us! Hide us from the face of the one who sits on the throne! Hide us from the anger of the Lamb! ¹⁷The great day of their anger has come. Who can live through it?"

144,000 People Are Marked With the Seal of the Living God

7 After this I saw four angels. They were standing at the four corners of the earth. They were holding back the four winds of the earth. This kept the winds from blowing on the land or the sea or on any tree. ²Then I saw another angel coming up from the east. He brought the official seal of the living God.

He called out in a loud voice to the four angels. They had been allowed to harm the land and the sea. ³ "Do not harm the land or the sea or the trees," he said. "Wait until we mark with this seal the foreheads of those who serve our God." ⁴ Then I heard how many people were marked with the seal. There were 144,000 from all the tribes of Israel.

⁵ From the tribe of Judah, 12,000 were marked with the seal.

From the tribe of Reuben, 12,000.

From the tribe of Gad, 12,000.

⁶ From the tribe of Asher, 12,000.

From the tribe of Naphtali, 12,000.

From the tribe of Manasseh, 12,000.

⁷ From the tribe of Simeon, 12,000.

From the tribe of Levi, 12,000.

From the tribe of Issachar, 12,000.

⁸ From the tribe of Zebulun, 12,000.

From the tribe of Joseph, 12,000.

From the tribe of Benjamin, 12,000.

The Huge Crowd Wearing White Robes

⁹ After this I looked, and there in front of me was a huge crowd of people. They stood in front of the throne and in front of the Lamb. There were so many that no one could count them. They came from every nation, tribe and people. That's true no matter what language they spoke. They were wearing white robes. In their hands they were holding palm branches. ¹⁰ They cried out in a loud voice,

"Salvation belongs to our God,
who sits on the throne.
Salvation also belongs to the Lamb."

¹¹ All the angels were standing around the throne. They were standing around the elders and the four living creatures. They fell down on their faces in front of the throne and worshiped God. ¹² They said,

"Amen!
May praise and glory
and wisdom be given to our God for ever and ever.
Give him thanks and honor and power and strength.
Amen!"

¹³ Then one of the elders spoke to me. "Who are these people dressed in white robes?" he asked. "Where did they come from?"

¹⁴ I answered, "Sir, you know."

He said, "They are the ones who have come out of the time of terrible suffering. They have washed their robes and made them white in the blood of the Lamb. ¹⁵ So

"they are in front of the throne of God.
They serve him day and night in his temple.

The one who sits on the
    throne
  will be with them to keep
    them safe.
16 'Never again will they be
    hungry.
  Never again will they be
    thirsty.
The sun will not beat down
    on them.'   *(Isaiah 49:10)*
  The heat of the desert will
    not harm them.
17 The Lamb, who is at the
    center of the area around
    the throne,
  will be their shepherd.
  'He will lead them to springs
    of living water.' *(Isaiah 49:10)*
  'And God will wipe away
    every tear from their
    eyes.'"   *(Isaiah 25:8)*

The Seventh Seal and the Gold Cup

8 The Lamb opened the seventh seal. Then there was silence in heaven for about half an hour.

2 I saw the seven angels who stand in front of God. Seven trumpets were given to them.

3 Another angel came and stood at the altar. He had a shallow gold cup for burning incense. He was given a lot of incense to offer on the golden altar. The altar was in front of the throne. With the incense he offered the prayers of all God's people. 4 The smoke of the incense rose up from the angel's hand. The prayers of God's people rose up together with it. The smoke and the prayers went up in front of God. 5 Then the angel took the gold cup and filled it with fire from the altar. He threw it down on the earth. There were rumblings and thunder, flashes of lightning, and an earthquake.

The Trumpets

6 Then the seven angels who had the seven trumpets got ready to blow them.

7 The first angel blew his trumpet. Hail and fire mixed with blood were thrown down on the earth. A third of the earth was burned up. A third of the trees were burned up. All the green grass was burned up.

8 The second angel blew his trumpet. Something that looked like a huge mountain on fire was thrown into the sea. A third of the sea turned into blood. 9 A third of the living creatures in the sea died. A third of the ships were destroyed.

10 The third angel blew his trumpet. Then a great star fell from the sky. It looked like a blazing torch. It fell on a third of the rivers and on the springs of water. 11 The name of the star is Wormwood. A third of the water turned bitter. Many people died from it.

12 The fourth angel blew his trumpet. Then a third of the sun was struck. A third of the moon was struck. A third of the stars were struck. So a third of each of them turned dark. Then a third of the day had no light. The same thing happened to a third of the night.

13 As I watched, I heard an

eagle that was flying high in the air. It called out in a loud voice, "How terrible! How terrible it will be for those living on the earth! How terrible! They will suffer as soon as the next three angels blow their trumpets!"

9 The fifth angel blew his trumpet. Then I saw a star that had fallen from the sky to the earth. The star was given the key to the tunnel leading down into a bottomless pit. The pit was called the Abyss. [2] The star opened the Abyss. Then smoke rose up from it like the smoke from a huge furnace. The sun and sky were darkened by the smoke from the Abyss. [3] Out of the smoke came locusts. They came down on the earth. They were given power like the power of scorpions of the earth. [4] They were told not to harm the grass of the earth or any plant or tree. They were supposed to harm only the people without God's official seal on their foreheads. [5] The locusts were not allowed to kill these people. But the locusts could hurt them over and over for five months. The pain the people suffered was like the sting of a scorpion when it strikes. [6] In those days, people will look for a way to die but won't find it. They will want to die, but death will escape them.

[7] The locusts looked like horses ready for battle. On their heads they wore something like crowns of gold. Their faces looked like human faces. [8] Their hair was like women's hair. Their teeth were like lions' teeth. [9] Their chests were covered with something that looked like armor made out of iron. The sound of their wings was like the thundering of many horses and chariots rushing into battle. [10] They had tails that could sting people like scorpions do. And in their tails they had power to hurt people over and over for five months. [11] Their king was the angel of the Abyss. In the Hebrew language his name is Abaddon. In Greek it is Apollyon. His name means Destroyer.

[12] The first terrible judgment is past. Two others are still coming.

[13] The sixth angel blew his trumpet. Then I heard a voice coming from the four corners of the golden altar. The altar stands in front of God. [14] The voice spoke to the sixth angel who had the trumpet. The voice said, "Set the four angels free who are held at the great river Euphrates." [15] The four angels had been ready for this very hour and day and month and year. They were set free to kill a third of all people. [16] The number of troops on horseback was 200,000,000. I heard how many there were.

[17] The horses and riders I saw in my vision had armor on their chests. It was red like fire, dark blue, and yellow like sulfur. The heads of the horses looked like lions' heads. Out of their mouths came fire, smoke and sulfur. [18] A third of all people were killed by the three plagues of fire, smoke

and sulfur that came out of the horses' mouths. ¹⁹ The power of the horses was in their mouths and in their tails. The tails were like snakes whose heads could bite.

²⁰ There were people who were not killed by these plagues. But they still didn't turn away from what they had been doing. They did not stop worshiping demons. They kept worshiping statues of gods made out of gold, silver, bronze, stone and wood. These statues can't see or hear or walk. ²¹ The people also did not turn away from their murders, witchcraft, sexual sins and stealing.

The Angel and the Little Scroll

10 Then I saw another mighty angel coming down from heaven. He was wearing a cloud like a robe. There was a rainbow above his head. His face was like the sun. His legs were like pillars of fire. ² He was holding a little scroll. It was lying open in his hand. The angel put his right foot on the sea and his left foot on the land. ³ Then he gave a loud shout like the roar of a lion. When he shouted, the voices of the seven thunders spoke. ⁴ When they had spoken, I was getting ready to write. But I heard a voice from heaven say, "Seal up what the seven thunders have said. Do not write it down."

⁵ I had seen an angel standing on the sea and on the land. This angel raised his right hand to heaven. ⁶ He made a promise in the name of the God who lives for ever and ever. This is the God who created the sky, earth and sea and all that is in them. The angel said, "There will be no more waiting! ⁷ God's plan will be carried out. This will happen when the seventh angel is ready to blow his trumpet. God told all this to the prophets who served him long ago."

⁸ Then the voice I had heard from heaven spoke to me again. It said, "The angel is standing on the sea and on the land. Go and take the scroll from him. It is lying open in his hand."

⁹ So I went to the angel and asked him to give me the little scroll. He said to me, "Take it and eat it. It will become sour in your stomach. But 'in your mouth it will taste as sweet as honey.' " *(Ezekiel 3:3)* ¹⁰ I took the little scroll from the angel's hand and ate it. In my mouth it tasted as sweet as honey. But when I had eaten it, it became sour in my stomach. ¹¹ Then I was told, "You must prophesy again about many peoples, nations, languages and kings."

The Two Witnesses

11 I was given a long stick that looked like a measuring rod. I was told, "Go and measure the temple of God. And measure the altar where the people are worshiping. ² But do not measure the outer courtyard. That's because it has been given to the Gentiles. They will take over the holy city for 42 months. ³ I will appoint my two witnesses. And they will prophesy for 1,260 days. They will be dressed in the rough clothes people wear when they're sad." ⁴The witnesses are "the two olive trees" and the two lampstands. And "they stand in front of the Lord of the earth." *(Zechariah 4:3,11,14)* ⁵If anyone tries to harm them, fire comes from their mouths and eats up their enemies. This is how anyone who wants to harm them must die. ⁶These witnesses have power to close up the sky. Then it will not rain while they are prophesying. They also have power to turn the waters into blood. And they can strike the earth with every kind of plague. They can do this as often as they want to. ⁷When they have finished speaking, the beast that comes up from the Abyss will attack them. He will overpower them and kill them. ⁸Their bodies will lie in the main street of the great city. It is also the city where their Lord was nailed to a cross. The city is sometimes compared to Sodom or Egypt. ⁹For three and a half days, people will stare at their bodies. These people will be from every tribe and nation, no matter what language they speak. They will refuse to bury them. ¹⁰Those who live on the earth will be happy about this. That's because those two prophets had made them suffer. The people will celebrate by sending one another gifts.

¹¹But after the three and a half days, the breath of life from God entered the witnesses. They both stood up. Terror struck those who saw them. ¹²Then the two witnesses heard a loud voice from heaven. It said to them, "Come up here." They went up to heaven in a cloud. Their enemies watched it happen.

¹³At that same time there was a powerful earthquake. A tenth of the city crumbled and fell. In the earthquake, 7,000 people were killed. Those who lived through it were terrified. They gave glory to the God of heaven.

¹⁴The second terrible judgment has passed. The third is coming soon.

The Seventh Trumpet

¹⁵The seventh angel blew his trumpet. There were loud voices in heaven. They said,

"The kingdom of the world
    has become
  the kingdom of our Lord
    and of his Messiah.
  He will rule for ever and
    ever."

¹⁶The 24 elders were sitting on their thrones in front of God. They fell on their faces and worshiped God. ¹⁷They said,

"Lord God who rules over all,
    we give thanks to you.
  You are the God who is and
    who was.
  We give you thanks.
    That's because you have
      begun to rule with your
      great power.
¹⁸The nations were angry,
  and the time for your anger
    has come.

The time has come to judge
   the dead.
It is time to reward your
   servants the prophets
   and your people who
   honor you.
There is a reward for all your
   people,
   both great and small.
It is time to destroy those
   who destroy the earth."

[19] Then God's temple in heaven was opened. Inside it the wooden chest called the ark of his covenant could be seen. There were flashes of lightning, rumblings and thunder, an earthquake and a severe hailstorm.

The Woman and the Dragon

12 A great sign appeared in heaven. It was a woman wearing the sun like clothes. The moon was under her feet. On her head she wore a crown of 12 stars. [2] She was pregnant. She cried out in pain because she was about to have a baby. [3] Then another sign appeared in heaven. It was a huge red dragon. It had seven heads and ten horns. On its seven heads it wore seven crowns. [4] The dragon's tail swept a third of the stars out of the sky. It threw the stars down to earth. The dragon stood in front of the woman who was about to have a baby. The dragon wanted to eat her child the moment he was born. [5] She gave birth to a son. He "will rule all the nations with an iron scepter." *(Psalm 2:9)* And her child was taken up to God and to his throne. [6] The woman escaped into the desert where God had a place prepared for her. There she would be taken care of for 1,260 days.

[7] Then a war began in heaven. Michael and his angels fought against the dragon. And the dragon and his angels fought back. [8] But the dragon wasn't strong enough. Both he and his angels lost their place in heaven. [9] The great dragon was thrown down to the earth, and his angels with him. The dragon is that old serpent called the devil, or Satan. He leads the whole world astray.

[10] Then I heard a loud voice in heaven. It said,

"Now the salvation and the
   power and the kingdom
   of our God have come.
The authority of his
   Messiah has come.
Satan, who brings charges
   against our brothers and
   sisters,
   has been thrown down.
He brings charges against
   them in front of our God
   day and night.
[11] They had victory over him
   by the blood the Lamb
   spilled for them.
They had victory over him
   by speaking the truth
   about Jesus to others.
They were willing to risk
   their lives,
   even if it led to death.
[12] So be joyful, you heavens!
   Be glad, all you who live
   there!
But how terrible it will be for
   the earth and the sea!

> The devil has come down
>   to you.
> He is very angry.
> He knows his time is
>   short."

[13] The dragon saw that he had been thrown down to the earth. So he chased the woman who had given birth to the boy. [14] The woman was given the two wings of a great eagle. She was given these wings so that she could fly away. She could fly to the place prepared for her in the desert. There she would be taken care of for three and a half years. She would be out of the serpent's reach. [15] Then out of his mouth the serpent spit water like a river. He wanted to catch the woman and sweep her away in the flood. [16] But the earth helped the woman. It opened its mouth and swallowed the river that the dragon had spit out. [17] The dragon was very angry with the woman. He went off to make war against the rest of her children. They obey God's commands. And they hold firmly to the truth they have said about Jesus.

The Beast Who Comes Out of the Sea

13 The dragon stood on the seashore. I saw a beast coming out of the sea. It had ten horns and seven heads. There were ten crowns on its horns. On each head was an evil name that brought shame to God. [2] The beast I saw looked like a leopard. But it had feet like a bear and a mouth like a lion. The dragon gave the beast his power, his throne, and great authority. [3] One of the beast's heads seemed to have had a deadly wound. But the wound had been healed. The whole world was amazed and followed the beast. [4] People worshiped the dragon, because he had given authority to the beast. They also worshiped the beast. They asked, "Who is like the beast? Who can make war against it?"

[5] The beast was given a mouth to brag and speak evil things against God. The beast was allowed to use its authority for 42 months. [6] The beast opened its mouth to speak evil things against God. It told lies about God and about the place where God lives. And it told lies about those who live in heaven with him. [7] The beast was allowed to make war against God's holy people and to overcome them. It was given authority over every tribe, people and nation, no matter what language they spoke. [8] Many people who live on the earth will worship the beast. They are the ones whose names are not written in the Lamb's book of life. The Lamb is the one whose death was planned before the world was created.

[9] Whoever has ears should listen.

[10] "Everyone who is supposed
>   to be captured
>   will be captured.
> Everyone who is supposed to
>   be killed by a sword
>   will be killed by a sword."

(Jeremiah 15:2)

So God's people must be patient and faithful.

The Beast Who Comes Out of the Earth

[11] Then I saw a second beast. This one came out of the earth. It had two horns like a lamb. But it spoke like a dragon. [12] This beast had all the authority of the first beast. It did what the first beast wanted. It made the earth and all who live on it worship the first beast. The first beast was the one whose deadly wound had been healed. [13] The second beast performed great signs. It even made fire come from heaven to the earth. And the fire was seen by everyone. [14] The first beast had given the second beast the power to perform these signs. By these signs, the second beast tricked those who live on the earth. The second beast ordered people to set up a statue to honor the first beast. The first beast was the one who had been wounded by a sword and still lived. [15] The second beast was allowed to give breath to this statue so it could speak. The statue could kill all who refused to worship it. [16] It also forced everyone to receive a mark on their right hand or on their forehead. People great or small, rich or poor, free or slave had to receive the mark. [17] They could not buy or sell anything unless they had the mark. The mark is the name of the beast or the number of its name.

[18] This problem requires wisdom. Anyone who is wise should figure out what the beast's number means. It is the number of a man. And that number is 666.

The Lamb and the 144,000

14 I looked, and there in front of me was the Lamb. He was standing on Mount Zion. With him were 144,000 people. Written on their foreheads were his name and his Father's name. [2] I heard a sound from heaven. It was like the roar of rushing waters and loud thunder. The sound I heard was like the music of harps being played. [3] Then everyone sang a new song in front of the throne. They sang it in front of the four living creatures and the elders. No one could learn the song except the 144,000. They had been set free from the evil of the earth. [4] They had not committed sexual sins with women. They had kept themselves pure. They follow the Lamb wherever he goes. They were purchased from among human beings as a first offering to God and the Lamb. [5] They told no lies. They are without blame.

The Three Angels

[6] I saw another angel. He was flying high in the air. He came to tell everyone on earth the good news that will always be true. He told it to every nation, tribe and people, no matter what language they spoke. [7] In a loud voice he said, "Have respect for God. Give him glory. The hour has come for God to judge. Worship him who made the heavens and the earth. Worship him who

made the sea and the springs of water."

[8] A second angel followed him. He said, " 'Fallen! Babylon the Great has fallen!' *(Isaiah 21:9)* The city of Babylon made all the nations drink the strong wine of her terrible sins."

[9] A third angel followed them. He said in a loud voice, "There will be trouble for anyone who worships the beast and its statue! There will be trouble for anyone who has its mark on their forehead or their hand! [10] They, too, will drink the wine of God's great anger. His wine has been poured full strength into the cup of his anger. They will be burned with flaming sulfur. The holy angels and the Lamb will see it happen. [11] The smoke of their terrible suffering will rise for ever and ever. Day and night, there will be no rest for anyone who worships the beast and its statue. There will be no rest for anyone who receives the mark of its name." [12] God's people need to be very patient. They are the ones who obey God's commands. And they remain faithful to Jesus.

[13] Then I heard a voice from heaven. "Write this," it said. "Blessed are the dead who die as believers in the Lord from now on."

"Yes," says the Holy Spirit. "They will rest from their labor. What they have done will not be forgotten."

The Harvest of the Earth

[14] I looked, and there in front of me was a white cloud. Sitting on the cloud was one who looked "like a son of man." *(Daniel 7:13)* He wore a gold crown on his head. In his hand was a sharp, curved blade for cutting grain. [15] Then another angel came out of the temple. He called in a loud voice to the one sitting on the cloud. "Take your blade," he said. "Cut the grain. The time has come. The earth is ready to be harvested." [16] So the one sitting on the cloud swung his blade over the earth. And the earth was harvested.

[17] Another angel came out of the temple in heaven. He too had a sharp, curved blade. [18] Still another angel came from the altar. He was in charge of the fire on the altar. He called out in a loud voice to the angel who had the sharp blade. "Take your blade," he said, "and gather the bunches of grapes from the earth's vine. Its grapes are ripe." [19] So the angel swung his blade over the earth. He gathered its grapes. Then he threw them into a huge winepress. The winepress stands for God's anger. [20] In the winepress outside the city, the grapes were stomped on. Blood flowed out of the winepress. It spread over the land for about 180 miles. It rose as high as the horses' heads.

Seven Angels With Seven Plagues

15 I saw in heaven another great and wonderful sign. Seven angels were about to bring the seven last plagues. The plagues would complete

God's anger. [2] Then I saw something that looked like a sea of glass glowing with fire. Standing beside the sea were those who had won the battle over the beast. They had also overcome its statue and the number of its name. They held harps given to them by God. [3] They sang the song of God's servant Moses and of the Lamb. They sang,

"Lord God who rules over
    all,
    everything you do is great
        and wonderful.
King of the nations,
    your ways are true and
        fair.
[4] Lord, who will not have
        respect for you?
    Who will not bring glory to
        your name?
You alone are holy.
All nations will come
    and worship you.
They see that the things you
    do are right."

[5] After this I looked, and I saw the temple in heaven. And it was opened. The temple is the holy tent where the tablets of the covenant law were kept. [6] Out of the temple came the seven angels who were bringing the seven plagues. They were dressed in clean, shining linen. They wore gold strips of cloth around their chests. [7] Then one of the four living creatures gave seven golden bowls to the seven angels. The bowls were filled with the anger of God, who lives for ever and ever. [8] The temple was filled with smoke that came from the glory and power of God. No one could enter the temple at that time. They had to wait until the seven plagues of the seven angels were completed.

The Seven Bowls of God's Great Anger

16 Then I heard a loud voice from the temple speaking to the seven angels. "Go," it said. "Pour out the seven bowls of God's great anger on the earth."

[2] The first angel went and poured out his bowl on the land. Ugly and painful sores broke out on people. Those people had the mark of the beast and worshiped its statue.

[3] The second angel poured out his bowl on the sea. It turned into blood like the blood of a dead person. Every living thing in the sea died.

[4] The third angel poured out his bowl on the rivers and springs of water. They became blood. [5] Then I heard the angel who was in charge of the waters. He said,

"Holy One, the way you judge
    is fair.
    You are the God who is and
        who was.
[6] Those who worship the beast
        have poured out blood.
    They have poured out
        the life's blood of your
            holy people and your
                prophets.
So you have given blood
        to drink to those who
            worship the beast.
    That's exactly what they
        should get."

⁷Then I heard the altar reply. It said,

"Lord God who rules over all,
    the way you judge is true
    and fair."

⁸The fourth angel poured out his bowl on the sun. The sun was allowed to burn people with fire. ⁹They were burned by the blazing heat. So they spoke evil things against the name of God, who controlled these plagues. But they refused to turn away from their sins. They did not give glory to God.

¹⁰The fifth angel poured out his bowl on the throne of the beast. The kingdom of the beast became very dark. People chewed on their tongues because they were suffering so much. ¹¹They spoke evil things against the God of heaven. They did this because of their pains and their sores. But they refused to turn away from the sins they had committed.

¹²The sixth angel poured out his bowl on the great river Euphrates. Its water dried up to prepare the way for the kings from the East. ¹³Then I saw three evil spirits that looked like frogs. They came out of the mouths of the dragon, the beast and the false prophet. ¹⁴They are spirits of demons that perform signs. They go out to gather the kings of the whole world for battle. This battle will take place on the great day of the God who rules over all.

¹⁵"Look! I am coming like a thief! Blessed is anyone who stays awake and keeps their clothes on. Then they will be ready. They will not be caught naked and so be put to shame."

¹⁶Then the evil spirits gathered the kings together. In the Hebrew language, the place where the kings met is called Armageddon.

¹⁷The seventh angel poured out his bowl into the air. Out of the temple came a loud voice from the throne. It said, "It is done!" ¹⁸Then there came flashes of lightning, rumblings, thunder and a powerful earthquake. There has never been an earthquake as terrible as this. One like this hasn't happened while human beings have lived on earth. ¹⁹The great city split into three parts. The cities of the nations crumbled and fell. God remembered Babylon the Great. He gave Babylon the cup filled with the wine of his terrible anger. ²⁰Every island ran away. The mountains could not be found. ²¹Huge hailstones weighing about 100 pounds each fell from the sky. The hail crushed people. And they spoke evil things against God because of the plague. That's because the plague of hail was so terrible.

Babylon the Great Prostitute Sits on the Beast

17 One of the seven angels who had the seven bowls came to me. He said, "Come. I will show you how the great prostitute will be punished. She

is the one who sits by many waters. [2] The kings of the earth took part in her evil ways. The people living on earth were drunk with the wine of her terrible sins."

[3] Then in a vision the angel carried me away to a desert. There the Holy Spirit showed me a woman sitting on a bright red beast. It was covered with names that say evil things about God. It had seven heads and ten horns. [4] The woman was dressed in purple and bright red. She was gleaming with gold, jewels and pearls. In her hand she held a golden cup filled with things that God hates. It was filled with her terrible, dirty sins. [5] The name written on her forehead was a mystery. Here is what it said.

THE GREAT CITY OF BABYLON
THE MOTHER OF PROSTITUTES
THE MOTHER OF EVERYTHING
ON EARTH THAT GOD HATES

[6] I saw that the woman was drunk with the blood of God's holy people. They are the ones who are witnesses about Jesus.

When I saw her, I was very amazed. [7] Then the angel said to me, "Why are you amazed? I will explain to you the mystery of the woman. And I will explain the mystery of the beast she rides on. The beast is the one who has the seven heads and ten horns. [8] The beast that you saw used to exist and now does not. Yet it will come up out of the Abyss and be destroyed. Some people on the earth will be amazed when they see the beast. Their names have not been written in the book of life from the time the world was created. They will be amazed at the beast. That's because it will come again even though it used to exist and now does not.

[9] "Here is a problem that you have to be wise to understand. The seven heads are seven hills that the woman sits on. [10] They are also seven kings. Five have fallen, one is ruling, and the other has still not come. When he does come, he must remain for only a little while. [11] The beast who used to exist, and now does not, is an eighth king. He belongs to the other seven. He will be destroyed.

[12] "The ten horns you saw are ten kings. They have not yet received a kingdom. But for one hour they will receive authority to rule together with the beast. [13] They have only one purpose. So they will give their power and authority to the beast. [14] They will make war against the Lamb. But the Lamb will have victory over them. That's because he is the most powerful Lord of all and the greatest King of all. His appointed, chosen and faithful followers will be with him."

[15] Then the angel spoke to me. "You saw the waters the prostitute sits on," he said. "They stand for all the nations of the world, no matter what their race or language is. [16] The beast and the ten horns you saw will hate the prostitute. They will destroy her and leave her naked. They

will eat her flesh and burn her with fire. [17] God has put it into their hearts to carry out his purpose. So they agreed to give the beast their royal authority. They will give him this authority until God's words come true. [18] The woman you saw stands for the great city of Babylon. That city rules over the kings of the earth."

Weeping When Babylon Falls

18 After these things I saw another angel coming down from heaven. He had great authority. His glory filled the earth with light. [2] With a mighty voice he shouted,

> "'Fallen! Babylon the Great
>   has fallen!'　*(Isaiah 21:9)*
> She has become a place
>   where demons live.
> She has become a den for
>   every evil spirit.
> She has become a place
>   where every 'unclean'
>   bird is found.
> She has become a place
>   where every 'unclean'
>   and hated animal is
>   found.
> [3] All the nations have drunk
>   the strong wine of her
>   terrible sins.
> The kings of the earth took
>   part in her evil ways.
> The traders of the world
>   grew rich from her great
>   wealth."

Warning to Run from Babylon's Judgment

[4] Then I heard another voice from heaven. It said,

> "'Come out of her, my
>   people.'　*(Jeremiah 51:45)*
> Then you will not take part
>   in her sins.
> You will not suffer from
>   any of her plagues.
> [5] Her sins are piled up to
>   heaven.
> God has remembered her
>   crimes.
> [6] Do to her as she has done to
>   others.
> Pay her back double for
>   what she has done.
> Pour her a double dose of
>   what she has poured for
>   others.
> [7] Give her as much pain and
>   suffering
> as the glory and wealth she
>   gave herself.
> She brags to herself,
>   'I rule on a throne like a
>   queen.
> I am not a widow.
>   I will never mourn.'
>   *(Isaiah 47:7,8)*
> [8] But she will be plagued by
>   death, sadness and
>   hunger.
> In a single day she will
>   suffer all these plagues.
> She will be burned up by fire.
> That's because the Lord
>   God who judges her is
>   mighty.

How Terrible When Babylon Falls!

[9] "The kings of the earth who committed terrible sins with her will weep. They will mourn because they used to share her riches. They will see the smoke rising as she burns. [10] They will

be terrified by her suffering. They will stand far away from her. And they will cry out,

> "'How terrible! How terrible
> it is for you, great city!
> How terrible for you,
> mighty city of Babylon!
> In just one hour you have
> been destroyed!'

[11] "The traders of the world will weep and mourn over her. No one buys what they sell anymore. [12] Here is what they had for sale.

> Gold, silver, jewels, pearls.
> Fine linen, purple, silk,
> bright red cloth.
> Every kind of citron wood.
> All sorts of things made out
> of ivory, valuable wood,
> bronze, iron, marble.
> [13] Cinnamon, spice, incense,
> myrrh, frankincense.
> Wine, olive oil, fine flour,
> wheat.
> Cattle, sheep, horses, car-
> riages, and human be-
> ings sold as slaves.

[14] "The merchants will say, 'The pleasure you longed for has left you. All your riches and glory have disappeared forever.' [15] The traders who sold these things became rich because of Babylon. When she suffers, they will stand far away. Her suffering will terrify them. They will weep and mourn. [16] They will cry out,

> "'How terrible! How terrible
> it is for you, great city,
> dressed in fine linen,
> purple and bright red!

> How terrible for you, great
> city, gleaming with gold,
> jewels and pearls!
> [17] In just one hour your
> great wealth has been
> destroyed!'

"Every sea captain and all who travel by ship will stand far away. So will the sailors and all who earn their living from the sea. [18] They will see the smoke rising as Babylon burns. They will ask, 'Was there ever a city like this great city?' [19] They will throw dust on their heads. They will weep and mourn. They will cry out,

> "'How terrible! How terrible
> it is for you, great city!
> All who had ships on the
> sea
> became rich because of her
> wealth!
> In just one hour she has been
> destroyed!'

> [20] "You heavens, be glad for this!
> You people of God, be glad!
> You apostles and prophets,
> be glad!
> God has judged her
> with the judgment she gave
> to you."

Babylon's Judgment Is Final

[21] Then a mighty angel picked up a huge rock. It was the size of a large millstone. He threw it into the sea. Then he said,

> "That is how
> the great city of Babylon
> will be thrown down.
> Never again will it be
> found.

22 The songs of musicians will
   never be heard in you
   again.
Gone will be the music
   of harps, flutes and
   trumpets.
No worker of any kind
   will ever be found in you
   again.
The sound of a millstone
   will never be heard in you
   again.
23 The light of a lamp
   will never shine in you
   again.
The voices of brides and
   grooms
   will never be heard in you
   again.
Your traders were among the
   world's most important
   people.
By your magic spell all
   the nations were led
   astray.
24 You were guilty of the murder
   of prophets and God's
   holy people.
You were guilty of the
   blood of all who have
   been killed on the
   earth."

*Three Hallelujahs for the Fall
of Babylon!*

19 After these things I
   heard a roar in heaven.
It sounded like a huge crowd
shouting,

"Hallelujah!
Salvation and glory and
   power belong to our
   God.
2   The way he judges is true
   and fair.

He has judged the great
   prostitute.
She made the earth impure
   with her terrible sins.
God has paid her back for
   killing those who served
   him."

3 Again they shouted,

"Hallelujah!
The smoke from her fire
   goes up for ever and
   ever."

4 The 24 elders and the four
living creatures bowed down.
They worshiped God, who was
sitting on the throne. They cried
out,

"Amen! Hallelujah!"

5 Then a voice came from the
throne. It said,

"Praise our God,
   all you who serve him!
Praise God, all you who have
   respect for him,
   both great and small!"

6 Then I heard the noise of a
huge crowd. It sounded like the
roar of rushing waters and like
loud thunder. The people were
shouting,

"Hallelujah!
   Our Lord God is the King
   who rules over all.
7 Let us be joyful and glad!
   Let us give him glory!
It is time for the Lamb's
   wedding.
   His bride has made herself
   ready.
8 Fine linen, bright and clean,
   was given to her to wear."

Fine linen stands for the right things that God's holy people do.

⁹Here is what the angel told me to write. "Blessed are those invited to the wedding supper of the Lamb!" Then he added, "These are the true words of God."

¹⁰When I heard this, I fell at his feet to worship him. But he said to me, "Don't do that! I serve God, just as you do. I am God's servant, just like believers who hold firmly to what Jesus has taught. Worship God! The Spirit of prophecy tells the truth about Jesus."

The Heavenly Warrior Has Victory Over the Beast

¹¹I saw heaven standing open. There in front of me was a white horse. Its rider is called Faithful and True. When he judges or makes war, he is always fair. ¹²His eyes are like blazing fire. On his head are many crowns. A name is written on him that only he knows. ¹³He is dressed in a robe dipped in blood. His name is the Word of God. ¹⁴The armies of heaven were following him, riding on white horses. They were dressed in fine linen, white and clean. ¹⁵Coming out of the rider's mouth is a sharp sword. He will strike down the nations with the sword. Scripture says, "He will rule them with an iron scepter." *(Psalm 2:9)* He stomps on the grapes of God's winepress. The winepress stands for the terrible anger of the God who rules over all.

¹⁶Here is the name that is written on the rider's robe and on his thigh.

THE GREATEST KING OF ALL AND THE MOST POWERFUL LORD OF ALL

¹⁷I saw an angel standing in the sun. He shouted to all the birds flying high in the air, "Come! Gather together for the great supper of God. ¹⁸Come and eat the dead bodies of kings, generals, and other mighty people. Eat the bodies of horses and their riders. Eat the bodies of all people, free and slave, great and small."

¹⁹Then I saw the beast and the kings of the earth with their armies. They had gathered together to make war against the rider on the horse and his army. ²⁰But the beast and the false prophet were captured. The false prophet had done signs for the beast. In this way the false prophet had tricked some people. Those people had received the mark of the beast and had worshiped its statue. The beast and the false prophet were thrown alive into the lake of fire. The lake of fire burns with sulfur. ²¹The rest were killed by the sword that came out of the rider's mouth. All the birds stuffed themselves with the dead bodies.

The Thousand Years

20 I saw an angel coming down out of heaven. He had the key to the Abyss. In his hand he held a heavy chain. ²He grabbed the dragon, that old serpent. The serpent is also called the devil, or Satan. The angel put him in chains for 1,000 years. ³Then he threw him into the Abyss. He locked it and sealed him in. This was to keep Satan from causing the nations to believe his lies anymore. Satan will be locked away until the 1,000 years are ended. After that, he must be set free for a short time.

⁴I saw thrones. Those who had been given authority to judge were sitting on them. I also saw the souls of those whose heads had been cut off. They had been killed because they had spoken what was true about Jesus. They had also been killed because of the word of God. They had not worshiped the beast or its statue. They had not received its mark on their foreheads or hands. They came to life and ruled with Christ for 1,000 years. ⁵This is the first resurrection. The rest of the dead did not come to life until the 1,000 years were ended. ⁶Blessed and holy are those who share in the first resurrection. The second death has no power over them. They will be priests of God and of Christ. They will rule with him for 1,000 years.

Satan Is Judged

⁷When the 1,000 years are over, Satan will be set free from his prison. ⁸He will go out to cause the nations to believe lies. He will gather them from the four corners of the earth. He will bring Gog and Magog together for battle. Their troops are as many as the grains of sand on the seashore. ⁹They marched across the whole earth. They surrounded the place where God's holy people were camped. It was the city he loves. But fire came down from heaven and burned them up. ¹⁰The devil had caused them to believe lies. He was thrown into the lake of burning sulfur. That is where the beast and the false prophet had been thrown. They will all suffer day and night for ever and ever.

The Dead Are Judged

¹¹I saw a great white throne. And I saw God sitting on it. When the earth and sky saw his face, they ran away. There was no place for them. ¹²I saw the dead, great and small, standing in front of the throne. Books were opened. Then another book was opened. It was the book of life. The dead were judged by what they had done. The things they had done were written in the books. ¹³The sea gave up the dead that were in it. And Death and Hell gave up their dead. Each person was judged by what they had done. ¹⁴Then Death and Hell were thrown into the lake of fire. The lake of fire is the second death. ¹⁵Anyone whose name was not written in the book of life was thrown into the lake of fire.

A New Heaven and a New Earth

21 I saw "a new heaven and a new earth." *(Isaiah 65:17)* The first heaven and the first earth

were completely gone. There was no longer any sea. [2] I saw the Holy City, the new Jerusalem. It was coming down out of heaven from God. It was prepared like a bride beautifully dressed for her husband. [3] I heard a loud voice from the throne. It said, "Look! God now makes his home with the people. He will live with them. They will be his people. And God himself will be with them and be their God. [4] 'He will wipe away every tear from their eyes. There will be no more death.' *(Isaiah 25:8)* And there will be no more sadness. There will be no more crying or pain. Things are no longer the way they used to be."

[5] He who was sitting on the throne said, "I am making everything new!" Then he said, "Write this down. You can trust these words. They are true."

[6] He said to me, "It is done. I am the Alpha and the Omega, the Beginning and the End. I will give water to anyone who is thirsty. The water will come from the spring of the water of life. It doesn't cost anything! [7] Those who have victory will receive all this from me. I will be their God, and they will be my children. [8] But others will be thrown into the lake of fire that burns with sulfur. Those who are afraid and those who do not believe will be there. Murderers and those who make themselves impure will join them. Those who commit sexual sins and those who practice witchcraft will go there. Those who worship statues of gods and all who tell lies will be there too. The lake of fire is the second death."

The New Jerusalem is the Bride of the Lamb

[9] One of the seven angels who had the seven bowls came and spoke to me. The bowls were filled with the seven last plagues. The angel said, "Come. I will show you the bride, the wife of the Lamb." [10] Then he carried me away in a vision. The Spirit took me to a huge, high mountain. He showed me Jerusalem, the Holy City. It was coming down out of heaven from God. [11] It shone with the glory of God. It gleamed like a very valuable jewel. It was like a jasper, as clear as crystal. [12] The city had a huge, high wall with 12 gates. Twelve angels were at the gates, one at each of them. On the gates were written the names of the 12 tribes of Israel. [13] There were three gates on the east and three on the north. There were three gates on the south and three on the west. [14] The wall of the city had 12 foundations. Written on them were the names of the 12 apostles of the Lamb.

[15] The angel who talked with me had a gold measuring rod. He used it to measure the city, its gates and its walls. [16] The city was laid out like a square. It was as long as it was wide. The angel measured the city with the rod. It was 1,400 miles long. It was as wide and high as it was

long. [17]The angel measured the wall as human beings measure things. It was 200 feet thick. [18]The wall was made out of jasper. The city was made out of pure gold, as pure as glass. [19]The foundations of the city walls were decorated with every kind of jewel. The first foundation was made out of jasper. The second was made out of sapphire. The third was made out of agate. The fourth was made out of emerald. [20]The fifth was made out of onyx. The sixth was made out of ruby. The seventh was made out of chrysolite. The eighth was made out of beryl. The ninth was made out of topaz. The tenth was made out of turquoise. The eleventh was made out of jacinth. The twelfth was made out of amethyst. [21]The 12 gates were made from 12 pearls. Each gate was made out of a single pearl. The main street of the city was made out of gold. It was gold as pure as glass that people can see through clearly.

[22]I didn't see a temple in the city. That's because the Lamb and the Lord God who rules over all are its temple. [23]The city does not need the sun or moon to shine on it. God's glory is its light, and the Lamb is its lamp. [24]The nations will walk by the light of the city. The kings of the world will bring their glory into it. [25]Its gates will never be shut, because there will be no night there. [26]The glory and honor of the nations will be brought into it. [27]Only what is pure will enter the city. No one who causes people to believe lies will enter it. No one who does shameful things will enter it either. Only those whose names are written in the Lamb's book of life will enter the city.

The Earth Is Made Like New Again

22 Then the angel showed me the river of the water of life. It was as clear as crystal. It flowed from the throne of God and of the Lamb. [2]It flowed down the middle of the city's main street. On each side of the river stood the tree of life, bearing 12 crops of fruit. Its fruit was ripe every month. The leaves of the tree bring healing to the nations. [3]There will no longer be any curse. The throne of God and of the Lamb will be in the city. God's servants will serve him. [4]They will see his face. His name will be on their foreheads. [5]There will be no more night. They will not need the light of a lamp or the light of the sun. The Lord God will give them light. They will rule for ever and ever.

John and the Angel

[6]The angel said to me, "You can trust these words. They are true. The Lord is the God who gives messages to the prophets. He sent his angel to show his servants the things that must soon take place."

[7]"Look! I am coming soon! Words of prophecy are written in this book. Blessed is the person who obeys them."

⁸ I, John, am the one who heard and saw these things. After that, I fell down to worship at the feet of the angel. He is the one who had been showing me these things. ⁹ But he said to me, "Don't do that! I serve God, just as you do. I am God's servant, just like the other prophets. And I serve God along with all who obey the words of this book. Worship God!"

¹⁰ Then he told me, "Do not seal up the words of the prophecy in this book. These things are about to happen. ¹¹ Let the person who does wrong keep on doing wrong. Let the evil person continue to be evil. Let the person who does right keep on doing what is right. And let the holy person continue to be holy."

The Revelation Ends With Warnings and Blessings

¹² "Look! I am coming soon! I bring my rewards with me. I will reward each person for what they have done. ¹³ I am the Alpha and the Omega. I am the First and the Last. I am the Beginning and the End.

¹⁴ "Blessed are those who wash their robes. They will have the right to come to the tree of life. They will be allowed to go through the gates into the city. ¹⁵ Outside the city are those who are impure. These people include those who practice witchcraft. Outside are also those who commit sexual sins and murder. Outside are those who worship statues of gods. And outside is everyone who loves and does what is false.

¹⁶ "I, Jesus, have sent my angel to give you this witness for the churches. I am the Root and the Son of David. I am the bright Morning Star."

¹⁷ The Holy Spirit and the bride say, "Come!" And the person who hears should say, "Come!" Anyone who is thirsty should come. Anyone who wants to take the free gift of the water of life should do so.

¹⁸ I am warning everyone who hears the words of the prophecy of this book. Suppose someone adds anything to them. Then God will add to that person the plagues told about in this book. ¹⁹ Suppose someone takes away any words from this book of prophecy. Then God will take away from that person the blessings told about in this book. God will take away their share in the tree of life. God will also take away their place in the Holy City.

²⁰ Jesus is a witness about these things. He says, "Yes. I am coming soon."

Amen. Come, Lord Jesus!

²¹ May the grace of the Lord Jesus be with God's people. Amen.

Dictionary

A

Abyss
A deep pit where evil spirits live. Satan will be held there in chains.

adultery
Having a sexual relationship with someone who is not your husband or wife.

altar
A table or raised place on which a gift, or sacrifice, was offered to God.

Amen
A word that means "it is true" or "let it be true."

angel
A spirit who is God's helper. A spirit who tells people God's words. See also *cherubim*.

anoint
1. To pour olive oil on people or things. This sets them apart for God. 2. To pour oil on people as part of praying for their healing.

anointed
To be set apart as God's special servant.

apostle
One of the twelve men who spent about three years with Jesus. They taught others about Jesus, too. See also *disciple*.

Aramaic
A language spoken by many people during Bible times. The Jews in Jesus' time most often spoke this language.

ark of the covenant
A large gold box that held the stone tablets of the Ten Commandments. The ark was God's throne on earth.

armor
A special outer covering like clothes made of metal. People wore it to help keep them safe in battle.

Asherah
A false god. People thought she was the Canaanite mother goddess and goddess of the sea.

B

Baal
The name of the most popular false god of Canaan.

Babel
A city where people tried to build a tower up to the sky.

Babylon
1. The capital city of the empire of Babylonia. 2. Any powerful, sinful city.

baptize
To sprinkle, pour on or cover a person with water. It is a sign that the person belongs to Jesus.

Beelzebub
Another name for the devil. Satan.

believe
To accept as true. To trust. See also *faith*.

blessed
1. Made joyful. 2. Helped by God.

C

cast lots
Something done to find out what God wants. It is like drawing straws to see who will go first.

chariot
A cart with two wheels pulled by horses. People, especially soldiers, rode in them.

cherubim
1. Spirits like angels who have large wings. They were and are a sign that God is sitting on his throne. 2. Spirits who serve God.

chief priest
See *high priest*.

Christ
A Greek word that means "the Anointed One." It is one of the names given to Jesus. It means the same thing as the Hebrew word *Messiah*. See also *Jesus*.

circumcision
Cutting off a male's foreskin (a piece of skin at the end of a penis). It was a sign that the person belonged to God.

clean
1. Something that God accepts. 2. Something that doesn't have sin.

clean animals
Animals that God said were acceptable to eat or to give as offerings.

commandment
A law or rule that God gives. See also *law*.

concubine
A woman who belonged to a man but was not his legal wife.

Council
See *Sanhedrin*.

covenant
1. A treaty, or promise, between two persons or groups. In the Bible it is a promise made between God and the people. 2. Promises from God for salvation.

cross
A wooden post with a bar near the top that extends to the right and left. A cross looks like the letter "T." The Romans killed people by nailing them to crosses.

crucify
To kill people by nailing them to crosses.

cud
Food that is chewed again. An animal such as a cow brings its food back from its stomach to its mouth. This food, or cud, can be chewed again. God told the people of Israel they could eat any animal that chews the cud and has hoofs that are separated.

curse
1. A call for God to punish someone. 2. A command of God that punishment will come on someone or something.

D

deacon
A church leader who helps people in Jesus' name.

dedicate
To set apart for a special purpose, often for God's use.

demon
An evil spirit.

devil
The one who tempts people to sin. See also *Satan*.

disciple
A person who follows a teacher. This person does what their teacher says to do. See also *apostle*. See also *Twelve, the*.

divorce
The end of a husband and wife's marriage.

doubt
A lack of faith or trust in something or someone. To not be sure.

E

Eden
The place where God made a garden for Adam and Eve.

elder
The leader of a church, town or nation. This person makes important decisions.

eternal
Forever. Without beginning or end.

evangelist
A person who tells others the Good News of Jesus.

evil
Bad. Wicked. Doing things that do not please God.

evil spirit
A demon. One of the devil's helpers.

F

faith
Trust and belief in God. Knowing that God is real, even though one can't see him. See also *believe*.

faithful
Able to be trusted or counted on.

famine
A time when there is not enough food to eat.

fast
Going without food and/or drink for a special reason.

Feast of Booths
A celebration or festival when the Israelites thanked God for the harvest of their crops. During the feast they lived in little tents for seven days to help remember when they traveled to Canaan.

Feast of Hanukkah
A celebration praising God that the Israelites and Jews today have to remember the cleaning and rededication of the temple. The temple had been made "unclean" by an enemy.

Feast of Weeks
A festival or celebration day at the beginning of the wheat harvest when the Israelites gave thanks to God. See also *Pentecost*.

Feast of Passover
See *Passover*.

Feast of Unleavened Bread
A week for remembering when God set the Israelites free from Egypt. It began the day after the Feast of Passover. During this time the people ate bread made without yeast, like they did when they left Egypt in a hurry.

fig
A sweet fruit that grows on trees in warm countries like Israel.

G

glory
1. God's greatness. 2. Praise and honor.

God
The maker and ruler of the world and all people.

grace
The kindness and forgiveness God gives to people. This is a gift. It cannot be earned.

H

hallelujah
A Hebrew word that means "praise the Lord."

Hanukkah
See *Feast of Hanukkah*.

harvest
Picking a crop when it is ripe.

heaven
1. God's home. 2. The sky. 3. Where Christians go after they die.

Hebrew
1. Another name for an Israelite. 2. The language spoken by the Israelites. The Old Testament is written in this language.

hell
A place of punishment for people who don't follow Jesus. They go there after they die.

Herod
The first name of five rulers from the same family. They ruled over Israel during the time of the New Testament.

high places
Places where people worshiped false gods. These places were found on top of hills.

high priest
A person from the family line of Aaron. He was in charge of everything in the holy tent or in the temple. He was in charge of everyone who came there to work and worship, too.

holy
Set apart for God. Belonging to God. Pure.

holy bread
Twelve loaves of bread placed in the Holy Room of the holy tent each week. They were a gift to God.

Holy Spirit
God's Spirit who creates life. He helps people do God's work. He helps people to believe in Jesus, to love him and to live like him.

holy tent
Also called the Tent of Meeting. A place where the Israelites worshiped God. They used this tent after they left Egypt and while they were in the desert for 40 years. Years later Solomon built the first temple. Then the people worshiped God there and not in the tent.

honor
To show respect to. To give credit to.

hosanna
A Hebrew word used to praise God.

hymn
A song of praise to God.

hyssop
A plant that smelled like mint. Its branches were used to shake water or blood on something to make it pure.

I

Immanuel
A name for Jesus that means "God with us."

incense
Spices that give a pleasing smell when they are burned. It was placed on the altar in the holy tent.

Israel
1. The new name God gave to Abraham's grandson Jacob. 2. The nation that came from the family line of Jacob. 3. The northern tribes that broke away from Judah to serve their own king.

Israelites
People from the nation of Israel. God's chosen people.

J

jealous
1. How God feels when people worship other things. 2. How we feel when someone else has something we want.

Jesus
The Greek form of the Hebrew name Joshua. It means "the LORD saves." See also *Christ*. See also *Immanuel*. See also *Savior*.

Jews
Another name for the people of Israel. This name was used after 600 B.C.

Jubilee
See *Year of Jubilee*.

judge
1. To decide if something is right or wrong. 2. A person who decides what is right or wrong in legal matters.

K

kingdom
An area or group of people ruled by a king.

L

law
Rules about what is right and wrong that God gave the people of Israel. See also *Law, the*.

Law, the
The first five books of the Bible.

Levites
Men from the tribe of Levi. They took care of the holy tent and the temple.

locust
A type of insect similar to a grasshopper. A huge number of them sometimes eats and destroys crops.

Lord
A personal name for God or Christ. It shows respect to him as our master and ruler.

lots
See *cast lots*.

M

manger
A food box for animals.

manna
Special food sent from heaven. It tasted like wafers, or crackers, sweetened with honey. God gave it to the Israelites in the desert, after they left Egypt.

mercy
More kindness and forgiveness than people deserve to get.

Messiah
A Hebrew word that means, "The Anointed One." It means the same thing as the Greek word *Christ*. See also *Jesus*.

millstone
A heavy rock used to crush grain to make flour.

miracle
An amazing thing that happens that only God can do. This includes such things as calming a storm or bringing someone back to life.

miraculous signs
Amazing things that God does to point us to him. These things cannot be explained by the laws of nature.

myrrh
A spice with a sweet smell. It came from plants and was made into perfume, incense and medicine.

N

nard
A costly oil made from a plant grown in India. It was used as a perfume to make skin smell good.

Nazarene
A person who came from the town of Nazareth. Jesus was called a Nazarene.

Nazirite
A person who was set apart to God in a special way. Or, a person who promised to do something special for God. They were not allowed to cut their hair, drink any wine or grape juice, eat grapes or raisins, or touch a dead body.

O

oath
A promise made before God.

obey
To do what you are told to do. To carry out God's commands.

offering
Something people give to God. It was and is a part of their worship. See also *sacrifice*.

oxen
Large cattle that are very strong. They were used to pull carts or plows.

P

papyrus
A tall, grassy plant that grows in shallow water. People made boats with these plants and paper from their stems.

Passover
A feast that happened every year. It reminded the people of the time when God "passed over" their homes in Egypt. Since the people put blood on the doorways, God did not hurt them.

paradise
A perfect place. Another name used for heaven.

pasture
A field of grassy land where cows or sheep may eat.

Pentecost

1. A celebration that was and is held 50 days after Passover. 2. The day the Holy Spirit came in a special way to live in Christians.

Pharaoh

The title of the ruler of Egypt in Bible times.

Pharisees

A group of Jews who carefully followed God's laws and their own rules about God's laws. Some Pharisees were also known as "teachers of the law."

Philistines

Strong enemies of Israel, especially during Saul and David's time.

pierce

To poke through with a sharp instrument.

pillar

1. A tall, upright post that helped to hold up a building. 2. A pillar could also mark a special place.

pillar of cloud

A cloud God used to lead the people of Israel. They could see it all day long when they were in the desert.

pillar of fire

A column of fire God used to lead the people of Israel. They could see it all night long when they were in the desert.

plague

1. A sickness that kills many people. 2. Anything that brings a lot of suffering or loss.

plumb line

A string that has a weight tied to the end of it. It is used to tell whether a wall is straight or not.

pomegranate

A round fruit with a tough skin, many seeds and a juicy red center.

praise

To give glory or honor to someone. To say good things about someone or something.

pregnant

Carrying a baby inside a woman's body until the baby is born.

Preparation Day

The day before the Sabbath day. A day to get all work done so that a person could rest on the Sabbath.

priest

A person who worked in the holy tent or the temple. He was responsible to give his own as well as other people's gifts and prayers to God.

prophecy

Important words or messages that God gives to his people. God gives these words through a special person called a prophet.

prophesy
1. To give a message from God.
2. To tell what the future will be.

prophet
A person who hears messages from God and tells them to others.

prostitutes
People who get paid to let other people have sexual relationships with them.

proverb
A wise saying.

psalm
A poem of praise, prayer or teaching. The book of Psalms is full of these poems.

Purim
A feast in which the Israelites remembered when God helped Queen Esther save the Jews.

R

Rabbi
The title of a teacher of Jewish law.

Raca
A word that made someone feel bad. It meant that they were foolish or stupid.

resurrection
Coming back to life in a whole new way and never dying again.

right hand
A place of honor and power. Jesus is at the right hand of God.

Rome
1. The empire that controlled a lot of the world when Jesus lived here on the earth. 2. The capital city of that empire. It is in Italy.

S

Sabbath
The seventh day of the week. On that day the Israelites rested from their work and turned their thoughts toward God.

sacred
Set apart for God. Holy.

sacrifice
1. To give something to God as a gift. 2. Something that is given to God as a gift of worship. See also *offering*.

Sadducees
A group of Jewish leaders. They followed only the first five books of the Bible. They did not believe that people rise from the dead.

salvation
Free from the guilt of sin. Jesus died for our sins and rose up from the dead. With this sacrifice, he paid for our sin. He has saved us if we believe in him.

Sanhedrin
A group of 71 Jewish leaders. They were led by the high priest. They were the most important Jewish court of law in Jesus' time.

Satan
God's most powerful enemy in the spirit world. Also called the devil.

saved
Set free from danger or sin.

Savior
The One who sets us free from our sins. A name belonging to Jesus Christ. See also *Jesus*.

Scripture
God's written Word to us. We also call this the Bible.

scroll
A long strip of paper or animal skin to write on. It was rolled up on two sticks to make it easy to use and store.

seal
1. A tool or a ring with a drawing or pattern cut into it
2. A mark made by pressing this tool into clay, wax or paper.

seer
A person who can tell the future with God's help. See also *prophet*.

shepherd
A person who takes care of sheep or goats.

sin
To disobey or displease God.

Sodom and Gomorrah
Two cities that God destroyed. The people who lived there were very evil.

Son of Man
A name Jesus gave to himself. It shows he is the Messiah. See also *Messiah*.

soul
A person's true inner self.

spiritual
Having to do with the things of God or the Bible.

staff
A stick a shepherd uses to take care of sheep or goats.

synagogue
A Jewish place of worship and teaching.

T

tambourine
A hand-held drum with metal pieces around the edge. It rattles when it is shaken or tapped.

tassels
Hanging groups of thread that are tied together at one end. God told the Israelites to sew tassels onto their clothing to remind them of God's commands.

temple
1. Any place of worship. 2. The building where the people of Israel worshiped God and brought their sacrifices. God was present there in a special way.

tempt
To try to get someone to do bad things.

Tent of Meeting
See *holy tent*.

threshing floor
A place where heads, or tops, of grain are beaten or stepped on. This is done to knock the seeds of grain from the stems.

tomb
A place to put dead bodies. It was often a cave with a big stone door.

treaty
An agreement between two people or groups or nations.

Twelve, the
The men who Jesus chose to be his special followers. See also *disciple*.

U

unclean
Something that God does not accept. Not pure. Not pleasing to God.

Urim and Thummim
Objects that were worn on the high priest's vest. They were used by the high priest to get a message from God.

V

vineyard
A place where grapes grow and are picked.

virgin
A woman who has never had a sexual relationship with a man.

vision
A dream from God. The person who saw it was usually awake. God gave these kinds of dreams to people to show them what he was going to do.

W

wafer
A thin, crisp cracker. Wafers were one kind of offering the Israelites brought to the Lord.

widow
A woman whose husband has died.

winepress
A place where juice is pressed out of grapes to make wine.

wisdom
Understanding that comes from God. Wise thinking.

worship
To give praise, honor and glory to God.

Y

Year of Jubilee
A special year that was to happen every 50 years in Israel. No crops could be planted. Any money that was owed was forgiven. Slaves were set free. Property was given back to its first owner.

yeast
Something added to bread dough to make the bread rise.

yoke
1. A strong piece of wood. It fit on the necks of two oxen so that they could pull carts or plows. 2. A piece of wood put on the neck of a slave or a prisoner.

Z

Zealot
A Jew who was willing to fight to get rid of the Roman rulers. Simon may have been part of this group before becoming one of Jesus' twelve disciples.

Zion
1. The city of Jerusalem. 2. The hill on which King David's house and the temple once stood. 3. Another name sometimes used for heaven.

150 Famous Bible Stories

Bible stories are the world's most important stories. They were written a long time ago, but they still teach us lots of things today. Much can be learned about people and about God from reading Bible stories.

Here is a list of some famous Bible stories. Try to read as many as you can. Check off the box next to each story once you have read it. There are many other great stories in the Bible. When you have completed reading all that are on the list, look for others.

FROM THE BEGINNING

☐ The Beginning   Genesis 1:1 — 2:3
☐ Adam and Eve   Genesis 2:15 — 3:24
☐ Cain and Abel   Genesis 4:1 – 16
☐ The Flood   Genesis 6:9 — 9:17
☐ The Tower of Babel   Genesis 11:1 – 9

STORIES OF THE PATRIARCHS

☐ God Chooses Abraham   Genesis 12:1 – 9; 17:1 – 8
☐ The Three Visitors   Genesis 18:1 – 15
☐ Sodom and Gomorrah Destroyed   Genesis 19:15 – 29
☐ Hagar and Ishmael Sent Away   Genesis 21:8 – 21
☐ Abraham Tested   Genesis 22:1 – 19
☐ Isaac and Rebekah   Genesis 24
☐ Jacob and Esau   Genesis 25:19 – 34
☐ Jacob Gets Isaac's Blessing   Genesis 27:1 – 40
☐ Jacob's Dream at Bethel   Genesis 28:10 – 22
☐ Jacob Marries Leah and Rachel   Genesis 29:14 – 30
☐ Joseph and His Brothers   Genesis 37
☐ The Wine Taster and the Baker   Genesis 40
☐ Pharaoh's Dreams   Genesis 41
☐ Joseph's Brothers Go to Egypt   Genesis 42 – 45

DELIVERANCE FROM EGYPT

☐ The Birth of Moses   Exodus 1:8 — 2:10
☐ Moses and the Burning Bush   Exodus 3:1 – 15
☐ The Ten Plagues   Exodus 7:6 — 11:10

☐ A Wise Ruling	1 Kings 3:16 – 28
☐ Solomon Builds the Temple	1 Kings 6
☐ The Queen of Sheba Visits Solomon	1 Kings 10:1 – 13
☐ Israel Rebels Against Rehoboam	1 Kings 12:1 – 24

ELIJAH AND ELISHA

☐ Elijah Fed by Ravens	1 Kings 17:1 – 6
☐ The Widow of Zarephath	1 Kings 17:7 – 24
☐ Elijah on Mount Carmel	1 Kings 18:16 – 46
☐ The LORD Appears to Elijah	1 Kings 19
☐ Naboth's Vineyard	1 Kings 21
☐ Ahab Killed at Ramoth Gilead	1 Kings 22:29 – 40
☐ Elijah Taken Up to Heaven	2 Kings 2:1 – 12
☐ Elisha's Miracles	2 Kings 2:13 – 25
☐ Naaman Healed of Leprosy	2 Kings 5

TROUBLED YEARS

☐ Jehu Anointed King of Israel	2 Kings 9
☐ A Seven-Year-Old King	2 Kings 11
☐ The Book of the Law Found	2 Kings 22:1 — 23:3
☐ The Lord Appoints Isaiah to Speak for Him	Isaiah 6:1 – 8
☐ Isaiah's Prophecy	Isaiah 53
☐ Jehoiakim Burns Jeremiah's Scroll	Jeremiah 36
☐ Jeremiah Thrown Into an Empty Well	Jeremiah 38:1 – 13
☐ Jonah and the Great Fish	Jonah 1 – 4

BABYLONIAN EXILE AND AFTER

☐ The Valley of Dry Bones	Ezekiel 37:1 – 14
☐ Nebuchadnezzar's Dream	Daniel 2
☐ The Image of Gold and the Fiery Furnace	Daniel 3
☐ The Writing on the Wall	Daniel 5
☐ Daniel in the Den of Lions	Daniel 6
☐ Rebuilding the Temple	Ezra 3:7 – 13
☐ Nehemiah Returns to Jerusalem	Nehemiah 2:1 – 18
☐ Esther Saves Her People	Esther 2:5 – 18; 3:12 — 5:8; 7:1 – 10
☐ Trials and Blessings of Job	Job 1,2,42

NEW TESTAMENT

THE EARLY CHURCH

REVELATION

WORLD OF THE PATRIARCHS

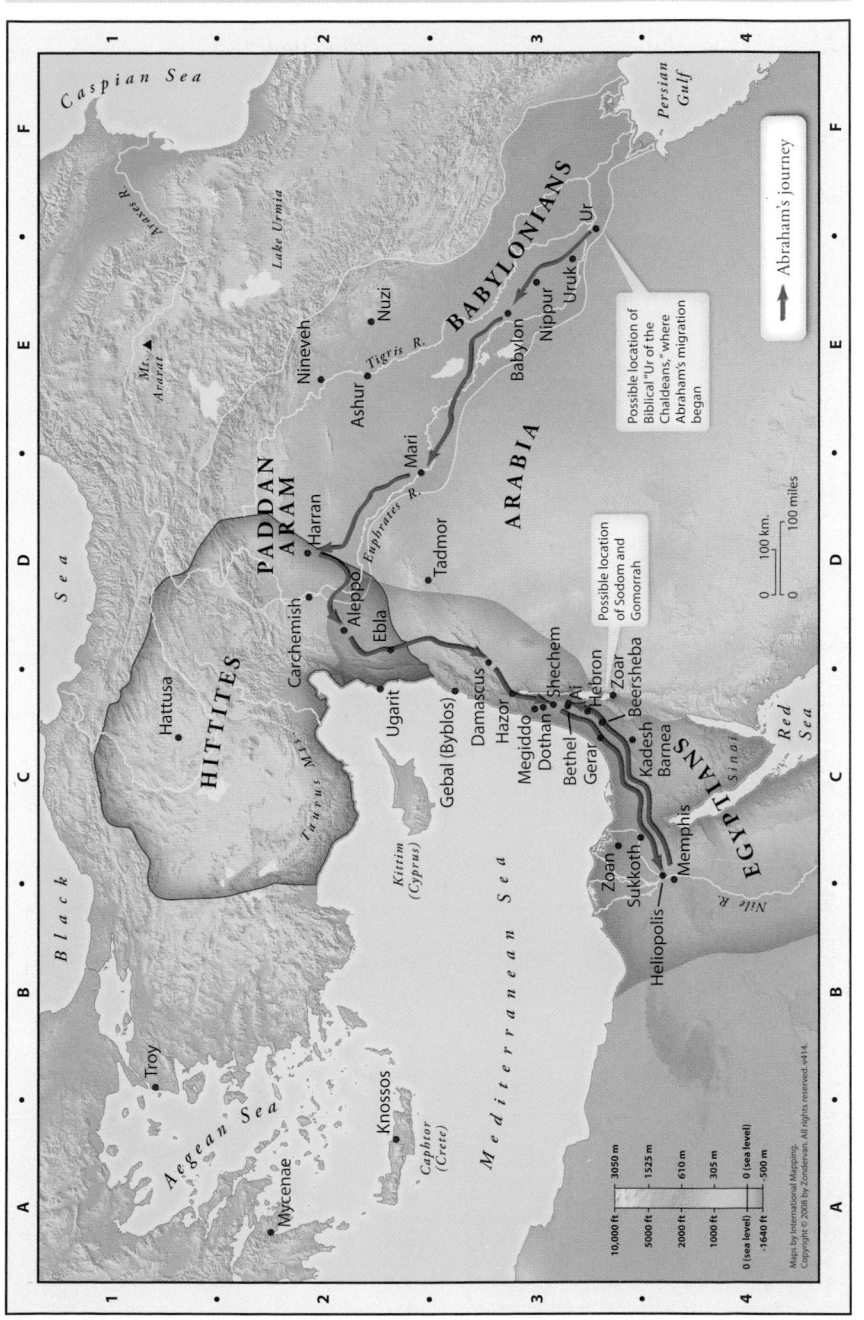

Maps by International Mapping.
Copyright © 2008 by Zondervan. All rights reserved. v414.

EXODUS AND CONQUEST OF CANAAN

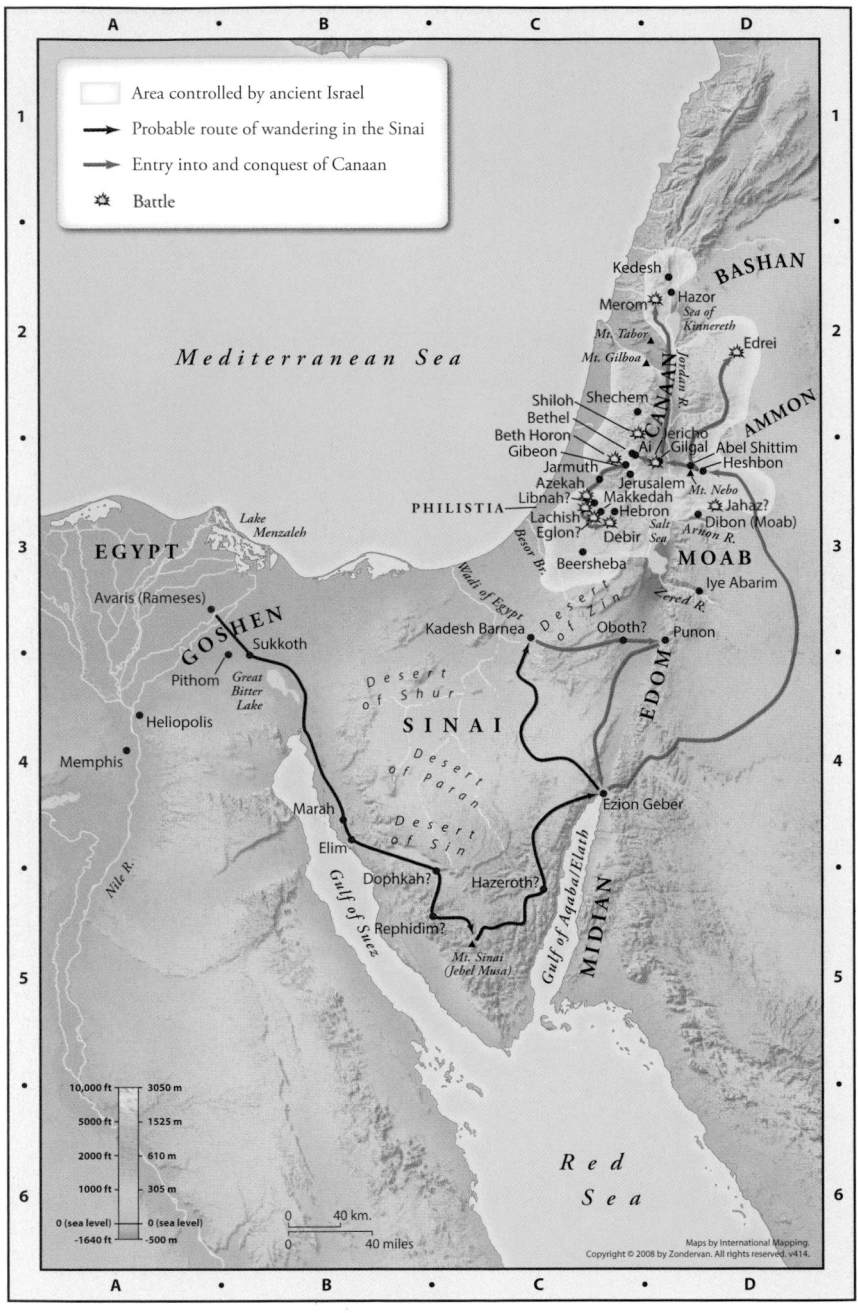

Area controlled by ancient Israel
Probable route of wandering in the Sinai
Entry into and conquest of Canaan
Battle

Mediterranean Sea

Kedesh
Merom · Hazor
Sea of Kinnereth
Mt. Tabor
Mt. Gilboa
BASHAN
Edrei
AMMON

Shiloh · Shechem
Bethel
Beth Horon
Gibeon
Jarmuth
Azekah
Libnah?
Lachish
Eglon?
Debir
Beersheba

Ai · Jericho
Gilgal · Abel Shittim
Heshbon
Jerusalem
Makkedah
Hebron
Mt. Nebo
Salt Sea
Jahaz?
Dibon (Moab)
Arnon R.

PHILISTIA

CANAAN

Jordan R.

MOAB
Iye Abarim

EGYPT
Lake Menzaleh

Avaris (Rameses)
GOSHEN
Sukkoth
Pithom
Great Bitter Lake
Heliopolis

Memphis

Nile R.

Marah
Elim
Dophkah?
Rephidim?
Mt. Sinai (Jebel Musa)

Desert of Shur
SINAI
Desert of Paran
Desert of Sin

Hazeroth?

Kadesh Barnea
Desert of Zin
Besor Br.
Wadi of Egypt

Oboth?
Punon

Zered R.

EDOM

Ezion Geber

Gulf of Suez
Gulf of Aqaba/Elath
MIDIAN

Red Sea

10,000 ft — 3050 m
5000 ft — 1525 m
2000 ft — 610 m
1000 ft — 305 m
0 (sea level) — 0 (sea level)
-1640 ft — -500 m

0 ____ 40 km.
0 ____ 40 miles

Maps by International Mapping.
Copyright © 2008 by Zondervan. All rights reserved. v414.

LAND OF THE TWELVE TRIBES

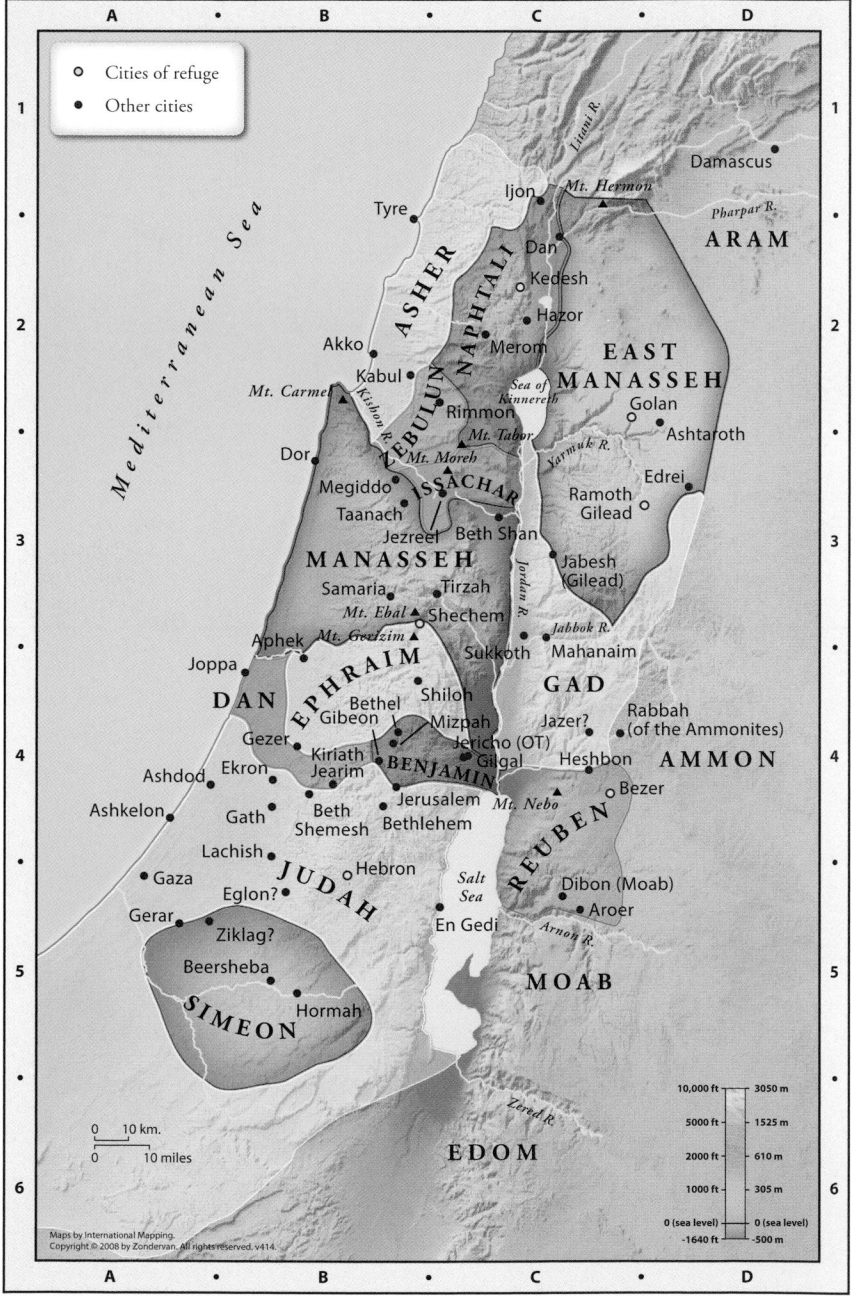

Cities of refuge
Other cities

A B C D

1

Damascus

Tyre   Ijon   Mt. Hermon
Pharpar R.
Litani R.
ARAM

Dan
Kedesh
Hazor

Akko   Merom   EAST
Kabul   MANASSEH
Mt. Carmel   Sea of
Kinnereth   Golan
Rimmon   Ashtaroth
Mt. Tabor   Yarmuk R.
Dor   Mt. Moreh   Edrei
Megiddo   ISSACHAR   Ramoth
Taanach   Gilead
Jezreel   Beth Shan
MANASSEH   Jabesh
Samaria   Tirzah   (Gilead)
Mt. Ebal   Shechem
Aphek   Mt. Gerizim   Sukkoth   Mahanaim
Joppa   GAD
DAN   EPHRAIM   Shiloh
Bethel   Rabbah
Gezer   Gibeon   Mizpah   Jazer?   (of the Ammonites)
Kiriath   Jericho (OT)
Ashdod   Ekron   Jearim   BENJAMIN   Gilgal   Heshbon   AMMON
Gath   Beth   Jerusalem   Mt. Nebo   Bezer
Ashkelon   Shemesh   Bethlehem   REUBEN
Lachish   Dibon (Moab)
Gaza   Eglon?   Hebron   Salt   Aroer
Gerar   Ziklag?   JUDAH   Sea   Arnon R.
Beersheba   En Gedi
SIMEON   Hormah   MOAB

Mediterranean Sea

ASHER
ZEBULUN
NAPHTALI
Kishon R.
Jordan R.
Jabbok R.

Zered R.

EDOM

0   10 km.
0   10 miles

10,000 ft   3050 m
5000 ft   1525 m
2000 ft   610 m
1000 ft   305 m
0 (sea level)   0 (sea level)
-1640 ft   -500 m

Maps by International Mapping.
Copyright © 2008 by Zondervan. All rights reserved. v414.

KINGDOM OF DAVID AND SOLOMON

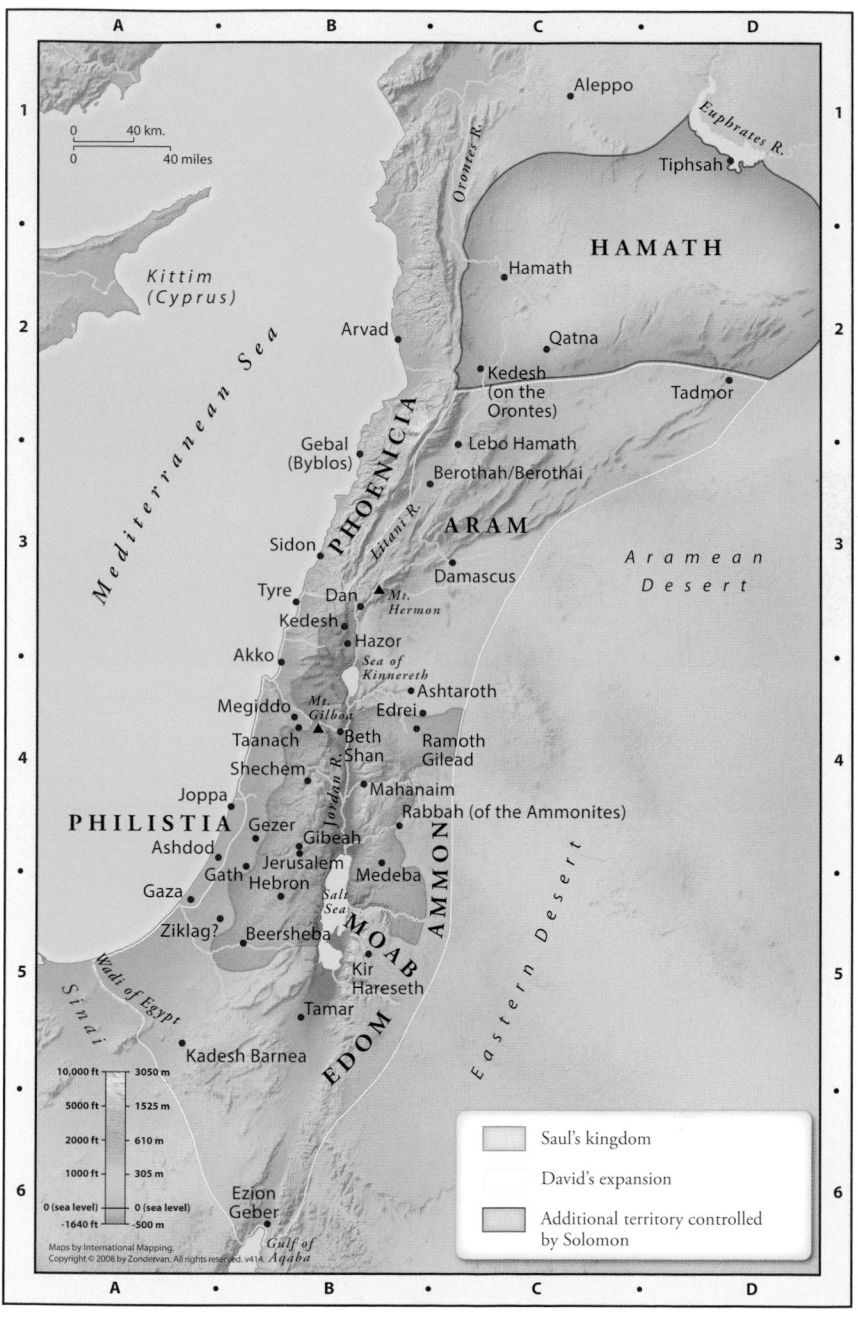

Aleppo

Euphrates R.

Tiphsah

HAMATH

Orontes R.

Kittim (Cyprus)

Hamath

Arvad

Qatna

Kedesh (on the Orontes)

Tadmor

Mediterranean Sea

Gebal (Byblos)

Lebo Hamath

Berothah/Berothai

PHOENICIA

Litani R.

ARAM

Aramean Desert

Sidon

Damascus

Tyre

Dan

Mt. Hermon

Kedesh

Hazor

Akko

Sea of Kinnereth

Megiddo

Mt. Gilboa

Ashtaroth

Edrei

Taanach

Beth Shan

Ramoth Gilead

Shechem

Jordan R.

Joppa

Mahanaim

PHILISTIA

Gezer

Rabbah (of the Ammonites)

Ashdod

Gibeah

AMMON

Gath

Jerusalem

Medeba

Gaza

Hebron

Salt Sea

Eastern Desert

Ziklag?

Beersheba

MOAB

Kir Hareseth

Wadi of Egypt

Tamar

Sinai

EDOM

Kadesh Barnea

0 40 km.
0 40 miles

10,000 ft — 3050 m
5000 ft — 1525 m
2000 ft — 610 m
1000 ft — 305 m
0 (sea level) — 0 (sea level)
-1640 ft — -500 m

Ezion Geber

Gulf of Aqaba

Maps by International Mapping.
Copyright © 2008 by Zondervan. All rights reserved. v414

Saul's kingdom

David's expansion

Additional territory controlled by Solomon

JESUS' MINISTRY

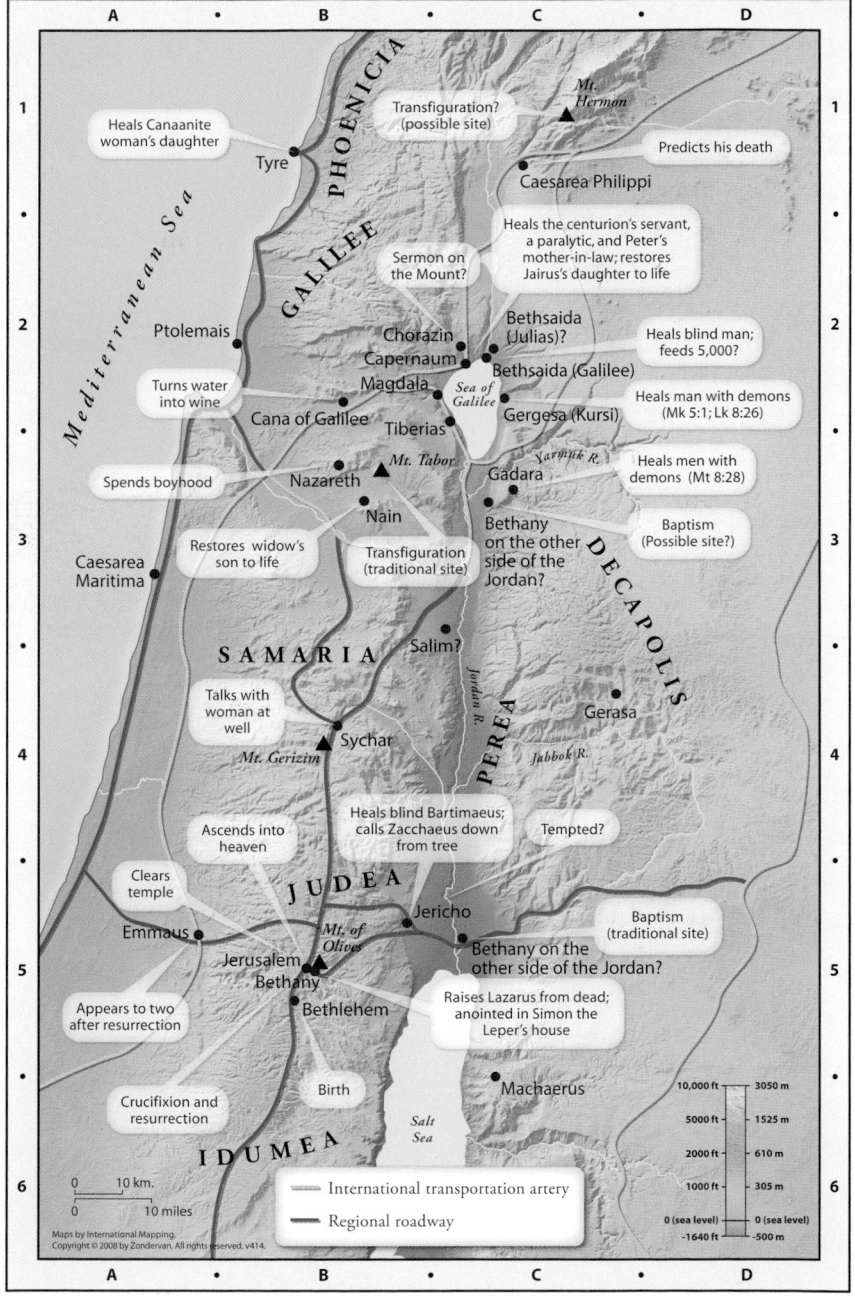

Heals Canaanite woman's daughter

Tyre

PHOENICIA

Transfiguration? (possible site)

Mt. Hermon

Predicts his death

Caesarea Philippi

GALILEE

Sermon on the Mount?

Heals the centurion's servant, a paralytic, and Peter's mother-in-law; restores Jairus's daughter to life

Ptolemais

Chorazin

Bethsaida (Julias)?

Heals blind man; feeds 5,000?

Capernaum

Bethsaida (Galilee)

Turns water into wine

Magdala

Sea of Galilee

Heals man with demons (Mk 5:1; Lk 8:26)

Cana of Galilee

Tiberias

Gergesa (Kursi)

Mediterranean Sea

Mt. Tabor

Yarmuk R.

Heals men with demons (Mt 8:28)

Spends boyhood

Nazareth

Gadara

Baptism (Possible site?)

Nain

Bethany on the other side of the Jordan?

DECAPOLIS

Caesarea Maritima

Restores widow's son to life

Transfiguration (traditional site)

SAMARIA

Salim?

Jordan R.

Talks with woman at well

Sychar

PEREA

Gerasa

Mt. Gerizim

Jabbok R.

Heals blind Bartimaeus; calls Zacchaeus down from tree

Tempted?

Ascends into heaven

JUDEA

Clears temple

Jericho

Baptism (traditional site)

Emmaus

Mt. of Olives

Bethany on the other side of the Jordan?

Jerusalem

Bethany

Appears to two after resurrection

Bethlehem

Raises Lazarus from dead; anointed in Simon the Leper's house

Crucifixion and resurrection

Birth

Machaerus

10,000 ft	3050 m
5000 ft	1525 m
2000 ft	610 m
1000 ft	305 m
0 (sea level)	0 (sea level)
-1640 ft	-500 m

IDUMEA

Salt Sea

0   10 km.
0   10 miles

International transportation artery

Regional roadway

Maps by International Mapping.
Copyright © 2008 by Zondervan. All rights reserved. v414.

PAUL'S MISSIONARY JOURNEYS

First missionary journey (A.D. 46–48)
Second missionary journey (A.D. 49–52)
Third missionary journey (A.D. 53–57)
Trip to Rome (A.D. 59–60)

Maps by International Mapping.
Copyright © 2008 by Zondervan. All rights reserved. v414.

JERUSALEM IN THE TIME OF JESUS

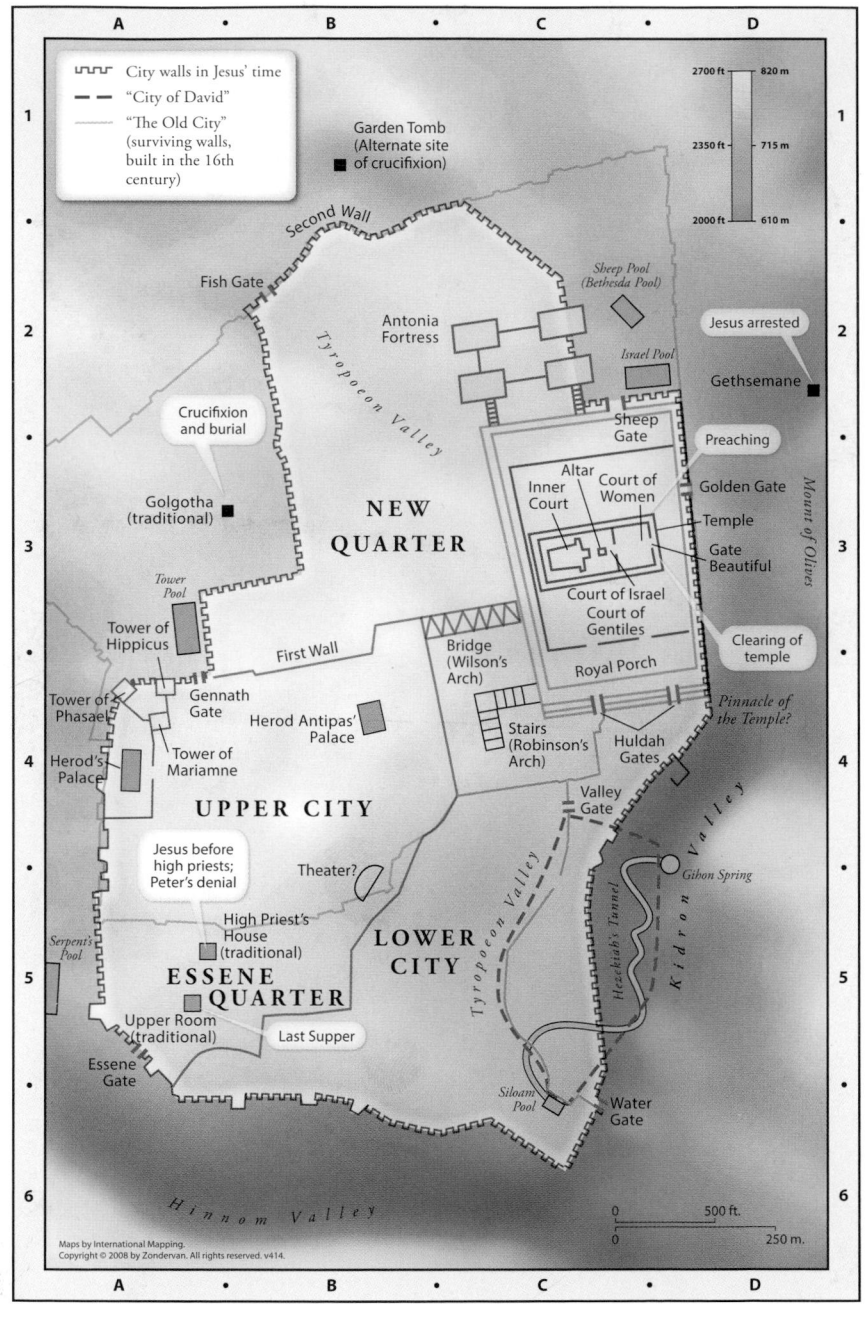

Legend:
- City walls in Jesus' time
- "City of David"
- "The Old City" (surviving walls, built in the 16th century)

Garden Tomb (Alternate site of crucifixion)

2700 ft — 820 m
2350 ft — 715 m
2000 ft — 610 m

Second Wall

Fish Gate

Sheep Pool (Bethesda Pool)

Antonia Fortress

Israel Pool

Jesus arrested

Gethsemane

Tyropoeon Valley

Crucifixion and burial

Golgotha (traditional)

NEW QUARTER

Sheep Gate

Altar
Inner Court
Court of Women

Preaching

Golden Gate

Temple

Gate Beautiful

Court of Israel
Court of Gentiles

Clearing of temple

Tower Pool

Tower of Hippicus

First Wall

Bridge (Wilson's Arch)

Royal Porch

Pinnacle of the Temple?

Tower of Phasael

Gennath Gate

Herod Antipas' Palace

Stairs (Robinson's Arch)

Huldah Gates

Tower of Mariamne

Herod's Palace

UPPER CITY

Valley Gate

Kidron Valley

Mount of Olives

Jesus before high priests; Peter's denial

Theater?

Gihon Spring

High Priest's House (traditional)

LOWER CITY

Hezekiah's Tunnel

Serpent's Pool

ESSENE QUARTER

Upper Room (traditional)

Last Supper

Tyropoeon Valley

Essene Gate

Siloam Pool

Water Gate

Hinnom Valley

0 — 500 ft.
0 — 250 m.

Maps by International Mapping.
Copyright © 2008 by Zondervan. All rights reserved. v414.